SELECTED FEDERAL TAXATION STATUTES AND REGULATIONS

2014 EDITION

Selected and Edited by

Daniel J. Lathrope

Distinguished E.L. Wiegand Professor of Law
University of San Francisco
School of Law

WEST®

Mat #41484955

ISBN: 978–0–314–28898–1

Printed in the United States of America

PREFACE

This volume is for student use in courses studying the provisions of the Internal Revenue Code. It contains selected and edited sections of the Internal Revenue Code (Title 26 of the United States Code), Treasury Regulations (Title 26 of the Code of Federal Regulations), proposed regulations, and, in the Appendix, various items that the Internal Revenue Service has issued.

The purpose of the volume is to provide a reasonably compact, convenient, and economical set of materials. It is not a complete source of the Code and Regulations. The entire text of the Code and Regulations is over 10,000 pages, the bulk of which students do not use.

This edition is current through May 20, 2013. The Appendix includes excerpts from Rev. Proc. 87–57 (depreciation allowances under § 168), excerpts from Instructions for IRS Form 4562 (depreciation allowances under § 168), excerpts from actuarial Values: Book Aleph, and Internal Revenue Service pronouncements setting forth cost-of-living and inflation adjustments for 2013.

Comments and suggestions about the materials are appreciated. Any ideas for improvement are welcome.

I want to express my gratitude to Benjamin J. Rubelmann, a second-year student at the University of San Francisco School of Law, for his assistance in the preparation of this volume.

DANIEL J. LATHROPE

San Francisco, California
May 2013

SUMMARY OF CONTENTS

SELECTED FEDERAL TAXATION STATUTES AND REGULATIONS

INTERNAL REVENUE TITLE

TABLE OF SUBTITLES

* Omitted entirely.

TABLE OF CHAPTERS IN SUBTITLES

Subtitle A. Income Taxes

Subtitle B. Estate and Gift Taxes

Subtitle C. Employment Taxes

Subtitle D. Miscellaneous Excise Taxes

Subtitle E. Alcohol, Tobacco, and Certain Other Excise Taxes *

* Omitted entirely.

Subtitle F. Procedure and Administration

Subtitle G. The Joint Committee on Taxation *

Subtitle H. Financing of Presidential Election Campaigns*

Subtitle I. Trust Fund Code *

Subtitle J. Coal Industry Health Benefits *

* Omitted entirely.

TABLE OF SUBCHAPTERS, PARTS AND SUBPARTS IN CHAPTERS

SUBTITLE A. INCOME TAXES

* Omitted entirely.

* Omitted entirely.

* Omitted entirely.

INTERNAL REVENUE TITLE

* Omitted entirely.

SUBTITLE B. ESTATE AND GIFT TAXES

* Omitted entirely.

SUBTITLE C. EMPLOYMENT TAXES

SUBTITLE D. MISCELLANEOUS EXCISE TAXES

SUBTITLE E. ALCOHOL, TOBACCO, AND CERTAIN OTHER EXCISE TAXES *

* * *

SUBTITLE F. PROCEDURE AND ADMINISTRATION

* Omitted entirely.

* Omitted entirely.

INTERNAL REVENUE TITLE

* Omitted entirely.

SUBTITLE G. THE JOINT COMMITTEE ON TAXATION *

* * *

SUBTITLE H. FINANCING OF PRESIDENTIAL ELECTION CAMPAIGNS *

* * *

SUBTITLE I. TRUST FUND CODE*

* * *

SUBTITLE J. COAL INDUSTRY HEALTH BENEFITS*

* * *

* Omitted entirely.

INTERNAL REVENUE TITLE

SUBTITLE A—INCOME TAXES

Chapter

1. Normal taxes and surtaxes.
2. Tax on self-employment income.*
3. Withholding of tax on nonresident aliens and foreign corporations.*
4. Rules applicable to recovery of excessive profits on government contracts.*
5. Tax on transfers to avoid income tax.*
6. Consolidated returns.

CHAPTER 1—NORMAL TAXES AND SURTAXES

Subchapter

A. Determination of tax liability.
B. Computation of taxable income.
C. Corporate distributions and adjustments.
D. Deferred compensation, etc.
E. Accounting periods and methods of accounting.
F. Exempt organizations.
G. Corporations used to avoid income tax on shareholders.
H. Banking institutions.*
I. Natural resources.
J. Estates, trusts, beneficiaries, and decedents.
K. Partners and partnerships.
L. Insurance companies.*
M. Regulated investment companies and real estate investment trusts.*
N. Tax based on income from sources within or without the United States.
O. Gain or loss on disposition of property.
P. Capital gains and losses.
Q. Readjustment of tax between years and special limitations.
[R. Repealed]
S. Tax treatment of S corporations and their shareholders.
T. Cooperatives and their patrons.*
[U. Repealed]
V. Title 11 cases.

SUBCHAPTER A—DETERMINATION OF TAX LIABILITY

Part

I. Tax on individuals.
II. Tax on corporations.
III. Changes in rates during a taxable year.*
IV. Credits against tax.
[V. Repealed]
VI. Alternative minimum tax.
VII. Environmental tax.*

* Omitted entirely.

PART I—TAX ON INDIVIDUALS

§ 1. Tax imposed

(a) Married individuals filing joint returns and surviving spouses.—There is hereby imposed on the taxable income of—

(1) every married individual (as defined in section 7703) who makes a single return jointly with his spouse under section 6013, and

(2) every surviving spouse (as defined in section 2(a)), a tax determined in accordance with the following table:

If taxable income is:	The tax is:
Not over $36,900	15% of taxable income.
Over $36,900 but not over $89,150	$5,535, plus 28% of the excess over $36,900.
Over $89,150 but not over $140,000	$20,165, plus 31% of the excess over $89,150.
Over $140,000 but not over $250,000	$35,928.50, plus 36% of the excess over $140,000.
Over $250,000	$75,528.50, plus 39.6% of the excess over $250,000.

(b) Heads of households.—There is hereby imposed on the taxable income of every head of a household (as defined in section 2(b)) a tax determined in accordance with the following table:

If taxable income is:	The tax is:
Not over $29,600	15% of taxable income.
Over $29,600 but not over $76,400	$4,440, plus 28% of the excess over $29,600.
Over $76,400 but not over $127,500	$17,544, plus 31% of the excess over $76,400.
Over $127,500 but not over $250,000	$33,385, plus 36% of the excess over $127,500.
Over $250,000	$77,485, plus 39.6% of the excess over $250,000.

(c) Unmarried individuals (other than surviving spouses and heads of households).—There is hereby imposed on the taxable income of every individual (other than a surviving spouse as defined in section 2(a) or the head of a household as defined in section 2(b)) who is not a married individual (as defined in section 7703) a tax determined in accordance with the following table:

If taxable income is:	The tax is:
Not over $22,100	15% of taxable income.
Over $22,100 but not over $53,500	$3,315, plus 28% of the excess over $22,100.
Over $53,500 but not over $115,000	$12,107, plus 31% of the excess over $53,500.
Over $115,000 but not over $250,000	$31,172, plus 36% of the excess over $115,000.
Over $250,000	$79,772, plus 39.6% of the excess over $250,000.

(d) Married individuals filing separate returns.—There is hereby imposed on the taxable income of every married individual (as defined in section 7703) who does not make a single return jointly with his spouse under section 6013, a tax determined in accordance with the following table:

If taxable income is:	The tax is:
Not over $18,450	15% of taxable income.
Over $18,450 but not over $44,575	$2,767.50, plus 28% of the excess over $18,450.
Over $44,575 but not over $70,000	$10,082.50, plus 31% of the excess over $44,575.

If taxable income is:	The tax is:
Over $70,000 but not over $125,000	$17,964.25, plus 36% of the excess over $70,000.
Over $125,000	$37,764.25, plus 39.6% of the excess over $125,000.

(e) Estates and trusts.—There is hereby imposed on the taxable income of—

(1) every estate, and

(2) every trust,

taxable under this subsection a tax determined in accordance with the following table:

If taxable income is:	The tax is:
Not over $1,500	15% of taxable income.
Over $1,500 but not over $3,500	$225, plus 28% of the excess over $1,500.
Over $3,500 but not over $5,500	$785, plus 31% of the excess over $3,500.
Over $5,500 but not over $7,500	$1,405, plus 36% of the excess over $5,500.
Over $7,500	$2,125, plus 39.6% of the excess over $7,500.

(f) Phaseout of marriage penalty in 15–percent bracket; adjustments in tax tables so that inflation will not result in tax increases.—

(1) In general.—Not later than December 15 of 1993, and each subsequent calendar year, the Secretary shall prescribe tables which shall apply in lieu of the tables contained in subsections (a), (b), (c), (d), and (e) with respect to taxable years beginning in the succeeding calendar year.

(2) Method of prescribing tables.—The table which under paragraph (1) is to apply in lieu of the table contained in subsection (a), (b), (c), (d), or (e), as the case may be, with respect to taxable years beginning in any calendar year shall be prescribed—

(A) except as provided in paragraph (8), by increasing the minimum and maximum dollar amounts for each rate bracket for which a tax is imposed under such table by the cost-of-living adjustment for such calendar year,

(B) by not changing the rate applicable to any rate bracket as adjusted under subparagraph (A), and

(C) by adjusting the amounts setting forth the tax to the extent necessary to reflect the adjustments in the rate brackets.

* * *

(8) Elimination of marriage penalty in 15–percent bracket.—With respect to taxable years beginning after December 31, 2003, in prescribing the tables under paragraph (1)—

(A) the maximum taxable income in the 15–percent rate bracket in the table contained in subsection (a) (and the minimum taxable income in the next higher taxable income bracket in such table) shall be 200 percent of the maximum taxable income in the 15–percent rate bracket in the table contained in subsection (c) (after any other adjustment under this subsection), and

(B) the comparable taxable income amounts in the table contained in subsection (d) shall be 1/2 of the amounts determined under subparagraph (A).

(g) Certain unearned income of children taxed as if parent's income.—

(1) In general.—In the case of any child to whom this subsection applies, the tax imposed by this section shall be equal to the greater of—

(A) the tax imposed by this section without regard to this subsection, or

(B) the sum of—

(i) the tax which would be imposed by this section if the taxable income of such child for the taxable year were reduced by the net unearned income of such child, plus

(ii) such child's share of the allocable parental tax.

(2) Child to whom subsection applies.—This subsection shall apply to any child for any taxable year if—

(A) such child—

(i) has not attained age 18 before the close of the taxable year, or

(ii)(I) has attained age 18 before the close of the taxable year and meets the age requirements of section 152(c)(3) (determined without regard to subparagraph (B) thereof), and

(II) whose earned income (as defined in section 911(d)(2)) for such taxable year does not exceed one-half of the amount of the individual's support (within the meaning of section 152(c)(1)(D) after the application of section 152(f)(5) (without regard to subparagraph (A) thereof)) for such taxable year,

(B) either parent of such child is alive at the close of the taxable year, and

(C) such child does not file a joint return for the taxable year.

(3) Allocable parental tax.—For purposes of this subsection—

(A) In general.—The term "allocable parental tax" means the excess of—

(i) the tax which would be imposed by this section on the parent's taxable income if such income included the net unearned income of all children of the parent to whom this subsection applies, over

(ii) the tax imposed by this section on the parent without regard to this subsection.

For purposes of clause (i), net unearned income of all children of the parent shall not be taken into account in computing any exclusion, deduction, or credit of the parent.

(B) Child's share.—A child's share of any allocable parental tax of a parent shall be equal to an amount which bears the same ratio to the total allocable parental tax as the child's net unearned income bears to the aggregate net unearned income of all children of such parent to whom this subsection applies.

(C) Special rule where parent has different taxable year.—Except as provided in regulations, if the parent does not have the same taxable year as the child, the allocable parental tax shall be determined on the basis of the taxable year of the parent ending in the child's taxable year.

(4) Net unearned income.—For purposes of this subsection—

(A) In general.—The term "net unearned income" means the excess of—

(i) the portion of the adjusted gross income for the taxable year which is not attributable to earned income (as defined in section 911(d)(2)), over

(ii) the sum of—

(I) the amount in effect for the taxable year under section 63(c)(5)(A) (relating to limitation on standard deduction in the case of certain dependents), plus

(II) the greater of the amount described in subclause (I) or, if the child itemizes his deductions for the taxable year, the amount of the itemized deductions allowed by this chapter for the taxable year which are directly connected with the production of the portion of adjusted gross income referred to in clause (i).

(B) Limitation based on taxable income.—The amount of the net unearned income for any taxable year shall not exceed the individual's taxable income for such taxable year.

* * *

(5) Special rules for determining parent to whom subsection applies.—For purposes of this subsection, the parent whose taxable income shall be taken into account shall be—

(A) in the case of parents who are not married (within the meaning of section 7703), the custodial parent (within the meaning of section 152(e)) of the child, and

(B) in the case of married individuals filing separately, the individual with the greater taxable income.

(6) Providing of parent's TIN.—The parent of any child to whom this subsection applies for any taxable year shall provide the TIN of such parent to such child and such child shall include such TIN on the child's return of tax imposed by this section for such taxable year.

(7) Election to claim certain unearned income of child on parent's return.—

(A) In general.—If—

(i) any child to whom this subsection applies has gross income for the taxable year only from interest and dividends (including Alaska Permanent Fund dividends),

(ii) such gross income is more than the amount described in paragraph (4)(A)(ii)(I) and less than 10 times the amount so described,

(iii) no estimated tax payments for such year are made in the name and TIN of such child, and no amount has been deducted and withheld under section 3406, and

(iv) the parent of such child (as determined under paragraph (5)) elects the application of subparagraph (B),

such child shall be treated (other than for purposes of this paragraph) as having no gross income for such year and shall not be required to file a return under section 6012.

(B) Income included on parent's return.—In the case of a parent making the election under this paragraph—

(i) the gross income of each child to whom such election applies (to the extent the gross income of such child exceeds twice the amount described in paragraph (4)(A)(ii)(I)) shall be included in such parent's gross income for the taxable year,

(ii) the tax imposed by this section for such year with respect to such parent shall be the amount equal to the sum of—

(I) the amount determined under this section after the application of clause (i), plus

(II) for each such child, 10 percent of the lesser of the amount described in paragraph (4)(A)(ii)(I) or the excess of the gross income of such child over the amount so described, and

(iii) any interest which is an item of tax preference under section 57(a)(5) of the child shall be treated as an item of tax preference of such parent (and not of such child).

(C) Regulations.—The Secretary shall prescribe such regulations as may be necessary or appropriate to carry out the purposes of this paragraph.

(h) Maximum capital gains rate.—

(1) In general.—If a taxpayer has a net capital gain for any taxable year, the tax imposed by this section for such taxable year shall not exceed the sum of—

(A) a tax computed at the rates and in the same manner as if this subsection had not been enacted on the greater of—

(i) taxable income reduced by the net capital gain; or

(ii) the lesser of—

(I) the amount of taxable income taxed at a rate below 25 percent; or

(II) taxable income reduced by the adjusted net capital gain;

(B) 0 percent of so much of the adjusted net capital gain (or, if less, taxable income) as does not exceed the excess (if any) of—

(i) the amount of taxable income which would (without regard to this paragraph) be taxed at a rate below 25 percent, over

(ii) the taxable income reduced by the adjusted net capital gain;

(C) 15 percent of the lesser of—

(i) so much of the adjusted net capital gain (or, if less, taxable income) as exceeds the amount on which a tax is determined under subparagraph (B), or

(ii) the excess of—

(I) the amount of taxable income which would (without regard to this paragraph) be taxed at a rate below 39.6 percent, over

(II) the sum of the amounts on which a tax is determined under subparagraphs (A) and (B),

(D) 20 percent of the adjusted net capital gain (or, if less, taxable income) in excess of the sum of the amounts on which tax is determined under subparagraphs (B) and (C),

(E) 25 percent of the excess (if any) of—

(i) the unrecaptured section 1250 gain (or, if less, the net capital gain (determined without regard to paragraph (11))), over

(ii) the excess (if any) of—

(I) the sum of the amount on which tax is determined under subparagraph (A) plus the net capital gain, over

(II) taxable income; and

(F) 28 percent of the amount of taxable income in excess of the sum of the amounts on which tax is determined under the preceding subparagraphs of this paragraph.

(2) Net capital gain taken into account as investment income.—For purposes of this subsection, the net capital gain for any taxable year shall be reduced (but not below zero) by the amount which the taxpayer takes into account as investment income under section 163(d)(4)(B)(iii).

(3) Adjusted net capital gain.—For purposes of this subsection, the term "adjusted net capital gain" means net capital gain reduced (but not below zero) by the sum of—

(A) net capital gain (determined without regard to paragraph (11)) reduced (but not below zero) by the sum of—

(i) unrecaptured section 1250 gain; and

(ii) 28–percent rate gain, plus

(B) qualified dividend income (as defined in paragraph (11)).

(4) 28-percent rate gain.—For purposes of this subsection, the term "28-percent rate gain" means the excess (if any) of—

(A) the sum of—

(i) collectibles gain; and

(ii) section 1202 gain, over

(B) the sum of—

(i) collectibles loss;

(ii) the net short-term capital loss; and

(iii) the amount of long-term capital loss carried under section 1212(b)(1)(B) to the taxable year.

(5) Collectibles gain and loss.—For purposes of this subsection.

(A) In general.—The terms "collectibles gain" and "collectibles loss" mean gain or loss (respectively) from the sale or exchange of a collectible (as defined in section 408(m) without regard to paragraph (3) thereof) which is a capital asset held for more than 1 year but only to the extent such gain is taken into account in computing gross income and such loss is taken into account in computing taxable income.

(B) Partnerships, etc.—For purposes of subparagraph (A), any gain from the sale of an interest in a partnership, S corporation, or trust which is attributable to unrealized appreciation in the value of collectibles shall be treated as gain from the sale or exchange of a collectible. Rules similar to the rules of section 751 shall apply for purposes of the preceding sentence.

(6) Unrecaptured section 1250 gain.—For purposes of this subsection.

(A) In general.—The term "unrecaptured section 1250 gain" means the excess (if any) of—

(i) the amount of long-term capital gain (not otherwise treated as ordinary income) which would be treated as ordinary income if section 1250(b)(1) included all depreciation and the applicable percentage under section 1250(a) were 100 percent, over

(ii) the excess (if any) of—

(I) the amount described in paragraph (4)(B); over

(II) the amount described in paragraph (4)(A).

(B) Limitation with respect to section 1231 property.—The amount described in subparagraph (A)(i) from sales, exchanges, and conversions described in section 1231(a)(3)(A) for any taxable year shall not exceed the net section 1231 gain (as defined in section 1231(c)(3)) for such year.

(7) Section 1202 gain.—For purposes of this subsection, the term "section 1202 gain" means the excess of—

(A) the gain which would be excluded from gross income under section 1202 but for the percentage limitation in section 1202(a), over

(B) the gain excluded from gross income under section 1202.

(8) Coordination with recapture of net ordinary losses under section 1231.—If any amount is treated as ordinary income under section 1231(c), such amount shall be allocated among the separate categories of net section 1231 gain (as defined in section 1231(c)(3)) in such manner as the Secretary may by forms or regulations prescribe.

(9) Regulations.—The Secretary may prescribe such regulations as are appropriate (including regulations requiring reporting) to apply this subsection in the case of sales and exchanges by pass-thru entities and of interests in such entities.

(10) Pass-thru entity defined.—For purposes of this subsection, the term "pass-thru entity" means—

(A) a regulated investment company;

(B) a real estate investment trust;

(C) an S corporation;

(D) a partnership;

(E) an estate or trust;

(F) a common trust fund; and

* * *

(11) Dividends taxed as net capital gain.—

(A) In general.—For purposes of this subsection, the term "net capital gain" means net capital gain (determined without regard to this paragraph) increased by qualified dividend income.

(B) Qualified dividend income.—For purposes of this paragraph—

(i) In general.—The term "qualified dividend income" means dividends received during the taxable year from—

(I) domestic corporations, and

(II) qualified foreign corporations.

(ii) Certain dividends excluded.—Such term shall not include—

(I) any dividend from a corporation which for the taxable year of the corporation in which the distribution is made, or the preceding taxable year, is a corporation exempt from tax under section 501 or 521,

(II) any amount allowed as a deduction under section 591 (relating to deduction for dividends paid by mutual savings banks, etc.), and

(III) any dividend described in section 404(k).

(iii) Coordination with section 246(c).—Such term shall not include any dividend on any share of stock—

(I) with respect to which the holding period requirements of section 246(c) are not met (determined by substituting in section 246(c)(1) "60 days" for "45 days" each place it appears and by substituting "121–day period" for "91–day period"), or

(II) to the extent that the taxpayer is under an obligation (whether pursuant to a short sale or otherwise) to make related payments with respect to positions in substantially similar or related property.

(C) Qualified foreign corporations.—

(i) In general.—Except as otherwise provided in this paragraph, the term "qualified foreign corporation" means any foreign corporation if—

(I) such corporation is incorporated in a possession of the United States, or

(II) such corporation is eligible for benefits of a comprehensive income tax treaty with the United States which the Secretary determines is satisfactory for purposes of this paragraph and which includes an exchange of information program.

(ii) Dividends on stock readily tradable on United States securities market.—A foreign corporation not otherwise treated as a qualified foreign corporation under clause (i) shall be so treated with respect to any dividend paid by such corporation if the stock with respect to which such dividend is paid is readily tradable on an established securities market in the United States.

(iii) Exclusion of dividends of certain foreign corporations.—Such term shall not include any foreign corporation which for the taxable year of the corporation in which the dividend was paid, or the preceding taxable year, is a passive foreign investment company (as defined in section 1297).

(iv) Coordination with foreign tax credit limitation.—Rules similar to the rules of section 904(b)(2)(B) shall apply with respect to the dividend rate differential under this paragraph.

(D) Special rules.—

(i) Amounts taken into account as investment income.—Qualified dividend income shall not include any amount which the taxpayer takes into account as investment income under section 163(d)(4)(B).

(ii) Extraordinary dividends.—If a taxpayer to whom this section applies receives, with respect to any share of stock, qualified dividend income from 1 or more dividends which are extraordinary dividends (within the meaning of section 1059(c)), any loss on the sale or exchange of such share shall, to the extent of such dividends, be treated as long-term capital loss.

(iii) Treatment of dividends from regulated investment companies and real estate investment trusts.—A dividend received from a regulated investment company or a real estate investment trust shall be subject to the limitations prescribed in sections 854 and 857.

(i) Rate reductions after 2000.—

(1) 10-percent rate bracket.—

(A) In general.—In the case of taxable years beginning after December 31, 2000—

(i) the rate of tax under subsections (a), (b), (c), and (d) on taxable income not over the initial bracket amount shall be 10 percent, and

(ii) the 15 percent rate of tax shall apply only to taxable income over the initial bracket amount but not over the maximum dollar amount for the 15-percent rate bracket.

(B) Initial bracket amount.—For purposes of this paragraph, the initial bracket amount is—

(i) $14,000 in the case of subsection (a),

(ii) $10,000 in the case of subsection (b), and

(iii) ½ the amount applicable under clause (i) (after adjustment, if any, under subparagraph (C)) in the case of subsections (c) and (d).

(C) Inflation adjustment.—In prescribing the tables under subsection (f) which apply with respect to taxable years beginning in calendar years after 2003—

(i) the cost-of-living adjustment shall be determined under subsection (f)(3) by substituting "2002" for "1992" in subparagraph (B) thereof, and

(ii) the adjustments under clause (i) shall not apply to the amount referred to in subparagraph (B)(iii).

If any amount after adjustment under the preceding sentence is not a multiple of $50, such amount shall be rounded to the next lowest multiple of $50.

(2) 25–, 28–, and 33–percent rate brackets.—The tables under subsections (a), (b), (c), (d), and (e) shall be applied—

(A) by substituting "25%" for "28%" each place it appears (before the application of subparagraph (B)),

(B) by substituting "28%" for "31%" each place it appears, and

(C) by substituting "33%" for "36%" each place it appears.

(3) Modifications to income tax brackets for high-income taxpayers.—

(A) 35–percent rate bracket.—In the case of taxable years beginning after December 31, 2012—

(i) the rate of tax under subsections (a), (b), (c), and (d) on a taxpayer's taxable income in the highest rate bracket shall be 35 percent to the extent such income does not exceed an amount equal to the excess of—

(I) the applicable threshold, over

(II) the dollar amount at which such bracket begins, and

(ii) the 39.6 percent rate of tax under such subsections shall apply only to the taxpayer's taxable income in such bracket in excess of the amount to which clause (i) applies.

(B) Applicable threshold.—For purposes of this paragraph, the term "applicable threshold" means—

(i) $450,000 in the case of subsection (a),

(ii) $425,000 in the case of subsection (b),

(iii) $400,000 in the case of subsection (c), and

(iv) 1/2 the amount applicable under clause (i) (after adjustment, if any, under subparagraph (C)) in the case of subsection (d).

(C) Inflation adjustment.—For purposes of this paragraph, with respect to taxable years beginning in calendar years after 2013, each of the dollar amounts under clauses (i), (ii), and (iii) of subparagraph (B) shall be adjusted in the same manner as under paragraph (1)(C)(i), except that subsection (f)(3)(B) shall be applied by substituting "2012" for "1992".

(4) Adjustment of tables.—The Secretary shall adjust the tables prescribed under subsection (f) to carry out this subsection.

§ 2. Definitions and special rules

(a) Definition of surviving spouse.—

(1) In general.—For purposes of section 1, the term "surviving spouse" means a taxpayer—

(A) whose spouse died during either of his two taxable years immediately preceding the taxable year, and

(B) who maintains as his home a household which constitutes for the taxable year the principal place of abode (as a member of such household) of a dependent (i) who (within the meaning of section 152 determined without regard to subsections (b)(1), (b)(2), and (d)(1)(B) thereof) is a son, stepson, daughter, or stepdaughter of the taxpayer, and (ii) with respect to whom the taxpayer is entitled to a deduction for the taxable year under section 151.

For purposes of this paragraph, an individual shall be considered as maintaining a household only if over half of the cost of maintaining the household during the taxable year is furnished by such individual.

(2) Limitations.—Notwithstanding paragraph (1), for purposes of section 1 a taxpayer shall not be considered to be a surviving spouse—

(A) if the taxpayer has remarried at any time before the close of the taxable year, or

(B) unless, for the taxpayer's taxable year during which his spouse died, a joint return could have been made under the provisions of section 6013 (without regard to subsection (a)(3) thereof).

* * *

(b) Definition of head of household.—

(1) In general.—For purposes of this subtitle, an individual shall be considered a head of a household if, and only if, such individual is not married at the close of his taxable year, is not a surviving spouse (as defined in subsection (a)), and either—

(A) maintains as his home a household which constitutes for more than one-half of such taxable year the principal place of abode, as a member of such household, of—

(i) a qualifying child of the individual (as defined in section 152(c), determined without regard to section 152(e)), but not if such child—

(I) is married at the close of the taxpayer's taxable year, and

(II) is not a dependent of such individual by reason of section 152(b)(2) or 152(b)(3), or both, or

(ii) any other person who is a dependent of the taxpayer, if the taxpayer is entitled to a deduction for the taxable year for such person under section 151, or

(B) maintains a household which constitutes for such taxable year the principal place of abode of the father or mother of the taxpayer, if the taxpayer is entitled to a deduction for the taxable year for such father or mother under section 151.

For purposes of this paragraph, an individual shall be considered as maintaining a household only if over half of the cost of maintaining the household during the taxable year is furnished by such individual.

(2) Determination of status.—For purposes of this subsection—

(A) an individual who is legally separated from his spouse under a decree of divorce or of separate maintenance shall not be considered as married;

(B) a taxpayer shall be considered as not married at the close of his taxable year if at any time during the taxable year his spouse is a nonresident alien; and

(C) a taxpayer shall be considered as married at the close of his taxable year if his spouse (other than a spouse described in subparagraph (B)) died during the taxable year.

(3) Limitations.—Notwithstanding paragraph (1), for purposes of this subtitle a taxpayer shall not be considered to be a head of a household—

(A) if at any time during the taxable year he is a nonresident alien; or

(B) by reason of an individual who would not be a dependent for the taxable year but for—

(i) subparagraph (H) of section 152(d)(2), or

(ii) paragraph (3) of section 152(d).

(c) Certain married individuals living apart.—For purposes of this part, an individual shall be treated as not married at the close of the taxable year if such individual is so treated under the provisions of section 7703(b).

* * *

§ 3. Tax tables for individuals

(a) Imposition of tax table tax.—

(1) In general.—In lieu of the tax imposed by section 1, there is hereby imposed for each taxable year on the taxable income of every individual—

(A) who does not itemize his deductions for the taxable year, and

(B) whose taxable income for such taxable year does not exceed the ceiling amount,

a tax determined under tables, applicable to such taxable year, which shall be prescribed by the Secretary and which shall be in such form as he determines appropriate. In the table so prescribed, the amounts of the tax shall be computed on the basis of the rates prescribed by section 1.

(2) Ceiling amount defined.—For purposes of paragraph (1), the term "ceiling amount" means, with respect to any taxpayer, the amount (not less than $20,000) determined by the Secretary for the tax rate category in which such taxpayer falls.

(3) Authority to prescribe tables for taxpayers who itemize deductions.—The Secretary may provide that this section shall apply also for any taxable year to individuals who itemize their deductions. Any tables prescribed under the preceding sentence shall be on the basis of taxable income.

(b) Section inapplicable to certain individuals.—This section shall not apply to—

(1) an individual making a return under section 443(a)(1) for a period of less than 12 months on account of a change in annual accounting period, and

(2) an estate or trust.

(c) Tax treated as imposed by section 1.—For purposes of this title, the tax imposed by this section shall be treated as tax imposed by section 1.

(d) Taxable income.—Whenever it is necessary to determine the taxable income of an individual to whom this section applies, the taxable income shall be determined under section 63.

* * *

PART II—TAX ON CORPORATIONS

§ 11. Tax imposed

(a) Corporations in general.—A tax is hereby imposed for each taxable year on the taxable income of every corporation.

(b) Amount of tax.—

(1) In general.—The amount of the tax imposed by subsection (a) shall be the sum of—

(A) 15 percent of so much of the taxable income as does not exceed $50,000,

(B) 25 percent of so much of the taxable income as exceeds $50,000 but does not exceed $75,000,

(C) 34 percent of so much of the taxable income as exceeds $75,000 but does not exceed $10,000,000, and

(D) 35 percent of so much of the taxable income as exceeds $10,000,000.

In the case of a corporation which has taxable income in excess of $100,000 for any taxable year, the amount of tax determined under the preceding sentence for such taxable year shall be increased by the lesser of (i) 5 percent of such excess, or (ii) $11,750. In the case of a corporation which has taxable income in excess of $15,000,000, the amount of the tax determined under the foregoing provisions of this paragraph shall be increased by an additional amount equal to the lesser of (i) 3 percent of such excess, or (ii) $100,000.

(2) Certain personal service corporations not eligible for graduated rates.—Notwithstanding paragraph (1), the amount of the tax imposed by subsection (a) on the taxable income of a qualified personal service corporation (as defined in section 448(d)(2)) shall be equal to 35 percent of the taxable income.

* * *

PART IV—CREDITS AGAINST TAX

Subpart

Subpart A—Nonrefundable Personal Credits

§ 21. Expenses for household and dependent care services necessary for gainful employment

(a) Allowance of credit.—

(1) In general.—In the case of an individual for which there are 1 or more qualifying individuals (as defined in subsection (b)(1)) with respect to such individual, there shall be allowed as a credit against the tax imposed by this chapter for the taxable year an amount equal to the applicable percentage of the employment-related expenses (as defined in subsection (b)(2)) paid by such individual during the taxable year.

(2) Applicable percentage defined.—For purposes of paragraph (1), the term "applicable percentage" means 35 percent reduced (but not below 20 percent) by 1 percentage point for each $2,000 (or fraction thereof) by which the taxpayer's adjusted gross income for the taxable year exceeds $15,000.

(b) Definitions of qualifying individual and employment-related expenses.—For purposes of this section—

(1) Qualifying individual.—The term "qualifying individual" means—

(A) a dependent of the taxpayer (as defined in section 152(a)(1)) who has not attained age 13,

(B) a dependent of the taxpayer (as defined in section 152, determined without regard to subsections (b)(1), (b)(2), and (d)(1)(B)) who is physically or mentally

* Omitted entirely.

incapable of caring for himself or herself and who has the same principal place of abode as the taxpayer for more than one-half of such taxable year, or

(C) the spouse of the taxpayer, if the spouse is physically or mentally incapable of caring for himself or herself and who has the same principal place of abode as the taxpayer for more than one-half of such taxable year.

(2) Employment-related expenses.—

(A) In general.—The term "employment-related expenses" means amounts paid for the following expenses, but only if such expenses are incurred to enable the taxpayer to be gainfully employed for any period for which there are 1 or more qualifying individuals with respect to the taxpayer:

(i) expenses for household services, and

(ii) expenses for the care of a qualifying individual.

Such term shall not include any amount paid for services outside the taxpayer's household at a camp where the qualifying individual stays overnight.

(B) Exception.—Employment-related expenses described in subparagraph (A) which are incurred for services outside the taxpayer's household shall be taken into account only if incurred for the care of—

(i) a qualifying individual described in paragraph (1)(A), or

(ii) a qualifying individual (not described in paragraph (1)(A)) who regularly spends at least 8 hours each day in the taxpayer's household.

(C) Dependent care centers.—Employment-related expenses described in subparagraph (A) which are incurred for services provided outside the taxpayer's household by a dependent care center (as defined in subparagraph (D)) shall be taken into account only if—

(i) such center complies with all applicable laws and regulations of a State or unit of local government, and

(ii) the requirements of subparagraph (B) are met.

(D) Dependent care center defined.—For purposes of this paragraph, the term "dependent care center" means any facility which—

(i) provides care for more than six individuals (other than individuals who reside at the facility), and

(ii) receives a fee, payment, or grant for providing services for any of the individuals (regardless of whether such facility is operated for profit).

(c) Dollar limit on amount creditable.—The amount of the employment-related expenses incurred during any taxable year which may be taken into account under subsection (a) shall not exceed—

(1) $3,000 if there is 1 qualifying individual with respect to the taxpayer for such taxable year, or

(2) $6,000 if there are 2 or more qualifying individuals with respect to the taxpayer for such taxable year.

The amount determined under paragraph (1) or (2) (whichever is applicable) shall be reduced by the aggregate amount excludable from gross income under section 129 for the taxable year.

(d) Earned income limitation.—

(1) In general.—Except as otherwise provided in this subsection, the amount of the employment-related expenses incurred during any taxable year which may be taken into account under subsection (a) shall not exceed—

(A) in the case of an individual who is not married at the close of such year, such individual's earned income for such year, or

(B) in the case of an individual who is married at the close of such year, the lesser of such individual's earned income or the earned income of his spouse for such year.

(2) Special rule for spouse who is a student or incapable of caring for himself.—In the case of a spouse who is a student or a qualifying individual described in subsection (b)(1)(C), for purposes of paragraph (1), such spouse shall be deemed for each month during which such spouse is a full-time student at an educational institution, or is such a qualifying individual, to be gainfully employed and to have earned income of not less than—

(A) $250 if subsection (c)(1) applies for the taxable year, or

(B) $500 if subsection (c)(2) applies for the taxable year.

In the case of any husband and wife, this paragraph shall apply with respect to only one spouse for any one month.

(e) Special rules.—For purposes of this section—

(1) Place of abode.—An individual shall not be treated as having the same principal place of abode of the taxpayer if at any time during the taxable year of the taxpayer the relationship between the individual and the taxpayer is in violation of local law.

(2) Married couples must file joint return.—If the taxpayer is married at the close of the taxable year, the credit shall be allowed under subsection (a) only if the taxpayer and his spouse file a joint return for the taxable year.

(3) Marital status.—An individual legally separated from his spouse under a decree of divorce or of separate maintenance shall not be considered as married.

(4) Certain married individuals living apart.—If—

(A) an individual who is married and who files a separate return—

(i) maintains as his home a household which constitutes for more than one-half of the taxable year the principal place of abode of a qualifying individual, and

(ii) furnishes over half of the cost of maintaining such household during the taxable year, and

(B) during the last 6 months of such taxable year such individual's spouse is not a member of such household,

such individual shall not be considered as married.

(5) Special dependency test in case of divorced parents, etc.—If—

(A) section 152(e) applies to any child with respect to any calendar year, and

(B) such child is under the age of 13 or is physically or mentally incapable of caring for himself,

in the case of any taxable year beginning in such calendar year, such child shall be treated as a qualifying individual described in subparagraph (A) or (B) of subsection (b)(1) (whichever is appropriate) with respect to the custodial parent (as defined in section 152(e)(4)(A)), and shall not be treated as a qualifying individual with respect to the noncustodial parent.

(6) Payments to related individuals.—No credit shall be allowed under subsection (a) for any amount paid by the taxpayer to an individual—

(A) with respect to whom, for the taxable year, a deduction under section 151(c) (relating to deduction for personal exemptions for dependents) is allowable either to the taxpayer or his spouse, or

(B) who is a child of the taxpayer (within the meaning of section 152(f)(1)) who has not attained the age of 19 at the close of the taxable year.

For purposes of this paragraph, the term "taxable year" means the taxable year of the taxpayer in which the service is performed.

(7) Student.—The term "student" means an individual who during each of 5 calendar months during the taxable year is a full-time student at an educational organization.

(8) Educational organization.—The term "educational organization" means an educational organization described in section 170(b)(1)(A)(ii).

(9) Identifying information required with respect to service provider.—No credit shall be allowed under subsection (a) for any amount paid to any person unless—

(A) the name, address, and taxpayer identification number of such person are included on the return claiming the credit, or

(B) if such person is an organization described in section 501(c)(3) and exempt from tax under section 501(a), the name and address of such person are included on the return claiming the credit.

In the case of a failure to provide the information required under the preceding sentence, the preceding sentence shall not apply if it is shown that the taxpayer exercised due diligence in attempting to provide the information so required.

(10) Identifying information required with respect to qualifying individuals.—No credit shall be allowed under this section with respect to any qualifying individual unless the TIN of such individual is included on the return claiming the credit.

(f) Regulations.—The Secretary shall prescribe such regulations as may be necessary to carry out the purposes of this section.

§ 23. Adoption expenses

(a) Allowance of credit.—

(1) In general.—In the case of an individual, there shall be allowed as a credit against the tax imposed by this chapter the amount of the qualified adoption expenses paid or incurred by the taxpayer.

(2) Year credit allowed.—The credit under paragraph (1) with respect to any expense shall be allowed—

(A) in the case of any expense paid or incurred before the taxable year in which such adoption becomes final, for the taxable year following the taxable year during which such expense is paid or incurred, and

(B) in the case of an expense paid or incurred during or after the taxable year in which such adoption becomes final, for the taxable year in which such expense is paid or incurred.

(3) $10,000 credit for adoption of child with special needs regardless of expenses.—In the case of an adoption of a child with special needs which becomes final during a taxable year, the taxpayer shall be treated as having paid during such year qualified adoption expenses with respect to such adoption in an amount equal to the excess (if any) of $10,000 over the aggregate qualified adoption expenses actually paid or incurred by the taxpayer with respect to such adoption during such taxable year and all prior taxable years.

(b) Limitations.—

(1) Dollar limitation.—The aggregate amount of qualified adoption expenses which may be taken into account under subsection (a) for all taxable years with respect to the adoption of a child by the taxpayer shall not exceed $10,000.

(2) Income limitation.—

(A) In general.—The amount allowable as a credit under subsection (a) for any taxable year (determined without regard to subsection (c)) shall be reduced (but not below zero) by an amount which bears the same ratio to the amount so allowable (determined without regard to this paragraph but with regard to paragraph (1)) as—

(i) the amount (if any) by which the taxpayer's adjusted gross income exceeds $150,000, bears to

(ii) $40,000.

(B) Determination of adjusted gross income.—For purposes of subparagraph (A), adjusted gross income shall be determined without regard to section 911, 931, and 933.

(3) Denial of double benefit.—

(A) In general.—No credit shall be allowed under subsection (a) for any expense for which a deduction or credit is allowed under any other provision of this chapter.

(B) Grants.—No credit shall be allowed under subsection (a) for any expense to the extent that funds for such expense are received under any Federal, State, or local program.

(c) Carryforwards of unused credit.—

(1) In general.—If the credit allowable under subsection (a) for any taxable year exceeds the limitation imposed by section 26(a) for such taxable year reduced by the sum of the credits allowable under this subpart (other than this section and sections 25D and 1400C), such excess shall be carried to the succeeding taxable year and added to the credit allowable under subsection (a) for such taxable year.

(2) Limitation.—No credit may be carried forward under this subsection to any taxable year following the fifth taxable year after the taxable year in which the credit arose. For purposes of the preceding sentence, credits shall be treated as used on a first-in first-out basis.

(d) Definitions.—For purposes of this section—

(1) Qualified adoption expenses.—The term "qualified adoption expenses" means reasonable and necessary adoption fees, court costs, attorney fees, and other expenses—

(A) which are directly related to, and the principal purpose of which is for, the legal adoption of an eligible child by the taxpayer,

(B) which are not incurred in violation of State or Federal law or in carrying out any surrogate parenting arrangement,

(C) which are not expenses in connection with the adoption by an individual of a child who is the child of such individual's spouse, and

(D) which are not reimbursed under an employer program or otherwise.

(2) Eligible child.—The term "eligible child" means any individual who—

(A) has not attained age 18, or

(B) is physically or mentally incapable of caring for himself.

(3) Child with special needs.—The term "child with special needs" means any child if—

(A) a State has determined that the child cannot or should not be returned to the home of his parents,

(B) such State has determined that there exists with respect to the child a specific factor or condition (such as his ethnic background, age, or membership in a minority or sibling group, or the presence of factors such as medical conditions or physical, mental, or emotional handicaps) because of which it is reasonable to conclude that such child cannot be placed with adoptive parents without providing adoption assistance, and

(C) such child is a citizen or resident of the United States (as defined in section 217(h)(3)).

(e) Special rules for foreign adoptions.—In the case of an adoption of a child who is not a citizen or resident of the United States (as defined in section 217(h)(3))—

(1) subsection (a) shall not apply to any qualified adoption expense with respect to such adoption unless such adoption becomes final, and

(2) any such expense which is paid or incurred before the taxable year in which such adoption becomes final shall be taken into account under this section as if such expense were paid or incurred during such year.

(f) Filing requirements.—

(1) Married couples must file joint returns.—Rules similar to the rules of paragraphs (2), (3), and (4) of section 21(e) shall apply for purposes of this section.

(2) Taxpayer must include TIN.—

(A) In general.—No credit shall be allowed under this section with respect to any eligible child unless the taxpayer includes (if known) the name, age, and TIN of such child on the return of tax for the taxable year.

* * *

(g) Basis adjustments.—For purposes of this subtitle, if a credit is allowed under this section for any expenditure with respect to any property, the increase in the basis of such property which would (but for this subsection) result from such expenditure shall be reduced by the amount of the credit so allowed.

(h) Adjustments for inflation.—In the case of a taxable year beginning after December 31, 2002, each of the dollar amounts in subsection (a)(3) and paragraphs (1) and (2)(A)(i) of subsection (b) shall be increased by an amount equal to—

(1) such dollar amount, multiplied by

(2) the cost-of-living adjustment determined under section 1(f)(3) for the calendar year in which the taxable year begins, determined by substituting "calendar year 2001" for "calendar year 1992" in subparagraph (B) thereof.

If any amount as increased under the preceding sentence is not a multiple of $10, such amount shall be rounded to the nearest multiple of $10.

(i) Regulations.—The Secretary shall prescribe such regulations as may be appropriate to carry out this section and section 137, including regulations which treat unmarried individuals who pay or incur qualified adoption expenses with respect to the same child as 1 taxpayer for purposes of applying the dollar amounts in subsections (a)(3) and (b)(1) of this section and in section 137(b)(1).

§ 24. Child tax credit

(a) Allowance of credit.—There shall be allowed as a credit against the tax imposed by this chapter for the taxable year with respect to each qualifying child of the taxpayer for which the taxpayer is allowed a deduction under section 151 an amount equal to $1,000.

(b) Limitation.—

(1) Limitation based on adjusted gross income.—The amount of the credit allowable under subsection (a) shall be reduced (but not below zero) by $50 for each $1,000 (or fraction thereof) by which the taxpayer's modified adjusted gross income exceeds the threshold amount. For purposes of the preceding sentence, the term "modified adjusted gross income" means adjusted gross income increased by any amount excluded from gross income under section 911, 931, or 933.

(2) Threshold amount.—For purposes of paragraph (1), the term "threshold amount" means—

(A) $110,000 in the case of a joint return,

(B) $75,000 in the case of an individual who is not married, and

(C) $55,000 in the case of a married individual filing a separate return.

For purposes of this paragraph, marital status shall be determined under section 7703.

(c) Qualifying child.—For purposes of this section—

(1) In general.—The term "qualifying child" means a qualifying child of the taxpayer (as defined in section 152(c)) who has not attained age 17.

(2) Exception for certain noncitizens.—The term "qualifying child" shall not include any individual who would not be a dependent if subparagraph (A) of section 152(b)(3) were applied without regard to all that follows "resident of the United States".

(d) Portion of credit refundable.—

(1) In general.—The aggregate credits allowed to a taxpayer under subpart C shall be increased by the lesser of—

(A) the credit which would be allowed under this section without regard to this subsection and the limitation under section 26(a) or

(B) the amount by which the aggregate amount of credits allowed by this subpart (determined without regard to this subsection) would increase if the limitation imposed by section 26(a) were increased by the greater of—

(i) 15 percent of so much of the taxpayer's earned income (within the meaning of section 32) which is taken into account in computing taxable income for the taxable year as exceeds $10,000, or

(ii) in the case of a taxpayer with 3 or more qualifying children, the excess (if any) of—

(I) the taxpayer's social security taxes for the taxable year, over

(II) the credit allowed under section 32 for the taxable year.

The amount of the credit allowed under this subsection shall not be treated as a credit allowed under this subpart and shall reduce the amount of credit otherwise allowable under subsection (a) without regard to section 26(a). For purposes of subparagraph (B), any amount excluded from gross income by reason of section 112 shall be treated as earned income which is taken into account in computing taxable income for the taxable year.

(2) Social security taxes.—For purposes of paragraph (1)—

(A) In general—The term "social security taxes" means, with respect to any taxpayer for any taxable year—

(i) the amount of the taxes imposed by section 3101 and 3201(a) on amounts received by the taxpayer during the calendar year in which the taxable year begins,

(ii) 50 percent of the taxes imposed by section 1401 on the self-employment income of the taxpayer for the taxable year, and

(iii) 50 percent of the taxes imposed by section 3211(a)(1) on amounts received by the taxpayer during the calendar year in which the taxable year begins.

(B) Coordination with special refund of social security taxes.—The term "social security taxes" shall not include any taxes to the extent the taxpayer is entitled to a special refund of such taxes under section 6413(c).

(C) Special rule.—Any amounts paid pursuant to an agreement under section 3121(*l*) (relating to agreements entered into by American employers with respect to foreign affiliates) which are equivalent to the taxes referred to in subparagraph (A)(i) shall be treated as taxes referred to in such paragraph.

(3) Inflation adjustment—In the case of any taxable year beginning in a calendar year after 2001, the $10,000 amount contained in paragraph (1)(B) shall be increased by an amount equal to—

(A) such dollar amount, multiplied by

(B) the cost-of-living adjustment determined under section 1(f)(3) for the calendar year in which the taxable year begins, determined by substituting "calendar year 2000" for "calendar year 1992" in subparagraph (B) thereof. Any increase determined under the preceding sentence shall be rounded to the nearest multiple of $50.

(4) Special rule for certain years.—Notwithstanding paragraph (3), in the case of any taxable year beginning after 2008 and before 2018, the dollar amount in effect for such taxable year under paragraph (1)(B)(i) shall be $3,000.

(e) Identification requirement.—No credit shall be allowed under this section to a taxpayer with respect to any qualifying child unless the taxpayer includes the name and taxpayer identification number of such qualifying child on the return of tax for the taxable year.

(f) Taxable year must be full taxable year.—Except in the case of a taxable year closed by reason of the death of the taxpayer, no credit shall be allowable under this section in the case of a taxable year covering a period of less than 12 months.

§ 25A. Hope and Lifetime Learning Credits

(a) Allowance of credit.—In the case of an individual, there shall be allowed as a credit against the tax imposed by this chapter for the taxable year the amount equal to the sum of—

(1) the Hope Scholarship Credit, plus

(2) the Lifetime Learning Credit.

(b) Hope Scholarship Credit.—

(1) Per student credit.—In the case of any eligible student for whom an election is in effect under this section for any taxable year, the Hope Scholarship Credit is an amount equal to the sum of—

(A) 100 percent of so much of the qualified tuition and related expenses paid by the taxpayer during the taxable year (for education furnished to the eligible student during any academic period beginning in such taxable year) as does not exceed $1,000, plus

(B) 50 percent of such expenses so paid as exceeds $1,000 but does not exceed the applicable limit.

(2) Limitations applicable to Hope Scholarship Credit.—

(A) Credit allowed only for 2 taxable years.—An election to have this section apply with respect to any eligible student for purposes of the Hope Scholarship Credit under subsection (a)(1) may not be made for any taxable year if such an election (by the taxpayer or any other individual) is in effect with respect to such student for any 2 prior taxable years.

(B) Credit allowed for year only if individual is at least ½ time student for portion of year.—The Hope Scholarship Credit under subsection (a)(1) shall not be allowed for a taxable year with respect to the qualified tuition and related expenses of an individual unless such individual is an eligible student for at least one academic period which begins during such year.

(C) Credit allowed only for first 2 years of post-secondary education.— The Hope Scholarship Credit under subsection (a)(1) shall not be allowed for a taxable year with respect to the qualified tuition and related expenses of an eligible student if the student has completed (before the beginning of such taxable year) the first 2 years of postsecondary education at an eligible educational institution.

(D) Denial of credit if student convicted of a felony drug offense.—The Hope Scholarship Credit under subsection (a)(1) shall not be allowed for qualified tuition and related expenses for the enrollment or attendance of a student for any academic period if such student has been convicted of a Federal or State felony offense consisting of the possession or distribution of a controlled substance before the end of the taxable year with or within which such period ends.

(3) Eligible student.—For purposes of this subsection, the term "eligible student" means, with respect to any academic period, a student who—

(A) meets the requirements of section 484(a)(1) of the Higher Education Act of 1965 (20 U.S.C. 1091(a)(1)), as in effect on the date of the enactment of this section, and

(B) is carrying at least ½ the normal full-time work load for the course of study the student is pursuing.

(4) Applicable limit.—For purposes of paragraph (1)(B), the applicable limit for any taxable year is an amount equal to 2 times the dollar amount in effect under paragraph (1)(A) for such taxable year.

(c) Lifetime Learning Credit.—

(1) Per taxpayer credit.—The Lifetime Learning Credit for any taxpayer for any taxable year is an amount equal to 20 percent of so much of the qualified tuition and related expenses paid by the taxpayer during the taxable year (for education furnished during any academic period beginning in such taxable year) as does not exceed $10,000 ($5,000 in the case of taxable years beginning before January 1, 2003).

(2) Special rules for determining expenses.—

(A) Coordination with Hope Scholarship.—The qualified tuition and related expenses with respect to an individual who is an eligible student for whom a

Hope Scholarship Credit under subsection (a)(1) is allowed for the taxable year shall not be taken into account under this subsection.

(B) Expenses eligible for Lifetime Learning Credit.—For purposes of paragraph (1), qualified tuition and related expenses shall include expenses described in subsection (f)(1) with respect to any course of instruction at an eligible educational institution to acquire or improve job skills of the individual.

(d) Limitation based on modified adjusted gross income.—

(1) In general.—The amount which would (but for this subsection) be taken into account under subsection (a) for the taxable year shall be reduced (but not below zero) by the amount determined under paragraph (2).

(2) Amount of reduction.—The amount determined under this paragraph is the amount which bears the same ratio to the amount which would be so taken into account as—

(A) the excess of—

(i) the taxpayer's modified adjusted gross income for such taxable year, over

(ii) $40,000 ($80,000 in the case of a joint return), bears to

(B) $10,000 ($20,000 in the case of a joint return).

(3) Modified adjusted gross income.—The term "modified adjusted gross income" means the adjusted gross income of the taxpayer for the taxable year increased by any amount excluded from gross income under section 911, 931, or 933.

(e) Election not to have section apply.—A taxpayer may elect not to have this section apply with respect to the qualified tuition and related expenses of an individual for any taxable year.

(f) Definitions.—For purposes of this section—

(1) Qualified tuition and related expenses.—

(A) In general.—The term "qualified tuition and related expenses" means tuition and fees required for the enrollment or attendance of—

(i) the taxpayer,

(ii) the taxpayer's spouse, or

(iii) any dependent of the taxpayer with respect to whom the taxpayer is allowed a deduction under section 151,

at an eligible educational institution for courses of instruction of such individual at such institution.

(B) Exception for education involving sports, etc.—Such term does not include expenses with respect to any course or other education involving sports, games, or hobbies, unless such course or other education is part of the individual's degree program.

(C) Exception for nonacademic fees.—Such term does not include student activity fees, athletic fees, insurance expenses, or other expenses unrelated to an individual's academic course of instruction.

(2) Eligible educational institution.—The term "eligible educational institution" means an institution—

(A) which is described in section 481 of the Higher Education Act of 1965 (20 U.S.C. 1088), as in effect on the date of the enactment of this section, and

(B) which is eligible to participate in a program under title IV of such Act.

(g) Special rules.—

(1) Identification requirement.—No credit shall be allowed under subsection (a) to a taxpayer with respect to the qualified tuition and related expenses of an individual unless the taxpayer includes the name and taxpayer identification number of such individual on the return of tax for the taxable year.

(2) Adjustment for certain scholarships, etc.—The amount of qualified tuition and related expenses otherwise taken into account under subsection (a) with respect to an individual for an academic period shall be reduced (before the application of subsections (b), (c), and (d)) by the sum of any amounts paid for the benefit of such individual which are allocable to such period as—

(A) a qualified scholarship which is excludable from gross income under section 117,

(B) an educational assistance allowance under chapter 30, 31, 32, 34, or 35 of title 38, United States Code, or under chapter 1606 of title 10, United States Code, and

(C) a payment (other than a gift, bequest, devise, or inheritance within the meaning of section 102(a)) for such individual's educational expenses, or attributable to such individual's enrollment at an eligible educational institution, which is excludable from gross income under any law of the United States.

(3) Treatment of expenses paid by dependent.—If a deduction under section 151 with respect to an individual is allowed to another taxpayer for a taxable year beginning in the calendar year in which such individual's taxable year begins—

(A) no credit shall be allowed under subsection (a) to such individual for such individual's taxable year, and

(B) qualified tuition and related expenses paid by such individual during such individual's taxable year shall be treated for purposes of this section as paid by such other taxpayer.

(4) Treatment of certain prepayments.—If qualified tuition and related expenses are paid by the taxpayer during a taxable year for an academic period which begins during the first 3 months following such taxable year, such academic period shall be treated for purposes of this section as beginning during such taxable year.

(5) Denial of double benefit.—No credit shall be allowed under this section for any expense for which a deduction is allowed under any other provision of this chapter.

(6) No credit for married individuals filing separate returns.—If the taxpayer is a married individual (within the meaning of section 7703), this section shall apply only if the taxpayer and the taxpayer's spouse file a joint return for the taxable year.

(7) Nonresident aliens.—If the taxpayer is a nonresident alien individual for any portion of the taxable year, this section shall apply only if such individual is treated as a resident alien of the United States for purposes of this chapter by reason of an election under subsection (g) or (h) of section 6013.

(h) Inflation adjustments.—

(1) Dollar limitation on amount of credit.—

(A) In general.—In the case of a taxable year beginning after 2001, each of the $1,000 amounts under subsection (b)(1) shall be increased by an amount equal to—

(i) such dollar amount, multiplied by

(ii) the cost-of-living adjustment determined under section 1(f)(3) for the calendar year in which the taxable year begins, determined by substituting "calendar year 2000" for "calendar year 1992" in subparagraph (B) thereof.

(B) Rounding.—If any amount as adjusted under subparagraph (A) is not a multiple of $100, such amount shall be rounded to the next lowest multiple of $100.

(2) Income limits.—

(A) In general.—In the case of a taxable year beginning after 2001, the $40,000 and $80,000 amounts in subsection (d)(2) shall each be increased by an amount equal to—

(i) such dollar amount, multiplied by

(ii) the cost-of-living adjustment determined under section 1(f)(3) for the calendar year in which the taxable year begins, determined by substituting "calendar year 2000" for "calendar year 1992" in subparagraph (B) thereof.

(B) Rounding.—If any amount as adjusted under subparagraph (A) is not a multiple of $1,000, such amount shall be rounded to the next lowest multiple of $1,000.

(i) American Opportunity Tax Credit.—In the case of any taxable year beginning after 2008 and before 2018—

(1) Increase in credit— The Hope Scholarship Credit shall be an amount equal to the sum of—

(A) 100 percent of so much of the qualified tuition and related expenses paid by the taxpayer during the taxable year (for education furnished to the eligible student during any academic period beginning in such taxable year) as does not exceed $2,000, plus

(B) 25 percent of such expenses so paid as exceeds $2,000 but does not exceed $4,000.

(2) Credit allowed for first 4 years of post-secondary education.— Subparagraphs (A) and (C) of subsection (b)(2) shall be applied by substituting "4" for "2".

(3) Qualified tuition and related expenses to include required course materials.— Subsection (f)(1)(A) shall be applied by substituting "tuition, fees, and course materials" for "tuition and fees".

(4) Increase in AGI limits for hope scholarship credit.— In lieu of applying subsection (d) with respect to the Hope Scholarship Credit, such credit (determined without regard to this paragraph) shall be reduced (but not below zero) by the amount which bears the same ratio to such credit (as so determined) as—

(A) the excess of—

(i) the taxpayer's modified adjusted gross income (as defined in subsection (d)(3)) for such taxable year, over

(ii) $80,000 ($160,000 in the case of a joint return), bears to

(B) $10,000 ($20,000 in the case of a joint return).

(5) Portion of credit made refundable.— 40 percent of so much of the credit allowed under subsection (a) as is attributable to the Hope Scholarship Credit (determined after application of paragraph (4) and without regard to this paragraph and section 26(a)) shall be treated as a credit allowable under subpart C (and not allowed under subsection (a)). The preceding sentence shall not apply to any taxpayer for any taxable year if such taxpayer is a child to whom subsection (g) of section 1 applies for such taxable year.

* * *

(j) Regulations.—The Secretary may prescribe such regulations as may be necessary or appropriate to carry out this section, including regulations providing for a recapture of the credit allowed under this section in cases where there is a refund in a subsequent taxable year of any amount which was taken into account in determining the amount of such credit.

§ 26. Limitation based on tax liability; definition of tax liability

(a) Limitation based on amount of tax.—The aggregate amount of credits allowed by this subpart for the taxable year shall not exceed the sum of—

(1) the taxpayer's regular tax liability for the taxable year reduced by the foreign tax credit allowable under section 27(a) and

(2) the tax imposed by section 55(a) for the taxable year.

(b) Regular tax liability.—For purposes of this part—

(1) In general.—The term "regular tax liability" means the tax imposed by this chapter for the taxable year.

(2) Exception for certain taxes.—For purposes of paragraph (1), any tax imposed by any of the following provisions shall not be treated as tax imposed by this chapter:

(A) section 55 (relating to minimum tax),

(B) section 59A (relating to environmental tax),

(C) subsection (m)(5)(B), (q), (t), or (v) of section 72 (relating to additional taxes on certain distributions),

* * *

(c) Tentative minimum tax.—For purposes of this part, the term "tentative minimum tax" means the amount determined under section 55(b)(1).

Subpart C—Refundable Credits

§ 31. Tax withheld on wages

(a) Wage withholding for income tax purposes.—

(1) In general.—The amount withheld as tax under chapter 24 shall be allowed to the recipient of the income as a credit against the tax imposed by this subtitle.

(2) Year of credit.—The amount so withheld during any calendar year shall be allowed as a credit for the taxable year beginning in such calendar year. If more than one taxable year begins in a calendar year, such amount shall be allowed as a credit for the last taxable year so beginning.

* * *

§ 32. Earned income

(a) Allowance of credit.—

(1) In general.—In the case of an eligible individual, there shall be allowed as a credit against the tax imposed by this subtitle for the taxable year an amount equal to the credit percentage of so much of the taxpayer's earned income for the taxable year as does not exceed the earned income amount.

(2) Limitation.—The amount of the credit allowable to a taxpayer under paragraph (1) for any taxable year shall not exceed the excess (if any) of—

(A) the credit percentage of the earned income amount, over

(B) the phaseout percentage of so much of the adjusted gross income (or, if greater, the earned income) of the taxpayer for the taxable year as exceeds the phaseout amount.

(b) Percentages and amounts.—For purposes of subsection (a)—

(1) Percentages.—The credit percentage and the phaseout percentage shall be determined as follows:

(A) In general.—In the case of taxable years beginning after 1995:

In the case of an eligible individual with:	**The credit percentage is:**	**The phaseout percentage is:**
1 qualifying child	34	15.98
2 or more qualifying children	40	21.06
No qualifying children	7.65	7.65

* * *

(2) Amounts—

(A) In general.—Subject to subparagraph (B), the earned income amount and the phaseout amount shall be determined as follows:

In the case of an eligible individual with:	**The earned** amount is:	**The phaseout** amount is:
1 qualifying child	$6,330	$11,610
2 or more qualifying children	$8,890	$11,610
No qualifying children	$4,220	$ 5,280

(B) Joint returns.—In the case of a joint return filed by an eligible individual and such individual's spouse, the phaseout amount determined under subparagraph (A) shall be increased by—

(i) $1,000 in the case of taxable years beginning in 2002, 2003, and 2004,

(ii) $2,000 in the case of taxable years beginning in 2005, 2006, and 2007, and

(iii) $3,000 in the case of taxable years beginning after 2007.

(3) Special rules for certain years.— In the case of any taxable year beginning after 2008 and before 2018—

(A) Increased credit percentage for 3 or more qualifying children.—In the case of a taxpayer with 3 or more qualifying children, the credit percentage is 45 percent.

(B) Reduction of marriage penalty.—

(i) In general.—The dollar amount in effect under paragraph (2)(B) shall be $5,000.

(ii) Inflation adjustment.—In the case of any taxable year beginning in 2010, the $5,000 amount in clause (i) shall be increased by an amount equal to—

(I) such dollar amount, multiplied by

(II) the cost of living adjustment determined under section 1(f)(3) for the calendar year in which the taxable year begins determined by substituting "calendar year 2008" for "calendar year 1992" in subparagraph (B) thereof.

(iii) Rounding.—Subparagraph (A) of subsection (j)(2) shall apply after taking into account any increase under clause (ii).

(c) Definitions and special rules.—For purposes of this section—

(1) Eligible individual.—

(A) In general.—The term "eligible individual" means—

(i) any individual who has a qualifying child for the taxable year, or

(ii) any other individual who does not have a qualifying child for the taxable year, if—

(I) such individual's principal place of abode is in the United States for more than one-half of such taxable year,

(II) such individual (or, if the individual is married, either the individual or the individual's spouse) has attained age 25 but not attained age 65 before the close of the taxable year, and

(III) such individual is not a dependent for whom a deduction is allowable under section 151 to another taxpayer for any taxable year beginning in the same calendar year as such taxable year.

For purposes of the preceding sentence, marital status shall be determined under section 7703.

(B) Qualifying child ineligible.—If an individual is the qualifying child of a taxpayer for any taxable year of such taxpayer beginning in a calendar year, such individual shall not be treated as an eligible individual for any taxable year of such individual beginning in such calendar year.

(C) Exception for individual claiming benefits under section 911.—The term "eligible individual" does not include any individual who claims the benefits of section 911 (relating to citizens or residents living abroad) for the taxable year.

* * *

(E) Identification number requirement.—No credit shall be allowed under this section to an eligible individual who does not include on the return of tax for the taxable year—

(i) such individual's taxpayer identification number, and

(ii) if the individual is married (within the meaning of section 7703), the taxpayer identification number of such individual's spouse.

(F) Individuals who do not include TIN, etc., of any qualifying child.—No credit shall be allowed under this section to any eligible individual who has one or more qualifying children if no qualifying child of such individual is taken into account under subsection (b) by reason of paragraph (3)(D).

(2) Earned income.—

(A) The term "earned income" means—

(i) wages, salaries, tips, and other employee compensation, but only if such amounts are includible in gross income for the taxable year, plus

(ii) the amount of the taxpayer's net earnings from self-employment for the taxable year (within the meaning of section 1402(a)), but such net earnings shall be determined with regard to the deduction allowed to the taxpayer by section 164(f).

(B) For purposes of subparagraph (A)—

(i) the earned income of an individual shall be computed without regard to any community property laws,

(ii) no amount received as a pension or annuity shall be taken into account,

(iii) no amount to which section 871(a) applies (relating to income of nonresident alien individuals not connected with United States business) shall be taken into account,

(iv) no amount received for services provided by an individual while the individual is an inmate at a penal institution shall be taken into account,

(v) no amount described in subparagraph (A) received for service performed in work activities as defined in paragraph (4) or (7) of section 407(d) of the Social Security Act to which the taxpayer is assigned under any State program under part A of title IV of such Act shall be taken into account, but only to the extent such amount is subsidized under such State program, and

(vi) a taxpayer may elect to treat amounts excluded from gross income by reason of section 112 as earned income.

(3) Qualifying child.—

(A) In general.—The term "qualifying child" means a qualifying child of the taxpayer (as defined in section 152(c), determined without regard to paragraph (1)(D) thereof and section 152(e)).

(B) Married individual.—The term "qualifying child" shall not include an individual who is married as of the close of the taxpayer's taxable year unless the taxpayer is entitled to a deduction under section 151 for such taxable year with respect to such individual (or would be so entitled but for section 152(e)).

(C) Place of abode.—For purposes of subparagraph (A), the requirements of section 152(c)(1)(B) shall be met only if the principal place of abode is in the United States.

(D) Identification requirements.—

(i) In general.—A qualifying child shall not be taken into account under subsection (b) unless the taxpayer includes the name, age, and TIN of the qualifying child on the return of tax for the taxable year.

(ii) Other methods.—The Secretary may prescribe other methods for providing the information described in clause (i).

(4) Treatment of military personnel stationed outside the United States.—For purposes of paragraphs (1)(A)(ii)(I) and (3)(C), the principal place of abode of a member of the Armed Forces of the United States shall be treated as in the United States during any period during which such member is stationed outside the United States while serving on extended active duty with the Armed Forces of the United States. For purposes of the preceding sentence, the term "extended active duty" means any period of active duty pursuant to a call or order to such duty for a period in excess of 90 days or for an indefinite period.

* * *

(d) Married individuals.—In the case of an individual who is married (within the meaning of section 7703), this section shall apply only if a joint return is filed for the taxable year under section 6013.

(e) Taxable year must be full taxable year.—Except in the case of a taxable year closed by reason of the death of the taxpayer, no credit shall be allowable under this section in the case of a taxable year covering a period of less than 12 months.

(f) Amount of credit to be determined under tables.—

(1) In general.—The amount of the credit allowed by this section shall be determined under tables prescribed by the Secretary.

(2) Requirements for tables.—The tables prescribed under paragraph (1) shall reflect the provisions of subsections (a) and (b) and shall have income brackets of not greater than $50 each—

(A) for earned income between $0 and the amount of earned income at which the credit is phased out under subsection (b), and

(B) for adjusted gross income between the dollar amount at which the phaseout begins under subsection (b) and the amount of adjusted gross income at which the credit is phased out under subsection (b).

* * *

(i) Denial of credit for individuals having excessive investment income.—

(1) In general.—No credit shall be allowed under subsection (a) for the taxable year if the aggregate amount of disqualified income of the taxpayer for the taxable year exceeds $2,200.

(2) Disqualified income.—For purposes of paragraph (1), the term "disqualified income" means—

(A) interest or dividends to the extent includible in gross income for the taxable year,

(B) interest received or accrued during the taxable year which is exempt from tax imposed by this chapter,

(C) the excess (if any) of—

(i) gross income from rents or royalties not derived in the ordinary course of a trade or business, over

(ii) the sum of—

(I) the deductions (other than interest) which are clearly and directly allocable to such gross income, plus

(II) interest deductions properly allocable to such gross income,

(D) the capital gain net income (as defined in section 1222) of the taxpayer for such taxable year, and

(E) the excess (if any) of—

(i) the aggregate income from all passive activities for the taxable year (determined without regard to any amount included in earned income under subsection (c)(2) or described in a preceding subparagraph), over

(ii) the aggregate losses from all passive activities for the taxable year (as so determined).

For purposes of subparagraph (E), the term "passive activity" has the meaning given such term by section 469.

(j) Inflation adjustments.—

(1) In general.—In the case of any taxable year beginning after 1996, each of the dollar amounts in subsections (b)(2) and (i)(1) shall be increased by an amount equal to—

(A) such dollar amount, multiplied by

(B) the cost-of-living adjustment determined under section 1(f)(3) for the calendar year in which the taxable year begins * * *.

* * *

(k) Restrictions on taxpayers who improperly claimed credit in prior year

(1) Taxpayers making prior fraudulent or reckless claims

(A) In general.—No credit shall be allowed under this section for any taxable year in the disallowance period.

(B) Disallowance period.—For purposes of paragraph (1), the disallowance period is—

(i) the period of 10 taxable years after the most recent taxable year for which there was a final determination that the taxpayer's claim of credit under this section was due to fraud, and

(ii) the period of 2 taxable years after the most recent taxable year for which there was a final determination that the taxpayer's claim of credit under this section was due to reckless or intentional disregard of rules and regulations (but not due to fraud).

(2) Taxpayers making improper prior claims.—In the case of a taxpayer who is denied credit under this section for any taxable year as a result of the deficiency procedures under subchapter B of chapter 63, no credit shall be allowed under this section for any subsequent taxable year unless the taxpayer provides such information as the Secretary may require to demonstrate eligibility for such credit.

(*l*) Coordination with certain means-tested programs.—For purposes of—

(1) the United States Housing Act of 1937,

(2) title V of the Housing Act of 1949,

(3) section 101 of the Housing and Urban Development Act of 1965,

(4) sections 221(d)(3), 235, and 236 of the National Housing Act, and

(5) the Food Stamp Act of 1977,

any refund made to an individual (or the spouse of an individual) by reason of this section, and any payment made to such individual (or such spouse) by an employer under section 3507, shall not be treated as income (and shall not be taken into account in determining resources for the month of its receipt and the following month).

(m) Identification numbers.—Solely for purposes of subsections (c)(1)(E) and (c)(3)(D), a taxpayer identification number means a social security number issued to an individual by the Social Security Administration (other than a social security number issued pursuant to clause (II) (or that portion of clause (III) that relates to clause (II)) of section 205(c)(2)(B)(i) of the Social Security Act).

* * *

Subpart D—Business Related Credits

§ 38. General business credit

(a) Allowance of credit.—There shall be allowed as a credit against the tax imposed by this chapter for the taxable year an amount equal to the sum of—

(1) the business credit carryforwards carried to such taxable year,

(2) the amount of the current year business credit, plus

(3) the business credit carrybacks carried to such taxable year.

(b) Current year business credit.—For purposes of this subpart, the amount of the current year business credit is the sum of the following credits determined for the taxable year:

(1) the investment credit determined under section 46,

* * *

(5) the low-income housing credit determined under section 42(a),

* * *

(c) Limitation based on amount of tax.—

(1) In general.—The credit allowed under subsection (a) for any taxable year shall not exceed the excess (if any) of the taxpayer's net income tax over the greater of—

(A) the tentative minimum tax for the taxable year, or

(B) 25 percent of so much of the taxpayer's net regular tax liability as exceeds $25,000.

For purposes of the preceding sentence, the term "net income tax" means the sum of the regular tax liability and the tax imposed by section 55, reduced by the credits allowable under subparts A and B of this part, and the term "net regular tax liability" means the regular tax liability reduced by the sum of the credits allowable under subparts A and B of this part.

* * *

§ 42. Low-income housing credit

(a) In general.—For purposes of section 38, the amount of the low-income housing credit determined under this section for any taxable year in the credit period shall be an amount equal to—

(1) the applicable percentage of

(2) the qualified basis of each qualified low-income building.

(b) Applicable percentage: 70 percent present value credit for certain new buildings; 30 percent present value credit for certain other buildings.—

(1) Determination of applicable percentage.—For purposes of this section, the term applicable percentage means, with respect to any building, the appropriate percentage prescribed by the Secretary for the earlier of—

(i) the month in which such building is placed in service, or

(ii) at the election of the taxpayer—

(I) the month in which the taxpayer and the housing credit agency enter into an agreement with respect to such building (which is binding on such agency, the taxpayer, and all successors in interest) as to the housing credit dollar amount to be allocated to such building, or

(II) in the case of any building to which subsection (h)(4)(B) applies, the month in which the tax-exempt obligations are issued.

A month may be elected under clause (ii) only if the election is made not later than the 5th day after the close of such month. Such an election, once made, shall be irrevocable.

(B) method of prescribing percentages.—The percentages prescribed by the Secretary for any month shall be percentages which will yield over a 10–year period amounts of credit under subsection (a) which have a present value equal to—

(i) 70 percent of the qualified basis of a new building which is not federally subsidized for the taxable year, and

(ii) 30 percent of the qualified basis of a building not described in clause (i).

* * *

(2) Temporary minimum credit rate for non-Federally subsidized new buildings.— In the case of any new building—

(A) which is placed in service by the taxpayer after the date of the enactment of this paragraph with respect to housing credit dollar amount allocations made before January 1, 2014, and

(B) which is not federally subsidized for the taxable year,

the applicable percentage shall not be less than 9 percent.

(c) Qualified basis; qualified low-income building.—For purposes of this section—

* * *

(2) Qualified low-income building.—The term "qualified low-income building" means any building—

(A) which is part of a qualified low-income housing project at all times during the period—

(i) beginning on the 1st day in the compliance period on which such building is part of such a project, and

(ii) ending on the last day of the compliance period with respect to such building, and

(B) to which the amendments made by section 201(a) of the Tax Reform Act of 1986 apply.

(d) Eligible basis.—For purposes of this section—

* * *

(5) Special rules for determining eligible bases.—

* * *

(B) Increase in credit for buildings in high cost areas.—

(i) In general.—In the case of any building located in a qualified census tract or difficult development area which is designated for purposes of this subparagraph—

(I) in the case of a new building, the eligible basis of such building shall be 130 percent of such basis determined without regard to this subparagraph, and

(II) in the case of an existing building, the rehabilitation expenditures taken into account under subsection (e) shall be 130 percent of such expenditures determined without regard to this subparagraph.

* * *

(f) Definition and special rules relating to credit period.—

(1) Credit period defined.—For purposes of this section, the term "credit period" means, with respect to any building, the period of 10 taxable years beginning with—

(A) the taxable year in which the building is placed in service, or

(B) at the election of the taxpayer, the succeeding taxable year,

but only if the building is a qualified low-income building as of the close of the 1st year of such period. The election under subparagraph (B), once made, shall be irrevocable.

* * *

(g) Qualified low-income housing project.—For purposes of this section—

(1) In general.—The term "qualified low-income housing project" means any project for residential rental property if the project meets the requirements of subparagraph (A) or (B) whichever is elected by the taxpayer:

(A) 20–50 test.—The project meets the requirements of this subparagraph if 20 percent or more of the residential units in such project are both rent-restricted and occupied by individuals whose income is 50 percent or less of area median gross income.

(B) 40–60 test.—The project meets the requirements of this subparagraph if 40 percent or more of the residential units in such project are both rent-restricted and occupied by individuals whose income is 60 percent or less of area median gross income.

Any election under this paragraph, once made, shall be irrevocable. For purposes of this paragraph, any property shall not be treated as failing to be residential rental property merely because part of the building in which such property is located is used for purposes other than residential rental purposes.

* * *

Subpart E—Rules for Computing Investment Credit

§ 46. Amount of credit

For purposes of section 38, the amount of the investment credit determined under this section for any taxable year shall be the sum of—

(1) the rehabilitation credit,

(2) the energy credit,

* * *

§ 47. Rehabilitation credit

(a) General rule.—For purposes of section 46, the rehabilitation credit for any taxable year is the sum of—

(1) 10 percent of the qualified rehabilitation expenditures with respect to any qualified rehabilitated building other than a certified historic structure, and

(2) 20 percent of the qualified rehabilitation expenditures with respect to any certified historic structure.

* * *

(c) Definitions.—For purposes of this section—

(1) Qualified rehabilitated building.—

(A) In general.—The term "qualified rehabilitated building" means any building (and its structural components) if—

(i) such building has been substantially rehabilitated,

(ii) such building was placed in service before the beginning of the rehabilitation,

(iii) in the case of any building other than a certified historic structure, in the rehabilitation process—

(I) 50 percent or more of the existing external walls of such building are retained in place as external walls,

(II) 75 percent of more of the existing external walls of such building are retained in place as internal or external walls, and

(III) 75 percent or more of the existing internal structural framework of such building is retained in place, and

(iv) depreciation (or amortization in lieu of depreciation) is allowable with respect to such building.

(B) Building must be first placed in service before 1936.—In the case of a building other than a certified historic structure, a building shall not be a qualified rehabilitated building unless the building was first placed in service before 1936.

(C) Substantially rehabilitated defined.—

(i) In general.—For purposes of subparagraph (A)(i), a building shall be treated as having been substantially rehabilitated only if the qualified rehabilitation expenditures during the 24–month period selected by the taxpayer (at the time and in the manner prescribed by regulation) and ending with or within the taxable year exceed the greater of—

(I) the adjusted basis of such building (and its structural components), or

(II) $5,000.

* * *

§ 49. At-risk rules

(a) General rule.—

(1) Certain nonrecourse financing excluded from credit base.—

(A) Limitation.—The credit base of any property to which this paragraph applies shall be reduced by the nonqualified nonrecourse financing with respect to such credit base (as of the close of the taxable year in which placed in service).

(B) Property to which paragraph applies.—This paragraph applies to any property which—

(i) is placed in service during the taxable year by a taxpayer described in section 465(a)(1), and

(ii) is used in connection with an activity with respect to which any loss is subject to limitation under section 465.

(C) Credit base defined.—For purposes of this paragraph, the term "credit base" means—

(i) the portion of the basis of any qualified rehabilitated building attributable to qualified rehabilitation expenditures,

(ii) the basis of any energy property,

* * *

(D) Nonqualified nonrecourse financing.—

(i) In general.—For purposes of this paragraph and paragraph (2), the term "nonqualified nonrecourse financing" means any nonrecourse financing which is not qualified commercial financing.

(ii) Qualified commercial financing.—For purposes of this paragraph, the term "qualified commercial financing" means any financing with respect to any property if—

(I) such property is acquired by the taxpayer from a person who is not a related person,

(II) the amount of the nonrecourse financing with respect to such property does not exceed 80 percent of the credit base of such property, and

(III) such financing is borrowed from a qualified person or represents a loan from any Federal, State, or local government or instrumentality thereof, or is guaranteed by any Federal, State, or local government.

Such term shall not include any convertible debt.

(iii) Nonrecourse financing.—For purposes of this subparagraph, the term "nonrecourse financing" includes—

(I) any amount with respect to which the taxpayer is protected against loss through guarantees, stop-loss agreements, or other similar arrangements, and

(II) except to the extent provided in regulations, any amount borrowed from a person who has an interest (other than as a creditor) in the activity in which the property is used or from a related person to a person (other than the taxpayer) having such an interest.

In the case of amounts borrowed by a corporation from a shareholder, subclause (II) shall not apply to an interest as a shareholder.

(iv) Qualified person.—For purposes of this paragraph, the term "qualified person" means any person which is actively and regularly engaged in the business of lending money and which is not—

(I) a related person with respect to the taxpayer,

(II) a person from which the taxpayer acquired the property (or a related person to such person), or

(III) a person who receives a fee with respect to the taxpayer's investment in the property (or a related person to such person).

(v) Related person.—For purposes of this subparagraph, the term "related person" has the meaning given such term by section 465(b)(3)(C). Except as otherwise provided in regulations prescribed by the Secretary, the determination of whether a person is a related person shall be made as of the close of the taxable year in which the property is placed in service.

(E) Application to partnerships and S corporations.—For purposes of this paragraph and paragraph (2)—

(i) In general.—Except as otherwise provided in this subparagraph, in the case of any partnership or S corporation, the determination of whether a partner's or shareholder's allocable share of any financing is nonqualified nonrecourse financing shall be made at the partner or shareholder level.

(ii) Special rule for certain recourse financing of S corporation.—A shareholder of an S corporation shall be treated as liable for his allocable share of any financing provided by a qualified person to such corporation if—

(I) such financing is recourse financing (determined at the corporate level), and

(II) such financing is provided with respect to qualified business property of such corporation.

(iii) Qualified business property.—For purposes of clause (ii), the term "qualified business property" means any property if—

(I) such property is used by the corporation in the active conduct of a trade or business,

(II) during the entire 12–month period ending on the last day of the taxable year, such corporation had at least 3 full-time employees who were not owner-employees (as defined in section 465(c)(7)(E)(i)) and substantially all the services of whom were services directly related to such trade or business, and

(III) during the entire 12-month period ending on the last day of such taxable year, such corporation had at least 1 full-time employee substantially all the services of whom were in the active management of the trade or business.

* * *

Subpart G—Credit Against Regular Tax for Prior Year Minimum Tax Liability

§ 53. Credit for prior year minimum tax liability

(a) Allowance of credit.—There shall be allowed as a credit against the tax imposed by this chapter for any taxable year an amount equal to the minimum tax credit for such taxable year.

(b) Minimum tax credit.—For purposes of subsection (a), the minimum tax credit for any taxable year is the excess (if any) of—

(1) the adjusted net minimum tax imposed for all prior taxable years beginning after 1986, over

(2) the amount allowable as a credit under subsection (a) for such prior taxable years.

(c) Limitation.—The credit allowable under subsection (a) for any taxable year shall not exceed the excess (if any) of—

(1) the regular tax liability of the taxpayer for such taxable year reduced by the sum of the credits allowable under subparts A, B, D, E, and F of this part, over

(2) the tentative minimum tax for the taxable year.

(d) Definitions.—For purposes of this section—

(1) Net minimum tax.—

(A) In general.—The term "net minimum tax" means the tax imposed by section 55.

(B) Credit not allowed for exclusion preferences.—

(i) Adjusted net minimum tax.—The adjusted net minimum tax for any taxable year is—

(I) the amount of the net minimum tax for such taxable year, reduced by

(II) the amount which would be the net minimum tax for such taxable year if the only adjustments and items of tax preference taken into account were those specified in clause (ii).

(ii) Specified items.—The following are specified in this clause—

(I) the adjustments provided for in subsection (b)(1) of section 56, and

(II) the items of tax preference described in paragraphs (5) and (7) of section 57(a).

* * *

(2) Tentative minimum tax.—The term "tentative minimum tax" has the meaning given to such term by section 55(b).

(e) Special rule for individuals with long-term unused credits.—

(1) In general.—If an individual has a long-term unused minimum tax credit for any taxable year beginning before January 1, 2013, the amount determined under subsection (c) for such taxable year shall not be less than the AMT refundable credit amount for such taxable year.

(2) AMT refundable credit amount.—For purposes of paragraph (1), the term "AMT refundable credit amount" means, with respect to any taxable year, the amount (not in excess of the long-term unused minimum tax credit for such taxable year) equal to the greater of—(A) 50 percent of the long-term unused minimum tax credit for such taxable year, or (B) the amount (if any) of the AMT refundable credit amount determined under this paragraph for the taxpayer's preceding taxable year (determined without regard to subsection (f)(2)).

(3) Long-term unused minimum tax credit.—

(A) In general.—For purposes of this subsection, the term "long-term unused minimum tax credit" means, with respect to any taxable year, the portion of the minimum tax credit determined under subsection (b) attributable to the adjusted net minimum tax for taxable years before the 3rd taxable year immediately preceding such taxable year.

(B) First-in, first-out ordering rule.—For purposes of subparagraph (A), credits shall be treated as allowed under subsection (a) on a first-in, first-out basis.

(4) Credit refundable.—For purposes of this title (other than this section), the credit allowed by reason of this subsection shall be treated as if it were allowed under subpart C.

PART VI—ALTERNATIVE MINIMUM TAX

§ 55. Alternative minimum tax imposed

(a) General rule.—There is hereby imposed (in addition to any other tax imposed by this subtitle) a tax equal to the excess (if any) of—

(1) the tentative minimum tax for the taxable year, over

(2) the regular tax for the taxable year.

(b) Tentative minimum tax.—For purposes of this part—

(1) Amount of tentative tax.—

(A) Noncorporate taxpayers.—

(i) In general.—In the case of a taxpayer other than a corporation, the tentative minimum tax for the taxable year is the sum of—

(I) 26 percent of so much of the taxable excess as does not exceed $175,000, plus

(II) 28 percent of so much of the taxable excess as exceeds $175,000.

The amount determined under the preceding sentence shall be reduced by the alternative minimum tax foreign tax credit for the taxable year.

(ii) Taxable excess.—For purposes of this subsection, the term "taxable excess" means so much of the alternative minimum taxable income for the taxable year as exceeds the exemption amount.

(iii) Married individual filing separate return.—In the case of a married individual filing a separate return, clause (i) shall be applied by substituting 50 percent of the dollar amount otherwise applicable under subclause (I) and subclause (II) thereof. For purposes of the preceding sentence, marital status shall be determined under section 7703.

(B) Corporations.—In the case of a corporation, the tentative minimum tax for the taxable year is—

(i) 20 percent of so much of the alternative minimum taxable income for the taxable year as exceeds the exemption amount, reduced by

(ii) the alternative minimum tax foreign tax credit for the taxable year.

(2) Alternative minimum taxable income.—The term "alternative minimum taxable income" means the taxable income of the taxpayer for the taxable year—

(A) determined with the adjustments provided in section 56 and section 58, and

(B) increased by the amount of the items of tax preference described in section 57.

If a taxpayer is subject to the regular tax, such taxpayer shall be subject to the tax imposed by this section (and, if the regular tax is determined by reference to an amount other than taxable income, such amount shall be treated as the taxable income of such taxpayer for purposes of the preceding sentence).

(3) Maximum rate of tax on net capital gain of noncorporate taxpayers.—The amount determined under the first sentence of paragraph (1)(A)(i) shall not exceed the sum of—

(A) the amount determined under such first sentence computed at the rates and in the same manner as if this paragraph had not been enacted on the taxable excess reduced by the lesser of—

(i) the net capital gain, or

(ii) the sum of—

(I) the adjusted net capital gain, plus

(II) the unrecaptured section 1250 gain, plus

(B) 0 percent of so much of the adjusted net capital gain (or, if less, taxable excess) as does not exceed an amount equal to the excess described in section 1(h)(1)(B), plus

(C) 15 percent of the lesser of—

(i) so much of the adjusted net capital gain (or, if less, taxable excess) as exceeds the amount on which tax is determined under subparagraph (B), or

(ii) the excess described in section 1(h)(1)(C)(ii), plus

(D) 20 percent of the adjusted net capital gain (or, if less, taxable excess) in excess of the sum of the amounts on which tax is determined under subparagraphs (B) and (C), plus

(E) 25 percent of the amount of taxable excess in excess of the sum of the amounts on which tax is determined under the preceding subparagraphs of this paragraph.

Terms used in this paragraph which are also used in section 1(h) shall have the respective meanings given such terms by section 1(h).

* * *

(c) Regular tax.—

(1) In general.—For purposes of this section, the term "regular tax" means the regular tax liability for the taxable year (as defined in section 26(b)) reduced by the foreign tax credit allowable * * *.

* * *

(d) Exemption amount.—For purposes of this section—

(1) Exemption amount for taxpayers other than corporations.—In the case of a taxpayer other than a corporation, the term "exemption amount" means—

(A) $78,750 in the case of—

(i) a joint return, or

(ii) a surviving spouse,

(B) $50,600 in the case of an individual who—

(i) is not a married individual, and

(ii) is not a surviving spouse, and

(C) 50 percent of the dollar amount applicable under paragraph (1)(A) in the case of a married individual who files a separate return, and

(D) $22,500 in the case of an estate or trust.

For purposes of this paragraph, the term "surviving spouse" has the meaning given to such term by section 2(a), and marital status shall be determined under section 7703.

(2) Corporations.—In the case of a corporation, the term "exemption amount" means $40,000.

(3) Phase-out of exemption amount.—The exemption amount of any taxpayer shall be reduced (but not below zero) by an amount equal to 25 percent of the amount by which the alternative minimum taxable income of the taxpayer exceeds—

(A) $150,000 in the case of a taxpayer described in paragraph (1)(A),

(B) $112,500 in the case of a taxpayer described in paragraph (1)(B),

(C) 50 percent of the dollar amount applicable under subparagraph (A) in the case of a taxpayer described in subparagraph (C) or (D) of paragraph (1), and

(D) $150,000 in the case of a taxpayer described in paragraph (2).

(4) Inflation adjustment.—

(A) In general.—In the case of any taxable year beginning in a calendar year after 2012, the amounts described in subparagraph (B) shall each be increased by an amount equal to—

(i) such dollar amount, multiplied by

(ii) the cost-of-living adjustment determined under section 1(f)(3) for the calendar year in which the taxable year begins, determined by substituting "calendar year 2011" for "calendar year 1992" in subparagraph (B) thereof.

(B) Amounts described.—The amounts described in this subparagraph are—

(i) each of the dollar amounts contained in subsection (b)(1)(A)(i),

(ii) each of the dollar amounts contained in paragraph (1), and

(iii) each of the dollar amounts in subparagraphs (A) and (B) of paragraph (3).

(C) Rounding.—Any increase determined under subparagraph (A) shall be rounded to the nearest multiple of $100.

(e) Exemption for small corporations

(1) In general.—

(A) $7,500,000 gross receipts test.—The tentative minimum tax of a corporation shall be zero for any taxable year if the corporation's average annual gross receipts for all 3–taxable-year periods ending before such taxable year does not exceed $7,500,000. For purposes of the preceding sentence, only taxable years beginning after December 31, 1993, shall be taken into account.

(B) $5,000,000 gross receipts test for first 3–year period.—Subparagraph (A) shall be applied by substituting "$5,000,000" for "$7,500,000" for the first 3–

taxable-year period (or portion thereof) of the corporation which is taken into account under subparagraph (A).

(C) First taxable year corporation in existence.—If such taxable year is the first taxable year that such corporation is in existence, the tentative minimum tax of such corporations for such year shall be zero.

(D) Special rules.—For purposes of this paragraph, the rules of paragraphs (2) and (3) of section 448(c) shall apply.

* * *

§ 56. Adjustments in computing alternative minimum taxable income

(a) Adjustments applicable to all taxpayers.—In determining the amount of the alternative minimum taxable income for any taxable year the following treatment shall apply (in lieu of the treatment applicable for purposes of computing the regular tax):

(1) Depreciation.—

(A) In general.—

(i) Property other than certain personal property.—Except as provided in clause (ii), the depreciation deduction allowable under section 167 with respect to any tangible property placed in service after December 31, 1986, shall be determined under the alternative system of section 168(g). In the case of property placed in service after December 31, 1998, the preceding sentence shall not apply but clause (ii) shall continue to apply.

(ii) 150-percent declining balance method for certain property.—The method of depreciation used shall be—

(I) the 150 percent declining balance method,

(II) switching to the straight line method for the 1st taxable year for which using the straight line method with respect to the adjusted basis as of the beginning of the year will yield a higher allowance.

The preceding sentence shall not apply to any section 1250 property (as defined in section 1250(c)) (and the straight line method shall be used for such section 1250 property) or to any other property if the depreciation deduction determined under section 168 with respect to such other property for purposes of the regular tax is determined by using the straight line method.

(B) Exception for certain property.—This paragraph shall not apply to property described in paragraph (1), (2), (3), or (4) of section 168(f), or in section 168(e)(3)(C)(iv).

* * *

(3) Treatment of certain long-term contracts.—In the case of any long-term contract entered into by the taxpayer on or after March 1, 1986, the taxable income from such contract shall be determined under the percentage of completion method of accounting (as modified by section 460(b)). For purposes of the preceding sentence, in the case of a contract described in section 460(e)(1), the percentage of the contract completed shall be determined under section 460(b)(1) by using the simplified procedures for allocation of costs prescribed under section 460(b)(3). The first sentence of this paragraph shall not apply to any home construction contract (as defined in section 460(e)(6)).

(4) Alternative tax net operating loss deduction.—The alternative tax net operating loss deduction shall be allowed in lieu of the net operating loss deduction allowed under section 172.

* * *

(6) Adjusted basis.—The adjusted basis of any property to which paragraph (1) or (5) applies (or with respect to which there are any expenditures to which paragraph (2) or subsection (b)(2) applies) shall be determined on the basis of the treatment prescribed in paragraph (1), (2), or (5), or subsection (b)(2), whichever applies.

* * *

(b) Adjustments applicable to individuals.—In determining the amount of the alternative minimum taxable income of any taxpayer (other than a corporation), the following treatment shall apply (in lieu of the treatment applicable for purposes of computing the regular tax):

(1) Limitation on itemized deductions.—

(A) In general.—No deduction shall be allowed—

(i) for any miscellaneous itemized deduction (as defined in section 67(b)), or

(ii) for any taxes described in paragraph (1), (2), or (3) of section 164(a) or clause (ii) of section 164(b)(5)(A).

Clause (ii) shall not apply to any amount allowable in computing adjusted gross income.

(B) Medical expenses.—In determining the amount allowable as a deduction under section 213, subsection (a) of section 213 shall be applied without regard to subsection (f) of such section.

(C) Interest.—In determining the amount allowable as a deduction for interest, subsections (d) and (h) of section 163 shall apply, except that—

(i) in lieu of the exception under section 163(h)(2)(D), the term "personal interest" shall not include any qualified housing interest (as defined in subsection (e)),

(ii) sections 163(d)(6) and 163(h)(5) (relating to phase-ins) shall not apply,

(iii) interest on any specified private activity bond (and any amount treated as interest on a specified private activity bond under section 57(a)(5)(B)), and any deduction referred to in section 57(a)(5)(A), shall be treated as includible in gross income (or as deductible) for purposes of applying section 163(d),

(iv) in lieu of the exception under section 163(d)(3)(B)(i), the term "investment interest" shall not include any qualified housing interest (as defined in subsection (e)), and

(v) the adjustments of this section and sections 57 and 58 shall apply in determining net investment income under section 163(d).

(D) Treatment of certain recoveries.—No recovery of any tax to which subparagraph (A)(ii) applied shall be included in gross income for purposes of determining alternative minimum taxable income.

(E) Standard deduction and deduction for personal exemptions not allowed.—The standard deduction under section 63(c), the deduction for personal exemptions under section 151, and the deduction under section 642(b) shall not be allowed. The preceding sentence shall not apply to so much of the standard deduction as is determined under subparagraphs (D) and (E) of section 63(c)(1).

(F) Section 68 not applicable.—Section 68 shall not apply.

* * *

(3) Treatment of incentive stock options.—Section 421 shall not apply to the transfer of stock acquired pursuant to the exercise of an incentive stock option (as defined in section 422). Section 422(c)(2) shall apply in any case where the disposition and the inclusion for purposes of this part are within the same taxable year and such section shall not apply in any other case. The adjusted basis of any stock so acquired shall be determined on the basis of the treatment prescribed by this paragraph.

(c) Adjustments applicable to corporations.—In determining the amount of the alternative minimum taxable income of a corporation, the following treatment shall apply:

(1) Adjustment for adjusted current earnings.—Alternative minimum taxable income shall be adjusted as provided in subsection (g).

* * *

(d) Alternative tax net operating loss deduction defined.—

(1) In general.—For purposes of subsection (a)(4), the term "alternative tax net operating loss deduction" means the net operating loss deduction allowable for the taxable year under section 172, except that—

(A) the amount of such deduction shall not exceed the sum of—

(i) the lesser of—

(I) the amount of such deduction attributable to net operating losses (other than the deduction described in clause (ii)(I)), or

(II) 90 percent of alternative minimum taxable income determined without regard to such deduction and the deduction under section 199, plus

(ii) the lesser of—

(I) the amount of such deduction attributable to an applicable net operating loss with respect to which an election is made under section 172(b)(1)(H), or

(II) alternative minimum taxable income determined without regard to such deduction and the deduction under section 199 reduced by the amount determined under clause (i), and

(B) in determining the amount of such deduction—

(i) the net operating loss (within the meaning of section 172(c)) for any loss year shall be adjusted as provided in paragraph (2), and

(ii) appropriate adjustments in the application of section 172(b)(2) shall be made to take into account the limitation of subparagraph (A).

(2) Adjustments to net operating loss computation.—

(A) Post–1986 loss years.—In the case of a loss year beginning after December 31, 1986, the net operating loss for such year under section 172(c) shall—

(i) be determined with the adjustments provided in this section and section 58, and

(ii) be reduced by the items of tax preference determined under section 57 for such year.

An item of tax preference shall be taken into account under clause (ii) only to the extent such item increased the amount of the net operating loss for the taxable year under section 172(c).

* * *

(e) Qualified housing interest.—For purposes of this part—

(1) In general.—The term "qualified housing interest" means interest which is qualified residence interest (as defined in section 163(h)(3)) and is paid or accrued during the taxable year on indebtedness which is incurred in acquiring, constructing, or substantially improving any property which—

(A) is the principal residence (within the meaning of section 121) of the taxpayer at the time such interest accrues, or

(B) is a qualified dwelling which is a qualified residence (within the meaning of section 163(h)(4)).

Such term also includes interest on any indebtedness resulting from the refinancing of indebtedness meeting the requirements of the preceding sentence; but only to the extent that the amount of the indebtedness resulting from such refinancing does not exceed the amount of the refinanced indebtedness immediately before the refinancing.

(2) Qualified dwelling.—The term "qualified dwelling" means any—

(A) house,

(B) apartment,

(C) condominium, or

(D) mobile home not used on a transient basis (within the meaning of section 7701(a)(19)(C)(v)),

including all structures or other property appurtenant thereto.

* * *

(g) Adjustments based on adjusted current earnings.—

(1) In general.—The alternative minimum taxable income of any corporation for any taxable year shall be increased by 75 percent of the excess (if any) of—

(A) the adjusted current earnings of the corporation, over

(B) the alternative minimum taxable income (determined without regard to this subsection and the alternative tax net operating loss deduction).

(2) Allowance of negative adjustments.—

(A) In general.—The alternative minimum taxable income for any corporation of any taxable year, shall be reduced by 75 percent of the excess (if any) of—

(i) the amount referred to in subparagraph (B) of paragraph (1), over

(ii) the amount referred to in subparagraph (A) of paragraph (1).

(B) Limitation.—The reduction under subparagraph (A) for any taxable year shall not exceed the excess (if any) of—

(i) the aggregate increases in alternative minimum taxable income under paragraph (1) for prior taxable years, over

(ii) the aggregate reductions under subparagraph (A) of this paragraph for prior taxable years.

(3) Adjusted current earnings.—For purposes of this subsection, the term "adjusted current earnings" means the alternative minimum taxable income for the taxable year—

(A) determined with the adjustments provided in paragraph (4), and

(B) determined without regard to this subsection and the alternative tax net operating loss deduction.

* * *

(4) Adjustments.—In determining adjusted current earnings, the following adjustments shall apply:

(A) Depreciation.—

(i) Property placed in service after 1989.—The depreciation deduction with respect to any property placed in service in a taxable year beginning after 1989 shall be determined under the alternative system of section 168(g). The preceding sentence shall not apply to any property placed in service after December 31, 1993, and the depreciation deduction with respect to such property shall be determined under the rules of subsection (a)(1)(A).

* * *

(B) Inclusion of items included for purposes of computing earnings and profits.—

(i) In general.—In the case of any amount which is excluded from gross income for purposes of computing alternative minimum taxable income but is taken into account in determining the amount of earnings and profits—

(I) such amount shall be included in income in the same manner as if such amount were includible in gross income for purposes of computing alternative minimum taxable income, and

(II) the amount of such income shall be reduced by any deduction which would have been allowable in computing alternative minimum taxable income if such amount were includible in gross income.

The preceding sentence shall not apply in the case of any amount excluded from gross income under section 108 (or the corresponding provisions of prior law) or under section 139A or 1357. * * *

* * *

(C) Disallowance of items not deductible in computing earnings and profits.—

(i) In general.—A deduction shall not be allowed for any item if such item would not be deductible for any taxable year for purposes of computing earnings and profits.

(ii) Special rule for certain dividends.—

(I) In general.—Clause (i) shall not apply to any deduction allowable under section 243 or 245 for any dividend which is a 100–percent dividend or which is received from a 20–percent owned corporation (as defined in section 243(c)(2)), but only to the extent such dividend is attributable to income of the paying corporation which is subject to tax under this chapter (determined after the application of sections 30A, 936 (including subsections (a)(4), (i), and (j) thereof) and 921 (as in effect before its repeal * * *.)).

(II) 100–percent dividend.—For purposes of subclause (I), the term "100 percent dividend" means any dividend if the percentage used for purposes of determining the amount allowable as a deduction under section 243 or 245 with respect to such dividend is 100 percent.

* * *

(v) Deduction for domestic production.—Clause (i) shall not apply to any amount allowable as a deduction under section 199.

* * *

(D) Certain other earnings and profits adjustments.—

(i) Intangible drilling costs.—The adjustments provided in section 312(n)(2)(A) shall apply in the case of amounts paid or incurred in taxable years beginning after December 31, 1989. In the case of a taxpayer other than an integrated oil company (as defined in section 291(b)(4)), in the case of any oil or gas well, this clause shall not apply in the case of amounts paid or incurred in taxable years beginning after December 31, 1992.

(ii) Certain amortization provisions not to apply.—Sections 173 and 248 shall not apply to expenditures paid or incurred in taxable years beginning after December 31, 1989.

(iii) LIFO inventory adjustments.—The adjustments provided in section 312(n)(4) shall apply, but only with respect to taxable years beginning after December 31, 1989.

* * *

(H) Adjusted basis.—The adjusted basis of any property with respect to which an adjustment under this paragraph applies shall be determined by applying the treatment prescribed in this paragraph.

* * *

(6) Exception for certain corporations.—This subsection shall not apply to any S corporation, * * *.

§ 57. Items of tax preference

(a) General rule.—For purposes of this part, the items of tax preference determined under this section are—

(1) Depletion.—With respect to each property (as defined in section 614), the excess of the deduction for depletion allowable under section 611 for the taxable year over the adjusted basis of the property at the end of the taxable year (determined without regard to the depletion deduction for the taxable year). Effective with respect to taxable years beginning after December 31, 1992, this paragraph shall not apply to any deduction for depletion computed in accordance with section 613A(c).

(2) Intangible drilling costs.—

(A) In general.—With respect to all oil, gas, and geothermal properties of the taxpayer, the amount (if any) by which the amount of the excess intangible drilling costs arising in the taxable year is greater than 65 percent of the net income of the taxpayer from oil, gas, and geothermal properties for the taxable year.

(B) Excess intangible drilling costs.—For purposes of subparagraph (A), the amount of the excess intangible drilling costs arising in the taxable year is the excess of—

(i) the intangible drilling and development costs paid or incurred in connection with oil, gas, and geothermal wells (other than costs incurred in drilling a nonproductive well) allowable under section 263(c) or 291(b) for the taxable year, over

(ii) the amount which would have been allowable for the taxable year if such costs had been capitalized and straight line recovery of intangibles (as defined in subsection (b)) had been used with respect to such costs.

(C) Net income from oil, gas, and geothermal properties.—For purposes of subparagraph (A), the amount of the net income of the taxpayer from oil, gas, and geothermal properties for the taxable year is the excess of—

(i) the aggregate amount of gross income (within the meaning of section 613(a)) from all oil, gas, and geothermal properties of the taxpayer received or accrued by the taxpayer during the taxable year, over

(ii) the amount of any deductions allocable to such properties reduced by the excess described in subparagraph (B) for such taxable year.

(D) Paragraph applied separately with respect to geothermal properties and oil and gas properties.—This paragraph shall be applied separately with respect to—

(i) all oil and gas properties which are not described in clause (ii), and

(ii) all properties which are geothermal deposits (as defined in section 613(e)(2)).

(E) Exception for independent producers.—In the case of any oil or gas well—

(i) In general.—In the case of any taxable year beginning after December 31, 1992, this paragraph shall not apply to any taxpayer which is not an integrated oil company (as defined in section 291(b)(4)).

(ii) Limitation on benefit.—The reduction in alternative minimum taxable income by reason of clause (i) for any taxable year shall not exceed 40 percent (30 percent in case of taxable years beginning in 1993) of the alternative minimum taxable income for such year determined without regard to clause (i) and the alternative tax net operating loss deduction under section 56(a)(4).

* * *

(5) Tax-exempt interest.—

(A) In general.—Interest on specified private activity bonds reduced by any deduction (not allowable in computing the regular tax) which would have been allowable if such interest were includible in gross income.

* * *

(C) Specified private activity bonds.—

(i) In general.—For purposes of this part, the term "specified private activity bond" means any private activity bond (as defined in section 141) which is issued after August 7, 1986, and the interest on which is not includible in gross income under section 103.

* * *

(vi) Exception for bonds issued in 2009 and 2010.—

(I) In general.—For purposes of clause (i), the term "private activity bond" shall not include any bond issued after December 31, 2008, and before January 1, 2011.

* * *

(6) Accelerated depreciation or amortization on certain property placed in service before January 1, 1987.—The amounts which would be treated as items of tax preference with respect to the taxpayer under paragraphs (2), (3), (4), and (12) of this subsection (as in effect on the day before the date of the enactment of the Tax Reform Act of 1986). The preceding sentence shall not apply to any property to which section 56(a)(1) or (5) applies.

(7) Exclusion for gains on sale of certain small business stock.—An amount equal to 7 percent of the amount excluded from gross income for the taxable year under section 1202.

(b) Straight line recovery of intangibles defined.—For purposes of paragraph (2) of subsection (a)—

(1) In general.—The term "straight line recovery of intangibles", when used with respect to intangible drilling and development costs for any well, means (except in the case of an election under paragraph (2)) ratable amortization of such costs over the 120–month period beginning with the month in which production from such well begins.

(2) Election.—If the taxpayer elects with respect to the intangible drilling and development costs for any well, the term "straight line recovery of intangibles" means any method which would be permitted for purposes of determining cost depletion with respect to such well and which is selected by the taxpayer for purposes of subsection (a)(2).

§ 58. Denial of certain losses

(a) Denial of farm loss.—

(1) In general.—For purposes of computing the amount of the alternative minimum taxable income for any taxable year of a taxpayer other than a corporation—

(A) Disallowance of farm loss.—No loss of the taxpayer for such taxable year from any tax shelter farm activity shall be allowed.

(B) Deduction in succeeding taxable year.—Any loss from a tax shelter farm activity disallowed under subparagraph (A) shall be treated as a deduction allocable to such activity in the 1st succeeding taxable year.

* * *

(b) Disallowance of passive activity loss.—In computing the alternative minimum taxable income of the taxpayer for any taxable year, section 469 shall apply, except that in applying section 469—

(1) the adjustments of sections 56 and 57 shall apply,

(2) the provisions of section 469(m) (relating to phase-in of disallowance) shall not apply, and

(3) in lieu of applying section 469(j)(7), the passive activity loss of a taxpayer shall be computed without regard to qualified housing interest (as defined in section 56(e)).

(c) Special rules.—For purposes of this section—

(1) Special rule for insolvent taxpayers.—

(A) In general.—The amount of losses to which subsection (a) or (b) applies shall be reduced by the amount (if any) by which the taxpayer is insolvent as of the close of the taxable year.

(B) Insolvent.—For purposes of this paragraph, the term "insolvent" means the excess of liabilities over the fair market value of assets.

(2) Loss allowed for year of disposition of farm shelter activity.—If the taxpayer disposes of his entire interest in any tax shelter farm activity during any taxable year, the amount of the loss attributable to such activity (determined after carryovers under subsection (a)(1)(B)) shall (to the extent otherwise allowable) be allowed for such taxable year in computing alternative minimum taxable income and not treated as a loss from a tax shelter farm activity.

SUBCHAPTER B—COMPUTATION OF TAXABLE INCOME

PART I—DEFINITION OF GROSS INCOME, ADJUSTED GROSS INCOME, TAXABLE INCOME, ETC.

§ 61. Gross income defined

(a) General definition.—Except as otherwise provided in this subtitle, gross income means all income from whatever source derived, including (but not limited to) the following items:

(1) Compensation for services, including fees, commissions, fringe benefits, and similar items;

(2) Gross income derived from business;

(3) Gains derived from dealings in property;

(4) Interest;

(5) Rents;

(6) Royalties;

(7) Dividends;

(8) Alimony and separate maintenance payments;

(9) Annuities;

(10) Income from life insurance and endowment contracts;

(11) Pensions;

(12) Income from discharge of indebtedness;

(13) Distributive share of partnership gross income;

(14) Income in respect of a decedent; and

(15) Income from an interest in an estate or trust.

(b) Cross references.—

For items specifically included in gross income, see part II (sec. 71 and following).
For items specifically excluded from gross income, see part III (sec. 101 and following).

* Omitted entirely.

§ 62. Adjusted gross income defined

(a) General rule.—For purposes of this subtitle, the term "adjusted gross income" means, in the case of an individual, gross income minus the following deductions:

(1) Trade and business deductions.—The deductions allowed by this chapter (other than by part VII of this subchapter) which are attributable to a trade or business carried on by the taxpayer, if such trade or business does not consist of the performance of services by the taxpayer as an employee.

(2) Certain trade and business deductions of employees.—

(A) Reimbursed expenses of employees.—The deductions allowed by part VI (section 161 and following) which consist of expenses paid or incurred by the taxpayer, in connection with the performance by him of services as an employee, under a reimbursement or other expense allowance arrangement with his employer. The fact that the reimbursement may be provided by a third party shall not be determinative of whether or not the preceding sentence applies.

(B) Certain expenses of performing artists.—The deductions allowed by section 162 which consist of expenses paid or incurred by a qualified performing artist in connection with the performances by him of services in the performing arts as an employee.

(C) Certain expenses of officials.—The deductions allowed by section 162 which consist of expenses paid or incurred with respect to services performed by an official as an employee of a State or a political subdivision thereof in a position compensated in whole or in part on a fee basis.

(D) Certain expenses of elementary and secondary school teachers.—In the case of taxable years beginning during 2002, 2003, 2004, 2005, 2006, 2007, 2008, 2009, 2010, 2011, 2012, or 2013 the deductions allowed by section 162 which consist of expenses, not in excess of $250, paid or incurred by an eligible educator in connection with books, supplies (other than nonathletic supplies for courses of instruction in health or physical education), computer equipment (including related software and services) and other equipment, and supplementary materials used by the eligible educator in the classroom.

(3) Losses from sale or exchange of property.—The deductions allowed by part VI (sec. 161 and following) as losses from the sale or exchange of property.

(4) Deductions attributable to rents and royalties.—The deductions allowed by part VI (sec. 161 and following), by section 212 (relating to expenses for production of income), and by section 611 (relating to depletion) which are attributable to property held for the production of rents or royalties.

(5) Certain deductions of life tenants and income beneficiaries of property.—In the case of a life tenant of property, or an income beneficiary of property held in trust, or an heir, legatee, or devisee of an estate, the deduction for depreciation allowed by section 167 and the deduction allowed by section 611.

(6) Pension, profit-sharing, and annuity plans of self-employed individuals.—In the case of an individual who is an employee within the meaning of section 401(c)(1), the deduction allowed by section 404.

(7) Retirement savings.—The deduction allowed by section 219 (relating to deduction of certain retirement savings).

* * *

(10) Alimony.—The deduction allowed by section 215.

* * *

(15) Moving expenses.—The deduction allowed by section 217.

* * *

(17) Interest on education loans.—The deduction allowed by section 221.

(18) Higher education expenses.—The deduction allowed by section 222.

Nothing in this section shall permit the same item to be deducted more than once.

(19) Health savings accounts.—The deduction allowed by section 223.

(20) Costs involving discrimination suits, etc.—Any deduction allowable under this chapter for attorney fees and court costs paid by, or on behalf of, the taxpayer in connection with any action involving a claim of unlawful discrimination (as defined in subsection (e)) or a claim of a violation of subchapter III of chapter 37 of title 31, United States Code or a claim made under section 1862(b)(3)(A) of the Social Security Act (42 U.S.C. 1395y(b)(3)(A)). The preceding sentence shall not apply to any deduction in excess of the amount includible in the taxpayer's gross income for the taxable year on account of a judgment or settlement (whether by suit or agreement and whether as lump sum or periodic payments) resulting from such claim.

* * *

(c) Certain arrangements not treated as reimbursement arrangements.—For purposes of subsection (a)(2)(A), an arrangement shall in no event be treated as a reimbursement or other expense allowance arrangement if—

(1) such arrangement does not require the employee to substantiate the expenses covered by the arrangement to the person providing the reimbursement, or

(2) such arrangement provides the employee the right to retain any amount in excess of the substantiated expenses covered under the arrangement.

The substantiation requirements of the preceding sentence shall not apply to any expense to the extent that substantiation is not required under section 274(d) for such expense by reason of the regulations prescribed under the 2nd sentence thereof.

(d) Definition; special rules.—

(1) Eligible educator.—

(A) In general.—For purposes of subsection (a)(2)(D), the term "eligible educator" means, with respect to any taxable year, an individual who is a kindergarten through grade 12 teacher, instructor, counselor, principal, or aide in a school for at least 900 hours during a school year.

(B) School.—The term "school" means any school which provides elementary education or secondary education (kindergarten through grade 12), as determined under State law.

(2) Coordination with exclusions.—A deduction shall be allowed under subsection (a)(2)(D) for expenses only to the extent the amount of such expenses exceeds the amount excludable under section 135, 529(c)(1), or 530(d)(2) for the taxable year.

(e) Unlawful discrimination defined.—For purposes of subsection (a)(20), the term "unlawful discrimination" means an act that is unlawful under any of the following:

(1) Section 302 of the Civil Rights Act of 1991 (2 U.S.C. 1202).

(2) Section 201, 202, 203, 204, 205, 206, or 207 of the Congressional Accountability Act of 1995 (2 U.S.C. 1311, 1312, 1313, 1314, 1315, 1316, or 1317).

(3) The National Labor Relations Act (29 U.S.C. 151 et seq.).

(4) The Fair Labor Standards Act of 1938 (29 U.S.C. 201 et seq.).

(5) Section 4 or 15 of the Age Discrimination in Employment Act of 1967 (29 U.S.C. 623 or 633a).

(6) Section 501 or 504 of the Rehabilitation Act of 1973 (29 U.S.C. 791 or 794).

(7) Section 510 of the Employee Retirement Income Security Act of 1974 (29 U.S.C. 1140).

(8) Title IX of the Education Amendments of 1972 (20 U.S.C. 1681 et seq.).

(9) The Employee Polygraph Protection Act of 1988 (29 U.S.C. 2001 et seq.).

(10) The Worker Adjustment and Retraining Notification Act (29 U.S.C. 2102 et seq.).

(11) Section 105 of the Family and Medical Leave Act of 1993 (29 U.S.C. 2615).

(12) Chapter 43 of title 38, United States Code (relating to employment and reemployment rights of members of the uniformed services).

(13) Section 1977, 1979, or 1980 of the Revised Statutes (42 U.S.C. 1981, 1983, or 1985).

(14) Section 703, 704, or 717 of the Civil Rights Act of 1964 (42 U.S.C. 2000e–2, 2000e–3, or 2000e–16).

(15) Section 804, 805, 806, 808, or 818 of the Fair Housing Act (42 U.S.C. 3604, 3605, 3606, 3608, or 3617).

(16) Section 102, 202, 302, or 503 of the Americans with Disabilities Act of 1990 (42 U.S.C. 12112, 12132, 12182, or 12203).

(17) Any provision of Federal law (popularly known as whistleblower protection provisions) prohibiting the discharge of an employee, the discrimination against an employee, or any other form of retaliation or reprisal against an employee for asserting rights or taking other actions permitted under Federal law.

(18) Any provision of Federal, State, or local law, or common law claims permitted under Federal, State, or local law—

(i) providing for the enforcement of civil rights, or

(ii) regulating any aspect of the employment relationship, including claims for wages, compensation, or benefits, or prohibiting the discharge of an employee, the discrimination against an employee, or any other form of retaliation or reprisal against an employee for asserting rights or taking other actions permitted by law.

§ 63. Taxable income defined

(a) In general.—Except as provided in subsection (b), for purposes of this subtitle, the term "taxable income" means gross income minus the deductions allowed by this chapter (other than the standard deduction).

(b) Individuals who do not itemize their deductions.—In the case of an individual who does not elect to itemize his deductions for the taxable year, for purposes of this subtitle, the term "taxable income" means adjusted gross income, minus—

(1) the standard deduction, and

(2) the deduction for personal exemptions provided in section 151.

(c) Standard deduction.—For purposes of this subtitle—

(1) In general.—Except as otherwise provided in this subsection, the term "standard deduction" means the sum of—

(A) the basic standard deduction,

(B) the additional standard deduction,

* * *

(2) Basic standard deduction.—For purposes of paragraph (1), the basic standard deduction is—

(A) 200 percent of the dollar amount in effect under subparagraph (C) for the taxable year in the case of—

(i) a joint return, or

(ii) a surviving spouse (as defined in section 2(a)),

(B) $4,400 in the case of a head of household (as defined in section 2(b)), or

(C) $3,000 in any other case.

(3) Additional standard deduction for aged and blind.—For purposes of paragraph (1), the additional standard deduction is the sum of each additional amount to which the taxpayer is entitled under subsection (f).

(4) Adjustments for inflation.—In the case of any taxable year beginning in a calendar year after 1988, each dollar amount contained in paragraph (2)(B), (2)(C) or (5) or subsection (f) shall be increased by an amount equal to—

(A) such dollar amount, multiplied by

(B) the cost-of-living adjustment determined under section 1(f)(3) * * *—

* * *

(5) Limitation on basic standard deduction in the case of certain dependents.—In the case of an individual with respect to whom a deduction under section 151 is allowable to another taxpayer for a taxable year beginning in the calendar year in which the individual's taxable year begins, the basic standard deduction applicable to such individual for such individual's taxable year shall not exceed the greater of—

(A) $500, or

(B) the sum of $250 and such individual's earned income.

(6) Certain individuals, etc., not eligible for standard deduction.—In the case of—

(A) a married individual filing a separate return where either spouse itemizes deductions,

(B) a nonresident alien individual,

(C) an individual making a return under section 443(a)(1) for a period of less than 12 months on account of a change in his annual accounting period, or

(D) an estate or trust, common trust fund, or partnership,

the standard deduction shall be zero.

* * *

(8) Disaster loss deduction.—For the purposes of paragraph (1), the term "disaster loss deduction" means the net disaster loss (as defined in section 165(h)(3)(B)).

(9) Motor vehicle sales tax deduction.—For purposes of paragraph (1), the term "motor vehicle sales tax deduction" means the amount allowable as a deduction under section 164(a)(6). Such term shall not include any amount taken into account under section 62(a).

(d) Itemized deductions.—For purposes of this subtitle, the term "itemized deductions" means the deductions allowable under this chapter other than—

(1) the deductions allowable in arriving at adjusted gross income, and

(2) the deduction for personal exemptions provided by section 151.

(e) Election to itemize.—

(1) In general.—Unless an individual makes an election under this subsection for the taxable year, no itemized deduction shall be allowed for the taxable year. For purposes of this subtitle, the determination of whether a deduction is allowable under this chapter shall be made without regard to the preceding sentence.

(2) Time and manner of election.—Any election under this subsection shall be made on the taxpayer's return, and the Secretary shall prescribe the manner of signifying such election on the return.

(3) Change of election.—Under regulations prescribed by the Secretary, a change of election with respect to itemized deductions for any taxable year may be made after the filing of the return for such year. If the spouse of the taxpayer filed a separate return for any taxable year corresponding to the taxable year of the taxpayer, the change shall not be allowed unless, in accordance with such regulations—

(A) the spouse makes a change of election with respect to itemized deductions, for the taxable year covered in such separate return, consistent with the change of treatment sought by the taxpayer, and

(B) the taxpayer and his spouse consent in writing to the assessment (within such period as may be agreed on with the Secretary) of any deficiency, to the extent attributable to such change of election, even though at the time of the filing of such consent the assessment of such deficiency would otherwise be prevented by the operation of any law or rule of law.

This paragraph shall not apply if the tax liability of the taxpayer's spouse for the taxable year corresponding to the taxable year of the taxpayer has been compromised under section 7122.

(f) Aged or blind additional amounts.—

(1) Additional amounts for the aged.—The taxpayer shall be entitled to an additional amount of $600—

(A) for himself if he has attained age 65 before the close of his taxable year, and

(B) for the spouse of the taxpayer if the spouse has attained age 65 before the close of the taxable year and an additional exemption is allowable to the taxpayer for such spouse under section 151(b).

(2) Additional amount for blind.—The taxpayer shall be entitled to an additional amount of $600—

(A) for himself if he is blind at the close of the taxable year, and

(B) for the spouse of the taxpayer if the spouse is blind as of the close of the taxable year and an additional exemption is allowable to the taxpayer for such spouse under section 151(b).

For purposes of subparagraph (B), if the spouse dies during the taxable year the determination of whether such spouse is blind shall be made as of the time of such death.

(3) Higher amount for certain unmarried individuals.—In the case of an individual who is not married and is not a surviving spouse, paragraphs (1) and (2) shall be applied by substituting "$750" for "$600".

(4) Blindness defined.—For purposes of this subsection, an individual is blind only if his central visual acuity does not exceed 20/200 in the better eye with correcting lenses, or if his visual acuity is greater than 20/200 but is accompanied by a limitation in the fields of vision such that the widest diameter of the visual field subtends an angle no greater than 20 degrees.

(g) Marital status.—For purposes of this section, marital status shall be determined under section 7703.

§ 64. Ordinary income defined

For purposes of this subtitle, the term "ordinary income" includes any gain from the sale or exchange of property which is neither a capital asset nor property described in section 1231(b). Any gain from the sale or exchange of property which is treated or considered, under other provisions of this subtitle, as "ordinary income" shall be treated as gain from the sale or exchange of property which is neither a capital asset nor property described in section 1231(b).

§ 65. Ordinary loss defined

For purposes of this subtitle, the term "ordinary loss" includes any loss from the sale or exchange of property which is not a capital asset. Any loss from the sale or exchange of property which is treated or considered, under other provisions of this subtitle, as "ordinary loss" shall be treated as loss from the sale or exchange of property which is not a capital asset.

§ 66. Treatment of community income

(a) Treatment of community income where spouses live apart.—If—

(1) 2 individuals are married to each other at any time during a calendar year;

(2) such individuals—

(A) live apart at all times during the calendar year, and

(B) do not file a joint return under section 6013 with each other for a taxable year beginning or ending in the calendar year;

(3) one or both of such individuals have earned income for the calendar year which is community income; and

(4) no portion of such earned income is transferred (directly or indirectly) between such individuals before the close of the calendar year,

then, for purposes of this title, any community income of such individuals for the calendar year shall be treated in accordance with the rules provided by section 879(a).

(b) Secretary may disregard community property laws where spouse not notified of community income.—The Secretary may disallow the benefits of any community property law to any taxpayer with respect to any income if such taxpayer acted as if solely entitled to such income and failed to notify the taxpayer's spouse before the due date (including extensions) for filing the return for the taxable year in which the income was derived of the nature and amount of such income.

(c) Spouse relieved of liability in certain other cases.—Under regulations prescribed by the Secretary, if—

(1) an individual does not file a joint return for any taxable year,

(2) such individual does not include in gross income for such taxable year an item of community income properly includible therein which, in accordance with the rules contained in section 879(a), would be treated as the income of the other spouse,

(3) the individual establishes that he or she did not know of, and had no reason to know of, such item of community income, and

(4) taking into account all facts and circumstances, it is inequitable to include such item of community income in such individual's gross income,

then, for purposes of this title, such item of community income shall be included in the gross income of the other spouse (and not in the gross income of the individual). Under procedures prescribed by the Secretary, if, taking into account all the facts and circumstances, it is inequitable to hold the individual liable for any unpaid tax or deficiency (or any portion of either) attributable to any item for which relief is not available under the preceding sentence, the Secretary may relieve such individual of such liability.

(d) Definitions.—For purposes of this section—

(1) Earned income.—The term "earned income" has the meaning given to such term by section 911(d)(2).

(2) Community income.—The term "community income" means income which, under applicable community property laws, is treated as community income.

(3) Community property laws.—The term "community property laws" means the community property laws of a State, a foreign country, or a possession of the United States.

§ 67. 2-percent floor on miscellaneous itemized deductions

(a) General Rule.—In the case of an individual, the miscellaneous itemized deductions for any taxable year shall be allowed only to the extent that the aggregate of such deductions exceeds 2 percent of adjusted gross income.

(b) Miscellaneous itemized deductions.—For purposes of this section, the term "miscellaneous itemized deductions" means the itemized deductions other than—

(1) the deduction under section 163 (relating to interest),

(2) the deduction under section 164 (relating to taxes),

(3) the deduction under section 165(a) for casualty or theft losses described in paragraph (2) or (3) of section 165(c) or for losses described in section 165(d),

(4) the deductions under section 170 (relating to charitable, etc., contributions and gifts) and section 642(c) (relating to deduction for amounts paid or permanently set aside for a charitable purpose),

(5) the deduction under section 213 (relating to medical, dental, etc., expenses),

(6) any deduction allowable for impairment-related work expenses,

(7) the deduction under section 691(c) (relating to deduction for estate tax in case of income in respect of the decedent),

(8) any deduction allowable in connection with personal property used in a short sale,

(9) the deduction under section 1341 (relating to computation of tax where taxpayer restores substantial amount held under claim of right),

(10) the deduction under section 72(b)(3) (relating to deduction where annuity payments cease before investment recovered),

(11) the deduction under section 171 (relating to deduction for amortizable bond premium), and

(12) the deduction under section 216 (relating to deductions in connection with cooperative housing corporations).

(c) Disallowance of indirect deduction through pass-thru entity.—

(1) In general.—The Secretary shall prescribe regulations which prohibit the indirect deduction through pass-thru entities of amounts which are not allowable as a deduction if paid or incurred directly by an individual and which contain such reporting requirements as may be necessary to carry out the purposes of this subsection.

* * *

(3) Treatment of certain other entities.—Paragraph (1) shall not apply—

(A) with respect to cooperatives and real estate investment trusts, and

(B) except as provided in regulations, with respect to estates and trusts.

* * *

(e) Determination of adjusted gross income in case of estates and trusts.—For purposes of this section, the adjusted gross income of an estate or trust shall be computed in the same manner as in the case of an individual, except that—

(1) the deductions for costs which are paid or incurred in connection with the administration of the estate or trust and which would not have been incurred if the property were not held in such trust or estate, and

(2) the deductions allowable under sections 642(b), 651, and 661,

shall be treated as allowable in arriving at adjusted gross income. Under regulations, appropriate adjustments shall be made in the application of part I of subchapter J of this chapter to take into account the provisions of this section.

(f) Coordination with other limitation.—This section shall be applied before the application of the dollar limitation of the second sentence of section 162(a) (relating to trade or business expenses).

§ 68. Overall limitation on itemized deductions

(a) General rule.—In the case of an individual whose adjusted gross income exceeds the applicable amount, the amount of the itemized deductions otherwise allowable for the taxable year shall be reduced by the lesser of—

(1) 3 percent of the excess of adjusted gross income over the applicable amount, or

(2) 80 percent of the amount of the itemized deductions otherwise allowable for such taxable year.

(b) Applicable amount.—

(1) In general.—For purposes of this section, the term "applicable amount" means—

(A) $300,000 in the case of a joint return or a surviving spouse (as defined in section 2(a)),

(B) $275,000 in the case of a head of household (as defined in section 2(b)),

(C) $250,000 in the case of an individual who is not married and who is not a surviving spouse or head of household, and

(D) 1/2 the amount applicable under subparagraph (A) (after adjustment, if any, under paragraph (2)) in the case of a married individual filing a separate return.

For purposes of this paragraph, marital status shall be determined under section 7703.

(2) Inflation adjustment.—In the case of any taxable year beginning in calendar years after 2013, each of the dollar amounts under subparagraphs (A), (B), and (C) of paragraph (1) shall be shall be increased by an amount equal to—

(A) such dollar amount, multiplied by

(B) the cost-of-living adjustment determined under section 1(f)(3) for the calendar year in which the taxable year begins, except that section 1(f)(3)(B) shall be applied by substituting "2012" for "1992".

If any amount after adjustment under the preceding sentence is not a multiple of $50, such amount shall be rounded to the next lowest multiple of $50.

(c) Exception for certain itemized deductions.—For purposes of this section, the term "itemized deductions" does not include—

(1) the deduction under section 213 (relating to medical, etc. expenses),

(2) any deduction for investment interest (as defined in section 163(d)), and

(3) the deduction under section 165(a) for casualty or theft losses described in paragraph (2) or (3) of section 165(c) or for losses described in section 165(d).

(d) Coordination with other limitations.—This section shall be applied after the application of any other limitation on the allowance of any itemized deduction.

(e) Exception for estates and trusts.—This section shall not apply to any estate or trust.

PART II—ITEMS SPECIFICALLY INCLUDED IN GROSS INCOME

§ 71. Alimony and separate maintenance payments

(a) General rule.—Gross income includes amounts received as alimony or separate maintenance payments.

(b) Alimony or separate maintenance payments defined.—For purposes of this section—

(1) In general.—The term "alimony or separate maintenance payment" means any payment in cash if—

(A) such payment is received by (or on behalf of) a spouse under a divorce or separation instrument,

(B) the divorce or separation instrument does not designate such payment as a payment which is not includible in gross income under this section and not allowable as a deduction under section 215,

(C) in the case of an individual legally separated from his spouse under a decree of divorce or of separate maintenance, the payee spouse and the payor spouse are not members of the same household at the time such payment is made, and

(D) there is no liability to make any such payment for any period after the death of the payee spouse and there is no liability to make any payment (in cash or property) as a substitute for such payments after the death of the payee spouse.

(2) Divorce or separation instrument.—The term "divorce or separation instrument" means—

(A) a decree of divorce or separate maintenance or a written instrument incident to such a decree,

(B) a written separation agreement, or

(C) a decree (not described in subparagraph (A)) requiring a spouse to make payments for the support or maintenance of the other spouse.

(c) Payments to support children.—

(1) In general.—Subsection (a) shall not apply to that part of any payment which the terms of the divorce or separation instrument fix (in terms of an amount of money or a part of the payment) as a sum which is payable for the support of children of the payor spouse.

(2) Treatment of certain reductions related to contingencies involving child.—For purposes of paragraph (1), if any amount specified in the instrument will be reduced—

(A) on the happening of a contingency specified in the instrument relating to a child (such as attaining a specified age, marrying, dying, leaving school, or a similar contingency), or

(B) at a time which can clearly be associated with a contingency of a kind specified in subparagraph (A),

an amount equal to the amount of such reduction will be treated as an amount fixed as payable for the support of children of the payor spouse.

(3) Special rule where payment is less than amount specified in instrument.—For purposes of this subsection, if any payment is less than the amount specified in the instrument, then so much of such payment as does not exceed the sum payable for support shall be considered a payment for such support.

(d) Spouse.—For purposes of this section, the term "spouse" includes a former spouse.

(e) Exception for joint returns.—This section and section 215 shall not apply if the spouses make a joint return with each other.

(f) Recomputation where excess front-loading of alimony payments—

(1) In general.—If there are excess alimony payments—

(A) the payor spouse shall include the amount of such excess payments in gross income for the payor spouse's taxable year beginning in the 3rd post-separation year, and

(B) the payee spouse shall be allowed a deduction in computing adjusted gross income for the amount of such excess payments for the payee's taxable year beginning in the 3rd post-separation year.

(2) Excess alimony payments.—For purposes of this subsection, the term "excess alimony payments" mean the sum of—

(A) the excess payments for the 1st post-separation year, and

(B) the excess payments for the 2nd post-separation year.

(3) Excess payments for 1st post-separation year.—For purposes of this subsection, the amount of the excess payments for the 1st post-separation year is the excess (if any) of—

(A) the amount of the alimony or separate maintenance payments paid by the payor spouse during the 1st post-separation year, over

(B) the sum of—

(i) the average of—

(I) the alimony or separate maintenance payments paid by the payor spouse during the 2nd post-separation year, reduced by the excess payments for the 2nd post-separation year, and

(II) the alimony or separate maintenance payments paid by the payor spouse during the 3rd post-separation year, plus

(ii) $15,000.

(4) Excess payments for 2nd post-separation year.—For purposes of this subsection, the amount of the excess payments for the 2nd post-separation year is the excess (if any) of—

(A) the amount of the alimony or separate maintenance payments paid by the payor spouse during the 2nd post-separation year, over

(B) the sum of—

(i) the amount of the alimony or separate maintenance payments paid by the payor spouse during the 3rd post-separation year, plus

(ii) $15,000.

(5) Exceptions.—

(A) Where payment ceases by reason of death or remarriage.—Paragraph (1) shall not apply if—

(i) either spouse dies before the close of the 3rd post-separation year, or the payee spouse remarries before the close of the 3rd post-separation year, and

(ii) the alimony or separate maintenance payments cease by reason of such death or remarriage.

(B) Support payments.—For purposes of this subsection, the term "alimony or separate maintenance payment" shall not include any payment received under a decree described in subsection (b)(2)(C).

(C) Fluctuating payments not within control of payor spouse.—For purposes of this subsection, the term "alimony or separate maintenance payment" shall not include any payment to the extent it is made pursuant to a continuing liability (over a period of not less than 3 years) to pay a fixed portion or portions of the income from a business or property or from compensation for employment or self-employment.

(6) Post-separation years.—For purposes of this subsection, the term "1st post-separation years" means the 1st calendar year in which the payor spouse paid to the payee spouse alimony or separate maintenance payments to which this section applies. The 2nd and 3rd post-separation years shall be the 1st and 2nd succeeding calendar years, respectively.

(g) Cross references.—

(1) For deduction of alimony or separate maintenance payments, see section 215.

(2) For taxable status of income of an estate or trust in the case of divorce, etc., see section 682.

§ 72. Annuities; certain proceeds of endowment and life insurance contracts

(a) General rules for annuities.—

(1) Income inclusion.—Except as otherwise provided in this chapter, gross income includes any amount received as an annuity (whether for a period certain or during one or more lives) under an annuity, endowment, or life insurance contract.

(2) Partial annuitization.—If any amount is received as an annuity for a period of 10 years or more or during one or more lives under any portion of an annuity, endowment, or life insurance contract—

(A) such portion shall be treated as a separate contract for purposes of this section,

(B) for purposes of applying subsections (b), (c), and (e), the investment in the contract shall be allocated pro rata between each portion of the contract from which amounts are received as an annuity and the portion of the contract from which amounts are not received as an annuity, and

(C) a separate annuity starting date under subsection (c)(4) shall be determined with respect to each portion of the contract from which amounts are received as an annuity.

(b) Exclusion ratio.—

(1) In general.—Gross income does not include that part of any amount received as an annuity under an annuity, endowment, or life insurance contract which bears the same ratio to such amount as the investment in the contract (as of the annuity starting date) bears to the expected return under the contract (as of such date).

(2) Exclusion limited to investment.—The portion of any amount received as an annuity which is excluded from gross income under paragraph (1) shall not exceed the unrecovered investment in the contract immediately before the receipt of such amount.

(3) Deduction where annuity payments cease before entire investment recovered.—

(A) In general.—If—

(i) after the annuity starting date, payments as an annuity under the contract cease by reason of the death of an annuitant, and

(ii) as of the date of such cessation, there is unrecovered investment in the contract,

the amount of such unrecovered investment (in excess of any amount specified in subsection (e)(5) which was not included in gross income) shall be allowed as a deduction to the annuitant for his last taxable year.

(B) Payments to other persons.—In the case of any contract which provides for payments meeting the requirements of subparagraphs (B) and (C) of subsection (c)(2), the deduction under subparagraph (A) shall be allowed to the person entitled to such payments for the taxable year in which such payments are received.

(C) Net operating loss deductions provided.—For purposes of section 172, a deduction allowed under this paragraph shall be treated as if it were attributable to a trade or business of the taxpayer.

(4) Unrecovered investment.—For purposes of this subsection, the unrecovered investment in the contract as of any date is—

(A) the investment in the contract (determined without regard to subsection (c)(2)) as of the annuity starting date, reduced by

(B) the aggregate amount received under the contract on or after such annuity starting date and before the date as of which the determination is being made, to the extent such amount was excludable from gross income under this subtitle.

(c) Definitions.—

(1) Investment in the contract.—For purposes of subsection (b), the investment in the contract as of the annuity starting date is—

(A) the aggregate amount of premiums or other consideration paid for the contract, minus

(B) the aggregate amount received under the contract before such date, to the extent that such amount was excludable from gross income under this subtitle or prior income tax laws.

(2) Adjustment in investment where there is refund feature.—If—

(A) the expected return under the contract depends in whole or in part on the life expectancy of one or more individuals;

(B) the contract provides for payments to be made to a beneficiary (or to the estate of an annuitant) on or after the death of the annuitant or annuitants; and

(C) such payments are in the nature of a refund of the consideration paid,

then the value (computed without discount for interest) of such payments on the annuity starting date shall be subtracted from the amount determined under paragraph (1). Such value shall be computed in accordance with actuarial tables prescribed by the Secretary. For purposes of this paragraph and of subsection (e)(2)(A), the term "refund of the consideration paid" includes amounts payable after the death of an annuitant by reason of a provision in the contract for a life annuity with minimum period of payments certain, but (if part of the consideration was contributed by an employer) does not include that part of any payment to a beneficiary (or to the estate of the annuitant) which is not attributable to the consideration paid by the employee for the contract as determined under paragraph (1)(A).

(3) Expected return.—For purposes of subsection (b), the expected return under the contract shall be determined as follows:

(A) Life expectancy.—If the expected return under the contract, for the period on and after the annuity starting date, depends in whole or in part on the life expectancy of one or more individuals, the expected return shall be computed with reference to actuarial tables prescribed by the Secretary.

(B) Installment payments.—If subparagraph (A) does not apply, the expected return is the aggregate of the amounts receivable under the contract as an annuity.

(4) Annuity starting date.—For purposes of this section, the annuity starting date in the case of any contract is the first day of the first period for which an amount is received as an annuity under the contract; except that if such date was before January 1, 1954, then the annuity starting date is January 1, 1954.

(d) Special rules for qualified employer retirement plans.—

(1) Simplified method of taxing annuity payments.—

(A) In general.—In the case of any amount received as an annuity under a qualified employer retirement plan—

(i) subsection (b) shall not apply, and

(ii) the investment in the contract shall be recovered as provided in this paragraph.

(B) Method of recovering investment in contract.—

(i) In general.—Gross income shall not include so much of any monthly annuity payment under a qualified employer retirement plan as does not exceed the amount obtained by dividing—

(I) the investment in the contract (as of the annuity starting date), by

(II) the number of anticipated payments determined under the table contained in clause (iii) (or, in the case of a contract to which subsection (c)(3)(B) applies, the number of monthly annuity payments under such contract).

(ii) Certain rules made applicable.—Rules similar to the rules of paragraphs (2) and (3) of subsection (b) shall apply for purposes of this paragraph.

(iii) Number of anticipated payments.—If the annuity is payable over the life of a single individual, the number of anticipated payments shall be determined as follows:

If the age of the annuitant on the annuity starting date is:	The number of anticipated payments is:
Not more than 55	360
More than 55 but not more than 60	310
More than 60 but not more than 65	260
More than 65 but not more than 70	210
More than 70	160.

(iv) Number of anticipated payments where more than one life.—If the annuity is payable over the lives of more than 1 individual, the number of anticipated payments shall be determined as follows:

If the combined ages of annuitants are:	The number is:
Not more than 110	410
More than 110 but not more than 120	360
More than 120 but not more than 130	310
More than 130 but not more than 140	260
More than 140	210.

(C) Adjustment for refund feature not applicable.—For purposes of this paragraph, investment in the contract shall be determined under subsection (c)(1) without regard to subsection (c)(2).

(D) Special rule where lump sum paid in connection with commencement of annuity payments.—If, in connection with the commencement of annuity payments under any qualified employer retirement plan, the taxpayer receives a lump-sum payment—

(i) such payment shall be taxable under subsection (e) as if received before the annuity starting date, and

(ii) the investment in the contract for purposes of this paragraph shall be determined as if such payment had been so received.

(E) Exception.—This paragraph shall not apply in any case where the primary annuitant has attained age 75 on the annuity starting date unless there are fewer than 5 years of guaranteed payments under the annuity.

(F) Adjustment where annuity payments not on monthly basis.—In any case where the annuity payments are not made on a monthly basis, appropriate adjustments in the application of this paragraph shall be made to take into account the period on the basis of which such payments are made.

(G) Qualified employer retirement plan.—For purposes of this paragraph, the term "qualified employer retirement plan" means any plan or contract described in paragraph (1), (2), or (3) of section 4974(c).

(2) Treatment of employee contributions under defined contribution plans.—For purposes of this section, employee contributions (and any income allocable thereto) under a defined contribution plan may be treated as a separate contract.

(e) Amounts not received as annuities.—

(1) Application of subsection.—

(A) In general.—This subsection shall apply to any amount which—

(i) is received under an annuity, endowment, or life insurance contract, and

(ii) is not received as an annuity,

if no provision of this subtitle (other than this subsection) applies with respect to such amount.

(B) Dividends.—For purposes of this section, any amount received which is in the nature of a dividend or similar distribution shall be treated as an amount not received as an annuity.

(2) General rule.—Any amount to which this subsection applies—

(A) if received on or after the annuity starting date, shall be included in gross income, or

(B) if received before the annuity starting date—

(i) shall be included in gross income to the extent allocable to income on the contract, and

(ii) shall not be included in gross income to the extent allocable to the investment in the contract.

(3) Allocation of amounts to income and investment.—For purposes of paragraph (2)(B)—

(A) Allocation to income.—Any amount to which this subsection applies shall be treated as allocable to income on the contract to the extent that such amount does not exceed the excess (if any) of—

(i) the cash value of the contract (determined without regard to any surrender charge) immediately before the amount is received, over

(ii) the investment in the contract at such time.

(B) Allocation to investment.—Any amount to which this subsection applies shall be treated as allocable to investment in the contract to the extent that such amount is not allocated to income under subparagraph (A).

(4) Special rules for application of paragraph (2)(B).—For purposes of paragraph (2)(B)—

(A) Loans treated as distributions.—If, during any taxable year, an individual—

(i) receives (directly or indirectly) any amount as a loan under any contract to which this subsection applies, or

(ii) assigns or pledges (or agrees to assign or pledge) any portion of the value of any such contract,

such amount or portion shall be treated as received under the contract as an amount not received as an annuity. The preceding sentence shall not apply for purposes of determining investment in the contract, except that the investment in the contract shall be increased by any amount included in gross income by reason of the amount treated as received under the preceding sentence.

(B) Treatment of policyholder dividends.—Any amount described in paragraph (1)(B) shall not be included in gross income under paragraph (2)(B)(i) to the extent such amount is retained by the insurer as a premium or other consideration paid for the contract.

(C) Treatment of transfers without adequate consideration.—

(i) In general.—If an individual who holds an annuity contract transfers it without full and adequate consideration, such individual shall be treated as receiving an amount equal to the excess of—

(I) the cash surrender value of such contract at the time of transfer, over

(II) the investment in such contract at such time, under the contract as an amount not received as an annuity.

(ii) Exception for certain transfers between spouses or former spouses.—Clause (i) shall not apply to any transfer to which section 1041(a) (relating to transfers of property between spouses or incident to divorce) applies.

(iii) Adjustment to investment in contract of transferee.—If under clause (i) an amount is included in the gross income of the transferor of an annuity contract, the investment in the contract of the transferee in such contract shall be increased by the amount so included.

(5) Retention of existing rules in certain cases.—

(A) In general.—In any case to which this paragraph applies—

(i) paragraphs (2)(B) and (4)(A) shall not apply, and

(ii) if paragraph (2)(A) does not apply,

the amount shall be included in gross income, but only to the extent it exceeds the investment in the contract.

(B) Existing contracts.—This paragraph shall apply to contracts entered into before August 14, 1982. Any amount allocable to investment in the contract after August 13, 1982, shall be treated as from a contract entered into after such date.

(C) Certain life insurance and endowment contracts.—Except as provided in paragraph (10) and except to the extent prescribed by the Secretary by regulations, this paragraph shall apply to any amount not received as an annuity which is received under a life insurance or endowment contract.

(D) Contracts under qualified plans.—Except as provided in paragraph (8), this paragraph shall apply to any amount received—

(i) from a trust described in section 401(a) which is exempt from tax under section 501(a),

(ii) from a contract—

(I) purchased by a trust described in clause (i),

(II) purchased as part of a plan described in section 403(a),

(III) described in section 403(b), or

(IV) provided for employees of a life insurance company under a plan described in section 818(a)(3), or

(iii) from an individual retirement account or an individual retirement annuity.

Any dividend described in section 404(k) which is received by a participant or beneficiary shall, for purposes of this subparagraph, be treated as paid under a separate contract to which clause (ii)(I) applies.

(E) Full refunds, surrenders, redemptions, and maturities.—This paragraph shall apply to—

(i) any amount received, whether in a single sum or otherwise, under a contract in full discharge of the obligation under the contract which is in the nature of a refund of the consideration paid for the contract, and

(ii) any amount received under a contract on its complete surrender, redemption, or maturity.

In the case of any amount to which the preceding sentence applies, the rule of paragraph (2)(A) shall not apply.

(6) Investment in the contract.—For purposes of this subsection, the investment in the contract as of any date is—

(A) the aggregate amount of premiums or other consideration paid for the contract before such date, minus

(B) the aggregate amount received under the contract before such date, to the extent that such amount was excludable from gross income under this subtitle or prior income tax laws.

[(7) Repealed.]

(8) Extension of paragraph (2)(b) to qualified plans.—

(A) In general.—Notwithstanding any other provision of this subsection, in the case of any amount received before the annuity starting date from a trust or contract described in paragraph (5)(D), paragraph (2)(B) shall apply to such amounts.

(B) Allocation of amount received.—For purposes of paragraph (2)(B), the amount allocated to the investment in the contract shall be the portion of the amount described in subparagraph (A) which bears the same ratio to such amount as the investment in the contract bears to the account balance. The determination under the preceding sentence shall be made as of the time of the distribution or at such other time as the Secretary may prescribe.

(C) Treatment of forfeitable rights.—If an employee does not have a nonforfeitable right to any amount under any trust or contract to which subparagraph (A) applies, such amount shall not be treated as part of the account balance.

(D) Investment in the contract before 1987.—In the case of a plan which on May 5, 1986, permitted withdrawal of any employee contributions before separation from service, subparagraph (A) shall apply only to the extent that amounts received before the annuity starting date (when increased by amounts previously received under the contract after December 31, 1986) exceed the investment in the contract as of December 31, 1986.

(9) Extension of paragraph (2)(b) to qualified tuition programs and Coverdell education savings accounts.—Notwithstanding any other provision of this subsection, paragraph (2)(B) shall apply to amounts received under a qualified tuition program (as defined in section 529(b)) or under a Coverdell education savings account (as defined in section 530(b)). The rule of paragraph (8)(B) shall apply for purposes of this paragraph.

* * *

(f) Special rules for computing employees' contributions.—In computing, for purposes of subsection (c)(1)(A), the aggregate amount of premiums or other consideration paid for the contract, and for purposes of subsection (e)(6), the aggregate premiums or other consideration paid, amounts contributed by the employer shall be included, but only to the extent that—

(1) such amounts were includible in the gross income of the employee under this subtitle or prior income tax laws; or

(2) if such amounts had been paid directly to the employee at the time they were contributed, they would not have been includible in the gross income of the employee under the law applicable at the time of such contribution.

* * *

(C) Adjustment for refund feature not applicable.—For purposes of this paragraph, investment in the contract shall be determined under subsection (c)(1) without regard to subsection (c)(2).

(D) Special rule where lump sum paid in connection with commencement of annuity payments.—If, in connection with the commencement of annuity payments under any qualified employer retirement plan, the taxpayer receives a lump-sum payment—

(i) such payment shall be taxable under subsection (e) as if received before the annuity starting date, and

(ii) the investment in the contract for purposes of this paragraph shall be determined as if such payment had been so received.

(E) Exception.—This paragraph shall not apply in any case where the primary annuitant has attained age 75 on the annuity starting date unless there are fewer than 5 years of guaranteed payments under the annuity.

(F) Adjustment where annuity payments not on monthly basis.—In any case where the annuity payments are not made on a monthly basis, appropriate adjustments in the application of this paragraph shall be made to take into account the period on the basis of which such payments are made.

(G) Qualified employer retirement plan.—For purposes of this paragraph, the term "qualified employer retirement plan" means any plan or contract described in paragraph (1), (2), or (3) of section 4974(c).

(2) Treatment of employee contributions under defined contribution plans.—For purposes of this section, employee contributions (and any income allocable thereto) under a defined contribution plan may be treated as a separate contract.

(g) Rules for transferee where transfer was for value.—Where any contract (or any interest therein) is transferred (by assignment or otherwise) for a valuable consideration, to the extent that the contract (or interest therein) does not, in the hands of the transferee, have a basis which is determined by reference to the basis in the hands of the transferor, then—

(1) for purposes of this section, only the actual value of such consideration, plus the amount of the premiums and other consideration paid by the transferee after the transfer, shall be taken into account in computing the aggregate amount of the premiums or other consideration paid for the contract;

(2) for purposes of subsection (c)(1)(B), there shall be taken into account only the aggregate amount received under the contract by the transferee before the annuity starting date, to the extent that such amount was excludable from gross income under this subtitle or prior income tax laws; and

(3) the annuity starting date is January 1, 1954, or the first day of the first period for which the transferee received an amount under the contract as an annuity, whichever is the later.

For purposes of this subsection, the term "transferee" includes a beneficiary of, or the estate of, the transferee.

(h) Option to receive annuity in lieu of lump sum.—If—

(1) a contract provides for payment of a lump sum in full discharge of an obligation under the contract, subject to an option to receive an annuity in lieu of such lump sum;

(2) the option is exercised within 60 days after the day on which such lump sum first became payable; and

(3) part or all of such lump sum would (but for this subsection) be includible in gross income by reason of subsection (e)(1),

then, for purposes of this subtitle, no part of such lump sum shall be considered as includible in gross income at the time such lump sum first became payable.

[(i) Repealed.]

(j) Interest.—Notwithstanding any other provision of this section, if any amount is held under an agreement to pay interest thereon, the interest payments shall be included in gross income.

[(k) Repealed.]

* * *

(m) Special rules applicable to employee annuities and distributions under employee plans.—

[(1) Repealed.]

(2) Computation of consideration paid by the employee.—In computing—

(A) the aggregate amount of premiums or other consideration paid for the contract for purposes of subsection (c)(1)(A) (relating to the investment in the contract), and

(B) the aggregate premiums or other consideration paid for purposes of subsection (e)(6) (relating to certain amounts not received as an annuity),

any amount allowed as a deduction with respect to the contract under section 404 which was paid while the employee was an employee within the meaning of section 401(c) (1) shall be treated as consideration contributed by the employer, and there shall not be taken into account any portion of the premiums or other consideration for the contract paid while the employee was an owner-employee which is properly allocable (as determined under regulations prescribed by the Secretary) to the cost of life, accident, health, or other insurance.

(3) Life insurance contracts.—

(A) This paragraph shall apply to any life insurance contract—

(i) purchased as a part of a plan described in section 403(a), or

(ii) purchased by a trust described in section 401(a) which is exempt from tax under section 501(a) if the proceeds of such contract are payable directly or indirectly to a participant in such trust or to a beneficiary of such participant.

(B) Any contribution to a plan described in subparagraph (A)(i) or a trust described in subparagraph (A)(ii) which is allowed as a deduction under section 404, and any income of a trust described in subparagraph (A)(ii), which is determined in accordance with regulations prescribed by the Secretary to have been applied to purchase the life insurance protection under a contract described in subparagraph (A), is includible in the gross income of the participant for the taxable year when so applied.

(C) In the case of the death of an individual insured under a contract described in subparagraph (A), an amount equal to the cash surrender value of the contract immediately before the death of the insured shall be treated as a payment under such plan or a distribution by such trust, and the excess of the amount payable by reason of the death of the insured over such cash surrender value shall not be includible in gross income under this section and shall be treated as provided in section 101.

[(4) Repealed.]

(5) Penalties applicable to certain amounts received by 5–percent owners.—

(A) This paragraph applies to amounts which are received from a qualified trust described in section 401(a) or under a plan described in section 403(a) at any time by an individual who is, or has been, a 5–percent owner, or by a successor of such an individual, but only to the extent such amounts are determined, under regulations prescribed by the Secretary, to exceed the benefits provided for such individual under the plan formula.

(B) If a person receives an amount to which this paragraph applies, his tax under this chapter for the taxable year in which such amount is received shall be increased by an amount equal to 10 percent of the portion of the amount so received which is includible in his gross income for such taxable year.

(C) For purposes of this paragraph, the term "5–percent owner" means any individual who, at any time during the 5 plan years preceding the plan year ending in the taxable year in which the amount is received, is a 5–percent owner (as defined in section 416(i)(1)(B)).

(6) Owner-employee defined.—For purposes of this subsection, the term "owner-employee" has the meaning assigned to it by section 401(c)(3) and includes an individual for whose benefit an individual retirement account or annuity described in section 408(a) or (b) is maintained. For purposes of the preceding sentence, the term "owner-employee" shall include an employee within the meaning of section 401(c)(1).

(7) Meaning of disabled.—For purposes of this section, an individual shall be considered to be disabled if he is unable to engage in any substantial gainful activity by reason of any medically determinable physical or mental impairment which can be expected to result in death or to be of long-continued and indefinite duration. An individual shall not be considered to be disabled unless he furnishes proof of the existence thereof in such form and manner as the Secretary may require.

[(8) Repealed.]

[(9) Repealed.]

(10) Determination of investment in the contract in the case of qualified domestic relations orders.—Under regulations prescribed by the Secretary, in the case of a distribution or payment made to an alternative payee who is the spouse or former spouse of a participant pursuant to a qualified domestic relations order (as defined in section 414(p)), the investment in the contract as of the date prescribed in such regulations shall be allocated on a pro rata basis between the present value of such distribution or payment and the present value of all other benefits payable with respect to the participant to which such order relates.

* * *

(*o*) Special rules for distributions from qualified plans to which employee made deductible contributions.—

(1) Treatment of contributions.—For purposes of this section and sections 402 and 403, notwithstanding section 414(h), any deductible employee contribution made to a qualified employer plan or government plan shall be treated as an amount contributed by the employer which is not includible in the gross income of the employee.

[(2) Repealed.]

(3) Amounts constructively received.—

(A) In general.—For purposes of this subsection, rules similar to the rules provided by subsection (p) (other than the exception contained in paragraph (2) thereof) shall apply.

(B) Purchase of life insurance.—To the extent any amount of accumulated deductible employee contributions of an employee are applied to the purchase of life insurance contracts, such amount shall be treated as distributed to the employee in the year so applied.

(4) Special rule for treatment of rollover amounts.—For purposes of sections 402(c), 403(a)(4), 403(b)(8), 408(d)(3), and 457(e)(16), the Secretary shall prescribe regulations providing for such allocations of amounts attributable to accumulated deductible employee contributions, and for such other rules, as may be necessary to insure that such accumulated deductible employee contributions do not become eligible for additional tax benefits (or freed from limitations) through the use of rollovers.

(5) Definitions and special rules.—For purposes of this subsection—

(A) Deductible employee contributions.—The term "deductible employee contributions" means any qualified voluntary employee contribution (as defined in section 219(e)(2)) made after December 31, 1981, in a taxable year beginning after such date and made for a taxable year beginning before January 1, 1987, and allowable as a deduction under section 219(a) for such taxable year.

(B) Accumulated deductible employee contributions.—The term "accumulated deductible employee contributions" means the deductible employee contributions—

(i) increased by the amount of income and gain allocable to such contributions, and

(ii) reduced by the sum of the amount of loss and expense allocable to such contributions and the amounts distributed with respect to the employee which are attributable to such contributions (or income or gain allocable to such contributions).

* * *

(6) Ordering rules.—Unless the plan specifies otherwise, any distribution from such plan shall not be treated as being made from the accumulated deductible employee contributions until all other amounts to the credit of the employee have been distributed.

(p) Loans treated as distributions.—For purposes of this section—

(1) Treatment as distributions.—

(A) Loans.—If during any taxable year a participant or beneficiary receives (directly or indirectly) any amount as a loan from a qualified employer plan, such amount shall be treated as having been received by such individual as a distribution under such plan.

(B) Assignments or pledges.—If during any taxable year a participant or beneficiary assigns (or agrees to assign) or pledges (or agrees to pledge) any portion of his interest in a qualified employer plan, such portion shall be treated as having been received by such individual as a loan from such plan.

(2) Exception for certain loans.—

(A) General rule.—Paragraph (1) shall not apply to any loan to the extent that such loan (when added to the outstanding balance of all other loans from such plan whether made on, before, or after August 13, 1982), does not exceed the lesser of—

(i) $50,000, reduced by the excess (if any) of—

(I) the highest outstanding balance of loans from the plan during the 1-year period ending on the day before the date on which such loan was made, over

(II) the outstanding balance of loans from the plan on the date on which such loan was made, or

(ii) the greater of (I) one-half of the present value of the nonforfeitable accrued benefit of the employee under the plan, or (II) $10,000.

For purposes of clause (ii), the present value of the nonforfeitable accrued benefit shall be determined without regard to any accumulated deductible employee contributions (as defined in subsection *(o)*(5)(B)).

(B) Requirement that loan be repayable within 5 years.—

(i) In general.—Subparagraph (A) shall not apply to any loan unless such loan, by its terms, is required to be repaid within 5 years.

(ii) Exception for home loans.—Clause (i) shall not apply to any loan used to acquire any dwelling unit which within a reasonable time is to be used (determined at the time the loan is made) as the principal residence of the participant.

(C) Requirement of level amortization.—Except as provided in regulations, this paragraph shall not apply to any loan unless substantially level amortization of such loan (with payments not less frequently than quarterly) is required over the term of the loan.

(D) Related employers and related plans.—For purposes of this paragraph—

(i) the rules of subsections (b), (c), and (m) of section 414 shall apply, and

(ii) all plans of an employer (determined after the application of such subsections) shall be treated as 1 plan.

(3) Denial of interest deductions in certain cases.—

(A) In general.—No deduction otherwise allowable under this chapter shall be allowed under this chapter for any interest paid or accrued on any loan to which paragraph (1) does not apply by reason of paragraph (2) during the period described in subparagraph (B).

(B) Period to which subparagraph (A) applies.—For purposes of subparagraph (A), the period described in this subparagraph is the period—

(i) on or after the 1st day on which the individual to whom the loan is made is a key employee (as defined in section 416(i)), or

(ii) such loan is secured by amounts attributable to elective deferrals described in subparagraph (A) or (C) of section 402(g)(3).

(4) Qualified employer plan, etc.—For purposes of this subsection—

(A) Qualified employer plan.—

(i) In general.—The term "qualified employer plan" means—

(I) a plan described in section 401(a) which includes a trust exempt from tax under section 501(a),

(II) an annuity plan described in section 403(a), and

(III) a plan under which amounts are contributed by an individual's employer for an annuity contract described in section 403(b).

(ii) Special rule.—The term "qualified employer plan" shall include any plan which was (or was determined to be) a qualified employer plan or a government plan.

(B) Government plan.—The term "government plan" means any plan, whether or not qualified, established and maintained for its employees by the United States, by a State or political subdivision thereof, or by an agency or instrumentality of any of the foregoing.

(5) Special rules for loans, etc., from certain contracts.—For purposes of this subsection, any amount received as a loan under a contract purchased under a qualified employer plan (and any assignment or pledge with respect to such a contract) shall be treated as a loan under such employer plan.

(q) 10-percent penalty for premature distributions from annuity contracts.—

(1) Imposition of penalty.—If any taxpayer receives any amount under an annuity contract, the taxpayer's tax under this chapter for the taxable year in which such amount is received shall be increased by an amount equal to 10 percent of the portion of such amount which is includible in gross income.

(2) Subsection not to apply to certain distributions.—Paragraph (1) shall not apply to any distribution—

(A) made on or after the date on which the taxpayer attains age 59½,

(B) made on or after the death of the holder (or, where the holder is not an individual, the death of the primary annuitant (as defined in subsection (s)(6)(B))),

(C) attributable to the taxpayer's becoming disabled within the meaning of subsection (m)(7),

(D) which is a part of a series of substantially equal periodic payments (not less frequently than annually) made for the life (or life expectancy) of the taxpayer or the joint lives (or joint life expectancies) of such taxpayer and his designated beneficiary,

(E) from a plan, contract, account, trust, or annuity described in subsection (e)(5)(D),

(F) allocable to investment in the contract before August 14, 1982,

(G) under a qualified funding asset (within the meaning of section 130(d), but without regard to whether there is a qualified assignment),

(H) to which subsection (t) applies (without regard to paragraph (2) thereof),

(I) under an immediate annuity contract (within the meaning of section 72(u)(4)), or

(J) which is purchased by an employer upon the termination of a plan described in section 401(a) or 403(a) and which is held by the employer until such time as the employee separates from service.

(3) Change in substantially equal payments.—If—

(A) paragraph (1) does not apply to a distribution by reason of paragraph (2)(D), and

(B) the series of payments under such paragraph are subsequently modified (other than by reason of death or disability)—

(i) before the close of the 5-year period beginning on the date of the first payment and after the taxpayer attains age 59½, or

(ii) before the taxpayer attains age 59½,

the taxpayer's tax for the 1st taxable year in which such modification occurs shall be increased by an amount, determined under regulations, equal to the tax which (but for paragraph (2)(D)) would have been imposed, plus interest for the deferral period (within the meaning of subsection (t)(4)(B)).

* * *

(s) Required distributions where holder dies before entire interest is distributed.—

(1) In general.—A contract shall not be treated as an annuity contract for purposes of this title unless it provides that—

(A) if any holder of such contract dies on or after the annuity starting date and before the entire interest in such contract has been distributed, the remaining portion of such interest will be distributed at least as rapidly as under the method of distributions being used as of the date of his death, and

(B) if any holder of such contract dies before the annuity starting date, the entire interest in such contract will be distributed within 5 years after the death of such holder.

(2) Exception for certain amounts payable over life of beneficiary.—If—

(A) any portion of the holder's interest is payable to (or for the benefit of) a designated beneficiary,

(B) such portion will be distributed (in accordance with regulations) over the life of such designated beneficiary (or over a period not extending beyond the life expectancy of such beneficiary), and

(C) such distributions begin not later than 1 year after the date of the holder's death or such later date as the Secretary may by regulations prescribe,

then for purposes of paragraph (1), the portion referred to in subparagraph (A) shall be treated as distributed on the day on which such distributions begin.

(3) Special rule where surviving spouse beneficiary.—If the designated beneficiary referred to in paragraph (2)(A) is the surviving spouse of the holder of the contract, paragraphs (1) and (2) shall be applied by treating such spouse as the holder of such contract.

(4) Designated beneficiary.—For purposes of this subsection, the term "designated beneficiary" means any individual designated a beneficiary by the holder of the contract.

(5) Exception for certain annuity contracts.—This subsection shall not apply to any annuity contract—

(A) which is provided—

(i) under a plan described in section 401(a) which includes a trust exempt from tax under section 501, or

(ii) under a plan described in section 403(a),

(B) which is described in section 403(b),

(C) which is an individual retirement annuity or provided under an individual retirement account or annuity, or

(D) which is a qualified funding asset (as defined in section 130(d), but without regard to whether there is a qualified assignment).

(6) Special rule where holder is corporation or other non-individual.—

(A) In general.—For purposes of this subsection, if the holder of the contract is not an individual, the primary annuitant shall be treated as the holder of the contract.

(B) Primary annuitant.—For purposes of subparagraph (A), the term "primary annuitant" means the individual, the events in the life of whom are of primary importance in affecting the timing or amount of the payout under the contract.

(7) Treatment of changes in primary annuitant where holder of contract is not an individual.—For purposes of this subsection, in the case of a holder of an annuity contract which is not an individual, if there is a change in a primary annuitant (as defined in paragraph (6)(B)), such change shall be treated as the death of the holder.

(t) 10–percent additional tax on early distributions from qualified retirement plans.—

(1) Imposition of additional tax.—If any taxpayer receives any amount from a qualified retirement plan (as defined in section 4974(c)), the taxpayer's tax under this chapter for the taxable year in which such amount is received shall be increased by an amount equal to 10 percent of the portion of such amount which is includible in gross income.

(2) Subsection not to apply to certain distributions.—Except as provided in paragraphs (3) and (4), paragraph (1) shall not apply to any of the following distributions:

(A) In general.—Distributions which are—

(i) made on or after the date on which the employee attains age 59½,

(ii) made to a beneficiary (or to the estate of the employee) on or after the death of the employee,

(iii) attributable to the employee's being disabled within the meaning of subsection (m)(7),

(iv) part of a series of substantially equal periodic payments (not less frequently than annually) made for the life (or life expectancy) of the employee or the joint lives (or joint life expectancies) of such employee and his designated beneficiary,

(v) made to an employee after separation from service after attainment of age 55,

* * *

(B) Medical expenses.—Distributions made to the employee (other than distributions described in subparagraph (A), (C), or (D)) to the extent such distributions do not exceed the amount allowable as a deduction under section 213 to the employee for amounts paid during the taxable year for medical care (determined without regard to whether the employee itemizes deductions for such taxable year).

(C) Payments to alternate payees pursuant to qualified domestic relations orders.—Any distribution to an alternate payee pursuant to a qualified domestic relations order (within the meaning of section 414(p)(1)).

(D) Distributions to unemployed individuals for health insurance premiums.—

(i) In general.—Distributions from an individual retirement plan to an individual after separation from employment—

(I) if such individual has received unemployment compensation for 12 consecutive weeks under any Federal or State unemployment compensation law by reason of such separation,

(II) if such distributions are made during any taxable year during which such unemployment compensation is paid or the succeeding taxable year, and

(III) to the extent such distributions do not exceed the amount paid during the taxable year for insurance described in section 213(d)(1)(D) with respect to the individual and the individual's spouse and dependents (as defined in section 152, determined without regard to subsections (b)(1), (b)(2), and (d)(1)(B) thereof).

(ii) Distributions after reemployment.—Clause (i) shall not apply to any distribution made after the individual has been employed for at least 60 days after the separation from employment to which clause (i) applies.

(iii) Self-employed individuals.—To the extent provided in regulations, a self-employed individual shall be treated as meeting the requirements of clause (i)(I) if, under Federal or State law, the individual would have received unemployment compensation but for the fact the individual was self-employed.

(E) Distributions from individual retirement plans for higher education expenses.—Distributions to an individual from an individual retirement plan to the extent such distributions do not exceed the qualified higher education expenses (as defined in paragraph (7)) of the taxpayer for the taxable year. Distributions shall not be taken into account under the preceding sentence if such distributions are described in subparagraph (A), (C), or (D) or to the extent paragraph (1) does not apply to such distributions by reason of subparagraph (B).

(F) Distributions from certain plans for first home purchases.—Distributions to an individual from an individual retirement plan which are qualified first-time homebuyer distributions (as defined in paragraph (8)). Distributions shall not be taken into account under the preceding sentence if such distributions are described in subparagraph (A), (C), (D), or (E) or to the extent paragraph (1) does not apply to such distributions by reason of subparagraph (B).

* * *

(3) Limitations.—

(A) Certain exceptions not to apply to individual retirement plans.—Subparagraphs (A)(v) and (C) of paragraph (2) shall not apply to distributions from an individual retirement plan.

(B) Periodic payments under qualified plans must begin after separation.—Paragraph (2)(A)(iv) shall not apply to any amount paid from a trust described in section 401(a) which is exempt from tax under section 501(a) or from a contract described in section 72(e)(5)(D)(ii) unless the series of payments begins after the employee separates from service.

(4) Change in substantially equal payments.—

(A) In general.—If—

(i) paragraph (1) does not apply to a distribution by reason of paragraph (2)(A)(iv), and

(ii) the series of payments under such paragraph are subsequently modified (other than by reason of death or disability)—

(I) before the close of the 5-year period beginning with the date of the first payment and after the employee attains age 59½, or

(II) before the employee attains age 59½, the taxpayer's tax for the 1st taxable year in which such modification occurs shall be increased by an amount, determined under regulations, equal to the tax which (but for paragraph (2)(A)(iv)) would have been imposed, plus interest for the deferral period.

(B) Deferral period.—For purposes of this paragraph, the term "deferral period" means the period beginning with the taxable year in which (without regard to paragraph (2)(A)(iv)) the distribution would have been includible in gross income and ending with the taxable year in which the modification described in subparagraph (A) occurs.

(5) Employee.—For purposes of this subsection, the term "employee" includes any participant, and in the case of an individual retirement plan, the individual for whose benefit such plan was established.

(6) Special rules for simple retirement accounts.—In the case of any amount received from a simple retirement account (within the meaning of section 408(p)) during the 2-year period beginning on the date such individual first participated in any qualified salary reduction arrangement maintained by the individual's employer under section 408(p)(2), paragraph (1) shall be applied by substituting "25 percent" for "10 percent".

(7) Qualified higher education expenses.—For purposes of paragraph (2)(E)—

(A) In general.—The term "qualified higher education expenses" means qualified higher education expenses (as defined in section 529(e)(3)) for education furnished to—

(i) the taxpayer,

(ii) the taxpayer's spouse, or

(iii) any child (as defined in section 152(f)(1)) or grandchild of the taxpayer or the taxpayer's spouse, at an eligible educational institution (as defined in section 529(e)(5)).

(B) Coordination with other benefits.—The amount of qualified higher education expenses for any taxable year shall be reduced as provided in section 25A(g)(2).

(8) Qualified first-time homebuyer distributions.—For purposes of paragraph (2)(F)—

(A) In general.—The term "qualified first-time homebuyer distribution" means any payment or distribution received by an individual to the extent such payment or distribution is used by the individual before the close of the 120th day after the day on which such payment or distribution is received to pay qualified acquisition costs with respect to a principal residence of a first-time homebuyer who is such individual, the spouse of such individual, or any child, grandchild, or ancestor of such individual or the individual's spouse.

(B) Lifetime dollar limitation.—The aggregate amount of payments or distributions received by an individual which may be treated as qualified first-time homebuyer distributions for any taxable year shall not exceed the excess (if any) of—

(i) $10,000, over

(ii) the aggregate amounts treated as qualified first-time homebuyer distributions with respect to such individual for all prior taxable years.

(C) Qualified acquisition costs.—For purposes of this paragraph, the term "qualified acquisition costs" means the costs of acquiring, constructing, or reconstructing a residence. Such term includes any usual or reasonable settlement, financing, or other closing costs.

(D) First-time homebuyer; other definitions.—For purposes of this paragraph—

(i) First-time homebuyer.—The term "first-time homebuyer" means any individual if—

(I) such individual (and if married, such individual's spouse) had no present ownership interest in a principal residence during the 2-year period ending on the date of acquisition of the principal residence to which this paragraph applies, and

(II) subsection (h) or (k) of section 1034 (as in effect on the day before the date of the enactment of this paragraph) did not suspend the running of any period of time specified in section 1034 (as so in effect) with respect to such individual on the day before the date the distribution is applied pursuant to subparagraph (A).

(ii) Principal residence.—The term "principal residence" has the same meaning as when used in section 121.

(iii) Date of acquisition.—The term "date of acquisition" means the date—

(I) on which a binding contract to acquire the principal residence to which subparagraph (A) applies is entered into, or

(II) on which construction or reconstruction of such a principal residence is commenced.

(E) Special rule where delay in acquisition.—If any distribution from any individual retirement plan fails to meet the requirements of subparagraph (A) solely by reason of a delay or cancellation of the purchase or construction of the residence, the amount of the distribution may be contributed to an individual retirement plan as provided in section 408(d)(3)(A)(i) (determined by substituting "120th day" for "60th day" in such section), except that—

(i) section 408(d)(3)(B) shall not be applied to such contribution, and

(ii) such amount shall not be taken into account in determining whether section 408(d)(3)(B) applies to any other amount.

* * *

(u) Treatment of annuity contracts not held by natural persons.—

(1) In general.—If any annuity contract is held by a person who is not a natural person—

(A) such contract shall not be treated as an annuity contract for purposes of this subtitle (other than subchapter L), and

(B) the income on the contract for any taxable year of the policyholder shall be treated as ordinary income received or accrued by the owner during such taxable year.

For purposes of this paragraph, holding by a trust or other entity as an agent for a natural person shall not be taken into account.

(2) Income on the contract.—

(A) In general.—For purposes of paragraph (1), the term "income on the contract" means, with respect to any taxable year of the policyholder, the excess of—

(i) the sum of the net surrender value of the contract as of the close of the taxable year plus all distributions under the contract received during the taxable year or any prior taxable year, reduced by

(ii) the sum of the amount of net premiums under the contract for the taxable year and prior taxable years and amounts includible in gross income for prior taxable years with respect to such contract under this subsection.

Where necessary to prevent the avoidance of this subsection, the Secretary may substitute "fair market value of the contract" for "net surrender value of the contract" each place it appears in the preceding sentence.

(B) Net premiums.—For purposes of this paragraph, the term "net premiums" means the amount of premiums paid under the contract reduced by any policyholder dividends.

(3) Exceptions.—This subsection shall not apply to any annuity contract which—

(A) is acquired by the estate of a decedent by reason of the death of the decedent,

(B) is held under a plan described in section 401(a) or 403(a), under a program described in section 403(b), or under an individual retirement plan,

(C) is a qualified funding asset (as defined in section 130(d), but without regard to whether there is a qualified assignment),

(D) is purchased by an employer upon the termination of a plan described in section 401(a) or 403(a) and which is held by the employer until all amounts under such contract are distributed to the employee for whom such contract was purchased or the employee's beneficiary, or

(E) is an immediate annuity.

(4) Immediate annuity.—For purposes of this subsection, the term "immediate annuity" means an annuity—

(A) which is purchased with a single premium or annuity consideration,

(B) the annuity starting date (as defined in subsection (c)(4)) of which commences no later than 1 year from the date of the purchase of the annuity, and

(C) which provides for a series of substantially equal periodic payments (to be made not less frequently than annually) during the annuity period.

(v) 10-percent additional tax for taxable distributions from modified endowment contracts.—

(1) Imposition of additional tax.—If any taxpayer receives any amount under a modified endowment contract (as defined in section 7702A), the taxpayer's tax under this chapter for the taxable year in which such amount is received shall be increased by an amount equal to 10 percent of the portion of such amount which is includible in gross income.

(2) Subsection not to apply to certain distributions.—Paragraph (1) shall not apply to any distribution—

(A) made on or after the date on which the taxpayer attains age 59½,

(B) which is attributable to the taxpayer's becoming disabled (within the meaning of subsection (m)(7)), or

(C) which is part of a series of substantially equal periodic payments (not less frequently than annually) made for the life (or life expectancy) of the taxpayer or the joint lives (or joint life expectancies) of such taxpayer and his beneficiary.

* * *

§ 73. Services of child

(a) Treatment of amounts received.—Amounts received in respect of the services of a child shall be included in his gross income and not in the gross income of the parent, even though such amounts are not received by the child.

(b) Treatment of expenditures.—All expenditures by the parent or the child attributable to amounts which are includible in the gross income of the child (and not of the parent) solely by reason of subsection (a) shall be treated as paid or incurred by the child.

(c) Parent defined.—For purposes of this section, the term "parent" includes an individual who is entitled to the services of a child by reason of having parental rights and duties in respect of the child.

* * *

§ 74. Prizes and awards

(a) General rule.—Except as otherwise provided in this section or in section 117 (relating to qualified scholarships), gross income includes amounts received as prizes and awards.

(b) Exception for certain prizes and awards transferred to charities.—Gross income does not include amounts received as prizes and awards made primarily in recognition of religious, charitable, scientific, educational, artistic, literary, or civic achievement, but only if—

(1) the recipient was selected without any action on his part to enter the contest or proceeding;

(2) the recipient is not required to render substantial future services as a condition to receiving the prize or award; and

(3) the prize or award is transferred by the payor to a governmental unit or organization described in paragraph (1) or (2) of section 170(c) pursuant to a designation made by the recipient.

(c) Exception for certain employee achievement awards.—

(1) In general.—Gross income shall not include the value of an employee achievement award (as defined in section 274(j)) received by the taxpayer if the cost to the employer of the employee achievement award does not exceed the amount allowable as a deduction to the employer for the cost of the employee achievement award.

(2) Excess deduction award.—If the cost to the employer of the employee achievement award received by the taxpayer exceeds the amount allowable as a deduction to the employer, then gross income includes the greater of—

(A) an amount equal to the portion of the cost to the employer of the award that is not allowable as a deduction to the employer (but not in excess of the value of the award), or

(B) the amount by which the value of the award exceeds the amount allowable as a deduction to the employer.

The remaining portion of the value of such award shall not be included in the gross income of the recipient.

(3) Treatment of tax-exempt employers.—In the case of an employer exempt from taxation under this subtitle, any reference in this subsection to the amount allowable as a deduction to the employer shall be treated as a reference to the amount which would be allowable as a deduction to the employer if the employer were not exempt from taxation under this subtitle.

(4) Cross reference.—

For provisions excluding certain de minimis fringes from gross income, see section 132(e).

§ 77. Commodity credit loans

(a) Election to include loans in income.—Amounts received as loans from the Commodity Credit Corporation shall, at the election of the taxpayer, be considered as income and shall be included in gross income for the taxable year in which received.

(b) Effect of election on adjustments for subsequent years.—If a taxpayer exercises the election provided for in subsection (a) for any taxable year, then the method of computing income so adopted shall be adhered to with respect to all subsequent taxable years unless with the approval of the Secretary a change to a different method is authorized.

§ 79. Group-term life insurance purchased for employees

(a) General rule.—There shall be included in the gross income of an employee for the taxable year an amount equal to the cost of group-term life insurance on his life provided for part or all of such year under a policy (or policies) carried directly or indirectly by his employer (or employers); but only to the extent that such cost exceeds the sum of—

(1) the cost of $50,000 of such insurance, and

(2) the amount (if any) paid by the employee toward the purchase of such insurance.

(b) Exceptions.—Subsection (a) shall not apply to—

(1) the cost of group-term life insurance on the life of an individual which is provided under a policy carried directly or indirectly by an employer after such individual has terminated his employment with such employer and is disabled (within the meaning of section 72(m)(7)),

(2) the cost of any portion of the group-term life insurance on the life of an employee provided during part or all of the taxable year of the employee under which—

(A) the employer is directly or indirectly the beneficiary, or

(B) a person described in section 170(c) is the sole beneficiary, for the entire period during such taxable year for which the employee receives such insurance, and

(3) the cost of any group-term life insurance which is provided under a contract to which section 72(m)(3) applies.

(c) Determination of cost of insurance.—For purposes of this section and section 6052, the cost of group-term insurance on the life of an employee provided during any period shall be determined on the basis of uniform premiums (computed on the basis of 5–year age brackets) prescribed by regulations by the Secretary.

(d) Nondiscrimination requirements.—

(1) In general.—In the case of a discriminatory group-term life insurance plan—

(A) subsection (a)(1) shall not apply with respect to any key employee, and

(B) the cost of group-term life insurance on the life of any key employee shall be the greater of—

(i) such cost determined without regard to subsection (c), or

(ii) such cost determined with regard to subsection (c).

(2) Discriminatory group-term life insurance plan.—For purposes of this subsection, the term "discriminatory group-term life insurance plan" means any plan of an employer for providing group-term life insurance unless—

(A) the plan does not discriminate in favor of key employees as to eligibility to participate, and

(B) the type and amount of benefits available under the plan do not discriminate in favor of participants who are key employees.

(3) Nondiscriminatory eligibility classification.—

(A) In general.—A plan does not meet requirements of subparagraph (A) of paragraph (2) unless—

(i) such plan benefits 70 percent or more of all employees of the employer,

(ii) at least 85 percent of all employees who are participants under the plan are not key employees,

(iii) such plan benefits such employees as qualify under a classification set up by the employer and found by the Secretary not to be discriminatory in favor of key employees, or

(iv) in the case of a plan which is part of a cafeteria plan, the requirements of section 125 are met.

(B) Exclusion of certain employees.—For purposes of subparagraph (A), there may be excluded from consideration—

(i) employees who have not completed 3 years of service;

(ii) part-time or seasonal employees;

(iii) employees not included in the plan who are included in a unit of employees covered by an agreement between employee representatives and one or more employers which the Secretary finds to be a collective bargaining agreement, if the benefits provided under the plan were the subject of good faith bargaining between such employee representatives and such employer or employers; and

(iv) employees who are nonresident aliens and who receive no earned income (within the meaning of section 911(d)(2)) from the employer which constitutes income from sources within the United States (within the meaning of section 861(a)(3)).

(4) Nondiscriminatory benefits.—A plan does not meet the requirements of paragraph (2)(B) unless all benefits available to participants who are key employees are available to all other participants.

(5) Special rule.—A plan shall not fail to meet the requirements of paragraph (2)(B) merely because the amount of life insurance on behalf of the employees under the plan bears a uniform relationship to the total compensation or the basic or regular rate of compensation of such employees.

(6) Key employee defined.—For purposes of this subsection, the term "key employee" has the meaning given to such term by paragraph (1) of section 416(i). Such term also includes any former employee if such employee when he retired or separated from service was a key employee.

* * *

(8) Treatment of former employees.—To the extent provided in regulations, this subsection shall be applied separately with respect to former employees.

(e) Employee includes former employee.—For purposes of this section the term "employee" includes a former employee.

* * *

§ 82. Reimbursement for expenses of moving

Except as provided in section 132(a)(6), there shall be included in gross income (as compensation for services) any amount received or accrued, directly or indirectly, by an individual as a payment for or reimbursement of expenses of moving from one residence to another residence which is attributable to employment or self-employment.

§ 83. Property transferred in connection with performance of services

(a) General rule.—If, in connection with the performance of services, property is transferred to any person other than the person for whom such services are performed, the excess of—

(1) the fair market value of such property (determined without regard to any restriction other than a restriction which by its terms will never lapse) at the first time the rights of the person having the beneficial interest in such property are transferable or are not subject to a substantial risk of forfeiture, whichever occurs earlier, over

(2) the amount (if any) paid for such property,

shall be included in the gross income of the person who performed such services in the first taxable year in which the rights of the person having the beneficial interest in such property are transferable or are not subject to a substantial risk of forfeiture, whichever is applicable. The preceding sentence shall not apply if such person sells or otherwise disposes of such property in an arm's length transaction before his rights in such property become transferable or not subject to a substantial risk of forfeiture.

(b) Election to include in gross income in year of transfer.—

(1) In general.—Any person who performs services in connection with which property is transferred to any person may elect to include in his gross income, for the taxable year in which such property is transferred, the excess of—

(A) the fair market value of such property at the time of transfer (determined without regard to any restriction other than a restriction which by its terms will never lapse), over

(B) the amount (if any) paid for such property.

If such election is made, subsection (a) shall not apply with respect to the transfer of such property, and if such property is subsequently forfeited, no deduction shall be allowed in respect of such forfeiture.

(2) Election.—An election under paragraph (1) with respect to any transfer of property shall be made in such manner as the Secretary prescribes and shall be made not later than 30 days after the date of such transfer. Such election may not be revoked except with the consent of the Secretary.

(c) Special rules.—For purposes of this section—

(1) Substantial risk of forfeiture.—The rights of a person in property are subject to a substantial risk of forfeiture if such person's rights to full enjoyment of such property are conditioned upon the future performance of substantial services by any individual.

(2) Transferability of property.—The rights of a person in property are transferable only if the rights in such property of any transferee are not subject to a substantial risk of forfeiture.

(3) Sales which may give rise to suit under section 16(b) of the Securities Exchange Act of 1934.—So long as the sale of property at a profit could subject a person to suit under section 16(b) of the Securities Exchange Act of 1934, such person's rights in such property are—

(A) subject to a substantial risk of forfeiture, and

(B) not transferable.

* * *

(d) Certain restrictions which will never lapse.—

(1) Valuation.—In the case of property subject to a restriction which by its terms will never lapse, and which allows the transferee to sell such property only at a price determined under a formula, the price so determined shall be deemed to be the fair market value of the property unless established to the contrary by the Secretary, and the burden of proof shall be on the Secretary with respect to such value.

(2) Cancellation.—If, in the case of property subject to a restriction which by its terms will never lapse, the restriction is canceled, then, unless the taxpayer establishes—

(A) that such cancellation was not compensatory, and

(B) that the person, if any, who would be allowed a deduction if the cancellation were treated as compensatory, will treat the transaction as not compensatory, as evidenced in such manner as the Secretary shall prescribe by regulations,

the excess of the fair market value of the property (computed without regard to the restrictions) at the time of cancellation over the sum of—

(C) the fair market value of such property (computed by taking the restriction into account) immediately before the cancellation, and

(D) the amount, if any, paid for the cancellation,

shall be treated as compensation for the taxable year in which such cancellation occurs.

(e) Applicability of section.—This section shall not apply to—

(1) a transaction to which section 421 applies,

(2) a transfer to or from a trust described in section 401(a) or a transfer under an annuity plan which meets the requirements of section 404(a)(2),

(3) the transfer of an option without a readily ascertainable fair market value,

(4) the transfer of property pursuant to the exercise of an option with a readily ascertainable fair market value at the date of grant, or

(5) group-term life insurance to which section 79 applies.

(f) Holding period.—In determining the period for which the taxpayer has held property to which subsection (a) applies, there shall be included only the period beginning at the first time his rights in such property are transferable or are not subject to a substantial risk of forfeiture, whichever occurs earlier.

(g) Certain exchanges.—If property to which subsection (a) applies is exchanged for property subject to restrictions and conditions substantially similar to those to which the property given in such exchange was subject, and if section 354, 355, 356, or 1036 (or so much of section 1031 as relates to section 1036) applied to such exchange, or if such exchange was pursuant to the exercise of a conversion privilege—

(1) such exchange shall be disregarded for purposes of subsection (a), and

(2) the property received shall be treated as property to which subsection (a) applies.

(h) Deduction by employer.—In the case of a transfer of property to which this section applies or a cancellation of a restriction described in subsection (d), there shall be allowed as a deduction under section 162, to the person for whom were performed the services in connection with which such property was transferred, an amount equal to the amount included under subsection (a), (b), or (d)(2) in the gross income of the person who performed such services. Such deduction shall be allowed for the taxable year of such person in which or with which ends the taxable year in which such amount is included in the gross income of the person who performed such services.

§ 84. Transfer of appreciated property to political organization

(a) General rule.—If—

(1) any person transfers property to a political organization, and

(2) the fair market value of such property exceeds its adjusted basis,

then for purposes of this chapter the transferor shall be treated as having sold such property to the political organization on the date of the transfer, and the transferor shall be treated as having realized an amount equal to the fair market value of such property on such date.

(b) Basis of property.—In the case of a transfer of property to a political organization to which subsection (a) applies, the basis of such property in the hands of the political organization shall be the same as it would be in the hands of the transferor, increased by the amount of gain recognized to the transferor by reason of such transfer.

(c) Political organization defined.—For purposes of this section, the term "political organization" has the meaning given to such term by section 527(e)(1).

§ 85. Unemployment compensation

(a) General rule.—In the case of an individual, gross income includes unemployment compensation.

(b) Unemployment compensation defined.—For purposes of this section, the term "unemployment compensation" means any amount received under a law of the United States or of a State which is in the nature of unemployment compensation.

(c) Special Rule for 2009.— In the case of any taxable year beginning in 2009, gross income shall not include so much of the unemployment compensation received by an individual as does not exceed $2,400.

§ 86. Social security and tier 1 railroad retirement benefits

(a) In general—

(1) In general—Except as provided in paragraph (2), gross income for the taxable year of any taxpayer described in subsection (b) (notwithstanding section 207 of the Social Security Act) includes social security benefits in an amount equal to the lesser of—

(A) one-half of the social security benefits received during the taxable year, or

(B) one-half of the excess described in subsection (b)(1).

(2) Additional amount—In the case of a taxpayer with respect to whom the amount determined under subsection (b)(1)(A) exceeds the adjusted base amount, the amount included in gross income under this section shall be equal to the lesser of—

(A) the sum of—

(i) 85 percent of such excess, plus

(ii) the lesser of the amount determined under paragraph (1) or an amount equal to one-half of the difference between the adjusted base amount and the base amount of the taxpayer, or

(B) 85 percent of the social security benefits received during the taxable year.

(b) Taxpayers to whom subsection (a) applies.—

(1) In general.—A taxpayer is described in this subsection if—

(A) the sum of—

(i) the modified adjusted gross income of the taxpayer for the taxable year, plus

(ii) one-half of the social security benefits received during the taxable year, exceeds

(B) the base amount.

(2) Modified adjusted gross income.—For purposes of this subsection, the term "modified adjusted gross income" means adjusted gross income—

(A) determined without regard to this section and sections 135, 137, 199, 221, 222, 911, 931, and 933, and

(B) increased by the amount of interest received or accrued by the taxpayer during the taxable year which is exempt from tax.

(c) Base amount and adjusted base amount.—For purposes of this section—

(1) Base amount.—The term "base amount" means—

(A) except as otherwise provided in this paragraph, $25,000,

(B) $32,000 in the case of a joint return, and

(C) zero in the case of a taxpayer who—

(i) is married as of the close of the taxable year (within the meaning of section 7703) but does not file a joint return for such year, and

(ii) does not live apart from his spouse at all times during the taxable year.

(2) Adjusted base amount.—The term "adjusted base amount" means—

(A) except as otherwise provided in this paragraph, $34,000,

(B) $44,000 in the case of a joint return, and

(C) zero in the case of a taxpayer described in paragraph (1)(C).

(d) Social security benefit.—

(1) In general.—For purposes of this section, the term "social security benefit" means any amount received by the taxpayer by reason of entitlement to—

(A) a monthly benefit under title II of the Social Security Act, or

(B) a tier 1 railroad retirement benefit.

* * *

PART III—ITEMS SPECIFICALLY EXCLUDED FROM GROSS INCOME

§ 101. Certain death benefits

(a) Proceeds of life insurance contracts payable by reason of death.—

(1) General rule.—Except as otherwise provided in paragraph (2), subsection (d), subsection (f), and subsection (j), gross income does not include amounts received (whether in a single sum or otherwise) under a life insurance contract, if such amounts are paid by reason of the death of the insured.

(2) Transfer for valuable consideration.—In the case of a transfer for a valuable consideration, by assignment or otherwise, of a life insurance contract or any interest therein, the amount excluded from gross income by paragraph (1) shall not exceed an amount equal to the sum of the actual value of such consideration and the premiums and other amounts subsequently paid by the transferee. The preceding sentence shall not apply in the case of such a transfer—

(A) if such contract or interest therein has a basis for determining gain or loss in the hands of a transferee determined in whole or in part by reference to such basis of such contract or interest therein in the hands of the transferor, or

(B) if such transfer is to the insured, to a partner of the insured, to a partnership in which the insured is a partner, or to a corporation in which the insured is a shareholder or officer.

The term "other amounts" in the first sentence of this paragraph includes interest paid or accrued by the transferee on indebtedness with respect to such contract or any interest therein if such interest paid or accrued is not allowable as a deduction by reason of section 264(a)(4).

[(b) Repealed.]

(c) Interest.—If any amount excluded from gross income by subsection (a) is held under an agreement to pay interest thereon, the interest payments shall be included in gross income.

(d) Payment of life insurance proceeds at a date later than death.—

(1) General rule.—The amounts held by an insurer with respect to any beneficiary shall be prorated (in accordance with such regulations as may be prescribed by the Secretary) over the period or periods with respect to which such payments are to be made. There shall be excluded from the gross income of such beneficiary in the taxable year received any amount determined by such proration. Gross income includes, to the extent not excluded by the preceding sentence, amounts received under agreements to which this subsection applies.

(2) Amount held by an insurer.—An amount held by an insurer with respect to any beneficiary shall mean an amount to which subsection (a) applies which is—

(A) held by any insurer under an agreement provided for in the life insurance contract, whether as an option or otherwise, to pay such amount on a date or dates later than the death of the insured, and

(B) equal to the value of such agreement to such beneficiary

(i) as of the date of death of the insured (as if any option exercised under the life insurance contract were exercised at such time), and

(ii) as discounted on the basis of the interest rate used by the insurer in calculating payments under the agreement and mortality tables prescribed by the Secretary.

(3) Application of subsection.—This subsection shall not apply to any amount to which subsection (c) is applicable.

* * *

(g) Treatment of certain accelerated death benefits.—

(1) In general.—For purposes of this section, the following amounts shall be treated as an amount paid by reason of the death of an insured:

(A) Any amount received under a life insurance contract on the life of an insured who is a terminally ill individual.

(B) Any amount received under a life insurance contract on the life of an insured who is a chronically ill individual.

(2) Treatment of viatical settlements.—

(A) In general.—If any portion of the death benefit under a life insurance contract on the life of an insured described in paragraph (1) is sold or assigned to a viatical settlement provider, the amount paid for the sale or assignment of such portion shall be treated as an amount paid under the life insurance contract by reason of the death of such insured.

(B) Viatical settlement provider.—

(i) In general.—The term "viatical settlement provider" means any person regularly engaged in the trade or business of purchasing, or taking assignments of, life insurance contracts on the lives of insureds described in paragraph (1) if—

(I) such person is licensed for such purposes (with respect to insureds described in the same subparagraph of paragraph (1) as the insured) in the State in which the insured resides, or

(II) in the case of an insured who resides in a State not requiring the licensing of such persons for such purposes with respect to such insured, such person meets the requirements of clause (ii) or (iii), whichever applies to such insured.

(ii) Terminally ill insureds.—A person meets the requirements of this clause with respect to an insured who is a terminally ill individual if such person—

(I) meets the requirements of sections 8 and 9 of the Viatical Settlements Model Act of the National Association of Insurance Commissioners, and

(II) meets the requirements of the Model Regulations of the National Association of Insurance Commissioners (relating to standards for evaluation of reasonable payments) in determining amounts paid by such person in connection with such purchases or assignments.

(iii) Chronically ill insureds.—A person meets the requirements of this clause with respect to an insured who is a chronically ill individual if such person—

(I) meets requirements similar to the requirements referred to in clause (ii)(I), and

(II) meets the standards (if any) of the National Association of Insurance Commissioners for evaluating the reasonableness of amounts paid by such person in connection with such purchases or assignments with respect to chronically ill individuals.

(3) Special rules for chronically ill insureds.—In the case of an insured who is a chronically ill individual—

(A) In general.—Paragraphs (1) and (2) shall not apply to any payment received for any period unless—

(i) such payment is for costs incurred by the payee (not compensated for by insurance or otherwise) for qualified long-term care services provided for the insured for such period, and

(ii) the terms of the contract giving rise to such payment satisfy—

(I) the requirements of section 7702B(b)(1)(B), and

(II) the requirements (if any) applicable under subparagraph (B).

For purposes of the preceding sentence, the rule of section 7702B(b)(2)(B) shall apply.

(B) Other requirements.—The requirements applicable under this subparagraph are—

(i) those requirements of section 7702B(g) and section 4980C which the Secretary specifies as applying to such a purchase, assignment, or other arrangement,

(ii) standards adopted by the National Association of Insurance Commissioners which specifically apply to chronically ill individuals (and, if such standards are adopted, the analogous requirements specified under clause (i) shall cease to apply), and

(iii) standards adopted by the State in which the policyholder resides (and if such standards are adopted, the analogous requirements specified under clause (i) and (subject to section 4980C(f)) standards under clause (ii), shall cease to apply).

(C) Per diem payments.—A payment shall not fail to be described in subparagraph (A) by reason of being made on a per diem or other periodic basis without regard to the expenses incurred during the period to which the payment relates.

(D) Limitation on exclusion for periodic payments.—For limitation on amount of periodic payments which are treated as described in paragraph (1), see section 7702B(d).

(4) Definitions.—For purposes of this subsection—

(A) Terminally ill individual.—The term "terminally ill individual" means an individual who has been certified by a physician as having an illness or physical condition which can reasonably be expected to result in death in 24 months or less after the date of the certification.

(B) Chronically ill individual.—The term "chronically ill individual" has the meaning given such term by section 7702B(c)(2); except that such term shall not include a terminally ill individual.

(C) Qualified long-term care services.—The term "qualified long-term care services" has the meaning given such term by section 7702B(c).

(D) Physician.—The term "physician" has the meaning given to such term by section 1861(r)(1) of the Social Security Act (42 U.S.C. 1395x(r)(1)).

(5) Exception for business-related policies.—This subsection shall not apply in the case of any amount paid to any taxpayer other than the insured if such taxpayer has an insurable interest with respect to the life of the insured by reason of the insured being a director, officer, or employee of the taxpayer or by reason of the insured being financially interested in any trade or business carried on by the taxpayer.

* * *

§ 102. Gifts and inheritances

(a) General rule.—Gross income does not include the value of property acquired by gift, bequest, devise, or inheritance.

(b) Income.—Subsection (a) shall not exclude from gross income—

(1) the income from any property referred to in subsection (a); or

(2) where the gift, bequest, devise, or inheritance is of income from property, the amount of such income.

Where, under the terms of the gift, bequest, devise, or inheritance, the payment, crediting, or distribution thereof is to be made at intervals, then, to the extent that it is paid or credited or to be distributed out of income from property, it shall be treated for purposes of paragraph (2) as a gift, bequest, devise, or inheritance of income from property. Any amount included in the gross income of a beneficiary under subchapter

J shall be treated for purposes of paragraph (2) as a gift, bequest, devise, or inheritance of income from property.

(c) Employee gifts.—

(1) In general.—Subsection (a) shall not exclude from gross income any amount transferred by or for an employer to, or for the benefit of, an employee.

(2) Cross references.—

For provisions excluding certain employee achievement awards from gross income, see section 74(c).

For provisions excluding certain de minimis fringes from gross income, see section 132(e).

§ 103. Interest on state and local bonds

(a) Exclusion.—Except as provided in subsection (b), gross income does not include interest on any State or local bond.

(b) Exceptions.—Subsection (a) shall not apply to—

(1) Private activity bond which is not a qualified bond.—Any private activity bond which is not a qualified bond (within the meaning of section 141).

(2) Arbitrage bond.—Any arbitrage bond (within the meaning of section 148).

(3) Bond not in registered form, etc.—Any bond unless such bond meets the applicable requirements of section 149.

(c) Definitions.—For purposes of this section and part IV—

(1) State or local bond.—The term "State or local bond" means an obligation of a State or political subdivision thereof.

(2) State.—The term "State" includes the District of Columbia and any possession of the United States.

§ 104. Compensation for injuries or sickness

(a) In general.—Except in the case of amounts attributable to (and not in excess of) deductions allowed under section 213 (relating to medical, etc., expenses) for any prior taxable year, gross income does not include—

(1) amounts received under workmen's compensation acts as compensation for personal injuries or sickness;

(2) the amount of any damages (other than punitive damages) received (whether by suit or agreement and whether as lump sums or as periodic payments) on account of personal physical injuries or physical sickness;

(3) amounts received through accident or health insurance (or through an arrangement having the effect of accident or health insurance) for personal injuries or sickness (other than amounts received by an employee, to the extent such amounts (A) are attributable to contributions by the employer which were not includible in the gross income of the employee, or (B) are paid by the employer);

(4) amounts received as a pension, annuity, or similar allowance for personal injuries or sickness resulting from active service in the armed forces of any country or in the Coast and Geodetic Survey or the Public Health Service, or as a disability annuity payable under the provisions of section 808 of the Foreign Service Act of 1980; and

(5) amounts received by an individual as disability income attributable to injuries incurred as a direct result of a terroristic or military action (as defined in section 692(c)(2)).

For purposes of paragraph (3), in the case of an individual who is, or has been, an employee within the meaning of section 401(c)(1) (relating to self-employed individuals), contributions made on behalf of such individual while he was such an employee to a trust described in section 401(a) which is exempt from tax under section 501(a), or under a plan described in section 403(a), shall, to the extent allowed as deductions under section 404, be treated as contributions by the employer which were not includible in the gross income of the employee. For purposes of paragraph (2), emotional distress shall not be treated as a physical injury or physical sickness. The preceding sentence shall not apply to an amount of damages not in excess of the amount paid for medical care (described in subparagraph (A) or (B) of section 213(d)(1)) attributable to emotional distress.

(b) Termination of application of subsection (a)(4) in certain cases.—

(1) In general.—Subsection (a)(4) shall not apply in the case of any individual who is not described in paragraph (2).

(2) Individuals to whom subsection (a)(4) continues to apply.—An individual is described in this paragraph if—

(A) on or before September 24, 1975, he was entitled to receive any amount described in subsection (a)(4),

(B) on September 24, 1975, he was a member of any organization (or reserve component thereof) referred to in subsection (a)(4) or under a binding written commitment to become such a member,

(C) he receives an amount described in subsection (a)(4) by reason of a combat-related injury, or

(D) on application therefor, he would be entitled to receive disability compensation from the Veterans' Administration.

* * *

(c) Application of prior law in certain cases.—The phrase "(other than punitive damages)" shall not apply to punitive damages awarded in a civil action—

(1) which is a wrongful death action, and

(2) with respect to which applicable State law (as in effect on September 13, 1995 and without regard to any modification after such date) provides, or has been construed to provide by a court of competent jurisdiction pursuant to a decision issued on or before September 13, 1995, that only punitive damages may be awarded in such an action.

This subsection shall cease to apply to any civil action filed on or after the first date on which the applicable State law ceases to provide (or is no longer construed to provide) the treatment described in paragraph (2).

(d) Cross references.—

(1) For exclusion from employee's gross income of employer contributions to accident and health plans, see section 106.

(2) For exclusion of part of disability retirement pay from the application of subsection (a)(4) of this section, see section 1403 of title 10, United States Code (relating to career compensation laws).

§ 105. Amounts received under accident and health plans

(a) Amounts attributable to employer contributions.—Except as otherwise provided in this section, amounts received by an employee through accident or health insurance for personal injuries or sickness shall be included in gross income to the extent such amounts (1) are attributable to contributions by the employer which were not includible in the gross income of the employee, or (2) are paid by the employer.

(b) Amounts expended for medical care.—Except in the case of amounts attributable to (and not in excess of) deductions allowed under section 213 (relating to medical, etc., expenses) for any prior taxable year, gross income does not include amounts referred to in subsection (a) if such amounts are paid, directly or indirectly, to the taxpayer to reimburse the taxpayer for expenses incurred by him for the medical care (as defined in section 213(d)) of the taxpayer, his spouse, his dependents (as defined in section 152, determined without regard to subsections (b)(1), (b)(2), and (d)(1)(B) thereof), and any child (as defined in section 152(f)(1)) of the taxpayer who as of the end of the taxable year has not attained age 27. Any child to whom section 152(e) applies shall be treated as a dependent of both parents for purposes of this subsection.

(c) Payments unrelated to absence from work.—Gross income does not include amounts referred to in subsection (a) to the extent such amounts—

(1) constitute payment for the permanent loss or loss of use of a member or function of the body, or the permanent disfigurement, of the taxpayer, his spouse, or a dependent (as defined in section 152, determined without regard to subsections (b)(1), (b)(2), and (d)(1)(B) thereof), and

(2) are computed with reference to the nature of the injury without regard to the period the employee is absent from work.

[(d) Repealed.]

(e) Accident and health plans.—For purposes of this section and section 104—

(1) amounts received under an accident or health plan for employees, and

(2) amounts received from a sickness and disability fund for employees maintained under the law of a State or the District of Columbia,

shall be treated as amounts received through accident or health insurance.

(f) Rules for application of section 213.—For purposes of section 213(a) (relating to medical, dental, etc., expenses) amounts excluded from gross income under subsection (c) or (d) shall not be considered as compensation (by insurance or otherwise) for expenses paid for medical care.

(g) Self-employed individual not considered an employee.—For purposes of this section, the term "employee" does not include an individual who is an employee within the meaning of section 401(c)(1) (relating to self-employed individuals).

(h) Amount paid to highly compensated individuals under a discriminatory self-insured medical expense reimbursement plan.—

(1) In general.—In the case of amounts paid to a highly compensated individual under a self-insured medical reimbursement plan which does not satisfy the requirements of paragraph (2) for a plan year, subsection (b) shall not apply to such amounts to the extent they constitute an excess reimbursement of such highly compensated individual.

(2) Prohibition of discrimination.—A self-insured medical reimbursement plan satisfies the requirements of this paragraph only if—

(A) the plan does not discriminate in favor of highly compensated individuals as to eligibility to participate; and

(B) the benefits provided under the plan do not discriminate in favor of participants who are highly compensated individuals.

(3) Nondiscriminatory eligibility classifications.—

(A) In general.—A self-insured medical reimbursement plan does not satisfy the requirements of subparagraph (A) of paragraph (2) unless such plan benefits—

(i) 70 percent or more of all employees, or 80 percent or more of all the employees who are eligible to benefit under the plan if 70 percent or more of all employees are eligible to benefit under the plan; or

(ii) such employees as qualify under a classification set up by the employer and found by the Secretary not to be discriminatory in favor of highly compensated individuals.

(B) Exclusion of certain employees.—For purposes of subparagraph (A), there may be excluded from consideration—

(i) employees who have not completed 3 years of service;

(ii) employees who have not attained age 25;

(iii) part-time or seasonal employees;

(iv) employees not included in the plan who are included in a unit of employees covered by an agreement between employee representatives and one or more employers which the Secretary finds to be a collective bargaining agreement, if accident and health benefits were the subject of good faith bargaining between such employee representatives and such employer or employers; and

(v) employees who are nonresident aliens and who receive no earned income (within the meaning of section 911(d)(2)) from the employer which constitutes income from sources within the United States (within the meaning of section 861(a)(3)).

(4) Nondiscriminatory benefits.—A self-insured medical reimbursement plan does not meet the requirements of subparagraph (B) of paragraph (2) unless all benefits provided for participants who are highly compensated individuals are provided for all other participants.

(5) Highly compensated individual defined.—For purposes of this subsection, the term "highly compensated individual" means an individual who is—

(A) one of the 5 highest paid officers,

(B) a shareholder who owns (with the application of section 318) more than 10 percent in value of the stock of the employer, or

(C) among the highest paid 25 percent of all employees (other than employees described in paragraph (3)(B) who are not participants).

(6) Self-insured medical reimbursement plan.—The term "self-insured medical reimbursement plan" means a plan of an employer to reimburse employees for expenses referred to in subsection (b) for which reimbursement is not provided under a policy of accident and health insurance.

(7) Excess reimbursement of highly compensated individual.—For purposes of this section, the excess reimbursement of a highly compensated individual which is attributable to a self-insured medical reimbursement plan is—

(A) in the case of a benefit available to highly compensated individuals but not to all other participants (or which otherwise fails to satisfy the requirements of paragraph (2)(B)), the amount reimbursed under the plan to the employee with respect to such benefit, and

(B) in the case of benefits (other than benefits described in subparagraph (A)) paid to a highly compensated individual by a plan which fails to satisfy the requirements of paragraph (2), the total amount reimbursed to the highly compensated individual for the plan year multiplied by a fraction—

(i) the numerator of which is the total amount reimbursed to all participants who are highly compensated individuals under the plan for the plan year, and

(ii) the denominator of which is the total amount reimbursed to all employees under the plan for such plan year.

In determining the fraction under subparagraph (B), there shall not be taken into account any reimbursement which is attributable to a benefit described in subparagraph (A).

(8) Certain controlled groups, etc.—All employees who are treated as employed by a single employer under subsection (b), (c), or (m) of section 414 shall be treated as employed by a single employer for purposes of this section.

(9) Regulations.—The Secretary shall prescribe such regulations as may be necessary to carry out the provisions of this section.

(10) Time of inclusion.—Any amount paid for a plan year that is included in income by reason of this subsection shall be treated as received or accrued in the taxable year of the participant in which the plan year ends.

* * *

§ 106. Contributions by employer to accident and health plans

(a) General rule.—Except as otherwise provided in this section, gross income of an employee does not include employer-provided coverage under an accident or health plan.

* * *

(c) Inclusion of long-term care benefits provided through flexible spending arrangements.—

(1) In general.—Effective on and after January 1, 1997, gross income of an employee shall include employer-provided coverage for qualified long-term care services (as defined in section 7702B(c)) to the extent that such coverage is provided through a flexible spending or similar arrangement.

(2) Flexible spending arrangement.—For purposes of this subsection, a flexible spending arrangement is a benefit program which provides employees with coverage under which—

(A) specified incurred expenses may be reimbursed (subject to reimbursement maximums and other reasonable conditions), and

(B) the maximum amount of reimbursement which is reasonably available to a participant for such coverage is less than 500 percent of the value of such coverage.

In the case of an insured plan, the maximum amount reasonably available shall be determined on the basis of the underlying coverage.

(d) Contributions to health savings accounts.—

(1) In general.—In the case of an employee who is an eligible individual (as defined in section 223(c)(1)), amounts contributed by such employee's employer to any health savings account (as defined in section 223(d)) of such employee shall be treated as employer-provided coverage for medical expenses under an accident or health plan to the extent such amounts do not exceed the limitation under section 223(b) (determined without regard to this subsection) which is applicable to such employee for such taxable year.

(2) Special rules.—Rules similar to the rules of paragraphs (2), (3), (4), and (5) of subsection (b) shall apply for purposes of this subsection.

(3) Cross reference.—For penalty on failure by employer to make comparable contributions to the health savings accounts of comparable employees, see section 4980G.

* * *

(f) Reimbursements for medicine restricted to prescribed drugs and insulin.— For purposes of this section and section 105, reimbursement for expenses incurred for a medicine or a drug shall be treated as a reimbursement for medical expenses only if such medicine or drug is a prescribed drug (determined without regard to whether such drug is available without a prescription) or is insulin.

§ 107. Rental value of parsonages

In the case of a minister of the gospel, gross income does not include—

(1) the rental value of a home furnished to him as part of his compensation; or

(2) the rental allowance paid to him as part of his compensation, to the extent used by him to rent or provide a home and to the extent such allowance does not exceed the fair rental value of the home, including furnishings and appurtenances such as a garage, plus the cost of utilities.

§ 108. Income from discharge of indebtedness

(a) Exclusion from gross income.—

(1) In general.—Gross income does not include any amount which (but for this subsection) would be includible in gross income by reason of the discharge (in whole or in part) of indebtedness of the taxpayer if—

(A) the discharge occurs in a title 11 case,

(B) the discharge occurs when the taxpayer is insolvent,

(C) the indebtedness discharged is qualified farm indebtedness,

(D) in the case of a taxpayer other than a C corporation, the indebtedness discharged is qualified real property business indebtedness, or

(E) the indebtedness discharged is qualified principal residence indebtedness which is discharged before January 1, 2014.

(2) Coordination of exclusions.—

(A) Title 11 exclusion takes precedence.—Subparagraphs (B), (C), (D), and (E) of paragraph (1) shall not apply to a discharge which occurs in a title 11 case.

(B) Insolvency exclusion takes precedence over qualified farm exclusion and qualified real property business exclusion.—Subparagraphs (C) and (D) of paragraph (1) shall not apply to a discharge to the extent the taxpayer is insolvent.

(C) Principal residence exclusion takes precedence over insolvency exclusion unless elected otherwise.—Paragraph (1)(B) shall not apply to a discharge to which paragraph (1)(E) applies unless the taxpayer elects to apply paragraph (1)(B) in lieu of paragraph (1)(E).

(3) Insolvency exclusion limited to amount of insolvency.—In the case of a discharge to which paragraph (1)(B) applies, the amount excluded under paragraph (1)(B) shall not exceed the amount by which the taxpayer is insolvent.

(b) Reduction of tax attributes.—

(1) In general.—The amount excluded from gross income under subparagraph (A), (B), or (C) of subsection (a)(1) shall be applied to reduce the tax attributes of the taxpayer as provided in paragraph (2).

(2) Tax attributes affected; order of reduction.—Except as provided in paragraph (5), the reduction referred to in paragraph (1) shall be made in the following tax attributes in the following order:

(A) NOL.—Any net operating loss for the taxable year of the discharge, and any net operating loss carryover to such taxable year.

(B) General business credit.—Any carryover to or from the taxable year of a discharge of an amount for purposes for determining the amount allowable as a credit under section 38 (relating to general business credit).

(C) Minimum tax credit.—The amount of the minimum tax credit available under section 53(b) as of the beginning of the taxable year immediately following the taxable year of the discharge.

(D) Capital loss carryovers.—Any net capital loss for the taxable year of the discharge, and any capital loss carryover to such taxable year under section 1212.

(E) Basis reduction.—

(i) In general.—The basis of the property of the taxpayer.

(ii) Cross reference.—

For provisions for making the reduction described in clause (i), see section 1017.

(F) Passive activity loss and credit carryovers.—Any passive activity loss or credit carryover of the taxpayer under section 469(b) from the taxable year of the discharge.

* * *

(3) Amount of reduction.—

(A) In general.—Except as provided in subparagraph (B), the reductions described in paragraph (2) shall be one dollar for each dollar excluded by subsection (a).

(B) Credit carryover reduction.—The reductions described in subparagraphs (B), (C), and (G) shall be 33⅓ cents for each dollar excluded by subsection (a). The reduction described in subparagraph (F) in any passive activity credit carryover shall be 33⅓ cents for each dollar excluded by subsection (a).

(4) Ordering rules.—

(A) Reductions made after determination of tax for year.—The reductions described in paragraph (2) shall be made after the determination of the tax imposed by this chapter for the taxable year of the discharge.

(B) Reductions under subparagraph (A) or (D) of paragraph (2).—The reductions described in subparagraph (A) or (D) of paragraph (2) (as the case may be) shall be made first in the loss for the taxable year of the discharge and then in the carryovers to such taxable year in the order of the taxable years from which each such carryover arose.

(C) Reductions under subparagraphs (B) and (G) of paragraph (2).—The reductions described in subparagraphs (B) and (G) of paragraph (2) shall be made in the order in which carryovers are taken into account under this chapter for the taxable year of the discharge.

(5) Election to apply reduction first against depreciable property.—

(A) In general.—The taxpayer may elect to apply any portion of the reduction referred to in paragraph (1) to the reduction under section 1017 of the basis of the depreciable property of the taxpayer.

(B) Limitation.—The amount to which an election under subparagraph (A) applies shall not exceed the aggregate adjusted bases of the depreciable property held by the taxpayer as of the beginning of the taxable year following the taxable year in which the discharge occurs.

(C) Other tax attributes not reduced.—Paragraph (2) shall not apply to any amount to which an election under this paragraph applies.

(c) Treatment of discharge of qualified real property business indebtedness.—

(1) Basis reduction.—

(A) In general.—The amount excluded from gross income under subparagraph (D) of subsection (a)(1) shall be applied to reduce the basis of the depreciable real property of the taxpayer.

(B) Cross reference.—

For provisions making the reduction described in subparagraph (A), see section 1017.

(2) Limitations.—

(A) Indebtedness in excess of value.—The amount excluded under subparagraph (D) of subsection (a)(1) with respect to any qualified real property business indebtedness shall not exceed the excess (if any) of—

(i) the outstanding principal amount of such indebtedness (immediately before the discharge), over

(ii) the fair market value of the real property described in paragraph (3)(A) (as of such time), reduced by the outstanding principal amount of any other qualified real property business indebtedness secured by such property (as of such time).

(B) Overall limitation.—The amount excluded under subparagraph (D) of subsection (a)(1) shall not exceed the aggregate adjusted bases of depreciable real property (determined after any reductions under subsections (b) and (g)) held by the taxpayer immediately before the discharge (other than depreciable real property acquired in contemplation of such discharge).

(3) Qualified real property business indebtedness.—The term "qualified real property business indebtedness" means indebtedness which—

(A) was incurred or assumed by the taxpayer in connection with real property used in a trade or business and is secured by such real property,

(B) was incurred or assumed before January 1, 1993, or if incurred or assumed on or after such date, is qualified acquisition indebtedness, and

(C) with respect to which such taxpayer makes an election to have this paragraph apply.

Such term shall not include qualified farm indebtedness. Indebtedness under subparagraph (B) shall include indebtedness resulting from the refinancing of indebtedness under subparagraph (B) (or this sentence), but only to the extent it does not exceed the amount of the indebtedness being refinanced.

(4) Qualified acquisition indebtedness.—For purposes of paragraph (3)(B), the term "qualified acquisition indebtedness" means, with respect to any real property described in paragraph (3)(A), indebtedness incurred or assumed to acquire, construct, reconstruct, or substantially improve such property.

(5) Regulations.—The Secretary shall issue such regulations as are necessary to carry out this subsection, including regulations preventing the abuse of this subsection through cross-collateralization or other means.

(d) Meaning of terms; special rules relating to certain provisions.—

(1) Indebtedness of taxpayer.—For purposes of this section, the term "indebtedness of the taxpayer" means any indebtedness—

(A) for which the taxpayer is liable, or

(B) subject to which the taxpayer holds property.

(2) Title 11 case.—For purposes of this section, the term "title 11 case" means a case under title 11 of the United States Code (relating to bankruptcy), but only if the taxpayer is under the jurisdiction of the court in such case and the discharge of indebtedness is granted by the court or is pursuant to a plan approved by the court.

(3) Insolvent.—For purposes of this section, the term "insolvent" means the excess of liabilities over the fair market value of assets. With respect to any discharge, whether or not the taxpayer is insolvent, and the amount by which the taxpayer is insolvent, shall be determined on the basis of the taxpayer's assets and liabilities immediately before the discharge.

[**(4) Repealed.**]

(5) Depreciable property.—The term "depreciable property" has the same meaning as when used in section 1017.

(6) Certain provisions to be applied at partner level.—In the case of a partnership, subsections (a), (b), (c), and (g) shall be applied at the partner level.

(7) Special rules for S corporation.—

(A) Certain provisions to be applied at corporate level.—In the case of an S corporation, subsections (a), (b), (c), and (g) shall be applied at the corporate level, including by not taking into account under section 1366(a) any amount excluded under subsection (a) of this section.

(B) Reduction in carryover of disallowed losses and deductions.—In the case of an S corporation, for purposes of subparagraph (A) of subsection (b)(2), any loss or deduction which is disallowed for the taxable year of the discharge under section 1366(d)(1) shall be treated as a net operating loss for such taxable year. The preceding sentence shall not apply to any discharge to the extent that subsection (a)(1)(D) applies to such discharge.

(C) Coordination with basis adjustments under section 1367(b)(2).—For purposes of subsection (e)(6), a shareholder's adjusted basis in indebtedness of an S corporation shall be determined without regard to any adjustments made under section 1367(b)(2).

(8) Reductions of tax attributes in title 11 cases of individuals to be made by estate.—In any case under chapter 7 or 11 of title 11 of the United States Code to which section 1398 applies, for purposes of paragraphs (1) and (5) of subsection (b) the estate (and not the individual) shall be treated as the taxpayer. The preceding sentence shall not apply for purposes of applying section 1017 to property transferred by the estate to the individual.

(9) Time for making election, etc.—

(A) Time.—An election under paragraph (5) of subsection (b) or under paragraph (3)(C) of subsection (c) shall be made on the taxpayer's return for the taxable year in which the discharge occurs or at such other time as may be permitted in regulations prescribed by the Secretary.

(B) Revocation only with consent.—An election referred to in subparagraph (A), once made, may be revoked only with the consent of the Secretary.

(C) Manner.—An election referred to in subparagraph (A) shall be made in such manner as the Secretary may by regulations prescribe.

(10) Cross reference.—

For provision that no reduction is to be made in the basis of exempt property of an individual debtor, see section 1017(c)(1).

(e) General rules for discharge of indebtedness (including discharges not in Title 11 cases or insolvency).—For purposes of this title—

(1) No other insolvency exception.—Except as otherwise provided in this section, there shall be no insolvency exception from the general rule that gross income includes income from the discharge of indebtedness.

(2) Income not realized to extent of lost deductions.—No income shall be realized from the discharge of indebtedness to the extent that payment of the liability would have given rise to a deduction.

(3) Adjustments for unamortized premium and discount.—The amount taken into account with respect to any discharge shall be properly adjusted for unamortized premium and unamortized discount with respect to the indebtedness discharged.

(4) Acquisition of indebtedness by person related to debtor.—

(A) Treated as acquisition by debtor.—For purposes of determining income of the debtor from discharge of indebtedness, to the extent provided in regulations prescribed by the Secretary, the acquisition of outstanding indebtedness by a person bearing a relationship to the debtor specified in section 267(b) or 707(b)(1) from a person who does not bear such a relationship to the debtor shall be treated as the acquisition of such indebtedness by the debtor. Such regulations shall provide for such adjustments in the treatment of any subsequent transactions involving the indebtedness as may be appropriate by reason of the application of the preceding sentence.

(B) Members of family.—For purposes of this paragraph, sections 267(b) and 707(b)(1) shall be applied as if section 267(c)(4) provided that the family of an individual consists of the individual's spouse, the individual's children, grandchildren, and parents, and any spouse of the individual's children or grandchildren.

(C) Entities under common control treated as related.—For purposes of this paragraph, two entities which are treated as a single employer under subsection (b) or (c) of section 414 shall be treated as bearing a relationship to each other which is described in section 267(b).

(5) Purchase-money debt reduction for solvent debtor treated as price reduction.—If—

(A) the debt of a purchaser of property to the seller of such property which arose out of the purchase of such property is reduced,

(B) such reduction does not occur—

(i) in a title 11 case, or

(ii) when the purchaser is insolvent, and

(C) but for this paragraph, such reduction would be treated as income to the purchaser from the discharge of indebtedness,

then such reduction shall be treated as a purchase price adjustment.

(6) Indebtedness contributed to capital.—Except as provided in regulations, for purposes of determining income of the debtor from discharge of indebtedness, if a debtor corporation acquires its indebtedness from a shareholder as a contribution to capital—

(A) section 118 shall not apply, but

(B) such corporation shall be treated as having satisfied the indebtedness with an amount of money equal to the shareholder's adjusted basis in the indebtedness.

(7) Recapture of gain on subsequent sale of stock.—

(A) In general.—If a creditor acquires stock of a debtor corporation in satisfaction of such corporation's indebtedness, for purposes of section 1245—

(i) such stock (and any other property the basis of which is determined in whole or in part by reference to the adjusted basis of such stock) shall be treated as section 1245 property,

(ii) the aggregate amount allowed to the creditor—

(I) as deductions under subsection (a) or (b) of section 166 (by reason of the worthlessness or partial worthlessness of the indebtedness), or

(II) as an ordinary loss on the exchange,

shall be treated as an amount allowed as a deduction for depreciation, and

(iii) an exchange of such stock qualifying under section 354(a), 355(a), or 356(a) shall be treated as an exchange to which section 1245(b)(3) applies.

The amount determined under clause (ii) shall be reduced by the amount (if any) included in the creditor's gross income on the exchange.

(B) Special rule for cash basis taxpayers.—In the case of any creditor who computes his taxable income under the cash receipts and disbursements method, proper adjustment shall be made in the amount taken into account under clause (ii) of subparagraph (A) for any amount which was not included in the creditor's gross income but which would have been included in such gross income if such indebtedness had been satisfied in full.

(C) Stock of parent corporation.—For purposes of this paragraph, stock of a corporation in control (within the meaning of section 368(c)) of the debtor corporation shall be treated as stock of the debtor corporation.

(D) Treatment of successor corporation.—For purposes of this paragraph, the term "debtor corporation" includes a successor corporation.

(E) Partnership rule.—Under regulations prescribed by the Secretary, rules similar to the rules of the foregoing subparagraphs of this paragraph shall apply with respect to the indebtedness of a partnership.

(8) Indebtedness satisfied by corporate stock or partnership interest.—For purposes of determining income of a debtor from discharge of indebtedness, if—

(A) a debtor corporation transfers stock, or

(B) a debtor partnership transfers a capital or profits interest in such partnership,

to a creditor in satisfaction of its recourse or nonrecourse indebtedness, such corporation or partnership shall be treated as having satisfied the indebtedness with an amount of money equal to the fair market value of the stock or interest. In the case of any partnership, any discharge of indebtedness income recognized under this paragraph shall be included in the distributive shares of taxpayers which were the partners in the partnership immediately before such discharge.

* * *

(10) Indebtedness satisfied by issuance of debt instrument.—

(A) In general.—For purposes of determining income of a debtor from discharge of indebtedness, if a debtor issues a debt instrument in satisfaction of indebtedness, such debtor shall be treated as having satisfied the indebtedness with an amount of money equal to the issue price of such debt instrument.

(B) Issue price.—For purposes of subparagraph (A), the issue price of any debt instrument shall be determined under sections 1273 and 1274. For purposes of the preceding sentence, section 1273(b)(4) shall be applied by reducing the stated redemption price of any instrument by the portion of such stated redemption price which is treated as interest for purposes of this chapter.

(f) Student loans.—

(1) In general.—In the case of an individual, gross income does not include any amount which (but for this subsection) would be includible in gross income by reason of the discharge (in whole or in part) of any student loan if such discharge was pursuant to a provision of such loan under which all or part of the indebtedness of the individual would be discharged if the individual worked for a certain period of time in certain professions for any of a broad class of employers.

(2) Student loan.—For purposes of this subsection, the term "student loan" means any loan to an individual to assist the individual in attending an educational organization described in section 170(b)(1)(A)(ii) made by—

(A) the United States, or an instrumentality or agency thereof,

(B) a State, territory, or possession of the United States, or the District of Columbia, or any political subdivision thereof, or

(C) a public benefit corporation—

(i) which is exempt from taxation under section 501(c)(3),

(ii) which has assumed control over a State, county, or municipal hospital, and

(iii) whose employees have been deemed to be public employees under State law, or

(D) any educational organization described in section 170(b)(1)(A)(ii) if such loan is made—

(i) pursuant to an agreement with any entity described in subparagraph (A), (B), or (C) under which the funds from which the loan was made were provided to such educational organization, or

(ii) pursuant to a program of such educational organization which is designed to encourage its students to serve in occupations with unmet needs or in areas with unmet needs and under which the services provided by the students (or former students) are for or under the direction of a governmental unit or an organization described in section 501(c)(3) and exempt from tax under section 501(a).

The term "student loan" includes any loan made by an educational organization described in section 170(b)(1)(A)(ii) or by an organization exempt from tax under section 501(a) to refinance a loan to an individual to assist the individual in attending any such educational organization but only if the refinancing loan is pursuant to a program of the refinancing organization which is designed as described in subparagraph (D)(ii).

(3) Exception for discharges on account of services performed for certain lenders.—Paragraph (1) shall not apply to the discharge of a loan made by an organization described in paragraph (2)(D) if the discharge is on account of services performed for either such organization.

(4) Payments under National Health Service Corps loan repayment program and certain state loan repayment programs.—In the case of an individual, gross income shall not include any amount received under section 338B(g) of the Public Health Service Act, under a State program described in section 338I of such Act, or under any other State loan repayment or loan forgiveness program that is intended to provide for the increased availability of health care services in underserved or health professional shortage areas (as determined by such State).

(g) Special rules for discharge of qualified farm indebtedness.—

(1) Discharge must be by qualified person.—

(A) In general.—Subparagraph (C) of subsection (a)(1) shall apply only if the discharge is by a qualified person.

(B) Qualified person.—For purposes of subparagraph (A), the term "qualified person" has the meaning given to such term by section 49(a)(1)(D)(iv); except that such term shall include any Federal, State, or local government or agency or instrumentality thereof.

(2) Qualified farm indebtedness.—For purposes of this section, indebtedness of a taxpayer shall be treated as qualified farm indebtedness if—

(A) such indebtedness was incurred directly in connection with the operation by the taxpayer of the trade or business of farming, and

(B) 50 percent or more of the aggregate gross receipts of the taxpayer for the 3 taxable years preceding the taxable year in which the discharge of such indebtedness occurs is attributable to the trade or business of farming.

(3) Amount excluded cannot exceed sum of tax attributes and business and investment assets.—

(A) In general.—The amount excluded under subparagraph (C) of subsection (a)(1) shall not exceed the sum of—

(i) the adjusted tax attributes of the taxpayer, and

(ii) the aggregate adjusted bases of qualified property held by the taxpayer as of the beginning of the taxable year following the taxable year in which the discharge occurs.

(B) Adjusted tax attributes.—For purposes of subparagraph (A), the term "adjusted tax attributes" means the sum of the tax attributes described in subparagraphs (A), (B), (C), (D), (F), and (G) of subsection (b)(2) determined by taking into account $3 for each $1 of the attributes described in subparagraphs (B), (C), and (G) of subsection (b)(2) and the attribute described in subparagraph (F) of subsection (b)(2) to the extent attributable to any passive activity credit carryover.

(C) Qualified property.—For purposes of this paragraph, the term "qualified property" means any property which is used or is held for use in a trade or business or for the production of income.

(D) Coordination with insolvency exclusion.—For purposes of this paragraph, the adjusted basis of any qualified property and the amount of the adjusted tax attributes shall be determined after any reduction under subsection (b) by reason of amounts excluded from gross income under subsection (a)(1)(B).

(h) Special rules relating to qualified principal residence indebtedness.—

(1) Basis reduction.—The amount excluded from gross income by reason of subsection (a)(1)(E) shall be applied to reduce (but not below zero) the basis of the principal residence of the taxpayer.

(2) Qualified principal residence indebtedness.—For purposes of this section, the term "qualified principal residence indebtedness" means acquisition indebtedness (within the meaning of section 163(h)(3)(B)), applied by substituting "$2,000,000 ($1,000,000" for "$1,000,000 ($500,000" in clause (ii) thereof)) with respect to the principal residence of the taxpayer.

(3) Exception for certain discharges not related to taxpayer's financial condition.—Subsection (a)(1)(E) shall not apply to the discharge of a loan if the discharge is on account of services performed for the lender or any other factor not directly related to a decline in the value of the residence or to the financial condition of the taxpayer.

(4) Ordering rule.—If any loan is discharged, in whole or in part, and only a portion of such loan is qualified principal residence indebtedness, subsection (a)(1)(E) shall apply only to so much of the amount discharged as exceeds the amount of the loan (as determined immediately before such discharge) which is not qualified principal residence indebtedness.

(5) Principal residence.—For purposes of this subsection, the term "principal residence" has the same meaning as when used in section 121.

(i) Deferral and ratable inclusion of income arising from business indebtedness discharged by the reacquisition of a debt instrument.—

(1) In general.—At the election of the taxpayer, income from the discharge of indebtedness in connection with the reacquisition after December 31, 2008, and before January 1, 2011, of an applicable debt instrument shall be includible in gross income ratably over the 5–taxable-year period beginning with—

(A) in the case of a reacquisition occurring in 2009, the fifth taxable year following the taxable year in which the reacquisition occurs, and

(B) in the case of a reacquisition occurring in 2010, the fourth taxable year following the taxable year in which the reacquisition occurs.

(2) Deferral of deduction for original issue discount in debt for debt exchanges.—

(A) In general.—If, as part of a reacquisition to which paragraph (1) applies, any debt instrument is issued for the applicable debt instrument being reacquired (or is treated as so issued under subsection (e)(4) and the regulations thereunder) and there is any original issue discount determined under subpart A of part V of subchapter P of this chapter with respect to the debt instrument so issued—

(i) except as provided in clause (ii), no deduction otherwise allowable under this chapter shall be allowed to the issuer of such debt instrument with respect to the portion of such original issue discount which—

(I) accrues before the 1st taxable year in the 5–taxable-year period in which income from the discharge of indebtedness attributable to the reacquisition of the debt instrument is includible under paragraph (1), and

(II) does not exceed the income from the discharge of indebtedness with respect to the debt instrument being reacquired, and

(ii) the aggregate amount of deductions disallowed under clause (i) shall be allowed as a deduction ratably over the 5–taxable-year period described in clause (i)(I).

If the amount of the original issue discount accruing before such 1st taxable year exceeds the income from the discharge of indebtedness with respect to the applicable debt instrument being reacquired, the deductions shall be disallowed in the order in which the original issue discount is accrued.

* * *

(3) Applicable debt instrument.—For purposes of this subsection—

(A) Applicable debt instrument.—The term "applicable debt instrument" means any debt instrument which was issued by—

(i) a C corporation, or

(ii) any other person in connection with the conduct of a trade or business by such person.

* * *

(5) Other definitions and rules.—For purposes of this subsection—

* * *

(C) Coordination with other exclusions.—If a taxpayer elects to have this subsection apply to an applicable debt instrument, subparagraphs (A), (B), (C), and (D) of subsection (a)(1) shall not apply to the income from the discharge of such indebtedness for the taxable year of the election or any subsequent taxable year.

* * *

§ 109. Improvements by lessee on lessor's property

Gross income does not include income (other than rent) derived by a lessor of real property on the termination of a lease, representing the value of such property attributable to buildings erected or other improvements made by the lessee.

§ 111. Recovery of tax benefit items

(a) Deductions.—Gross income does not include income attributable to the recovery during the taxable year of any amount deducted in any prior taxable year to the extent such amount did not reduce the amount of tax imposed by this chapter.

(b) Credits.—

(1) In general.—If—

(A) a credit was allowable with respect to any amount for any prior taxable year, and

(B) during the taxable year there is a downward price adjustment or similar adjustment,

the tax imposed by this chapter for the taxable year shall be increased by the amount of the credit attributable to the adjustment.

(2) Exception where credit did not reduce tax.—Paragraph (1) shall not apply to the extent that the credit allowable for the recovered amount did not reduce the amount of tax imposed by this chapter.

* * *

(c) Treatment of carryovers.—For purposes of this section, an increase in a carryover which has not expired before the beginning of the taxable year in which the recovery or adjustment takes place shall be treated as reducing tax imposed by this chapter.

* * *

§ 112. Certain combat zone compensation of members of the Armed Forces

(a) Enlisted personnel.—Gross income does not include compensation received for active service as a member below the grade of commissioned officer in the Armed Forces of the United States for any month during any part of which such member—

(1) served in a combat zone, or

(2) was hospitalized as a result of wounds, disease, or injury incurred while serving in a combat zone; but this paragraph shall not apply for any month beginning more than 2 years after the date of the termination of combatant activities in such zone.

* * *

§ 115. Income of states, municipalities, etc.

Gross income does not include—

(1) income derived from any public utility or the exercise of any essential governmental function and accruing to a State or any political subdivision thereof, or the District of Columbia; or

(2) income accruing to the government of any possession of the United States, or any political subdivision thereof.

§ 117. Qualified scholarships

(a) General rule.—Gross income does not include any amount received as a qualified scholarship by an individual who is a candidate for a degree at an educational organization described in section 170(b)(1)(A)(ii).

(b) Qualified scholarship.—For purposes of this section—

(1) In general.—The term "qualified scholarship" means any amount received by an individual as a scholarship or fellowship grant to the extent the individual establishes that, in accordance with the conditions of the grant, such amount was used for qualified tuition and related expenses.

(2) Qualified tuition and related expenses.—For purposes of paragraph (1), the term "qualified tuition and related expenses" means—

(A) tuition and fees required for the enrollment or attendance of a student at an educational organization described in section 170(b)(1)(A)(ii), and

(B) fees, books, supplies, and equipment required for courses of instruction at such an educational organization.

(c) Limitation.—

(1) In general.—Except as provided in paragraph (2), subsections (a) and (d) shall not apply to that portion of any amount received which represents payment for teaching, research, or other services by the student required as a condition for receiving the qualified scholarship or qualified tuition reduction.

(2) Exceptions.—Paragraph (1) shall not apply to any amount received by an individual under—

(A) The National Health Service Corps Scholarship Program under section 338A(g)(1)(A) of the Public Health Service Act, or

(B) The Armed Forces Health Professions Scholarship and Financial Assistance program under subchapter I of chapter 105 of title 10, United States Code.

(d) Qualified tuition reduction.—

(1) In general.—Gross income shall not include any qualified tuition reduction.

(2) Qualified tuition reduction.—For purposes of this subsection, the term "qualified tuition reduction" means the amount of any reduction in tuition provided to an employee of an organization described in section 170(b)(1)(A)(ii) for the education (below the graduate level) at such organization (or another organization described in section 170(b)(1)(A)(ii)) of—

(A) such employee, or

(B) any person treated as an employee (or whose use is treated as an employee use) under the rules of section 132(h).

(3) Reduction must not discriminate in favor of highly compensated, etc.—Paragraph (1) shall apply with respect to any qualified tuition reduction provided with respect to any highly compensated employee only if such reduction is available on substantially the same terms to each member of a group of employees which is defined under a reasonable classification set up by the employer which does not discriminate in favor of highly compensated employees (within the meaning of section 414(q)). For purposes of this paragraph, the term "highly compensated employee" has the meaning given such term by section 414(q).

[(4) Repealed.]

(5) Special rules for teaching and research assistants.—In the case of the education of an individual who is a graduate student at an educational organization described in section 170(b)(1)(A)(ii) and who is engaged in teaching or research activities for such organization, paragraph (2) shall be applied as if it did not contain the phrase "(below the graduate level)".

§ 118. Contributions to the capital of a corporation

(a) General rule.—In the case of a corporation, gross income does not include any contribution to the capital of the taxpayer.

(b) Contributions in aid of construction, etc.—For purposes of subsection (a), * * *, the term "contribution to the capital of the taxpayer" does not include any contribution in aid of construction or any other contribution as a customer or potential customer.

* * *

(e) Cross references.—

(1) For basis of property acquired by a corporation through a contribution to its capital, see section 362.

(2) For special rules in the case of contributions of indebtedness, see section 108(e)(6).

§ 119. Meals or lodging furnished for the convenience of the employer

(a) Meals and lodging furnished to employee, his spouse, and his dependents, pursuant to employment.—There shall be excluded from gross income of an employee the value of any meals or lodging furnished to him, his spouse, or any of his dependents by or on behalf of his employer for the convenience of the employer, but only if—

(1) in the case of meals, the meals are furnished on the business premises of the employer, or

(2) in the case of lodging, the employee is required to accept such lodging on the business premises of his employer as a condition of his employment.

(b) Special rules.—For purposes of subsection (a)—

(1) Provisions of employment contract or state statute not to be determinative.—In determining whether meals or lodging are furnished for the convenience of the employer, the provisions of an employment contract or of a State statute fixing terms of employment shall not be determinative of whether the meals or lodging are intended as compensation.

(2) Certain factors not taken into account with respect to meals.—In determining whether meals are furnished for the convenience of the employer, the fact that a charge is made for such meals, and the fact that the employee may accept or decline such meals, shall not be taken into account.

(3) Certain fixed charges for meals.—

(A) In general.—If—

(i) an employee is required to pay on a periodic basis a fixed charge for his meals, and

(ii) such meals are furnished by the employer for the convenience of the employer,

there shall be excluded from the employee's gross income an amount equal to such fixed charge.

(B) Application of subparagraph (A).—Subparagraph (A) shall apply—

(i) whether the employee pays the fixed charge out of his stated compensation or out of his own funds, and

(ii) only if the employee is required to make the payment whether he accepts or declines the meals.

(4) Meals furnished to employees on business premises where meals of most employees are otherwise excludable.—All meals furnished on the business premises of an employer to such employer's employees shall be treated as furnished for the convenience of the employer if, without regard to this paragraph, more than half of the employees to whom such meals are furnished on such premises are furnished such meals for the convenience of the employer.

* * *

(d) Lodging furnished by certain educational institutions to employees.—

(1) In general.—In the case of an employee of an educational institution, gross income shall not include the value of qualified campus lodging furnished to such employee during the taxable year.

(2) Exception in cases of inadequate rent.—Paragraph (1) shall not apply to the extent of the excess of—

(A) the lesser of—

(i) 5 percent of the appraised value of the qualified campus lodging, or

(ii) the average of the rentals paid by individuals (other than employees or students of the educational institution) during such calendar year for lodging provided by the educational institution which is comparable to the qualified campus lodging provided to the employee, over

(B) the rent paid by the employee for the qualified campus lodging during such calendar year.

The appraised value under subparagraph (A)(i) shall be determined as of the close of the calendar year in which the taxable year begins, or, in the case of a rental period not greater than 1 year, at any time during the calendar year in which such period begins.

(3) Qualified campus lodging.—For purposes of this subsection, the term "qualified campus lodging" means lodging to which subsection (a) does not apply and which is—

(A) located on, or in the proximity of, a campus of the educational institution, and

(B) furnished to the employee, his spouse, and any of his dependents by or on behalf of such institution for use as a residence.

(4) Educational institution, etc.—For purposes of this subsection—

(A) In general.—The term "educational institution" means—

(i) an institution described in section 170(b)(1)(A)(ii) (or an entity organized under State law and composed of public institutions so described), or

(ii) an academic health center.

(B) Academic health center.—For purposes of subparagraph (A), the term "academic health center" means an entity—

(i) which is described in section 170(b)(1)(A)(iii),

(ii) which receives (during the calendar year in which the taxable year of the taxpayer begins) payments under subsection (d)(5)(B) or (h) of section 1886 of the Social Security Act (relating to graduate medical education), and

(iii) which has as one of its principal purposes or functions the providing and teaching of basic and clinical medical science and research with the entity's own faculty.

§ 121. Exclusion of gain from sale of principal residence

(a) Exclusion.—Gross income shall not include gain from the sale or exchange of property if, during the 5–year period ending on the date of the sale or exchange, such property has been owned and used by the taxpayer as the taxpayer's principal residence for periods aggregating 2 years or more.

(b) Limitations.—

(1) In general.—The amount of gain excluded from gross income under subsection (a) with respect to any sale or exchange shall not exceed $250,000.

(2) Special rules for joint returns.—In the case of a husband and wife who make a joint return for the taxable year of the sale or exchange of the property—

(A) $500,000 limitation for certain joint returns.—Paragraph (1) shall be applied by substituting "$500,000" for "$250,000" if.—

(i) either spouse meets the ownership requirements of subsection (a) with respect to such property;

(ii) both spouses meet the use requirements of subsection (a) with respect to such property; and

(iii) neither spouse is ineligible for the benefits of subsection (a) with respect to such property by reason of paragraph (3).

(B) Other joint returns.—If such spouses do not meet the requirements of subparagraph (A), the limitation under paragraph (1) shall be the sum of the limitations under paragraph (1) to which each spouse would be entitled if such spouses had not been married. For purposes of the preceding sentence, each spouse shall be treated as owning the property during the period that either spouse owned the property.

(3) Application to only 1 sale or exchange every 2 years.—

(A) In general.—Subsection (a) shall not apply to any sale or exchange by the taxpayer if, during the 2–year period ending on the date of such sale or exchange, there was any other sale or exchange by the taxpayer to which subsection (a) applied.

(B) Pre–May 7, 1997, sales not taken into account.—Subparagraph (A) shall be applied without regard to any sale or exchange before May 7, 1997.

(4) Special rule for certain sales by surviving spouses.—In the case of a sale or exchange of property by an unmarried individual whose spouse is deceased on the date of such sale, paragraph (1) shall be applied by substituting "$500,000" for "$250,000" if such sale occurs not later than 2 years after the date of death of such spouse and the requirements of paragraph (2)(A) were met immediately before such date of death.

(4) [5 Ed.] Exclusion of gain allocated to nonqualified use.—

(A) In general.—Subsection (a) shall not apply to so much of the gain from the sale or exchange of property as is allocated to periods of nonqualified use.

(B) Gain allocated to periods of nonqualified use.—For purposes of subparagraph (A), gain shall be allocated to periods of nonqualified use based on the ratio which—

(i) the aggregate periods of nonqualified use during the period such property was owned by the taxpayer, bears to

(ii) the period such property was owned by the taxpayer.

(C) Period of nonqualified use.—For purposes of this paragraph—

(i) In general.—The term "period of nonqualified use" means any period (other than the portion of any period preceding January 1, 2009) during which the property is not used as the principal residence of the taxpayer or the taxpayer's spouse or former spouse.

(ii) Exceptions.—The term "period of nonqualified use" does not include—

(I) any portion of the 5–year period described in subsection (a) which is after the last date that such property is used as the principal residence of the taxpayer or the taxpayer's spouse,

(II) any period (not to exceed an aggregate period of 10 years) during which the taxpayer or the taxpayer's spouse is serving on qualified official extended duty (as defined in subsection (d)(9)(C)) described in clause (i), (ii), or (iii) of subsection (d)(9)(A), and

(III) any other period of temporary absence (not to exceed an aggregate period of 2 years) due to change of employment, health conditions, or such other unforeseen circumstances as may be specified by the Secretary.

(D) Coordination with recognition of gain attributable to depreciation.—For purposes of this paragraph—

(i) subparagraph (A) shall be applied after the application of subsection (d)(6), and

(ii) subparagraph (B) shall be applied without regard to any gain to which subsection (d)(6) applies.

(c) Exclusion for taxpayers failing to meet certain requirements.—

(1) In general.—In the case of a sale or exchange to which this subsection applies, the ownership and use requirements of subsection (a), and subsection (b)(3), shall not apply; but the dollar limitation under paragraph (1) or (2) of subsection (b), whichever is applicable, shall be equal to—

(A) the amount which bears the same ratio to such limitation (determined without regard to this paragraph) as

(B)(i) the shorter of—

(I) the aggregate periods, during the 5–year period ending on the date of such sale or exchange, such property has been owned and used by the taxpayer as the taxpayer's principal residence; or

(II) the period after the date of the most recent prior sale or exchange by the taxpayer to which subsection (a) applied and before the date of such sale or exchange, bears to

(ii) 2 years.

(2) Sales and exchanges to which subsection applies.—This subsection shall apply to any sale or exchange if—

(A) subsection (a) would not (but for this subsection) apply to such sale or exchange by reason of—

(i) a failure to meet the ownership and use requirements of subsection (a), or

(ii) subsection (b)(3), and

(B) such sale or exchange is by reason of a change in place of employment, health, or, to the extent provided in regulations, unforeseen circumstances.

(d) Special rules.—

(1) Joint returns.—If a husband and wife make a joint return for the taxable year of the sale or exchange of the property, subsections (a) and (c) shall apply if either spouse meets the ownership and use requirements of subsection (a) with respect to such property.

(2) Property of deceased spouse.—For purposes of this section, in the case of an unmarried individual whose spouse is deceased on the date of the sale or exchange of property, the period such unmarried individual owned and used such property shall include the period such deceased spouse owned and used such property before death.

(3) Property owned by spouse or former spouse.—For purposes of this section—

(A) Property transferred to individual from spouse or former spouse.—In the case of an individual holding property transferred to such individual in a transaction described in section 1041(a), the period such individual owns such property shall include the period the transferor owned the property.

(B) Property used by former spouse pursuant to divorce decree, etc.—Solely for purposes of this section, an individual shall be treated as using property as such individual's principal residence during any period of ownership while such individual's spouse or former spouse is granted use of the property under a divorce or separation instrument (as defined in section 71(b)(2)).

(4) Tenant-stockholder in cooperative housing corporation.—For purposes of this section, if the taxpayer holds stock as a tenant-stockholder (as defined in section 216) in a cooperative housing corporation (as defined in such section), then—

(A) the holding requirements of subsection (a) shall be applied to the holding of such stock, and

(B) the use requirements of subsection (a) shall be applied to the house or apartment which the taxpayer was entitled to occupy as such stockholder.

(5) Involuntary conversions.—

(A) In general.—For purposes of this section, the destruction, theft, seizure, requisition, or condemnation of property shall be treated as the sale of such property.

(B) Application of section 1033.—In applying section 1033 (relating to involuntary conversions), the amount realized from the sale or exchange of property shall be treated as being the amount determined without regard to this section, reduced by the amount of gain not included in gross income pursuant to this section.

(C) Property acquired after involuntary conversion.—If the basis of the property sold or exchanged is determined (in whole or in part) under section 1033(b) (relating to basis of property acquired through involuntary conversion), then the holding and use by the taxpayer of the converted property shall be treated as holding and use by the taxpayer of the property sold or exchanged.

(6) Recognition of gain attributable to depreciation.—Subsection (a) shall not apply to so much of the gain from the sale of any property as does not exceed the portion of the depreciation adjustments (as defined in section 1250(b)(3)) attributable to periods after May 6, 1997, in respect of such property.

(7) Determination of use during periods of out-of-residence care.—In the case of a taxpayer who—

(A) becomes physically or mentally incapable of selfcare, and

(B) owns property and uses such property as the taxpayer's principal residence during the 5–year period described in subsection (a) for periods aggregating at least 1 year,

then the taxpayer shall be treated as using such property as the taxpayer's principal residence during any time during such 5–year period in which the taxpayer owns the property and resides in any facility (including a nursing home) licensed by a State or political subdivision to care for an individual in the taxpayer's condition.

(8) Sales of remainder interests.—For purposes of this section—

(A) In general.—At the election of the taxpayer, this section shall not fail to apply to the sale or exchange of an interest in a principal residence by reason of such interest being a remainder interest in such residence, but this section shall not apply to any other interest in such residence which is sold or exchanged separately.

(B) Exception for sales to related parties.—Subparagraph (A) shall not apply to any sale to, or exchange with, any person who bears a relationship to the taxpayer which is described in section 267(b) or 707(b).

* * *

(10) Property acquired in like-kind exchange.—If a taxpayer acquires property in an exchange with respect to which gain is not recognized (in whole or in part) to the taxpayer under subsection (a) or (b) of section 1031, subsection (a) shall not apply to the sale or exchange of such property by such taxpayer (or by any person whose basis in such property is determined, in whole or in part, by reference to the basis in the hands of such taxpayer) during the 5–year period beginning with the date of such acquisition.

* * *

(e) Denial of exclusion for expatriates.—This section shall not apply to any sale or exchange by an individual if the treatment provided by section 877(a)(1) applies to such individual.

(f) Election to have section not apply.—This section shall not apply to any sale or exchange with respect to which the taxpayer elects not to have this section apply.

(g) Residences acquired in rollovers under section 1034.—For purposes of this section, in the case of property the acquisition of which by the taxpayer resulted under section 1034 (as in effect on the day before the date of the enactment of this section) in the nonrecognition of any part of the gain realized on the sale or exchange of another residence, in determining the period for which the taxpayer has owned and used such property as the taxpayer's principal residence, there shall be included the aggregate periods for which such other residence (and each prior residence taken into account under section 1223(6) in determining the holding period of such property) had been so owned and used.

§ 123. Amounts received under insurance contracts for certain living expenses

(a) General rule.—In the case of an individual whose principal residence is damaged or destroyed by fire, storm, or other casualty, or who is denied access to his principal residence by governmental authorities because of the occurrence or threat of occurrence of such a casualty, gross income does not include amounts received by such individual under an insurance contract which are paid to compensate or reimburse such individual for living expenses incurred for himself and members of his household resulting from the loss of use or occupancy of such residence.

(b) Limitation.—Subsection (a) shall apply to amounts received by the taxpayer for living expenses incurred during any period only to the extent the amounts received do not exceed the amount by which—

(1) the actual living expenses incurred during such period for himself and members of his household resulting from the loss of use or occupancy of their residence, exceed

(2) the normal living expenses which would have been incurred for himself and members of his household during such period.

§ 125. Cafeteria plans

(a) In general.—Except as provided in subsection (b), no amount shall be included in the gross income of a participant in a cafeteria plan solely because, under the plan, the participant may choose among the benefits of the plan.

(b) Exception for highly compensated participants and key employees.—

(1) Highly compensated participants.—In the case of a highly compensated participant, subsection (a) shall not apply to any benefit attributable to a plan year for which the plan discriminates in favor of—

(A) highly compensated individuals as to eligibility to participate, or

(B) highly compensated participants as to contributions and benefits.

(2) Key employees.—In the case of a key employee (within the meaning of section 416(i)(1)), subsection (a) shall not apply to any benefit attributable to a plan for which the statutory nontaxable benefits provided to key employees exceed 25 percent of the aggregate of such benefits provided for all employees under the plan. For purposes of the preceding sentence, statutory nontaxable benefits shall be determined without regard to the second sentence of subsection (f).

(3) Year of inclusion.—For purposes of determining the taxable year of inclusion, any benefit described in paragraph (1) or (2) shall be treated as received or accrued in the taxable year of the participant or key employee in which the plan year ends.

(c) Discrimination as to benefits or contributions.—For purposes of subparagraph (B) of subsection (b)(1), a cafeteria plan does not discriminate where qualified benefits and total benefits (or employer contributions allocable to qualified benefits and employer contributions for total benefits) do not discriminate in favor of highly compensated participants.

(d) Cafeteria plan defined.—For purposes of this section—

(1) In general.—The term "cafeteria plan" means a written plan under which—

(A) all participants are employees, and

(B) the participants may choose among 2 or more benefits consisting of cash and qualified benefits.

(2) Deferred compensation plans excluded.—

(A) In general.—The term "cafeteria plan" does not include any plan which provides for deferred compensation.

(B) Exception for cash and deferred arrangements.—Subparagraph (A) shall not apply to a profit-sharing or stock bonus plan or rural cooperative plan (within the meaning of section 401(k)(7)) which includes a qualified cash or deferred arrangement (as defined in section 401(k)(2)) to the extent of amounts which a covered employee may elect to have the employer pay as contributions to a trust under such plan on behalf of the employee.

(C) Exception for certain plans maintained by educational institutions.—Subparagraph (A) shall not apply to a plan maintained by an educational organization described in section 170(b)(1)(A)(ii) to the extent of amounts which a covered employee may elect to have the employer pay as contributions for post-retirement group life insurance if—

(i) all contributions for such insurance must be made before retirement, and

(ii) such life insurance does not have a cash surrender value at any time.

For purposes of section 79, any life insurance described in the preceding sentence shall be treated as group-term life insurance.

(D) Exception for Health Savings Accounts.—Subparagraph A shall not apply to a plan to the extent of amounts which a covered employee may elect to have the employer pay as contributions to a health savings account established on behalf of the employee.

(e) Highly compensated participant and individual defined.—For purposes of this section—

(1) Highly compensated participant.—The term "highly compensated participant" means a participant who is—

(A) an officer,

(B) a shareholder owning more than 5 percent of the voting power or value of all classes of stock of the employer,

(C) highly compensated, or

(D) a spouse or dependent (within the meaning of section 152, determined without regard to subsections (b)(1), (b)(2), and (d)(1)(B) thereof) of an individual described in subparagraph (A), (B), or (C).

(2) Highly compensated individual.—The term "highly compensated individual" means an individual who is described in subparagraphs (A), (B), (C), or (D) of paragraph (1).

§ 125(f), below, applies to taxable years beginning before January 1, 2014.

(f) Qualified benefits defined.—For purposes of this section, the term "qualified benefit" means any benefit which, with the application of subsection (a), is not includible in the gross income of the employee by reason of an express provision of this chapter (other than section 106(b), 117, 127, or 132). Such term includes any group term life insurance which is includible in gross income only because it exceeds the dollar limitation of section 79 and such term includes any other benefit permitted under regulations. Such term shall not include any product which is advertised, marketed, or offered as long-term care insurance.

§ 125(f), below, applies to taxable years beginning after December 31, 2013.

(f) Qualified benefits defined.—For purposes of this section—

(1) In general.—The term "qualified benefit" means any benefit which, with the application of subsection (a), is not includible in the gross income of the employee by reason of an express provision of this chapter (other than section 106(b), 117, 127, or 132). Such term includes any group term life insurance which is includible in gross income only because it exceeds the dollar limitation of section 79 and such term includes any other benefit permitted under regulations.

(2) Long-term care insurance not qualified.—The term "qualified benefit" shall not include any product which is advertised, marketed, or offered as long-term care insurance.

(3) Certain exchange-participating qualified health plans not qualified.—

(A) In general.—The term "qualified benefit" shall not include any qualified health plan (as defined in section 1301(a) of the Patient Protection and Affordable Care Act) [42 U.S.C. 18021(a)] offered through an Exchange established under section 1311 of such Act [42 U.S.C. 18031].

(B) Exception for exchange-eligible employers.—Subparagraph (A) shall not apply with respect to any employee if such employee's employer is a qualified employer (as defined in section 1312(f)(2) of the Patient Protection and Affordable Care Act [42 U.S.C. 18032(f)(2)]) offering the employee the opportunity to enroll through such an Exchange in a qualified health plan in a group market.

(g) Special rules.—

* * *

(2) Health benefits.—For purposes of subparagraph (B) of subsection (b)(1), a cafeteria plan which provides health benefits shall not be treated as discriminatory if—

(A) contributions under the plan on behalf of each participant include an amount which—

(i) equals 100 percent of the cost of the health benefit coverage under the plan of the majority of the highly compensated participants similarly situated, or

(ii) equals or exceeds 75 percent of the cost of the health benefit coverage of the participant (similarly situated) having the highest cost health benefit coverage under the plan, and

(B) contributions or benefits under the plan in excess of those described in subparagraph (A) bear a uniform relationship to compensation.

(3) Certain participation eligibility rules not treated as discriminatory.—For purposes of subparagraph (A) of subsection (b)(1), a classification shall not be treated as discriminatory if the plan—

(A) benefits a group of employees described in section 410(b)(2)(A)(i), and

(B) meets the requirements of clauses (i) and (ii):

(i) No employee is required to complete more than 3 years of employment with the employer or employers maintaining the plan as a condition of participation in the plan, and the employment requirement for each employee is the same.

(ii) Any employee who has satisfied the employment requirement of clause (i) and who is otherwise entitled to participate in the plan commences participation no later than the first day of the first plan year beginning after the date the employment requirement was satisfied unless the employee was separated from service before the first day of that plan year.

(4) Certain controlled groups, etc.—All employees who are treated as employed by a single employer under subsection (b), (c), or (m) of section 414 shall be treated as employed by a single employer for purposes of this section.

* * *

(i) Limitation on Health Flexible Spending Arrangements—

(1) In general.—For purposes of this section, if a benefit is provided under a cafeteria plan through employer contributions to a health flexible spending arrangement, such benefit shall not be treated as a qualified benefit unless the cafeteria plan provides that an employee may not elect for any taxable year to have salary reduction contributions in excess of $2,500 made to such arrangement.

(2) Adjustment for inflation.—In the case of any taxable year beginning after December 31, 2013, the dollar amount in paragraph (1) shall be increased by an amount equal to—

(A) such amount, multiplied by

(B) the cost-of-living adjustment determined under section 1(f)(3) for the calendar year in which such taxable year begins by substituting "calendar year 2012" for "calendar year 1992" in subparagraph (B) thereof.

If any increase determined under this paragraph is not a multiple of $50, such increase shall be rounded to the next lowest multiple of $50.

* * *

(*l*) Regulations.—The Secretary shall prescribe such regulations as may be necessary to carry out the provisions of this section.

§ 127. Educational assistance programs

(a) Exclusion from gross income.—

(1) In general.—Gross income of an employee does not include amounts paid or expenses incurred by the employer for educational assistance to the employee if the assistance is furnished pursuant to a program which is described in subsection (b).

(2) $5,250 maximum exclusion.—If, but for this paragraph, this section would exclude from gross income more than $5,250 of educational assistance furnished to an individual during a calendar year, this section shall apply only to the first $5,250 of such assistance so furnished.

(b) Educational assistance program.—

(1) In general.—For purposes of this section an educational assistance program is a separate written plan of an employer for the exclusive benefit of his employees to provide such employees with educational assistance. The program must meet the requirements of paragraphs (2) through (6) of this subsection.

(2) Eligibility.—The program shall benefit employees who qualify under a classification set up by the employer and found by the Secretary not to be discriminatory in favor of employees who are highly compensated employees (within the meaning of section 414(q)) or their dependents. For purposes of this paragraph, there shall be excluded from consideration employees not included in the program who are included in a unit of employees covered by an agreement which the Secretary of Labor finds to be a collective bargaining agreement between employee representatives and one or more employers, if there is evidence that educational assistance benefits were the subject of good faith bargaining between such employee representatives and such employer or employers.

(3) Principal shareholders or owners.—Not more than 5 percent of the amounts paid or incurred by the employer for educational assistance during the year may be provided for the class of individuals who are shareholders or owners (or their spouses or dependents), each of whom (on any day of the year) owns more than 5 percent of the stock or of the capital or profits interest in the employer.

(4) Other benefits as an alternative.—A program must not provide eligible employees with a choice between educational assistance and other remuneration includible in gross income. For purposes of this section, the business practices of the employer (as well as the written program) will be taken into account.

(5) No funding required.—A program referred to in paragraph (1) is not required to be funded.

(6) Notification of employees.—Reasonable notification of the availability and terms of the program must be provided to eligible employees.

(c) Definitions; special rules.—For purposes of this section—

(1) Educational assistance.—The term "educational assistance" means—

(A) the payment, by an employer, of expenses incurred by or on behalf of an employee for education of the employee (including, but not limited to, tuition, fees, and similar payments, books, supplies, and equipment), and

(B) the provision, by an employer, of courses of instruction for such employee (including books, supplies, and equipment),

but does not include payment for, or the provision of, tools or supplies which may be retained by the employee after completion of a course of instruction, or meals, lodging, or transportation. The term "educational assistance" also does not include any payment for, or the provision of any benefits with respect to, any course or other education involving sports, games, or hobbies.

(2) Employee.—The term "employee" includes, for any year, an individual who is an employee within the meaning of section 401(c)(1) (relating to self-employed individuals).

(3) Employer.—An individual who owns the entire interest in an unincorporated trade or business shall be treated as his own employer. A partnership shall be treated as the employer of each partner who is an employee within the meaning of paragraph (2).

(4) Attribution rules.—

(A) Ownership of stock.—Ownership of stock in a corporation shall be determined in accordance with the rules provided under subsections (d) and (e) of section 1563 (without regard to section 1563(e)(3)(C)).

(B) Interest in unincorporated trade or business.—The interest of an employee in a trade or business which is not incorporated shall be determined in accordance with regulations prescribed by the Secretary, which shall be based on principles similar to the principles which apply in the case of subparagraph (A).

(5) Certain tests not applicable.—An educational assistance program shall not be held or considered to fail to meet any requirements of subsection (b) merely because—

(A) of utilization rates for the different types of educational assistance made available under the program; or

(B) successful completion, or attaining a particular course grade, is required for or considered in determining reimbursement under the program.

(6) Relationship to current law.—This section shall not be construed to affect the deduction or inclusion in income of amounts (not within the exclusion under this section) which are paid or incurred, or received as reimbursement, for educational expenses under section 117, 162 or 212.

(7) Disallowance of excluded amounts as credit or deduction.—No deduction or credit shall be allowed to the employee under any other section of this chapter for any amount excluded from income by reason of this section.

* * *

§ 129. Dependent care assistance programs

(a) Exclusion.—

(1) In general.—Gross income of an employee does not include amounts paid or incurred by the employer for dependent care assistance provided to such employee if the assistance is furnished pursuant to a program which is described in subsection (d).

(2) Limitation of exclusion.—

(A) In general.—The amount which may be excluded under paragraph (1) for dependent care assistance with respect to dependent care services provided during a taxable year shall not exceed $5,000 ($2,500 in the case of a separate return by a married individual).

(B) Year of inclusion.—The amount of any excess under subparagraph (A) shall be included in gross income in the taxable year in which the dependent care services were provided (even if payment of dependent care assistance for such services occurs in a subsequent taxable year).

(C) Marital status.—For purposes of this paragraph, marital status shall be determined under the rules of paragraphs (3) and (4) of section 21(e).

For purposes of the preceding sentence, marital status shall be determined under the rules of paragraphs (3) and (4) of section 21(e).

(b) Earned income limitation.—

(1) In general.—The amount excluded from the income of an employee under subsection (a) for any taxable year shall not exceed—

(A) in the case of an employee who is not married at the close of such taxable year, the earned income of such employee for such taxable year, or

(B) in the case of an employee who is married at the close of such taxable year, the lesser of—

(i) the earned income of such employee for such taxable year, or

(ii) the earned income of the spouse of such employee for such taxable year.

(2) Special rule for certain spouses.—For purposes of paragraph (1), the provisions of section 21(d)(2) shall apply in determining the earned income of a spouse who is a student or incapable or caring for himself.

(c) Payments to related individuals.—No amount paid or incurred during the taxable year of an employee by an employer in providing dependent care assistance to such employee shall be excluded under subsection (a) if such amount was paid or incurred to an individual—

(1) with respect to whom, for such taxable year, a deduction is allowable under section 151(c) (relating to personal exemptions for dependents) to such employee or the spouse of such employee, or

(2) who is a child of such employee (within the meaning of section 152(f)(1)) under the age of 19 at the close of such taxable year.

(d) Dependent care assistance program.—

(1) In general.—For purposes of this section a dependent care assistance program is a separate written plan of an employer for the exclusive benefit of his employees to provide such employees with dependent care assistance which meets the requirements of paragraphs (2) through (8) of this subsection. If any plan would qualify as a dependent care assistance program but for a failure to meet the requirements of this subsection, then, notwithstanding such failure, such plan shall be treated as a dependent care assistance program in the case of employees who are not highly compensated employees.

(2) Discrimination.—The contributions or benefits provided under the plan shall not discriminate in favor of employees who are highly compensated employees (within the meaning of section 414(q)) or their dependents.

(3) Eligibility.—The program shall benefit employees who qualify under a classification set up by the employer and found by the Secretary not to be discriminatory in favor of employees described in paragraph (2), or their dependents.

(4) Principal shareholders or owners.—Not more than 25 percent of the amounts paid or incurred by the employer for dependent care assistance during the year may be provided for the class of individuals who are shareholders or owners (or their spouses or dependents), each of whom (on any day of the year) owns more than 5 percent of the stock or of the capital or profits interest in the employer.

(5) No funding required.—A program referred to in paragraph (1) is not required to be funded.

(6) Notification of eligible employees.—Reasonable notification of the availability and terms of the program shall be provided to eligible employees.

(7) Statement of expenses.—The plan shall furnish to an employee, on or before January 31, a written statement showing the amounts paid or expenses incurred by the employer in providing dependent care assistance to such employee during the previous calendar year.

(8) Benefits.—

(A) In general.—A plan meets the requirements of this paragraph if the average benefits provided to employees who are not highly compensated employees under all plans of the employer is at least 55 percent of the average benefits provided to highly compensated employees under all plans of the employer.

(B) Salary reduction agreements.—For purposes of subparagraph (A), in the case of any benefits provided through a salary reduction agreement, a plan may disregard any employees whose compensation is less than $25,000. For purposes of this subparagraph, the term "compensation" has the meaning given such term by section 414(q)(4), except that, under rules prescribed by the Secretary, an employer may elect to determine compensation on any other basis which does not discriminate in favor of highly compensated employees.

(9) Excluded employees.—For purposes of paragraphs (3) and (8), there shall be excluded from consideration—

(A) subject to rules similar to the rules of section 410(b)(4), employees who have not attained the age of 21 and completed 1 year of service (as defined in section 410(a)(3)), and

(B) employees not included in a dependent care assistance program who are included in a unit of employees covered by an agreement which the Secretary finds to be a collective bargaining agreement between employee representatives and 1 or more employees, if there is evidence that dependent care benefits were the subject of good faith bargaining between such employee representatives and such employer or employers.

* * *

§ 132. Certain fringe benefits

(a) Exclusion from gross income.—Gross income shall not include any fringe benefit which qualifies as a—

(1) no-additional-cost service,

(2) qualified employee discount,

(3) working condition fringe,

(4) de minimis fringe,

(5) qualified transportation fringe,

(6) qualified moving expense reimbursement,

(7) qualified retirement planning services, or

* * *

(b) No-additional-cost service defined.—For purposes of this section, the term "no-additional-cost service" means any service provided by an employer to an employee for use by such employee if—

(1) such service is offered for sale to customers in the ordinary course of the line of business of the employer in which the employee is performing services, and

(2) the employer incurs no substantial additional cost (including forgone revenue) in providing such service to the employee (determined without regard to any amount paid by the employee for such service).

(c) Qualified employee discount defined.—For purposes of this section—

(1) Qualified employee discount.—The term "qualified employee discount" means any employee discount with respect to qualified property or services to the extent such discount does not exceed—

(A) in the case of property, the gross profit percentage of the price at which the property is being offered by the employer to customers, or

(B) in the case of services, 20 percent of the price at which the services are being offered by the employer to customers.

(2) Gross profit percentage.—

(A) In general.—The term "gross profit percentage" means the percent which—

(i) the excess of the aggregate sales price of property sold by the employer to customers over the aggregate cost of such property to the employer, is of

(ii) the aggregate sale price of such property.

(B) Determination of gross profit percentage.—Gross profit percentage shall be determined on the basis of—

(i) all property offered to customers in the ordinary course of the line of business of the employer in which the employee is performing services (or a reasonable classification of property selected by the employer), and

(ii) the employer's experience during a representative period.

(3) Employee discount defined.—The term "employee discount" means the amount by which—

(A) the price at which the property or services are provided by the employer to an employee for use by such employee, is less than

(B) the price at which such property or services are being offered by the employer to customers.

(4) Qualified property or services.—The term "qualified property or services" means any property (other than real property and other than personal property of a kind held for investment) or services which are offered for sale to customers in the ordinary course of the line of business of the employer in which the employee is performing services.

(d) Working condition fringe defined.—For purposes of this section, the term "working condition fringe" means any property or services provided to an employee of the employer to the extent that, if the employee paid for such property or services, such payment would be allowable as a deduction under section 162 or 167.

(e) De minimis fringe defined.—For purposes of this section—

(1) In general.—The term "de minimis fringe" means any property or service the value of which is (after taking into account the frequency with which similar fringes are provided by the employer to the employer's employees) so small as to make accounting for it unreasonable or administratively impracticable.

(2) Treatment of certain eating facilities.—The operation by an employer of any eating facility for employees shall be treated as a de minimis fringe if—

(A) such facility is located on or near the business premises of the employer, and

(B) revenue derived from such facility normally equals or exceeds the direct operating costs of such facility.

The preceding sentence shall apply with respect to any highly compensated employee only if access to the facility is available on substantially the same terms to each member of a group of employees which is defined under a reasonable classification set up by the employer which does not discriminate in favor of highly compensated employees. For purposes of subparagraph (B), an employee entitled under section 119 to exclude the value of a meal provided at such facility shall be treated as having paid an amount for such meal equal to the direct operating costs of the facility attributable to such meal.

(f) Qualified transportation fringe.—

(1) In general.—For purposes of this section, the term "qualified transportation fringe" means any of the following provided by an employer to an employee:

(A) Transportation in a commuter highway vehicle if such transportation is in connection with travel between the employee's residence and place of employment.

(B) Any transit pass.

(C) Qualified parking.

(D) Any qualified bicycle commuting reimbursement.

(2) Limitation on exclusion.—The amount of the fringe benefits which are provided by an employer to any employee and which may be excluded from gross income under subsection (a)(5) shall not exceed—

(A) $100 per month in the case of the aggregate of the benefits described in subparagraphs (A) and (B) of paragraph (1),

(B) $175 per month in the case of qualified parking, and

(C) The applicable annual limitation in the case of any qualified bicycle commuting reimbursement.

In the case of any month beginning on or after the date of the enactment of this sentence and before January 1, 2014, paragraph (A) shall be applied as if the dollar amount therein were the same as the dollar amount in effect for such month under subparagraph (B).

(3) Cash reimbursements.—For purposes of this subsection, the term "qualified transportation fringe" includes a cash reimbursement by an employer to an employee for a benefit described in paragraph (1). The preceding sentence shall apply to a cash reimbursement for any transit pass only if a voucher or similar item which may be exchanged only for a transit pass is not readily available for direct distribution by the employer to the employee.

(4) No constructive receipt.—No amount shall be included in the gross income of an employee solely because the employee may choose between any qualified transportation fringe (other than a qualified bicycle commuting reimbursement) and compensation which would otherwise be includible in gross income of such employee.

(5) Definitions.—For purposes of this subsection—

(A) Transit pass.—The term "transit pass" means any pass, token, farecard, voucher, or similar item entitling a person to transportation (or transportation at a reduced price) if such transportation is—

(i) on mass transit facilities (whether or not publicly owned), or

(ii) provided by any person in the business of transporting persons for compensation or hire if such transportation is provided in a vehicle meeting the requirements of subparagraph (B)(i).

(B) Commuter highway vehicle.—The term "commuter highway vehicle" means any highway vehicle—

(i) the seating capacity of which is at least 6 adults (not including the driver), and

(ii) at least 80 percent of the mileage use of which can reasonably be expected to be—

(I) for purposes of transporting employees in connection with travel between their residences and their place of employment, and

(II) on trips during which the number of employees transported for such purposes is at least ½ of the adult seating capacity of such vehicle (not including the driver).

(C) Qualified parking.—The term "qualified parking" means parking provided to an employee on or near the business premises of the employer or on or near a location from which the employee commutes to work by transportation described in subparagraph (A), in a commuter highway vehicle, or by carpool. Such term shall not include any parking on or near property used by the employee for residential purposes.

(D) Transportation provided by employer.—Transportation referred to in paragraph (1)(A) shall be considered to be provided by an employer if such transportation is furnished in a commuter highway vehicle operated by or for the employer.

(E) Employee.—For purposes of this subsection, the term "employee" does not include an individual who is an employee within the meaning of section 401(c)(1).

(F) Definitions related to bicycle commuting reimbursement.—

(i) Qualified bicycle commuting reimbursement.—The term "qualified bicycle commuting reimbursement" means, with respect to any calendar year, any employer reimbursement during the 15–month period beginning with the first day of such calendar year for reasonable expenses incurred by the employee during such calendar year for the purchase of a bicycle and bicycle improvements, repair, and storage, if such bicycle is regularly used for travel between the employee's residence and place of employment.

(ii) Applicable annual limitation.—The term "applicable annual limitation" means, with respect to any employee for any calendar year, the product of $20 multiplied by the number of qualified bicycle commuting months during such year.

(iii) Qualified bicycle commuting month.—The term "qualified bicycle commuting month" means, with respect to any employee, any month during which such employee—

(I) regularly uses the bicycle for a substantial portion of the travel between the employee's residence and place of employment, and

(II) does not receive any benefit described in subparagraph (A), (B), or (C) of paragraph (1).

(6) Inflation adjustment.—

(A) In general.—In the case of any taxable year beginning in a calendar year after 1993, the dollar amounts contained in subparagraphs (A) and (B) of paragraph (2) shall be increased by an amount equal to—

(i) such dollar amount, multiplied by

(ii) the cost-of-living adjustment determined under section 1(f)(3) for the calendar year in which the taxable year begins, by substituting "calendar year 1998" for "calendar year 1992".

In the case of any taxable year beginning in a calendar year after 2002, clause (ii) shall be applied by substituting "calendar year 2001" for "calendar year 1998" for purposes of adjusting the dollar amount contained in paragraph (2)(A).

(B) Rounding. If any increase determined under subparagraph (A) is not a multiple of $5, such increase shall be rounded to the next lowest multiple of $5.

(7) Coordination with other provisions.—For purposes of this section, the terms "working condition fringe" and "de minimis fringe" shall not include any qualified transportation fringe (determined without regard to paragraph (2)).

(g) Qualified moving expense reimbursement.—For purposes of this section, the term "qualified moving expense reimbursement" means any amount received (directly or indirectly) by an individual from an employer as a payment for (or a reimbursement of) expenses which would be deductible as moving expenses under section 217 if directly paid or incurred by the individual. Such term shall not include any payment for (or reimbursement of) an expense actually deducted by the individual in a prior taxable year.

(h) Certain individuals treated as employees for purposes of subsections (a)(1) and (2).—For purposes of paragraphs (1) and (2) of subsection (a)—

(1) Retired and disabled employees and surviving spouse of employee treated as employee.—With respect to a line of business of an employer, the term "employee" includes—

(A) any individual who was formerly employed by such employer in such line of business and who separated from service with such employer in such line of business by reason of retirement or disability, and

(B) any widow or widower of any individual who died while employed by such employer in such line of business or while an employee within the meaning of subparagraph (A).

(2) Spouse and dependent children.—

(A) In general.—Any use by the spouse or a dependent child of the employee shall be treated as use by the employee.

(B) Dependent child.—For purposes of subparagraph (A), the term "dependent child" means any child (as defined in section 152(f)(1)) of the employee—

(i) who is a dependent of the employee, or

(ii) both of whose parents are deceased and who has not attained age 25.

For purposes of the preceding sentence, any child to whom section 152(e) applies shall be treated as the dependent of both parents.

(3) Special rule for parents in the case of air transportation.—Any use of air transportation by a parent of an employee (determined without regard to paragraph (1)(B)) shall be treated as use by the employee.

(i) Reciprocal agreements.—For purposes of paragraph (1) of subsection (a), any service provided by an employer to an employee of another employer shall be treated as provided by the employer of such employee if—

(1) such service is provided pursuant to a written agreement between such employers, and

(2) neither of such employers incurs any substantial additional costs (including foregone revenue) in providing such service or pursuant to such agreement.

(j) Special rules.—

(1) Exclusions under subsection (a)(1) and (2) apply to officers, etc., only if no discrimination.—Paragraphs (1) and (2) of subsection (a) shall apply with respect to any fringe benefit described therein provided with respect to any highly compensated employee only if such fringe benefit is available on substantially the same terms to each member of a group of employees which is defined under a reasonable classification set up by the employer which does not discriminate in favor of highly compensated employees. * * *

* * *

(3) Auto salesmen.—

(A) In general.—For purposes of subsection (a)(3), qualified automobile demonstration use shall be treated as a working condition fringe.

(B) Qualified automobile demonstration use.—For purposes of subparagraph (A), the term "qualified automobile demonstration use" means any use of an automobile by a full-time automobile salesman in the sales area in which the automobile dealer's sales office is located if—

(i) such use is provided primarily to facilitate the salesman's performance of services for the employer, and

(ii) there are substantial restrictions on the personal use of such automobile by such salesman.

(4) On-premises gyms and other athletic facilities.—

(A) In general.—Gross income shall not include the value of any on-premises athletic facility provided by an employer to his employees.

(B) On-premises athletic facility.—For purposes of this paragraph, the term "on-premises athletic facility" means any gym or other athletic facility—

(i) which is located on the premises of the employer,

(ii) which is operated by the employer, and

(iii) substantially all the use of which is by employees of the employer, their spouses, and their dependent children (within the meaning of subsection (h)).

* * *

(6) Highly compensated employee.—For purposes of this section, the term "highly compensated employee" has the meaning given such term by section 414(q).

(7) Air cargo.—For purposes of subsection (b), the transportation of cargo by air and the transportation of passengers by air shall be treated as the same service.

* * *

(k) Customers not to include employees.—For purposes of this section (other than subsection (c)(2)), the term "customers" shall only include customers who are not employees.

(*l*) Section not to apply to fringe benefits expressly provided for elsewhere.—This section (other than subsections (e) and (g)) shall not apply to any fringe benefits of a type the tax treatment of which is expressly provided for in any other section of this chapter.

(m) Qualified retirement planning services.—

(1) In general.—For purposes of this section, the term "qualified retirement planning services" means any retirement planning advice or information provided to an employee and his spouse by an employer maintaining a qualified employer plan.

(2) Nondiscrimination rule.—Subsection (a)(7) shall apply in the case of highly compensated employees only if such services are available on substantially the same terms to each member of the group of employees normally provided education and information regarding the employer's qualified employer plan.

(3) Qualified employer plan.—For purposes of this subsection, the term "qualified employer plan" means a plan, contract, pension, or account described in section 219(g)(5).

* * *

(*o*) Regulations.—The Secretary shall prescribe such regulations as may be necessary or appropriate to carry out the purposes of this section.

§ 135. Income from United States savings bonds used to pay higher education tuition and fees

(a) General rule.—In the case of an individual who pays qualified higher education expenses during the taxable year, no amount shall be includible in gross income by reason of the redemption during such year of any qualified United States savings bond.

(b) Limitations.—

(1) Limitation where redemption proceeds exceed higher education expenses.—

(A) In general.—If—

(i) the aggregate proceeds of qualified United States savings bonds redeemed by the taxpayer during the taxable year exceed

(ii) the qualified higher education expenses paid by the taxpayer during such taxable year, the amount excludable from gross income under subsection (a) shall not exceed the applicable fraction of the amount excludable from gross income under subsection (a) without regard to this subsection.

(B) Applicable fraction.—For purposes of subparagraph (A), the term "applicable fraction" means the fraction the numerator of which is the amount described in subparagraph (A)(ii) and the denominator of which is the amount described in subparagraph (A)(i).

(2) Limitation based on modified adjusted gross income.—

(A) In general.—If the modified adjusted gross income of the taxpayer for the taxable year exceeds $40,000 ($60,000 in the case of a joint return), the amount which would (but for this paragraph) be excludable from gross income under subsection (a) shall be reduced (but not below zero) by the amount which bears the same ratio to the amount which would be so excludable as such excess bears to $15,000 ($30,000 in the case of a joint return).

(B) Inflation adjustment.—In the case of any taxable year beginning in a calendar year after 1990, the $40,000 and $60,000 amounts contained in subparagraph (A) shall be increased by an amount equal to—

(i) such dollar amount, multiplied by

(ii) the cost-of-living adjustment under section 1(f)(3) * * *.

* * *

(c) Definitions.—For purposes of this section—

(1) Qualified United States savings bond.—The term "qualified United States savings bond" means any United States savings bond issued—

(A) after December 31, 1989,

(B) to an individual who has attained age 24 before the date of issuance, and

(C) at discount under section 3105 of title 31, United States Code.

(2) Qualified higher education expenses.—

(A) In general.—The term "qualified higher education expenses" means tuition and fees required for the enrollment or attendance of—

(i) the taxpayer,

(ii) the taxpayer's spouse, or

(iii) any dependent of the taxpayer with respect to whom the taxpayer is allowed a deduction under section 151,

at an eligible educational institution.

(B) Exception for education involving sports, etc.—Such term shall not include expenses with respect to any course or other education involving sports, games, or hobbies other than as part of a degree program.

(C) Contributions to qualified tuition program and Coverdell education savings accounts.—Such term shall include any contribution to a qualified tuition program (as defined in section 529) on behalf of a designated beneficiary (as defined in such section), or to a Coverdell education savings account (as defined in section 530) on behalf of an account beneficiary, who is an individual described in subparagraph (A); but there shall be no increase in the investment in the contract for purposes of applying section 529(c)(3)(A) by reason of any portion of such contribution which is not includible in gross income by reason of this subparagraph.

(3) Eligible educational institution.—The term "eligible educational institution" has the meaning given such term by section 529(e)(5).

(4) Modified adjusted gross income.—The term "modified adjusted gross income" means the adjusted gross income of the taxpayer for the taxable year determined—

(A) without regard to this section and sections 137, 199, 221, 222, 911, 931, and 933, and

(B) after the application of sections 86, 469, and 219.

(d) Special rules.—

(1) Adjustment for certain scholarships and veterans benefits.—The amount of qualified higher education expenses otherwise taken into account under subsection (a) with respect to the education of an individual shall be reduced (before the application of subsection (b)) by the sum of the amounts received with respect to such individual for the taxable year as—

(A) a qualified scholarship which under section 117 is not includable in gross income,

* * *

(C) a payment (other than a gift, bequest, devise, or inheritance within the meaning of section 102(a)) for educational expenses, or attributable to attendance at an eligible educational institution, which is exempt from income taxation by any law of the United States, or

(D) a payment, waiver or reimbursement of qualified higher education expenses under a qualified tuition program (within the meaning of section 529(b)).

(2) Coordination with other higher education benefits.—The amount of the qualified higher education expenses otherwise taken into account under subsection (a) with respect to the education of an individual shall be reduced (before the application of subsection (b)) by—

(A) the amount of such expenses which are taken into account in determining the credit allowed to the taxpayer or any other person under section 25A with respect to such expenses; and

(B) the amount of such expenses which are taken into account in determining the exclusions under sections 529(c)(3)(B) and 530(d)(2).

(3) No exclusion for married individuals filing separate returns.—If the taxpayer is a married individual (within the meaning of section 7703), this section shall apply only if the taxpayer and his spouse file a joint return for the taxable year.

(4) Regulations.—The Secretary may prescribe such regulations as may be necessary or appropriate to carry out this section, including regulations requiring record keeping and information reporting.

§ 137. Adoption assistance programs

(a) Exclusion.—

(1) In general.—Gross income of an employee does not include amounts paid or expenses incurred by the employer for qualified adoption expenses in connection with the adoption of a child by an employee if such amounts are furnished pursuant to an adoption assistance program.

(2) $10,000 exclusion for adoption of child with special needs regardless of expenses.—In the case of an adoption of a child with special needs which becomes final during a taxable year, the qualified adoption expenses with respect to such adoption for such year shall be increased by an amount equal to the excess (if any) of $10,000 over the actual aggregate qualified adoption expenses with respect to such adoption during such taxable year and all prior taxable years.

(b) Limitations—

(1) Dollar limitation.—The aggregate of the amounts paid or expenses incurred which may be taken into account under subsection (a) for all taxable years with respect to the adoption of a child by the taxpayer shall not exceed $10,000.

(2) Income limitation.—The amount excludable from gross income under subsection (a) for any taxable year shall be reduced (but not below zero) by an amount which bears the same ratio to the amount so excludable (determined without regard to this paragraph but with regard to paragraph (1)) as—

(A) the amount (if any) by which the taxpayer's adjusted gross income exceeds $150,000, bears to

(B) $40,000.

(3) Determination of adjusted gross income.—For purposes of paragraph (2), adjusted gross income shall be determined—

(A) without regard to this section and sections 199, 221, 222, 911, 931, and 933, and

(B) after the application of sections 86, 135, 219, and 469.

(c) Adoption assistance program.—For purposes of this section, an adoption assistance program is a separate written plan of an employer for the exclusive benefit of such employer's employees—

(1) under which the employer provides such employees with adoption assistance, and

(2) which meets requirements similar to the requirements of paragraphs (2), (3), (5), and (6) of section 127(b).

* * *

(d) Qualified adoption expenses.—For purposes of this section, the term "qualified adoption expenses" has the meaning given such term by section 23(d) (determined without regard to reimbursements under this section).

(e) Certain rules to apply.—Rules similar to the rules of subsections (e), (f), and (g) of section 23 shall apply for purposes of this section.

(f) Adjustments for inflation.—In the case of a taxable year beginning after December 31, 2002, each of the dollar amounts in subsection (a)(2) and paragraphs (1) and (2)(A) of subsection (b) shall be increased by an amount equal to—

(1) such dollar amount, multiplied by

(2) the cost-of-living adjustment determined under section 1(f)(3) for the calendar year in which the taxable year begins, determined by substituting "calendar year 2001" for "calendar year 1992" in subparagraph (B) thereof.

If any amount as increased under the preceding sentence is not a multiple of $10, such amount shall be rounded to the nearest multiple of $10.

§ 139. Disaster relief payments.

(a) General rule.—Gross income shall not include any amount received by an individual as a qualified disaster relief payment.

(b) Qualified disaster relief payment defined.—For purposes of this section, the term "qualified disaster relief payment" means any amount paid to or for the benefit of an individual—

(1) to reimburse or pay reasonable and necessary personal, family, living, or funeral expenses incurred as a result of a qualified disaster,

(2) to reimburse or pay reasonable and necessary expenses incurred for the repair or rehabilitation of a personal residence or repair or replacement of its contents to the extent that the need for such repair, rehabilitation, or replacement is attributable to a qualified disaster,

(3) by a person engaged in the furnishing or sale of transportation as a common carrier by reason of the death or personal physical injuries incurred as a result of a qualified disaster, or

(4) if such amount is paid by a Federal, State, or local government, or agency or instrumentality thereof, in connection with a qualified disaster in order to promote the general welfare, but only to the extent any expense compensated by such payment is not otherwise compensated for by insurance or otherwise.

(c) Qualified disaster defined.—For purposes of this section, the term "qualified disaster" means—

(1) a disaster which results from a terroristic or military action (as defined in section 692(c)(2)),

(2) federally declared disaster (as defined by section 165(h)(3)(C)(i)),

(3) a disaster which results from an accident involving a common carrier, or from any other event, which is determined by the Secretary to be of a catastrophic nature, or

(4) with respect to amounts described in subsection (b)(4), a disaster which is determined by an applicable Federal, State, or local authority (as determined by the Secretary) to warrant assistance from the Federal, State, or local government or agency or instrumentality thereof.

(d) Coordination with employment taxes.—For purposes of chapter 2 and subtitle C, qualified disaster relief payments and qualified disaster mitigation payments shall not be treated as net earnings from self-employment, wages, or compensation subject to tax.

(e) No relief for certain individuals.—Subsections (a), (f) and (g) shall not apply with respect to any individual identified by the Attorney General to have been a participant or conspirator in a terroristic action (as so defined), or a representative of such individual.

(f) Exclusion of certain additional payments.—Gross income shall not include any amount received as payment under section 406 of the Air Transportation Safety and System Stabilization Act.

(g) Qualified disaster mitigation payments.—

(1) In general.—Gross income shall not include any amount received as a qualified disaster mitigation payment.

(2) Qualified disaster mitigation payment defined.—For purposes of this section, the term "qualified disaster mitigation payment" means any amount which is paid pursuant to the Robert T. Stafford Disaster Relief and Emergency Assistance Act (as in effect on the date of the enactment of this subsection) or the National Flood Insurance Act (as in effect on such date) to or for the benefit of the owner of any property for hazard mitigation with respect to such property. Such term shall not include any amount received for the sale or disposition of any property.

(3) No increase in basis.—Notwithstanding any other provision of this subtitle, no increase in the basis or adjusted basis of any property shall result from any amount excluded under this subsection with respect to such property.

(h) Denial of double benefit.—Notwithstanding any other provision of this subtitle, no deduction or credit shall be allowed (to the person for whose benefit a qualified disaster relief payment or qualified disaster mitigation payment is made) for, or by reason of, any expenditure to the extent of the amount excluded under this section with respect to such expenditure.

§ 139A. Federal subsidies for prescription drug plans

Gross income shall not include any special subsidy payment received under section 1860D–22 of the Social Security Act. This section shall not be taken into account for purposes of determining whether any deduction is allowable with respect to any cost taken into account in determining such payment.

PART IV—TAX EXEMPTION REQUIREMENTS FOR STATE AND LOCAL BONDS

Subpart A—Private Activity Bonds

§ 141. Private activity bond; qualified bond

(a) Private activity bond.—For purposes of this title, the term "private activity bond" means any bond issued as part of an issue—

(1) which meets—

(A) the private business use test of paragraph (1) of subsection (b), and

(B) the private security or payment test of paragraph (2) of subsection (b), or

(2) which meets the private loan financing test of subsection (c).

(b) Private business tests.—

(1) Private business use test.—Except as otherwise provided in this subsection, an issue meets the test of this paragraph if more than 10 percent of the proceeds of the issue are to be used for any private business use.

(2) Private security or payment test.—Except as otherwise provided in this subsection, an issue meets the test of this paragraph if the payment of the principal of, or the interest on, more than 10 percent of the proceeds of such issue is (under the terms of such issue or any underlying arrangement) directly or indirectly—

(A) secured by any interest in—

(i) property used or to be used for a private business use, or

(ii) payments in respect of such property, or

(B) to be derived from payments (whether or not to the issuer) in respect of property, or borrowed money, used or to be used for a private business use.

* * *

(e) Qualified bond.—For purposes of this part, the term "qualified bond" means any private activity bond if—

(1) In general.—Such bond is—

(A) an exempt facility bond,

(B) a qualified mortgage bond,

(C) a qualified veterans' mortgage bond,

* Omitted entirely.

(D) a qualified small issue bond,

(E) a qualified student loan bond,

(F) a qualified redevelopment bond, or

(G) a qualified 501(c)(3) bond.

* * *

§ 142. Exempt facility bond

(a) General rule.—For purposes of this part, the term "exempt facility bond" means any bond issued as part of an issue 95 percent or more of the net proceeds of which are to be used to provide—

(1) airports,

(2) docks and wharves,

(3) mass commuting facilities,

(4) facilities for the furnishing of water,

(5) sewage facilities,

(6) solid waste disposal facilities,

(7) qualified residential rental projects,

(8) facilities for the local furnishing of electric energy or gas,

* * *

(13) qualified public educational facilities,

* * *

Subpart B—Requirements Applicable to All State and Local Bonds

§ 148. Arbitrage

(a) Arbitrage bond defined.—For purposes of section 103, the term "arbitrage bond" means any bond issued as part of an issue any portion of the proceeds of which are reasonably expected (at the time of issuance of the bond) to be used directly or indirectly—

(1) to acquire higher yielding investments, or

(2) to replace funds which were used directly or indirectly to acquire higher yielding investments.

For purposes of this subsection, a bond shall be treated as an arbitrage bond if the issuer intentionally uses any portion of the proceeds of the issue of which such bond is a part in a manner described in paragraph (1) or (2).

* * *

§ 149. Bonds must be registered to be tax exempt; other requirements

(a) Bonds must be registered to be tax exempt.—

(1) General rule.—Nothing in section 103(a) or in any other provision of law shall be construed to provide an exemption from Federal income tax for interest on any registration-required bond unless such bond is in registered form.

(2) Registration-required bond.—For purposes of paragraph (1), the term "registration-required bond" means any bond other than a bond which—

(A) is not of a type offered to the public, or

(B) has a maturity (at issue) of not more than 1 year.

* * *

PART V—DEDUCTIONS FOR PERSONAL EXEMPTIONS

§ 151. Allowance of deductions for personal exemptions

(a) Allowance of deductions.—In the case of an individual, the exemptions provided by this section shall be allowed as deductions in computing taxable income.

(b) Taxpayer and spouse.—An exemption of the exemption amount for the taxpayer; and an additional exemption of the exemption amount for the spouse of the taxpayer if a joint return is not made by the taxpayer and his spouse, and if the spouse, for the calendar year in which the taxable year of the taxpayer begins, has no gross income and is not the dependent of another taxpayer.

(c) Additional exemption for dependents.—An exemption of the exemption amount for each individual who is a dependent (as defined in section 152) of the taxpayer for the taxable year.

(d) Exemption amount.—For purposes of this section—

(1) In general.—Except as otherwise provided in this subsection, the term "exemption amount" means $2,000.

(2) Exemption amount disallowed in case of certain dependents.—In the case of an individual with respect to whom a deduction under this section is allowable to another taxpayer for a taxable year beginning in the calendar year in which the individual's taxable year begins, the exemption amount applicable to such individual for such individual's taxable year shall be zero.

(3) Phaseout.—

(A) In general.—In the case of any taxpayer whose adjusted gross income for the taxable year exceeds the applicable amount in effect under section 68(b), the exemption amount shall be reduced by the applicable percentage.

(B) Applicable percentage.—For purposes of subparagraph (A), the term "applicable percentage" means 2 percentage points for each $2,500 (or fraction thereof) by which the taxpayer's adjusted gross income for the taxable year exceeds the threshold amount. In the case of a married individual filing a separate return, the preceding sentence shall be applied by substituting "$1,250" for "$2,500". In no event shall the applicable percentage exceed 100 percent.

(C) Coordination with other provisions.—The provisions of this paragraph shall not apply for purposes of determining whether a deduction under this section with respect to any individual is allowable to another taxpayer for any taxable year.

(4) Inflation adjustments.—In the case of any taxable year beginning in a calendar year after 1989, the dollar amount contained in paragraph (1) shall be increased by an amount equal to—

(A) such dollar amount, multiplied by

(B) the cost-of-living adjustment determined under section 1(f)(3) * * *.

(e) Identifying information required.—No exemption shall be allowed under this section with respect to any individual unless the TIN of such individual is included on the return claiming the exemption.

§ 152. Dependent defined

(a) In general.—For purposes of this subtitle, the term "dependent" means—

(1) a qualifying child, or

(2) a qualifying relative.

(b) Exceptions.—For purposes of this section—

(1) Dependents ineligible.—If an individual is a dependent of a taxpayer for any taxable year of such taxpayer beginning in a calendar year, such individual shall be treated as having no dependents for any taxable year of such individual beginning in such calendar year.

(2) Married dependents.—An individual shall not be treated as a dependent of a taxpayer under subsection (a) if such individual has made a joint return with the individual's spouse under section 6013 for the taxable year beginning in the calendar year in which the taxable year of the taxpayer begins.

(3) Citizens or nationals of other countries.—

(A) In general.—The term "dependent" does not include an individual who is not a citizen or national of the United States unless such individual is a resident of the United States or a country contiguous to the United States.

(B) Exception for adopted child.—Subparagraph (A) shall not exclude any child of a taxpayer (within the meaning of subsection (f)(1)(B)) from the definition of "dependent" if—

(i) for the taxable year of the taxpayer, the child has the same principal place of abode as the taxpayer and is a member of the taxpayer's household, and

(ii) the taxpayer is a citizen or national of the United States.

(c) Qualifying child.—For purposes of this section—

(1) In general.—The term "qualifying child" means, with respect to any taxpayer for any taxable year, an individual—

(A) who bears a relationship to the taxpayer described in paragraph (2),

(B) who has the same principal place of abode as the taxpayer for more than one-half of such taxable year,

(C) who meets the age requirements of paragraph (3),

(D) who has not provided over one-half of such individual's own support for the calendar year in which the taxable year of the taxpayer begins, and

(E) who has not filed a joint return (other than only for a claim of refund) with the individual's spouse under section 6013 for the taxable year beginning in the calendar year in which the taxable year of the taxpayer begins.

(2) Relationship.—For purposes of paragraph (1)(A), an individual bears a relationship to the taxpayer described in this paragraph if such individual is—

(A) a child of the taxpayer or a descendant of such a child, or

(B) a brother, sister, stepbrother, or stepsister of the taxpayer or a descendant of any such relative.

(3) Age requirements.—

(A) In general.—For purposes of paragraph (1)(C), an individual meets the requirements of this paragraph if such individual is younger than the taxpayer claiming such individual as a qualifying child and—

(i) has not attained the age of 19 as of the close of the calendar year in which the taxable year of the taxpayer begins, or

(ii) is a student who has not attained the age of 24 as of the close of such calendar year.

(B) Special rule for disabled.—In the case of an individual who is permanently and totally disabled (as defined in section 22(e)(3)) at any time during such calendar year, the requirements of subparagraph (A) shall be treated as met with respect to such individual.

(4) Special rule relating to 2 or more who can claim the same qualifying child.—

(A) In general.—Except as provided in subparagraphs (B) and (C), if (but for this paragraph) an individual may be claimed as a qualifying child by 2 or more taxpayers for a taxable year beginning in the same calendar year, such individual shall be treated as the qualifying child of the taxpayer who is—

(i) a parent of the individual, or

(ii) if clause (i) does not apply, the taxpayer with the highest adjusted gross income for such taxable year.

(B) More than 1 parent claiming qualifying child.—If the parents claiming any qualifying child do not file a joint return together, such child shall be treated as the qualifying child of—

(i) the parent with whom the child resided for the longest period of time during the taxable year, or

(ii) if the child resides with both parents for the same amount of time during such taxable year, the parent with the highest adjusted gross income.

(C) No parent claiming qualifying child.—If the parents of an individual may claim such individual as a qualifying child but no parent so claims the individual, such individual may be claimed as the qualifying child of another taxpayer but only if the adjusted gross income of such taxpayer is higher than the highest adjusted gross income of any parent of the individual.

(d) Qualifying relative.—For purposes of this section—

(1) In general.—The term "qualifying relative" means, with respect to any taxpayer for any taxable year, an individual—

(A) who bears a relationship to the taxpayer described in paragraph (2),

(B) whose gross income for the calendar year in which such taxable year begins is less than the exemption amount (as defined in section 151(d)),

(C) with respect to whom the taxpayer provides over one-half of the individual's support for the calendar year in which such taxable year begins, and

(D) who is not a qualifying child of such taxpayer or of any other taxpayer for any taxable year beginning in the calendar year in which such taxable year begins.

(2) Relationship.—For purposes of paragraph (1)(A), an individual bears a relationship to the taxpayer described in this paragraph if the individual is any of the following with respect to the taxpayer:

(A) A child or a descendant of a child.

(B) A brother, sister, stepbrother, or stepsister.

(C) The father or mother, or an ancestor of either.

(D) A stepfather or stepmother.

(E) A son or daughter of a brother or sister of the taxpayer.

(F) A brother or sister of the father or mother of the taxpayer.

(G) A son-in-law, daughter-in-law, father-in-law, mother-in-law, brother-in-law, or sister-in-law.

(H) An individual (other than an individual who at any time during the taxable year was the spouse, determined without regard to section 7703, of the taxpayer) who, for the taxable year of the taxpayer, has the same principal place of abode as the taxpayer and is a member of the taxpayer's household.

(3) Special rule relating to multiple support agreements.—For purposes of paragraph (1)(C), over one-half of the support of an individual for a calendar year shall be treated as received from the taxpayer if—

(A) no one person contributed over one-half of such support,

(B) over one-half of such support was received from 2 or more persons each of whom, but for the fact that any such person alone did not contribute over one-half of such support, would have been entitled to claim such individual as a dependent for a taxable year beginning in such calendar year,

(C) the taxpayer contributed over 10 percent of such support, and

(D) each person described in subparagraph (B) (other than the taxpayer) who contributed over 10 percent of such support files a written declaration (in such manner and form as the Secretary may by regulations prescribe) that such person will not claim such individual as a dependent for any taxable year beginning in such calendar year.

(4) Special rule relating to income of handicapped dependents.—

(A) In general.—For purposes of paragraph (1)(B), the gross income of an individual who is permanently and totally disabled (as defined in section 22(e)(3)) at any time during the taxable year shall not include income attributable to services performed by the individual at a sheltered workshop if—

(i) the availability of medical care at such workshop is the principal reason for the individual's presence there, and

(ii) the income arises solely from activities at such workshop which are incident to such medical care.

(B) Sheltered workshop defined.—For purposes of subparagraph (A), the term "sheltered workshop" means a school—

(i) which provides special instruction or training designed to alleviate the disability of the individual, and

(ii) which is operated by an organization described in section 501(c)(3) and exempt from tax under section 501(a), or by a State, a possession of the United States, any political subdivision of any of the foregoing, the United States, or the District of Columbia.

(5) Special rules for support.—For purposes of this subsection—

(A) payments to a spouse which are includible in the gross income of such spouse under section 71 or 682 shall not be treated as a payment by the payor spouse for the support of any dependent, and

(B) in the case of the remarriage of a parent, support of a child received from the parent's spouse shall be treated as received from the parent.

(e) Special rule for divorced parents, etc.—

(1) In general.—Notwithstanding subsection (c)(1)(B), (c)(4), or (d)(1)(C), if—

(A) a child receives over one-half of the child's support during the calendar year from the child's parents—

(i) who are divorced or legally separated under a decree of divorce or separate maintenance,

(ii) who are separated under a written separation agreement, or

(iii) who live apart at all times during the last 6 months of the calendar year, and—

(B) such child is in the custody of 1 or both of the child's parents for more than one-half of the calendar year, such child shall be treated as being the qualifying child or qualifying relative of the noncustodial parent for a calendar year if the requirements described in paragraph (2) or (3) are met.

(2) Exception where custodial parent releases claim to exemption for the year.—For purposes of paragraph (1), the requirements described in this paragraph are met with respect to any calendar year if—

(A) the custodial parent signs a written declaration (in such manner and form as the Secretary may by regulations prescribe) that such custodial parent will not claim such child as a dependent for any taxable year beginning in such calendar year, and

(B) the noncustodial parent attaches such written declaration to the noncustodial parent's return for the taxable year beginning during such calendar year.

(3) Exception for certain pre–1985 instruments.—

(A) In general.—For purposes of paragraph (1), the requirements described in this paragraph are met with respect to any calendar year if—

(i) a qualified pre–1985 instrument between the parents applicable to the taxable year beginning in such calendar year provides that the noncustodial parent shall be entitled to any deduction allowable under section 151 for such child, and

(ii) the noncustodial parent provides at least $600 for the support of such child during such calendar year.

For purposes of this subparagraph, amounts expended for the support of a child or children shall be treated as received from the noncustodial parent to the extent that such parent provided amounts for such support.

(B) Qualified pre–1985 instrument.—For purposes of this paragraph, the term "qualified pre–1985 instrument" means any decree of divorce or separate maintenance or written agreement—

(i) which is executed before January 1, 1985,

(ii) which on such date contains the provision described in subparagraph (A)(i), and

(iii) which is not modified on or after such date in a modification which expressly provides that this paragraph shall not apply to such decree or agreement.

(4) Custodial parent and noncustodial parent.—For purposes of this subsection—

(A) Custodial parent.—The term "custodial parent" means the parent having custody for the greater portion of the calendar year.

(B) Noncustodial parent.—The term "noncustodial parent" means the parent who is not the custodial parent.

(5) Exception for multiple-support agreement.—This subsection shall not apply in any case where over one-half of the support of the child is treated as having been received from a taxpayer under the provision of subsection (d)(3).

(6) Special rule for support received from new spouse of parent.—For purposes of this subsection, in the case of the remarriage of a parent, support of a child received from the parent's spouse shall be treated as received from the parent.

(f) Other definitions and rules.—For purposes of this section—

(1) Child defined.—

(A) In general.—The term "child" means an individual who is—

(i) a son, daughter, stepson, or stepdaughter of the taxpayer, or

(ii) an eligible foster child of the taxpayer.

(B) Adopted child.—In determining whether any of the relationships specified in subparagraph (A)(i) or paragraph (4) exists, a legally adopted individual of the taxpayer, or an individual who is lawfully placed with the taxpayer for legal adoption by the taxpayer, shall be treated as a child of such individual by blood.

(C) Eligible foster child.—For purposes of subparagraph (A)(ii), the term "eligible foster child" means an individual who is placed with the taxpayer by an authorized placement agency or by judgment, decree, or other order of any court of competent jurisdiction.

(2) Student defined.—The term "student" means an individual who during each of 5 calendar months during the calendar year in which the taxable year of the taxpayer begins—

(A) is a full-time student at an educational organization described in section 170(b)(1)(A)(ii), or

(B) is pursuing a full-time course of institutional on-farm training under the supervision of an accredited agent of an educational organization described in section 170(b)(1)(A)(ii) or of a State or political subdivision of a State.

(3) Determination of household status.—An individual shall not be treated as a member of the taxpayer's household if at any time during the taxable year of the taxpayer the relationship between such individual and the taxpayer is in violation of local law.

(4) Brother and sister.—The terms "brother" and "sister" include a brother or sister by the half blood.

(5) Special support test in case of students.—For purposes of subsections (c)(1)(D) and (d)(1)(C), in the case of an individual who is—

(A) a child of the taxpayer, and

(B) a student,

amounts received as scholarships for study at an educational organization described in section 170(b)(1)(A)(ii) shall not be taken into account.

(6) Treatment of missing children.—

(A) In general.—Solely for the purposes referred to in subparagraph (B), a child of the taxpayer—

(i) who is presumed by law enforcement authorities to have been kidnapped by someone who is not a member of the family of such child or the taxpayer, and

(ii) who had, for the taxable year in which the kidnapping occurred, the same principal place of abode as the taxpayer for more than one-half of the portion of such year before the date of the kidnapping, shall be treated as meeting the requirement of subsection (c)(1)(B) with respect to a taxpayer for all taxable years ending during the period that the child is kidnapped.

(B) Purposes.—Subparagraph (A) shall apply solely for purposes of determining—

(i) the deduction under section 151(c),

(ii) the credit under section 24 (relating to child tax credit),

(iii) whether an individual is a surviving spouse or a head of a household (as such terms are defined in section 2), and

(iv) the earned income credit under section 32.

(C) Comparable treatment of certain qualifying relatives.—For purposes of this section, a child of the taxpayer—

(i) who is presumed by law enforcement authorities to have been kidnapped by someone who is not a member of the family of such child or the taxpayer, and

(ii) who was (without regard to this paragraph) a qualifying relative of the taxpayer for the portion of the taxable year before the date of the kidnapping,

shall be treated as a qualifying relative of the taxpayer for all taxable years ending during the period that the child is kidnapped.

(D) Termination of treatment.—Subparagraphs (A) and (C) shall cease to apply as of the first taxable year of the taxpayer beginning after the calendar year in which there is a determination that the child is dead (or, if earlier, in which the child would have attained age 18).

(7) Cross references.—For provision treating child as dependent of both parents for purposes of certain provisions, see sections 105(b), 132(h)(2)(B), and 213(d)(5).

§ 153. Cross references

(1) For deductions of estates and trusts, in lieu of the exemptions under section 151, see section 642(b).

* * *

(3) For determination of marital status, see section 7703.

PART VI—ITEMIZED DEDUCTIONS FOR INDIVIDUALS AND CORPORATIONS

§ 161. Allowance of deductions

In computing taxable income under section 63, there shall be allowed as deductions the items specified in this part, subject to the exceptions provided in part IX (sec. 261 and following, relating to items not deductible).

§ 162. Trade or business expenses

(a) In general.—There shall be allowed as a deduction all the ordinary and necessary expenses paid or incurred during the taxable year in carrying on any trade or business, including—

(1) a reasonable allowance for salaries or other compensation for personal services actually rendered;

(2) traveling expenses (including amounts expended for meals and lodging other than amounts which are lavish or extravagant under the circumstances) while away from home in the pursuit of a trade or business; and

(3) rentals or other payments required to be made as a condition to the continued use or possession, for purposes of the trade or business, of property to which the taxpayer has not taken or is not taking title or in which he has no equity.

For purposes of the preceding sentence, the place of residence of a Member of Congress (including any Delegate and Resident Commissioner) within the State, congressional district, or possession which he represents in Congress shall be considered his home, but amounts expended by such Members within each taxable year for living expenses shall not be deductible for income tax purposes in excess of $3,000. For purposes of paragraph (2), the taxpayer shall not be treated as being temporarily away from home during any period of employment if such period exceeds 1 year. The preceding sentence shall not apply to any Federal employee during any period for which such employee is certified by the Attorney General (or the designee thereof) as traveling on behalf of the United States in temporary duty status to investigate or prosecute, or provide support services for the investigation or prosecution of, a Federal crime.

(b) Charitable contributions and gifts excepted.—No deduction shall be allowed under subsection (a) for any contribution or gift which would be allowable as a deduction under section 170 were it not for the percentage limitations, the dollar limitations, or the requirements as to the time of payment, set forth in such section.

(c) Illegal bribes, kickbacks, and other payments.—

(1) Illegal payments to government officials or employees.—No deduction shall be allowed under subsection (a) for any payment made, directly or indirectly, to an official or employee of any government, or of any agency or instrumentality of any government, if the payment constitutes an illegal bribe or kickback or, if the payment is to an official or employee of a foreign government, the payment is unlawful under the Foreign Corrupt Practices Act of 1977. The burden of proof in respect of the issue, for the purposes of this paragraph, as to whether a payment constitutes an illegal bribe or kickback (or is unlawful under the Foreign Corrupt Practices Act of 1977) shall be upon the Secretary to the same extent as he bears the burden of proof under section 7454 (concerning the burden of proof when the issue relates to fraud).

(2) Other illegal payments.—No deduction shall be allowed under subsection (a) for any payment (other than a payment described in paragraph (1)) made, directly or indirectly, to any person, if the payment constitutes an illegal bribe, illegal kickback, or other illegal payment under any law of the United States, or under any law of a State (but only if such State law is generally enforced), which subjects the payor to a criminal penalty or the loss of license or privilege to engage in a trade or business. For purposes of this paragraph, a kickback includes a payment in consideration of the referral of a client, patient, or customer. The burden of proof in respect of the issue, for purposes of this paragraph, as to whether a payment constitutes an illegal bribe, illegal kickback, or other illegal payment shall be upon the Secretary to the same extent as he bears the burden of proof under section 7454 (concerning the burden of proof when the issue relates to fraud).

(3) Kickbacks, rebates, and bribes under medicare and medicaid.—No deduction shall be allowed under subsection (a) for any kickback, rebate, or bribe made by any provider of services, supplier, physician, or other person who furnishes items or services for which payment is or may be made under the Social Security Act, or in whole or in part out of Federal funds under a State plan approved under such Act, if such kickback, rebate, or bribe is made in connection with the furnishing of such items or services or the making or receipt of such payments. For purposes of this paragraph, a kickback includes a payment in consideration of the referral of a client, patient, or customer.

* * *

(e) Denial of deduction for certain lobbying and political expenditures.—

(1) In general.—No deduction shall be allowed under subsection (a) for any amount paid or incurred in connection with—

(A) influencing legislation,

(B) participation in, or intervention in, any political campaign on behalf of (or in opposition to) any candidate for public office,

(C) any attempt to influence the general public, or segments thereof, with respect to elections, legislative matters, or referendums, or

(D) any direct communication with a covered executive branch official in an attempt to influence the official actions or positions of such official.

(2) Exception for local legislation.—In the case of any legislation of any local council or similar governing body—

(A) paragraph (1)(A) shall not apply, and

(B) the deduction allowed by subsection (a) shall include all ordinary and necessary expenses (including, but not limited to, traveling expenses described in subsection (a)(2) and the cost of preparing testimony) paid or incurred during the taxable year in carrying on any trade or business—

(i) in direct connection with appearances before, submission of statements to, or sending communications to the committees, or individual members, of such council or body with respect to legislation or proposed legislation of direct interest to the taxpayer, or

(ii) in direct connection with communication of information between the taxpayer and an organization of which the taxpayer is a member with respect to any such legislation or proposed legislation which is of direct interest to the taxpayer and to such organization,

and that portion of the dues so paid or incurred with respect to any organization of which the taxpayer is a member which is attributable to the expenses of the activities described in clauses (i) and (ii) carried on by such organization.

(3) Application to dues of tax-exempt organizations.—No deduction shall be allowed under subsection (a) for the portion of dues or other similar amounts paid by the taxpayer to an organization which is exempt from tax under this subtitle which the organization notifies the taxpayer under section 6033(e)(1)(A)(ii) is allocable to expenditures to which paragraph (1) applies.

(4) Influencing legislation.—For purposes of this subsection—

(A) In general.—The term "influencing legislation" means any attempt to influence any legislation through communication with any member or employee of a legislative body, or with any government official or employee who may participate in the formulation of legislation.

(B) Legislation.—The term "legislation" has the meaning given such term by section 4911(e)(2).

(5) Other special rules.—

(A) Exception for certain taxpayers.—In the case of any taxpayer engaged in the trade or business of conducting activities described in paragraph (1), paragraph (1) shall not apply to expenditures of the taxpayer in conducting such activities directly on behalf of another person (but shall apply to payments by such other person to the taxpayer for conducting such activities).

(B) De minimis exception.—

(i) In general.—Paragraph (1) shall not apply to any in-house expenditures for any taxable year if such expenditures do not exceed $2,000. In determining whether a taxpayer exceeds the $2,000 limit under this clause, there shall not be taken into account overhead costs otherwise allocable to activities described in paragraphs (1)(A) and (D).

(ii) In-house expenditures.—For purposes of clause (i), the term ''in-house expenditures'' means expenditures described in paragraphs (1)(A) and (D) other than—

(I) payments by the taxpayer to a person engaged in the trade or business of conducting activities described in paragraph (1) for the conduct of such activities on behalf of the taxpayer, or

(II) dues or other similar amounts paid or incurred by the taxpayer which are allocable to activities described in paragraph (1).

(C) Expenses incurred in connection with lobbying and political activities.—Any amount paid or incurred for research for, or preparation, planning, or coordination of, any activity described in paragraph (1) shall be treated as paid or incurred in connection with such activity.

(6) Covered executive branch official.—For purposes of this subsection, the term ''covered executive branch official'' means—

(A) the President,

(B) the Vice President,

(C) any officer or employee of the White House Office of the Executive Office of the President, and the 2 most senior level officers of each of the other agencies in such Executive Office, and

(D) **(i)** any individual serving in a position in level I of the Executive Schedule under section 5312 of title 5, United States Code, (ii) any other individual designated by the President as having Cabinet level status, and (iii) any immediate deputy of an individual described in clause (i) or (ii).

(7) Special rule for Indian tribal governments.—For purposes of this subsection, an Indian tribal government shall be treated in the same manner as a local council or similar governing body.

* * *

(f) Fines and penalties.—No deduction shall be allowed under subsection (a) for any fine or similar penalty paid to a government for the violation of any law.

(g) Treble damage payments under the antitrust laws.—If in a criminal proceeding a taxpayer is convicted of a violation of the antitrust laws, or his plea of guilty or nolo contendere to an indictment or information charging such a violation is entered or accepted in such a proceeding, no deduction shall be allowed under subsection (a) for two-thirds of any amount paid or incurred—

(1) on any judgment for damages entered against the taxpayer under section 4 of the Act entitled ''An Act to supplement existing laws against unlawful restraints and monopolies, and for other purposes'', approved October 15, 1914 (commonly known as the Clayton Act), on account of such violation or any related violation of the antitrust laws which occurred prior to the date of the final judgment of such conviction, or

(2) in settlement of any action brought under such section 4 on account of such violation or related violation.

* * *

(h) State legislators' travel expenses away from home.—

(1) In general.—For purposes of subsection (a), in the case of any individual who is a State legislator at any time during the taxable year and who makes an election under this subsection for the taxable year—

(A) the place of residence of such individual within the legislative district which he represented shall be considered his home,

(B) he shall be deemed to have expended for living expenses (in connection with his trade or business as a legislator) an amount equal to the sum of the amounts determined by multiplying each legislative day of such individual during the taxable year by the greater of—

(i) the amount generally allowable with respect to such day to employees of the State of which he is a legislator for per diem while away from home, to the extent such amount does not exceed 110 percent of the amount described in clause (ii) with respect to such day, or

(ii) the amount generally allowable with respect to such day to employees of the executive branch of the Federal Government for per diem while away from home but serving in the United States, and

(C) he shall be deemed to be away from home in the pursuit of a trade or business on each legislative day.

(2) Legislative days.—For purposes of paragraph (1), a legislative day during any taxable year for any individual shall be any day during such year on which—

(A) the legislature was in session (including any day in which the legislature was not in session for a period of 4 consecutive days or less), or

(B) the legislature was not in session but the physical presence of the individual was formally recorded at a meeting of a committee of such legislature.

(3) Election.—An election under this subsection for any taxable year shall be made at such time and in such manner as the Secretary shall by regulations prescribe.

(4) Section not to apply to legislators who reside near capitol.—For taxable years beginning after December 31, 1980, this subsection shall not apply to any legislator whose place of residence within the legislative district which he represents is 50 or fewer miles from the capitol building of the State.

* * *

(k) Stock reacquisition expenses.—

(1) In general.—Except as provided in paragraph (2), no deduction otherwise allowable shall be allowed under this chapter for any amount paid or incurred by a corporation in connection with the reacquisition of its stock or of the stock of any related person (as defined in section 465(b)(3)(C)).

(2) Exceptions.—Paragraph (1) shall not apply to—

(A) Certain specific deductions.—Any—

(i) deduction allowable under section 163 (relating to interest),

(ii) deduction for amounts which are properly allocable to indebtedness and amortized over the term of such indebtedness, or

(iii) deduction for dividends paid (within the meaning of section 561).

(B) Stock of certain regulated investment companies.—Any amount paid or incurred in connection with the redemption of any stock in a regulated investment company which issues only stock which is redeemable upon the demand of the shareholder.

(*l*) Special rules for health insurance costs of self-employed individuals.—

(1) Allowance of deduction.—In the case of a taxpayer who is an employee within the meaning of section 401(c)(1), there shall be allowed as a deduction under this section an amount equal to the amount paid during the taxable year for insurance which constitutes medical care for—

(A) the taxpayer,

(B) the taxpayer's spouse,

(C) the taxpayer's dependents, and

(D) any child (as defined in section 152(f)(1)) of the taxpayer who as of the end of the taxable year has not attained age 27.

(2) Limitations.—

(A) Dollar amount.—No deduction shall be allowed under paragraph (1) to the extent that the amount of such deduction exceeds the taxpayer's earned income (within the meaning of section 401(c)) derived by the taxpayer from the trade or business with respect to which the plan providing the medical care coverage is established.

(B) Other coverage.—Paragraph (1) shall not apply to any taxpayer for any calendar month for which the taxpayer is eligible to participate in any subsidized health plan maintained by any employer of the taxpayer or of the spouse of, or any dependent, or individual described in subparagraph (D) of paragraph (1) with respect to, the taxpayer.* * *

* * *

(3) Coordination with medical deduction.—Any amount paid by a taxpayer for insurance to which paragraph (1) applies shall not be taken into account in computing the amount allowable to the taxpayer as a deduction under section 213(a).

(4) Deduction not allowed for self-employment tax purposes.—The deduction allowable by reason of this subsection shall not be taken into account in determining an individual's net earnings from self-employment (within the meaning of section 1402(a)) for purposes of chapter 2 * * *.

(5) Treatment of certain S corporation shareholders.—This subsection shall apply in the case of any individual treated as a partner under section 1372(a), except that—

(A) for purposes of this subsection, such individual's wages (as defined in section 3121) from the S corporation shall be treated as such individual's earned income (within the meaning of section 401(c)(1)), and

(B) there shall be such adjustments in the application of this subsection as the Secretary may by regulations prescribe.

(m) Certain excessive employee remuneration.—

(1) In general.—In the case of any publicly held corporation, no deduction shall be allowed under this chapter for applicable employee remuneration with respect to any covered employee to the extent that the amount of such remuneration for the taxable year with respect to such employee exceeds $1,000,000.

(2) Publicly held corporation.—For purposes of this subsection, the term "publicly held corporation" means any corporation issuing any class of common equity securities required to be registered under section 12 of the Securities Exchange Act of 1934.

(3) Covered employee.—For purposes of this subsection, the term "covered employee" means any employee of the taxpayer if—

(A) as of the close of the taxable year, such employee is the chief executive officer of the taxpayer or is an individual acting in such a capacity, or

(B) the total compensation of such employee for the taxable year is required to be reported to shareholders under the Securities Exchange Act of 1934 by reason of such employee being among the 4 highest compensated officers for the taxable year (other than the chief executive officer).

(4) Applicable employee remuneration.—For purposes of this subsection—

(A) In general.—Except as otherwise provided in this paragraph, the term "applicable employee remuneration" means, with respect to any covered employee for any taxable year, the aggregate amount allowable as a deduction under this chapter for such taxable year (determined without regard to this subsection) for remuneration for services performed by such employee (whether or not during the taxable year).

(B) Exception for remuneration payable on commission basis.—The term "applicable employee remuneration" shall not include any remuneration payable on a commission basis solely on account of income generated directly by the individual performance of the individual to whom such remuneration is payable.

(C) Other performance-based compensation.—The term "applicable employee remuneration" shall not include any remuneration payable solely on account of the attainment of one or more performance goals, but only if—

(i) the performance goals are determined by a compensation committee of the board of directors of the taxpayer which is comprised solely of 2 or more outside directors,

(ii) the material terms under which the remuneration is to be paid, including the performance goals, are disclosed to shareholders and approved by a majority of the vote in a separate shareholder vote before the payment of such remuneration, and

(iii) before any payment of such remuneration, the compensation committee referred to in clause (i) certifies that the performance goals and any other material terms were in fact satisfied.

* * *

§ 163. Interest

(a) General rule.—There shall be allowed as a deduction all interest paid or accrued within the taxable year on indebtedness.

(b) Installment purchases where interest charge is not separately stated.—

(1) General rule.—If personal property or educational services are purchased under a contract—

(A) which provides that payment of part or all of the purchase price is to be made in installments, and

(B) in which carrying charges are separately stated but the interest charge cannot be ascertained,

then the payments made during the taxable year under the contract shall be treated for purposes of this section as if they included interest equal to 6 percent of the average unpaid balance under the contract during the taxable year. For purposes of the preceding sentence, the average unpaid balance is the sum of the unpaid balance outstanding on the first day of each month beginning during the taxable year, divided by 12. For purposes of this paragraph, the term "educational services" means any service (including lodging) which is purchased from an educational organization described in section 170(b)(1)(A)(ii) and which is provided for a student of such organization.

(2) Limitation.—In the case of any contract to which paragraph (1) applies, the amount treated as interest for any taxable year shall not exceed the aggregate carrying charges which are properly attributable to such taxable year.

(c) Redeemable ground rents.—For purposes of this subtitle, any annual or periodic rental under a redeemable ground rent (excluding amounts in redemption thereof) shall be treated as interest on an indebtedness secured by a mortgage.

(d) Limitation on investment interest.—

(1) In general.—In the case of a taxpayer other than a corporation, the amount allowed as a deduction under this chapter for investment interest for any taxable year shall not exceed the net investment income of the taxpayer for the taxable year.

(2) Carryforward of disallowed interest.—The amount not allowed as a deduction for any taxable year by reason of paragraph (1) shall be treated as investment interest paid or accrued by the taxpayer in the succeeding taxable year.

(3) Investment interest.—For purposes of this subsection—

(A) In general.—The term "investment interest" means any interest allowable as a deduction under this chapter (determined without regard to paragraph (1)) which is paid or accrued on indebtedness properly allocable to property held for investment.

(B) Exceptions.—The term "investment interest" shall not include—

(i) any qualified residence interest (as defined in subsection (h)(3)), or

(ii) any interest which is taken into account under section 469 in computing income or loss from a passive activity of the taxpayer.

(C) Personal property used in short sale.—For purposes of this paragraph, the term "interest" includes any amount allowable as a deduction in connection with personal property used in a short sale.

(4) Net investment income.—For purposes of this subsection—

(A) In general.—The term "net investment income" means the excess of—

(i) investment income, over

(ii) investment expenses.

(B) Investment income.—The term "investment income" means the sum of—

(i) gross income from property held for investment (other than any gain taken into account under clause (ii)(I)),

(ii) the excess (if any) of—

(I) the net gain attributable to the disposition of property held for investment, over

(II) the net capital gain determined by only taking into account gains and losses from dispositions of property held for investment, plus

(iii) so much of the net capital gain referred to in clause (ii)(II) (or, if lesser, the net gain referred to in clause (ii)(I)) as the taxpayer elects to take into account under this clause.

Such term shall include qualified dividend income (as defined in section 1(h)(11)(B)) only to the extent the taxpayer elects to treat such income as investment income for purposes of this subsection.

(C) Investment expenses.—The term "investment expenses" means the deductions allowed under this chapter (other than for interest) which are directly connected with the production of investment income.

(D) Income and expenses from passive activities.—Investment income and investment expenses shall not include any income or expenses taken into account under section 469 in computing income or loss from a passive activity.

* * *

(5) Property held for investment.—For purposes of this subsection—

(A) In general.—The term "property held for investment" shall include—

(i) any property which produces income of a type described in section 469(e)(1), and

(ii) any interest held by a taxpayer in an activity involving the conduct of a trade or business—

(I) which is not a passive activity, and

(II) with respect to which the taxpayer does not materially participate.

(B) Investment expenses.—In the case of property described in subparagraph (A)(i), expenses shall be allocated to such property in the same manner as under section 469.

(C) Terms.—For purposes of this paragraph, the terms "activity", "passive activity", and "materially participate" have the meanings given such terms by section 469.

* * *

(e) Original issue discount.—

(1) In general.—In the case of any debt instrument issued after July 1, 1982, the portion of the original issue discount with respect to such debt instrument which is allowable as a deduction to the issuer for any taxable year shall be equal to the aggregate daily portions of the original issue discount for days during such taxable year.

(2) Definitions and special rules.—For purposes of this subsection—

(A) Debt instrument.—The term "debt instrument" has the meaning given such term by section 1275(a)(1).

(B) Daily portions.—The daily portion of the original issue discount for any day shall be determined under section 1272(a) (without regard to paragraph (7) thereof and without regard to section 1273(a)(3)).

(C) Short-term obligations.—In the case of an obligor of a short-term obligation (as defined in section 1283(a)(1)(A)) who uses the cash receipts and disbursements method of accounting, the original issue discount (and any other interest payable) on such obligation shall be deductible only when paid.

* * *

(4) Exceptions.—This subsection shall not apply to any debt instrument described in—

(A) subparagraph (D) of section 1272(a)(2) (relating to obligations issued by natural persons before March 2, 1984), and

(B) subparagraph (E) of section 1272(a)(2) (relating to loans between natural persons).

(5) Special rules for original issue discount on certain high yield obligations.—

(A) In general.—In the case of an applicable high yield discount obligation issued by a corporation—

(i) no deduction shall be allowed under this chapter for the disqualified portion of the original issue discount on such obligation, and

(ii) the remainder of such original issue discount shall not be allowable as a deduction until paid.

For purposes of this paragraph, rules similar to the rules of subsection (i)(3)(B) shall apply in determining the amount of the original issue discount and when the original issue discount is paid.

(B) Disqualified portion treated as stock distribution for purposes of dividend received deduction.—

(i) In general.—Solely for purposes of sections 243, 245, 246, and 246A, the dividend equivalent portion of any amount includible in gross income of a corporation under section 1272(a) in respect of an applicable high yield discount obligation shall be treated as a dividend received by such corporation from the corporation issuing such obligation.

(ii) Dividend equivalent portion.—For purposes of clause (i), the dividend equivalent portion of any amount includible in gross income under section 1272(a) in respect of an applicable high yield discount obligation is the portion of the amount so includible—

(I) which is attributable to the disqualified portion of the original issue discount on such obligation, and

(II) which would have been treated as a dividend if it had been a distribution made by the issuing corporation with respect to stock in such corporation.

(C) Disqualified portion.—

(i) In general.—For purposes of this paragraph, the disqualified portion of the original issue discount on any applicable high yield discount obligation is the lesser of—

(I) the amount of such original issue discount, or

(II) the portion of the total return on such obligation which bears the same ratio to such total return as the disqualified yield on such obligation bears to the yield to maturity on such obligation.

(ii) Definitions.—For purposes of clause (i), the term "disqualified yield" means the excess of the yield to maturity on the obligation over the sum referred to subsection (i)(1)(B) plus 1 percentage point, and the term "total return" is the amount which would have been the original issue discount on the obligation if interest described in the parenthetical in section 1273(a)(2) were included in the stated redemption price at maturity.

(D) Exception for S corporations.—This paragraph shall not apply to any obligation issued by any corporation for any period for which such corporation is an S corporation.

(E) Effect on earnings and profits.—This paragraph shall not apply for purposes of determining earnings and profits; except that, for purposes of determining the dividend equivalent portion of any amount includible in gross income under section 1272(a) in respect of an applicable high yield discount obligation, no reduction shall be made for any amount attributable to the disqualified portion of any original issue discount on such obligation.

(F) Suspension of application of paragraph.—

(i) Temporary suspension.—This paragraph shall not apply to any applicable high yield discount obligation issued during the period beginning on September 1, 2008, and ending on December 31, 2009, in exchange (including an exchange resulting from a modification of the debt instrument) for an obligation which is not an applicable high yield discount obligation and the issuer (or obligor) of which is the same as the issuer (or obligor) of such applicable high yield discount obligation. The preceding sentence shall not apply to any obligation the interest on which is interest described in section 871(h)(4) (without regard to subparagraph (D) thereof) or to any obligation issued to a related person (within the meaning of section 108(e)(4)).

(ii) Successive application.—Any obligation to which clause (i) applies shall not be treated as an applicable high yield discount obligation for purposes of applying this subparagraph to any other obligation issued in exchange for such obligation.

(iii) Secretarial authority to suspend application.—The Secretary may apply this paragraph with respect to debt instruments issued in periods following the period described in clause (i) if the Secretary determines that such application is appropriate in light of distressed conditions in the debt capital markets.

(G) Cross reference.—

For definition of applicable high yield discount obligation, see subsection (i).

(6) Cross references.—

For provision relating to deduction of original issue discount on tax-exempt obligation, see section 1288.

For special rules in the case of the borrower under certain loans for personal use, see section 1275(b).

(f) Denial of deduction for interest on certain obligations not in registered form.—

(1) In general.—Nothing in subsection (a) or in any other provision of law shall be construed to provide a deduction for interest on any registration-required obligation unless such obligation is in registered form.

(2) Registration-required obligation.—For purposes of this section—

(A) In general.—The term "registration-required obligation" means any obligation (including any obligation issued by a governmental entity) other than an obligation which—

(i) is issued by a natural person,

(ii) is not of a type offered to the public, or

(iii) has a maturity (at issue) of not more than 1 year.

* * *

(h) Disallowance of deduction for personal interest.—

(1) In general.—In the case of a taxpayer other than a corporation, no deduction shall be allowed under this chapter for personal interest paid or accrued during the taxable year.

(2) Personal interest.—For purposes of this subsection, the term "personal interest" means any interest allowable as a deduction under this chapter other than—

(A) interest paid or accrued on indebtedness properly allocable to a trade or business (other than the trade or business of performing services as an employee),

(B) any investment interest (within the meaning of subsection (d)),

(C) any interest which is taken into account under section 469 in computing income or loss from a passive activity of the taxpayer,

(D) any qualified residence interest (within the meaning of paragraph (3)),

(E) any interest payable under section 6601 on any unpaid portion of the tax imposed by section 2001 for the period during which an extension of time for payment of such tax is in effect under section 6163, and

(F) any interest allowable as a deduction under section 221 (relating to interest on educational loans).

(3) Qualified residence interest.—For purposes of this subsection—

(A) In general.—The term "qualified residence interest" means any interest which is paid or accrued during the taxable year on—

(i) acquisition indebtedness with respect to any qualified residence of the taxpayer, or

(ii) home equity indebtedness with respect to any qualified residence of the taxpayer.

For purposes of the preceding sentence, the determination of whether any property is a qualified residence of the taxpayer shall be made as of the time the interest is accrued.

(B) Acquisition indebtedness.—

(i) In general.—The term "acquisition indebtedness" means any indebtedness which—

(I) is incurred in acquiring, constructing, or substantially improving any qualified residence of the taxpayer, and

(II) is secured by such residence.

Such term also includes any indebtedness secured by such residence resulting from the refinancing of indebtedness meeting the requirements of the preceding sentence (or this sentence); but only to the extent the amount of the indebtedness resulting from such refinancing does not exceed the amount of the refinanced indebtedness.

(ii) $1,000,000 Limitation.—The aggregate amount treated as acquisition indebtedness for any period shall not exceed $1,000,000 ($500,000 in the case of a married individual filing a separate return).

(C) Home equity indebtedness.—

(i) In general.—The term "home equity indebtedness" means any indebtedness (other than acquisition indebtedness) secured by a qualified residence to the extent the aggregate amount of such indebtedness does not exceed—

(I) the fair market value of such qualified residence, reduced by

(II) the amount of acquisition indebtedness with respect to such residence.

(ii) Limitation.—The aggregate amount treated as home equity indebtedness for any period shall not exceed $100,000 ($50,000 in the case of a separate return by a married individual).

(D) Treatment of indebtedness incurred on or before October 13, 1987.—

(i) In general.—In the case of any pre-October 13, 1987, indebtedness—

(I) such indebtedness shall be treated as acquisition indebtedness, and

(II) the limitation of subparagraph (B)(ii) shall not apply.

(ii) Reduction in $1,000,000 Limitation.—The limitation of subparagraph (B)(ii) shall be reduced (but not below zero) by the aggregate amount of outstanding pre-October 13, 1987, indebtedness.

(iii) Pre–October 13, 1987, indebtedness.—The term "pre-October 13, 1987, indebtedness" means—

(I) any indebtedness which was incurred on or before October 13, 1987, and which was secured by a qualified residence on October 13, 1987, and at all times thereafter before the interest is paid or accrued, or

(II) any indebtedness which is secured by the qualified residence and was incurred after October 13, 1987, to refinance indebtedness described in subclause (I) (or refinanced indebtedness meeting the requirements of this subclause) to the extent (immediately after the refinancing) the principal amount of the indebtedness resulting from the refinancing does not exceed the principal amount of the refinanced indebtedness (immediately before the refinancing).

(iv) Limitation on period of refinancing.—Subclause (II) of clause (iii) shall not apply to any indebtedness after—

(I) the expiration of the term of the indebtedness described in clause (iii)(I), or

(II) if the principal of the indebtedness described in clause (iii)(I) is not amortized over its term, the expiration of the term of the 1st refinancing of such indebtedness (or if earlier, the date which is 30 years after the date of such 1st refinancing).

* * *

(4) Other definitions and special rules.—For purposes of this subsection—

(A) Qualified residence.—

(i) In general.—The term "qualified residence" means—

(I) the principal residence (within the meaning of section 121) of the taxpayer, and

(II) 1 other residence of the taxpayer which is selected by the taxpayer for purposes of this subsection for the taxable year and which is used by the taxpayer as a residence (within the meaning of section 280A(d)(1)).

(ii) Married individuals filing separate returns.—If a married couple does not file a joint return for the taxable year—

(I) such couple shall be treated as 1 taxpayer for purposes of clause (i), and

(II) each individual shall be entitled to take into account 1 residence unless both individuals consent in writing to 1 individual taking into account the principal residence and 1 other residence.

(iii) Residence not rented.—For purposes of clause (i)(II), notwithstanding section 280A(d)(1), if the taxpayer does not rent a dwelling unit at any time during a taxable year, such unit may be treated as a residence for such taxable year.

(B) Special rule for cooperative housing corporations.—Any indebtedness secured by stock held by the taxpayer as a tenant-stockholder (as defined in section 216) in a cooperative housing corporation (as so defined) shall be treated as secured by the house or apartment which the taxpayer is entitled to occupy as such a tenant-stockholder. If stock described in the preceding sentence may not be used to secure indebtedness, indebtedness shall be treated as so secured if the taxpayer establishes to the satisfaction of the Secretary that such indebtedness was incurred to acquire such stock.

(C) Unenforceable security interests.—Indebtedness shall not fail to be treated as secured by any property solely because, under any applicable State or local homestead or other debtor protection law in effect on August 16, 1986, the security interest is ineffective or the enforceability of the security interest is restricted.

(D) Special rules for estates and trusts.—For purposes of determining whether any interest paid or accrued by an estate or trust is qualified residence interest, any residence held by such estate or trust shall be treated as a qualified residence of such estate or trust if such estate or trust establishes that such residence is a qualified residence of a beneficiary who has a present interest in such estate or trust or an interest in the residuary of such estate or trust.

* * *

(i) Applicable high yield discount obligation.—

(1) In general.—For purposes of this section, the term "applicable high yield discount obligation" means any debt instrument if—

(A) the maturity date of such instrument is more than 5 years from the date of issue,

(B) the yield to maturity on such instrument equals or exceeds the sum of—

(i) the applicable Federal rate in effect under section 1274(d) for the calendar month in which the obligation is issued, plus

(ii) 5 percentage points, and

(C) such instrument has significant original issue discount.

For purposes of subparagraph (B)(i), the Secretary may by regulation (i) permit a rate to be used with respect to any debt instrument which is higher than the applicable Federal rate if the taxpayer establishes to the satisfaction of the Secretary that such higher rate is based on the same principles as the applicable Federal rate and is appropriate for the term of the instrument, or (ii) permit, on a temporary basis, a rate to be used with respect to any debt instrument which is higher than the applicable Federal rate if the Secretary determines that such rate is appropriate in light of distressed conditions in the debt capital markets.

(2) Significant original issue discount.—For purposes of paragraph (1)(C), a debt instrument shall be treated as having significant original issue discount if—

(A) the aggregate amount which would be includible in gross income with respect to such instrument for periods before the close of any accrual period (as defined in section 1272(a)(5)) ending after the date 5 years after the date of issue, exceeds—

(B) the sum of—

(i) the aggregate amount of interest to be paid under the instrument before the close of such accrual period, and

(ii) the product of the issue price of such instrument (as defined in sections 1273(b) and 1274(a)) and its yield to maturity.

(3) Special rules.—For purposes of determining whether a debt instrument is an applicable high yield discount obligation—

(A) any payment under the instrument shall be assumed to be made on the last day permitted under the instrument, and

(B) any payment to be made in the form of another obligation (or stock) of the issuer (or a related person within the meaning of section 453(f)(1)) shall be assumed to be made when such obligation (or stock) is required to be paid in cash or in property other than such obligation (or stock).

Except for purposes of paragraph (1)(B), any reference to an obligation in subparagraph (B) of this paragraph shall be treated as including a reference to stock.

(4) Debt instrument.—For purposes of this subsection, the term "debt instrument" means any instrument which is a debt instrument as defined in section 1275(a).

(5) Regulations.—The Secretary shall prescribe such regulations as may be appropriate to carry out the purposes of this subsection and subsection (e)(5), including—

(A) regulations providing for modifications to the provisions of this subsection and subsection (e)(5) in the case of varying rates of interest, put or call options, indefinite maturities, contingent payments, assumptions of debt instruments, conversion rights, or other circumstances where such modifications are appropriate to carry out the purposes of this subsection and subsection (e)(5), and

(B) regulations to prevent avoidance of the purposes of this subsection and subsection (e)(5) through the use of issuers other than C corporations, agreements to borrow amounts due under the debt instrument, or other arrangements.

(j) Limitation on deduction for interest on certain indebtedness.—

(1) Limitation.—

(A) In general.—If this subsection applies to any corporation for any taxable year, no deduction shall be allowed under this chapter for disqualified interest paid or accrued by such corporation during such taxable year. The amount disallowed under the preceding sentence shall not exceed the corporation's excess interest expense for the taxable year.

(B) Disallowed amount carried to succeeding taxable year.—Any amount disallowed under subparagraph (A) for any taxable year shall be treated as disqualified interest paid or accrued in the succeeding taxable year (and clause (ii) of paragraph (2)(A) shall not apply for purposes of applying this subsection to the amount so treated).

(2) Corporations to which subsection applies.—

(A) In general.—This subsection shall apply to any corporation for any taxable year if—

(i) such corporation has excess interest expense for such taxable year, and

(ii) the ratio of debt to equity of such corporation as of the close of such taxable year (or on any other day during the taxable year as the Secretary may by regulations prescribe) exceeds 1.5 to 1.

(B) Excess interest expense.—

(i) In general.—For purposes of this subsection, the term "excess interest expense" means the excess (if any) of—

(I) the corporation's net interest expense, over

(II) the sum of 50 percent of the adjusted taxable income of the corporation plus any excess limitation carryforward under clause (ii).

(ii) Excess limitation carryforward.—If a corporation has an excess limitation for any taxable year, the amount of such excess limitation shall be an excess limitation carryforward to the 1st succeeding taxable year and to the 2nd and 3rd succeeding taxable years to the extent not previously taken into account under this clause. The amount of such a carryforward taken into account for any such succeeding taxable year shall not exceed the excess interest expense for such succeeding taxable year (determined without regard to the carryforward from the taxable year of such excess limitation).

(iii) Excess limitation.—For purposes of clause (ii), the term "excess limitation" means the excess (if any) of—

(I) 50 percent of the adjusted taxable income of the corporation, over

(II) the corporation's net interest expense.

(C) Ratio of debt to equity.—For purposes of this paragraph, the term "ratio of debt to equity" means the ratio which the total indebtedness of the corporation bears to the sum of its money and all other assets reduced (but not below zero) by such total indebtedness. For purposes of the preceding sentence—

(i) the amount taken into account with respect to any asset shall be the adjusted basis thereof for purposes of determining gain,

(ii) the amount taken into account with respect to any indebtedness with original issue discount shall be its issue price plus the portion of the original issue discount previously accrued as determined under the rules of section 1272 (determined without regard to subsection (a)(7) or (b)(4) thereof), and

(iii) there shall be such other adjustments as the Secretary may by regulations prescribe.

(3) Disqualified interest.—For purposes of this subsection, the term "disqualified interest" means—

(A) any interest paid or accrued by the taxpayer (directly or indirectly) to a related person if no tax is imposed by this subtitle with respect to such interest,

(B) any interest paid or accrued by the taxpayer with respect to any indebtedness to a person who is not a related person if—

(i) there is a disqualified guarantee of such indebtedness, and

(ii) no gross basis tax is imposed by this subtitle with respect to such interest, and

* * *

(4) Related person.—For purposes of this subsection—

(A) In general.—Except as provided in subparagraph (B), the term "related person" means any person who is related (within the meaning of section 267(b) or 707(b)(1)) to the taxpayer.

(B) Special rule for certain partnerships.—

(i) In general.—Any interest paid or accrued to a partnership which (without regard to this subparagraph) is a related person shall not be treated as paid or accrued to a related person if less than 10 percent of the profits and capital interests in such partnership are held by persons with respect to whom no tax is imposed by this subtitle on such interest. The preceding sentence shall not apply to any interest allocable to any partner in such partnership who is a related person to the taxpayer.

(ii) Special rule where treaty reduction.—If any treaty between the United States and any foreign country reduces the rate of tax imposed by this subtitle on a partner's share of any interest paid or accrued to a partnership, such partner's interests in such partnership shall, for purposes of clause (i), be treated as held in part by a tax-exempt person and in part by a taxable person under rules similar to the rules of paragraph (5)(B).

(5) Special rules for determining whether interest is subject to tax.—

(A) Treatment of pass-thru entities.—In the case of any interest paid or accrued to a partnership, the determination of whether any tax is imposed by this subtitle on such interest shall be made at the partner level. Rules similar to the rules of the preceding sentence shall apply in the case of any pass-thru entity other than a partnership and in the case of tiered partnerships and other entities.

(B) Interest treated as tax-exempt to extent of treaty reduction.—If any treaty between the United States and any foreign country reduces the rate of tax imposed by this subtitle on any interest paid or accrued by the taxpayer, such interest shall be treated as interest on which no tax is imposed by this subtitle to the extent of the same proportion of such interest as—

(i) the rate of tax imposed without regard to such treaty, reduced by the rate of tax imposed under the treaty, bears to

(ii) the rate of tax imposed without regard to the treaty.

(6) Other definitions and special rules.—For purposes of this subsection—

(A) Adjusted taxable income.—The term "adjusted taxable income" means the taxable income of the taxpayer—

(i) computed without regard to—

(I) any deduction allowable under this chapter for the net interest expense.

(II) the amount of any net operating loss deduction under section 172, and

(III) any deduction allowable for depreciation, amortization, or depletion, and

(ii) computed with such other adjustments as the Secretary may by regulations prescribe.

(B) Net interest expense.—The term "net interest expense" means the excess (if any) of—

(i) the interest paid or accrued by the taxpayer during the taxable year, over

(ii) the amount of interest includible in the gross income of such taxpayer for such taxable year.

The Secretary may by regulations provide for adjustments in determining the amount of net interest expense.

(C) Treatment of affiliated group.—All members of the same affiliated group (within the meaning of section 1504(a)) shall be treated as 1 taxpayer.

(D) Disqualified guarantee.—

(i) In general.—Except as provided in clause (ii), the term "disqualified guarantee" means any guarantee by a related person which is—

(I) an organization exempt from taxation under this subtitle, or

(II) a foreign person.

(ii) Exceptions.—The term "disqualified guarantee" shall not include a guarantee—

(I) in any circumstances identified by the Secretary by regulation, where the interest on the indebtedness would have been subject to a net basis tax if the interest had been paid to the guarantor, or

(II) if the taxpayer owns a controlling interest in the guarantor.

For purposes of subclause (II), except as provided in regulations, the term "a controlling interest" means direct or indirect ownership of at least 80 percent of the total voting power and value of all classes of stock of a corporation, or 80 percent of the profit and capital interests in any other entity. For purposes of the preceding sentence, the rules of paragraphs (1) and (5) of section 267(c) shall apply; except that such rules shall also apply to interest in entities other than corporations.

(iii) Guarantee.—Except as provided in regulations, the term "guarantee" includes any arrangement under which a person (directly or indirectly through an entity or otherwise) assures, on a conditional or unconditional basis, the payment of another person's obligation under any indebtedness.

(E) Gross basis and net basis taxation.—

(i) Gross basis tax.—The term "gross basis tax" means any tax imposed by this subtitle which is determined by reference to the gross amount of any item of income without any reduction for any deduction allowed by this subtitle.

(ii) Net basis tax.—The term "net basis tax" means any tax imposed by this subtitle which is not a gross basis tax.

(7) Coordination with passive loss rules, etc.—This subsection shall be applied before sections 465 and 469.

* * *

(9) Regulations.—The Secretary shall prescribe such regulations as may be appropriate to carry out the purposes of this subsection, including—

(A) such regulations as may be appropriate to prevent the avoidance of the purposes of this subsection,

(B) regulations providing such adjustments in the case of corporations which are members of an affiliated group as may be appropriate to carry out the purposes of this subsection,

* * *

(k) Section 6166 interest.—No deduction shall be allowed under this section for any interest payable under section 6601 on any unpaid portion of the tax imposed by section 2001 for the period during which an extension of time for payment of such tax is in effect under section 6166.

(*l*) Disallowance of deduction on certain debt instruments of corporations.—

(1) In general.—No deduction shall be allowed under this chapter for any interest paid or accrued on a disqualified debt instrument.

(2) Disqualified debt instrument.—For purposes of this subsection, the term "disqualified debt instrument" means any indebtedness of a corporation which is payable in equity of the issuer or a related party or equity held by the issuer (or any related party) in any other person.

(3) Special rules for amounts payable in equity.—For purposes of paragraph (2), indebtedness shall be treated as payable in equity of the issuer or a related party only if—

(A) a substantial amount of the principal or interest is required to be paid or converted, or at the option of the issuer or a related party is payable in, or convertible into, such equity,

(B) a substantial amount of the principal or interest is required to be determined, or at the option of the issuer or a related party is determined, by reference to the value of such equity, or

(C) the indebtedness is part of an arrangement which is reasonably expected to result in a transaction described in subparagraph (A) or (B).

For purposes of this paragraph, principal or interest shall be treated as required to be so paid, converted, or determined if it may be required at the option of the holder or a related party and there is a substantial certainty the option will be exercised.

(4) Capitalization allowed with respect to equity of persons other than issuer and related parties.—If the disqualified debt instrument of a corporation is payable in equity held by the issuer (or any related party) in any other person (other than a related party), the basis of such equity shall be increased by the amount not allowed as a deduction by reason of paragraph (1) with respect to the instrument.

(5) Exception for certain instruments issued by dealers in securities.—For purposes of this subsection, the term "disqualified debt instrument" does not include indebtedness issued by a dealer in securities (or a related party) which is payable in, or by reference to, equity (other than equity of the issuer or a related party) held by such dealer in its capacity as a dealer in securities. For purposes of this paragraph, the term "dealer in securities" has the meaning given such term by section 475.

(6) Related party.—For purposes of this subsection, a person is a related party with respect to another person if such person bears a relationship to such other person described in section 267(b) or 707(b).

(7) Regulations.—The Secretary shall prescribe such regulations as may be necessary or appropriate to carry out the purposes of this subsection, including regulations preventing avoidance of this subsection through the use of an issuer other than a corporation.

(m) Cross references.—

(1) For disallowance of certain amounts paid in connection with insurance, endowment, or annuity contracts, see section 264.

(2) For disallowance of deduction for interest relating to tax-exempt income, see section 265(a)(2).

(3) For disallowance of deduction for carrying charges chargeable to capital account, see section 266.

(4) For disallowance of interest with respect to transactions between related taxpayers, see section 267.

* * *

§ 164. Taxes

(a) General rule.—Except as otherwise provided in this section, the following taxes shall be allowed as a deduction for the taxable year within which paid or accrued:

(1) State and local, and foreign, real property taxes.

(2) State and local personal property taxes.

(3) State and local, and foreign, income, war profits, and excess profits taxes.

(4) The GST tax imposed on income distributions.

(5) The environmental tax imposed by section 59A.

* * *

In addition, there shall be allowed as a deduction State and local, and foreign, taxes not described in the preceding sentence which are paid or accrued within the taxable year in carrying on a trade or business or an activity described in section 212 (relating to expenses for production of income). Notwithstanding the preceding sentence, any tax (not described in the first sentence of this subsection) which is paid or accrued by the taxpayer in connection with an acquisition or disposition of property shall be treated as part of the cost of the acquired property or, in the case of a disposition, as a reduction in the amount realized on the disposition.

(b) Definitions and special rules.—For purposes of this section—

(1) Personal property taxes.—The term "personal property tax" means an ad valorem tax which is imposed on an annual basis in respect of personal property.

(2) State or local taxes.—A State or local tax includes only a tax imposed by a State, a possession of the United States, or a political subdivision of any of the foregoing, or by the District of Columbia.

(3) Foreign taxes.—A foreign tax includes only a tax imposed by the authority of a foreign country.

(4) Special rules for GST tax.—

(A) In general.—The GST tax imposed on income distributions is—

(i) the tax imposed by section 2601, and

(ii) any State tax described in section 2604,

but only to the extent such tax is imposed on a transfer which is included in the gross income of the distributee and to which section 666 does not apply.

(B) Special rule for tax paid before due date.—Any tax referred to in subparagraph (A) imposed with respect to a transfer occurring during the taxable year of the distributee (or, in the case of a taxable termination, the trust) which is paid not later than the time prescribed by law (including extensions) for filing the return with respect to such transfer shall be treated as having been paid on the last day of the taxable year in which the transfer was made.

(5) General sales taxes.—For purposes of subsection (a)—

(A) Election to deduct State and local sales taxes in lieu of State and local income taxes.—At the election of the taxpayer for the taxable year, subsection (a) shall be applied—

(i) without regard to the reference to State and local income taxes, and

(ii) as if State and local general sales taxes were referred to in a paragraph thereof.

(B) Definition of general sales tax.—The term "general sales tax" means a tax imposed at one rate with respect to the sale at retail of a broad range of classes of items.

(C) Special rules for food, etc.—In the case of items of food, clothing, medical supplies, and motor vehicles–

(i) the fact that the tax does not apply with respect to some or all of such items shall not be taken into account in determining whether the tax applies with respect to a broad range of classes of items, and

(ii) the fact that the rate of tax applicable with respect to some or all of such items is lower than the general rate of tax shall not be taken into account in \determining whether the tax is imposed at one rate.

(D) Items taxed at different rates.—Except in the case of a lower rate of tax applicable with respect to an item described in subparagraph (C), no deduction shall be allowed under this paragraph for any general sales tax imposed with respect to an item at a rate other than the general rate of tax.

(E) Compensating use taxes.—A compensating use tax with respect to an item shall be treated as a general sales tax. For purposes of the preceding sentence, the term "compensating use tax" means, with respect to any item, a tax which—

(i) is imposed on the use, storage, or consumption of such item, and

(ii) is complementary to a general sales tax, but only if a deduction is allowable under this paragraph with respect to items sold at retail in the taxing jurisdiction which are similar to such item.

(F) Special rule for motor vehicles.—In the case of motor vehicles, if the rate of tax exceeds the general rate, such excess shall be disregarded and the general rate shall be treated as the rate of tax.

(G) Separately stated general sales taxes.—If the amount of any general sales tax is separately stated, then, to the extent that the amount so stated is paid by the consumer (other than in connection with the consumer's trade or business) to the seller, such amount shall be treated as a tax imposed on, and paid by, such consumer.

(H) Amount of deduction may be determined under tables.—

(i) In general.—At the election of the taxpayer for the taxable year, the amount of the deduction allowed under this paragraph for such year shall be—

(I) the amount determined under this paragraph (without regard to this subparagraph) with respect to motor vehicles, boats, and other items specified by the Secretary, and

(II) the amount determined under tables prescribed by the Secretary with respect to items to which subclause (I) does not apply.

(ii) Requirements for tables.—The tables prescribed under clause (i)—

(I) shall reflect the provisions of this paragraph,

(II) shall be based on the average consumption by taxpayers on a State-by-State basis (as determined by the Secretary) of items to which clause (i)(I) does not apply, taking into account filing status, number of dependents, adjusted gross income, and rates of State and local general sales taxation, and

(III) need only be determined with respect to adjusted gross incomes up to the applicable amount (as determined under section 68(b)).

(I) Application of paragraph.—This paragraph shall apply to taxable years beginning after December 31, 2003, and before January 1, 2014.

* * *

(c) Deduction denied in case of certain taxes.—No deduction shall be allowed for the following taxes:

(1) Taxes assessed against local benefits of a kind tending to increase the value of the property assessed; but this paragraph shall not prevent the deduction of so much of such taxes as is properly allocable to maintenance or interest charges.

(2) Taxes on real property, to the extent that subsection (d) requires such taxes to be treated as imposed on another taxpayer.

(d) Apportionment of taxes on real property between seller and purchaser.—

(1) General rule.—For purposes of subsection (a), if real property is sold during any real property tax year, then—

(A) so much of the real property tax as is properly allocable to that part of such year which ends on the day before the date of the sale shall be treated as a tax imposed on the seller, and

(B) so much of such tax as is properly allocable to that part of such year which begins on the date of the sale shall be treated as a tax imposed on the purchaser.

(2) Special rules.—

(A) In the case of any sale of real property, if—

(i) a taxpayer may not, by reason of his method of accounting, deduct any amount for taxes unless paid, and

(ii) the other party to the sale is (under the law imposing the real property tax) liable for the real property tax for the real property tax year,

then for purposes of subsection (a) the taxpayer shall be treated as having paid, on the date of the sale, so much of such tax as, under paragraph (1) of this subsection, is treated as imposed on the taxpayer. For purposes of the preceding sentence, if neither party is liable for the tax, then the party holding the property at the time the tax becomes a lien on the property shall be considered liable for the real property tax for the real property tax year.

(B) In the case of any sale of real property, if the taxpayer's taxable income for the taxable year during which the sale occurs is computed under an accrual method of accounting, and if no election under section 461(c) (relating to the accrual of real property taxes) applies, then, for purposes of subsection (a), that portion of such tax which—

(i) is treated, under paragraph (1) of this subsection, as imposed on the taxpayer, and

(ii) may not, by reason of the taxpayer's method of accounting, be deducted by the taxpayer for any taxable year,

shall be treated as having accrued on the date of the sale.

(e) Taxes of shareholder paid by corporation.—Where a corporation pays a tax imposed on a shareholder on his interest as a shareholder, and where the shareholder does not reimburse the corporation, then—

(1) the deduction allowed by subsection (a) shall be allowed to the corporation; and

(2) no deduction shall be allowed the shareholder for such tax.

(f) Deduction for one-half of self-employment taxes.—

(1) In general.—In the case of an individual, in addition to the taxes described in subsection (a), there shall be allowed as a deduction for the taxable year an amount equal to one-half of the taxes imposed by section 1401 for such taxable year.

(2) Deduction treated as attributable to trade or business.—For purposes of this chapter, the deduction allowed by paragraph (1) shall be treated as attributable to a trade or business carried on by the taxpayer which does not consist of the performance of services by the taxpayer as an employee.

* * *

§ 165. Losses

(a) General rule.—There shall be allowed as a deduction any loss sustained during the taxable year and not compensated for by insurance or otherwise.

(b) Amount of deduction.—For purposes of subsection (a), the basis for determining the amount of the deduction for any loss shall be the adjusted basis provided in section 1011 for determining the loss from the sale or other disposition of property.

(c) Limitation on losses of individuals.—In the case of an individual, the deduction under subsection (a) shall be limited to—

(1) losses incurred in a trade or business;

(2) losses incurred in any transaction entered into for profit, though not connected with a trade or business; and

(3) except as provided in subsection (h), losses of property not connected with a trade or business or a transaction entered into for profit, if such losses arise from fire, storm, shipwreck, or other casualty, or from theft.

(d) Wagering losses.—Losses from wagering transactions shall be allowed only to the extent of the gains from such transactions.

(e) Theft losses.—For purposes of subsection (a), any loss arising from theft shall be treated as sustained during the taxable year in which the taxpayer discovers such loss.

(f) Capital losses.—Losses from sales or exchanges of capital assets shall be allowed only to the extent allowed in sections 1211 and 1212.

(g) Worthless securities.—

(1) General rule.—If any security which is a capital asset becomes worthless during the taxable year, the loss resulting therefrom shall, for purposes of this subtitle, be treated as a loss from the sale or exchange, on the last day of the taxable year, of a capital asset.

(2) Security defined.—For purposes of this subsection, the term "security" means—

(A) a share of stock in a corporation;

(B) a right to subscribe for, or to receive, a share of stock in a corporation; or

(C) a bond, debenture, note, or certificate, or other evidence of indebtedness, issued by a corporation or by a government or political subdivision thereof, with interest coupons or in registered form.

(3) Securities in affiliated corporation.—For purposes of paragraph (1), any security in a corporation affiliated with a taxpayer which is a domestic corporation shall not be treated as a capital asset. For purposes of the preceding sentence, a corporation shall be treated as affiliated with the taxpayer only if—

(A) the taxpayer owns directly stock in such corporation meeting the requirements of section 1504(a)(2), and,

(B) more than 90 percent of the aggregate of its gross receipts for all taxable years has been from sources other than royalties, rents (except rents derived from rental of properties to employees of the corporation in the ordinary course of its operating business), dividends, interest (except interest received on deferred purchase price of operating assets sold), annuities, and gains from sales or exchanges of stocks and securities.

In computing gross receipts for purposes of the preceding sentence, gross receipts from sales or exchanges of stocks and securities shall be taken into account only to the extent of gains therefrom.

(h) Treatment of casualty gains and losses.—

(1) $100 limitation per casualty.—Any loss of an individual described in subsection (c)(3) shall be allowed only to the extent that the amount of the loss to such individual arising from each casualty, or from each theft, exceeds $500 ($100 for taxable years beginning after December 31, 2009).

(2) Net casualty loss allowed only to the extent it exceeds 10 percent of adjusted gross income.—

(A) In general.—If the personal casualty losses for any taxable year exceed the personal casualty gains for such taxable year, such losses shall be allowed for the taxable year only to the extent of the sum of—

(i) the amount of the personal casualty gains for the taxable year, plus

(ii) so much of such excess as exceeds 10 percent of the adjusted gross income of the individual.

(B) Special rule where personal casualty gains exceed personal casualty losses.—If the personal casualty gains for any taxable year exceed the personal casualty losses for such taxable year—

(i) all such gains shall be treated as gains from sales or exchanges of capital assets, and

(ii) all such losses shall be treated as losses from sales or exchanges of capital assets.

* * *

(4) Definitions of personal casualty gain and personal casualty loss.—For purposes of this subsection—

(A) Personal casualty gain.—The term "personal casualty gain" means the recognized gain from any involuntary conversion of property which is described in subsection (c)(3) arising from fire, storm, shipwreck, or other casualty, or from theft.

(B) Personal casualty loss.—The term "personal casualty loss" means any loss described in subsection (c)(3). For purposes of paragraphs (2) and (3), the amount of any personal casualty loss shall be determined after the application of paragraph (1).

(5) Special rules.—

(A) Personal casualty losses allowable in computing adjusted gross income to the extent of personal casualty gains.—In any case to which paragraph (2)(A) applies, the deduction for personal casualty losses for any taxable year shall be treated as a deduction allowable in computing adjusted gross income to the extent such losses do not exceed the personal casualty gains for the taxable year.

(B) Joint returns.—For purposes of this subsection, a husband and wife making a joint return for the taxable year shall be treated as 1 individual.

(C) Determination of adjusted gross income in case of estates and trusts.—For purposes of paragraph (2), the adjusted gross income of an estate or trust shall be computed in the same manner as in the case of an individual, except that the deductions for costs paid or incurred in connection with the administration of the estate or trust shall be treated as allowable in arriving at adjusted gross income.

(D) Coordination with estate tax.—No loss described in subsection (c)(3) shall be allowed if, at the time of filing the return, such loss has been claimed for estate tax purposes in the estate tax return.

(E) Claim required to be filed in certain cases.—Any loss of an individual described in subsection (c)(3) to the extent covered by insurance shall be taken into account under this section only if the individual files a timely insurance claim with respect to such loss.

(i) Disaster losses.—

(1) Election to take deduction for preceding year.—Notwithstanding the provisions of subsection (a), any loss occurring in a disaster area (as defined by clause (ii) of subsection (h)(3)(C)) and attributable to a federally declared disaster (as defined by clause (i) of such subsection) may, at the election of the taxpayer, be taken into account for the taxable year immediately preceding the taxable year in which the disaster occurred.

(2) Year of loss.—If an election is made under this subsection, the casualty resulting in the loss shall be treated for purposes of this title as having occurred in the taxable year for which the deduction is claimed.

(3) Amount of loss.—The amount of the loss taken into account in the preceding taxable year by reason of paragraph (1) shall not exceed the uncompensated amount determined on the basis of the facts existing at the date the taxpayer claims the loss.

* * *

(j) Denial of deduction for losses on certain obligations not in registered form.—

(1) In general.—Nothing in subsection (a) or in any other provision of law shall be construed to provide a deduction for any loss sustained on any registration-required obligation unless such obligation is in registered form * * *.

(2) Definitions.—For purposes of this subsection—

(A) Registration-required obligation.—The term "registration-required obligation" has the meaning given to such term by section 163(f)(2).

(B) Registered form.—The term "registered form" has the same meaning as when used in section 163(f).

(3) Exceptions.—The Secretary may, by regulations, provide that this subsection and section 1287 shall not apply with respect to obligations held by any person if—

(A) such person holds such obligations in connection with a trade or business outside the United States,

(B) such person holds such obligations as a broker dealer (registered under Federal or State law) for sale to customers in the ordinary course of his trade or business,

(C) such person complies with reporting requirements with respect to ownership, transfers, and payments as the Secretary may require, or

(D) such person promptly surrenders the obligation to the issuer for the issuance of a new obligation in registered form,

but only if such obligations are held under arrangements provided in regulations or otherwise which are designed to assure that such obligations are not delivered to any United States person other than a person described in subparagraph (A), (B), or (C).

(k) Treatment as disaster loss where taxpayer ordered to demolish or relocate residence in disaster area because of disaster.—In the case of a taxpayer whose residence is located in an area which has been determined by the President of the United States to warrant assistance by the Federal Government under the Robert T. Stafford Disaster Relief and Emergency Assistance Act, if—

(1) not later than the 120th day after the date of such determination, the taxpayer is ordered, by the government of the State or any political subdivision thereof in which such residence is located, to demolish or relocate such residence, and

(2) the residence has been rendered unsafe for use as a residence by reason of the disaster,

any loss attributable to such disaster shall be treated as a loss which arises from a casualty and which is described in subsection (i).

* * *

§ 166. Bad debts

(a) General rule.—

(1) Wholly worthless debts.—There shall be allowed as a deduction any debt which becomes worthless within the taxable year.

(2) Partially worthless debts.—When satisfied that a debt is recoverable only in part, the Secretary may allow such debt, in an amount not in excess of the part charged off within the taxable year, as a deduction.

(b) Amount of deduction.—For purposes of subsection (a), the basis for determining the amount of the deduction for any bad debt shall be the adjusted basis provided in section 1011 for determining the loss from the sale or other disposition of property.

[(c) Repealed.]

(d) Nonbusiness debts.—

(1) General rule.—In the case of a taxpayer other than a corporation—

(A) subsection (a) shall not apply to any nonbusiness debt; and

(B) where any nonbusiness debt becomes worthless within the taxable year, the loss resulting therefrom shall be considered a loss from the sale or exchange, during the taxable year, of a capital asset held for not more than 1 year.

(2) Nonbusiness debt defined.—For purposes of paragraph (1), the term "nonbusiness debt" means a debt other than—

(A) a debt created or acquired (as the case may be) in connection with a trade or business of the taxpayer; or

(B) a debt the loss from the worthlessness of which is incurred in the taxpayer's trade or business.

(e) Worthless securities.—This section shall not apply to a debt which is evidenced by a security as defined in section 165(g)(2)(C).

* * *

§ 167. Depreciation

(a) General rule.—There shall be allowed as a depreciation deduction a reasonable allowance for the exhaustion, wear and tear (including a reasonable allowance for obsolescence)—

(1) of property used in the trade or business, or

(2) of property held for the production of income.

(b) Cross reference.—

For determination of depreciation deduction in case of property to which section 168 applies, see section 168.

(c) Basis for depreciation.—

(1) In general.—The basis on which exhaustion, wear and tear, and obsolescence are to be allowed in respect of any property shall be the adjusted basis provided in section 1011, for the purpose of determining the gain on the sale or other disposition of such property.

(2) Special rule for property subject to lease.—If any property is acquired subject to a lease—

(A) no portion of the adjusted basis shall be allocated to the leasehold interest, and

(B) the entire adjusted basis shall be taken into account in determining the depreciation deduction (if any) with respect to the property subject to the lease.

(d) Life tenants and beneficiaries of trusts and estates.—In the case of property held by one person for life with remainder to another person, the deduction shall be computed as if the life tenant were the absolute owner of the property and shall be allowed to the life tenant. In the case of property held in trust, the allowable deduction shall be apportioned between the income beneficiaries and the trustee in accordance with the pertinent provisions of the instrument creating the trust, or, in the absence of such provisions, on the basis of the trust income allocable to each. In the case of an estate, the allowable deduction shall be apportioned between the estate and the heirs, legatees, and devisees on the basis of the income of the estate allocable to each.

(e) Certain term interests not depreciable.—

(1) In general.—No depreciation deduction shall be allowed under this section (and no depreciation or amortization deduction shall be allowed under any other provision of this subtitle) to the taxpayer for any term interest in property for any period during which the remainder interest in such property is held (directly or indirectly) by a related person.

(2) Coordination with other provisions.—

(A) Section 273.—This subsection shall not apply to any term interest to which section 273 applies.

(B) Section 305(e).—This subsection shall not apply to the holder of the dividend rights which were separated from any stripped preferred stock to which section 305(e)(1) applies.

(3) Basis adjustments.—If, but for this subsection, a depreciation or amortization deduction would be allowable to the taxpayer with respect to any term interest in property—

(A) the taxpayer's basis in such property shall be reduced by any depreciation or amortization deductions disallowed under this subsection, and

(B) the basis of the remainder interest in such property shall be increased by the amount of such disallowed deductions (properly adjusted for any depreciation deductions allowable under subsection (d) to the taxpayer).

(4) Special rules.—

(A) Denial of increase in basis of remainderman.—No increase in the basis of the remainder interest shall be made under paragraph (3)(B) for any disallowed deductions attributable to periods during which the term interest was held—

(i) by an organization exempt from tax under this subtitle, or

* * *

(B) Coordination with subsection (d).—If, but for this subsection, a depreciation or amortization deduction would be allowable to any person with respect to any term interest in property, the principles of subsection (d) shall apply to such person with respect to such term interest.

(5) Definitions.—For purposes of this subsection—

(A) Term interest in property.—The term "term interest in property" has the meaning given such term by section 1001(e)(2).

(B) Related persons.—The term "related person" means any person bearing a relationship to the taxpayer described in subsection (b) or (e) of section 267.

(6) Regulations.—The Secretary shall prescribe such regulations as may be necessary to carry out the purposes of this subsection, including regulations preventing avoidance of this subsection through cross-ownership arrangements or otherwise.

(f) Treatment of certain property excluded from section 197.—

(1) Computer software.—

(A) In general.—If a depreciation deduction is allowable under subsection (a) with respect to any computer software, such deduction shall be computed by using the straight line method and a useful life of 36 months.

(B) Computer software.—For purposes of this section, the term "computer software" has the meaning given to such term by section 197(e)(3)(B); except that such term shall not include any such software which is an amortizable section 197 intangible.

* * *

(2) Certain interests or rights acquired separately.—If a depreciation deduction is allowable under subsection (a) with respect to any property described in subparagraph (B), (C), or (D) of section 197(e)(4), such deduction shall be computed in accordance with regulations prescribed by the Secretary. * * *

(3) Mortgage servicing rights.—If a depreciation deduction is allowable under subsection (a) with respect to any right described in section 197(e)(6), such deduction shall be computed by using the straight line method and a useful life of 108 months.

* * *

(i) Cross references.—

(1) For additional rule applicable to depreciation of improvements in the case of mines, oil and gas wells, other natural deposits, and timber, see section 611.

(2) For amortization of goodwill and certain other intangibles, see section 197.

§ 168. Accelerated cost recovery system

(a) General rule.—Except as otherwise provided in this section, the depreciation deduction provided by section 167(a) for any tangible property shall be determined by using—

(1) the applicable depreciation method,

(2) the applicable recovery period, and

(3) the applicable convention.

(b) Applicable depreciation method.—For purposes of this section—

(1) In general.—Except as provided in paragraphs (2) and (3), the applicable depreciation method is—

(A) the 200 percent declining balance method,

(B) switching to the straight line method for the 1st taxable year for which using the straight line method with respect to the adjusted basis as of the beginning of such year will yield a larger allowance.

(2) 150 percent declining balance method in certain cases.—Paragraph (1) shall be applied by substituting "150 percent" for "200 percent" in the case of—

(A) any 15–year or 20–year property,

(B) any property used in a farming business (within the meaning of section 263A(e)(4)),

* * *

(D) any property (other than property described in paragraph (3)) with respect to which the taxpayer elects under paragraph (5) to have the provisions of this paragraph apply.

(3) Property to which straight line method applies.—The applicable depreciation method shall be the straight line method in the case of the following property:

(A) Nonresidential real property.

(B) Residential rental property.

(C) Any railroad grading or tunnel bore.

(D) Property with respect to which the taxpayer elects under paragraph (5) to have the provisions of this paragraph apply.

(E) Property described in subsection (e)(3)(D)(ii).

* * *

(4) Salvage value treated as zero.—Salvage value shall be treated as zero.

(5) Election.—An election under paragraph (2)(C) or (3)(D) may be made with respect to 1 or more classes of property for any taxable year and once made with respect to any class shall apply to all property in such class placed in service during such taxable year. Such an election, once made, shall be irrevocable.

(c) Applicable recovery period.—For purposes of this section, the applicable recovery period shall be determined in accordance with the following table:

In the case of:	**The applicable recovery period is:**
3–year property	3 years
5–year property	5 years
7–year property	7 years
10–year property	10 years
15–year property	15 years
20–year property	20 years
Water utility property	25 years
Residential rental property	27.5 years
Nonresidential real property	39 years
Any railroad grading or tunnel bore	50 years

(d) Applicable convention.—For purposes of this section—

(1) In general.—Except as otherwise provided in this subsection, the applicable convention is the half-year convention.

(2) Real property.—In the case of—

(A) nonresidential real property,

(B) residential rental property, and

(C) any railroad grading or tunnel bore,

the applicable convention is the mid-month convention.

(3) Special rule where substantial property placed in service during last 3 months of taxable year.—

(A) In general.—Except as provided in regulations, if during any taxable year—

(i) the aggregate bases of property to which this section applies placed in service during the last 3 months of the taxable year, exceed

(ii) 40 percent of the aggregate bases of property to which this section applies placed in service during such taxable year,

the applicable convention for all property to which this section applies placed in service during such taxable year shall be the mid-quarter convention.

(B) Certain property not taken into account.—For purposes of subparagraph (A) there shall not be taken into account—

(i) any nonresidential real property, residential rental property, and railroad grading or tunnel bore, and

(ii) any other property placed in service and disposed of during the same taxable year.

(4) Definitions.—

(A) Half-year convention.—The half-year convention is a convention which treats all property placed in service during any taxable year (or disposed of during any taxable year) as placed in service (or disposed of) on the mid-point of such taxable year.

(B) Mid-month convention.—The mid-month convention is a convention which treats all property placed in service during any month (or disposed of during any month) as placed in service (or disposed of) on the mid-point of such month.

(C) Mid-quarter convention.—The mid-quarter convention is a convention which treats all property placed in service during any quarter of a taxable year (or disposed of during any quarter of a taxable year) as placed in service (or disposed of) on the mid-point of such quarter.

(e) Classification of property.—For purposes of this section—

(1) In general.—Except as otherwise provided in this subsection, property shall be classified under the following table:

Property shall be treated as:	If such property has a class life (in years) of:
3-year property	4 or less
5-year property	More than 4 but less than 10
7-year property	10 or more but less than 16
10-year property	16 or more but less than 20
15-year property	20 or more but less than 25
20-year property	25 or more

(2) Residential rental or nonresidential real property.—

(A) Residential rental property.—

(i) Residential rental property.—The term "residential rental property" means any building or structure if 80 percent or more of the gross rental income from such building or structure for the taxable year is rental income from dwelling units.

(ii) Definitions.—For purposes of clause (i)—

(I) the term "dwelling unit" means a house or apartment used to provide living accommodations in a building or structure, but does not include a unit in a hotel, motel, or other establishment more than one-half of the units in which are used on a transient basis, and

(II) if any portion of the building or structure is occupied by the taxpayer, the gross rental income from such building or structure shall include the rental value of the portion so occupied.

(B) Nonresidential real property.—The term "nonresidential real property" means section 1250 property which is not—

(i) residential rental property, or

(ii) property with a class life of less than 27.5 years.

(3) Classification of certain property.—

(A) 3-year property.—The term "3-year property" includes—

(i) any race horse—

(I) which is placed in service before January 1, 2014, and

(II) which is placed in service after December 31, 2013, and which is more than 2 years old at the time such horse is placed in service by the purchaser,

(ii) any horse other than a race horse which is more than 12 years old at the time it is placed in service, and

* * *

(B) 5-year property.—The term "5-year property" includes—

(i) any automobile or light general purpose truck,

(ii) any semi-conductor manufacturing equipment,

(iii) any computer-based telephone central office switching equipment,

(iv) any qualified technological equipment,

(v) any section 1245 property used in connection with research and experimentation,

* * *

(C) 7-year property.—The term "7-year property" includes—

(i) any railroad track, and

(ii) any motorsports entertainment complex,

(iii) any Alaska natural gas pipeline,

(iv) any natural gas gathering line the original use of which commences with the taxpayer after April 11, 2005, and

(v) any property which—

(I) does not have a class life, and

(II) is not otherwise classified under paragraph (2) or this paragraph.

(D) 10-year property.—The term "10-year property" includes—

(i) any single purpose agricultural or horticultural structure (within the meaning of subsection (i)(13)),

(ii) any tree or vine bearing fruit or nuts.

* * *

(E) 15-year property.—The term "15-year property" includes—

(i) any municipal wastewater treatment plant, and

(ii) any telephone distribution plant and comparable equipment used for 2-way exchange of voice and data communications.

(iii) any section 1250 property which is a retail motor fuels outlet (whether or not food or other convenience items are sold at the outlet),

* * *

(f) Property to which section does not apply.—This section shall not apply to—

(1) Certain methods of depreciation.—Any property if—

(A) the taxpayer elects to exclude such property from the application of this section, and

(B) for the 1st taxable year for which a depreciation deduction would be allowable with respect to such property in the hands of the taxpayer, the property is properly depreciated under the unit-of-production method or any method of depreciation not expressed in a term of years (other than the retirement-replacement-betterment method or similar method).

* * *

(3) Films and video tape.—Any motion picture film or video tape.

(4) Sound recordings.—Any works which result from the fixation of a series of musical, spoken, or other sounds, regardless of the nature of the material (such as discs, tapes, or other photorecordings) in which such sounds are embodied.

(5) Certain property placed in service in churning transactions.—

(A) In general.—Property—

(i) described in paragraph (4) of section 168(e) (as in effect before the amendments made by the Tax Reform Act of 1986), or

(ii) which would be described in such paragraph if such paragraph were applied by substituting "1987" for "1981" and "1986" for "1980" each place such terms appear.

(B) Subparagraph (A)(ii) not to apply.—Clause (ii) of subparagraph (A) shall not apply to—

(i) any residential rental property or nonresidential real property,

(ii) any property if, for the 1st taxable year in which such property is placed in service—

(I) the amount allowable as a deduction under this section (as in effect before the date of the enactment of this paragraph) with respect to such property is greater than

(II) the amount allowable as a deduction under this section (as in effect on or after such date and using the half-year convention) for such taxable year, or

(iii) any property to which this section (as amended by the Tax Reform Act of 1986) applied in the hands of the transferor.

(C) Special rule.—In the case of any property to which this section would apply but for this paragraph, the depreciation deduction under section 167 shall be determined under the provisions of this section as in effect before the amendments made by section 201 of the Tax Reform Act of 1986.

(g) Alternative depreciation system for certain property.—

(1) In general.—In the case of—

(A) any tangible property which during the taxable year is used predominantly outside the United States,

(B) any tax-exempt use property,

(C) any tax-exempt bond financed property,

(D) any imported property covered by an Executive order under paragraph (6), and

(E) any property to which an election under paragraph (7) applies,

the depreciation deduction provided by section 167(a) shall be determined under the alternative depreciation system.

(2) Alternative depreciation system.—For purposes of paragraph (1), the alternative depreciation system is depreciation determined by using—

(A) the straight line method (without regard to salvage value),

(B) the applicable convention determined under subsection (d), and

(C) a recovery period determined under the following table:

In the case of:	The recovery period shall be:
(i) Property not described in clause (ii) or (iii)	The class life
(ii) Personal property with no class life	12 years
(iii) Nonresidential real and residential rental property	40 years
(iv) Any railroad grading or tunnel bore or water utility property	50 years

(3) Special rules for determining class life.—

(A) Tax-exempt use property subject to lease.—In the case of any tax-exempt use property subject to a lease, the recovery period used for purposes of paragraph (2) shall (notwithstanding any other subparagraph of this paragraph) in no event be less than 125 percent of the lease term.

(B) Special rule for certain property assigned to classes.—For purposes of paragraph (2), in the case of property described in any of the following subparagraphs of subsection (e)(3), the class life shall be determined as follows:

If property is described in subparagraph:	The class life is:
(A)(iii)	4
(B)(ii)	5
(B)(iii)	9.5
(B)(iv)	10
(C)(i)	10
(C)(iii)	22
(C)(iv)	14
(D)(i)	15
(D)(ii)	20
(E)(i)	24
(E)(ii)	24
(E)(iii)	20
(E)(iv)	39
(E)(v)	39
(E)(vi)	20
(E)(vii)	30
(E)(viii)	35
(E)(ix)	39
(F)	25

(C) Qualified technological equipment.—In the case of any qualified technological equipment, the recovery period used for purposes of paragraph (2) shall be 5 years.

(D) Automobiles, etc.—In the case of any automobile or light general purpose truck, the recovery period used for purposes of paragraph (2) shall be 5 years.

(E) Certain real property.—In the case of any section 1245 property which is real property with no class life, the recovery period used for purposes of paragraph (2) shall be 40 years.

* * *

(7) Election to use alternative depreciation system.—

(A) In general.—If the taxpayer makes an election under this paragraph with respect to any class of property for any taxable year, the alternative depreciation system under this subsection shall apply to all property in such class placed in service during such taxable year. Notwithstanding the preceding sentence, in the case of nonresidential real property or residential rental property, such election may be made separately with respect to each property.

(B) Election irrevocable.—An election under subparagraph (A), once made, shall be irrevocable.

* * *

(i) Definitions and special rules.—For purposes of this section—

(1) Class life.—Except as provided in this section, the term "class life" means the class life (if any) which would be applicable with respect to any property as of January 1, 1986, under subsection (m) of section 167 (determined without regard to paragraph (4) and as if the taxpayer had made an election under such subsection). The Secretary, through an office established in the Treasury, shall monitor and analyze actual experience with respect to all depreciable assets. The reference in this paragraph to subsection (m) of section 167 shall be treated as a reference to such subsection as in effect on the day before the date of the enactment of the Revenue Reconciliation Act of 1990.

(2) Qualified technological equipment.—

(A) In general.—The term "qualified technological equipment" means—

(i) any computer or peripheral equipment,

(ii) any high technology telephone station equipment installed on the customer's premises, and

(iii) any high technology medical equipment.

(B) Computer or peripheral equipment defined.—For purposes of this paragraph—

(i) In general.—The term "computer or peripheral equipment" means—

(I) any computer, and

(II) any related peripheral equipment.

(ii) Computer.—The term "computer" means a programmable electronically activated device which—

(I) is capable of accepting information, applying prescribed processes to the information, and supplying the results of these processes with or without human intervention, and

(II) consists of a central processing unit containing extensive storage, logic, arithmetic, and control capabilities.

(iii) Related peripheral equipment.—The term "related peripheral equipment" means any auxiliary machine (whether on-line or off-line) which is designed to be placed under the control of the central processing unit of a computer.

(iv) Exceptions.—The term "computer or peripheral equipment" shall not include—

(I) any equipment which is an integral part of other property which is not a computer,

(II) typewriters, calculators, adding and accounting machines, copiers, duplicating equipment, and similar equipment, and

(III) equipment of a kind used primarily for amusement or entertainment of the user.

(C) High technology medical equipment.—For purposes of this paragraph, the term ''high technology medical equipment'' means any electronic, electromechanical, or computer-based high technology equipment used in the screening, monitoring, observation, diagnosis, or treatment of patients in a laboratory, medical, or hospital environment.

(3) Lease term.—

(A) In general.—In determining a lease term—

(i) there shall be taken into account options to renew, and

(ii) the term of a lease shall include the term of any service contract or similar arrangement (whether or not treated as a lease under section 7701(e))—

(I) which is part of the same transaction (or series of related transactions) which includes the lease, and

(II) which is with respect to the property subject to the lease or substantially similar property, and

(iii) 2 or more successive leases which are part of the same transaction (or a series of related transactions) with respect to the same or substantially similar property shall be treated as 1 lease.

(B) Special rule for fair rental options on nonresidential real property or residential rental property.—For purposes of clause (i) of subparagraph (A), in the case of nonresidential real property or residential rental property, there shall not be taken into account any option to renew at fair market value, determined at the time of renewal.

(4) General asset accounts.—Under regulations, a taxpayer may maintain 1 or more general asset accounts for any property to which this section applies. Except as provided in regulations, all proceeds realized on any disposition of property in a general asset account shall be included in income as ordinary income.

(5) Changes in use.—The Secretary shall, by regulations, provide for the method of determining the deduction allowable under section 167(a) with respect to any tangible property for any taxable year (and the succeeding taxable years) during which such property changes status under this section but continues to be held by the same person.

(6) Treatments of additions or improvements to property.—In the case of any addition to (or improvement of) any property—

(A) any deduction under subsection (a) for such addition or improvement shall be computed in the same manner as the deduction for such property would be computed if such property had been placed in service at the same time as such addition or improvement, and

(B) the applicable recovery period for such addition or improvement shall begin on the later of—

(i) the date on which such addition (or improvement) is placed in service, or

(ii) the date on which the property with respect to which such addition (or improvement) was made is placed in service.

(7) Treatment of certain transferees.—

(A) In general.—In the case of any property transferred in a transaction described in subparagraph (B), the transferee shall be treated as the transferor for purposes of computing the depreciation deduction determined under this section with respect to so much of the basis in the hands of the transferee as does not exceed the adjusted basis in the hands of the transferor. In any case where this section as in effect before the amendments made by section 201 of the Tax Reform

Act of 1986 applied to the property in the hands of the transferor, the reference in the preceding sentence to this section shall be treated as a reference to this section as so in effect.

(B) Transactions covered.—The transactions described in this subparagraph are—

(i) any transaction described in section 332, 351, 361, 721, or 731, and

(ii) any transaction between members of the same affiliated group during any taxable year for which a consolidated return is made by such group.

Subparagraph (A) shall not apply in the case of a termination of a partnership under section 708(b)(1)(B).

(C) Property reacquired by the taxpayer.—Under regulations, property which is disposed of and then reacquired by the taxpayer shall be treated for purposes of computing the deduction allowable under subsection (a) as if such property had not been disposed of.

(8) Treatment of leasehold improvements.—

(A) In general.—In the case of any building erected (or improvements made) on leased property, if such building or improvement is property to which this section applies, the depreciation deduction shall be determined under the provisions of this section.

(B) Treatment of lessor improvements which are abandoned at termination of lease.—An improvement—

(i) which is made by the lessor of leased property for the lessee of such property, and

(ii) which is irrevocably disposed of or abandoned by the lessor at the termination of the lease by such lessee,

shall be treated for purposes of determining gain or loss under this title as disposed of by the lessor when so disposed of or abandoned.

* * *

(12) Sections 1245 and 1250 property.—The terms "section 1245 property" and "section 1250 property" have the meanings given such terms by sections 1245(a)(3) and 1250(c), respectively.

* * *

(k) Special allowance for certain property acquired after December 31, 2007, and before January 1, 2014.—

(1) Additional allowance.—In the case of any qualified property—

(A) the depreciation deduction provided by section 167(a) for the taxable year in which such property is placed in service shall include an allowance equal to 50 percent of the adjusted basis of the qualified property, and

(B) the adjusted basis of the qualified property shall be reduced by the amount of such deduction before computing the amount otherwise allowable as a depreciation deduction under this chapter for such taxable year and any subsequent taxable year.

(2) Qualified property.—For purposes of this subsection—

(A) In general.—The term "qualified property" means property—

(i)(I) to which this section applies which has a recovery period of 20 years or less,

(II) which is computer software (as defined in section 167(f)(1)(B)) for which a deduction is allowable under section 167(a) without regard to this subsection,

(III) which is water utility property, or

(IV) which is qualified leasehold improvement property,

(ii) the original use of which commences with the taxpayer after December 31, 2007,

(iii) which is—

(I) acquired by the taxpayer after December 31, 2007, and before January 1, 2014, but only if no written binding contract for the acquisition was in effect before January 1, 2008, or

(II) acquired by the taxpayer pursuant to a written binding contract which was entered into after December 31, 2007, and before January 1, 2014, and

(iv) which is placed in service by the taxpayer before January 1, 2014, or, in the case of property described in subparagraph (B) or (C), before January 1, 2015.

(B) Certain property having longer production periods treated as qualified property.—

(i) In general.—The term "qualified property" includes any property if such property—

(I) meets the requirements of clauses (i), (ii), (iii), and (iv) of subparagraph (A),

(II) has a recovery period of at least 10 years or is transportation property,

(III) is subject to section 263A, and

(IV) meets the requirements of clause (iii) of section 263A(f)(1)(B) (determined as if such clauses also apply to property which has a long useful life (within the meaning of section 263A(f))).

(ii) Only pre-January 1, 2014, basis eligible for additional allowance.—In the case of property which is qualified property solely by reason of clause (i), paragraph (1) shall apply only to the extent of the adjusted basis thereof attributable to manufacture, construction, or production before January 1, 2014.

(iii) Transportation property.—For purposes of this subparagraph, the term "transportation property" means tangible personal property used in the trade or business of transporting persons or property.

(iv) Application of subparagraph.—This subparagraph shall not apply to any property which is described in subparagraph (C).

(C) Certain aircraft.—The term "qualified property" includes property—

(i) which meets the requirements of clauses (ii), (iii), and (iv) of subparagraph (A),

(ii) which is an aircraft which is not a transportation property (as defined in subparagraph (B)(iii)) other than for agricultural or firefighting purposes,

(iii) which is purchased and on which such purchaser, at the time of the contract for purchase, has made a nonrefundable deposit of the lesser of—

(I) 10 percent of the cost, or

(II) $100,000, and

(iv) which has—

(I) an estimated production period exceeding 4 months, and

(II) a cost exceeding $200,000.

(D) Exceptions.—

(i) Alternative depreciation property.—The term "qualified property" shall not include any property to which the alternative depreciation system under subsection (g) applies, determined—

(I) without regard to paragraph (7) of subsection (g) (relating to election to have system apply), and

(II) after application of section 280F(b) (relating to listed property with limited business use).

* * *

(iii) Election out.—If a taxpayer makes an election under this clause with respect to any class of property for any taxable year, this subsection shall not apply to all property in such class placed in service during such taxable year.

(E) Special rules.—

(i) Self-constructed property.—In the case of a taxpayer manufacturing, constructing, or producing property for the taxpayer's own use, the requirements of clause (iii) of subparagraph (A) shall be treated as met if the taxpayer begins manufacturing, constructing, or producing the property after December 31, 2007, and before January 1, 2014.

(ii) Sale-leasebacks.—For purposes of clause (iii) and subparagraph (A)(ii), if property is—

(I) originally placed in service after December 31, 2007, by a person, and

(II) sold and leased back by such person within 3 months after the date such property was originally placed in service,

such property shall be treated as originally placed in service not earlier than the date on which such property is used under the leaseback referred to in subclause (II).

* * *

(iv) Limitations related to users and related parties.—The term "qualified property" shall not include any property if—

(I) the user of such property (as of the date on which such property is originally placed in service) or a person which is related (within the meaning of section 267(b) or 707(b)) to such user or to the taxpayer had a written binding contract in effect for the acquisition of such property at any time on or before December 31, 2007, or

(II) in the case of property manufactured, constructed, or produced for such user's or person's own use, the manufacture, construction, or production of such property began at any time on or before December 31, 2007.

(F) Coordination with section 280F.—For purposes of section 280F—

(i) Automobiles.—In the case of a passenger automobile (as defined in section 280F(d)(5)) which is qualified property, the Secretary shall increase the limitation under section 280F(a)(1)(A)(i) by $8,000.

(ii) Listed property.—The deduction allowable under paragraph (1) shall be taken into account in computing any recapture amount under section 280F(b)(2).

(G) Deduction allowed in computing minimum tax.—For purposes of determining alternative minimum taxable income under section 55, the deduction under subsection (a) for qualified property shall be determined under this section without regard to any adjustment under section 56.

(3) Qualified leasehold improvement property.—For purposes of this subsection—

(A) In general.—The term "qualified leasehold improvement property" means any improvement to an interior portion of a building which is nonresidential real property if—

(i) such improvement is made under or pursuant to a lease (as defined in subsection (h)(7))—

(I) by the lessee (or any sublessee) of such portion, or

(II) by the lessor of such portion,

(ii) such portion is to be occupied exclusively by the lessee (or any sublessee) of such portion, and

(iii) such improvement is placed in service more than 3 years after the date the building was first placed in service.

(B) Certain improvements not included.—Such term shall not include any improvement for which the expenditure is attributable to—

(i) the enlargement of the building,

(ii) any elevator or escalator,

(iii) any structural component benefiting a common area, and

(iv) the internal structural framework of the building.

(C) Definitions and special rules.—For purposes of this paragraph—

(i) Commitment to lease treated as lease.—A commitment to enter into a lease shall be treated as a lease, and the parties to such commitment shall be treated as lessor and lessee, respectively.

(ii) Related persons.—A lease between related persons shall not be considered a lease. For purposes of the preceding sentence, the term "related persons" means—

(I) members of an affiliated group (as defined in section 1504), and

(II) persons having a relationship described in subsection (b) of section 267; except that, for purposes of this clause, the phrase "80 percent or more" shall be substituted for the phrase "more than 50 percent" each place it appears in such subsection.

* * *

(5) Special rule for property acquired during certain pre-2012 periods.— In the case of qualified property acquired by the taxpayer (under rules similar to the rules of clauses (ii) and (iii) of paragraph (2)(A)) after September 8, 2010, and before January 1, 2012, and which is placed in service by the taxpayer before January 1, 2012 (January 1, 2013, in the case of property described in subparagraph (2)(B) or (2)(C)), paragraph (1)(A) shall be applied by substituting "100 percent" for "50 percent".

§ 169. Amortization of pollution control facilities

(a) Allowance of deduction.—Every person, at his election, shall be entitled to a deduction with respect to the amortization of the amortizable basis of any certified pollution control facility (as defined in subsection (d)), based on a period of 60 months. Such amortization deduction shall be an amount, with respect to each month of such period within the taxable year, equal to the amortizable basis of the pollution control facility at the end of such month divided by the number of months (including the month for which the deduction is computed) remaining in the period. Such amortizable basis at the end of the month shall be computed without regard to the amortization deduction for such month. The amortization deduction provided by this section with respect to any month shall be in lieu of the depreciation deduction with respect to such pollution control facility for such month provided by section 167. The 60–month period shall begin, as to any pollution control facility, at the election of the taxpayer, with the month following the month in which such facility was completed or acquired, or with the succeeding taxable year.

(b) Election of amortization.—The election of the taxpayer to take the amortization deduction and to begin the 60–month period with the month following the month in which the facility is completed or acquired, or with the taxable year succeeding the taxable year in which such facility is completed or acquired, shall be made by filing with the Secretary, in such manner, in such form, and within such time, as the Secretary may by regulations prescribe, a statement of such election.

* * *

(f) Amortizable basis.—

(1) Defined.—For purposes of this section, the term "amortizable basis" means that portion of the adjusted basis (for determining gain) of a certified pollution control facility which may be amortized under this section.

(2) Special rules.—

(A) If a certified pollution control facility has a useful life (determined as of the first day of the first month for which a deduction is allowable under this section) in excess of 15 years, the amortizable basis of such facility shall be equal to an amount which bears the same ratio to the portion of the adjusted basis of such facility, which would be eligible for amortization but for the application of this subparagraph, as 15 bears to the number of years of useful life of such facility.

(B) The amortizable basis of a certified pollution control facility with respect to which an election under this section is in effect shall not be increased, for purposes of this section, for additions or improvements after the amortization period has begun.

(g) Depreciation deduction.—The depreciation deduction provided by section 167 shall, despite the provisions of subsection (a), be allowed with respect to the portion of the adjusted basis which is not the amortizable basis.

* * *

§ 170. Charitable, etc., contributions and gifts

(a) Allowance of deduction.—

(1) General rule.—There shall be allowed as a deduction any charitable contribution (as defined in subsection (c)) payment of which is made within the taxable year. A charitable contribution shall be allowable as a deduction only if verified under regulations prescribed by the Secretary.

(2) Corporations on accrual basis.—In the case of a corporation reporting its taxable income on the accrual basis, if—

(A) the board of directors authorizes a charitable contribution during any taxable year, and

(B) payment of such contribution is made after the close of such taxable year and on or before the 15th day of the third month following the close of such taxable year, then the taxpayer may elect to treat such contribution as paid during such taxable year. The election may be made only at the time of the filing of the return for such taxable year, and shall be signified in such manner as the Secretary shall by regulations prescribe.

(3) Future interests in tangible personal property.—For purposes of this section, payment of a charitable contribution which consists of a future interest in tangible personal property shall be treated as made only when all intervening interests in, and rights to the actual possession or enjoyment of, the property have expired or are held by persons other than the taxpayer or those standing in a relationship to the taxpayer described in section 267(b) or 707(b). For purposes of the preceding sentence, a fixture which is intended to be severed from the real property shall be treated as tangible personal property.

(b) Percentage limitations.—

(1) Individuals.—In the case of an individual, the deduction provided in subsection (a) shall be limited as provided in the succeeding subparagraphs.

(A) General rule.—Any charitable contribution to—

(i) a church or a convention or association of churches,

(ii) an educational organization which normally maintains a regular faculty and curriculum and normally has a regularly enrolled body of pupils or students in attendance at the place where its educational activities are regularly carried on,

(iii) an organization the principal purpose or functions of which are the providing of medical or hospital care or medical education or medical research, if the organization is a hospital, or if the organization is a medical research organization directly engaged in the continuous active conduct of medical research in conjunction with a hospital, and during the calendar year in which the contribution is made such organization is committed to spend such contributions for such research before January 1 of the fifth calendar year which begins after the date such contribution is made,

(iv) an organization which normally receives a substantial part of its support (exclusive of income received in the exercise or performance by such organization of its charitable, educational, or other purpose or function constituting the basis for its exemption under section 501(a)) from the United States or any State or political subdivision thereof or from direct or indirect contributions from the general public, and which is organized and operated exclusively to receive, hold, invest, and administer property and to make expenditures to or for the benefit of a college or university which is an organization referred to in clause (ii) of this subparagraph and which is an agency or instrumentality of a State or political subdivision thereof, or which is owned or operated by a State or political subdivision thereof or by an agency or instrumentality of one or more States or political subdivisions,

(v) a governmental unit referred to in subsection (c)(1),

(vi) an organization referred to in subsection (c)(2) which normally receives a substantial part of its support (exclusive of income received in the exercise or performance by such organization of its charitable, educational, or other purpose or function constituting the basis for its exemption under section 501(a)) from a governmental unit referred to in subsection (c)(1) or from direct or indirect contributions from the general public,

(vii) a private foundation described in subparagraph (F), or

(viii) an organization described in section 509(a)(2) or (3), shall be allowed to the extent that the aggregate of such contributions does not exceed 50 percent of the taxpayer's contribution base for the taxable year.

(B) Other contributions.—Any charitable contribution other than a charitable contribution to which subparagraph (A) applies shall be allowed to the extent that the aggregate of such contributions does not exceed the lesser of—

(i) 30 percent of the taxpayer's contribution base for the taxable year, or

(ii) the excess of 50 percent of the taxpayer's contribution base for the taxable year over the amount of charitable contributions allowable under subparagraph (A) (determined without regard to subparagraph (C)).

If the aggregate of such contributions exceeds the limitation of the preceding sentence, such excess shall be treated (in a manner consistent with the rules of subsection (d)(1)) as a charitable contribution (to which subparagraph (A) does not apply) in each of the 5 succeeding taxable years in order of time.

(C) Special limitation with respect to contributions described in subparagraph (A) of certain capital gain property.—

(i) In the case of charitable contributions described in subparagraph (A) of capital gain property to which subsection (e)(1)(B) does not apply, the total amount of contributions of such property which may be taken into account under subsection (a) for any taxable year shall not exceed 30 percent of the taxpayer's contribution base for such year. For purposes of this subsection, contributions of capital gain property to which this subparagraph applies shall be taken into account after all other charitable contributions (other than charitable contributions to which subparagraph (D) applies).

(ii) If charitable contributions described in subparagraph (A) of capital gain property to which clause (i) applies exceeds 30 percent of the taxpayer's contribution base for any taxable year, such excess shall be treated, in a manner consistent with the rules of subsection (d)(1), as a charitable contribution of capital gain property to which clause (i) applies in each of the 5 succeeding taxable years in order of time.

(iii) At the election of the taxpayer (made at such time and in such manner as the Secretary prescribes by regulations), subsection (e)(1) shall apply to all contributions of capital gain property (to which subsection (e)(1)(B) does not otherwise apply) made by the taxpayer during the taxable year. If such an election is made, clauses (i) and (ii) shall not apply to contributions of capital gain property made during the taxable year, and, in applying subsection (d) (1) for such taxable year with respect to contributions of capital gain property made in any prior contribution year for which an election was not made under this clause, such contributions shall be reduced as if subsection (e) (1) had applied to such contributions in the year in which made.

(iv) For purposes of this paragraph, the term "capital gain property" means, with respect to any contribution, any capital asset the sale of which at its fair market value at the time of the contribution would have resulted in gain which would have been long-term capital gain. For purposes of the preceding sentence, any property which is property used in the trade or business (as defined in section 1231(b)) shall be treated as a capital asset.

(D) Special limitation with respect to contributions of capital gain property to organizations not described in subparagraph (A).—

(i) In general.—In the case of charitable contributions (other than charitable contributions to which subparagraph (A) applies) of capital gain property, the total amount of such contributions of such property taken into account under subsection (a) for any taxable year shall not exceed the lesser of—

(I) 20 percent of the taxpayer's contribution base for the taxable year, or

(II) the excess of 30 percent of the taxpayer's contribution base for the taxable year over the amount of the contributions of capital gain property to which subparagraph (C) applies.

For purposes of this subsection, contributions of capital gain property to which this subparagraph applies shall be taken into account after all other charitable contributions.

(ii) Carryover.—If the aggregate amount of contributions described in clause (i) exceeds the limitation of clause (i), such excess shall be treated (in a manner consistent with the rules of subsection (d)(1)) as a charitable contribution of capital gain property to which clause (i) applies in each of the 5 succeeding taxable years in order of time.

* * *

(G) Contribution base defined.—For purposes of this section, the term "contribution base" means adjusted gross income (computed without regard to any net operating loss carryback to the taxable year under section 172).

(2) Corporations.—In the case of a corporation—

(A) In general.—The total deductions under subsection (a) for any taxable year (other than for contributions to which subparagraph (B) applies) shall not exceed 10 percent of the taxpayer's taxable income.

* * *

(C) Taxable income.—For purposes of this paragraph, taxable income shall be computed without regard to—

(i) this section,

(ii) part VIII (except section 248),

(iii) any net operating loss carryback to the taxable year under section 172,

(iv) section 199, and

(v) any capital loss carryback to the taxable year under section 1212(a)(1).

* * *

(c) Charitable contribution defined.—For purposes of this section, the term "charitable contribution" means a contribution or gift to or for the use of—

(1) A State, a possession of the United States, or any political subdivision of any of the foregoing, or the United States or the District of Columbia, but only if the contribution or gift is made for exclusively public purposes.

(2) A corporation, trust, or community chest, fund, or foundation—

(A) created or organized in the United States or in any possession thereof, or under the law of the United States, any State, the District of Columbia, or any possession of the United States;

(B) organized and operated exclusively for religious, charitable, scientific, literary, or educational purposes, or to foster national or international amateur sports competition (but only if no part of its activities involve the provision of athletic facilities or equipment), or for the prevention of cruelty to children or animals;

(C) no part of the net earnings of which inures to the benefit of any private shareholder or individual; and

(D) which is not disqualified for tax exemption under section 501(c)(3) by reason of attempting to influence legislation, and which does not participate in, or intervene in (including the publishing or distributing of statements), any political campaign on behalf of (or in opposition to) any candidate for public office.

A contribution or gift by a corporation to a trust, chest, fund, or foundation shall be deductible by reason of this paragraph only if it is to be used within the United States or any of its possessions exclusively for purposes specified in subparagraph (B). * * *

(3) A post or organization of war veterans, or an auxiliary unit or society of, or trust or foundation for, any such post or organization—

(A) organized in the United States or any of its possessions, and

(B) no part of the net earnings of which inures to the benefit of any private shareholder or individual.

(4) In the case of a contribution or gift by an individual, a domestic fraternal society, order, or association, operating under the lodge system, but only if such contribution or gift is to be used exclusively for religious, charitable, scientific, literary, or educational purposes, or for the prevention of cruelty to children or animals.

(5) A cemetery company owned and operated exclusively for the benefit of its members, or any corporation chartered solely for burial purposes as a cemetery corporation and not permitted by its charter to engage in any business not necessarily incident to that purpose, if such company or corporation is not operated for profit and no part of the net earnings of such company or corporation inures to the benefit of any private shareholder or individual.

For purposes of this section, the term "charitable contribution" also means an amount treated under subsection (g) as paid for the use of an organization described in paragraph (2), (3), or (4).

(d) Carryovers of excess contributions.—

(1) Individuals.—

(A) In general.—In the case of an individual, if the amount of charitable contributions described in subsection (b)(1)(A) payment of which is made within a taxable year (hereinafter in this paragraph referred to as the "contribution year") exceeds 50 percent of the taxpayer's contribution base for such year, such excess shall be treated as a charitable contribution described in subsection (b)(1)(A) paid in each of the 5 succeeding taxable years in order of time, but, with respect to any such succeeding taxable year, only to the extent of the lesser of the two following amounts:

(i) the amount by which 50 percent of the taxpayer's contribution base for such succeeding taxable year exceeds the sum of the charitable contributions described in subsection (b)(1)(A) payment of which is made by the taxpayer within such succeeding taxable year (determined without regard to this subparagraph) and the charitable contributions described in subsection (b)(1)(A) payment of which was made in taxable years before the contribution year which are treated under this subparagraph as having been paid in such succeeding taxable year; or

(ii) in the case of the first succeeding taxable year, the amount of such excess, and in the case of the second, third, fourth, or fifth succeeding taxable year, the portion of such excess not treated under this subparagraph as a charitable contribution described in subsection (b)(1)(A) paid in any taxable year intervening between the contribution year and such succeeding taxable year.

(B) Special rule for net operating loss carryovers.—In applying subparagraph (A), the excess determined under subparagraph (A) for the contribution year shall be reduced to the extent that such excess reduces taxable income (as computed for purposes of the second sentence of section 172(b)(2)) and increases the net operating loss deduction for a taxable year succeeding the contribution year.

(2) Corporations.—

(A) In general.—Any contribution made by a corporation in a taxable year (hereinafter in this paragraph referred to as the "contribution year") in excess of the amount deductible for such year under subsection (b)(2)(A) shall be deductible for each of the 5 succeeding taxable years in order of time, but only to the extent of the lesser of the two following amounts: (i) the excess of the maximum amount deductible for such succeeding taxable year under subsection (b)(2)(A) over the sum of the contributions made in such year plus the aggregate of the excess contributions which were made in taxable years before the contribution year and which are deductible under this subparagraph for such succeeding taxable year; or (ii) in the case of the first succeeding taxable year, the amount of such excess contribution, and in the case of the second, third, fourth, or fifth succeeding taxable year, the portion of such excess contribution not deductible under this subparagraph for any taxable year intervening between the contribution year and such succeeding taxable year.

(B) Special rule for net operating loss carryovers.—For purposes of subparagraph (A), the excess of—

(i) the contributions made by a corporation in a taxable year to which this section applies, over

(ii) the amount deductible in such year under the limitation in subsection (b)(2)(A),

shall be reduced to the extent that such excess reduces taxable income (as computed for purposes of the second sentence of section 172(b)(2)) and increases a net operating loss carryover under section 172 to a succeeding taxable year.

(e) Certain contributions of ordinary income and capital gain property.—

(1) General rule.—The amount of any charitable contribution of property otherwise taken into account under this section shall be reduced by the sum of—

(A) the amount of gain which would not have been long-term capital gain (determined without regard to section 1221(b)(3)) if the property contributed had been sold by the taxpayer at its fair market value (determined at the time of such contribution), and

(B) in the case of a charitable contribution—

(i) of tangible personal property—

(I) if the use by the donee is unrelated to the purpose or function constituting the basis for its exemption under section 501 (or, in the case of a governmental unit, to any purpose or function described in subsection (c)), or

(II) which is applicable property (as defined in paragraph (7)(C), but without regard to clause (ii) thereof) which is sold, exchanged, or otherwise disposed of by the donee before the last day of the taxable year in which the contribution was made and with respect to which the donee has not made a certification in accordance with paragraph (7)(D),

(ii) to or for the use of a private foundation (as defined in section 509(a)), other than a private foundation described in subsection (b)(1)(F),

(iii) of any patent, copyright (other than a copyright described in section 1221(a)(3) or 1231(b)(1)(C)), trademark, trade name, trade secret, know-how, software (other than software described in section 197(e)(3)(A)(i)), or similar property, or applications or registrations of such property,

* * *

the amount of gain which would have been long-term capital gain if the property contributed had been sold by the taxpayer at its fair market value (determined at the time of such contribution).

For purposes of applying this paragraph (other than in the case of gain to which section 617(d)(1), 1245(a), 1250(a), 1252(a), or 1254(a) applies), property which is property used in the trade or business (as defined in section 1231(b)) shall be treated as a capital asset. For purposes of applying this paragraph in the case of a charitable contribution of stock in an S corporation, rules similar to the rules of section 751 shall apply in determining whether gain on such stock would have been long-term capital gain if such stock were sold by the taxpayer.

(2) Allocation of basis.—For purposes of paragraph (1), in the case of a charitable contribution of less than the taxpayer's entire interest in the property contributed, the taxpayer's adjusted basis in such property shall be allocated between the interest contributed and any interest not contributed in accordance with regulations prescribed by the Secretary.

(3) Special rule for certain contributions of inventory and other property.—

(A) Qualified contributions.—For purposes of this paragraph, a qualified contribution shall mean a charitable contribution of property described in paragraph (1) or (2) of section 1221(a), by a corporation (other than a corporation which is an S corporation) to an organization which is described in section 501(c)(3) and is exempt under section 501(a) (other than a private foundation, as defined in section 509(a), which is not an operating foundation, as defined in section 4942(j)(3)), but only if—

(i) the use of the property by the donee is related to the purpose or function constituting the basis for its exemption under section 501 and the property is to be used by the donee solely for the care of the ill, the needy, or infants;

(ii) the property is not transferred by the donee in exchange for money, other property, or services;

(iii) the taxpayer receives from the donee a written statement representing that its use and disposition of the property will be in accordance with the provisions of clauses (i) and (ii); and

(iv) in the case where the property is subject to regulation under the Federal Food, Drug, and Cosmetic Act, as amended, such property must fully satisfy the applicable requirements of such Act and regulations promulgated thereunder on the date of transfer and for one hundred and eighty days prior thereto.

(B) Amount of reduction.—The reduction under paragraph (1)(A) for any qualified contribution (as defined in subparagraph (A)) shall be no greater than the sum of—

(i) one-half of the amount computed under paragraph (1)(A) (computed without regard to this paragraph), and

(ii) the amount (if any) by which the charitable contribution deduction under this section for any qualified contribution (computed by taking into account the amount determined in clause (i), but without regard to this clause) exceeds twice the basis of such property.

* * *

(E) This paragraph shall not apply to so much of the amount of the gain described in paragraph (1)(A) which would be long-term capital gain but for the application of sections 617, 1245, 1250, or 1252.

* * *

(5) Special rule for contributions of stock for which market quotations are readily available.—

(A) In general.—Subparagraph (B)(ii) of paragraph (1) shall not apply to any contribution of qualified appreciated stock.

(B) Qualified appreciated stock.—Except as provided in subparagraph (C), for purposes of this paragraph, the term "qualified appreciated stock" means any stock of a corporation—

(i) for which (as of the date of the contribution) market quotations are readily available on an established securities market, and

(ii) which is capital gain property (as defined in subsection (b)(1)(C)(iv)).

(C) Donor may not contribute more than 10 percent of stock of corporation.—

(i) In general.—In the case of any donor, the term "qualified appreciated stock" shall not include any stock of a corporation contributed by the donor in a contribution to which paragraph (1)(B)(ii) applies (determined without regard to this paragraph) to the extent that the amount of the stock so contributed (when increased by the aggregate amount of all prior such contributions by the donor of stock in such corporation) exceeds 10 percent (in value) of all of the outstanding stock of such corporation.

(ii) Special rule.—For purposes of clause (i), an individual shall be treated as making all contributions made by any member of his family (as defined in section 267(c)(4)).

* * *

(7) Recapture of deduction on certain dispositions of exempt use property.—

(A) In general.—In the case of an applicable disposition of applicable property, there shall be included in the income of the donor of such property for the taxable year of such donor in which the applicable disposition occurs an amount equal to the excess (if any) of—

(i) the amount of the deduction allowed to the donor under this section with respect to such property, over

(ii) the donor's basis in such property at the time such property was contributed.

(B) Applicable disposition.—For purposes of this paragraph, the term "applicable disposition" means any sale, exchange, or other disposition by the donee of applicable property—

(i) after the last day of the taxable year of the donor in which such property was contributed, and

(ii) before the last day of the 3–year period beginning on the date of the contribution of such property,

unless the donee makes a certification in accordance with subparagraph (D).

(C) Applicable property.—For purposes of this paragraph, the term "applicable property" means charitable deduction property (as defined in section 6050L(a)(2)(A))—

(i) which is tangible personal property the use of which is identified by the donee as related to the purpose or function constituting the basis of the donee's exemption under section 501, and

(ii) for which a deduction in excess of the donor's basis is allowed.

(D) Certification.—A certification meets the requirements of this subparagraph if it is a written statement which is signed under penalty of perjury by an officer of the donee organization and—

(i) which—

(I) certifies that the use of the property by the donee was substantial and related to the purpose or function constituting the basis for the donee's exemption under section 501, and

(II) describes how the property was used and how such use furthered such purpose or function, or

(ii) which—

(I) states the intended use of the property by the donee at the time of the contribution, and

(II) certifies that such intended use has become impossible or infeasible to implement.

(f) Disallowance of deduction in certain cases and special rules.—

(1) In general.—No deduction shall be allowed under this section for a contribution to or for the use of an organization or trust described in section 508(d) or 4948(c)(4) subject to the conditions specified in such sections.

(2) Contributions of property placed in trust.—

(A) Remainder interest.—In the case of property transferred in trust, no deduction shall be allowed under this section for the value of a contribution of a remainder interest unless the trust is a charitable remainder annuity trust or a charitable remainder unitrust (described in section 664), or a pooled income fund (described in section 642(c)(5)).

(B) Income interests, etc.—No deduction shall be allowed under this section for the value of any interest in property (other than a remainder interest) transferred in trust unless the interest is in the form of a guaranteed annuity or the trust instrument specifies that the interest is a fixed percentage distributed yearly of the fair market value of the trust property (to be determined yearly) and the grantor is treated as the owner of such interest for purposes of applying section 671. If the donor ceases to be treated as the owner of such an interest for purposes of applying section 671, at the time the donor ceases to be so treated, the donor shall for purposes of this chapter be considered as having received an amount of income equal to the amount of any deduction he received under this section for the contribution reduced by the discounted value of all amounts of income earned by the trust and taxable to him before the time at which he ceases to be treated as the owner of the interest. Such amounts of income shall be discounted to the date of the contribution. The Secretary shall prescribe such regulations as may be necessary to carry out the purposes of this subparagraph.

(C) Denial of deduction in case of payments by certain trusts.—In any case in which a deduction is allowed under this section for the value of an interest in property described in subparagraph (B), transferred in trust, no deduction shall be allowed under this section to the grantor or any other person for the amount of any contribution made by the trust with respect to such interest.

(D) Exception.—This paragraph shall not apply in a case in which the value of all interests in property transferred in trust are deductible under subsection (a).

(3) Denial of deduction in case of certain contributions of partial interests in property.—

(A) In general.—In the case of a contribution (not made by a transfer in trust) of an interest in property which consists of less than the taxpayer's entire interest in such property, a deduction shall be allowed under this section only to the extent that the value of the interest contributed would be allowable as a deduction under this section if such interest had been transferred in trust. For purposes of this subparagraph, a contribution by a taxpayer of the right to use property shall be treated as a contribution of less than the taxpayer's entire interest in such property.

(B) Exceptions.—Subparagraph (A) shall not apply to—

(i) a contribution of a remainder interest in a personal residence or farm,

(ii) a contribution of an undivided portion of the taxpayer's entire interest in property, and

(iii) a qualified conservation contribution.

(4) Valuation of remainder interest in real property.—For purposes of this section, in determining the value of a remainder interest in real property, depreciation (computed on the straight line method) and depletion of such property shall be taken into account, and such value shall be discounted at a rate of 6 percent per annum, except that the Secretary may prescribe a different rate.

(5) Reduction for certain interest.—If, in connection with any charitable contribution, a liability is assumed by the recipient or by any other person, or if a charitable contribution is of property which is subject to a liability, then, to the extent necessary to avoid the duplication of amounts, the amount taken into account for purposes of this section as the amount of the charitable contribution—

(A) shall be reduced for interest (i) which has been paid (or is to be paid) by the taxpayer, (ii) which is attributable to the liability, and (iii) which is attributable to any period after the making of the contribution, and

(B) in the case of a bond, shall be further reduced for interest (i) which has been paid (or is to be paid) by the taxpayer on indebtedness incurred or continued to purchase or carry such bond, and (ii) which is attributable to any period before the making of the contribution.

The reduction pursuant to subparagraph (B) shall not exceed the interest (including interest equivalent) on the bond which is attributable to any period before the making of the contribution and which is not (under the taxpayer's method of accounting) includible in the gross income of the taxpayer for any taxable year. For purposes of this paragraph, the term "bond" means any bond, debenture, note, or certificate or other evidence of indebtedness.

(6) Deductions for out-of-pocket expenditures.—No deduction shall be allowed under this section for an out-of-pocket expenditure made by any person on behalf of an organization described in subsection (c) (other than an organization described in section 501(h)(5) (relating to churches, etc.)) if the expenditure is made for the purpose of influencing legislation (within the meaning of section 501(c)(3)).

(7) Reformations to comply with paragraph (2).—

(A) In general. A deduction shall be allowed under subsection (a) in respect of any qualified reformation (within the meaning of section 2055(e)(3)(B)).

(B) Rules similar to section 2055(e)(3) to apply.—For purposes of this paragraph, rules similar to the rules of section 2055(e)(3) shall apply.

(8) Substantiation requirement for certain contributions.—

(A) General rule.—No deduction shall be allowed under subsection (a) for any contribution of $250 or more unless the taxpayer substantiates the contribution by a contemporaneous written acknowledgment of the contribution by the donee organization that meets the requirements of subparagraph (B).

(B) Content of acknowledgement.—An acknowledgement meets the requirements of this subparagraph if it includes the following information:

(i) The amount of cash and a description (but not value) of any property other than cash contributed.

(ii) Whether the donee organization provided any goods or services in consideration, in whole or in part, for any property described in clause (i).

(iii) A description and good faith estimate of the value of any goods or services referred to in clause (ii) or, if such goods or services consist solely of intangible religious benefits, a statement to that effect.

For purposes of this subparagraph, the term "intangible religious benefit" means any intangible religious benefit which is provided by an organization organized exclusively for religious purposes and which generally is not sold in a commercial transaction outside the donative context.

(C) Contemporaneous.—For purposes of subparagraph (A), an acknowledgment shall be considered to be contemporaneous if the taxpayer obtains the acknowledgment on or before the earlier of—

(i) the date on which the taxpayer files a return for the taxable year in which the contribution was made, or

(ii) the due date (including extensions) for filing such return.

(D) Substantiation not required for contributions reported by the donee organization.—Subparagraph (A) shall not apply to a contribution if the donee organization files a return, on such form and in accordance with such regulations as the Secretary may prescribe, which includes the information described in subparagraph (B) with respect to the contribution.

(E) Regulations.—The Secretary shall prescribe such regulations as may be necessary or appropriate to carry out the purposes of this paragraph, including regulations that may provide that some or all of the requirements of this paragraph do not apply in appropriate cases.

(9) Denial of deduction where contribution for lobbying activities.—No deduction shall be allowed under this section for a contribution to an organization which conducts activities to which section 162(e)(1) applies on matters of direct financial interest to the donor's trade or business, if a principal purpose of the contribution was to avoid Federal income tax by securing a deduction for such activities under this section which would be disallowed by reason of section 162(e) if the donor had conducted such activities directly. No deduction shall be allowed under section 162(a) for any amount for which a deduction is disallowed under the preceding sentence.

* * *

(11) Qualified appraisal and other documentation for certain contributions.—

(A) In general.—

(i) Denial of deduction.—In the case of an individual, partnership, or corporation, no deduction shall be allowed under subsection (a) for any contribution of property for which a deduction of more than $500 is claimed unless such person meets the requirements of subparagraphs (B), (C), and (D), as the case may be, with respect to such contribution.

(ii) Exceptions.—

(I) Readily valued property.—Subparagraphs (C) and (D) shall not apply to cash, property described in subsection (e)(1)(B)(iii) or section 1221(a)(1), publicly traded securities (as defined in section 6050L(a)(2)(B)), and any qualified vehicle described in paragraph (12)(A)(ii) for which an acknowledgement under paragraph (12)(B)(iii) is provided.

(II) Reasonable cause.—Clause (i) shall not apply if it is shown that the failure to meet such requirements is due to reasonable cause and not to willful neglect.

(B) Property description for contributions of more than $500—In the case of contributions of property for which a deduction of more than $500 is claimed, the requirements of this subparagraph are met if the individual, partnership or corporation includes with the return for the taxable year in which the contribution is made a description of such property and such other information as the Secretary may require. The requirements of this subparagraph shall not apply to a C corporation which is not a personal service corporation or a closely held C corporation.

(C) Qualified appraisal for contributions of more than $5,000—In the case of contributions of property for which a deduction of more than $5,000 is claimed, the requirements of this subparagraph are met if the individual, partnership, or corporation obtains a qualified appraisal of such property and attaches to the return for the taxable year in which such contribution is made such information regarding such property and such appraisal as the Secretary may require.

(D) Substantiation for contributions of more than $500,000.—In the case of contributions of property for which a deduction of more than $500,000 is claimed, the requirements of this subparagraph are met if the individual, partnership, or corporation attaches to the return for the taxable year a qualified appraisal of such property.

(E) Qualified appraisal and appraiser.—For purposes of this paragraph—

(i) Qualified appraisal.—The term "qualified appraisal" means, with respect to any property, an appraisal of such property which—

(I) is treated for purposes of this paragraph as a qualified appraisal under regulations or other guidance prescribed by the Secretary, and

(II) is conducted by a qualified appraiser in accordance with generally accepted appraisal standards and any regulations or other guidance prescribed under subclause (I).

(ii) Qualified appraiser.—Except as provided in clause (iii), the term "qualified appraiser" means an individual who—

(I) has earned an appraisal designation from a recognized professional appraiser organization or has otherwise met minimum education and experience requirements set forth in regulations prescribed by the Secretary,

(II) regularly performs appraisals for which the individual receives compensation, and

(III) meets such other requirements as may be prescribed by the Secretary in regulations or other guidance.

(iii) Specific appraisals.—An individual shall not be treated as a qualified appraiser with respect to any specific appraisal unless—

(I) the individual demonstrates verifiable education and experience in valuing the type of property subject to the appraisal, and

(II) the individual has not been prohibited from practicing before the Internal Revenue Service by the Secretary under section 330(c) of title 31, United States Code, at any time during the 3-year period ending on the date of the appraisal.

(F) Aggregation of similar items of property.—For purposes of determining thresholds under this paragraph, property and all similar items of property donated to 1 or more donees shall be treated as 1 property.

(G) Special rule for pass-thru entities.—In the case of a partnership or S corporation, this paragraph shall be applied at the entity level, except that the deduction shall be denied at the partner or shareholder level.

(H) Regulations.—The Secretary may prescribe such regulations as may be necessary or appropriate to carry out the purposes of this paragraph, including regulations that may provide that some or all of the requirements of this paragraph do not apply in appropriate cases.

(12) Contributions of used motor vehicles, boats, and airplanes.—

(A) In general.—In the case of a contribution of a qualified vehicle the claimed value of which exceeds $500—

(i) paragraph (8) shall not apply and no deduction shall be allowed under subsection (a) for such contribution unless the taxpayer substantiates the contribution by a contemporaneous written acknowledgement of the contribution by the donee organization that meets the requirements of subparagraph (B) and includes the acknowledgement with the taxpayer's return of tax which includes the deduction, and

(ii) if the organization sells the vehicle without any significant intervening use or material improvement of such vehicle by the organization, the amount of the deduction allowed under subsection (a) shall not exceed the gross proceeds received from such sale.

(B) Content of acknowledgement.—An acknowledgement meets the requirements of this subparagraph if it includes the following information:

(i) The name and taxpayer identification number of the donor.

(ii) The vehicle identification number or similar number.

(iii) In the case of a qualified vehicle to which subparagraph (A)(ii) applies—

(I) a certification that the vehicle was sold in an arm's length transaction between unrelated parties,

(II) the gross proceeds from the sale, and

(III) a statement that the deductible amount may not exceed the amount of such gross proceeds.

(iv) In the case of a qualified vehicle to which subparagraph (A)(ii) does not apply–

(I) a certification of the intended use or material improvement of the vehicle and the intended duration of such use, and

(II) a certification that the vehicle would not be transferred in exchange for money, other property, or services before completion of such use or improvement.

(v) Whether the donee organization provided any goods or services in consideration, in whole or in part, for the qualified vehicle.

(vi) A description and good faith estimate of the value of any goods or services referred to in clause (v) or, if such goods or services consist solely of intangible religious benefits (as defined in paragraph (8)(B)), a statement to that effect.

(C) Contemporaneous.—For purposes of subparagraph (A), an acknowledgement shall be considered to be contemporaneous if the donee organization provides it within 30 days of—

(i) the sale of the qualified vehicle, or

(ii) in the case of an acknowledgement including a certification described in subparagraph (B)(iv), the contribution of the qualified vehicle.

(D) Information to Secretary.—A donee organization required to provide an acknowledgement under this paragraph shall provide to the Secretary the information contained in the acknowledgement. Such information shall be provided at such time and in such manner as the Secretary may prescribe.

(E) Qualified vehicle.—For purposes of this paragraph, the term "qualified vehicle" means any—

(i) motor vehicle manufactured primarily for use on public streets, roads, and highways,

(ii) boat, or

(iii) airplane.

Such term shall not include any property which is described in section 1221(a)(1).

(F) Regulations or other guidance.—The Secretary shall prescribe such regulations or other guidance as may be necessary to carry out the purposes of this paragraph. The Secretary may prescribe regulations or other guidance which exempts sales by the donee organization which are in direct furtherance of such organization's charitable purpose from the requirements of subparagraphs (A)(ii) and (B)(iv)(II).

* * *

(16) Contributions of clothing and household items.—

(A) In general.—In the case of an individual, partnership, or corporation, no deduction shall be allowed under subsection (a) for any contribution of clothing or a household item unless such clothing or household item is in good used condition or better.

(B) Items of minimal value.—Notwithstanding subparagraph (A), the Secretary may by regulation deny a deduction under subsection (a) for any contribution of clothing or a household item which has minimal monetary value.

(C) Exception for certain property.—Subparagraphs (A) and (B) shall not apply to any contribution of a single item of clothing or a household item for which a deduction of more than $500 is claimed if the taxpayer includes with the taxpayer's return a qualified appraisal with respect to the property.

(D) Household items.—For purposes of this paragraph—

(i) In general.—The term "household items" includes furniture, furnishings, electronics, appliances, linens, and other similar items.

(ii) Excluded items.—Such term does not include—

(I) food,

(II) paintings, antiques, and other objects of art,

(III) jewelry and gems, and

(IV) collections.

(E) Special rule for pass-thru entities.—In the case of a partnership or S corporation, this paragraph shall be applied at the entity level, except that the deduction shall be denied at the partner or shareholder level.

(17) Recordkeeping.—No deduction shall be allowed under subsection (a) for any contribution of a cash, check, or other monetary gift unless the donor maintains as a record of such contribution a bank record or a written communication from the donee showing the name of the donee organization, the date of the contribution, and the amount of the contribution.

* * *

(g) Amounts paid to maintain certain students as members of taxpayer's household.—

(1) In general.—Subject to the limitations provided by paragraph (2), amounts paid by the taxpayer to maintain an individual (other than a dependent, as defined in section 152 (determined without regard to subsections (b)(1), (b)(2) and (d)(1)(B) thereof), or a relative of the taxpayer) as a member of his household during the period that such individual is—

(A) a member of the taxpayer's household under a written agreement between the taxpayer and an organization described in paragraph (2), (3), or (4) of subsection (c) to implement a program of the organization to provide educational opportunities for pupils or students in private homes, and

(B) a full-time pupil or student in the twelfth or any lower grade at an educational organization described in section 170(b)(1)(A)(ii) located in the United States,

shall be treated as amounts paid for the use of the organization.

(2) Limitations.—

(A) Amount.—Paragraph (1) shall apply to amounts paid within the taxable year only to the extent that such amounts do not exceed $50 multiplied by the number of full calendar months during the taxable year which fall within the period described in paragraph (1). For purposes of the preceding sentence, if 15 or more days of a calendar month fall within such period such month shall be considered as a full calendar month.

(B) Compensation or reimbursement.—Paragraph (1) shall not apply to any amount paid by the taxpayer within the taxable year if the taxpayer receives any money or other property as compensation or reimbursement for maintaining the individual in his household during the period described in paragraph (1).

(3) Relative defined.—For purposes of paragraph (1), the term "relative of the taxpayer" means an individual who, with respect to the taxpayer, bears any of the relationships described in subparagraphs (A) through (G) of section 152(d)(2).

(4) No other amount allowed as deduction.—No deduction shall be allowed under subsection (a) for any amount paid by a taxpayer to maintain an individual as a member of his household under a program described in paragraph (1)(A) except as provided in this subsection.

(h) Qualified conservation contribution.—

(1) In general.—For purposes of subsection (f)(3)(B)(iii), the term "qualified conservation contribution" means a contribution—

(A) of a qualified real property interest,

(B) to a qualified organization,

(C) exclusively for conservation purposes.

(2) Qualified real property interest.—For purposes of this subsection, the term "qualified real property interest" means any of the following interests in real property:

(A) the entire interest of the donor other than a qualified mineral interest,

(B) a remainder interest, and

(C) a restriction (granted in perpetuity) on the use which may be made of the real property.

(3) Qualified organization.—For purposes of paragraph (1), the term "qualified organization" means an organization which—

(A) is described in clause (v) or (vi) of subsection (b)(1)(A), or

(B) is described in section 501(c)(3) and—

(i) meets the requirements of section 509(a)(2), or

(ii) meets the requirements of section 509(a)(3) and is controlled by an organization described in subparagraph (A) or in clause (i) of this subparagraph.

(4) Conservation purpose defined.—

(A) In general.—For purposes of this subsection, the term "conservation purpose" means—

(i) the preservation of land areas for outdoor recreation by, or the education of, the general public,

(ii) the protection of a relatively natural habitat of fish, wildlife, or plants, or similar ecosystem,

(iii) the preservation of open space (including farmland and forest land) where such preservation is—

(I) for the scenic enjoyment of the general public, or

(II) pursuant to a clearly delineated Federal, State, or local governmental conservation policy,

and will yield a significant public benefit, or

(iv) the preservation of an historically important land area or a certified historic structure.

(B) Special rules with respect to buildings in registered historic districts.— In the case of any contribution of a qualified real property interest which is a restriction with respect to the exterior of a building described in subparagraph (C)(ii), such contribution shall not be considered to be exclusively for conservation purposes unless—

(i) such interest—

(I) includes a restriction which preserves the entire exterior of the building (including the front, sides, rear, and height of the building), and

(II) prohibits any change in the exterior of the building which is inconsistent with the historical character of such exterior,

(ii) the donor and donee enter into a written agreement certifying, under penalty of perjury, that the donee—

(I) is a qualified organization (as defined in paragraph (3)) with a purpose of environmental protection, land conservation, open space preservation, or historic preservation, and

(II) has the resources to manage and enforce the restriction and a commitment to do so, and

(iii) in the case of any contribution made in a taxable year beginning after the date of the enactment of this subparagraph, the taxpayer includes with the taxpayer's return for the taxable year of the contribution—

(I) a qualified appraisal (within the meaning of subsection (f)(11)(E)) of the qualified property interest,

(II) photographs of the entire exterior of the building, and

(III) a description of all restrictions on the development of the building.

(C) Certified historic structure.—For purposes of subparagraph (A)(iv), the term "certified historic structure" means—

(i) any building, structure, or land area which is listed in the National Register, or

(ii) any building which is located in a registered historic district (as defined in section 47(c)(3)(B)) and is certified by the Secretary of the Interior to the Secretary as being of historic significance to the district.

A building, structure, or land area satisfies the preceding sentence if it satisfies such sentence either at the time of the transfer or on the due date (including extensions) for filing the transferor's return under this chapter for the taxable year in which the transfer is made.

(5) Exclusively for conservation purposes.—For purposes of this subsection—

(A) Conservation purpose must be protected.—A contribution shall not be treated as exclusively for conservation purposes unless the conservation purpose is protected in perpetuity.

* * *

(i) Standard mileage rate for use of passenger automobile.—For purposes of computing the deduction under this section for use of a passenger automobile the standard mileage rate shall be 14 cents per mile.

(j) Denial of deduction for certain travel expenses.—No deduction shall be allowed under this section for traveling expenses (including amounts expended for meals and lodging) while away from home, whether paid directly or by reimbursement, unless there is no significant element of personal pleasure, recreation, or vacation in such travel.

* * *

(*l*) Treatment of certain amounts paid to or for the benefit of institutions of higher education.—

(1) In general.—For purposes of this section, 80 percent of any amount described in paragraph (2) shall be treated as a charitable contribution.

(2) Amount described.—For purposes of paragraph (1), an amount is described in this paragraph if—

(A) the amount is paid by the taxpayer to or for the benefit of an educational organization—

(i) which is described in subsection (b)(1)(A)(ii), and

(ii) which is an institution of higher education (as defined in section 3304(f)), and

(B) such amount would be allowable as a deduction under this section but for the fact that the taxpayer receives (directly or indirectly) as a result of paying such amount the right to purchase tickets for seating at an athletic event in an athletic stadium of such institution.

If any portion of a payment is for the purchase of such tickets, such portion and the remaining portion (if any) of such payment shall be treated as separate amounts for purposes of this subsection.

(m) Certain donee income from intellectual property treated as an additional charitable contribution.—

(1) Treatment as additional contribution.—In the case of a taxpayer who makes a qualified intellectual property contribution, the deduction allowed under subsection (a) for each taxable year of the taxpayer ending on or after the date of such contribution shall be increased (subject to the limitations under subsection (b)) by the applicable percentage of qualified donee income with respect to such contribution which is properly allocable to such year under this subsection.

(2) Reduction in additional deductions to extent of initial deduction.— With respect to any qualified intellectual property contribution, the deduction allowed under subsection (a) shall be increased under paragraph (1) only to the extent that the aggregate amount of such increases with respect to such contribution exceed the amount allowed as a deduction under subsection (a) with respect to such contribution determined without regard to this subsection.

(3) Qualified donee income.—For purposes of this subsection, the term "qualified donee income" means any net income received by or accrued to the donee which is properly allocable to the qualified intellectual property.

(4) Allocation of qualified donee income to taxable years of donor.—For purposes of this subsection, qualified donee income shall be treated as properly allocable to a taxable year of the donor if such income is received by or accrued to the donee for the taxable year of the donee which ends within or with such taxable year of the donor.

(5) 10–year limitation.—Income shall not be treated as properly allocable to qualified intellectual property for purposes of this subsection if such income is received by or accrued to the donee after the 10–year period beginning on the date of the contribution of such property.

(6) Benefit limited to life of intellectual property.—Income shall not be treated as properly allocable to qualified intellectual property for purposes of this subsection if such income is received by or accrued to the donee after the expiration of the legal life of such property.

(7) Applicable percentage.—For purposes of this subsection, the term "applicable percentage" means the percentage determined under the following table which corresponds to a taxable year of the donor ending on or after the date of the qualified intellectual property contribution:

Taxable Year of Donor Ending on or After Date of Contribution:	**Applicable Percentage:**
1st	100
2nd	100
3rd	90
4th	80
5th	70
6th	60
7th	50
8th	40
9th	30
10th	20
11th	10

Taxable Year of Donor Ending on or After Date of Contribution:	Applicable Percentage:
12th	10.

(8) Qualified intellectual property contribution—For purposes of this subsection, the term "qualified intellectual property contribution" means any charitable contribution of qualified intellectual property—

(A) the amount of which taken into account under this section is reduced by reason of subsection (e)(1), and

(B) with respect to which the donor informs the donee at the time of such contribution that the donor intends to treat such contribution as a qualified intellectual property contribution for purposes of this subsection and section 6050L.

(9) Qualified intellectual property—For purposes of this subsection, the term "qualified intellectual property" means property described in subsection (e)(1)(B)(iii) (other than property contributed to or for the use of an organization described in subsection (e)(1)(B)(ii)).

(10) Other special rules—

(A) Application of limitations on charitable contributions—Any increase under this subsection of the deduction provided under subsection (a) shall be treated for purposes of subsection (b) as a deduction which is attributable to a charitable contribution to the donee to which such increase relates.

(B) Net income determined by donee—The net income taken into account under paragraph (3) shall not exceed the amount of such income reported under section 6050L(b)(1).

(C) Deduction limited to 12 taxable years.—Except as may be provided under subparagraph (D)(i), this subsection shall not apply with respect to any qualified intellectual property contribution for any taxable year of the donor after the 12th taxable year of the donor which ends on or after the date of such contribution.

(D) Regulations—The Secretary may issue regulations or other guidance to carry out the purposes of this subsection, including regulations or guidance—

(i) modifying the application of this subsection in the case of a donor or donee with a short taxable year, and

(ii) providing for the determination of an amount to be treated as net income of the donee which is properly allocable to qualified intellectual property in the case of a donee who uses such property to further a purpose or function constituting the basis of the donee's exemption under section 501 (or, in the case of a governmental unit, any purpose described in section 170(c)) and does not possess a right to receive any payment from a third party with respect to such property.

* * *

(*o*) Special rules for fractional gifts.—

(1) Denial of deduction in certain cases.—

(A) In general.—No deduction shall be allowed for a contribution of an undivided portion of a taxpayer's entire interest in tangible personal property unless all interests in the property are held immediately before such contribution by—

(i) the taxpayer, or

(ii) the taxpayer and the donee.

(B) Exceptions.—The Secretary may, by regulation, provide for exceptions to subparagraph (A) in cases where all persons who hold an interest in the property make proportional contributions of an undivided portion of the entire interest held by such persons.

(2) Valuation of subsequent gifts.—In the case of any additional contribution, the fair market value of such contribution shall be determined by using the lesser of—

(A) the fair market value of the property at the time of the initial fractional contribution, or

(B) the fair market value of the property at the time of the additional contribution.

(3) Recapture of deduction in certain cases; addition to tax.—

(A) Recapture.—The Secretary shall provide for the recapture of the amount of any deduction allowed under this section (plus interest) with respect to any contribution of an undivided portion of a taxpayer's entire interest in tangible personal property—

(i) in any case in which the donor does not contribute all of the remaining interests in such property to the donee (or, if such donee is no longer in existence, to any person described in section 170(c)) on or before the earlier of—

(I) the date that is 10 years after the date of the initial fractional contribution, or

(II) the date of the death of the donor, and

(ii) in any case in which the donee has not, during the period beginning on the date of the initial fractional contribution and ending on the date described in clause (i)—

(I) had substantial physical possession of the property, and

(II) used the property in a use which is related to a purpose or function constituting the basis for the organizations' exemption under section 501.

(B) Addition to tax.—The tax imposed under this chapter for any taxable year for which there is a recapture under subparagraph (A) shall be increased by 10 percent of the amount so recaptured.

(4) Definitions.—For purposes of this subsection—

(A) Additional contribution.—The term "additional contribution" means any charitable contribution by the taxpayer of any interest in property with respect to which the taxpayer has previously made an initial fractional contribution.

(B) Initial fractional contribution.—The term "initial fractional contribution" means, with respect to any taxpayer, the first charitable contribution of an undivided portion of the taxpayer's entire interest in any tangible personal property.

* * *

§ 171. Amortizable bond premium

(a) General rule.—In the case of any bond, as defined in subsection (d), the following rules shall apply to the amortizable bond premium (determined under subsection (b)) on the bond:

(1) Taxable bonds.—In the case of a bond (other than a bond the interest on which is excludable from gross income), the amount of the amortizable bond premium for the taxable year shall be allowed as a deduction.

(2) Tax-exempt bonds.—In the case of any bond the interest on which is excludable from gross income, no deduction shall be allowed for the amortizable bond premium for the taxable year.

(3) Cross reference.—

For adjustment to basis on account of amortizable bond premium, see section 1016(a)(5).

(b) Amortizable bond premium.—

(1) Amount of bond premium.—For purposes of paragraph (2), the amount of bond premium, in the case of the holder of any bond, shall be determined—

(A) with reference to the amount of the basis (for determining loss on sale or exchange) of such bond,

(B)(i) with reference to the amount payable on maturity or on earlier call date, in the case of any bond other than a bond to which clause (ii) applies, or and

(ii) with reference to the amount payable on maturity (or if it results in a smaller amortizable bond premium attributable to the period of earlier call date, with reference to the amount payable on earlier call date), in the case of any bond described in subsection (a)(1) which is acquired after December 31, 1957, and

(C) with adjustments proper to reflect unamortized bond premium, with respect to the bond, for the period before the date as of which subsection (a) becomes applicable with respect to the taxpayer with respect to such bond.

In no case shall the amount of bond premium on a convertible bond include any amount attributable to the conversion features of the bond.

(2) Amount amortizable.—The amortizable bond premium of the taxable year shall be the amount of the bond premium attributable to such year. In the case of a bond to which paragraph (1)(B)(ii) applies and which has a call date, the amount of bond premium attributable to the taxable year in which the bond is called shall include an amount equal to the excess of the amount of the adjusted basis (for determining loss on sale or exchange) of such bond as of the beginning of the taxable year over the amount received on redemption of the bond or (if greater) the amount payable on maturity.

(3) Method of determination.—

(A) In general.—Except as provided in regulations prescribed by the Secretary, the determinations required under paragraphs (1) and(2) shall be made on the basis of the taxpayer's yield to maturity determined by—

(i) using the taxpayer's basis (for purposes of determining loss on sale or exchange) of the obligation, and

(ii) compounding at the close of each accrual period (as defined in section 1272(a)(5)).

(B) Special rule where earlier call date is used.—For purposes of subparagraph (A), if the amount payable on an earlier call date is used under paragraph (1)(B)(ii) in determining the amortizable bond premium attributable to the period before the earlier call date, such bond shall be treated as maturing on such date for the amount so payable and then reissued on such date for the amount so payable.

(4) Treatment of certain bonds acquired in exchange for other property.—

(A) In general.—If—

(i) a bond is acquired by any person in exchange for other property, and

(ii) the basis of such bond is determined (in whole or in part) by reference to the basis of such other property,

for purposes of applying this subsection to such bond while held by such person, the basis of such bond shall not exceed its fair market value immediately after the exchange. A similar rule shall apply in the case of such bond while held by any other person whose basis is determined (in whole or in part) by reference to the basis in the hands of the person referred to in clause (i).

(B) Special rule where bond exchanged in reorganization.—Subparagraph (A) shall not apply to an exchange by the taxpayer of a bond for another bond if such exchange is a part of a reorganization (as defined in section 368). If any portion of the basis of the taxpayer in a bond transferred in such an exchange is not taken into account in determining bond premium by reason of this paragraph, such portion shall not be taken into account in determining the amount of bond premium on any bond received in the exchange.

(c) Election as to taxable bonds.—

(1) Eligibility to elect; bonds with respect to which election permitted.—In the case of bonds the interest on which is not excludible from gross income, this section shall apply only if the taxpayer has so elected.

(2) Manner and effect of election.—The election authorized under this subsection shall be made in accordance with such regulations as the Secretary shall prescribe. If such election is made with respect to any bond (described in paragraph (1)) of the taxpayer, it shall also apply to all such bonds held by the taxpayer at the beginning of the first taxable year to which the election applies and to all such bonds thereafter acquired by him and shall be binding for all subsequent taxable years with respect to all such bonds of the taxpayer, unless, on application by the taxpayer, the Secretary permits him, subject to such conditions as the Secretary deems necessary, to revoke such election. In the case of bonds held by a common trust fund, as defined in section 584(a), the election authorized under this subsection shall be exercisable with respect to such bonds only by the common trust fund. In case of bonds held by an estate or trust, the election authorized under this subsection shall be exercisable with respect to such bonds only by the fiduciary.

(d) Bond defined.—For purposes of this section, the term "bond" means any bond, debenture, note, or certificate or other evidence of indebtedness, but does not include any such obligation which constitutes stock in trade of the taxpayer or any such obligation of a kind which would properly be included in the inventory of the taxpayer if on hand at the close of the taxable year, or any such obligation held by the taxpayer primarily for sale to customers in the ordinary course of his trade or business.

(e) Treatment as offset to interest payments.—Except as provided in regulations, in the case of any taxable bond—

(1) the amount of any bond premium shall be allocated among the interest payments on the bond under rules similar to the rules of subsection (b)(3), and

(2) in lieu of any deduction under subsection (a), the amount of any premium so allocated to any interest payment shall be applied against (and operate to reduce) the amount of such interest payment.

For purposes of the preceding sentence, the term "taxable bond" means any bond the interest of which is not excludable from gross income.

* * *

§ 172. Net operating loss deduction

(a) Deduction allowed.—There shall be allowed as a deduction for the taxable year an amount equal to the aggregate of (1) the net operating loss carryovers to such year, plus (2) the net operating loss carrybacks to such year. For purposes of this subtitle, the term "net operating loss deduction" means the deduction allowed by this subsection.

(b) Net operating loss carrybacks and carryovers.—

(1) Years to which loss may be carried.—

(A) General rule.—Except as otherwise provided in this paragraph, a net operating loss for any taxable year—

(i) shall be a net operating loss carryback to each of the 2 taxable years preceding the taxable year of such loss, and

(ii) shall be a net operating loss carryover to each of the 20 taxable years following the taxable year of the loss.

* * *

(2) Amount of carrybacks and carryovers.—The entire amount of the net operating loss for any taxable year (hereinafter in this section referred to as the "loss year") shall be carried to the earliest of the taxable years to which (by reason of paragraph (1)) such loss may be carried. The portion of such loss which shall be carried to each of the other taxable years shall be the excess, if any, of the amount of such loss over the sum of the taxable income for each of the prior taxable years to which such loss may be carried. For purposes of the preceding sentence, the taxable income for any such prior taxable year shall be computed—

(A) with the modifications specified in subsection (d) other than paragraphs (1), (4), and (5) thereof, and

(B) by determining the amount of the net operating loss deduction without regard to the net operating loss for the loss year or for any taxable year thereafter,

and the taxable income so computed shall not be considered to be less than zero.

(3) Election to waive carryback.—Any taxpayer entitled to a carryback period under paragraph (1) may elect to relinquish the entire carryback period with respect to a net operating loss for any taxable year. Such election shall be made in such manner as may be prescribed by the Secretary, and shall be made by the due date (including extensions of time) for filing the taxpayer's return for the taxable year of the net operating loss for which the election is to be in effect. Such election, once made for any taxable year, shall be irrevocable for such taxable year.

(c) Net operating loss defined.—For purposes of this section, the term "net operating loss" means the excess of the deductions allowed by this chapter over the gross income. Such excess shall be computed with the modifications specified in subsection (d).

(d) Modifications.—The modifications referred to in this section are as follows:

(1) Net operating loss deduction.—No net operating loss deduction shall be allowed.

(2) Capital gains and losses of taxpayers other than corporations.—In the case of a taxpayer other than a corporation—

(A) the amount deductible on account of losses from sales or exchanges of capital assets shall not exceed the amount includable on account of gains from sales or exchanges of capital assets; and

(B) the exclusion provided by section 1202 shall not be allowed.

(3) Deduction for personal exemptions.—No deduction shall be allowed under section 151 (relating to personal exemptions). No deduction in lieu of any such deduction shall be allowed.

(4) Nonbusiness deductions of taxpayers other than corporations.—In the case of a taxpayer other than a corporation, the deductions allowable by this chapter which are not attributable to a taxpayer's trade or business shall be allowed only to the extent of the amount of the gross income not derived from such trade or business. For purposes of the preceding sentence—

(A) any gain or loss from the sale or other disposition of—

(i) property, used in the trade or business, of a character which is subject to the allowance for depreciation provided in section 167, or

(ii) real property used in the trade or business,

shall be treated as attributable to the trade or business;

(B) the modifications specified in paragraphs (1), (2)(B), and (3) shall be taken into account;

(C) any deduction for casualty or theft losses allowable under paragraph (2) or (3) of section 165(c) shall be treated as attributable to the trade or business; and

(D) any deduction allowed under section 404 to the extent attributable to contributions which are made on behalf of an individual who is an employee within the meaning of section 401(c)(1) shall not be treated as attributable to the trade or business of such individual.

* * *

(7) Manufacturing deduction.—The deduction under section 199 shall not be allowed.

(e) Law applicable to computations.—In determining the amount of any net operating loss carryback or carryover to any taxable year, the necessary computations involving any other taxable year shall be made under the law applicable to such other taxable year.

* * *

(k) Cross references.—

(1) For treatment of net operating loss carryovers in certain corporate acquisitions, see section 381.

(2) For special limitation on net operating loss carryovers in case of a corporate change of ownership, see section 382.

§ 173. Circulation expenditures

(a) General rule.—Notwithstanding section 263, all expenditures (other than expenditures for the purchase of land or depreciable property or for the acquisition of circulation through the purchase of any part of the business of another publisher of a newspaper, magazine, or other periodical) to establish, maintain, or increase the circulation of a newspaper, magazine or other periodical shall be allowed as a deduction; except that the deduction shall not be allowed with respect to the portion of such expenditures as, under regulations prescribed by the Secretary, is chargeable to capital account if the taxpayer elects, in accordance with such regulations, to treat such portion as so chargeable. Such election, if made, must be for the total amount of such portion of the expenditures which is so chargeable to capital account, and shall be binding for all subsequent taxable years unless, upon application by the taxpayer, the Secretary permits a revocation of such election subject to such conditions as he deems necessary.

* * *

§ 174. Research and experimental expenditures

(a) Treatment as expenses.—

(1) In general.—A taxpayer may treat research or experimental expenditures which are paid or incurred by him during the taxable year in connection with his trade or business as expenses which are not chargeable to capital account. The expenditures so treated shall be allowed as a deduction.

(2) When method may be adopted.—

(A) Without consent.—A taxpayer may, without the consent of the Secretary, adopt the method provided in this subsection for his first taxable year—

(i) which begins after December 31, 1953, and ends after August 16, 1954, and

(ii) for which expenditures described in paragraph (1) are paid or incurred.

(B) With consent.—A taxpayer may, with the consent of the Secretary, adopt at any time the method provided in this subsection.

(3) Scope.—The method adopted under this subsection shall apply to all expenditures described in paragraph (1). The method adopted shall be adhered to in computing taxable income for the taxable year and for all subsequent taxable years unless, with the approval of the Secretary, a change to a different method is authorized with respect to part or all of such expenditures.

(b) Amortization of certain research and experimental expenditures.—

(1) In general.—At the election of the taxpayer, made in accordance with regulations prescribed by the Secretary, research or experimental expenditures which are—

(A) paid or incurred by the taxpayer in connection with his trade or business,

(B) not treated as expenses under subsection (a), and

(C) chargeable to capital account but not chargeable to property of a character which is subject to the allowance under section 167 (relating to allowance for depreciation, etc.) or section 611 (relating to allowance for depletion),

may be treated as deferred expenses. In computing taxable income, such deferred expenses shall be allowed as a deduction ratably over such period of not less than 60 months as may be selected by the taxpayer (beginning with the month in which the taxpayer first realizes benefits from such expenditures). Such deferred expenses are expenditures properly chargeable to capital account for purposes of section 1016(a)(1) (relating to adjustments to basis of property).

(2) Time for and scope of election.—The election provided by paragraph (1) may be made for any taxable year beginning after December 31, 1953, but only if made not later than the time prescribed by law for filing the return for such taxable year (including extensions thereof). The method so elected, and the period selected by the taxpayer, shall be adhered to in computing taxable income for the taxable year for which the election is made and for all subsequent taxable years unless, with the approval of the Secretary, a change to a different method (or to a different period) is authorized with respect to part or all of such expenditures. The election shall not apply to any expenditure paid or incurred during any taxable year before the taxable year for which the taxpayer makes the election.

(c) Land and other property.—This section shall not apply to any expenditure for the acquisition or improvement of land, or for the acquisition or improvement of property to be used in connection with the research or experimentation and of a character which is subject to the allowance under section 167 (relating to allowance for depreciation, etc.) or section 611 (relating to allowance for depletion); but for purposes of this section allowances under section 167, and allowances under section 611, shall be considered as expenditures.

(d) Exploration expenditures.—This section shall not apply to any expenditure paid or incurred for the purpose of ascertaining the existence, location, extent, or quality of any deposit of ore or other mineral (including oil and gas).

(e) Only reasonable research expenditures eligible.—This section shall apply to a research or experimental expenditure only to the extent that the amount thereof is reasonable under the circumstances.

* * *

§ 178. Amortization of cost of acquiring a lease

(a) General rule.—In determining the amount of the deduction allowable to a lessee for exhaustion, wear and tear, obsolescence, or amortization in respect of any cost of acquiring the lease, the term of the lease shall be treated as including all renewal options (and any other period for which the parties reasonably expect the lease to be renewed) if less than 75 percent of such cost is attributable to the period of the term of the lease remaining on the date of its acquisition.

(b) Certain periods excluded.—For purposes of subsection (a), in determining the period of the term of the lease remaining on the date of acquisition, there shall not be taken into account any period for which the lease may subsequently be renewed, extended, or continued pursuant to an option exercisable by the lessee.

§ 179. Election to expense certain depreciable business assets

(a) Treatment as expenses.—A taxpayer may elect to treat the cost of any section 179 property as an expense which is not chargeable to capital account. Any cost so treated shall be allowed as a deduction for the taxable year in which the section 179 property is placed in service.

(b) Limitations.—

(1) Dollar limitation.—The aggregate cost which may be taken into account under subsection (a) for any taxable year shall not exceed—

(A) $250,000 in the case of taxable years beginning after 2007 and before 2010,

(B) $500,000 in the case of taxable years beginning in 2010, 2011, 2012, 2013, and

(C) $25,000 in the case of taxable years beginning after 2013.

(2) Reduction in limitation.—The limitation under paragraph (1) for any taxable year shall be reduced (but not below zero) by the amount by which the cost of section 179 property placed in service during such taxable year exceeds—

(A) $800,000 in the case of taxable years beginning after 2007 and before 2010,

(B) $2,000,000 in the case of taxable years beginning in 2010, 2011, 2012, 2013, and

(C) $200,000 in the case of taxable years beginning after 2013.

(3) Limitation based on income from trade or business.—

(A) In general.—The amount allowed as a deduction under subsection (a) for any taxable year (determined after the application of paragraphs (1) and (2)) shall not exceed the aggregate amount of taxable income of the taxpayer for such taxable year which is derived from the active conduct by the taxpayer of any trade or business during such taxable year.

(B) Carryover of disallowed deduction.—The amount allowable as a deduction under subsection (a) for any taxable year shall be increased by the lesser of—

(i) the aggregate amount disallowed under subparagraph (A) for all prior taxable years (to the extent not previously allowed as a deduction by reason of this subparagraph), or

(ii) the excess (if any) of—

(I) the limitation of paragraphs (1) and (2) (or if lesser, the aggregate amount of taxable income referred to in subparagraph (A)), over

(II) the amount allowable as a deduction under subsection (a) for such taxable year without regard to this subparagraph.

(C) Computation of taxable income.—For purposes of this paragraph, taxable income derived from the conduct of a trade or business shall be computed without regard to the deduction allowable under this section.

(4) Married individuals filing separately.—In the case of a husband and wife filing separate returns for the taxable year—

(A) such individuals shall be treated as 1 taxpayer for purposes of paragraphs (1) and (2), and

(B) unless such individuals elect otherwise, 50 percent of the cost which may be taken into account under subsection (a) for such taxable year (before application of paragraph (3)) shall be allocated to each such individual.

(5) Limitation on cost taken into account for certain passenger vehicles.—

(A) In general.—The cost of any sport utility vehicle for any taxable year which may be taken into account under this section shall not exceed $25,000.

(B) Sport utility vehicle.—For purposes of subparagraph (A)—

(i) In general.—The term "sport utility vehicle" means any 4-wheeled vehicle—

(I) which is primarily designed or which can be used to carry passengers over public streets, roads, or highways (except any vehicle operated exclusively on a rail or rails),

(II) which is not subject to section 280F, and

(III) which is rated at not more than 14,000 pounds gross vehicle weight.

(ii) Certain vehicles excluded.—Such term does not include any vehicle which—

(I) is designed to have a seating capacity of more than 9 persons behind the driver's seat,

(II) is equipped with a cargo area of at least 6 feet in interior length which is an open area or is designed for use as an open area but is enclosed by a cap and is not readily accessible directly from the passenger compartment, or

(III) has an integral enclosure, fully enclosing the driver compartment and load carrying device, does not have seating rearward of the driver's seat, and has no body section protruding more than 30 inches ahead of the leading edge of the windshield.

(c) Election.—

(1) In general.—An election under this section for any taxable year shall—

(A) specify the items of section 179 property to which the election applies and the portion of the cost of each of such items which is to be taken into account under subsection (a), and

(B) be made on the taxpayer's return of the tax imposed by this chapter for the taxable year.

Such election shall be made in such manner as the Secretary may by regulations prescribe.

(2) Election irrevocable.—Any election made under this section, and any specification contained in any such election, may not be revoked except with the consent of the Secretary. Any such election or specification with respect to any taxable year beginning after 2002 and before 2014 may be revoked by the taxpayer with respect to any property, and such revocation, once made, shall be irrevocable.

(d) Definitions and special rules.—

(1) Section 179 property.—For purposes of this section, the term "section 179 property" means property—

(A) which is—

(i) tangible property (to which section 168 applies), or

(ii) computer software (as defined in section 197(e)(3)(B)) which is described in section 197(e)(3)(A)(i), to which section 167 applies, and which is placed in service in a taxable year beginning after 2002 and before 2014,

(B) which is section 1245 property (as defined in section 1245(a)(3)), and

(C) which is acquired by purchase for use in the active conduct of a trade or business.

Such term shall not include any property described in section 50(b) and shall not include air conditioning or heating units.

(2) Purchase defined.—For purposes of paragraph (1), the term "purchase" means any acquisition of property, but only if—

(A) the property is not acquired from a person whose relationship to the person acquiring it would result in the disallowance of losses under section 267 or 707(b) (but, in applying section 267(b) and (c) for purposes of this section, paragraph (4) of section 267(c) shall be treated as providing that the family of an individual shall include only his spouse, ancestors, and lineal descendants),

(B) the property is not acquired by one component member of a controlled group from another component member of the same controlled group, and

(C) the basis of the property in the hands of the person acquiring it is not determined—

(i) in whole or in part by reference to the adjusted basis of such property in the hands of the person from whom acquired, or

(ii) under section 1014(a) (relating to property acquired from a decedent).

(3) Cost.—For purposes of this section, the cost of property does not include so much of the basis of such property as is determined by reference to the basis of other property held at any time by the person acquiring such property.

(4) Section not to apply to estates and trusts.—This section shall not apply to estates and trusts.

(5) Section not to apply to certain noncorporate lessors.—This section shall not apply to any section 179 property which is purchased by a person who is not a corporation and with respect to which such person is the lessor unless—

(A) the property subject to the lease has been manufactured or produced by the lessor, or

(B) the term of the lease (taking into account options to renew) is less than 50 percent of the class life of the property (as defined in section 168(i)(1)), and for the period consisting of the first 12 months after the date on which the property is transferred to the lessee the sum of the deductions with respect to such property which are allowable to the lessor solely by reason of section 162 (other than rents and reimbursed amounts with respect to such property) exceeds 15 percent of the rental income produced by such property.

(6) Dollar limitation of controlled group.—For purposes of subsection (b) of this section—

(A) all component members of a controlled group shall be treated as one taxpayer, and

(B) the Secretary shall apportion the dollar limitation contained in subsection (b)(1) among the component members of such controlled group in such manner as he shall by regulations prescribe.

(7) Controlled group defined.—For purposes of paragraphs (2) and (6), the term "controlled group" has the meaning assigned to it by section 1563(a), except that, for such purposes, the phrase "more than 50 percent" shall be substituted for the phrase "at least 80 percent" each place it appears in section 1563(a)(1).

(8) Treatment of partnerships and S corporations.—In the case of a partnership, the limitations of subsection (b) shall apply with respect to the partnership and with respect to each partner. A similar rule shall apply in the case of an S corporation and its shareholders.

* * *

(10) Recapture in certain cases.—The Secretary shall, by regulations, provide for recapturing the benefit under any deduction allowable under subsection (a) with respect to any property which is not used predominantly in a trade or business at any time.

* * *

§ 183. Activities not engaged in for profit

(a) General rule.—In the case of an activity engaged in by an individual or an S corporation, if such activity is not engaged in for profit, no deduction attributable to such activity shall be allowed under this chapter except as provided in this section.

(b) Deductions allowable.—In the case of an activity not engaged in for profit to which subsection (a) applies, there shall be allowed—

(1) the deductions which would be allowable under this chapter for the taxable year without regard to whether or not such activity is engaged in for profit, and

(2) a deduction equal to the amount of the deductions which would be allowable under this chapter for the taxable year only if such activity were engaged in for profit, but only to the extent that the gross income derived from such activity for the taxable year exceeds the deductions allowable by reason of paragraph (1).

(c) Activity not engaged in for profit defined.—For purposes of this section, the term "activity not engaged in for profit" means any activity other than one with respect to which deductions are allowable for the taxable year under section 162 or under paragraph (1) or (2) of section 212.

(d) Presumption.—If the gross income derived from an activity for 3 or more of the taxable years in the period of 5 consecutive taxable years which ends with the taxable year exceeds the deductions attributable to such activity (determined without regard to whether or not such activity is engaged in for profit), then, unless the Secretary establishes to the contrary, such activity shall be presumed for purposes of this chapter for such taxable year to be an activity engaged in for profit. In the case of an activity which consists in major part of the breeding, training, showing, or racing of horses, the preceding sentence shall be applied by substituting "2" for "3" and "7" for "5".

(e) Special rule.—

(1) In general.—A determination as to whether the presumption provided by subsection (d) applies with respect to any activity shall, if the taxpayer so elects, not be made before the close of the fourth taxable year (sixth taxable year, in the case of an activity described in the last sentence of such subsection) following the taxable year in which the taxpayer first engages in the activity. For purposes of the preceding sentence, a taxpayer shall be treated as not having engaged in an activity during any taxable year beginning before January 1, 1970.

(2) Initial period.—If the taxpayer makes an election under paragraph (1), the presumption provided by subsection (d) shall apply to each taxable year in the 5–taxable year (or 7–taxable year) period beginning with the taxable year in which the taxpayer first engages in the activity, if the gross income derived from the activity for 3 (or 2 if applicable) or more of the taxable years in such period exceeds the deductions attributable to the activity (determined without regard to whether or not the activity is engaged in for profit).

(3) Election.—An election under paragraph (1) shall be made at such time and manner, and subject to such terms and conditions, as the Secretary may prescribe.

(4) Time for assessing deficiency attributable to activity.—If a taxpayer makes an election under paragraph (1) with respect to an activity, the statutory period for the assessment of any deficiency attributable to such activity shall not expire before the expiration of 2 years after the date prescribed by law (determined without extensions) for filing the return of tax under chapter 1 for the last taxable year in the period of 5 taxable years (or 7 taxable years) to which the election relates. Such deficiency may be assessed notwithstanding the provisions of any law or rule of law which would otherwise prevent such an assessment.

§ 186. Recoveries of damages for antitrust violations, etc.

(a) Allowance of deduction.—If a compensatory amount which is included in gross income is received or accrued during the taxable year for a compensable injury, there shall be allowed as a deduction for the taxable year an amount equal to the lesser of—

(1) the amount of such compensatory amount, or

(2) the amount of the unrecovered losses sustained as a result of such compensable injury.

(b) Compensable injury.—For purposes of this section, the term "compensable injury" means—

(1) injuries sustained as a result of an infringement of a patent issued by the United States,

(2) injuries sustained as a result of a breach of contract or a breach of fiduciary duty or relationship, or

(3) injuries sustained in business, or to property, by reason of any conduct forbidden in the antitrust laws for which a civil action may be brought under section 4 of the Act entitled "An Act to supplement existing laws against unlawful restraints and monopolies, and for other purposes", approved October 15, 1914 (commonly known as the Clayton Act).

(c) Compensatory amount.—For purposes of this section, the term "compensatory amount" means the amount received or accrued during the taxable year as damages as a result of an award in, or in settlement of, a civil action for recovery for a compensable injury, reduced by any amounts paid or incurred in the taxable year in securing such award or settlement.

(d) Unrecovered losses—

(1) In general.—For purposes of this section, the amount of any unrecovered loss sustained as a result of any compensable injury is—

(A) the sum of the amount of the net operating losses (as determined under section 172) for each taxable year in whole or in part within the injury period, to the extent that such net operating losses are attributable to such compensable injury, reduced by

(B) the sum of—

(i) the amount of the net operating losses described in subparagraph (A) which were allowed for any prior taxable year as a deduction under section 172 as a net operating loss carryback or carryover to such taxable year, and

(ii) the amounts allowed as a deduction under subsection (a) for any prior taxable year for prior recoveries of compensatory amounts for such compensable injury.

(2) Injury period.—For purposes of paragraph (1), the injury period is—

(A) with respect to any infringement of a patent, the period in which such infringement occurred,

(B) with respect to a breach of contract or breach of fiduciary duty or relationship, the period during which amounts would have been received or accrued but for the breach of contract or breach of fiduciary duty or relationship, and

(C) with respect to injuries sustained by reason of any conduct forbidden in the antitrust laws, the period in which such injuries were sustained.

(3) Net operating losses attributable to compensable injuries.—For purposes of paragraph (1)—

(A) a net operating loss for any taxable year shall be treated as attributable to a compensable injury to the extent of the compensable injury sustained during such taxable year, and

(B) if only a portion of a net operating loss for any taxable year is attributable to a compensable injury, such portion shall (in applying section 172 for purposes of this section) be considered to be a separate net operating loss for such year to be applied after the other portion of such net operating loss.

(e) Effect on net operating loss carryovers.—If for the taxable year in which a compensatory amount is received or accrued any portion of a net operating loss carryover to such year is attributable to the compensable injury for which such amount is received or accrued, such portion of such net operating loss carryover shall be reduced by an amount equal to—

(1) the deduction allowed under subsection (a) with respect to such compensatory amount, reduced by

(2) any portion of the unrecovered losses sustained as a result of the compensable injury with respect to which the period for carryover under section 172 has expired.

§ 195. Start-up expenditures

(a) Capitalization of expenditures.—Except as otherwise provided in this section, no deduction shall be allowed for start-up expenditures.

(b) Election to deduct.—

(1) Allowance of deduction.—If a taxpayer elects the application of this subsection with respect to any start-up expenditures—

(A) the taxpayer shall be allowed a deduction for the taxable year in which the active trade or business begins in an amount equal to the lesser of—

(i) the amount of start-up expenditures with respect to the active trade or business, or

(ii) $5,000, reduced (but not below zero) by the amount by which such start-up expenditures exceed $50,000, and

(B) the remainder of such start-up expenditures shall be allowed as a deduction ratably over the 180–month period beginning with the month in which the active trade or business begins.

(2) Dispositions before close of amortization period.—In any case in which a trade or business is completely disposed of by the taxpayer before the end of the period to which paragraph (1) applies, any deferred expenses attributable to such trade or business which were not allowed as a deduction by reason of this section may be deducted to the extent allowable under section 165.

* * *

(c) Definitions.—For purposes of this section—

(1) Start-up expenditures.—The term "start-up expenditure" means any amount—

(A) paid or incurred in connection with—

(i) investigating the creation or acquisition of an active trade or business, or

(ii) creating an active trade or business, or

(iii) any activity engaged in for profit and for the production of income before the date on which the active trade or business begins, in anticipation of such activity becoming an active trade or business, and

(B) which, if paid or incurred in connection with the operation of an existing active trade or business (in the same field as the trade or business referred to in subparagraph (A)), would be allowable as a deduction for the taxable year in which paid or incurred.

The term "start-up expenditure" does not include any amount with respect to which a deduction is allowable under section 163(a), 164, or 174.

(2) Beginning of trade or business.—

(A) In general.—Except as provided in subparagraph (B), the determination of when an active trade or business begins shall be made in accordance with such regulations as the Secretary may prescribe.

(B) Acquired trade or business.—An acquired active trade or business shall be treated as beginning when the taxpayer acquires it.

(d) Election.—

(1) Time for making election.—An election under subsection (b) shall be made not later than the time prescribed by law for filing the return for the taxable year in which the trade or business begins (including extensions thereof).

(2) Scope of election.—The period selected under subsection (b) shall be adhered to in computing taxable income for the taxable year for which the election is made and all subsequent taxable years.

§ 197. Amortization of goodwill and certain other intangibles

(a) General rule.—A taxpayer shall be entitled to an amortization deduction with respect to any amortizable section 197 intangible. The amount of such deduction shall be determined by amortizing the adjusted basis (for purposes of determining gain) of such intangible ratably over the 15–year period beginning with the month in which such intangible was acquired.

(b) No other depreciation or amortization deduction allowable.—Except as provided in subsection (a), no depreciation or amortization deduction shall be allowable with respect to any amortizable section 197 intangible.

(c) Amortizable section 197 intangible.—For purposes of this section—

(1) In general.—Except as otherwise provided in this section, the term ''amortizable section 197 intangible'' means any section 197 intangible—

(A) which is acquired by the taxpayer after the date of the enactment of this section, and

(B) which is held in connection with the conduct of a trade or business or an activity described in section 212.

(2) Exclusion of self-created intangibles, etc.—The term ''amortizable section 197 intangible'' shall not include any section 197 intangible—

(A) which is not described in subparagraph (D), (E), or (F) of subsection (d)(1), and

(B) which is created by the taxpayer.

This paragraph shall not apply if the intangible is created in connection with a transaction (or series of related transactions) involving the acquisition of assets constituting a trade or business or substantial portion thereof.

(3) Anti–churning rules.—

For exclusion of intangibles acquired in certain transactions, see subsection (f)(9).

(d) Section 197 intangible.—For purposes of this section—

(1) In general.—Except as otherwise provided in this section, the term ''section 197 intangible'' means—

(A) goodwill,

(B) going concern value,

(C) any of the following intangible items:

(i) workforce in place including its composition and terms and conditions (contractual or otherwise) of its employment,

(ii) business books and records, operating systems, or any other information base (including lists or other information with respect to current or prospective customers),

(iii) any patent, copyright, formula, process, design, pattern, knowhow, format, or other similar item,

(iv) any customer-based intangible,

(v) any supplier-based intangible, and

(vi) any other similar item,

(D) any license, permit, or other right granted by a governmental unit or an agency or instrumentality thereof,

(E) any covenant not to compete (or other arrangement to the extent such arrangement has substantially the same effect as a covenant not to compete) entered into in connection with an acquisition (directly or indirectly) of an interest in a trade or business or substantial portion thereof, and

(F) any franchise, trademark, or trade name.

(2) Customer-based intangible.—

(A) In general.—The term "customer-based intangible" means—

(i) composition of market,

(ii) market share, and

(iii) any other value resulting from future provision of goods or services pursuant to relationships (contractual or otherwise) in the ordinary course of business with customers.

(B) Special rule for financial institutions.—In the case of a financial institution, the term "customer-based intangible" includes deposit base and similar items.

(3) Supplier-based intangible.—The term "supplier-based intangible" means any value resulting from future acquisitions of goods or services pursuant to relationships (contractual or otherwise) in the ordinary course of business with suppliers of goods or services to be used or sold by the taxpayer.

(e) Exceptions.—For purposes of this section, the term "section 197 intangible" shall not include any of the following:

(1) Financial interests.—Any interest—

(A) in a corporation, partnership, trust, or estate, or

(B) under an existing futures contract, foreign currency contract, notional principal contract, or other similar financial contract.

(2) Land.—Any interest in land.

(3) Computer software.—

(A) In general.—Any—

(i) computer software which is readily available for purchase by the general public, is subject to a nonexclusive license, and has not been substantially modified, and

(ii) other computer software which is not acquired in a transaction (or series of related transactions) involving the acquisition of assets constituting a trade or business or substantial portion thereof.

(B) Computer software defined.—For purposes of subparagraph (A), the term "computer software" means any program designed to cause a computer to perform a desired function. Such term shall not include any data base or similar item unless the data base or item is in the public domain and is incidental to the operation of otherwise qualifying computer software.

(4) Certain interests or rights acquired separately.—Any of the following not acquired in a transaction (or series of related transactions) involving the acquisition of assets constituting a trade business or substantial portion thereof:

(A) Any interest in a film, sound recording, video tape, book, or similar property.

(B) Any right to receive tangible property or services under a contract or granted by a governmental unit or agency or instrumentality thereof.

(C) Any interest in a patent or copyright.

(D) To the extent provided in regulations, any right under a contract (or granted by a governmental unit or an agency or instrumentality thereof) if such right—

(i) has a fixed duration of less than 15 years, or

(ii) is fixed as to amount and, without regard to this section, would be recoverable under a method similar to the unit-of-production method.

(5) Interests under leases and debt instruments.—Any interest under—

(A) an existing lease of tangible property, or

(B) except as provided in subsection (d)(2)(B), any existing indebtedness.

(6) Mortgage servicing.—Any right to service indebtedness which is secured by residential real property unless such right is acquired in a transaction (or series of related transactions) involving the acquisition of assets (other than rights described in this paragraph) constituting a trade or business or substantial portion thereof.

(7) Certain transaction costs.—Any fees for professional services, and any transaction costs, incurred by parties to a transaction with respect to which any portion of the gain or loss is not recognized under part III of subchapter C.

(f) Special rules.—

(1) Treatment of certain dispositions, etc.—

(A) In general.—If there is a disposition of any amortizable section 197 intangible acquired in a transaction or series of related transactions (or any such intangible becomes worthless) and one or more other amortizable section 197 intangibles acquired in such transaction or series of related transactions are retained—

(i) no loss shall be recognized by reason of such disposition (or such worthlessness), and

(ii) appropriate adjustments to the adjusted bases of such retained intangibles shall be made for any loss not recognized under clause (i).

(B) Special rule for covenants not to compete.—In the case of any section 197 intangible which is a covenant not to compete (or other arrangement) described in subsection (d)(1)(E), in no event shall such covenant or other arrangement be treated as disposed of (or becoming worthless) before the disposition of the entire interest described in such subsection in connection with which such covenant (or other arrangement) was entered into.

(C) Special rule.—All persons treated as a single taxpayer under section 41(f)(1) shall be so treated for purposes of this paragraph.

(2) Treatment of certain transfers.—

(A) In general.—In the case of any section 197 intangible transferred in a transaction described in subparagraph (B), the transferee shall be treated as the transferor for purposes of applying this section with respect to so much of the adjusted basis in the hands of the transferee as does not exceed the adjusted basis in the hands of the transferor.

(B) Transactions covered.—The transactions described in this subparagraph are—

(i) any transaction described in section 332, 351, 361, 721, 731, 1031, or 1033, and

(ii) any transaction between members of the same affiliated group during any taxable year for which a consolidated return is made by such group.

(3) Treatment of amounts paid pursuant to covenants not to compete, etc.—Any amount paid or incurred pursuant to a covenant or arrangement referred to in subsection (d)(1)(E) shall be treated as an amount chargeable to capital account.

(4) Treatment of franchises, etc.—

(A) Franchise.—The term "franchise" has the meaning given to such term by section 1253(b)(1).

(B) Treatment of renewals.—Any renewal of a franchise, trademark, or trade name (or of a license, a permit, or other right referred to in subsection (d)(1)(D) shall be treated as an acquisition). The preceding sentence shall only apply with respect to costs incurred in connection with such renewal.

(C) Certain amounts not taken into account.—Any amount to which section 1253(d)(1) applies shall not be taken into account under this section.

(5) Treatment of certain reinsurance transactions.—In the case of any amortizable section 197 intangible resulting from an assumption reinsurance transaction, the amount taken into account as the adjusted basis of such intangible under this section shall be the excess of—

(A) the amount paid or incurred by the acquirer under the assumption reinsurance transaction, over

(B) the amount required to be capitalized under section 848 in connection with such transaction.

Subsection (b) shall not apply to any amount required to be capitalized under section 848.

(6) Treatment of certain subleases.—For purposes of this section, a sublease shall be treated in the same manner as a lease of the underlying property involved.

(7) Treatment as depreciable.—For purposes of this chapter, any amortizable section 197 intangible shall be treated as property which is of a character subject to the allowance for depreciation provided in section 167.

(8) Treatment of certain increments in value.—This section shall not apply to any increment in value if, without regard to this section, such increment is properly taken into account in determining the cost of property which is not a section 197 intangible.

(9) Anti-churning rules.—For purposes of this section—

(A) In general.—The term "amortizable section 197 intangible" shall not include any section 197 intangible which is described in subparagraph (A) or (B) of subsection (d)(1) (or for which depreciation or amortization would not have been allowable but for this section) and which is acquired by the taxpayer after the date of the enactment of this section, if—

(i) the intangible was held or used at any time on or after July 25, 1991, and on or before such date of enactment by the taxpayer or a related person,

(ii) the intangible was acquired from a person who held such intangible at any time on or after July 25, 1991, and on or before such date of enactment, and, as part of the transaction, the user of such intangible does not change, or

(iii) the taxpayer grants the right to use such intangible to a person (or a person related to such person) who held or used such intangible at any time on or after July 25, 1991, and on or before such date of enactment.

For purposes of this subparagraph, the determination of whether the user of property changes as part of a transaction shall be determined in accordance with regulations prescribed by the Secretary. For purposes of this subparagraph, deductions allowable under section 1253(d) shall be treated as deductions allowable for amortization.

(B) Exception where gain recognized.—If—

(i) subparagraph (A) would not apply to an intangible acquired by the taxpayer but for the last sentence of subparagraph (C)(i), and

(ii) the person from whom the taxpayer acquired the intangible elects, notwithstanding any other provision of this title—

(I) to recognize gain on the disposition of the intangible, and

(II) to pay a tax on such gain which, when added to any other income tax on such gain under this title, equals such gain multiplied by the highest rate of income tax applicable to such person under this title,

then subparagraph (A) shall apply to the intangible only to the extent that the taxpayer's adjusted basis in the intangible exceeds the gain recognized under clause (ii)(I).

(C) Related person defined.—For purposes of this paragraph—

(i) Related person.—A person (hereinafter in this paragraph referred to as the "related person") is related to any person if—

(I) the related person bears a relationship to such person specified in section 267(b) or section 707(b)(1), or

(II) the related person and such person are engaged in trades or businesses under common control (within the meaning of subparagraphs (A) and (B) of section 41(f)(1)).

For purposes of subclause (I), in applying section 267(b) or 707(b)(1), "20 percent" shall be substituted for "50 percent".

(ii) Time for making determination.—A person shall be treated as related to another person if such relationship exists immediately before or immediately after the acquisition of the intangible involved.

(D) Acquisitions by reason of death.—Subparagraph (A) shall not apply to the acquisition of any property by the taxpayer if the basis of the property in the hands of the taxpayer is determined under section 1014(a).

(E) Special rule for partnerships.—With respect to any increase in the basis of partnership property under section 732, 734, or 743, determinations under this paragraph shall be made at the partner level and each partner shall be treated as having owned and used such partner's proportionate share of the partnership assets.

(F) Anti-abuse rules.—The term "amortizable section 197 intangible" does not include any section 197 intangible acquired in a transaction, one of the principal purposes of which is to avoid the requirement of subsection (c)(1) that the intangible be acquired after the date of the enactment of this section or to avoid the provisions of subparagraph (A).

(10) Tax-exempt use property subject to lease.—In the case of any section 197 intangible which would be tax-exempt use property as defined in subsection (h) of section 168 if such section applied to such intangible, the amortization period under this section shall not be less than 125 percent of the lease term (within the meaning of section 168(i)(3)).

(g) Regulations.—The Secretary shall prescribe such regulations as may be appropriate to carry out the purposes of this section, including such regulations as may be appropriate to prevent avoidance of the purposes of this section through related persons or otherwise.

§ 199. Income attributable to domestic production activities

(a) Allowance of deduction.—

(1) In general.—There shall be allowed as a deduction an amount equal to 9 percent of the lesser of—

(A) the qualified production activities income of the taxpayer for the taxable year, or

(B) taxable income (determined without regard to this section) for the taxable year.

(2) Phasein.—In the case of any taxable year beginning after 2004 and before 2010, paragraph (1) shall be applied by substituting for the percentage contained therein the transition percentage determined under the following table:

For taxable years beginning in:	The transition percentage is:
2005 or 2006	3
2007, 2008, or 2009	6.

(b) Deduction limited to wages paid.—

(1) In general.—The amount of the deduction allowable under subsection (a) for any taxable year shall not exceed 50 percent of the W–2 wages of the taxpayer for the taxable year.

(2) W–2 wages.—For purposes of this section—

(A) In general.—The term "W–2 wages" means, with respect to any person for any taxable year of such person, the sum of the amounts described in paragraphs (3) and (8) of section 6051(a) paid by such person with respect to employment of employees by such person during the calendar year ending during such taxable year.

(B) Limitation to wages attributable to domestic production.—Such term shall not include any amount which is not properly allocable to domestic production gross receipts for purposes of subsection (c)(1).

(C) Return requirement.—Such term shall not include any amount which is not properly included in a return filed with the Social Security Administration on or before the 60th day after the due date (including extensions) for such return.

(D) Special rule for qualified film.—In the case of a qualified film, such term shall include compensation for services performed in the United states by actors, production personnel, directors, and producers.

(3) Acquisitions and dispositions.—The Secretary shall provide for the application of this subsection in cases where the taxpayer acquires, or disposes of, the major portion of a trade or business or the major portion of a separate unit of a trade or business during the taxable year.

(c) Qualified production activities income.—For purposes of this section—

(1) In general.—The term "qualified production activities income" for any taxable year means an amount equal to the excess (if any) of—

(A) the taxpayer's domestic production gross receipts for such taxable year, over

(B) the sum of—

(i) the cost of goods sold that are allocable to such receipts, and

(ii) other expenses, losses, or deductions (other than the deduction allowed under this section), which are properly allocable to such receipts.

(2) Allocation method.—The Secretary shall prescribe rules for the proper allocation of items described in paragraph (1) for purposes of determining qualified production activities income. Such rules shall provide for the proper allocation of items whether or not such items are directly allocable to domestic production gross receipts.

(3) Special rules for determining costs.—

(A) In general.—For purposes of determining costs under clause (i) of paragraph (1)(B), any item or service brought into the United States shall be treated as acquired by purchase, and its cost shall be treated as not less than its value immediately after it entered the United States. A similar rule shall apply in determining the adjusted basis of leased or rented property where the lease or rental gives rise to domestic production gross receipts.

(B) Exports for further manufacture.—In the case of any property described in subparagraph (A) that had been exported by the taxpayer for further manufacture, the increase in cost or adjusted basis under subparagraph (A) shall not exceed the difference between the value of the property when exported and the value of the property when brought back into the United States after the further manufacture.

(4) Domestic production gross receipts.—

(A) In general.—The term "domestic production gross receipts" means the gross receipts of the taxpayer which are derived from—

(i) any lease, rental, license, sale, exchange, or other disposition of–

(I) qualifying production property which was manufactured, produced, grown, or extracted by the taxpayer in whole or in significant part within the United States,

(II) any qualified film produced by the taxpayer, or

(III) electricity, natural gas, or potable water produced by the taxpayer in the United States,

(ii) in the case of a taxpayer engaged in the active conduct of a construction trade or business, construction of real property performed in the United States by the taxpayer in the ordinary course of such trade or business, or

(iii) in the case of a taxpayer engaged in the active conduct of an engineering or architectural services trade or business, engineering or architectural services performed in the United States by the taxpayer in the ordinary course of such trade or business with respect to the construction of real property in the United States.

(B) Exceptions.—Such term shall not include gross receipts of the taxpayer which are derived from—

(i) the sale of food and beverages prepared by the taxpayer at a retail establishment,

(ii) the transmission or distribution of electricity, natural gas, or potable water, or

(iii) the lease, rental, license, sale, exchange, or other disposition of land.

* * *

(5) Qualifying production property.—The term "qualifying production property" means—

(A) tangible personal property,

(B) any computer software, and

(C) any property described in section 168(f)(4).

(6) Qualified film.—The term "qualified film" means any property described in section 168(f)(3) if not less than 50 percent of the total compensation relating to the production of such property is compensation for services performed in the United States by actors, production personnel, directors, and producers. Such term does not include property with respect to which records are required to be maintained under section 2257 of title 18, United States Code. A qualified film shall include any copyrights, trademarks, or other intangibles with respect to such film. The methods and means of distributing a qualified film shall not affect the availability of the deduction under this section.

(7) Related persons.—

(A) In general.—The term "domestic production gross receipts" shall not include any gross receipts of the taxpayer derived from property leased, licensed, or rented by the taxpayer for use by any related person.

(B) Related person.—For purposes of subparagraph (A), a person shall be treated as related to another person if such persons are treated as a single employer under subsection (a) or (b) of section 52 or subsection (m) or (*o*) of section 414, except that determinations under subsections (a) and (b) of section 52 shall be made without regard to section 1563(b).

(d) Definitions and special rules.—

(1) Application of section to pass-thru entities.—

(A) Partnerships and S corporations.—In the case of a partnership or S corporation–

(i) this section shall be applied at the partner or shareholder level,

(ii) each partner or shareholder shall take into account such person's allocable share of each item described in subparagraph (A) or (B) of subsection (c)(1) (determined without regard to whether the items described in such subparagraph (A) exceed the items described in such subparagraph (B)),

(iii) each partner or shareholder shall be treated for purposes of subsection (b) as having W–2 wages for the taxable year in an amount equal to such person's allocable share of the W–2 wages of the partnership or S corporation for the taxable year (as determined under regulations prescribed by the Secretary), and

(iv) in the case of each partner of a partnership, or shareholder of an S corporation, who owns (directly or indirectly) at least 20 percent of the capital interests in such partnership or of the stock of such S corporation—

(I) such partner or shareholder shall be treated as having engaged directly in any film produced by such partnership or S corporation, and

(II) such partnership or S corporation shall be treated as having engaged directly in any film produced by such partner or shareholder.

(B) Trusts and estates.—In the case of a trust or estate—

(i) the items referred to in subparagraph (A)(ii) (as determined therein) and the W–2 wages of the trust or estate for the taxable year, shall be apportioned between the beneficiaries and the fiduciary (and among the beneficiaries) under regulations prescribed by the Secretary, and

(ii) for purposes of paragraph (2), adjusted gross income of the trust or estate shall be determined as provided in section 67(e) with the adjustments described in such paragraph.

(C) Regulations.—The Secretary may prescribe rules requiring or restricting the allocation of items and wages under this paragraph and may prescribe such reporting requirements as the Secretary determines appropriate.

(2) Application to individuals.—In the case of an individual, subsections (a)(1)(B) and (d)(9)(A)(iii) shall be applied by substituting "adjusted gross income" for "taxable income". For purposes of the preceding sentence, adjusted gross income shall be determined—

(A) after application of sections 86, 135, 137, 219, 221, 222, and 469, and

(B) without regard to this section.

* * *

(4) Special rule for affiliated groups.—

(A) In general.—All members of an expanded affiliated group shall be treated as a single corporation for purposes of this section.

(B) Expanded affiliated group.—For purposes of this section, the term "expanded affiliated group" means an affiliated group as defined in section 1504(a), determined–

(i) by substituting "more than 50 percent" for "at least 80 percent" each place it appears, and

(ii) without regard to paragraphs (2) and (4) of section 1504(b).

(C) Allocation of deduction.—Except as provided in regulations, the deduction under subsection (a) shall be allocated among the members of the expanded affiliated group in proportion to each member's respective amount (if any) of qualified production activities income.

(5) Trade or business requirement.—This section shall be applied by only taking into account items which are attributable to the actual conduct of a trade or business.

(6) Coordination with minimum tax.—For purposes of determining alternative minimum taxable income under section 55—

(A) qualified production activities income shall be determined without regard to any adjustments under sections 56 through 59, and

(B) in the case of a corporation, subsection (a)(1)(B) shall be applied by substituting "alternative minimum taxable income" for "taxable income".

* * *

(10) Regulations.—The Secretary shall prescribe such regulations as are necessary to carry out the purposes of this section, including regulations which prevent more than 1 taxpayer from being allowed a deduction under this section with respect to any activity described in subsection (c)(4)(A)(i).

PART VII—ADDITIONAL ITEMIZED DEDUCTIONS FOR INDIVIDUALS

§ 211. Allowance of deductions

In computing taxable income under section 63, there shall be allowed as deductions the items specified in this part, subject to the exceptions provided in part IX (section 261 and following, relating to items not deductible).

§ 212. Expenses for production of income

In the case of an individual, there shall be allowed as a deduction all the ordinary and necessary expenses paid or incurred during the taxable year—

(1) for the production or collection of income;

(2) for the management, conservation, or maintenance of property held for the production of income; or

(3) in connection with the determination, collection, or refund of any tax.

§ 213. Medical, dental, etc., expenses

(a) Allowance of deduction.—There shall be allowed as a deduction the expenses paid during the taxable year, not compensated for by insurance or otherwise, for medical care of the taxpayer, his spouse, or a dependent (as defined in section 152, determined without regard to subsections (b)(1), (b)(2), and (d)(1)(B) thereof), to the extent that such expenses exceed 10 percent of adjusted gross income.

(b) Limitation with respect to medicine and drugs.—An amount paid during the taxable year for medicine or a drug shall be taken into account under subsection (a) only if such medicine or drug is a prescribed drug or is insulin.

(c) Special rule for decedents.—

(1) Treatment of expenses paid after death.—For purposes of subsection (a), expenses for the medical care of the taxpayer which are paid out of his estate during the 1–year period beginning with the day after the date of his death shall be treated as paid by the taxpayer at the time incurred.

(2) Limitation.—Paragraph (1) shall not apply if the amount paid is allowable under section 2053 as a deduction in computing the taxable estate of the decedent, but this paragraph shall not apply if (within the time and in the manner and form prescribed by the Secretary) there is filed—

(A) a statement that such amount has not been allowed as a deduction under section 2053, and

(B) a waiver of the right to have such amount allowed at any time as a deduction under section 2053.

(d) Definitions.—For purposes of this section—

(1) The term "medical care" means amounts paid—

(A) for the diagnosis, cure, mitigation, treatment, or prevention of disease, or for the purpose of affecting any structure or function of the body,

(B) for transportation primarily for and essential to medical care referred to in subparagraph (A),

(C) for qualified long-term care services (as defined in section 7702B(c)), or

(D) for insurance (including amounts paid as premiums under part B of title XVIII of the Social Security Act, relating to supplementary medical insurance for the aged) covering medical care referred to in subparagraphs (A) and (B) or for any qualified long-term care insurance contract (as defined in section 7702B(b)).

In the case of a qualified long-term care insurance contract (as defined in section 7702B(b)), only eligible long-term care premiums (as defined in paragraph (10)) shall be taken into account under subparagraph (D).

(2) Amounts paid for certain lodging away from home treated as paid for medical care.—Amounts paid for lodging (not lavish or extravagant under the circumstances) while away from home primarily for and essential to medical care referred to in paragraph (1)(A) shall be treated as amounts paid for medical care if—

(A) the medical care referred to in paragraph (1)(A) is provided by a physician in a licensed hospital (or in a medical care facility which is related to, or the equivalent of, a licensed hospital), and

(B) there is no significant element of personal pleasure, recreation, or vacation in the travel away from home.

The amount taken into account under the preceding sentence shall not exceed $50 for each night for each individual.

(3) Prescribed drug.—The term "prescribed drug" means a drug or biological which requires a prescription of a physician for its use by an individual.

(4) Physician.—The term "physician" has the meaning given to such term by section 1861(r) of the Social Security Act (42 U.S.C. 1395x(r)).

(5) Special rule in the case of child of divorced parents, etc.—Any child to whom section 152(e) applies shall be treated as a dependent of both parents for purposes of this section.

(6) In the case of an insurance contract under which amounts are payable for other than medical care referred to in subparagraphs (A), (B), and (C) of paragraph (1)—

(A) no amount shall be treated as paid for insurance to which paragraph (1)(D) applies unless the charge for such insurance is either separately stated in the contract, or furnished to the policyholder by the insurance company in a separate statement,

(B) the amount taken into account as the amount paid for such insurance shall not exceed such charge, and

(C) no amount shall be treated as paid for such insurance if the amount specified in the contract (or furnished to the policyholder by the insurance company in a separate statement) as the charge for such insurance is unreasonably large in relation to the total charges under the contract.

(7) Subject to the limitations of paragraph (6), premiums paid during the taxable year by a taxpayer before he attains the age of 65 for insurance covering medical care (within the meaning of subparagraphs (A), (B), and (C) of paragraph (1)) for the taxpayer, his spouse, or a dependent after the taxpayer attains the age of 65 shall be treated as expenses paid during the taxable year for insurance which constitutes medical care if premiums for such insurance are payable (on a level payment basis) under the contract for a period of 10 years or more or until the year in which the taxpayer attains the age of 65 (but in no case for a period of less than 5 years).

(8) The determination of whether an individual is married at any time during the taxable year shall be made in accordance with the provisions of section 6013(d) (relating to determination of status as husband and wife).

(9) Cosmetic surgery.—

(A) In general.—The term "medical care" does not include cosmetic surgery or other similar procedures, unless the surgery or procedure is necessary to ameliorate a deformity arising from, or directly related to, a congenital abnormality, a personal injury resulting from an accident or trauma, or disfiguring disease.

(B) Cosmetic surgery defined.—For purposes of this paragraph, the term "cosmetic surgery" means any procedure which is directed at improving the patient's appearance and does not meaningfully promote the proper function of the body or prevent or treat illness or disease.

(10) Eligible long-term care premiums.—

(A) In general.—For purposes of this section, the term "eligible long-term care premiums" means the amount paid during a taxable year for any qualified long-term care insurance contract (as defined in section 7702B(b)) covering an individual, to the extent such amount does not exceed the limitation determined under the following table:

In the case of an individual with an attained age before the close of the taxable year of:	**The limitation is:**
40 or less	$ 200
More than 40 but not more than 50	375
More than 50 but not more than 60	750
More than 60 but not more than 70	2,000
More than 70	2,500

* * *

(11) Certain payments to relatives treated as not paid for medical care.—An amount paid for a qualified long-term care service (as defined in section 7702B(c)) provided to an individual shall be treated as not paid for medical care if such service is provided—

(A) by the spouse of the individual or by a relative (directly or through a partnership, corporation, or other entity) unless the service is provided by a licensed professional with respect to such service, or

(B) by a corporation or partnership which is related (within the meaning of section 267(b) or 707(b)) to the individual.

For purposes of this paragraph, the term "relative" means an individual bearing a relationship to the individual which is described in any of subparagraphs (A) through (G) of section 152(d)(2). This paragraph shall not apply for purposes of section 105(b) with respect to reimbursements through insurance.

(e) Exclusion of amounts allowed for care of certain dependents.—Any expense allowed as a credit under section 21 shall not be treated as an expense paid for medical care.

(f) Special rule for 2013, 2014, 2015, and 2016. In the case of any taxable year beginning after December 31, 2012, and ending before January 1, 2017, subsection (a) shall be applied with respect to a taxpayer by substituting "7.5 percent" for "10 percent" if such taxpayer or such taxpayer's spouse has attained age 65 before the close of such taxable year.

§ 215. Alimony, etc., payments

(a) General rule.—In the case of an individual, there shall be allowed as a deduction an amount equal to the alimony or separate maintenance payments paid during such individual's taxable year.

(b) Alimony or separate maintenance payments defined.—For purposes of this section, the term "alimony or separate maintenance payment" means any alimony or separate maintenance payment (as defined in section 71(b)) which is includible in the gross income of the recipient under section 71.

(c) Requirement of identification number.—The Secretary may prescribe regulations under which—

(1) any individual receiving alimony or separate maintenance payments is required to furnish such individual's taxpayer identification number to the individual making such payments, and

(2) the individual making such payments is required to include such taxpayer identification number on such individual's return for the taxable year in which such payments are made.

(d) Coordination with section 682.—No deduction shall be allowed under this section with respect to any payment if, by reason of section 682 (relating to income of alimony trusts), the amount thereof is not includible in such individual's gross income.

§ 217. Moving expenses

(a) Deduction allowed.—There shall be allowed as a deduction moving expenses paid or incurred during the taxable year in connection with the commencement of work by the taxpayer as an employee or as a self-employed individual at a new principal place of work.

(b) Definition of moving expenses.—

(1) In general.—For purposes of this section, the term "moving expenses" means only the reasonable expenses—

(A) of moving household goods and personal effects from the former residence to the new residence, and

(B) of traveling (including lodging) from the former residence to the new place of residence.

Such term shall not include any expenses for meals.

(2) Individuals other than taxpayer.—In the case of any individual other than the taxpayer, expenses referred to in paragraph (1) shall be taken into account only if such individual has both the former residence and the new residence as his principal place of abode and is a member of the taxpayer's household.

(c) Conditions for allowance.—No deduction shall be allowed under this section unless—

(1) the taxpayer's new principal place of work—

(A) is at least 50 miles farther from his former residence than was his former principal place of work, or

(B) if he had no former principal place of work, is at least 50 miles from his former residence, and

(2) either—

(A) during the 12–month period immediately following his arrival in the general location of his new principal place of work, the taxpayer is a full-time employee, in such general location, during at least 39 weeks, or

(B) during the 24–month period immediately following his arrival in the general location of his new principal place of work, the taxpayer is a full-time employee or performs services as a self-employed individual on a full-time basis, in such general location, during at least 78 weeks, of which not less than 39 weeks are during the 12–month period referred to in subparagraph (A).

For purposes of paragraph (1), the distance between two points shall be the shortest of the more commonly traveled routes between such two points.

(d) Rules for application of subsection (c)(2).—

(1) The condition of subsection (c)(2) shall not apply if the taxpayer is unable to satisfy such condition by reason of—

(A) death or disability, or

(B) involuntary separation (other than for willful misconduct) from the service of, or transfer for the benefit of, an employer after obtaining full-time employment in which the taxpayer could reasonably have been expected to satisfy such condition.

(2) If a taxpayer has not satisfied the condition of subsection (c)(2) before the time prescribed by law (including extensions thereof) for filing the return for the taxable year during which he paid or incurred moving expenses which would otherwise be deductible under this section, but may still satisfy such condition, then such expenses may (at the election of the taxpayer) be deducted for such taxable year notwithstanding subsection (c)(2).

(3) If—

(A) for any taxable year moving expenses have been deducted in accordance with the rule provided in paragraph (2), and

(B) the condition of subsection (c)(2) cannot be satisfied at the close of a subsequent taxable year,

then an amount equal to the expenses which were so deducted shall be included in gross income for the first such subsequent taxable year.

(e) Repealed.

(f) Self-employed individual.—For purposes of this section, the term "self-employed individual" means an individual who performs personal services—

(1) as the owner of the entire interest in an unincorporated trade or business, or

(2) as a partner in a partnership carrying on a trade or business.

(g) Rules for members of the Armed Forces of the United States.—In the case of a member of the Armed Forces of the United States on active duty who moves pursuant to a military order and incident to a permanent change of station—

(1) the limitations under subsection (c) shall not apply;

(2) any moving and storage expenses which are furnished in kind (or for which reimbursement or an allowance is provided, but only to the extent of the expenses paid or incurred) to such member, his spouse, or his dependents, shall not be includible in gross income, and no reporting with respect to such expenses shall be required by the Secretary of Defense or the Secretary of Transportation, as the case may be; and

(3) if moving and storage expenses are furnished in kind (or if reimbursement or an allowance for such expenses is provided) to such member's spouse and his dependents with regard to moving to a location other than the one to which such member moves (or from a location other than the one from which such member moves), this section shall apply with respect to the moving expenses of his spouse and dependents—

(A) as if his spouse commenced work as an employee at a new principal place of work at such location; and

(B) without regard to the limitations under subsection (c).

(h) Special rules for foreign moves.—

(1) Allowance of certain storage fees.—In the case of a foreign move, for purposes of this section, the moving expenses described in subsection (b)(1)(A) include the reasonable expenses—

(A) of moving household goods and personal effects to and from storage, and

(B) of storing such goods and effects for part or all of the period during which the new place of work continues to be the taxpayer's principal place of work.

(2) Foreign move.—For purposes of this subsection, the term "foreign move" means the commencement of work by the taxpayer at a new principal place of work located outside the United States.

(3) United States defined.—For purposes of this subsection and subsection (i), the term "United States" includes the possessions of the United States.

* * *

(j) Regulations.—The Secretary shall prescribe such regulations as may be necessary to carry out the purposes of this section.

§ 219. Retirement savings

(a) Allowance of deduction.—In the case of an individual, there shall be allowed as a deduction an amount equal to the qualified retirement contributions of the individual for the taxable year.

(b) Maximum amount of deduction.—

(1) In general.—The amount allowable as a deduction under subsection (a) to any individual for any taxable year shall not exceed the lesser of—

(A) the deductible amount, or

(B) an amount equal to the compensation includible in the individual's gross income for such taxable year.

* * *

(4) Special rule for simple retirement accounts.—This section shall not apply with respect to any amount contributed to a simple retirement account established under section 408(p).

(5) Deductible amount.—For purposes of paragraph (1)(A)—

(A) In general.—The deductible amount shall be determined in accordance with the following table:

For taxable years beginning in:	The deductible amount is:
2002 through 2004	$3,000
2005 through 2007	$4,000
2008 and thereafter	$5,000

(B) Catch-up contributions for individuals 50 or older.—

(i) In general.—In the case of an individual who has attained the age of 50 before the close of the taxable year, the deductible amount for such taxable year shall be increased by the applicable amount.

(ii) Applicable amount.—For purposes of clause (i), the applicable amount shall be the amount determined in accordance with the following table:

For taxable years beginning in:	The applicable amount is:
2002 through 2005	$ 500
2006 and thereafter	$1,000

* * *

(D) Cost-of-living adjustment.—

(i) In general.—In the case of any taxable year beginning in a calendar year after 2008, the $5,000 amount under subparagraph (A) shall be increased by an amount equal to—

(I) such dollar amount, multiplied by

(II) the cost-of-living adjustment determined under section 1(f)(3) * * *.

(ii) Rounding rules.—If any amount after adjustment under clause (i) is not a multiple of $500, such amount shall be rounded to the next lower multiple of $500.

(c) Special rules for certain married individuals.—

(1) In general.—In the case of an individual to whom this paragraph applies for the taxable year, the limitation of paragraph (1) of subsection (b) shall be equal to the lesser of—

(A) the dollar amount in effect under subsection (b)(1)(A) for the taxable year, or

(B) the sum of—

(i) the compensation includible in such individual's gross income for the taxable year, plus

(ii) the compensation includible in the gross income of such individual's spouse for the taxable year reduced by—

(I) the amount allowed as a deduction under subsection (a) to such spouse for such taxable year,

(II) the amount of any designated nondeductible contribution (as defined in section 408(*o*)) on behalf of such spouse for such taxable year, and

(III) the amount of any contribution on behalf of such spouse to a Roth IRA under section 408A for such taxable year.

(2) Individuals to whom paragraph (1) applies.—Paragraph (1) shall apply to any individual if—

(A) such individual files a joint return for the taxable year, and

(B) the amount of compensation (if any) includible in such individual's gross income for the taxable year is less than the compensation includible in the gross income of such individual's spouse for the taxable year.

(d) Other limitations and restrictions.—

(1) Beneficiary must be under age 70½.—No deduction shall be allowed under this section with respect to any qualified retirement contribution for the benefit of an individual if such individual has attained age 70½ before the close of such individual's taxable year for which the contribution was made.

* * *

(e) Qualified retirement contribution.—For purposes of this section, the term "qualified retirement contribution" means—

(1) any amount paid in cash for the taxable year by or on behalf of an individual to an individual retirement plan for such individual's benefit, and

* * *

(f) Other definitions and special rules.—

(1) Compensation.—For purposes of this section, the term "compensation" includes earned income (as defined in section 401(c)(2)). The term "compensation" does not include any amount received as a pension or annuity and does not include any amount received as deferred compensation. The term "compensation" shall include any amount includible in the individual's gross income under section 71 with respect to a divorce or separation instrument described in subparagraph (A) of section 71(b)(2). For purposes of this paragraph, section 401(c)(2) shall be applied as if the term trade or business for purposes of section 1402 included service described in subsection (c)(6). The term compensation includes any differential wage payment (as defined in section 3401(h)(2)).

(2) Married individuals.—The maximum deduction under subsection (b) shall be computed separately for each individual, and this section shall be applied without regard to any community property laws.

(3) Time when contributions deemed made.—For purposes of this section, a taxpayer shall be deemed to have made a contribution to an individual retirement plan on the last day of the preceding taxable year if the contribution is made on account of such taxable year and is made not later than the time prescribed by law for filing the return for such taxable year (not including extensions thereof).

* * *

(g) Limitation on deduction for active participants in certain pension plans.—

(1) In general.—If (for any part of any plan year ending with or within a taxable year) an individual or an individual's spouse is an active participant, each of the dollar limitations contained in subsections (b)(1)(A) and (c)(1)(A) for such taxable year shall be reduced (but not below zero) by the amount determined under paragraph (2).

(2) Amount of reduction.—

(A) In general.—The amount determined under this paragraph with respect to any dollar limitation shall be the amount which bears the same ratio to such limitation as—

(i) the excess of—

(I) the taxpayer's adjusted gross income for such taxable year, over

(II) the applicable dollar amount, bears to

(ii) $10,000 ($20,000 in the case of a joint return for a taxable year beginning after December 31, 2006).

* * *

(3) Adjusted gross income; applicable dollar amount.—For purposes of this subsection—

(A) Adjusted gross income.—Adjusted gross income of any taxpayer shall be determined—

(i) after application of sections 86 and 469, and

(ii) without regard to sections 135, 137, 199, 221, 222, and 911 or the deduction allowable under this section.

(B) Applicable dollar amount.—The term "applicable dollar amount" means the following:

(i) In the case of a taxpayer filing a joint return:

For taxable years beginning in:	The applicable dollar amount is:
* * *	
2007 and thereafter	$80,000.

(ii) In the case of any other taxpayer (other than a married individual filing a separate return):

For taxable years beginning in:	The applicable dollar amount is:
* * *	
2005 and thereafter	$50,000.

(iii) In the case of a married individual filing a separate return, zero.

(4) Special rule for married individuals filing separately and living apart.—A husband and wife who—

(A) file separate returns for any taxable year, and

(B) live apart at all times during such taxable year,

shall not be treated as married individuals for purposes of this subsection.

(5) Active participant.—For purposes of this subsection, the term "active participant" means, with respect to any plan year, an individual—

(A) who is an active participant in—

(i) a plan described in section 401(a) which includes a trust exempt from tax under section 501(a),

(ii) an annuity plan described in section 403(a),

(iii) a plan established for its employees by the United States, by a State or political subdivision thereof, or by an agency or instrumentality of any of the foregoing,

(iv) an annuity contract described in section 403(b),

(v) a simplified employee pension (within the meaning of section 408(k)), or

(vi) any simple retirement account (within the meaning of section 408(p)), or

(B) who makes deductible contributions to a trust described in section 501(c)(18).

The determination of whether an individual is an active participant shall be made without regard to whether or not such individual's rights under a plan, trust, or contract are nonforfeitable. An eligible deferred compensation plan (within the meaning of section 457(b)) shall not be treated as a plan described in subparagraph (A)(iii).

* * *

(7) Special rule for spouses who are not active participants.—If this subsection applies to an individual for any taxable year solely because their spouse is an active participant, then, in applying this subsection to the individual (but not their spouse).—

(A) the applicable dollar amount under paragraph (3)(B)(i) shall be $150,000; and

(B) the amount applicable under paragraph (2)(A)(ii) shall be $10,000.

(8) Inflation adjustment.—In the case of any taxable year beginning in a calendar year after 2006, the dollar amount in the last row of the table contained in paragraph (3)(B)(i), the dollar amount in the last row of the table contained in paragraph (3)(B)(ii), and the dollar amount contained in paragraph (7)(A), shall each be increased by an amount equal to—

(A) such dollar amount, multiplied by

(B) the cost-of-living adjustment determined under section 1(f)(3) for the calendar year in which the taxable year begins, determined by substituting "calendar year 2005" for "calendar year 1992" in subparagraph (B) thereof.

Any increase determined under the preceding sentence shall be rounded to the nearest multiple of $1,000.

* * *

§ 221. Interest on education loans

(a) Allowance of deduction.—In the case of an individual, there shall be allowed as a deduction for the taxable year an amount equal to the interest paid by the taxpayer during the taxable year on any qualified education loan.

(b) Maximum deduction.—

(1) In general.—Except as provided in paragraph (2), the deduction allowed by subsection (a) for the taxable year shall not exceed the amount determined in accordance with the following table:

In the case of taxable years beginning in:	The dollar amount is:
1998	$1,000
1999	$1,500
2000	$2,000
2001 or thereafter	$2,500.

(2) Limitation based on modified adjusted gross income.—

(A) In general.—The amount which would (but for this paragraph) be allowable as a deduction under this section shall be reduced (but not below zero) by the amount determined under subparagraph (B).

(B) Amount of reduction.—The amount determined under this subparagraph is the amount which bears the same ratio to the amount which would be so taken into account as—

(i) the excess of—

(I) the taxpayer's modified adjusted gross income for such taxable year, over

(II) $50,000 ($100,000 in the case of a joint return), bears to

(ii) $15,000 ($30,000 in the case of a joint return).

(C) Modified adjusted gross income.—The term "modified adjusted gross income" means adjusted gross income determined—

(i) without regard to this section and sections 199, 222, 911, 931, and 933, and

(ii) after application of sections 86, 135, 137, 219, and 469.

(c) Dependents not eligible for deduction.—No deduction shall be allowed by this section to an individual for the taxable year if a deduction under section 151 with respect to such individual is allowed to another taxpayer for the taxable year beginning in the calendar year in which such individual's taxable year begins.

(d) Definitions.—For purposes of this section—

(1) Qualified education loan.—The term "qualified education loan" means any indebtedness incurred by the taxpayer solely to pay qualified higher education expenses—

(A) which are incurred on behalf of the taxpayer, the taxpayer's spouse, or any dependent of the taxpayer as of the time the indebtedness was incurred,

(B) which are paid or incurred within a reasonable period of time before or after the indebtedness is incurred, and

(C) which are attributable to education furnished during a period during which the recipient was an eligible student.

Such term includes indebtedness used to refinance indebtedness which qualifies as a qualified education loan. The term "qualified education loan" shall not include any indebtedness owed to a person who is related (within the meaning of section 267(b) or 707(b)(1)) to the taxpayer or to any person by reason of a loan under any qualified employer plan (as defined in section 72(p)(4)) or under any contract referred to in section 72(p)(5).

(2) Qualified higher education expenses.—The term "qualified higher education expenses" means the cost of attendance (as defined in section 472 of the Higher Education Act of 1965, 20 U.S.C. 1087*ll*, as in effect on the day before the date of the enactment of the Taxpayer Relief Act of 1997) at an eligible educational institution, reduced by the sum of—

(A) the amount excluded from gross income under section 127, 135, 529, or 530 by reason of such expenses, and

(B) the amount of any scholarship, allowance, or payment described in section 25A(g)(2).

For purposes of the preceding sentence, the term "eligible educational institution" has the same meaning given such term by section 25A(f)(2), except that such term shall also include an institution conducting an internship or residency program leading to a degree or certificate awarded by an institution of higher education, a hospital, or a health care facility which offers postgraduate training.

(3) Eligible student.—The term "eligible student" has the meaning given such term by section 25A(b)(3).

(4) Dependent.—The term "dependent" has the meaning given such term by section 152 (determined without regard to subsections (b)(1), (b)(2), and (d)(1)(B) thereof).

(e) Special rules.—

(1) Denial of double benefit.—No deduction shall be allowed under this section for any amount for which a deduction is allowable under any other provision of this chapter.

(2) Married couples must file joint return.—If the taxpayer is married at the close of the taxable year, the deduction shall be allowed under subsection (a) only if the taxpayer and the taxpayer's spouse file a joint return for the taxable year.

(3) Marital status.—Marital status shall be determined in accordance with section 7703.

(f) Inflation adjustments.—

(1) In general.—In the case of a taxable year beginning after 2002, the $50,000 and $100,000 amounts in subsection (b)(2) shall each be increased by an amount equal to—

(A) such dollar amount, multiplied by

(B) the cost-of-living adjustment determined under section 1(f)(3) for the calendar year in which the taxable year begins, determined by substituting "calendar year 2001" for "calendar year 1992" in subparagraph (B) thereof.

(2) Rounding.—If any amount as adjusted under paragraph (1) is not a multiple of $5,000, such amount shall be rounded to the next lowest multiple of $5,000.

§ 222. Qualified tuition and related expenses.

(a) Allowance of deduction.—In the case of an individual, there shall be allowed as a deduction an amount equal to the qualified tuition and related expenses paid by the taxpayer during the taxable year.

(b) Dollar limitations.—

(1) In general.—The amount allowed as a deduction under subsection (a) with respect to the taxpayer for any taxable year shall not exceed the applicable dollar limit.

(2) Applicable dollar limit.—

* * *

(B) After 2003.—In the case of any taxable year beginning after 2003, the applicable dollar amount shall be equal to—

(i) in the case of a taxpayer whose adjusted gross income for the taxable year does not exceed $65,000 ($130,000 in the case of a joint return), $4,000,

(ii) in the case of a taxpayer not described in clause (i) whose adjusted gross income for the taxable year does not exceed $80,000 ($160,000 in the case of a joint return), $2,000, and

(iii) in the case of any other taxpayer, zero.

(C) Adjusted gross income.—For purposes of this paragraph, adjusted gross income shall be determined—

(i) without regard to this section and sections 199, 911, 931, and 933, and

(ii) after application of sections 86, 135, 137, 219, 221, and 469.

(c) No double benefit.—

(1) In general.—No deduction shall be allowed under subsection (a) for any expense for which a deduction is allowed to the taxpayer under any other provision of this chapter.

(2) Coordination with other education incentives.—

(A) Denial of deduction if credit elected.—No deduction shall be allowed under subsection (a) for a taxable year with respect to the qualified tuition and related expenses with respect to an individual if the taxpayer or any other person elects to have section 25A apply with respect to such individual for such year.

(B) Coordination with exclusions.—The total amount of qualified tuition and related expenses shall be reduced by the amount of such expenses taken into account in determining any amount excluded under section 135, 529(c)(1), or 530(d)(2). For purposes of the preceding sentence, the amount taken into account in determining the amount excluded under section 529(c)(1) shall not include that portion of the distribution which represents a return of any contributions to the plan.

(3) Dependents.—No deduction shall be allowed under subsection (a) to any individual with respect to whom a deduction under section 151 is allowable to another taxpayer for a taxable year beginning in the calendar year in which such individual's taxable year begins.

(d) Definitions and special rules.—For purposes of this section—

(1) Qualified tuition and related expenses.—The term "qualified tuition and related expenses" has the meaning given such term by section 25A(f). Such expenses shall be reduced in the same manner as under section 25A(g)(2).

(2) Identification requirement.—No deduction shall be allowed under subsection (a) to a taxpayer with respect to the qualified tuition and related expenses of an individual unless the taxpayer includes the name and taxpayer identification number of the individual on the return of tax for the taxable year.

(3) Limitation on taxable year of deduction.—

(A) In general.—A deduction shall be allowed under subsection (a) for qualified tuition and related expenses for any taxable year only to the extent such expenses are in connection with enrollment at an institution of higher education during the taxable year.

(B) Certain prepayments allowed.—Subparagraph (A) shall not apply to qualified tuition and related expenses paid during a taxable year if such expenses are in connection with an academic term beginning during such taxable year or during the first 3 months of the next taxable year.

(4) No deduction for married individuals filing separate returns.—If the taxpayer is a married individual (within the meaning of section 7703), this section shall apply only if the taxpayer and the taxpayer's spouse file a joint return for the taxable year.

* * *

(6) Regulations.—The Secretary may prescribe such regulations as may be necessary or appropriate to carry out this section, including regulations requiring recordkeeping and information reporting.

(e) Termination.—This section shall not apply to taxable years beginning after December 31, 2013.

§ 223. Health savings accounts

(a) Deduction allowed.—In the case of an individual who is an eligible individual for any month during the taxable year, there shall be allowed as a deduction for the taxable year an amount equal to the aggregate amount paid in cash during such taxable year by or on behalf of such individual to a health savings account of such individual.

(b) Limitations.—

(1) In general.—The amount allowable as a deduction under subsection (a) to an individual for the taxable year shall not exceed the sum of the monthly limitations for months during such taxable year that the individual is an eligible individual.

* * *

(4) Coordination with other contributions.—The limitation which would (but for this paragraph) apply under this subsection to an individual for any taxable year shall be reduced (but not below zero) by the sum of—

(A) the aggregate amount paid for such taxable year to Archer MSAs of such individual,

(B) the aggregate amount contributed to health savings accounts of such individual which is excludable from the taxpayer's gross income for such taxable year under section 106(d) (and such amount shall not be allowed as a deduction under subsection (a)) * * *

* * *

(6) Denial of deduction to dependents.—No deduction shall be allowed under this section to any individual with respect to whom a deduction under section 151 is allowable to another taxpayer for a taxable year beginning in the calendar year in which such individual's taxable year begins.

* * *

(c) Definitions and special rules.—For purposes of this section—

(1) Eligible individual.—

(A) In general.—The term "eligible individual" means, with respect to any month, any individual if—

(i) such individual is covered under a high deductible health plan as of the 1st day of such month, and

(ii) such individual is not, while covered under a high deductible health plan, covered under any health plan—

(I) which is not a high deductible health plan, and

(II) which provides coverage for any benefit which is covered under the high deductible health plan.

(B) Certain coverage disregarded.—Subparagraph (A)(ii) shall be applied without regard to—

(i) coverage for any benefit provided by permitted insurance, and

(ii) coverage (whether through insurance or otherwise) for accidents, disability, dental care, vision care, or long-term care. * * *

(2) High deductible health plan.—

(A) In general.—The term "high deductible health plan" means a health plan—

(i) which has an annual deductible which is not less than—

(I) $1,000 for self-only coverage, and

(II) twice the dollar amount in subclause (I) for family coverage, and

(ii) the sum of the annual deductible and the other annual out-of-pocket expenses required to be paid under the plan (other than for premiums) for covered benefits does not exceed—

(I) $5,000 for self-only coverage, and

(II) twice the dollar amount in subclause (I) for family coverage.

(B) Exclusion of certain plans.—Such term does not include a health plan if substantially all of its coverage is coverage described in paragraph (1)(B).

(C) Safe harbor for absence of preventive care deductible.—A plan shall not fail to be treated as a high deductible health plan by reason of failing to have a deductible for preventive care (within the meaning of section 1871 of the Social Security Act, except as otherwise provided by the Secretary).

(D) Special rules for network plans.—In the case of a plan using a network of providers—

(i) Annual out-of-pocket limitation.—Such plan shall not fail to be treated as a high deductible health plan by reason of having an out-of-pocket limitation for services provided outside of such network which exceeds the applicable limitation under subparagraph (A)(ii).

(ii) Annual deductible.—Such plan's annual deductible for services provided outside of such network shall not be taken into account for purposes of subsection (b)(2).

(3) Permitted insurance.—The term "permitted insurance" means—

(A) insurance if substantially all of the coverage provided under such insurance relates to—

(i) liabilities incurred under workers' compensation laws,

(ii) tort liabilities,

(iii) liabilities relating to ownership or use of property, or

(iv) such other similar liabilities as the Secretary may specify by regulations,

(B) insurance for a specified disease or illness, and

(C) insurance paying a fixed amount per day (or other period) of hospitalization.

(4) Family coverage.—The term "family coverage" means any coverage other than self-only coverage.

(5) Archer MSA.—The term "Archer MSA" has the meaning given such term in section 220(d).

(d) Health savings account.—For purposes of this section—

(1) In general.—The term "health savings account" means a trust created or organized in the United States as a health savings account exclusively for the purpose of paying the qualified medical expenses of the account beneficiary, but only if the written governing instrument creating the trust meets the following requirements:

(A) Except in the case of a rollover contribution described in subsection (f)(5) or section 220(f)(5), no contribution will be accepted—

(i) unless it is in cash, or

(ii) to the extent such contribution, when added to previous contributions to the trust for the calendar year, exceeds the sum of—

(I) the dollar amount in effect under subsection (b)(2)(B), and

(II) the dollar amount in effect under subsection (b)(3)(B).

(B) The trustee is a bank (as defined in section 408(n)), an insurance company (as defined in section 816), or another person who demonstrates to the satisfaction of the Secretary that the manner in which such person will administer the trust will be consistent with the requirements of this section.

(C) No part of the trust assets will be invested in life insurance contracts.

(D) The assets of the trust will not be commingled with other property except in a common trust fund or common investment fund.

(E) The interest of an individual in the balance in his account is nonforfeitable.

(2) Qualified medical expenses.—

(A) In general.—The term "qualified medical expenses" means, with respect to an account beneficiary, amounts paid by such beneficiary for medical care (as defined in section 213(d) for such individual), the spouse of such individual, and any dependent (as defined in section 152, determined without regard to subsections (b)(1), (b)(2), and (d)(1)(B) thereof) of such individual, but only to the extent such amounts are not compensated for by insurance or otherwise. Such term shall include an amount paid for medicine or a drug only if such medicine or drug is a prescribed drug (determined without regard to whether such drug is available without a prescription) or is insulin.

(B) Health insurance may not be purchased from account.—Subparagraph (A) shall not apply to any payment for insurance.

(C) Exceptions.—Subparagraph (B) shall not apply to any expense for coverage under—

(i) a health plan during any period of continuation coverage required under any Federal law,

(ii) a qualified long-term care insurance contract (as defined in section 7702B(b)),

(iii) a health plan during a period in which the individual is receiving unemployment compensation under any Federal or State law, or

(iv) in the case of an account beneficiary who has attained the age specified in section 1811 of the Social Security Act, any health insurance other than a medicare supplemental policy (as defined in section 1882 of the Social Security Act).

(3) Account beneficiary.—The term "account beneficiary" means the individual on whose behalf the health savings account was established.

(4) Certain rules to apply.—Rules similar to the following rules shall apply for purposes of this section:

(A) Section 219(d)(2) (relating to no deduction for rollovers).

(B) Section 219(f)(3) (relating to time when contributions deemed made).

(C) Except as provided in section 106(d), section 219(f)(5) (relating to employer payments).

(D) Section 408(g) (relating to community property laws).

(E) Section 408(h) (relating to custodial accounts).

(e) Tax treatment of accounts.—

(1) In general.—A health savings account is exempt from taxation under this subtitle unless such account has ceased to be a health savings account. Notwithstanding the preceding sentence, any such account is subject to the taxes imposed by section 511 (relating to imposition of tax on unrelated business income of charitable, etc. organizations).

(2) Account terminations.—Rules similar to the rules of paragraphs (2) and (4) of section 408(e) shall apply to health savings accounts, and any amount treated as distributed under such rules shall be treated as not used to pay qualified medical expenses.

(f) Tax treatment of distributions.—

(1) Amounts used for qualified medical expenses.—Any amount paid or distributed out of a health savings account which is used exclusively to pay qualified medical expenses of any account beneficiary shall not be includible in gross income.

(2) Inclusion of amounts not used for qualified medical expenses.—Any amount paid or distributed out of a health savings account which is not used exclusively to pay the qualified medical expenses of the account beneficiary shall be included in the gross income of such beneficiary.

* * *

(4) Additional tax on distributions not used for qualified medical expenses.—

(A) In general.—The tax imposed by this chapter on the account beneficiary for any taxable year in which there is a payment or distribution from a health savings account of such beneficiary which is includible in gross income under paragraph (2) shall be increased by 20 percent of the amount which is so includible.

(B) Exception for disability or death.—Subparagraph (A) shall not apply if the payment or distribution is made after the account beneficiary becomes disabled within the meaning of section 72(m)(7) or dies.

(C) Exception for distributions after medicare eligibility.—Subparagraph (A) shall not apply to any payment or distribution after the date on which the account beneficiary attains the age specified in section 1811 of the Social Security Act.

(5) Rollover contribution.—An amount is described in this paragraph as a rollover contribution if it meets the requirements of subparagraphs (A) and (B).

(A) In general.—Paragraph (2) shall not apply to any amount paid or distributed from a health savings account to the account beneficiary to the extent the amount received is paid into a health savings account for the benefit of such beneficiary not later than the 60th day after the day on which the beneficiary receives the payment or distribution.

(B) Limitation.—This paragraph shall not apply to any amount described in subparagraph (A) received by an individual from a health savings account if, at any time during the 1-year period ending on the day of such receipt, such individual received any other amount described in subparagraph (A) from a health savings account which was not includible in the individual's gross income because of the application of this paragraph.

(6) Coordination with medical expense deduction.—For purposes of determining the amount of the deduction under section 213, any payment or distribution out of a health savings account for qualified medical expenses shall not be treated as an expense paid for medical care.

(7) Transfer of account incident to divorce.—The transfer of an individual's interest in a health savings account to an individual's spouse or former spouse under a divorce or separation instrument described in subparagraph (A) of section 71(b)(2) shall not be considered a taxable transfer made by such individual notwithstanding any other provision of this subtitle, and such interest shall, after such transfer, be treated as a health savings account with respect to which such spouse is the account beneficiary.

(8) Treatment after death of account beneficiary.—

(A) Treatment if designated beneficiary is spouse.—If the account beneficiary's surviving spouse acquires such beneficiary's interest in a health savings account by reason of being the designated beneficiary of such account at the death of the account beneficiary, such health savings account shall be treated as if the spouse were the account beneficiary.

(B) Other cases.—

(i) In general.—If, by reason of the death of the account beneficiary, any person acquires the account beneficiary's interest in a health savings account in a case to which subparagraph (A) does not apply—

(I) such account shall cease to be a health savings account as of the date of death, and

(II) an amount equal to the fair market value of the assets in such account on such date shall be includible if such person is not the estate of such beneficiary, in such person's gross income for the taxable year which includes such date, or if such person is the estate of such beneficiary, in such beneficiary's gross income for the last taxable year of such beneficiary.

(ii) Special rules.—

(I) Reduction of inclusion for predeath expenses.—The amount includible in gross income under clause (i) by any person (other than the estate) shall be reduced by the amount of qualified medical expenses which were incurred by the decedent before the date of the decedent's death and paid by such person within 1 year after such date.

(II) Deduction for estate taxes.—An appropriate deduction shall be allowed under section 691(c) to any person (other than the decedent or the decedent's spouse) with respect to amounts included in gross income under clause (i) by such person.

(g) Cost-of-living adjustment.—

(1) In general.—Each dollar amount in subsections (b)(2) and (c)(2)(A) shall be increased by an amount equal to—

(A) such dollar amount, multiplied by

(B) the cost-of-living adjustment determined under section 1(f)(3) * * *.

* * *

PART VIII—SPECIAL DEDUCTIONS FOR CORPORATIONS

§ 241. Allowance of special deductions

In addition to the deductions provided in part VI (sec. 161 and following), there shall be allowed as deductions in computing taxable income the items specified in this part.

§ 243. Dividends received by corporations

(a) General rule.—In the case of a corporation, there shall be allowed as a deduction an amount equal to the following percentages of the amount received as dividends from a domestic corporation which is subject to taxation under this chapter:

(1) 70 percent, in the case of dividends other than dividends described in paragraph (2) or (3);

(2) 100 percent, in the case of dividends received by a small business investment company operating under the Small Business Investment Act of 1958 (15 U.S.C. 661 and following); and

(3) 100 percent, in the case of qualifying dividends (as defined in subsection (b)(1)).

(b) Qualifying dividends.—

(1) In general.—For purposes of this section, the term "qualifying dividend" means any dividend received by a corporation—

(A) if at the close of the day on which such dividend is received, such corporation is a member of the same affiliated group as the corporation distributing such dividend, and

(B) if—

(i) such dividend is distributed out of the earnings and profits of a taxable year of the distributing corporation which ends after December 31, 1963, for which an election under section 1562 was not in effect, and on each day of which the distributing corporation and the corporation receiving the dividend were members of such affiliated group, or

(ii) such dividend is paid by a corporation with respect to which an election under section 936 is in effect for the taxable year in which such dividend is paid.

(2) Affiliated group.—For purposes of this subsection:

(A) In general.—The term "affiliated group" has the meaning given such term by section 1504(a), except that for such purposes sections 1504(b)(2), 1504(b)(4), and 1504(c) shall not apply.

* * *

(c) Retention of 80–percent dividends received deduction for dividends from 20–percent owned corporations.—

(1) In general.—In the case of any dividend received from a 20–percent owned corporation—

(A) subsection (a)(1) of this section, and

(B) subsections (a)(3) and (b)(2) of section 244,

shall be applied by substituting "80 percent" for "70 percent".

(2) 20–percent owned corporation.—For purposes of this section, the term "20–percent owned corporation" means any corporation if 20 percent or more of the stock of such corporation (by vote and value) is owned by the taxpayer. For purposes of the preceding sentence, stock described in section 1504(a)(4) shall not be taken into account.

* * *

§ 246. Rules applying to deductions for dividends received

(a) Deduction not allowed for dividends from certain corporations.—

(1) In general.—The deductions allowed by sections 243, 244, and 245 shall not apply to any dividend from a corporation which, for the taxable year of the corporation in which the distribution is made, or for the next preceding taxable year of the corporation, is a corporation exempt from tax under section 501 (relating to certain charitable, etc., organizations) or section 521 (relating to farmers' cooperative associations).

* * *

(b) Limitation on aggregate amount of deductions.—

(1) General rule.—Except as provided in paragraph (2), the aggregate amount of the deductions allowed by sections 243(a)(1), 244(a), and subsection (a) or (b) of section 245 shall not exceed the percentage determined under paragraph (3) of the taxable income computed without regard to the deductions allowed by sections 172, 199, 243(a)(1), 244(a), subsection (a) or (b) of section 245, and 247, without regard to any adjustment under section 1059, and without regard to any capital loss carryback to the taxable year under section 1212(a)(1).

(2) Effect of net operating loss.—Paragraph (1) shall not apply for any taxable year for which there is a net operating loss (as determined under section 172).

(3) Special rules.—The provisions of paragraph (1) shall be applied—

(A) first separately with respect to dividends from 20–percent owned corporations (as defined in section 243(c)(2)) and the percentage determined under this paragraph shall be 80 percent, and

(B) then separately with respect to dividends not from 20–percent owned corporations and the percentage determined under this paragraph shall be 70 percent and the taxable income shall be reduced by the aggregate amount of dividends from 20–percent owned corporations (as so defined).

(c) Exclusion of certain dividends.—

(1) In general.—No deduction shall be allowed under section 243, 244, or 245, in respect of any dividend on any share of stock—

(A) which is held by the taxpayer for 45 days or less during the 91–day period beginning on the date which is 45 days before the date on which such share becomes ex-dividend with respect to such dividend, or

(B) to the extent that the taxpayer is under an obligation (whether pursuant to a short sale or otherwise) to make related payments with respect to positions in substantially similar or related property.

(2) 90–day rule in the case of certain preference dividends.—In the case of stock having preference in dividends, if the taxpayer receives dividends with respect to such stock which are attributable to a period or periods aggregating in excess of 366 days, paragraph (1)(A) shall be applied—

(A) by substituting "90 days" for "45 days" each place it appears, and

(B) by substituting "181–day period" for "91–day period".

(3) Determination of holding periods.—For purposes of this subsection, in determining the period for which the taxpayer has held any share of stock—

(A) the day of disposition, but not the day of acquisition, shall be taken into account, and

(B) paragraph (3) of section 1223 shall not apply.

(4) Holding period reduced for periods where risk of loss diminished.—The holding periods determined for purposes of this subsection shall be appropriately reduced (in the manner provided in regulations prescribed by the Secretary) for any period (during such periods) in which—

(A) the taxpayer has an option to sell, is under a contractual obligation to sell, or has made (and not closed) a short sale of, substantially identical stock or securities,

(B) the taxpayer is the grantor of an option to buy substantially identical stock or securities, or

(C) under regulations prescribed by the Secretary, a taxpayer has diminished his risk of loss by holding 1 or more other positions with respect to substantially similar or related property.

The preceding sentence shall not apply in the case of any qualified covered call (as defined in section 1092(c)(4) but without regard to the requirement that gain or loss with respect to the option not be ordinary income or loss), other than a qualified covered call option to which section 1092(f) applies.

* * *

§ 246A. Dividends received deduction reduced where portfolio stock is debt financed

(a) General rule.—In the case of any dividend on debt-financed portfolio stock, there shall be substituted for the percentage which (but for this subsection) would be used in determining the amount of the deduction allowable under section 243, 244, or 245(a) a percentage equal to the product of—

(1) 70 percent (80 percent in the case of any dividend from a 20–percent owned corporation as defined in section 243(c)(2)), and

(2) 100 percent minus the average indebtedness percentage.

(b) Section not to apply to dividends for which 100 percent dividends received deduction allowable.—Subsection (a) shall not apply to—

(1) qualifying dividends (as defined in section 243(b) without regard to section 243(d)(4)), and

(2) dividends received by a small business investment company operating under the Small Business Investment Act of 1958.

(c) Debt financed portfolio stock.—For purposes of this section—

(1) In general.—The term "debt financed portfolio stock" means any portfolio stock if at some time during the base period there is portfolio indebtedness with respect to such stock.

(2) Portfolio stock.—The term "portfolio stock" means any stock of a corporation unless—

(A) as of the beginning of the ex-dividend date, the taxpayer owns stock of such corporation—

(i) possessing at least 50 percent of the total voting power of the stock of such corporation, and

(ii) having a value equal to at least 50 percent of the total value of the stock of such corporation, or

(B) as of the beginning of the ex-dividend date—

(i) the taxpayer owns stock of such corporation which would meet the requirements of subparagraph (A) if "20 percent" were substituted for "50 percent" each place it appears in such subparagraph, and

(ii) stock meeting the requirements of subparagraph (A) is owned by 5 or fewer corporate shareholders.

* * *

(4) Treatment of certain preferred stock.—For purposes of determining whether the requirements of subparagraph (A) or (B) of paragraph (2) or of subparagraph (A) of paragraph (3) are met, stock described in section 1504(a)(4) shall not be taken into account.

(d) Average indebtedness percentage.—For purposes of this section—

(1) In general.—Except as provided in paragraph (2), the term "average indebtedness percentage" means the percentage obtained by dividing—

(A) the average amount (determined under regulations prescribed by the Secretary) of the portfolio indebtedness with respect to the stock during the base period, by

(B) the average amount (determined under regulations prescribed by the Secretary) of the adjusted basis of the stock during the base period.

(2) Special rule where stock not held throughout base period.—In the case of any stock which was not held by the taxpayer throughout the base period, paragraph (1) shall be applied as if the base period consisted only of that portion of the base period during which the stock was held by the taxpayer.

(3) Portfolio indebtedness.—

(A) In general.—The term "portfolio indebtedness" means any indebtedness directly attributable to investment in the portfolio stock.

(B) Certain amounts received from short sale treated as indebtedness.—For purposes of subparagraph (A), any amount received from a short sale shall be treated as indebtedness for the period beginning on the day on which such amount is received and ending on the day the short sale is closed.

(4) Base period.—The term "base period" means, with respect to any dividend, the shorter of—

(A) the period beginning on the ex-dividend date for the most recent previous dividend on the stock and ending on the day before the ex-dividend date for the dividend involved, or

(B) the 1–year period ending on the day before the ex-dividend date for the dividend involved.

(e) Reduction in dividends received deduction not to exceed allocable interest.—Under regulations prescribed by the Secretary, any reduction under this section in the amount allowable as a deduction under section 243, 244, or 245 with respect to any dividend shall not exceed the amount of any interest deduction (including any deductible short sale expense) allocable to such dividend.

(f) Regulations.—The regulations prescribed for purposes of this section under section 7701(f) shall include regulations providing for the disallowance of interest deductions or other appropriate treatment (in lieu of reducing the dividend received deduction) where the obligor of the indebtedness is a person other than the person receiving the dividend.

§ 248. Organizational expenditures

(a) Election to deduct.—If a corporation elects the application of this subsection (in accordance with regulations prescribed by the Secretary) with respect to any organizational expenditures—

(1) the corporation shall be allowed a deduction for the taxable year in which the corporation begins business in an amount equal to the lesser of—

(A) the amount of organizational expenditures with respect to the taxpayer, or

(B) $5,000, reduced (but not below zero) by the amount by which such organizational expenditures exceed $50,000, and

(2) the remainder of such organizational expenditures shall be allowed as a deduction ratably over the 180–month period beginning with the month in which the corporation begins business.

(b) Organizational expenditures defined.—The term "organizational expenditures" means any expenditure which—

(1) is incident to the creation of the corporation;

(2) is chargeable to capital account; and

(3) is of a character which, if expended incident to the creation of a corporation having a limited life, would be amortizable over such life.

(c) Time for and scope of election.—The election provided by subsection (a) may be made for any taxable year beginning after December 31, 1953, but only if made not later than the time prescribed by law for filing the return for such taxable year (including extensions thereof). The period so elected shall be adhered to in computing the taxable income of the corporation for the taxable year for which the election is made and all subsequent taxable years. * * *

§ 249. Limitation on deduction of bond premium on repurchase

(a) General rule.—No deduction shall be allowed to the issuing corporation for any premium paid or incurred upon the repurchase of a bond, debenture, note, or certificate or other evidence of indebtedness which is convertible into the stock of the issuing corporation, or a corporation in the same parent-subsidiary controlled controlled group (within the meaning of section 1563(a)(1)) as the issuing corporation, to the extent the repurchase price exceeds an amount equal to the adjusted issue price plus a normal call premium on bonds or other evidences of indebtedness which are not convertible. The preceding sentence shall not apply to the extent that the corporation can demonstrate to the satisfaction of the Secretary that such excess is attributable to the cost of borrowing and is not attributable to the conversion feature.

(b) Adjusted issue price.—For purposes of subsection (a), the adjusted issue price is the issue price (as defined in sections 1273(b) and 1274) increased by any amount of discount deducted before repurchase, or, in the case of bonds or other evidences of indebtedness issued after February 28, 1913, decreased by any amount of premium included in gross income before repurchase by the issuing corporation.

PART IX—ITEMS NOT DEDUCTIBLE

§ 261. General rule for disallowance of deductions

In computing taxable income no deduction shall in any case be allowed in respect of the items specified in this part.

§ 262. Personal, living, and family expenses

(a) General rule.—Except as otherwise expressly provided in this chapter, no deduction shall be allowed for personal, living, or family expenses.

(b) Treatment of certain phone expenses.—For purposes of subsection (a), in the case of an individual, any charge (including taxes thereon) for basic local telephone service with respect to the 1st telephone line provided to any residence of the taxpayer shall be treated as a personal expense.

§ 263. Capital expenditures

(a) General rule.—No deduction shall be allowed for—

(1) Any amount paid out for new buildings or for permanent improvements or betterments made to increase the value of any property or estate. This paragraph shall not apply to—

(A) expenditures for the development of mines or deposits deductible under section 616,

(B) research and experimental expenditures deductible under section 174,

(C) soil and water conservation expenditures deductible under section 175,

(D) expenditures by farmers for fertilizer, etc., deductible under section 180,

(E) expenditures for removal of architectural and transportation barriers to the handicapped and elderly which the taxpayer elects to deduct under section 190,

* * *

(G) expenditures for which a deduction is allowed under section 179;

* * *

(2) Any amount expended in restoring property or in making good the exhaustion thereof for which an allowance is or has been made.

[**(b) Repealed.**]

(c) Intangible drilling and development costs in the case of oil and gas wells and geothermal wells.—Notwithstanding subsection (a), and except as provided in subsection (i), regulations shall be prescribed by the Secretary under this subtitle corresponding to the regulations which granted the option to deduct as expenses intangible drilling and development costs in the case of oil and gas wells and which were recognized and approved by the Congress in House Concurrent Resolution 50, Seventy-ninth Congress. Such regulations shall also grant the option to deduct as expenses intangible drilling and development costs in the case of wells drilled for any geothermal deposit (as defined in section 613(e)(2)) to the same extent and in the same manner as such expenses are deductible in the case of oil and gas wells. This subsection shall not apply with respect to any costs to which any deduction is allowed under section 59(e) or 291.

* * *

§ 263A. Capitalization and inclusion in inventory costs of certain expenses

(a) Nondeductibility of certain direct and indirect costs.—

(1) In general.—In the case of any property to which this section applies, any costs described in paragraph (2)—

(A) in the case of property which is inventory in the hands of the taxpayer, shall be included in inventory costs, and

(B) in the case of any other property, shall be capitalized.

(2) Allocable costs.—The costs described in this paragraph with respect to any property are—

(A) the direct costs of such property, and

(B) such property's proper share of those indirect costs (including taxes) part or all of which are allocable to such property.

Any cost which (but for this subsection) could not be taken into account in computing taxable income for any taxable year shall not be treated as a cost described in this paragraph.

(b) Property to which section applies.—Except as otherwise provided in this section, this section shall apply to—

(1) Property produced by taxpayer.—Real or tangible personal property produced by the taxpayer.

(2) Property acquired for resale.—

(A) In general.—Real or personal property described in section 1221(a)(1) which is acquired by the taxpayer for resale.

(B) Exception for taxpayer with gross receipts of $10,000,000 or less.—Subparagraph (A) shall not apply to any personal property acquired during any taxable year by the taxpayer for resale if the average annual gross receipts of the taxpayer (or any predecessor) for the 3–taxable year period ending with the taxable year preceding such taxable year do not exceed $10,000,000.

(C) Aggregation rules, etc.—For purposes of subparagraph (B), rules similar to the rules of paragraphs (2) and (3) of section 448(c) shall apply.

For purposes of paragraph (1), the term "tangible personal property" shall include a film, sound recording, video tape, book, or similar property.

(c) General exceptions.—

(1) Personal use property.—This section shall not apply to any property produced by the taxpayer for use by the taxpayer other than in a trade or business or an activity conducted for profit.

(2) Research and experimental expenditures.—This section shall not apply to any amount allowable as a deduction under section 174.

(3) Certain development and other costs of oil and gas wells or other mineral property.—This section shall not apply to any cost allowable as a deduction under section 167(h), 179B, 263(c), 263(i), 291(b)(2), 616, or 617.

(4) Coordination with long-term contract rules.—This section shall not apply to any property produced by the taxpayer pursuant to a long-term contract.

(5) Timber and certain ornamental trees.—This section shall not apply to—

(A) trees raised, harvested, or grown by the taxpayer other than trees described in clause (ii) of subsection (e)(4)(B) (after application of the last sentence thereof), and

(B) any real property underlying such trees.

* * *

(d) Exception for farming businesses.—

(1) Section not to apply to certain property.—

(A) In general.—This section shall not apply to any of the following which is produced by the taxpayer in a farming business:

(i) Any animal.

(ii) Any plant which has a preproductive period of 2 years or less.

(B) Exception for taxpayers required to use accrual method.—Subparagraph (A) shall not apply to any corporation, partnership, or tax shelter required to use an accrual method of accounting under section 447 or 448(a)(3).

* * *

(3) Election to have this section not apply.—

(A) In general.—If a taxpayer makes an election under this paragraph, this section shall not apply to any plant produced in any farming business carried on by such taxpayer.

(B) Certain persons not eligible.—No election may be made under this paragraph by a corporation, partnership, or tax shelter, if such corporation, partnership, or tax shelter is required to use an accrual method of accounting under section 447 or 448(a)(3).

(i) by a corporation, partnership, or tax shelter, if such corporation, partnership, or tax shelter is required to use an accrual method of accounting under section 447 or 448(a)(3), or

(ii) with respect to the planting, cultivation, maintenance, or development of pistachio trees.

(C) Special rule for citrus and almond growers.—An election under this paragraph shall not apply with respect to any item which is attributable to the planting, cultivation, maintenance, or development of any citrus or almond grove (or part thereof) and which is incurred before the close of the 4th taxable year beginning with the taxable year in which the trees were planted. For purposes of the preceding sentence, the portion of a citrus or almond grove planted in 1 taxable year shall be treated separately from the portion of such grove planted in another taxable year.

(D) Election.—Unless the Secretary otherwise consents, an election under this paragraph may be made only for the taxpayer's 1st taxable year which begins after December 31, 1986, and during which the taxpayer engages in a farming business. Any such election, once made, may be revoked only with the consent of the Secretary.

(e) Definitions and special rules for purposes of subsection (d).—

(1) Recapture of expensed amounts on disposition.—

(A) In general.—In the case of any plant with respect to which amounts would have been capitalized under subsection (a) but for an election under subsection (d)(3)—

(i) such plant (if not otherwise section 1245 property) shall be treated as section 1245 property, and

(ii) for purposes of section 1245, the recapture amount shall be treated as a deduction allowed for depreciation with respect to such property.

(B) Recapture amount.—For purposes of subparagraph (A), the term "recapture amount" means any amount allowable as a deduction to the taxpayer which, but for an election under subsection (d)(3), would have been capitalized with respect to the plant.

(2) Effects of election on depreciation.—

(A) In general.—If the taxpayer (or any related person) makes an election under subsection (d)(3), the provisions of section 168(g)(2) (relating to alternative depreciation) shall apply to all property of the taxpayer used predominantly in the farming business and placed in service in any taxable year during which any such election is in effect.

(B) Related person.—For purposes of subparagraph (A), the term "related person" means—

(i) the taxpayer and members of the taxpayer's family,

(ii) any corporation (including an S corporation) if 50 percent or more (in value) of the stock of such corporation is owned (directly or through the application of section 318) by the taxpayer or members of the taxpayer's family,

(iii) a corporation and any other corporation which is a member of the same controlled group described in section 1563(a)(1), and

(iv) any partnership if 50 percent or more (in value) of the interests in such partnership is owned directly or indirectly by the taxpayer or members of the taxpayer's family.

(C) Members of family.—For purposes of this paragraph, the term "family" means the taxpayer, the spouse of the taxpayer, and any of their children who have not attained age 18 before the close of the taxable year.

(3) Preproductive period.—

(A) In general.—For purposes of this section, the term "preproductive period" means—

(i) in the case of a plant which will have more than 1 crop or yield, the period before the 1st marketable crop or yield from such plant, or

(ii) in the case of any other plant, the period before such plant is reasonably expected to be disposed of.

For purposes of this subparagraph, use by the taxpayer in a farming business of any supply produced in such business shall be treated as a disposition.

(B) Rule for determining period.—In the case of a plant grown in commercial quantities in the United States, the preproductive period for such plant if grown in the United States shall be based on the nationwide weighted average preproductive period for such plant.

(4) Farming business.—For purposes of this section—

(A) In general.—The term "farming business" means the trade or business of farming.

(B) Certain trades and businesses included.—The term "farming business" shall include the trade or business of—

(i) operating a nursery or sod farm, or

(ii) the raising or harvesting of trees bearing fruit, nuts, or other crops, or ornamental trees.

For purposes of clause (ii), an evergreen tree which is more than 6 years old at the time severed from the roots shall not be treated as an ornamental tree.

(5) Certain inventory valuation methods permitted.—The Secretary shall by regulations permit the taxpayer to use reasonable inventory valuation methods to compute the amount required to be capitalized under subsection (a) in the case of any plant.

(f) Special rules for allocation of interest to property produced by the taxpayer.—

(1) Interest capitalized only in certain cases.—Subsection (a) shall only apply to interest costs which are—

(A) paid or incurred during the production period, and

(B) allocable to property which is described in subsection (b)(1) and which has—

(i) a long useful life,

(ii) an estimated production period exceeding 2 years, or

(iii) an estimated production period exceeding 1 year and a cost exceeding $1,000,000.

(2) Allocation rules.—

(A) In general.—In determining the amount of interest required to be capitalized under subsection (a) with respect to any property—

(i) interest on any indebtedness directly attributable to production expenditures with respect to such property shall be assigned to such property, and

(ii) interest on any other indebtedness shall be assigned to such property to the extent that the taxpayer's interest costs could have been reduced if production expenditures (not attributable to indebtedness described in clause (i)) had not been incurred.

(B) Exception for qualified residence interest.—Subparagraph (A) shall not apply to any qualified residence interest (within the meaning of section 163(h)).

(C) Special rule for flow-through entities.—Except as provided in regulations, in the case of any flow-through entity, this paragraph shall be applied first at the entity level and then at the beneficiary level.

(3) Interest relating to property used to produce property.—This subsection shall apply to any interest on indebtedness allocable (as determined under paragraph (2)) to property used to produce property to which this subsection applies to the extent such interest is allocable (as so determined) to the produced property.

(4) Definitions.—For purposes of this subsection—

(A) Long useful life.—Property has a long useful life if such property is—

(i) real property, or

(ii) property with a class life of 20 years or more (as determined under section 168).

(B) Production period.—The term "production period" means, when used with respect to any property, the period—

(i) beginning on the date on which production of the property begins, and

(ii) ending on the date on which the property is ready to be placed in service or is ready to be held for sale.

(C) Production expenditures.—The term "production expenditures" means the costs (whether or not incurred during the production period) required to be capitalized under subsection (a) with respect to the property.

(g) Production.—For purposes of this section—

(1) In general.—The term "produce" includes construct, build, install, manufacture, develop, or improve.

(2) Treatment of property produced under contract for the taxpayer.—The taxpayer shall be treated as producing any property produced for the taxpayer under a contract with the taxpayer; except that only costs paid or incurred by the taxpayer (whether under such contract or otherwise) shall be taken into account in applying subsection (a) to the taxpayer.

(h) Exemption for free lance authors, photographers, and artists.—

(1) In general.—Nothing in this section shall require the capitalization of any qualified creative expense.

(2) Qualified creative expense.—For purposes of this subsection, the term "qualified creative expense" means any expense—

(A) which is paid or incurred by an individual in the trade or business of such individual (other than as an employee) of being a writer, photographer, or artist, and

(B) which, without regard to this section, would be allowable as a deduction for the taxable year.

Such term does not include any expense related to printing, photographic plates, motion picture films, video tapes, or similar items.

(3) Definitions.—For purposes of this subsection—

(A) Writer.—The term "writer" means any individual if the personal efforts of such individual create (or may reasonably be expected to create) a literary manuscript, musical composition (including any accompanying words), or dance score.

(B) Photographer.—The term "photographer" means any individual if the personal efforts of such individual create (or may reasonably be expected to create) a photograph or photographic negative or transparency.

(C) Artist.—

(i) In general.—The term "artist" means any individual if the personal efforts of such individual create (or may reasonably be expected to create) a picture, painting, sculpture, statue, etching, drawing, cartoon, graphic design, or original print edition.

(ii) Criteria.—In determining whether any expense is paid or incurred in the trade or business of being an artist, the following criteria shall be taken into account:

(I) The originality and uniqueness of the item created (or to be created).

(II) The predominance of aesthetic value over utilitarian value of the item created (or to be created).

* * *

§ 264. Certain amounts paid in connection with insurance contracts

(a) General rule.—No deduction shall be allowed for—

(1) Premiums on any life insurance policy, or endowment or annuity contract, if the taxpayer is directly or indirectly a beneficiary under the policy or contract.

(2) Any amount paid or accrued on indebtedness incurred or continued to purchase or carry a single premium life insurance, endowment, or annuity contract.

(3) Except as provided in subsection (d), any amount paid or accrued on indebtedness incurred or continued to purchase or carry a life insurance, endowment, or annuity contract (other than a single premium contract or a contract treated as a single premium contract) pursuant to a plan of purchase which contemplates the systematic direct or indirect borrowing of part or all of the increases in the cash value of such contract (either from the insurer or otherwise).

(4) Except as provided in subsection (e), any interest paid or accrued on any indebtedness with respect to 1 or more life insurance policies owned by the taxpayer covering the life of any individual, or any endowment or annuity contracts owned by the taxpayer covering any individual.

Paragraph (2) shall apply in respect of annuity contracts only as to contracts purchased after March 1, 1954. Paragraph (3) shall apply only in respect of contracts purchased after August 6, 1963. Paragraph (4) shall apply with respect to contracts purchased after June 20, 1986.

* * *

(e) Special rules for application of subsection (a)(4).—

(1) Exception for key persons.—Subsection (a)(4) shall not apply to any interest paid or accrued on any indebtedness with respect to policies or contracts covering an individual who is a key person to the extent that the aggregate amount of such indebtedness with respect to policies and contracts covering such individual does not exceed $50,000.

(2) Interest rate cap on key persons and pre-1986 contracts.—

* * *

(3) Key person.—For purposes of paragraph (1), the term "key person" means an officer or 20–percent owner, except that the number of individuals who may be treated as key persons with respect to any taxpayer shall not exceed the greater of—

(A) 5 individuals, or

(B) the lesser of 5 percent of the total officers and employees of the taxpayer or 20 individuals.

(4) 20–percent owner.—For purposes of this subsection, the term "20–percent owner" means—

(A) if the taxpayer is a corporation, any person who owns directly 20 percent or more of the outstanding stock of the corporation or stock possessing 20 percent or more of the total combined voting power of all stock of the corporation, or

(B) if the taxpayer is not a corporation, any person who owns 20 percent or more of the capital or profits interest in the taxpayer.

* * *

(f) Pro rata allocation of interest expense to policy cash values.—

(1) In general.—No deduction shall be allowed for that portion of the taxpayer's interest expense which is allocable to unborrowed policy cash values.

(2) Allocation.—For purposes of paragraph (1), the portion of the taxpayer's interest expense which is allocable to unborrowed policy cash values is an amount which bears the same ratio to such interest expense as—

(A) the taxpayer's average unborrowed policy cash values of life insurance policies, and annuity and endowment contracts, issued after June 8, 1997, bears to

(B) the sum of—

(i) in the case of assets of the taxpayer which are life insurance policies or annuity or endowment contracts, the average unborrowed policy cash values of such policies and contracts, and

(ii) in the case of assets of the taxpayer not described in clause (i), the average adjusted bases (within the meaning of section 1016) of such assets.

(3) Unborrowed policy cash value.—For purposes of this subsection, the term "unborrowed policy cash value" means, with respect to any life insurance policy or annuity or endowment contract, the excess of—

(A) the cash surrender value of such policy or contract determined without regard to any surrender charge, over

(B) the amount of any loan with respect to such policy or contract.

If the amount described in subparagraph (A) with respect to any policy or contract does not reasonably approximate its actual value, the amount taken into account under subparagraph (A) shall be the greater of the amount of the insurance company liability or the insurance company reserve with respect to such policy or contract (as determined for purposes of the annual statement approved by the National Association of Insurance Commissioners) or shall be such other amount as is determined by the Secretary.

(4) Exception for certain policies and contracts.—

(A) Policies and contracts covering 20–percent owners, officers, directors, and employees.—Paragraph (1) shall not apply to any policy or contract owned by an entity engaged in a trade or business if such policy or contract covers only 1 individual and if such individual is (at the time first covered by the policy or contract)—

(i) a 20–percent owner of such entity, or

(ii) an individual (not described in clause (i)) who is an officer, director, or employee of such trade or business.

A policy or contract covering a 20–percent owner of such entity shall not be treated as failing to meet the requirements of the preceding sentence by reason of covering the joint lives of such owner and such owner's spouse.

(B) Contracts subject to current income inclusion.—Paragraph (1) shall not apply to any annuity contract to which section 72(u) applies.

(C) Coordination with paragraph (2).—Any policy or contract to which paragraph (1) does not apply by reason of this paragraph shall not be taken into account under paragraph (2).

(D) 20–Percent owner.—For purposes of subparagraph (A), the term "20–percent owner" has the meaning given such term by subsection (e)(4).

(E) Master contracts.—If coverage for each insured under a master contract is treated as a separate contract for purposes of sections 817(h), 7702, and 7702A, coverage for each such insured shall be treated as a separate contract for purposes of subparagraph (A). For purposes of the preceding sentence, the term "master contract" shall not include any group life insurance contract (as defined in section 848(e)(2)).

(5) Exception for policies and contracts held by natural persons; treatment of partnerships and S corporations.—

(A) Policies and contracts held by natural persons.—

(i) In general.—This subsection shall not apply to any policy or contract held by a natural person.

(ii) Exception where business is beneficiary.—If a trade or business is directly or indirectly the beneficiary under any policy or contract, such policy or contract shall be treated as held by such trade or business and not by a natural person.

(iii) Special rules.—

(I) Certain trades or businesses not taken into account.—Clause (ii) shall not apply to any trade or business carried on as a sole proprietorship and to any trade or business performing services as an employee.

(II) Limitation on unborrowed cash value.—The amount of the unborrowed cash value of any policy or contract which is taken into account by reason of clause (ii) shall not exceed the benefit to which the trade or business is directly or indirectly entitled under the policy or contract.

(iv) Reporting.—The Secretary shall require such reporting from policyholders and issuers as is necessary to carry out clause (ii).

(B) Treatment of partnerships and S corporations.—In the case of a partnership or S corporation, this subsection shall be applied at the partnership and corporate levels.

(6) Special rules.—

(A) Coordination with subsection (a) and section 265.—If interest on any indebtedness is disallowed under subsection (a) or section 265—

(i) such disallowed interest shall not be taken into account for purposes of applying this subsection, and

(ii) the amount otherwise taken into account under paragraph (2)(B) shall be reduced (but not below zero) by the amount of such indebtedness.

(B) Coordination with section 263A.—This subsection shall be applied before the application of section 263A (relating to capitalization of certain expenses where taxpayer produces property).

(7) Interest expense.—The term "interest expense" means the aggregate amount allowable to the taxpayer as a deduction for interest (within the meaning of section 265(b)(4)) for the taxable year (determined without regard to this subsection, section 265(b), and section 291).

* * *

§ 265. Expenses and interest relating to tax-exempt income

(a) General rule.—No deduction shall be allowed for—

(1) Expenses.—Any amount otherwise allowable as a deduction which is allocable to one or more classes of income other than interest (whether or not any amount of income of that class or classes is received or accrued) wholly exempt from the taxes imposed by this subtitle, or any amount otherwise allowable under section 212 (relating to expenses for production of income) which is allocable to interest (whether or not any amount of such interest is received or accrued) wholly exempt from the taxes imposed by this subtitle.

(2) Interest.—Interest on indebtedness incurred or continued to purchase or carry obligations the interest on which is wholly exempt from the taxes imposed by this subtitle.

(3) Certain regulated investment companies.—In the case of a regulated investment company which distributes during the taxable year an exempt-interest dividend (including exempt-interest dividends paid after the close of the taxable year as described in section 855), that portion of any amount otherwise allowable as a deduction which the amount of the income of such company wholly exempt from taxes under this subtitle bears to the total of such exempt income and its gross income (excluding from gross income, for this purpose, capital gain net income, as defined in section 1222(9)).

(4) Interest related to exempt-interest dividends.—Interest on indebtedness incurred or continued to purchase or carry shares of stock of a regulated investment company which during the taxable year of the holder thereof distributes exempt-interest dividends.

* * *

(6) Section not to apply with respect to parsonage and military housing allowances.—No deduction shall be denied under this section for interest on a mortgage on, or real property taxes on, the home of the taxpayer by reason of the receipt of an amount as—

(A) a military housing allowance, or

(B) a parsonage allowance excludable from gross income under section 107.

* * *

§ 266. Carrying charges

No deduction shall be allowed for amounts paid or accrued for such taxes and carrying charges as, under regulations prescribed by the Secretary, are chargeable to capital account with respect to property, if the taxpayer elects, in accordance with such regulations, to treat such taxes or charges as so chargeable.

§ 267. Losses, expenses, and interest with respect to transactions between related taxpayers

(a) In general.—

(1) Deduction for losses disallowed.—No deduction shall be allowed in respect of any loss from the sale or exchange of property, directly or indirectly, between persons specified in any of the paragraphs of subsection (b). The preceding sentence shall not apply to any loss of the distributing corporation (or the distributee) in the case of a distribution in complete liquidation.

(2) Matching of deduction and payee income item in the case of expenses and interest.—If—

(A) by reason of the method of accounting of the person to whom the payment is to be made, the amount thereof is not (unless paid) includible in the gross income of such person, and

(B) at the close of the taxable year of the taxpayer for which (but for this paragraph) the amount would be deductible under this chapter, both the taxpayer and the person to whom the payment is to be made are persons specified in any of the paragraphs of subsection (b),

then any deduction allowable under this chapter in respect of such amount shall be allowable as of the day as of which such amount is includible in the gross income of the person to whom the payment is made (or, if later, as of the day on which it would be so allowable but for this paragraph). For purposes of this paragraph, in the case of a personal service corporation (within the meaning of section 441(i)(2)), such corporation and any employee-owner (within the meaning of section 269A(b)(2), as modified by section 441(i)(2)) shall be treated as persons specified in subsection (b).

* * *

(b) Relationships.—The persons referred to in subsection (a) are:

(1) Members of a family, as defined in subsection (c)(4);

(2) An individual and a corporation more than 50 percent in value of the outstanding stock of which is owned, directly or indirectly, by or for such individual;

(3) Two corporations which are members of the same controlled group (as defined in subsection (f));

(4) A grantor and a fiduciary of any trust;

(5) A fiduciary of a trust and a fiduciary of another trust, if the same person is a grantor of both trusts;

(6) A fiduciary of a trust and a beneficiary of such trust;

(7) A fiduciary of a trust and a beneficiary of another trust, if the same person is a grantor of both trusts;

(8) A fiduciary of a trust and a corporation more than 50 percent in value of the outstanding stock of which is owned, directly or indirectly, by or for the trust or by or for a person who is a grantor of the trust;

(9) A person and an organization to which section 501 (relating to certain educational and charitable organizations which are exempt from tax) applies and which is controlled directly or indirectly by such person or (if such person is an individual) by members of the family of such individual;

(10) A corporation and a partnership if the same persons own—

(A) more than 50 percent in value of the outstanding stock of the corporation, and

(B) more than 50 percent of the capital interest, or the profits interest, in the partnership;

(11) An S corporation and another S corporation if the same persons own more than 50 percent in value of the outstanding stock of each corporation;

(12) An S corporation and a C corporation, if the same persons own more than 50 percent in value of the outstanding stock of each corporation; or

(13) Except in the case of a sale or exchange in satisfaction of a pecuniary bequest, an executor of an estate and a beneficiary of such estate.

(c) Constructive ownership of stock.—For purposes of determining, in applying subsection (b), the ownership of stock—

(1) Stock owned, directly or indirectly, by or for a corporation, partnership, estate, or trust shall be considered as being owned proportionately by or for its shareholders, partners, or beneficiaries;

(2) An individual shall be considered as owning the stock owned, directly or indirectly, by or for his family;

(3) An individual owning (otherwise than by the application of paragraph (2)) any stock in a corporation shall be considered as owning the stock owned, directly or indirectly, by or for his partner;

(4) The family of an individual shall include only his brothers and sisters (whether by the whole or half blood), spouse, ancestors, and lineal descendants; and

(5) Stock constructively owned by a person by reason of the application of paragraph (1) shall, for the purpose of applying paragraph (1), (2), or (3), be treated as actually owned by such person, but stock constructively owned by an individual by reason of the application of paragraph (2) or (3) shall not be treated as owned by him for the purpose of again applying either of such paragraphs in order to make another the constructive owner of such stock.

(d) Amount of gain where loss previously disallowed.—If—

(1) in the case of a sale or exchange of property to the taxpayer a loss sustained by the transferor is not allowable to the transferor as a deduction by reason of subsection (a)(1) * * *; and

(2) after December 31, 1953, the taxpayer sells or otherwise disposes of such property (or of other property the basis of which in his hands is determined directly or indirectly by reference to such property) at a gain,

then such gain shall be recognized only to the extent that it exceeds so much of such loss as is properly allocable to the property sold or otherwise disposed of by the taxpayer. This subsection applies with respect to taxable years ending after December 31, 1953. This subsection shall not apply if the loss sustained by the transferor is not allowable to the transferor as a deduction by reason of section 1091 (relating to wash sales) * * *.

(e) Special rules for pass-thru entities.—

(1) In general.—In the case of any amount paid or incurred by, to, or on behalf of, a pass-thru entity, for purposes of applying subsection (a)(2)—

(A) such entity,

(B) in the case of—

(i) a partnership, any person who owns (directly or indirectly) any capital interest or profits interest of such partnership, or

(ii) an S corporation, any person who owns (directly or indirectly) any of the stock of such corporation,

(C) any person who owns (directly or indirectly) any capital interest or profits interest of a partnership in which such entity owns (directly or indirectly) any capital interest or profits interest, and

(D) any person related (within the meaning of subsection (b) of this section or section 707(b)(1)) to a person described in subparagraph (B) or (C),

shall be treated as persons specified in a paragraph of subsection (b). Subparagraph (C) shall apply to a transaction only if such transaction is related either to the operations of the partnership described in such subparagraph or to an interest in such partnership.

(2) Pass-thru entity.—For purposes of this section, the term "pass-thru entity" means—

(A) a partnership, and

(B) an S corporation.

(3) Constructive ownership in the case of partnerships.—For purposes of determining ownership of a capital interest or profits interest of a partnership, the principles of subsection (c) shall apply, except that—

(A) paragraph (3) of subsection (c) shall not apply, and

(B) interests owned (directly or indirectly) by or for a C corporation shall be considered as owned by or for any shareholder only if such shareholder owns (directly or indirectly) 5 percent or more in value of the stock of such corporation.

(4) Subsection (a)(2) not to apply to certain guaranteed payments of partnerships.—In the case of any amount paid or incurred by a partnership, subsection (a)(2) shall not apply to the extent that section 707(c) applies to such amount.

(5) Exception for certain expenses and interest of partnerships owning low-income housing.—

(A) In general.—This subsection shall not apply with respect to qualified expenses and interest paid or incurred by a partnership owning low-income housing to—

(i) any qualified 5–percent or less partner of such partnership, or

(ii) any person related (within the meaning of subsection (b) of this section or section 707(b)(1)) to any qualified 5–percent or less partner of such partnership.

(B) Qualified 5–percent or less partner.—For purposes of this paragraph, the term "qualified 5–percent or less partner" means any partner who has (directly or indirectly) an interest of 5 percent or less in the aggregate capital and profits interests of the partnership but only if—

(i) such partner owned the low-income housing at all times during the 2–year period ending on the date such housing was transferred to the partnership, or

(ii) such partnership acquired the low-income housing pursuant to a purchase, assignment, or other transfer from the Department of Housing and Urban Development or any State or local housing authority.

For purposes of the preceding sentence, a partner shall be treated as holding any interest in the partnership which is held (directly or indirectly) by any person related (within the meaning of subsection (b) of this section or section 707(b)(1)) to such partner.

(C) Qualified expenses and interest.—For purpose of this paragraph, the term "qualified expenses and interest" means any expense or interest incurred by the partnership with respect to low-income housing held by the partnership but—

(i) only if the amount of such expense or interest (as the case may be) is unconditionally required to be paid by the partnership not later than 10 years after the date such amount was incurred, and

(ii) in the case of such interest, only if such interest is incurred at an annual rate not in excess of 12 percent.

(D) Low-income housing.—For purposes of this paragraph, the term "low-income housing" means—

(i) any interest in property described in clause (i), (ii), (iii), or (iv) of section 1250(a)(1)(B), and

(ii) any interest in a partnership owning such property.

(6) Cross reference.—

For additional rules relating to partnerships, see section 707(b).

(f) Controlled group defined; special rules applicable to controlled groups.—

(1) Controlled group defined.—For purposes of this section, the term "controlled group" has the meaning given to such term by section 1563(a), except that—

(A) "more than 50 percent" shall be substituted for "at least 80 percent" each place it appears in section 1563(a), and

(B) the determination shall be made without regard to subsections (a)(4) and (e)(3)(C) of section 1563.

(2) Deferral (rather than denial) of loss from sale or exchange between members.—In the case of any loss from the sale or exchange of property which is between members of the same controlled group and to which subsection (a)(1) applies (determined without regard to this paragraph but with regard to paragraph (3))—

(A) subsections (a)(1) and (d) shall not apply to such loss, but

(B) such loss shall be deferred until the property is transferred outside such controlled group and there would be recognition of loss under consolidated return principles or until such other time as may be prescribed in regulations.

* * *

(4) Determination of relationship resulting in disallowance of loss, for purposes of other provisions.—For purposes of any other section of this title which refers to a relationship which would result in a disallowance of losses under this section, deferral under paragraph (2) shall be treated as disallowance.

(g) Coordination with section 1041.—Subsection (a)(1) shall not apply to any transfer described in section 1041(a) (relating to transfers of property between spouses or incident to divorce).

§ 269. Acquisitions made to evade or avoid income tax

(a) In general.—If—

(1) any person or persons acquire, or acquired on or after October 8, 1940, directly or indirectly, control of a corporation, or

(2) any corporation acquires, or acquired on or after October 8, 1940, directly or indirectly, property of another corporation, not controlled, directly or indirectly, immediately before such acquisition, by such acquiring corporation or its stockholders, the basis of which property, in the hands of the acquiring corporation, is determined by reference to the basis in the hands of the transferor corporation,

and the principal purpose for which such acquisition was made is evasion or avoidance of Federal income tax by securing the benefit of a deduction, credit, or other allowance which such person or corporation would not otherwise enjoy, then the Secretary may disallow such deduction, credit, or other allowance. For purposes of paragraphs (1) and (2), control means the ownership of stock possessing at least 50 percent of the total combined voting power of all classes of stock entitled to vote or at least 50 percent of the total value of shares of all classes of stock of the corporation.

(b) Certain liquidations after qualified stock purchases.—

(1) In general.—If—

(A) there is a qualified stock purchase by a corporation of another corporation,

(B) an election is not made under section 338 with respect to such purchase,

(C) the acquired corporation is liquidated pursuant to a plan of liquidation adopted not more than 2 years after the acquisition date, and

(D) the principal purpose for such liquidation is the evasion or avoidance of Federal income tax by securing the benefit of a deduction, credit, or other allowance which the acquiring corporation would not otherwise enjoy,

then the Secretary may disallow such deduction, credit, or other allowance.

(2) Meaning of terms.—For purposes of paragraph (1), the terms "qualified stock purchase" and "acquisition date" have the same respective meanings as when used in section 338.

(c) Power of Secretary to allow deduction, etc., in part.—In any case to which subsection (a) or (b) applies the Secretary is authorized—

(1) to allow as a deduction, credit, or allowance any part of any amount disallowed by such subsection, if he determines that such allowance will not result in the evasion or avoidance of Federal income tax for which the acquisition was made; or

(2) to distribute, apportion, or allocate gross income, and distribute, apportion, or allocate the deductions, credits, or allowances the benefit of which was sought to be secured, between or among the corporations, or properties, or parts thereof, involved, and to allow such deductions, credits, or allowances so distributed, apportioned, or allocated, but to give effect to such allowance only to such extent as he determines will not result in the evasion or avoidance of Federal income tax for which the acquisition was made; or

(3) to exercise his powers in part under paragraph (1) and in part under paragraph (2).

§ 269A. Personal service corporations formed or availed of to avoid or evade income tax

(a) General rule—If—

(1) substantially all of the services of a personal service corporation are performed for (or on behalf of) 1 other corporation, partnership, or other entity, and

(2) the principal purpose for forming, or availing of, such personal service corporation is the avoidance or evasion of Federal income tax by reducing the income of, or securing the benefit of any expense, deduction, credit, exclusion, or other allowance for, any employee-owner which would not otherwise be available,

then the Secretary may allocate all income, deductions, credits, exclusions, and other allowances between such personal service corporation and its employee-owners, if such allocation is necessary to prevent avoidance or evasion of Federal income tax or clearly to reflect the income of the personal service corporation or any of its employee-owners.

(b) Definitions.—For purposes of this section—

(1) Personal service corporation.—The term "personal service corporation" means a corporation the principal activity of which is the performance of personal services and such services are substantially performed by employee-owners.

(2) Employee-owner.—The term "employee-owner" means any employee who owns, on any day during the taxable year, more than 10 percent of the outstanding stock of the personal service corporation. For purposes of the preceding sentence, section 318 shall apply, except that "5 percent" shall be substituted for "50 percent" in section 318(a)(2)(C).

* * *

§ 271. Debts owed by political parties, etc.

(a) General rule.—In the case of a taxpayer (other than a bank as defined in section 581) no deduction shall be allowed under section 166 (relating to bad debts) or under section 165(g) (relating to worthlessness of securities) by reason of the worthlessness of any debt owed by a political party.

* * *

§ 273. Holders of life or terminable interest

Amounts paid under the laws of a State, the District of Columbia, a possession of the United States, or a foreign country as income to the holder of a life or terminable interest acquired by gift, bequest, or inheritance shall not be reduced or diminished by any deduction for shrinkage (by whatever name called) in the value of such interest due to the lapse of time.

§ 274. Disallowance of certain entertainment, etc., expenses

(a) Entertainment, amusement, or recreation.—

(1) In general.—No deduction otherwise allowable under this chapter shall be allowed for any item—

(A) Activity.—With respect to an activity which is of a type generally considered to constitute entertainment, amusement, or recreation, unless the taxpayer establishes that the item was directly related to, or, in the case of an item directly preceding or following a substantial and bona fide business discussion (including business meetings at a convention or otherwise), that such item was associated with, the active conduct of the taxpayer's trade or business, or

(B) Facility.—With respect to a facility used in connection with an activity referred to in subparagraph (A).

In the case of an item described in subparagraph (A), the deduction shall in no event exceed the portion of such item which meets the requirements of subparagraph (A).

(2) Special rules.—For purposes of applying paragraph (1)—

(A) Dues or fees to any social, athletic, or sporting club or organization shall be treated as items with respect to facilities.

(B) An activity described in section 212 shall be treated as a trade or business.

(C) In the case of a club, paragraph (1)(B) shall apply unless the taxpayer establishes that the facility was used primarily for the furtherance of the taxpayer's trade or business and that the item was directly related to the active conduct of such trade or business.

(3) Denial of deduction for club dues.—Notwithstanding the preceding provisions of this subsection, no deduction shall be allowed under this chapter for amounts paid or incurred for membership in any club organized for business, pleasure, recreation, or other social purpose.

(b) Gifts.—

(1) Limitation.—No deduction shall be allowed under section 162 or section 212 for any expense for gifts made directly or indirectly to any individual to the extent that such expense, when added to prior expenses of the taxpayer for gifts made to such individual during the same taxable year, exceeds $25. For purposes of this section, the term "gift" means any item excludable from gross income of the recipient under section 102 which is not excludable from his gross income under any other provision of this chapter, but such term does not include—

(A) an item having a cost to the taxpayer not in excess of $4.00 on which the name of the taxpayer is clearly and permanently imprinted and which is one of a number of identical items distributed generally by the taxpayer, or

(B) a sign, display rack, or other promotional material to be used on the business premises of the recipient.

(2) Special rules.—

(A) In the case of a gift by a partnership, the limitation contained in paragraph (1) shall apply to the partnership as well as to each member thereof.

(B) For purposes of paragraph (1), a husband and wife shall be treated as one taxpayer.

(c) Certain foreign travel.—

(1) In general.—In the case of any individual who travels outside the United States away from home in pursuit of a trade or business or in pursuit of an activity described in section 212, no deduction shall be allowed under section 162 or section 212 for that portion of the expenses of such travel otherwise allowable under such section which, under regulations prescribed by the Secretary, is not allocable to such trade or business or to such activity.

(2) Exception.—Paragraph (1) shall not apply to the expenses of any travel outside the United States away from home if—

(A) such travel does not exceed one week, or

(B) the portion of the time of travel outside the United States away from home which is not attributable to the pursuit of the taxpayer's trade or business or an activity described in section 212 is less than 25 percent of the total time on such travel.

(3) Domestic travel excluded.—For purposes of this subsection, travel outside the United States does not include any travel from one point in the United States to another point in the United States.

(d) Substantiation required.—No deduction or credit shall be allowed—

(1) under section 162 or 212 for any traveling expense (including meals and lodging while away from home),

(2) for any item with respect to an activity which is of a type generally considered to constitute entertainment, amusement, or recreation, or with respect to a facility used in connection with such an activity,

(3) any expense for gifts, or

(4) with respect to any listed property (as defined in section 280F(d)(4)),

unless the taxpayer substantiates by adequate records or by sufficient evidence corroborating the taxpayer's own statement (A) the amount of such expense or other item, (B) the time and place of the travel, entertainment, amusement, recreation or use of the facility or property, or the date and description of the gift, (C) the business purpose of the expense or other item, and (D) the business relationship to the taxpayer of persons entertained, using the facility or property, or receiving the gift. The Secretary may by regulations provide that some or all of the requirements of the preceding sentence shall not apply in the case of an expense which does not exceed an amount prescribed pursuant to such regulations. This subsection shall not apply to any qualified nonpersonal use vehicle (as defined in subsection (i)).

(e) Specific exceptions to application of subsection (a).—Subsection (a) shall not apply to—

(1) Food and beverages for employees.—Expenses for food and beverages (and facilities used in connection therewith) furnished on the business premises of the taxpayer primarily for his employees.

(2) Expenses treated as compensation.—

(A) In general.—Except as provided in subparagraph (B), expenses for goods, services, and facilities, to the extent that the expenses are treated by the taxpayer, with respect to the recipient of the entertainment, amusement, or recreation, as compensation to an employee on the taxpayer's return of tax under this chapter and as wages to such employee for purposes of chapter 24 (relating to withholding of income tax at source on wages).

(B) Specified individuals.—

(i) In general.—In the case of a recipient who is a specified individual, subparagraph (A) and paragraph (9) shall each be applied by substituting "to the extent that the expenses do not exceed the amount of the expenses which" for "to the extent that the expenses".

(ii) Specified individual.—For purposes of clause (i), the term "specified individual" means any individual who—

(I) is subject to the requirements of section 16(a) of the Securities Exchange Act of 1934 with respect to the taxpayer or a related party to the taxpayer, or

(II) would be subject to such requirements if the taxpayer (or such related party) were an issuer of equity securities referred to in such section.

For purposes of this clause, a person is a related party with respect to another person if such person bears a relationship to such other person described in section 267(b) or 707(b).

(3) Reimbursed expenses.—Expenses paid or incurred by the taxpayer, in connection with the performance by him of services for another person (whether or not such other person is his employer), under a reimbursement or other expense allowance arrangement with such other person, but this paragraph shall apply—

(A) where the services are performed for an employer, only if the employer has not treated such expenses in the manner provided in paragraph (2), or

(B) where the services are performed for a person other than an employer, only if the taxpayer accounts (to the extent provided by subsection (d)) to such person.

(4) Recreational, etc., expenses for employees.—Expenses for recreational, social, or similar activities (including facilities therefor) primarily for the benefit of employees (other than employees who are highly compensated employees) (within the meaning of section 414(q)). For purposes of this paragraph, an individual owning less than a 10–percent interest in the taxpayer's trade or business shall not be considered a shareholder or other owner, and for such purposes an individual shall be treated as owning any interest owned by a member of his family (within the meaning of section 267(c)(4)). This paragraph shall not apply for purposes of subsection (a)(3).

(5) Employee, stockholder, etc., business meetings.—Expenses incurred by a taxpayer which are directly related to business meetings of his employees, stockholders, agents, or directors.

(6) Meetings of business leagues, etc.—Expenses directly related and necessary to attendance at a business meeting or convention of any organization described in section 501(c)(6) (relating to business leagues, chambers of commerce, real estate boards, and boards of trade) and exempt from taxation under section 501(a).

(7) Items available to public.—Expenses for goods, services, and facilities made available by the taxpayer to the general public.

(8) Entertainment sold to customers.—Expenses for goods or services (including the use of facilities) which are sold by the taxpayer in a bona fide transaction for an adequate and full consideration in money or money's worth.

(9) Expenses includible in income of persons who are not employees.—Expenses paid or incurred by the taxpayer for goods, services, and facilities to the extent that the expenses are includible in the gross income of a recipient of the entertainment, amusement, or recreation who is not an employee of the taxpayer as compensation for services rendered or as a prize or award under section 74. The preceding sentence shall not apply to any amount paid or incurred by the taxpayer if such amount is required to be included (or would be so required except that the amount is less than $600) in any information return filed by such taxpayer under part III of subchapter A of chapter 61 and is not so included.

For purposes of this subsection, any item referred to in subsection (a) shall be treated as an expense.

(f) Interest, taxes, casualty losses, etc.—This section shall not apply to any deduction allowable to the taxpayer without regard to its connection with his trade or business (or with his income-producing activity). In the case of a taxpayer which is not an individual, the preceding sentence shall be applied as if it were an individual.

(g) Treatment of entertainment, etc., type facility.—For purposes of this chapter, if deductions are disallowed under subsection (a) with respect to any portion of a facility, such portion shall be treated as an asset which is used for personal, living, and family purposes (and not as an asset used in the trade or business).

(h) Attendance at conventions, etc.—

(1) In general.—In the case of any individual who attends a convention, seminar, or similar meeting which is held outside the North American area, no deduction shall be allowed under section 162 for expenses allocable to such meeting unless the taxpayer establishes that the meeting is directly related to the active conduct of his trade or business and that, after taking into account in the manner provided by regulations prescribed by the Secretary—

(A) the purpose of such meeting and the activities taking place at such meeting,

(B) the purposes and activities of the sponsoring organizations or groups,

(C) the residences of the active members of the sponsoring organization and the places at which other meetings of the sponsoring organization or groups have been held or will be held, and

(D) such other relevant factors as the taxpayer may present, it is as reasonable for the meeting to be held outside the North American area as within the North American area.

(2) Conventions on cruise ships.—In the case of any individual who attends a convention, seminar, or other meeting which is held on any cruise ship, no deduction shall be allowed under section 162 for expenses allocable to such meeting, unless the taxpayer meets the requirements of paragraph (5) and establishes that the meeting is directly related to the active conduct of his trade or business and that—

(A) the cruise ship is a vessel registered in the United States; and

(B) all ports of call of such cruise ship are located in the United States or in possessions of the United States.

With respect to cruises beginning in any calendar year, not more than $2,000 of the expenses attributable to an individual attending one or more meetings may be taken into account under section 162 by reason of the preceding sentence.

(3) Definitions.—For purposes of this subsection—

(A) North American area.—The term "North American area" means the United States, its possessions, and the Trust Territory of the Pacific Islands, and Canada and Mexico.

(B) Cruise ship.—The term "cruise ship" means any vessel sailing within or without the territorial waters of the United States.

(4) Subsection to apply to employer as well as to traveler.—

(A) Except as provided in subparagraph (B), this subsection shall apply to deductions otherwise allowable under section 162 to any person, whether or not such person is the individual attending the convention, seminar, or similar meeting.

(B) This subsection shall not deny a deduction to any person other than the individual attending the convention, seminar, or similar meeting with respect to any amount paid by such person to or on behalf of such individual if includible in the gross income of such individual. The preceding sentence shall not apply if the amount is required to be included in any information return filed by such person under part III of subchapter A of chapter 61 and is not so included.

(5) Reporting requirements.—No deduction shall be allowed under section 162 for expenses allocable to attendance at a convention, seminar, or similar meeting on any cruise ship unless the taxpayer claiming the deduction attaches to the return of tax on which the deduction is claimed—

(A) a written statement signed by the individual attending the meeting which includes—

(i) information with respect to the total days of the trip, excluding the days of transportation to and from the cruise ship port, and the number of hours of each day of the trip which such individual devoted to scheduled business activities,

(ii) a program of the scheduled business activities of the meeting, and

(iii) such other information as may be required in regulations prescribed by the Secretary; and

(B) a written statement signed by an officer of the organization or group sponsoring the meeting which includes—

(i) a schedule of the business activities of each day of the meeting,

(ii) the number of hours which the individual attending the meeting attended such scheduled business activities, and

(iii) such other information as may be required in regulations prescribed by the Secretary.

* * *

(7) Seminars, etc. for section 212 purposes.—No deduction shall be allowed under section 212 for expenses allocable to a convention, seminar, or similar meeting.

(i) Qualified nonpersonal use vehicle.—For purposes of subsection (d), the term "qualified nonpersonal use vehicle" means any vehicle which, by reason of its nature, is not likely to be used more than a de minimis amount for personal purposes.

(j) Employee achievement awards.—

(1) General rule.—No deduction shall be allowed under section 162 or section 212 for the cost of an employee achievement award except to the extent that such cost does not exceed the deduction limitations of paragraph (2).

(2) Deduction limitations.—The deduction for the cost of an employee achievement award made by an employer to an employee—

(A) which is not a qualified plan award, when added to the cost to the employer for all other employee achievement awards made to such employee during the taxable year which are not qualified plan awards, shall not exceed $400, and

(B) which is a qualified plan award, when added to the cost to the employer for all other employee achievement awards made to such employee during the taxable year (including employee achievement awards which are not qualified plan awards), shall not exceed $1,600.

(3) Definitions.—For purposes of this subsection—

(A) Employee achievement award.—The term "employee achievement award" means an item of tangible personal property which is—

(i) transferred by an employer to an employee for length of service achievement or safety achievement,

(ii) awarded as part of a meaningful presentation, and

(iii) awarded under conditions and circumstances that do not create a significant likelihood of the payment of disguised compensation.

(B) Qualified plan award.—

(i) In general.—The term "qualified plan award" means an employee achievement award awarded as part of an established written plan or program of the taxpayer which does not discriminate in favor of highly compensated employees (within the meaning of section 414(q)) as to eligibility or benefits.

(ii) Limitation.—An employee achievement award shall not be treated as a qualified plan award for any taxable year if the average cost of all employee achievement awards which are provided by the employer during the year, and which would be qualified plan awards but for this subparagraph, exceeds $400. For purposes of the preceding sentence, average cost shall be determined by including the entire cost of qualified plan awards, without taking into account employee achievement awards of nominal value.

(4) Special rules.—For purposes of this subsection—

(A) Partnerships.—In the case of an employee achievement award made by a partnership, the deduction limitations contained in paragraph (2) shall apply to the partnership as well as to each member thereof.

(B) Length of service awards.—An item shall not be treated as having been provided for length of service achievement if the item is received during the recipient's 1st 5 years of employment or if the recipient received a length of service achievement award (other than an award excludable under section 132(e)(1)) during that year or any of the prior 4 years.

(C) Safety achievement awards.—An item provided by an employer to an employee shall not be treated as having been provided for safety achievement if—

(i) during the taxable year, employee achievement awards (other than awards excludable under section 132(e)(1)) for safety achievement have previously been awarded by the employer to more than 10 percent of the employees of the employer (excluding employees described in clause (ii)), or

(ii) such item is awarded to a manager, administrator, clerical employee, or other professional employee.

(k) Business meals.—

(1) In general.—No deduction shall be allowed under this chapter for the expense of any food or beverages unless—

(A) such expense is not lavish or extravagant under the circumstances, and

(B) the taxpayer (or an employee of the taxpayer) is present at the furnishing of such food or beverages.

(2) Exceptions.—Paragraph (1) shall not apply to—

(A) any expense described in paragraph (2), (3), (4), (7), (8), or (9) of subsection (e), and

(B) any other expense to the extent provided in regulations.

(*l*) Additional limitations on entertainment tickets.—

(1) Entertainment tickets.—

(A) In general.—In determining the amount allowable as a deduction under this chapter for any ticket for any activity or facility described in subsection (d)(2), the amount taken into account shall not exceed the face value of such ticket.

(B) Exception for certain charitable sports events.—Subparagraph (A) shall not apply to any ticket for any sports event—

(i) which is organized for the primary purpose of benefiting an organization which is described in section 501(c)(3) and exempt from tax under section 501(a),

(ii) all of the net proceeds of which are contributed to such organization, and

(iii) which utilizes volunteers for substantially all of the work performed in carrying out such event.

(2) Skyboxes, etc.—In the case of a skybox or other private luxury box leased for more than 1 event, the amount allowable as a deduction under this chapter with respect to such events shall not exceed the sum of the face value of non-luxury box seat tickets for the seats in such box covered by the lease. For purposes of the preceding sentence, 2 or more related leases shall be treated as 1 lease.

(m) Additional limitations on travel expenses.—

(1) Luxury water transportation.—

(A) In general.—No deduction shall be allowed under this chapter for expenses incurred for transportation by water to the extent such expenses exceed twice the aggregate per diem amounts for days of such transportation. For purposes of the preceding sentence, the term "per diem amounts" means the highest amount generally allowable with respect to a day to employees of the executive branch of the Federal Government for per diem while away from home but serving in the United States.

(B) Exceptions.—Subparagraph (A) shall not apply to—

(i) any expense allocable to a convention, seminar, or other meeting which is held on any cruise ship, and

(ii) any expense described in paragraph (2), (3), (4), (7), (8), or (9) of subsection (e).

(2) Travel as form of education.—No deduction shall be allowed under this chapter for expenses for travel as a form of education.

(3) Travel expenses of spouse, dependent, or others.—No deduction shall be allowed under this chapter (other than section 217) for travel expenses paid or incurred with respect to a spouse, dependent, or other individual accompanying the taxpayer (or an officer or employee of the taxpayer) on business travel, unless—

(A) the spouse, dependent, or other individual is an employee of the taxpayer,

(B) the travel of the spouse, dependent, or other individual is for a bona fide business purpose, and

(C) such expenses would otherwise be deductible by the spouse, dependent, or other individual.

(n) Only 50 percent of meal and entertainment expenses allowed as deduction.—

(1) In general.—The amount allowable as a deduction under this chapter for—

(A) any expense for food or beverages, and

(B) any item with respect to an activity which is of a type generally considered to constitute entertainment, amusement, or recreation, or with respect to a facility used in connection with such activity,

shall not exceed 50 percent of the amount of such expense or item which would (but for this paragraph) be allowable as a deduction under this chapter.

(2) Exceptions.—Paragraph (1) shall not apply to any expense if—

(A) such expense is described in paragraph (2), (3), (4), (7), (8), or (9) of subsection (e),

(B) in the case of an expense for food or beverages, such expense is excludable from the gross income of the recipient under section 132 by reason of subsection (e) thereof (relating to de minimis fringes),

(C) such expense is covered by a package involving a ticket described in subsection (*l*)(1)(B),

(D) in the case of an employer who pays or reimburses moving expenses of an employee, such expenses are includible in the income of the employee under section 82, or

(E) such expense is for food or beverages—

(i) required by any Federal law to be provided to crew members of a commercial vessel,

(ii) provided to crew members of a commercial vessel—

(I) which is operating on the Great Lakes, the Saint Lawrence Seaway, or any inland waterway of the United States, and

(II) which is of a kind which would be required by Federal law to provide food and beverages to crew members if it were operated at sea,

(iii) provided on an oil or gas platform or drilling rig if the platform or rig is located offshore, or

(iv) provided on an oil or gas platform or drilling rig, or at a support camp which is in proximity and integral to such platform or rig, if the platform or rig is located in the United States north of 54 degrees north latitude.

Clauses (i) and (ii) of subparagraph (E) shall not apply to vessels primarily engaged in providing luxury water transportation (determined under the principles of subsection (m)). In the case of the employee, the exception of subparagraph (A) shall not apply to expenses described in subparagraph (D).

* * *

(*o*) Regulatory authority.—The Secretary shall prescribe such regulations as he may deem necessary to carry out the purposes of this section, including regulations prescribing whether subsection (a) or subsection (b) applies in cases where both such subsections would otherwise apply.

§ 275. Certain taxes

(a) General rule.—No deduction shall be allowed for the following taxes:

(1) Federal income taxes, including—

(A) the tax imposed by section 3101 (relating to the tax on employees under the Federal Insurance Contributions Act);

* * *

(C) the tax withheld at source on wages under section 3402.

* * *

(3) Estate, inheritance, legacy, succession, and gift taxes.

* * *

(5) Taxes on real property, to the extent that section 164(d) requires such taxes to be treated as imposed on another taxpayer.

(6) Taxes imposed by chapters 41, 42, 43, 44, 45, 46, and 54.

Paragraph (1) shall not apply to any taxes to the extent such taxes are allowable as a deduction under section 164(f).

(b) Cross reference.—

For disallowance of certain other taxes, see section 164(c).

§ 276. Certain indirect contributions to political parties

(a) Disallowance of deduction.—No deduction otherwise allowable under this chapter shall be allowed for any amount paid or incurred for—

(1) advertising in a convention program of a political party, or in any other publication if any part of the proceeds of such publication directly or indirectly inures (or is intended to inure) to or for the use of a political party or a political candidate,

(2) admission to any dinner or program, if any part of the proceeds of such dinner or program directly or indirectly inures (or is intended to inure) to or for the use of a political party or a political candidate, or

(3) admission to an inaugural ball, inaugural gala, inaugural parade, or inaugural concert, or to any similar event which is identified with a political party or a political candidate.

* * *

§ 279. Interest on indebtedness incurred by corporation to acquire stock or assets of another corporation

(a) General rule.—No deduction shall be allowed for any interest paid or incurred by a corporation during the taxable year with respect to its corporate acquisition indebtedness to the extent that such interest exceeds—

(1) $5,000,000, reduced by

(2) the amount of interest paid or incurred by such corporation during such year on obligations (A) issued after December 31, 1967, to provide consideration for an acquisition described in paragraph (1) of subsection (b), but (B) which are not corporate acquisition indebtedness.

(b) Corporate acquisition indebtedness.—For purposes of this section, the term "corporate acquisition indebtedness" means any obligation evidenced by a bond, debenture, note, or certificate or other evidence of indebtedness issued after October 9, 1969, by a corporation (hereinafter in this section referred to as "issuing corporation") if—

(1) such obligation is issued to provide consideration for the acquisition of—

(A) stock in another corporation (hereinafter in this section referred to as "acquired corporation"), or

(B) assets of another corporation (hereinafter in this section referred to as "acquired corporation") pursuant to a plan under which at least two-thirds (in value) of all the assets (excluding money) used in trades and businesses carried on by such corporation are acquired,

(2) such obligation is either—

(A) subordinated to the claims of trade creditors of the issuing corporation generally, or

(B) expressly subordinated in right of payment to the payment of any substantial amount of unsecured indebtedness, whether outstanding or subsequently issued, of the issuing corporation,

(3) the bond or other evidence of indebtedness is either—

(A) convertible directly or indirectly into stock of the issuing corporation, or

(B) part of an investment unit or other arrangement which includes, in addition to such bond or other evidence of indebtedness, an option to acquire, directly or indirectly, stock in the issuing corporation, and

(4) as of a day determined under subsection (c)(1), either—

(A) the ratio of debt to equity (as defined in subsection (c)(2) of the issuing corporation exceeds 2 to 1), or

(B) the projected earnings (as defined in subsection (c)(3)) do not exceed 3 times the annual interest to be paid or incurred (determined under subsection (c)(4)).

* * *

(j) Effect on other provisions.—No inference shall be drawn from any provision in this section that any instrument designated as a bond, debenture, note, or certificate or other evidence of indebtedness by its issuer represents an obligation or indebtedness of such issuer in applying any other provision of this title.

§ 280A. Disallowance of certain expenses in connection with business use of home, rental of vacation homes, etc.

(a) General rule.—Except as otherwise provided in this section, in the case of a taxpayer who is an individual or an S corporation, no deduction otherwise allowable under this chapter shall be allowed with respect to the use of a dwelling unit which is used by the taxpayer during the taxable year as a residence.

(b) Exception for interest, taxes, casualty losses, etc.—Subsection (a) shall not apply to any deduction allowable to the taxpayer without regard to its connection with his trade or business (or with his income-producing activity).

(c) Exceptions for certain business or rental use; limitation on deductions for such use.—

(1) Certain business use.—Subsection (a) shall not apply to any item to the extent such item is allocable to a portion of the dwelling unit which is exclusively used on a regular basis—

(A) as the principal place of business for any trade or business of the taxpayer,

(B) as a place of business which is used by patients, clients, or customers in meeting or dealing with the taxpayer in the normal course of his trade or business, or

(C) in the case of a separate structure which is not attached to the dwelling unit, in connection with the taxpayer's trade or business.

In the case of an employee, the preceding sentence shall apply only if the exclusive use referred to in the preceding sentence is for the convenience of his employer. For purposes of subparagraph (A), the term "principal place of business" includes a place of business which is used by the taxpayer for the administrative or management activities of any trade or business of the taxpayer if there is no other fixed location of such trade or business where the taxpayer conducts substantial administrative or management activities of such trade or business.

(2) Certain storage use.—Subsection (a) shall not apply to any item to the extent such item is allocable to space within the dwelling unit which is used on a regular basis as a storage unit for the inventory or product samples of the taxpayer held for use in the taxpayer's trade or business of selling products at retail or wholesale, but only if the dwelling unit is the sole fixed location of such trade or business.

(3) Rental use.—Subsection (a) shall not apply to any item which is attributable to the rental of the dwelling unit or portion thereof (determined after the application of subsection (e)).

(4) Use in providing day care services.—

(A) In general.—Subsection (a) shall not apply to any item to the extent that such item is allocable to the use of any portion of the dwelling unit on a regular basis in the taxpayer's trade or business of providing day care for children, for individuals who have attained age 65, or for individuals who are physically or mentally incapable of caring for themselves.

(B) Licensing, etc., requirement.—Subparagraph (A) shall apply to items accruing for a period only if the owner or operator of the trade or business referred to in subparagraph (A)—

(i) has applied for (and such application has not been rejected),

(ii) has been granted (and such granting has not been revoked), or

(iii) is exempt from having,

a license, certification, registration, or approval as a day care center or as a family or group day care home under the provisions of any applicable State law. This subparagraph shall apply only to items accruing in periods beginning on or after the first day of the first month which begins more than 90 days after the date of the enactment of the Tax Reduction and Simplification Act of 1977.

(C) Allocation formula.—If a portion of the taxpayer's dwelling unit used for the purposes described in subparagraph (A) is not used exclusively for those purposes, the amount of the expenses attributable to that portion shall not exceed an amount which bears the same ratio to the total amount of the items allocable to such portion as the number of hours the portion is used for such purposes bears to the number of hours the portion is available for use.

(5) Limitation on deductions.—In the case of a use described in paragraph (1), (2), or (4), and in the case of a use described in paragraph (3) where the dwelling unit is used by the taxpayer during the taxable year as a residence, the deductions allowed under this chapter for the taxable year by reason of being attributed to such use shall not exceed the excess of—

(A) the gross income derived from such use for the taxable year, over

(B) the sum of—

(i) the deductions allocable to such use which are allowable under this chapter for the taxable year whether or not such unit (or portion thereof) was so used, and

(ii) the deductions allocable to the trade or business (or rental activity) in which such use occurs (but which are not allocable to such use) for such taxable year.

Any amount not allowable as a deduction under this chapter by reason of the preceding sentence shall be taken into account as a deduction (allocable to such use) under this chapter for the succeeding taxable year. Any amount taken into account for any taxable year under the preceding sentence shall be subject to the limitation of the 1st sentence of this paragraph whether or not the dwelling unit is used as a residence during such taxable year.

(6) Treatment of rental to employer.—Paragraphs (1) and (3) shall not apply to any item which is attributable to the rental of the dwelling unit (or any portion thereof) by the taxpayer to his employer during any period in which the taxpayer uses the dwelling unit (or portion) in performing services as an employee of the employer.

(d) Use as residence.—

(1) In general.—For purposes of this section, a taxpayer uses a dwelling unit during the taxable year as a residence if he uses such unit (or portion thereof) for personal purposes for a number of days which exceeds the greater of—

(A) 14 days, or

(B) 10 percent of the number of days during such year for which such unit is rented at a fair rental.

For purposes of subparagraph (B), a unit shall not be treated as rented at a fair rental for any day for which it is used for personal purposes.

(2) Personal use of unit.—For purposes of this section, the taxpayer shall be deemed to have used a dwelling unit for personal purposes for a day if, for any part of such day, the unit is used—

(A) for personal purposes by the taxpayer or any other person who has an interest in such unit, or by any member of the family (as defined in section 267(c)(4)) of the taxpayer or such other person;

(B) by any individual who uses the unit under an arrangement which enables the taxpayer to use some other dwelling unit (whether or not a rental is charged for the use of such other unit); or

(C) by any individual (other than an employee with respect to whose use section 119 applies), unless for such day the dwelling unit is rented for a rental which, under the facts and circumstances, is fair rental.

The Secretary shall prescribe regulations with respect to the circumstances under which use of the unit for repairs and annual maintenance will not constitute personal use under this paragraph, except that if the taxpayer is engaged in repair and maintenance on a substantially full time basis for any day, such authority shall not allow the Secretary to treat a dwelling unit as being used for personal use by the taxpayer on such day merely because other individuals who are on the premises on such day are not so engaged.

(3) Rental to family member, etc., for use as principal residence.—

(A) In general.—A taxpayer shall not be treated as using a dwelling unit for personal purposes by reason of a rental arrangement for any period if for such period such dwelling unit is rented, at a fair rental, to any person for use as such person's principal residence.

(B) Special rules for rental to person having interest in unit.—

(i) Rental must be pursuant to shared equity financing agreement.—Subparagraph (A) shall apply to a rental to a person who has an interest in the dwelling unit only if such rental is pursuant to a shared equity financing agreement.

(ii) Determination of fair rental.—In the case of a rental pursuant to a shared equity financing agreement, fair rental shall be determined as of the time the agreement is entered into and by taking into account the occupant's qualified ownership interest.

(C) Shared equity financing agreement.—For purposes of this paragraph, the term "shared equity financing agreement" means an agreement under which—

(i) 2 or more persons acquire qualified ownership interests in a dwelling unit, and

(ii) the person (or persons) holding 1 or more of such interests—

(I) is entitled to occupy the dwelling unit for use as a principal residence, and

(II) is required to pay rent to 1 or more other persons holding qualified ownership interests in the dwelling unit.

(D) Qualified ownership interest.—For purposes of this paragraph, the term "qualified ownership interest" means an undivided interest for more than 50 years in the entire dwelling unit and appurtenant land being acquired in the transaction to which the shared equity financing agreement relates.

(4) Rental of principal residence.—

(A) In general.—For purposes of applying subsection (c)(5) to deductions allocable to a qualified rental period, a taxpayer shall not be considered to have used a dwelling unit for personal purposes for any day during the taxable year which occurs before or after a qualified rental period described in subparagraph (B)(i), or before a qualified rental period described in subparagraph (B)(ii), if with respect to such day such unit constitutes the principal residence (within the meaning of section 121) of the taxpayer.

(B) Qualified rental period.—For purposes of subparagraph (A), the term "qualified rental period" means a consecutive period of—

(i) 12 or more months which begins or ends in such taxable year, or

(ii) less than 12 months which begins in such taxable year and at the end of which such dwelling unit is sold or exchanged, and

for which such unit is rented, or is held for rental, at a fair rental.

(e) Expenses attributable to rental.—

(1) In general.—In any case where a taxpayer who is an individual or an S corporation uses a dwelling unit for personal purposes on any day during the taxable year (whether or not he is treated under this section as using such unit as a residence), the amount deductible under this chapter with respect to expenses attributable to the rental of the unit (or portion thereof) for the taxable year shall not exceed an amount which bears the same relationship to such expenses as the number of days during each year that the unit (or portion thereof) is rented at a fair rental bears to the total number of days during such year that the unit (or portion thereof) is used.

(2) Exception for deductions otherwise allowable.—This subsection shall not apply with respect to deductions which would be allowable under this chapter for the taxable year whether or not such unit (or portion thereof) was rented.

(f) Definitions and special rules.—

(1) Dwelling unit defined.—For purposes of this section—

(A) In general.—The term "dwelling unit" includes a house, apartment, condominium, mobile home, boat, or similar property, and all structures or other property appurtenant to such dwelling unit.

(B) Exception.—The term "dwelling unit" does not include that portion of a unit which is used exclusively as a hotel, motel, inn, or similar establishment.

(2) Personal use by shareholders of S corporation.—In the case of an S corporation, subparagraphs (A) and (B) of subsection (d)(2) shall be applied by substituting "any shareholder of the S corporation" for "the taxpayer" each place it appears.

(3) Coordination with section 183.—If subsection (a) applies with respect to any dwelling unit (or portion thereof) for the taxable year—

(A) section 183 (relating to activities not engaged in for profit) shall not apply to such unit (or portion thereof) for such year, but

(B) such year shall be taken into account as a taxable year for purposes of applying subsection (d) of section 183 (relating to 5–year presumption).

(4) Coordination with section 162(a)(2).—Nothing in this section shall be construed to disallow any deduction allowable under section 162(a)(2) (or any deduction which meets the tests of section 162(a)(2) but is allowable under another provision of this title) by reason of the taxpayer's being away from home in the pursuit of a trade or business (other than the trade or business of renting dwelling units).

(g) Special rule for certain rental use.—Notwithstanding any other provision of this section or section 183, if a dwelling unit is used during the taxable year by the taxpayer as a residence and such dwelling unit is actually rented for less than 15 days during the taxable year, then—

(1) no deduction otherwise allowable under this chapter because of the rental use of such dwelling unit shall be allowed, and

(2) the income derived from such use for the taxable year shall not be included in the gross income of such taxpayer under section 61.

§ 280B. Demolition of structures

In the case of the demolition of any structure—

(1) no deduction otherwise allowable under this chapter shall be allowed to the owner or lessee of such structure for—

(A) any amount expended for such demolition, or

(B) any loss sustained on account of such demolition; and

(2) amounts described in paragraph (1) shall be treated as properly chargeable to capital account with respect to the land on which the demolished structure was located.

§ 280E. Expenditures in connection with the illegal sale of drugs

No deduction or credit shall be allowed for any amount paid or incurred during the taxable year in carrying on any trade or business if such trade or business (or the activities which comprise such trade or business) consists of trafficking in controlled substances (within the meaning of schedule I and II of the Controlled Substances Act) which is prohibited by Federal law or the law of any State in which such trade or business is conducted.

§ 280F. Limitation on depreciation for luxury automobiles; limitation where certain property used for personal purposes

(a) Limitation on amount of depreciation for luxury automobiles.—

(1) Depreciation.—

(A) Limitation.—The amount of the depreciation deduction for any taxable year for any passenger automobile shall not exceed—

(i) $2,560 for the 1st taxable year in the recovery period,

(ii) $4,100 for the 2nd taxable year in the recovery period,

(iii) $2,450 for the 3rd taxable year in the recovery period, and

(iv) $1,475 for each succeeding taxable year in the recovery period.

(B) Disallowed deductions allowed for years after recovery period.—

(i) In general.—Except as provided in clause (ii), the unrecovered basis of any passenger automobile shall be treated as an expense for the 1st taxable year after the recovery period. Any excess of the unrecovered basis over the limitation of clause (ii) shall be treated as an expense in the succeeding taxable year.

(ii) $1,475 limitation.—The amount treated as an expense under clause (i) for any taxable year shall not exceed $1,475.

(iii) Property must be depreciable.—No amount shall be allowable as a deduction by reason of this subparagraph with respect to any property for any taxable year unless a depreciation deduction would be allowable with respect to such property for such taxable year.

(iv) Amount treated as recovery deduction.—For purposes of this subtitle, any amount allowable as a deduction by reason of this subparagraph shall be treated as a depreciation deduction allowable under section 168.

* * *

(2) Coordination with reductions in amount allowable by reason of personal use, etc.—This subsection shall be applied before—

(A) the application of subsection (b), and

(B) the application of any other reduction in the amount of any depreciation deduction allowable under section 168 by reason of any use not qualifying the property for such credit or depreciation deduction.

(b) Limitation where business use of listed property not greater than 50 percent.—

(1) Depreciation.—If any listed property is not predominantly used in a qualified business use for any taxable year, the deduction allowed under section 168 with respect to such property for such taxable year and any subsequent taxable year shall be determined under section 168(g) (relating to alternative depreciation system).

(2) Recapture.—

(A) Where business use percentage does not exceed 50 percent.—If—

(i) property is predominantly used in a qualified business use in a taxable year in which it is placed in service, and

(ii) such property is not predominantly used in a qualified business use for any subsequent taxable year,

then any excess depreciation shall be included in gross income for the taxable year referred to in clause (ii), and the depreciation deduction for the taxable year referred to in clause (ii) and any subsequent taxable years shall be determined under section 168(g) (relating to alternative depreciation system).

(B) Excess depreciation.—For purposes of subparagraph (A), the term "excess depreciation" means the excess (if any) of—

(i) the amount of the depreciation deductions allowable with respect to the property for taxable years before the 1st taxable year in which the property was not predominantly used in a qualified business use, over

(ii) the amount which would have been so allowable if the property had not been predominantly used in a qualified business use for the taxable year in which it was placed in service.

(3) Property predominantly used in qualified business use.—For purposes of this subsection, property shall be treated as predominantly used in a qualified business use for any taxable year if the business use percentage for such taxable year exceeds 50 percent.

(c) Treatment of leases.—

(1) Lessor's deductions not affected.—This section shall not apply to any listed property leased or held for leasing by any person regularly engaged in the business of leasing such property.

(2) Lessee's deductions reduced.—For purposes of determining the amount allowable as a deduction under this chapter for rentals or other payments under a lease for a period of 30 days or more of listed property, only the allowable percentage of such payments shall be taken into account.

(3) Allowable percentage.—For purposes of paragraph (2), the allowable percentage shall be determined under tables prescribed by the Secretary. Such tables shall be prescribed so that the reduction in the deduction under paragraph (2) is substantially equivalent to the applicable restrictions contained in subsections (a) and (b).

(4) Lease term.—In determining the term of any lease for purposes of paragraph (2), the rules of section 168(i)(3)(A) shall apply.

(5) Lessee recapture.—Under regulations prescribed by the Secretary, rules similar to the rules of subsection (b)(3) shall apply to any lessee to which paragraph (2) applies.

(d) Definitions and special rules.—For purposes of this section—

(1) Coordination with section 179.—Any deduction allowable under section 179 with respect to any listed property shall be subject to the limitations of subsections (a) and (b), and the limitation of paragraph (3) of this subsection, in the same manner as if it were a depreciation deduction allowable under section 168.

(2) Subsequent depreciation deductions reduced for deductions allocable to personal use.—Solely for purposes of determining the amount of the depreciation deduction for subsequent taxable years, if less than 100 percent of the use of any listed property during any taxable year is use in a trade or business (including the holding for the production of income), all of the use of such property during such taxable year shall be treated as use so described.

(3) Deductions of employee.—

(A) In general.—Any employee use of listed property shall not be treated as use in a trade or business for purposes of determining the amount of any depreciation deduction allowable to the employee (or the amount of any deduction allowable to the employee for rentals or other payments under a lease of listed property) unless such use is for the convenience of the employer and required as a condition of employment.

(B) Employee use.—For purposes of subparagraph (A), the term "employee use" means any use in connection with the performance of services as an employee.

(4) Listed property.—

(A) In general.—Except as provided in subparagraph (B), the term "listed property" means—

(i) any passenger automobile,

(ii) any other property used as a means of transportation,

(iii) any property of a type generally used for purposes of entertainment, recreation, or amusement,

(iv) any computer or peripheral equipment (as defined in section 168(i)(2)(B)), and

(v) any other property of a type specified by the Secretary by regulations.

(B) Exception for certain computers.—The term "listed property" shall not include any computer or peripheral equipment (as so defined) used exclusively at a regular business establishment and owned or leased by the person operating such establishment. For purposes of the preceding sentence, any portion of a dwelling unit shall be treated as a regular business establishment if (and only if) the requirements of section 280A(c)(1) are met with respect to such portion.

(C) Exception for property used in business of transporting persons or property.—Except to the extent provided in regulations, clause (ii) of subparagraph (A) shall not apply to any property substantially all of the use of which is in a trade or business of providing to unrelated persons services consisting of the transportation of persons or property for compensation or hire.

(5) Passenger automobile.—

(A) In general.—Except as provided in subparagraph (B), the term "passenger automobile" means any 4–wheeled vehicle—

(i) which is manufactured primarily for use on public streets, roads, and highways, and

(ii) which is rated at 6,000 pounds unloaded gross vehicle weight or less.

In the case of a truck or van, clause (ii) shall be applied by substituting "gross vehicle weight" for "unloaded gross vehicle weight".

(B) Exception for certain vehicles.—The term "passenger automobile" shall not include—

(i) any ambulance, hearse, or combination ambulance-hearse used by the taxpayer directly in a trade or business,

(ii) any vehicle used by the taxpayer directly in the trade or business of transporting persons or property for compensation or hire, and

(iii) under regulations, any truck or van.

(6) Business use percentage.—

(A) In general.—The term "business use percentage" means the percentage of the use of any listed property during any taxable year which is a qualified business use.

(B) Qualified business use.—Except as provided in subparagraph (C), the term "qualified business use" means any use in a trade or business of the taxpayer.

(C) Exception for certain use by 5–percent owners and related persons.—

(i) In general.—The term "qualified business use" shall not include—

(I) leasing property to any 5–percent owner or related person,

(II) use of property provided as compensation for the performance of services by a 5–percent owner or related person, or

(III) use of property provided as compensation for the performance of services by any person not described in subclause (II) unless an amount is included in the gross income of such person with respect to such use, and, where required, there was withholding under chapter 24.

(ii) Special rule for aircraft.—Clause (i) shall not apply with respect to any aircraft if at least 25 percent of the total use of the aircraft during the taxable year consists of qualified business use not described in clause (i).

(D) Definitions.—For purposes of this paragraph—

(i) 5–percent owner.—The term "5–percent owner" means any person who is a 5–percent owner with respect to the taxpayer (as defined in section 416(i)(1)(B)(i)).

(ii) Related person.—The term "related person" means any person related to the taxpayer (within the meaning of section 267(b)).

* * *

(8) Unrecovered basis.—For purposes of subsection (a)(2), the term "unrecovered basis" means the adjusted basis of the passenger automobile determined after the application of subsection (a) and as if all use during the recovery period were use in a trade or business (including the holding of property for the production of income).

(9) All taxpayers holding interests in passenger automobile treated as 1 taxpayer.—All taxpayers holding interests in any passenger automobile shall be treated as 1 taxpayer for purposes of applying subsection (a) to such automobile, and the limitations of subsection (a) shall be allocated among such taxpayers in proportion to their interests in such automobile.

* * *

§ 280G. Golden parachute payments

(a) General rule.—No deduction shall be allowed under this chapter for any excess parachute payment.

(b) Excess parachute payment.—For purposes of this section—

(1) In general.—The term "excess parachute payment" means an amount equal to the excess of any parachute payment over the portion of the base amount allocated to such payment.

(2) Parachute payment defined.—

(A) In general.—The term "parachute payment" means any payment in the nature of compensation to (or for the benefit of) a disqualified individual if—

(i) such payment is contingent on a change—

(I) in the ownership or effective control of the corporation, or

(II) in the ownership of a substantial portion of the assets of the corporation, and

(ii) the aggregate present value of the payments in the nature of compensation to (or for the benefit of) such individual which are contingent on such change equals or exceeds an amount equal to 3 times the base amount.

For purposes of clause (ii), payments not treated as parachute payments under paragraph (4)(A), (5), or (6) shall not be taken into account.

(B) Agreements.—The term "parachute payment" shall also include any payment in the nature of compensation to (or for the benefit of) a disqualified individual if such payment is made pursuant to an agreement which violates any generally enforced securities laws or regulations. In any proceeding involving the issue of whether any payment made to a disqualified individual is a parachute payment on account of a violation of any generally enforced securities laws or regulations, the burden of proof with respect to establishing the occurrence of a violation of such a law or regulation shall be upon the Secretary.

* * *

(3) Base amount.—

(A) In general.—The term "base amount" means the individual's annualized includible compensation for the base period.

(B) Allocation.—The portion of the base amount allocated to any parachute payment shall be an amount which bears the same ratio to the base amount as—

(i) the present value of such payment, bears to

(ii) the aggregate present value of all such payments.

(4) Treatment of amounts which taxpayer establishes as reasonable compensation.—In the case of any payment described in paragraph (2)(A)—

(A) the amount treated as a parachute payment shall not include the portion of such payment which the taxpayer establishes by clear and convincing evidence is reasonable compensation for personal services to be rendered on or after the date of the change described in paragraph (2)(A)(i), and

(B) the amount treated as an excess parachute payment shall be reduced by the portion of such payment which the taxpayer establishes by clear and convincing evidence is reasonable compensation for personal services actually rendered before the date of the change described in paragraph (2)(A)(i).

For purposes of subparagraph (B), reasonable compensation for services actually rendered before the date of the change described in paragraph (2)(A)(i) shall be first offset against the base amount.

* * *

PART XI—SPECIAL RULES RELATING TO CORPORATE PREFERENCE ITEMS

§ 291. Special rules relating to corporate preference items

(a) Reduction in certain preference items, etc.—For purposes of this subtitle, in the case of a corporation—

(1) Section 1250 capital gain treatment.—In the case of section 1250 property which is disposed of during the taxable year, 20 percent of the excess (if any) of—

(A) the amount which would be treated as ordinary income if such property was section 1245 property, over

(B) the amount treated as ordinary income under section 1250 (determined without regard to this paragraph),

shall be treated as gain which is ordinary income under section 1250 and shall be recognized notwithstanding any other provision of this title. Under regulations prescribed by the Secretary, the provisions of this paragraph shall not apply to the disposition of any property to the extent section 1250(a) does not apply to such disposition by reason of section 1250(d).

(2) Reduction in percentage depletion.—In the case of iron ore and coal (including lignite), the amount allowable as a deduction under section 613 with respect to any property (as defined in section 614) shall be reduced by 20 percent of the amount of the excess (if any) of—

(A) the amount of the deduction allowable under section 613 for the taxable year (determined without regard to this paragraph), over

(B) the adjusted basis of the property at the close of the taxable year (determined without regard to the depletion deduction for the taxable year).

* * *

(b) Special rules for treatment of intangible drilling costs and mineral exploration and development costs.—For purposes of this subtitle, in the case of a corporation—

(1) In general.—The amount allowable as a deduction for any taxable year (determined without regard to this section)—

(A) under section 263(c) in the case of an integrated oil company, or

(B) under section 616(a) or 617(a),

shall be reduced by 30 percent.

(2) Amortization of amounts not allowable as deductions under paragraph (1).—The amount not allowable as a deduction under section 263(c), 616(a), or 617(a) (as the case may be) for any taxable year by reason of paragraph (1) shall be allowable as a deduction ratably over the 60-month period beginning with the month in which the costs are paid or incurred.

(3) Dispositions.—For purposes of section 1254, any deduction under paragraph (2) shall be treated as a deduction allowable under section 263(c), 616(a), or 617(a) (whichever is appropriate).

(4) Integrated oil company defined.—For purposes of this subsection, the term "integrated oil company" means, with respect to any taxable year, any producer of crude oil to whom subsection (c) of section 613A does not apply by reason of paragraph (2) or (4) of section 613A(d).

(5) Coordination with cost depletion.—The portion of the adjusted basis of any property which is attributable to amounts to which paragraph (1) applied shall not be taken into account for purposes of determining depletion under section 611.

* * *

SUBCHAPTER C—CORPORATE DISTRIBUTIONS AND ADJUSTMENTS

PART I—DISTRIBUTIONS BY CORPORATIONS

Subpart A—Effects on Recipients

§ 301. Distributions of property

(a) In general.—Except as otherwise provided in this chapter, a distribution of property (as defined in section 317(a)) made by a corporation to a shareholder with respect to its stock shall be treated in the manner provided in subsection (c).

(b) Amount distributed.—

(1) General rule.—For purposes of this section, the amount of any distribution shall be the amount of money received, plus the fair market value of the other property received.

(2) Reduction for liabilities.—The amount of any distribution determined under paragraph (1) shall be reduced (but not below zero) by—

(A) the amount of any liability of the corporation assumed by the shareholder in connection with the distribution, and

(B) the amount of any liability to which the property received by the shareholder is subject immediately before, and immediately after, the distribution.

* Omitted entirely.

(3) Determination of fair market value.—For purposes of this section, fair market value shall be determined as of the date of the distribution.

(c) Amount taxable.—In the case of a distribution to which subsection (a) applies—

(1) Amount constituting dividend.—That portion of the distribution which is a dividend (as defined in section 316) shall be included in gross income.

(2) Amount applied against basis.—That portion of the distribution which is not a dividend shall be applied against and reduce the adjusted basis of the stock.

(3) Amount in excess of basis.—

(A) In general.—Except as provided in subparagraph (B), that portion of the distribution which is not a dividend, to the extent that it exceeds the adjusted basis of the stock, shall be treated as gain from the sale or exchange of property.

(B) Distributions out of increase in value accrued before March 1, 1913.—That portion of the distribution which is not a dividend, to the extent that it exceeds the adjusted basis of the stock and to the extent that it is out of increase in value accrued before March 1, 1913, shall be exempt from tax.

(d) Basis.—The basis of property received in a distribution to which subsection (a) applies shall be the fair market value of such property.

(e) Special rule for certain distributions received by 20 percent corporate shareholder.—

(1) In general.—Except to the extent otherwise provided in regulations, solely for purposes of determining the taxable income of any 20 percent corporate shareholder (and its adjusted basis in the stock of the distributing corporation), section 312 shall be applied with respect to the distributing corporation as if it did not contain subsections (k) and (n) thereof.

(2) 20 percent corporate shareholder.—For purposes of this subsection, the term "20 percent corporate shareholder" means, with respect to any distribution, any corporation which owns (directly or through the application of section 318)—

(A) stock in the corporation making the distribution possessing at least 20 percent of the total combined voting power of all classes of stock entitled to vote, or

(B) at least 20 percent of the total value of all stock of the distributing corporation (except nonvoting stock which is limited and preferred as to dividends),

but only if, but for this subsection, the distributee corporation would be entitled to a deduction under section 243, 244, or 245 with respect to such distribution.

(3) Application of section 312(n)(7) not affected.—The reference in paragraph (1) to subsection (n) of section 312 shall be treated as not including a reference to paragraph (7) of such subsection.

(4) Regulations.—The Secretary shall prescribe such regulations as may be necessary or appropriate to carry out the purposes of this subsection.

(f) Special rules.—

(1) For distributions in redemption of stock, see section 302.

(2) For distributions in complete liquidation, see part II (sec. 331 and following).

(3) For distributions in corporate organizations and reorganizations, see part III (sec. 351 and following).

(4) For taxation of dividends received by individuals at capital gains rates, see section 1(h)(11).

§ 302. Distributions in redemption of stock

(a) General rule.—If a corporation redeems its stock (within the meaning of section 317(b)), and if paragraph (1), (2), (3), (4), or (5) of subsection (b) applies, such redemption shall be treated as a distribution in part or full payment in exchange for the stock.

(b) Redemptions treated as exchanges.—

(1) Redemptions not equivalent to dividends.—Subsection (a) shall apply if the redemption is not essentially equivalent to a dividend.

(2) Substantially disproportionate redemption of stock.—

(A) In general.—Subsection (a) shall apply if the distribution is substantially disproportionate with respect to the shareholder.

(B) Limitation.—This paragraph shall not apply unless immediately after the redemption the shareholder owns less than 50 percent of the total combined voting power of all classes of stock entitled to vote.

(C) Definitions.—For purposes of this paragraph, the distribution is substantially disproportionate if—

(i) the ratio which the voting stock of the corporation owned by the shareholder immediately after the redemption bears to all of the voting stock of the corporation at such time,

is less than 80 percent of—

(ii) the ratio which the voting stock of the corporation owned by the shareholder immediately before the redemption bears to all of the voting stock of the corporation at such time.

For purposes of this paragraph, no distribution shall be treated as substantially disproportionate unless the shareholder's ownership of the common stock of the corporation (whether voting or nonvoting) after and before redemption also meets the 80 percent requirement of the preceding sentence. For purposes of the preceding sentence, if there is more than one class of common stock, the determinations shall be made by reference to fair market value.

(D) Series of redemptions.—This paragraph shall not apply to any redemption made pursuant to a plan the purpose or effect of which is a series of redemptions resulting in a distribution which (in the aggregate) is not substantially disproportionate with respect to the shareholder.

(3) Termination of shareholder's interest.—Subsection (a) shall apply if the redemption is in complete redemption of all of the stock of the corporation owned by the shareholder.

(4) Redemption from noncorporate shareholder in partial liquidation.—Subsection (a) shall apply to a distribution if such distribution is—

(A) in redemption of stock held by a shareholder who is not a corporation, and

(B) in partial liquidation of the distributing corporation.

* * *

(6) Application of paragraphs.—In determining whether a redemption meets the requirements of paragraph (1), the fact that such redemption fails to meet the requirements of paragraph (2), (3) or (4) shall not be taken into account. If a redemption meets the requirements of paragraph (3) and also the requirements of paragraph (1), (2), or (4), then so much of subsection (c)(2) as would (but for this sentence) apply in respect of the acquisition of an interest in the corporation within the 10–year period beginning on the date of the distribution shall not apply.

(c) Constructive ownership of stock.—

(1) In general.—Except as provided in paragraph (2) of this subsection, section 318(a) shall apply in determining the ownership of stock for purposes of this section.

(2) For determining termination of interest.—

(A) In the case of a distribution described in subsection (b)(3), section 318(a)(1) shall not apply if—

(i) immediately after the distribution the distributee has no interest in the corporation (including an interest as officer, director, or employee), other than an interest as a creditor,

(ii) the distributee does not acquire any such interest (other than stock acquired by bequest or inheritance) within 10 years from the date of such distribution, and

(iii) the distributee, at such time and in such manner as the Secretary by regulations prescribes, files an agreement to notify the Secretary of any acquisition described in clause (ii) and to retain such records as may be necessary for the application of this paragraph.

If the distributee acquires such an interest in the corporation (other than by bequest or inheritance) within 10 years from the date of the distribution, then the periods of limitation provided in sections 6501 and 6502 on the making of an assessment and the collection by levy or a proceeding in court shall, with respect to any deficiency (including interest and additions to the tax) resulting from such acquisition, include one year immediately following the date on which the distributee (in accordance with regulations prescribed by the Secretary) notifies the Secretary of such acquisition; and such assessment and collection may be made notwithstanding any provision of law or rule of law which otherwise would prevent such assessment and collection.

(B) Subparagraph (A) of this paragraph shall not apply if—

(i) any portion of the stock redeemed was acquired, directly or indirectly, within the 10–year period ending on the date of the distribution by the distributee from a person the ownership of whose stock would (at the time of distribution) be attributable to the distributee under section 318(a), or

(ii) any person owns (at the time of the distribution) stock the ownership of which is attributable to the distributee under section 318(a) and such person acquired any stock in the corporation, directly or indirectly, from the distributee within the 10–year period ending on the date of the distribution, unless such stock so acquired from the distributee is redeemed in the same transaction.

The preceding sentence shall not apply if the acquisition (or, in the case of clause (ii), the disposition) by the distributee did not have as one of its principal purposes the avoidance of Federal income tax.

(C) Special rule for waivers by entities.—

(i) In general.—Subparagraph (A) shall not apply to a distribution to any entity unless—

(I) such entity and each related person meet the requirements of clauses (i), (ii), and (iii) of subparagraph (A), and

(II) each related person agrees to be jointly and severally liable for any deficiency (including interest and additions to tax) resulting from an acquisition described in clause (ii) of subparagraph (A).

In any case to which the preceding sentence applies, the second sentence of subparagraph (A) and subparagraph (B)(ii) shall be applied by substituting "distributee or any related person" for "distributee" each place it appears.

(ii) Definitions.—For purposes of this subparagraph—

(I) the term "entity" means a partnership, estate, trust, or corporation; and

(II) the term "related person" means any person to whom ownership of stock in the corporation is (at the time of the distribution) attributable under section 318(a)(1) if such stock is further attributable to the entity under section 318(a)(3).

(d) Redemptions treated as distributions of property.—Except as otherwise provided in this subchapter, if a corporation redeems its stock (within the meaning of section 317(b)), and if subsection (a) of this section does not apply, such redemption shall be treated as a distribution of property to which section 301 applies.

(e) Partial liquidation defined.—

(1) In general.—For purposes of subsection (b)(4), a distribution shall be treated as in partial liquidation of a corporation if—

(A) the distribution is not essentially equivalent to a dividend (determined at the corporate level rather than at the shareholder level), and

(B) the distribution is pursuant to a plan and occurs within the taxable year in which the plan is adopted or within the succeeding taxable year.

(2) Termination of business.—The distributions which meet the requirements of paragraph (1)(A) shall include (but shall not be limited to) a distribution which meets the requirements of subparagraphs (A) and (B) of this paragraph:

(A) The distribution is attributable to the distributing corporation's ceasing to conduct, or consists of the assets of, a qualified trade or business.

(B) Immediately after the distribution, the distributing corporation is actively engaged in the conduct of a qualified trade or business.

(3) Qualified trade or business.—For purposes of paragraph (2), the term "qualified trade or business" means any trade or business which—

(A) was actively conducted throughout the 5-year period ending on the date of the redemption, and

(B) was not acquired by the corporation within such period in a transaction in which gain or loss was recognized in whole or in part.

(4) Redemption may be pro rata.—Whether or not a redemption meets the requirements of subparagraphs (A) and (B) of paragraph (2) shall be determined without regard to whether or not the redemption is pro rata with respect to all of the shareholders of the corporation.

(5) Treatment of certain pass-thru entities.—For purposes of determining under subsection (b)(4) whether any stock is held by a shareholder who is not a corporation, any stock held by a partnership, estate, or trust shall be treated as if it were actually held proportionately by its partners or beneficiaries.

(f) Cross references.—

For special rules relating to redemption—

(1) Death Taxes.—Of stock to pay death taxes, see section 303.

(2) Section 306 Stock.—Of section 306 stock, see section 306.

(3) Liquidations.—Of stock in complete liquidation, see section 331.

§ 303. Distributions in redemption of stock to pay death taxes

(a) In general.—A distribution of property to a shareholder by a corporation in redemption of part or all of the stock of such corporation which (for Federal estate tax purposes) is included in determining the gross estate of a decedent, to the extent that the amount of such distribution does not exceed the sum of—

(1) the estate, inheritance, legacy, and succession taxes (including any interest collected as a part of such taxes) imposed because of such decedent's death, and

(2) the amount of funeral and administration expenses allowable as deductions to the estate under section 2053 (or under section 2106 in the case of the estate of a decedent nonresident, not a citizen of the United States),

shall be treated as a distribution in full payment in exchange for the stock so redeemed.

(b) Limitations on application of subsection (a).—

(1) Period for distribution.—Subsection (a) shall apply only to amounts distributed after the death of the decedent and—

(A) within the period of limitations provided in section 6501(a) for the assessment of the Federal estate tax (determined without the application of any provision other than section 6501(a)), or within 90 days after the expiration of such period,

(B) if a petition for redetermination of a deficiency in such estate tax has been filed with the Tax Court within the time prescribed in section 6213, at any time before the expiration of 60 days after the decision of the Tax Court becomes final, or

(C) if an election has been made under section 6166 and if the time prescribed by this subparagraph expires at a later date than the time prescribed by subparagraph (B) of this paragraph, within the time determined under section 6166 for the payment of the installments.

(2) Relationship of stock to decedent's estate.—

(A) In general.—Subsection (a) shall apply to a distribution by a corporation only if the value (for Federal estate tax purposes) of all of the stock of such corporation which is included in determining the value of the decedent's gross estate exceeds 35 percent of the excess of—

(i) the value of the gross estate of such decedent, over

(ii) the sum of the amounts allowable as a deduction under section 2053 or 2054.

(B) Special rule for stock in 2 or more corporations.—For purposes of subparagraph (A), stock of 2 or more corporations, with respect to each of which there is included in determining the value of the decedent's gross estate 20 percent or more in value of the outstanding stock, shall be treated as the stock of a single corporation. For purposes of the 20–percent requirement of the preceding sentence, stock which, at the decedent's death, represents the surviving spouse's interest in property held by the decedent and the surviving spouse as community property or as joint tenants, tenants by the entirety, or tenants in common shall be treated as having been included in determining the value of the decedent's gross estate.

(3) Relationship of shareholder to estate tax.—Subsection (a) shall apply to a distribution by a corporation only to the extent that the interest of the shareholder is reduced directly (or through a binding obligation to contribute) by any payment of an amount described in paragraph (1) or (2) of subsection (a).

(4) Additional requirements for distributions made more than 4 years after decedent's death.—In the case of amounts distributed more than 4 years after the date of the decedent's death, subsection (a) shall apply to a distribution by a corporation only to the extent of the lesser of—

(A) the aggregate of the amounts referred to in paragraph (1) or (2) of subsection (a) which remained unpaid immediately before the distribution, or

(B) the aggregate of the amounts referred to in paragraph (1) or (2) of subsection (a) which are paid during the 1-year period beginning on the date of such distribution.

(c) Stock with substituted basis.—If—

(1) a shareholder owns stock of a corporation (referred to in this subsection as "new stock") the basis of which is determined by reference to the basis of stock of a corporation (referred to in this subsection as "old stock"),

(2) the old stock was included (for Federal estate tax purposes) in determining the gross estate of a decedent, and

(3) subsection (a) would apply to a distribution of property to such shareholder in redemption of the old stock,

then, subject to the limitations specified in subsection (b), subsection (a) shall apply in respect of a distribution in redemption of the new stock.

(d) Special rules for generation-skipping transfers.—Where stock in a corporation is the subject of a generation-skipping transfer (within the meaning of section 2611(a)) occurring at the same time as and as a result of the death of an individual—

(1) the stock shall be deemed to be included in the gross estate of such individual;

(2) taxes of the kind referred to in subsection (a)(1) which are imposed because of the generation-skipping transfer shall be treated as imposed because of such individual's death (and for this purpose the tax imposed by section 2601 shall be treated as an estate tax);

(3) the period of distribution shall be measured from the date of the generation-skipping transfer; and

(4) the relationship of stock to the decedent's estate shall be measured with reference solely to the amount of the generation-skipping transfer.

§ 304. Redemption through use of related corporations

(a) Treatment of certain stock purchases.—

(1) Acquisition by related corporation (other than subsidiary).—For purposes of sections 302 and 303, if—

(A) one or more persons are in control of each of two corporations, and

(B) in return for property, one of the corporations acquires stock in the other corporation from the person (or persons) so in control,

then (unless paragraph (2) applies) such property shall be treated as a distribution in redemption of the stock of the corporation acquiring such stock. To the extent that such distribution is treated as a distribution to which section 301 applies, the transferor and the acquiring corporation shall be treated in the same manner as if the transferor had transferred the stock so acquired to the acquiring corporation in exchange for stock of the acquiring corporation in a transaction to which section 351(a) applies, and then the acquiring corporation had redeemed the stock it was treated as issuing in such transaction.

(2) Acquisition by subsidiary.—For purposes of sections 302 and 303, if—

(A) in return for property, one corporation acquires from a shareholder of another corporation stock in such other corporation, and

(B) the issuing corporation controls the acquiring corporation,

then such property shall be treated as a distribution in redemption of the stock of the issuing corporation.

(b) Special rules for application of subsection (a).—

(1) Rule for determinations under section 302(b).—In the case of any acquisition of stock to which subsection (a) of this section applies, determinations as to whether the acquisition is, by reason of section 302(b), to be treated as a distribution in part or full payment in exchange for the stock shall be made by reference to the stock of the issuing corporation. In applying section 318(a) (relating to constructive ownership of stock) with respect to section 302(b) for purposes of this paragraph, sections 318(a)(2)(C) and 318(a)(3)(C) shall be applied without regard to the 50 percent limitation contained therein.

(2) Amount constituting dividend.—In the case of any acquisition of stock to which subsection (a) applies, the determination of the amount which is a dividend (and the source thereof) shall be made as if the property were distributed—

(A) by the acquiring corporation to the extent of its earnings and profits, and

(B) then by the issuing corporation to the extent of its earnings and profits.

(3) Coordination with section 351.—

(A) Property treated as received in redemption.—Except as otherwise provided in this paragraph, subsection (a) (and not section 351 and not so much of sections 357 and 358 as relates to section 351) shall apply to any property received in a distribution described in subsection (a).

(B) Certain assumptions of liability, etc.—

(i) In general.—In the case of an acquisition described in section 351, subsection (a) shall not apply to any liability—

(I) assumed by the acquiring corporation, or

(II) to which the stock is subject,

if such liability was incurred by the transferor to acquire the stock. For purposes of the preceding sentence, the term "stock" means stock referred to in paragraph (1)(B) or (2)(A) of subsection (a).

(ii) Extension of obligations, etc.—For purposes of clause (i), an extension, renewal, or refinancing of a liability which meets the requirements of clause (i) shall be treated as meeting such requirements.

(iii) Clause (i) does not apply to stock acquired from related person except where complete termination.—Clause (i) shall apply only to stock acquired by the transferor from a person—

(I) none of whose stock is attributable to the transferor under section 318(a) (other than paragraph (4) thereof), or

(II) who satisfies rules similar to the rules of section 302(c)(2) with respect to both the acquiring and the issuing corporations (determined as if such person were a distributee of each such corporation).

* * *

(4) Treatment of certain intragroup transactions.—

(A) In general.—In the case of any transfer described in subsection (a) of stock from 1 member of an affiliated group to another member of such group, proper adjustments shall be made to—

(i) the adjusted basis of any intragroup stock, and

(ii) the earnings and profits of any member of such group,

to the extent necessary to carry out the purposes of this section.

(B) Definitions.—For purposes of this paragraph—

(i) Affiliated group.—The term "affiliated group" has the meaning given such term by section 1504(a).

(ii) Intragroup stock.—The term "intragroup stock" means any stock which—

(I) is in a corporation which is a member of an affiliated group, and

(II) is held by another member of such group.

* * *

(c) Control.—

(1) In general.—For purposes of this section, control means the ownership of stock possessing at least 50 percent of the total combined voting power of all classes of stock entitled to vote, or at least 50 percent of the total value of shares of all classes of stock. If a person (or persons) is in control (within the meaning of the preceding sentence) of a corporation which in turn owns at least 50 percent of the total combined voting power of all stock entitled to vote of another corporation, or owns at least 50 percent of the total value of the shares of all classes of stock of another corporation, then such person (or persons) shall be treated as in control of such other corporation.

(2) Stock acquired in the transaction.—For purposes of subsection (a)(1)—

(A) General rule.—Where 1 or more persons in control of the issuing corporation transfer stock of such corporation in exchange for stock of the acquiring corporation, the stock of the acquiring corporation received shall be taken into account in determining whether such person or persons are in control of the acquiring corporation.

(B) Definition of control group.—Where 2 or more persons in control of the issuing corporation transfer stock of such corporation to the acquiring corporation and, after the transfer, the transferors are in control of the acquiring corporation, the person or persons in control of each corporation shall include each of the persons who so transfer stock.

(3) Constructive ownership.—

(A) In general.—Section 318(a) (relating to constructive ownership of stock) shall apply for purposes of determining control under this section.

(B) Modification of 50–percent limitations in section 318.—For purposes of subparagraph (A)—

(i) paragraph (2)(C) of section 318(a) shall be applied by substituting "5 percent" for "50 percent", and

(ii) paragraph (3)(C) of section 318(a) shall be applied—

(I) by substituting "5 percent" for "50 percent", and

(II) in any case where such paragraph would not apply but for subclause (I), by considering a corporation as owning the stock (other than stock in such corporation) owned by or for any shareholder of such corporation in that proportion which the value of the stock which such shareholder owned in such corporation bears to the value of all stock in such corporation.

§ 305. Distributions of stock and stock rights

(a) General rule.—Except as otherwise provided in this section, gross income does not include the amount of any distribution of the stock of a corporation made by such corporation to its shareholders with respect to its stock.

(b) Exceptions.—Subsection (a) shall not apply to a distribution by a corporation of its stock, and the distribution shall be treated as a distribution of property to which section 301 applies—

(1) Distributions in lieu of money.—If the distribution is, at the election of any of the shareholders (whether exercised before or after the declaration thereof), payable either—

(A) in its stock, or

(B) in property.

(2) Disproportionate distributions.—If the distribution (or a series of distributions of which such distribution is one) has the result of—

(A) the receipt of property by some shareholders, and

(B) an increase in the proportionate interests of other shareholders in the assets or earnings and profits of the corporation.

(3) Distributions of common and preferred stock.—If the distribution (or a series of distributions of which such distribution is one) has the result of—

(A) the receipt of preferred stock by some common shareholders, and

(B) the receipt of common stock by other common shareholders.

(4) Distributions on preferred stock.—If the distribution is with respect to preferred stock, other than an increase in the conversion ratio of convertible preferred stock made solely to take account of a stock dividend or stock split with respect to the stock into which such convertible stock is convertible.

(5) Distributions of convertible preferred stock.—If the distribution is of convertible preferred stock, unless it is established to the satisfaction of the Secretary that such distribution will not have the result described in paragraph (2).

(c) Certain transactions treated as distributions.—For purposes of this section and section 301, the Secretary shall prescribe regulations under which a change in conversion ratio, a change in redemption price, a difference between redemption price and issue price, a redemption which is treated as a distribution to which section 301 applies, or any transaction (including a recapitalization) having a similar effect on the interest of any shareholder shall be treated as a distribution with respect to any shareholder whose proportionate interest in the earnings and profits or assets of the corporation is increased by such change, difference, redemption, or similar transaction. Regulations prescribed under the preceding sentence shall provide that—

(1) where the issuer of stock is required to redeem the stock at a specified time or the holder of stock has the option to require the issuer to redeem the stock, a redemption premium resulting from such requirement or option shall be treated as reasonable only if the amount of such premium does not exceed the amount determined under the principles of section 1273(a)(3),

(2) a redemption premium shall not fail to be treated as a distribution (or series of distributions) merely because the stock is callable, and

(3) in any case in which a redemption premium is treated as a distribution (or series of distributions), such premium shall be taken into account under principles similar to the principles of section 1272(a).

(d) Definitions.—

(1) Rights to acquire stock.—For purposes of this section, the term "stock" includes rights to acquire such stock.

(2) Shareholders.—For purposes of subsections (b) and (c), the term "shareholder" includes a holder of rights or of convertible securities.

(e) Treatment of purchaser of stripped preferred stock.—

(1) In general.—If any person purchases after April 30, 1993, any stripped preferred stock, then such person, while holding such stock, shall include in gross income amounts equal to the amounts which would have been so includible if such stripped preferred stock were a bond issued on the purchase date and having original issue discount equal to the excess, if any, of—

(A) the redemption price for such stock, over

(B) the price at which such person purchased such stock.

The preceding sentence shall also apply in the case of any person whose basis in such stock is determined by reference to the basis in the hands of such purchaser.

(2) Basis adjustments.—Appropriate adjustments to basis shall be made for amounts includible in gross income under paragraph (1).

(3) Tax treatment of person stripping stock.—If any person strips the rights to 1 or more dividends from any stock described in paragraph (5)(B) and after April 30, 1993, disposes of such dividend rights, for purposes of paragraph (1), such person shall be treated as having purchased the stripped preferred stock on the date of such disposition for a purchase price equal to such person's adjusted basis in such stripped preferred stock.

(4) Amounts treated as ordinary income.—Any amount included in gross income under paragraph (1) shall be treated as ordinary income.

(5) Stripped preferred stock.—For purposes of this subsection—

(A) In general.—The term "stripped preferred stock" means any stock described in subparagraph (B) if there has been a separation in ownership between such stock and any dividend on such stock which has not become payable.

(B) Description of stock.—Stock is described in this subsection if such stock—

(i) is limited and preferred as to dividends and does not participate in corporate growth to any significant extent, and

(ii) has a fixed redemption price.

(6) Purchase.—For purposes of this subsection, the term "purchase" means—

(A) any acquisition of stock, where

(B) the basis of such stock is not determined in whole or in part by the reference to the adjusted basis of such stock in the hands of the person from whom acquired.

* * *

(f) Cross references.—

For special rules—

(1) Relating to the receipt of stock and stock rights in corporate organizations and reorganizations, see part III (sec. 351 and following).

(2) In the case of a distribution which results in a gift, see section 2501 and following.

(3) In the case of a distribution which has the effect of the payment of compensation, see section 61(a)(1).

§ 306. Dispositions of certain stock

(a) General rule.—If a shareholder sells or otherwise disposes of section 306 stock (as defined in subsection (c))—

(1) Dispositions other than redemptions.—If such disposition is not a redemption (within the meaning of section 317(b))—

(A) The amount realized shall be treated as ordinary income. This subparagraph shall not apply to the extent that—

(i) the amount realized, exceeds

(ii) such stock's ratable share of the amount which would have been a dividend at the time of distribution if (in lieu of section 306 stock) the corporation had distributed money in an amount equal to the fair market value of the stock at the time of distribution.

(B) Any excess of the amount realized over the sum of—

(i) the amount treated under subparagraph (A) as ordinary income, plus

(ii) the adjusted basis of the stock,

shall be treated as gain from the sale of such stock.

(C) No loss shall be recognized.

(D) Treatment as dividend.—For purposes of section 1(h)(11) and such other provisions as the Secretary may specify, any amount treated as ordinary income under this paragraph shall be treated as a dividend received from the corporation.

(2) Redemption.—If the disposition is a redemption, the amount realized shall be treated as a distribution of property to which section 301 applies.

(b) Exceptions.—Subsection (a) shall not apply—

(1) Termination of shareholder's interest, etc.—

(A) Not in redemption.—If the disposition—

(i) is not a redemption;

(ii) is not, directly or indirectly, to a person the ownership of whose stock would (under section 318(a)) be attributable to the shareholder; and

(iii) terminates the entire stock interest of the shareholder in the corporation (and for purposes of this clause, section 318(a) shall apply).

(B) In redemption.—If the disposition is a redemption and paragraph (3) or (4) of section 302(b) applies.

(2) Liquidations.—If the section 306 stock is redeemed in a distribution in complete liquidation to which part II (sec. 331 and following) applies.

(3) Where gain or loss is not recognized.—To the extent that, under any provision of this subtitle, gain or loss to the shareholder is not recognized with respect to the disposition of the section 306 stock.

(4) Transactions not in avoidance.—If it is established to the satisfaction of the Secretary—

(A) that the distribution, and the disposition or redemption, or

(B) in the case of a prior or simultaneous disposition (or redemption) of the stock with respect to which the section 306 stock disposed of (or redeemed) was issued, that the disposition (or redemption) of the section 306 stock,

was not in pursuance of a plan having as one of its principal purposes the avoidance of Federal income tax.

(c) Section 306 stock defined.—

(1) In general.—For purposes of this subchapter, the term "section 306 stock" means stock which meets the requirements of subparagraph (A), (B), or (C) of this paragraph.

(A) Distributed to seller.—Stock (other than common stock issued with respect to common stock) which was distributed to the shareholder selling or otherwise disposing of such stock if, by reason of section 305(a), any part of such distribution was not includible in the gross income of the shareholder.

(B) Received in a corporate reorganization or separation.—Stock which is not common stock and—

(i) which was received, by the shareholder selling or otherwise disposing of such stock, in pursuance of a plan of reorganization (within the meaning of section 368(a)), or in a distribution or exchange to which section 355 (or so much of section 356 as relates to section 355) applied, and

(ii) with respect to the receipt of which gain or loss to the shareholder was to any extent not recognized by reason of part III, but only to the extent that either the effect of the transaction was substantially the same as the receipt of a stock dividend, or the stock was received in exchange for section 306 stock.

For purposes of this section, a receipt of stock to which the foregoing provisions of this subparagraph apply shall be treated as a distribution of stock.

(C) Stock having transferred or substituted basis.—Except as otherwise provided in subparagraph (B), stock the basis of which (in the hands of the shareholder selling or otherwise disposing of such stock) is determined by reference to the basis (in the hands of such shareholder or any other person) of section 306 stock.

(2) Exception where no earnings and profits.—For purposes of this section, the term "section 306 stock" does not include any stock no part of the distribution of which would have been a dividend at the time of the distribution if money had been distributed in lieu of the stock.

(3) Certain stock acquired in section 351 exchange.—The term "section 306 stock" also includes any stock which is not common stock acquired in an exchange to which section 351 applied if receipt of money (in lieu of the stock) would have been treated as a dividend to any extent. Rules similar to the rules of section 304(b)(2) shall apply—

(A) for purposes of the preceding sentence, and

(B) for purposes of determining the application of this section to any subsequent disposition of stock which is section 306 stock by reason of an exchange described in the preceding sentence.

(4) Application of attribution rules for certain purposes.—For purposes of paragraphs (1)(B)(ii) and (3), section 318(a) shall apply. For purposes of applying the preceding sentence to paragraph (3), the rules of section 304(c)(3)(B) shall apply.

(d) Stock rights.—For purposes of this section—

(1) stock rights shall be treated as stock, and

(2) stock acquired through the exercise of stock rights shall be treated as stock distributed at the time of the distribution of the stock rights, to the extent of the fair market value of such rights at the time of the distribution.

(e) Convertible stock.—For purposes of subsection (c)—

(1) if section 306 stock was issued with respect to common stock and later such section 306 stock is exchanged for common stock in the same corporation (whether or not such exchange is pursuant to a conversion privilege contained in the section 306 stock), then (except as provided in paragraph (2)) the common stock so received shall not be treated as section 306 stock; and

(2) common stock with respect to which there is a privilege of converting into stock other than common stock (or into property), whether or not the conversion privilege is contained in such stock, shall not be treated as common stock.

* * *

(g) Change in terms and conditions of stock.—If a substantial change is made in the terms and conditions of any stock, then, for purposes of this section—

(1) the fair market value of such stock shall be the fair market value at the time of the distribution or at the time of such change, whichever such value is higher;

(2) such stock's ratable share of the amount which would have been a dividend if money had been distributed in lieu of stock shall be determined as of the time of distribution or as of the time of such change, whichever such ratable share is higher; and

(3) subsection (c)(2) shall not apply unless the stock meets the requirements of such subsection both at the time of such distribution and at the time of such change.

§ 307. Basis of stock and stock rights acquired in distributions

(a) General rule.—If a shareholder in a corporation receives its stock or rights to acquire its stock (referred to in this subsection as "new stock") in a distribution to which section 305(a) applies, then the basis of such new stock and of the stock with respect to which it is distributed (referred to in this section as "old stock"), respectively, shall, in the shareholder's hands, be determined by allocating between the old stock and the new stock the adjusted basis of the old stock. Such allocation shall be made under regulations prescribed by the Secretary.

(b) Exception for certain stock rights.—

(1) In general.—If—

(A) a corporation distributes rights to acquire its stock to a shareholder in a distribution to which section 305(a) applies, and

(B) the fair market value of such rights at the time of the distribution is less than 15 percent of the fair market value of the old stock at such time,

then subsection (a) shall not apply and the basis of such rights shall be zero, unless the taxpayer elects under paragraph (2) of this subsection to determine the basis of the old stock and of the stock rights under the method of allocation provided in subsection (a).

(2) Election.—The election referred to in paragraph (1) shall be made in the return filed within the time prescribed by law (including extensions thereof) for the taxable year in which such rights were received. Such election shall be made in such manner as the Secretary may by regulations prescribe, and shall be irrevocable when made.

* * *

Subpart B—Effects on Corporation

§ 311. Taxability of corporation on distribution

(a) General rule.—Except as provided in subsection (b), no gain or loss shall be recognized to a corporation on the distribution (not in complete liquidation) with respect to its stock, of—

(1) its stock (or rights to acquire its stock), or

(2) property.

(b) Distributions of appreciated property.—

(1) In general.—If—

(A) a corporation distributes property (other than an obligation of such corporation) to a shareholder in a distribution to which subpart A applies, and

(B) the fair market value of such property exceeds its adjusted basis (in the hands of the distributing corporation),

then gain shall be recognized to the distributing corporation as if such property were sold to the distributee at its fair market value.

(2) Treatment of liabilities.—Rules similar to the rules of section 336(b) shall apply for purposes of this subsection.

(3) Special rule for certain distributions of partnership or trust interests.—If the property distributed consists of an interest in a partnership or trust, the Secretary may by regulations provide that the amount of the gain recognized under paragraph (1) shall be computed without regard to any loss attributable to property contributed to the partnership or trust for the principal purpose of recognizing such loss on the distribution.

§ 312. Effect on earnings and profits

(a) General rule.—Except as otherwise provided in this section, on the distribution of property by a corporation with respect to its stock, the earnings and profits of the corporation (to the extent thereof) shall be decreased by the sum of—

(1) the amount of money,

(2) the principal amount of the obligations of such corporation (or, in the case of obligations having original issue discount, the aggregate issue price of such obligations), and

(3) the adjusted basis of the other property, so distributed.

(b) Distributions of appreciated property.—On the distribution by a corporation, with respect to its stock, of any property (other than an obligation of such corporation) the fair market value of which exceeds the adjusted basis thereof—

(1) the earnings and profits of the corporation shall be increased by the amount of such excess, and

(2) subsection (a)(3) shall be applied by substituting "fair market value" for "adjusted basis".

For purposes of this subsection and subsection (a), the adjusted basis of any property is its adjusted basis as determined for purposes of computing earnings and profits.

(c) Adjustments for liabilities.—In making the adjustments to the earnings and profits of a corporation under subsection (a) or (b), proper adjustment shall be made for—

(1) the amount of any liability to which the property distributed is subject, and

(2) the amount of any liability of the corporation assumed by a shareholder in connection with the distribution.

(d) Certain distributions of stock and securities.—

(1) In general.—The distribution to a distributee by or on behalf of a corporation of its stock or securities, of stock or securities in another corporation, or of property, in a distribution to which this title applies, shall not be considered a distribution of the earnings and profits of any corporation—

(A) if no gain to such distributee from the receipt of such stock or securities, or property, was recognized under this title, or

(B) if the distribution was not subject to tax in the hands of such distributee by reason of section 305(a).

(2) Prior distributions.—In the case of a distribution of stock or securities, or property, to which section 115(h) of the Internal Revenue Code of 1939 (or the corresponding provision of prior law) applied, the effect on earnings and profits of such distribution shall be determined under such section 115(h), or the corresponding provision of prior law, as the case may be.

(3) Stock or securities.—For purposes of this subsection, the term "stock or securities" includes rights to acquire stock or securities.

[(e) Repealed.]

(f) Effect on earnings and profits of gain or loss and of receipt of tax-free distributions.—

(1) Effect on earnings and profits of gain or loss.—The gain or loss realized from the sale or other disposition (after February 28, 1913) of property by a corporation—

(A) for the purpose of the computation of the earnings and profits of the corporation, shall (except as provided in subparagraph (B)) be determined by using as the adjusted basis the adjusted basis (under the law applicable to the year in which the sale or other disposition was made) for determining gain, except that no regard shall be had to the value of the property as of March 1, 1913; but

(B) for purposes of the computation of the earnings and profits of the corporation for any period beginning after February 28, 1913, shall be determined by using as the adjusted basis the adjusted basis (under the law applicable to the year in which the sale or other disposition was made) for determining gain.

Gain or loss so realized shall increase or decrease the earnings and profits to, but not beyond, the extent to which such a realized gain or loss was recognized in computing taxable income under the law applicable to the year in which such sale or disposition was made. Where, in determining the adjusted basis used in computing such realized gain or loss, the adjustment to the basis differs from the adjustment proper for the purpose of determining earnings and profits, then the latter adjustment shall be used in determining the increase or decrease above provided. For purposes of this subsection, a loss with respect to which a deduction is disallowed under section 1091 (relating to wash sales of stock or securities), or the corresponding provision of prior law, shall not be deemed to be recognized.

(2) Effect on earnings and profits of receipt of tax-free distributions.—Where a corporation receives (after February 28, 1913) a distribution from a second corporation which (under the law applicable to the year in which the distribution was made) was not a taxable dividend to the shareholders of the second corporation, the amount of such distribution shall not increase the earnings and profits of the first corporation in the following cases:

(A) no such increase shall be made in respect of the part of such distribution which (under such law) is directly applied in reduction of the basis of the stock in respect of which the distribution was made; and

(B) no such increase shall be made if (under such law) the distribution causes the basis of the stock in respect of which the distribution was made to be allocated between such stock and the property received (or such basis would, but for section 307(b), be so allocated).

* * *

(h) Allocation in certain corporate separations and reorganizations.—

(1) Section 355.—In the case of a distribution or exchange to which section 355 (or so much of section 356 as relates to section 355) applies, proper allocation with respect to the earnings and profits of the distributing corporation and the controlled corporation (or corporations) shall be made under regulations prescribed by the Secretary.

(2) Section 368(a)(1)(C) or (D).—In the case of a reorganization described in subparagraph (C) or (D) of section 368(a)(1), proper allocation with respect to the earnings and profits of the acquired corporation shall, under regulations prescribed by the Secretary, be made between the acquiring corporation and the acquired corporation (or any corporation which had control of the acquired corporation before the reorganization).

* * *

(k) Effect of depreciation on earnings and profits.—

(1) General rule.—For purposes of computing the earnings and profits of a corporation for any taxable year beginning after June 30, 1972, the allowance for depreciation (and amortization, if any) shall be deemed to be the amount which would be allowable for such year if the straight line method of depreciation had been used for each taxable year beginning after June 30, 1972.

(2) Exception.—If for any taxable year a method of depreciation was used by the taxpayer which the Secretary has determined results in a reasonable allowance under section 167(a) and which is the unit-of-production method or other method not expressed in a term of years, then the adjustment to earnings and profits for depreciation for such year shall be determined under the method so used (in lieu of the straight line method).

(3) Exception for tangible property.—

(A) In general.—Except as provided in subparagraph (B), in the case of tangible property to which section 168 applies, the adjustment to earnings and profits for depreciation for any taxable year shall be determined under the alternative depreciation system (within the meaning of section 168(g)(2)).

(B) Treatment of amounts deductible under section 179, 179A, 179B, 179C, 179D, or 179E.—For purposes of computing the earnings and profits of a corporation, any amount deductible under section 179, 179A, 179B, 179C, 179D, or 179E shall be allowed as a deduction ratably over the period of 5 taxable years (beginning with the taxable year for which such amount is deductible under section 179, 179A, 179B, 179C, 179D, or 179E, as the case may be).

* * *

(*l*) Discharge of indebtedness income.—

(1) Does not increase earnings and profits if applied to reduce basis.— The earnings and profits of a corporation shall not include income from the discharge of indebtedness to the extent of the amount applied to reduce basis under section 1017.

(2) Reduction of deficit in earnings and profits in certain cases.—If—

(A) the interest of any shareholder of a corporation is terminated or extinguished in a title 11 or similar case (within the meaning of section 368(a)(3)(A)), and

(B) there is a deficit in the earnings and profits of the corporation,

then such deficit shall be reduced by an amount equal to the paid-in capital which is allocable to the interest of the shareholder which is so terminated or extinguished.

(m) No adjustment for interest paid on certain registration-required obligations not in registered form.—The earnings and profits of any corporation shall not be decreased by any interest with respect to which a deduction is not or would not be allowable by reason of section 163(f), unless at the time of issuance the issuer is a foreign corporation that is not a controlled foreign corporation (within the meaning of section 957), and the issuance did not have as a purpose the avoidance of section 163(f) of this subsection.

(n) Adjustments to earnings and profits to more accurately reflect economic gain and loss.—For purposes of computing the earnings and profits of a corporation, the following adjustments shall be made:

(1) Construction period carrying charges.—

(A) In general.—In the case of any amount paid or incurred for construction period carrying charges—

(i) no deduction shall be allowed with respect to such amount, and

(ii) the basis of the property with respect to which such charges are allocable shall be increased by such amount.

(B) Construction period carrying charges defined.—For purposes of this paragraph, the term "construction period carrying charges" means all—

(i) interest paid or accrued on indebtedness incurred or continued to acquire, construct, or carry property,

(ii) property taxes, and

(iii) similar carrying charges,

to the extent such interest, taxes, or charges are attributable to the construction period for such property and would be allowable as a deduction in determining taxable income under this chapter for the taxable year in which paid or incurred.

(C) Construction period.—The term "construction period" has the meaning given the term production period under section 263A(f)(4)(B).

(2) Intangible drilling costs and mineral exploration and development costs.—

(A) Intangible drilling costs.—Any amount allowable as a deduction under section 263(c) in determining taxable income (other than costs incurred in connection with a nonproductive well)—

(i) shall be capitalized, and

(ii) shall be allowed as a deduction ratably over the 60–month period beginning with the month in which such amount was paid or incurred.

(B) Mineral exploration and development costs.—Any amount allowable as a deduction under section 616(a) or 617 in determining taxable income—

(i) shall be capitalized, and

(ii) shall be allowed as a deduction ratably over the 120–month period beginning with the later of—

(I) the month in which production from the deposit begins, or

(II) the month in which such amount was paid or incurred.

(3) Certain amortization provisions not to apply.—Sections 173 and 248 shall not apply.

(4) **LIFO inventory adjustments.**—

(A) **In general.**—Earnings and profits shall be increased or decreased by the amount of any increase or decrease in the LIFO recapture amount as of the close of each taxable year; except that any decrease below the LIFO recapture amount as of the close of the taxable year preceding the 1st taxable year to which this paragraph applies to the taxpayer shall be taken into account only to the extent provided in regulations prescribed by the Secretary.

(B) **LIFO recapture amount.**—For purposes of this paragraph, the term "LIFO recapture amount" means the amount (if any) by which—

(i) the inventory amount of the inventory assets under the first-in, first-out method authorized by section 471, exceeds

(ii) the inventory amount of such assets under the LIFO method.

(C) **Definitions.**—For purposes of this paragraph—

(i) **LIFO method.**—The term "LIFO method" means the method authorized by section 472 (relating to last-in, first-out inventories).

(ii) **Inventory assets.**—The term "inventory assets" means stock in trade of the corporation, or other property of a kind which would properly be included in the inventory of the corporation if on hand at the close of the taxable year.

(iii) **Inventory amount.**—The inventory amount of assets under the first-in, first-out method authorized by section 471 shall be determined—

(I) if the corporation uses the retail method of valuing inventories under section 472, by using such method, or

(II) if subclause (I) does not apply, by using cost or market, whichever is lower.

(5) **Installment sales.**—In the case of any installment sale, earnings and profits shall be computed as if the corporation did not use the installment method.

(6) **Completed contract method of accounting.**—In the case of a taxpayer who uses the completed contract method of accounting, earnings and profits shall be computed as if such taxpayer used the percentage of completion method of accounting.

(7) **Redemptions.**—If a corporation distributes amounts in a redemption to which section 302(a) or 303 applies, the part of such distribution which is properly chargeable to earnings and profits shall be an amount which is not in excess of the ratable share of the earnings and profits of such corporation accumulated after February 28, 1913, attributable to the stock so redeemed.

* * *

(*o*) Definition of original issue discount and issue price for purposes of subsection (a)(2).—For purposes of subsection (a)(2), the terms "original issue discount" and "issue price" have the same respective meanings as when used in subpart A of part V of subchapter P of this chapter.

Subpart C—Definitions; Constructive Ownership of Stock

§ 316. Dividend defined

(a) General rule.—For purposes of this subtitle, the term "dividend" means any distribution of property made by a corporation to its shareholders—

(1) out of its earnings and profits accumulated after February 28, 1913, or

(2) out of its earnings and profits of the taxable year (computed as of the close of the taxable year without diminution by reason of any distributions made during the

taxable year), without regard to the amount of the earnings and profits at the time the distribution was made.

Except as otherwise provided in this subtitle, every distribution is made out of earnings and profits to the extent thereof, and from the most recently accumulated earnings and profits. To the extent that any distribution is, under any provision of this subchapter, treated as a distribution of property to which section 301 applies, such distribution shall be treated as a distribution of property for purposes of this subsection.

(b) Special rules.—

(1) Certain insurance company dividends.—The definition in subsection (a) shall not apply to the term "dividend" as used in subchapter L in any case where the reference is to dividends of insurance companies paid to policyholders as such.

(2) Distributions by personal holding companies.—

(A) In the case of a corporation which—

(i) under the law applicable to the taxable year in which the distribution is made, is a personal holding company (as defined in section 542), or

(ii) for the taxable year in respect of which the distribution is made under section 563(b) (relating to dividends paid after the close of the taxable year), or section 547 (relating to deficiency dividends), or the corresponding provisions of prior law, is a personal holding company under the law applicable to such taxable year,

the term "dividend" also means any distribution of property (whether or not a dividend as defined in subsection (a)) made by the corporation to its shareholders, to the extent of its undistributed personal holding company income (determined under section 545 without regard to distributions under this paragraph) for such year.

(B) For purposes of subparagraph (A), the term "distribution of property" includes a distribution in complete liquidation occurring within 24 months after the adoption of a plan of liquidation, but—

(i) only to the extent of the amounts distributed to distributees other than corporate shareholders, and

(ii) only to the extent that the corporation designates such amounts as a dividend distribution and duly notifies such distributees of such designation, under regulations prescribed by the Secretary, but

(iii) not in excess of the sum of such distributees' allocable share of the undistributed personal holding company income for such year, computed without regard to this subparagraph or section 562(b).

* * *

§ 317. Other definitions

(a) Property.—For purposes of this part, the term "property" means money, securities, and any other property; except that such term does not include stock in the corporation making the distribution (or rights to acquire such stock).

(b) Redemption of stock.—For purposes of this part, stock shall be treated as redeemed by a corporation if the corporation acquires its stock from a shareholder in exchange for property, whether or not the stock so acquired is cancelled, retired, or held as treasury stock.

§ 318. Constructive ownership of stock

(a) General rule.—For purposes of those provisions of this subchapter to which the rules contained in this section are expressly made applicable—

(1) Members of family.—

(A) In general.—An individual shall be considered as owning the stock owned, directly or indirectly, by or for—

(i) his spouse (other than a spouse who is legally separated from the individual under a decree of divorce or separate maintenance), and

(ii) his children, grandchildren, and parents.

(B) Effect of adoption.—For purposes of subparagraph (A) (ii), a legally adopted child of an individual shall be treated as a child of such individual by blood.

(2) Attribution from partnerships, estates, trusts, and corporations.—

(A) From partnerships and estates.—Stock owned, directly or indirectly, by or for a partnership or estate shall be considered as owned proportionately by its partners or beneficiaries.

(B) From trusts.—

(i) Stock owned, directly or indirectly, by or for a trust (other than an employees' trust described in section 401(a) which is exempt from tax under section 501(a)) shall be considered as owned by its beneficiaries in proportion to the actuarial interest of such beneficiaries in such trust.

(ii) Stock owned, directly or indirectly, by or for any portion of a trust of which a person is considered the owner under subpart E of part I of subchapter J (relating to grantors and others treated as substantial owners) shall be considered as owned by such person.

(C) From corporations.—If 50 percent or more in value of the stock in a corporation is owned, directly or indirectly, by or for any person, such person shall be considered as owning the stock owned, directly or indirectly, by or for such corporation, in that proportion which the value of the stock which such person so owns bears to the value of all the stock in such corporation.

(3) Attribution to partnerships, estates, trusts, and corporations.—

(A) To partnerships and estates.—Stock owned, directly or indirectly, by or for a partner or a beneficiary of an estate shall be considered as owned by the partnership or estate.

(B) To trusts.—

(i) Stock owned, directly or indirectly, by or for a beneficiary of a trust (other than an employees' trust described in section 401(a) which is exempt from tax under section 501(a)) shall be considered as owned by the trust, unless such beneficiary's interest in the trust is a remote contingent interest. For purposes of this clause, a contingent interest of a beneficiary in a trust shall be considered remote if, under the maximum exercise of discretion by the trustee in favor of such beneficiary, the value of such interest, computed actuarially, is 5 percent or less of the value of the trust property.

(ii) Stock owned, directly or indirectly, by or for a person who is considered the owner of any portion of a trust under subpart E of part I of subchapter J (relating to grantors and others treated as substantial owners) shall be considered as owned by the trust.

(C) To corporations.—If 50 percent or more in value of the stock in a corporation is owned, directly or indirectly, by or for any person, such corporation shall be considered as owning the stock owned, directly or indirectly, by or for such person.

(4) Options.—If any person has an option to acquire stock, such stock shall be considered as owned by such person. For purposes of this paragraph, an option to acquire such an option, and each one of a series of such options, shall be considered as an option to acquire such stock.

(5) Operating rules.—

(A) In general.—Except as provided in subparagraphs (B) and (C), stock constructively owned by a person by reason of the application of paragraph (1), (2), (3), or (4), shall, for purposes of applying paragraphs (1), (2), (3), and (4), be considered as actually owned by such person.

(B) Members of family.—Stock constructively owned by an individual by reason of the application of paragraph (1) shall not be considered as owned by him for purposes of again applying paragraph (1) in order to make another the constructive owner of such stock.

(C) Partnerships, estates, trusts, and corporations.—Stock constructively owned by a partnership, estate, trust, or corporation by reason of the application of paragraph (3) shall not be considered as owned by it for purposes of applying paragraph (2) in order to make another the constructive owner of such stock.

(D) Option rule in lieu of family rule.—For purposes of this paragraph, if stock may be considered as owned by an individual under paragraph (1) or (4), it shall be considered as owned by him under paragraph (4).

(E) S corporation treated as partnership.—For purposes of this subsection—

(i) an S corporation shall be treated as a partnership, and

(ii) any shareholder of the S corporation shall be treated as a partner of such partnership.

The preceding sentence shall not apply for purposes of determining whether stock in the S corporation is constructively owned by any person.

(b) Cross references.—

For provisions to which the rules contained in subsection (a) apply, see—

(1) section 302 (relating to redemption of stock);

(2) section 304 (relating to redemption by related corporations);

(3) section 306(b)(1)(A) (relating to disposition of section 306 stock);

(4) section 338(h)(3) (defining purchase);

(5) section 382(*l*)(3) (relating to special limitations on net operating loss carryovers);

* * *

PART II—CORPORATE LIQUIDATIONS

Subpart

A. Effects on recipients.

B. Effects on corporation.

C. [Repealed].

D. Definition and special rule.

Subpart A—Effects on Recipients

§ 331. Gain or loss to shareholders in corporate liquidations

(a) Distributions in complete liquidation treated as exchanges.—Amounts received by a shareholder in a distribution in complete liquidation of a corporation shall be treated as in full payment in exchange for the stock.

(b) Nonapplication of section 301.—Section 301 (relating to effects on shareholder of distributions of property) shall not apply to any distribution of property (other than a distribution referred to in paragraph (2)(B) of section 316(b)) in complete liquidation.

(c) Cross reference.—

For general rule for determination of the amount of gain or loss recognized, see section 1001.

§ 332. Complete liquidations of subsidiaries

(a) General rule.—No gain or loss shall be recognized on the receipt by a corporation of property distributed in complete liquidation of another corporation.

(b) Liquidations to which section applies.—For purposes of this section, a distribution shall be considered to be in complete liquidation only if—

(1) the corporation receiving such property was, on the date of the adoption of the plan of liquidation, and has continued to be at all times until the receipt of the property, the owner of stock (in such other corporation) meeting the requirements of section 1504(a)(2); and either

(2) the distribution is by such other corporation in complete cancellation or redemption of all its stock, and the transfer of all the property occurs within the taxable year; in such case the adoption by the shareholders of the resolution under which is authorized the distribution of all the assets of such corporation in complete cancellation or redemption of all its stock shall be considered an adoption of a plan of liquidation, even though no time for the completion of the transfer of the property is specified in such resolution; or

(3) such distribution is one of a series of distributions by such other corporation in complete cancellation or redemption of all its stock in accordance with a plan of liquidation under which the transfer of all the property under the liquidation is to be completed within 3 years from the close of the taxable year during which is made the first of the series of distributions under the plan, except that if such transfer is not completed within such period, or if the taxpayer does not continue qualified under paragraph (1) until the completion of such transfer, no distribution under the plan shall be considered a distribution in complete liquidation.

If such transfer of all the property does not occur within the taxable year, the Secretary may require of the taxpayer such bond, or waiver of the statute of limitations on assessment and collection, or both, as he may deem necessary to insure, if the transfer of the property is not completed within such 3–year period, or if the taxpayer does not continue qualified under paragraph (1) until the completion of such transfer, the assessment and collection of all income taxes then imposed by law for such taxable year or subsequent taxable years, to the extent attributable to property so received. A distribution otherwise constituting a distribution in complete liquidation within the meaning of this subsection shall not be considered as not constituting such a distribution merely because it does not constitute a distribution or liquidation within the meaning of the corporate law under which the distribution is made; and for purposes of this subsection a transfer of property of such other corporation to the taxpayer shall not be considered as not constituting a distribution (or one of a series of distributions) in complete cancellation or redemption of all the stock of such other corporation, merely because the carrying out of the plan involves (A) the transfer under the plan to the taxpayer by such other corporation of property, not attributable to shares owned by the taxpayer, on an exchange described in section 361, and (B) the complete cancellation or redemption under the plan, as a result of exchanges described in section 354, of the shares not owned by the taxpayer.

* * *

§ 334. Basis of property received in liquidations

(a) General rule.—If property is received in a distribution in complete liquidation, and if gain or loss is recognized on receipt of such property, then the basis of the property in the hands of the distributee shall be the fair market value of such property at the time of the distribution.

(b) Liquidation of subsidiary.—

(1) In general.—If property is received by a corporate distributee in a distribution in a complete liquidation to which section 332 applies (or in a transfer described in section 337(b)(1)), the basis of such property in the hands of such distributee shall be the same as it would be in the hands of the transferor; except that, in the hands of such distributee—

(A) the basis of such property shall be the fair market value of the property at the time of the distribution in any case in which gain or loss is recognized by the liquidating corporation with respect to such property, and

(B) the basis of any property described in section 362(e)(1)(B) shall be the fair market value of the property at the time of the distribution in any case in which such distributee's aggregate adjusted basis of such property would (but for this subparagraph) exceed the fair market value of such property immediately after such liquidation.

(2) Corporate distributee.—For purposes of this subsection, the term "corporate distributee" means only the corporation which meets the stock ownership requirements specified in section 332(b).

Subpart B—Effects on Corporation

§ 336. Gain or loss recognized on property distributed in complete liquidation

(a) General rule.—Except as otherwise provided in this section or section 337, gain or loss shall be recognized to a liquidating corporation on the distribution of property in complete liquidation as if such property were sold to the distributee at its fair market value.

(b) Treatment of liabilities.—If any property distributed in the liquidation is subject to a liability or the shareholder assumes a liability of the liquidating corporation in connection with the distribution, for purposes of subsection (a) and section 337, the fair market value of such property shall be treated as not less than the amount of such liability.

(c) Exception for liquidations which are part of a reorganization.—For provision providing that this subpart does not apply to distributions in pursuance of a plan of reorganization, see section 361(c)(4).

(d) Limitations on recognition of loss.—

(1) No loss recognized in certain distributions to related persons.—

(A) In general.—No loss shall be recognized to a liquidating corporation on the distribution of any property to a related person (within the meaning of section 267) if—

(i) such distribution is not pro rata, or

(ii) such property is disqualified property.

(B) Disqualified property.—For purposes of subparagraph (A), the term "disqualified property" means any property which is acquired by the liquidating corporation in a transaction to which section 351 applied, or as a contribution to capital, during the 5–year period ending on the date of the distribution. Such term includes any property if the adjusted basis of such property is determined (in whole or in part) by reference to the adjusted basis of property described in the preceding sentence.

(2) Special rule for certain property acquired in certain carryover basis transactions.—

(A) In general.—For purposes of determining the amount of loss recognized by any liquidating corporation on any sale, exchange, or distribution of property described in subparagraph (B), the adjusted basis of such property shall be reduced (but not below zero) by the excess (if any) of—

(i) the adjusted basis of such property immediately after its acquisition by such corporation, over

(ii) the fair market value of such property as of such time.

(B) Description of property.—

(i) In general.—For purposes of subparagraph (A), property is described in this subparagraph if—

(I) such property is acquired by the liquidating corporation in a transaction to which section 351 applied or as a contribution to capital, and

(II) the acquisition of such property by the liquidating corporation was part of a plan a principal purpose of which was to recognize loss by the liquidating corporation with respect to such property in connection with the liquidation.

Other property shall be treated as so described if the adjusted basis of such other property is determined (in whole or in part) by reference to the adjusted basis of property described in the preceding sentence.

(ii) Certain acquisitions treated as part of plan.—For purposes of clause (i), any property described in clause (i)(I) acquired by the liquidated corporation after the date 2 years before the date of the adoption of the plan of complete liquidation shall, except as provided in regulations, be treated as acquired as part of a plan described in clause (i)(II).

(C) Recapture in lieu of disallowance.—The Secretary may prescribe regulations under which, in lieu of disallowing a loss under subparagraph (A) for a prior taxable year, the gross income of the liquidating corporation for the taxable year in which the plan of complete liquidation is adopted shall be increased by the amount of the disallowed loss.

(3) Special rule in case of liquidation to which section 332 applies.—In the case of any liquidation to which section 332 applies, no loss shall be recognized to the liquidating corporation on any distribution in such liquidation. The preceding sentence shall apply to any distribution to the 80–percent distributee only if subsection (a) or (b)(1) of section 337 applies to such distribution.

(e) Certain stock sales and distributions may be treated as asset transfers.—Under regulations prescribed by the Secretary, if—

(1) a corporation owns stock in another corporation meeting the requirements of section 1504(a)(2), and

(2) such corporation sells, exchanges, or distributes all of such stock,

an election may be made to treat such sale, exchange, or distribution as a disposition of all of the assets of such other corporation, and no gain or loss shall be recognized on the sale, exchange, or distribution of such stock.

§ 337. Nonrecognition for property distributed to parent in complete liquidation of subsidiary

(a) In general.—No gain or loss shall be recognized to the liquidating corporation on the distribution to the 80–percent distributee of any property in a complete liquidation to which section 332 applies.

(b) Treatment of indebtedness of subsidiary, etc.—

(1) Indebtedness of subsidiary to parent.—If—

(A) a corporation is liquidated in a liquidation to which section 332 applies, and

(B) on the date of the adoption of the plan of liquidation, such corporation was indebted to the 80–percent distributee,

for purposes of this section and section 336, any transfer of property to the 80–percent distributee in satisfaction of such indebtedness shall be treated as a distribution to such distributee in such liquidation.

* * *

(c) 80–percent distributee.—For purposes of this section, the term "80–percent distributee" means only the corporation which meets the 80–percent stock ownership requirements specified in section 332(b). For purposes of this section, the determination of whether any corporation is an 80–percent distributee shall be made without regard to any consolidated return regulation.

(d) Regulations.—The Secretary shall prescribe such regulations as may be necessary or appropriate to carry out the purposes of the amendments made by subtitle D of title VI of the Tax Reform Act of 1986, including—

(1) regulations to ensure that such purposes may not be circumvented through the use of any provision of law or regulations (including the consolidated return regulations and part III of this subchapter) or through the use of a regulated investment company, real estate investment trust, or tax-exempt entity, and

* * *

§ 338. Certain stock purchases treated as asset acquisitions

(a) General rule.—For purposes of this subtitle, if a purchasing corporation makes an election under this section (or is treated under subsection (e) as having made such an election), then, in the case of any qualified stock purchase, the target corporation—

(1) shall be treated as having sold all of its assets at the close of the acquisition date at fair market value in a single transaction, and

(2) shall be treated as a new corporation which purchased all of the assets referred to in paragraph (1) as of the beginning of the day after the acquisition date.

(b) Basis of assets after deemed purchase.—

(1) In general.—For purposes of subsection (a), the assets of the target corporation shall be treated as purchased for an amount equal to the sum of—

(A) the grossed-up basis of the purchasing corporation's recently purchased stock, and

(B) the basis of the purchasing corporation's nonrecently purchased stock.

(2) Adjustment for liabilities and other relevant items.—The amount described in paragraph (1) shall be adjusted under regulations prescribed by the Secretary for liabilities of the target corporation and other relevant items.

(3) Election to step-up the basis of certain target stock.—

(A) In general.—Under regulations prescribed by the Secretary, the basis of the purchasing corporation's nonrecently purchased stock shall be the basis amount determined under subparagraph (B) of this paragraph if the purchasing corporation makes an election to recognize gain as if such stock were sold on the acquisition date for an amount equal to the basis amount determined under subparagraph (B).

(B) Determination of basis amount.—For purposes of subparagraph (A), the basis amount determined under this subparagraph shall be an amount equal to the grossed-up basis determined under subparagraph (A) of paragraph (1) multiplied by a fraction—

(i) the numerator of which is the percentage of stock (by value) in the target corporation attributable to the purchasing corporation's nonrecently purchased stock, and

(ii) the denominator of which is 100 percent minus the percentage referred to in clause (i).

(4) Grossed-up basis.—For purposes of paragraph (1), the grossed-up basis shall be an amount equal to the basis of the corporation's recently purchased stock, multiplied by a fraction—

(A) the numerator of which is 100 percent, minus the percentage of stock (by value) in the target corporation attributable to the purchasing corporation's nonrecently purchased stock, and

(B) the denominator of which is the percentage of stock (by value) in the target corporation attributable to the purchasing corporation's recently purchased stock.

(5) Allocation among assets.—The amount determined under paragraphs (1) and (2) shall be allocated among the assets of the target corporation under regulations prescribed by the Secretary.

(6) Definitions of recently purchased stock and nonrecently purchased stock.—For purposes of this subsection—

(A) Recently purchased stock.—The term "recently purchased stock" means any stock in the target corporation which is held by the purchasing corporation on the acquisition date and which was purchased by such corporation during the 12–month acquisition period.

(B) Nonrecently purchased stock.—The term "nonrecently purchased stock" means any stock in the target corporation which is held by the purchasing corporation on the acquisition date and which is not recently purchased stock.

[(c) Repealed.]

(d) Purchasing corporation; target corporation; qualified stock purchase.—For purposes of this section—

(1) Purchasing corporation.—The term "purchasing corporation" means any corporation which makes a qualified stock purchase of stock of another corporation.

(2) Target corporation.—The term "target corporation" means any corporation the stock of which is acquired by another corporation in a qualified stock purchase.

(3) Qualified stock purchase.—The term "qualified stock purchase" means any transaction or series of transactions in which stock (meeting the requirements of section 1504(a)(2)) of 1 corporation is acquired by another corporation by purchase during the 12–month acquisition period.

(e) Deemed election where purchasing corporation acquires asset of target corporation.—

(1) In general.—A purchasing corporation shall be treated as having made an election under this section with respect to any target corporation if, at any time during the consistency period, it acquires any asset of the target corporation (or a target affiliate).

(2) Exceptions.—Paragraph (1) shall not apply with respect to any acquisition by the purchasing corporation if—

(A) such acquisition is pursuant to a sale by the target corporation (or the target affiliate) in the ordinary course of its trade or business,

(B) the basis of the property acquired is determined (wholly) by reference to the adjusted basis of such property in the hands of the person from whom acquired,

(C) such acquisition was before September 1, 1982, or

(D) such acquisition is described in regulations prescribed by the Secretary and meets such conditions as such regulations may provide.

(3) Anti-avoidance rule.—Whenever necessary to carry out the purpose of this subsection and subsection (f), the Secretary may treat stock acquisitions which are pursuant to a plan and which meet the requirements of section 1504(a)(2) as qualified stock purchases.

(f) Consistency required for all stock acquisitions from same affiliated group.—If a purchasing corporation makes qualified stock purchases with respect to the target corporation and 1 or more target affiliates during any consistency period, then (except as otherwise provided in subsection (e))—

(1) any election under this section with respect to the first such purchase shall apply to each other such purchase, and

(2) no election may be made under this section with respect to the second or subsequent such purchase if such an election was not made with respect to the first such purchase.

(g) Election.—

(1) When made.—Except as otherwise provided in regulations, an election under this section shall be made not later than the 15th day of the 9th month beginning after the month in which the acquisition date occurs.

(2) Manner.—An election by the purchasing corporation under this section shall be made in such manner as the Secretary shall by regulations prescribe.

(3) Election irrevocable.—An election by a purchasing corporation under this section, once made, shall be irrevocable.

(h) Definitions and special rules.—For purposes of this section—

(1) 12–month acquisition period.—The term "12–month acquisition period" means the 12–month period beginning with the date of the first acquisition by purchase of stock included in a qualified stock purchase (or, if any of such stock was acquired in an acquisition which is a purchase by reason of subparagraph (C) of paragraph (3), the date on which the acquiring corporation is first considered under section 318(a) (other than paragraph (4) thereof) as owning stock owned by the corporation from which such acquisition was made).

(2) Acquisition date.—The term "acquisition date" means, with respect to any corporation, the first day on which there is a qualified stock purchase with respect to the stock of such corporation.

(3) Purchase.—

(A) In general.—The term "purchase" means any acquisition of stock, but only if—

(i) the basis of the stock in the hands of the purchasing corporation is not determined (I) in whole or in part by reference to the adjusted basis of such stock in the hands of the person from whom acquired, or (II) under section 1014(a) (relating to property acquired from a decedent),

(ii) the stock is not acquired in an exchange to which section 351, 354, 355, or 356 applies and is not acquired in any other transaction described in regulations in which the transferor does not recognize the entire amount of the gain or loss realized on the transaction, and

(iii) the stock is not acquired from a person the ownership of whose stock would, under section 318(a) (other than paragraph (4) thereof), be attributed to the person acquiring such stock.

(B) Deemed purchase under subsection (a).—The term "purchase" includes any deemed purchase under subsection (a)(2). The acquisition date for a corporation which is deemed purchased under subsection (a)(2) shall be determined under regulations prescribed by the Secretary.

(C) Certain stock acquisitions from related corporations.—

(i) In general.—Clause (iii) of subparagraph (A) shall not apply to an acquisition of stock from a related corporation if at least 50 percent in value of the stock of such related corporation was acquired by purchase (within the meaning of subparagraphs (A) and (B)).

(ii) Certain distributions.—Clause (i) of subparagraph (A) shall not apply to an acquisition of stock described in clause (i) of this subparagraph if the corporation acquiring such stock—

(I) made a qualified stock purchase of stock of the related corporation, and

(II) made an election under this section (or is treated under subsection (e) as having made such an election) with respect to such qualified stock purchase.

(iii) Related corporation defined.—For purposes of this subparagraph, a corporation is a related corporation if stock owned by such corporation is treated (under section 318(a) other than paragraph (4) thereof) as owned by the corporation acquiring the stock.

(4) Consistency period.—

(A) In general.—Except as provided in subparagraph (B), the term "consistency period" means the period consisting of—

(i) the 1–year period before the beginning of the 12–month acquisition period for the target corporation,

(ii) such acquisition period (up to and including the acquisition date), and

(iii) the 1–year period beginning on the day after the acquisition date.

(B) Extension where there is plan.—The period referred to in subparagraph (A) shall also include any period during which the Secretary determines that there was in effect a plan to make a qualified stock purchase plus 1 or more other qualified stock purchases (or asset acquisitions described in subsection (e)) with respect to the target corporation or any target affiliate.

(5) Affiliated group.—The term "affiliated group" has the meaning given to such term by section 1504(a) (determined without regard to the exceptions contained in section 1504(b)).

(6) Target affiliate.—

(A) In general.—A corporation shall be treated as a target affiliate of the target corporation if each of such corporations was, at any time during so much of the consistency period as ends on the acquisition date of the target corporation, a member of an affiliated group which had the same common parent.

* * *

[(7) Repealed.]

(8) Acquisitions by affiliated group treated as made by 1 corporation.—Except as provided in regulations prescribed by the Secretary, stock and asset acquisitions made by members of the same affiliated group shall be treated as made by 1 corporation.

(9) Target not treated as member of affiliated group.—Except as otherwise provided in paragraph (10) or in regulations prescribed under this paragraph, the target corporation shall not be treated as a member of an affiliated group with respect to the sale described in subsection (a)(1).

(10) Elective recognition of gain or loss by target corporation, together with nonrecognition of gain or loss on stock sold by selling consolidated group.—

(A) In general.—Under regulations prescribed by the Secretary, an election may be made under which if—

(i) the target corporation was, before the transaction, a member of the selling consolidated group, and

(ii) the target corporation recognizes gain or loss with respect to the transaction as if it sold all of its assets in a single transaction,

then the target corporation shall be treated as a member of the selling consolidated group with respect to such sale, and (to the extent provided in regulations) no gain or loss will be recognized on stock sold or exchanged in the transaction by members of the selling consolidated group.

(B) Selling consolidated group.—For purposes of subparagraph (A), the term "selling consolidated group" means any group of corporations which (for the taxable period which includes the transaction)—

(i) includes the target corporation, and

(ii) files a consolidated return.

To the extent provided in regulations, such term also includes any affiliated group of corporations which includes the target corporation (whether or not such group files a consolidated return).

(C) Information required to be furnished to the Secretary.—Under regulations, where an election is made under subparagraph (A), the purchasing corporation and the common parent of the selling consolidated group shall, at such times and in such manner as may be provided in regulations, furnish to the Secretary the following information:

(i) The amount allocated under subsection (b)(5) to goodwill or going concern value.

(ii) Any modification of the amount described in clause (i).

(iii) Any other information as the Secretary deems necessary to carry out the provisions of this paragraph.

(11) Elective formula for determining fair market value.—For purposes of subsection (a)(1), fair market value may be determined on the basis of a formula provided in regulations prescribed by the Secretary which takes into account liabilities and other relevant items.

* * *

(15) Combined deemed sale return.—Under regulations prescribed by the Secretary, a combined deemed sale return may be filed by all target corporations acquired by a purchasing corporation on the same acquisition date if such target corporations were members of the same selling consolidated group (as defined in subparagraph (B) of paragraph (10)).

* * *

(i) Regulations.—The Secretary shall prescribe such regulations as may be necessary or appropriate to carry out the purposes of this section, including—

(1) regulations to ensure that the purpose of this section to require consistency of treatment of stock and asset sales and purchases may not be circumvented through the use of any provision of law or regulations (including the consolidated return regulations) and

(2) regulations providing for the coordination of the provisions of this section with the provision of this title relating to foreign corporations and their shareholders.

Subpart D—Definition and Special Rule

§ 346. Definition and special rule

(a) Complete liquidation.—For purposes of this subchapter, a distribution shall be treated as in complete liquidation of a corporation if the distribution is one of a series of distributions in redemption of all of the stock of the corporation pursuant to a plan.

(b) Transactions which might reach same result as partial liquidations.—The Secretary shall prescribe such regulations as may be necessary to ensure that the purposes of subsections (a) and (b) of section 222 of the Tax Equity and Fiscal Responsibility Act of 1982 (which repeal the special tax treatment for partial liquidations) may not be circumvented through the use of section 355, 351, or any other provision of law or regulations (including the consolidated return regulations).

PART III—CORPORATE ORGANIZATIONS AND REORGANIZATIONS

Subpart
A. Corporate organizations.
B. Effects on shareholders and security holders.
C. Effects on corporation.
D. Special rule; definitions.

Subpart A—Corporate Organizations

§ 351. Transfer to corporation controlled by transferor

(a) General rule.—No gain or loss shall be recognized if property is transferred to a corporation by one or more persons solely in exchange for stock in such corporation and immediately after the exchange such person or persons are in control (as defined in section 368(c)) of the corporation.

(b) Receipt of property.—If subsection (a) would apply to an exchange but for the fact that there is received, in addition to the stock permitted to be received under subsection (a), other property or money, then—

(1) gain (if any) to such recipient shall be recognized, but not in excess of—

(A) the amount of money received, plus

(B) the fair market value of such other property received; and

(2) no loss to such recipient shall be recognized.

(c) Special rules where distribution to shareholders.—

(1) In general.—In determining control for purposes of this section, the fact that any corporate transferor distributes part or all of the stock in the corporation which it receives in the exchange to its shareholders shall not be taken into account.

(2) Special rule for section 355.—If the requirements of section 355 (or so much of section 356 as relates to section 355) are met with respect to a distribution described in paragraph (1), then, solely for purposes of determining the tax treatment of the transfers of property to the controlled corporation by the distributing corporation, the fact that the shareholders of the distributing corporation dispose of part or all of the distributed stock, or the fact that the corporation whose stock was distributed issues additional stock, shall not be taken into account in determining control for purposes of this section.

(d) Services, certain indebtedness, and accrued interest not treated as property.—For purposes of this section, stock issued for—

(1) services,

(2) indebtedness of the transferee corporation which is not evidenced by a security, or

(3) interest on indebtedness of the transferee corporation which accrued on or after the beginning of the transferor's holding period for the debt,

shall not be considered as issued in return for property.

(e) Exceptions.—This section shall not apply to—

(1) Transfer of property to an investment company.—A transfer of property to an investment company. For purposes of the preceding sentence, the determination of whether a company is an investment company shall be made—

(A) by taking into account all stock and securities held by the company, and

(B) by treating as stock and securities—

(i) money,

(ii) stocks and other equity interests in a corporation, evidences of indebtedness, options, forward or futures contracts, notional principal contracts and derivatives,

(iii) any foreign currency,

(iv) any interest in a real estate investment trust, a common trust fund, a regulated investment company, a publicly-traded partnership (as defined in section 7704(b)) or any other equity interest (other than in a corporation) which pursuant to its terms or any other arrangement is readily convertible into, or exchangeable for, any asset described in any preceding clause, this clause or clause (v) or (viii),

(v) except to the extent provided in regulations prescribed by the Secretary, any interest in a precious metal, unless such metal is used or held in the active conduct of a trade or business after the contribution,

(vi) except as otherwise provided in regulations prescribed by the Secretary, interests in any entity if substantially all of the assets of such entity consist (directly or indirectly) of any assets described in any preceding clause or clause (viii),

(vii) to the extent provided in regulations prescribed by the Secretary, any interest in any entity not described in clause (vi), but only to the extent of the value of such interest that is attributable to assets listed in clauses (i) through (v) or clause (viii), or

(viii) any other asset specified in regulations prescribed by the Secretary.

The Secretary may prescribe regulations that, under appropriate circumstances, treat any asset described in clauses (i) through (v) as not so listed.

(2) Title 11 or similar case.—A transfer of property of a debtor pursuant to a plan while the debtor is under the jurisdiction of a court in a title 11 or similar case (within the meaning of section 368(a)(3)(A)), to the extent that the stock received in the exchange is used to satisfy the indebtedness of such debtor.

(f) Treatment of controlled corporation.—If—

(1) property is transferred to a corporation (hereinafter in this subsection referred to as the "controlled corporation") in an exchange with respect to which gain or loss is not recognized (in whole or in part) to the transferor under this section, and

(2) such exchange is not in pursuance of a plan of reorganization,

section 311 shall apply to any transfer in such exchange by the controlled corporation in the same manner as if such transfer were a distribution to which subpart A of part I applies.

(g) Nonqualified preferred stock not treated as stock.—

(1) In general.—In the case of a person who transfers property to a corporation and receives nonqualified preferred stock—

(A) subsection (a) shall not apply to such transferor, and

(B) if (and only if) the transferor receives stock other than nonqualified preferred stock—

(i) subsection (b) shall apply to such transferor; and

(ii) such nonqualified preferred stock shall be treated as other property for purposes of applying subsection (b).

(2) Nonqualified preferred stock.—For purposes of paragraph (1)—

(A) In general.—The term "nonqualified preferred stock" means preferred stock if—

(i) the holder of such stock has the right to require the issuer or a related person to redeem or purchase the stock,

(ii) the issuer or a related person is required to redeem or purchase such stock,

(iii) the issuer or a related person has the right to redeem or purchase the stock and, as of the issue date, it is more likely than not that such right will be exercised, or

(iv) the dividend rate on such stock varies in whole or in part (directly or indirectly) with reference to interest rates, commodity prices, or other similar indices.

(B) Limitations.—Clauses (i), (ii), and (iii) of subparagraph (A) shall apply only if the right or obligation referred to therein may be exercised within the 20–year period beginning on the issue date of such stock and such right or obligation is not subject to a contingency which, as of the issue date, makes remote the likelihood of the redemption or purchase.

(C) Exceptions for certain rights or obligations.—

(i) In general.—A right or obligation shall not be treated as described in clause (i), (ii), or (iii) of subparagraph (A) if—

(I) it may be exercised only upon the death, disability, or mental incompetency of the holder, or

(II) in the case of a right or obligation to redeem or purchase stock transferred in connection with the performance of services for the issuer or a related person (and which represents reasonable compensation), it may be exercised only upon the holder's separation from service from the issuer or a related person.

(ii) Exception.—Clause (i)(I) shall not apply if the stock relinquished in the exchange, or the stock acquired in the exchange is in—

(I) a corporation if any class of stock in such corporation or a related party is readily tradable on an established securities market or otherwise, or

(II) any other corporation if such exchange is part of a transaction or series of transactions in which such corporation is to become a corporation described in subclause (I).

(3) Definitions.—For purposes of this subsection—

(A) Preferred stock.—The term "preferred stock" means stock which is limited and preferred as to dividends and does not participate in corporate growth to any significant extent. Stock shall not be treated as participating in corporate growth to any significant extent unless there is a real and meaningful likelihood of the shareholder actually participating in the earnings and growth of the corporation. If there is not a real and meaningful likelihood that dividends beyond any limitation or preference will actually be paid, the possibility of such payments will be disregarded in determining whether stock is limited and preferred as to dividends.

(B) Related person.—A person shall be treated as related to another person if they bear a relationship to such other person described in section 267(b) or 707(b).

(4) Regulations.—The Secretary may prescribe such regulations as may be necessary or appropriate to carry out the purposes of this subsection and sections 354(a)(2)(C), 355(a)(3)(D), and 356(e). The Secretary may also prescribe regulations, consistent with the treatment under this subsection and such sections, for the treatment of nonqualified preferred stock under other provisions of this title.

(h) Cross references.—

(1) For special rule where another party to the exchange assumes a liability, see section 357.

(2) For the basis of stock or property received in an exchange to which this section applies, see sections 358 and 362.

(3) For special rule in the case of an exchange described in this section but which results in a gift, see section 2501 and following.

(4) For special rule in the case of an exchange described in this section but which has the effect of the payment of compensation by the corporation or by a transferor, see section 61(a)(1).

(5) For coordination of this section with section 304, see section 304(b)(3).

Subpart B—Effects on Shareholders and Security Holders

§ 354. Exchanges of stock and securities in certain reorganizations

(a) General rule.—

(1) In general.—No gain or loss shall be recognized if stock or securities in a corporation a party to a reorganization are, in pursuance of the plan of reorganization, exchanged solely for stock or securities in such corporation or in another corporation a party to the reorganization.

(2) Limitations.—

(A) Excess principal amount.—Paragraph (1) shall not apply if—

(i) the principal amount of any such securities received exceeds the principal amount of any such securities surrendered, or

(ii) any such securities are received and no such securities are surrendered.

(B) Property attributable to accrued interest.—Neither paragraph (1) nor so much of section 356 as relates to paragraph (1) shall apply to the extent that any stock (including nonqualified preferred stock, as defined in section 351(g)(2)), securities, or other property received is attributable to interest which has accrued on securities on or after the beginning of the holder's holding period.

(C) Nonqualified preferred stock.—

(i) In general.—Nonqualified preferred stock (as defined in section 351(g)(2)) received in exchange for stock other than nonqualified preferred stock (as so defined) shall not be treated as stock or securities.

(ii) Recapitalizations of family-owned corporations.—

(I) In general.—Clause (i) shall not apply in the case of a recapitalization under section 368(a)(1)(E) of a family-owned corporation.

(II) Family-owned corporation.—For purposes of this clause, except as provided in regulations, the term "family-owned corporation" means any corporation which is described in clause (i) of section 447(d)(2)(C) throughout the 8–year period beginning on the date which is 5 years before the date of the recapitalization. For purposes of the preceding sentence, stock shall not be treated as owned by a family member during any period described in section 355(d)(6)(B).

(III) Extension of statute of limitations.—The statutory period for the assessment of any deficiency attributable to a corporation failing to be a family-owned corporation shall not expire before the expiration of 3 years after the date the Secretary is notified by the corporation (in such manner as the Secretary may prescribe) of such failure, and such deficiency may be assessed before the expiration of such 3–year period notwithstanding the provisions of any other law or rule of law which would otherwise prevent such assessment.

(3) Cross references.—

(A) For treatment of the exchange if any property is received which is not permitted to be received under this subsection (including an excess principal amount of securities received over securities surrendered, but not including nonqualified preferred stock and property to which paragraph (2)(B) applies), see section 356.

(B) For treatment of accrued interest in the case of an exchange described in paragraph (2)(B), see section 61.

(b) Exception.—

(1) In general.—Subsection (a) shall not apply to an exchange in pursuance of a plan of reorganization within the meaning of subparagraph (D) or (G) of section 368(a)(1), unless—

(A) the corporation to which the assets are transferred acquires substantially all of the assets of the transferor of such assets; and

(B) the stock, securities, and other properties received by such transferor, as well as the other properties of such transferor, are distributed in pursuance of the plan of reorganization.

(2) Cross reference.—

For special rules for certain exchanges in pursuance of plans of reorganization within the meaning of subparagraph (D) or (G) of section 368(a)(1), see section 355.

* * *

§ 355. Distribution of stock and securities of a controlled corporation

(a) Effect on distributees.—

(1) General rule.—If—

(A) a corporation (referred to in this section as the "distributing corporation")—

(i) distributes to a shareholder, with respect to its stock, or

(ii) distributes to a security holder, in exchange for its securities,

solely stock or securities of a corporation (referred to in this section as "controlled corporation") which it controls immediately before the distribution,

(B) the transaction was not used principally as a device for the distribution of the earnings and profits of the distributing corporation or the controlled corporation or both (but the mere fact that subsequent to the distribution stock or securities in one or more of such corporations are sold or exchanged by all or some of the distributees (other than pursuant to an arrangement negotiated or agreed upon prior to such distribution) shall not be construed to mean that the transaction was used principally as such a device),

(C) the requirements of subsection (b) (relating to active businesses) are satisfied, and

(D) as part of the distribution, the distributing corporation distributes—

(i) all of the stock and securities in the controlled corporation held by it immediately before the distribution, or

(ii) an amount of stock in the controlled corporation constituting control within the meaning of section 368(c), and it is established to the satisfaction of the Secretary that the retention by the distributing corporation of stock (or stock and securities) in the controlled corporation was not in pursuance of a plan having as one of its principal purposes the avoidance of Federal income tax,

then no gain or loss shall be recognized to (and no amount shall be includible in the income of) such shareholder or security holder on the receipt of such stock or securities.

(2) Non pro rata distributions, etc.—Paragraph (1) shall be applied without regard to the following:

(A) whether or not the distribution is pro rata with respect to all of the shareholders of the distributing corporation,

(B) whether or not the shareholder surrenders stock in the distributing corporation, and

(C) whether or not the distribution is in pursuance of a plan of reorganization (within the meaning of section 368(a)(1)(D)).

(3) Limitations.—

(A) Excess principal amount.—Paragraph (1) shall not apply if—

(i) the principal amount of the securities in the controlled corporation which are received exceeds the principal amount of the securities which are surrendered in connection with such distribution, or

(ii) securities in the controlled corporation are received and no securities are surrendered in connection with such distribution.

(B) Stock acquired in taxable transactions within 5 years treated as boot.—For purposes of this section (other than paragraph (1)(D) of this subsection) and so much of section 356 as relates to this section, stock of a controlled corporation acquired by the distributing corporation by reason of any transaction—

(i) which occurs within 5 years of the distribution of such stock, and

(ii) in which gain or loss was recognized in whole or in part,

shall not be treated as stock of such controlled corporation, but as other property.

(C) Property attributable to accrued interest.—Neither paragraph (1) nor so much of section 356 as relates to paragraph (1) shall apply to the extent that any stock (including nonqualified preferred stock, as defined in section 351(g)(2)), securities, or other property received is attributable to interest which has accrued on securities on or after the beginning of the holder's holding period.

(D) Nonqualified preferred stock.—Nonqualified preferred stock (as defined in section 351(g)(2)) received in a distribution with respect to stock other than nonqualified preferred stock (as so defined) shall not be treated as stock or securities.

(4) Cross references.—

(A) For treatment of the exchange if any property is received which is not permitted to be received under this subsection (including an excess principal amount of securities received over securities surrendered, but not including nonqualified preferred stock and property to which paragraph (3)(C) applies), see section 356.

(B) For treatment of accrued interest in the case of an exchange described in paragraph (3)(C), see section 61.

(b) Requirements as to active business.—

(1) In general.—Subsection (a) shall apply only if either—

(A) the distributing corporation, and the controlled corporation (or, if stock of more than one controlled corporation is distributed, each of such corporations), is engaged immediately after the distribution in the active conduct of a trade or business, or

(B) immediately before the distribution, the distributing corporation had no assets other than stock or securities in the controlled corporations and each of the controlled corporations is engaged immediately after the distribution in the active conduct of a trade or business.

(2) Definition.—For purposes of paragraph (1), a corporation shall be treated as engaged in the active conduct of a trade or business if and only if—

(A) it is engaged in the active conduct of a trade or business,

(B) such trade or business has been actively conducted throughout the 5-year period ending on the date of the distribution,

(C) such trade or business was not acquired within the period described in subparagraph (B) in a transaction in which gain or loss was recognized in whole or in part, and

(D) control of a corporation which (at the time of acquisition of control) was conducting such trade or business—

(i) was not acquired by any distributee corporation directly (or through 1 or more corporations, whether through the distributing corporation or otherwise) within the period described in subparagraph (B) and was not acquired by the distributing corporation directly (or through 1 or more corporations) within such period, or

(ii) was so acquired by any such corporation within such period, but, in each case in which such control was so acquired, it was so acquired, only by reason of transactions in which gain or loss was not recognized in whole or in part, or only by reason of such transactions combined with acquisitions before the beginning of such period.

For purposes of subparagraph (D), all distributee corporations which are members of the same affiliated group (as defined in section 1504(a) without regard to section 1504(b)) shall be treated as 1 distributee corporation.

(3) Special rules for determining active conduct in the case of affiliated groups.—

(A) In general.—For purposes of determining whether a corporation meets the requirements of paragraph (2)(A), all members of such corporation's separate affiliated group shall be treated as one corporation.

(B) Separate affiliated group.—For purposes of this paragraph, the term "separate affiliated group" means, with respect to any corporation, the affiliated group which would be determined under section 1504(a) if such corporation were the common parent and section 1504(b) did not apply.

(C) Treatment of trade or business conducted by acquired member.—If a corporation became a member of a separate affiliated group as a result of one or more transactions in which gain or loss was recognized in whole or in part, any trade or business conducted by such corporation (at the time that such corporation became such a member) shall be treated for purposes of paragraph (2) as acquired in a transaction in which gain or loss was recognized in whole or in part.

(D) Regulations.—The Secretary shall prescribe such regulations as are necessary or appropriate to carry out the purposes of this paragraph, including regulations which provide for the proper application of subparagraphs (B), (C), and (D) of paragraph (2), and modify the application of subsection (a)(3)(B), in connection with the application of this paragraph.

(c) Taxability of corporation on distribution.—

(1) In general.—Except as provided in paragraph (2), no gain or loss shall be recognized to a corporation on any distribution to which this section (or so much of section 356 as relates to this section) applies and which is not in pursuance of a plan of reorganization.

(2) Distribution of appreciated property.—

(A) In general.—If—

(i) in a distribution referred to in paragraph (1), the corporation distributes property other than qualified property, and

(ii) the fair market value of such property exceeds its adjusted basis (in the hands of the distributing corporation),

then gain shall be recognized to the distributing corporation as if such property were sold to the distributee at its fair market value.

(B) Qualified property.—For purposes of subparagraph (A), the term "qualified property" means any stock or securities in the controlled corporation.

(C) Treatment of liabilities.—If any property distributed in the distribution referred to in paragraph (1) is subject to a liability or the shareholder assumes a liability of the distributing corporation in connection with the distribution, then, for purposes of subparagraph (A), the fair market value of such property shall be treated as not less than the amount of such liability.

(3) Coordination with sections 311 and 336(a).—Sections 311 and 336(a) shall not apply to any distribution referred to in paragraph (1).

(d) Recognition of gain on certain distributions of stock or securities in controlled corporation.—

(1) In general.—In the case of a disqualified distribution, any stock or securities in the controlled corporation shall not be treated as qualified property for purposes of subsection (c)(2) of this section or section 361(c)(2).

(2) Disqualified distribution.—For purposes of this subsection, the term "disqualified distribution" means any distribution to which this section (or so much of section 356 as relates to this section) applies if, immediately after the distribution—

(A) any person holds disqualified stock in the distributing corporation which constitutes a 50–percent or greater interest in such corporation, or

(B) any person holds disqualified stock in the controlled corporation (or, if stock of more than 1 controlled corporation is distributed, in any controlled corporation) which constitutes a 50–percent or greater interest in such corporation.

(3) Disqualified stock.—For purposes of this subsection, the term "disqualified stock" means—

(A) any stock in the distributing corporation acquired by purchase after October 9, 1990, and during the 5–year period ending on the date of the distribution, and

(B) any stock in any controlled corporation—

(i) acquired by purchase after October 9, 1990, and during the 5–year period ending on the date of the distribution, or

(ii) received in the distribution to the extent attributable to distributions on—

(I) stock described in subparagraph (A), or

(II) any securities in the distributing corporation acquired by purchase after October 9, 1990, and during the 5–year period ending on the date of the distribution.

(4) 50–percent or greater interest.—For purposes of this subsection, the term "50–percent or greater interest" means stock possessing at least 50 percent of the total combined voting power of all classes of stock entitled to vote or at least 50 percent of the total value of shares of all classes of stock.

(5) Purchase.—For purposes of this subsection—

(A) In general.—Except as otherwise provided in this paragraph, the term "purchase" means any acquisition but only if—

(i) the basis of the property acquired in the hands of the acquirer is not determined (I) in whole or in part by reference to the adjusted basis of such property in the hands of the person from whom acquired, or (II) under section 1014(a), and

(ii) the property is not acquired in an exchange to which section 351, 354, 355, or 356 applies.

(B) Certain section 351 exchanges treated as purchases.—The term "purchase" includes any acquisition of property in an exchange to which section 351 applies to the extent such property is acquired in exchange for—

(i) any cash or cash item,

(ii) any marketable stock or security, or

(iii) any debt of the transferor.

(C) Carryover basis transactions.—If—

(i) any person acquires property from another person who acquired such property by purchase (as determined under this paragraph with regard to this subparagraph), and

(ii) the adjusted basis of such property in the hands of such acquirer is determined in whole or in part by reference to the adjusted basis of such property in the hands of such other person,

such acquirer shall be treated as having acquired such property by purchase on the date it was so acquired by such other person.

(6) Special rule where substantial diminution of risk.—

(A) In general.—If this paragraph applies to any stock or securities for any period, the running of any 5–year period set forth in subparagraph (A) or (B) of paragraph (3) (whichever applies) shall be suspended during such period.

(B) Property to which suspension applies.—This paragraph applies to any stock or securities for any period during which the holder's risk of loss with respect to such stock or securities, or with respect to any portion of the activities of the corporation, is (directly or indirectly) substantially diminished by—

(i) an option,

(ii) a short sale,

(iii) any special class of stock, or

(iv) any other device or transaction.

(7) Aggregation rules.—

(A) In general.—For purposes of this subsection, a person and all persons related to such person (within the meaning of section 267(b) or 707(b)(1)) shall be treated as one person.

(B) Persons acting pursuant to plans or arrangements.—If two or more persons act pursuant to a plan or arrangement with respect to acquisitions of stock or securities in the distributing corporation or controlled corporation, such persons shall be treated as one person for purposes of this subsection.

(8) Attribution from entities.—

(A) In general.—Paragraph (2) of section 318(a) shall apply in determining whether a person holds stock or securities in any corporation (determined by substituting "10 percent" for "50 percent" in subparagraph (C) of such paragraph (2) and by treating any reference to stock as including a reference to securities).

(B) Deemed purchase rule.—If—

(i) any person acquires by purchase an interest in any entity, and

(ii) such person is treated under subparagraph (A) as holding any stock or securities by reason of holding such interest,

such stock or securities shall be treated as acquired by purchase by such person on the later of the date of the purchase of the interest in such entity or the date such stock or securities are acquired by purchase by such entity.

(9) Regulations.—The Secretary shall prescribe such regulations as may be necessary to carry out the purposes of this subsection, including—

(A) regulations to prevent the avoidance of the purposes of this subsection through the use of related persons, intermediaries, pass-thru entities, options, or other arrangements, and

(B) regulations modifying the definition of the term "purchase".

(e) Recognition of gain on certain distributions of stock or securities in connection with acquisitions.—

(1) General rule.—If there is a distribution to which this subsection applies, any stock or securities in the controlled corporation shall not be treated as qualified property for purposes of subsection (c)(2) of this section or section 361(c)(2).

(2) Distributions to which subsection applies.—

(A) In general.—This subsection shall apply to any distribution—

(i) to which this section (or so much of section 356 as relates to this section) applies, and

(ii) which is part of a plan (or series of related transactions) pursuant to which 1 or more persons acquire directly or indirectly stock representing a 50–percent or greater interest in the distributing corporation or any controlled corporation.

(B) Plan presumed to exist in certain cases.—If 1 or more persons acquire directly or indirectly stock representing a 50–percent or greater interest in the distributing corporation or any controlled corporation during the 4–year period beginning on the date which is 2 years before the date of the distribution, such acquisition shall be treated as pursuant to a plan described in subparagraph (A)(ii) unless it is established that the distribution and the acquisition are not pursuant to a plan or series of related transactions.

(C) Certain plans disregarded.—A plan (or series of related transactions) shall not be treated as described in subparagraph (A)(ii) if, immediately after the completion of such plan or transactions, the distributing corporation and all controlled corporations are members of a single affiliated group (as defined in section 1504 without regard to subsection (b) thereof).

(D) Coordination with subsection (d).—This subsection shall not apply to any distribution to which subsection (d) applies.

(3) Special rules relating to acquisitions.—

(A) Certain acquisitions not taken into account.—Except as provided in regulations, the following acquisitions shall not be taken into account in applying paragraph (2)(A)(ii):

(i) The acquisition of stock in any controlled corporation by the distributing corporation.

(ii) The acquisition by a person of stock in any controlled corporation by reason of holding stock or securities in the distributing corporation.

(iii) The acquisition by a person of stock in any successor corporation of the distributing corporation or any controlled corporation by reason of holding stock or securities in such distributing or controlled corporation.

(iv) The acquisition of stock in the distributing corporation or any controlled corporation to the extent that the percentage of stock owned directly or indirectly in such corporation by each person owning stock in such corporation immediately before the acquisition does not decrease.

This subparagraph shall not apply to any acquisition if the stock held before the acquisition was acquired pursuant to a plan (or series of related transactions) described in paragraph (2)(A)(ii).

(B) Asset acquisitions.—Except as provided in regulations, for purposes of this subsection, if the assets of the distributing corporation or any controlled corporation are acquired by a successor corporation in a transaction described in subparagraph (A), (C), or (D) of section 368(a)(1) or any other transaction specified in regulations by the Secretary, the shareholders (immediately before the acquisition) of the corporation acquiring such assets shall be treated as acquiring stock in the corporation from which the assets were acquired.

(4) Definition and special rules.—For purposes of this subsection—

(A) 50–percent or greater interest.—The term "50–percent or greater interest" has the meaning given such term by subsection (d)(4).

(B) Distributions in title 11 or similar case.—Paragraph (1) shall not apply to any distribution made in a title 11 or similar case (as defined in section 368(a)(3)).

(C) Aggregation and attribution rules.—

(i) Aggregation.—The rules of paragraph (7)(A) of subsection (d) shall apply.

(ii) Attribution.—Section 318(a)(2) shall apply in determining whether a person holds stock or securities in any corporation. Except as provided in regulations, section 318(a)(2)(C) shall be applied without regard to the phrase "50 percent or more in value" for purposes of the preceding sentence.

(D) Successors and predecessors.—For purposes of this subsection, any reference to a controlled corporation or a distributing corporation shall include a reference to any predecessor or successor of such corporation.

(E) Statute of limitations.—If there is a distribution to which paragraph (1) applies—

(i) the statutory period for the assessment of any deficiency attributable to any part of the gain recognized under this subsection by reason of such distribution shall not expire before the expiration of 3 years from the date the Secretary is notified by the taxpayer (in such manner as the Secretary may by regulations prescribe) that such distribution occurred, and

(ii) such deficiency may be assessed before the expiration of such 3–year period notwithstanding the provisions of any other law or rule of law which would otherwise prevent such assessment.

(5) Regulations.—The Secretary shall prescribe such regulations as may be necessary to carry out the purposes of this subsection, including regulations—

(A) providing for the application of this subsection where there is more than 1 controlled corporation,

(B) treating 2 or more distributions as 1 distribution where necessary to prevent the avoidance of such purposes, and

(C) providing for the application of rules similar to the rules of subsection (d)(6) where appropriate for purposes of paragraph (2)(B).

(f) Section not to apply to certain intragroup distributions.—Except as provided in regulations, this section (or so much of section 356 as relates to this section) shall not apply to the distribution of stock from 1 member of an affiliated group (as defined in section 1504(a)) to another member of such group if such distribution is part of a plan (or series of related transactions) described in subsection (e)(2)(A)(ii) (determined after the application of subsection (e)).

(g) Section Not to Apply to Distributions Involving Disqualified Investment Corporations.—

(1) In general.—This section (and so much of section 356 as relates to this section) shall not apply to any distribution which is part of a transaction if—

(A) either the distributing corporation or controlled corporation is, immediately after the transaction, a disqualified investment corporation, and

(B) any person holds, immediately after the transaction, a 50-percent or greater interest in any disqualified investment corporation, but only if such person did not hold such an interest in such corporation immediately before the transaction.

(2) Disqualified investment corporation.—For purposes of this subsection—

(A) In general.—The term "disqualified investment corporation" means any distributing or controlled corporation if the fair market value of the investment assets of the corporation is—

(i) in the case of distributions after the end of the 1-year period beginning on the date of the enactment of this subsection, 2/3 or more of the fair market value of all assets of the corporation, and

(ii) in the case of distributions during such 1-year period, 3/4 or more of the fair market value of all assets of the corporation.

(B) Investment assets.—

(i) In general.—Except as otherwise provided in this subparagraph, the term "investment assets" means—

(I) cash,

(II) any stock or securities in a corporation,

(III) any interest in a partnership,

(IV) any debt instrument or other evidence of indebtedness,

(V) any option, forward or futures contract, notional principal contract, or derivative,

(VI) foreign currency, or

(VII) any similar asset.

(ii) Exception for assets used in active conduct of certain financial trades or businesses.—Such term shall not include any asset which is held for use in the active and regular conduct of—

(I) a lending or finance business (within the meaning of section 954(h)(4)),

(II) a banking business through a bank (as defined in section 581), a domestic building and loan association (within the meaning of section 7701(a)(19)), or any similar institution specified by the Secretary, or

(III) an insurance business if the conduct of the business is licensed, authorized, or regulated by an applicable insurance regulatory body.

This clause shall only apply with respect to any business if substantially all of the income of the business is derived from persons who are not related (within the meaning of section 267(b) or 707(b)(1)) to the person conducting the business.

(iii) Exception for securities marked to market.—Such term shall not include any security (as defined in section 475(c)(2)) which is held by a dealer in securities and to which section 475(a) applies.

(iv) Stock or securities in a 20–percent controlled entity.—

(I) In general.—Such term shall not include any stock and securities in, or any asset described in subclause (IV) or (V) of clause (i) issued by, a corporation which is a 20–percent controlled entity with respect to the distributing or controlled corporation.

(II) Look-thru rule.—The distributing or controlled corporation shall, for purposes of applying this subsection, be treated as owning its ratable share of the assets of any 20–percent controlled entity.

(III) 20–percent controlled entity.—For purposes of this clause, the term "20–percent controlled entity" means, with respect to any distributing or controlled corporation, any corporation with respect to which the distributing or controlled corporation owns directly or indirectly stock meeting the requirements of section 1504(a)(2), except that such section shall be applied by substituting "20 percent" for "80 percent" and without regard to stock described in section 1504(a)(4).

(v) Interests in certain partnerships.—

(I) In general.—Such term shall not include any interest in a partnership, or any debt instrument or other evidence of indebtedness, issued by the partnership, if 1 or more of the trades or businesses of the partnership are (or, without regard to the 5–year requirement under subsection (b)(2)(B), would be) taken into account by the distributing or controlled corporation, as the case may be, in determining whether the requirements of subsection (b) are met with respect to the distribution.

(II) Look-thru rule.—The distributing or controlled corporation shall, for purposes of applying this subsection, be treated as owning its ratable share of the assets of any partnership described in subclause (I).

(3) 50–percent or greater interest.—For purposes of this subsection—

(A) In general.—The term "50–percent or greater interest" has the meaning given such term by subsection (d)(4).

(B) Attribution rules.—The rules of section 318 shall apply for purposes of determining ownership of stock for purposes of this paragraph.

(4) Transaction.—For purposes of this subsection, the term "transaction" includes a series of transactions.

(5) Regulations.—The Secretary shall prescribe such regulations as may be necessary to carry out, or prevent the avoidance of, the purposes of this subsection, including regulations—

(A) to carry out, or prevent the avoidance of, the purposes of this subsection in cases involving—

(i) the use of related persons, intermediaries, pass-thru entities, options, or other arrangements, and

(ii) the treatment of assets unrelated to the trade or business of a corporation as investment assets if, prior to the distribution, investment assets were used to acquire such unrelated assets,

(B) which in appropriate cases exclude from the application of this subsection a distribution which does not have the character of a redemption which would be treated as a sale or exchange under section 302, and

(C) which modify the application of the attribution rules applied for purposes of this subsection.

§ 356. Receipt of additional consideration

(a) Gain on exchanges.—

(1) Recognition of gain.—If—

(A) section 354 or 355 would apply to an exchange but for the fact that

(B) the property received in the exchange consists not only of property permitted by section 354 or 355 to be received without the recognition of gain but also of other property or money,

then the gain, if any, to the recipient shall be recognized, but in an amount not in excess of the sum of such money and the fair market value of such other property.

(2) Treatment as dividend.—If an exchange is described in paragraph (1) but has the effect of the distribution of a dividend (determined with the application of section 318(a)), then there shall be treated as a dividend to each distributee such an amount of the gain recognized under paragraph (1) as is not in excess of his ratable share of the undistributed earnings and profits of the corporation accumulated after February 28, 1913. The remainder, if any, of the gain recognized under paragraph (1) shall be treated as gain from the exchange of property.

(b) Additional consideration received in certain distributions.—If—

(1) section 355 would apply to a distribution but for the fact that

(2) the property received in the distribution consists not only of property permitted by section 355 to be received without the recognition of gain, but also of other property or money,

then an amount equal to the sum of such money and the fair market value of such other property shall be treated as a distribution of property to which section 301 applies.

(c) Loss.—If—

(1) section 354 would apply to an exchange, or section 355 would apply to an exchange or distribution, but for the fact that

(2) the property received in the exchange or distribution consists not only of property permitted by section 354 or 355 to be received without the recognition of gain or loss, but also of other property or money,

then no loss from the exchange or distribution shall be recognized.

(d) Securities as other property.—For purposes of this section—

(1) In general.—Except as provided in paragraph (2), the term "other property" includes securities.

(2) Exceptions.—

(A) Securities with respect to which nonrecognition of gain would be permitted.—The term "other property" does not include securities to the extent that, under section 354 or 355, such securities would be permitted to be received without the recognition of gain.

(B) Greater principal amount in section 354 exchange.—If—

(i) in an exchange described in section 354 (other than subsection (c) thereof), securities of a corporation a party to the reorganization are surrendered and securities of any corporation a party to the reorganization are received, and

(ii) the principal amount of such securities received exceeds the principal amount of such securities surrendered,

then, with respect to such securities received, the term "other property" means only the fair market value of such excess. For purposes of this subparagraph and subparagraph (C), if no securities are surrendered, the excess shall be the entire principal amount of the securities received.

(C) Greater principal amount in section 355 transaction.—If, in an exchange or distribution described in section 355, the principal amount of the securities in the controlled corporation which are received exceeds the principal amount of the securities in the distributing corporation which are surrendered, then, with respect to such securities received, the term "other property" means only the fair market value of such excess.

(e) Nonqualified preferred stock treated as other property.—For purposes of this section—

(1) In general.—Except as provided in paragraph (2), the term "other property" includes nonqualified preferred stock (as defined in section 351(g)(2)).

(2) Exception.—The term "other property" does not include nonqualified preferred stock (as so defined) to the extent that, under section 354 or 355, such preferred stock would be permitted to be received without the recognition of gain.

(f) Exchanges for section 306 stock.—Notwithstanding any other provision of this section, to the extent that any of the other property (or money) is received in exchange for section 306 stock, an amount equal to the fair market value of such other property (or the amount of such money) shall be treated as a distribution of property to which section 301 applies.

(g) Transactions involving gift or compensation.—

For special rules for a transaction described in section 354, 355, or this section, but which—

(1) results in a gift, see section 2501 and following, or

(2) has the effect of the payment of compensation, see section 61(a)(1).

§ 357. Assumption of liability

(a) General rule.—Except as provided in subsections (b) and (c), if—

(1) the taxpayer receives property which would be permitted to be received under section 351 or 361 without the recognition of gain if it were the sole consideration, and

(2) as part of the consideration, another party to the exchange assumes a liability of the taxpayer,

then such assumption shall not be treated as money or other property, and shall not prevent the exchange from being within the provisions of section 351 or 361 as the case may be.

(b) Tax avoidance purpose.—

(1) In general.—If, taking into consideration the nature of the liability and the circumstances in the light of which the arrangement for the assumption was made, it appears that the principal purpose of the taxpayer with respect to the assumption described in subsection (a)—

(A) was a purpose to avoid Federal income tax on the exchange, or

(B) if not such purpose, was not a bona fide business purpose,

then such assumption (in the total amount of the liability assumed pursuant to such exchange) shall, for purposes of section 351 or 361 (as the case may be), be considered as money received by the taxpayer on the exchange.

(2) Burden of proof.—In any suit or proceeding where the burden is on the taxpayer to prove such assumption is not to be treated as money received by the taxpayer, such burden shall not be considered as sustained unless the taxpayer sustains such burden by the clear preponderance of the evidence.

(c) Liabilities in excess of basis.—

(1) In general.—In the case of an exchange—

(A) to which section 351 applies, or

(B) to which section 361 applies by reason of a plan of reorganization within the meaning of section 368(a)(1)(D) with respect to which stock or securities of the corporation to which the assets are transferred are distributed in a transaction which qualifies under section 355,

if the sum of the amount of the liabilities assumed, exceeds the total of the adjusted basis of the property transferred pursuant to such exchange, then such excess shall be considered as a gain from the sale or exchange of a capital asset or of property which is not a capital asset, as the case may be.

(2) Exceptions.—Paragraph (1) shall not apply to any exchange—

(A) to which subsection (b)(1) of this section applies, or

(B) which is pursuant to a plan of reorganization within the meaning of section 368(a)(1)(G) where no former shareholder of the transferor corporation receives any consideration for his stock.

(3) Certain liabilities excluded.—

(A) In general.—If a taxpayer transfers, in an exchange to which section 351 applies, a liability the payment of which either—

(i) would give rise to a deduction, or

(ii) would be described in section 736(a),

then, for purposes of paragraph (1), the amount of such liability shall be excluded in determining the amount of liabilities assumed.

(B) Exception.—Subparagraph (A) shall not apply to any liability to the extent that the incurrence of the liability resulted in the creation of, or an increase in, the basis of any property.

(d) Determination of amount of liability assumed—

(1) In general—For purposes of this section, section 358(d), section 358(h), section 361(b)(3), section 362(d), section 368(a)(1)(C), and section 368(a)(2)(B), except as provided in regulations—

(A) a recourse liability (or portion thereof) shall be treated as having been assumed if, as determined on the basis of all facts and circumstances, the transferee has agreed to, and is expected to, satisfy such liability (or portion), whether or not the transferor has been relieved of such liability; and

(B) except to the extent provided in paragraph (2), a nonrecourse liability shall be treated as having been assumed by the transferee of any asset subject to such liability.

(2) Exception for nonrecourse liability— The amount of the nonrecourse liability treated as described in paragraph (1)(B) shall be reduced by the lesser of—

(A) the amount of such liability which an owner of other assets not transferred to the transferee and also subject to such liability has agreed with the transferee to, and is expected to, satisfy; or

(B) the fair market value of such other assets (determined without regard to section 7701(g)).

(3) Regulations— The Secretary shall prescribe such regulations as may be necessary to carry out the purposes of this subsection and section 362(d). The Secretary may also prescribe regulations which provide that the manner in which a liability is treated as assumed under this subsection is applied, where appropriate, elsewhere in this title.

§ 358. Basis to distributees

(a) General rule.—In the case of an exchange to which section 351, 354, 355, 356, or 361 applies—

(1) Nonrecognition property.—The basis of the property permitted to be received under such section without the recognition of gain or loss shall be the same as that of the property exchanged—

(A) decreased by—

(i) the fair market value of any other property (except money) received by the taxpayer,

(ii) the amount of any money received by the taxpayer, and

(iii) the amount of loss to the taxpayer which was recognized on such exchange, and

(B) increased by—

(i) the amount which was treated as a dividend, and

(ii) the amount of gain to the taxpayer which was recognized on such exchange (not including any portion of such gain which was treated as a dividend).

(2) Other property.—The basis of any other property (except money) received by the taxpayer shall be its fair market value.

(b) Allocation of basis.—

(1) In general.—Under regulations prescribed by the Secretary, the basis determined under subsection (a)(1) shall be allocated among the properties permitted to be received without the recognition of gain or loss.

(2) Special rule for section 355.—In the case of an exchange to which section 355 (or so much of section 356 as relates to section 355) applies, then in making the allocation under paragraph (1) of this subsection, there shall be taken into account not only the property so permitted to be received without the recognition of gain or loss, but also the stock or securities (if any) of the distributing corporation which are retained, and the allocation of basis shall be made among all such properties.

(c) Section 355 transactions which are not exchanges.—For purposes of this section, a distribution to which section 355 (or so much of section 356 as relates to section 355) applies shall be treated as an exchange, and for such purposes the stock and securities of the distributing corporation which are retained shall be treated as surrendered, and received back, in the exchange.

(d) Assumption of liability.—

(1) In general.—Where, as part of the consideration to the taxpayer, another party to the exchange assumed a liability of the taxpayer, such assumption shall, for purposes of this section, be treated as money received by the taxpayer on the exchange.

(2) Exception.—Paragraph (1) shall not apply to the amount of any liability excluded under section 357(c)(3).

(e) Exception.—This section shall not apply to property acquired by a corporation by the exchange of its stock or securities (or the stock or securities of a corporation which is in control of the acquiring corporation) as consideration in whole or in part for the transfer of the property to it.

(f) Definition of nonrecognition property in case of section 361 exchange.—For purposes of this section, the property permitted to be received under section 361 without the recognition of gain or loss shall be treated as consisting only of stock or securities in another corporation a party to the reorganization.

(g) Adjustments in intragroup transactions involving section 355.—In the case of a distribution to which section 355 (or so much of section 356 as relates to section 355) applies and which involves the distribution of stock from 1 member of an affiliated group (as defined in section 1504(a) without regard to subsection (b) thereof) to another member of such group, the Secretary may, notwithstanding any other provision of this section, provide adjustments to the adjusted basis of any stock which—

(1) is in a corporation which is a member of such group, and

(2) is held by another member of such group,

to appropriately reflect the proper treatment of such distribution.

(h) Special rules for assumption of liabilities to which subsection (d) does not apply.—

(1) In general.—If, after application of the other provisions of this section to an exchange or series of exchanges, the basis of property to which subsection (a)(1) applies exceeds the fair market value of such property, then such basis shall be reduced (but not below such fair market value) by the amount (determined as of the date of the exchange) of any liability—

(A) which is assumed by another person as part of the exchange, and

(B) with respect to which subsection (d)(1) does not apply to the assumption.

(2) Exceptions.—Except as provided by the Secretary, paragraph (1) shall not apply to any liability if—

(A) the trade or business with which the liability is associated is transferred to the person assuming the liability as part of the exchange, or

(B) substantially all of the assets with which the liability is associated are transferred to the person assuming the liability as part of the exchange.

(3) Liability.—For purposes of this subsection, the term "liability" shall include any fixed or contingent obligation to make payment, without regard to whether the obligation is otherwise taken into account for purposes of this title.

Subpart C—Effects on Corporation

§ 361. Nonrecognition of gain or loss to corporations; treatment of distributions

(a) General rule.—No gain or loss shall be recognized to a corporation if such corporation is a party to a reorganization and exchanges property, in pursuance of the plan of reorganization, solely for stock or securities in another corporation a party to the reorganization.

(b) Exchanges not solely in kind.—

(1) Gain.—If subsection (a) would apply to an exchange but for the fact that the property received in exchange consists not only of stock or securities permitted by subsection (a) to be received without the recognition of gain, but also of other property or money, then—

(A) Property distributed.—If the corporation receiving such other property or money distributes it in pursuance of the plan of reorganization, no gain to the corporation shall be recognized from the exchange, but

(B) Property not distributed.—If the corporation receiving such other property or money does not distribute it in pursuance of the plan of reorganization, the gain, if any, to the corporation shall be recognized.

The amount of gain recognized under subparagraph (B) shall not exceed the sum of the money and the fair market value of the other property so received which is not so distributed.

(2) Loss.—If subsection (a) would apply to an exchange but for the fact that the property received in exchange consists not only of property permitted by subsection (a) to be received without the recognition of gain or loss, but also of other property or money, then no loss from the exchange shall be recognized.

(3) Treatment of transfers to creditors.—For purposes of paragraph (1), any transfer of the other property or money received in the exchange by the corporation to its creditors in connection with the reorganization shall be treated as a distribution in pursuance of the plan of reorganization. The Secretary may prescribe such regulations as may be necessary to prevent avoidance of tax through abuse of the preceding sentence or subsection (c)(3). In the case of a reorganization described in section 368(a)(1)(D) with respect to which stock or securities of the corporation to which the assets are transferred are distributed in a transaction which qualifies under section 355, this paragraph shall apply only to the extent that the sum of the money and the fair market value of other property transferred to such creditors does not exceed the adjusted bases of such assets transferred (reduced by the amount of the liabilities assumed (within the meaning of section 357(c))).

(c) Treatment of distributions.—

(1) In general.—Except as provided in paragraph (2), no gain or loss shall be recognized to a corporation a party to a reorganization on the distribution to its shareholders of property in pursuance of the plan of reorganization.

(2) Distributions of appreciated property.—

(A) In general.—If—

(i) in a distribution referred to in paragraph (1), the corporation distributes property other than qualified property, and

(ii) the fair market value of such property exceeds its adjusted basis (in the hands of the distributing corporation), then gain shall be recognized to the distributing corporation as if such property were sold to the distributee at its fair market value.

(B) Qualified property.—For purposes of this subsection, the term "qualified property" means—

(i) any stock in (or right to acquire stock in) the distributing corporation or obligation of the distributing corporation, or

(ii) any stock in (or right to acquire stock in) another corporation which is a party to the reorganization or obligation of another corporation which is such a party if such stock (or right) or obligation is received by the distributing corporation in the exchange.

(C) Treatment of liabilities.—If any property distributed in the distribution referred to in paragraph (1) is subject to a liability or the shareholder assumes a liability of the distributing corporation in connection with the distribution, then, for purposes of subparagraph (A), the fair market value of such property shall be treated as not less than the amount of such liability.

(3) Treatment of certain transfers to creditors.—For purposes of this subsection, any transfer of qualified property by the corporation to its creditors in connection with the reorganization shall be treated as a distribution to its shareholders pursuant to the plan of reorganization.

(4) Coordination with other provisions.—Section 311 and subpart B of part II of this subchapter shall not apply to any distribution referred to in paragraph (1).

(5) Cross reference.—

For provision providing for recognition of gain in certain distributions, see section 355(d).

§ 362. Basis to corporations

(a) Property acquired by issuance of stock or as paid-in surplus.—If property was acquired on or after June 22, 1954, by a corporation—

(1) in connection with a transaction to which section 351 (relating to transfer of property to corporation controlled by transferor) applies, or

(2) as paid-in surplus or as a contribution to capital,

then the basis shall be the same as it would be in the hands of the transferor, increased in the amount of gain recognized to the transferor on such transfer.

(b) Transfers to corporations.—If property was acquired by a corporation in connection with a reorganization to which this part applies, then the basis shall be the same as it would be in the hands of the transferor, increased in the amount of gain recognized to the transferor on such transfer. This subsection shall not apply if the property acquired consists of stock or securities in a corporation a party to the reorganization, unless acquired by the exchange of stock or securities of the transferee (or of a corporation which is in control of the transferee) as the consideration in whole or in part for the transfer.

(c) Special rule for certain contributions to capital.—

(1) Property other than money.—Notwithstanding subsection (a)(2), if property other than money—

(A) is acquired by a corporation, on or after June 22, 1954, as a contribution to capital, and

(B) is not contributed by a shareholder as such,

then the basis of such property shall be zero.

(2) Money.—Notwithstanding subsection (a)(2), if money—

(A) is received by a corporation, on or after June 22, 1954, as a contribution to capital, and

(B) is not contributed by a shareholder as such,

then the basis of any property acquired with such money during the 12–month period beginning on the day the contribution is received shall be reduced by the amount of such contribution. The excess (if any) of the amount of such contribution over the amount of the reduction under the preceding sentence shall be applied to the reduction (as of the last day of the period specified in the preceding sentence) of the basis of any other property held by the taxpayer. The particular properties to which the reductions required by this paragraph shall be allocated shall be determined under regulations prescribed by the Secretary.

(d) Limitation on basis increase attributable to assumption of liability—

(1) In general.—In no event shall the basis of any property be increased under subsection (a) or (b) above the fair market value of such property (determined without regard to section 7701(g)) by reason of any gain recognized to the transferor as a result of the assumption of a liability.

(2) Treatment of gain not subject to tax.—Except as provided in regulations, if—

(A) gain is recognized to the transferor as a result of an assumption of a nonrecourse liability by a transferee which is also secured by assets not transferred to such transferee; and

(B) no person is subject to tax under this title on such gain,

then, for purposes of determining basis under subsections (a) and (b), the amount of gain recognized by the transferor as a result of the assumption of the liability shall be determined as if the liability assumed by the transferee equaled such transferee's ratable portion of such liability determined on the basis of the relative fair market values (determined without regard to section 7701(g)) of all of the assets subject to such liability.

(e) Limitations on built-in losses.—

(1) Limitation on importation of built-in losses.—

(A) In general.—If in any transaction described in subsection (a) or (b) there would (but for this subsection) be an importation of a net built-in loss, the basis of each property described in subparagraph (B) which is acquired in such transaction shall (notwithstanding subsections (a) and (b)) be its fair market value immediately after such transaction.

(B) Property described.—For purposes of subparagraph (A), property is described in this subparagraph if—

(i) gain or loss with respect to such property is not subject to tax under this subtitle in the hands of the transferor immediately before the transfer, and

(ii) gain or loss with respect to such property is subject to such tax in the hands of the transferee immediately after such transfer.

In any case in which the transferor is a partnership, the preceding sentence shall be applied by treating each partner in such partnership as holding such partner's proportionate share of the property of such partnership.

(C) Importation of net built-in loss.—For purposes of subparagraph (A), there is an importation of a net built-in loss in a transaction if the transferee's aggregate adjusted bases of property described in subparagraph (B) which is transferred in such transaction would (but for this paragraph) exceed the fair market value of such property immediately after such transaction.

(2) Limitation on transfer of built-in losses in section 351 transactions.—

(A) In general.—If—

(i) property is transferred by a transferor in any transaction which is described in subsection (a) and which is not described in paragraph (1) of this subsection, and

(ii) the transferee's aggregate adjusted bases of such property so transferred would (but for this paragraph) exceed the fair market value of such property immediately after such transaction,

then, notwithstanding subsection (a), the transferee's aggregate adjusted bases of the property so transferred shall not exceed the fair market value of such property immediately after such transaction.

(B) Allocation of basis reduction.—The aggregate reduction in basis by reason of subparagraph (A) shall be allocated among the property so transferred in proportion to their respective built-in losses immediately before the transaction.

(C) Election to apply limitation to transferor's stock basis.—

(i) In general.—If the transferor and transferee of a transaction described in subparagraph (A) both elect the application of this subparagraph—

(I) subparagraph (A) shall not apply, and

(II) the transferor's basis in the stock received for property to which subparagraph (A) does not apply by reason of the election shall not exceed its fair market value immediately after the transfer.

(ii) Election.—Any election under clause (i) shall be made at such time and in such form and manner as the Secretary may prescribe, and, once made, shall be irrevocable.

Subpart D—Special Rule; Definitions

§ 368. Definitions relating to corporate reorganizations

(a) Reorganization.—

(1) In general.—For purposes of parts I and II and this part, the term "reorganization" means—

(A) a statutory merger or consolidation;

(B) the acquisition by one corporation, in exchange solely for all or a part of its voting stock (or in exchange solely for all or a part of the voting stock of a corporation which is in control of the acquiring corporation), of stock of another corporation if, immediately after the acquisition, the acquiring corporation has control of such other corporation (whether or not such acquiring corporation had control immediately before the acquisition);

(C) the acquisition by one corporation, in exchange solely for all or a part of its voting stock (or in exchange solely for all or a part of the voting stock of a corporation which is in control of the acquiring corporation), of substantially all of the properties of another corporation, but in determining whether the exchange is solely for stock the assumption by the acquiring corporation of a liability of the other shall be disregarded;

(D) a transfer by a corporation of all or a part of its assets to another corporation if immediately after the transfer the transferor, or one or more of its shareholders (including persons who were shareholders immediately before the transfer), or any combination thereof, is in control of the corporation to which the assets are transferred; but only if, in pursuance of the plan, stock or securities of the corporation to which the assets are transferred are distributed in a transaction which qualifies under section 354, 355, or 356;

(E) a recapitalization;

(F) a mere change in identity, form, or place of organization of one corporation, however effected; or

(G) a transfer by a corporation of all or part of its assets to another corporation in a title 11 or similar case; but only if, in pursuance of the plan, stock or securities of the corporation to which the assets are transferred are distributed in a transaction which qualifies under section 354, 355, or 356.

(2) Special rules relating to paragraph (1).—

(A) Reorganizations described in both paragraph (1)(C) and paragraph (1)(D).—If a transaction is described in both paragraph (1)(C) and paragraph (1)(D), then, for purposes of this subchapter (other than for purposes of subparagraph (c)), such transaction shall be treated as described only in paragraph (1)(D).

(B) Additional consideration in certain paragraph (1)(C) cases.—If—

(i) one corporation acquires substantially all of the properties of another corporation,

(ii) the acquisition would qualify under paragraph (1)(C) but for the fact that the acquiring corporation exchanges money or other property in addition to voting stock, and

(iii) the acquiring corporation acquires, solely for voting stock described in paragraph (1)(C), property of the other corporation having a fair market value which is at least 80 percent of the fair market value of all of the property of the other corporation,

then such acquisition shall (subject to subparagraph (A) of this paragraph) be treated as qualifying under paragraph (1)(C). Solely for the purpose of determining whether clause (iii) of the preceding sentence applies, the amount of any liability assumed by the acquiring corporation shall be treated as money paid for the property.

(C) Transfers of assets or stock to subsidiaries in certain paragraph (1)(A), (1)(B), (1)(C), and (1)(G) cases.—A transaction otherwise qualifying under paragraph (1)(A), (1)(B), or (1)(C) shall not be disqualified by reason of the fact that part or all of the assets or stock which were acquired in the transaction are transferred to a corporation controlled by the corporation acquiring such assets or stock. A similar rule shall apply to a transaction otherwise qualifying under paragraph (1)(G) where the requirements of subparagraphs (A) and (B) of section 354(b)(1) are met with respect to the acquisition of the assets.

(D) Use of stock of controlling corporation in paragraph (1)(A) and (1)(G) cases.—The acquisition by one corporation, in exchange for stock of a corporation (referred to in this subparagraph as "controlling corporation") which is in control of the acquiring corporation, of substantially all of the properties of another corporation shall not disqualify a transaction under paragraph (1)(A) or (1)(G) if—

(i) no stock of the acquiring corporation is used in the transaction, and

(ii) in the case of a transaction under paragraph (1)(A), such transaction would have qualified under paragraph (1)(A) had the merger been into the controlling corporation.

(E) Statutory merger using voting stock of corporation controlling merged corporation.—A transaction otherwise qualifying under paragraph (1)(A) shall not be disqualified by reason of the fact that stock of a corporation (referred to in this subparagraph as the "controlling corporation") which before the merger was in control of the merged corporation is used in the transaction, if—

(i) after the transaction, the corporation surviving the merger holds substantially all of its properties and of the properties of the merged corporation (other than stock of the controlling corporation distributed in the transaction); and

(ii) in the transaction, former shareholders of the surviving corporation exchanged, for an amount of voting stock of the controlling corporation, an amount of stock in the surviving corporation which constitutes control of such corporation.

* * *

(G) Distribution requirement for paragraph (1)(C).—

(i) In general.—A transaction shall fail to meet the requirements of paragraph (1)(C) unless the acquired corporation distributes the stock, securities, and other properties it receives, as well as its other properties, in pursuance of the plan of reorganization. For purposes of the preceding sentence, if the acquired corporation is liquidated pursuant to the plan of reorganization, any distribution to its creditors in connection with such liquidation shall be treated as pursuant to the plan of reorganization.

(ii) Exception.—The Secretary may waive the application of clause (i) to any transaction subject to any conditions the Secretary may prescribe.

(H) Special rules for determining whether certain transactions are qualified under paragraph (1)(D).—For purposes of determining whether a transaction qualifies under paragraph (1)(D)—

(i) in the case of a transaction with respect to which the requirements of subparagraphs (A) and (B) of section 354(b)(1) are met, the term "control" has the meaning given such term by section 304(c), and

(ii) in the case of a transaction with respect to which the requirements of section 355 (or so much of section 356 as relates to section 355) are met, the fact that the shareholders of the distributing corporation dispose of part or all of the distributed stock, or the fact that the corporation whose stock was distributed issues additional stock, shall not be taken into account.

(3) Additional rules relating to title 11 and similar cases.—

(A) Title 11 or similar case defined.—For purposes of this part, the term "title 11 or similar case" means—

(i) a case under title 11 of the United States Code, or

(ii) a receivership, foreclosure, or similar proceeding in a Federal or State court.

(B) Transfer of assets in a title 11 or similar case.—In applying paragraph (1)(G), a transfer of the assets of a corporation shall be treated as made in a title 11 or similar case if and only if—

(i) any party to the reorganization is under the jurisdiction of the court in such case, and

(ii) the transfer is pursuant to a plan of reorganization approved by the court.

(C) Reorganizations qualifying under paragraph (1)(G) and another provision.—If a transaction would (but for this subparagraph) qualify both—

(i) under subparagraph (G) of paragraph (1), and

(ii) under any other subparagraph of paragraph (1) or under section 332 or 351,

then, for purposes of this subchapter (other than section 357(c)(1)), such transaction shall be treated as qualifying only under subparagraph (G) of paragraph (1).

* * *

(E) Application of paragraph (2)(E)(ii).—In the case of a title 11 or similar case, the requirement of clause (ii) of paragraph (2)(E) shall be treated as met if—

(i) no former shareholder of the surviving corporation received any consideration for his stock, and

(ii) the former creditors of the surviving corporation exchanged, for an amount of voting stock of the controlling corporation, debt of the surviving corporation which had a fair market value equal to 80 percent or more of the total fair market value of the debt of the surviving corporation.

(b) Party to a reorganization.—For purposes of this part, the term "a party to a reorganization" includes—

(1) a corporation resulting from a reorganization, and

(2) both corporations, in the case of a reorganization resulting from the acquisition by one corporation of stock or properties of another.

In the case of a reorganization qualifying under paragraph (1)(B) or (1)(C) of subsection (a), if the stock exchanged for the stock or properties is stock of a corporation which is in control of the acquiring corporation, the term "a party to a reorganization" includes the corporation so controlling the acquiring corporation. In the case of a reorganization qualifying under paragraph (1)(A), (1)(B), (1)(C), or (1)(G) of subsection (a) by reason of paragraph (2)(C) of subsection (a), the term "a party to a reorganization" includes the corporation controlling the corporation to which the acquired assets or stock are transferred. In the case of a reorganization qualifying under paragraph (1)(A) or (1)(G) of subsection (a) by reason of paragraph (2)(D) of that subsection, the term "a party to a reorganization" includes the controlling corporation referred to in such paragraph (2)(D). In the case of a reorganization qualifying under subsection (a)(1)(A) by reason of subsection (a)(2)(E), the term "party to a reorganization" includes the controlling corporation referred to in subsection (a)(2)(E).

(c) Control defined.—For purposes of part I (other than section 304), part II, and this part, the term "control" means the ownership of stock possessing at least 80 percent of the total combined voting power of all classes of stock entitled to vote and at least 80 percent of the total number of shares of all other classes of stock of the corporation.

PART V—CARRYOVERS

§ 381. Carryovers in certain corporate acquisitions

(a) General rule.—In the case of the acquisition of assets of a corporation by another corporation—

(1) in a distribution to such other corporation to which section 332 (relating to liquidations of subsidiaries) applies; or

(2) in a transfer to which section 361 (relating to nonrecognition of gain or loss to corporations) applies, but only if the transfer is in connection with a reorganization described in subparagraph (A), (C), (D), (F), or (G) of section 368(a)(1), the acquiring corporation shall succeed to and take into account, as of the close of the day of distribution or transfer, the items described in subsection (c) of the distributor or transferor corporation, subject to the conditions and limitations specified in subsections (b) and (c). For purposes of the preceding sentence, a reorganization shall be treated as meeting the requirements of subparagraph (D) or (G) of section 368(a)(1) only if the requirements of subparagraphs (A) and (B) of section 354(b)(1) are met.

(b) Operating rules.—Except in the case of an acquisition in connection with a reorganization described in subparagraph (F) of section 368(a)(1)—

(1) The taxable year of the distributor or transferor corporation shall end on the date of distribution or transfer.

(2) For purposes of this section, the date of distribution or transfer shall be the day on which the distribution or transfer is completed; except that, under regulations prescribed by the Secretary, the date when substantially all of the property has been distributed or transferred may be used if the distributor or transferor corporation ceases all operations, other than liquidating activities, after such date.

(3) The corporation acquiring property in a distribution or transfer described in subsection (a) shall not be entitled to carry back a net operating loss or a net capital loss for a taxable year ending after the date of distribution or transfer to a taxable year of the distributor or transferor corporation.

(c) Items of the distributor or transferor corporation.—The items referred to in subsection (a) are:

(1) Net operating loss carryovers.—The net operating loss carryovers determined under section 172, subject to the following conditions and limitations:

(A) The taxable year of the acquiring corporation to which the net operating loss carryovers of the distributor or transferor corporation are first carried shall be the first taxable year ending after the date of distribution or transfer.

(B) In determining the net operating loss deduction, the portion of such deduction attributable to the net operating loss carryovers of the distributor or transferor corporation to the first taxable year of the acquiring corporation ending after the date of distribution or transfer shall be limited to an amount which bears the same ratio to the taxable income (determined without regard to a net operating loss deduction) of the acquiring corporation in such taxable year as the number of days in the taxable year after the date of distribution or transfer bears to the total number of days in the taxable year.

(C) For the purpose of determining the amount of the net operating loss carryovers under section 172(b)(2), a net operating loss for a taxable year (hereinafter in this subparagraph referred to as the "loss year") of a distributor or transferor corporation which ends on or before the end of a loss year of the acquiring corporation shall be considered to be a net operating loss for a year prior to such loss year of the acquiring corporation. For the same purpose, the taxable income for a "prior taxable year" (as the term is used in section 172(b)(2)) shall be computed as provided in such section; except that, if the date of distribution or transfer is on a day other than the last day of a taxable year of the acquiring corporation—

(i) such taxable year shall (for the purpose of this subparagraph only) be considered to be 2 taxable years (hereinafter in this subparagraph referred to as the "pre-acquisition part year" and the "post-acquisition part year");

(ii) the pre-acquisition part year shall begin on the same day as such taxable year begins and shall end on the date of distribution or transfer;

(iii) the post-acquisition part year shall begin on the day following the date of distribution or transfer and shall end on the same day as the end of such taxable year;

(iv) the taxable income for such taxable year (computed with the modifications specified in section 172(b)(2)(A) but without a net operating loss deduction) shall be divided between the pre-acquisition part year and the post-acquisition part year in proportion to the number of days in each;

(v) the net operating loss deduction for the pre-acquisition part year shall be determined as provided in section 172(b)(2)(B), but without regard to a net operating loss year of the distributor or transferor corporation; and

(vi) the net operating loss deduction for the post-acquisition part year shall be determined as provided in section 172(b)(2)(B).

(2) Earnings and profits.—In the case of a distribution or transfer described in subsection (a)—

(A) the earnings and profits or deficit in earnings and profits, as the case may be, of the distributor or transferor corporation shall, subject to subparagraph (B), be deemed to have been received or incurred by the acquiring corporation as of the close of the date of the distribution or transfer; and

(B) a deficit in earnings and profits of the distributor, transferor, or acquiring corporation shall be used only to offset earnings and profits accumulated after the date of transfer. For this purpose, the earnings and profits for the taxable year of the acquiring corporation in which the distribution or transfer occurs shall be deemed to have been accumulated after such distribution or transfer in an amount which bears the same ratio to the undistributed earnings and profits of the acquiring corporation for such taxable year (computed without regard to any earnings and profits received from the distributor or transferor corporation, as described in subparagraph (A) of this paragraph) as the number of days in the taxable year after the date of distribution or transfer bears to the total number of days in the taxable year.

(3) Capital loss carryover.—The capital loss carryover determined under section 1212, subject to the following conditions and limitations:

(A) The taxable year of the acquiring corporation to which the capital loss carryover of the distributor or transferor corporation is first carried shall be the first taxable year ending after the date of distribution or transfer.

(B) The capital loss carryover shall be a short-term capital loss in the taxable year determined under subparagraph (A) but shall be limited to an amount which bears the same ratio to the capital gain net income (determined without regard to a short-term capital loss attributable to capital loss carryover), if any, of the acquiring corporation in such taxable year as the number of days in the taxable year after the date of distribution or transfer bears to the total number of days in the taxable year.

(C) For purposes of determining the amount of such capital loss carryover to taxable years following the taxable year determined under subparagraph (A), the capital gain net income in the taxable year determined under subparagraph (A) shall be considered to be an amount equal to the amount determined under subparagraph (B).

(4) Method of accounting.—The acquiring corporation shall use the method of accounting used by the distributor or transferor corporation on the date of distribution or transfer unless different methods were used by several distributor or transferor corporations or by a distributor or transferor corporation and the acquiring corporation. If different methods were used, the acquiring corporation shall use the method or combination of methods of computing taxable income adopted pursuant to regulations prescribed by the Secretary.

(5) Inventories.—In any case in which inventories are received by the acquiring corporation, such inventories shall be taken by such corporation (in determining its income) on the same basis on which such inventories were taken by the distributor or transferor corporation, unless different methods were used by several distributor or transferor corporations or by a distributor or transferor corporation and the acquiring corporation. If different methods were used, the acquiring corporation shall use the method or combination of methods of taking inventory adopted pursuant to regulations prescribed by the Secretary.

(6) Method of computing depreciation allowance.—The acquiring corporation shall be treated as the distributor or transferor corporation for purposes of computing the depreciation allowance under sections 167 and 168 on property acquired in a distribution or transfer with respect to so much of the basis in the hands of the acquiring corporation as does not exceed the adjusted basis in the hands of the distributor or transferor corporation.

[(7) Repealed.]

(8) Installment method.—If the acquiring corporation acquires installment obligations (the income from which the distributor or transferor corporation reports on the installment basis under section 453) the acquiring corporation shall, for purposes of section 453, be treated as if it were the distributor or transferor corporation.

(9) Amortization of bond discount or premium.—If the acquiring corporation assumes liability for bonds of the distributor or transferor corporation issued at a discount or premium, the acquiring corporation shall be treated as the distributor or transferor corporation after the date of distribution or transfer for purposes of determining the amount of amortization allowable or includible with respect to such discount or premium.

(10) Treatment of certain mining development and exploration expenses of distributor or transferor corporation.—The acquiring corporation shall be entitled to deduct, as if it were the distributor or transferor corporation, expenses deferred under section 616 (relating to certain development expenditures) if the distributor or transferor corporation has so elected.

(11) Contributions to pension plans, employees' annuity plans, and stock bonus and profit-sharing plans.—The acquiring corporation shall be considered to be the distributor or transferor corporation after the date of distribution or transfer for the purpose of determining the amounts deductible under section 404 with respect to pension plans, employees' annuity plans, and stock bonus and profit-sharing plans.

(12) Recovery of tax benefit items.—If the acquiring corporation is entitled to the recovery of any amounts previously deducted by (or allowable as credits to) the distributor or transferor corporation, the acquiring corporation shall succeed to the treatment under section 111 which would apply to such amounts in the hands of the distributor or transferor corporation.

(13) Involuntary conversions under section 1033.—The acquiring corporation shall be treated as the distributor or transferor corporation after the date of distribution or transfer for purposes of applying section 1033.

(14) Dividend carryover to personal holding company.—The dividend carryover (described in section 564) to taxable years ending after the date of distribution or transfer.

[(15) Repealed.]

(16) Certain obligations of distributor or transferor corporation.—If the acquiring corporation—

(A) assumes an obligation of the distributor or transferor corporation which, after the date of the distribution or transfer, gives rise to a liability, and

(B) such liability, if paid or accrued by the distributor or transferor corporation, would have been deductible in computing its taxable income,

the acquiring corporation shall be entitled to deduct such items when paid or accrued, as the case may be, as if such corporation were the distributor or transferor corporation. A corporation which would have been an acquiring corporation under this section if the date of distribution or transfer had occurred on or after the effective date of the provisions of this subchapter applicable to a liquidation or reorganization, as the case may be, shall be entitled, even though the date of distribution or transfer occurred before such effective date, to apply this paragraph with respect to amounts paid or accrued in taxable years beginning after December 31, 1953, on account of such obligations of the distributor or transferor corporation. This paragraph shall not apply if such obligations are reflected in the amount of stock, securities, or property transferred by the acquiring corporation to the transferor corporation for the property of the transferor corporation.

(17) Deficiency dividend of personal holding company.—If the acquiring corporation pays a deficiency dividend (as defined in section 547(d)) with respect to the distributor or transferor corporation, such distributor or transferor corporation shall, with respect to such payments, be entitled to the deficiency dividend deduction provided in section 547.

(18) Percentage depletion on extraction of ores or minerals from the waste or residue of prior mining.—The acquiring corporation shall be considered to be the distributor or transferor corporation for the purpose of determining the applicability of section 613(c)(3) (relating to extraction of ores or minerals from the ground).

(19) Charitable contributions in excess of prior years' limitations.—Contributions made in the taxable year ending on the date of distribution or transfer and the 4 prior taxable years by the distributor or transferor corporation in excess of the amount deductible under section 170(b)(2) for such taxable years shall be deductible by the acquiring corporation for its taxable years which begin after the date of distribution or transfer, subject to the limitations imposed in section 170(b)(2). In applying the preceding sentence, each taxable year of the distributor or transferor corporation beginning on or before the date of distribution or transfer shall be treated as a prior taxable year with reference to the acquiring corporation's taxable years beginning after such date.

* * *

§ 382. Limitation on net operating loss carryforwards and certain built-in losses following ownership change

(a) General rule.—The amount of the taxable income of any new loss corporation for any post-change year which may be offset by pre-change losses shall not exceed the section 382 limitation for such year.

(b) Section 382 limitation.—For purposes of this section—

(1) In general.—Except as otherwise provided in this section, the section 382 limitation for any post-change year is an amount equal to—

(A) the value of the old loss corporation, multiplied by

(B) the long-term tax-exempt rate.

(2) Carryforward of unused limitation.—If the section 382 limitation for any post-change year exceeds the taxable income of the new loss corporation for such year which was offset by pre-change losses, the section 382 limitation for the next post-change year shall be increased by the amount of such excess.

(3) Special rule for post-change year which includes change date.—In the case of any post-change year which includes the change date—

(A) Limitation does not apply to taxable income before change.—Subsection (a) shall not apply to the portion of the taxable income for such year which is allocable to the period in such year on or before the change date. Except as provided in subsection (h)(5) and in regulations, taxable income shall be allocated ratably to each day in the year.

(B) Limitation for period after change.—For purposes of applying the limitation of subsection (a) to the remainder of the taxable income for such year, the section 382 limitation shall be an amount which bears the same ratio to such limitation (determined without regard to this paragraph) as—

(i) the number of days in such year after the change date, bears to

(ii) the total number of days in such year.

(c) Carryforwards disallowed if continuity of business requirements not met.—

(1) In general.—Except as provided in paragraph (2), if the new loss corporation does not continue the business enterprise of the old loss corporation at all times during the 2–year period beginning on the change date, the section 382 limitation for any post-change year shall be zero.

(2) Exception for certain gains.—The section 382 limitation for any post-change year shall not be less than the sum of—

(A) any increase in such limitation under—

(i) subsection (h)(1)(A) for recognized built-in gains for such year, and

(ii) subsection (h)(1)(C) for gain recognized by reason of an election under section 338, plus

(B) any increase in such limitation under subsection (b)(2) for amounts described in subparagraph (A) which are carried forward to such year.

(d) Pre-change loss and post-change year.—For purposes of this section—

(1) Pre-change loss.—The term "pre-change loss" means—

(A) any net operating loss carryforward of the old loss corporation to the taxable year ending with the ownership change or in which the change date occurs, and

(B) the net operating loss of the old loss corporation for the taxable year in which the ownership change occurs to the extent such loss is allocable to the period in such year on or before the change date.

Except as provided in subsection (h)(5) and in regulations, the net operating loss shall, for purposes of subparagraph (B), be allocated ratably to each day in the year.

(2) Post-change year.—The term "post-change year" means any taxable year ending after the change date.

(e) Value of old loss corporation.—For purposes of this section—

(1) In general.—Except as otherwise provided in this subsection, the value of the old loss corporation is the value of the stock of such corporation (including any stock described in section 1504(a)(4)) immediately before the ownership change.

(2) Special rule in the case of redemption or other corporate contraction.—If a redemption or other corporate contraction occurs in connection with an ownership change, the value under paragraph (1) shall be determined after taking such redemption or other corporate contraction into account.

* * *

(f) Long-term tax-exempt rate.—For purposes of this section—

(1) In general.—The long-term tax-exempt rate shall be the highest of the adjusted Federal long-term rates in effect for any month in the 3–calendar-month period ending with the calendar month in which the change date occurs.

(2) Adjusted federal long-term rate.—For purposes of paragraph (1), the term "adjusted Federal long-term rate" means the Federal long-term rate determined under section 1274(d), except that—

(A) paragraphs (2) and (3) thereof shall not apply, and

(B) such rate shall be properly adjusted for differences between rates on long-term taxable and tax-exempt obligations.

(g) Ownership change.—For purposes of this section—

(1) In general.—There is an ownership change if, immediately after any owner shift involving a 5–percent shareholder or any equity structure shift—

(A) the percentage of the stock of the loss corporation owned by 1 or more 5–percent shareholders has increased by more than 50 percentage points, over

(B) the lowest percentage of stock of the loss corporation (or any predecessor corporation) owned by such shareholders at any time during the testing period.

(2) Owner shift involving 5–percent shareholder.—There is an owner shift involving a 5–percent shareholder if—

(A) there is any change in the respective ownership of stock of a corporation, and

(B) such change affects the percentage of stock of such corporation owned by any person who is a 5–percent shareholder before or after such change.

(3) Equity structure shift defined.—

(A) In general.—The term "equity structure shift" means any reorganization (within the meaning of section 368). Such term shall not include—

(i) any reorganization described in subparagraph (D) or (G) of section 368(a)(1) unless the requirements of section 354(b)(1) are met, and

(ii) any reorganization described in subparagraph (F) of section 368(a)(1).

(B) Taxable reorganization-type transactions, etc.—To the extent provided in regulations, the term "equity structure shift" includes taxable reorganization-type transactions, public offerings, and similar transactions.

(4) Special rules for application of subsection.—

(A) Treatment of less than 5–percent shareholders.—Except as provided in subparagraphs (B)(i) and (C), in determining whether an ownership change has occurred, all stock owned by shareholders of a corporation who are not 5–percent shareholders of such corporation shall be treated as stock owned by 1 5–percent shareholder of such corporation.

(B) Coordination with equity structure shifts.—For purposes of determining whether an equity structure shift (or subsequent transaction) is an ownership change—

(i) Less than 5–percent shareholders.—Subparagraph (A) shall be applied separately with respect to each group of shareholders (immediately before such equity structure shift) of each corporation which was a party to the reorganization involved in such equity structure shift.

(ii) Acquisitions of stock.—Unless a different proportion is established, acquisitions of stock after such equity structure shift shall be treated as being made proportionately from all shareholders immediately before such acquisition.

(C) Coordination with other owner shifts.—Except as provided in regulations, rules similar to the rules of subparagraph (B) shall apply in determining whether there has been an owner shift involving a 5–percent shareholder and whether such shift (or subsequent transaction) results in an ownership change.

(D) Treatment of worthless stock.—If any stock held by a 50–percent shareholder is treated by such shareholder as becoming worthless during any taxable year of such shareholder and such stock is held by such shareholder as of the close of such taxable year, for purposes of determining whether an ownership change occurs after the close of such taxable year, such shareholder—

(i) shall be treated as having acquired such stock on the 1st day of his 1st succeeding taxable year, and

(ii) shall not be treated as having owned such stock during any prior period.

For purposes of the preceding sentence, the term ''50–percent shareholder'' means any person owning 50 percent or more of the stock of the corporation at any time during the 3–year period ending on the last day of the taxable year with respect to which the stock was so treated.

(h) Special rules for built-in gains and losses and section 338 gains.—For purposes of this section—

(1) In general.—

(A) Net unrealized built-in gain.—

(i) In general.—If the old loss corporation has a net unrealized built-in gain, the section 382 limitation for any recognition period taxable year shall be increased by the recognized built-in gains for such taxable year.

(ii) Limitation.—The increase under clause (i) for any recognition period taxable year shall not exceed—

(I) the net unrealized built-in gain, reduced by

(II) recognized built-in gains for prior years ending in the recognition period.

(B) Net unrealized built-in loss.—

(i) In general.—If the old loss corporation has a net unrealized built-in loss, the recognized built-in loss for any recognition period taxable year shall be subject to limitation under this section in the same manner as if such loss were a pre-change loss.

(ii) Limitation.—Clause (i) shall apply to recognized built-in losses for any recognition period taxable year only to the extent such losses do not exceed—

(I) the net unrealized built-in loss, reduced by

(II) recognized built-in losses for prior taxable years ending in the recognition period.

(C) Special rules for certain section 338 gains.—If an election under section 338 is made in connection with an ownership change and the net unrealized built-in gain is zero by reason of paragraph (3)(B), then, with respect to such change, the section 382 limitation for the post-change year in which gain is recognized by reason of such election shall be increased by the lesser of—

(i) the recognized built-in gains by reason of such election, or

(ii) the net unrealized built-in gain (determined without regard to paragraph (3)(B)).

(2) Recognized built-in gain and loss.—

(A) Recognized built-in gain.—The term "recognized built-in gain" means any gain recognized during the recognition period on the disposition of any asset to the extent the new loss corporation establishes that—

(i) such asset was held by the old loss corporation immediately before the change date, and

(ii) such gain does not exceed the excess of—

(I) the fair market value of such asset on the change date, over

(II) the adjusted basis of such asset on such date.

(B) Recognized built-in loss.—The term "recognized built-in loss" means any loss recognized during the recognition period on the disposition of any asset except to the extent the new loss corporation establishes that—

(i) such asset was not held by the old loss corporation immediately before the change date, or

(ii) such loss exceeds the excess of—

(I) the adjusted basis of such asset on the change date, over

(II) the fair market value of such asset on such date.

Such term includes any amount allowable as depreciation, amortization, or depletion for any period within the recognition period except to the extent the new loss corporation establishes that the amount so allowable is not attributable to the excess described in clause (ii).

(3) Net unrealized built-in gain and loss defined.—

(A) Net unrealized built-in gain and loss.—

(i) In general.—The terms "net unrealized built-in gain" and "net unrealized built-in loss" mean, with respect to any old loss corporation, the amount by which—

(I) the fair market value of the assets of such corporation immediately before an ownership change is more or less, respectively, than

(II) the aggregate adjusted basis of such assets at such time.

(ii) Special rule for redemptions or other corporate contractions.—If a redemption or other corporate contraction occurs in connection with an ownership change, to the extent provided in regulations, determinations under clause (i) shall be made after taking such redemption or other corporate contraction into account.

(B) Threshold requirement.—

(i) In general.—If the amount of the net unrealized built-in gain or net unrealized built-in loss (determined without regard to this subparagraph) of any old loss corporation is not greater than the lesser of—

(I) 15 percent of the amount determined for purposes of subparagraph (A)(i)(I), or

(II) $10,000,000,

the net unrealized built-in gain or net unrealized built-in loss shall be zero.

(ii) Cash and cash items not taken into account.—In computing any net unrealized built-in gain or net unrealized built-in loss under clause (i), except as provided in regulations, there shall not be taken into account—

(I) any cash or cash item, or

(II) any marketable security which has a value which does not substantially differ from adjusted basis.

(4) Disallowed loss allowed as a carryforward.—If a deduction for any portion of a recognized built-in loss is disallowed for any post-change year, such portion—

(A) shall be carried forward to subsequent taxable years under rules similar to the rules for the carrying forward of net operating losses (or to the extent the amount so disallowed is attributable to capital losses, under rules similar to the rules for the carrying forward of net capital losses), but

(B) shall be subject to limitation under this section in the same manner as a pre-change loss.

(5) Special rules for post-change year which includes change date.—For purposes of subsection (b)(3)—

(A) in applying subparagraph (A) thereof, taxable income shall be computed without regard to recognized built-in gains to the extent such gains increased the section 382 limitation for the year (or recognized built-in losses to the extent such losses are treated as pre-change losses), and gain described in paragraph (1)(C), for the year, and

(B) in applying subparagraph (B) thereof, the section 382 limitation shall be computed without regard to recognized built-in gains, and gain described in paragraph (1)(C), for the year.

(6) Treatment of certain built-in items.—

(A) Income items.—Any item of income which is properly taken into account during the recognition period but which is attributable to periods before the change date shall be treated as a recognized built-in gain for the taxable year in which it is properly taken into account.

(B) Deduction items.—Any amount which is allowable as a deduction during the recognition period (determined without regard to any carryover) but which is attributable to periods before the change date shall be treated as a recognized built-in loss for the taxable year for which it is allowable as a deduction.

(C) Adjustments.—The amount of the net unrealized built-in gain or loss shall be properly adjusted for amounts which would be treated as recognized built-in gains or losses under this paragraph if such amounts were properly taken into account (or allowable as a deduction) during the recognition period.

(7) Recognition period, etc.—

(A) Recognition period.—The term "recognition period" means, with respect to any ownership change, the 5–year period beginning on the change date.

(B) Recognition period taxable year.—The term "recognition period taxable year" means any taxable year any portion of which is in the recognition period.

(8) Determination of fair market value in certain cases.—If 80 percent or more in value of the stock of a corporation is acquired in 1 transaction (or in a series of related transactions during any 12–month period), for purposes of determining the net unrealized built-in loss, the fair market value of the assets of such corporation shall not exceed the grossed up amount paid for such stock properly adjusted for indebtedness of the corporation and other relevant items.

(9) Tax-free exchanges or transfers.—The Secretary shall prescribe such regulations as may be necessary to carry out the purposes of this subsection where property held on the change date was acquired (or is subsequently transferred) in a transaction where gain or loss is not recognized (in whole or in part).

(i) Testing period.—For purposes of this section—

(1) 3–year period.—Except as otherwise provided in this section, the testing period is the 3–year period ending on the day of any owner shift involving a 5–percent shareholder or equity structure shift.

(2) Shorter period where there has been recent ownership change.—If there has been an ownership change under this section, the testing period for determining whether a 2nd ownership change has occurred shall not begin before the 1st day following the change date for such earlier ownership change.

(3) Shorter period where all losses arise after 3–year period begins.—The testing period shall not begin before the earlier of the 1st day of the 1st taxable year from which there is a carryforward of a loss or of an excess credit to the 1st post-change year or the taxable year in which the transaction being tested occurs. Except as provided in regulations, this paragraph shall not apply to any loss corporation which has a net unrealized built-in loss (determined after application of subsection (h)(3)(B)).

(j) Change date.—For purposes of this section, the change date is—

(1) in the case where the last component of an ownership change is an owner shift involving a 5–percent shareholder, the date on which such shift occurs, and

(2) in the case where the last component of an ownership change is an equity structure shift, the date of the reorganization.

(k) Definitions and special rules.—For purposes of this section—

(1) Loss corporation.—The term "loss corporation" means a corporation entitled to use a net operating loss carryover or having a net operating loss for the taxable year in which the ownership change occurs. Except to the extent provided in regulations, such term includes any corporation with a net unrealized built-in loss.

(2) Old loss corporation.—The term "old loss corporation" means any corporation—

(A) with respect to which there is an ownership change, and

(B) which (before the ownership change) was a loss corporation.

(3) New loss corporation.—The term "new loss corporation" means a corporation which (after an ownership change) is a loss corporation. Nothing in this section shall be treated as implying that the same corporation may not be both the old loss corporation and the new loss corporation.

(4) Taxable income.—Taxable income shall be computed with the modifications set forth in section 172(d).

(5) Value.—The term "value" means fair market value.

(6) Rules relating to stock.—

(A) Preferred stock.—Except as provided in regulations and subsection (e), the term "stock" means stock other than stock described in section 1504(a)(4).

(B) Treatment of certain rights, etc.—The Secretary shall prescribe such regulations as may be necessary—

(i) to treat warrants, options, contracts to acquire stock, convertible debt interests, and other similar interests as stock, and

(ii) to treat stock as not stock.

(C) Determinations on basis of value.—Determinations of the percentage of stock of any corporation held by any person shall be made on the basis of value.

(7) 5–percent shareholder.—The term "5–percent shareholder" means any person holding 5 percent or more of the stock of the corporation at any time during the testing period.

(*l*) Certain additional operating rules.—For purposes of this section—

(1) Certain capital contributions not taken into account.—

(A) In general.—Any capital contribution received by an old loss corporation as part of a plan a principal purpose of which is to avoid or increase any limitation under this section shall not be taken into account for purposes of this section.

(B) Certain contributions treated as part of plan.—For purposes of subparagraph (A), any capital contribution made during the 2–year period ending on the change date shall, except as provided in regulations, be treated as part of a plan described in subparagraph (A).

(2) Ordering rules for application of section.—

(A) Coordination with section 172(b) carryover rules.—In the case of any pre-change loss for any taxable year (hereinafter in this subparagraph referred to as the "loss year") subject to limitation under this section, for purposes of determining under the 2nd sentence of section 172(b)(2) the amount of such loss which may be carried to any taxable year, taxable income for any taxable year shall be treated as not greater than—

(i) the section 382 limitation for such taxable year, reduced by

(ii) the unused pre-change losses for taxable years preceding the loss year.

Similar rules shall apply in the case of any credit or loss subject to limitation under section 383.

(B) Ordering rule for losses carried from same taxable year.—In any case in which—

(i) a pre-change loss of a loss corporation for any taxable year is subject to a section 382 limitation, and

(ii) a net operating loss of such corporation from such taxable year is not subject to such limitation,

taxable income shall be treated as having been offset first by the loss subject to such limitation.

(3) Operating rules relating to ownership of stock.—

(A) Constructive ownership.—Section 318 (relating to constructive ownership of stock) shall apply in determining ownership of stock, except that—

(i) paragraphs (1) and (5)(B) of section 318(a) shall not apply and an individual and all members of his family described in paragraph (1) of section 318(a) shall be treated as 1 individual for purposes of applying this section,

(ii) paragraph (2) of section 318(a) shall be applied—

(I) without regard to the 50–percent limitation contained in subparagraph (C) thereof, and

(II) except as provided in regulations, by treating stock attributed thereunder as no longer being held by the entity from which attributed,

(iii) paragraph (3) of section 318(a) shall be applied only to the extent provided in regulations,

(iv) except to the extent provided in regulations, an option to acquire stock shall be treated as exercised if such exercise results in an ownership change, and

(v) in attributing stock from an entity under paragraph (2) of section 318(a), there shall not be taken into account—

(I) in the case of attribution from a corporation, stock which is not treated as stock for purposes of this section, or

(II) in the case of attribution from another entity, an interest in such entity similar to stock described in subclause (I).

A rule similar to the rule of clause (iv) shall apply in the case of any contingent purchase, warrant, convertible debt, put, stock subject to a risk of forfeiture, contract to acquire stock, or similar interests.

(B) Stock acquired by reason of death, gift, divorce, separation, etc.—If—

(i) the basis of any stock in the hands of any person is determined—

(I) under section 1014 (relating to property acquired from a decedent),

(II) section 1015 (relating to property acquired by a gift or transfer in trust), or

(III) section 1041(b)(2) (relating to transfers of property between spouses or incident to divorce),

(ii) stock is received by any person in satisfaction of a right to receive a pecuniary bequest, or

(iii) stock is acquired by a person pursuant to any divorce or separation instrument (within the meaning of section 71(b)(2)),

such person shall be treated as owning such stock during the period such stock was owned by the person from whom it was acquired.

(C) Certain changes in percentage ownership which are attributable to fluctuations in value not taken into account.—Except as provided in regulations, any change in proportionate ownership which is attributable solely to fluctuations in the relative fair market values of different classes of stock shall not be taken into account.

(4) Reduction in value where substantial nonbusiness assets.—

(A) In general.—If, immediately after an ownership change, the new loss corporation has substantial nonbusiness assets, the value of the old loss corporation shall be reduced by the excess (if any) of—

(i) the fair market value of the nonbusiness assets of the old loss corporation, over

(ii) the nonbusiness asset share of indebtedness for which such corporation is liable.

(B) Corporation having substantial nonbusiness assets.—For purposes of subparagraph (A)—

(i) In general.—The old loss corporation shall be treated as having substantial nonbusiness assets if at least ⅓ of the value of the total assets of such corporation consists of nonbusiness assets.

* * *

(C) Nonbusiness assets.—For purposes of this paragraph, the term "nonbusiness assets" means assets held for investment.

(D) Nonbusiness asset share.—For purposes of this paragraph, the nonbusiness asset share of the indebtedness of the corporation is an amount which bears the same ratio to such indebtedness as—

(i) the fair market value of the nonbusiness assets of the corporation, bears to

(ii) the fair market value of all assets of such corporation.

(E) Treatment of subsidiaries.—For purposes of this paragraph, stock and securities in any subsidiary corporation shall be disregarded and the parent corporation shall be deemed to own its ratable share of the subsidiary's assets. For purposes of the preceding sentence, a corporation shall be treated as a subsidiary if the parent owns 50 percent or more of the combined voting power of all classes of stock entitled to vote, and 50 percent or more of the total value of shares of all classes of stock.

(5) Title 11 or similar case.—

(A) In general.—Subsection (a) shall not apply to any ownership change if—

(i) the old loss corporation is (immediately before such ownership change) under the jurisdiction of the court in a title 11 or similar case, and

(ii) the shareholders and creditors of the old loss corporation (determined immediately before such ownership change) own (after such ownership change and as a result of being shareholders or creditors immediately before such change) stock of the new loss corporation (or stock of a controlling corporation if also in bankruptcy) which meets the requirements of section 1504(a)(2) (determined by substituting "50 percent" for "80 percent" each place it appears).

(B) Reduction for interest payments to creditors becoming shareholders.—In any case to which subparagraph (A) applies, the pre-change losses and excess credits (within the meaning of section 383(a)(2)) which may be carried to a post-change year shall be computed as if no deduction was allowable under this chapter for the interest paid or accrued by the old loss corporation on indebtedness which was converted into stock pursuant to title 11 or similar case during—

(i) any taxable year ending during the 3–year period preceding the taxable year in which the ownership change occurs, and

(ii) the period of the taxable year in which the ownership change occurs on or before the change date.

(C) Coordination with section 108.—In applying section 108(e)(8) to any case to which subparagraph (A) applies, there shall not be taken into account any indebtedness for interest described in subparagraph (B).

(D) Section 382 limitation zero if another change within 2 years.—If, during the 2–year period immediately following an ownership change to which this paragraph applies, an ownership change of the new loss corporation occurs, this paragraph shall not apply and the section 382 limitation with respect to the 2nd ownership change for any post-change year ending after the change date of the 2nd ownership change shall be zero.

(E) Only certain stock taken into account.—For purposes of subparagraph (A)(ii), stock transferred to a creditor shall be taken into account only to the extent such stock is transferred in satisfaction of indebtedness and only if such indebtedness—

(i) was held by the creditor at least 18 months before the date of the filing of the title 11 or similar case, or

(ii) arose in the ordinary course of the trade or business of the old loss corporation and is held by the person who at all times held the beneficial interest in such indebtedness.

* * *

(G) Title 11 or similar case.—For purposes of this paragraph, the term "title 11 or similar case" has the meaning given such term by section 368(a)(3)(A).

(H) Election not to have paragraph apply.—A new loss corporation may elect, subject to such terms and conditions as the Secretary may prescribe, not to have the provisions of this paragraph apply.

(6) Special rule for insolvency transactions.—If paragraph (5) does not apply to any reorganization described in subparagraph (G) of section 368(a)(1) or any exchange of debt for stock in a title 11 or similar case (as defined in section 368(a)(3)(A)), the value under subsection (e) shall reflect the increase (if any) in value of the old loss corporation resulting from any surrender or cancellation of creditors' claims in the transaction.

(7) Coordination with alternative minimum tax.—The Secretary shall by regulation provide for the application of this section to the alternative tax net operating loss deduction under section 56(d).

(8) Predecessor and successor entities.—Except as provided in regulations, any entity and any predecessor or successor entities of such entity shall be treated as 1 entity.

(m) Regulations.—The Secretary shall prescribe such regulations as may be necessary or appropriate to carry out the purposes of this section and section 383, including (but not limited to) regulations—

(1) providing for the application of this section and section 383 where an ownership change with respect to the old loss corporation is followed by an ownership change with respect to the new loss corporation, and

(2) providing for the application of this section and section 383 in the case of a short taxable year,

(3) providing for such adjustments to the application of this section and section 383 as is necessary to prevent the avoidance of the purposes of this section and section 383, including the avoidance of such purposes through the use of related persons, pass-thru entities, or other intermediaries,

(4) providing for the application of subsection (g)(4) where there is only 1 corporation involved, and

(5) providing, in the case of any group of corporations described in section 1563(a) (determined by substituting "50 percent" for "80 percent" each place it appears and determined without regard to paragraph (4) thereof), appropriate adjustments to value, built-in gain or loss, and other items so that items are not omitted or taken into account more than once.

* * *

§ 383. Special limitations on certain excess credits, etc.

(a) Excess credits.—

(1) In general.—Under regulations, if an ownership change occurs with respect to a corporation, the amount of any excess credit for any taxable year which may be used in any post-change year shall be limited to an amount determined on the basis of the tax liability which is attributable to so much of the taxable income as does not exceed the section 382 limitation for such post-change year to the extent available after the application of section 382 and subsections (b) and (c) of this section.

(2) Excess credit.—For purposes of paragraph (1), the term "excess credit" means—

(A) any unused general business credit of the corporation under section 39, and

(B) any unused minimum tax credit of the corporation under section 53.

(b) Limitation on net capital loss.—If an ownership change occurs with respect to a corporation, the amount of any net capital loss under section 1212 for any taxable year before the 1st post-change year which may be used in any post-change year shall be limited under regulations which shall be based on the principles applicable under section 382. Such regulations shall provide that any such net capital loss used in a post-change year shall reduce the section 382 limitation which is applied to pre-change losses under section 382 for such year.

* * *

(d) Pro ration rules for year which includes change.—For purposes of this section, rules similar to the rules of subsections (b)(3) and (d)(1)(B) of section 382 shall apply.

(e) Definitions.—Terms used in this section shall have the same respective meanings as when used in section 382, except that appropriate adjustments shall be made to take into account that the limitations of this section apply to credits and net capital losses.

§ 384. Limitation on use of preacquisition losses to offset built-in gains

(a) General rule.—If—

(1)(A) a corporation acquires directly (or through 1 or more other corporations) control of another corporation, or

(B) the assets of a corporation are acquired by another corporation in a reorganization described in subparagraph (A), (C), or (D) of section 368(a)(1), and

(2) either of such corporations is a gain corporation,

income for any recognition period taxable year (to the extent attributable to recognized built-in gains) shall not be offset by any preacquisition loss (other than a preacquisition loss of the gain corporation).

(b) Exception where corporations under common control.—

(1) In general.—Subsection (a) shall not apply to the preacquisition loss of any corporation if such corporation and the gain corporation were members of the same controlled group at all times during the 5-year period ending on the acquisition date.

(2) Controlled group.—For purposes of this subsection, the term "controlled group" means a controlled group of corporations (as defined in section 1563(a)); except that—

(A) "more than 50 percent" shall be substituted for "at least 80 percent" each place it appears,

(B) the ownership requirements of section 1563(a) must be met both with respect to voting power and value, and

(C) the determination shall be made without regard to subsection (a)(4) of section 1563.

(3) Shorter period where corporations not in existence for 5 years.—If either of the corporations referred to in paragraph (1) was not in existence throughout the 5–year period referred to in paragraph (1), the period during which such corporation was in existence (or if both, the shorter of such periods) shall be substituted for such 5–year period.

(c) Definitions.—For purposes of this section—

(1) Recognized built-in gain.—

(A) In general.—The term "recognized built-in gain" means any gain recognized during the recognition period on the disposition of any asset except to the extent the gain corporation (or, in any case described in subsection (a)(1)(B), the acquiring corporation) establishes that—

(i) such asset was not held by the gain corporation on the acquisition date, or

(ii) such gain exceeds the excess (if any) of—

(I) the fair market value of such asset on the acquisition date, over

(II) the adjusted basis of such asset on such date.

(B) Treatment of certain income items.—Any item of income which is properly taken into account for any recognition period taxable year but which is attributable to periods before the acquisition date shall be treated as a recognized built-in gain for the taxable year in which it is properly taken into account and shall be taken into account in determining the amount of the net unrealized built-in gain.

(C) Limitation.—The amount of the recognized built-in gains for any recognition period taxable year shall not exceed—

(i) the net unrealized built-in gain, reduced by

(ii) the recognized built-in gains for prior years ending in the recognition period which (but for this section) would have been offset by preacquisition losses.

(2) Acquisition date.—The term "acquisition date" means—

(A) in any case described in subsection (a)(1)(A), the date on which the acquisition of control occurs, or

(B) in any case described in subsection (a)(1)(B), the date of the transfer in the reorganization.

(3) Preacquisition loss.—

(A) In general.—The term "preacquisition loss" means—

(i) any net operating loss carryforward to the taxable year in which the acquisition date occurs, and

(ii) any net operating loss for the taxable year in which the acquisition date occurs to the extent such loss is allocable to the period in such year on or before the acquisition date.

Except as provided in regulations, the net operating loss shall, for purposes of clause (ii), be allocated ratably to each day in the year.

(B) Treatment of recognized built-in loss.—In the case of a corporation with a net unrealized built-in loss, the term "preacquisition loss" includes any recognized built-in loss.

(4) Gain corporation.—The term "gain corporation" means any corporation with a net unrealized built-in gain.

(5) Control.—The term "control" means ownership of stock in a corporation which meets the requirements of section 1504(a)(2).

(6) Treatment of members of same group.—Except as provided in regulations and except for purposes of subsection (b), all corporations which are members of the same affiliated group immediately before the acquisition date shall be treated as 1 corporation. To the extent provided in regulations, section 1504 shall be applied without regard to subsection (b) thereof for purposes of the preceding sentence.

(7) Treatment of predecessors and successors.—Any reference in this section to a corporation shall include a reference to any predecessor or successor thereof.

(8) Other definitions.—Except as provided in regulations, the terms "net unrealized built-in gain", "net unrealized built-in loss", "recognized built-in loss", "recognition period", and "recognition period taxable year", have the same respective meanings as when used in section 382(h), except that the acquisition date shall be taken into account in lieu of the change date.

(d) Limitation also to apply to excess credits or net capital losses.—Rules similar to the rules of subsection (a) shall also apply in the case of any excess credit (as defined in section 383(a)(2)) or net capital loss.

(e) Ordering rules for net operating losses, etc.—

(1) Carryover rules.—If any preacquisition loss may not offset a recognized built-in gain by reason of this section, such gain shall not be taken into account in determining under section 172(b)(2) the amount of such loss which may be carried to other taxable years. A similar rule shall apply in the case of any excess credit or net capital loss limited by reason of subsection (d).

(2) Ordering rule for losses carried from same taxable year.—In any case in which—

(A) a preacquisition loss for any taxable year is subject to limitation under subsection (a), and

(B) a net operating loss from such taxable year is not subject to such limitation,

taxable income shall be treated as having been offset 1st by the loss subject to such limitation.

(f) Regulations.—The Secretary shall prescribe such regulations as may be necessary to carry out the purposes of this section, including regulations to ensure that the purposes of this section may not be circumvented through—

(1) the use of any provision of law or regulations (including subchapter K of this chapter), or

(2) contributions of property to a corporation.

PART VI—TREATMENT OF CERTAIN CORPORATE INTERESTS AS STOCK OR INDEBTEDNESS

§ 385. Treatment of certain interests in corporations as stock or indebtedness

(a) Authority to prescribe regulations.—The Secretary is authorized to prescribe such regulations as may be necessary or appropriate to determine whether an interest in a corporation is to be treated for purposes of this title as stock or indebtedness (or as in part stock and in part indebtedness).

(b) Factors.—The regulations prescribed under this section shall set forth factors which are to be taken into account in determining with respect to a particular factual situation whether a debtor-creditor relationship exists or a corporation-shareholder relationship exists. The factors so set forth in the regulations may include among other factors:

(1) whether there is a written unconditional promise to pay on demand or on a specified date a sum certain in money in return for an adequate consideration in money or money's worth, and to pay a fixed rate of interest,

(2) whether there is subordination to or preference over any indebtedness of the corporation,

(3) the ratio of debt to equity of the corporation,

(4) whether there is convertibility into the stock of the corporation, and

(5) the relationship between holdings of stock in the corporation and holdings of the interest in question.

(c) Effect of classification by issuer.—

(1) In general.—The characterization (as of the time of issuance) by the issuer as to whether an interest in a corporation is stock or indebtedness shall be binding on such issuer and on all holders of such interest (but shall not be binding on the Secretary).

(2) Notification of inconsistent treatment.—Except as provided in regulations, paragraph (1) shall not apply to any holder of an interest if such holder on his return discloses that he is treating such interest in a manner inconsistent with the characterization referred to in paragraph (1).

(3) Regulations.—The Secretary is authorized to require such information as the Secretary determines to be necessary to carry out the provisions of this subsection.

SUBCHAPTER D—DEFERRED COMPENSATION, ETC.

PART I—PENSION, PROFIT-SHARING, STOCK BONUS PLANS, ETC.

Subpart A—General Rule

§ 401. Qualified pension, profit-sharing, and stock bonus plans

(a) Requirements for qualification.—A trust created or organized in the United States and forming part of a stock bonus, pension, or profit-sharing plan of an employer for the exclusive benefit of his employees or their beneficiaries shall constitute a qualified trust under this section—

(1) if contributions are made to the trust by such employer, or employees, or both, or by another employer who is entitled to deduct his contributions under section 404(a)(3)(B) (relating to deduction for contributions to profit-sharing and stock bonus plans), or by a charitable remainder trust pursuant to a qualified gratuitous

* Omitted entirely.

transfer (as defined in section 664(g)(1)), for the purpose of distributing to such employees or their beneficiaries the corpus and income of the fund accumulated by the trust in accordance with such plan;

(2) if under the trust instrument it is impossible, at any time prior to the satisfaction of all liabilities with respect to employees and their beneficiaries under the trust, for any part of the corpus or income to be (within the taxable year or thereafter) used for, or diverted to, purposes other than for the exclusive benefit of his employees or their beneficiaries (but this paragraph shall not be construed, in the case of a multiemployer plan, to prohibit the return of a contribution within 6 months after the plan administrator determines that the contribution was made by a mistake of fact or law (other than a mistake relating to whether the plan is described in section 401(a) or the trust which is part of such plan is exempt from taxation under section 501(a), or the return of any withdrawal liability payment determined to be an overpayment within 6 months of such determination));

(3) if the plan of which such trust is a part satisfies the requirements of section 410 (relating to minimum participation standards); and

(4) if the contributions or benefits provided under the plan do not discriminate in favor of highly compensated employees (within the meaning of section 414(q)). For purposes of this paragraph, there shall be excluded from consideration employees described in section 410(b)(3)(A) and (C).

(5) Special rules relating to nondiscrimination requirements.—

(A) Salaried or clerical employees.—A classification shall not be considered discriminatory within the meaning of paragraph (4) or section 410(b)(2)(A)(i) merely because it is limited to salaried or clerical employees.

(B) Contributions and benefits may bear uniform relationship to compensation.—A plan shall not be considered discriminatory within the meaning of paragraph (4) merely because the contributions or benefits of, or on behalf of, the employees under the plan bear a uniform relationship to the compensation (within the meaning of section 414(s)) of such employees.

(C) Certain disparity permitted.—A plan shall not be considered discriminatory within the meaning of paragraph (4) merely because the contributions or benefits of, or on behalf of, the employees under the plan favor highly compensated employees (as defined in section 414(q)) in the manner permitted under subsection (*l*).

(D) Integrated defined benefit plan.—

(i) In general.—A defined benefit plan shall not be considered discriminatory within the meaning of paragraph (4) merely because the plan provides that the employer-derived accrued retirement benefit for any participant under the plan may not exceed the excess (if any) of—

(I) the participant's final pay with the employer, over

(II) the employer-derived retirement benefit created under Federal law attributable to service by the participant with the employer.

For purposes of this clause, the employer-derived retirement benefit created under Federal law shall be treated as accruing ratably over 35 years.

(ii) Final pay.—For purposes of this subparagraph, the participant's final pay is the compensation (as defined in section 414(q)(4)) paid to the participant by the employer for any year—

(I) which ends during the 5–year period ending with the year in which the participant separated from service for the employer, and

(II) for which the participant's total compensation from the employer was highest.

* * *

(7) A trust shall not constitute a qualified trust under this section unless the plan of which such trust is a part satisfies the requirements of section 411 (relating to minimum vesting standards).

(8) A trust forming part of a defined benefit plan shall not constitute a qualified trust under this section unless the plan provides that forfeitures must not be applied to increase the benefits any employee would otherwise receive under the plan.

(9) Required distributions.—

(A) In general.—A trust shall not constitute a qualified trust under this subsection unless the plan provides that the entire interest of each employee—

(i) will be distributed to such employee not later than the required beginning date, or

(ii) will be distributed, beginning not later than the required beginning date, in accordance with regulations, over the life of such employee or over the lives of such employee and a designated beneficiary (or over a period not extending beyond the life expectancy of such employee or the life expectancy of such employee and a designated beneficiary).

(B) Required distribution where employee dies before entire interest is distributed.—

(i) Where distributions have begun under subparagraph (A)(ii).—A trust shall not constitute a qualified trust under this section unless the plan provides that if—

(I) the distribution of the employee's interest has begun in accordance with subparagraph (A)(ii), and

(II) the employee dies before his entire interest has been distributed to him,

the remaining portion of such interest will be distributed at least as rapidly as under the method of distributions being used under subparagraph (A)(ii) as of the date of his death.

(ii) 5-year rule for other cases.—A trust shall not constitute a qualified trust under this section unless the plan provides that, if an employee dies before the distribution of the employee's interest has begun in accordance with subparagraph (A)(ii), the entire interest of the employee will be distributed within 5 years after the death of such employee.

(iii) Exception to 5-year rule for certain amounts payable over life of beneficiary.—If—

(I) any portion of the employee's interest is payable to (or for the benefit of) a designated beneficiary,

(II) such portion will be distributed (in accordance with regulations) over the life of such designated beneficiary (or over a period not extending beyond the life expectancy of such beneficiary), and

(III) such distributions begin not later than 1 year after the date of the employee's death or such later date as the Secretary may by regulations prescribe,

for purposes of clause (ii), the portion referred to in subclause (I) shall be treated as distributed on the date on which such distributions begin.

(iv) Special rule for surviving spouse of employee.—If the designated beneficiary referred to in clause (iii)(I) is the surviving spouse of the employee—

(I) the date on which the distributions are required to begin under clause (iii)(III) shall not be earlier than the date on which the employee would have attained age 70½, and

(II) if the surviving spouse dies before the distributions to such spouse begin, this subparagraph shall be applied as if the surviving spouse were the employee.

(C) Required beginning date.—For purposes of this paragraph—

(i) In general.—The term "required beginning date" means April 1 of the calendar year following the later of—

(I) the calendar year in which the employee attains age 70½, or

(II) the calendar year in which the employee retires.

* * *

(10) Other requirements.—

(A) Plans benefiting owner-employees.—In the case of any plan which provides contributions or benefits for employees some or all of whom are owner-employees (as defined in subsection (c)(3)), a trust forming part of such plan shall constitute a qualified trust under this section only if the requirements of subsection (d) are also met.

(B) Top-heavy plans.—

(i) In general.—In the case of any top-heavy plan, a trust forming part of such plan shall constitute a qualified trust under this section only if the requirements of section 416 are met.

(ii) Plans which may become top-heavy.—Except to the extent provided in regulations, a trust forming part of a plan (whether or not a top-heavy plan) shall constitute a qualified trust under this section only if such plan contains provisions—

(I) which will take effect if such plan becomes a top-heavy plan, and

(II) which meet the requirements of section 416.

* * *

(11) Requirement of joint and survivor annuity and preretirement survivor annuity.—

(A) In general.—In the case of any plan to which this paragraph applies, except as provided in section 417, a trust forming part of such plan shall not constitute a qualified trust under this section unless—

(i) in the case of a vested participant who does not die before the annuity starting date, the accrued benefit payable to such participant is provided in the form of a qualified joint and survivor annuity, and

(ii) in the case of a vested participant who dies before the annuity starting date and who has a surviving spouse, a qualified preretirement survivor annuity is provided to the surviving spouse of such participant.

(B) Plans to which paragraph applies.—This paragraph shall apply to—

(i) any defined benefit plan,

(ii) any defined contribution plan which is subject to the funding standards of section 412, and

(iii) any participant under any other defined contribution plan unless—

(I) such plan provides that the participant's nonforfeitable accrued benefit (reduced by any security interest held by the plan by reason of a loan outstanding to such participant) is payable in full, on the death of the participant, to the participant's surviving spouse (or, if there is no surviving spouse or the surviving spouse consents in the manner required under section 417(a)(2), to a designated beneficiary),

(II) such participant does not elect a payment of benefits in the form of a life annuity, and

(III) with respect to such participant, such plan is not a direct or indirect transferee (in a transfer after December 31, 1984) of a plan which is described in clause (i) or (ii) or to which this clause applied with respect to the participant.

Clause (iii)(III) shall apply only with respect to the transferred assets (and income therefrom) if the plan separately accounts for such assets and any income therefrom.

* * *

(D) Special rule where participant and spouse married less than 1 year.—A plan shall not be treated as failing to meet the requirements of subparagraphs (B)(iii) or (C) merely because the plan provides that benefits will not be payable to the surviving spouse of the participant unless the participant and such spouse had been married throughout the 1-year period ending on the earlier of the participant's annuity starting date or the date of the participant's death.

* * *

(13) Assignment and alienation.—

(A) In general.—A trust shall not constitute a qualified trust under this section unless the plan of which such trust is a part provides that benefits provided under the plan may not be assigned or alienated. For purposes of the preceding sentence, there shall not be taken into account any voluntary and revocable assignment of not to exceed 10 percent of any benefit payment made by any participant who is receiving benefits under the plan unless the assignment or alienation is made for purposes of defraying plan administration costs. For purposes of this paragraph a loan made to a participant or beneficiary shall not be treated as an assignment or alienation if such loan is secured by the participant's accrued nonforfeitable benefit and is exempt from the tax imposed by section 4975 (relating to tax on prohibited transactions) by reason of section 4975(d)(1). This paragraph shall take effect on January 1, 1976 and shall not apply to assignments which were irrevocable on September 2, 1974.

(B) Special rules for domestic relations orders.—Subparagraph (A) shall apply to the creation, assignment, or recognition of a right to any benefit payable with respect to a participant pursuant to a domestic relations order, except that subparagraph (A) shall not apply if the order is determined to be a qualified domestic relations order.

* * *

(16) A trust shall not constitute a qualified trust under this section if the plan of which such trust is a part provides for benefits or contributions which exceed the limitations of section 415.

(17) Compensation limit.—

(A) In general.—A trust shall not constitute a qualified trust under this section unless, under the plan of which such trust is a part, the annual compensation of each employee taken into account under the plan for any year does not exceed $200,000.

(B) Cost-of-living adjustment.—The Secretary shall adjust annually the $200,000 amount in subparagraph (A) for increases in the cost-of-living at the same time and in the same manner as adjustments under section 415(d); except that the base period shall be the calendar quarter beginning July 1, 2001, and any increase which is not a multiple of $5,000 shall be rounded to the next lowest multiple of $5,000.

* * *

(26) Additional participation requirements.—

(A) In general.—In the case of a trust which is a part of a defined benefit plan, such trust shall not constitute a qualified trust under this subsection unless on each day of the plan year such trust benefits at least the lesser of—

(i) 50 employees of the employer, or

(ii) the greater of—

(I) 40 percent of all employees of the employer, or

(II) 2 employees (or if there is only 1 employee, such employee).

* * *

(27) Determinations as to profit-sharing plans.—

(A) Contributions need not be based on profits.—The determination of whether the plan under which any contributions are made is a profit-sharing plan shall be made without regard to current or accumulated profits of the employer and without regard to whether the employer is a tax-exempt organization.

(B) Plan must designate type.—In the case of a plan which is intended to be a money purchase pension plan or a profit-sharing plan, a trust forming part of such plan shall not constitute a qualified trust under this subsection unless the plan designates such intent at such time and in such manner as the Secretary may prescribe.

* * *

(c) Definitions and rules relating to self-employed individuals and owner-employees.—For purposes of this section—

(1) Self-employed individual treated as employee.—

(A) In general.—The term "employee" includes, for any taxable year, an individual who is a self-employed individual for such taxable year.

(B) Self-employed individual.—The term "self-employed individual" means, with respect to any taxable year, an individual who has earned income (as defined in paragraph (2)) for such taxable year. To the extent provided in regulations prescribed by the Secretary, such term also includes, for any taxable year—

(i) an individual who would be a self-employed individual within the meaning of the preceding sentence but for the fact that the trade or business carried on by such individual did not have net profits for the taxable year, and

(ii) an individual who has been a self-employed individual within the meaning of the preceding sentence for any prior taxable year.

(2) Earned income.—

(A) In general.—The term "earned income" means the net earnings from self-employment (as defined in section 1402(a)), but such net earnings shall be determined—

(i) only with respect to a trade or business in which personal services of the taxpayer are a material income-producing factor,

(ii) without regard to paragraphs (4) and (5) of section 1402(c),

(iii) in the case of any individual who is treated as an employee under sections 3121(d)(3)(A), (C), or (D), without regard to paragraph (2) of section 1402(c),

(iv) without regard to items which are not included in gross income for purposes of this chapter, and the deductions properly allocable to or chargeable against such items,

(v) with regard to the deductions allowed by section 404 to the taxpayer, and

(vi) with regard to the deduction allowed to the taxpayer by section 164(f).

For purposes of this subparagraph, section 1402, as in effect for a taxable year ending on December 31, 1962, shall be treated as having been in effect for all taxable years ending before such date. For purposes of this part only (other than sections 419 and 419A), this subparagraph shall be applied as if the term "trade or business" for purposes of section 1402 included service described in section 1402(c)(6).

[(B) Repealed.]

(C) Income from disposition of certain property.—For purposes of this section, the term "earned income" includes gains (other than any gain which is treated under any provision of this chapter as gain from the sale or exchange of a capital asset) and net earnings derived from the sale or other disposition of, the transfer of any interest in, or the licensing of the use of property (other than good will) by an individual whose personal efforts created such property.

(3) Owner-employee.—The term "owner-employee" means an employee who—

(A) owns the entire interest in an unincorporated trade or business, or

(B) in the case of a partnership, is a partner who owns more than 10 percent of either the capital interest or the profits interest in such partnership.

To the extent provided in regulations prescribed by the Secretary, such term also means an individual who has been an owner-employee within the meaning of the preceding sentence.

(4) Employer.—An individual who owns the entire interest in an unincorporated trade or business shall be treated as his own employer. A partnership shall be treated as the employer of each partner who is an employee within the meaning of paragraph (1).

(5) Contributions on behalf of owner-employees.—The term "contribution on behalf of an owner-employee" includes, except as the context otherwise requires, a contribution under a plan—

(A) by the employer for an owner-employee, and

(B) by an owner-employee as an employee.

* * *

(d) Contribution limit on owner-employees.—A trust forming part of a pension or profit-sharing plan which provides contributions or benefits for employees some or all of whom are owner-employees shall constitute a qualified trust under this section only if, in addition to meeting the requirements of subsection (a), the plan provides that contributions on behalf of any owner-employee may be made only with respect to the earned income of such owner-employee which is derived from the trade or business with respect to which such plan is established.

* * *

(k) Cash or deferred arrangements.—

(1) General rule.—A profit-sharing or stock bonus plan, a pre-ERISA money purchase plan, or a rural cooperative plan shall not be considered as not satisfying the requirements of subsection (a) merely because the plan includes a qualified cash or deferred arrangement.

(2) Qualified cash or deferred arrangement.—A qualified cash or deferred arrangement is any arrangement which is part of a profit-sharing or stock bonus plan, a pre-ERISA money purchase plan, or a rural cooperative plan which meets the requirements of subsection (a)—

(A) under which a covered employee may elect to have the employer make payments as contributions to a trust under the plan on behalf of the employee, or to the employee directly in cash;

(B) under which amounts held by the trust which are attributable to employer contributions made pursuant to the employee's election—

(i) may not be distributable to participants or other beneficiaries earlier than—

(I) severance from service, death, or disability,

(II) an event described in paragraph (10),

(III) in the case of a profit-sharing or stock bonus plan, the attainment of age 59½, or

(IV) in the case of contributions to a profit-sharing or stock bonus plan to which section 402(e)(3) applies, upon hardship of the employee, and

* * *

(ii) will not be distributable merely by reason of the completion of a stated period of participation or the lapse of a fixed number of years;

(C) which provides that an employee's right to his accrued benefit derived from employer contributions made to the trust pursuant to his election is nonforfeitable, and

(D) which does not require, as a condition of participation in the arrangement, that an employee complete a period of service with the employer (or employers) maintaining the plan extending beyond the period permitted under section 410(a)(1) (determined without regard to subparagraph (B)(i) thereof).

(3) Application of participation and discrimination standards.—

(A) A cash or deferred arrangement shall not be treated as a qualified cash or deferred arrangement unless—

(i) those employees eligible to benefit under the arrangement satisfy the provisions of section 410(b)(1), and

(ii) the actual deferral percentage for eligible highly compensated employees (as defined in paragraph (5)) for the plan year bears a relationship to the actual deferral percentage for all other eligible employees for the preceding plan year which meets either of the following tests:

(I) The actual deferral percentage for the group of eligible highly compensated employees is not more than the actual deferral percentage of all other eligible employees multiplied by 1.25.

(II) The excess of the actual deferral percentage for the group of eligible highly compensated employees over that of all other eligible employees is not more than 2 percentage points, and the actual deferral percentage for the group of eligible highly compensated employees is not more than the actual deferral percentage of all other eligible employees multiplied by 2.

If 2 or more plans which include cash or deferred arrangements are considered as 1 plan for purposes of section 401(a)(4) or 410(b), the cash or deferred arrangements included in such plans shall be treated as 1 arrangement for purposes of this subparagraph.

If any highly compensated employee is a participant under 2 or more cash or deferred arrangements of the employer, for purposes of determining the deferral percentage with respect to such employee, all such cash or deferred arrangements shall be treated as 1 cash or deferred arrangement. An arrangement may apply clause (ii) by using the plan year rather than the preceding plan year if the employer so elects, except that if such an election is made, it may not be changed except as provided by the Secretary.

(B) For purposes of subparagraph (A), the actual deferral percentage for a specified group of employees for a plan year shall be the average of the ratios (calculated separately for each employee in such group) of—

(i) the amount of employer contributions actually paid over to the trust on behalf of each such employee for such plan year, to

(ii) the employee's compensation for such plan year.

(C) A cash or deferred arrangement shall be treated as meeting the requirements of subsection (a)(4) with respect to contributions if the requirements of subparagraph (A)(ii) are met.

(D) For purposes of subparagraph (B), the employer contributions on behalf of any employee—

(i) shall include any employer contributions made pursuant to the employee's election under paragraph (2), and

(ii) under such rules as the Secretary may prescribe, may, at the election of the employer, include—

(I) matching contributions (as defined in 401(m)(4)(A)) which meet the requirements of paragraph (2)(B) and (C), and

(II) qualified nonelective contributions (within the meaning of section 401(m)(4)(C)).

(E) For purposes of this paragraph, in the case of the first plan year of any plan (other than a successor plan), the amount taken into account as the actual deferral percentage of nonhighly compensated employees for the preceding plan year shall be—

(i) 3 percent, or

(ii) if the employer makes an election under this subclause, the actual deferral percentage of nonhighly compensated employees determined for such first plan year.

* * *

(4) Other requirements.—

(A) Benefits (other than matching contributions) must not be contingent on election to defer.—A cash or deferred arrangement of any employer shall not be treated as a qualified cash or deferred arrangement if any other benefit is conditioned (directly or indirectly) on the employee electing to have the employer make or not make contributions under the arrangement in lieu of receiving cash. The preceding sentence shall not apply to any matching contribution (as defined in section 401(m)) made by reason of such an election.

(B) Eligibility of State and local governments and tax-exempt organizations.—

(i) Tax-exempts eligible.—Except as provided in clause (ii), any organization exempt from tax under this subtitle may include a qualified cash or deferred arrangement as part of a plan maintained by it.

(ii) Governments ineligible.—A cash or deferred arrangement shall not be treated as a qualified cash or deferred arrangement if it is part of a plan maintained by a State or local government or political subdivision thereof, or any agency or instrumentality thereof. This clause shall not apply to a rural cooperative plan or to a plan of an employer described in clause (iii).

* * *

(C) Coordination with other plans.—Except as provided in section 401(m), any employer contribution made pursuant to an employee's election under a qualified cash or deferred arrangement shall not be taken into account for purposes of determining whether any other plan meets the requirements of section 401(a) or 410(b). This subparagraph shall not apply for purposes of determining whether a plan meets the average benefit requirement of section 410(b)(2)(A)(ii).

(5) Highly compensated employee.—For purposes of this subsection, the term "highly compensated employee" has the meaning given such term by section 414(q).

* * *

(11) Adoption of simple plan to meet nondiscrimination tests.—

(A) In general.—A cash or deferred arrangement maintained by an eligible employer shall be treated as meeting the requirements of paragraph (3)(A)(ii) if such arrangement meets—

(i) the contribution requirements of subparagraph (B),

(ii) the exclusive plan requirements of subparagraph (C), and

(iii) the vesting requirements of section 408(p)(3).

(B) Contribution requirements.—

(i) In general.—The requirements of this subparagraph are met if, under the arrangement—

(I) an employee may elect to have the employer make elective contributions for the year on behalf of the employee to a trust under the plan in an amount which is expressed as a percentage of compensation of the employee but which in no event exceeds the amount in effect under section 408(p)(2)(A)(ii),

(II) the employer is required to make a matching contribution to the trust for the year in an amount equal to so much of the amount the employee elects under subclause (I) as does not exceed 3 percent of compensation for the year, and

(III) no other contributions may be made other than contributions described in subclause (I) or (II).

(ii) Employer may elect 2–percent nonelective contribution.—An employer shall be treated as meeting the requirements of clause (i)(II) for any year if, in lieu of the contributions described in such clause, the employer elects (pursuant to the terms of the arrangement) to make nonelective contributions of 2 percent of compensation for each employee who is eligible to participate in the arrangement and who has at least $5,000 of compensation from the employer for the year. If an employer makes an election under this subparagraph for any year, the employer shall notify employees of such election within a reasonable period of time before the 60th day before the beginning of such year.

(iii) Administrative requirements.—

(I) In general.—Rules similar to the rules of subparagraphs (B) and (C) of section 408(p)(5) shall apply for purposes of this subparagraph.

(II) Notice of election period.—The requirements of this subparagraph shall not be treated as met with respect to any year unless the employer notifies each employee eligible to participate, within a reasonable period of time before the 60th day before the beginning of such year (and, for the first year the employee is so eligible, the 60th day before the first day such employee is so eligible), of the rules similar to the rules of section 408(p)(5)(C) which apply by reason of subclause (I).

(C) Exclusive plan requirement.—The requirements of this subparagraph are met for any year to which this paragraph applies if no contributions were made, or benefits were accrued, for services during such year under any qualified plan of the employer on behalf of any employee eligible to participate in the cash or deferred arrangement, other than contributions described in subparagraph (B).

(D) Definitions and special rule.—

(i) Definitions.—For purposes of this paragraph, any term used in this paragraph which is also used in section 408(p) shall have the meaning given such term by such section.

(ii) Coordination with top-heavy rules.—A plan meeting the requirements of this paragraph for any year shall not be treated as a top-heavy plan under section 416 for such year if such plan allows only contributions required under this paragraph.

(12) Alternative methods of meeting nondiscrimination requirements.—

(A) In general.—A cash or deferred arrangement shall be treated as meeting the requirements of paragraph (3)(A)(ii) if such arrangement—

(i) meets the contribution requirements of subparagraph (B) or (C), and

(ii) meets the notice requirements of subparagraph (D).

(B) Matching contributions.—

(i) In general.—The requirements of this subparagraph are met if, under the arrangement, the employer makes matching contributions on behalf of each employee who is not a highly compensated employee in an amount equal to—

(I) 100 percent of the elective contributions of the employee to the extent such elective contributions do not exceed 3 percent of the employee's compensation, and

(II) 50 percent of the elective contributions of the employee to the extent that such elective contributions exceed 3 percent but do not exceed 5 percent of the employee's compensation.

(ii) Rate for highly compensated employees.—The requirements of this subparagraph are not met if, under the arrangement, the rate of matching contribution with respect to any elective contribution of a highly compensated employee at any rate of elective contribution is greater than that with respect to an employee who is not a highly compensated employee.

(iii) Alternative plan designs.—If the rate of any matching contribution with respect to any rate of elective contribution is not equal to the percentage required under clause (i), an arrangement shall not be treated as failing to meet the requirements of clause (i) if—

(I) the rate of an employer's matching contribution does not increase as an employee's rate of elective contributions increase, and

(II) the aggregate amount of matching contributions at such rate of elective contribution is at least equal to the aggregate amount of matching contributions which would be made if matching contributions were made on the basis of the percentages described in clause (i).

(C) Nonelective contributions.—The requirements of this subparagraph are met if, under the arrangement, the employer is required, without regard to whether the employee makes an elective contribution or employee contribution, to make a contribution to a defined contribution plan on behalf of each employee who is not a highly compensated employee and who is eligible to participate in the arrangement in an amount equal to at least 3 percent of the employee's compensation.

(D) Notice requirement.—An arrangement meets the requirements of this paragraph if, under the arrangement, each employee eligible to participate is, within a reasonable period before any year, given written notice of the employee's rights and obligations under the arrangement which—

(i) is sufficiently accurate and comprehensive to apprise the employee of such rights and obligations, and

(ii) is written in a manner calculated to be understood by the average employee eligible to participate.

(E) Other requirements.—

(i) Withdrawal and vesting restrictions.—An arrangement shall not be treated as meeting the requirements of subparagraph (B) or (C) of this paragraph unless the requirements of subparagraphs (B) and (C) of paragraph (2) are met with respect to all employer contributions (including matching contributions) taken into account in determining whether the requirements of subparagraphs (B) and (C) of this paragraph are met.

(ii) Social security and similar contributions not taken into account.—An arrangement shall not be treated as meeting the requirements of subparagraph (B) or (C) unless such requirements are met without regard to subsection (*l*), and, for purposes of subsection (*l*), employer contributions under subparagraph (B) or (C) shall not be taken into account.

(F) Other plans.—An arrangement shall be treated as meeting the requirements under subparagraph (A)(i) if any other plan maintained by the employer meets such requirements with respect to employees eligible under the arrangement.

(13) Alternative method for automatic contribution arrangements to meet nondiscrimination requirements.—

(A) In general.—A qualified automatic contribution arrangement shall be treated as meeting the requirements of paragraph (3)(A)(ii).

(B) Qualified automatic contribution arrangement.—For purposes of this paragraph, the term "qualified automatic contribution arrangement" means any cash or deferred arrangement which meets the requirements of subparagraphs (C) through (E).

(C) Automatic deferral.—

(i) In general.—The requirements of this subparagraph are met if, under the arrangement, each employee eligible to participate in the arrangement is treated as having elected to have the employer make elective contributions in an amount equal to a qualified percentage of compensation.

(ii) Election out.—The election treated as having been made under clause (i) shall cease to apply with respect to any employee if such employee makes an affirmative election—

(I) to not have such contributions made, or

(II) to make elective contributions at a level specified in such affirmative election.

(iii) Qualified percentage.—For purposes of this subparagraph, the term "qualified percentage" means, with respect to any employee, any percentage determined under the arrangement if such percentage is applied uniformly, does not exceed 10 percent, and is at least—

(I) 3 percent during the period ending on the last day of the first plan year which begins after the date on which the first elective contribution described in clause (i) is made with respect to such employee,

(II) 4 percent during the first plan year following the plan year described in subclause (I),

(III) 5 percent during the second plan year following the plan year described in subclause (I), and

(IV) 6 percent during any subsequent plan year.

(iv) Automatic deferral for current employees not required.—Clause (i) may be applied without taking into account any employee who—

(I) was eligible to participate in the arrangement (or a predecessor arrangement) immediately before the date on which such arrangement becomes a qualified automatic contribution arrangement (determined after application of this clause), and

(II) had an election in effect on such date either to participate in the arrangement or to not participate in the arrangement.

(D) Matching or nonelective contributions.—

(i) In general.—The requirements of this subparagraph are met if, under the arrangement, the employer—

(I) makes matching contributions on behalf of each employee who is not a highly compensated employee in an amount equal to the sum of 100 percent of the elective contributions of the employee to the extent that such contributions do not exceed 1 percent of compensation plus 50 percent of so much of such contributions as exceed 1 percent but do not exceed 6 percent of compensation, or

(II) is required, without regard to whether the employee makes an elective contribution or employee contribution, to make a contribution to a defined contribution plan on behalf of each employee who is not a highly compensated employee and who is eligible to participate in the arrangement in an amount equal to at least 3 percent of the employee's compensation.

(ii) Application of rules for matching contributions.—The rules of clauses (ii) and (iii) of paragraph (12)(B) shall apply for purposes of clause (i)(I).

(iii) Withdrawal and vesting restrictions.—An arrangement shall not be treated as meeting the requirements of clause (i) unless, with respect to employer contributions (including matching contributions) taken into account in determining whether the requirements of clause (i) are met—

(I) any employee who has completed at least 2 years of service (within the meaning of section 411(a)) has a nonforfeitable right to 100 percent of the employee's accrued benefit derived from such employer contributions, and

(II) the requirements of subparagraph (B) of paragraph (2) are met with respect to all such employer contributions.

(iv) Application of certain other rules.—The rules of subparagraphs (E)(ii) and (F) of paragraph (12) shall apply for purposes of subclauses (I) and (II) of clause (i).

(E) Notice requirements.—

(i) In general.—The requirements of this subparagraph are met if, within a reasonable period before each plan year, each employee eligible to participate in the arrangement for such year receives written notice of the employee's rights and obligations under the arrangement which—

(I) is sufficiently accurate and comprehensive to apprise the employee of such rights and obligations, and

(II) is written in a manner calculated to be understood by the average employee to whom the arrangement applies.

(ii) Timing and content requirements.—A notice shall not be treated as meeting the requirements of clause (i) with respect to an employee unless—

(I) the notice explains the employee's right under the arrangement to elect not to have elective contributions made on the employee's behalf (or to elect to have such contributions made at a different percentage),

(II) in the case of an arrangement under which the employee may elect among 2 or more investment options, the notice explains how contributions made under the arrangement will be invested in the absence of any investment election by the employee, and

(III) the employee has a reasonable period of time after receipt of the notice described in subclauses (I) and (II) and before the first elective contribution is made to make either such election.

(*l*) Permitted disparity in plan contributions or benefits.—

(1) In general.—The requirements of this subsection are met with respect to a plan if—

(A) in the case of a defined contribution plan, the requirements of paragraph (2) are met, and

(B) in the case of a defined benefit plan, the requirements of paragraph (3) are met.

(2) Defined contribution plan.—

(A) In general.—A defined contribution plan meets the requirements of this paragraph if the excess contribution percentage does not exceed the base contribution percentage by more than the lesser of—

(i) the base contribution percentage, or

(ii) the greater of—

(I) 5.7 percentage points, or

(II) the percentage equal to the portion of the rate of tax under section 3111(a) (in effect as of the beginning of the year) which is attributable to old-age insurance.

(B) Contribution percentages.—For purposes of this paragraph—

(i) Excess contribution percentage.—The term "excess contribution percentage" means the percentage of compensation which is contributed by the employer under the plan with respect to that portion of each participant's compensation in excess of the integration level.

(ii) Base contribution percentage.—The term "base contribution percentage" means the percentage of compensation contributed by the employer under the plan with respect to that portion of each participant's compensation not in excess of the integration level.

(3) Defined benefit plan.—A defined benefit plan meets the requirements of this paragraph if—

(A) Excess plans.—

(i) In general.—In the case of a plan other than an offset plan—

(I) the excess benefit percentage does not exceed the base benefit percentage by more than the maximum excess allowance,

(II) any optional form of benefit, preretirement benefit, actuarial factor, or other benefit or feature provided with respect to compensation in excess of the integration level is provided with respect to compensation not in excess of such level, and

(III) benefits are based on average annual compensation.

(ii) Benefit percentages.—For purposes of this subparagraph, the excess and base benefit percentages shall be computed in the same manner as the excess and base contribution percentages under paragraph (2)(B), except that such determination shall be made on the basis of benefits attributable to employer contributions rather than contributions.

(B) Offset plans.—In the case of an offset plan, the plan provides that—

(i) a participant's accrued benefit attributable to employer contributions (within the meaning of section 411(c)(1)) may not be reduced (by reason of the offset) by more than the maximum offset allowance, and

(ii) benefits are based on average annual compensation.

(4) Definitions relating to paragraph (3).—For purposes of paragraph (3)—

(A) Maximum excess allowance.—The maximum excess allowance is equal to—

(i) in the case of benefits attributable to any year of service with the employer taken into account under the plan, ¾ of a percentage point, and

(ii) in the case of total benefits, ¾ of a percentage point, multiplied by the participant's years of service (not in excess of 35) with the employer taken into account under the plan.

In no event shall the maximum excess allowance exceed the base benefit percentage.

(B) Maximum offset allowance.—The maximum offset allowance is equal to—

(i) in the case of benefits attributable to any year of service with the employer taken into account under the plan, ¾ percent of the participant's final average compensation, and

(ii) in the case of total benefits, ¾ percent of the participant's final average compensation, multiplied by the participant's years of service (not in excess of 35) with the employer taken into account under the plan.

In no event shall the maximum offset allowance exceed 50 percent of the benefit which would have accrued without regard to the offset reduction.

(C) Reductions.—

(i) In general.—The Secretary shall prescribe regulations requiring the reduction of the ¾ percentage factor under subparagraph (A) or (B)—

(I) in the case of a plan other than an offset plan which has an integration level in excess of covered compensation, or

(II) with respect to any participant in an offset plan who has final average compensation in excess of covered compensation.

(ii) Basis of reductions.—Any reductions under clause (i) shall be based on the percentages of compensation replaced by the employer-derived portions of primary insurance amounts under the Social Security Act for participants with compensation in excess of covered compensation.

(D) Offset plan.—The term "offset plan" means any plan with respect to which the benefit attributable to employer contributions for each participant is reduced by an amount specified in the plan.

(5) Other definitions and special rules.—For purposes of this subsection—

(A) Integration level.—

(i) In general.—The term "integration level" means the amount of compensation specified under the plan (by dollar amount or formula) at or below which the rate at which contributions or benefits are provided (expressed as a percentage) is less than such rate above such amount.

(ii) Limitation.—The integration level for any year may not exceed the contribution and benefit base in effect under section 230 of the Social Security Act for such year.

(iii) Level to apply to all participants.—A plan's integration level shall apply with respect to all participants in the plan.

(iv) Multiple integration levels.—Under rules prescribed by the Secretary, a defined benefit plan may specify multiple integration levels.

(B) Compensation.—The term "compensation" has the meaning given such term by section 414(s).

(C) Average annual compensation.—The term "average annual compensation" means the participant's highest average annual compensation for—

(i) any period of at least 3 consecutive years, or

(ii) if shorter, the participant's full period of service.

(D) Final average compensation.—

(i) In general.—The term "final average compensation" means the participant's average annual compensation for—

(I) the 3–consecutive year period ending with the current year, or

(II) if shorter, the participant's full period of service.

(ii) Limitation.—A participant's final average compensation shall be determined by not taking into account in any year compensation in excess of the contribution and benefit base in effect under section 230 of the Social Security Act for such year.

(E) Covered compensation.—

(i) In general.—The term "covered compensation" means, with respect to an employee, the average of the contribution and benefit bases in effect under section 230 of the Social Security Act for each year in the 35–year period ending with the year in which the employee attains the social security retirement age.

(ii) Computation for any year.—For purposes of clause (i), the determination for any year preceding the year in which the employee attains the social security retirement age shall be made by assuming that there is no increase in the bases described in clause (i) after the determination year and before the employee attains social security retirement age.

(iii) Social security retirement age.—For purposes of this subparagraph, the term "social security retirement age" has the meaning given such term by section 415(b)(8).

* * *

(m) Nondiscrimination test for matching contributions and employee contributions.—

(1) In general.—A defined contribution plan shall be treated as meeting the requirements of subsection (a)(4) with respect to the amount of any matching contribution or employee contribution for any plan year only if the contribution percentage requirement of paragraph (2) of this subsection is met for such plan year.

(2) Requirements.—

(A) Contribution percentage requirement.—A plan meets the contribution percentage requirement of this paragraph for any plan year only if the contribution percentage for eligible highly compensated employees for such plan year does not exceed the greater of—

(i) 125 percent of such percentage for all other eligible employees for the preceding plan year, or

(ii) the lesser of 200 percent of such percentage for all other eligible employees for the preceding plan year, or such percentage for all other eligible employees for the preceding plan year plus 2 percentage points.

This subparagraph may be applied by using the plan year rather than the preceding plan year if the employer so elects, except that if such an election is made, it may not be changed except as provided by the Secretary.

(B) Multiple plans treated as a single plan.—If two or more plans of an employer to which matching contributions, employee contributions, or elective deferrals are made are treated as one plan for purposes of section 410(b), such plans shall be treated as one plan for purposes of this subsection. If a highly compensated employee participates in two or more plans of an employer to which contributions to which this subsection applies are made, all such contributions shall be aggregated for purposes of this subsection.

(3) Contribution percentage.—For purposes of paragraph (2), the contribution percentage for a specified group of employees for a plan year shall be the average of the ratios (calculated separately for each employee in such group) of—

(A) the sum of the matching contributions and employee contributions paid under the plan on behalf of each such employee for such plan year, to

(B) the employee's compensation (within the meaning of section 414(s)) for such plan year.

Under regulations, an employer may elect to take into account (in computing the contribution percentage) elective deferrals and qualified nonelective contributions under the plan or any other plan of the employer. If matching contributions are taken into account for purposes of subsection (k)(3)(A)(ii) for any plan year, such contributions shall not be taken into account under subparagraph (A) for such year. Rules similar to the rules of subsection (k)(3)(E) shall apply for purposes of this subsection.

* * *

§ 402. Taxability of beneficiary of employees' trust

(a) Taxability of beneficiary of exempt trust.—Except as otherwise provided in this section, any amount actually distributed to any distributee by any employees' trust described in section 401(a) which is exempt from tax under section 501(a) shall be taxable to the distributee, in the taxable year of the distributee in which distributed, under section 72 (relating to annuities).

(b) Taxability of beneficiary of nonexempt trust.—

(1) Contributions.—Contributions to an employees' trust made by an employer during a taxable year of the employer which ends with or within a taxable year of the trust for which the trust is not exempt from tax under section 501(a) shall be included in the gross income of the employee in accordance with section 83 (relating to property transferred in connection with performance of services), except that the value of the employee's interest in the trust shall be substituted for the fair market value of the property for purposes of applying such section.

(2) Distributions.—The amount actually distributed or made available to any distributee by any trust described in paragraph (1) shall be taxable to the distributee, in the taxable year in which so distributed or made available, under section 72 (relating to annuities), except that distributions of income of such trust before the annuity starting date (as defined in section 72(c)(4)) shall be included in the gross income of the employee without regard to section 72(e)(5) (relating to amounts not received as annuities).

(3) Grantor trusts.—A beneficiary of any trust described in paragraph (1) shall not be considered the owner of any portion of such trust under subpart E of part I of subchapter J (relating to grantors and others treated as substantial owners).

(4) Failure to meet requirements of section 410(b).—

(A) Highly compensated employees.—If 1 of the reasons a trust is not exempt from tax under section 501(a) is the failure of the plan of which it is a part to meet the requirements of section 401(a)(26) or 410(b), then a highly compensated employee shall, in lieu of the amount determined under paragraph (1) or (2) include in gross income for the taxable year with or within which the taxable year of the trust ends an amount equal to the vested accrued benefit of such employee (other than the employee's investment in the contract) as of the close of such taxable year of the trust.

(B) Failure to meet coverage tests.—If a trust is not exempt from tax under section 501(a) for any taxable year solely because such trust is part of a plan which fails to meet the requirements of section 401(a)(26) or 410(b), paragraphs (1) and (2) shall not apply by reason of such failure to any employee who was not a highly compensated employee during—

(i) such taxable year, or

(ii) any preceding period for which service was creditable to such employee under the plan.

(C) Highly compensated employee.—For purposes of this paragraph, the term "highly compensated employee" has the meaning given such term by section 414(q).

(c) Rules applicable to rollovers from exempt trusts.—

(1) Exclusion from income.—If—

(A) any portion of the balance to the credit of an employee in a qualified trust is paid to the employee in an eligible rollover distribution,

(B) the distributee transfers any portion of the property received in such distribution to an eligible retirement plan, and

(C) in the case of a distribution of property other than money, the amount so transferred consists of the property distributed,

then such distribution (to the extent so transferred) shall not be includible in gross income for the taxable year in which paid.

(2) Maximum amount which may be rolled over.—In the case of any eligible rollover distribution, the maximum amount transferred to which paragraph (1) applies shall not exceed the portion of such distribution which is includible in gross income (determined without regard to paragraph (1)). The preceding sentence shall not apply to such distribution to the extent—

(A) such portion is transferred in a direct trustee-to-trustee transfer to a qualified trust or to an annuity contract described in section 403(b) and such trust or contract provides for separate accounting for amounts so transferred (and earnings hereon), including separately accounting for the portion of such distribution which is includible in gross income and the portion of such distribution which is not so includible, or

(B) such portion is transferred to an eligible retirement plan described in clause (i) or (ii) of paragraph (8)(B).

In the case of a transfer described in subparagraph (A) or (B), the amount transferred shall be treated as consisting first of the portion of such distribution that is includible in gross income (determined without regard to paragraph (1)).

(3) Transfer must be made with 60 days of receipt.—

(A) In general.—Except as provided in subparagraph (B), paragraph (1) shall not apply to any transfer of a distribution made after the 60th day following the day on which the distributee received the property distributed.

(B) Hardship exception.—The Secretary may waive the 60–day requirement under subparagraph (A) where the failure to waive such requirement would be against equity or good conscience, including casualty, disaster, or other event beyond the reasonable control of the individual subject to such requirement.

(4) Eligible rollover distribution.—For purposes of this subsection, the term "eligible rollover distribution" means any distribution to an employee of all or any portion of the balance to the credit of the employee in a qualified trust; except that such term shall not include—

(A) any distribution which is one of a series of substantially equal periodic payments (not less frequently than annually) made—

(i) for the life (or life expectancy) of the employee or the joint lives (or joint life expectancies) of the employee and the employee's designated beneficiary, or

(ii) for a specified period of 10 years or more,

(B) any distribution to the extent such distribution is required under section 401(a)(9), and

(C) any distribution which is made upon hardship of the employee.

If all or any portion of a distribution during 2009 is treated as an eligible rollover distribution but would not be so treated if the minimum distribution requirements under section 401(a)(9) had applied during 2009, such distribution shall not be treated as an eligible rollover distribution for purposes of section 401(a)(31) or 3405(c) or subsection (f) of this section.

(5) Transfer treated as rollover contribution under section 408.—For purposes of this title, a transfer to an eligible retirement plan described in clause (i)

or (ii) of paragraph (8)(B) resulting in any portion of a distribution being excluded from gross income under paragraph (1) shall be treated as a rollover contribution described in section 408(d)(3).

* * *

(8) Definitions.—For purposes of this subsection—

(A) Qualified trust.—The term "qualified trust" means an employees' trust described in section 401(a) which is exempt from tax under section 501(a).

(B) Eligible retirement plan.—The term "eligible retirement plan" means—

(i) an individual retirement account described in section 408(a),

(ii) an individual retirement annuity described in section 408(b) (other than an endowment contract),

(iii) a qualified trust,

(iv) an annuity plan described in section 403(a),

* * *

(vi) an annuity contract described in section 403(b).

If any portion of an eligible rollover distribution is attributable to payments or distributions from a designated Roth account (as defined in section 402A), an eligible retirement plan with respect to such portion shall include only another designated Roth account and a Roth IRA.

(9) Rollover where spouse receives distribution after death of employee.—If any distribution attributable to an employee is paid to the spouse of the employee after the employee's death, the preceding provisions of this subsection shall apply to such distribution in the same manner as if the spouse were the employee.

* * *

(11) Distributions to inherited individual retirement plan of nonspouse beneficiary.—

(A) In general.—If, with respect to any portion of a distribution from an eligible retirement plan described in paragraph (8)(B)(iii) of a deceased employee, a direct trustee-to-trustee transfer is made to an individual retirement plan described in clause (i) or (ii) of paragraph (8)(B) established for the purposes of receiving the distribution on behalf of an individual who is a designated beneficiary (as defined by section 401(a)(9)(E)) of the employee and who is not the surviving spouse of the employee—

(i) the transfer shall be treated as an eligible rollover distribution,

(ii) the individual retirement plan shall be treated as an inherited individual retirement account or individual retirement annuity (within the meaning of section 408(d)(3)(C)) for purposes of this title, and

(iii) section 401(a)(9)(B) (other than clause (iv) thereof) shall apply to such plan.

(B) Certain trusts treated as beneficiaries.—For purposes of this paragraph, to the extent provided in rules prescribed by the Secretary, a trust maintained for the benefit of one or more designated beneficiaries shall be treated in the same manner as a designated beneficiary.

* * *

(e) Other rules applicable to exempt trusts.—

(1) Alternate payees.—

(A) Alternate payee treated as distributee.—For purposes of subsection (a) and section 72, an alternate payee who is the spouse or former spouse of the participant shall be treated as the distributee of any distribution or payment made to the alternate payee under a qualified domestic relations order (as defined in section 414(p)).

(B) Rollovers.—If any amount is paid or distributed to an alternate payee who is the spouse or former spouse of the participant by reason of any qualified domestic relations order (within the meaning of section 414(p)), subsection (c) shall apply to such distribution in the same manner as if such alternate payee were the employee.

* * *

(3) Cash or deferred arrangements.—For purposes of this title, contributions made by an employer on behalf of an employee to a trust which is a part of a qualified cash or deferred arrangement (as defined in section 401(k)(2)) or which is part of a salary reduction agreement under section 403(b) shall not be treated as distributed or made available to the employee nor as contributions made to the trust by the employee merely because the arrangement includes provisions under which the employee has an election whether the contribution will be made to the trust or received by the employee in cash.

* * *

(g) Limitation on exclusion for elective deferrals.—

(1) In general.—

(A) Limitation.—Notwithstanding subsections (e)(3) and (h)(1)(B), the elective deferrals of any individual for any taxable year shall be included in such individual's gross income to the extent the amount of such deferrals for the taxable year exceeds the applicable dollar amount. The preceding sentence shall not apply the portion of such excess as does exceed the designated Roth contributions of the individual for the taxable year.

(B) Applicable dollar amount.—For purposes of subparagraph (A), the applicable dollar amount shall be the amount determined in accordance with the following table:

For taxable years beginning in: calendar year:	The applicable dollar amount is:
2002	$11,000
2003	$12,000
2004	$13,000
2005	$14,000
2006 or thereafter	$15,000

(C) Catch-up contributions.—In addition to subparagraph (A), in the case of an eligible participant (as defined in section 414(v)), gross income shall not include elective deferrals in excess of the applicable dollar amount under subparagraph (B) to the extent that the amount of such elective deferrals does not exceed the applicable dollar amount under section 414(v)(2)(B)(i) for the taxable year (without regard to the treatment of the elective deferrals by an applicable employer under section 414(v)).

* * *

(4) Cost-of-living adjustment.—In the case of taxable years beginning after December 31, 2006, the Secretary shall adjust the $15,000 amount under (1)(B) at the same time and in the same manner as under section 415(d) * * *.

* * *

(5) Disregard of community property laws.—This subsection shall be applied without regard to community property laws.

(6) Coordination with section 72.—For purposes of applying section 72, any amount includible in gross income for any taxable year under this subsection but which is not distributed from the plan during such taxable year shall not be treated as investment in the contract.

* * *

(i) Treatment of self-employed individuals.—For purposes of this section, except as otherwise provided in subparagraph (A) of subsection (d)(4), the term "employee" includes a self-employed individual (as defined in section 401(c)(1)(B)) and the employer of such individual shall be the person treated as his employer under section 401(c)(4).

* * *

(k) Treatment of simple retirement accounts.—Rules similar to the rules of paragraphs (1) and (3) of subsection (h) shall apply to contributions and distributions with respect to a simple retirement account under section 408(p).

* * *

§ 402A. Optional treatment of elective deferrals as Roth contributions

(a) General rule.—If an applicable retirement plan includes a qualified Roth contribution program—

(1) any designated Roth contribution made by an employee pursuant to the program shall be treated as an elective deferral for purposes of this chapter, except that such contribution shall not be excludable from gross income, and

(2) such plan (and any arrangement which is part of such plan) shall not be treated as failing to meet any requirement of this chapter solely by reason of including such program.

(b) Qualified Roth contribution program.—For purposes of this section—

(1) In general.—The term "qualified Roth contribution program" means a program under which an employee may elect to make designated Roth contributions in lieu of all or a portion of elective deferrals the employee is otherwise eligible to make under the applicable retirement plan.

(2) Separate accounting required.—A program shall not be treated as a qualified Roth contribution program unless the applicable retirement plan–

(A) establishes separate accounts ("designated Roth accounts") for the designated Roth contributions of each employee and any earnings properly allocable to the contributions, and

(B) maintains separate recordkeeping with respect to each account.—

(c) Definitions and rules relating to designated Roth contributions.—For purposes of this section—

(1) Designated Roth contribution.—The term "designated Roth contribution" means any elective deferral which–

(A) is excludable from gross income of an employee without regard to this section, and

(B) the employee designates (at such time and in such manner as the Secretary may prescribe) as not being so excludable.

(2) Designation limits.—The amount of elective deferrals which an employee may designate under paragraph (1) shall not exceed the excess (if any) of—

(A) the maximum amount of elective deferrals excludable from gross income of the employee for the taxable year (without regard to this section), over

(B) the aggregate amount of elective deferrals of the employee for the taxable year which the employee does not designate under paragraph (1).

(3) Rollover contributions.—

(A) In general.—A rollover contribution of any payment or distribution from a designated Roth account which is otherwise allowable under this chapter may be made only if the contribution is to—

(i) another designated Roth account of the individual from whose account the payment or distribution was made, or

(ii) a Roth IRA of such individual.

(B) Coordination with limit.—Any rollover contribution to a designated Roth account under subparagraph (A) shall not be taken into account for purposes of paragraph (1).

(4) Taxable rollovers to designated Roth accounts.—

(A) In general.—Notwithstanding sections 402(c), 403(b)(8), and 457(e)(16), in the case of any distribution to which this paragraph applies—

(i) there shall be included in gross income any amount which would be includible were it not part of a qualified rollover contribution,

(ii) section 72(t) shall not apply, and

(iii) unless the taxpayer elects not to have this clause apply, any amount required to be included in gross income for any taxable year beginning in 2010 by reason of this paragraph shall be so included ratably over the 2-taxable-year period beginning with the first taxable year beginning in 2011.

Any election under clause (iii) for any distributions during a taxable year may not be changed after the due date for such taxable year.

(B) Distributions to which paragraph applies.—In the case of an applicable retirement plan which includes a qualified Roth contribution program, this paragraph shall apply to a distribution from such plan other than from a designated Roth account which is contributed in a qualified rollover contribution (within the meaning of section 408A(e)) to the designated Roth account maintained under such plan for the benefit of the individual to whom the distribution is made.

(C) Coordination with limit.—Any distribution to which this paragraph applies shall not be taken into account for purposes of paragraph (1).

(D) Other rules.—The rules of subparagraphs (D), (E), and (F) of section 408A(d)(3) (as in effect for taxable years beginning after 2009) shall apply for purposes of this paragraph.

(E) Special rule for certain transfers.—In the case of an applicable retirement plan which includes a qualified Roth contribution program—

(i) the plan may allow an individual to elect to have the plan transfer any amount not otherwise distributable under the plan to a designated Roth account maintained for the benefit of the individual,

(ii) such transfer shall be treated as a distribution to which this paragraph applies which was contributed in a qualified rollover contribution (within the meaning of section 408A(e)) to such account, and

(iii) the plan shall not be treated as violating the provisions of section 401(k)(2)(B)(i), 403(b)(7)(A)(i), 403(b)(11), or 457(d)(1)(A), or of section 8433 of title 5, United States Code, solely by reason of such transfer.

(d) Distribution rules.—For purposes of this title—

(1) Exclusion.—Any qualified distribution from a designated Roth account shall not be includible in gross income.

(2) Qualified distribution.—For purposes of this subsection—

(A) In general.—The term "qualified distribution" has the meaning given such term by section 408A(d)(2)(A) (without regard to clause (iv) thereof).

(B) Distributions within nonexclusion period.—A payment or distribution from a designated Roth account shall not be treated as a qualified distribution if such payment or distribution is made within the 5–taxable-year period beginning with the earlier of—

(i) the first taxable year for which the individual made a designated Roth contribution to any designated Roth account established for such individual under the same applicable retirement plan, or

(ii) if a rollover contribution was made to such designated Roth account from a designated Roth account previously established for such individual under another applicable retirement plan, the first taxable year for which the individual made a designated Roth contribution to such previously established account.

(C) Distributions of excess deferrals and contributions and earnings thereon.— The term "qualified distribution" shall not include any distribution of any excess deferral under section 402(g)(2) or any excess contribution under section 401(k)(8), and any income on the excess deferral or contribution.

(3) Treatment of distributions of certain excess deferrals.—Notwithstanding section 72, if any excess deferral under section 402(g)(2) attributable to a designated Roth contribution is not distributed on or before the 1st April 15 following the close of the taxable year in which such excess deferral is made, the amount of such excess deferral shall—

(A) not be treated as investment in the contract, and

(B) be included in gross income for the taxable year in which such excess is distributed.

(4) Aggregation rules.—Section 72 shall be applied separately with respect to distributions and payments from a designated Roth account and other distributions and payments from the plan.

(e) Other definitions.—For purposes of this section—

(1) Applicable retirement plan.—The term "applicable retirement plan" means—

(A) an employees' trust described in section 401(a) which is exempt from tax under section 501(a),

(B) a plan under which amounts are contributed by an individual's employer for an annuity contract described in section 403(b), and

(C) an eligible deferred compensation plan (as defined in section 457(b)) of an eligible employer described in section 457(e)(1)(A).

(2) Elective deferral.—The term "elective deferral" means—

(A) any elective deferral described in subparagraph (A) or (C) of section 402(g)(3), and

(B) any elective deferral of compensation by an individual under an eligible deferred compensation plan (as defined in section 457(b)) of an eligible employer described in section 457(e)(1)(A).

§ 403. Taxation of employee annuities

(a) Taxability of beneficiary under a qualified annuity plan.—

(1) Distributee taxable under section 72.—If an annuity contract is purchased by an employer for an employee under a plan which meets the requirements of section 404(a)(2) (whether or not the employer deducts the amounts paid for the contract under such section), the amount actually distributed to any distributee under the contract shall be taxable to the distributee (in the year in which so distributed) under section 72 (relating to annuities).

* * *

(3) Self-employed individuals.—For purposes of this subsection, the term "employee" includes an individual who is an employee within the meaning of section 401(c)(1), and the employer of such individual is the person treated as his employer under section 401(c)(4).

(4) Rollover amounts.—

(A) General rule.—If—

(i) any portion of the balance to the credit of an employee in an employee annuity described in paragraph (1) is paid to him in an eligible rollover distribution (within the meaning of section 402(c)(4)),

(ii) the employee transfers any portion of the property he receives in such distribution to an eligible retirement plan, and

(iii) in the case of a distribution of property other than money, the amount so transferred consists of the property distributed,

then such distribution (to the extent so transferred) shall not be includible in gross income for the taxable year in which paid.

(B) Certain rules made applicable.—The rules of paragraphs (2) through (7) and (11) and (9) of section 402(c) and section 402(f) shall apply for purposes of subparagraph (A).

(5) Direct trustee-to-trustee transfer.—Any amount transferred in a direct trustee-to-trustee transfer in accordance with section 401(a)(31) shall not be includible in gross income for the taxable year of such transfer.

(b) Taxability of beneficiary under annuity purchased by section 501(c)(3) organization or public school.—

(1) General rule.—If—

(A) an annuity contract is purchased—

(i) for an employee by an employer described in section 501(c)(3) which is exempt from tax under section 501(a),

(ii) for an employee (other than an employee described in clause (i)), who performs services for an educational organization described in section 170(b)(1)(A)(ii), by an employer which is a State, a political subdivision of a State, or an agency or instrumentality of any one or more of the foregoing, or

* * *

(B) such annuity contract is not subject to subsection (a),

(C) the employee's rights under the contract are nonforfeitable, except for failure to pay future premiums,

* * *

(E) in the case of a contract purchased under a salary reduction agreement, the contract meets the requirements of section 401(a)(30),

then contributions and other additions by such employer for such annuity contract shall be excluded from the gross income of the employee for the taxable year to the extent that the aggregate of such contributions and additions (when expressed as an annual addition (within the meaning of section 415(c)(2))) does not exceed the applicable limit under section 415. The amount actually distributed to any distributee under such contract shall be taxable to the distributee (in the year in which so distributed) under section 72 (relating to annuities). For purposes of applying the rules of this subsection to contributions and other additions by an employer for a taxable year, amounts transferred to a contract described in this paragraph by reason of a rollover contribution described in paragraph (8) of this subsection or section 408(d)(3)(A)(ii) shall not be considered contributed by such employer.

* * *

(c) Taxability of beneficiary under nonqualified annuities or under annuities purchased by exempt organizations.—Premiums paid by an employer for an annuity contract which is not subject to subsection (a) shall be included in the gross income of the employee in accordance with section 83 (relating to property transferred in connection with performance of services), except that the value of such contract shall be substituted for the fair market value of the property for purposes of applying such section. The preceding sentence shall not apply to that portion of the premiums paid which is excluded from gross income under subsection (b). In the case of any portion of any contract which is attributable to premiums to which this subsection applies, the amount actually paid or made available under such contract to any beneficiary which is attributable to such premiums shall be taxable to the beneficiary (in the year in which so paid or made available) under section 72 (relating to annuities).

§ 404. Deduction for contributions of an employer to an employees' trust or annuity plan and compensation under a deferred-payment plan

(a) General rule.—If contributions are paid by an employer to or under a stock bonus, pension, profit-sharing, or annuity plan, or if compensation is paid or accrued on account of any employee under a plan deferring the receipt of such compensation, such contributions or compensation shall not be deductible under this chapter; but, if they would otherwise be deductible, they shall be deductible under this section, subject, however, to the following limitations as to the amounts deductible in any year:

(1) Pension trusts.—

(A) In general.—In the taxable year when paid, if the contributions are paid into a pension trust (other than a trust to which paragraph (3) applies), and if such taxable year ends within or with a taxable year of the trust for which the trust is exempt under section 501(a), * * * in an amount determined as follows:

(i) the amount necessary to satisfy the minimum funding standard provided by section 412(a) for plan years ending within or with such taxable year (or for any prior plan year), if such amount is greater than the amount determined under clause (ii) or (iii) (whichever is applicable with respect to the plan),

(ii) the amount necessary to provide with respect to all of the employees under the trust the remaining unfunded cost of their past and current service credits distributed as a level amount, or a level percentage of compensation, over the remaining future service of each such employee, as determined under regulations prescribed by the Secretary, but if such remaining unfunded cost with respect to any 3 individuals is more than 50 percent of such remaining unfunded cost, the amount of such unfunded cost attributable to such individuals shall be distributed over a period of at least 5 taxable years,

(iii) an amount equal to the normal cost of the plan, as determined under regulations prescribed by the Secretary, plus, if past service or other supplementary pension or annuity credits are provided by the plan, an amount necessary to amortize the unfunded costs attributable to such credits in equal annual payments (until fully amortized) over 10 years, as determined under regulations prescribed by the Secretary.

In determining the amount deductible in such year under the foregoing limitations the funding method and the actuarial assumptions used shall be those used for such year under section 431, and the maximum amount deductible for such year shall be an amount equal to the full funding limitation for such year determined under section 431.

* * *

(2) Employees' annuities.—In the taxable year when paid, in an amount determined in accordance with paragraph (1), if the contributions are paid toward the purchase of retirement annuities, or retirement annuities and medical benefits as described in section 401(h), and such purchase is a part of a plan which meets the requirements of section 401(a)(3), (4), (5), (6), (7), (8), (9), (11), (12), (13), (14), (15), (16), (17), (19), (20), (22), (26), (27), (31), and (37) and, if applicable, the requirements of section 401(a)(10) and of section 401(d), and if refunds of premiums, if any, are applied within the current taxable year or next succeeding taxable year towards the purchase of such retirement annuities, or such retirement annuities and medical benefits.

(3) Stock bonus and profit-sharing trusts.—

(A) Limits on deductible contributions.—

(i) In general.—In the taxable year when paid, if the contributions are paid into a stock bonus or profit-sharing trust, and if such taxable year ends within or with a taxable year of the trust with respect to which the trust is exempt under section 501(a), in an amount not in excess of the greater of—

(I) 25 percent of the compensation otherwise paid or accrued during the taxable year to the beneficiaries under the stock bonus or profit-sharing plan, or

(II) the amount such employer is required to contribute to such trust under section 401(k)(11) for such year.

(ii) Carryover of excess contributions.—Any amount paid into the trust in any taxable year in excess of the limitation of clause (i) (or the corresponding provision of prior law) shall be deductible in the succeeding taxable years in order of time, but the amount so deductible under this clause in any 1 such succeeding taxable year together with the amount allowable under clause (i) shall not exceed the amount described in subclause (I) or (II) of clause (i), whichever is greater, with respect to such taxable year.

(iii) Certain retirement plans excluded.—For purposes of this subparagraph, the term "stock bonus or profit-sharing trust" shall not include any trust designed to provided benefits upon retirement and covering a period of years, if under the plan the amounts to be contributed by the employer can be determined actuarially as provided in paragraph (1).

(iv) 2 or more trusts treated as 1 trust.—If the contributions are made to 2 or more stock bonus or profit-sharing trusts, such trusts shall be considered a single trust for purposes of applying the limitations in this subparagraph.

(v) Defined contribution plan subject to the funding standards.—Except as provided by the Secretary, a defined contribution plan which is subject to the funding standards of section 412 shall be treated in the same manner as a stock bonus or profit-sharing plan for purposes of this subparagraph.

* * *

(5) Other plans.—If the plan is not one included in paragraph (1), (2), or (3), in the taxable year in which an amount attributable to the contribution is includible in the gross income of employees participating in the plan, but, in the case of a plan in which more than one employee participates only if separate accounts are maintained for each employee. For purposes of this section, any vacation pay which is treated as deferred compensation shall be deductible for the taxable year of the employer in which paid to the employee.

* * *

(7) Limitation on deductions where combination of defined contribution plan and defined benefit plan.—

(A) In general.—If amounts are deductible under the foregoing paragraphs of this subsection (other than paragraph (5)) in connection with 1 or more defined contribution plans and 1 or more defined benefit plans, or in connection with trusts or plans described in 2 or more of such paragraphs, the total amount deductible in a taxable year under such plans shall not exceed the greater of—

(i) 25 percent of the compensation otherwise paid or accrued during the taxable year to the beneficiaries under such plans, or

(ii) the amount of contributions made to or under the defined benefit plans to the extent such contributions do not exceed the amount of employer contributions necessary to satisfy the minimum funding standard provided by section 412 with respect to any such defined benefit plans for the plan year which ends with or within such taxable year (or for any prior plan year).

A defined contribution plan which is a pension plan shall not be treated as failing to provide definitely determinable benefits merely by limiting employer contributions to amounts deductible under this section. * * *

(B) Carryover of contributions in excess of the deductible limit.—Any amount paid under the plans in any taxable year in excess of the limitation of subparagraph (A) shall be deductible in the succeeding taxable years in order of time, but the amount so deductible under this subparagraph in any 1 such succeeding taxable year together with the amount allowable under subparagraph (A) shall not exceed 25 percent of the compensation otherwise paid or accrued during such taxable year to the beneficiaries under the plans.

(C) Paragraph not to apply in certain cases.—

(i) Beneficiary test.—This paragraph shall not have the effect of reducing the amount otherwise deductible under paragraphs (1), (2), and (3), if no employee is a beneficiary under more than 1 trust or under a trust and an annuity plan.

(ii) Elective deferrals.—If, in connection with 1 or more defined contribution plans and 1 or more defined benefit plans, no amounts (other than elective deferrals (as defined in section 402(g)(3))) are contributed to any of the defined contribution plans for the taxable year, then subparagraph (A) shall not apply with respect to any of such defined contribution plans and defined benefit plans.

* * *

(8) Self-employed individuals.—In the case of a plan included in paragraph (1), (2), or (3) which provides contributions or benefits for employees some or all of whom are employees within the meaning of section 401(c)(1), for purposes of this section—

(A) the term "employee" includes an individual who is an employee within the meaning of section 401(c)(1), and the employer of such individual is the person treated as his employer under section 401(c)(4);

(B) the term "earned income" has the meaning assigned to it by section 401(c)(2);

(C) the contributions to such plan on behalf of an individual who is an employee within the meaning of section 401(c)(1) shall be considered to satisfy the conditions of section 162 or 212 to the extent that such contributions do not exceed the earned income of such individual (determined without regard to the deductions allowed by this section) derived from the trade or business with respect to which such plan is established, and to the extent that such contributions are not allocable (determined in accordance with regulations prescribed by the Secretary) to the purchase of life, accident, health, or other insurance; and

(D) any reference to compensation shall, in the case of an individual who is an employee within the meaning of section 401(c)(1), be considered to be a reference to the earned income of such individual derived from the trade or business with respect to which the plan is established.

* * *

(11) Determinations relating to deferred compensation.—For purposes of determining under this section—

(A) whether compensation of an employee is deferred compensation; and

(B) when deferred compensation is paid,

no amount shall be treated as received by the employee, or paid, until it is actually received by the employee.

* * *

(b) Method of contributions, etc., having the effect of a plan; certain deferred benefits.—

(1) Method of contributions, etc., having the effect of a plan.—If—

(A) there is no plan, but

(B) there is a method or arrangement of employer contributions or compensation which has the effect of a stock bonus, pension, profit-sharing, or annuity plan, or other plan deferring the receipt of compensation (including a plan described in paragraph (2)),

subsection (a) shall apply as if there were such a plan.

(2) Plans providing certain deferred benefits.—

(A) In general.—For purposes of this section, any plan providing for deferred benefits (other than compensation) for employees, their spouses, or their dependents shall be treated as a plan deferring the receipt of compensation. In the case of such a plan, for purposes of this section, the determination of when an amount is includible in gross income shall be made without regard to any provisions of this chapter excluding such benefits from gross income.

(B) Exception.—Subparagraph (A) shall not apply to any benefit provided through a welfare benefit fund (as defined in section 419(e)).

* * *

(d) Deductibility of payments of deferred compensation, etc., to independent contractors.—If a plan would be described in so much of subsection (a) as precedes paragraph (1) thereof (as modified by subsection (b)) but for the fact that there is no employer-employee relationship, the contributions or compensation—

(1) shall not be deductible by the payor thereof under this chapter, but

(2) shall (if they would be deductible under this chapter but for paragraph (1)) be deductible under this subsection for the taxable year in which an amount attributable to the contribution or compensation is includible in the gross income of the persons participating in the plan.

* * *

(j) Special rules relating to application with section 415.—

(1) No deduction in excess of section 415 limitation.—In computing the amount of any deduction allowable under paragraph (1), (2), (3), (4), (7), or (9) of subsection (a) for any year—

(A) in the case of a defined benefit plan, there shall not be taken into account any benefits for any year in excess of any limitation on such benefits under section 415 for such year, or

(B) in the case of a defined contribution plan, the amount of any contributions otherwise taken into account shall be reduced by any annual additions in excess of the limitation under section 415 for such year.

(2) No advance funding of cost-of-living adjustments.—For purposes of clause (i), (ii) or (iii) of subsection (a)(1)(A), and in computing the full funding limitation, there shall not be taken into account any adjustments under section 415(d)(1) for any year before the year for which such adjustment first takes effect.

* * *

(*l*) Limitation on amount of annual compensation taken into account.—For purposes of applying the limitations of this section, the amount of annual compensation of each employee taken into account under the plan for any year shall not exceed $200,000. The Secretary shall adjust the $200,000 amount at the same time and in the same manner as under section 401(a)(17)(B). For purposes of clause (i), (ii), or (iii) of subsection (a)(1)(A), and in computing the full funding limitation, any adjustment under the preceding sentence shall not be taken into account for any year before the year for which such adjustment first takes effect.

(m) Special rules for simple retirement accounts.—

(1) In general.—Employer contributions to a simple retirement account shall be treated as if they are made to a plan subject to the requirements of this section.

(2) Timing.—

(A) Deduction.—Contributions described in paragraph (1) shall be deductible in the taxable year of the employer with or within which the calendar year for which the contributions were made ends.

(B) Contributions after end of year.—For purposes of this subsection, contributions shall be treated as made for a taxable year if they are made on account of the taxable year and are made not later than the time prescribed by law for filing the return for the taxable year (including extensions thereof).

(n) Elective deferrals not taken into account for purposes of deduction limits.—Elective deferrals (as defined in section 402(g)(3)) shall not be subject to any limitation contained in paragraph (3), (7), or (9) of subsection (a) or paragraph (1)(C) of subsection (h), and such elective deferrals shall not be taken into account in applying any such limitation to any other contributions.

* * *

§ 408. Individual retirement accounts

(a) Individual retirement account.—For purposes of this section, the term "individual retirement account" means a trust created or organized in the United States for the exclusive benefit of an individual or his beneficiaries, but only if the written governing instrument creating the trust meets the following requirements:

(1) Except in the case of a rollover contribution described in subsection (d)(3), in section 402(c), 403(a)(4), 403(b)(8), or 457(e)(16), no contribution will be accepted unless it is in cash, and contributions will not be accepted for the taxable year on behalf of any individual in excess of the amount in effect for such taxable year under section 219(b)(1)(A).

(2) The trustee is a bank (as defined in subsection (n)) or such other person who demonstrates to the satisfaction of the Secretary that the manner in which such other person will administer the trust will be consistent with the requirements of this section.

(3) No part of the trust funds will be invested in life insurance contracts.

(4) The interest of an individual in the balance in his account is nonforfeitable.

(5) The assets of the trust will not be commingled with other property except in a common trust fund or common investment fund.

(6) Under regulations prescribed by the Secretary, rules similar to the rules of section 401(a)(9) and the incidental death benefit requirements of section 401(a) shall apply to the distribution of the entire interest of an individual for whose benefit the trust is maintained.

* * *

(d) Tax treatment of distributions.—

(1) In general.—Except as otherwise provided in this subsection, any amount paid or distributed out of an individual retirement plan shall be included in gross income by the payee or distributee, as the case may be, in the manner provided under section 72.

(2) Special rules for applying section 72.—For purposes of applying section 72 to any amount described in paragraph (1)—

(A) all individual retirement plans shall be treated as 1 contract,

(B) all distributions during any taxable year shall be treated as 1 distribution, and

(C) the value of the contract, income on the contract, and investment in the contract shall be computed as of the close of the calendar year in which the taxable year begins.

For purposes of subparagraph (C), the value of the contract shall be increased by the amount of any distributions during the calendar year.

(3) Rollover contribution.—An amount is described in this paragraph as a rollover contribution if it meets the requirements of subparagraphs (A) and (B).

(A) In general.—Paragraph (1) does not apply to any amount paid or distributed out of an individual retirement account or individual retirement annuity to the individual for whose benefit the account or annuity is maintained if—

(i) the entire amount received (including money and any other property) is paid into an individual retirement account or individual retirement annuity (other than an endowment contract) for the benefit of such individual not later than the 60th day after the day on which he receives the payment or distribution; or

(ii) the entire amount received (including money and any other property) is paid into an eligible retirement plan for the benefit of such individual not later than the 60th day after the date on which the payment or distribution is received, except that the maximum amount which may be paid into such plan may not exceed the portion of the amount received which is includible in gross income (determined without regard to this paragraph).

For purposes of (ii), the term "eligible retirement plan" means an eligible retirement plan described in clause (iii), (iv), or (vi) of section 402(c)(8)(B).

(B) Limitation.—This paragraph does not apply to any amount described in subparagraph (A)(i) received by an individual from an individual retirement account, or individual retirement annuity if at any time during the 1-year period ending on the day of such receipt such individual received any other amount described in that subparagraph from an individual retirement account, or an individual retirement annuity which was not includible in his gross income because of the application of this paragraph.

(C) Denial of rollover treatment for inherited accounts, etc.—

(i) In general.—In the case of an inherited individual retirement account or individual retirement annuity—

(I) this paragraph shall not apply to any amount received by an individual from such an account or annuity (and no amount transferred from such account or annuity to another individual retirement account or annuity shall be excluded from gross income by reason of such transfer), and

(II) such inherited account or annuity shall not be treated as an individual retirement account or annuity for purposes of determining whether any other amount is a rollover contribution.

(ii) Inherited individual retirement account or annuity.—An individual retirement account or individual retirement annuity shall be treated as inherited if—

(I) the individual for whose benefit the account or annuity is maintained acquired such account by reason of a death of another individual, and

(II) such individual was not the surviving spouse of such other individual.

* * *

(G) Simple retirement accounts.—In the case of any payment or distribution out of a simple retirement account (as defined in subsection (p)) to which section 72(t)(6) applies, this paragraph shall not apply unless such payment or distribution is paid into another simple retirement account.

(H) Application of section 72.—

(i) In general.—If—

(I) a distribution is made from an individual retirement plan, and

(II) a rollover contribution is made to an eligible retirement plan described in section 402(c)(8)(B)(iii), (iv), (v), or (vi) with respect to all or part of such distribution,

then, notwithstanding paragraph (2), the rules of clause (ii) shall apply for purposes of applying section 72.

(ii) Applicable rules.—In the case of a distribution described in clause (i)—

(I) section 72 shall be applied separately to such distribution,

(II) notwithstanding the pro rata allocation of income on, and investment in, the contract to distributions under section 72, the portion of such distribution rolled over to an eligible retirement plan described in clause (i) shall be treated as from income on the contract (to the extent of the aggregate income on the contract from all individual retirement plans of the distributee), and

(III) appropriate adjustments shall be made in applying section 72 to other distributions in such taxable year and subsequent taxable years.

(I) Waiver of 60-day requirement.—The Secretary may waive the 60-day requirement under subparagraphs (A) and (D) where the failure to waive such requirement would be against equity or good conscience, including casualty, disaster, or other events beyond the reasonable control of the individual subject to such requirement.

* * *

(6) Transfer of account incident to divorce.—The transfer of an individual's interest in an individual retirement account or an individual retirement annuity to his spouse or former spouse under a divorce or separation instrument described in subparagraph (A) of section 71(b)(2) is not to be considered a taxable transfer made by such individual notwithstanding any other provision of this subtitle, and such interest at the time of the transfer is to be treated as an individual retirement account of such spouse, and not of such individual. Thereafter such account or annuity for purposes of this subtitle is to be treated as maintained for the benefit of such spouse.

* * *

(8) Distributions for charitable purposes.—

(A) In general.—So much of the aggregate amount of qualified charitable distributions with respect to a taxpayer made during any taxable year which does not exceed $100,000 shall not be includible in gross income of such taxpayer for such taxable year.

(B) Qualified charitable distribution.—For purposes of this paragraph, the term "qualified charitable distribution" means any distribution from an individual retirement plan (other than a plan described in subsection (k) or (p))—

(i) which is made directly by the trustee to an organization described in section 170(b)(1)(A) (other than any organization described in section 509(a)(3) or any fund or account described in section 4966(d)(2)), and

(ii) which is made on or after the date that the individual for whose benefit the plan is maintained has attained age 70 1/2.

A distribution shall be treated as a qualified charitable distribution only to the extent that the distribution would be includible in gross income without regard to subparagraph (A).

(C) Contributions must be otherwise deductible.—For purposes of this paragraph, a distribution to an organization described in subparagraph (B)(i) shall be treated as a qualified charitable distribution only if a deduction for the entire distribution would be allowable under section 170 (determined without regard to subsection (b) thereof and this paragraph).

(D) Application of section 72.—Notwithstanding section 72, in determining the extent to which a distribution is a qualified charitable distribution, the entire amount of the distribution shall be treated as includible in gross income without regard to subparagraph (A) to the extent that such amount does not exceed the aggregate amount which would have been so includible if all amounts in all individual retirement plans of the individual were distributed during such taxable year and all such plans were treated as 1 contract for purposes of determining under section 72 the aggregate amount which would have been so includible. Proper adjustments shall be made in applying section 72 to other distributions in such taxable year and subsequent taxable years.

(E) Denial of deduction.—Qualified charitable distributions which are not includible in gross income pursuant to subparagraph (A) shall not be taken into account in determining the deduction under section 170.

(F) Termination.—This paragraph shall not apply to distributions made in taxable years beginning after December 31, 2013.

* * *

(e) Tax treatment of accounts and annuities.—

(1) Exemption from tax.—Any individual retirement account is exempt from taxation under this subtitle unless such account has ceased to be an individual retirement account by reason of paragraph (2) or (3). Notwithstanding the preceding sentence, any such account is subject to the taxes imposed by section 511 (relating to imposition of tax on unrelated business income of charitable, etc. organizations).

* * *

(i) Reports.—The trustee of an individual retirement account and the issuer of an endowment contract described in subsection (b) or an individual retirement annuity shall make such reports regarding such account, contract, or annuity to the Secretary and to the individuals for whom the account, contract, or annuity is, or is to be, maintained with respect to contributions (and the years to which they relate), distributions aggregating $10 or more in any calendar year, and such other matters as the Secretary may require. The reports required by this subsection—

(1) shall be filed at such time and in such manner as the Secretary prescribes, and

(2) shall be furnished to individuals—

(A) not later than January 31 of the calendar year following the calendar year to which such reports relate, and

(B) in such manner as the Secretary prescribes.

In the case of a simple retirement account under subsection (p), only one report under this subsection shall be required to be submitted each calendar year to the Secretary (at the time provided under paragraph (2)) but, in addition to the report under this subsection, there shall be furnished, within 31 days after each calendar year, to the individual on whose behalf the account is maintained a statement with respect to the account balance as of the close of, and the account activity during, such calendar year.

(j) Increase in maximum limitations for simplified employee pensions.—In the case of any simplified employee pension, subsections (a)(1) and (b)(2) of this section shall be applied by increasing the amounts contained therein by the amount of the limitation in effect under section 415(c)(1)(A).

(k) Simplified employee pension defined.—

(1) In general.—For purposes of this title, the term "simplified employee pension" means an individual retirement account or individual retirement annuity—

(A) with respect to which the requirements of paragraphs (2), (3), (4), and (5) of this subsection are met, and

(B) if such account or annuity is part of a top-heavy plan (as defined in section 416), with respect to which the requirements of section 416(c)(2) are met.

(2) Participation requirements.—This paragraph is satisfied with respect to a simplified employee pension for a year only if for such year the employer contributes to the simplified employee pension of each employee who—

(A) has attained age 21,

(B) has performed service for the employer during at least 3 of the immediately preceding 5 years, and

(C) received at least $450 in compensation (within the meaning of section 414(q)(4)) from the employer for the year.

For purposes of this paragraph, there shall be excluded from consideration employees described in subparagraph (A) or (C) of section 410(b)(3). For purposes of any arrangement described in subsection (k)(6), any employee who is eligible to have employer contributions made on the employee's behalf under such arrangement shall be treated as if such a contribution was made.

(3) Contributions may not discriminate in favor of the highly compensated, etc.—

(A) In general.—The requirements of this paragraph are met with respect to a simplified employee pension for a year if for such year the contributions made by the employer to simplified employee pensions for his employees do not discriminate in favor of any highly compensated employee (within the meaning of section 414(q)).

(B) Special rules.—For purposes of subparagraph (A), there shall be excluded from consideration employees described in subparagraph (A) or (C) of section 410(b)(3).

(C) Contributions must bear uniform relationship to total compensation.—For purposes of subparagraph (A), and except as provided in subparagraph (D), employer contributions to simplified employee pensions (other than contributions under an arrangement described in paragraph (6)) shall be considered discriminatory unless contributions thereto bear a uniform relationship to the compensation (not in excess of the first $200,000) of each employee maintaining a simplified employee pension.

(D) Permitted disparity.—For purposes of subparagraph (C), the rules of section 401(*l*)(2) shall apply to contributions to simplified employee pensions (other than contributions under an arrangement described in paragraph (6)).

(4) Withdrawals must be permitted.—A simplified employee pension meets the requirements of this paragraph only if—

(A) employer contributions thereto are not conditioned on the retention in such pension of any portion of the amount contributed, and

(B) there is no prohibition imposed by the employer on withdrawals from the simplified employee pension.

(5) Contributions must be made under written allocation formula.—The requirements of this paragraph are met with respect to a simplified employee pension only if employer contributions to such pension are determined under a definite written allocation formula which specifies—

(A) the requirements which an employee must satisfy to share in an allocation, and

(B) the manner in which the amount allocated is computed.

* * *

(7) Definitions.—For purposes of this subsection and subsection (*l*)—

(A) Employee, employer, or owner-employee.—The terms "employee", "employer", and "owner-employee" shall have the respective meanings given such terms by section 401(c).

(B) Compensation.—Except as provided in paragraph (2)(C), the term "compensation" has the meaning given such term by section 414(s).

(C) Year.—The term "year" means—

(i) the calendar year, or

(ii) if the employer elects, subject to such terms and conditions as the Secretary may prescribe, to maintain the simplified employee pension on the basis of the employer's taxable year.

* * *

(m) Investment in collectibles treated as distributions.—

* * *

(2) Collectible defined.—For purposes of this subsection, the term "collectible" means—

(A) any work of art,

(B) any rug or antique,

(C) any metal or gem,

(D) any stamp or coin,

(E) any alcoholic beverage, or

(F) any other tangible personal property specified by the Secretary for purposes of this subsection.

* * *

(*o*) Definitions and rules relating to nondeductible contributions to individual retirement plans.—

(1) In general.—Subject to the provisions of this subsection, designated nondeductible contributions may be made on behalf of an individual to an individual retirement plan.

(2) Limits on amounts which may be contributed.—

(A) In general.—The amount of the designated nondeductible contributions made on behalf of any individual for any taxable year shall not exceed the nondeductible limit for such taxable year.

(B) Nondeductible limit.—For purposes of this paragraph—

(i) In general.—The term "nondeductible limit" means the excess of—

(I) the amount allowable as a deduction under section 219 (determined without regard to section 219(g)), over

(II) the amount allowable as a deduction under section 219 (determined with regard to section 219(g)).

(ii) Taxpayer may elect to treat deductible contributions as nondeductible.—If a taxpayer elects not to deduct an amount which (without regard to this clause) is allowable as a deduction under section 219 for any taxable year, the nondeductible limit for such taxable year shall be increased by such amount.

(C) Designated nondeductible contributions.—

(i) In general.—For purposes of this paragraph, the term "designated nondeductible contribution" means any contribution to an individual retirement plan for the taxable year which is designated (in such manner as the Secretary may prescribe) as a contribution for which a deduction is not allowable under section 219.

(ii) Designation.—Any designation under clause (i) shall be made on the return of tax imposed by chapter 1 for the taxable year.

(3) Time when contributions made.—In determining for which taxable year a designated nondeductible contribution is made, the rule of section 219(f)(3) shall apply.

(4) Individual required to report amount of designated nondeductible contributions.—

(A) In general.—Any individual who—

(i) makes a designated nondeductible contribution to any individual retirement plan for any taxable year, or

(ii) receives any amount from any individual retirement plan for any taxable year,

shall include on his return of the tax imposed by chapter 1 for such taxable year and any succeeding taxable year (or on such other form as the Secretary may prescribe for any such taxable year) information described in subparagraph (B).

(B) Information required to be supplied.—The following information is described in this subparagraph:

(i) The amount of designated nondeductible contributions for the taxable year.

(ii) The amount of distributions from individual retirement plans for the taxable year.

(iii) The excess (if any) of—

(I) the aggregate amount of designated nondeductible contributions for all preceding taxable years, over

(II) the aggregate amount of distributions from individual retirement plans which was excludable from gross income for such taxable years.

(iv) The aggregate balance of all individual retirement plans of the individual as of the close of the calendar year in which the taxable year begins.

(v) Such other information as the Secretary may prescribe.

* * *

(p) Simple retirement accounts.—

(1) In general.—For purposes of this title, the term "simple retirement account" means an individual retirement plan (as defined in section 7701(a)(37))—

(A) with respect to which the requirements of paragraphs (3), (4), and (5) are met; and

(B) with respect to which the only contributions allowed are contributions under a qualified salary reduction arrangement.

(2) Qualified salary reduction arrangement.—

(A) In general.—For purposes of this subsection, the term "qualified salary reduction arrangement" means a written arrangement of an eligible employer under which—

(i) an employee eligible to participate in the arrangement may elect to have the employer make payments—

(I) as elective employer contributions to a simple retirement account on behalf of the employee, or

(II) to the employee directly in cash,

(ii) the amount which an employee may elect under clause (i) for any year is required to be expressed as a percentage of compensation and may not exceed a total of the applicable dollar amount for any year,

(iii) the employer is required to make a matching contribution to the simple retirement account for any year in an amount equal to so much of the amount the employee elects under clause (i)(I) as does not exceed the applicable percentage of compensation for the year, and

(iv) no contributions may be made other than contributions described in clause (i) or (iii).

(B) Employer may elect 2–percent nonelective contribution.—

(i) In general.—An employer shall be treated as meeting the requirements of subparagraph (A)(iii) for any year if, in lieu of the contributions described in such clause, the employer elects to make nonelective contributions of 2 percent of compensation for each employee who is eligible to participate in the arrangement and who has at least $5,000 of compensation from the employer for the year. If an employer makes an election under this subparagraph for any year, the employer shall notify employees of such election within a reasonable period of time before the 60–day period for such year under paragraph (5)(C).

(ii) Compensation limitation.—The compensation taken into account under clause (i) for any year shall not exceed the limitation in effect for such year under section 401(a)(17).

(C) Definitions.—For purposes of this subsection—

(i) Eligible employer.—

(I) In general.—The term "eligible employer" means, with respect to any year, an employer which had no more than 100 employees who received at least $5,000 of compensation from the employer for the preceding year.

(II) 2–year grace period.—An eligible employer who establishes and maintains a plan under this subsection for 1 or more years and who fails to be an eligible employer for any subsequent year shall be treated as an eligible employer for the 2 years following the last year the employer was an eligible employer. If such failure is due to any acquisition, disposition, or similar transaction involving an eligible employer, the preceding sentence shall not apply.

(ii) Applicable percentage.—

(I) In general.—The term "applicable percentage" means 3 percent.

(II) Election of lower percentage.—An employer may elect to apply a lower percentage (not less than 1 percent) for any year for all employees eligible to participate in the plan for such year if the employer notifies the employees of such lower percentage within a reasonable period of time before the 60–day election period for such year under paragraph (5)(C). An employer may not elect a lower percentage under this subclause for any year if that election would result in the applicable percentage being lower than 3 percent in more than 2 of the years in the 5–year period ending with such year.

(III) Special rule for years arrangement not in effect.—If any year in the 5–year period described in subclause (II) is a year prior to the first year for which any qualified salary reduction arrangement is in effect with respect to the employer (or any predecessor), the employer shall be treated as if the level of the employer matching contribution was at 3 percent of compensation for such prior year.

* * *

(E) Applicable dollar amount; cost-of-living adjustment.—

(i) In general.—For purposes of subparagraph (A)(ii), the applicable dollar amount shall be the amount determined in accordance with the following table:

For years beginning in calendar year:	The applicable dollar amount:
2002	$ 7,000
2003	$ 8,000
2004	$ 9,000
2005 or thereafter	$10,000

(ii) Cost-of-living adjustment.—In the case of a year beginning after December 31, 2005, the Secretary shall adjust the $10,000 amount under clause (i) at the same time and in the same manner as under section 415(d), * * *.

(3) Vesting requirements.—The requirements of this paragraph are met with respect to a simple retirement account if the employee's rights to any contribution to the simple retirement account are nonforfeitable. For purposes of this paragraph, rules similar to the rules of subsection (k)(4) shall apply.

(4) Participation requirements.—

(A) In general.—The requirements of this paragraph are met with respect to any simple retirement account for a year only if, under the qualified salary reduction arrangement, all employees of the employer who—

(i) received at least $5,000 in compensation from the employer during any 2 preceding years, and

(ii) are reasonably expected to receive at least $5,000 in compensation during the year,

are eligible to make the election under paragraph (2)(A)(i) or receive the nonelective contribution described in paragraph (2)(B).

(B) Excludable employees.—An employer may elect to exclude from the requirement under subparagraph (A) employees described in section 410(b)(3).

* * *

(6) Definitions.—For purposes of this subsection—

(A) Compensation.—

(i) In general.—The term "compensation" means amounts described in paragraphs (3) and (8) of section 6051(a). For purposes of the preceding sentence, amounts described in section 6051(a)(3) shall be determined without regard to section 3401(a)(3).

(ii) Self-employed.—In the case of an employee described in subparagraph (B), the term "compensation" means net earnings from self-employment determined under section 1402(a) without regard to any contribution under this subsection. The preceding sentence shall be applied as if the term "trade or business" for purposes of section 1402 included service described in section 1402(c)(6).

(B) Employee.—The term "employee" includes an employee as defined in section 401(c)(1).

(C) Year.—The term "year" means the calendar year.

* * *

§ 408A. Roth IRAs

(a) General rule.—Except as provided in this section, a Roth IRA shall be treated for purposes of this title in the same manner as an individual retirement plan.

(b) Roth IRA.—For purposes of this title, the term "Roth IRA" means an individual retirement plan (as defined in section 7701(a)(37)) which is designated (in such manner as the Secretary may prescribe) at the time of establishment of the plan as a Roth IRA. Such designation shall be made in such manner as the Secretary may prescribe.

(c) Treatment of contributions.—

(1) No deduction allowed.—No deduction shall be allowed under section 219 for a contribution to a Roth IRA.

(2) Contribution limit.—The aggregate amount of contributions for any taxable year to all Roth IRAs maintained for the benefit of an individual shall not exceed the excess (if any) of—

(A) the maximum amount allowable as a deduction under section 219 with respect to such individual for such taxable year (computed without regard to subsection (d)(1) or (g) of such section), over

(B) the aggregate amount of contributions for such taxable year to all other individual retirement plans (other than Roth IRAs) maintained for the benefit of the individual.

(3) Limits based on modified adjusted gross income.—

(A) Dollar limit.—The amount determined under paragraph (2) for any taxable year shall not exceed an amount equal to the amount determined under paragraph (2)(A) for such taxable year, reduced (but not below zero) by the amount which bears the same ratio to such amount as—

(i) the excess of—

(I) the taxpayer's adjusted gross income for such taxable year, over

(II) the applicable dollar amount, bears to

(ii) $15,000 ($10,000 in the case of a joint return or a married individual filing a separate return).

The rules of subparagraphs (B) and (C) of section 219(g)(2) shall apply to any reduction under this subparagraph.

(B) Definitions.—For purposes of this paragraph—

(i) adjusted gross income shall be determined in the same manner as under section 219(g)(3), except that any amount included in gross income under subsection (d)(3) shall not be taken into account, and

(ii) the applicable dollar amount is—

(I) in the case of a taxpayer filing a joint return, $150,000,

(II) in the case of any other taxpayer (other than a married individual filing a separate return), $95,000, and

(III) in the case of a married individual filing a separate return, zero.

(C) Marital status.—Section 219(g)(4) shall apply for purposes of this paragraph.

(D) Inflation adjustment.—In the case of any taxable year beginning in a calendar year after 2006, the dollar amounts in subclauses (I) and (II) of subparagraph (B)(ii) shall each be increased by an amount equal to—

(i) such dollar amount, multiplied by

(ii) the cost-of-living adjustment determined under section 1(f)(3) for the calendar year in which the taxable year begins, determined by substituting "calendar year 2005" for "calendar year 1992" in subparagraph (B) thereof. Any increase determined under the preceding sentence shall be rounded to the nearest multiple of $1,000.

(4) Contributions permitted after age 70½.—Contributions to a Roth IRA may be made even after the individual for whom the account is maintained has attained age 70½.

(5) Mandatory distribution rules not to apply before death.—Notwithstanding subsections (a)(6) and (b)(3) of section 408 (relating to required distributions), the following provisions shall not apply to any Roth IRA:

(A) Section 401(a)(9)(A).

(B) The incidental death benefit requirements of section 401(a).

(6) Rollover contributions.—

(A) In general.—No rollover contribution may be made to a Roth IRA unless it is a qualified rollover contribution.

(B) Coordination with limit.—A qualified rollover contribution shall not be taken into account for purposes of paragraph (2).

(7) Time when contributions made.—For purposes of this section, the rule of section 219(f)(3) shall apply.

(d) Distribution rules.—For purposes of this title—

(1) Exclusion.—Any qualified distribution from a Roth IRA shall not be includible in gross income.

(2) Qualified distribution.—For purposes of this subsection—

(A) In general.—The term "qualified distribution" means any payment or distribution—

(i) made on or after the date on which the individual attains age 59½,

(ii) made to a beneficiary (or to the estate of the individual) on or after the death of the individual,

(iii) attributable to the individual's being disabled (within the meaning of section 72(m)(7)), or

(iv) which is a qualified special purpose distribution.

(B) Distributions within nonexclusion period.—A payment or distribution from a Roth IRA shall not be treated as a qualified distribution under subparagraph (A) if such payment or distribution is made within the 5-taxable year period beginning with the first taxable year for which the individual made a contribution to a Roth IRA (or such individual's spouse made a contribution to a Roth IRA) established for such individual.

(C) Distributions of excess contributions and earnings.—The term "qualified distribution" shall not include any distribution of any contribution described in section 408(d)(4) and any net income allocable to the contribution.

(3) Rollovers from an eligible retirement plan other than a Roth IRA.—

(A) In general.—Notwithstanding sections 402(c), 403(b)(8), 408(d)(3), and 457(e)(16), in the case of any distribution to which this paragraph applies—

(i) there shall be included in gross income any amount which would be includible were it not part of a qualified rollover contribution,

(ii) section 72(t) shall not apply, and

(iii) unless the taxpayer elects not to have this clause apply, any amount required to be included in gross income for any taxable year beginning in 2010 by reason of this paragraph shall be so included ratably over the 2–taxable-year period beginning with the first taxable year beginning in 2011.

Any election under clause (iii) for any distributions during a taxable year may not be changed after the due date for such taxable year.

(B) Distributions to which paragraph applies.—This paragraph shall apply to a distribution from an eligible retirement plan (as defined by section 402(c)(8)(B)) maintained for the benefit of an individual which is contributed to a Roth IRA maintained for the benefit of such individual in a qualified rollover contribution. This paragraph shall not apply to a distribution which is a qualified rollover contribution from a Roth IRA or a qualified rollover contribution from a designated Roth account which is a rollover contribution described in section 402A(c)(3)(A).

(C) Conversions.—The conversion of an individual retirement plan (other than a Roth IRA) to a Roth IRA shall be treated for purposes of this paragraph as a distribution to which this paragraph applies.

(D) Additional reporting requirements.—Trustees of Roth IRAs, trustees of individual retirement plans, persons subject to section 6047(d)(1), or all of the foregoing persons, whichever is appropriate, shall include such additional information in reports required under section 408(i) or 6047 as the Secretary may require to ensure that amounts required to be included in gross income under subparagraph (A) are so included.

(E) Special rules for contributions to which 2–year averaging applies.—In the case of a qualified rollover contribution to a Roth IRA of a distribution to which subparagraph (A)(iii) applied, the following rules shall apply:

(i) Acceleration of inclusion.—

(I) In general.—The amount otherwise required to be included in gross income for any taxable year beginning in 2010 or the first taxable year in the 2–year period under subparagraph (A)(iii) shall be increased by the aggregate distributions from Roth IRAs for such taxable year which are allocable under paragraph (4) to the portion of such qualified rollover contribution required to be included in gross income under subparagraph (A)(i).

(II) Limitation on aggregate amount included.—The amount required to be included in gross income for any taxable year under subparagraph (A)(iii) shall not exceed the aggregate amount required to be included in gross income under subparagraph (A)(iii) for all taxable years in the 2–year period (without regard to subclause (I)) reduced by amounts included for all preceding taxable years.

(ii) Death of distributee.—

(I) In general.—If the individual required to include amounts in gross income under such subparagraph dies before all of such amounts are included, all remaining amounts shall be included in gross income for the taxable year which includes the date of death.

(II) Special rule for surviving spouse.—If the spouse of the individual described in subclause (I) acquires the individual's entire interest in any Roth IRA to which such qualified rollover contribution is properly allocable, the spouse may elect to treat the remaining amounts described in subclause (I) as includible in the spouse's gross income in the taxable years of the spouse ending with or within the taxable years of such individual in which such amounts would otherwise have been includible. Any such election may not be made or changed after the due date for the spouse's taxable year which includes the date of death.

(F) Special rule for applying section 72.—

(i) In general.—If—

(I) any portion of a distribution from a Roth IRA is properly allocable to a qualified rollover contribution described in this paragraph; and

(II) such distribution is made within the 5–taxable year period beginning with the taxable year in which such contribution was made, then section 72(t) shall be applied as if such portion were includible in gross income.

(ii) Limitation.—Clause (i) shall apply only to the extent of the amount of the qualified rollover contribution includible in gross income under subparagraph (A)(i).

(4) Aggregation and ordering rules.—

(A) Aggregation rules.—Section 408(d)(2) shall be applied separately with respect to Roth IRAs and other individual retirement plans.

(B) Ordering rules.—For purposes of applying this section and section 72 to any distribution from a Roth IRA, such distribution shall be treated as made—

(i) from contributions to the extent that the amount of such distribution, when added to all previous distributions from the Roth IRA, does not exceed the aggregate contributions to the Roth IRA; and

(ii) from such contributions in the following order:

(I) Contributions other than qualified rollover contributions to which paragraph (3) applies.

(II) Qualified rollover contributions to which paragraph (3) applies on a first-in, first-out basis.

Any distribution allocated to a qualified rollover contribution under clause (ii)(II) shall be allocated first to the portion of such contribution required to be included in gross income.

(5) Qualified special purpose distribution.—For purposes of this section, the term "qualified special purpose distribution" means any distribution to which subparagraph (F) of section 72(t)(2) applies.

(6) Taxpayer may make adjustments before due date.—

(A) In general.—Except as provided by the Secretary, if, on or before the due date for any taxable year, a taxpayer transfers in a trustee-to-trustee transfer any contribution to an individual retirement plan made during such taxable year from such plan to any other individual retirement plan, then, for purposes of this chapter, such contribution shall be treated as having been made to the transferee plan (and not the transferor plan).

(B) Special rules.—

(i) Transfer of earnings.—Subparagraph (A) shall not apply to the transfer of any contribution unless such transfer is accompanied by any net income allocable to such contribution.

(ii) No deduction.—Subparagraph (A) shall apply to the transfer of any contribution only to the extent no deduction was allowed with respect to the contribution to the transferor plan.

(7) Due date.—For purposes of this subsection, the due date for any taxable year is the date prescribed by law (including extensions of time) for filing the taxpayer's return for such taxable year.

(e) Qualified rollover contribution.—For purposes of this section–

(1) In general.—The term "qualified rollover contribution" means a rollover contribution—

(A) to a Roth IRA from another such account,

(B) from an eligible retirement plan, but only if—

(i) in the case of an individual retirement plan, such rollover contribution meets the requirements of section 408(d)(3), and

(ii) in the case of any eligible retirement plan (as defined in section 402(c)(8)(B) other than clauses (i) and (ii) thereof), such rollover contribution meets the requirements of section 402(c), 403(b)(8), or 457(e)(16), as applicable.

For purposes of section 408(d)(3)(B), there shall be disregarded any qualified rollover contribution from an individual retirement plan (other than a Roth IRA) to a Roth IRA.

* * *

(f) Individual retirement plan.—For purposes of this section—

(1) a simplified employee pension or a simple retirement account may not be designated as a Roth IRA; and

(2) contributions to any such pension or account shall not be taken into account for purposes of subsection (c)(2)(B).

§ 409A. Inclusion in gross income of deferred compensation under nonqualified deferred compensation plans

(a) Rules relating to constructive receipt.—

(1) Plan failures.—

(A) Gross income inclusion.—

(i) In general.—If at any time during a taxable year a nonqualified deferred compensation plan—

(I) fails to meet the requirements of paragraphs (2), (3), and (4), or

(II) is not operated in accordance with such requirements,

all compensation deferred under the plan for the taxable year and all preceding taxable years shall be includible in gross income for the taxable year to the extent not subject to a substantial risk of forfeiture and not previously included in gross income.

(ii) Application only to affected participants.—Clause (i) shall only apply with respect to all compensation deferred under the plan for participants with respect to whom the failure relates.

(B) Interest and additional tax payable with respect to previously deferred compensation.—

(i) In general.—If compensation is required to be included in gross income under subparagraph (A) for a taxable year, the tax imposed by this chapter for the taxable year shall be increased by the sum of—

(I) the amount of interest determined under clause (ii), and

(II) an amount equal to 20 percent of the compensation which is required to be included in gross income.

(ii) Interest.—For purposes of clause (i), the interest determined under this clause for any taxable year is the amount of interest at the underpayment rate plus 1 percentage point on the underpayments that would have occurred had the deferred compensation been includible in gross income for the taxable year in which first deferred or, if later, the first taxable year in which such deferred compensation is not subject to a substantial risk of forfeiture.

(2) Distributions.—

(A) In general.—The requirements of this paragraph are met if the plan provides that compensation deferred under the plan may not be distributed earlier than—

(i) separation from service as determined by the Secretary (except as provided in subparagraph (B)(i)),

(ii) the date the participant becomes disabled (within the meaning of subparagraph (C)),

(iii) death,

(iv) a specified time (or pursuant to a fixed schedule) specified under the plan at the date of the deferral of such compensation,

(v) to the extent provided by the Secretary, a change in the ownership or effective control of the corporation, or in the ownership of a substantial portion of the assets of the corporation, or

(vi) the occurrence of an unforeseeable emergency.

(B) Special rules.—

(i) Specified employees.—In the case of any specified employee, the requirement of subparagraph (A)(i) is met only if distributions may not be made before the date which is 6 months after the date of separation from service (or, if earlier, the date of death of the employee). For purposes of the preceding sentence, a specified employee is a key employee (as defined in section 416(i) without regard to paragraph (5) thereof) of a corporation any stock in which is publicly traded on an established securities market or otherwise.

(ii) Unforeseeable emergency.—For purposes of subparagraph (A)(vi)—

(I) In general.—The term "unforeseeable emergency" means a severe financial hardship to the participant resulting from an illness or accident of the participant, the participant's spouse, or a dependent (as defined in section 152(a)) of the participant, loss of the participant's property due to casualty, or other similar extraordinary and unforeseeable circumstances arising as a result of events beyond the control of the participant.

(II) Limitation on distributions.—The requirement of subparagraph (A)(vi) is met only if, as determined under regulations of the Secretary, the amounts distributed with respect to an emergency do not exceed the amounts necessary to satisfy such emergency plus amounts necessary to pay taxes reasonably anticipated as a result of the distribution, after taking into account the extent to which such hardship is or may be relieved through reimbursement or compensation by insurance or otherwise or by liquidation of the participant's assets (to the extent the liquidation of such assets would not itself cause severe financial hardship).

(C) Disabled.—For purposes of subparagraph (A)(ii), a participant shall be considered disabled if the participant—

(i) is unable to engage in any substantial gainful activity by reason of any medically determinable physical or mental impairment which can be expected to result in death or can be expected to last for a continuous period of not less than 12 months, or

(ii) is, by reason of any medically determinable physical or mental impairment which can be expected to result in death or can be expected to last for a continuous period of not less than 12 months, receiving income replacement benefits for a period of not less than 3 months under an accident and health plan covering employees of the participant's employer.

(3) Acceleration of benefits.—The requirements of this paragraph are met if the plan does not permit the acceleration of the time or schedule of any payment under the plan, except as provided in regulations by the Secretary.

(4) Elections.—

(A) In general.—The requirements of this paragraph are met if the requirements of subparagraphs (B) and (C) are met.

(B) Initial deferral decision.—

(i) In general.—The requirements of this subparagraph are met if the plan provides that compensation for services performed during a taxable year may be deferred at the participant's election only if the election to defer such compensation is made not later than the close of the preceding taxable year or at such other time as provided in regulations.

(ii) First year of eligibility.—In the case of the first year in which a participant becomes eligible to participate in the plan, such election may be made with respect to services to be performed subsequent to the election within 30 days after the date the participant becomes eligible to participate in such plan.

(iii) Performance-based compensation.—In the case of any performance-based compensation based on services performed over a period of at least 12 months, such election may be made no later than 6 months before the end of the period.

(C) Changes in time and form of distribution.—The requirements of this subparagraph are met if, in the case of a plan which permits under a subsequent election a delay in a payment or a change in the form of payment—

(i) the plan requires that such election may not take effect until at least 12 months after the date on which the election is made,

(ii) in the case of an election related to a payment not described in clause (ii), (iii), or (vi) of paragraph (2)(A), the plan requires that the payment with respect to which such election is made be deferred for a period of not less than 5 years from the date such payment would otherwise have been made, and

(iii) the plan requires that any election related to a payment described in paragraph (2)(A)(iv) may not be made less than 12 months prior to the date of the first scheduled payment under such paragraph.

(b) Rules relating to funding.—

(1) Offshore property in a trust.—In the case of assets set aside (directly or indirectly) in a trust (or other arrangement determined by the Secretary) for purposes of paying deferred compensation under a nonqualified deferred compensation plan, for purposes of section 83 such assets shall be treated as property transferred in connection with the performance of services whether or not such assets are available to satisfy claims of general creditors—

(A) at the time set aside if such assets (or such trust or other arrangement) are located outside of the United States, or

(B) at the time transferred if such assets (or such trust or other arrangement) are subsequently transferred outside of the United States.

This paragraph shall not apply to assets located in a foreign jurisdiction if substantially all of the services to which the nonqualified deferred compensation relates are performed in such jurisdiction.

(2) Employer's financial health.—In the case of compensation deferred under a nonqualified deferred compensation plan, there is a transfer of property within the meaning of section 83 with respect to such compensation as of the earlier of—

(A) the date on which the plan first provides that assets will become restricted to the provision of benefits under the plan in connection with a change in the employer's financial health, or

(B) the date on which assets are so restricted, whether or not such assets are available to satisfy claims of general creditors.

* * *

(4) Income inclusion for offshore trusts and employer's financial health.—For each taxable year that assets treated as transferred under this subsection remain set aside in a trust or other arrangement subject to paragraph (1), (2) or (3), any increase in value in, or earnings with respect to, such assets shall be treated as an additional transfer of property under this subsection (to the extent not previously included in income).

(5) Interest on tax liability payable with respect to transferred property.—

(A) In general.—If amounts are required to be included in gross income by reason of paragraph (1), (2), or (3) for a taxable year, the tax imposed by this chapter for such taxable year shall be increased by the sum of—

(i) the amount of interest determined under subparagraph (B), and

(ii) an amount equal to 20 percent of the amounts required to be included in gross income.

(B) Interest.—For purposes of subparagraph (A), the interest determined under this subparagraph for any taxable year is the amount of interest at the underpayment rate plus 1 percentage point on the underpayments that would have occurred had the amounts so required to be included in gross income by paragraph (1), (2) or (3) been includible in gross income for the taxable year in which first deferred or, if later, the first taxable year in which such amounts are not subject to a substantial risk of forfeiture.

(c) No inference on earlier income inclusion or requirement of later inclusion.—Nothing in this section shall be construed to prevent the inclusion of amounts in gross income under any other provision of this chapter or any other rule of law earlier than the time provided in this section. Any amount included in gross income under this section shall not be required to be included in gross income under any other provision of this chapter or any other rule of law later than the time provided in this section.

(d) Other definitions and special rules.—For purposes of this section:

(1) Nonqualified deferred compensation plan.—The term "nonqualified deferred compensation plan" means any plan that provides for the deferral of compensation, other than—

(A) a qualified employer plan, and

(B) any bona fide vacation leave, sick leave, compensatory time, disability pay, or death benefit plan.

(2) Qualified employer plan.—The term "qualified employer plan" means—

(A) any plan, contract, pension, account, or trust described in subparagraph (A) or (B) of section 219(g)(5) (without regard to subparagraph (A)(iii)),

(B) any eligible deferred compensation plan (within the meaning of section 457(b)), and

(C) any plan described in section 415(m).

(3) Plan includes arrangements, etc.—The term "plan" includes any agreement or arrangement, including an agreement or arrangement that includes one person.

(4) Substantial risk of forfeiture.—The rights of a person to compensation are subject to a substantial risk of forfeiture if such person's rights to such compensation are conditioned upon the future performance of substantial services by any individual.

(5) Treatment of earnings.—References to deferred compensation shall be treated as including references to income (whether actual or notional) attributable to such compensation or such income.

(6) Aggregation rules.—Except as provided by the Secretary, rules similar to the rules of subsections (b) and (c) of section 414 shall apply.

(e) Regulations.—The Secretary shall prescribe such regulations as may be necessary or appropriate to carry out the purposes of this section, including regulations—

(1) providing for the determination of amounts of deferral in the case of a nonqualified deferred compensation plan which is a defined benefit plan,

(2) relating to changes in the ownership and control of a corporation or assets of a corporation for purposes of subsection (a)(2)(A)(v),

(3) exempting arrangements from the application of subsection (b) if such arrangements will not result in an improper deferral of United States tax and will not result in assets being effectively beyond the reach of creditors,

(4) defining financial health for purposes of subsection (b)(2), and

(5) disregarding a substantial risk of forfeiture in cases where necessary to carry out the purposes of this section.

Subpart B—Special Rules

§ 410. Minimum participation standards

(a) Participation.—

(1) Minimum age and service conditions.—

(A) General rule.—A trust shall not constitute a qualified trust under section 401(a) if the plan of which it is a part requires, as a condition of participation in the plan, that an employee complete a period of service with the employer or employers maintaining the plan extending beyond the later of the following dates—

(i) the date on which the employee attains the age of 21; or

(ii) the date on which he completes 1 year of service.

(B) Special rules for certain plans.—

(i) In the case of any plan which provides that after not more than 2 years of service each participant has a right to 100 percent of his accrued benefit under the plan which is nonforfeitable (within the meaning of section 411) at the time such benefit accrues, clause (ii) of subparagraph (A) shall be applied by substituting "2 years of service" for "1 year of service".

(ii) In the case of any plan maintained exclusively for employees of an educational institution (as defined in section 170(b)(1)(A)(ii)) by an employer which is exempt from tax under section 501(a) which provides that each participant having at least 1 year of service has a right to 100 percent of his accrued benefit under the plan which is nonforfeitable (within the meaning of section 411) at the time such benefit accrues, clause (i) of subparagraph (A) shall be applied by substituting "26" for "21". This clause shall not apply to any plan to which clause (i) applies.

(2) Maximum age conditions.—A trust shall not constitute a qualified trust under section 401(a) if the plan of which it is a part excludes from participation (on the basis of age) employees who have attained a specified age.

(3) Definition of year of service.—

(A) General rule.—For purposes of this subsection, the term "year of service" means a 12–month period during which the employee has not less than 1,000 hours of service. For purposes of this paragraph, computation of any 12–month period shall be made with reference to the date on which the employee's employment commenced, except that, under regulations prescribed by the Secretary of Labor, such computation may be made by reference to the first day of a plan year in the case of an employee who does not complete 1,000 hours of service during the 12–month period beginning on the date his employment commenced.

* * *

(4) Time of participation.—A plan shall be treated as not meeting the requirements of paragraph (1) unless it provides that any employee who has satisfied the minimum age and service requirements specified in such paragraph, and who is otherwise entitled to participate in the plan, commences participation in the plan no later than the earlier of—

(A) the first day of the first plan year beginning after the date on which such employee satisfied such requirements, or

(B) the date 6 months after the date on which he satisfied such requirements,

unless such employee was separated from the service before the date referred to in subparagraph (A) or (B), whichever is applicable.

* * *

(b) Minimum coverage requirements.—

(1) In general.—A trust shall not constitute a qualified trust under section 401(a) unless such trust is designated by the employer as part of a plan which meets 1 of the following requirements:

(A) The plan benefits at least 70 percent of employees who are not highly compensated employees.

(B) The plan benefits—

(i) a percentage of employees who are not highly compensated employees which is at least 70 percent of

(ii) the percentage of highly compensated employees benefiting under the plan.

(C) The plan meets the requirements of paragraph (2).

(2) Average benefit percentage test.—

(A) In general.—A plan shall be treated as meeting the requirements of this paragraph if—

(i) the plan benefits such employees as qualify under a classification set up by the employer and found by the Secretary not to be discriminatory in favor of highly compensated employees, and

(ii) the average benefit percentage for employees who are not highly compensated employees is at least 70 percent of the average benefit percentage for highly compensated employees.

(B) Average benefit percentage.—For purposes of this paragraph, the term "average benefit percentage" means, with respect to any group, the average of the benefit percentages calculated separately with respect to each employee in such group (whether or not a participant in any plan).

(C) Benefit percentage.—For purposes of this paragraph—

(i) In general.—The term "benefit percentage" means the employer-provided contribution or benefit of an employee under all qualified plans maintained by the employer, expressed as a percentage of such employee's compensation (within the meaning of section 414(s)).

(ii) Period for computing percentage.—At the election of an employer, the benefit percentage for any plan year shall be computed on the basis of contributions or benefits for—

(I) such plan year, or

(II) any consecutive plan year period (not greater than 3 years) which ends with such plan year and which is specified in such election.

An election under this clause, once made, may be revoked or modified only with the consent of the Secretary.

(D) Employees taken into account.—For purposes of determining who is an employee for purposes of determining the average benefit percentage under subparagraph (B)—

(i) except as provided in clause (ii), paragraph (4)(A) shall not apply, or

(ii) if the employer elects, paragraph (4)(A) shall be applied by using the lowest age and service requirements of all qualified plans maintained by the employer.

(E) Qualified plan.—For purposes of this paragraph, the term "qualified plan" means any plan which (without regard to this subsection) meets the requirements of section 401(a).

* * *

§ 411. Minimum vesting standards

(a) General rule.—A trust shall not constitute a qualified trust under section 401(a) unless the plan of which such trust is a part provides that an employee's right to his normal retirement benefit is nonforfeitable upon the attainment of normal retirement age (as defined in paragraph (8)) and in addition satisfies the requirements of paragraphs (1), (2), and (11) of this subsection and the requirements of subsection (b)(3), and also satisfies, in the case of a defined benefit plan, the requirements of subsection (b)(1) and, in the case of a defined contribution plan, the requirements of subsection (b)(2).

(1) Employee contributions.—A plan satisfies the requirements of this paragraph if an employee's rights in his accrued benefit derived from his own contributions are nonforfeitable.

(2) Employer contributions.—

(A) Defined benefit plans.—

(i) In general.—In the case of a defined benefit plan, a plan satisfies the requirements of this paragraph if it satisfies the requirements of clause (ii) or (iii).

(ii) 5-year vesting.—A plan satisfies the requirements of this clause if an employee who has completed at least 5 years of service has a nonforfeitable right to 100 percent of the employee's accrued benefit derived from employer contributions.

(iii) 3 to 7 year vesting.—A plan satisfies the requirements of this clause if an employee has a nonforfeitable right to a percentage of the employee's accrued benefit derived from employer contributions determined under the following table:

Years of service:	The nonforfeitable percentage is:
3	20
4	40
5	60
6	80
7 or more	100.

(B) Defined contribution plans.—

(i) In general.—In the case of a defined contribution plan, a plan satisfies the requirements of this paragraph if it satisfies the requirements of clause (ii) or (iii).

(ii) 3-year vesting.—A plan satisfies the requirements of this clause if an employee who has completed at least 3 years of service has a nonforfeitable right to 100 percent of the employee's accrued benefit derived from employer contributions.

(iii) 2 to 6 year vesting.—A plan satisfies the requirements of this clause if an employee has a nonforfeitable right to a percentage of the employee's accrued benefit derived from employer contributions determined under the following table:

Years of service:	The nonforfeitable percentage is:
3	20
4	40
5	60
6	80
7 or more	100.

(3) Certain permitted forfeitures, suspensions, etc.—For purposes of this subsection—

(A) Forfeiture on account of death.—A right to an accrued benefit derived from employer contributions shall not be treated as forfeitable solely because the plan provides that it is not payable if the participant dies (except in the case of a survivor annuity which is payable as provided in section 401(a)(11)).

* * *

(4) Service included in determination of nonforfeitable percentage.—In computing the period of service under the plan for purposes of determining the nonforfeitable percentage under paragraph (2), all of an employee's years of service with the employer or employers maintaining the plan shall be taken into account, except that the following may be disregarded:

(A) years of service before age 18, except that in the case of a plan which does not satisfy subparagraph (A) or (B) of paragraph (2), the plan may not disregard any such year of service during which the employee was a participant;

(B) years of service during a period for which the employee declined to contribute to a plan requiring employee contributions;

(C) years of service with an employer during any period for which the employer did not maintain the plan or a predecessor plan (as defined under regulations prescribed by the Secretary);

(D) service not required to be taken into account under paragraph (6);

(E) years of service before January 1, 1971, unless the employee has had at least 3 years of service after December 31, 1970;

(F) years of service before the first plan year to which this section applies, if such service would have been disregarded under the rules of the plan with regard to breaks in service as in effect on the applicable date; and

* * *

(5) Year of service.—

(A) General rule.—For purposes of this subsection, except as provided in subparagraph (C), the term "year of service" means a calendar year, plan year, or other 12–consecutive month period designated by the plan (and not prohibited under regulations prescribed by the Secretary of Labor) during which the participant has completed 1,000 hours of service.

* * *

(6) Breaks in service.—

(A) Definition of 1–year break in service.—For purposes of this paragraph, the term "1–year break in service" means a calendar year, plan year, or other 12–consecutive-month period designated by the plan (and not prohibited under regulations prescribed by the Secretary of Labor) during which the participant has not completed more than 500 hours of service.

(B) 1 year of service after 1–year break in service.—For purposes of paragraph (4), in the case of any employee who has any 1–year break in service, years of service before such break shall not be required to be taken into account until he has completed a year of service after his return.

* * *

(7) Accrued benefit.—

(A) In general.—For purposes of this section, the term "accrued benefit" means—

(i) in the case of a defined benefit plan, the employee's accrued benefit determined under the plan and, except as provided in subsection (c) (3), expressed in the form of an annual benefit commencing at normal retirement age, or

(ii) in the case of a plan which is not a defined benefit plan, the balance of the employee's account.

* * *

(8) Normal retirement age.—For purposes of this section, the term "normal retirement age" means the earlier of—

(A) the time a plan participant attains normal retirement age under the plan, or

(B) the later of—

(i) the time a plan participant attains age 65, or

(ii) the 5th anniversary of the time a plan participant commenced participation in the plan.

* * *

(10) Changes in vesting schedule.—

(A) General rule.—A plan amendment changing any vesting schedule under the plan shall be treated as not satisfying the requirements of paragraph (2) if the nonforfeitable percentage of the accrued benefit derived from employer contributions (determined as of the later of the date such amendment is adopted, or the date such amendment becomes effective) of any employee who is a participant in the plan is less than such nonforfeitable percentage computed under the plan without regard to such amendment.

(B) Election of former schedule.—A plan amendment changing any vesting schedule under the plan shall be treated as not satisfying the requirements of paragraph (2) unless each participant having not less than 3 years of service is permitted to elect, within a reasonable period after the adoption of such amendment, to have his nonforfeitable percentage computed under the plan without regard to such amendment.

(11) Restrictions on certain mandatory distributions.—

(A) In general.—If the present value of any nonforfeitable accrued benefit exceeds $5,000, a plan meets the requirements of this paragraph only if such plan provides that such benefit may not be immediately distributed without the consent of the participant.

* * *

(b) Accrued benefit requirements.—

(1) Defined benefit plans.—

(A) 3-percent method.—A defined benefit plan satisfies the requirements of this paragraph if the accrued benefit to which each participant is entitled upon his separation from the service is not less than—

(i) 3 percent of the normal retirement benefit to which he would be entitled if he commenced participation at the earliest possible entry age under the plan and served continuously until the earlier of age 65 or the normal retirement age specified under the plan, multiplied by

(ii) the number of years (not in excess of 33⅓) of his participation in the plan.

In the case of a plan providing retirement benefits based on compensation during any period, the normal retirement benefit to which a participant would be entitled shall be determined as if he continued to earn annually the average rate of compensation which he earned during consecutive years of service, not in excess of 10, for which his compensation was the highest. For purposes of this subparagraph, social security benefits and all other relevant factors used to compute benefits shall be treated as remaining constant as of the current year for all years after such current year.

(B) 133⅓ percent rule.—A defined benefit plan satisfies the requirements of this paragraph for a particular plan year if under the plan the accrued benefit payable at the normal retirement age is equal to the normal retirement benefit and the annual rate at which any individual who is or could be a participant can accrue the retirement benefits payable at normal retirement age under the plan for any later plan year is not more than 133⅓ percent of the annual rate at which he can accrue benefits for any plan year beginning on or after such particular plan year and before such later plan year. * * *

(C) Fractional rule.—A defined benefit plan satisfies the requirements of this paragraph if the accrued benefit to which any participant is entitled upon his separation from the service is not less than a fraction of the annual benefit commencing at normal retirement age to which he would be entitled under the plan as in effect on the date of his separation if he continued to earn annually until normal retirement age the same rate of compensation upon which his normal retirement benefit would be computed under the plan, determined as if he had attained normal retirement age on the date on which any such determination is made (but taking into account no more than the 10 years of service immediately preceding his separation from service). Such fraction shall be a fraction, not exceeding 1, the numerator of which is the total number of his years of participation in the plan (as of the date of his separation from the service) and the denominator of which is the total number of years he would have participated in the plan if he separated from the service at the normal retirement age. For purposes of this subparagraph, social security benefits and all other relevant factors used to compute benefits shall be treated as remaining constant as of the current year for all years after such current year.

* * *

(2) Defined contribution plans.—

(A) In general.—A defined contribution plan satisfies the requirements of this paragraph if, under the plan, allocations to the employee's account are not ceased, and the rate at which amounts are allocated to the employee's account is not reduced, because of the attainment of any age.

(B) Application to target benefit plans.—The Secretary shall provide by regulation for the application of the requirements of this paragraph to target benefit plans.

(C) Coordination with other requirements.—The Secretary may provide by regulation for the coordination of the requirements of this paragraph with the requirements of subsection (a), sections 404, 410, and 415, and the provisions of this subchapter precluding discrimination in favor of highly compensated employees.

(D) Coordination with other requirements.—The Secretary may provide by regulation for the coordination of the requirements of this subparagraph with the requirements of subsection (a), sections 404, 410, and 415, and the provisions of this subchapter precluding discrimination in favor of highly compensated employees.

(3) Separate accounting required in certain cases.—A plan satisfies the requirements of this paragraph if—

(A) in the case of a defined benefit plan, the plan requires separate accounting for the portion of each employee's accrued benefit derived from any voluntary employee contributions permitted under the plan; and

(B) in the case of any plan which is not a defined benefit plan, the plan requires separate accounting for each employee's accrued benefit.

* * *

§ 414. Definitions and special rules

(a) Service for predecessor employer.—For purposes of this part—

(1) in any case in which the employer maintains a plan of a predecessor employer, service for such predecessor shall be treated as service for the employer, and

(2) in any case in which the employer maintains a plan which is not the plan maintained by a predecessor employer, service for such predecessor shall, to the extent provided in regulations prescribed by the Secretary, be treated as service for the employer.

* * *

(i) Defined contribution plan.—For purposes of this part, the term "defined contribution plan" means a plan which provides for an individual account for each participant and for benefits based solely on the amount contributed to the participant's account, and any income, expenses, gains and losses, and any forfeitures of accounts of other participants which may be allocated to such participant's account.

(j) Defined benefit plan.—For purposes of this part, the term "defined benefit plan" means any plan which is not a defined contribution plan.

(k) Certain plans.—A defined benefit plan which provides a benefit derived from employer contributions which is based partly on the balance of the separate account of a participant shall—

(1) for purposes of section 410 (relating to minimum participation standards), be treated as a defined contribution plan,

(2) for purposes of sections 72(d) (relating to treatment of employee contributions as separate contract), 411(a)(7)(A) (relating to minimum vesting standards), 415 (relating to limitations on benefits and contributions under qualified plans), and 401(m) (relating to nondiscrimination tests for matching requirements and employee contributions), be treated as consisting of a defined contribution plan to the extent benefits are based on the separate account of a participant and as a defined benefit plan with respect to the remaining portion of benefits under the plan, and

* * *

(p) Qualified domestic relations order defined.—For purposes of this subsection and section 401(a)(13)—

(1) In general.—

(A) Qualified domestic relations order.—The term "qualified domestic relations order" means a domestic relations order—

(i) which creates or recognizes the existence of an alternate payee's right to, or assigns to an alternate payee the right to, receive all or a portion of the benefits payable with respect to a participant under a plan, and

(ii) with respect to which the requirements of paragraphs (2) and (3) are met.

(B) Domestic relations order.—The term "domestic relations order" means any judgment, decree, or order (including approval of a property settlement agreement) which—

(i) relates to the provision of child support, alimony payments, or marital property rights to a spouse, former spouse, child, or other dependent of a participant, and

(ii) is made pursuant to a State domestic relations law (including a community property law).

(2) Order must clearly specify certain facts.—A domestic relations order meets the requirements of this paragraph only if such order clearly specifies—

(A) the name and the last known mailing address (if any) of the participant and the name and mailing address of each alternate payee covered by the order,

(B) the amount or percentage of the participant's benefits to be paid by the plan to each such alternate payee, or the manner in which such amount or percentage is to be determined,

(C) the number of payments or period to which such order applies, and

(D) each plan to which such order applies.

(3) Order may not alter amount, form, etc., of benefits.—A domestic relations order meets the requirements of this paragraph only if such order—

(A) does not require a plan to provide any type or form of benefit, or any option, not otherwise provided under the plan,

(B) does not require the plan to provide increased benefits (determined on the basis of actuarial value), and

(C) does not require the payment of benefits to an alternate payee which are required to be paid to another alternate payee under another order previously determined to be a qualified domestic relations order.

(4) Exception for certain payments made after earliest retirement age.—

(A) In general.—A domestic relations order shall not be treated as failing to meet the requirements of subparagraph (A) of paragraph (3) solely because such order requires that payment of benefits be made to an alternate payee—

(i) on or in the case of any payment before a participant has separated from service, before the date on which the participant attains (or would have attained) the earliest retirement age,

(ii) as if the participant had retired on the date on which such payment is to begin under such order (but taking into account only the present value of the benefits actually accrued and not taking into account the present value of any employer subsidy for early retirement), and

(iii) in any form in which such benefits may be paid under the plan to the participant (other than in the form of a joint and survivor annuity with respect to the alternate payee and his or her subsequent spouse).

For purposes of clause (ii), the interest rate assumption used in determining the present value shall be the interest rate specified in the plan or, if no rate is specified, 5 percent.

(B) Earliest retirement age.—For purposes of this paragraph, the term "earliest retirement age" means the earlier of—

(i) the date on which the participant is entitled to a distribution under the plan, or

(ii) the later of—

(I) the date the participant attains age 50, or

(II) the earliest date on which the participant could begin receiving benefits under the plan if the participant separated from service.

* * *

(6) Plan procedures with respect to orders.—

(A) Notice and determination by administrator.—In the case of any domestic relations order received by a plan—

(i) the plan administrator shall promptly notify the participant and each alternate payee of the receipt of such order and the plan's procedures for determining the qualified status of domestic relations orders, and

(ii) within a reasonable period after receipt of such order, the plan administrator shall determine whether such order is a qualified domestic relations order and notify the participant and each alternate payee of such determination.

(B) Plan to establish reasonable procedures.—Each plan shall establish reasonable procedures to determine the qualified status of domestic relations orders and to administer distributions under such qualified orders.

(7) Procedures for period during which determination is being made.—

(A) In general.—During any period in which the issue of whether a domestic relations order is a qualified domestic relations order is being determined (by the plan administrator, by a court a competent jurisdiction, or otherwise), the plan administrator shall separately account for the amounts (hereinafter in this paragraph referred to as the "segregated amounts") which would have been payable to the alternate payee during such period if the order had been determined to be a qualified domestic relations order.

(B) Payment to alternate payee if order determined to be qualified domestic relations order.—If within the 18–month period described in subparagraph (E) the order (or modification thereof) is determined to be a qualified domestic relations order, the plan administrator shall pay the segregated amounts (including any interest thereon) to the person or persons entitled thereto.

(C) Payment to plan participant in certain cases.—If within the 18–month period described in subparagraph (E)—

(i) it is determined that the order is not a qualified domestic relations order, or

(ii) the issue as to whether such order is a qualified domestic relations order is not resolved,

then the plan administrator shall pay the segregated amounts (including any interest thereon) to the person or persons who would have been entitled to such amounts if there had been no order.

(D) Subsequent determination or order to be applied prospectively only.—Any determination that an order is a qualified domestic relations order which is made after the close of the 18–month period described in subparagraph (E) period shall be applied prospectively only.

(E) Determination of 18–month period.—For purposes of this paragraph, the 18–month period described in this subparagraph is the 18–month period beginning with the date on which the first payment would be required to be made under the domestic relations order.

(8) Alternate payee defined.—The term "alternate payee" means any spouse, former spouse, child or other dependent of a participant who is recognized by a domestic relations order as having a right to receive all, or a portion of, the benefits payable under a plan with respect to such participant.

(9) Subsection not to apply to plans to which section 401(a)(13) does not apply.—This subsection shall not apply to any plan to which section 401(a)(13) does not apply. For purposes of this title, except as provided in regulations, any distribution from an annuity contract under section 403(b) pursuant to a qualified domestic relations order shall be treated in the same manner as a distribution from a plan to which section 401(a)(13) applies.

(10) Waiver of certain distribution requirements.—With respect to the requirements of subsections (a) and (k) of section 401, section 403(b), section 409(d), and section 457(d), a plan shall not be treated as failing to meet such requirements solely by reason of payments to an alternative payee pursuant to a qualified domestic relations order.

* * *

(q) Highly compensated employee.—

(1) In general.—The term "highly compensated employee" means any employee who—

(A) was a 5-percent owner at any time during the year or the preceding year, or

(B) for the preceding year—

(i) had compensation from the employer in excess of $80,000, and

(ii) if the employer elects the application of this clause for such preceding year, was in the top-paid group of employees for such preceding year.

The Secretary shall adjust the $80,000 amount under subparagraph (B) at the same time and in the same manner as under section 415(d), except that the base period shall be the calendar quarter ending September 30, 1996.

(2) 5-percent owner.—An employee shall be treated as a 5-percent owner for any year if at any time during such year such employee was a 5-percent owner (as defined in section 416(i)(1)) of the employer.

(3) Top-paid group.—An employee is in the top-paid group of employees for any year if such employee is in the group consisting of the top 20 percent of the employees when ranked on the basis of compensation paid during such year.

* * *

(v) Catch-up contributions for individuals age 50 or over.—

(1) In general.—An applicable employer plan shall not be treated as failing to meet any requirement of this title solely because the plan permits an eligible participant to make additional elective deferrals in any plan year.

(2) Limitation on amount of additional deferrals.—

(A) In general.—A plan shall not permit additional elective deferrals under paragraph (1) for any year in an amount greater than the lesser of—

(i) the applicable dollar amount, or

(ii) the excess (if any) of—

(I) the participant's compensation (as defined in section 415(c)(3)) for the year, over

(II) any other elective deferrals of the participant for such year which are made without regard to this subsection.

(B) Applicable dollar amount.—For purposes of this paragraph—

(i) In the case of an applicable employer plan other than a plan described in section 401(k)(11) or 408(p), the applicable dollar amount shall be determined in accordance with the following table:

For taxable years beginning in:	**The applicable dollar amount is:**
2002	$1,000

2003	$2,000
2004	$3,000
2005	$4,000
2006 and thereafter	$5,000

(ii) In the case of an applicable employer plan described in section 401(k)(11) or 408(p), the applicable dollar amount shall be determined in accordance with the following table:

For taxable years beginning in:	The applicable dollar amount is:
2002	$ 500
2003	$1,000
2004	$1,500
2005	$2,000
2006 and thereafter	$2,500

(C) Cost–of–living adjustment.—In the case of a year beginning after December 31, 2006, the Secretary shall adjust annually the $5,000 amount in subparagraph (B)(i) and the $2,500 amount in subparagraph (B)(ii) for increases in the cost-of-living at the same time and in the same manner as adjustments under section 415(d); * * *.

* * *

(3) Treatment of contributions.—In the case of any contribution to a plan under paragraph (1)—

(A) such contribution shall not, with respect to the year in which the contribution is made—

(i) be subject to any otherwise applicable limitation contained in section 401(a)(30), 402(h), 403(b), 408, 415(c), and 457(b)(2) (determined without regard to section 457(b)(3)), or

(ii) be taken into account in applying such limitations to other contributions or benefits under such plan or any other such plan, and

(B) except as provided in paragraph (4), such plan shall not be treated as failing to meet the requirements of section 401(a)(4), 401(k)(3), 401(k)(11), 403(b)(12), 408(k), 410(b), or 416 by reason of the making of (or the right to make) such contribution.

(4) Application of nondiscrimination rules.—

(A) In general.—An applicable employer plan shall be treated as failing to meet the nondiscrimination requirements under section 401(a)(4) with respect to benefits, rights, and features unless the plan allows all eligible participants to make the same election with respect to the additional elective deferrals under this subsection.

(B) Aggregation.—For purposes of subparagraph (A), all plans maintained by employers who are treated as a single employer under subsection (b), (c), (m), or (*o*) of section 414 shall be treated as 1 plan, except that a plan described in clause (i) of section 410(b)(6)(C) shall not be treated as a plan of the employer until the expiration of the transition period with respect to such plan (as determined under clause (ii) of such section).

(5) Eligible participant.—For purposes of this subsection, the term "eligible participant" means, with respect to any plan year, a participant in a plan—

(A) who would attain age 50 by the end of the taxable year,

(B) with respect to whom no other elective deferrals may (without regard to this subsection) be made to the plan for the plan (or other applicable) year by reason of the application of any limitation or other restriction described in paragraph (3) or comparable limitation or restriction contained in the terms of the plan.

(6) Other definitions and rules.—For purposes of this subsection—

(A) Applicable employer plan.—The term "applicable employer plan" means—

(i) an employees' trust described in section 401(a) which is exempt from tax under section 501(a),

(ii) a plan under which amounts are contributed by an individual's employer for an annuity contract described in section 403(b),

(iii) an eligible deferred compensation plan under section 457 of an eligible employer described in section 457(e)(1)(A), and

(iv) an arrangement meeting the requirements of section 408 (k) or (p).

(B) Elective deferral.—The term "elective deferral" has the meaning given such term by subsection (u)(2)(C).

* * *

§ 415. Limitations on benefits and contribution under qualified plans

(a) General rule.—

(1) Trusts.—A trust which is a part of a pension, profit-sharing, or stock bonus plan shall not constitute a qualified trust under section 401(a) if—

(A) in the case of a defined benefit plan, the plan provides for the payment of benefits with respect to a participant which exceed the limitation of subsection (b),

(B) in the case of a defined contribution plan, contributions and other additions under the plan with respect to any participant for any taxable year exceed the limitation of subsection (c), * * *

* * *

(2) Section applies to certain annuities and accounts.—In the case of—

(A) an employee annuity plan described in section 403(a),

(B) an annuity contract described in section 403(b), or

(C) a simplified employee pension described in section 408(k),

such a contract, plan, or pension shall not be considered to be described in section 403(a), 403(b), or 408(k), as the case may be, unless it satisfies the requirements of subparagraph (A) or subparagraph (B) of paragraph (1), whichever is appropriate, and has not been disqualified under subsection (g). In the case of an annuity contract described in section 403(b), the preceding sentence shall apply only to the portion of the annuity contract which exceeds the limitation of subsection (b) or the limitation of subsection (c), whichever is appropriate.

(b) Limitation for defined benefit plans.—

(1) In general.—Benefits with respect to a participant exceed the limitation of this subsection if, when expressed as an annual benefit (within the meaning of paragraph (2)), such annual benefit is greater than the lesser of—

(A) $160,000, or

(B) 100 percent of the participant's average compensation for his high 3 years.

(2) Annual benefit.—

(A) In general.—For purposes of paragraph (1), the term "annual benefit" means a benefit payable annually in the form of a straight life annuity (with no ancillary benefits) under a plan to which employees do not contribute and under which no rollover contributions (as defined in sections 402(c), 403(a)(4), 403(b)(8), 408(d)(3)), and 457(e)(16) are made.

* * *

(c) Limitation for defined contribution plans.—

(1) In general.—Contributions and other additions with respect to a participant exceed the limitation of this subsection if, when expressed as an annual addition (within the meaning of paragraph (2)) to the participant's account, such annual addition is greater than the lesser of—

(A) $40,000, or

(B) 100 percent of the participant's compensation.

(2) Annual addition.—For purposes of paragraph (1), the term "annual addition" means the sum for any year of—

(A) employer contributions,

(B) the employee contributions, and

(i) the amount of the employee contributions in excess of 6 percent of his compensation, or

(ii) one-half of the employee contributions, and

(C) forfeitures.

For the purposes of this paragraph, employee contributions under subparagraph (B) are determined without regard to any rollover contributions (as defined in sections 402(c), 403(a)(4), 403(b)(8), 408(d)(3) and 457(e)(16)) without regard to employee contributions to a simplified employee pension which are excludable from gross income under section 408(k)(6). Subparagraph (B) of paragraph (1) shall not apply to any contribution for medical benefits (within the meaning of section 419A(f)(2)) after separation from service which is treated as an annual addition.

(3) Participant's compensation.—For purposes of paragraph (1)—

(A) In general.—The term "participant's compensation" means the compensation of the participant from the employer for the year.

(B) Special rule for self-employed individuals.—In the case of an employee within the meaning of section 401(c)(1), subparagraph (A) shall be applied by substituting "the participant's earned income (within the meaning of section 401(c)(2) but determined without regard to any exclusion under section 911)" for "compensation of the participant from the employer".

* * *

(d) Cost-of-living adjustments.—

(1) In general.—The Secretary shall adjust annually—

(A) the $160,000 amount in subsection (b)(1)(A),

(B) in the case of a participant who separated from service, the amount taken into account under subsection (b)(1)(B), and

(C) the $40,000 amount in subsection (c)(1)(A),

for increases in the cost-of-living in accordance with regulations prescribed by the Secretary.

(2) Method.—The regulations prescribed under paragraph (1) shall provide for—

(A) an adjustment with respect to any calendar year based on the increase in the applicable index for the calendar quarter ending September 30 of the preceding calendar year over such index for the base period, and

(B) adjustment procedures which are similar to the procedures used to adjust benefit amounts under section 215(i)(2)(A) of the Social Security Act.

(3) Base period.—For purposes of paragraph (2)—

(A) $160,000 Amount.—The base period taken into account for purposes of paragraph (1)(A) is the calendar quarter beginning July 1, 2001.

* * *

(D) $40,000 Amount.—The base period taken into account for purposes of paragraph (1)(C) is the calendar quarter beginning July 1, 2001.

(4) Rounding.—

(A) $160,000 amount.—Any increase under subparagraph (A) of paragraph (1) which is not a multiple of $5,000 shall be rounded to the next lowest multiple of $5,000. This subparagraph shall also apply for purposes of any provision of this title that provides for adjustments in accordance with the method contained in this subsection, except to the extent provided in such provision.

(B) $40,000 amount.—Any increase under subparagraph (C) of paragraph (1) which is not a multiple of $1,000 shall be rounded to the next lowest multiple of $1,000.

* * *

§ 416. Special rules for top-heavy plans

(a) General rule.—A trust shall not constitute a qualified trust under section 401(a) for any plan year if the plan of which it is a part is a top-heavy plan for such plan year unless such plan meets—

(1) the vesting requirements of subsection (b), and

(2) the minimum benefit requirements of subsection (c).

(b) Vesting requirements.—

(1) In general.—A plan satisfies the requirements of this subsection if it satisfies the requirements of either of the following subparagraphs:

(A) 3-year vesting.—A plan satisfies the requirements of this subparagraph if an employee who has completed at least 3 years of service with the employer or employers maintaining the plan has a nonforfeitable right to 100 percent of his accrued benefit derived from employer contributions.

(B) 6-year graded vesting.—A plan satisfies the requirements of this subparagraph if an employee has a nonforfeitable right to a percentage of his accrued benefit derived from employer contributions determined under the following table:

Years of service:	The nonforfeitable percentage is:
2	20
3	40
4	60
5	80
6 or more	100

(2) Certain rules made applicable.—Except to the extent inconsistent with the provisions of this subsection, the rules of section 411 shall apply for purposes of this subsection.

(c) Plan must provide minimum benefits.—

(1) Defined benefit plans.—

(A) In general.—A defined benefit plan meets the requirements of this subsection if the accrued benefit derived from employer contributions of each participant who is a non-key employee, when expressed as an annual retirement benefit, is not less than the applicable percentage of the participant's average compensation for years in the testing period.

(B) Applicable percentage.—For purposes of subparagraph (A), the term "applicable percentage" means the lesser of—

(i) 2 percent multiplied by the number of years of service with the employer, or

(ii) 20 percent.

(C) Years of service.—For purposes of this paragraph—

(i) In general.—Except as provided in clause (ii) or (iii), years of service shall be determined under the rules of paragraphs (4), (5), and (6) of section 411(a).

(ii) Exception for years during which plan was not top-heavy.—A year of service with the employer shall not be taken into account under this paragraph if—

(I) the plan was not a top-heavy plan for any plan year ending during such year of service, or

(II) such year of service was completed in a plan year beginning before January 1, 1984.

(iii) Exception for plan under which no key employee (or former key employee) benefits for plan year.—For purposes of determining an employee's years of service with the employer, any service with the employer shall be disregarded to the extent that such service occurs during a plan year when the plan benefits (within the meaning of section 410(b)) no key employee or former key employee.

(D) Average compensation for high 5 years.—For purposes of this paragraph—

(i) In general.—A participant's testing period shall be the period of consecutive years (not exceeding 5) during which the participant had the greatest aggregate compensation from the employer.

(ii) Year must be included in year of service.—The years taken into account under clause (i) shall be properly adjusted for years not included in a year of service.

(iii) Certain years not taken into account.—Except to the extent provided in the plan, a year shall not be taken into account under clause (i) if—

(I) such year ends in a plan year beginning before January 1, 1984, or

(II) such year begins after the close of the last year in which the plan was a top-heavy plan.

(E) Annual retirement benefit.—For purposes of this paragraph, the term "annual retirement benefit" means a benefit payable annually in the form of a single life annuity (with no ancillary benefits) beginning at the normal retirement age under the plan.

(2) Defined contribution plans.—

(A) In general.—A defined contribution plan meets the requirements of the subsection if the employer contribution for the year for each participant who is a non-key employee is not less than 3 percent of such participant's compensation (within the meaning of section 415). Employer matching contributions (as defined in section 401(m)(4)(A) shall be taken into account for purposes of this subparagraph) (and any reduction under this sentence shall not be taken into accounting in determining whether section 401(k)(4)(A) applies).

(B) Special rule where maximum contribution less than 3 percent.—

(i) In general.—The percentage referred to in subparagraph (A) for any year shall not exceed the percentage at which contributions are made (or required to be made) under the plan for the year for the key employee for whom such percentage is the highest for the year.

(ii) Treatment of aggregation groups.—

(I) For purposes of this subparagraph, all defined contribution plans required to be included in an aggregation group under subsection (g)(2)(A)(i) shall be treated as one plan.

(II) This subparagraph shall not apply to any plan required to be included in an aggregation group if such plan enables a defined benefit plan required to be included in such group to meet the requirements of section 401(a)(4) or 410.

* * *

(g) Top-heavy plan defined.—For purposes of this section—

(1) In general.—

(A) Plans not required to be aggregated.—Except as provided in subparagraph (B), the term "top-heavy plan" means, with respect to any plan year—

(i) any defined benefit plan if, as of the determination date, the present value of the cumulative accrued benefits under the plan for key employees exceeds 60 percent of the present value of the cumulative accrued benefits under the plan for all employees, and

(ii) any defined contribution plan if, as of the determination date, the aggregate of the accounts of key employees under the plan exceeds 60 percent of the aggregate of the accounts of all employees under such plan.

* * *

(4) Other special rules.—For purposes of this subsection—

* * *

(G) Simple retirement accounts.—The term "top-heavy plan" shall not include a simple retirement account under section 408(p).

* * *

(i) Definitions.—For purposes of this section—

(1) Key employee.—

(A) In general.—The term "key employee" means an employee who, at any time during the plan year, is—

(i) an officer of the employer having an annual compensation greater than $130,000,

(ii) a 5-percent owner of the employer, or

(iii) a 1-percent owner of the employer having an annual compensation from the employer of more than $150,000.

For purposes of clause (i), no more than 50 employees (or, if lesser, the greater of 3 or 10 percent of the employees) shall be treated as officers. In the case of plan years beginning after December 31, 2002, the $130,000 amount in clause (i) shall be adjusted at the same time and in the same manner as under section 415(d), * * *. Such term shall not include any officer or employee of an entity referred to in section 414(d) (relating to governmental plans). For purposes of determining the number of officers taken into account under clause (i), employees described in section 414(q)(5) shall be excluded.

(B) Percentage owners.—

(i) 5-percent owner.—For purposes of this paragraph, the term "5-percent owner" means—

(I) if the employer is a corporation, any person who owns (or is considered as owning within the meaning of section 318) more than 5 percent of the outstanding stock of the corporation or stock possessing more than 5 percent of the total combined voting power of all stock of the corporation, or

(II) if the employer is not a corporation, any person who owns more than 5 percent of the capital or profits interest in the employer.

(ii) 1-percent owner.—For purposes of this paragraph, the term "1-percent owner" means any person who would be described in clause (i) if "1 percent" were substituted for "5 percent" each place it appears in clause (i).

(iii) Constructive ownership rules.—For purposes of this subparagraph—

(I) subparagraph (C) of section 318(a)(2) shall be applied by substituting "5 percent" for "50 percent", and

(II) in the case of any employer which is not a corporation, ownership in such employer shall be determined in accordance with regulations prescribed by the Secretary which shall be based on principles similar to the principles of section 318 (as modified by subclause (I)).

(C) Aggregation rules do not apply for purposes of determining ownership in the employer.—The rules of subsections (b), (c), and (m) of section 414 shall not apply for purposes of determining ownership in the employer.

(D) Compensation.—For purposes of this paragraph, the term "compensation" has the meaning given such term by section 414(q)(4).

(2) Non-key employee.—The term "non-key employee" means any employee who is not a key employee.

(3) Self-employed individuals.—In the case of a self-employed individual described in section 401(c)(1)—

(A) such individual shall be treated as an employee, and

(B) such individual's earned income (within the meaning of section 401(c)(2)) shall be treated as compensation.

* * *

(5) Treatment of beneficiaries.—The terms "employee" and "key employee" include their beneficiaries.

* * *

§ 417. Definitions and special rules for purposes of minimum survivor annuity requirements

(a) Election to waive qualified joint and survivor annuity or qualified preretirement survivor annuity.—

(1) In general.—A plan meets the requirements of section 401(a)(11) only if—

(A) under the plan, each participant—

(i) may elect at any time during the applicable election period to waive the qualified joint and survivor annuity form of benefit or the qualified preretirement survivor annuity form of benefit (or both), and

(ii) if the participant elects a waiver under clause (i), may elect the qualified optional survivor annuity at any time during the applicable election period, and

(iii) may revoke any such election at any time during the applicable election period, and

(B) the plan meets the requirements of paragraphs (2), (3), and (4) of this subsection.

(2) Spouse must consent to election.—Each plan shall provide that an election under paragraph (1)(A)(i) shall not take effect unless—

(A)(i) the spouse of the participant consents in writing to such election, (ii) such election designates a beneficiary (or a form of benefits) which may not be changed without spousal consent (or the consent of the spouse expressly permits designations by the participant without any requirement of further consent by the spouse), and (iii) the spouse's consent acknowledges the effect of such election and is witnessed by a plan representative or a notary public, or

(B) it is established to the satisfaction of a plan representative that the consent required under subparagraph (A) may not be obtained because there is no spouse, because the spouse cannot be located, or because of such other circumstances as the Secretary may by regulations prescribe.

Any consent by a spouse (or establishment that the consent of a spouse may not be obtained) under the preceding sentence shall be effective only with respect to such spouse.

(3) Plan to provide written explanations.—

(A) Explanation of joint and survivor annuity.—Each plan shall provide to each participant, within a reasonable period of time before the annuity starting date (and consistent with such regulations as the Secretary may prescribe), a written explanation of—

(i) the terms and conditions of the qualified joint and survivor annuity and of the qualified optional survivor annuity,

(ii) the participant's right to make, and the effect of, an election under paragraph (1) to waive the joint and survivor annuity form of benefit,

(iii) the rights of the participant's spouse under paragraph (2), and

(iv) the right to make, and the effect of, a revocation of an election under paragraph (1).

(B) Explanation of qualified preretirement survivor annuity.—

(i) In general.—Each plan shall provide to each participant, within the applicable period with respect to such participant (and consistent with such regulations as the Secretary may prescribe), a written explanation with respect to the qualified preretirement survivor annuity comparable to that required under subparagraph (A).

(ii) Applicable period.—For purposes of clause (i), the term "applicable period" means, with respect to a participant, whichever of the following periods ends last:

(I) The period beginning with the first day of the plan year in which the participant attains age 32 and ending with the close of the plan year preceding the plan year in which the participant attains age 35.

(II) A reasonable period after the individual becomes a participant.

(III) A reasonable period ending after paragraph (5) ceases to apply to the participant.

(IV) A reasonable period ending after section 401(a)(11) applies to the participant.

In the case of a participant who separates from service before attaining age 35, the applicable period shall be a reasonable period after separation.

(4) Requirement of spousal consent for using plan assets as security for loans.—Each plan shall provide that, if section 401(a)(11) applies to a participant when part or all of the participant's accrued benefit is to be used as security for a loan, no portion of the participant's accrued benefit may be used as security for such loan unless—

(A) the spouse of the participant (if any) consents in writing to such use during the 90–day period ending on the date on which the loan is to be so secured, and

(B) requirements comparable to the requirements of paragraph (2) are met with respect to such consent.

* * *

PART II—CERTAIN STOCK OPTIONS

§ 421. General rules

(a) Effect of qualifying transfer.—If a share of stock is transferred to an individual in a transfer in respect of which the requirements of section 422(a) or 423(a) are met—

(1) no income shall result at the time of the transfer of such share to the individual upon his exercise of the option with respect to such share;

(2) no deduction under section 162 (relating to trade or business expenses) shall be allowable at any time to the employer corporation, a parent or subsidiary corporation of such corporation, or a corporation issuing or assuming a stock option in a transaction to which section 424(a) applies, with respect to the share so transferred; and

(3) no amount other than the price paid under the option shall be considered as received by any of such corporations for the share so transferred.

(b) Effect of disqualifying disposition.—If the transfer of a share of stock to an individual pursuant to his exercise of an option would otherwise meet the requirements of section 422(a) or 423(a) except that there is a failure to meet any of the holding period requirements of section 422(a)(1) or 423(a)(1), then any increase in the income of such individual or deduction from the income of his employer corporation for the taxable year in which such exercise occurred attributable to such disposition, shall be treated as an increase in income or a deduction from income in the taxable year of such individual or of such employer corporation in which such disposition occurred.
* * *

* * *

§ 422. Incentive stock options

(a) In general.—Section 421(a) shall apply with respect to the transfer of a share of stock to an individual pursuant to his exercise of an incentive stock option if—

(1) no disposition of such share is made by him within 2 years from the date of the granting of the option nor within 1 year after the transfer of such share to him, and

(2) at all times during the period beginning on the date of the granting of the option and ending on the day 3 months before the date of such exercise, such individual was an employee of either the corporation granting such option, a parent or subsidiary corporation of such corporation, or a corporation or a parent or subsidiary corporation of such corporation issuing or assuming a stock option in a transaction to which section 424(a) applies.

(b) Incentive stock option.—For purposes of this part, the term "incentive stock option" means an option granted to an individual for any reason connected with his employment by a corporation, if granted by the employer corporation or its parent or subsidiary corporation, to purchase stock of any of such corporations, but only if—

(1) the option is granted pursuant to a plan which includes the aggregate number of shares which may be issued under options and the employees (or class of employees) eligible to receive options, and which is approved by the stockholders of the granting corporation within 12 months before or after the date such plan is adopted;

(2) such option is granted within 10 years from the date such plan is adopted, or the date such plan is approved by the stockholders, whichever is earlier;

(3) such option by its terms is not exercisable after the expiration of 10 years from the date such option is granted;

(4) the option price is not less than the fair market value of the stock at the time such option is granted;

(5) such option by its terms is not transferable by such individual otherwise than by will or the laws of descent and distribution, and is exercisable, during his lifetime, only by him; and

(6) such individual, at the time the option is granted, does not own stock possessing more than 10 percent of the total combined voting power of all classes of stock of the employer corporation or of its parent or subsidiary corporation.

Such term shall not include any option if (as of the time the option is granted) the terms of such option provide that it will not be treated as an incentive stock option.

* * *

(d) $100,000 per year limitation.—

(1) In general.—To the extent that the aggregate fair market value of stock with respect to which incentive stock options (determined without regard to this subsection) are exercisable for the 1st time by any individual during any calendar year (under all plans of the individual's employer corporation and its parent and subsidiary corporations) exceeds $100,000, such options shall be treated as options which are not incentive stock options.

(2) Ordering rule.—Paragraph (1) shall be applied by taking options into account in the order in which they were granted.

(3) Determination of fair market value.—For purposes of paragraph (1), the fair market value of any stock shall be determined as of the time the option with respect to such stock is granted.

§ 423. Employee stock purchase plans

(a) General rule.—Section 421(a) shall apply with respect to the transfer of a share of stock to an individual pursuant to his exercise of an option granted after December 31, 1963, under an employee stock purchase plan (as defined in subsection (b)) if—

(1) no disposition of such share is made by him within 2 years after the date of the granting of the option nor within 6 months after the transfer of such share to him; and

(2) at all times during the period beginning with the date of the granting of the option and ending on the day 3 months before the date of such exercise, he is an employee of the corporation granting such option, a parent or subsidiary corporation of such corporation, or a corporation or a parent or subsidiary corporation of such corporation issuing or assuming a stock option in a transaction to which section 424(a) applies.

* * *

§ 424. Definitions and special rules

(a) Corporate reorganizations, liquidations, etc.—For purposes of this part, the term "issuing or assuming a stock option in a transaction to which section 424(a) applies" means a substitution of a new option for the old option, or an assumption of the old option, by an employer corporation, or a parent or subsidiary of such corporation, by reason of a corporate merger, consolidation, acquisition of property or stock, separation, reorganization, or liquidation, if—

(1) the excess of the aggregate fair market value of the shares subject to the option immediately after the substitution or assumption over the aggregate option price of such shares is not more than the excess of the aggregate fair market value of all shares subject to the option immediately before such substitution or assumption over the aggregate option price of such shares, and

(2) the new option or the assumption of the old option does not give the employee additional benefits which he did not have under the old option.

For purposes of this subsection, the parent-subsidiary relationship shall be determined at the time of any such transaction under this subsection.

(b) Acquisition of new stock.—For purposes of this part, if stock is received by an individual in a distribution to which section 305, 354, 355, 356, or 1036 (or so much of section 1031 as relates to section 1036) applies, and such distribution was made with respect to stock transferred to him upon his exercise of the option, such stock shall be considered as having been transferred to him on his exercise of such option. A similar rule shall be applied in the case of a series of such distributions.

(c) Disposition.—

(1) In general.—Except as provided in paragraphs (2), (3), and (4), for purposes of this part, the term "disposition" includes a sale, exchange, gift, or a transfer of legal title, but does not include—

(A) a transfer from a decedent to an estate or a transfer by bequest or inheritance;

(B) an exchange to which section 354, 355, 356, or 1036 (or so much of section 1031 as relates to section 1036) applies; or

(C) a mere pledge or hypothecation.

* * *

SUBCHAPTER E—ACCOUNTING PERIODS AND METHODS OF ACCOUNTING

PART I—ACCOUNTING PERIODS

§ 441. Period for computation of taxable income

(a) Computation of taxable income.—Taxable income shall be computed on the basis of the taxpayer's taxable year.

(b) Taxable year.—For purposes of this subtitle, the term "taxable year" means—

(1) the taxpayer's annual accounting period, if it is a calendar year or a fiscal year;

(2) the calendar year, if subsection (g) applies;

(3) the period for which the return is made, if a return is made for a period of less than 12 months; or

* * *

(c) Annual accounting period.—For purposes of this subtitle, the term "annual accounting period" means the annual period on the basis of which the taxpayer regularly computes his income in keeping his books.

(d) Calendar year.—For purposes of this subtitle, the term "calendar year" means a period of 12 months ending on December 31.

(e) Fiscal year.—For purposes of this subtitle, the term "fiscal year" means a period of 12 months ending on the last day of any month other than December. In the case of any taxpayer who has made the election provided by subsection (f), the term means the annual period (varying from 52 to 53 weeks) so elected.

(f) Election of year consisting of 52–53 weeks.—

(1) General rule.—A taxpayer who, in keeping his books, regularly computes his income on the basis of an annual period which varies from 52 to 53 weeks and ends always on the same day of the week and ends always—

(A) on whatever date such same day of the week last occurs in a calendar month, or

(B) on whatever date such same day of the week falls which is nearest to the last day of a calendar month,

may (in accordance with the regulations prescribed under paragraph (3)) elect to compute his taxable income for purposes of this subtitle on the basis of such annual period. This paragraph shall apply to taxable years ending after the date of the enactment of this title.

* * *

(3) Special rule for partnerships, S corporations, and personal service corporations.—The Secretary may by regulation provide terms and conditions for the application of this subsection to a partnership, S corporation, or personal service corporation (within the meaning of section 441(i)(2)).

(4) Regulations.—The Secretary shall prescribe such regulations as he deems necessary for the application of this subsection.

(g) No books kept; no accounting period.—Except as provided in section 443 (relating to returns for periods of less than 12 months), the taxpayer's taxable year shall be the calendar year if—

(1) the taxpayer keeps no books;

(2) the taxpayer does not have an annual accounting period; or

(3) the taxpayer has an annual accounting period, but such period does not qualify as a fiscal year.

* * *

(i) Taxable year of personal service corporations.—

(1) In general.—For purposes of this subtitle, the taxable year of any personal service corporation shall be the calendar year unless the corporation establishes, to the satisfaction of the Secretary, a business purpose for having a different period for its taxable year. For purposes of this paragraph, any deferral of income to shareholders shall not be treated as a business purpose.

(2) Personal service corporation.—For purposes of this subsection, the term "personal service corporation" has the meaning given such term by section 269A(b)(1), except that section 269A(b)(2) shall be applied—

(A) by substituting "any" for "more than 10 percent", and

(B) by substituting "any" for "50 percent or more in value" in section 318(a)(2)(C).

A corporation shall not be treated as a personal service corporation unless more than 10 percent of the stock (by value) in such corporation is held by employee-owners (within the meaning of section 269A(b)(2), as modified by the preceding sentence). If a corporation is a member of an affiliated group filing a consolidated return, all members of such group shall be taken into account in determining whether such corporation is a personal service corporation.

§ 442. Change of annual accounting period

If a taxpayer changes his annual accounting period, the new accounting period shall become the taxpayer's taxable year only if the change is approved by the Secretary. For purposes of this subtitle, if a taxpayer to whom section 441(g) applies adopts an annual accounting period (as defined in section 441(c)) other than a calendar year, the taxpayer shall be treated as having changed his annual accounting period.

§ 443. Returns for a period of less than 12 months

(a) Returns for short period.—A return for a period of less than 12 months (referred to in this section as "short period") shall be made under any of the following circumstances:

(1) Change of annual accounting period.—When the taxpayer, with the approval of the Secretary, changes his annual accounting period. In such a case, the return shall be made for the short period beginning on the day after the close of the former taxable year and ending at the close of the day before the day designated as the first day of the new taxable year.

(2) Taxpayer not in existence for entire taxable year.—When the taxpayer is in existence during only part of what would otherwise be his taxable year.

(b) Computation of tax on change of annual accounting period.—

(1) General rule.—If a return is made under paragraph (1) of subsection (a), the taxable income for the short period shall be placed on an annual basis by multiplying the modified taxable income for such short period by 12, dividing the result by the number of months in the short period. The tax shall be the same part of the tax computed on the annual basis as the number of months in the short period is of 12 months.

(2) Exception.—

(A) Computation based on 12–month period.—If the taxpayer applies for the benefits of this paragraph and establishes the amount of his taxable income for the 12–month period described in subparagraph (B), computed as if that period were a taxable year and under the law applicable to that year, then the tax for the short period, computed under paragraph (1), shall be reduced to the greater of the following:

(i) an amount which bears the same ratio to the tax computed on the taxable income for the 12–month period as the modified taxable income computed on the basis of the short period bears to the modified taxable income for the 12–month period; or

(ii) the tax computed on the modified taxable income for the short period.

The taxpayer (other than a taxpayer to whom subparagraph (B)(ii) applies) shall compute the tax and file his return without the application of this paragraph.

(B) 12–month period.—The 12–month period referred to in subparagraph (A) shall be—

(i) the period of 12 months beginning on the first day of the short period, or

(ii) the period of 12 months ending at the close of the last day of the short period, if at the end of the 12 months referred to in clause (i) the taxpayer is not in existence or (if a corporation) has theretofore disposed of substantially all of its assets.

(C) Application for benefits.—Application for the benefits of this paragraph shall be made in such manner and at such time as the regulations prescribed under subparagraph (D) may require; except that the time so prescribed shall not be later than the time (including extensions) for filing the return for the first taxable year which ends on or after the day which is 12 months after the first day of the short period. Such application, in case the return was filed without regard to this paragraph, shall be considered a claim for credit or refund with respect to the amount by which the tax is reduced under this paragraph.

(D) Regulations.—The Secretary shall prescribe such regulations as he deems necessary for the application of this paragraph.

(3) Modified taxable income defined.—For purposes of this subsection the term "modified taxable income" means, with respect to any period, the gross income for such period minus the deductions allowed by this chapter for such period (but, in the case of a short period, only the adjusted amount of the deductions for personal exemptions).

(c) Adjustment in deduction for personal exemption.—In the case of a taxpayer other than a corporation, if a return is made for a short period by reason of subsection (a)(1) and if the tax is not computed under subsection (b)(2), then the exemptions allowed as a deduction under section 151 (and any deduction in lieu thereof) shall be reduced to amounts which bear the same ratio to the full exemptions as the number of months in the short period bears to 12.

(d) Adjustment in computing minimum tax and tax preferences.—If a return is made for a short period by reason of subsection (a)—

(1) the alternative minimum taxable income for the short period shall be placed on an annual basis by multiplying such amount by 12 and dividing the result by the number of months in the short period, and

(2) the amount computed under paragraph (1) of section 55(a) shall bear the same relation to the tax computed on the annual basis as the number of months in the short period bears to 12.

* * *

§ 444. Election of taxable year other than required taxable year

(a) General rule.—Except as otherwise provided in this section, a partnership, S corporation, or personal service corporation may elect to have a taxable year other than the required taxable year.

(b) Limitations on taxable years which may be elected.—

(1) In general.—Except as provided in paragraphs (2) and (3), an election may be made under subsection (a) only if the deferral period of the taxable year elected is not longer than 3 months.

(2) Changes in taxable year.—Except as provided in paragraph (3), in the case of an entity changing a taxable year, an election may be made under subsection (a) only if the deferral period of the taxable year elected is not longer than the shorter of—

(A) 3 months, or

(B) the deferral period of the taxable year which is being changed.

(3) Special rule for entities retaining 1986 taxable years.—In the case of an entity's 1st taxable year beginning after December 31, 1986, an entity may elect a taxable year under subsection (a) which is the same as the entity's last taxable year beginning in 1986.

(4) Deferral period.—For purposes of this subsection, except as provided in regulations, the term "deferral period" means, with respect to any taxable year of the entity, the months between—

(A) the beginning of such year, and

(B) the close of the 1st required taxable year ending within such year.

(c) Effect of election.—If an entity makes an election under subsection (a), then—

(1) in the case of a partnership or S corporation, such entity shall make the payments required by section 7519, and

(2) in the case of a personal service corporation, such corporation shall be subject to the deduction limitations of section 280H.

(d) Elections.—

(1) Person making election.—An election under subsection (a) shall be made by the partnership, S corporation, or personal service corporation.

(2) Period of election.—

(A) In general.—Any election under subsection (a) shall remain in effect until the partnership, S corporation, or personal service corporation changes its taxable year or otherwise terminates such election. Any change to a required taxable year may be made without the consent of the Secretary.

(B) No further election.—If an election is terminated under subparagraph (A) or paragraph (3)(A), the partnership, S corporation, or personal service corporation may not make another election under subsection (a).

(3) Tiered structures, etc.—

(A) In general.—Except as otherwise provided in this paragraph—

(i) no election may be under subsection (a) with respect to any entity which is part of a tiered structure, and

(ii) an election under subsection (a) with respect to any entity shall be terminated if such entity becomes part of a tiered structure.

(B) Exceptions for structures consisting of certain entities with same taxable year.—Subparagraph (A) shall not apply to any tiered structure which consists only of partnerships or S corporations (or both) all of which have the same taxable year.

(e) Required taxable year.—For purposes of this section, the term "required taxable year" means the taxable year determined under section 706(b), 1378, or 441(i) without taking into account any taxable year which is allowable by reason of business purposes. Solely for purposes of the preceding sentence, sections 706(b), 1378, and 441(i) shall be treated as in effect for taxable years beginning before January 1, 1987.

(f) Personal service corporation.—For purposes of this section, the term "personal service corporation" has the meaning given to such term by section 441(i)(2).

(g) Regulations.—The Secretary shall prescribe such regulations as may be necessary to carry out the provisions of this section, including regulations to prevent the avoidance of subsection (b)(2)(B) or (d)(2)(B) through the change in form of an entity.

PART II—METHODS OF ACCOUNTING

Subpart A—Methods of Accounting in General

§ 446. General rule for methods of accounting

(a) General rule.—Taxable income shall be computed under the method of accounting on the basis of which the taxpayer regularly computes his income in keeping his books.

(b) Exceptions.—If no method of accounting has been regularly used by the taxpayer, or if the method used does not clearly reflect income, the computation of taxable income shall be made under such method as, in the opinion of the Secretary, does clearly reflect income.

(c) Permissible methods.—Subject to the provisions of subsections (a) and (b), a taxpayer may compute taxable income under any of the following methods of accounting—

(1) the cash receipts and disbursements method;

(2) an accrual method;

(3) any other method permitted by this chapter; or

(4) any combination of the foregoing methods permitted under regulations prescribed by the Secretary.

(d) Taxpayer engaged in more than one business.—A taxpayer engaged in more than one trade or business may, in computing taxable income, use a different method of accounting for each trade or business.

(e) Requirement respecting change of accounting method.—Except as otherwise expressly provided in this chapter, a taxpayer who changes the method of accounting on the basis of which he regularly computes his income in keeping his books shall, before computing his taxable income under the new method, secure the consent of the Secretary.

(f) Failure to request change of method of accounting.—If the taxpayer does not file with the Secretary a request to change the method of accounting, the absence of the consent of the Secretary to a change in the method of accounting shall not be taken into account—

(1) to prevent the imposition of any penalty, or the addition of any amount to tax, under this title, or

(2) to diminish the amount of such penalty or addition to tax.

§ 447. Method of accounting for corporations engaged in farming

(a) General rule.—Except as otherwise provided by law, the taxable income from farming of—

(1) a corporation engaged in the trade or business of farming, or

(2) a partnership engaged in the trade or business of farming, if a corporation is a partner in such partnership,

shall be computed on an accrual method of accounting. This section shall not apply to the trade or business of operating a nursery or sod farm or to the raising or harvesting of trees (other than fruit and nut trees).

(b) Preproductive period expenses.—

For rules requiring capitalization of certain preproductive period expenses, see section 263A.

(c) Exception for certain corporations.—For purposes of subsection (a), a corporation shall be treated as not being a corporation if it is—

(1) an S corporation, or

(2) a corporation the gross receipts of which meet the requirements of subsection (d).

(d) Gross receipts requirements.—

(1) In general.—A corporation meets the requirements of this subsection if, for each prior taxable year beginning after December 31, 1975, such corporation (and any predecessor corporation) did not have gross receipts exceeding $1,000,000. For purposes of the preceding sentence, all corporations which are members of the same controlled group of corporations (within the meaning of section 1563(a)) shall be treated as 1 corporation.

(2) Special rules for family corporations.—

(A) In general.—In the case of a family corporation, paragraph (1) shall be applied—

(i) by substituting "December 31, 1985," for "December 31, 1975,"; and

(ii) by substituting "$25,000,000" for "$1,000,000".

* * *

§ 448. Limitation on use of cash method of accounting

(a) General rule.—Except as otherwise provided in this section, in the case of a—

(1) C corporation,

(2) partnership which has a C corporation as a partner, or

(3) tax shelter,

taxable income shall not be computed under the cash receipts and disbursements method of accounting.

(b) Exceptions.—

(1) Farming business.—Paragraphs (1) and (2) of subsection (a) shall not apply to any farming business.

(2) Qualified personal service corporations.—Paragraphs (1) and (2) of subsection (a) shall not apply to a qualified personal service corporation, and such a corporation shall be treated as an individual for purposes of determining whether paragraph (2) of subsection (a) applies to any partnership.

(3) Entities with gross receipts of not more than $5,000,000.—Paragraphs (1) and (2) of subsection (a) shall not apply to any corporation or partnership for any taxable year if, for all prior taxable years beginning after December 31, 1985, such entity (or any predecessor) met the $5,000,000 gross receipts test of subsection (c).

(c) $5,000,000 gross receipts test.—For purposes of this section—

(1) In general.—A corporation or partnership meets the $5,000,000 gross receipts test of this subsection for any prior taxable year if the average annual gross receipts of such entity for the 3–taxable-year period ending with such prior taxable year does not exceed $5,000,000.

(2) Aggregation rules.—All persons treated as a single employer under subsection (a) or (b) of section 52 or subsection (m) or (*o*) of section 414 shall be treated as one person for purposes of paragraph (1).

(3) Special rules.—For purposes of this subsection—

(A) Not in existence for entire 3–year period.—If the entity was not in existence for the entire 3–year period referred to in paragraph (1), such paragraph shall be applied on the basis of the period during which such entity (or trade or business) was in existence.

(B) Short taxable years.—Gross receipts for any taxable year of less than 12 months shall be annualized by multiplying the gross receipts for the short period by 12 and dividing the result by the number of months in the short period.

(C) Gross receipts.—Gross receipts for any taxable year shall be reduced by returns and allowances made during such year.

(D) Treatment of predecessors.—Any reference in this subsection to an entity shall include a reference to any predecessor of such entity.

(d) Definitions and special rules.—For purposes of this section—

(1) Farming business.—

(A) In general.—The term "farming business" means the trade or business of farming (within the meaning of section 263A(e)(4)).

(B) Timber and ornamental trees.—The term "farming business" includes the raising, harvesting, or growing of trees to which section 263A(c)(5) applies.

(2) Qualified personal service corporation.—The term "qualified personal service corporation" means any corporation—

(A) substantially all of the activities of which involve the performance of services in the fields of health, law, engineering, architecture, accounting, actuarial science, performing arts, or consulting, and

(B) substantially all of the stock of which (by value) is held directly (or indirectly through 1 or more partnerships, S corporations, or qualified personal service corporations not described in paragraph (2) or (3) of subsection (a)) by—

(i) employees performing services for such corporation in connection with the activities involving a field referred to in subparagraph (A),

(ii) retired employees who had performed such services for such corporation,

(iii) the estate of any individual described in clause (i) or (ii), or

(iv) any other person who acquired such stock by reason of the death of an individual described in clause (i) or (ii) (but only for the 2–year period beginning on the date of the death of such individual).

To the extent provided in regulations which shall be prescribed by the Secretary, indirect holdings through a trust shall be taken into account under subparagraph (B).

(3) Tax shelter defined.—The term "tax shelter" has the meaning given such term by section 461(i)(3) (determined after application of paragraph (4) thereof). An S corporation shall not be treated as a tax shelter for purposes of this section merely by reason of being required to file a notice of exemption from registration with a State agency described in section 461(i)(3)(A), but only if there is a requirement applicable to all corporations offering securities for sale in the State that to be exempt from such registration the corporation must file such a notice.

* * *

(5) Special rule for certain services.—

(A) In general.—In the case of any person using an accrual method of accounting with respect to amounts to be received for the performance of services by such person, such person shall not be required to accrue any portion of such amounts which (on the basis of such person's experience) will not be collected if—

(i) such services are in fields referred to in paragraph (2)(A), or

(ii) such person meets the gross receipts test of subsection (c) for all prior taxable years.

(B) Exception.—This paragraph shall not apply to any amount if interest is required to be paid on such amount or there is any penalty for failure to timely pay such amount.

(C) Regulations.—The Secretary shall prescribe regulations to permit taxpayers to determine amounts referred to in subparagraph (A) using computations or formulas which, based on experience, accurately reflect the amount of income that will not be collected by such person. A taxpayer may adopt, or request consent of the Secretary to change to, a computation or formula that clearly reflects the taxpayer's experience. A request under the preceding sentence shall be approved if such computation or formula clearly reflects the taxpayer's experience.

* * *

(7) Coordination with section 481.—In the case of any taxpayer required by this section to change its method of accounting for any taxable year—

(A) such change shall be treated as initiated by the taxpayer,

(B) such change shall be treated as made with the consent of the Secretary, and

(C) the period for taking into account the adjustments under section 481 by reason of such change—

(i) except as provided in clause (ii), shall not exceed 4 years, and

(ii) in the case of a hospital, shall be 10 years.

(8) Use of related parties, etc.—The Secretary shall prescribe such regulations as may be necessary to prevent the use of related parties, pass-thru entities, or intermediaries to avoid the application of this section.

Subpart B—Taxable Year for Which Items of Gross Income Included

§ 451. General rule for taxable year of inclusion

(a) General rule.—The amount of any item of gross income shall be included in the gross income for the taxable year in which received by the taxpayer, unless, under the method of accounting used in computing taxable income, such amount is to be properly accounted for as of a different period.

(b) Special rule in case of death.—In the case of the death of a taxpayer whose taxable income is computed under an accrual method of accounting, any amount accrued only by reason of the death of the taxpayer shall not be included in computing taxable income for the period in which falls the date of the taxpayer's death.

(c) Special rule for employee tips.—For purposes of subsection (a), tips included in a written statement furnished an employer by an employee pursuant to section 6053(a) shall be deemed to be received at the time the written statement including such tips is furnished to the employer.

(d) Special rule for crop insurance proceeds or disaster payments.—In the case of insurance proceeds received as a result of destruction or damage to crops, a taxpayer reporting on the cash receipts and disbursements method of accounting may elect to include such proceeds in income for the taxable year following the taxable year of destruction or damage, if he establishes that, under his practice, income from such crops would have been reported in a following taxable year. For purposes of the preceding sentence, payments received under the Agricultural Act of 1949, as amended, or title II of the Disaster Assistance Act of 1988, as a result of (1) destruction or damage to crops caused by drought, flood, or any other natural disaster, or (2) the inability to plant crops because of such a natural disaster shall be treated as insurance proceeds received as a result of destruction or damage to crops. An election under this subsection for any taxable year shall be made at such time and in such manner as the Secretary prescribes.

* * *

(h) Special rule for cash options for receipt of qualified prizes.—

(1) In general.—For purposes of this title, in the case of an individual on the cash receipts and disbursements methods of accounting, a qualified prize option shall be disregarded in determining the taxable year for which any portion of the qualified prize is properly includible in gross income of the taxpayer.

(2) Qualified prize option; qualified prize.—For purposes of this subsection—

(A) In general.—The term "qualified prize option" means an option which—

(i) entitles an individual to receive a single cash payment in lieu of receiving a qualified prize (or remaining portion thereof), and

(ii) is exercisable not later than 60 days after such individual becomes entitled to the qualified prize.

(B) Qualified prize.—The term "qualified prize" means any prize or award which—

(i) is awarded as a part of a contest, lottery, jackpot, game, or other similar arrangement,

(ii) does not relate to any past services performed by the recipient and does not require the recipient to perform any substantial future service, and

(iii) is payable over a period of at least 10 years.

(3) Partnership, etc.—The Secretary shall provide for the application of this subsection in the case of a partnership or other pass-through entity consisting entirely of individuals described in paragraph (1).

* * *

§ 453. Installment method

(a) General rule.—Except as otherwise provided in this section, income from an installment sale shall be taken into account for purposes of this title under the installment method.

(b) Installment sale defined.—For purposes of this section—

(1) In general.—The term "installment sale" means a disposition of property where at least 1 payment is to be received after the close of the taxable year in which the disposition occurs.

(2) Exceptions.—The term "installment sale" does not include—

(A) Dealer dispositions.—Any dealer disposition (as defined in subsection (*l*)).

(B) Inventories of personal property.—A disposition of personal property of a kind which is required to be included in the inventory of the taxpayer if on hand at the close of the taxable year.

(c) Installment method defined.—For purposes of this section, the term "installment method" means a method under which the income recognized for any taxable year from a disposition is that proportion of the payments received in that year which the gross profit (realized or to be realized when payment is completed) bears to the total contract price.

(d) Election out.—

(1) In general.—Subsection (a) shall not apply to any disposition if the taxpayer elects to have subsection (a) not apply to such disposition.

(2) Time and manner for making election.—Except as otherwise provided by regulations, an election under paragraph (1) with respect to a disposition may be made only on or before the due date prescribed by law (including extensions) for filing the taxpayer's return of the tax imposed by this chapter for the taxable year in which the disposition occurs. Such an election shall be made in the manner prescribed by regulations.

(3) Election revocable only with consent.—An election under paragraph (1) with respect to any disposition may be revoked only with the consent of the Secretary.

(e) Second dispositions by related persons.—

(1) In general.—If—

(A) any person disposes of property to a related person (hereinafter in this subsection referred to as the "first disposition"), and

(B) before the person making the first disposition receives all payments with respect to such disposition, the related person disposes of the property (hereinafter in this subsection referred to as the "second disposition"),

then, for purposes of this section, the amount realized with respect to such second disposition shall be treated as received at the time of the second disposition by the person making the first disposition.

(2) 2–year cutoff for property other than marketable securities.—

(A) In general.—Except in the case of marketable securities, paragraph (1) shall apply only if the date of the second disposition is not more than 2 years after the date of the first disposition.

(B) Substantial diminishing of risk of ownership.—The running of the 2–year period set forth in subparagraph (A) shall be suspended with respect to any property for any period during which the related person's risk of loss with respect to the property is substantially diminished by—

(i) the holding of a put with respect to such property (or similar property),

(ii) the holding by another person of a right to acquire the property, or

(iii) a short sale or any other transaction.

(3) Limitation on amount treated as received.—The amount treated for any taxable year as received by the person making the first disposition by reason of paragraph (1) shall not exceed the excess of—

(A) the lesser of—

(i) the total amount realized with respect to any second disposition of the property occurring before the close of the taxable year, or

(ii) the total contract price for the first disposition, over

(B) the sum of—

(i) the aggregate amount of payments received with respect to the first disposition before the close of such year, plus

(ii) the aggregate amount treated as received with respect to the first disposition for prior taxable years by reason of this subsection.

(4) Fair market value where disposition is not sale or exchange.—For purposes of this subsection, if the second disposition is not a sale or exchange, an amount equal to the fair market value of the property disposed of shall be substituted for the amount realized.

(5) Later payments treated as receipt of tax paid amounts.—If paragraph (1) applies for any taxable year, payments received in subsequent taxable years by the person making the first disposition shall not be treated as the receipt of payments with respect to the first disposition to the extent that the aggregate of such payments does not exceed the amount treated as received by reason of paragraph (1).

(6) Exception for certain dispositions.—For purposes of this subsection—

(A) Reacquisitions of stock by issuing corporation not treated as first dispositions.—Any sale or exchange of stock to the issuing corporation shall not be treated as a first disposition.

(B) Involuntary conversions not treated as second dispositions.—A compulsory or involuntary conversion (within the meaning of section 1033) and any transfer thereafter shall not be treated as a second disposition if the first disposition occurred before the threat or imminence of the conversion.

(C) Dispositions after death.—Any transfer after the earlier of—

(i) the death of the person making the first disposition, or

(ii) the death of the person acquiring the property in the first disposition,

and any transfer thereafter shall not be treated as a second disposition.

(7) Exception where tax avoidance not a principal purpose.—This subsection shall not apply to a second disposition (and any transfer thereafter) if it is established to the satisfaction of the Secretary that neither the first disposition nor the second disposition had as one of its principal purposes the avoidance of Federal income tax.

(8) Extension of statute of limitations.—The period for assessing a deficiency with respect to a first disposition (to the extent such deficiency is attributable to the application of this subsection) shall not expire before the day which is 2 years after the date on which the person making the first disposition furnishes (in such manner as the Secretary may by regulations prescribe) a notice that there was a second disposition of the property to which this subsection may have applied. Such deficiency may be assessed notwithstanding the provisions of any law or rule of law which would otherwise prevent such assessment.

(f) Definitions and special rules.—For purposes of this section—

(1) Related person.—Except for purposes of subsections (g) and (h), the term "related person" means—

(A) a person whose stock would be attributed under section 318(a) (other than paragraph (4) thereof) to the person first disposing of the property, or

(B) a person who bears a relationship described in section 267(b) to the person first disposing of the property.

(2) Marketable securities.—The term "marketable securities" means any security for which, as of the date of the disposition, there was a market on an established securities market or otherwise.

(3) Payment.—Except as provided in paragraph (4), the term "payment" does not include the receipt of evidences of indebtedness of the person acquiring the property (whether or not payment of such indebtedness is guaranteed by another person).

(4) Purchaser evidences of indebtedness payable on demand or readily tradable.—Receipt of a bond or other evidence of indebtedness which—

(A) is payable on demand, or

(B) is readily tradable,

shall be treated as receipt of payment.

(5) Readily tradable defined.—For purposes of paragraph (4), the term "readily tradable" means a bond or other evidence of indebtedness which is issued—

(A) with interest coupons attached or in registered form (other than one in registered form which the taxpayer establishes will not be readily tradable in an established securities market), or

(B) in any other form designed to render such bond or other evidence of indebtedness readily tradable in an established securities market.

(6) Like-kind exchanges.—In the case of any exchange described in section 1031(b)—

(A) the total contract price shall be reduced to take into account the amount of any property permitted to be received in such exchange without recognition of gain,

(B) the gross profit from such exchange shall be reduced to take into account any amount not recognized by reason of section 1031(b), and

(C) the term "payment", when used in any provision of this section other than subsection (b)(1), shall not include any property permitted to be received in such exchange without recognition of gain.

Similar rules shall apply in the case of an exchange which is described in section 356(a) and is not treated as a dividend.

(7) Depreciable property.—The term "depreciable property" means property of a character which (in the hands of the transferee) is subject to the allowance for depreciation provided in section 167.

(8) Payments to be received defined.—The term "payments to be received" includes—

(A) the aggregate amount of all payments which are not contingent as to amount, and

(B) the fair market value of any payments which are contingent as to amount.

(g) Sale of depreciable property to controlled entity.—

(1) In general.—In the case of an installment sale of depreciable property between related persons—

(A) subsection (a) shall not apply,

(B) for purposes of this title—

(i) except as provided in clause (ii), all payments to be received shall be treated as received in the year of the disposition, and

(ii) in the case of any payments which are contingent as to the amount but with respect to which the fair market value may not be reasonably ascertained, the basis shall be recovered ratably, and

(C) the purchaser may not increase the basis of any property acquired in such sale by any amount before the time such amount is includible in the gross income of the seller.

(2) Exception where tax avoidance not a principal purpose.—Paragraph (1) shall not apply if it is established to the satisfaction of the Secretary that the disposition did not have as one of its principal purposes the avoidance of Federal income tax.

(3) Related persons.—For purposes of this subsection, the term "related persons" has the meaning given to such term by section 1239(b), except that such term shall include 2 or more partnerships having a relationship to each other described in section 707(b)(1)(B).

(h) Use of installment method by shareholders in certain liquidations.—

(1) Receipt of obligations not treated as receipt of payment.—

(A) In general.—If, in a liquidation to which section 331 applies, the shareholder receives (in exchange for the shareholder's stock) an installment obligation acquired in respect of a sale or exchange by the corporation during the 12–month period beginning on the date a plan of complete liquidation is adopted and the liquidation is completed during such 12–month period, then, for purposes of this section, the receipt of payments under such obligation (but not the receipt of such obligation) by the shareholder shall be treated as the receipt of payment for the stock.

(B) Obligations attributable to sale of inventory must result from bulk sale.—Subparagraph (A) shall not apply to an installment obligation acquired in respect of a sale or exchange of—

(i) stock in trade of the corporation,

(ii) other property of a kind which would properly be included in the inventory of the corporation if on hand at the close of the taxable year, and

(iii) property held by the corporation primarily for sale to customers in the ordinary course of its trade or business,

unless such sale or exchange is to 1 person in 1 transaction and involves substantially all of such property attributable to a trade or business of the corporation.

(C) Special rule where obligor and shareholder are related persons.—If the obligor of any installment obligation and the shareholder are married to each other or are related persons (within the meaning of section 1239(b)), to the extent such installment obligation is attributable to the disposition by the corporation of depreciable property—

(i) subparagraph (A) shall not apply to such obligation, and

(ii) for purposes of this title, all payments to be received by the shareholder shall be deemed received in the year the shareholder receives the obligation.

(D) Coordination with subsection (e)(1)(A).—For purposes of subsection (e)(1)(A), disposition of property by the corporation shall be treated also as disposition of such property by the shareholder.

(E) Sales by liquidating subsidiaries.—For purposes of subparagraph (A), in the case of a controlling corporate shareholder (within the meaning of section 368(c)) of a selling corporation, an obligation acquired in respect of a sale or exchange by the selling corporation shall be treated as so acquired by such controlling corporate shareholder. The preceding sentence shall be applied successively to each controlling corporate shareholder above such controlling corporate shareholder.

(2) Distributions received in more than 1 taxable year of shareholder.—If—

(A) paragraph (1) applies with respect to any installment obligation received by a shareholder from a corporation, and

(B) by reason of the liquidation such shareholder receives property in more than 1 taxable year,

then, on completion of the liquidation, basis previously allocated to property so received shall be reallocated for all such taxable years so that the shareholder's basis in the stock of the corporation is properly allocated among all property received by such shareholder in such liquidation.

(i) Recognition of recapture income in year of disposition.—

(1) In general.—In the case of any installment sale of property to which subsection (a) applies—

(A) notwithstanding subsection (a), any recapture income shall be recognized in the year of the disposition, and

(B) any gain in excess of the recapture income shall be taken into account under the installment method.

(2) Recapture income.—For purposes of paragraph (1), the term "recapture income" means, with respect to any installment sale, the aggregate amount which would be treated as ordinary income under section 1245 or 1250 (or so much of section 751 as relates to section 1245 or 1250) for the taxable year of the disposition if all payments to be received were received in the taxable year of disposition.

(j) Regulations.—

(1) In general.—The Secretary shall prescribe such regulations as may be necessary or appropriate to carry out the provisions of this section.

(2) Selling price not readily ascertainable.—The regulations prescribed under paragraph (1) shall include regulations providing for ratable basis recovery in transactions where the gross profit or the total contract price (or both) cannot be readily ascertained.

(k) Current inclusion in case of revolving credit plans, etc.—In the case of—

(1) any disposition of personal property under a revolving credit plan, or

(2) any installment obligation arising out of a sale of—

(A) stock or securities which are traded on an established securities market, or

(B) to the extent provided in regulations, property (other than stock or securities) of a kind regularly traded on an established market,

subsection (a) shall not apply, and, for purposes of this title, all payments to be received shall be treated as received in the year of disposition. The Secretary may provide for the application of this subsection in whole or in part for transactions in which the rules of this subsection otherwise would be avoided through the use of related parties, pass-thru entities, or intermediaries.

(*l*) Dealer dispositions.—For purposes of subsection (b)(2)(A)—

(1) In general.—The term "dealer disposition" means any of the following dispositions:

(A) Personal property.—Any disposition of personal property by a person who regularly sells or otherwise disposes of personal property of the same type on the installment plan.

(B) Real property.—Any disposition of real property which is held by the taxpayer for sale to customers in the ordinary course of the taxpayer's trade or business.

(2) Exceptions.—The term "dealer disposition" does not include—

(A) Farm property.—The disposition on the installment plan of any property used or produced in the trade or business of farming (within the meaning of section 2032A(e)(4) or (5)).

(B) Timeshares and residential lots.—

(i) In general.—Any dispositions described in clause (ii) on the installment plan if the taxpayer elects to have paragraph (3) apply to any installment obligations which arise from such dispositions. An election under this paragraph shall not apply with respect to an installment obligation which is guaranteed by any person other than an individual.

(ii) Dispositions to which subparagraph applies.—A disposition is described in this clause if it is a disposition in the ordinary course of the taxpayer's trade or business to an individual of—

(I) a timeshare right to use or a timeshare ownership interest in residential real property for not more than 6 weeks per year, or a right to use specified campgrounds for recreational purposes, or

(II) any residential lot, but only if the taxpayer (or any related person) is not to make any improvements with respect to such lot.

For purposes of subclause (I), a timeshare right to use (or timeshare ownership interest in) property held by the spouse, children, grandchildren, or parents of an individual shall be treated as held by such individual.

(C) Carrying charges or interest.—Any carrying charges or interest with respect to a disposition described in subparagraph (A) or (B) which are added on the books of account of the seller to the established cash selling price of the property shall be included in the total contract price of the property and, if such charges or interest are not so included, any payments received shall be treated as applying first against such carrying charges or interest.

(3) Payment of interest on timeshares and residential lots.—

(A) In general.—In the case of any installment obligation to which paragraph (2)(B) applies, the tax imposed by this chapter for any taxable year for which payment is received on such obligation shall be increased by the amount of interest determined in the manner provided under subparagraph (B).

(B) Computation of interest.—

(i) In general.—The amount of interest referred to in subparagraph (A) for any taxable year shall be determined—

(I) on the amount of the tax for such taxable year which is attributable to the payments received during such taxable year on installment obligations to which this subsection applies,

(II) for the period beginning on the date of sale, and ending on the date such payment is received, and

(III) by using the applicable Federal rate under section 1274 (without regard to subsection (d)(2) thereof) in effect at the time of the sale compounded semiannually.

(ii) Interest not taken into account.—For purposes of clause (i), the portion of any tax attributable to the receipt of any payment shall be determined without regard to any interest imposed under subparagraph (A).

(iii) Taxable year of sale.—No interest shall be determined for any payment received in the taxable year of the disposition from which the installment obligation arises.

(C) Treatment as interest.—Any amount payable under this paragraph shall be taken into account in computing the amount of any deduction allowable to the taxpayer for interest paid or accrued during such taxable year.

§ 453A. Special rules for nondealers

(a) General rule.—In the case of an installment obligation to which this section applies—

(1) interest shall be paid on the deferred tax liability with respect to such obligation in the manner provided under subsection (c), and

(2) the pledging rules under subsection (d) shall apply.

(b) Installment obligations to which section applies.—

(1) In general.—This section shall apply to any obligation which arises from the disposition of any property under the installment method, but only if the sales price of such property exceeds $150,000.

(2) Special rule for interest payments.—For purposes of subsection (a)(1), this section shall apply to an obligation described in paragraph (1) arising during a taxable year only if—

(A) such obligation is outstanding as of the close of such taxable year, and

(B) the face amount of all such obligations held by the taxpayer which arose during, and are outstanding as of the close of, such taxable year exceeds $5,000,000.

Except as provided in regulations, all persons treated as a single employer under subsection (a) or (b) of section 52 shall be treated as one person for purposes of this paragraph and subsection (c)(4).

(3) Exception for personal use and farm property.—An installment obligation shall not be treated as described in paragraph (1) if it arises from the disposition—

(A) by an individual of personal use property (within the meaning of section 1275(b)(3)), or

(B) of any property used or produced in the trade or business of farming (within the meaning of section 2032A(e)(4) or (5)).

(4) Special rule for timeshares and residential lots.—An installment obligation shall not be treated as described in paragraph (1) if it arises from a disposition described in section 453(l)(2)(B), but the provisions of section 453(l)(3) (relating to interest payments on timeshares and residential lots) shall apply to such obligation.

(5) Sales price.—For purposes of paragraph (1), all sales or exchanges which are part of the same transaction (or a series of related transactions) shall be treated as 1 sale or exchange.

(c) Interest on deferred tax liability.—

(1) In general.—If an obligation to which this section applies is outstanding as of the close of any taxable year, the tax imposed by this chapter for such taxable year shall be increased by the amount of interest determined in the manner provided under paragraph (2).

(2) Computation of interest.—For purposes of paragraph (1), the interest for any taxable year shall be an amount equal to the product of—

(A) the applicable percentage of the deferred tax liability with respect to such obligation, multiplied by

(B) the underpayment rate in effect under section 6621(a)(2) for the month with or within which the taxable year ends.

(3) Deferred tax liability.—For purposes of this section, the term "deferred tax liability" means, with respect to any taxable year, the product of—

(A) the amount of gain with respect to an obligation which has not been recognized as of the close of such taxable year, multiplied by

(B) the maximum rate of tax in effect under section 1 or 11, whichever is appropriate, for such taxable year.

For purposes of applying the preceding sentence with respect to so much of the gain which, when recognized, will be treated as long-term capital gain, the maximum rate on net capital gain under section 1(h) or 1201 (whichever is appropriate) shall be taken into account.

(4) Applicable percentage.—For purposes of this subsection, the term "applicable percentage" means, with respect to obligations arising in any taxable year, the percentage determined by dividing—

(A) the portion of the aggregate face amount of such obligations outstanding as of the close of such taxable year in excess of $5,000,000, by

(B) the aggregate face amount of such obligations outstanding as of the close of such taxable year.

(5) Treatment as interest.—Any amount payable under this subsection shall be taken into account in computing the amount of any deduction allowable to the taxpayer for interest paid or accrued during the taxable year.

(6) Regulations.—The Secretary shall prescribe such regulations as may be necessary to carry out the provisions of this subsection including regulations providing for the application of this subsection in the case of contingent payments, short taxable years, and pass-thru entities.

(d) Pledges, etc., of installment obligations.—

(1) In general.—For purposes of section 453, if any indebtedness (hereinafter in this subsection referred to as "secured indebtedness") is secured by an installment obligation to which this section applies, the net proceeds of the secured indebtedness shall be treated as a payment received on such installment obligation as of the later of—

(A) the time the indebtedness becomes secured indebtedness, or

(B) the time the proceeds of such indebtedness are received by the taxpayer.

(2) Limitation based on total contract price.—The amount treated as received under paragraph (1) by reason of any secured indebtedness shall not exceed the excess (if any) of—

(A) the total contract price, over

(B) any portion of the total contract price received under the contract before the later of the times referred to in subparagraph (A) or (B) of paragraph (1) (including amounts previously treated as received under paragraph (1) but not including amounts not taken into account by reason of paragraph (3)).

(3) Later payments treated as receipt of tax paid amounts.—If any amount is treated as received under paragraph (1) with respect to any installment obligation, subsequent payments received on such obligation shall not be taken into account for purposes of section 453 to the extent that the aggregate of such subsequent payments does not exceed the aggregate amount treated as received under paragraph (1).

(4) Secured indebtedness.—For purposes of this subsection indebtedness is secured by an installment obligation to the extent that payment of principal or interest on such indebtedness is directly secured (under the terms of the indebtedness or any underlying arrangements) by any interest in such installment obligation. A payment shall be treated as directly secured by an interest in an installment obligation to the extent an arrangement allows the taxpayer to satisfy all or a portion of the indebtedness with the installment obligation.

(e) Regulations.—The Secretary shall prescribe such regulations as may be necessary to carry out the purposes of this section, including regulations—

(1) disallowing the use of the installment method in whole or in part for transactions in which the rules of this section otherwise would be avoided through the use of related persons, pass-thru entities, or intermediaries, and

(2) providing that the sale of an interest in a partnership or other pass-thru entity will be treated as a sale of the proportionate share of the assets of the partnership or other entity.

§ 453B. Gain or loss disposition of installment obligations

(a) General rule.—If an installment obligation is satisfied at other than its face value or distributed, transmitted, sold, or otherwise disposed of, gain or loss shall result to the extent of the difference between the basis of the obligation and—

(1) the amount realized, in the case of satisfaction at other than face value or a sale or exchange, or

(2) the fair market value of the obligation at the time of distribution, transmission, or disposition, in the case of the distribution, transmission, or disposition otherwise than by sale or exchange.

Any gain or loss so resulting shall be considered as resulting from the sale or exchange of the property in respect of which the installment obligation was received.

(b) Basis of obligation.—The basis of an installment obligation shall be the excess of the face value of the obligation over an amount equal to the income which would be returnable were the obligation satisfied in full.

(c) Special rule for transmission at death.—Except as provided in section 691 (relating to recipients of income in respect of decedents), this section shall not apply to the transmission of installment obligations at death.

(d) Exception for distributions to which section 337(a) applies.—Subsection (a) shall not apply to any distribution to which section 337(a) applies.

* * *

(f) Obligation becomes unenforceable.—For purposes of this section, if any installment obligation is canceled or otherwise becomes unenforceable—

(1) the obligation shall be treated as if it were disposed of in a transaction other than a sale or exchange, and

(2) if the obligor and obligee are related persons (within the meaning of section 453(f)(1)), the fair market value of the obligation shall be treated as not less than its face amount.

(g) Transfers between spouses or incident to divorce.—In the case of any transfer described in subsection (a) of section 1041 (other than a transfer in trust)—

(1) subsection (a) of this section shall not apply, and

(2) the same tax treatment with respect to the transferred installment obligation shall apply to the transferee as would have applied to the transferor.

(h) Certain liquidating distributions by S corporations.—If—

(1) an installment obligation is distributed by an S corporation in a complete liquidation, and

(2) receipt of the obligation is not treated as payment for the stock by reason of section 453(h)(1),

then, except for purposes of any tax imposed by subchapter S, no gain or loss with respect to the distribution of the obligation shall be recognized by the distributing corporation. Under regulations prescribed by the Secretary, the character of the gain or loss to the shareholder shall be determined in accordance with the principles of section 1366(b).

§ 454. Obligations issued at discount

(a) Non-interest-bearing obligations issued at a discount.—If, in the case of a taxpayer owning any non-interest-bearing obligation issued at a discount and redeemable for fixed amounts increasing at stated intervals or owning an obligation described in paragraph (2) of subsection (c), the increase in the redemption price of such obligation occurring in the taxable year does not (under the method of accounting used in computing his taxable income) constitute income to him in such year, such taxpayer may, at his election made in his return for any taxable year, treat such increase as income received in such taxable year. If any such election is made with respect to any such obligation, it shall apply also to all such obligations owned by the taxpayer at the beginning of the first taxable year to which it applies and to all such obligations thereafter acquired by him and shall be binding for all subsequent taxable years, unless on application by the taxpayer the Secretary permits him, subject to such conditions as the Secretary deems necessary, to change to a different method. In the case of any such obligations owned by the taxpayer at the beginning of the first taxable year to which his election applies, the increase in the redemption price of such obligations occurring between the date of acquisition (or, in the case of an obligation described in paragraph (2) of subsection (c), the date of acquisition of the series E bond involved) and the first day of such taxable year shall also be treated as income received in such taxable year.

(b) Short-term obligations issued on discount basis.—In the case of any obligation—

(1) of the United States; or

(2) of a State or a possession of the United States, or any political subdivision of any of the foregoing, or of the District of Columbia,

which is issued on a discount basis and payable without interest at a fixed maturity date not exceeding 1 year from the date of issue, the amount of discount at which such obligation is originally sold shall not be considered to accrue until the date on which such obligation is paid at maturity, sold, or otherwise disposed of.

(c) Matured United States savings bonds.—In the case of a taxpayer who—

(1) holds a series E United States savings bond at the date of maturity, and

(2) pursuant to regulations prescribed under chapter 31 of title 31 (A) retains his investment in such series E bond in an obligation of the United States, other than a current income obligation, or (B) exchanges such series E bond for another non-transferable obligation of the United States in an exchange upon which gain or loss is not recognized because of section 1037 (or so much of section 1031 as relates to section 1037),

the increase in redemption value (to the extent not previously includible in gross income) in excess of the amount paid for such series E bond shall be includible in gross income in the taxable year in which the obligation is finally redeemed or in the taxable year of final maturity, whichever is earlier. This subsection shall not apply to a corporation, and shall not apply in the case of any taxable year for which the taxpayer's taxable income is computed under an accrual method of accounting or for which an election made by the taxpayer under subsection (a) applies.

§ 455. Prepaid subscription income

(a) Year in which included.—Prepaid subscription income to which this section applies shall be included in gross income for the taxable years during which the liability described in subsection (d)(2) exists.

(b) Where taxpayer's liability ceases.—In the case of any prepaid subscription income to which this section applies—

(1) If the liability described in subsection (d)(2) ends, then so much of such income as was not includible in gross income under subsection (a) for preceding taxable years shall be included in gross income for the taxable year in which the liability ends.

(2) If the taxpayer dies or ceases to exist, then so much of such income as was not includible in gross income under subsection (a) for preceding taxable years shall be included in gross income for the taxable year in which such death, or such cessation of existence, occurs.

(c) Prepaid subscription income to which this section applies.—

(1) Election of benefits.—This section shall apply to prepaid subscription income if and only if the taxpayer makes an election under this section with respect to the trade or business in connection with which such income is received. The election shall be made in such manner as the Secretary may by regulations prescribe. No election may be made with respect to a trade or business if in computing taxable income the cash receipts and disbursements method of accounting is used with respect to such trade or business.

(2) Scope of election.—An election made under this section shall apply to all prepaid subscription income received in connection with the trade or business with respect to which the taxpayer has made the election; except that the taxpayer may, to the extent permitted under regulations prescribed by the Secretary, include in gross income for the taxable year of receipt the entire amount of any prepaid subscription income if the liability from which it arose is to end within 12 months after the date of receipt. An election made under this section shall not apply to any prepaid subscription income received before the first taxable year for which the election is made.

* * *

(d) Definitions.—For purposes of this section—

(1) Prepaid subscription income.—The term "prepaid subscription income" means any amount (includible in gross income) which is received in connection with, and is directly attributable to, a liability which extends beyond the close of the taxable year in which such amount is received, and which is income from a subscription to a newspaper, magazine, or other periodical.

(2) Liability.—The term "liability" means a liability to furnish or deliver a newspaper, magazine, or other periodical.

(3) Receipt of prepaid subscription income.—Prepaid subscription income shall be treated as received during the taxable year for which it is includible in gross income under section 451 (without regard to this section).

(e) Deferral of income under established accounting procedures.—Notwithstanding the provisions of this section, any taxpayer who has, for taxable years prior to the first taxable year to which this section applies, reported his income under an established and consistent method or practice of accounting for prepaid subscription income (to which this section would apply if an election were made) may continue to report his income for taxable years to which this title applies in accordance with such method or practice.

§ 456. Prepaid dues income of certain membership organizations

(a) Year in which included.—Prepaid dues income to which this section applies shall be included in gross income for the taxable years during which the liability described in subsection (e)(2) exists.

(b) Where taxpayer's liability ceases.—In the case of any prepaid dues income to which this section applies—

(1) If the liability described in subsection (e)(2) ends, then so much of such income as was not includible in gross income under subsection (a) for preceding taxable years shall be included in gross income for the taxable year in which the liability ends.

(2) If the taxpayer ceases to exist, then so much of such income as was not includible in gross income under subsection (a) for preceding taxable years shall be included in gross income for the taxable year in which such cessation of existence occurs.

(c) Prepaid dues income to which this section applies.—

(1) Election of benefits.—This section shall apply to prepaid dues income if and only if the taxpayer makes an election under this section with respect to the trade or business in connection with which such income is received. The election shall be made in such manner as the Secretary may by regulations prescribe. No election may be made with respect to a trade or business if in computing taxable income the cash receipts and disbursements method of accounting is used with respect to such trade or business.

(2) Scope of election.—An election made under this section shall apply to all prepaid dues income received in connection with the trade or business with respect to which the taxpayer has made the election; except that the taxpayer may, to the extent permitted under regulations prescribed by the Secretary, include in gross income for the taxable year of receipt the entire amount of any prepaid dues income if the liability from which it arose is to end within 12 months after the date of receipt. Except as provided in subsection (d), an election made under this section shall not apply to any prepaid dues income received before the first taxable year for which the election is made.

* * *

(e) Definitions.—For purposes of this section—

(1) Prepaid dues income.—The term "prepaid dues income" means any amount (includible in gross income) which is received by a membership organization in connection with, and is directly attributable to, a liability to render services or make available membership privileges over a period of time which extends beyond the close of the taxable year in which such amount is received.

(2) Liability.—The term "liability" means a liability to render services or make available membership privileges over a period of time which does not exceed 36 months, which liability shall be deemed to exist ratably over the period of time that such services are required to be rendered, or that such membership privileges are required to be made available.

(3) Membership organization.—The term "membership organization" means a corporation, association, federation, or other organization—

(A) organized without capital stock of any kind, and

(B) no part of the net earnings of which is distributable to any member.

(4) Receipt of prepaid dues income.—Prepaid dues income shall be treated as received during the taxable year for which it is includible in gross income under section 451 (without regard to this section).

§ 458. Magazines, paperbacks, and records returned after the close of the taxable year

(a) Exclusion from gross income.—A taxpayer who is on an accrual method of accounting may elect not to include in the gross income for the taxable year the income attributable to the qualified sale of any magazine, paperback, or record which is returned to the taxpayer before the close of the merchandise return period.

* * *

(c) Qualified sales to which section applies.—

(1) Election of benefits.—This section shall apply to qualified sales of magazines, paperbacks, or records, as the case may be, if and only if the taxpayer makes an election under this section with respect to the trade or business in connection with which such sales are made. An election under this section may be made without the consent of the Secretary. The election shall be made in such manner as the Secretary may by regulations prescribe and shall be made for any taxable year not later than the time prescribed by law for filing the return for such taxable year (including extensions thereof).

(2) Scope of election.—An election made under this section shall apply to all qualified sales of magazines, paperbacks, or records, as the case may be, made in connection with the trade or business with respect to which the taxpayer has made the election.

(3) Period to which election applies.—An election under this section shall be effective for the taxable year for which it is made and for all subsequent taxable years, unless the taxpayer secures the consent of the Secretary to the revocation of such election.

(4) Treatment as method of accounting.—Except to the extent inconsistent with the provisions of this section, for purposes of this subtitle, the computation of taxable income under an election made under this section shall be treated as a method of accounting.

* * *

§ 460. Special rules for long-term contracts

(a) Requirement that percentage of completion method be used.—In the case of any long-term contract, the taxable income from such contract shall be determined under the percentage of completion method (as modified by subsection (b)).

(b) Percentage of completion method.—

(1) Requirements of percentage of completion method.—Except as provided in paragraph (3), in the case of any long-term contract with respect to which the percentage of completion method is used—

(A) the percentage of completion shall be determined by comparing costs allocated to the contract under subsection (c) and incurred before the close of the taxable year with the estimated total contract costs, and

(B) upon completion of the contract (or, with respect to any amount properly taken into account after completion of the contract, when such amount is so properly taken into account), the taxpayer shall pay (or shall be entitled to receive) interest computed under the look-back method of paragraph (2).

In the case of any long-term contract with respect to which the percentage of completion method is used, except for purposes of applying the look-back method of paragraph (2), any income under the contract (to the extent not previously includible in gross income) shall be included in gross income for the taxable year following the taxable year in which the contract was completed.

For purposes of subtitle F (other than sections 6654 and 6655), any interest required to be paid by the taxpayer under subparagraph (B) shall be treated as an increase in the tax imposed by this chapter for the taxable year in which the contract is completed (or, in the case of interest payable with respect to any amount properly taken into account after completion of the contract, for the taxable year in which the amount is so properly taken into account).

* * *

(c) Allocation of costs to contract.—

(1) Direct and certain indirect costs.—In the case of a long-term contract, all costs (including research and experimental costs) which directly benefit, or are incurred by reason of, the long-term contract activities of the taxpayer shall be allocated to such contract in the same manner as costs are allocated to extended period long-term contracts under section 451 and the regulations thereunder.

* * *

(f) Long-term contract.—For purposes of this section—

(1) In general.—The term "long-term contract" means any contract for the manufacture, building, installation, or construction of property if such contract is not completed within the taxable year in which such contract is entered into.

(2) Special rule for manufacturing contracts.—A contract for the manufacture of property shall not be treated as a long-term contract unless such contract involves the manufacture of—

(A) any unique item of a type which is not normally included in the finished goods inventory of the taxpayer, or

(B) any item which normally requires more than 12 calendar months to complete (without regard to the period of the contract).

(3) Aggregation, etc.—For purposes of this subsection, under regulations prescribed by the Secretary—

(A) 2 or more contracts which are interdependent (by reason of pricing or otherwise) may be treated as 1 contract, and

(B) a contract which is properly treated as an aggregation of separate contracts may be so treated.

(g) Contract commencement date. For purposes of this section, the term "contract commencement date" means, with respect to any contract, the first date on which any costs (other than bidding expenses or expenses incurred in connection with negotiating the contract) allocable to such contract are incurred.

(h) Regulations.—The Secretary shall prescribe such regulations as may be necessary or appropriate to carry out the purposes of this section, including regulations to prevent the use of related parties, pass-thru entities, intermediaries, options, or other similar arrangements to avoid the application of this section.

Subpart C—Taxable Year for Which Deductions Taken

§ 461. General rule for taxable year of deduction

(a) General rule.—The amount of any deduction or credit allowed by this subtitle shall be taken for the taxable year which is the proper taxable year under the method of accounting used in computing taxable income.

(b) Special rule in case of death.—In the case of the death of a taxpayer whose taxable income is computed under an accrual method of accounting, any amount accrued as a deduction or credit only by reason of the death of the taxpayer shall not be allowed in computing taxable income for the period in which falls the date of the taxpayer's death.

(c) Accrual of real property taxes.—

(1) In general.—If the taxable income is computed under an accrual method of accounting, then, at the election of the taxpayer, any real property tax which is related to a definite period of time shall be accrued ratably over that period.

(2) When election may be made.—

(A) Without consent.—A taxpayer may, without the consent of the Secretary, make an election under this subsection for his first taxable year in which he incurs real property taxes. Such an election shall be made not later than the time prescribed by law for filing the return for such year (including extensions thereof).

(B) With consent.—A taxpayer may, with the consent of the Secretary, make an election under this subsection at any time.

(d) Limitation on acceleration of accrual of taxes.—

(1) General rule.—In the case of a taxpayer whose taxable income is computed under an accrual method of accounting, to the extent that the time for accruing taxes is earlier than it would be but for any action of any taxing jurisdiction taken after December 31, 1960, then, under regulations prescribed by the Secretary, such taxes shall be treated as accruing at the time they would have accrued but for such action by such taxing jurisdiction.

(2) Limitation.—Under regulations prescribed by the Secretary, paragraph (1) shall be inapplicable to any item of tax to the extent that its application would (but for this paragraph) prevent all persons (including successors in interest) from ever taking such item into account.

* * *

(f) Contested liabilities.—If—

(1) the taxpayer contests an asserted liability,

(2) the taxpayer transfers money or other property to provide for the satisfaction of the asserted liability,

(3) the contest with respect to the asserted liability exists after the time of the transfer, and

(4) but for the fact that the asserted liability is contested, a deduction would be allowed for the taxable year of the transfer (or for an earlier taxable year) determined after application of subsection (h),

then the deduction shall be allowed for the taxable year of the transfer. This subsection shall not apply in respect of the deduction for income, war profits, and excess profits taxes imposed by the authority of any foreign country or possession of the United States.

(g) Prepaid interest.—

(1) In general.—If the taxable income of the taxpayer is computed under the cash receipts and disbursements method of accounting, interest paid by the taxpayer which, under regulations prescribed by the Secretary, is properly allocable to any period—

(A) with respect to which the interest represents a charge for the use or forbearance of money, and

(B) which is after the close of the taxable year in which paid,

shall be charged to capital account and shall be treated as paid in the period to which so allocable.

(2) Exception.—This subsection shall not apply to points paid in respect of any indebtedness incurred in connection with the purchase or improvement of, and secured by, the principal residence of the taxpayer to the extent that, under regulations prescribed by the Secretary, such payment of points is an established business practice in the area in which such indebtedness is incurred, and the amount of such payment does not exceed the amount generally charged in such area.

(h) Certain liabilities not incurred before economic performance.—

(1) In general.—For purposes of this title, in determining whether an amount has been incurred with respect to any item during any taxable year, the all events test shall not be treated as met any earlier than when economic performance with respect to such item occurs.

(2) Time when economic performance occurs.—Except as provided in regulations prescribed by the Secretary, the time when economic performance occurs shall be determined under the following principles:

(A) Services and property provided to the taxpayer.—If the liability of the taxpayer arises out of—

(i) the providing of services to the taxpayer by another person, economic performance occurs as such person provides such services,

(ii) the providing of property to the taxpayer by another person, economic performance occurs as the person provides such property, or

(iii) the use of the property by the taxpayer, economic performance occurs as the taxpayer uses such property.

(B) Services and property provided by the taxpayer.—If the liability of the taxpayer requires the taxpayer to provide property or services, economic performance occurs as the taxpayer provides such property or services.

(C) Workers compensation and tort liabilities of the taxpayer.—If the liability of the taxpayer requires a payment to another person and—

(i) arises under any workers compensation act, or

(ii) arises out of any tort,

economic performance occurs as the payments to such person are made. Subparagraphs (A) and (B) shall not apply to any liability described in the preceding sentence.

(D) Other items.—In the case of any other liability of the taxpayer, economic performance occurs at the time determined under regulations prescribed by the Secretary.

(3) Exception for certain recurring items.—

(A) In general.—Notwithstanding paragraph (1) an item shall be treated as incurred during any taxable year if—

(i) the all events test with respect to such item is met during such taxable year (determined without regard to paragraph (1)),

(ii) economic performance with respect to such item occurs within the shorter of—

(I) a reasonable period after the close of such taxable year, or

(II) 8½ months after the close of such taxable year,

(iii) such item is recurring in nature and the taxpayer consistently treats items of such kind as incurred in the taxable year in which the requirements of clause (i) are met, and

(iv) either—

(I) such item is not a material item, or

(II) the accrual of such item in the taxable year in which the requirements of clause (i) are met results in a more proper match against income than accruing such item in the taxable year in which economic performance occurs.

(B) Financial statements considered under subparagraph (A)(iv).—In making a determination under subparagraph (A)(iv), the treatment of such item on financial statements shall be taken into account.

(C) Paragraph not to apply to workers compensation and tort liabilities.—This paragraph shall not apply to any item described in subparagraph (C) of paragraph (2).

(4) All events test.—For purposes of this subsection, the all events test is met with respect to any item if all events have occurred which determine the fact of liability and the amount of such liability can be determined with reasonable accuracy.

(5) Subsection not to apply to certain items.—This subsection shall not apply to any item for which a deduction is allowable under a provision of this title which specifically provides for a deduction for a reserve for estimated expenses.

(i) Special rules for tax shelters.—

(1) Recurring item exception not to apply.—In the case of a tax shelter, economic performance shall be determined without regard to paragraph (3) of subsection (h).

* * *

(3) Tax shelter defined.—For purposes of this subsection, the term "tax shelter" means—

(A) any enterprise (other than a C corporation) if at any time interests in such enterprise have been offered for sale in any offering required to be registered with any Federal or State agency having the authority to regulate the offering of securities for sale,

(B) any syndicate (within the meaning of section 1256(e)(3)(B)), and

(C) any tax shelter (as defined in section 6662(d)(2)(C)(ii)).

(4) Special rules for farming.—In the case of the trade or business of farming (as defined in section 464(e)), in determining whether an entity is a tax shelter, the definition of farming syndicate in section 464(c) shall be substituted for subparagraphs (A) and (B) of paragraph (3).

(5) Economic performance.—For purposes of this subsection, the term "economic performance" has the meaning given such term by subsection (h).

* * *

§ 464. Limitations on deductions for certain farming

(a) General rule.—In the case of any farming syndicate (as defined in subsection (c)), a deduction (otherwise allowable under this chapter) for amounts paid for feed, seed, fertilizer, or other similar farm supplies shall only be allowed for the taxable year in which such feed, seed, fertilizer, or other supplies are actually used or consumed, or, if later, for the taxable year for which allowable as a deduction (determined without regard to this section).

* * *

(c) Farming syndicate defined.—

(1) In general.—For purposes of this section, the term "farming syndicate" means—

(A) a partnership or any other enterprise other than a corporation which is not an S corporation engaged in the trade or business of farming, if at any time interests in such partnership or enterprise have been offered for sale in any offering required to be registered with any Federal or State agency having authority to regulate the offering of securities for sale, or

(B) a partnership or any other enterprise other than a corporation which is not an S corporation engaged in the trade or business of farming, if more than 35 percent of the losses during any period are allocable to limited partners or limited entrepreneurs.

* * *

(e) Definitions.—For purposes of this section—

(1) Farming.—The term "farming" means the cultivation of land or the raising or harvesting of any agricultural or horticultural commodity including the raising, shearing, feeding, caring for, training, and management of animals. For purposes of the preceding sentence, trees (other than trees bearing fruit or nuts) shall not be treated as an agricultural or horticultural commodity.

(2) Limited entrepreneur.—The term "limited entrepreneur" means a person who—

(A) has an interest in an enterprise other than as a limited partner, and

(B) does not actively participate in the management of such enterprise.

* * *

§ 465. Deductions limited to amount at risk

(a) Limitation to amount at risk.—

(1) In general.—In the case of—

(A) an individual, and

(B) a C corporation with respect to which the stock ownership requirement of paragraph (2) of section 542(a) is met,

engaged in an activity to which this section applies, any loss from such activity for the taxable year shall be allowed only to the extent of the aggregate amount with respect to which the taxpayer is at risk (within the meaning of subsection (b)) for such activity at the close of the taxable year.

(2) Deduction in succeeding year.—Any loss from an activity to which this section applies not allowed under this section for the taxable year shall be treated as a deduction allocable to such activity in the first succeeding taxable year.

(3) Special rules for applying paragraph (1)(B).—For purposes of paragraph (1)(B)—

(A) section 544(a)(2) shall be applied as if such section did not contain the phrase "or by or for his partner"; and

(B) sections 544(a)(4)(A) and 544(b)(1) shall be applied by substituting "the corporation meet the stock ownership requirements of section 542(a)(2)" for "the corporation a personal holding company".

(b) Amounts considered at risk.—

(1) In general.—For purposes of this section, a taxpayer shall be considered at risk for an activity with respect to amounts including—

(A) the amount of money and the adjusted basis of other property contributed by the taxpayer to the activity, and

(B) amounts borrowed with respect to such activity (as determined under paragraph (2)).

(2) Borrowed amounts.—For purposes of this section, a taxpayer shall be considered at risk with respect to amounts borrowed for use in an activity to the extent that he—

(A) is personally liable for the repayment of such amounts, or

(B) has pledged property, other than property used in such activity, as security for such borrowed amount (to the extent of the net fair market value of the taxpayer's interest in such property).

No property shall be taken into account as security if such property is directly or indirectly financed by indebtedness which is secured by property described in paragraph (1).

(3) Certain borrowed amounts excluded.—

(A) In general.—Except to the extent provided in regulations, for purposes of paragraph (1)(B), amounts borrowed shall not be considered to be at risk with respect to an activity if such amounts are borrowed from any person who has an interest in such activity or from a related person to a person (other than the taxpayer) having such an interest.

(B) Exceptions.—

(i) Interest as creditor.—Subparagraph (A) shall not apply to an interest as a creditor in the activity.

(ii) Interest as shareholder with respect to amounts borrowed by corporation.—In the case of amounts borrowed by a corporation from a shareholder, subparagraph (A) shall not apply to an interest as a shareholder.

(C) Related person.—For purposes of this subsection, a person (hereinafter in this paragraph referred to as the "related person") is related to any person if—

(i) the related person bears a relationship to such person specified in section 267(b) or section 707(b)(1), or

* * *

For purposes of clause (i), in applying section 267(b) or 707(b)(1), "10 percent" shall be substituted for "50 percent".

(4) Exception.—Notwithstanding any other provision of this section, a taxpayer shall not be considered at risk with respect to amounts protected against loss through nonrecourse financing, guarantees, stop loss agreements, or other similar arrangements.

(5) Amounts at risk in subsequent years.—If in any taxable year the taxpayer has a loss from an activity to which subsection (a) applies, the amount with respect to which a taxpayer is considered to be at risk (within the meaning of subsection (b)) in subsequent taxable years with respect to that activity shall be reduced by that portion of the loss which (after the application of subsection (a)) is allowable as a deduction.

(6) Qualified nonrecourse financing treated as amount at risk.—For purposes of this section—

(A) In general.—Notwithstanding any other provision of this subsection, in the case of an activity of holding real property, a taxpayer shall be considered at risk with respect to the taxpayer's share of any qualified nonrecourse financing which is secured by real property used in such activity.

(B) Qualified nonrecourse financing.—For purposes of this paragraph, the term "qualified nonrecourse financing" means any financing—

(i) which is borrowed by the taxpayer with respect to the activity of holding real property,

(ii) which is borrowed by the taxpayer from a qualified person or represents a loan from any Federal, State, or local government or instrumentality thereof, or is guaranteed by any Federal, State, or local government,

(iii) except to the extent provided in regulations, with respect to which no person is personally liable for repayment, and

(iv) which is not convertible debt.

(C) Special rule for partnerships.—In the case of a partnership, a partner's share of any qualified nonrecourse financing of such partnership shall be determined on the basis of the partner's share of liabilities of such partnership incurred in connection with such financing (within the meaning of section 752).

(D) Qualified person defined.—For purposes of this paragraph—

(i) In general.—The term "qualified person" has the meaning given such term by section 49(a)(1)(D)(iv).

(ii) Certain commercially reasonable financing from related persons.—For purposes of clause (i), section 49(a)(1)(D)(iv) shall be applied without regard to subclause (I) thereof (relating to financing from related persons) if the financing from the related person is commercially reasonable and on substantially the same terms as loans involving unrelated persons.

(E) Activity of holding real property.—For purposes of this paragraph—

(i) Incidental personal property and services.—The activity of holding real property includes the holding of personal property and the providing of services which are incidental to making real property available as living accommodations.

(ii) Mineral property.—The activity of holding real property shall not include the holding of mineral property.

(c) Activities to which section applies.—

(1) Types of activities.—This section applies to any taxpayer engaged in the activity of—

(A) holding, producing, or distributing motion picture films or video tapes,

(B) farming (as defined in section 464(e)),

(C) leasing any section 1245 property (as defined in section 1245(a)(3)),

(D) exploring for, or exploiting, oil and gas resources, or

(E) exploring for, or exploiting, geothermal deposits (as defined in section 613(e)(2)).

(2) Separate activities.—For purposes of this section—

(A) In general.—Except as provided in subparagraph (B), a taxpayer's activity with respect to each—

(i) film or video tape,

(ii) section 1245 property which is leased or held for leasing,

(iii) farm,

(iv) oil and gas property (as defined under section 614), or

(v) geothermal property (as defined under section 614),

shall be treated as a separate activity.

(B) Aggregation rules.—

(i) Special rule for leases of section 1245 property by partnerships or S corporations.—In the case of any partnership or S corporation, all activities with respect to section 1245 properties which—

(I) are leased or held for lease, and

(II) are placed in service in any taxable year of the partnership or S corporation,

shall be treated as a single activity.

(ii) Other aggregation rules.—Rules similar to the rules of subparagraphs (B) and (C) of paragraph (3) shall apply for purposes of this paragraph.

(3) Extension to other activities.—

(A) In general.—In the case of taxable years beginning after December 31, 1978, this section also applies to each activity—

(i) engaged in by the taxpayer in carrying on a trade or business or for the production of income, and

(ii) which is not described in paragraph (1).

(B) Aggregation of activities where taxpayer actively participates in management of trade or business.—Except as provided in subparagraph (C), for purposes of this section, activities described in subparagraph (A) which constitute a trade or business shall be treated as one activity if—

(i) the taxpayer actively participates in the management of such trade or business, or

(ii) such trade or business is carried on by a partnership or an S corporation and 65 percent or more of the losses for the taxable year is allocable to persons who actively participate in the management of the trade or business.

(C) Aggregation or separation of activities under regulations.—The Secretary shall prescribe regulations under which activities described in subparagraph (A) shall be aggregated or treated as separate activities.

(D) Application of subsection (b)(3).—In the case of an activity described in subparagraph (A), subsection (b)(3) shall apply only to the extent provided in regulations prescribed by the Secretary.

(4) Exclusion for certain equipment leasing by closely-held corporations.—

(A) In general.—In the case of a corporation described in subsection (a)(1)(B) actively engaged in equipment leasing—

(i) the activity of equipment leasing shall be treated as a separate activity, and

(ii) subsection (a) shall not apply to losses from such activity.

(B) 50-percent gross receipts test.—For purposes of subparagraph (A), a corporation shall not be considered to be actively engaged in equipment leasing unless 50 percent or more of the gross receipts of the corporation for the taxable year is attributable, under regulations prescribed by the Secretary, to equipment leasing.

(C) Component members of controlled group treated as a single corporation.—For purposes of subparagraph (A), the component members of a controlled group of corporations shall be treated as a single corporation.

* * *

(6) Definitions relating to paragraphs (4) and (5).—For purposes of paragraphs (4) and (5)—

(A) Equipment leasing.—The term ''equipment leasing'' means—

(i) the leasing of equipment which is section 1245 property, and

(ii) the purchasing, servicing, and selling of such equipment.

(B) Leasing of master sound recordings, etc., excluded.—The term ''equipment leasing'' does not include the leasing of master sound recordings, and other similar contractual arrangements with respect to tangible or intangible assets associated with literary, artistic, or musical properties.

(C) Controlled group of corporations; component member.—The terms ''controlled group of corporations'' and ''component member'' have the same meanings as when used in section 1563. The determination of the taxable years taken into account with respect to any controlled group of corporations shall be made in a manner consistent with the manner set forth in section 1563.

(7) Exclusion of active businesses of qualified C corporations.—

(A) In general.—In the case of a taxpayer which is a qualified C corporation—

(i) each qualifying business carried on by such taxpayer shall be treated as a separate activity, and

(ii) subsection (a) shall not apply to losses from such business.

(B) Qualified C corporation.—For purposes of subparagraph (A), the term ''qualified C corporation'' means any corporation described in subparagraph (B) of subsection (a)(1) which is not—

(i) a personal holding company (as defined in section 542(a)), or

(ii) a personal service corporation (as defined in section 269A(b) but determined by substituting ''5 percent'' for ''10 percent'' in section 269A(b)(2)).

(C) Qualifying business.—For purposes of this paragraph, the term ''qualifying business'' means any active business if—

(i) during the entire 12-month period ending on the last day of the taxable year, such corporation had at least 1 full-time employee substantially all the services of whom were in the active management of such business,

(ii) during the entire 12-month period ending on the last day of the taxable year, such corporation had at least 3 full-time, nonowner employees substantially all of the services of whom were services directly related to such business,

(iii) the amount of the deductions attributable to such business which are allowable to the taxpayer solely by reason of sections 162 and 404 for the taxable year exceeds 15 percent of the gross income from such business for such year, and

(iv) such business is not an excluded business.

(D) Special rules for application of subparagraph (C).—

(i) Partnerships in which taxpayer is a qualified corporate partner.—In the case of an active business of a partnership, if—

(I) the taxpayer is a qualified corporate partner in the partnership, and

(II) during the entire 12-month period ending on the last day of the partnership's taxable year, there was at least 1 full-time employee of the partnership (or of a qualified corporate partner) substantially all the services of whom were in the active management of such business,

then the taxpayer's proportionate share (determined on the basis of its profits interest) of the activities of the partnership in such business shall be treated as activities of the taxpayer (and clause (i) of subparagraph (C) shall not apply in determining whether such business is a qualifying business of the taxpayer).

(ii) Qualified corporate partner.—For purposes of clause (i), the term "qualified corporate partner" means any corporation if—

(I) such corporation is a general partner in the partnership,

(II) such corporation has an interest of 10 percent or more in the profits and losses of the partnership, and

(III) such corporation has contributed property to the partnership in an amount not less than the lesser of $500,000 or 10 percent of the net worth of the corporation.

For purposes of subclause (III), any contribution of property other than money shall be taken into account at its fair market value.

(iii) Deduction for owner employee compensation not taken into account.—For purposes of clause (iii) of subparagraph (C), there shall not be taken into account any deduction in respect of compensation for personal services rendered by any employee (other than a non-owner employee) of the taxpayer or any member of such employee's family (within the meaning of section 318(a)(1)).

* * *

(E) Definitions.—For purposes of this paragraph—

(i) Non-owner employee.—The term "non-owner employee" means any employee who does not own, at any time during the taxable year, more than 5 percent in value of the outstanding stock of the taxpayer. For purposes of the preceding sentence, section 318 shall apply, except that "5 percent" shall be substituted for "50 percent" in section 318(a)(2)(C).

(ii) Excluded business.—The term "excluded business" means—

(I) equipment leasing (as defined in paragraph (6)), and

(II) any business involving the use, exploitation, sale, lease, or other disposition of master sound recordings, motion picture films, video tapes, or tangible or intangible assets associated with literary, artistic, musical, or similar properties.

* * *

(F) Affiliated group treated as 1 taxpayer.—For purposes of this paragraph—

(i) In general.—Except as provided in subparagraph (G), the component members of an affiliated group of corporations shall be treated as a single taxpayer.

(ii) Affiliated group of corporations.—The term "affiliated group of corporations" means an affiliated group (as defined in section 1504(a)) which files or is required to file consolidated income tax returns.

(iii) Component member.—The term "component member" means an includible corporation (as defined in section 1504) which is a member of the affiliated group.

(G) Loss of 1 member of affiliated group may not offset income of personal holding company or personal service corporation.—Nothing in this paragraph shall permit any loss of a member of an affiliated group to be used as an offset against the income of any other member of such group which is a personal holding company (as defined in section 542(a)) or a personal service corporation (as defined in section 269A(b) but determined by substituting "5 percent" for "10 percent" in section 269A(b)(2)).

(d) Definition of loss.—For purposes of this section, the term "loss" means the excess of the deductions allowable under this chapter for the taxable year (determined without regard to the first sentence of subsection (a)) and allocable to an activity to which this section applies over the income received or accrued by the taxpayer during the taxable year from such activity (determined without regard to subsection (e)(1)(A)).

(e) Recapture of losses where amount at risk is less than zero.—

(1) In general.—If zero exceeds the amount for which the taxpayer is at risk in any activity at the close of any taxable year—

(A) the taxpayer shall include in his gross income for such taxable year (as income from such activity) an amount equal to such excess, and

(B) an amount equal to the amount so included in gross income shall be treated as a deduction allocable to such activity for the first succeeding taxable year.

(2) Limitation.—The excess referred to in paragraph (1) shall not exceed—

(A) the aggregate amount of the reductions required by subsection (b) (5) with respect to the activity by reason of losses for all prior taxable years beginning after December 31, 1978, reduced by

(B) the amounts previously included in gross income with respect to such activity under this subsection.

§ 467. Certain payments for the use of property or services

(a) Accrual method on present value basis.—In the case of the lessor or lessee under any section 467 rental agreement, there shall be taken into account for purposes of this title for any taxable year the sum of—

(1) the amount of the rent which accrues during such taxable year as determined under subsection (b), and

(2) interest for the year on the amounts which were taken into account under this subsection for prior taxable years and which are unpaid.

(b) Accrual of rental payments.—

(1) Allocation follows agreement.—Except as provided in paragraph (2), the determination of the amount of the rent under any section 467 rental agreement which accrues during any taxable year shall be made—

(A) by allocating rents in accordance with the agreement, and

(B) by taking into account any rent to be paid after the close of the period in an amount determined under regulations which shall be based on present value concepts.

(2) Constant rental accrual in case of certain tax avoidance transactions, etc.—In the case of any section 467 rental agreement to which this paragraph applies, the portion of the rent which accrues during any taxable year shall be that portion of the constant rental amount with respect to such agreement which is allocable to such taxable year.

(3) Agreements to which paragraph (2) applies.—Paragraph (2) applies to any rental payment agreement if—

(A) such agreement is a disqualified leaseback or long-term agreement, or

(B) such agreement does not provide for the allocation referred to in paragraph (1)(A).

(4) Disqualified leaseback or long-term agreement.—For purposes of this subsection, the term "disqualified leaseback or long-term agreement" means any section 467 rental agreement if—

(A) such agreement is part of a leaseback transaction or such agreement is for a term in excess of 75 percent of the statutory recovery period for the property, and

(B) a principal purpose for providing increasing rents under the agreement is the avoidance of tax imposed by this subtitle.

(5) Exceptions to disqualification in certain cases.—The Secretary shall prescribe regulations setting forth circumstances under which agreements will not be treated as disqualified leaseback or long-term agreements, including circumstances relating to—

(A) changes in amounts paid determined by reference to price indices,

(B) rents based on a fixed percentage of lessee receipts or similar amounts,

(C) reasonable rent holidays, or

(D) changes in amounts paid to unrelated 3rd parties.

(c) Recapture of prior understated inclusions under leaseback or long-term agreements.—

(1) In general.—If—

(A) the lessor under any section 467 rental agreement disposes of any property subject to such agreement during the term of such agreement, and

(B) such agreement is a leaseback or long-term agreement to which paragraph (2) of subsection (b) did not apply,

the recapture amount shall be treated as ordinary income. Such gain shall be recognized notwithstanding any other provision of this subtitle.

(2) Recapture amount.—For purposes of paragraph (1), the term "recapture amount" means the lesser of—

(A) the prior understated inclusions, or

(B) the excess of the amount realized (or in the case of a disposition other than a sale, exchange, or involuntary conversion, the fair market value of the property) over the adjusted basis of such property.

The amount determined under subparagraph (B) shall be reduced by the amount of any gain treated as ordinary income on the disposition under any other provision of this subtitle.

(3) Prior understated inclusions.—For purposes of this subsection, the term "prior understated inclusion" means the excess (if any) of—

(A) the amount which would have been taken into account by the lessor under subsection (a) for periods before the disposition if subsection (b)(2) had applied to the agreement, over

(B) the amount taken into account under subsection (a) by the lessor for periods before the disposition.

(4) Leaseback or long-term agreement.—For purposes of this subsection, the term "leaseback or long-term agreement" means any agreement described in subsection (b)(4)(A).

(5) Special rules.—Under regulations prescribed by the Secretary—

(A) exceptions similar to the exceptions applicable under section 1245 or 1250 (whichever is appropriate) shall apply for purposes of this subsection,

(B) any transferee in a disposition excepted by reason of subparagraph (A) who has a transferred basis in the property shall be treated in the same manner as the transferor, and

(C) for purposes of sections 170(e) and 751(c), amounts treated as ordinary income under this section shall be treated in the same manner as amounts treated as ordinary income under section 1245 or 1250.

(d) Section 467 rental agreements.—

(1) In general.—Except as otherwise provided in this subsection, the term "section 467 rental agreements" means any rental agreement for the use of tangible property under which—

(A) there is at least one amount allocable to the use of property during a calendar year which is to be paid after the close of the calendar year following the calendar year in which such use occurs, or

(B) there are increases in the amount to be paid as rent under the agreement.

(2) Section not to apply to agreements involving payments of $250,000 or less.—This section shall not apply to any amount to be paid for the use of property if the sum of the following amounts does not exceed $250,000—

(A) the aggregate amount of payments received as consideration for such use of property, and

(B) the aggregate value of any other consideration to be received for such use of property.

For purposes of the preceding sentence, rules similar to the rules of clauses (ii) and (iii) of section 1274(c)(4)(C) shall apply.

(e) Definitions.—For purposes of this section—

(1) Constant rental amount.—The term "constant rental amount" means, with respect to any section 467 rental agreement, the amount which, if paid as of the close of each lease period under the agreement, would result in an aggregate present value equal to the present value of the aggregate payments required under the agreement.

(2) Leaseback transaction.—A transaction is a leaseback transaction if it involves a leaseback to any person who had an interest in such property at any time within 2 years before such leaseback (or to a related person).

(3) Statutory recovery period.—

(A) In general.—

In the case of property which is:	The statutory recovery period is:
3–year property	3 years
5–year property	5 years
7–year property	7 years
10–year property	10 years
15–year and 20–year property	15 years
Residential rental property and nonresidential real property	19 years
Any railroad grading or tunnel bore	50 years

(B) Special rule for property not depreciable under section 168.—In the case of property to which section 168 does not apply, subparagraph (A) shall be applied as if section 168 applies to such property.

(4) Discount and interest rate.—For purposes of computing present value and interest under subsection (a)(2), the rate used shall be equal to 110 percent of the applicable Federal rate determined under section 1274(d) (compounded semiannually) which is in effect at the time the agreement is entered into with respect to debt instruments having a maturity equal to the term of the agreement.

(5) Related person.—The term "related person" has the meaning given to such term by section 465(b)(3)(C).

(6) Certain options of lessee to renew not taken into account.—Except as provided in regulations prescribed by the Secretary, there shall not be taken into account in computing the term of any agreement for purposes of this section any extension which is solely at the option of the lessee.

(f) Comparable rules where agreement for decreasing payments.—Under regulations prescribed by the Secretary, rules comparable to the rules of this section shall also apply in the case of any agreement where the amount paid under the agreement for the use of property decreases during the term of the agreement.

(g) Comparable rules for services.—Under regulations prescribed by the Secretary, rules comparable to the rules of subsection (a)(2) shall also apply in the case of payments for services which meet requirements comparable to the requirements of subsection (d). The preceding sentence shall not apply to any amount to which section 404 or 404A (or any other provision specified in regulations) applies.

(h) Regulations.—The Secretary shall prescribe such regulations as may be appropriate to carry out the purposes of this section, including regulations providing for the application of this section in the case of contingent payments.

§ 469. Passive activity losses and credits limited

(a) Disallowance.—

(1) In general.—If for any taxable year the taxpayer is described in paragraph (2), neither—

(A) the passive activity loss, nor

(B) the passive activity credit,

for the taxable year shall be allowed.

(2) Persons described.—The following are described in this paragraph:

(A) any individual, estate, or trust,

(B) any closely held C corporation, and

(C) any personal service corporation.

(b) Disallowed loss or credit carried to next year.—Except as otherwise provided in this section, any loss or credit from an activity which is disallowed under subsection (a) shall be treated as a deduction or credit allocable to such activity in the next taxable year.

(c) Passive activity defined.—For purposes of this section—

(1) In general.—The term "passive activity" means any activity—

(A) which involves the conduct of any trade or business, and

(B) in which the taxpayer does not materially participate.

(2) Passive activity includes any rental activity.—The term "passive activity" includes any rental activity.

(3) Working interests in oil and gas property.—

(A) In general.—The term "passive activity" shall not include any working interest in any oil or gas property which the taxpayer holds directly or through an entity which does not limit the liability of the taxpayer with respect to such interest.

* * *

(4) Material participation not required for paragraphs (2) and (3).—Paragraphs (2) and (3) shall be applied without regard to whether or not the taxpayer materially participates in the activity.

(5) Trade or business includes research and experimentation activity.—For purposes of paragraph (1)(A), the term "trade or business" includes any activity involving research or experimentation (within the meaning of section 174).

(6) Activity in connection with trade or business or production of income.—To the extent provided in regulations, for purposes of paragraph (1)(A), the term "trade or business" includes—

(A) any activity in connection with a trade or business, or

(B) any activity with respect to which expenses are allowable as a deduction under section 212.

(7) Special rules for taxpayers in real property business.—

(A) In general.—If this paragraph applies to any taxpayer for a taxable year—

(i) paragraph (2) shall not apply to any rental real estate activity of such taxpayer for such taxable year, and

(ii) this section shall be applied as if each interest of the taxpayer in rental real estate were a separate activity.

Notwithstanding clause (ii), a taxpayer may elect to treat all interests in rental real estate as one activity. Nothing in the preceding provisions of this subparagraph shall be construed as affecting the determination of whether the taxpayer materially participates with respect to any interest in a limited partnership as a limited partner.

(B) Taxpayers to whom paragraph applies.—This paragraph shall apply to a taxpayer for a taxable year if—

(i) more than one-half of the personal services performed in trades or businesses by the taxpayer during such taxable year are performed in real property trades or businesses in which the taxpayer materially participates, and

(ii) such taxpayer performs more than 750 hours of services during the taxable year in real property trades or businesses in which the taxpayer materially participates.

In the case of a joint return, the requirements of the preceding sentence are satisfied if and only if either spouse separately satisfies such requirements. For purposes of the preceding sentence, activities in which a spouse materially participates shall be determined under subsection (h).

(C) Real property trade or business.—For purposes of this paragraph, the term "real property trade or business" means any real property development, redevelopment, construction, reconstruction, acquisition, conversion, rental, operation, management, leasing, or brokerage trade or business.

(D) Special rules for subparagraph (B).—

(i) Closely held C corporations.—In the case of a closely held C corporation, the requirements of subparagraph (B) shall be treated as met for any taxable year if more than 50 percent of the gross receipts of such corporation for such taxable year are derived from real property trades or businesses in which the corporation materially participates.

(ii) Personal services as an employee.—For purposes of subparagraph (B), personal services performed as an employee shall not be treated as performed in real property trades or businesses. The preceding sentence shall not apply if such employee is a 5–percent owner (as defined in section 416(i)(1)(B)) in the employer.

(d) Passive activity loss and credit defined.—For purposes of this section—

(1) Passive activity loss.—The term "passive activity loss" means the amount (if any) by which—

(A) the aggregate losses from all passive activities for the taxable year, exceed

(B) the aggregate income from all passive activities for such year.

(2) Passive activity credit.—The term "passive activity credit" means the amount (if any) by which—

(A) the sum of the credits from all passive activities allowable for the taxable year under—

(i) subpart D of part IV of subchapter A, or

(ii) subpart B * * * of such part IV, exceeds

(B) the regular tax liability of the taxpayer for the taxable year allocable to all passive activities.

(e) Special rules for determining income or loss from a passive activity.—For purposes of this section—

(1) Certain income not treated as income from passive activity.—In determining the income or loss from any activity—

(A) In general.—There shall not be taken into account—

(i) any—

(I) gross income from interest, dividends, annuities, or royalties not derived in the ordinary course of a trade or business,

(II) expenses (other than interest) which are clearly and directly allocable to such gross income, and

(III) interest expense properly allocable to such gross income, and

(ii) gain or loss not derived in the ordinary course of a trade or business which is attributable to the disposition of property—

(I) producing income of a type described in clause (i), or

(II) held for investment.

For purposes of clause (ii), any interest in a passive activity shall not be treated as property held for investment.

(B) Return on working capital.—For purposes of subparagraph (A), any income, gain, or loss which is attributable to an investment of working capital shall be treated as not derived in the ordinary course of a trade or business.

(2) Passive losses of certain closely held corporations may offset active income.—

(A) In general.—If a closely held C corporation (other than a personal service corporation) has net active income for any taxable year, the passive activity loss of such taxpayer for such taxable year (determined without regard to this paragraph)—

(i) shall be allowable as a deduction against net active income, and

(ii) shall not be taken into account under subsection (a) to the extent so allowable as a deduction.

A similar rule shall apply in the case of any passive activity credit of the taxpayer.

(B) Net active income.—For purposes of this paragraph, the term "net active income" means the taxable income of the taxpayer for the taxable year determined without regard to—

(i) any income or loss from a passive activity, and

(ii) any item of gross income, expense, gain, or loss described in paragraph (1)(A).

(3) Compensation for personal services.—Earned income (within the meaning of section 911(d)(2)(A)) shall not be taken into account in computing the income or loss from a passive activity for any taxable year.

(4) Dividends reduced by dividends received deduction.—For purposes of paragraphs (1) and (2), income from dividends shall be reduced by the amount of any dividends received deduction under section 243, 244, or 245.

(f) Treatment of former passive activities.—For purposes of this section—

(1) In general.—If an activity is a former passive activity for any taxable year—

(A) any unused deduction allocable to such activity under subsection (b) shall be offset against the income from such activity for the taxable year,

(B) any unused credit allocable to such activity under subsection (b) shall be offset against the regular tax liability (computed after the application of paragraph (1)) allocable to such activity for the taxable year, and

(C) any such deduction or credit remaining after the application of subparagraphs (A) and (B) shall continue to be treated as arising from a passive activity.

(2) Change in status of closely held C corporation or personal service corporation.—If a taxpayer ceases for any taxable year to be a closely held C corporation or personal service corporation, this section shall continue to apply to losses and credits to which this section applied for any preceding taxable year in the same manner as if such taxpayer continued to be a closely held C corporation or personal service corporation, whichever is applicable.

(3) Former passive activity.—The term "former passive activity" means any activity which, with respect to the taxpayer—

(A) is not a passive activity for the taxable year, but

(B) was a passive activity for any prior taxable year.

(g) Dispositions of entire interest in passive activity.—If during the taxable year a taxpayer disposes of his entire interest in any passive activity (or former passive activity), the following rules shall apply:

(1) Fully taxable transaction.—

(A) In general.—If all gain or loss realized on such disposition is recognized, the excess of—

(i) any loss from such activity for such taxable year (determined after the application of subsection (b)), over

(ii) any net income or gain for such taxable year from all other passive activities (determined after the application of subsection (b)),

shall be treated as a loss which is not from a passive activity.

(B) Subparagraph (A) not to apply to disposition involving related party.—If the taxpayer and the person acquiring the interest bear a relationship to each other described in section 267(b) or section 707(b)(1), then subparagraph (A) shall not apply to any loss of the taxpayer until the taxable year in which such interest is acquired (in a transaction described in subparagraph (A)) by another person who does not bear such a relationship to the taxpayer.

(C) Income from prior years.—To the extent provided in regulations, income or gain from the activity for preceding taxable years shall be taken into account under subparagraph (A)(ii) for the taxable year to the extent necessary to prevent the avoidance of this section.

(2) Disposition by death. –If an interest in the activity is transferred by reason of the death of the taxpayer—

(A) paragraph (1)(A) shall apply to losses described in paragraph (1)(A) to the extent such losses are greater than the excess (if any) of—

(i) the basis of such property in the hands of the transferee, over

(ii) the adjusted basis of such property immediately before the death of the taxpayer, and

(B) any losses to the extent of the excess described in subparagraph (A) shall not be allowed as a deduction for any taxable year.

(3) Installment sale of entire interest.—In the case of an installment sale of an entire interest in an activity to which section 453 applies, paragraph (1) shall apply to the portion of such losses for each taxable year which bears the same ratio to all such losses as the gain recognized on such sale during such taxable year bears to the gross profit from such sale (realized or to be realized when payment is completed).

(h) Material participation defined.—For purposes of this section—

(1) In general.—A taxpayer shall be treated as materially participating in an activity only if the taxpayer is involved in the operations of the activity on a basis which is—

(A) regular,

(B) continuous, and

(C) substantial.

(2) Interests in limited partnerships.—Except as provided in regulations, no interest in a limited partnership as a limited partner shall be treated as an interest with respect to which a taxpayer materially participates.

(3) Treatment of certain retired individuals and surviving spouses.—A taxpayer shall be treated as materially participating in any farming activity for a taxable year if paragraph (4) or (5) of section 2032A(b) would cause the requirements of section 2032A(b)(1)(C)(ii) to be met with respect to real property used in such activity if such taxpayer had died during the taxable year.

(4) Certain closely held C corporations and personal service corporations.—A closely held C corporation or personal service corporation shall be treated as materially participating in an activity only if—

(A) 1 or more shareholders holding stock representing more than 50 percent (by value) of the outstanding stock of such corporation materially participate in such activity, or

(B) in the case of a closely held C corporation (other than a personal service corporation), the requirements of section 465(c)(7)(C) (without regard to clause (iv)) are met with respect to such activity.

(5) Participation by spouse.—In determining whether a taxpayer materially participates, the participation of the spouse of the taxpayer shall be taken into account.

(i) $25,000 offset for rental real estate activities.—

(1) In general.—In the case of any natural person, subsection (a) shall not apply to that portion of the passive activity loss or the deduction equivalent (within the meaning of subsection (j)(5)) of the passive activity credit for any taxable year which is attributable to all rental real estate activities with respect to which such individual actively participated in such taxable year (and if any portion of such loss or credit arose in another taxable year, in such other taxable year).

(2) Dollar limitation.—The aggregate amount to which paragraph (1) applies for any taxable year shall not exceed $25,000.

(3) Phase-out of exemption.—

(A) In general.—In the case of any taxpayer, the $25,000 amount under paragraph (2) shall be reduced (but not below zero) by 50 percent of the amount by which the adjusted gross income of the taxpayer for the taxable year exceeds $100,000.

(B) Special phase-out of rehabilitation credit.—In the case of any portion of the passive activity credit for any taxable year which is attributable to the rehabilitation credit determined under section 47, subparagraph (A) shall be applied by substituting "$200,000" for "$100,000".

* * *

(D) Exception for low-income housing credit.—Subparagraph (A) shall not apply to any portion of the passive activity credit for any taxable year which is attributable to any credit determined under section 42.

* * *

(F) Adjusted gross income.—For purposes of this paragraph, adjusted gross income shall be determined without regard to—

(i) any amount includible in gross income under section 86,

(ii) the amounts excludable from gross income under sections 135 and 137.

(iii) any amount allowable as a deduction under sections 199, 219, 221, and 222 and

(iv) any passive activity loss or any loss allowable by reason of subsection (c)(7).

(4) Special rule for estates.—

(A) In general.—In the case of taxable years of an estate ending less than 2 years after the date of the death of the decedent, this subsection shall apply to all rental real estate activities with respect to which such decedent actively participated before his death.

(B) Reduction for surviving spouse's exemption.—For purposes of subparagraph (A), the $25,000 amount under paragraph (2) shall be reduced by the amount of the exemption under paragraph (1) (without regard to paragraph (3)) allowable to the surviving spouse of the decedent for the taxable year ending with or within the taxable year of the estate.

(5) Married individuals filing separately.—

(A) In general.—Except as provided in subparagraph (B), in the case of any married individual filing a separate return, this subsection shall be applied by substituting—

(i) "$12,500" for "$25,000" each place it appears,

(ii) "$50,000" for "$100,000" in paragraph (3)(A), and

(iii) "$100,000" for "$200,000" in paragraph (3)(B).

(B) Taxpayers not living apart.—This subsection shall not apply to a taxpayer who—

(i) is a married individual filing a separate return for any taxable year, and

(ii) does not live apart from his spouse at all times during such taxable year.

(6) Active participation.—

(A) In general.—An individual shall not be treated as actively participating with respect to any interest in any rental real estate activity for any period if, at any time during such period, such interest (including any interest of the spouse of the individual) is less than 10 percent (by value) of all interests in such activity.

(B) No participation requirement for low-income housing or rehabilitation credit.—Paragraphs (1) and (4)(A) shall be applied without regard to the active participation requirement in the case of—

(i) any credit determined under section 42 for any taxable year, or

(ii) any rehabilitation credit determined under section 47.

(C) Interest as a limited partner.—Except as provided in regulations, no interest as a limited partner in a limited partnership shall be treated as an interest with respect to which the taxpayer actively participates.

(D) Participation by spouse.—In determining whether a taxpayer actively participates, the participation of the spouse of the taxpayer shall be taken into account.

(j) Other definitions and special rules.—For purposes of this section—

(1) Closely held C corporation.—The term "closely held C corporation" means any C corporation described in section 465(a)(1)(B).

(2) Personal service corporation.—The term "personal service corporation" has the meaning given such term by section 269A(b)(1), except that section 269A(b)(2) shall be applied—

(A) by substituting "any" for "more than 10 percent", and

(B) by substituting "any" for "50 percent or more in value" in section 318(a)(2)(C).

A corporation shall not be treated as a personal service corporation unless more than 10 percent of the stock (by value) in such corporation is held by employee-owners (within the meaning of section 269A(b)(2), as modified by the preceding sentence).

(3) Regular tax liability.—The term "regular tax liability" has the meaning given such term by section 26(b).

(4) Allocation of passive activity loss and credit.—The passive activity loss and the passive activity credit (and the $25,000 amount under subsection (i)) shall be allocated to activities, and within activities, on a pro rata basis in such manner as the Secretary may prescribe.

(5) Deduction equivalent.—The deduction equivalent of credits from a passive activity for any taxable year is the amount which (if allowed as a deduction) would reduce the regular tax liability for such taxable year by an amount equal to such credits.

(6) Special rule for gifts.—In the case of a disposition of any interest in a passive activity by gift—

(A) the basis of such interest immediately before the transfer shall be increased by the amount of any passive activity losses allocable to such interest with respect to which a deduction has not been allowed by reason of subsection (a), and

(B) such losses shall not be allowable as a deduction for any taxable year.

(7) Qualified residence interest.—The passive activity loss of a taxpayer shall be computed without regard to qualified residence interest (within the meaning of section 163(h)(3)).

(8) Rental activity.—The term "rental activity" means any activity where payments are principally for the use of tangible property.

(9) Election to increase basis of property by amount of disallowed credit.—For purposes of determining gain or loss from a disposition of any property to which subsection (g)(1) applies, the transferor may elect to increase the basis of such property immediately before the transfer by an amount equal to the portion of any unused credit allowable under this chapter which reduced the basis of such property for the taxable year in which such credit arose. If the taxpayer elects the application of this paragraph, such portion of the passive activity credit of such taxpayer shall not be allowed for any taxable year.

(10) Coordination with section 280A.—If a passive activity involves the use of a dwelling unit to which section 280A(c)(5) applies for any taxable year, any income, deduction, gain, or loss allocable to such use shall not be taken into account for purposes of this section for such taxable year.

(11) Aggregation of members of affiliated groups.—Except as provided in regulations, all members of an affiliated group which files a consolidated return shall be treated as 1 corporation.

(12) Special rule for distributions by estates or trusts.—If any interest in a passive activity is distributed by an estate or trust—

(A) the basis of such interest immediately before such distribution shall be increased by the amount of any passive activity losses allocable to such interest, and

(B) such losses shall not be allowable as a deduction for any taxable year.

(k) Separate application of section in case of publicly traded partnerships.—

(1) In general.—This section shall be applied separately with respect to items attributable to each publicly traded partnership (and subsection (i) shall not apply with respect to items attributable to any such partnership). * * *

(2) Publicly traded partnership.—For purposes of this section, the term "publicly traded partnership" means any partnership if—

(A) interests in such partnership are traded on an established securities market, or

(B) interests in such partnership are readily tradable on a secondary market (or the substantial equivalent thereof).

(3) Coordination with subsection (g).—For purposes of subsection (g), a taxpayer shall not be treated as having disposed of his entire interest in an activity of a publicly traded partnership until he disposes of his entire interest in such partnership.

* * *

(*l*) Regulations.—The Secretary shall prescribe such regulations as may be necessary or appropriate to carry out provisions of this section, including regulations—

(1) which specify what constitutes an activity, material participation, or active participation for purposes of this section,

(2) which provide that certain items of gross income will not be taken into account in determining income or loss from any activity (and the treatment of expenses allocable to such income),

(3) requiring net income or gain from a limited partnership or other passive activity to be treated as not from a passive activity,

(4) which provide for the determination of the allocation of interest expense for purposes of this section, and

(5) which deal with changes in marital status and changes between joint returns and separate returns.

* * *

Subpart D—Inventories

§ 471. General rule for inventories

(a) General rule.—Whenever in the opinion of the Secretary the use of inventories is necessary in order clearly to determine the income of any taxpayer, inventories shall be taken by such taxpayer on such basis as the Secretary may prescribe as conforming as nearly as may be to the best accounting practice in the trade or business and as most clearly reflecting the income.

(b) Estimates of inventory shrinkage permitted.—A method of determining inventories shall not be treated as failing to clearly reflect income solely because it utilizes estimates of inventory shrinkage that are confirmed by a physical count only after the last day of the taxable year if—

(1) the taxpayer normally does a physical count of inventories at each location on a regular and consistent basis, and

(2) the taxpayer makes proper adjustments to such inventories and to its estimating methods to the extent such estimates are greater than or less than the actual shrinkage.

(c) Cross reference.—

For rules relating to capitalization of direct and indirect costs of property, see section 263A.

§ 472. Last-in, first-out inventories

(a) Authorization.—A taxpayer may use the method provided in subsection (b) (whether or not such method has been prescribed under section 471) in inventorying goods specified in an application to use such method filed at such time and in such manner as the Secretary may prescribe. The change to, and the use of, such method shall be in accordance with such regulations as the Secretary may prescribe as necessary in order that the use of such method may clearly reflect income.

(b) Method applicable.—In inventorying goods specified in the application described in subsection (a), the taxpayer shall:

(1) Treat those remaining on hand at the close of the taxable year as being: First, those included in the opening inventory of the taxable year (in the order of acquisition) to the extent thereof; and second, those acquired in the taxable year;

(2) Inventory them at cost; and

(3) Treat those included in the opening inventory of the taxable year in which such method is first used as having been acquired at the same time and determine their cost by the average cost method.

(c) Condition.—Subsection (a) shall apply only if the taxpayer establishes to the satisfaction of the Secretary that the taxpayer has used no procedure other than that specified in paragraphs (1) and (3) of subsection (b) in inventorying such goods to ascertain the income, profit, or loss of the first taxable year for which the method described in subsection (b) is to be used, for the purpose of a report or statement covering such taxable year—

(1) to shareholders, partners, or other proprietors, or to beneficiaries, or

(2) for credit purposes.

* * *

§ 475. Mark to market accounting method for dealers in securities

(a) General rule.—Notwithstanding any other provision of this subpart, the following rules shall apply to securities held by a dealer in securities:

(1) Any security which is inventory in the hands of the dealer shall be included in inventory at its fair market value.

(2) In the case of any security which is not inventory in the hands of the dealer and which is held at the close of any taxable year—

(A) the dealer shall recognize gain or loss as if such security were sold for its fair market value on the last business day of such taxable year, and

(B) any gain or loss shall be taken into account for such taxable year.

Proper adjustment shall be made in the amount of any gain or loss subsequently realized for gain or loss taken into account under the preceding sentence. The Secretary may provide by regulations for the application of this paragraph at times other than the times provided in this paragraph.

(b) Exceptions.—

(1) In general.—Subsection (a) shall not apply to—

(A) any security held for investment,

(B)(i) any security described in subsection (c)(2)(C) which is acquired (including originated) by the taxpayer in the ordinary course of a trade or business of the taxpayer and which is not held for sale, and (ii) any obligation to acquire a security described in clause (i) if such obligation is entered into in the ordinary course of such trade or business and is not held for sale, and

(C) any security which is a hedge with respect to—

(i) a security to which subsection (a) does not apply, or

(ii) a position, right to income, or a liability which is not a security in the hands of the taxpayer.

To the extent provided in regulations, subparagraph (C) shall not apply to any security held by a person in its capacity as a dealer in securities.

(2) Identification required.—A security shall not be treated as described in subparagraph (A), (B), or (C) of paragraph (1), as the case may be, unless such security is clearly identified in the dealer's records as being described in such subparagraph before the close of the day on which it was acquired, originated, or entered into (or such other time as the Secretary may by regulations prescribe).

(3) Securities subsequently not exempt.—If a security ceases to be described in paragraph (1) at any time after it was identified as such under paragraph (2), subsection (a) shall apply to any changes in value of the security occurring after the cessation.

(4) Special rule for property held for investment.—To the extent provided in regulations, subparagraph (A) of paragraph (1) shall not apply to any security described in subparagraph (D) or (E) of subsection (c)(2) which is held by a dealer in such securities.

(c) Definitions.—For purposes of this section—

(1) Dealer in securities defined.—The term "dealer in securities" means a taxpayer who—

(A) regularly purchases securities from or sells securities to customers in the ordinary course of a trade or business; or

(B) regularly offers to enter into, assume, offset, assign or otherwise terminate positions in securities with customers in the ordinary course of a trade or business.

(2) Security defined.—The term "security" means any—

(A) share of stock in a corporation;

(B) partnership or beneficial ownership interest in a widely held or publicly traded partnership or trust;

(C) note, bond, debenture, or other evidence of indebtedness;

(D) interest rate, currency, or equity notional principal contract;

(E) evidence of an interest in, or a derivative financial instrument in, any security described in subparagraph (A), (B), (C), or (D), or any currency, including any option, forward contract, short position, and any similar financial instrument in such a security or currency; and

(F) position which—

(i) is not a security described in subparagraph (A), (B), (C), (D), or (E),

(ii) is a hedge with respect to such a security, and

(iii) is clearly identified in the dealer's records as being described in this subparagraph before the close of the day on which it was acquired or entered into (or such other time as the Secretary may by regulations prescribe).

Subparagraph (E) shall not include any contract to which section 1256(a) applies.

(3) Hedge.—The term "hedge" means any position which manages the dealer's risk of interest rate or price changes or currency fluctuations, including any position which is reasonably expected to become a hedge within 60 days after the acquisition of the position.

(4) Special rules for certain receivables.—

(A) In general.—Paragraph (2)(C) shall not include any nonfinancial customer paper.

(B) Nonfinancial customer paper.—For purposes of subparagraph (A), the term "nonfinancial customer paper" means any receivable which—

(i) is a note, bond, debenture, or other evidence of indebtedness;

(ii) arises out of the sale of nonfinancial goods or services by a person the principal activity of which is the selling or providing of nonfinancial goods or services; and

(iii) is held by such person (or a person who bears a relationship to such person described in section 267(b) or 707(b)) at all times since issue.

(d) Special rules.—For purposes of this section—

(1) Coordination with certain rules.—The rules of sections 263(g), 263A, and 1256(a) shall not apply to securities to which subsection (a) applies, and section 1091 shall not apply (and section 1092 shall apply) to any loss recognized under subsection (a).

(2) Improper identification.—If a taxpayer—

(A) identifies any security under subsection (b)(2) as being described in subsection (b)(1) and such security is not so described, or

(B) fails under subsection (c)(2)(F)(iii) to identify any position which is described in subsection (c)(2)(F) (without regard to clause (iii) thereof) at the time such identification is required,

the provisions of subsection (a) shall apply to such security or position, except that any loss under this section prior to the disposition of the security or position shall be recognized only to the extent of gain previously recognized under this section (and not previously taken into account under this paragraph) with respect to such security or position.

(3) Character of gain or loss.—

(A) In general.—Except as provided in subparagraph (B) or section 1236(b)—

(i) In general.—Any gain or loss with respect to a security under subsection (a)(2) shall be treated as ordinary income or loss.

(ii) Special rule for dispositions.—If—

(I) gain or loss is recognized with respect to a security before the close of the taxable year, and

(II) subsection (a)(2) would have applied if the security were held as of the close of the taxable year,

such gain or loss shall be treated as ordinary income or loss.

(B) Exception.—Subparagraph (A) shall not apply to any gain or loss which is allocable to a period during which—

(i) the security is described in subsection (b)(1)(C) (without regard to subsection (b)(2)),

(ii) the security is held by a person other than in connection with its activities as a dealer in securities, or

(iii) the security is improperly identified (within the meaning of subparagraph (A) or (B) of paragraph (2)).

* * *

(g) Regulatory authority.—The Secretary shall prescribe such regulations as may be necessary or appropriate to carry out the purposes of this section, including rules—

(1) to prevent the use of year-end transfers, related parties, or other arrangements to avoid the provisions of this section,

(2) to provide for the application of this section to any security which is a hedge which cannot be identified with a specific security, position, right to income, or liability, and

(3) to prevent the use by taxpayers of subsection (c)(4) to avoid the application of this section to a receivable that is inventory in the hands of the taxpayer (or a person who bears a relationship to the taxpayer described in section 267(b) or 707(b)).

PART III—ADJUSTMENTS

§ 481. Adjustments required by changes in method of accounting

(a) General rule.—In computing the taxpayer's taxable income for any taxable year (referred to in this section as the "year of the change")—

(1) if such computation is under a method of accounting different from the method under which the taxpayer's taxable income for the preceding taxable year was computed, then

(2) there shall be taken into account those adjustments which are determined to be necessary solely by reason of the change in order to prevent amounts from being duplicated or omitted, except there shall not be taken into account any adjustment in respect of any taxable year to which this section does not apply unless the adjustment is attributable to a change in the method of accounting initiated by the taxpayer.

(b) Limitation on tax where adjustments are substantial.—

(1) Three year allocation.—If—

(A) the method of accounting from which the change is made was used by the taxpayer in computing his taxable income for the 2 taxable years preceding the year of the change, and

(B) the increase in taxable income for the year of the change which results solely by reason of the adjustments required by subsection (a)(2) exceeds $3,000,

then the tax under this chapter attributable to such increase in taxable income shall not be greater than the aggregate increase in the taxes under this chapter (or under the corresponding provisions of prior revenue laws) which would result if one-third of such increase in taxable income were included in taxable income for the year of the change and one-third of such increase were included for each of the 2 preceding taxable years.

(2) Allocation under new method of accounting.—If—

(A) the increase in taxable income for the year of the change which results solely by reason of the adjustments required by subsection (a)(2) exceeds $3,000, and

(B) the taxpayer establishes his taxable income (under the new method of accounting) for one or more taxable years consecutively preceding the taxable year of the change for which the taxpayer in computing taxable income used the method of accounting from which the change is made,

then the tax under this chapter attributable to such increase in taxable income shall not be greater than the net increase in the taxes under this chapter (or under the corresponding provisions of prior revenue laws) which would result if the adjustments required by subsection (a)(2) were allocated to the taxable year or years specified in subparagraph (B) to which they are properly allocable under the new method of accounting and the balance of the adjustments required by subsection (a)(2) was allocated to the taxable year of the change.

(3) Special rules for computations under paragraphs (1) and (2).—For purposes of this subsection—

(A) There shall be taken into account the increase or decrease in tax for any taxable year preceding the year of the change to which no adjustment is allocated under paragraph (1) or (2) but which is affected by a net operating loss (as defined in section 172) or by a capital loss carryback or carryover (as defined in section

1212), determined with reference to taxable years with respect to which adjustments under paragraph (1) or (2) are allocated.

(B) The increase or decrease in the tax for any taxable year for which an assessment of any deficiency, or a credit or refund of any overpayment, is prevented by any law or rule of law, shall be determined by reference to the tax previously determined (within the meaning of section 1314(a)) for such year.

* * *

(c) Adjustments under regulations.—In the case of any change described in subsection (a), the taxpayer may, in such manner and subject to such conditions as the Secretary may by regulations prescribe, take the adjustments required by subsection (a)(2) into account in computing the tax imposed by this chapter for the taxable year or years permitted under such regulations.

§ 482. Allocation of income and deductions among taxpayers

In any case of two or more organizations, trades, or businesses (whether or not incorporated, whether or not organized in the United States, and whether or not affiliated) owned or controlled directly or indirectly by the same interests, the Secretary may distribute, apportion, or allocate gross income, deductions, credits, or allowances between or among such organizations, trades, or businesses, if he determines that such distribution, apportionment, or allocation is necessary in order to prevent evasion of taxes or clearly to reflect the income of any of such organizations, trades, or businesses. In the case of any transfer (or license) of intangible property (within the meaning of section 936(h)(3)(B)), the income with respect to such transfer or license shall be commensurate with the income attributable to the intangible.

§ 483. Interest on certain deferred payments

(a) Amount constituting interest.—For purposes of this title, in the case of any payment—

(1) under any contract for the sale or exchange of any property, and

(2) to which this section applies,

there shall be treated as interest that portion of the total unstated interest under such contract which, as determined in a manner consistent with the method of computing interest under section 1272(a), is properly allocable to such payment.

(b) Total unstated interest.—For purposes of this section, the term "total unstated interest" means, with respect to a contract for the sale or exchange of property, an amount equal to the excess of—

(1) the sum of the payments to which this section applies which are due under the contract, over

(2) the sum of the present values of such payments and the present values of any interest payments due under the contract.

For purposes of the preceding sentence, the present value of a payment shall be determined under the rules of section 1274(b)(2) using a discount rate equal to the applicable Federal rate determined under section 1274(d).

(c) Payments to which subsection (a) applies.—

(1) In general.—Except as provided in subsection (d), this section shall apply to any payment on account of the sale or exchange of property which constitutes part or all of the sales price and which is due more than 6 months after the date of such sale or exchange under a contract—

(A) under which some or all of the payments are due more than 1 year after the date of such sale or exchange, and

(B) under which there is total unstated interest.

(2) Treatment of other debt instruments.—For purposes of this section, a debt instrument of the purchaser which is given in consideration for the sale or exchange of property shall not be treated as a payment, and any payment due under such debt instrument shall be treated as due under the contract for the sale or exchange.

(3) Debt instrument defined.—For purposes of this subsection, the term "debt instrument" has the meaning given such term by section 1275(a)(1).

(d) Exceptions and limitations.—

(1) Coordination with original issue discount rules.—This section shall not apply to any debt instrument for which an issue price is determined under section 1273(b) (other than paragraph (4) thereof) or section 1274.

(2) Sales prices of $3,000 or less.—This section shall not apply to any payment on account of the sale or exchange of property if it can be determined at the time of such sale or exchange that the sales price cannot exceed $3,000.

(3) Carrying charges.—In the case of the purchaser, the tax treatment of amounts paid on account of the sale or exchange of property shall be made without regard to this section if any such amounts are treated under section 163(b) as if they included interest.

(4) Certain sales of patents.—In the case of any transfer described in section 1235(a) (relating to sale or exchange of patents), this section shall not apply to any amount contingent on the productivity, use, or disposition of the property transferred.

(e) Maximum rate of interest on certain transfers of land between related parties.—

(1) In general.—In the case of any qualified sale, the discount rate used in determining the total unstated interest rate under subsection (b) shall not exceed 6 percent, compounded semiannually.

(2) Qualified sale.—For purposes of this subsection, the term "qualified sale" means any sale or exchange of land by an individual to a member of such individual's family (within the meaning of section 267(c)(4)).

(3) $500,000 limitation.—Paragraph (1) shall not apply to any qualified sale between individuals made during any calendar year to the extent that the sales price for such sale (when added to the aggregate sales price for prior qualified sales between such individuals during the calendar year) exceeds $500,000.

(4) Nonresident alien individuals.—Paragraph (1) shall not apply to any sale or exchange if any party to such sale or exchange is a nonresident alien individual.

(f) Regulations.—The Secretary shall prescribe such regulations as may be necessary or appropriate to carry out the purposes of this section including regulations providing for the application of this section in the case of—

(1) any contract for the sale or exchange of property under which the liability for, or the amount or due date of, a payment cannot be determined at the time of the sale or exchange, or

(2) any change in the liability for, or the amount or due date of, any payment (including interest) under a contract for the sale or exchange of property.

(g) Cross references.—

(1) For treatment of assumptions, see section 1274(c)(4).

(2) For special rules for certain transactions where stated principal amount does not exceed $2,800,000, see section 1274A.

(3) For special rules in case of the borrower under certain loans for personal use, see section 1275(b).

SUBCHAPTER F—EXEMPT ORGANIZATIONS

PART I—GENERAL RULE

§ 501. Exemption from tax on corporations, certain trusts, etc.

(a) Exemption from taxation.—An organization described in subsection (c) or (d) or section 401(a) shall be exempt from taxation under this subtitle unless such exemption is denied under section 502 or 503.

(b) Tax on unrelated business income and certain other activities.—An organization exempt from taxation under subsection (a) shall be subject to tax to the extent provided in parts II, III, and VI of this subchapter, but (notwithstanding parts II, III, and VI of this subchapter) shall be considered an organization exempt from income taxes for the purpose of any law which refers to organizations exempt from income taxes.

(c) List of exempt organizations.—The following organizations are referred to in subsection (a):

* * *

(3) Corporations, and any community chest, fund, or foundation, organized and operated exclusively for religious, charitable, scientific, testing for public safety, literary, or educational purposes, or to foster national or international amateur sports competition (but only if no part of its activities involve the provision of athletic facilities or equipment), or for the prevention of cruelty to children or animals, no part of the net earnings of which inures to the benefit of any private shareholder or individual, no substantial part of the activities of which is carrying on propaganda, or otherwise attempting, to influence legislation (except as otherwise provided in subsection (h)), and which does not participate in, or intervene in (including the publishing or distributing of statements), any political campaign on behalf of (or in opposition to) any candidate for public office.

(4)(A) Civic leagues or organizations not organized for profit but operated exclusively for the promotion of social welfare, or local associations of employees, the membership of which is limited to the employees of a designated person or persons in a particular municipality, and the net earnings of which are devoted exclusively to charitable, educational, or recreational purposes.

* Omitted entirely.

(B) Subparagraph (A) shall not apply to an entity unless no part of the net earnings of such entity inures to the benefit of any private shareholder or individual.

(5) Labor, agricultural, or horticultural organizations.

(6) Business leagues, chambers of commerce, real-estate boards, boards of trade, or professional football leagues (whether or not administering a pension fund for football players), not organized for profit and no part of the net earnings of which inures to the benefit of any private shareholder or individual.

(7) Clubs organized for pleasure, recreation, and other nonprofitable purposes, substantially all of the activities of which are for such purposes and no part of the net earnings of which inures to the benefit of any private shareholder.

(8) Fraternal beneficiary societies, orders, or associations—

(A) operating under the lodge system or for the exclusive benefit of the members of a fraternity itself operating under the lodge system, and

(B) providing for the payment of life, sick, accident, or other benefits to the members of such society, order, or association or their dependents.

(9) Voluntary employees' beneficiary associations providing for the payment of life, sick, accident, or other benefits to the members of such association or their dependents or designated beneficiaries, if no part of the net earnings of such association inures (other than through such payments) to the benefit of any private shareholder or individual. For purposes of providing for the payment of sick and accident benefits to members of such an association and their dependents, the term "dependent" shall include any individual who is a child (as defined in section 152(f)(1)) of a member who as of the end of the calendar year has not attained age 27.

(10) Domestic fraternal societies, orders, or associations, operating under the lodge system—

(A) the net earnings of which are devoted exclusively to religious, charitable, scientific, literary, educational, and fraternal purposes, and

(B) which do not provide for the payment of life, sick, accident, or other benefits.

* * *

(19) A post or organization of past or present members of the Armed Forces of the United States, or an auxiliary unit or society of, or a trust or foundation for, any such post or organization—

(A) organized in the United States or any of its possessions,

(B) at least 75 percent of the members of which are past or present members of the Armed Forces of the United States and substantially all of the other members of which are individuals who are cadets or are spouses, widows, widowers, ancestors, or lineal descendants of past or present members of the Armed Forces of the United States or of cadets, and

(C) no part of the net earnings of which inures to the benefit of any private shareholder or individual.

* * *

(h) Expenditures by public charities to influence legislation.—

(1) General rule.—In the case of an organization to which this subsection applies, exemption from taxation under subsection (a) shall be denied because a substantial part of the activities of such organization consists of carrying on propaganda, or otherwise attempting, to influence legislation, but only if such organization normally—

(A) makes lobbying expenditures in excess of the lobbying ceiling amount for such organization for each taxable year, or

(B) makes grass roots expenditures in excess of the grass roots ceiling amount for such organization for each taxable year.

(2) Definitions.—For purposes of this subsection—

(A) Lobbying expenditures.—The term "lobbying expenditures" means expenditures for the purpose of influencing legislation (as defined in section 4911(d)).

(B) Lobbying ceiling amount.—The lobbying ceiling amount for any organization for any taxable year is 150 percent of the lobbying nontaxable amount for such organization for such taxable year, determined under section 4911.

(C) Grass roots expenditures.—The term "grass roots expenditures" means expenditures for the purpose of influencing legislation (as defined in section 4911(d) without regard to paragraph (1)(B) thereof).

(D) Grass roots ceiling amount.—The grass roots ceiling amount for any organization for any taxable year is 150 percent of the grass roots nontaxable amount for such organization for such taxable year, determined under section 4911.

(3) Organizations to which this subsection applies.—This subsection shall apply to any organization which has elected (in such manner and at such time as the Secretary may prescribe) to have the provisions of this subsection apply to such organization and which, for the taxable year which includes the date the election is made, is described in subsection (c)(3) and—

(A) is described in paragraph (4), and

(B) is not a disqualified organization under paragraph (5).

(4) Organizations permitted to elect to have this subsection apply.—An organization is described in this paragraph if it is described in—

(A) section 170(b)(1)(A)(ii) (relating to educational institutions),

(B) section 170(b)(1)(A)(iii) (relating to hospitals and medical research organizations),

(C) section 170(b)(1)(A)(iv) (relating to organizations supporting government schools),

(D) section 170(b)(1)(A)(vi) (relating to organizations publicly supported by charitable contributions),

(E) section 509(a)(2) (relating to organizations publicly supported by admissions, sales, etc.), or

(F) section 509(a)(3) (relating to organizations supporting certain types of public charities) except that for purposes of this subparagraph, section 509(a)(3) shall be applied without regard to the last sentence of section 509(a).

(5) Disqualified organizations.—For purposes of paragraph (3) an organization is a disqualified organization if it is—

(A) described in section 170(b)(1)(A)(i) (relating to churches),

(B) an integrated auxiliary of a church or of a convention or association of churches, or

* * *

(i) Prohibition of discrimination by certain social clubs.—Notwithstanding subsection (a), an organization which is described in subsection (c)(7) shall not be exempt from taxation under subsection (a) for any taxable year if, at any time during such taxable year, the charter, bylaws, or other governing instrument, of such organization or any written policy statement of such organization contains a provision which provides for discrimination against any person on the basis of race, color, or religion. The preceding sentence to the extent it relates to discrimination on the basis of religion shall not apply to—

(1) an auxiliary of a fraternal beneficiary society if such society—

(A) is described in subsection (c)(8) and exempt from tax under subsection (a), and

(B) limits its membership to the members of a particular religion, or

(2) a club which in good faith limits its membership to the members of a particular religion in order to further the teachings or principles of that religion, and not to exclude individuals of a particular race or color.

* * *

(k) Treatment of certain organizations providing child care.—For purposes of subsection (c)(3) of this section and sections 170(c)(2), 2055(a)(2), and 2522(a)(2), the term "educational purposes" includes the providing of care of children away from their homes if—

(1) substantially all of the care provided by the organization is for purposes of enabling individuals to be gainfully employed, and

(2) the services provided by the organization are available to the general public.

* * *

PART II—PRIVATE FOUNDATIONS

§ 507. Termination of private foundation status

(a) General rule.—Except as provided in subsection (b), the status of any organization as a private foundation shall be terminated only if—

(1) such organization notifies the Secretary (at such time and in such manner as the Secretary may by regulations prescribe) of its intent to accomplish such termination, or

(2)(A) with respect to such organization, there have been either willful repeated acts (or failures to act), or a willful and flagrant act (or failure to act), giving rise to liability for tax under chapter 42, and

(B) the Secretary notifies such organization that, by reason of subparagraph (A), such organization is liable for the tax imposed by subsection (c),

and either such organization pays the tax imposed by subsection (c) (or any portion not abated under subsection (g)) or the entire amount of such tax is abated under subsection (g).

(b) Special rules.—

(1) Transfer to, or operation as, public charity.—The status as a private foundation of any organization, with respect to which there have not been either willful repeated acts (or failures to act) or a willful and flagrant act (or failure to act) giving rise to liability for tax under chapter 42, shall be terminated if—

(A) such organization distributes all of its net assets to one or more organizations described in section 170(b)(1)(A) (other than in clauses (vii) and (viii)) each of which has been in existence and so described for a continuous period of at least 60 calendar months immediately preceding such distribution, or

(B)(i) such organization meets the requirements of paragraph (1), (2), or (3) of section 509(a) by the end of the 12–month period beginning with its first taxable year which begins after December 31, 1969, or for a continuous period of 60 calendar months beginning with the first day of any taxable year which begins after December 31, 1969,

(ii) such organization notifies the Secretary (in such manner as the Secretary may by regulations prescribe) before the commencement of such 12–month or 60–month period (or before the 90th day after the day on which regulations first prescribed under this subsection become final) that it is terminating its private foundation status, and

(iii) such organization establishes to the satisfaction of the Secretary (in such manner as the Secretary may by regulations prescribe) immediately after the expiration of such 12–month or 60–month period that such organization has complied with clause (i).

If an organization gives notice under subparagraph (B)(ii) of the commencement of a 60–month period and such organization fails to meet the requirements of paragraph (1), (2), or (3) of section 509(a) for the entire 60–month period, this part and chapter 42 shall not apply to such organization for any taxable year within such 60–month period for which it does meet such requirements.

(2) Transferee foundations.—For purposes of this part, in the case of a transfer of assets of any private foundation to another private foundation pursuant to any liquidation, merger, redemption, recapitalization, or other adjustment, organization, or reorganization, the transferee foundation shall not be treated as a newly created organization.

(c) Imposition of tax.—There is hereby imposed on each organization which is referred to in subsection (a) a tax equal to the lower of—

(1) the amount which the private foundation substantiates by adequate records or other corroborating evidence as the aggregate tax benefit resulting from the section 501(c)(3) status of such foundation, or

(2) the value of the net assets of such foundation.

(d) Aggregate tax benefit.—

(1) In general.—For purposes of subsection (c), the aggregate tax benefit resulting from the section 501(c)(3) status of any private foundation is the sum of—

(A) the aggregate increases in tax under chapters 1, 11, and 12 (or the corresponding provisions of prior law) which would have been imposed with respect to all substantial contributors to the foundation if deductions for all contributions made by such contributors to the foundation after February 28, 1913, had been disallowed, and

(B) the aggregate increases in tax under chapter 1 (or the corresponding provisions of prior law) which would have been imposed with respect to the income of the private foundation for taxable years beginning after December 31, 1912, if (i) it had not been exempt from tax under section 501(a) (or the corresponding provisions of prior law), and (ii) in the case of a trust, deductions under section 642(c) (or the corresponding provisions of prior law) had been limited to 20 percent of the taxable income of the trust (computed without the benefit of section 642(c) but with the benefit of section 170(b)(1)(A)), and

(C) interest on the increases in tax determined under subparagraphs (A) and (B) from the first date on which each such increase would have been due and payable to the date on which the organization ceases to be a private foundation.

(2) Substantial contributor.—

(A) Definition.—For purposes of paragraph (1), the term "substantial contributor" means any person who contributed or bequeathed an aggregate amount of more than $5,000 to the private foundation, if such amount is more than 2 percent of the total contributions and bequests received by the foundation before the close of the taxable year of the foundation in which the contribution or bequest is received by the foundation from such person. In the case of a trust, the term "substantial contributor" also means the creator of the trust.

(B) Special rules.—For purposes of subparagraph (A)—

(i) each contribution or bequest shall be valued at fair market value on the date it was received,

(ii) in the case of a foundation which is in existence on October 9, 1969, all contributions and bequests received on or before such date shall be treated (except for purposes of clause (i)) as if received on such date,

(iii) an individual shall be treated as making all contributions and bequests made by his spouse, and

(iv) any person who is a substantial contributor on any date shall remain a substantial contributor for all subsequent periods.

(C) Person ceases to be substantial contributor in certain cases.—

(i) In general.—A person shall cease to be treated as a substantial contributor with respect to any private foundation as of the close of any taxable year of such foundation if—

(I) during the 10–year period ending at the close of such taxable year such person (and all related persons) have not made any contribution to such private foundation,

(II) at no time during such 10–year period was such person (or any related person) a foundation manager of such private foundation, and

(III) the aggregate contributions made by such person (and related persons) are determined by the Secretary to be insignificant when compared to the aggregate amount of contributions to such foundation by one other person.

For purposes of subclause (III), appreciation on contributions while held by the foundation shall be taken into account.

(ii) Related person.—For purposes of clause (i), the term "related person" means, with respect to any person, any other person who would be a disqualified person (within the meaning of section 4946) by reason of his relationship to such person. In the case of a contributor which is a corporation, the term also includes any officer or director of such corporation.

(3) Regulations.—For purposes of this section, the determination as to whether and to what extent there would have been any increase in tax shall be made in accordance with regulations prescribed by the Secretary.

(e) Value of assets.—For purposes of subsection (c), the value of the net assets shall be determined at whichever time such value is higher: (1) the first day on which action is taken by the organization which culminates in its ceasing to be a private foundation, or (2) the date on which it ceases to be a private foundation.

(f) Liability in case of transfers of assets from private foundation.—For purposes of determining liability for the tax imposed by subsection (c) in the case of assets transferred by the private foundation, such tax shall be deemed to have been imposed on the first day on which action is taken by the organization which culminates in its ceasing to be a private foundation.

(g) Abatement of taxes.—The Secretary may abate the unpaid portion of the assessment of any tax imposed by subsection (c), or any liability in respect thereof, if—

(1) the private foundation distributes all of its net assets to one or more organizations described in section 170(b)(1)(A) (other than in clauses (vii) and (viii)) each of which has been in existence and so described for a continuous period of at least 60 calendar months, or

(2) following the notification prescribed in section 6104(c) to the appropriate State officer, such State officer within one year notifies the Secretary, in such manner as the Secretary may by regulations prescribe, that corrective action has been initiated pursuant to State law to insure that the assets of such private foundation are preserved for such charitable or other purposes specified in section 501(c)(3) as may be ordered or approved by a court of competent jurisdiction, and upon completion of the corrective action, the Secretary receives certification from the appropriate State officer that such action has resulted in such preservation of assets.

§ 508. Special rules with respect to section 501(c)(3) organizations

(a) New organizations must notify Secretary that they are applying for recognition of section 501(c)(3) status.—Except as provided in subsection (c), an organization organized after October 9, 1969, shall not be treated as an organization described in section 501(c)(3)—

(1) unless it has given notice to the Secretary, in such manner as the Secretary may by regulations prescribe, that it is applying for recognition of such status, or

(2) for any period before the giving of such notice, if such notice is given after the time prescribed by the Secretary by regulations for giving notice under this subsection.

(b) Presumption that organizations are private foundations.—Except as provided in subsection (c), any organization (including an organization in existence on October 9, 1969) which is described in section 501(c)(3) and which does not notify the Secretary, at such time and in such manner as the Secretary may by regulations prescribe, that it is not a private foundation shall be presumed to be a private foundation.

(c) Exceptions.—

(1) Mandatory exceptions.—Subsections (a) and (b) shall not apply to—

(A) churches, their integrated auxiliaries, and conventions or associations of churches, or

(B) any organization which is not a private foundation (as defined in section 509(a)) and the gross receipts of which in each taxable year are normally not more than $5,000.

(2) Exceptions by regulations.—The Secretary may by regulations exempt (to the extent and subject to such conditions as may be prescribed in such regulations) from the provisions of subsection (a) or (b) or both—

(A) educational organizations described in section 170(b)(1)(A)(ii), and

(B) any other class of organizations with respect to which the Secretary determines that full compliance with the provisions of subsections (a) and (b) is not necessary to the efficient administration of the provisions of this title relating to private foundations.

(d) Disallowance of certain charitable, etc., deductions.—

(1) Gift or bequest to organizations subject to section 507(c) tax.—No gift or bequest made to an organization upon which the tax provided by section 507(c) has been imposed shall be allowed as a deduction under section 170, 545(b)(2), 642(c), 2055, 2106(a)(2), or 2522, if such gift or bequest is made—

(A) by any person after notification is made under section 507(a), or

(B) by a substantial contributor (as defined in section 507(d)(2)) in his taxable year which includes the first day on which action is taken by such organization which culminates in the imposition of tax under section 507(c) and any subsequent taxable year.

(2) Gift or bequest to taxable private foundation, section 4947 trust, etc.—No gift or bequest made to an organization shall be allowed as a deduction under section 170, 545(b)(2), 642(c), 2055, 2106(a)(2), or 2522, if such gift or bequest is made—

(A) to a private foundation or a trust described in section 4947 in a taxable year for which it fails to meet the requirements of subsection (e) (determined without regard to subsection (e)(2)), or

(B) to any organization in a period for which it is not treated as an organization described in section 501(c)(3) by reason of subsection (a).

(3) Exception.—Paragraph (1) shall not apply if the entire amount of the unpaid portion of the tax imposed by section 507(c) is abated by the Secretary under section 507(g).

(e) Governing instruments.—

(1) General rule.—A private foundation shall not be exempt from taxation under section 501(a) unless its governing instrument includes provisions the effects of which are—

(A) to require its income for each taxable year to be distributed at such time and in such manner as not to subject the foundation to tax under section 4942, and

(B) to prohibit the foundation from engaging in any act of self-dealing (as defined in section 4941(d)), from retaining any excess business holdings (as defined in section 4943(c)), from making any investments in such manner as to subject the foundation to tax under section 4944, and from making any taxable expenditures (as defined in section 4945(d)).

* * *

§ 509. Private foundation defined

(a) General rule.—For purposes of this title, the term "private foundation" means a domestic or foreign organization described in section 501(c)(3) other than—

(1) an organization described in section 170(b)(1)(A) (other than in clauses (vii) and (viii));

(2) an organization which—

(A) normally receives more than one-third of its support in each taxable year from any combination of—

(i) gifts, grants, contributions, or membership fees, and

(ii) gross receipts from admissions, sales of merchandise, performance of services, or furnishing of facilities, in an activity which is not an unrelated trade or business (within the meaning of section 513), not including such receipts from any person, or from any bureau or similar agency of a governmental unit (as described in section 170(c)(1)), in any taxable year to the extent such receipts exceed the greater of $5,000 or 1 percent of the organization's support in such taxable year,

from persons other than disqualified persons (as defined in section 4946) with respect to the organization, from governmental units described in section 170(c)(1), or from organizations described in section 170(b)(1)(A) (other than in clauses (vii) and (viii)), and

(B) normally receives not more than one-third of its support in each taxable year from the sum of—

(i) gross investment income (as defined in subsection (e)) and

(ii) the excess (if any) of the amount of the unrelated business taxable income (as defined in section 512) over the amount of the tax imposed by section 511;

(3) an organization which—

(A) is organized, and at all times thereafter is operated, exclusively for the benefit of, to perform the functions of, or to carry out the purposes of one or more specified organizations described in paragraph (1) or (2),

(B) is—

(i) operated, supervised, or controlled by one or more organizations described in paragraph (1) or (2),

(ii) supervised or controlled in connection with one or more such organizations, or

(iii) operated in connection with one or more such organizations, and

(C) is not controlled directly or indirectly by one or more disqualified persons (as defined in section 4946) other than foundation managers and other than one or more organizations described in paragraph (1) or (2); and

(4) an organization which is organized and operated exclusively for testing for public safety.

For purposes of paragraph (3), an organization described in paragraph (2) shall be deemed to include an organization described in section 501(c)(4), (5), or (6) which would be described in paragraph (2) if it were an organization described in section 501(c)(3).

(b) Continuation of private foundation status.—For purposes of this title, if an organization is a private foundation (within the meaning of subsection (a)) on October 9, 1969, or becomes a private foundation on any subsequent date, such organization shall be treated as a private foundation for all periods after October 9, 1969, or after such subsequent date, unless its status as such is terminated under section 507.

(c) Status of organization after termination of private foundation status.—For purposes of this part, an organization the status of which as a private foundation is terminated under section 507 shall (except as provided in section 507(b)(2)) be treated as an organization created on the day after the date of such termination.

(d) Definition of support.—For purposes of this part and chapter 42, the term "support" includes (but is not limited to)—

(1) gifts, grants, contributions, or membership fees,

(2) gross receipts from admissions, sales of merchandise, performance of services, or furnishing of facilities in any activity which is not an unrelated trade or business (within the meaning of section 513),

(3) net income from unrelated business activities, whether or not such activities are carried on regularly as a trade or business,

(4) gross investment income (as defined in subsection (e)),

(5) tax revenues levied for the benefit of an organization and either paid to or expended on behalf of such organization, and

(6) the value of services or facilities (exclusive of services or facilities generally furnished to the public without charge) furnished by a governmental unit referred to in section 170(c)(1) to an organization without charge.

Such term does not include any gain from the sale or other disposition of property which would be considered as gain from the sale or exchange of a capital asset, or the value of exemption from any Federal, State, or local tax or any similar benefit.

(e) Definition of gross investment income.—For purposes of subsection (d), the term "gross investment income" means the gross amount of income from interest, dividends, payments with respect to securities loans (as defined in section 512(a)(5)), rents, and royalties, but not including any such income to the extent included in computing the tax imposed by section 511.

(f) Requirements for supporting organizations.—

(1) Type III supporting organizations.—For purposes of subsection (a)(3)(B)(iii), an organization shall not be considered to be operated in connection with any organization described in paragraph (1) or (2) of subsection (a) unless such organization meets the following requirements:

(A) Responsiveness.—For each taxable year beginning after the date of the enactment of this subsection, the organization provides to each supported organization such information as the Secretary may require to ensure that such organization is responsive to the needs or demands of the supported organization.

(B) Foreign supported organizations.—

(i) In general.—The organization is not operated in connection with any supported organization that is not organized in the United States.

(ii) Transition rule for existing organizations.—If the organization is operated in connection with an organization that is not organized in the United States on the date of the enactment of this subsection, clause (i) shall not apply until the first day of the third taxable year of the organization beginning after the date of the enactment of this subsection.

(2) Organizations controlled by donors.—

(A) In general.—For purposes of subsection (a)(3)(B), an organization shall not be considered to be–

(i) operated, supervised, or controlled by any organization described in paragraph (1) or (2) of subsection (a), or

(ii) operated in connection with any organization described in paragraph (1) or (2) of subsection (a),

if such organization accepts any gift or contribution from any person described in subparagraph (B).

(B) Person described.—A person is described in this subparagraph if, with respect to a supported organization of an organization described in subparagraph (A), such person is—

(i) a person (other than an organization described in paragraph (1), (2), or (4) of section 509(a)) who directly or indirectly controls, either alone or together with persons described in clauses (ii) and (iii), the governing body of such supported organization,

(ii) a member of the family (determined under section 4958(f)(4)) of an individual described in clause (i), or

(iii) a 35–percent controlled entity (as defined in section 4958(f)(3) by substituting "persons described in clause (i) or (ii) of section 509(f)(2)(B)" for "persons described in subparagraph (A) or (B) of paragraph (1)" in subparagraph (A)(i) thereof).

(3) Supported organization.—For purposes of this subsection, the term "supported organization" means, with respect to an organization described in subsection (a)(3), an organization described in paragraph (1) or (2) of subsection (a)—

(A) for whose benefit the organization described in subsection (a)(3) is organized and operated, or

(B) with respect to which the organization performs the functions of, or carries out the purposes of.

PART III—TAXATION OF BUSINESS INCOME OF CERTAIN EXEMPT ORGANIZATIONS

§ 511. Imposition of tax on unrelated business income of charitable, etc., organizations

(a) Charitable, etc., organizations taxable at corporation rates.—

(1) Imposition of tax.—There is hereby imposed for each taxable year on the unrelated business taxable income (as defined in section 512) of every organization described in paragraph (2) a tax computed as provided in section 11. In making such computation for purposes of this section, the term "taxable income" as used in section 11 shall be read as "unrelated business taxable income".

(2) Organizations subject to tax.—

(A) Organizations described in sections 401(a) and 501(c).—The tax imposed by paragraph (1) shall apply in the case of any organization (other than a trust described in subsection (b) or an organization described in section 501(c)(1)) which is exempt, except as provided in this part or part II (relating to private foundations), from taxation under this subtitle by reason of section 501(a).

(B) State colleges and universities.—The tax imposed by paragraph (1) shall apply in the case of any college or university which is an agency or instrumentality of any government or any political subdivision thereof, or which is owned or operated by a government or any political subdivision thereof, or by any agency or instrumentality of one or more governments or political subdivisions. Such tax shall also apply in the case of any corporation wholly owned by one or more such colleges or universities.

(b) Tax on charitable, etc., trusts.—

(1) Imposition of tax.—There is hereby imposed for each taxable year on the unrelated business taxable income of every trust described in paragraph (2) a tax computed as provided in section 1(e). In making such computation for purposes of this section, the term "taxable income" as used in section 1 shall be read as "unrelated business taxable income" as defined in section 512.

(2) Charitable, etc., trusts subject to tax.—The tax imposed by paragraph (1) shall apply in the case of any trust which is exempt, except as provided in this part or part II (relating to private foundations), from taxation under this subtitle by reason of section 501(a) and which, if it were not for such exemption, would be subject to subchapter J (sec. 641 and following, relating to estates, trusts, beneficiaries, and decedents).

* * *

§ 512. Unrelated business taxable income

(a) Definition.—For purposes of this title—

(1) General rule.—Except as otherwise provided in this subsection, the term "unrelated business taxable income" means the gross income derived by any organization from any unrelated trade or business (as defined in section 513) regularly carried on by it, less the deductions allowed by this chapter which are directly connected with the carrying on of such trade or business, both computed with the modifications provided in subsection (b).

* * *

(b) Modifications.—The modifications referred to in subsection (a) are the following:

(1) There shall be excluded all dividends, interest, payments with respect to securities loans (as defined in section 512(a)(5)), amounts received or accrued as consideration for entering into agreements to make loans, and annuities, and all deductions directly connected with such income.

(2) There shall be excluded all royalties (including overriding royalties) whether measured by production or by gross or taxable income from the property, and all deductions directly connected with such income.

(3) In the case of rents—

(A) Except as provided in subparagraph (B), there shall be excluded—

(i) all rents from real property (including property described in section 1245(a)(3)(C)), and

(ii) all rents from personal property (including for purposes of this paragraph as personal property any property described in section 1245(a)(3)(B)) leased with such real property, if the rents attributable to such personal property are an incidental amount of the total rents received or accrued under the lease, determined at the time the personal property is placed in service.

(B) Subparagraph (A) shall not apply—

(i) if more than 50 percent of the total rent received or accrued under the lease is attributable to personal property described in subparagraph (A)(ii), or

(ii) if the determination of the amount of such rent depends in whole or in part on the income or profits derived by any person from the property leased (other than an amount based on a fixed percentage or percentages of receipts or sales).

(C) There shall be excluded all deductions directly connected with rents excluded under subparagraph (A).

(4) Notwithstanding paragraph (1), (2), (3), or (5), in the case of debt-financed property (as defined in section 514) there shall be included, as an item of gross income derived from an unrelated trade or business, the amount ascertained under section 514(a)(1), and there shall be allowed, as a deduction, the amount ascertained under section 514(a)(2).

(5) There shall be excluded all gains or losses from the sale, exchange, or other disposition of property other than—

(A) stock in trade or other property of a kind which would properly be includible in inventory if on hand at the close of the taxable year, or

(B) property held primarily for sale to customers in the ordinary course of the trade or business.

There shall also be excluded all gains or losses recognized, in connection with the organization's investment activities, from the lapse or termination of options to buy or sell securities (as defined in section 1236(c)) or real property and all gains or losses from the forfeiture of good-faith deposits (that are consistent with established business practice) for the purchase, sale, or lease of real property in connection with the organization's investment activities. This paragraph shall not apply with respect to the cutting of timber which is considered, on the application of section 631, as a sale or exchange of such timber.

(6) The net operating loss deduction provided in section 172 shall be allowed, except that—

(A) the net operating loss for any taxable year, the amount of the net operating loss carryback or carryover to any taxable year, and the net operating loss deduction for any taxable year shall be determined under section 172 without taking into account any amount of income or deduction which is excluded under this part in computing the unrelated business taxable income; and

(B) the terms "preceding taxable year" and "preceding taxable years" as used in section 172 shall not include any taxable year for which the organization was not subject to the provisions of this part.

(7) There shall be excluded all income derived from research for (A) the United States, or any of its agencies or instrumentalities, or (B) any State or political subdivision thereof; and there shall be excluded all deductions directly connected with such income.

(8) In the case of a college, university, or hospital, there shall be excluded all income derived from research performed for any person, and all deductions directly connected with such income.

(9) In the case of an organization operated primarily for purposes of carrying on fundamental research the results of which are freely available to the general public, there shall be excluded all income derived from research performed for any person, and all deductions directly connected with such income.

(10) In the case of any organization described in section 511(a), the deduction allowed by section 170 (relating to charitable etc. contributions and gifts) shall be allowed (whether or not directly connected with the carrying on of the trade or business), but shall not exceed 10 percent of the unrelated business taxable income computed without the benefit of this paragraph.

(11) In the case of any trust described in section 511(b), the deduction allowed by section 170 (relating to charitable etc. contributions and gifts) shall be allowed (whether or not directly connected with the carrying on of the trade or business), and for such purpose a distribution made by the trust to a beneficiary described in section 170 shall be considered as a gift or contribution. The deduction allowed by this paragraph shall be allowed with the limitations prescribed in section 170(b)(1)(A) and (B) determined with reference to the unrelated business taxable income computed without the benefit of this paragraph (in lieu of with reference to adjusted gross income).

(12) Except for purposes of computing the net operating loss under section 172 and paragraph (6), there shall be allowed a specific deduction of $1,000. In the case of a diocese, province of a religious order, or a convention or association of churches, there shall also be allowed, with respect to each parish, individual church, district, or other local unit, a specific deduction equal to the lower of—

(A) $1,000, or

(B) the gross income derived from any unrelated trade or business regularly carried on by such local unit.

* * *

§ 513. Unrelated trade or business

(a) General rule.—The term "unrelated trade or business" means, in the case of any organization subject to the tax imposed by section 511, any trade or business the conduct of which is not substantially related (aside from the need of such organization for income or funds or the use it makes of the profits derived) to the exercise or performance by such organization of its charitable, educational, or other purpose or function constituting the basis for its exemption under section 501 (or, in the case of an organization described in section 511(a)(2)(B), to the exercise or performance of any purpose or function described in section 501(c)(3)), except that such term does not include any trade or business—

(1) in which substantially all the work in carrying on such trade or business is performed for the organization without compensation; or

(2) which is carried on, in the case of an organization described in section 501(c)(3) or in the case of a college or university described in section 511(a)(2)(B), by the organization primarily for the convenience of its members, students, patients, officers, or employees, or, in the case of a local association of employees described in section 501(c)(4) organized before May 27, 1969, which is the selling by the organization of items of work-related clothes and equipment and items normally sold through vending machines, through food dispensing facilities, or by snack bars, for the convenience of its members at their usual places of employment; or

(3) which is the selling of merchandise, substantially all of which has been received by the organization as gifts or contributions.

* * *

§ 514. Unrelated debt-financed income

(a) Unrelated debt-financed income and deductions.—In computing under section 512 the unrelated business taxable income for any taxable year—

(1) Percentage of income taken into account.—There shall be included with respect to each debt-financed property as an item of gross income derived from an unrelated trade or business an amount which is the same percentage (but not in excess of 100 percent) of the total gross income derived during the taxable year from or on account of such property as (A) the average acquisition indebtedness (as defined in subsection (c)(7)) for the taxable year with respect to the property is of (B) the average amount (determined under regulations prescribed by the Secretary) of the adjusted basis of such property during the period it is held by the organization during such taxable year.

(2) Percentage of deductions taken into account.—There shall be allowed as a deduction with respect to each debt-financed property an amount determined by applying (except as provided in the last sentence of this paragraph) the percentage derived under paragraph (1) to the sum determined under paragraph (3). The percentage derived under this paragraph shall not be applied with respect to the deduction of any capital loss resulting from the carryback or carryover of net capital losses under section 1212.

(3) Deductions allowable.—The sum referred to in paragraph (2) is the sum of the deductions under this chapter which are directly connected with the debt-financed property or the income therefrom, except that if the debt-financed property is of a character which is subject to the allowance for depreciation provided in section 167, the allowance shall be computed only by use of the straight-line method.

(b) Definition of debt-financed property.—

(1) In general.—For purposes of this section, the term "debt-financed property" means any property which is held to produce income and with respect to which there is an acquisition indebtedness (as defined in subsection (c)) at any time during the taxable year (or, if the property was disposed of during the taxable year, with respect to which there was an acquisition indebtedness at any time during the 12–month period ending with the date of such disposition), except that such term does not include—

(A)(i) any property substantially all the use of which is substantially related (aside from the need of the organization for income or funds) to the exercise or performance by such organization of its charitable, educational, or other purpose or function constituting the basis for its exemption under section 501 (or, in the case of an organization described in section 511(a)(2)(B), to the exercise or performance of any purpose or function designated in section 501(c)(3)), or (ii) any property to which clause (i) does not apply, to the extent that its use is so substantially related;

* * *

PART VIII—HIGHER EDUCATION SAVINGS ENTITIES

§ 529. Qualified tuition programs

(a) General rule.—A qualified tuition program shall be exempt from taxation under this subtitle. Notwithstanding the preceding sentence, such program shall be subject to the taxes imposed by section 511 (relating to imposition of tax on unrelated business income of charitable organizations).

(b) Qualified tuition program.—For purposes of this section—

(1) In general.—The term "qualified tuition program" means a program established and maintained by a State or agency or instrumentality thereof or by 1 or more eligible educational institutions—

(A) under which a person—

(i) may purchase tuition credits or certificates on behalf of a designated beneficiary which entitle the beneficiary to the waiver or payment of qualified higher education expenses of the beneficiary, or

(ii) in the case of a program established and maintained by a State or agency or instrumentality thereof, may make contributions to an account which is established for the purpose of meeting the qualified higher education expenses of the designated beneficiary of the account, and

(B) which meets the other requirements of this subsection.

Except to the extent provided in regulations, a program established and maintained by 1 or more eligible educational institutions shall not be treated as a qualified tuition program unless such program provides that amounts are held in a qualified trust and such program has received a ruling or determination that such program meets the applicable requirements for a qualified tuition program. For purposes of the preceding sentence, the term "qualified trust" means a trust which is created or organized in the United States for the exclusive benefit of designated beneficiaries and with respect to which the requirements of paragraphs (2) and (5) of section 408(a) are met.

(2) Cash contributions.—A program shall not be treated as a qualified tuition program unless it provides that purchases or contributions may only be made in cash.

(3) Separate accounting.—A program shall not be treated as a qualified State tuition program unless it provides separate accounting for each designated beneficiary.

(4) No investment direction.—A program shall not be treated as a qualified tuition program unless it provides that any contributor to, or designated beneficiary under, such program may not directly or indirectly direct the investment of any contributions to the program (or any earnings thereon).

(5) No pledging of interest as security.—A program shall not be treated as a qualified tuition program if it allows any interest in the program or any portion thereof to be used as security for a loan.

(6) Prohibition on excess contributions.—A program shall not be treated as a qualified tuition program unless it provides adequate safeguards to prevent contributions on behalf of a designated beneficiary in excess of those necessary to provide for the qualified higher education expenses of the beneficiary.

(c) Tax treatment of designated beneficiaries and contributors.—

(1) In general.—Except as otherwise provided in this subsection, no amount shall be includible in gross income of—

(A) a designated beneficiary under a qualified tuition program, or

(B) a contributor to such program on behalf of a designated beneficiary,

with respect to any distribution or earnings under such program.

(2) Gift tax treatment of contributions.—For purposes of chapters 12 and 13—

(A) In general.—Any contribution to a qualified tuition program on behalf of any designated beneficiary—

(i) shall be treated as a completed gift to such beneficiary which is not a future interest in property, and

(ii) shall not be treated as a qualified transfer under section 2503(e).

(B) Treatment of excess contributions.—If the aggregate amount of contributions described in subparagraph (A) during the calendar year by a donor exceeds the limitation for such year under section 2503(b), such aggregate amount shall, at the election of the donor, be taken into account for purposes of such section ratably over the 5–year period beginning with such calendar year.

(3) Distributions.—

(A) In general.—Any distribution under a qualified tuition program shall be includible in the gross income of the distributee in the manner as provided under section 72 to the extent not excluded from gross income under any other provision of this chapter.

(B) Distributions for qualified higher education expenses.—For purposes of this paragraph—

(i) In–kind distributions.—No amount shall be includible in gross income under subparagraph (A) by reason of a distribution which consists of providing a benefit to the distributee which, if paid for by the distributee, would constitute payment of a qualified higher education expense.

(ii) Cash distributions.—In the case of distributions not described in clause (i), if—

(I) such distributions do not exceed the qualified higher education expenses (reduced by expenses described in clause (i)), no amount shall be includible in gross income, and

(II) in any other case, the amount otherwise includible in gross income shall be reduced by an amount which bears the same ratio to such amount as such expenses bear to such distributions.

(iii) Exception for institutional programs.—In the case of any taxable year beginning before January 1, 2004, clauses (i) and (ii) shall not apply with respect to any distribution during such taxable year under a qualified tuition program established and maintained by 1 or more eligible educational institutions.

(iv) Treatment as distributions.—Any benefit furnished to a designated beneficiary under a qualified tuition program shall be treated as a distribution to the beneficiary for purposes of this paragraph.

(v) Coordination with hope and lifetime learning credits.—The total amount of qualified higher education expenses with respect to an individual for the taxable year shall be reduced—

(I) as provided in section 25A(g)(2), and

(II) by the amount of such expenses which were taken into account in determining the credit allowed to the taxpayer or any other person under section 25A.

(vi) Coordination with Coverdell education savings accounts.—If, with respect to an individual for any taxable year—

(I) the aggregate distributions to which clauses (i) and (ii) and section 530(d)(2)(A) apply, exceed

(II) the total amount of qualified higher education expenses otherwise taken into account under clauses (i) and (ii) (after the application of clause (v)) for such year,

the taxpayer shall allocate such expenses among such distributions for purposes of determining the amount of the exclusion under clauses (i) and (ii) and section 530(d)(2)(A).

(C) Change in beneficiaries or programs.—

(i) Rollovers.—Subparagraph (A) shall not apply to that portion of any distribution which, within 60 days of such distribution, is transferred—

(I) to another qualified tuition program for the benefit of the designated beneficiary, or

(II) to the credit of another designated beneficiary under a qualified tuition program who is a member of the family of the designated beneficiary with respect to which the distribution was made.

(ii) Change in designated beneficiaries.—Any change in the designated beneficiary of an interest in a qualified tuition program shall not be treated as a distribution for purposes of subparagraph (A) if the new beneficiary is a member of the family of the old beneficiary.

(iii) Limitation on certain rollovers.—Clause (i)(I) shall not apply to any transfer if such transfer occurs within 12 months from the date of a previous transfer to any qualified tuition program for the benefit of the designated beneficiary.

(D) Operating rules.—For purposes of applying section 72—

(i) to the extent provided by the Secretary, all qualified tuition programs of which an individual is a designated beneficiary shall be treated as one program,

(ii) except to the extent provided by the Secretary, all distributions during a taxable year shall be treated as one distribution, and

(iii) except to the extent provided by the Secretary, the value of the contract, income on the contract, and investment in the contract shall be computed as of the close of the calendar year in which the taxable year begins.

(4) Estate tax treatment.—

(A) In general.—No amount shall be includible in the gross estate of any individual for purposes of chapter 11 by reason of an interest in a qualified tuition program.

(B) Amounts includible in estate of designated beneficiary in certain cases.—Subparagraph (A) shall not apply to amounts distributed on account of the death of a beneficiary.

(C) Amounts includible in estate of donor making excess contributions.—In the case of a donor who makes the election described in paragraph (2)(B) and who dies before the close of the 5-year period referred to in such paragraph, notwithstanding subparagraph (A), the gross estate of the donor shall include the portion of such contributions properly allocable to periods after the date of death of the donor.

(5) Other gift tax rules.—For purposes of chapters 12 and 13—

(A) Treatment of distributions.—Except as provided in subparagraph (B), in no event shall a distribution from a qualified tuition program be treated as a taxable gift.

(B) Treatment of designation of new beneficiary.—The taxes imposed by chapters 12 and 13 shall apply to a transfer by reason of a change in the designated beneficiary under the program (or a rollover to the account of a new beneficiary) unless the new beneficiary is—

(i) assigned to the same generation as (or a higher generation than) the old beneficiary (determined in accordance with section 2651), and

(ii) a member of the family of the old beneficiary.

(6) Additional tax.—The tax imposed by section 530(d)(4) shall apply to any payment or distribution from a qualified tuition program in the same manner as such tax applies to a payment or distribution from an Coverdell education savings account. This paragraph shall not apply to any payment or distribution in any taxable year beginning before January 1, 2004, which is includible in gross income but used for qualified higher education expenses of the designated beneficiary.

(d) Reports.—Each officer or employee having control of the qualified tuition program or their designee shall make such reports regarding such program to the Secretary and to designated beneficiaries with respect to contributions, distributions, and such other matters as the Secretary may require. The reports required by this subsection shall be filed at such time and in such manner and furnished to such individuals at such time and in such manner as may be required by the Secretary.

(e) Other definitions and special rules.—For purposes of this section—

(1) Designated beneficiary.—The term "designated beneficiary" means—

(A) the individual designated at the commencement of participation in the qualified tuition program as the beneficiary of amounts paid (or to be paid) to the program,

(B) in the case of a change in beneficiaries described in subsection (c)(3)(C), the individual who is the new beneficiary, and

(C) in the case of an interest in a qualified tuition program purchased by a State or local government (or agency or instrumentality thereof) or an organization described in section 501(c)(3) and exempt from taxation under section 501(a) as part of a scholarship program operated by such government or organization, the individual receiving such interest as a scholarship.

(2) Member of family.—The term "member of the family" means, with respect to any designated beneficiary—

(A) the spouse of such beneficiary;

(B) an individual who bears a relationship to such beneficiary which is described in subparagraphs (A) through (G) of section 152(d)(2);

(C) the spouse of any individual described in subparagraph (B); and

(D) any first cousin of such beneficiary.

(3) Qualified higher education expenses.—

(A) In general.—The term "qualified higher education expenses" means—

(i) tuition, fees, books, supplies, and equipment required for the enrollment or attendance of a designated beneficiary at an eligible educational institution;

(ii) expenses for special needs services in the case of a special needs beneficiary which are incurred in connection with such enrollment or attendance.

(iii) expenses paid or incurred in 2009 or 2010 for the purchase of any computer technology or equipment (as defined in section 170(e)(6)(F)(i)) or Internet access and related services, if such technology, equipment, or services are to be used by the beneficiary and the beneficiary's family during any of the years the beneficiary is enrolled at an eligible educational institution.

Clause (iii) shall not include expenses for computer software designed for sports, games, or hobbies unless the software is predominantly educational in nature.

(B) Room and board included for students who are at least half-time.—

(i) In general.—In the case of an individual who is an eligible student (as defined in section 25A(b)(3)) for any academic period, such term shall also include reasonable costs for such period (as determined under the qualified tuition program) incurred by the designated beneficiary for room and board while attending such institution. For purposes of subsection (b)(6), a designated beneficiary shall be treated as meeting the requirements of this clause.

(ii) Limitation.—The amount treated as qualified higher education expenses by reason of clause (i) shall not exceed—

(I) the allowance (applicable to the student) for room and board included in the cost of attendance (as defined in section 472 of the Higher Education Act of 1965 (20 U.S.C. 1087ll), as in effect on the date of the enactment of the Economic Growth and Tax Relief Reconciliation Act of 2001) as determined by the eligible educational institution for such period, or

(II) if greater, the actual invoice amount the student residing in housing owned or operated by the eligible educational institution is charged by such institution for room and board costs for such period.

(4) Application of section 514.—An interest in a qualified tuition program shall not be treated as debt for purposes of section 514.

(5) Eligible educational institution.—The term "eligible educational institution" means an institution—

(A) which is described in section 481 of the Higher Education Act of 1965 (20 U.S.C. 1088), as in effect on the date of the enactment of this paragraph, and

(B) which is eligible to participate in a program under title IV of such Act.

(f) Regulations.—Notwithstanding any other provision of this section, the Secretary shall prescribe such regulations as may be necessary or appropriate to carry out the purposes of this section and to prevent abuse of such purposes, including regulations under chapters 11, 12, and 13 of this title.

§ 530. Coverdell education savings accounts

(a) General rule.—A Coverdell education savings account shall be exempt from taxation under this subtitle. Notwithstanding the preceding sentence, the Coverdell education savings account shall be subject to the taxes imposed by section 511 (relating to imposition of tax on unrelated business income of charitable organizations).

(b) Definitions and special rules.—For purposes of this section—

(1) Coverdell education savings account.—The term "Coverdell education savings account" means a trust created or organized in the United States exclusively for the purpose of paying the qualified education expenses of an individual who is the designated beneficiary of the trust (and designated as Coverdell education savings account at the time created or organized), but only if the written governing instrument creating the trust meets the following requirements:

(A) No contribution will be accepted—

(i) unless it is in cash,

(ii) after the date on which such beneficiary attains age 18, or

(iii) except in the case of rollover contributions, if such contribution would result in aggregate contributions for the taxable year exceeding $2,000.

(B) The trustee is a bank (as defined in section 408(n)) or another person who demonstrates to the satisfaction of the Secretary that the manner in which that person will administer the trust will be consistent with the requirements of this section or who has so demonstrated with respect to any individual retirement plan.

(C) No part of the trust assets will be invested in life insurance contracts.

(D) The assets of the trust shall not be commingled with other property except in a common trust fund or common investment fund.

(E) Except as provided in subsection (d)(7), any balance to the credit of the designated beneficiary on the date on which the beneficiary attains age 30 shall be distributed within 30 days after such date to the beneficiary or, if the beneficiary dies before attaining age 30, shall be distributed within 30 days after the date of death of such beneficiary.

The age limitations in subparagraphs (A)(ii) and (E), and paragraphs (5) and (6) of subsection (d), shall not apply to any designated beneficiary with special needs (as determined under regulations prescribed by the Secretary).

(2) Qualified education expenses.—

(A) In general.—The term "qualified education expenses" means—

(i) qualified higher education expenses (as defined in section 529(e)(3)), and

(ii) qualified elementary and secondary education expenses (as defined in paragraph (3)).

(B) Qualified state tuition programs.—Such term shall include any contribution to a qualified State tuition program (as defined in section 529(b)) on behalf of the designated beneficiary (as defined in section 529(e)(1)); but there shall be no increase in the investment in the contract for purposes of applying section 72 by reason of any portion of such contribution which is not includible in gross income by reason of subsection (d)(2).

(3) Qualified elementary and secondary education expenses.—

(A) In general.—The term "qualified elementary and secondary education expenses" means—

(i) expenses for tuition, fees, academic tutoring, special needs services in the case of a special needs beneficiary, books, supplies, and other equipment which are incurred in connection with the enrollment or attendance of the designated beneficiary of the trust as an elementary or secondary school student at a public, private, or religious school,

(ii) expenses for room and board, uniforms, transportation, and supplementary items and services (including extended day programs) which are required or provided by a public, private, or religious school in connection with such enrollment or attendance, and

(iii) expenses for the purchase of any computer technology or equipment (as defined in section 170(e)(6)(F)(i)) or Internet access and related services, if such technology, equipment, or services are to be used by the beneficiary and the beneficiary's family during any of the years the beneficiary is in school.

Clause (iii) shall not include expenses for computer software designed for sports, games, or hobbies unless the software is predominantly educational in nature.

(B) School.—The term "school" means any school which provides elementary education or secondary education (kindergarten through grade 12), as determined under State law.

(4) Time when contributions deemed made.—An individual shall be deemed to have made a contribution to a Coverdell education savings account on the last day of the preceding taxable year if the contribution is made on account of such taxable year and is made not later than the time prescribed by law for filing the return for such taxable year (not including extensions thereof).

(c) Reduction in permitted contributions based on adjusted gross income.—

(1) In general.—In the case of a contributor who is an individual, the maximum amount the contributor could otherwise make to an account under this section shall be reduced by an amount which bears the same ratio to such maximum amount as—

(A) the excess of—

(i) the contributor's modified adjusted gross income for such taxable year, over

(ii) $95,000 ($190,000 in the case of a joint return), bears to

(B) $15,000 ($30,000 in the case of a joint return).

(2) Modified adjusted gross income.—For purposes of paragraph (1), the term "modified adjusted gross income" means the adjusted gross income of the taxpayer for the taxable year increased by any amount excluded from gross income under section 911, 931, or 933.

(d) Tax treatment of distributions.—

(1) In general.—Any distribution shall be includible in the gross income of the distributee in the manner as provided in section 72.

(2) Distributions for qualified education expenses.—

(A) In general.—No amount shall be includible in gross income under paragraph (1) if the qualified education expenses of the designated beneficiary during the taxable year are not less than the aggregate distributions during the taxable year.

(B) Distributions in excess of expenses.—If such aggregate distributions exceed such expenses during the taxable year, the amount otherwise includible in gross income under paragraph (1) shall be reduced by the amount which bears the same ratio to the amount which would be includible in gross income under paragraph (1) (without regard to this subparagraph) as the qualified education expenses bear to such aggregate distributions.

(C) Coordination with hope and lifetime learning credits and qualified tuition programs.—For purposes of subparagraph (A)—

(i) Credit coordination.—The total amount of qualified education expenses with respect to an individual for the taxable year shall be reduced—

(I) as provided in section 25A(g)(2), and

(II) by the amount of such expenses which were taken into account in determining the credit allowed to the taxpayer or any other person under section 25A.

(ii) Coordination with qualified tuition programs.—If, with respect to an individual for any taxable year—

(I) the aggregate distributions during such year to which subparagraph (A) and section 529(c)(3)(B) apply, exceed

(II) the total amount of qualified education expenses (after the application of clause (i)) for such year,

the taxpayer shall allocate such expenses among such distributions for purposes of determining the amount of the exclusion under paragraph (A) and section 529(c)(3)(B).

(D) Disallowance of excluded amounts as deduction, credit, or exclusion.—No deduction, credit, or exclusion shall be allowed to the taxpayer under any other section of this chapter for any qualified education expenses to the extent taken into account in determining the amount of the exclusion under this paragraph.

(3) Special rules for applying estate and gift taxes with respect to account.—Rules similar to the rules of paragraphs (2), (4), and (5) of section 529(c) shall apply for purposes of this section.

(4) Additional tax for distributions not used for educational expenses.—

(A) In general.—The tax imposed by this chapter for any taxable year on any taxpayer who receives a payment or distribution from a Coverdell education savings account which is includible in gross income shall be increased by 10 percent of the amount which is so includible.

(B) Exceptions.—Subparagraph (A) shall not apply if the payment or distribution is—

(i) made to a beneficiary (or to the estate of the designated beneficiary) on or after the death of the designated beneficiary,

(ii) attributable to the designated beneficiary's being disabled (within the meaning of section 72(m)(7)),

(iii) made on account of a scholarship, allowance, or payment described in section 25A(g)(2) received by the designated beneficiary to the extent the amount of the payment or distribution does not exceed the amount of the scholarship, allowance, or payment,

* * *

(v) an amount which is includible in gross income solely by applicatIon of paragraph (2)(C)(i)(II) for the taxable year.

(C) Contributions returned before certain date.—Subparagraph (A) shall not apply to the distribution of any contribution made during a taxable year on behalf of a designated beneficiary if—

(i) such distribution is made before the first day of the sixth month of the taxable year following the taxable year, and

(ii) such distribution is accompanied by the amount of net income attributable to such excess contribution.

Any net income described in clause (ii) shall be included in gross income for the taxable year in which such excess contribution was made.

(5) Rollover contributions.—Paragraph (1) shall not apply to any amount paid or distributed from a Coverdell education savings account to the extent that the amount received is paid, not later than the 60th day after the date of such payment or distribution, into another Coverdell education savings account for the benefit of the same beneficiary or a member of the family (within the meaning of section 529(e)(2)) of such beneficiary who has not attained age 30 as of such date. The preceding sentence shall not apply to any payment or distribution if it applied to any prior payment or distribution during the 12–month period ending on the date of the payment or distribution.

(6) Change in beneficiary.—Any change in the beneficiary of a Coverdell education savings account shall not be treated as a distribution for purposes of paragraph (1) if the new beneficiary is a member of the family (as so defined) of the old beneficiary and has not attained age 30 as of the date of such change.

(7) Special rules for death and divorce.—Rules similar to the rules of paragraphs (7) and (8) of section 220(f) shall apply. In applying the preceding sentence, members of the family (as so defined) of the designated beneficiary shall be treated in the same manner as the spouse under such paragraph (8).

(8) Deemed distribution on required distribution date.—In any case in which a distribution is required under subsection (b)(1)(E), any balance to the credit of a designated beneficiary as of the close of the 30–day period referred to in such subsection for making such distribution shall be deemed distributed at the close of such period.

* * *

(e) Tax treatment of accounts.—Rules similar to the rules of paragraphs (2) and (4) of section 408(e) shall apply to any Coverdell education savings account.

(f) Community property laws.—This section shall be applied without regard to any community property laws.

(g) Custodial accounts.—For purposes of this section, a custodial account shall be treated as a trust if the assets of such account are held by a bank (as defined in section 408(n)) or another person who demonstrates, to the satisfaction of the Secretary, that the manner in which he will administer the account will be consistent with the requirements of this section, and if the custodial account would, except for the fact that it is not a trust, constitute an account described in subsection (b)(1). For purposes of this title, in the case of a custodial account treated as a trust by reason of the preceding sentence, the custodian of such account shall be treated as the trustee thereof.

(h) Reports.—The trustee of a Coverdell education savings account shall make such reports regarding such account to the Secretary and to the beneficiary of the account with respect to contributions, distributions, and such other matters as the Secretary may require. The reports required by this subsection shall be filed at such time and in such manner and furnished to such individuals at such time and in such manner as may be required.

SUBCHAPTER G—CORPORATIONS USED TO AVOID INCOME TAX ON SHAREHOLDERS

Part

I. Corporations improperly accumulating surplus.
II. Personal holding companies.
III. Foreign personal holding companies.*
IV. Deduction for dividends paid.

PART I—CORPORATIONS IMPROPERLY ACCUMULATING SURPLUS

§ 531. Imposition of accumulated earnings tax

In addition to other taxes imposed by this chapter, there is hereby imposed for each taxable year on the accumulated taxable income (as defined in section 535) of each corporation described in section 532, an accumulated earnings tax equal to 20 percent of the accumulated taxable income.

§ 532. Corporations subject to accumulated earnings tax

(a) General rule.—The accumulated earnings tax imposed by section 531 shall apply to every corporation (other than those described in subsection (b)) formed or availed of for the purpose of avoiding the income tax with respect to its shareholders or the shareholders of any other corporation, by permitting earnings and profits to accumulate instead of being divided or distributed.

(b) Exceptions.—The accumulated earnings tax imposed by section 531 shall not apply to—

(1) a personal holding company (as defined in section 542),

(2) a corporation exempt from tax under subchapter F (section 501 and following), or

* * *

(c) Application determined without regard to number of shareholders.—The application of this part to a corporation shall be determined without regard to the number of shareholders of such corporation.

§ 533. Evidence of purpose to avoid income tax

(a) Unreasonable accumulation determinative of purpose.—For purposes of section 532, the fact that the earnings and profits of a corporation are permitted to accumulate beyond the reasonable needs of the business shall be determinative of the purpose to avoid the income tax with respect to shareholders, unless the corporation by the preponderance of the evidence shall prove to the contrary.

* Omitted entirely.

(b) Holding or investment company.—The fact that any corporation is a mere holding or investment company shall be prima facie evidence of the purpose to avoid the income tax with respect to shareholders.

§ 534. Burden of proof

(a) General rule.—In any proceeding before the Tax Court involving a notice of deficiency based in whole or in part on the allegation that all or any part of the earnings and profits have been permitted to accumulate beyond the reasonable needs of the business, the burden of proof with respect to such allegation shall—

(1) if notification has not been sent in accordance with subsection (b), be on the Secretary, or

(2) if the taxpayer has submitted the statement described in subsection (c), be on the Secretary with respect to the grounds set forth in such statement in accordance with the provisions of such subsection.

(b) Notification by Secretary.—Before mailing the notice of deficiency referred to in subsection (a), the Secretary may send by certified mail or registered mail a notification informing the taxpayer that the proposed notice of deficiency includes an amount with respect to the accumulated earnings tax imposed by section 531.

(c) Statement by taxpayer.—Within such time (but not less than 30 days) after the mailing of the notification described in subsection (b) as the Secretary may prescribe by regulations, the taxpayer may submit a statement of the grounds (together with facts sufficient to show the basis thereof) on which the taxpayer relies to establish that all or any part of the earnings and profits have not been permitted to accumulate beyond the reasonable needs of the business.

* * *

§ 535. Accumulated taxable income

(a) Definition.—For purposes of this subtitle, the term "accumulated taxable income" means the taxable income, adjusted in the manner provided in subsection (b), minus the sum of the dividends paid deduction (as defined in section 561) and the accumulated earnings credit (as defined in subsection (c)).

(b) Adjustments to taxable income.—For purposes of subsection (a), taxable income shall be adjusted as follows:

(1) Taxes.—There shall be allowed as a deduction Federal income and excess profits taxes and income, war profits, and excess profits taxes of foreign countries and possessions of the United States (to the extent not allowable as a deduction under section 275(a) (4)), accrued during the taxable year or deemed to be paid by a domestic corporation under section 902(a) or 960(a) (1) for the taxable year, but not including the accumulated earnings tax imposed by section 531, the personal holding company tax imposed by section 541, or the taxes imposed by corresponding sections of a prior income tax law.

(2) Charitable contributions.—The deduction for charitable contributions provided under section 170 shall be allowed without regard to section 170(b) (2).

(3) Special deductions disallowed.—The special deductions for corporations provided in part VIII (except section 248) of subchapter B (section 241 and following, relating to the deduction for dividends received by corporations, etc.) shall not be allowed.

(4) Net operating loss.—The net operating loss deduction provided in section 172 shall not be allowed.

(5) Capital losses.—

(A) In general.—Except as provided in subparagraph (B), there shall be allowed as a deduction an amount equal to the net capital loss for the taxable year (determined without regard to paragraph (7)(A)).

(B) Recapture of previous deductions for capital gains.—The aggregate amount allowable as a deduction under subparagraph (A) for any taxable year shall be reduced by the lesser of—

(i) the nonrecaptured capital gains deductions, or

(ii) the amount of the accumulated earnings and profits of the corporation as of the close of the preceding taxable year.

(C) Nonrecaptured capital gains deductions.—For purposes of subparagraph (B), the term "nonrecaptured capital gains deductions" means the excess of—

(i) the aggregate amount allowable as a deduction under paragraph (6) for preceding taxable years beginning after July 18, 1984, over

(ii) the aggregate of the reductions under subparagraph (B) for preceding taxable years.

(6) Net capital gains.—

(A) In general.—There shall be allowed as a deduction—

(i) the net capital gain for the taxable year (determined with the application of paragraph (7)), reduced by

(ii) the taxes attributable to such net capital gain.

(B) Attributable taxes.—For purposes of subparagraph (A), the taxes attributable to the net capital gain shall be an amount equal to the difference between—

(i) the taxes imposed by this subtitle (except the tax imposed by this part) for the taxable year, and

(ii) such taxes computed for such year without including in taxable income the net capital gain for the taxable year (determined without the application of paragraph (7)).

(7) Capital loss carryovers.—

(A) Unlimited carryforward.—The net capital loss for any taxable year shall be treated as a short-term capital loss in the next taxable year.

(B) Section 1212 inapplicable.—No allowance shall be made for the capital loss carryback or carryforward provided in section 1212.

(8) Special rules for mere holding or investment companies.—In the case of a mere holding or investment company—

(A) Capital loss deduction, etc., not allowed.—Paragraphs (5) and (7)(A) shall not apply.

(B) Deduction for certain offsets.—There shall be allowed as a deduction the net short-term capital gain for the taxable year to the extent such gain does not exceed the amount of any capital loss carryover to such taxable year under section 1212 (determined without regard to paragraph (7)(B)).

(C) Earnings and profits.—For purposes of subchapter C, the accumulated earnings and profits at any time shall not be less than they would be if this subsection had applied to the computation of earnings and profits for all taxable years beginning after July 18, 1984.

* * *

(c) Accumulated earnings credit.—

(1) General rule.—For purposes of subsection (a), in the case of a corporation other than a mere holding or investment company the accumulated earnings credit is (A) an amount equal to such part of the earnings and profits for the taxable year as are retained for the reasonable needs of the business, minus (B) the deduction allowed by subsection (b)(6). For purposes of this paragraph, the amount of the earnings and profits for the taxable year which are retained is the amount by which the earnings and profits for the taxable year exceed the dividends paid deduction (as defined in section 561) for such year.

(2) Minimum credit.—

(A) In general.—The credit allowable under paragraph (1) shall in no case be less than the amount by which $250,000 exceeds the accumulated earnings and profits of the corporation at the close of the preceding taxable year.

(B) Certain service corporations.—In the case of a corporation the principal function of which is the performance of services in the field of health, law, engineering, architecture, accounting, actuarial science, performing arts, or consulting, subparagraph (A) shall be applied by substituting "$150,000" for "$250,000".

(3) Holding and investment companies.—In the case of a corporation which is a mere holding or investment company, the accumulated earnings credit is the amount (if any) by which $250,000 exceeds the accumulated earnings and profits of the corporation at the close of the preceding taxable year.

(4) Accumulated earnings and profits.—For purposes of paragraphs (2) and (3), the accumulated earnings and profits at the close of the preceding taxable year shall be reduced by the dividends which under section 563(a) (relating to dividends paid after the close of the taxable year) are considered as paid during such taxable year.

(5) Cross reference.—

For denial of credit provided in paragraph (2) or (3) where multiple corporations are formed to avoid tax, see section 1551, and for limitation on such credit in the case of certain controlled corporations, see section 1561.

* * *

§ 537. Reasonable needs of the business

(a) General rule.—For purposes of this part, the term "reasonable needs of the business" includes—

(1) the reasonably anticipated needs of the business,

(2) the section 303 redemption needs of the business, and

(3) the excess business holdings redemption needs of the business.

(b) Special rules.—For purposes of subsection (a)—

(1) Section 303 redemption needs.—The term "section 303 redemption needs" means, with respect to the taxable year of the corporation in which a shareholder of the corporation died or any taxable year thereafter, the amount needed (or reasonably anticipated to be needed) to make a redemption of stock included in the gross estate of the decedent (but not in excess of the maximum amount of stock to which section 303(a) may apply).

* * *

(3) Obligations incurred to make redemptions.—In applying paragraphs (1) and (2), the discharge of any obligation incurred to make a redemption described in such paragraphs shall be treated as the making of such redemption.

* * *

(5) No inference as to prior taxable years.—The application of this part to any taxable year before the first taxable year specified in paragraph (1) shall be made without regard to the fact that distributions in redemption coming within the terms of such paragraphs were subsequently made.

PART II—PERSONAL HOLDING COMPANIES

§ 541. Imposition of personal holding company tax

In addition to other taxes imposed by this chapter, there is hereby imposed for each taxable year on the undistributed personal holding company income (as defined in section 545) of every personal holding company (as defined in section 542) a personal holding company tax equal to 20 percent of the undistributed personal holding company income.

§ 542. Definition of personal holding company

(a) General rule.—For purposes of this subtitle, the term "personal holding company" means any corporation (other than a corporation described in subsection (c)) if—

(1) Adjusted ordinary gross income requirement.—At least 60 percent of its adjusted ordinary gross income (as defined in section 543(b)(2)) for the taxable year is personal holding company income (as defined in section 543(a)), and

(2) Stock ownership requirement.—At any time during the last half of the taxable year more than 50 percent in value of its outstanding stock is owned, directly or indirectly, by or for not more than 5 individuals. For purposes of this paragraph, an organization described in section 401(a), 501(c)(17), or 509(a) or a portion of a trust permanently set aside or to be used exclusively for the purposes described in section 642(c) or a corresponding provision of a prior income tax law shall be considered an individual.

* * *

(c) Exceptions.—The term "personal holding company" as defined in subsection (a) does not include—

(1) a corporation exempt from tax under subchapter F (sec. 501 and following);

(2) a bank as defined in section 581, or a domestic building and loan association within the meaning of section 7701(a)(19);

(3) a life insurance company;

* * *

(6) a lending or finance company if—

(A) 60 percent or more of its ordinary gross income (as defined in section 543(b)(1)) is derived directly from the active and regular conduct of a lending or finance business;

(B) the personal holding company income for the taxable year (computed without regard to income described in subsection (d)(3) and income derived directly from the active and regular conduct of a lending or finance business, and computed by including as personal holding company income the entire amount of the gross income from rents, royalties, produced film rents, and compensation for use of corporate property by shareholders) is not more than 20 percent of the ordinary gross income;

(C) the sum of the deductions which are directly allocable to the active and regular conduct of its lending or finance business equals or exceeds the sum of—

(i) 15 percent of so much of the ordinary gross income derived therefrom as does not exceed $500,000, plus

(ii) 5 percent of so much of the ordinary gross income derived therefrom as exceeds $500,000; and

(D) the loans to a person who is a shareholder in such company during the taxable year by or for whom 10 percent or more in value of its outstanding stock is owned directly or indirectly (including, in the case of an individual, stock owned by members of his family as defined in section 544(a)(2)), outstanding at any time during such year do not exceed $5,000 in principal amount;

* * *

(8) a corporation which is subject to the jurisdiction of the court in a title 11 or similar case (within the meaning of section 368(a)(3)(A)) unless a major purpose of instituting or continuing such case is the avoidance of the tax imposed by section 541.

* * *

§ 543. Personal holding company income

(a) General rule.—For purposes of this subtitle, the term "personal holding company income" means the portion of the adjusted ordinary gross income which consists of:

(1) Dividends, etc.—Dividends, interest, royalties (other than mineral, oil, or gas royalties or copyright royalties), and annuities. This paragraph shall not apply to—

(A) interest constituting rent (as defined in subsection (b)(3)),

* * *

(C) active business computer software royalties (within the meaning of subsection (d)), and

(D) interest received by a broker or dealer (within the meaning of section 3(a)(4) or (5) of the Securities and Exchange Act of 1934) in connection with—

(i) any securities or money market instruments held as property described in section 1221(a)(1),

(ii) margin accounts, or

(iii) any financing for a customer secured by securities or money market instruments.

(2) Rents.—The adjusted income from rents; except that such adjusted income shall not be included if—

(A) such adjusted income constitutes 50 percent or more of the adjusted ordinary gross income, and

(B) the sum of—

(i) the dividends paid during the taxable year (determined under section 562),

(ii) the dividends considered as paid on the last day of the taxable year under section 563(d) (as limited by the second sentence of section 563(b)), and

(iii) the consent dividends for the taxable year (determined under section 565),

equals or exceeds the amount, if any, by which the personal holding company income for the taxable year (computed without regard to this paragraph and paragraph (6), and computed by including as personal holding company income copyright royalties and the adjusted income from mineral, oil, and gas royalties) exceeds 10 percent of the ordinary gross income.

(3) Mineral, oil, and gas royalties.—The adjusted income from mineral, oil, and gas royalties; except that such adjusted income shall not be included if—

(A) such adjusted income constitutes 50 percent or more of the adjusted ordinary gross income,

(B) the personal holding company income for the taxable year (computed without regard to this paragraph, and computed by including as personal holding company income copyright royalties and the adjusted income from rents) is not more than 10 percent of the ordinary gross income, and

(C) the sum of the deductions which are allowable under section 162 (relating to trade or business expenses) other than—

(i) deductions for compensation for personal services rendered by the shareholders, and

(ii) deductions which are specifically allowable under sections other than section 162,

equals or exceeds 15 percent of the adjusted ordinary gross income.

(4) Copyright royalties.—Copyright royalties; except that copyright royalties shall not be included if—

(A) such royalties (exclusive of royalties received for the use of, or right to use, copyrights or interests in copyrights on works created in whole, or in part, by any shareholder) constitute 50 percent or more of the ordinary gross income,

(B) the personal holding company income for the taxable year computed—

(i) without regard to copyright royalties, other than royalties received for the use of, or right to use, copyrights or interests in copyrights in works created in whole, or in part, by any shareholder owning more than 10 percent of the total outstanding capital stock of the corporation,

(ii) without regard to dividends from any corporation in which the taxpayer owns at least 50 percent of all classes of stock entitled to vote and at least 50 percent of the total value of all classes of stock and which corporation meets the requirements of this subparagraph and subparagraphs (A) and (C), and

(iii) by including as personal holding company income the adjusted income from rents and the adjusted income from mineral, oil, and gas royalties,

is not more than 10 percent of the ordinary gross income, and

(C) the sum of the deductions which are properly allocable to such royalties and which are allowable under section 162, other than—

(i) deductions for compensation for personal services rendered by the shareholders,

(ii) deductions for royalties paid or accrued, and

(iii) deductions which are specifically allowable under sections other than section 162,

equals or exceeds 25 percent of the amount by which the ordinary gross income exceeds the sum of the royalties paid or accrued and the amounts allowable as deductions under section 167 (relating to depreciation) with respect to copyright royalties.

For purposes of this subsection, the term "copyright royalties" means compensation, however designated, for the use of, or the right to use, copyrights in works protected by copyright issued under title 17 of the United States Code and to which copyright protection is also extended by the laws of any country other than the United States of America by virtue of any international treaty, convention, or agreement, or interests in any such copyrighted works, and includes payments from any person for performing rights in any such copyrighted work and payments (other than produced film rents as defined in paragraph (5)(B)) received for the use of, or right to use, films. For purposes of this paragraph, the term "shareholder" shall include any person who owns stock within the meaning of section 544. This paragraph shall not apply to active business computer software royalties.

(5) Produced film rents.—

(A) Produced film rents; except that such rents shall not be included if such rents constitute 50 percent or more of the ordinary gross income.

(B) For purposes of this section, the term "produced film rents" means payments received with respect to an interest in a film for the use of, or right to use, such film, but only to the extent that such interest was acquired before substantial completion of production of such film. In the case of a producer who actively participates in the production of the film, such term includes an interest in the proceeds or profits from the film, but only to the extent such interest is attributable to such active participation.

(6) Use of corporate property by shareholder.—

(A) Amounts received as compensation (however designated and from whomever received) for the use of, or the right to use, tangible property of the corporation in any case where, at any time during the taxable year, 25 percent or more in value of the outstanding stock of the corporation is owned, directly or indirectly, by or for an individual entitled to the use of the property (whether such right is obtained directly from the corporation or by means of a sublease or other arrangement).

(B) Subparagraph (A) shall apply only to a corporation which has personal holding company income in excess of 10 percent of its ordinary gross income.

(C) For purposes of the limitation in subparagraph (B), personal holding company income shall be computed—

(i) without regard to subparagraph (A) or paragraph (2),

(ii) by excluding amounts received as compensation for the use of (or right to use) intangible property (other than mineral, oil, or gas royalties or copyright royalties) if a substantial part of the tangible property used in connection with such intangible property is owned by the corporation and all such tangible and intangible property is used in the active conduct of a trade or business by an individual or individuals described in subparagraph (A), and

(iii) by including copyright royalties and adjusted income from mineral, oil, and gas royalties.

(7) Personal service contracts.—

(A) Amounts received under a contract under which the corporation is to furnish personal services; if some person other than the corporation has the right to designate (by name or by description) the individual who is to perform the services, or if the individual who is to perform the services is designated (by name or by description) in the contract; and

(B) amounts received from the sale or other disposition of such a contract.

This paragraph shall apply with respect to amounts received for services under a particular contract only if at some time during the taxable year 25 percent or more in value of the outstanding stock of the corporation is owned, directly or indirectly, by or for the individual who has performed, is to perform, or may be designated (by name or by description) as the one to perform, such services.

(8) Estates and trusts.—Amounts includible in computing the taxable income of the corporation under part I of subchapter J (sec. 641 and following, relating to estates, trusts, and beneficiaries).

(b) Definitions.—For purposes of this part—

(1) Ordinary gross income.—The term "ordinary gross income" means the gross income determined by excluding—

(A) all gains from the sale or other disposition of capital assets, and

(B) all gains (other than those referred to in subparagraph (A)) from the sale or other disposition of property described in section 1231(b).

(2) Adjusted ordinary gross income.—The term "adjusted ordinary gross income" means the ordinary gross income adjusted as follows:

(A) Rents.—From the gross income from rents (as defined in the second sentence of paragraph (3) of this subsection) subtract the amount allowable as deductions for—

(i) exhaustion, wear and tear, obsolescence, and amortization of property other than tangible personal property which is not customarily retained by any one lessee for more than three years,

(ii) property taxes,

(iii) interest, and

(iv) rent,

to the extent allocable, under regulations prescribed by the Secretary, to such gross income from rents. The amount subtracted under this subparagraph shall not exceed such gross income from rents.

(B) Mineral royalties, etc.—From the gross income from mineral, oil, and gas royalties described in paragraph (4), and from the gross income from working interests in an oil or gas well, subtract the amount allowable as deductions for—

(i) exhaustion, wear and tear, obsolescence, amortization, and depletion,

(ii) property and severance taxes,

(iii) interest, and

(iv) rent,

to the extent allocable, under regulations prescribed by the Secretary, to such gross income from royalties or such gross income from working interests in oil or gas wells. The amount subtracted under this subparagraph with respect to royalties shall not exceed the gross income from such royalties, and the amount subtracted under this subparagraph with respect to working interests shall not exceed the gross income from such working interests.

(C) Interest.—There shall be excluded—

(i) interest received on a direct obligation of the United States held for sale to customers in the ordinary course of trade or business by a regular dealer who is making a primary market in such obligations, and

(ii) interest on a condemnation award, a judgment, and a tax refund.

(D) Certain excluded rents.—From the gross income consisting of compensation described in subparagraph (D) of paragraph (3) subtract the amount allowable as deductions for the items described in clauses (i), (ii), (iii), and (iv) of subparagraph (A) to the extent allocable, under regulations prescribed by the Secretary, to such gross income. The amount subtracted under this subparagraph shall not exceed such gross income.

(3) Adjusted income from rents.—The term "adjusted income from rents" means the gross income from rents, reduced by the amount subtracted under paragraph (2) (A) of this subsection. For purposes of the preceding sentence, the term "rents" means compensation, however designated, for the use of, or right to use, property, and the interest on debts owed to the corporation, to the extent such debts represent the price for which real property held primarily for sale to customers in the ordinary course of its trade or business was sold or exchanged by the corporation; but such term does not include—

(A) amounts constituting personal holding company income under subsection (a)(6),

(B) copyright royalties (as defined in subsection (a)(4)),

(C) produced film rents (as defined in subsection (a)(5)(B)),

(D) compensation, however designated, for the use of, or the right to use, any tangible personal property manufactured or produced by the taxpayer, if during the taxable year the taxpayer is engaged in substantial manufacturing or production of tangible personal property of the same type, or

(E) active business computer software royalties (as defined in subsection (d)).

(4) Adjusted income from mineral, oil, and gas royalties.—The term "adjusted income from mineral, oil, and gas royalties" means the gross income from mineral, oil, and gas royalties (including production payments and overriding royalties), reduced by the amount subtracted under paragraph (2)(B) of this subsection in respect of such royalties.

* * *

§ 544. Rules for determining stock ownership

(a) Constructive ownership.—For purposes of determining whether a corporation is a personal holding company, insofar as such determination is based on stock ownership under section 542(a)(2), section 543(a)(7), section 543(a)(6), or section 543(a)(4)—

(1) Stock not owned by individual.—Stock owned, directly or indirectly, by or for a corporation, partnership, estate, or trust shall be considered as being owned proportionately by its shareholders, partners, or beneficiaries.

(2) Family and partnership ownership.—An individual shall be considered as owning the stock owned, directly or indirectly, by or for his family or by or for his partner. For purposes of this paragraph, the family of an individual includes only his brothers and sisters (whether by the whole or half blood), spouse, ancestors, and lineal descendants.

(3) Options.—If any person has an option to acquire stock, such stock shall be considered as owned by such person. For purposes of this paragraph, an option to acquire such an option, and each one of a series of such options, shall be considered as an option to acquire such stock.

(4) Application of family-partnership and option rules.—Paragraphs (2) and (3) shall be applied—

(A) for purposes of the stock ownership requirement provided in section 542(a)(2), if, but only if, the effect is to make the corporation a personal holding company;

(B) for purposes of section 543(a)(7) (relating to personal service contracts), of section 543(a)(6) (relating to use of property by shareholders), or of section 543(a)(4) (relating to copyright royalties), if, but only if, the effect is to make the amounts therein referred to includible under such paragraph as personal holding company income.

(5) Constructive ownership as actual ownership.—Stock constructively owned by a person by reason of the application of paragraph (1) or (3) shall, for purposes of applying paragraph (1) or (2), be treated as actually owned by such person; but stock constructively owned by an individual by reason of the application of paragraph (2) shall not be treated as owned by him for purposes of again applying such paragraph in order to make another the constructive owner of such stock.

(6) Option rule in lieu of family and partnership rule.—If stock may be considered as owned by an individual under either paragraph (2) or (3) it shall be considered as owned by him under paragraph (3).

* * *

§ 545. Undistributed personal holding company income

(a) Definition.—For purposes of this part, the term "undistributed personal holding company income" means the taxable income of a personal holding company adjusted in the manner provided in subsections (b), (c), and (d), minus the dividends paid deduction as defined in section 561. In the case of a personal holding company which is a foreign corporation, not more than 10 percent in value of the outstanding stock of which is owned (within the meaning of section 958(a)) during the last half of the taxable year by United States persons, the term "undistributed personal holding company income" means the amount determined by multiplying the undistributed personal holding company income (determined without regard to this sentence) by the percentage in value of its outstanding stock which is the greatest percentage in value of its outstanding stock so owned by United States persons on any one day during such period.

(b) Adjustments to taxable income.—For the purposes of subsection (a), the taxable income shall be adjusted as follows:

(1) Taxes.—There shall be allowed as a deduction Federal income and excess profits taxes and income, war profits and excess profits taxes of foreign countries and possessions of the United States (to the extent not allowable as a deduction under section 275(a)(4)), accrued during the taxable year or deemed to be paid by a domestic corporation under section 902(a) or 960(a)(1) for the taxable year, but not including the accumulated earnings tax imposed by section 531, the personal holding company tax imposed by section 541, or the taxes imposed by corresponding sections of a prior income tax law.

(2) Charitable contributions.—The deduction for charitable contributions provided under section 170 shall be allowed, but in computing such deduction the limitations in section 170(b)(1)(A), (B), (D), and (E) shall apply, and section 170(b)(2) and (d)(1) shall not apply. For purposes of this paragraph, the term "contribution base" when used in section 170(b)(1) means the taxable income computed with the adjustments (other than the 10–percent limitation) provided in section 170(b)(2) and (d)(1) and without deduction of the amount disallowed under paragraph (6) of this subsection.

(3) Special deductions disallowed.—The special deductions for corporations provided in part VIII (except section 248) of subchapter B (section 241 and following, relating to the deduction for dividends received by corporations, etc.) shall not be allowed.

(4) Net operating loss.—The net operating loss deduction provided in section 172 shall not be allowed, but there shall be allowed as a deduction the amount of the net operating loss (as defined in section 172(c)) for the preceding taxable year computed without the deductions provided in part VIII (except section 248) of subchapter B.

(5) Net capital gains.—There shall be allowed as a deduction the net capital gain for the taxable year, minus the taxes imposed by this subtitle attributable to such net capital gain. The taxes attributable to such net capital gain shall be an amount equal to the difference between—

(A) the taxes imposed by this subtitle (except the tax imposed by this part) for such year, and

(B) such taxes computed for such year without including such net capital gain in taxable income.

(6) Expenses and depreciation applicable to property of the taxpayer.—The aggregate of the deductions allowed under section 162 (relating to trade or business expenses) and section 167 (relating to depreciation), which are allocable to the operation and maintenance of property owned or operated by the corporation, shall be allowed only in an amount equal to the rent or other compensation received for the use of, or the right to use, the property, unless it is established (under regulations prescribed by the Secretary) to the satisfaction of the Secretary—

(A) that the rent or other compensation received was the highest obtainable, or, if none was received, that none was obtainable;

(B) that the property was held in the course of a business carried on bona fide for profit; and

(C) either that there was reasonable expectation that the operation of the property would result in a profit, or that the property was necessary to the conduct of the business.

* * *

§ 547. Deduction for deficiency dividends

(a) General rule.—If a determination (as defined in subsection (c)) with respect to a taxpayer establishes liability for personal holding company tax imposed by section 541 (or by a corresponding provision of a prior income tax law) for any taxable year, a deduction shall be allowed to the taxpayer for the amount of deficiency dividends (as defined in subsection (d)) for the purpose of determining the personal holding company tax for such year, but not for the purpose of determining interest, additional amounts, or assessable penalties computed with respect to such personal holding company tax.

(b) Rules for application of section.—

(1) Allowance of deduction.—The deficiency dividend deduction shall be allowed as of the date the claim for the deficiency dividend deduction is filed.

(2) Credit or refund.—If the allowance of a deficiency dividend deduction results in an overpayment of personal holding company tax for any taxable year, credit or refund with respect to such overpayment shall be made as if on the date of the determination 2 years remained before the expiration of the period of limitation on the filing of claim for refund for the taxable year to which the overpayment relates. No interest shall be allowed on a credit or refund arising from the application of this section.

(c) Determination.—For purposes of this section, the term "determination" means—

(1) a decision by the Tax Court or a judgment, decree, or other order by any court of competent jurisdiction, which has become final;

(2) a closing agreement made under section 7121; or

(3) under regulations prescribed by the Secretary, an agreement signed by the Secretary and by, or on behalf of, the taxpayer relating to the liability of such taxpayer for personal holding company tax.

(d) Deficiency dividends.—

(1) Definition.—For purposes of this section, the term "deficiency dividends" means the amount of the dividends paid by the corporation on or after the date of the determination and before filing claim under subsection (e), which would have been includible in the computation of the deduction for dividends paid under section 561 for the taxable year with respect to which the liability for personal holding company tax exists, if distributed during such taxable year. No dividends shall be considered as deficiency dividends for purposes of subsection (a) unless distributed within 90 days after the determination.

(2) Effect on dividends paid deduction.—

(A) For taxable year in which paid.—Deficiency dividends paid in any taxable year (to the extent of the portion thereof taken into account under subsection (a) in determining personal holding company tax) shall not be included in the amount of dividends paid for such year for purposes of computing the dividends paid deduction for such year and succeeding years.

(B) For prior taxable year.—Deficiency dividends paid in any taxable year (to the extent of the portion thereof taken into account under subsection (a) in determining personal holding company tax) shall not be allowed for purposes of section 563(b) in the computation of the dividends paid deduction for the taxable year preceding the taxable year in which paid.

(e) Claim required.—No deficiency dividend deduction shall be allowed under subsection (a) unless (under regulations prescribed by the Secretary) claim therefor is filed within 120 days after the determination.

(f) Suspension of statute of limitations and stay of collection.—

(1) Suspension of running of statute.—If the corporation files a claim, as provided in subsection (e), the running of the statute of limitations provided in section 6501 on the making of assessments, and the bringing of distraint or a proceeding in court for collection, in respect of the deficiency and all interest, additional amounts, or assessable penalties, shall be suspended for a period of 2 years after the date of the determination.

(2) Stay of collection.—In the case of any deficiency with respect to the tax imposed by section 541 established by a determination under this section—

(A) the collection of the deficiency and all interest, additional amounts, and assessable penalties shall, except in cases of jeopardy, be stayed until the expiration of 120 days after the date of the determination, and

(B) if claim for deficiency dividend deduction is filed under subsection (e), the collection of such part of the deficiency as is not reduced by the deduction for deficiency dividends provided in subsection (a) shall be stayed until the date the claim is disallowed (in whole or in part), and if disallowed in part collection shall be made only with respect to the part disallowed.

No distraint or proceeding in court shall be begun for the collection of an amount the collection of which is stayed under subparagraph (A) or (B) during the period for which the collection of such amount is stayed.

(g) Deduction denied in case of fraud, etc.—No deficiency dividend deduction shall be allowed under subsection (a) if the determination contains a finding that any part of the deficiency is due to fraud with intent to evade tax, or to wilful failure to file an income tax return within the time prescribed by law or prescribed by the Secretary in pursuance of law.

PART IV—DEDUCTION FOR DIVIDENDS PAID

§ 561. Definition of deduction for dividends paid

(a) General rule.—The deduction for dividends paid shall be the sum of—

(1) the dividends paid during the taxable year,

(2) the consent dividends for the taxable year (determined under section 565), and

(3) in the case of a personal holding company, the dividend carryover described in section 564.

(b) Special rules applicable.—In determining the deduction for dividends paid, the rules provided in section 562 (relating to rules applicable in determining dividends eligible for dividends paid deduction) and section 563 (relating to dividends paid after the close of the taxable year) shall be applicable.

§ 562. Rules applicable in determining dividends eligible for dividends paid deduction

(a) General rule.—For purposes of this part, the term "dividend" shall, except as otherwise provided in this section, include only dividends described in section 316 (relating to definition of dividends for purposes of corporate distributions).

(b) Distributions in liquidation.—

(1) Except in the case of a personal holding company described in section 542—

(A) in the case of amounts distributed in liquidation, the part of such distribution which is properly chargeable to earnings and profits accumulated after February 28, 1913, shall be treated as a dividend for purposes of computing the dividends paid deduction, and

(B) in the case of a complete liquidation occurring within 24 months after the adoption of a plan of liquidation, any distribution within such period pursuant to such plan shall, to the extent of the earnings and profits (computed without regard to capital losses) of the corporation for the taxable year in which such distribution is made, be treated as a dividend for purposes of computing the dividends paid deduction.

Except to the extent provided in regulations, the preceding sentence shall not apply in the case of any mere holding or investment company which is not a regulated investment company.

(2) In the case of a complete liquidation of a personal holding company, occurring within 24 months after the adoption of a plan of liquidation, the amount of any distribution within such period pursuant to such plan shall be treated as a dividend for purposes of computing the dividends paid deduction, to the extent that such amount is distributed to corporate distributees and represents such corporate distributees' allocable share of the undistributed personal holding company income for the taxable year of such distribution computed without regard to this paragraph and without regard to subparagraph (B) of section 316(b)(2).

(c) Preferential dividends.—Except in the case of a publicly offered regulated investment company (as defined in section 67(c)(2)(8)), the amount of any distribution shall not be considered as a dividend for purposes of computing the dividends paid deduction, unless such distribution is pro rata, with no preference to any share of stock as compared with other shares of the same class, and with no preference to one class of stock as compared with another class except to the extent that the former is entitled (without reference to waivers of their rights by shareholders) to such preference. In the case of a distribution by a regulated investment company (other than a publicly offered regulated investment company (as so defined)) to a shareholder who made an initial investment of at least $10,000,000 in such company, such distribution shall not be treated as not being pro rata or as being preferential solely by reason of an increase in the distribution by reason of reductions in administrative expenses of the company.

* * *

§ 563. Rules relating to dividends paid after close of taxable year

(a) Accumulated earnings tax.—In the determination of the dividends paid deduction for purposes of the accumulated earnings tax imposed by section 531, a dividend paid after the close of any taxable year and on or before the 15th day of the third month following the close of such taxable year shall be considered as paid during such taxable year.

(b) Personal holding company tax.—In the determination of the dividends paid deduction for purposes of the personal holding company tax imposed by section 541, a dividend paid after the close of any taxable year and on or before the 15th day of the third month following the close of such taxable year shall, to the extent the taxpayer elects in its return for the taxable year, be considered as paid during such taxable year. The amount allowed as a dividend by reason of the application of this subsection with respect to any taxable year shall not exceed either—

(1) The undistributed personal holding company income of the corporation for the taxable year, computed without regard to this subsection, or

(2) 20 percent of the sum of the dividends paid during the taxable year, computed without regard to this subsection.

(c) Dividends considered as paid on last day of taxable year.—For the purpose of applying section 562(a), with respect to distributions under subsection (a) or (b) of this section, a distribution made after the close of a taxable year and on or before the 15th day of the third month following the close of the taxable year shall be considered as made on the last day of such taxable year.

§ 564. Dividend carryover

(a) General rule.—For purposes of computing the dividends paid deduction under section 561, in the case of a personal holding company the dividend carryover for any taxable year shall be the dividend carryover to such taxable year, computed as provided in subsection (b), from the two preceding taxable years.

(b) Computation of dividend carryover.—The dividend carryover to the taxable year shall be determined as follows:

(1) For each of the 2 preceding taxable years there shall be determined the taxable income computed with the adjustments provided in section 545 (whether or not the taxpayer was a personal holding company for either of such preceding taxable years), and there shall also be determined for each such year the deduction for dividends paid during such year as provided in section 561 (but determined without regard to the dividend carryover to such year).

(2) There shall be determined for each such taxable year whether there is an excess of such taxable income over such deduction for dividends paid or an excess of such deduction for dividends paid over such taxable income, and the amount of each such excess.

(3) If there is an excess of such deductions for dividends paid over such taxable income for the first preceding taxable year, such excess shall be allowed as a dividend carryover to the taxable year.

(4) If there is an excess of such deduction for dividends paid over such taxable income for the second preceding taxable year, such excess shall be reduced by the amount determined in paragraph (5), and the remainder of such excess shall be allowed as a dividend carryover to the taxable year.

(5) The amount of the reduction specified in paragraph (4) shall be the amount of the excess of the taxable income, if any, for the first preceding taxable year over such deduction for dividends paid, if any, for the first preceding taxable year.

§ 565. Consent dividends

(a) General rule.—If any person owns consent stock (as defined in subsection (f)(1)) in a corporation on the last day of the taxable year of such corporation, and such person agrees, in a consent filed with the return of such corporation in accordance with regulations prescribed by the Secretary, to treat as a dividend the amount specified in such consent, the amount so specified shall, except as provided in subsection (b), constitute a consent dividend for purposes of section 561 (relating to the deduction for dividends paid).

(b) Limitations.—A consent dividend shall not include—

(1) an amount specified in a consent which, if distributed in money, would constitute, or be part of, a distribution which would be disqualified for purposes of the dividends paid deduction under section 562(c) (relating to preferential dividends), or

(2) an amount specified in a consent which would not constitute a dividend (as defined in section 316) if the total amounts specified in consents filed by the corporation had been distributed in money to shareholders on the last day of the taxable year of such corporation.

(c) Effect of consent.—The amount of a consent dividend shall be considered, for purposes of this title—

(1) as distributed in money by the corporation to the shareholder on the last day of the taxable year of the corporation, and

(2) as contributed to the capital of the corporation by the shareholder on such day.

(d) Consent dividends and other distributions.—If a distribution by a corporation consists in part of consent dividends and in part of money or other property, the entire amount specified in the consents and the amount of such money or other property shall be considered together for purposes of applying this title.

* * *

(f) Definitions.—

(1) Consent stock.—Consent stock, for purposes of this section, means the class or classes of stock entitled, after the payment of preferred dividends, to a share in the distribution (other than in complete or partial liquidation) within the taxable year of all the remaining earnings and profits, which share constitutes the same proportion of such distribution regardless of the amount of such distribution.

(2) Preferred dividends.—Preferred dividends, for purposes of this section, means a distribution (other than in complete or partial liquidation), limited in amount, which must be made on any class of stock before a further distribution (other than in complete or partial liquidation) of earnings and profits may be made within the taxable year.

SUBCHAPTER I—NATURAL RESOURCES

PART I—DEDUCTIONS

§ 611. Allowance of deduction for depletion

(a) General rule.—In the case of mines, oil and gas wells, other natural deposits, and timber, there shall be allowed as a deduction in computing taxable income a reasonable allowance for depletion and for depreciation of improvements, according to the peculiar conditions in each case; such reasonable allowance in all cases to be made under regulations prescribed by the Secretary. For purposes of this part, the term "mines" includes deposits of waste or residue, the extraction of ores or minerals from which is treated as mining under section 613(c). In any case in which it is ascertained as a result of operations or of development work that the recoverable units are greater or less than the prior estimate thereof, then such prior estimate (but not the basis for depletion) shall be revised and the allowance under this section for subsequent taxable years shall be based on such revised estimate.

(b) Special rules.—

(1) Leases.—In the case of a lease, the deduction under this section shall be equitably apportioned between the lessor and lessee.

(2) Life tenant and remainderman.—In the case of property held by one person for life with remainder to another person, the deduction under this section shall be computed as if the life tenant were the absolute owner of the property and shall be allowed to the life tenant.

(3) Property held in trust.—In the case of property held in trust, the deduction under this section shall be apportioned between the income beneficiaries and the trustee in accordance with the pertinent provisions of the instrument creating the trust, or, in the absence of such provisions, on the basis of the trust income allocable to each.

(4) Property held by estate.—In the case of an estate, the deduction under this section shall be apportioned between the estate and the heirs, legatees, and devisees on the basis of the income of the estate allocable to each.

* * *

* Omitted entirely.

§ 612. Basis for cost depletion

Except as otherwise provided in this subchapter, the basis on which depletion is to be allowed in respect of any property shall be the adjusted basis provided in section 1011 for the purpose of determining the gain upon the sale or other disposition of such property.

§ 613. Percentage depletion

(a) General rule.—In the case of the mines, wells, and other natural deposits listed in subsection (b), the allowance for depletion under section 611 shall be the percentage, specified in subsection (b), of the gross income from the property excluding from such gross income an amount equal to any rents or royalties paid or incurred by the taxpayer in respect of the property. Such allowance shall not exceed 50 percent (100 percent in the case of oil and gas properties) of the taxpayer's taxable income from the property (computed without allowance for depletion and without the deduction under section 199). For purposes of the preceding sentence, the allowable deductions taken into account with respect to expenses of mining in computing the taxable income from the property shall be decreased by an amount equal to so much of any gain which (1) is treated under section 1245 (relating to gain from disposition of certain depreciable property) as ordinary income, and (2) is properly allocable to the property. In no case shall the allowance for depletion under section 611 be less than it would be if computed without reference to this section.

(b) Percentage depletion rates.—The mines, wells, and other natural deposits, and the percentages, referred to in subsection (a) are as follows:

(1) 22 percent—

(A) sulphur and uranium; and

(B) if from deposits in the United States—anorthosite, clay, laterite, and nephelite syenite (to the extent that alumina and aluminum compounds are extracted therefrom), asbestos, bauxite, celestite, chromite, corundum, fluorspar, graphite, ilmenite, kyanite, mica, olivine, quartz crystals (radio grade), rutile, block steatite talc, and zircon, and ores of the following metals: antimony, beryllium, bismuth, cadmium, cobalt, columbium, lead, lithium, manganese, mercury, molybdenum, nickel, platinum and platinum group metals, tantalum, thorium, tin, titanium, tungsten, vanadium, and zinc.

(2) 15 percent—If from deposits in the United States—

(A) gold, silver, copper, and iron ore, and

(B) oil shale (except shale described in paragraph (5)).

(3) 14 percent—

(A) metal mines (if paragraph (1)(B) or (2)(A) does not apply), rock asphalt, and vermiculite; and

(B) if paragraph (1)(B), (5), or (6)(B) does not apply, ball clay, bentonite, china clay, sagger clay, and clay used or sold for use for purposes dependent on its refractory properties.

(4) 10 percent—asbestos (if paragraph (1)(B) does not apply), brucite, coal, lignite, perlite, sodium chloride, and wollastonite.

(5) 7½ percent—clay and shale used or sold for use in the manufacture of sewer pipe or brick, and clay, shale, and slate used or sold for use as sintered or burned lightweight aggregates.

(6) 5 percent—

(A) gravel, peat, pumice, sand, scoria, shale (except shale described in paragraph (2)(B) or (5)), and stone (except stone described in paragraph (7));

(B) clay used, or sold for use, in the manufacture of drainage and roofing tile, flower pots, and kindred products; and

(C) if from brine wells—bromine, calcium chloride, and magnesium chloride.

(7) 14 percent—all other minerals, including, but not limited to, aplite, barite, borax, calcium carbonates, diatomaceous earth, dolomite, feldspar, fullers earth, garnet, gilsonite, granite, limestone, magnesite, magnesium carbonates, marble, mollusk shells (including clam shells and oyster shells), phosphate rock, potash, quartzite, slate, soapstone, stone (used or sold for use by the mine owner or operator as dimension stone or ornamental stone), thenardite, tripoli, trona, and (if paragraph (1)(B) does not apply) bauxite, flake graphite, fluorspar, lepidolite, mica, spodumene, and talc (including pyrophyllite), except that, unless sold on bid in direct competition with a bona fide bid to sell a mineral listed in paragraph (3), the percentage shall be 5 percent for any such other mineral (other than slate to which paragraph (5) applies) when used, or sold for use, by the mine owner or operator as rip rap, ballast, road material, rubble, concrete aggregates, or for similar purposes. For purposes of this paragraph, the term "all other minerals" does not include—

(A) soil, sod, dirt, turf, water, or mosses;

(B) minerals from sea water, the air, or similar inexhaustible sources; or

(C) oil and gas wells.

For the purposes of this subsection, minerals (other than sodium chloride) extracted from brines pumped from a saline perennial lake within the United States shall not be considered minerals from an inexhaustible source.

(c) Definition of gross income from property.—For purposes of this section—

(1) Gross income from the property.—The term "gross income from the property" means, in the case of a property other than an oil or gas well and other than a geothermal deposit, the gross income from mining.

(2) Mining.—The term "mining" includes not merely the extraction of the ores or minerals from the ground but also the treatment processes considered as mining described in paragraph (4) (and the treatment processes necessary or incidental thereto), and so much of the transportation of ores or minerals (whether or not by common carrier) from the point of extraction from the ground to the plants or mills in which such treatment processes are applied thereto as is not in excess of 50 miles unless the Secretary finds that the physical and other requirements are such that the ore or mineral must be transported a greater distance to such plants or mills.

(3) Extraction of the ores or minerals from the ground.—The term "extraction of the ores or minerals from the ground" includes the extraction by mine owners or operators of ores or minerals from the waste or residue of prior mining. The preceding sentence shall not apply to any such extraction of the mineral or ore by a purchaser of such waste or residue or of the rights to extract ores or minerals therefrom.

* * *

(d) Denial of percentage depletion in case of oil and gas wells.—Except as provided in section 613A, in the case of any oil or gas well, the allowance for depletion shall be computed without reference to this section.

* * *

§ 613A. Limitations on percentage depletion in case of oil and gas wells

(a) General rule.—Except as otherwise provided in this section, the allowance for depletion under section 611 with respect to any oil or gas well shall be computed without regard to section 613.

(b) Exemption for certain domestic gas wells.—

(1) In general.—The allowance for depletion under section 611 shall be computed in accordance with section 613 with respect to—

(A) regulated natural gas, and

(B) natural gas sold under a fixed contract,

and 22 percent shall be deemed to be specified in subsection (b) of section 613 for purposes of subsection (a) of that section.

* * *

(c) Exemption for independent producers and royalty owners.—

(1) In general.—Except as provided in subsection (d), the allowance for depletion under section 611 shall be computed in accordance with section 613 with respect to—

(A) so much of the taxpayer's average daily production of domestic crude oil as does not exceed the taxpayer's depletable oil quantity; and

(B) so much of the taxpayer's average daily production of domestic natural gas as does not exceed the taxpayer's depletable natural gas quantity;

and 15 percent shall be deemed to be specified in subsection (b) of section 613 for purposes of subsection (a) of that section.

(2) Average daily production.—For purposes of paragraph (1)—

(A) the taxpayer's average daily production of domestic crude oil or natural gas for any taxable year, shall be determined by dividing his aggregate production of domestic crude oil or natural gas, as the case may be, during the taxable year by the number of days in such taxable year, and

(B) in the case of a taxpayer holding a partial interest in the production from any property (including an interest held in a partnership) such taxpayer's production shall be considered to be that amount of such production determined by multiplying the total production of such property by the taxpayer's percentage participation in the revenues from such property.

(3) Depletable oil quantity.—

(A) In general.—For purposes of paragraph (1), the taxpayer's depletable oil quantity shall be equal to—

(i) the tentative quantity determined under subparagraph (B), reduced (but not below zero) by

(ii) except in the case of a taxpayer making an election under paragraph (6)(B), the taxpayer's average daily marginal production for the taxable year.

(B) Tentative quantity.—For purposes of subparagraph (A), the tentative quantity is 1,000 barrels.

(4) Daily depletable natural gas quantity.—For purposes of paragraph (1), the depletable natural gas quantity of any taxpayer for any taxable year shall be equal to 6,000 cubic feet multiplied by the number of barrels of the taxpayer's depletable oil quantity to which the taxpayer elects to have this paragraph apply.

The taxpayer's depletable oil quantity for any taxable year shall be reduced by the number of barrels with respect to which an election under this paragraph applies. Such election shall be made at such time and in such manner as the Secretary shall by regulations prescribe.

* * *

(8) Businesses under common control; members of the same family.—

(A) Component members of controlled group treated as one taxpayer.—For purposes of this subsection, persons who are members of the same controlled group of corporations shall be treated as one taxpayer.

(B) Aggregation of business entities under common control.—If 50 percent or more of the beneficial interest in two or more corporations, trusts, or estates is owned by the same or related persons (taking into account only persons who own at least 5 percent of such beneficial interest), the tentative quantity determined under paragraph (3)(B) shall be allocated among all such entities in proportion to the respective production of domestic crude oil during the period in question by such entities.

(C) Allocation among members of the same family.—In the case of individuals who are members of the same family, the tentative quantity determined under paragraph (3)(B) shall be allocated among such individuals in proportion to the respective production of domestic crude oil during the period in question by such individuals.

(D) Definition and special rules.—For purposes of this paragraph—

(i) the term "controlled group of corporations" has the meaning given to such term by section 1563(a), except that section 1563(b)(2) shall not apply and except that "more than 50 percent" shall be substituted for "at least 80 percent" each place it appears in section 1563(a),

(ii) a person is a related person to another person if such persons are members of the same controlled group of corporations or if the relationship between such persons would result in a disallowance of losses under section 267 or 707(b), except that for this purpose the family of an individual includes only his spouse and minor children,

(iii) the family of an individual includes only his spouse and minor children, and

(iv) each 6,000 cubic feet of domestic natural gas shall be treated as 1 barrel of domestic crude oil.

* * *

(10) Certain production not taken into account.—In applying this subsection, there shall not be taken into account the production of natural gas with respect to which subsection (b) applies.

(11) Subchapter S corporations.—

(A) Computation of depletion allowance at shareholder level.—In the case of an S corporation, the allowance for depletion with respect to any oil or gas property shall be computed separately by each shareholder.

(B) Allocation of basis.—The S corporation shall allocate to each shareholder his pro rata share of the adjusted basis of the S corporation in each oil or gas property held by the S corporation. The allocation shall be made as of the later of the date of acquisition of the property by the S corporation, or the first day of the first taxable year of the S corporation to which the Subchapter S Revision Act of 1982 applies. Each shareholder shall separately keep records of his share of the adjusted basis in each oil and gas property of the S corporation, adjust such share of the adjusted basis for any depletion taken on such property, and use such adjusted basis each year in the computation of his cost depletion or in the computation of his gain or loss on the disposition of such property by the S corporation. In the case of any distribution of oil or gas property to its shareholders by the S corporation, the corporation's adjusted basis in the property shall be an amount equal to the sum of the shareholders' adjusted bases in such property, as determined under this subparagraph.

(d) Limitations on application of subsection (c).—

(1) Limitation based on taxable income.—The deduction for the taxable year attributable to the application of subsection (c) shall not exceed 65 percent of the taxpayer's taxable income for the year computed without regard to—

(A) any depletion on production from an oil or gas property which is subject to the provisions of subsection (c),

(B) any deduction allowable under section 199,

(C) any net operating loss carryback to the taxable year under section 172,

(D) any capital loss carryback to the taxable year under section 1212, and

(E) in the case of a trust, any distributions to its beneficiary, except in the case of any trust where any beneficiary of such trust is a member of the family (as defined in section 267(c) (4)) of a settlor who created inter vivos and testamentary trusts for members of the family and such settlor died within the last six days of the fifth month in 1970, and the law in the jurisdiction in which such trust was created requires all or a portion of the gross or net proceeds of any royalty or other interest in oil, gas, or other mineral representing any percentage depletion allowance to be allocated to the principal of the trust.

If an amount is disallowed as a deduction for the taxable year by reason of application of the preceding sentence, the disallowed amount shall be treated as an amount allowable as a deduction under subsection (c) for the following taxable year, subject to the application of the preceding sentence to such taxable year. For purposes of basis adjustments and determining whether cost depletion exceeds percentage depletion with respect to the production from a property, any amount disallowed as a deduction on the application of this paragraph shall be allocated to the respective properties from which the oil or gas was produced in proportion to the percentage depletion otherwise allowable to such properties under subsection (c).

* * *

(e) Definitions.—For purposes of this section—

(1) Crude oil.—The term "crude oil" includes a natural gas liquid recovered from a gas well in lease separators or field facilities.

(2) Natural gas.—The term "natural gas" means any product (other than crude oil) of an oil or gas well if a deduction for depletion is allowable under section 611 with respect to such product.

(3) Domestic.—The term "domestic" refers to production from an oil or gas well located in the United States or in a possession of the United States.

(4) Barrel.—The term "barrel" means 42 United States gallons.

§ 614. Definition of property

(a) General rule.—For the purpose of computing the depletion allowance in the case of mines, wells, and other natural deposits, the term "property" means each separate interest owned by the taxpayer in each mineral deposit in each separate tract or parcel of land.

(b) Special rules as to operating mineral interests in oil and gas wells or geothermal deposits.—In the case of oil and gas wells or geothermal deposits—

(1) In general.—Except as otherwise provided in this subsection—

(A) all of the taxpayer's operating mineral interests in a separate tract or parcel of land shall be combined and treated as one property, and

(B) the taxpayer may not combine an operating mineral interest in one tract or parcel of land with an operating mineral interest in another tract or parcel of land.

(2) Election to treat operating mineral interests as separate properties.—If the taxpayer has more than one operating mineral interest in a single tract or parcel of land, he may elect to treat one or more of such operating mineral interests as separate properties. The taxpayer may not have more than one combination of operating mineral interests in a single tract or parcel of land. If the taxpayer makes the election provided in this paragraph with respect to any interest in a tract or parcel of land, each operating mineral interest which is discovered or acquired by the taxpayer in such tract or parcel of land after the taxable year for which the election is made shall be treated—

(A) if there is no combination of interests in such tract or parcel, as a separate property unless the taxpayer elects to combine it with another interest, or

(B) if there is a combination of interests in such tract or parcel, as part of such combination unless the taxpayer elects to treat it as a separate property.

(3) Certain unitization or pooling arrangements.—

(A) In general.—Under regulations prescribed by the Secretary, if one or more of the taxpayer's operating mineral interests participate, under a voluntary or compulsory unitization or pooling agreement, in a single cooperative or unit plan of operation, then for the period of such participation—

(i) they shall be treated for all purposes of this subtitle as one property, and

(ii) the application of paragraphs (1), (2), and (4) in respect of such interests shall be suspended.

(B) Limitation.—Subparagraph (A) shall apply to a voluntary agreement only if all the operating mineral interests covered by such agreement—

(i) are in the same deposit, or are in 2 or more deposits the joint development or production of which is logical from the standpoint of geology, convenience, economy, or conservation, and

(ii) are in tracts or parcels of land which are contiguous or in close proximity.

* * *

(4) Manner, time, and scope of election.—

(A) Manner and time.—Any election provided in paragraph (2) shall be made for each operating mineral interest, in the manner prescribed by the Secretary by regulations, not later than the time prescribed by law for filing the return (including extensions thereof) for whichever of the following taxable years is the later: The first taxable year beginning after December 31, 1963, or the first taxable year in which any expenditure for development or operation in respect of such operating mineral interest is made by the taxpayer after the acquisition of such interest.

(B) Scope.—Any election under paragraph (2) shall be for all purposes of this subtitle and shall be binding on the taxpayer for all subsequent taxable years.

* * *

(c) Special rules as to operating mineral interests in mines.—

(1) Election to aggregate separate interests.—Except in the case of oil and gas wells and geothermal deposits, if a taxpayer owns two or more separate operating mineral interests which constitute part or all of an operating unit, he may elect (for all purposes of this subtitle)—

(A) to form an aggregation of, and to treat as one property, all such interests owned by him which comprise any one mine or any two or more mines; and

(B) to treat as a separate property each such interest which is not included within an aggregation referred to in subparagraph (A).

For purposes of this paragraph, separate operating mineral interests which constitute part or all of an operating unit may be aggregated whether or not they are included in a single tract or parcel of land and whether or not they are included in contiguous tracts or parcels. For purposes of this paragraph, a taxpayer may elect to form more than one aggregation of operating mineral interests within any one operating unit; but no aggregation may include any operating mineral interest which is a part of a mine without including all of the operating mineral interests which are a part of such mine in the first taxable year for which the election to aggregate is effective, and any operating mineral interest which thereafter becomes a part of such mine shall be included in such aggregation.

(2) Election to treat a single interest as more than one property.—Except in the case of oil and gas wells and geothermal deposits, if a single tract or parcel of land contains a mineral deposit which is being extracted, or will be extracted, by means of two or more mines for which expenditures for development or operation have been made by the taxpayer, then the taxpayer may elect to allocate to such mines, under regulations prescribed by the Secretary, all of the tract or parcel of land and of the mineral deposit contained therein, and to treat as a separate property that portion of the tract or parcel of land and of the mineral deposit so allocated to each mine. A separate property formed pursuant to an election under this paragraph shall be treated as a separate property for all purposes of this subtitle (including this paragraph). A separate property so formed may, under regulations prescribed by the Secretary, be included as a part of an aggregation in accordance with paragraphs (1) and (3). The election provided by this paragraph may not be made with respect to any property which is a part of an aggregation formed by the taxpayer under paragraph (1) except with the consent of the Secretary.

(3) Manner and scope of election.—The elections provided by paragraphs (1) and (2) shall be made, in accordance with regulations prescribed by the Secretary, not later than the time prescribed for filing the return (including extensions thereof) for the first taxable year—

(A) in which, in the case of an election under paragraph (1), any expenditure for development or operation in respect of the separate operating mineral interest is made by the taxpayer after the acquisition of such interest, or

(B) in which, in the case of an election under paragraph (2), expenditures for development or operation of more than one mine in respect of a property are made by the taxpayer after the acquisition of the property.

An election made under paragraph (1) or (2) for a taxable year shall be binding upon the taxpayer for such year and all subsequent taxable years, except that the Secretary may consent to a different treatment of any interest with respect to which an election has been made.

(d) Operating mineral interests defined.—For purposes of this section, the term "operating mineral interest" includes only an interest in respect of which the costs of production of the mineral are required to be taken into account by the taxpayer for purposes of computing the taxable income limitation provided for in section 613, or would be so required if the mine, well, or other natural deposit were in the production stage.

(c) Special rule as to nonoperating mineral interests.—

(1) Aggregation of separate interests.—If a taxpayer owns two or more separate nonoperating mineral interests in a single tract or parcel of land or in two or more adjacent tracts or parcels of land, the Secretary shall, on showing by the taxpayer that a principal purpose is not the avoidance of tax, permit the taxpayer to treat (for all purposes of this subtitle) all such mineral interests in each separate kind of mineral deposit as one property. If such permission is granted for any taxable year, the taxpayer shall treat such interests as one property for all subsequent taxable years unless the Secretary consents to a different treatment.

(2) Nonoperating mineral interests defined.—For purposes of this subsection, the term "nonoperating mineral interests" includes only interests which are not operating mineral interests.

§ 616. Development expenditures

(a) In general.—Except as provided in subsections (b) and (d), there shall be allowed as a deduction in computing taxable income all expenditures paid or incurred during the taxable year for the development of a mine or other natural deposit (other than an oil or gas well) if paid or incurred after the existence of ores or minerals in commercially marketable quantities has been disclosed. This section shall not apply to expenditures for the acquisition or improvement of property of a character which is subject to the allowance for depreciation provided in section 167, but allowances for depreciation shall be considered, for purposes of this section, as expenditures.

(b) Election of taxpayer.—At the election of the taxpayer, made in accordance with regulations prescribed by the Secretary, expenditures described in subsection (a) paid or incurred during the taxable year shall be treated as deferred expenses and shall be deductible on a ratable basis as the units of produced ores or minerals benefited by such expenditures are sold. In the case of such expenditures paid or incurred during the development stage of the mine or deposit, the election shall apply only with respect to the excess of such expenditures during the taxable year over the net receipts during the taxable year from the ores or minerals produced from such mine or deposit. The election under this subsection, if made, must be for the total amount of such expenditures, or the total amount of such excess, as the case may be, with respect to the mine or deposit, and shall be binding for such taxable year.

(c) Adjusted basis of mine or deposit.—The amount of expenditures which are treated under subsection (b) as deferred expenses shall be taken into account in computing the adjusted basis of the mine or deposit, except that such amount, and the adjustments to basis provided in section 1016(a)(9), shall be disregarded in determining the adjusted basis of the property for the purpose of computing a deduction for depletion under section 611.

* * *

§ 617. Deduction and recapture of certain mining exploration expenditures

(a) Allowance of deduction.—

(1) General rule.—At the election of the taxpayer, expenditures paid or incurred during the taxable year for the purpose of ascertaining the existence, location, extent, or quality of any deposit of ore or other mineral, and paid or incurred before the beginning of the development stage of the mine, shall be allowed as a deduction in computing taxable income. This subsection shall apply only with respect to the amount of such expenditures which, but for this subsection, would not be allowable as a deduction for the taxable year. This subsection shall not apply to expenditures for the acquisition or improvement of property of a character which is subject to the allowance for depreciation provided in section 167, but allowances for depreciation shall be considered, for purposes of this subsection, as expenditures paid or incurred. In no case shall this subsection apply with respect to amounts paid or incurred for the purpose of ascertaining the existence, location, extent, or quality of any deposit of oil or gas or of any mineral with respect to which a deduction for percentage depletion is not allowable under section 613.

(2) Elections.—

(A) Method.—Any election under this subsection shall be made in such manner as the Secretary may by regulations prescribe.

(B) Time and scope.—The election provided by paragraph (1) for the taxable year may be made at any time before the expiration of the period prescribed for making a claim for credit or refund of the tax imposed by this chapter for the taxable year. Such an election for the taxable year shall apply to all expenditures described in paragraph (1) paid or incurred by the taxpayer during the taxable year or during any subsequent taxable year. Such an election may not be revoked unless the Secretary consents to such revocation.

(C) Deficiencies.—The statutory period for the assessment of any deficiency for any taxable year, to the extent such deficiency is attributable to an election or revocation of an election under this subsection, shall not expire before the last day of the 2–year period beginning on the day after the date on which such election or revocation of election is made; and such deficiency may be assessed at any time before the expiration of such 2–year period, notwithstanding any law or rule of law which would otherwise prevent such assessment.

(b) Recapture on reaching producing stage.—

(1) Recapture.—If, in any taxable year, any mine with respect to which expenditures were deducted pursuant to subsection (a) reaches the producing stage, then—

(A) If the taxpayer so elects with respect to all such mines reaching the producing stage during the taxable year, he shall include in gross income for the taxable year an amount equal to the adjusted exploration expenditures with respect to such mines, and the amount so included in income shall be treated for purposes of this subtitle as expenditures which (i) are paid or incurred on the respective dates on which the mines reach the producing stage, and (ii) are properly chargeable to capital account.

(B) If subparagraph (A) does not apply with respect to any such mine, then the deduction for depletion under section 611 with respect to the property shall be disallowed until the amount of depletion which would be allowable but for this subparagraph equals the amount of the adjusted exploration expenditures with respect to such mine.

(2) Elections.—

(A) Method.—Any election under this subsection shall be made in such manner as the Secretary may by regulations prescribe.

(B) Time and scope.—The election provided by paragraph (1) for any taxable year may be made or changed not later than the time prescribed by law for filing the return (including extensions thereof) for such taxable year.

(c) Recapture in case of bonus or royalty.—If an election has been made under subsection (a) with respect to expenditures relating to a mining property and the taxpayer receives or accrues a bonus or a royalty with respect to such property, then the deduction for depletion under section 611 with respect to the bonus or royalty shall be disallowed until the amount of depletion which would be allowable but for this subsection equals the amount of the adjusted exploration expenditures with respect to the property to which the bonus or royalty relates.

(d) Gain from dispositions of certain mining property.—

(1) General rule.—Except as otherwise provided in this subsection, if mining property is disposed of the lower of—

(A) the adjusted exploration expenditures with respect to such property, or

(B) the excess of—

(i) the amount realized (in the case of a sale, exchange, or involuntary conversion), or the fair market value (in the case of any other disposition), over

(ii) the adjusted basis of such property,

shall be treated as ordinary income. Such gain shall be recognized notwithstanding any other provision of this subtitle.

(2) Disposition of portion of property.—For purposes of paragraph (1)—

(A) In the case of the disposition of a portion of a mining property (other than an undivided interest), the entire amount of the adjusted exploration expenditures with respect to such property shall be treated as attributable to such portion to the extent of the amount of the gain to which paragraph (1) applies.

(B) In the case of the disposition of an undivided interest in a mining property (or a portion thereof), a proportionate part of the adjusted exploration expenditures with respect to such property shall be treated as attributable to such undivided interest to the extent of the amount of the gain to which paragraph (1) applies.

This paragraph shall not apply to any expenditure to the extent the taxpayer establishes to the satisfaction of the Secretary that such expenditure relates neither to the portion (or interest therein) disposed of nor to any mine, in the property held by the taxpayer before the disposition, which has reached the producing stage.

(3) Exceptions and limitations.—Paragraphs (1), (2), and (3) of section 1245(b) (relating to exceptions and limitations with respect to gain from disposition of certain depreciable property) shall apply in respect of this subsection in the same manner and with the same effect as if references in section 1245(b) to section 1245 or any provision thereof were references to this subsection or the corresponding provisions of this subsection and as if references to section 1245 property were references to mining property.

(4) Application of subsection.—This subsection shall apply notwithstanding any other provision of this subtitle.

(5) Coordination with section 1254.—This subsection shall not apply to any disposition to which section 1254 applies.

(e) Basis of property.—

(1) Basis.—The basis of any property shall not be reduced by the amount of any depletion which would be allowable but for the application of this section.

(2) Adjustments.—The Secretary shall prescribe such regulations as he may deem necessary to provide for adjustments to the basis of property to reflect gain recognized under subsection (d)(1).

(f) Definitions.—For purposes of this section—

(1) Adjusted exploration expenditures.—The term "adjusted exploration expenditures" means, with respect to any property or mine—

(A) the amount of the expenditures allowed for the taxable year and all preceding taxable years as deductions under subsection (a) to the taxpayer or any other person which are properly chargeable to such property or mine and which (but for the election under subsection (a)) would be reflected in the adjusted basis of such property or mine, reduced by

(B) for the taxable year and for each preceding taxable year, the amount (if any) by which (i) the amount which would have been allowable for percentage depletion under section 613 but for the deduction of such expenditures, exceeds (ii) the amount allowable for depletion under section 611,

properly adjusted for any amounts included in gross income under subsection (b) or (c) and for any amounts of gain to which subsection (d) applied.

(2) Mining property.—The term "mining property" means any property (within the meaning of section 614 after the application of subsections (c) and (e) thereof) with respect to which any expenditures allowed as a deduction under subsection (a)(1) are properly chargeable.

(3) Disposal of coal or domestic iron ore with a retained economic interest.—A transaction which constitutes a disposal of coal or iron ore under section 631(c) shall be treated as a disposition. In such a case, the excess referred to in subsection (d)(1)(B) shall be treated as equal to the gain (if any) referred to in section 631(c).

(g) Special rules relating to partnership property.—

(1) Property distributed to partner.—In the case of any property or mine received by the taxpayer in a distribution with respect to part or all of his interest in a partnership, the adjusted exploration expenditures with respect to such property or mine include the adjusted exploration expenditures (not otherwise included under subsection (f)(1)) with respect to such property or mine immediately prior to such distribution, but the adjusted exploration expenditures with respect to any such property or mine shall be reduced by the amount of gain to which section 751(b) applied realized by the partnership (as constituted after the distribution) on the distribution of such property or mine.

(2) Property retained by partnership.—In the case of any property or mine held by a partnership after a distribution to a partner to which section 751(b) applied, the adjusted exploration expenditures with respect to such property or mine shall, under regulations prescribed by the Secretary, be reduced by the amount of gain to which section 751(b) applied realized by such partner with respect to such distribution on account of such property or mine.

* * *

PART III—SALES AND EXCHANGES

§ 631. Gain or loss in the case of timber, coal, or domestic iron ore

(a) Election to consider cutting as sale or exchange.—If the taxpayer so elects on his return for a taxable year, the cutting of timber (for sale or for use in the taxpayer's trade or business) during such year by the taxpayer who owns, or has a contract right to cut, such timber (providing he has owned such timber or has held such contract right on the first day of such year and for a period of more than 1 year before such cutting) shall be considered as a sale or exchange of such timber cut during such year. If such election has been made, gain or loss to the taxpayer shall be recognized in an amount equal to the difference between the fair market value of such timber, and the adjusted basis for depletion of such timber in the hands of the taxpayer. Such fair market value shall be the fair market value as of the first day of the taxable year in which such timber is cut, and shall thereafter be considered as the cost of such cut timber to the taxpayer for all purposes for which such cost is a necessary factor. If a taxpayer makes an election under this subsection, such election shall apply with respect to all timber which is owned by the taxpayer or which the taxpayer has a contract right to cut and shall be binding on the taxpayer for the taxable year for which the election is made and for all subsequent years, unless the Secretary, on showing of undue hardship, permits the taxpayer to revoke his election; such revocation, however, shall preclude any further elections under this subsection except with the consent of the Secretary. For purposes of this subsection and subsection (b), the term "timber" includes evergreen trees which are more than 6 years old at the time severed from the roots and are sold for ornamental purposes.

(b) Disposal of timber.—In the case of the disposal of timber held for more than 1 year before such disposal, by the owner thereof under any form or type of contract by virtue of which such owner either retains an economic interest in such timber or makes an outright sale of such timber, the difference between the amount realized from the disposal of such timber and the adjusted depletion basis thereof, shall be considered as though it were a gain or loss, as the case may be, on the sale of such timber. In determining the gross income, the adjusted gross income, or the taxable income of the lessee, the deductions allowable with respect to rents and royalties shall be determined without regard to the provisions of this subsection. In the case of disposal of timber with a retained economic interest, the date of disposal of such timber shall be deemed to be the date such timber is cut, but if payment is made to the owner under the contract before such timber is cut the owner may elect to treat the date of such payment as the date of disposal of such timber. For purposes of this subsection, the term "owner" means any person who owns an interest in such timber, including a sublessor and a holder of a contract to cut timber.

(c) Disposal of coal or domestic iron ore with a retained economic interest.—In the case of the disposal of coal (including lignite), or iron ore mined in the United States, held for more than 1 year before such disposal, by the owner thereof under any form of contract by virtue of which such owner retains an economic interest in such coal or iron ore, the difference between the amount realized from the disposal of such coal or iron ore and the adjusted depletion basis thereof plus the deductions disallowed for the taxable year under section 272 shall be considered as though it were a gain or loss, as the case may be, on the sale of such coal or iron ore. If for the taxable year of such gain or loss the maximum rate of tax imposed by this chapter on any net capital gain is less than such maximum rate for ordinary income, such owner shall not be entitled to the allowance for percentage depletion provided in section 613 with respect to such coal or iron ore. This subsection shall not apply to income realized by any owner as a co-adventurer, partner, or principal in the mining of such coal or iron ore, and the word "owner" means any person who owns an economic interest in coal or iron ore in place, including a sublessor. The date of disposal of such coal or iron ore shall be deemed to be the date such coal or iron ore is mined. In determining the gross income, the adjusted gross income, or the taxable income of the lessee, the deductions allowable with respect to rents and royalties shall be determined without regard to the provisions of this subsection. This subsection shall have no application, for purposes of applying subchapter G, relating to corporations used to avoid income tax on shareholders (including the determinations of the amount of the deductions under section 535(b)(6) or section 545(b)(5)). This subsection shall not apply to any disposal of iron ore or coal—

(1) to a person whose relationship to the person disposing of such iron ore would result in the disallowance of losses under section 267 or 707(b), or

(2) to a person owned or controlled directly or indirectly by the same interests which own or control the person disposing of such iron ore or coal.

PART IV—MINERAL PRODUCTION PAYMENTS

§ 636. Income tax treatment of mineral production payments

(a) Carved-out production payment.—A production payment carved out of mineral property shall be treated, for purposes of this subtitle, as if it were a mortgage loan on the property, and shall not qualify as an economic interest in the mineral property. In the case of a production payment carved out for exploration or development of a mineral property, the preceding sentence shall apply only if and to the extent gross income from the property (for purposes of section 613) would be realized, in the absence of the application of such sentence, by the person creating the production payment.

(b) Retained production payment on sale of mineral property.—A production payment retained on the sale of a mineral property shall be treated, for purposes of this subtitle, as if it were a purchase money mortgage loan and shall not qualify as an economic interest in the mineral property.

(c) Retained production payment on lease of mineral property.—A production payment retained in a mineral property by the lessor in a leasing transaction shall be treated, for purposes of this subtitle, insofar as the lessee (or his successors in interest) is concerned, as if it were a bonus granted by the lessee to the lessor payable in installments. The treatment of the production payment in the hands of the lessor shall be determined without regard to the provisions of this subsection.

(d) Definition.—As used in this section, the term "mineral property" has the meaning assigned to the term "property" in section 614(a).

(e) Regulations.—The Secretary shall prescribe such regulations as may be necessary to carry out the purposes of this section.

SUBCHAPTER J—ESTATES, TRUSTS, BENEFICIARIES, AND DECEDENTS

Part

PART I—ESTATES, TRUSTS, AND BENEFICIARIES

Subpart

Subpart A—General Rules for Taxation of Estates and Trusts

§ 641. Imposition of tax

(a) Application of tax.—The tax imposed by section 1(e) shall apply to the taxable income of estates or of any kind of property held in trust, including—

(1) income accumulated in trust for the benefit of unborn or unascertained persons or persons with contingent interests, and income accumulated or held for future distribution under the terms of the will or trust;

(2) income which is to be distributed currently by the fiduciary to the beneficiaries, and income collected by a guardian of an infant which is to be held or distributed as the court may direct;

(3) income received by estates of deceased persons during the period of administration or settlement of the estate; and

(4) income which, in the discretion of the fiduciary, may be either distributed to the beneficiaries or accumulated.

(b) Computation and payment.—The taxable income of an estate or trust shall be computed in the same manner as in the case of an individual, except as otherwise provided in this part. The tax shall be computed on such taxable income and shall be paid by the fiduciary. For purposes of this subsection, a foreign trust or foreign estate shall be treated as a nonresident alien individual who is not present in the United States at any time.

(c) Special rules for taxation of electing small business trusts.—

(1) In general.—For purposes of this chapter—

(A) the portion of any electing small business trust which consists of stock in 1 or more S corporations shall be treated as a separate trust, and

(B) the amount of the tax imposed by this chapter on such separate trust shall be determined with the modifications of paragraph (2).

(2) Modifications.—For purposes of paragraph (1), the modifications of this paragraph are the following:

(A) Except as provided in section 1(h), the amount of the tax imposed by section 1(e) shall be determined by using the highest rate of tax set forth in section 1(e).

(B) The exemption amount under section 55(d) shall be zero.

(C) The only items of income, loss, deduction, or credit to be taken into account are the following:

(i) The items required to be taken into account under section 1366.

(ii) Any gain or loss from the disposition of stock in an S corporation.

(iii) To the extent provided in regulations, State or local income taxes or administrative expenses to the extent allocable to items described in clauses (i) and (ii).

(iv) Any interest expense paid or accrued on indebtedness incurred to acquire stock in an S corporation.

No deduction or credit shall be allowed for any amount not described in this paragraph, and no item described in this paragraph shall be apportioned to any beneficiary.

(D) No amount shall be allowed under paragraph (1) or (2) of section 1211(b).

(3) Treatment of remainder of trust and distributions.—For purposes of determining—

(A) the amount of the tax imposed by this chapter on the portion of any electing small business trust not treated as a separate trust under paragraph (1), and

(B) the distributable net income of the entire trust, the items referred to in paragraph (2)(C) shall be excluded. Except as provided in the preceding sentence, this subsection shall not affect the taxation of any distribution from the trust.

(4) Treatment of unused deductions where termination of separate trust.—If a portion of an electing small business trust ceases to be treated as a separate trust under paragraph (1), any carryover or excess deduction of the separate trust which is referred to in section 642(h) shall be taken into account by the entire trust.

(5) Electing small business trust.—For purposes of this subsection, the term "electing small business trust" has the meaning given such term by section 1361(e)(1).

§ 642. Special rules for credits and deductions

* * *

(b) Deduction for personal exemption.—

(1) Estates.—An estate shall be allowed a deduction of $600.

(2) Trusts.—

(A) In general.—Except as otherwise provided in this paragraph, a trust shall be allowed a deduction of $100.

(B) Trusts distributing income currently.—A trust which, under its governing instrument, is required to distribute all of its income currently shall be allowed a deduction of $300.

* * *

(3) Deductions in lieu of personal exemption.—The deductions allowed by this subsection shall be in lieu of the deductions allowed under section 151 (relating to deduction for personal exemption).

(c) Deduction for amounts paid or permanently set aside for a charitable purpose.—

(1) General rule.—In the case of an estate or trust (other than a trust meeting the specifications of subpart B), there shall be allowed as a deduction in computing its taxable income (in lieu of the deduction allowed by section 170(a), relating to deduction for charitable, etc., contributions and gifts) any amount of the gross income, without limitation, which pursuant to the terms of the governing instrument is, during the taxable year, paid for a purpose specified in section 170(c) (determined without regard to section 170(c)(2)(A)). If a charitable contribution is paid after the close of such taxable year and on or before the last day of the year following the close of such taxable year, then the trustee or administrator may elect to treat such contribution as paid during such taxable year. The election shall be made at such time and in such manner as the Secretary prescribes by regulations.

(2) Amounts permanently set aside.—In the case of an estate, and in the case of a trust (other than a trust meeting the specifications of subpart B) required by the terms of its governing instrument to set aside amounts which was—

(A) created on or before October 9, 1969, if—

(i) an irrevocable remainder interest is transferred to or for the use of an organization described in section 170(c), or

(ii) the grantor is at all times after October 9, 1969, under a mental disability to change the terms of the trust; or

(B) established by a will executed on or before October 9, 1969, if—

(i) the testator dies before October 9, 1972, without having republished the will after October 9, 1969, by codicil or otherwise,

(ii) the testator at no time after October 9, 1969, had the right to change the portions of the will which pertain to the trust, or

(iii) the will is not republished by codicil or otherwise before October 9, 1972, and the testator is on such date and at all times thereafter under a mental disability to republish the will by codicil or otherwise,

there shall also be allowed as a deduction in computing its taxable income any amount of the gross income, without limitation, which pursuant to the terms of the governing instrument is, during the taxable year, permanently set aside for a purpose specified in section 170(c), or is to be used exclusively for religious, charitable, scientific, literary, or educational purposes, or for the prevention of cruelty to children or animals, or for the establishment, acquisition, maintenance, or operation of a public cemetery not operated for profit. In the case of a trust, the preceding sentence shall apply only to gross income earned with respect to amounts transferred to the trust before October 9, 1969, or transferred under a will to which subparagraph (B) applies.

(3) Pooled income funds.—In the case of a pooled income fund (as defined in paragraph (5)), there shall also be allowed as a deduction in computing its taxable income any amount of the gross income attributable to gain from the sale of a capital asset held for more than 1 year, without limitation, which pursuant to the terms of the governing instrument is, during the taxable year, permanently set aside for a purpose specified in section 170(c).

(4) Adjustments.—To the extent that the amount otherwise allowable as a deduction under this subsection consists of gain described in section 1202(a), proper adjustment shall be made for any exclusion allowable to the estate or trust under section 1202. In the case of a trust, the deduction allowed by this subsection shall be subject to section 681 (relating to unrelated business income).

(5) Definition of pooled income fund.—For purposes of paragraph (3), a pooled income fund is a trust—

(A) to which each donor transfers property, contributing an irrevocable remainder interest in such property to or for the use of an organization described in section 170(b)(1)(A) (other than in clauses (vii) or (viii)), and retaining an income interest for the life of one or more beneficiaries (living at the time of such transfer),

(B) in which the property transferred by each donor is commingled with property transferred by other donors who have made or make similar transfers,

(C) which cannot have investments in securities which are exempt from the taxes imposed by this subtitle,

(D) which includes only amounts received from transfers which meet the requirements of this paragraph,

(E) which is maintained by the organization to which the remainder interest is contributed and of which no donor or beneficiary of an income interest is a trustee, and

(F) from which each beneficiary of an income interest receives income, for each year for which he is entitled to receive the income interest referred to in subparagraph (A), determined by the rate of return earned by the trust for such year.

For purposes of determining the amount of any charitable contribution allowable by reason of a transfer of property to a pooled fund, the value of the income interest shall be determined on the basis of the highest rate of return earned by the fund for any of the 3 taxable years immediately preceding the taxable year of the fund in which the transfer is made. In the case of funds in existence less than 3 taxable years preceding the taxable year of the fund in which a transfer is made, the rate of return shall be deemed to be 6 percent per annum, except that the Secretary may prescribe a different rate of return.

(6) Taxable private foundations.—In the case of a private foundation which is not exempt from taxation under section 501(a) for the taxable year, the provisions of this subsection shall not apply and the provisions of section 170 shall apply.

(d) Net operating loss deduction.—The benefit of the deduction for net operating losses provided by section 172 shall be allowed to estates and trusts under regulations prescribed by the Secretary.

(e) Deduction for depreciation and depletion.—An estate or trust shall be allowed the deduction for depreciation and depletion only to the extent not allowable to beneficiaries under sections 167(d) and 611(b).

(f) Amortization deductions.—The benefit of the deductions for amortization provided by sections 169 and 197 shall be allowed to estates and trusts in the same manner as in the case of an individual. The allowable deduction shall be apportioned between the income beneficiaries and the fiduciary under regulations prescribed by the Secretary.

(g) Disallowance of double deductions.—Amounts allowable under section 2053 or 2054 as a deduction in computing the taxable estate of a decedent shall not be allowed as a deduction (or as an offset against the sales price of property in determining gain or loss) in computing the taxable income of the estate or of any other person, unless there is filed, within the time and in the manner and form prescribed by the Secretary, a statement that the amounts have not been allowed as deductions under section 2053 or 2054 and a waiver of the right to have such amounts allowed at any time as deductions under section 2053 or 2054. Rules similar to the rules of the preceding sentence shall apply to amounts which may be taken into account under section 2621(a)(2) or 2622(b). This subsection shall not apply with respect to deductions allowed under part II (relating to income in respect of decedents).

(h) Unused loss carryovers and excess deductions on termination available to beneficiaries.—If on the termination of an estate or trust, the estate or trust has—

(1) a net operating loss carryover under section 172 or a capital loss carryover under section 1212, or

(2) for the last taxable year of the estate or trust deductions (other than the deductions allowed under subsections (b) or (c)) in excess of gross income for such year,

then such carryover or such excess shall be allowed as a deduction, in accordance with regulations prescribed by the Secretary, to the beneficiaries succeeding to the property of the estate or trust.

* * *

§ 643. Definitions applicable to subparts A, B, C, and D

(a) Distributable net income.—For purposes of this part, the term "distributable net income" means, with respect to any taxable year, the taxable income of the estate or trust computed with the following modifications—

(1) Deduction for distributions.—No deduction shall be taken under sections 651 and 661 (relating to additional deductions).

(2) Deduction for personal exemption.—No deduction shall be taken under section 642(b) (relating to deduction for personal exemptions).

(3) Capital gains and losses.—Gains from the sale or exchange of capital assets shall be excluded to the extent that such gains are allocated to corpus and are not (A) paid, credited, or required to be distributed to any beneficiary during the taxable year, or (B) paid, permanently set aside, or to be used for the purposes specified in section 642(c). Losses from the sale or exchange of capital assets shall be excluded, except to the extent such losses are taken into account in determining the amount of gains from the sale or exchange of capital assets which are paid, credited, or required to be distributed to any beneficiary during the taxable year. The exclusion under section 1202 shall not be taken into account.

(4) Extraordinary dividends and taxable stock dividends.—For purposes only of subpart B (relating to trusts which distribute current income only), there shall be excluded those items of gross income constituting extraordinary dividends or taxable stock dividends which the fiduciary, acting in good faith, does not pay or credit to any beneficiary by reason of his determination that such dividends are allocable to corpus under the terms of the governing instrument and applicable local law.

(5) Tax-exempt interest.—There shall be included any tax-exempt interest to which section 103 applies, reduced by any amounts which would be deductible in respect of disbursements allocable to such interest but for the provisions of section 265 (relating to disallowance of certain deductions).

* * *

(7) Abusive transactions.—The Secretary shall prescribe such regulations as may be necessary or appropriate to carry out the purposes of this part, including regulations to prevent avoidance of such purposes.

If the estate or trust is allowed a deduction under section 642(c), the amount of the modifications specified in paragraphs (5) and (6) shall be reduced to the extent that the amount of income which is paid, permanently set aside, or to be used for the purposes specified in section 642(c) is deemed to consist of items specified in those paragraphs. For this purpose, such amount shall (in the absence of specific provisions in the governing instrument) be deemed to consist of the same proportion of each class of items of income of the estate or trust as the total of each class bears to the total of all classes.

(b) Income.—For purposes of this subpart and subparts B, C, and D, the term "income", when not preceded by the words "taxable", "distributable net", "undistributed net", or "gross", means the amount of income of the estate or trust for the taxable year determined under the terms of the governing instrument and applicable local law. Items of gross income constituting extraordinary dividends or taxable stock dividends which the fiduciary, acting in good faith, determines to be allocable to corpus under the terms of the governing instrument and applicable local law shall not be considered income.

(c) Beneficiary.—For purposes of this part, the term "beneficiary" includes heir, legatee, devisee.

* * *

(e) Treatment of property distributed in kind.—

(1) Basis of beneficiary.—The basis of any property received by a beneficiary in a distribution from an estate or trust shall be—

(A) the adjusted basis of such property in the hands of the estate or trust immediately before the distribution, adjusted for

(B) any gain or loss recognized to the estate or trust on the distribution.

(2) Amount of distribution.—In the case of any distribution of property (other than cash), the amount taken into account under sections 661(a)(2) and 662(a)(2) shall be the lesser of—

(A) the basis of such property in the hands of the beneficiary (as determined under paragraph (1)), or

(B) the fair market value of such property.

(3) Election to recognize gain.—

(A) In general.—In the case of any distribution of property (other than cash) to which an election under this paragraph applies—

(i) paragraph (2) shall not apply,

(ii) gain or loss shall be recognized by the estate or trust in the same manner as if such property had been sold to the distributee at its fair market value, and

(iii) the amount taken into account under sections 661(a)(2) and 662(a)(2) shall be the fair market value of such property.

(B) Election.—Any election under this paragraph shall apply to all distributions made by the estate or trust during a taxable year and shall be made on the return of such estate or trust for such taxable year.

Any such election, once made, may be revoked only with the consent of the Secretary.

(4) Exception for distributions described in section 663(a).—This subsection shall not apply to any distribution described in section 663(a).

(f) Treatment of multiple trusts.—For purposes of this subchapter, under regulations prescribed by the Secretary, 2 or more trusts shall be treated as 1 trust if—

(1) such trusts have substantially the same grantor or grantors and substantially the same primary beneficiary or beneficiaries, and

(2) a principal purpose of such trusts is the avoidance of the tax imposed by this chapter.

For purposes of the preceding sentence, a husband and wife shall be treated as 1 person.

(g) Certain payments of estimated tax treated as paid by beneficiary.—

(1) In general.—In the case of a trust—

(A) the trustee may elect to treat any portion of a payment of estimated tax made by such trust for any taxable year of the trust as a payment made by a beneficiary of such trust,

(B) any amount so treated shall be treated as paid or credited to the beneficiary on the last day of such taxable year, and

(C) for purposes of subtitle F, the amount so treated—

(i) shall not be treated as a payment of estimated tax made by the trust, but

(ii) shall be treated as a payment of estimated tax made by such beneficiary on January 15 following the taxable year.

(2) Time for making election.—An election under paragraph (1) shall be made on or before the 65th day after the close of the taxable year of the trust and in such manner as the Secretary may prescribe.

(3) Extension to last year of estate.—In the case of a taxable year reasonably expected to be the last taxable year of an estate—

(A) any reference in this subsection to a trust shall be treated as including a reference to an estate, and

(B) the fiduciary of the estate shall be treated as the trustee.

* * *

§ 644. Taxable year of trusts

(a) In general.—For purposes of this subtitle, the taxable year of any trust shall be the calendar year.

(b) Exception for trusts exempt from tax and charitable trusts.—Subsection (a) shall not apply to a trust exempt from taxation under section 501(a) or to a trust described in section 4947(a)(1).

§ 645. Certain revocable trusts treated as part of estate

(a) General rule.—For purposes of this subtitle, if both the executor (if any) of an estate and the trustee of a qualified revocable trust elect the treatment provided in this section, such trust shall be treated and taxed as part of such estate (and not as a separate trust) for all taxable years of the estate ending after the date of the decedent's death and before the applicable date.

(b) Definitions.—For purposes of subsection (a)—

(1) Qualified revocable trust.—The term "qualified revocable trust" means any trust (or portion thereof) which was treated under section 676 as owned by the decedent of the estate referred to in subsection (a) by reason of a power in the grantor (determined without regard to section 672(e)).

(2) Applicable date.—The term "applicable date" means—

(A) if no return of tax imposed by chapter 11 is required to be filed, the date which is 2 years after the date of the decedent's death, and

(B) if such a return is required to be filed, the date which is 6 months after the date of the final determination of the liability for tax imposed by chapter 11.

(c) Election.—The election under subsection (a) shall be made not later than the time prescribed for filing the return of tax imposed by this chapter for the first taxable year of the estate (determined with regard to extensions) and, once made, shall be irrevocable.

Subpart B—Trusts Which Distribute Current Income Only

§ 651. Deduction for trusts distributing current income only

(a) Deduction.—In the case of any trust the terms of which—

(1) provide that all of its income is required to be distributed currently, and

(2) do not provide that any amounts are to be paid, permanently set aside, or used for the purposes specified in section 642(c) (relating to deduction for charitable, etc., purposes), there shall be allowed as a deduction in computing the taxable income of the trust the amount of the income for the taxable year which is required to be distributed currently. This section shall not apply in any taxable year in which the trust distributes amounts other than amounts of income described in paragraph (1).

(b) Limitation on deduction.—If the amount of income required to be distributed currently exceeds the distributable net income of the trust for the taxable year, the deduction shall be limited to the amount of the distributable net income. For this purpose, the computation of distributable net income shall not include items of income which are not included in the gross income of the trust and the deductions allocable thereto.

§ 652. Inclusion of amounts in gross income of beneficiaries of trusts distributing current income only

(a) Inclusion.—Subject to subsection (b), the amount of income for the taxable year required to be distributed currently by a trust described in section 651 shall be included in the gross income of the beneficiaries to whom the income is required to be distributed, whether distributed or not. If such amount exceeds the distributable net income, there shall be included in the gross income of each beneficiary an amount which bears the same ratio to distributable net income as the amount of income required to be distributed to such beneficiary bears to the amount of income required to be distributed to all beneficiaries.

(b) Character of amounts.—The amounts specified in subsection (a) shall have the same character in the hands of the beneficiary as in the hands of the trust. For this purpose, the amounts shall be treated as consisting of the same proportion of each class of items entering into the computation of distributable net income of the trust as the total of each class bears to the total distributable net income of the trust, unless the terms of the trust specifically allocate different classes of income to different beneficiaries. In the application of the preceding sentence, the items of deduction entering into the computation of distributable net income shall be allocated among the items of distributable net income in accordance with regulations prescribed by the Secretary.

(c) Different taxable years.—If the taxable year of a beneficiary is different from that of the trust, the amount which the beneficiary is required to include in gross income in accordance with the provisions of this section shall be based upon the amount of income of the trust for any taxable year or years of the trust ending within or with his taxable year.

Subpart C—Estates and Trusts Which May Accumulate Income or Which Distribute Corpus

§ 661. Deduction for estates and trusts accumulating income or distributing corpus

(a) Deduction.—In any taxable year there shall be allowed as a deduction in computing the taxable income of an estate or trust (other than a trust to which subpart B applies), the sum of—

(1) any amount of income for such taxable year required to be distributed currently (including any amount required to be distributed which may be paid out of income or corpus to the extent such amount is paid out of income for such taxable year); and

(2) any other amounts properly paid or credited or required to be distributed for such taxable year;

but such deduction shall not exceed the distributable net income of the estate or trust.

(b) Character of amounts distributed.—The amount determined under subsection (a) shall be treated as consisting of the same proportion of each class of items entering into the computation of distributable net income of the estate or trust as the total of each class bears to the total distributable net income of the estate or trust in the absence of the allocation of different classes of income under the specific terms of the governing instrument. In the application of the preceding sentence, the items of deduction entering into the computation of distributable net income (including the deduction allowed under section 642(c)) shall be allocated among the items of distributable net income in accordance with regulations prescribed by the Secretary.

(c) Limitation on deduction.—No deduction shall be allowed under subsection (a) in respect of any portion of the amount allowed as a deduction under that subsection (without regard to this subsection) which is treated under subsection (b) as consisting of any item of distributable net income which is not included in the gross income of the estate or trust.

§ 662. Inclusion of amounts in gross income of beneficiaries of estates and trusts accumulating income or distributing corpus

(a) Inclusion.—Subject to subsection (b), there shall be included in the gross income of a beneficiary to whom an amount specified in section 661(a) is paid, credited, or required to be distributed (by an estate or trust described in section 661), the sum of the following amounts:

(1) Amounts required to be distributed currently.—The amount of income for the taxable year required to be distributed currently to such beneficiary, whether distributed or not. If the amount of income required to be distributed currently to all beneficiaries exceeds the distributable net income (computed without the deduction allowed by section 642(c), relating to deduction for charitable, etc., purposes) of the estate or trust, then, in lieu of the amount provided in the preceding sentence, there shall be included in the gross income of the beneficiary an amount which bears the same ratio to distributable net income (as so computed) as the amount of income required to be distributed currently to such beneficiary bears to the amount required to be distributed currently to all beneficiaries. For purposes of this section, the phrase "the amount of income for the taxable year required to be distributed currently" includes any amount required to be paid out of income or corpus to the extent such amount is paid out of income for such taxable year.

(2) Other amounts distributed.—All other amounts properly paid, credited, or required to be distributed to such beneficiary for the taxable year. If the sum of—

(A) the amount of income for the taxable year required to be distributed currently to all beneficiaries, and

(B) all other amounts properly paid, credited, or required to be distributed to all beneficiaries

exceeds the distributable net income of the estate or trust, then, in lieu of the amount provided in the preceding sentence, there shall be included in the gross income of the beneficiary an amount which bears the same ratio to distributable net income (reduced by the amounts specified in (A)) as the other amounts properly paid, credited or required to be distributed to the beneficiary bear to the other amounts properly paid, credited, or required to be distributed to all beneficiaries.

(b) Character of amounts.—The amounts determined under subsection (a) shall have the same character in the hands of the beneficiary as in the hands of the estate or trust. For this purpose, the amounts shall be treated as consisting of the same proportion of each class of items entering into the computation of distributable net income as the total of each class bears to the total distributable net income of the estate or trust unless the terms of the governing instrument specifically allocate different classes of income to different beneficiaries. In the application of the preceding sentence, the items of deduction entering into the computation of distributable net income (including the deduction allowed under section 642(c)) shall be allocated among the items of distributable net income in accordance with regulations prescribed by the Secretary. In the application of this subsection to the amount determined under paragraph (1) of subsection (a), distributable net income shall be computed without regard to any portion of the deduction under section 642(c) which is not attributable to income of the taxable year.

(c) Different taxable years.—If the taxable year of a beneficiary is different from that of the estate or trust, the amount to be included in the gross income of the beneficiary shall be based on the distributable net income of the estate or trust and the amounts properly paid, credited, or required to be distributed to the beneficiary during any taxable year or years of the estate or trust ending within or with his taxable year.

§ 663. Special rules applicable to sections 661 and 662

(a) Exclusions.—There shall not be included as amounts falling within section 661(a) or 662(a)—

(1) Gifts, bequests, etc.—Any amount which, under the terms of the governing instrument, is properly paid or credited as a gift or bequest of a specific sum of money or of specific property and which is paid or credited all at once or in not more than 3 installments. For this purpose an amount which can be paid or credited only from the income of the estate or trust shall not be considered as a gift or bequest of a specific sum of money.

(2) Charitable, etc., distributions.—Any amount paid or permanently set aside or otherwise qualifying for the deduction provided in section 642(c) (computed without regard to sections 508(d), 681, and 4948(c)(4)).

(3) Denial of double deduction.—Any amount paid, credited, or distributed in the taxable year, if section 651 or section 661 applied to such amount for a preceding taxable year of an estate or trust because credited or required to be distributed in such preceding taxable year.

(b) Distributions in first sixty-five days of taxable year.—

(1) General rule.—If within the first 65 days of any taxable year of an estate or a trust, an amount is properly paid or credited, such amount shall be considered paid or credited on the last day of the preceding taxable year.

(2) Limitation.—Paragraph (1) shall apply with respect to any taxable year of an estate or a trust only if the executor of such estate or the fiduciary of such trust (as the case may be) elects, in such manner and at such time as the Secretary prescribes by regulations, to have paragraph (1) apply for such taxable year.

(c) Separate shares treated as separate trusts.—For the sole purpose of determining the amount of distributable net income in the application of sections 661 and 662, in the case of a single trust having more than one beneficiary, substantially separate and independent shares of different beneficiaries in the trust shall be treated as separate trusts. Rules similar to the rules of the preceding provisions of this subsection shall apply to treat substantially separate and independent shares of different beneficiaries in an estate having more than 1 beneficiary as separate estates. The existence of such substantially separate and independent shares and the manner of treatment as separate trusts, including the application of subpart D, shall be determined in accordance with regulations prescribed by the Secretary.

§ 664. Charitable remainder trusts

(a) General rule.—Notwithstanding any other provision of this subchapter, the provisions of this section shall, in accordance with regulations prescribed by the Secretary, apply in the case of a charitable remainder annuity trust and a charitable remainder unitrust.

(b) Character of distributions.—Amounts distributed by a charitable remainder annuity trust or by a charitable remainder unitrust shall be considered as having the following characteristics in the hands of a beneficiary to whom is paid the annuity described in subsection (d)(1)(A) or the payment described in subsection (d)(2)(A):

(1) First, as amounts of income (other than gains, and amounts treated as gains, from the sale or other disposition of capital assets) includible in gross income to the extent of such income of the trust for the year and such undistributed income of the trust for prior years;

(2) Second, as a capital gain to the extent of the capital gain of the trust for the year and the undistributed capital gain of the trust for prior years;

(3) Third, as other income to the extent of such income of the trust for the year and such undistributed income of the trust for prior years; and

(4) Fourth, as a distribution of trust corpus.

For purposes of this section, the trust shall determine the amount of its undistributed capital gain on a cumulative net basis.

(c) Taxation of trusts.—

(1) Income tax.—A charitable remainder annuity trust and a charitable remainder unitrust shall, for any taxable year, not be subject to any tax imposed by this subtitle.

(2) Excise tax.—

(A) In general.—In the case of a charitable remainder annuity trust or a charitable remainder unitrust which has unrelated business taxable income (within the meaning of section 512, determined as if part III of subchapter F applied to such trust) for a taxable year, there is hereby imposed on such trust or unitrust an excise tax equal to the amount of such unrelated business taxable income.

(B) Certain rules to apply.—The tax imposed by subparagraph (A) shall be treated as imposed by chapter 42 for purposes of this title other than subchapter E of chapter 42.

(C) Tax court proceedings.—For purposes of this paragraph, the references in section 6212(c)(1) to section 4940 shall be deemed to include references to this paragraph.

(d) Definitions.—

(1) Charitable remainder annuity trust.—For purposes of this section, a charitable remainder annuity trust is a trust—

(A) from which a sum certain (which is not less than 5 percent nor more than 50 percent of the initial net fair market value of all property placed in trust) is to be paid, not less often than annually, to one or more persons (at least one of which is not an organization described in section 170(c) and, in the case of individuals, only to an individual who is living at the time of the creation of the trust) for a term of years (not in excess of 20 years) or for the life or lives of such individual or individuals,

(B) from which no amount other than the payments described in subparagraph (A) and other than qualified gratuitous transfers described in subparagraph (C)

may be paid to or for the use of any person other than an organization described in section 170(c),

(C) following the termination of the payments described in subparagraph (A), the remainder interest in the trust is to be transferred to, or for the use of, an organization described in section 170(c) or is to be retained by the trust for such a use or, to the extent the remainder interest is in qualified employer securities (as defined in subsection (g)(4)), all or part of such securities are to be transferred to an employee stock ownership plan (as defined in section 4975(e)(7)) in a qualified gratuitous transfer (as defined by subsection (g)), and

(D) the value (determined under section 7520) of such remainder interest is at least 10 percent of the initial net fair market value of all property placed in the trust.

(2) Charitable remainder unitrust.—For purposes of this section, a charitable remainder unitrust is a trust—

(A) from which a fixed percentage (which is not less than 5 percent nor more than 50 percent) of the net fair market value of its assets, valued annually, is to be paid, not less often than annually, to one or more persons (at least one of which is not an organization described in section 170(c) and, in the case of individuals, only to an individual who is living at the time of the creation of the trust) for a term of years (not in excess of 20 years) or for the life or lives of such individual or individuals,

(B) from which no amount other than the payments described in subparagraph (A) and other than qualified gratuitous transfers described in subparagraph (C) may be paid to or for the use of any person other than an organization described in section 170(c),

(C) following the termination of the payments described in subparagraph (A), the remainder interest in the trust is to be transferred to, or for the use of, an organization described in section 170(c) or is to be retained by the trust for such a use or, to the extent the remainder interest is in qualified employer securities (as defined in subsection (g)(4)), all or part of such securities are to be transferred to an employee stock ownership plan (as defined in section 4975(e)(7)) in a qualified gratuitous transfer (as defined by subsection (g)), and

(D) with respect to each contribution of property to the trust, the value (determined under section 7520) of such remainder interest in such property is at least 10 percent of the net fair market value of such property as of the date such property is contributed to the trust.

(3) Exception.—Notwithstanding the provisions of paragraphs (2)(A) and (B), the trust instrument may provide that the trustee shall pay the income beneficiary for any year—

(A) the amount of the trust income, if such amount is less than the amount required to be distributed under paragraph (2)(A), and

(B) any amount of the trust income which is in excess of the amount required to be distributed under paragraph (2)(A), to the extent that (by reason of subparagraph (A)) the aggregate of the amounts paid in prior years was less than the aggregate of such required amounts.

(4) Severance of certain additional contributions.—If—

(A) any contribution is made to a trust which before the contribution is a charitable remainder unitrust, and

(B) such contribution would (but for this paragraph) result in such trust ceasing to be a charitable unitrust by reason of paragraph (2)(D), such contribution shall be treated as a transfer to a separate trust under regulations prescribed by the Secretary.

(e) Valuation for purposes of charitable contribution.—For purposes of determining the amount of any charitable contribution, the remainder interest of a charitable remainder annuity trust or charitable remainder unitrust shall be computed on the basis that an amount equal to 5 percent of the net fair market value of its assets (or a greater amount, if required under the terms of the trust instrument) is to be distributed each year.

(f) Certain contingencies permitted.—

(1) General rule.—If a trust would, but for a qualified contingency, meet the requirements of paragraph (1)(A) or (2)(A) of subsection (d), such trust shall be treated as meeting such requirements.

(2) Value determined without regard to qualified contingency.—For purposes of determining the amount of any charitable contribution (or the actuarial value of any interest), a qualified contingency shall not be taken into account.

(3) Qualified contingency.—For purposes of this subsection, the term "qualified contingency" means any provision of a trust which provides that, upon the happening of a contingency, the payments described in paragraph (1)(A) or (2)(A) of subsection (d) (as the case may be) will terminate not later than such payments would otherwise terminate under the trust.

* * *

Subpart D—Treatment of Excess Distributions by Trusts

§ 665. Definitions applicable to subpart D

(a) Undistributed net income.—For purposes of this subpart, the term "undistributed net income" for any taxable year means the amount by which the distributable net income of the trust for such taxable year exceeds the sum of—

(1) the amounts for such taxable year specified in paragraphs (1) and (2) of section 661(a), and

(2) the amount of taxes imposed on the trust attributable to such distributable net income.

(b) Accumulation distribution.—For purposes of this subpart, except as provided in subsection (c), the term "accumulation distribution" means, for any taxable year of the trust, the amount by which—

(1) the amounts specified in paragraph (2) of section 661(a) for such taxable year, exceed

(2) distributable net income for such year reduced (but not below zero) by the amounts specified in paragraph (1) of section 661(a).

For purposes of section 667 (other than subsection (c) thereof, relating to multiple trusts), the amounts specified in paragraph (2) of section 661(a) shall not include amounts properly paid, credited, or required to be distributed to a beneficiary from a trust (other than a foreign trust) as income accumulated before the birth of such beneficiary or before such beneficiary attains the age of 21. If the amounts properly paid, credited, or required to be distributed by the trust for the taxable year do not exceed the income of the trust for such year, there shall be no accumulation distribution for such year.

(c) Exception for accumulation distributions from certain domestic trusts.—For purposes of this subpart—

(1) In general.—In the case of a qualified trust, any distribution in any taxable year beginning after the date of the enactment of this subsection shall be computed without regard to any undistributed net income.

(2) Qualified trust.—For purposes of this subsection, the term "qualified trust" means any trust other than—

(A) a foreign trust (or, except as provided in regulations, a domestic trust which at any time was a foreign trust), or

(B) a trust created before March 1, 1984, unless it is established that the trust would not be aggregated with other trusts under section 643(f) if such section applied to such trust.

(d) Taxes imposed on the trust.—For purposes of this subpart—

(1) In general.—The term "taxes imposed on the trust" means the amount of the taxes which are imposed for any taxable year of the trust under this chapter (without regard to this subpart or part IV of subchapter A) and which, under regulations prescribed by the Secretary, are properly allocable to the undistributed portions of distributable net income and gains in excess of losses from sales or exchanges of capital assets. The amount determined in the preceding sentence shall be reduced by any amount of such taxes deemed distributed under section 666(b) and (c) to any beneficiary.

* * *

(e) Preceding taxable year.—For purposes of this subpart—

(1) In the case of a foreign trust created by a United States person, the term "preceding taxable year" does not include any taxable year of the trust to which this part does not apply.

(2) In the case of a preceding taxable year with respect to which a trust qualified, without regard to this subpart, under the provisions of subpart B, for purposes of the application of this subpart to such trust for such taxable year, such trust shall, in accordance with regulations prescribed by the Secretary, be treated as a trust to which subpart C applies.

§ 666. Accumulation distribution allocated to preceding years

(a) Amount allocated.—In the case of a trust which is subject to subpart C, the amount of the accumulation distribution of such trust for a taxable year shall be deemed to be an amount within the meaning of paragraph (2) of section 661(a) distributed on the last day of each of the preceding taxable years, commencing with the earliest of such years, to the extent that such amount exceeds the total of any undistributed net income for all earlier preceding taxable years. The amount deemed to be distributed in any such preceding taxable year under the preceding sentence shall not exceed the undistributed net income for such preceding taxable year. For purposes of this subsection, undistributed net income for each of such preceding taxable years shall be computed without regard to such accumulation distribution and without regard to any accumulation distribution determined for any succeeding taxable year.

(b) Total taxes deemed distributed.—If any portion of an accumulation distribution for any taxable year is deemed under subsection (a) to be an amount within the meaning of paragraph (2) of section 661(a) distributed on the last day of any preceding taxable year, and such portion of such distribution is not less than the undistributed net income for such preceding taxable year, the trust shall be deemed to have distributed on the last day of such preceding taxable year an additional amount within the meaning of paragraph (2) of section 661(a). Such additional amount shall be equal to the taxes (other than the tax imposed by section 55) imposed on the trust for such preceding taxable year attributable to the undistributed net income. For purposes of this subsection, the undistributed net income and the taxes imposed on the trust for such preceding taxable year attributable to such undistributed net income shall be computed without regard to such accumulation distribution and without regard to any accumulation distribution determined for any succeeding taxable year.

(c) Pro rata portion of taxes deemed distributed.—If any portion of an accumulation distribution for any taxable year is deemed under subsection (a) to be an amount within the meaning of paragraph (2) of section 661(a) distributed on the last day of any preceding taxable year and such portion of the accumulation distribution is less than the undistributed net income for such preceding taxable year, the trust shall be deemed to have distributed on the last day of such preceding taxable year an additional amount within the meaning of paragraph (2) of section 661(a). Such additional amount shall be equal to the taxes (other than the tax imposed by section 55) imposed on the trust for such taxable year attributable to the undistributed net income multiplied by the ratio of the portion of the accumulation distribution to the undistributed net income of the trust for such year. For purposes of this subsection, the undistributed net income and the taxes imposed on the trust for such preceding taxable year attributable to such undistributed net income shall be computed without regard to the accumulation distribution and without regard to any accumulation distribution determined for any succeeding taxable year.

(d) Rule when information is not available.—If adequate records are not available to determine the proper application of this subpart to an amount distributed by a trust, such amount shall be deemed to be an accumulation distribution consisting of undistributed net income earned during the earliest preceding taxable year of the trust in which it can be established that the trust was in existence.

(e) Denial of refund to trusts and beneficiaries.—No refund or credit shall be allowed to a trust or a beneficiary of such trust for any preceding taxable year by reason of a distribution deemed to have been made by such trust in such year under this section.

§ 667. Treatment of amounts deemed distributed by trust in preceding years

(a) General rule.—The total of the amounts which are treated under section 666 as having been distributed by a trust in a preceding taxable year shall be included in the income of a beneficiary of the trust when paid, credited, or required to be distributed to the extent that such total would have been included in the income of such beneficiary under section 662(a)(2) (and, with respect to any tax-exempt interest to which section 103 applies, under section 662(b)) if such total had been paid to such beneficiary on the last day of such preceding taxable year. The tax imposed by this subtitle on a beneficiary for a taxable year in which any such amount is included in his income shall be determined only as provided in this section and shall consist of the sum of—

(1) a partial tax computed on the taxable income reduced by an amount equal to the total of such amounts, at the rate and in the manner as if this section had not been enacted,

(2) a partial tax determined as provided in subsection (b) of this section, and

* * *

(b) Tax on distribution.—

(1) In general.—The partial tax imposed by subsection (a)(2) shall be determined—

(A) by determining the number of preceding taxable years of the trust on the last day of which an amount is deemed under section 666(a) to have been distributed,

(B) by taking from the 5 taxable years immediately preceding the year of the accumulation distribution the 1 taxable year for which the beneficiary's taxable income was the highest and the 1 taxable year for which his taxable income was the lowest,

(C) by adding to the beneficiary's taxable income for each of the 3 taxable years remaining after the application of subparagraph (B) an amount determined by dividing the amount deemed distributed under section 666 and required to be included in income under subsection (a) by the number of preceding taxable years determined under subparagraph (A), and

(D) by determining the average increase in tax for the 3 taxable years referred to in subparagraph (C) resulting from the application of such subparagraph.

The partial tax imposed by subsection (a)(2) shall be the excess (if any) of the average increase in tax determined under subparagraph (D), multiplied by the number of preceding taxable years determined under subparagraph (A), over the amount of taxes (other than the amount of taxes described in section 665(d) (2)) deemed distributed to the beneficiary under sections 666(b) and (c).

(2) Treatment of loss years.—For purposes of paragraph (1), the taxable income of the beneficiary for any taxable year shall be deemed to be not less than zero.

(3) Certain preceding taxable years not taken into account.—For purposes of paragraph (1), if the amount of the undistributed net income deemed distributed in any preceding taxable year of the trust is less than 25 percent of the amount of the accumulation distribution divided by the number of preceding taxable years to which the accumulation distribution is allocated under section 666(a), the number of preceding taxable years of the trust with respect to which an amount is deemed distributed to a beneficiary under section 666(a) shall be determined without regard to such year.

(4) Effect of other accumulation distributions.—In computing the partial tax under paragraph (1) for any beneficiary, the income of such beneficiary for each of his prior taxable years shall include amounts previously deemed distributed to such beneficiary in such year under section 666 as a result of prior accumulation distributions (whether from the same or another trust).

(5) Multiple distributions in the same taxable year.—In the case of accumulation distributions made from more than one trust which are includible in the income of a beneficiary in the same taxable year, the distributions shall be deemed to have been made consecutively in whichever order the beneficiary shall determine.

(6) Adjustment in partial tax for estate and generation-skipping transfer taxes attributable to partial tax.—

(A) In general.—The partial tax shall be reduced by an amount which is equal to the pre-death portion of the partial tax multiplied by a fraction—

(i) the numerator of which is that portion of the tax imposed by chapter 11 or 13, as the case may be, which is attributable (on a proportionate basis) to amounts included in the accumulation distribution, and

(ii) the denominator of which is the amount of the accumulation distribution which is subject to the tax imposed by chapter 11 or 13, as the case may be.

(B) Partial tax determined without regard to this paragraph.—For purposes of this paragraph, the term "partial tax" means the partial tax imposed by subsection (a)(2) determined under this subsection without regard to this paragraph.

(C) Pre-death portion.—For purposes of this paragraph, the pre-death portion of the partial tax shall be an amount which bears the same ratio to the partial tax as the portion of the accumulation distribution which is attributable to the period before the date of the death of the decedent or the date of the generation-skipping transfer bears to the total accumulation distribution.

(c) Special rule for multiple trusts.—

(1) In general.—If, in the same prior taxable year of the beneficiary in which any part of the accumulation distribution from a trust (hereinafter in this paragraph referred to as "third trust") is deemed under section 666(a) to have been distributed to such beneficiary, some part of prior distributions by each of 2 or more other trusts is deemed under section 666(a) to have been distributed to such beneficiary, then subsections (b) and (c) of section 666 shall not apply with respect to such part of the accumulation distribution from such third trust.

(2) Accumulation distributions from trust not taken into account unless they equal or exceed $1,000.—For purposes of paragraph (1), an accumulation distribution from a trust to a beneficiary shall be taken into account only if such distribution, when added to any prior accumulation distributions from such trust which are deemed under section 666(a) to have been distributed to such beneficiary for the same prior taxable year of the beneficiary, equals or exceeds $1,000.

* * *

Subpart E—Grantors and Others Treated as Substantial Owners

§ 671. Trust income, deductions, and credits attributable to grantors and others as substantial owners

Where it is specified in this subpart that the grantor or another person shall be treated as the owner of any portion of a trust, there shall then be included in computing the taxable income and credits of the grantor or the other person those items of income, deductions, and credits against tax of the trust which are attributable to that portion of the trust to the extent that such items would be taken into account under this chapter in computing taxable income or credits against the tax of an individual. Any remaining portion of the trust shall be subject to subparts A through D. No items of a trust shall be included in computing the taxable income and credits of the grantor or of any other person solely on the grounds of his dominion and control over the trust under section 61 (relating to definition of gross income) or any other provision of this title, except as specified in this subpart.

§ 672. Definitions and rules

(a) Adverse party.—For purposes of this subpart, the term "adverse party" means any person having a substantial beneficial interest in the trust which would be adversely affected by the exercise or nonexercise of the power which he possesses respecting the trust. A person having a general power of appointment over the trust property shall be deemed to have a beneficial interest in the trust.

(b) Nonadverse party.—For purposes of this subpart, the term "nonadverse party" means any person who is not an adverse party.

(c) Related or subordinate party.—For purposes of this subpart, the term "related or subordinate party" means any nonadverse party who is—

(1) the grantor's spouse if living with the grantor;

(2) any one of the following: The grantor's father, mother, issue, brother or sister; an employee of the grantor; a corporation or any employee of a corporation in which the stock holdings of the grantor and the trust are significant from the viewpoint of voting control; a subordinate employee of a corporation in which the grantor is an executive.

For purposes of subsection (f) and sections 674 and 675, a related or subordinate party shall be presumed to be subservient to the grantor in respect of the exercise or nonexercise of the powers conferred on him unless such party is shown not to be subservient by a preponderance of the evidence.

(d) Rule where power is subject to condition precedent.—A person shall be considered to have a power described in this subpart even though the exercise of the power is subject to a precedent giving of notice or takes effect only on the expiration of a certain period after the exercise of the power.

(e) Grantor treated as holding any power or interest of grantor's spouse.—

(1) In general.—For purposes of this subpart, a grantor shall be treated as holding any power or interest held by—

(A) any individual who was the spouse of the grantor at the time of the creation of such power or interest, or

(B) any individual who became the spouse of the grantor after the creation of such power or interest, but only with respect to periods after such individual became the spouse of the grantor.

(2) Marital status.—For purposes of paragraph (1)(A), an individual legally separated from his spouse under a decree of divorce or of separate maintenance shall not be considered as married.

(f) Subpart not to result in foreign ownership.—

(1) In general.—Notwithstanding any other provision of this subpart, this subpart shall apply only to the extent such application results in an amount (if any) being currently taken into account (directly or through 1 or more entities) under this chapter in computing the income of a citizen or resident of the United States or a domestic corporation.

(2) Exceptions.—

(A) Certain revocable and irrevocable trusts.—Paragraph (1) shall not apply to any portion of a trust if—

(i) the power to revest absolutely in the grantor title to the trust property to which such portion is attributable is exercisable solely by the grantor without the approval or consent of any other person or with the consent of a related or subordinate party who is subservient to the grantor, or

(ii) the only amounts distributable from such portion (whether income or corpus) during the lifetime of the grantor are amounts distributable to the grantor or the spouse of the grantor.

(B) Compensatory trusts.—Except as provided in regulations, paragraph (1) shall not apply to any portion of a trust distributions from which are taxable as compensation for services rendered.

(3) Special rules.—Except as otherwise provided in regulations prescribed by the Secretary—

(A) a controlled foreign corporation (as defined in section 957) shall be treated as a domestic corporation for purposes of paragraph (1), and

(B) paragraph (1) shall not apply for purposes of applying section 1297.

(4) Recharacterization of purported gifts.—In the case of any transfer directly or indirectly from a partnership or foreign corporation which the transferee treats as a gift or bequest, the Secretary may recharacterize such transfer in such circumstances as the Secretary determines to be appropriate to prevent the avoidance of the purposes of this subsection.

(5) Special rule where grantor is foreign person.—If—

(A) but for this subsection, a foreign person would be treated as the owner of any portion of a trust, and

(B) such trust has a beneficiary who is a United States person,

such beneficiary shall be treated as the grantor of such portion to the extent such beneficiary has made (directly or indirectly) transfers of property (other than in a sale for full and adequate consideration) to such foreign person. For purposes of the preceding sentence, any gift shall not be taken into account to the extent such gift would be excluded from taxable gifts under section 2503(b).

(6) Regulations.—The Secretary shall prescribe such regulations as may be necessary or appropriate to carry out the purposes of this subsection, including regulations providing that paragraph (1) shall not apply in appropriate cases.

§ 673. Reversionary interests

(a) General rule.—The grantor shall be treated as the owner of any portion of a trust in which he has a reversionary interest in either the corpus or the income therefrom, if, as of the inception of that portion of the trust, the value of such interest exceeds 5 percent of the value of such portion.

(b) Reversionary interest taking effect at death of minor lineal descendant beneficiary.—In the case of any beneficiary who—

(1) is a lineal descendant of the grantor, and

(2) holds all of the present interests in any portion of a trust,

the grantor shall not be treated under subsection (a) as the owner of such portion solely by reason of a reversionary interest in such portion which takes effect upon the death of such beneficiary before such beneficiary attains age 21.

(c) Special rule for determining value of reversionary interest.—For purposes of subsection (a), the value of the grantor's reversionary interest shall be determined by assuming the maximum exercise of discretion in favor of the grantor.

(d) Postponement of date specified for reacquisition.—Any postponement of the date specified for the reacquisition of possession or enjoyment of the reversionary interest shall be treated as a new transfer in trust commencing with the date on which the postponement is effective and terminating with the date prescribed by the postponement. However, income for any period shall not be included in the income of the grantor by reason of the preceding sentence if such income would not be so includible in the absence of such postponement.

§ 674. Power to control beneficial enjoyment

(a) General rule.—The grantor shall be treated as the owner of any portion of a trust in respect of which the beneficial enjoyment of the corpus or the income therefrom is subject to a power of disposition, exercisable by the grantor or a nonadverse party, or both, without the approval or consent of any adverse party.

(b) Exceptions for certain powers.—Subsection (a) shall not apply to the following powers regardless of by whom held:

(1) Power to apply income to support of a dependent.—A power described in section 677(b) to the extent that the grantor would not be subject to tax under that section.

(2) Power affecting beneficial enjoyment only after occurrence of events.—A power, the exercise of which can only affect the beneficial enjoyment of the income for a period commencing after the occurrence of an event such that a grantor would not be treated as the owner under section 673 if the power were a reversionary interest; but the grantor may be treated as the owner after the occurrence of the event unless the power is relinquished.

(3) Power exercisable only by will.—A power exercisable only by will, other than a power in the grantor to appoint by will the income of the trust where the income is accumulated for such disposition by the grantor or may be so accumulated in the discretion of the grantor or a nonadverse party, or both, without the approval or consent of any adverse party.

(4) Power to allocate among charitable beneficiaries.—A power to determine the beneficial enjoyment of the corpus or the income therefrom if the corpus or income is irrevocably payable for a purpose specified in section 170(c) (relating to definition of charitable contributions) * * *.

(5) Power to distribute corpus.—A power to distribute corpus either—

(A) to or for a beneficiary or beneficiaries or to or for a class of beneficiaries (whether or not income beneficiaries) provided that the power is limited by a reasonably definite standard which is set forth in the trust instrument; or

(B) to or for any current income beneficiary, provided that the distribution of corpus must be chargeable against the proportionate share of corpus held in trust for the payment of income to the beneficiary as if the corpus constituted a separate trust.

A power does not fall within the powers described in this paragraph if any person has a power to add to the beneficiary or beneficiaries or to a class of beneficiaries designated to receive the income or corpus, except where such action is to provide for after-born or after-adopted children.

(6) Power to withhold income temporarily.—A power to distribute or apply income to or for any current income beneficiary or to accumulate the income for him, provided that any accumulated income must ultimately be payable—

(A) to the beneficiary from whom distribution or application is withheld, to his estate, or to his appointees (or persons named as alternate takers in default of appointment) provided that such beneficiary possesses a power of appointment which does not exclude from the class of possible appointees any person other than the beneficiary, his estate, his creditors, or the creditors of his estate, or

(B) on termination of the trust, or in conjunction with a distribution of corpus which is augmented by such accumulated income, to the current income beneficiaries in shares which have been irrevocably specified in the trust instrument.

Accumulated income shall be considered so payable although it is provided that if any beneficiary does not survive a date of distribution which could reasonably have been expected to occur within the beneficiary's lifetime, the share of the deceased beneficiary is to be paid to his appointees or to one or more designated alternate takers (other than the grantor or the grantor's estate) whose shares have been irrevocably specified. A power does not fall within the powers described in this paragraph if any person has a power to add to the beneficiary or beneficiaries or to a class of beneficiaries designated to receive the income or corpus except where such action is to provide for after-born or after-adopted children.

(7) Power to withhold income during disability of a beneficiary.—A power exercisable only during—

(A) the existence of a legal disability of any current income beneficiary, or

(B) the period during which any income beneficiary shall be under the age of 21 years,

to distribute or apply income to or for such beneficiary or to accumulate and add the income to corpus. A power does not fall within the powers described in this paragraph if any person has a power to add to the beneficiary or beneficiaries or to a class of beneficiaries designated to receive the income or corpus, except where such action is to provide for after-born or after-adopted children.

(8) Power to allocate between corpus and income.—A power to allocate receipts and disbursements as between corpus and income, even though expressed in broad language.

(c) Exception for certain powers of independent trustees.—Subsection (a) shall not apply to a power solely exercisable (without the approval or consent of any other person) by a trustee or trustees, none of whom is the grantor, and no more than half of whom are related or subordinate parties who are subservient to the wishes of the grantor—

(1) to distribute, apportion, or accumulate income to or for a beneficiary or beneficiaries, or to, for, or within a class of beneficiaries; or

(2) to pay out corpus to or for a beneficiary or beneficiaries or to or for a class of beneficiaries (whether or not income beneficiaries).

A power does not fall within the powers described in this subsection if any person has a power to add to the beneficiary or beneficiaries or to a class of beneficiaries designated to receive the income or corpus, except where such action is to provide for after-born or after-adopted children. For periods during which an individual is the spouse of the grantor (within the meaning of section 672(e)(2)), any reference in this subsection to the grantor shall be treated as including a reference to such individual.

(d) Power to allocate income if limited by a standard.—Subsection (a) shall not apply to a power solely exercisable (without the approval or consent of any other person) by a trustee or trustees, none of whom is the grantor or spouse living with the grantor, to distribute, apportion, or accumulate income to or for a beneficiary or beneficiaries, or to, for, or within a class of beneficiaries, whether or not the conditions of paragraph (6) or (7) of subsection (b) are satisfied, if such power is limited by a reasonably definite external standard which is set forth in the trust instrument. A power does not fall within the powers described in this subsection if any person has a power to add to the beneficiary or beneficiaries or to a class of beneficiaries designated to receive the income or corpus except where such action is to provide for after-born or after-adopted children.

§ 675. Administrative powers

The grantor shall be treated as the owner of any portion of a trust in respect of which—

(1) Power to deal for less than adequate and full consideration.—A power exercisable by the grantor or a nonadverse party, or both, without the approval or consent of any adverse party enables the grantor or any person to purchase, exchange, or otherwise deal with or dispose of the corpus or the income therefrom for less than an adequate consideration in money or money's worth.

(2) Power to borrow without adequate interest or security.—A power exercisable by the grantor or a nonadverse party, or both, enables the grantor to borrow the corpus or income, directly or indirectly, without adequate interest or without adequate security except where a trustee (other than the grantor) is authorized under a general lending power to make loans to any person without regard to interest or security.

(3) Borrowing of the trust funds.—The grantor has directly or indirectly borrowed the corpus or income and has not completely repaid the loan, including any interest, before the beginning of the taxable year. The preceding sentence shall not apply to a loan which provides for adequate interest and adequate security, if such loan is made by a trustee other than the grantor and other than a related or subordinate trustee subservient to the grantor. For periods during which an individual is the spouse of the grantor (within the meaning of section 672(e)(2)), any reference in this paragraph to the grantor shall be treated as including a reference to such individual.

(4) General powers of administration.—A power of administration is exercisable in a nonfiduciary capacity by any person without the approval or consent of any person in a fiduciary capacity. For purposes of this paragraph, the term "power of administration" means any one or more of the following powers: (A) a power to vote or direct the voting of stock or other securities of a corporation in which the holdings of the grantor and the trust are significant from the viewpoint of voting control; (B) a power to control the investment of the trust funds either by directing investments or reinvestments, or by vetoing proposed investments or reinvestments, to the extent that the trust funds consist of stocks or securities of corporations in which the holdings of the grantor and the trust are significant from the viewpoint of voting control; or (C) a power to reacquire the trust corpus by substituting other property of an equivalent value.

§ 676. Power to revoke

(a) General rule.—The grantor shall be treated as the owner of any portion of a trust, whether or not he is treated as such owner under any other provision of this part, where at any time the power to revest in the grantor title to such portion is exercisable by the grantor or a non-adverse party, or both.

(b) Power affecting beneficial enjoyment only after occurrence of event.—Subsection (a) shall not apply to a power the exercise of which can only affect the beneficial enjoyment of the income for a period commencing after the occurrence of an event such that a grantor would not be treated as the owner under section 673 if the power were a reversionary interest. But the grantor may be treated as the owner after the occurrence of such event unless the power is relinquished.

§ 677. Income for benefit of grantor

(a) General rule.—The grantor shall be treated as the owner of any portion of a trust, whether or not he is treated as such owner under section 674, whose income without the approval or consent of any adverse party is, or, in the discretion of the grantor or a nonadverse party, or both, may be—

(1) distributed to the grantor or the grantor's spouse;

(2) held or accumulated for future distribution to the grantor or the grantor's spouse; or

(3) applied to the payment of premiums on policies of insurance on the life of the grantor or the grantor's spouse (except policies of insurance irrevocably payable for a purpose specified in section 170(c) (relating to definition of charitable contributions)).

This subsection shall not apply to a power the exercise of which can only affect the beneficial enjoyment of the income for a period commencing after the occurrence of an event such that the grantor would not be treated as the owner under section 673 if the power were a reversionary interest; but the grantor may be treated as the owner after the occurrence of the event unless the power is relinquished.

(b) Obligations of support.—Income of a trust shall not be considered taxable to the grantor under subsection (a) or any other provision of this chapter merely because such income in the discretion of another person, the trustee, or the grantor acting as trustee or co-trustee, may be applied or distributed for the support or maintenance of a beneficiary (other than the grantor's spouse) whom the grantor is legally obligated to support or maintain, except to the extent that such income is so applied or distributed. In cases where the amounts so applied or distributed are paid out of corpus or out of other than income for the taxable year, such amounts shall be considered to be an amount paid or credited within the meaning of paragraph (2) of section 661(a) and shall be taxed to the grantor under section 662.

§ 678. Person other than grantor treated as substantial owner

(a) General rule.—A person other than the grantor shall be treated as the owner of any portion of a trust with respect to which:

(1) such person has a power exercisable solely by himself to vest the corpus or the income therefrom in himself, or

(2) such person has previously partially released or otherwise modified such a power and after the release or modification retains such control as would, within the principles of sections 671 to 677, inclusive, subject a grantor of a trust to treatment as the owner thereof.

(b) Exception where grantor is taxable.—Subsection (a) shall not apply with respect to a power over income, as originally granted or thereafter modified, if the grantor of the trust or a transferor (to whom section 679 applies) is otherwise treated as the owner under the provisions of this subpart other than this section.

(c) Obligations of support.—Subsection (a) shall not apply to a power which enables such person, in the capacity of trustee or co-trustee, merely to apply the income of the trust to the support or maintenance of a person whom the holder of the power is obligated to support or maintain except to the extent that such income is so applied. In cases where the amounts so applied or distributed are paid out of corpus or out of other than income of the taxable year, such amounts shall be considered to be an amount paid or credited within the meaning of paragraph (2) of section 661(a) and shall be taxed to the holder of the power under section 662.

(d) Effect of renunciation or disclaimer.—Subsection (a) shall not apply with respect to a power which has been renounced or disclaimed within a reasonable time after the holder of the power first became aware of its existence.

(e) Cross reference.—

For provision under which beneficiary of trust is treated as owner of the portion of the trust which consists of stock in an S corporation, see section 1361(d).

§ 679. Foreign trusts having one or more United States beneficiaries

(a) Transferor treated as owner.—

(1) In general.—A United States person who directly or indirectly transfers property to a foreign trust (other than a trust described in section 6048(a)(3)(B)(ii)) shall be treated as the owner for his taxable year of the portion of such trust attributable to such property if for such year there is a United States beneficiary of any portion of such trust.

(2) Exceptions.—Paragraph (1) shall not apply—

(A) Transfers by reason of death.—To any transfer by reason of the death of the transferor.

(B) Transfers at fair market value.—To any transfer of property to a trust in exchange for consideration of at least the fair market value of the transferred property. For purposes of the preceding sentence, consideration other than cash shall be taken into account at its fair market value.

(3) Certain obligations not taken into account under fair market value exception.—

(A) In general.—In determining whether paragraph (2)(B) applies to any transfer by a person described in clause (ii) or (iii) of subparagraph (C), there shall not be taken into account—

(i) except as provided in regulations, any obligation of a person described in subparagraph (C), and

(ii) to the extent provided in regulations, any obligation which is guaranteed by a person described in subparagraph (C).

(B) Treatment of principal payments on obligation.—Principal payments by the trust on any obligation referred to in subparagraph (A) shall be taken into account on and after the date of the payment in determining the portion of the trust attributable to the property transferred.

(C) Persons described.—The persons described in this subparagraph are—

(i) the trust,

(ii) any grantor, owner, or beneficiary of the trust, and

(iii) any person who is related (within the meaning of section 643(i)(2)(B)) to any grantor, owner, or beneficiary of the trust.

(4) Special rules applicable to foreign grantor who later becomes a United States person.—

(A) In general.—If a nonresident alien individual has a residency starting date within 5 years after directly or indirectly transferring property to a foreign trust, this section and section 6048 shall be applied as if such individual transferred to such trust on the residency starting date an amount equal to the portion of such trust attributable to the property transferred by such individual to such trust in such transfer.

(B) Treatment of undistributed income.—For purposes of this section, undistributed net income for periods before such individual's residency starting date shall be taken into account in determining the portion of the trust which is attributable to property transferred by such individual to such trust but shall not otherwise be taken into account.

(C) Residency starting date.—For purposes of this paragraph, an individual's residency starting date is the residency starting date determined under section 7701(b)(2)(A).

(5) Outbound trust migrations.—If—

(A) an individual who is a citizen or resident of the United States transferred property to a trust which was not a foreign trust, and

(B) such trust becomes a foreign trust while such individual is alive, then this section and section 6048 shall be applied as if such individual transferred to such trust on the date such trust becomes a foreign trust an amount equal to the portion of such trust attributable to the property previously transferred by such individual to such trust. A rule similar to the rule of paragraph (4)(B) shall apply for purposes of this paragraph.

(b) Trusts acquiring United States beneficiaries.—If—

(1) subsection (a) applies to a trust for the transferor's taxable year, and

(2) subsection (a) would have applied to the trust for his immediately preceding taxable year but for the fact that for such preceding taxable year there was no United States beneficiary for any portion of the trust,

then, for purposes of this subtitle, the transferor shall be treated as having income for the taxable year (in addition to his other income for such year) equal to the undistributed net income (at the close of such immediately preceding taxable year) attributable to the portion of the trust referred to in subsection (a).

(c) Trusts treated as having a United States beneficiary.—

(1) In general.—For purposes of this section, a trust shall be treated as having a United States beneficiary for the taxable year unless—

(A) under the terms of the trust, no part of the income or corpus of the trust may be paid or accumulated during the taxable year to or for the benefit of a United States person, and

(B) if the trust were terminated at any time during the taxable year, no part of the income or corpus of such trust could be paid to or for the benefit of a United States person.

For purposes of subparagraph (A), an amount shall be treated as accumulated for the benefit of a United States person even if the United States person's interest in the trust is contingent on a future event.

(2) Attribution of ownership.—For purposes of paragraph (1), an amount shall be treated as paid or accumulated to or for the benefit of a United States person if such amount is paid to or accumulated for a foreign corporation, foreign partnership, or foreign trust or estate, and—

(A) in the case of a foreign corporation, such corporation is a controlled foreign corporation (as defined in section 957(a)),

(B) in the case of a foreign partnership, a United States person is a partner of such partnership, or

(C) in the case of a foreign trust or estate, such trust or estate has a United States beneficiary (within the meaning of paragraph (1)).

(3) Certain United States beneficiaries disregarded.—A beneficiary shall not be treated as a United States person in applying this section with respect to any transfer of property to foreign trust if such beneficiary first became a United States person more than 5 years after the date of such transfer.

(4) Special rule in case of discretion to identify beneficiaries.—For purposes of paragraph (1)(A), if any person has the discretion (by authority given in the trust agreement, by power of appointment, or otherwise) of making a distribution from the trust to, or for the benefit of, any person, such trust shall be treated as having a beneficiary who is a United States person unless—

(A) the terms of the trust specifically identify the class of persons to whom such distributions may be made, and

(B) none of those persons are United States persons during the taxable year.

(5) Certain agreements and understandings treated as terms of the trust.— For purposes of paragraph (1)(A), if any United States person who directly or indirectly transfers property to the trust is directly or indirectly involved in any agreement or understanding (whether written, oral, or otherwise) that may result in the income or corpus of the trust being paid or accumulated to or for the benefit of a United States person, such agreement or understanding shall be treated as a term of the trust.

(6) Uncompensated use of trust property treated as a payment.—For purposes of this subsection, a loan of cash or marketable securities (or the use of any other trust property) directly or indirectly to or by any United States person (whether or not a beneficiary under the terms of the trust) shall be treated as paid or accumulated for the benefit of a United States person. The preceding sentence shall not apply to the extent that the United States person repays the loan at a market rate of interest (or pays the fair market value of the use of such property) within a reasonable period of time.

(d) Presumption that foreign trust has United States beneficiary.—If a United States person directly or indirectly transfers property to a foreign trust (other than a trust described in section 6048(a)(3)(B)(ii)), the Secretary may treat such trust as having a United States beneficiary for purposes of applying this section to such transfer unless such person—

(1) submits such information to the Secretary as the Secretary may require with respect to such transfer, and

(2) demonstrates to the satisfaction of the Secretary that such trust satisfies the requirements of subparagraphs (A) and (B) of subsection (c)(1).

(e) Regulations.—The Secretary shall prescribe such regulations as may be necessary or appropriate to carry out the purposes of this section.

Subpart F—Miscellaneous

§ 681. Limitation on charitable deduction

(a) Trade or business income.—In computing the deduction allowable under section 642(c) to a trust, no amount otherwise allowable under section 642(c) as a deduction shall be allowed as a deduction with respect to income of a taxable year which is allocable to its unrelated business income for such year. For purposes of the preceding sentence, the term "unrelated business income" means an amount equal to the amount which, if such trust were exempt from tax under section 501(a) by reason of section 501(c)(3), would be computed as its unrelated business taxable income under section 512 (relating to income derived from certain business activities and from certain property acquired with borrowed funds).

* * *

§ 682. Income of an estate or trust in case of divorce, etc.

(a) Inclusion in gross income of wife.—There shall be included in the gross income of a wife who is divorced or legally separated under a decree of divorce or of separate maintenance (or who is separated from her husband under a written separation agreement) the amount of the income of any trust which such wife is entitled to receive and which, except for this section, would be includible in the gross income of her husband, and such amount shall not, despite any other provision of this subtitle, be includible in the gross income of such husband. This subsection shall not apply to that part of any such income of the trust which the terms of the decree, written separation agreement, or trust instrument fix, in terms of an amount of money or a portion of such income, as a sum which is payable for the support of minor children of such husband. In case such income is less than the amount specified in the decree, agreement, or instrument, for the purpose of applying the preceding sentence, such income, to the extent of such sum payable for such support, shall be considered a payment for such support.

(b) Wife considered a beneficiary.—For purposes of computing the taxable income of the estate or trust and the taxable income of a wife to whom subsection (a) applies, such wife shall be considered as the beneficiary specified in this part.

(c) Cross reference.—

For definitions of "husband" and "wife", as used in this section, see section 7701(a)(17).

§ 684. Recognition of gain on certain transfers to certain foreign trusts and estates

(a) In general.—Except as provided in regulations, in the case of any transfer of property by a United States person to a foreign estate or trust, for purposes of this subtitle, such transfer shall be treated as a sale or exchange for an amount equal to the fair market value of the property transferred, and the transferor shall recognize as gain the excess of—

(1) the fair market value of the property so transferred, over

(2) the adjusted basis (for purposes of determining gain) of such property in the hands of the transferor.

(b) Exception.—Subsection (a) shall not apply to a transfer to a trust by a United States person to the extent that any person is treated as the owner of such trust under section 671.

(c) Treatment of trusts which become foreign trusts.—If a trust which is not a foreign trust becomes a foreign trust, such trust shall be treated for purposes of this section as having transferred, immediately before becoming a foreign trust, all of its assets to a foreign trust.

PART II—INCOME IN RESPECT OF DECEDENTS

§ 691. Recipients of income in respect of decedents

(a) Inclusion in gross income.—

(1) General rule.—The amount of all items of gross income in respect of a decedent which are not properly includible in respect of the taxable period in which falls the date of his death or a prior period (including the amount of all items of gross income in respect of a prior decedent, if the right to receive such amount was acquired by reason of the death of the prior decedent or by bequest, devise, or inheritance from the prior decedent) shall be included in the gross income, for the taxable year when received, of:

(A) the estate of the decedent, if the right to receive the amount is acquired by the decedent's estate from the decedent;

(B) the person who, by reason of the death of the decedent, acquires the right to receive the amount, if the right to receive the amount is not acquired by the decedent's estate from the decedent; or

(C) the person who acquires from the decedent the right to receive the amount by bequest, devise, or inheritance, if the amount is received after a distribution by the decedent's estate of such right.

(2) Income in case of sale, etc.—If a right, described in paragraph (1), to receive an amount is transferred by the estate of the decedent or a person who received such right by reason of the death of the decedent or by bequest, devise, or inheritance from the decedent, there shall be included in the gross income of the estate or such person, as the case may be, for the taxable period in which the transfer occurs, the fair market value of such right at the time of such transfer plus the amount by which any consideration for the transfer exceeds such fair market value. For purposes of this paragraph, the term "transfer" includes sale, exchange, or other disposition, or the satisfaction of an installment obligation at other than face value, but does not include transmission at death to the estate of the decedent or a transfer to a person pursuant to the right of such person to receive such amount by reason of the death of the decedent or by bequest, devise, or inheritance from the decedent.

(3) Character of income determined by reference to decedent.—The right, described in paragraph (1), to receive an amount shall be treated, in the hands of the estate of the decedent or any person who acquired such right by reason of the death of the decedent, or by bequest, devise, or inheritance from the decedent, as if it had been acquired by the estate or such person in the transaction in which the right to receive the income was originally derived and the amount includible in gross income under paragraph (1) or (2) shall be considered in the hands of the estate or such person to have the character which it would have had in the hands of the decedent if the decedent had lived and received such amount.

(4) Installment obligations acquired from decedent.—In the case of an installment obligation reportable by the decedent on the installment method under section 453, if such obligation is acquired by the decedent's estate from the decedent or by any person by reason of the death of the decedent or by bequest, devise, or inheritance from the decedent—

(A) an amount equal to the excess of the face amount of such obligation over the basis of the obligation in the hands of the decedent (determined under section 453B) shall, for the purpose of paragraph (1), be considered as an item of gross income in respect of the decedent; and

(B) such obligation shall, for purposes of paragraphs (2) and (3), be considered a right to receive an item of gross income in respect of the decedent, but the amount includible in gross income under paragraph (2) shall be reduced by an amount equal to the basis of the obligation in the hands of the decedent (determined under section 453B).

(5) Other rules relating to installment obligations.—

(A) In general.—In the case of an installment obligation reportable by the decedent on the installment method under section 453, for purposes of paragraph (2)—

(i) the second sentence of paragraph (2) shall be applied by inserting "(other than the obligor)" after "or a transfer to a person",

(ii) any cancellation of such an obligation shall be treated as a transfer, and

(iii) any cancellation of such an obligation occurring at the death of the decedent shall be treated as a transfer by the estate of the decedent (or, if held by a person other than the decedent before the death of the decedent, by such person).

(B) Face amount treated as fair market value in certain cases.—In any case to which the first sentence of paragraph (2) applies by reason of subparagraph (A), if the decedent and the obligor were related persons (within the meaning of section 453(f)(1)), the fair market value of the installment obligation shall be treated as not less than its face amount.

(C) Cancellation includes becoming unenforceable.—For purposes of subparagraph (A), an installment obligation which becomes unenforceable shall be treated as if it were canceled.

(b) Allowance of deductions and credit.—The amount of any deduction specified in section 162, 163, 164, 212, or 611 (relating to deductions for expenses, interest, taxes, and depletion) or credit specified in section 27 (relating to foreign tax credit), in respect of a decedent which is not properly allowable to the decedent in respect of the taxable period in which falls the date of his death, or a prior period, shall be allowed:

(1) Expenses, interest, and taxes.—In the case of a deduction specified in section 162, 163, 164, or 212 and a credit specified in section 27, in the taxable year when paid—

(A) to the estate of the decedent; except that

(B) if the estate of the decedent is not liable to discharge the obligation to which the deduction or credit relates, to the person who, by reason of the death of the decedent or by bequest, devise, or inheritance acquires, subject to such obligation, from the decedent an interest in property of the decedent.

(2) Depletion.—In the case of the deduction specified in section 611, to the person described in subsection (a)(1)(A), (B), or (C) who, in the manner described therein, receives the income to which the deduction relates, in the taxable year when such income is received.

(c) Deduction for estate tax.—

(1) Allowance of deduction.—

(A) General rule.—A person who includes an amount in gross income under subsection (a) shall be allowed, for the same taxable year, as a deduction an amount which bears the same ratio to the estate tax attributable to the net value for estate tax purposes of all the items described in subsection (a)(1) as the value for estate tax purposes of the items of gross income or portions thereof in respect of which such person included the amount in gross income (or the amount included in gross income, whichever is lower) bears to the value for estate tax purposes of all the items described in subsection (a)(1).

(B) Estates and trusts.—In the case of an estate or trust, the amount allowed as a deduction under subparagraph (A) shall be computed by excluding from the gross income of the estate or trust the portion (if any) of the items described in subsection (a)(1) which is properly paid, credited, or to be distributed to the beneficiaries during the taxable year.

(2) Method of computing deduction.—For purposes of paragraph (1)—

(A) The term "estate tax" means the tax imposed on the estate of the decedent or any prior decedent under section 2001 or 2101, reduced by the credits against such tax.

(B) The net value for estate tax purposes of all the items described in subsection (a)(1) shall be the excess of the value for estate tax purposes of all the items described in subsection (a)(1) over the deductions from the gross estate in respect of claims which represent the deductions and credit described in subsection (b). Such net value shall be determined with respect to the provisions of section 421(c)(2), relating to the deduction for estate tax with respect to stock options to which part II of subchapter D applies.

(C) The estate tax attributable to such net value shall be an amount equal to the excess of the estate tax over the estate tax computed without including in the gross estate such net value.

(3) Special rule for generation-skipping transfers.—In the case of any tax imposed by chapter 13 on a taxable termination or a direct skip occurring as a result of the death of the transferor, there shall be allowed a deduction (under principles similar to the principles of this subsection) for the portion of such tax attributable to items of gross income of the trust which were not properly includible in the gross income of the trust for periods before the date of such termination.

(4) Coordination with capital gain provisions.—For purposes of sections 1(h), 1201, 1202, and 1211, the amount taken into account with respect to any item described in subsection (a)(1) shall be reduced (but not below zero) by the amount of the deduction allowable under paragraph (1) of this subsection with respect to such item.

(5) Coordination with section 402(d).—For purposes of section 402(d) (other than paragraph (1)(C) thereof), the total taxable amount of any lump sum distribution shall be reduced by the amount of the deduction allowable under paragraph (1) of this subsection which is attributable to the total taxable amount (determined without regard to this paragraph).

(d) Amounts received by surviving annuitant under joint and survivor annuity contract.—

(1) Deduction for estate tax.—For purposes of computing the deduction under subsection (c)(1)(A), amounts received by a surviving annuitant—

(A) as an annuity under a joint and survivor annuity contract where the decedent annuitant died after December 31, 1953, and after the annuity starting date (as defined in section 72(c)(4)), and

(B) during the surviving annuitant's life expectancy period,

shall, to the extent included in gross income under section 72, be considered as amounts included in gross income under subsection (a).

(2) Net value for estate tax purposes.—In determining the net value for estate tax purposes under subsection (c)(2)(B) for purposes of this subsection, the value for estate tax purposes of the items described in paragraph (1) of this subsection shall be computed—

(A) by determining the excess of the value of the annuity at the date of the death of the deceased annuitant over the total amount excludable from the gross income of the surviving annuitant under section 72 during the surviving annuitant's life expectancy period, and

(B) by multiplying the figure so obtained by the ratio which the value of the annuity for estate tax purposes bears to the value of the annuity at the date of the death of the deceased.

(3) Definitions.—For purposes of this subsection—

(A) The term "life expectancy period" means the period beginning with the first day of the first period for which an amount is received by the surviving annuitant under the contract and ending with the close of the taxable year with or in which falls the termination of the life expectancy of the surviving annuitant. For purposes of this subparagraph, the life expectancy of the surviving annuitant shall be determined, as of the date of the death of the deceased annuitant, with reference to actuarial tables prescribed by the Secretary.

(B) The surviving annuitant's expected return under the contract shall be computed, as of the death of the deceased annuitant, with reference to actuarial tables prescribed by the Secretary.

(e) Cross reference.—

For application of this section to income in respect of a deceased partner, see section 753.

SUBCHAPTER K—PARTNERS AND PARTNERSHIPS

PART I—DETERMINATION OF TAX LIABILITY

§ 701. Partners, not partnership, subject to tax

A partnership as such shall not be subject to the income tax imposed by this chapter. Persons carrying on business as partners shall be liable for income tax only in their separate or individual capacities.

§ 702. Income and credits of partner

(a) General rule.—In determining his income tax, each partner shall take into account separately his distributive share of the partnership's—

(1) gains and losses from sales or exchanges of capital assets held for not more than 1 year,

(2) gains and losses from sales or exchanges of capital assets held for more than 1 year,

(3) gains and losses from sales or exchanges of property described in section 1231 (relating to certain property used in a trade or business and involuntary conversions),

(4) charitable contributions (as defined in section 170(c)),

(5) dividends with respect to which section 1(h)(11) or part VIII of Subchapter B applies,

(6) taxes, described in section 901, paid or accrued to foreign countries and to possessions of the United States,

(7) other items of income, gain, loss, deduction, or credit, to the extent provided by regulations prescribed by the Secretary, and

(8) taxable income or loss, exclusive of items requiring separate computation under other paragraphs of this subsection.

(b) Character of items constituting distributive share.—The character of any item of income, gain, loss, deduction, or credit included in a partner's distributive share under paragraphs (1) through (7) of subsection (a) shall be determined as if such item were realized directly from the source from which realized by the partnership, or incurred in the same manner as incurred by the partnership.

(c) Gross income of a partner.—In any case where it is necessary to determine the gross income of a partner for purposes of this title, such amount shall include his distributive share of the gross income of the partnership.

(d) Cross reference.—

For rules relating to procedures for determining the tax treatment of partnership items see subchapter C of chapter 63 (section 6221 and following).

§ 703. Partnership computations

(a) Income and deductions.—The taxable income of a partnership shall be computed in the same manner as in the case of an individual except that—

(1) the items described in section 702(a) shall be separately stated, and

(2) the following deductions shall not be allowed to the partnership:

(A) the deductions for personal exemptions provided in section 151,

(B) the deduction for taxes provided in section 164(a) with respect to taxes, described in section 901, paid or accrued to foreign countries and to possessions of the United States,

(C) the deduction for charitable contributions provided in section 170,

(D) the net operating loss deduction provided in section 172,

(E) the additional itemized deductions for individuals provided in part VII of subchapter B (sec. 211 and following), and

(F) the deduction for depletion under section 611 with respect to oil and gas wells.

(b) Elections of the partnership.—Any election affecting the computation of taxable income derived from a partnership shall be made by the partnership, except that any election under—

(1) subsection (b)(5) or (c)(3) of section 108 (relating to income from discharge of indebtedness),

(2) section 617 (relating to deduction and recapture of certain mining exploration expenditures), or

* * *

shall be made by each partner separately.

§ 704. Partner's distributive share

(a) Effect of partnership agreement.—A partner's distributive share of income, gain, loss, deduction, or credit shall, except as otherwise provided in this chapter, be determined by the partnership agreement.

(b) Determination of distributive share.—A partner's distributive share of income, gain, loss, deduction, or credit (or item thereof) shall be determined in accordance with the partner's interest in the partnership (determined by taking into account all facts and circumstances), if—

(1) the partnership agreement does not provide as to the partner's distributive share of income, gain, loss, deduction, or credit (or item thereof), or

(2) the allocation to a partner under the agreement of income, gain, loss, deduction, or credit (or item thereof) does not have substantial economic effect.

(c) Contributed property.—

(1) In general.—Under regulations prescribed by the Secretary—

(A) income, gain, loss, and deduction with respect to property contributed to the partnership by a partner shall be shared among the partners so as to take account of the variation between the basis of the property to the partnership and its fair market value at the time of contribution,

(B) if any property so contributed is distributed (directly or indirectly) by the partnership (other than to the contributing partner) within 7 years of being contributed—

(i) the contributing partner shall be treated as recognizing gain or loss (as the case may be) from the sale of such property in an amount equal to the gain or loss which would have been allocated to such partner under subparagraph (A) by reason of the variation described in subparagraph (A) if the property had been sold at its fair market value at the time of the distribution,

(ii) the character of such gain or loss shall be determined by reference to the character of the gain or loss which would have resulted if such property had been sold by the partnership to the distributee, and

(iii) appropriate adjustments shall be made to the adjusted basis of the contributing partner's interest in the partnership and to the adjusted basis of the property distributed to reflect any gain or loss recognized under this subparagraph, and

(C) if any property so contributed has a built-in loss—

(i) such built-in loss shall be taken into account only in determining the amount of items allocated to the contributing partner, and

(ii) except as provided in regulations, in determining the amount of items allocated to other partners, the basis of the contributed property in the hands of the partnership shall be treated as being equal to its fair market value at the time of contribution.

(2) Special rule for distributions where gain or loss would not be recognized outside partnerships.—Under regulations prescribed by the Secretary, if—

(A) property contributed by a partner (hereinafter referred to as the "contributing partner") is distributed by the partnership to another partner, and

(B) other property of a like kind (within the meaning of section 1031) is distributed by the partnership to the contributing partner not later than the earlier of—

(i) the 180th day after the date of the distribution described in subparagraph (A), or

(ii) the due date (determined with regard to extensions) for the contributing partner's return of the tax imposed by this chapter for the taxable year in which the distribution described in subparagraph (A) occurs,

then to the extent of the value of the property described in subparagraph (B), paragraph (1)(B) shall be applied as if the contributing partner had contributed to the partnership the property described in subparagraph (B).

(3) Other rules.—Under regulations prescribed by the Secretary, rules similar to the rules of paragraph (1) shall apply to contributions by a partner (using the cash receipts and disbursements method of accounting) of accounts payable and other accrued but unpaid items. Any reference in paragraph (1) or (2) to the contributing partner shall be treated as including a reference to any successor of such partner.

(d) Limitation on allowance of losses.—A partner's distributive share of partnership loss (including capital loss) shall be allowed only to the extent of the adjusted basis of such partner's interest in the partnership at the end of the partnership year in which such loss occurred. Any excess of such loss over such basis shall be allowed as a deduction at the end of the partnership year in which such excess is repaid to the partnership.

(e) Family partnerships.—

(1) Recognition of interest created by purchase or gift.—A person shall be recognized as a partner for purposes of this subtitle if he owns a capital interest in a partnership in which capital is a material income-producing factor, whether or not such interest was derived by purchase or gift from any other person.

(2) Distributive share of donee includible in gross income.—In the case of any partnership interest created by gift, the distributive share of the donee under the partnership agreement shall be includible in his gross income, except to the extent that such share is determined without allowance of reasonable compensation for services rendered to the partnership by the donor, and except to the extent that the portion of such share attributable to donated capital is proportionately greater than the share of the donor attributable to the donor's capital. The distributive share of a partner in the earnings of the partnership shall not be diminished because of absence due to military service.

(3) Purchase of interest by member of family.—For purposes of this section, an interest purchased by one member of a family from another shall be considered to be created by gift from the seller, and the fair market value of the purchased interest shall be considered to be donated capital. The "family" of any individual shall include only his spouse, ancestors, and lineal descendants, and any trusts for the primary benefit of such persons.

(f) Cross reference.—

For rules in the case of the sale, exchange, liquidation, or reduction of a partner's interest, see section 706(c)(2).

§ 705. Determination of basis of partner's interest

(a) General rule.—The adjusted basis of a partner's interest in a partnership shall, except as provided in subsection (b), be the basis of such interest determined under section 722 (relating to contributions to a partnership) or section 742 (relating to transfers of partnership interests)—

(1) increased by the sum of his distributive share for the taxable year and prior taxable years of—

(A) taxable income of the partnership as determined under section 703(a),

(B) income of the partnership exempt from tax under this title, and

(C) the excess of the deductions for depletion over the basis of the property subject to depletion;

(2) decreased (but not below zero) by distributions by the partnership as provided in section 733 and by the sum of his distributive share for the taxable year and prior taxable years of—

(A) losses of the partnership, and

(B) expenditures of the partnership not deductible in computing its taxable income and not properly chargeable to capital account; and

(3) decreased (but not below zero) by the amount of the partner's deduction for depletion for any partnership oil and gas property to the extent such deduction does not exceed the proportionate share of the adjusted basis of such property allocated to such partner under section 613A(c)(7)(D).

(b) Alternative rule.—The Secretary shall prescribe by regulations the circumstances under which the adjusted basis of a partner's interest in a partnership may be determined by reference to his proportionate share of the adjusted basis of partnership property upon a termination of the partnership.

§ 706. Taxable years of partner and partnership

(a) Year in which partnership income is includible.—In computing the taxable income of a partner for a taxable year, the inclusions required by section 702 and section 707(c) with respect to a partnership shall be based on the income, gain, loss, deduction, or credit of the partnership for any taxable year of the partnership ending within or with the taxable year of the partner.

(b) Taxable year.—

(1) Partnership's taxable year.—

(A) Partnership treated as taxpayer.—The taxable year of a partnership shall be determined as though the partnership were a taxpayer.

(B) Taxable year determined by reference to partners.—Except as provided in subparagraph (C), a partnership shall not have a taxable year other than—

(i) the majority interest taxable year (as defined in paragraph (4)),

(ii) if there is no taxable year described in clause (i), the taxable year of all the principal partners of the partnership, or

(iii) if there is no taxable year described in clause (i) or (ii), the calendar year unless the Secretary by regulations prescribes another period.

(C) Business purpose.—A partnership may have a taxable year not described in subparagraph (B) if it establishes, to the satisfaction of the Secretary, a business purpose therefor. For purposes of this subparagraph, any deferral of income to partners shall not be treated as a business purpose.

(2) Partner's taxable year.—A partner may not change to a taxable year other than that of a partnership in which he is a principal partner unless he establishes, to the satisfaction of the Secretary, a business purpose therefor.

(3) Principal partner.—For the purpose of this subsection, a principal partner is a partner having an interest of 5 percent or more in partnership profits or capital.

(4) Majority interest taxable year; limitation on required changes.—

(A) Majority interest taxable year defined.—For purposes of paragraph (1)(B)(i)—

(i) In general.—The term "majority interest taxable year" means the taxable year (if any) which, on each testing day, constituted the taxable year of 1 or more partners having (on such day) an aggregate interest in partnership profits and capital of more than 50 percent.

(ii) Testing days.—The testing days shall be—

(I) the 1st day of the partnership taxable year (determined without regard to clause (i)), or

(II) the days during such representative period as the Secretary may prescribe.

(B) Further change not required for 3 years.—Except as provided in regulations necessary to prevent the avoidance of this section, if, by reason of paragraph (1)(B)(i), the taxable year of a partnership is changed, such partnership shall not be required to change to another taxable year for either of the 2 taxable years following the year of change.

(5) Application with other sections.—Except as provided in regulations, for purposes of determining the taxable year to which a partnership is required to change by reason of this subsection, changes in taxable years of other persons required by this subsection, section 441(i), section 584(h), section 644, or section 1378(a) shall be taken into account.

(c) Closing of partnership year.—

(1) General rule.—Except in the case of a termination of a partnership and except as provided in paragraph (2) of this subsection, the taxable year of a partnership shall not close as the result of the death of a partner, the entry of a new partner, the liquidation of a partner's interest in the partnership, or the sale or exchange of a partner's interest in the partnership.

(2) Treatment of dispositions.—

(A) Disposition of entire interest.—The taxable year of a partnership shall close with respect to a partner whose entire interest in the partnership terminates (whether by reason of death, liquidation, or otherwise).

(B) Disposition of less than entire interest.—The taxable year of a partnership shall not close (other than at the end of a partnership's taxable year as determined under subsection (b)(1)) with respect to a partner who sells or exchanges less than his entire interest in the partnership or with respect to a partner whose interest is reduced (whether by entry of a new partner, partial liquidation of a partner's interest, gift, or otherwise).

(d) Determination of distributive share when partner's interest changes.—

(1) In general.—Except as provided in paragraphs (2) and (3), if during any taxable year of the partnership there is a change in any partner's interest in the partnership, each partner's distributive share of any item of income, gain, loss, deduction, or credit of the partnership for such taxable year shall be determined by the use of any method prescribed by the Secretary by regulations which takes into account the varying interests of the partners in the partnership during such taxable year.

(2) Certain cash basis items prorated over period to which attributable.—

(A) In general.—If during any taxable year of the partnership there is a change in any partner's interest in the partnership, then (except to the extent provided in regulations) each partner's distributive share of any allocable cash basis item shall be determined—

(i) by assigning the appropriate portion of such item to each day in the period to which it is attributable, and

(ii) by allocating the portion assigned to any such day among the partners in proportion to their interests in the partnership at the close of such day.

(B) Allocable cash basis item.—For purposes of this paragraph, the term "allocable cash basis item" means any of the following items with respect to which the partnership uses the cash receipts and disbursements method of accounting:

(i) Interest.

(ii) Taxes.

(iii) Payments for services or for the use of property.

(iv) Any other item of a kind specified in regulations prescribed by the Secretary as being an item with respect to which the application of this paragraph is appropriate to avoid significant misstatements of the income of the partners.

(C) Items attributable to periods not within taxable year.—If any portion of any allocable cash basis item is attributable to—

(i) any period before the beginning of the taxable year, such portion shall be assigned under subparagraph (A)(i) to the first day of the taxable year, or

(ii) any period after the close of the taxable year, such portion shall be assigned under subparagraph (A)(i) to the last day of the taxable year.

(D) Treatment of deductible items attributable to prior periods.—If any portion of a deductible cash basis item is assigned under subparagraph (C)(i) to the first day of any taxable year—

(i) such portion shall be allocated among persons who are partners in the partnership during the period to which such portion is attributable in accordance with their varying interests in the partnership during such period, and

(ii) any amount allocated under clause (i) to a person who is not a partner in the partnership on such first day shall be capitalized by the partnership and treated in the manner provided for in section 755.

(3) Items attributable to interest in lower tier partnership prorated over entire taxable year.—If—

(A) during any taxable year of the partnership there is a change in any partner's interest in the partnership (hereinafter in this paragraph referred to as the "upper tier partnership"), and

(B) such partnership is a partner in another partnership (hereinafter in this paragraph referred to as the "lower tier partnership"),

then (except to the extent provided in regulations) each partner's distributive share of any item of the upper tier partnership attributable to the lower tier partnership shall be determined by assigning the appropriate portion (determined by applying principles similar to the principles of subparagraphs (C) and (D) of paragraph (2)) of each such item to the appropriate days during which the upper tier partnership is a partner in the lower tier partnership and by allocating the portion assigned to any such day among the partners in proportion to their interests in the upper tier partnership at the close of such day.

(4) Taxable year determined without regard to subsection (c)(2)(A).—For purposes of this subsection, the taxable year of a partnership shall be determined without regard to subsection (c)(2)(A).

§ 707. Transactions between partner and partnership

(a) Partner not acting in capacity as partner.—

(1) In general.—If a partner engages in a transaction with a partnership other than in his capacity as a member of such partnership, the transaction shall, except as otherwise provided in this section, be considered as occurring between the partnership and one who is not a partner.

(2) Treatment of payments to partners for property or services.—Under regulations prescribed by the Secretary—

(A) Treatment of certain services and transfers of property.—If—

(i) a partner performs services for a partnership or transfers property to a partnership,

(ii) there is a related direct or indirect allocation and distribution to such partner, and

(iii) the performance of such services (or such transfer) and the allocation and distribution, when viewed together, are properly characterized as a transaction occurring between the partnership and a partner acting other than in his capacity as a member of the partnership,

such allocation and distribution shall be treated as a transaction described in paragraph (1).

(B) Treatment of certain property transfers.—If—

(i) there is a direct or indirect transfer of money or other property by a partner to a partnership,

(ii) there is a related direct or indirect transfer of money or other property by the partnership to such partner (or another partner), and

(iii) the transfers described in clauses (i) and (ii), when viewed together, are properly characterized as a sale or exchange of property,

such transfers shall be treated either as a transaction described in paragraph (1) or as a transaction between 2 or more partners acting other than in their capacity as members of the partnership.

(b) Certain sales or exchanges of property with respect to controlled partnerships.—

(1) Losses disallowed.—No deduction shall be allowed in respect of losses from sales or exchanges of property (other than an interest in the partnership), directly or indirectly, between—

(A) a partnership and a person owning, directly or indirectly, more than 50 percent of the capital interest, or the profits interest, in such partnership, or

(B) two partnerships in which the same persons own, directly or indirectly, more than 50 percent of the capital interests or profits interests.

In the case of a subsequent sale or exchange by a transferee described in this paragraph, section 267(d) shall be applicable as if the loss were disallowed under section 267(a)(1). For purposes of section 267(a)(2), partnerships described in subparagraph (B) of this paragraph shall be treated as persons specified in section 267(b).

(2) Gains treated as ordinary income.—In the case of a sale or exchange, directly or indirectly, of property, which in the hands of the transferee, is property other than a capital asset as defined in section 1221—

(A) between a partnership and a person owning, directly or indirectly, more than 50 percent of the capital interest, or profits interest, in such partnership, or

(B) between two partnerships in which the same persons own, directly or indirectly, more than 50 percent of the capital interests or profits interests,

any gain recognized shall be considered as ordinary income.

(3) Ownership of a capital or profits interest.—For purposes of paragraphs (1) and (2) of this subsection, the ownership of a capital or profits interest in a partnership shall be determined in accordance with the rules for constructive ownership of stock provided in section 267(c) other than paragraph (3) of such section.

(c) Guaranteed payments.—To the extent determined without regard to the income of the partnership, payments to a partner for services or the use of capital shall be considered as made to one who is not a member of the partnership, but only for the purposes of section 61(a) (relating to gross income) and, subject to section 263, for purposes of section 162(a) (relating to trade or business expenses).

§ 708. Continuation of partnership

(a) General rule.—For purposes of this subchapter, an existing partnership shall be considered as continuing if it is not terminated.

(b) Termination.—

(1) General rule.—For purposes of subsection (a), a partnership shall be considered as terminated only if—

(A) no part of any business, financial operation, or venture of the partnership continues to be carried on by any of its partners in a partnership, or

(B) within a 12–month period there is a sale or exchange of 50 percent or more of the total interest in partnership capital and profits.

(2) Special rules.—

(A) Merger or consolidation.—In the case of the merger or consolidation of two or more partnerships, the resulting partnership shall, for purposes of this section, be considered the continuation of any merging or consolidating partnership whose members own an interest of more than 50 percent in the capital and profits of the resulting partnership.

(B) Division of a partnership.—In the case of a division of a partnership into two or more partnerships, the resulting partnerships (other than any resulting partnership the members of which had an interest of 50 percent or less in the capital and profits of the prior partnership) shall, for purposes of this section, be considered a continuation of the prior partnership.

§ 709. Treatment of organization and syndication fees

(a) General rule.—Except as provided in subsection (b), no deduction shall be allowed under this chapter to the partnership or to any partner for any amounts paid or incurred to organize a partnership or to promote the sale of (or to sell) an interest in such partnership.

(b) Deduction of organization fees.—

(1) Allowance of deduction.—If a partnership elects the application of this subsection (in accordance with regulations prescribed by the Secretary) with respect to any organizational expenses—

(A) the partnership shall be allowed a deduction for the taxable year in which the partnership begins business in an amount equal to the lesser of—

(i) the amount of organizational expenses with respect to the partnership, or

(ii) $5,000, reduced (but not below zero) by the amount by which such organizational expenses exceed $50,000, and

(B) the remainder of such organizational expenses shall be allowed as a deduction ratably over the 180–month period beginning with the month in which the partnership begins business.

(2) Dispositions before close of amortization period.—In any case in which a partnership is liquidated before the end of the period to which paragraph (1)(B) applies, any deferred expenses attributable to the partnership which were not allowed as a deduction by reason of this section may be deducted to the extent allowable under section 165.

(3) Organizational expenses defined.—The organizational expenses to which paragraph (1) applies, are expenditures which—

(A) are incident to the creation of the partnership;

(B) are chargeable to capital account; and

(C) are of a character which, if expended incident to the creation of a partnership having an ascertainable life, would be amortized over such life.

PART II—CONTRIBUTIONS, DISTRIBUTIONS, AND TRANSFERS

Subpart A—Contributions to a Partnership

§ 721. Nonrecognition of gain or loss on contribution

(a) General rule.—No gain or loss shall be recognized to a partnership or to any of its partners in the case of a contribution of property to the partnership in exchange for an interest in the partnership.

(b) Special rule.—Subsection (a) shall not apply to gain realized on a transfer of property to a partnership which would be treated as an investment company (within the meaning of section 351) if the partnership were incorporated.

(c) Regulations relating to certain transfers to partnerships.—The Secretary may provide by regulations that subsection (a) shall not apply to gain realized on the transfer of property to a partnership if such gain, when recognized, will be includible in the gross income of a person other than a United States person.

* * *

§ 722. Basis of contributing partner's interest

The basis of an interest in a partnership acquired by a contribution of property, including money, to the partnership shall be the amount of such money and the adjusted basis of such property to the contributing partner at the time of the contribution increased by the amount (if any) of gain recognized under section 721(b) to the contributing partner at such time.

§ 723. Basis of property contributed to partnership

The basis of property contributed to a partnership by a partner shall be the adjusted basis of such property to the contributing partner at the time of the contribution increased by the amount (if any) of gain recognized under section 721(b) to the contributing partner at such time.

§ 724. Character of gain or loss on contributed unrealized receivables, inventory items, and capital loss property

(a) Contributions of unrealized receivables.—In the case of any property which—

(1) was contributed to the partnership by a partner, and

(2) was an unrealized receivable in the hands of such partner immediately before such contribution,

any gain or loss recognized by the partnership on the disposition of such property shall be treated as ordinary income or ordinary loss, as the case may be.

(b) Contributions of inventory items.—In the case of any property which—

(1) was contributed to the partnership by a partner, and

(2) was an inventory item in the hands of such partner immediately before such contribution,

any gain or loss recognized by the partnership on the disposition of such property during the 5-year period beginning on the date of such contribution shall be treated as ordinary income or ordinary loss, as the case may be.

(c) Contributions of capital loss property.—In the case of any property which—

(1) was contributed by a partner to the partnership, and

(2) was a capital asset in the hands of such partner immediately before such contribution,

any loss recognized by the partnership on the disposition of such property during the 5-year period beginning on the date of such contribution shall be treated as a loss from the sale of a capital asset to the extent that, immediately before such contribution, the adjusted basis of such property in the hands of the partner exceeded the fair market value of such property.

(d) Definitions.—For purposes of this section—

(1) Unrealized receivable.—The term "unrealized receivable" has the meaning given such term by section 751(c) (determined by treating any reference to the partnership as referring to the partner).

(2) Inventory item.—The term "inventory item" has the meaning given such term by section 751(d) (determined by treating any reference to the partnership as referring to the partner and by applying section 1231 without regard to any holding period therein provided).

(3) Substituted basis property.—

(A) In general.—If any property described in subsection (a), (b), or (c) is disposed of in a nonrecognition transaction, the tax treatment which applies to such property under such subsection shall also apply to any substituted basis property resulting from such transaction. A similar rule shall also apply in the case of a series of non-recognition transactions.

(B) Exception for stock in C corporation.—Subparagraph (A) shall not apply to any stock in a C corporation received in an exchange described in section 351.

Subpart B—Distributions by a Partnership

§ 731. Extent of recognition of gain or loss on distribution

(a) Partners.—In the case of a distribution by a partnership to a partner—

(1) gain shall not be recognized to such partner, except to the extent that any money distributed exceeds the adjusted basis of such partner's interest in the partnership immediately before the distribution, and

(2) loss shall not be recognized to such partner, except that upon a distribution in liquidation of a partner's interest in a partnership where no property other than that described in subparagraph (A) or (B) is distributed to such partner, loss shall be recognized to the extent of the excess of the adjusted basis of such partner's interest in the partnership over the sum of—

(A) any money distributed, and

(B) the basis to the distributee, as determined under section 732, of any unrealized receivables (as defined in section 751(c)) and inventory (as defined in section 751(d)).

Any gain or loss recognized under this subsection shall be considered as gain or loss from the sale or exchange of the partnership interest of the distributee partner.

(b) Partnerships.—No gain or loss shall be recognized to a partnership on a distribution to a partner of property, including money.

(c) Treatment of marketable securities.—

(1) In general.—For purposes of subsection (a)(1) and section 737—

(A) the term "money" includes marketable securities, and

(B) such securities shall be taken into account at their fair market value as of the date of the distribution.

(2) Marketable securities.—For purposes of this subsection:

(A) In general.—The term "marketable securities" means financial instruments and foreign currencies which are, as of the date of the distribution, actively traded (within the meaning of section 1092(d)(1)).

(B) Other property.—Such term includes—

(i) any interest in—

(I) a common trust fund, or

(II) a regulated investment company which is offering for sale or has outstanding any redeemable security (as defined in section 2(a)(32) of the Investment Company Act of 1940) of which it is the issuer,

(ii) any financial instrument which, pursuant to its terms or any other arrangement, is readily convertible into, or exchangeable for, money or marketable securities,

(iii) any financial instrument the value of which is determined substantially by reference to marketable securities,

(iv) except to the extent provided in regulations prescribed by the Secretary, any interest in a precious metal which, as of the date of the distribution, is actively traded (within the meaning of section 1092(d)(1)) unless such metal was produced, used, or held in the active conduct of a trade or business by the partnership,

(v) except as otherwise provided in regulations prescribed by the Secretary, interests in any entity if substantially all of the assets of such entity consist (directly or indirectly) of marketable securities, money, or both, and

(vi) to the extent provided in regulations prescribed by the Secretary, any interest in an entity not described in clause (v) but only to the extent of the value of such interest which is attributable to marketable securities, money, or both.

(C) Financial instrument.—The term "financial instrument" includes stocks and other equity interests, evidences of indebtedness, options, forward or futures contracts, notional principal contracts, and derivatives.

(3) Exceptions.—

(A) In general.—Paragraph (1) shall not apply to the distribution from a partnership of a marketable security to a partner if—

(i) the security was contributed to the partnership by such partner, except to the extent that the value of the distributed security is attributable to marketable securities or money contributed (directly or indirectly) to the entity to which the distributed security relates,

(ii) to the extent provided in regulations prescribed by the Secretary, the property was not a marketable security when acquired by such partnership, or

(iii) such partnership is an investment partnership and such partner is an eligible partner thereof.

(B) Limitation on gain recognized.—In the case of a distribution of marketable securities to a partner, the amount taken into account under paragraph (1) shall be reduced (but not below zero) by the excess (if any) of—

(i) such partner's distributive share of the net gain which would be recognized if all of the marketable securities of the same class and issuer as the distributed securities held by the partnership were sold (immediately before the transaction to which the distribution relates) by the partnership for fair market value, over

(ii) such partner's distributive share of the net gain which is attributable to the marketable securities of the same class and issuer as the distributed securities held by the partnership immediately after the transaction, determined by using the same fair market value as used under clause (i).

Under regulations prescribed by the Secretary, all marketable securities held by the partnership may be treated as marketable securities of the same class and issuer as the distributed securities.

(C) Definitions relating to investment partnerships.—For purposes of subparagraph (A)(iii):

(i) Investment partnership.—The term "investment partnership" means any partnership which has never been engaged in a trade or business and substantially all of the assets (by value) of which have always consisted of—

(I) money,

(II) stock in a corporation,

(III) notes, bonds, debentures, or other evidences of indebtedness,

(IV) interest rate, currency, or equity notional principal contracts,

(V) foreign currencies,

(VI) interests in or derivative financial instruments (including options, forward or futures contracts, short positions, and similar financial instruments) in any asset described in any other subclause of this clause or in any commodity traded on or subject to the rules of a board of trade or commodity exchange,

(VII) other assets specified in regulations prescribed by the Secretary, or

(VIII) any combination of the foregoing.

(ii) Exception for certain activities.—A partnership shall not be treated as engaged in a trade or business by reason of—

(I) any activity undertaken as an investor, trader, or dealer in any asset described in clause (i), or

(II) any other activity specified in regulations prescribed by the Secretary.

(iii) Eligible partner.—

(I) In general.—The term "eligible partner" means any partner who, before the date of the distribution, did not contribute to the partnership any property other than assets described in clause (i).

(II) Exception for certain nonrecognition transactions.—The term "eligible partner" shall not include the transferor or transferee in a nonrecognition transaction involving a transfer of any portion of an interest in a partnership with respect to which the transferor was not an eligible partner.

(iv) Look-thru of partnership tiers.—Except as otherwise provided in regulations prescribed by the Secretary—

(I) a partnership shall be treated as engaged in any trade or business engaged in by, and as holding (instead of a partnership interest) a proportionate share of the assets of, any other partnership in which the partnership holds a partnership interest, and

(II) a partner who contributes to a partnership an interest in another partnership shall be treated as contributing a proportionate share of the assets of the other partnership.

If the preceding sentence does not apply under such regulations with respect to any interest held by a partnership in another partnership, the interest in such other partnership shall be treated as if it were specified in a subclause of clause (i).

(4) Basis of securities distributed.—

(A) In general.—The basis of marketable securities with respect to which gain is recognized by reason of this subsection shall be—

(i) their basis determined under section 732, increased by

(ii) the amount of such gain.

(B) Allocation of basis increase.—Any increase in basis attributable to the gain described in subparagraph (A)(ii) shall be allocated to marketable securities in proportion to their respective amounts of unrealized appreciation before such increase.

(5) Subsection disregarded in determining basis of partner's interest in partnership and of basis of partnership property.—Sections 733 and 734 shall be applied as if no gain were recognized, and no adjustment were made to the basis of property, under this subsection.

(6) Character of gain recognized.—In the case of a distribution of a marketable security which is an unrealized receivable (as defined in section 751(c)) or an inventory item (as defined in section 751(d)), any gain recognized under this subsection shall be treated as ordinary income to the extent of any increase in the basis of such security attributable to the gain described in paragraph (4)(A)(ii).

(7) Regulations.—The Secretary shall prescribe such regulations as may be necessary or appropriate to carry out the purposes of this subsection, including regulations to prevent the avoidance of such purposes.

(d) Exceptions.—This section shall not apply to the extent otherwise provided by section 736 (relating to payments to a retiring partner or a deceased partner's successor in interest), section 751 (relating to unrealized receivables and inventory items), and section 737 (relating to recognition of precontribution gain in case of certain distributions).

§ 732. Basis of distributed property other than money

(a) Distributions other than in liquidation of a partner's interest.—

(1) General rule.—The basis of property (other than money) distributed by a partnership to a partner other than in liquidation of the partner's interest shall, except as provided in paragraph (2), be its adjusted basis to the partnership immediately before such distribution.

(2) Limitation.—The basis to the distributee partner of property to which paragraph (1) is applicable shall not exceed the adjusted basis of such partner's interest in the partnership reduced by any money distributed in the same transaction.

(b) Distributions in liquidation.—The basis of property (other than money) distributed by a partnership to a partner in liquidation of the partner's interest shall be an amount equal to the adjusted basis of such partner's interest in the partnership reduced by any money distributed in the same transaction.

(c) Allocation of basis.—

(1) In general.—The basis of distributed properties to which subsection (a)(2) or (b) is applicable shall be allocated—

(A)(i) first to any unrealized receivables (as defined in section 751(c)) and inventory items (as defined in section 751(d)) in an amount equal to the adjusted basis of each such property to the partnership, and

(ii) if the basis to be allocated is less than the sum of the adjusted bases of such properties to the partnership, then, to the extent any decrease is required in order to have the adjusted bases of such properties equal the basis to be allocated, in the manner provided in paragraph (3), and

(B) to the extent of any basis remaining after the allocation under subparagraph (A), to other distributed properties—

(i) first by assigning to each such other property such other property's adjusted basis to the partnership, and

(ii) then, to the extent any increase or decrease in basis is required in order to have the adjusted bases of such other distributed properties equal such remaining basis, in the manner provided in paragraph (2) or (3), whichever is appropriate.

(2) Method of allocating increase.—Any increase required under paragraph (1)(B) shall be allocated among the properties—

(A) first to properties with unrealized appreciation in proportion to their respective amounts of unrealized appreciation before such increase (but only to the extent of each property's unrealized appreciation), and

(B) then, to the extent such increase is not allocated under subparagraph (A), in proportion to their respective fair market values.

(3) Method of allocating decrease.—Any decrease required under paragraph (1)(A) or (1)(B) shall be allocated—

(A) first to properties with unrealized depreciation in proportion to their respective amounts of unrealized depreciation before such decrease (but only to the extent of each property's unrealized depreciation), and

(B) then, to the extent such decrease is not allocated under subparagraph (A), in proportion to their respective adjusted bases (as adjusted under subparagraph (A)).

(d) Special partnership basis to transferee.—For purposes of subsections (a), (b), and (c), a partner who acquired all or a part of his interest by a transfer with respect to which the election provided in section 754 is not in effect, and to whom a distribution of property (other than money) is made with respect to the transferred interest within 2 years after such transfer, may elect, under regulations prescribed by the Secretary, to treat as the adjusted partnership basis of such property the adjusted basis such property would have if the adjustment provided in section 743(b) were in effect with respect to the partnership property. The Secretary may by regulations require the application of this subsection in the case of a distribution to a transferee partner, whether or not made within 2 years after the transfer, if at the time of the transfer the fair market value of the partnership property (other than money) exceeded 110 percent of its adjusted basis to the partnership.

(e) Exception.—This section shall not apply to the extent that a distribution is treated as a sale or exchange of property under section 751(b) (relating to unrealized receivables and inventory items).

(f) Corresponding adjustment to basis of assets of a distributed corporation controlled by a corporate partner.—

(1) In general.—If—

(A) a corporation (hereafter in this subsection referred to as the "corporate partner") receives a distribution from a partnership of stock in another corporation (hereafter in this subsection referred to as the "distributed corporation"),

(B) the corporate partner has control of the distributed corporation immediately after the distribution or at any time thereafter, and

(C) the partnership's adjusted basis in such stock immediately before the distribution exceeded the corporate partner's adjusted basis in such stock immediately after the distribution,

then an amount equal to such excess shall be applied to reduce (in accordance with subsection (c)) the basis of property held by the distributed corporation at such time (or, if the corporate partner does not control the distributed corporation at such time, at the time the corporate partner first has such control).

(2) Exception for certain distributions before control acquired.—Paragraph (1) shall not apply to any distribution of stock in the distributed corporation if—

(A) the corporate partner does not have control of such corporation immediately after such distribution, and

(B) the corporate partner establishes to the satisfaction of the Secretary that such distribution was not part of a plan or arrangement to acquire control of the distributed corporation.

(3) Limitations on basis reduction.—

(A) In general.—The amount of the reduction under paragraph (1) shall not exceed the amount by which the sum of the aggregate adjusted bases of the property and the amount of money of the distributed corporation exceeds the corporate partner's adjusted basis in the stock of the distributed corporation.

(B) Reduction not to exceed adjusted basis of property.— No reduction under paragraph (1) in the basis of any property shall exceed the adjusted basis of such property (determined without regard to such reduction).

(4) Gain recognition where reduction limited.—If the amount of any reduction under paragraph (1) (determined after the application of paragraph (3)(A)) exceeds the aggregate adjusted bases of the property of the distributed corporation—

(A) such excess shall be recognized by the corporate partner as long-term capital gain, and

(B) the corporate partner's adjusted basis in the stock of the distributed corporation shall be increased by such excess.

(5) Control.— For purposes of this subsection, the term "control" means ownership of stock meeting the requirements of section 1504(a)(2).

(6) Indirect distributions.—For purposes of paragraph (1), if a corporation acquires (other than in a distribution from a partnership) stock the basis of which is determined (by reason of being distributed from a partnership) in whole or in part by reference to subsection (a)(2) or (b), the corporation shall be treated as receiving a distribution of such stock from a partnership.

(7) Special rule for stock in controlled corporation.—If the property held by a distributed corporation is stock in a corporation which the distributed corporation controls, this subsection shall be applied to reduce the basis of the property of such controlled corporation. This subsection shall be reapplied to any property of any controlled corporation which is stock in a corporation which it controls.

(8) Regulations.—The Secretary shall prescribe such regulations as may be necessary to carry out the purposes of this subsection, including regulations to avoid double counting and to prevent the abuse of such purposes.

§ 733. Basis of distributee partner's interest

In the case of a distribution by a partnership to a partner other than in liquidation of a partner's interest, the adjusted basis to such partner of his interest in the partnership shall be reduced (but not below zero) by—

(1) the amount of any money distributed to such partner, and

(2) the amount of the basis to such partner of distributed property other than money, as determined under section 732.

§ 734. Optional adjustment to basis of undistributed partnership property

(a) General rule.—The basis of partnership property shall not be adjusted as the result of a distribution of property to a partner unless the election, provided in section 754 (relating to optional adjustment to basis of partnership property), is in effect with respect to such partnership or unless there is a substantial basis reduction.

(b) Method of adjustment.—In the case of a distribution of property to a partner by a partnership with respect to which the election provided in section 754 is in effect or with respect to which there is a substantial basis reduction, the partnership shall—

(1) increase the adjusted basis of partnership property by—

(A) the amount of any gain recognized to the distributee partner with respect to such distribution under section 731(a)(1), and

(B) in the case of distributed property to which section 732(a)(2) or (b) applies, the excess of the adjusted basis of the distributed property to the partnership immediately before the distribution (as adjusted by section 732(d)) over the basis of the distributed property to the distributee, as determined under section 732, or

(2) decrease the adjusted basis of partnership property by—

(A) the amount of any loss recognized to the distributee partner with respect to such distribution under section 731(a)(2), and

(B) in the case of distributed property to which section 732(b) applies, the excess of the basis of the distributed property to the distributee, as determined under section 732, over the adjusted basis of the distributed property to the partnership immediately before such distribution (as adjusted by section 732(d)).

Paragraph (1)(B) shall not apply to any distributed property which is an interest in another partnership with respect to which the election provided in section 754 is not in effect.

(c) Allocation of basis.—The allocation of basis among partnership properties where subsection (b) is applicable shall be made in accordance with the rules provided in section 755.

(d) Substantial basis reduction.—

(1) In general.—For purposes of this section, there is a substantial basis reduction with respect to a distribution if the sum of the amounts described in subparagraphs (A) and (B) of subsection (b)(2) exceeds $250,000.

(2) Regulations.—For regulations to carry out this subsection, see section 743(d)(2).

(e) Exception for securitization partnerships.—For purposes of this section, a securitization partnership (as defined in section 743(f)) shall not be treated as having a substantial basis reduction with respect to any distribution of property to a partner.

§ 735. Character of gain or loss on disposition of distributed property

(a) Sale or exchange of certain distributed property.—

(1) Unrealized receivables.—Gain or loss on the disposition by a distributee partner of unrealized receivables (as defined in section 751(c)) distributed by a partnership, shall be considered as ordinary income or as ordinary loss, as the case may be.

(2) Inventory items.—Gain or loss on the sale or exchange by a distributee partner of inventory items (as defined in section 751(d)) distributed by a partnership shall, if sold or exchanged within 5 years from the date of the distribution, be considered as ordinary income or as ordinary loss, as the case may be.

(b) Holding period for distributed property.—In determining the period for which a partner has held property received in a distribution from a partnership (other than for purposes of subsection (a)(2)), there shall be included the holding period of the partnership, as determined under section 1223, with respect to such property.

(c) Special rules.—

(1) Waiver of holding periods contained in section 1231.—For purposes of this section, section 751(d) (defining inventory item) shall be applied without regard to any holding period in section 1231(b).

(2) Substituted basis property.—

(A) In general.—If any property described in subsection (a) is disposed of in a nonrecognition transaction, the tax treatment which applies to such property under such subsection shall also apply to any substituted basis property resulting from such transaction. A similar rule shall also apply in the case of a series of nonrecognition transactions.

(B) Exception for stock in C corporation.—Subparagraph (A) shall not apply to any stock in a C corporation received in an exchange described in section 351.

§ 736. Payments to a retiring partner or a deceased partner's successor in interest

(a) Payments considered as distributive share or guaranteed payment.—Payments made in liquidation of the interest of a retiring partner or a deceased partner shall, except as provided in subsection (b), be considered—

(1) as a distributive share to the recipient of partnership income if the amount thereof is determined with regard to the income of the partnership, or

(2) as a guaranteed payment described in section 707(c) if the amount thereof is determined without regard to the income of the partnership.

(b) Payments for interest in partnership.—

(1) General rule.—Payments made in liquidation of the interest of a retiring partner or a deceased partner shall, to the extent such payments (other than payments described in paragraph (2)) are determined, under regulations prescribed by the Secretary, to be made in exchange for the interest of such partner in partnership property, be considered as a distribution by the partnership and not as a distributive share or guaranteed payment under subsection (a).

(2) Special rules.—For purposes of this subsection, payments in exchange for an interest in partnership property shall not include amounts paid for—

(A) unrealized receivables of the partnership (as defined in section 751(c)), or

(B) good will of the partnership, except to the extent that the partnership agreement provides for a payment with respect to good will.

(3) Limitation on application of paragraph (2).—Paragraph (2) shall apply only if—

(A) capital is not a material income-producing factor for the partnership, and

(B) the retiring or deceased partner was a general partner in the partnership.

§ 737. Recognition of precontribution gain in case of certain distributions to contributing partner

(a) General rule.—In the case of any distribution by a partnership to a partner, such partner shall be treated as recognizing gain in an amount equal to the lesser of—

(1) the excess (if any) of (A) the fair market value of property (other than money) received in the distribution over (B) the adjusted basis of such partner's interest in the partnership immediately before the distribution reduced (but not below zero) by the amount of money received in the distribution, or

(2) the net precontribution gain of the partner.

Gain recognized under the preceding sentence shall be in addition to any gain recognized under section 731. The character of such gain shall be determined by reference to the proportionate character of the net precontribution gain.

(b) Net precontribution gain.—For purposes of this section, the term "net precontribution gain" means the net gain (if any) which would have been recognized by the distributee partner under section 704(c)(1)(B) if all property which—

(1) had been contributed to the partnership by the distributee partner within 7 years of the distribution, and

(2) is held by such partnership immediately before the distribution,

had been distributed by such partnership to another partner.

(c) Basis rules.—

(1) Partner's interest.—The adjusted basis of a partner's interest in a partnership shall be increased by the amount of any gain recognized by such partner under subsection (a). For purposes of determining the basis of the distributed property (other than money), such increase shall be treated as occurring immediately before the distribution.

(2) Partnership's basis in contributed property.—Appropriate adjustments shall be made to the adjusted basis of the partnership in the contributed property referred to in subsection (b) to reflect gain recognized under subsection (a).

(d) Exceptions.—

(1) Distributions of previously contributed property.—If any portion of the property distributed consists of property which had been contributed by the distributee partner to the partnership, such property shall not be taken into account under subsection (a)(1) and shall not be taken into account in determining the amount of the net precontribution gain. If the property distributed consists of an interest in an entity, the preceding sentence shall not apply to the extent that the value of such interest is attributable to property contributed to such entity after such interest had been contributed to the partnership.

(2) Coordination with section 751.—This section shall not apply to the extent section 751(b) applies to such distribution.

* * *

Subpart C—Transfers of Interests in a Partnership

§ 741. Recognition and character of gain or loss on sale or exchange

In the case of a sale or exchange of an interest in a partnership, gain or loss shall be recognized to the transferor partner. Such gain or loss shall be considered as gain or loss from the sale or exchange of a capital asset, except as otherwise provided in section 751 (relating to unrealized receivables and inventory items).

§ 742. Basis of transferee partner's interest

The basis of an interest in a partnership acquired other than by contribution shall be determined under part II of subchapter O (sec. 1011 and following).

§ 743. Optional adjustment to basis of partnership property

(a) General rule.—The basis of partnership property shall not be adjusted as the result of a transfer of an interest in a partnership by sale or exchange or on the death of a partner unless the election provided by section 754 (relating to optional adjustment to basis of partnership property) is in effect with respect to such partnership or unless the partnership has a substantial built-in loss immediately after such transfer.

(b) Adjustment to basis of partnership property.—In the case of a transfer of an interest in a partnership by sale or exchange or upon the death of a partner, a partnership with respect to which the election provided in section 754 is in effect or which has a has a substantial built-in loss immediately after such transfer shall—

(1) increase the adjusted basis of the partnership property by the excess of the basis to the transferee partner of his interest in the partnership over his proportionate share of the adjusted basis of the partnership property, or

(2) decrease the adjusted basis of the partnership property by the excess of the transferee partner's proportionate share of the adjusted basis of the partnership property over the basis of his interest in the partnership.

Under regulations prescribed by the Secretary, such increase or decrease shall constitute an adjustment to the basis of partnership property with respect to the transferee partner only. A partner's proportionate share of the adjusted basis of partnership property shall be determined in accordance with his interest in partnership capital and, in the case of property contributed to the partnership by a partner, section 704(c) (relating to contributed property) shall apply in determining such share. In the case of an adjustment under this subsection to the basis of partnership property subject to depletion, any depletion allowable shall be determined separately for the transferee partner with respect to his interest in such property.

(c) Allocation of basis.—The allocation of basis among partnership properties where subsection (b) is applicable shall be made in accordance with the rules provided in section 755.

(d) Substantial built-in loss.—

(1) In general.—For purposes of this section, a partnership has a substantial built-in loss with respect to a transfer of an interest in a partnership if the partnership's adjusted basis in the partnership property exceeds by more than $250,000 the fair market value of such property.

(2) Regulations.—The Secretary shall prescribe such regulations as may be appropriate to carry out the purposes of paragraph (1) and section 734(d), including regulations aggregating related partnerships and disregarding property acquired by the partnership in an attempt to avoid such purposes.

(e) Alternative rules for electing investment partnerships.—

(1) No adjustment of partnership basis.—For purposes of this section, an electing investment partnership shall not be treated as having a substantial built-in loss with respect to any transfer occurring while the election under paragraph (6)(A) is in effect.

(2) Loss deferral for transferee partner.—In the case of a transfer of an interest in an electing investment partnership, the transferee partner's distributive share of losses (without regard to gains) from the sale or exchange of partnership property shall not be allowed except to the extent that it is established that such losses exceed the loss (if any) recognized by the transferor (or any prior transferor to the extent not fully offset by a prior disallowance under this paragraph) on the transfer of the partnership interest.

(3) No reduction in partnership basis.—Losses disallowed under paragraph (2) shall not decrease the transferee partner's basis in the partnership interest.

(4) Effect of termination of partnership.—This subsection shall be applied without regard to any termination of a partnership under section 708(b)(1)(B).

(5) Certain basis reductions treated as losses.—In the case of a transferee partner whose basis in property distributed by the partnership is reduced under section 732(a)(2), the amount of the loss recognized by the transferor on the transfer of the partnership interest which is taken into account under paragraph (2) shall be reduced by the amount of such basis reduction.

(6) Electing investment partnership.—For purposes of this subsection, the term "electing investment partnership" means any partnership if—

(A) the partnership makes an election to have this subsection apply,

(B) the partnership would be an investment company under section 3(a)(1)(A) of the Investment Company Act of 1940 but for an exemption under paragraph (1) or (7) of section 3(c) of such Act,

(C) such partnership has never been engaged in a trade or business,

(D) substantially all of the assets of such partnership are held for investment,

(E) at least 95 percent of the assets contributed to such partnership consist of money,

(F) no assets contributed to such partnership had an adjusted basis in excess of fair market value at the time of contribution,

(G) all partnership interests of such partnership are issued by such partnership pursuant to a private offering before the date which is 24 months after the date of the first capital contribution to such partnership,

(H) the partnership agreement of such partnership has substantive restrictions on each partner's ability to cause a redemption of the partner's interest, and

(I) the partnership agreement of such partnership provides for a term that is not in excess of 15 years.

The election described in subparagraph (A), once made, shall be irrevocable except with the consent of the Secretary.

(7) Regulations.—The Secretary shall prescribe such regulations as may be appropriate to carry out the purposes of this subsection, including regulations for applying this subsection to tiered partnerships.

(f) Exception for securitization partnerships.—

(1) No adjustment of partnership basis.—For purposes of this section, a securitization partnership shall not be treated as having a substantial built-in loss with respect to any transfer.

(2) Securitization partnership.—For purposes of paragraph (1), the term "securitization partnership" means any partnership the sole business activity of which is to issue securities which provide for a fixed principal (or similar) amount and which are primarily serviced by the cash flows of a discrete pool (either fixed or revolving) of receivables or other financial assets that by their terms convert into cash in a finite period, but only if the sponsor of the pool reasonably believes that the receivables and other financial assets comprising the pool are not acquired so as to be disposed of.

Subpart D—Provisions Common to Other Subparts

§ 751. Unrealized receivables and inventory items

(a) Sale or exchange of interest in partnership.—The amount of any money, or the fair market value of any property, received by a transferor partner in exchange for all or a part of his interest in the partnership attributable to—

(1) unrealized receivables of the partnership, or

(2) inventory items of the partnership,

shall be considered as an amount realized from the sale or exchange of property other than a capital asset.

(b) Certain distributions treated as sales or exchanges.—

(1) General rule.—To the extent a partner receives in a distribution—

(A) partnership property which is—

(i) unrealized receivables, or

(ii) inventory items which have appreciated substantially in value,

in exchange for all or a part of his interest in other partnership property (including money), or

(B) partnership property (including money) other than property described in subparagraph (A)(i) or (ii) in exchange for all or a part of his interest in partnership property described in subparagraph (A)(i) or (ii),

such transactions shall, under regulations prescribed by the Secretary, be considered as a sale or exchange of such property between the distributee and the partnership (as constituted after the distribution).

(2) Exceptions.—Paragraph (1) shall not apply to—

(A) a distribution of property which the distributee contributed to the partnership, or

(B) payments, described in section 736(a), to a retiring partner or successor in interest of a deceased partner.

(3) Substantial appreciation.—For purposes of paragraph (1)—

(A) In general.—Inventory items of the partnership shall be considered to have appreciated substantially in value if their fair market value exceeds 120 percent of the adjusted basis to the partnership of such property.

(B) Certain property excluded.—For purposes of subparagraph (A), there shall be excluded any inventory property if a principal purpose for acquiring such property was to avoid the provisions of this subsection relating to inventory items.

(c) Unrealized receivables.—For purposes of this subchapter, the term "unrealized receivables" includes, to the extent not previously includible in income under the method of accounting used by the partnership, any rights (contractual or otherwise) to payment for—

(1) goods delivered, or to be delivered, to the extent the proceeds therefrom would be treated as amounts received from the sale or exchange of property other than a capital asset, or

(2) services rendered, or to be rendered.

For purposes of this section and sections 731, 732, and 741 (but not for purposes of section 736), such term also includes mining property (as defined in section 617(f)(2)), stock in a DISC (as described in section 992(a)), section 1245 property (as defined in section 1245(a)(3)), stock in certain foreign corporations (as described in section 1248), section 1250 property (as defined in section 1250(c)), farm land (as defined in section 1252(a)), franchises, trademarks, or trade names (referred to in section 1253(a)), and an oil, gas, or geothermal property (described in section 1254) but only to the extent of the amount which would be treated as gain to which section 617(d)(1), 995(c), 1245(a), 1248(a), 1250(a), 1252(a), 1253(a), or 1254(a) would apply if (at the time of the transaction described in this section or sections 731, 732, or 741, as the case may be) such property had been sold by the partnership at its fair market value. For purposes of this section and sections 731, 732, and 741 (but not for purposes of section 736), such term also includes any market discount bond (as defined in section 1278) and any short-term obligation (as defined in section 1283) but only to the extent of the amount which would be treated as ordinary income if (at the time of the transaction described in this section or section 731, 732, or 741, as the case may be) such property had been sold by the partnership.

(d) Inventory items.—For purposes of this subchapter, the term "inventory items" means—

(1) property of the partnership of the kind described in section 1221(a)(1),

(2) any other property of the partnership which, on sale or exchange by the partnership, would be considered property other than a capital asset and other than property described in section 1231, and

(3) any other property held by the partnership which, if held by the selling or distributee partner, would be considered property of the type described in paragraph (1), or (2).

* * *

(f) Special rules in the case of tiered partnerships, etc.—In determining whether property of a partnership is—

(1) an unrealized receivable, or

(2) an inventory item,

such partnership shall be treated as owning its proportionate share of the property of any other partnership in which it is a partner. Under regulations, rules similar to the rules of the preceding sentence shall also apply in the case of interests in trusts.

§ 752. Treatment of certain liabilities

(a) Increase in partner's liabilities.—Any increase in a partner's share of the liabilities of a partnership, or any increase in a partner's individual liabilities by reason of the assumption by such partner of partnership liabilities, shall be considered as a contribution of money by such partner to the partnership.

(b) Decrease in partner's liabilities.—Any decrease in a partner's share of the liabilities of a partnership, or any decrease in a partner's individual liabilities by reason of the assumption by the partnership of such individual liabilities, shall be considered as a distribution of money to the partner by the partnership.

(c) Liability to which property is subject.—For purposes of this section, a liability to which property is subject shall, to the extent of the fair market value of such property, be considered as a liability of the owner of the property.

(d) Sale or exchange of an interest.—In the case of a sale or exchange of an interest in a partnership, liabilities shall be treated in the same manner as liabilities in connection with the sale or exchange of property not associated with partnerships.

§ 753. Partner receiving income in respect of decedent

The amount includible in the gross income of a successor in interest of a deceased partner under section 736(a) shall be considered income in respect of a decedent under section 691.

§ 754. Manner of electing optional adjustment to basis of partnership property

If a partnership files an election, in accordance with regulations prescribed by the Secretary, the basis of partnership property shall be adjusted, in the case of a distribution of property, in the manner provided in section 734 and, in the case of a transfer of a partnership interest, in the manner provided in section 743. Such an election shall apply with respect to all distributions of property by the partnership and to all transfers of interests in the partnership during the taxable year with respect to which such election was filed and all subsequent taxable years. Such election may be revoked by the partnership, subject to such limitations as may be provided by regulations prescribed by the Secretary.

§ 755. Rules for allocation of basis

(a) General rule.—Any increase or decrease in the adjusted basis of partnership property under section 734(b) (relating to the optional adjustment to the basis of undistributed partnership property) or section 743(b) (relating to the optional adjustment to the basis of partnership property in the case of a transfer of an interest in a partnership) shall, except as provided in subsection (b), be allocated—

(1) in a manner which has the effect of reducing the difference between the fair market value and the adjusted basis of partnership properties, or

(2) in any other manner permitted by regulations prescribed by the Secretary.

(b) Special rule.—In applying the allocation rules provided in subsection (a), increases or decreases in the adjusted basis of partnership property arising from a distribution of, or a transfer of an interest attributable to, property consisting of—

(1) capital assets and property described in section 1231(b), or

(2) any other property of the partnership,

shall be allocated to partnership property of a like character except that the basis of any such partnership property shall not be reduced below zero. If, in the case of a distribution, the adjustment to basis of property described in paragraph (1) or (2) is prevented by the absence of such property or by insufficient adjusted basis for such property, such adjustment shall be applied to subsequently acquired property of a like character in accordance with regulations prescribed by the Secretary.

* * *

PART III—DEFINITIONS

§ 761. Terms defined

(a) Partnership.—For purposes of this subtitle, the term "partnership" includes a syndicate, group, pool, joint venture, or other unincorporated organization through or by means of which any business, financial operation, or venture is carried on, and which is not, within the meaning of this title, a corporation or a trust or estate. Under regulations the Secretary may, at the election of all the members of an unincorporated organization, exclude such organization from the application of all or part of this subchapter, if it is availed of—

(1) for investment purposes only and not for the active conduct of a business,

(2) for the joint production, extraction, or use of property, but not for the purpose of selling services or property produced or extracted, or

(3) by dealers in securities for a short period for the purpose of underwriting, selling, or distributing a particular issue of securities,

if the income of the members of the organization may be adequately determined without the computation of partnership taxable income.

(b) Partner.—For purposes of this subtitle, the term "partner" means a member of a partnership.

(c) Partnership agreement.—For purposes of this subchapter, a partnership agreement includes any modifications of the partnership agreement made prior to, or at, the time prescribed by law for the filing of the partnership return for the taxable year (not including extensions) which are agreed to by all the partners, or which are adopted in such other manner as may be provided by the partnership agreement.

(d) Liquidation of a partner's interest.—For purposes of this subchapter, the term "liquidation of a partner's interest" means the termination of a partner's entire interest in a partnership by means of a distribution, or a series of distributions, to the partner by the partnership.

(e) Distributions partnership interests treated as exchanges.—Except as otherwise provided in regulations, for purposes of—

(1) section 708 (relating to continuation of partnership),

(2) section 743 (relating to optional adjustment to basis of partnership property), and

(3) any other provision of this subchapter specified in regulations prescribed by the Secretary, any distribution of an interest in a partnership (not otherwise treated as an exchange) shall be treated as an exchange.

(f) Qualified joint venture.—

(1) In general.—In the case of a qualified joint venture conducted by a husband and wife who file a joint return for the taxable year, for purposes of this title—

(A) such joint venture shall not be treated as a partnership,

(B) all items of income, gain, loss, deduction, and credit shall be divided between the spouses in accordance with their respective interests in the venture, and

(C) each spouse shall take into account such spouse's respective share of such items as if they were attributable to a trade or business conducted by such spouse as a sole proprietor.

(2) Qualified joint venture.—For purposes of paragraph (1), the term "qualified joint venture" means any joint venture involving the conduct of a trade or business if—

(A) the only members of such joint venture are a husband and wife,

(B) both spouses materially participate (within the meaning of section 469(h) without regard to paragraph (5) thereof) in such trade or business, and

(C) both spouses elect the application of this subsection.

(g) Cross reference.—

For rules in the case of the sale, exchange, liquidation, or reduction of a partner's interest, see sections 704(b) and 706(c)(2).

PART IV—SPECIAL RULES FOR ELECTING LARGE PARTNERSHIPS

§ 771. Application of subchapter to electing large partnerships

The preceding provisions of this subchapter to the extent inconsistent with the provisions of this part shall not apply to an electing large partnership and its partners.

§ 772. Simplified flow-through

(a) General rule.—In determining the income tax of a partner of an electing large partnership, such partner shall take into account separately such partner's distributive share of the partnership's—

(1) taxable income or loss from passive loss limitation activities,

(2) taxable income or loss from other activities,

(3) net capital gain (or net capital loss)—

(A) to the extent allocable to passive loss limitation activities, and

(B) to the extent allocable to other activities,

(4) tax-exempt interest,

(5) applicable net AMT adjustment separately computed for—

(A) passive loss limitation activities, and

(B) other activities,

(6) general credits,

(7) low-income housing credit determined under section 42,

(8) rehabilitation credit determined under section 47,

(9) foreign income taxes, and

(10) other items to the extent that the Secretary determines that the separate treatment of such items is appropriate.

(b) Separate computations.—In determining the amounts required under subsection (a) to be separately taken into account by any partner, this section and section 773 shall be applied separately with respect to such partner by taking into account such partner's distributive share of the items of income, gain, loss, deduction, or credit of the partnership.

(c) Treatment at partner level.—

(1) In general.—Except as provided in this subsection, rules similar to the rules of section 702(b) shall apply to any partner's distributive share of the amounts referred to in subsection (a).

(2) Income or loss from passive loss limitation activities.—For purposes of this chapter, any partner's distributive share of any income or loss described in subsection (a)(1) shall be treated as an item of income or loss (as the case may be) from the conduct of a trade or business which is a single passive activity (as defined in section 469). A similar rule shall apply to a partner's distributive share of amounts referred to in paragraphs (3)(A) and (5)(A) of subsection (a).

(3) Income or loss from other activities.—

(A) In general.—For purposes of this chapter, any partner's distributive share of any income or loss described in subsection (a)(2) shall be treated as an item of income or expense (as the case may be) with respect to property held for investment.

(B) Deductions for loss not subject to section 67.—The deduction under section 212 for any loss described in subparagraph (A) shall not be treated as a miscellaneous itemized deduction for purposes of section 67.

* * *

(d) Operating rules.—For purposes of this section—

(1) Passive loss limitation activity.—The term "passive loss limitation activity" means—

(A) any activity which involves the conduct of a trade or business, and

(B) any rental activity.

For purposes of the preceding sentence, the term "trade or business" includes any activity treated as a trade or business under paragraph (5) or (6) of section 469(c).

* * *

(f) Special rules for applying passive loss limitations.—If any person holds an interest in an electing large partnership other than as a limited partner—

(1) paragraph (2) of subsection (c) shall not apply to such partner, and

(2) such partner's distributive share of the partnership items allocable to passive loss limitation activities shall be taken into account separately to the extent necessary to comply with the provisions of section 469.

The preceding sentence shall not apply to any items allocable to an interest held as a limited partner.

§ 773. Computations at partnership level

(a) General rule.—

(1) Taxable income.—The taxable income of an electing large partnership shall be computed in the same manner as in the case of an individual except that—

(A) the items described in section 772(a) shall be separately stated, and

(B) the modifications of subsection (b) shall apply.

(2) Elections.—All elections affecting the computation of the taxable income of an electing large partnership or the computation of any credit of an electing large partnership shall be made by the partnership; except that the election under section 901, and any election under section 108, shall be made by each partner separately.

(3) Limitations, etc.—

(A) In general.—Except as provided in subparagraph (B), all limitations and other provisions affecting the computation of the taxable income of an electing large partnership or the computation of any credit of an electing large partnership shall be applied at the partnership level (and not at the partner level).

(B) Certain limitations applied at partner level.—The following provisions shall be applied at the partner level (and not at the partnership level):

(i) Section 68 (relating to overall limitation on itemized deductions).

(ii) Sections 49 and 465 (relating to at risk limitations).

(iii) Section 469 (relating to limitation on passive activity losses and credits).

(iv) Any other provision specified in regulations.

(4) Coordination with other provisions.—Paragraphs (2) and (3) shall apply notwithstanding any other provision of this chapter other than this part.

(b) Modifications to determination of taxable income.—In determining the taxable income of an electing large partnership—

(1) Certain deductions not allowed.—The following deductions shall not be allowed:

(A) The deduction for personal exemptions provided in section 151.

(B) The net operating loss deduction provided in section 172.

(C) The additional itemized deductions for individuals provided in part VII of subchapter B (other than section 212 thereof).

(2) Charitable deductions.—In determining the amount allowable under section 170, the limitation of section 170(b)(2) shall apply.

(3) Coordination with section 67.—In lieu of applying section 67, 70 percent of the amount of the miscellaneous itemized deductions shall be disallowed.

(c) Special rules for income from discharge of indebtedness.—If an electing large partnership has income from the discharge of any indebtedness—

(1) such income shall be excluded in determining the amounts referred to in section 772(a), and

(2) in determining the income tax of any partner of such partnership—

(A) such income shall be treated as an item required to be separately taken into account under section 772(a), and

(B) the provisions of section 108 shall be applied without regard to this part.

§ 774. Other modifications

(a) Treatment of certain optional adjustments, etc.—In the case of an electing large partnership—

(1) computations under section 773 shall be made without regard to any adjustment under section 743(b) or 108(b), but

(2) a partner's distributive share of any amount referred to in section 772(a) shall be appropriately adjusted to take into account any adjustment under section 743(b) or 108(b) with respect to such partner.

* * *

(c) Partnership not terminated by reason of change in ownership.—Subparagraph (B) of section 708(b)(1) shall not apply to an electing large partnership.

* * *

§ 775. Electing large partnership defined

(a) General rule.—For purposes of this part—

(1) In general.—The term "electing large partnership" means, with respect to any partnership taxable year, any partnership if—

(A) the number of persons who were partners in such partnership in the preceding partnership taxable year equaled or exceeded 100, and

(B) such partnership elects the application of this part.

To the extent provided in regulations, a partnership shall cease to be treated as an electing large partnership for any partnership taxable year if in such taxable year fewer than 100 persons were partners in such partnership.

(2) Election.—The election under this subsection shall apply to the taxable year for which made and all subsequent taxable years unless revoked with the consent of the Secretary.

(b) Special rules for certain service partnerships.—

(1) Certain partners not counted.—For purposes of this section, the term "partner" does not include any individual performing substantial services in connection with the activities of the partnership and holding an interest in such partnership, or an individual who formerly performed substantial services in connection with such activities and who held an interest in such partnership at the time the individual performed such services.

(2) Exclusion.—For purposes of this part, an election under subsection (a) shall not be effective with respect to any partnership if substantially all the partners of such partnership—

(A) are individuals performing substantial services in connection with the activities of such partnership or are personal service corporations (as defined in section 269A(b)) the owner-employees (as defined in section 269A(b)) of which perform such substantial services,

(B) are retired partners who had performed such substantial services, or

(C) are spouses of partners who are performing (or had previously performed) such substantial services.

* * *

§ 777. Regulations

The Secretary shall prescribe such regulations as may be appropriate to carry out the purposes of this part.

SUBCHAPTER N—TAX BASED ON INCOME FROM SOURCES WITHIN OR WITHOUT THE UNITED STATES

PART III—INCOME FROM SOURCES WITHOUT THE UNITED STATES

Subpart B—Earned Income of Citizens or Residents of United States

§ 911. Citizens or residents of the United States living abroad

(a) Exclusion form gross income.—At the election of a qualified individual (made separately with respect to paragraphs (1) and (2)), there shall be excluded from the gross income of such individual, and exempt from taxation under this subtitle, for any taxable year—

(1) the foreign earned income of such individual, and

(2) the housing cost amount of such individual.

(b) Foreign earned income.—

(1) Definition.—For purposes of this section—

(A) In general.—The term "foreign earned income" with respect to any individual means the amount received by such individual from sources within a foreign country or countries which constitute earned income attributable to services performed by such individual during the period described in subparagraph (A) or (B) of subsection (d)(1), whichever is applicable.

(B) Certain amounts not included in foreign earned income.—The foreign earned income for an individual shall not include amounts—

(i) received as a pension or annuity,

(ii) paid by the United States or an agency thereof to an employee of the United States or an agency thereof,

(iii) included in gross income by reason of section 402(b) (relating to taxability of beneficiary of nonexempt trust) or section 403(c) (relating to taxability of beneficiary under a nonqualified annuity), or

* Omitted entirely.

(iv) received after the close of the taxable year following the taxable year in which the services to which the amounts are attributable are performed.

(2) Limitation on foreign earned income.—

(A) In general.—The foreign earned income of an individual which may be excluded under subsection (a)(1) for any taxable year shall not exceed the amount of foreign earned income computed on a daily basis at an annual rate equal to the exclusion amount for the calendar year in which such taxable year begins.

(B) Attribution to year in which services are performed.—For purposes of applying subparagraph (A), amounts received shall be considered received in the taxable year in which the services to which the amounts are attributable are performed.

(C) Treatment of community income.—In applying subparagraph (A) with respect to amounts received from services performed by a husband or wife which are community income under community property laws applicable to such income, the aggregate amount which may be excludable from the gross income of such husband and wife under subsection (a)(1) for any taxable year shall equal the amount which would be so excludable if such amounts did not constitute community income.

(D) Exclusion amount.—

(i) In general.—The exclusion amount for any calendar year is the exclusion amount determined in accordance with the following table (as adjusted by clause (ii)):

For calendar year—	The exclusion amount is—
1998	$72,000
1999	74,000
2000	76,000
2001	78,000
2002 and thereafter	80,000.

* * *

(c) Housing cost amount.—For purposes of this section—

(1) In general.—The term "housing cost amount" means an amount equal to the excess of—

(A) the housing expenses of an individual for the taxable year to the extent such expenses do not exceed the amount determined under paragraph (2), over

(B) an amount equal to the product of—

(i) 16 percent of the amount (computed on a daily basis) in effect under subsection (b)(2)(D) for the calendar year in which such taxable year begins, multiplied by

(ii) the number of days of such taxable year within the applicable period described in subparagraph (A) or (B) of subsection (d)(1).

(2) Limitation.—

(A) In general.—The amount determined under this paragraph is an amount equal to the product of—

(i) 30 percent (adjusted as may be provided under subparagraph (B)) of the amount (computed on a daily basis) in effect under subsection (b)(2)(D) for the calendar year in which the taxable year of the individual begins, multiplied by

(ii) the number of days of such taxable year within the applicable period described in subparagraph (A) or (B) of subsection (d)(1).

(B) Regulations.—The Secretary may issue regulations or other guidance providing for the adjustment of the percentage under subparagraph (A)(i) on the basis of geographic differences in housing costs relative to housing costs in the United States.

(3) Housing expenses.—

(A) In general.—The term "housing expenses" means the reasonable expenses paid or incurred during the taxable year by or on behalf of an individual for housing for the individual (and, if they reside with him, for his spouse and dependents) in a foreign county. The term—

(i) includes expenses attributable to the housing (such as utilities and insurance), but

(ii) does not include interest and taxes of the kind deductible under section 163 or 164 or any amount allowable as a deduction under section 216(a).

Housing expenses shall not be treated as reasonable to the extent such expenses are lavish or extravagant under the circumstances.

(B) Second foreign household.—

(i) In general.—Except as provided in clause (ii), only housing expenses incurred with respect to that abode which bears the closest relationship to the tax home of the individual shall be taken into account under paragraph (1).

(ii) Separate household for spouse and dependents.—If an individual maintains a separate abode outside the United States for his spouse and dependents and they do not reside with him because of living conditions which are dangerous, unhealthful, or otherwise adverse, then—

(I) the words "if they reside with him" in subparagraph (A) shall be disregarded, and

(II) the housing expenses incurred with respect to such abode shall be taken into account under paragraph (1).

(4) Special rules where housing expenses not provided by employer.—

(A) In general.—To the extent the housing cost amount of any individual for any taxable year is not attributable to employer provided amounts, such amount shall be treated as a deduction allowable in computing adjusted gross income to the extent of the limitation of subparagraph (B).

(B) Limitation.—For purposes of subparagraph (A), the limitation of this subparagraph is the excess of—

(i) the foreign earned income of the individual for the taxable year, over

(ii) the amount of such income excluded from gross income under subsection (a) for the taxable year.

(C) 1-year carryover of housing amounts not allowed by reason of subparagraph (B).—

(i) In general.—The amount not allowable as a deduction for any taxable year under subparagraph (A) by reason of the limitation of subparagraph (B) shall be treated as a deduction allowable in computing adjusted gross income for the succeeding taxable year (and only for the succeeding taxable year) to the extent of the limitation of clause (ii) for such succeeding taxable year.

(ii) Limitation.—For purposes of clause (i), the limitation of this clause for any taxable year is the excess of—

(I) the limitation of subparagraph (B) for such taxable year, over

(II) amounts treated as a deduction under subparagraph (A) for such taxable year.

(D) Employer provided amounts.—For purposes of this paragraph, the term "employer provided amounts" means any amount paid or incurred on behalf of the individual by the individual's employer which is foreign earned income included in the individual's gross income for the taxable year (without regard to this section).

(E) Foreign earned income.—For purposes of this paragraph, an individual's foreign earned income for any taxable year shall be determined without regard to the limitation of subparagraph (A) of subsection (b)(2).

(d) Definitions and special rules.—For purposes of this section—

(1) Qualified individual.—The term "qualified individual" means an individual whose tax home is in a foreign county and who is—

(A) a citizen of the United States and establishes to the satisfaction of the Secretary that he has been a bona fide resident of a foreign county or countries for an uninterrupted period which includes an entire taxable year, or

(B) a citizen or resident of the United States and who, during any period of 12 consecutive months, is present in a foreign country or countries during at least 330 full days in such period.

(2) Earned income.—

(A) In general.—The term "earned income" means wages, salaries, or professional fees, and other amounts received as compensation for personal services actually rendered, but does not include that part of the compensation derived by the taxpayer for personal services rendered by him to a corporation which represents a distribution of earnings or profits rather than a reasonable allowance as compensation for the personal services actually rendered.

(B) Taxpayer engaged in trade or business.—In the case of a taxpayer engaged in a trade or business in which both personal services and capital are material income-producing factors, under regulations prescribed by the Secretary, a reasonable allowance as compensation for the personal services rendered by the taxpayer, not in excess of 30 percent of his share of the net profits of such trade or business, shall be considered as earned income.

(3) Tax home.—The term "tax home" means, with respect to any individual, such individual's home for purposes of section 162(a)(2) (relating to traveling expenses while away from home). An individual shall not be treated as having a tax home in a foreign country for any period for which his abode is within the United States.

* * *

(5) Test of bona fide residence.—If—

(A) an individual who has earned income from sources within a foreign country submits a statement to the authorities of that country that he is not a resident of that country, and

(B) such individual is held not subject as a resident of that country to the income tax of that country by its authorities with respect to such earnings,

then such individual shall not be considered a bona fide resident of that country for purposes of paragraph (1)(A).

(6) Denial of double benefits.—No deduction or exclusion from gross income under this subtitle or credit against the tax imposed by this chapter (including any credit or deduction for the amount of taxes paid or accrued to a foreign country or possession of the United States) shall be allowed to the extent such deduction, exclusion, or credit is properly allocable to or chargeable against amounts excluded from gross income under subsection (a).

(7) Aggregate benefit cannot exceed foreign earned income.—The sum of the amount excluded under subsection (a) and the amount deducted under subsection (c)(3)(A) for the taxable year shall not exceed the individual's foreign earned income for such year.

* * *

SUBCHAPTER O—GAIN OR LOSS ON DISPOSITION OF PROPERTY

PART I—DETERMINATION OF AMOUNT OF AND RECOGNITION OF GAIN OR LOSS

§ 1001. Determination of amount of and recognition of gain or loss

(a) Computation of gain or loss.—The gain from the sale or other disposition of property shall be the excess of the amount realized therefrom over the adjusted basis provided in section 1011 for determining gain, and the loss shall be the excess of the adjusted basis provided in such section for determining loss over the amount realized.

(b) Amount realized.—The amount realized from the sale or other disposition of property shall be the sum of any money received plus the fair market value of the property (other than money) received. In determining the amount realized—

(1) there shall not be taken into account any amount received as reimbursement for real property taxes which are treated under section 164(d) as imposed on the purchaser, and

(2) there shall be taken into account amounts representing real property taxes which are treated under section 164(d) as imposed on the taxpayer if such taxes are to be paid by the purchaser.

(c) Recognition of gain or loss.—Except as otherwise provided in this subtitle, the entire amount of the gain or loss, determined under this section, on the sale or exchange of property shall be recognized.

(d) Installment sales.—Nothing in this section shall be construed to prevent (in the case of property sold under contract providing for payment in installments) the taxation of that portion of any installment payment representing gain or profit in the year in which such payment is received.

(e) Certain term interests.—

(1) In general.—In determining gain or loss from the sale or other disposition of a term interest in property, that portion of the adjusted basis of such interest which

* Omitted entirely.

is determined pursuant to section 1014, 1015, or 1041 (to the extent that such adjusted basis is a portion of the entire adjusted basis of the property) shall be disregarded.

(2) Term interest in property defined.—For purposes of paragraph (1), the term "term interest in property" means—

(A) a life interest in property,

(B) an interest in property for a term of years, or

(C) an income interest in a trust.

(3) Exception.—Paragraph (1) shall not apply to a sale or other disposition which is a part of a transaction in which the entire interest in property is transferred to any person or persons.

PART II—BASIS RULES OF GENERAL APPLICATION

§ 1011. Adjusted basis for determining gain or loss

(a) General rule.—The adjusted basis for determining the gain or loss from the sale or other disposition of property, whenever acquired, shall be the basis (determined under section 1012 or other applicable sections of this subchapter and subchapters C (relating to corporate distributions and adjustments), K (relating to partners and partnerships), and P (relating to capital gains and losses)), adjusted as provided in section 1016.

(b) Bargain sale to a charitable organization.—If a deduction is allowable under section 170 (relating to charitable contributions) by reason of a sale, then the adjusted basis for determining the gain from such sale shall be that portion of the adjusted basis which bears the same ratio to the adjusted basis as the amount realized bears to the fair market value of the property.

§ 1012. Basis of property—cost

(a) In general.—The basis of property shall be the cost of such property, except as otherwise provided in this subchapter and subchapters C (relating to corporate distributions and adjustments), K (relating to partners and partnerships), and P (relating to capital gains and losses).

(b) Special rule for apportioned real estate taxes.—The cost of real property shall not include any amount in respect of real property taxes which are treated under section 164(d) as imposed on the taxpayer.

(c) Determinations by account.—

(1) In general.—In the case of the sale, exchange, or other disposition of a specified security on or after the applicable date, the conventions prescribed by regulations under this section shall be applied on an account by account basis.

(2) Application to certain funds.—

(A) In general.—Except as provided in subparagraph (B), any stock for which an average basis method is permissible under section 1012 which is acquired before January 1, 2012, shall be treated as a separate account from any such stock acquired on or after such date.

(B) Election fund for treatment as single account.—If a fund described in subparagraph (A) elects to have this subparagraph apply with respect to one or more of its stockholders—

(i) subparagraph (A) shall not apply with respect to any stock in such fund held by such stockholders, and

(ii) all stock in such fund which is held by such stockholders shall be treated as covered securities described in section 6045(g)(3) without regard to the date of the acquisition of such stock.

A rule similar to the rule of the preceding sentence shall apply with respect to a broker holding such stock as a nominee.

(3) Definitions.—For purposes of this section, the terms "specified security" and "applicable date" shall have the meaning given such terms in section 6045(g).

(d) Average basis for stock acquired pursuant to a dividend reinvestment plan.—

(1) In general.—In the case of any stock acquired after December 31, 2010, in connection with a dividend reinvestment plan, the basis of such stock while held as part of such plan shall be determined using one of the methods which may be used for determining the basis of stock in an open-end fund.

(2) Treatment after transfer.—In the case of the transfer to another account of stock to which paragraph (1) applies, such stock shall have a cost basis in such other account equal to its basis in the dividend reinvestment plan immediately before such transfer (properly adjusted for any fees or other charges taken into account in connection with such transfer).

(3) Separate accounts; election for treatment as single account.—Rules similar to the rules of subsection (c)(2) shall apply for purposes of this subsection.

(4) Dividend reinvestment plan.—For purposes of this subsection—

(A) In general.—The term "dividend reinvestment plan" means any arrangement under which dividends on any stock are reinvested in stock identical to the stock with respect to which the dividends are paid.

(B) Initial stock acquisition treated as acquired in connection with plan.—Stock shall be treated as acquired in connection with a dividend reinvestment plan if such stock is acquired pursuant to such plan or if the dividends paid on such stock are subject to such plan.

§ 1014. Basis of property acquired from a decedent

(a) In general.—Except as otherwise provided in this section, the basis of property in the hands of a person acquiring the property from a decedent or to whom the property passed from a decedent shall, if not sold, exchanged, or otherwise disposed of before the decedent's death by such person, be—

(1) the fair market value of the property at the date of the decedent's death, or

(2) in the case of an election under either section 2032 or section 811(j) of the Internal Revenue Code of 1939 where the decedent died after October 21, 1942, its value at the applicable valuation date prescribed by those sections,

(3) in the case of an election under section 2032A, its value determined under such section, or

(4) to the extent of the applicability of the exclusion described in section 2031(c), the basis in the hands of the decedent.

(b) Property acquired from the decedent.—For purposes of subsection (a), the following property shall be considered to have been acquired from or to have passed from the decedent:

(1) Property acquired by bequest, devise, or inheritance, or by the decedent's estate from the decedent;

(2) Property transferred by the decedent during his lifetime in trust to pay the income for life to or on the order or direction of the decedent, with the right reserved to the decedent at all times before his death to revoke the trust;

(3) In the case of decedents dying after December 31, 1951, property transferred by the decedent during his lifetime in trust to pay the income for life to or on the order or direction of the decedent with the right reserved to the decedent at all times before his death to make any change in the enjoyment thereof through the exercise of a power to alter, amend, or terminate the trust;

(4) Property passing without full and adequate consideration under a general power of appointment exercised by the decedent by will;

* * *

(6) In the case of decedents dying after December 31, 1947, property which represents the surviving spouse's one-half share of community property held by the decedent and the surviving spouse under the community property laws of any State, or possession of the United States or any foreign country, if at least one-half of the whole of the community interest in such property was includible in determining the value of the decedent's gross estate under chapter 11 of subtitle B (section 2001 and following, relating to estate tax) or section 811 of the Internal Revenue Code of 1939;

* * *

(9) In the case of decedents dying after December 31, 1953, property acquired from the decedent by reason of death, form of ownership, or other conditions (including property acquired through the exercise or non-exercise of a power of appointment), if by reason thereof the property is required to be included in determining the value of the decedent's gross estate under chapter 11 of subtitle B * * *. In such case, if the property is acquired before the death of the decedent, the basis shall be the amount determined under subsection (a) reduced by the amount allowed to the taxpayer as deductions in computing taxable income under this subtitle * * * for exhaustion, wear and tear, obsolescence, amortization, and depletion on such property before the death of the decedent. Such basis shall be applicable to the property commencing on the death of the decedent. This paragraph shall not apply to—

(A) annuities described in section 72;

* * *

(C) property described in any other paragraph of this subsection.

(10) Property includible in the gross estate of the decedent under section 2044 (relating to certain property for which marital deduction was previously allowed). In any such case, the last 3 sentences of paragraph (9) shall apply as if such property were described in the first sentence of paragraph (9).

(c) Property representing income in respect of a decedent.—This section shall not apply to property which constitutes a right to receive an item of income in respect of a decedent under section 691.

* * *

(e) Appreciated property acquired by decedent by gift within 1 year of death.—

(1) In general.—In the case of a decedent dying after December 31, 1981, if—

(A) appreciated property was acquired by the decedent by gift during the 1–year period ending on the date of the decedent's death, and

(B) such property is acquired from the decedent by (or passes from the decedent to) the donor of such property (or the spouse of such donor), the basis of such property in the hands of such donor (or spouse) shall be the adjusted basis of such property in the hands of the decedent immediately before the death of the decedent.

(2) Definitions.—For purposes of paragraph (1)—

(A) Appreciated property.—The term "appreciated property" means any property if the fair market value of such property on the day it was transferred to the decedent by gift exceeds its adjusted basis.

(B) Treatment of certain property sold by estate.—In the case of any appreciated property described in subparagraph (A) of paragraph (1) sold by the estate of the decedent or by a trust of which the decedent was the grantor, rules similar to the rules of paragraph (1) shall apply to the extent the donor of such property (or the spouse of such donor) is entitled to the proceeds from such sale.

§ 1015. Basis of property acquired by gifts and transfers in trust

(a) Gifts after December 31, 1920.—If the property was acquired by gift after December 31, 1920, the basis shall be the same as it would be in the hands of the donor or the last preceding owner by whom it was not acquired by gift, except that if such basis (adjusted for the period before the date of the gift as provided in section 1016) is greater than the fair market value of the property at the time of the gift, then for the purpose of determining loss the basis shall be such fair market value. If the facts necessary to determine the basis in the hands of the donor or the last preceding owner are unknown to the donee, the Secretary shall, if possible, obtain such facts from such donor or last preceding owner, or any other person cognizant thereof. If the Secretary finds it impossible to obtain such facts, the basis in the hands of such donor or last preceding owner shall be the fair market value of such property as found by the Secretary as of the date or approximate date at which, according to the best information that the Secretary is able to obtain, such property was acquired by such donor or last preceding owner.

(b) Transfer in trust after December 31, 1920.—If the property was acquired after December 31, 1920, by a transfer in trust (other than by a transfer in trust by a gift, bequest, or devise), the basis shall be the same as it would be in the hands of the grantor increased in the amount of gain or decreased in the amount of loss recognized to the grantor on such transfer under the law applicable to the year in which the transfer was made.

(c) Gift or transfer in trust before January 1, 1921.—If the property was acquired by gift or transfer in trust on or before December 31, 1920, the basis shall be the fair market value of such property at the time of such acquisition.

(d) Increased basis for gift tax paid.—

(1) In general.—If—

(A) the property is acquired by gift on or after September 2, 1958, the basis shall be the basis determined under subsection (a), increased (but not above the fair market value of the property at the time of the gift) by the amount of gift tax paid with respect to such gift, or

(B) the property was acquired by gift before September 2, 1958, and has not been sold, exchanged, or otherwise disposed of before such date, the basis of the property shall be increased on such date by the amount of gift tax paid with respect to such gift, but such increase shall not exceed an amount equal to the amount by which the fair market value of the property at the time of the gift exceeded the basis of the property in the hands of the donor at the time of the gift.

(2) Amount of tax paid with respect to gift.—For purposes of paragraph (1), the amount of gift tax paid with respect to any gift is an amount which bears the same ratio to the amount of gift tax paid under chapter 12 with respect to all gifts made by the donor for the calendar year (or preceding calendar period) in which such gift is made as the amount of such gift bears to the taxable gifts (as defined in section 2503(a) but computed without the deduction allowed by section 2521) made by the donor during such calendar year or period. For purposes of the preceding sentence, the amount of any gift shall be the amount included with respect to such gift in determining (for the purposes of section 2503(a)) the total amount of gifts made during the calendar year or period, reduced by the amount of any deduction allowed with respect to such gift under section 2522 (relating to charitable deduction) or under section 2523 (relating to marital deduction).

(3) Gifts treated as made one-half by each spouse.—For purposes of paragraph (1), where the donor and his spouse elected, under section 2513 to have the gift considered as made one-half by each, the amount of gift tax paid with respect to such gift under chapter 12 shall be the sum of the amounts of tax paid with respect to each half of such gift (computed in the manner provided in paragraph (2)).

(4) Treatment as adjustment to basis.—For purposes of section 1016(b), an increase in basis under paragraph (1) shall be treated as an adjustment under section 1016(a).

* * *

(6) Special rule for gifts made after December 31, 1976.—

(A) In general.—In the case of any gift made after December 31, 1976, the increase in basis provided by this subsection with respect to any gift for the gift tax paid under chapter 12 shall be an amount (not in excess of the amount of tax so paid) which bears the same ratio to the amount of tax so paid as—

(i) the net appreciation in value of the gift, bears to

(ii) the amount of the gift.

(B) Net appreciation.—For purposes of paragraph (1), the net appreciation in value of any gift is the amount by which the fair market value of the gift exceeds the donor's adjusted basis immediately before the gift.

(e) Gifts between spouses.—In the case of any property acquired by gift in a transfer described in section 1041(a), the basis of such property in the hands of the transferee shall be determined under section 1041(b)(2) and not this section.

§ 1016. Adjustments to basis

(a) General rule.—Proper adjustment in respect of the property shall in all cases be made—

(1) for expenditures, receipts, losses, or other items, properly chargeable to capital account, but no such adjustment shall be made—

(A) for taxes or other carrying charges described in section 266, or

(B) for expenditures described in section 173 (relating to circulation expenditures),

for which deductions have been taken by the taxpayer in determining taxable income for the taxable year or prior taxable years;

(2) in respect of any period since February 28, 1913, for exhaustion, wear and tear, obsolescence, amortization, and depletion, to the extent of the amount—

(A) allowed as deductions in computing taxable income under this subtitle or prior income tax laws, and

(B) resulting (by reason of the deductions so allowed) in a reduction for any taxable year of the taxpayer's taxes under this subtitle (other than chapter 2, relating to tax on self-employment income), or prior income, war-profits, or excess-profits tax laws,

but not less than the amount allowable under this subtitle or prior income tax laws. Where no method has been adopted under section 167 (relating to depreciation deduction), the amount allowable shall be determined under the straight line method. * * * Where for any taxable year before the taxable year 1932 the depletion allowance was based on discovery value or a percentage of income, then the adjustment for depletion for such year shall be based on the depletion which would have been allowable for such year if computed without reference to discovery value or a percentage of income;

* * *

(5) in the case of any bond (as defined in section 171(d)) the interest on which is wholly exempt from the tax imposed by this subtitle, to the extent of the amortizable bond premium disallowable as a deduction pursuant to section 171(a)(2), and in the case of any other bond (as defined in section 171(d)) to the extent of the deductions allowable pursuant to section 171(a)(1) (or the amount applied to reduce interest payments under section 171(e)(2)) with respect thereto;

* * *

(7) in the case of a residence the acquisition of which resulted, under section 1034 (as in effect on the day before the date of the enactment of the Taxpayer Relief Act of 1997), in the nonrecognition of any part of the gain realized on the sale, exchange, or involuntary conversion of another residence, to the extent provided in section 1034(e) (as so in effect);

* * *

(9) for amounts allowed as deductions as deferred expenses under section 616(b) (relating to certain expenditures in the development of mines) and resulting in a reduction of the taxpayer's taxes under this subtitle, but not less than the amounts allowable under such section for the taxable year and prior years;

[(10) Repealed.]

(11) for deductions to the extent disallowed under section 268 (relating to sale of land with unharvested crops), notwithstanding the provisions of any other paragraph of this subsection;

* * *

(14) for amounts allowed as deductions as deferred expenses under section 174(b)(1) (relating to research and experimental expenditures) and resulting in a reduction of the taxpayers' taxes under this subtitle, but not less than the amounts allowable under such section for the taxable year and prior years;

* * *

(17) to the extent provided in section 1376 in the case of stock of, and indebtedness owed to, shareholders of an S corporation;

* * *

(21) to the extent provided in section 1059 (relating to reduction in basis for extraordinary dividends);

* * *

(b) Substituted basis.—Whenever it appears that the basis of property in the hands of the taxpayer is a substituted basis, then the adjustments provided in subsection (a) shall be made after first making in respect of such substituted basis proper adjustments of a similar nature in respect of the period during which the property was held by the transferor, donor, or grantor, or during which the other property was held by the person for whom the basis is to be determined. A similar rule shall be applied in the case of a series of substituted bases.

(c) Increase in basis of property on which additional estate tax is imposed.—

(1) Tax imposed with respect to entire interest.—If an additional estate tax is imposed under section 2032A(c)(1) with respect to any interest in property and the qualified heir makes an election under this subsection with respect to the imposition of such tax, the adjusted basis of such interest shall be increased by an amount equal to the excess of—

(A) the fair market value of such interest on the date of the decedent's death (or the alternate valuation date under section 2032, if the executor of the decedent's estate elected the application of such section), over

(B) the value of such interest determined under section 2032A(a).

(2) Partial dispositions.—

(A) In general.—In the case of any partial disposition for which an election under this subsection is made, the increase in basis under paragraph (1) shall be an amount—

(i) which bears the same ratio to the increase which would be determined under paragraph (1) (without regard to this paragraph) with respect to the entire interest, as

(ii) the amount of the tax imposed under section 2032A(c)(1) with respect to such disposition bears to the adjusted tax difference attributable to the entire interest (as determined under section 2032A(c)(2)(B)).

(B) Partial disposition.—For purposes of subparagraph (A), the term "partial disposition" means any disposition or cessation to which subsection (c)(2)(D), (h)(1)(B), or (i)(1)(B) of section 2032A applies.

(3) Time adjustment made.—Any increase in basis under this subsection shall be deemed to have occurred immediately before the disposition or cessation resulting in the imposition of the tax under section 2032A(c)(1).

(4) Special rule in the case of substituted property.—If the tax under section 2032A(c)(1) is imposed with respect to qualified replacement property (as defined in section 2032A(h)(3)(B)) or qualified exchange property (as defined in section 2032A(i)(3)), the increase in basis under paragraph (1) shall be made by reference to the property involuntarily converted or exchanged (as the case may be).

(5) Election.—

(A) In general.—An election under this subsection shall be made at such time and in such manner as the Secretary shall by regulations prescribe. Such an election, once made, shall be irrevocable.

(B) Interest on recaptured amount.—If an election is made under this subsection with respect to any additional estate tax imposed under section 2032A(c)(1), for purposes of section 6601 (relating to interest on underpayments), the last date prescribed for payment of such tax shall be deemed to be the last date prescribed for payment of the tax imposed by section 2001 with respect to the estate of the decedent (as determined for purposes of section 6601).

* * *

§ 1017. Discharge of indebtedness

(a) General rule.—If—

(1) an amount is excluded from gross income under subsection (a) of section 108 (relating to discharge of indebtedness), and

(2) under subsection (b)(2)(E), (b)(5), or (c)(1) of section 108, any portion of such amount is to be applied to reduce basis,

then such portion shall be applied in reduction of the basis of any property held by the taxpayer at the beginning of the taxable year following the taxable year in which the discharge occurs.

(b) Amount and properties determined under regulations.—

(1) In general.—The amount of reduction to be applied under subsection (a) (not in excess of the portion referred to in subsection (a)), and the particular properties the bases of which are to be reduced, shall be determined under regulations prescribed by the Secretary.

(2) Limitation in Title 11 case or insolvency.—In the case of a discharge to which subparagraph (A) or (B) of section 108(a)(1) applies, the reduction in basis under subsection (a) of this section shall not exceed the excess of—

(A) the aggregate of the bases of the property held by the taxpayer immediately after the discharge, over

(B) the aggregate of the liabilities of the taxpayer immediately after the discharge.

The preceding sentence shall not apply to any reduction in basis by reason of an election under section 108(b)(5).

(3) Certain reductions may only be made in the basis of depreciable property.—

(A) In general.—Any amount which under subsection (b)(5) or (c)(1) of section 108 is to be applied to reduce basis shall be applied only to reduce the basis of depreciable property held by the taxpayer.

(B) Depreciable property.—For purposes of this section, the term "depreciable property" means any property of a character subject to the allowance for depreciation, but only if a basis reduction under subsection (a) will reduce the amount of depreciation or amortization which otherwise would be allowable for the period immediately following such reduction.

(C) Special rule for partnership interests.—For purposes of this section, any interest of a partner in a partnership shall be treated as depreciable property to the extent of such partner's proportionate interest in the depreciable property held by such partnership. The preceding sentence shall apply only if there is a corresponding reduction in the partnership's basis in depreciable property with respect to such partner.

(D) Special rule in case of affiliated group.—For purposes of this section, if—

(i) a corporation holds stock in another corporation (hereinafter in this subparagraph referred to as the "subsidiary"), and

(ii) such corporations are members of the same affiliated group which file a consolidated return under section 1501 for the taxable year in which the discharge occurs, then such stock shall be treated as depreciable property to the extent that such subsidiary consents to a corresponding reduction in the basis of its depreciable property.

(E) Election to treat certain inventory as depreciable property.—

(i) In general.—At the election of the taxpayer, for purposes of this section, the term "depreciable property" includes any real property which is described in section 1221(a)(1).

(ii) Election.—An election under clause (i) shall be made on the taxpayer's return for the taxable year in which the discharge occurs or at such other time as may be permitted in regulations prescribed by the Secretary. Such an election, once made, may be revoked only with the consent of the Secretary.

(F) Special rules for qualified real property business indebtedness.—In the case of any amount which under section 108(c)(1) is to be applied to reduce basis—

(i) depreciable property shall only include depreciable real property for purposes of subparagraphs (A) and (C),

(ii) subparagraph (E) shall not apply, and

(iii) in the case of property taken into account under section 108(c)(2)(B), the reduction with respect to such property shall be made as of the time immediately before disposition if earlier than the time under subsection (a).

(4) Special rules for qualified farm indebtedness.—

(A) In general.—Any amount which under subsection (b)(2)(E) of section 108 is to be applied to reduce basis and which is attributable to an amount excluded under subsection (a)(1)(C) of section 108—

(i) shall be applied only to reduce the basis of qualified property held by the taxpayer, and

(ii) shall be applied to reduce the basis of qualified property in the following order:

(I) First the basis of qualified property which is depreciable property.

(II) Second the basis of qualified property which is land used or held for use in the trade or business of farming.

(III) Then the basis of other qualified property.

(B) Qualified property.—For purposes of this paragraph, the term "qualified property" has the meaning given to such term by section 108(g)(3)(C).

(C) Certain rules made applicable.—Rules similar to the rules of subparagraphs (C), (D), and (E) of paragraph (3) shall apply for purposes of this paragraph and section 108(g).

(c) Special rules.—

(1) Reduction not to be made in exempt property.—In the case of an amount excluded from gross income under section 108(a)(1)(A), no reduction in basis shall be made under this section in the basis of property which the debtor treats as exempt property under section 522 of title 11 of the United States Code.

(2) Reductions in basis not treated as dispositions.—For purposes of this title, a reduction in basis under this section shall not be treated as a disposition.

(d) Recapture of reductions.—

(1) In general.—For purposes of sections 1245 and 1250—

(A) any property the basis of which is reduced under this section and which is neither section 1245 property nor section 1250 property shall be treated as section 1245 property, and

(B) any reduction under this section shall be treated as a deduction allowed for depreciation.

(2) Special rule for section 1250.—For purposes of section 1250(b), the determination of what would have been the depreciation adjustments under the straight line method shall be made as if there had been no reduction under this section.

§ 1019. Property on which lessee has made improvements

Neither the basis nor the adjusted basis of any portion of real property shall, in the case of the lessor of such property, be increased or diminished on account of income derived by the lessor in respect of such property and excludable from gross income under section 109 (relating to improvements by lessee on lessor's property). If an amount representing any part of the value of real property attributable to buildings erected or other improvements made by a lessee in respect of such property was included in gross income of the lessor for any taxable year beginning before January 1, 1942, the basis of each portion of such property shall be properly adjusted for the amount so included in gross income.

PART III—COMMON NONTAXABLE EXCHANGES

§ 1031. Exchange of property held for productive use or investment

(a) Nonrecognition of gain or loss from exchanges solely in kind.—

(1) In general.—No gain or loss shall be recognized on the exchange of property held for productive use in a trade or business or for investment if such property is exchanged solely for property of like kind which is to be held either for productive use in a trade or business or for investment.

(2) Exception.—This subsection shall not apply to any exchange of—

(A) stock in trade or other property held primarily for sale,

(B) stocks, bonds, or notes,

(C) other securities or evidences of indebtedness or interest,

(D) interests in a partnership,

(E) certificates of trust or beneficial interests, or

(F) choses in action.

For purposes of this section, an interest in a partnership which has in effect a valid election under section 761(a) to be excluded from the application of all of subchapter K shall be treated as an interest in each of the assets of such partnership and not as an interest in a partnership.

(3) Requirement that property be identified and that exchange be completed not more than 180 days after transfer of exchanged property.—For purposes of this subsection, any property received by the taxpayer shall be treated as property which is not like-kind property if—

(A) such property is not identified as property to be received in the exchange on or before the day which is 45 days after the date on which the taxpayer transfers the property relinquished in the exchange, or

(B) such property is received after the earlier of—

(i) the day which is 180 days after the date on which the taxpayer transfers the property relinquished in the exchange, or

(ii) the due date (determined with regard to extension) for the transferor's return of the tax imposed by this chapter for the taxable year in which the transfer of the relinquished property occurs.

(b) Gain from exchanges not solely in kind.—If an exchange would be within the provisions of subsection (a), of section 1035(a), of section 1036(a), or of section 1037(a), if it were not for the fact that the property received in exchange consists not only of property permitted by such provisions to be received without the recognition of gain, but also of other property or money, then the gain, if any, to the recipient shall be recognized, but in an amount not in excess of the sum of such money and the fair market value of such other property.

(c) Loss from exchanges not solely in kind.—If an exchange would be within the provisions of subsection (a), of section 1035(a), of section 1036(a), or of section 1037(a), if it were not for the fact that the property received in exchange consists not only of property permitted by such provisions to be received without the recognition of gain or loss, but also of other property or money, then no loss from the exchange shall be recognized.

(d) Basis.—If property was acquired on an exchange described in this section, section 1035(a), section 1036(a), or section 1037(a), then the basis shall be the same as that of the property exchanged, decreased in the amount of any money received by the taxpayer and increased in the amount of gain or decreased in the amount of loss to the taxpayer that was recognized on such exchange. If the property so acquired consisted in part of the type of property permitted by this section, section 1035(a), section 1036(a), or section 1037(a), to be received without the recognition of gain or loss, and in part of other property, the basis provided in this subsection shall be allocated between the properties (other than money) received, and for the purpose of the allocation there shall be assigned to such other property an amount equivalent to its fair market value at the date of the exchange. For purposes of this section, section 1035(a), and section 1036(a), where as part of the consideration to the taxpayer another party to the exchange assumed (as determined under section 357(d)) a liability of the taxpayer, such assumption shall be considered as money received by the taxpayer on the exchange.

(e) Exchanges of livestock of different sexes.—For purposes of this section, livestock of different sexes are not property of a like kind.

(f) Special rules for exchanges between related persons.—

(1) In general.—If—

(A) a taxpayer exchanges property with a related person,

(B) there is nonrecognition of gain or loss to the taxpayer under this section with respect to the exchange of such property (determined without regard to this subsection), and

(C) before the date 2 years after the date of the last transfer which was part of such exchange—

(i) the related person disposes of such property, or

(ii) the taxpayer disposes of the property received in the exchange from the related person which was of like kind to the property transferred by the taxpayer,

there shall be no nonrecognition of gain or loss under this section to the taxpayer with respect to such exchange; except that any gain or loss recognized by the taxpayer by reason of this subsection shall be taken into account as of the date on which the disposition referred to in subparagraph (C) occurs.

(2) Certain dispositions not taken into account.—For purposes of paragraph (1)(C), there shall not be taken into account any disposition—

(A) after the earlier of the death of the taxpayer or the death of the related person,

(B) in a compulsory or involuntary conversion (within the meaning of section 1033) if the exchange occurred before the threat or imminence of such conversion, or

(C) with respect to which it is established to the satisfaction of the Secretary that neither the exchange nor such disposition had as one of its principal purposes the avoidance of Federal income tax.

(3) Related person.—For purposes of this subsection, the term "related person" means any person bearing a relationship to the taxpayer described in section 267(b) or 707(b)(1).

(4) Treatment of certain transactions.—This section shall not apply to any exchange which is part of a transaction (or series of transactions) structured to avoid the purposes of this subsection.

(g) Special rule where substantial diminution of risk.—

(1) In general.—If paragraph (2) applies to any property for any period, the running of the period set forth in subsection (f)(1)(C) with respect to such property shall be suspended during such period.

(2) Property to which subsection applies.—This paragraph shall apply to any property for any period during which the holder's risk of loss with respect to the property is substantially diminished by—

(A) the holding of a put with respect to such property,

(B) the holding by another person of a right to acquire such property, or

(C) a short sale or any other transaction.

(h) Special rules for foreign real and personal property.—For purposes of this section—

(1) Real property.—Real property located in the United States and real property located outside the United States are not property of a like kind.

(2) Personal property.—

(A) In general.—Personal property used predominantly within the United States and personal property used predominantly outside the United States are not property of a like kind.

(B) Predominant use.—Except as provided in subparagraphs (C) and (D), the predominant use of any property shall be determined based on—

(i) in the case of the property relinquished in the exchange, the 2–year period ending on the date of such relinquishment, and

(ii) in the case of the property acquired in the exchange, the 2–year period beginning on the date of such acquisition.

(C) Property held for less than 2 years.—Except in the case of an exchange which is part of a transaction (or series of transactions) structured to avoid the purposes of this subsection—

(i) only the periods the property was held by the person relinquishing the property (or any related person) shall be taken into account under subparagraph (B)(i), and

(ii) only the periods the property was held by the person acquiring the property (or any related person) shall be taken into account under subparagraph (B)(ii).

(D) Special rule for certain property.—Property described in any subparagraph of section 168(g)(4) shall be treated as used predominantly in the United States.

* * *

§ 1032. Exchange of stock for property

(a) Nonrecognition of gain or loss.—No gain or loss shall be recognized to a corporation on the receipt of money or other property in exchange for stock (including treasury stock) of such corporation. No gain or loss shall be recognized by a corporation with respect to any lapse or acquisition of an option, or with respect to a securities futures contract (as defined in section 1234B), to buy or sell its stock (including treasury stock).

(b) Basis.—

For basis of property acquired by a corporation in certain exchanges for its stock, see section 362.

§ 1033. Involuntary conversions

(a) General rule.—If property (as a result of its destruction in whole or in part, theft, seizure, or requisition or condemnation or threat or imminence thereof) is compulsorily or involuntarily converted—

(1) Conversion into similar property.—Into property similar or related in service or use to the property so converted, no gain shall be recognized.

(2) Conversion into money.—Into money or into property not similar or related in service or use to the converted property, the gain (if any) shall be recognized except to the extent hereinafter provided in this paragraph:

(A) Nonrecognition of gain.—If the taxpayer during the period specified in subparagraph (B), for the purpose of replacing the property so converted, purchases other property similar or related in service or use to the property so converted, or purchases stock in the acquisition of control of a corporation owning such other property, at the election of the taxpayer the gain shall be recognized only to the extent that the amount realized upon such conversion (regardless of whether such amount is received in one or more taxable years) exceeds the cost of such other property or such stock. Such election shall be made at such time and in such manner as the Secretary may by regulations prescribe. For purposes of this paragraph—

(i) no property or stock acquired before the disposition of the converted property shall be considered to have been acquired for the purpose of replacing such converted property unless held by the taxpayer on the date of such disposition; and

(ii) the taxpayer shall be considered to have purchased property or stock only if, but for the provisions of subsection (b) of this section, the unadjusted basis of such property or stock would be its cost within the meaning of section 1012.

(B) Period within which property must be replaced.—The period referred to in subparagraph (A) shall be the period beginning with the date of the disposition of the converted property, or the earliest date of the threat or imminence of requisition or condemnation of the converted property, whichever is the earlier, and ending—

(i) 2 years after the close of the first taxable year in which any part of the gain upon the conversion is realized, or

(ii) subject to such terms and conditions as may be specified by the Secretary, at the close of such later date as the Secretary may designate on application by the taxpayer. Such application shall be made at such time and in such manner as the Secretary may by regulations prescribe.

(C) Time for assessment of deficiency attributable to gain upon conversion.—If a taxpayer has made the election provided in subparagraph (A), then—

(i) the statutory period for the assessment of any deficiency, for any taxable year in which any part of the gain on such conversion is realized, attributable to such gain shall not expire prior to the expiration of 3 years from the date the Secretary is notified by the taxpayer (in such manner as the Secretary may by regulations prescribe) of the replacement of the converted property or of an intention not to replace, and

(ii) such deficiency may be assessed before the expiration of such 3-year period notwithstanding the provisions of section 6212(c) or the provisions of any other law or rule of law which would otherwise prevent such assessment.

(D) Time for assessment of other deficiencies attributable to election.—If the election provided in subparagraph (A) is made by the taxpayer and such other property or such stock was purchased before the beginning of the last taxable year in which any part of the gain upon such conversion is realized, any deficiency, to the extent resulting from such election, for any taxable year ending before such last taxable year may be assessed (notwithstanding the provisions of section 6212(c) or 6501 or the provisions of any other law or rule of law which would otherwise prevent such assessment) at any time before the expiration of the period within which a deficiency for such last taxable year may be assessed.

(E) Definitions. For purposes of this paragraph—

(i) Control.—The term "control" means the ownership of stock possessing at least 80 percent of the total combined voting power of all classes of stock entitled to vote and at least 80 percent of the total number of shares of all other classes of stock of the corporation.

(ii) Disposition of the converted property.—The term "disposition of the converted property" means the destruction, theft, seizure, requisition, or condemnation of the converted property, or the sale or exchange of such property under threat or imminence of requisition or condemnation.

(b) Basis of property acquired through involuntary conversion.—

(1) Conversions described in subsection (a)(1).—If the property was acquired as the result of a compulsory or involuntary conversion described in subsection (a)(1), the basis shall be the same as in the case of the property so converted—

(A) decreased in the amount of any money received by the taxpayer which was not expended in accordance with the provisions of law (applicable to the year in which such conversion was made) determining the taxable status of the gain or loss upon such conversion, and

(B) increased in the amount of gain or decreased in the amount of loss to the taxpayer recognized upon such conversion under the law applicable to the year in which such conversion was made.

(2) Conversions described in subsection (a)(2).—In the case of property purchased by the taxpayer in a transaction described in subsection (a)(2) which resulted in the nonrecognition of any part of the gain realized as the result of a compulsory or involuntary conversion, the basis shall be the cost of such property decreased in the amount of the gain not so recognized; and if the property purchased consists of more than 1 piece of property, the basis determined under this sentence shall be allocated to the purchased properties in proportion to their respective costs.

(3) Property held by corporation the stock of which is replacement property.—

(A) In general.—If the basis of stock in a corporation is decreased under paragraph (2), an amount equal to such decrease shall also be applied to reduce the basis of property held by the corporation at the time the taxpayer acquired control (as defined in subsection (a)(2)(E)) of such corporation.

(B) Limitation.—Subparagraph (A) shall not apply to the extent that it would (but for this subparagraph) require a reduction in the aggregate adjusted bases of the property of the corporation below the taxpayer's adjusted basis of the stock in the corporation (determined immediately after such basis is decreased under paragraph (2)).

(C) Allocation of basis reduction.—The decrease required under subparagraph (A) shall be allocated—

(i) first to property which is similar or related in service or use to the converted property,

(ii) second to depreciable property (as defined in section 1017(b)(3)(B)) not described in clause (i), and

(iii) then to other property.

(D) Special rules.—

(i) Reduction not to exceed adjusted basis of property.—No reduction in the basis of any property under this paragraph shall exceed the adjusted basis of such property (determined without regard to such reduction).

(ii) Allocation of reduction among properties.—If more than 1 property is described in a clause of subparagraph (C), the reduction under this paragraph shall be allocated among such property in proportion to the adjusted bases of such property (as so determined).

(c) Property sold pursuant to reclamation laws.—For purposes of this subtitle, if property lying within an irrigation project is sold or otherwise disposed of in order to conform to the acreage limitation provisions of Federal reclamation laws, such sale or disposition shall be treated as an involuntary conversion to which this section applies.

(d) Livestock destroyed by disease.—For purposes of this subtitle, if livestock are destroyed by or on account of disease, or are sold or exchanged because of disease, such destruction or such sale or exchange shall be treated as an involuntary conversion to which this section applies.

* * *

(g) Condemnation of real property held for productive use in trade or business or for investment.—

(1) Special rule.—For purposes of subsection (a), if real property (not including stock in trade or other property held primarily for sale) held for productive use in trade or business or for investment is (as the result of its seizure, requisition, or condemnation, or threat or imminence thereof) compulsorily or involuntarily converted, property of a like kind to be held either for productive use in trade or business or for investment shall be treated as property similar or related in service or use to the property so converted.

(2) Limitation.—Paragraph (1) shall not apply to the purchase of stock in the acquisition of control of a corporation described in subsection (a)(2)(A).

* * *

(4) Special rule.—In the case of a compulsory or involuntary conversion described in paragraph (1), subsection (a)(2)(B)(i) shall be applied by substituting "3 years" for "2 years".

(h) Special rules for property damaged by presidentially declared disasters.—

* * *

(2) Trade or business and investment property.—If a taxpayer's property held for productive use in a trade or business or for investment located in a disaster area and compulsorily or involuntarily converted as a result of a federally declared disaster, tangible property of a type held for productive use in a trade or business shall be treated for purposes of subsection (a) as property similar or related in service or use to the property so converted.

(3) Federally declared disaster; disaster area.—The terms "federally declared disaster" and "disaster area" shall have the respective meaning given such terms by section 165(h)(3)(C).

* * *

(i) Replacement property must be acquired from unrelated person in certain cases.—

(1) In general.—If the property which is involuntarily converted is held by a taxpayer to which this subsection applies, subsection (a) shall not apply if the replacement property or stock is acquired from a related person. The preceding sentence shall not apply to the extent that the related person acquired the replacement property or stock from an unrelated person during the period applicable under subsection (a)(2)(B).

(2) Taxpayers to which subsection applies.—This subsection shall apply to—

(A) a C corporation,

(B) a partnership in which 1 or more C corporations own, directly or indirectly (determined in accordance with section 707(b)(3)), more than 50 percent of the capital interest, or profits interest, in such partnership at the time of the involuntary conversion, and

(C) any other taxpayer if, with respect to property which is involuntarily converted during the taxable year, the aggregate of the amount of realized gain on such property on which there is realized gain exceeds $100,000.

In the case of a partnership, subparagraph (C) shall apply with respect to the partnership and with respect to each partner. A similar rule shall apply in the case of an S corporation and its shareholders.

(3) Related person.—For purposes of this subsection, a person is related to another person if the person bears a relationship to the other person described in section 267(b) or 707(b)(1).

* * *

(*l*) Cross references.—

(1) For determination of the period for which the taxpayer has held property involuntarily converted, see section 1223.

(2) For treatment of gains from involuntary conversions as capital gains in certain cases, see section 1231(a).

(3) For exclusion from gross income of gain from involuntary conversion of principal residence, see section 121.

§ 1035. Certain exchanges of insurance policies

(a) General rules.—No gain or loss shall be recognized on the exchange of—

(1) a contract of life insurance for another contract of life insurance or for an endowment or annuity contract or for a qualified long-term care insurance contract; or

(2) a contract of endowment insurance (A) for another contract of endowment insurance which provides for regular payments beginning at a date not later than the date payments would have begun under the contract exchanged, or (B) for an annuity contract, or (C) for a qualified long-term care insurance contract;

(3) an annuity contract for an annuity contract or for a qualified long-term care insurance contract; or

(4) a qualified long-term care insurance contract for a qualified long-term care insurance contract.

(b) Definitions.—For the purpose of this section—

(1) Endowment contract.—A contract of endowment insurance is a contract with an insurance company which depends in part on the life expectancy of the insured, but which may be payable in full in a single payment during his life.

(2) Annuity contract.—An annuity contract is a contract to which paragraph (1) applies but which may be payable during the life of the annuitant only in installments. For purposes of the preceding sentence, a contract shall not fail to be treated as an annuity contract solely because a qualified long-term care insurance contract is a part of or a rider on such contract.

(3) Life insurance contract.—A contract of life insurance is a contract to which paragraph (1) applies but which is not ordinarily payable in full during the life of the insured. For purposes of the preceding sentence, a contract shall not fail to be treated as a life insurance contract solely because a qualified long-term care insurance contract is a part of or a rider on such contract.

(c) Exchanges involving foreign persons.—To the extent provided in regulations, subsection (a) shall not apply to any exchange having the effect of transferring property to any person other than a United States person.

(d) Cross references.—

(1) For rules relating to recognition of gain or loss where an exchange is not solely in kind, see subsections (b) and (c) of section 1031.

(2) For rules relating to the basis of property acquired in an exchange described in subsection (a), see subsection (d) of section 1031.

§ 1036. Stock for stock of same corporation

(a) General rule.—No gain or loss shall be recognized if common stock in a corporation is exchanged solely for common stock in the same corporation, or if preferred stock in a corporation is exchanged solely for preferred stock in the same corporation.

(b) Nonqualified preferred stock not treated as stock.—For purposes of this section, nonqualified preferred stock (as defined in section 351(g)(2)) shall be treated as property other than stock.

(c) Cross references.—

(1) For rules relating to recognition of gain or loss where an exchange is not solely in kind, see subsections (b) and (c) of section 1031.

(2) For rules relating to the basis of property acquired in an exchange described in subsection (a), see subsection (d) of section 1031.

§ 1038. Certain reacquisitions of real property

(a) General rule.—If—

(1) a sale of real property gives rise to indebtedness to the seller which is secured by the real property sold, and

(2) the seller of such property reacquires such property in partial or full satisfaction of such indebtedness,

then, except as provided in subsections (b) and (d), no gain or loss shall result to the seller from such reacquisition, and no debt shall become worthless or partially worthless as a result of such reacquisition.

(b) Amount of gain resulting.—

(1) In general.—In the case of a reacquisition of real property to which subsection (a) applies, gain shall result from such reacquisition to the extent that—

(A) the amount of money and the fair market value of other property (other than obligations of the purchaser) received, prior to such reacquisition, with respect to the sale of such property, exceeds

(B) the amount of the gain on the sale of such property returned as income for periods prior to such reacquisition.

(2) Limitation.—The amount of gain determined under paragraph (1) resulting from a reacquisition during any taxable year beginning after the date of the enactment of this section shall not exceed the amount by which the price at which the real property was sold exceeded its adjusted basis, reduced by the sum of—

(A) the amount of the gain on the sale of such property returned as income for periods prior to the reacquisition of such property, and

(B) the amount of money and the fair market value of other property (other than obligations of the purchaser received with respect to the sale of such property) paid or transferred by the seller in connection with the reacquisition of such property.

For purposes of this paragraph, the price at which real property is sold is the gross sales price reduced by the selling commissions, legal fees, and other expenses incident to the sale of such property which are properly taken into account in determining gain or loss on such sale.

(3) Gain recognized.—Except as provided in this section, the gain determined under this subsection resulting from a reacquisition to which subsection (a) applies shall be recognized, notwithstanding any other provision of this subtitle.

(c) Basis of reacquired real property.—If subsection (a) applies to the reacquisition of any real property, the basis of such property upon such reacquisition shall be the adjusted basis of the indebtedness to the seller secured by such property (determined as of the date of reacquisition), increased by the sum of—

(1) the amount of the gain determined under subsection (b) resulting from such reacquisition, and

(2) the amount described in subsection (b)(2)(B).

If any indebtedness to the seller secured by such property is not discharged upon the reacquisition of such property, the basis of such indebtedness shall be zero.

* * *

(e) Principal residences.—If—

(1) subsection (a) applies to a reacquisition of real property with respect to the sale of which gain was not recognized under section 121 (relating to gain on sale of principal residence); and

(2) within 1 year after the date of the reacquisition of such property by the seller, such property is resold by him,

then, under regulations prescribed by the Secretary, subsections (b), (c), and (d) of this section shall not apply to the reacquisition of such property and, for purposes of applying section 121, the resale of such property shall be treated as a part of the transaction constituting the original sale of such property.

[(f) Repealed.]

(g) Acquisition by estate, etc., of seller.—Under regulations prescribed by the Secretary, if an installment obligation is indebtedness to the seller which is described in subsection (a), and if such obligation is, in the hands of the taxpayer, an obligation with respect to which section 691(a)(4)(B) applies, then—

(1) for purposes of subsection (a), acquisition of real property by the taxpayer shall be treated as reacquisition by the seller, and

(2) the basis of the real property acquired by the taxpayer shall be increased by an amount equal to the deduction under section 691(c) which would (but for this subsection) have been allowable to the taxpayer with respect to the gain on the exchange of the obligation for the real property.

§ 1040. Transfer of certain farm, etc., real property

(a) General rule.—If the executor of the estate of any decedent transfers to a qualified heir (within the meaning of section 2032A(e)(1)) any property with respect to which an election was made under section 2032A, then gain on such transfer shall be recognized to the estate only to the extent that, on the date of such transfer, the fair market value of such property exceeds the value of such property for purposes of chapter 11 (determined without regard to section 2032A).

(b) Similar rule for certain trusts.—To the extent provided in regulations prescribed by the Secretary, a rule similar to the rule provided in subsection (a) shall apply where the trustee of a trust (any portion of which is included in the gross estate of the decedent) transfers property with respect to which an election was made under section 2032A.

(c) Basis of property acquired in transfer described in subsection (a) or (b).—The basis of property acquired in a transfer with respect to which gain realized is not recognized by reason of subsection (a) or (b) shall be the basis of such property immediately before the transfer increased by the amount of the gain recognized to the estate or trust on the transfer.

§ 1041. Transfers of property between spouses or incident to divorce

(a) General rule.—No gain or loss shall be recognized on a transfer of property from an individual to (or in trust for the benefit of)—

(1) a spouse, or

(2) a former spouse, but only if the transfer is incident to the divorce.

(b) Transfer treated as gift; transferee has transferor's basis.—In the case of any transfer of property described in subsection (a)—

(1) for purposes of this subtitle, the property shall be treated as acquired by the transferee by gift, and

(2) the basis of the transferee in the property shall be the adjusted basis of the transferor.

(c) Incident to divorce.—For purposes of subsection (a)(2), a transfer of property is incident to the divorce if such transfer—

(1) occurs within 1 year after the date on which the marriage ceases, or

(2) is related to the cessation of the marriage.

* * *

(e) Transfers in trust where liability exceeds basis.—Subsection (a) shall not apply to the transfer of property in trust to the extent that—

(1) the sum of the amount of the liabilities assumed, plus the amount of the liabilities to which the property is subject, exceeds

(2) the total of the adjusted basis of the property transferred.

Proper adjustment shall be made under subsection (b) in the basis of the transferee in such property to take into account gain recognized by reason of the preceding sentence.

PART IV—SPECIAL RULES

§ 1059. Corporate shareholder's basis in stock reduced by nontaxed portion of extraordinary dividends

(a) General rule.—If any corporation receives any extraordinary dividend with respect to any share of stock and such corporation has not held such stock for more than 2 years before the dividend announcement date—

(1) Reduction in basis.—The basis of such corporation in such stock shall be reduced (but not below zero) by the nontaxed portion of such dividends.

(2) Amounts in excess of basis.—If the nontaxed portion of such dividends exceeds such basis, such excess shall be treated as gain from the sale or exchange of such stock for the taxable year in which the extraordinary dividend is received.

(b) Nontaxed portion.—For purposes of this section—

(1) In general.—The nontaxed portion of any dividend is the excess (if any) of—

(A) the amount of such dividend, over

(B) the taxable portion of such dividend.

(2) Taxable portion.—The taxable portion of any dividend is—

(A) the portion of such dividend includible in gross income, reduced by

(B) the amount of any deduction allowable with respect to such dividend under section 243, 244, or 245.

(c) Extraordinary dividend defined.—For purposes of this section—

(1) In general.—The term "extraordinary dividend" means any dividend with respect to a share of stock if the amount of such dividend equals or exceeds the threshold percentage of the taxpayer's adjusted basis in such share of stock.

(2) Threshold percentage.—The term "threshold percentage" means—

(A) 5 percent in the case of stock which is preferred as to dividends, and

(B) 10 percent in the case of any other stock.

(3) Aggregation of dividends.—

(A) Aggregation within 85–day period.—All dividends—

(i) which are received by the taxpayer (or a person described in subparagraph (C)) with respect to any share of stock, and

(ii) which have ex-dividend dates within the same period of 85 consecutive days,

shall be treated as 1 dividend.

(B) Aggregation within 1 year where dividends exceed 20 percent of adjusted basis.—All dividends—

(i) which are received by the taxpayer (or a person described in subparagraph (C)) with respect to any share of stock, and

(ii) which have ex-dividend dates during the same period of 365 consecutive days,

shall be treated as extraordinary dividends if the aggregate of such dividends exceeds 20 percent of the taxpayer's adjusted basis in such stock (determined without regard to this section).

(C) Substituted basis transactions.—In the case of any stock, a person is described in this subparagraph if—

(i) the basis of such stock in the hands of such person is determined in whole or in part by reference to the basis of such stock in the hands of the taxpayer, or

(ii) the basis of such stock in the hands of the taxpayer is determined in whole or in part by reference to the basis of such stock in the hands of such person.

(4) Fair market value determination.—If the taxpayer establishes to the satisfaction of the Secretary the fair market value of any share of stock as of the day before the ex-dividend date, the taxpayer may elect to apply paragraphs (1) and (3) by substituting such value for the taxpayer's adjusted basis.

(d) Special rules.—For purposes of this section—

(1) Time for reduction.—Any reduction in basis under subsection (a)(1) shall be treated as occurring at the beginning of the ex-dividend date of the extraordinary dividend to which the reduction relates.

(2) Distributions in kind.—To the extent any dividend consists of property other than cash, the amount of such dividend shall be treated as the fair market value of such property (as of the date of the distribution) reduced as provided in section 301(b)(2).

(3) Determination of holding period.—For purposes of determining the holding period of stock under subsection (a), rules similar to the rules of paragraphs (3) and (4) of section 246(c) shall apply; except that "2 years" shall be substituted for the number of days specified in subparagraph (B) of section 246(c)(3).

(4) Ex-dividend date.—The term "ex-dividend date" means the date on which the share of stock becomes ex-dividend.

(5) Dividend announcement date.—The term "dividend announcement date" means, with respect to any dividend, the date on which the corporation declares, announces, or agrees to amount or the payment of such dividend, whichever is the earliest.

(6) Exception where stock held during entire existence of corporation.—

(A) In general.—Subsection (a) shall not apply to any extraordinary dividend with respect to any share of stock of a corporation if—

(i) such stock was held by the taxpayer during the entire period such corporation was in existence, and

(ii) except as provided in regulations, no earnings and profits of such corporation were attributable to transfers of property from (or earnings and profits of) a corporation which is not a qualified corporation.

(B) Qualified corporation.—For purposes of subparagraph (A), the term "qualified corporation" means any corporation (including a predecessor corporation)—

(i) with respect to which the taxpayer holds directly or indirectly during the entire period of such corporation's existence at least the same ownership interest as the taxpayer holds in the corporation distributing the extraordinary dividend, and

(ii) which has no earnings and profits—

(I) which were earned by, or

(II) which are attributable to gain on property which accrued during a period the corporation holding the property was,

a corporation not described in clause (i).

(C) Application of paragraph.—This paragraph shall not apply to any extraordinary dividend to the extent such application is inconsistent with the purposes of this section.

(e) Special rules for certain distributions.—

(1) Treatment of partial liquidations and certain redemptions.—Except as otherwise provided in regulations—

(A) Redemptions.—In the case of any redemption of stock—

(i) which is part of a partial liquidation (within the meaning of section 302(e)) of the redeeming corporation,

(ii) which is not pro rata as to all shareholders, or

(iii) which would not have been treated (in whole or in part) as a dividend if—

(I) any options had not been taken into account under section 318(a)(4), or

(II) section 304(a) had not applied,

any amount treated as a dividend with respect to such redemption shall be treated as an extraordinary dividend to which paragraphs (1) and (2) of subsection (a) apply without regard to the period the taxpayer held such stock. In the case of a redemption described in clause (iii), only the basis in the stock redeemed shall be taken into account under subsection (a).

(B) Reorganizations, etc.—An exchange described in section 356 which is treated as a dividend shall be treated as a redemption of stock for purposes of applying subparagraph (A).

(2) Qualifying dividends.—

(A) In general.—Except as provided in regulations, the term "extraordinary dividend" does not include any qualifying dividend (within the meaning of section 243).

(B) Exception.—Subparagraph (A) shall not apply to any portion of a dividend which is attributable to earnings and profits which—

(i) were earned by a corporation during a period it was not a member of the affiliated group, or

(ii) are attributable to gain on property which accrued during a period the corporation holding the property was not a member of the affiliated group.

(3) Qualified preferred dividends.—

(A) In general.—In the case of 1 or more qualified preferred dividends with respect to any share of stock—

(i) this section shall not apply to such dividends if the taxpayer holds such stock for more than 5 years, and

(ii) if the taxpayer disposes of such stock before it has been held for more than 5 years, the aggregate reduction under subsection (a)(1) with respect to such dividends shall not be greater than the excess (if any) of—

(I) the qualified preferred dividends paid with respect to such stock during the period the taxpayer held such stock, over

(II) the qualified preferred dividends which would have been paid during such period on the basis of the stated rate of return.

(B) Rate of return.—For purposes of this paragraph—

(i) Actual rate of return.—The actual rate of return shall be the rate of return for the period for which the taxpayer held the stock, determined—

(I) by only taking into account dividends during such period, and

(II) by using the lesser of the adjusted basis of the taxpayer in such stock or the liquidation preference of such stock.

(ii) Stated rate of return.—The stated rate of return shall be the annual rate of the qualified preferred dividend payable with respect to any share of stock (expressed as a percentage of the amount described in clause (i)(II)).

(C) Definitions and special rules.—For purposes of this paragraph—

(i) Qualified preferred dividend.—The term "qualified preferred dividend" means any fixed dividend payable with respect to any share of stock which—

(I) provides for fixed preferred dividends payable not less frequently than annually, and

(II) is not in arrears as to dividends at the time the taxpayer acquires the stock.

Such term shall not include any dividend payable with respect to any share of stock if the actual rate of return on such stock exceeds 15 percent.

(ii) Holding period.—In determining the holding period for purposes of subparagraph (A)(ii), subsection (d)(3) shall be applied by substituting "5 years" for "2 years".

(f) Treatment of dividends on certain preferred stock.—

(1) In general.—Any dividend with respect to disqualified preferred stock shall be treated as an extraordinary dividend to which paragraphs (1) and (2) of subsection (a) apply without regard to the period the taxpayer held the stock.

(2) Disqualified preferred stock.—For purposes of this subsection, the term "disqualified preferred stock" means any stock which is preferred as to dividends if—

(A) when issued, such stock has a dividend rate which declines (or can reasonably be expected to decline) in the future,

(B) the issue price of such stock exceeds its liquidation rights or its stated redemption price, or

(C) such stock is otherwise structured—

(i) to avoid the other provisions of this section, and

(ii) to enable corporate shareholders to reduce tax through a combination of dividend received deductions and loss on the disposition of the stock.

(g) Regulations.—The Secretary shall prescribe such regulations as may be appropriate to carry out the purposes of this section, including regulations—

(1) providing for the application of this section in the case of stock dividends, stock splits, reorganizations, and other similar transactions, in the case of stock held by pass-thru entities, and in the case of consolidated groups, and

(2) providing that the rules of subsection (f) shall apply in the case of stock which is not preferred as to dividends in cases where stock is structured to avoid the purposes of this section.

§ 1060. Special allocation rules for certain asset acquisitions

(a) General rule.—In the case of any applicable asset acquisition, for purposes of determining both—

(1) the transferee's basis in such assets, and

(2) the gain or loss of the transferor with respect to such acquisition,

the consideration received for such assets shall be allocated among such assets acquired in such acquisition in the same manner as amounts are allocated to assets under section 338(b)(5). If in connection with an applicable asset acquisition, the transferee and transferor agree in writing as to the allocation of any consideration, or as to the fair market value of any of the assets, such agreement shall be binding on both the transferee and transferor unless the Secretary determines that such allocation (or fair market value) is not appropriate.

(b) Information required to be furnished to Secretary.—Under regulations, the transferor and transferee in an applicable asset acquisition shall, at such times and in such manner as may be provided in such regulations, furnish to the Secretary the following information:

(1) The amount of the consideration received for the assets which is allocated to section 197 intangibles.

(2) Any modification of the amount described in paragraph (1).

(3) Any other information with respect to other assets transferred in such acquisition as the Secretary deems necessary to carry out the provisions of this section.

(c) Applicable asset acquisition.—For purposes of this section, the term "applicable asset acquisition" means any transfer (whether directly or indirectly)—

(1) of assets which constitute a trade or business, and

(2) with respect to which the transferee's basis in such assets is determined wholly by reference to the consideration paid for such assets.

A transfer shall not be treated as failing to be an applicable asset acquisition merely because section 1031 applies to a portion of the assets transferred.

(d) Treatment of certain partnership transactions.—In the case of a distribution of partnership property or a transfer of an interest in a partnership—

(1) the rules of subsection (a) shall apply but only for purposes of determining the value of section 197 intangibles for purposes of applying section 755, and

(2) if section 755 applies, such distribution or transfer (as the case may be) shall be treated as an applicable asset acquisition for purposes of subsection (b).

(e) Information required in case of certain transfers of interests in entities.—

(1) In general.—If—

(A) a person who is a 10–percent owner with respect to any entity transfers an interest in such entity, and

(B) in connection with such transfer, such owner (or a related person) enters into an employment contract, covenant not to compete, royalty or lease agreement, or other agreement with the transferee,

such owner and the transferee shall, at such time and in such manner as the Secretary may prescribe, furnish such information as the Secretary may require.

(2) 10–percent owner.—For purposes of this subsection—

(A) In general.—The term ''10–percent owner'' means, with respect to any entity, any person who holds 10 percent or more (by value) of the interests in such entity immediately before the transfer.

(B) Constructive ownership.—Section 318 shall apply in determining ownership of stock in a corporation. Similar principles shall apply in determining the ownership of interests in any other entity.

(3) Related person.—For purposes of this subsection, the term ''related person'' means any person who is related (within the meaning of section 267(b) or 707(b)(1)) to the 10–percent owner.

* * *

PART VII—WASH SALES; STRADDLES

§ 1091. Loss from wash sales of stock or securities

(a) Disallowance of loss deduction.—In the case of any loss claimed to have been sustained from any sale or other disposition of shares of stock or securities where it appears that, within a period beginning 30 days before the date of such sale or disposition and ending 30 days after such date, the taxpayer has acquired (by purchase or by an exchange on which the entire amount of gain or loss was recognized by law), or has entered into a contract or option so to acquire, substantially identical stock or securities, then no deduction shall be allowed under section 165 unless the taxpayer is a dealer in stock or securities and the loss is sustained in a transaction made in the ordinary course of such business. For purposes of this section, the term ''stock or securities'' shall, except as provided in regulations, include contracts or options to acquire or sell stock or securities.

(b) Stock acquired less than stock sold.—If the amount of stock or securities acquired (or covered by the contract or option to acquire) is less than the amount of stock or securities sold or otherwise disposed of, then the particular shares of stock or securities the loss from the sale or other disposition of which is not deductible shall be determined under regulations prescribed by the Secretary.

(c) Stock acquired not less than stock sold.—If the amount of stock or securities acquired (or covered by the contract or option to acquire) is not less than the amount of stock or securities sold or otherwise disposed of, then the particular shares of stock or securities the acquisition of which (or the contract or option to acquire which) resulted in the nondeductibility of the loss shall be determined under regulations prescribed by the Secretary.

(d) Unadjusted basis in case of wash sale of stock.—If the property consists of stock or securities the acquisition of which (or the contract or option to acquire which) resulted in the nondeductibility (under this section or corresponding provisions of prior internal revenue laws) of the loss from the sale or other disposition of substantially identical stock or securities, then the basis shall be the basis of the stock or securities so sold or disposed of, increased or decreased, as the case may be, by the difference, if any, between the price at which the property was acquired and the price at which such substantially identical stock or securities were sold or otherwise disposed of.

(e) Certain short sales of stock or securities and securities futures contracts to sell.—Rules similar to the rules of subsection (a) shall apply to any loss realized on the closing of a short sale of (or the sale, exchange, or termination of a securities futures contract to sell) stock or securities if, within a period beginning 30 days before the date of such closing and ending 30 days after such date—

(1) substantially identical stock or securities were sold, or

(2) another short sale of (or securities futures contracts to sell) substantially identical stock or securities was entered into.

For purposes of this subsection, the term "securities future contract" has the meaning provided by section 1234B(c).

(f) Cash settlement.—This section shall not fail to apply to a contract or option to acquire or sell stock or securities solely by reason of the fact that the contract or option settles in (or could be settled in) cash or property other than stock or securities.

SUBCHAPTER P—CAPITAL GAINS AND LOSSES

Part

PART I—TREATMENT OF CAPITAL GAINS

§ 1201. Alternative tax for corporations

(a) General rule.—If for any taxable year a corporation has a net capital gain and any rate of tax imposed by section 11, 511, or 831(a) or (b) (whichever is applicable) exceeds 35 percent (determined without regard to the last 2 sentences of section 11(b)(1)), then, in lieu of any such tax, there is hereby imposed a tax (if such tax is less than the tax imposed by such sections) which shall consist of the sum of—

(1) a tax computed on the taxable income reduced by the amount of the net capital gain, at the rates and in the manner as if this subsection had not been enacted, plus

(2) a tax of 35 percent of the net capital gain (or, if less, taxable income).

* * *

§ 1202. 50-percent exclusion for gain from certain small business stock

(a) Exclusion.—

* Editorially supplied.

(1) In general.—In the case of a taxpayer other than a corporation, gross income shall not include 50 percent of any gain from the sale or exchange of qualified small business stock held for more than 5 years.

* * *

(3) Special rules for 2009 and certain periods in 2010.—In the case of qualified small business stock acquired after the date of the enactment of this paragraph and on or before the date of the enactment of the Creating Small Business Jobs Act of 2010—

(A) paragraph (1) shall be applied by substituting "75 percent" for "50 percent", and

(B) paragraph (2) shall not apply.

In the case of any stock which would be described in the preceding sentence (but for this sentence), the acquisition date for purposes of this subsection shall be the first day on which such stock was held by the taxpayer determined after the application of section 1223.

(4) 100 percent exclusion for stock acquired during certain periods in 2010, 2011, 2012, and 2013.—In the case of qualified small business stock acquired after the date of the enactment of the Creating Small Business Jobs Act of 2010 and before January 1, 2014—

(A) paragraph (1) shall be applied by substituting "100 percent" for "50 percent",

(B) paragraph (2) shall not apply, and

(C) paragraph (7) of section 57(a) shall not apply.

In the case of any stock which would be described in the preceding sentence (but for this sentence), the acquisition date for purposes of this subsection shall be the first day on which such stock was held by the taxpayer determined after the application of section 1223.

(b) Per-issuer limitation on taxpayer's eligible gain.—

(1) In general.—If the taxpayer has eligible gain for the taxable year from 1 or more dispositions of stock issued by any corporation, the aggregate amount of such gain from dispositions of stock issued by such corporation which may be taken into account under subsection (a) for the taxable year shall not exceed the greater of—

(A) $10,000,000 reduced by the aggregate amount of eligible gain taken into account by the taxpayer under subsection (a) for prior taxable years and attributable to dispositions of stock issued by such corporation, or

(B) 10 times the aggregate adjusted bases of qualified small business stock issued by such corporation and disposed of by the taxpayer during the taxable year.

For purposes of subparagraph (B), the adjusted basis of any stock shall be determined without regard to any addition to basis after the date on which such stock was originally issued.

(2) Eligible gain.—For purposes of this subsection, the term "eligible gain" means any gain from the sale or exchange of qualified small business stock held for more than 5 years.

(3) Treatment of married individuals.—

(A) Separate returns.—In the case of a separate return by a married individual, paragraph (1)(A) shall be applied by substituting "$5,000,000" for "$10,000,000".

(B) Allocation of exclusion.—In the case of any joint return, the amount of gain taken into account under subsection (a) shall be allocated equally between the spouses for purposes of applying this subsection to subsequent taxable years.

(C) Marital status.—For purposes of this subsection, marital status shall be determined under section 7703.

(c) Qualified small business stock.—For purposes of this section—

(1) In general.—Except as otherwise provided in this section, the term "qualified small business stock" means any stock in a C corporation which is originally issued after the date of the enactment of the Revenue Reconciliation Act of 1993, if—

(A) as of the date of issuance, such corporation is a qualified small business, and

(B) except as provided in subsections (f) and (h), such stock is acquired by the taxpayer at its original issue (directly or through an underwriter)—

(i) in exchange for money or other property (not including stock), or

(ii) as compensation for services provided to such corporation (other than services performed as an underwriter of such stock).

(2) Active business requirement; etc.—

(A) In general.—Stock in a corporation shall not be treated as qualified small business stock unless, during substantially all of the taxpayer's holding period for such stock, such corporation meets the active business requirements of subsection (e) and such corporation is a C corporation.

(B) Special rule for certain small business investment companies.—

(i) Waiver of active business requirement.—Notwithstanding any provision of subsection (e), a corporation shall be treated as meeting the active business requirements of such subsection for any period during which such corporation qualifies as a specialized small business investment company.

(ii) Specialized small business investment company.—For purposes of clause (i), the term "specialized small business investment company" means any eligible corporation (as defined in subsection (e)(4)) which is licensed to operate under section 301(d) of the Small Business Investment Act of 1958 (as in effect on May 13, 1993).

(3) Certain purchases by corporation of its own stock.—

(A) Redemptions from taxpayer or related person.—Stock acquired by the taxpayer shall not be treated as qualified small business stock if, at any time during the 4–year period beginning on the date 2 years before the issuance of such stock, the corporation issuing such stock purchased (directly or indirectly) any of its stock from the taxpayer or from a person related (within the meaning of section 267(b) or 707(b)) to the taxpayer.

(B) Significant redemptions.—Stock issued by a corporation shall not be treated as qualified business stock if, during the 2–year period beginning on the date 1 year before the issuance of such stock, such corporation made 1 or more purchases of its stock with an aggregate value (as of the time of the respective purchases) exceeding 5 percent of the aggregate value of all of its stock as of the beginning of such 2–year period.

(C) Treatment of certain transactions.—If any transaction is treated under section 304(a) as a distribution in redemption of the stock of any corporation, for purposes of subparagraphs (A) and (B), such corporation shall be treated as purchasing an amount of its stock equal to the amount treated as such a distribution under section 304(a).

(d) Qualified small business.—For purposes of this section—

(1) In general.—The term "qualified small business" means any domestic corporation which is a C corporation if—

(A) the aggregate gross assets of such corporation (or any predecessor thereof) at all times on or after the date of the enactment of the Revenue Reconciliation Act of 1993 and before the issuance did not exceed $50,000,000,

(B) the aggregate gross assets of such corporation immediately after the issuance (determined by taking into account amounts received in the issuance) do not exceed $50,000,000, and

(C) such corporation agrees to submit such reports to the Secretary and to shareholders as the Secretary may require to carry out the purposes of this section.

(2) Aggregate gross assets.—

(A) In general.—For purposes of paragraph (1), the term "aggregate gross assets" means the amount of cash and the aggregate adjusted bases of other property held by the corporation.

(B) Treatment of contributed property.—For purposes of subparagraph (A), the adjusted basis of any property contributed to the corporation (or other property with a basis determined in whole or in part by reference to the adjusted basis of property so contributed) shall be determined as if the basis of the property contributed to the corporation (immediately after such contribution) were equal to its fair market value as of the time of such contribution.

(3) Aggregation rules.—

(A) In general.—All corporations which are members of the same parent-subsidiary controlled group shall be treated as 1 corporation for purposes of this subsection.

(B) Parent-subsidiary controlled group.—For purposes of subparagraph (A), the term "parent-subsidiary controlled group" means any controlled group of corporations as defined in section 1563(a)(1), except that—

(i) "more than 50 percent" shall be substituted for "at least 80 percent" each place it appears in section 1563(a)(1), and

(ii) section 1563(a)(4) shall not apply.

(e) Active business requirement.—

(1) In general.—For purposes of subsection (c)(2), the requirements of this subsection are met by a corporation for any period if during such period—

(A) at least 80 percent (by value) of the assets of such corporation are used by such corporation in the active conduct of 1 or more qualified trades or businesses, and

(B) such corporation is an eligible corporation.

(2) Special rule for certain activities.—For purposes of paragraph (1), if, in connection with any future qualified trade or business, a corporation is engaged in—

(A) start-up activities described in section 195(c)(1)(A),

(B) activities resulting in the payment or incurring of expenditures which may be treated as research and experimental expenditures under section 174, or

(C) activities with respect to in-house research expenses described in section 41(b)(4), assets used in such activities shall be treated as used in the active conduct of a qualified trade or business. Any determination under this paragraph shall be made without regard to whether a corporation has any gross income from such activities at the time of the determination.

(3) Qualified trade or business.—For purposes of this subsection, the term "qualified trade or business" means any trade or business other than—

(A) any trade or business involving the performance of services in the fields of health, law, engineering, architecture, accounting, actuarial science, performing arts, consulting, athletics, financial services, brokerage services, or any trade or business where the principal asset of such trade or business is the reputation or skill of 1 or more of its employees,

(B) any banking, insurance, financing, leasing, investing, or similar business,

(C) any farming business (including the business of raising or harvesting trees),

(D) any business involving the production or extraction of products of a character with respect to which a deduction is allowable under section 613 or 613A, and

(E) any business of operating a hotel, motel, restaurant, or similar business.

* * *

(7) Maximum real estate holdings.—A corporation shall not be treated as meeting the requirements of paragraph (1) for any period during which more than 10 percent of the total value of its assets consists of real property which is not used in the active conduct of a qualified trade or business. For purposes of the preceding sentence, the ownership of, dealing in, or renting of real property shall not be treated as the active conduct of a qualified trade or business.

(8) Computer software royalties.—For purposes of paragraph (1), rights to computer software which produces active business computer software royalties (within the meaning of section 543(d)(1)) shall be treated as an asset used in the active conduct of a trade or business.

* * *

PART II—TREATMENT OF CAPITAL LOSSES

§ 1211. Limitation on capital losses

(a) Corporations.—In the case of a corporation, losses from sales or exchanges of capital assets shall be allowed only to the extent of gains from such sales or exchanges.

(b) Other taxpayers.—In the case of a taxpayer other than a corporation, losses from sales or exchanges of capital assets shall be allowed only to the extent of the gains from such sales or exchanges, plus (if such losses exceed such gains) the lower of—

(1) $3,000 ($1,500 in the case of a married individual filing a separate return), or

(2) the excess of such losses over such gains.

§ 1212. Capital loss carrybacks and carryovers

(a) Corporations.—

(1) In general.—If a corporation has a net capital loss for any taxable year (hereinafter in this paragraph referred to as the "loss year"), the amount thereof shall be—

(A) a capital loss carryback to each of the 3 taxable years preceding the loss year, but only to the extent—

* * *

(ii) the carryback of such loss does not increase or produce a net operating loss (as defined in section 172(c)) for the taxable year to which it is being carried back;

(B) except as provided in subparagraph (C), a capital loss carryover to each of the 5 taxable years succeeding the loss year; and

* * *

and shall be treated as a short-term capital loss in each such taxable year. The entire amount of the net capital loss for any taxable year shall be carried to the earliest of the taxable years to which such loss may be carried, and the portion of such loss which shall be carried to each of the other taxable years to which such loss may be carried shall be the excess, if any, of such loss over the total of the capital gain net income for each of the prior taxable years to which such loss may be carried. For purposes of the preceding sentence, the capital gain net income for any such prior taxable year shall be computed without regard to the net capital loss for the loss year or for any taxable year thereafter. In the case of any net capital loss which cannot be carried back in full to a preceding taxable year by reason of clause (ii) of subparagraph (A), the capital gain net income for such prior taxable year shall in no case be treated as greater than the amount of such loss which can be carried back to such preceding taxable year upon the application of such clause (ii).

* * *

(b) Other taxpayers.—

(1) In general.—If a taxpayer other than a corporation has a net capital loss for any taxable year—

(A) the excess of the net short-term capital loss over the net long-term capital gain for such year shall be a short-term capital loss in the succeeding taxable year, and

(B) the excess of the net long-term capital loss over the net short-term capital gain for such year shall be a long-term capital loss in the succeeding taxable year.

(2) Treatment of amounts allowed under section 1211(b)(1) or (2).—

(A) In general.—For purposes of determining the excess referred to in subparagraph (A) or (B) of paragraph (1), there shall be treated as a short-term capital gain in the taxable year an amount equal to the lesser of—

(i) the amount allowed for the taxable year under paragraph (1) or (2) of section 1211(b), or

(ii) the adjusted taxable income for such taxable year.

(B) Adjusted taxable income.—For purposes of subparagraph (A), the term "adjusted taxable income" means taxable income increased by the sum of—

(i) the amount allowed for the taxable year under paragraph (1) or (2) of section 1211(b), and

(ii) the deduction allowed for such year under section 151 or any deduction in lieu thereof.

For purposes of the preceding sentence, any excess of the deductions allowed for the taxable year over the gross income for such year shall be taken into account as negative taxable income.

* * *

PART III—GENERAL RULES FOR DETERMINING CAPITAL GAINS AND LOSSES

§ 1221. Capital asset defined

(a) In general.—For purposes of this subtitle, the term "capital asset" means property held by the taxpayer (whether or not connected with his trade or business), but does not include—

(1) stock in trade of the taxpayer or other property of a kind which would properly be included in the inventory of the taxpayer if on hand at the close of the taxable year, or property held by the taxpayer primarily for sale to customers in the ordinary course of his trade or business;

(2) property, used in his trade or business, of a character which is subject to the allowance for depreciation provided in section 167, or real property used in his trade or business;

(3) a copyright, a literary, musical, or artistic composition, a letter or memorandum, or similar property, held by—

(A) a taxpayer whose personal efforts created such property,

(B) in the case of a letter, memorandum, or similar property, a taxpayer for whom such property was prepared or produced, or

(C) a taxpayer in whose hands the basis of such property is determined, for purposes of determining gain from a sale or exchange, in whole or part by reference to the basis of such property in the hands of a taxpayer described in subparagraph (A) or (B);

(4) accounts or notes receivable acquired in the ordinary course of trade or business for services rendered or from the sale of property described in paragraph (1);

(5) a publication of the United States Government (including the Congressional Record) which is received from the United States Government or any agency thereof, other than by purchase at the price at which it is offered for sale to the public, and which is held by—

(A) a taxpayer who so received such publication, or

(B) a taxpayer in whose hands the basis of such publication is determined, for purposes of determining gain from a sale or exchange, in whole or in part by reference to the basis of such publication in the hands of a taxpayer described in subparagraph (A);

(6) any commodities derivative financial instrument held by a commodities derivatives dealer, unless—

(A) it is established to the satisfaction of the Secretary that such instrument has no connection to the activities of such dealer as a dealer, and

(B) such instrument is clearly identified in such dealer's records as being described in subparagraph (A) before the close of the day on which it was acquired, originated, or entered into (or such other time as the Secretary may by regulations prescribe);

(7) any hedging transaction which is clearly identified as such before the close of the day on which it was acquired, originated, or entered into (or such other time as the Secretary may by regulations prescribe); or

(8) supplies of a type regularly used or consumed by the taxpayer in the ordinary course of a trade or business of the taxpayer.

(b) Definitions and special rules.—

(1) Commodities derivative financial instruments.—For purposes of subsection (a)(6)—

(A) Commodities derivatives dealer.—The term "commodities derivatives dealer" means a person which regularly offers to enter into, assume, offset, assign, or terminate positions in commodities derivative financial instruments with customers in the ordinary course of a trade or business.

(B) Commodities derivative financial instrument.—

(i) In general.—The term "commodities derivative financial instrument" means any contract or financial instrument with respect to commodities (other than a share of stock in a corporation, a beneficial interest in a partnership or trust, a note, bond, debenture, or other evidence of indebtedness, or a section 1256 contract (as defined in section 1256(b))), the value or settlement price of which is calculated by or determined by reference to a specified index.

(ii) Specified index.—The term "specified index" means any one or more or any combination of—

(I) a fixed rate, price or amount, or

(II) a variable rate, price, or amount, which is based on any current, objectively determinable financial or economic information with respect to commodities which is not within the control of any of the parties to the contract or instrument and is not unique to any of the parties' circumstances.

(2) Hedging transaction.—

(A) In general.—For purposes of this section, the term "hedging transaction" means any transaction entered into by the taxpayer in the normal course of the taxpayer's trade or business primarily—

(i) to manage risk of price changes or currency fluctuations with respect to ordinary property which is held or to be held by the taxpayer,

(ii) to manage risk of interest rate or price changes or currency fluctuations with respect to borrowings made or to be made, or ordinary obligations incurred or to be incurred, by the taxpayer, or

(iii) to manage such other risks as the Secretary may prescribe in regulations.

(B) Treatment of nonidentification or improper identification of hedging transactions.—Notwithstanding subsection (a)(7), the Secretary shall prescribe regulations to properly characterize any income, gain, expense, or loss arising from a transaction—

(i) which is a hedging transaction but which was not identified as such in accordance with subsection (a)(7), or

(ii) which was so identified but is not a hedging transaction.

(3) Sale or exchange of self-created musical works.—At the election of the taxpayer, paragraphs (1) and (3) of subsection (a) shall not apply to musical compositions or copyrights in musical works sold or exchanged by a taxpayer described in subsection (a)(3).

(4) Regulations.—The Secretary shall prescribe such regulations as are appropriate to carry out the purposes of paragraph (6) and (7) of subsection (a) in the case of transactions involving related parties.

§ 1222. Other terms relating to capital gains and losses

For purposes of this subtitle—

(1) Short-term capital gain.—The term "short-term capital gain" means gain from the sale or exchange of a capital asset held for not more than 1 year, if and to the extent such gain is taken into account in computing gross income.

(2) Short-term capital loss.—The term "short-term capital loss" means loss from the sale or exchange of a capital asset held for not more than 1 year, if and to the extent that such loss is taken into account in computing taxable income.

(3) Long-term capital gain.—The term "long-term capital gain" means gain from the sale or exchange of a capital asset held for more than 1 year, if and to the extent such gain is taken into account in computing gross income.

(4) Long-term capital loss.—The term "long-term capital loss" means loss from the sale or exchange of a capital asset held for more than 1 year, if and to the extent that such loss is taken into account in computing taxable income.

(5) Net short-term capital gain.—The term "net short-term capital gain" means the excess of short-term capital gains for the taxable year over the short-term capital losses for such year.

(6) Net short-term capital loss.—The term "net short-term capital loss" means the excess of short-term capital losses for the taxable year over the short-term capital gains for such year.

(7) Net long-term capital gain.—The term "net long-term capital gain" means the excess of long-term capital gains for the taxable year over the long-term capital losses for such year.

(8) Net long-term capital loss.—The term "net long-term capital loss" means the excess of long-term capital losses for the taxable year over the long-term capital gains for such year.

(9) Capital gain net income.—The term "capital gain net income" means the excess of the gains from sales or exchanges of capital assets over the losses from such sales or exchanges.

(10) Net capital loss.—The term "net capital loss" means the excess of the losses from sales or exchanges of capital assets over the sum allowed under section 1211. In the case of a corporation, for the purpose of determining losses under this paragraph, amounts which are short-term capital losses under section 1212(a)(1) shall be excluded.

(11) Net capital gain.—The term "net capital gain" means the excess of the net long-term capital gain for the taxable year over the net short-term capital loss for such year.

* * *

§ 1223. Holding period of property

For purposes of this subtitle—

(1) In determining the period for which the taxpayer has held property received in an exchange, there shall be included the period for which he held the property exchanged if, under this chapter, the property has, for the purpose of determining gain or loss from a sale or exchange, the same basis in whole or in part in his hands as the property exchanged, and, in the case of such exchanges after March 1, 1954, the property exchanged at the time of such exchange was a capital asset as defined in section 1221 or property described in section 1231. For purposes of this paragraph—

(A) an involuntary conversion described in section 1033 shall be considered an exchange of the property converted for the property acquired, and

(B) a distribution to which section 355 (or so much of section 356 as relates to section 355) applies shall be treated as an exchange.

(2) In determining the period for which the taxpayer has held property however acquired there shall be included the period for which such property was held by any other person, if under this chapter such property has, for the purpose of determining gain or loss from a sale or exchange, the same basis in whole or in part in his hands as it would have in the hands of such other person.

(3) In determining the period for which the taxpayer has held stock or securities the acquisition of which (or the contract or option to acquire which) resulted in the nondeductibility (under section 1091 relating to wash sales) of the loss from the sale or other disposition of substantially identical stock or securities, there shall be included the period for which he held the stock or securities the loss from the sale or other disposition of which was not deductible.

(4) In determining the period for which the taxpayer has held stock or rights to acquire stock received on a distribution, if the basis of such stock or rights is determined under section 307 (or under so much of section 1052(c) as refers to section 113(a)(23) of the Internal Revenue Code of 1939), there shall (under regulations prescribed by the Secretary) be included the period for which he held the stock in the distributing corporation before the receipt of such stock or rights upon such distribution.

(5) In determining the period for which the taxpayer has held stock or securities acquired from a corporation by the exercise of rights to acquire such stock or securities, there shall be included only the period beginning with the date on which the right to acquire was exercised.

* * *

(7) In determining the period for which the taxpayer has held a commodity acquired in satisfaction of a commodity futures contract (other than a commodity futures contract to which section 1256 applies) there shall be included the period for which he held the commodity futures contract if such commodity futures contract was a capital asset in his hands.

* * *

(9) In the case of a person acquiring property from a decedent or to whom property passed from a decedent (within the meaning of section 1014(b)), if—

(A) the basis of such property in the hands of such person is determined under section 1014, and

(B) such property is sold or otherwise disposed of by such person within 1 year after the decedent's death,

then such person shall be considered to have held such property for more than 1 year.

(10) If—

(A) property is acquired by any person in a transfer to which section 1040 applies,

(B) such property is sold or otherwise disposed of by such person within 1 year after the decedent's death, and

(C) such sale or disposition is to a person who is a qualified heir (as defined in section 2032A(e)(1)) with respect to the decedent, then the person making such sale or other disposition shall be considered to have held such property for more than 1 year.

* * *

(14) If the security to which a securities futures contract (as defined in section 1234B) relates (other than a contract to which section 1256 applies) is acquired in satisfaction of such contract, in determining the period for which the taxpayer has held such security, there shall be included the period for which the taxpayer held such contract if such contract was a capital asset in the hands of the taxpayer.

* * *

PART IV—SPECIAL RULES FOR DETERMINING CAPITAL GAINS AND LOSSES

§ 1231. Property used in the trade or business and involuntary conversions

(a) General rule.—

(1) Gains exceed losses.—If—

(A) the section 1231 gains for any taxable year, exceed

(B) the section 1231 losses for such taxable year,

such gains and losses shall be treated as long-term capital gains or long-term capital losses, as the case may be.

(2) Gains do not exceed losses.—If—

(A) the section 1231 gains for any taxable year, do not exceed

(B) the section 1231 losses for such taxable year,

such gains and losses shall not be treated as gains and losses from sales or exchanges of capital assets.

(3) Section 1231 gains and losses.—For purposes of this subsection—

(A) Section 1231 gain.—The term "section 1231 gain" means—

(i) any recognized gain on the sale or exchange of property used in the trade or business, and

(ii) any recognized gain from the compulsory or involuntary conversion (as a result of destruction in whole or in part, theft or seizure, or an exercise of the power of requisition or condemnation or the threat or imminence thereof) into other property or money of—

(I) property used in the trade or business, or

(II) any capital asset which is held for more than 1 year and is held in connection with a trade or business or a transaction entered into for profit.

(B) Section 1231 loss.—The term "section 1231 loss" means any recognized loss from a sale or exchange or conversion described in subparagraph (A).

(4) Special rules.—For purposes of this subsection—

(A) In determining under this subsection whether gains exceed losses—

(i) the section 1231 gains shall be included only if and to the extent taken into account in computing gross income, and

(ii) the section 1231 losses shall be included only if and to the extent taken into account in computing taxable income, except that section 1211 shall not apply.

(B) Losses (including losses not compensated for by insurance or otherwise) on the destruction, in whole or in part, theft or seizure, or requisition or condemnation of—

(i) property used in the trade or business, or

(ii) capital assets which are held for more than 1 year and are held in connection with a trade or business or a transaction entered into for profit,

shall be treated as losses from a compulsory or involuntary conversion.

(C) In the case of any involuntary conversion (subject to the provisions of this subsection but for this sentence) arising from fire, storm, shipwreck, or other casualty, or from theft, of any—

(i) property used in the trade or business, or

(ii) any capital asset which is held for more than 1 year and is held in connection with a trade or business or a transaction entered into for profit,

this subsection shall not apply to such conversion (whether resulting in gain or loss) if during the taxable year the recognized losses from such conversions exceed the recognized gains from such conversions.

(b) Definition of property used in the trade or business.—For purposes of this section—

(1) General rule.—The term "property used in the trade or business" means property used in the trade or business, of a character which is subject to the allowance for depreciation provided in section 167, held for more than 1 year, and real property used in the trade or business, held for more than 1 year, which is not—

(A) property of a kind which would properly be includible in the inventory of the taxpayer if on hand at the close of the taxable year,

(B) property held by the taxpayer primarily for sale to customers in the ordinary course of his trade or business,

(C) a copyright, a literary, musical, or artistic composition, a letter or memorandum, or similar property, held by a taxpayer described in paragraph (3) of section 1221(a), or

(D) a publication of the United States Government (including the Congressional Record) which is received from the United States Government, or any agency thereof, other than by purchase at the price at which it is offered for sale to the public, and which is held by a taxpayer described in paragraph (5) of section 1221(a).

(2) Timber, coal, or domestic iron ore.—Such term includes timber, coal, and iron ore with respect to which section 631 applies.

(3) Livestock.—Such term includes—

(A) cattle and horses, regardless of age, held by the taxpayer for draft, breeding, dairy, or sporting purposes, and held by him for 24 months or more from the date of acquisition, and

(B) other livestock, regardless of age, held by the taxpayer for draft, breeding, dairy, or sporting purposes, and held by him for 12 months or more from the date of acquisition.

Such term does not include poultry.

(4) Unharvested crop.—In the case of an unharvested crop on land used in the trade or business and held for more than 1 year, if the crop and the land are sold or exchanged (or compulsorily or involuntarily converted) at the same time and to the same person, the crop shall be considered as "property used in the trade or business."

(c) Recapture of net ordinary losses.—

(1) In general.—The net section 1231 gain for any taxable year shall be treated as ordinary income to the extent such gain does not exceed the non-recaptured net section 1231 losses.

(2) Non-recaptured net section 1231 losses.—For purposes of this subsection, the term "non-recaptured net section 1231 losses" means the excess of—

(A) the aggregate amount of the net section 1231 losses for the 5 most recent preceding taxable years beginning after December 31, 1981, over

(B) the portion of such losses taken into account under paragraph (1) for such preceding taxable years.

(3) Net section 1231 gain.—For purposes of this subsection, the term "net section 1231 gain" means the excess of—

(A) the section 1231 gains, over

(B) the section 1231 losses.

(4) Net section 1231 loss.—For purposes of this subsection, the term "net section 1231 loss" means the excess of—

(A) the section 1231 losses, over

(B) the section 1231 gains.

(5) Special rules.—For purposes of determining the amount of the net section 1231 gain or loss for any taxable year, the rules of paragraph (4) of subsection (a) shall apply.

§ 1233. Gains and losses from short sales

(a) Capital assets.—For purposes of this subtitle, gain or loss from the short sale of property shall be considered as gain or loss from the sale or exchange of a capital asset to the extent that the property, including a commodity future, used to close the short sale constitutes a capital asset in the hands of the taxpayer.

(b) Short-term gains and holding periods.—If gain or loss from a short sale is considered as gain or loss from the sale or exchange of a capital asset under subsection (a) and if on the date of such short sale substantially identical property has been held by the taxpayer for not more than 1 year (determined without regard to the effect, under paragraph (2) of this subsection, of such short sale on the holding period), or if substantially identical property is acquired by the taxpayer after such short sale and on or before the date of the closing thereof—

(1) any gain on the closing of such short sale shall be considered as a gain on the sale or exchange of a capital asset held for not more than 1 year (notwithstanding the period of time any property used to close such short sale has been held); and

(2) the holding period of such substantially identical property shall be considered to begin (notwithstanding section 1223, relating to the holding period of property) on the date of the closing of the short sale, or on the date of a sale, gift, or other disposition of such property, whichever date occurs first. This paragraph shall apply to such substantially identical property in the order of the dates of the acquisition of such property, but only to so much of such property as does not exceed the quantity sold short.

For purposes of this subsection, the acquisition of an option to sell property at a fixed price shall be considered as a short sale, and the exercise or failure to exercise such option shall be considered as a closing of such short sale.

(c) Certain options to sell.—Subsection (b) shall not include an option to sell property at a fixed price acquired on the same day on which the property identified as intended to be used in exercising such option is acquired and which, if exercised, is exercised through the sale of the property so identified. If the option is not exercised, the cost of the option shall be added to the basis of the property with which the option is identified. * * *

(d) Long-term losses.—If on the date of such short sale substantially identical property has been held by the taxpayer for more than 1 year, any loss on the closing of such short sale shall be considered as a loss on the sale or exchange of a capital asset held for more than 1 year (notwithstanding the period of time any property used to close such short sale has been held, and notwithstanding section 1234).

(e) Rules for application of section.—

(1) Subsection (b)(1) or (d) shall not apply to the gain or loss, respectively, on any quantity of property used to close such short sale which is in excess of the quantity of the substantially identical property referred to in the applicable subsection.

(2) For purposes of subsections (b) and (d)—

(A) the term "property" includes only stocks and securities (including stocks and securities dealt with on a "when issued" basis), and commodity futures, which are capital assets in the hands of the taxpayer, * * *;

(B) in the case of futures transactions in any commodity on or subject to the rules of a board of trade or commodity exchange, a commodity future requiring delivery in 1 calendar month shall not be considered as property substantially identical to another commodity future requiring delivery in a different calendar month;

(C) in the case of a short sale of property by an individual, the term "taxpayer", in the application of this subsection and subsections (b) and (d), shall be read as "taxpayer or his spouse"; but an individual who is legally separated from the taxpayer under a decree of divorce or of separate maintenance shall not be considered as the spouse of the taxpayer;

(D) a securities futures contract (as defined in section 1234B) to acquire substantially identical property shall be treated as substantially identical property; and

(E) entering into a securities futures contract (as so defined) to sell shall be considered to be a short sale, and the settlement of such contract shall be considered to be the closing of such short sale.

(3) Where the taxpayer enters into 2 commodity futures transactions on the same day, one requiring delivery by him in one market and the other requiring delivery to him of the same (or substantially identical) commodity in the same calendar month in a different market, and the taxpayer subsequently closes both such transactions on the same day, subsections (b) and (d) shall have no application to so much of the commodity involved in either such transaction as does not exceed in quantity the commodity involved in the other.

(4)(A) In the case of a taxpayer who is a dealer in securities (within the meaning of section 1236)—

(i) if, on the date of a short sale of stock, substantially identical property which is a capital asset in the hands of the taxpayer has been held for not more than 1 year, and

(ii) if such short sale is closed more than 20 days after the date on which it was made,

subsection (b)(2) shall apply in respect of the holding period of such substantially identical property.

(B) For purposes of subparagraph (A)—

(i) the last sentence of subsection (b) applies; and

(ii) the term "stock" means any share or certificate of stock in a corporation, any bond or other evidence of indebtedness which is convertible into any such share or certificate, or any evidence of an interest in, or right to subscribe to or purchase, any of the foregoing.

* * *

(g) Hedging transactions.—This section shall not apply in the case of a hedging transaction in commodity futures.

* * *

§ 1234. Options to buy or sell

(a) Treatment of gain or loss in the case of the purchaser.—

(1) General rule.—Gain or loss attributable to the sale or exchange of, or loss attributable to failure to exercise, an option to buy or sell property shall be considered gain or loss from the sale or exchange of property which has the same character as the property to which the option relates has in the hands of the taxpayer (or would have in the hands of the taxpayer if acquired by him).

(2) Special rule for loss attributable to failure to exercise option.—For purposes of paragraph (1), if loss is attributable to failure to exercise an option, the option shall be deemed to have been sold or exchanged on the day it expired.

(3) Nonapplication of subsection.—This subsection shall not apply to—

(A) an option which constitutes property described in paragraph (1) of section 1221(a);

(B) in the case of gain attributable to the sale or exchange of an option, any income derived in connection with such option which, without regard to this subsection, is treated as other than gain from the sale or exchange of a capital asset; and

(C) a loss attributable to failure to exercise an option described in section 1233(c).

(b) Treatment of grantor of option in the case of stock, securities, or commodities.—

(1) General rule.—In the case of the grantor of the option, gain or loss from any closing transaction with respect to, and gain on lapse of, an option in property shall be treated as a gain or loss from the sale or exchange of a capital asset held not more than 1 year.

(2) Definitions.—For purposes of this subsection—

(A) Closing transaction.—The term "closing transaction" means any termination of the taxpayer's obligation under an option in property other than through the exercise or lapse of the option.

(B) Property.—The term "property" means stocks and securities (including stocks and securities dealt with on a "when issued" basis), commodities, and commodity futures.

(3) Nonapplication of subsection.—This subsection shall not apply to any option granted in the ordinary course of the taxpayer's trade or business of granting options.

(c) Treatment of options on section 1256 contracts and cash settlement options.—

(1) Section 1256 contracts.—Gain or loss shall be recognized on the exercise of an option on a section 1256 contract (within the meaning of section 1256(b)).

(2) Treatment of cash settlement options.—

(A) In general.—For purposes of subsections (a) and (b), a cash settlement option shall be treated as an option to buy or sell property.

(B) Cash settlement option.—For purposes of subparagraph (A), the term "cash settlement option" means any option which on exercise settles in (or could be settled in) cash or property other than the underlying property.

§ 1234A. Gains or losses from certain terminations

Gain or loss attributable to the cancellation, lapse, expiration, or other termination of—

(1) a right or obligation (other than a securities contract, as defined in section 1234B) with respect to property which is (or on acquisition would be) a capital asset in the hands of the taxpayer, or

(2) a section 1256 contract (as defined in section 1256) not described in paragraph (1) which is a capital asset in the hands of the taxpayer,

shall be treated as gain or loss from the sale of a capital asset. The preceding sentence shall not apply to the retirement of any debt instrument (whether or not through a trust or other participation arrangement).

§ 1234B. Gains or losses from securities futures contracts

(a) Treatment of gain or loss.—

(1) In general.—Gain or loss attributable to the sale, exchange, or termination of a securities futures contract shall be considered gain or loss from the sale or exchange of property which has the same character as the property to which the contract relates has in the hands of the taxpayer (or would have in the hands of the taxpayer if acquired by the taxpayer).

(2) Nonapplication of subsection.—This subsection shall not apply to—

(A) a contract which constitutes property described in paragraph (1) or (7) of section 1221(a), and

(B) any income derived in connection with a contract which, without regard to this subsection, is treated as other than gain from the sale or exchange of a capital asset.

(b) Short-term gains and losses.—Except as provided in the regulations under section 1092(b) or this section or in section 1233, if gain or loss on the sale, exchange, or termination of a securities futures contract to sell property is considered as gain or loss from the sale or exchange of a capital asset, such gain or loss shall be treated as short-term capital gain or loss.

(c) Securities futures contract.—For purposes of this section, the term "securities futures contract" means any security future (as defined in section 3(a)(55)(A) of the Securities Exchange Act of 1934, as in effect on the date of the enactment of this section). * * *

(d) Contracts not treated as commodity futures contracts.—For purposes of this title, a securities futures contract shall not be treated as a commodity futures contract.

(e) Regulations.—The Secretary shall prescribe such regulations as may be appropriate to provide for the proper treatment of securities futures contracts under this title.

* * *

§ 1235. Sale or exchange of patents

(a) General.—A transfer (other than by gift, inheritance, or devise) of property consisting of all substantial rights to a patent, or an undivided interest therein which includes a part of all such rights, by any holder shall be considered the sale or exchange of a capital asset held for more than 1 year, regardless of whether or not payments in consideration of such transfer are—

(1) payable periodically over a period generally coterminous with the transferee's use of the patent, or

(2) contingent on the productivity, use, or disposition of the property transferred.

(b) "Holder" defined.—For purposes of this section, the term "holder" means—

(1) any individual whose efforts created such property, or

(2) any other individual who has acquired his interest in such property in exchange for consideration in money or money's worth paid to such creator prior to actual reduction to practice of the invention covered by the patent, if such individual is neither—

(A) the employer of such creator, nor

(B) related to such creator (within the meaning of subsection (d)).

* * *

(d) Related persons.—Subsection (a) shall not apply to any transfer, directly or indirectly, between persons specified within any one of the paragraphs of section 267(b) or persons described in section 707(b); except that, in applying section 267(b) and (c) and section 707(b) for purposes of this section—

(1) the phrase "25 percent or more" shall be substituted for the phrase "more than 50 percent" each place it appears in section 267(b) or 707(b), and

(2) paragraph (4) of section 267(c) shall be treated as providing that the family of an individual shall include only his spouse, ancestors, and lineal descendants.

* * *

§ 1236. Dealers in securities

(a) Capital gains.—Gain by a dealer in securities from the sale or exchange of any security shall in no event be considered as gain from the sale or exchange of a capital asset unless—

(1) the security was, before the close of the day on which it was acquired (or such earlier time as the Secretary may prescribe by regulations), clearly identified in the dealer's records as a security held for investment; and

(2) the security was not, at any time after the close of such day (or such earlier time), held by such dealer primarily for sale to customers in the ordinary course of his trade or business.

(b) Ordinary losses.—Loss by a dealer in securities from the sale or exchange of any security shall, * * *, in no event be considered as ordinary loss if at any time after November 19, 1951, the security was clearly identified in the dealer's records as a security held for investment.

(c) Definition of security.—For purposes of this section, the term "security" means any share of stock in any corporation, certificate of stock or interest in any corporation, note, bond, debenture, or evidence of indebtedness, or any evidence of an interest in or right to subscribe to or purchase any of the foregoing.

* * *

(e) Special rule for options.—For purposes of subsection (a), any security acquired by a dealer pursuant to an option held by such dealer may be treated as held for investment only if the dealer, before the close of the day on which the option was acquired, clearly identified the option on his records as held for investment. For purposes of the preceding sentence, the term "option" includes the right to subscribe to or purchase any security.

§ 1237. Real property subdivided for sale

(a) General.—Any lot or parcel which is part of a tract of real property in the hands of a taxpayer other than a C corporation shall not be deemed to be held primarily for sale to customers in the ordinary course of trade or business at the time of sale solely because of the taxpayer having subdivided such tract for purposes of sale or because of any activity incident to such subdivision or sale, if—

(1) such tract, or any lot or parcel thereof, had not previously been held by such taxpayer primarily for sale to customers in the ordinary course of trade or business (unless such tract at such previous time would have been covered by this section) and, in the same taxable year in which the sale occurs, such taxpayer does not so hold any other real property; and

(2) no substantial improvement that substantially enhances the value of the lot or parcel sold is made by the taxpayer on such tract while held by the taxpayer or is made pursuant to a contract of sale entered into between the taxpayer and the buyer. For purposes of this paragraph, an improvement shall be deemed to be made by the taxpayer if such improvement was made by—

(A) the taxpayer or members of his family (as defined in section 267(c) (4)), by a corporation controlled by the taxpayer, an S corporation which included the taxpayer as a shareholder, or by a partnership which included the taxpayer as a partner; or

(B) a lessee, but only if the improvement constitutes income to the taxpayer; or

(C) Federal, State, or local government, or political subdivision thereof, but only if the improvement constitutes an addition to basis for the taxpayer; and

(3) such lot or parcel, except in the case of real property acquired by inheritance or devise, is held by the taxpayer for a period of 5 years.

(b) Special rules for application of section.—

(1) Gains.—If more than 5 lots or parcels contained in the same tract of real property are sold or exchanged, gain from any sale or exchange (which occurs in or after the taxable year in which the sixth lot or parcel is sold or exchanged) of any lot or parcel which comes within the provisions of paragraphs (1), (2) and (3) of subsection (a) of this section shall be deemed to be gain from the sale of property held primarily for sale to customers in the ordinary course of the trade or business to the extent of 5 percent of the selling price.

(2) Expenditures of sale.—For the purpose of computing gain under paragraph (1) of this subsection, expenditures incurred in connection with the sale or exchange of any lot or parcel shall neither be allowed as a deduction in computing taxable income, nor treated as reducing the amount realized on such sale or exchange; but so much of such expenditures as does not exceed the portion of gain deemed under paragraph (1) of this subsection to be gain from the sale of property held primarily for sale to customers in the ordinary course of trade or business shall be so allowed as a deduction, and the remainder, if any, shall be treated as reducing the amount realized on such sale or exchange.

(3) Necessary improvements.—No improvement shall be deemed a substantial improvement for purposes of subsection (a) if the lot or parcel is held by the taxpayer for a period of 10 years and if—

(A) such improvement is the building or installation of water, sewer, or drainage facilities or roads (if such improvement would except for this paragraph constitute a substantial improvement);

(B) it is shown to the satisfaction of the Secretary that the lot or parcel, the value of which was substantially enhanced by such improvement, would not have been marketable at the prevailing local price for similar building sites without such improvement; and

(C) the taxpayer elects, in accordance with regulations prescribed by the Secretary, to make no adjustment to basis of the lot or parcel, or of any other property owned by the taxpayer, on account of the expenditures for such improvements. Such election shall not make any item deductible which would not otherwise be deductible.

(c) Tract defined.—For purposes of this section, the term "tract of real property" means a single piece of real property, except that 2 or more pieces of real property shall be considered a tract if at any time they were contiguous in the hands of the taxpayer or if they would be contiguous except for the interposition of a road, street, railroad, stream, or similar property. If, following the sale or exchange of any lot or parcel from a tract of real property, no further sales or exchanges of any other lots or parcels from the remainder of such tract are made for a period of 5 years, such remainder shall be deemed a tract.

§ 1239. Gain from sale of depreciable property between certain related taxpayers

(a) Treatment of gain as ordinary income.—In the case of a sale or exchange of property, directly or indirectly, between related persons, any gain recognized to the transferor shall be treated as ordinary income if such property is, in the hands of the transferee, of a character which is subject to the allowance for depreciation provided in section 167.

(b) Related persons.—For purposes of subsection (a), the term "related persons" means—

(1) a person and all entities which are controlled entities with respect to such person,

(2) a taxpayer and any trust in which such taxpayer (or his spouse) is a beneficiary, unless such beneficiary's interest in the trust is a remote contingent interest (within the meaning of section 318(a)(3)(B)(i)), and

(3) except in the case of a sale or exchange in satisfaction of a pecuniary bequest, an executor of an estate and a beneficiary of such estate.

(c) Controlled entity defined.—

(1) General rule.—For purposes of this section, the term "controlled entity" means, with respect to any person—

(A) a corporation more than 50 percent of the value of the outstanding stock of which is owned (directly or indirectly) by or for such person,

(B) a partnership more than 50 percent of the capital interest or profits interest in which is owned (directly or indirectly) by or for such person, and

(C) any entity which is a related person to such person under paragraph (3), (10), (11), or (12) of section 267(b).

(2) Constructive ownership.—For purposes of this section, ownership shall be determined in accordance with rules similar to the rules under section 267(c) (other than paragraph (3) thereof).

(d) Employer and related employee association.—For purposes of subsection (a), the term "related person" also includes—

(1) an employer and any person related to the employer (within the meaning of subsection (b)), and

(2) a welfare benefit fund (within the meaning of section 419(e)) which is controlled directly or indirectly by persons referred to in paragraph (1).

(e) Patent applications treated as depreciable property.—For purposes of this section, a patent application shall be treated as property which, in the hands of the transferee, is of a character which is subject to the allowance for depreciation provided in section 167.

§ 1241. Cancellation of lease or distributor's agreement

Amounts received by a lessee for the cancellation of a lease, or by a distributor of goods for the cancellation of a distributor's agreement (if the distributor has a substantial capital investment in the distributorship), shall be considered as amounts received in exchange for such lease or agreement.

§ 1244. Losses on small business stock

(a) General rule.—In the case of an individual, a loss on section 1244 stock issued to such individual or to a partnership which would (but for this section) be treated as a loss from the sale or exchange of a capital asset shall, to the extent provided in this section, be treated as an ordinary loss.

(b) Maximum amount for any taxable year.—For any taxable year the aggregate amount treated by the taxpayer by reason of this section as an ordinary loss shall not exceed—

(1) $50,000, or

(2) $100,000, in the case of a husband and wife filing a joint return for such year under section 6013.

(c) Section 1244 stock defined.—

(1) In general.—For purposes of this section, the term "section 1244 stock" means stock in a domestic corporation if—

(A) at the time such stock is issued, such corporation was a small business corporation,

(B) such stock was issued by such corporation for money or other property (other than stock and securities), and

(C) such corporation, during the period of its 5 most recent taxable years ending before the date the loss on such stock was sustained, derived more than 50

percent of its aggregate gross receipts from sources other than royalties, rents, dividends, interests, annuities, and sales or exchanges of stocks or securities.

(2) Rules for application of paragraph (1)(C).—

(A) Period taken into account with respect to new corporations.—For purposes of paragraph (1)(C), if the corporation has not been in existence for 5 taxable years ending before the date the loss on the stock was sustained, there shall be substituted for such 5–year period—

(i) the period of the corporation's taxable years ending before such date, or

(ii) if the corporation has not been in existence for 1 taxable year ending before such date, the period such corporation has been in existence before such date.

(B) Gross receipts from sales of securities.—For purposes of paragraph (1)(C), gross receipts from the sales or exchanges of stock or securities shall be taken into account only to the extent of gains therefrom.

(C) Nonapplication where deductions exceed gross income.—Paragraph (1)(C) shall not apply with respect to any corporation if, for the period taken into account for purposes of paragraph (1)(C), the amount of the deductions allowed by this chapter (other than by sections 172, 243, 244, and 245) exceeds the amount of gross income.

(3) Small business corporation defined.—

(A) In general.—For purposes of this section, a corporation shall be treated as a small business corporation if the aggregate amount of money and other property received by the corporation for stock, as a contribution to capital, and as paid-in surplus, does not exceed $1,000,000. The determination under the preceding sentence shall be made as of the time of the issuance of the stock in question but shall include amounts received for such stock and for all stock theretofore issued.

(B) Amount taken into account with respect to property.—For purposes of subparagraph (A), the amount taken into account with respect to any property other than money shall be the amount equal to the adjusted basis to the corporation of such property for determining gain, reduced by any liability to which the property was subject or which was assumed by the corporation. The determination under the preceding sentence shall be made as of the time the property was received by the corporation.

(d) Special rules.—

(1) Limitations on amount of ordinary loss.—

(A) Contributions of property having basis in excess of value.—If—

(i) section 1244 stock was issued in exchange for property,

(ii) the basis of such stock in the hands of the taxpayer is determined by reference to the basis in his hands of such property, and

(iii) the adjusted basis (for determining loss) of such property immediately before the exchange exceeded its fair market value at such time,

then in computing the amount of the loss on such stock for purposes of this section the basis of such stock shall be reduced by an amount equal to the excess described in clause (iii).

(B) Increases in basis.—In computing the amount of the loss on stock for purposes of this section, any increase in the basis of such stock (through contributions to the capital of the corporation, or otherwise) shall be treated as allocable to stock which is not section 1244 stock.

(2) Recapitalizations, changes in name, etc.—To the extent provided in regulations prescribed by the Secretary, stock in a corporation, the basis of which (in the hands of a taxpayer) is determined in whole or in part by reference to the basis in his hands of stock in such corporation which meets the requirements of subsection (c)(1) (other than subparagraph (C) thereof), or which is received in a reorganization described in section 368(a)(1)(F) in exchange for stock which meets such requirements, shall be treated as meeting such requirements. For purposes of paragraphs (1)(C) and (3)(A) of subsection (c), a successor corporation in a reorganization described in section 368(a)(1)(F) shall be treated as the same corporation as its predecessor.

(3) Relationship to net operating loss deduction.—For purposes of section 172 (relating to the net operating loss deduction), any amount of loss treated by reason of this section as an ordinary loss shall be treated as attributable to a trade or business of the taxpayer.

(4) Individual defined.—For purposes of this section, the term "individual" does not include a trust or estate.

(e) Regulations.—The Secretary shall prescribe such regulations as may be necessary to carry out the purposes of this section.

§ 1245. Gain from dispositions of certain depreciable property

(a) General rule.—

(1) Ordinary income.—Except as otherwise provided in this section, if section 1245 property is disposed of the amount by which the lower of—

(A) the recomputed basis of the property, or

(B)(i) in the case of a sale, exchange, or involuntary conversion, the amount realized, or

(ii) in the case of any other disposition, the fair market value of such property,

exceeds the adjusted basis of such property shall be treated as ordinary income. Such gain shall be recognized notwithstanding any other provision of this subtitle.

(2) Recomputed basis.—For purposes of this section—

(A) In general.—The term "recomputed basis" means, with respect to any property, its adjusted basis recomputed by adding thereto all adjustments reflected in such adjusted basis on account of deductions (whether in respect of the same or other property) allowed or allowable to the taxpayer or to any other person for depreciation or amortization.

(B) Taxpayer may establish amount allowed.—For purposes of subparagraph (A), if the taxpayer can establish by adequate records or other sufficient evidence that the amount allowed for depreciation or amortization for any period was less than the amount allowable, the amount added for such period shall be the amount allowed.

(C) Certain deductions treated as amortization.—Any deduction allowable under section 179, 179A, 179B, 179C, 179D, 179E, 181, 190, 193, or 194 shall be treated as if it were a deduction allowable for amortization.

(3) Section 1245 property.—For purposes of this section, the term "section 1245 property" means any property which is or has been property of a character subject to the allowance for depreciation provided in section 167 and is either—

(A) personal property,

(B) other property (not including a building or its structural components) but only if such other property is tangible and has an adjusted basis in which there are reflected adjustments described in paragraph (2) for a period in which such property (or other property)—

(i) was used as an integral part of manufacturing, production, or extraction or of furnishing transportation, communications, electrical energy, gas, water, or sewage disposal services,

(ii) constituted a research facility used in connection with any of the activities referred to in clause (i), or

(iii) constituted a facility used in connection with any of the activities referred to in clause (i) for the bulk storage of fungible commodities (including commodities in a liquid or gaseous state),

(C) so much of any real property (other than any property described in subparagraph (B)) which has an adjusted basis in which there are reflected adjustments for amortization under section 169, 179, 179A, 179B, 179C, 179D, 179E, 185, 188 (as in effect before its repeal by the Revenue Reconciliation Act of 1990), 190, 193, or 194.

(D) a single purpose agricultural or horticultural structure (as defined in section 168(i)(13)),

(E) a storage facility (not including a building or its structural components) used in connection with the distribution of petroleum or any primary product of petroleum, or

* * *

(b) Exceptions and limitations.—

(1) Gifts.—Subsection (a) shall not apply to a disposition by gift.

(2) Transfers at death.—Except as provided in section 691 (relating to income in respect of a decedent), subsection (a) shall not apply to a transfer at death.

(3) Certain tax-free transactions.—If the basis of property in the hands of a transferee is determined by reference to its basis in the hands of the transferor by reason of the application of section 332, 351, 361, 721, or 731, then the amount of gain taken into account by the transferor under subsection (a)(1) shall not exceed the amount of gain recognized to the transferor on the transfer of such property (determined without regard to this section). Except as provided in paragraph (6), this paragraph shall not apply to a disposition to an organization (other than a cooperative described in section 521) which is exempt from the tax imposed by this chapter.

(4) Like kind exchanges; involuntary conversions, etc.—If property is disposed of and gain (determined without regard to this section) is not recognized in whole or in part under section 1031 or 1033, then the amount of gain taken into account by the transferor under subsection (a)(1) shall not exceed the sum of—

(A) the amount of gain recognized on such disposition (determined without regard to this section), plus

(B) the fair market value of property acquired which is not section 1245 property and which is not taken into account under subparagraph (A).

(5) Property distributed by a partnership to a partner.—

(A) In general.—For purposes of this section, the basis of section 1245 property distributed by a partnership to a partner shall be deemed to be determined by reference to the adjusted basis of such property to the partnership.

(B) Adjustments added back.—In the case of any property described in subparagraph (A), for purposes of computing the recomputed basis of such property the amount of the adjustments added back for periods before the distribution by the partnership shall be—

(i) the amount of the gain to which subsection (a) would have applied if such property had been sold by the partnership immediately before the distribution at its fair market value at such time, reduced by

(ii) the amount of such gain to which section 751(b) applied.

* * *

(8) Disposition of amortizable section 197 intangibles.—

(A) In general.—If a taxpayer disposes of more than 1 amortizable section 197 intangible (as defined in section 197(c)) in a transaction or a series of related transactions, all such amortizable 197 intangibles shall be treated as 1 section 1245 property for purposes of this section.

(B) Exception.—Subparagraph (A) shall not apply to any amortizable section 197 intangible (as so defined) with respect to which the adjusted basis exceeds the fair market value.

(c) Adjustments to basis.—The Secretary shall prescribe such regulations as he may deem necessary to provide for adjustments to the basis of property to reflect gain recognized under subsection (a).

(d) Application of section.—This section shall apply notwithstanding any other provision of this subtitle.

§ 1250. Gain from dispositions of certain depreciable realty

(a) General rule.—Except as otherwise provided in this section—

(1) Additional depreciation after December 31, 1975.—

(A) In general.—If section 1250 property is disposed of after December 31, 1975, then the applicable percentage of the lower of—

(i) that portion of the additional depreciation (as defined in subsection (b) (1) or (4)) attributable to periods after December 31, 1975, in respect of the property, or

(ii) the excess of the amount realized (in the case of a sale, exchange, or involuntary conversion), or the fair market value of such property (in the case of any other disposition), over the adjusted basis of such property,

shall be treated as gain which is ordinary income. Such gain shall be recognized notwithstanding any other provision of this subtitle.

(B) Applicable percentage.—For purposes of subparagraph (A), the term "applicable percentage" means—

(i) in the case of section 1250 property with respect to which a mortgage is insured under section 221(d)(3) or 236 of the National Housing Act, or housing financed or assisted by direct loan or tax abatement under similar provisions of State or local laws and with respect to which the owner is subject to the restrictions described in section 1039(b)(1)(B) (as in effect on the day before the date of the enactment of the Revenue Reconciliation Act of 1990), 100 percent minus 1 percentage point for each full month the property was held after the date the property was held 100 full months;

(ii) in the case of dwelling units which, on the average, were held for occupancy by families or individuals eligible to receive subsidies under section 8 of the United States Housing Act of 1937, as amended, or under the provisions of State or local law authorizing similar levels of subsidy for lower-income families, 100 percent minus 1 percentage point for each full month the property was held after the date the property was held 100 full months;

(iii) in the case of section 1250 property with respect to which a depreciation deduction for rehabilitation expenditures was allowed under section 167(k), 100 percent minus 1 percentage point for each full month in excess of 100 full months after the date on which such property was placed in service;

(iv) in the case of section 1250 property with respect to which a loan is made or insured under title V of the Housing Act of 1949, 100 percent minus 1 percentage point for each full month the property was held after the date the property was held 100 full months; and

(v) in the case of all other section 1250 property, 100 percent.

In the case of a building (or a portion of a building devoted to dwelling units), if, on the average, 85 percent or more of the dwelling units contained in such building (or portion thereof) are units described in clause (ii), such building (or portion thereof) shall be treated as property described in clause (ii). Clauses (i), (ii), and (iv) shall not apply with respect to the additional depreciation described in subsection (b)(4) which was allowed under section 167(k).

* * *

(b) Additional depreciation defined.—For purposes of this section—

(1) In general.—The term "additional depreciation" means, in the case of any property, the depreciation adjustments in respect of such property; except that, in the case of property held more than one year, it means such adjustments only to the extent that they exceed the amount of the depreciation adjustments which would have resulted if such adjustments had been determined for each taxable year under the straight line method of adjustment.

* * *

(3) Depreciation adjustments.—The term "depreciation adjustments" means, in respect of any property, all adjustments attributable to periods after December 31, 1963, reflected in the adjusted basis of such property on account of deductions (whether in respect of the same or other property) allowed or allowable to the taxpayer or to any other person for exhaustion, wear and tear, obsolescence, or amortization (other than amortization under section 168 (as in effect before its repeal by the Tax Reform Act of 1976), 169, 185 (as in effect before its repeal by the Tax Reform Act of 1986), 188 (as in effect before its repeal by the Revenue Reconciliation Act of 1990), 190, or 193). For purposes of the preceding sentence, if the taxpayer can establish by adequate records or other sufficient evidence that the amount allowed as a deduction for any period was less than the amount allowable, the amount taken into account for such period shall be the amount allowed.

* * *

(5) Method of computing straight line adjustments.—For purposes of paragraph (1), the depreciation adjustments which would have resulted for any taxable year under the straight line method shall be determined—

(A) in the case of property to which section 168 applies, by determining the adjustments which would have resulted for such year if the taxpayer had elected the straight line method for such year using the recovery period applicable to such property, and

(B) in the case of any property to which section 168 does not apply, if a useful life (or salvage value) was used in determining the amount allowable as a deduction for any taxable year, by using such life (or value).

(c) Section 1250 property.—For purposes of this section, the term "section 1250 property" means any real property (other than section 1245 property, as defined in section 1245(a)(3)) which is or has been property of a character subject to the allowance for depreciation provided in section 167.

(d) Exceptions and limitations.—

(1) Gifts.—Subsection (a) shall not apply to a disposition by gift.

(2) Transfers at death.—Except as provided in section 691 (relating to income in respect of a decedent), subsection (a) shall not apply to a transfer at death.

(3) Certain tax-free transactions.—If the basis of property in the hands of a transferee is determined by reference to its basis in the hands of the transferor by reason of the application of section 332, 351, 361, 721, or 731, then the amount of gain taken into account by the transferor under subsection (a) shall not exceed the amount of gain recognized to the transferor on the transfer of such property (determined without regard to this section). Except as provided in paragraph (9), this paragraph shall not apply to a disposition to an organization (other than a cooperative described in section 521) which is exempt from the tax imposed by this chapter.

(4) Like kind exchanges; involuntary conversions, etc.—

(A) Recognition limit.—If property is disposed of and gain (determined without regard to this section) is not recognized in whole or in part under section 1031 or 1033, then the amount of gain taken into account by the transferor under subsection (a) shall not exceed the greater of the following:

(i) the amount of gain recognized on the disposition (determined without regard to this section), increased as provided in subparagraph (B), or

(ii) the amount determined under subparagraph (C).

(B) Increase for certain stock.—With respect to any transaction, the increase provided by this subparagraph is the amount equal to the fair market value of any stock purchased in a corporation which (but for this paragraph) would result in nonrecognition of gain under section 1033(a)(2)(A).

(C) Adjustment where insufficient section 1250 property is acquired.—With respect to any transaction, the amount determined under this subparagraph shall be the excess of—

(i) the amount of gain which would (but for this paragraph) be taken into account under subsection (a), over

(ii) the fair market value (or cost in the case of a transaction described in section 1033(a)(2)) of the section 1250 property acquired in the transaction.

(D) Basis of property acquired.—In the case of property purchased by the taxpayer in a transaction described in section 1033(a)(2), in applying section 1033(b)(2), such sentence shall be applied—

(i) first solely to section 1250 properties and to the amount of gain not taken into account under subsection (a) by reason of this paragraph, and

(ii) then to all purchased properties to which such sentence applies and to the remaining gain not recognized on the transaction as if the cost of the section 1250 properties were the basis of such properties computed under clause (i).

In the case of property acquired in any other transaction to which this paragraph applies, rules consistent with the preceding sentence shall be applied under regulations prescribed by the Secretary.

(E) Additional depreciation with respect to property disposed of.—In the case of any transaction described in section 1031 or 1033, the additional depreciation in respect of the section 1250 property acquired which is attributable to the section 1250 property disposed of shall be an amount equal to the amount of the gain which was not taken into account under subsection (a) by reason of the application of this paragraph.

(5) Property distributed by a partnership to a partner.—

(A) In general.—For purposes of this section, the basis of section 1250 property distributed by a partnership to a partner shall be deemed to be determined by reference to the adjusted basis of such property to the partnership.

(B) Additional depreciation.—In respect of any property described in subparagraph (A), the additional depreciation attributable to periods before the distribution by the partnership shall be—

(i) the amount of the gain to which subsection (a) would have applied if such property had been sold by the partnership immediately before the distribution at its fair market value at such time and the applicable percentage for the property had been 100 percent, reduced by

(ii) if section 751(b) applied to any part of such gain, the amount of such gain to which section 751(b) would have applied if the applicable percentage for the property had been 100 percent.

* * *

(g) Adjustments to basis.—The Secretary shall prescribe such regulations as he may deem necessary to provide for adjustments to the basis of property to reflect gain recognized under subsection (a).

(h) Application of section.—This section shall apply notwithstanding any other provision of this subtitle.

§ 1252. Gain from disposition of farm land

(a) General rule.—

(1) Ordinary income.—Except as otherwise provided in this section, if farm land which the taxpayer has held for less than 10 years is disposed of during a taxable year beginning after December 31, 1969, the lower of—

(A) the applicable percentage of the aggregate of the deductions allowed under sections 175 (relating to soil and water conservation expenditures) and 182 (as in effect on the day before the date of the enactment of the Tax Reform Act of 1986) for expenditures made by the taxpayer after December 31, 1969, with respect to the farm land or

(B) the excess of—

(i) the amount realized (in the case of a sale, exchange, or involuntary conversion), or the fair market value of the farm land (in the case of any other disposition), over

(ii) the adjusted basis of such land,

shall be treated as ordinary income. Such gain shall be recognized notwithstanding any other provision of this subtitle.

(2) Farm land.—For purposes of this section, the term "farm land" means any land with respect to which deductions have been allowed under sections 175 (relating to soil and water conservation expenditures) or 182 (relating to expenditures by farmers for clearing land).

(3) Applicable percentage.—For purposes of this section—

If the farm land is disposed of—	The applicable percentage is—
Within 5 years after the date it was acquired	100 percent
Within the sixth year after it was acquired	80 percent
Within the seventh year after it was acquired	60 percent
Within the eighth year after it was acquired	40 percent
Within the ninth year after it was acquired	20 percent
10 years or more years after it was acquired	0 percent

(b) Special rules.—Under regulations prescribed by the Secretary, rules similar to the rules of section 1245 shall be applied for purposes of this section.

§ 1253. Transfers of franchises, trademarks, and trade names

(a) General rule.—A transfer of a franchise, trademark, or trade name shall not be treated as a sale or exchange of a capital asset if the transferor retains any significant power, right, or continuing interest with respect to the subject matter of the franchise, trademark, or trade name.

(b) Definitions.—For purposes of this section—

(1) Franchise.—The term "franchise" includes an agreement which gives one of the parties to the agreement the right to distribute, sell, or provide goods, services, or facilities, within a specified area.

(2) Significant power, right, or continuing interest.—The term "significant power, right, or continuing interest" includes, but is not limited to, the following rights with respect to the interest transferred:

(A) A right to disapprove any assignment of such interest, or any part thereof.

(B) A right to terminate at will.

(C) A right to prescribe the standards of quality of products used or sold, or of services furnished, and of the equipment and facilities used to promote such products or services.

(D) A right to require that the transferee sell or advertise only products or services of the transferor.

(E) A right to require that the transferee purchase substantially all of his supplies and equipment from the transferor.

(F) A right to payments contingent on the productivity, use, or disposition of the subject matter of the interest transferred, if such payments constitute a substantial element under the transfer agreement.

(3) Transfer.—The term "transfer" includes the renewal of a franchise, trademark, or trade name.

(c) Treatment of contingent payments by transferor.—Amounts received or accrued on account of a transfer, sale, or other disposition of a franchise, trademark, or trade name which are contingent on the productivity, use, or disposition of the franchise, trademark, or trade name transferred shall be treated as amounts received or accrued from the sale or other disposition of property which is not a capital asset.

(d) Treatment of payments by transferee.—

(1) Contingent serial payments.—

(A) In general.—Any amount described in subparagraph (B) which is paid or incurred during the taxable year on account of a transfer, sale, or other disposition of a franchise, trademark, or trade name shall be allowed as a deduction under section 162(a) (relating to trade or business expenses).

(B) Amounts to which paragraph applies.—An amount is described in this subparagraph if it—

(i) is contingent on the productivity, use, or disposition of the franchise, trademark, or trade name, and

(ii) is paid as part of a series of payments—

(I) which are payable not less frequently than annually throughout the entire term of the transfer agreement, and

(II) which are substantially equal in amount (or payable under a fixed formula).

(2) Other payments.—Any amount paid or incurred on account of a transfer, sale, or other disposition of a franchise, trademark, or trade name to which paragraph (1) does not apply shall be treated as an amount chargeable to capital account.

(3) Renewals, etc.—For purposes of determining the term of a transfer agreement under this section, there shall be taken into account all renewal options (and any other period for which the parties reasonably expect the agreement to be renewed).

§ 1254. Gain from disposition of interest in oil, gas, geothermal, or other mineral properties

(a) General rule.—

(1) Ordinary income.—If any section 1254 property is disposed of, the lesser of—

(A) the aggregate amount of—

(i) expenditures which have been deducted by the taxpayer or any person under section 263, 616, or 617 with respect to such property and which, but for such deduction, would have been included in the adjusted basis of such property, and

(ii) the deductions for depletion under section 611 which reduced the adjusted basis of such property, or

(B) the excess of—

(i) in the case of—

(I) a sale, exchange, or involuntary conversion, the amount realized, or

(II) in the case of any other disposition, the fair market value of such property, over

(ii) the adjusted basis of such property,

shall be treated as gain which is ordinary income. Such gain shall be recognized notwithstanding any other provision of this subtitle.

* * *

§ 1256. Section 1256 contracts marked to market

(a) General rule.—For purposes of this subtitle—

(1) each section 1256 contract held by the taxpayer at the close of the taxable year shall be treated as sold for its fair market value on the last business day of such taxable year (and any gain or loss shall be taken into account for the taxable year),

(2) proper adjustment shall be made in the amount of any gain or loss subsequently realized for gain or loss taken into account by reason of paragraph (1),

(3) any gain or loss with respect to a section 1256 contract shall be treated as—

(A) short-term capital gain or loss, to the extent of 40 percent of such gain or loss, and

(B) long-term capital gain or loss, to the extent of 60 percent of such gain or loss, and

(4) if all the offsetting positions making up any straddle consist of section 1256 contracts to which this section applies (and such straddle is not part of a larger straddle), sections 1092 and 263(g) shall not apply with respect to such straddle.

(b) Section 1256 contract defined.—

(1) In general.—For purposes of this section, the term "section 1256 contract" means—

(A) any regulated futures contract,

(B) any foreign currency contract,

(C) any nonequity option,

(D) any dealer equity option, and

(E) any dealer securities futures contract.

(2) Exceptions.—The term "section 1256 contract" shall not include—

(A) any securities futures contract or option on such a contract unless such contract or option is a dealer securities futures contract, or

(B) any interest rate swap, currency swap, basis swap, interest rate cap, interest rate floor, commodity swap, equity swap, equity index swap, credit default swap, or similar agreement.

* * *

(e) Mark to market not to apply to hedging transactions.—

(1) Section not to apply.—Subsection (a) shall not apply in the case of a hedging transaction.

(2) Definition of hedging transaction.— For purposes of this subsection, the term "hedging transaction" means any hedging transaction (as defined in section 1221(b)(2)(A)) if, before the close of the day on which such transaction was entered into (or such earlier time as the Secretary may prescribe by regulations), the taxpayer clearly identifies such transaction as being a hedging transaction.

(3) Special rule for syndicates.—

(A) In general.—Notwithstanding paragraph (2), the term "hedging transaction" shall not include any transaction entered into by or for a syndicate.

(B) Syndicate defined.—For purposes of subparagraph (A), the term "syndicate" means any partnership or other entity (other than a corporation which is not an S corporation) if more than 35 percent of the losses of such entity during the taxable year are allocable to limited partners or limited entrepreneurs (within the meaning of section 464(e)(2)).

(C) Holdings attributable to active management.—For purposes of subparagraph (B), an interest in an entity shall not be treated as held by a limited partner or a limited entrepreneur (within the meaning of section 464(e)(2))—

(i) for any period if during such period such interest is held by an individual who actively participates at all times during such period in the management of such entity,

(ii) for any period if during such period such interest is held by the spouse, children, grandchildren, and parents of an individual who actively participates at all times during such period in the management of such entity,

(iii) if such interest is held by an individual who actively participated in the management of such entity for a period of not less than 5 years,

(iv) if such interest is held by the estate of an individual who actively participated in the management of such entity or is held by the estate of an individual if with respect to such individual such interest was at any time described in clause (ii), or

(v) if the Secretary determines (by regulations or otherwise) that such interest should be treated as held by an individual who actively participates in the management of such entity, and that such entity and such interest are not used (or to be used) for tax-avoidance purposes.

For purposes of this subparagraph, a legally adopted child of an individual shall be treated as a child of such individual by blood.

* * *

(g) Definitions.—For purposes of this section—

(1) Regulated futures contracts defined.—The term "regulated futures contract" means a contract—

(A) with respect to which the amount required to be deposited and the amount which may be withdrawn depends on a system of marking to market, and

(B) which is traded on or subject to the rules of a qualified board or exchange.

(2) Foreign currency contract defined.—

(A) Foreign currency contract.—The term "foreign currency contract" means a contract—

(i) which requires delivery of, or the settlement of which depends on the value of, a foreign currency which is a currency in which positions are also traded through regulated futures contracts.

(ii) which is traded in the interbank market, and

(iii) which is entered into at arm's length at a price determined by reference to the price in the interbank market.

(B) Regulations.—The Secretary shall prescribe such regulations as may be necessary or appropriate to carry out the purposes of subparagraph (A), including regulations excluding from the application of subparagraph (A) any contract (or type of contract) if its application thereto would be inconsistent with such purposes.

(3) Nonequity option.—The term "nonequity option" means any listed option which is not an equity option.

(4) Dealer equity option.—The term "dealer equity option" means, with respect to an options dealer, any listed option which—

(A) is an equity option,

(B) is purchased or granted by such options dealer in the normal course of his activity of dealing in options, and

(C) is listed on the qualified board or exchange on which such options dealer is registered.

(5) Listed option.—The term "listed option" means any option (other than a right to acquire stock from the issuer) which is traded on (or subject to the rules of) a qualified board or exchange.

(6) Equity option.—The term "equity option" means any option—

(A) to buy or sell stock, or

(B) the value of which is determined directly or indirectly by reference to any stock or any narrow-based security index (as defined in section 3(a)(55) of the Securities Exchange Act of 1934, as in effect on the date of the enactment of this paragraph).

The term "equity option" includes such an option on a group of stocks only if such group meets the requirements for a narrow-based security index (as so defined). * * *

(7) Qualified board or exchange.—The term "qualified board or exchange" means—

(A) a national securities exchange which is registered with the Securities and Exchange Commission,

(B) a domestic board of trade designated as a contract market by the Commodity Futures Trading Commission, or

(C) any other exchange, board of trade, or other market which the Secretary determines has rules adequate to carry out the purposes of this section.

(8) Options dealer.—

(A) In general.—The term "options dealer" means any person registered with an appropriate national securities exchange as a market maker or specialist in listed options.

(B) Persons trading in other markets.—In any case in which the Secretary makes a determination under subparagraph (C) of paragraph (7), the term "options dealer" also includes any person whom the Secretary determines performs functions similar to the persons described in subparagraph (A). Such determinations shall be made to the extent appropriate to carry out the purposes of this section.

(9) Dealer securities futures contract.—

(A) In general.—The term "dealer securities futures contract" means, with respect to any dealer, any securities futures contract, and any option on such a contract, which—

(i) is entered into by such dealer (or, in the case of an option, is purchased or granted by such dealer) in the normal course of his activity of dealing in such contracts or options, as the case may be, and

(ii) is traded on a qualified board or exchange.

(B) Dealer.—For purposes of subparagraph (A), a person shall be treated as a dealer in securities futures contracts or options on such contracts if the Secretary determines that such person performs, with respect to such contracts or options, as the case may be, functions similar to the functions performed by persons described in paragraph (8)(A). Such determination shall be made to the extent appropriate to carry out the purposes of this section.

(C) Securities futures contract.—The term "securities futures contract" has the meaning given to such term by section 1234B.

§ 1258. Recharacterization of gain from certain financial transactions

(a) General rule.—In the case of any gain—

(1) which (but for this section) would be treated as gain from the sale or exchange of a capital asset, and

(2) which is recognized on the disposition or other termination of any position which was held as part of a conversion transaction,

such gain (to the extent such gain does not exceed the applicable imputed income amount) shall be treated as ordinary income.

(b) Applicable imputed income amount.—For purposes of subsection (a), the term "applicable imputed income amount" means, with respect to any disposition or other termination referred to in subsection (a), an amount equal to—

(1) the amount of interest which would have accrued on the taxpayer's net investment in the conversion transaction for the period ending on the date of such disposition or other termination (or, if earlier, the date on which the requirements of subsection (c) ceased to be satisfied) at a rate equal to 120 percent of the applicable rate, reduced by

(2) the amount treated as ordinary income under subsection (a) with respect to any prior disposition or other termination of a position which was held as a part of such transaction.

The Secretary shall by regulations provide for such reductions in the applicable imputed income amount as may be appropriate by reason of amounts capitalized under section 263(g), ordinary income received, or otherwise.

(c) Conversion transaction.—For purposes of this section, the term "conversion transaction" means any transaction—

(1) substantially all of the taxpayer's expected return from which is attributable to the time value of the taxpayer's net investment in such transaction, and

(2) which is—

(A) the holding of any property (whether or not actively traded), and the entering into a contract to sell such property (or substantially identical property) at a price determined in accordance with such contract, but only if such property was acquired and such contract was entered into on a substantially contemporaneous basis,

(B) an applicable straddle,

(C) any other transaction which is marketed or sold as producing capital gains from a transaction described in paragraph (1), or

(D) any other transaction specified in regulations prescribed by the Secretary.

(d) Definitions and special rules.—For purposes of this section—

(1) Applicable straddle.—The term "applicable straddle" means any straddle (within the meaning of section 1092(c)).

(2) Applicable rate.—The term "applicable rate" means—

(A) the applicable Federal rate determined under section 1274(d) (compounded semiannually) as if the conversion transaction were a debt instrument, or

(B) if the term of the conversion transaction is indefinite, the Federal short-term rates in effect under section 6621(b) during the period of the conversion transaction (compounded daily).

(3) Treatment of built-in losses.—

(A) In general.—If any position with a built-in loss becomes part of a conversion transaction—

(i) for purposes of applying this subtitle to such position for periods after such position becomes part of such transaction, such position shall be taken into account at its fair market value as of the time it became part of such transaction, except that

(ii) upon the disposition or other termination of such position in a transaction in which gain or loss is recognized, such built-in loss shall be recognized and shall have a character determined without regard to this section.

(B) Built-in loss.—For purposes of subparagraph (A), the term "built-in loss" means the loss (if any) which would have been realized if the position had been disposed of or otherwise terminated at its fair market value as of the time such position became part of the conversion transaction.

(4) Position taken into account at fair market value.—In determining the taxpayer's net investment in any conversion transaction, there shall be included the fair market value of any position which becomes part of such transaction (determined as of the time such position became part of such transaction).

(5) Special rule for options dealers and commodities traders.—

(A) In general.—Subsection (a) shall not apply to transactions—

(i) of an options dealer in the normal course of the dealer's trade or business of dealing in options, or

(ii) of a commodities trader in the normal course of the trader's trade or business of trading section 1256 contracts.

(B) Definitions.—For purposes of this paragraph—

(i) Options dealer.—The term "options dealer" has the meaning given such term by section 1256(g)(8).

(ii) Commodities trader.—The term "commodities trader" means any person who is a member (or, except as otherwise provided in regulations, is entitled to trade as a member) of a domestic board of trade which is designated as a contract market by the Commodity Futures Trading Commission.

(C) Limited partners and limited entrepreneurs.—In the case of any gain from a transaction recognized by an entity which is allocable to a limited partner or limited entrepreneur (within the meaning of section 464(e)(2)), subparagraph (A) shall not apply if—

(i) substantially all of the limited partner's (or limited entrepreneur's) expected return from the entity is attributable to the time value of the partner's (or entrepreneur's) net investment in such entity,

(ii) the transaction (or the interest in the entity) was marketed or sold as producing capital gains treatment from a transaction described in subsection (c)(1), or

(iii) the transaction (or the interest in the entity) is a transaction (or interest) specified in regulations prescribed by the Secretary.

§ 1259. Constructive sales treatment for appreciated financial positions

(a) In general.—If there is a constructive sale of an appreciated financial position—

(1) the taxpayer shall recognize gain as if such position were sold, assigned, or otherwise terminated at its fair market value on the date of such constructive sale (and any gain shall be taken into account for the taxable year which includes such date), and

(2) for purposes of applying this title for periods after the constructive sale—

(A) proper adjustment shall be made in the amount of any gain or loss subsequently realized with respect to such position for any gain taken into account by reason of paragraph (1), and

(B) the holding period of such position shall be determined as if such position were originally acquired on the date of such constructive sale.

(b) Appreciated financial position.—For purposes of this section—

(1) In general.—Except as provided in paragraph (2), the term "appreciated financial position" means any position with respect to any stock, debt instrument, or partnership interest if there would be gain were such position sold, assigned, or otherwise terminated at its fair market value.

(2) Exceptions.—The term "appreciated financial position" shall not include—

(A) any position with respect to debt if—

(i) the position unconditionally entitles the holder to receive a specified principal amount,

(ii) the interest payments (or other similar amounts) with respect to such position meet the requirements of clause (i) of section 860G(a)(1)(B), and

(iii) such position is not convertible (directly or indirectly) into stock of the issuer or any related person,

(B) any hedge with respect to a position described in subparagraph (A), and

(C) any position which is marked to market under any provision of this title or the regulations thereunder.

(3) Position.—The term "position" means an interest, including a futures or forward contract, short sale, or option.

(c) Constructive sale.—For purposes of this section—

(1) In general.—A taxpayer shall be treated as having made a constructive sale of an appreciated financial position if the taxpayer (or a related person)—

(A) enters into a short sale of the same or substantially identical property,

(B) enters into an offsetting notional principal contract with respect to the same or substantially identical property,

(C) enters into a futures or forward contract to deliver the same or substantially identical property,

(D) in the case of an appreciated financial position that is a short sale or a contract described in subparagraph (B) or (C) with respect to any property, acquires the same or substantially identical property, or

(E) to the extent prescribed by the Secretary in regulations, enters into 1 or more other transactions (or acquires 1 or more positions) that have substantially the same effect as a transaction described in any of the preceding subparagraphs.

(2) Exception for sales of nonpublicly traded property.—A taxpayer shall not be treated as having made a constructive sale solely because the taxpayer enters into a contract for sale of any stock, debt instrument, or partnership interest which is not a marketable security (as defined in section 453(f)) if the contract settles within 1 year after the date such contract is entered into.

(3) Exception for certain closed transactions.—

(A) In general.—In applying this section, there shall be disregarded any transaction (which would cause a constructive sale) during the taxable year if—

(i) such transaction is closed on or before the 30th day after the close of such taxable year,

(ii) the taxpayer holds the appreciated financial position throughout the 60–day period beginning on the date such transaction is closed, and

(iii) at no time during such 60–day period is the taxpayer's risk of loss with respect to such position reduced by reason of a circumstance which would be described in section 246(c)(4) if references to stock included references to such position.

(B) Treatment of certain closed transactions where risk of loss on appreciated financial position diminished.—If—

(i) a transaction, which would otherwise cause a constructive sale of an appreciated financial position, is closed during the taxable year or during the 30 days thereafter, and

(ii) another transaction is entered into during the 60–day period beginning on the date the transaction referred to in clause (i) is closed—

(I) which would (but for this subparagraph) cause the requirement of subparagraph (A)(iii) not to be met with respect to the transaction described in clause (i) of this subparagraph,

(II) which is closed on or before the 30th day after the close of the taxable year in which the transaction referred to in clause (i) occurs, and

(III) which meets the requirements of clauses (ii) and (iii) of subparagraph (A),

the transaction referred to in clause (ii) shall be disregarded for purposes of determining whether the requirements of subparagraph (A)(iii) are met with respect to the transaction described in clause (i).

(4) Related person.—A person is related to another person with respect to a transaction if—

(A) the relationship is described in section 267(b) or 707(b), and

(B) such transaction is entered into with a view toward avoiding the purposes of this section.

(d) Other definitions.—For purposes of this section—

(1) Forward contract.—The term "forward contract" means a contract to deliver a substantially fixed amount of property (including cash) for a substantially fixed price.

(2) Offsetting notional principal contract.—The term "offsetting notional principal contract" means, with respect to any property, an agreement which includes—

(A) a requirement to pay (or provide credit for) all or substantially all of the investment yield (including appreciation) on such property for a specified period, and

(B) a right to be reimbursed for (or receive credit for) all or substantially all of any decline in the value of such property.

(e) Special rules.—

(1) Treatment of subsequent sale of position which was deemed sold.—If—

(A) there is a constructive sale of any appreciated financial position,

(B) such position is subsequently disposed of, and

(C) at the time of such disposition, the transaction resulting in the constructive sale of such position is open with respect to the taxpayer or any related person, solely for purposes of determining whether the taxpayer has entered into a constructive sale of any other appreciated financial position held by the taxpayer, the taxpayer shall be treated as entering into such transaction immediately after such disposition. For purposes of the preceding sentence, an assignment or other termination shall be treated as a disposition.

(2) Certain trust instruments treated as stock.—For purposes of this section, an interest in a trust which is actively traded (within the meaning of section 1092(d)(1)) shall be treated as stock unless substantially all (by value) of the property held by the trust is debt described in subsection (b)(2)(A).

(3) Multiple positions in property.—If a taxpayer holds multiple positions in property, the determination of whether a specific transaction is a constructive sale and, if so, which appreciated financial position is deemed sold shall be made in the same manner as actual sales.

(f) Regulations.—The Secretary shall prescribe such regulations as may be necessary or appropriate to carry out the purposes of this section.

§ 1260. Gains from constructive ownership transactions.

(a) In general.—If the taxpayer has gain from a constructive ownership transaction with respect to any financial asset and such gain would (without regard to this section) be treated as a long-term capital gain—

(1) such gain shall be treated as ordinary income to the extent that such gain exceeds the net underlying long-term capital gain, and

(2) to the extent such gain is treated as a long-term capital gain after the application of paragraph (1), the determination of the capital gain rate (or rates) applicable to such gain under section 1(h) shall be determined on the basis of the respective rate (or rates) that would have been applicable to the net underlying long-term capital gain.

(b) Interest charge on deferral of gain recognition.—

(1) In general.—If any gain is treated as ordinary income for any taxable year by reason of subsection (a)(1), the tax imposed by this chapter for such taxable year shall be increased by the amount of interest determined under paragraph (2) with respect to each prior taxable year during any portion of which the constructive ownership transaction was open. Any amount payable under this paragraph shall be taken into account in computing the amount of any deduction allowable to the taxpayer for interest paid or accrued during such taxable year.

(2) Amount of interest.—The amount of interest determined under this paragraph with respect to a prior taxable year is the amount of interest which would have been imposed under section 6601 on the underpayment of tax for such year which would have resulted if the gain (which is treated as ordinary income by reason of subsection (a)(1)) had been included in gross income in the taxable years in which it accrued (determined by treating the income as accruing at a constant rate equal to the applicable Federal rate as in effect on the day the transaction closed). The period during which such interest shall accrue shall end on the due date (without extensions) for the return of tax imposed by this chapter for the taxable year in which such transaction closed.

(3) Applicable Federal rate.—For purposes of paragraph (2), the applicable Federal rate is the applicable Federal rate determined under section 1274(d) (compounded semiannually) which would apply to a debt instrument with a term equal to the period the transaction was open.

(4) No credits against increase in tax.—Any increase in tax under paragraph (1) shall not be treated as tax imposed by this chapter for purposes of determining—

(A) the amount of any credit allowable under this chapter, or

(B) the amount of the tax imposed by section 55.

(c) Financial asset.—For purposes of this section—

(1) In general.—The term "financial asset" means—

(A) any equity interest in any pass-thru entity, and

(B) to the extent provided in regulations—

(i) any debt instrument, and

(ii) any stock in a corporation which is not a pass-thru entity.

(2) Pass-thru entity.—For purposes of paragraph (1), the term "pass-thru entity" means—

(A) a regulated investment company,

(B) a real estate investment trust,

(C) an S corporation,

(D) a partnership,

(E) a trust,

(F) a common trust fund,

(G) a passive foreign investment company (as defined in section 1297 without regard to subsection (d) thereof), and

(H) a REMIC.

(d) Constructive ownership transaction.—For purposes of this section—

(1) In general.—The taxpayer shall be treated as having entered into a constructive ownership transaction with respect to any financial asset if the taxpayer—

(A) holds a long position under a notional principal contract with respect to the financial asset,

(B) enters into a forward or futures contract to acquire the financial asset,

(C) is the holder of a call option, and is the grantor of a put option, with respect to the financial asset and such options have substantially equal strike prices and substantially contemporaneous maturity dates, or

(D) to the extent provided in regulations prescribed by the Secretary, enters into one or more other transactions (or acquires one or more positions) that have substantially the same effect as a transaction described in any of the preceding subparagraphs.

(2) Exception for positions which are marked to market.—This section shall not apply to any constructive ownership transaction if all of the positions which are part of such transaction are marked to market under any provision of this title or the regulations thereunder.

(3) Long position under notional principal contract.— A person shall be treated as holding a long position under a notional principal contract with respect to any financial asset if such person—

(A) has the right to be paid (or receive credit for) all or substantially all of the investment yield (including appreciation) on such financial asset for a specified period, and

(B) is obligated to reimburse (or provide credit for) all or substantially all of any decline in the value of such financial asset.

(4) Forward contract.—The term "forward contract" means any contract to acquire in the future (or provide or receive credit for the future value of) any financial asset.

(e) Net underlying long-term capital gain.—For purposes of this section, in the case of any constructive ownership transaction with respect to any financial asset, the term "net underlying long-term capital gain" means the aggregate net capital gain that the taxpayer would have had if—

(1) the financial asset had been acquired for fair market value on the date such transaction was opened and sold for fair market value on the date such transaction was closed, and

(2) only gains and losses that would have resulted from the deemed ownership under paragraph (1) were taken into account.

The amount of the net underlying long-term capital gain with respect to any financial asset shall be treated as zero unless the amount thereof is established by clear and convincing evidence.

(f) Special rule where taxpayer takes delivery.—Except as provided in regulations prescribed by the Secretary, if a constructive ownership transaction is closed by reason of taking delivery, this section shall be applied as if the taxpayer had sold all the contracts, options, or other positions which are part of such transaction for fair market value on the closing date. The amount of gain recognized under the preceding sentence shall not exceed the amount of gain treated as ordinary income under subsection (a). Proper adjustments shall be made in the amount of any gain or loss subsequently realized for gain recognized and treated as ordinary income under this subsection.

(g) Regulations.—The Secretary shall prescribe such regulations as may be necessary or appropriate to carry out the purposes of this section, including regulations—

(1) to permit taxpayers to mark to market constructive ownership transactions in lieu of applying this section, and

(2) to exclude certain forward contracts which do not convey substantially all of the economic return with respect to a financial asset.

PART V—SPECIAL RULES FOR BONDS AND OTHER DEBT INSTRUMENTS

Subpart A—Original Issue Discount

§ 1271. Treatment of amounts received on retirement or sale or exchange of debt instruments

(a) General rule.—For purposes of this title—

* Omitted entirely.

(1) Retirement.—Amounts received by the holder on retirement of any debt instrument shall be considered as amounts received in exchange therefor.

(2) Ordinary income on sale or exchange where intention to call before maturity.—

(A) In general.—If at the time of original issue there was an intention to call a debt instrument before maturity, any gain realized on the sale or exchange thereof which does not exceed an amount equal to—

(i) the original issue discount, reduced by

(ii) the portion of original issue discount previously includible in the gross income of any holder (without regard to subsection (a)(7) or (b)(4) of section 1272 (or the corresponding provisions of prior law)),

shall be treated as ordinary income.

(B) Exceptions.—This paragraph (and paragraph (2) of subsection (c)) shall not apply to—

(i) any tax-exempt obligation, or

(ii) any holder who has purchased the debt instrument at a premium.

* * *

(b) Exception for certain obligations.—

(1) In general.—This section shall not apply to—

(A) any obligation issued by a natural person before June 9, 1997, and

(B) any obligation issued before July 2, 1982, by an issuer which is not a corporation and is not a government or political subdivision thereof.

(2) Termination.—Paragraph (1) shall not apply to any obligation purchased (within the meaning of section 1272(d)(1)) after June 8, 1997.

* * *

(d) Double inclusion in income not required.—This section and sections 1272 and 1286 shall not require the inclusion of any amount previously includible in gross income.

§ 1272. Current inclusion in income of original issue discount

(a) Original issue discount on debt instruments issued after July 1, 1982, included in income on basis of constant interest rate.—

(1) General rule.—For purposes of this title, there shall be included in the gross income of the holder of any debt instrument having original issue discount issued after July 1, 1982, an amount equal to the sum of the daily portions of the original issue discount for each day during the taxable year on which such holder held such debt instrument.

(2) Exceptions.—Paragraph (1) shall not apply to—

(A) Tax-exempt obligations.—Any tax-exempt obligation.

(B) United States savings bonds.—Any United States savings bond.

(C) Short-term obligations.—Any debt instrument which has a fixed maturity date not more than 1 year from the date of issue.

(D) Obligations issued by natural persons before March 2, 1984.—Any obligation issued by a natural person before March 2, 1984.

(E) Loans between natural persons.—

(i) In general.—Any loan made by a natural person to another natural person if—

(I) such loan is not made in the course of a trade or business of the lender, and

(II) the amount of such loan (when increased by the outstanding amount of prior loans by such natural person to such other natural person) does not exceed $10,000.

(ii) Clause (i) not to apply where tax avoidance a principal purpose.—Clause (i) shall not apply if the loan has as 1 of its principal purposes the avoidance of any Federal tax.

(iii) Treatment of husband and wife.—For purposes of this subparagraph, a husband and wife shall be treated as 1 person. The preceding sentence shall not apply where the spouses lived apart at all times during the taxable year in which the loan is made.

(3) Determination of daily portions.—For purposes of paragraph (1), the daily portion of the original issue discount on any debt instrument shall be determined by allocating to each day in any accrual period its ratable portion of the increase during such accrual period in the adjusted issue price of the debt instrument. For purposes of the preceding sentence, the increase in the adjusted issue price for any accrual period shall be an amount equal to the excess (if any) of—

(A) the product of—

(i) the adjusted issue price of the debt instrument at the beginning of such accrual period, and

(ii) the yield to maturity (determined on the basis of compounding at the close of each accrual period and properly adjusted for the length of the accrual period), over

(B) the sum of the amounts payable as interest on such debt instrument during such accrual period.

(4) Adjusted issue price.—For purposes of this subsection, the adjusted issue price of any debt instrument at the beginning of any accrual period is the sum of—

(A) the issue price of such debt instrument, plus

(B) the adjustments under this subsection to such issue price for all periods before the first day of such accrual period.

(5) Accrual period.—Except as otherwise provided in regulations prescribed by the Secretary, the term "accrual period" means a 6-month period (or shorter period from the date of original issue of the debt instrument) which ends on a day in the calendar year corresponding to the maturity date of the debt instrument or the date 6 months before such maturity date.

* * *

(b) Ratable inclusion retained for corporate debt instruments issued before July 2, 1982.—

(1) General rule.—There shall be included in the gross income of the holder of any debt instrument issued by a corporation after May 27, 1969, and before July 2, 1982—

(A) the ratable monthly portion of original issue discount, multiplied by

(B) the number of complete months (plus any fractional part of a month determined under paragraph (3)) such holder held such debt instrument during the taxable year.

* * *

(c) Exceptions.—This section shall not apply to any holder—

(1) who has purchased the debt instrument at a premium, or

* * *

(d) Definition and special rule.—

(1) Purchase defined.—For purposes of this section, the term "purchase" means—

(A) any acquisition of a debt instrument, where

(B) the basis of the debt instrument is not determined in whole or in part by reference to the adjusted basis of such debt instrument in the hands of the person from whom acquired.

(2) Basis adjustment.—The basis of any debt instrument in the hands of the holder thereof shall be increased by the amount included in his gross income pursuant to this section.

§ 1273. Determination of amount of original issue discount

(a) General rule.—For purposes of this subpart—

(1) In general.—The term "original issue discount" means the excess (if any) of—

(A) the stated redemption price at maturity, over

(B) the issue price.

(2) Stated redemption price at maturity.—The term "stated redemption price at maturity" means the amount fixed by the last modification of the purchase agreement and includes interest and other amounts payable at that time (other than any interest based on a fixed rate, and payable unconditionally at fixed periodic intervals of 1 year or less during the entire term of the debt instrument).

(3) ¼ of 1 percent de minimis rule.—If the original issue discount determined under paragraph (1) is less than—

(A) ¼ of 1 percent of the stated redemption price at maturity, multiplied by

(B) the number of complete years to maturity,

then the original issue discount shall be treated as zero.

(b) Issue price.—For purposes of this subpart—

(1) Publicly offered debt instruments not issued for property.—In the case of any issue of debt instruments—

(A) publicly offered, and

(B) not issued for property,

the issue price is the initial offering price to the public (excluding bond houses and brokers) at which price a substantial amount of such debt instruments was sold.

(2) Other debt instruments not issued for property.—In the case of any issue of debt instruments not issued for property and not publicly offered, the issue price of each such instrument is the price paid by the first buyer of such debt instrument.

(3) Debt instruments issued for property where there is public trading.—In the case of a debt instrument which is issued for property and which—

(A) is part of an issue a portion of which is traded on an established securities market, or

(B)(i) is issued for stock or securities which are traded on an established securities market, or

(ii) to the extent provided in regulations, is issued for property (other than stock or securities) of a kind regularly traded on an established market,

the issue price of such debt instrument shall be the fair market value of such property.

(4) Other cases.—Except in any case—

(A) to which paragraph (1), (2), or (3) of this subsection applies, or

(B) to which section 1274 applies,

the issue price of a debt instrument which is issued for property shall be the stated redemption price at maturity.

(5) Property.—In applying this subsection, the term "property" includes services and the right to use property, but such term does not include money.

* * *

§ 1274. Determination of issue price in the case of certain debt instruments issued for property

(a) In general.—In the case of any debt instrument to which this section applies, for purposes of this subpart, the issue price shall be—

(1) where there is adequate stated interest, the stated principal amount, or

(2) in any other case, the imputed principal amount.

(b) Imputed principal amount.—For purposes of this section—

(1) In general.—Except as provided in paragraph (3), the imputed principal amount of any debt instrument shall be equal to the sum of the present values of all payments due under such debt instrument.

(2) Determination of present value.—For purposes of paragraph (1), the present value of a payment shall be determined in the manner provided by regulations prescribed by the Secretary—

(A) as of the date of the sale or exchange, and

(B) by using a discount rate equal to the applicable Federal rate, compounded semiannually.

(3) Fair market value rule in potentially abusive situations.—

(A) In general.—In the case of any potentially abusive situation, the imputed principal amount of any debt instrument received in exchange for property shall be the fair market value of such property adjusted to take into account other consideration involved in the transaction.

(B) Potentially abusive situation defined.—For purposes of subparagraph (A), the term "potentially abusive situation" means—

(i) a tax shelter (as defined in section 6662(d)(2)(C)(iii)), and

(ii) any other situation which, by reason of—

(I) recent sales transactions,

(II) nonrecourse financing,

(III) financing with a term in excess of the economic life of the property, or

(IV) other circumstances,

is of a type which the Secretary specifies by regulations as having potential for tax avoidance.

(c) Debt instruments to which section applies.—

(1) In general.—Except as otherwise provided in this subsection, this section shall apply to any debt instrument given in consideration for the sale or exchange of property if—

(A) the stated redemption price at maturity for such debt instrument exceeds—

(i) where there is adequate stated interest, the stated principal amount, or

(ii) in any other case, the imputed principal amount of such debt instrument determined under subsection (b), and

(B) some or all of the payments due under such debt instrument are due more than 6 months after the date of such sale or exchange.

(2) Adequate stated interest.—For purposes of this section, there is adequate stated interest with respect to any debt instrument if the stated principal amount for such debt instrument is less than or equal to the imputed principal amount of such debt instrument determined under subsection (b).

(3) Exceptions.—This section shall not apply to—

(A) Sales for $1,000,000 or less of farms by individuals or small businesses.—

(i) In general.—Any debt instrument arising from the sale or exchange of a farm * * *—

(I) by an individual, estate, or testamentary trust,

(II) by a corporation which as of the date of the sale or exchange is a small business corporation (as defined in section 1244(c)(3)), or

(III) by a partnership which as of the date of the sale or exchange meets requirements similar to those of section 1244(c)(3).

(ii) $1,000,000 limitation.—Clause (i) shall apply only if it can be determined at the time of the sale or exchange that the sales price cannot exceed $1,000,000. For purposes of the preceding sentence, all sales and exchanges which are part of the same transaction (or a series of related transactions) shall be treated as 1 sale or exchange.

(B) Sales of principal residences.—Any debt instrument arising from the sale or exchange by an individual of his principal residence (within the meaning of section 121).

(C) Sales involving total payments of $250,000 or less.—

(i) In general.—Any debt instrument arising from the sale or exchange of property if the sum of the following amounts does not exceed $250,000:

(I) the aggregate amount of the payments due under such debt instrument and all other debt instruments received as consideration for the sale or exchange, and

(II) the aggregate amount of any other consideration to be received for the sale or exchange.

(ii) Consideration other than debt instrument taken into account at fair market value.—For purposes of clause (i), any consideration (other than a debt instrument) shall be taken into account at its fair market value.

(iii) Aggregation of transactions.—For purposes of this subparagraph, all sales and exchanges which are part of the same transaction (or a series of related transactions) shall be treated as 1 sale or exchange.

(D) Debt instruments which are publicly traded or issued for publicly traded property.—Any debt instrument to which section 1273(b)(3) applies.

(E) Certain sales of patents.—In the case of any transfer described in section 1235(a) (relating to sale or exchange of patents), any amount contingent on the productivity, use, or disposition of the property transferred.

(F) Sales or exchanges to which section 483(e) applies.—Any debt instrument to the extent section 483(e) (relating to certain land transfers between related persons) applies to such instrument.

(4) Exception for assumptions.—If any person—

(A) in connection with the sale or exchange of property, assumes any debt instrument, or

(B) acquires any property subject to any debt instrument,

in determining whether this section or section 483 applies to such debt instrument, such assumption (or such acquisition) shall not be taken into account unless the terms and conditions of such debt instrument are modified (or the nature of the transaction is changed) in connection with the assumption (or acquisition).

(d) Determination of applicable federal rate.—For purposes of this section—

(1) Applicable federal rate.—

(A) In general.—

In the case of a debt instrument with a term of:	The applicable Federal rate is:
Not over 3 years	The Federal short-term rate
Over 3 years but not over 9 years	The Federal mid-term rate
Over 9 years	The Federal long-term rate

(B) Determination of rates.—During each calendar month, the Secretary shall determine the Federal short-term rate, mid-term rate, and long-term rate which shall apply during the following calendar month.

(C) Federal rate for any calendar month.—For purposes of this paragraph—

(i) Federal short-term rate.—The Federal short-term rate shall be the rate determined by the Secretary based on the average market yield (during any 1–month period selected by the Secretary and ending in the calendar month in which the determination is made) on outstanding marketable obligations of the United States with remaining periods to maturity of 3 years or less.

(ii) Federal mid-term and long-term rates.—The Federal mid-term and long-term rate shall be determined in accordance with the principles of clause (i).

(D) Lower rate permitted in certain cases.—The Secretary may by regulations permit a rate to be used with respect to any debt instrument which is lower than the applicable Federal rate if the taxpayer establishes to the satisfaction of the Secretary that such lower rate is based on the same principles as the applicable Federal rate and is appropriate for the term of such instrument.

(2) Lowest 3–month rate applicable to any sale or exchange.—

(A) In general.—In the case of any sale or exchange, the applicable Federal rate shall be the lowest 3–month rate.

(B) Lowest 3–month rate.—For purposes of subparagraph (A), the term "lowest 3–month rate" means the lowest of the applicable Federal rates in effect for any month in the 3–calendar-month period ending with the 1st calendar month in which there is a binding contract in writing for such sale or exchange.

(3) Term of debt instrument.—In determining the term of a debt instrument for purposes of this subsection, under regulations prescribed by the Secretary, there shall be taken into account options to renew or extend.

(e) 110 percent rate where sale-leaseback involved.—

(1) In general.—In the case of any debt instrument to which this subsection applies, the discount rate used under subsection (b)(2)(B) or section 483(b) shall be 110 percent of the applicable Federal rate, compounded semiannually.

(2) Lower discount rates shall not apply.—Section 1274A shall not apply to any debt instrument to which this subsection applies.

(3) Debt instruments to which this subsection applies.—This subsection shall apply to any debt instrument given in consideration for the sale or exchange of any property if, pursuant to a plan, the transferor or any related person leases a portion of such property after such sale or exchange.

§ 1274A. Special rules for certain transactions where stated principal amount does not exceed $2,800,000

(a) Lower discount rate.—In the case of any qualified debt instrument, the discount rate used for purposes of sections 483 and 1274 shall not exceed 9 percent, compounded semiannually.

(b) Qualified debt instrument defined.—For purposes of this section, the term "qualified debt instrument" means any debt instrument given in consideration for the sale or exchange of property (other than new section 38 property within the meaning of section 48(b), as in effect on the day before the date of the enactment of the Revenue Reconciliation Act of 1990) if the stated principal amount of such instrument does not exceed $2,800,000.

(c) Election to use cash method where stated principal amount does not exceed $2,000,000.—

(1) In general.—In the case of any cash method debt instrument—

(A) section 1274 shall not apply, and

(B) interest on such debt instrument shall be taken into account by both the borrower and the lender under the cash receipts and disbursements method of accounting.

(2) Cash method debt instrument.—For purposes of paragraph (1), the term "cash method debt instrument" means any qualified debt instrument if—

(A) the stated principal amount does not exceed $2,000,000,

(B) the lender does not use an accrual method of accounting and is not a dealer with respect to the property sold or exchanged,

(C) section 1274 would have applied to such instrument but for an election under this subsection, and

(D) an election under this subsection is jointly made with respect to such debt instrument by the borrower and lender.

(3) Successors bound by election.—

(A) In general.—Except as provided in subparagraph (B), paragraph (1) shall apply to any successor to the borrower or lender with respect to a cash method debt instrument.

(B) Exception where lender transfers debt instrument to accrual method taxpayer.—If the lender (or any successor) transfers any cash method debt instrument to a taxpayer who uses an accrual method of accounting, this paragraph shall not apply with respect to such instrument for periods after such transfer.

(4) Fair market value rule in potentially abusive situations.—In the case of any cash method debt instrument, section 483 shall be applied as if it included provisions similar to the provisions of section 1274(b)(3).

(d) Other special rules.—

(1) Aggregation rules.—For purposes of this section—

(A) all sales or exchanges which are part of the same transaction (or a series of related transactions) shall be treated as 1 sale or exchange, and

(B) all debt instruments arising from the same transaction (or a series of related transactions) shall be treated as 1 debt instrument.

(2) Inflation adjustments.—

(A) In general.—In the case of any debt instrument arising out of a sale or exchange during any calendar year after 1989, each dollar amount contained in the preceding provisions of this section shall be increased by the inflation adjustment for such calendar year. Any increase under the preceding sentence shall be rounded to the nearest multiple of $100 (or, if such increase is multiple of $50, such increase shall be increased to the nearest multiple of $100).

(B) Inflation adjustment.—For purposes of subparagraph (A), the inflation adjustment for any calendar year is the percentage (if any) by which—

(i) the CPI for the preceding calendar year exceeds

(ii) the CPI for calendar year 1988.

For purposes of the preceding sentence, the CPI for any calendar year is the average of the Consumer Price Index as of the close of the 12–month period ending on September 30 of such calendar year.

(e) Regulations.—The Secretary shall prescribe such regulations as may be necessary to carry out the purposes of this subsection, including—

(1) regulations coordinating the provisions of this section with other provisions of this title,

(2) regulations necessary to prevent the avoidance of tax through the abuse of the provisions of subsection (c), and

(3) regulations relating to the treatment of transfers of cash method debt instruments.

§ 1275. Other definitions and special rules

(a) Definitions.—For purposes of this subpart—

(1) Debt instrument.—

(A) In general.—Except as provided in subparagraph (B), the term "debt instrument" means a bond, debenture, note, or certificate or other evidence of indebtedness.

(B) Exception for certain annuity contracts.—The term "debt instrument" shall not include any annuity contract to which section 72 applies and which—

(i) depends (in whole or in substantial part) on the life expectancy of 1 or more individuals, or

(ii) is issued by an insurance company subject to tax under subchapter L (or by an entity described in section 501(c) and exempt from tax under section 501(a) which would be subject to tax under subchapter L were it not so exempt)—

(I) in a transaction in which there is no consideration other than cash or another annuity contract meeting the requirements of this clause,

(II) pursuant to the exercise of an election under an insurance contract by a beneficiary thereof on the death of the insured party under such contract, or

(III) in a transaction involving a qualified pension or employee benefit plan.

(2) Issue date.—

(A) Publicly offered debt instruments.—In the case of any debt instrument which is publicly offered, the term "date of original issue" means the date on which the issue was first issued to the public.

(B) Issues not publicly offered and not issued for property.—In the case of any debt instrument to which section 1273(b)(2) applies, the term "date of original issue" means the date on which the debt instrument was sold by the issuer.

(C) Other debt instruments.—In the case of any debt instrument not described in subparagraph (A) or (B), the term "date of original issue" means the date on which the debt instrument was issued in a sale or exchange.

(3) Tax-exempt obligation.—The term "tax-exempt obligation" means any obligation if—

(A) the interest on such obligation is not includible in gross income under section 103, or

(B) the interest on such obligation is exempt from tax (without regard to the identity of the holder) under any other provision of law.

(4) Treatment of obligations distributed by corporations.—Any debt obligation of a corporation distributed by such corporation with respect to its stock shall be treated as if it had been issued by such corporation for property.

(b) Treatment of borrower in the case of certain loans for personal use.—

(1) Sections 1274 and 483 not to apply.—In the case of the obligor under any debt instrument given in consideration for the sale or exchange of property, sections 1274 and 483 shall not apply if such property is personal use property.

(2) Original issue discount deducted on cash basis in certain cases.—In the case of any debt instrument, if—

(A) such instrument—

(i) is incurred in connection with the acquisition or carrying of personal use property, and

(ii) has original issue discount (determined after the application of paragraph (1)), and

(B) the obligor under such instrument uses the cash receipts and disbursements method of accounting,

notwithstanding section 163(e), the original issue discount on such instrument shall be deductible only when paid.

(3) Personal use property.—For purposes of this subsection, the term "personal use property" means any property substantially all of the use of which by the taxpayer is not in connection with a trade or business of the taxpayer or an activity described in section 212. The determination of whether property is described in the preceding sentence shall be made as of the time of issuance of the debt instrument.

(c) Information requirements.—

(1) Information required to be set forth on instrument.—

(A) In general.—In the case of any debt instrument having original issue discount, the Secretary may by regulations require that—

(i) the amount of the original issue discount, and

(ii) the issue date,

be set forth on such instrument.

(B) Special rule for instruments not publicly offered.—In the case of any issue of debt instruments not publicly offered, the regulations prescribed under subparagraph (A) shall not require the information to be set forth on the debt instrument before any disposition of such instrument by the first buyer.

(2) Information required to be submitted to secretary.—In the case of any issue of publicly offered debt instruments having original issue discount, the issuer shall (at such time and in such manner as the Secretary shall by regulation prescribe) furnish the Secretary the following information:

(A) The amount of the original issue discount.

(B) The issue date.

(C) Such other information with respect to the issue as the Secretary may by regulations require.

For purposes of the preceding sentence, any person who makes a public offering of stripped bonds (or stripped coupons) shall be treated as the issuer of a publicly offered debt instrument having original issue discount.

(3) Exceptions.—This subsection shall not apply to any obligation referred to in section 1272(a)(2) (relating to exceptions from current inclusion of original issue discount).

* * *

(d) Regulation authority.—The Secretary may prescribe regulations providing that where, by reason of varying rates of interest, put or call options, indefinite maturities, contingent payments, assumptions of debt instruments, or other circumstances, the tax treatment under this subpart (or section 163(e)) does not carry out the purposes of this subpart (or section 163(e)), such treatment shall be modified to the extent appropriate to carry out the purposes of this subpart (or section 163(e)).

Subpart B—Market Discount on Bonds

§ 1276. Disposition gain representing accrued market discount treated as ordinary income

(a) Ordinary income.—

(1) In general.—Except as otherwise provided in this section, gain on the disposition of any market discount bond shall be treated as ordinary income to the extent it does not exceed the accrued market discount on such bond. Such gain shall be recognized notwithstanding any other provision of this subtitle.

(2) Dispositions other than sales, etc.—For purposes of paragraph (1), a person disposing of any market discount bond in any transaction other than a sale, exchange, or involuntary conversion shall be treated as realizing an amount equal to the fair market value of the bond.

* * *

(b) Accrued market discount.—For purposes of this section—

(1) Ratable accrual.—Except as otherwise provided in this subsection or subsection (c), the accrued market discount on any bond shall be an amount which bears the same ratio to the market discount on such bond as—

(A) the number of days which the taxpayer held the bond, bears to

(B) the number of days after the date the taxpayer acquired the bond and up to (and including) the date of its maturity.

(2) Election of accrual on basis of constant interest rate (in lieu of ratable accrual).—

(A) In general.—At the election of the taxpayer with respect to any bond, the accrued market discount on such bond shall be the aggregate amount which would have been includible in the gross income of the taxpayer under section 1272(a) (determined without regard to paragraph (2) thereof) with respect to such bond for all periods during which the bond was held by the taxpayer if such bond had been—

(i) originally issued on the date on which such bond was acquired by the taxpayer,

(ii) for an issue price equal to the basis of the taxpayer in such bond immediately after its acquisition.

(B) Coordination where bond has original issue discount.—In the case of any bond having original issue discount, for purposes of applying subparagraph (A)—

(i) the stated redemption price at maturity of such bond shall be treated as equal to its revised issue price, and

(ii) the determination of the portion of the original issue discount which would have been includible in the gross income of the taxpayer under section 1272(a) shall be made under regulations prescribed by the Secretary.

(C) Election irrevocable.—An election under subparagraph (A), once made with respect to any bond, shall be irrevocable.

(3) Special rule where partial principal payments.—In the case of a bond the principal of which may be paid in 2 or more payments, the amount of accrued market discount shall be determined under regulations prescribed by the Secretary.

(c) Treatment of nonrecognition transactions.—Under regulations prescribed by the Secretary—

(1) Transferred basis property.—If a market discount bond is transferred in a nonrecognition transaction and such bond is transferred basis property in the hands of the transferee, for purposes of determining the amount of the accrued market discount with respect to the transferee—

(A) the transferee shall be treated as having acquired the bond on the date on which it was acquired by the transferor for an amount equal to the basis of the transferor, and

(B) proper adjustments shall be made for gain recognized by the transferor on such transfer (and for any original issue discount or market discount included in the gross income of the transferor).

(2) Exchanged basis property.—If any market discount bond is disposed of by the taxpayer in a nonrecognition transaction and paragraph (1) does not apply to such transaction, any accrued market discount determined with respect to the property disposed of to the extent not theretofore treated as ordinary income under subsection (a)—

(A) shall be treated as accrued market discount with respect to the exchanged basis property received by the taxpayer in such transaction if such property is a market discount bond, and

(B) shall be treated as ordinary income on the disposition of the exchanged basis property received by the taxpayer in such exchange if such property is not a market discount bond.

(3) Paragraph (1) to apply to certain distributions by corporations or partnerships.—For purposes of paragraph (1), if the basis of any market discount bond in the hands of a transferee is determined under section 732(a), or 732(b), such property shall be treated as transferred basis property in the hands of such transferee.

(d) Special rules.—Under regulations prescribed by the Secretary—

(1) rules similar to the rules of subsection (b) of section 1245 shall apply for purposes of this section; except that—

(A) paragraph (1) of such subsection shall not apply,

(B) an exchange qualifying under section 354(a), 355(a), or 356(a) (determined without regard to subsection (a) of this section) shall be treated as an exchange described in paragraph (3) of such subsection, and

(C) paragraph (3) of section 1245(b) shall be applied as if it did not contain a reference to section 351, and

(2) appropriate adjustments shall be made to the basis of any property to reflect gain recognized under subsection (a).

§ 1277. Deferral of interest deduction allocable to accrued market discount

(a) General rule.—Except as otherwise provided in this section, the net direct interest expense with respect to any market discount bond shall be allowed as a deduction for the taxable year only to the extent that such expense exceeds the portion of the market discount allocable to the days during the taxable year on which such bond was held by the taxpayer (as determined under the rules of section 1276(b)).

(b) Disallowed deduction allowed for later years.—

(1) Election to take into account in later year where net interest income from bond.—

(A) In general.—If—

(i) there is net interest income for any taxable year with respect to any market discount bond, and

(ii) the taxpayer makes an election under this subparagraph with respect to such bond,

Any disallowed interest expense with respect to such bond shall be treated as interest paid or accrued by the taxpayer during such taxable year to the extent such disallowed interest expense does not exceed the net interest income with respect to such bond.

(B) Determination of disallowed interest expense.—For purposes of subparagraph (A), the amount of the disallowed interest expense—

(i) shall be determined as of the close of the preceding taxable year, and

(ii) shall not include any amount previously taken into account under subparagraph (A).

(C) Net interest income.—For purposes of this paragraph, the term "net interest income" means the excess of the amount determined under paragraph (2) of subsection (c) over the amount determined under paragraph (1) of subsection (c).

(2) Remainder of disallowed interest expense allowed for year of disposition.—

(A) In general.—Except as otherwise provided in this paragraph, the amount of the disallowed interest expense with respect to any market discount bond shall be treated as interest paid or accrued by the taxpayer in the taxable year in which such bond is disposed of.

(B) Nonrecognition transactions.—If any market discount bond is disposed of in a nonrecognition transaction—

(i) the disallowed interest expense with respect to such bond shall be treated as interest paid or accrued in the year of disposition only to the extent of the amount of gain recognized on such disposition, and

(ii) the disallowed interest expense with respect to such property (to the extent not so treated) shall be treated as disallowed interest expense—

(I) in the case of a transaction described in section 1276(c)(1), of the transferee with respect to the transferred basis property, or

(II) in the case of a transaction described in section 1276(c)(2), with respect to the exchanged basis property.

(C) Disallowed interest expense reduced for amounts previously taken into account under paragraph (1).—For purposes of this paragraph, the amount of the disallowed interest expense shall not include any amount previously taken into account under paragraph (1).

(3) Disallowed interest expense.—For purposes of this subsection, the term "disallowed interest expense" means the aggregate amount disallowed under subsection (a) with respect to the market discount bond.

(c) Net direct interest expense.—For purposes of this section, the term "net direct interest expense" means, with respect to any market discount bond, the excess (if any) of—

(1) the amount of interest paid or accrued during the taxable year on indebtedness which is incurred or continued to purchase or carry such bond, over

(2) the aggregate amount of interest (including original issue discount) includible in gross income for the taxable year with respect to such bond.

* * *

§ 1278. Definitions and special rules

(a) In general.—For purposes of this part—

(1) Market discount bond.—

(A) In general.—Except as provided in subparagraph (B), the term "market discount bond" means any bond having market discount.

(B) Exceptions.—The term "market discount bond" shall not include—

(i) Short-term obligations.—Any obligation with a fixed maturity date not exceeding 1 year from the date of issue.

(ii) United States savings bonds.—Any United States savings bond.

(iii) Installment obligations.—Any installment obligation to which section 453B applies.

(C) Section 1277 not applicable to tax-exempt obligations.—For purposes of section 1277, the term "market discount bond" shall not include any tax-exempt obligation (as defined in section 1275(a)(3)).

(D) Treatment of bonds acquired at original issue.—

(i) In general.—Except as otherwise provided in this subparagraph or in regulations, the term "market discount bond" shall not include any bond acquired by the taxpayer at its original issue.

(ii) Treatment of bonds acquired for less than issue price.—Clause (i) shall not apply to any bond if—

(I) the basis of the taxpayer in such bond is determined under section 1012, and

(II) such basis is less than the issue price of such bond determined under subpart A of this part.

(iii) Bonds acquired in certain reorganizations.—Clause (i) shall not apply to any bond issued pursuant to a plan of reorganization (within the meaning of section 368(a)(1)) in exchange for another bond having market discount. Solely for purposes of section 1276, the preceding sentence shall not apply if such other bond was issued on or before July 18, 1984 (the date of the enactment of section 1276) and if the bond issued pursuant to such plan of reorganization has the same term and the same interest rate as such other bond had.

(iv) Treatment of certain transferred basis property.—For purposes of clause (i), if the adjusted basis of any bond in the hands of the taxpayer is determined by reference to the adjusted basis of such bond in the hands of a person who acquired such bond at its original issue, such bond shall be treated as acquired by the taxpayer at its original issue.

(2) Market discount.—

(A) In general.—The term "market discount" means the excess (if any) of—

(i) the stated redemption price of the bond at maturity, over

(ii) the basis of such bond immediately after its acquisition by the taxpayer.

(B) Coordination where bond has original issue discount.—In the case of any bond having original issue discount, for purposes of subparagraph (A), the stated redemption price of such bond at maturity shall be treated as equal to its revised issue price.

(C) De minimis rule.—If the market discount is less than ¼ of 1 percent of the stated redemption price of the bond at maturity multiplied by the number of complete years to maturity (after the taxpayer acquired the bond), then the market discount shall be considered to be zero.

(3) Bond.—The term "bond" means any bond, debenture, note, certificate, or other evidence of indebtedness.

(4) Revised issue price.—The term "revised issue price" means the sum of—

(A) the issue price of the bond, and

(B) the aggregate amount of the original issue discount includible in the gross income of all holders for periods before the acquisition of the bond by the taxpayer (determined without regard to section 1272(a)(7) or (b)(4)) or, in the case of a tax-exempt obligation, the aggregate amount of the original issue discount which accrued in the manner provided by section 1272(a) (determined without regard to paragraph (7) thereof) during periods before the acquisition of the bond by the taxpayer.

(5) Original issue discount, etc.—The terms "original issue discount", "stated redemption price at maturity", and "issue price" have the respective meanings given such terms by subpart A of this part.

(b) Election to include market discount currently.—

(1) In general.—If the taxpayer makes an election under this subsection—

(A) sections 1276 and 1277 shall not apply, and

(B) market discount on any market discount bond shall be included in the gross income of the taxpayer for the taxable years to which it is attributable (as determined under the rules of subsection (b) of section 1276).

Except for purposes of sections 103, 871(a), 881, 1441, 1442, and 6049 (and such other provisions as may be specified in regulations), any amount included in gross income under subparagraph (B) shall be treated as interest for purposes of this title.

(2) Scope of election.—An election under this subsection shall apply to all market discount bonds acquired by the taxpayer on or after the 1st day of the 1st taxable year to which such election applies.

(3) Period to which election applies.—An election under this subsection shall apply to the taxable year for which it is made and for all subsequent taxable years, unless the taxpayer secures the consent of the Secretary to the revocation of such election.

(4) Basis adjustment.—The basis of any bond in the hands of the taxpayer shall be increased by the amount included in gross income pursuant to this subsection.

(c) Regulations.—The Secretary shall prescribe such regulations as may be necessary to carry out the purposes of this subpart, including regulations providing proper adjustments in the case of a bond the principal of which may be paid in 2 or more payments.

Subpart D—Miscellaneous Provisions

§ 1286. Tax treatment of stripped bonds

(a) Inclusion in income as if bond and coupons were original issue discount bonds.—If any person purchases after July 1, 1982, a stripped bond or a stripped coupon, then such bond or coupon while held by such purchaser (or by any other person whose basis is determined by reference to the basis in the hands of such purchaser) shall be treated for purposes of this part as a bond originally issued on the purchase date and having an original issue discount equal to the excess (if any) of—

(1) the stated redemption price at maturity (or, in the case of coupon, the amount payable on the due date of such coupon), over

(2) such bond's or coupon's ratable share of the purchase price.

For purposes of paragraph (2), ratable shares shall be determined on the basis of their respective fair market values on the date of purchase.

(b) Tax treatment of person stripping bond.—For purposes of this subtitle, if any person strips 1 or more coupons from a bond and after July 1, 1982, disposes of the bond or such coupon—

(1) such person shall include in gross income an amount equal to the sum of—

(A) the interest accrued on such bond while held by such person and before the time such coupon or bond was disposed of (to the extent such interest has not theretofore been included in such person's gross income), and

(B) the accrued market discount on such bond determined as of the time such coupon or bond was disposed of (to the extent such discount has not theretofore been included in such person's gross income),

(2) the basis of the bond and coupons shall be increased by the amount included in gross income under paragraph (1),

(3) the basis of the bond and coupons immediately before the disposition (as adjusted pursuant to paragraph (2)) shall be allocated among the items retained by such person and the items disposed of by such person on the basis of their respective fair market values, and

(4) for purposes of subsection (a), such person shall be treated as having purchased on the date of such disposition each such item which he retains for an amount equal to the basis allocated to such item under paragraph (3).

A rule similar to the rule of paragraph (4) shall apply in the case of any person whose basis in any bond or coupon is determined by reference to the basis of the person described in the preceding sentence.

* * *

(e) Definitions and special rules.—For purposes of this section—

(1) Bond.—The term "bond" means a bond, debenture, note, or certificate or other evidence of indebtedness.

(2) Stripped bond.—The term "stripped bond" means a bond issued at any time with interest coupons where there is a separation in ownership between the bond and any coupon which has not yet become payable.

(3) Stripped coupon.—The term "stripped coupon" means any coupon relating to a stripped bond.

(4) Stated redemption price at maturity.—The term "stated redemption price at maturity" has the meaning given such term by section 1273(a)(2).

(5) Coupon.—The term "coupon" includes any right to receive interest on a bond (whether or not evidenced by a coupon). This paragraph shall apply for purposes of subsection (c) only in the case of purchases after July 1, 1982.

(6) Purchase.—The term "purchase" has the meaning given such term by section 1272(d)(1).

* * *

(g) Regulation authority.—The Secretary may prescribe regulations providing that where, by reason of varying rates of interest, put or call options, or other circumstances, the tax treatment under this section does not accurately reflect the income of the holder of a stripped coupon or stripped bond, or of the person disposing of such bond or coupon, as the case may be, for any period, such treatment shall be modified to require that the proper amount of income be included for such period.

§ 1287. Denial of capital gain treatment for gains on certain obligations not in registered form

(a) In general.—If any registration-required obligation is not in registered form, any gain on the sale or other disposition of such obligation shall be treated as ordinary income * * *.

(b) Definitions.—For purposes of subsection (a)—

(1) Registration-required obligation.—The term "registration-required obligation" has the meaning given to such term by section 163(f)(2).

(2) Registered form.—The term "registered form" has the same meaning as when used in section 163(f).

§ 1288. Treatment of original issue discount on tax-exempt obligations

(a) General rule.—Original issue discount on any tax-exempt obligation shall be treated as accruing—

(1) for purposes of section 163, in the manner provided by section 1272(a) * * *, and

(2) for purposes of determining the adjusted basis of the holder, in the manner provided by section 1272(a) * * *.

(b) Definitions and special rules.—For purposes of this section—

(1) Original issue discount.—The term "original issue discount" has the meaning given to such term by section 1273(a) without regard to paragraph (3) thereof. In applying section 483 or 1274, under regulations prescribed by the Secretary, appropriate adjustments shall be made to the applicable Federal rate to take into account the tax exemption for interest on the obligation.

(2) Tax-exempt obligation.—The term "tax-exempt obligation" has the meaning given to such term by section 1275(a)(3).

* * *

SUBCHAPTER Q—READJUSTMENT OF TAX BETWEEN YEARS AND SPECIAL LIMITATIONS

PART I—INCOME AVERAGING

§ 1301. Averaging of farm income

(a) In general.—At the election of an individual engaged in a farming business or fishing business, the tax imposed by section 1 for such taxable year shall be equal to the sum of—

(1) a tax computed under such section on taxable income reduced by elected farm income, plus

(2) the increase in tax imposed by section 1 which would result if taxable income for each of the 3 prior taxable years were increased by an amount equal to one-third of the elected farm income.

* Omitted entirely.

Any adjustment under this section for any taxable year shall be taken into account in applying this section for any subsequent taxable year.

(b) Definitions.—In this section—

(1) Elected farm income.—

(A) In general.—The term "elected farm income" means so much of the taxable income for the taxable year—

(i) which is attributable to any farming business or fishing business; and

(ii) which is specified in the election under subsection (a).

(B) Treatment of gains.—For purposes of subparagraph (A), gain from the sale or other disposition of property (other than land) regularly used by the taxpayer in such a farming business or fishing business for a substantial period shall be treated as attributable to such a farming business or fishing business.

(2) Individual.—The term "individual" shall not include any estate or trust.

(3) Farming business.—The term "farming business" has the meaning given such term by section 263A(e)(4).

(4) Fishing business.—The term "fishing business" means the conduct of commercial fishing as defined in section 3 of the Magnuson–Stevens Fishery Conservation and Management Act (16 U.S.C. 1802).

(c) Regulations.—The Secretary shall prescribe such regulations as may be appropriate to carry out the purposes of this section, including regulations regarding—

(1) the order and manner in which items of income, gain, deduction, or loss, or limitations on tax, shall be taken into account in computing the tax imposed by this chapter on the income of any taxpayer to whom this section applies for any taxable year, and

(2) the treatment of any short taxable year.

PART II—MITIGATION OF EFFECT OF LIMITATIONS AND OTHER PROVISIONS

§ 1311. Correction of error

(a) General rule.—If a determination (as defined in section 1313) is described in one or more of the paragraphs of section 1312 and, on the date of the determination, correction of the effect of the error referred to in the applicable paragraph of section 1312 is prevented by the operation of any law or rule of law, other than this part and other than section 7122 (relating to compromises), then the effect of the error shall be corrected by an adjustment made in the amount and in the manner specified in section 1314.

(b) Conditions necessary for adjustment.—

(1) Maintenance of an inconsistent position.—Except in cases described in paragraphs (3)(B) and (4) of section 1312, an adjustment shall be made under this part only if—

(A) in case the amount of the adjustment would be credited or refunded in the same manner as an overpayment under section 1314, there is adopted in the determination a position maintained by the Secretary, or

(B) in case the amount of the adjustment would be assessed and collected in the same manner as a deficiency under section 1314, there is adopted in the determination a position maintained by the taxpayer with respect to whom the determination is made, and the position maintained by the Secretary in the case described in subparagraph (A) or maintained by the taxpayer in the case described in subparagraph (B) is inconsistent with the erroneous inclusion, exclusion, omission, allowance, disallowance, recognition, or nonrecognition, as the case may be.

(2) Correction not barred at time of erroneous action.—

(A) Determination described in section 1312(3)(B).—In the case of a determination described in section 1312(3)(B) (relating to certain exclusions from income), adjustment shall be made under this part only if assessment of a deficiency for the taxable year in which the item is includible or against the related taxpayer was not barred, by any law or rule of law, at the time the Secretary first maintained, in a notice of deficiency sent pursuant to section 6212 or before the Tax Court, that the item described in section 1312(3)(B) should be included in the gross income of the taxpayer for the taxable year to which the determination relates.

(B) Determination described in section 1312(4).—In the case of a determination described in section 1312(4) (relating to disallowance of certain deductions and credits), adjustment shall be made under this part only if credit or refund of the overpayment attributable to the deduction or credit described in such section which should have been allowed to the taxpayer or related taxpayer was not barred, by any law or rule of law, at the time the taxpayer first maintained before the Secretary or before the Tax Court, in writing, that he was entitled to such deduction or credit for the taxable year to which the determination relates.

(3) Existence of relationship.—In case the amount of the adjustment would be assessed and collected in the same manner as a deficiency (except for cases described in section 1312(3)(B)), the adjustment shall not be made with respect to a related taxpayer unless he stands in such relationship to the taxpayer at the time the latter first maintains the inconsistent position in a return, claim for refund, or petition (or amended petition) to the Tax Court for the taxable year with respect to which the determination is made, or if such position is not so maintained, then at the time of the determination.

§ 1312. Circumstances of adjustment

The circumstances under which the adjustment provided in section 1311 is authorized are as follows:

(1) Double inclusion of an item of gross income.—The determination requires the inclusion in gross income of an item which was erroneously included in the gross income of the taxpayer for another taxable year or in the gross income of a related taxpayer.

(2) Double allowance of a deduction or credit.—The determination allows a deduction or credit which was erroneously allowed to the taxpayer for another taxable year or to a related taxpayer.

(3) Double exclusion of an item of gross income.—

(A) Items included in income.—The determination requires the exclusion from gross income of an item included in a return filed by the taxpayer or with respect to which tax was paid and which was erroneously excluded or omitted from the gross income of the taxpayer for another taxable year, or from the gross income of a related taxpayer; or

(B) Items not included in income.—The determination requires the exclusion from gross income of an item not included in a return filed by the taxpayer and with respect to which the tax was not paid but which is includible in the gross income of the taxpayer for another taxable year or in the gross income of a related taxpayer.

(4) Double disallowance of a deduction or credit.—The determination disallows a deduction or credit which should have been allowed to, but was not allowed to, the taxpayer for another taxable year, or to a related taxpayer.

(5) Correlative deductions and inclusions for trusts or estates and legatees, beneficiaries, or heirs.—The determination allows or disallows any of the additional deductions allowable in computing the taxable income of estates or trusts, or requires or denies any of the inclusions in the computation of taxable income of beneficiaries, heirs, or legatees, specified in subparts A to E, inclusive (secs. 641 and following, relating to estates, trusts and beneficiaries) of part I of subchapter J of this chapter, or corresponding provisions of prior internal revenue laws, and the correlative inclusion or deduction, as the case may be, has been erroneously excluded, omitted, or included, or disallowed, omitted, or allowed, as the case may be, in respect of the related taxpayer.

(6) Correlative deductions and credits for certain related corporations.—The determination allows or disallows a deduction (including a credit) in computing the taxable income (or, as the case may be, net income, normal tax net income, or surtax net income) of a corporation, and a correlative deduction or credit has been erroneously allowed, omitted, or disallowed, as the case may be, in respect of a related taxpayer described in section 1313(c)(7).

(7) Basis of property after erroneous treatment of a prior transaction.—

(A) General rule.—The determination determines the basis of property, and in respect of any transaction on which such basis depends, or in respect of any transaction which was erroneously treated as affecting such basis, there occurred, with respect to a taxpayer described in subparagraph (B) of this paragraph, any of the errors described in subparagraph (C) of this paragraph.

(B) Taxpayers with respect to whom the erroneous treatment occurred.—The taxpayer with respect to whom the erroneous treatment occurred must be—

(i) the taxpayer with respect to whom the determination is made,

(ii) a taxpayer who acquired title to the property in the transaction and from whom, mediately or immediately, the taxpayer with respect to whom the determination is made derived title, or

(iii) a taxpayer who had title to the property at the time of the transaction and from whom, mediately or immediately, the taxpayer with respect to whom the determination is made derived title, if the basis of the property in the hands of the taxpayer with respect to whom the determination is made is determined under section 1015(a) (relating to the basis of property acquired by gift).

(C) Prior erroneous treatment.—With respect to a taxpayer described in subparagraph (B) of this paragraph—

(i) there was an erroneous inclusion in, or omission from, gross income,

(ii) there was an erroneous recognition, or nonrecognition, of gain or loss, or

(iii) there was an erroneous deduction of an item properly chargeable to capital account or an erroneous charge to capital account of an item properly deductible.

§ 1313. Definitions

(a) Determination.—For purposes of this part, the term "determination" means—

(1) a decision by the Tax Court or a judgment, decree, or other order by any court of competent jurisdiction, which has become final;

(2) a closing agreement made under section 7121;

(3) a final disposition by the Secretary of a claim for refund. For purposes of this part, a claim for refund shall be deemed finally disposed of by the Secretary—

(A) as to items with respect to which the claim was allowed, on the date of allowance of refund or credit or on the date of mailing notice of disallowance (by reason of offsetting items) of the claim for refund, and

(B) as to items with respect to which the claim was disallowed, in whole or in part, or as to items applied by the Secretary in reduction of the refund or credit, on expiration of the time for instituting suit with respect thereto (unless suit is instituted before the expiration of such time); or

(4) under regulations prescribed by the Secretary, an agreement for purposes of this part, signed by the Secretary and by any person, relating to the liability of such person (or the person for whom he acts) in respect of a tax under this subtitle for any taxable period.

(b) Taxpayer.—Notwithstanding section 7701(a)(14), the term "taxpayer" means any person subject to a tax under the applicable revenue law.

(c) Related taxpayer.—For purposes of this part, the term "related taxpayer" means a taxpayer who, with the taxpayer with respect to whom a determination is made, stood, in the taxable year with respect to which the erroneous inclusion, exclusion, omission, allowance, or disallowance was made, in one of the following relationships:

(1) husband and wife,

(2) grantor and fiduciary,

(3) grantor and beneficiary,

(4) fiduciary and beneficiary, legatee, or heir,

(5) decedent and decedent's estate,

(6) partner, or

(7) member of an affiliated group of corporations (as defined in section 1504).

§ 1314. Amount and method of adjustment

(a) Ascertainment of amount of adjustment.—In computing the amount of an adjustment under this part there shall first be ascertained the tax previously determined for the taxable year with respect to which the error was made. The amount of the tax previously determined shall be the excess of—

(1) the sum of—

(A) the amount shown as the tax by the taxpayer on his return (determined as provided in section 6211(b)(1), (3), and (4), relating to the definition of deficiency), if a return was made by the taxpayer and an amount was shown as the tax by the taxpayer thereon, plus

(B) the amounts previously assessed (or collected without assessment) as a deficiency, over—

(2) the amount of rebates, as defined in section 6211(b)(2), made.

There shall then be ascertained the increase or decrease in tax previously determined which results solely from the correct treatment of the item which was the subject of the error (with due regard given to the effect of the item in the computation of gross income, taxable income, and other matters under this subtitle). A similar computation shall be made for any other taxable year affected, or treated as affected, by a net operating loss deduction (as defined in section 172) or by a capital loss carryback or carryover (as defined in section 1212), determined with reference to the taxable year with respect to which the error was made. The amount so ascertained (together with any amounts wrongfully collected as additions to the tax or interest, as a result of such error) for each taxable year shall be the amount of the adjustment for that taxable year.

(b) Method of adjustment.—The adjustment authorized in section 1311(a) shall be made by assessing and collecting, or refunding or crediting, the amount thereof in the same manner as if it were a deficiency determined by the Secretary with respect to the taxpayer as to whom the error was made or an overpayment claimed by such taxpayer, as the case may be, for the taxable year or years with respect to which an amount is ascertained under subsection (a), and as if on the date of the determination one year remained before the expiration of the periods of limitation upon assessment or filing claim for refund for such taxable year or years. If, as a result of a determination described in section 1313(a)(4), an adjustment has been made by the assessment and collection of a deficiency or the refund or credit of an overpayment, and subsequently such determination is altered or revoked, the amount of the adjustment ascertained under subsection (a) of this section shall be redetermined on the basis of such alteration or revocation and any overpayment or deficiency resulting from such redetermination shall be refunded or credited, or assessed and collected, as the case may be, as an adjustment under this part. In the case of an adjustment resulting from an increase or decrease in a net operating loss or net capital loss which is carried back to the year of adjustment, interest shall not be collected or paid for any period prior to the close of the taxable year in which the net operating loss or net capital loss arises.

(c) Adjustment unaffected by other items.—The amount to be assessed and collected in the same manner as a deficiency, or to be refunded or credited in the same manner as an overpayment, under this part, shall not be diminished by any credit or set-off based upon any item other than the one which was the subject of the adjustment. The amount of the adjustment under this part, if paid, shall not be recovered by a claim or suit for refund or suit for erroneous refund based upon any item other than the one which was the subject of the adjustment.

* * *

PART V—CLAIM OF RIGHT

§ 1341. Computation of tax where taxpayer restores substantial amount held under claim of right

(a) General rule.—If—

(1) an item was included in gross income for a prior taxable year (or years) because it appeared that the taxpayer had an unrestricted right to such item;

(2) a deduction is allowable for the taxable year because it was established after the close of such prior taxable year (or years) that the taxpayer did not have an unrestricted right to such item or to a portion of such item; and

(3) the amount of such deduction exceeds $3,000,

then the tax imposed by this chapter for the taxable year shall be the lesser of the following:

(4) the tax for the taxable year computed with such deduction; or

(5) an amount equal to—

(A) the tax for the taxable year computed without such deduction, minus

(B) the decrease in tax under this chapter (or the corresponding provisions of prior revenue laws) for the prior taxable year (or years) which would result solely from the exclusion of such item (or portion thereof) from gross income for such prior taxable year (or years).

* * *

(b) Special rules.—

(1) If the decrease in tax ascertained under subsection (a)(5)(B) exceeds the tax imposed by this chapter for the taxable year (computed without the deduction) such excess shall be considered to be a payment of tax on the last day prescribed by law for the payment of tax for the taxable year, and shall be refunded or credited in the same manner as if it were an overpayment for such taxable year.

(2) Subsection (a) does not apply to any deduction allowable with respect to an item which was included in gross income by reason of the sale or other disposition of stock in trade of the taxpayer (or other property of a kind which would properly have been included in the inventory of the taxpayer if on hand at the close of the prior taxable year) or property held by the taxpayer primarily for sale to customers in the ordinary course of his trade or business. * * *

(3) If the tax imposed by this chapter for the taxable year is the amount determined under subsection (a)(5), then the deduction referred to in subsection (a)(2) shall not be taken into account for any purpose of this subtitle other than this section.

(4) For purposes of determining whether paragraph (4) or paragraph (5) of subsection (a) applies—

(A) in any case where the deduction referred to in paragraph (4) of subsection (a) results in a net operating loss, such loss shall, for purposes of computing the tax for the taxable year under such paragraph (4), be carried back to the same extent and in the same manner as is provided under section 172; and

(B) in any case where the exclusion referred to in paragraph (5)(B) of subsection (a) results in a net operating loss or capital loss for the prior taxable year (or years), such loss shall, for purposes of computing the decrease in tax for the prior taxable year (or years) under such paragraph (5)(B), be carried back and carried over to the same extent and in the same manner as is provided under section 172 or section 1212, except that no carryover beyond the taxable year shall be taken into account.

(5) For purposes of this chapter, the net operating loss described in paragraph (4)(A) of this subsection, or the net operating loss or capital loss described in paragraph (4)(B) of this subsection, as the case may be, shall (after the application of paragraph (4) or (5)(B) of subsection (a) for the taxable year) be taken into account under section 172 or 1212 for taxable years after the taxable year to the same extent and in the same manner as—

(A) a net operating loss sustained for the taxable year, if paragraph (4) of subsection (a) applied, or

(B) a net operating loss or capital loss sustained for the prior taxable year (or years), if paragraph (5)(B) of subsection (a) applied.

SUBCHAPTER S—TAX TREATMENT OF S CORPORATIONS AND THEIR SHAREHOLDERS

PART I—IN GENERAL

§ 1361. S corporation defined

(a) S corporation defined.—

(1) In general.—For purposes of this title, the term "S corporation" means, with respect to any taxable year, a small business corporation for which an election under section 1362(a) is in effect for such year.

(2) C corporation.—For purposes of this title, the term "C corporation" means, with respect to any taxable year, a corporation which is not an S corporation for such year.

(b) Small business corporation.—

(1) In general.—For purposes of this subchapter, the term "small business corporation" means a domestic corporation which is not an ineligible corporation and which does not—

(A) have more than 100 shareholders,

(B) have as a shareholder a person (other than an estate, a trust described in subsection (c)(2), or an organization described in subsection (c)(6)) who is not an individual,

(C) have a nonresident alien as a shareholder, and

(D) have more than 1 class of stock.

(2) Ineligible corporation defined.—For purposes of paragraph (1), the term "ineligible corporation" means any corporation which is—

(A) a financial institution which uses the reserve method of accounting for bad debts described in section 585,

(B) an insurance company subject to tax under subchapter L,

(C) a corporation to which an election under section 936 applies, or

(D) a DISC or former DISC.

[**(E)** Redesignated (D)]

(3) Treatment of certain wholly owned subsidiaries.—

(A) In general.—Except as provided in regulations prescribed by the Secretary, for purposes of this title—

(i) a corporation which is a qualified subchapter S subsidiary shall not be treated as a separate corporation, and

(ii) all assets, liabilities, and items of income, deduction, and credit of a qualified subchapter S subsidiary shall be treated as assets, liabilities, and such items (as the case may be) of the S corporation.

(B) Qualified subchapter S subsidiary.—For purposes of this paragraph, the term "qualified subchapter S subsidiary" means any domestic corporation which is not an ineligible corporation (as defined in paragraph (2)), if—

(i) 100 percent of the stock of such corporation is held by the S corporation, and

(ii) the S corporation elects to treat such corporation as a qualified subchapter S subsidiary.

(C) Treatment of terminations of qualified subchapter S subsidiary status.—

(i) In general.—For purposes of this title, if any corporation which was a qualified subchapter S subsidiary ceases to meet the requirements of subparagraph (B), such corporation shall be treated as a new corporation acquiring all of its assets (and assuming all of its liabilities) immediately before such cessation from the S corporation in exchange for its stock.

(ii) Termination by reason of sale of stock.—If the failure to meet the requirements of subparagraph (B) is by reason of the sale of stock of a corporation which is a qualified subchapter S subsidiary, the sale of such stock shall be treated as if—

(I) the sale were a sale of an undivided interest in the assets of such corporation (based on the percentage of the corporation's stock sold), and

(II) the sale were followed by an acquisition by such corporation of all of its assets (and the assumption by such corporation of all of its liabilities) in a transaction to which section 351 applies.

(D) Election after termination.—If a corporation's status as a qualified subchapter S subsidiary terminates, such corporation (and any successor corporation) shall not be eligible to make—

(i) an election under subparagraph (B)(ii) to be treated as a qualified subchapter S subsidiary, or

(ii) an election under section 1362(a) to be treated as an S corporation,

before its 5th taxable year which begins after the 1st taxable year for which such termination was effective, unless the Secretary consents to such election.

(E) Information returns.—Except to the extent provided by the Secretary, this paragraph shall not apply to part III of subchapter A of chapter 61 (relating to information returns).

(c) Special rules for applying subsection (b).—

(1) Members of a family treated as 1 shareholder.—

(A) In general.—For purposes of subsection (b)(1)(A), there shall be treated as one shareholder—

(i) a husband and wife (and their estates), and

(ii) all members of a family (and their estates).

(B) Members of a family.—For purposes of this paragraph—

(i) In general.—The term "members of a family" means a common ancestor, any lineal descendant of such common ancestor, and any spouse or former spouse of such common ancestor or any such lineal descendant.

(ii) Common ancestor.—An individual shall not be considered to be a common ancestor if, on the applicable date, the individual is more than 6 generations removed from the youngest generation of shareholders who would (but for this subparagraph) be members of the family. For purposes of the preceding sentence, a spouse (or former spouse) shall be treated as being of the same generation as the individual to whom such spouse is (or was) married.

(iii) Applicable date.—The term "applicable date" means the latest of—

(I) the date the election under section 1362(a) is made,

(II) the earliest date that an individual described in clause (i) holds stock in the S corporation, or

(III) October 22, 2004.

(C) Effect of adoption, etc.—Any legally adopted child of an individual, any child who is lawfully placed with an individual for legal adoption by the individual, and any eligible foster child of an individual (within the meaning of section 152(f)(1)(C)), shall be treated as a child of such individual by blood.

(2) Certain trusts permitted as shareholders.—

(A) In general.—For purposes of subsection (b)(1)(B), the following trusts may be shareholders:

(i) A trust all of which is treated (under subpart E of part I of subchapter J of this chapter) as owned by an individual who is a citizen or resident of the United States.

(ii) A trust which was described in clause (i) immediately before the death of the deemed owner and which continues in existence after such death, but only for the 2–year period beginning on the day of the deemed owner's death.

(iii) A trust with respect to stock transferred to it pursuant to the terms of a will, but only for the 2–year period beginning on the day on which such stock is transferred to it.

(iv) A trust created primarily to exercise the voting power of stock transferred to it.

(v) An electing small business trust.

* * *

This subparagraph shall not apply to any foreign trust.

(B) Treatment as shareholders.—For purposes of subsection (b)(1)—

(i) In the case of a trust described in clause (i) of subparagraph (A), the deemed owner shall be treated as the shareholder.

(ii) In the case of a trust described in clause (ii) of subparagraph (A), the estate of the deemed owner shall be treated as the shareholder.

(iii) In the case of a trust described in clause (iii) of subparagraph (A), the estate of the testator shall be treated as the shareholder.

(iv) In the case of a trust described in clause (iv) of subparagraph (A), each beneficiary of the trust shall be treated as a shareholder.

(v) In the case of a trust described in clause (v) of subparagraph (A), each potential current beneficiary of such trust shall be treated as a shareholder; except that, if for any period there is no potential current beneficiary of such trust, such trust shall be treated as the shareholder during such period.

* * *

(3) Estate of individual in bankruptcy may be shareholder.—For purposes of subsection (b)(1)(B), the term "estate" includes the estate of an individual in a case under title 11 of the United States Code.

(4) Differences in common stock voting rights disregarded.—For purposes of subsection (b)(1)(D), a corporation shall not be treated as having more than 1 class of stock solely because there are differences in voting rights among the shares of common stock.

(5) Straight debt safe harbor.—

(A) In general.—For purposes of subsection (b)(1)(D), straight debt shall not be treated as a second class of stock.

(B) Straight debt defined.—For purposes of this paragraph, the term "straight debt" means any written unconditional promise to pay on demand or on a specified date a sum certain in money if—

(i) the interest rate (and interest payment dates) are not contingent on profits, the borrower's discretion, or similar factors,

(ii) there is no convertibility (directly or indirectly) into stock, and

(iii) the creditor is an individual (other than a nonresident alien), an estate, a trust described in paragraph (2), or a person which is actively and regularly engaged in the business of lending money.

(C) Regulations.—The Secretary shall prescribe such regulations as may be necessary or appropriate to provide for the proper treatment of straight debt under this subchapter and for the coordination of such treatment with other provisions of this title.

(6) Certain exempt organizations permitted as shareholders.—For purposes of subsection (b)(1)(B), an organization which is—

(A) described in section 401(a) or 501(c)(3), and

(B) exempt from taxation under section 501(a),

may be a shareholder in an S corporation.

(d) Special rule for qualified subchapter S trust.—

(1) In general.—In the case of a qualified subchapter S trust with respect to which a beneficiary makes an election under paragraph (2)—

(A) such trust shall be treated as a trust described in subsection (c)(2)(A)(i),

(B) for purposes of section 678(a), the beneficiary of such trust shall be treated as the owner of that portion of the trust which consists of stock in an S corporation with respect to which the election under paragraph (2) is made, and

* * *

(2) Election.—

(A) In general.—A beneficiary of a qualified subchapter S trust (or his legal representative) may elect to have this subsection apply.

(B) Manner and time of election.—

(i) Separate election with respect to each corporation.—An election under this paragraph shall be made separately with respect to each corporation the stock of which is held by the trust.

(ii) Elections with respect to successive income beneficiaries.—If there is an election under this paragraph with respect to any beneficiary, an election under this paragraph shall be treated as made by each successive beneficiary unless such beneficiary affirmatively refuses to consent to such election.

(iii) Time, manner, and form of election.—Any election, or refusal, under this paragraph shall be made in such manner and form, and at such time, as the Secretary may prescribe.

(C) Election irrevocable.—An election under this paragraph, once made, may be revoked only with the consent of the Secretary.

(D) Grace period.—An election under this paragraph shall be effective up to 15 days and 2 months before the date of the election.

(3) Qualified subchapter S trust.—For purposes of this subsection, the term "qualified subchapter S trust" means a trust—

(A) the terms of which require that—

(i) during the life of the current income beneficiary, there shall be only 1 income beneficiary of the trust,

(ii) any corpus distributed during the life of the current income beneficiary may be distributed only to such beneficiary,

(iii) the income interest of the current income beneficiary in the trust shall terminate on the earlier of such beneficiary's death or the termination of the trust, and

(iv) upon the termination of the trust during the life of the current income beneficiary, the trust shall distribute all of its assets to such beneficiary, and

(B) all of the income (within the meaning of section 643(b)) of which is distributed (or required to be distributed) currently to 1 individual who is a citizen or resident of the United States.

A substantially separate and independent share of a trust within the meaning of section 663(c) shall be treated as a separate trust for purposes of this subsection and subsection (c).

(4) Trust ceasing to be qualified.—

(A) Failure to meet requirements of paragraph (3)(A).—If a qualified subchapter S trust ceases to meet any requirement of paragraph (3)(A), the provisions of this subsection shall not apply to such trust as of the date it ceases to meet such requirement.

(B) Failure to meet requirements of paragraph (3)(B).—If any qualified subchapter S trust ceases to meet any requirement of paragraph (3)(B) but continues to meet the requirements of paragraph (3)(A), the provisions of this subsection shall not apply to such trust as of the first day of the first taxable year beginning after the first taxable year for which it failed to meet the requirements of paragraph (3)(B).

(e) Electing small business trust defined.—

(1) Electing small business trust.—For purposes of this section—

(A) In general.—Except as provided in subparagraph (B), the term "electing small business trust" means any trust if—

(i) such trust does not have as a beneficiary any person other than (I) an individual, (II) an estate, (III) an organization described in paragraph (2), (3), (4), or (5) of section 170(c), or (IV) an organization described in section 170(c)(1) which holds a contingent interest in such trust and is not a potential current beneficiary,

(ii) no interest in such trust was acquired by purchase, and

(iii) an election under this subsection applies to such trust.

(B) Certain trusts not eligible.—The term "electing small business trust" shall not include—

(i) any qualified subchapter S trust (as defined in subsection (d)(3)) if an election under subsection (d)(2) applies to any corporation the stock of which is held by such trust,

(ii) any trust exempt from tax under this subtitle, and

(iii) any charitable remainder annuity trust or charitable remainder unitrust (as defined in section 664(d)).

(C) Purchase.—For purposes of subparagraph (A), the term "purchase" means any acquisition if the basis of the property acquired is determined under section 1012.

(2) Potential current beneficiary.—For purposes of this section, the term "potential current beneficiary" means, with respect to any period, any person who at any time during such period is entitled to, or at the discretion of any person may receive, a distribution from the principal or income of the trust (determined without regard to any power of appointment to the extent such power remains unexercised at the end of such period). If a trust disposes of all of the stock which it holds in an S corporation, then, with respect to such corporation, the term "potential current beneficiary" does not include any person who first met the requirements of the preceding sentence during the 60–day period ending on the date of such disposition.

(3) Election.—An election under this subsection shall be made by the trustee. Any such election shall apply to the taxable year of the trust for which made and all subsequent taxable years of such trust unless revoked with the consent of the Secretary.

(4) Cross reference.—

For special treatment of electing small business trusts, see section 641(c).

(f) Restricted bank director stock.—

(1) In general.—Restricted bank director stock shall not be taken into account as outstanding stock of the S corporation in applying this subchapter (other than section 1368(f)).

(2) Restricted bank director stock.—For purposes of this subsection, the term "restricted bank director stock" means stock in a bank (as defined in section 581) or a depository institution holding company (as defined in section 3(w)(1) of the Federal Deposit Insurance Act (12 U.S.C. 1813(w)(1))), if such stock—

(A) is required to be held by an individual under applicable Federal or State law in order to permit such individual to serve as a director, and

(B) is subject to an agreement with such bank or company (or a corporation which controls (within the meaning of section 368(c)) such bank or company) pursuant to which the holder is required to sell back such stock (at the same price as the individual acquired such stock) upon ceasing to hold the office of director.

(3) Cross reference.—For treatment of certain distributions with respect to restricted bank director stock, see section 1368(f).

* * *

§ 1362. Election; revocation; termination

(a) Election.—

(1) In general.—Except as provided in subsection (g), a small business corporation may elect, in accordance with the provisions of this section, to be an S corporation.

(2) All shareholders must consent to election.—An election under this subsection shall be valid only if all persons who are shareholders in such corporation on the day on which such election is made consent to such election.

(b) When made.—

(1) In general.—An election under subsection (a) may be made by a small business corporation for any taxable year—

(A) at any time during the preceding taxable year, or

(B) at any time during the taxable year and on or before the 15th day of the 3d month of the taxable year.

(2) Certain elections made during 1st 2½ months treated as made for next taxable year.—If—

(A) an election under subsection (a) is made for any taxable year during such year and on or before the 15th day of the 3d month of such year, but

(B) either—

(i) on 1 or more days in such taxable year before the day on which the election was made the corporation did not meet the requirements of subsection (b) of section 1361, or

(ii) 1 or more of the persons who held stock in the corporation during such taxable year and before the election was made did not consent to the election,

then such election shall be treated as made for the following taxable year.

(3) Election made after 1st 2½ months treated as made for following taxable year.—If—

(A) a small business corporation makes an election under subsection (a) for any taxable year, and

(B) such election is made after the 15th day of the 3d month of the taxable year and on or before the 15th day of the 3d month of the following taxable year,

then such election shall be treated as made for the following taxable year.

(4) Taxable years of 2½ months or less.—For purposes of this subsection, an election for a taxable year made not later than 2 months and 15 days after the first day of the taxable year shall be treated as timely made during such year.

(5) Authority to treat late elections, etc., as timely.—If—

(A) an election under subsection (a) is made for any taxable year (determined without regard to paragraph (3)) after the date prescribed by this subsection for making such election for such taxable year or no such election is made for any taxable year, and

(B) the Secretary determines that there was reasonable cause for the failure to timely make such election, the Secretary may treat such an election as timely made for such taxable year (and paragraph (3) shall not apply).

(c) Years for which effective.—An election under subsection (a) shall be effective for the taxable year of the corporation for which it is made and for all succeeding taxable years of the corporation, until such election is terminated under subsection (d).

(d) Termination.—

(1) By revocation.—

(A) In general.—An election under subsection (a) may be terminated by revocation.

(B) More than one-half of shares must consent to revocation.—An election may be revoked only if shareholders holding more than one-half of the shares of stock of the corporation on the day on which the revocation is made consent to the revocation.

(C) When effective.—Except as provided in subparagraph (D)—

(i) a revocation made during the taxable year and on or before the 15th day of the 3d month thereof shall be effective on the 1st day of such taxable year, and

(ii) a revocation made during the taxable year but after such 15th day shall be effective on the 1st day of the following taxable year.

(D) Revocation may specify prospective date.—If the revocation specifies a date for revocation which is on or after the day on which the revocation is made, the revocation shall be effective on and after the date so specified.

(2) By corporation ceasing to be small business corporation.—

(A) In general.—An election under subsection (a) shall be terminated whenever (at any time on or after the 1st day of the 1st taxable year for which the corporation is an S corporation) such corporation ceases to be a small business corporation.

(B) When effective.—Any termination under this paragraph shall be effective on and after the date of cessation.

(3) Where passive investment income exceeds 25 percent of gross receipts for 3 consecutive taxable years and corporation has accumulated earnings and profits.—

(A) Termination.—

(i) In general.—An election under subsection (a) shall be terminated whenever the corporation—

(I) has accumulated earnings and profits at the close of each of 3 consecutive taxable years, and

(II) has gross receipts for each of such taxable years more than 25 percent of which are passive investment income.

(ii) When effective.—Any termination under this paragraph shall be effective on and after the first day of the first taxable year beginning after the third consecutive taxable year referred to in clause (i).

(iii) Years taken into account.—A prior taxable year shall not be taken into account under clause (i) unless—

(I) such taxable year began after December 31, 1981, and

(II) the corporation was an S corporation for such taxable year.

(B) Gross receipts from the sales of certain assets.—For purposes of this paragraph—

(i) in the case of dispositions of capital assets (other than stock and securities), gross receipts from such dispositions shall be taken into account only to the extent of the capital gain net income therefrom, and

(ii) in the case of sales or exchanges of stock or securities, gross receipts shall be taken into account only to the extent of the gains therefrom.

(C) Passive investment income defined.—

(i) In general.—Except as otherwise provided in this subparagraph, the term "passive investment income" means gross receipts derived from royalties, rents, dividends, interest, and annuities.

(ii) Exception for interest on notes from sales of inventory.—The term "passive investment income" shall not include interest on any obligation acquired in the ordinary course of the corporation's trade or business from its sale of property described in section 1221(a)(1).

(iii) Treatment of certain lending or finance companies.—If the S corporation meets the requirements of section 542(c)(6) for the taxable year, the term "passive investment income" shall not include gross receipts for the taxable year which are derived directly from the active and regular conduct of a lending or finance business (as defined in section 542(d)(1)).

(iv) Treatment of certain dividends.—If an S corporation holds stock in a C corporation meeting the requirements of section 1504(a)(2), the term "passive investment income" shall not include dividends from such C corporation to the extent such dividends are attributable to the earnings and profits of such C corporation derived from the active conduct of a trade or business.

(v) Exception for banks, etc.—In the case of a bank (as defined in section 581) or a depository institution holding company (as defined in section 3(w)(1) of the Federal Deposit Insurance Act (12 U.S.C. 1813(w)(1))), the term "passive investment income" shall not include—

(I) interest income earned by such bank or company, or

(II) dividends on assets required to be held by such bank or company, including stock in the Federal Reserve Bank, the Federal Home Loan Bank, or the Federal Agricultural Mortgage Bank or participation certificates issued by a Federal Intermediate Credit Bank.

(e) Treatment of S termination year.—

(1) In general.—In the case of an S termination year, for purposes of this title—

(A) S short year.—The portion of such year ending before the 1st day for which the termination is effective shall be treated as a short taxable year for which the corporation is an S corporation.

(B) C short year.—The portion of such year beginning on such 1st day shall be treated as a short taxable year for which the corporation is a C corporation.

(2) Pro rata allocation.—Except as provided in paragraph (3) and subparagraphs (C) and (D) of paragraph (6), the determination of which items are to be taken into account for each of the short taxable years referred to in paragraph (1) shall be made—

(A) first by determining for the S termination year—

(i) the amount of each of the items of income, loss, deduction, or credit described in section 1366(a)(1)(A), and

(ii) the amount of the nonseparately computed income or loss, and

(B) then by assigning an equal portion of each amount determined under subparagraph (A) to each day of the S termination year.

(3) Election to have items assigned to each short taxable year under normal tax accounting rules.—

(A) In general.—A corporation may elect to have paragraph (2) not apply.

(B) Shareholders must consent to election.—An election under this subsection shall be valid only if all persons who are shareholders in the corporation at any time during the S short year and all persons who are shareholders in the corporation on the first day of the C short year consent to such election.

(4) S termination year.—For purposes of this subsection, the term "S termination year" means any taxable year of a corporation (determined without regard to this subsection) in which a termination of an election made under subsection (a) takes effect (other than on the 1st day thereof).

(5) Tax for C short year determined on annualized basis.—

(A) In general.—The taxable income for the short year described in subparagraph (B) of paragraph (1) shall be placed on an annual basis by multiplying the taxable income for such short year by the number of days in the S termination year and by dividing the result by the number of days in the short year. The tax shall be the same part of the tax computed on the annual basis as the number of days in such short year is of the number of days in the S termination year.

* * *

(6) Other special rules.—For purposes of this title—

(A) Short years treated as 1 year for carryover purposes.—The short taxable year described in subparagraph (A) of paragraph (1) shall not be taken into account for purposes of determining the number of taxable years to which any item may be carried back or carried forward by the corporation.

(B) Due date for S year.—The due date for filing the return for the short taxable year described in subparagraph (A) of paragraph (1) shall be the same as the due date for filing the return for the short taxable year described in subparagraph (B) of paragraph (1) (including extensions thereof).

(C) Paragraph (2) not to apply to items resulting from section 338.—Paragraph (2) shall not apply with respect to any item resulting from the application of section 338.

(D) Pro rata allocation for S termination year not to apply if 50–percent change in ownership.—Paragraph (2) shall not apply to an S termination year if there is a sale or exchange of 50 percent or more of the stock in such corporation during such year.

(f) Inadvertent invalid elections or terminations.—If—

(1) an election under subsection (a) or section 1361(b)(3)(B)(ii) by any corporation—

(A) was not effective for the taxable year for which made (determined without regard to subsection (b)(2)) by reason of a failure to meet the requirements of section 1361(b) or to obtain shareholder consents, or

(B) was terminated under paragraph (2) or (3) of subsection (d) or section 1361(b)(3)(C).

(2) the Secretary determines that the circumstances resulting in such ineffectiveness or termination were inadvertent,

(3) no later than a reasonable period of time after discovery of the circumstances resulting in such ineffectiveness or termination, steps were taken—

(A) so that the corporation for which the election was made or the termination occurred is a small business corporation or a qualified subchapter S subsidiary, as the case may be, or

(B) to acquire the required shareholder consents, and

(4) the corporation for which the election was made or the termination occurred, and each person who was a shareholder in such corporation at any time during the period specified pursuant to this subsection, agrees to make such adjustments (consistent with the treatment of the corporation as an S corporation or a qualified subchapter S subsidiary, as the case may be) as may be required by the Secretary with respect to such period, then, notwithstanding the circumstances resulting in such ineffectiveness or termination, such corporation shall be treated as an S corporation or a qualified subchapter S subsidiary, as the case may be during the period specified by the Secretary.

(g) Election after termination.—If a small business corporation has made an election under subsection (a) and if such election has been terminated under subsection (d), such corporation (and any successor corporation) shall not be eligible to make an election under subsection (a) for any taxable year before its 5th taxable year which begins after the 1st taxable year for which such termination is effective, unless the Secretary consents to such election.

§ 1363. Effect of election on corporation

(a) General rule.—Except as otherwise provided in this subchapter, an S corporation shall not be subject to the taxes imposed by this chapter.

(b) Computation of corporation's taxable income.—The taxable income of an S corporation shall be computed in the same manner as in the case of an individual, except that—

(1) the items described in section 1366(a)(1)(A) shall be separately stated,

(2) the deductions referred to in section 703(a)(2) shall not be allowed to the corporation,

(3) section 248 shall apply, and

(4) section 291 shall apply if the S corporation (or any predecessor) was a C corporation for any of the 3 immediately preceding taxable years.

(c) Elections of the S corporation.—

(1) In general.—Except as provided in paragraph (2), any election affecting the computation of items derived from an S corporation shall be made by the corporation.

(2) Exceptions.—In the case of an S corporation, elections under the following provisions shall be made by each shareholder separately—

(A) section 617 (relating to deduction and recapture of certain mining exploration expenditures), and

(B) section 901 (relating to taxes of foreign countries and possessions of the United States).

* * *

PART II—TAX TREATMENT OF SHAREHOLDERS

§ 1366. Pass-thru of items to shareholders

(a) Determination of shareholder's tax liability.—

(1) In general.—In determining the tax under this chapter of a shareholder for the shareholder's taxable year in which the taxable year of the S corporation ends (or for the final taxable year of a shareholder who dies, or of a trust or estate which terminates, before the end of the corporation's taxable year), there shall be taken into account the shareholder's pro rata share of the corporation's—

(A) items of income (including tax-exempt income), loss, deduction, or credit the separate treatment of which could affect the liability for tax of any shareholder, and

(B) nonseparately computed income or loss.

For purposes of the preceding sentence, the items referred to in subparagraph (A) shall include amounts described in paragraph (4) or (6) of section 702(a).

(2) Nonseparately computed income or loss defined.—For purposes of this subchapter, the term "nonseparately computed income or loss" means gross income minus the deductions allowed to the corporation under this chapter, determined by excluding all items described in paragraph (1)(A).

(b) Character passed thru.—The character of any item included in a shareholder's pro rata share under paragraph (1) of subsection (a) shall be determined as if such item were realized directly from the source from which realized by the corporation, or incurred in the same manner as incurred by the corporation.

(c) Gross income of a shareholder.—In any case where it is necessary to determine the gross income of a shareholder for purposes of this title, such gross income shall include the shareholder's pro rata share of the gross income of the corporation.

(d) Special rules for losses and deductions.—

(1) Cannot exceed shareholder's basis in stock and debt.—The aggregate amount of losses and deductions taken into account by a shareholder under subsection (a) for any taxable year shall not exceed the sum of—

(A) the adjusted basis of the shareholder's stock in the S corporation (determined with regard to paragraphs (1) and (2)(A) of section 1367(a) for the taxable year), and

(B) the shareholder's adjusted basis of any indebtedness of the S corporation to the shareholder (determined without regard to any adjustment under paragraph (2) of section 1367(b) for the taxable year).

(2) Indefinite carryover of disallowed losses and deductions.—

(A) In general.—Except as provided in subparagraph (B), any loss or deduction which is disallowed for any taxable year by reason of paragraph (1) shall be treated as incurred by the corporation in the succeeding taxable year with respect to that shareholder.

(B) Transfers of stock between spouses or incident to divorce.—In the case of any transfer described in section 1041(a) of stock of an S corporation, any loss or deduction described in subparagraph (A) with respect such stock shall be treated as incurred by the corporation in the succeeding taxable year with respect to the transferee.

(3) Carryover of disallowed losses and deductions to post-termination transition period.—

(A) In general.—If for the last taxable year of a corporation for which it was an S corporation a loss or deduction was disallowed by reason of paragraph (1), such loss or deduction shall be treated as incurred by the shareholder on the last day of any post-termination transition period.

(B) Cannot exceed shareholder's basis in stock.—The aggregate amount of losses and deductions taken into account by a shareholder under subparagraph (A) shall not exceed the adjusted basis of the shareholder's stock in the corporation (determined at the close of the last day of the post-termination transition period and without regard to this paragraph).

(C) Adjustment in basis of stock.—The shareholder's basis in the stock of the corporation shall be reduced by the amount allowed as a deduction by reason of this paragraph.

(D) At-risk limitations.—To the extent that any increase in adjusted basis described in subparagraph (B) would have increased the shareholder's amount at risk under section 465 if such increase had occurred on the day preceding the commencement of the post-termination transition period, rules similar to the rules described in subparagraphs (A) through (C) shall apply to any losses disallowed by reason of section 465(a).

(4) Application of limitation on charitable contributions.—In the case of any charitable contribution of property to which the second sentence of section 1367(a)(2) applies, paragraph (1) shall not apply to the extent of the excess (if any) of—

(A) the shareholder's pro rata share of such contribution, over

(B) the shareholder's pro rata share of the adjusted basis of such property.

(e) Treatment of family group.—If an individual who is a member of the family (within the meaning of section 704(e)(3)) of one or more shareholders of an S corporation renders services for the corporation or furnishes capital to the corporation without receiving reasonable compensation therefor, the Secretary shall make such adjustments in the items taken into account by such individual and such shareholders as may be necessary in order to reflect the value of such services or capital.

(f) Special rules.—

* * *

(2) Treatment of tax imposed on built-in gains.—If any tax is imposed under section 1374 for any taxable year on an S corporation, for purposes of subsection (a), the amount so imposed shall be treated as a loss sustained by the S corporation during such taxable year. The character of such loss shall be determined by allocating the loss proportionately among the recognized built-in gains giving rise to such tax.

(3) Reduction in pass-thru for tax imposed on excess net passive income.—If any tax is imposed under section 1375 for any taxable year on an S corporation, for purposes of subsection (a), each item of passive investment income shall be reduced by an amount which bears the same ratio to the amount of such tax as—

(A) the amount of such item, bears to

(B) the total passive investment income for the taxable year.

§ 1367. Adjustments to basis of stock of shareholders, etc.

(a) General rule.—

(1) Increases in basis.—The basis of each shareholder's stock in an S corporation shall be increased for any period by the sum of the following items determined with respect to that shareholder for such period:

(A) the items of income described in subparagraph (A) of section 1366(a)(1),

(B) any nonseparately computed income determined under subparagraph (B) of section 1366(a)(1), and

(C) the excess of the deductions for depletion over the basis of the property subject to depletion.

(2) Decreases in basis.—The basis of each shareholder's stock in an S corporation shall be decreased for any period (but not below zero) by the sum of the following items determined with respect to the shareholder for such period:

(A) distributions by the corporation which were not includible in the income of the shareholder by reason of section 1368,

(B) the items of loss and deduction described in subparagraph (A) of section 1366(a)(1),

(C) any nonseparately computed loss determined under subparagraph (B) of section 1366(a)(1),

(D) any expense of the corporation not deductible in computing its taxable income and not properly chargeable to capital account, and

(E) the amount of the shareholder's deduction for depletion for any oil and gas property held by the S corporation to the extent such deduction does not exceed the proportionate share of the adjusted basis of such property allocated to such shareholder under section 613A(c)(11)(B).

The decrease under subparagraph (B) by reason of a charitable contribution (as defined in section 170(c)) of property shall be the amount equal to the shareholder's pro rata share of the adjusted basis of such property. The preceding sentence shall not apply to contributions made in taxable years beginning after December 31, 2013.

(b) Special rules.—

(1) Income items.—An amount which is required to be included in the gross income of a shareholder and shown on his return shall be taken into account under subparagraph (A) or (B) of subsection (a)(1) only to the extent such amount is included in the shareholder's gross income on his return, increased or decreased by any adjustment of such amount in a redetermination of the shareholder's tax liability.

(2) Adjustments in basis of indebtedness.—

(A) Reduction of basis.—If for any taxable year the amounts specified in subparagraphs (B), (C), (D), and (E) of subsection (a)(2) exceed the amount which reduces the shareholder's basis to zero, such excess shall be applied to reduce (but not below zero) the shareholder's basis in any indebtedness of the S corporation to the shareholder.

(B) Restoration of basis.—If for any taxable year beginning after December 31, 1982, there is a reduction under subparagraph (A) in the shareholder's basis in the indebtedness of an S corporation to a shareholder, any net increase (after the application of paragraphs (1) and (2) of subsection (a)) for any subsequent taxable year shall be applied to restore such reduction in basis before any of it may be used to increase the shareholder's basis in the stock of the S corporation.

(3) Coordination with sections 165(g) and 166(d).—This section and section 1366 shall be applied before the application of sections 165(g) and 166(d) to any taxable year of the shareholder or the corporation in which the security or debt becomes worthless.

(4) Adjustments in case of inherited stock.—

(A) In general.—If any person acquires stock in an S corporation by reason of the death of a decedent or by bequest, devise, or inheritance, section 691 shall be applied with respect to any item of income of the S corporation in the same manner as if the decedent had held directly his pro rata share of such item.

(B) Adjustments to basis.—The basis determined under section 1014 of any stock in an S corporation shall be reduced by the portion of the value of the stock which is attributable to items constituting income in respect of the decedent.

§ 1368. Distributions

(a) General rule.—A distribution of property made by an S corporation with respect to its stock to which (but for this subsection) section 301(c) would apply shall be treated in the manner provided in subsection (b) or (c), whichever applies.

(b) S corporation having no earnings and profits.—In the case of a distribution described in subsection (a) by an S corporation which has no accumulated earnings and profits—

(1) Amount applied against basis.—The distribution shall not be included in gross income to the extent that it does not exceed the adjusted basis of the stock.

(2) Amount in excess of basis.—If the amount of the distribution exceeds the adjusted basis of the stock, such excess shall be treated as gain from the sale or exchange of property.

(c) S corporation having earnings and profits.—In the case of a distribution described in subsection (a) by an S corporation which has accumulated earnings and profits—

(1) Accumulated adjustments account.—That portion of the distribution which does not exceed the accumulated adjustments account shall be treated in the manner provided by subsection (b).

(2) Dividend.—That portion of the distribution which remains after the application of paragraph (1) shall be treated as a dividend to the extent it does not exceed the accumulated earnings and profits of the S corporation.

(3) Treatment of remainder.—Any portion of the distribution remaining after the application of paragraph (2) of this subsection shall be treated in the manner provided by subsection (b).

Except to the extent provided in regulations, if the distributions during the taxable year exceed the amount in the accumulated adjustments account at the close of the taxable year, for purposes of this subsection, the balance of such account shall be allocated among such distributions in proportion to their respective sizes.

(d) Certain adjustments taken into account.—Subsections (b) and (c) shall be applied by taking into account (to the extent proper)—

(1) the adjustments to the basis of the shareholder's stock described in section 1367, and

(2) the adjustments to the accumulated adjustments account which are required by subsection (e)(1).

In the case of any distribution made during any taxable year, the adjusted basis of the stock shall be determined with regard to the adjustments provided in paragraph (1) of section 1367(a) for the taxable year.

(e) Definitions and special rules.—For purposes of this section—

(1) Accumulated adjustments account.—

(A) In general.—Except as otherwise provided in this paragraph, the term "accumulated adjustments account" means an account of the S corporation which is adjusted for the S period in a manner similar to the adjustments under section 1367 (except that no adjustment shall be made for income (and related expenses) which is exempt from tax under this title and the phrase "(but not below zero)" shall be disregarded in section 1367(a)(2)) and no adjustment shall be made for Federal taxes attributable to any taxable year in which the corporation was a C corporation.

(B) Amount of adjustment in the case of redemptions.—In the case of any redemption which is treated as an exchange under section 302(a) or 303(a), the adjustment in the accumulated adjustments account shall be an amount which bears the same ratio to the balance in such account as the number of shares redeemed in such redemption bears to the number of shares of stock in the corporation immediately before such redemption.

(C) Net loss for year disregarded.—

(i) In general.—In applying this section to distributions made during any taxable year, the amount in the accumulated adjustments account as of the close of such taxable year shall be determined without regard to any net negative adjustment for such taxable year.

(ii) Net negative adjustment.—For purposes of clause (i), the term "net negative adjustment" means, with respect to any taxable year, the excess (if any) of—

(I) the reductions in the account for the taxable year (other than for distributions), over

(II) the increases in such account for such taxable year.

(2) S period.—The term "S period" means the most recent continuous period during which the corporation has been an S corporation. Such period shall not include any taxable year beginning before January 1, 1983.

(3) Election to distribute earnings first.—

(A) In general.—An S corporation may, with the consent of all of its affected shareholders, elect to have paragraph (1) of subsection (c) not apply to all distributions made during the taxable year for which the election is made.

(B) Affected shareholder.—For purposes of subparagraph (A), the term "affected shareholder" means any shareholder to whom a distribution is made by the S corporation during the taxable year.

(f) Restricted bank director stock.—If a director receives a distribution (not in part or full payment in exchange for stock) from an S corporation with respect to any restricted bank director stock (as defined in section 1361(f)), the amount of such distribution–

(1) shall be includible in gross income of the director, and

(2) shall be deductible by the corporation for the taxable year of such corporation in which or with which ends the taxable year in which such amount in included in the gross income of the director.

PART III—SPECIAL RULES

§ 1371. Coordination with subchapter C

(a) Application of subchapter C rules.—Except as otherwise provided in this title, and except to the extent inconsistent with this subchapter, subchapter C shall apply to an S corporation and its shareholders.

(b) No carryover between C year and S year.—

(1) From C year to S year.—No carryforward, and no carryback, arising for a taxable year for which a corporation is a C corporation may be carried to a taxable year for which such corporation is an S corporation.

(2) No carryover from S year.—No carryforward, and no carryback, shall arise at the corporate level for a taxable year for which a corporation is an S corporation.

(3) Treatment of S year as elapsed year.—Nothing in paragraphs (1) and (2) shall prevent treating a taxable year for which a corporation is an S corporation as a taxable year for purposes of determining the number of taxable years to which an item may be carried back or carried forward.

(c) Earnings and profits.—

(1) In general.—Except as provided in paragraphs (2) and (3) and subsection (d)(3), no adjustment shall be made to the earnings and profits of an S corporation.

(2) Adjustments for redemptions, liquidations, reorganizations, divisives, etc.—In the case of any transaction involving the application of subchapter C to any S corporation, proper adjustment to any accumulated earnings and profits of the corporation shall be made.

(3) Adjustments in case of distributions treated as dividends under section 1368(c)(2).—Paragraph (1) shall not apply with respect to that portion of a distribution which is treated as a dividend under section 1368(c)(2).

* * *

(e) Cash distributions during post-termination transition period.—

(1) In general.—Any distribution of money by a corporation with respect to its stock during a post-termination transition period shall be applied against and reduce the adjusted basis of the stock, to the extent that the amount of the distribution does not exceed the accumulated adjustments account (within the meaning of section 1368(e)).

(2) Election to distribute earnings first.—An S corporation may elect to have paragraph (1) not apply to all distributions made during a post-termination transition period described in section 1377(b)(1)(A). Such election shall not be effective unless all shareholders of the S corporation to whom distributions are made by the S corporation during such post-termination transition period consent to such election.

§ 1372. Partnership rules to apply for fringe benefit purposes

(a) General rule.—For purposes of applying the provisions of this subtitle which relate to employee fringe benefits—

(1) the S corporation shall be treated as a partnership, and

(2) any 2-percent shareholder of the S corporation shall be treated as a partner of such partnership.

(b) 2–percent shareholder defined.—For purposes of this section, the term "2–percent shareholder" means any person who owns (or is considered as owning within the meaning of section 318) on any day during the taxable year of the S corporation more than 2 percent of the outstanding stock of such corporation or stock possessing more than 2 percent of the total combined voting power of all stock of such corporation.

§ 1374. Tax imposed on certain built-in gains

(a) General Rule.—If for any taxable year beginning in the recognition period an S corporation has a net recognized built-in gain, there is hereby imposed a tax (computed under subsection (b)) on the income of such corporation for such taxable year.

(b) Amount of tax.—

(1) In general.—The amount of the tax imposed by subsection (a) shall be computed by applying the highest rate of tax specified in section 11(b) to the net recognized built-in gain of the S corporation for the taxable year.

(2) Net operating loss carryforwards from C years allowed.—Notwithstanding section 1371(b)(1), any net operating loss carryforward arising in a taxable year for which the corporation was a C corporation shall be allowed for purposes of this section as a deduction against the net recognized built-in gain of the S corporation for the taxable year. For purposes of determining the amount of any such loss which may be carried to subsequent taxable years, the amount of the net recognized built-in gain shall be treated as taxable income. Rules similar to the rules of the preceding sentences of this paragraph shall apply in the case of a capital loss carryforward arising in a taxable year for which the corporation was a C corporation.

(3) Credits.—

(A) In general.—Except as provided in subparagraph (B), no credit shall be allowable under part IV of subchapter A of this chapter (other than under section 34) against the tax imposed by subsection (a).

(B) Business credit carryforwards from C years allowed.—Notwithstanding section 1371(b)(1), any business credit carryforward under section 39 arising in a taxable year for which the corporation was a C corporation shall be allowed as a credit against the tax imposed by subsection (a) in the same manner as if it were imposed by section 11. A similar rule shall apply in the case of the minimum tax credit under section 53 to the extent attributable to taxable years for which the corporation was a C corporation.

(4) Coordination with section 1201(a).—For purposes of section 1201(a)—

(A) the tax imposed by subsection (a) shall be treated as if it were imposed by section 11, and

(B) the amount of the net recognized built-in gain shall be treated as the taxable income.

(c) Limitations.—

(1) Corporations which were always S corporations.—Subsection (a) shall not apply to any corporation if an election under section 1362(a) has been in effect with respect to such corporation for each of its taxable years. Except as provided in regulations, an S corporation and any predecessor corporation shall be treated as 1 corporation for purposes of the preceding sentence.

(2) Limitation on amount of net recognized built-in gain.—The amount of the net recognized built-in gain taken into account under this section for any taxable year shall not exceed the excess (if any) of—

(A) the net unrealized built-in gain, over

(B) the net recognized built-in gain for prior taxable years beginning in the recognition period.

(d) Definitions and special rules.—For purposes of this section—

(1) Net unrealized built-in gain.—The term "net unrealized built-in gain" means the amount (if any) by which—

(A) the fair market value of the assets of the S corporation as of the beginning of its 1st taxable year for which an election under section 1362(a) is in effect, exceeds

(B) the aggregate adjusted bases of such assets at such time.

(2) Net recognized built-in gain.—

(A) In general.—The term "net recognized built-in gain" means, with respect to any taxable year in the recognition period, the lesser of—

(i) the amount which would be the taxable income of the S corporation for such taxable year if only recognized built-in gains and recognized built-in losses were taken into account, or

(ii) such corporation's taxable income for such taxable year (determined as provided in section 1375(b)(1)(B)).

(B) Carryover.—If, for any taxable year described in subparagraph (A), the amount referred to in clause (i) of subparagraph (A) exceeds the amount referred to in clause (ii) of subparagraph (A), such excess shall be treated as a recognized built-in gain in the succeeding taxable year. The preceding sentence shall apply only in the case of a corporation treated as an S corporation by reason of an election made on or after March 31, 1988.

(3) Recognized built-in gain.—The term "recognized built-in gain" means any gain recognized during the recognition period on the disposition of any asset except to the extent that the S corporation establishes that—

(A) such asset was not held by the S corporation as of the beginning of the 1st taxable year for which it was an S corporation, or

(B) such gain exceeds the excess (if any) of—

(i) the fair market value of such asset as of the beginning of such 1st taxable year, over

(ii) the adjusted basis of the asset as of such time.

(4) Recognized built-in losses.—The term "recognized built-in loss" means any loss recognized during the recognition period on the disposition of any asset to the extent that the S corporation establishes that—

(A) such asset was held by the S corporation as of the beginning of the 1st taxable year referred to in paragraph (3), and

(B) such loss does not exceed the excess of—

(i) the adjusted basis of such asset as of the beginning of such 1st taxable year, over

(ii) the fair market value of such asset as of such time.

(5) Treatment of certain built-in items.—

(A) Income items.—Any item of income which is properly taken into account during the recognition period but which is attributable to periods before the 1st taxable year for which the corporation was an S corporation shall be treated as a recognized built-in gain for the taxable year in which it is properly taken into account.

(B) Deduction items.—Any amount which is allowable as a deduction during the recognition period (determined without regard to any carryover) but which is attributable to periods before the 1st taxable year referred to in subparagraph (A) shall be treated as a recognized built-in loss for the taxable year for which it is allowable as a deduction.

(C) Adjustment to net unrealized built-in gain.—The amount of the net unrealized built-in gain shall be properly adjusted for amounts treated as recognized built-in gains or losses under this paragraph if such amounts were properly taken into account (or allowable as a deduction) during the recognition period.

(6) Treatment of certain property.—If the adjusted basis of any asset is determined (in whole or in part) by reference to the adjusted basis of any other asset held by the S corporation as of the beginning of the 1st taxable year referred to in paragraph (3)—

(A) such asset shall be treated as held by the S corporation as of the beginning of such 1st taxable year, and

(B) any determination under paragraph (3)(B) or (4)(B) with respect to such asset shall be made by reference to the fair market value and adjusted basis of such other asset as of the beginning of such 1st taxable year.

(7) Recognition period.—

(A) In general.—The term "recognition period" means the 10-year period beginning with the 1st day of the 1st taxable year for which the corporation was an S corporation.

(B) Special rules for 2009, 2010, and 2011.—No tax shall be imposed on the net recognized built-in gain of an S corporation—

(i) in the case of any taxable year beginning in 2009 or 2010, if the 7th taxable year in the recognition period preceded such taxable year, or

(ii) in the case of any taxable year beginning in 2011, if the 5th year in the recognition period preceded such taxable year.

The preceding sentence shall be applied separately with respect to any asset to which paragraph (8) applies.

(C) Special rule for 2012 and 2013.—For purposes of determining the net recognized built-in gain for taxable years beginning in 2012 or 2013, subparagraphs (A) * * * shall be applied by substituting "5-year" for "10-year".

* * *

(E) Installment sales.—If an S corporation sells an asset and reports the income from the sale using the installment method under section 453, the treatment of all payments received shall be governed by the provisions of this paragraph applicable to the taxable year in which such sale was made.

(8) Treatment of transfer of assets from C corporation to S corporation.—

(A) In general.—Except to the extent provided in regulations, if—

(i) an S corporation acquires any asset, and

(ii) the S corporation's basis in such asset is determined (in whole or in part) by reference to the basis of such asset (or any other property) in the hands of a C corporation,

then a tax is hereby imposed on any net recognized built-in gain attributable to any such assets for any taxable year beginning in the recognition period. The amount of such tax shall be determined under the rules of this section as modified by subparagraph (B).

(B) Modifications.—For purposes of this paragraph, the modifications of this subparagraph are as follows:

(i) In general.—The preceding paragraphs of this subsection shall be applied by taking into account the day on which the assets were acquired by the S corporation in lieu of the beginning of the 1st taxable year for which the corporation was an S corporation.

(ii) Subsection (c)(1) not to apply.—Subsection (c)(1) shall not apply.

(9) Reference to 1st taxable year.—Any reference in this section to the 1st taxable year for which the corporation was an S corporation shall be treated as a reference to the 1st taxable year for which the corporation was an S corporation pursuant to its most recent election under section 1362.

(e) Regulations.—The Secretary shall prescribe such regulations as may be necessary to carry out the purposes of this section including regulations providing for the appropriate treatment of successor corporations.

§ 1375. Tax imposed when passive investment income of corporation having accumulated earnings and profits exceeds 25 percent of gross receipts

(a) General rule.—If for the taxable year an S corporation has—

(1) accumulated earnings and profits at the close of such taxable year, and

(2) gross receipts more than 25 percent of which are passive investment income,

then there is hereby imposed a tax on the income of such corporation for such taxable year. Such tax shall be computed by multiplying the excess net passive income by the highest rate of tax specified in section 11(b).

(b) Definitions.—For purposes of this section—

(1) Excess net passive income.—

(A) In general.—Except as provided in subparagraph (B), the term "excess net passive income" means an amount which bears the same ratio to the net passive income for the taxable year as—

(i) the amount by which the passive investment income for the taxable year exceeds 25 percent of the gross receipts for the taxable year, bears to

(ii) the passive investment income for the taxable year.

(B) Limitation.—The amount of the excess net passive income for any taxable year shall not exceed the amount of the corporation's taxable income for such taxable year as determined under section 63(a)—

(i) without regard to the deductions allowed by part VIII of subchapter B (other than the deduction allowed by section 248, relating to organization expenditures), and

(ii) without regard to the deduction under section 172.

(2) Net passive income.—The term "net passive income" means—

(A) passive investment income, reduced by

(B) the deductions allowable under this chapter which are directly connected with the production of such income (other than deductions allowable under section 172 and part VIII of subchapter B).

(3) Passive investment income, etc.—The terms "passive investment income" and "gross receipts" have the same respective meanings as when used in paragraph (3) of section 1362(d).

(4) Coordination with section 1374.—Notwithstanding paragraph (3), the amount of passive investment income shall be determined by not taking into account any recognized built-in gain or loss of the S corporation for any taxable year in the recognition period. Terms used in the preceding sentence shall have the same respective meanings as when used in section 1374.

(c) Credits not allowable.—No credit shall be allowed under part IV of subchapter A of this chapter (other than section 34) against the tax imposed by subsection (a).

(d) Waiver of tax in certain cases.—If the S corporation establishes to the satisfaction of the Secretary that—

(1) it determined in good faith that it had no accumulated earnings and profits at the close of a taxable year, and

(2) during a reasonable period of time after it was determined that it did have accumulated earnings and profits at the close of such taxable year such earnings and profits were distributed,

the Secretary may waive the tax imposed by subsection (a) for such taxable year.

PART IV—DEFINITIONS; MISCELLANEOUS

§ 1377. Definitions and special rule

(a) Pro rata share.—For purposes of this subchapter—

(1) In general.—Except as provided in paragraph (2), each shareholder's pro rata share of any item for any taxable year shall be the sum of the amounts determined with respect to the shareholder—

(A) by assigning an equal portion of such item to each day of the taxable year, and

(B) then by dividing that portion pro rata among the shares outstanding on such day.

(2) Election to terminate year.—

(A) In general.—Under regulations prescribed by the Secretary, if any shareholder terminates the shareholder's interest in the corporation during the taxable year and all affected shareholders and the corporation agree to the application of this paragraph, paragraph (1) shall be applied to the affected shareholders as if the taxable year consisted of 2 taxable years the first of which ends on the date of the termination.

(B) Affected shareholders.—For purposes of subparagraph (A), the term "affected shareholders" means the shareholder whose interest is terminated and all shareholders to whom such shareholder has transferred shares during the taxable year. If such shareholder has transferred shares to the corporation, the term "affected shareholders" shall include all persons who are shareholders during the taxable year.

(b) Post-termination transition period.—

(1) In general.—For purposes of this subchapter, the term "post-termination transition period" means—

(A) the period beginning on the day after the last day of the corporation's last taxable year as an S corporation and ending on the later of—

(i) the day which is 1 year after such last day, or

(ii) the due date for filing the return for such last year as an S corporation (including extensions),

(B) the 120–day period beginning on the date of any determination pursuant to an audit of the taxpayer which follows the termination of the corporation's election and which adjusts a subchapter S item of income, loss, or deduction of the corporation arising during the S period (as defined in section 1368(e)(2)), and

(C) the 120–day period beginning on the date of a determination that the corporation's election under section 1362(a) had terminated for a previous taxable year.

(2) Determination defined.—For purposes of paragraph (1), the term "determination" means—

(A) a determination as defined in section 1313(a), or

(B) an agreement between the corporation and the Secretary that the corporation failed to qualify as an S corporation.

(3) Special rules for audit related post-termination transition periods.—

(A) No application to carryovers.—Paragraph (1)(B) shall not apply for purposes of section 1366(d)(3).

(B) Limitation on application to distributions.—Paragraph (1)(B) shall apply to a distribution described in section 1371(e) only to the extent that the amount of such distribution does not exceed the aggregate increase (if any) in the accumulated adjustments account (within the meaning of section 1368(e)) by reason of the adjustments referred to in such paragraph.

(c) Manner of making elections, etc.—Any election under this subchapter, and any revocation under section 1362(d)(1), shall be made in such manner as the Secretary shall by regulations prescribe.

§ 1378. Taxable year of S corporation

(a) General rule.—For purposes of this subtitle, the taxable year of an S corporation shall be a permitted year.

(b) Permitted year defined.—For purposes of this section, the term "permitted year" means a taxable year which—

(1) is a year ending December 31, or

(2) is any other accounting period for which the corporation establishes a business purpose to the satisfaction of the Secretary.

For purposes of paragraph (2), any deferral of income to shareholders shall not be treated as a business purpose.

SUBCHAPTER V—TITLE 11 CASES

§ 1398. Rules relating to individuals' title 11 cases

(a) Cases to which section applies.—Except as provided in subsection (b), this section shall apply to any case under chapter 7 (relating to liquidations) or chapter 11 (relating to reorganizations) of title 11 of the United States Code in which the debtor is an individual.

(b) Exceptions where case is dismissed, etc.—

(1) Section does not apply where case is dismissed.—This section shall not apply if the case under chapter 7 or 11 of title 11 of the United States Code is dismissed.

(2) Section does not apply at partnership level.—For purposes of subsection (a), a partnership shall not be treated as an individual, but the interest in a partnership of a debtor who is an individual shall be taken into account under this section in the same manner as any other interest of the debtor.

(c) Computation and payment of tax; basic standard deduction.—

(1) Computation and payment of tax.—Except as otherwise provided in this section, the taxable income of the estate shall be computed in the same manner as for an individual. The tax shall be computed on such taxable income and shall be paid by the trustee.

(2) Tax rates.—The tax on the taxable income of the estate shall be determined under subsection (d) of section 1.

(3) Basic standard deduction.—In the case of an estate which does not itemize deductions, the basic standard deduction for the estate for the taxable year shall be the same as for a married individual filing a separate return for such year.

(d) Taxable year of debtors.—

(1) General rule.—Except as provided in paragraph (2), the taxable year of the debtor shall be determined without regard to the case under title 11 of the United States Code to which this section applies.

(2) Election to terminate debtor's year when case commences.—

(A) In general.—Notwithstanding section 442, the debtor may (without the approval of the Secretary) elect to treat the debtor's taxable year which includes the commencement date as 2 taxable years—

(i) the first of which ends on the day before the commencement date, and

(ii) the second of which begins on the commencement date.

(B) Spouse may join in election.—In the case of a married individual (within the meaning of section 7703), the spouse may elect to have the debtor's election under subparagraph (A) also apply to the spouse, but only if the debtor and the spouse file a joint return for the taxable year referred to in subparagraph (A)(i).

(C) No election where debtor has no assets.—No election may be made under subparagraph (A) by a debtor who has no assets other than property which the debtor may treat as exempt property under section 522 of title 11 of the United States Code.

(D) Time for making election.—An election under subparagraph (A) or (B) may be made only on or before the due date for filing the return for the taxable year referred to in subparagraph (A)(i). Any such election, once made, shall be irrevocable.

(E) Returns.—A return shall be made for each of the taxable years specified in subparagraph (A).

(F) Annualization.—For purposes of subsections (b), (c), and (d) of section 443, a return filed for either of the taxable years referred to in subparagraph (A) shall be treated as a return made under paragraph (1) of subsection (a) of section 443.

(3) Commencement date defined.—For purposes of this subsection, the term "commencement date" means the day on which the case under title 11 of the United States Code to which this section applies commences.

(e) Treatment of income, deductions, and credits.—

(1) Estate's share of debtor's income.—The gross income of the estate for each taxable year shall include the gross income of the debtor to which the estate is entitled under title 11 of the United States Code. The preceding sentence shall not apply to any amount received or accrued by the debtor before the commencement date (as defined in subsection (d)(3)).

(2) Debtor's share of debtor's income.—The gross income of the debtor for any taxable year shall not include any item to the extent that such item is included in the gross income of the estate by reason of paragraph (1).

(3) Rule for making determinations with respect to deductions, credits, and employment taxes.—Except as otherwise provided in this section, the determination of whether or not any amount paid or incurred by the estate—

(A) is allowable as a deduction or credit under this chapter, or

(B) is wages for purposes of subtitle C,

shall be made as if the amount were paid or incurred by the debtor and as if the debtor were still engaged in the trades and businesses, and in the activities, the debtor was engaged in before the commencement of the case.

(f) Treatment of transfers between debtor and estate.—

(1) Transfer to estate not treated as disposition.—A transfer (other than by sale or exchange) of an asset from the debtor to the estate shall not be treated as a disposition for purposes of any provision of this title assigning tax consequences to a disposition, and the estate shall be treated as the debtor would be treated with respect to such asset.

(2) Transfer from estate to debtor not treated as disposition.—In the case of a termination of the estate, a transfer (other than by sale or exchange) of an asset from the estate to the debtor shall not be treated as a disposition for purposes of any provision of this title assigning tax consequences to a disposition, and the debtor shall be treated as the estate would be treated with respect to such asset.

(g) Estate succeeds to tax attributes of debtor.—The estate shall succeed to and take into account the following items (determined as of the first day of the debtor's taxable year in which the case commences) of the debtor—

(1) Net operating loss carryovers.—The net operating loss carryovers determined under section 172.

(2) Charitable contributions carryovers.—The carryover of excess charitable contributions determined under section 170(d)(1).

(3) Recovery of tax benefit items.—Any amount to which section 111 (relating to recovery of tax benefit items) applies.

(4) Credit carryovers, etc.—The carryovers of any credit, and all other items which, but for the commencement of the case, would be required to be taken into account by the debtor with respect to any credit.

(5) Capital loss carryovers.—The capital loss carryover determined under section 1212.

(6) Basis, holding period, and character of assets.—In the case of any asset acquired (other than by sale or exchange) by the estate from the debtor, the basis, holding period, and character it had in the hands of the debtor.

(7) Method of accounting.—The method of accounting used by the debtor.

(8) Other attributes.—Other tax attributes of the debtor, to the extent provided in regulations prescribed by the Secretary as necessary or appropriate to carry out the purposes of this section.

(h) Administration, liquidation, and reorganization expenses; carryovers and carrybacks of certain excess expenses.—

(1) Administration, liquidation, and reorganization expenses.—Any administrative expense allowed under section 503 of title 11 of the United States Code, and any fee or charge assessed against the estate under chapter 123 of title 28 of the United States Code, to the extent not disallowed under any other provision of this title, shall be allowed as a deduction.

(2) Carryback and carryover of excess administrative costs, etc., to estate taxable years.—

(A) Deduction allowed.—There shall be allowed as a deduction for the taxable year an amount equal to the aggregate of (i) the administrative expense carryovers to such year, plus (ii) the administrative expense carrybacks to such year.

(B) Administrative expense loss, etc.—If a net operating loss would be created or increased for any estate taxable year if section 172(c) were applied without the modification contained in paragraph (4) of section 172(d), then the amount of the net operating loss so created (or the amount of the increase in the net operating loss) shall be an administrative expense loss for such taxable year which shall be an administrative expense carryback to each of the 3 preceding taxable years and an administrative expense carryover to each of the 7 succeeding taxable years.

(C) Determination of amount carried to each taxable year.—The portion of any administrative expense loss which may be carried to any other taxable year shall be determined under section 172(b)(2), except that for each taxable year the computation under section 172(b)(2) with respect to the net operating loss shall be made before the computation under this paragraph.

(D) Administrative expense deductions allowed only to estate.—The deductions allowable under this chapter solely by reason of paragraph (1), and the deduction provided by subparagraph (A) of this paragraph, shall be allowable only to the estate.

(i) Debtor succeeds to tax attributes of estate.—In the case of a termination of an estate, the debtor shall succeed to and take into account the items referred to in paragraphs (1), (2), (3), (4), (5), and (6) of subsection (g) in a manner similar to that provided in such paragraphs (but taking into account that the transfer is from the estate to the debtor instead of from the debtor to the estate). In addition, the debtor shall succeed to and take into account the other tax attributes of the estate, to the extent provided in regulations prescribed by the Secretary as necessary or appropriate to carry out the purposes of this section.

(j) Other special rules.—

(1) Change of accounting period without approval.—Notwithstanding section 442, the estate may change its annual accounting period one time without the approval of the Secretary.

(2) Treatment of certain carrybacks.—

(A) Carrybacks from estate.—If any carryback year of the estate is a taxable year before the estate's first taxable year, the carryback to such carryback year shall be taken into account for the debtor's taxable year corresponding to the carryback year.

(B) Carrybacks from debtor's activities.—The debtor may not carry back to a taxable year before the debtor's taxable year in which the case commences any carryback from a taxable year ending after the case commences.

(C) Carryback and carryback year defined.—For purposes of this paragraph—

(i) Carryback.—The term "carryback" means a net operating loss carryback under section 172 or a carryback of any credit provided by part IV of subchapter A.

(ii) Carryback year.—The term "carryback year" means the taxable year to which a carryback is carried.

§ 1399. No separate taxable entities for partnerships, corporations, etc.

Except in any case to which section 1398 applies, no separate taxable entity shall result from the commencement of a case under title 11 of the United States Code.

CHAPTER 2A—UNEARNED INCOME MEDICARE CONTRIBUTION

§ 1411. Imposition of tax

(a) In general.—Except as provided in subsection (e)—

(1) Application to individuals.—In the case of an individual, there is hereby imposed (in addition to any other tax imposed by this subtitle) for each taxable year a tax equal to 3.8 percent of the lesser of—

(A) net investment income for such taxable year, or

(B) the excess (if any) of—

(i) the modified adjusted gross income for such taxable year, over

(ii) the threshold amount.

(2) Application to estates and trusts.—In the case of an estate or trust, there is hereby imposed (in addition to any other tax imposed by this subtitle) for each taxable year a tax of 3.8 percent of the lesser of—

(A) the undistributed net investment income for such taxable year, or

(B) the excess (if any) of—

(i) the adjusted gross income (as defined in section 67(e)) for such taxable year, over

(ii) the dollar amount at which the highest tax bracket in section 1(e) begins for such taxable year.

(b) Threshold amount.—For purposes of this chapter, the term "threshold amount" means—

(1) in the case of a taxpayer making a joint return under section 6013 or a surviving spouse (as defined in section 2(a)), $250,000,

(2) in the case of a married taxpayer (as defined in section 7703) filing a separate return, 1/2 of the dollar amount determined under paragraph (1), and

(3) in any other case, $200,000.

(c) Net investment income.—For purposes of this chapter—

(1) In general.—The term "net investment income" means the excess (if any) of—

(A) the sum of—

(i) gross income from interest, dividends, annuities, royalties, and rents, other than such income which is derived in the ordinary course of a trade or business not described in paragraph (2),

(ii) other gross income derived from a trade or business described in paragraph (2), and

(iii) net gain (to the extent taken into account in computing taxable income) attributable to the disposition of property other than property held in a trade or business not described in paragraph (2), over

(B) the deductions allowed by this subtitle which are properly allocable to such gross income or net gain.

(2) Trades and businesses to which tax applies.—A trade or business is described in this paragraph if such trade or business is—

(A) a passive activity (within the meaning of section 469) with respect to the taxpayer, or

(B) a trade or business of trading in financial instruments or commodities (as defined in section 475(e)(2)).

(3) Income on investment of working capital subject to tax.—A rule similar to the rule of section 469(e)(1)(B) shall apply for purposes of this subsection.

(4) Exception for certain active interests in partnerships and S corporations.—In the case of a disposition of an interest in a partnership or S corporation—

(A) gain from such disposition shall be taken into account under clause (iii) of paragraph (1)(A) only to the extent of the net gain which would be so taken into account by the transferor if all property of the partnership or S corporation were sold for fair market value immediately before the disposition of such interest, and

(B) a rule similar to the rule of subparagraph (A) shall apply to a loss from such disposition.

(5) Exception for distributions from qualified plans.—The term "net investment income" shall not include any distribution from a plan or arrangement described in section 401(a), 403(a), 403(b), 408, 408A, or 457(b).

(6) Special rule.—Net investment income shall not include any item taken into account in determining self-employment income for such taxable year on which a tax is imposed by section 1401(b).

(d) Modified adjusted gross income.—For purposes of this chapter, the term "modified adjusted gross income" means adjusted gross income increased by the excess of—

(1) the amount excluded from gross income under section 911(a)(1), over

(2) the amount of any deductions (taken into account in computing adjusted gross income) or exclusions disallowed under section 911(d)(6) with respect to the amounts described in paragraph (1).

(e) Nonapplication of section.—This section shall not apply to—

(1) a nonresident alien, or

(2) a trust all of the unexpired interests in which are devoted to one or more of the purposes described in section 170(c)(2)(B).

CHAPTER 6—CONSOLIDATED RETURNS

SUBCHAPTER A—RETURNS AND PAYMENT OF TAX

§ 1501. Privilege to file consolidated returns

An affiliated group of corporations shall, subject to the provisions of this chapter, have the privilege of making a consolidated return with respect to the income tax imposed by chapter 1 for the taxable year in lieu of separate returns. The making of a consolidated return shall be upon the condition that all corporations which at any time during the taxable year have been members of the affiliated group consent to all the consolidated return regulations prescribed under section 1502 prior to the last day prescribed by law for the filing of such return. The making of a consolidated return shall be considered as such consent. In the case of a corporation which is a member of the affiliated group for a fractional part of the year, the consolidated return shall include the income of such corporation for such part of the year as it is a member of the affiliated group.

§ 1502. Regulations

The Secretary shall prescribe such regulations as he may deem necessary in order that the tax liability of any affiliated group of corporations making a consolidated return and of each corporation in the group, both during and after the period of affiliation, may be returned, determined, computed, assessed, collected, and adjusted, in such manner as clearly to reflect the income-tax liability and the various factors necessary for the determination of such liability, and in order to prevent avoidance of such tax liability. In carrying out the preceding sentence, the Secretary may prescribe rules that are different from the provisions of chapter 1 that would apply if such corporations filed separate returns.

§ 1503. Computation and payment of tax

[**(a) General rule.**—] * In any case in which a consolidated return is made or is required to be made, the tax shall be determined, computed, assessed, collected, and adjusted in accordance with the regulations under section 1502 prescribed before the last day prescribed by law for the filing of such return.

* * *

(e) Special rule for determining adjustments to basis.—

(1) In general.—Solely for purposes of determining gain or loss on the disposition of intragroup stock and the amount of any inclusion by reason of an excess loss account, in determining the adjustments to the basis of such intragroup stock on account of the earnings and profits of any member of an affiliated group for any consolidated year (and in determining the amount in such account)—

(A) such earnings and profits shall be determined as if section 312 were applied for such taxable year (and all preceding consolidated years of the member with respect to such group) without regard to subsections (k) and (n) thereof, and

(B) earnings and profits shall not include any amount excluded from gross income under section 108 to the extent the amount so excluded was not applied to reduce tax attributes (other than basis in property).

(2) Definitions.—For purposes of this subsection—

(A) Intragroup stock.—The term "intragroup stock" means any stock which—

(i) is in a corporation which is or was a member of an affiliated group of corporations, and

(ii) is held by another corporation which is or was a member of such group.

Such term includes any other property the basis of which is determined (in whole or in part) by reference to the basis of stock described in the preceding sentence.

(B) Consolidated year.—The term "consolidated year" means any taxable year for which the affiliated group makes a consolidated return.

(C) Application of section 312(n)(7) not affected.—The reference in paragraph (1) to subsection (n) of section 312 shall be treated as not including a reference to paragraph (7) of such subsection.

(3) Adjustments.—Under regulations prescribed by the Secretary, proper adjustments shall be made in the application of paragraph (1)—

(A) in the case of any property acquired by the corporation before consolidation, for the difference between the adjusted basis of such property for purposes of computing taxable income and its adjusted basis for purposes of computing earnings and profits, and

* * *

* Omitted entirely.

(4) Elimination of election to reduce basis of indebtedness.—Nothing in the regulations prescribed under section 1502 shall permit any reduction in the amount otherwise included in gross income by reason of an excess loss account if such reduction is on account of a reduction in the basis of indebtedness.

* * *

§ 1504. Definitions

(a) Affiliated group defined.—For purposes of this subtitle—

(1) In general.—The term "affiliated group" means—

(A) 1 or more chains of includible corporations connected through stock ownership with a common parent corporation which is an includible corporation, but only if—

(B)(i) the common parent owns directly stock meeting the requirements of paragraph (2) in at least 1 of the other includible corporations, and

(ii) stock meeting the requirements of paragraph (2) in each of the includible corporations (except the common parent) is owned directly by 1 or more of the other includible corporations.

(2) 80–percent voting and value test.—The ownership of stock of any corporation meets the requirements of this paragraph if it—

(A) possesses at least 80 percent of the total voting power of the stock of such corporation, and

(B) has a value equal to at least 80 percent of the total value of the stock of such corporation.

(3) 5 years must elapse before reconsolidation.—

(A) In general.—If—

(i) a corporation is included (or required to be included) in a consolidated return filed by an affiliated group for a taxable year which includes any period after December 31, 1984, and

(ii) such corporation ceases to be a member of such group in a taxable year beginning after December 31, 1984,

with respect to periods after such cessation, such corporation (and any successor of such corporation) may not be included in any consolidated return filed by the affiliated group (or by another affiliated group with the same common parent or a successor of such common parent) before the 61st month beginning after its first taxable year in which it ceased to be a member of such affiliated group.

(B) Secretary may waive application of subparagraph (A).—The Secretary may waive the application of subparagraph (A) to any corporation for any period subject to such conditions as the Secretary may prescribe.

(4) Stock not to include certain preferred stock.—For purposes of this subsection, the term "stock" does not include any stock which—

(A) is not entitled to vote,

(B) is limited and preferred as to dividends and does not participate in corporate growth to any significant extent,

(C) has redemption and liquidation rights which do not exceed the issue price of such stock (except for a reasonable redemption or liquidation premium), and

(D) is not convertible into another class of stock.

(5) Regulations.—The Secretary shall prescribe such regulations as may be necessary or appropriate to carry out the purposes of this subsection, including (but not limited to) regulations—

(A) which treat warrants, obligations convertible into stock, and other similar interests as stock, and stock as not stock,

(B) which treat options to acquire or sell stock as having been exercised,

(C) which provide that the requirements of paragraph (2)(B) shall be treated as met if the affiliated group, in reliance on a good faith determination of value, treated such requirements as met,

(D) which disregard an inadvertent ceasing to meet the requirements of paragraph (2)(B) by reason of changes in relative values of different classes of stock,

(E) which provide that transfers of stock within the group shall not be taken into account in determining whether a corporation ceases to be a member of an affiliated group, and

(F) which disregard changes in voting power to the extent such changes are disproportionate to related changes in value.

(b) Definition of "includible corporation".—As used in this chapter, the term "includible corporation" means any corporation except—

(1) Corporations exempt from taxation under section 501.

(2) Insurance companies subject to taxation under section 801.

(3) Foreign corporations.

* * *

(8) An S corporation.

* * *

SUBCHAPTER B—RELATED RULES

PART I—IN GENERAL

§ 1551. Disallowance of the benefits of the graduated corporate rates and accumulated earnings credit

(a) In general.—If—

(1) any corporation transfers, on or after January 1, 1951, and on or before June 12, 1963, all or part of its property (other than money) to a transferee corporation,

(2) any corporation transfers, directly or indirectly, after June 12, 1963, all or part of its property (other than money) to a transferee corporation, or

(3) five or fewer individuals who are in control of a corporation transfer, directly or indirectly, after June 12, 1963, property (other than money) to a transferee corporation,

and the transferee corporation was created for the purpose of acquiring such property or was not actively engaged in business at the time of such acquisition, and if after such transfer the transferor or transferors are in control of such transferee corporation during any part of the taxable year of such transferee corporation, then for such taxable year of such transferee corporation the Secretary may (except as may be otherwise determined under subsection (c)) disallow the benefits of the rates contained in section 11(b) which are lower than the highest rate specified in such section, or the accumulated earnings credit provided in paragraph (2) or (3) of section 535(c), unless such transferee corporation shall establish by the clear preponderance of the evidence that the securing of such benefits or credit was not a major purpose of such transfer.

(b) Control.—For purposes of subsection (a), the term "control" means—

(1) With respect to a transferee corporation described in subsection (a) (1) or (2), the ownership by the transferor corporation, its shareholders, or both, of stock possessing at least 80 percent of the total combined voting power of all classes of stock entitled to vote or at least 80 percent of the total value of shares of all classes of the stock; or

(2) With respect to each corporation described in subsection (a) (3), the ownership by the five or fewer individuals described in such subsection of stock possessing—

(A) at least 80 percent of the total combined voting power of all classes of stock entitled to vote or at least 80 percent of the total value of shares of all classes of the stock of each corporation, and

(B) more than 50 percent of the total combined voting power of all classes of stock entitled to vote or more than 50 percent of the total value of shares of all classes of stock of each corporation, taking into account the stock ownership of each such individual only to the extent such stock ownership is identical with respect to each such corporation.

For purposes of this subsection, section 1563(e) shall apply in determining the ownership of stock.

(c) Authority of the Secretary under this section.—The provisions of section 269(c), and the authority of the Secretary under such section, shall, to the extent not inconsistent with the provisions of this section, be applicable to this section.

§ 1552. Earnings and profits

(a) General rule.—Pursuant to regulations prescribed by the Secretary the earnings and profits of each member of an affiliated group required to be included in a consolidated return for such group filed for a taxable year shall be determined by allocating the tax liability of the group for such year among the members of the group in accord with whichever of the following methods the group shall elect in its first consolidated return filed for such a taxable year:

(1) The tax liability shall be apportioned among the members of the group in accordance with the ratio which that portion of the consolidated taxable income attributable to each member of the group having taxable income bears to the consolidated taxable income.

(2) The tax liability of the group shall be allocated to the several members of the group on the basis of the percentage of the total tax which the tax of such member if computed on a separate return would bear to the total amount of the taxes for all members of the group so computed.

(3) The tax liability of the group (excluding the tax increases arising from the consolidation) shall be allocated on the basis of the contribution of each member of the group to the consolidated taxable income of the group. Any tax increases arising from the consolidation shall be distributed to the several members in direct proportion to the reduction in tax liability resulting to such members from the filing of the consolidated return as measured by the difference between their tax liabilities determined on a separate return basis and their tax liabilities based on their contributions to the consolidated taxable income.

(4) The tax liability of the group shall be allocated in accord with any other method selected by the group with the approval of the Secretary.

(b) Failure to elect.—If no election is made in such first return, the tax liability shall be allocated among the several members of the group pursuant to the method prescribed in subsection (a)(1).

PART II—CERTAIN CONTROLLED CORPORATIONS

§ 1561. Limitations on certain multiple tax benefits in the case of certain controlled corporations

(a) General rule.—The component members of a controlled group of corporations on a December 31 shall, for their taxable years which include such December 31, be limited for purposes of this subtitle to—

(1) amounts in each taxable income bracket in the tax table in section 11(b)(1) which do not aggregate more than the maximum amount in such bracket to which a corporation which is not a component member of a controlled group is entitled,

(2) one $250,000 ($150,000 if any component member is a corporation described in section 535(c)(2)(B)) amount for purposes of computing the accumulated earnings credit under section 535(c)(2) and (3),

(3) one $40,000 exemption amount for purposes of computing the amount of the minimum tax, and

(4) one $2,000,000 amount for purposes of computing the tax imposed by section 59A.

The amounts specified in paragraph (1), the amount specified in paragraph (3), and the amount specified in paragraph (4) shall be divided equally among the component members of such group on such December 31 unless all of such component members consent (at such time and in such manner as the Secretary shall by regulations prescribe) to an apportionment plan providing for an unequal allocation of such amounts. The amounts specified in paragraph (2) shall be divided equally among the component members of such group on such December 31 unless the Secretary prescribes regulations permitting an unequal allocation of such amounts. Notwithstanding paragraph (1), in applying the last 2 sentences of section 11(b)(1) to such component members, the taxable income of all such component members shall be taken into account and any increase in tax under such last 2 sentences shall be divided among such component members in the same manner as amounts under paragraph (1). In applying section 55(d)(3), the alternative minimum taxable income of all component members shall be taken into account and any decrease in the exemption amount shall be allocated to the component members in the same manner as under paragraph (3).

* * *

§ 1563. Definitions and special rules

(a) Controlled group of corporations.—For purposes of this part, the term "controlled group of corporations" means any group of—

(1) Parent-subsidiary controlled group.—One or more chains of corporations connected through stock ownership with a common parent corporation if—

(A) stock possessing at least 80 percent of the total combined voting power of all classes of stock entitled to vote or at least 80 percent of the total value of shares of all classes of stock of each of the corporations, except the common parent corporation, is owned (within the meaning of subsection (d)(1)) by one or more of the other corporations; and

(B) the common parent corporation owns (within the meaning of subsection (d)(1)) stock possessing at least 80 percent of the total combined voting power of all classes of stock entitled to vote or at least 80 percent of the total value of shares of all classes of stock of at least one of the other corporations, excluding, in computing such voting power or value, stock owned directly by such other corporations.

(2) Brother-sister controlled group.—Two or more corporations if 5 or fewer persons who are individuals, estates, or trusts own (within the meaning of subsection (d)(2)) stock possessing more than 50 percent of the total combined voting power of all classes of stock entitled to vote or more than 50 percent of the total value of shares of all classes of stock of each corporation, taking into account the stock ownership of each such person only to the extent such stock ownership is identical with respect to each such corporation.

(3) Combined group.—Three or more corporations each of which is a member of a group of corporations described in paragraph (1) or (2), and one of which—

(A) is a common parent corporation included in a group of corporations described in paragraph (1), and also

(B) is included in a group of corporations described in paragraph (2).

* * *

(b) Component member.—

(1) General rule.—For purposes of this part, a corporation is a component member of a controlled group of corporations on a December 31 of any taxable year (and with respect to the taxable year which includes such December 31) if such corporation—

(A) is a member of such controlled group of corporations on the December 31 included in such year and is not treated as an excluded member under paragraph (2), or

(B) is not a member of such controlled group of corporations on the December 31 included in such year but is treated as an additional member under paragraph (3).

(2) Excluded members.—A corporation which is a member of a controlled group of corporations on December 31 of any taxable year shall be treated as an excluded member of such group for the taxable year including such December 31 if such corporation—

(A) is a member of such group for less than one-half the number of days in such taxable year which precede such December 31,

* * *

(3) Additional members.—A corporation which—

(A) was a member of a controlled group of corporations at any time during a calendar year,

(B) is not a member of such group on December 31 of such calendar year, and

(C) is not described, with respect to such group, in subparagraph (B), (C), (D), or (E) of paragraph (2),

shall be treated as an additional member of such group on December 31 for its taxable year including such December 31 if it was a member of such group for one-half (or more) of the number of days in such taxable year which precede such December 31.

(4) Overlapping groups.—If a corporation is a component member of more than one controlled group of corporations with respect to any taxable year, such corporation shall be treated as a component member of only one controlled group. The determination as to the group of which such corporation is a component member shall be made under regulations prescribed by the Secretary which are consistent with the purposes of this part.

(c) Certain stock excluded.—

(1) General rule.—For purposes of this part, the term "stock" does not include—

(A) nonvoting stock which is limited and preferred as to dividends,

(B) treasury stock, and

(C) stock which is treated as "excluded stock" under paragraph (2).

(2) Stock treated as "excluded stock".—

(A) Parent-subsidiary controlled group.—For purposes of subsection (a)(1), if a corporation (referred to in this paragraph as "parent corporation") owns (within the meaning of subsections (d)(1) and (e)(4)), 50 percent or more of the total combined voting power of all classes of stock entitled to vote or 50 percent or more of the total value of shares of all classes of stock in another corporation (referred to in this paragraph as "subsidiary corporation"), the following stock of the subsidiary corporation shall be treated as excluded stock—

(i) stock in the subsidiary corporation held by a trust which is part of a plan of deferred compensation for the benefit of the employees of the parent corporation or the subsidiary corporation,

(ii) stock in the subsidiary corporation owned by an individual (within the meaning of subsection (d)(2)) who is a principal stockholder or officer of the parent corporation. For purposes of this clause, the term "principal stockholder" of a corporation means an individual who owns (within the meaning of subsection (d)(2)) 5 percent or more of the total combined voting power of all classes of stock entitled to vote or 5 percent or more of the total value of shares of all classes of stock in such corporation,

(iii) stock in the subsidiary corporation owned (within the meaning of subsection (d)(2)) by an employee of the subsidiary corporation if such stock is subject to conditions which run in favor of such parent (or subsidiary) corporation and which substantially restrict or limit the employee's right (or if the employee constructively owns such stock, the direct owner's right) to dispose of such stock, or

(iv) stock in the subsidiary corporation owned (within the meaning of subsection (d)(2)) by an organization (other than the parent corporation) to which section 501 (relating to certain educational and charitable organizations which are exempt from tax) applies and which is controlled directly or indirectly by the parent corporation or subsidiary corporation, by an individual, estate, or trust that is a principal stockholder (within the meaning of clause (ii)) of the parent corporation, by an officer of the parent corporation, or by any combination thereof.

(B) Brother-sister controlled group.—For purposes of subsection (a)(2), if 5 or fewer persons who are individuals, estates, or trusts (referred to in this subparagraph as "common owners") own (within the meaning of subsection (d)(2)), 50 percent or more of the total combined voting power of all classes of stock entitled to vote or 50 percent or more of the total value of shares of all classes of stock in a corporation, the following stock of such corporation shall be treated as excluded stock—

(i) stock in such corporation held by an employees' trust described in section 401(a) which is exempt from tax under section 501(a), if such trust is for the benefit of the employees of such corporation,

(ii) stock in such corporation owned (within the meaning of subsection (d)(2)) by an employee of the corporation if such stock is subject to conditions which run in favor of any of such common owners (or such corporation) and which substantially restrict or limit the employee's right (or if the employee constructively owns such stock, the direct owner's right) to dispose of such stock. If a condition which limits or restricts the employee's right (or the direct owner's right) to dispose of such stock also applies to the stock held by any of the common owners pursuant to a bona fide reciprocal stock purchase arrangement, such condition shall not be treated as one which restricts or limits the employee's right to dispose of such stock, or

(iii) stock in such corporation owned (within the meaning of subsection (d)(2)) by an organization to which section 501 (relating to certain educational and charitable organizations which are exempt from tax) applies and which is controlled directly or indirectly by such corporation, by an individual, estate, or trust that is a principal stockholder (within the meaning of subparagraph (A)(ii)) of such corporation, by an officer of such corporation, or by any combination thereof.

(d) Rules for determining stock ownership.—

(1) Parent-subsidiary controlled group.—For purposes of determining whether a corporation is a member of a parent-subsidiary controlled group of corporations (within the meaning of subsection (a)(1)), stock owned by a corporation means—

(A) stock owned directly by such corporation, and

(B) stock owned with the application of paragraphs (1), (2), and (3) of subsection (e).

(2) Brother-sister controlled group.—For purposes of determining whether a corporation is a member of a brother-sister controlled group of corporations (within the meaning of subsection (a)(2)), stock owned by a person who is an individual, estate, or trust means—

(A) stock owned directly by such person, and

(B) stock owned with the application of subsection (e).

(e) Constructive ownership.—

(1) Options.—If any person has an option to acquire stock, such stock shall be considered as owned by such person. For purposes of this paragraph, an option to acquire such an option, and each one of a series of such options, shall be considered as an option to acquire such stock.

(2) Attribution from partnerships.—Stock owned, directly or indirectly, by or for a partnership shall be considered as owned by any partner having an interest of 5 percent or more in either the capital or profits of the partnership in proportion to his interest in capital or profits, whichever such proportion is the greater.

(3) Attribution from estates or trusts.—

(A) Stock owned, directly or indirectly, by or for an estate or trust shall be considered as owned by any beneficiary who has an actuarial interest of 5 percent or more in such stock, to the extent of such actuarial interest. For purposes of this subparagraph, the actuarial interest of each beneficiary shall be determined by assuming the maximum exercise of discretion by the fiduciary in favor of such beneficiary and the maximum use of such stock to satisfy his rights as a beneficiary.

(B) Stock owned, directly or indirectly, by or for any portion of a trust of which a person is considered the owner under subpart E of part I of subchapter J (relating to grantors and others treated as substantial owners) shall be considered as owned by such person.

(C) This paragraph shall not apply to stock owned by any employees' trust described in section 401(a) which is exempt from tax under section 501(a).

(4) Attribution from corporations.—Stock owned, directly or indirectly, by or for a corporation shall be considered as owned by any person who owns (within the meaning of subsection (d)) 5 percent or more in value of its stock in that proportion which the value of the stock which such person so owns bears to the value of all the stock in such corporation.

(5) Spouse.—An individual shall be considered as owning stock in a corporation owned, directly or indirectly, by or for his spouse (other than a spouse who is legally separated from the individual under a decree of divorce whether interlocutory or final, or a decree of separate maintenance), except in the case of a corporation with respect to which each of the following conditions is satisfied for its taxable year—

(A) The individual does not, at any time during such taxable year, own directly any stock in such corporation;

(B) The individual is not a director or employee and does not participate in the management of such corporation at any time during such taxable year;

(C) Not more than 50 percent of such corporation's gross income for such taxable year was derived from royalties, rents, dividends, interest, and annuities; and

(D) Such stock in such corporation is not, at any time during such taxable year, subject to conditions which substantially restrict or limit the spouse's right to dispose of such stock and which run in favor of the individual or his children who have not attained the age of 21 years.

(6) Children, grandchildren, parents, and grandparents.—

(A) Minor children.—An individual shall be considered as owning stock owned, directly or indirectly, by or for his children who have not attained the age of 21 years, and, if the individual has not attained the age of 21 years, the stock owned, directly or indirectly, by or for his parents.

(B) Adult children and grandchildren.—An individual who owns (within the meaning of subsection (d)(2), but without regard to this subparagraph) more than 50 percent of the total combined voting power of all classes of stock entitled to vote or more than 50 percent of the total value of shares of all classes of stock in a corporation shall be considered as owning the stock in such corporation owned, directly or indirectly, by or for his parents, grandparents, grandchildren, and children who have attained the age of 21 years.

(C) Adopted child.—For purposes of this section, a legally adopted child of an individual shall be treated as a child of such individual by blood.

(f) Other definitions and rules.—

(1) Employee defined.—For purposes of this section the term "employee" has the same meaning such term is given by paragraphs (1) and (2) of section 3121(d).

(2) Operating rules.—

(A) In general.—Except as provided in subparagraph (B), stock constructively owned by a person by reason of the application of paragraph (1), (2), (3), (4), (5), or (6) of subsection (e) shall, for purposes of applying such paragraphs, be treated as actually owned by such person.

(B) Members of family.—Stock constructively owned by an individual by reason of the application of paragraph (5) or (6) of subsection (e) shall not be treated as owned by him for purposes of again applying such paragraphs in order to make another the constructive owner of such stock.

(3) Special rules.—For purposes of this section—

(A) If stock may be considered as owned by a person under subsection (e)(1) and under any other paragraph of subsection (e), it shall be considered as owned by him under subsection (e)(1).

(B) If stock is owned (within the meaning of subsection (d)) by two or more persons, such stock shall be considered as owned by the person whose ownership of such stock results in the corporation being a component member of a controlled group. If by reason of the preceding sentence, a corporation would (but for this sentence) become a component member of two controlled groups, it shall be treated as a component member of one controlled group. The determination as to the group of which such corporation is a component member shall be made under regulations prescribed by the Secretary which are consistent with the purposes of this part.

(C) If stock is owned by a person within the meaning of subsection (d) and such ownership results in the corporation being a component member of a controlled group, such stock shall not be treated as excluded stock under subsection (c)(2), if by reason of treating such stock as excluded stock the result is that such corporation is not a component member of a controlled group of corporations.

* * *

(5) Brother-sister controlled group definition for provisions other than this part.—

(A) In general.—Except as specifically provided in an applicable provision, subsection (a)(2) shall be applied to an applicable provision as if it read as follows:

(2) Brother-sister controlled group.—Two or more corporations if 5 or fewer persons who are individuals, estates, or trusts own (within the meaning of subsection (d)(2)) stock possessing—

(A) at least 80 percent of the total combined voting power of all classes of stock entitled to vote, or at least 80 percent of the total value of shares of all classes of stock, of each corporation, and

(B) more than 50 percent of the total combined voting power of all classes of stock entitled to vote or more than 50 percent of the total value of shares of all classes of stock of each corporation, taking into account the stock ownership of each such person only to the extent such stock ownership is identical with respect to each such corporation.

(B) Applicable provision.—For purposes of this paragraph, an applicable provision is any provision of law (other than this part) which incorporates the definition of controlled group of corporations under subsection (a).

SUBTITLE B—ESTATE AND GIFT TAXES

CHAPTER 11—ESTATE TAX

SUBCHAPTER A—ESTATES OF CITIZENS OR RESIDENTS

PART I—TAX IMPOSED

§ 2001. Imposition and rate of tax

(a) Imposition.—A tax is hereby imposed on the transfer of the taxable estate of every decedent who is a citizen or resident of the United States.

(b) Computation of tax.—The tax imposed by this section shall be the amount equal to the excess (if any) of—

(1) a tentative tax computed under subsection (c) on the sum of—

(A) the amount of the taxable estate, and

(B) the amount of the adjusted taxable gifts, over

(2) the aggregate amount of tax which would have been payable under chapter 12 with respect to gifts made by the decedent after December 31, 1976, if the modifications described in subsection (g) had been applicable at the time of such gifts.

For purposes of paragraph (1)(B), the term "adjusted taxable gifts" means the total amount of the taxable gifts (within the meaning of section 2503) made by the decedent after December 31, 1976, other than gifts which are includible in the gross estate of the decedent.

(c) Rate schedule.—

If the amount with respect to which the tentative tax to be computed is:	The tentative tax is:
Not over $10,000	18 percent of such amount.
Over $10,000 but not over $20,000	$1,800, plus 20 percent of the excess of such amount over $10,000.

* Omitted entirely.

If the amount with respect to which the tentative tax to be computed is:	The tentative tax is:
Over $20,000 but not over $40,000	$3,800, plus 22 percent of the excess of such amount over $20,000.
Over $40,000 but not over $60,000	$8,200, plus 24 percent of the excess of such amount over $40,000.
Over $60,000 but not over $80,000	$13,000, plus 26 percent of the excess of such amount over $60,000.
Over $80,000 but not over $100,000	$18,200, plus 28 percent of the excess of such amount over $80,000.
Over $100,000 but not over $150,000	$23,800, plus 30 percent of the excess of such amount over $100,000.
Over $150,000 but not over $250,000	$38,800, plus 32 percent of the excess of such amount over $150,000.
Over $250,000 but not over $500,000	$70,800, plus 34 percent of the excess of such amount over $250,000.
Over $500,000 but not over $750,000	$155,800, plus 37 percent of the excess of such amount over $500,000.
Over $750,000 but not over $1,000,000	$248,300, plus 39 percent of the excess of such amount over $750,000.
Over $1,000,000	$345,800, plus 40 percent of the excess of such amount over $1,000,000.

(d) Adjustment for gift tax paid by spouse.—For purposes of subsection (b)(2), if—

(1) the decedent was the donor of any gift one-half of which was considered under section 2513 as made by the decedent's spouse, and

(2) the amount of such gift is includible in the gross estate of the decedent,

any tax payable by the spouse under chapter 12 on such gift (as determined under section 2012(d)) shall be treated as a tax payable with respect to a gift made by the decedent.

(e) Coordination of sections 2513 and 2035.—If—

(1) the decedent's spouse was the donor of any gift one-half of which was considered under section 2513 as made by the decedent, and

(2) the amount of such gift is includible in the gross estate of the decedent's spouse by reason of section 2035,

such gift shall not be included in the adjusted taxable gifts of the decedent for purposes of subsection (b)(1)(B), and the aggregate amount determined under subsection (b)(2) shall be reduced by the amount (if any) determined under subsection (d) which was treated as a tax payable by the decedent's spouse with respect to such gift.

(f) Valuation of gifts.—

(1) In general.—If the time has expired under section 6501 within which a tax may be assessed under chapter 12 (or under corresponding provisions of prior laws) on—

(A) the transfer of property by gift made during a preceding calendar period (as defined in section 2502(b)); or

(B) an increase in taxable gifts required under section 2701(d),

the value thereof shall, for purposes of computing the tax under this chapter, be the value as finally determined for purposes of chapter 12.

(2) Final determination.—For purposes of paragraph (1), a value shall be treated as finally determined for purposes of chapter 12 if—

(A) the value is shown on a return under such chapter and such value is not contested by the Secretary before the expiration of the time referred to in paragraph (1) with respect to such return;

(B) in a case not described in subparagraph (A), the value is specified by the Secretary and such value is not timely contested by the taxpayer; or

(C) the value is determined by a court or pursuant to a settlement agreement with the Secretary.

For purposes of subparagraph (A), the value of an item shall be treated as shown on a return if the item is disclosed in the return, or in a statement attached to the return, in a manner adequate to apprise the Secretary of the nature of such item.

(g) Modifications to gift tax payable to reflect different tax rates.—For purposes of applying subsection (b)(2) with respect to 1 or more gifts, the rates of tax under subsection (c) in effect at the decedent's death shall, in lieu of the rates of tax in effect at the time of such gifts, be used both to compute—

(1) the tax imposed by chapter 12 with respect to such gifts, and

(2) the credit allowed against such tax under section 2505, including in computing—

(A) the applicable credit amount under section 2505(a)(1), and

(B) the sum of the amounts allowed as a credit for all preceding periods under section 2505(a)(2).

§ 2002. Liability for payment

The tax imposed by this chapter shall be paid by the executor.

PART II—CREDITS AGAINST TAX

§ 2010. Unified credit against estate tax

(a) General rule.—A credit of the applicable credit amount shall be allowed to the estate of every decedent against the tax imposed by section 2001.

(b) Adjustment to credit for certain gifts made before 1977.—The amount of the credit allowable under subsection (a) shall be reduced by an amount equal to 20 percent of the aggregate amount allowed as a specific exemption under section 2521 (as in effect before its repeal by the Tax Reform Act of 1976) with respect to gifts made by the decedent after September 8, 1976.

(c) Applicable credit amount.—

(1) In general.—For purposes of this section, the applicable credit amount is the amount of the tentative tax which would be determined under section 2001(c) if the amount with respect to which such tentative tax is to be computed were equal to the applicable exclusion amount.

(2) Applicable exclusion amount.—For purposes of this subsection, the applicable exclusion amount is the sum of—

(A) the basic exclusion amount, and

(B) in the case of a surviving spouse, the deceased spousal unused exclusion amount.

(3) Basic exclusion amount.—

(A) In general.—For purposes of this subsection, the basic exclusion amount is $5,000,000.

(B) Inflation adjustment.—In the case of any decedent dying in a calendar year after 2011, the dollar amount in subparagraph (A) shall be increased by an amount equal to—

(i) such dollar amount, multiplied by

(ii) the cost-of-living adjustment determined under section 1(f)(3) for such calendar year by substituting "calendar year 2010" for "calendar year 1992" in subparagraph (B) thereof.

If any amount as adjusted under the preceding sentence is not a multiple of $10,000, such amount shall be rounded to the nearest multiple of $10,000.

(4) Deceased spousal unused exclusion amount.—For purposes of this subsection, with respect to a surviving spouse of a deceased spouse dying after December 31, 2010, the term "deceased spousal unused exclusion amount" means the lesser of—

(A) the basic exclusion amount, or

(B) the excess of—

(i) the applicable exclusion amount of the last such deceased spouse of such surviving spouse, over

(ii) the amount with respect to which the tentative tax is determined under section 2001(b)(1) on the estate of such deceased spouse.

(5) Special rules.—

(A) Election required.—A deceased spousal unused exclusion amount may not be taken into account by a surviving spouse under paragraph (2) unless the executor of the estate of the deceased spouse files an estate tax return on which such amount is computed and makes an election on such return that such amount may be so taken into account. Such election, once made, shall be irrevocable. No election may be made under this subparagraph if such return is filed after the time prescribed by law (including extensions) for filing such return.

(B) Examination of prior returns after expiration of period of limitations with respect to deceased spousal unused exclusion amount.—Notwithstanding any period of limitation in section 6501, after the time has expired under section 6501 within which a tax may be assessed under chapter 11 or 12 with respect to a deceased spousal unused exclusion amount, the Secretary may examine a return of the deceased spouse to make determinations with respect to such amount for purposes of carrying out this subsection.

(6) Regulations.—The Secretary shall prescribe such regulations as may be necessary or appropriate to carry out this subsection.

(d) Limitation based on amount of tax.—The amount of the credit allowed by subsection (a) shall not exceed the amount of the tax imposed by section 2001.

§ 2012. Credit for gift tax

(a) In general.—If a tax on a gift has been paid under chapter 12 (sec. 2501 and following), or under corresponding provisions of prior laws, and thereafter on the death of the donor any amount in respect of such gift is required to be included in the value of the gross estate of the decedent for purposes of this chapter, then there shall be credited against the tax imposed by section 2001 the amount of the tax paid on a gift under chapter 12, or under corresponding provisions of prior laws, with respect to so much of the property which constituted the gift as is included in the gross estate, except that the amount of such credit shall not exceed an amount which bears the same ratio to the tax imposed by section 2001 (after deducting from such tax the unified credit provided by section 2010) as the value (at the time of the gift or at the time of the death, whichever is lower) of so much of the property which constituted the gift as is included in the gross estate bears to the value of the entire gross estate reduced by the aggregate amount of the charitable and marital deductions allowed under sections 2055, 2056, and 2106(a)(2).

(b) Valuation reductions.—In applying, with respect to any gift, the ratio stated in subsection (a), the value at the time of the gift or at the time of the death, referred to in such ratio, shall be reduced—

(1) by such amount as will properly reflect the amount of such gift which was excluded in determining (for purposes of section 2503(a)), or of corresponding provisions of prior laws, the total amount of gifts made during the calendar quarter (or calendar year if the gift was made before January 1, 1971) in which the gift was made;

(2) if a deduction with respect to such gift is allowed under section 2056(a) (relating to marital deduction), then by the amount of such value, reduced as provided in paragraph (1); and

(3) if a deduction with respect to such gift is allowed under sections 2055 or 2106(a)(2) (relating to charitable deduction), then by the amount of such value, reduced as provided in paragraph (1) of this subsection.

(c) Where gift considered made one-half by spouse.—Where the decedent was the donor of the gift but, under the provisions of section 2513, or corresponding provisions of prior laws, the gift was considered as made one-half by his spouse—

(1) the term "the amount of the tax paid on a gift under chapter 12", as used in subsection (a), includes the amounts paid with respect to each half of such gift, the amount paid with respect to each being computed in the manner provided in subsection (d); and

(2) in applying, with respect to such gift, the ratio stated in subsection (a), the value at the time of the gift or at the time of the death, referred to in such ratio, includes such value with respect to each half of such gift, each such value being reduced as provided in paragraph (1) of subsection (b).

(d) Computation of amount of gift tax paid.—

(1) Amount of tax.—For purposes of subsection (a), the amount of tax paid on a gift under chapter 12, or under corresponding provisions of prior laws, with respect to any gift shall be an amount which bears the same ratio to the total tax paid for the calendar quarter (or calendar year if the gift was made before January 1, 1971) in which the gift was made as the amount of such gift bears to the total amount of taxable gifts (computed without deduction of the specific exemption) for such quarter or year.

(2) Amount of gift.—For purposes of paragraph (1), the "amount of such gift" shall be the amount included with respect to such gift in determining (for the purposes of section 2503(a), or of corresponding provisions of prior laws) the total amount of gifts made during such quarter or year, reduced by the amount of any deduction allowed with respect to such gift under section 2522, or under corresponding provisions of prior laws (relating to charitable deduction), or under section 2523 (relating to marital deduction).

(e) Section inapplicable to gifts made after December 31, 1976.—No credit shall be allowed under this section with respect to the amount of any tax paid under chapter 12 on any gift made after December 31, 1976.

§ 2013. Credit for tax on prior transfers

(a) General rule.—The tax imposed by section 2001 shall be credited with all or a part of the amount of the Federal estate tax paid with respect to the transfer of property (including property passing as a result of the exercise or non-exercise of a power of appointment) to the decedent by or from a person (herein designated as a "transferor") who died within 10 years before, or within 2 years after, the decedent's death. If the transferor died within 2 years of the death of the decedent, the credit shall be the amount determined under subsections (b) and (c). If the transferor predeceased the decedent by more than 2 years, the credit shall be the following percentage of the amount so determined—

(1) 80 percent, if within the third or fourth years preceding the decedent's death;

(2) 60 percent, if within the fifth or sixth years preceding the decedent's death;

(3) 40 percent, if within the seventh or eighth years preceding the decedent's death; and

(4) 20 percent, if within the ninth or tenth years preceding the decedent's death.

(b) Computation of credit.—Subject to the limitation prescribed in subsection (c), the credit provided by this section shall be an amount which bears the same ratio to the estate tax paid (adjusted as indicated hereinafter) with respect to the estate of the transferor as the value of the property transferred bears to the taxable estate of the transferor (determined for purposes of the estate tax) decreased by any death taxes paid with respect to such estate. For purposes of the preceding sentence, the estate tax paid shall be the Federal estate tax paid increased by any credits allowed against such estate tax under section 2012, or corresponding provisions of prior laws, on account of gift tax, and for any credits allowed against such estate tax under this section on account of prior transfers where the transferor acquired property from a person who died within 10 years before the death of the decedent.

(c) Limitation on credit.—

(1) In general.—The credit provided in this section shall not exceed the amount by which—

(A) the estate tax imposed by section 2001 or section 2101 (after deducting the credits provided for in sections 2010, 2012, and 2014) computed without regard to this section, exceeds

(B) such tax computed by excluding from the decedent's gross estate the value of such property transferred and, if applicable, by making the adjustment hereinafter indicated.

If any deduction is otherwise allowable under section 2055 or section 2106(a)(2) (relating to charitable deduction) then, for the purpose of the computation indicated in subparagraph (B), the amount of such deduction shall be reduced by that part of such deduction which the value of such property transferred bears to the decedent's entire gross estate reduced by the deductions allowed under sections 2053 and 2054, or section 2106(a)(1) (relating to deduction for expenses, losses, etc.). For purposes of this section, the value of such property transferred shall be the value as provided for in subsection (d) of this section.

(2) Two or more transferors.—If the credit provided in this section relates to property received from 2 or more transferors, the limitation provided in paragraph (1) of this subsection shall be computed by aggregating the value of the property so transferred to the decedent. The aggregate limitation so determined shall be apportioned in accordance with the value of the property transferred to the decedent by each transferor.

(d) Valuation of property transferred.—The value of property transferred to the decedent shall be the value used for the purpose of determining the Federal estate tax liability of the estate of the transferor but—

(1) there shall be taken into account the effect of the tax imposed by section 2001 or 2101, or any estate, succession, legacy, or inheritance tax, on the net value to the decedent of such property;

(2) where such property is encumbered in any manner, or where the decedent incurs any obligation imposed by the transferor with respect to such property, such encumbrance or obligation shall be taken into account in the same manner as if the amount of a gift to the decedent of such property was being determined; and

(3) if the decedent was the spouse of the transferor at the time of the transferor's death, the net value of the property transferred to the decedent shall be reduced by the amount allowed under section 2056 (relating to marital deductions) as a deduction from the gross estate of the transferor.

(e) Property defined.—For purposes of this section, the term "property" includes any beneficial interest in property, including a general power of appointment (as defined in section 2041).

(f) Treatment of additional tax imposed under section 2032A.—If section 2032A applies to any property included in the gross estate of the transferor and an additional tax is imposed with respect to such property under section 2032A(c) before the date which is 2 years after the date of the decedent's death, for purposes of this section—

(1) the additional tax imposed by section 2032A(c) shall be treated as a Federal estate tax payable with respect to the estate of the transferor; and

(2) the value of such property and the amount of the taxable estate of the transferor shall be determined as if section 2032A did not apply with respect to such property.

§ 2014. Credit for foreign death taxes

(a) In general.—The tax imposed by section 2001 shall be credited with the amount of any estate, inheritance, legacy, or succession taxes actually paid to any foreign country in respect of any property situated within such foreign country and included in the gross estate (not including any such taxes paid with respect to the estate of a person other than the decedent). The determination of the country within which property is situated shall be made in accordance with the rules applicable under subchapter B (sec. 2101 and following) in determining whether property is situated within or without the United States.

(b) Limitations on credit.—The credit provided in this section with respect to such taxes paid to any foreign country—

(1) shall not, with respect to any such tax, exceed an amount which bears the same ratio to the amount of such tax actually paid to such foreign country as the value of property which is—

(A) situated within such foreign country,

(B) subjected to such tax, and

(C) included in the gross estate

bears to the value of all property subjected to such tax; and

(2) shall not, with respect to all such taxes, exceed an amount which bears the same ratio to the tax imposed by section 2001 (after deducting from such tax the credits provided by sections 2010 and 2012) as the value of property which is—

(A) situated within such foreign country,

(B) subjected to the taxes of such foreign country, and

(C) included in the gross estate

bears to the value of the entire gross estate reduced by the aggregate amount of the deductions allowed under sections 2055 and 2056.

* * *

(e) Period of limitation.—The credit provided in this section shall be allowed only for such taxes as were actually paid and credit therefor claimed within 4 years after the filing of the return required by section 6018, except that—

(1) If a petition for redetermination of a deficiency has been filed with the Tax Court within the time prescribed in section 6213(a), then within such 4–year period or before the expiration of 60 days after the decision of the Tax Court becomes final.

(2) If, under section 6161, an extension of time has been granted for payment of the tax shown on the return, or of a deficiency, then within such 4–year period or before the date of the expiration of the period of the extension.

Refund based on such credit may (despite the provisions of sections 6511 and 6512) be made if claim therefor is filed within the period above provided. Any such refund shall be made without interest.

(f) Additional limitation in cases involving a deduction under section 2053(d).—In any case where a deduction is allowed under section 2053(d) for an estate, succession, legacy, or inheritance tax imposed by and actually paid to any foreign country upon a transfer by the decedent for public, charitable, or religious uses described in section 2055, the property described in subparagraphs (A), (B), and (C) of paragraphs (1) and (2) of subsection (b) of this section shall not include any property in respect of which such deduction is allowed under section 2053(d).

* * *

§ 2015. Credit for death taxes on remainders

Where an election is made under section 6163(a) to postpone payment of the tax imposed by section 2001 or 2101, such part of any estate, inheritance, legacy, or succession taxes allowable as a credit under section 2014, as is attributable to a reversionary or remainder interest may be allowed as a credit against the tax attributable to such interest, subject to the limitations on the amount of the credit contained in such sections, if such part is paid, and credit therefor claimed, at any time before the expiration of the time for payment of the tax imposed by section 2001 or 2101 as postponed and extended under section 6163.

§ 2016. Recovery of taxes claimed as credit

If any tax claimed as a credit under section 2014 is recovered from any foreign country, the executor, or any other person or persons recovering such amount, shall give notice of such recovery to the Secretary at such time and in such manner as may be required by regulations prescribed by him, and the Secretary shall (despite the provisions of section 6501) redetermine the amount of the tax under this chapter and the amount, if any, of the tax due on such redetermination, shall be paid by the executor or such person or persons, as the case may be, on notice and demand. No interest shall be assessed or collected on any amount of tax due on any redetermination by the Secretary, resulting from a refund to the executor of tax claimed as a credit under section 2014, for any period before the receipt of such refund, except to the extent interest was paid by the foreign country on such refund.

PART III—GROSS ESTATE

§ 2031. Definition of gross estate

(a) General.—The value of the gross estate of the decedent shall be determined by including to the extent provided for in this part, the value at the time of his death of all property, real or personal, tangible or intangible, wherever situated.

(b) Valuation of unlisted stock and securities.—In the case of stock and securities of a corporation the value of which, by reason of their not being listed on an exchange and by reason of the absence of sales thereof, cannot be determined with reference to bid and asked prices or with reference to sales prices, the value thereof shall be determined by taking into consideration, in addition to all other factors, the value of stock or securities of corporations engaged in the same or a similar line of business which are listed on an exchange.

(c) Estate tax with respect to land subject to a qualified conservation easement.—

(1) In general.—If the executor makes the election described in paragraph (6), then, except as otherwise provided in this subsection, there shall be excluded from the gross estate the lesser of—

(A) the applicable percentage of the value of land subject to a qualified conservation easement, reduced by the amount of any deduction under section 2055(f) with respect to such land, or

(B) the exclusion limitation.

(2) Applicable percentage.—For purposes of paragraph (1), the term "applicable percentage" means 40 percent reduced (but not below zero) by 2 percentage points for each percentage point (or fraction thereof) by which the value of the qualified conservation easement is less than 30 percent of the value of the land (determined without regard to the value of such easement and reduced by the value of any retained development right (as defined in paragraph (5))). The values taken into account under the preceding sentence shall be such values as of the date of the contribution referred to in paragraph (8)(B).

(3) Exclusion limitation.—For purposes of paragraph (1), the exclusion limitation is the limitation determined in accordance with the following table:

In the case of estates of decedents dying during:	The exclusion limitation is:
1998	$100,000
1999	200,000
2000	300,000
2001	400,000
2002 or thereafter	500,000.

(4) Treatment of certain indebtedness.—

(A) In general.—The exclusion provided in paragraph (1) shall not apply to the extent that the land is debt-financed property.

(B) Definitions.—For purposes of this paragraph—

(i) Debt-financed property.—The term "debt-financed property" means any property with respect to which there is an acquisition indebtedness (as defined in clause (ii)) on the date of the decedent's death.

(ii) Acquisition indebtedness.—The term "acquisition indebtedness" means, with respect to debt-financed property, the unpaid amount of—

(I) the indebtedness incurred by the donor in acquiring such property,

(II) the indebtedness incurred before the acquisition of such property if such indebtedness would not have been incurred but for such acquisition,

(III) the indebtedness incurred after the acquisition of such property if such indebtedness would not have been incurred but for such acquisition and the incurrence of such indebtedness was reasonably foreseeable at the time of such acquisition, and

(IV) the extension, renewal, or refinancing of an acquisition indebtedness.

(5) Treatment of retained development right.—

(A) In general.—Paragraph (1) shall not apply to the value of any development right retained by the donor in the conveyance of a qualified conservation easement.

(B) Termination of retained development right.—If every person in being who has an interest (whether or not in possession) in the land executes an agreement to extinguish permanently some or all of any development rights (as defined in subparagraph (D)) retained by the donor on or before the date for filing the return of the tax imposed by section 2001, then any tax imposed by section 2001 shall be reduced accordingly. Such agreement shall be filed with the return of the tax imposed by section 2001. The agreement shall be in such form as the Secretary shall prescribe.

(C) Additional tax.—Any failure to implement the agreement described in subparagraph (B) not later than the earlier of—

(i) the date which is 2 years after the date of the decedent's death, or

(ii) the date of the sale of such land subject to the qualified conservation easement,

shall result in the imposition of an additional tax in the amount of the tax which would have been due on the retained development rights subject to such agreement. Such additional tax shall be due and payable on the last day of the 6th month following such date.

(D) Development right defined.—For purposes of this paragraph, the term "development right" means any right to use the land subject to the qualified conservation easement in which such right is retained for any commercial purpose which is not subordinate to and directly supportive of the use of such land as a farm for farming purposes (within the meaning of section 2032A(e)(5)).

(6) Election.—The election under this subsection shall be made on or before the due date (including extensions) for filing the return of the tax imposed by section 2001 and shall be made on such return. Such an election, once made, shall be irrevocable.

(7) Calculation of estate tax due.—An executor making the election described in paragraph (6) shall, for purposes of calculating the amount of tax imposed by section 2001, include the value of any development right (as defined in paragraph (5)) retained by the donor in the conveyance of such qualified conservation easement. The computation of tax on any retained development right prescribed in this paragraph shall be done in such manner and on such forms as the Secretary shall prescribe.

(8) Definitions.—For purposes of this subsection—

(A) Land subject to a qualified conservation easement.—The term "land subject to a qualified conservation easement" means land—

(i) which is located in the United States or any possession of the United States,

(ii) which was owned by the decedent or a member of the decedent's family at all times during the 3–year period ending on the date of the decedent's death, and

(iii) with respect to which a qualified conservation easement has been made by an individual described in subparagraph (C), as of the date of the election described in paragraph (6).

(B) Qualified conservation easement.—The term "qualified conservation easement" means a qualified conservation contribution (as defined in section 170(h)(1)) of a qualified real property interest (as defined in section 170(h)(2)(C)), except that clause (iv) of section 170(h)(4)(A) shall not apply, and the restriction on the use of such interest described in section 170(h)(2)(C) shall include a prohibition on more than a de minimis use for a commercial recreational activity.

(C) Individual described.—An individual is described in this subparagraph if such individual is—

(i) the decedent,

(ii) a member of the decedent's family,

(iii) the executor of the decedent's estate, or

(iv) the trustee of a trust the corpus of which includes the land to be subject to the qualified conservation easement.

(D) Member of family.—The term "member of the decedent's family" means any member of the family (as defined in section 2032A(e)(2)) of the decedent.

(9) Treatment of easements granted after death.—In any case in which the qualified conservation easement is granted after the date of the decedent's death and on or before the due date (including extensions) for filing the return of tax imposed by section 2001, the deduction under section 2055(f) with respect to such easement shall be allowed to the estate but only if no charitable deduction is allowed under chapter 1 to any person with respect to the grant of such easement.

(10) Application of this section to interests in partnerships, corporations, and trusts.—This section shall apply to an interest in a partnership, corporation, or trust if at least 30 percent of the entity is owned (directly or indirectly) by the decedent, as determined under the rules described in section 2057(e)(3).

(d) Cross reference.—

For executor's right to be furnished on request a statement regarding any valuation made by the Secretary within the gross estate, see section 7517.

§ 2032. Alternate valuation

(a) General.—The value of the gross estate may be determined, if the executor so elects, by valuing all the property included in the gross estate as follows:

(1) In the case of property distributed, sold, exchanged, or otherwise disposed of, within 6 months after the decedent's death such property shall be valued as of the date of distribution, sale, exchange, or other disposition.

(2) In the case of property not distributed, sold, exchanged, or otherwise disposed of, within 6 months after the decedent's death such property shall be valued as of the date 6 months after the decedent's death.

(3) Any interest or estate which is affected by mere lapse of time shall be included at its value as of the time of death (instead of the later date) with adjustment for any difference in its value as of the later date not due to mere lapse of time.

(b) Special rules.—No deduction under this chapter of any item shall be allowed if allowance for such item is in effect given by the alternate valuation provided by this section. Wherever in any other subsection or section of this chapter reference is made to the value of property at the time of the decedent's death, such reference shall be deemed to refer to the value of such property used in determining the value of the gross estate. In case of an election made by the executor under this section, then—

(1) for purposes of the charitable deduction under section 2055 or 2106(a)(2), any bequest, legacy, devise, or transfer enumerated therein, and

(2) for the purpose of the marital deduction under section 2056, any interest in property passing to the surviving spouse,

shall be valued as of the date of the decedent's death with adjustment for any difference in value (not due to mere lapse of time or the occurrence or nonoccurrence of a contingency) of the property as of the date 6 months after the decedent's death (substituting, in the case of property distributed by the executor or trustee, or sold, exchanged, or otherwise disposed of, during such 6–month period, the date thereof).

(c) Election must decrease gross estate and estate tax.—No election may be made under this section with respect to an estate unless such election will decrease—

(1) the value of the gross estate, and

(2) the sum of the tax imposed by this chapter and the tax imposed by chapter 13 with respect to property includible in the decedent's gross estate (reduced by credits allowable against such taxes).

(d) Election.—

(1) In general.—The election provided for in this section shall be made by the executor on the return of the tax imposed by this chapter. Such election, once made, shall be irrevocable.

(2) Exception.—No election may be made under this section if such return is filed more than 1 year after the time prescribed by law (including extensions) for filing such return.

§ 2032A. Valuation of certain farm, etc., real property

(a) Value based on use under which property qualifies.—

(1) General rule.—If—

(A) the decedent was (at the time of his death) a citizen or resident of the United States, and

(B) the executor elects the application of this section and files the agreement referred to in subsection (d)(2),

then, for purposes of this chapter, the value of qualified real property shall be its value for the use under which it qualifies, under subsection (b), as qualified real property.

(2) Limitation on aggregate reduction in fair market value.—The aggregate decrease in the value of qualified real property taken into account for purposes of this chapter which results from the application of paragraph (1) with respect to any decedent shall not exceed $750,000.

* * *

(b) Qualified real property.—

(1) In general.—For purposes of this section, the term "qualified real property" means real property located in the United States which was acquired from or passed from the decedent to a qualified heir of the decedent and which, on the date of the decedent's death, was being used for a qualified use by the decedent or a member of the decedent's family, but only if—

(A) 50 percent or more of the adjusted value of the gross estate consists of the adjusted value of real or personal property which—

(i) on the date of the decedent's death, was being used for a qualified use by the decedent or a member of the decedent's family, and

(ii) was acquired from or passed from the decedent to a qualified heir of the decedent.

(B) 25 percent or more of the adjusted value of the gross estate consists of the adjusted value of real property which meets the requirements of subparagraphs (A)(ii) and (C),

(C) during the 8–year period ending on the date of the decedent's death there have been periods aggregating 5 years or more during which—

(i) such real property was owned by the decedent or a member of the decedent's family and used for a qualified use by the decedent or a member of the decedent's family, and

(ii) there was material participation by the decedent or a member of the decedent's family in the operation of the farm or other business, and

(D) such real property is designated in the agreement referred to in subsection (d)(2).

(2) Qualified use.—For purposes of this section, the term "qualified use" means the devotion of the property to any of the following:

(A) use as a farm for farming purposes, or

(B) use in a trade or business other than the trade or business of farming.

(3) Adjusted value.—For purposes of paragraph (1), the term "adjusted value" means—

(A) in the case of the gross estate, the value of the gross estate for purposes of this chapter (determined without regard to this section), reduced by any amounts allowable as a deduction under paragraph (4) of section 2053(a), or

(B) in the case of any real or personal property, the value of such property for purposes of this chapter (determined without regard to this section), reduced by any amounts allowable as a deduction in respect of such property under paragraph (4) of section 2053(a).

(4) Decedents who are retired or disabled.—

(A) In general.—If, on the date of the decedent's death, the requirements of paragraph (1)(C)(ii) with respect to the decedent for any property are not met, and the decedent—

(i) was receiving old-age benefits under title II of the Social Security Act for a continuous period ending on such date, or

(ii) was disabled for a continuous period ending on such date,

then paragraph (1)(C)(ii) shall be applied with respect to such property by substituting "the date on which the longer of such continuous periods began" for "the date of the decedent's death" in paragraph (1)(C).

(B) Disabled defined.—For purposes of subparagraph (A), an individual shall be disabled if such individual has a mental or physical impairment which renders him unable to materially participate in the operation of the farm or other business.

(C) Coordination with recapture.—For purposes of subsection (c)(6)(B)(i), if the requirements of paragraph (1)(C)(ii) are met with respect to any decedent by reason of subparagraph (A), the period ending on the date on which the continuous period taken into account under subparagraph (A) began shall be treated as the period immediately before the decedent's death.

(5) Special rules for surviving spouses.—

(A) In general.—If property is qualified real property with respect to a decedent (hereinafter in this paragraph referred to as the "first decedent") and such property was acquired from or passed from the first decedent to the surviving spouse of the first decedent, for purposes of applying this subsection and subsection (c) in the case of the estate of such surviving spouse, active management of the farm or other business by the surviving spouse shall be treated as material participation by such surviving spouse in the operation of such farm or business.

(B) Special rule.—For the purposes of subparagraph (A), the determination of whether property is qualified real property with respect to the first decedent shall be made without regard to subparagraph (D) of paragraph (1) and without regard to whether an election under this section was made.

(C) Coordination with paragraph (4).—In any case in which to do so will enable the requirements of paragraph (1)(C)(ii) to be met with respect to the surviving spouse, this subsection and subsection (c) shall be applied by taking into account any application of paragraph (4).

(c) Tax treatment of dispositions and failures to use for qualified use.—

(1) Imposition of additional estate tax.—If, within 10 years after the decedent's death and before the death of the qualified heir—

(A) the qualified heir disposes of any interest in the qualified real property (other than by a disposition to a member of his family), or

(B) the qualified heir ceases to use for the qualified use the qualified real property which was acquired (or passed) from the decedent,

then, there is hereby imposed an additional estate tax.

(2) Amount of additional tax.—

(A) In general.—The amount of the additional tax imposed by paragraph (1) with respect to any interest shall be the amount equal to the lesser of—

(i) the adjusted tax difference attributable to such interest, or

(ii) the excess of the amount realized with respect to the interest (or, in any case other than a sale or exchange at arm's length, the fair market value of the interest) over the value of the interest determined under subsection (a).

(B) Adjusted tax difference attributable to interest.—For purposes of subparagraph (A), the adjusted tax difference attributable to an interest is the amount which bears the same ratio to the adjusted tax difference with respect to the estate (determined under subparagraph (C)) as—

(i) the excess of the value of such interest for purposes of this chapter (determined without regard to subsection (a)) over the value of such interest determined under subsection (a), bears to

(ii) a similar excess determined for all qualified real property.

(C) Adjusted tax difference with respect to the estate.—For purposes of subparagraph (B), the term "adjusted tax difference with respect to the estate" means the excess of what would have been the estate tax liability but for subsection (a) over the estate tax liability. For purposes of this subparagraph, the term "estate tax liability" means the tax imposed by section 2001 reduced by the credits allowable against such tax.

(D) Partial dispositions.—For purposes of this paragraph, where the qualified heir disposes of a portion of the interest acquired by (or passing to) such heir (or a predecessor qualified heir) or there is a cessation of use of such a portion—

(i) the value determined under subsection (a) taken into account under subparagraph (A)(ii) with respect to such portion shall be its pro rata share of such value of such interest, and

(ii) the adjusted tax difference attributable to the interest taken into account with respect to the transaction involving the second or any succeeding portion shall be reduced by the amount of the tax imposed by this subsection with respect to all prior transactions involving portions of such interest.

* * *

(5) Liability for tax; furnishing of bond.—The qualified heir shall be personally liable for the additional tax imposed by this subsection with respect to his interest unless the heir has furnished bond which meets the requirements of subsection (e)(11).

(6) Cessation of qualified use.—For purposes of paragraph (1)(B), real property shall cease to be used for the qualified use if—

(A) such property ceases to be used for the qualified use set forth in subparagraph (A) or (B) of subsection (b)(2) under which the property qualified under subsection (b), or

(B) during any period of 8 years ending after the date of the decedent's death and before the date of the death of the qualified heir, there had been periods aggregating more than 3 years during which—

(i) in the case of periods during which the property was held by the decedent, there was no material participation by the decedent or any member of his family in the operation of the farm or other business, and

(ii) in the case of periods during which the property was held by any qualified heir, there was no material participation by such qualified heir or any member of his family in the operation of the farm or other business.

(7) Special rules.—

(A) No tax if use begins within 2 years.—If the date on which the qualified heir begins to use the qualified real property (hereinafter in this subparagraph referred to as the commencement date) is before the date 2 years after the decedent's death—

(i) no tax shall be imposed under paragraph (1) by reason of the failure by the qualified heir to so use such property before the commencement date, and

(ii) the 10–year period under paragraph (1) shall be extended by the period after the decedent's death and before the commencement date.

(B) Active management by eligible qualified heir treated as material participation.—For purposes of paragraph (6)(B)(ii), the active management of a farm or other business by—

(i) an eligible qualified heir, or

(ii) a fiduciary of an eligible qualified heir described in clause (ii) or (iii) of subparagraph (C),

shall be treated as material participation by such eligible qualified heir in the operation of such farm or business. In the case of an eligible qualified heir described in clause (ii), (iii), or (iv) of subparagraph (C), the preceding sentence shall apply only during periods during which such heir meets the requirements of such clause.

(C) Eligible qualified heir.—For purposes of this paragraph, the term "eligible qualified heir" means a qualified heir who—

(i) is the surviving spouse of the decedent,

(ii) has not attained the age of 21,

(iii) is disabled (within the meaning of subsection (b)(4)(B)), or

(iv) is a student.

(D) Student.—For purposes of subparagraph (C), an individual shall be treated as a student with respect to periods during any calendar year if (and only if) such individual is a student (within the meaning of section 152(f)(2)) for such calendar year.

(E) Certain rents treated as qualified use.—For purposes of this subsection, a surviving spouse or lineal descendant of the decedent shall not be treated as failing to use qualified real property in a qualified use solely because such spouse or descendant rents such property to a member of the family of such spouse or descendant on a net cash basis. For purposes of the preceding sentence, a legally adopted child of an individual shall be treated as the child of such individual by blood.

(8) Qualified conservation contribution is not a disposition.—A qualified conservation contribution (as defined in section 170(h)) by gift or otherwise shall not be deemed a disposition under subsection (c)(1)(A).

(d) Election; agreement.—

(1) Election.—The election under this section shall be made on the return of the tax imposed by section 2001. Such election shall be made in such manner as the Secretary shall by regulations prescribe. Such an election, once made, shall be irrevocable.

(2) Agreement.—The agreement referred to in this paragraph is a written agreement signed by each person in being who has an interest (whether or not in possession) in any property designated in such agreement consenting to the application of subsection (c) with respect to such property.

(3) Modification of election and agreement to be permitted.—The Secretary shall prescribe procedures which provide that in any case in which the executor makes an election under paragraph (1) (and submits the agreement referred to in paragraph (2)) within the time prescribed therefor, but—

(A) the notice of election, as filed, does not contain all required information, or

(B) signatures of 1 or more persons required to enter into the agreement described in paragraph (2) are not included on the agreement as filed, or the agreement does not contain all required information,

the executor will have a reasonable period of time (not exceeding 90 days) after notification of such failures to provide such information or signatures.

(e) Definitions; special rules.—For purposes of this section—

(1) Qualified heir.—The term "qualified heir" means, with respect to any property, a member of the decedent's family who acquired such property (or to whom such property passed) from the decedent. If a qualified heir disposes of any interest in qualified real property to any member of his family, such member shall thereafter be treated as the qualified heir with respect to such interest.

(2) Member of family.—The term "member of the family" means, with respect to any individual, only—

(A) an ancestor of such individual,

(B) the spouse of such individual,

(C) a lineal descendant of such individual, of such individual's spouse, or of a parent of such individual, or

(D) the spouse of any lineal descendant described in subparagraph (C).

For purposes of the preceding sentence, a legally adopted child of an individual shall be treated as the child of such individual by blood.

(3) Certain real property included.—In the case of real property which meets the requirements of subparagraph (C) of subsection (b)(1), residential buildings and related improvements on such real property occupied on a regular basis by the owner or lessee of such real property or by persons employed by such owner or lessee for the purpose of operating or maintaining such real property, and roads, buildings, and other structures and improvements functionally related to the qualified use shall be treated as real property devoted to the qualified use.

(4) Farm.—The term "farm" includes stock, dairy, poultry, fruit, furbearing animal, and truck farms, plantations, ranches, nurseries, ranges, greenhouses or other similar structures used primarily for the raising of agricultural or horticultural commodities, and orchards and woodlands.

(5) Farming purposes.—The term "farming purposes" means—

(A) cultivating the soil or raising or harvesting any agricultural or horticultural commodity (including the raising, shearing, feeding, caring for, training, and management of animals) on a farm;

(B) handling, drying, packing, grading, or storing on a farm any agricultural or horticultural commodity in its unmanufactured state, but only if the owner, tenant, or operator of the farm regularly produces more than one-half of the commodity so treated; and

(C)(i) the planting, cultivating, caring for, or cutting of trees, or

(ii) the preparation (other than milling) of trees for market.

(6) Material participation.—Material participation shall be determined in a manner similar to the manner used for purposes of paragraph (1) of section 1402(a) (relating to net earnings from self-employment).

(7) Method of valuing farms.—

(A) In general.—Except as provided in subparagraph (B), the value of a farm for farming purposes shall be determined by dividing—

(i) the excess of the average annual gross cash rental for comparable land used for farming purposes and located in the locality of such farm over the average annual State and local real estate taxes for such comparable land, by

(ii) the average annual effective interest rate for all new Federal Land Bank loans.

For purposes of the preceding sentence, each average annual computation shall be made on the basis of the 5 most recent calendar years ending before the date of the decedent's death.

(B) Value based on net share rental in certain cases.—

(i) In general.—If there is no comparable land from which the average annual gross cash rental may be determined but there is comparable land from which the average net share rental may be determined, subparagraph (A)(i) shall be applied by substituting "average annual net share rental" for "average annual gross cash rental".

(ii) Net share rental.—For purposes of this paragraph, the term "net share rental" means the excess of—

(I) the value of the produce received by the lessor of the land on which such produce is grown, over

(II) the cash operating expenses of growing such produce which, under the lease, are paid by the lessor.

(C) Exception.—The formula provided by subparagraph (A) shall not be used—

(i) where it is established that there is no comparable land from which the average annual gross cash rental may be determined and that there is no comparable land from which the average net share rental may be determined, or

(ii) where the executor elects to have the value of the farm for farming purposes determined under paragraph (8).

(8) Method of valuing closely held business interests, etc.—In any case to which paragraph (7)(A) does not apply, the following factors shall apply in determining the value of any qualified real property:

(A) The capitalization of income which the property can be expected to yield for farming or closely held business purposes over a reasonable period of time under prudent management using traditional cropping patterns for the area, taking into account soil capacity, terrain configuration, and similar factors,

(B) The capitalization of the fair rental value of the land for farmland or closely held business purposes,

(C) Assessed land values in a State which provides a differential or use value assessment law for farmland or closely held business,

(D) Comparable sales of other farm or closely held business land in the same geographical area far enough removed from a metropolitan or resort area so that nonagricultural use is not a significant factor in the sales price, and

(E) Any other factor which fairly values the farm or closely held business value of the property.

(9) Property acquired from decedent.—Property shall be considered to have been acquired from or to have passed from the decedent if—

(A) such property is so considered under section 1014(b) (relating to basis of property acquired from a decedent),

(B) such property is acquired by any person from the estate, or

(C) such property is acquired by any person from a trust (to the extent such property is includible in the gross estate of the decedent).

(10) Community property.— If the decedent and his surviving spouse at any time held qualified real property as community property, the interest of the surviving spouse in such property shall be taken into account under this section to the extent necessary to provide a result under this section with respect to such property which is consistent with the result which would have obtained under this section if such property had not been community property.

(11) Bond in lieu of personal liability.—If the qualified heir makes written application to the Secretary for determination of the maximum amount of the additional tax which may be imposed by subsection (c) with respect to the qualified heir's interest, the Secretary (as soon as possible, and in any event within 1 year after the making of such application) shall notify the heir of such maximum amount.

The qualified heir, on furnishing a bond in such amount and for such period as may be required, shall be discharged from personal liability for any additional tax imposed by subsection (c) and shall be entitled to a receipt or writing showing such discharge.

(12) Active management.—The term "active management" means the making of the management decisions of a business (other than the daily operating decisions).

* * *

§ 2033. Property in which the decedent had an interest

The value of the gross estate shall include the value of all property to the extent of the interest therein of the decedent at the time of his death.

§ 2034. Dower or curtesy interests

The value of the gross estate shall include the value of all property to the extent of any interest therein of the surviving spouse, existing at the time of the decedent's death as dower or curtesy, or by virtue of a statute creating an estate in lieu of dower or curtesy.

§ 2035. Adjustments for certain gifts made within 3 years of decedent's death

(a) Inclusion of certain property in gross estate.—If—

(1) the decedent made a transfer (by trust or otherwise) of an interest in any property, or relinquished a power with respect to any property, during the 3–year period ending on the date of the decedent's death, and

(2) the value of such property (or an interest therein) would have been included in the decedent's gross estate under section 2036, 2037, 2038, or 2042 if such transferred interest or relinquished power had been retained by the decedent on the date of his death,

the value of the gross estate shall include the value of any property (or interest therein) which would have been so included.

(b) Inclusion of gift tax on gifts made during 3 years before decedent's death.—The amount of the gross estate (determined without regard to this subsection) shall be increased by the amount of any tax paid under chapter 12 by the decedent or his estate on any gift made by the decedent or his spouse during the 3–year period ending on the date of the decedent's death.

(c) Other rules relating to transfers within 3 years of death.—

(1) In general.—For purposes of—

(A) section 303(b) (relating to distributions in redemption of stock to pay death taxes),

(B) section 2032A (relating to special valuation of certain farms, etc., real property), and

(C) subchapter C of chapter 64 (relating to lien for taxes),

the value of the gross estate shall include the value of all property to the extent of any interest therein of which the decedent has at any time made a transfer, by trust or otherwise, during the 3–year period ending on the date of the decedent's death.

(2) Coordination with section 6166.—An estate shall be treated as meeting the 35 percent of adjusted gross estate requirement of section 6166(a)(1) only if the estate meets such requirement both with and without the application of subsection (a).

(3) Marital and small transfers.—Paragraph (1) shall not apply to any transfer (other than a transfer with respect to a life insurance policy) made during a calendar year to any donee if the decedent was not required by section 6019 (other than by reason of section 6019(2)) to file any gift tax return for such year with respect to transfers to such donee.

(d) Exception.—Subsection (a) and paragraph (1) of subsection (c) shall not apply to any bona fide sale for an adequate and full consideration in money or money's worth.

(e) Treatment of certain transfers from revocable trusts.—For purposes of this section and section 2038, any transfer from any portion of a trust during any period that such portion was treated under section 676 as owned by the decedent by reason of a power in the grantor (determined without regard to section 672(e)) shall be treated as a transfer made directly by the decedent.

§ 2036. Transfers with retained life estate

(a) General rule.—The value of the gross estate shall include the value of all property to the extent of any interest therein of which the decedent has at any time made a transfer (except in case of a bona fide sale for an adequate and full consideration in money or money's worth), by trust or otherwise, under which he has retained for his life or for any period not ascertainable without reference to his death or for any period which does not in fact end before his death—

(1) the possession or enjoyment of, or the right to the income from, the property, or

(2) the right, either alone or in conjunction with any person, to designate the persons who shall possess or enjoy the property or the income therefrom.

(b) Voting rights.—

(1) In general.—For purposes of subsection (a)(1), the retention of the right to vote (directly or indirectly) shares of stock of a controlled corporation shall be considered to be a retention of the enjoyment of transferred property.

(2) Controlled corporation.—For purposes of paragraph (1), a corporation shall be treated as a controlled corporation if, at any time after the transfer of the property and during the 3–year period ending on the date of the decedent's death, the decedent owned (with the application of section 318), or had the right (either alone or in conjunction with any person) to vote, stock possessing at least 20 percent of the total combined voting power of all classes of stock.

(3) Coordination with section 2035.—For purposes of applying section 2035 with respect to paragraph (1), the relinquishment or cessation of voting rights shall be treated as a transfer of property made by the decedent.

* * *

§ 2037. Transfers taking effect at death

(a) General rule.—The value of the gross estate shall include the value of all property to the extent of any interest therein of which the decedent has at any time after September 7, 1916, made a transfer (except in case of a bona fide sale for an adequate and full consideration in money or money's worth), by trust or otherwise, if—

(1) possession or enjoyment of the property can, through ownership of such interest, be obtained only by surviving the decedent, and

(2) the decedent has retained a reversionary interest in the property (but in the case of a transfer made before October 8, 1949, only if such reversionary interest arose by the express terms of the instrument of transfer), and the value of such reversionary interest immediately before the death of the decedent exceeds 5 percent of the value of such property.

(b) Special rules.—For purposes of this section, the term "reversionary interest" includes a possibility that property transferred by the decedent—

(1) may return to him or his estate, or

(2) may be subject to a power of disposition by him,

but such term does not include a possibility that the income alone from such property may return to him or become subject to a power of disposition by him. The value of a reversionary interest immediately before the death of the decedent shall be determined (without regard to the fact of the decedent's death) by usual methods of valuation, including the use of tables of mortality and actuarial principles, under regulations prescribed by the Secretary. In determining the value of a possibility that property may be subject to a power of disposition by the decedent, such possibility shall be valued as if it were a possibility that such property may return to the decedent or his estate. Notwithstanding the foregoing, an interest so transferred shall not be included in the decedent's gross estate under this section if possession or enjoyment of the property could have been obtained by any beneficiary during the decedent's life through the exercise of a general power of appointment (as defined in section 2041) which in fact was exercisable immediately before the decedent's death.

§ 2038. Revocable transfers

(a) In general.—The value of the gross estate shall include the value of all property—

(1) Transfers after June 22, 1936.—To the extent of any interest therein of which the decedent has at any time made a transfer (except in case of a bona fide sale for an adequate and full consideration in money or money's worth), by trust or otherwise, where the enjoyment thereof was subject at the date of his death to any change through the exercise of a power (in whatever capacity exercisable) by the decedent alone or by the decedent in conjunction with any other person (without regard to when or from what source the decedent acquired such power), to alter, amend, revoke, or terminate, or where any such power is relinquished during the 3–year period ending on the date of the decedent's death.

(2) Transfers on or before June 22, 1936.—To the extent of any interest therein of which the decedent has at any time made a transfer (except in case of a bona fide sale for an adequate and full consideration in money or money's worth), by trust or otherwise, where the enjoyment thereof was subject at the date of his death to any change through the exercise of a power, either by the decedent alone or in conjunction with any person, to alter, amend, or revoke, or where the decedent relinquished any such power during the 3–year period ending on the date of the decedent's death. Except in the case of transfers made after June 22, 1936, no interest of the decedent of which he has made a transfer shall be included in the gross estate under paragraph (1) unless it is includible under this paragraph.

(b) Date of existence of power.—For purposes of this section, the power to alter, amend, revoke, or terminate shall be considered to exist on the date of the decedent's death even though the exercise of the power is subject to a precedent giving of notice or even though the alteration, amendment, revocation, or termination takes effect only on the expiration of a stated period after the exercise of the power, whether or not on or before the date of the decedent's death notice has been given or the power has been exercised. In such cases proper adjustment shall be made representing the interests which would have been excluded from the power if the decedent had lived, and for such purpose, if the notice has not been given or the power has not been exercised on or before the date of his death, such notice shall be considered to have been given, or the power exercised, on the date of his death.

§ 2039. Annuities

(a) General.—The gross estate shall include the value of an annuity or other payment receivable by any beneficiary by reason of surviving the decedent under any form of contract or agreement entered into after March 3, 1931 (other than as insurance under policies on the life of the decedent), if, under such contract or agreement, an annuity or other payment was payable to the decedent, or the decedent possessed the right to receive such annuity or payment, either alone or in conjunction with another for his life or for any period not ascertainable without reference to his death or for any period which does not in fact end before his death.

(b) Amount includible.—Subsection (a) shall apply to only such part of the value of the annuity or other payment receivable under such contract or agreement as is proportionate to that part of the purchase price therefor contributed by the decedent. For purposes of this section, any contribution by the decedent's employer or former employer to the purchase price of such contract or agreement (whether or not to an employee's trust or fund forming part of a pension, annuity, retirement, bonus or profit sharing plan) shall be considered to be contributed by the decedent if made by reason of his employment.

§ 2040. Joint interests

(a) General rule.—The value of the gross estate shall include the value of all property to the extent of the interest therein held as joint tenants with right of survivorship by the decedent and any other person, or as tenants by the entirety by the decedent and spouse, or deposited, with any person carrying on the banking business, in their joint names and payable to either or the survivor, except such part thereof as may be shown to have originally belonged to such other person and never to have been received or acquired by the latter from the decedent for less than an adequate and full consideration in money or money's worth: *Provided*, That where such property or any part thereof, or part of the consideration with which such property was acquired, is shown to have been at any time acquired by such other person from the decedent for less than an adequate and full consideration in money or money's worth, there shall be excepted only such part of the value of such property as is proportionate to the consideration furnished by such other person: *Provided further*, That where any property has been acquired by gift, bequest, devise, or inheritance, as a tenancy by the entirety by the decedent and spouse, then to the extent of one-half of the value thereof, or, where so acquired by the decedent and any other person as joint tenants with right of survivorship and their interests are not otherwise specified or fixed by law, then to the extent of the value of a fractional part to be determined by dividing the value of the property by the number of joint tenants with right of survivorship.

(b) Certain joint interests of husband and wife.—

(1) Interests of spouse excluded from gross estate.—Notwithstanding subsection (a), in the case of any qualified joint interest, the value included in the gross estate with respect to such interest by reason of this section is one-half of the value of such qualified joint interest.

(2) Qualified joint interest defined.—For purposes of paragraph (1), the term "qualified joint interest" means any interest in property held by the decedent and the decedent's spouse as—

(A) tenants by the entirety, or

(B) joint tenants with right of survivorship, but only if the decedent and the spouse of the decedent are the only joint tenants.

§ 2041. Powers of appointment

(a) In general.—The value of the gross estate shall include the value of all property—

(1) Powers of appointment created on or before October 21, 1942.—To the extent of any property with respect to which a general power of appointment created on or before October 21, 1942, is exercised by the decedent—

(A) by will, or

(B) by a disposition which is of such nature that if it were a transfer of property owned by the decedent, such property would be includible in the decedent's gross estate under sections 2035 to 2038, inclusive;

but the failure to exercise such a power or the complete release of such a power shall not be deemed an exercise thereof. If a general power of appointment created on or before October 21, 1942, has been partially released so that it is no longer a general power of appointment, the exercise of such power shall not be deemed to be the exercise of a general power of appointment if—

(i) such partial release occurred before November 1, 1951, or

(ii) the donee of such power was under a legal disability to release such power on October 21, 1942, and such partial release occurred not later than 6 months after the termination of such legal disability.

(2) Powers created after October 21, 1942.—To the extent of any property with respect to which the decedent has at the time of his death a general power of appointment created after October 21, 1942, or with respect to which the decedent has at any time exercised or released such a power of appointment by a disposition which is of such nature that if it were a transfer of property owned by the decedent, such property would be includible in the decedent's gross estate under sections 2035 to 2038, inclusive. For purposes of this paragraph (2), the power of appointment shall be considered to exist on the date of the decedent's death even though the exercise of the power is subject to a precedent giving of notice or even though the exercise of the power takes effect only on the expiration of a stated period after its exercise, whether or not on or before the date of the decedent's death notice has been given or the power has been exercised.

(3) Creation of another power in certain cases.—To the extent of any property with respect to which the decedent—

(A) by will, or

(B) by a disposition which is of such nature that if it were a transfer of property owned by the decedent such property would be includible in the decedent's gross estate under section 2035, 2036, or 2037,

exercises a power of appointment created after October 21, 1942, by creating another power of appointment which under the applicable local law can be validly exercised so as to postpone the vesting of any estate or interest in such property, or suspend the absolute ownership or power of alienation of such property, for a period ascertainable without regard to the date of the creation of the first power.

(b) Definitions.—For purposes of subsection (a)—

(1) General power of appointment.—The term "general power of appointment" means a power which is exercisable in favor of the decedent, his estate, his creditors, or the creditors of his estate; except that—

(A) A power to consume, invade, or appropriate property for the benefit of the decedent which is limited by an ascertainable standard relating to the health, education, support, or maintenance of the decedent shall not be deemed a general power of appointment.

(B) A power of appointment created on or before October 21, 1942, which is exercisable by the decedent only in conjunction with another person shall not be deemed a general power of appointment.

(C) In the case of a power of appointment created after October 21, 1942, which is exercisable by the decedent only in conjunction with another person—

(i) If the power is not exercisable by the decedent except in conjunction with the creator of the power—such power shall not be deemed a general power of appointment.

(ii) If the power is not exercisable by the decedent except in conjunction with a person having a substantial interest in the property, subject to the power, which is adverse to exercise of the power in favor of the decedent—such power shall not be deemed a general power of appointment. For the purposes of this clause a person who, after the death of the decedent, may be possessed of a power of appointment (with respect to the property subject to the decedent's power) which he may exercise in his own favor shall be deemed as having an interest in the property and such interest shall be deemed adverse to such exercise of the decedent's power.

(iii) If (after the application of clauses (i) and (ii)) the power is a general power of appointment and is exercisable in favor of such other person—such power shall be deemed a general power of appointment only in respect of a fractional part of the property subject to such power, such part to be determined by dividing the value of such property by the number of such persons (including the decedent) in favor of whom such power is exercisable.

For purposes of clauses (ii) and (iii), a power shall be deemed to be exercisable in favor of a person if it is exercisable in favor of such person, his estate, his creditors, or the creditors of his estate.

(2) Lapse of power.—The lapse of a power of appointment created after October 21, 1942, during the life of the individual possessing the power shall be considered a release of such power. The preceding sentence shall apply with respect to the lapse of powers during any calendar year only to the extent that the property, which could have been appointed by exercise of such lapsed powers, exceeded in value, at the time of such lapse, the greater of the following amounts:

(A) $5,000, or

(B) 5 percent of the aggregate value, at the time of such lapse, of the assets out of which, or the proceeds of which, the exercise of the lapsed powers could have been satisfied.

* * *

§ 2042. Proceeds of life insurance

The value of the gross estate shall include the value of all property—

(1) Receivable by the executor.—To the extent of the amount receivable by the executor as insurance under policies on the life of the decedent.

(2) Receivable by other beneficiaries.—To the extent of the amount receivable by all other beneficiaries as insurance under policies on the life of the decedent with respect to which the decedent possessed at his death any of the incidents of ownership, exercisable either alone or in conjunction with any other person. For purposes of the preceding sentence, the term "incident of ownership" includes a reversionary interest (whether arising by the express terms of the policy or other instrument or by operation of law) only if the value of such reversionary interest exceeded 5 percent of the value of the policy immediately before the death of the decedent. As used in this paragraph, the term "reversionary interest" includes a possibility that the policy, or the proceeds of the policy, may return to the decedent or his estate, or may be subject to a power of disposition by him. The value of a reversionary interest at any time shall be determined (without regard to the fact of the decedent's death) by usual methods of valuation, including the use of tables of mortality and actuarial principles, pursuant to regulations prescribed by the Secretary. In determining the value of a possibility that the policy or proceeds thereof may be subject to a power of disposition by the decedent, such possibility shall be valued as if it were a possibility that such policy or proceeds may return to the decedent or his estate.

§ 2043. Transfers for insufficient consideration

(a) In general.—If any one of the transfers, trusts, interests, rights, or powers enumerated and described in sections 2035 to 2038, inclusive, and section 2041 is made, created, exercised, or relinquished for a consideration in money or money's worth, but is not a bona fide sale for an adequate and full consideration in money or money's worth, there shall be included in the gross estate only the excess of the fair market value at the time of death of the property otherwise to be included on account of such transaction, over the value of the consideration received therefor by the decedent.

(b) Marital rights not treated as consideration.—

(1) In general.—For purposes of this chapter, a relinquishment or promised relinquishment of dower or curtesy, or of a statutory estate created in lieu of dower or curtesy, or of other marital rights in the decedent's property or estate, shall not be considered to any extent a consideration "in money or money's worth".

(2) Exception.—For purposes of section 2053 (relating to expenses, indebtedness, and taxes), a transfer of property which satisfies the requirements of paragraph (1) of section 2516 (relating to certain property settlements) shall be considered to be made for an adequate and full consideration in money or money's worth.

§ 2044. Certain property for which marital deduction was previously allowed

(a) General rule.—The value of the gross estate shall include the value of any property to which this section applies in which the decedent had a qualifying income interest for life.

(b) Property to which this section applies.—This section applies to any property if—

(1) a deduction was allowed with respect to the transfer of such property to the decedent—

(A) under section 2056 by reason of subsection (b)(7) thereof, or

(B) under section 2523 by reason of subsection (f) thereof, and

(2) section 2519 (relating to dispositions of certain life estates) did not apply with respect to a disposition by the decedent of part or all of such property.

(c) Property treated as having passed from decedent.—For purposes of this chapter and chapter 13, property includible in the gross estate of the decedent under subsection (a) shall be treated as property passing from the decedent.

§ 2045. Prior interests

Except as otherwise specifically provided by law, sections 2034 to 2042, inclusive, shall apply to the transfers, trusts, estates, interests, rights, powers, and relinquishment of powers, as severally enumerated and described therein, whenever made, created, arising, existing, exercised, or relinquished.

§ 2046. Disclaimers

For provisions relating to the effect of a qualified disclaimer for purposes of this chapter, see section 2518.

PART IV—TAXABLE ESTATE

§ 2051. Definition of taxable estate

For purposes of the tax imposed by section 2001, the value of the taxable estate shall be determined by deducting from the value of the gross estate the deductions provided for in this part.

§ 2053. Expenses, indebtedness, and taxes

(a) General rule.—For purposes of the tax imposed by section 2001, the value of the taxable estate shall be determined by deducting from the value of the gross estate such amounts—

(1) for funeral expenses,

(2) for administration expenses,

(3) for claims against the estate, and

(4) for unpaid mortgages on, or any indebtedness in respect of, property where the value of the decedent's interest therein, undiminished by such mortgage or indebtedness, is included in the value of the gross estate,

as are allowable by the laws of the jurisdiction, whether within or without the United States, under which the estate is being administered.

(b) Other administration expenses.—Subject to the limitations in paragraph (1) of subsection (c), there shall be deducted in determining the taxable estate amounts representing expenses incurred in administering property not subject to claims which is included in the gross estate to the same extent such amounts would be allowable as a deduction under subsection (a) if such property were subject to claims, and such amounts are paid before the expiration of the period of limitation for assessment provided in section 6501.

(c) Limitations.—

(1) Limitations applicable to subsections (a) and (b).—

(A) Consideration for claims.—The deduction allowed by this section in the case of claims against the estate, unpaid mortgages, or any indebtedness shall, when founded on a promise or agreement, be limited to the extent that they were contracted bona fide and for an adequate and full consideration in money or money's worth; except that in any case in which any such claim is founded on a promise or agreement of the decedent to make a contribution or gift to or for the use of any donee described in section 2055 for the purposes specified therein, the deduction for such claims shall not be so limited, but shall be limited to the extent that it would be allowable as a deduction under section 2055 if such promise or agreement constituted a bequest.

(B) Certain taxes.—Any income taxes on income received after the death of the decedent, or property taxes not accrued before his death, or any estate, succession, legacy, or inheritance taxes, shall not be deductible under this section.

(C) Certain claims by remaindermen.—No deduction shall be allowed under this section for a claim against the estate by a remainderman relating to any property described in section 2044.

(D) Section 6166 interest.—No deduction shall be allowed under this section for any interest payable under section 6601 on any unpaid portion of the tax imposed by section 2001 for the period during which an extension of time for payment of such tax is in effect under section 6166.

(2) Limitations applicable only to subsection (a).—In the case of the amounts described in subsection (a), there shall be disallowed the amount by which the deductions specified therein exceed the value, at the time of the decedent's death, of property subject to claims, except to the extent that such deductions represent amounts paid before the date prescribed for the filing of the estate tax return. For purposes of this section, the term "property subject to claims" means property includible in the gross estate of the decedent which, or the avails of which, would under the applicable law, bear the burden of the payment of such deductions in the final adjustment and settlement of the estate, except that the value of the property shall be reduced by the amount of the deduction under section 2054 attributable to such property.

(d) Certain foreign death taxes.—

(1) In general.—Notwithstanding the provisions of subsection (c)(1)(B), for purposes of the tax imposed by section 2001, the value of the taxable estate may be determined, if the executor so elects before the expiration of the period of limitation for assessment provided in section 6501, by deducting from the value of the gross estate the amount (as determined in accordance with regulations prescribed by the Secretary) of any estate, succession, legacy, or inheritance tax imposed by and actually paid to any foreign country, in respect of any property situated within such foreign country and included in the gross estate of a citizen or resident of the United States, upon a transfer by the decedent for public, charitable, or religious uses described in section 2055. The determination under this paragraph of the country within which property is situated shall be made in accordance with the rules applicable under subchapter B (sec. 2101 and following) in determining whether property is situated within or without the United States. Any election under this paragraph shall be exercised in accordance with regulations prescribed by the Secretary.

(2) Condition for allowance of deduction.—No deduction shall be allowed under paragraph (1) for a foreign death tax specified therein unless the decrease in the tax imposed by section 2001 which results from the deduction provided in paragraph (1) will inure solely for the benefit of the public, charitable, or religious transferees described in section 2055 or section 2106(a)(2). In any case where the tax imposed by section 2001 is equitably apportioned among all the transferees of property included in the gross estate, including those described in sections 2055 and 2106(a)(2) (taking into account any exemptions, credits, or deductions allowed by this chapter), in determining such decrease, there shall be disregarded any decrease in the Federal estate tax which any transferees other than those described in sections 2055 and 2106(a)(2) are required to pay.

(3) Effect on credit for foreign death taxes of deduction under this subsection.—

(A) Election.—An election under this subsection shall be deemed a waiver of the right to claim a credit, against the Federal estate tax, under a death tax convention with any foreign country for any tax or portion thereof in respect of which a deduction is taken under this subsection.

(B) Cross reference.—See section 2014(f) for the effect of a deduction taken under this paragraph on the credit for foreign death taxes.

(e) Marital rights.—

For provisions treating certain relinquishments of marital rights as consideration in money or money's worth, see section 2043(b)(2).

§ 2054. Losses

For purposes of the tax imposed by section 2001, the value of the taxable estate shall be determined by deducting from the value of the gross estate losses incurred during the settlement of estates arising from fires, storms, shipwrecks, or other casualties, or from theft, when such losses are not compensated for by insurance or otherwise.

§ 2055. Transfers for public, charitable, and religious uses

(a) In general.—For purposes of the tax imposed by section 2001, the value of the taxable estate shall be determined by deducting from the value of the gross estate the amount of all bequests, legacies, devises, or transfers—

(1) to or for the use of the United States, any State, any political subdivision thereof, or the District of Columbia, for exclusively public purposes;

(2) to or for the use of any corporation organized and operated exclusively for religious, charitable, scientific, literary, or educational purposes, including the encouragement of art, or to foster national or international amateur sports competition (but only if no part of its activities involve the provision of athletic facilities or equipment), and the prevention of cruelty to children or animals, no part of the net earnings of which inures to the benefit of any private stockholder or individual, which is not disqualified for tax exemption under section 501(c)(3) by reason of attempting to influence legislation, and which does not participate in, or intervene in (including the publishing or distributing of statements), any political campaign on behalf of (or in opposition to) any candidate for public office;

(3) to a trustee or trustees, or a fraternal society, order, or association operating under the lodge system, but only if such contributions or gifts are to be used by such trustee or trustees, or by such fraternal society, order, or association, exclusively for religious, charitable, scientific, literary, or educational purposes, or for the prevention of cruelty to children or animals, such trust, fraternal society, order, or association would not be disqualified for tax exemption under section 501(c)(3) by reason of attempting to influence legislation, and such trustee or trustees, or such fraternal society, order, or association, does not participate in, or intervene in (including the publishing or distributing of statements), any political campaign on behalf of (or in opposition to) any candidate for public office;

(4) to or for the use of any veterans' organization incorporated by Act of Congress, or of its departments or local chapters or posts, no part of the net earnings of which inures to the benefit of any private shareholder or individual; or

* * *

For purposes of this subsection, the complete termination before the date prescribed for the filing of the estate tax return of a power to consume, invade, or appropriate property for the benefit of an individual before such power has been exercised by reason of the death of such individual or for any other reason shall be considered and deemed to be a qualified disclaimer with the same full force and effect as though he had filed such qualified disclaimer. Rules similar to the rules of section 501(j) shall apply for purposes of paragraph (2).

(b) Powers of appointment.—Property includible in the decedent's gross estate under section 2041 (relating to powers of appointment) received by a donee described in this section shall, for purposes of this section, be considered a bequest of such decedent.

(c) Death taxes payable out of bequests.—If the tax imposed by section 2001, or any estate, succession, legacy, or inheritance taxes, are, either by the terms of the will, by the law of the jurisdiction under which the estate is administered, or by the law of the jurisdiction imposing the particular tax, payable in whole or in part out of the bequests, legacies, or devises otherwise deductible under this section, then the amount deductible under this section shall be the amount of such bequests, legacies, or devises reduced by the amount of such taxes.

(d) Limitation on deduction.—The amount of the deduction under this section for any transfer shall not exceed the value of the transferred property required to be included in the gross estate.

(e) Disallowance of deductions in certain cases.—

* * *

(2) Where an interest in property (other than an interest described in section 170(f)(3)(B)) passes or has passed from the decedent to a person, or for a use, described in subsection (a), and an interest (other than an interest which is extinguished upon the decedent's death) in the same property passes or has passed (for less than an adequate and full consideration in money or money's worth) from the decedent to a person, or for a use, not described in subsection (a), no deduction shall be allowed under this section for the interest which passes or has passed to the person, or for the use, described in subsection (a) unless—

(A) in the case of a remainder interest, such interest is in a trust which is a charitable remainder annuity trust or a charitable remainder unitrust (described in section 664) or a pooled income fund (described in section 642(c)(5)), or

(B) in the case of any other interest, such interest is in the form of a guaranteed annuity or is a fixed percentage distributed yearly of the fair market value of the property (to be determined yearly).

(3) Reformations to comply with paragraph (2).—

(A) In general.—A deduction shall be allowed under subsection (a) in respect of any qualified reformation.

(B) Qualified reformation.—For purposes of this paragraph, the term "qualified reformation" means a change of a governing instrument by reformation, amendment, construction, or otherwise which changes a reformable interest into a qualified interest but only if—

(i) any difference between—

(I) the actuarial value (determined as of the date of the decedent's death) of the qualified interest, and

(II) the actuarial value (as so determined) of the reformable interest,

does not exceed 5 percent of the actuarial value (as so determined) of the reformable interest,

(ii) in the case of—

(I) a charitable remainder interest, the nonremainder interest (before and after the qualified reformation) terminated at the same time, or

(II) any other interest, the reformable interest and the qualified interest are for the same period, and

(iii) such change is effective as of the date of the decedent's death.

A nonremainder interest (before reformation) for a term of years in excess of 20 years shall be treated as satisfying subclause (I) of clause (ii) if such interest (after reformation) is for a term of 20 years.

(C) Reformable interest.—For purposes of this paragraph—

(i) In general.—The term "reformable interest" means any interest for which a deduction would be allowable under subsection (a) at the time of the decedent's death but for paragraph (2).

(ii) Beneficiary's interest must be fixed.—The term "reformable interest" does not include any interest unless, before the remainder vests in possession, all payments to persons other than an organization described in subsection (a) are expressed either in specified dollar amounts or a fixed percentage of the fair market value of the property. For purposes of determining whether all such payments are expressed as a fixed percentage of the fair market value of the property, section 664(d)(3) shall be taken into account.

(iii) Special rule where timely commencement of reformation.—Clause (ii) shall not apply to any interest if a judicial proceeding is commenced to change such interest into a qualified interest not later than the 90th day after—

(I) if an estate tax return is required to be filed, the last date (including extensions) for filing such return, or

(II) if no estate tax return is required to be filed, the last date (including extensions) for filing the income tax return for the 1st taxable year for which such a return is required to be filed by the trust.

* * *

(D) Qualified interest.—For purposes of this paragraph, the term "qualified interest" means an interest for which a deduction is allowable under subsection (a).

* * *

(4) Works of art and their copyrights treated as separate properties in certain cases.—

(A) In general.—In the case of a qualified contribution of a work of art, the work of art and the copyright on such work of art shall be treated as separate properties for purposes of paragraph (2).

(B) Work of art defined.—For purposes of this paragraph, the term "work of art" means any tangible personal property with respect to which there is a copyright under Federal law.

(C) Qualified contribution defined.—For purposes of this paragraph, the term "qualified contribution" means any transfer of property to a qualified organization if the use of the property by the organization is related to the purpose or function constituting the basis for its exemption under section 501.

(D) Qualified organization defined.—For purposes of this paragraph, the term "qualified organization" means any organization described in section

501(c)(3) other than a private foundation (as defined in section 509). For purposes of the preceding sentence, a private operating foundation (as defined in section 4942(j)(3)) shall not be treated as a private foundation.

(5) Contributions to donor advised funds.—A deduction otherwise allowed under subsection (a) for any contribution to a donor advised fund (as defined in section 4966(d)(2)) shall only be allowed if—

(A) the sponsoring organization (as defined in section 4966(d)(1)) with respect to such donor advised fund is not—

(i) described in paragraph (3) or (4) of subsection (a), or

(ii) a type III supporting organization (as defined in section 4943(f)(5)(A)) which is not a functionally integrated type III supporting organization (as defined in section 4943(f)(5)(B)), and

(B) the taxpayer obtains a contemporaneous written acknowledgment (determined under rules similar to the rules of section 170(f)(8)(C)) from the sponsoring organization (as so defined) of such donor advised fund that such organization has exclusive legal control over the assets contributed.

(f) Special rule for irrevocable transfers of easements in real property.—A deduction shall be allowed under subsection (a) in respect of any transfer of a qualified real property interest (as defined in section 170(h)(2)(C)) which meets the requirements of section 170(h) (without regard to paragraph (4)(A) thereof).

* * *

§ 2056. Bequests, etc., to surviving spouse

(a) Allowance of marital deduction.—For purposes of the tax imposed by section 2001, the value of the taxable estate shall, except as limited by subsection (b), be determined by deducting from the value of the gross estate an amount equal to the value of any interest in property which passes or has passed from the decedent to his surviving spouse, but only to the extent that such interest is included in determining the value of the gross estate.

(b) Limitation in the case of life estate or other terminable interest.—

(1) General rule.—Where, on the lapse of time, on the occurrence of an event or contingency, or on the failure of an event or contingency to occur, an interest passing to the surviving spouse will terminate or fail, no deduction shall be allowed under this section with respect to such interest—

(A) if an interest in such property passes or has passed (for less than an adequate and full consideration in money or money's worth) from the decedent to any person other than such surviving spouse (or the estate of such spouse); and

(B) if by reason of such passing such person (or his heirs or assigns) may possess or enjoy any part of such property after such termination or failure of the interest so passing to the surviving spouse;

and no deduction shall be allowed with respect to such interest (even if such deduction is not disallowed under subparagraphs (A) and (B))—

(C) if such interest is to be acquired for the surviving spouse, pursuant to directions of the decedent, by his executor or by the trustee of a trust.

For purposes of this paragraph, an interest shall not be considered as an interest which will terminate or fail merely because it is the ownership of a bond, note, or similar contractual obligation, the discharge of which would not have the effect of an annuity for life or for a term.

(2) Interest in unidentified assets.—Where the assets (included in the decedent's gross estate) out of which, or the proceeds of which, an interest passing to the surviving spouse may be satisfied include a particular asset or assets with respect to which no deduction would be allowed if such asset or assets passed from the decedent to such spouse, then the value of such interest passing to such spouse shall, for purposes of subsection (a), be reduced by the aggregate value of such particular assets.

(3) Interest of spouse conditional on survival for limited period.—For purposes of this subsection, an interest passing to the surviving spouse shall not be considered as an interest which will terminate or fail on the death of such spouse if—

(A) such death will cause a termination or failure of such interest only if it occurs within a period not exceeding 6 months after the decedent's death, or only if it occurs as a result of a common disaster resulting in the death of the decedent and the surviving spouse, or only if it occurs in the case of either such event; and

(B) such termination or failure does not in fact occur.

(4) Valuation of interest passing to surviving spouse.—In determining for purposes of subsection (a) the value of any interest in property passing to the surviving spouse for which a deduction is allowed by this section—

(A) there shall be taken into account the effect which the tax imposed by section 2001, or any estate, succession, legacy, or inheritance tax, has on the net value to the surviving spouse of such interest; and

(B) where such interest or property is encumbered in any manner, or where the surviving spouse incurs any obligation imposed by the decedent with respect to the passing of such interest, such encumbrance or obligation shall be taken into account in the same manner as if the amount of a gift to such spouse of such interest were being determined.

(5) Life estate with power of appointment in surviving spouse.—In the case of an interest in property passing from the decedent, if his surviving spouse is entitled for life to all the income from the entire interest, or all the income from a specific portion thereof, payable annually or at more frequent intervals, with power in the surviving spouse to appoint the entire interest, or such specific portion (exercisable in favor of such surviving spouse, or of the estate of such surviving spouse, or in favor of either, whether or not in each case the power is exercisable in favor of others), and with no power in any other person to appoint any part of the interest, or such specific portion, to any person other than the surviving spouse—

(A) the interest or such portion thereof so passing shall, for purposes of subsection (a), be considered as passing to the surviving spouse, and

(B) no part of the interest so passing shall, for purposes of paragraph (1)(A), be considered as passing to any person other than the surviving spouse.

This paragraph shall apply only if such power in the surviving spouse to appoint the entire interest, or such specific portion thereof, whether exercisable by will or during life, is exercisable by such spouse alone and in all events.

(6) Life insurance or annuity payments with power of appointment in surviving spouse.—In the case of an interest in property passing from the decedent consisting of proceeds under a life insurance, endowment, or annuity contract, if under the terms of the contract such proceeds are payable in installments or are held by the insurer subject to an agreement to pay interest thereon (whether the proceeds, on the termination of any interest payments, are payable in a lump sum or in annual or more frequent installments), and such installment or interest payments are payable annually or at more frequent intervals, commencing not later than 13 months after the decedent's death, and all amounts, or a specific portion of all such amounts, payable during the life of the surviving spouse are payable only to such spouse, and such spouse has the power to appoint all amounts, or such specific portion, payable under such contract (exercisable in favor of such surviving spouse, or of the estate of such surviving spouse, or in favor of either, whether or not in each case the power is exercisable in favor of others), with no power in any other person to appoint such amounts to any person other than the surviving spouse—

(A) such amounts shall, for purposes of subsection (a), be considered as passing to the surviving spouse, and

(B) no part of such amounts shall, for purposes of paragraph (1)(A), be considered as passing to any person other than the surviving spouse.

This paragraph shall apply only if, under the terms of the contract, such power in the surviving spouse to appoint such amounts, whether exercisable by will or during life, is exercisable by such spouse alone and in all events.

(7) Election with respect to life estate for surviving spouse.—

(A) In general.—In the case of qualified terminable interest property—

(i) for purposes of subsection (a), such property shall be treated as passing to the surviving spouse, and

(ii) for purposes of paragraph (1)(A), no part of such property shall be treated as passing to any person other than the surviving spouse.

(B) Qualified terminable interest property defined.—For purposes of this paragraph—

(i) In general.—The term "qualified terminable interest property" means property—

(I) which passes from the decedent,

(II) in which the surviving spouse has a qualifying income interest for life, and

(III) to which an election under this paragraph applies.

(ii) Qualifying income interest for life.—The surviving spouse has a qualifying income interest for life if—

(I) the surviving spouse is entitled to all the income from the property, payable annually or at more frequent intervals, or has a usufruct interest for life in the property, and

(II) no person has a power to appoint any part of the property to any person other than the surviving spouse.

Subclause (II) shall not apply to a power exercisable only at or after the death of the surviving spouse. To the extent provided in regulations, an annuity shall be treated in a manner similar to an income interest in property (regardless of whether the property from which the annuity is payable can be separately identified).

(iii) Property includes interest therein.—The term "property" includes an interest in property.

(iv) Specific portion treated as separate property.—A specific portion of property shall be treated as separate property.

(v) Election.—An election under this paragraph with respect to any property shall be made by the executor on the return of tax imposed by section 2001. Such an election, once made, shall be irrevocable.

(C) Treatment of survivor annuities.—In the case of an annuity included in the gross estate of the decedent under section 2039 (or, in the case of an interest in an annuity arising under the community property laws of a State, included in the gross estate of the decedent under section 2033) where only the surviving spouse has the right to receive payments before the death of such surviving spouse—

(i) the interest of such surviving spouse shall be treated as a qualifying income interest for life, and

(ii) the executor shall be treated as having made an election under this subsection with respect to such annuity unless the executor otherwise elects on the return of tax imposed by section 2001.

An election under clause (ii), once made, shall be irrevocable.

(8) Special rule for charitable remainder trusts.—

(A) In general.—If the surviving spouse of the decedent is the only beneficiary of a qualified charitable remainder trust who is not a charitable beneficiary * * *, paragraph (1) shall not apply to any interest in such trust which passes or has passed from the decedent to such surviving spouse.

(B) Definitions.—For purposes of subparagraph (A)—

(i) Charitable beneficiary.—The term ''charitable beneficiary'' means any beneficiary which is an organization described in section 170(c).

* * *

(iii) Qualified charitable remainder trust.—The term ''qualified charitable remainder trust'' means a charitable remainder annuity trust or a charitable remainder unitrust (described in section 664).

(9) Denial of double deduction.—Nothing in this section or any other provision of this chapter shall allow the value of any interest in property to be deducted under this chapter more than once with respect to the same decedent.

(10) Specific portion.—For purposes of paragraphs (5), (6), and (7)(B)(iv), the term ''specific portion'' only includes a portion determined on a fractional or percentage basis.

(c) Definition.—For purposes of this section, an interest in property shall be considered as passing from the decedent to any person if and only if—

(1) such interest is bequeathed or devised to such person by the decedent;

(2) such interest is inherited by such person from the decedent;

(3) such interest is the dower or curtesy interest (or statutory interest in lieu thereof) of such person as surviving spouse of the decedent;

(4) such interest has been transferred to such person by the decedent at any time;

(5) such interest was, at the time of the decedent's death, held by such person and the decedent (or by them and any other person) in joint ownership with right of survivorship;

(6) the decedent had a power (either alone or in conjunction with any person) to appoint such interest and if he appoints or has appointed such interest to such person, or if such person takes such interest in default on the release or nonexercise of such power; or

(7) such interest consists of proceeds of insurance on the life of the decedent receivable by such person.

Except as provided in paragraph (5) or (6) of subsection (b), where at the time of the decedent's death it is not possible to ascertain the particular person or persons to whom an interest in property may pass from the decedent, such interest shall, for purposes of subparagraphs (A) and (B) of subsection (b)(1), be considered as passing from the decedent to a person other than the surviving spouse.

(d) Disallowance of marital deduction where surviving spouse not United States citizen.—

(1) In general.—Except as provided in paragraph (2), if the surviving spouse of the decedent is not a citizen of the United States—

(A) no deduction shall be allowed under subsection (a), and

(B) section 2040(b) shall not apply.

(2) Marital deduction allowed for certain transfers in trust.—

(A) In general.—Paragraph (1) shall not apply to any property passing to the surviving spouse in a qualified domestic trust.

(B) Special rule.—If any property passes from the decedent to the surviving spouse of the decedent, for purposes of subparagraph (A), such property shall be treated as passing to such spouse in a qualified domestic trust if—

(i) such property is transferred to such a trust before the date on which the return of the tax imposed by this chapter is made, or

(ii) such property is irrevocably assigned to such a trust under an irrevocable assignment made on or before such date which is enforceable under local law.

(3) Allowance of credit to certain spouses.—If—

(A) property passes to the surviving spouse of the decedent (hereinafter in this paragraph referred to as the "first decedent"),

(B) without regard to this subsection, a deduction would be allowable under subsection (a) with respect to such property, and

(C) such surviving spouse dies and the estate of such surviving spouse is subject to the tax imposed by this chapter,

the Federal estate tax paid (or treated as paid under section 2056A(b)(7)) by the first decedent with respect to such property shall be allowed as a credit under section 2013 to the estate of such surviving spouse and the amount of such credit shall be determined under such section without regard to when the first decedent died and without regard to subsection (d)(3) of such section.

(4) Special rule where resident spouse becomes citizen.— Paragraph (1) shall not apply if—

(A) the surviving spouse of the decedent becomes a citizen of the United States before the day on which the return of the tax imposed by this chapter is made, and

(B) such spouse was a resident of the United States at all times after the date of the death of the decedent and before becoming a citizen of the United States.

(5) Reformations permitted.—

(A) In general.—In the case of any property with respect to which a deduction would be allowable under subsection (a) but for this subsection, the determination of whether a trust is a qualified domestic trust shall be made—

(i) as of the date on which the return of the tax imposed by this chapter is made, or

(ii) if a judicial proceeding is commenced on or before the due date (determined with regard to extensions) for filing such return to change such trust into a trust which is a qualified domestic trust, as of the time when the changes pursuant to such proceeding are made.

(B) Statute of limitations.—If a judicial proceeding described in subparagraph (A)(ii) is commenced with respect to any trust, the period for assessing any deficiency of tax attributable to any failure of such trust to be a qualified domestic trust shall not expire before the date 1 year after the date on which the Secretary is notified that the trust has been changed pursuant to such judicial proceeding or that such proceeding has been terminated.

§ 2056A. Qualified domestic trust

(a) Qualified domestic trust defined.—For purposes of this section and section 2056(d), the term "qualified domestic trust" means, with respect to any decedent, any trust if—

(1) the trust instrument—

(A) except as provided in regulations prescribed by the Secretary, requires that at least 1 trustee of the trust be an individual citizen of the United States or a domestic corporation, and

(B) provides that no distribution (other than a distribution of income) may be made from the trust unless a trustee who is an individual citizen of the United States or a domestic corporation has the right to withhold from such distribution the tax imposed by this section on such distribution.

(2) such trust meets such requirements as the Secretary may by regulations prescribe to ensure the collection of any tax imposed by subsection (b), and

(3) an election under this section by the executor of the decedent applies to such trust.

(b) Tax treatment of trust.—

(1) Imposition of estate tax.—There is hereby imposed an estate tax on—

(A) any distribution before the date of the death of the surviving spouse from a qualified domestic trust, and

(B) the value of the property remaining in a qualified domestic trust on the date of the death of the surviving spouse.

(2) Amount of tax.—

(A) In general.—In the case of any taxable event, the amount of the estate tax imposed by paragraph (1) shall be the amount equal to—

(i) the tax which would have been imposed under section 2001 on the estate of the decedent if the taxable estate of the decedent had been increased by the sum of—

(I) the amount involved in such taxable event, plus

(II) the aggregate amount involved in previous taxable events with respect to qualified domestic trusts of such decedent, reduced by

(ii) the tax which would have been imposed under section 2001 on the estate of the decedent if the taxable estate of the decedent had been increased by the amount referred to in clause (i)(II).

(B) Tentative tax where tax of decedent not finally determined.—

(i) In general.—If the tax imposed on the estate of the decedent under section 2001 is not finally determined before the taxable event, the amount of the tax imposed by paragraph (1) on such event shall be determined by using the highest rate of tax in effect under section 2001 as of the date of the decedent's death.

(ii) Refund of excess when tax finally determined.—If—

(I) the amount of the tax determined under clause (i), exceeds

(II) the tax determined under subparagraph (A) on the basis of the final determination of the tax imposed by section 2001 on the estate of the decedent,

such excess shall be allowed as a credit or refund (with interest) if claim therefor is filed not later than 1 year after the date of such final determination.

(C) Special rule where decedent has more than 1 qualified domestic trust.—If there is more than 1 qualified domestic trust with respect to any decedent, the amount of the tax imposed by paragraph (1) with respect to such trusts shall be determined by using the highest rate of tax in effect under section 2001 as of the date of the decedent's death (and the provisions of paragraph (3)(B) shall not apply) unless, pursuant to a designation made by the decedent's executor, there is 1 person—

(i) who is an individual citizen of the United States or a domestic corporation and is responsible for filing all returns of tax imposed under paragraph (1) with respect to such trusts and for paying all tax so imposed, and

(ii) who meets such requirements as the Secretary may by regulations prescribe.

(3) Certain lifetime distributions exempt from tax.—

(A) Income distributions.—No tax shall be imposed by paragraph (1)(A) on any distribution of income to the surviving spouse.

(B) Hardship exemption.—No tax shall be imposed by paragraph (1)(A) on any distribution to the surviving spouse on account of hardship.

(4) Tax where trust ceases to qualify.—If any qualified domestic trust ceases to meet the requirements of paragraphs (1) and (2) of subsection (a), the tax imposed by paragraph (1) shall apply as if the surviving spouse died on the date of such cessation.

(5) Due date.—

(A) Tax on distributions.—The estate tax imposed by paragraph (1)(A) shall be due and payable on the 15th day of the 4th month following the calendar year in which the taxable event occurs; except that the estate tax imposed by paragraph (1)(A) on distributions during the calendar year in which the surviving spouse dies shall be due and payable not later than the date on which the estate tax imposed by paragraph (1)(B) is due and payable.

(B) Tax at death of spouse.—The estate tax imposed by paragraph (1)(B) shall be due and payable on the date 9 months after the date of such death.

(6) Liability for tax.—Each trustee shall be personally liable for the amount of the tax imposed by paragraph (1). Rules similar to the rules of section 2204 shall apply for purposes of the preceding sentence.

(7) Treatment of tax.—For purposes of section 2056(d), any tax paid under paragraph (1) shall be treated as a tax paid under section 2001 with respect to the estate of the decedent.

(8) Lien for tax.—For purposes of section 6324, any tax imposed by paragraph (1) shall be treated as an estate tax imposed under this chapter with respect to a decedent dying on the date of the taxable event (and the property involved shall be treated as the gross estate of such decedent).

(9) Taxable event.—The term "taxable event" means the event resulting in tax being imposed under paragraph (1).

(10) Certain benefits allowed.—

(A) In general.—If any property remaining in the qualified domestic trust on the date of the death of the surviving spouse is includible in the gross estate of such spouse for purposes of this chapter (or would be includible if such spouse were a citizen or resident of the United States), any benefit which is allowable (or would be allowable if such spouse were a citizen or resident of the United States) with respect to such property to the estate of such spouse under section 2014, 2032, 2032A, 2055, 2056, 2058 or 6166 shall be allowed for purposes of the tax imposed by paragraph (1)(B).

(B) Section 303.—If the estate of the surviving spouse meets the requirements of section 303 with respect to any property described in subparagraph (A), for purposes of section 303, the tax imposed by paragraph (1)(B) with respect to such property shall be treated as a Federal estate tax payable with respect to the estate of the surviving spouse.

(C) Section 6161(a)(2).—The provisions of section 6161(a)(2) shall apply with respect to the tax imposed by paragraph (1)(B), and the reference in such section to the executor shall be treated as a reference to the trustees of the trust.

(11) Special rule where distribution tax paid out of trust.—For purposes of this subsection, if any portion of the tax imposed by paragraph (1)(A) with respect to any distribution is paid out of the trust, an amount equal to the portion so paid shall be treated as a distribution described in paragraph (1)(A).

(12) Special rule where spouse becomes citizen.—If the surviving spouse of the decedent becomes a citizen of the United States and if—

(A) such spouse was a resident of the United States at all times after the date of the death of the decedent and before such spouse becomes a citizen of the United States,

(B) no tax was imposed by paragraph (1)(A) with respect to any distribution before such spouse becomes such a citizen, or

(C) such spouse elects—

(i) to treat any distribution on which tax was imposed by paragraph (1)(A) as a taxable gift made by such spouse for purposes of—

(I) section 2001, and

(II) determining the amount of the tax imposed by section 2501 on actual taxable gifts made by such spouse during the year in which the spouse becomes a citizen or any subsequent year, and

(ii) to treat any reduction in the tax imposed by paragraph (1)(A) by reason of the credit allowable under section 2010 with respect to the decedent as a credit allowable to such surviving spouse under section 2505 for purposes of determining the amount of the credit allowable under section 2505 with respect to taxable gifts made by the surviving spouse during the year in which the spouse becomes a citizen or any subsequent year,

paragraph (1)(A) shall not apply to any distributions after such spouse becomes such a citizen (and paragraph (1)(B) shall not apply).

(13) Coordination with section 1015.—For purposes of section 1015, any distribution on which tax is imposed by paragraph (1)(A) shall be treated as a transfer by gift, and any tax paid under paragraph (1)(A) shall be treated as a gift tax.

(14) Coordination with terminable interest rules.—Any interest in a qualified domestic trust shall not be treated as failing to meet the requirements of paragraph (5) or (7) of section 2056(b) merely by reason of any provision of the trust instrument permitting the withholding from any distribution of an amount to pay the tax imposed by paragraph (1) on such distribution.

(15) No tax on certain distributions.—No tax shall be imposed by paragraph (1) on any distribution to the surviving spouse to the extent such distribution is to reimburse such surviving spouse for any tax imposed by subtitle A on any item of income of the trust to which such surviving spouse is not entitled under the terms of the trust.

(c) Definitions.—For purposes of this section—

(1) Property includes interest therein.—The term "property" includes an interest in property.

(2) Income.—The term "income" has the meaning given to such term by section 643(b).

(3) Trust.—To the extent provided in regulations prescribed by the Secretary, the term "trust" includes other arrangements which have substantially the same effect as a trust.

(d) Election.—An election under this section with respect to any trust shall be made by the executor on the return of the tax imposed by section 2001. Such an election, once made, shall be irrevocable. No election may be made under this section on any return if such return is filed more than one year after the time prescribed by law (including extensions) for filing such return.

(e) Regulations.—The Secretary shall prescribe such regulations as may be necessary or appropriate to carry out the purposes of this section, including regulations under which there may be treated as a qualified domestic trust any annuity or other payment which is includible in the decedent's gross estate and is by its terms payable for life or a term of years.

§ 2058. State death taxes

(a) Allowance of deduction.—For purposes of the tax imposed by section 2001, the value of the taxable estate shall be determined by deducting from the value of the gross estate the amount of any estate, inheritance, legacy, or succession taxes actually paid to any State or the District of Columbia, in respect of any property included in the gross estate (not including any such taxes paid with respect to the estate of a person other than the decedent).

(b) Period of limitations.—The deduction allowed by this section shall include only such taxes as were actually paid and deduction therefor claimed before the later of—

(1) 4 years after the filing of the return required by section 6018, or

(2) if—

(A) a petition for redetermination of a deficiency has been filed with the Tax Court within the time prescribed in section 6213(a), the expiration of 60 days after the decision of the Tax Court becomes final,

(B) an extension of time has been granted under section 6161 or 6166 for payment of the tax shown on the return, or of a deficiency, the date of the expiration of the period of the extension, or

(C) a claim for refund or credit of an overpayment of tax imposed by this chapter has been filed within the time prescribed in section 6511, the latest of the expiration of—

(i) 60 days from the date of mailing by certified mail or registered mail by the Secretary to the taxpayer of a notice of the disallowance of any part of such claim,

(ii) 60 days after a decision by any court of competent jurisdiction becomes final with respect to a timely suit instituted upon such claim, or

(iii) 2 years after a notice of the waiver of disallowance is filed under section 6532(a)(3).

Notwithstanding sections 6511 and 6512, refund based on the deduction may be made if the claim for refund is filed within the period provided in the preceding sentence. Any such refund shall be made without interest.

SUBCHAPTER C—MISCELLANEOUS

§ 2203. Definition of executor

The term "executor" wherever it is used in this title in connection with the estate tax imposed by this chapter means the executor or administrator of the decedent, or, if there is no executor or administrator appointed, qualified, and acting within the United States, then any person in actual or constructive possession of any property of the decedent.

§ 2204. Discharge of fiduciary from personal liability

(a) General rule.—If the executor makes written application to the Secretary for determination of the amount of the tax and discharge from personal liability therefor, the Secretary (as soon as possible, and in any event within 9 months after the making of such application, or, if the application is made before the return is filed, then within 9 months after the return is filed, but not after the expiration of the period prescribed for the assessment of the tax in section 6501) shall notify the executor of the amount of the tax. The executor, on payment of the amount of which he is notified (other than any amount the time for payment of which is extended under section 6161, 6163, or 6166), and on furnishing any bond which may be required for any amount for which the time for payment is extended, shall be discharged from personal liability for any deficiency in tax thereafter found to be due and shall be entitled to a receipt or writing showing such discharge.

(b) Fiduciary other than the executor.—If a fiduciary (not including a fiduciary in respect of the estate of a nonresident decedent) other than the executor makes written application to the Secretary for determination of the amount of any estate tax for which the fiduciary may be personally liable, and for discharge from personal liability therefor, the Secretary upon the discharge of the executor from personal liability under subsection (a), or upon the expiration of 6 months after the making of such application by the fiduciary, if later, shall notify the fiduciary (1) of the amount of such tax for which it has been determined the fiduciary is liable, or (2) that it has been determined that the fiduciary is not liable for any such tax. Such application shall be accompanied by a copy of the instrument, if any, under which such fiduciary is acting, a description of the property held by the fiduciary, and such other information for purposes of carrying out the provisions of this section as the Secretary may require by regulations. On payment of the amount of such tax for which it has been determined the fiduciary is liable (other than any amount the time for payment of which has been extended under section 6161, 6163, or 6166), and on furnishing any bond which may be required for any amount for which the time for payment has been extended, or on receipt by him of notification of a determination that he is not liable for any such tax, the fiduciary shall be discharged from personal liability for any deficiency in such tax thereafter found to be due and shall be entitled to a receipt or writing evidencing such discharge.

* * *

(d) Good faith reliance on gift tax returns.—If the executor in good faith relies on gift tax returns furnished under section 6103(e)(3) for determining the decedent's adjusted taxable gifts, the executor shall be discharged from personal liability with respect to any deficiency of the tax imposed by this chapter which is attributable to adjusted taxable gifts which—

(1) are made more than 3 years before the date of the decedent's death, and

(2) are not shown on such returns.

§ 2205. Reimbursement out of estate

If the tax or any part thereof is paid by, or collected out of, that part of the estate passing to or in the possession of any person other than the executor in his capacity as such, such person shall be entitled to reimbursement out of any part of the estate still undistributed or by a just and equitable contribution by the persons whose interest in the estate of the decedent would have been reduced if the tax had been paid before the distribution of the estate or whose interest is subject to equal or prior liability for the payment of taxes, debts, or other charges against the estate, it being the purpose and intent of this chapter that so far as is practicable and unless otherwise directed by the will of the decedent the tax shall be paid out of the estate before its distribution.

§ 2206. Liability of life insurance beneficiaries

Unless the decedent directs otherwise in his will, if any part of the gross estate on which tax has been paid consists of proceeds of policies of insurance on the life of the decedent receivable by a beneficiary other than the executor, the executor shall be entitled to recover from such beneficiary such portion of the total tax paid as the proceeds of such policies bear to the taxable estate. If there is more than one such beneficiary, the executor shall be entitled to recover from such beneficiaries in the same ratio. In the case of such proceeds receivable by the surviving spouse of the decedent for which a deduction is allowed under section 2056 (relating to marital deduction), this section shall not apply to such proceeds except as to the amount thereof in excess of the aggregate amount of the marital deductions allowed under such section.

§ 2207. Liability of recipient of property over which decedent had power of appointment

Unless the decedent directs otherwise in his will, if any part of the gross estate on which the tax has been paid consists of the value of property included in the gross estate under section 2041, the executor shall be entitled to recover from the person receiving such property by reason of the exercise, nonexercise, or release of a power of appointment such portion of the total tax paid as the value of such property bears to the taxable estate. If there is more than one such person, the executor shall be entitled to recover from such persons in the same ratio. In the case of such property received by the surviving spouse of the decedent for which a deduction is allowed under section 2056 (relating to marital deduction), this section shall not apply to such property except as to the value thereof reduced by an amount equal to the excess of the aggregate amount of the marital deductions allowed under section 2056 over the amount of proceeds of insurance upon the life of the decedent receivable by the surviving spouse for which proceeds a marital deduction is allowed under such section.

§ 2207A. Right of recovery in the case of certain marital deduction property

(a) Recovery with respect to estate tax.—

(1) In general.—If any part of the gross estate consists of property the value of which is includible in the gross estate by reason of section 2044 (relating to certain property for which marital deduction was previously allowed), the decedent's estate shall be entitled to recover from the person receiving the property the amount by which—

(A) the total tax under this chapter which has been paid, exceeds

(B) the total tax under this chapter which would have been payable if the value of such property had not been included in the gross estate.

(2) Decedent may otherwise direct.—Paragraph (1) shall not apply with respect to any property to the extent that the decedent in his will (or a revocable trust) specifically indicates an intent to waive any right of recovery under this subchapter with respect to such property.

(b) Recovery with respect to gift tax.—If for any calendar year tax is paid under chapter 12 with respect to any person by reason of property treated as transferred by such person under section 2519, such person shall be entitled to recover from the person receiving the property the amount by which—

(1) the total tax for such year under chapter 12, exceeds

(2) the total tax which would have been payable under such chapter for such year if the value of such property had not been taken into account for purposes of chapter 12.

(c) More than one recipient of property.—For purposes of this section, if there is more than one person receiving the property, the right of recovery shall be against each such person.

(d) Taxes and interest.—In the case of penalties and interest attributable to additional taxes described in subsections (a) and (b), rules similar to subsections (a), (b), and (c) shall apply.

§ 2207B. Right of recovery where decedent retained interest

(a) Estate tax.—

(1) In general.—If any part of the gross estate on which tax has been paid consists of the value of property included in the gross estate by reason of section 2036 (relating to transfers with retained life estate), the decedent's estate shall be entitled to recover from the person receiving the property the amount which bears the same ratio to the total tax under this chapter which has been paid as—

(A) the value of such property, bears to

(B) the taxable estate.

(2) Decedent may otherwise direct.—Paragraph (1) shall not apply with respect to any property to the extent that the decedent in his will (or a revocable trust) specifically indicates an intent to waive any right of recovery under this subchapter with respect to such property.

(b) More than one recipient.—For purposes of this section, if there is more than 1 person receiving the property, the right of recovery shall be against each such person.

(c) Penalties and interest.—In the case of penalties and interest attributable to the additional taxes described in subsection (a), rules similar to the rules of subsections (a) and (b) shall apply.

(d) No right of recovery against charitable remainder trusts.—No person shall be entitled to recover any amount by reason of this section from a trust to which section 664 applies (determined without regard to this section).

CHAPTER 12—GIFT TAX

Subchapter
A. Determination of tax liability.
B. Transfers.
C. Deductions.

SUBCHAPTER A—DETERMINATION OF TAX LIABILITY

§ 2501. Imposition of tax

(a) Taxable transfers.—

(1) General rule.—A tax, computed as provided in section 2502, is hereby imposed for each calendar year on the transfer of property by gift during such calendar year by any individual, resident or nonresident.

* * *

(4) Transfers to political organizations.—Paragraph (1) shall not apply to the transfer of money or other property to a political organization (within the meaning of section 527(e)(1)) for the use of such organization.

* * *

(d) Cross references.—

(1) For increase in basis of property acquired by gift for gift tax paid, see section 1015(d).

* * *

§ 2502. Rate of tax

(a) Computation of tax.—The tax imposed by section 2501 for each calendar year shall be an amount equal to the excess of—

(1) a tentative tax, computed under section 2001(c), on the aggregate sum of the taxable gifts for such calendar year and for each of the preceding calendar periods, over

(2) a tentative tax, computed under such section, on the aggregate sum of the taxable gifts for each of the preceding calendar periods.

(b) Preceding calendar period.—Whenever used in this title in "connection with the gift" tax imposed by this chapter, the term preceding calendar period means—

(1) calendar years 1932 and 1970 and all calendar years intervening between calendar year 1932 and calendar year 1970,

(2) the first calendar quarter of calendar year 1971 and all calendar quarters intervening between such calendar quarter and the first calendar quarter of calendar year 1982, and

(3) all calendar years after 1981 and before the calendar year for which the tax is being computed.

For purposes of paragraph (1), the term "calendar year 1932" includes only that portion of such year after June 6, 1932.

(c) Tax to be paid by donor.—The tax imposed by section 2501 shall be paid by the donor.

§ 2503. Taxable gifts

(a) General definition.—The term "taxable gifts" means the total amount of gifts made during the calendar year, less the deductions provided in subchapter C (section 2522 and following).

(b) Exclusion from gifts.—

(1) In general.—In the case of gifts (other than gifts of future interests in property) made to any person by the donor during the calendar year, the first $10,000 of such gifts to such person shall not, for purposes of subsection (a), be included in the total amount of gifts made during such year. Where there has been a transfer to any person of a present interest in property, the possibility that such interest may be diminished by the exercise of a power shall be disregarded in applying this subsection, if no part of such interest will at any time pass to any other person.

(2) Inflation adjustment.—In the case of gifts made in a calendar year after 1998, the $10,000 amount contained in paragraph (1) shall be increased by an amount equal to—

(A) $10,000, multiplied by

(B) the cost-of-living adjustment determined under section 1(f)(3) for such calendar year by substituting "calendar year 1997" for "calendar year 1992" in subparagraph (B) thereof.

If any amount as adjusted under the preceding sentence is not a multiple of $1,000, such amount shall be rounded to the next lowest multiple of $1,000.

(c) Transfer for the benefit of minor.—No part of a gift to an individual who has not attained the age of 21 years on the date of such transfer shall be considered a gift of a future interest in property for purposes of subsection (b) if the property and the income therefrom—

(1) may be expended by, or for the benefit of, the donee before his attaining the age of 21 years, and

(2) will to the extent not so expended—

(A) pass to the donee on his attaining the age of 21 years, and

(B) in the event the donee dies before attaining the age of 21 years, be payable to the estate of the donee or as he may appoint under a general power of appointment as defined in section 2514(c).

[(d) Repealed.]

(e) Exclusion for certain transfers for educational expenses or medical expenses.—

(1) In general.—Any qualified transfer shall not be treated as a transfer of property by gift for purposes of this chapter.

(2) Qualified transfer.—For purposes of this subsection, the term "qualified transfer" means any amount paid on behalf of an individual—

(A) as tuition to an educational organization described in section 170(b)(1)(A)(ii) for the education or training of such individual, or

(B) to any person who provides medical care (as defined in section 213(d)) with respect to such individual as payment for such medical care.

(f) Waiver of certain pension rights.—If any individual waives, before the death of a participant, any survivor benefit, or right to such benefit, under section 401(a)(11) or 417, such waiver shall not be treated as a transfer of property by gift for purposes of this chapter.

(g) Treatment of certain loans of artworks.—

(1) In general.—For purposes of this subtitle, any loan of a qualified work of art shall not be treated as a transfer (and the value of such qualified work of art shall be determined as if such loan had not been made) if—

(A) such loan is to an organization described in section 501(c)(3) and exempt from tax under section 501(c) (other than a private foundation), and

(B) the use of such work by such organization is related to the purpose or function constituting the basis for its exemption under section 501.

(2) Definitions.—For purposes of this section—

(A) Qualified work of art.—The term "qualified work of art" means any archaeological, historic, or creative tangible personal property.

* * *

§ 2504. Taxable gifts for preceding calendar periods

(a) In general.—In computing taxable gifts for preceding calendar periods for purposes of computing the tax for any calendar year—

(1) there shall be treated as gifts such transfers as were considered to be gifts under the gift tax laws applicable to the calendar period in which the transfers were made,

(2) there shall be allowed such deductions as were provided for under such laws, and

(3) the specific exemption in the amount (if any) allowable under section 2521 (as in effect before its repeal by the Tax Reform Act of 1976) shall be applied in all computations in respect of preceding calendar periods ending before January 1, 1977, for purposes of computing the tax for any calendar year.

(b) Exclusions from gifts for preceding calendar periods.—In the case of gifts made to any person by the donor during preceding calendar periods, the amount excluded, if any, by the provisions of gift tax laws applicable to the periods in which the gifts were made shall not, for purposes of subsection (a), be included in the total amount of the gifts made during such preceding calendar periods.

(c) Valuation of gifts.—If the time has expired under section 6501 within which a tax may be assessed under this chapter 12 (or under corresponding provisions of prior laws) on.—

(1) the transfer of property by gift made during a preceding calendar period (as defined in section 2502(b)); or

(2) an increase in taxable gifts required under section 2701(d),

the value thereof shall, for purposes of computing the tax under this chapter, be the value as finally determined (within the meaning of section 2001(f)(2)) for purposes of this chapter.

(d) Net gifts.—The term "net gifts" as used in corresponding provisions of prior laws shall be read as "taxable gifts" for purposes of this chapter.

§ 2505. Unified credit against gift tax

(a) General rule.—In the case of a citizen or resident of the United States, there shall be allowed as a credit against the tax imposed by section 2501 for each calendar year an amount equal to—

(1) the applicable credit amount in effect under section 2010(c) which would apply if the donor died as of the end of the calendar year, reduced by

(2) the sum of the amounts allowable as a credit to the individual under this section for all preceding calendar periods.

For purposes of applying paragraph (2) for any calendar year, the rates of tax in effect under section 2502(a)(2) for such calendar year shall, in lieu of the rates of tax in effect for preceding calendar periods, be used in determining the amounts allowable as a credit under this section for all preceding calendar periods.

(b) Adjustment to credit for certain gifts made before 1977.—The amount allowable under subsection (a) shall be reduced by an amount equal to 20 percent of the aggregate amount allowed as a specific exemption under section 2521 (as in effect before its repeal by the Tax Reform Act of 1976) with respect to gifts made by the individual after September 8, 1976.

(c) Limitation based on amount of tax.—The amount of the credit allowed under subsection (a) for any calendar year shall not exceed the amount of the tax imposed by section 2501 for such calendar year.

SUBCHAPTER B—TRANSFERS

§ 2511. Transfers in general

(a) Scope.—Subject to the limitations contained in this chapter, the tax imposed by section 2501 shall apply whether the transfer is in trust or otherwise, whether the gift is direct or indirect, and whether the property is real or personal, tangible or intangible; but in the case of a nonresident not a citizen of the United States, shall apply to a transfer only if the property is situated within the United States.

* * *

§ 2512. Valuation of gifts

(a) If the gift is made in property, the value thereof at the date of the gift shall be considered the amount of the gift.

(b) Where property is transferred for less than an adequate and full consideration in money or money's worth, then the amount by which the value of the property exceeded the value of the consideration shall be deemed a gift, and shall be included in computing the amount of gifts made during the calendar year.

(c) Cross reference.—

For individual's right to be furnished on request a statement regarding any valuation made by the Secretary of a gift by that individual, see section 7517.

§ 2513. Gift by husband or wife to third party

(a) Considered as made one-half by each.—

(1) In general.—A gift made by one spouse to any person other than his spouse shall, for the purposes of this chapter, be considered as made one-half by him and one-half by his spouse, but only if at the time of the gift each spouse is a citizen or resident of the United States. This paragraph shall not apply with respect to a gift by a spouse of an interest in property if he creates in his spouse a general power of appointment, as defined in section 2514(c), over such interest. For purposes of this section, an individual shall be considered as the spouse of another individual only if he is married to such individual at the time of the gift and does not remarry during the remainder of the calendar year.

(2) Consent of both spouses.—Paragraph (1) shall apply only if both spouses have signified (under the regulations provided for in subsection (b)) their consent to the application of paragraph (1) in the case of all such gifts made during the calendar year by either while married to the other.

(b) Manner and time of signifying consent.—

(1) Manner.—A consent under this section shall be signified in such manner as is provided under regulations prescribed by the Secretary.

(2) Time.—Such consent may be so signified at any time after the close of the calendar year in which the gift was made, subject to the following limitations—

(A) The consent may not be signified after the 15th day of April following the close of such year, unless before such 15th day no return has been filed for such year by either spouse, in which case the consent may not be signified after a return for such year is filed by either spouse.

(B) The consent may not be signified after a notice of deficiency with respect to the tax for such year has been sent to either spouse in accordance with section 6212(a).

(c) Revocation of consent.—Revocation of a consent previously signified shall be made in such manner as is provided under regulations prescribed by the Secretary, but the right to revoke a consent previously signified with respect to a calendar year—

(1) shall not exist after the 15th day of April following the close of such year if the consent was signified on or before such 15th day; and

(2) shall not exist if the consent was not signified until after such 15th day.

(d) Joint and several liability for tax.—If the consent required by subsection (a)(2) is signified with respect to a gift made in any calendar year, the liability with respect to the entire tax imposed by this chapter of each spouse for such year shall be joint and several.

§ 2514. Powers of appointment

(a) Powers created on or before October 21, 1942.—An exercise of a general power of appointment created on or before October 21, 1942, shall be deemed a transfer of property by the individual possessing such power; but the failure to exercise such a power or the complete release of such a power shall not be deemed an exercise thereof. If a general power of appointment created on or before October 21, 1942, has been partially released so that it is no longer a general power of appointment, the subsequent exercise of such power shall not be deemed to be the exercise of a general power of appointment if—

(1) such partial release occurred before November 1, 1951, or

(2) the donee of such power was under a legal disability to release such power on October 21, 1942, and such partial release occurred not later than six months after the termination of such legal disability.

(b) Powers created after October 21, 1942.—The exercise or release of a general power of appointment created after October 21, 1942, shall be deemed a transfer of property by the individual possessing such power.

(c) Definition of general power of appointment.—For purposes of this section, the term "general power of appointment" means a power which is exercisable in favor of the individual possessing the power (hereafter in this subsection referred to as the "possessor"), his estate, his creditors, or the creditors of his estate; except that—

(1) A power to consume, invade, or appropriate property for the benefit of the possessor which is limited by an ascertainable standard relating to the health, education, support, or maintenance of the possessor shall not be deemed a general power of appointment.

(2) A power of appointment created on or before October 21, 1942, which is exercisable by the possessor only in conjunction with another person shall not be deemed a general power of appointment.

(3) In the case of a power of appointment created after October 21, 1942, which is exercisable by the possessor only in conjunction with another person—

(A) if the power is not exercisable by the possessor except in conjunction with the creator of the power—such power shall not be deemed a general power of appointment;

(B) if the power is not exercisable by the possessor except in conjunction with a person having a substantial interest, in the property subject to the power, which is adverse to exercise of the power in favor of the possessor—such power shall not be deemed a general power of appointment. For the purposes of this subparagraph a person who, after the death of the possessor, may be possessed of a power of appointment (with respect to the property subject to the possessor's power) which he may exercise in his own favor shall be deemed as having an interest in the property and such interest shall be deemed adverse to such exercise of the possessor's power;

(C) if (after the application of subparagraphs (A) and (B)) the power is a general power of appointment and is exercisable in favor of such other person—such power shall be deemed a general power of appointment only in respect of a fractional part of the property subject to such power, such part to be determined by dividing the value of such property by the number of such persons (including the possessor) in favor of whom such power is exercisable.

For purposes of subparagraphs (B) and (C), a power shall be deemed to be exercisable in favor of a person if it is exercisable in favor of such person, his estate, his creditors, or the creditors of his estate.

(d) Creation of another power in certain cases.—If a power of appointment created after October 21, 1942, is exercised by creating another power of appointment which, under the applicable local law, can be validly exercised so as to postpone the vesting of any estate or interest in the property which was subject to the first power, or suspend the absolute ownership or power of alienation of such property, for a period ascertainable without regard to the date of the creation of the first power, such exercise of the first power shall, to the extent of the property subject to the second power, be deemed a transfer of property by the individual possessing such power.

(e) Lapse of power.—The lapse of a power of appointment created after October 21, 1942, during the life of the individual possessing the power shall be considered a release of such power. The rule of the preceding sentence shall apply with respect to the lapse of powers during any calendar year only to the extent that the property which could have been appointed by exercise of such lapsed powers exceeds in value the greater of the following amounts:

(1) $5,000, or

(2) 5 percent of the aggregate value of the assets out of which, or the proceeds of which, the exercise of the lapsed powers could be satisfied.

* * *

§ 2515. Treatment of generation-skipping transfer tax

In the case of any taxable gift which is a direct skip (within the meaning of chapter 13), the amount of such gift shall be increased by the amount of any tax imposed on the transferor under chapter 13 with respect to such gift.

§ 2516. Certain property settlements

Where husband and wife enter into a written agreement relative to their marital and property rights and divorce occurs within the 3–year period beginning on the date 1 year before such agreement is entered into (whether or not such agreement is approved by the divorce decree), any transfers of property or interests in property made pursuant to such agreement—

(1) to either spouse in settlement of his or her marital or property rights, or

(2) to provide a reasonable allowance for the support of issue of the marriage during minority,

shall be deemed to be transfers made for a full and adequate consideration in money or money's worth.

§ 2518. Disclaimers

(a) General rule.—For purposes of this subtitle, if a person makes a qualified disclaimer with respect to any interest in property, this subtitle shall apply with respect to such interest as if the interest had never been transferred to such person.

(b) Qualified disclaimer defined.—For purposes of subsection (a), the term "qualified disclaimer" means an irrevocable and unqualified refusal by a person to accept an interest in property but only if—

(1) such refusal is in writing,

(2) such writing is received by the transferor of the interest, his legal representative, or the holder of the legal title to the property to which the interest relates not later than the date which is 9 months after the later of—

(A) the day on which the transfer creating the interest in such person is made, or

(B) the day on which such person attains age 21,

(3) such person has not accepted the interest or any of its benefits, and

(4) as a result of such refusal, the interest passes without any direction on the part of the person making the disclaimer and passes either—

(A) to the spouse of the decedent, or

(B) to a person other than the person making the disclaimer.

(c) Other rules.—For purposes of subsection (a)—

(1) Disclaimer of undivided portion of interest.—A disclaimer with respect to an undivided portion of an interest which meets the requirements of the preceding sentence shall be treated as a qualified disclaimer of such portion of the interest.

(2) Powers.—A power with respect to property shall be treated as an interest in such property.

(3) Certain transfers treated as disclaimers.—A written transfer of the transferor's entire interest in the property—

(A) which meets requirements similar to the requirements of paragraphs (2) and (3) of subsection (b), and

(B) which is to a person or persons who would have received the property had the transferor made a qualified disclaimer (within the meaning of subsection (b)),

shall be treated as a qualified disclaimer.

§ 2519. Dispositions of certain life estates

(a) General rule.—For purposes of this chapter and chapter 11, any disposition of all or part of a qualifying income interest for life in any property to which this section applies shall be treated as a transfer of all interests in such property other than the qualifying income interest.

(b) Property to which this subsection applies.—This section applies to any property if a deduction was allowed with respect to the transfer of such property to the donor—

(1) under section 2056 by reason of subsection (b)(7) thereof, or

(2) under section 2523 by reason of subsection (f) thereof.

(c) Cross reference.—

For right of recovery for gift tax in the case of property treated as transferred under this section, see section 2207A(b).

SUBCHAPTER C—DEDUCTIONS

§ 2522. Charitable and similar gifts

(a) Citizens or residents.—In computing taxable gifts for the calendar year, there shall be allowed as a deduction in the case of a citizen or resident the amount of all gifts made during such year to or for the use of—

(1) the United States, any State, or any political subdivision thereof, or the District of Columbia, for exclusively public purposes;

(2) a corporation, or trust, or community chest, fund, or foundation, organized and operated exclusively for religious, charitable, scientific, literary, or educational purposes, or to foster national or international amateur sports competition (but only if no part of its activities involve the provision of athletic facilities or equipment), including the encouragement of art and the prevention of cruelty to children or animals, no part of the net earnings of which inures to the benefit of any private shareholder or individual, which is not disqualified for tax exemption under section 501(c)(3) by reason of attempting to influence legislation, and which does not participate in, or intervene in (including the publishing or distributing of statements), any political campaign on behalf of (or in opposition to) any candidate for public office;

(3) a fraternal society, order, or association, operating under the lodge system, but only if such gifts are to be used exclusively for religious, charitable, scientific, literary, or educational purposes, including the encouragement of art and the prevention of cruelty to children or animals;

(4) posts or organizations of war veterans, or auxiliary units or societies of any such posts or organizations, if such posts, organizations, units, or societies are organized in the United States or any of its possessions, and if no part of their net earnings inures to the benefit of any private shareholder or individual.

* * *

* * *

(c) Disallowance of deductions in certain cases.—

* * *

(2) Where a donor transfers an interest in property (other than an interest described in section 170(f)(3)(B)) to a person, or for a use, described in subsection (a) or (b) and an interest in the same property is retained by the donor, or is transferred or has been transferred (for less than an adequate and full consideration in money or money's worth) from the donor to a person, or for a use, not described in subsection (a) or (b), no deduction shall be allowed under this section for the interest which is, or has been transferred to the person, or for the use, described in subsection (a) or (b), unless—

(A) in the case of a remainder interest, such interest is in a trust which is a charitable remainder annuity trust or a charitable remainder unitrust (described in section 664) or a pooled income fund (described in section 642(c)(5)), or

(B) in the case of any other interest, such interest is in the form of a guaranteed annuity or is a fixed percentage distributed yearly of the fair market value of the property (to be determined yearly).

* * *

(d) Special rule for irrevocable transfers of easements in real property.—A deduction shall be allowed under subsection (a) in respect of any transfer of a qualified real property interest (as defined in section 170(h)(2)(C)) which meets the requirements of section 170(h) (without regard to paragraph (4)(A) thereof).

(e) Special rules for fractional gifts.—

(1) Denial of deduction in certain cases.—

(A) In general.—No deduction shall be allowed for a contribution of an undivided portion of a taxpayer's entire interest in tangible personal property unless all interests in the property are held immediately before such contribution by—

(i) the taxpayer, or

(ii) the taxpayer and the donee.

(B) Exceptions.—The Secretary may, by regulation, provide for exceptions to subparagraph (A) in cases where all persons who hold an interest in the property make proportional contributions of an undivided portion of the entire interest held by such persons.

* * *

§ 2523. Gift to spouse

(a) Allowance of deduction.—Where a donor transfers during the calendar year by gift an interest in property to a donee who at the time of the gift is the donor's spouse, there shall be allowed as a deduction in computing taxable gifts for the calendar year an amount with respect to such interest equal to its value.

(b) Life estate or other terminable interest.—Where, on the lapse of time, on the occurrence of an event or contingency, or on the failure of an event or contingency to occur, such interest transferred to the spouse will terminate or fail, no deduction shall be allowed with respect to such interest—

(1) if the donor retains in himself, or transfers or has transferred (for less than an adequate and full consideration in money or money's worth) to any person other than such donee spouse (or the estate of such spouse), an interest in such property, and if by reason of such retention or transfer the donor (or his heirs or assigns) or such person (or his heirs or assigns) may possess or enjoy any part of such property after such termination or failure of the interest transferred to the donee spouse; or

(2) if the donor immediately after the transfer to the donee spouse has a power to appoint an interest in such property which he can exercise (either alone or in conjunction with any person) in such manner that the appointee may possess or enjoy any part of such property after such termination or failure of the interest transferred to the donee spouse. For purposes of this paragraph, the donor shall be considered as having immediately after the transfer to the donee spouse such power to appoint even though such power cannot be exercised until after the lapse of time, upon the occurrence of an event or contingency, or on the failure of an event or contingency to occur.

An exercise or release at any time by the donor, either alone or in conjunction with any person, of a power to appoint an interest in property, even though not otherwise a transfer, shall, for purposes of paragraph (1), be considered as a transfer by him. Except as provided in subsection (e), where at the time of the transfer it is impossible to ascertain the particular person or persons who may receive from the donor an interest in property so transferred by him, such interest shall, for purposes of paragraph (1), be considered as transferred to a person other than the donee spouse.

(c) Interest in unidentified assets.—Where the assets out of which, or the proceeds of which, the interest transferred to the donee spouse may be satisfied include a particular asset or assets with respect to which no deduction would be allowed if such asset or assets were transferred from the donor to such spouse, then the value of the interest transferred to such spouse shall, for purposes of subsection (a), be reduced by the aggregate value of such particular assets.

(d) Joint interests.—If the interest is transferred to the donee spouse as sole joint tenant with the donor or as tenant by the entirety, the interest of the donor in the property which exists solely by reason of the possibility that the donor may survive the donee spouse, or that there may occur a severance of the tenancy, shall not be considered for purposes of subsection (b) as an interest retained by the donor in himself.

(e) Life estate with power of appointment in donee spouse.—Where the donor transfers an interest in property, if by such transfer his spouse is entitled for life to all of the income from the entire interest, or all the income from a specific portion thereof, payable annually or at more frequent intervals, with power in the donee spouse to appoint the entire interest, or such specific portion (exercisable in favor of such donee spouse, or of the estate of such donee spouse, or in favor of either, whether or not in each case the power is exercisable in favor of others), and with no power in any other person to appoint any part of such interest, or such portion, to any person other than the donee spouse—

(1) the interest, or such portion, so transferred shall, for purposes of subsection (a) be considered as transferred to the donee spouse, and

(2) no part of the interest, or such portion, so transferred shall, for purposes of subsection (b)(1), be considered as retained in the donor or transferred to any person other than the donee spouse.

This subsection shall apply only if, by such transfer, such power in the donee spouse to appoint the interest, or such portion, whether exercisable by will or during life, is exercisable by such spouse alone and in all events. For purposes of this subsection, the term "specific portion" only includes a portion determined on a fractional or percentage basis.

(f) Election with respect to life estate for donee spouse.—

(1) In general.—In the case of qualified terminable interest property—

(A) for purposes of subsection (a), such property shall be treated as transferred to the donee spouse, and

(B) for purposes of subsection (b)(1), no part of such property shall be considered as retained in the donor or transferred to any person other than the donee spouse.

(2) Qualified terminable interest property.—For purposes of this subsection, the term "qualified terminable interest property" means any property—

(A) which is transferred by the donor spouse,

(B) in which the donee spouse has a qualifying income interest for life, and

(C) to which an election under this subsection applies.

(3) Certain rules made applicable.—For purposes of this subsection, rules similar to the rules of clauses (ii), (iii), and (iv) of section 2056(b)(7)(B) shall apply and the rules of section 2056(b)(10) shall apply.

(4) Election.—

(A) Time and manner.—An election under this subsection with respect to any property shall be made on or before the date prescribed by section 6075(b) for filing a gift tax return with respect to the transfer (determined without regard to section 6019(2)) and shall be made in such manner as the Secretary shall by regulations prescribe.

(B) Election irrevocable.—An election under this subsection, once made, shall be irrevocable.

(5) Treatment of interest retained by donor spouse.—

(A) In general.—In the case of any qualified terminable interest property—

(i) such property shall not be includible in the gross estate of the donor spouse, and

(ii) any subsequent transfer by the donor spouse of an interest in such property shall not be treated as a transfer for purposes of this chapter.

(B) Subparagraph (A) not to apply after transfer by donee spouse.— Subparagraph (A) shall not apply with respect to any property after the donee spouse is treated as having transferred such property under section 2519, or such property is includible in the donee spouse's gross estate under section 2044.

(6) Treatment of joint and survivor annuities.—In the case of a joint and survivor annuity where only the donor spouse and donee spouse have the right to receive payments before the death of the last spouse to die—

(A) the donee spouse's interest shall be treated as a qualifying income interest for life,

(B) the donor spouse shall be treated as having made an election under this subsection with respect to such annuity unless the donor spouse otherwise elects on or before the date specified in paragraph (4)(A),

(C) paragraph (5) and section 2519 shall not apply to the donor spouse's interest in the annuity, and

(D) if the donee spouse dies before the donor spouse, no amount shall be includible in the gross estate of the donee spouse under section 2044 with respect to such annuity.

An election under subparagraph (B), once made, shall be irrevocable.

(g) Special rule for charitable remainder trusts.—

(1) In general.—If, after the transfer, the donee spouse is the only noncharitable beneficiary (other than the donor) of a qualified charitable remainder trust, subsection (b) shall not apply to the interest in such trust which is transferred to the donee spouse.

(2) Definitions.—For purposes of paragraph (1), the terms "noncharitable beneficiary" and "qualified charitable remainder trust" have the meanings given to such terms by section 2056(b)(8)(B).

(h) Denial of double deduction.—Nothing in this section or any other provision of this chapter shall allow the value of any interest in property to be deducted under this chapter more than once with respect to the same donor.

(i) Disallowance of marital deduction where spouse not citizen.—If the spouse of the donor is not a citizen of the United States—

(1) no deduction shall be allowed under this section,

(2) section 2503(b) shall be applied with respect to gifts which are made by the donor to such spouse and with respect to which a deduction would be allowable under this section but for paragraph (1) by substituting "$100,000" for "$10,000", and

(3) the principles of sections 2515 and 2515A (as such sections were in effect before their repeal by the Economic Recovery Tax Act of 1981) shall apply, except that the provisions of such section 2515 providing for an election shall not apply.

This subsection shall not apply to any transfer resulting from the acquisition of rights under a joint and survivor annuity described in subsection (f)(6).

§ 2524. Extent of deductions

The deductions provided in sections 2522 and 2523 shall be allowed only to the extent that the gifts therein specified are included in the amount of gifts against which such deductions are applied.

CHAPTER 13—TAX ON GENERATION-SKIPPING TRANSFERS

SUBCHAPTER A—TAX IMPOSED

§ 2601. Tax imposed

A tax is hereby imposed on every generation-skipping transfer (within the meaning of subchapter B).

§ 2602. Amount of tax

The amount of the tax imposed by section 2601 is—

(1) the taxable amount (determined under subchapter C), multiplied by

(2) the applicable rate (determined under subchapter E).

§ 2603. Liability for tax

(a) Personal liability.—

(1) Taxable distributions.—In the case of a taxable distribution, the tax imposed by section 2601 shall be paid by the transferee.

(2) Taxable termination.—In the case of a taxable termination or a direct skip from a trust, the tax shall be paid by the trustee.

(3) Direct skip.—In the case of a direct skip (other than a direct skip from a trust), the tax shall be paid by the transferor.

(b) Source of tax.—Unless otherwise directed pursuant to the governing instrument by specific reference to the tax imposed by this chapter, the tax imposed by this chapter on a generation-skipping transfer shall be charged to the property constituting such transfer.

(c) Cross reference.—

For provisions making estate and gift tax provisions with respect to transferee liability, liens, and related matters applicable to the tax imposed by section 2601, see section 2661.

SUBCHAPTER B—GENERATION–SKIPPING TRANSFERS

§ 2611. Generation-skipping transfer defined

(a) In general.—For purposes of this chapter, the term "generation-skipping transfer" means—

(1) a taxable distribution,

(2) a taxable termination, and

(3) a direct skip.

(b) Certain transfers excluded.—The term "generation-skipping transfer" does not include—

(1) any transfer which, if made inter vivos by an individual, would not be treated as a taxable gift by reason of section 2503(e) (relating to exclusion of certain transfers for educational or medical expenses), and

(2) any transfer to the extent—

(A) the property transferred was subject to a prior tax imposed under this chapter,

(B) the transferee in the prior transfer was assigned to the same generation as (or a lower generation than) the generation assignment of the transferee in this transfer, and

(C) such transfers do not have the effect of avoiding tax under this chapter with respect to any transfer.

§ 2612. Taxable termination; taxable distribution; direct skip

(a) Taxable termination.—

(1) General rule.—For purposes of this chapter, the term "taxable termination" means the termination (by death, lapse of time, release of power, or otherwise) of an interest in property held in a trust unless—

(A) immediately after such termination, a non-skip person has an interest in such property, or

(B) at no time after such termination may a distribution (including distributions on termination) be made from such trust to a skip person.

(2) Certain partial terminations treated as taxable.—If, upon the termination of an interest in property held in trust by reason of the death of a lineal descendant of the transferor, a specified portion of the trust's assets are distributed to 1 or more skip persons (or 1 or more trusts for the exclusive benefit of such persons), such termination shall constitute a taxable termination with respect to such portion of the trust property.

(b) Taxable distribution.—For purposes of this chapter, the term "taxable distribution" means any distribution from a trust to a skip person (other than a taxable termination or a direct skip).

(c) Direct skip.—For purposes of this chapter—

(1) In general.—The term "direct skip" means a transfer subject to a tax imposed by chapter 11 or 12 of an interest in property to a skip person.

(2) Look–thru rules not to apply.—Solely for purposes of determining whether any transfer to a trust is a direct skip, the rules of section 2651(f)(2) shall not apply.

§ 2613. Skip person and non-skip person defined

(a) Skip person.—For purposes of this chapter, the term "skip person" means—

(1) a natural person assigned to a generation which is 2 or more generations below the generation assignment of the transferor, or

(2) a trust—

(A) if all interests in such trust are held by skip persons, or

(B) if—

(i) there is no person holding an interest in such trust, and

(ii) at no time after such transfer may a distribution (including distributions on termination) be made from such trust to a non-skip person.

(b) Non-skip person.—For purposes of this chapter, the term "non-skip person" means any person who is not a skip person.

SUBCHAPTER C—TAXABLE AMOUNT

§ 2621. Taxable amount in case of taxable distribution

(a) In general.—For purposes of this chapter, the taxable amount in the case of any taxable distribution shall be—

(1) the value of the property received by the transferee, reduced by

(2) any expense incurred by the transferee in connection with the determination, collection, or refund of the tax imposed by this chapter with respect to such distribution.

(b) Payment of GST tax treated as taxable distribution.—For purposes of this chapter, if any of the tax imposed by this chapter with respect to any taxable distribution is paid out of the trust, an amount equal to the portion so paid shall be treated as a taxable distribution.

§ 2622. Taxable amount in case of taxable termination

(a) In general.—For purposes of this chapter, the taxable amount in the case of a taxable termination shall be—

(1) the value of all property with respect to which the taxable termination has occurred, reduced by

(2) any deduction allowed under subsection (b).

(b) Deduction for certain expenses.—For purposes of subsection (a), there shall be allowed a deduction similar to the deduction allowed by section 2053 (relating to expenses, indebtedness, and taxes) for amounts attributable to the property with respect to which the taxable termination has occurred.

§ 2623. Taxable amount in case of direct skip

For purposes of this chapter, the taxable amount in the case of a direct skip shall be the value of the property received by the transferee.

§ 2624. Valuation

(a) General rule.—Except as otherwise provided in this chapter, property shall be valued as of the time of the generation-skipping transfer.

(b) Alternate valuation and special use valuation elections apply to certain direct skips.—In the case of any direct skip of property which is included in the transferor's gross estate, the value of such property for purposes of this chapter shall be the same as its value for purposes of chapter 11 (determined with regard to sections 2032 and 2032A).

(c) Alternate valuation election permitted in the case of taxable terminations occurring at death.—If 1 or more taxable terminations with respect to the same trust occur at the same time as and as a result of the death of an individual, an election may be made to value all of the property included in such terminations in accordance with section 2032.

(d) Reduction for consideration provided by transferee.—For purposes of this chapter, the value of the property transferred shall be reduced by the amount of any consideration provided by the transferee.

SUBCHAPTER D—GST EXEMPTION

§ 2631. GST exemption

(a) General rule.—For purposes of determining the inclusion ratio, every individual shall be allowed a GST exemption amount which may be allocated by such individual (or his executor) to any property with respect to which such individual is the transferor.

(b) Allocations irrevocable.—Any allocation under subsection (a), once made, shall be irrevocable.

(c) GST exemption amount.—For purposes of subsection (a), the GST exemption amount for any calendar year shall be equal to the basic exclusion amount under section 2010(c) for such calendar year.

§ 2632. Special rules for allocation of GST exemption

(a) Time and manner of allocation.—

(1) Time.—Any allocation by an individual of his GST exemption under section 2631(a) may be made at any time on or before the date prescribed for filing the estate tax return for such individual's estate (determined with regard to extensions), regardless of whether such a return is required to be filed.

(2) Manner.—The Secretary shall prescribe by forms or regulations the manner in which any allocation referred to in paragraph (1) is to be made.

(b) Deemed allocation to certain lifetime direct skips.—

(1) In general.—If any individual makes a direct skip during his lifetime, any unused portion of such individual's GST exemption shall be allocated to the property transferred to the extent necessary to make the inclusion ratio for such property zero. If the amount of the direct skip exceeds such unused portion, the entire unused portion shall be allocated to the property transferred.

(2) Unused portion.—For purposes of paragraph (1), the unused portion of an individual's GST exemption is that portion of such exemption which has not previously been allocated by such individual (or treated as allocated under paragraph (1) or subsection (c)(1)).

(3) Subsection not to apply in certain cases.—An individual may elect to have this subsection not apply to a transfer.

(c) Deemed allocation to certain lifetime transfers to GST trusts.—

(1) In general.—If any individual makes an indirect skip during such individual's lifetime, any unused portion of such individual's GST exemption shall be allocated to the property transferred to the extent necessary to make the inclusion ratio for such property zero. If the amount of the indirect skip exceeds such unused portion, the entire unused portion shall be allocated to the property transferred.

(2) Unused portion.—For purposes of paragraph (1), the unused portion of an individual's GST exemption is that portion of such exemption which has not previously been—

(A) allocated by such individual,

(B) treated as allocated under subsection (b) with respect to a direct skip occurring during or before the calendar year in which the indirect skip is made, or

(C) treated as allocated under paragraph (1) with respect to a prior indirect skip.

(3) Definitions.—

(A) Indirect skip.—For purposes of this subsection, the term "indirect skip" means any transfer of property (other than a direct skip) subject to the tax imposed by chapter 12 made to a GST trust.

(B) GST trust.—The term "GST trust" means a trust that could have a generation-skipping transfer with respect to the transferor unless—

(i) the trust instrument provides that more than 25 percent of the trust corpus must be distributed to or may be withdrawn by one or more individuals who are non-skip persons—

(I) before the date that the individual attains age 46,

(II) on or before one or more dates specified in the trust instrument that will occur before the date that such individual attains age 46, or

(III) upon the occurrence of an event that, in accordance with regulations prescribed by the Secretary, may reasonably be expected to occur before the date that such individual attains age 46,

(ii) the trust instrument provides that more than 25 percent of the trust corpus must be distributed to or may be withdrawn by one or more individuals who are non-skip persons and who are living on the date of death of another person identified in the instrument (by name or by class) who is more than 10 years older than such individuals,

(iii) the trust instrument provides that, if one or more individuals who are non-skip persons die on or before a date or event described in clause (i) or (ii), more than 25 percent of the trust corpus either must be distributed to the estate or estates of one or more of such individuals or is subject to a general power of appointment exercisable by one or more of such individuals,

(iv) the trust is a trust any portion of which would be included in the gross estate of a non-skip person (other than the transferor) if such person died immediately after the transfer,

(v) the trust is a charitable lead annuity trust (within the meaning of section 2642(e)(3)(A)) or a charitable remainder annuity trust or a charitable remainder unitrust (within the meaning of section 664(d)), or

(vi) the trust is a trust with respect to which a deduction was allowed under section 2522 for the amount of an interest in the form of the right to receive annual payments of a fixed percentage of the net fair market value of the trust property (determined yearly) and which is required to pay principal to a non-skip person if such person is alive when the yearly payments for which the deduction was allowed terminate.

For purposes of this subparagraph, the value of transferred property shall not be considered to be includible in the gross estate of a non-skip person or subject to a right of withdrawal by reason of such person holding a right to withdraw so much of such property as does not exceed the amount referred to in section 2503(b) with respect to any transferor, and it shall be assumed that powers of appointment held by non-skip persons will not be exercised.

(4) Automatic allocations to certain GST trusts.—For purposes of this subsection, an indirect skip to which section 2642(f) applies shall be deemed to have been made only at the close of the estate tax inclusion period. The fair market value of such transfer shall be the fair market value of the trust property at the close of the estate tax inclusion period.

(5) Applicability and effect.—

(A) In general.—An individual—

(i) may elect to have this subsection not apply to—

(I) an indirect skip, or

(II) any or all transfers made by such individual to a particular trust, and

(ii) may elect to treat any trust as a GST trust for purposes of this subsection with respect to any or all transfers made by such individual to such trust.

(B) Elections.—

(i) Elections with respect to indirect skips.—An election under subparagraph (A)(i)(I) shall be deemed to be timely if filed on a timely filed gift tax return for the calendar year in which the transfer was made or deemed to have been made pursuant to paragraph (4) or on such later date or dates as may be prescribed by the Secretary.

(ii) Other elections.—An election under clause (i)(II) or (ii) of subparagraph (A) may be made on a timely filed gift tax return for the calendar year for which the election is to become effective.

(d) Retroactive allocations.—

(1) In general.—If—

(A) a non-skip person has an interest or a future interest in a trust to which any transfer has been made,

(B) such person—

(i) is a lineal descendant of a grandparent of the transferor or of a grandparent of the transferor's spouse or former spouse, and

(ii) is assigned to a generation below the generation assignment of the transferor, and

(C) such person predeceases the transferor,

then the transferor may make an allocation of any of such transferor's unused GST exemption to any previous transfer or transfers to the trust on a chronological basis.

(2) Special rules.—If the allocation under paragraph (1) by the transferor is made on a gift tax return filed on or before the date prescribed by section 6075(b) for gifts made within the calendar year within which the non-skip person's death occurred—

(A) the value of such transfer or transfers for purposes of section 2642(a) shall be determined as if such allocation had been made on a timely filed gift tax return for each calendar year within which each transfer was made,

(B) such allocation shall be effective immediately before such death, and

(C) the amount of the transferor's unused GST exemption available to be allocated shall be determined immediately before such death.

(3) Future interest.—For purposes of this subsection, a person has a future interest in a trust if the trust may permit income or corpus to be paid to such person on a date or dates in the future.

(e) Allocation of unused GST exemption.—

(1) In general.—Any portion of an individual's GST exemption which has not been allocated within the time prescribed by subsection (a) shall be deemed to be allocated as follows—

(A) first, to property which is the subject of a direct skip occurring at such individual's death, and

(B) second, to trusts with respect to which such individual is the transferor and from which a taxable distribution or a taxable termination might occur at or after such individual's death.

(2) Allocation within categories.—

(A) In general.—The allocation under paragraph (1) shall be made among the properties described in subparagraph (A) thereof and the trusts described in subparagraph (B) thereof, as the case may be, in proportion to the respective amounts (at the time of allocation) of the nonexempt portions of such properties or trusts.

(B) Nonexempt portion.—For purposes of subparagraph (A), the term "nonexempt portion" means the value (at the time of allocation) of the property or trust, multiplied by the inclusion ratio with respect to such property or trust.

SUBCHAPTER E—APPLICABLE RATE; INCLUSION RATIO

§ 2641. Applicable rate

(a) General rule.—For purposes of this chapter, the term "applicable rate" means, with respect to any generation-skipping transfer, the product of—

(1) the maximum Federal estate tax rate, and

(2) the inclusion ratio with respect to the transfer.

(b) Maximum federal estate tax rate.—For purposes of subsection (a), the term "maximum Federal estate tax rate" means the maximum rate imposed by section 2001 on the estates of decedents dying at the time of the taxable distribution, taxable termination, or direct skip, as the case may be.

§ 2642. Inclusion ratio

(a) Inclusion ratio defined.—For purposes of this chapter—

(1) In general.—Except as otherwise provided in this section, the inclusion ratio with respect to any property transferred in a generation-skipping transfer shall be the excess (if any) of 1 over—

(A) except as provided in subparagraph (B), the applicable fraction determined for the trust from which such transfer is made, or

(B) in the case of a direct skip, the applicable fraction determined for such skip.

(2) Applicable fraction.—For purposes of paragraph (1), the applicable fraction is a fraction—

(A) the numerator of which is the amount of the GST exemption allocated to the trust (or in the case of a direct skip, allocated to the property transferred in such skip), and

(B) the denominator of which is—

(i) the value of the property transferred to the trust (or involved in the direct skip), reduced by

(ii) the sum of—

(I) any Federal estate tax or State death tax actually recovered from the trust attributable to such property, and

(II) any charitable deduction allowed under section 2055 or 2522 with respect to such property.

Except as provided in paragraphs (3) and (4) of subsection (b), the value determined under subparagraph (B)(i) shall be of the property as of the time of the transfer to the trust (or the direct skip).

(3) Severing of trusts.—

(A) In general.—If a trust is severed in a qualified severance, the trusts resulting from such severance shall be treated as separate trusts thereafter for purposes of this chapter.

(B) Qualified severance.—For purposes of subparagraph (A)—

(i) In general.—The term "qualified severance" means the division of a single trust and the creation (by any means available under the governing instrument or under local law) of two or more trusts if—

(I) the single trust was divided on a fractional basis, and

(II) the terms of the new trusts, in the aggregate, provide for the same succession of interests of beneficiaries as are provided in the original trust.

(ii) Trusts with inclusion ratio greater than zero.—If a trust has an inclusion ratio of greater than zero and less than 1, a severance is a qualified severance only if the single trust is divided into two trusts, one of which receives a fractional share of the total value of all trust assets equal to the applicable fraction of the single trust immediately before the severance. In such case, the trust receiving such fractional share shall have an inclusion ratio of zero and the other trust shall have an inclusion ratio of 1.

(iii) Regulations.—The term "qualified severance" includes any other severance permitted under regulations prescribed by the Secretary.

(C) Timing and manner of severances.—A severance pursuant to this paragraph may be made at any time. The Secretary shall prescribe by forms or regulations the manner in which the qualified severance shall be reported to the Secretary.

(b) Valuation rules, etc.—Except as provided in subsection (f)—

(1) Gifts for which gift tax return filed or deemed allocation made.—If the allocation of the GST exemption to any transfers of property is made on a gift tax return filed on or before the date prescribed by section 6075(b) for such transfer or is deemed to be made under section 2632 (b)(1) or (c)(1)—

(A) the value of such property for purposes of subsection (a) shall be its value as finally determined for purposes of chapter 12 (within the meaning of section 2001(f)(2)), or, in the case of an allocation deemed to have been made at the close of an estate tax inclusion period, its value at the time of the close of the estate tax inclusion period, and

(B) such allocation shall be effective on and after the date of such transfer, or, in the case of an allocation deemed to have been made at the close of an estate tax inclusion period, on and after the close of such estate tax inclusion period.

(2) Transfers and allocations at or after death.—

(A) Transfers at death.—If property is transferred as a result of the death of the transferor, the value of such property for purposes of subsection (a) shall be its value as finally determined for purposes of chapter 11; except that, if the requirements prescribed by the Secretary respecting allocation of post-death changes in value are not met, the value of such property shall be determined as of the time of the distribution concerned.

(B) Allocations to property transferred at death of transferor.—Any allocation to property transferred as a result of the death of the transferor shall be effective on and after the date of the death of the transferor.

(3) Allocations to inter vivos transfers not made on timely filed gift tax return.—If any allocation of the GST exemption to any property not transferred as a result of the death of the transferor is not made on a gift tax return filed on or before the date prescribed by section 6075(b) and is not deemed to be made under section 2632(b)(1)—

(A) the value of such property for purposes of subsection (a) shall be determined as of the time such allocation is filed with the Secretary, and

(B) such allocation shall be effective on and after the date on which such allocation is filed with the Secretary.

(4) QTIP trusts.—If the value of property is included in the estate of a spouse by virtue of section 2044, and if such spouse is treated as the transferor of such property under section 2652(a), the value of such property for purposes of subsection (a) shall be its value for purposes of chapter 11 in the estate of such spouse.

(c) Treatment of certain direct skips which are nontaxable gifts.—

(1) In general.—In the case of a direct skip which is a nontaxable gift, the inclusion ratio shall be zero.

(2) Exception for certain transfers in trust.—Paragraph (1) shall not apply to any transfer to a trust for the benefit of an individual unless—

(A) during the life of such individual, no portion of the corpus or income of the trust may be distributed to (or for the benefit of) any person other than such individual, and

(B) if the trust does not terminate before the individual dies, the assets of such trust will be includible in the gross estate of such individual.

Rules similar to the rules of section 2652(c)(3) shall apply for purposes of subparagraph (A).

(3) Nontaxable gift.—For purposes of this subsection, the term "nontaxable gift" means any transfer of property to the extent such transfer is not treated as a taxable gift by reason of—

(A) section 2503(b) (taking into account the application of section 2513), or

(B) section 2503(e).

(d) Special rules where more than 1 transfer made to trust.—

(1) In general.—If a transfer of property is made to a trust in existence before such transfer, the applicable fraction for such trust shall be recomputed as of the time of such transfer in the manner provided in paragraph (2).

(2) Applicable fraction.—In the case of any such transfer, the recomputed applicable fraction is a fraction—

(A) the numerator of which is the sum of—

(i) the amount of the GST exemption allocated to property involved in such transfer, plus

(ii) the nontax portion of such trust immediately before such transfer, and

(B) the denominator of which is the sum of—

(i) the value of the property involved in such transfer reduced by the sum of—

(I) any Federal estate tax or State death tax actually recovered from the trust attributable to such property, and

(II) any charitable deduction allowed under section 2055 or 2522 with respect to such property, and

(ii) the value of all of the property in the trust (immediately before such transfer).

(3) Nontax portion.—For purposes of paragraph (2), the term "nontax portion" means the product of—

(A) the value of all of the property in the trust, and

(B) the applicable fraction in effect for such trust.

(4) Similar recomputation in case of certain late allocations.—If—

(A) any allocation of the GST exemption to property transferred to a trust is not made on a timely filed gift tax return required by section 6019, and

(B) there was a previous allocation with respect to property transferred to such trust,

the applicable fraction for such trust shall be recomputed as of the time of such allocation under rules similar to the rules of paragraph (2).

(e) Special rules for charitable lead annuity trusts.—

(1) In general.—For purposes of determining the inclusion ratio for any charitable lead annuity trust, the applicable fraction shall be a fraction—

(A) the numerator of which is the adjusted GST exemption, and

(B) the denominator of which is the value of all of the property in such trust immediately after the termination of the charitable lead annuity.

(2) Adjusted GST exemption.—For purposes of paragraph (1), the adjusted GST exemption is an amount equal to the GST exemption allocated to the trust increased by interest determined—

(A) at the interest rate used in determining the amount of the deduction under section 2055 or 2522 (as the case may be) for the charitable lead annuity, and

(B) for the actual period of the charitable lead annuity.

(3) Definitions.—For purposes of this subsection—

(A) Charitable lead annuity trust.—The term "charitable lead annuity trust" means any trust in which there is a charitable lead annuity.

(B) Charitable lead annuity.—The term "charitable lead annuity" means any interest in the form of a guaranteed annuity with respect to which a deduction was allowed under section 2055 or 2522 (as the case may be).

(4) Coordination with subsection (d).—Under regulations, appropriate adjustments shall be made in the application of subsection (d) to take into account the provisions of this subsection.

(f) Special rules for certain inter vivos transfers.—Except as provided in regulations—

(1) In general.—For purposes of determining the inclusion ratio, if—

(A) an individual makes an inter vivos transfer of property, and

(B) the value of such property would be includible in the gross estate of such individual under chapter 11 if such individual died immediately after making such transfer (other than by reason of section 2035),

any allocation of GST exemption to such property shall not be made before the close of the estate tax inclusion period (and the value of such property shall be determined under paragraph (2)). If such transfer is a direct skip, such skip shall be treated as occurring as of the close of the estate tax inclusion period.

(2) Valuation.—In the case of any property to which paragraph (1) applies, the value of such property shall be—

(A) if such property is includible in the gross estate of the transferor (other than by reason of section 2035), its value for purposes of chapter 11, or

(B) if subparagraph (A) does not apply, its value as of the close of the estate tax inclusion period (or, if any allocation of GST exemption to such property is not made on a timely filed gift tax return for the calendar year in which such period ends, its value as of the time such allocation is filed with the Secretary).

(3) Estate tax inclusion period.—For purposes of this subsection, the term "estate tax inclusion period" means any period after the transfer described in paragraph (1) during which the value of the property involved in such transfer would be includible in the gross estate of the transferor under chapter 11 if he died. Such period shall in no event extend beyond the earlier of—

(A) the date on which there is a generation-skipping transfer with respect to such property, or

(B) the date of the death of the transferor.

(4) Treatment of spouse.—Except as provided in regulations, any reference in this subsection to an individual or transferor shall be treated as including a reference to the spouse of such individual or transferor.

(5) Coordination with subsection (d).—Under regulations, appropriate adjustments shall be made in the application of subsection (d) to take into account the provisions of this subsection.

(g) Relief provisions.—

(1) Relief from late elections.—

(A) In general.—The Secretary shall by regulation prescribe such circumstances and procedures under which extensions of time will be granted to make—

(i) an allocation of GST exemption described in paragraph (1) or (2) of subsection (b), and

(ii) an election under subsection (b)(3) or (c)(5) of section 2632.

Such regulations shall include procedures for requesting comparable relief with respect to transfers made before the date of the enactment of this paragraph.

(B) Basis for determinations.—In determining whether to grant relief under this paragraph, the Secretary shall take into account all relevant circumstances, including evidence of intent contained in the trust instrument or instrument of transfer and such other factors as the Secretary deems relevant. For purposes of determining whether to grant relief under this paragraph, the time for making the allocation (or election) shall be treated as if not expressly prescribed by statute.

(2) Substantial compliance.—An allocation of GST exemption under section 2632 that demonstrates an intent to have the lowest possible inclusion ratio with respect to a transfer or a trust shall be deemed to be an allocation of so much of the transferor's unused GST exemption as produces the lowest possible inclusion ratio. In determining whether there has been substantial compliance, all relevant circumstances shall be taken into account, including evidence of intent contained in the trust instrument or instrument of transfer and such other factors as the Secretary deems relevant.

SUBCHAPTER F—OTHER DEFINITIONS AND SPECIAL RULES

§ 2651. Generation assignment

(a) In general.—For purposes of this chapter, the generation to which any person (other than the transferor) belongs shall be determined in accordance with the rules set forth in this section.

(b) Lineal descendants.—

(1) In general.—An individual who is a lineal descendant of a grandparent of the transferor shall be assigned to that generation which results from comparing the number of generations between the grandparent and such individual with the number of generations between the grandparent and the transferor.

(2) On spouse's side.—An individual who is a lineal descendant of a grandparent of a spouse (or former spouse) of the transferor (other than such spouse) shall be assigned to that generation which results from comparing the number of generations between such grandparent and such individual with the number of generations between such grandparent and such spouse.

(3) Treatment of legal adoptions, etc.—For purposes of this subsection—

(A) Legal adoptions.—A relationship by legal adoption shall be treated as a relationship by blood.

(B) Relationships by half-blood.—A relationship by the half-blood shall be treated as a relationship of the whole-blood.

(c) Marital relationship.—

(1) Marriage to transferor.—An individual who has been married at any time to the transferor shall be assigned to the transferor's generation.

(2) Marriage to other lineal descendants.—An individual who has been married at any time to an individual described in subsection (b) shall be assigned to the generation of the individual so described.

(d) Persons who are not lineal descendants.—An individual who is not assigned to a generation by reason of the foregoing provisions of this section shall be assigned to a generation on the basis of the date of such individual's birth with—

(1) an individual born not more than 12½ years after the date of the birth of the transferor assigned to the transferor's generation,

(2) an individual born more than 12½ years but not more than 37½ years after the date of the birth of the transferor assigned to the first generation younger than the transferor, and

(3) similar rules for a new generation every 25 years.

(e) Special rule for persons with a deceased parent.—

(1) In general.—For purposes of determining whether any transfer is a generation-skipping transfer, if—

(A) an individual is a descendant of a parent of the transferor (or the transferor's spouse or former spouse), and

(B) such individual's parent who is a lineal descendant of the parent of the transferor (or the transferor's spouse or former spouse) is dead at the time the transfer (from which an interest of such individual is established or derived) is subject to a tax imposed by chapter 11 or 12 upon the transferor (and if there shall be more than 1 such time, then at the earliest such time),

such individual shall be treated as if such individual were a member of the generation which is 1 generation below the lower of the transferor's generation or the generation assignment of the youngest living ancestor of such individual who is also a descendant of the parent of the transferor (or the transferor's spouse or former spouse), and the generation assignment of any descendant of such individual shall be adjusted accordingly.

(2) Limited application of subsection to collateral heirs.—This subsection shall not apply with respect to a transfer to any individual who is not a lineal descendant of the transferor (or the transferor's spouse or former spouse) if, at the time of the transfer, such transferor has any living lineal descendant.

(f) Other special rules.—

(1) Individuals assigned to more than 1 generation.—Except as provided in regulations, an individual who, but for this subsection, would be assigned to more than 1 generation shall be assigned to the youngest such generation.

(2) Interests through entities.—Except as provided in paragraph (3), if an estate, trust, partnership, corporation, or other entity has an interest in property, each individual having a beneficial interest in such entity shall be treated as having an interest in such property and shall be assigned to a generation under the foregoing provisions of this subsection.

(3) Treatment of certain charitable organizations and governmental entities.—Any—

(A) organization described in section 511(a)(2),

(B) charitable trust described in section 511(b)(2), and

(C) governmental entity,

shall be assigned to the transferor's generation.

§ 2652. Other definitions

(a) Transferor.—For purposes of this chapter—

(1) In general.—Except as provided in this subsection or section 2653(a), the term "transferor" means—

(A) in the case of any property subject to the tax imposed by chapter 11, the decedent, and

(B) in the case of any property subject to the tax imposed by chapter 12, the donor.

An individual shall be treated as transferring any property with respect to which such individual is the transferor.

(2) Gift-splitting by married couples.—If, under section 2513, one-half of a gift is treated as made by an individual and one-half of such gift is treated as made by the spouse of such individual, such gift shall be so treated for purposes of this chapter.

(3) Special election for qualified terminable interest property.—In the case of—

(A) any trust with respect to which a deduction is allowed to the decedent under section 2056 by reason of subsection (b)(7) thereof, and

(B) any trust with respect to which a deduction to the donor spouse is allowed under section 2523 by reason of subsection (f) thereof,

the estate of the decedent or the donor spouse, as the case may be, may elect to treat all of the property in such trust for purposes of this chapter as if the election to be treated as qualified terminable interest property had not been made.

(b) Trust and trustee.—

(1) Trust.—The term "trust" includes any arrangement (other than an estate) which, although not a trust, has substantially the same effect as a trust.

(2) Trustee.—In the case of an arrangement which is not a trust but which is treated as a trust under this subsection, the term "trustee" shall mean the person in actual or constructive possession of the property subject to such arrangement.

(3) Examples.—Arrangements to which this subsection applies include arrangements involving life estates and remainders, estates for years, and insurance and annuity contracts.

(c) Interest.—

(1) In general.—A person has an interest in property held in trust if (at the time the determination is made) such person—

(A) has a right (other than a future right) to receive income or corpus from the trust,

(B) is a permissible current recipient of income or corpus from the trust and is not described in section 2055(a), or

(C) is described in section 2055(a) and the trust is—

(i) a charitable remainder annuity trust,

(ii) a charitable remainder unitrust within the meaning of section 664, or

(iii) a pooled income fund within the meaning of section 642(c)(5).

(2) Certain interests disregarded.—For purposes of paragraph (1), an interest which is used primarily to postpone or avoid any tax imposed by this chapter shall be disregarded.

(3) Certain support obligations disregarded.—The fact that income or corpus of the trust may be used to satisfy an obligation of support arising under State law shall be disregarded in determining whether a person has an interest in the trust, if—

(A) such use is discretionary, or

(B) such use is pursuant to the provisions of any State law substantially equivalent to the Uniform Gifts to Minors Act.

(d) Executor.—For purposes of this chapter, the term "executor" has the meaning given such term by section 2203.

§ 2653. Taxation of multiple skips

(a) General rule.—For purposes of this chapter, if—

(1) there is a generation-skipping transfer of any property, and

(2) immediately after such transfer such property is held in trust,

for purposes of applying this chapter (other than section 2651) to subsequent transfers from the portion of such trust attributable to such property, the trust will be treated as if the transferor of such property were assigned to the first generation above the highest generation of any person who has an interest in such trust immediately after the transfer.

(b) Trust retains inclusion ratio.—

(1) In general.—Except as provided in paragraph (2), the provisions of subsection (a) shall not affect the inclusion ratio determined with respect to any trust. Under regulations prescribed by the Secretary, notwithstanding the preceding sentence, proper adjustment shall be made to the inclusion ratio with respect to such trust to take into account any tax under this chapter borne by such trust which is imposed by this chapter on the transfer described in subsection (a).

(2) Special rule for pour-over trust.—

(A) In general.—If the generation-skipping transfer referred to in subsection (a) involves the transfer of property from 1 trust to another trust (hereinafter in this paragraph referred to as the "pour-over trust"), the inclusion ratio for the pour-over trust shall be determined by treating the nontax portion of such distribution as if it were a part of a GST exemption allocated to such trust.

(B) Nontax portion.—For purposes of subparagraph (A), the nontax portion of any distribution is the amount of such distribution multiplied by the applicable fraction which applies to such distribution.

§ 2654. Special rules

(a) Basis adjustment.—

(1) In general.—Except as provided in paragraph (2), if property is transferred in a generation-skipping transfer, the basis of such property shall be increased (but not above the fair market value of such property) by an amount equal to that portion of the tax imposed by section 2601 (computed without regard to section 2604) with respect to the transfer which is attributable to the excess of the fair market value of such property over its adjusted basis immediately before the transfer. The preceding shall be applied after any basis adjustment under section 1015 with respect to the transfer.

(2) Certain transfers at death.—If property is transferred in a taxable termination which occurs at the same time as and as a result of the death of an individual, the basis of such property shall be adjusted in a manner similar to the manner provided under section 1014(a); except that, if the inclusion ratio with respect to such property is less than 1, any increase or decrease in basis shall be limited by multiplying such increase or decrease (as the case may be) by the inclusion ratio.

(b) Certain trusts treated as separate trusts.—For purposes of this chapter—

(1) the portions of a trust attributable to transfers from different transferors shall be treated as separate trusts, and

(2) substantially separate and independent shares of different beneficiaries in a trust shall be treated as separate trusts.

Except as provided in the preceding sentence, nothing in this chapter shall be construed as authorizing a single trust to be treated as 2 or more trusts. For purposes of this subsection, a trust shall be treated as part of an estate during any period that the trust is so treated under section 645.

(c) Disclaimers.—

For provisions relating to the effect of a qualified disclaimer for purposes of this chapter, see section 2518.

(d) Limitation on personal liability of trustee.—A trustee shall not be personally liable for any increase in the tax imposed by section 2601 which is attributable to the fact that—

(1) section 2642(c) (relating to exemption of certain nontaxable gifts) does not apply to a transfer to the trust which was made during the life of the transferor and for which a gift tax return was not filed, or

(2) the inclusion ratio with respect to the trust is greater than the amount of such ratio as computed on the basis of the return on which was made (or was deemed made) an allocation of the GST exemption to property transferred to such trust.

The preceding sentence shall not apply if the trustee has knowledge of facts sufficient reasonably to conclude that a gift tax return was required to be filed or that the inclusion ratio was erroneous.

SUBCHAPTER G—ADMINISTRATION

§ 2661. Administration

Insofar as applicable and not inconsistent with the provisions of this chapter—

(1) except as provided in paragraph (2), all provisions of subtitle F (including penalties) applicable to the gift tax, to chapter 12, or to section 2501, are hereby made applicable in respect of the generation-skipping transfer tax, this chapter, or section 2601, as the case may be, and

(2) in the case of a generation-skipping transfer occurring at the same time as and as a result of the death of an individual, all provisions of subtitle F (including penalties) applicable to the estate tax, to chapter 11, or to section 2001 are hereby made applicable in respect of the generation-skipping transfer tax, this chapter, or section 2601 (as the case may be).

§ 2662. Return requirements

(a) In general.—The Secretary shall prescribe by regulations the person who is required to make the return with respect to the tax imposed by this chapter and the time by which any such return must be filed. To the extent practicable, such regulations shall provide that—

(1) the person who is required to make such return shall be the person liable under section 2603(a) for payment of such tax, and

(2) the return shall be filed—

(A) in the case of a direct skip (other than from a trust), on or before the date on which an estate or gift tax return is required to be filed with respect to the transfer, and

(B) in all other cases, on or before the 15th day of the 4th month after the close of the taxable year of the person required to make such return in which such transfer occurs.

(b) Information returns.—The Secretary may by regulations require a return to be filed containing such information as he determines to be necessary for purposes of this chapter.

§ 2663. Regulations

The Secretary shall prescribe such regulations as may be necessary or appropriate to carry out the purposes of this chapter, including—

(1) such regulations as may be necessary to coordinate the provisions of this chapter with the recapture tax imposed under section 2032A(c),

(2) regulations (consistent with the principles of chapters 11 and 12) providing for the application of this chapter in the case of transferors who are nonresidents not citizens of the United States, and

(3) regulations providing for such adjustments as may be necessary to the application of this chapter in the case of any arrangement which, although not a trust, is treated as a trust under section 2652(b).

CHAPTER 14—SPECIAL VALUATION RULES

§ 2701. Special valuation rules in case of transfers of certain interests in corporations or partnerships

(a) Valuation rules.—

(1) In general.—Solely for purposes of determining whether a transfer of an interest in a corporation or partnership to (or for the benefit of) a member of the transferor's family is a gift (and the value of such transfer), the value of any right—

(A) which is described in subparagraph (A) or (B) of subsection (b)(1), and

(B) which is with respect to any applicable retained interest that is held by the transferor or an applicable family member immediately after the transfer,

shall be determined under paragraph (3). This paragraph shall not apply to the transfer of any interest for which market quotations are readily available (as of the date of transfer) on an established securities market.

(2) Exceptions for marketable retained interests, etc.—Paragraph (1) shall not apply to any right with respect to an applicable retained interest if—

(A) market quotations are readily available (as of the date of the transfer) for such interest on an established securities market,

(B) such interest is of the same class as the transferred interest, or

(C) such interest is proportionally the same as the transferred interest, without regard to nonlapsing differences in voting power (or, for a partnership, nonlapsing differences with respect to management and limitations on liability).

Subparagraph (C) shall not apply to any interest in a partnership if the transferor or an applicable family member has the right to alter the liability of the transferee of the transferred property. Except as provided by the Secretary, any difference described in subparagraph (C) which lapses by reason of any Federal or State law shall be treated as a nonlapsing difference for purposes of such subparagraph.

(3) Valuation of rights to which paragraph (1) applies.—

(A) In general.—The value of any right described in paragraph (1), other than a distribution right which consists of a right to receive a qualified payment, shall be treated as being zero.

(B) Valuation of certain qualified payments.—If—

(i) any applicable retained interest confers a distribution right which consists of the right to a qualified payment, and

(ii) there are 1 or more liquidation, put, call, or conversion rights with respect to such interest,

the value of all such rights shall be determined as if each liquidation, put, call, or conversion right were exercised in the manner resulting in the lowest value being determined for all such rights.

(C) Valuation of qualified payments where no liquidation, etc. rights.—In the case of an applicable retained interest which is described in subparagraph (B)(i) but not subparagraph (B)(ii), the value of the distribution right shall be determined without regard to this section.

(4) Minimum valuation of junior equity.—

(A) In general.—In the case of a transfer described in paragraph (1) of a junior equity interest in a corporation or partnership, such interest shall in no event be valued at an amount less than the value which would be determined if the total value of all of the junior equity interests in the entity were equal to 10 percent of the sum of—

(i) the total value of all of the equity interests in such entity, plus

(ii) the total amount of indebtedness of such entity to the transferor (or an applicable family member).

(B) Definitions.—For purposes of this paragraph—

(i) Junior equity interest.—The term "junior equity interest" means common stock or, in the case of a partnership, any partnership interest under which the rights as to income and capital (or, to the extent provided in regulations, the rights as to either income or capital) are junior to the rights of all other classes of equity interests.

(ii) Equity interest.—The term "equity interest" means stock or any interest as a partner, as the case may be.

(b) Applicable retained interests.—For purposes of this section—

(1) In general.—The term "applicable retained interest" means any interest in an entity with respect to which there is—

(A) a distribution right, but only if, immediately before the transfer described in subsection (a)(1), the transferor and applicable family members hold (after application of subsection (e)(3)) control of the entity, or

(B) a liquidation, put, call, or conversion right.

(2) Control.—For purposes of paragraph (1)—

(A) Corporations.—In the case of a corporation, the term "control" means the holding of at least 50 percent (by vote or value) of the stock of the corporation.

(B) Partnerships.—In the case of a partnership, the term "control" means—

(i) the holding of at least 50 percent of the capital or profits interests in the partnership, or

(ii) in the case of a limited partnership, the holding of any interest as a general partner.

(C) Applicable family member.—For purposes of this subsection, the term "applicable family member" includes any lineal descendant of any parent of the transferor or the transferor's spouse.

(c) Distribution and other rights; qualified payments.—For purposes of this section—

(1) Distribution right.—

(A) In general.—The term "distribution right" means—

(i) a right to distributions from a corporation with respect to its stock, and

(ii) a right to distributions from a partnership with respect to a partner's interest in the partnership.

(B) Exceptions.—The term "distribution right" does not include—

(i) a right to distributions with respect to any interest which is junior to the rights of the transferred interest,

(ii) any liquidation, put, call, or conversion right, or

(iii) any right to receive any guaranteed payment described in section 707(c) of a fixed amount.

(2) Liquidation, etc. rights.—

(A) In general.—The term "liquidation, put, call, or conversion right" means any liquidation, put, call, or conversion right, or any similar right, the exercise or nonexercise of which affects the value of the transferred interest.

(B) Exception for fixed rights.—

(i) In general.—The term "liquidation, put, call, or conversion right" does not include any right which must be exercised at a specific time and at a specific amount.

(ii) Treatment of certain rights.—If a right is assumed to be exercised in a particular manner under subsection (a)(3)(B), such right shall be treated as so exercised for purposes of clause (i).

(C) Exception for certain rights to convert.—The term "liquidation, put, call, or conversion right" does not include any right which—

(i) is a right to convert into a fixed number (or a fixed percentage) of shares of the same class of stock in a corporation as the transferred stock in such corporation under subsection (a)(1) (or stock which would be of the same class but for nonlapsing differences in voting power),

(ii) is nonlapsing,

(iii) is subject to proportionate adjustments for splits, combinations, reclassifications, and similar changes in the capital stock, and

(iv) is subject to adjustments similar to the adjustments under subsection (d) for accumulated but unpaid distributions.

A rule similar to the rule of the preceding sentence shall apply for partnerships.

(3) Qualified payment.—

(A) In general.—Except as otherwise provided in this paragraph, the term "qualified payment" means any dividend payable on a periodic basis under any cumulative preferred stock (or a comparable payment under any partnership interest) to the extent that such dividend (or comparable payment) is determined at a fixed rate.

(B) Treatment of variable rate payments.—For purposes of subparagraph (A), a payment shall be treated as fixed as to rate if such payment is determined at a rate which bears a fixed relationship to a specified market interest rate.

(C) Elections.—

(i) In general.—Payments under any interest held by a transferor which (without regard to this subparagraph) are qualified payments shall be treated as qualified payments unless the transferor elects not to treat such payments as qualified payments. Payments described in the preceding sentence which are held by an applicable family member shall be treated as qualified payments only if such member elects to treat such payments as qualified payments.

(ii) A transferor or applicable family member holding any distribution right which (without regard to this subparagraph) is not a qualified payment may elect to treat such right as a qualified payment, to be paid in the amounts and at the times specified in such election. The preceding sentence shall apply only to the extent that the amounts and times so specified are not inconsistent with the underlying legal instrument giving rise to such right.

(iii) Elections irrevocable.—Any election under this subparagraph with respect to an interest shall, once made, be irrevocable.

(d) Transfer tax treatment of cumulative but unpaid distributions.—

(1) In general.—If a taxable event occurs with respect to any distribution right to which subsection (a)(3)(B) or (C) applied, the following shall be increased by the amount determined under paragraph (2):

(A) The taxable estate of the transferor in the case of a taxable event described in paragraph (3)(A)(i).

(B) The taxable gifts of the transferor for the calendar year in which the taxable event occurs in the case of a taxable event described in paragraph (3)(A)(ii) or (iii).

(2) Amount of increase.—

(A) In general.—The amount of the increase determined under this paragraph shall be the excess (if any) of—

(i) the value of the qualified payments payable during the period beginning on the date of the transfer under subsection (a)(1) and ending on the date of the taxable event determined as if—

(I) all such payments were paid on the date payment was due, and

(II) all such payments were reinvested by the transferor as of the date of payment at a yield equal to the discount rate used in determining the value of the applicable retained interest described in subsection (a)(1), over

(ii) the value of such payments paid during such period computed under clause (i) on the basis of the time when such payments were actually paid.

(B) Limitation on amount of increase.—

(i) In general.—The amount of the increase under subparagraph (A) shall not exceed the applicable percentage of the excess (if any) of—

(I) the value (determined as of the date of the taxable event) of all equity interests in the entity which are junior to the applicable retained interest, over

(II) the value of such interests (determined as of the date of the transfer to which subsection (a)(1) applied).

(ii) Applicable percentage.—For purposes of clause (i), the applicable percentage is the percentage determined by dividing—

(I) the number of shares in the corporation held (as of the date of the taxable event) by the transferor which are applicable retained interests of the same class, by

(II) the total number of shares in such corporation (as of such date) which are of the same class as the class described in subclause (I).

A similar percentage shall be determined in the case of interests in a partnership.

(iii) Definition.—For purposes of this subparagraph, the term "equity interest" has the meaning given such term by subsection (a)(4)(B).

(C) Grace period.—For purposes of subparagraph (A), any payment of any distribution during the 4–year period beginning on its due date shall be treated as having been made on such due date.

(3) Taxable events.—For purposes of this subsection—

(A) In general.—The term "taxable event" means any of the following:

(i) The death of the transferor if the applicable retained interest conferring the distribution right is includible in the estate of the transferor.

(ii) The transfer of such applicable retained interest.

(iii) At the election of the taxpayer, the payment of any qualified payment after the period described in paragraph (2)(C), but only with respect to such payment.

(B) Exception where spouse is transferee.—

(i) Deathtime transfers.—Subparagraph (A)(i) shall not apply to any interest includible in the gross estate of the transferor if a deduction with respect to such interest is allowable under section 2056 or 2106(a)(3).

(ii) Lifetime transfers.—A transfer to the spouse of the transferor shall not be treated as a taxable event under subparagraph (A)(ii) if such transfer does not result in a taxable gift by reason of—

(I) any deduction allowed under section 2523, or the exclusion under section 2503(b), or

(II) consideration for the transfer provided by the spouse.

(iii) Spouse succeeds to treatment of transferor.—If an event is not treated as a taxable event by reason of this subparagraph, the transferee spouse or surviving spouse (as the case may be) shall be treated in the same manner as the transferor in applying this subsection with respect to the interest involved.

(4) Special rules for applicable family members.—

(A) Family member treated in same manner as transferor.—For purposes of this subsection, an applicable family member shall be treated in the same manner as the transferor with respect to any distribution right retained by such family member to which subsection (a)(3)(B) or (C) applied.

(B) Transfer to applicable family member.—In the case of a taxable event described in paragraph (3)(A)(ii) involving the transfer of an applicable retained interest to an applicable family member (other than the spouse of the transferor), the applicable family member shall be treated in the same manner as the transferor in applying this subsection to distributions accumulating with respect to such interest after such taxable event.

(C) Transfer to transferors.—In the case of a taxable event described in paragraph (3)(A)(ii) involving a transfer of an applicable retained interest from an applicable family member to a transferor, this subsection shall continue to apply to the transferor during any period the transferor holds such interest.

(5) Transfer to include termination.—For purposes of this subsection, any termination of an interest shall be treated as a transfer.

(e) Other definitions and rules.—For purposes of this section—

(1) Member of the family.—The term "member of the family" means, with respect to any transferor—

(A) the transferor's spouse,

(B) a lineal descendant of the transferor or the transferor's spouse, and

(C) the spouse of any such descendant.

(2) Applicable family member.—The term "applicable family member" means, with respect to any transferor—

(A) the transferor's spouse,

(B) an ancestor of the transferor or the transferor's spouse, and

(C) the spouse of any such ancestor.

(3) Attribution of indirect holdings and transfers.—An individual shall be treated as holding any interest to the extent such interest is held indirectly by such individual through a corporation, partnership, trust, or other entity. If any individual is treated as holding any interest by reason of the preceding sentence, any transfer which results in such interest being treated as no longer held by such individual shall be treated as a transfer of such interest.

(4) Effect of adoption.—A relationship by legal adoption shall be treated as a relationship by blood.

(5) Certain changes treated as transfers.—Except as provided in regulations, a contribution to capital or a redemption, recapitalization, or other change in the capital structure of a corporation or partnership shall be treated as a transfer of an interest in such entity to which this section applies if the taxpayer or an applicable family member—

(A) receives an applicable retained interest in such entity pursuant to such transaction, or

(B) under regulations, otherwise holds, immediately after such transaction, an applicable retained interest in such entity.

This paragraph shall not apply to any transaction (other than a contribution to capital) if the interests in the entity held by the transferor, applicable family members, and members of the transferor's family before and after the transaction are substantially identical.

(6) Adjustments.—Under regulations prescribed by the Secretary, if there is any subsequent transfer, or inclusion in the gross estate, of any applicable retained interest which was valued under the rules of subsection (a), appropriate adjustments shall be made for purposes of chapter 11, 12, or 13 to reflect the increase in the amount of any prior taxable gift made by the transferor or decedent by reason of such valuation or to reflect the application of subsection (d).

(7) Treatment as separate interests.—The Secretary may by regulation provide that any applicable retained interest shall be treated as 2 or more separate interests for purposes of this section.

§ 2702. Special valuation rules in case of transfers of interests in trusts

(a) Valuation rules.—

(1) In general.—Solely for purposes of determining whether a transfer of an interest in trust to (or for the benefit of) a member of the transferor's family is a gift (and the value of such transfer), the value of any interest in such trust retained by the transferor or any applicable family member (as defined in section 2701(e)(2)) shall be determined as provided in paragraph (2).

(2) Valuation of retained interests.—

(A) In general.—The value of any retained interest which is not a qualified interest shall be treated as being zero.

(B) Valuation of qualified interest.—The value of any retained interest which is a qualified interest shall be determined under section 7520.

(3) Exceptions.—

(A) In general.—This subsection shall not apply to any transfer—

(i) if such transfer is an incomplete gift,

(ii) if such transfer involves the transfer of an interest in trust all the property in which consists of a residence to be used as a personal residence by persons holding term interests in such trust, or

(iii) to the extent that regulations provide that such transfer is not inconsistent with the purposes of this section.

(B) Incomplete gift.—For purposes of subparagraph (A), the term "incomplete gift" means any transfer which would not be treated as a gift whether or not consideration was received for such transfer.

(b) Qualified interest.—For purposes of this section, the term "qualified interest" means—

(1) any interest which consists of the right to receive fixed amounts payable not less frequently than annually,

(2) any interest which consists of the right to receive amounts which are payable not less frequently than annually and are a fixed percentage of the fair market value of the property in the trust (determined annually), and

(3) any noncontingent remainder interest if all of the other interests in the trust consist of interests described in paragraph (1) or (2).

(c) Certain property treated as held in trust.—For purposes of this section—

(1) In general.—The transfer of an interest in property with respect to which there is 1 or more term interests shall be treated as a transfer of an interest in a trust.

(2) Joint purchases.—If 2 or more members of the same family acquire interests in any property described in paragraph (1) in the same transaction (or a series of related transactions), the person (or persons) acquiring the term interests in such property shall be treated as having acquired the entire property and then transferred to the other persons the interests acquired by such other persons in the transaction (or series of transactions). Such transfer shall be treated as made in exchange for the consideration (if any) provided by such other persons for the acquisition of their interests in such property.

(3) Term interest.—The term "term interest" means—

(A) a life interest in property, or

(B) an interest in property for a term of years.

(4) Valuation rule for certain term interests.—If the nonexercise of rights under a term interest in tangible property would not have a substantial effect on the valuation of the remainder interest in such property—

(A) subparagraph (A) of subsection (a)(2) shall not apply to such term interest, and

(B) the value of such term interest for purposes of applying subsection (a)(1) shall be the amount which the holder of the term interest establishes as the amount for which such interest could be sold to an unrelated third party.

(d) Treatment of transfers of interests in portion of trust.—In the case of a transfer of an income or remainder interest with respect to a specified portion of the property in a trust, only such portion shall be taken into account in applying this section to such transfer.

(e) Member of the family.—For purposes of this section, the term "member of the family" shall have the meaning given such term by section 2704(c)(2).

§ 2703. Certain rights and restrictions disregarded

(a) General rule.—For purposes of this subtitle, the value of any property shall be determined without regard to—

(1) any option, agreement, or other right to acquire or use the property at a price less than the fair market value of the property (without regard to such option, agreement, or right), or

(2) any restriction on the right to sell or use such property.

(b) Exceptions.—Subsection (a) shall not apply to any option, agreement, right, or restriction which meets each of the following requirements:

(1) It is a bona fide business arrangement.

(2) It is not a device to transfer such property to members of the decedent's family for less than full and adequate consideration in money or money's worth.

(3) Its terms are comparable to similar arrangements entered into by persons in an arms' length transaction.

§ 2704. Treatment of certain lapsing rights and restrictions

(a) Treatment of lapsed voting or liquidation rights.—

(1) In general.—For purposes of this subtitle, if—

(A) there is a lapse of any voting or liquidation right in a corporation or partnership, and

(B) the individual holding such right immediately before the lapse and members of such individual's family hold, both before and after the lapse, control of the entity,

such lapse shall be treated as a transfer by such individual by gift, or a transfer which is includible in the gross estate of the decedent, whichever is applicable, in the amount determined under paragraph (2).

(2) Amount of transfer.—For purposes of paragraph (1), the amount determined under this paragraph is the excess (if any) of—

(A) the value of all interests in the entity held by the individual described in paragraph (1) immediately before the lapse (determined as if the voting and liquidation rights were nonlapsing), over

(B) the value of such interests immediately after the lapse.

(3) Similar rights.—The Secretary may by regulations apply this subsection to rights similar to voting and liquidation rights.

(b) Certain restrictions on liquidation disregarded.—

(1) In general.—For purposes of this subtitle, if—

(A) there is a transfer of an interest in a corporation or partnership to (or for the benefit of) a member of the transferor's family, and

(B) the transferor and members of the transferor's family hold, immediately before the transfer, control of the entity,

any applicable restriction shall be disregarded in determining the value of the transferred interest.

(2) Applicable restriction.—For purposes of this subsection, the term "applicable restriction" means any restriction—

(A) which effectively limits the ability of the corporation or partnership to liquidate, and

(B) with respect to which either of the following applies:

(i) The restriction lapses, in whole or in part, after the transfer referred to in paragraph (1).

(ii) The transferor or any member of the transferor's family, either alone or collectively, has the right after such transfer to remove, in whole or in part, the restriction.

(3) Exceptions.—The term "applicable restriction" shall not include—

(A) any commercially reasonable restriction which arises as part of any financing by the corporation or partnership with a person who is not related to the transferor or transferee, or a member of the family of either, or

(B) any restriction imposed, or required to be imposed, by any Federal or State law.

(4) Other restrictions.—The Secretary may by regulations provide that other restrictions shall be disregarded in determining the value of the transfer of any interest in a corporation or partnership to a member of the transferor's family if such restriction has the effect of reducing the value of the transferred interest for purposes of this subtitle but does not ultimately reduce the value of such interest to the transferee.

(c) Definitions and special rules.—For purposes of this section—

(1) Control.—The term "control" has the meaning given such term by section 2701(b)(2).

(2) Member of the family.—The term "member of the family" means, with respect to any individual—

(A) such individual's spouse,

(B) any ancestor or lineal descendant of such individual or such individual's spouse,

(C) any brother or sister of the individual, and

(D) any spouse of any individual described in subparagraph (B) or (C).

(3) Attribution.—The rule of section 2701(e)(3) shall apply for purposes of determining the interests held by any individual.

SUBTITLE C—EMPLOYMENT TAXES

CHAPTER 24—COLLECTION OF INCOME TAX AT SOURCE ON WAGES

§ 3401. Definitions

(a) Wages.—For purposes of this chapter, the term "wages" means all remuneration (other than fees paid to a public official) for services performed by an employee for his employer, including the cash value of all remuneration (including benefits) paid in any medium other than cash; except that such term shall not include remuneration paid—

* * *

(3) for domestic service in a private home, local college club, or local chapter of a college fraternity or sorority; or

(4) for service not in the course of the employer's trade or business performed in any calendar quarter by an employee, unless the cash remuneration paid for such service is $50 or more and such service is performed by an individual who is regularly employed by such employer to perform such service. For purposes of this paragraph, an individual shall be deemed to be regularly employed by an employer during a calendar quarter only if—

(A) on each of some 24 days during such quarter such individual performs for such employer for some portion of the day service not in the course of the employer's trade or business; or

(B) such individual was regularly employed (as determined under subparagraph (A)) by such employer in the performance of such service during the preceding calendar quarter; or

(5) for services by a citizen or resident of the United States for a foreign government or an international organization; or

* * *

(9) for services performed by a duly ordained, commissioned, or licensed minister of a church in the exercise of his ministry or by a member of a religious order in the exercise of duties required by such order; or

(10)(A) for services performed by an individual under the age of 18 in the delivery or distribution of newspapers or shopping news, not including delivery or distribution to any point for subsequent delivery or distribution; or

(B) for services performed by an individual in, and at the time of, the sale of newspapers or magazines to ultimate consumers, under an arrangement under which the newspapers or magazines are to be sold by him at a fixed price, his compensation being based on the retention of the excess of such price over the amount at which the newspapers or magazines are charged to him, whether or not

* Omitted entirely.

he is guaranteed a minimum amount of compensation for such services, or is entitled to be credited with the unsold newspapers or magazines turned back; or

(11) for services not in the course of the employer's trade or business, to the extent paid in any medium other than cash; or

(12) to, or on behalf of, an employee or his beneficiary—

(A) from or to a trust described in section 401(a) which is exempt from tax under section 501(a) at the time of such payment unless such payment is made to an employee of the trust as remuneration for services rendered as such employee and not as a beneficiary of the trust; or

(B) under or to an annuity plan which, at the time of such payment, is a plan described in section 403(a); or

(C) for a payment described in section 402(h)(1) and (2) if, at the time of such payment, it is reasonable to believe that the employee will be entitled to an exclusion under such section for payment; or

(D) under an arrangement to which section 408(p) applies; or

* * *

(13) pursuant to any provision of law other than section 5(c) or 6(1) of the Peace Corps Act, for service performed as a volunteer or volunteer leader within the meaning of such Act; or

(14) in the form of group-term life insurance on the life of an employee; or

(15) to or on behalf of an employee if (and to the extent that) at the time of the payment of such remuneration it is reasonable to believe that a corresponding deduction is allowable under section 217 (determined without regard to section 274(n)); or

(16)(A) as tips in any medium other than cash;

(B) as cash tips to an employee in any calendar month in the course of his employment by an employer unless the amount of such cash tips is $20 or more;

* * *

(19) for any benefit provided to or on behalf of an employee if at the time such benefit is provided it is reasonable to believe that the employee will be able to exclude such benefit from income under section 74(c), 108(f)(4), 117, or 132; or

(20) for any medical care reimbursement made to or for the benefit of an employee under a self-insured medical reimbursement plan (within the meaning of section 105(h)(6));

(21) for any payment made to or for the benefit of an employee if at the time of such payment it is reasonable to believe that the employee will be able to exclude such payment from income under section 106(b),

(22) any payment made to or for the benefit of an employee if at the time of such payment it is reasonable to believe that the employee will be able to exclude such payment from income under section 106(d), or

* * *

The term "wages" includes any amount includible in gross income of an employee under section 409A and payment of such amount shall be treated as having been made in the taxable year in which the amount is so includible.

* * *

§ 3402. Income tax collected at source

(a) Requirement of withholding.—

(1) In general.—Except as otherwise provided in this section, every employer making payment of wages shall deduct and withhold upon such wages a tax determined in accordance with tables or computational procedures prescribed by the Secretary. Any tables or procedures prescribed under this paragraph shall—

(A) apply with respect to the amount of wages paid during such periods as the Secretary may prescribe, and

(B) be in such form, and provide for such amounts to be deducted and withheld, as the Secretary determines to be most appropriate to carry out the purposes of this chapter and to reflect the provisions of chapter 1 applicable to such periods.

(2) Amount of wages.—For purposes of applying tables or procedures prescribed under paragraph (1), the term "the amount of wages" means the amount by which the wages exceed the number of withholding exemptions claimed multiplied by the amount of one such exemption. The amount of each withholding exemption shall be equal to the amount of one personal exemption provided in section 151(b), prorated to the payroll period. The maximum number of withholding exemptions permitted shall be calculated in accordance with regulations prescribed by the Secretary under this section, taking into account any reduction in withholding to which an employee is entitled under this section.

* * *

§ 3403. Liability for tax

The employer shall be liable for the payment of the tax required to be deducted and withheld under this chapter, and shall not be liable to any person for the amount of any such payment.

SUBTITLE D—MISCELLANEOUS EXCISE TAXES

CHAPTER 43—QUALIFIED PENSION, ETC., PLANS

§ 4972. Tax on nondeductible contributions to qualified employer plans

(a) Tax imposed.—In the case of any qualified employer plan, there is hereby imposed a tax equal to 10 percent of the nondeductible contributions under the plan (determined as of the close of the taxable year of the employer).

(b) Employer liable for tax.—The tax imposed by this section shall be paid by the employer making the contributions.

(c) Nondeductible contributions.—For purposes of this section—

(1) In general.—The term "nondeductible contributions" means, with respect to any qualified employer plan, the sum of—

(A) the excess (if any) of—

(i) the amount contributed for the taxable year by the employer to or under such plan, over

(ii) the amount allowable as a deduction under section 404 for such contributions (determined without regard to subsection (e) thereof), and

(B) the amount determined under this subsection for the preceding taxable year reduced by the sum of—

(i) the portion of the amount so determined returned to the employer during the taxable year, and

(ii) the portion of the amount so determined deductible under section 404 for the taxable year (determined without regard to subsection (e) thereof).

(2) Ordering rule for section 404.—For purposes of paragraph (1), the amount allowable as a deduction under section 404 for any taxable year shall be treated as—

* Omitted entirely.

(A) first from carryforwards to such taxable year from preceding taxable years (in order of time), and

(B) then from contributions made during such taxable year.

(3) Contributions which may be returned to employer.—In determining the amount of nondeductible contributions for any taxable year, there shall not be taken into account any contribution for such taxable year which is distributed to the employer in a distribution described in section 4980(c)(2)(B)(ii) if such distribution is made on or before the last day on which a contribution may be made for such taxable year under section 404(a)(6).

(4) Special rule for self-employed individuals.—For purposes of paragraph (1), if—

(A) the amount which is required to be contributed to a plan under section 412 on behalf of an individual who is an employee (within the meaning of section 401(c)(1)), exceeds

(B) the earned income (within the meaning of section 404(a)(8)) of such individual derived from the trade or business with respect to which such plan is established,

such excess shall be treated as an amount allowable as a deduction under section 404.

* * *

(d) Definitions.—For purposes of this section—

(1) Qualified employer plan.—

(A) In general.—The term "qualified employer plan" means—

(i) any plan meeting the requirements of section 401(a) which includes a trust exempt from tax under section 501(a),

(ii) an annuity plan described in section 403(a),

(iii) any simplified employee pension (within the meaning of section 408(k)), and

(iv) any simple retirement account (within the meaning of section 408(p)).

(B) Exemption for governmental and tax exempt plans.—The term "qualified employer plan" does not include a plan described in subparagraph (A) or (B) of section 4980(c)(1).

(2) Employer.—In the case of a plan which provides contributions or benefits for employees some or all of whom are self-employed individuals within the meaning of section 401(c)(1), the term "employer" means the person treated as the employer under section 401(c)(4).

§ 4973. Tax on excess contributions to certain tax-favored accounts and annuities

(a) Tax imposed.—In the case of—

(1) an individual retirement account (within the meaning of section 408(a)),

* * *

(3) an individual retirement annuity (within the meaning of section 408(b)), a custodial account treated as an annuity contract under section 403(b)(7)(A) (relating to custodial accounts for regulated investment company stock),

(4) a Coverdell education savings account (as defined in section 530), or

(5) a health savings account (within the meaning of section 223(d)), there is imposed for each taxable year a tax in an amount equal to 6 percent of the amount of the excess contributions to such individual's accounts or annuities (determined as of the close of the taxable year). The amount of such tax for any taxable year shall not exceed 6 percent of the value of the account or annuity (determined as of the close of the taxable year). In the case of an endowment contract described in section 408(b), the tax imposed by this section does not apply to any amount allocable to life, health, accident, or other insurance under such contract. The tax imposed by this subsection shall be paid by such individual.

(b) Excess contributions.—For purposes of this section, in the case of individual retirement accounts or individual retirement annuities, the term "excess contributions" means the sum of—

(1) the excess (if any) of—

(A) the amount contributed for the taxable year to the accounts or for the annuities (other than a contribution to a Roth IRA or a rollover contribution described in section 402(c), 403(a)(4), 403(b)(8), 408(d)(3), or 457(e)(16)), over

(B) the amount allowable as a deduction under section 219 for such contributions, and

(2) the amount determined under this subsection for the preceding taxable year reduced by the sum of—

(A) the distributions out of the account for the taxable year which were included in the gross income of the payee under section 408(d)(1),

(B) the distributions out of the account for the taxable year to which section 408(d)(5) applies, and

(C) the excess (if any) of the maximum amount allowable as a deduction under section 219 for the taxable year over the amount contributed (determined without regard to section 219(f)(6)) to the accounts or for the annuities (including the amount contributed to a Roth IRA) for the taxable year.

For purposes of this subsection, any contribution which is distributed from the individual retirement account or the individual retirement annuity in a distribution to which section 408(d)(4) applies shall be treated as an amount not contributed. For purposes of paragraphs (1)(B) and (2)(C), the amount allowable as a deduction under section 219 shall be computed without regard to section 219(g).

(c) Section 403(b) contracts.—For purposes of this section, in the case of a custodial account referred to in subsection (a)(3), the term "excess contributions" means the sum of—

(1) the excess (if any) of the amount contributed for the taxable year to such account (other than a rollover contribution described in section 403(b)(8) or 408(d)(3)(A)(iii)), over the lesser of the amount excludable from gross income under section 403(b) or the amount permitted to be contributed under the limitations contained in section 415 (or under whichever such section is applicable, if only one is applicable), and

(2) the amount determined under this subsection for the preceding taxable year, reduced by—

(A) the excess (if any) of the lesser of (i) the amount excludable from gross income under section 403(b) or (ii) the amount permitted to be contributed under the limitations contained in section 415 over the amount contributed to the account for the taxable year (or under whichever such section is applicable, if only one is applicable), and

(B) the sum of the distributions out of the account (for all prior taxable years) which are included in gross income under section 72(e).

* * *

§ 4977. Tax on certain fringe benefits provided by an employer

(a) Imposition of tax.—In the case of an employer to whom an election under this section applies for any calendar year, there is hereby imposed a tax for such calendar year equal to 30 percent of the excess fringe benefits.

(b) Excess fringe benefits.—For purposes of subsection (a), the term "excess fringe benefits" means, with respect to any calendar year—

(1) the aggregate value of the fringe benefits provided by the employer during the calendar year which were not includible in gross income under paragraphs (1) and (2) of section 132(a), over

(2) 1 percent of the aggregate amount of compensation—

(A) which was paid by the employer during such calendar year to employees, and

(B) was includible in gross income for purposes of chapter 1.

(c) Effect of election on section 132(a).—If—

(1) an election under this section is in effect with respect to an employer for any calendar year, and

(2) at all times on or after January 1, 1984, and before the close of the calendar year involved, substantially all of the employees of the employer were entitled to employee discounts on goods or services provided by the employer in 1 line of business,

for purposes of paragraphs (1) and (2) of section 132(a) (but not for purposes of section 132(h)), all employees of any line of business of the employer which was in existence on January 1, 1984, shall be treated as employees of the line of business referred to in paragraph (2).

(d) Period of election.—An election under this section shall apply to the calendar year for which made and all subsequent calendar years unless revoked by the employer.

(e) Treatment of controlled groups.—All employees treated as employed by a single employer under subsection (b), (c), or (m) of section 414 shall be treated as employed by a single employer for purposes of this section.

(f) Section to apply only to employment within the United States.—Except as otherwise provided in regulations, this section shall apply only with respect to employment within the United States.

§ 4979. Tax on certain excess contributions

(a) General rule.—In the case of any plan, there is hereby imposed a tax for the taxable year equal to 10 percent of the sum of—

(1) any excess contributions under such plan for the plan year ending in such taxable year, and

(2) any excess aggregate contributions under the plan for the plan year ending in such taxable year.

(b) Liability for tax.—The tax imposed by subsection (a) shall be paid by the employer.

(c) Excess contributions.—For purposes of this section, the term "excess contributions" has the meaning given such term by sections 401(k)(8)(B), 408(k)(6)(C), and 501(c)(18).

(d) Excess aggregate contribution.—For purposes of this section, the term "excess aggregate contribution" has the meaning given to such term by section 401(m)(6)(B). For purposes of determining excess aggregate contributions under an annuity contract described in section 403(b), such contract shall be treated as a plan described in subsection (e)(1).

(e) Plan.—For purposes of this section, the term "plan" means—

(1) a plan described in section 401(a) which includes a trust exempt from tax under section 501(a),

(2) any annuity plan described in section 403(a),

(3) any annuity contract described in section 403(b),

(4) a simplified employee pension of an employer which satisfies the requirements of section 408(k), and

(5) a plan described in section 501(c)(18).

Such term includes any plan which, at any time, has been determined by the Secretary to be such a plan.

(f) No tax where excess distributed within specified period after close of year.—

(1) In general.—No tax shall be imposed under this section on any excess contribution or excess aggregate contribution, as the case may be, to the extent such contribution (together with any income allocable thereto through the end of the plan year for which the contribution was made) is distributed (or, if forfeitable, is forfeited) before the close of the first 2 1/2 months (6 months in the case of an excess contribution or excess aggregate contribution to an eligible automatic contribution arrangement (as defined in section 414(w)(3))) of the following plan year.

(2) Year of inclusion.—Any amount distributed as provided in paragraph (1) shall be treated as earned and received by the recipient in the recipient's taxable year in which such distributions were made.

SUBTITLE F—PROCEDURE AND ADMINISTRATION

Chapter
61. Information and returns.
62. Time and place for paying tax.
63. Assessment.
64. Collection.
65. Abatements, credits, and refunds.*
66. Limitations.
67. Interest.
68. Additions to the tax, additional amounts, and assessable penalties.
69. General provisions relating to stamps.*
70. Jeopardy, receiverships, etc.
71. Transferees and fiduciaries.
72. Licensing and registration.*
73. Bonds.*
74. Closing agreements and compromises.
75. Crimes, other offenses, and forfeitures.
76. Judicial proceedings.
77. Miscellaneous provisions.
78. Discovery of liability and enforcement of title.*
79. Definitions.
80. General rules.

CHAPTER 61—INFORMATION AND RETURNS

Subchapter
A. Returns and records.
B. Miscellaneous provisions.

SUBCHAPTER A—RETURNS AND RECORDS

Part
I. Records, statements, and special returns.
II. Tax returns or statements.
III. Information returns.
IV. Signing and verifying of returns and other documents.*
V. Time for filing returns and other documents.
VI. Extension of time for filing returns.
VII. Place for filing returns or other documents.*
VIII. Designation of income tax payments to Presidential Election Campaign Fund.*

PART I—RECORDS, STATEMENTS, AND SPECIAL RETURNS

§ 6001. Notice or regulations requiring records, statements, and special returns

Every person liable for any tax imposed by this title, or for the collection thereof, shall keep such records, render such statements, make such returns, and comply with such rules and regulations as the Secretary may from time to time prescribe. Whenever in the judgment of the Secretary it is necessary, he may require any person,

* Omitted entirely.

by notice served upon such person or by regulations, to make such returns, render such statements, or keep such records, as the Secretary deems sufficient to show whether or not such person is liable for tax under this title. The only records which an employer shall be required to keep under this section in connection with charged tips shall be charge receipts, records necessary to comply with section 6053(c), and copies of statements furnished by employees under section 6053(a).

PART II—TAX RETURNS OR STATEMENTS

Subpart A—General Requirement

§ 6011. General requirement of return, statement, or list

(a) General rule.—When required by regulations prescribed by the Secretary any person made liable for any tax imposed by this title, or with respect to the collection thereof, shall make a return or statement according to the forms and regulations prescribed by the Secretary. Every person required to make a return or statement shall include therein the information required by such forms or regulations.

* * *

Subpart B—Income Tax Returns

§ 6012. Persons required to make returns of income

(a) General rule.—Returns with respect to income taxes under subtitle A shall be made by the following:

(1)(A) Every individual having for the taxable year gross income which equals or exceeds the exemption amount, except that a return shall not be required of an individual—

(i) who is not married (determined by applying section 7703), is not a surviving spouse (as defined in section 2(a)), is not a head of a household (as defined in section 2(b)), and for the taxable year has gross income of less than the sum of the exemption amount plus the basic standard deduction applicable to such an individual,

(ii) who is a head of a household (as so defined) and for the taxable year has gross income of less than the sum of the exemption amount plus the basic standard deduction applicable to such an individual,

(iii) who is a surviving spouse (as so defined) and for the taxable year has gross income of less than the sum of the exemption amount plus the basic standard deduction applicable to such an individual, or

(iv) who is entitled to make a joint return and whose gross income, when combined with the gross income of his spouse, is, for the taxable year, less than the sum of twice the exemption amount plus the basic standard deduction applicable to a joint return, but only if such individual and his spouse, at the close of the taxable year, had the same household as their home.

* Omitted entirely.

Clause (iv) shall not apply if for the taxable year such spouse makes a separate return or any other taxpayer is entitled to an exemption for such spouse under section 151(c).

(B) The amount specified in clause (i), (ii), or (iii) of subparagraph (A) shall be increased by the amount of 1 additional standard deduction (within the meaning of section 63(c)(3)) in the case of an individual entitled to such deduction by reason of section 63(f)(1)(A) (relating to individuals age 65 or more), and the amount specified in clause (iv) of subparagraph (A) shall be increased by the amount of the additional standard deduction for each additional standard deduction to which the individual or his spouse is entitled by reason of section 63(f)(1).

(C) The exception under subparagraph (A) shall not apply to any individual—

(i) who is described in section 63(c)(5) and who has—

(I) income (other than earned income) in excess of the sum of the amount in effect under section 63(c)(5)(A) plus the additional standard deduction (if any) to which the individual is entitled, or

(II) total gross income in excess of the standard deduction, or

(ii) for whom the standard deduction is zero under section 63(c)(6).

(D) For purposes of this subsection—

(i) The terms "standard deduction", "basic standard deduction" and "additional standard deduction" have the respective meanings given such terms by section 63(c).

(ii) The term "exemption amount" has the meaning given such term by section 151(d). In the case of an individual described in section 151(d)(2), the exemption amount shall be zero.

(2) Every corporation subject to taxation under subtitle A;

(3) Every estate the gross income of which for the taxable year is $600 or more;

(4) Every trust having for the taxable year any taxable income, or having gross income of $600 or over, regardless of the amount of taxable income;

* * *

(b) Returns made by fiduciaries and receivers.—

(1) Returns of decedents.—If an individual is deceased, the return of such individual required under subsection (a) shall be made by his executor, administrator, or other person charged with the property of such decedent.

(2) Persons under a disability.—If an individual is unable to make a return required under subsection (a), the return of such individual shall be made by a duly authorized agent, his committee, guardian, fiduciary or other person charged with the care of the person or property of such individual. The preceding sentence shall not apply in the case of a receiver appointed by authority of law in possession of only a part of the property of an individual.

(3) Receivers, trustees and assignees for corporation.—In a case where a receiver, trustee in a case under title 11 of the United States Code, or assignee, by order of a court of competent jurisdiction, by operation of law or otherwise, has possession of or holds title to all or substantially all the property or business of a corporation, whether or not such property or business is being operated, such receiver, trustee, or assignee shall make the return of income for such corporation in the same manner and form as corporations are required to make such returns.

(4) Returns of estates and trusts.—Returns of an estate, a trust, or an estate of an individual under chapter 7 or 11 of title 11 of the United States Code shall be made by the fiduciary thereof.

(5) Joint fiduciaries.—Under such regulations as the Secretary may prescribe, a return made by one of two or more joint fiduciaries shall be sufficient compliance with the requirements of this section. A return made pursuant to this paragraph shall contain a statement that the fiduciary has sufficient knowledge of the affairs of the person for whom the return is made to enable him to make the return, and that the return is, to the best of his knowledge and belief, true and correct.

* * *

(c) Certain income earned abroad or from sale of residence.—For purposes of this section, gross income shall be computed without regard to the exclusion provided for in section 121 (relating to gain from sale of principal residence) and without regard to the exclusion provided for in section 911 (relating to citizens or residents of United States living abroad).

(d) Tax-exempt interest required to be shown on return.—Every person required to file a return under this section for the taxable year shall include on such return the amount of interest received or accrued during the taxable year which is exempt from the tax imposed by chapter 1.

(e) Consolidated returns.—

For provisions relating to consolidated returns by affiliated corporations, see chapter 6.

§ 6013. Joint returns of income tax by husband and wife

(a) Joint returns.—A husband and wife may make a single return jointly of income taxes under subtitle A, even though one of the spouses has neither gross income nor deductions, except as provided below:

* * *

(2) no joint return shall be made if the husband and wife have different taxable years; except that if such taxable years begin on the same day and end on different days because of the death of either or both, then the joint return may be made with respect to the taxable year of each. The above exception shall not apply if the surviving spouse remarries before the close of his taxable year, nor if the taxable year of either spouse is a fractional part of a year under section 443(a)(1);

(3) in the case of death of one spouse or both spouses the joint return with respect to the decedent may be made only by his executor or administrator; except that in the case of the death of one spouse the joint return may be made by the surviving spouse with respect to both himself and the decedent if no return for the taxable year has been made by the decedent, no executor or administrator has been appointed, and no executor or administrator is appointed before the last day prescribed by law for filing the return of the surviving spouse. If an executor or administrator of the decedent is appointed after the making of the joint return by the surviving spouse, the executor or administrator may disaffirm such joint return by making, within 1 year after the last day prescribed by law for filing the return of the surviving spouse, a separate return for the taxable year of the decedent with respect to which the joint return was made, in which case the return made by the survivor shall constitute his separate return.

(b) Joint return after filing separate return.—

(1) In general.—Except as provided in paragraph (2), if an individual has filed a separate return for a taxable year for which a joint return could have been made by him and his spouse under subsection (a) and the time prescribed by law for filing the return for such taxable year has expired, such individual and his spouse may nevertheless make a joint return for such taxable year. A joint return filed by the husband and wife under this subsection shall constitute the return of the husband

and wife for such taxable year, and all payments, credits, refunds, or other repayments made or allowed with respect to the separate return of either spouse for such taxable year shall be taken into account in determining the extent to which the tax based upon the joint return has been paid. If a joint return is made under this subsection, any election (other than the election to file a separate return) made by either spouse in his separate return for such taxable year with respect to the treatment of any income, deduction, or credit of such spouse shall not be changed in the making of the joint return where such election would have been irrevocable if the joint return had not been made. If a joint return is made under this subsection after the death of either spouse, such return with respect to the decedent can be made only by his executor or administrator.

(2) Limitations for making of election.—The election provided for in paragraph (1) may not be made—

(A) after the expiration of 3 years from the last date prescribed by law for filing the return for such taxable year (determined without regard to any extension of time granted to either spouse); or

(B) after there has been mailed to either spouse, with respect to such taxable year, a notice of deficiency under section 6212, if the spouse, as to such notice, files a petition with the Tax Court within the time prescribed in section 6213; or

(C) after either spouse has commenced a suit in any court for the recovery of any part of the tax for such taxable year; or

(D) after either spouse has entered into a closing agreement under section 7121 with respect to such taxable year, or after any civil or criminal case arising against either spouse with respect to such taxable year has been compromised under section 7122.

* * *

(c) Treatment of joint return after death of either spouse.—For purposes of sections 15, 443, and 7851(a)(1)(A), where the husband and wife have different taxable years because of the death of either spouse, the joint return shall be treated as if the taxable years of both spouses ended on the date of the closing of the surviving spouse's taxable year.

(d) Special rules.—For purposes of this section—

(1) the status as husband and wife of two individuals having taxable years beginning on the same day shall be determined—

(A) if both have the same taxable year—as of the close of such year; or

(B) if one dies before the close of the taxable year of the other—as of the time of such death;

(2) an individual who is legally separated from his spouse under a decree of divorce or of separate maintenance shall not be considered as married; and

(3) if a joint return is made, the tax shall be computed on the aggregate income and the liability with respect to the tax shall be joint and several.

* * *

§ 6015. Relief from joint and several liability on joint return

(a) In general.—Notwithstanding section 6013(d)(3)—

(1) an individual who has made a joint return may elect to seek relief under the procedures prescribed under subsection (b); and

(2) if such individual is eligible to elect the application of subsection (c), such individual may, in addition to any election under paragraph (1), elect to limit such individual's liability for any deficiency with respect to such joint return in the manner prescribed under subsection (c).

Any determination under this section shall be made without regard to community property laws.

(b) Procedures for relief from liability applicable to all joint filers.—

(1) In general.—Under procedures prescribed by the Secretary, if—

(A) a joint return has been made for a taxable year;

(B) on such return there is an understatement of tax attributable to erroneous items of one individual filing the joint return;

(C) the other individual filing the joint return establishes that in signing the return he or she did not know, and had no reason to know, that there was such understatement;

(D) taking into account all the facts and circumstances, it is inequitable to hold the other individual liable for the deficiency in tax for such taxable year attributable to such understatement; and

(E) the other individual elects (in such form as the Secretary may prescribe) the benefits of this subsection not later than the date which is 2 years after the date the Secretary has begun collection activities with respect to the individual making the election,

then the other individual shall be relieved of liability for tax (including interest, penalties, and other amounts) for such taxable year to the extent such liability is attributable to such understatement.

(2) Apportionment of relief.—If an individual who, but for paragraph (1)(C), would be relieved of liability under paragraph (1), establishes that in signing the return such individual did not know, and had no reason to know, the extent of such understatement, then such individual shall be relieved of liability for tax (including interest, penalties, and other amounts) for such taxable year to the extent that such liability is attributable to the portion of such understatement of which such individual did not know and had no reason to know.

(3) Understatement—For purposes of this subsection, the term "understatement" has the meaning given to such term by section 6662(d)(2)(A).

(c) Procedures to limit liability for taxpayers no longer married or taxpayers legally separated or not living together.—

(1) In general.—Except as provided in this subsection, if an individual who has made a joint return for any taxable year elects the application of this subsection, the individual's liability for any deficiency which is assessed with respect to the return shall not exceed the portion of such deficiency properly allocable to the individual under subsection (d).

(2) Burden of proof.—Except as provided in subparagraph (A)(ii) or (C) of paragraph (3), each individual who elects the application of this subsection shall have the burden of proof with respect to establishing the portion of any deficiency allocable to such individual.

(3) Election.—

(A) Individuals eligible to make election.—

(i) In general.—An individual shall only be eligible to elect the application of this subsection if—

(I) at the time such election is filed, such individual is no longer married to, or is legally separated from, the individual with whom such individual filed the joint return to which the election relates; or

(II) such individual was not a member of the same household as the individual with whom such joint return was filed at any time during the 12-month period ending on the date such election is filed.

(ii) Certain taxpayers ineligible to elect.—If the Secretary demonstrates that assets were transferred between individuals filing a joint return as part of a fraudulent scheme by such individuals, an election under this subsection by either individual shall be invalid (and section 6013(d)(3) shall apply to the joint return).

(B) Time for election.—An election under this subsection for any taxable year may be made at any time after a deficiency for such year is asserted but not later than 2 years after the date on which the Secretary has begun collection activities with respect to the individual making the election.

(C) Election not valid with respect to certain deficiencies.—If the Secretary demonstrates that an individual making an election under this subsection had actual knowledge, at the time such individual signed the return, of any item giving rise to a deficiency (or portion thereof) which is not allocable to such individual under subsection (d), such election shall not apply to such deficiency (or portion). This subparagraph shall not apply where the individual with actual knowledge establishes that such individual signed the return under duress.

(4) Liability increased by reason of transfers of property to avoid tax—

(A) In general.—Notwithstanding any other provision of this subsection, the portion of the deficiency for which the individual electing the application of this subsection is liable (without regard to this paragraph) shall be increased by the value of any disqualified asset transferred to the individual.

(B) Disqualified asset.—For purposes of this paragraph—

(i) In general.—The term "disqualified asset" means any property or right to property transferred to an individual making the election under this subsection with respect to a joint return by the other individual filing such joint return if the principal purpose of the transfer was the avoidance of tax or payment of tax.

(ii) Presumption.—

(I) In general.—For purposes of clause (i), except as provided in subclause (II), any transfer which is made after the date which is 1 year before the date on which the first letter of proposed deficiency which allows the taxpayer an opportunity for administrative review in the Internal Revenue Service Office of Appeals is sent shall be presumed to have as its principal purpose the avoidance of tax or payment of tax.

(II) Exceptions.—Subclause (I) shall not apply to any transfer pursuant to a decree of divorce or separate maintenance or a written instrument incident to such a decree or to any transfer which an individual establishes did not have as its principal purpose the avoidance of tax or payment of tax.

(d) Allocation of deficiency.—For purposes of subsection (c).—

(1) In general.—The portion of any deficiency on a joint return allocated to an individual shall be the amount which bears the same ratio to such deficiency as the net amount of items taken into account in computing the deficiency and allocable to the individual under paragraph (3) bears to the net amount of all items taken into account in computing the deficiency.

(2) Separate treatment of certain items.—If a deficiency (or portion thereof) is attributable to—

(A) the disallowance of a credit; or

(B) any tax (other than tax imposed by section 1 or 55) required to be included with the joint return;

and such item is allocated to one individual under paragraph (3), such deficiency (or portion) shall be allocated to such individual. Any such item shall not be taken into account under paragraph (1).

(3) Allocation of items giving rise to the deficiency.—For purposes of this subsection—

(A) In general.—Except as provided in paragraphs (4) and (5), any item giving rise to a deficiency on a joint return shall be allocated to individuals filing the return in the same manner as it would have been allocated if the individuals had filed separate returns for the taxable year.

(B) Exception where other spouse benefits.—Under rules prescribed by the Secretary, an item otherwise allocable to an individual under subparagraph (A) shall be allocated to the other individual filing the joint return to the extent the item gave rise to a tax benefit on the joint return to the other individual.

(C) Exception for fraud.—The Secretary may provide for an allocation of any item in a manner not prescribed by subparagraph (A) if the Secretary establishes that such allocation is appropriate due to fraud of one or both individuals.

(4) Limitations on separate returns disregarded.—If an item of deduction or credit is disallowed in its entirety solely because a separate return is filed, such disallowance shall be disregarded and the item shall be computed as if a joint return had been filed and then allocated between the spouses appropriately. A similar rule shall apply for purposes of section 86.

(5) Child's liability.—If the liability of a child of a taxpayer is included on a joint return, such liability shall be disregarded in computing the separate liability of either spouse and such liability shall be allocated appropriately between the spouses.

(e) Petition for review by Tax Court.—

(1) In general.—In the case of an individual against whom a deficiency has been asserted and who elects to have subsection (b) or (c) apply, or in the case of an individual who requests equitable relief under subsection (f)—

(A) In general.—In addition to any other remedy provided by law, the individual may petition the Tax Court (and the Tax Court shall have jurisdiction) to determine the appropriate relief available to the individual under this section if such petition is filed—

(i) at any time after the earlier of—

(I) the date the Secretary mails, by certified or registered mail to the taxpayer's last known address, notice of the Secretary's final determination of relief available to the individual, or

(II) the date which is 6 months after the date such election is filed or request is made with the Secretary, and

(ii) not later than the close of the 90th day after the date described in clause (i)(I).

(B) Restrictions applicable to collection of assessment.—

(i) In general.—Except as otherwise provided in section 6851 or 6861, no levy or proceeding in court shall be made, begun, or prosecuted against the individual making an election under subsection (b) or (c) or requesting equitable relief under subsection (f) for collection of any assessment to which such election or request relates until the close of the 90th day referred to in subparagraph (A)(ii), or, if a petition has been filed with the Tax Court under subparagraph (A), until the decision of the Tax Court has become final. Rules similar to the rules of section 7485 shall apply with respect to the collection of such assessment.

(ii) Authority to enjoin collection actions.—Notwithstanding the provisions of section 7421(a), the beginning of such levy or proceeding during the time the prohibition under clause (i) is in force may be enjoined by a proceeding in the proper court, including the Tax Court. The Tax Court shall have no jurisdiction under this subparagraph to enjoin any action or proceeding unless a timely petition has been filed under subparagraph (A) and then only in respect of the amount of the assessment to which the election under subsection (b) or (c) relates or to which the request under subsection (f) relates.

(2) Suspension of running of period of limitations.—The running of the period of limitations in section 6502 on the collection of the assessment to which the petition under paragraph (1)(A) relates shall be suspended—

(A) for the period during which the Secretary is prohibited by paragraph (1)(B) from collecting by levy or a proceeding in court and for 60 days thereafter, and

(B) if a waiver under paragraph (5) is made, from the date the claim for relief was filed until 60 days after the waiver is filed with the Secretary.

(3) Limitation on Tax Court jurisdiction.—If a suit for refund is begun by either individual filing the joint return pursuant to section 6532—

(A) the Tax Court shall lose jurisdiction of the individual's action under this section to whatever extent jurisdiction is acquired by the district court or the United States Court of Federal Claims over the taxable years that are the subject of the suit for refund, and

(B) the court acquiring jurisdiction shall have jurisdiction over the petition filed under the subsection.

(4) Notice to other spouse.—The Tax Court shall establish rules which provide the individual filing a joint return but not making the election under subsection (b) or (c) or the request for equitable relief under subsection (f) with adequate notice and an opportunity to become a party to a proceeding under either such subsection.

(5) Waiver.—An individual who elects the application of subsection (b) or (c) or who requests equitable relief under subsection (f) (and who agrees with the Secretary's determination of relief) may waive in writing at any time the restrictions in paragraph (1)(B) with respect to collection of the outstanding assessment (whether or not a notice of the Secretary's final determination of relief has been mailed).

(f) Equitable relief.—Under procedures prescribed by the Secretary, if—

(1) taking into account all the facts and circumstances, it is inequitable to hold the individual liable for any unpaid tax or any deficiency (or any portion of either); and

(2) relief is not available to such individual under subsection (b) or (c), the Secretary may relieve such individual of such liability.

(g) Credits and refunds.—

(1) In general.—Except as provided in paragraphs (2) and (3), notwithstanding any other law or rule of law (other than section 6511, 6512(b), 7121, or 7122), credit or refund shall be allowed or made to the extent attributable to the application of this section.

(2) Res judicata.—In the case of any election under subsection (b) or (c) or any request for equitable relief under subsection (f), if a decision of a court in any prior proceeding for the same taxable year has become final, such decision shall be conclusive except with respect to the qualification of the individual for relief which was not an issue in such proceeding. The exception contained in the preceding sentence shall not apply if the court determines that the individual participated meaningfully in such prior proceeding.

(3) Credit and refund not allowed under subsection (c).—No credit or refund shall be allowed as a result of an election under subsection (c).

(h) Regulations.—The Secretary shall prescribe such regulations as are necessary to carry out the provisions of this section, including—

(1) regulations providing methods for allocation of items other than the methods under subsection (d)(3); and

(2) regulations providing the opportunity for an individual to have notice of, and an opportunity to participate in, any administrative proceeding with respect to an election made under subsection (b) or (c) or a request for equitable relief made under subsection (f) by the other individual filing the joint return.

Subpart C—Estate and Gift Tax Returns

§ 6018. Estate tax returns

(a) Returns by executor.—

(1) Citizens or residents.—In all cases where the gross estate at the death of a citizen or resident exceeds the basic exclusion amount in effect under section 2010(c) for the calendar year which includes the date of death, the executor shall make a return with respect to the estate tax imposed by subtitle B.

* * *

(3) Adjustment for certain gifts.—The amount applicable under paragraph (1) and the amount set forth in paragraph (2) shall each be reduced (but not below zero) by the sum of—

(A) the amount of the adjusted taxable gifts (within the meaning of section 2001(b)) made by the decedent after December 31, 1976, plus

(B) the aggregate amount allowed as a specific exemption under section 2521 (as in effect before its repeal by the Tax Reform Act of 1976) with respect to gifts made by the decedent after September 8, 1976.

(b) Returns by beneficiaries.—If the executor is unable to make a complete return as to any part of the gross estate of the decedent, he shall include in his return a description of such part and the name of every person holding a legal or beneficial interest therein. Upon notice from the Secretary such person shall in like manner make a return as to such part of the gross estate.

§ 6019. Gift tax returns

Any individual who in any calendar year makes any transfer by gift other than—

(1) a transfer which under subsection (b) or (e) of section 2503 is not to be included in the total amount of gifts for such year,

(2) a transfer of an interest with respect to which a deduction is allowed under section 2523, or

(3) a transfer with respect to which a deduction is allowed under section 2522 but only if—

(A)(i) such transfer is of the donor's entire interest in the property transferred, and

(ii) no other interest in such property is or has been transferred (for less than adequate and full consideration in money or money's worth) from the donor to a person, or for a use, not described in subsection (a) or (b) of section 2522, or

(B) such transfer is described in section 2522(d),

shall make a return for such year with respect to the gift tax imposed by subtitle B.

PART III—INFORMATION RETURNS

Subpart A—Information Concerning Persons Subject to Special Provisions

§ 6031. Return of partnership income

(a) General rule.—Every partnership (as defined in section 761(a)) shall make a return for each taxable year, stating specifically the items of its gross income and the deductions allowable by subtitle A, and such other information for the purpose of carrying out the provisions of subtitle A as the Secretary may by forms and regulations prescribe, and shall include in the return the names and addresses of the individuals who would be entitled to share in the taxable income if distributed and the amount of the distributive share of each individual.

(b) Copies to partners.—Each partnership required to file a return under subsection (a) for any partnership taxable year shall (on or before the day on which the return for such taxable year was required to be filed) furnish to each person who is a partner or who holds an interest in such partnership as a nominee for another person at any time during such taxable year a copy of such information required to be shown on such return as may be required by regulations. * * *

* * *

§ 6036. Notice of qualification as executor or receiver

Every receiver, trustee in a case under title 11 of the United States Code, assignee for benefit of creditors, or other like fiduciary, and every executor (as defined in section 2203), shall give notice of his qualification as such to the Secretary in such manner and at such time as may be required by regulations of the Secretary. The Secretary may by regulation provide such exemptions from the requirements of this section as the Secretary deems proper.

§ 6037. Return of S corporation

(a) In general.—Every S corporation shall make a return for each taxable year, stating specifically the items of its gross income and the deductions allowable by subtitle A, the names and addresses of all persons owning stock in the corporation at

* Omitted entirely.

any time during the taxable year, the number of shares of stock owned by each shareholder at all times during the taxable year, the amount of money and other property distributed by the corporation during the taxable year to each shareholder, the date of each such distribution, each shareholder's pro rata share of each item of the corporation for the taxable year, and such other information, for the purpose of carrying out the provisions of subchapter S of chapter 1, as the Secretary may by forms and regulations prescribe. Any return filed pursuant to this section shall, for purposes of chapter 66 (relating to limitations), be treated as a return filed by the corporation under section 6012.

(b) Copies to shareholders.—Each S corporation required to file a return under subsection (a) for any taxable year shall (on or before the day on which the return for such taxable year was filed) furnish to each person who is a shareholder at any time during such taxable year a copy of such information shown on such return as may be required by regulations.

(c) Shareholder's return must be consistent with corporate return or Secretary notified of inconsistency.—

(1) In general.—A shareholder of an S corporation shall, on such shareholder's return, treat a subchapter S item in a manner which is consistent with the treatment of such item on the corporate return.

(2) Notification of inconsistent treatment.—

(A) In general.—In the case of any subchapter S item, if—

(i)(I) the corporation has filed a return but the shareholder's treatment on his return is (or may be) inconsistent with the treatment of the item on the corporate return, or

(II) the corporation has not filed a return, and

(ii) the shareholder files with the Secretary a statement identifying the inconsistency,

paragraph (1) shall not apply to such item.

(B) Shareholder receiving incorrect information.—A shareholder shall be treated as having complied with clause (ii) of subparagraph (A) with respect to a subchapter S item if the shareholder—

(i) demonstrates to the satisfaction of the Secretary that the treatment of the subchapter S item on the shareholder's return is consistent with the treatment of the item on the schedule furnished to the shareholder by the corporation, and

(ii) elects to have this paragraph apply with respect to that item.

(3) Effect of failure to notify.—In any case—

(A) described in subparagraph (A)(i)(I) of paragraph (2), and

(B) in which the shareholder does not comply with subparagraph (A)(ii) of paragraph (2),

any adjustment required to make the treatment of the items by such shareholder consistent with the treatment of the items on the corporate return shall be treated as arising out of mathematical or clerical errors and assessed according to section 6213(b)(1). Paragraph (2) of section 6213(b) shall not apply to any assessment referred to in the preceding sentence.

(4) Subchapter S item.—For purposes of this subsection, the term "subchapter S item" means any item of an S corporation to the extent that regulations prescribed by the Secretary provide that, for purposes of this subtitle, such item is more appropriately determined at the corporation level than at the shareholder level.

(5) Addition to tax for failure to comply with section.—

For addition to tax in the case of a shareholder's negligence in connection with, or disregard of, the requirements of this section, see part II of subchapter A of chapter 68.

Subpart B—Information Concerning Transactions With Other Persons

§ 6043. Liquidating, etc., transactions

(a) Corporate liquidating, etc., transactions.—Every corporation shall—

(1) Within 30 days after the adoption by the corporation of a resolution or plan for the dissolution of the corporation or for the liquidation of the whole or any part of its capital stock, make a return setting forth the terms of such resolution or plan and such other information as the Secretary shall by forms or regulations prescribe; and

(2) When required by the Secretary, make a return regarding its distributions in liquidation, stating the name and address of, the number and class of shares owned by, and the amount paid to, each shareholder, or, if the distribution is in property other than money, the fair market value (as of the date the distribution is made) of the property distributed to each shareholder.

* * *

(c) Changes in control and recapitalizations.—If—

(1) control (as defined in section 304(c)(1)) of a corporation is acquired by any person (or group of persons) in a transaction (or series of related transactions), or

(2) there is a recapitalization of a corporation or other substantial change in the capital structure of a corporation,

when required by the Secretary, such corporation shall make a return (at such time and in such manner as the Secretary may prescribe) setting forth the identity of the parties to the transaction, the fees involved, the changes in the capital structure involved, and such other information as the Secretary may require with respect to such transaction.

§ 6043A. Returns relating to taxable mergers and acquisitions

(a) In general.—According to the forms or regulations prescribed by the Secretary, the acquiring corporation in any taxable acquisition shall make a return setting forth—

(1) a description of the acquisition,

(2) the name and address of each shareholder of the acquired corporation who is required to recognize gain (if any) as a result of the acquisition,

(3) the amount of money and the fair market value of other property transferred to each such shareholder as part of such acquisition, and

(4) such other information as the Secretary may prescribe.

To the extent provided by the Secretary, the requirements of this section applicable to the acquiring corporation shall be applicable to the acquired corporation and not to the acquiring corporation.

* * *

(c) Taxable acquisition.—For purposes of this section, the term "taxable acquisition" means any acquisition by a corporation of stock in or property of another corporation if any shareholder of the acquired corporation is required to recognize gain (if any) as a result of such acquisition.

* * *

PART V—TIME FOR FILING RETURNS AND OTHER DOCUMENTS

§ 6072. Time for filing income tax returns

(a) General rule.—In the case of returns under section 6012, 6013, 6017, or 6031 (relating to income tax under subtitle A), returns made on the basis of the calendar year shall be filed on or before the 15th day of April following the close of the calendar year and returns made on the basis of a fiscal year shall be filed on or before the 15th day of the fourth month following the close of the fiscal year, except as otherwise provided in the following subsections of this section.

(b) Returns of corporations.—Returns of corporations under section 6012 made on the basis of the calendar year shall be filed on or before the 15th day of March following the close of the calendar year, and such returns made on the basis of a fiscal year shall be filed on or before the 15th day of the third month following the close of the fiscal year. * * *

* * *

§ 6075. Time for filing estate and gift tax returns

(a) Estate tax returns.—Returns made under section 6018(a) (relating to estate taxes) shall be filed within 9 months after the date of the decedent's death.

(b) Gift tax returns.—

(1) General rule.—Returns made under section 6019 (relating to gift taxes) shall be filed on or before the 15th day of April following the close of the calendar year.

(2) Extension where taxpayer granted extension for filing income tax return.—Any extension of time granted the taxpayer for filing the return of income taxes imposed by subtitle A for any taxable year which is a calendar year shall be deemed to be also an extension of time granted the taxpayer for filing the return under section 6019 for such calendar year.

(3) Coordination with due date for estate tax return.—Notwithstanding paragraphs (1) and (2), the time for filing the return made under section 6019 for the calendar year which includes the date of death of the donor shall not be later than the time (including extensions) for filing the return made under section 6018 (relating to estate tax returns) with respect to such donor.

PART VI—EXTENSION OF TIME FOR FILING RETURNS

§ 6081. Extension of time for filing returns

(a) General rule.—The Secretary may grant a reasonable extension of time for filing any return, declaration, statement, or other document required by this title or by regulations. Except in the case of taxpayers who are abroad, no such extension shall be for more than 6 months.

(b) Automatic extension for corporation income tax returns.—An extension of 3 months for the filing of the return of income taxes imposed by subtitle A shall be allowed any corporation if, in such manner and at such time as the Secretary may by regulations prescribe, there is filed on behalf of such corporation the form prescribed by the Secretary, and if such corporation pays, on or before the date prescribed for payment of the tax, the amount properly estimated as its tax; but this extension may be terminated at any time by the Secretary by mailing to the taxpayer notice of such termination at least 10 days prior to the date for termination fixed in such notice.

* * *

SUBCHAPTER B—MISCELLANEOUS PROVISIONS

§ 6113. Disclosure of nondeductibility of contributions

(a) General rule.—Each fundraising solicitation by (or on behalf of) an organization to which this section applies shall contain an express statement (in a conspicuous and easily recognizable format) that contributions or gifts to such organization are not deductible as charitable contributions for Federal income tax purposes.

(b) Organizations to which section applies.—

(1) In general.—Except as otherwise provided in this subsection, this section shall apply to any organization which is not described in section 170(c) and which—

(A) is described in subsection (c) (other than paragraph (1) thereof) or (d) of section 501 and exempt from taxation under section 501(a),

(B) is a political organization (as defined in section 527(e)), or

(C) was an organization described in subparagraph (A) or (B) at any time during the 5–year period ending on the date of the fundraising solicitation or is a successor to an organization so described at any time during such 5–year period.

(2) Exception for small organizations.—

(A) Annual gross receipts do not exceed $100,000.—This section shall not apply to any organization the gross receipts of which in each taxable year are normally not more than $100,000.

(B) Multiple organization rule.—The Secretary may treat any group of 2 or more organizations as 1 organization for purposes of subparagraph (A) where necessary or appropriate to prevent the avoidance of this section through the use of multiple organizations.

(3) Special rule for certain fraternal organizations.—For purposes of paragraph (1), an organization described in section 170(c)(4) shall be treated as described in section 170(c) only with respect to solicitations for contributions or gifts which are to be used exclusively for purposes referred to in section 170(c)(4).

(c) Fundraising solicitation.—For purposes of this section—

(1) In general.—Except as provided in paragraph (2), the term "fundraising solicitation" means any solicitation of contributions or gifts which is made—

(A) in written or printed form,

(B) by television or radio, or

(C) by telephone.

(2) Exception for certain letters or calls.—The term "fundraising solicitation" shall not include any letter or telephone call if such letter or call is not part of a coordinated fundraising campaign soliciting more than 10 persons during the calendar year.

§ 6115. Disclosure related to quid pro quo contributions

(a) Disclosure requirement.—If an organization described in section 170(c) (other than paragraph (1) thereof) receives a quid pro quo contribution in excess of $75, the organization shall, in connection with the solicitation or receipt of the contribution, provide a written statement which—

(1) informs the donor that the amount of the contribution that is deductible for Federal income tax purposes is limited to the excess of the amount of any money and the value of any property other than money contributed by the donor over the value of the goods or services provided by the organization, and

(2) provides the donor with a good faith estimate of the value of such goods or services.

(b) Quid pro quo contribution.—For purposes of this section, the term "quid pro quo contribution" means a payment made partly as a contribution and partly in consideration for goods or services provided to the payor by the donee organization. A quid pro quo contribution does not include any payment made to an organization, organized exclusively for religious purposes, in return for which the taxpayer receives solely an intangible religious benefit that generally is not sold in a commercial transaction outside the donative context.

CHAPTER 62—TIME AND PLACE FOR PAYING TAX

SUBCHAPTER B—EXTENSIONS OF TIME FOR PAYMENT

§ 6161. Extension of time for paying tax

(a) Amount determined by taxpayer on return.—

(1) General rule.—The Secretary, except as otherwise provided in this title, may extend the time for payment of the amount of the tax shown, or required to be shown, on any return or declaration required under authority of this title (or any installment thereof), for a reasonable period not to exceed 6 months (12 months in the case of estate tax) from the date fixed for payment thereof. Such extension may exceed 6 months in the case of a taxpayer who is abroad.

(2) Estate tax.—The Secretary may, for reasonable cause, extend the time for payment of—

(A) any part of the amount determined by the executor as the tax imposed by chapter 11, or

(B) any part of any installment under section 6166 (including any part of a deficiency prorated to any installment under such section),

for a reasonable period not in excess of 10 years from the date prescribed by section 6151(a) for payment of the tax (or, in the case of an amount referred to in subparagraph (B), if later, not beyond the date which is 12 months after the due date for the last installment).

* * *

§ 6163. Extension of time for payment of estate tax on value of reversionary or remainder interest in property

(a) Extension permitted.—If the value of a reversionary or remainder interest in property is included under chapter 11 in the value of the gross estate, the payment of

* Omitted entirely.

the part of the tax under chapter 11 attributable to such interest may, at the election of the executor, be postponed until 6 months after the termination of the precedent interest or interests in the property, under such regulations as the Secretary may prescribe.

(b) Extension for reasonable cause.—At the expiration of the period of postponement provided for in subsection (a), the Secretary may, for reasonable cause, extend the time for payment for a reasonable period or periods not in excess of 3 years from the expiration of the period of postponement provided in subsection (a).

* * *

§ 6164. Extension of time for payment of taxes by corporations expecting carrybacks

(a) In general.—If a corporation, in any taxable year, files with the Secretary a statement, as provided in subsection (b), with respect to an expected net operating loss carryback from such taxable year, the time for payment of all or part of any tax imposed by subtitle A for the taxable year immediately preceding such taxable year shall be extended, to the extent and subject to the conditions and limitations hereinafter provided in this section.

* * *

§ 6166. Extension of time for payment of estate tax where estate consists largely of interest in closely held business

(a) 5–year deferral; 10–year installment payment.—

(1) In general.—If the value of an interest in a closely held business which is included in determining the gross estate of a decedent who was (at the date of his death) a citizen or resident of the United States exceeds 35 percent of the adjusted gross estate, the executor may elect to pay part or all of the tax imposed by section 2001 in 2 or more (but not exceeding 10) equal installments.

(2) Limitation.—The maximum amount of tax which may be paid in installments under this subsection shall be an amount which bears the same ratio to the tax imposed by section 2001 (reduced by the credits against such tax) as—

(A) the closely held business amount, bears to

(B) the amount of the adjusted gross estate.

(3) Date for payment of installments.—If an election is made under paragraph (1), the first installment shall be paid on or before the date selected by the executor which is not more than 5 years after the date prescribed by section 6151(a) for payment of the tax, and each succeeding installment shall be paid on or before the date which is 1 year after the date prescribed by this paragraph for payment of the preceding installment.

(b) Definitions and special rules.—

(1) Interest in closely held business.—For purposes of this section, the term "interest in a closely held business" means—

(A) an interest as a proprietor in a trade or business carried on as a proprietorship;

(B) an interest as a partner in a partnership carrying on a trade or business, if—

(i) 20 percent or more of the total capital interest in such partnership is included in determining the gross estate of the decedent, or

(ii) such partnership had 45 or fewer partners; or

(C) stock in a corporation carrying on a trade or business if—

(i) 20 percent or more in value of the voting stock of such corporation is included in determining the gross estate of the decedent, or

(ii) such corporation had 45 or fewer shareholders.

* * *

(3) Farmhouses and certain other structures taken into account.—For purposes of the 35–percent requirement of subsection (a)(1), an interest in a closely held business which is the business of farming includes an interest in residential buildings and related improvements on the farm which are occupied on a regular basis by the owner or lessee of the farm or by persons employed by such owner or lessee for purposes of operating or maintaining the farm.

(4) Value.—For purposes of this section, value shall be value determined for purposes of chapter 11 (relating to estate tax).

(5) Closely held business amount.—For purposes of this section, the term "closely held business amount" means the value of the interest in a closely held business which qualifies under subsection (a)(1).

(6) Adjusted gross estate.—For purposes of this section, the term, "adjusted gross estate" means the value of the gross estate reduced by the sum of the amounts allowable as a deduction under section 2053 or 2054. Such sum shall be determined on the basis of the facts and circumstances in existence on the date (including extensions) for filing the return of tax imposed by section 2001 (or, if earlier, the date on which such return is filed).

(7) Partnership interests and stock which is not readily tradable.—

(A) In general.—If the executor elects the benefits of this paragraph (at such time and in such manner as the Secretary shall by regulations prescribe), then—

(i) for purposes of paragraph (1)(B)(i) or (1)(C)(i) (whichever is appropriate) and for purposes of subsection (c), any capital interest in a partnership and any non-readily-tradable stock which (after the application of paragraph (2)) is treated as owned by the decedent shall be treated as included in determining the value of the decedent's gross estate,

(ii) the executor shall be treated as having selected under subsection (a)(3) the date prescribed by section 6151(a), and

(iii) for purposes of applying section 6601(j), the 2–percent portion (as defined in such section) shall be treated as being zero.

(B) Non-readily-tradable stock defined.—For purposes of this paragraph, the term "non-readily-tradable stock" means stock for which, at the time of the decedent's death, there was no market on a stock exchange or in an over-the-counter market.

* * *

(9) Deferral not available for passive assets.—

(A) In general.—For purposes of subsection (a)(1) and determining the closely held business amount (but not for purposes of subsection (g)), the value of any interest in a closely held business shall not include the value of that portion of such interest which is attributable to passive assets held by the business.

(B) Passive asset defined.—For purposes of this paragraph—

(i) In general.—The term "passive asset" means any asset other than an asset used in carrying on a trade or business.

(ii) Stock treated as passive asset.—The term "passive asset" includes any stock in another corporation unless—

(I) such stock is treated as held by the decedent by reason of an election under paragraph (8), and

(II) such stock qualified under subsection (a)(1).

(iii) Exception for active corporations.—If—

(I) a corporation owns 20 percent or more in value of the voting stock of another corporation, or such other corporation has 45 or fewer shareholders, and

(II) 80 percent or more of the value of the assets of each such corporation is attributable to assets used in carrying on a trade or business,

then such corporations shall be treated as 1 corporation for purposes of clause (ii). For purposes of applying subclause (II) to the corporation holding the stock of the other corporation, such stock shall not be taken into account.

* * *

(c) Special rule for interests in 2 or more closely held businesses.—For purposes of this section, interests in 2 or more closely held businesses, with respect to each of which there is included in determining the value of the decedent's gross estate 20 percent or more of the total value of each such business, shall be treated as an interest in a single closely held business. For purposes of the 20–percent requirement of the preceding sentence, an interest in a closely held business which represents the surviving spouse's interest in property held by the decedent and the surviving spouse as community property or as joint tenants, tenants by the entirety, or tenants in common shall be treated as having been included in determining the value of the decedent's gross estate.

(d) Election.—Any election under subsection (a) shall be made not later than the time prescribed by section 6075(a) for filing the return of tax imposed by section 2001 (including extensions thereof), and shall be made in such manner as the Secretary shall by regulations prescribe. If an election under subsection (a) is made, the provisions of this subtitle shall apply as though the Secretary were extending the time for payment of the tax.

* * *

(f) Time for payment of interest.—If the time for payment of any amount of tax has been extended under this section—

(1) Interest for first 5 years.—Interest payable under section 6601 of any unpaid portion of such amount attributable to the first 5 years after the date prescribed by section 6151(a) for payment of the tax shall be paid annually.

(2) Interest for periods after first 5 years.—Interest payable under section 6601 on any unpaid portion of such amount attributable to any period after the 5–year period referred to in paragraph (1) shall be paid annually at the same time as, and as a part of, each installment payment of the tax.

* * *

(g) Acceleration of payment.—

(1) Disposition of interest; withdrawal of funds from business.—

(A) If—

(i)(I) any portion of an interest in a closely held business which qualifies under subsection (a)(1) is distributed, sold, exchanged, or otherwise disposed of, or

(II) money and other property attributable to such an interest is withdrawn from such trade or business, and

(ii) the aggregate of such distributions, sales, exchanges, or other dispositions and withdrawals equals or exceeds 50 percent of the value of such interest,

then the extension of time for payment of tax provided in subsection (a) shall cease to apply, and the unpaid portion of the tax payable in installments shall be paid upon notice and demand from the Secretary.

(B) In the case of a distribution in redemption of stock to which section 303 (or so much of section 304 as relates to section 303) applies—

(i) the redemption of such stock, and the withdrawal of money and other property distributed in such redemption, shall not be treated as a distribution or withdrawal for purposes of subparagraph (A), and

(ii) for purposes of subparagraph (A), the value of the interest in the closely held business shall be considered to be such value reduced by the value of the stock redeemed.

This subparagraph shall apply only if, on or before the date prescribed by subsection (a)(3) for the payment of the first installment which becomes due after the date of the distribution (or, if earlier, on or before the day which is 1 year after the date of the distribution), there is paid an amount of the tax imposed by section 2001 not less than the amount of money and other property distributed.

(C) Subparagraph (A)(i) does not apply to an exchange of stock pursuant to a plan of reorganization described in subparagraph (D), (E), or (F) of section 368(a)(1) nor to an exchange to which section 355 (or so much of section 356 as relates to section 355) applies; but any stock received in such an exchange shall be treated for purposes of subparagraph (A)(i) as an interest qualifying under subsection (a)(1).

(D) Subparagraph (A)(i) does not apply to a transfer of property of the decedent to a person entitled by reason of the decedent's death to receive such property under the decedent's will, the applicable law of descent and distribution, or a trust created by the decedent. A similar rule shall apply in the case of a series of subsequent transfers of the property by reason of death so long as each transfer is to a member of the family (within the meaning of section 267(c)(4)) of the transferor in such transfer.

* * *

(F) Changes in interest in business company.—If any stock in a holding company is treated as stock in a business company by reason of subsection (b)(8)(A)—

(i) any disposition of any interest in such stock in the business company by such holding company, or

(ii) any withdrawal of any money or other property from such business company attributable to such stock by such holding company owning such stock,

shall be treated for purposes of subparagraph (a) as a disposition of (or a withdrawal with respect to) the stock qualifying under subsection (a)(1).

(2) Undistributed income of estate.—

(A) If an election is made under this section and the estate has undistributed net income for any taxable year ending on or after the due date for the first installment, the executor shall, on or before the date prescribed by law for filing the income tax return for such taxable year (including extensions thereof), pay an amount equal to such undistributed net income in liquidation of the unpaid portion of the tax payable in installments.

(B) For purposes of subparagraph (A), the undistributed net income of the estate for any taxable year is the amount by which the distributable net income of the estate for such taxable year (as defined in section 643) exceeds the sum of—

(i) the amounts for such taxable year specified in paragraphs (1) and (2) of section 661(a) (relating to deductions for distributions, etc.);

(ii) the amount of tax imposed for the taxable year on the estate under chapter 1; and

(iii) the amount of the tax imposed by section 2001 (including interest) paid by the executor during the taxable year (other than any amount paid pursuant to this paragraph).

* * *

(i) Special rule for certain direct skips.—To the extent that an interest in a closely held business is the subject of a direct skip (within the meaning of section 2612(c)) occurring at the same time as and as a result of the decedent's death, then for purposes of this section any tax imposed by section 2601 on the transfer of such interest shall be treated as if it were additional tax imposed by section 2001.

* * *

CHAPTER 63—ASSESSMENT

Subchapter
A. In general.*
B. Deficiency procedures in the case of income, estate, gift, and certain excise taxes.
C. Tax treatment of partnership items.
D. Electing large partnerships*

SUBCHAPTER B—DEFICIENCY PROCEDURES IN THE CASE OF INCOME, ESTATE, GIFT, AND CERTAIN EXCISE TAXES

§ 6211. Definition of a deficiency

(a) In general.—For purposes of this title in the case of income, estate, and gift taxes imposed by subtitles A and B * * *, the term "deficiency" means the amount by which the tax imposed by subtitle A or B, * * *, exceeds the excess of—

(1) the sum of—

(A) the amount shown as the tax by the taxpayer upon his return, if a return was made by the taxpayer and an amount was shown as the tax by the taxpayer thereon, plus

(B) the amounts previously assessed (or collected without assessment) as a deficiency, over—

(2) the amount of rebates, as defined in subsection (b)(2), made.

* * *

§ 6212. Notice of deficiency

(a) In general.—If the Secretary determines that there is a deficiency in respect of any tax imposed by subtitles A or B * * *, he is authorized to send notice of such deficiency to the taxpayer by certified mail or registered mail. Such notice shall include

* Omitted entirely.

a notice to the taxpayer of the taxpayer's right to contact a local office of the taxpayer advocate and the location and phone number of the appropriate office.

(b) Address for notice of deficiency.—

(1) Income and gift taxes and certain excise taxes.—In the absence of notice to the Secretary under section 6903 of the existence of a fiduciary relationship, notice of a deficiency in respect of a tax imposed by subtitle A, chapter 12, * * *, if mailed to the taxpayer at his last known address, shall be sufficient for purposes of subtitle A, chapter 12, * * * even if such taxpayer is deceased, or is under a legal disability, or, in the case of a corporation, has terminated its existence.

(2) Joint income tax return.—In the case of a joint income tax return filed by husband and wife, such notice of deficiency may be a single joint notice, except that if the Secretary has been notified by either spouse that separate residences have been established, then, in lieu of the single joint notice, a duplicate original of the joint notice shall be sent by certified mail or registered mail to each spouse at his last known address.

(3) Estate tax.—In the absence of notice to the Secretary under section 6903 of the existence of a fiduciary relationship, notice of a deficiency in respect of a tax imposed by chapter 11, if addressed in the name of the decedent or other person subject to liability and mailed to his last known address, shall be sufficient for purposes of chapter 11 and of this chapter.

(c) Further deficiency letters restricted.—

(1) General rule.—If the Secretary has mailed to the taxpayer a notice of deficiency as provided in subsection (a), and the taxpayer files a petition with the Tax Court within the time prescribed in section 6213(a), the Secretary shall have no right to determine any additional deficiency of income tax for the same taxable year, of gift tax for the same calendar year, of estate tax in respect of the taxable estate of the same decedent, * * *.

* * *

(d) Authority to rescind notice of deficiency with taxpayer's consent.—The Secretary may, with the consent of the taxpayer, rescind any notice of deficiency mailed to the taxpayer. Any notice so rescinded shall not be treated as a notice of deficiency for purposes of subsection (c)(1) (relating to further deficiency letters restricted), section 6213(a) (relating to restrictions applicable to deficiencies; petition to Tax Court), and section 6512(a) (relating to limitations in case of petition to Tax Court), and the taxpayer shall have no right to file a petition with the Tax Court based on such notice. Nothing in this subsection shall affect any suspension of the running of any period of limitations during any period during which the rescinded notice was outstanding.

§ 6213. Restrictions applicable to deficiencies; petition to Tax Court

(a) Time for filing petition and restriction on assessment.—Within 90 days, or 150 days if the notice is addressed to a person outside the United States, after the notice of deficiency authorized in section 6212 is mailed (not counting Saturday, Sunday, or a legal holiday in the District of Columbia as the last day), the taxpayer may file a petition with the Tax Court for a redetermination of the deficiency. * * * Any petition filed with the Tax Court on or before the last date specified for filing such petition by the Secretary in the notice of deficiency shall be treated as timely filed.

* * *

(c) Failure to file petition.—If the taxpayer does not file a petition with the Tax Court within the time prescribed in subsection (a), the deficiency, notice of which has been mailed to the taxpayer, shall be assessed, and shall be paid upon notice and demand from the Secretary.

(d) Waiver of restrictions.—The taxpayer shall at any time (whether or not a notice of deficiency has been issued) have the right, by a signed notice in writing filed with the Secretary, to waive the restrictions provided in subsection (a) on the assessment and collection of the whole or any part of the deficiency.

* * *

SUBCHAPTER C—TAX TREATMENT OF PARTNERSHIP ITEMS

§ 6221. Tax treatment determined at partnership level

Except as otherwise provided in this subchapter, the tax treatment of any partnership item (and the applicability of any penalty, addition to tax, or additional amount which relates to an adjustment to a partnership item) shall be determined at the partnership level.

§ 6222. Partner's return must be consistent with partnership return or Secretary notified of inconsistency

(a) In general.—A partner shall, on the partner's return, treat a partnership item in a manner which is consistent with the treatment of such partnership item on the partnership return.

(b) Notification of inconsistent treatment.—

(1) In general.—In the case of any partnership item, if—

(A)(i) the partnership has filed a return but the partner's treatment on his return is (or may be) inconsistent with the treatment of the item on the partnership return, or

(ii) the partnership has not filed a return, and

(B) the partner files with the Secretary a statement identifying the inconsistency,

subsection (a) shall not apply to such item.

(2) Partner receiving incorrect information.—A partner shall be treated as having complied with subparagraph (B) of paragraph (1) with respect to a partnership item if the partner—

(A) demonstrates to the satisfaction of the Secretary that the treatment of the partnership item on the partner's return is consistent with the treatment of the item on the schedule furnished to the partner by the partnership, and

(B) elects to have this paragraph apply with respect to that item.

(c) Effect of failure to notify.—In any case—

(1) described in paragraph (1)(A)(i) of subsection (b), and

(2) in which the partner does not comply with paragraph (1)(B) of subsection (b),

section 6225 shall not apply to any part of a deficiency attributable to any computational adjustment required to make the treatment of the items by such partner consistent with the treatment of the items on the partnership return.

* * *

§ 6223. Notice to partners of proceedings

(a) Secretary must give partners notice of beginning and completion of administrative proceedings.—The Secretary shall mail to each partner whose name and address is furnished to the Secretary notice of—

(1) the beginning of an administrative proceeding at the partnership level with respect to a partnership item, and

(2) the final partnership administrative adjustment resulting from any such proceeding.

A partner shall not be entitled to any notice under this subsection unless the Secretary has received (at least 30 days before it is mailed to the tax matters partner) sufficient information to enable the Secretary to determine that such partner is entitled to such notice and to provide such notice to such partner.

* * *

(g) Tax matters partner must keep partners informed of proceedings.—To the extent and in the manner provided by regulations, the tax matters partner of a partnership shall keep each partner informed of all administrative and judicial proceedings for the adjustment at the partnership level of partnership items.

* * *

§ 6224. Participation in administrative proceedings; waivers; agreements

(a) Participation in administrative proceedings.—Any partner has the right to participate in any administrative proceeding relating to the determination of partnership items at the partnership level.

(b) Partner may waive rights.—

(1) In general.—A partner may at any time waive—

(A) any right such partner has under this subchapter, and

(B) any restriction under this subchapter on action by the Secretary.

(2) Form.—Any waiver under paragraph (1) shall be made by a signed notice in writing filed with the Secretary.

(c) Settlement agreement.—In the absence of a showing of fraud, malfeasance, or misrepresentation of fact—

(1) Binds all parties.—A settlement agreement between the Secretary or the Attorney General (or his delegate) and 1 or more partners in a partnership with respect to the determination of partnership items for any partnership taxable year shall (except as otherwise provided in such agreement) be binding on all parties to such agreement with respect to the determination of partnership items for such partnership taxable year. An indirect partner is bound by any such agreement entered into by the pass-thru partner unless the indirect partner has been identified as provided in section 6223(c)(3).

* * *

(3) Tax matters partner may bind certain other partners.—

(A) In general.—A partner who is not a notice partner (and not a member of a notice group described in subsection (b)(2) of section 6223) shall be bound by any settlement agreement—

(i) which is entered into by the tax matters partner, and

(ii) in which the tax matters partner expressly states that such agreement shall bind the other partners.

(B) Exception.—Subparagraph (A) shall not apply to any partner who (within the time prescribed by the Secretary) files a statement with the Secretary providing that the tax matters partner shall not have the authority to enter into a settlement agreement on behalf of such partner.

§ 6225. Assessments made only after partnership level proceedings are completed

(a) Restriction on assessment and collection.—Except as otherwise provided in this subchapter, no assessment of a deficiency attributable to any partnership item may be made (and no levy or proceeding in any court for the collection of any such deficiency may be made, begun, or prosecuted) before—

(1) the close of the 150th day after the day on which a notice of a final partnership administrative adjustment was mailed to the tax matters partner, and

(2) if a proceeding is begun in the Tax Court under section 6226 during such 150–day period, the decision of the court in such proceeding has become final.

(b) Premature action may be enjoined.—Notwithstanding section 7421(a), any action which violates subsection (a) may be enjoined in the proper court, including the Tax Court. The Tax Court shall have no jurisdiction to enjoin any action or proceeding under this subsection unless a timely petition for a readjustment of the partnership items for the taxable year has been filed and then only in respect of the adjustments that are the subject of such petition.

* * *

§ 6226. Judicial review of final partnership administrative adjustments

(a) Petition by tax matters partner.—Within 90 days after the day on which a notice of a final partnership administrative adjustment is mailed to the tax matters partner, the tax matters partner may file a petition for a readjustment of the partnership items for such taxable year with—

(1) the Tax Court,

(2) the district court of the United States for the district in which the partnership's principal place of business is located, or

(3) the Claims Court.

(b) Petition by partner other than tax matters partner.—

(1) In general.—If the tax matters partner does not file a readjustment petition under subsection (a) with respect to any final partnership administrative adjustment, any notice partner (and any 5–percent group) may, within 60 days after the close of the 90–day period set forth in subsection (a), file a petition for a readjustment of the partnership items for the taxable year involved with any of the courts described in subsection (a).

* * *

(c) Partners treated as parties.—If an action is brought under subsection (a) or (b) with respect to a partnership for any partnership taxable year—

(1) each person who was a partner in such partnership at any time during such year shall be treated as a party to such action, and

(2) the court having jurisdiction of such action shall allow each such person to participate in the action.

* * *

§ 6229. Period of limitations for making assessments

(a) General rule.—Except as otherwise provided in this section, the period for assessing any tax imposed by subtitle A with respect to any person which is attributable to any partnership item (or affected item) for a partnership taxable year shall not expire before the date which is 3 years after the later of—

(1) the date on which the partnership return for such taxable year was filed, or

(2) the last day for filing such return for such year (determined without regard to extensions).

* * *

(c) Special rule in case of fraud, etc.—

(1) False return.—If any partner has, with the intent to evade tax, signed or participated directly or indirectly in the preparation of a partnership return which includes a false or fraudulent item—

(A) in the case of partners so signing or participating in the preparation of the return, any tax imposed by subtitle A which is attributable to any partnership item (or affected item) for the partnership taxable year to which the return relates may be assessed at any time, and

(B) in the case of all other partners, subsection (a) shall be applied with respect to such return by substituting "6 years" for "3 years".

(2) Substantial omission of income.—If any partnership omits from gross income an amount properly includible therein and such amount is described in clause (i) or (ii) of section 6501(e)(1)(A), subsection (a) shall be applied by substituting "6 years" for "3 years."

(3) No return.—In the case of a failure by a partnership to file a return for any taxable year, any tax attributable to a partnership item (or affected item) arising in such year may be assessed at any time.

(4) Return filed by Secretary.—For purposes of this section, a return executed by the Secretary under subsection (b) of section 6020 on behalf of the partnership shall not be treated as a return of the partnership.

* * *

§ 6231. Definitions and special rules

(a) Definitions.—For purposes of this subchapter—

(1) Partnership.—

(A) In general.—Except as provided in subparagraph (B), the term "partnership" means any partnership required to file a return under section 6031(a).

(B) Exception for small partnerships.—

(i) In general.—The term "partnership" shall not include any partnership having 10 or fewer partners each of whom is an individual (other than a nonresident alien), a C corporation, or an estate of a deceased partner. For purposes of the preceding sentence, a husband and wife (and their estates) shall be treated as 1 partner.

(I) such partnership has 10 or fewer partners each of whom is a natural person (other than a nonresident alien) or an estate, and

(II) each partner's share of each partnership item is the same as his share of every other item.

For purposes of the preceding sentence, a husband and wife (and their estates) shall be treated as 1 partner.

(ii) Election to have subchapter apply.—A partnership (within the meaning of subparagraph (A)) may for any taxable year elect to have clause (i) not apply. Such election shall apply for such taxable year and all subsequent taxable years unless revoked with the consent of the Secretary.

(2) Partner.—The term "partner" means—

(A) a partner in the partnership, and

(B) any other person whose income tax liability under subtitle A is determined in whole or in part by taking into account directly or indirectly partnership items of the partnership.

(3) Partnership item.—The term "partnership item" means, with respect to a partnership, any item required to be taken into account for the partnership's taxable year under any provision of subtitle A to the extent regulations prescribed by the Secretary provide that, for purposes of this subtitle, such item is more appropriately determined at the partnership level than at the partner level.

(4) Nonpartnership item.—The term "nonpartnership item" means an item which is (or is treated as) not a partnership item.

(5) Affected item.—The term "affected item" means any item to the extent such item is affected by a partnership item.

(6) Computational adjustment.—The term "computational adjustment" means the change in the tax liability of a partner which properly reflects the treatment under this subchapter of a partnership item. All adjustments required to apply the results of a proceeding with respect to a partnership under this subchapter to an indirect partner shall be treated as computational adjustments.

(7) Tax matters partner.—The tax matters partner of any partnership is—

(A) the general partner designated as the tax matters partner as provided in regulations, or

(B) if there is no general partner who has been so designated, the general partner having the largest profits interest in the partnership at the close of the taxable year involved (or, where there is more than 1 such partner, the 1 of such partners whose name would appear first in an alphabetical listing).

If there is no general partner designated under subparagraph (A) and the Secretary determines that it is impracticable to apply subparagraph (B), the partner selected by the Secretary shall be treated as the tax matters partner. The Secretary shall, within 30 days of selecting a tax matters partner under the preceding sentence, notify all partners required to receive notice under section 6223(a) of the name and address of the person selected.

(8) Notice partner.—The term "notice partner" means a partner who, at the time in question, would be entitled to notice under subsection (a) of section 6223 (determined without regard to subsections (b)(2) and (e)(1)(B) thereof).

(9) Pass-thru partner.—The term "pass-thru partner" means a partnership, estate, trust, S corporation, nominee, or other similar person through whom other persons hold an interest in the partnership with respect to which proceedings under this subchapter are conducted.

(10) Indirect partner.—The term "indirect partner" means a person holding an interest in a partnership through 1 or more pass-thru partners.

* * *

CHAPTER 64—COLLECTION

SUBCHAPTER A—GENERAL PROVISIONS

§ 6301. Collection authority

The Secretary shall collect the taxes imposed by the internal revenue laws.

§ 6302. Mode or time of collection

(a) Establishment by regulations.—If the mode or time for collecting any tax is not provided for by this title, the Secretary may establish the same by regulations.

* * *

SUBCHAPTER C—LIEN FOR TAXES

§ 6320. Notice and opportunity for hearing upon filing of notice of lien.

(a) Requirement of notice.—

(1) In general.—The Secretary shall notify in writing the person described in section 6321 of the filing of a notice of lien under section 6323.

(2) Time and method for notice.—The notice required under paragraph (1) shall be—

(A) given in person;

(B) left at the dwelling or usual place of business of such person; or

(C) sent by certified or registered mail to such person's last known address, not more than 5 business days after the day of the filing of the notice of lien.

(3) Information included with notice.—The notice required under paragraph (1) shall include in simple and nontechnical terms—

(A) the amount of unpaid tax;

(B) the right of the person to request a hearing during the 30–day period beginning on the day after the 5–day period described in paragraph (2);

(C) the administrative appeals available to the taxpayer with respect to such lien and the procedures relating to such appeals; and

(D) the provisions of this title and procedures relating to the release of liens on property.

* Omitted entirely.

(b) Right to fair hearing.—

(1) In general.—If the person requests a hearing in writing under subsection (a)(3)(B) and states the grounds for the requested hearing, such hearing shall be held by the Internal Revenue Service Office of Appeals.

(2) One hearing per period.— A person shall be entitled to only one hearing under this section with respect to the taxable period to which the unpaid tax specified in subsection (a)(3)(A) relates.

(3) Impartial officer.—The hearing under this subsection shall be conducted by an officer or employee who has had no prior involvement with respect to the unpaid tax specified in subsection (a)(3)(A) before the first hearing under this section or section 6330. A taxpayer may waive the requirement of this paragraph.

(4) Coordination with 6330.—To the extent practicable, a hearing under this section shall be held in conjunction with a hearing under section 6330.

(c) Conduct of hearing; review; suspensions.—For purposes of this section, subsections (c), (d) (other than paragraph (2)(B) thereof), (e) and (g) of section 6330 shall apply.

§ 6321. Lien for taxes

If any person liable to pay any tax neglects or refuses to pay the same after demand, the amount (including any interest, additional amount, addition to tax, or assessable penalty, together with any costs that may accrue in addition thereto) shall be a lien in favor of the United States upon all property and rights to property, whether real or personal, belonging to such person.

§ 6322. Period of lien

Unless another date is specifically fixed by law, the lien imposed by section 6321 shall arise at the time the assessment is made and shall continue until the liability for the amount so assessed (or a judgment against the taxpayer arising out of such liability) is satisfied or becomes unenforceable by reason of lapse of time.

§ 6324. Special liens for estate and gift taxes

(a) Liens for estate tax.—Except as otherwise provided in subsection (c)—

(1) Upon gross estate.—Unless the estate tax imposed by chapter 11 is sooner paid in full, or becomes unenforceable by reason of lapse of time, it shall be a lien upon the gross estate of the decedent for 10 years from the date of death, except that such part of the gross estate as is used for the payment of charges against the estate and expenses of its administration, allowed by any court having jurisdiction thereof, shall be divested of such lien.

(2) Liability of transferees and others.—If the estate tax imposed by chapter 11 is not paid when due, then the spouse, transferee, trustee (except the trustee of an employees' trust which meets the requirements of section 401(a)), surviving tenant, person in possession of the property by reason of the exercise, nonexercise, or release of a power of appointment, or beneficiary, who receives, or has on the date of the decedent's death, property included in the gross estate under sections 2034 to 2042, inclusive, to the extent of the value, at the time of the decedent's death, of such property, shall be personally liable for such tax. Any part of such property transferred by (or transferred by a transferee of) such spouse, transferee, trustee, surviving tenant, person in possession, or beneficiary, to a purchaser or holder of a security interest shall be divested of the lien provided in paragraph (1) and a like lien shall then attach to all the property of such spouse, transferee, trustee, surviving tenant, person in possession, or beneficiary, or transferee of any such person, except any part transferred to a purchaser or a holder of a security interest.

(3) Continuance after discharge of fiduciary.—The provisions of section 2204 (relating to discharge of fiduciary from personal liability) shall not operate as a release of any part of the gross estate from the lien for any deficiency that may thereafter be determined to be due, unless such part of the gross estate (or any interest therein) has been transferred to a purchaser or a holder of a security interest, in which case such part (or such interest) shall not be subject to a lien or to any claim or demand for any such deficiency, but the lien shall attach to the consideration received from such purchaser or holder of a security interest, by the heirs, legatees, devisees, or distributees.

(b) Lien for gift tax.—Except as otherwise provided in subsection (c), unless the gift tax imposed by chapter 12 is sooner paid in full or becomes unenforceable by reason of lapse of time, such tax shall be a lien upon all gifts made during the period for which the return was filed, for 10 years from the date the gifts are made. If the tax is not paid when due, the donee of any gift shall be personally liable for such tax to the extent of the value of such gift. Any part of the property comprised in the gift transferred by the donee (or by a transferee of the donee) to a purchaser or holder of a security interest shall be divested of the lien imposed by this subsection and such lien, to the extent of the value of such gift, shall attach to all the property (including after-acquired property) of the donee (or the transferee) except any part transferred to a purchaser or holder of a security interest.

* * *

SUBCHAPTER D—SEIZURE OF PROPERTY FOR COLLECTION OF TAXES

§ 6330. Notice and opportunity for hearing before levy

(a) Requirement of notice before levy.—

(1) In general.—No levy may be made on any property or right to property of any person unless the Secretary has notified such person in writing of their right to a hearing under this section before such levy is made. Such notice shall be required only once for the taxable period to which the unpaid tax specified in paragraph (3)(A) relates.

(2) Time and method for notice.—The notice required under paragraph (1) shall be—

(A) given in person;

(B) left at the dwelling or usual place of business of such person; or

(C) sent by certified or registered mail, return receipt requested, to such person's last known address;

not less than 30 days before the day of the first levy with respect to the amount of the unpaid tax for the taxable period.

(3) Information included with notice.—The notice required under paragraph (1) shall include in simple and nontechnical terms—

(A) the amount of unpaid tax;

(B) the right of the person to request a hearing during the 30–day period under paragraph (2); and

(C) the proposed action by the Secretary and the rights of the person with respect to such action, including a brief statement which sets forth—

(i) the provisions of this title relating to levy and sale of property;

(ii) the procedures applicable to the levy and sale of property under this title;

(iii) the administrative appeals available to the taxpayer with respect to such levy and sale and the procedures relating to such appeals;

(iv) the alternatives available to taxpayers which could prevent levy on property (including installment agreements under section 6159); and

(v) the provisions of this title and procedures relating to redemption of property and release of liens on property.

(b) Right to fair hearing.—

(1) In general.—If the person requests a hearing in writing under subsection (a)(3)(B) and states the grounds for the requested hearing, such hearing shall be held by the Internal Revenue Service Office of Appeals.

(2) One hearing per period.—A person shall be entitled to only one hearing under this section with respect to the taxable period to which the unpaid tax specified in subsection (a)(3)(A) relates.

(3) Impartial officer.—The hearing under this subsection shall be conducted by an officer or employee who has had no prior involvement with respect to the unpaid tax specified in subsection (a)(3)(A) before the first hearing under this section or section 6320. A taxpayer may waive the requirement of this paragraph.

(c) Matters considered at hearing.—In the case of any hearing conducted under this section—

(1) Requirement of investigation.—The appeals officer shall at the hearing obtain verification from the Secretary that the requirements of any applicable law or administrative procedure have been met.

(2) Issues at hearing.—

(A) In general.—The person may raise at the hearing any relevant issue relating to the unpaid tax or the proposed levy, including—

(i) appropriate spousal defenses;

(ii) challenges to the appropriateness of collection actions; and

(iii) offers of collection alternatives, which may include the posting of a bond, the substitution of other assets, an installment agreement, or an offer-in-compromise.

(B) Underlying liability.—The person may also raise at the hearing challenges to the existence or amount of the underlying tax liability for any tax period if the person did not receive any statutory notice of deficiency for such tax liability or did not otherwise have an opportunity to dispute such tax liability.

(3) Basis for the determination.—The determination by an appeals officer under this subsection shall take into consideration—

(A) the verification presented under paragraph (1);

(B) the issues raised under paragraph (2); and

(C) whether any proposed collection action balances the need for the efficient collection of taxes with the legitimate concern of the person that any collection action be no more intrusive than necessary.

(4) Certain issues precluded.—An issue may not be raised at the hearing if—

(A)(i) the issue was raised and considered at a previous hearing under section 6320 or in any other previous administrative or judicial proceeding; and

(ii) the person seeking to raise the issue participated meaningfully in such hearing or proceeding; or

(B) the issue meets the requirement of clause(i) or (ii) of section 6702(b)(2)(A).

This paragraph shall not apply to any issue with respect to which subsection (d)(2)(B) applies.

(d) Proceeding after hearing.—

(1) Judicial review of determination.—The person may, within 30 days of a determination under this section, appeal such determination to the Tax Court (and the Tax Court shall have jurisdiction with respect to such matter).

(2) Jurisdiction retained at IRS Office of Appeals.—The Internal Revenue Service Office of Appeals shall retain jurisdiction with respect to any determination made under this section, including subsequent hearings requested by the person who requested the original hearing on issues regarding—

(A) collection actions taken or proposed with respect to such determination; and

(B) after the person has exhausted all administrative remedies, a change in circumstances with respect to such person which affects such determination.

(e) Suspension of collections and statute of limitations.—

(1) In general.—Except as provided in paragraph (2), if a hearing is requested under subsection (a)(3)(B), the levy actions which are the subject of the requested hearing and the running of any period of limitations under section 6502 (relating to collection after assessment), section 6531 (relating to criminal prosecutions), or section 6532 (relating to other suits) shall be suspended for the period during which such hearing, and appeals therein, are pending. In no event shall any such period expire before the 90th day after the day on which there is a final determination in such hearing. Notwithstanding the provisions of section of 7421(a), the beginning of a levy or proceeding during the time the suspension under this paragraph is in force may be enjoined by a proceeding in the proper court, including the Tax Court. The Tax Court shall have no jurisdiction under this paragraph to enjoin any action or proceeding unless a timely appeal has been filed under subsection (d)(1) and then only in respect of the unpaid tax or proposed levy to which the determination being appealed relates.

(2) Levy upon appeal.—Paragraph (1) shall not apply to a levy action while an appeal is pending if the underlying tax liability is not at issue in the appeal and the court determines that the Secretary has shown good cause not to suspend the levy.

(f) Exceptions.—If—

(1) the Secretary has made a finding under the last sentence of section 6331(a) that the collection of tax is in jeopardy,

(2) the Secretary has served a levy on a State to collect a Federal tax liability from a State tax refund,

(3) the Secretary has served a disqualified employment tax levy, or

(4) the Secretary has served a Federal contractor levy,

this section shall not apply, except that the taxpayer shall be given the opportunity for the hearing described in this section within a reasonable period of time after the levy.

(g) Frivolous requests for hearing, etc.—Notwithstanding any other provision of this section, if the Secretary determines that any portion of a request for a hearing under this section or section 6320 meets the requirement of clause (i) or (ii) of section

6702(b)(2)(A), then the Secretary may treat such portion as if it were never submitted and such portion shall not be subject to any further administrative or judicial review.

(h) Definitions related to exceptions.—For purposes of subsection (f)—

(1) Disqualified employment tax levy.—A disqualified employment tax levy is any levy in connection with the collection of employment taxes for any taxable period if the person subject to the levy (or any predecessor thereof) requested a hearing under this section with respect to unpaid employment taxes arising in the most recent 2–year period before the beginning of the taxable period with respect to which the levy is served. For purposes of the preceding sentence, the term "employment taxes" means any taxes under chapter 21, 22, 23, or 24.

(2) Federal contractor levy.—A Federal contractor levy is any levy if the person whose property is subject to the levy (or any predecessor thereof) is a Federal contractor.

§ 6331. Levy and distraint

(a) Authority of Secretary.—If any person liable to pay any tax neglects or refuses to pay the same within 10 days after notice and demand, it shall be lawful for the Secretary to collect such tax (and such further sum as shall be sufficient to cover the expenses of the levy) by levy upon all property and rights to property (except such property as is exempt under section 6334) belonging to such person or on which there is a lien provided in this chapter for the payment of such tax. Levy may be made upon the accrued salary or wages of any officer, employee, or elected official, of the United States, the District of Columbia, or any agency or instrumentality of the United States or the District of Columbia, by serving a notice of levy on the employer (as defined in section 3401(d)) of such officer, employee, or elected official. If the Secretary makes a finding that the collection of such tax is in jeopardy, notice and demand for immediate payment of such tax may be made by the Secretary and, upon failure or refusal to pay such tax, collection thereof by levy shall be lawful without regard to the 10–day period provided in this section.

(b) Seizure and sale of property.—The term "levy" as used in this title includes the power of distraint and seizure by any means. Except as otherwise provided in subsection (e), a levy shall extend only to property possessed and obligations existing at the time thereof. In any case in which the Secretary may levy upon property or rights to property, he may seize and sell such property or rights to property (whether real or personal, tangible or intangible).

(c) Successive seizures.—Whenever any property or right to property upon which levy has been made by virtue of subsection (a) is not sufficient to satisfy the claim of the United States for which levy is made, the Secretary may, thereafter, and as often as may be necessary, proceed to levy in like manner upon any other property liable to levy of the person against whom such claim exists, until the amount due from him, together with all expenses, is fully paid.

(d) Requirement of notice before levy.—

(1) In general.—Levy may be made under subsection (a) upon the salary or wages or other property of any person with respect to any unpaid tax only after the Secretary has notified such person in writing of his intention to make such levy.

(2) 30–day requirement.—The notice required under paragraph (1) shall be—

(A) given in person,

(B) left at the dwelling or usual place of business of such person, or

(C) sent by certified or registered mail to such person's last known address,

no less than 30 days before the day of the levy.

(3) Jeopardy.—Paragraph (1) shall not apply to a levy if the Secretary has made a finding under the last sentence of subsection (a) that the collection of tax is in jeopardy.

(4) Information included with notice.—The notice required under paragraph (1) shall include a brief statement which sets forth in simple and nontechnical terms—

(A) the provisions of this title relating to levy and sale of property,

(B) the procedures applicable to the levy and sale of property under this title,

(C) the administrative appeals available to the taxpayer with respect to such levy and sale and the procedures relating to such appeals,

(D) the alternatives available to taxpayers which could prevent levy on the property (including installment agreements under section 6159),

(E) the provisions of this title relating to redemption of property and release of liens on property, and

(F) the procedures applicable to the redemption of property and the release of a lien on property under this title.

(e) Continuing levy on salary and wages.—The effect of a levy on salary or wages payable to or received by a taxpayer shall be continuous from the date such levy is first made until such levy is released under section 6343.

* * *

§ 6334. Property exempt from levy

(a) Enumeration.—There shall be exempt from levy—

* * *

(4) Unemployment benefits.—Any amount payable to an individual with respect to his unemployment (including any portion thereof payable with respect to dependents) under an unemployment compensation law of the United States, of any State, or of the District of Columbia or of the Commonwealth of Puerto Rico.

* * *

(8) Judgments for support of minor children.—If the taxpayer is required by judgment of a court of competent jurisdiction, entered prior to the date of levy, to contribute to the support of his minor children, so much of his salary, wages, or other income as is necessary to comply with such judgment.

(9) Minimum exemption for wages, salary, and other income.—Any amount payable to or received by an individual as wages or salary for personal services, or as income derived from other sources, during any period, to the extent that the total of such amounts payable to or received by him during such period does not exceed the applicable exempt amount determined under subsection (d).

* * *

(11) Certain public assistance payments.—Any amount payable to an individual as a recipient of public assistance under—

(A) title IV (relating to aid to families with dependent children) or title XVI (relating to supplemental security income for the aged, blind, and disabled) of the Social Security Act, or

(B) State or local government public assistance or public welfare programs for which eligibility is determined by a needs or income test.

* * *

(13) Residences exempt in small deficiency cases and principal residences and certain business assets exempt in absence of certain approval or jeopardy.—

(A) Residences in small deficiency cases.—If the amount of the levy does not exceed $5,000—

(i) any real property used as a residence by the taxpayer; or

(ii) any real property of the taxpayer (other than real property which is rented) used by any other individual as a residence.

(B) Principal residences and certain business assets.—Except to the extent provided in subsection (e)—

(i) the principal residence of the taxpayer (within the meaning of section 121); and

(ii) tangible personal property or real property (other than real property which is rented) used in the trade or business of an individual taxpayer.

* * *

(d) Exempt amount of wages, salary, or other income.—

(1) Individuals on weekly basis.—In the case of an individual who is paid or receives all of his wages, salary, and other income on a weekly basis, the amount of the wages, salary, and other income payable to or received by him during any week which is exempt from levy under subsection (a)(9) shall be the exempt amount.

(2) Exempt amount.—For purposes of paragraph (1), the term "exempt amount" means an amount equal to—

(A) the sum of—

(i) the standard deduction, and

(ii) the aggregate amount of the deductions for personal exemptions allowed the taxpayer under section 151 in the taxable year in which such levy occurs, divided by

(B) 52.

Unless the taxpayer submits to the Secretary a written and properly verified statement specifying the facts necessary to determine the proper amount under subparagraph (A), subparagraph (A) shall be applied as if the taxpayer were a married individual filing a separate return with only 1 personal exemption.

(3) Individuals on basis other than weekly.—In the case of any individual not described in paragraph (1), the amount of the wages, salary, and other income payable to or received by him during any applicable pay period or other fiscal period (as determined under regulations prescribed by the Secretary) which is exempt from levy under subsection (a)(9) shall be an amount (determined under such regulations) which as nearly as possible will result in the same total exemption from levy for such individual over a period of time as he would have under paragraph (1) if (during such period of time) he were paid or received such wages, salary, and other income on a regular weekly basis.

(e) Levy allowed on principal residences and certain business assets in certain circumstances.—

(1) Principal residences.—

(A) Approval required.—A principal residence shall not be exempt from levy if a judge or magistrate of a district court of the United States approves (in writing) the levy of such residence.

(B) Jurisdiction.—The district courts of the United States shall have exclusive jurisdiction to approve a levy under subparagraph (A).

(2) Certain business assets.—Property (other than a principal residence) described in subsection (a)(13)(B) shall not be exempt from levy if—

(A) a district director or assistant district director of the Internal Revenue Service personally approves (in writing) the levy of such property; or

(B) the Secretary finds that the collection of tax is in jeopardy.

An official may not approve a levy under subparagraph (A) unless the official determines that the taxpayer's other assets subject to collection are insufficient to pay the amount due, together with expenses of the proceedings.

* * *

CHAPTER 66—LIMITATIONS

SUBCHAPTER A—LIMITATIONS ON ASSESSMENT AND COLLECTION

§ 6501. Limitations on assessment and collection

(a) General rule.—Except as otherwise provided in this section, the amount of any tax imposed by this title shall be assessed within 3 years after the return was filed (whether or not such return was filed on or after the date prescribed) or, if the tax is payable by stamp, at any time after such tax became due and before the expiration of 3 years after the date on which any part of such tax was paid, and no proceeding in court without assessment for the collection of such tax shall be begun after the expiration of such period. For purposes of this chapter, the term "return" means the return required to be filed by the taxpayer (and does not include a return of any person from whom the taxpayer has received an item of income, gain, loss, deduction, or credit).

(b) Time return deemed filed.—

(1) Early return.—For purposes of this section, a return of tax imposed by this title, except tax imposed by chapter 3, 21, or 24, filed before the last day prescribed by law or by regulations promulgated pursuant to law for the filing thereof, shall be considered as filed on such last day.

* * *

(c) Exceptions.—

(1) False return.—In the case of a false or fraudulent return with the intent to evade tax, the tax may be assessed, or a proceeding in court for collection of such tax may be begun without assessment, at any time.

(2) Willful attempt to evade tax.—In case of a willful attempt in any manner to defeat or evade tax imposed by this title (other than tax imposed by subtitle A or B), the tax may be assessed, or a proceeding in court for the collection of such tax may be begun without assessment, at any time.

* Omitted entirely.

(3) No return.—In the case of failure to file a return, the tax may be assessed, or a proceeding in court for the collection of such tax may be begun without assessment, at any time.

(4) Extension by agreement.—

(A) In general.—Where, before the expiration of the time prescribed in this section for the assessment of any tax imposed by this title, except the estate tax provided in chapter 11, both the Secretary and the taxpayer have consented in writing to its assessment after such time, the tax may be assessed at any time prior to the expiration of the period agreed upon. The period so agreed upon may be extended by subsequent agreements in writing made before the expiration of the period previously agreed upon.

(B) Notice to taxpayer of right to refuse or limit extension.—The Secretary shall notify the taxpayer of the taxpayer's right to refuse to extend the period of limitations, or to limit such extension to particular issues or to a particular period of time, on each occasion when the taxpayer is requested to provide such consent.

* * *

(9) Gift tax on certain gifts not shown on return.—If any gift of property the value of which (or any increase in taxable gifts required under section 2701(d) which) is required to be shown on a return of tax imposed by chapter 12 (without regard to section 2503(b)), and is not shown on such return, any tax imposed by chapter 12 on such gift may be assessed, or a proceeding in court for the collection of such tax may be begun without assessment, at any time. The preceding sentence shall not apply to any item which is disclosed in such return, or in a statement attached to the return, in a manner adequate to apprise the Secretary of the nature of such item.

* * *

(d) Request for prompt assessment.—Except as otherwise provided in subsection (c), (e), or (f), in the case of any tax (other than the tax imposed by chapter 11 of subtitle B, relating to estate taxes) for which return is required in the case of a decedent, or by his estate during the period of administration, or by a corporation, the tax shall be assessed, and any proceeding in court without assessment for the collection of such tax shall be begun, within 18 months after written request therefor (filed after the return is made and filed in such manner and such form as may be prescribed by regulations of the Secretary) by the executor, administrator, or other fiduciary representing the estate of such decedent, or by the corporation, but not after the expiration of 3 years after the return was filed. This subsection shall not apply in the case of a corporation unless—

(1)(A) such written request notifies the Secretary that the corporation contemplates dissolution at or before the expiration of such 18–month period, (B) the dissolution is in good faith begun before the expiration of such 18–month period, and (C) the dissolution is completed;

(2)(A) such written request notifies the Secretary that a dissolution has in good faith been begun, and (B) the dissolution is completed; or

(3) a dissolution has been completed at the time such written request is made.

(e) Substantial omission of items.—Except as otherwise provided in subsection (c)—

(1) Income taxes.—In the case of any tax imposed by subtitle A—

(A) General rule.—If the taxpayer omits from gross income an amount properly includible therein and—

(i) such amount is in excess of 25 percent of the amount of gross income stated in the return, or

(ii) such amount—

(I) is attributable to one or more assets with respect to which information is required to be reported under section 6038D (or would be so required if such section were applied without regard to the dollar threshold specified in subsection (a) thereof and without regard to any exceptions provided pursuant to subsection (h)(1) thereof), and

(II) is in excess of $5,000,

the tax may be assessed, or a proceeding in court for collection of such tax may be begun without assessment, at any time within 6 years after the return was filed.

(B) Determination of gross income.—For purposes of subparagraph (A)—

(i) In the case of a trade or business, the term "gross income" means the total of the amounts received or accrued from the sale of goods or services (if such amounts are required to be shown on the return) prior to diminution by the cost of such sales or services; and

(ii) In determining the amount omitted from gross income, there shall not be taken into account any amount which is omitted from gross income stated in the return if such amount is disclosed in the return, or in a statement attached to the return, in a manner adequate to apprise the Secretary of the nature and amount of such item.

* * *

(2) Estate and gift taxes.—In the case of a return of estate tax under chapter 11 or a return of gift tax under chapter 12, if the taxpayer omits from the gross estate or from the total amount of the gifts made during the period for which the return was filed items includible in such gross estate or such total gifts, as the case may be, as exceed in amount 25 percent of the gross estate stated in the return or the total amount of gifts stated in the return, the tax may be assessed, or a proceeding in court for the collection of such tax may be begun without assessment, at any time within 6 years after the return was filed. In determining the items omitted from the gross estate or the total gifts, there shall not be taken into account any item which is omitted from the gross estate or from the total gifts stated in the return if such item is disclosed in the return, or in a statement attached to the return, in a manner adequate to apprise the Secretary of the nature and amount of such item.

* * *

(f) Personal holding company tax.—If a corporation which is a personal holding company for any taxable year fails to file with its return under chapter 1 for such year a schedule setting forth—

(1) the items of gross income and adjusted ordinary gross income, described in section 543, received by the corporation during such year, and

(2) the names and addresses of the individuals who owned, within the meaning of section 544 (relating to rules for determining stock ownership), at any time during the last half of such year more than 50 percent in value of the outstanding capital stock of the corporation,

the personal holding company tax for such year may be assessed, or a proceeding in court for the collection of such tax may be begun without assessment, at any time within 6 years after the return for such year was filed.

(g) Certain income tax returns of corporations.—

(1) **Trusts or partnerships.**—If a taxpayer determines in good faith that it is a trust or partnership and files a return as such under subtitle A, and if such taxpayer is thereafter held to be a corporation for the taxable year for which the return is filed, such return shall be deemed the return of the corporation for purposes of this section.

* * *

(h) **Net operating loss or capital loss carrybacks.**—In the case of a deficiency attributable to the application to the taxpayer of a net operating loss carryback or a capital loss carryback (including deficiencies which may be assessed pursuant to the provisions of section 6213(b)(3)), such deficiency may be assessed at any time before the expiration of the period within which a deficiency for the taxable year of the net operating loss or net capital loss which results in such carryback may be assessed.

* * *

§ 6502. Collection after assessment

(a) **Length of period.**—Where the assessment of any tax imposed by this title has been made within the period of limitation properly applicable thereto, such tax may be collected by levy or by a proceeding in court, but only if the levy is made or the proceeding begun—

(1) within 10 years after the assessment of the tax, or

(2) if—

(A) there is an installment agreement between the taxpayer and the Secretary, prior to the date which is 90 days after the expiration of any period for collection agreed upon in writing by the Secretary and the taxpayer at the time the installment agreement was entered into; or

(B) there is a release of levy under section 6343 after such 10–year period, prior to the expiration of any period for collection agreed upon in writing by the Secretary and the taxpayer before such release.

If a timely proceeding in court for the collection of a tax is commenced, the period during which such tax may be collected by levy shall be extended and shall not expire until the liability for the tax (or a judgment against the taxpayer arising from such liability) is satisfied or becomes unenforceable.

* * *

§ 6503. Suspension of running of period of limitation

(a) **Issuance of statutory notice of deficiency.**—

(1) **General rule.**—The running of the period of limitations provided in section 6501 * * * on the making of assessments or the collection by levy or a proceeding in court, in respect of any deficiency as defined in section 6211 (relating to income, estate, gift and certain excise taxes), shall (after the mailing of a notice under section 6212(a)) be suspended for the period during which the Secretary is prohibited from making the assessment or from collecting by levy or a proceeding in court (and in any event, if a proceeding in respect of the deficiency is placed on the docket of the Tax Court, until the decision of the Tax Court becomes final), and for 60 days thereafter.

* * *

SUBCHAPTER B—LIMITATIONS ON CREDIT OR REFUND

§ 6511. Limitations on credit or refund

(a) Period of limitation on filing claim.—Claim for credit or refund of an overpayment of any tax imposed by this title in respect of which tax the taxpayer is required to file a return shall be filed by the taxpayer within 3 years from the time the return was filed or 2 years from the time the tax was paid, whichever of such periods expires the later, or if no return was filed by the taxpayer, within 2 years from the time the tax was paid. Claim for credit or refund of an overpayment of any tax imposed by this title which is required to be paid by means of a stamp shall be filed by the taxpayer within 3 years from the time the tax was paid.

(b) Limitation on allowance of credits and refunds.—

(1) Filing of claim within prescribed period.—No credit or refund shall be allowed or made after the expiration of the period of limitation prescribed in subsection (a) for the filing of a claim for credit or refund, unless a claim for credit or refund is filed by the taxpayer within such period.

(2) Limit on amount of credit or refund.—

(A) Limit where claim filed within 3-year period.—If the claim was filed by the taxpayer during the 3-year period prescribed in subsection (a), the amount of the credit or refund shall not exceed the portion of the tax paid within the period, immediately preceding the filing of the claim, equal to 3 years plus the period of any extension of time for filing the return. If the tax was required to be paid by means of a stamp, the amount of the credit or refund shall not exceed the portion of the tax paid within the 3 years immediately preceding the filing of the claim.

(B) Limit where claim not filed within 3-year period.—If the claim was not filed within such 3-year period, the amount of the credit or refund shall not exceed the portion of the tax paid during the 2 years immediately preceding the filing of the claim.

(C) Limit if no claim filed.—If no claim was filed, the credit or refund shall not exceed the amount which would be allowable under subparagraph (A) or (B), as the case may be, if claim was filed on the date the credit or refund is allowed.

(c) Special rules applicable in case of extension of time by agreement.—If an agreement under the provisions of section 6501(c)(4) extending the period for assessment of a tax imposed by this title is made within the period prescribed in subsection (a) for the filing of a claim for credit or refund—

(1) Time for filing claim.—The period for filing claim for credit or refund or for making credit or refund if no claim is filed, provided in subsections (a) and (b)(1), shall not expire prior to 6 months after the expiration of the period within which an assessment may be made pursuant to the agreement or any extension thereof under section 6501(c)(4).

(2) Limit on amount.—If a claim is filed, or a credit or refund is allowed when no claim was filed, after the execution of the agreement and within 6 months after the expiration of the period within which an assessment may be made pursuant to the agreement or any extension thereof, the amount of the credit or refund shall not exceed the portion of the tax paid after the execution of the agreement and before the filing of the claim or the making of the credit or refund, as the case may be, plus the portion of the tax paid within the period which would be applicable under subsection (b)(2) if a claim had been filed on the date the agreement was executed.

(3) Claims not subject to special rule.—This subsection shall not apply in the case of a claim filed, or credit or refund allowed if no claim is filed, either—

(A) prior to the execution of the agreement or

(B) more than 6 months after the expiration of the period within which an assessment may be made pursuant to the agreement or any extension thereof.

(d) Special rules applicable to income taxes.—

(1) Seven-year period of limitation with respect to bad debts and worthless securities.—If the claim for credit or refund relates to an overpayment of tax imposed by subtitle A on account of—

(A) The deductibility by the taxpayer, under section 166 or section 832(c), of a debt as a debt which became worthless, or, under section 165(g), of a loss from worthlessness of a security, or

(B) The effect that the deductibility of a debt or loss described in subparagraph (A) has on the application to the taxpayer of a carryover,

in lieu of the 3–year period of limitation prescribed in subsection (a), the period shall be 7 years from the date prescribed by law for filing the return for the year with respect to which the claim is made. If the claim for credit or refund relates to an overpayment on account of the effect that the deductibility of such a debt or loss has on the application to the taxpayer of a carryback, the period shall be either 7 years from the date prescribed by law for filing the return for the year of the net operating loss which results in such carryback or the period prescribed in paragraph (2) of this subsection, whichever expires the later. In the case of a claim described in this paragraph the amount of the credit or refund may exceed the portion of the tax paid within the period prescribed in subsection (b)(2) or (c), whichever is applicable, to the extent of the amount of the overpayment attributable to the deductibility of items described in this paragraph.

(2) Special period of limitation with respect to net operating loss or capital loss carrybacks.—

(A) Period of limitation.—If the claim for credit or refund relates to an overpayment attributable to a net operating loss carryback or a capital loss carryback, in lieu of the 3–year period of limitation prescribed in subsection (a), the period shall be that period which ends 3 years after the time prescribed by law for filing the return (including extensions thereof) for the taxable year of the net operating loss or net capital loss which results in such carryback, or the period prescribed in subsection (c) in respect of such taxable year, whichever expires later. In the case of such a claim, the amount of the credit or refund may exceed the portion of the tax paid within the period provided in subsection (b)(2) or (c), whichever is applicable, to the extent of the amount of the overpayment attributable to such carryback.

(B) Applicable rules.—

(i) In general.—If the allowance of a credit or refund of an overpayment of tax attributable to a net operating loss carryback or a capital loss carryback is otherwise prevented by the operation of any law or rule of law other than section 7122 (relating to compromises), such credit or refund may be allowed or made, if claim therefor is filed within the period provided in subparagraph (A) of this paragraph.

(ii) Tentative carryback adjustments.—If the allowance of an application, credit, or refund of a decrease in tax determined under section 6411(b) is otherwise prevented by the operation of any law or rule of law other than section 7122, such application, credit, or refund may be allowed or made if application for a tentative carryback adjustment is made within the period provided in section 6411(a).

(iii) Determinations by courts to be conclusive.—In the case of any such claim for credit or refund or any such application for a tentative carryback adjustment, the determination by any court, including the Tax Court, in any proceeding in which the decision of the court has become final, shall be conclusive except with respect to—

(I) the net operating loss deduction and the effect of such deduction, and

(II) the determination of a short-term capital loss and the effect of such short-term capital loss, to the extent that such deduction or short-term capital loss is affected by a carryback which was not an issue in such proceeding.

* * *

(h) Running of periods of limitation suspended while taxpayer is unable to manage financial affairs due to disability.—

(1) In general.—In the case of an individual, the running of the periods specified in subsections (a), (b), and (c) shall be suspended during any period of such individual's life that such individual is financially disabled.

(2) Financially disabled.—

(A) In general.—For purposes of paragraph (1), an individual is financially disabled if such individual is unable to manage his financial affairs by reason of a medically determinable physical or mental impairment of the individual which can be expected to result in death or which has lasted or can be expected to last for a continuous period of not less than 12 months. An individual shall not be considered to have such an impairment unless proof of the existence thereof is furnished in such form and manner as the Secretary may require.

(B) Exception where individual has guardian, etc.—An individual shall not be treated as financially disabled during any period that such individual's spouse or any other person is authorized to act on behalf of such individual in financial matters.

* * *

§ 6512. Limitations in case of petition to Tax Court

(a) Effect of petition to Tax Court.—If the Secretary has mailed to the taxpayer a notice of deficiency under section 6212(a) (relating to deficiencies of income, estate, gift, and certain excise taxes) and if the taxpayer files a petition with the Tax Court within the time prescribed in section 6213(a) (or 7481(c) with respect to a determination of statutory interest or section 7481(d) solely with respect to a determination of estate tax by the Tax Court), no credit or refund of income tax for the same taxable year, of gift tax for the same calendar year or calendar quarter, of estate tax in respect of the taxable estate of the same decedent, or of tax imposed by chapter 41, 42, 43, or 44 with respect to any act (or failure to act) to which such petition relates, in respect of which the Secretary has determined the deficiency shall be allowed or made and no suit by the taxpayer for the recovery of any part of the tax shall be instituted in any court except—

(1) As to overpayments determined by a decision of the Tax Court which has become final, and

(2) As to any amount collected in excess of an amount computed in accordance with the decision of the Tax Court which has become final, and

(3) As to any amount collected after the period of limitation upon the making of levy or beginning a proceeding in court for collection has expired; but in any such claim for credit or refund or in any such suit for refund the decision of the Tax Court which has become final, as to whether such period has expired before the notice of deficiency was mailed, shall be conclusive, and

(4) As to overpayments attributable to partnership items, in accordance with subchapter C of chapter 63, and

(5) As to any amount collected within the period during which the Secretary is prohibited from making the assessment or from collecting by levy or through a proceeding in court under the provisions of section 6213(a), and

(6) As to overpayments the Secretary is authorized to refund or credit pending appeal as provided in subsection (b).

(b) Overpayment determined by Tax Court.—

(1) Jurisdiction to determine.—Except as provided by paragraph (3) and by section 7463, if the Tax Court finds that there is no deficiency and further finds that the taxpayer has made an overpayment of income tax for the same taxable year, of gift tax for the same calendar year or calendar quarter, of estate tax in respect of the taxable estate of the same decedent, or of tax imposed by chapter 41, 42, 43, or 44 with respect to any act (or failure to act) to which such petition relates, in respect of which the Secretary determined the deficiency, or finds that there is a deficiency but that the taxpayer has made an overpayment of such tax, the Tax Court shall have jurisdiction to determine the amount of such overpayment, and such amount shall, when the decision of the Tax Court has become final, be credited or refunded to the taxpayer. If a notice of appeal in respect of the decision of the Tax Court is filed under section 7483, the Secretary is authorized to refund or credit the overpayment determined by the Tax Court to the extent the overpayment is not contested on appeal.

* * *

§ 6513. Time return deemed filed and tax considered paid

(a) Early return or advance payment of tax.—For purposes of section 6511, any return filed before the last day prescribed for the filing thereof shall be considered as filed on such last day. For purposes of section 6511(b)(2) and (c), payment of any portion of the tax made before the last day prescribed for the payment of the tax shall be considered made on such last day. For purposes of this subsection, the last day prescribed for filing the return or paying the tax shall be determined without regard to any extension of time granted the taxpayer and without regard to any election to pay the tax in installments.

* * *

§ 6514. Credits or refunds after period of limitation

(a) Credits or refunds after period of limitation.—A refund of any portion of an internal revenue tax shall be considered erroneous and a credit of any such portion shall be considered void—

(1) Expiration of period for filing claim.—If made after the expiration of the period of limitation for filing claim therefor, unless within such period claim was filed: or

(2) Disallowance of claim and expiration of period for filing suit.—In the case of a claim filed within the proper time and disallowed by the Secretary, if the credit or refund was made after the expiration of the period of limitation for filing suit, unless within such period suit was begun by the taxpayer.

* * *

(b) Credit after period of limitation.—Any credit against a liability in respect of any taxable year shall be void if any payment in respect of such liability would be considered an overpayment under section 6401(a).

SUBCHAPTER D—PERIODS OF LIMITATION IN JUDICIAL PROCEEDINGS

§ 6531. Periods of limitation on criminal prosecutions

No person shall be prosecuted, tried, or punished for any of the various offenses arising under the internal revenue laws unless the indictment is found or the information instituted within 3 years next after the commission of the offense, except that the period of limitation shall be 6 years—

(1) for offenses involving the defrauding or attempting to defraud the United States or any agency thereof, whether by conspiracy or not, and in any manner;

(2) for the offense of willfully attempting in any manner to evade or defeat any tax or the payment thereof;

(3) for the offense of willfully aiding or assisting in, or procuring, counseling, or advising, the preparation or presentation under, or in connection with any matter arising under, the internal revenue laws, of a false or fraudulent return, affidavit, claim, or document (whether or not such falsity or fraud is with the knowledge or consent of the person authorized or required to present such return, affidavit, claim, or document);

(4) for the offense of willfully failing to pay any tax, or make any return (other than a return required under authority of part III of subchapter A of chapter 61) at the time or times required by law or regulations;

(5) for offenses described in sections 7206(1) * * *;

* * *

§ 6532. Periods of limitation on suits

(a) Suits by taxpayers for refund.—

(1) General rule.—No suit or proceeding under section 7422(a) for the recovery of any internal revenue tax, penalty, or other sum, shall be begun before the expiration of 6 months from the date of filing the claim required under such section unless the Secretary renders a decision thereon within that time, nor after the expiration of 2 years from the date of mailing by certified mail or registered mail by the Secretary to the taxpayer of a notice of the disallowance of the part of the claim to which the suit or proceeding relates.

(2) Extension of time.—The 2–year period prescribed in paragraph (1) shall be extended for such period as may be agreed upon in writing between the taxpayer and the Secretary.

(3) Waiver of notice of disallowance.—If any person files a written waiver of the requirement that he be mailed a notice of disallowance, the 2–year period prescribed in paragraph (1) shall begin on the date such waiver is filed.

(4) Reconsideration after mailing of notice.—Any consideration, reconsideration, or action by the Secretary with respect to such claim following the mailing of a notice by certified mail or registered mail of disallowance shall not operate to extend the period within which suit may be begun.

* * *

CHAPTER 67—INTEREST

SUBCHAPTER A—INTEREST ON UNDERPAYMENTS

§ 6601. Interest on underpayment, nonpayment, or extensions of time for payment, of tax

(a) General rule.—If any amount of tax imposed by this title (whether required to be shown on a return, or to be paid by stamp or by some other method) is not paid on or before the last date prescribed for payment, interest on such amount at the underpayment rate established under section 6621 shall be paid for the period from such last date to the date paid.

(b) Last date prescribed for payment.—For purposes of this section, the last date prescribed for payment of the tax shall be determined under chapter 62 with the application of the following rules:

(1) Extensions of time disregarded.—The last date prescribed for payment shall be determined without regard to any extension of time for payment or any installment agreement entered into under section 6159.

(2) Installment payments.—In the case of an election under section 6156(a) to pay the tax in installments—

(A) The date prescribed for payment of each installment of the tax shown on the return shall be determined under section 6156(b), and

(B) The last date prescribed for payment of the first installment shall be deemed the last date prescribed for payment of any portion of the tax not shown on the return.

(3) Jeopardy.—The last date prescribed for payment shall be determined without regard to any notice and demand for payment issued, by reason of jeopardy (as provided in chapter 70), prior to the last date otherwise prescribed for such payment.

(4) Accumulated earnings tax.—In the case of the tax imposed by section 531 for any taxable year, the last date prescribed for payment shall be deemed to be the due date (without regard to extensions) for the return of tax imposed by subtitle A for such taxable year.

(5) Last date for payment not otherwise prescribed.—In the case of taxes payable by stamp and in all other cases in which the last date for payment is not otherwise prescribed, the last date for payment shall be deemed to be the date the liability for tax arises (and in no event shall be later than the date notice and demand for the tax is made by the Secretary).

* * *

(e) Applicable rules.—Except as otherwise provided in this title—

(1) Interest treated as tax.—Interest prescribed under this section on any tax shall be paid upon notice and demand, and shall be assessed, collected, and paid in the same manner as taxes. Any reference in this title (except subchapter B of

* Omitted entirely.

chapter 63, relating to deficiency procedures) to any tax imposed by this title shall be deemed also to refer to interest imposed by this section on such tax.

(2) Interest on penalties, additional amounts, or additions to the tax.—

(A) In general.—Interest shall be imposed under subsection (a) in respect of any assessable penalty, additional amount, or addition to the tax (other than an addition to tax imposed under section 6651(a)(1) or 6653 or under part II of subchapter A of chapter 68) only if such assessable penalty, additional amount, or addition to the tax is not paid within 21 calendar days from the date of notice and demand therefor (10 business days if the amount for which such notice and demand is made equals or exceeds $100,000), and in such case interest shall be imposed only for the period from the date of the notice and demand to the date of payment.

(B) Interest on certain additions to tax.—Interest shall be imposed under this section with respect to any addition to tax imposed by section 6651(a)(1) or 6653 or under part II of subchapter A of chapter 68 for the period which—

(i) begins on the date on which the return of the tax with respect to which such addition to tax is imposed is required to be filed (including any extensions), and

(ii) ends on the date of payment of such addition to tax.

(3) Payments made within specified period after notice and demand.—If notice and demand is made for payment of any amount and if such amount is paid within 21 calendar days (10 business days if the amount for which such notice and demand is made equals or exceeds $100,000) after the date of such notice and demand, interest under this section on the amount so paid shall not be imposed for the period after the date of such notice and demand.

* * *

(j) 2–percent rate on certain portion of estate tax extended under section 6166.—

(1) In general.—If the time for payment of an amount of tax imposed by chapter 11 is extended as provided in section 6166, then in lieu of the annual rate provided by subsection (a)—

(A) interest on the 2–percent portion of such amount shall be paid at the rate of 2 percent, and

(B) interest on so much of such amount as exceeds the 2–percent portion shall be paid at a rate equal to 45 percent of the annual rate provided by subsection (a).

For purposes of this subsection, the amount of any deficiency which is prorated to installments payable under section 6166 shall be treated as an amount of tax payable in installments under such section.

(2) 2–percent portion.—For purposes of this subsection, the term "2–percent portion" means the lesser of—

(A)(i) the amount of the tentative tax which would be determined under the rate schedule set forth in section 2001(c) if the amount with respect to which such tentative tax is to be computed were the sum of $1,000,000 and the applicable exclusion amount in effect under section 2010(c), reduced by

(ii) the applicable credit amount in effect under section 2010(c), or

(B) the amount of the tax imposed by chapter 11 which is extended as provided in section 6166.

§ 6603. Deposits made to suspend running of interest on potential underpayments, etc.

(a) Authority to make deposits other than as payment of tax.—A taxpayer may make a cash deposit with the Secretary which may be used by the Secretary to pay any tax imposed under subtitle A or B or chapter 41, 42, 43, or 44 which has not been assessed at the time of the deposit. Such a deposit shall be made in such manner as the Secretary shall prescribe.

(b) No interest imposed.—To the extent that such deposit is used by the Secretary to pay tax, for purposes of section 6601 (relating to interest on underpayments), the tax shall be treated as paid when the deposit is made.

(c) Return of deposit.—Except in a case where the Secretary determines that collection of tax is in jeopardy, the Secretary shall return to the taxpayer any amount of the deposit (to the extent not used for a payment of tax) which the taxpayer requests in writing.

* * *

SUBCHAPTER B—INTEREST ON OVERPAYMENTS

§ 6611. Interest on overpayments

(a) Rate.—Interest shall be allowed and paid upon any overpayment in respect of any internal revenue tax at the overpayment rate established under section 6621.

(b) Period.—Such interest shall be allowed and paid as follows:

(1) Credits.—In the case of a credit, from the date of the overpayment to the due date of the amount against which the credit is taken.

(2) Refunds.—In the case of a refund, from the date of the overpayment to a date (to be determined by the Secretary) preceding the date of the refund check by not more than 30 days, whether or not such refund check is accepted by the taxpayer after tender of such check to the taxpayer. The acceptance of such check shall be without prejudice to any right of the taxpayer to claim any additional overpayment and interest thereon.

(3) Late returns.—Notwithstanding paragraph (1) or (2) in the case of a return of tax which is filed after the last date prescribed for filing such return (determined with regard to extensions), no interest shall be allowed or paid for any day before the date on which the return is filed.

* * *

SUBCHAPTER C—DETERMINATION OF INTEREST RATE; COMPOUNDING OF INTEREST

§ 6621. Determination of rate of interest

(a) General Rule.—

(1) Overpayment rate.—The overpayment rate established under this section shall be the sum of—

(A) the Federal short-term rate determined under subsection (b), plus

(B) 3 percentage points (2 percentage points in the case of a corporation).

* * *

(2) Underpayment rate.—The underpayment rate established under this section shall be the sum of—

(A) the Federal short-term rate determined under subsection (b), plus

(B) 3 percentage points.

(b) Federal short-term rate.—For purposes of this section—

(1) General rule.—The Secretary shall determine the Federal short-term rate for the first month in each calendar quarter.

(2) Period during which rate applies.—

(A) In general.—Except as provided in subparagraph (B), the Federal short-term rate determined under paragraph (1) for any month shall apply during the first calendar quarter beginning after such month.

(B) Special rule for individual estimated tax.—In determining the addition to tax under section 6654 for failure to pay estimated tax for any taxable year, the Federal short-term rate which applies during the 3rd month following such taxable year shall also apply during the first 15 days of the 4th month following such taxable year.

(3) Federal short-term rate.—The Federal short-term rate for any month shall be the Federal short-term rate determined during such month by the Secretary in accordance with section 1274(d). Any such rate shall be rounded to the nearest full percent (or, if a multiple of ½ of 1 percent such rate shall be increased to the next highest full percent).

* * *

§ 6622. Interest compounded daily

(a) General rule.—In computing the amount of any interest required to be paid under this title or sections 1961(c)(1) or 2411 of title 28, United States Code, by the Secretary or by the taxpayer, or any other amount determined by reference to such amount of interest, such interest and such amount shall be compounded daily.

(b) Exception for penalty for failure to file estimated tax.—Subsection (a) shall not apply for purposes of computing the amount of any addition to tax under section 6654 or 6655.

CHAPTER 68—ADDITIONS TO THE TAX, ADDITIONAL AMOUNTS, AND ASSESSABLE PENALTIES

SUBCHAPTER A—ADDITIONS TO THE TAX AND ADDITIONAL AMOUNTS

PART I—GENERAL PROVISIONS

§ 6651. Failure to file tax return or to pay tax

(a) Addition to the tax.—In case of failure—

(1) to file any return required under authority of subchapter A of chapter 61 (other than part III thereof), subchapter A of chapter 51 (relating to distilled spirits, wines, and beer), or of subchapter A of chapter 52 (relating to tobacco, cigars, cigarettes, and cigarette papers and tubes), or of subchapter A of chapter 53 (relating to machine guns and certain other firearms), on the date prescribed therefor (determined with regard to any extension of time for filing), unless it is shown that such failure is due to reasonable cause and not due to willful neglect, there shall be added to the amount required to be shown as tax on such return 5 percent of the amount of such tax if the failure is for not more than 1 month, with an additional 5 percent for each additional month or fraction thereof during which such failure continues, not exceeding 25 percent in the aggregate;

(2) to pay the amount shown as tax on any return specified in paragraph (1) on or before the date prescribed for payment of such tax (determined with regard to any extension of time for payment), unless it is shown that such failure is due to reasonable cause and not due to willful neglect, there shall be added to the amount shown as tax on such return 0.5 percent of the amount of such tax if the failure is for not more than 1 month, with an additional 0.5 percent for each additional month or fraction thereof during which such failure continues, not exceeding 25 percent in the aggregate; or

(3) to pay any amount in respect of any tax required to be shown on a return specified in paragraph (1) which is not so shown (including an assessment made pursuant to section 6213(b)) within 21 calendar days from the date of notice and demand therefor (10 business days if the amount for which such notice and demand is made equals or exceeds $100,000), unless it is shown that such failure is due to reasonable cause and not due to willful neglect, there shall be added to the amount of tax stated in such notice and demand 0.5 percent of the amount of such tax if the failure is for not more than 1 month, with an additional 0.5 percent for each additional month or fraction thereof during which such failure continues, not exceeding 25 percent in the aggregate.

In the case of a failure to file a return of tax imposed by chapter 1 within 60 days of the date prescribed for filing of such return (determined with regard to any extensions of time for filing), unless it is shown that such failure is due to reasonable cause and not due to willful neglect, the addition to tax under paragraph (1) shall not be less than the lesser of $135 or 100 percent of the amount required to be shown as tax on such return.

(b) Penalty imposed on net amount due.—For purposes of—

(1) subsection (a)(1), the amount of tax required to be shown on the return shall be reduced by the amount of any part of the tax which is paid on or before the date prescribed for payment of the tax and by the amount of any credit against the tax which may be claimed on the return,

(2) subsection (a)(2), the amount of tax shown on the return shall, for purposes of computing the addition for any month, be reduced by the amount of any part of the tax which is paid on or before the beginning of such month and by the amount of any credit against the tax which may be claimed on the return, and

(3) subsection (a)(3), the amount of tax stated in the notice and demand shall, for the purpose of computing the addition for any month, be reduced by the amount of any part of the tax which is paid before the beginning of such month.

* * *

(f) Increase in penalty for fraudulent failure to file.—If any failure to file any return is fraudulent, paragraph (1) of subsection (a) shall be applied—

(1) by substituting "15 percent" for "5 percent" each place it appears, and

(2) by substituting "75 percent" for "25 percent".

* * *

§ 6654. Failure by individual to pay estimated income tax

(a) Addition to the tax.—Except as otherwise provided in this section, in the case of any underpayment of estimated tax by an individual, there shall be added to the tax under chapter 1 and the tax under chapter 2 for the taxable year an amount determined by applying—

(1) the underpayment rate established under section 6621,

(2) to the amount of the underpayment,

(3) for the period of the underpayment.

(b) Amount of underpayment; period of underpayment.—For purposes of subsection (a)—

(1) Amount.—The amount of the underpayment shall be the excess of—

(A) the required installment, over

(B) the amount (if any) of the installment paid on or before the due date for the installment.

(2) Period of underpayment.—The period of the underpayment shall run from the due date for the installment to whichever of the following dates is the earlier—

(A) the 15th day of the 4th month following the close of the taxable year, or

(B) with respect to any portion of the underpayment, the date on which such portion is paid.

(3) Order of crediting payments.—For purposes of paragraph (2)(B), a payment of estimated tax shall be credited against unpaid required installments in the order in which such installments are required to be paid.

(c) Number of required installments; due dates.—For purposes of this section—

(1) Payable in 4 installments.—There shall be 4 required installments for each taxable year.

(2) Time for payment of installments.—

In the case of the following required installments:	The due date is:
1st	April 15
2nd	June 15
3rd	September 15
4th	January 15 of the following taxable year

(d) Amount of required installments.—For purposes of this section—

(1) Amount.—

(A) In general.—Except as provided in paragraph (2), the amount of any required installment shall be 25 percent of the required annual payment.

(B) Required annual payment.—For purposes of subparagraph (A), the term "required annual payment" means the lesser of—

(i) 90 percent of the tax shown on the return for the taxable year (or, if no return is filed, 90 percent of the tax for such year), or

(ii) 100 percent of the tax shown on the return of the individual for the preceding taxable year.

Clause (ii) shall not apply if the preceding taxable year was not a taxable year of 12 months or if the individual did not file a return for such preceding taxable year.

* * *

(e) Exceptions.—

(1) Where tax is small amount.—No addition to tax shall be imposed under subsection (a) for any taxable year if the tax shown on the return for such taxable year (or, if no return is filed, the tax), reduced by the credit allowable under section 31, is less than $1,000.

(2) Where no tax liability for preceding taxable year.—No addition to tax shall be imposed under subsection (a) for any taxable year if—

(A) the preceding taxable year was a taxable year of 12 months,

(B) the individual did not have any liability for tax for the preceding taxable year, and

(C) the individual was a citizen or resident of the United States throughout the preceding taxable year.

* * *

(g) Application of section in case of tax withheld on wages.—

(1) In general.—For purposes of applying this section, the amount of the credit allowed under section 31 for the taxable year shall be deemed a payment of estimated tax, and an equal part of such amount shall be deemed paid on each due date for such taxable year, unless the taxpayer establishes the dates on which all amounts were actually withheld, in which case the amounts so withheld shall be deemed payments of estimated tax on the dates on which such amounts were actually withheld.

(2) Separate application.—The taxpayer may apply paragraph (1) separately with respect to—

(A) wage withholding, and

(B) all other amounts withheld for which credit is allowed under section 31.

(h) Special rule where return filed on or before January 31.—If, on or before January 31 of the following taxable year, the taxpayer files a return for the taxable year and pays in full the amount computed on the return as payable, then no addition to tax shall be imposed under subsection (a) with respect to any underpayment of the 4th required installment for the taxable year.

* * *

(*l*) Estates and trusts.—

(1) In general.—Except as otherwise provided in this subsection, this section shall apply to any estate or trust.

(2) Exception for estates and certain trusts.—With respect to any taxable year ending before the date 2 years after the date of the decedent's death, this section shall not apply to—

(A) the estate of such decedent, or

(B) any trust—

(i) all of which was treated (under subpart E of part I of subchapter J of chapter 1) as owned by the decedent, and

(ii) to which the residue of the decedent's estate will pass under his will (or, if no will is admitted to probate, which is the trust primarily responsible for paying debts, taxes, and expenses of administration).

* * *

PART II—ACCURACY-RELATED AND FRAUD PENALTIES

§ 6662. Imposition of accuracy-related penalty on underpayments

(a) Imposition of penalty.—If this section applies to any portion of an underpayment of tax required to be shown on a return, there shall be added to the tax an amount equal to 20 percent of the portion of the underpayment to which this section applies.

(b) Portion of underpayment to which section applies.—This section shall apply to the portion of any underpayment which is attributable to 1 or more of the following:

(1) Negligence or disregard of rules or regulations.

(2) Any substantial understatement of income tax.

(3) Any substantial valuation misstatement under chapter 1.

(4) Any substantial overstatement of pension liabilities.

(5) Any substantial estate or gift tax valuation understatement.

(6) Any disallowance of claimed tax benefits by reason of a transaction lacking economic substance (within the meaning of section 7701(*o*)) or failing to meet the requirements of any similar rule of law.

* * *

This section shall not apply to any portion of an underpayment on which a penalty is imposed under section 6663. Except as provided in paragraph (1) or (2)(B) of section 6662A(e), this section shall not apply to the portion of any underpayment which is attributable to a reportable transaction understatement on which a penalty is imposed under section 6662A.

(c) Negligence.—For purposes of this section, the term "negligence" includes any failure to make a reasonable attempt to comply with the provisions of this title, and the term "disregard" includes any careless, reckless, or intentional disregard.

(d) Substantial understatement of income tax.—

(1) Substantial understatement.—

(A) In general.—For purposes of this section, there is a substantial understatement of income tax for any taxable year if the amount of the understatement for the taxable year exceeds the greater of—

(i) 10 percent of the tax required to be shown on the return for the taxable year, or

(ii) $5,000.

(B) Special rule for corporations.—In the case of a corporation other than an S corporation or a personal holding company (as defined in section 542), there is a substantial understatement of income tax for any taxable year if the amount of the understatement for the taxable year exceeds the lesser of—

(i) 10 percent of the tax required to be shown on the return for the taxable year (or, if greater, $10,000), or

(ii) $10,000,000.

(2) Understatement.—

(A) In general.—For purposes of paragraph (1), the term "understatement" means the excess of—

(i) the amount of the tax required to be shown on the return for the taxable year, over

(ii) the amount of the tax imposed which is shown on the return, reduced by any rebate (within the meaning of section 6211(b)(2)).

The excess under the preceding sentence shall be determined without regard to items to which section 6662A applies.

(B) Reduction for understatement due to position of taxpayer or disclosed item.—The amount of the understatement under subparagraph (A) shall be reduced by that portion of the understatement which is attributable to—

(i) the tax treatment of any item by the taxpayer if there is or was substantial authority for such treatment, or

(ii) any item if—

(I) the relevant facts affecting the item's tax treatment are adequately disclosed in the return or in a statement attached to the return, and

(II) there is a reasonable basis for the tax treatment of such item by the taxpayer.

For purposes of clause (ii)(II), in no event shall a corporation be treated as having a reasonable basis for its tax treatment of an item attributable to a multiple-party financing transaction if such treatment does not clearly reflect the income of the corporation.

(C) Reduction not to apply to tax shelters.—

(i) In general.—Subparagraph (B) shall not apply to any item attributable to a tax shelter.

(ii) Tax shelter.—For purposes of clause (i), the term "tax shelter" means–

(I) a partnership or other entity,

(II) any investment plan or arrangement, or

(III) any other plan or arrangement,

if a significant purpose of such partnership, entity, plan, or arrangement is the avoidance or evasion of Federal income tax.

(3) Secretarial list.—The Secretary may prescribe a list of positions which the Secretary believes do not meet 1 or more of the standards specified in paragraph (2)(B)(i), section 6664(d)(2), and section 6694(a)(1). Such list (and any revisions thereof) shall be published in the Federal Register or the Internal Revenue Bulletin.

(e) Substantial valuation misstatement under chapter 1.—

(1) In general.—For purposes of this section, there is a substantial valuation misstatement under chapter 1 if—

(A) the value of any property (or the adjusted basis of any property) claimed on any return of tax imposed by chapter 1 is 150 percent or more of the amount determined to be the correct amount of such valuation or adjusted basis (as the case may be), or

(B)(i) the price for any property or services (or for the use of property) claimed on any such return in connection with any transaction between persons described in section 482 is 200 percent or more (or 50 percent or less) of the amount determined under section 482 to be the correct amount of such price, or

(ii) the net section 482 transfer price adjustment for the taxable year exceeds the lesser of $5,000,000 or 10 percent of the taxpayer's gross receipts.

(2) Limitation.—No penalty shall be imposed by reason of subsection (b)(3) unless the portion of the underpayment for the taxable year attributable to substantial valuation misstatements under chapter 1 exceeds $5,000 ($10,000 in the case of a corporation other than an S corporation or a personal holding company (as defined in section 542)).

* * *

(g) Substantial estate or gift tax valuation understatement.—

(1) In general.—For purposes of this section, there is a substantial estate or gift tax valuation understatement if the value of any property claimed on any return of tax imposed by subtitle B is 65 percent or less of the amount determined to be the correct amount of such valuation.

(2) Limitation.—No penalty shall be imposed by reason of subsection (b)(5) unless the portion of the underpayment attributable to substantial estate or gift tax valuation understatements for the taxable period (or, in the case of the tax imposed by chapter 11, with respect to the estate of the decedent) exceeds $5,000.

(h) Increase in penalty in case of gross valuation misstatements.—

(1) In general.—To the extent that a portion of the underpayment to which this section applies is attributable to one or more gross valuation misstatements, subsection (a) shall be applied with respect to such portion by substituting "40 percent" for "20 percent".

(2) Gross valuation misstatements.—The term "gross valuation misstatements" means—

(A) any substantial valuation misstatement under chapter 1 as determined under subsection (e) by substituting—

(i) in paragraph (1)(A), "200 percent" for "150 percent",

(ii) in paragraph (1)(B)(i)—

(I) "400 percent" for "200 percent", and

(II) "25 percent" for "50 percent", and

(iii) in paragraph (1)(B)(ii)—

(I) "$20,000,000" for "$5,000,000", and

(II) "20 percent" for "10 percent".

(B) any substantial overstatement of pension liabilities as determined under subsection (f) by substituting "400 percent" for "200 percent", and

(C) any substantial estate or gift tax valuation understatement as determined under subsection (g) by substituting "40 percent" for "65 percent".

(i) Increase in Penalty in Case of Nondisclosed Noneconomic Substance Transactions.—

(1) In general.—In the case of any portion of an underpayment which is attributable to one or more nondisclosed noneconomic substance transactions, subsection (a) shall be applied with respect to such portion by substituting "40 percent" for "20 percent".

(2) Nondisclosed noneconomic substance transactions.—For purposes of this subsection, the term "nondisclosed noneconomic substance transaction" means any portion of a transaction described in subsection (b)(6) with respect to which the relevant facts affecting the tax treatment are not adequately disclosed in the return nor in a statement attached to the return.

(3) Special rule for amended returns.—In no event shall any amendment or supplement to a return of tax be taken into account for purposes of this subsection if the amendment or supplement is filed after the earlier of the date the taxpayer is first contacted by the Secretary regarding the examination of the return or such other date as is specified by the Secretary.

* * *

§ 6663. Imposition of fraud penalty

(a) Imposition of penalty.—If any part of any underpayment of tax required to be shown on a return is due to fraud, there shall be added to the tax an amount equal to 75 percent of the portion of the underpayment which is attributable to fraud.

(b) Determination of portion attributable to fraud.—If the Secretary establishes that any portion of an underpayment is attributable to fraud, the entire underpayment shall be treated as attributable to fraud, except with respect to any portion of the underpayment which the taxpayer establishes (by a preponderance of the evidence) is not attributable to fraud.

(c) Special rule for joint returns.—In the case of a joint return, this section shall not apply with respect to a spouse unless some part of the underpayment is due to the fraud of such spouse.

§ 6664. Definitions and special rules

(a) Underpayment.—For purposes of this part, the term "underpayment" means the amount by which any tax imposed by this title exceeds the excess of—

(1) the sum of—

(A) the amount shown as the tax by the taxpayer on his return, plus

(B) amounts not so shown previously assessed (or collected without assessment), over

(2) the amount of rebates made.

For purposes of paragraph (2), the term "rebate" means so much of an abatement, credit, refund, or other repayment, as was made on the ground that the tax imposed was less than the excess of the amount specified in paragraph (1) over the rebates previously made.

(b) Penalties applicable only where return filed.—The penalties provided in this part shall apply only in cases where a return of tax is filed (other than a return prepared by the Secretary under the authority of section 6020(b)).

(c) Reasonable cause exception for underpayments.—

(1) In general.—No penalty shall be imposed under section 6662 or 6663 with respect to any portion of an underpayment if it is shown that there was a reasonable cause for such portion and that the taxpayer acted in good faith with respect to such portion.

(2) Exception.—Paragraph (1) shall not apply to any portion of an underpayment which is attributable to one or more transactions described in section 6662(b)(6).

(3) Special rule for certain valuation overstatements.—In the case of any underpayment attributable to a substantial or gross valuation overstatement under chapter 1 with respect to charitable deduction property, paragraph (1) shall not apply. The preceding sentence shall not apply to a substantial valuation overstatement under chapter 1 if—

(A) the claimed value of the property was based on a qualified appraisal made by a qualified appraiser, and

(B) in addition to obtaining such appraisal, the taxpayer made a good faith investigation of the value of the contributed property.

(4) Definitions.—For purposes of this subsection—

(A) Charitable deduction property.—The term "charitable deduction property" means any property contributed by the taxpayer in a contribution for which a deduction was claimed under section 170. For purposes of paragraph (3), such term shall not include any securities for which (as of the date of the contribution) market quotations are readily available on an established securities market.

(B) Qualified appraisal.—The term "qualified appraisal" has the meaning given such term by section 170(f)(11)(E)(i).

(C) Qualified appraiser.—The term "qualified appraiser" has the meaning given such term by section 170(f)(11)(E)(ii).

* * *

PART III—APPLICABLE RULES

§ 6665. Applicable rules

(a) Additions treated as tax.—Except as otherwise provided in this title—

(1) the additions to the tax, additional amounts, and penalties provided by this chapter shall be paid upon notice and demand and shall be assessed, collected, and paid in the same manner as taxes; and

(2) any reference in this title to "tax" imposed by this title shall be deemed also to refer to the additions to the tax, additional amounts, and penalties provided by this chapter.

(b) Procedure for assessing certain additions to tax.—For purposes of subchapter B of chapter 63 (relating to deficiency procedures for income, estate, gift, and certain excise taxes), subsection (a) shall not apply to any addition to tax under section 6651, 6654, or 6655; except that it shall apply—

(1) in the case of an addition described in section 6651, to that portion of such addition which is attributable to a deficiency in tax described in section 6211; or

(2) to an addition described in section 6654 or 6655, if no return is filed for the taxable year.

SUBCHAPTER B—ASSESSABLE PENALTIES

PART I—GENERAL PROVISIONS

* Omitted entirely.

§ 6671. Rules for application of assessable penalties

(a) Penalty assessed as tax.—The penalties and liabilities provided by this subchapter shall be paid upon notice and demand by the Secretary, and shall be assessed and collected in the same manner as taxes. Except as otherwise provided, any reference in this title to "tax" imposed by this title shall be deemed also to refer to the penalties and liabilities provided by this subchapter.

(b) Person defined.—The term "person", as used in this subchapter, includes an officer or employee of a corporation, or a member or employee of a partnership, who as such officer, employee, or member is under a duty to perform the act in respect of which the violation occurs.

§ 6672. Failure to collect and pay over tax, or attempt to evade or defeat tax

(a) General rule.—Any person required to collect, truthfully account for, and pay over any tax imposed by this title who willfully fails to collect such tax, or truthfully account for and pay over such tax, or willfully attempts in any manner to evade or defeat any such tax or the payment thereof, shall, in addition to other penalties provided by law, be liable to a penalty equal to the total amount of the tax evaded, or not collected, or not accounted for and paid over. No penalty shall be imposed under section 6653 or part II of subchapter A of chapter 68 for any offense to which this section is applicable.

(b) Preliminary notice requirement.—

(1) In general.—No penalty shall be imposed under subsection (a) unless the Secretary notifies the taxpayer in writing by mail to an address as determined under section 6212(b) or in person that the taxpayer shall be subject to an assessment of such penalty.

(2) Timing of notice.—The mailing of the notice described in paragraph (1) (or, in the case of such a notice delivered in person, such delivery) shall precede any notice and demand of any penalty under subsection (a) by at least 60 days.

(3) Statute of limitations.—If a notice described in paragraph (1) with respect to any penalty is mailed or delivered in person before the expiration of the period provided by section 6501 for the assessment of such penalty (determined without regard to this paragraph), the period provided by such section for the assessment of such penalty shall not expire before the later of—

(A) the date 90 days after the date on which such notice was mailed or delivered in person, or

(B) if there is a timely protest of the proposed assessment, the date 30 days after the Secretary makes a final administrative determination with respect to such protest.

(4) Exception for jeopardy.—This subsection shall not apply if the Secretary finds that the collection of the penalty is in jeopardy.

* * *

(d) Right of contribution where more than 1 person liable for penalty.—If more than 1 person is liable for the penalty under subsection (a) with respect to any tax, each person who paid such penalty shall be entitled to recover from other persons who are liable for such penalty an amount equal to the excess of the amount paid by such person over such person's proportionate share of the penalty. Any claim for such a recovery may be made only in a proceeding which is separate from, and is not joined or consolidated with—

(1) an action for collection of such penalty brought by the United States, or

(2) a proceeding in which the United States files a counterclaim or third-party complaint for the collection of such penalty.

(e) Exception for voluntary board members of tax-exempt organizations.— No penalty shall be imposed by subsection (a) on any unpaid, volunteer member of any board of trustees or directors of an organization exempt from tax under subtitle A if such member—

(1) is solely serving in an honorary capacity,

(2) does not participate in the day-to-day or financial operations of the organization, and

(3) does not have actual knowledge of the failure on which such penalty is imposed.

The preceding sentence shall not apply if it results in no person being liable for the penalty imposed by subsection (a).

§ 6673. Sanctions and costs awarded by courts

(a) Tax Court proceedings.—

(1) Procedures instituted primarily for delay, etc.—Whenever it appears to the Tax Court that—

(A) proceedings before it have been instituted or maintained by the taxpayer primarily for delay,

(B) the taxpayer's position in such proceeding is frivolous or groundless, or

(C) the taxpayer unreasonably failed to pursue available administrative remedies,

the Tax Court, in its decision, may require the taxpayer to pay to the United States a penalty not in excess of $25,000.

(2) Counsel's liability for excessive costs.—Whenever it appears to the Tax Court that any attorney or other person admitted to practice before the Tax Court has multiplied the proceedings in any case unreasonably and vexatiously, the Tax Court may require—

(A) that such attorney or other person pay personally the excess costs, expenses, and attorneys' fees reasonably incurred because of such conduct, or

(B) if such attorney is appearing on behalf of the Commissioner of Internal Revenue, that the United States pay such excess costs, expenses, and attorneys' fees in the same manner as such an award by a district court.

(b) Proceedings in other courts.—

(1) Claims under section 7433.—Whenever it appears to the court that the taxpayer's position in the proceedings before the court instituted or maintained by such taxpayer under section 7433 is frivolous or groundless the court may require the taxpayer to pay to the United States a penalty not in excess of $10,000.

(2) Collection of sanctions and costs.—In any civil proceeding before any court (other than the Tax Court) which is brought by or against the United States in connection with the determination, collection, or refund of any tax, interest, or penalty under this title, any monetary sanctions, penalties, or costs awarded by the court to the United States may be assessed by the Secretary and, upon notice and demand, may be collected in the same manner as a tax.

(3) Sanctions and costs awarded by a Court of Appeals.—In connection with any appeal from a proceeding in the Tax Court or a civil proceeding described in paragraph (2), an order of a United States Court of Appeals or the Supreme Court awarding monetary sanctions, penalties or court costs to the United States may be registered in a district court upon filing a certified copy of such order and shall be enforceable as other district court judgments. Any such sanctions, penalties, or costs may be assessed by the Secretary and, upon notice and demand, may be collected in the same manner as a tax.

§ 6694. Understatement of taxpayer's liability by income tax return preparer

(a) Understatement due to unreasonable positions.—

(1) In general.—If a tax return preparer—

(A) prepares any return or claim of refund with respect to which any part of an understatement of liability is due to a position described in paragraph (2), and

(B) knew (or reasonably should have known) of the position, such tax return preparer shall pay a penalty with respect to each such return or claim in an amount equal to the greater of $1,000 or 50 percent of the income derived (or to be derived) by the tax return preparer with respect to the return or claim.

(2) Unreasonable position.—

(A) In general.—Except as otherwise provided in this paragraph, a position is described in this paragraph unless there is or was substantial authority for the position.

(B) Disclosed positions.—If the position was disclosed as provided in section 6662(d)(2)(B)(ii)(I) and is not a position to which subparagraph (C) applies, the position is described in this paragraph unless there is a reasonable basis for the position.

(C) Tax shelters and reportable transactions.—If the position is with respect to a tax shelter (as defined in section 6662(d)(2)(C)(ii)) or a reportable transaction to which section 6662A applies, the position is described in this paragraph unless it is reasonable to believe that the position would more likely than not be sustained on its merits.

(3) Reasonable cause exception.—No penalty shall be imposed under this subsection if it is shown that there is reasonable cause for the understatement and the tax return preparer acted in good faith.

(b) Understatement due to willful or reckless conduct.—

(1) In general.—Any tax return preparer who prepares any return or claim for refund with respect to which any part of an understatement of liability is due to a conduct described in paragraph (2) shall pay a penalty with respect to each such return or claim in an amount equal to the greater of—

(A) $5,000, or

(B) 50 percent of the income derived (or to be derived) by the tax return preparer with respect to the return or claim.

(2) Willful or reckless conduct.—Conduct described in this paragraph is conduct by the tax return preparer which is—

(A) a willful attempt in any manner to understate the liability for tax on the return or claim, or

(B) a reckless or intentional disregard of rules or regulations.

(3) Reduction in penalty.—The amount of any penalty payable by any person by reason of this subsection for any return or claim for refund shall be reduced by the amount of the penalty paid by such person by reason of subsection (a).

(c) Extension of period of collection where preparer pays 15 percent of penalty.—

(1) In general.—If, within 30 days after the day on which notice and demand of any penalty under subsection (a) or (b) is made against any person who is a tax return preparer, such person pays an amount which is not less than 15 percent of the amount of such penalty and files a claim for refund of the amount so paid, no levy or proceeding in court for the collection of the remainder of such penalty shall be made, begun, or prosecuted until the final resolution of a proceeding begun as provided in paragraph (2). Notwithstanding the provisions of section 7421(a), the beginning of such proceeding or levy during the time such prohibition is in force may be enjoined by a proceeding in the proper court. Nothing in this paragraph shall be construed to prohibit any counterclaim for the remainder of such penalty in a proceeding begun as provided in paragraph (2).

(2) Preparer must bring suit in district court to determine his liability for penalty.—If, within 30 days after the day on which his claim for refund of any partial payment of any penalty under subsection (a) or (b) is denied (or, if earlier, within 30 days after the expiration of 6 months after the day on which he filed the claim for refund), the tax return preparer fails to begin a proceeding in the appropriate United States district court for the determination of his liability for such penalty, paragraph (1) shall cease to apply with respect to such penalty, effective on the day following the close of the applicable 30–day period referred to in this paragraph.

(3) Suspension of running of period of limitations on collection.—The running of the period of limitations provided in section 6502 on the collection by levy or by a proceeding in court in respect of any penalty described in paragraph (1) shall be suspended for the period during which the Secretary is prohibited from collecting by levy or a proceeding in court.

(d) Abatement of penalty where taxpayer's liability not understated.—If at any time there is a final administrative determination or a final judicial decision that there was no understatement of liability in the case of any return or claim for refund with respect to which a penalty under subsection (a) or (b) has been assessed, such assessment shall be abated, and if any portion of such penalty has been paid the amount so paid shall be refunded to the person who made such payment as an overpayment of tax without regard to any period of limitations which, but for this subsection, would apply to the making of such refund.

(e) Understatement of liability defined.—For purposes of this section, the term "understatement of liability" means any understatement of the net amount payable with respect to any tax imposed by this title or any overstatement of the net amount creditable or refundable with respect to any such tax. Except as otherwise provided in subsection (d), the determination of whether or not there is an understatement of liability shall be made without regard to any administrative or judicial action involving the taxpayer.

(f) Cross reference.—For definition of tax return preparer, see section 7701(a)(36).

§ 6698. Failure to file partnership return

(a) General rule.—In addition to the penalty imposed by section 7203 (relating to willful failure to file return, supply information, or pay tax), if any partnership required to file a return under section 6031 for any taxable year—

(1) fails to file such return at the time prescribed therefor (determined with regard to any extension of time for filing), or

(2) files a return which fails to show the information required under section 6031,

such partnership shall be liable for a penalty determined under subsection (b) for each month (or fraction thereof) during which such failure continues (but not to exceed 12 months), unless it is shown that such failure is due to reasonable cause.

(b) Amount per month.—For purposes of subsection (a), the amount determined under this subsection for any month is the product of—

(1) $195, multiplied by

(2) the number of persons who were partners in the partnership during any part of the taxable year.

(c) Assessment of penalty.—The penalty imposed by subsection (a) shall be assessed against the partnership.

(d) Deficiency procedures not to apply.—Subchapter B of chapter 63 (relating to deficiency procedures for income, estate, gift, and certain excise taxes) shall not apply in respect of the assessment or collection of any penalty imposed by subsection (a).

§ 6701. Penalties for aiding and abetting understatement of tax liability

(a) Imposition of penalty.—Any person—

(1) who aids or assists in, procures, or advises with respect to, the preparation or presentation of any portion of a return, affidavit, claim, or other document,

(2) who knows (or has reason to believe) that such portion will be used in connection with any material matter arising under the internal revenue laws, and

(3) who knows that such portion (if so used) would result in an understatement of the liability for tax of another person,

shall pay a penalty with respect to each such document in the amount determined under subsection (b).

(b) Amount of penalty.—

(1) In general.—Except as provided in paragraph (2), the amount of the penalty imposed by subsection (a) shall be $1,000.

(2) Corporations.—If the return, affidavit, claim, or other document relates to the tax liability of a corporation, the amount of the penalty imposed by subsection (a) shall be $10,000.

(3) Only 1 penalty per person per period.—If any person is subject to a penalty under subsection (a) with respect to any document relating to any taxpayer for any taxable period (or where there is no taxable period, any taxable event), such person shall not be subject to a penalty under subsection (a) with respect to any other document relating to such taxpayer for such taxable period (or event).

* * *

§ 6702. Frivolous tax submissions

(a) Civil penalty for frivolous tax returns.—A person shall pay a penalty of $5,000 if—

(1) Such person files what purports to be a return of a tax imposed by this title but which—

(A) does not contain information on which the substantial correctness of the self-assessment may be judged, or

(B) contains information that on its face indicates that the self-assessment is substantially incorrect, and

(2) the conduct referred to in paragraph (1)—

(A) is based on a position which the Secretary has identified as frivolous under subsection (c), or

(B) reflects a desire to delay or impede the administration of Federal tax laws.

(b) Civil penalty for specified frivolous submissions.—

(1) Imposition of penalty.—Except as provided in paragraph (3), any person who submits a specified frivolous submission shall pay a penalty of $5,000.

(2) Specified frivolous submission.—For purposes of this section—

(A) Specified frivolous submission.—The term "specified frivolous submission" means a specified submission if any portion of such submission—

(i) is based on a position which the Secretary has identified as frivolous under subsection (c), or

(ii) reflects a desire to delay or impede the administration of Federal tax laws.

(B) Specified submission.—The term "specified submission" means—

(i) a request for a hearing under—

(I) section 6320 (relating to notice and opportunity for hearing upon filing of notice of lien), or

(II) section 6330 (relating to notice and opportunity for hearing before levy), and

(ii) an application under—

(I) section 6159 (relating to agreements for payment of tax liability in installments),

(II) section 7122 (relating to compromises), or

(III) section 7811 (relating to taxpayer assistance orders).

(3) Opportunity to withdraw submission.—If the Secretary provides a person with notice that a submission is a specified frivolous submission and such person withdraws such submission within 30 days after such notice, the penalty imposed under paragraph (1) shall not apply with respect to such submission.

(c) Listing of frivolous positions.—The Secretary shall prescribe (and periodically revise) a list of positions which the Secretary has identified as being frivolous for purposes of this subsection. The Secretary shall not include in such list any position that the Secretary determines meets the requirement of section 6662(d)(2)(B)(ii)(II).

(d) Reduction of penalty.—The Secretary may reduce the amount of any penalty imposed under this section if the Secretary determines that such reduction would promote compliance with and administration of the Federal tax laws.

(e) Penalties in addition to other penalties.—The penalties imposed by this section shall be in addition to any other penalty provided by law.

§ 6706. Original issue discount information requirements

(a) Failure to show information on debt instrument.—In the case of a failure to set forth on a debt instrument the information required to be set forth on such instrument under section 1275(c)(1), unless it is shown that such failure is due to reasonable cause and not to willful neglect, the issuer shall pay a penalty of $50 for each instrument with respect to which such a failure exists.

(b) Failure to furnish information to Secretary.—Any issuer who fails to furnish information required under section 1275(c)(2) with respect to any issue of debt instruments on the date prescribed therefor (determined with regard to any extension of time for filing) shall pay a penalty equal to 1 percent of the aggregate issue price of such issue, unless it is shown that such failure is due to reasonable cause and not willful neglect. The amount of the penalty imposed under the preceding sentence with respect to any issue of debt instruments shall not exceed $50,000 for such issue.

(c) Deficiency procedures not to apply.—Subchapter B of chapter 63 (relating to deficiency procedures for income, estate, gift, and certain excise taxes) shall not apply in respect of the assessment or collection of any penalty imposed by this section.

SUBCHAPTER C—PROCEDURAL REQUIREMENTS

§ 6751. Procedural requirements

(a) Computation of penalty included in notice.—The Secretary shall include with each notice of penalty under this title information with respect to the name of the penalty, the section of this title under which the penalty is imposed, and a computation of the penalty.

(b) Approval of assessment.—

(1) In general.—No penalty under this title shall be assessed unless the initial determination of such assessment is personally approved (in writing) by the immediate supervisor of the individual making such determination or such higher level official as the Secretary may designate.

(2) Exceptions.—Paragraph (1) shall not apply to—

(A) any addition to tax under section 6651, 6654, or 6655; or

(B) any other penalty automatically calculated through electronic means.

(c) Penalties.—For purposes of this section, the term "penalty" includes any addition to tax or any additional amount.

CHAPTER 70—JEOPARDY, RECEIVERSHIPS, ETC.

SUBCHAPTER A—JEOPARDY

PART I—TERMINATION OF TAXABLE YEAR

§ 6851. Termination assessments of income tax

(a) Authority for making—

(1) In general.—If the Secretary finds that a taxpayer designs quickly to depart from the United States or to remove his property therefrom, or to conceal himself or his property therein, or to do any other act (including in the case of a corporation distributing all or a part of its assets in liquidation or otherwise) tending to prejudice or to render wholly or partially ineffectual proceedings to collect the income tax for the current or the immediately preceding taxable year unless such proceeding be brought without delay, the Secretary shall immediately make a determination of tax for the current taxable year or for the preceding taxable year, or both, as the case may be, and notwithstanding any other provision of law, such tax shall become immediately due and payable. The Secretary shall immediately assess the amount of the tax so determined (together with all interest, additional amounts, and additions to the tax provided by law) for the current taxable year or such preceding taxable year, or both, as the case may be, and shall cause notice of such determination and assessment to be given the taxpayer, together with a demand for immediate payment of such tax.

* * *

PART II—JEOPARDY ASSESSMENTS

§ 6861. Jeopardy assessments of income, estate, gift, and certain excise taxes

(a) Authority for making.—If the Secretary believes that the assessment or collection of a deficiency, as defined in section 6211, will be jeopardized by delay, he shall, notwithstanding the provisions of section 6213(a), immediately assess such deficiency (together with all interest, additional amounts, and additions to the tax provided for by law), and notice and demand shall be made by the Secretary for the payment thereof.

(b) Deficiency letters.—If the jeopardy assessment is made before any notice in respect of the tax to which the jeopardy assessment relates has been mailed under section 6212(a), then the Secretary shall mail a notice under such subsection within 60 days after the making of the assessment.

* * *

CHAPTER 71—TRANSFEREES AND FIDUCIARIES

§ 6901. Transferred assets

(a) Method of collection.—The amounts of the following liabilities shall, except as hereinafter in this section provided, be assessed, paid, and collected in the same manner and subject to the same provisions and limitations as in the case of the taxes with respect to which the liabilities were incurred:

(1) Income, estate, and gift taxes.—

(A) Transferees.—The liability, at law or in equity, of a transferee of property—

(i) of a taxpayer in the case of a tax imposed by subtitle A (relating to income taxes),

(ii) of a decedent in the case of a tax imposed by chapter 11 (relating to estate taxes), or

(iii) of a donor in the case of a tax imposed by chapter 12 (relating to gift taxes),

in respect of the tax imposed by subtitle A or B.

(B) Fiduciaries.—The liability of a fiduciary under section 3713(b) of title 31, United States Code in respect of the payment of any tax described in subparagraph (A) from the estate of the taxpayer, the decedent, or the donor, as the case may be.

(2) Other taxes.—The liability, at law or in equity of a transferee of property of any person liable in respect of any tax imposed by this title (other than a tax imposed by subtitle A or B), but only if such liability arises on the liquidation of a partnership or corporation, or on a reorganization within the meaning of section 368(a).

(b) Liability.—Any liability referred to in subsection (a) may be either as to the amount of tax shown on a return or as to any deficiency or underpayment of any tax.

* * *

(h) Definition of transferee.—As used in this section, the term "transferee" includes donee, heir, legatee, devisee, and distributee, and with respect to estate taxes, also includes any person who, under section 6324(a)(2), is personally liable for any part of such tax.

* * *

§ 6903. Notice of fiduciary relationship

(a) Rights and obligations of fiduciary.—Upon notice to the Secretary that any person is acting for another person in a fiduciary capacity, such fiduciary shall assume the powers, rights, duties, and privileges of such other person in respect of a tax imposed by this title (except as otherwise specifically provided and except that the tax shall be collected from the estate of such other person), until notice is given that the fiduciary capacity has terminated.

(b) Manner of notice.—Notice under this section shall be given in accordance with regulations prescribed by the Secretary.

§ 6905. Discharge of executor from personal liability for decedent's income and gift taxes

(a) Discharge of liability.—In the case of liability of a decedent for taxes imposed by subtitle A or by chapter 12, if the executor makes written application (filed after the return with respect to such taxes is made and filed in such manner and such form as may be prescribed by regulations of the Secretary) for release from personal liability for such taxes, the Secretary may notify the executor of the amount of such taxes. The executor, upon payment of the amount of which he is notified, or 9 months after receipt of the application if no notification is made by the Secretary before such date, shall be discharged from personal liability for any deficiency in such tax thereafter found to be due and shall be entitled to a receipt or writing showing such discharge.

(b) Definition of executor.—For purposes of this section, the term "executor" means the executor or administrator of the decedent appointed, qualified, and acting within the United States.

* * *

CHAPTER 74—CLOSING AGREEMENTS AND COMPROMISES

§ 7121. Closing agreements

(a) Authorization.—The Secretary is authorized to enter into an agreement in writing with any person relating to the liability of such person (or of the person or estate for whom he acts) in respect of any internal revenue tax for any taxable period.

(b) Finality.—If such agreement is approved by the Secretary (within such time as may be stated in such agreement, or later agreed to) such agreement shall be final and conclusive, and, except upon a showing of fraud or malfeasance, or misrepresentation of a material fact—

(1) the case shall not be reopened as to the matters agreed upon or the agreement modified by any officer, employee, or agent of the United States, and

(2) in any suit, action, or proceeding, such agreement, or any determination, assessment, collection, payment, abatement, refund, or credit made in accordance therewith, shall not be annulled, modified, set aside, or disregarded.

§ 7122. Compromises

(a) Authorization.—The Secretary may compromise any civil or criminal case arising under the internal revenue laws prior to reference to the Department of Justice for prosecution or defense; and the Attorney General or his delegate may compromise any such case after reference to the Department of Justice for prosecution or defense.

* * *

CHAPTER 75—CRIMES, OTHER OFFENSES, AND FORFEITURES

Subchapter

A. Crimes.
B. Other offenses.*
C. Forfeitures.*
D. Miscellaneous penalty and forfeiture provisions.*

SUBCHAPTER A—CRIMES

Part

I. General provisions.
II. Penalties applicable to certain taxes.*

PART I—GENERAL PROVISIONS

§ 7201. Attempt to evade or defeat tax

Any person who willfully attempts in any manner to evade or defeat any tax imposed by this title or the payment thereof shall, in addition to other penalties provided by law, be guilty of a felony and, upon conviction thereof, shall be fined not more than $100,000 ($500,000 in the case of a corporation), or imprisoned not more than 5 years, or both, together with the costs of prosecution.

§ 7203. Willful failure to file return, supply information, or pay tax

Any person required under this title to pay any estimated tax or tax, or required by this title or by regulations made under authority thereof to make a return, keep any records, or supply any information, who willfully fails to pay such estimated tax or tax, make such return, keep such records, or supply such information, at the time or times required by law or regulations, shall, in addition to other penalties provided by law, be

* Omitted entirely.

guilty of a misdemeanor and, upon conviction thereof, shall be fined not more than $25,000 ($100,000 in the case of a corporation), or imprisoned not more than 1 year, or both, together with the costs of prosecution. In the case of any person with respect to whom there is a failure to pay any estimated tax, this section shall not apply to such person with respect to such failure if there is no addition to tax under section 6654 or 6655 with respect to such failure. * * *

§ 7206. Fraud and false statements

Any person who—

(1) Declaration under penalties of perjury.—Willfully makes and subscribes any return, statement, or other document, which contains or is verified by a written declaration that it is made under the penalties of perjury, and which he does not believe to be true and correct as to every material matter; or

(2) Aid or assistance.—Willfully aids or assists in, or procures, counsels, or advises the preparation or presentation under, or in connection with any matter arising under, the internal revenue laws, of a return, affidavit, claim, or other document, which is fraudulent or is false as to any material matter, whether or not such falsity or fraud is with the knowledge or consent of the person authorized or required to present such return, affidavit, claim, or document; or

* * *

shall be guilty of a felony and, upon conviction thereof, shall be fined not more than $100,000 ($500,000 in the case of a corporation), or imprisoned not more than 3 years, or both, together with the costs of prosecution.

CHAPTER 76—JUDICIAL PROCEEDINGS

Subchapter

SUBCHAPTER B—PROCEEDINGS BY TAXPAYERS AND THIRD PARTIES

§ 7421. Prohibition of suits to restrain assessment or collection

(a) Tax.—Except as provided in sections 6015(e), 6212(a) and (c), 6213(a), 6225(b), 6246(b), 6330(e)(1), 6331(i), 6672(c), 6694(c), 7426(a) and (b)(1), 7429(b), and 7436 no suit for the purpose of restraining the assessment or collection of any tax shall be maintained in any court by any person, whether or not such person is the person against whom such tax was assessed.

(b) Liability of transferee or fiduciary.—No suit shall be maintained in any court for the purpose of restraining the assessment or collection (pursuant to the provisions of chapter 71) of—

(1) the amount of the liability, at law or in equity, of a transferee of property of a taxpayer in respect of any internal revenue tax, or

(2) the amount of the liability of a fiduciary under section 3713(b) of title 31, United States Code in respect of any such tax.

* Omitted entirely.

§ 7422. Civil actions for refund

(a) No suit prior to filing claim for refund.—No suit or proceeding shall be maintained in any court for the recovery of any internal revenue tax alleged to have been erroneously or illegally assessed or collected, or of any penalty claimed to have been collected without authority, or of any sum alleged to have been excessive or in any manner wrongfully collected, until a claim for refund or credit has been duly filed with the Secretary, according to the provisions of law in that regard, and the regulations of the Secretary established in pursuance thereof.

(b) Protest or duress.—Such suit or proceeding may be maintained whether or not such tax, penalty, or sum has been paid under protest or duress.

* * *

(e) Stay of proceedings.—If the Secretary prior to the hearing of a suit brought by a taxpayer in a district court or the United States Claims Court for the recovery of any income tax, estate tax, gift tax, or tax imposed by chapter 41, 42, 43, or 44 (or any penalty relating to such taxes) mails to the taxpayer a notice that a deficiency has been determined in respect of the tax which is the subject matter of taxpayer's suit, the proceedings in taxpayer's suit shall be stayed during the period of time in which the taxpayer may file a petition with the Tax Court for a redetermination of the asserted deficiency, and for 60 days thereafter. If the taxpayer files a petition with the Tax Court, the district court or the United States Claims Court, as the case may be, shall lose jurisdiction of taxpayer's suit to whatever extent jurisdiction is acquired by the Tax Court of the subject matter of taxpayer's suit for refund. If the taxpayer does not file a petition with the Tax Court for a redetermination of the asserted deficiency, the United States may counterclaim in the taxpayer's suit, or intervene in the event of a suit as described in subsection (c) (relating to suits against officers or employees of the United States), within the period of the stay of proceedings notwithstanding that the time for such pleading may have otherwise expired. The taxpayer shall have the burden of proof with respect to the issues raised by such counterclaim or intervention of the United States except as to the issue of whether the taxpayer has been guilty of fraud with intent to evade tax. This subsection shall not apply to a suit by a taxpayer which, prior to the date of enactment of this title, is commenced, instituted, or pending in a district court or the United States Claims Court for the recovery of any income tax, estate tax, or gift tax (or any penalty relating to such taxes).

* * *

§ 7430. Awarding of costs and certain fees

(a) In general.—In any administrative or court proceeding which is brought by or against the United States in connection with the determination, collection, or refund of any tax, interest, or penalty under this title, the prevailing party may be awarded a judgment or a settlement for—

(1) reasonable administrative costs incurred in connection with such administrative proceeding within the Internal Revenue Service, and

(2) reasonable litigation costs incurred in connection with such court proceeding.

(b) Limitations.—

(1) Requirement that administrative remedies be exhausted.—A judgment for reasonable litigation costs shall not be awarded under subsection (a) in any court proceeding unless the court determines that the prevailing party has exhausted the administrative remedies available to such party within the Internal Revenue Service. Any failure to agree to an extension of the time for the assessment of any tax shall not be taken into account for purposes of determining whether the prevailing party meets the requirements of the preceding sentence.

(2) Only costs allocable to the United States.—An award under subsection (a) shall be made only for reasonable litigation and administrative costs which are allocable to the United States and not to any other party.

(3) Costs denied where party prevailing protracts proceedings.—No award for reasonable litigation and administrative costs may be made under subsection (a) with respect to any portion of the administrative or court proceeding during which the prevailing party has unreasonably protracted such proceeding.

(4) Period for applying to IRS for administrative costs.—An award may be made under subsection (a) by the Internal Revenue Service for reasonable administrative costs only if the prevailing party files an application with the Internal Revenue Service for such costs before the 91st day after the date on which the final decision of the Internal Revenue Service as to the determination of the tax, interest, or penalty is mailed to such party.

(c) Definitions.—For purposes of this section—

(1) Reasonable litigation costs.—The term "reasonable litigation costs" includes—

(A) reasonable court costs, and

(B) based upon prevailing market rates for the kind or quality of services furnished—

(i) the reasonable expenses of expert witnesses in connection with a court proceeding, except that no expert witness shall be compensated at a rate in excess of the highest rate of compensation for expert witnesses paid by the United States,

(ii) the reasonable cost of any study, analysis, engineering report, test, or project which is found by the court to be necessary for the preparation of the party's case, and

(iii) reasonable fees paid or incurred for the services of attorneys in connection with the court proceeding, except that such fees shall not be in excess of $125 per hour unless the court determines that a special factor, such as the limited availability of qualified attorneys for such proceeding, the difficulty of the issues presented in court, or the local availability of tax expertise, justifies a higher rate.

In the case of any calendar year beginning after 1996, the dollar amount referred to in clause (iii) shall be increased by an amount equal to such dollar amount multiplied by the cost-of-living adjustment determined under section 1(f)(3) for such calendar year, by substituting "calendar year 1995" for "calendar year 1992" in subparagraph (B) thereof. If any dollar amount after being increased under the preceding sentence is not a multiple of $10, such dollar amount shall be rounded to the nearest multiple of $10.

(2) Reasonable administrative costs.—The term "reasonable administrative costs" means—

(A) any administrative fees or similar charges imposed by the Internal Revenue Service, and

(B) expenses, costs, and fees described in paragraph (1)(B), except that any determination made by the court under clause (ii) or (iii) thereof shall be made by the Internal Revenue Service in cases where the determination under paragraph (4)(C) of the awarding of reasonable administrative costs is made by the Internal Revenue Service.

Such term shall only include costs incurred on or after whichever of the following is the earliest: (i) the date of the receipt by the taxpayer of the notice of the decision of the Internal Revenue Service Office of Appeals; (ii) the date of the notice of deficiency; or (iii) the date on which the first letter of proposed deficiency which allows the taxpayer an opportunity for administrative review in the Internal Revenue Service Office of Appeals is sent.

(3) Attorneys' fees.—

(A) In general.—For purposes of paragraphs (1) and (2), fees for the services of an individual (whether or not an attorney) who is authorized to practice before the Tax Court or before the Internal Revenue Service shall be treated as fees for the services of an attorney.

(B) Pro bono services.—The court may award reasonable attorneys' fees under subsection (a) in excess of the attorneys' fees paid or incurred if such fees are less than the reasonable attorneys' fees because an individual is representing the prevailing party for no fee or for a fee which (taking into account all the facts and circumstances) is no more than a nominal fee. This subparagraph shall apply only if such award is paid to such individual or such individual's employer.

(4) Prevailing party.—

(A) In general.—The term "prevailing party" means any party in any proceeding to which subsection (a) applies (other than the United States or any creditor of the taxpayer involved)—

(i) which—

(I) has substantially prevailed with respect to the amount in controversy, or

(II) has substantially prevailed with respect to the most significant issue or set of issues presented, and

(ii) which meets the requirements of the 1st sentence of section 2412(d)(1)(B) of title 28, United States Code (as in effect on October 22, 1986) except to the extent differing procedures are established by rule of court and meets the requirements of section 2412(d)(2)(B) of such title 28 (as so in effect).

(B) Exception if United States establishes that its position was substantially justified.—

(i) General rule.—A party shall not be treated as the prevailing party in a proceeding to which subsection (a) applies if the United States establishes that the position of the United States in the proceeding was substantially justified.

(ii) Presumption of no justification if Internal Revenue Service did not follow certain published guidance.—For purposes of clause (i), the position of the United States shall be presumed not to be substantially justified if the Internal Revenue Service did not follow its applicable published guidance in the administrative proceeding. Such presumption may be rebutted.

(iii) Effect of losing on substantially similar issues.—In determining for purposes of clause (i) whether the position of the United States was substantially justified, the court shall take into account whether the United States has lost in courts of appeal for other circuits on substantially similar issues.

(iv) Applicable published guidance.—For purposes of clause (ii), the term "applicable published guidance" means—

(I) regulations, revenue rulings, revenue procedures, information releases, notices, and announcements, and

(II) any of the following which are issued to the taxpayer: private letter rulings, technical advice memoranda, and determination letters.

(C) Determination as to prevailing party.—Any determination under this paragraph as to whether a party is a prevailing party shall be made by agreement of the parties or—

(i) in the case where the final determination with respect to the tax, interest, or penalty is made at the administrative level, by the Internal Revenue Service, or

(ii) in the case where such final determination is made by a court, the court.

* * *

SUBCHAPTER C—THE TAX COURT

PART I—ORGANIZATION AND JURISDICTION

§ 7441. Status

There is hereby established, under article I of the Constitution of the United States, a court of record to be known as the United States Tax Court. The members of the Tax Court shall be the chief judge and the judges of the Tax Court.

§ 7443. Membership

(a) Number.—The Tax Court shall be composed of 19 members.

(b) Appointment.—Judges of the Tax Court shall be appointed by the President, by and with the advice and consent of the Senate, solely on the grounds of fitness to perform the duties of the office.

* * *

PART II—PROCEDURE

§ 7454. Burden of proof in fraud, foundation manager, and transferee cases

(a) Fraud.—In any proceeding involving the issue whether the petitioner has been guilty of fraud with intent to evade tax, the burden of proof in respect of such issue shall be upon the Secretary.

* * *

§ 7463. Disputes involving $50,000 or less

(a) In general.—In the case of any petition filed with the Tax Court for a redetermination of a deficiency where neither the amount of the deficiency placed in dispute, nor the amount of any claimed overpayment, exceeds—

(1) $50,000 for any one taxable year, in the case of the taxes imposed by subtitle A,

(2) $50,000, in the case of the tax imposed by chapter 11,

(3) $50,000 for any one calendar year, in the case of the tax imposed by chapter 12, or

(4) $50,000 for any 1 taxable period (or, if there is no taxable period, taxable event) in the case of any tax imposed by subtitle D which is described in section 6212(a) (relating to a notice of deficiency),

at the option of the taxpayer concurred in by the Tax Court or a division thereof before the hearing of the case, proceedings in the case shall be conducted under this section. Notwithstanding the provisions of section 7453, such proceedings shall be conducted in accordance with such rules of evidence, practice, and procedure as the Tax Court may prescribe. A decision, together with a brief summary of the reasons therefor, in any such case shall satisfy the requirements of sections 7459(b) and 7460.

* * *

PART IV—DECLARATORY JUDGMENTS

§ 7477. Declaratory judgments relating to value of certain gifts

(a) Creation of remedy.—In a case of an actual controversy involving a determination by the Secretary of the value of any gift shown on the return of tax imposed by chapter 12 or disclosed on such return or in any statement attached to such return, upon the filing of an appropriate pleading, the Tax Court may make a declaration of the value of such gift. Any such declaration shall have the force and effect of a decision of the Tax Court and shall be reviewable as such.

(b) Limitations

(1) Petitioner.—A pleading may be filed under this section only by the donor.

(2) Exhaustion of administrative remedies.—The court shall not issue a declaratory judgment or decree under this section in any proceeding unless it determines that the petitioner has exhausted all available administrative remedies within the Internal Revenue Service.

(3) Time for bringing action.—If the Secretary sends by certified or registered mail notice of his determination as described in subsection (a) to the petitioner, no proceeding may be initiated under this section unless the pleading is filed before the 91st day after the date of such mailing.

§ 7479. Declaratory judgments relating to eligibility of estate with respect to installment payments under section 6166

(a) Creation of remedy.—In a case of actual controversy involving a determination by the Secretary of (or a failure by the Secretary to make a determination with respect to)—

(1) whether an election may be made under section 6166 (relating to extension of time for payment of estate tax where estate consists largely of interest in closely held business) with respect to an estate (or with respect to any property included therein), or

(2) whether the extension of time for payment of tax provided in section 6166(a) has ceased to apply with respect to an estate (or with respect to any property included therein),

upon the filing of an appropriate pleading, the Tax Court may make a declaration with respect to whether such election may be made or whether such extension has ceased to apply. Any such declaration shall have the force and effect of a decision of the Tax Court and shall be reviewable as such.

(b) Limitations

(1) Petitioner.—A pleading may be filed under this section, with respect to any estate, only—

(A) by the executor of such estate, or

(B) by any person who has assumed an obligation to make payments under section 6166 with respect to such estate (but only if each other such person is joined as a party).

(2) Exhaustion of administrative remedies.—The court shall not issue a declaratory judgment or decree under this section in any proceeding unless it determines that the petitioner has exhausted all available administrative remedies within the Internal Revenue Service. A petitioner shall be deemed to have exhausted its administrative remedies with respect to a failure of the Secretary to make a determination at the expiration of 180 days after the date on which the request for such determination was made if the petitioner has taken, in a timely manner, all reasonable steps to secure such determination.

(3) Time for bringing action.—If the Secretary sends by certified or registered mail notice of his determination as described in subsection (a) to the petitioner, no proceeding may be initiated under this section unless the pleading is filed before the 91st day after the date of such mailing.

(c) Extension of time to file refund suit.—The 2-year period in section 6532(a)(1) for filing suit for refund after disallowance of a claim shall be suspended during the 90-day period after the mailing of the notice referred to in subsection (b)(3) and, if a pleading has been filed with the Tax Court under this section, until the decision of the Tax Court has become final.

SUBCHAPTER D—COURT REVIEW OF TAX COURT DECISIONS

§ 7482. Courts of review

(a) Jurisdiction.—

(1) In general.—The United States Courts of Appeals (other than the United States Court of Appeals for the Federal Circuit) shall have exclusive jurisdiction to review the decisions of the Tax Court, except as provided in section 1254 of Title 28 of the United States Code, in the same manner and to the same extent as decisions of the district courts in civil actions tried without a jury; and the judgment of any such court shall be final, except that it shall be subject to review by the Supreme Court of the United States upon certiorari, in the manner provided in section 1254 of Title 28 of the United States Code.

* * *

(b) Venue.—

(1) In general.—Except as otherwise provided in paragraphs (2) and (3), such decisions may be reviewed by the United States court of appeals for the circuit in which is located—

(A) in the case of a petitioner seeking redetermination of tax liability other than a corporation, the legal residence of the petitioner,

(B) in the case of a corporation seeking redetermination of tax liability, the principal place of business or principal office or agency of the corporation, or, if it has no principal place of business or principal office or agency in any judicial circuit, then the office to which was made the return of the tax in respect of which the liability arises,

* * *

If for any reason no subparagraph of the preceding sentence applies, then such decisions may be reviewed by the Court of Appeals for the District of Columbia. For purposes of this paragraph, the legal residence, principal place of business, or principal office or agency referred to herein shall be determined as of the time the petition seeking redetermination of tax liability was filed with the Tax Court or as of the time the petition seeking a declaratory decision under section 7428 or 7476, or the petition under section 6226, 6228(a), or 6234(c), was filed with the Tax Court.

(2) By agreement.—Notwithstanding the provisions of paragraph (1), such decisions may be reviewed by any United States Court of Appeals which may be designated by the Secretary and the taxpayer by stipulation in writing.

* * *

(c) Powers.—

(1) To affirm, modify, or reverse.—Upon such review, such courts shall have power to affirm or, if the decision of the Tax Court is not in accordance with law, to modify or to reverse the decision of the Tax Court, with or without remanding the case for a rehearing, as justice may require.

(2) To make rules.—Rules for review of decisions of the Tax Court shall be those prescribed by the Supreme Court under section 2072 of title 28 of the United States Code.

(3) To require additional security.—Nothing in section 7483 shall be construed as relieving the petitioner from making or filing such undertakings as the court may require as a condition of or in connection with the review.

(4) To impose damages.—The United States Court of Appeals and the Supreme Court shall have power to require the taxpayer to pay to the United States a penalty in any case where the decision of the Tax Court is affirmed and it appears that the appeal was instituted or maintained primarily for delay or that the taxpayer's position in the appeal is frivolous or groundless.

SUBCHAPTER E—BURDEN OF PROOF

§ 7491. Burden of proof

(a) Burden shifts where taxpayer produces credible evidence.—

(1) General rule.—If, in any court proceeding, a taxpayer introduces credible evidence with respect to any factual issue relevant to ascertaining the liability of the taxpayer for any tax imposed by subtitle A or B, the Secretary shall have the burden of proof with respect to such issue.

(2) Limitations.—Paragraph (1) shall apply with respect to an issue only if—

(A) the taxpayer has complied with the requirements under this title to substantiate any item;

(B) the taxpayer has maintained all records required under this title and has cooperated with reasonable requests by the Secretary for witnesses, information, documents, meetings, and interviews; and

(C) in the case of a partnership, corporation, or trust, the taxpayer is described in section 7430(c)(4)(A)(ii).

(3) Coordination.—Paragraph (1) shall not apply to any issue if any other provision of this title provides for a specific burden of proof with respect to such issue.

Subparagraph (C) shall not apply to any qualified revocable trust (as defined in section 645(b) (1)) with respect to liability for tax for any taxable year ending after the date of the decedent's death and before the applicable date (as defined in section 645(b)(2)).

(b) Use of statistical information on unrelated taxpayers.—In the case of an individual taxpayer, the Secretary shall have the burden of proof in any court proceeding with respect to any item of income which was reconstructed by the Secretary solely through the use of statistical information on unrelated taxpayers.

(c) Penalties.—Notwithstanding any other provision of this title, the Secretary shall have the burden of production in any court proceeding with respect to the liability of any individual for any penalty, addition to tax, or additional amount imposed by this title.

CHAPTER 77—MISCELLANEOUS PROVISIONS

§ 7502. Timely mailing treated as timely filing and paying

(a) General rule.—

(1) Date of delivery.—If any return, claim, statement, or other document required to be filed, or any payment required to be made, within a prescribed period or on or before a prescribed date under authority of any provision of the internal revenue laws is, after such period or such date, delivered by United States mail to the agency, officer, or office with which such return, claim, statement, or other document is required to be filed, or to which such payment is required to be made, the date of the United States postmark stamped on the cover in which such return, claim, statement, or other document, or payment, is mailed shall be deemed to be the date of delivery or the date of payment, as the case may be.

(2) Mailing requirements.—This subsection shall apply only if—

(A) the postmark date falls within the prescribed period or on or before the prescribed date—

(i) for the filing (including any extension granted for such filing) of the return, claim, statement, or other document, or

(ii) for making the payment (including any extension granted for making such payment), and

(B) the return, claim, statement, or other document, or payment was, within the time prescribed in subparagraph (A), deposited in the mail in the United States in an envelope or other appropriate wrapper, postage prepaid, properly addressed to the agency, officer, or office with which the return, claim, statement, or other document is required to be filed, or to which such payment is required to be made.

(b) Postmarks.—This section shall apply in the case of postmarks not made by the United States Postal Service only if and to the extent provided by regulations prescribed by the Secretary.

(c) Registered and certified mailing; electronic filing.—

(1) Registered mail.—For purposes of this section, if any such return, claim, statement, or other document, or payment, is sent by United States registered mail—

(A) such registration shall be prima facie evidence that the return, claim, statement, or other document was delivered to the agency, officer, or office to which addressed, and

(B) the date of registration shall be deemed the postmark date.

(2) Certified mail; electronic filing.—The Secretary is authorized to provide by regulations the extent to which the provisions of paragraph (1) with respect to prima facie evidence of delivery and the postmark date shall apply to certified mail and electronic filing.

* * *

(f) Treatment of private delivery services.—

(1) In general.—Any reference in this section to the United States mail shall be treated as including a reference to any designated delivery service, and any reference in this section to a postmark by the United States Postal Service shall be treated as including a reference to any date recorded or marked as described in paragraph (2)(C) by any designated delivery service.

* * *

§ 7517. Furnishing on request of statement explaining estate or gift valuation

(a) General rule.—If the Secretary makes a determination or a proposed determination of the value of an item of property for purposes of the tax imposed under chapter 11, 12, or 13, he shall furnish, on the written request of the executor, donor, or the person required to make the return of the tax imposed by chapter 13 (as the case may be), to such executor, donor, or person a written statement containing the material required by subsection (b). Such statement shall be furnished not later than 45 days after the later of the date of such request or the date of such determination or proposed determination.

(b) Contents of statement.—A statement required to be furnished under subsection (a) with respect to the value of an item of property shall—

(1) explain the basis on which the valuation was determined or proposed,

(2) set forth any computation used in arriving at such value, and

(3) contain a copy of any expert appraisal made by or for the Secretary.

(c) Effect of statement.—Except to the extent otherwise provided by law, the value determined or proposed by the Secretary with respect to which a statement is furnished under this section, and the method used in arriving at such value, shall not be binding on the Secretary.

§ 7519. Required payments for entities electing not to have required taxable year

(a) General rule.—This section applies to a partnership or S corporation for any taxable year, if—

(1) an election under section 444 is in effect for the taxable year, and

(2) the required payment determined under subsection (b) for such taxable year (or any preceding taxable year) exceeds $500.

(b) Required payment.—For purposes of this section, the term "required payment" means, with respect to any applicable election year of a partnership or S corporation, an amount equal to—

(1) the excess of the product of—

(A) the applicable percentage of the adjusted highest section 1 rate, multiplied by

(B) the net base year income of the entity, over

(2) the net required payment balance.

For purposes of paragraph (1)(A), the term "adjusted highest section 1 rate" means the highest rate of tax in effect under section 1 as of the end of the base year plus 1 percentage point (or, in the case of applicable election years beginning in 1987, 36 percent).

* * *

§ 7520. Valuation tables

(a) General rule.—For purposes of this title, the value of any annuity, any interest for life or a term of years, or any remainder or reversionary interest shall be determined—

(1) under tables prescribed by the Secretary, and

(2) by using an interest rate (rounded to the nearest 2/10ths of 1 percent) equal to 120 percent of the Federal midterm rate in effect under section 1274(d)(1) for the month in which the valuation date falls.

If an income, estate, or gift tax charitable contribution is allowable for any part of the property transferred, the taxpayer may elect to use such Federal midterm rate for either of the 2 months preceding the month in which the valuation date falls for purposes of paragraph (2). In the case of transfers of more than 1 interest in the same property with respect to which the taxpayer may use the same rate under paragraph (2), the taxpayer shall use the same rate with respect to each such interest.

(b) Section not to apply for certain purposes.—This section shall not apply for purposes of part I of subchapter D of chapter 1 or any other provision specified in regulations.

(c) Tables.—

(1) In general.—The tables prescribed by the Secretary for purposes of subsection (a) shall contain valuation factors for a series of interest rate categories.

* * *

§ 7525. Confidentiality privileges relating to taxpayer communications

(a) Uniform application to taxpayer communications with federally authorized practitioners.—

(1) General rule.—With respect to tax advice, the same common law protections of confidentiality which apply to a communication between a taxpayer and an attorney shall also apply to a communication between a taxpayer and any federally authorized tax practitioner to the extent the communication would be considered a privileged communication if it were between a taxpayer and an attorney.

(2) Limitations.—Paragraph (1) may only be asserted in—

(A) any noncriminal tax matter before the Internal Revenue Service; and

(B) any noncriminal tax proceeding in Federal court brought by or against the United States.

(3) Definitions.—For purposes of this subsection—

(A) Federally authorized tax practitioner.—The term "federally authorized tax practitioner" means any individual who is authorized under Federal law to practice before the Internal Revenue Service if such practice is subject to Federal regulation under section 330 of title 31, United States Code.

(B) **Tax advice.**—The term "tax advice" means advice given by an individual with respect to a matter which is within the scope of the individual's authority to practice described in subparagraph (A).

(b) **Section not to apply to communications regarding tax shelters.**—The privilege under subsection (a) shall not apply to any written communication which is—

(1) between a federally authorized tax practitioner and—

(A) any person,

(B) any director, officer, employee, agent, or representative of the person, or

(C) any other person holding a capital or profits interest in the person, and

(2) in connection with the promotion of the direct or indirect participation of the person in any tax shelter (as defined in section 6662(d)(2)(C)(ii)).

CHAPTER 79—DEFINITIONS

§ 7701. Definitions

(a) When used in this title, where not otherwise distinctly expressed or manifestly incompatible with the intent thereof—

(1) **Person.**—The term "person" shall be construed to mean and include an individual, a trust, estate, partnership, association, company or corporation.

(2) **Partnership and partner.**—The term "partnership" includes a syndicate, group, pool, joint venture, or other unincorporated organization, through or by means of which any business, financial operation, or venture is carried on, and which is not, within the meaning of this title, a trust or estate or a corporation; and the term "partner" includes a member in such a syndicate, group, pool, joint venture, or organization.

(3) **Corporation.**—The term "corporation" includes associations, joint-stock companies, and insurance companies.

(4) **Domestic.**—The term "domestic" when applied to a corporation or partnership means created or organized in the United States or under the law of the United States or of any State unless, in the case of a partnership, the Secretary provides otherwise by regulations.

(5) **Foreign.**—The term "foreign" when applied to a corporation or partnership means a corporation or partnership which is not domestic.

(6) **Fiduciary.**—The term "fiduciary" means a guardian, trustee, executor, administrator, receiver, conservator, or any person acting in any fiduciary capacity for any person.

(7) **Stock.**—The term "stock" includes shares in an association, joint-stock company, or insurance company.

(8) **Shareholder.**—The term "shareholder" includes a member in an association, joint-stock company, or insurance company.

(9) **United States.**—The term "United States" when used in a geographical sense includes only the States and the District of Columbia.

(10) **State.**—The term "State" shall be construed to include the District of Columbia, where such construction is necessary to carry out provisions of this title.

(11) **Secretary of the Treasury and Secretary.**—

(A) Secretary of the Treasury.—The term "Secretary of the Treasury" means the Secretary of the Treasury, personally, and shall not include any delegate of his.

(B) Secretary.—The term "Secretary" means the Secretary of the Treasury or his delegate.

(12) Delegate.—

(A) In general.—The term "or his delegate"—

(i) when used with reference to the Secretary of the Treasury, means any officer, employee, or agency of the Treasury Department duly authorized by the Secretary of the Treasury directly, or indirectly by one or more redelegations of authority, to perform the function mentioned or described in the context; and

(ii) when used with reference to any other official of the United States, shall be similarly construed.

* * *

(13) Commissioner.—The term "Commissioner" means the Commissioner of Internal Revenue.

(14) Taxpayer.—The term "taxpayer" means any person subject to any internal revenue tax.

* * *

(17) Husband and wife.—As used in sections 682, and 2516, if the husband and wife therein referred to are divorced, wherever appropriate to the meaning of such sections, the term "wife" shall be read "former wife" and the term "husband" shall be read "former husband"; and, if the payments described in such sections are made by or on behalf of the wife or former wife to the husband or former husband instead of vice versa, wherever appropriate to the meaning of such sections, the term "husband" shall be read "wife" and the term "wife" shall be read "husband."

* * *

(21) Levy.—The term "levy" includes the power of distraint and seizure by any means.

(22) Attorney General.—The term "Attorney General" means the Attorney General of the United States.

(23) Taxable year.—The term "taxable year" means the calendar year, or the fiscal year ending during such calendar year, upon the basis of which the taxable income is computed under subtitle A. "Taxable year" means, in the case of a return made for a fractional part of a year under the provisions of subtitle A or under regulations prescribed by the Secretary, the period for which such return is made.

(24) Fiscal year.—The term "fiscal year" means an accounting period of 12 months ending on the last day of any month other than December.

(25) Paid or incurred, paid or accrued.—The terms "paid or incurred" and "paid or accrued" shall be construed according to the method of accounting upon the basis of which the taxable income is computed under subtitle A.

(26) Trade or business.—The term "trade or business" includes the performance of the functions of a public office.

(27) Tax Court.—The term "Tax Court" means the United States Tax Court.

(28) Other terms.—Any term used in this subtitle with respect to the application of, or in connection with, the provisions of any other subtitle of this title shall have the same meaning as in such provisions.

* * *

(30) United States person.—The term "United States person" means—

(A) a citizen or resident of the United States,

(B) a domestic partnership,

(C) a domestic corporation,

(D) any estate (other than a foreign estate, within the meaning of paragraph (31)), and

(E) any trust if—

(i) a court within the United States is able to exercise primary supervision over the administration of the trust, and

(ii) one or more United States persons have the authority to control all substantial decisions of the trust.

(31) Foreign estate or trust.—

(A) Foreign estate.—The term "foreign estate" means an estate the income of which, from sources without the United States which is not effectively connected with the conduct of a trade or business within the United States, is not includible in gross income under subtitle A.

(B) Foreign trust.—The term "foreign trust" means any trust other than a trust described in subparagraph (E) of paragraph (30).

* * *

(36) Tax return preparer.—

(A) In general.—The term "tax return preparer" means any person who prepares for compensation, or who employs one or more persons to prepare for compensation, any return of tax imposed by this title or any claim for refund of tax imposed by this title. For purposes of the preceding sentence, the preparation of a substantial portion of a return or claim for refund shall be treated as if it were the preparation of such return or claim for refund.

(B) Exceptions.—A person shall not be an "tax return preparer" merely because such person—

(i) furnishes typing, reproducing, or other mechanical assistance,

(ii) prepares a return or claim for refund of the employer (or of an officer or employee of the employer) by whom he is regularly and continuously employed,

(iii) prepares as a fiduciary a return or claim for refund for any person, or

(iv) prepares a claim for refund for a taxpayer in response to any notice of deficiency issued to such taxpayer or in response to any waiver of restriction after the commencement of an audit of such taxpayer or another taxpayer if a determination in such audit of such other taxpayer directly or indirectly affects the tax liability of such taxpayer.

(37) Individual retirement plan.—The term "individual retirement plan" means—

(A) an individual retirement account described in section 408(a), and

(B) an individual retirement annuity described in section 408(b).

(38) Joint return.—The term "joint return" means a single return made jointly under section 6013 by a husband and wife.

* * *

(41) TIN.—The term "TIN" means the identifying number assigned to a person under section 6109.

(42) Substituted basis property.—The term "substituted basis property" means property which is—

(A) transferred basis property, or

(B) exchanged basis property.

(43) Transferred basis property.—The term "transferred basis property" means property having a basis determined under any provision of subtitle A (or under any corresponding provision of prior income tax law) providing that the basis shall be determined in whole or in part by reference to the basis in the hands of the donor, grantor, or other transferor.

(44) Exchanged basis property.—The term "exchanged basis property" means property having a basis determined under any provision of subtitle A (or under any corresponding provision of prior income tax law) providing that the basis shall be determined in whole or in part by reference to other property held at any time by the person for whom the basis is to be determined.

(45) Nonrecognition transaction.—The term "nonrecognition transaction" means any disposition of property in a transaction in which gain or loss is not recognized in whole or in part for purposes of subtitle A.

* * *

(c) Includes and including.—The terms "includes" and "including" when used in a definition contained in this title shall not be deemed to exclude other things otherwise within the meaning of the term defined.

* * *

(g) Clarification of fair market value in the case of nonrecourse indebtedness.—For purposes of subtitle A, in determining the amount of gain or loss (or deemed gain or loss) with respect to any property, the fair market value of such property shall be treated as being not less than the amount of any nonrecourse indebtedness to which such property is subject.

* * *

(*l*) Regulations relating to conduit arrangements.—The Secretary may prescribe regulations recharacterizing any multiple-party financing transaction as a transaction directly among any 2 or more of such parties where the Secretary determines that such recharacterization is appropriate to prevent avoidance of any tax imposed by this title.

* * *

(*o*) Clarification of Economic Substance Doctrine.—

(1) Application of doctrine.—In the case of any transaction to which the economic substance doctrine is relevant, such transaction shall be treated as having economic substance only if—

(A) the transaction changes in a meaningful way (apart from Federal income tax effects) the taxpayer's economic position, and

(B) the taxpayer has a substantial purpose (apart from Federal income tax effects) for entering into such transaction.

(2) Special rule where taxpayer relies on profit potential.—

(A) In general.—The potential for profit of a transaction shall be taken into account in determining whether the requirements of subparagraphs (A) and (B) of paragraph (1) are met with respect to the transaction only if the present value of the reasonably expected pre-tax profit from the transaction is substantial in relation to the present value of the expected net tax benefits that would be allowed if the transaction were respected.

(B) Treatment of fees and foreign taxes.—Fees and other transaction expenses shall be taken into account as expenses in determining pre-tax profit under subparagraph (A). The Secretary shall issue regulations requiring foreign taxes to be treated as expenses in determining pre-tax profit in appropriate cases.

(3) State and local tax benefits.—For purposes of paragraph (1), any State or local income tax effect which is related to a Federal income tax effect shall be treated in the same manner as a Federal income tax effect.

(4) Financial accounting benefits.—For purposes of paragraph (1)(B), achieving a financial accounting benefit shall not be taken into account as a purpose for entering into a transaction if the origin of such financial accounting benefit is a reduction of Federal income tax.

(5) Definitions and special rules.—For purposes of this subsection—

(A) Economic substance doctrine.—The term "economic substance doctrine" means the common law doctrine under which tax benefits under subtitle A with respect to a transaction are not allowable if the transaction does not have economic substance or lacks a business purpose.

(B) Exception for personal transactions of individuals.—In the case of an individual, paragraph (1) shall apply only to transactions entered into in connection with a trade or business or an activity engaged in for the production of income.

(C) Determination of application of doctrine not affected.—The determination of whether the economic substance doctrine is relevant to a transaction shall be made in the same manner as if this subsection had never been enacted.

(D) Transaction.—The term "transaction" includes a series of transactions.

(p) Cross references.—

(1) Other definitions.—

For other definitions, see the following sections of Title 1 of the United States Code:

(1) Singular as including plural, section 1.

(2) Plural as including singular, section 1.

(3) Masculine as including feminine, section 1.

* * *

§ 7702. Life insurance contract defined

(a) General rule.—For purposes of this title, the term "life insurance contract" means any contract which is a life insurance contract under the applicable law, but only if such contract—

(1) meets the cash value accumulation test of subsection (b), or

(2)(A) meets the guideline premium requirements of subsection (c), and

(B) falls within the cash value corridor of subsection (d).

(b) Cash value accumulation test for subsection (a)(1).—

(1) In general.—A contract meets the cash value accumulation test of this subsection if, by the terms of the contract, the cash surrender value of such contract may not at any time exceed the net single premium which would have to be paid at such time to fund future benefits under the contract.

(2) Rules for applying paragraph (1).—Determinations under paragraph (1) shall be made—

(A) on the basis of interest at the greater of an annual effective rate of 4 percent or the rate or rates guaranteed on issuance of the contract,

(B) on the basis of the rules of subparagraph (B)(i) (and, in the case of qualified additional benefits, subparagraph (B)(ii)) of subsection (c)(3), and

(C) by taking into account under subparagraphs (A) and (D) of subsection (e)(1) only current and future death benefits and qualified additional benefits.

(c) Guideline premium requirements.—For purposes of this section—

(1) In general.—A contract meets the guideline premium requirements of this subsection if the sum of the premiums paid under such contract does not at any time exceed the guideline premium limitation as of such time.

(2) Guideline premium limitation.—The term "guideline premium limitation" means, as of any date, the greater of—

(A) the guideline single premium, or

(B) the sum of the guideline level premiums to such date.

(3) Guideline single premium.—

(A) In general.—The term "guideline single premium" means the premium at issue with respect to future benefits under the contract.

(B) Basis on which determination is made.—The determination under subparagraph (A) shall be based on—

(i) reasonable mortality charges which meet the requirements (if any) prescribed in regulations and which (except as provided in regulations) do not exceed the mortality charges specified in the prevailing commissioners' standard tables (as defined in section 807(d)(5)) as of the time the contract is issued,

(ii) any reasonable charges (other than mortality charges) which (on the basis of the company's experience, if any, with respect to similar contracts) are reasonably expected to be actually paid, and

(iii) interest at the greater of an annual effective rate of 6 percent or the rate or rates guaranteed on issuance of the contract.

* * *

§ 7702B. Treatment of qualified long-term care insurance

(a) In general.—For purposes of this title—

(1) a qualified long-term care insurance contract shall be treated as an accident and health insurance contract,

(2) amounts (other than policyholder dividends, as defined in section 808, or premium refunds) received under a qualified long-term care insurance contract shall be treated as amounts received for personal injuries and sickness and shall be treated as reimbursement for expenses actually incurred for medical care (as defined in section 213(d)),

(3) any plan of an employer providing coverage under a qualified long-term care insurance contract shall be treated as an accident and health plan with respect to such coverage,

(4) except as provided in subsection (e)(3), amounts paid for a qualified long-term care insurance contract providing the benefits described in subsection (b)(2)(A) shall be treated as payments made for insurance for purposes of section 213(d)(1)(D), and

* * *

(b) Qualified long-term care insurance contract.—For purposes of this title—

(1) In general.—The term "qualified long-term care insurance contract" means any insurance contract if—

(A) the only insurance protection provided under such contract is coverage of qualified long-term care services,

(B) such contract does not pay or reimburse expenses incurred for services or items to the extent that such expenses are reimbursable under title XVIII of the Social Security Act or would be so reimbursable but for the application of a deductible or coinsurance amount,

(C) such contract is guaranteed renewable,

(D) such contract does not provide for a cash surrender value or other money that can be—

(i) paid, assigned, or pledged as collateral for a loan, or

(ii) borrowed,

other than as provided in subparagraph (E) or paragraph (2)(C),

(E) all refunds of premiums, and all policyholder dividends or similar amounts, under such contract are to be applied as a reduction in future premiums or to increase future benefits, and

(F) such contract meets the requirements of subsection (g).

(2) Special rules.—

(A) Per diem, etc. payments permitted.—A contract shall not fail to be described in subparagraph (A) or (B) of paragraph (1) by reason of payments being made on a per diem or other periodic basis without regard to the expenses incurred during the period to which the payments relate.

(B) Special rules relating to medicare.—

(i) Paragraph (1)(B) shall not apply to expenses which are reimbursable under title XVIII of the Social Security Act only as a secondary payor.

(ii) No provision of law shall be construed or applied so as to prohibit the offering of a qualified long-term care insurance contract on the basis that the contract coordinates its benefits with those provided under such title.

(C) Refunds of premiums.—Paragraph (1)(E) shall not apply to any refund on the death of the insured, or on a complete surrender or cancellation of the contract, which cannot exceed the aggregate premiums paid under the contract. Any refund on a complete surrender or cancellation of the contract shall be includible in gross income to the extent that any deduction or exclusion was allowable with respect to the premiums.

(c) Qualified long-term care services.—For purposes of this section—

(1) In general.—The term "qualified long-term care services" means necessary diagnostic, preventive, therapeutic, curing, treating, mitigating, and rehabilitative services, and maintenance or personal care services, which—

(A) are required by a chronically ill individual, and

(B) are provided pursuant to a plan of care prescribed by a licensed health care practitioner.

(2) Chronically ill individual.—

(A) In general.—The term "chronically ill individual" means any individual who has been certified by a licensed health care practitioner as—

(i) being unable to perform (without substantial assistance from another individual) at least 2 activities of daily living for a period of at least 90 days due to a loss of functional capacity,

(ii) having a level of disability similar (as determined under regulations prescribed by the Secretary in consultation with the Secretary of Health and Human Services) to the level of disability described in clause (i), or

(iii) requiring substantial supervision to protect such individual from threats to health and safety due to severe cognitive impairment.

Such term shall not include any individual otherwise meeting the requirements of the preceding sentence unless within the preceding 12–month period a licensed health care practitioner has certified that such individual meets such requirements.

(B) Activities of daily living.—For purposes of subparagraph (A), each of the following is an activity of daily living:

(i) Eating.

(ii) Toileting.

(iii) Transferring.

(iv) Bathing.

(v) Dressing.

(vi) Continence.

A contract shall not be treated as a qualified long-term care insurance contract unless the determination of whether an individual is a chronically ill individual described in subparagraph (A)(i) takes into account at least 5 of such activities.

(3) Maintenance or personal care services.—The term "maintenance or personal care services" means any care the primary purpose of which is the provision of needed assistance with any of the disabilities as a result of which the individual is a chronically ill individual (including the protection from threats to health and safety due to severe cognitive impairment).

(4) Licensed health care practitioner.—The term "licensed health care practitioner" means any physician (as defined in section 1861(r)(1) of the Social Security Act) and any registered professional nurse, licensed social worker, or other individual who meets such requirements as may be prescribed by the Secretary.

* * *

§ 7703. Determination of marital status

(a) General rule.—For purposes of part V of subchapter B of chapter 1 and those provisions of this title which refer to this subsection—

(1) the determination of whether an individual is married shall be made as of the close of his taxable year; except that if his spouse dies during his taxable year such determination shall be made as of the time of such death; and

(2) an individual legally separated from his spouse under a decree of divorce or of separate maintenance shall not be considered as married.

(b) Certain married individuals living apart.—For purposes of these provisions of this title which refer to this subsection, if—

(1) an individual who is married (within the meaning of subsection (a)) and who files a separate return maintains as his home a household which constitutes for more than one-half of the taxable year the principal place of abode of a child (within the meaning of section 152(f)(1)) with respect to whom such individual is entitled to a deduction for the taxable year under section 151 (or would be so entitled but for section 152(e)),

(2) such individual furnishes over one-half of the cost of maintaining such household during the taxable year, and

(3) during the last 6 months of the taxable year, such individual's spouse is not a member of such household,

such individual shall not be considered as married.

§ 7704. Certain publicly traded partnerships treated as corporations

(a) General rule.—For purposes of this title, except as provided in subsection (c), a publicly traded partnership shall be treated as a corporation.

(b) Publicly traded partnership.—For purposes of this section, the term ''publicly traded partnership'' means any partnership if—

(1) interests in such partnership are traded on an established securities market, or

(2) interests in such partnership are readily tradable on a secondary market (or the substantial equivalent thereof).

(c) Exception for partnerships with passive-type income.—

(1) In general.—Subsection (a) shall not apply to any publicly traded partnership for any taxable year if such partnership met the gross income requirements of paragraph (2) for such taxable year and each preceding taxable year beginning after December 31, 1987, during which the partnership (or any predecessor) was in existence. For purposes of the preceding sentence, a partnership shall not be treated as being in existence during any period before the 1st taxable year in which such partnership (or a predecessor) was a publicly traded partnership.

(2) Gross income requirements.—A partnership meets the gross income requirements of this paragraph for any taxable year if 90 percent or more of the gross income of such partnership for such taxable year consists of qualifying income.

* * *

(d) Qualifying income.—For purposes of this section—

(1) In general.—Except as otherwise provided in this subsection, the term ''qualifying income'' means—

(A) interest,

(B) dividends,

(C) real property rents,

(D) gain from the sale or other disposition of real property (including property described in section 1221(a)(1)),

(E) income and gains derived from the exploration, development, mining or production, processing, refining, transportation (including pipelines transporting gas, oil, or products thereof), or the marketing of any mineral or natural resource (including fertilizer, geothermal energy, and timber), industrial source carbon dioxide, or the transportation or storage of any fuel described in subsection (b), (c), (d), or (e) of section 6426, or any alcohol fuel defined in section 6426(b)(4)(A) or any biodiesel fuel as defined in section 40A(d)(1),

(F) any gain from the sale or disposition of a capital asset (or property described in section 1231(b)) held for the production of income described in any of the foregoing subparagraphs of this paragraph, and

(G) in the case of a partnership described in the second sentence of subsection (c)(3), income and gains from commodities (not described in section 1221(a)(1)) or futures, forwards, and options with respect to commodities.

For purposes of subparagraph (E), the term "mineral or natural resource" means any product of a character with respect to which a deduction for depletion is allowable under section 611; except that such term shall not include any product described in subparagraph (A) or (B) of section 613(b)(7).

* * *

(5) Special rule for determining gross income from certain real property sales.—In the case of the sale or other disposition of real property described in section 1221(a)(1), gross income shall not be reduced by inventory costs.

* * *

(f) Effect of becoming corporation.—As of the 1st day that a partnership is treated as a corporation under this section, for purposes of this title, such partnership shall be treated as—

(1) transferring all of its assets (subject to its liabilities) to a newly formed corporation in exchange for the stock of the corporation, and

(2) distributing such stock to its partners in liquidation of their interests in the partnership.

* * *

CHAPTER 80—GENERAL RULES

SUBCHAPTER A—APPLICATION OF INTERNAL REVENUE LAWS

§ 7805. Rules and regulations

(a) Authorization.—Except where such authority is expressly given by this title to any person other than an officer or employee of the Treasury Department, the Secretary shall prescribe all needful rules and regulations for the enforcement of this title, including all rules and regulations as may be necessary by reason of any alteration of law in relation to internal revenue.

(b) Retroactivity of regulations.—

(1) In general.—Except as otherwise provided in this subsection, no temporary, proposed, or final regulation relating to the internal revenue laws shall apply to any taxable period ending before the earliest of the following dates:

(A) The date on which such regulation is filed with the Federal Register.

(B) In the case of any final regulation, the date on which any proposed or temporary regulation to which such final regulation relates was filed with the Federal Register.

(C) The date on which any notice substantially describing the expected contents of any temporary, proposed, or final regulation is issued to the public.

(2) Exception for promptly issued regulations.—Paragraph (1) shall not apply to regulations filed or issued within 18 months of the date of the enactment of the statutory provision to which the regulation relates.

(3) Prevention of abuse.—The Secretary may provide that any regulation may take effect or apply retroactively to prevent abuse.

(4) Correction of procedural defects.—The Secretary may provide that any regulation may apply retroactively to correct a procedural defect in the issuance of any prior regulation.

(5) Internal regulations.—The limitation of paragraph (1) shall not apply to any regulation relating to internal Treasury Department policies, practices, or procedures.

(6) Congressional authorization.—The limitation of paragraph (1) may be superseded by a legislative grant from Congress authorizing the Secretary to prescribe the effective date with respect to any regulation.

(7) Election to apply retroactively.—The Secretary may provide for any taxpayer to elect to apply any regulation before the dates specified in paragraph (1).

(8) Application to rulings.—The Secretary may prescribe the extent, if any, to which any ruling (including any judicial decision or any administrative determination other than by regulation) relating to the internal revenue laws shall be applied without retroactive effect.

(c) Preparation and distribution of regulations, forms, stamps, and other matters.—The Secretary shall prepare and distribute all the instructions, regulations, directions, forms, blanks, stamps, and other matters pertaining to the assessment and collection of internal revenue.

(d) Manner of making elections prescribed by Secretary.—Except to the extent otherwise provided by this title, any election under this title shall be made at such time and in such manner as the Secretary shall prescribe.

(e) Temporary regulations.—

(1) Issuance.—Any temporary regulation issued by the Secretary shall also be issued as a proposed regulation.

(2) 3-year duration.—Any temporary regulation shall expire within 3 years after the date of issuance of such regulation.

* * *

§ 7806. Construction of title

(a) Cross references.—The cross references in this title to other portions of the title, or other provisions of law, where the word "see" is used, are made only for convenience, and shall be given no legal effect.

(b) Arrangement and classification.—No inference, implication, or presumption of legislative construction shall be drawn or made by reason of the location or grouping of any particular section or provision or portion of this title, nor shall any table of contents, table of cross references, or similar outline, analysis, or descriptive matter relating to the contents of this title be given any legal effect. The preceding sentence also applies to the sidenotes and ancillary tables contained in the various prints of this Act before its enactment into law.

SUBCHAPTER C—PROVISIONS AFFECTING MORE THAN ONE SUBTITLE

§ 7872. Treatment of loans with below-market interest rates

(a) Treatment of gift loans and demand loans.—

(1) In general.—For purposes of this title, in the case of any below-market loan to which this section applies and which is a gift loan or a demand loan, the forgone interest shall be treated as—

(A) transferred from the lender to the borrower, and

(B) retransferred by the borrower to the lender as interest.

(2) Time when transfers made.—Except as otherwise provided in regulations prescribed by the Secretary, any forgone interest attributable to periods during any calendar year shall be treated as transferred (and retransferred) under paragraph (1) on the last day of such calendar year.

(b) Treatment of other below-market loans.—

(1) In general.—For purposes of this title, in the case of any below-market loan to which this section applies and to which subsection (a)(1) does not apply, the lender shall be treated as having transferred on the date the loan was made (or, if later, on the first day on which this section applies to such loan), and the borrower shall be treated as having received on such date, cash in an amount equal to the excess of—

(A) the amount loaned, over

(B) the present value of all payments which are required to be made under the terms of the loan.

(2) Obligation treated as having original issue discount.—For purposes of this title—

(A) In general.—Any below-market loan to which paragraph (1) applies shall be treated as having original issue discount in an amount equal to the excess described in paragraph (1).

(B) Amount in addition to other original issue discount.—Any original issue discount which a loan is treated as having by reason of subparagraph (A) shall be in addition to any other original issue discount on such loan (determined without regard to subparagraph (A)).

(c) Below-market loans to which section applies.—

(1) In general.—Except as otherwise provided in this subsection and subsection (g), this section shall apply to—

(A) Gifts.—Any below-market loan which is a gift loan.

(B) Compensation-related loans.—Any below-market loan directly or indirectly between—

(i) an employer and an employee, or

(ii) an independent contractor and a person for whom such independent contractor provides services.

(C) Corporation-shareholder loans.—Any below-market loan directly or indirectly between a corporation and any shareholder of such corporation.

(D) Tax avoidance loans.—Any below-market loan 1 of the principal purposes of the interest arrangements of which is the avoidance of any Federal tax.

(E) Other below-market loans.—To the extent provided in regulations, any below-market loan which is not described in subparagraph (A), (B), (C), or (F) if the interest arrangements of such loan have a significant effect on any Federal tax liability of the lender or the borrower.

(F) Loans to qualified continuing care facilities.—Any loan to any qualified continuing care facility pursuant to a continuing care contract.

(2) $10,000 de minimis exception for gift loans between individuals.—

(A) In general.—In the case of any gift loan directly between individuals, this section shall not apply to any day on which the aggregate outstanding amount of loans between such individuals does not exceed $10,000.

(B) De minimis exception not to apply to loans attributable to acquisition of income-producing assets.—Subparagraph (A) shall not apply to any gift loan directly attributable to the purchase or carrying of income-producing assets.

(C) Cross reference.—

For limitation on amount treated as interest where loans do not exceed $100,000, see subsection (d)(1).

(3) $10,000 de minimis exception for compensation-related and corporate-shareholder loans.—

(A) In general.—In the case of any loan described in subparagraph (B) or (C) of paragraph (1), this section shall not apply to any day on which the aggregate outstanding amount of loans between the borrower and lender does not exceed $10,000.

(B) Exception not to apply where 1 of principal purposes is tax avoidance.—Subparagraph (A) shall not apply to any loan the interest arrangements of which have as 1 of their principal purposes the avoidance of any Federal tax.

(d) Special rules for gift loans.—

(1) Limitation on interest accrual for purposes of income taxes where loans do not exceed $100,000.—

(A) In general.—For purposes of subtitle A, in the case of a gift loan directly between individuals, the amount treated as retransferred by the borrower to the lender as of the close of any year shall not exceed the borrower's net investment income for such year.

(B) Limitation not to apply where 1 of principal purposes is tax avoidance.—Subparagraph (A) shall not apply to any loan the interest arrangements of which have as 1 of their principal purposes the avoidance of any Federal tax.

(C) Special rule where more than 1 gift loan outstanding.—For purposes of subparagraph (A), in any case in which a borrower has outstanding more than 1 gift loan, the net investment income of such borrower shall be allocated among such loans in proportion to the respective amounts which would be treated as retransferred by the borrower without regard to this paragraph.

(D) Limitation not to apply where aggregate amount of loans exceed $100,000.—This paragraph shall not apply to any loan made by a lender to a borrower for any day on which the aggregate outstanding amount of loans between the borrower and lender exceeds $100,000.

(E) Net investment income.—For purposes of this paragraph—

(i) In general.—The term "net investment income" has the meaning given such term by section 163(d)(4).

(ii) De minimis rule.—If the net investment income of any borrower for any year does not exceed $1,000, the net investment income of such borrower for such year shall be treated as zero.

(iii) Additional amounts treated as interest.—In determining the net investment income of a person for any year, any amount which would be included in the gross income of such person for such year by reason of section 1272 if such section applied to all deferred payment obligations shall be treated as interest received by such person for such year.

(iv) Deferred payment obligations.—The term "deferred payment obligation" includes any market discount bond, short-term obligation, United States savings bond, annuity, or similar obligation.

(2) Special rule for gift tax.—In the case of any gift loan which is a term loan, subsection (b)(1) (and not subsection (a)) shall apply for purposes of chapter 12.

(e) Definitions of below-market loan and forgone interest.—For purposes of this section—

(1) Below-market loan.—The term "below-market loan" means any loan if—

(A) in the case of a demand loan, interest is payable on the loan at a rate less than the applicable Federal rate, or

(B) in the case of a term loan, the amount loaned exceeds the present value of all payments due under the loan.

(2) Forgone interest.—The term "forgone interest" means, with respect to any period during which the loan is outstanding, the excess of—

(A) the amount of interest which would have been payable on the loan for the period if interest accrued on the loan at the applicable Federal rate and were payable annually on the day referred to in subsection (a)(2), over

(B) any interest payable on the loan properly allocable to such period.

(f) Other definitions and special rules.—For purposes of this section—

(1) Present value.—The present value of any payment shall be determined in the manner provided by regulations prescribed by the Secretary—

(A) as of the date of the loan, and

(B) by using a discount rate equal to the applicable Federal rate.

(2) Applicable federal rate.—

(A) Term loans.—In the case of any term loan, the applicable Federal rate shall be the applicable Federal rate in effect under section 1274(d) (as of the day on which the loan was made), compounded semiannually.

(B) Demand loans.—In the case of a demand loan, the applicable Federal rate shall be the Federal short-term rate in effect under section 1274(d) for the period for which the amount of forgone interest is being determined, compounded semiannually.

(3) Gift loan.—The term "gift loan" means any below-market loan where the forgoing of interest is in the nature of a gift.

(4) Amount loaned.—The term "amount loaned" means the amount received by the borrower.

(5) Demand loan.—The term "demand loan" means any loan which is payable in full at any time on the demand of the lender. Such term also includes (for purposes other than determining the applicable Federal rate under paragraph (2)) any loan if the benefits of the interest arrangements of such loan are not transferable and are conditioned on the future performance of substantial services by an individual. To the extent provided in regulations, such term also includes any loan with an indefinite maturity.

(6) Term loan.—The term "term loan" means any loan which is not a demand loan.

(7) Husband and wife treated as 1 person.—A husband and wife shall be treated as 1 person.

(8) Loans to which section 483, 643(i), or 1274 applies.—This section shall not apply to any loan to which section 483, 643(i), or 1274 applies.

(9) No withholding.—No amount shall be withheld under chapter 24 with respect to—

(A) any amount treated as transferred or retransferred under subsection (a), and

(B) any amount treated as received under subsection (b).

(10) Special rule for term loans.—If this section applies to any term loan on any day, this section shall continue to apply to such loan notwithstanding paragraphs (2) and (3) of subsection (c). In the case of a gift loan, the preceding sentence shall only apply for purposes of chapter 12.

(11) Time for determining rate applicable to employee relocation loans.—

(A) In general.—In the case of any term loan made by an employer to an employee the proceeds of which are used by the employee to purchase a principal residence (within the meaning of section 121), the determination of the applicable Federal rate shall be made as of the date the written contract to purchase such residence was entered into.

(B) Paragraph only to apply to cases to which section 217 applies.—Subparagraph (A) shall only apply to the purchase of a principal residence in connection with the commencement of work by an employee or a change in the principal place of work of an employee to which section 217 applies.

* * *

(i) Regulations.—

(1) In general.—The Secretary shall prescribe such regulations as may be necessary or appropriate to carry out the purposes of this section, including—

(A) regulations providing that where, by reason of varying rates of interest, conditional interest payments, waivers of interest, disposition of the lender's or borrower's interest in the loan, or other circumstances, the provisions of this section do not carry out the purposes of this section, adjustments to the provisions of this section will be made to the extent necessary to carry out the purposes of this section,

(B) regulations for the purpose of assuring that the positions of the borrower and lender are consistent as to the application (or nonapplication) of this section, and

(C) regulations exempting from the application of this section any class of transactions the interest arrangements of which have no significant effect on any Federal tax liability of the lender or the borrower.

(2) Estate tax coordination.—Under regulations prescribed by the Secretary, any loan which is made with donative intent and which is a term loan shall be taken into account for purposes of chapter 11 in a manner consistent with the provisions of subsection (b).

TREASURY REGULATIONS

INCOME TAXES

DETERMINATION OF TAX LIABILITY

§ 1.1(h)–1 Capital gains look-through rule for sales or exchanges of interests in a partnership, S corporation, or trust.

(a) In general. When an interest in a partnership held for more than one year is sold or exchanged, the transferor may recognize ordinary income (e.g., section 751(a)), collectibles gain, section 1250 capital gain, and residual long-term capital gain or loss. When stock in an S corporation held for more than one year is sold or exchanged, the transferor may recognize ordinary income (e.g., sections 304, 306, 341, 1254), collectibles gain, and residual long-term capital gain or loss. When an interest in a trust held for more than one year is sold or exchanged, a transferor who is not treated as the owner of the portion of the trust attributable to the interest sold or exchanged (sections 673 through 679) (a non-grantor transferor) may recognize collectibles gain and residual long-term capital gain or loss.

(b) Look-through capital gain—(1) In general. Look-through capital gain is the share of collectibles gain allocable to an interest in a partnership, S corporation, or trust, plus the share of section 1250 capital gain allocable to an interest in a partnership, determined under paragraphs (b)(2) and (3) of this section.

(2) Collectibles gain—(i) Definition. For purposes of this section, *collectibles gain* shall be treated as gain from the sale or exchange of a collectible (as defined in section 408(m) without regard to section 408(m)(3)) that is a capital asset held for more than 1 year.

(ii) Share of collectibles gain allocable to an interest in a partnership, S corporation, or trust. When an interest in a partnership, S corporation, or trust held for more than one year is sold or exchanged in a transaction in which all realized gain is recognized, the transferor shall recognize as collectibles gain the amount of net gain (but not net loss) that would be allocated to that partner (taking into account any remedial allocation under § 1.704–3(d)), shareholder, or beneficiary (to the extent attributable to the portion of the partnership interest, S corporation stock, or trust interest transferred that was held for more than one year) if the partnership, S corporation, or trust transferred all of its collectibles for cash equal to the fair market value of the assets in a fully taxable transaction immediately before the transfer of the interest in the partnership, S corporation, or trust. If less than all of the realized gain is recognized upon the sale or exchange of an interest in a partnership, S corporation, or trust, the same methodology shall apply to determine the collectibles gain recognized by the transferor, except that the partnership, S corporation, or trust shall be treated as transferring only a proportionate amount of each of its collectibles determined as a fraction that is the amount of gain recognized in the sale or exchange over the amount of gain realized in the sale or exchange. With respect to the transfer of an interest in a trust, this paragraph (b)(2) applies only to transfers by non-grantor transferors (as defined in paragraph (a) of this section). This paragraph (b)(2) does not apply to a transaction that is treated, for Federal income tax purposes, as a redemption of an interest in a partnership, S corporation, or trust.

(3) Section 1250 capital gain—(i) Definition. For purposes of this section, *section 1250 capital gain* means the capital gain (not otherwise treated as ordinary income) that would be treated as ordinary income if section 1250(b)(1) included all depreciation and the applicable percentage under section 1250(a) were 100 percent.

(ii) Share of section 1250 capital gain allocable to interest in partnership. When an interest in a partnership held for more than one year is sold or exchanged in a transaction in which all realized gain is recognized, there shall be taken into account under section 1(h)(7)(A)(i) in determining the partner's unrecaptured section 1250 gain the amount of section 1250 capital gain that would be allocated (taking into account any remedial allocation under § 1.704–3(d)) to that partner (to the extent attributable to the portion of the partnership interest transferred that was held for more than one year) if the partnership transferred all of its section 1250 property in a fully taxable transaction for cash equal to the fair market value of the assets immediately before the transfer of the interest in the partnership. If less than all of the realized gain is recognized upon the sale or exchange of an interest in a partnership, the same methodology shall apply to determine the section 1250 gain recognized by the transferor, except that the partnership shall be treated as transferring only a proportionate amount of each section 1250 property determined as a fraction that is the amount of gain recognized in the sale or exchange over the amount of gain realized in the sale or exchange. This paragraph (b)(3) does not apply to a transaction that is treated, for Federal income tax purposes, as a redemption of a partnership interest.

(iii) Limitation with respect to net section 1231 gain. In determining a transferor partner's net section 1231 gain (as defined in section 1231(c)(3)) for purposes of section 1(h)(7)(B), the transferor partner's allocable share of section 1250 capital gain in partnership property shall not be treated as section 1231 gain, regardless of whether the partnership property is used in the trade or business (as defined in section 1231(b)).

(c) Residual long-term capital gain or loss. The amount of residual long-term capital gain or loss recognized by a partner, shareholder of an S corporation, or beneficiary of a trust on account of the sale or exchange of an interest in a partnership, S corporation, or trust shall equal the amount of long-term capital gain or loss that the partner would recognize under section 741, that the shareholder would recognize upon the sale or exchange of stock of an S corporation, or that the beneficiary would recognize upon the sale or exchange of an interest in a trust (pre-look through long-term capital gain or loss) minus the amount of long-term capital gain determined under paragraph (b) of this section (look-through capital gain).

* * *

(f) Examples. The following examples illustrate the requirements of this section:

Example 1. Collectibles gain. (i) A and B are equal partners in a personal service partnership (PRS). B transfers B's interest in PRS to T for $15,000 when PRS's balance sheet (reflecting a cash receipts and disbursements method of accounting) is as follows:

ASSETS

	Adjusted Basis	Market Value
Cash	$ 3,000	$ 3,000
Loans Owed to Partnership	10,000	10,000
Collectibles	1,000	3,000
Other Capital Assets	6,000	2,000
Capital Assets	7,000	5,000
Unrealized Receivables	0	14,000
Total	$20,000	$32,000

LIABILITIES AND CAPITAL

Liabilities	$ 2,000	$ 2,000
Capital:		
A	9,000	15,000
B	9,000	15,000
	$20,000	$32,000

(ii) At the time of the transfer, *B* has held the interest in *PRS* for more than one year, and *B's* basis for the partnership interest is $10,000 ($9,000 plus $1,000, *B's* share of partnership liabilities). None of the property owned by *PRS* is section 704(c) property. The total amount realized by *B* is $16,000, consisting of the cash received, $15,000 plus $1,000, *B's* share of the partnership liabilities assumed by T. See section 752. *B's* undivided one-half interest in *PRS* includes a one-half interest in the partnership's unrealized receivables and a one-half interest in the partnership's collectibles.

(iii) If *PRS* were to sell all of its section 751 property in a fully taxable transaction for cash equal to the fair market value of the assets immediately prior to the transfer of *B's* partnership interest to *T*, *B* would be allocated $7,000 of ordinary income from the sale of *PRS's* unrealized receivables. Therefore, *B* will recognize $7,000 of ordinary income with respect to the unrealized receivables. The difference between the amount of capital gain or loss that the partner would realize in the absence of section 751 ($6,000) and the amount of ordinary income or loss determined under § 1.751–1(a)(2) ($7,000) is the partner's capital gain or loss on the sale of the partnership interest under section 741. In this case, the transferor has a $1,000 pre-look-through long-term capital loss.

(iv) If *PRS* were to sell all of its collectibles in a fully taxable transaction for cash equal to the fair market value of the assets immediately prior to the transfer of *B's* partnership interest to T, *B* would be allocated $1,000 of gain from the sale of the collectibles. Therefore, *B* will recognize $1,000 of collectibles gain on account of the collectibles held by *PRS*.

(v) The difference between the transferor's pre-look-through long-term capital gain or loss (–$1,000) and the look-through capital gain determined under this section ($1,000) is the transferor's residual long-term capital gain or loss on the sale of the partnership interest. Under these facts, *B* will recognize a $2,000 residual long-term capital loss on account of the sale or exchange of the interest in *PRS*.

Example 2. Special allocations. Assume the same facts as in *Example 1,* except that under the partnership agreement, all gain from the sale of the collectibles is specially allocated to *B*, and *B* transfers *B's* interest to *T* for $16,000. All items of income, gain, loss, or deduction of *PRS*, other than the collectibles gain, are divided equally between *A* and *B*. Under these facts, *B's* amount realized is $17,000, consisting of the cash received, $16,000, plus $1,000, *B's* share of the partnership liabilities assumed by *T*. See section 752. *B* will recognize $7,000 of ordinary income with respect to the unrealized receivables (determined under § 1.751–1(a)(2)). Accordingly, *B*'s pre-look-through long-term capital gain would be $0. If *PRS* were to sell all of its collectibles in a fully taxable transaction for cash equal to the fair market value of the assets immediately prior to the transfer of *B's* partnership interest to *T*, *B* would be allocated $2,000 of gain from the sale of the collectibles. Therefore, *B* will recognize $2,000 of collectibles gain on account of the collectibles held by *PRS*. *B* also will recognize a $2,000 residual long-term capital loss on account of the sale of *B*'s interest in *PRS*.

Example 3. Net collectibles loss ignored. Assume the same facts as in *Example 1*, except that the collectibles held by *PRS* have an adjusted basis of $3,000 and a fair market value of $1,000, and the other capital assets have an adjusted basis of $4,000 and a fair market value of $4,000. (The total adjusted basis and fair market value of the partnership's capital assets are the same as in *Example 1*). If *PRS* were to sell all of its collectibles in a fully taxable transaction for cash equal to the fair market value of the assets immediately prior to the transfer of *B*'s partnership interest to *T, B* would be allocated $1,000 of loss from the dale of collectibles. Because none of the gain from the sale of the interest in *PRS* is attributable to unrealized appreciation in the value of collectibles held by *PRS*, the net loss in collectibles held by *PRS* is not recognized at the time *B* transfers the interest in *PRS*. *B* will recognize $7,000 of ordinary income (determined under § 1.751–1(a)(2)) and a $1,000 long-term capital loss on account of the sale of *B*'s interest in *PRS*.

Example 4. Collectibles gain in an S corporation. **(i)** A corporation *(X)* has always been an S corporation and is owned by individuals A, *B*, and *C*. In 1996, *X* invested in antiques. Subsequent to their purchase, the antiques appreciated in value by $300. A owns one-third of the shares of *X* stock and has held that stock for more than one year. A's adjusted basis in the *X* stock is $100. If A were to sell all of A's *X* stock to *T* for $150, A would realize $50 of pre-look-through long-term capital gain.

(ii) If *X* were to sell its antiques in a fully taxable transaction for cash equal to the fair market value of the assets immediately before the transfer to *T*, A would be allocated $100 of gain on account of the sale. Therefore, A will recognize $100 of collectibles gain (look-through capital gain) on account of the collectibles held by *X*.

(iii) The difference between the transferor's pre-look-through long-term capital gain or loss ($50) and the look-through capital gain determined under this section ($100) is the transferor's residual long-term capital gain or loss on the sale of the S corporation stock. Under these facts, A will recognize $100 of collectibles gain and a $50 residual long-term capital loss on account of the sale of A's interest in *X*.

Example 5. Sale or exchange of partnership interest where part of the interest has a short-term holding period. **(i)** A, B and C form an equal partnership (PRS). In connection with the formation, A contributes $5,000 in cash and a capital asset with a fair market value of $5,000 and a basis of $2,000; B contributes $7,000 in cash and a collectible with a fair market value of $3,000 and a basis of $3,000; and C contributes $10,000 in cash. At the time of the contribution, A had held the contributed property for two years. Six months later, when A's basis in PRS is $7,000, A transfers A's interest in PRS to T for $14,000 at a time when PRS's balance sheet (reflecting a cash receipts and disbursements method of accounting) is as follows:

ASSETS

	Adjusted Basis	Market Value
Cash	$22,000	$22,000
Unrealized Receivables	0	6,000
Capital Asset	2,000	5,000
Collectible	3,000	9,000
Capital Assets	5,000	14,000
Total	$27,000	$42,000

(ii) Although at the time of the transfer A has not held A's interest in PRS for more than one year, 50 percent of the fair market value of A's interest in PRS was received in exchange for a capital asset with a long-term holding period. Therefore, 50 percent of A's interest in PRS has a long-term holding period. See § 1.1223–3(b)(1).

(iii) If PRS were to sell all of its section 751 property in a fully taxable transaction immediately before A's transfer of the partnership interest, A would be allocated $2,000 of ordinary income. Accordingly, A will recognize $2,000 ordinary income and $5,000 ($7,000–$2,000) of capital gain on account of the transfer to T of A's interest in PRS. Fifty percent ($2,500) of that gain is long-term capital gain and 50 percent ($2,500) is short-term capital gain. See § 1.1223–3(c)(1).

(iv) If the collectible were sold or exchanged in a fully taxable transaction immediately before A's transfer of the partnership interest, A would be allocated $2,000 of gain attributable to the collectible. The gain attributable to the collectible that is allocable to the portion of the transferred interest in PRS with a long-term holding period is $1,000 (50 percent of $2,000). Accordingly, A will recognize $1,000 of collectibles gain on account of the transfer of A's interest in PRS.

(v) The difference between the amount of prelook-through long-term capital gain or loss ($2,500) and the look-through capital gain or loss ($1,000) is the amount of residual long-term capital gain or loss that A will recognize on account of the transfer of A's interest in PRS. Under these facts, A will recognize a residual long-term capital gain of $1,500 and a short-term capital gain of $2,500.

* * *

[T.D. 8902, 65 FR 57092, Sept. 21, 2000]

COMPUTATION OF TAXABLE INCOME

§ 1.61–1 Gross income.

(a) General definition. Gross income means all income from whatever source derived, unless excluded by law. Gross income includes income realized in any form, whether in money, property, or services. Income may be realized, therefore, in the form of services, meals, accommodations, stock, or other property, as well as in cash. Section 61 lists the more common items of gross income for purposes of illustration. For purposes of further illustration, § 1.61–14 mentions several miscellaneous items of gross income not listed specifically in section 61. Gross income, however, is not limited to the items so enumerated.

(b) Cross references. Cross references to other provisions of the Code are to be found throughout the regulations under section 61. The purpose of these cross references is to direct attention to the more common items which are included in or excluded from gross income entirely, or treated in some special manner. To the extent that another section of the Code or of the regulations thereunder, provides specific treatment for any item of income, such other provision shall apply notwithstanding section 61 and the regulations thereunder. The cross references do not cover all possible items.

(1) For examples of items specifically included in gross income, see part II (section 71 and following), subchapter B, chapter 1 of the Code.

(2) For examples of items specifically excluded from gross income, see part III (section 101 and following), subchapter B, chapter 1 of the Code.

(3) For general rules as to the taxable year for which an item is to be included in gross income, see section 451 and the regulations thereunder.

§ 1.61–2 Compensation for services, including fees, commissions, and similar items.

(a) In general. **(1)** Wages, salaries, commissions paid salesmen, compensation for services on the basis of a percentage of profits, commissions on insurance premiums, tips, bonuses (including Christmas bonuses), termination or severance pay, rewards, jury fees, marriage fees and other contributions received by a clergyman for services, pay of persons in the military or naval forces of the United States, retired pay of employees, pensions, and retirement allowances are income to the recipients unless excluded by law. * * *

* * *

(c) Payment to charitable, etc., organization on behalf of person rendering services. The value of services is not includible in gross income when such services are rendered directly and gratuitously to an organization described in section 170(c). Where, however, pursuant to an agreement or understanding, services are rendered to a person for the benefit of an organization described in section 170(c) and an amount for such services is paid to such organization by the person to whom the services are rendered, the amount so paid constitutes income to the person performing the services.

(d) Compensation paid other than in cash—(1) In general. Except as otherwise provided in paragraph (d)(6)(i) of this section (relating to certain property transferred after June 30, 1969), if services are paid for in property, the fair market value of the property taken in payment must be included in income as compensation. If services are paid for in exchange for other services, the fair market value of such other services taken in payment must be included in income as compensation. If the services are rendered at a stipulated price, such price will be presumed to be the fair market value of the compensation received in the absence of evidence to the contrary. * * *

(2) Property transferred to employee or independent contractor. **(i)** * * * if property is transferred by an employer to an employee or if property is transferred to an independent contractor, as compensation for services, for an amount less than its fair market value, then regardless of whether the transfer is in the form of a sale or exchange, the difference between the amount paid for the property and the amount of its fair market value at the time of the transfer is compensation and shall be included in the gross income of the employee or independent contractor. In computing the gain or loss from the subsequent sale of such property, its basis shall be the amount paid for the property increased by the amount of such difference included in gross income.

(ii) (a) Cost of life insurance on the life of the employee. Generally, life insurance premiums paid by an employer on the life of his employee where the proceeds of such insurance are payable to the beneficiary of such employee are part of the gross income of the employee. * * * For the special rules relating to the includibility in an employee's gross income of an amount equal to the cost of certain group term life insurance on the employee's life which is carried directly or indirectly by his employer, see section 79 and the regulations thereunder. For special rules relating to the exclusion of contributions by an employer to accident and health plans for the employee, see section 106 and the regulations thereunder. * * *

* * *

(4) Stock and notes transferred to employee or independent contractor. Except as otherwise provided by section 421 and the regulations thereunder and § 1.61–15 (relating to stock options), and paragraph (d)(6)(i) of this section, if a corporation transfers its own stock to an employee or independent contractor as compensation for services, the fair market value of the stock at the time of transfer shall be included in the gross income of the employee or independent contractor. Notes or other evidences of indebtedness received in payment for services constitute income in the amount of their fair market value at the time of the transfer. A taxpayer receiving as compensation a note regarded as good for its face value at maturity, but not bearing interest, shall treat as income as of the time of receipt its fair discounted value computed at the prevailing rate. As payments are received on such a note, there shall be included in income that portion of each payment which represents the proportionate part of the discount originally taken on the entire note.

* * *

(6) Certain property transferred, premiums paid, and contributions made in connection with the performance of services after June 30, 1969—(i) Exception. * * * If section 83 applies to a transfer of property, and the property is not subject to a restriction that has a significant effect on the fair market value of such property, then the rules contained in paragraph (d)(1), (2), and (4) of this section * * * shall also apply to such transfer to the extent such rules are not inconsistent with section 83.

* * *

[T.D. 6500, 25 FR 11402, Nov. 26, 1960, as amended by T.D. 6696, 28 FR 13450, Dec. 12, 1963; T.D. 6856, 30 FR 13316, Oct. 20, 1965; T.D. 6888, 31 FR 9200, July 6, 1966; T.D. 7544, 43 FR 31913, July 24, 1978; T.D. 7623, 44 FR 28800, May 17, 1979; T.D. 8256, 54 FR 28582, July 6, 1989; T.D. 9092, 68 FR 54336, Sept. 17, 2003]

§ 1.61–3 Gross income derived from business.

(a) In general. In a manufacturing, merchandising, or mining business, "gross income" means the total sales, less the cost of goods sold, plus any income from investments and from incidental or outside operations or sources. Gross income is determined without subtraction of depletion allowances based on a percentage of income to the extent that it exceeds cost depletion which may be required to be included in the amount of inventoriable costs as provided in § 1.471–11 and without subtraction of selling expenses, losses or other items not ordinarily used in computing costs of goods sold or amounts which are of a type for which a deduction would be disallowed under section 162(c), (f), or (g) in the case of a business expense. The cost of goods sold should be determined in accordance with the method of accounting consistently used by the taxpayer. Thus, for example, an amount cannot be taken into account in the computation of cost of goods sold any earlier than the taxable year in which economic performance occurs with respect to the amount (see § 1.446–1(c)(1)(ii)).

* * *

[T.D. 6500, 25 FR 11402, Nov. 26, 1960; 25 FR 14021, Dec. 31, 1960, as amended by T.D. 7207, 37 FR 20767, Oct. 5, 1972; T.D. 7285, 38 FR 26184, Sept. 19, 1973; T.D. 8408, 57 FR 12419, Apr. 10, 1992]

§ 1.61–4 Gross income of farmers.

(a) Farmers using the cash method of accounting. A farmer using the cash receipts and disbursements method of accounting shall include in his gross income for the taxable year—

(1) The amount of cash and the value of merchandise or other property received during the taxable year from the sale of livestock and produce which he raised,

(2) The profits from the sale of any livestock or other items which were purchased,

(3) All amounts received from breeding fees, fees from rent of teams, machinery, or land, and other incidental farm income,

(4) All subsidy and conservation payments received which must be considered as income, and

(5) Gross income from all other sources.

The profit from the sale of livestock or other items which were purchased is to be ascertained by deducting the cost from the sales price in the year in which the sale occurs, except that in the case of the sale of purchased animals held for draft, breeding, or dairy purposes, the profits shall be the amount of any excess of the sales price over the amount representing the difference between the cost and the depreciation allowed or allowable (determined in accordance with the rules applicable under section 1016(a) and the regulations thereunder). However, see section 162 and the regulations thereunder with respect to the computation of taxable income on other than the crop method where the cost of seeds or young plants purchased for further development and cultivation prior to sale is involved. Crop shares (whether or not considered rent under State law) shall be included in gross income as of the year in which the crop shares are reduced to money or the equivalent of money. See section 263A for rules regarding costs that are required to be capitalized.

(b) Farmers using an accrual method of accounting. A farmer using an accrual method of accounting must use inventories to determine his gross income. His gross income on an accrual method is determined by adding the total of the items described in subparagraphs (1) through (5) of this paragraph and subtracting therefrom the total of the items described in subparagraphs (6) and (7) of this paragraph. These items are as follows:

(1) The sales price of all livestock and other products held for sale and sold during the year;

(2) The inventory value of livestock and products on hand and not sold at the end of the year;

(3) All miscellaneous items of income, such as breeding fees, fees from the rent of teams, machinery, or land, or other incidental farm income;

(4) Any subsidy or conservation payments which must be considered as income;

(5) Gross income from all other sources;

(6) The inventory value of the livestock and products on hand and not sold at the beginning of the year; and

(7) The cost of any livestock or products purchased during the year (except livestock held for draft, dairy, or breeding purposes, unless included in inventory).

All livestock raised or purchased for sale shall be added in the inventory at their proper valuation determined in accordance with the method authorized and adopted for the purpose. Livestock acquired for draft, breeding, or dairy purposes and not for sale may be included in the inventory (see subparagraphs (2), (6), and (7) of this paragraph) instead of being treated as capital assets subject to depreciation, provided such practice is followed consistently from year to year by the taxpayer. When any livestock included in an inventory are sold, their cost must not be taken as an additional deduction in computing taxable income, because such deduction is reflected in the inventory. See the regulations under section 471. See section 263A for rules regarding costs that are required to be capitalized. Crop shares (whether or not considered rent under State law) shall be included in gross income as of the year in which the crop shares are reduced to money or the equivalent of money.

(c) Special rules for certain receipts. In the case of the sale of machinery, farm equipment, or any other property (except stock in trade of the taxpayer, or property of a kind which would properly be included in the inventory of the taxpayer if on hand at the close of the taxable year, or property held by the taxpayer primarily for sale to customers in the ordinary course of his trade or business), any excess of the proceeds of the sale over the adjusted basis of such property shall be included in the taxpayer's gross income for the taxable year in which such sale is made. See, however, section 453 and the regulations thereunder for special rules relating to certain installment sales. If farm produce is exchanged for merchandise, groceries, or the like, the market value of the article received in exchange is to be included in gross income. * * *

(d) Definition of "farm". As used in this section, the term "farm" embraces the farm in the ordinarily accepted sense, and includes stock, dairy, poultry, fruit, and truck farms; also plantations, ranches, and all land used for farming operations. All individuals, partnerships, or corporations that cultivate, operate, or manage farms for gain or profit, either as owners or tenants, are designated as farmers. * * *

* * *

[T.D. 6500, 25 FR 11402, Nov. 26, 1960; 25 FR 14021, Dec. 31, 1960, as amended by T.D. 7198, 37 FR 13679, July 13, 1972; T.D. 8729, 62 FR 44546, Aug. 22, 1997]

§ 1.61–6 Gains derived from dealings in property.

(a) In general. Gain realized on the sale or exchange of property is included in gross income, unless excluded by law. For this purpose property includes tangible items, such as a building, and intangible items, such as goodwill. Generally, the gain is the excess of the amount realized over the unrecovered cost or other basis for the property sold or exchanged. The specific rules for computing the amount of gain or loss are contained in section 1001 and the regulations thereunder. When a part of a larger property is sold, the cost or other basis of the entire property shall be equitably apportioned among the several parts, and the gain realized or loss sustained on the part of the entire property sold is the difference between the selling price and the cost or other basis allocated to such part. The sale of each part is treated as a separate transaction and gain or loss shall be computed separately on each part. Thus, gain or loss shall be determined at the time of sale of each part and not deferred until the entire property has been disposed of. This rule may be illustrated by the following examples:

Example (1). A, a dealer in real estate, acquires a 10-acre tract for $10,000, which he divides into 20 lots. The $10,000 cost must be equitably apportioned among the lots so that on the sale of each A can determine his taxable gain or deductible loss.

Example (2). B purchases for $25,000 property consisting of a used car lot and adjoining filling station. At the time, the fair market value of the filling station is $15,000 and the fair market value of the used car lot is $10,000. Five years later B sells the filling station for $20,000 at a time when $2,000 has been properly allowed as depreciation thereon. B's gain on this sale is $7,000, since $7,000 is the amount by which the selling price of the filling station exceeds the portion of the cost equitably allocable to the filling station at the time of purchase reduced by the depreciation properly allowed.

(b) Nontaxable exchanges. Certain realized gains or losses on the sale or exchange of property are not "recognized", that is, are not included in or deducted from gross income at the time the transaction occurs. Gain or loss from such sales or exchanges is generally recognized at some later time. Examples of such sales or exchanges are the following:

(1) Certain formations, reorganizations, and liquidations of corporations, see sections 331, 333, 337, 351, 354, 355, and 361;

(2) Certain formations and distributions of partnerships, see sections 721 and 731;

(3) Exchange of certain property held for productive use or investment for property of like kind, see section 1031;

(4) A corporation's exchange of its stock for property, see section 1032;

(5) Certain involuntary conversions of property if replaced, see section 1033;

(6) Sale or exchange of residence if replaced, see section 1034;

(7) Certain exchanges of insurance policies and annuity contracts, see section 1035; and

(8) Certain exchanges of stock for stock in the same corporation, see section 1036.

(c) Character of recognized gain. Under subchapter P, chapter 1 of the Code, relating to capital gains and losses, certain gains derived from dealings in property are treated specially * * *. Generally, the property subject to this treatment is a "capital asset", or treated as a "capital asset". For definition of such assets, see sections 1221 and 1231, and the regulations thereunder. For some of the rules either granting or denying this special treatment, see the following sections and the regulations thereunder:

(1) Transactions between partner and partnership, section 707;

(2) Sale or exchange of property used in the trade or business and involuntary conversions, section 1231;

* * *

§ 1.61–7 Interest.

(a) In general. As a general rule, interest received by or credited to the taxpayer constitutes gross income and is fully taxable. Interest income includes interest on savings or other bank deposits; interest on coupon bonds; interest on an open account, a promissory note, a mortgage, or a corporate bond or debenture; the interest portion of a condemnation award; usurious interest (unless by State law it is automatically converted to a payment on the principal); interest on legacies; interest on life insurance proceeds held under an agreement to pay interest thereon; and interest on refunds of Federal taxes. * * *

* * *

[T.D. 6500, 25 FR 11402, Nov. 26, 1960, as amended by T.D. 6723, 29 FR 5342, April 21, 1964; T.D. 6873, 31 FR 941, Jan. 25, 1966]

§ 1.61–8 Rents and royalties.

(a) In general. Gross income includes rentals received or accrued for the occupancy of real estate or the use of personal property. * * * Gross income includes royalties. Royalties may be received from books, stories, plays, copyrights, trademarks, formulas, patents, and from the exploitation of natural resources, such as coal, gas, oil, copper, or timber. Payments received as a result of the transfer of patent rights may under some circumstances constitute capital gain instead of ordinary income. See section 1235 and the regulations thereunder. For special rules for certain income from natural resources, see subchapter I (section 611 and following), chapter 1 of the Code, and the regulations thereunder.

(b) Advance rentals; cancellation payments. Except as provided in section 467 and the regulations thereunder, and except as otherwise provided by the Commissioner in published guidance (see § 601.601(d)(2) of this chapter), gross income includes advance rentals, which must be included in income for the year of receipt regardless of the period covered or the method of accounting employed by the taxpayer. An amount received by a lessor from a lessee for cancelling a lease constitutes gross income for the year in which it is received, since it is essentially a substitute for rental payments. As to amounts received by a lessee for the cancellation of a lease, see section 1241 and the regulations thereunder.

(c) Expenditures by lessee. As a general rule, if a lessee pays any of the expenses of his lessor such payments are additional rental income of the lessor. If a lessee places improvements on real estate which constitute, in whole or in part, a substitute for rent, such improvements constitute rental income to the lessor. Whether or not improvements made by a lessee result in rental income to the lessor in a particular case depends upon the intention of the parties, which may be indicated either by the terms of the lease or by the surrounding circumstances. For the exclusion from gross income of income (other than rent) derived by a lessor of real property on the termination of a lease, representing the value of such property attributable to buildings erected or other improvements made by a lessee, see section 109 and the regulations thereunder. * * *

[T.D. 6500, 25 FR 11402, Nov. 26, 1960, as amended by T.D. 8820, 64 FR 26845, May 18, 1999; T.D. 9135, 69 FR 41192, July 8, 2004]

§ 1.61–9 Dividends.

(a) In general. Except as otherwise specifically provided, dividends are included in gross income under sections 61 and 301. For the principal rules with respect to dividends includible in gross income, see section 316 and the regulations thereunder. * * *

* * *

(c) Dividends on stock sold. When stock is sold, and a dividend is both declared and paid after the sale, such dividend is not gross income to the seller. When stock is sold after the declaration of a dividend and after the date as of which the seller becomes entitled to the dividend, the dividend ordinarily is income to the seller. When stock is sold between the time of declaration and the time of payment of the dividend, and the sale takes place at such time that the purchaser becomes entitled to the dividend, the dividend ordinarily is income to him. The fact that the purchaser may have included the amount of the dividend in his purchase price in contemplation of receiving the dividend does not exempt him from tax. Nor can the purchaser deduct the added amount he advanced to the seller in anticipation of the dividend. That added amount is merely part of the purchase price of the stock. In some cases, however, the purchaser may be considered to be the recipient of the dividend even though he has not received the legal title to the stock itself and does not himself receive the dividend. For example, if the seller retains the legal title to the stock as trustee solely for the purpose of securing the payment of the purchase price, with the understanding that he is to apply the dividends received from time to time in reduction of the purchase price, the dividends are considered to be income to the purchaser.

[T.D. 6500, 25 FR 11402, Nov. 26, 1960, as amended by T.D. 6777, 29 FR 17807, Dec. 16, 1964]

§ 1.61–10 Alimony and separate maintenance payments; annuities; income from life insurance and endowment contracts.

(a) In general. Alimony and separate maintenance payments, annuities, and income from life insurance and endowment contracts in general constitute gross income, unless excluded by law. Annuities paid by religious, charitable, and educational corporations are generally taxable to the same extent as other annuities. * * *

(b) Cross references. For the detailed rules relating to—

(1) Alimony and separate maintenance payments, see section 71 and the regulations thereunder;

(2) Annuities, certain proceeds of endowment and life insurance contracts, see section 72 and the regulations thereunder;

(3) Life insurance proceeds paid by reason of death of insured, * * *, see section 101 and the regulations thereunder;

(4) Annuities paid by employees' trusts, see section 402 and the regulations thereunder;

(5) Annuities purchased for employee by employer, see section 403 and the regulations thereunder.

§ 1.61–11 Pensions.

(a) In general. Pensions and retirement allowances paid either by the Government or by private persons constitute gross income unless excluded by law. Usually, where the taxpayer did not contribute to the cost of a pension and was not taxable on his employer's contributions, the full amount of the pension is to be included in his gross income. But see sections 72, 402, and 403, and the regulations thereunder. When amounts are received from other types of pensions, a portion of the payment may be excluded from gross income. * * *

* * *

[T.D. 6500, 25 FR 11402, Nov. 26, 1960, as amended by T.D. 6856, 30 FR 13316, Oct. 20, 1965]

§ 1.61–12 Income from discharge of indebtedness.

(a) In general. The discharge of indebtedness, in whole or in part, may result in the realization of income. If, for example, an individual performs services for a creditor, who in consideration thereof cancels the debt, the debtor realizes income in the amount of the debt as compensation for his services. A taxpayer may realize income by the payment or purchase of his obligations at less than their face value. In general, if a shareholder in a corporation which is indebted to him gratuitously forgives the debt, the transaction amounts to a contribution to the capital of the corporation to the extent of the principal of the debt.

* * *

[T.D. 6500, 25 FR 11402, Nov. 26, 1960, as amended by T.D. 6984, 33 FR 19174, Dec. 24, 1968; T.D. 7741, 45 FR 81745, Dec. 12, 1980; T.D. 8746, 62 FR 68173, Dec. 31, 1997]

§ 1.61–13 Distributive share of partnership gross income; income in respect of a decedent; income from an interest in an estate or trust.

(a) In general. A partner's distributive share of partnership gross income (under section 702(c)) constitutes gross income to him. Income in respect of a decedent (under section 691) constitutes gross income to the recipient. Income from an interest in an estate or trust constitutes gross income under the detailed rules of part I (section 641 and following), subchapter J, chapter 1 of the Code. In many cases, these sections also determine who is to include in his gross income the income from an estate or trust.

* * *

[T.D. 6500, 25 FR 11402, Nov. 26, 1960]

§ 1.61–14 Miscellaneous items of gross income.

(a) In general. In addition to the items enumerated in section 61(a), there are many other kinds of gross income. For example, punitive damages such as treble damages under the antitrust laws and exemplary damages for fraud are gross income. Another person's payment of the taxpayer's income taxes constitutes gross income to the taxpayer unless excluded by law. Illegal gains constitute gross income. Treasure trove, to the extent of its value in United States currency, constitutes gross income for the taxable year in which it is reduced to undisputed possession.

* * *

[T.D. 6500, 25 FR 11402, Nov. 26, 1960, as amended by T.D. 6856, 30 FR 13316, Oct. 20, 1965; T.D. 8491, 58 FR 53127, Oct. 14, 1993]

§ 1.61–21 Taxation of fringe benefits.

(a) Fringe benefits—(1) In general. Section 61(a)(1) provides that, except as otherwise provided in subtitle A of the Internal Revenue Code of 1986, gross income includes compensation for services, including fees, commissions, fringe benefits, and similar items. For an outline of the regulations under this section relating to fringe benefits, see paragraph (a)(7) of this section. Examples of fringe benefits include: an employer-provided automobile, a flight on an employer-provided aircraft, an employer-provided free or discounted commercial airline flight, an employer-provided vacation, an employer-provided discount on property or services, an employer-provided membership in a country club or other social club, and an employer-provided ticket to an entertainment or sporting event.

(2) Fringe benefits excluded from income. To the extent that a particular fringe benefit is specifically excluded from gross income pursuant to another section of subtitle A of the Internal Revenue Code of 1986, that section shall govern the treatment of that fringe benefit. Thus, if the requirements of the governing section are satisfied, the fringe benefits may be excludable from gross income. Examples of excludable fringe benefits include qualified tuition reductions provided to an employee (section 117(d)); meals or lodging furnished to an employee for the convenience of the employer (section 119); benefits provided under a dependent care assistance program (section 129); and no-additional-cost services, qualified employee discounts, working condition fringes, and de minimis fringes (section 132). Similarly, the value of the use by an employee of an employer-provided vehicle or a flight provided to an employee on an employer-provided aircraft may be excludable from income under section 105 (because, for example, the transportation is provided for medical reasons) if and to the extent that the requirements of that section are satisfied. Section 134 excludes from gross income "qualified military benefits." An example of a benefit that is not a qualified military benefit is the personal use of an employer-provided vehicle. The fact that another section of subtitle A of the Internal Revenue Code addresses the taxation of a particular fringe benefit will not preclude section 61 and the regulations thereunder from applying, to the extent that they are not inconsistent with such other section. For example, many fringe benefits specifically addressed in other sections of subtitle A of the Internal Revenue Code are excluded from gross income only to the extent that they do not exceed specific dollar or percentage limits, or only if certain other requirements are met. If the limits are exceeded or the requirements are not met, some or all of the fringe benefit may be includible in gross income pursuant to section 61. See paragraph (b)(3) of this section.

(3) Compensation for services. A fringe benefit provided in connection with the performance of services shall be considered to have been provided as compensation for such services. Refraining from the performance of services (such as pursuant to a covenant not to compete) is deemed to be the performance of services for purposes of this section.

(4) Person to whom fringe benefit is taxable—(i) In general. A taxable fringe benefit is included in the income of the person performing the services in connection with which the fringe benefit is furnished. Thus, a fringe benefit may be taxable to a person even though that person did not actually receive the fringe benefit. If a fringe benefit is furnished to someone other than the service provider such benefit is considered in this section as furnished to the service provider, and use by the other person is considered use by the service provider. For example, the provision of an automobile by an employer to an employee's spouse in connection with the performance of services by the employee is taxable to the employee. The automobile is considered available to the employee and use by the employee's spouse is considered use by the employee.

(ii) All persons to whom benefits are taxable referred to as employees. The person to whom a fringe benefit is taxable need not be an employee of the provider of the fringe benefit, but may be, for example, a partner, director, or an independent contractor. For convenience, the term "employee" includes any person performing services in connection with which a fringe benefit is furnished, unless otherwise specifically provided in this section.

(5) Provider of a fringe benefit referred to as an employer. The "provider" of a fringe benefit is that person for whom the services are performed, regardless of whether that person actually provides the fringe benefit to the recipient. The provider of a fringe benefit need not be the employer of the recipient of the fringe benefit, but may be, for example, a client or customer of the employer or of an independent contractor. For convenience, the term "employer" includes any provider of a fringe benefit in connection with payment for the performance of services, unless otherwise specifically provided in this section.

* * *

(b) Valuation of fringe benefits—(1) In general. An employee must include in gross income the amount by which the fair market value of the fringe benefit exceeds the sum of—

(i) The amount, if any, paid for the benefit by or on behalf of the recipient, and

(ii) The amount, if any, specifically excluded from gross income by some other section of subtitle A of the Internal Revenue Code of 1986.

Therefore, for example, if the employee pays fair market value for what is received, no amount is includible in the gross income of the employee. In general, the determination of the fair market value of a fringe benefit must be made before subtracting out the amount, if any, paid for the benefit and the amount, if any, specifically excluded from gross income by another section of subtitle A. * * *

(2) Fair market value. In general, fair market value is determined on the basis of all the facts and circumstances. Specifically, the fair market value of a fringe benefit is the amount that an individual would have to pay for the particular fringe benefit in an arm's-length transaction. Thus, for example, the effect of any special relationship that may exist between the employer and the employee must be disregarded. Similarly, an employee's subjective perception of the value of a fringe benefit is not relevant to the determination of the fringe benefit's fair market value nor is the cost incurred by the employer determinative of its fair market value. * * *

(3) Exclusion from income based on cost. If a statutory exclusion phrased in terms of cost applies to the provision of a fringe benefit, section 61 does not require the inclusion in the recipient's gross income of the difference between the fair market value and the excludable cost of that fringe benefit. For example, section 129 provides an exclusion from an employee's gross income for amounts contributed by an employer to a dependent care assistance program for employees. Even if the fair market value of the dependent care assistance exceeds the employer's cost, the excess is not subject to inclusion under section 61 and this section. However, if the statutory cost exclusion is a limited amount, the fair market value of the fringe benefit attributable to any excess cost is subject to inclusion. This would be the case, for example, where an employer pays or incurs a cost of more than $5,000 to provide dependent care assistance to an employee.

(4) Fair market value of the availability of an employer-provided vehicle—(i) In general. If the vehicle special valuation rules of paragraph (d), (e), or (f) of this section do not apply with respect to an employer-provided vehicle, the value of the availability of that vehicle is determined under the general valuation principles set forth in this section. In general, that value equals the amount that an individual would have to pay in an arm's-length transaction to lease the same or comparable vehicle on the same or comparable conditions in the geographic area in which the vehicle is available for use. An example of a comparable condition is the amount of time that the vehicle is available to the employee for use, e.g., a one-year period. Unless the employee can substantiate that the same or comparable vehicle could have been leased on a cents-per-mile basis, the value of the availability of the vehicle cannot be computed by applying a cents-per-mile rate to the number of miles the vehicle is driven.

(ii) Certain equipment excluded. The fair market value of a vehicle does not include the fair market value of any specialized equipment not susceptible to personal use or any telephone that is added to or carried in the vehicle, provided that the presence of that equipment or telephone is necessitated by, and attributable to, the business needs of the employer. However, the value of specialized equipment must be included, if the employee to whom the vehicle is available uses the specialized equipment in a trade or business of the employee other than the employee's trade or business of being an employee of the employer.

* * *

(f) Commuting valuation rule—(1) In general. Under the commuting valuation rule of this paragraph (f), the value of the commuting use of an employer-provided vehicle may be determined pursuant to paragraph (f)(3) of this section if the following criteria are met by the employer and employees with respect to the vehicle:

(i) The vehicle is owned or leased by the employer and is provided to one or more employees for use in connection with the employer's trade or business and is used in the employer's trade or business;

(ii) For bona fide noncompensatory business reasons, the employer requires the employee to commute to and/or from work in the vehicle;

(iii) The employer has established a written policy under which neither the employee, nor any individual whose use would be taxable to the employee, may use the vehicle for personal purposes, other than for commuting or de minimis personal use (such as a stop fora personal errand on the way between a business delivery and the employee's home);

(iv) Except for de minimis personal use, the employee does not use the vehicle for any personal purpose other than commuting; and

(v) The employee required to use the vehicle for commuting is not a control employee of the employer (as defined in paragraphs (f)(5) and (6) of this section).

Personal use of a vehicle is all use of the vehicle by an employee that is not used in the employee's trade or business of being an employee of the employer. An employer-provided vehicle that is generally used each workday to transport at least three employees of the employer to and from work in an employer-sponsored commuting vehicle pool is deemed to meet the requirements of paragraphs (f)(1)(i) and (ii) of this section.

* * *

(3) Commuting value—(i) $1.50 per one-way commute. If the requirements of this paragraph (f) are satisfied, the value of the commuting use of an employer-provided vehicle is $1.50 per one-way commute (e.g., from home to work or from work to home). The value provided in this paragraph (f)(3) includes the value of any goods or services directly related to the vehicle (e.g., fuel).

(ii) Value per employee. If there is more than one employee who commutes in the vehicle, such as in the case of an employer-sponsored commuting vehicle pool, the amount includible in the income of each employee is $1.50 per one-way commute. Thus, the amount includible for each round-trip commute is $3.00 per employee. * * *

(4) Definition of vehicle. For purposes of this paragraph (f), the term "vehicle" means any motorized wheeled vehicle manufactured primarily for use on public streets, roads, and highways. * * *

(5) Control employee defined—Non-government employer. For purposes of this paragraph (f), a control employee of a non-government employer is any employee—

(i) Who is a Board- or shareholder-appointed, confirmed, or elected officer of the employer whose compensation equals or exceeds $50,000,

(ii) Who is a director of the employer,

(iii) Whose compensation equals or exceeds $100,000, or

(iv) Who owns a one-percent or greater equity, capital, or profits interest in the employer.

For purposes of determining who is a one-percent owner under paragraph (f)(5)(iv) of this section, any individual who owns (or is considered as owning under section 318(a) or principles similar to section 318(a) for entities other than corporations) one percent or more of the fair market value of an entity (the "owned entity") is considered a one-percent owner of all entities which would be aggregated with the owned entity under the rules of section 414(b), (c), (m), or (*o*). For purposes of determining who is an officer or director with respect to an employer under this paragraph (f)(5), notwithstanding anything in this section to the contrary, if an entity would be aggregated with other entities under the rules of section 414(b), (c), (m), or (*o*), the officer definition (but not the compensation requirement) and the director definition apply to each such separate entity rather than to the aggregated employer. An employee who is an officer or a director of an entity (the "first entity") shall be treated as an officer or a director of all entities aggregated with the first entity under the rules of section 414(b), (c), (m), or (*o*). Instead of applying the control employee definition of this paragraph (f)(5), an employer may treat all, and only, employees who are "highly compensated" employees (as defined in § 1.132–8(g)) as control employees for purposes of this paragraph (f).

* * *

(j) Valuation of meals provided at an employer-operated eating facility for employees—(1) In general. The valuation rule of this paragraph (j) may be used to value a meal provided at an employer-operated eating facility for employees (as defined in § 1.132–7). For rules relating to an exclusion for the value of meals provided at an employer-operated eating facility for employees, see section 132(e)(2) and § 1.132–7.

(2) Valuation formula—(i) In general. The value of all meals provided at an employer-operated eating facility for employees during a calendar year ("total meal value") is 150 percent of the direct operating costs of the eating facility determined separately with respect to such eating facility whether or not the direct operating costs test is applied separately to such eating facility under § 1.132–7(b)(2). For purposes of this paragraph (j), the definition of direct operating costs provided in § 1.132–7(b) and the adjustments specified in § 1.132–7(a)(2) apply. The taxable value of meals provided at an eating facility may be determined in two ways. The "individual meal subsidy" may be treated as the taxable value of a meal provided at the eating facility (see paragraph (j)(2)(ii) of this section) to a particular employee. Alternatively, the employer may allocate the "total meal subsidy" among employees (see paragraph (j)(2)(iii) of this section).

(ii) "Individual meal subsidy" defined. The "individual meal subsidy" is determined by multiplying the amount paid by the employee for a particular meal by a fraction, the numerator of which is the total meal value and the denominator of which is the gross receipts of the eating facility for the calendar year and then subtracting the amount paid by the employee for the meal. The taxable value of meals provided to a particular employee during a calendar year, therefore, is the sum of the individual meal subsidies provided to the employee during the calendar year. This rule is available only if there is a charge for each meal selection and if each employee is charged the same price for any given meal selection.

(iii) Allocation of "total meal subsidy." Instead of using the individual meal subsidy method provided in paragraph (j)(2)(ii) of this section, the employer may allocate the "total meal subsidy" (total meal value less the gross receipts of the facility) among employees in any manner reasonable under the circumstances. It will be presumed reasonable for an employer to allocate the total meal subsidy on a per-employee basis if the employer has information that would substantiate to the satisfaction of the Commissioner that each employee was provided approximately the same number of meals at the facility.

(k) Commuting valuation rule for certain employees—(1) In general. Under the rule of this paragraph (k), the value of the commuting use of employer-provided transportation may be determined under paragraph (k)(3) of this section if the following criteria are met by the employer and employee with respect to the transportation:

(i) The transportation is provided, solely because of unsafe conditions, to an employee who would ordinarily walk or use public transportation for commuting to or from work;

(ii) The employer has established a written policy (e.g., in the employer's personnel manual) under which the transportation is not provided for the employee's personal purposes other than for commuting due to unsafe conditions and the employer's practice in fact corresponds with the policy;

(iii) The transportation is not used for personal purposes other than commuting due to unsafe conditions; and

(iv) The employee receiving the employer-provided transportation is a qualified employee of the employer (as defined in paragraph (k)(6) of this section).

(2) Trip-by-trip basis. The special valuation rule of this paragraph (k) applies on a trip-by-trip basis. If an employer and employee fail to meet the criteria of paragraph (k)(1) of this section with respect to any trip, the value of the transportation for that trip is not determined under paragraph (k)(3) of this section and the amount includible in the employee's income is determined by reference to the fair market value of the transportation.

(3) Commuting value—(i) $1.50 per one-way commute. If the requirements of this paragraph (k) are satisfied, the value of the commuting use of the employer-provided transportation is $1.50 per one-way commute (i.e., from home to work or from work to home).

(ii) Value per employee. If transportation is provided to more than one qualified employee at the same time, the amount includible in the income of each employee is $1.50 per one-way commute.

(4) Definition of employer-provided transportation. For purposes of this paragraph (k), "employer-provided transportation" means transportation by vehicle (as defined in paragraph (f)(4) of this section) that is purchased by the employer (or that is purchased by the employee and reimbursed by the employer) from a party that is not related to the employer for the purpose of transporting a qualified employee to or from work. Reimbursements made by an employer to an employee to cover the cost of purchasing transportation (e.g., hiring cabs) must be made under a bona fide reimbursement arrangement.

(5) Unsafe conditions. Unsafe conditions exist if a reasonable person would, under the facts and circumstances, consider it unsafe for the employee to walk to or from home, or to walk to or use public transportation at the time of day the employee must commute. One of the factors indicating whether it is unsafe is the history of crime in the geographic area surrounding the employee's workplace or residence at the time of day the employee must commute.

* * *

[T.D. 8256, 54 FR 28582, July 6, 1989; as amended by T.D. 8389, 57 FR 1870, Jan. 16, 1992, and T.D. 8457, 57 FR 62192, Dec. 30, 1992; T.D. 9597, 77 FR 45480, Aug. 1, 2012]

§ 1.62–1T Adjusted gross income.

(a) Basis for determining the amount of certain deductions. The term "adjusted gross income" means the gross income computed under section 61 minus such of the deductions allowed by chapter 1 of the Code as are specified in section 62(a). Adjusted gross income is used as the basis for determining the following:

(1) The limitation on the amount of miscellaneous itemized deductions (under section 67),

(2) The limitation on the amount of the deduction for casualty losses (under section 165(h)(2)),

(3) The limitation on the amount of the deduction for charitable contributions (under section 170(b)(1)),

(4) The limitation on the amount of the deduction for medical and dental expenses (under section 213),

(5) The limitation on the amount of the deduction for qualified retirement contributions for active participants in certain pension plans (under section 219(g)), and

(6) The phase-out of the exemption from the disallowance of passive activity losses and credits (under section 469(i)(3)).

(b) Double deduction not permitted. Section 62(a) merely specifies which of the deductions provided in chapter 1 of the Code shall be allowed in computing adjusted gross income. It does not create any new deductions. The fact that a particular item may be described in more than one of the paragraphs under section 62(a) does not permit the item to be deducted twice in computing adjusted gross income or taxable income.

* * *

(d) Expenses directly related to a trade or business. For the purpose of the deductions specified in section 62, the performance of personal services as an employee does not constitute the carrying on of a trade or business, except as otherwise expressly provided. The practice of a profession, not as an employee, is considered the conduct of a trade or business within the meaning of such section. To be deductible for the purposes of determining adjusted gross income, expenses must be those directly, and not those merely remotely, connected with the conduct of a trade or business. For example, taxes are deductible in arriving at adjusted gross income only if they constitute expenditures directly attributable to a trade or business or to property from which rents or royalties are derived. Thus, property taxes paid or incurred on real property used in a trade or business are deductible, but state taxes on net income are not deductible even though the taxpayer's income is derived from the conduct of a trade or business.

(e) Reimbursed and unreimbursed employee expenses—(1) In general. Expenses paid or incurred by an employee that are deductible from gross income under part VI in computing taxable income (determined without regard to section 67) and for which the employee is reimbursed by the employer, its agent, or third party (for whom the employee performs a benefit as an employee of the employer) under an express agreement for reimbursement or pursuant to an express expense allowance arrangement may be deducted from gross income in computing adjusted gross income. * * *

* * *

(g) Moving expenses. For taxable years beginning after December 31, 1986, a taxpayer described in section 217(a) shall not take into account the deduction described in section 217 relating to moving expenses in computing adjusted gross income under section 62 even if the taxpayer is reimbursed for his or her moving expenses. Such a taxpayer shall include the amount of any reimbursement for moving expenses in income pursuant to section 82. The deduction described in section 217 shall be taken into account in computing the taxable income of the taxpayer under section 63. Pursuant to section 67(b)(6), the 2-percent floor described in section 67(a) does not apply to moving expenses.

* * *

[T.D. 8189, 53 FR 9873, Mar. 28, 1988, as amended by T.D. 8276, 54 FR 51024, Dec. 12, 1989; T.D. 8324, 55 FR 51691, Dec. 17, 1990; T.D. 8451, 57 FR 57668, Dec. 7, 1992]

§ 1.62–2 Reimbursements and other expense allowance arrangements.

* * *

(c) Reimbursement or other expense allowance arrangement—(1) Defined. * * *

(2) Accountable plans—(i) In general. Except as provided in paragraph (c)(2)(ii) of this section, if an arrangement meets the requirements of paragraphs (d), (e), and (f) of this section, all amounts paid under the arrangement are treated as paid under an "accountable plan."

* * *

(4) Treatment of payments under accountable plans. Amounts treated as paid under an accountable plan are excluded from the employee's gross income, are not reported as wages or other compensation on the employee's Form W–2, and are exempt from the withholding and payment of employment taxes (Federal Insurance Contributions Act (FICA), Federal Unemployment Tax Act (FUTA), Railroad Retirement Tax Act (RRTA), Railroad Unemployment Repayment Tax (RURT), and income tax.) See paragraph (*l*) of this section for cross references.

(5) Treatment of payments under nonaccountable plans. Amounts treated as paid under a nonaccountable plan are included in the employee's gross income, must be reported as wages or other compensation on the employee's Form W–2, and are subject to withholding and payment of employment taxes (FICA, FUTA, RRTA, RURT, and income tax). See paragraph (h) of this section. Expenses attributable to amounts included in the employee's gross income may be deducted, provided the employee can substantiate the full amount of his or her expenses (i.e., the amount of the expenses, if any, the reimbursement for which is treated as paid under an accountable plan as well as those for which the employee is claiming the deduction) in accordance with §§ 1.274–5T and 1.274(d)–1 or 1.162–17, but only as a miscellaneous itemized deduction subject to the limitations applicable to such expenses (e.g., the 80-percent limitation on meal and entertainment expenses provided in section 274(n) and the 2-percent floor provided in section 67).

(d) Business connection—(1) In general. Except as provided in paragraphs (d)(2) and (d)(3) of this section, an arrangement meets the requirements of this paragraph (d) if it provides advances, allowances (including per diem allowances, allowances only for meals and incidental expenses, and mileage allowances), or reimbursements only for business expenses that are allowable as deductions by part VI (section 161 and the following), subchapter B, chapter 1 of the Code, and that are paid or incurred by the employee in connection with the performance of services as an employee of the employer. The payment may be actually received from the employer, its agent, or a third party for whom the employee performs a service as an employee of the employer, and may include amounts charged directly or indirectly to the payor through credit card systems or otherwise. In addition, if both wages and the reimbursement or other expense allowance are combined in a single payment, the reimbursement or other expense allowance must be identified either by making a separate payment or by specifically identifying the amount of the reimbursement or other expense allowance.

* * *

(e) Substantiation—(1) In general. An arrangement meets the requirements of this paragraph (e) if it requires each business expense to be substantiated to the payor in accordance with paragraph (e)(2) or (e)(3) of this section, whichever is applicable, within a reasonable period of time. * * *

* * *

(f) Returning amounts in excess of expenses—(1) In general. Except as provided in paragraph (f)(2) of this section, an arrangement meets the requirements of this paragraph (f) if it requires the employee to return to the payor within a reasonable period of time may amount paid under the arrangement in excess of the expenses substantiated in accordance with paragraph (e) of this section. The determination of whether an arrangement requires an employee to return amounts in excess of substantiated expenses will depend on the facts and circumstances. An arrangement whereby money is advanced to an employee to defray expenses will be treated as satisfying the requirements of this paragraph (f) only if the amount of money advanced is reasonably calculated not to exceed the amount of anticipated expenditures, the advance of money is made on a day within a reasonable period of the day that the anticipated expenditures are paid or incurred, and any amounts in excess of the expenses substantiated in accordance with paragraph (e) of this section are required to be returned to the payor within a reasonable period of time after the advance is received.

(2) Per diem or mileage allowances. The Commissioner may, in his discretion, prescribe rules in pronouncements of general applicability under which a reimbursement or other expense allowance arrangement that provides per diem allowances providing for ordinary and necessary expenses of traveling away from home (exclusive of transportation costs to and from destination) or mileage allowances providing for ordinary and necessary expenses of local travel and transportation while traveling away from home will be treated as satisfying the requirements of this paragraph (f), even though the arrangement does not require the employee to return the portion of such an allowance that relates to the days or miles of travel substantiated and that exceeds the amount of the employee's expenses deemed substantiated pursuant to rules prescribed under section 274(d), provided the allowance is paid at a rate for each day or mile of travel that is reasonably calculated not to exceed the amount of the employee's expenses or anticipated expenses and the employee is required to return to the payor within a reasonable period of time any portion of such allowance which relates to days or miles of travel not substantiated in accordance with paragraph (e) of this section.

* * *

[T.D. 8324, 55 FR 51691, Dec. 17, 1990; T.D. 8324, 56 FR 8911, Mar. 4, 1991; T.D. 8451, 57 FR 57668, Dec. 7, 1992; T.D. 8666, 61 FR 27005, May 30, 1996; T.D. 9064, 68 FR 39011, July 1, 2003]

§ 1.67–1T 2–percent floor on miscellaneous itemized deductions.

(a) Type of expenses subject to the floor—(1) In general. With respect to individuals, section 67 disallows deductions for miscellaneous itemized deductions (as defined in paragraph (b) of this section) in computing taxable income (*i.e.,* so-called "below-the-line" deductions) to the extent that such otherwise allowable deductions do not exceed 2 percent of the individual's adjusted gross income (as defined in section 62 and the regulations thereunder). Examples of expenses that, if otherwise deductible, are subject to the 2–percent floor include but are not limited to—

(i) Unreimbursed employee expenses, such as expenses for transportation, travel fares and lodging while away from home, business meals and entertainment, continuing education courses, subscriptions to professional journals, union or professional dues, professional uniforms, job hunting, and the business use of the employee's home,

(ii) Expenses for the production or collection of income for which a deduction is otherwise allowable under section 212(1) and (2), such as investment advisory fees, subscriptions to investment advisory publications, certain attorneys' fees, and the cost of safe deposit boxes,

(iii) Expenses for the determination of any tax for which a deduction is otherwise allowable under section 212(3), such as tax counsel fees and appraisal fees, and

(iv) Expenses for an activity for which a deduction is otherwise allowable under section 183. See section 62 with respect to deductions that are allowable in computing adjusted gross income (*i.e.,* so-called "above-the-line" deductions).

(2) Other limitations. Except as otherwise provided in paragraph (d) of this section, to the extent that any limitation or restriction is placed on the amount of a miscellaneous itemized deduction, that limitation shall apply prior to the application of the 2-percent floor. * * *

* * *

(c) Allocation of expenses. If a taxpayer incurs expenses that relate to both a trade or business activity (within the meaning of section 162) and a production of income or tax preparation activity (within the meaning of section 212), the taxpayer shall allocate such expenses between the activities on a reasonable basis.

* * *

[T.D. 8189, 53 FR 9875, Mar. 28, 1988]

§ 1.71–1 Alimony and separate maintenance payments; income to wife or former wife.

(a) In general. Section 71 provides rules for treatment in certain cases of payments in the nature of or in lieu of alimony or an allowance for support as between spouses who are divorced or separated. For convenience, the payee spouse will hereafter in this section be referred to as the "wife" and the spouse from whom she is divorced or separated as the "husband." See section 7701(a)(17). * * * For rules relative to the taxable status of income of an estate or trust in case of divorce, etc., see section 682 and the regulations thereunder.

(b) Alimony or separate maintenance payments received from the husband—(1) Decree of divorce or separate maintenance. (i) In the case of divorce or legal separation, paragraph (1) of section 71(a) requires the inclusion in the gross income of the wife of periodic payments (whether or not made at regular intervals) received by her after a decree of divorce or of separate maintenance. Such periodic payments must be made in discharge of a legal obligation imposed upon or incurred by the husband because of the marital or family relationship under a court order or decree divorcing or legally separating the husband and wife or a written instrument incident to the divorce status or legal separation status.

* * *

(2) Written separation agreement. (i) Where the husband and wife are separated and living apart and do not file a joint income tax return for the taxable year, paragraph (2) of section 71(a) requires the inclusion in the gross income of the wife of periodic payments (whether or not made at regular intervals) received by her pursuant to a written separation agreement executed after August 16, 1954. The periodic payments must be made under the terms of the written separation agreement after its execution and because of the marital or family relationship. Such payments are includible in the wife's gross income whether or not the agreement is a legally enforceable instrument. Moreover, if the wife is divorced or legally separated subsequent to the written separation agreement, payments made under such agreement continue to fall within the provisions of section 71(a)(2).

* * *

(3) Decree for support. (i) Where the husband and wife are separated and living apart and do not file a joint income tax return for the taxable year, paragraph (3) of section 71(a) requires the inclusion in the gross income of the wife of periodic payments (whether or not made at regular intervals) received by her after August 16, 1954, from her husband under any type of court order or decree (including an interlocutory decree of divorce or a decree of alimony pendente lite) entered after March 1, 1954, requiring the husband to make the payments for her support or maintenance. It is not necessary for the wife to be legally separated or divorced from her husband under a court order or decree; nor is it necessary for the order or decree for support to be for the purpose of enforcing a written separation agreement.

* * *

[T.D. 6500, 25 FR 11402, Nov. 26, 1960]

§ 1.71–1T Alimony and separate maintenance payments.

(a) In general.

Q–1. What is the income tax treatment of alimony or separate maintenance payments?

A–1. Alimony or separate maintenance payments are, under section 71, included in the gross income of the payee spouse and, under section 215, allowed as a deduction from the gross income of the payor spouse.

Q–2. What is an alimony or separate maintenance payment?

A–2. An alimony or separate maintenance payment is any payment received by or on behalf of a spouse (which for this purpose includes a former spouse) of the payor under a divorce or separation instrument that meets all of the following requirements:

(a) The payment is in cash (see A–5).

(b) The payment is not designated as a payment which is excludible from the gross income of the payee and nondeductible by the payor (see A–8).

(c) In the case of spouses legally separated under a decree of divorce or separate maintenance, the spouses are not members of the same household at the time the payment is made (see A–9).

(d) The payor has no liability to continue to make any payment after the death of the payee (or to make any payment as a substitute for such payment) * * * (see A–10).

(e) The payment is not treated as child support (see A–15).

* * *

Q–3. In order to be treated as alimony or separate maintenance payments, must the payments be "periodic" as that term was defined prior to enactment of the Tax Reform Act of 1984 or be made in discharge of a legal obligation of the payor to support the payee arising out of a marital or family relationship?

A–3. No. The Tax Reform Act of 1984 replaces the old requirements with the requirements described in A–2 above. Thus, the requirements that alimony or separate maintenance payments be "periodic" and be made in discharge of a legal obligation to support arising out of a marital or family relationship have been eliminated.

Q–4. Are the instruments described in section 71(a) of prior law the same as divorce or separation instruments described in section 71, as amended by the Tax Reform Act of 1984?

A–4. Yes.

(b) Specific requirements.

Q–5. May alimony or separate maintenance payments be made in a form other than cash?

A–5. No. Only cash payments (including checks and money orders payable on demand) qualify as alimony or separate maintenance payments. Transfers of services or property (including a debt instrument of a third party or an annuity contract), execution of a debt instrument by the payor, or the use of property of the payor do not qualify as alimony or separate maintenance payments.

Q–6. May payments of cash to a third party on behalf of a spouse qualify as alimony or separate maintenance payments if the payments are pursuant to the terms of a divorce or separation instrument?

A–6. Yes. Assuming all other requirements are satisfied, a payment of cash by the payor spouse to a third party under the terms of the divorce or separation instrument will qualify as a payment of cash which is received "on behalf of a spouse". For example, cash payments of rent, mortgage, tax, or tuition liabilities of the payee spouse made under the terms of the divorce or separation instrument will qualify as alimony or separate maintenance payments. Any payments to maintain property owned by the payor spouse and used by the payee spouse (including mortgage payments, real estate taxes and insurance premiums) are not payments on behalf of a spouse even if those payments are made pursuant to the terms of the divorce or separation instrument. Premiums paid by the payor spouse for term or whole life insurance on the payor's life made under the terms of the divorce or separation instrument will qualify as payments on behalf of the payee spouse to the extent that the payee spouse is the owner of the policy.

Q–7. May payments of cash to a third party on behalf of a spouse qualify as alimony or separate maintenance payments if the payments are made to the third party at the written request of the payee spouse?

A–7. Yes. For example, instead of making an alimony or separate maintenance payment directly to the payee, the payor spouse may make a cash payment to a charitable organization if such payment is pursuant to the written request, consent or ratification of the payee spouse. Such request, consent or ratification must state that the parties intend the payment to be treated as an alimony or separate maintenance payment to the payee spouse subject to the rules of section 71, and must be received by the payor spouse prior to the date of filing of the payor's first return of tax for the taxable year in which the payment was made.

Q–8. How may spouses designate that payments otherwise qualifying as alimony or separate maintenance payments shall be excludible from the gross income of the payee and nondeductible by the payor?

A–8. The spouses may designate that payments otherwise qualifying as alimony or separate maintenance payments shall be nondeductible by the payor and excludible from gross income by the payee by so providing in a divorce or separation instrument (as defined in section 71(b)(2)). If the spouses have executed a written separation agreement (as described in section 71(b)(2)(B)), any writing signed by both spouses which designates otherwise qualifying alimony or separate maintenance payments as nondeductible and excludible and which refers to the written separation agreement will be treated as a written separation agreement (and thus a divorce or separation instrument) for purposes of the preceding sentence. If the spouses are subject to temporary support orders (as described in section 71(b)(2)(C)), the designation of otherwise qualifying alimony or separate payments as nondeductible and excludible must be made in the original or a subsequent temporary support order. A copy of the instrument containing the designation of payments as not alimony or separate maintenance payments must be attached to the payee's first filed return of tax (Form 1040) for each year in which the designation applies.

Q–9. What are the consequences if, at the time a payment is made, the payor and payee spouses are members of the same household?

A–9. Generally, a payment made at the time when the payor and payee spouses are members of the same household cannot qualify as an alimony or separate maintenance payment if the spouses are legally separated under a decree of divorce or of separate maintenance. For purposes of the preceding sentence, a dwelling unit formerly shared by both spouses shall not be considered two separate households even if the spouses physically separate themselves within the dwelling unit. The spouses will not be treated as members of the same household if one spouse is preparing to depart from the household of the other spouse, and does depart not more than one month after the date the payment is made. If the spouses are not legally separated under a decree of divorce or separate maintenance, a payment under a written separation agreement or a decree described in section 71(b)(2)(C) may qualify as an alimony or separate maintenance payment notwithstanding that the payor and payee are members of the same household at the time the payment is made.

Q–10. Assuming all other requirements relating to the qualification of certain payments as alimony or separate maintenance payments are met, what are the consequences if the payor spouse is required to continue to make the payments after the death of the payee spouse?

A–10. None of the payments before (or after) the death of the payee spouse qualify as alimony or separate maintenance payments.

* * *

Q–13. What are the consequences if the payor spouse is required to make one or more payments (in cash or property) after the death of the payee spouse as a substitute for the continuation of pre-death payments which would otherwise qualify as alimony or separate maintenance payments?

A–13. If the payor spouse is required to make any such substitute payments, none of the otherwise qualifying payments will qualify as alimony or separate maintenance payments. The divorce or separation instrument need not state, however, that there is no liability to make any such substitute payment.

Q–14. Under what circumstances will one or more payments (in cash or property) which are to occur after the death of the payee spouse be treated as a substitute for the continuation of payments which would otherwise qualify as alimony or separate maintenance payments?

A–14. To the extent that one or more payments are to begin to be made, increase in amount, or become accelerated in time as a result of the death of the payee spouse, such payments may be treated as a substitute for the continuation of payments terminating on the death of the payee spouse which would otherwise qualify as alimony or separate maintenance payments. The determination of whether or not such payments are a substitute for the continuation of payments which would otherwise qualify as alimony or separate maintenance payments, and of the amount of the otherwise qualifying alimony or separate maintenance payments for which any such payments are a substitute, will depend on all of the facts and circumstances.

Example (1). Under the terms of a divorce decree, A is obligated to make annual alimony payments to B of $30,000, terminating on the earlier of the expiration of 6 years or the death of B. B maintains custody of the minor children of A and B. The decree provides that at the death of B, if there are minor children of A and B remaining, A will be obligated to make annual payments of $10,000 to a trust, the income and corpus of which are to be used for the benefit of the children until the youngest child attains the age of majority. These facts indicate that A's liability to make annual $10,000 payments in trust for the benefit of his minor children upon the death of B is a substitute for $10,000 of the $30,000 annual payments to B. Accordingly, $10,000 of each of the $30,000 annual payments to B will not qualify as alimony or separate maintenance payments.

Example (2). Under the terms of a divorce decree, A is obligated to make annual alimony payments to B of $30,000, terminating on the earlier of the expiration of 15 years or the death of B. The divorce decree provides that if B dies before the expiration of the 15 year period, A will pay to B's estate the difference between the total amount that A would have paid had B survived, minus the amount actually paid. For example, if B dies at the end of the 10th year in which payments are made, A will pay to B's estate $150,000 ($450,000–$300,000). These facts indicate that A's liability to make a lump sum payment to B's estate upon the death of B is a substitute for the full amount of each of the annual $30,000 payments to B. Accordingly, none of the annual $30,000 payments to B will qualify as alimony or separate maintenance payments. The result would be the same if the lump sum payable at B's death were discounted by an appropriate interest factor to account for the prepayment.

(c) Child support payments.

Q–15. What are the consequences of a payment which the terms of the divorce or separation instrument fix as payable for the support of a child of the payor spouse?

A–15. A payment which under the terms of the divorce or separation instrument is fixed (or treated as fixed) as payable for the support of a child of the payor spouse does not qualify as an alimony or separate maintenance payment. Thus, such a payment is not deductible by the payor spouse or includible in the income of the payee spouse.

Q–16. When is a payment fixed (or treated as fixed) as payable for the support of a child of the payor spouse?

A–16. A payment is fixed as payable for the support of a child of the payor spouse if the divorce or separation instrument specifically designates some sum or portion (which sum or portion may fluctuate) as payable for the support of a child of the payor spouse. A payment will be treated as fixed as payable for the support of a child of the payor spouse if the payment is reduced (a) on the happening of a contingency relating to a child of the payor, or (b) at a time which can clearly be associated with such a contingency. A payment may be treated as fixed as payable for the support of a child of the payor spouse even if other separate payments specifically are designated as payable for the support of a child of the payor spouse.

Q–17. When does a contingency relate to a child of the payor?

A–17. For this purpose, a contingency relates to a child of the payor if it depends on any event relating to that child, regardless of whether such event is certain or likely to occur. Events that relate to a child of the payor include the following: the child's attaining a specified age or income level, dying, marrying, leaving school, leaving the spouse's household, or gaining employment.

Q–18. When will a payment be treated as to be reduced at a time which can clearly be associated with the happening of a contingency relating to a child of the payor?

A–18. There are two situations, described below, in which payments which would otherwise qualify as alimony or separate maintenance payments will be presumed to be reduced at a time clearly associated with the happening of a contingency relating to a child of the payor. In all other situations, reductions in payments will not be treated as clearly associated with the happening of a contingency relating to a child of the payor.

The first situation referred to above is where the payments are to be reduced not more than 6 months before or after the date the child is to attain the age of 18, 21, or local age of majority. The second situation is where the payments are to be reduced on two or more occasions which occur not more than one year before or after a different child of the payor spouse attains a certain age between the ages of 18 and 24, inclusive. The certain age referred to in the preceding sentence must be the same for each such child, but need not be a whole number of years.

The presumption in the two situations described above that payments are to be reduced at a time clearly associated with the happening of a contingency relating to a child of the payor may be rebutted (either by the Service or by taxpayers) by showing that the time at which the payments are to be reduced was determined independently of any contingencies relating to the children of the payor. The presumption in the first situation will be rebutted conclusively if the reduction is a complete cessation of alimony or separate maintenance payments during the sixth post-separation year (described in A–21) or upon the expiration of a 72-month period. The presumption may also be rebutted in other circumstances, for example, by showing that alimony payments are to be made for a period customarily provided in the local jurisdiction, such as a period equal to one-half the duration of the marriage.

Example: A and B are divorced on July 1, 1985, when their children, C (born July 15, 1970) and D (born September 23, 1972), are 14 and 12, respectively. Under the divorce decree, A is to make alimony payments to B of $2,000 per month. Such payments are to be reduced to $1,500 per month on January 1, 1991 and to $1,000 per month on January 1, 1995. On January 1, 1991, the date of the first reduction in payments, C will be 20 years 5 months and 17 days old. On January 1, 1995, the date of the second reduction in payments, D will be 22 years 3 months and 9 days old. Each of the reductions in payments is to occur not more than one year before or after a different child of A attains the age of 21 years and 4 months. (Actually, the reductions are to occur not more than one year before or after C and D attain any of the ages 21 years 3 months and 9 days through 21 years 5 months and 17 days). Accordingly, the reductions will be presumed to clearly be associated with the happening of a contingency relating to C and D. Unless this presumption is rebutted, payments under the divorce decree equal to the sum of the reduction ($1,000 per month) will be treated as fixed for the support of the children of A and therefore will not qualify as alimony or separate maintenance payments.

* * *

[T.D. 7973, 49 FR 34455, Aug. 31, 1984; 49 FR 36645, Sept. 19, 1984]

§ 1.72–1 Introduction.

(a) General principle. Section 72 prescribes rules relating to the inclusion in gross income of amounts received under a life insurance, endowment, or annuity contract unless such amounts are specifically excluded from gross income under other provisions of chapter 1 of the Code. In general, these rules provide that amounts subject to the provisions of section 72 are includible in the gross income of the recipient except to the extent that they are considered to represent a reduction or return of premiums or other consideration paid.

(b) Amounts to be considered as a return of premiums. For the purpose of determining the extent to which amounts received represent a reduction or return of premiums or other consideration paid, the provisions of section 72 distinguish between "amounts received as an annuity" and "amounts not received as an annuity". In general, "amounts received as an annuity" are amounts which are payable at regular intervals over a period of more than one full year from the date on which they are deemed to begin, provided the total of the amounts so payable or the period for which they are to be paid can be determined as of that date. * * *

Any other amounts to which the provisions of section 72 apply are considered to be "amounts not received as an annuity". * * *

* * *

[T.D. 6500, 25 FR 11402, Nov. 26, 1960, as amended by T.D. 6676, 28 FR 10134, Sept. 17, 1963]

§ 1.72–4 Exclusion ratio.

(a) General rule. **(1)(i)** To determine the proportionate part of the total amount received each year as an annuity which is excludable from the gross income of a recipient in the taxable year of receipt * * *, an exclusion ratio is to be determined for each contract. In general, this ratio is determined by dividing the investment in the contract as found under § 1.72–6 by the expected return under such contract as found under § 1.72–5. Where a single consideration is given for a particular contract which provides for two or more annuity elements, an exclusion ratio shall be determined for the contract as a whole by dividing the investment in such contract by the aggregate of the expected returns under all the annuity elements provided thereunder. * * *

(ii) The exclusion ratio for the particular contract is then applied to the total amount received as an annuity during the taxable year by each recipient. * * * Any excess of the total amount received as an annuity during the taxable year over the amount determined by the application of the exclusion ratio to such total amount shall be included in the gross income of the recipient for the taxable year of receipt.

(2) The principles of subparagraph (1) may be illustrated by the following example:

Example. Taxpayer A purchased an annuity contract providing for payments of $100 per month for a consideration of $12,650. Assuming that the expected return under this contract is $16,000 the exclusion ratio to be used by A is $12,650 ÷ 16,000; or 79.1 percent (79.06 rounded to the nearest tenth). If 12 such monthly payments are received by A during his taxable year, the total amount he may exclude from his gross income in such year is $949.20 ($1,200 × 79.1 percent). The balance of $250.80 ($1,200 less $949.20) is the amount to be included in gross income. If A instead received only five such payments during the year, he should exclude $395.50 (500 × 79.1 percent) of the total amounts received.

* * *

* * *

[T.D. 6500, 25 FR 11402, Nov. 26, 1960, as amended by T.D. 7043, 35 FR 8477, June 2, 1970; T.D. 7352, 40 FR 16663, April 14, 1975; T.D. 8115, 51 FR 45690, Dec. 19, 1986; 52 FR 10223, Mar. 31, 1987]

§ 1.72–5 Expected return.

(a) Expected return for but one life. **(1)** If a contract to which section 72 applies provides that one annuitant is to receive a fixed monthly income for life, the expected return is determined by multiplying the total of the annuity payments to be received annually by the multiple shown in Table I or V (whichever is applicable) of § 1.72–9 under the age (as of the annuity starting date) and, if applicable, sex of the measuring life (usually the annuitant's). Thus, where a male purchases a contract before July 1, 1986, providing for an immediate annuity of $100 per month for his life and, as of the annuity starting date (in this case the date of purchase), the annuitant's age at his nearest birthday is 66, the expected return is computed as follows:

Monthly payment of $100 × 12 months equals annual payment of	$ 1,200
Multiple shown in Table I male, age 66	14.4
Expected return (1,200 × 14.4)	17,280

If, however, the taxpayer had purchased the contract after June 30, 1986, the expected return would be $23,040, determined by multiplying 19.2 (multiple shown in Table V, age 66) by $1,200.

* * *

[T.D. 6500, 25 FR 11402, Nov. 26, 1960, as amended by T.D. 8115, 51 FR 45690, Dec. 19, 1986]

§ 1.72–6 Investment in the contract.

(a) General rule. **(1)** For the purpose of computing the "investment in the contract", it is first necessary to determine the "aggregate amount of premiums or other consideration paid" for such contract. See section 72(c)(1). This determination is made as of the later of the annuity starting date of the contract or the date on which an amount is first received thereunder as an annuity. The amount so found is then reduced by the sum of the following amounts in order to find the investment in the contract:

(i) The total amount of any return of premiums or dividends received (including unrepaid loans or dividends applied against the principal or interest on such loans) on or before the date on which the foregoing determination is made, and

(ii) The total of any other amounts received with respect to the contract on or before such date which were excludable from the gross income of the recipient under the income tax law applicable at the time of receipt.

* * *

* * *

[T.D. 6500, 25 FR 11402, Nov. 26, 1960, as amended by T.D. 6676, 28 FR 10134, Sept. 17, 1963; TD 7311, 39 FR 11880, April 1, 1974; T.D. 8115, 51 FR 45690, Dec. 19, 1986; 52 FR 10223, Mar. 31, 1987]

§ 1.72–9 Tables

The following tables are to be used in connection with computations under section 72 and the regulations thereunder. Tables I, II, IIA, III, and IV are to be used if the investment in the contract does not include a post-June 1986 investment in the contract (as defined in § 1.72–6(d)(3)). Tables V, VI, VIA, VII, and VIII are to be used if the investment in the contract includes a post-June 1986 investment in the contract (as defined in § 1.72–6(d)(3)). In the case of a contract under which amounts are received as an annuity after June 30, 1986, a taxpayer receiving such amounts may elect to treat the entire investment in the contract as post-June 1986 investment in the contract and thus apply Tables V through VIII. A taxpayer may make the election for any taxable year in which such amounts are received by attaching to the taxpayer's return for such taxable year a statement that the taxpayer is electing under § 1.72–9 to treat the entire investment in the contract as post-June 1986 investment in the contract. The statement must contain the taxpayer's name, address, and taxpayer identification number. The election is irrevocable and applies with respect to all amounts that the taxpayer receives as an annuity under the contract in the taxable year for which the election is made or in any subsequent taxable year. (Note that for purposes of the examples in §§ 1.72–4 through 1.72–11 the election described in this section is disregarded, (i.e., it is assumed that the taxpayer does not make an election under this section).) * * *

TABLE I—ORDINARY LIFE ANNUITIES ONE LIFE—EXPECTED RETURN MULTIPLES

Ages		
Male	Female	Multiples
	* * *	
35	40	38.2
36	41	37.3
37	42	36.5
38	43	35.6
39	44	34.7
40	45	33.8
41	46	33.0
42	47	32.1
43	48	31.2
44	49	30.4
45	50	29.6
46	51	28.7
47	52	27.9
48	53	27.1
49	54	26.3
50	55	25.5
51	56	24.7
52	57	24.0
53	58	23.2
54	59	22.4
55	60	21.7
56	61	21.0
57	62	20.3
58	63	19.6
59	64	18.9
60	65	18.2
61	66	17.5
62	67	16.9
63	68	16.2
64	69	15.6
65	70	15.0
66	71	14.4
67	72	13.8
68	73	13.2
69	74	12.6
70	75	12.1
71	76	11.6
72	77	11.0
73	78	10.5
74	79	10.1
75	80	9.6
76	81	9.1
77	82	8.7
78	83	8.3
79	84	7.8

* * *

TABLE V—ORDINARY LIFE ANNUITIES ONE LIFE—EXPECTED RETURN MULTIPLES

AGE	MULTIPLE
* * *	
35	47.3
36	46.4
37	45.4
38	44.4
39	43.5
40	42.5
41	41.5
42	40.6
43	39.6
44	38.7

TABLE V—ORDINARY LIFE ANNUITIES
ONE LIFE—EXPECTED RETURN
MULTIPLES

AGE	MULTIPLE
45	37.7
46	36.8
47	35.9
48	34.9
49	34.0
50	33.1
51	32.2
52	31.3
53	30.4
54	29.5
55	28.6
56	27.7
57	26.8
58	25.9
59	25.0
60	24.2
61	23.3
62	22.5
63	21.6
64	20.8
65	20.0
66	19.2
67	18.4
68	17.6
69	16.8
70	16.0
71	15.3
72	14.6
73	13.9
74	13.2
75	12.5
76	11.9
77	11.2
78	10.6
79	10.0

* * *

TABLE VI—ORDINARY JOINT LIFE AND LAST SURVIVOR ANNUITIES;
TWO LIVES—EXPECTED RETURN MULTIPLES

AGES	45	46	47	48	49	50	51	52	53	54
45	44.1	43.6	43.2	42.7	42.3	42.0	41.6	41.3	41.0	40.7
46	43.6	43.1	42.6	42.2	41.8	41.4	41.0	40.6	40.3	40.0
47	43.2	42.6	42.1	41.7	41.2	40.8	40.4	40.0	39.7	39.3
48	42.7	42.2	41.7	41.2	40.7	40.2	39.8	39.4	39.0	38.7
49	42.3	41.8	41.2	40.7	40.2	39.7	39.3	38.8	38.4	38.1
50	42.0	41.4	40.8	40.2	39.7	39.2	38.7	38.3	37.9	37.5
51	41.6	41.0	40.4	39.8	39.3	38.7	38.2	37.8	37.3	36.9
52	41.3	40.6	40.0	39.4	38.8	38.3	37.8	37.3	36.8	36.4
53	41.0	40.3	39.7	39.0	38.4	37.9	37.3	36.8	36.3	35.8
54	40.7	40.0	39.3	38.7	38.1	37.5	36.9	36.4	35.8	35.3
55	40.4	39.7	39.0	38.4	37.7	37.1	36.5	35.9	35.4	34.9
56	40.2	39.5	38.7	38.1	37.4	36.8	36.1	35.6	35.0	34.4
57	40.0	39.2	38.5	37.8	37.1	36.4	35.8	35.2	34.6	34.0
58	39.7	39.0	38.2	37.5	36.8	36.1	35.5	34.8	34.2	33.6
59	39.6	38.8	38.0	37.3	36.6	35.9	35.2	34.5	33.9	33.3
60	39.4	38.6	37.8	37.1	36.3	35.6	34.9	34.2	33.6	32.9
61	39.2	38.4	37.6	36.9	36.1	35.4	34.6	33.9	33.3	32.6
62	39.1	38.3	37.5	36.7	35.9	35.1	34.4	33.7	33.0	32.3
63	38.9	38.1	37.3	36.5	35.7	34.9	34.2	33.5	32.7	32.0
64	38.8	38.0	37.2	36.3	35.5	34.8	34.0	33.2	32.5	31.8
65	38.7	37.9	37.0	36.2	35.4	34.6	33.8	33.0	32.3	31.6
66	38.6	37.8	36.9	36.1	35.2	34.4	33.6	32.9	32.1	31.4
67	38.5	37.7	36.8	36.0	35.1	34.3	33.5	32.7	31.9	31.2
68	38.4	37.6	36.7	35.8	35.0	34.2	33.4	32.5	31.8	31.0
69	38.4	37.5	36.6	35.7	34.9	34.1	33.2	32.4	31.6	30.8

* * *

[T.D. 6500, 25 FR 11402, Nov. 26, 1960, as amended by T.D. 8115, 51 FR 45690, Dec. 19, 1986; 60 FR 16381, Mar. 30, 1995]

§ 1.73–1 Services of child.

(a) Compensation for personal services of a child shall, regardless of the provisions of State law relating to who is entitled to the earnings of the child, and regardless of whether the income is in fact received by the child, be deemed to be the gross income of the child and not the gross income of the parent of the child. Such compensation, therefore, shall be included in the gross income of the child and shall be reflected in the return rendered by or for such child. The income of a minor child is not required to be included in the gross income of the parent for income tax purposes. For requirements for making the return by such child, or for such child by his guardian, or other person charged with the care of his person or property, see section 6012.

(b) In the determination of taxable income or adjusted gross income, as the case may be, all expenditures made by the parent or the child attributable to amounts which are includible in the gross income of the child and not of the parent solely by reason of section 73 are deemed to have been paid or incurred by the child. In such determination, the child is entitled to take deductions not only for expenditures made on his behalf by his parent which would be commonly considered as business expenses, but also for other expenditures such as charitable contributions made by the parent in the name of the child and out of the child's earnings.

(c) For purposes of section 73, the term "parent" includes any individual who is entitled to the services of the child by reason of having parental rights and duties in respect of the child. * * *

[T.D. 6500, 25 FR 11402, Nov. 26, 1960]

§ 1.74–1 Prizes and awards.

(a) Inclusion in gross income. (1) Section 74(a) requires the inclusion in gross income of all amounts received as prizes and awards, unless such prizes or awards qualify as an exclusion from gross income under subsection (b), or unless such prize or award is a scholarship or fellowship grant excluded from gross income by section 117. Prizes and awards which are includible in gross income include (but are not limited to) amounts received from radio and television giveaway shows, door prizes, and awards in contests of all types, as well as any prizes and awards from an employer to an employee in recognition of some achievement in connection with his employment.

(2) If the prize or award is not made in money but is made in goods or services, the fair market value of the goods or services is the amount to be included in income.

* * *

(c) Scholarships and fellowship grants. See section 117 and the regulations thereunder for provisions relating to scholarships and fellowship grants.

[T.D. 6500, 25 FR 11402, Nov. 26, 1960]

§ 1.74–1 (*Proposed, published 1-9-89.*) Prizes and awards.

(b) Exclusion from gross income. * * * and (4) the payor transfers the prize or award (and the prize or award is, in fact, transferred) to one or more governmental units or organizations described in paragraph (1) or (2) of section 170(c) pursuant to a designation by the recipient. Accordingly, awards such as the Nobel prize and the Pulitzer prize will qualify for the exclusion if the award is transferred by the payor to one or more qualifying organizations pursuant to a qualified designation by the recipient.

(c) Designation by recipient.—(1) In general. To qualify for the exclusion under this section, the recipient must make a qualifying designation, in writing, within 45 days of the date the prize or award is granted (see paragraph (e)(3) of this section for a definition of "granted"). A qualifying designation is required to indicate only that a designation is being made. The document does not need to state on its face that the organization(s) are entities described in paragraph (1) and/or (2) of section 170(c) to result in a qualified designation. Furthermore, it is not necessary that the document do more than identify a class of entities from which the payor may select a recipient. However, designation of a specific nonqualified donee organization or designation of a class of recipients that may include nonqualified donee organizations is not a qualified designation. The following example illustrates the application of this section:

A distinguished ophthalmologist, S, is awarded the Nobel prize for medicine. S may designate that the prize money be given to a particular university that is described in section 170(c)(1), or to any university that is described in that section. However, S cannot designate that the award be given to a donee that is not described in section 170(c)(1), such as a foreign medical school. Selection of such a donee or inclusion of such a donee on a list of possible donees on S's designation would disqualify the designation.

(2) Prizes and awards granted before 60 days after date of publication of final regulations. In the case of prizes and awards granted before 60 days after the date of publication of final regulations, a qualifying designation may be made at any time prior to 105 days after date of publication of final regulations.

(d) Transferred by payor. An exclusion will not be available under this section unless the designated items or amounts are transferred by the payor to one or more qualified donee organizations. The provisions of this paragraph shall not be satisfied unless the items or amounts are transferred by the payor to one or more qualifying donee organizations no later than the due date of the return (without regard to extensions) for the taxable year in which the items or amounts would otherwise be includible in the recipient's gross income. A transfer may be accomplished by any method that results in the receipt of the items or amounts by one or more qualified donee organizations from the payor and does not involve a disqualifying use of the items or amounts. Delivery of items or amounts by a person associated with a payor (e.g., a contractual agent, licensee, or other representative of the payor) will satisfy the requirements of this section so long as the items or amounts are received by, or on behalf of, one or more qualified donee organizations. Possession of a prize or award by any person before a designation is made will not result in the disallowance of an exclusion unless a disqualifying use of the items or amounts is made before the items or amounts are returned to the payor for transfer to one or more qualified donee organizations (see paragraph (e)(2) of this section for a definition of "disqualifying use"). Accordingly, transfer of an item or amount to a nonqualified donee organization will not result in an ineffective transfer under this section if the item or amount is timely returned to the payor by the nonqualified donee organization before a disqualifying use of the item or amount is made and the item or amount is then transferred to a qualifying organization.

(e) Definitions.—(1) For purposes of this section, "qualified donee organizations" means entities defined in section 170(c)(1) or (2) of the Code.

(2) For purposes of this section, the term "disqualifying use" means, in the case of cash or other intangibles, spending, depositing, investing or otherwise using the prize or award so as to enure to the benefit of the recipient or any person other than the grantor or an entity described in section 170(c)(1) or (2). In the case of tangible items, the term "disqualifying use" means physical possession of the item for more than a brief period of time by any person other than the grantor or an entity described in section 170(c)(1) or (2). Thus, physical possession by the recipient or a person associated with the recipient may constitute a disqualifying use if the item is kept for more than a brief period of time. For example, receipt of an unexpected tangible award at a ceremony that otherwise comports with the requirements of this section will not constitute a disqualifying use unless the recipient fails to return the item to the payor as soon as practicable after receipt.

(3) For purposes of this section, an item will be considered "granted" when it is subject to the recipient's dominion and control to such an extent that it otherwise would be includible in the recipient's gross income.

(f) Charitable deduction not allowable. Neither the payor nor the recipient will be allowed a charitable deduction for the value of any prize or award that is excluded under this section.

(g) Qualified scholarships. See section 117 and the regulations thereunder for provisions relating to qualified scholarships.

§ 1.74–2 (*Proposed, published 1–9–89.*) Special exclusion for certain employee achievement awards.

(a) General rule—(1) Section 74(c) provides an exclusion from gross income for the value of an employee achievement award (as defined in section 274(j)) received by an employee if the cost to the employer of the award does not exceed the amount allowable as a deduction to the employer for the cost of the award. Thus, where the cost to the employer of an employee achievement award is fully deductible after considering the limitation under section 274(j), the value representing the employer's cost of the award is excludable from the employee's gross income.

(2) Where the cost of an award to the employer is so disproportionate to the fair market value of the award that there is a significant likelihood that the award was given as disguised compensation, no portion of the award will qualify as an employee achievement award excludable under the provisions of this section * * *.

(b) Excess deduction award. Where the cost to the employer of an employee achievement award exceeds the amount allowable as a deduction to the employer, the recipient must include in gross income an amount which is the greater of (1) the excess of such cost over the amount that is allowable as a deduction (but not to exceed the fair market value of the award) or (2) the excess of the fair market value of the award over the amount allowable as a deduction to the employer.

(c) Examples. The operation of this section may be illustrated by the following examples:

Example (1). An employer makes a qualifying length of service award to an employee in the form of a television set. Assume that the deduction limitation under § 274(j)(2) applicable to the award is $400. Assume also that the cost of the television set to the employer was $350, and that the fair market value of the television set is $475. The amount excludable is $475 (the full fair market value of the television set). This is true even though the fair market value exceeds both the cost of the television set to the employer and the $400 deduction allowable to the employer for non-qualified plan awards under section 274(j)(2)(A).

Example (2). Assume the same facts as in example (1) except that the fair market value of the television set is $900. Under these circumstances, the fair market value of the television set is so disproportionate to the cost of the item to the employer that the item will be considered payment of disguised compensation. As a result, no portion of the award will qualify as an employee achievement award. Since no portion of the award is excludable by the employee, the employer must report the full fair market value of the award as compensation on the employee's Form W–2.

* * *

Example (4). An employer invites its employees to attend a party it is sponsoring to benefit a charity. In order to encourage the employees to attend the party and to make contributions to the charity, the employer promises to match the employees' contributions and also provides expensive prizes to be awarded to contributing employees selected at random. Each employee receiving a prize must include the full fair market value of the prize in gross income because the prizes are not qualifying achievement awards under section 274(j) or de minimis fringe benefits under section 132(e). Since the prizes are not excludable, the employer must report the full fair market value of the prize as compensation on the employee's Form W–2.

(d) Special rules—(1) The exclusion provided by this section shall not be available for any award made by a sole-proprietorship to the sole proprietor.

(2) In the case of an employer exempt from taxation under subtitle A of the Code, any reference in this section to the amount allowable as a deduction to the employer shall be treated as a reference to the amount which would be allowable as a deduction to the employer if the employer were not exempt from taxation under Subtitle A of the Code.

(e) Exclusion for certain de minimis fringe benefits. Nothing contained in this section shall preclude the exclusion of the value of an employee award that is otherwise qualified for exclusion under section 132(e).

§ 1.79–1 Group-term life insurance—general rules.

(a) What is group-term life insurance? Life insurance is not group-term life insurance for purposes of section 79 unless it meets the following conditions: **(1)** It provides a general death benefit that is excludable from gross income under section 101(a).

(2) It is provided to a group of employees.

(3) It is provided under a policy carried directly or indirectly by the employer.

(4) The amount of insurance provided to each employee is computed under a formula that precludes individual selection. This formula must be based on factors such as age, years of service, compensation, or position. This condition may be satisfied even if the amount of insurance provided is determined under a limited number of alternative schedules that are based on the amount each employee elects to contribute. However, the amount of insurance provided under each schedule must be computed under a formula that precludes individual selection.

* * *

[T.D. 6888, 31 FR 9201, July 6, 1966, as amended by T.D. 6999, 34 FR 995.5011, Jan. 23, 1969; T.D. 7132, 36 FR 13091, July 14, 1971; T.D. 7236, 37 FR 28624, 38 FR 2417, Dec. 28, 1972; T.D. 7623, 44 FR 28797, May 17, 1979; T.D. 7917, 48 FR 45761, Oct. 7, 1983; T.D. 7924, 48 FR 54594, Dec. 6, 1983; T.D. 8821, 64 FR 29790, June 3, 1999; T.D. 9223, 70 FR 50971, Aug. 29, 2005]

§ 1.79–3 Determination of amount equal to cost of group-term life insurance.

* * *

(d) The cost of the portion of the group-term life insurance on an employee's life. (1) * * * Table 1, which is set forth in subparagraph (2) of this paragraph, determines the cost for each $1,000 of such portion of the group-term life insurance on the employee's life for each one-month period. The cost of the portion of the group-term life insurance on the employee's life for each period of coverage of one month is obtained by multiplying the number of thousand dollars of such insurance computed to the nearest tenth which is provided during such period by the appropriate amount set forth in Table 1. In any case in which group-term life insurance is provided for a period of coverage of less than one month, the amount set forth in Table 1 is prorated over such period of coverage.

(2) For the cost of group-term life insurance provided after June 30, 1999, the following table sets forth the cost of $1,000 of group-term life insurance provided for one month, computed on the basis of 5–year age brackets. * * * For purposes of Table I, the age of the employee is the employee's attained age on the last day of the employee's taxable year.

Table I.—Uniform Premiums for $1,000 of Group–Term Life Insurance Protection

5–year age bracket	Cost per $1,000 of protection for 1 month
Under 25	$0.05
25 to 30	.06
30 to 34	.08
35 to 39	.09
40 to 44	.10
45 to 49	.15
50 to 54	.23
55 to 59	.43
60 to 64	.64
65 to 69	1.27
70 and above	2.06

(3) The net premium cost of group-term life insurance as provided in Table 1 of subparagraph (2) of this paragraph applies only to the cost of group-term life insurance subject to the rule of inclusion set forth in section 79(a). Therefore, such net premium cost is not applicable to the determination of the cost of group-term life insurance provided under a policy which is not subject to such rule of inclusion.

* * *

[T.D. 6888, 31 FR 9203, July 6, 1966, as amended by T.D. 7623, 44 FR 28800, May 17, 1979; T.D. 7924, 48 FR 54595, Dec. 6, 1983; T.D. 8273, 54 FR 47979, Nov. 20, 1989; T.D. 8424, 57 FR 33635, July 30, 1992; T.D. 8821, 64 FR 29788, June 3, 1999]

§ 1.82–1 Payments for or reimbursements of expenses of moving from one residence to another residence attributable to employment or self-employment.

(a) Reimbursements in gross income—(1) In general. Any amount received or accrued, directly or indirectly, by an individual as a payment for or reimbursement of expenses of moving from one residence to another residence attributable to employment or self-employment is includible in gross income under section 82 as compensation for services in the taxable year received or accrued. For rules relating to the year a deduction may be allowed for expenses of moving from one residence to another residence, see section 217 and the regulations thereunder.

* * *

[T.D. 7195, 37 FR 13533, July 11, 1972, as amended by T.D. 7578, 43 FR 59355, Dec. 20, 1978]

§ 1.83–1 Property transferred in connection with the performance of services.

(a) Inclusion in gross income—(1) General rule. Section 83 provides rules for the taxation of property transferred to an employee or independent contractor (or beneficiary thereof) in connection with the performance of services by such employee or independent contractor. In general, such property is not taxable under section 83(a) until it has been transferred (as defined in § 1.83–3(a)) to such person and become substantially vested (as defined in § 1.83–3(b)) in such person. In that case, the excess of—

(i) The fair market value of such property (determined without regard to any lapse restriction, as defined in § 1.83–3(i)) at the time that the property becomes substantially vested, over

(ii) The amount (if any) paid for such property,

shall be included as compensation in the gross income of such employee or independent contractor for the taxable year in which the property becomes substantially vested. Until such property becomes substantially vested, the transferor shall be regarded as the owner of such property, and any income from such property received by the employee or independent contractor (or beneficiary thereof) or the right to the use of such property by the employee or independent contractor constitutes additional compensation and shall be included in the gross income of such employee or independent contractor for the taxable year in which such income is received or such use is made available. This paragraph applies to a transfer of property in connection with the performance of services even though the transferor is not the person for whom such services are performed.

* * *

(b) Subsequent sale, forfeiture, or other disposition of nonvested property. (1) If substantially nonvested property (that has been transferred in connection with the performance of services) is subsequently sold or otherwise disposed of to a third party in an arm's length transaction while still substantially nonvested, the person who performed such services shall realize compensation in an amount equal to the excess of—

(i) The amount realized on such sale or other disposition, over

(ii) The amount (if any) paid for such property.

Such amount of compensation is includible in his gross income in accordance with his method of accounting. Two preceding sentences also apply when the person disposing of the property has received it in a non-arm's length transaction described in paragraph (c) of this section. In addition, section 83(a) and paragraph (a) of this section shall thereafter cease to apply with respect to such property.

(2) If substantially nonvested property that has been transferred in connection with the performance of services to the person performing such services is forfeited while still substantially nonvested and held by such person, the difference between the amount paid (if any) and the amount received upon forfeiture (if any) shall be treated as an ordinary gain or loss. This paragraph (b)(2) does not apply to property to which § 1.83-2(a) applies.

(3) This paragraph (b) shall not apply to, and no gain shall be recognized on, any sale, forfeiture, or other disposition described in this paragraph to the extent that any property received in exchange therefor is substantially nonvested. Instead, section 83 and this section shall apply with respect to such property received (as if it were substituted for the property disposed of).

(c) Dispositions of nonvested property not at arm's length. If substantially nonvested property (that has been transferred in connection with the performance of services) is disposed of in a transaction which is not at arm's length and the property remains substantially nonvested, the person who performed such services realizes compensation equal in amount to the sum of any money and the fair market value of any substantially vested property received in such disposition. Such amount of compensation is includible in his gross income in accordance with his method of accounting. However, such amount of compensation shall not exceed the fair market value of the property disposed of at the time of disposition (determined without regard to any lapse restriction), reduced by the amount paid for such property. In addition, section 83 and these regulations shall continue to apply with respect to such property, except that any amount previously includible in gross income under this paragraph (c) shall thereafter be treated as an amount paid for such property. For example, if in 1971 an employee pays $50 for a share of stock which has a fair market value of $100 and is substantially nonvested at that time and later in 1971 (at a time when the property still has a fair market value of $100 and is still substantially nonvested) the employee disposes of, in a transaction not at arm's length, the share of stock to his wife for $10, the employee realizes compensation of $10 in 1971. If in 1972, when the share of stock has a fair market value of $120, it becomes substantially vested, the employee realizes additional compensation in 1972 in the amount of $60 (the $120 fair market value of the stock less both the $50 price paid for the stock and the $10 taxed as compensation in 1971). For purposes of this paragraph, if substantially nonvested property has been transferred to a person other than the person who performed the services, and the transferee dies holding the property while the property is still substantially nonvested and while the person who performed the services is alive, the transfer which results by reason of the death of such transferee is a transfer not at arm's length.

* * *

(e) Forfeiture after substantial vesting. If a person is taxable under section 83(a) when the property transferred becomes substantially vested and thereafter the person's beneficial interest in such property is nevertheless forfeited pursuant to a lapse restriction, any loss incurred by such person (but not by a beneficiary of such person) upon such forfeiture shall be an ordinary loss to the extent the basis in such property has been increased as a result of the recognition of income by such person under section 83(a) with respect to such property.

(f) Examples. The provisions of this section may be illustrated by the following examples:

Example (1). On November 1, 1978, X corporation sells to E, an employee, 100 shares of X corporation stock at $10 per share. At the time of such sale the fair market value of the X corporation stock is $100 per share. Under the terms of the sale each share of stock is subject to a substantial risk of forfeiture which will not lapse until November 1, 1988. Evidence of this restriction is stamped on the face of E's stock certificates, which are therefore nontransferable (within the meaning of § 1.83-3(d)).

Since in 1978 E's stock is substantially nonvested, E does not include any of such amount in his gross income as compensation in 1978. On November 1, 1988, the fair market value of the X corporation stock is $250 per share. Since the X corporation stock becomes substantially vested in 1988, E must include $24,000 (100 shares of X corporation stock × $250 fair market value per share less $10 price paid by E for each share) as compensation for 1988. Dividends paid by X to E on E's stock after it was transferred to E on November 1, 1973, are taxable to E as additional compensation during the period E's stock is substantially nonvested and are deductible as such by X.

Example (2). Assume the facts are the same as in example (1), except that on November 1, 1985, each share of stock of X corporation in E's hands could as a matter of law be transferred to a bona fide purchaser who would not be required to forfeit the stock if the risk of forfeiture materialized. In the event, however, that the risk materializes, E would be liable in damages to X. On November 1, 1985, the fair market value of the X corporation stock is $230 per share. Since E's stock is transferable within the meaning of § 1.83–3(d) in 1985, the stock is substantially vested and E must include $22,000 (100 shares of X corporation stock × $230 fair market value per share less $10 price paid by E for each share) as compensation for 1985.

Example (3). Assume the facts are the same as in example (1) except that, in 1984 E sells his 100 shares of X corporation stock in an arm's length sale to I, an investment company, for $120 per share. At the time of this sale each share of X corporation's stock has a fair market value of $200. Under paragraph (b) of this section, E must include $11,000 (100 shares of X corporation stock × $120 amount realized per share less $10 price paid by E per share) as compensation for 1984 notwithstanding that the stock remains nontransferable and is still subject to a substantial risk of forfeiture at the time of such sale. Under § 1.83–4(b)(2), I's basis in the X corporation stock is $120 per share.

[T.D. 7554, 43 FR 31913, July 24, 1978; as amended by T.D. 9092, 68 FR 54336, Sept. 17, 2003]

§ 1.83–2 Election to include in gross income in year of transfer.

(a) In general. If property is transferred (within the meaning of § 1.83–3(a)) in connection with the performance of services, the person performing such services may elect to include in gross income under section 83(b) the excess (if any) of the fair market value of the property at the time of transfer (determined without regard to any lapse restriction, as defined in § 1.83–3(i)) over the amount (if any) paid for such property, as compensation for services. The fact that the transferee has paid full value for the property transferred, realizing no bargain element in the transaction, does not preclude the use of the election as provided for in this section. If this election is made, the substantial vesting rules of section 83(a) and the regulations thereunder do not apply with respect to such property, and except as otherwise provided in section 83(d)(2) and the regulations thereunder (relating to the cancellation of a nonlapse restriction), any subsequent appreciation in the value of the property is not taxable as compensation to the person who performed the services. Thus, property with respect to which this election is made shall be includible in gross income as of the time of transfer, even though such property is substantially nonvested (as defined in § 1.83–3(b)) at the time of transfer, and no compensation will be includible in gross income when such property becomes substantially vested (as defined in § 1.83–3(b)). In computing the gain or loss from the subsequent sale or exchange of such property, its basis shall be the amount paid for the property increased by the amount included in gross income under section 83(b). If property for which a section 83(b) election is in effect is forfeited while substantially nonvested, such forfeiture shall be treated as a sale or exchange upon which there is realized a loss equal to the excess (if any) of—

(1) The amount paid (if any) for such property, over,

(2) The amount realized (if any) upon such forfeiture.

If such property is a capital asset in the hands of the taxpayer, such loss shall be a capital loss. A sale or other disposition of the property that is in substance a forfeiture, or is made in contemplation of a forfeiture, shall be treated as a forfeiture under the two immediately preceding sentences.

(b) Time for making election. Except as provided in the following sentence, the election referred to in paragraph (a) of this section shall be filed not later than 30 days after the date the property was transferred (or, if later, January 29, 1970) and may be filed prior to the date of transfer. Any statement filed before February 15, 1970, which was amended not later than February 16, 1970, in order to make it conform to the requirements of paragraph (e) of this section, shall be deemed a proper election under section 83(b).

(c) Manner of making election. The election referred to in paragraph (a) of this section is made by filing one copy of a written statement with the internal revenue office with whom the person who performed the services files his return. In addition, one copy of such statement shall be submitted with this income tax return for the taxable year in which such property was transferred.

(d) Additional copies. The person who performed the services shall also submit a copy of the statement referred to in paragraph (c) of this section to the person for whom the services are performed. In addition, if the person who performs the services and the transferee of such property are not the same person, the person who performs the services shall submit a copy of such statement to the transferee of the property.

(e) Content of statement. The statement shall be signed by the person making the election and shall indicate that it is being made under section 83(b) of the Code, and shall contain the following information:

(1) The name, address and taxpayer identification number of the taxpayer;

(2) A description of each property with respect to which the election is being made;

(3) The date or dates on which the property is transferred and the taxable year (for example, "calendar year 1970" or "fiscal year ending May 31, 1970") for which such election was made;

(4) The nature of the restriction or restrictions to which the property is subject;

(5) The fair market value at the time of transfer (determined without regard to any lapse restriction, as defined in § 1.83–3(i)) of each property with respect to which the election is being made;

(6) The amount (if any) paid for such property; and

(7) With respect to elections made after July 21, 1978, a statement to the effect that copies have been furnished to other persons as provided in paragraph (d) of this section.

(f) Revocability of election. An election under section 83(b) may not be revoked except with the consent of the Commissioner. Consent will be granted only in the case where the transferee is under a mistake of fact as to the underlying transaction and must be requested within 60 days of the date on which the mistake of fact first became known to the person who made the election. In any event, a mistake as to the value, or decline in the value, of the property with respect to which an election under section 83(b) has been made or a failure to perform an act contemplated at the time of transfer of such property does not constitute a mistake of fact.

[T.D. 7554, 43 FR 31915, July 24, 1978]

§ 1.83–3 Meaning and use of certain terms.

(a) Transfer—(1) In general. For purposes of section 83 and the regulations thereunder, a transfer of property occurs when a person acquires a beneficial ownership interest in such property (disregarding any lapse restriction, as defined in § 1.83-3(i)) * * *.

(2) Option. The grant of an option to purchase certain property does not constitute a transfer of such property. However, see § 1.83–7 for the extent to which the grant of the option itself is subject to section 83. In addition, if the amount paid for the transfer of property is an indebtedness secured by the transferred property, on which there is no personal liability to pay all or a substantial part of such indebtedness, such transaction may be in substance the same as the grant of an option. The determination of the substance of the transaction shall be based upon all the facts and circumstances. The factors to be taken into account include the type of property involved, the extent to which the risk that the property will decline in value has been transferred, and the likelihood that the purchase price will, in fact, be paid. See also § 1.83–4(c) for the treatment of forgiveness of indebtedness that has constituted an amount paid.

(3) Requirement that property be returned. Similarly, no transfer may have occurred where property is transferred under conditions that require its return upon the happening of an event that is certain to occur, such as the termination of employment. In such a case, whether there is, in fact, a transfer depends upon all the facts and circumstances. Factors which indicate that no transfer has occurred are described in paragraph (a)(4), (5), and (6) of this section.

(4) Similarity to option. An indication that no transfer has occurred is the extent to which the conditions relating to a transfer are similar to an option.

(5) Relationship to fair market value. An indication that no transfer has occurred is the extent to which the consideration to be paid the transferee upon surrendering the property does not approach the fair market value of the property at the time of surrender. For purposes of paragraph (a)(5) and (6) of this section, fair market value includes fair market value determined under the rules of § 1.83–5(a)(1), relating to the valuation of property subject to nonlapse restrictions. Therefore, the existence of a nonlapse restriction referred to in § 1.83–5(a)(1) is not a factor indicating no transfer has occurred.

(6) Risk of loss. An indication that no transfer has occurred is the extent to which the transferee does not incur the risk of a beneficial owner that the value of the property at the time of transfer will decline substantially. Therefore, for purposes of this (6), risk of decline in property value is not limited to the risk that any amount paid for the property may be lost.

(7) Examples. The provisions of this paragraph may be illustrated by the following examples:

Example (1). On January 3, 1971, X corporation sells for $500 to S, a salesman of X, 10 shares of stock in X corporation with a fair market value of $1,000. The stock is nontransferable and subject to return to the corporation (for $500) if S's sales do not reach a certain level by December 31, 1971. Disregarding the restriction concerning S's sales (since the restrictions is a lapse restriction), S's interest in the stock is that of a beneficial owner and therefore a transfer occurs on January 3, 1971.

Example (2). On November 17, 1972, W sells to E 100 shares of stock in W corporation with a fair market value of $10,000 in exchange for a $10,000 note without personal liability. The note requires E to make yearly payments of $2,000 commencing in 1973. E collects the dividends, votes the stock and pays the interest on the note. However, he makes no payments toward the face amount of the note. Because E has no personal liability on the note, and since E is making no payments towards the face amount of the note, the likelihood of E paying the full purchase price is in substantial doubt. As a result E has not incurred the risks of a beneficial owner that the value of the stock will decline. Therefore, no transfer of the stock has occurred on November 17, 1972, but an option to purchase the stock has been granted to E.

Example (3). On January 3, 1971, X corporation purports to transfer to E, an employee, 100 shares of stock in X corporation. The X stock is subject to the sole restriction that E must sell such stock to X on termination of employment for any reason for an amount which is equal to the excess (if any) of the book value of the X stock at termination of employment over book value on January 3, 1971. The stock is not transferable by E and the restrictions on transfer are stamped on the certificate. Under these facts and circumstances, there is no transfer of the X stock within the meeting of section 83.

Example (4). Assume the same facts as in example (3) except that E paid $3,000 for the stock and that the restriction required E upon termination of employment to sell the stock to M for the total amount of dividends that have been declared on the stock since September 2, 1971, or $3,000 whichever is higher. Again, under the facts and circumstances, no transfer of the X stock has occurred.

Example (5). On July 4, 1971, X corporation purports to transfer to G, an employee, 100 shares of X stock. The stock is subject to the sole restriction that upon termination of employment G must sell the stock to X for the greater of its fair market value at such time or $100, the amount G paid for the stock. On July 4, 1971 the X stock has a fair market value of $100. Therefore, G does not incur the risk of a beneficial owner that the value of the stock at the time of transfer ($100) will decline substantially. Under these facts and circumstances, no transfer has occurred.

(b) Substantially vested and substantially nonvested property. For purposes of section 83 and the regulations thereunder, property is substantially nonvested when it is subject to a substantial risk of forfeiture, within the meaning of paragraph (c) of this section, and is nontransferable, within the meaning of paragraph (d) of this section. Property is substantially vested for such purposes when it is either transferable or not subject to a substantial risk of forfeiture.

(c) Substantial risk of forfeiture—(1) In general. For purposes of section 83 and the regulations thereunder, whether a risk of forfeiture is substantial or not depends upon the facts and circumstances. A substantial risk of forfeiture exists where rights in property that are transferred are conditioned, directly or indirectly, upon the future performance (or refraining from performance) of substantial services by any person, or the occurrence of a condition related to a purpose of the transfer, and the possibility of forfeiture is substantial if such condition is not satisfied.

Property is not transferred subject to a substantial risk of forfeiture to the extent that the employer is required to pay the fair market value of a portion of such property to the employee upon the return of such property. The risk that the value of property will decline during a certain period of time does not constitute a substantial risk of forfeiture. A nonlapse restriction, standing by itself, will not result in a substantial risk of forfeiture.

(2) Illustrations of substantial risks of forfeiture. The regularity of the performance of services and the time spent in performing such services tend to indicate whether services required by a condition are substantial. The fact that the person performing services has the right to decline to perform such services without forfeiture may tend to establish that services are insubstantial. Where stock is transferred to an underwriter prior to a public offering and the full enjoyment of such stock is expressly or impliedly conditioned upon the successful completion of the underwriting, the stock is subject to a substantial risk of forfeiture. Where an employee receives property from an employer subject to a requirement that it be returned if the total earnings of the employer do not increase, such property is subject to a substantial risk of forfeiture. On the other hand, requirements that the property be returned to the employer if the employee is discharged for cause or for committing a crime will not be considered to result in a substantial risk of forfeiture. An enforceable requirement that the property be returned to the employer if the employee accepts a job with a competing firm will not ordinarily be considered to result in a substantial risk of forfeiture unless the particular facts and circumstances indicate to the contrary. Factors which may be taken into account in determining whether a covenant not to compete constitutes a substantial risk of forfeiture are the age of the employee, the availability of alternative employment opportunities, the likelihood of the employee's obtaining such other employment, the degree of skill possessed by the employee, the employee's health, and the practice (if any) of the employer to enforce such covenants. Similarly, rights in property transferred to a retiring employee subject to the sole requirement that it be returned unless he renders consulting services upon the request of his former employer will not be considered subject to a substantial risk of forfeiture unless he is in fact expected to perform substantial services.

(3) Enforcement of forfeiture condition. In determining whether the possibility of forfeiture is substantial in the case of rights in property transferred to an employee of a corporation who owns a significant amount of the total combined voting power or value of all classes of stock of the employer corporation or of its parent corporation, there will be taken into account (i) the employee's relationship to other stockholders and the extent of their control, potential control and possible loss of control of the corporation, (ii) the position of the employee in the corporation and the extent to which he is subordinate to other employees, (iii) the employee's relationship to the officers and directors of the corporation, (iv) the person or persons who must approve the employee's discharge, and (v) past actions of the employer in enforcing the provisions of the restrictions. For example, if an employee would be considered as having received rights in property subject to a substantial risk of forfeiture, but for the fact that the employee owns 20 percent of the single class of stock in the transferor corporation, and if the remaining 80 percent of the class of stock is owned by an unrelated individual (or members of such an individual's family) so that the possibility of the corporation enforcing a restriction on such rights is substantial, then such rights are subject to a substantial risk of forfeiture. On the other hand, if 4 percent of the voting power of all the stock of a corporation is owned by the president of such corporation and the remaining stock is so diversely held by the public that the president, in effect, controls the corporation, then the possibility of the corporation enforcing a restriction on rights in property transferred to the president is not substantial, and such rights are not subject to a substantial risk of forfeiture.

(4) Examples. The rules contained in paragraph (c)(1) of this section may be illustrated by the following examples. In each example it is assumed that, if the conditions on transfer are not satisfied, the forfeiture provision will be enforced.

Example (1). On November 1, 1971, corporation X transfers in connection with the performance of services to E, an employee, 100 shares of corporation X stock for $90 per share. Under the terms of the transfer, E will be subject to a binding commitment to resell the stock to corporation X at $90 per share if he leaves the employment of corporation X for any reason prior to the expiration of a 2-year period from the date of such transfer. Since E must perform substantial services for corporation X and will not be paid more than $90 for the stock, regardless of its value, if he fails to perform such services during such 2-year period, E's rights in the stock are subject to a substantial risk of forfeiture during such period.

Example (2). On November 10, 1971, corporation X transfers in connection with the performance of services to a trust for the benefit of employees, $100x. Under the terms of the trust any child of an employee who is an enrolled full-time student at an accredited educational institution as a candidate for a degree will receive an annual grant of cash for each academic year the student completes as a student in good standing, up to a maximum of four years. E, an employee, has a child who is enrolled as a full-time student at an accredited college as a candidate for a degree. Therefore, E has a beneficial interest in the assets of the trust equalling the value of four cash grants. Since E's child must complete one year of college in order to receive a cash grant, E's interest in the trust assets are subject to a substantial risk of forfeiture to the extent E's child has not become entitled to any grants.

Example (3). On November 25, 1971, corporation X gives to E, an employee, in connection with his performance of services to corporation X, a bonus of 100 shares of corporation X stock. Under the terms of the bonus arrangement E is obligated to return the corporation X stock to corporation X if he terminates his employment for any reason. However, for each year occurring after November 25, 1971, during which E remains employed with corporation X, E ceases to be obligated to return 10 shares of the corporation X stock. Since in each year occurring after November 25, 1971, for which E remains employed he is not required to return 10 shares of corporation X's stock, E's rights in 10 shares each year for 10 years cease to be subject to a substantial risk of forfeiture for each year he remains so employed.

Example (4). **(a)** Assume the same facts as in example (3) except that for each year occurring after November 25, 1971, for which E remains employed with corporation X, X agrees to pay, in redemption of the bonus shares given to E if he terminates employment for any reason, 10 percent of the fair market value of each share of stock on the date of such termination of employment. Since corporation X will pay E 10 percent of the value of his bonus stock for each of the 10 years after November 25, 1971, in which he remains employed by X, and the risk of a decline in value is not a substantial risk of forfeiture, E's interest in 10 percent of such bonus stock becomes substantially vested in each of those years.

(b) The following chart illustrates the fair market value of the bonus stock and the fair market value of the portion of bonus stock that becomes substantially vested on November 25, for the following years:

	Fair market value of	
Year	All stock	Portion of stock that becomes vested
1972	$200	$20
1973	300	30
1974	150	15
1975	150	15
1976	100	10

If E terminates his employment on July 1, 1977, when the fair market value of the bonus stock is $100, E must return the bonus stock to X, and X must pay, in redemption of the bonus stock, $50 (50 percent of the value of the bonus stock on the date of termination of employment). E has recognized income under section 83(a) and § 1.83–1(a) with respect to 50 percent of the bonus stock, and E's basis in that portion of the stock equals the amount of income recognized, $90. Under § 1.83–1(e), the $40 loss E incurred upon forfeiture ($90 basis less $50 redemption payment) is an ordinary loss.

Example (5). On January 7, 1971, corporation X, a computer service company, transfers to E, 100 shares of corporation X stock for $50. E is a highly compensated salesman who sold X's products in a three-state area since 1960. At the time of transfer each share of X stock has a fair market value of $100. The stock is transferred to E in connection with his termination of employment with X. Each share of X stock is subject to the sole condition that E can keep such share only if he does not engage in competition with X for a 5-year period in the three-state area where E had previously sold X's products. E, who is 45 years old, has no intention of retiring from the work force. In order to earn a salary comparable to his current compensation, while preventing the risk of forfeiture from arising, E will have to expend a substantial amount of time and effort in another industry or market to establish the necessary business contacts. Thus, under these facts and circumstances E's rights in the stock are subject to a substantial risk of forfeiture.

(d) Transferability of property. For purposes of section 83 and the regulations thereunder, the rights of a person in property are transferable if such person can transfer any interest in the property to any person other than the transferor of the property, but only if the rights in such property of such transferee are not subject to a substantial risk of forfeiture. Accordingly, property is transferable if the person performing the services or receiving the property can sell, assign, or pledge (as collateral for a loan, or as security for the performance of an obligation, or for any other purpose) his interest in the property to any person other than the transferor of such property and if the transferee is not required to give up the property or its value in the event the substantial risk of forfeiture materializes. On the other hand, property is not considered to be transferable merely because the person performing the services or receiving the property may designate a beneficiary to receive the property in the event of his death.

(e) Property. For purposes of section 83 and the regulations thereunder, the term "property" includes real and personal property other than either money or an unfunded and unsecured promise to pay money or property in the future. The term also includes a beneficial interest in assets (including money) which are transferred or set aside from the claims of creditors of the transferor, for example, in a trust or escrow account. See, however, § 1.83–8(a) with respect to employee trusts and annuity plans subject to section 402(b) and section 403(c). * * *

(f) Property transferred in connection with the performance of services. Property transferred to an employee or an independent contractor (or beneficiary thereof) in recognition of the performance of, or the refraining from performance of, services is considered transferred in connection with the performance of services within the meaning of section 83. The existence of other persons entitled to buy stock on the same terms and conditions as an employee, whether pursuant to a public or private offering may, however, indicate that in such circumstances a transfer to the employee is not in recognition of the performance of, or the refraining from performance of, services. The transfer of property is subject to section 83 whether such transfer is in respect of past, present, or future services.

(g) Amount paid. For purposes of section 83 and the regulations thereunder, the term "amount paid" refers to the value of any money or property paid for the transfer of property to which section 83 applies, and does not refer to any amount paid for the right to use such property or to receive the income therefrom. Such value does not include any stated or unstated interest payments. For rules regarding the calculation of the amount of unstated interest payments, see § 1.483–1(c). When section 83 applies to the transfer of property pursuant to the exercise of an option, the term "amount paid" refers to any amount paid for the grant of the option plus any amount paid as the exercise price of the option. For rules regarding the forgiveness of indebtedness treated as an amount paid, see § 1.83-4(c).

(h) Nonlapse restriction. For purposes of section 83 and the regulations thereunder, a restriction which by its terms will never lapse (also referred to as a "nonlapse restriction") is a permanent limitation on the transferability of property—

(1) Which will require the transferee of the property to sell, or offer to sell, such property at a price determined under a formula, and

(2) Which will continue to apply to and be enforced against the transferee or any subsequent holder (other than the transferor).

A limitation subjecting the property to a permanent right of first refusal in a particular person at a price determined under a formula is a permanent nonlapse restriction. Limitations imposed by registration requirements of State or Federal security laws or similar laws imposed with respect to sales or other dispositions of stock or securities are not nonlapse restrictions. An obligation to resell or to offer to sell property transferred in connection with the performance of services to a specific person or persons at its fair market value at the time of such sale is not a nonlapse restriction. See § 1.83-5(c) for examples of nonlapse restrictions.

(i) Lapse restriction. For purposes of section 83 and the regulations thereunder, the term "lapse restriction" means a restriction other than a nonlapse restriction as defined in paragraph (h) of this section, and includes (but is not limited to) a restriction that carries a substantial risk of forfeiture.

* * *

[T.D. 7554, 43 FR 31916, July 24, 1978, as amended by T.D. 8042, 50 FR 31713, Aug. 6, 1985; 50 FR 39664, Sept. 30, 1985; T.D. 9092, 68 FR 54336, Sept. 17, 2003; T.D. 9223, 70 FR 50971, Aug. 29, 2005]

§ 1.83-4 Special rules.

(a) Holding period. Under section 83(f), the holding period of transferred property to which section 83(a) applies shall begin just after such property is substantially vested. However, if the person who has performed the services in connection with which property is transferred has made an election under section 83(b), the holding period of such property shall begin just after the date such property is transferred. If property to which section 83 and the regulations thereunder apply is transferred at arm's length, the holding period of such property in the hands of the transferee shall be determined in accordance with the rules provided in section 1223.

(b) Basis. **(1)** Except as provided in paragraph (b)(2) of this section, if property to which section 83 and the regulations thereunder apply is acquired by any person (including a person who acquires such property in a subsequent transfer which is not at arm's length), while such property is still substantially nonvested, such person's basis for the property shall reflect any amount paid for such property and any amount includible in the gross income of the person who performed the services (including any amount so includible as a result of a disposition by the person who acquired such property.) Such basis shall also reflect any adjustments to basis provided under sections 1015 and 1016.

(2) If property to which § 1.83-1 applies is transferred at arm's length, the basis of the property in the hands of the transferee shall be determined under section 1012 and the regulations thereunder.

(c) Forgiveness of indebtedness treated as an amount paid. If an indebtedness that has been treated as an amount paid under § 1.83-1(a)(1)(ii) is subsequently cancelled, forgiven or satisfied for an amount less than the amount of such indebtedness, the amount that is not, in fact, paid shall be includible in the gross income of the service provider in the taxable year in which such cancellation, forgiveness or satisfaction occurs.

[T.D. 7554, 43 FR 31918, July 24, 1978]

§ 1.83-5 Restrictions that will never lapse.

(a) Valuation. For purposes of section 83 and the regulations thereunder, in the case of property subject to a nonlapse restriction (as defined in § 1.83-3(h)), the price determined under the formula price will be considered to be the fair market value of the property unless established to the contrary by the Commissioner, and the burden of proof shall be on the Commissioner with respect to such value. If stock in a corporation is subject to a nonlapse restriction which requires the transferee to sell such stock only at a formula price based on book value, a reasonable multiple of earnings or a reasonable combination thereof, the price so determined will ordinarily be regarded as determinative of the fair market value of such property for purposes of section 83. However, in certain circumstances the formula price will not be considered to be the fair market value of property subject to such a formula price restriction, even though the formula price restriction is a substantial factor in determining such value. For example, where the formula price is the current book value of stock, the book value of the stock at some time in the future may be a more accurate measure of the value of the stock than the current book value of the stock for purposes of determining the fair market value of the stock at the time the stock becomes substantially vested.

(b) Cancellation—(1) In general. Under section 83(d)(2), if a nonlapse restriction imposed on property that is subject to section 83 is cancelled, then, unless the taxpayer establishes—

(i) That such cancellation was not compensatory, and

(ii) That the person who would be allowed a deduction, if any, if the cancellation were treated as compensatory, will treat the transaction as not compensatory, as provided in paragraph (c)(2) of this section,

the excess of the fair market value of such property (computed without regard to such restriction) at the time of cancellation, over the sum of—

(iii) The fair market value of such property (computed by taking the restriction into account) immediately before the cancellation, and

(iv) The amount, if any, paid for the cancellation,

shall be treated as compensation for the taxable year in which such cancellation occurs. Whether there has been a noncompensatory cancellation of a nonlapse restriction under section 83(d)(2) depends upon the particular facts and circumstances. Ordinarily the fact that the employee or independent contractor is required to perform additional services or that the salary or payment of such a person is adjusted to take the cancellation into account indicates that such cancellation has a compensatory purpose. On the other hand, the fact that the original purpose of a restriction no longer exists may indicate that the purpose of such cancellation is noncompensatory. Thus, for example, if a so-called "buy-sell" restriction was imposed on a corporation's stock to limit ownership of such stock and is being cancelled in connection with a public offering of the stock, such cancellation will generally be regarded as noncompensatory. However, the mere fact that the employer is willing to forego a deduction under section 83(h) is insufficient evidence to establish a noncompensatory cancellation of a nonlapse restriction. The refusal by a corporation or shareholder to repurchase stock of the corporation which is subject to a permanent right of first refusal will generally be treated as a cancellation of a nonlapse restriction. The preceding sentence shall not apply where there is no nonlapse restriction, for example, where the price to be paid for the stock subject to the right of first refusal is the fair market value of the stock. Section 83(d)(2) and this (1) do not apply where immediately after the cancellation of a nonlapse restriction the property is still substantially nonvested and no section 83(b) election has been made with respect to such property. In such a case the rules of section 83(a) and § 1.83–1 shall apply to such property.

(2) Evidence of noncompensatory cancellation. In addition to the information necessary to establish the factors described in paragraph (b)(1) of this section, the taxpayer shall request the employer to furnish the taxpayer with a written statement indicating that the employer will not treat the cancellation of the nonlapse restriction as a compensatory event, and that no deduction will be taken with respect to such cancellation. The taxpayer shall file such written statement with his income tax return for the taxable year in which or with which such cancellation occurs.

(c) Examples. The provisions of this section may be illustrated by the following examples:

Example (1). On November 1, 1971, X corporation whose shares are closely held and not regularly traded, transfers to E, an employee, 100 shares of X corporation stock subject to the condition that, if he desires to dispose of such stock during the period of his employment, he must resell the stock to his employer at its then existing book value. In addition, E or E's estate is obligated to offer to sell the stock at his retirement or death to his employer at its then existing book value. Under these facts and circumstances, the restriction to which the shares of X corporation stock are subject is a nonlapse restriction. Consequently, the fair market value of the X stock is includible in E's gross income as compensation for taxable year 1971. However, in determining the fair market value of the X stock, the book value formula price will ordinarily be regarded as being determinative of such value.

Example (2). Assume the facts are the same as in example (1), except that the X stock is subject to the condition that if E desires to dispose of the stock during the period of his employment he must resell the stock to his employer at a multiple of earnings per share that is in this case a reasonable approximation of value at the time of transfer to E. In addition, E or E's estate is obligated to offer to sell the stock at his retirement or death to his employer at the same multiple of earnings. Under these facts and circumstances, the restriction to which the X corporation stock is subject is a nonlapse restriction. Consequently, the fair market value of the X stock is includible in E's gross income for taxable year 1971. However, in determining the fair market value of the X stock, the multiple-of-earnings formula price will ordinarily be regarded as determinative of such value.

Example (3). On January 4, 1971, X corporation transfers to E, an employee, 100 shares of stock in X corporation. Each such share of stock is subject to an agreement between X and E whereby E agrees that such shares are to be held solely for investment purposes and not for resale (a so-called investment letter restriction). E's rights in such stock are substantially vested upon transfer, causing the fair market value of each share of X corporation stock to be includible in E's gross income as compensation for taxable year 1971. Since such an investment letter restriction does not constitute a nonlapse restriction, in determining the fair market value of each share, the investment letter restriction is disregarded.

Example (4). On September 1, 1971, X corporation transfers to B, an independent contractor, 500 shares of common stock in X corporation in exchange for B's agreement to provide services in the construction of an office building on property owned by X corporation. X corporation has 100 shares of preferred stock outstanding and an additional 500 shares of common stock outstanding. The preferred stock has a liquidation value of $1,000x, which is equal to the value of all assets owned by X. Therefore, the book value of the common stock in X corporation is $0. Under the terms of the transfer, if B wishes to dispose of the stock, B must offer to sell the stock to X for 150 percent of the then existing book value of B's common stock. The stock is also subject to a substantial risk of forfeiture until B performs the agreed-upon services. B makes a timely election under section 83(b) to include the value of the stock in gross income in 1971. Under these facts and circumstances, the restriction to which the shares of X corporation common stock are subject is a nonlapse restriction. In determining the fair market value of the X common stock at the time of transfer, the book value formula price would ordinarily be regarded as determinative of such value. However, the fair market value of X common stock at the time of transfer, subject to the book value restriction, is greater than $0 since B was willing to agree to provide valuable personal services in exchange for the stock. In determining the fair market value of the stock, the expected book value after construction of the office building would be given great weight. The likelihood of completion of construction would be a factor in determining the expected book value after completion of construction.

[T.D. 7554, 43 FR 31918, July 24, 1978]

§ 1.83–6 Deduction by employer.

(a) Allowance of deduction—(1) General rule. In the case of a transfer of property in connection with the performance of services, or a compensatory cancellation of a nonlapse restriction described in section 83(d) and § 1.83–5, a deduction is allowable under section 162 or 212 to the person for whom the services were performed. The amount of the deduction is equal to the amount included as compensation in the gross income of the service provider under section 83(a), (b), or (d)(2), but only to the extent the amount meets the requirements of section 162 or 212 and the regulations thereunder. The deduction is allowed only for the taxable year of that person in which or with which ends the taxable year of the service provider in which the amount is included as compensation. For purposes of this paragraph, any amount excluded from gross income under section 79 or section 101(b) or subchapter N is considered to have been included in gross income.

(2) Special rule. For purposes of paragraph (a)(1) of this section, the service provider is deemed to have included the amount as compensation in gross income if the person for whom the services were performed satisfies in a timely manner all requirements of section 6041 or section 6041A, and the regulations thereunder, with respect to that amount of compensation. For purposes of the preceding sentence, whether a person for whom services were performed satisfies all requirements of section 6041 or section 6041A, and the regulations thereunder, is determined without regard to § 1.6041–3(c) (exception for payments to corporations). In the case of a disqualifying disposition of stock described in section 421(b), an employer that otherwise satisfies all requirements of section 6041 and the regulations thereunder will be considered to have done so timely for purposes of this paragraph (a)(2) if Form W–2 or Form W–2c, as appropriate, is furnished to the employee or former employee, and is filed with the federal government, on or before the date on which the employer files the tax return claiming the deduction relating to the disqualifying disposition.

* * *

(4) Capital expenditure, etc. No deduction is allowed under section 83(h) to the extent that the transfer of property constitutes a capital expenditure, an item of deferred expense, or an amount properly includible in the value of inventory items. In the case of a capital expenditure, for example, the basis of the property to which such capital expenditure relates shall be increased at the same time and to the same extent as any amount includible in the employee's gross income in respect of such transfer. Thus, for example, no deduction is allowed to a corporation in respect of a transfer of its stock to a promoter upon its organization, notwithstanding that such promoter must include the value of such stock in his gross income in accordance with the rules under section 83.

***

(b) Recognition of gain or loss. Except as provided in section 1032, at the time of a transfer of property in connection with the performance of services the transferor recognizes gain to the extent that the transferor receives an amount that exceeds the transferor's basis in the property. In addition, at the time a deduction is allowed under section 83(h) and paragraph (a) of this section, gain or loss is recognized to the extent of the difference between (i) the sum of the amount paid plus the amount allowed as a deduction under section 83(h), and (ii) the sum of the taxpayer's basis in the property plus any amount recognized pursuant to the previous sentence.

(c) Forfeitures. If, under section 83(h) and paragraph (a) of this section, a deduction, an increase in basis, or a reduction of gross income was allowable (disregarding the reasonableness of the amount of compensation) in respect of a transfer of property and such property is subsequently forfeited, the amount of such deduction, increase in basis or reduction of gross income shall be includible in the gross income of the person to whom it was allowable for the taxable year of forfeiture. The basis of such property in the hands of the person to whom it is forfeited shall include any such amount includible in the gross income of such person, as well as any amount such person pays upon forfeiture.

(d) Special rules for transfers by shareholders—(1) Transfers. If a shareholder of a corporation transfers property to an employee of such corporation or to an independent contractor (or to a beneficiary thereof), in consideration of services performed for the corporation, the transaction shall be considered to be a contribution of such property to the capital of such corporation by the shareholder, and immediately thereafter a transfer of such property by the corporation to the employee or independent contractor under paragraphs (a) and (b) of this section. For purposes of this (1), such a transfer will be considered to be in consideration for services performed for the corporation if either the property transferred is substantially nonvested at the time of transfer or an amount is includible in the gross income of the employee or independent contractor at the time of transfer under § 1.83–1(a)(1) or § 1.83–2(a). In the case of such a transfer, any money or other property paid to the shareholder for such stock shall be considered to be paid to the corporation and transferred immediately thereafter by the corporation to the shareholder as a distribution to which section 302 applies. For special rules that may apply to a corporation's transfer of its own stock to any person in consideration of services performed for another corporation or partnership, see § 1.1032–3. * * *.

(2) Forfeiture. If, following a transaction described in paragraph (d)(1) of this section, the transferred property is forfeited to the shareholder, paragraph (c) of this section shall apply both with respect to the shareholder and with respect to the corporation. In addition, the corporation shall in the taxable year of forfeiture be allowed a loss (or realize a gain) to offset any gain (or loss) realized under paragraph (b) of this section. For example, if a shareholder transfers property to an employee of the corporation as compensation, and as a result the shareholder's basis of $200x in such property is allocated to his stock in such corporation and such corporation recognizes a short-term capital gain of $800x, and is allowed a deduction of $1,000x on such transfer, upon a subsequent forfeiture of the property to the shareholder, the shareholder shall take $200x into gross income, and the corporation shall take $1,000x into gross income and be allowed a short-term capital loss of $800x.

* * *

[T.D. 7554, 43 FR 31919, July 24, 1978, as amended by T.D. 8599, 60 FR 36995, July 19, 1995; T.D. 8883, 65 FR 31073, May 16, 2000; T.D. 9092, 68 FR 54336, Sept. 17, 2003]

§ 1.83–7 Taxation of nonqualified stock options.

(a) In general. If there is granted to an employee or independent contractor (or beneficiary thereof) in connection with the performance of services, an option to which section 421 (relating generally to certain qualified and other options) does not apply, section 83(a) shall apply to such grant if the option has a readily ascertainable fair market value (determined in accordance with paragraph (b) of this section) at the time the option is granted. The person who performed such services realizes compensation upon such grant at the time and in the amount determined under section 83(a). If section 83(a) does not apply to the grant of such an option because the option does not have a readily ascertainable fair market value at the time of grant, sections 83(a) and 83(b) shall apply at the time the option is exercised or otherwise disposed of, even though the fair market value of such option may have become readily ascertainable before such time. If the option is exercised, sections 83(a) and 83(b) apply to the transfer of property pursuant to such exercise, and the employee or independent contractor realizes compensation upon such transfer at the time and in the amount determined under section 83(a) or 83(b). If the option is sold or otherwise disposed of in an arm's length transaction, sections 83(a) and 83(b) apply to the transfer of money or other property received in the same manner as sections 83(a) and 83(b) would have applied to the transfer of property pursuant to an exercise of the option. The preceding sentence does not apply to a sale or other disposition of the option to a person related to the service provider that occurs on or after July 2, 2003. For this purpose, a person is related to the service provider if—

(1) The person and the service provider bear a relationship to each other that is specified in section 267(b) or 707(b)(1), subject to the modifications that the language "20 percent" is used instead of "50 percent" each place it appears in sections 267(b) and 707(b)(1), and section 267(c)(4) is applied as if the family of an individual includes the spouse of any member of the family; or

(2) The person and the service provider are engaged in trades or businesses under common control (within the meaning of section 52(a) and (b)); provided that a person is not related to the service provider if the person is the service recipient with respect to the option or the grantor of the option.

(b) Readily ascertainable defined—(1) Actively traded on an established market. Options have a value at the time they are granted, but that value is ordinarily not readily ascertainable unless the option is actively traded on an established market. If an option is actively traded on an established market, the fair market value of such option is readily ascertainable for purposes of this section by applying the rules of valuation set forth in § 20.2031–2.

(2) Not actively traded on an established market. When an option is not actively traded on an established market, it does not have a readily ascertainable fair market value unless its fair market value can otherwise be measured with reasonable accuracy. For purposes of this section, if an option is not actively traded on an established market, the option does not have a readily ascertainable fair market value when granted unless the taxpayer can show that all of the following conditions exist:

(i) The option is transferable by the optionee;

(ii) The option is exercisable immediately in full by the optionee;

(iii) The option or the property subject to the option is not subject to any restriction or condition (other than a lien or other condition to secure the payment of the purchase price) which has a significant effect upon the fair market value of the option; and

(iv) The fair market value of the option privilege is readily ascertainable in accordance with paragraph (b)(3) of this section.

(3) Option privilege. The option privilege in the case of an option to buy is the opportunity to benefit during the option's exercise period from any increase in the value of property subject to the option during such period, without risking any capital. Similarly, the option privilege in the case of an option to sell is the opportunity to benefit during the exercise period from a decrease in the value of property subject to the option. For example, if at some time during the exercise period of an option to buy, the fair market value of the property subject to the option is greater than the option's exercise price, a profit may be realized by exercising the option and immediately selling the property so acquired for its higher fair market value. Irrespective of whether any such gain may be realized immediately at the time an option is granted, the fair market value of an option to buy includes the value of the right to benefit from any future increase in the value of the property subject to the option (relative to the option exercise price), without risking any capital. Therefore, the fair market value of an option is not merely the difference that may exist at a particular time between the option's exercise price and the value of the property subject to the option, but also includes the value of the option privilege for the remainder of the exercise period. Accordingly, for purposes of this section, in determining whether the fair market value of an option is readily ascertainable, it is necessary to consider whether the value of the entire option privilege can be measured with reasonable accuracy. In determining whether the value of the option privilege is readily ascertainable, and in determining the amount of such value when such value is readily ascertainable, it is necessary to consider—

(i) Whether the value of the property subject to the option can be ascertained;

(ii) The probability of any ascertainable value of such property increasing or decreasing; and

(iii) The length of the period during which the option can be exercised.

* * *

[T.D. 7554, 43 FR 31920, July 24, 1978, as amended by T.D. 9067, 68 FR 39453, July 1, 2003; T.D. 9148, 69 FR 48392, Aug. 10, 2004]

§ 1.101–1 Exclusion from gross income of proceeds of life insurance contracts payable by reason of death.

(a)(1) In general. Section 101(a)(1) states the general rule that the proceeds of life insurance policies, if paid by reason of the death of the insured, are excluded from the gross income of the recipient. Death benefit payments having the characteristics of life insurance proceeds payable by reason of death under contracts, such as workmen's compensation insurance contracts, endowment contracts, or accident and health insurance contracts, are covered by this provision. * * * The exclusion from gross income allowed by section 101(a) applies whether payment is made to the estate of the insured or to any beneficiary (individual, corporation, or partnership) and whether it is made directly or in trust. The extent to which this exclusion applies in cases where life insurance policies have been transferred for a valuable consideration is stated in section 101(a)(2) and in paragraph (b) of this section. In cases where the proceeds of a life insurance policy, payable by reason of the death of the insured, are paid other than in a single sum at the time of such death, the amounts to be excluded from gross income may be affected by the provisions of section 101(c) (relating to amounts held under agreements to pay interest) or section 101(d) (relating to amounts payable at a date later than death). See §§ 1.101–3 and 1.101–4. However, neither section 101(c) nor section 101(d) applies to a single sum payment which does not exceed the amount payable at the time of death even though such amount is actually paid at a date later than death.

* * *

(b) Transfers of life insurance policies. **(1)** In the case of a transfer, by assignment or otherwise, of a life insurance policy or any interest therein for a valuable consideration, the amount of the proceeds attributable to such policy or interest which is excludable from the transferee's gross income is generally limited to the sum of (i) the actual value of the consideration for such transfer, and (ii) the premiums and other amounts subsequently paid by the transferee * * *. However, this limitation on the amount excludable from the transferee's gross income does not apply (except in certain special cases involving a series of transfers), where the basis of the policy or interest transferred, for the purpose of determining gain or loss with respect to the transferee, is determinable, in whole or in part, by reference to the basis of such policy or interest in the hands of the transferor * * *. Neither does the limitation apply where the policy or interest therein is transferred to the insured, to a partner of the insured, to a partnership in which the insured is a partner, or to a corporation in which the insured is a shareholder or officer (see section 101(a)(2)(B)). * * *

(2) In the case of a gratuitous transfer, by assignment or otherwise, of a life insurance policy or any interest therein, as a general rule the amount of the proceeds attributable to such policy or interest which is excludable from the transferee's gross income under section 101(a) is limited to the sum of (i) the amount which would have been excludable by the transferor (in accordance with this section) if no such transfer had taken place, and (ii) any premiums and other amounts subsequently paid by the transferee. * * * However, where the gratuitous transfer in question is made by or to the insured, a partner of the insured, a partnership in which the insured is a partner, or a corporation in which the insured is a shareholder or officer, the entire amount of the proceeds attributable to the policy or interest transferred shall be excludable from the transferee's gross income * * *.

* * *

[T.D. 6500, 25 FR 11402, Nov. 26, 1960, as amended by T.D. 6783, 29 FR 18356, Dec. 24, 1964; T.D. 7836, 47 FR 42337, Sept. 27, 1982; T.D. 9340, 72 FR 41159, July 26, 2007]

§ 1.101–3 Interest payments.

(a) Applicability of section 101(c). Section 101(c) provides that if any amount excluded from gross income by section 101(a) (relating to life insurance proceeds) or section 101(b) (relating to employees' death benefits) is held under an agreement to pay interest thereon, the interest payments shall be included in gross income. This provision applies to payments made (either by an insurer or by or on behalf of an employer) of interest earned on any amount so excluded from gross income which is held without substantial diminution of the principal amount during the period when such interest payments are being made or credited to the beneficiaries or estate of the insured or the employee. For example, if a monthly payment is $100, of which $99 represents interest and $1 represents diminution of the principal amount, the principal amount shall be considered held under an agreement to pay interest thereon and the interest payment shall be included in the gross income of the recipient. Section 101(c) applies whether the election to have an amount held under an agreement to pay interest thereon is made by the insured or employee or by his beneficiaries or estate, and whether or not an interest rate is explicitly stated in the agreement. Section 101(d), relating to the payment of life insurance proceeds at a date later than death, shall not apply to any amount to which section 101(c) applies. See section 101(d)(4). However, both section 101(c) and section 101(d) may apply to payments received under a single life insurance contract. * * *

(b) Determination of "present value". For the purpose of determining whether section 101(c) or section 101(d) applies, the present value (at the time of the insured's death) of any amount which is to be paid at a date later than death shall be determined by the use of the interest rate and mortality tables used by the insurer in determining the size of the payments to be made.

[T.D. 6500, 25 FR 11402, Nov. 26, 1960, as amended by T.D. 6577, 26 FR 10127, Oct. 28, 1961]

§ 1.101–4 Payment of life insurance proceeds at a date later than death.

(a) In general. (1)(i) Section 101(d) states the provisions governing the exclusion from gross income of amounts (other than those to which section 101(c) applies) received under a life insurance contract and paid by reason of the death of the insured which are paid to a beneficiary on a date or dates later than the death of the insured. However, if the amounts payable as proceeds of life insurance to which section 101(a)(1) applies cannot in any event exceed the amount payable at the time of the insured's death, such amounts are fully excludable from the gross income of the recipient (or recipients) without regard to the actual time of payment and no further determination need be made under this section. Section 101(d)(1)(A) provides an exclusion from gross income of any amount determined by a proration, under applicable regulations, of "an amount held by an insurer with respect to any beneficiary". The quoted phrase is defined in section 101(d)(2). For the regulations governing the method of computation of this proration, see paragraphs (c) through (f) of this section. The prorated amounts are to be excluded from the gross income of the beneficiary regardless of the taxable year in which they are actually received * * *.

* * *

(b) Amount held by an insurer. (1) For the purpose of the proration referred to in section 101(d)(1), an "amount held by an insurer with respect to any beneficiary" means an amount equal to the present value to such beneficiary (as of the date of death of the insured) of an agreement by the insurer under a life insurance policy (whether as an option or otherwise) to pay such beneficiary an amount or amounts at a date or dates later than the death of the insured (section 101(d)(2)). The present value of such agreement is to be computed as if the agreement under the life insurance policy had been entered into on the date of death of the insured, except that such value shall be determined by the use of the mortality table and interest rate used by the insurer in calculating payments to be made to the beneficiary under such agreement. Where an insurance policy provides an option for the payment of a specific amount upon the death of the insured in full discharge of the contract, such lump sum is the amount held by the insurer with respect to all beneficiaries (or their beneficiaries) under the contract. See, however, paragraph (e) of this section.

(2) In the case of two or more beneficiaries, the "amount held by the insurer" with respect to each beneficiary depends on the relationship of the different benefits payable to such beneficiaries. Where the amounts payable to two or more beneficiaries are independent of each other, the "amount held by the insurer with respect to each beneficiary" shall be determined and prorated over the periods involved independently. Thus, if a certain amount per month is to be paid to A for his life, and, concurrently, another amount per month is to be paid to B for his life, the "amount held by the insurer" shall be determined and prorated for both A and B independently, but the aggregate shall not exceed the total present value of such payments to both. On the other hand, if the obligation to pay B was contingent on his surviving A, the "amount held by the insurer" shall be considered an amount held with respect to both beneficiaries simultaneously. Furthermore, it is immaterial whether B is a named beneficiary or merely the ultimate recipient of payments for a term of years. For the special rules governing the computation of the proration of the "amount held by an insurer" in determining amounts excludable under the provisions of section 101(d), see paragraphs (c) to (f), inclusive, of this section.

(3) Notwithstanding any other provision of this section, if the policy was transferred for a valuable consideration, the total "amount held by an insurer" cannot exceed the sum of the consideration paid plus any premiums or other consideration paid subsequent to the transfer if the provisions of section 101(a)(2) and paragraph (b) of § 1.101–1 limit the excludability of the proceeds to such total.

(c) Treatment of payments for life to a sole beneficiary. If the contract provides for the payment of a specified lump sum, but, pursuant to an agreement between the beneficiary and the insurer, payments are to be made during the life of the beneficiary in lieu of such lump sum, the lump sum shall be divided by the life expectancy of the beneficiary determined in accordance with the mortality table used by the insurer in determining the benefits to be paid. However, if payments are to be made to the estate or beneficiary of the primary beneficiary in the event that the primary beneficiary dies before receiving a certain number of payments or a specified total amount, such lump sum shall be reduced by the present value (at the time of the insured's death) of amounts which may be paid by reason of the guarantee, in accordance with the provisions of paragraph (e) of this section, before making this calculation. To the extent that payments received in each taxable year do not exceed the amount found from the above calculation, they are "prorated amounts" of the "amount held by an insurer" and are excludable from the gross income of the beneficiary without regard to whether he lives beyond the life expectancy used in making the calculation. If the contract in question does not provide for the payment of a specific lump sum upon the death of the insured as one of the alternative methods of payment, the present value (at the time of the death of the insured) of the payments to be made the beneficiary, determined in accordance with the interest rate and mortality table used by the insurer in determining the benefits to be paid, shall be used in the above calculation in lieu of a lump sum.

* * *

[T.D. 6500, 25 FR 11402, Nov. 26, 1960, as amended by T.D. 6577, 26 FR 10127, Oct. 28, 1961; 26 FR 10275, Nov. 2, 1961]

§ 1.102–1 Gifts and inheritances.

(a) General rule. Property received as a gift, or received under a will or under statutes of descent and distribution, is not includible in gross income, although the income from such property is includible in gross income. An amount of principal paid under a marriage settlement is a gift. However, see section 71 and the regulations thereunder for rules relating to alimony or allowances paid upon divorce or separation. Section 102 does not apply to prizes and awards (see section 74 and § 1.74–1) nor to scholarships and fellowship grants (see section 117 and the regulations thereunder).

(b) Income from gifts and inheritances. The income from any property received as a gift, or under a will or statute of descent and distribution shall not be excluded from gross income under paragraph (a) of this section.

(c) Gifts and inheritances of income. If the gift, bequest, devise, or inheritance is of income from property, it shall not be excluded from gross income under paragraph (a) of this section. Section 102 provides a special rule for the treatment of certain gifts, bequests, devises, or inheritances which by their terms are to be paid, credited, or distributed at intervals. Except as provided in section 663(a)(1) and paragraph (d) of this section, to the extent any such gift, bequest, devise, or inheritance is paid, credited, or to be distributed out of income from property, it shall be considered a gift, bequest, devise, or inheritance of income from property. Section 102 provides the same treatment for amounts of income from property which is paid, credited, or to be distributed under a gift or bequest whether the gift or bequest is in terms of a right to payments at intervals (regardless of income) or is in terms of a right to income. To the extent the amounts in either case are paid, credited, or to be distributed at intervals out of income, they are not to be excluded under section 102 from the taxpayer's gross income.

(d) Effect of subchapter J. Any amount required to be included in the gross income of a beneficiary under sections 652, 662, or 668 shall be treated for purposes of this section as a gift, bequest, devise, or inheritance of income from property. On the other hand, any amount excluded from the gross income of a beneficiary under section 663(a)(1) shall be treated for purposes of this section as property acquired by gift, bequest, devise, or inheritance.

(e) Income taxed to grantor or assignor. Section 102 is not intended to tax a donee upon the same income which is taxed to the grantor of a trust or assignor of income under section 61 or sections 671 through 677, inclusive.

[T.D. 6500, 25 FR 11402, Nov. 26, 1960]

§ 1.102–1 (*Proposed, published 1–9–89.*) Gifts and inheritances.

* * *

(f) Exclusions—(1) In general. Section 102 does not apply to prizes and awards (including employee achievement awards) (see section 74); certain de minimis fringe benefits (see section 132);

any amount transferred by or for an employer to, or for the benefit of, an employee (see section 102(c)); or to qualified scholarships (see section 117).

(2) Employer/Employee transfers. For purposes of section 102(c), extraordinary transfers to the natural objects of an employer's bounty will not be considered transfers to, or for the benefit of, an employee if the employee can show that the transfer was not made in recognition of the employee's employment. Accordingly, section 102(c) shall not apply to amounts transferred between related parties (e.g., father and son) if the purpose of the transfer can be substantially attributed to the familial relationship of the parties and not to the circumstances of their employment.

§ 1.103–1 Interest upon obligations of a State, territory, etc.

(a) Interest upon obligations of a State, territory, a possession of the United States, the District of Columbia, or any political subdivision thereof (hereinafter collectively or individually referred to as "State or local governmental unit") is not includable in gross income, except as provided * * *.

(b) Obligations issued by or on behalf of any State or local governmental unit by constituted authorities empowered to issue such obligations are the obligations of such a unit. * * * Certificates issued by a political subdivision for public improvements (such as sewers, sidewalks, streets, etc.) which are evidence of special assessments against specific property, which assessments become a lien against such property and which the political subdivision is required to enforce, are, for purposes of this section, obligations of the political subdivision even though the obligations are to be satisfied out of special funds and not out of general funds or taxes. The term "political subdivision", for purposes of this section denotes any division of any State or local governmental unit which is a municipal corporation or which has been delegated the right to exercise part of the sovereign power of the unit. As thus defined, a political subdivision of any State or local governmental unit may or may not, for purposes of this section, include special assessment districts so created, such as road, water, sewer, gas, light, reclamation, drainage, irrigation, levee, school, harbor, port improvement, and similar districts and divisions of any such unit.

[T.D. 6500, 25 FR 11402, Nov. 26, 1960, as amended by T.D. 7199, 37 FR 15486, Aug. 3, 1972]

§ 1.104–1 Compensation for injuries or sickness.

(a) In general. Section 104(a) provides an exclusion from gross income with respect to certain amounts * * *, which are received for personal injuries or sickness, except to the extent that such amounts are attributable to (but not in excess of) deductions allowed under section 213 (relating to medical, etc., expenses) for any prior taxable year. See section 213 and the regulations thereunder.

(b) Amounts received under workmen's compensation acts. Section 104(a)(1) excludes from gross income amounts which are received by an employee under a workmen's compensation act (such as the Longshoremen's and Harbor Workers' Compensation Act, 33 U.S.C., c. 18), or under a statute in the nature of a workmen's compensation act which provides compensation to employees for personal injuries or sickness incurred in the course of employment. Section 104(a)(1) also applies to compensation which is paid under a workmen's compensation act to the survivor or survivors of a deceased employee. However, section 104(a)(1) does not apply to a retirement pension or annuity to the extent that it is determined by reference to the employee's age or length of service, or the employee's prior contributions, even though the employee's retirement is occasioned by an occupational injury or sickness. Section 104(a)(1) also does not apply to amounts which are received as compensation for a nonoccupational injury or sickness nor to amounts received as compensation for an occupational injury or sickness to the extent that they are in excess of the amount provided in the applicable workmen's compensation act or acts. See, however, §§ 1.105–1 through 1.105–5 for rules relating to exclusion of such amounts from gross income.

(c) Damages received on account of personal physical injuries or physical sickness—(1) In general. Section 104(a)(2) excludes from gross income the amount of any damages (other than punitive damages) received (whether by suit or agreement and whether as lump sums or as periodic payments) on account of personal physical injuries or physical sickness. Emotional distress is not considered a physical injury or physical sickness. However, damages for emotional distress attributable to a physical injury or physical sickness are excluded from income under section 104(a)(2). Section 104(a)(2) also excludes damages not in excess of the amount paid for medical care (described in section 213(d)(1)(A) or (B)) for emotional distress. For purposes of this paragraph (c), the term damages means an amount received (other than workers' compensation) through prosecution of a legal suit or action, or through a settlement agreement entered into in lieu of prosecution.

(2) Cause of action and remedies. The section 104(a)(2) exclusion may apply to damages recovered for a personal physical injury or physical sickness under a statute, even if that statute does not provide for a broad range of remedies. The injury need not be defined as a tort under state or common law.

* * *

(d) Accident or health insurance. Section 104(a)(3) excludes from gross income amounts received through accident or health insurance for personal injuries or sickness (other than amounts received by an employee, to the extent that such amounts (1) are attributable to contributions of the employer which were not includible in the gross income of the employee, or (2) are paid by the employer). Similar treatment is also accorded to amounts received under accident or health plans and amounts received from sickness or disability funds. See section 105(e) and § 1.105–5. If, therefore, an individual purchases a policy accident or health insurance out of his own funds, amounts received thereunder for personal injuries or sickness are excludable from his gross income under section 104(a)(3). See, however, section 213 and the regulations thereunder as to the inclusion in gross income of amounts attributable to deductions allowed under section 213 for any prior taxable year. Section 104(a)(3) also applies to amounts received by an employee for personal injuries or sickness from a fund which is maintained exclusively by employee contributions. Conversely, if an employer is either the sole contributor to such a fund, or is the sole purchaser of a policy of accident or health insurance for his employees (on either a group or individual basis), the exclusion provided under section 104(a)(3) does not apply to any amounts received by his employees through such fund or insurance. If the employer and his employees contribute to a fund or purchase insurance which pays accident or health benefits to employees, section 104(a)(3) does not apply to amounts received thereunder by employees to the extent that such amounts are attributable to the employer's contributions. See § 1.105–1 for rules relating to the determination of the amount attributable to employer contributions. * * *

* * *

[T.D. 6500, 25 FR 11402, Nov. 26, 1960, as amended by T.D. 6722, 29 FR 5070, April 14, 1964; T.D. 7043, 35 FR 8477, June 2, 1970; T.D. 9573, 77 FR 3107, Jan. 23, 2012]

§ 1.105–1 Amounts attributable to employer contributions.

(a) In general. Under section 105(a), amounts received by an employee through accident or health insurance for personal injuries or sickness must be included in his gross income to the extent that such amounts (1) are attributable to contributions of the employer which were not includible in the gross income of the employee, or (2) are paid by the employer, unless such amounts are excluded therefrom * * *. For purposes of this section, the term "amounts received by an employee through an accident or health plan" refers to any amounts received through accident or health insurance, and also to any amounts which, under section 105(e), are treated as being so received. * * * A self-employed individual is not an employee for purposes of section 105 * * *. * * * Thus, such an individual will not be treated as an employee with respect to benefits described in section 105 received from a plan in which he participates as an employee within the meaning of section 401(c)(1) at the time he, his spouse, or any of his dependents becomes entitled to receive such benefits.

(b) Noncontributory plans. All amounts received by employees through an accident or health plan which is financed solely by their employer, either by payment of premiums on an accident or health insurance policy (whether on a group or individual basis), by contributions to a fund which pays accident or health benefits, or by direct payment of the benefits under the plan, are subject to the provisions of section 105(a), except to the extent that they are excludable under section 105(b), (c), or (d). This rule may be illustrated by the following examples:

Example (1). Employer A maintains a plan for his employees which provides that he will continue to pay regular wages to employees who are absent from work due to sickness or personal injuries. Employees make no contributions to the plan and all benefits are paid by the employer. Amounts received by employees under the plan are subject to section 105(a), and must be included in gross income unless excluded therefrom under section 105(b), (c), or (d).

Example (2). Pursuant to a State nonoccupational disability benefits law, employer B maintains an accident and health plan for his employees. Although under the State law B is authorized to withhold from his employees' wages a specified amount for employee contributions to the State fund, in actual practice B does not so withhold and makes all contributions out of his own funds. All amounts received by B's employees from the State fund are subject to section 105(a), and must be included in gross income unless excluded therefrom under section 105(b), (c), or (d).

* * *

[T.D. 6500, 25 FR 11402, Nov. 26, 1960, as amended by T.D. 6722, 29 FR 5071, April 14, 1964]

§ 1.105–2 Amounts expended for medical care.

Section 105(b) provides an exclusion from gross income with respect to the amounts referred to in section 105(a) (see § 1.105–1) which are paid, directly or indirectly, to the taxpayer to reimburse him for expenses incurred for the medical care (as defined in section 213(e)) of the taxpayer, his spouse, and his dependents (as defined in section 152). However, the exclusion does not apply to amounts which are attributable to (and not in excess of) deductions allowed under section 213 (relating to medical, etc., expenses) for any prior taxable year. See section 213 and the regulations thereunder. Section 105(b) applies only to amounts which are paid specifically to reimburse the taxpayer for expenses incurred by him for the prescribed medical care. Thus, section 105(b) does not apply to amounts which the taxpayer would be entitled to receive irrespective of whether or not he incurs expenses for medical care. For example, if under a wage continuation plan the taxpayer is entitled to regular wages during a period of absence from work due to sickness or injury, amounts received under such plan are not excludable from his gross income under section 105(b) even though the taxpayer may have incurred medical expenses during the period of illness. * * * If the amounts are paid to the taxpayer solely to reimburse him for expenses which he incurred for the prescribed medical care, section 105(b) is applicable even though such amounts are paid without proof of the amount of the actual expenses incurred by the taxpayer, but section 105(b) is not applicable to the extent that such amounts exceed the amount of the actual expenses for such medical care. If the taxpayer incurs an obligation for medical care, payment to the obligee in discharge of such obligation shall constitute indirect payment to the taxpayer as reimbursement for medical care. Similarly, payment to or on behalf of the taxpayer's spouse or dependents shall constitute indirect payment to the taxpayer.

[T.D. 6500, 25 FR 11402, Nov. 26, 1960]

§ 1.105–3 Payments unrelated to absence from work.

Section 105(c) provides an exclusion from gross income with respect to the amounts referred to in section 105(a) to the extent that such amounts (a) constitute payments for the permanent loss or permanent loss of use of a member or function of the body, or the permanent disfigurement, of the taxpayer, his spouse, or a dependent (as defined in section 152), and (b) are computed with reference to the nature of the injury without regard to the period the employee is absent from work. Loss of use or disfigurement shall be considered permanent when it may reasonably be expected to continue for the life of the individual. For purposes of section 105(c), loss or loss of use of a member or function of the body includes the loss or loss of use of an appendage of the body, the loss of an eye, the loss of substantially all of the vision of an eye, and the loss of substantially all of the hearing in one or both ears. The term "disfigurement" shall be given a reasonable interpretation in the light of all the particular facts and circumstances. Section 105(c) does not apply if the amount of the benefits is determined by reference to the period the employee is absent from work. For example, if an employee is absent from work as a result of the loss of an arm, and under the accident and health plan established by his employer, he is to receive $125 a week so long as he is absent from work for a period not in excess of 52 weeks, section 105(c) is not applicable to such payments. * * * However, for purposes of section 105(c), it is immaterial whether an amount is paid in a lump sum or in installments. Section 105(c) does not apply to amounts which are treated as workmen's compensation under paragraph (b) of § 1.104–1, or to amounts paid by reason of the death of the employee (see section 101).

[T.D. 6500, 25 FR 11402, Nov. 26, 1960]

§ 1.105–5 Accident and health plans.

(a) In general. Sections 104(a)(3) and 105(b), (c), * * * exclude from gross income certain amounts received through accident or health insurance. Section 105(e) provides that for purposes of sections 104 and 105 amounts received through an accident or health plan for employees, and amounts received from a sickness and disability fund for employees maintained under the law of a State, a Territory, or the District of Columbia, shall be treated as amounts received through accident or health insurance. In general, an accident or health plan is an arrangement for the payment of amounts to employees in the event of personal injuries or sickness. A plan may cover one or more employees, and there may be different plans for different employees or classes of employees. An accident or health plan may be either insured or noninsured, and it is not necessary that the plan be in writing or that the employee's rights to benefits under the plan be enforceable. However, if the employee's rights are not enforceable, an amount will be deemed to be received under a plan only if, on the date the employee became sick or injured, the employee was covered by a plan (or a program, policy, or custom having the effect of a plan) providing for the payment of amounts to the employee in the event of personal injuries or sickness, and notice or knowledge of such plan was reasonably available to the employee. It is immaterial who makes payment of the benefits provided by the plan. For example, payment may be made by the employer, a welfare fund, a State sickness or disability benefits fund, an association of employers or employees, or by an insurance company.

(b) Self-employed individuals. Under section 105(g), a self-employed individual is not treated as an employee for purposes of section 105. Therefore, for example, benefits paid under an accident or health plan as referred to in section 105(e) to or on behalf of an individual who is self-employed in the business with respect to which the plan is established will not be treated as received through accident and health insurance for purposes of sections 104(a)(3) and 105.

[T.D. 6722, 29 FR 5071, April 14, 1964]

§ 1.106-1 Contributions by employer to accident and health plans.

The gross income of an employee does not include contributions which his employer makes to an accident or health plan for compensation (through insurance or otherwise) to the employee for personal injuries or sickness incurred by him, his spouse, or his dependents, as defined in section 152. The employer may contribute to an accident or health plan either by paying the premium (or a portion of the premium) on a policy of accident or health insurance covering one or more of his employees, or by contributing to a separate trust or fund (including a fund referred to in section 105(e)) which provides accident or health benefits directly or through insurance to one or more of his employees. However, if such insurance policy, trust, or fund provides other benefits in addition to accident or health benefits, section 106 applies only to the portion of the employer's contribution which is allocable to accident or health benefits. See paragraph (d) of § 1.104-1 and §§ 1.105-1 through 1.105-5, inclusive, for regulations relating to exclusion from an employee's gross income of amounts received through accident or health insurance and through accident or health plans.

[T.D. 6500, 25 FR 11402, Nov. 26, 1960]

§ 1.107-1 Rental value of parsonages.

(a) In the case of a minister of the gospel, gross income does not include (1) the rental value of a home, including utilities, furnished to him as a part of his compensation, or (2) the rental allowance paid to him as part of his compensation to the extent such allowance is used by him to rent or otherwise provide a home. In order to qualify for the exclusion, the home or rental allowance must be provided as remuneration for services which are ordinarily the duties of a minister of the gospel. * * * Examples of specific services the performance of which will be considered duties of a minister for purposes of section 107 include the performance of sacerdotal functions, the conduct of religious worship, the administration and maintenance of religious organizations and their integral agencies, and the performance of teaching and administrative duties at theological seminaries. Also, the service performed by a qualified minister as an employee of the United States (other than as a chaplain in the Armed Forces, whose service is considered to be that of a commissioned officer in his capacity as such, and not as a minister in the exercise of his ministry), or a State, Territory, or possession of the United States, or a political subdivision of any of the foregoing, or the District of Columbia, is in the exercise of his ministry provided the service performed includes such services as are ordinarily the duties of a minister.

* * *

(c) A rental allowance must be included in the minister's gross income in the taxable year in which it is received, to the extent that such allowance is not used by him during such taxable year to rent or otherwise provide a home. Circumstances under which a rental allowance will be deemed to have been used to rent or provide a home will include cases in which the allowance is expended (1) for rent of a home, (2) for purchase of a home, and (3) for expenses directly related to providing a home. Expenses for food and servants are not considered for this purpose to be directly related to providing a home. Where the minister rents, purchases, or owns a farm or other business property in addition to a home, the portion of the rental allowance expended in connection with the farm or business property shall not be excluded from his gross income.

[T.D. 6500, 25 FR 11402, Nov. 26, 1960, as amended by T.D. 6691, 28 FR 12817, Dec. 3, 1963]

§ 1.108–2 Acquisition of indebtedness by a person related to the debtor.

(a) General rules. The acquisition of outstanding indebtedness by a person related to the debtor from a person who is not related to the debtor results in the realization by the debtor of income from discharge of indebtedness (to the extent required by section 61(a)(12) and section 108) in an amount determined under paragraph (f) of this section. Income realized pursuant to the preceding sentence is excludible from gross income to the extent provided in section 108(a). The rules of this paragraph apply if indebtedness is acquired directly by a person related to the debtor in a direct acquisition (as defined in paragraph (b) of this section) or if a holder of indebtedness becomes related to the debtor in an indirect acquisition (as defined in paragraph (c) of this section).

(b) Direct acquisition. An acquisition of outstanding indebtedness is a direct acquisition under this section if a person related to the debtor (or a person who becomes related to the debtor on the date the indebtedness is acquired) acquires the indebtedness from a person who is not related to the debtor. Notwithstanding the foregoing, the Commissioner may provide by Revenue Procedure or other published guidance that certain acquisitions of indebtedness described in the preceding sentence are not direct acquisitions for purposes of this section.

* * *

[T.D. 8460, 57 FR 61808, Dec. 29, 1992]

§ 1.109–1 Exclusion from gross income of lessor of real property of value of improvements erected by lessee.

(a) Income derived by a lessor of real property upon the termination, through forfeiture or otherwise, of the lease of such property and attributable to buildings erected or other improvements made by the lessee upon the leased property is excluded from gross income. However, where the facts disclose that such buildings or improvements represent in whole or in part a liquidation in kind of lease rentals, the exclusion from gross income shall not apply to the extent that such buildings or improvements represent such liquidation. The exclusion applies only with respcct to thc income realized by the lessor upon the termination of the lease and has no application to income, if any, in the form of rent, which may be derived by a lessor during the period of the lease and attributable to buildings erected or other improvements made by the lessee. It has no application to income which may be realized by the lessor upon the termination of the lease but not attributable to the value of such buildings or improvements. Neither does it apply to income derived by the lessor subsequent to the termination of the lease incident to the ownership of such buildings or improvements.

* * *

[T.D. 6500, 25 FR 11402, Nov. 26, 1960]

§ 1.111–1 Recovery of certain items previously deducted or credited.

(a) General. Section 111 provides that income attributable to the recovery during any taxable year of bad debts, prior taxes, and delinquency amounts shall be excluded from gross income to the extent of the "recovery exclusion" with respect to such items. The rule of exclusion so prescribed by statute applies equally with respect to all other losses, expenditures and accruals made the basis of deductions from gross income for prior taxable years, * * *, but not including deductions with respect to depreciation, depletion, amortization, or amortizable bond premiums. The term "recovery exclusion" as used in this section means an amount equal to the portion of the bad debts, prior taxes, and delinquency amounts (the items specifically referred to in section 111), and of all other items subject to the rule of exclusion which, when deducted or credited for a prior taxable year, did not result in a reduction of any tax of the taxpayer under subtitle A (other than the accumulated earnings tax imposed by section 531 or the personal holding company tax imposed by section 541) * * *.

* * *

[T.D. 6500, 25 FR 11402, Nov. 26, 1960]

§ 1.117–1 Exclusion of amounts received as a scholarship or fellowship grant.

(a) In general. * * * The exclusion from gross income of an amount which is a scholarship or fellowship grant is controlled solely by section 117. * * *

[T.D. 6500, 25 FR 11402, Nov. 26, 1960]

§ 1.117–3 Definitions.

(a) Scholarship. A scholarship generally means an amount paid or allowed to, or for the benefit of, a student, whether an undergraduate or a graduate, to aid such individual in pursuing his studies. * * * If an educational institution maintains or participates in a plan whereby the tuition of a child of a faculty member of such institution is remitted by any other participating educational institution attended by such child, the amount of the tuition so remitted shall be considered to be an amount received as a scholarship.

(b) Educational organization. * * *. * * * for purposes of section 117 the term "educational organization" means only an educational organization which normally maintains a regular faculty and curriculum and normally has a regularly organized body of students in attendance at the place where its educational activities are carried on. * * *

(c) Fellowship grant. A fellowship grant generally means an amount paid or allowed to, or for the benefit of, an individual to aid him in the pursuit of study or research. * * * The term also includes any amount received in the nature of a family allowance as a part of a fellowship grant. However, the term does not include any amount provided by an individual to aid a relative, friend, or other individual in the pursuit of study or research where the grantor is motivated by family or philanthropic considerations.

* * *

(e) Candidate for a degree. The term "candidate for a degree" means an individual, whether an undergraduate or a graduate, who is pursuing studies or conducting research to meet the requirements for an academic or professional degree conferred by colleges or universities. It is not essential that such study or research be pursued or conducted at an educational institution which confers such degrees if the purpose thereof is to meet the requirements for a degree of a college or university which does confer such degrees. A student who receives a scholarship for study at a secondary school or other educational institution is considered to be a "candidate for a degree."

[T.D. 6500, 25 FR 11402, Nov. 26, 1960, as amended by T.D. 8032, 50 FR 27232, July 2, 1985]

§ 1.117–4 Items not considered as scholarships or fellowship grants.

The following payments or allowances shall not be considered to be amounts received as a scholarship or a fellowship grant for the purpose of section 117:

* * *

(c) Amounts paid as compensation for services or primarily for the benefit of the grantor. **(1)** * * * any amount paid or allowed to, or on behalf of, an individual to enable him to pursue studies or research, if such amount represents either compensation for past, present, or future employment services or represents payment for services which are subject to the direction or supervision of the grantor.

(2) Any amount paid or allowed to, or on behalf of, an individual to enable him to pursue studies or research primarily for the benefit of the grantor.

However, amounts paid or allowed to, or on behalf of, an individual to enable him to pursue studies or research are considered to be amounts received as a scholarship or fellowship grant for the purpose of section 117 if the primary purpose of the studies or research is to further the education and training of the recipient in his individual capacity and the amount provided by the grantor for such purpose does not represent compensation or payment for the services described in subparagraph (1) of this paragraph. Neither the fact that the recipient is required to furnish reports of his progress to the grantor, nor the fact that the results of his studies or research may be of some incidental benefits to the grantor shall, of itself, be considered to destroy the essential character of such amount as a scholarship or fellowship grant.

[T.D. 6500, 25 FR 11402, Nov. 26, 1960, as amended by T.D. 8032, 50 FR 27232, July 2, 1985]

§ 1.117–6 (*Proposed, published 6–9–88.*) Qualified scholarships.

* * *

(b) Exclusion of qualified scholarships—(1) Gross income does not include any amount received as a qualified scholarship by an individual who is a candidate for a degree at an educational organization described in section 170(b)(1)(A)(ii), subject to the rules set forth in paragraph (d) of this section. Generally, any amount of a scholarship or fellowship grant that is not excludable under section 117 is includable in the gross income of the recipient for the taxable year in which such amount is received, notwithstanding the provisions of section 102 (relating to exclusion from gross income of gifts). However, see section 127 and the regulations thereunder for rules permitting an exclusion from gross income for certain educational assistance payments. See also section 162 and the regulations thereunder for the deductibility as a trade or business expense of the educational expenses of an individual who is not a candidate for a degree.

(2) If the amount of a scholarship or fellowship grant eligible to be excluded as a qualified scholarship under this paragraph cannot be determined when the grant is received because expenditures for qualified tuition and related expenses have not yet been incurred, then that portion of any amount received as a scholarship or fellowship grant that is not used for qualified tuition and related expenses within the academic period to which the scholarship or fellowship grant applies must be included in the gross income of the recipient for the taxable year in which such academic period ends.

(c) Definitions—(1) Qualified scholarship. For purposes of this section, a qualified scholarship is any amount received by an individual as a scholarship or fellowship grant (as defined in paragraph (c)(3) of this section), to the extent the individual establishes that, in accordance with the conditions of the grant, such amount was used for qualified tuition and related expenses (as defined in paragraph (c)(2) of this section). To be considered a qualified scholarship, the terms of the scholarship or fellowship grant need not expressly require that the amounts received be used for tuition and related expenses. However, to the extent that the terms of the grant specify that any portion of the grant cannot be used for tuition and related expenses or designate any portion of the grant for purposes other than tuition and related expenses (such as for room and board, or for a meal allowance), such amounts are not amounts received as a qualified scholarship. See paragraph (e) of this section for rules relating to recordkeeping requirements for establishing amounts used for qualified tuition and related expenses.

(2) Qualified tuition and related expenses. For purposes of this section, qualified tuition and related expenses are—

(i) Tuition and fees required for the enrollment or attendance of a student at an educational organization described in section 170(b)(1)(A)(ii); and

(ii) Fees, books, supplies, and equipment required for courses of instruction at such an educational organization.

In order to be treated as related expenses under this section, the fees, books, supplies, and equipment must be required of all students in the particular course of instruction. Incidental expenses are not considered related expenses. Incidental expenses include expenses incurred for room and board, travel, research, clerical help, and equipment and other expenses that are not required for either enrollment or attendance at an educational organization, or in a course of instruction at such educational organization. See paragraph (c)(6), Example (1) of this section.

(3) Scholarship or fellowship grant—(i) In general. Generally, a scholarship or fellowship grant is a cash amount paid or allowed to, or for the benefit of, an individual to aid such individual in the pursuit of study or research. A scholarship or fellowship grant also may be in the form of a reduction in the amount owed by the recipient to an educational organization for tuition, room and board, or any other fee. A scholarship or fellowship grant may be funded by a governmental agency, college or university, charitable organization, business, or any other source. To be considered a scholarship or fellowship grant for purposes of this section, any amount received need not be formally designated as a scholarship. For example, an "allowance" is treated as a scholarship if it meets the definition set forth in this paragraph. However, a scholarship or fellowship grant does not include any amount provided by an individual to aid a relative, friend, or other individual in the pursuit of study or research if the grantor is motivated by family or philanthropic considerations.

* * *

(4) Candidate for a degree. For purposes of this section, a candidate for a degree is—

(i) A primary or secondary school student;

(ii) An undergraduate or graduate student at a college or university who is pursuing studies or conducting research to meet the requirement for an academic or professional degree; or

(iii) A full-time or part-time student at an educational organization described in section 170(b)(1)(A)(ii) that—

(A) Provides an educational program that is acceptable for full credit towards a bachelor's or higher degree, or offers a program of training to prepare students for gainful employment in a recognized occupation, and

(B) Is authorized under Federal or State law to provide such a program and is accredited by a nationally recognized accreditation agency.

The student may pursue studies or conduct research at an educational organization other than the one conferring the degree provided that such study or research meets the requirements of the educational organization granting the degree. * * *

(d) Inclusion of qualified scholarships and qualified tuition reductions representing payment for services—(1) In general. The exclusion from gross income under this section does not apply to that portion of any amount received as a qualified scholarship or qualified tuition reduction (as defined under section 117(d)) that represents payment for teaching, research, or other services by the student required as a condition to receiving the qualified scholarship or qualified tuition reduction, regardless of whether all candidates for the degree are required to perform such services. The provisions of this paragraph (d) apply not only to cash amounts received in return for such services, but also to amounts by which the tuition or related expenses of the person who performs services are reduced, whether or not pursuant to a tuition reduction plan described in section 117(d).

(2) Payment for services. For purposes of this section, a scholarship or fellowship grant represents payment for services when the grantor requires the recipient to perform services in return for the granting of the scholarship or fellowship. A requirement that the recipient pursue studies, research, or other activities primarily for the benefit of the grantor is treated as a requirement to perform services. A requirement that a recipient furnish periodic reports to the grantor for the purpose of keeping the grantor informed as to the general progress of the individual, however, does not constitute the performance of services. A scholarship or fellowship grant conditioned upon either past, present, or future teaching, research, or other services by the recipient represents payment for services under this section. * * *

(3) Determination of amount of scholarship or fellowship grant representing payment for services. If only a portion of a scholarship or fellowship grant represents payment for services, the grantor must determine the amount of the scholarship or fellowship grant (including any reduction in tuition or related expenses) to be allocated to payment for services. Factors to be taken into account in making this allocation include, but are not limited to, compensation paid by—

(i) The grantor for similar services performed by students with qualifications comparable to those of the scholarship recipient, but who do not receive scholarship or fellowship grants;

(ii) The grantor for similar services performed by full-time or part-time employees of the grantor who are not students; and

(iii) Educational organizations, other than the grantor of the scholarship or fellowship, for similar services performed either by students or other employees.

If the recipient includes in gross income the amount allocated by the grantor to payment for services and such amount represents reasonable compensation for those services, then any additional amount of a scholarship or fellowship grant received from the same grantor that meets the requirements of paragraph (b) of this section is excludable from gross income. * * *

* * *

(e) Recordkeeping requirements. In order to be eligible to exclude from gross income any amount received as a qualified scholarship (as defined in paragraph (c)(1) of this section), the recipient must maintain records that establish amounts used for qualified tuition and related expenses (as defined in paragraph (c)(2) of this section) as well as the total amount of qualified tuition and related expenses. Such amounts may be established by providing to the Service, upon request, copies of relevant bills, receipts, cancelled checks, or other documentation or records that clearly reflect the use of the money. The recipient must also submit, upon request, documentation that establishes receipt of the grant, notification date of the grant, and the conditions and requirements of the particular grant. Subject to the rules set forth in paragraph (d) of this section, qualified scholarship amounts are excludable without the need to trace particular grant dollars to particular expenditures for qualified tuition and related expenses.

* * *

§ 1.118-1 Contributions to the capital of a corporation.

In the case of a corporation, section 118 provides an exclusion from gross income with respect to any contribution of money or property to the capital of the taxpayer. Thus, if a corporation requires additional funds for conducting its business and obtains such funds through voluntary pro rata payments by its shareholders, the amounts so received being credited to its surplus account or to a special account, such amounts do not constitute income, although there is no increase in the outstanding shares of stock of the corporation. In such a case the payments are in the nature of assessments upon, and represent an additional price paid for, the shares of stock held by the individual shareholders, and will be treated as an addition to and as a part of the operating capital of the company. Section 118 also applies to contributions to capital made by persons other than shareholders. For example, the exclusion applies to the value of land or other property contributed to a corporation by a governmental unit or by a civic group for the purpose of inducing the corporation to locate its business in a particular community, or for the purpose of enabling the corporation to expand its operating facilities. However, the exclusion does not apply to any money or property transferred to the corporation in consideration for goods or services rendered, or to subsidies paid for the purpose of inducing the taxpayer to limit production. See section 362 for the basis of property acquired by a corporation through a contribution to its capital by its stockholders or by nonstockholders.

[T.D. 6500, 25 FR 11402, Nov. 26, 1960]

§ 1.119-1 Meals and lodging furnished for the convenience of the employer.

(a) Meals—(1) In general. The value of meals furnished to an employee by his employer shall be excluded from the employee's gross income if two tests are met: (i) The meals are furnished on the business premises of the employer, and (ii) the meals are furnished for the convenience of the employer. The question of whether meals are furnished for the convenience of the employer is one of fact to be determined by analysis of all the facts and circumstances in each case. If the tests described in subdivisions (i) and (ii) of this subparagraph are met, the exclusion shall apply irrespective of whether under an employment contract or a statute fixing the terms of employment such meals are furnished as compensation.

(2) Meals furnished without a charge. (i) Meals furnished by an employer without charge to the employee will be regarded as furnished for the convenience of the employer if such meals are furnished for a substantial noncompensatory business reason of the employer. If an employer furnishes meals as a means of providing additional compensation to his employee (and not for a substantial noncompensatory business reason of the employer), the meals so furnished will not be regarded as furnished for the convenience of the employer. Conversely, if the employer furnishes meals to his employee for a substantial noncompensatory business reason, the meals so furnished will be regarded as furnished for the convenience of the employer, even though such meals are also furnished for a compensatory reason. In determining the reason of an employer for furnishing meals, the mere declaration that meals are furnished for a noncompensatory business reason is not sufficient to prove that meals are furnished for the convenience of the employer, but such determination will be based upon an examination of all the surrounding facts and circumstances. In subdivision (ii) of this subparagraph, there are set forth some of the substantial noncompensatory business reasons which occur frequently and which justify the conclusion that meals furnished for such a reason are furnished for the convenience of the employer. In subdivision (iii) of this subparagraph, there are set forth some of the business reasons which are considered to be compensatory and which, in the absence of a substantial noncompensatory business reason, justify the conclusion that meals furnished for such a reason are not furnished for the convenience of the employer. Generally, meals furnished before or after the working hours of the employee will not be regarded as furnished for the convenience of the employer, but see subdivision (ii)(d) and (f) of this subparagraph for some exceptions to this general rule. Meals furnished on nonworking days do not qualify for the exclusion under section 119. If the employee is required to occupy living quarters on the business premises of his employer as a condition of his employment (as defined in paragraph (b) of this section), the exclusion applies to the value of any meal furnished without charge to the employee on such premises.

(ii)(a) Meals will be regarded as furnished for a substantial noncompensatory business reason of the employer when the meals are furnished to the employee during his working hours to have the employee available for emergency call during his meal period. In order to demonstrate that meals are furnished to the employee to have the employee available for emergency call during the meal period, it must be shown that emergencies have actually occurred, or can reasonably be expected to occur, in the employer's business which have resulted, or will result, in the employer calling on the employee to perform his job during his meal period.

(b) Meals will be regarded as furnished for a substantial noncompensatory business reason of the employer when the meals are furnished to the employee during his working hours because the employer's business is such that the employee must be restricted to a short meal period, such as 30 or 45 minutes, and because the employee could not be expected to eat elsewhere in such a short meal period. For example, meals may qualify under this subdivision when the employer is engaged in a business in which the peak work load occurs during the normal lunch hours. However, meals cannot qualify under this subdivision (b) when the reason for restricting the time of the meal period is so that the employee can be let off earlier in the day.

(c) Meals will be regarded as furnished for a substantial noncompensatory business reason of the employer when the meals are furnished to the employee during his working hours because the employee could not otherwise secure proper meals within a reasonable meal period. For example, meals may qualify under this subdivision (c) when there are insufficient eating facilities in the vicinity of the employer's premises.

(d) A meal furnished to a restaurant employee or other food service employee for each meal period in which the employee works will be regarded as furnished for a substantial noncompensatory business reason of the employer, irrespective of whether the meal is furnished during, immediately before, or immediately after the working hours of the employee.

(e) If the employer furnishes meals to employees at a place of business and the reason for furnishing the meals to each of substantially all of the employees who are furnished the meals is a substantial noncompensatory business reason of the employer, the meals furnished to each other employee will also be regarded as furnished for a substantial noncompensatory business reason of the employer.

(f) If an employer would have furnished a meal to an employee during his working hours for a substantial noncompensatory business reason, a meal furnished to such an employee immediately after his working hours because his duties prevented him from obtaining a meal during his working hours will be regarded as furnished for a substantial noncompensatory business reason.

(iii) Meals will be regarded as furnished for a compensatory business reason of the employer when the meals are furnished to the employee to promote the morale or goodwill of the employee, or to attract prospective employees.

(3) Meals furnished with a charge. **(i)** If an employer provides meals which an employee may or may not purchase, the meals will not be regarded as furnished for the convenience of the employer. Thus, meals for which a charge is made by the employer will not be regarded as furnished for the convenience of the employer if the employee has a choice of accepting the meals and paying for them or of not paying for them and providing his meals in another manner.

(ii) If an employer furnishes an employee meals for which the employee is charged an unvarying amount (for example, by subtraction from his stated compensation) irrespective of whether he accepts the meals, the amount of such flat charge made by the employer for such meals is not, as such, part of the compensation includible in the gross income of the employee; whether the value of the meals so furnished is excludable under section 119 is determined by applying the rules of subparagraph (2) of this paragraph. If meals furnished for an unvarying amount are not furnished for the convenience of the employer in accordance with the rules of subparagraph (2) of this paragraph, the employee shall include in gross income the value of the meals regardless of whether the value exceeds or is less than the amount charged for such meals. In the absence of evidence to the contrary, the value of the meals may be deemed to be equal to the amount charged for them.

(b) Lodging. The value of lodging furnished to an employee by the employer shall be excluded from the employee's gross income if three tests are met:

(1) The lodging is furnished on the business premises of the employer,

(2) The lodging is furnished for the convenience of the employer, and

(3) The employee is required to accept such lodging as a condition of his employment.

The requirement of subparagraph (3) of this paragraph that the employee is required to accept such lodging as a condition of his employment means that he be required to accept the lodging in order to enable him properly to perform the duties of his employment. Lodging will be regarded as furnished to enable the employee properly to perform the duties of his employment when, for example, the lodging is furnished because the employee is required to be available for duty at all times or because the employee could not perform the services required of him unless he is furnished such lodging. If the tests described in subparagraphs (1), (2), and (3) of this paragraph are met, the exclusion shall apply irrespective of whether a charge is made, or whether, under an employment contract or statute fixing the terms of employment, such lodging is furnished as compensation. If the employer furnishes the employee lodging for which the employee is charged an unvarying amount irrespective of whether he accepts the lodging, the amount of the charge made by the employer for such lodging is not, as such, part of the compensation includible in the gross income of the employee; whether the value of the lodging is excludable from gross income under section 119 is determined by applying the other rules of this paragraph. If the tests described in subparagraph (1), (2), and (3) of this paragraph are not met, the employee shall include in gross income the value of the lodging regardless of whether it exceeds or is less than the amount charged. In the absence of evidence to the contrary, the value of the lodging may be deemed to be equal to the amount charged.

(c) Business premises of the employer.—(1) In general. For purposes of this section, the term "business premises of the employer" generally means the place of employment of the employee. For example, meals and lodging furnished in the employer's home to a domestic servant would constitute meals and lodging furnished on the business premises of the employer. Similarly, meals furnished to cowhands while herding their employer's cattle on leased land would be regarded as furnished on the business premises of the employer.

* * *

(e) Rules. The exclusion provided by section 119 applies only to meals and lodging furnished in kind by an employer to his employee. If the employee has an option to receive additional compensation in lieu of meals or lodging in kind, the value of such meals and lodging is not excluded from gross income. However, the mere fact that an employee, at his option, may decline to accept meals tendered in kind will not of itself require inclusion of the value thereof in gross income. Cash allowances for meals or lodging received by an employee are includible in gross income to the extent that such allowances constitute compensation.

(f) Examples. The provisions of section 119 may be illustrated by the following examples:

Example (1). A waitress who works from 7 a.m. to 4 p.m. is furnished without charge two meals a work day. The employer encourages the waitress to have her breakfast on his business premises before starting work, but does not require her to have breakfast there. She is required, however, to have her lunch on such premises. Since the waitress is a food service employee and works during the normal breakfast and lunch periods, the waitress is permitted to exclude from her gross income both the value of the breakfast and the value of the lunch.

Example (2). The waitress in example (1) is allowed to have meals on the employer's premises without charge on her days off. The waitress is not permitted to exclude the value of such meals from her gross income.

Example (3). A bank teller who works from 9 a.m. to 5 p.m. is furnished his lunch without charge in a cafeteria which the bank maintains on its premises. The bank furnishes the teller such meals in order to limit his lunch period to 30 minutes since the bank's peak work load occurs during the normal lunch period. If the teller had to obtain his lunch elsewhere, it would take him considerably longer than 30 minutes for lunch, and the bank strictly enforces the 30-minute time limit. The bank teller may exclude from his gross income the value of such meals obtained in the bank cafeteria.

* * *

Example (5). A Civil Service employee of a State is employed at an institution and is required by his employer to be available for duty at all times. The employer furnishes the employee with meals and lodging at the institution without charge. Under the applicable State statute, his meals and lodging are regarded as part of the employee's compensation. The employee would nevertheless be entitled to exclude the value of such meals and lodging from his gross income.

Example (6). An employee of an institution is given the choice of residing at the institution free of charge, or of residing elsewhere and receiving a cash allowance in addition to his regular salary. If he elects to reside at the institution, the value to the employee of the lodging furnished by the employer will be includible in the employee's gross income because his residence at the institution is not required in order for him to perform properly the duties of his employment.

Example (7). A construction worker is employed at a construction project at a remote job site in Alaska. Due to the inaccessibility of facilities for the employees who are working at the job site to obtain food and lodging and the prevailing weather conditions, the employer is required to furnish meals and lodging to the employee at the camp site in order to carry on the construction project. The employee is required to pay $40 a week for the meals and lodging. The weekly charge of $40 is not, as such, part of the compensation includible in the gross income of the employee, and under paragraphs (a) and (b) of this section the value of the meals and lodging is excludable from his gross income.

Example (8). A manufacturing company provides a cafeteria on its premises at which its employees can purchase their lunch. There is no other eating facility located near the company's premises, but the employee can furnish his own meal by bringing his lunch. The amount of compensation which any employee is required to include in gross income is not reduced by the amount charged for the meals, and the meals are not considered to be furnished for the convenience of the employer.

Example (9). A hospital maintains a cafeteria on its premises where all of its 230 employees may obtain a meal during their working hours. No charge is made for these meals. The hospital furnishes such meals in order to have each of 210 of the employees available for any emergencies that may occur, and it is shown that each such employee is at times called upon to perform services during his meal period. Although the hospital does not require such employees to remain on the premises during meal periods, they rarely leave the hospital during their meal period. Since the hospital furnishes meals to each of substantially all of its employees in order to have each of them available for emergency call during his meal period, all of the hospital employees who obtain their meals in the hospital cafeteria may exclude from their gross income the value of such meals.

[T.D. 6500, 25 FR 11402, Nov. 26, 1960; T.D. 6745, 29 FR 9380, July 9, 1964; T.D. 8006, 50 FR 2964, Jan. 23, 1985]

§ 1.121–1 Exclusion of gain from sale or exchange of a principal residence.

(a) In general. Section 121 provides that, under certain circumstances, gross income does not include gain realized on the sale or exchange of property that was owned and used by a taxpayer as the taxpayer's principal residence. Subject to the other provisions of section 121, a taxpayer may exclude gain only if, during the 5–year period ending on the date of the sale or exchange, the taxpayer owned and used the property as the taxpayer's principal residence for periods aggregating 2 years or more.

(b) Residence—(1) In general. Whether property is used by the taxpayer as the taxpayer's residence depends upon all the facts and circumstances. A property used by the taxpayer as the taxpayer's residence may include a houseboat, a house trailer, or the house or apartment that the taxpayer is entitled to occupy as a tenant-stockholder in a cooperative housing corporation (as those terms are defined in section 216(b)(1) and (2)). Property used by the taxpayer as the taxpayer's residence does not include personal property that is not a fixture under local law.

(2) Principal residence. In the case of a taxpayer using more than one property as a residence, whether property is used by the taxpayer as the taxpayer's principal residence depends upon all the facts and circumstances. If a taxpayer alternates between 2 properties, using each as a residence for successive periods of time, the property that the taxpayer uses a majority of the time during the year ordinarily will be considered the taxpayer's principal residence. In addition to the taxpayer's use of the property, relevant factors in determining a taxpayer's principal residence, include, but are not limited to—

(i) The taxpayer's place of employment;

(ii) The principal place of abode of the taxpayer's family members;

(iii) The address listed on the taxpayer's federal and state tax returns, driver's license, automobile registration, and voter registration card;

(iv) The taxpayer's mailing address for bills and correspondence;

(v) The location of the taxpayer's banks; and

(vi) The location of religious organizations and recreational clubs with which the taxpayer is affiliated.

(3) Vacant land—(i) In general. The sale or exchange of vacant land is not a sale or exchange of the taxpayer's principal residence unless—

(A) The vacant land is adjacent to land containing the dwelling unit of the taxpayer's principal residence;

(B) The taxpayer owned and used the vacant land as part of the taxpayer's principal residence;

(C) The taxpayer sells or exchanges the dwelling unit in a sale or exchange that meets the requirements of section 121 within 2 years before or 2 years after the date of the sale or exchange of the vacant land; and

(D) The requirements of section 121 have otherwise been met with respect to the vacant land.

(ii) Limitations—(A) Maximum limitation amount. For purposes of section 121(b)(1) and (2) (relating to the maximum limitation amount of the section 121 exclusion), the sale or exchange of the dwelling unit and the vacant land are treated as one sale or exchange. Therefore, only one maximum limitation amount of $250,000 ($500,000 for certain joint returns) applies to the combined sales or exchanges of vacant land and the dwelling unit. In applying the maximum limitation amount to sales or exchanges that occur in different taxable years, gain from the sale or exchange of the dwelling unit, up to the maximum limitation amount under section 121(b)(1) or (2), is excluded first and each spouse is treated as excluding one-half of the gain from a sale or exchange to which section 121(b)(2)(A) and § 1.121–2(a)(3)(i) (relating to the limitation for certain joint returns) apply.

(B) Sale or exchange of more than one principal residence in 2–year period. If a dwelling unit and vacant land are sold or exchanged in separate transactions that qualify for the section 121 exclusion under this paragraph (b)(3), each of the transactions is disregarded in applying section 121(b)(3) (restricting the application of section 121 to only 1 sale or exchange every 2 years) to the other transactions but is taken into account as a sale or exchange of a principal residence on the date of the transaction in applying section 121(b)(3) to that transaction and the sale or exchange of any other principal residence.

(C) Sale or exchange of vacant land before dwelling unit. If the sale or exchange of the dwelling unit occurs in a later taxable year than the sale or exchange of the vacant land and after the date prescribed by law (including extensions) for the filing of the return for the taxable year of the sale or exchange of the vacant land, any gain from the sale or exchange of the vacant land must be treated as taxable on the taxpayer's return for the taxable year of the sale or exchange of the vacant land. If the taxpayer has reported gain from the sale or exchange of the vacant land as taxable, after satisfying the requirements of this paragraph (b)(3) the taxpayer may claim the section 121 exclusion with regard to the sale or exchange of the vacant land (for any period for which the period of limitation under section 6511 has not expired) by filing an amended return.

(4) Examples. The provisions of this paragraph (b) are illustrated by the following examples:

Example 1. Taxpayer A owns 2 residences, one in New York and one in Florida. From 1999 through 2004, he lives in the New York residence for 7 months and the Florida residence for 5 months of each year. In the absence of facts and circumstances indicating otherwise, the New York residence is A's principal residence. A would be eligible for the section 121 exclusion of gain from the sale or exchange of the New York residence, but not the Florida residence.

Example 2. Taxpayer B owns 2 residences, one in Virginia and one in Maine. During 1999 and 2000, she lives in the Virginia residence. During 2001 and 2002, she lives in the Maine residence. During 2003, she lives in the Virginia residence. B's principal residence during 1999, 2000, and 2003 is the Virginia residence. B's principal residence during 2001 and 2002 is the Maine residence. B would be eligible for the 121 exclusion of gain from the sale or exchange of either residence (but not both) during 2003.

Example 3. In 1991 Taxpayer C buys property consisting of a house and 10 acres that she uses as her principal residence. In May 2005 C sells 8 acres of the land and realizes a gain of $110,000. C does not sell the dwelling unit before the due date for filing C's 2005 return, therefore C is not eligible to exclude the $110,000 of gain. In March 2007 C sells the house and remaining 2 acres realizing a gain of $180,000 from the sale of the house. C may exclude the $180,000 of gain. Because the sale of the 8 acres occurred within 2 years from the date of the sale of the dwelling unit, the sale of the 8 acres is treated as a sale of the taxpayer's principal residence under paragraph (b)(3) of this section. C may file an amended return for 2005 to claim an exclusion for $70,000 ($250,000–$180,000 gain previously excluded) of the $110,000 gain from the sale of the 8 acres.

Example 4. In 1998 Taxpayer D buys a house and 1 acre that he uses as his principal residence. In 1999 D buys 29 acres adjacent to his house and uses the vacant land as part of his principal residence. In 2003 D sells the house and 1 acre and the 29 acres in 2 separate transactions. D sells the house and 1 acre at a loss of $25,000. D realizes $270,000 of gain from the sale of the 29 acres. D may exclude the $245,000 gain from the 2 sales.

(c) Ownership and use requirements—(1) In general. The requirements of ownership and use for periods aggregating 2 years or more may be satisfied by establishing ownership and use for 24 full months or for 730 days (365 x 2). The requirements of ownership and use may be satisfied during nonconcurrent periods if both the ownership and use tests are met during the 5–year period ending on the date of the sale or exchange.

(2) Use. (i) In establishing whether a taxpayer has satisfied the 2–year use requirement, occupancy of the residence is required. However, short temporary absences, such as for vacation or other seasonal absence (although accompanied with rental of the residence), are counted as periods of use.

(ii) Determination of use during periods of out-of-residence care. If a taxpayer has become physically or mentally incapable of self-care and the taxpayer sells or exchanges property that the taxpayer owned and used as the taxpayer's principal residence for periods aggregating at least 1 year during the 5–year period preceding the sale or exchange, the taxpayer is treated as using the property as the taxpayer's principal residence for any period of time during the 5–year period in which the taxpayer owns the property and resides in any facility (including a nursing home) licensed by a State or political subdivision to care for an individual in the taxpayer's condition.

(3) Ownership—(i) Trusts. If a residence is owned by a trust, for the period that a taxpayer is treated under sections 671 through 679 (relating to the treatment of grantors and others as substantial owners) as the owner of the trust or the portion of the trust that includes the residence, the taxpayer will be treated as owning the residence for purposes of satisfying the 2–year ownership requirement of section 121, and the sale or exchange by the trust will be treated as if made by the taxpayer.

(ii) Certain single owner entities. If a residence is owned by an eligible entity (within the meaning of § 301.7701–3(a) of this chapter) that has a single owner and is disregarded for federal tax purposes as an entity separate from its owner under § 301.7701–3 of this chapter, the owner will be treated as owning the residence for purposes of satisfying the 2–year ownership requirement of section 121, and the sale or exchange by the entity will be treated as if made by the owner.

(4) Examples. The provisions of this paragraph (c) are illustrated by the following examples. The examples assume that § 1.121–3 (relating to the reduced maximum exclusion) does not apply to the sale of the property. The examples are as follows:

Example 1. Taxpayer A has owned and used his house as his principal residence since 1986. On January 31, 1998, A moves to another state. A rents his house to tenants from that date until April 18, 2000, when he sells it. A is eligible for the section 121 exclusion because he has owned and used the house as his principal residence for at least 2 of the 5 years preceding the sale.

Example 2. Taxpayer B owns and uses a house as her principal residence from 1986 to the end of 1997. On January 4, 1998, B moves to another state and ceases to use the house. B's son moves into the house in March 1999 and uses the residence until it is sold on July 1, 2001. B may not exclude gain from the sale under section 121 because she did not use the property as her principal residence for at least 2 years out of the 5 years preceding the sale.

Example 3. Taxpayer C lives in a townhouse that he rents from 1993 through 1996. On January 18, 1997, he purchases the townhouse. On February 1, 1998, C moves into his daughter's home. On May 25, 2000, while still living in his daughter's home, C sells his townhouse. The section 121 exclusion will apply to gain from the sale because C owned the townhouse for at least 2 years out of the 5 years preceding the sale (from January 19, 1997 until May 25, 2000) and he used the townhouse as his principal residence for at least 2 years during the 5–year period preceding the sale (from May 25, 1995 until February 1, 1998).

Example 4. Taxpayer D, a college professor, purchases and moves into a house on May 1, 1997. He uses the house as his principal residence continuously until September 1, 1998, when he goes abroad for a 1–year sabbatical leave. On October 1, 1999, 1 month after returning from the leave, D sells the house. Because his leave is not considered to be a short temporary absence under paragraph (c)(2) of this section, the period of the sabbatical leave may not be included in determining whether D used the house for periods aggregating 2 years during the 5–year period ending on the date of the sale. Consequently, D is not entitled to exclude gain under section 121 because he did not use the residence for the requisite period.

Example 5. Taxpayer E purchases a house on February 1, 1998, that he uses as his principal residence. During 1998 and 1999, E leaves his residence for a 2–month summer vacation. E sells the house on March 1, 2000. Although, in the 5–year period preceding the date of sale, the total time E used his residence is less than 2 years (21 months), the section 121 exclusion will apply to gain from the sale of the residence because, under paragraph (c)(2) of this section, the 2–month vacations are short temporary absences and are counted as periods of use in determining whether E used the residence for the requisite period.

(d) Depreciation taken after May 6, 1997—(1) In general. The section 121 exclusion does not apply to so much of the gain from the sale or exchange of property as does not exceed the portion of the depreciation adjustments (as defined in section 1250(b)(3)) attributable to the property for periods after May 6, 1997. Depreciation adjustments allocable to any portion of the property to which the section 121 exclusion does not apply under paragraph (e) of this section are not taken into account for this purpose.

(2) Example. The provisions of this paragraph (d) are illustrated by the following example:

Example. On July 1, 1999, Taxpayer A moves into a house that he owns and had rented to tenants since July 1, 1997. A took depreciation deductions totaling $14,000 for the period that he rented the property. After using the residence as his principal residence for 2 full years, A sells the property on August 1, 2001. A's gain realized from the sale is $40,000. A has no other section 1231 or capital gains or losses for 2001. Only $26,000 ($40,000 gain realized—$14,000 depreciation deductions) may be excluded under section 121. Under section 121(d)(6) and paragraph (d)(1) of this section, A must recognize $14,000 of the gain as unrecaptured section 1250 gain within the meaning of section 1(h).

(e) Property used in part as a principal residence—(1) Allocation required. Section 121 will not apply to the gain allocable to any portion (separate from the dwelling unit) of property sold or exchanged with respect to which a taxpayer does not satisfy the use requirement. Thus, if a portion of the property was used for residential purposes and a portion of the property (separate from the dwelling unit) was used for non-residential purposes, only the gain allocable to the residential portion is excludable under section 121. No allocation is required if both the residential and nonresidential portions of the property are within the same dwelling unit. However, section 121 does not apply to the gain allocable to the residential portion of the property to the extent provided by paragraph (d) of this section.

(2) Dwelling unit. For purposes of this paragraph (e), the term dwelling unit has the same meaning as in section 280A(f)(1), but does not include appurtenant structures or other property.

(3) Method of allocation. For purposes of determining the amount of gain allocable to the residential and non-residential portions of the property, the taxpayer must allocate the basis and the amount realized between the residential and the non-residential portions of the property using the same method of allocation that the taxpayer used to determine depreciation adjustments (as defined in section 1250(b)(3)), if applicable.

(4) Examples. The provisions of this paragraph (e) are illustrated by the following examples:

Example 1. Non-residential use of property not within the dwelling unit. (i) Taxpayer A owns a property that consists of a house, a stable and 35 acres. A uses the stable and 28 acres for non-residential purposes for more than 3 years during the 5–year period preceding the sale. A uses the entire house and the remaining 7 acres as his principal residence for at least 2 years during the 5–year period preceding the sale. For periods after May 6, 1997, A claims depreciation deductions of $9,000 for the non-residential use of the stable. A sells the entire property in 2004, realizing a gain of $24,000. A has no other section 1231 or capital gains or losses for 2004.

(ii) Because the stable and the 28 acres used in the business are separate from the dwelling unit, the allocation rules under this paragraph (e) apply and A must allocate the basis and amount realized between the portion of the property that he used as his principal residence and the portion of the property that he used for non-residential purposes. A determines that $14,000 of the gain is allocable to the non-residential-use portion of the property and that $10,000 of the gain is allocable to the portion of the property used as his residence. A must recognize the $14,000 of gain allocable to the non-residential-use portion of the property ($9,000 of which is unrecaptured section 1250 gain within the meaning of section 1(h), and $5,000 of which is adjusted net capital gain). A may exclude $10,000 of the gain from the sale of the property.

Example 2. Non-residential use of property not within the dwelling unit and rental of the entire property. (i) In 1998 Taxpayer B buys a property that includes a house, a barn, and 2 acres. B uses the house and 2 acres as her principal residence and the barn for an antiques business. In 2002, B moves out of the house and rents it to tenants. B sells the property in 2004, realizing a gain of $21,000. Between 1998 and 2004 B claims depreciation deductions of $4,800 attributable to the antiques business. Between 2002 and 2004 B claims depreciation deductions of $3,000 attributable to the house. B has no other section 1231 or capital gains or losses for 2004.

(ii) Because the portion of the property used in the antiques business is separate from the dwelling unit, the allocation rules under this paragraph (e) apply. B must allocate basis and amount realized between the portion of the property that she used as her principal residence and the portion of the property that she used for non-residential purposes. B determines that $4,000 of the gain is allocable to the non-residential portion of the property and that $17,000 of the gain is allocable to the portion of the property that she used as her principal residence.

(iii) B must recognize the $4,000 of gain allocable to the non-residential portion of the property (all of which is unrecaptured section 1250 gain within the meaning of section 1(h)). In addition, the section 121 exclusion does not apply to the gain allocable to the residential portion of the property to the extent of the depreciation adjustments attributable to the residential portion of the property for periods after May 6, 1997 ($3,000). Therefore, B may exclude $14,000 of the gain from the sale of the property.

Example 3. Non-residential use of a separate dwelling unit. (i) In 2002 Taxpayer C buys a 3–story townhouse and converts the basement level, which has a separate entrance, into a separate apartment by installing a kitchen and bathroom and removing the interior stairway that leads from the basement to the upper floors. After the conversion, the property constitutes 2 dwelling units within the meaning of paragraph (e)(2) of this section. C uses the first and second floors of the townhouse as his principal residence and rents the basement level to tenants from 2003 to 2007. C claims depreciation deductions of $2,000 for that period with respect to the basement apartment. C sells the entire property in 2007, realizing gain of $18,000. C has no other section 1231 or capital gains or losses for 2007.

(ii) Because the basement apartment and the upper floors of the townhouse are separate dwelling units, C must allocate the gain between the portion of the property that he used as his principal residence and the portion of the property that he used for non-residential purposes under paragraph (e) of this section. After allocating the basis and the amount realized between the residential and non-residential portions of the property, C determines that $6,000 of the gain is allocable to the non-residential portion of the property and that $12,000 of the gain is allocable to the portion of the property used as his residence. C must recognize the $6,000 of gain allocable to the non-residential portion of the property ($2,000 of which is unrecaptured section 1250 gain within the meaning of section 1(h), and $4,000 of which is adjusted net capital gain). C may exclude $12,000 of the gain from the sale of the property.

Example 4. Separate dwelling unit converted to residential use. The facts are the same as in Example 3 except that in 2007 C incorporates the basement of the townhouse into his principal residence by eliminating the kitchen and building a new interior stairway to the upper floors. C uses all 3 floors of the townhouse as his principal residence for 2 full years and sells the townhouse in 2010, realizing a gain of $20,000. Under section 121(d)(6) and paragraph (d) of this section, C must recognize $2,000 of the gain as unrecaptured section 1250 gain within the meaning of section 1(h). Because C used the entire 3 floors of the townhouse as his principal residence for 2 of the 5 years preceding the sale of the property, C may exclude the remaining $18,000 of the gain from the sale of the house.

Example 5. Non-residential use within the dwelling unit, property depreciated. Taxpayer D, an attorney, buys a house in 2003. The house constitutes a single dwelling unit but D uses a portion of the house as a law office. D claims depreciation deductions of $2,000 during the period that she owns the house. D sells the house in 2006, realizing a gain of $13,000. D has no other section

1231 or capital gains or losses for 2006. Under section 121(d)(6) and paragraph (d) of this section, D must recognize $2,000 of the gain as unrecaptured section 1250 gain within the meaning of section 1(h). D may exclude the remaining $11,000 of the gain from the sale of her house because, under paragraph (e)(1) of this section, she is not required to allocate gain to the business use within the dwelling unit.

Example 6. Non-residential use within the dwelling unit, property not depreciated. The facts are the same as in Example 5, except that D is not entitled to claim any depreciation deductions with respect to her business use of the house. D may exclude $13,000 of the gain from the sale of her house because, under paragraph (e)(1) of this section, she is not required to allocate gain to the business use within the dwelling unit.

* * *

[T.D.9030, 67 FR 78358, Dec. 24, 2002]

§ 1.121–2 Limitations.

(a) Dollar limitations—(1) In general. A taxpayer may exclude from gross income up to $250,000 of gain from the sale or exchange of the taxpayer's principal residence. A taxpayer is eligible for only one maximum exclusion per principal residence.

(2) Joint owners. If taxpayers jointly own a principal residence but file separate returns, each taxpayer may exclude from gross income up to $250,000 of gain that is attributable to each taxpayer's interest in the property, if the requirements of section 121 have otherwise been met.

(3) Special rules for joint returns—(i) In general. A husband and wife who make a joint return for the year of the sale or exchange of a principal residence may exclude up to $500,000 of gain if—

(A) Either spouse meets the 2–year ownership requirements of § 1.121–1(a) and (c);

(B) Both spouses meet the 2–year use requirements of § 1.121–1(a) and (c); and

(C) Neither spouse excluded gain from a prior sale or exchange of property under section 121 within the last 2 years (as determined under paragraph (b) of this section).

(ii) Other joint returns. For taxpayers filing jointly, if either spouse fails to meet the requirements of paragraph (a)(3)(i) of this section, the maximum limitation amount to be claimed by the couple is the sum of each spouse's limitation amount determined on a separate basis as if they had not been married. For this purpose, each spouse is treated as owning the property during the period that either spouse owned the property.

(4) Examples. The provisions of this paragraph (a) are illustrated by the following examples. The examples assume that § 1.121–3 (relating to the reduced maximum exclusion) does not apply to the sale of the property. The examples are as follows:

Example 1. Unmarried Taxpayers A and B own a house as joint owners, each owning a 50 percent interest in the house. They sell the house after owning and using it as their principal residence for 2 full years. The gain realized from the sale is $256,000. A and B are each eligible to exclude $128,000 of gain because the amount of realized gain allocable to each of them from the sale does not exceed each taxpayer's available limitation amount of $250,000.

Example 2. The facts are the same as in Example 1, except that A and B are married taxpayers who file a joint return for the taxable year of the sale. A and B are eligible to exclude the entire amount of realized gain ($256,000) from gross income because the gain realized from the sale does not exceed the limitation amount of $500,000 available to A and B as taxpayers filing a joint return.

Example 3. During 1999, married Taxpayers H and W each sell a residence that each had separately owned and used as a principal residence before their marriage. Each spouse meets the ownership and use tests for his or her respective residence. Neither spouse meets the use requirement for the other spouse's residence. H and W file a joint return for the year of the sales. The gain realized from the sale of H's residence is $200,000. The gain realized from the sale of W's residence is $300,000. Because the ownership and use requirements are met for each residence by each respective spouse, H and W are each eligible to exclude up to $250,000 of gain from the sale of their individual residences. However, W may not use H's unused exclusion to exclude gain in excess of her limitation amount. Therefore, H and W must recognize $50,000 of the gain realized on the sale of W's residence.

Example 4. Married Taxpayers H and W sell their residence and file a joint return for the year of the sale. W, but not H, satisfies the requirements of section 121. They are eligible to exclude up to $250,000 of the gain from the sale of the residence because that is the sum of each spouse's dollar limitation amount determined on a separate basis as if they had not been married ($0 for H, $250,000 for W).

Example 5. Married Taxpayers H and W have owned and used their principal residence since 1998. On February 16, 2001, H dies. On September 24, 2001, W sells the residence and realizes a gain of $350,000. Pursuant to section 6013(a)(3), W and H's executor make a joint return for 2001. All $350,000 of the gain from the sale of the residence may be excluded.

Example 6. Assume the same facts as Example 5, except that W does not sell the residence until January 31, 2002. Because W's filing status for the taxable year of the sale is single, the special rules for joint returns under paragraph (a)(3) of this section do not apply and W may exclude only $250,000 of the gain.

(b) Application of section 121 to only 1 sale or exchange every 2 years—(1) In general. Except as otherwise provided in § 1.121–3 (relating to the reduced maximum exclusion), a taxpayer may not exclude from gross income gain from the sale or exchange of a principal residence if, during the 2–year period ending on the date of the sale or exchange, the taxpayer sold or exchanged other property for which gain was excluded under section 121. For purposes of this paragraph (b)(1), any sale or exchange before May 7, 1997, is disregarded.

(2) Example. The following example illustrates the rules of this paragraph (b). The example assumes that § 1.121–3 (relating to the reduced maximum exclusion) does not apply to the sale of the property. The example is as follows:

Example. Taxpayer A owns a townhouse that he uses as his principal residence for 2 full years, 1998 and 1999. A buys a house in 2000 that he owns and uses as his principal residence. A sells the townhouse in 2002 and excludes gain realized on its sale under section 121. A sells the house in 2003. Although A meets the 2–year ownership and use requirements of section 121, A is not eligible to exclude gain from the sale of the house because A excluded gain within the last 2 years under section 121 from the sale of the townhouse.

* * *

[T.D.9030, 67 FR 78358, Dec. 24, 2002]

§ 1.121–3 Reduced maximum exclusion for taxpayers failing to meet certain requirements.

(a) In general. In lieu of the limitation under section 121(b) and § 1.121–2, a reduced maximum exclusion limitation may be available for a taxpayer who sells or exchanges property used as the taxpayer's principal residence but fails to satisfy the ownership and use requirements described in § 1.121–1(a) and (c) or the 2–year limitation described in § 1.121–2(b).

(b) Primary reason for sale or exchange. In order for a taxpayer to claim a reduced maximum exclusion under section 121(c), the sale or exchange must be by reason of a change in place of employment, health, or unforeseen circumstances. If a safe harbor described in this section applies, a sale or exchange is deemed to be by reason of a change in place of employment, health, or unforeseen circumstances. If a safe harbor described in this section does not apply, a sale or exchange is by reason of a change in place of employment, health, or unforeseen circumstances only if the primary reason for the sale or exchange is a change in place of employment (within the meaning of paragraph (c) of this section), health (within the meaning of paragraph (d) of this section), or unforeseen circumstances (within the meaning of paragraph (e) of this section). Whether the requirements of this section are satisfied depends upon all the facts and circumstances. Factors that may be relevant in determining the taxpayer's primary reason for the sale or exchange include (but are not limited to) the extent to which—

(1) The sale or exchange and the circumstances giving rise to the sale or exchange are proximate in time;

(2) The suitability of the property as the taxpayer's principal residence materially changes;

(3) The taxpayer's financial ability to maintain the property is materially impaired;

(4) The taxpayer uses the property as the taxpayer's residence during the period of the taxpayer's ownership of the property;

(5) The circumstances giving rise to the sale or exchange are not reasonably foreseeable when the taxpayer begins using the property as the taxpayer's principal residence; and

(6) The circumstances giving rise to the sale or exchange occur during the period of the taxpayer's ownership and use of the property as the taxpayer's principal residence.

(c) Sale or exchange by reason of a change in place of employment—(1) In general. A sale or exchange is by reason of a change in place of employment if, in the case of a qualified individual described in paragraph (f) of this section, the primary reason for the sale or exchange is a change in the location of the individual's employment.

(2) Distance safe harbor. A sale or exchange is deemed to be by reason of a change in place of employment (within the meaning of paragraph (c)(1) of this section) if—

(i) The change in place of employment occurs during the period of the taxpayer's ownership and use of the property as the taxpayer's principal residence; and

(ii) The qualified individual's new place of employment is at least 50 miles farther from the residence sold or exchanged than was the former place of employment, or, if there was no former place of employment, the distance between the qualified individual's new place of employment and the residence sold or exchanged is at least 50 miles.

(3) Employment. For purposes of this paragraph (c), employment includes the commencement of employment with a new employer, the continuation of employment with the same employer, and the commencement or continuation of self-employment.

(4) Examples. The following examples illustrate the rules of this paragraph (c):

Example 1. A is unemployed and owns a townhouse that she has owned and used as her principal residence since 2003. In 2004 A obtains a job that is 54 miles from her townhouse, and she sells the townhouse. Because the distance between A's new place of employment and the townhouse is at least 50 miles, the sale is within the safe harbor of paragraph (c)(2) of this section and A is entitled to claim a reduced maximum exclusion under section 121(c)(2).

Example 2. B is an officer in the United States Air Force stationed in Florida. B purchases a house in Florida in 2002. In May 2003 B moves out of his house to take a 3–year assignment in Germany. B sells his house in January 2004. Because B's new place of employment in Germany is at least 50 miles farther from the residence sold than is B's former place of employment in Florida, the sale is within the safe harbor of paragraph (c)(2) of this section and B is entitled to claim a reduced maximum exclusion under section 121(c)(2).

Example 3. C is employed by Employer R at R's Philadelphia office. C purchases a house in February 2002 that is 35 miles from R's Philadelphia office. In May 2003 C begins a temporary assignment at R's Wilmington office that is 72 miles from C's house, and moves out of the house. In June 2005 C is assigned to work in R's London office. C sells her house in August 2005 as a result of the assignment to London. The sale of the house is not within the safe harbor of paragraph (c)(2) of this section by reason of the change in place of employment from Philadelphia to Wilmington because the Wilmington office is not 50 miles farther from C's house than is the Philadelphia office. Furthermore, the sale is not within the safe harbor by reason of the change in place of employment to London because C is not using the house as her principal residence when she moves to London. However, C is entitled to claim a reduced maximum exclusion under section 121(c)(2) because, under the facts and circumstances, the primary reason for the sale is the change in C's place of employment.

Example 4. In July 2003 D, who works as an emergency medicine physician, buys a condominium that is 5 miles from her place of employment and uses it as her principal residence. In February 2004, D obtains a job that is located 51 miles from D's condominium. D may be called in to work unscheduled hours and, when called, must be able to arrive at work quickly. Because of the demands of the new job, D sells her condominium and buys a townhouse that is 4 miles from her new place of employment. Because D's new place of employment is only 46 miles farther from the condominium than is D's former place of employment, the sale is not within the safe harbor of paragraph (c)(2) of this section. However, D is entitled to claim a reduced maximum exclusion under section 121(c)(2) because, under the facts and circumstances, the primary reason for the sale is the change in D's place of employment.

(d) Sale or exchange by reason of health—(1) In general. A sale or exchange is by reason of health if the primary reason for the sale or exchange is to obtain, provide, or facilitate the diagnosis, cure, mitigation, or treatment of disease, illness, or injury of a qualified individual described in paragraph (f) of this section, or to obtain or provide medical or personal care for a qualified individual suffering from a disease, illness, or injury. A sale or exchange that is merely beneficial to the general health or well-being of an individual is not a sale or exchange by reason of health.

(2) Physician's recommendation safe harbor. A sale or exchange is deemed to be by reason of health if a physician (as defined in section 213(d)(4)) recommends a change of residence for reasons of health (as defined in paragraph (d)(1) of this section).

(3) Examples. The following examples illustrate the rules of this paragraph (d):

Example 1. In 2003 A buys a house that she uses as her principal residence. A is injured in an accident and is unable to care for herself. A sells her house in 2004 and moves in with her daughter so that the daughter can provide the care that A requires as a result of her injury. Because, under the facts and circumstances, the primary reason for the sale of A's house is A's health, A is entitled to claim a reduced maximum exclusion under section 121(c)(2).

Example 2. H's father has a chronic disease. In 2003 H and W purchase a house that they use as their principal residence. In 2004 H and W sell their house in order to move into the house of H's father so that they can provide the care he requires as a result of his disease. Because, under the facts and circumstances, the primary reason for the sale of their house is the health of H's father, H and W are entitled to claim a reduced maximum exclusion under section 121(c)(2).

Example 3. H and W purchase a house in 2003 that they use as their principal residence. Their son suffers from a chronic illness that requires regular medical care. Later that year their son begins a new treatment that is available at a hospital 100 miles away from their residence. In 2004 H and W sell their house so that they can be closer to the hospital to facilitate their son's treatment. Because, under the facts and circumstances, the primary reason for the sale is to facilitate the treatment of their son's chronic illness, H and W are entitled to claim a reduced maximum exclusion under section 121(c)(2).

Example 4. B, who has chronic asthma, purchases a house in Minnesota in 2003 that he uses as his principal residence. B's doctor tells B that moving to a warm, dry climate would mitigate B's asthma symptoms. In 2004 B sells his house and moves to Arizona to relieve his asthma symptoms. The sale is within the safe harbor of paragraph (d)(2) of this section and B is entitled to claim a reduced maximum exclusion under section 121(c)(2).

Example 5. In 2003 H and W purchase a house in Michigan that they use as their principal residence. H's doctor tells H that he should get more outdoor exercise, but H is not suffering from any disease that can be treated or mitigated by outdoor exercise. In 2004 H and W sell their house and move to Florida so that H can increase his general level of exercise by playing golf year-round. Because the sale of the house is merely beneficial to H's general health, the sale of the house is not by reason of H's health. H and W are not entitled to claim a reduced maximum exclusion under section 121(c)(2).

(e) Sale or exchange by reason of unforeseen circumstances—(1) In general. A sale or exchange is by reason of unforeseen circumstances if the primary reason for the sale or exchange is the occurrence of an event that the taxpayer could not reasonably have anticipated before purchasing and occupying the residence. A sale or exchange by reason of unforeseen circumstances (other than a sale or exchange deemed to be by reason of unforeseen circumstances under paragraph (e)(2) or (3) of this section) does not qualify for the reduced maximum exclusion if the primary reason for the sale or exchange is a preference for a different residence or an improvement in financial circumstances.

(2) Specific event safe harbors. A sale or exchange is deemed to be by reason of unforeseen circumstances (within the meaning of paragraph (e)(1) of this section) if any of the events specified in paragraphs (e)(2)(i) through (iii) of this section occur during the period of the taxpayer's ownership and use of the residence as the taxpayer's principal residence:

(i) The involuntary conversion of the residence.

(ii) Natural or man-made disasters or acts of war or terrorism resulting in a casualty to the residence (without regard to deductibility under section 165(h)).

(iii) In the case of a qualified individual described in paragraph (f) of this section—

(A) Death;

(B) The cessation of employment as a result of which the qualified individual is eligible for unemployment compensation (as defined in section 85(b));

(C) A change in employment or self-employment status that results in the taxpayer's inability to pay housing costs and reasonable basic living expenses for the taxpayer's household (including amounts for food, clothing, medical expenses, taxes, transportation, court-ordered payments, and expenses reasonably necessary to the production of income, but not for the maintenance of an affluent or luxurious standard of living);

(D) Divorce or legal separation under a decree of divorce or separate maintenance; or

(E) Multiple births resulting from the same pregnancy.

(3) Designation of additional events as unforeseen circumstances. The Commissioner may designate other events or situations as unforeseen circumstances in published guidance of general applicability and may issue rulings addressed to specific taxpayers identifying other events or situations as unforeseen circumstances with regard to those taxpayers (see § 601.601(d)(2) of this chapter).

(4) Examples. The following examples illustrate the rules of this paragraph (e):

Example 1. In 2003 A buys a house in California. After A begins to use the house as her principal residence, an earthquake causes damage to A's house. A sells the house in 2004. The sale is within the safe harbor of paragraph (e)(2)(ii) of this section and A is entitled to claim a reduced maximum exclusion under section 121(c)(2).

Example 2. H works as a teacher and W works as a pilot. In 2003 H and W buy a house that they use as their principal residence. Later that year W is furloughed from her job for six months. H and W are unable to pay their mortgage and reasonable basic living expenses for their household during the period W is furloughed. H and W sell their house in 2004. The sale is within the safe harbor of paragraph (e)(2)(iii)(C) of this section and H and W are entitled to claim a reduced maximum exclusion under section 121(c)(2).

Example 3. In 2003 H and W buy a two-bedroom condominium that they use as their principal residence. In 2004 W gives birth to twins and H and W sell their condominium and buy a four-bedroom house. The sale is within the safe harbor of paragraph (e)(2)(iii)(E) of this section, and H and W are entitled to claim a reduced maximum exclusion under section 121(c)(2).

Example 4. In 2003 B buys a condominium in a high-rise building and uses it as his principal residence. B's monthly condominium fee is $X. Three months after B moves into the condominium, the condominium association replaces the building's roof and heating system. Six months later, B's monthly condominium fee doubles in order to pay for the repairs. B sells the condominium in 2004 because he is unable to afford the new condominium fee along with a monthly mortgage payment. The safe harbors of paragraph (e)(2) of this section do not apply. However, under the facts and circumstances, the primary reason for the sale, the doubling of the condominium fee, is an unforeseen circumstance because B could not reasonably have anticipated that the condominium fee would double at the time he purchased and occupied the property. Consequently, the sale of the condominium is by reason of unforeseen circumstances and B is entitled to claim a reduced maximum exclusion under section 121(c)(2).

Example 5. In 2003 C buys a house that he uses as his principal residence. The property is located on a heavily traveled road. C sells the property in 2004 because C is disturbed by the traffic. The safe harbors of paragraph (e)(2) of this section do not apply. Under the facts and circumstances, the primary reason for the sale, the traffic, is not an unforeseen circumstance because C could reasonably have anticipated the traffic at the time he purchased and occupied the house. Consequently, the sale of the house is not by reason of unforeseen circumstances and C is not entitled to claim a reduced maximum exclusion under section 121(c)(2).

Example 6. In 2003 D and her fiance E buy a house and live in it as their principal residence. In 2004 D and E cancel their wedding plans and E moves out of the house. Because D cannot afford to make the monthly mortgage payments alone, D and E sell the house in 2004. The safe harbors of paragraph (e)(2) of this section do not apply. However, under the facts and circumstances, the primary reason for the sale, the broken engagement, is an unforeseen circumstance because D and E could not reasonably have anticipated the broken engagement at the time they purchased and occupied the house. Consequently, the sale is by reason of unforeseen circumstances and D and E are each entitled to claim a reduced maximum exclusion under section 121(c)(2).

Example 7. In 2003 F buys a small condominium that she uses as her principal residence. In 2005 F receives a promotion and a large increase in her salary. F sells the condominium in 2004 and purchases a house because she can now afford the house. The safe harbors of paragraph (e)(2) of this section do not apply. Under the facts and circumstances, the primary reason for the sale of the house, F's salary increase, is an improvement in F's financial circumstances. Under paragraph (e)(1) of this section, an improvement in financial circumstances, even if the result of unforeseen circumstances, does not qualify for the reduced maximum exclusion by reason of unforeseen circumstances under section 121(c)(2).

Example 8. In April 2003 G buys a house that he uses as his principal residence. G sells his house in October 2004 because the house has greatly appreciated in value, mortgage rates have substantially decreased, and G can afford a bigger house. The safe harbors of paragraph (e)(2) of this section do not apply. Under the facts and circumstances, the primary reasons for the sale of the house, the changes in G's house value and in the mortgage rates, are an improvement in G's financial circumstances. Under paragraph (e)(1) of this section, an improvement in financial circumstances, even if the result of unforeseen circumstances, does not qualify for the reduced maximum exclusion by reason of unforeseen circumstances under section 121(c)(2).

Example 9. H works as a police officer for City X. In 2003 H buys a condominium that he uses as his principal residence. In 2004 H is assigned to City X's K–9 unit and is required to care for the police service dog at his home. Because H's condominium association does not permit H to have a dog in his condominium, in 2004 he sells the condominium and buys a house. The safe harbors of paragraph (e)(2) of this section do not apply. However, under the facts and circumstances, the primary reason for the sale, H's assignment to the K–9 unit, is an unforeseen circumstance because H could not reasonably have anticipated his assignment to the K–9 unit at the time he purchased and occupied the condominium. Consequently, the sale of the condominium is by reason of unforeseen circumstances and H is entitled to claim a reduced maximum exclusion under section 121(c)(2).

Example 10. In 2003, J buys a small house that she uses as her principal residence. After J wins the lottery, she sells the small house in 2004 and buys a bigger, more expensive house. The safe harbors of paragraph (e)(2) of this section do not apply. Under the facts and circumstances, the primary reason for the sale of the house, winning the lottery, is an improvement in J's financial circumstances. Under paragraph (e)(1) of this section, an improvement in financial circumstances, even if the result of unforeseen circumstances, does not qualify for the reduced maximum exclusion under section 121(c)(2).

(f) Qualified individual. For purposes of this section, qualified individual means—

(1) The taxpayer;

(2) The taxpayer's spouse;

(3) A co-owner of the residence;

(4) A person whose principal place of abode is in the same household as the taxpayer; or

(5) For purposes of paragraph (d) of this section, a person bearing a relationship specified in sections 152(a)(1) through 152(a)(8) (without regard to qualification as a dependent) to a qualified individual described in paragraphs (f)(1) through (4) of this section, or a descendant of the taxpayer's grandparent.

(g) Computation of reduced maximum exclusion. (1) The reduced maximum exclusion is computed by multiplying the maximum dollar limitation of $250,000 ($500,000 for certain joint filers) by a fraction. The numerator of the fraction is the shortest of the period of time that the taxpayer owned the property during the 5–year period ending on the date of the sale or exchange; the period of time that the taxpayer used the property as the taxpayer's principal residence during the 5–year period ending on the date of the sale or exchange; or the period of time between the date of a prior sale or exchange of property for which the taxpayer excluded gain under section 121 and the date of the current sale or exchange. The numerator of the fraction may be expressed in days or months. The denominator of the fraction is 730 days or 24 months (depending on the measure of time used in the numerator).

(2) Examples. The following examples illustrate the rules of this paragraph (g):

Example 1. Taxpayer A purchases a house that she uses as her principal residence. Twelve months after the purchase, A sells the house due to a change in place of her employment. A has not excluded gain under section 121 on a prior sale or exchange of property within the last 2 years. A is eligible to exclude up to $125,000 of the gain from the sale of her house (12/24 x $250,000).

Example 2. (i) Taxpayer H owns a house that he has used as his principal residence since 1996. On January 15, 1999, H and W marry and W begins to use H's house as her principal residence. On January 15, 2000, H sells the house due to a change in W's place of employment. Neither H nor W has excluded gain under section 121 on a prior sale or exchange of property within the last 2 years.

(ii) Because H and W have not each used the house as their principal residence for at least 2 years during the 5-year period preceding its sale, the maximum dollar limitation amount that may be claimed by H and W will not be $500,000, but the sum of each spouse's limitation amount determined on a separate basis as if they had not been married. (See § 1.121–2(a)(3)(ii).)

(iii) H is eligible to exclude up to $250,000 of gain because he meets the requirements of section 121. W is not eligible to exclude the maximum dollar limitation amount. Instead, because the sale of the house is due to a change in place of employment, W is eligible to claim a reduced maximum exclusion of up to $125,000 of the gain (365/730 x $250,000). Therefore, H and W are eligible to exclude up to $375,000 of gain ($250,000 + $125,000) from the sale of the house.

* * *

[T.D. 9030, 67 FR 78365, Dec. 24, 2002; T.D. 9152, 69 FR 50304, Aug. 16, 2004]

§ 1.121–4 Special rules.

(a) Property of deceased spouse—(1) In general. For purposes of satisfying the ownership and use requirements of section 121, a taxpayer is treated as owning and using property as the taxpayer's principal residence during any period that the taxpayer's deceased spouse owned and used the property as a principal residence before death if—

(i) The taxpayer's spouse is deceased on the date of the sale or exchange of the property; and

(ii) The taxpayer has not remarried at the time of the sale or exchange of the property.

(2) Example. The provisions of this paragraph (a) are illustrated by the following example. The example assumes that § 1.121–3 (relating to the reduced maximum exclusion) does not apply to the sale of the property. The example is as follows:

Example. Taxpayer H has owned and used a house as his principal residence since 1987. H and W marry on July 1, 1999 and from that date they use H's house as their principal residence. H dies on August 15, 2000, and W inherits the property. W sells the property on September 1, 2000, at which time she has not remarried. Although W has owned and used the house for less than 2 years, W will be considered to have satisfied the ownership and use requirements of section 121 because W's period of ownership and use includes the period that H owned and used the property before death.

(b) Property owned by spouse or former spouse—(1) Property transferred to individual from spouse or former spouse. If a taxpayer obtains property from a spouse or former spouse in a transaction described in section 1041(a), the period that the taxpayer owns the property will include the period that the spouse or former spouse owned the property.

(2) Property used by spouse or former spouse. A taxpayer is treated as using property as the taxpayer's principal residence for any period that the taxpayer has an ownership interest in the property and the taxpayer's spouse or former spouse is granted use of the property under a divorce or separation instrument (as defined in section 71(b)(2)), provided that the spouse or former spouse uses the property as his or her principal residence.

(c) Tenant-stockholder in cooperative housing corporation. A taxpayer who holds stock as a tenant-stockholder in a cooperative housing corporation (as those terms are defined in sections 216(b)(1) and (2)) may be eligible to exclude gain under section 121 on the sale or exchange of the stock. In determining whether the taxpayer meets the requirements of section 121, the ownership requirements are applied to the holding of the stock and the use requirements are applied to the house or apartment that the taxpayer is entitled to occupy by reason of the taxpayer's stock ownership.

(d) Involuntary conversions—(1) In general. For purposes of section 121, the destruction, theft, seizure, requisition, or condemnation of property is treated as a sale of the property.

(2) Application of section 1033. In applying section 1033 (relating to involuntary conversions), the amount realized from the sale or exchange of property used as the taxpayer's principal residence is treated as being the amount determined without regard to section 121, reduced by the amount of gain excluded from the taxpayer's gross income under section 121.

(3) Property acquired after involuntary conversion. If the basis of the property acquired as a result of an involuntary conversion is determined (in whole or in part) under section 1033(b) (relating to the basis of property acquired through an involuntary conversion), then for purposes of satisfying the requirements of section 121, the taxpayer will be treated as owning and using the acquired property as the taxpayer's principal residence during any period of time that the taxpayer owned and used the converted property as the taxpayer's principal residence.

(4) Example. The provisions of this paragraph (d) are illustrated by the following example:

Example. (i) On February 18, 1999, fire destroys Taxpayer A's house which has an adjusted basis of $80,000. A had owned and used this property as her principal residence for 20 years prior to its destruction. A's insurance company pays A $400,000 for the house. A realizes a gain of $320,000 ($400,000—$80,000). On August 27, 1999, A purchases a new house at a cost of $100,000.

(ii) Because the destruction of the house is treated as a sale for purposes of section 121, A will exclude $250,000 of the realized gain from A's gross income. For purposes of section 1033, the amount realized is then treated as being $150,000 ($400,000—$250,000) and the gain realized is $70,000 ($150,000 amount realized—$80,000 basis). A elects under section 1033 to recognize only $50,000 of the gain ($150,000 amount realized—$100,000 cost of new house). The remaining $20,000 of gain is deferred and A's basis in the new house is $80,000 ($100,000 cost—$20,000 gain not recognized).

(iii) A will be treated as owning and using the new house as A's principal residence during the 20-year period that A owned and used the destroyed house.

(e) Sales or exchanges of partial interests—(1) Partial interests other than remainder interests—(i) In general. Except as provided in paragraph (e)(2) of this section (relating to sales or exchanges of remainder interests), a taxpayer may apply the section 121 exclusion to gain from the sale or exchange of an interest in the taxpayer's principal residence that is less than the taxpayer's entire interest if the interest sold or exchanged includes an interest in the dwelling unit. For rules relating to the sale or exchange of vacant land, see § 1.121–1(b)(3).

(ii) Limitations—(A) Maximum limitation amount. For purposes of section 121(b)(1) and (2) (relating to the maximum limitation amount of the section 121 exclusion), sales or exchanges of partial interests in the same principal residence are treated as one sale or exchange. Therefore, only one maximum limitation amount of $250,000 ($500,000 for certain joint returns) applies to the combined sales or exchanges of the partial interests. In applying the maximum limitation amount to sales or exchanges that occur in different taxable years, a taxpayer may exclude gain from the first sale or exchange of a partial interest up to the taxpayer's full maximum limitation amount and may exclude gain from the sale or exchange of any other partial interest in the same principal residence to the extent of any remaining maximum limitation amount, and each spouse is treated as excluding one-half of the gain from a sale or exchange to which section 121(b)(2)(A) and § 1.121–2(a)(3)(i)(relating to the limitation for certain joint returns) apply.

(B) Sale or exchange of more than one principal residence in 2-year period. For purposes of applying section 121(b)(3) (restricting the application of section 121 to only 1 sale or exchange every 2 years), each sale or exchange of a partial interest is disregarded with respect to other sales or exchanges of partial interests in the same principal residence, but is taken into account as of the date of the sale or exchange in applying section 121(b)(3) to that sale or exchange and the sale or exchange of any other principal residence.

(2) Sales or exchanges of remainder interests—(i) In general. A taxpayer may elect to apply the section 121 exclusion to gain from the sale or exchange of a remainder interest in the taxpayer's principal residence.

(ii) Limitations—(A) Sale or exchange of any other interest. If a taxpayer elects to exclude gain from the sale or exchange of a remainder interest in the taxpayer's principal residence, the section 121 exclusion will not apply to a sale or exchange of any other interest in the residence that is sold or exchanged separately.

(B) Sales or exchanges to related parties. This paragraph (e)(2) will not apply to a sale or exchange to any person that bears a relationship to the taxpayer that is described in section 267(b) or 707(b).

(iii) Election. The taxpayer makes the election under this paragraph (e)(2) by filing a return for the taxable year of the sale or exchange that does not include the gain from the sale or exchange of the remainder interest in the taxpayer's gross income. A taxpayer may make or revoke the election at any time before the expiration of a 3-year period beginning on the last date prescribed by law (determined without regard to extensions) for the filing of the return for the taxable year in which the sale or exchange occurred.

(3) Example. The provisions of this paragraph (e) are illustrated by the following example:

Example. In 1991 Taxpayer A buys a house that A uses as his principal residence. In 2004 A's friend B moves into A's house and A sells B a 50% interest in the house realizing a gain of $136,000. A may exclude the $136,000 of gain. In 2005 A sells his remaining 50% interest in the home to B realizing a gain of $138,000. A may exclude $114,000 ($250,000—$136,000 gain previously excluded) of the $138,000 gain from the sale of the remaining interest.

(f) No exclusion for expatriates. The section 121 exclusion will not apply to any sale or exchange by an individual if the provisions of section 877(a) (relating to the treatment of expatriates) applies to the individual.

(g) Election to have section not apply. A taxpayer may elect to have the section 121 exclusion not apply to a sale or exchange of property. The taxpayer makes the election by filing a return for the taxable year of the sale or exchange that includes the gain from the sale or exchange of the taxpayer's principal residence in the taxpayer's gross income. A taxpayer may make an election under this paragraph (g) to have section 121 not apply (or revoke an election to have section 121 not apply) at any time before the expiration of a 3–year period beginning on the last date prescribed by law (determined without regard to extensions) for the filing of the return for the taxable year in which the sale or exchange occurred.

(h) Residences acquired in rollovers under section 1034. If a taxpayer acquires property in a transaction that qualifies under section 1034 (section 1034 property) for the nonrecognition of gain realized on the sale or exchange of another property and later sells or exchanges such property, in determining the period of the taxpayer's ownership and use of the property under section 121 the taxpayer may include the periods that the taxpayer owned and used the section 1034 property as the taxpayer's principal residence (and each prior residence taken into account under section 1223(7) in determining the holding period of the section 1034 property).

(i) [Reserved].

(j) Election to apply regulations retroactively. Taxpayers who would otherwise qualify under §§ 1.121–1 through 1.121–4 to exclude gain from a sale or exchange of a principal residence before December 24, 2002 but on or after May 7, 1997, may elect to apply §§ 1.121–1 through 1.121–4 for any years for which the period of limitation under section 6511 has not expired. The taxpayer makes the election under this paragraph (j) by filing a return for the taxable year of the sale or exchange that does not include the gain from the sale or exchange of the taxpayer's principal residence in the taxpayer's gross income. Taxpayers who have filed a return for the taxable year of the sale or exchange may elect to apply the provisions of these regulations for any years for which the period of limitation under section 6511 has not expired by filing an amended return.

(k) Audit protection. The Internal Revenue Service will not challenge a taxpayer's position that a sale or exchange of a principal residence occurring before December 24, 2002 but on or after May 7, 1997, qualifies for the section 121 exclusion if the taxpayer has made a reasonable, good faith effort to comply with the requirements of section 121. Compliance with the provisions of the regulations project under section 121 (REG–105235–99 (2000–2 C.B. 447)) generally will be considered a reasonable, good faith effort to comply with the requirements of section 121.

* * *

[T.D.9030, 67 FR 78358, Dec. 24, 2002; 68 FR 6350, Feb. 7, 2003]

§ 1.132–1 Exclusion from gross income for certain fringe benefits.

* * *

(b) Definition of employee—(1) No-additional-cost services and qualified employee discounts. For purposes of section 132(a)(1) (relating to no-additional-cost services) and section 132(a)(2) (relating to qualified employee discounts), the term "employee" (with respect to a line of business of an employer) means—

(i) Any individual who is currently employed by the employer in the line of business,

(ii) Any individual who was formerly employed by the employer in the line of business and who separated from service with the employer in the line of business by reason of retirement or disability, and

(iii) Any widow or widower of an individual who died while employed by the employer in the line of business or who separated from service with the employer in the line of business by reason of retirement or disability.

For purposes of this paragraph (b)(1), any partner who performs services for a partnership is considered employed by the partnership. In addition, any use by the spouse or dependent child (as defined in paragraph (b)(5) of this section) of the employee will be treated as use by the employee. For purposes of section 132(a)(1) (relating to no-additional-cost services), any use of air transportation by a parent of an employee (determined without regard to section 132(f)(1)(B) and paragraph (b)(1)(iii) of this section) will be treated as use by the employee.

(2) Working condition fringes. For purposes of section 132(a)(3) (relating to working condition fringes), the term "employee" means—

(i) Any individual who is currently employed by the employer,

(ii) Any partner who performs services for the partnership,

(iii) Any director of the employer, and

(iv) Any independent contractor who performs services for the employer.

Notwithstanding anything in this paragraph (b)(2) to the contrary, an independent contractor who performs services for the employer cannot exclude the value of parking or the use of consumer goods provided pursuant to a product testing program under § 1.132–5(n); in addition, any director of the employer cannot exclude the value of the use of consumer goods provided pursuant to a product testing program under § 1.132–5(n).

(3) On-premises athletic facilities. For purposes of section 132(h)(5) (relating to on-premises athletic facilities), the term "employee" means—

(i) Any individual who is currently employed by the employer,

(ii) Any individual who was formerly employed by the employer and who separated from service with the employer by reason of retirement or disability, and

(iii) Any widow or widower of an individual who died while employed by the employer or who separated from service with the employer by reason of retirement or disability.

For purposes of this paragraph (b)(3), any partner who performs services for a partnership is considered employed by the partnership. In addition, any use by the spouse or dependent child (as defined in paragraph (b)(5) of this section) of the employee will be treated as use by the employee.

(4) De minimis fringes. For purposes of section 132(a)(4) (relating to de minimis fringes), the term "employee" means any recipient of a fringe benefit.

(5) Dependent child. The term "dependent child" means any son, stepson, daughter, or stepdaughter of the employee who is a dependent of the employee, or both of whose parents are deceased and who has not attained age 25. Any child to whom section 152(e) applies will be treated as the dependent of both parents.

* * *

(d) Customers not to include employees. For purposes of section 132 and the regulations thereunder, the term "customer" means any customer who is not an employee. However, the preceding sentence does not apply to section 132(c)(2) (relating to the gross profit percentage for determining a qualified employee discount). Thus, an employer that provides employee discounts cannot exclude sales made to employees in determining the aggregate sales to customers.

(e) Treatment of on-premises athletic facilities—(1) In general. Gross income does not include the value of any on-premises athletic facility provided by an employer to its employees. For purposes of section 132(h)(5) and this paragraph (e), the term "on-premises athletic facility" means any gym or other athletic facility (such as a pool, tennis court, or golf course)—

(i) Which is located on the premises of the employer,

(ii) Which is operated by the employer, and

(iii) Substantially all of the use of which during the calendar year is by employees of the employer, their spouses, and their dependent children.

For purposes of paragraph (e)(1)(iii) of this section, the term "dependent children" has the same meaning as the plural of the term "dependent child" in paragraph (b)(5) of this section. The exclusion of this paragraph (e) does not apply to any athletic facility if access to the facility is made available to the general public through the sale of memberships, the rental of the facility, or a similar arrangement.

(2) Premises of the employer. The athletic facility need not be located on the employer's business premises. However, the athletic facility must be located on premises of the employer. The exclusion provided in this paragraph (e) applies whether the premises are owned or leased by the employer; in addition, the exclusion is available even if the employer is not a named lessee on the lease so long as the employer pays reasonable rent. The exclusion provided in this paragraph (e) does not apply to any athletic facility that is a facility for residential use. Thus, for example, a resort with accompanying athletic facilities (such as tennis courts, pool, and gym) would not qualify for the exclusion provided in this paragraph (e). An athletic facility is considered to be located on the employer's premises if the facility is located on the premises of a voluntary employees' beneficiary association funded by the employer.

(3) Application of rules to membership in an athletic facility. The exclusion provided in this paragraph (e) does not apply to any membership in an athletic facility (including health clubs or country clubs) unless the facility is owned (or leased) and operated by the employer and substantially all the use of the facility is by employees of the employer, their spouses, and their dependent children. Therefore, membership in a health club or country club not meeting the rules provided in this paragraph (e) would not qualify for the exclusion.

(4) Operation by the employer. An employer is considered to operate the athletic facility if the employer operates the facility through its own employees, or if the employer contracts out to another to operate the athletic facility. For example, if an employer hires an independent contractor to operate the athletic facility for the employer's employees, the facility is considered to be operated by the employer. In addition, if an athletic facility is operated by more than one employer, it is considered to be operated by each employer. For purposes of paragraph (e)(1)(iii) of this section, substantially all of the use of a facility that is operated by more than one employer must be by employees of the various employers, their spouses, and their dependent children. Where the facility is operated by more than one employer, an employer that pays rent either directly to the owner of the premises or to a sublessor of the premises is eligible for the exclusion. If an athletic facility is operated by a voluntary employees' beneficiary association funded by an employer, the employer is considered to operate the facility.

(5) Nonapplicability of nondiscrimination rules. The nondiscrimination rules of section 132 and § 1.132–8 do not apply to on-premises athletic facilities.

(f) Nonapplicability of section 132 in certain cases—(1) Tax treatment provided for in another section. If the tax treatment or a particular fringe benefit is expressly provided for in another section of Chapter 1 of the Internal Revenue Code of 1986, section 132 and the applicable regulations (except for section 132(e) and the regulations thereunder) do not apply to such fringe benefit. For example, because section 129 provides an exclusion from gross income for amounts paid or incurred by an employer for dependent care assistance for an employee, the exclusions under section 132 and this section do not apply to the provision by an employer to an employee of dependent care assistance. Similarly, because section 117(d) applies to tuition reductions, the exclusions under section 132 do not apply to free or discounted tuition provided to an employee by an organization operated by the employer, whether the tuition is for study at or below the graduate level. Of course, if the amounts paid by the employer are for education relating to the employee's trade or business of being an employee of the employer so that, if the employee paid for the education, the amount paid could be deducted under section 162, the costs of the education may be eligible for exclusion as a working condition fringe.

(2) Limited statutory exclusions. If another section of Chapter 1 of the Internal Revenue Code of 1986 provides an exclusion from gross income based on the cost of the benefit provided to the employee and such exclusion is a limited amount, section 132 and the regulations thereunder may apply to the extent the cost of the benefit exceeds the statutory exclusion.

* * *

[T.D. 8256, 54 FR 28601, July 6, 1989; T.D. 8457, 57 FR 62196, Dec. 30, 1992; 58 FR 7296, Feb. 5, 1993]

§ 1.132–2 No-additional-cost services.

(a) In general—(1) Definition. Gross income does not include the value of a no-additional-cost service. A "no-additional-cost service" is any service provided by an employer to an employee for the employee's personal use if—

(i) The service is offered for sale by the employer to its customers in the ordinary course of the line of business of the employer in which the employee performs substantial services, and

(ii) The employer incurs no substantial additional cost in providing the service to the employee (including foregone revenue and excluding any amount paid by or on behalf of the employee for the service).

For rules relating to the line of business limitation, see § 1.132–4. For purposes of this section, a service will not be considered to be offered for sale by the employer to its customers if that service is primarily provided to employees and not to the employer's customers.

(2) Excess capacity services. Services that are eligible for treatment as no-additional-cost services include excess capacity services such as hotel accommodations; transportation by aircraft, train, bus, subway, or cruise line; and telephone services. Services that are not eligible for treatment as no-additional-cost services are non-excess capacity services such as the facilitation by a stock brokerage firm of the purchase of stock. Employees who receive non-excess capacity services may, however, be eligible for a qualified employee discount of up to 20 percent of the value of the service provided. See § 1.132–3.

(3) Cash rebates. The exclusion for a no-additional-cost service applies whether the service is provided at no charge or at a reduced price. The exclusion also applies if the benefit is provided through a partial or total cash rebate of an amount paid for the service.

(4) Applicability of nondiscrimination rules. The exclusion for a no-additional-cost service applies to highly compensated employees only if the service is available on substantially the same terms to each member of a group of employees that is defined under a reasonable classification set up by the employer that does not discriminate in favor of highly compensated employees. See § 1.132–8.

(5) No substantial additional cost—(i) In general. The exclusion for a no-additional-cost service applies only if the employer does not incur substantial additional cost in providing the service to the employee. For purposes of the preceding sentence, the term "cost" includes revenue that is forgone because the service is provided to an employee rather than a nonemployee. (For purposes of determining whether any revenue is forgone, it is assumed that the employee would not have purchased the service unless it were available to the employee at the actual price charged to the employee.) Whether an employer incurs substantial additional cost must be determined without regard to any amount paid by the employee for the service. Thus, any reimbursement by the employee for the cost of providing the service does not affect the determination of whether the employer incurs substantial additional cost.

(ii) Labor intensive services. An employer must include the cost of labor incurred in providing services to employees when determining whether the employer has incurred substantial additional cost. An employer incurs substantial additional cost, whether non-labor costs are incurred, if a substantial amount of time is spent by the employer or its employees in providing the service to employees. This would be the result whether the time spent by the employer or its employees in providing the services would have been "idle," or if the services were provided outside normal business hours. An employer generally incurs no substantial additional cost, however, if the services provided to the employee are merely incidental to the primary service being provided by the employer. For example, the in-flight services of a flight attendant and the cost of in-flight meals provided to airline employees traveling on a space-available basis are merely incidental to the primary service being provided (i.e., air transportation). Similarly, maid service provided to hotel employees renting hotel rooms on a space-available basis is merely incidental to the primary service being provided (i.e., hotel accommodations).

* * *

(b) Reciprocal agreements. For purposes of the exclusion from gross income for a no-additional-cost service, an exclusion is available to an employee of one employer for a no-additional-cost service provided by an unrelated employer only if all of the following requirements are satisfied—

(1) The service provided to such employee by the unrelated employer is the same type of service generally provided to nonemployee customers by both the line of business in which the employee works and the line of business in which the service is provided to such employee (so that the employee would be permitted to exclude from gross income the value of the service if such service were provided directly by the employee's employer);

(2) Both employers are parties to a written reciprocal agreement under which a group of employees of each employer, all of whom perform substantial services in the same line of business, may receive no-additional-cost services from the other employer; and

(3) Neither employer incurs any substantial additional cost (including forgone revenue) in providing such service to the employees of the other employer, or pursuant to such agreement. If one employer receives a substantial payment from the other employer with respect to the reciprocal agreement, the paying employer will be considered to have incurred a substantial additional cost pursuant to the agreement, and consequently services performed under the reciprocal agreement will not qualify for exclusion as no-additional-cost services.

(c) Example. The rules of this section are illustrated by the following example:

Example. Assume that a commercial airline permits its employees to take personal flights on the airline at no charge and receive reserved seating. Because the employer foregoes potential revenue by permitting the employees to reserve seats, employees receiving such free flights are not eligible for the no-additional-cost exclusion.

[T.D. 8256, 54 FR 28602, July 6, 1989]

§ 1.132–3 Qualified employee discounts.

(a) In general—(1) Definition. Gross income does not include the value of a qualified employee discount. A "qualified employee discount" is any employee discount with respect to qualified property or services provided by an employer to an employee for use by the employee to the extent the discount does not exceed—

(i) The gross profit percentage multiplied by the price at which the property is offered to customers in the ordinary course of the employer's line of business, for discounts on property, or

(ii) Twenty percent of the price at which the service is offered to customers, for discounts on services.

(2) Qualified property or services—(i) In general. The term "qualified property or services" means any property or services that are offered for sale to customers in the ordinary course of the line of business of the employer in which the employee performs substantial services. For rules relating to the line of business limitation, see § 1.132–4.

(ii) Exception for certain property. The term "qualified property" does not include real property and it does not include personal property (whether tangible or intangible) of a kind commonly held for investment. Thus, an employee may not exclude from gross income the amount of an employee discount provided on the purchase of securities, commodities, or currency, or of either residential or commercial real estate, whether or not the particular purchase is made for investment purposes.

(iii) Property and services not offered in ordinary course of business. The term "qualified property or services" does not include any property or services of a kind that is not offered for sale to customers in the ordinary course of the line of business of the employer. For example, employee discounts provided on property or services that are offered for sale primarily to employees and their families (such as merchandise sold at an employee store or through an employer-provided catalog service) may not be excluded from gross income. For rules relating to employer-operated eating facilities, see § 1.132–7, and for rules relating to employer-operated on-premises athletic facilities, see § 1.132–1(e).

(3) No reciprocal agreement exception. The exclusion for a qualified employee discount does not apply to property or services provided by another employer pursuant to a written reciprocal agreement that exists between employers to provide discounts on property and services to employees of the other employer.

(4) Property or services provided without charge, at a reduced price, or by rebates. The exclusion for a qualified employee discount applies whether the property or service is provided at no charge (in which case only part of the discount may be excludable as a qualified employee discount) or at a reduced price. The exclusion also applies if the benefit is provided through a partial or total cash rebate of an amount paid for the property or service.

(5) Property or services provided directly by the employer or indirectly through a third party. A qualified employee discount may be provided either directly by the employer or indirectly through a third party. For example, an employee of an appliance manufacturer may receive a qualified employee discount on the manufacturer's appliances purchased at a retail store that offers such appliances for sale to customers. The employee may exclude the amount of the qualified employee discount whether the employee is provided the appliance at no charge or purchases it at a reduced price, or whether the employee receives a partial or total cash rebate from either the employer-manufacturer or the retailer. If an employee receives additional rights associated with the property that are not provided by the employee's employer to customers in the ordinary course of the line of business in which the employee performs substantial services (such as the right to return or exchange the property or special warranty rights), the employee may only receive a qualified employee discount with respect to the property and not the additional rights. Receipt of such additional rights may occur, for example, when an employee of a manufacturer purchases property manufactured by the employee's employer at a retail outlet.

(6) Applicability of nondiscrimination rules. The exclusion for a qualified employee discount applies to highly compensated employees only if the discount is available on substantially the same terms to each member of a group of employees that is defined under a reasonable classification set up by the employer that does not discriminate in favor of highly compensated employees. See § 1.132–8.

(b) Employee discount—(1) Definition. The term "employee discount" means the excess of—

(i) The price at which the property or service is being offered by the employer for sale to customers, over

(ii) The price at which the property or service is provided by the employer to an employee for use by the employee. A transfer of property by an employee without consideration is treated as use by the employee for purposes of this section. Thus, for example, if an employee receives a discount on property offered for sale by his employer to customers and the employee makes a gift of the property to his parent, the property will be considered to be provided for use by the employee; thus, the discount will be eligible for exclusion as a qualified employee discount.

(2) Price to customers—(i) Determined at time of sale. In determining the amount of an employee discount, the price at which the property or service is being offered to customers at the time of the employee's purchase is controlling. For example, assume that an employer offers a product to customers for $20 during the first six months of a calendar year, but at the time the employee purchases the product at a discount, the price at which the product is being offered to customers is $25. In this case, the price from which the employee discount is measured is $25. Assume instead that, at the time the employee purchases the product at a discount, the price at which the product is being offered to customers is $15 and the price charged the employee is $12. The employee discount is measured from $15, the price at which the product is offered for sale to customers at the time of the employee purchase. Thus, the employee discount is $15 − $12, or $3.

(ii) Quantity discount not reflected. The price at which a property or service is being offered to customers cannot reflect any quantity discount unless the employee actually purchases the requisite quantity of the property or service.

(iii) Price to employer's customers controls. In determining the amount of an employee discount, the price at which a property or service is offered to customers of the employee's employer is controlling. Thus, the price at which the property is sold to the wholesale customers of a manufacturer will generally be lower than the price at which the same property is sold to the customers of a retailer. However, see paragraph (a)(5) of this section regarding the effect of a wholesaler providing to its employees additional rights not provided to customers of the wholesaler in the ordinary course of its business.

(iv) Discounts to discrete customer or consumer groups. Subject to paragraph (2)(ii) of this section, if an employer offers for sale property or services at one or more discounted prices to discrete customer or consumer groups, and sales at all such discounted prices comprise at least 35 percent of the employer's gross sales for a representative period, then in determining the amount of an employee discount, the price at which such property or service is being offered to customers for purposes of this section is a discounted price. The applicable discounted price is the current undiscounted price, reduced by the percentage discount at which the greatest percentage of the employer's discounted gross sales are made for such representative period. If sales at different percentage discounts equal the same percentage of the employer's gross sales, the price at which the property or service is being provided to customers may be reduced by the average of the discounts offered to each of the two groups. For purposes of this section, a representative period is the taxable year of the employer immediately preceding the taxable year in which the property or service is provided to the employee at a discount. If more than one employer would be aggregated under section 414(b), (c), (m), or (*o*), and not all of the employers have the same taxable year, the employers required to be aggregated must designate the 12–month period to be used in determining gross sales for a representative period. The 12–month period designated, however, must be used on a consistent basis.

(v) Examples. The rules provided in this paragraph (b)(2) are illustrated by the following examples:

Example (1). Assume that a wholesale employer offers property for sale to two discrete customer groups at differing prices. Assume further that during the prior taxable year of the employer, 70 percent of the employer's gross sales are made at a 15 percent discount and 30 percent at no discount. For purposes of this paragraph (b)(2), the current undiscounted price at which the property or service is being offered by the employer for sale to customers may be reduced by the 15 percent discount.

Example (2). Assume that a retail employer offers a 20 percent discount to members of the American Bar Association, a 15 percent discount to members of the American Medical Association, and a ten percent discount to employees of the Federal Government. Assume further that during the prior taxable year of the employer, sales to American Bar Association members equal 15 percent of the employer's gross sales, sales to American Medical Association members equal 20 percent of the employer's gross sales, and sales to Federal Government employees equal 25 percent of the employer's gross sales. For purposes of this paragraph (b)(2), the current undiscounted price at which the property or service is being offered by the employer for sale to customers may be reduced by the ten percent Federal Government discount.

(3) Damaged, distressed, or returned goods. If an employee pays at least fair market value for damaged, distressed, or returned property, such employee will not have income attributable to such purchase.

(c) Gross profit percentage—(1) In general—(i) General rule. An exclusion from gross income for an employee discount on qualified property is limited to the price at which the property is being offered to customers in the ordinary course of the employer's line of business, multiplied by the employer's gross profit percentage. The term "gross profit percentage" means the excess of the aggregate sales price of the property sold by the employer to customers (including employees) over the employer's aggregate cost of the property, then divided by the aggregate sales price.

(ii) Calculation of gross profit percentage. The gross profit percentage must be calculated separately for each line of business based on the aggregate sales price and aggregate cost of property in that line of business for a representative period. For purposes of this section, a representative period is the taxable year of the employer immediately preceding the taxable year in which the discount is available. For example, if the aggregate amount of sales of property in an employer's line of business for the prior taxable year was $800,000, and the aggregate cost of the property for the year was $600,000, the gross profit percentage would be 25 percent ($800,000 minus $600,000, then divided by $800,000). If two or more employers are required to aggregate under section 414(b), (c), (m), or (*o*) (aggregated employer), and if all of the aggregated employers do not share the same taxable year, then the aggregated employers must designate the 12–month period to be used in determining the gross profit percentage. The 12–month period designated, however, must be used on a consistent basis. If an employee performs substantial services in more than one line of business, the gross profit percentage of the line of business in which the property is sold determines the amount of the excludable employee discount.

(iii) Special rule for employers in their first year of existence. An employer in its first year of existence may estimate the gross profit percentage of a line of business based on its mark-up from cost. Alternatively, an employer in its first year of existence may determine the gross profit percentage by reference to an appropriate industry average.

(iv) Redetermination of gross profit percentage. If substantial changes in an employer's business indicate at any time that it is inappropriate for the prior year's gross profit percentage to be used for the current year, the employer must, within a reasonable period, redetermine the gross profit percentage for the remaining portion of the current year as if such portion of the year were the first year of the employer's existence.

(2) Line of business. In general, an employer must determine the gross profit percentage on the basis of all property offered to customers (including employees) in each separate line of business. An employer may instead select a classification of property that is narrower than the applicable line of business. However, the classification must be reasonable. For example, if an employer computes gross profit percentage according to the department in which products are sold, such classification is reasonable. Similarly, it is reasonable to compute gross profit percentage on the basis of the type of merchandise sold (such as high mark-up and low mark-up classifications). It is not reasonable, however, for an employer to classify certain low mark-up products preferred by certain employees (such as highly compensated employees) with high mark-up products or to classify certain high mark-up products preferred by other employees with low mark-up products.

(3) Generally accepted accounting principles. In general, the aggregate sales price of property must be determined in accordance with generally accepted accounting principles. An employer must compute the aggregate cost of property in the same manner in which it is computed for the employer's Federal income tax liability; thus, for example, section 263A and the regulations thereunder apply in determining the cost of property.

* * *

(e) Excess discounts. Unless excludable under a provision of the Internal Revenue Code of 1986 other than section 132(a)(2), an employee discount provided on property is excludable to the extent of the gross profit percentage multiplied by the price at which the property is being offered for sale to customers. If an employee discount exceeds the gross profit percentage, the excess discount is includible in the employee's income. For example, if the discount on employer-purchased property is 30 percent and the employer's gross profit percentage for the period in the relevant line of business is 25 percent, then 5 percent of the price at which the property is being offered for sale to customers is includible in the employee's income. With respect to services, an employee discount of up to 20 percent may be excludable. If an employee discount exceeds 20 percent, the excess discount is includible in the employee's income. For example, assume that a commercial airline provides a pass to each of its employees permitting the employees to obtain a free round-trip coach ticket with a confirmed seat to any destination the airline services. Neither the exclusion of section 132(a)(1) (relating to no-additional-cost services) nor any other statutory exclusion applies to a flight taken primarily for personal purposes by an employee under this program.

However, an employee discount of up to 20 percent may be excluded as a qualified employee discount. Thus, if the price charged to customers for the flight taken is $300 (under restrictions comparable to those actually placed on travel associated with the employee airline ticket), $60 is excludible from gross income as a qualified employee discount and $240 is includible in gross income.

[T.D. 8256, 54 FR 28603, July 6, 1989]

§ 1.132–4 Line of business limitation.

(a) In general—(1) Applicability—(i) General rule. A no-additional-cost service or a qualified employee discount provided to an employee is only available with respect to property or services that are offered for sale to customers in the ordinary course of the same line of business in which the employee receiving the property or service performs substantial services. Thus, an employee who does not perform substantial services in a particular line of business of the employer may not exclude from income under section 132(a)(1) or (a)(2) the value of services or employee discounts received on property or services in that line of business. For rules that relax the line of business requirement, see paragraphs (b) through (g) of this section.

(ii) Property and services sold to employees rather than customers. Because the property or services must be offered for sale to customers in the ordinary course of the same line of business in which the employee performs substantial services, the line of business limitation is not satisfied if the employer's products or services are sold primarily to employees of the employer, rather than to customers. Thus, for example, an employer in the banking line of business is not considered in the variety store line of business if the employer establishes an employee store that offers variety store items for sale to the employer's employees. See § 1.132–7 for rules relating to employer-operated eating facilities, and see § 1.132–1(e) for rules relating to employer-operated on-premises athletic facilities.

(iii) Performance of substantial services in more than one line of business. An employee who performs services in more than one of the employer's lines of business may only exclude no-additional-cost services and qualified employee discounts in the lines of business in which the employee performs substantial services.

(iv) Performance of services that directly benefit more than one line of business—(A) In general. An employee who performs substantial services that directly benefit more than one line of business of an employer is treated as performing substantial services in all such lines of business. For example, an employee who maintains accounting records for an employer's three lines of business may receive qualified employee discounts in all three lines of business. Similarly, if an employee of a minor line of business of an employer that is significantly interrelated with a major line of business of the employer performs substantial services that directly benefit both the major and the minor lines of business, the employee is treated as performing substantial services for both the major and the minor lines of business.

(B) Examples. The rules provided in this paragraph (a)(1)(iv) are illustrated by the following examples:

Example (1). Assume that employees of units of an employer provide repair or financing services, or sell by catalog, with respect to retail merchandise sold by the employer. Such employees may be considered to perform substantial services for the retail merchandise line of business under paragraph (a)(1)(iv)(A) of this section.

Example (2). Assume that an employer operates a hospital and a laundry service. Assume further that some of the gross receipts of the laundry service line of business are from laundry services sold to customers other than the hospital employer. Only the employees of the laundry service who perform substantial services which directly benefit the hospital line of business (through the provision of laundry services to the hospital) will be treated as performing substantial services for the hospital line of business. Other employees of the laundry service line of business will not be treated as employees of the hospital line of business.

Example (3). Assume the same facts as in example (2), except that the employer also operates a chain of dry cleaning stores. Employees who perform substantial services which directly benefit the dry cleaning stores but who do not perform substantial services that directly benefit the hospital line of business will not be treated as performing substantial services for the hospital line of business.

(2) Definition—(i) In general. An employer's line of business is determined by reference to the Enterprise Standard Industrial Classification Manual (ESIC Manual) prepared by the Statistical Policy Division of the U.S. Office of Management and Budget. An employer is considered to have more than one line of business if the employer offers for sale to customers property or services in more than one two-digit code classification referred to in the ESIC Manual.

(ii) Examples. Examples of two-digit classifications are general retail merchandise stores; hotels and other lodging places; auto repair, services, and garages; and food stores.

(3) Aggregation of two-digit classifications. If, pursuant to paragraph (a)(2) of this section, an employer has more than one line of business, such lines of business will be treated as a single line of business where and to the extent that one or more of the following aggregation rules apply:

(i) If it is uncommon in the industry of the employer for any of the separate lines of business of the employer to be operated without the others, the separate lines of business are treated as one line of business.

(ii) If it is common for a substantial number of employees (other than those employees who work at the headquarters or main office of the employer) to perform substantial services for more than one line of business of the employer, so that determination of which employees perform substantial services for which line or lines of business would be difficult, then the separate lines of business of the employer in which such employees perform substantial services are treated as one line of business. For example, assume that an employer operates a delicatessen with an attached service counter at which food is sold for consumption on the premises. Assume further that most but not all employees work both at the delicatessen and at the service counter. Under the aggregation rule of this paragraph (a)(3)(ii), the delicatessen and the service counter are treated as one line of business.

(iii) If the retail operations of an employer that are located on the same premises are in separate lines of business but would be considered to be within one line of business under paragraph (a)(2) of this section if the merchandise offered for sale in such lines of business were offered for sale at a department store, then the operations are treated as one line of business. For example, assume that on the same premises an employer sells both women's apparel and jewelry. Because, if sold together at a department store, the operations would be part of the same line of business, the operations are treated as one line of business.

* * *

(h) Line of business requirement does not expand benefits eligible for exclusion. The line of business requirement limits the benefits eligible for the no-additional-cost service and qualified employee discount exclusions to property or services provided by an employer to its customers in the ordinary course of the line of business of the employer in which the employee performs substantial services. The requirement is intended to ensure that employers do not offer, on a tax-free or reduced basis, property or services to employees that are not offered to the employer's customers, even if the property or services offered to the customers and the employees are within the same line of business (as defined in this section).

[T.D. 8256, 54 FR 28606, July 6, 1989]

§ 1.132–5 Working condition fringes.

(a) In general—(1) Definition. Gross income does not include the value of a working condition fringe. A "working condition fringe" is any property or service provided to an employee of an employer to the extent that, if the employee paid for the property or service, the amount paid would be allowable as a deduction under section 162 or 167.

(i) A service or property offered by an employer in connection with a flexible spending account is not excludable from gross income as a working condition fringe. For purposes of the preceding sentence, a flexible spending account is an agreement (whether or not written) entered into between an employer and an employee that makes available to the employee over a time period a certain level of unspecified non-cash benefits with a pre-determined cash value.

(ii) If, under section 274 or any other section, certain substantiation requirements must be met in order for a deduction under section 162 or 167 to be allowable, then those substantiation requirements apply when determining whether a property or service is excludable as a working condition fringe.

(iii) An amount that would be deductible by the employee under a section other than section 162 or 167, such as section 212, is not a working condition fringe.

(iv) A physical examination program provided by the employer is not excludable as a working condition fringe even if the value of such program might be deductible to the employee under section 213. The previous sentence applies without regard to whether the employer makes the program mandatory to some or all employees.

(v) A cash payment made by an employer to an employee will not qualify as a working condition fringe unless the employer requires the employee to—

(A) Use the payment for expenses in connection with a specific or pre-arranged activity or undertaking for which a deduction is allowable under section 162 or 167,

(B) Verify that the payment is actually used for such expenses, and

(C) Return to the employer any part of the payment not so used.

(vi) The limitation of section 67(a) (relating to the two-percent floor on miscellaneous itemized deductions) is not considered when determining the amount of a working condition fringe. For example, assume that an employer provides a $1,000 cash advance to Employee A and that the conditions of paragraph (a)(1)(v) of this section are not satisfied. Even to the extent A uses the allowance for expenses for which a deduction is allowable under sections 162 and 167, because such cash payment is not a working condition fringe, section 67(a) applies. The $1,000 payment is includible in A's gross income and subject to income and employment tax withholding. If, however, the conditions of paragraph (a)(1)(v) of this section are satisfied with respect to the payment, then the amount of A's working condition fringe is determined without regard to section 67(a). The $1,000 payment is excludible from A's gross income and not subject to income and employment tax reporting and withholding.

(2) Trade or business of the employee—(i) General. If the hypothetical payment for a property or service would be allowable as a deduction with respect to a trade or business of an employee other than the employee's trade or business of being an employee of the employer, it cannot be taken into account for purposes of determining the amount, if any, of the working condition fringe.

(ii) Examples. The rule of paragraph (a)(2)(i) of this section may be illustrated by the following examples:

Example (1). Assume that, unrelated to company X's trade or business and unrelated to employee A's trade or business of being an employee of company X, A is a member of the board of directors of company Y. Assume further that company X provides A with air transportation to a company Y board of director's meeting. A may not exclude from gross income the value of the air transportation to the meeting as a working condition fringe. A may, however, deduct such amount under section 162 if the section 162 requirements are satisfied. The result would be the same whether the air transportation was provided in the form of a flight on a commercial airline or a seat on a company X airplane.

Example (2). Assume the same facts as in example (1) except that A serves on the board of directors of company Z and company Z regularly purchases a significant amount of goods and services from company X. Because of the relationship between Company Z and A's employer, A's membership on Company Z's board of directors is related to A's trade or business of being an employee of Company X. Thus, A may exclude from gross income the value of air transportation to board meetings as a working condition fringe.

Example (3). Assume the same facts as in example (1) except that A serves on the board of directors of a charitable organization. Assume further that the service by A on the charity's board is substantially related to company X's trade or business. In this case, A may exclude from gross income the value of air transportation to board meetings as a working condition fringe.

Example (4). Assume the same facts as in example (3) except that company X also provides A with the use of a company X conference room which A uses for monthly meetings relating to the charitable organization. Also assume that A uses company X's copy machine and word processor each month in connection with functions of the charitable organization. Because of the substantial business benefit that company X derives from A's service on the board of the charity, A may exclude as a working condition fringe the value of the use of company X property in connection with the charitable organization.

(b) Vehicle allocation rules—(1) In general—(i) General rule. In general, with respect to an employer-provided vehicle, the amount excludable as a working condition fringe is the amount that would be allowable as a deduction under section 162 or 167 if the employee paid for the availability of the vehicle. For example, assume that the value of the availability of an employer-provided vehicle for a full year is $2,000, without regard to any working condition fringe (i.e., assuming all personal use). Assume further that the employee drives the vehicle 6,000 miles for his employer's business and 2,000 miles for reasons other than the employer's business. In this situation, the value of the working condition fringe is $2,000 multiplied by a fraction, the numerator of which is the business-use mileage (6,000 miles) and the denominator of which is the total mileage (8,000 miles). Thus, the value of the working condition fringe is $1,500. The total amount includible in the employee's gross income on account of the availability of the vehicle is $500 ($2,000 − $1,500). * * * Generally, when determining the amount of an employee's working condition fringe, miles accumulated on the vehicle by all employees of the employer during the period in which the vehicle is available to the employee are considered. For example, assume that during the year in which the vehicle is available to the employee in the above example, other employees accumulate 2,000 additional miles on the vehicle (while the employee is not in the automobile). In this case, the value of the working condition fringe is $2,000 multiplied by a fraction, the numerator of which is the business-use mileage by the employee (including all mileage (business and personal) accumulated by other employees) (8,000 miles) and the denominator of which is the total mileage (including all mileage accumulated by other employees) (10,000 miles). Thus, the value of the working condition fringe is $1,600; the total amount includible in the employee's gross income on account of the availability of the vehicle is $400 ($2,000 – $1,600). If, however, substantially all of the use of the automobile by other employees in the employer's business is limited to a certain period, such as the last three months of the year, the miles driven by the other employees during that period would not be considered when determining the employee's working condition fringe exclusion. Similarly, miles driven by other employees are not considered if the pattern of use of the employer-provided automobiles is designed to reduce Federal taxes. For example, assume that an employer provides employees A and B each with the availability of an employer-provided automobile and that A uses the automobile assigned to him 80 percent for the employer's business and that B uses the automobile assigned to him 30 percent for the employer's business. If A and B alternate the use of their assigned automobiles each week in such a way as to achieve a reduction in federal taxes, then the employer may count only miles placed on the automobile by the employee to whom the automobile is assigned when determining each employee's working condition fringe.

(ii) Use by an individual other than the employee. For purposes of this section, if the availability of a vehicle to an individual would be taxed to an employee, use of the vehicle by the individual is included in references to use by the employee.

(iii) Provision of an expensive vehicle for personal use. If an employer provides an employee with a vehicle that an employee may use in part for personal purposes, there is no working condition fringe exclusion with respect to the personal miles driven by the employee; if the employee paid for the availability of the vehicle, he would not be entitled to deduct under section 162 or 167 any part of the payment attributable to personal miles. The amount of the inclusion is not affected by the fact that the employee would have chosen the availability of a less expensive vehicle. Moreover, the result is the same even though the decision to provide an expensive rather than an inexpensive vehicle is made by the employer for bona fide noncompensatory business reasons.

* * *

(c) Applicability of substantiation requirements of sections 162 and 274(d)–(1) In general. The value of property or services provided to an employee may not be excluded from the employee's gross income as a working condition fringe, by either the employer or the employee, unless the applicable substantiation requirements of either section 274(d) or section 162 (whichever is applicable) and the regulations thereunder are satisfied. The substantiation requirements of section 274(d) apply to an employee even if the requirements of section 274 do not apply to the employee's employer for deduction purposes (such as when the employer is a tax-exempt organization or a governmental unit).

(2) Section 274(d) requirements. The substantiation requirements of section 274(d) are satisfied by "adequate records or sufficient evidence corroborating the [employee's] own statement". Therefore, such records or evidence provided by the employee, and relied upon by the employer to the extent permitted by the regulations promulgated under section 274(d), will be sufficient to substantiate a working condition fringe exclusion.

* * *

(s) Application of section 274(a)(3)—(1) In general. If an employer's deduction under section 162(a) for dues paid or incurred for membership in any club organized for business, pleasure, recreation, or other social purpose is disallowed by section 274(a)(3), the amount, if any, of an employee's working condition fringe benefit relating to an employer-provided membership in the club is determined without regard to the application of section 274(a) to the employee. To be excludible as a working condition fringe benefit, however, the amount must otherwise qualify for deduction by the employee under section 162(a). If an employer treats the amount paid or incurred for membership in any club organized for business, pleasure, recreation, or other social purpose as compensation under section 274(e)(2), then the expense is deductible by the employer as compensation and no amount may be excluded from the employee's gross income as a working condition fringe benefit. See § 1.274–2(f)(2)(iii)(A).

* * *

(3) Examples. The following examples illustrate this paragraph (s):

Example 1. Assume that Company X provides Employee B with a country club membership for which it paid $20,000. B substantiates, within the meaning of paragraph (c) of this section, that the club was used 40 percent for business purposes. The business use of the club (40 percent) may be considered a working condition fringe benefit, notwithstanding that the employer's deduction for the dues allocable to the business use is disallowed by section 274(a)(3), if X does not treat the club membership as compensation under section 274(e)(2). Thus, B may exclude from gross income $8,000 (40 percent of the club dues, which reflects B's business use). X must report $12,000 as wages subject to withholding and payment of employment taxes (60 percent of the value of the club dues, which reflects B's personal use). B must include $12,000 in gross income. X may deduct as compensation the amount it paid for the club dues which reflects B's personal use provided the amount satisfies the other requirements for a salary or compensation deduction under section 162.

Example 2. Assume the same facts as Example 1 except that Company X treats the $20,000 as compensation to B under section 274(e)(2). No portion of the $20,000 will be considered a working condition fringe benefit because the section 274(a)(3) disallowance will apply to B. Therefore, B must include $20,000 in gross income.

(t) Application of section 274(m)(3)—(1) In general. If an employer's deduction under section 162(a) for amounts paid or incurred for the travel expenses of a spouse, dependent, or other individual accompanying an employee is disallowed by section 274(m)(3), the amount, if any, of the employee's working condition fringe benefit relating to the employer-provided travel is determined without regard to the application of section 274(m)(3). To be excludible as a working condition fringe benefit, however, the amount must otherwise qualify for deduction by the employee under section 162(a). The amount will qualify for deduction and for exclusion as a working condition fringe benefit if it can be adequately shown that the spouse's, dependent's, or other accompanying individual's presence on the employee's business trip has a bona fide business purpose and if the employee substantiates the travel within the meaning of paragraph (c) of this section. If the travel does not qualify as a working condition fringe benefit, the employee must include in gross income as a fringe benefit the value of the employer's payment of travel expenses with respect to a spouse, dependent, or other individual accompanying the employee on business travel. See §§ 1.61–21(a)(4) and 1.162–2(c). If an employer treats as compensation under section 274(e)(2) the amount paid or incurred for the travel expenses of a spouse, dependent, or other individual accompanying an employee, then the expense is deductible by the employer as compensation and no amount may be excluded from the employee's gross income as a working condition fringe benefit. See § 1.274–2(f)(2)(iii)(A).

* * *

[T.D. 8256, 54 FR 28608, July 6, 1989, as amended by T.D. 8457, 57 FR 62192, Dec. 30, 1992; T.D. 8666, 61 FR 27005, May 30, 1996; T.D. 8933, 66 FR 2244, Jan. 11, 2001; T.D. 9483, 72 FR 27936, May 19, 2010]

§ 1.132–6 De minimis fringes.

(a) In general. Gross income does not include the value of a de minimis fringe provided to an employee. The term "de minimis fringe" means any property or service the value of which is (after taking into account the frequency with which similar fringes are provided by the employer to the employer's employees) so small as to make accounting for it unreasonable or administratively impracticable.

(b) Frequency—(1) Employee-measured frequency. Generally, the frequency with which similar fringes are provided by the employer to the employer's employees is determined by reference to the frequency with which the employer provides the fringes to each individual employee. For example, if an employer provides a free meal in kind to one employee on a daily basis, but not to any other employee, the value of the meals is not de minimis with respect to that one employee even though with respect to the employer's entire workforce the meals are provided "infrequently."

(2) Employer-measured frequency. Notwithstanding the rule of paragraph (b)(1) of this section, except for purposes of applying the special rules of paragraph (d)(2) of this section, where it would be administratively difficult to determine frequency with respect to individual employees, the frequency with which similar fringes are provided by the employer to the employer's employees is determined by reference to the frequency with which the employer provides the fringes to the workforce as a whole. Therefore, under this rule, the frequency with which any individual employee receives such a fringe benefit is not relevant and in some circumstances, the de minimis fringe exclusion may apply with respect to a benefit even though a particular employee receives the benefit frequently. For example, if an employer exercises sufficient control and imposes significant restrictions on the personal use of a company copying machine so that at least 85 percent of the use of the machine is for business purposes, any personal use of the copying machine by particular employees is considered to be a de minimis fringe.

(c) Administrability. Unless excluded by a provision of chapter 1 of the Internal Revenue Code of 1986 other than section 132(a)(4), the value of any fringe benefit that would not be unreasonable or administratively impracticable to account for is includible in the employee's gross income. Thus, except as provided in paragraph (d)(2) of this section, the provision of any cash fringe benefit is never excludable under section 132(a) as a de minimis fringe benefit. Similarly except as otherwise provided in paragraph (d) of this section, a cash equivalent fringe benefit (such as a fringe benefit provided to an employee through the use of a gift certificate or charge or credit card) is generally not excludable under section 132(a) even if the same property or service acquired (if provided in kind) would be excludable as a de minimis fringe benefit. For example, the provision of cash to an employee for a theatre ticket that would itself be excludable as a de minimis fringe (see paragraph (e)(1) of this section) is not excludable as a de minimis fringe.

(d) Special rules—* * *

(2) Occasional meal money or local transportation fare—(i) General rule. Meals, meal money or local transportation fare provided to an employee is excluded as a de minimis fringe benefit if the benefit provided is reasonable and is provided in a manner that satisfies the following three conditions:

(A) Occasional basis. The meals, meal money or local transportation fare is provided to the employee on an occasional basis. Whether meal money or local transportation fare is provided to an employee on an occasional basis will depend upon the frequency i.e. the availability of the benefit and regularity with which the benefit is provided by the employer to the employee. Thus, meals, meal money, or local transportation fare or a combination of such benefits provided to an employee on a regular or routine basis is not provided on an occasional basis.

(B) Overtime. The meals, meal money or local transportation fare is provided to an employee because overtime work necessitates an extension of the employee's normal work schedule. This condition does not fail to be satisfied merely because the circumstances giving rise to the need for overtime work are reasonably foreseeable.

(C) Meal money. In the case of a meal or meal money, the meal or meal money is provided to enable the employee to work overtime. Thus, for example, meals provided on the employer's premises that are consumed during the period that the employee works overtime or meal money provided for meals consumed during such period satisfy this condition.

In no event shall meal money or local transportation fare calculated on the basis of the number of hours worked (e.g., $1.00 per hour for each hour over eight hours) be considered a de minimis fringe benefit.

(ii) Applicability of other exclusions for certain meals and for transportation provided for security concerns. The value of meals furnished to an employee, an employee's spouse, or any of the employee's dependents by or on behalf of the employee's employer for the convenience of the employer is excluded from the employee's gross income if the meals are furnished on the business premises of the employer (see section 119). (For purposes of the exclusion under section 119, the definitions of an employee under § 1.132–1(b) do not apply.) If, for a bona fide business-oriented security concern, an employer provides an employee vehicle transportation that is specially designed for security (for example, the vehicle is equipped with bulletproof glass and armor plating), and the conditions of § 1.132–5(m) are satisfied, the value of the special security design is excludable from gross income as a working condition fringe if the employee would not have had such special security design but for the bona fide business-oriented security concern.

(iii) Special rule for employer-provided transportation provided in certain circumstances. (A) Partial exclusion of value. If an employer provides transportation (such as taxi fare) to an employee for use in commuting to and/or from work because of unusual circumstances and because, based on the facts and circumstances, it is unsafe for the employee to use other available means of transportation, the excess of the value of each one-way trip over $1.50 per one-way commute is excluded from gross income. The rule of this paragraph (d)(2)(iii) is not available to a control employee as defined in § 1.61–21(f)(5) and (6).

(B) "Unusual circumstances". Unusual circumstances are determined with respect to the employee receiving the transportation and are based on all facts and circumstances. An example of unusual circumstances would be when an employee is asked to work outside of his normal work hours (such as being called to the workplace at 1:00 am when the employee normally works from 8:00 am to 4:00 pm). Another example of unusual circumstances is a temporary change in the employee's work schedule (such as working from 12 midnight to 8:00 am rather than from 8:00 am to 4:00 pm for a two-week period).

(C) "Unsafe conditions". Factors indicating whether it is unsafe for an employee to use other available means of transportation are the history of crime in the geographic area surrounding the employee's workplace or residence and the time of day during which the employee must commute.

(3) Use of special rules or examples to establish a general rule. The special rules provided in this paragraph (d) or examples provided in paragraph (e) of this section may not be used to establish any general rule permitting exclusion as a de minimis fringe. For example, the fact that $252 (i.e., $21 per month for 12 months) worth of public transit passes can be excluded from gross income as a *de minimis* fringe in 1992 does not mean that any fringe benefit with a value equal to or less than $252 may be excluded as a *de minimis* fringe. As another example, the fact that the commuting use of an employer-provided vehicle more than one day a month is an example of a benefit not excludable as a de minimis fringe (see paragraph (e)(2) of this section) does not mean that the commuting use of a vehicle up to 12 times per year is excludable from gross income as a de minimis fringe.

(4) Benefits exceeding value and frequency limits. If a benefit provided to an employee is not de minimis because either the value or frequency exceeds a limit provided in this paragraph (d), no amount of the benefit is considered to be a de minimis fringe. For example, if, in 1992, an employer provides a $50 monthly public transit pass, the entire $50 must be included in income, not just the excess value over $21.

(e) Examples—(1) Benefits excludable from income. Examples of de minimis fringe benefits are occasional typing of personal letters by a company secretary; occasional personal use of an employer's copying machine, provided that the employer exercises sufficient control and imposes significant restrictions on the personal use of the machine so that at least 85 percent of the use of the machine is for business purposes; occasional cocktail parties, group meals, or picnics for employees and their guests; traditional birthday or holiday gifts of property (not cash) with a low fair market value; occasional theater or sporting event tickets; coffee, doughnuts, and soft drinks; local telephone calls; and flowers, fruit, books, or similar property provided to employees under special circumstances (e.g., on account of illness, outstanding performance, or family crisis).

(2) Benefits not excludable as de minimis fringes. Examples of fringe benefits that are not excludable from gross income as de minimis fringes are: season tickets to sporting or theatrical events; the commuting use of an employer-provided automobile or other vehicle more than one day a month; membership in a private country club or athletic facility, regardless of the frequency with which the employee uses the facility; employer-provided group-term life insurance on the life of the spouse or child of an employee; and use of employer-owned or leased facilities (such as an apartment, hunting lodge, boat, etc.) for a weekend. Some amount of the value of certain of these fringe benefits may be excluded from income under other statutory provisions, such as the exclusion for working condition fringes. See § 1.132–5.

(f) Nonapplicability of nondiscrimination rules. Except to the extent provided in § 1.132–7, the nondiscrimination rules of section 132(h)(1) and § 1.132–8 do not apply in determining the amount, if any, of a de minimis fringe. Thus, a fringe benefit may be excludable as a de minimis fringe even if the benefit is provided exclusively to highly compensated employees of the employer.

[T.D. 8256, 54 FR 28615, July 6, 1989, as amended by T.D. 8389, 57 FR 1871, Jan. 16, 1992; T.D. 8389, 57 FR 5982, Feb. 19, 1992]

§ 1.132–7 Employer-operated eating facilities.

(a) In general—(1) Condition for exclusion—(i) General rule. The value of meals provided to employees at an employer-operated eating facility for employees is excludable from gross income as a de minimis fringe only if on an annual basis, the revenue from the facility equals or exceeds the direct operating costs of the facility.

(ii) Additional condition for highly compensated employees. With respect to any highly compensated employee, an exclusion is available under this section only if the condition set out in paragraph (a)(1)(i) of this section is satisfied and access to the facility is available on substantially the same terms to each member of a group of employees that is defined under a reasonable classification set up by the employer that does not discriminate in favor of highly compensated employees. See § 1.132–8. For purposes of this paragraph (a)(1)(ii), each dining room or cafeteria in which meals are served is treated as a separate eating facility, whether each such dining room or cafeteria has its own kitchen or other food-preparation area.

(2) Employer-operated eating facility for employees. An employer-operated eating facility for employees is a facility that meets all of the following conditions—

(i) The facility is owned or leased by the employer,

(ii) The facility is operated by the employer,

(iii) The facility is located on or near the business premises of the employer, and

(iv) The meals furnished at the facility are provided during, or immediately before or after, the employee's workday.

For purposes of this section, the term "meals" means food, beverages, and related services provided at the facility. If an employer can reasonably determine the number of meals that are excludable from income by the recipient employees under section 119, the employer may, in determining whether the requirement of paragraph (a)(1)(i) of this section is satisfied, disregard all costs and revenues attributable to such meals provided to such employees. If an employer can reasonably determine the number of meals received by volunteers who receive food and beverages at a hospital, free or at a discount, the employer may, in determining whether the requirement of paragraph (a)(1)(i) of this section is satisfied, disregard all costs and revenues attributable to such meals provided to such volunteers. If an employer charges nonemployees a greater amount than employees, in determining whether the requirement of paragraph (a)(1)(i) of this section is satisfied, the employer must disregard all costs and revenues attributable to such meals provided to such nonemployees.

(3) Operation by the employer. If an employer contracts with another to operate an eating facility for its employees, the facility is considered to be operated by the employer for purposes of this section. If an eating facility is operated by more than one employer, it is considered to be operated by each employer.

(4) Example. The provisions of this paragraph (a)(2) may be illustrated by the following example:

Example (1). Assume that a not-for-profit hospital system maintains cafeterias for the use of its employees and volunteers. Only the employees are charged for food service at the cafeteria and the policy of the hospital is to charge the employees only for the costs of food, beverage and labor directly attributable to the meal. Most of the cafeterias within the system furnish more free meals to volunteers than they serve paid meals to employees. For purposes of this paragraph, as long as the employer can accurately determine the number of meals received free or at a discount by volunteers, the employer may disregard all the costs and revenues attributable to such meals provided to volunteers. Therefore, for purposes of this paragraph, the costs of the hospital system for furnishing meals to employees who pay for them are the costs to be compared to determine if the revenues from the facility equal or exceed direct operating costs of the facility's service to employees.

(b) Direct operating costs—(1) In general. For purposes of this section, the direct operating costs of an eating facility are—

(i) The cost of food and beverages, and

(ii) The cost of labor for personnel whose services relating to the facility are performed primarily on the premises of the eating facility. Direct operating costs do not include the labor cost attributable to personnel whose services relating to the facility are not performed primarily on the premises of the eating facility. Thus, for example, the labor costs attributable to cooks, waiters, and waitresses are included in direct operating costs, but the labor cost attributable to a manager of an eating facility whose services relating to the facility are not primarily performed on the premises of the eating facility is not included in direct operating costs. If an employee performs services relating to the facility both on and off the premises of the eating facility, only the portion of the total labor cost of the employee relating to the facility that bears the same proportion to such total labor cost as time spent on the premises bears to total time spent performing services relating to the facility is included in direct operating costs. For example, assume that 60 percent of the services of a cook in the above example are not related to the eating facility. Only 40 percent of the total labor cost of the cook is includible in direct operating costs. For purposes of this section, labor costs include all compensation required to be reported on a Form W–2 for income tax purposes and related employment taxes paid by the employer. In determining the direct operating costs of an eating facility, the employer may include as part of the facility, vending machines that are provided by the employer and located on the same premises as the other eating facilities operated by the employer.

(2) Multiple dining rooms or cafeterias. The direct operating costs test may be applied separately for each dining room or cafeteria. Alternatively, the direct operating costs test may be applied with respect to all the eating facilities operated by the employer.

(3) Payment to operator of facility. If an employer contracts with another to operate an eating facility for its employees, the direct operating costs of the facility consist both of direct operating costs, if any, incurred by the employer and the amount paid to the operator of the facility to the extent that such amount is attributable to what would be direct operating costs if the employer operated the facility directly.

(c) Valuation of non-excluded meals provided at an employer-operated eating facility for employees. If the exclusion for meals provided at an employer-operated eating facility for employees is not available, the recipient of meals provided at such facility must include in income the amount by which the fair market value of the meals provided exceeds the sum of—

(1) The amount, if any, paid for the meals, and

(2) The amount, if any, specifically excluded by another section of chapter 1 of this subtitle.

For special valuation rules relating to such meals, see § 1.61–21(j).

[T.D. 8256, 54 FR 28617, July 6, 1989]

§ 1.132–8 Fringe benefit nondiscrimination rules.

(a) Application of nondiscrimination rules—(1) General rule. A highly compensated employee who receives a no-additional-cost service, a qualified employee discount or a meal provided at an employer-operated eating facility for employees shall not be permitted to exclude such benefit from his or her income unless the benefit is available on substantially the same terms to:

(i) All employees of the employer; or

(ii) A group of employees of the employer which is defined under a reasonable classification set up by the employer that does not discriminate in favor of highly compensated employees. See paragraph (f) of this section for the definition of a highly compensated employee.

(2) Consequences of discrimination—(i) In general. If an employer maintains more than one fringe benefit program, i.e., either different fringe benefits being provided to the same group of employees, or different classifications of employees or the same fringe benefit being provided to two or more classifications of employees, the nondiscrimination requirements of section 132 will generally be applied separately to each such program. Thus, a determination that one fringe benefit program discriminates in favor of highly compensated employees generally will not cause other fringe benefit programs covering the same highly compensated employees to be treated as discriminatory. If the fringe benefits provided to a highly compensated individual do not satisfy the nondiscrimination rules provided in this section, such individual shall be unable to exclude from gross income any portion of the benefit. For example, if an employer offers a 20 percent discount (which otherwise satisfies the requirements for a qualified employee discount) to all non-highly compensated employees and a 35 percent discount to all highly compensated employees, the entire value of the 35 percent discount (not just the excess over 20 percent) is includible in the gross income and wages of the highly compensated employees who make purchases at a discount.

(ii) Exception—(A) Related fringe benefit programs. If one of a group of fringe benefit programs discriminates in favor of highly compensated employees, no related fringe benefit provided to such highly compensated employees under any other fringe benefit program may be excluded from the gross income of such highly compensated employees. For example, assume a department store provides a 20 percent merchandise discount to all employees under one fringe benefit program. Assume further that under a second fringe benefit program, the department store provides an additional 15 percent merchandise discount to a group of employees defined under a classification which discriminates in favor of highly compensated employees. Because the second fringe benefit program is discriminatory, the 15 percent merchandise discount provided to the highly compensated employees is not a qualified employee discount. In addition, because the 20 percent merchandise discount provided under the first fringe benefit program is related to the fringe benefit provided under the second fringe benefit program, the 20 percent merchandise discount provided the highly compensated employees is not a qualified employee discount. Thus, the entire 35 percent merchandise discount provided to the highly compensated employees is includible in such employees' gross incomes.

(B) Employer operated eating facilities for employees. For purposes of paragraph (a)(2)(ii)(A) of this section, meals at different employer-operated eating facilities for employees are not related fringe benefits, so that a highly compensated employee may exclude from gross income the value of a meal at a nondiscriminatory facility even though any meals provided to him or her at a discriminatory facility cannot be excluded.

(3) Scope of the nondiscrimination rules provided in this section. The nondiscrimination rules provided in this section apply only to fringe benefits provided pursuant to section 132(a)(1), (a)(2), and (e)(2). These rules have no application to any other employee benefit that may be subject to nondiscrimination requirements under any other section of the Code.

(b) Aggregation of employees—(1) Section 132(a)(1) and (2). For purposes of determining whether the exclusions for no-additional-cost services and qualified employee discounts are available to highly compensated employees, the nondiscrimination rules of this section are applied by aggregating the employees of all related employers (as defined in § 1.132-1(c)), except that employees in different lines of business (as defined in § 1.132-4) are not to be aggregated. Thus, in general, for purposes of this section, the term "employees of the employer" refers to all employees of the employer and any other entity that is a member of a group described in section 414(b), (c), (m), or (*o*) and that performs services within the same line of business as the employer which provides the particular fringe benefit. Employees in different lines of business will be aggregated, however, if the line of business limitation has been relaxed pursuant to paragraphs (b) through (g) of § 1.132-4.

(2) Section 132(e)(2). For purposes of determining whether the exclusions for meals provided at employer-operated eating facilities are available to highly compensated employees, the nondiscrimination rules of this section are applied by aggregating the employees of all related employers (as defined in section § 1.132-1(c)) who regularly work at or near the premises on which the eating facility is located, except that employees in different lines of business (as defined in § 1.132-4) are not to be aggregated. The nondiscrimination rules of this section are applied separately to each eating facility. Each dining room or cafeteria in which meals are served is treated as a separate eating facility, regardless of whether each such dining room or cafeteria has its own kitchen or other food-preparation area.

* * *

(c) Availability on substantially the same terms—(1) General rule. The determination of whether a benefit is available on substantially the same terms shall be made upon the basis of the facts and circumstances of each situation. In general, however, if any one of the terms or conditions governing the availability of a particular benefit to one or more employees varies from any one of the terms or conditions governing the availability of a benefit made available to one or more other employees, such benefit shall not be considered to be available on substantially the same terms except to the extent otherwise provided in paragraph (c)(2) of this section. For example, if a department store provides a 20 percent qualified employee discount to all of its employees on all merchandise, the substantially the same terms requirement will be satisfied. Similarly, if the discount provided to all employees is 30 percent on certain merchandise (such as apparel), and 20 percent on all other merchandise, the substantially the same terms requirement will be satisfied. However, if a department store provides a 20 percent qualified employee discount to all employees, but as to the employees in certain departments, the discount is available upon hire, and as to the remaining departments, the discount is only available when an employee has completed a specified term of service, the 20 percent discount is not available on substantially the same terms to all of the employees of the employer. Similarly, if a greater discount is given to employees with more seniority, full-time work status, or a particular job description, such benefit (i.e., the discount) would not be available to all employees eligible for the discount on substantially the same terms, except to the extent otherwise provided in paragraph (c)(2) of this section. These examples also apply to no-additional-cost services. Thus, if an employer charges non-highly compensated employees for a no-additional-cost service and does not charge highly compensated employees (or charges highly compensated employees a lesser amount), the substantially the same terms requirement will not be satisfied.

(2) Certain terms relating to priority. Certain fringe benefits made available to employees are available only in limited quantities that may be insufficient to meet employee demand. This situation may occur either because of employer policy (such as where an employer determines that only a certain number of units of a specific product will be made available to employees each year) or because of the nature of the fringe benefit (such as where an employer provides a no-additional-cost transportation service that is limited to the number of seats available just before departure). Under these circumstances, an employer may find it necessary to establish some method of allocating the limited fringe benefits among the employees eligible to receive the fringe benefits. The employer may establish the priorities described below.

(i) Priority on a first come, first served, or similar basis. A benefit shall not fail to be treated as available to a group of employees on substantially the same terms merely because the employer allocates the benefit among such employees on a "first come, first served" or lottery basis, provided that the same notice of the terms of availability is given to all employees in the group and the terms under which the benefit is provided to employees within the group are otherwise the same with respect to all employees. For purposes of the preceding sentence, a program that gives priority to employees who are the first to submit written requests for the benefit will constitute priority on a "first come, first served" basis. Similarly, if the employer regularly engages in the practice of allocating benefits on a priority basis to employees demonstrating a critical need, such benefit shall not fail to be treated as available on substantially the same terms to all of the employees with respect to whom such priority status is available as long as the determination is based upon uniform and objective criteria which have been communicated to all employees in the group of eligible employees. An example of a critical need would be priority transportation given to an employee in the event of a medical emergency involving the employee (or a member of the employee's immediate family) or a recent death in the employee's immediate family. Frustrated vacation plans or forfeited deposits would not be treated as giving rise to particularly critical needs.

(ii) Priority on the basis of seniority. Solely for purposes of § 1.132–8, a benefit shall not fail to be treated as available to a group of employees of the employer on substantially the same terms merely because the employer allocates the benefit among such employees on a seniority basis provided that:

(A) The same notice of the terms of availability is given to all employees in the group; and

(B) The average value of the benefit provided for each nonhighly compensated employee is at least 75% of that provided for each highly compensated employee. For purposes of this test, the average value of the benefit provided for each nonhighly compensated (highly compensated) employee is determined by taking the sum of the fair market values of such benefit provided to all the nonhighly compensated (highly compensated) employees, determined in accordance with § 1.61–21, and then dividing that sum by the total number of nonhighly compensated (highly compensated) employees of the employer. For purposes of determining the average value of the benefit provided for each employee, all employee's of the employer are counted, including those who are not eligible to receive the benefit from the employer.

(d) Testing for discrimination.

(1) Classification test. In the event that a benefit described in section 132(a)(1), (a)(2) or (e)(2) is not available on substantially the same terms to all of the employees of the employer, no exclusion shall be available to a highly compensated employee for such benefit unless the program under which the benefit is provided satisfies the nondiscrimination standards set forth in this section. The nondiscrimination standard of this section will be satisfied only if the benefit is available on substantially the same terms to a group of employees of the employer which is defined under a reasonable classification established by the employer that does not discriminate in favor of highly compensated employees. The determination of whether a particular classification is discriminatory will generally depend upon the facts and circumstances involved, based upon principles similar to those applied for purposes of section 410(b)(2)(A)(i) or, for years commencing prior to January 1, 1988, section 410(b)(1)(B). Thus, in general, except as otherwise provided in this section, if a benefit is available on substantially the same terms to a group of employees which, when compared with all of the other employees of the employer, constitutes a nondiscriminatory classification under section 410(b)(2)(A)(i) (or, if applicable, section 410(b)(1)(B)), it shall be deemed to be nondiscriminatory.

(2) Classifications that are per se discriminatory. A classification that, on its face, makes fringe benefits available principally to highly compensated employees is per se discriminatory. In addition, a classification that is based on either an amount or rate of compensation is per se discriminatory if it favors those with the higher amount or rate of compensation. On the other hand, a classification that is based on factors such as seniority, full-time vs. part-time employment, or job description is not per se discriminatory but may be discriminatory as applied to the workforce of a particular employer.

(3) Former employees. When determining whether a classification is discriminatory, former employees shall be tested separately from other employees of the employer. Therefore, a classification is not discriminatory solely because the employer does not make fringe benefits available to any former employee. Whether a classification of former employees discriminates in favor of highly compensated employees will depend upon the particular facts and circumstances.

(4) Restructuring of benefits. For purposes of testing whether a particular group of employees would constitute a discriminatory classification for purposes of this section, an employer may restructure its fringe benefit program as described in this paragraph. If a fringe benefit is provided to more than one group of employees, and one or more such groups would constitute a discriminatory classification if considered by itself, then for purposes of this section, the employer may restructure its fringe benefit program so that all or some of the members of such group may be aggregated with another group, provided that each member of the restructured group will have available to him or her the same benefit upon the same terms and conditions. For example, assume that all highly compensated employees of an employer have fewer than five years of service and all nonhighly compensated employees have over five years of service. If the employer provided a five percent discount to employees with under five years of service and a ten percent discount to employees with over five years of service, the discount program available to the highly compensated employees would not satisfy the nondiscriminatory classification test; however, as a result of the rule described in this paragraph (d)(4), the employer could structure the program to consist of a five percent discount for all employees and a five percent additional discount for nonhighly compensated employees.

(5) Employer-operated eating facilities for employees—(i) General rule. If access to an employer-operated eating facility for employees is available to a classification of employees that discriminates in favor of highly compensated employees, then the classification will not be treated as discriminating in favor of highly compensated employees unless the facility is used by one or more executive group employees more than a de minimis amount.

(ii) Executive group employee. For purposes of this paragraph (d)(5), an employee is an "executive group employee" if the definition of paragraph (f)(1) of this section is satisfied. For purposes of identifying such employees, the phrase "top one percent of the employees" is substituted for the phrase "top ten percent of the employees" in section 414(q)(4) (relating to the definition of "top-paid group").

(e) Cash bonuses or rebates. A cash bonus or rebate provided to an employee by an employer that is determined with reference to the value of employer-provided property or services purchased by the employee, is treated as an equivalent employee discount. For example, assume a department store provides a 20 percent merchandise discount to all employees under a fringe benefit program. In addition, assume that the department store provides cash bonuses to a group of employees defined under a classification which discriminates in favor of highly compensated employees. Assume further that such cash bonuses equal 15 percent of the value of merchandise purchased by each employee. This arrangement is substantively identical to the example described in paragraph (e)(2)(i) of this section concerning related fringe benefit programs. Thus, both the 20 percent merchandise discount and the 15 percent cash bonus provided to the highly compensated employees are includible in such employees' gross incomes.

(f) Highly compensated employee—(1) Government and nongovernment employees. A highly compensated employee of any employer is any employee who, during the year or the preceding year—

(i) Was a 5–percent owner,

(ii) Received compensation from the employer in excess of $75,000,

(iii) Received compensation from the employer in excess of $50,000 and was in the top-paid group of employees for such year, or

(iv) Was at any time an officer and received compensation greater than 150 percent of the amount in effect under section 415(c)(1)(A) for such year.

For purposes of determining whether an employee is a highly compensated employee, the rules of sections 414(q), (s), and (t) apply.

(2) Former employees. A former employee shall be treated as a highly compensated employee if—

(i) The employee was a highly compensated employee when the employee separated from service, or

(ii) The employee was a highly compensated employee at any time after attaining age 55.

[T.D. 8256, 54 FR 28618, July 6, 1989]

§ 1.151–1 Deductions for personal exemptions.

* * *

(b) Exemptions for individual taxpayer and spouse (so-called personal exemptions). Section 151(b) allows an exemption for the taxpayer and an additional exemption for the spouse of the taxpayer if a joint return is not made by the taxpayer and his spouse, and if the spouse, for the calendar year in which the taxable year of the taxpayer begins, has no gross income and is not the dependent of another taxpayer. Thus, a husband is not entitled to an exemption for his wife on his separate return for the taxable year beginning in a calendar year during which she has any gross income (though insufficient to require her to file a return). Since, in the case of a joint return, there are two taxpayers (although under section 6013 there is only one income for the two taxpayers on such return, *i.e.*, their aggregate income), two exemptions are allowed on such return, one for each taxpayer spouse. If in any case a joint return is made by the taxpayer and his spouse, no other person is allowed an exemption for such spouse even though such other person would have been entitled to claim an exemption for such spouse as a dependent if such joint return had not been made.

(c) Exemptions for taxpayer attaining the age of 65 and spouse attaining the age of 65 (so-called old-age exemptions). (1) * * *

(2) In determining the age of an individual for the purposes of the exemption for old age, the last day of the taxable year of the taxpayer is the controlling date. Thus, in the event of a separate return by a husband, no additional exemption for old age may be claimed for his spouse unless such spouse has attained the age of 65 on or before the close of the taxable year of the husband. In no event shall the additional exemption for old age be allowed with respect to a spouse who dies before attaining the age of 65 even though such spouse would have attained the age of 65 before the close of the taxable year of the taxpayer. For the purposes of the old-age exemption, an individual attains the age of 65 on the first moment of the day preceding his sixty-fifth birthday. Accordingly, an individual whose sixty-fifth birthday falls on January 1 in a given year attains the age of 65 on the last day of the calendar year immediately preceding.

* * *

[T.D. 6500, 25 FR 11402, Nov. 26, 1960, as amended by T.D. 7114, 36 FR 9018, May 18, 1971; T.D. 7230, 37 FR 28288, Dec. 22, 1972]

§ 1.152–1 General definition of a dependent.

(a)(1) * * *

(2)(i) For purposes of determining whether or not an individual received, for a given calendar year, over half of his support from the taxpayer, there shall be taken into account the amount of support received from the taxpayer as compared to the entire amount of support which the individual received from all sources, including support which the individual himself supplied. The term "support" includes food, shelter, clothing, medical and dental care, education, and the like. Generally, the amount of an item of support will be the amount of expense incurred by the one furnishing such item. If the item of support furnished an individual is in the form of property or lodging, it will be necessary to measure the amount of such item of support in terms of its fair market value.

(ii) In computing the amount which is contributed for the support of an individual, there must be included any amount which is contributed by such individual for his own support, including income which is ordinarily excludable from gross income, such as benefits received under the Social Security Act (42 U.S.C. ch. 7). * * *

(iii)(a) For purposes of determining the amount of support furnished for a child (or children) by a taxpayer for a given calendar year, an arrearage payment made in a year subsequent to a calendar year for which there is an unpaid liability shall not be treated as paid either during that calendar year or in the year of payment, but no amount shall be treated as an arrearage payment to the extent that there is an unpaid liability (determined without regard to such payment) with respect to the support of a child for the taxable year of payment; and

(b) Similarly, payments made prior to any calendar year (whether or not made in the form of a lump sum payment in settlement of the parent's liability for support) shall not be treated as made during such calendar year, but payments made during any calendar year from amounts set aside in trust by a parent in a prior year, shall be treated as made during the calendar year in which paid.

(b) Section 152(a)(9) applies to any individual (other than an individual who at any time during the taxable year was the spouse, determined without regard to section 153, of the taxpayer) who lives with the taxpayer and is a member of the taxpayer's household during the entire taxable year of the taxpayer. An individual is not a member of the taxpayer's household if at any time during the taxable year of the taxpayer the relationship between such individual and the taxpayer is in violation of local law. It is not necessary under section 152(a)(9) that the dependent be related to the taxpayer. For example, foster children may qualify as dependents. It is necessary, however, that the taxpayer both maintain and occupy the household. The taxpayer and dependent will be considered as occupying the household for such entire taxable year notwithstanding temporary absences from the household due to special circumstances. A nonpermanent failure to occupy the common abode by reason of illness, education, business, vacation, military service, or a custody agreement under which the dependent is absent for less than six months in the taxable year of the taxpayer, shall be considered temporary absence due to special circumstances. The fact that the dependent dies during the year shall not deprive the taxpayer of the deduction if the dependent lived in the household for the entire part of the year preceding his death. Likewise, the period during the taxable year preceding the birth of an individual shall not prevent such individual from qualifying as a dependent under section 152(a)(9). Moreover, a child who actually becomes a member of the taxpayer's household during the taxable year shall not be prevented from being considered a member of such household for the entire taxable year, if the child is required to remain in a hospital for a period following its birth, and if such child would otherwise have been a member of the taxpayer's household during such period.

* * *

[T.D. 6500, 25 FR 11402, Nov. 26, 1960, as amended by T.D. 6603, 28 FR 7094, July 11, 1963; T.D. 7099, 36 FR 5337, Mar. 20, 1971; T.D. 7114, 36 FR 9019, May 18, 1971]

§ 1.152–4 Special rule for a child of divorced or separated parents or parents who live apart.

(a) In general. A taxpayer may claim a dependency deduction for a child (as defined in section 152(f)(1)) only if the child is the qualifying child of the taxpayer under section 152(c) or the qualifying relative of the taxpayer under section 152(d). Section 152(c)(4)(B) provides that a child who is claimed as a qualifying child by parents who do not file a joint return together is treated as the qualifying child of the parent with whom the child resides for a longer period of time during the taxable year or, if the child resides with both parents for an equal period of time, of the parent with the higher adjusted gross income. However, a child is treated as the qualifying child or qualifying relative of the noncustodial parent if the custodial parent releases a claim to the exemption under section 152(e) and this section.

(b) Release of claim by custodial parent—(1) In general. Under section 152(e)(1), notwithstanding section 152(c)(1)(B), (c)(4), or (d)(1)(C), a child is treated as the qualifying child or qualifying relative of the noncustodial parent (as defined in paragraph (d) of this section) if the requirements of paragraphs (b)(2) and (b)(3) of this section are met.

(2) Support, custody, and parental status—(i) In general. The requirements of this paragraph (b)(2) are met if the parents of the child provide over one-half of the child's support for the calendar year, the child is in the custody of one or both parents for more than one-half of the calendar year, and the parents—

(A) Are divorced or legally separated under a decree of divorce or separate maintenance;

(B) Are separated under a written separation agreement; or

(C) Live apart at all times during the last 6 months of the calendar year whether or not they are or were married.

(ii) Multiple support agreement. The requirements of this paragraph (b)(2) are not met if over one-half of the support of the child is treated as having been received from a taxpayer under section 152(d)(3).

(3) Release of claim to child. The requirements of this paragraph (b)(3) are met for a calendar year if—

(i) The custodial parent signs a written declaration that the custodial parent will not claim the child as a dependent for any taxable year beginning in that calendar year and the noncustodial parent attaches the declaration to the noncustodial parent's return for the taxable year; or

(ii) A qualified pre–1985 instrument, as defined in section 152(e)(3)(B), applicable to the taxable year beginning in that calendar year, provides that the noncustodial parent is entitled to the dependency exemption for the child and the noncustodial parent provides at least $600 for the support of the child during the calendar year.

(c) Custody. A child is in the custody of one or both parents for more than one-half of the calendar year if one or both parents have the right under state law to physical custody of the child for more than one-half of the calendar year.

(d) Custodial parent—(1) In general. The custodial parent is the parent with whom the child resides for the greater number of nights during the calendar year, and the noncustodial parent is the parent who is not the custodial parent. A child is treated as residing with neither parent if the child is emancipated under state law. For purposes of this section, a child resides with a parent for a night if the child sleeps—

(i) At the residence of that parent (whether or not the parent is present); or

(ii) In the company of the parent, when the child does not sleep at a parent's residence (for example, the parent and child are on vacation together).

(2) Night straddling taxable years. A night that extends over two taxable years is allocated to the taxable year in which the night begins.

(3) Absences. (i) Except as provided in paragraph (d)(3)(ii) of this section, for purposes of this paragraph (d), a child who does not reside (within the meaning of paragraph (d)(1) of this section) with a parent for a night is treated as residing with the parent with whom the child would have resided for the night but for the absence.

(ii) A child who does not reside (within the meaning of paragraph (d)(1) of this section) with a parent for a night is treated as not residing with either parent for that night if it cannot be determined with which parent the child would have resided or if the child would not have resided with either parent for the night.

(4) Special rule for equal number of nights. If a child is in the custody of one or both parents for more than one-half of the calendar year and the child resides with each parent for an equal number of nights during the calendar year, the parent with the higher adjusted gross income for the calendar year is treated as the custodial parent.

(5) Exception for a parent who works at night. If, in a calendar year, due to a parent's nighttime work schedule, a child resides for a greater number of days but not nights with the parent who works at night, that parent is treated as the custodial parent. On a school day, the child is treated as residing at the primary residence registered with the school.

(e) Written declaration—(1) Form of declaration—(i) In general. The written declaration under paragraph (b)(3)(i) of this section must be an unconditional release of the custodial parent's claim to the child as a dependent for the year or years for which the declaration is effective. A declaration is not unconditional if the custodial parent's release of the right to claim the child as a dependent requires the satisfaction of any condition, including the noncustodial parent's meeting of an obligation such as the payment of support. A written declaration must name the noncustodial parent to whom the exemption is released. A written declaration must specify the year or years for which it is effective. A written declaration that specifies all future years is treated as specifying the first taxable year after the taxable year of execution and all subsequent taxable years.

(ii) Form designated by IRS. A written declaration may be made on Form 8332, Release/Revocation of Release of Claim to Exemption for Child by Custodial Parent, or successor form designated by the IRS. A written declaration not on the form designated by the IRS must conform to the substance of that form and must be a document executed for the sole purpose of serving as a written declaration under this section. A court order or decree or a separation agreement may not serve as a written declaration.

(2) Attachment to return. A noncustodial parent must attach a copy of the written declaration to the parent's return for each taxable year in which the child is claimed as a dependent.

(3) Revocation of written declaration—(i) In general. A parent may revoke a written declaration described in paragraph (e)(1) of this section by providing written notice of the revocation to the other parent. The parent revoking the written declaration must make reasonable efforts to provide actual notice to the other parent. The revocation may be effective no earlier than the taxable year that begins in the first calendar year after the calendar year in which the parent revoking the written declaration provides, or makes reasonable efforts to provide, the written notice.

(ii) Form of revocation. The revocation may be made on Form 8332, Release/Revocation of Release of Claim to Exemption for Child by Custodial Parent, or successor form designated by the IRS whether or not the written declaration was made on a form designated by the IRS. A revocation not on that form must conform to the substance of the form and must be a document executed for the sole purpose of serving as a revocation under this section. The revocation must specify the year or years for which the revocation is effective. A revocation that specifies all future years is treated as specifying the first taxable year after the taxable year the revocation is executed and all subsequent taxable years.

(iii) Attachment to return. The parent revoking the written declaration must attach a copy of the revocation to the parent's return for each taxable year for which the parent claims a child as a dependent as a result of the revocation. The parent revoking the written declaration must keep a copy of the revocation and evidence of delivery of the notice to the other parent, or of the reasonable efforts to provide actual notice.

(4) Ineffective declaration or revocation. A written declaration or revocation that fails to satisfy the requirements of this paragraph (e) has no effect.

(5) Written declaration executed in a taxable year beginning on or before July 2, 2008. A written declaration executed in a taxable year beginning on or before July 2, 2008, that satisfies the requirements for the form of a written declaration in effect at the time the written declaration is executed, will be treated as meeting the requirements of paragraph (e)(1) of this section. Paragraph (e)(3) of this section applies without regard to whether a custodial parent executed the written declaration in a taxable year beginning on or before July 2, 2008.

(f) Coordination with other sections. If section 152(e) and this section apply, a child is treated as the dependent of both parents for purposes of sections 105(b), 132(h)(2)(B), and 213(d)(5).

(g) Examples. The provisions of this section are illustrated by the following examples that assume, unless otherwise provided, that each taxpayer's taxable year is the calendar year, one or both of the child's parents provide over one-half of the child's support for the calendar year, one or both parents have the right under state law to physical custody of the child for more than one-half of the calendar year, and the child otherwise meets the requirements of a qualifying child under section 152(c) or a qualifying relative under section 152(d). In addition, in each of the examples, no qualified pre–1985 instrument or multiple support agreement is in effect. The examples are as follows:

Example 1. **(i)** B and C are the divorced parents of Child. In 2009, Child resides with B for 210 nights and with C for 155 nights. B executes a Form 8332 for 2009 releasing B's right to claim Child as a dependent for that year, which C attaches to C's 2009 return.

(ii) Under paragraph (d) of this section, B is the custodial parent of Child in 2009 because B is the parent with whom Child resides for the greater number of nights in 2009. Because the requirements of paragraphs (b)(2) and (3) of this section are met, C may claim Child as a dependent.

Example 2. The facts are the same as in Example 1 except that B does not execute a Form 8332 or similar declaration for 2009. Therefore, section 152(e) and this section do not apply. Whether Child is the qualifying child or qualifying relative of B or C is determined under section 152(c) or (d).

Example 3. **(i)** D and E are the divorced parents of Child. Under a custody decree, Grandmother has the right under state law to physical custody of Child from January 1 to July 31, 2009.

(ii) Because D and E do not have the right under state law to physical custody of Child for over one-half of the 2009 calendar year, under paragraph (c) of this section, Child is not in the custody of one or both parents for over one-half of the calendar year. Therefore, section 152(e) and this section do not apply, and whether Child is the qualifying child or qualifying relative of D, E, or Grandmother is determined under section 152(c) or (d).

Example 4. **(i)** The facts are the same as in Example 3, except that Grandmother has the right to physical custody of Child from January 1 to March 31, 2009, and, as a result, Child resides with Grandmother during this period. D and E jointly have the right to physical custody of Child from April 1 to December 31, 2009. During this period, Child resides with D for 180 nights and with E for 95 nights. D executes a Form 8332 for 2009 releasing D's right to claim Child as a dependent for that year, which E attaches to E's 2009 return.

(ii) Under paragraph (c) of this section, Child is in the custody of D and E for over one-half of the calendar year, because D and E have the right under state law to physical custody of Child for over one-half of the calendar year.

(iii) Under paragraph (d)(3)(ii) of this section, the nights that Child resides with Grandmother are not allocated to either parent. Child resides with D for a greater number of nights than with E during the calendar year and, under paragraph (d)(1) of this section, D is the custodial parent.

(iv) Because the requirements of paragraphs (b)(2) and (3) of this section are met, section 152(e) and this section apply, and E may claim Child as a dependent.

Example 5. **(i)** The facts are the same as in Example 4, except that D is away on military service from April 10 to June 15, 2009, and September 6 to October 20, 2009. During these periods Child resides with Grandmother in Grandmother's residence. Child would have resided with D if D had not been away on military service. Grandmother claims Child as a dependent on Grandmother's 2009 return.

(ii) Under paragraph (d)(3)(i) of this section, Child is treated as residing with D for the nights that D is away on military service. Because the requirements of paragraphs (b)(2) and (3) of this section are met, section 152(e) and this section apply, and E, not Grandmother, may claim Child as a dependent.

* * *

Example 8. H and J are the divorced parents of Child. Child generally resides with H during the week and with J every other weekend. Child resides with J in H's residence for 10 consecutive nights while H is hospitalized. Under paragraph (d)(1)(i) of this section, Child resides with H for the 10 nights.

Example 9. K and L, who are separated under a written separation agreement, are the parents of Child. In August 2009, K and Child spend 10 nights together in a hotel while on vacation. Under paragraph (d)(1)(ii) of this section, Child resides with K for the 10 nights that K and Child are on vacation.

* * *

Example 11. O and P, who never married, are the parents of Child. In 2009, Child spends alternate weeks residing with O and P. During a week that Child is residing with O, O gives Child permission to spend a night at the home of a friend. Under paragraph (d)(3)(i) of this section, the night Child spends at the friend's home is treated as a night that Child resides with O.

Example 12. The facts are the same as in Example 11, except that Child also resides at summer camp for 6 weeks. Because Child resides with each parent for alternate weeks, Child would have resided with O for 3 weeks and with P for 3 weeks of the period that Child is at camp. Under paragraph (d)(3)(i) of this section, Child is treated as residing with O for 3 weeks and with P for 3 weeks.

Example 13. The facts are the same as in Example 12, except that Child does not spend alternate weeks residing with O and P, and it cannot be determined whether Child would have resided with O or P for the period that Child is at camp. Under paragraph (d)(3)(ii) of this section, Child is treated as residing with neither parent for the 6 weeks.

* * *

[T.D. 9408, 73 FR 37797, July 2, 2008]

§ 1.161–1 Allowance of deductions.

Section 161 provides for the allowance as deductions, in computing taxable income under section 63(a), of the items specified in part VI (section 161 and following), subchapter B, chapter 1 of the Code, subject to the exceptions provided in part IX (section 261 and following), of such subchapter B, relating to items not deductible. Double deductions are not permitted. * * *

[T.D. 6500, 25 FR 11402, Nov. 26, 1960]

§ 1.162–1 Business expenses.

(a) In general. Business expenses deductible from gross income include the ordinary and necessary expenditures directly connected with or pertaining to the taxpayer's trade or business, except items which are used as the basis for a deduction or a credit under provisions of law other than section 162. The cost of goods purchased for resale, with proper adjustment for opening and closing inventories, is deducted from gross sales in computing gross income. * * * Among the items included in business expenses are management expenses, commissions (but see section 263 and the regulations thereunder), labor, supplies, incidental repairs, operating expenses of automobiles used in the trade or business, traveling expenses while away from home solely in the pursuit of a trade or business (see § 1.162–2), advertising and other selling expenses, together with insurance premiums against fire, storm, theft, accident, or other similar losses in the case of a business, and rental for the use of business property. No such item shall be included in business expenses, however, to the extent that it is used by the taxpayer in computing the cost of property included in its inventory or used in determining the gain or loss basis of its plant, equipment, or other property. * * * A deduction for an expense paid or incurred after December 30, 1969, which would otherwise be allowable under section 162 shall not be denied on the grounds that allowance of such deduction would frustrate a sharply defined public policy. See section 162(c), (f), and (g) and the regulations thereunder. The full amount of the allowable deduction for ordinary and necessary expenses in carrying on a business is deductible, even though such expenses exceed the gross income derived during the taxable year from such business. * * *

* * *

[T.D. 6500, 25 FR 11402, Nov. 26, 1960, as amended by T.D. 6690, 28 FR 12253, Nov. 19, 1963; T.D. 6996, 34 FR 835, Jan. 18, 1969; T.D. 7315, 39 FR 20203, June 7, 1974; T.D. 7345, 40 FR 7437, Feb. 20, 1975; T.D. 8189, 53 FR 9881, Mar. 28, 1988; T.D. 8491, 58 FR 53127, Oct. 14, 1993]

§ 1.162–2 Traveling expenses.

(a) Traveling expenses include travel fares, meals and lodging, and expenses incident to travel such as expenses for sample rooms, telephone and telegraph, public stenographers, etc. Only such traveling expenses as are reasonable and necessary in the conduct of the taxpayer's business and directly attributable to it may be deducted. If the trip is undertaken for other than business purposes, the travel fares and expenses incident to travel are personal expenses and the meals and lodging are living expenses. If the trip is solely on business, the reasonable and necessary traveling expenses, including travel fares, meals and lodging, and expenses incident to travel, are business expenses. * * *

(b)(1) If a taxpayer travels to a destination and while at such destination engages in both business and personal activities, traveling expenses to and from such destination are deductible only if the trip is related primarily to the taxpayer's trade or business. If the trip is primarily personal in nature, the traveling expenses to and from the destination are not deductible even though the taxpayer engages in business activities while at such destination. However, expenses while at the destination which are properly allocable to the taxpayer's trade or business are deductible even though the traveling expenses to and from the destination are not deductible.

(2) Whether a trip is related primarily to the taxpayer's trade or business or is primarily personal in nature depends on the facts and circumstances in each case. The amount of time during the period of the trip which is spent on personal activity compared to the amount of time spent on activities directly relating to the taxpayer's trade or business is an important factor in determining whether the trip is primarily personal. If, for example, a taxpayer spends one week while at a destination on activities which are directly related to his trade or business and subsequently spends an additional five weeks for vacation or other personal activities, the trip will be considered primarily personal in nature in the absence of a clear showing to the contrary.

* * *

(d) Expenses paid or incurred by a taxpayer in attending a convention or other meeting may constitute an ordinary and necessary business expense under section 162 depending upon the facts and circumstances of each case. No distinction will be made between self-employed persons and employees. The fact that an employee uses vacation or leave time or that his attendance at the convention is voluntary will not necessarily prohibit the allowance of the deduction. The allowance of deductions for such expenses will depend upon whether there is a sufficient relationship between the taxpayer's trade of business and his attendance at the convention or other meeting so that he is benefiting or advancing the interests of his trade or business by such attendance. If the convention is for political, social or other purposes unrelated to the taxpayer's trade or business, the expenses are not deductible.

(e) Commuters' fares are not considered as business expenses and are not deductible.

* * *

[T.D. 6500, 25 FR 11402, Nov. 26, 1960]

§ 1.162–3T Materials and supplies (temporary).

(a) In general—(1) Non-incidental materials and supplies. Amounts paid to acquire or produce materials and supplies are deductible in the taxable year in which the materials and supplies are used or consumed in the taxpayer's operations.

(2) Incidental materials and supplies. Amounts paid to acquire or produce incidental materials and supplies that are carried on hand and for which no record of consumption is kept or of which physical inventories at the beginning and end of the taxable year are not taken, are deductible in the taxable year in which these amounts are paid, provided taxable income is clearly reflected.

* * *

(b) Coordination with other provisions of the Internal Revenue Code. Nothing in this section changes the treatment of any amount that is specifically provided for under any provision of the Internal Revenue Code or regulations other than section 162(a) or section 212 and the regulations under those sections. For example, see section § 1.263(a)–3T, which requires taxpayers to capitalize amounts paid to improve tangible property and section 263A and the regulations under section 263A, which require taxpayers to capitalize the direct and allocable indirect costs, including the cost of materials and supplies, to property produced or to property acquired for resale. See also § 1.471–1, which requires taxpayers to include in inventory certain materials and supplies.

(c) Definitions—(1) Materials and supplies. For purposes of this section, materials and supplies means tangible property that is used or consumed in the taxpayer's operations that is not inventory and that—

(i) Is a component acquired to maintain, repair, or improve a unit of tangible property (as determined under § 1.263(a)–3T(e)) owned, leased, or serviced by the taxpayer and that is not acquired as part of any single unit of tangible property;

(ii) Consists of fuel, lubricants, water, and similar items, that are reasonably expected to be consumed in 12 months or less, beginning when used in taxpayer's operations;

(iii) Is a unit of property as determined under § 1.263(a)–3T(e) that has an economic useful life of 12 months or less, beginning when the property is used or consumed in the taxpayer's operations;

(iv) Is a unit of property as determined under § 1.263(a)–3T(e) that has an acquisition cost or production cost (as determined under section 263A) of $100 or less (or other amount as identified in published guidance in the Federal Register or in the

Internal Revenue Bulletin (see § 601.601(d)(2)(ii)(b) of this chapter)); or

(v) Is identified in published guidance in the Federal Register or in the Internal Revenue Bulletin (see § 601.601(d)(2)(ii)(b) of this chapter) as materials and supplies for which treatment is permitted under this section.

* * *

(3) Economic useful life—(i) General rule. The economic useful life of a unit of property is not necessarily the useful life inherent in the property but is the period over which the property may reasonably be expected to be useful to the taxpayer or, if the taxpayer is engaged in a trade or business or an activity for the production of income, the period over which the property may reasonably be expected to be useful to the taxpayer in its trade or business or for the production of income, as applicable. See § 1.167(a)–1(b) for the factors to be considered in determining this period.

* * *

(d) Election to capitalize and depreciate—(1) In general. A taxpayer may elect to treat as a capital expenditure and to treat as an asset subject to the allowance for depreciation the cost of any material or supply as defined in paragraph (c)(1) of this section.* * *

* * *

(f) Election to apply de minimis rule—(1) In general. A taxpayer may elect to apply the de minimis rule under § 1.263(a)–2T(g) to any material or supply defined in paragraph (c)(1) this section.* * *

* * *

(g) Sale or disposition of materials and supplies. Upon sale or other disposition, materials and supplies as defined in this section are not treated as a capital asset under section 1221 or as property used in the trade or business under section 1231. Any asset for which the taxpayer makes the election to capitalize and depreciate under paragraph (d) of this section shall not be treated as a material or supply.

* * *

[T.D. 9564, 76 FR 81080, Dec. 27, 2011; 77 FR 18687, Mar. 28, 2012; 77 FR 74584, Dec. 17, 2012]

§ 1.162–4T Repairs (temporary).

(a) In general. A taxpayer may deduct amounts paid for repairs and maintenance to tangible property if the amounts paid are not otherwise required to be capitalized.

* * *

[T.D. 9564, 76 FR 81084, Dec. 27, 2011; 77 FR 74584, Dec. 17, 2012]

§ 1.162–5 Expenses for education.

(a) General rule. Expenditures made by an individual for education (including research undertaken as part of his educational program) which are not expenditures of a type described in paragraph (b)(2) or (3) of this section are deductible as ordinary and necessary business expenses (even though the education may lead to a degree) if the education—

(1) Maintains or improves skills required by the individual in his employment or other trade or business, or

(2) Meets the express requirements of the individual's employer, or the requirements of applicable law or regulations, imposed as a condition to the retention by the individual of an established employment relationship, status, or rate of compensation.

(b) Nondeductible educational expenditures—(1) In general. Educational expenditures described in subparagraphs (2) and (3) of this paragraph are personal expenditures or constitute an inseparable aggregate of personal and capital expenditures and, therefore, are not deductible as ordinary and necessary business expenses even though the education may maintain or improve skills required by the individual in his employment or other trade or business or may meet the express requirements of the individual's employer or of applicable law or regulations.

(2) Minimum educational requirements. (i) The first category of nondeductible educational expenses within the scope of subparagraph (1) of this paragraph are expenditures made by an individual for education which is required of him in order to meet the minimum educational requirements for qualification in his employment or other trade or business. The minimum education necessary to qualify for a position or other trade or business must be determined from a consideration of such factors as the requirements of the employer, the applicable law and regulations, and the standards of the profession, trade, or business involved. The fact that an individual is already performing service in an employment status does not establish that he has met the minimum educational requirements for qualification in that employment. Once an individual has met the minimum educational requirements for qualification in his employment or other trade or business (as in effect when he enters the employment or trade or business), he shall be treated as continuing to meet those requirements even though they are changed.

(ii) The minimum educational requirements for qualification of a particular individual in a position in an educational institution is the minimum level of education (in terms of aggregate college hours or degree) which under the applicable laws or regulations, in effect at the time this individual is first employed in such position, is normally required of an individual initially being employed in such a position. If there are no normal requirements as to the minimum level of education required for a position in an educational institution, then an individual in such a position shall be considered to have met the minimum educational requirements for qualification in that position when he becomes a member of the faculty of the educational institution. The determination of whether an individual is a member of the faculty of an educational institution must be made on the basis of the particular practices of the institution. However, an individual will ordinarily be considered to be a member of the faculty of an institution if (a) he has tenure or his years of service are being counted toward obtaining tenure; (b) the institution is making contributions to a retirement plan (other than Social Security or a similar program) in respect of his employment; or (c) he has a vote in faculty affairs.

(iii) The application of this subparagraph may be illustrated by the following examples:

Example (1). General facts: State X requires a bachelor's degree for beginning secondary school teachers which must include 30 credit hours of professional educational courses. In addition, in order to retain his position, a secondary school teacher must complete a fifth year of preparation within 10 years after beginning his employment. If an employing school official certifies to the State Department of Education that applicants having a bachelor's degree and the required courses in professional education cannot be found, he may hire individuals as secondary school teachers if they have completed a minimum of 90 semester hours of college work. However, to be retained in his position, such an individual must obtain his bachelor's degree and complete the required professional educational courses within 3 years after his employment commences. Under these facts, a bachelor's degree, without regard to whether it includes 30 credit hours of professional educational courses, is considered to be the minimum educational requirement for qualification as a secondary school teacher in State X. This is the case notwithstanding the number of teachers who are actually hired without such a degree. The following are examples of the application of these facts in particular situations:

Situation 1. A, at the time he is employed as a secondary school teacher in State X, has a bachelor's degree including 30 credit hours of professional educational courses. After his employment, A completes a fifth college year of education and, as a result, is issued a standard certificate. The fifth college year of education undertaken by A is not education required to meet the minimum educational requirements for qualification as a secondary school teacher. Accordingly, the expenditures for such education are deductible unless the expenditures are for education which is part of a program of study being pursued by A which will lead to qualifying him in a new trade or business.

Situation 2. Because of a shortage of applicants meeting the stated requirements, B, who has a bachelor's degree, is employed as a secondary school teacher in State X even though he has only 20 credit hours of professional educational courses. After his employment, B takes an additional 10 credit hours of professional educational courses. Since these courses do not constitute education required to meet the minimum educational requirements for qualification as a secondary school teacher which is a bachelor's degree and will not lead to qualifying B in a new trade or business, the expenditures for such courses are deductible.

Situation 3. Because of a shortage of applicants meeting the stated requirements, C is employed as a secondary school teacher in State X although he has only 90 semester hours of college work toward his bachelor's degree. After his employment, C undertakes courses leading to a bachelor's degree. These courses (including any courses in professional education) constitute education required to meet the minimum educational requirements for qualification as a secondary school teacher. Accordingly, the expenditures for such education are not deductible.

Situation 4. Subsequent to the employment of A, B, and C, but before they have completed a fifth college year of education, State X changes its requirements affecting secondary school teachers to provide that beginning teachers must have completed 5 college years of preparation. In the cases of A, B, and C, a fifth college year of education is not considered to be education undertaken to meet the minimum educational requirements for qualifications as a secondary school teacher. Accordingly, expenditures for a fifth year of college will be deductible unless the expenditures are for education which is part of a program being pursued by A, B, or C which will lead to qualifying him in a new trade or business.

Example (2). D, who holds a bachelor's degree, obtains temporary employment as an instructor at University Y and undertakes graduate courses as a candidate for a graduate degree. D may become a faculty member only if he obtains a graduate degree and may continue to hold a position as instructor only so long as he shows satisfactory progress towards obtaining this graduate degree. The graduate courses taken by D constitute education required to meet the minimum educational requirements for qualification in D's trade or business and, thus, the expenditures for such courses are not deductible.

Example (3). E, who has completed 2 years of a normal 3-year law school course leading to a bachelor of laws degree (LL.B.), is hired by a law firm to do legal research and perform other functions on a full-time basis. As a condition to continued employment, E is required to obtain an LL.B. and pass the State bar examination. E completes his law school education by attending night law school, and he takes a bar review course in order to prepare for the State bar examination. The law courses and bar review course constitute education required to meet the minimum educational requirements for qualification in E's trade or business and, thus, the expenditures for such courses are not deductible.

(3) Qualification for new trade or business. **(i)** The second category of nondeductible educational expenses within the scope of subparagraph (1) of this paragraph are expenditures made by an individual for education which is part of a program of study being pursued by him which will lead to qualifying him in a new trade or business. In the case of an employee, a change of duties does not constitute a new trade or business if the new duties involve the same general type of work as is involved in the individual's present employment. For this purpose, all teaching and related duties shall be considered to involve the same general type of work. The following are examples of changes in duties which do not constitute new trades or businesses:

(a) Elementary to secondary school classroom teacher.

(b) Classroom teacher in one subject (such as mathematics) to classroom teacher in another subject (such as science).

(c) Classroom teacher to guidance counselor.

(d) Classroom teacher to principal.

(ii) The application of this subparagraph to individuals other than teachers may be illustrated by the following examples:

Example (1). A, a self-employed individual practicing a profession other than law, for example, engineering, accounting, etc., attends law school at night and after completing his law school studies receives a bachelor of laws degree. The expenditures made by A in attending law school are nondeductible because this course of study qualifies him for a new trade or business.

Example (2). Assume the same facts as in example (1) except that A has the status of an employee rather than a self-employed individual, and that his employer requires him to obtain a bachelor of laws degree. A intends to continue practicing his nonlegal profession as an employee of such employer. Nevertheless, the expenditures made by A in attending law school are not deductible since this course of study qualifies him for a new trade or business.

Example (3). B, a general practitioner of medicine, takes a 2-week course reviewing new developments in several specialized fields of medicine. B's expenses for the course are deductible because the course maintains or improves skills required by him in his trade or business and does not qualify him for a new trade or business.

Example (4). C, while engaged in the private practice of psychiatry, undertakes a program of study and training at an accredited psychoanalytic institute which will lead to qualifying him to practice psychoanalysis. C's expenditures for such study and training are deductible because the study and training maintains or improves skills required by him in his trade or business and does not qualify him for a new trade or business.

(c) Deductible educational expenditures—(1) Maintaining or improving skills. The deduction under the category of expenditures for education which maintains or improves skills required by the individual in his employment or other trade or business includes refresher courses or courses dealing with current developments as well as academic or vocational courses provided the expenditures for the courses are not within either category of nondeductible expenditures described in paragraph (b)(2) or (3) of this section.

(2) Meeting requirements of employer. An individual is considered to have undertaken education in order to meet the express requirements of his employer, or the requirements of applicable law or regulations, imposed as a condition to the retention by the taxpayer of his established employment relationship, status, or rate of compensation only if such requirements are imposed for a bona fide business purpose of the individual's employer. Only the minimum education necessary to the retention by the individual of his established employment relationship, status, or rate of compensation may be considered as undertaken to meet the express requirements of the taxpayer's employer. However, education in excess of such minimum education may qualify as education undertaken in order to maintain or improve the skills required by the taxpayer in his employment or other trade or business (see subparagraph (1) of this paragraph). In no event, however, is a deduction allowable for expenditures for education which, even though for education required by the employer or applicable law or regulations, are within one of the categories of nondeductible expenditures described in paragraph (b)(2) and (3) of this section.

* * *

(e) Travel away from home. **(1)** If an individual travels away from home primarily to obtain education the expenses of which are deductible under this section, his expenditures for travel, meals, and lodging while away from home are deductible. However, if as an incident of such trip the individual engages in some personal activity such as sightseeing, social visiting, or entertaining, or other recreation, the portion of the expenses attributable to such personal activity constitutes nondeductible personal or living expenses and is not allowable as a deduction. If the individual's travel away from home is primarily personal, the individual's expenditures for travel, meals and lodging (other than meals and lodging during the time spent in participating in deductible education pursuits) are not deductible. Whether a particular trip is primarily personal or primarily to obtain education the expenses of which are deductible under this section depends upon all the facts and circumstances of each case. An important factor to be taken into consideration in making the determination is the relative amount of time devoted to personal activity as compared with the time devoted to educational pursuits. The rules set forth in this paragraph are subject to the provisions of section 162(a)(2), relating to deductibility of certain traveling expenses, and section 274(c) and (d), relating to allocation of certain foreign travel expenses and substantiation required, respectively, and the regulations thereunder.

(2) Examples. The application of this subsection may be illustrated by the following examples:

Example (1). A, a self-employed tax practitioner, decides to take a 1-week course in new developments in taxation, which is offered in City X, 500 miles away from his home. His primary purpose in going to X is to take the course, but he also takes a side trip to City Y (50 miles from X) for 1 day, takes a sightseeing trip while in X, and entertains some personal friends. A's transportation expenses to City X and return to his home are deductible but his transportation expenses to City Y are not deductible. A's expenses for meals and lodging while away from home will be allocated between his educational pursuits and his personal activities. Those expenses which are entirely personal, such as sightseeing and entertaining friends, are not deductible to any extent.

Example (2). The facts are the same as in example (1) except that A's primary purpose in going to City X is to take a vacation. This purpose is indicated by several factors, one of which is the fact that he spends only 1 week attending the tax course and devotes 5 weeks entirely to personal activities. None of A's transportation expenses are deductible and his expenses for meals and lodging while away from home are not deductible to the extent attributable to personal activities. His expenses for meals and lodging allocable to the week attending the tax course are, however, deductible.

Example (3). B, a high school mathematics teacher in New York City, in the summertime travels to a university in California in order to take a mathematics course the expense of which is deductible under this section. B pursues only one-fourth of a full course of study and the remainder of her time is devoted to personal activities the expense of which is not deductible. Absent a showing by B of a substantial nonpersonal reason for taking the course in the university in California, the trip is considered taken primarily for personal reasons and the cost of traveling from New York City to California and return would not be deductible. However, one-fourth of the cost of B's meals and lodging while attending the university in California may be considered properly allocable to deductible educational pursuits and, therefore, is deductible.

[T.D. 6500, 25 FR 11402, Nov. 26, 1960, as amended by T.D. 6918, 32 FR 6679, May 2, 1967]

§ 1.162–7 Compensation for personal services.

(a) There may be included among the ordinary and necessary expenses paid or incurred in carrying on any trade or business a reasonable allowance for salaries or other compensation for personal services actually rendered. The test of deductibility in the case of compensation payments is whether they are reasonable and are in fact payments purely for services.

(b) The test set forth in paragraph (a) of this section and its practical application may be further stated and illustrated as follows:

(1) Any amount paid in the form of compensation, but not in fact as the purchase price of services, is not deductible. An ostensible salary paid by a corporation may be a distribution of a dividend on stock. This is likely to occur in the case of a corporation having few shareholders, practically all of whom draw salaries. If in such a case the salaries are in excess of those ordinarily paid for similar services and the excessive payments correspond or bear a close relationship to the stockholdings of the officers or employees, it would seem likely that the salaries are not paid wholly for services rendered, but that the excessive payments are a distribution of earnings upon the stock. An ostensible salary may be in part payment for property. This may occur, for example, where a partnership sells out to a corporation, the former partners agreeing to continue in the service of the corporation. In such a case it may be found that the salaries of the former partners are not merely for services, but in part constitute payment for the transfer of their business.

(2) The form or method of fixing compensation is not decisive as to deductibility. While any form of contingent compensation invites scrutiny as a possible distribution of earnings of the enterprise, it does not follow that payments on a contingent basis are to be treated fundamentally on any basis different from that applying to compensation at a flat rate. Generally speaking, if contingent compensation is paid pursuant to a free bargain between the employer and the individual made before the services are rendered, not influenced by any consideration on the part of the employer other than that of securing on fair and advantageous terms the services of the individual, it should be allowed as a deduction even though in the actual working out of the contract it may prove to be greater than the amount which would ordinarily be paid.

(3) In any event the allowance for the compensation paid may not exceed what is reasonable under all the circumstances. It is, in general, just to assume that reasonable and true compensation is only such amount as would ordinarily be paid for like services by like enterprises under like circumstances. The circumstances to be taken into consideration are those existing at the date when the contract for services was made, not those existing at the date when the contract is questioned.

* * *

[T.D. 6500, 25 FR 11402, Nov. 26, 1960]

§ 1.162–8 Treatment of excessive compensation.

The income tax liability of the recipient in respect of an amount ostensibly paid to him as compensation, but not allowed to be deducted as such by the payor, will depend upon the circumstances of each case. Thus, in the case of excessive payments by corporations, if such payments correspond or bear a close relationship to stockholdings, and are found to be a distribution of earnings or profits, the excessive payments will be treated as a dividend. If such payments constitute payment for property, they should be treated by the payor as a capital expenditure and by the recipient as part of the purchase price. In the absence of evidence to justify other treatment, excessive payments for salaries or other compensation for personal services will be included in gross income of the recipient.

[T.D. 6500, 25 FR 11402, Nov. 26, 1960]

§ 1.162–9 Bonuses to employees.

Bonuses to employees will constitute allowable deductions from gross income when such payments are made in good faith and as additional compensation for the services actually rendered by the employees, provided such payments, when added to the stipulated salaries, do not exceed a reasonable compensation for the services rendered. It is immaterial whether such bonuses are paid in cash or in kind or partly in cash and partly in kind. Donations made to employees and others, which do not have in them the element of compensation or which are in excess of reasonable compensation for services, are not deductible from gross income.

[T.D. 6500, 25 FR 11402, Nov. 26, 1960]

§ 1.162–11 Rentals.

(a) Acquisition of a leasehold. If a leasehold is acquired for business purposes for a specified sum, the purchaser may take as a deduction in his return an aliquot part of such sum each year, based on the number of years the lease has to run. Taxes paid by a tenant to or for a landlord for business property are additional rent and constitute a deductible item to the tenant and taxable income to the landlord, the amount of the tax being deductible by the latter. * * * See section 178 * * * for rules governing the effect to be given renewal options in amortizing the costs incurred after July 28, 1958, of acquiring a lease. See § 1.197–2 for rules governing the amortization of costs to acquire limited interests in section 197 intangibles.

* * *

[T.D. 6500, 25 FR 11402, Nov. 26, 1960, as amended by T.D. 6520, 25 FR 13692, Dec. 24, 1960; T.D. 8865, 65 FR 3820, Jan. 25, 2000; T.D. 9564, 76 FR 81084, Dec. 27, 2011]

§ 1.162–11T Rentals (temporary).

(a) [Reserved]. For further guidance, see § 1.162–11(a).

(b) Improvements by lessee on lessor's property. The cost to a taxpayer of erecting buildings or making permanent improvements on property of which the taxpayer is a lessee is a capital expenditure and is not deductible as a business expense. For the rules regarding improvements to leased property where the improvements are tangible property, see § 1.263(a)–3T(f)(1). For the rules regarding depreciation or amortization deductions for leasehold improvements, see § 1.167(a)–4T.

* * *

[T.D. 9564, 76 FR 81084, Dec. 27, 2011; 77 FR 74584, Dec. 17, 2012]

§ 1.162–12 Expenses of farmers.

(a) Farms engaged in for profit. A farmer who operates a farm for profit is entitled to deduct from gross income as necessary expenses all amounts actually expended in the carrying on of the business of farming. The cost of ordinary tools of short life or small cost, such as hand tools, including shovels, rakes, etc., may be deducted. The purchase of feed and other costs connected with raising livestock may be treated as expense deductions insofar as such costs represent actual outlay, but not including the value of farm produce grown upon the farm or the labor of the taxpayer. * * * If a farmer does not compute income upon the crop method, the cost of seeds and young plants which are purchased for further development and cultivation prior to sale in later years may be deducted as an expense for the year of purchase, provided the farmer follows a consistent practice of deducting such costs as an expense from year to year. * * * The cost of farm machinery, equipment, and farm buildings represents a capital investment and is not an allowable deduction as an item of expense. Amounts expended in the development of farms, orchards, and ranches prior to the time when the productive state is reached may, at the election of the taxpayer, be regarded as investments of capital. * * * Amounts expended in purchasing work, breeding, dairy, or sporting animals are regarded as investments of capital, * * *. The purchase price of an automobile, even when wholly used in carrying on farming operations, is not deductible, but is regarded as an investment of capital. The cost of gasoline, repairs, and upkeep of an automobile if used wholly in the business of farming is deductible as an expense; if used partly for business purposes and partly for the pleasure or convenience of the taxpayer or his family, such cost may be apportioned according to the extent of the use for purposes of business and pleasure or convenience, and only the proportion of such cost justly attributable to business purposes is deductible as a necessary expense.

* * *

[T.D. 6500, 25 FR 11402, Nov. 26, 1960, as amended by T.D. 6548, 26 FR 1486, Feb. 22, 1961; T.D. 7198, 37 FR 13679, July 13, 1972; T.D. 8729, 62 FR 44546, Aug. 22, 1997; T.D. 8897, 65 FR 50643, Aug. 21, 2000]

§ 1.162–15 Contributions, dues, etc.

(a) Contributions to organizations described in section 170—(1) In general. No deduction is allowable under section 162(a) for a contribution or gift by an individual or a corporation if any part thereof is deductible under section 170. For example, if a taxpayer makes a contribution of $5,000 and only $4,000 of this amount is deductible under section 170(a) (whether because of the percentage limitation under either section 170(b)(1) or (2), the requirement as to time of payment, or both) no deduction is allowable under section 162(a) for the remaining $1,000.

(2) Scope of limitations. The limitations provided in section 162(b) and this paragraph apply only to payments which are in fact contributions or gifts to organizations described in section 170. For example, payments by a transit company to a local hospital (which is a charitable organization within the meaning of section 170) in consideration of a binding obligation on the part of the hospital to provide hospital services and facilities for the company's employees are not contributions or gifts within the meaning of section 170 and may be deductible under section 162(a) if the requirements of section 162(a) are otherwise satisfied.

(b) Other contributions. Donations to organizations other than those described in section 170 which bear a direct relationship to the taxpayer's business and are made with a reasonable expectation of a financial return commensurate with the amount of the donation may constitute allowable deductions as business expenses, * * *. For example, a transit company may donate a sum of money to an organization (of a class not referred to in section 170) intending to hold a convention in the city in which it operates, with a reasonable expectation that the holding of such convention will augment its income through a greater number of people using its transportation facilities.

(c) Dues. Dues and other payments to an organization, such as a labor union or a trade association, which otherwise meet the requirements of the regulations under section 162, are deductible in full. For limitations on the deductibility of dues and other payments, see paragraph (b) and (c) of § 1.162–20.

(d) Cross reference. For provisions dealing with expenditures for institutional or "good will" advertising, see § 1.162–20.

[T.D. 6500, 25 FR 11402, Nov. 26, 1960, as amended by T.D. 6819, 30 FR 5580, April 20, 1965]

§ 1.162–17 Reporting and substantiation of certain business expenses of employees.

(a) Introductory. The purpose of the regulations in this section is to provide rules for the reporting of information on income tax returns by taxpayers who pay or incur ordinary and necessary business expenses in connection with the performance of services as an employee and to furnish guidance as to the type of records which will be useful in compiling such information and in its substantiation, if required. The rules prescribed in this section do not apply to expenses paid or incurred for incidentals, such as office supplies for the employer or local transportation in connection with an errand. Employees incurring such incidental expenses are not required to provide substantiation for such amounts. The term "ordinary and necessary business expenses" means only those expenses which are ordinary and necessary in the conduct of the taxpayer's business and are directly attributable to such business. The term does not include nondeductible personal, living or family expenses.

(b) Expenses for which the employee is required to account to his employer—(1) Reimbursements equal to expenses. The employee need not report on his tax return (either itemized or in total amount) expenses for travel, transportation, entertainment, and similar purposes paid or incurred by him solely for the benefit of his employer for which he is required to account and does account to his employer and which are charged directly or indirectly to the employer (for example, through credit cards) or for which the employee is paid through advances, reimbursements, or otherwise, provided the total amount of such advances, reimbursements, and charges is equal to such expenses. In such a case the taxpayer need only state in his return that the total of amounts charged directly or indirectly to his employer through credit cards or otherwise and received from the employer as advances or reimbursements did not exceed the ordinary and necessary business expenses paid or incurred by the employee.

(2) Reimbursements in excess of expenses. In case the total of amounts charged directly or indirectly to the employer and received from the employer as advances, reimbursements, or otherwise, exceeds the ordinary and necessary business expenses paid or incurred by the employee and the employee is required to and does account to his employer for such expenses, the taxpayer must include such excess in income and state on his return that he has done so.

(3) Expenses in excess of reimbursements. If the employee's ordinary and necessary business expenses exceed the total of the amounts charged directly or indirectly to the employer and received from the employer as advances, reimbursements, or otherwise, and the employee is required to and does account to his employer for such expenses, the taxpayer may make the statement in his return required by subparagraph (1) of this paragraph unless he wishes to claim a deduction for such excess. If, however, he wishes to secure a deduction for such excess, he must submit a statement showing the following information as part of his tax return:

(i) The total of any charges paid or borne by the employer and of any other amounts received from the employer for payment of expenses whether by means of advances, reimbursements or otherwise; and

(ii) The nature of his occupation, the number of days away from home on business, and the total amount of ordinary and necessary business expenses paid or incurred by him (including those charged directly or indirectly to the employer through credit cards or otherwise) broken down into such broad categories as transportation, meals and lodging while away from home overnight, entertainment expenses, and other business expenses.

(4) To "account" to his employer as used in this section means to submit an expense account or other required written statement to the employer showing the business nature and the amount of all the employee's expenses (including those charged directly or indirectly to the employer through credit cards or otherwise) broken down into such broad categories as transportation, meals and lodging while away from home overnight, entertainment expenses, and other business expenses. For this purpose, the Commissioner in his discretion may approve reasonable business practices under which mileage, per diem in lieu of subsistence, and similar allowances providing for ordinary and necessary business expenses in accordance with a fixed scale may be regarded as equivalent to an accounting to the employer.

(c) Expenses for which the employee is not required to account to his employer. If the employee is not required to account to his employer for his ordinary and necessary business expenses, e.g., travel, transportation, entertainment, and similar items, or, though required, fails to account for such expenses, he must submit, as a part of his tax return, a statement showing the following information:

(1) The total of all amounts received as advances or reimbursements from his employer in connection with the ordinary and necessary business expenses of the employee, including amounts charged directly or indirectly to the employer through credit cards or otherwise; and

(2) The nature of his occupation, the number of days away from home on business, and the total amount of ordinary and necessary business expenses paid or incurred by him (including those charged directly or indirectly to the employer through credit cards or otherwise) broken down into such broad categories as transportation, meals and lodging while away from home overnight, entertainment expenses, and other business expenses.

* * *

(e) Applicability. * * *

(3) For taxable years beginning on or after January 1, 1989, the provisions of this section are superseded by the regulations under section 62(c) to the extent this section is inconsistent with those regulations. See § 1.62–2.

[T.D. 6500, 25 FR 11402, Nov. 26, 1960, as amended by T.D. 6630, 27 FR 12935, Dec. 29, 1962; T.D. 8276, 54 FR 51026, Dec. 12, 1989; T.D. 8324, 55 FR 51695, Dec. 17, 1990]

§ 1.162–18 Illegal bribes and kickbacks.

(a) Illegal payments to government officials or employees—(1) In general. No deduction shall be allowed under section 162(a) for any amount paid or incurred, directly or indirectly, to an official or employee of any government, or of any agency or other instrumentality of any government, if—

(i) In the case of a payment made to an official or employee of a government other than a foreign government described in subparagraph (3)(ii) or (iii) of this paragraph, the payment constitutes an illegal bribe or kickback, or

(ii) In the case of a payment made to an official or employee of a foreign government described in subparagraph (3)(ii) or (iii) of this paragraph, the making of the payment would be unlawful under the laws of the United States (if such laws were applicable to the payment and to the official or employee at the time the expenses were paid or incurred).

No deduction shall be allowed for an accrued expense if the eventual payment thereof would fall within the prohibition of this section. The place where the expenses are paid or incurred is immaterial. For purposes of subdivision (ii) of this subparagraph, lawfulness, or unlawfulness of the payment under the laws of the foreign country is immaterial.

(2) Indirect payment. For purposes of this paragraph, an indirect payment to an individual shall include any payment which inures to his benefit or promotes his interests, regardless of the medium in which the payment is made and regardless of the identity of the immediate recipient or payor. Thus, for example, payment made to an agent, relative, or independent contractor of an official or employee, or even directly into the general treasury of a foreign country of which the beneficiary is an official or employee, may be treated as an indirect payment to the official or employee, if in fact such payment inures or will inure to his benefit or promotes or will promote his financial or other interests. A payment made by an agent or independent contractor of the taxpayer which benefits the taxpayer shall be treated as an indirect payment by the taxpayer to the official or employee.

* * *

(4) Laws of the United States. The term "laws of the United States", to which reference is made in paragraph (a)(1)(ii) of this section, shall be deemed to include only Federal statutes, including State laws which are assimilated into Federal law by Federal statute, and legislative and interpretative regulations thereunder. The term shall also be limited to statutes which prohibit some act or acts, for the violation of which there is a civil or criminal penalty.

* * *

(b) Other illegal payments—(1) In general. No deduction shall be allowed under section 162(a) for any payment (other than a payment described in paragraph (a) of this section) made, directly or indirectly, to any person, if the payment constitutes an illegal bribe, illegal kickback, or other illegal payment under the laws of the United States (as defined in paragraph (a)(4) of this section), or under any State law (but only if such State law is generally enforced), which subjects the payor to a criminal penalty or the loss (including a suspension) of license or privilege to engage in a trade or business (whether or not such penalty or loss is actually imposed upon the taxpayer). For purposes of this paragraph, a kickback includes a payment in consideration of the referral of a client, patient, or customer. This paragraph applies only to payments made after December 30, 1969.

(2) State law. For purposes of this paragraph, State law means a statute of a State or the District of Columbia.

(3) Generally enforced. For purposes of this paragraph, a State law shall be considered to be generally enforced unless it is never enforced or the only persons normally charged with violations thereof in the State (or the District of Columbia) enacting the law are infamous or those whose violations are extraordinarily flagrant. For example, a criminal statute of a State shall be considered to be generally enforced unless violations of the statute which are brought to the attention of appropriate authorities do not result in any enforcement action in the absence of unusual circumstances.

* * *

(c) Kickbacks, rebates, and bribes under medicare and medicaid. No deduction shall be allowed under section 162(a) for any kickback, rebate, or bribe (whether or not illegal) made on or after December 10, 1971, by any provider of services, supplier, physician, or other person who furnishes items or services for which payment is or may be made under the Social Security Act, as amended, or in whole or in part out of Federal funds under a State plan approved under such Act, if such kickback, rebate, or bribe is made in connection with the furnishing of such items or services or the making or receipt of such payments. For purposes of this paragraph, a kickback includes a payment in consideration of the referral of a client, patient, or customer.

[T.D. 6500, 25 FR 11402, Nov. 26, 1960, as amended by T.D. 7345, 40 FR 7437, Feb. 20, 1975; 40 FR 8948, March 4, 1975]

§ 1.162-20 Expenditures attributable to lobbying, political campaigns, attempts to influence legislation, etc., and certain advertising.

(a) In general—(1) Scope of section. * * *

* * *

(2) Institutional or "good will" advertising. Expenditures for institutional or "good will" advertising which keeps the taxpayer's name before the public are generally deductible as ordinary and necessary business expenses provided the expenditures are related to the patronage the taxpayer might reasonably expect in the future. For example, a deduction will ordinarily be allowed for the cost of advertising which keeps the taxpayer's name before the public in connection with encouraging contributions to such organizations as the Red Cross, the purchase of United States Savings Bonds, or participation in similar causes. In like fashion, expenditures for advertising which presents views on economic, financial, social, or other subjects of a general nature, but which does not involve any of the activities specified in paragraph (b) or (c) of this section for which a deduction is not allowable, are deductible if they otherwise meet the requirements of the regulations under section 162.

* * *

[T.D. 6819, 30 FR 5581, April 20, 1965, as amended by T.D. 6996, 34 FR 835, Jan. 18, 1969; T.D. 8602, 60 FR 37573, July 21, 1995]

§ 1.162-21 Fines and penalties.

* * *

(b) Definition. (1) For purposes of this section a fine or similar penalty includes an amount—

(i) Paid pursuant to conviction or a plea of guilty or *nolo contendere* for a crime (felony or misdemeanor) in a criminal proceeding;

(ii) Paid as a civil penalty imposed by Federal, State, or local law, including additions to tax and additional amounts and assessable penalties imposed by chapter 68 of the Internal Revenue Code of 1954;

(iii) Paid in settlement of the taxpayer's actual or potential liability for a fine or penalty (civil or criminal); or

(iv) Forfeited as collateral posted in connection with a proceeding which could result in imposition of such a fine or penalty.

(2) The amount of a fine or penalty does not include legal fees and related expenses paid or incurred in the defense of a prosecution or civil action arising from a violation of the law imposing the fine or civil penalty, nor court costs assessed against the taxpayer, or stenographic and printing charges. Compensatory damages (including damages under section 4A of the Clayton Act (15 U.S.C. 15a), as amended) paid to a government do not constitute a fine or penalty.

(c) Examples. The application of this section may be illustrated by the following examples:

Example (1). M Corp. was indicted under section 1 of the Sherman Anti-Trust Act (15 U.S.C. 1) for fixing and maintaining prices of certain electrical products. M Corp. was convicted and was fined $50,000. The United States sued M Corp. under section 4A of the Clayton Act (15 U.S.C. 15a) for $100,000, the amount of the actual damages resulting from the price fixing of which M Corp. was convicted. Pursuant to a final judgment entered in the civil action M Corp. paid the United States $100,000 in damages. Section 162(f) precludes M Corp. from deducting the fine of $50,000 as a trade or business expense. Section 162(f) does not preclude it from deducting the $100,000 paid to the United States as actual damages.

Example (2). N Corp. was found to have violated 33 U.S.C. 1321(b)(3) when a vessel it operated discharged oil in harmful quantities into the navigable waters of the United States. A civil penalty under 33 U.S.C. 1321(b)(6) of $5,000 was assessed against N Corp. with respect to the discharge. N Corp. paid $5,000 to the Coast Guard in payment of the civil penalty. Section 162(f) precludes N Corp. from deducting the $5,000 penalty.

Example (3). O Corp., a manufacturer of motor vehicles, was found to have violated 42 U.S.C. 1857f–2(a)(1) by selling a new motor vehicle which was not covered by the required certificate of conformity. Pursuant to 42 U.S.C. 1857f–4, O Corp. was required to pay, and did pay, a civil penalty of $10,000. In addition, pursuant to 42 U.S.C. 1857f–5a(c)(1), O Corp. was required to expend, and did expend, $500 in order to remedy the nonconformity of that motor vehicle. Section 162(f) precludes O Corp. from deducting the $10,000 penalty as a trade or business expense, but does not preclude it from deducting the $500 which it expended to remedy the nonconformity.

Example (4). P Corp. was the operator of a coal mine in which occurred a violation of a mandatory safety standard prescribed by the Federal Coal Mine Health and Safety Act of 1969 (30 U.S.C. 801 et seq.). Pursuant to 30 U.S.C. 819(a), a civil penalty of $10,000 was assessed against P Corp., and P Corp. paid the penalty. Section 162(f) precludes P Corp. from deducting the $10,000 penalty.

* * *

[T.D. 7345, 40 FR 7437, Feb. 20, 1975; 40 FR 8948, March 4, 1975, as amended by T.D. 7366, 40 FR 29290, July 11, 1975]

§ 1.162–25T Deductions with respect to noncash fringe benefits.

(a) Employer. If an employer includes the value of a noncash fringe benefit in an employee's gross income, the employer may not deduct this amount as compensation for services, but rather may deduct only the costs incurred by the employer in providing the benefit to the employee. The employer may be allowed a cost recovery deduction under section 168 or a deduction under section 179 for an expense not chargeable to capital account, or, if the noncash fringe benefit is property leased by the employer, a deduction for the ordinary and necessary business expense of leasing the property.

* * *

[T.D. 8004, 50 FR 755, Jan. 7, 1985; T.D. 8061, 50 FR 46013, Nov. 6, 1985; T.D. 8063, 50 FR 52312, Dec. 23, 1985; T.D. 8276, 54 FR 51026, Dec. 12, 1989; T.D. 8451, 57 FR 57668, Dec. 7, 1992]

§ 1.162–29 Influencing legislation.

(a) Scope. This section provides rules for determining whether an activity is influencing legislation for purposes of section 162(e)(1)(A). * * *

(b) Definitions. For purposes of this section—

(1) Influencing legislation. Influencing legislation means—

(i) Any attempt to influence any legislation through a lobbying communication; and

(ii) All activities, such as research, preparation, planning, and coordination, including deciding whether to make a lobbying communication, engaged in for a purpose of making or supporting a lobbying communication, even if not yet made. See paragraph (c) of this section for rules for determining the purposes for engaging in an activity.

(2) Attempt to influence legislation. An attempt to influence any legislation through a lobbying communication is making the lobbying communication.

(3) Lobbying communication. A lobbying communication is any communication (other than any communication compelled by subpoena, or otherwise compelled by Federal or State law) with any member or employee of a legislative body or any other government official or employee who may participate in the formulation of the legislation that—

(i) Refers to specific legislation and reflects a view on that legislation; or

(ii) Clarifies, amplifies, modifies, or provides support for views reflected in a prior lobbying communication.

(4) Legislation. Legislation includes any action with respect to Acts, bills, resolutions, or other similar items by a legislative body. Legislation includes a proposed treaty required to be submitted by the President to the Senate for its advice and consent from the time the President's representative begins to negotiate its position with the prospective parties to the proposed treaty.

(5) Specific legislation. Specific legislation includes a specific legislative proposal that has not been introduced in a legislative body.

(6) Legislative bodies. Legislative bodies are Congress, state legislatures, and other similar governing bodies, excluding local councils (and similar governing bodies), and executive, judicial, or administrative bodies. For this purpose, administrative bodies include school boards, housing authorities, sewer and water districts, zoning boards, and other similar Federal, State, or local special purpose bodies, whether elective or appointive.

(7) Examples. The provisions of this paragraph (b) are illustrated by the following examples.

Example 1. Taxpayer P's employee, A, is assigned to approach members of Congress to gain their support for a pending bill. A drafts and P prints a position letter on the bill. P distributes the letter to members of Congress. Additionally, A personally contacts several members of Congress or their staffs to seek support for P's position on the bill. The letter and the personal contacts are lobbying communications. Therefore, P is influencing legislation.

Example 2. Taxpayer R is invited to provide testimony at a congressional oversight hearing concerning the implementation of The Financial Institutions Reform, Recovery, and Enforcement Act of 1989. Specifically, the hearing concerns a proposed regulation increasing the threshold value of commercial and residential real estate transactions for which an appraisal by a state licensed or certified appraiser is required. In its testimony, R states that it is in favor of the proposed regulation. Because R does not refer to any specific legislation or reflect a view on any such legislation, R has not made a lobbying communication. Therefore, R is not influencing legislation.

Example 3. State X enacts a statute that requires the licensing of all day- care providers. Agency B in State X is charged with writing rules to implement the statute. After the enactment of the statute, Taxpayer § sends a letter to Agency B providing detailed proposed rules that § recommends Agency B adopt to implement the statute on licensing of day-care providers. Because the letter to Agency B neither refers to nor reflects a view on any specific legislation, it is not a lobbying communication. Therefore, § is not influencing legislation.

Example 4. Taxpayer T proposes to a State Park Authority that it purchase a particular tract of land for a new park. Even if T's proposal would necessarily require the State Park Authority eventually to seek appropriations to acquire the land and develop the new park, T has not made a lobbying communication because there has been no reference to, nor any view reflected on, any specific legislation. Therefore, T's proposal is not influencing legislation.

Example 5. **(i)** Taxpayer U prepares a paper that asserts that lack of new capital is hurting State X's economy. The paper indicates that State X residents either should invest more in local businesses or increase their savings so that funds will be available to others interested in making investments. U forwards a summary of the unpublished paper to legislators in State X with a cover letter that states in part:

You must take action to improve the availability of new capital in the state.

(ii) Because neither the summary nor the cover letter refers to any specific legislative proposal and no other facts or circumstances indicate that they refer to an existing legislative proposal, forwarding the summary to legislators in State X is not a lobbying communication. Therefore, U is not influencing legislation.

(iii) Q, a member of the legislature of State X, calls U to request a copy of the unpublished paper from which the summary was prepared. U forwards the paper with a cover letter that simply refers to the enclosed materials. Because U's letter to Q and the unpublished paper do not refer to any specific legislation or reflect a view on any such legislation, the letter is not a lobbying communication. Therefore, U is not influencing legislation.

Example 6. **(i)** Taxpayer V prepares a paper that asserts that lack of new capital is hurting the national economy. The paper indicates that lowering the capital gains rate would increase the availability of capital and increase tax receipts from the capital gains tax. V forwards the paper to its representatives in Congress with a cover letter that says, in part:

I urge you to support a reduction in the capital gains tax rate.

(ii) V's communication is a lobbying communication because it refers to and reflects a view on a specific legislative proposal (i.e., lowering the capital gains rate). Therefore, V is influencing legislation.

Example 7. Taxpayer W, based in State A, notes in a letter to a legislator of State A that State X has passed a bill that accomplishes a stated purpose and then says that State A should pass such a bill. No such bill has been introduced into the State A legislature. The communication is a lobbying communication because it refers to and reflects a view on a specific legislative proposal. Therefore, W is influencing legislation.

Example 8. **(i)** Taxpayer Y represents citrus fruit growers. Y writes a letter to a United States senator discussing how pesticide O has benefited citrus fruit growers and disputing problems linked to its use. The letter discusses a bill pending in Congress and states in part:

This bill would prohibit the use of pesticide O. If citrus growers are unable to use this pesticide, their crop yields will be severely reduced, leading to higher prices for consumers and lower profits, even bankruptcy, for growers.

(ii) Y's views on the bill are reflected in this statement. Thus, the communication is a lobbying communication, and Y is influencing legislation.

Example 9. **(i)** B, the president of Taxpayer Z, an insurance company, meets with Q, who chairs the X state legislature's committee with jurisdiction over laws regulating insurance companies, to discuss the possibility of legislation to address current problems with surplus-line companies. B recommends that legislation be introduced that would create minimum capital and surplus requirements for surplus-line companies and create clearer guidelines concerning the risks that surplus-line companies can insure. B's discussion with Q is a lobbying communication because B refers to and reflects a view on a specific legislative proposal. Therefore, Z is influencing legislation.

(ii) Q is not convinced that the market for surplus-line companies is substantial enough to warrant such legislation and requests that B provide information on the amount and types of risks covered by surplus-line companies. After the meeting, B has employees of Z prepare estimates of the percentage of property and casualty insurance risks handled by surplus-line companies. B sends the estimates with a cover letter that simply refers to the enclosed materials. Although B's follow-up letter to Q does not refer to specific legislation or reflect a view on such legislation, B's letter supports the views reflected in the earlier communication. Therefore, the letter is a lobbying communication and Z is influencing legislation.

(c) Purpose for engaging in an activity—(1) In general. The purposes for engaging in an activity are determined based on all the facts and circumstances. Facts and circumstances include, but are not limited to—

(i) Whether the activity and the lobbying communication are proximate in time;

(ii) Whether the activity and the lobbying communication relate to similar subject matter;

(iii) Whether the activity is performed at the request of, under the direction of, or on behalf of a person making the lobbying communication;

(iv) Whether the results of the activity are also used for a nonlobbying purpose; and

(v) Whether, at the time the taxpayer engages in the activity, there is specific legislation to which the activity relates.

(2) Multiple purposes. If a taxpayer engages in an activity both for the purpose of making or supporting a lobbying communication and for some nonlobbying purpose, the taxpayer must treat the activity as engaged in partially for a lobbying purpose and partially for a nonlobbying purpose. This division of the activity must result in a reasonable allocation of costs to influencing legislation. See § 1.162–28 (allocation rules for certain expenditures to which section 162(e)(1) applies). A taxpayer's treatment of these multiple-purpose activities will, in general, not result in a reasonable allocation if it allocates to influencing legislation—

(i) Only the incremental amount of costs that would not have been incurred but for the lobbying purpose; or

(ii) An amount based solely on the number of purposes for engaging in that activity without regard to the relative importance of those purposes.

(3) Activities treated as having no purpose to influence legislation. A taxpayer that engages in any of the following activities is treated as having done so without a purpose of making or supporting a lobbying communication—

(i) Before evidencing a purpose to influence any specific legislation referred to in paragraph (c)(3)(i)(A) or (B) of this section (or similar legislation)—

(A) Determining the existence or procedural status of specific legislation, or the time, place, and subject of any hearing to be held by a legislative body with respect to specific legislation; or

(B) Preparing routine, brief summaries of the provisions of specific legislation;

(ii) Performing an activity for purposes of complying with the requirements of any law (for example, satisfying state or federal securities law filing requirements);

(iii) Reading any publications available to the general public or viewing or listening to other mass media communications; and

(iv) Merely attending a widely attended speech.

(4) Examples. The provisions of this paragraph (c) are illustrated by the following examples.

Example 1. (i) Facts. In 1997, Agency F issues proposed regulations relating to the business of Taxpayer W. There is no specific legislation during 1997 that is similar to the regulatory proposal. W undertakes a study of the impact of the proposed regulations on its business. W incorporates the results of that study in comments sent to Agency F in 1997. In 1998, legislation is introduced in Congress that is similar to the regulatory proposal. Also in 1998, W writes a letter to Senator P stating that it opposes the proposed legislation. W encloses with the letter a copy of the comments it sent to Agency F.

(ii) Analysis. W's letter to Senator P refers to and reflects a view on specific legislation and therefore is a lobbying communication. Although W's study of the impact of the proposed regulations is proximate in time and similar in subject matter to its lobbying communication, W performed the study and incorporated the results in comments sent to Agency F when no legislation with a similar subject matter was pending (a nonlobbying use). On these facts, W engaged in the study solely for a nonlobbying purpose.

Example 2. (i) Facts. The governor of State Q proposes a budget that includes a proposed sales tax on electricity. Using its records of electricity consumption, Taxpayer Y estimates the additional costs that the budget proposal would impose upon its business. In the same year, Y writes to members of the state legislature and explains that it opposes the proposed sales tax. In its letter, Y includes its estimate of the costs that the sales tax would impose on its business. Y does not demonstrate any other use of its estimates.

(ii) Analysis. The letter is a lobbying communication (because it refers to and reflects a view on specific legislation, the governor's proposed budget). Y's estimate of additional costs under the proposal supports the lobbying communication, is proximate in time and similar in subject matter to a specific legislative proposal then in existence, and is not used for a nonlobbying purpose. Based on these facts, Y estimated its additional costs under the budget proposal solely to support the lobbying communication.

Example 3. (i) Facts. A senator in the State Q legislature announces her intention to introduce legislation to require health insurers to cover a particular medical procedure in all policies sold in the state. Taxpayer Y has different policies for two groups of employees, one of which covers the procedure and one of which does not. After the bill is introduced, Y's legislative affairs staff asks Y's human resources staff to estimate the additional cost to cover the procedure for both groups of employees. Y's human resources staff prepares a study estimating Y's increased costs and forwards it to the legislative affairs staff. Y's legislative staff then writes to members of the state legislature and explains that it opposes the proposed change in insurance coverage based on the study. Y's legislative affairs staff thereafter forwards the study, prepared for its use in opposing the statutory proposal, to its labor relations staff for use in negotiations with employees scheduled to begin later in the year.

(ii) Analysis. The letter to legislators is a lobbying communication (because it refers to and reflects a view on specific legislation). The activity of estimating Y's additional costs under the proposed legislation relate to the same subject as the lobbying communication, occurs close in time to the lobbying communication, is conducted at the request of a person making a lobbying communication, and relates to specific legislation then in existence. Although Y used the study in its labor negotiations, mere use for that purpose does not establish that Y estimated its additional costs under the proposed legislation in part for a nonlobbying purpose. Thus, based on all the facts and circumstances, Y estimated the additional costs it would incur under the proposal solely to make or support the lobbying communication.

Example 4. (i) Facts. After several years of developmental work under various contracts, in 1996, Taxpayer A contracts with the Department of Defense (DOD) to produce a prototype of a new generation military aircraft. A is aware that DOD will be able to fund the contract only if Congress appropriates an amount for that purpose in the upcoming appropriations process. In 1997, A conducts simulation tests of the aircraft and revises the specifications of the aircraft's expected performance capabilities, as required under the contract. A submits the results of the tests and the revised specifications to DOD. In 1998, Congress considers legislation to appropriate funds for the contract. In that connection, A summarizes the results of the simulation tests and of the aircraft's expected performance capabilities, and submits the summary to interested members of Congress with a cover letter that encourages them to support appropriations of funds for the contract.

(ii) Analysis. The letter is a lobbying communication (because it refers to specific legislation (i.e., appropriations) and requests passage). The described activities in 1996, 1997, and 1998 relate to the same subject as the lobbying communication. The summary was prepared specifically for, and close in time to, that communication. Based on these facts, the summary was prepared solely for a lobbying purpose. In contrast, A conducted the tests and revised the specifications to comply with its production contract with DOD. A conducted the tests and revised the specifications solely for a nonlobbying purpose.

Example 5. (i) Facts. C, president of Taxpayer W, travels to the state capital to attend a two-day conference on new manufacturing processes. C plans to spend a third day in the capital meeting with state legislators to explain why W opposes a pending bill unrelated to the subject of the conference. At the meetings with the legislators, C makes lobbying communications by referring to and reflecting a view on the pending bill.

(ii) Analysis. C's traveling expenses (transportation and meals and lodging) are partially for the purpose of making or supporting the lobbying communications and partially for a nonlobbying purpose. As a result, under paragraph (c)(2) of this section, W must reasonably allocate C's traveling expenses between these two purposes. Allocating to influencing legislation only C's incremental transportation expenses (i.e., the taxi fare to meet with the state legislators) does not result in a reasonable allocation of traveling expenses.

Example 6. (i) Facts. On February 1, 1997, a bill is introduced in Congress that would affect Company E. Employees in E's legislative affairs department, as is customary, prepare a brief summary of the bill and periodically confirm the procedural status of the bill through conversations with employees and members of Congress. On March 31, 1997, the head of E's legislative affairs department meets with E's President to request that B, a chemist, temporarily help the legislative affairs department analyze the bill. The President agrees, and suggests that B also be assigned to draft a position letter in opposition to the bill. Employees of the legislative affairs department continue to confirm periodically the procedural status of the bill. On October 31, 1997, B's position letter in opposition to the bill is delivered to members of Congress.

(ii) Analysis. B's letter is a lobbying communication because it refers to and reflects a view on specific legislation. Under paragraph (c)(3)(i) of this section, the assignment of B to assist the legislative affairs department in analyzing the bill and in drafting a position letter in opposition to the bill evidences a purpose to influence legislation. Neither the activity of periodically confirming the procedural status of the bill nor the activity of preparing the routine, brief summary of the bill before March 31 constitutes influencing legislation. In contrast, periodically confirming the procedural status of the bill on or after March 31 relates to the same subject as, and is close in time to, the lobbying communication and is used for no nonlobbying purpose. Consequently, after March 31, E determined the procedural status of the bill for the purpose of supporting the lobbying communication by B.

(d) Lobbying communication made by another. If a taxpayer engages in activities for a purpose of supporting a lobbying communication to be made by another person (or by a group of persons), the taxpayer's activities are treated under paragraph (b) of this section as influencing legislation. For example, if a taxpayer or an employee of the taxpayer (as a volunteer or otherwise) engages in an activity to assist a trade association in preparing its lobbying communication, the taxpayer's activities are influencing legislation even if the lobbying communication is made by the trade association and not the taxpayer. If, however, the taxpayer's employee, acting outside the employee's scope of employment, volunteers to engage in those activities, then the taxpayer is not influencing legislation.

* * *

[T.D. 8602, 60 FR 37568, July 21, 1995]

§ 1.163–1 Interest deduction in general.

* * *

(b) Interest paid by the taxpayer on a mortgage upon real estate of which he is the legal or equitable owner, even though the taxpayer is not directly liable upon the bond or note secured by such mortgage, may be deducted as interest on his indebtedness. * * *

* * *

[T.D. 6500, 25 FR 11402, Nov. 26, 1960, as amended by T.D. 6821, 30 FR 6216, May 4, 1965; T.D. 6873, 31 FR 941, Jan. 25, 1966; T.D. 7408, 41 FR 9547, March 5, 1976]

§ 1.163–7 Deduction for OID on certain debt instruments.

(a) General rule. Except as otherwise provided in paragraph (b) of this section, an issuer (including a transferee) determines the amount of OID that is deductible each year under section 163(e)(1) by using the constant yield method described in § 1.1272–1(b). This determination, however, is made without regard to section 1272(a)(7) (relating to acquisition premium) and § 1.1273–1(d) (relating to de minimis OID). An issuer is permitted a deduction under section 163(e)(1) only to the extent the issuer is primarily liable on the debt instrument. For certain limitations on the deductibility of OID, see sections 163(e) and 1275(b)(2). * * *

(b) Special rules for de minimis OID—(1) Stated interest. If a debt instrument has a de minimis amount of OID (within the meaning of § 1.1273–1(d)), the issuer treats all stated interest on the debt instrument as qualified stated interest. See §§ 1.446–2(b) and 1.461–1 for the treatment of qualified stated interest.

(2) Deduction of de minimis OID on other than a constant yield basis. In lieu of deducting de minimis OID under the general rule of paragraph (a) of this section, an issuer of a debt instrument with a de minimis amount of OID (other than a de minimis amount treated as qualified stated interest under paragraph (b)(1) of this section) may choose to deduct the OID at maturity, on a straight-line basis over the term of the debt instrument, or in proportion to stated interest payments. The issuer makes this choice by reporting the de minimis OID in a manner consistent with the method chosen on the issuer's timely filed Federal income tax return for the taxable year in which the debt instrument is issued.

* * *

[T.D. 8517, 59 FR 4804, Feb. 2, 1994, as amended by T.D. 8674, 61 FR 30138, June 14, 1996; T.D. 8934, 66 FR 2815, Jan. 12, 2001]

§ 1.163–8T Allocation of interest expense among expenditures.

(a) In general—(1) Application. This section prescribes rules for allocating interest expense for purposes of applying sections 469 (the "passive loss limitation") and 163(d) and (h) (the "non-business interest limitations").

* * *

(3) Manner of allocation. In general, interest expense on a debt is allocated in the same manner as the debt to which such interest expense relates is allocated. Debt is allocated by tracing disbursements of the debt proceeds to specific expenditures. This section prescribes rules for tracing debt proceeds to specific expenditures.

(4) Treatment of interest expenses—(i) General rule. Except as otherwise provided in paragraph (m) of this section (relating to limitations on interest expense other than the passive loss and nonbusiness interest limitations), interest expense allocated under the rules of this section is treated in the following manner:

(A) Interest expense allocated to a trade or business expenditure (as defined in paragraph (b)(7) of this section) is taken into account under section 163(h)(2)(A);

(B) Interest expense allocated to a passive activity expenditure (as defined in paragraph (b)(4) of this section) or a former passive activity expenditure (as defined in paragraph (b)(2) of this section) is taken into account for purposes of section 469 in determining the income or loss from the activity to which such expenditure relates;

(C) Interest expense allocated to an investment expenditure (as defined in paragraph (b)(3) of this section) is treated for purposes of section 163(d) as investment interest;

(D) Interest expense allocated to a personal expenditure (as defined in paragraph (b)(5) of this section) is treated for purposes of section 163(h) as personal interest; and

(E) Interest expense allocated to a portfolio expenditure (as defined in paragraph (b)(6) of this section) is treated for purposes of section 469(e)(2)(B)(ii) as interest expense described in section 469(e)(1)(A)(i)(III).

(ii) Examples. The following examples illustrate the application of this paragraph (a)(4):

Example (1). Taxpayer A, an individual, incurs interest expense allocated under the rules of this section to the following expenditures:

$6,000	Passive activity expenditure.
$4,000	Personal expenditure.

The $6,000 interest expense allocated to the passive activity expenditure is taken into account for purposes of section 469 in computing A's income or loss from the activity to which such interest relates. Pursuant to section 163(h), A may not deduct the $4,000 interest expense allocated to the personal expenditure (except to the extent such interest is qualified residence interest, within the meaning of section 163(h)(3)).

Example (2). **(i)** Corporation M, a closely held C corporation (within the meaning of section 469(j)(1)) has $10,000 of interest expense for a taxable year. Under the rules of this section, M's interest expense is allocated to the following expenditures:

$2,000	Passive activity expenditure.
$3,000	Portfolio expenditure.
$5,000	Other expenditures.

(ii) Under section 163(d)(3)(D) and this paragraph (a)(4), the $2,000 interest expense allocated to the passive activity expenditure is taken into account in computing M's passive activity loss for the taxable year, but, pursuant to section 469(e)(1) and this paragraph (a)(4), the interest expense allocated to the portfolio expenditure and the other expenditures is not taken into account for such purposes.

(iii) Since M is a closely held C corporation, its passive activity loss is allowable under section 469(e)(2)(A) as a deduction from net active income. Under section 469(e)(2)(B) and this paragraph (a)(4), the $5,000 interest expense allocated to other expenditures is taken into account in computing M's net active income, but the interest expense allocated to the passive activity expenditure and the portfolio expenditure is not taken into account for such purposes.

(iv) Since M is a corporation, the $3,000 interest expense allocated to the portfolio expenditure is allowable without regard to section 163(d). If M were an individual, however, the interest expense allocated to the portfolio expenditure would be treated as investment interest for purposes of applying the limitation of section 163(d).

(b) Definitions. For purposes of this section—

(1) "Former passive activity" means an activity described in section 469(f)(3), but only if an unused deduction or credit (within the meaning of section 469(f)(1)(A) or (B)) is allocable to the activity under section 469(b) for the taxable year.

(2) "Former passive activity expenditure" means an expenditure that is taken into account under section 469 in computing the income or loss from a former passive activity of the taxpayer or an expenditure (including an expenditure properly chargeable to capital account) that would be so taken into account if such expenditure were otherwise deductible.

(3) "Investment expenditure" means an expenditure (other than a passive activity expenditure) properly chargeable to capital account with respect to property held for investment (within the meaning of section 163(d)(5)(A)) or an expenditure in connection with the holding of such property.

(4) "Passive activity expenditure" means an expenditure that is taken into account under section 469 in computing income or loss from a passive activity of the taxpayer or an expenditure (including an expenditure properly chargeable to capital account) that would be so taken into account if such expenditure were otherwise deductible. For purposes of this section, the term "passive activity expenditure" does not include any expenditure with respect to any low-income housing project in any taxable year in which any benefit is allowed with respect to such project under section 502 of the Tax Reform Act of 1986.

(5) "Personal expenditure" means an expenditure that is not a trade or business expenditure, a passive activity expenditure, or an investment expenditure.

(6) "Portfolio expenditure" means an investment expenditure properly chargeable to capital account with respect to property producing income of a type described in section 469(e)(1)(A) or an investment expenditure for an expense clearly and directly allocable to such income.

(7) "Trade or business expenditure" means an expenditure (other than a passive activity expenditure or an investment expenditure) in connection with the conduct of any trade or business other than the trade or business of performing services as an employee.

(c) Allocation of debt and interest expense—(1) Allocation in accordance with use of proceeds. Debt is allocated to expenditures in accordance with the use of the debt proceeds and, except as provided in paragraph (m) of this section, interest expense accruing on a debt during any period is allocated to expenditures in the same manner as the debt is allocated from time to time during such period. Except as provided in paragraph (m) of this section, debt proceeds and related interest expense are allocated solely by reference to the use of such proceeds, and the allocation is not affected by the use of an interest in any property to secure the repayment of such debt or interest. The following example illustrates the principles of this paragraph (c)(1):

Example. Taxpayer A, an individual, pledges corporate stock held for investment as security for a loan and uses the debt proceeds to purchase an automobile for personal use. Interest expense accruing on the debt is allocated to the personal expenditure to purchase the automobile even though the debt is secured by investment property.

(2) Allocation period—(i) Allocation of debt. Debt is allocated to an expenditure for the period beginning on the date the proceeds of the debt are used or treated as used under the rules of this section to make the expenditure and ending on the earlier of—

(A) The date the debt is repaid; or

(B) The date the debt is reallocated in accordance with the rules in paragraphs (c)(4) and (j) of this section.

(ii) Allocation of interest expense—(A) In general. Except as otherwise provided in paragraph (m) of this section, interest expense accruing on a debt for any period is allocated in the same manner as the debt is allocated from time to time, regardless of when the interest is paid.

(B) Effect of compounding. Accrued interest is treated as a debt until it is paid and any interest accruing on unpaid interest is allocated in the same manner as the unpaid interest is allocated. For the taxable year in which a debt is reallocated under the rules in paragraphs (c)(4) and (j) of this section, however, compound interest accruing on such debt (other than compound interest accruing on interest that accrued before the beginning of the year) may be allocated between the original expenditure and the new expenditure on a straight-line basis (i.e., by allocating an equal amount of such interest expense to each day during the taxable year). In addition, a taxpayer may treat a year as consisting of 12 30–day months for purposes of allocating interest on a straight-line basis.

(C) Accrual of interest expense. For purposes of this paragraph (c)(2)(ii), the amount of interest expense that accrues during any period is determined by taking into account relevant provisions of the loan agreement and any applicable law such as sections 163(e), 483, and 1271 through 1275.

* * *

(3) Allocation of debt; proceeds not disbursed to borrower—(i) Third-party financing. If a lender disburses debt proceeds to a person other than the borrower in consideration for the sale or use of property, for services, or for any other purpose, the debt is treated for purposes of this section as if the borrower used an amount of the debt proceeds equal to such disbursement to make an expenditure for such property, services, or other purpose.

(ii) Debt assumptions not involving cash disbursements. If a taxpayer incurs or assumes a debt in consideration for the sale or use of property, for services, or for any other purpose, or takes property subject to a debt, and no debt proceeds are disbursed to the taxpayer, the debt is treated for purposes of this section as if the taxpayer used an amount of the debt proceeds equal to the balance of the debt outstanding at such time to make an expenditure for such property, services, or other purpose.

(4) Allocation of debt; proceeds deposited in borrower's account—(i) Treatment of deposit. For purposes of this section, a deposit of debt proceeds in an account is treated as an investment expenditure, and amounts held in an account (whether or not interest bearing) are treated as property held for investment. Debt allocated to an account under this paragraph (c)(4)(i) must be reallocated as required by paragraph (j) of this section whenever debt proceeds held in the account are used for another expenditure. This paragraph (c)(4) provides rules for determining when debt proceeds are expended from the account. The following example illustrates the principles of this paragraph (c)(4)(i):

Example. Taxpayer C, a calendar year taxpayer, borrows $100,000 on January 1 and immediately uses the proceeds to open a noninterest-bearing checking account. No other amounts are deposited in the account during the year, and no portion of the principal amount of the debt is repaid during the year. On April 1, C uses $20,000 of the debt proceeds held in the account for a passive activity expenditure. On September 1, C uses an additional $40,000 of the debt proceeds held in the account for a personal expenditure. Under this paragraph (c)(4)(i), from January 1 through March 31 the entire $100,000 debt is allocated to an investment expenditure for the account. From April 1 through August 31, $20,000 of the debt is allocated to the passive activity expenditure, and

$80,000 of the debt is allocated to the investment expenditure for the account. From September 1 through December 31, $40,000 of the debt is allocated to the personal expenditure, $20,000 is allocated to the passive activity expenditure, and $40,000 is allocated to an investment expenditure for the account.

(ii) Expenditures from account; general ordering rule. Except as provided in paragraph (c)(4)(iii)(B) or (C) of this section, debt proceeds deposited in an account are treated as expended before—

(A) Any unborrowed amounts held in the account at the time such debt proceeds are deposited; and

(B) Any amounts (borrowed or unborrowed) that are deposited in the account after such debt proceeds are deposited.

The following example illustrates the application of this paragraph (c)(4)(ii):

Example. On January 10, taxpayer E opens a checking account, depositing $500 of proceeds of Debt A and $1,000 of unborrowed funds. The following chart summarizes the transactions which occur during the year with respect to the account:

Date	Transaction
Jan. 10	$500 proceeds of Debt A and $1,000 unborrowed funds deposited.
Jan. 11	$500 proceeds of Debt B deposited.
Feb. 17	$800 personal expenditure.
Feb. 26	$700 passive activity expenditure.
June 21	$1,000 proceeds of Debt C deposited.
Nov. 24	$800 investment expenditure.
Dec. 20	$600 personal expenditure.

The $800 personal expenditure is treated as made from the $500 proceeds of Debt A and $300 of the proceeds of Debt B. The $700 passive activity expenditure is treated as made from the remaining $200 proceeds of Debt B and $500 of unborrowed funds. The $800 investment expenditure is treated as made entirely from the proceeds of Debt C. The $600 personal expenditure is treated as made from the remaining $200 proceeds of Debt C and $400 of unborrowed funds. Under paragraph (c)(4)(i) of this section, debt is allocated to an investment expenditure for periods during which debt proceeds are held in the account.

(iii) Expenditures from account; supplemental ordering rules—(A) Checking or similar accounts. Except as otherwise provided in this paragraph (c)(4)(iii), an expenditure from a checking or similar account is treated as made at the time the check is written on the account, provided the check is delivered or mailed to the payee within a reasonable period after the writing of the check. For this purpose, the taxpayer may treat checks written on the same day as written in any order. In the absence of evidence to the contrary, a check is presumed to be written on the date appearing on the check and to be delivered or mailed to the payee within a reasonable period thereafter. Evidence to the contrary may include the fact that a check does not clear within a reasonable period after the date appearing on the check.

(B) Expenditures within 15 days after deposit of borrowed funds. The taxpayer may treat any expenditure made from an account within 15 days after debt proceeds are deposited in such account as made from such proceeds to the extent thereof even if under paragraph (c)(4)(ii) of this section the debt proceeds would be treated as used to make one or more other expenditures. Any such expenditures and the debt proceeds from which such expenditures are treated as made are disregarded in applying paragraph (c)(4)(ii) of this section. The following examples illustrate the application of this paragraph (c)(4)(iii)(B):

Example (1). Taxpayer D incurs a $1,000 debt on June 5 and immediately deposits the proceeds in an account ("Account A"). On June 17, D transfers $2,000 from Account A to another account ("Account B"). On June 30, D writes a $1,500 check on Account B for a passive activity expenditure. In addition, numerous deposits of borrowed and unborrowed amounts and expenditures occur with respect to both accounts throughout the month of June. Notwithstanding these other transactions, D may treat $1,000 of the deposit to Account B on June 17 as an expenditure from the debt proceeds deposited in Account A on June 5. In addition, D may similarly treat $1,000 of the passive activity expenditure on June 30 as made from debt proceeds treated as deposited in Account B on June 17.

Example (2). The facts are the same as in the example in paragraph (c)(4)(ii) of this section, except that the proceeds of Debt B are deposited on February 11 rather than on January 11. Since the $700 passive activity expenditure occurs within 15 days after the proceeds of Debt B are deposited in the account, E may treat such expenditure as being made from the proceeds of Debt B to the extent thereof. If E treats the passive activity expenditure in this manner, the expenditures from the account are treated as follows: The $800 personal expenditure is treated as made from the $500 proceeds of Debt A and $300 of unborrowed funds. The $700 passive activity expenditure is treated as made from the $500 proceeds of Debt B and $200 of unborrowed funds. The remaining expenditures are treated as in the example in paragraph (c)(4)(ii) of this section.

(C) Interest on segregated account. In the case of an account consisting solely of the proceeds of a debt and interest earned on such account, the taxpayer may treat any expenditure from such account as made first from amounts constituting interest (rather than debt proceeds) to the extent of the balance of such interest in the account at the time of the expenditure, determined by applying the rules in this paragraph (c)(4). To the extent any expenditure is treated as made from interest under this paragraph (c)(4)(iii)(C), the expenditure is disregarded in applying paragraph (c)(4)(ii) of this section.

(iv) Optional method for determining date of reallocation. Solely for the purpose of determining the date on which debt allocated to an account under paragraph (c)(4)(i) of this section is reallocated, the taxpayer may treat all expenditures made during any calendar month from debt proceeds in the account as occurring on the later of the first day of such month or the date on which such debt proceeds are deposited in the account. This paragraph (c)(4)(iv) applies only if all expenditures from an account during the same calendar month are similarly treated. The following example illustrates the application of this paragraph (c)(4)(iv):

Example. On January 10, taxpayer G opens a checking account, depositing $500 of proceeds of Debt A and $1,000 of unborrowed funds. The following chart summarizes the transactions which occur during the year with respect to the account (note that these facts are the same as the facts of the example in paragraph (c)(4)(ii) of this section):

Date	Transaction
Jan. 10	$500 proceeds of Debt A and $1,000 unborrowed funds deposited.
Jan. 11	$500 proceeds of Debt B deposited.
Feb. 17	$800 personal expenditure.
Feb. 26	$700 passive activity expenditure.
June 21	$1,000 proceeds of Debt C deposited.
Nov. 24	$800 investment expenditure.
Dec. 20	$600 personal expenditure.

Assume that G chooses to apply the optional rule of this paragraph (c)(4)(iv) to all expenditures. For purposes of determining the date on which debt is allocated to the $800 personal expenditure made on February 17, the $500 treated as made from the proceeds of Debt A and the $300 treated as made from the proceeds of Debt B are treated as expenditures occurring on February 1. Accordingly, Debt A is allocated to an investment expenditure for the account from January 10 through January 31 and to the personal expenditure from February 1 through December 31, and $300 of Debt B is allocated to an investment expenditure for the account from January 11 through January 31 and to the personal expenditure from February 1 through December 31. The remaining $200 of Debt B is allocated to an investment expenditure for the account from January 11 through January 31 and to the passive activity expenditure from February 1 through December 31. The $800 of Debt C used to make the investment expenditure on November 24 is allocated to an investment expenditure for the account from June 21 through October 31 and to an investment expenditure from November 1 through December 31. The remaining $200 of Debt C is allocated to an investment expenditure for the account from June 21 through November 30 and to a personal expenditure from December 1 through December 31.

(v) Simultaneous deposits—(A) In general. If the proceeds of two or more debts are deposited in an account simultaneously, such proceeds are treated for purposes of this paragraph (c)(4) as deposited in the order in which the debts were incurred.

(B) Order in which debts incurred. If two or more debts are incurred simultaneously or are treated under applicable law as incurred simultaneously, the debts are treated for purposes of this paragraph (c)(4)(v) as incurred in any order the taxpayer selects.

(C) Borrowings on which interest accrues at different rates. If interest does not accrue at the same fixed or variable rate on the entire amount of a borrowing, each portion of the borrowing on which interest accrues at a different fixed or variable rate is treated as a separate debt for purposes of this paragraph (c)(4)(v).

(vi) Multiple accounts. The rules in this paragraph (c)(4) apply separately to each account of a taxpayer.

(5) Allocation of debt; proceeds received in cash—(i) Expenditure within 15 days of receiving debt proceeds. If a taxpayer receives the proceeds of a debt in cash, the taxpayer may treat any cash expenditure made within 15 days after receiving the cash as made from such debt proceeds to the extent thereof and may treat such expenditure as made on the date the taxpayer received the cash. The following example illustrates the rule in this paragraph (c)(5)(i):

Example. Taxpayer F incurs a $1,000 debt on August 4 and receives the debt proceeds in cash. F deposits $1,500 cash in an account on August 15 and on August 27 writes a check on the account for a passive activity expenditure. In addition, F engages in numerous other cash transactions throughout the month of August, and numerous deposits of borrowed and unborrowed amounts and expenditures occur with respect to the account during the same period. Notwithstanding these other transactions, F may treat $1,000 of the deposit on August 15 as an expenditure made from the debt proceeds on August 4. In addition, under the rule in paragraph (c)(4)(v)(B) of this section, F may treat the passive activity expenditure on August 27 as made from the $1,000 debt proceeds treated as deposited in the account.

(ii) Other expenditures. Except as provided in paragraphs (c)(5)(i) and (iii) of this section, any debt proceeds a taxpayer (other than a corporation) receives in cash are treated as used to make personal expenditures. For purposes of this paragraph (c)(5), debt proceeds are received in cash if, for example, a withdrawal of cash from an account is treated under the rules of this section as an expenditure of debt proceeds.

* * *

(d) Debt repayments—(1) General ordering rule. If, at the time any portion of a debt is repaid, such debt is allocated to more than one expenditure, the debt is treated for purposes of this section as repaid in the following order:

(i) Amounts allocated to personal expenditures;

(ii) Amounts allocated to investment expenditures and passive activity expenditures (other than passive activity expenditures described in paragraph (d)(1)(iii) of this section);

(iii) Amounts allocated to passive activity expenditures in connection with a rental real estate activity with respect to which the taxpayer actively participates (within the meaning of section 469(i));

(iv) Amounts allocated to former passive activity expenditures; and

(v) Amounts allocated to trade or business expenditures and to expenditures described in the last sentence of paragraph (b)(4) of this section.

* * *

(m) Coordination with other provisions—(1) Effect of other limitations—(i) In general. All debt is allocated among expenditures pursuant to the rules in this section, without regard to any limitations on the deductibility of interest expense on such debt. The applicability of the passive loss and nonbusiness interest limitations to interest on such debt, however, may be affected by other limitations on the deductibility of interest expense.

* * *

(2) Effect on other limitations—(i) General rule. Except as provided in paragraph (m)(2)(ii) of this section, any limitation on the deductibility of an item (other than the passive loss and nonbusiness interest limitations) applies without regard to the manner in which debt is allocated under this section. Thus, for example, interest expense treated under section 265(a)(2) as interest on indebtedness incurred or continued to purchase or carry obligations the interest on which is wholly exempt from Federal income tax is not deductible regardless of the expenditure to which the underlying debt is allocated under this section.

* * *

(3) Qualified residence interest. Qualified residence interest (within the meaning of section 163(h)(3)) is allowable as a deduction without regard to the manner in which such interest expense is allocated under the rules of this section. In addition, qualified residence interest is not taken into account in determining the income or loss from any activity for purposes of section 469 or in determining the amount of investment interest for purposes of section 163(d). The following example illustrates the rule in this paragraph (m)(3):

Example. Taxpayer E, an individual, incurs a $20,000 debt secured by a residence and immediately uses the proceeds to purchase an automobile exclusively for E's personal use. Under the rules in this section, the debt and interest expense on the debt are allocated to a personal expenditure. If, however, the interest on the debt is qualified residence interest within the meaning of section 163(h)(3), the interest is not treated as personal interest for purposes of section 163(h).

* * *

[T.D. 8145, 52 FR 24999, July 2, 1987, 62 FR 40270, July 28, 1997]

§ 1.163–9T Personal interest.

(a) In general. No deduction under any provision of Chapter 1 of the Internal Revenue Code shall be allowed for personal interest paid or accrued during the taxable year by a taxpayer other than a corporation.

(b) Personal interest—(1) Definition. For purposes of this section, personal interest is any interest expense other than—

(i) Interest paid or accrued on indebtedness properly allocable (within the meaning of § 1.163–8T) to the conduct of trade or business (other than the trade or business of performing services as an employee),

(ii) Any investment interest (within the meaning of section 163(d)(3)),

(iii) Any interest that is taken into account under section 469 in computing income or loss from a passive activity of the taxpayer,

(iv) Any qualified residence interest (within the meaning of section 163(h)(3) * * *); and

(v) Any interest payable under section 6601 with respect to the unpaid portion of the tax imposed by section 2001 for the period during which an extension of time for payment of such tax is in effect under section 6163, 6166, or 6166A (as in effect before its repeal by the Economic Recovery Tax Act of 1981).

(2) Interest relating to taxes—(i) In general. Except as provided in paragraph (b)(2)(iii) of this section, personal interest includes interest—

(A) Paid on underpayments of individual Federal, State or local income taxes and on indebtedness used to pay such taxes (within the meaning of § 1.163–8T), regardless of the source of the income generating the tax liability;

(B) Paid under section 453(e)(4)(B) (interest on deferred tax resulting from certain installment sales) * * *; or

(C) Paid by a trust, S corporation, or other pass-through entity on underpayments of State or local income taxes and on indebtedness used to pay such taxes.

(ii) Example. A, an individual, owns stock of an S corporation. On its return for 1987, the corporation under reports its taxable income. Consequently, A under reports A's share of that income on A's tax return. In 1989, A pays the resulting deficiency plus interest to the Internal Revenue Service. The interest paid by A in 1989 on the tax deficiency is personal interest, notwithstanding the fact that the additional tax liability may have arisen out of income from a trade or business. The result would be the same if A's business had been operated as a sole proprietorship.

(iii) Certain other taxes. Personal interest does not include interest—

(A) Paid with respect to sales, excise and similar taxes that are incurred in connection with a trade or business or an investment activity;

(B) Paid by an S corporation with respect to an underpayment of income tax from a year in which the S corporation was a C corporation or with respect to an underpayment of the taxes imposed by sections 1374 or 1375, or similar provision of State law; or

(C) Paid by a transferee under section 6901 (tax liability resulting from transferred assets), or a similar provision of State law, with respect to a C corporation's underpayment of income tax.

* * *

[T.D. 8168, 52 FR 48409, Dec. 22, 1987; 68 FR 13226, Mar. 19, 2003]

§ 1.164–1 Deduction for taxes.

(a) In general. Only the following taxes shall be allowed as a deduction under this section for the taxable year within which paid or accrued, according to the method of accounting used in computing taxable income:

(1) State and local, and foreign, real property taxes.

(2) State and local personal property taxes.

(3) State and local, and foreign, income, war profits, and excess profits taxes.

* * *

In addition, there shall be allowed as a deduction under this section State and local and foreign taxes not described in * * * this paragraph which are paid or accrued within the taxable year in carrying on a trade or business or an activity described in section 212 (relating to expenses for production of income). For example, dealers or investors in securities and dealers or investors in real estate may deduct State stock transfer and real estate transfer taxes, respectively, under section 164, to the extent they are expenses incurred in carrying on a trade or business or an activity for the production of income. In general, taxes are deductible only by the person upon whom they are imposed. * * *

* * *

[T.D. 6500, 25 FR 11402, Nov. 26, 1960, as amended by T.D. 6780, 29 FR 18145, Dec. 22, 1964; T.D. 7577, 43 FR 59357, Dec. 20, 1978]

§ 1.164–2 Deduction denied in case of certain taxes.

This section and § 1.275 describe certain taxes for which no deduction is allowed. * * * In the case of taxable years beginning after December 31, 1963, the denial is governed by sections 164 and 275. No deduction is allowed for the following taxes:

(a) Federal income taxes. Federal income taxes, including the taxes imposed by section 3101, relating to the tax on employees under the Federal Insurance Contributions Act (chapter 21 of the Code); sections 3201 and 3211, relating to the taxes on railroad employees and railroad employee representatives; section 3402, relating to the tax withheld at source on wages; * * *

* * *

(g) Taxes for local benefits. Except as provided in § 1.164–4, taxes assessed against local benefits of a kind tending to increase the value of the property assessed.

* * *

[T.D. 6500, 25 FR 11402, Nov. 26, 1960, as amended by T.D. 6780, 29 FR 18145, Dec. 22, 1964; T.D. 7767, 46 FR 11263, Feb. 6, 1981]

§ 1.164–3 Definitions and special rules.

* * *

(a) State or local taxes. A State or local tax includes only a tax imposed by a State, a possession of the United States, or a political subdivision of any of the foregoing, or by the District of Columbia.

(b) Real property taxes. The term "real property taxes" means taxes imposed on interests in real property and levied for the general public welfare, but it does not include taxes assessed against local benefits. See § 1.164–4.

(c) Personal property taxes. The term "personal property tax" means an ad valorem tax which is imposed on an annual basis in respect of personal property. To qualify as a personal property tax, a tax must meet the following three tests:

(1) The tax must be ad valorem—that is, substantially in proportion to the value of the personal property. A tax which is based on criteria other than value does not qualify as ad valorem. For example, a motor vehicle tax based on weight, model year, and horsepower, or any of these characteristics is not an ad valorem tax. However, a tax which is partly based on value and partly based on other criteria may qualify in part. For example, in the case of a motor vehicle tax of 1 percent of value plus 40 cents per hundredweight, the part of the tax equal to 1 percent of value qualifies as an ad valorem tax and the balance does not qualify.

(2) The tax must be imposed on an annual basis, even if collected more frequently or less frequently.

(3) The tax must be imposed in respect of personal property. A tax may be considered to be imposed in respect of personal property even if in form it is imposed on the exercise of a privilege. Thus, for taxable years beginning after December 31, 1963, State and local taxes on the registration or licensing of highway motor vehicles are not deductible as personal property taxes unless and to the extent that the tests prescribed in this subparagraph are met. For example, an annual ad valorem tax qualifies as a personal property tax although it is denominated a registration fee imposed for the privilege of registering motor vehicles or of using them on the highways.

(d) Foreign taxes. The term "foreign tax" includes only a tax imposed by the authority of a foreign country. A tax-imposed by a political subdivision of a foreign country is considered to be imposed by the authority of that foreign country.

* * *

[T.D. 6500, 25 FR 11402, Nov. 26, 1960, as amended by T.D. 6780, 29 FR 18146, Dec. 22, 1964]

§ 1.164–4 Taxes for local benefits.

(a) So-called taxes for local benefits * * *, more properly assessments, paid for local benefits such as street, sidewalk, and other like improvements, imposed because of and measured by some benefit inuring directly to the property against which the assessment is levied are not deductible as taxes. A tax is considered assessed against local benefits when the property subject to the tax is limited to property benefited. Special assessments are not deductible, even though an incidental benefit may inure to the public welfare. The real property taxes deductible are those levied for the general public welfare by the proper taxing authorities at a like rate against all property in the territory over which such authorities have jurisdiction. Assessments under the statutes of California relating to irrigation, and of Iowa relating to drainage, and under certain statutes of Tennessee relating to levees, are limited to property benefited, and if the assessments are so limited, the amounts paid thereunder are not deductible as taxes. For treatment of assessments for local benefits as adjustments to the basis of property, see section 1016(a)(1) and the regulations thereunder.

(b)(1) Insofar as assessments against local benefits are made for the purpose of maintenance or repair or for the purpose of meeting interest charges with respect to such benefits, they are deductible. In such cases, the burden is on the taxpayer to show the allocation of the amounts assessed to the different purposes. If the allocation cannot be made, none of the amount so paid is deductible.

* * *

[T.D. 6500, 25 FR 11402, Nov. 26, 1960, as amended by T.D. 6780, 29 FR 18147, Dec. 22, 1964]

§ 1.164–6 Apportionment of taxes on real property between seller and purchaser.

(a) Scope. Except as provided otherwise in section 164(f) and § 1.164–8, when real property is sold, section 164(d)(1) governs the deduction by the seller and the purchaser of current real property taxes. Section 164(d)(1) performs two functions: (1) It provides a method by which a portion of the taxes for the real property tax year in which the property is sold may be deducted by the seller and a portion by the purchaser; and (2) it limits the deduction of the seller and the purchaser to the portion of the taxes corresponding to the part of the real property tax year during which each was the owner of the property. These functions are accomplished by treating a portion of the taxes for the real property tax year in which the property is sold as imposed on the seller and a portion as imposed on the purchaser. To the extent that the taxes are treated as imposed on the seller and the purchaser, each shall be allowed a deduction, under section 164(a), in the taxable year such tax is paid or accrued, or treated as paid or accrued under section 164(d)(2)(A) or (D) and this section. No deduction is allowed for taxes on real property to the extent that they are imposed on another taxpayer, or are treated as imposed on another taxpayer under section 164(d). For the election to accrue real property taxes ratably see section 461(c) and the regulations thereunder.

(b) Application of rule of apportionment. (1)(i) For purposes of the deduction provided by section 164(a), if real property is sold during any real property tax year, the portion of the real property tax properly allocable to that part of the real property tax year which ends on the day before the date of the sale shall be treated as a tax imposed on the seller, and the portion of such tax properly allocable to that part of such real property tax year which begins on the date of the sale shall be treated as a tax imposed on the purchaser. For definition of "real property tax year" see paragraph (c) of this section. This rule shall apply whether or not the seller and the purchaser apportion such tax. The rule of apportionment contained in section 164(d)(1) applies even though the same real property is sold more than once during the real property tax year. (See paragraph (d)(5) of this section for rule requiring inclusion in gross income of excess deductions.)

(ii) Where the real property tax becomes a personal liability or a lien before the beginning of the real property tax year to which it relates and the real property is sold subsequent to the time the tax becomes a personal liability or a lien but prior to the beginning of the related real property tax year—

(a) The seller may not deduct any amount for real property taxes for the related real property tax year, and

(b) To the extent that he holds the property for such real property tax year, the purchaser may deduct the amount of such taxes for the taxable year they are paid (or amounts representing such taxes are paid to the seller, mortgagee, trustee or other person having an interest in the property as security) or accrued by him according to his method of accounting.

(iii) Similarly, where the real property tax becomes a personal liability or a lien after the end of the real property tax year to which it relates and the real property is sold prior to the time the tax becomes a personal liability or a lien but after the end of the related real property tax year—

(a) The purchaser may not deduct any amount for real property taxes for the related real property tax year, and

(b) To the extent that he holds the property for such real property tax year, the seller may deduct the amount of such taxes for the taxable year they are paid (or amounts representing such taxes are paid to the purchaser, mortgagee, trustee, or other person having an interest in the property as security) or accrued by him according to his method of accounting.

(iv) Where the real property is sold (or purchased) during the related real property tax year the real property taxes for such year are apportioned between the parties to such sale and may be deducted by such parties in accordance with the provisions of paragraph (d) of this section.

(2) Section 164(d) does not apply to delinquent real property taxes for any real property tax year prior to the real property tax year in which the property is sold.

(3) The provisions of this paragraph may be illustrated by the following examples:

Example (1). The real property tax year in County R is April 1 to March 31. A, the owner on April 1, 1954, of real property located in County R sells the real property to B on June 30, 1954. B owns the real property from June 30, 1954, through March 31, 1955. The real property tax for the real property tax year April 1, 1954—March 31, 1955 is $365. For purposes of section 164(a), $90 (90/365 × $365, April 1, 1954—June 29, 1954) of the real property tax is treated as imposed on A, the seller, and $275 (275/365 × $365, June 30, 1954—March 31, 1955) of such real property tax is treated as imposed on B, the purchaser.

Example (2). In County S the real property tax year is the calendar year. The real property tax becomes a lien on June 1 and is payable on July 1 of the current real property tax year, but there is no personal liability for such tax. On April 30, 1955, C, the owner of real property in County S on January 1, 1955, sells the real property to D. On July 1, 1955, D pays the 1955 real property tax. On August 31, 1955, D sells the same real property to E. C, D, and E use the cash receipts and disbursements method of accounting. Under the provisions of section 164(d)(1), 119/365 (January 1–April 29, 1955) of the real property tax payable on July 1, 1955, for the 1955 real property tax year is treated as imposed on C, and, under the provisions of section 164(d)(2)(A), such portion is treated as having been paid by him on the date of sale. Under the provisions of section 164(d)(1), 123/365 (April 30–August 30, 1955) of the real property tax paid July 1, 1955, for the 1955 real property tax year is treated as imposed on D and may be deducted by him. Under the provisions of section 164(d)(1), 123/365 (August 31–December 31, 1955) of the real property tax due and paid on July 1, 1955, for the 1955 real property tax year is treated as imposed on E and, under the provisions of section 164(d)(2)(A) such portion is treated as having been paid by him on the date of sale.

Example (3). In State X the real property tax year is the calendar year. The real property tax becomes a lien on November 1 of the preceding calendar year. On November 15, 1955, F sells real property in State X to G. G owns the real property through December 31, 1956. Under section 164(d)(1), the real property tax (which became a lien on November 1, 1954) for the 1955 real property tax year is apportioned between F and G. No part of the real property tax for the 1956 real property tax year may be deducted by F. The entire real property tax for the 1956 real property tax year may be deducted by G when paid or accrued, depending upon the method of accounting used by him. See subparagraph (6) of paragraph (d) and section 461(c) and the regulations thereunder.

(c) Real property tax year. As used in section 164(d), the term "real property tax year" refers to the period which, under the law imposing the tax, is regarded as the period to which the tax imposed relates. Where the State and one or more local governmental units each imposes a tax on real property, the real property tax year for each tax must be determined for purposes of applying the rule of apportionment of section 164(d)(1) to each tax. The time when the tax rate is determined, the time when the assessment is made, the time when the tax becomes a lien, or the time when the tax becomes due or delinquent does not necessarily determine the real property tax year. The real property tax year may or may not correspond to the fiscal year of the governmental unit imposing the tax. In each case the State or local law determines what constitutes the real property tax year. Although the seller and the purchaser may or may not make an allocation of real property taxes, the meaning of "real property tax year" in section 164(d) and the application of section 164(d) do not depend upon what real property taxes were allocated nor the method of allocation used by the parties.

(d) Special rules—(1) Seller using cash receipts and disbursements method of accounting. Under the provisions of section 164(d), if the seller by reason of his method of accounting may not deduct any amount for taxes unless paid, and—

(i) The purchaser (under the law imposing the real property tax) is liable for the real property tax for the real property tax year, or

(ii) The seller (under the law imposing the real property tax) is liable for the real property tax for the real property tax year and the tax is not payable until after the date of sale,

then the portion of the tax treated under section 164(d)(1) as imposed upon the seller (whether or not actually paid by him in the taxable year in which the sale occurs) shall be considered as having been paid by him in such taxable year. Such portion may be deducted by him for the taxable year in which the sale occurs, or, if at a later time, for the taxable year (which would be proper under the taxpayer's method of accounting) in which the tax is actually paid, or an amount representing such tax is paid to the purchaser, mortgagee, trustee, or other person having an interest in the property as security.

(2) Purchasers using the cash receipts and disbursements method of accounting. Under the provisions of section 164(d), if the purchaser by reason of his method of accounting may not deduct any amount for taxes unless paid and the seller (under the law imposing the real property tax) is liable for the real property tax for the real property tax year, the portion of the tax treated under section 164(d)(1) as imposed upon the purchaser (whether or not actually paid by him in the taxable year in which the sale occurs) shall be considered as having been paid by him in such taxable year. Such portion may be deducted by him for the taxable year in which the sale occurs, or, if at a later time, for the taxable year (which would be proper under the taxpayer's method of accounting) in which the tax is actually paid, or an amount representing such tax is paid to the seller, mortgagee, trustee, or other person having an interest in the property as security.

(3) Persons considered liable for tax. Where the tax is not a liability of any person, the person who holds the property at the time the tax becomes a lien on the property shall be considered liable for the tax. As to a particular sale, in determining:

(i) Whether the other party to the sale is liable for the tax or,

(ii) The person who holds the property at the time the tax becomes a lien on the property (where the tax is not a liability of any person),

prior or subsequent sales of the property during the real property tax year shall be disregarded.

(4) Examples. The provisions of subparagraphs (1), (2), and (3) of this paragraph may be illustrated as follows:

Example (1). In County X the real property tax year is the calendar year. The real property tax is a personal liability of the owner of the real property on June 30 of the current real property tax year, but is not payable until February 28 of the following real property tax year. A, the owner of real property in County X on January 1, 1955, uses the cash receipts and disbursements method of accounting. On May 30, 1955, A sells the real property to B, who also uses the cash receipts and disbursements method of accounting. B retains ownership of the real property for the balance of the 1955 calendar year. Under the provisions of section 164(d)(1), $^{149}/_{365}$ (January 1–May 29, 1955) of the real property tax payable on February 28, 1956, for the 1955 real property tax year is treated as imposed on A, the seller, and under the provisions of section 164(d)(2)(A) such portion is treated as having been paid by him on the date of sale and may be deducted by him for his taxable year in which the sale occurs (whether or not such portion is actually paid by him in that year) or for his taxable year in which the tax is actually paid or an amount representing such tax is paid. Under the provisions of section 164(d)(1), $^{216}/_{365}$ (May 30–December 31, 1955) of the real property tax payable on February 28, 1956, for the 1955 real property tax year is treated as imposed on B, the purchaser, and may be deducted by him for his taxable year in which the tax is actually paid, or an amount representing such tax is paid.

Example (2). In County Y, the real property tax year is the calendar year. The real property tax becomes a lien on January 1, 1955, and is payable on April 30, 1955. There is no personal liability for the real property tax imposed by County Y. On April 30, 1955, C, the owner of real property in County Y on January 1, 1955, pays the real property tax for the 1955 real property tax year. On May 1, 1955, C sells the real property to D. On September 1, 1955, D sells the real property to E. C, D, and E use the cash receipts and disbursements method of accounting. Under the provisions of section 164(d)(1), $^{120}/_{365}$ (January 1–April 30, 1955) of the real property tax is treated as imposed upon C and may be deducted by him for his taxable year in which the tax is actually paid. Under section 164(d)(1), $^{123}/_{365}$ (May 1–August 31, 1955) of the real property tax is treated as imposed upon D and, under the provisions of section 164(d)(2)(A), is treated as having been paid by him on May 1, 1955, and may be deducted by D for his taxable year in which the sale from C to him occurs (whether or not such portion is actually paid by him in that year), or for his taxable year in which an amount representing such tax is paid. Since, according to paragraph (d)(3) of this section, the prior sale by C to D is disregarded, under the provisions of section 164(d)(1), $^{122}/_{365}$ (September 1–December 31, 1955) of the real property tax is treated as imposed on E and, under the provisions of section 164(d)(2)(A), is treated as having been paid by him on September 1, 1955, and may be deducted by E for his taxable year in which the sale from D to him occurs (whether or not such portion is actually paid by him in that year), or for his taxable year in which an amount representing such tax is paid.

Example (3). In County X the real property tax year is the calendar year and the real property taxes are assessed and become a lien on June 30 of the current real property tax year, but are not payable until September 1 of that year. There is no personal liability for the real property tax imposed by County X. A, the owner on January 1, 1955, of real property in County X, uses the cash receipts and disbursements method of accounting. On July 15, 1955, A sells the real property to B. Under the provisions of section 164(d)(1), $^{195}/_{365}$ (January 1–July 14, 1955) of the real property tax payable on September 1, 1955, for the 1955 real property tax year is treated as imposed on A, and may be deducted by him for his taxable year in which the sale occurs (whether or not such portion is actually paid by him in that year) or for his taxable year in which the tax is actually paid or an amount representing such tax is paid. Under the provisions of section 164(d)(1), $^{170}/_{365}$ (July 15–December 31, 1955) of the real property tax is treated as imposed on B and may be deducted by him for his taxable year in which the sale occurs (whether or not such portion is actually paid by him in that year), or for his taxable year in which the tax is actually paid or an amount representing such tax is paid.

* * *

(6) Persons using an accrual method of accounting. Where real property is sold and the seller or the purchaser computes his taxable income (for the taxable year during which the sale occurs) on an accrual method of accounting then, if the seller or the purchaser has not made the election provided in section 461(c) (relating to the accrual of real property taxes), the portion of any real property tax which is treated as imposed on him and which may not be deducted by him for any taxable year by reason of his method of accounting shall be treated as having accrued on the date of sale. The provisions of this subparagraph may be illustrated as follows:

Example. In County X the real property tax becomes a lien on property and is assessed on November 30 for the current calendar year, which is also the real property tax year. There is no personal liability for the real property tax imposed by County X. A owns, on January 1, 1955, real property in County X. A uses an accrual method of accounting and has not made any election under section 461(c) to accrue ratably real property taxes. A sells real property on June 30, 1955. By reason of A's method of accounting, he could not deduct any part of the real property tax for 1955 on the real property since he sold the real property prior to November 30, 1955, the accrual date. Under section 164(d)(1), $^{180}/_{365}$ (January 1–June 29, 1955) of the real property tax for the 1955 real property tax year is treated as imposed on A, and under section 164(d)(2)(D) that portion is treated as having accrued on June 30, 1955, and may be deducted by A for his taxable year in which such date falls. B, the purchaser from A, who uses an accrual method of accounting, has likewise not made an election under section 461(c) to accrue real property taxes ratably. Under section 164(d)(1), $^{185}/_{365}$ of the real property taxes may be accrued by B on November 30, 1955, and deducted for his taxable year in which such date falls.

* * *

[T.D. 6500, 25 FR 11402, Nov. 26, 1960]

§ 1.165–1 Losses.

(a) Allowance of deduction. Section 165(a) provides that, in computing taxable income under section 63, any loss actually sustained during the taxable year and not made good by insurance or some other form of compensation shall be allowed as a deduction subject to any provision of the internal revenue laws which prohibits or limits the amount of the deduction. This deduction for losses sustained shall be taken in accordance with section 165 and the regulations thereunder. * * *

(b) Nature of loss allowable. To be allowable as a deduction under section 165(a), a loss must be evidenced by closed and completed transactions, fixed by identifiable events, and * * * actually sustained during the taxable year. Only a bona fide loss is allowable. Substance and not mere form shall govern in determining a deductible loss.

(c) Amount deductible. **(1)** The amount of loss allowable as a deduction under section 165(a) shall not exceed the amount prescribed by § 1.1011–1 as the adjusted basis for determining the loss from the sale or other disposition of the property involved. In the case of each such deduction claimed, therefore, the basis of the property must be properly adjusted as prescribed by § 1.1011–1 for such items as expenditures, receipts, or losses, properly chargeable to capital account, and for such items as depreciation, obsolescence, amortization, and depletion, in order to determine the amount of loss allowable as a deduction. * * *

* * *

(3) A loss from the sale or exchange of a capital asset shall be allowed as a deduction under section 165(a) but only to the extent allowed in section 1211 (relating to limitation on capital losses) and section 1212 (relating to capital loss carrybacks and carryovers), and in the regulations under those sections.

(4) In determining the amount of loss actually sustained for purposes of section 165(a), proper adjustment shall be made for any salvage value and for any insurance or other compensation received.

(d) Year of deduction. **(1)** A loss shall be allowed as a deduction under section 165(a) only for the taxable year in which the loss is sustained. For this purpose, a loss shall be treated as sustained during the taxable year in which the loss occurs as evidenced by closed and completed transactions and as fixed by identifiable events occurring in such taxable year. For provisions relating to situations where a loss attributable to a disaster will be treated as sustained in the taxable year immediately preceding the taxable year in which the disaster actually occurred, see section 165(h)* and § 1.165–11.

(2)(i) If a casualty or other event occurs which may result in a loss and, in the year of such casualty or event, there exists a claim for reimbursement with respect to which there is a reasonable prospect of recovery, no portion of the loss with respect to which reimbursement may be received is sustained, for purposes of section 165, until it can be ascertained with reasonable certainty whether or not such reimbursement will be received. Whether a reasonable prospect of recovery exists with respect to a claim for reimbursement of a loss is a question of fact to be determined upon an examination of all facts and circumstances. Whether or not such reimbursement will be received may be ascertained with reasonable certainty, for example, by a settlement of the claim, by an adjudication of the claim, or by an abandonment of the claim. When a taxpayer claims that the taxable year in which a loss is sustained is fixed by his abandonment of the claim for reimbursement, he must be able to produce objective evidence of his having abandoned the claim, such as the execution of a release.

(ii) If in the year of the casualty or other event a portion of the loss is not covered by a claim for reimbursement with respect to which there is a reasonable prospect of recovery, then such portion of the loss is sustained during the taxable year in which the casualty or other event occurs. For example, if property having an adjusted basis of $10,000 is completely destroyed by fire in 1961, and if the taxpayer's only claim for reimbursement consists of an insurance claim for $8,000 which is settled in 1962, the taxpayer sustains a loss of $2,000 in 1961. However, if the taxpayer's automobile is completely destroyed in 1961 as a result of the negligence of another person and there exists a reasonable prospect of recovery on a claim for the full value of the automobile against such person, the taxpayer does not sustain any loss until the taxable year in which the claim is adjudicated or otherwise settled. If the automobile had an adjusted basis of $5,000 and the taxpayer secures a judgment of $4,000 in 1962, $1,000 is deductible for the taxable year 1962. If in 1963 it becomes reasonably certain that only $3,500 can ever be collected on such judgment, $500 is deductible for the taxable year 1963.

(iii) If the taxpayer deducted a loss in accordance with the provisions of this paragraph and in a subsequent taxable year receives reimbursement for such loss, he does not recompute the tax for the taxable year in which the deduction was taken but includes the amount of such reimbursement in his gross income for the taxable year in which received, subject to the provisions of section 111, relating to recovery of amounts previously deducted.

(3) Any loss arising from theft shall be treated as sustained during the taxable year in which the taxpayer discovers the loss (see § 1.165–8, relating to theft losses). However, if in the year of discovery there exists a claim for reimbursement with respect to which there is a reasonable prospect of recovery, no portion of the loss with respect to which reimbursement may be received is sustained, for purposes of section 165, until the taxable year in which it can be ascertained with reasonable certainty whether or not such reimbursement will be received.

* * *

(e) Limitation on losses of individuals. In the case of an individual, the deduction for losses granted by section 165(a) shall, subject to the provisions of section 165(c) and paragraph (a) of this section, be limited to:

(1) Losses incurred in a trade or business;

(2) Losses incurred in any transaction entered into for profit, though not connected with a trade or business; and

(3) Losses of property not connected with a trade or business and not incurred in any transaction entered into for profit, if such losses arise from fire, storm, shipwreck, or other casualty, or from theft, and if the loss involved has not been allowed for estate tax purposes in the estate tax return. For additional provisions pertaining to the allowance of casualty and theft losses, see §§ 1.165–7 and 1.165–8, respectively.

* * *

[T.D. 6500, 25 FR 11402, Nov. 26, 1960, as amended by T.D. 6735, 29 FR 6493, May 19, 1964; T.D. 6996, 34 FR 835, Jan. 18, 1969; T.D. 7301, 39 FR 963, Jan. 4, 1974; T.D. 7522, 42 FR 63411, Dec. 16, 1977]

§ 1.165–2 Obsolescence of nondepreciable property.

(a) Allowance of deduction. A loss incurred in a business or in a transaction entered into for profit and arising from the sudden termination of the usefulness in such business or transaction of any nondepreciable property, in a case where such business or transaction is discontinued or where such property is permanently discarded from use therein, shall be allowed as a deduction under section 165(a) for the taxable year in which the loss is actually sustained. For this purpose, the taxable year in which the loss is sustained is not necessarily the taxable year in which the overt act of abandonment, or the loss of title to the property, occurs.

(b) Exceptions. This section does not apply to losses sustained upon the sale or exchange of property, losses sustained upon the obsolescence or worthlessness of depreciable property, casualty losses, or losses reflected in inventories required to be taken under section 471. The limitations contained in sections 1211 and 1212 upon losses from the sale or exchange of capital assets do not apply to losses allowable under this section.

* * *

[T.D. 6500, 25 FR 11402, Nov. 26, 1960; T.D. 9564, 76 FR 81084, Dec. 27, 2011]

§ 1.165–4 Decline in value of stock.

(a) Deduction disallowed. No deduction shall be allowed under section 165(a) solely on account of a decline in the value of stock owned by the taxpayer when the decline is due to a fluctuation in the market price of the stock or to other similar cause. A mere shrinkage in the value of stock owned by the taxpayer, even though extensive, does not give rise to a deduction under section 165(a) if the stock has any recognizable value on the date claimed as the date of loss. No loss for a decline in the value of stock owned by the taxpayer shall be allowed as a deduction under section 165(a) except insofar as the loss is recognized under § 1.1002–1 upon the sale or exchange of the stock and except as otherwise provided in § 1.165–5 with respect to stock which becomes worthless during the taxable year.

* * *

(d) Definition. As used in this section, the term "stock" means a share of stock in a corporation or a right to subscribe for, or to receive, a share of stock in a corporation.

[T.D. 6500, 25 FR 11402, Nov. 26, 1960; 25 FR 14021, Dec. 21, 1960]

§ 1.165–5 Worthless securities.

(a) Definition of security. As used in section 165(g) and this section, the term "security" means:

(1) A share of stock in a corporation;

(2) A right to subscribe for, or to receive, a share of stock in a corporation; or

(3) A bond, debenture, note, or certificate, or other evidence of indebtedness to pay a fixed or determinable sum of money, which has been issued with interest coupons or in registered form by a domestic or foreign corporation or by any government or political subdivision thereof.

(b) Ordinary loss. If any security which is not a capital asset becomes wholly worthless during the taxable year, the loss resulting therefrom may be deducted under section 165(a) as an ordinary loss.

(c) Capital loss. If any security which is a capital asset becomes wholly worthless at any time during the taxable year, the loss resulting therefrom may be deducted under section 165(a) but only as though it were a loss from a sale or exchange, on the last day of the taxable year, of a capital asset. See section 165(g)(1). The amount so allowed as a deduction shall be subject to the limitations upon capital losses described in paragraph (c)(3) of § 1.165–1.

(d) Loss on worthless securities of an affiliated corporation—(1) Deductible as an ordinary loss. If a taxpayer which is a domestic corporation owns any security of a domestic or foreign corporation which is affiliated with the taxpayer within the meaning of subparagraph (2) of this paragraph and such security becomes wholly worthless during the taxable year, the loss resulting therefrom may be deducted under section 165(a) as an ordinary loss in accordance with paragraph (b) of this section. The fact that the security is in fact a capital asset of the taxpayer is immaterial for this purpose, since section 165(g)(3) provides that such security shall be treated as though it were not a capital asset for the purposes of section 165(g)(1). A debt which becomes wholly worthless during the taxable year shall be as an ordinary loss in accordance with the provisions of this subparagraph, to the extent that such debt is a security within the meaning of paragraph (a)(3) of this section.

(2) Affiliated corporation defined. For purposes of this paragraph, a corporation shall be treated as affiliated with the taxpayer owning the security if—

(i)(a) In the case of a taxable year beginning on or after January 1, 1970, the taxpayer owns directly—

(1) Stock possessing at least 80 percent of the voting power of all classes of such corporation's stock, and

(2) At least 80 percent of each class of such corporation's nonvoting stock excluding for purposes of this subdivision (i)(a) nonvoting stock which is limited and preferred as to dividends (see section 1504(a)), or

* * *

(ii) None of the stock of such corporation was acquired by the taxpayer solely for the purpose of converting a capital loss sustained by reason of the worthlessness of any such stock into an ordinary loss under section 165(g)(3), and

(iii) More than 90 percent of the aggregate of the gross receipts of such corporation for all the taxable years during which it has been in existence has been from sources other than royalties, rents (except rents derived from rental of properties to employees of such corporation in the ordinary course of its operating business), dividends, interest (except interest received on the deferred purchase price of operating assets sold), annuities, and gains from sales or exchanges of stocks and securities. For this purpose, the term "gross receipts" means total receipts determined without any deduction for cost of goods sold, and gross receipts from sales or exchanges of stocks and securities shall be taken into account only to the extent of gains from such sales or exchanges.

* * *

[T.D. 6500, 25 FR 11402, Nov. 26, 1960; 25 FR 14021, Dec. 31, 1960, as amended by T.D. 7224, 37 FR 25928, Dec. 6, 1972; T.D. 9386, 73 FR 13124 (Mar. 11, 2008)]

§ 1.165–6 Farming losses.

(a) Allowance of losses. (1) Except as otherwise provided in this section, any loss incurred in the operation of a farm as a trade or business shall be allowed as a deduction under section 165(a) or as a net operating loss deduction in accordance with the provisions of section 172. * * *

(2) If the taxpayer owns and operates a farm for profit in addition to being engaged in another trade or business, but sustains a loss from the operation of the farming business, then the amount of loss sustained in the operation of the farm may be deducted from gross income, if any, from all other sources.

(3) Loss incurred in the operation of a farm for recreation or pleasure shall not be allowed as a deduction from gross income. * * *

(b) Loss from shrinkage. If, in the course of the business of farming, farm products are held for a favorable market, no deduction shall be allowed under section 165(a) in respect of such products merely because of shrinkage in weight, decline in value, or deterioration in storage.

(c) Loss of prospective crop. The total loss by frost, storm, flood, or fire of a prospective crop being grown in the business of farming shall not be allowed as a deduction under section 165(a).

(d) Loss of livestock—(1) Raised stock. A taxpayer engaged in the business of raising and selling livestock, such as cattle, sheep, or horses, may not deduct as a loss under section 165(a) the value of animals that perish from among those which were raised on the farm.

(2) Purchased stock. The loss sustained upon the death by disease, exposure, or injury of any livestock purchased and used in the trade or business of farming shall be allowed as a deduction under section 165(a). See, also, paragraph (e) of this section.

(e) Loss due to compliance with orders of governmental authority. The loss sustained upon the destruction by order of the United States, a State, or any other governmental authority, of any livestock, or other property, purchased and used in the trade or business of farming shall be allowed as a deduction under section 165(a).

(f) Amount deductible—(1) Expenses of operation. The cost of any feed, pasture, or care which is allowed under section 162 as an expense of operating a farm for profit shall not be included as a part of the cost of livestock for purposes of determining the amount of loss deductible under section 165(a) and this section. For the deduction of farming expenses, see § 1.162–12.

(2) Losses reflected in inventories. If inventories are taken into account in determining the income from the trade or business of farming, no deduction shall be allowed under this section for losses sustained during the taxable year upon livestock or other products, whether purchased for resale or produced on the farm, to the extent such losses are reflected in the inventory on hand at the close of the taxable year. Nothing in this section shall be construed to disallow the deduction of any loss reflected in the inventories of the taxpayer. For provisions relating to inventories of farmers, see section 471 * * *.

* * *

§ 1.165–7 Casualty losses.

(a) In general—(1) Allowance of deduction. Except as otherwise provided in paragraphs (b)(4) and (c) of this section, any loss arising from fire, storm, shipwreck, or other casualty is allowable as a deduction under section 165(a) for the taxable year in which the loss is sustained. * * * The manner of determining the amount of a casualty loss allowable as a deduction in computing taxable income under section 63 is the same whether the loss has been incurred in a trade or business or in any transaction entered into for profit, or whether it has been a loss of property not connected with a trade or business and not incurred in any transaction entered into for profit. The amount of a casualty loss shall be determined in accordance with paragraph (b) of this section. * * *

(2) Method of valuation. (i) In determining the amount of loss deductible under this section, the fair market value of the property immediately before and immediately after the casualty shall generally be ascertained by competent appraisal. This appraisal must recognize the effects of any general market decline affecting undamaged as well as damaged property which may occur simultaneously with the casualty, in order that any deduction under this section shall be limited to the actual loss resulting from damage to the property.

(ii) The cost of repairs to the property damaged is acceptable as evidence of the loss of value if the taxpayer shows that (a) the repairs are necessary to restore the property to its condition immediately before the casualty, (b) the amount spent for such repairs is not excessive, (c) the repairs do not care for more than the damage suffered, and (d) the value of the property after the repairs does not as a result of the repairs exceed the value of the property immediately before the casualty.

(3) Damage to automobiles. An automobile owned by the taxpayer, whether used for business purposes or maintained for recreation or pleasure, may be the subject of a casualty loss, including those losses specifically referred to in subparagraph (1) of this paragraph. In addition, a casualty loss occurs when an automobile owned by the taxpayer is damaged and when:

(i) The damage results from the faulty driving of the taxpayer or other person operating the automobile but is not due to the willful act or willful negligence of the taxpayer or of one acting in his behalf or

(ii) The damage results from the faulty driving of the operator of the vehicle with which the automobile of the taxpayer collides.

* * *

(5) Property converted from personal use. In the case of property which originally was not used in the trade or business or for income-producing purposes and which is thereafter converted to either of such uses, the fair market value of the property on the date of conversion, if less than the adjusted basis of the property at such time, shall be used, after making proper adjustments in respect of basis, as the basis for determining the amount of loss under paragraph (b)(1) of this section. See paragraph (b) of § 1.165–9, and § 1.167(g)–1.

(6) Theft losses. A loss which arises from theft is not considered a casualty loss for purposes of this section. See § 1.165–8, relating to theft losses.

(b) Amount deductible—(1) General rule. In the case of any casualty loss whether or not incurred in a trade or business or in any transaction entered into for profit, the amount of loss to be taken into account for purposes of section 165(a) shall be the lesser of either—

(i) The amount which is equal to the fair market value of the property immediately before the casualty reduced by the fair market value of the property immediately after the casualty; or

(ii) The amount of the adjusted basis prescribed in § 1.1011–1 for determining the loss from the sale or other disposition of the property involved.

However, if property used in a trade or business or held for the production of income is totally destroyed by casualty, and if the fair market value of such property immediately before the casualty is less than the adjusted basis of such property, the amount of the adjusted basis of such property shall be treated as the amount of the loss for purposes of section 165(a).

(2) Aggregation of property for computing loss. **(i)** A loss incurred in a trade or business or in any transaction entered into for profit shall be determined under subparagraph (1) of this paragraph by reference to the single, identifiable property damaged or destroyed. Thus, for example, in determining the fair market value of the property before and after the casualty in a case where damage by casualty has occurred to a building and ornamental or fruit trees used in a trade or business, the decrease in value shall be measured by taking the building and trees into account separately, and not together as an integral part of the realty, and separate losses shall be determined for such building and trees.

(ii) In determining a casualty loss involving real property and improvements thereon not used in a trade or business or in any transaction entered into for profit, the improvements (such as buildings and ornamental trees and shrubbery) to the property damaged or destroyed shall be considered an integral part of the property, for purposes of subparagraph (1) of this paragraph, and no separate basis need be apportioned to such improvements.

(3) Examples. The application of this paragraph may be illustrated by the following examples:

Example (1). In 1956 B purchases for $3,600 an automobile which he uses for nonbusiness purposes. In 1959 the automobile is damaged in an accidental collision with another automobile. The fair market value of B's automobile is $2,000 immediately before the collision and $1,500 immediately after the collision. B receives insurance proceeds of $300 to cover the loss. The amount of the deduction allowable under section 165(a) for the taxable year 1959 is $200, computed as follows:

Value of automobile immediately before casualty	$2,000
Less: Value of automobile immediately after casualty	1,500
Value of property actually destroyed	500
Loss to be taken into account for purposes of section 165(a): Lesser amount of property actually destroyed ($500) or adjusted basis of property ($3,600)	500
Less: Insurance received	300
Deduction allowable	200

Example (2). In 1958 A purchases land containing an office building for the lump sum of $90,000. The purchase price is allocated between the land ($18,000) and the building ($72,000) for purposes of determining basis. After the purchase A planted trees and ornamental shrubs on the grounds surrounding the building. In 1961 the land, building, trees, and shrubs are damaged by hurricane. At the time of the casualty the adjusted basis of the land is $18,000 and the adjusted basis of the building is $66,000. At that time the trees and shrubs have an adjusted basis of $1,200. The fair market value of the land and building immediately before the casualty is $18,000 and $70,000, respectively, and immediately after the casualty is $18,000 and $52,000, respectively. The fair market value of the trees and shrubs immediately before the casualty is $2,000 and immediately after the casualty is $400. In 1961 insurance of $5,000 is received to cover the loss to the building. A has no other gains or losses in 1961 subject to section 1231 and § 1.1231–1. The amount of the deduction allowable under section 165(a) with respect to the building for the taxable year 1961 is $13,000, computed as follows:

Value of property immediately before casualty	$70,000
Less: Value of property immediately after casualty	52,000
Value of property actually destroyed	18,000
Less: Insurance received	5,000
Loss to be taken into account for purposes of section 165(a): Lesser amount of property actually destroyed ($18,000) or adjusted basis of property ($66,000)	18,000
Less: Insurance received	5,000
Deduction allowable	13,000

The amount of the deduction allowable under section 165(a) with respect to the trees and shrubs for the taxable year 1961 is $1,200, computed as follows:

Value of property immediately before casualty	$2,000
Less: Value of property immediately after casualty	400
Value of property actually destroyed	1,600
Loss to be taken into account for purposes of section 165(a): Lesser amount of property actually destroyed ($1,600) or adjusted basis of property ($1,200)	1,200

Example (3). Assume the same facts as in example (2) except that A purchases land containing a house instead of an office building. The house is used as his private residence. Since the property is used for personal purposes, no allocation of the purchase price is necessary for the land and house. Likewise, no individual determination of the fair market values of the land, house, trees, and shrubs is necessary. The amount of the deduction allowable under section 165(a) with respect to the land, house, trees, and shrubs for the taxable year 1961 is $14,600, computed as follows:

Value of property immediately before casualty	$90,000
Less: Value of property immediately after casualty	70,400
Value of property actually destroyed	19,600
Loss to be taken into account for purposes of section 165(a): Lesser amount of property actually destroyed ($19,600) or adjusted basis of property ($91,200)	19,600
Less: Insurance received	5,000
Deduction allowable	14,600

* * *

(c) Loss sustained by an estate. A casualty loss of property not connected with a trade or business and not incurred in any transaction entered into for profit which is sustained during the settlement of an estate shall be allowed as a deduction under sections 165(a) and 641(b) in computing the taxable income of the estate if the loss has not been allowed under section 2054 in computing the taxable estate of the decedent and if the statement has been filed in accordance with § 1.642(g)–1. See section 165(c)(3).

* * *

[T.D. 6500, 25 FR 11402, Nov. 26, 1960, as amended by T.D. 6712, 29 FR 3652, March 24, 1964; T.D. 6735, 29 FR 6493, May 19, 1964; T.D. 6786, 29 FR 18501, Dec. 29, 1964; T.D. 7522, 42 FR 63411, Dec. 16, 1977]

§ 1.165–8 Theft losses.

(a) Allowance of deduction. **(1)** Except as otherwise provided in paragraphs (b) and (c) of this section, any loss arising from theft is allowable as a deduction under section 165(a) for the taxable year in which the loss is sustained. See section 165(c)(3).

(2) A loss arising from theft shall be treated under section 165(a) as sustained during the taxable year in which the taxpayer discovers the loss. See section 165(e). Thus, a theft loss is not deductible under section 165(a) for the taxable year in which the theft actually occurs unless that is also the year in which the taxpayer discovers the loss. However, if in the year of discovery there exists a claim for reimbursement with respect to which there is a reasonable prospect of recovery, see paragraph (d) of § 1.165–1.

(3) * * * See section 7852(c), relating to items not to be twice deducted from income.

* * *

(c) Amount deductible. The amount deductible under this section in respect of a theft loss shall be determined consistently with the manner prescribed in § 1.165–7 for determining the amount of casualty loss allowable as a deduction under section 165(a). In applying the provisions of paragraph (b) of § 1.165–7 for this purpose, the fair market value of the property immediately after the theft shall be considered to be zero. * * *

(d) Definition. For purposes of this section the term "theft" shall be deemed to include, but shall not necessarily be limited to, larceny, embezzlement, and robbery.

* * *

[T.D. 6500, 25 FR 11402, Nov. 26, 1960, as amended by T.D. 6786, 29 FR 18502, Dec. 29, 1964]

§ 1.165–9 Sale of residential property.

(a) Losses not allowed. A loss sustained on the sale of residential property purchased or constructed by the taxpayer for use as his personal residence and so used by him up to the time of the sale is not deductible under section 165(a).

(b) Property converted from personal use. **(1)** If property purchased or constructed by the taxpayer for use as his personal residence is, prior to its sale, rented or otherwise appropriated to income-producing purposes and is used for such purposes up to the time of its sale, a loss sustained on the sale of the property shall be allowed as a deduction under section 165(a).

(2) The loss allowed under this paragraph upon the sale of the property shall be the excess of the adjusted basis prescribed in § 1.1011–1 for determining loss over the amount realized from the sale. For this purpose, the adjusted basis for determining loss shall be the lesser of either of the following amounts, adjusted as prescribed in § 1.1011–1 for the period subsequent to the conversion of the property to income-producing purposes:

(i) The fair market value of the property at the time of conversion, or

(ii) The adjusted basis for loss, at the time of conversion, determined under § 1.1011–1 but without reference to the fair market value.

* * *

(c) Examples. The application of paragraph (b) of this section may be illustrated by the following examples:

Example (1). Residential property is purchased by the taxpayer in 1943 for use as his personal residence at a cost of $25,000, of which $15,000 is allocable to the building. The taxpayer uses the property as his personal residence until January 1, 1952, at which time its fair market value is $22,000, of which $12,000 is allocable to the building. The taxpayer rents the property from January 1, 1952, until January 1, 1955, at which time it is sold for $16,000. On January 1, 1952, the building has an estimated useful life of 20 years. It is assumed that the building has no estimated salvage value and that there are no adjustments in respect of basis other than depreciation, which is computed on the straight-line method. The loss to be taken into account for purposes of section 165(a) for the taxable year 1955 is $4,200, computed as follows:

Basis of property at time of conversion for purposes of this section (that is, the lesser of $25,000 cost or $22,000 fair market value)	$22,000
Less: Depreciation allowable from January 1, 1952, to January 1, 1955 (3 years at 5 percent based on $12,000, the value of the building at time of conversion, as prescribed by § 1.167(g)–1)	1,800
Adjusted basis prescribed in § 1.1011–1 for determining loss on sale of the property	20,200
Less: Amount realized on sale	16,000
Loss to be taken into account for purposes of section 165(a)	4,200

In this example the value of the building at the time of conversion is used as the basis for computing depreciation. See example (2) of this paragraph wherein the adjusted basis of the building is required to be used for such purpose.

Example (2). Residential property is purchased by the taxpayer in 1940 for use as his personal residence at a cost of $23,000, of which $10,000 is allocable to the building. The taxpayer uses the property as his personal residence until January 1, 1953, at which time its fair market value is $20,000, of which $12,000 is allocable to the building. The taxpayer rents the property from January 1, 1953, until January 1, 1957, at which time it is sold for $17,000. On January 1, 1953, the building has an estimated useful life of 20 years. It is assumed that the building has no estimated salvage value and that there are no adjustments in respect of basis other than depreciation, which is computed on the straight-line method. The loss to be taken into account for purposes of section 165(a) for the taxable year 1957 is $1,000, computed as follows:

Basis of property at time of conversion for purposes of this section (that is, the lesser of $23,000 cost or $20,000 fair market value)	$20,000
Less: Depreciation allowable from January 1, 1953, to January 1, 1957 (4 years at 5 percent based on $10,000, the cost of the building, as prescribed by § 1.167(g)–1)	2,000
Adjusted basis prescribed in § 1.1011–1 for determining loss on sale of the property	18,000
Less: Amount realized on sale	17,000
Loss to be taken into account for purposes of section 165(a)	1,000

[T.D. 6500, 25 FR 11402, Nov. 26, 1960, as amended by T.D. 6712, 29 FR 3652, March 24, 1964]

§ 1.165–11 Election in respect of losses attributable to a disaster.

(a) In general. Section 165(h) provides that a taxpayer who has sustained a disaster loss which is allowable as a deduction under section 165(a) may, under certain circumstances, elect to deduct such loss for the taxable year immediately preceding the taxable year in which the disaster actually occurred.

* * *

(d) Scope and effect of election. An election made pursuant to section 165(h) and this section in respect of a loss arising from a particular disaster shall apply to the entire loss sustained by the taxpayer from such disaster during the period specified in paragraph (b)(1) of this section in the area specified in paragraph (b)(2) of this section. If such an election is made, the disaster to which the election relates will be deemed to have occurred in the taxable year immediately preceding the taxable year in which the disaster actually occurred, and the loss to which the election applies will be deemed to have been sustained in such preceding taxable year.

* * *

[T.D. 6735, 29 FR 6493, May 19, 1964, as amended by T.D. 7224, 37 FR 25928, Dec. 6, 1972; T.D. 7522, 42 FR 63411, Dec. 16, 1977]

§ 1.166–1 Bad debts.

* * *

(c) Bona fide debt required. Only a bona fide debt qualifies for purposes of section 166. A bona fide debt is a debt which arises from a debtor-creditor relationship based upon a valid and enforceable obligation to pay a fixed or determinable sum of money. A debt arising out of the receivables of an accrual method taxpayer is deemed to be an enforceable obligation for purposes of the preceding sentence to the extent that the income such debt represents have been included in the return of income for the year for which the deduction as a bad debt is claimed or for a prior taxable year. For example, a debt arising out of gambling receivables that are unenforceable under state or local law, which an accrual method taxpayer includes in income under section 61, is an enforceable obligation for purposes of this paragraph. A gift or contribution to capital shall not be considered a debt for purposes of section 166. * * *

(d) Amount deductible—(1) General rule. * * * the basis for determining the amount of deduction under section 166 in respect of a bad debt shall be the same as the adjusted basis prescribed by § 1.1011–1 for determining the loss from the sale or other disposition of property. * * *

(2) Specific cases. Subject to any provision of section 166 and the regulations thereunder which provides to the contrary, the following amounts are deductible as bad debts:

(i) Notes or accounts receivable. **(a)** If, in computing taxable income, a taxpayer values his notes or accounts receivable at their fair market value when received, the amount deductible as a bad debt under section 166 in respect of such receivables shall be limited to such fair market value even though it is less than their face value.

(b) A purchaser of accounts receivable which become worthless during the taxable year shall be entitled under section 166 to a deduction which is based upon the price he paid for such receivables but not upon their face value.

(ii) Bankruptcy claim. Only the difference between the amount received in distribution of the assets of a bankrupt and the amount of the claim may be deducted under section 166 as a bad debt.

(iii) Claim against decedent's estate. The excess of the amount of the claim over the amount received by a creditor of a decedent in distribution of the assets of the decedent's estate may be considered a worthless debt under section 166.

(e) Prior inclusion in income required. Worthless debts arising from unpaid wages, salaries, fees, rents, and similar items of taxable income shall not be allowed as a deduction under section 166 unless the income such items represent has been included in the return of income for the year for which the deduction as a bad debt is claimed or for a prior taxable year.

(f) Recovery of bad debts. Any amount attributable to the recovery during the taxable year of a bad debt, or of a part of a bad debt, which was allowed as a deduction from gross income in a prior taxable year shall be included in gross income for the taxable year of recovery, except to the extent that the recovery is excluded from gross income * * *.

(g) Worthless securities. **(1)** Section 166 and the regulations thereunder do not apply to a debt which is evidenced by a bond, debenture, note, or certificate, or other evidence of indebtedness, issued by a corporation or by a government or political subdivision thereof, with interest coupons or in registered form. See section 166(e). For provisions allowing the deduction of a loss resulting from the worthlessness of such a debt, see § 1.165–5.

* * *

[T.D. 6500, 25 FR 11402, Nov. 26, 1960, as amended by T.D. 6996, 34 FR 835, Jan. 18, 1969; T.D. 7902, 48 FR 33260, July 21, 1983; T.D. 8071, 51 FR 2479, Jan. 17, 1986]

§ 1.166–2 Evidence of worthlessness.

(a) General rule. In determining whether a debt is worthless in whole or in part the district director will consider all pertinent evidence, including the value of the collateral, if any, securing the debt and the financial condition of the debtor.

(b) Legal action not required. Where the surrounding circumstances indicate that a debt is worthless and uncollectible and that legal action to enforce payment would in all probability not result in the satisfaction of execution on a judgment, a showing of these facts will be sufficient evidence of the worthlessness of the debt for purposes of the deduction under section 166.

(c) Bankruptcy—(1) General rule. Bankruptcy is generally an indication of the worthlessness of at least a part of an unsecured and unpreferred debt.

(2) Year of deduction. In bankruptcy cases a debt may become worthless before settlement in some instances; and in others, only when a settlement in bankruptcy has been reached. In either case, the mere fact that bankruptcy proceedings instituted against the debtor are terminated in a later year, thereby confirming the conclusion that the debt is worthless, shall not authorize the shifting of the deduction under section 166 to such later year.

* * *

[T.D. 6500, 25 FR 11402, Nov. 26, 1960; 25 FR 14021, Dec. 31, 1960, as amended by T.D. 7254, 38 FR 2418, Jan. 26, 1973; T.D. 8492, 58 FR 53658, Oct. 18, 1993]

§ 1.166–3 Partial or total worthlessness.

(a) Partial worthlessness—(1) Applicable to specific debts only. A deduction under section 166(a)(2) on account of partially worthless debts shall be allowed with respect to specific debts only.

(2) Charge-off required. (i) If, from all the surrounding and attending circumstances, the district director is satisfied that a debt is partially worthless, the amount which has become worthless shall be allowed as a deduction under section 166(a)(2) but only to the extent charged off during the taxable year.

(ii) If a taxpayer claims a deduction for a part of a debt for the taxable year within which that part of the debt is charged off and the deduction is disallowed for that taxable year, then, in a case where the debt becomes partially worthless after the close of that taxable year, a deduction under section 166(a)(2) shall be allowed for a subsequent taxable year but not in excess of the amount charged off in the prior taxable year plus any amount charged off in the subsequent taxable year. In such instance, the charge-off in the prior taxable year shall, if consistently maintained as such, be sufficient to that extent to meet the charge-off requirement of section 166(a)(2) with respect to the subsequent taxable year.

(iii) Before a taxpayer may deduct a debt in part, he must be able to demonstrate to the satisfaction of the district director the amount thereof which is worthless and the part thereof which has been charged off.

* * *

(b) Total worthlessness. If a debt becomes wholly worthless during the taxable year, the amount thereof which has not been allowed as a deduction from gross income for any prior taxable year shall be allowed as a deduction for the current taxable year.

[T.D. 6500, 25 FR 11402, Nov. 26, 1960; T.D. 8763, 63 FR 4396, Jan. 29, 1998; 63 FR 5834, Feb. 4, 1998]

§ 1.166–5 Nonbusiness debts.

(a) Allowance of deduction as capital loss. (1) The loss resulting from any nonbusiness debt's becoming partially or wholly worthless within the taxable year shall not be allowed as a deduction under * * * section 166(a) * * * in determining the taxable income of a taxpayer other than a corporation. See section 166(d)(1)(A).

(2) If, in the case of a taxpayer other than a corporation, a nonbusiness debt becomes wholly worthless within the taxable year, the loss resulting therefrom shall be treated as a loss from the sale or exchange, during the taxable year, of a capital asset held for not more than 1 year * * *. Such a loss is subject to the limitations provided in section 1211, relating to the limitation on capital losses, and section 1212, relating to the capital loss carryover, and in the regulations under those sections. A loss on a nonbusiness debt shall be treated as sustained only if and when the debt has become totally worthless, and no deduction shall be allowed for a nonbusiness debt which is recoverable in part during the taxable year.

(b) Nonbusiness debt defined. For purposes of section 166 and this section, a nonbusiness debt is any debt other than—

(1) A debt which is created, or acquired, in the course of a trade or business of the taxpayer, determined without regard to the relationship of the debt to a trade or business of the taxpayer at the time when the debt becomes worthless; or

(2) A debt the loss from the worthlessness of which is incurred in the taxpayer's trade or business.

The question whether a debt is a nonbusiness debt is a question of fact in each particular case. The determination of whether the loss on a debt's becoming worthless has been incurred in a trade or business of the taxpayer shall, for this purpose, be made in substantially the same manner for determining whether a loss has been incurred in a trade or business for purposes of section 165(c)(1). For purposes of subparagraph (2) of this paragraph, the character of the debt is to be determined by the relation which the loss resulting from the debt's becoming worthless bears to the trade or business of the taxpayer. If that relation is a proximate one in the conduct of the trade or business in which the taxpayer is engaged at the time the debt becomes worthless, the debt comes within the exception provided by that subparagraph. The use to which the borrowed funds are put by the debtor is of no consequence in making a determination under this paragraph. For purposes of section 166 and this section, a nonbusiness debt does not include a debt described in section 165(g)(2)(C). See § 1.165–5, relating to losses on worthless securities.

(c) Guaranty of obligations. For provisions treating a loss sustained by a guarantor of obligations as a loss resulting from the worthlessness of a debt, see §§ 1.66–8 and 1.166–9.

(d) Examples. The application of this section may be illustrated by the following examples involving a case where A, an individual who is engaged in the grocery business and who makes his return on the basis of the calendar year, extends credit to B in 1955 on an open account:

Example (1). In 1956 A sells the business but retains the claim against B. The claim becomes worthless in A's hands in 1957. A's loss is not controlled by the nonbusiness debt provisions, since the original consideration has been advanced by A in his trade or business.

Example (2). In 1956 A sells the business to C but sells the claim against B to the taxpayer, D. The claim becomes worthless in D's hands in 1957. During 1956 and 1957, D is not engaged in any trade or business. D's loss is controlled by the nonbusiness debt provisions even though the original consideration has been advanced by A in his trade or business, since the debt has not been created or acquired in connection with a trade or business of D and since in 1957 D is not engaged in a trade or business incident to the conduct of which a loss from the worthlessness of such claim is a proximate result.

Example (3). In 1956 A dies, leaving the business, including the accounts receivable, to his son, C, the taxpayer. The claim against B becomes worthless in C's hands in 1957. C's loss is not controlled by the nonbusiness debt provisions. While C does not advance any consideration for the claim, or create or acquire it in connection with his trade or business, the loss is sustained as a proximate incident to the conduct of the trade or business in which he is engaged at the time the debt becomes worthless.

Example (4). In 1956 A dies, leaving the business to his son, C, but leaving the claim against B to his son, D, the taxpayer. The claim against B becomes worthless in D's hands in 1957. During 1956 and 1957, D is not engaged in any trade or business. D's loss is controlled by the nonbusiness debt provisions even though the original consideration has been advanced by A in his trade or business, since the debt has not been created or acquired in connection with a trade or business of D and since in 1957 D is not engaged in a trade or business incident to the conduct of which a loss from the worthlessness of such claim is a proximate result.

Example (5). In 1956 A dies; and, while his executor, C, is carrying on the business, the claim against B becomes worthless in 1957. The loss sustained by A's estate is not controlled by the nonbusiness debt provisions. While C does not advance any consideration for the claim on behalf of the estate, or create or acquire it in connection with a trade or business in which the estate is engaged, the loss is sustained as a proximate incident to the conduct of the trade or business in which the estate is engaged at the time the debt becomes worthless.

* * *

[T.D. 6500, 25 FR 11402, Nov. 26, 1960, as amended by T.D. 7657, 44 FR 68464, Nov. 29, 1979; T.D. 7728, 45 FR 72650, Nov. 3, 1980]

§ 1.166–9 Losses of guarantors, endorsers, and indemnitors incurred, on agreements made after December 31, 1975, in taxable years beginning after such date.

(a) Payment treated as worthless business debt. This paragraph applies to taxpayers who, after December 31, 1975, enter into an agreement in the course of their trade or business to act as (or in a manner essentially equivalent to) a guarantor, endorser, or indemnitor of (or other secondary obligor upon) a debt obligation. Subject to the provisions of paragraphs (c), (d), and (e) of this section, a payment of principal or interest made during a taxable year beginning after December 31, 1975, by the taxpayer in discharge of part or all of the taxpayer's obligation as a guarantor, endorser, or indemnitor is treated as a business debt becoming worthless in the taxable year in which the payment is made or in the taxable year described in paragraph (e)(2) of this section. Neither section 163 (relating to interest) nor section 165 (relating to losses) shall apply with respect to such a payment.

(b) Payment treated as worthless nonbusiness debt. This paragraph applies to taxpayers (other than corporations) who, after December 31, 1975, enter into a transaction for profit, but not in the course of their trade or business, to act as (or in a manner essentially equivalent to) a guarantor, endorser, or indemnitor of (or other secondary obligator upon) a debt obligation. Subject to the provisions of paragraphs (c), (d), and (e) of this section, a payment of principal or interest made during a taxable year beginning after December 31, 1975, by the taxpayer in discharge of part or all of the taxpayer's obligation as a guarantor, endorser, or indemnitor is treated as a worthless nonbusiness debt in the taxable year in which the payment is made or in the taxable year described in paragraph (e)(2) of this section. Neither section 163 nor section 165 shall apply with respect to such a payment.

(c) Obligations issued by corporations. No treatment as a worthless debt is allowed with respect to a payment made by the taxpayer in discharge of part or all of the taxpayer's obligation as a guarantor, endorser, or indemnitor of an obligation issued by a corporation if, on the basis of the facts and circumstances at the time the obligation was entered into, the payment constitutes a contribution to capital by a shareholder. The rule of this paragraph (c) applies to payments whenever made * * *.

(d) Certain payments treated as worthless debts. A payment in discharge of part or all of taxpayer's agreement to act as guarantor, endorser, or indemnitor of an obligation is to be treated as a worthless debt only if—

(1) The agreement was entered into in the course of the taxpayer's trade or business or a transaction for profit;

(2) There was an enforceable legal duty upon the taxpayer to make the payment (except that legal action need not have been brought against the taxpayer); and

(3) The agreement was entered into before the obligation became worthless (or partially worthless in the case of an agreement entered into in the course of the taxpayer's trade or business). See §§ 1.166–2 and 1.166–3 for rules on worthless and partially worthless debts. For purposes of this paragraph (d)(3), an agreement is considered as entered into before the obligation became worthless (or partially worthless) if there was a reasonable expectation on the part of the taxpayer at the time the agreement was entered into that the taxpayer would not be called upon to pay the debt (subject to such agreement) without full reimbursement from the issuer of the obligation.

(e) Special rules—(1) Reasonable consideration required. Treatment as a worthless debt of a payment made by a taxpayer in discharge of part or all of the taxpayer's agreement to act as a guarantor, endorser, or indemnitor of an obligation is allowed only if the taxpayer demonstrates that reasonable consideration was received for entering into the agreement. For purposes of this paragraph (e)(1), reasonable consideration is not limited to direct consideration in the form of cash or property. Thus, where a taxpayer can demonstrate that the agreement was given without direct consideration in the form of cash or property but in accordance with normal business practice or for a good faith business purpose, worthless debt treatment is allowed with respect to a payment in discharge of part or all of the agreement if the conditions of this section are met. However, consideration received from a taxpayer's spouse or any individual listed in section 152(a) must be direct consideration in the form of cash or property.

(2) Right of subrogation. With respect to a payment made by a taxpayer in discharge of part or all of the taxpayer's agreement to act as a guarantor, endorser, or indemnitor where the agreement provides for a right of subrogation or other similar right against the issuer, treatment as a worthless debt is not allowed until the taxable year in which the right of subrogation or other similar right becomes totally worthless (or partially worthless in the case of an agreement which arose in the course of the taxpayer's trade or business).

* * *

(4) Taxpayer defined. For purposes of this section, except as otherwise provided, the term "taxpayer" means any taxpayer and includes individuals, corporations, partnerships, trusts and estates.

* * *

[T.D. 7657, 44 FR 68465, Nov. 29, 1979, as amended by T.D. 7747, 45 FR 86445, Dec. 31, 1980; T.D. 7920, 48 FR 50712, Nov. 3, 1983]

§ 1.167(a)–1 Depreciation in general.

(a) Reasonable allowance. Section 167(a) provides that a reasonable allowance for the exhaustion, wear and tear, and obsolescence of property used in the trade or business or of property held by the taxpayer for the production of income shall be allowed as a depreciation deduction. * * * The allowance shall not reflect amounts representing a mere reduction in market value. * * *

* * *

[T.D. 6500, 25 FR 11402, Nov. 26, 1960, as amended by T.D. 6712, 29 FR 3653, March 24, 1964; T.D. 7203, 37 FR 17133, Aug. 25, 1972]

§ 1.167(a)–2 Tangible property.

The depreciation allowance in the case of tangible property applies only to that part of the property which is subject to wear and tear, to decay or decline from natural causes, to exhaustion, and to obsolescence. The allowance does not apply to inventories or stock in trade, or to land apart from the improvements or physical development added to it. The allowance does not apply to natural resources which are subject to the allowance for depletion provided in section 611. No deduction for depreciation shall be allowed on automobiles or other vehicles used solely for pleasure, on a building used by the taxpayer solely as his residence, or on furniture or furnishings therein, personal effects, or clothing; but properties and costumes used exclusively in a business, such as a theatrical business, may be depreciated.

[T.D. 6500, 25 FR 11402, Nov. 26, 1960]

§ 1.167(a)–3 Intangibles.

(a) In general. If an intangible asset is known from experience or other factors to be of use in the business or in the production of income for only a limited period, the length of which can be estimated with reasonable accuracy, such an intangible asset may be the subject of a depreciation allowance. Examples are patents and copyrights. * * * For rules with respect to organizational expenditures, see section 248 and the regulations thereunder. * * * See sections 197 and 167(f) and, to the extent applicable, §§ 1.197–2 and 1.167–14 for amortization of goodwill and certain other intangibles acquired after August 10, 1993, or after July 25, 1991, if a valid retroactive election under § 1.197–1T has been made.

(b) Safe harbor amortization for certain intangible assets—(1) Useful life. Solely for purposes of determining the depreciation allowance referred to in paragraph (a) of this section, a taxpayer may treat an intangible asset as having a useful life equal to 15 years unless—

(i) An amortization period or useful life for the intangible asset is specifically prescribed or prohibited by the Internal Revenue Code, the regulations thereunder (other than by this paragraph (b)), or other published guidance in the Internal Revenue Bulletin (see § 601.601(d)(2) of this chapter);

(ii) The intangible asset is described in § 1.263(a)–4(c) (relating to intangibles acquired from another person) or § 1.263(a)–4(d)(2) (relating to created financial interests);

(iii) The intangible asset has a useful life the length of which can be estimated with reasonable accuracy; or

(iv) The intangible asset is described in § 1.263(a)–4(d)(8) (relating to certain benefits arising from the provision, production, or improvement of real property), in which case the taxpayer may treat the intangible asset as having a useful life equal to 25 years solely for purposes of determining the depreciation allowance referred to in paragraph (a) of this section.

(2) Applicability to acquisitions of a trade or business, changes in the capital structure of a business entity, and certain other transactions. The safe harbor useful life provided by paragraph (b)(1) of this section does not apply to an amount required to be capitalized by § 1.263(a)–5 (relating to amounts paid to facilitate an acquisition of a trade or business, a change in the capital structure of a business entity, and certain other transactions).

(3) Depreciation method. A taxpayer that determines its depreciation allowance for an intangible asset using the 15–year useful life prescribed by paragraph (b)(1) of this section (or the 25–year useful life in the case of an intangible asset described in § 1.263(a)–4(d)(8)) must determine the allowance by amortizing the basis of the intangible asset (as determined under section 167(c) and without regard to salvage value) ratably over the useful life beginning on the first day of the month in which the intangible asset is placed in service by the taxpayer. The intangible asset is not eligible for amortization in the month of disposition.

(4) Effective date. This paragraph (b) applies to intangible assets created on or after December 31, 2003.

[T.D. 6500, 25 FR 11402, Nov. 26, 1960, as amended by T.D. 8865, 65 FR 3820, Jan. 25, 2000; T.D. 9107, 69 FR 435, Jan. 5, 2004]

§ 1.167(a)–8 Retirements.

(a) Gains and losses on retirements. * * *

* * *

(4) Where an asset is retired by actual physical abandonment (as, for example, in the case of a building condemned as unfit for further occupancy or other use), loss will be recognized measured by the amount of the adjusted basis of the asset abandoned at the time of such abandonment. In order to qualify for the recognition of loss from physical abandonment, the intent of the taxpayer must be irrevocably to discard the asset so that it will neither be used again by him nor retrieved by him for sale, exchange, or other disposition. * * *

* * *

[T.D. 6500, 25 FR 11402, Nov. 26, 1960; T.D. 9564, 76 FR 81084, Dec. 27, 2011]

§ 1.167(a)–10 When depreciation deduction is allowable.

(a) A taxpayer should deduct the proper depreciation allowance each year and may not increase his depreciation allowances in later years by reason of his failure to deduct any depreciation allowance or of his action in deducting an allowance plainly inadequate under the known facts in prior years. The inadequacy of the depreciation allowance for property in prior years shall be determined on the basis of the allowable method of depreciation used by the taxpayer for such property or under the straight line method if no allowance has ever been claimed for such property. The preceding sentence shall not be construed as precluding application of any method provided in section 167(b) if taxpayer's failure to claim any allowance for depreciation was due solely to erroneously treating as a deductible expense an item properly chargeable to capital account. For rules relating to adjustments to basis, see section 1016 and the regulations thereunder.

(b) The period for depreciation of an asset shall begin when the asset is placed in service and shall end when the asset is retired from service. A proportionate part of one year's depreciation is allowable for that part of the first and last year during which the asset was in service. However, in the case of a multiple asset account, the amount of depreciation may be determined by using what is commonly described as an ''averaging convention'', that is, by using an assumed timing of additions and retirements. For example, it might be assumed that all additions and retirements to the asset account occur uniformly throughout the taxable year, in which case depreciation is computed on the average of the beginning and ending balances of the asset account for the taxable year. * * * Among still other averaging conventions which may be used is the one under which it is assumed that all additions and retirements during the first half of a given year were made on the first day of that year and that all additions and retirements during the second half of the year were made on the first day of the following year. Thus, a full year's depreciation would be taken on additions in the first half of the year and no depreciation would be taken on additions in the second half. Moreover, under this convention, no depreciation would be taken on retirements in the first half of the year and a full year's depreciation would be taken on the retirements in the second half. An averaging convention, if used, must be consistently followed as to the account or accounts for which it is adopted, and must be applied to both additions and retirements. In any year in which an averaging convention substantially distorts the depreciation allowance for the taxable year, it may not be used.

§ 1.167(a)–14 Treatment of certain intangible property excluded from section 197.

(a) Overview. This section provides rules for the amortization of certain intangibles that are excluded from section 197 (relating to the amortization of goodwill and certain other intangibles). These excluded intangibles * * * include certain computer software and certain other separately acquired rights, such as rights to receive tangible property or services, patents and copyrights, certain mortgage servicing rights, and rights of fixed duration or amount. Intangibles for which an amortization amount is determined under section 167(f) and intangibles otherwise excluded from section 197 are amortizable only if they qualify as property subject to the allowance for depreciation under section 167(a).

(b) Computer software—(1) In general. The amount of the deduction for computer software described in section 167(f)(1) and § 1.197–2(c)(4) is determined by amortizing the cost or other basis of the computer software using the straight line method described in § 1.167(b)–1 (except that its salvage value is treated as zero) and an amortization period of 36 months beginning on the first day of the month that the computer software is placed in service. Before determining the amortization deduction allowable under this paragraph (b), the cost or other basis of computer software that is section 179 property, as defined in section 179(d)(1)(A)(ii), must be reduced for any portion of the basis the taxpayer properly elects to treat as an expense under section 179. * * * If costs for developing computer software that the taxpayer properly elects to defer under section 174(b) result in the development of property subject to the allowance for depreciation under section 167, the rules of this paragraph (b) will apply to the unrecovered costs. In addition, this paragraph (b) applies to the cost of separately acquired computer software if the cost to acquire the software is separately stated and the cost is required to be capitalized under section 263(a).

(2) Exceptions. Paragraph (b)(1) of this section does not apply to the cost of computer software properly and consistently taken into account under § 1.162–11. The cost of acquiring an interest in computer software that is included, without being separately stated, in the cost of the hardware or other tangible property is treated as part of the cost of the hardware or other tangible property that is capitalized and depreciated under other applicable sections of the Internal Revenue Code.

* * *

(c) Certain interests or rights not acquired as part of a purchase of a trade or business—(1) Certain rights to receive tangible property or services. The amount of the deduction for a right (other than a right acquired as part of a purchase of a trade or business) to receive tangible property or services under a contract or from a governmental unit (as specified in section 167(f)(2) and § 1.197–2(c)(6)) is determined as follows:

(i) Amortization of fixed amounts. The basis of a right to receive a fixed amount of tangible property or services is amortized for each taxable year by multiplying the basis of the right by a fraction, the numerator of which is the amount of tangible property or services received during the taxable year and the denominator of which is the total amount of tangible property or services received or to be received under the terms of the contract or governmental grant. For example, if a taxpayer acquires a favorable contract right to receive a fixed amount of raw materials during an unspecified period, the taxpayer must amortize the cost of acquiring the contract right by multiplying the total cost by a fraction, the numerator of which is the amount of raw materials received under the contract during the taxable year and the denominator of which is the total amount of raw materials received or to be received under the contract.

(ii) Amortization of unspecified amount over fixed period. The cost or other basis of a right to receive an unspecified amount of tangible property or services over a fixed period is amortized ratably over the period of the right. (See paragraph (c)(3) of this section regarding renewals).

(iii) Amortization in other cases. [Reserved]

(2) Rights of fixed duration or amount. The amount of the deduction for a right (other than a right acquired as part of a purchase of a trade or business) of fixed duration or amount received under a contract or granted by a governmental unit (specified in section 167(f)(2) and § 1.197–2(c)(13)) and not covered by paragraph (c)(1) of this section is determined as follows:

(i) rights to a fixed amount. The basis of a right to a fixed amount is amortized for each taxable year by multiplying the basis by a fraction, the numerator of which is the amount received during the taxable year and the denominator of which is the total amount received or to be received under the terms of the contract or governmental grant.

(ii) Rights to an unspecified amount over fixed duration of less than 15 years. The basis of a right to an unspecified amount over a fixed duration of less than 15 years is amortized ratably over the period of the right.

(3) Application of renewals. (i) For purposes of paragraphs (c)(1) and (2) of this section, the duration of a right under a contract (or granted by a governmental unit) includes any renewal period if, based on all of the facts and circumstances in existence at any time during the taxable year in which the right is acquired, the facts clearly indicate a reasonable expectancy of renewal.

(ii) The mere fact that a taxpayer will have the opportunity to renew a contract right or other right on the same terms as are available to others, in a competitive auction or similar process that is designed to reflect fair market value and in which the taxpayer is not contractually advantaged, will generally not be taken into account in determining the duration of such right provided that the bidding produces a fair market value price comparable to the price that would be obtained if the rights were purchased immediately after renewal from a person (other than the person granting the renewal) in an arm's length transaction.

(iii) The cost of a renewal not included in the terms of the contract or governmental grant is treated as the acquisition of a separate intangible asset

(4) Patents and copyrights. If the purchase price of a interest (other than an interest acquired as part of a purchase of a trade or business) in a patent or copyright described in section 167(f)(2) and § 1.197–2(c)(7) is payable on at least an annual basis as either a fixed amount per use or a fixed percentage of the revenue derived from the use of the patent or copyright, the depreciation deduction for a taxable year is equal to the amount of the purchase price paid or incurred during the year. Otherwise, the basis of such patent or copyright (or an interest therein) is depreciated either ratably over its remaining useful life or under section 167(g) (income forecast method). If a patent or copyright becomes valueless in any year before its legal expiration, the adjusted basis may be deducted in that year.

(5) Additional rules. The period of amortization under paragraphs (c)(1) through (4) of this section begins when the intangible is placed in service. * * *

* * *

[T.D. 8865, 65 FR 3820, Jan. 25, 2000, as amended by T.D. 9091, 68 FR 52985, Sept. 8, 2003 T.D. 9283, 71 FR 51737, Aug. 31, 2006]

§ 1.167(b)–0 Methods of computing depreciation.

(a) In general. Any reasonable and consistently applied method of computing depreciation may be used or continued in use under section 167. Regardless of the method used in computing depreciation, deductions for depreciation shall not exceed such amounts as may be necessary to recover the unrecovered cost or other basis less salvage during the remaining useful life of the property. The reasonableness of any claim for depreciation shall be determined upon the basis of conditions known to exist at the end of the period for which the return is made. It is the responsibility of the taxpayer to establish the reasonableness of the deduction for depreciation claimed. Generally, depreciation deductions so claimed will be changed only where there is a clear and convincing basis for a change.

* * *

[T.D. 6500, 26 FR 11402, Nov. 26, 1960]

§ 1.167(b)–1 Straight line method.

(a) Application of methods. Under the straight line method the cost or other basis of the property less its estimated salvage value is deductible in equal annual amounts over the period of the estimated useful life of the property. The allowance for depreciation for the taxable year is determined by dividing the adjusted basis of the property at the beginning of the taxable year, less salvage value, by the remaining useful life of the property at such time. For convenience, the allowance so determined may be reduced to a percentage or fraction. The straight line method may be used in determining a reasonable allowance for depreciation for any property which is subject to depreciation under section 167 and it shall be used in all cases where the taxpayer has not adopted a different acceptable method with respect to such property.

* * *

[T.D. 6500, 25 FR 11402, Nov. 26, 1960]

§ 1.167(b)–2 Declining balance method.

(a) Application of method. Under the declining balance method a uniform rate is applied each year to the unrecovered cost or other basis of the property. * * * The declining balance rate may be determined without resort to formula. Such rate * * * shall not exceed twice the appropriate straight line rate computed without adjustment for salvage. While salvage is not taken into account in determining the annual allowances under this method, in no event shall an asset (or an account) be depreciated below a reasonable salvage value. * * *

(b) Illustrations. The declining balance method is illustrated by the following examples:

Example (1). A new asset having an estimated useful life of 20 years was purchased on January 1, 1954, for $1,000. The normal straight line rate (without adjustment for salvage) is 5 percent, and the declining balance rate at twice the normal straight line is 10 percent. The annual depreciation allowances for 1954, 1955, and 1956 are as follows:

Year	Basis	Declining balance rate (percent)	Depreciation allowance
1954	$1,000	10	$100
1955	900	10	90
1956	810	10	81

* * *

[T.D. 6500, 25 FR 11402, Nov. 26, 1960, as amended by T.D. 6712, 29 FR 3653, March 24, 1964]

§ 1.167(g)-1 Basis for depreciation.

The basis upon which the allowance for depreciation is to be computed with respect to any property shall be the adjusted basis provided in section 1011 for the purpose of determining gain on the sale or other disposition of such property. In the case of property which has not been used in the trade or business or held for the production of income and which is thereafter converted to such use, the fair market value on the date of such conversion, if less than the adjusted basis of the property at that time, is the basis for computing depreciation.

[T.D. 6500, 25 FR 11402, Nov. 26, 1960; redesignated by T.D. 6712, 29 FR 3653, March 24, 1964]

§ 1.167(h)-1 Life tenants and beneficiaries of trusts and estates.

(a) Life tenants. In the case of property held by one person for life with remainder to another person, the deduction for depreciation shall be computed as if the life tenant were the absolute owner of the property so that he will be entitled to the deduction during his life, and thereafter the deduction, if any, shall be allowed to the remainderman.

(b) Trusts. If property is held in trust, the allowable deduction is to be apportioned between the income beneficiaries and the trustee on the basis of the trust income allocable to each, unless the governing instrument (or local law) requires or permits the trustee to maintain a reserve for depreciation in any amount. In the latter case, the deduction is first allocated to the trustee to the extent that income is set aside for a depreciation reserve, and any part of the deduction in excess of the income set aside for the reserve shall be apportioned between the income beneficiaries and the trustee on the basis of the trust income (in excess of the income set aside for the reserve) allocable to each. For example:

(1) If under the trust instrument or local law the income of a trust computed without regard to depreciation is to be distributed to a named beneficiary, the beneficiary is entitled to the deduction to the exclusion of the trustee.

(2) If under the trust instrument or local law the income of a trust is to be distributed to a named beneficiary, but the trustee is directed to maintain a reserve for depreciation in any amount, the deduction is allowed to the trustee (except to the extent that income set aside for the reserve is less than the allowable deduction). The same result would follow if the trustee sets aside income for a depreciation reserve pursuant to discretionary authority to do so in the governing instrument.

No effect shall be given to any allocation of the depreciation deduction which gives any beneficiary or the trustee a share of such deduction greater than his pro rata share of the trust income, irrespective of any provisions in the trust instrument except as otherwise provided in this paragraph when the trust instrument or local law requires or permits the trustee to maintain a reserve for depreciation.

(c) Estates. In the case of an estate the allowable deduction shall be apportioned between the estate and the heirs legatees, and devisees on the basis of income of the estate which is allocable to each.

[T.D. 6500, 25 FR 11402, Nov. 26, 1960; redesignated by T.D. 6712, 29 FR 3653, March 24, 1964]

§ 1.168(a)-1 Modified accelerated cost recovery system.

(a) Section 168 determines the depreciation allowance for tangible property that is of a character subject to the allowance for depreciation provided in section 167(a) and that is placed in service after December 31, 1986 (or after July 31, 1986, if the taxpayer made an election under section 203(a)(1)(B) of the Tax Reform Act of 1986; 100 Stat. 2143). Except for property excluded from the application of section 168 as a result of section 168(f) or as a result of a transitional rule, the provisions of section 168 are mandatory for all eligible property. The allowance for depreciation under section 168 constitutes the amount of depreciation allowable under section 167(a). The determination of whether tangible property is property of a character subject to the allowance for depreciation is made under section 167 and the regulations under section 167.

* * *

[T.D. 9314, 72 FR 9245, March 1, 2007]

§ 1.170A–1 Charitable, etc., contributions and gifts; allowance of deduction.

(a) Allowance of deduction. Any charitable contribution, as defined in section 170(c), actually paid during the taxable year is allowable as a deduction in computing taxable income irrespective of the method of accounting employed or of the date on which the contribution is pledged. However, charitable contributions by corporations may under certain circumstances be deductible even though not paid during the taxable year as provided in section 170(a)(2) * * *.

* * *

(b) Time of making contribution. Ordinarily, a contribution is made at the time delivery is effected. The unconditional delivery or mailing of a check which subsequently clears in due course will constitute an effective contribution on the date of delivery or mailing. If a taxpayer unconditionally delivers or mails a properly endorsed stock certificate to a charitable donee or the donee's agent, the gift is completed on the date of delivery or, if such certificate is received in the ordinary course of the mails, on the date of mailing. If the donor delivers the stock certificate to his bank or broker as the donor's agent, or to the issuing corporation or its agent, for transfer into the name of the donee, the gift is completed on the date the stock is transferred on the books of the corporation. For rules relating to the date of payment of a contribution consisting of a future interest in tangible personal property, see section 170(a)(3) and § 1.170A–5.

(c) Value of a contribution in property. (1) If a charitable contribution is made in property other than money, the amount of the contribution is the fair market value of the property at the time of the contribution reduced as provided in section 170(e)(1) * * *.

(2) The fair market value is the price at which the property would change hands between a willing buyer and a willing seller, neither being under any compulsion to buy or sell and both having reasonable knowledge of relevant facts. If the contribution is made in property of a type which the taxpayer sells in the course of his business, the fair market value is the price which the taxpayer would have received if he had sold the contributed property in the usual market in which he customarily sells, at the time and place of the contribution and, in the case of a contribution of goods in quantity, in the quantity contributed. The usual market of a manufacturer or other producer consists of the wholesalers or other distributors to or through whom he customarily sells, but if he sells only at retail the usual market consists of his retail customers.

(3) If a donor makes a charitable contribution of property, such as stock in trade, at a time when he could not reasonably have been expected to realize its usual selling price, the value of the gift is not the usual selling price but is the amount for which the quantity of property contributed would have been sold by the donor at the time of the contribution.

(4) Any costs and expenses pertaining to the contributed property which were incurred in taxable years preceding the year of contribution and are properly reflected in the opening inventory for the year of contribution must be removed from inventory and are not a part of the cost of goods sold for purposes of determining gross income for the year of contribution. Any costs and expenses pertaining to the contributed property which are incurred in the year of contribution and would, under the method of accounting used, be properly reflected in the cost of goods sold for such year are to be treated as part of the costs of goods sold for such year. If costs and expenses incurred in producing or acquiring the contributed property are, under the method of accounting used, properly deducted under section 162 or other section of the Code, such costs and expenses will be allowed as deductions for the taxable year in which they are paid or incurred whether or not such year is the year of the contribution. Any such costs and expenses which are treated as part of the cost of goods sold for the year of contribution, and any such costs and expenses which are properly deducted under section 162 or other section of the Code, are not to be treated under any section of the Code as resulting in any basis for the contributed property. Thus, for example, the contributed property has no basis for purposes of determining under section 170(e)(1)(A) * * * the amount of gain which would have been recognized if such property had been sold by the donor at its fair market value at the time of its contribution. The amount of any charitable contribution for the taxable year is not to be reduced by the amount of any costs or expenses pertaining to the contributed property which was properly deducted under section 162 or other section of the Code for any taxable year preceding the year of the contribution. This subparagraph applies only to property which was held by the taxpayer for sale in the course of a trade or business. * * *

* * *

(5) Transfers of property to an organization described in section 170(c) which bear a direct relationship to the taxpayer's trade or business and which are made with a reasonable expectation of financial return commensurate with the amount of the transfer may constitute allowable deductions as trade or business expenses rather than as charitable contributions. See section 162 and the regulations thereunder.

* * *

(e) Transfers subject to a condition or power. If as of the date of a gift a transfer for charitable purposes is dependent upon the performance of some act or the happening of a precedent event in order that it might become effective, no deduction is allowable unless the possibility that the charitable transfer will not become effective is so remote as to be negligible. If an interest in property passes to, or is vested in, charity on the date of the gift and the interest would be defeated by the subsequent performance of some act or the happening of some event, the possibility of occurrence of which appears on the date of the gift to be so remote as to be negligible, the deduction is allowable. For example, A transfers land to a city government for as long as the land is used by the city for a public park. If on the date of the gift the city does plan to use the land for a park and the possibility that the city will not use the land for a public park is so remote as to be negligible, A is entitled to a deduction under section 170 for his charitable contribution.

* * *

(g) Contributions of services. No deduction is allowable under section 170 for a contribution of services. However, unreimbursed expenditures made incident to the rendition of services to an organization contributions to which are deductible may constitute a deductible contribution. For example, the cost of a uniform without general utility which is required to be worn in performing donated services is deductible. Similarly, out-of-pocket transportation expenses necessarily incurred in performing donated services are deductible. Reasonable expenditures for meals and lodging necessarily incurred while away from home in the course of performing donated services also are deductible. For the purposes of this paragraph, the phrase "while away from home" has the same meaning as that phrase is used for purposes of section 162 and the regulations thereunder.

(h) Payment in exchange for consideration—(1) Burden on taxpayer to show that all or part of payment is a charitable contribution or gift. No part of a payment that a taxpayer makes to or for the use of an organization described in section 170(c) that is in consideration for (as defined in § 1.170A–13(f)(6)) goods or services (as defined in § 1.170A–13(f)(5)) is a contribution or gift within the meaning of section 170(c) unless the taxpayer—

(i) Intends to make a payment in an amount that exceeds the fair market value of the goods or services; and

(ii) Makes a payment in an amount that exceeds the fair market value of the goods or services.

(2) Limitation on amount deductible—(i) In general. The charitable contribution deduction under section 170(a) for a payment a taxpayer makes partly in consideration for goods or services may not exceed the excess of—

(A) The amount of any cash paid and the fair market value of any property (other than cash) transferred by the taxpayer to an organization described in section 170(c); over

(B) The fair market value of the goods or services the organization provides in return.

(ii) Special rules. For special limits on the deduction for charitable contributions of ordinary income and capital gain property, see section 170(e) and §§ 1.170A–4 and 1.170A–4A.

(3) Certain goods or services disregarded. For purposes of section 170(a) and paragraphs (h)(1) and (h)(2) of this section, goods or services described in § 1.170A–13(f)(8)(i) or § 1.170A–13(f)(9)(i) are disregarded.

(4) Donee estimates of the value of goods or services may be treated as fair market value—(i) In general. For purposes of section 170(a), a taxpayer may rely on either a contemporaneous written acknowledgment provided under section 170(f)(8) and § 1.170A–13(f) or a written disclosure statement provided under section 6115 for the fair market value of any goods or services provided to the taxpayer by the donee organization.

(ii) Exception. A taxpayer may not treat an estimate of the value of goods or services as their fair market value if the taxpayer knows, or has reason to know, that such treatment is unreasonable. For example, if a taxpayer knows, or has reason to know, that there is an error in an estimate provided by an organization described in section 170(c) pertaining to goods or services that have a readily ascertainable value, it is unreasonable for the taxpayer to treat the estimate as the fair market value of the goods or services. Similarly, if a taxpayer is a dealer in the type of goods or services provided in consideration for the taxpayer's payment and knows, or has reason to know, that the estimate is in error, it is unreasonable for the taxpayer to treat the estimate as the fair market value of the goods or services.

(5) Examples. The following examples illustrate the rules of this paragraph (h).

Example (1). Certain goods or services disregarded. Taxpayer makes a $50 payment to Charity B, an organization described in section 170(c), in exchange for a family membership. The family membership entitles Taxpayer and members of Taxpayer's family to certain benefits. These benefits include free admission to weekly poetry readings, discounts on merchandise sold by B in its gift shop or by mail order, and invitations to special events for members only, such as lectures or informal receptions. When B first offers its membership package for the year, B reasonably projects that each special event for members will have a cost to B, excluding any allocable overhead, of $5 or less per person attending the event. Because the family membership benefits are disregarded pursuant to § 1.170A–13(f)(8)(i), Taxpayer may treat the $50 payment as a contribution or gift within the meaning of section 170(c), regardless of Taxpayer's intent and whether or not the payment exceeds the fair market value of the goods or services. Furthermore, any charitable contribution deduction available to Taxpayer may be calculated without regard to the membership benefits.

Example (2). Treatment of good faith estimate at auction as the fair market value. Taxpayer attends an auction held by Charity C, an organization described in section 170(c). Prior to the auction, C publishes a catalog that meets the requirements for a written disclosure statement under section 6115(a) (including C's good faith estimate of the value of items that will be available for bidding). A representative of C gives a copy of the catalog to each individual (including Taxpayer) who attends the auction. Taxpayer notes that in the catalog C's estimate of the value of a vase is $100. Taxpayer has no reason to doubt the accuracy of this estimate. Taxpayer successfully bids and pays $500 for the vase. Because Taxpayer knew, prior to making her payment, that the estimate in the catalog was less than the amount of her payment, Taxpayer satisfies the requirement of paragraph (h)(1)(i) of this section. Because Taxpayer makes a payment in an amount that exceeds that estimate, Taxpayer satisfies the requirements of paragraph (h)(1)(ii) of this section. Taxpayer may treat C's estimate of the value of the vase as its fair market value in determining the amount of her charitable contribution deduction.

Example (3). Good faith estimate not in error. Taxpayer makes a $200 payment to Charity D, an organization described in section 170(c). In return for Taxpayer's payment, D gives Taxpayer a book that Taxpayer could buy at retail prices typically ranging from $18 to $25. D provides Taxpayer with a good faith estimate, in a written disclosure statement under section 6115(a), of $20 for the value of the book. Because the estimate is within the range of typical retail prices for the book, the estimate contained in the written disclosure statement is not in error. Although Taxpayer knows that the book is sold for as much as $25, Taxpayer may treat the estimate of $20 as the fair market value of the book in determining the amount of his charitable contribution deduction.

* * *

[T.D. 7207, 37 FR 20771, Oct. 4, 1972, as amended by T.D. 7340, 40 FR 1238, Jan. 7, 1975; T.D. 7807, 47 FR 4508, Feb. 1, 1982; T.D. 8002, 49 FR 50666, Dec. 31, 1984; T.D. 8308, 55 FR 35587, Aug. 31, 1990; T.D. 8690, 61 FR 65946, Dec. 16, 1996; T.D. 9194, 70 FR 18928, April 11, 2005; T.D. 9391, 73 FR 19358, April 9, 2008]

§ 1.170A–4 Reduction in amount of charitable contributions of certain appreciated property.

(a) Amount of reduction. Section 170(e)(1) requires that the amount of the charitable contribution which would be taken into account under section 170(a) without regard to section 170(e) shall be reduced before applying the percentage limitations under section 170(b):

(1) In the case of a contribution by an individual or by a corporation of ordinary income property, as defined in paragraph (b)(1) of this section, by the amount of gain (hereinafter in this section referred to as ordinary income) which would have been recognized as gain which is not long-term capital gain if the property had been sold by the donor at its fair market value at the time of its contribution to the charitable organization,

(2) In the case of a contribution by an individual of section 170(e) capital gain property, as defined in paragraph (b)(2) of this section, by 50 percent of the amount of gain (hereinafter in this section referred to as long-term capital gain) which would have been recognized as long-term capital gain if the property had been sold by the donor at its fair market value at the time of its contribution to the charitable organization, and

(3) In the case of a contribution by a corporation of section 170(e) capital gain property, as defined in paragraph (b)(2) of this section, by 62½ percent of the amount of gain (hereinafter in this section referred to as long-term capital gain) which would have been recognized as long-term capital gain if the property had been sold by the donor at its fair market value at the time of its contribution to the charitable organization.

Section 170(e)(1) and this paragraph do not apply to reduce the amount of the charitable contribution where, by reason of the transfer of the contributed property, ordinary income or capital gain is recognized by the donor in the same taxable year in which the contribution is made. Thus, where income or gain is recognized under section 453(d) upon the transfer of an installment obligation to a charitable organization, or under section 454(b) upon the transfer of an obligation issued at a discount to such an organization, or upon the assignment of income to such an organization, section 170(e)(1) and this paragraph do not apply if recognition of the income or gain occurs in the same taxable year in which the contribution is made. Section 170(e)(1) and this paragraph apply to a charitable contribution of an interest in ordinary income property or section 170(e) capital gain property which is described in paragraph (b) of § 1.170A-6, or paragraph (b) of § 1.170A-7. For purposes of applying section 170(e)(1) and this paragraph it is immaterial whether the charitable contribution is made "to" the charitable organization or whether it is made "for the use of" the charitable organization. See § 1.170A-8(a)(2).

(b) Definitions and other rules. For purposes of this section:

(1) Ordinary income property. The term "ordinary income property" means property any portion of the gain on which would not have been long term capital gain if the property had been sold by the donor at its fair market value at the time of its contribution to the charitable organization. Such term includes, for example, property held by the donor primarily for sale to customers in the ordinary course of his trade or business, a work of art created by the donor, a manuscript prepared by the donor, letters and memorandums prepared by or for the donor, a capital asset held by the donor for not more than 1 year (6 months for taxable years beginning before 1977; 9 months for taxable years beginning in 1977), and stock described in section 306(a), 341(a), or 1248(a) to the extent that, after applying such section, gain on its disposition would not have been long-term capital gain. The term does not include an income interest in respect of which a deduction is allowed under section 170(f)(2)(B) and paragraph (c) of § 1.170A-6.

(2) Section 170(e) capital gain property. The term "section 170(e) capital gain property" means property any portion of the gain on which would have been treated as long-term capital gain if the property had been sold by the donor at its fair market value at the time of its contribution to the charitable organization and which:

(i) Is contributed to or for the use of a private foundation, as defined in section 509(a) and the regulations thereunder, other than a private foundation described in section 170(b)(1)(E),

(ii) Constitutes tangible personal property contributed to or for the use of a charitable organization, other than a private foundation to which subdivision (i) of this subparagraph applies, which is put to an unrelated use by the charitable organization within the meaning of subparagraph (3) of this paragraph, or

(iii) Constitutes property not described in subdivision (i) or (ii) of this subparagraph which is 30-percent capital gain property to which an election under paragraph (d)(2) of § 1.170A-8 applies.

For purposes of this subparagraph a fixture which is intended to be severed from real property shall be treated as tangible personal property.

(3) Unrelated use—(i) In general. The term "unrelated use" means a use which is unrelated to the purpose or function constituting the basis of the charitable organization's exemption under section 501 or, in the case of a contribution of property to a governmental unit, the use of such property by such unit for other than exclusively public purposes. For example, if a painting contributed to an educational institution is used by that organization for educational purposes by being placed in its library for display and study by art students, the use is not an unrelated use; but if the painting is sold and the proceeds used by the organization for educational purposes, the use of the property is an unrelated use. If furnishings contributed to a charitable organization are used by it in its offices and buildings in the course of carrying out its functions, the use of the property is not an unrelated use. If a set or collection of items of tangible personal property is contributed to a charitable organization or governmental unit, the use of the set or collection is not an unrelated use if the donee sells or otherwise disposes of only an insubstantial portion of the set or collection. The use by a trust of tangible personal property contributed to it for the benefit of a charitable organization is an unrelated use if the use by the trust is one which would have been unrelated if made by the charitable organization.

(ii) Proof of use. For purposes of applying subparagraph (2)(ii) of this paragraph, a taxpayer who makes a charitable contribution of tangible personal property to or for the use of a charitable organization or governmental unit may treat such property as not being put to an unrelated use by the donee if:

(a) He establishes that the property is not in fact put to an unrelated use by the donee, or

(b) At the time of the contribution or at the time the contribution is treated as made, it is reasonable to anticipate that the property will not be put to an unrelated use by the donee. In the case of a contribution of tangible personal property to or for the use of a museum, if the object donated is of a general type normally retained by such museum or other museums for museum purposes, it will be reasonable for the donor to anticipate, unless he has actual knowledge to the contrary, that the object will not be put to an unrelated use by the donee, whether or not the object is later sold or exchanged by the donee.

* * *

(c) Allocation of basis and gain—(1) In general. Except as provided in subparagraph (2) of this paragraph:

(i) If a taxpayer makes a charitable contribution of less than his entire interest in appreciated property, whether or not the transfer is made in trust, as, for example, in the case of a transfer of appreciated property to a pooled income fund described in section 642(c)(5) and § 1.642(c)–5, and is allowed a deduction under section 170 for a portion of the fair market value of such property, then for purposes of applying the reduction rules of section 170(e)(1) and this section to the contributed portion of the property the taxpayer's adjusted basis in such property at the time of the contribution shall be allocated under section 170(e)(2) between the contributed portion of the property and the non-contributed portion.

(ii) The adjusted basis of the contributed portion of the property shall be that portion of the adjusted basis of the entire property which bears the same ratio to the total adjusted basis as the fair market value of the contributed portion of the property bears to the fair market value of the entire property.

(iii) The ordinary income and the long-term capital gain which shall be taken into account in applying section 170(e)(1) and paragraph (a) of this section to the contributed portion of the property shall be the amount of gain which would have been recognized as ordinary income and long-term capital gain if such contributed portion had been sold by the donor at its fair market value at the time of its contribution to the charitable organization.

(2) Bargain sale. (i) Section 1011(b) and § 1.1011–2 apply to bargain sales of property to charitable organizations. For purposes of applying the reduction rules of section 170(e)(1) and this section to the contributed portion of the property in the case of a bargain sale, there shall be allocated under section 1011(b) to the contributed portion of the property that portion of the adjusted basis of the entire property that bears the same ratio to the total adjusted basis as the fair market value of the contributed portion of the property bears to the fair market value of the entire property. For purposes of applying section 170(e)(1) and paragraph (a) of this section to the contributed portion of the property in such a case, there shall be allocated to the contributed portion the amount of gain that is not recognized on the bargain sale but that would have been recognized if such contributed portion had been sold by the donor at its fair market value at the time of its contribution to the charitable organization.

(ii) The term "bargain sale", as used in this subparagraph, means a transfer of property which is in part a sale or exchange of the property and in part a charitable contribution, as defined in section 170(c), of the property.

(3) Ratio of ordinary income and capital gain. For purposes of applying subparagraphs (1)(iii) and (2)(i) of this paragraph, the amount of ordinary income (or long-term capital gain) which would have been recognized if the contributed portion of the property had been sold by the donor at its fair market value at the time of its contribution shall be that amount which bears the same ratio to the ordinary income (or long-term capital gain) which would have been recognized if the entire property had been sold by the donor at its fair market value at the time of its contribution as (i) the fair market value of the contributed portion at such time bears to (ii) the fair market value of the entire property at such time. In the case of a bargain sale, the fair market value of the contributed portion for purposes of subdivision (i) is the amount determined by subtracting from the fair market value of the entire property the amount realized on the sale.

* * *

[T.D. 7207, 37 FR 20776, Oct. 4, 1972; 37 FR 22982, Oct. 27, 1972, as amended by T.D. 7728, 45 FR 72650, Nov. 3, 1980; T.D. 7807, 47 FR 4510, Feb. 1, 1982; T.D. 8176, 53 FR 5569, Feb. 25, 1988; T.D. 8540, 59 FR 30100, June 10, 1994]

§ 1.170A–5 Future interests in tangible personal property.

(a) In general. **(1)** A contribution consisting of a transfer of a future interest in tangible personal property shall be treated as made only when all intervening interests in, and rights to the actual possession or enjoyment of, the property—

(i) Have expired, or

(ii) Are held by persons other than the taxpayer or those standing in a relationship to the taxpayer described in section 267(b) and the regulations thereunder, relating to losses, expenses, and interest with respect to transactions between related taxpayers.

(2) Section 170(a)(3) and this section have no application in respect of a transfer of an undivided present interest in property. For example, a contribution of an undivided one-quarter interest in a painting with respect to which the donee is entitled to possession during 3 months of each year shall be treated as made upon the receipt by the donee of a formally executed and acknowledged deed of gift. However, the period of initial possession by the donee may not be deferred in time for more than 1 year.

(3) Section 170(a)(3) and this section have no application in respect of a transfer of a future interest in intangible personal property or in real property. However, a fixture which is intended to be severed from real property shall be treated as tangible personal property. For example, a contribution of a future interest in a chandelier which is attached to a building is considered a contribution which consists of a future interest in tangible personal property if the transferor intends that it be detached from the building at or prior to the time when the charitable organization's right to possession or enjoyment of the chandelier is to commence.

(4) For purposes of section 170(a)(3) and this section, the term "future interest" has generally the same meaning as it has when used in section 2503 and § 25.2503–3 of this chapter (Gift Tax Regulations); it includes reversions, remainders, and other interests or estates, whether vested or contingent, and whether or not supported by a particular interest or estate, which are limited to commence in use, possession, or enjoyment at some future date or time. The term "future interest" includes situations in which a donor purports to give tangible personal property to a charitable organization, but has an understanding, arrangement, agreement, etc., whether written or oral, with the charitable organization which has the effect of reserving to, or retaining in, such donor a right to the use, possession, or enjoyment of the property.

(5) In the case of a charitable contribution of a future interest to which section 170(a)(3) and this section apply the other provisions of section 170 and the regulations thereunder are inapplicable to the contribution until such time as the contribution is treated as made under section 170(a)(3).

(b) Illustrations. The application of this section may be illustrated by the following examples:

Example (1). On December 31, 1970, A, an individual who reports his income on the calendar year basis, conveys by deed of gift to a museum title to a painting, but reserves to himself the right to the use, possession, and enjoyment of the painting during his lifetime. It is assumed that there was no intention to avoid the application of section 170(f)(3)(A) by the conveyance. At the time of the gift the value of the painting is $90,000. Since the contribution consists of a future interest in tangible personal property in which the donor has retained an intervening interest, no contribution is considered to have been made in 1970.

Example (2). Assume the same facts as in example (1) except that on December 31, 1971, A relinquishes all of his right to the use, possession, and enjoyment of the painting and delivers the painting to the museum. Assuming that the value of the painting has increased to $95,000, A is treated as having made a charitable contribution of $95,000 in 1971 for which a deduction is allowable without regard to section 170(f)(3)(A).

Example (3). Assume the same facts as in example (1) except A dies without relinquishing his right to the use, possession, and enjoyment of the painting. Since A did not relinquish his right to the use, possession, and enjoyment of the property during his life, A is treated as not having made a charitable contribution of the painting for income tax purposes.

* * *

[T.D. 7207, 37 FR 20779, Oct. 4, 1972; T.D. 8540, 59 FR 30100, June 10, 1994]

§ 1.170A–7 Contributions not in trust of partial interests in property.

(a) In general. **(1)** In the case of a charitable contribution, not made by a transfer in trust, of any interest in property which consists of less than the donor's entire interest in such property, no deduction is allowed under section 170 for the value of such interest unless the interest is an interest described in paragraph (b) of this section. See section 170(f)(3)(A). For purposes of this section, a contribution of the right to use property which the donor owns, for example, a rent-free lease, shall be treated as a contribution of less than the taxpayer's entire interest in such property.

* * *

[T.D. 7207, 37 FR 20782, Oct. 4, 1972; 37 FR 22982, Oct. 27, 1972, as amended by T.D. 7955, 49 FR 19975, May 11, 1984; T.D. 8069, 51 FR 1498, Jan. 14, 1986; T.D. 8540, 59 FR 30100, June 10, 1994]

§ 1.170A–13 Recordkeeping and return requirements for deductions for charitable contributions.

* * *

(f) Substantiation of charitable contributions of $250 or more—(1) In general. No deduction is allowed under section 170(a) for all or part of any contribution of $250 or more unless the taxpayer substantiates the contribution with a contemporaneous written acknowledgment from the donee organization. A taxpayer who makes more than one contribution of $250 or more to a donee organization in a taxable year may substantiate the contributions with one or more contemporaneous written acknowledgments. Section 170(f)(8) does not apply to a payment of $250 or more if the amount contributed (as determined under § 1.170A–1(h)) is less than $250. Separate contributions of less than $250 are not subject to the requirements of section 170(f)(8), regardless of whether the sum of the contributions made by a taxpayer to a donee organization during a taxable year equals $250 or more.

(2) Written acknowledgment. Except as otherwise provided in paragraphs (f)(8) through (f)(11) and (f)(13) of this section, a written acknowledgment from a donee organization must provide the following information—

(i) The amount of any cash the taxpayer paid and a description (but not necessarily the value) of any property other than cash the taxpayer transferred to the donee organization;

(ii) A statement of whether or not the donee organization provides any goods or services in consideration, in whole or in part, for any of the cash or other property transferred to the donee organization;

(iii) If the donee organization provides any goods or services other than intangible religious benefits (as described in section 170(f)(8)), a description and good faith estimate of the value of those goods or services; and

(iv) If the donee organization provides any intangible religious benefits, a statement to that effect.

(3) Contemporaneous. A written acknowledgment is contemporaneous if it is obtained by the taxpayer on or before the earlier of—

(i) The date the taxpayer files the original return for the taxable year in which the contribution was made; or

(ii) The due date (including extensions) for filing the taxpayer's original return for that year.

(4) Donee organization. For purposes of this paragraph (f), a donee organization is an organization described in section 170(c).

(5) Goods or services. Goods or services means cash, property, services, benefits, and privileges.

(6) In consideration for. A donee organization provides goods or services in consideration for a taxpayer's payment if, at the time the taxpayer makes the payment to the donee organization, the taxpayer receives or expects to receive goods or services in exchange for that payment. Goods or services a donee organization provides in consideration for a payment by a taxpayer include goods or services provided in a year other than the year in which the taxpayer makes the payment to the donee organization.

(7) Good faith estimate. For purposes of this section, good faith estimate means a donee organization's estimate of the fair market value of any goods or services, without regard to the manner in which the organization in fact made that estimate. See § 1.170A–1(h)(4) for rules regarding when a taxpayer may treat a donee organization's estimate of the value of goods or services as the fair market value.

(8) Certain goods or services disregarded—(i) In general. For purposes of section 170(f)(8), the following goods or services are disregarded—

(A) Goods or services that have insubstantial value under the guidelines provided in Revenue Procedures 90–12, 1990–1 C.B. 471, 92–49, 1992–1 C.B. 987, and any successor documents. (See § 601.601(d)(2)(ii) of the Statement of Procedural Rules, 26 CFR part 601.); and

(B) Annual membership benefits offered to a taxpayer in exchange for a payment of $75 or less per year that consist of—

(1) Any rights or privileges, other than those described in section 170(*l*), that the taxpayer can exercise frequently during the membership period. Examples of such rights and privileges may include, but are not limited to, free or discounted admission to the organization's facilities or events, free or discounted parking, preferred access to goods or services, and discounts on the purchase of goods or services; and

(2) Admission to events during the membership period that are open only to members of a donee organization and for which the donee organization reasonably projects that the cost per person (excluding any allocable overhead) attending each such event is within the limits established for "low cost articles" under section 513(h)(2). The projected cost to the donee organization is determined at the time the organization first offers its membership package for the year (using section 3.07 of Revenue Procedure 90–12, or any successor documents, to determine the cost of any items or services that are donated).

(ii) Examples. The following examples illustrate the rules of this paragraph (f)(8).

Example (1). Membership benefits disregarded. Performing Arts Center E is an organization described in section 170(c). In return for a payment of $75, E offers a package of basic membership benefits that includes the right to purchase tickets to performances one week before they go on sale to the general public, free parking in E's garage during evening and weekend performances, and a 10% discount on merchandise sold in E's gift shop. In return for a payment of $150, E offers a package of preferred membership benefits that includes all of the benefits in the $75 package as well as a poster that is sold in E's gift shop for $20. The basic membership and the preferred membership are each valid for twelve months, and there are approximately 50 performances of various productions at E during a twelve-month period. E's gift shop is open for several hours each week and at performance times. F, a patron of the arts, is solicited by E to make a contribution. E offers F the preferred membership benefits in return for a payment of $150 or more. F makes a payment of $300 to E.F can satisfy the substantiation requirement of section 170(f)(8) by obtaining a contemporaneous written acknowledgment from E that includes a description of the poster and a good faith estimate of its fair market value ($20) and disregards the remaining membership benefits.

Example (2). Contemporaneous written acknowledgment need not mention rights or privileges that can be disregarded. The facts are the same as in Example 1, except that F made a payment of $300 and received only a basic membership. F can satisfy the section 170(f)(8) substantiation requirement with a contemporaneous written acknowledgment stating that no goods or services were provided.

Example (3). Rights or privileges that cannot be exercised frequently. Community Theater Group G is an organization described in section 170(c). Every summer, G performs four different plays. Each play is performed two times. In return for a membership fee of $60, G offers its members free admission to any of its performances. Nonmembers may purchase tickets on a performance by performance basis for $15 a ticket. H, an individual who is a sponsor of the theater, is solicited by G to make a contribution. G tells H that the membership benefit will be provided in return for any payment of $60 or more. H chooses to make a payment of $350 to G and receives in return the membership benefit. G's membership benefit of free admission is not described in paragraph (f)(8)(i)(B) of this section because it is not a privilege that can be exercised frequently (due to the limited number of performances offered by G). Therefore, to meet the requirements of section 170(f)(8), a contemporaneous written acknowledgment of H's $350 payment must include a description of the free admission benefit and a good faith estimate of its value.

Example (4). Multiple memberships. In December of each year, K, an individual, gives each of her six grandchildren a junior membership in Dinosaur Museum, an organization described in section 170(c). Each junior membership costs $50, and K makes a single payment of $300 for all six memberships. A junior member is entitled to free admission to the museum and to weekly films, slide shows, and lectures about dinosaurs. In addition, each junior member receives a bi-monthly, non-commercial quality newsletter with information about dinosaurs and upcoming events. K's contemporaneous written acknowledgment from Dinosaur Museum may state that no goods or services were provided in exchange for K's payment.

(9) Goods or services provided to employees or partners of donors—(i) Certain goods or services disregarded. For purposes of section 170(f)(8), goods or services provided by a donee organization to employees of a donor, or to partners of a partnership that is a donor, in return for a payment to the organization may be disregarded to the extent that the goods or services provided to each employee or partner are the same as those described in paragraph (f)(8)(i) of this section.

(ii) No good faith estimate required for other goods or services. If a taxpayer makes a contribution of $250 or more to a donee organization and, in return, the donee organization offers the taxpayer's employees or partners goods or services other than those described in paragraph (f)(9)(i) of this section, the contemporaneous written acknowledgment of the taxpayer's contribution is not required to include a good faith estimate of the value of such goods or services but must include a description of those goods or services.

(iii) Example. The following example illustrates the rules of this paragraph (f)(9).

Example. Museum J is an organization described in section 170(c). For a payment of $40, J offers a package of basic membership benefits that includes free admission and a 10% discount on merchandise sold in J's gift shop. J's other membership categories are for supporters who contribute $100 or more. Corporation K makes a payment of $50,000 to J and, in return, J offers K's employees free admission for one year, a tee-shirt with J's logo that costs J $4.50, and a gift shop discount of 25% for one year. The free admission for K's employees is the same as the benefit made available to holders of the $40 membership and is otherwise described in paragraph (f)(8)(i)(B) of this section. The tee-shirt given to each of K's employees is described in paragraph (f)(8)(i)(A) of this section. Therefore, the contemporaneous written acknowledgment of K's payment is not required to include a description or good faith estimate of the value of the free admission or the tee-shirts. However, because the gift shop discount offered to K's employees is different than that offered to those who purchase the $40 membership, the discount is not described in paragraph (f)(8)(i) of this section. Therefore, the contemporaneous written acknowledgment of K's payment is required to include a description of the 25% discount offered to K's employees.

(10) Substantiation of out-of-pocket expenses. A taxpayer who incurs unreimbursed expenditures incident to the rendition of services, within the meaning of § 1.170A–1(g), is treated as having obtained a contemporaneous written acknowledgment of those expenditures if the taxpayer—

(i) Has adequate records under paragraph (a) of this section to substantiate the amount of the expenditures; and

(ii) Obtains by the date prescribed in paragraph (f)(3) of this section a statement prepared by the donee organization containing—

(A) A description of the services provided by the taxpayer;

(B) A statement of whether or not the donee organization provides any goods or services in consideration, in whole or in part, for the unreimbursed expenditures; and

(C) The information required by paragraphs (f)(2)(iii) and (iv) of this section.

(11) Contributions made by payroll deduction—(i) Form of substantiation. A contribution made by means of withholding from a taxpayer's wages and payment by the taxpayer's employer to a donee organization may be substantiated, for purposes of section 170(f)(8), by both—

(A) A pay stub, Form W–2, or other document furnished by the employer that sets forth the amount withheld by the employer for the purpose of payment to a donee organization; and

(B) A pledge card or other document prepared by or at the direction of the donee organization that includes a statement to the effect that the organization does not provide goods or services in whole or partial consideration for any contributions made to the organization by payroll deduction.

(ii) Application of $250 threshold. For the purpose of applying the $250 threshold provided in section 170(f)(8)(A) to contributions made by the means described in paragraph (f)(11)(i) of this section, the amount withheld from each payment of wages to a taxpayer is treated as a separate contribution.

(12) Distributing organizations as donees. An organization described in section 170(c), or an organization described in 5 CFR 950.105 (a Principal Combined Fund Organization for purposes of the Combined Federal Campaign) and acting in that capacity, that receives a payment made as a contribution is treated as a donee organization solely for purposes of section 170(f)(8), even if the organization (pursuant to the donor's instructions or otherwise) distributes the amount received to one or more organizations described in section 170(c). This paragraph (f)(12) does not apply, however, to a case in which the distributee organization provides goods or services as part of a transaction structured with a view to avoid taking the goods or services into account in determining the amount of the deduction to which the donor is entitled under section 170.

(13) Transfers to certain trusts. Section 170(f)(8) does not apply to a transfer of property to a trust described in section 170(f)(2)(B), a charitable remainder annuity trust (as defined in section 664(d)(1)), or a charitable remainder unitrust (as defined in section 664(d)(2) or (d)(3) or

§ 1.664(3)(a)(1)(i)(b)). Section 170(f)(8) does apply, however, to a transfer to a pooled income fund (as defined in section 642(c)(5)); for such a transfer, the contemporaneous written acknowledgment must state that the contribution was transferred to the donee organization's pooled income fund and indicate whether any goods or services (in addition to an income interest in the fund) were provided in exchange for the transfer. The contemporaneous written acknowledgment is not required to include a good faith estimate of the income interest.

(14) Substantiation of payments to a college or university for the right to purchase tickets to athletic events. For purposes of paragraph (f)(2)(iii) of this section, the right to purchase tickets for seating at an athletic event in exchange for a payment described in section 170(*l*) is treated as having a value equal to twenty percent of such payment. For example, when a taxpayer makes a payment of $312.50 for the right to purchase tickets for seating at an athletic event, the right to purchase tickets is treated as having a value of $62.50. The remaining $250 is treated as a charitable contribution, which the taxpayer must substantiate in accordance with the requirements of this section.

(15) Substantiation of charitable contributions made by a partnership or an S corporation. If a partnership or an S corporation makes a charitable contribution of $250 or more, the partnership or S corporation will be treated as the taxpayer for purposes of section 170(f)(8). Therefore, the partnership or S corporation must substantiate the contribution with a contemporaneous written acknowledgment from the donee organization before reporting the contribution on its income tax return for the year in which the contribution was made and must maintain the contemporaneous written acknowledgment in its records. A partner of a partnership or a shareholder of an S corporation is not required to obtain any additional substantiation for his or her share of the partnership's or S corporation's charitable contribution.

(16) Purchase of an annuity. If a taxpayer purchases an annuity from a charitable organization and claims a charitable contribution deduction of $250 or more for the excess of the amount paid over the value of the annuity, the contemporaneous written acknowledgment must state whether any goods or services in addition to the annuity were provided to the taxpayer. The contemporaneous written acknowledgment is not required to include a good faith estimate of the value of the annuity. See § 1.170A–1(d)(2) for guidance in determining the value of the annuity.

(17) Substantiation of matched payments—(i) In general. For purposes of section 170, if a taxpayer's payment to a donee organization is matched, in whole or in part, by another payor, and the taxpayer receives goods or services in consideration for its payment and some or all of the matching payment, those goods or services will be treated as provided in consideration for the taxpayer's payment and not in consideration for the matching payment.

(ii) Example. The following example illustrates the rules of this paragraph (f)(17).

Example. Taxpayer makes a $400 payment to Charity L, a donee organization. Pursuant to a matching payment plan, Taxpayer's employer matches Taxpayer's $400 payment with an additional payment of $400. In consideration for the combined payments of $800, L gives Taxpayer an item that it estimates has a fair market value of $100. L does not give the employer any goods or services in consideration for its contribution. The contemporaneous written acknowledgment provided to the employer must include a statement that no goods or services were provided in consideration for the employer's $400 payment. The contemporaneous written acknowledgment provided to Taxpayer must include a statement of the amount of Taxpayer's payment, a description of the item received by Taxpayer, and a statement that L's good faith estimate of the value of the item received by Taxpayer is $100.

(18) Effective date. This paragraph (f) applies to contributions made on or after December 16, 1996. However, taxpayers may rely on the rules of this paragraph (f) for contributions made on or after January 1, 1994.

[T.D. 8002, 49 FR 50664, 50666, Dec. 31, 1984, as amended by T.D. 8003, 49 FR 50659, Dec. 31, 1984; T.D. 8199, 53 FR 16080, May 5, 1988; T.D. 8199, 53 FR 18372, May 23, 1988; T.D. 8623, 60 FR 53128, Oct. 12, 1995; T.D. 8690, 61 FR 65952, Dec. 16, 1996]

§ 1.174–2 Definition of research and experimental expenditures.

(a) In general. (1) The term research or experimental expenditures, as used in section 174, means expenditures incurred in connection with the taxpayer's trade or business which represent research and development costs in the experimental or laboratory sense. The term generally includes all such costs incident to the development or improvement of a product. The term includes the costs of obtaining a patent, such as attorneys' fees expended in making and perfecting a patent application. Expenditures represent research and development costs in the experimental or laboratory sense if they are for activities intended to discover information that would eliminate uncertainty concerning the development or improvement of a product. Uncertainty exists if the information available to the taxpayer does not establish the capability or method for developing or improving the product or the appropriate design of the product. Whether expenditures qualify as research or experimental expenditures depends on the nature of the activity to which the expenditures relate, not the nature of the product or improvement being developed or the level of technological advancement the product or improvement represents.

(2) For purposes of this section, the term product includes any pilot model, process, formula, invention, technique, patent, or similar property, and includes products to be used by the taxpayer in its trade or business as well as products to be held for sale, lease, or license.

(3) The term research or experimental expenditures does not include expenditures for—

(i) The ordinary testing or inspection of materials or products for quality control (quality control testing);

(ii) Efficiency surveys;

(iii) Management studies;

(iv) Consumer surveys;

(v) Advertising or promotions;

(vi) The acquisition of another's patent, model, production or process; or

(vii) Research in connection with literary, historical, or similar projects.

(4) For purposes of paragraph (a)(3)(i) of this section, testing or inspection to determine whether particular units of materials or products conform to specified parameters is quality control testing. However, quality control testing does not include testing to determine if the design of the product is appropriate.

(5) See section 263A and the regulations thereunder for cost capitalization rules which apply to expenditures paid or incurred for research in connection with literary, historical, or similar projects involving the production of property, including the production of films, sound recordings, video tapes, books, or similar properties.

(6) Section 174 applies to a research or experimental expenditure only to the extent that the amount of the expenditure is reasonable under the circumstances. In general, the amount of an expenditure for research or experimental activities is reasonable if the amount would ordinarily be paid for like activities by like enterprises under like circumstances. Amounts supposedly paid for research that are not reasonable under the circumstances may be characterized as disguised dividends, gifts, loans, or similar payments. The reasonableness requirement of this paragraph (a)(6) does not apply to the reasonableness of the type or nature of the activities themselves.

* * *

[T.D. 6500, 25 FR 11402, Nov. 26, 1960; T.D. 8131, 52 FR 10084, March 30, 1987; T.D. 8562, 59 FR 50159, Oct. 3, 1994]

§ 1.179–1 Election to expense certain depreciable assets.

* * *

(e) Change in use; recapture—(1) In general. If a taxpayer's section 179 property is not used predominantly in a trade or business of the taxpayer at any time before the end of the property's recovery period, the taxpayer must recapture in the taxable year in which the section 179 property is not used predominantly in a trade or business any benefit derived from expensing such property. The benefit derived from expensing the property is equal to the excess of the amount expensed under this section over the total amount that would have been allowable for prior taxable years and the taxable year of recapture as a deduction under section 168 (had section 179 not been elected) for the portion of the cost of the property to which the expensing relates (regardless of whether such excess reduced the taxpayer's tax liability). For purposes of the preceding sentence (i) the "amount expensed under this section" shall not include any amount that was not allowed as a deduction to a taxpayer because the taxpayer's aggregate amount of allowable section 179 expenses exceeded the section 179(b) dollar limitation, and (ii) in the case of an individual who does not elect to itemize deductions under section 63(g) in the taxable year of recapture, the amount allowable as a deduction under section 168 in the taxable year of recapture shall be determined by treating property used in the production of income other than rents or royalties as being property used for personal purposes. The amount to be recaptured shall be treated as ordinary income for the taxable year in which the property is no longer used predominantly in a trade or business of the taxpayer. For taxable years following the year of recapture, the taxpayer's deductions under section 168(a) shall be determined as if no section 179 election with respect to the property had been made. However, see section 280F(d)(1) relating to the coordination of section 179 with the limitation on the amount of depreciation for luxury automobiles and where certain property is used for personal purposes. If the recapture rules of both section 280F(b)(2) and this paragraph (e)(1) apply to an item of section 179 property, the amount of recapture for such property shall be determined only under the rules of section 280F(b)(2).

(2) Predominant use. Property will be treated as not used predominantly in a trade or business of the taxpayer if 50 percent or more of the use of such property during any taxable year within the recapture period is for a use other than in a trade or business of the taxpayer. * * *

(3) Basis; application with section 1245. The basis of property with respect to which there is recapture under paragraph (e)(1) of this section shall be increased immediately before the event resulting in such recapture by the amount recaptured. If section 1245(a) applies to a disposition of property, there is no recapture under paragraph (e)(1) of this section.

* * *

(5) Example. The following example illustrates the provisions of paragraphs (e)(1) through (e)(4) of this section.

Example. A, a calendar-year taxpayer, purchases and places in service on January 1, 1991, section 179 property costing $15,000. The property is 5–year property for section 168 purposes and is the only item of depreciable property placed in service by A during 1991. A properly elects to expense $10,000 of the cost and elects under section 168(b)(5) to depreciate the remaining cost under the straight-line method. On January 1, 1992, A converts the property from use in A's business to use for the production of income, and A uses the property in the latter capacity for the entire year. A elects to itemize deductions for 1992. Because the property was not predominantly used in A's trade or business in 1992, A must recapture any benefit derived from expensing the property under section 179. Had A not elected to expense the $10,000 in 1991, A would have been entitled to deduct, under section 168, 10 percent of the $10,000 in 1991, and 20 percent of the $10,000 in 1992. Therefore, A must include $7,000 in ordinary income for the 1992 taxable year, the excess of $10,000 (the section 179 expense amount) over $3,000 (30 percent of $10,000).

(f) Basis—(1) In general. A taxpayer who elects to expense under section 179 must reduce the unadjusted basis of the section 179 property by the amount of the section 179 expense deduction. * * *

(2) Special rules for partnerships and S corporations. Generally, the basis of a partnership or S corporation's section 179 property must be reduced to reflect the amount of section 179 expense elected by the partnership or S corporation. * * *

(3) Special rules with respect to trusts and estates which are partners or S corporation shareholders. Since the section 179 election is not available for trusts or estates, a partner or S corporation shareholder that is a trust or estate may not deduct its allocable share of the section 179 expense elected by the partnership or S corporation. The partnership or S corporation's basis in section 179 property shall not be reduced to reflect any portion of the section 179 expense that is allocable to the trust or estate. * * *

[T.D. 6507, 25 FR 12341, Dec. 2, 1960, as amended by T.D. 6712, 29 FR 3655, March 24, 1964; T.D. 7116, 36 FR 9017, May 18, 1971, as amended by T.D. 7137, 36 FR 14735, Aug. 11, 1971; T.D. 8121, 52 FR 410, Jan. 6, 1987; as amended by T.D. 8455, 57 FR 61313, Dec. 24, 1992]

§ 1.183–1 Activities not engaged in for profit.

(a) In general. * * * Whether an activity is engaged in for profit is determined under section 162 and section 212(1) and (2) except insofar as section 183(d) creates a presumption that the activity is engaged in for profit. If deductions are not allowable under sections 162 and 212(1) and (2), the deduction allowance rules of section 183(b) and this section apply. Pursuant to section 641(b), the taxable income of an estate or trust is computed in the same manner as in the case of an individual, with certain exceptions not here relevant. Accordingly, where an estate or trust engages in an activity or activities which are not for profit, the rules of section 183 and this section apply in computing the allowable deductions of such trust or estate. No inference is to be drawn from the provisions of section 183 and the regulations thereunder that any activity of a corporation (other than an electing small business corporation) is or is not a business or engaged in for profit. * * *

(b) Deductions allowable—(1) Manner and extent. If an activity is not engaged in for profit, deductions are allowable under section 183(b) in the following order and only to the following extent:

(i) Amounts allowable as deductions during the taxable year under chapter 1 of the Code without regard to whether the activity giving rise to such amounts was engaged in for profit are allowable to the full extent allowed by the relevant sections of the Code, determined after taking into account any limitations or exceptions with respect to the allowability of such amounts. For example, the allowability-of-interest expenses incurred with respect to activities not engaged in for profit is limited by the rules contained in section 163(d).

(ii) Amounts otherwise allowable as deductions during the taxable year under chapter 1 of the Code, but only if such allowance does not result in an adjustment to the basis of property, determined as if the activity giving rise to such amounts was engaged in for profit, are allowed only to the extent the gross income attributable to such activity exceeds the deductions allowed or allowable under subdivision (i) of this subparagraph.

(iii) Amounts otherwise allowable as deductions for the taxable year under chapter 1 of the Code which result in (or if otherwise allowed would have resulted in) an adjustment to the basis of property, determined as if the activity giving rise to such deductions was engaged in for profit, are allowed only to the extent the gross income attributable to such activity exceeds the deductions allowed or allowable under subdivisions (i) and (ii) of this subparagraph. Deductions falling within this subdivision include such items as depreciation, partial losses with respect to property, partially worthless debts, amortization, and amortizable bond premium.

(2) Rule for deductions involving basis adjustments—(i) In general. If deductions are allowed under subparagraph (1)(iii) of this paragraph, and such deductions are allowed with respect to more than one asset, the deduction allowed with respect to each asset shall be determined separately in accordance with the computation set forth in subdivision (ii) of this subparagraph.

(ii) Basis adjustment fraction. The deduction allowed under subparagraph (1)(iii) of this paragraph is computed by multiplying the amount which would have been allowed, had the activity been engaged in for profit, as a deduction with respect to each particular asset which involves a basis adjustment, by the basis adjustment fraction—

(a) The numerator of which is the total of deductions allowable under subparagraph (1)(iii) of this paragraph, and

(b) The denominator of which is the total of deductions which involve basis adjustments which would have been allowed with respect to the activity had the activity been engaged in for profit.

The amount resulting from this computation is the deduction allowed under subparagraph (1)(iii) of this paragraph with respect to the particular asset. The basis of such asset is adjusted only to the extent of such deduction.

* * *

(c) Presumption that activity is engaged in for profit—(1) In general. If for—

(i) Any 2 of 7 consecutive taxable years, in the case of an activity which consists in major part of the breeding, training, showing, or racing of horses, or

(ii) Any 2* of 5 consecutive taxable years, in the case of any other activity, the gross income derived from an activity exceeds the deductions attributable to such activity which would be allowed or allowable if the activity were engaged in for profit, such activity is presumed, unless the Commissioner establishes to the contrary, to be engaged in for profit. * * * Such presumption applies with respect to the second profit year and all years subsequent to the second profit year within the 5- or 7-year period beginning with the first profit year. This presumption arises only if the activity is substantially the same activity for each of the relevant taxable years, including the taxable year in question. If the taxpayer does not meet the requirements of section 183(d) and this paragraph, no inference that the activity is not engaged in for profit shall arise by reason of the provisions of section 183. For purposes of this paragraph, a net operating loss deduction is not taken into account as a deduction. For purposes of this subparagraph a short taxable year constitutes a taxable year.

* * *

* Omitted entirely.

(d) Activity defined—(1) Ascertainment of activity. In order to determine whether, and to what extent, section 183 and the regulations thereunder apply, the activity or activities of the taxpayer must be ascertained. For instance, where the taxpayer is engaged in several undertakings, each of these may be a separate activity, or several undertakings may constitute one activity. In ascertaining the activity or activities of the taxpayer, all the facts and circumstances of the case must be taken into account. Generally, the most significant facts and circumstances in making this determination are the degree of organizational and economic interrelationship of various undertakings, the business purpose which is (or might be) served by carrying on the various undertakings separately or together in a trade or business or in an investment setting, and the similarity of various undertakings. Generally, the Commissioner will accept the characterization by the taxpayer of several undertakings either as a single activity or as separate activities. The taxpayer's characterization will not be accepted, however, when it appears that his characterization is artificial and cannot be reasonably supported under the facts and circumstances of the case. If the taxpayer engages in two or more separate activities, deductions and income from each separate activity are not aggregated either in determining whether a particular activity is engaged in for profit or in applying section 183. Where land is purchased or held primarily with the intent to profit from increase in its value, and the taxpayer also engages in farming on such land, the farming and the holding of the land will ordinarily be considered a single activity only if the farming activity reduces the net cost of carrying the land for its appreciation in value. Thus, the farming and holding of the land will be considered a single activity only if the income derived from farming exceeds the deductions attributable to the farming activity which are not directly attributable to the holding of the land (that is, deductions other than those directly attributable to the holding of the land such as interest on a mortgage secured by the land, annual property taxes attributable to the land and improvements, and depreciation of improvements to the land).

(2) Rules for allocation of expenses. If the taxpayer is engaged in more than one activity, an item of deduction or income may be allocated between two or more of these activities. Where property is used in several activities, and one or more of such activities is determined not to be engaged in for profit, deductions relating to such property must be allocated between the various activities on a reasonable and consistently applied basis.

(3) Example. The provisions of this paragraph may be illustrated by the following example:

Example. (i) A, an individual, owns a small house located near the beach in a resort community. Visitors come to the area for recreational purposes during only 3 months of the year. During the remaining 9 months of the year houses such as A's are not rented. Customarily, A arranges that the house will be leased for 2 months of 3–month recreational season to vacationers and reserves the house for his own vacation during the remaining month of the recreational season. In 1971, A leases the house for 2 months for $1,000 per month and actually uses the house for his own vacation during the other month of the recreational season. For 1971, the expenses attributable to the house are $1,200 interest, $600 real estate taxes, $600 maintenance, $300 utilities, and $1,200 which would have been allowed as depreciation had the activity been engaged in for profit. Under these facts and circumstances, A is engaged in a single activity, holding the beach house primarily for personal purposes, which is an "activity not engaged in for profit" within the meaning of section 183(c). See paragraph (b)(9) of § 1.183–2.

(ii) Since the $1,200 of interest and the $600 of real estate taxes are specifically allowable as deductions under sections 163 and 164(a) without regard to whether the beach house activity is engaged in for profit, no allocation of these expenses between the uses of the beach house is necessary. However, since section 262 specifically disallows personal, living, and family expenses as deductions, the maintenance and utilities expenses and the depreciation from the activity must be allocated between the rental use and the personal use of the beach house. Under the particular facts and circumstances, ⅔ (2 months of rental use over 3 months of total use) of each of these expenses are allocated to the rental use, and ⅓ (1 month of personal use over 3 months of total use) of each of these expenses are allocated to the personal use as follows:

	Rental use ⅔—expenses allocable to section 183(b)(2)	Personal use ⅓—expenses allocable to section 262
Maintenance expense $600	$ 400	$200
Utilities expense $300	200	100
Depreciation $1,200	800	400
Total	1,400	700

The $700 of expenses and depreciation allocated to the personal use of the beach house are disallowed as a deduction under section 262. In addition, the allowability of each of the expenses and the depreciation allocated to section 183(b)(2) is determined under paragraph (b)(1)(ii) and (iii) of this section. Thus, the maximum amount allowable as a deduction under section 183(b)(2) is $200 ($2,000 gross income from activity, less $1,800 deductions under section 183(b)(1)). Since the amounts described in section 183(b)(2) ($1,400) exceed the maximum amount allowable ($200), and since the amounts described in paragraph (b)(1)(ii) of this section ($600) exceed such maximum amount allowable ($200), none of the depreciation (an amount described in paragraph (b)(1)(iii) of this section) is allowable as a deduction.

(e) Gross income from activity not engaged in for profit defined. For purposes of section 183 and the regulations thereunder, gross income derived from an activity not engaged in for profit includes the total of all gains from the sale, exchange, or other disposition of property, and all other gross receipts derived from such activity. Such gross income shall include, for instance, capital gains, and rents received for the use of property which is held in connection with the activity. The taxpayer may determine gross income from any activity by subtracting the cost of goods sold from the gross receipts so long as he consistently does so and follows generally accepted methods of accounting in determining such gross income.

(f) Rule for electing small business corporations. Section 183 and this section shall be applied at the corporate level in determining the allowable deductions of an electing small business corporation.

[T.D. 7198, 37 FR 13680, July 13, 1972]

§ 1.183–2 Activity not engaged in for profit defined.

(a) In general. For purposes of section 183 and the regulations thereunder, the term "activity not engaged in for profit" means any activity other than one with respect to which deductions are allowable for the taxable year under section 162 or under paragraph (1) or (2) of section 212. Deductions are allowable under section 162 for expenses of carrying on activities which constitute a trade or business of the taxpayer and under section 212 for expenses incurred in connection with activities engaged in for the production or collection of income or for the management, conservation, or maintenance of property held for the production of income. Except as provided in section 183 and § 1.183–1, no deductions are allowable for expenses incurred in connection with activities which are not engaged in for profit. Thus, for example, deductions are not allowable under section 162 or 212 for activities which are carried on primarily as a sport, hobby, or for recreation. The determination whether an activity is engaged in for profit is to be made by reference to objective standards, taking into account all of the facts and circumstances of each case. Although a reasonable expectation of profit is not required, the facts and circumstances must indicate that the taxpayer entered into the activity, or continued the activity, with the objective of making a profit. In determining whether such an objective exists, it may be sufficient that there is a small chance of making a large profit. Thus it may be found that an investor in a wildcat oil well who incurs very substantial expenditures is in the venture for profit even though the expectation of a profit might be considered unreasonable. In determining whether an activity is engaged in for profit, greater weight is given to objective facts than to the taxpayer's mere statement of his intent.

(b) Relevant factors. In determining whether an activity is engaged in for profit, all facts and circumstances with respect to the activity are to be taken into account. No one factor is determinative in making this determination. In addition, it is not intended that only the factors described in this paragraph are to be taken into account in making the determination, or that a determination is to be made on the basis that the number of factors (whether or not listed in this paragraph) indicating a lack of profit objective exceeds the number of factors indicating a profit objective, or vice versa. Among the factors which should normally be taken into account are the following:

(1) Manner in which the taxpayer carries on the activity. The fact that the taxpayer carries on the activity in a businesslike manner and maintains complete and accurate books and records may indicate that the activity is engaged in for profit. Similarly, where an activity is carried on in a manner substantially similar to other activities of the same nature which are profitable, a profit motive may be indicated. A change of operating methods, adoption of new techniques or abandonment of unprofitable methods in a manner consistent with an intent to improve profitability may also indicate a profit motive.

(2) The expertise of the taxpayer or his advisors. Preparation for the activity by extensive study of its accepted business, economic, and scientific practices, or consultation with those who are expert therein, may indicate that the taxpayer has a profit motive where the taxpayer carries on the activity in accordance with such practices. Where a taxpayer has such preparation or procures such expert advice, but does not carry on the activity in accordance with such practices, a lack of intent to derive profit may be indicated unless it appears that the taxpayer is attempting to develop new or superior techniques which may result in profits from the activity.

(3) The time and effort expended by the taxpayer in carrying on the activity. The fact that the taxpayer devotes much of his personal time and effort to carrying on an activity, particularly if the activity does not have substantial personal or recreational aspects, may indicate an intention to derive a profit. A taxpayer's withdrawal from another occupation to devote most of his energies to the activity may also be evidence that the activity is engaged in for profit. The fact that the taxpayer devotes a limited amount of time to an activity does not necessarily indicate a lack of profit motive where the taxpayer employs competent and qualified persons to carry on such activity.

(4) Expectation that assets used in activity may appreciate in value. The term "profit" encompasses appreciation in the value of assets, such as land, used in the activity. Thus, the taxpayer may intend to derive a profit from the operation of the activity, and may also intend that, even if no profit from current operations is derived, an overall profit will result when appreciation in the value of land used in the activity is realized since income from the activity together with the appreciation of land will exceed expenses of operation. See, however, paragraph (d) of § 1.183–1 for definition of an activity in this connection.

(5) The success of the taxpayer in carrying on other similar or dissimilar activities. The fact that the taxpayer has engaged in similar activities in the past and converted them from unprofitable to profitable enterprises may indicate that he is engaged in the present activity for profit, even though the activity is presently unprofitable.

(6) The taxpayer's history of income or losses with respect to the activity. A series of losses during the initial or start-up stage of an activity may not necessarily be an indication that the activity is not engaged in for profit. However, where losses continue to be sustained beyond the period which customarily is necessary to bring the operation to profitable status such continued losses, if not explainable, as due to customary business risks or reverses, may be indicative that the activity is not being engaged in for profit. If losses are sustained because of unforeseen or fortuitous circumstances which are beyond the control of the taxpayer, such as drought, disease, fire, theft, weather damages, other involuntary conversions, or depressed market conditions, such losses would not be an indication that the activity is not engaged in for profit. A series of years in which net income was realized would of course be strong evidence that the activity is engaged in for profit.

(7) The amount of occasional profits, if any, which are earned. The amount of profits in relation to the amount of losses incurred, and in relation to the amount of the taxpayer's investment and the value of the assets used in the activity, may provide useful criteria in determining the taxpayer's intent. An occasional small profit from an activity generating large losses, or from an activity in which the taxpayer has made a large investment, would not generally be determinative that the activity is engaged in for profit. However, substantial profit, though only occasional, would generally be indicative that an activity is engaged in for profit, where the investment or losses are comparatively small. Moreover, an opportunity to earn a substantial ultimate profit in a highly speculative venture is ordinarily sufficient to indicate that the activity is engaged in for profit even though losses or only occasional small profits are actually generated.

(8) The financial status of the taxpayer. The fact that the taxpayer does not have substantial income or capital from sources other than the activity may indicate that an activity is engaged in for profit. Substantial income from sources other than the activity (particularly if the losses from the activity generate substantial tax benefits) may indicate that the activity is not engaged in for profit especially if there are personal or recreational elements involved.

(9) Elements of personal pleasure or recreation. The presence of personal motives in carrying on of an activity may indicate that the activity is not engaged in for profit, especially where there are recreational or personal elements involved. On the other hand, a profit motivation may be indicated where an activity lacks any appeal other than profit. It is not, however, necessary that an activity be engaged in with the exclusive intention of deriving a profit or with the intention of maximizing profits. For example, the availability of other investments which would yield a higher return, or which would be more likely to be profitable, is not evidence that an activity is not engaged in for profit. An activity will not be treated as not engaged in for profit merely because the taxpayer has purposes or motivations other than solely to make a profit. Also, the fact that the taxpayer derives personal pleasure from engaging in the activity is not sufficient to cause the activity to be classified as not engaged in for profit if the activity is in fact engaged in for profit as evidenced by other factors whether or not listed in this paragraph.

(c) Examples. The provisions of this section may be illustrated by the following examples:

Example (1). The taxpayer inherited a farm from her husband in an area which was becoming largely residential, and is now nearly all so. The farm had never made a profit before the taxpayer inherited it, and the farm has since had substantial losses in each year. The decedent from whom the taxpayer inherited the farm was a stockbroker, and he also left the taxpayer substantial stock holdings which yield large income from dividends. The taxpayer lives on an area of the farm which is set aside exclusively for living purposes. A farm manager is employed to operate the farm, but modern methods are not used in operating the farm. The taxpayer was born and raised on a farm, and expresses a strong preference for living on a farm. The taxpayer's activity of farming, based on all the facts and circumstances, could be found not to be engaged in for profit.

Example (2). The taxpayer is a wealthy individual who is greatly interested in philosophy. During the past 30 years he has written and published at his own expense several pamphlets, and he has engaged in extensive lecturing activity, advocating and disseminating his ideas. He has made a profit from these activities in only occasional years, and the profits in those years were small in relation to the amounts of the losses in all other years. The taxpayer has very sizable income from securities (dividends and capital gains) which constitutes the principal source of his livelihood. The activity of lecturing, publishing pamphlets, and disseminating his ideas is not an activity engaged in by the taxpayer for profit.

Example (3). The taxpayer, very successful in the business of retailing soft drinks, raises dogs and horses. He began raising a particular breed of dogs many years ago in the belief that the breed was in danger of declining, and he has raised and sold the dogs in each year since. The taxpayer recently began raising and racing thoroughbred horses. The losses from thc taxpayer's dog and horse activities have increased in magnitude over the years, and he has not made a profit on these operations during any of the last 15 years. The taxpayer generally sells the dogs only to friends, does not advertise the dogs for sale, and shows the dogs only infrequently. The taxpayer races his horses only at the "prestige" tracks at which he combines his racing activities with social and recreational activities. The horse and dog operations are conducted at a large residential property on which the taxpayer also lives, which includes substantial living quarters and attractive recreational facilities for the taxpayer and his family. Since (i) the activity of raising dogs and horses and racing the horses is of a sporting and recreational nature, (ii) the taxpayer has substantial income from his business activities of retailing soft drinks, (iii) the horse and dog operations are not conducted in a businesslike manner, and (iv) such operations have a continuous record of losses, it could be determined that the horse and dog activities of the taxpayer are not engaged in for profit.

Example (4). The taxpayer inherited a farm of 65 acres from his parents when they died 6 years ago. The taxpayer moved to the farm from his house in a small nearby town, and he operates it in the same manner as his parents operated the farm before they died. The taxpayer is employed as a skilled machine operator in a nearby factory, for which he is paid approximately $8,500 per year. The farm has not been profitable for the past 15 years because of rising costs of operating farms in general, and because of the decline in the price of the produce of this farm in particular. The taxpayer consults the local agent of the State agricultural service from time to time, and the suggestions of the agent have generally been followed. The manner in which the farm is operated by the taxpayer is substantially similar to the manner in which farms of similar size, and which grow similar crops in the area, are operated. Many of these other farms do not make profits. The taxpayer does much of the required labor around the farm himself, such as fixing fences, planting crops, etc. The activity of farming could be found, based on all the facts and circumstances, to be engaged in by the taxpayer for profit.

Example (5). A, an independent oil and gas operator, frequently engages in the activity of searching for oil on undeveloped and unexplored land which is not near proven fields. He does so in a manner substantially similar to that of others who engage in the same activity. The chances, based on the experience of A and others who engaged in this activity, are strong that A will not find a commercially profitable oil deposit when he drills on land not established geologically to be proven oil bearing land. However, on the rare occasions that these activities do result in discovering a well, the operator generally realizes a very large return from such activity. Thus, there is a small chance that A will make a large profit from his soil exploration activity. Under these circumstances, A is engaged in the activity of oil drilling for profit.

* * *

[T.D. 7198, 37 FR 13683, July 13, 1972]

§ 1.195–1 Election to amortize start-up expenditures.

* * *

(b) Time and manner of making election. A taxpayer is deemed to have made an election under section 195(b) to amortize start-up expenditures as defined in section 195(c)(1) for the taxable year in which the active trade or business to which the expenditures relate begins. A taxpayer may choose to forgo the deemed election by affirmatively electing to capitalize its start-up expenditures on a timely filed Federal income tax return (including extensions) for the taxable year in which the active trade or business to which the expenditures relate begins. The election either to amortize start-up expenditures under section 195(b) or to capitalize start-up expenditures is irrevocable and applies to all start-up expenditures that are related to the active trade or business. A change in the characterization of an item as a start-up expenditure is a change in method of accounting to which sections 446 and 481(a) apply if the taxpayer treated the item consistently for two or more taxable years. A change in the determination of the taxable year in which the active trade or business begins also is treated as a change in method of accounting if the taxpayer amortized start-up expenditures for two or more taxable years.

* * *

[T.D. 9411, 73 FR 38913, July 8, 2008; T.D. 9542, 76 FR 50888, Aug. 17, 2011]

§ 1.197–2 Amortization of goodwill and certain other intangibles.

(a) Overview—(1) In general. * * *

(2) Section 167(f) property. Section 167(f) prescribes rules for computing the depreciation deduction for certain property to which section 197 does not apply. See § 1.167(a)–14 for rules under section 167(f) * * *.

* * *

(c) Section 197 intangibles; exceptions. The term section 197 intangible does not include property described in section 197(e). The following rules and definitions provide guidance concerning property to which the exceptions apply:

* * *

(13) Rights of fixed duration or amount. (i) Section 197 intangibles do not include any right under a contract or any license, permit, or other right granted by a governmental unit if the right—

(A) Is acquired in the ordinary course of a trade or business (or an activity described in section 212) and not as part of a purchase of a trade or business;

(B) Is not described in section 197(d)(1)(A), (B), (E), or (F);

(C) Is not a customer-based intangible, a customer-related information base, or any other similar item; and

(D) Either—

(1) Has a fixed duration of less than 15 years; or

(2) Is fixed as to amount and the adjusted basis thereof is properly recoverable (without regard to this section) under a method similar to the unit-of-production method.

(ii) See § 1.167(a)–14(c)(2) and (3) for applicable rules.

(d) Amortizable section 197 intangibles—(1) Definition. Except as otherwise provided in this paragraph (d), the term amortizable section 197 intangible means any section 197 intangible acquired after August 10, 1993 (or after July 25, 1991, if a valid retroactive election under § 1.197–1T has been made), and held in connection with the conduct of a trade or business or an activity described in section 212.

(2) Exception for self-created intangibles—(i) In general. Except as provided in paragraph (d)(2)(iii) of this section, amortizable section 197 intangibles do not include any section 197 intangible created by the taxpayer (a self-created intangible).

(ii) Created by the taxpayer—(A) Defined. A section 197 intangible is created by the taxpayer to the extent the taxpayer makes payments or otherwise incurs costs for its creation, production, development, or improvement, whether the actual work is performed by the taxpayer or by another person under a contract with the taxpayer entered into before the contracted creation, production, development, or improvement occurs. For example, a technological process developed specifically for a taxpayer under an arrangement with another person pursuant to which the taxpayer retains all rights to the process is created by the taxpayer.

(B) Contracts for the use of intangibles. A section 197 intangible is not a self-created intangible to the extent that it results from the entry into (or renewal of) a contract for the use of an existing section 197 intangible. Thus, for example, the exception for self-created intangibles does not apply to capitalized costs, such as legal and other professional fees, incurred by a licensee in connection with the entry into (or renewal of) a contract for the use of know-how or similar property.

(C) Improvements and modifications. If an existing section 197 intangible is improved or otherwise modified by the taxpayer or by another person under a contract with the taxpayer, the existing intangible and the capitalized costs (if any) of the improvements or other modifications are each treated as a separate section 197 intangible for purposes of this paragraph (d).

(iii) Exceptions. (A) The exception for self-created intangibles does not apply to any section 197 intangible described in section 197(d)(1)(D) (relating to licenses, permits or other rights granted by a governmental unit), 197(d)(1)(E) (relating to covenants not to compete), or 197(d)(1)(F) (relating to franchises, trademarks, and trade names). Thus, for example, capitalized costs incurred in the development, registration, or defense of a trademark or trade name do not qualify for the exception and are amortized over 15 years under section 197.

(B) The exception for self-created intangibles does not apply to any section 197 intangible created in connection with the purchase of a trade or business (as defined in paragraph (e) of this section).

(C) If a taxpayer disposes of a self-created intangible and subsequently reacquires the intangible in an acquisition described in paragraph (h)(5)(ii) of this section, the exception for self-created intangibles does not apply to the reacquired intangible.

(3) Exception for property subject to anti-churning rules. Amortizable section 197 intangibles do not include any property to which the anti-churning rules of section 197(f)(9) and paragraph (h) of this section apply.

(e) Purchase of a trade or business. Several of the exceptions in section 197 apply only to property that is not acquired in (or created in connection with) a transaction or series of related transactions involving the acquisition of assets constituting a trade or business or a substantial portion thereof. Property acquired in (or created in connection with) such a transaction or series of related transactions is referred to in this section as property acquired as part of (or created in connection with) a purchase of a trade or business. For purposes of section 197 and this section, the applicability of the limitation is determined under the following rules:

(1) Goodwill or going concern value. An asset or group of assets constitutes a trade or business or a substantial portion thereof if their use would constitute a trade or business under section 1060 (that is, if goodwill or going concern value could under any circumstances attach to the assets). See § 1.1060–1(b)(2). For this purpose, all the facts and circumstances, including any employee relationships that continue (or covenants not to compete that are entered into) as part of the transfer of the assets, are taken into account in determining whether goodwill or going concern value could attach to the assets.

(2) Franchise, trademark, or trade name—(i) In general. The acquisition of a franchise, trademark, or trade name constitutes the acquisition of a trade or business or a substantial portion thereof.

(ii) Exceptions. For purposes of this paragraph (e)(2)—

(A) A trademark or trade name is disregarded if it is included in computer software under paragraph (c)(4) of this section or in an interest in a film, sound recording, video tape, book, or other similar property under paragraph (c)(5) of this section;

(B) A franchise, trademark, or trade name is disregarded if its value is nominal or the taxpayer irrevocably disposes of it immediately after its acquisition; and

(C) The acquisition of a right or interest in a trademark or trade name is disregarded if the grant of the right or interest is not, under the principles of section 1253, a transfer of all substantial rights to such property or of an undivided interest in all substantial rights to such property.

(3) Acquisitions to be included. The assets acquired in a transaction (or series of related transactions) include only assets (including a beneficial or other indirect interest in assets where the interest is of a type described in paragraph (c)(1) of this section) acquired by the taxpayer and persons related to the taxpayer from another person and persons related to that other person. For purposes of this paragraph (e)(3), persons are related only if their relationship is described in section 267(b) or 707(b) or they are engaged in trades or businesses under common control within the meaning of section 41(f)(1).

(4) Substantial portion. The determination of whether acquired assets constitute a substantial portion of a trade or business is to be based on all of the facts and circumstances, including the nature and the amount of the assets acquired as well as the nature and amount of the assets retained by the transferor. The value of the assets acquired relative to the value of the assets retained by the transferor is not determinative of whether the acquired assets constitute a substantial portion of a trade or business.

* * *

(g) Special rules—(1) Treatment of certain dispositions—(i) Loss disallowance rules—(A) In general. No loss is recognized on the disposition of an amortizable section 197 intangible if the taxpayer has any retained intangibles. The retained intangibles with respect to the disposition of any amortizable section 197 intangible (the transferred intangible) are all amortizable section 197 intangibles, or rights to use or interests (including beneficial or other indirect interests) in amortizable section 197 intangibles (including the transferred intangible) that were acquired in the same transaction or series of related transactions as the transferred intangible and are retained after its disposition. Except as otherwise provided in paragraph (g)(1)(iv)(B) of this section, the adjusted basis of each of the retained intangibles is increased by the product of—

(1) The loss that is not recognized solely by reason of this rule; and

(2) A fraction, the numerator of which is the adjusted basis of the retained intangible on the date of the disposition and the denominator of which is the total adjusted bases of all the retained intangibles on that date.

* * *

(k) Examples. The following examples illustrate the application of this section:

Example 1. Advertising costs. (i) Q manufactures and sells consumer products through a series of wholesalers and distributors. In order to increase sales of its products by encouraging consumer loyalty to its products and to enhance the value of the goodwill, trademarks, and trade names of the business, Q advertises its products to the consuming public. It regularly incurs costs to develop radio, television, and print advertisements. These costs generally consist of employee costs and amounts paid to independent advertising agencies. Q also incurs costs to run these advertisements in the various media for which they were developed.

(ii) The advertising costs are not chargeable to capital account under paragraph (f)(3) of this section (relating to costs incurred for covenants not to compete, rights granted by governmental units, and contracts for the use of section 197 intangibles) and are currently deductible as ordinary and necessary expenses under section 162. Accordingly, under paragraph (a)(3) of this section, section 197 does not apply to these costs.

* * *

Example 6. Acquisition and amortization of covenant not to compete. (i) As part of the acquisition of a trade or business from C, B and C enter into an agreement containing a covenant not to compete. Under this agreement, C agrees that it will not compete with the business acquired by B within a prescribed geographical territory for a period of three years after the date on which the business is sold to B. In exchange for this agreement, B agrees to pay C $90,000 per year for each year in the term of the agreement. The agreement further provides that, in the event of a breach by C of his obligations under the agreement, B may terminate the agreement, cease making any of the payments due thereafter, and pursue any other legal or equitable remedies available under applicable law. The amounts payable to C under the agreement are not contingent payments for purposes of § 1.1275–4. The present fair market value of B's rights under the agreement is $225,000. The aggregate consideration paid excluding any amount treated as interest or original issue discount under applicable provisions of the Internal Revenue Code, for all assets acquired in the transaction (including the covenant not to compete) exceeds the sum of the amount of Class I assets and the aggregate fair market value of all Class II, Class III, Class IV, Class V, and Class VI assets by $50,000. See § 1.338–6(b) for rules for determining the assets in each class.

(ii) Because the covenant is acquired in an applicable asset acquisition (within the meaning of section 1060(c)), paragraph (f)(4)(ii) of this section applies and the basis of B in the covenant is determined pursuant to section 1060(a) and the regulations thereunder. Under §§ 1.1060–1(c)(2) and 1.338–6(c)(1), B's basis in the covenant cannot exceed its fair market value. Thus, B's basis in the covenant immediately after the acquisition is $225,000. This basis is amortized ratably over the 15-year period beginning on the first day of the month in which the agreement is entered into. All of the remaining consideration after allocation to the covenant and other Class VI assets ($50,000) is allocated to Class VII assets (goodwill and going concern value). See §§ 1.1060–1(c)(2) and 1.338–6(b).

* * *

[T.D. 8865, 65 FR 3827, Jan. 25, 2000; 65 FR 16318, March 28, 2000; 65 FR 60585, Oct. 12, 2000; T.D. 8907, 65 FR 69671, Nov. 20, 2000; T.D. 8940, 66 FR 9929, Feb. 13, 2001; 66 FR 17363, March 30, 2001; 66 FR 22286, May 3, 2001; T.D. 9256, 71 FR 17996, April 10, 2006; T.D. 9377, 73 FR 3869, Jan. 23, 2008; T.D. 9533, 76 FR 39280, July 6, 2011]

§ 1.212–1 Nontrade or nonbusiness expenses.

(a) An expense may be deducted under section 212 only if—

(1) It has been paid or incurred by the taxpayer during the taxable year (i) for the production or collection of income which, if and when realized, will be required to be included in income for Federal income tax purposes, or (ii) for the management, conservation, or maintenance of property held for the production of such income, or (iii) in connection with the determination, collection, or refund of any tax; and

(2) It is an ordinary and necessary expense for any of the purposes stated in subparagraph (1) of this paragraph.

(b) The term "income" for the purpose of section 212 includes not merely income of the taxable year but also income which the taxpayer has realized in a prior taxable year or may realize in subsequent taxable years; and is not confined to recurring income but applies as well to gains from the disposition of property. For example, if defaulted bonds, the interest from which if received would be includible in income, are purchased with the expectation of realizing capital gain on their resale, even though no current yield thereon is anticipated, ordinary and necessary expenses thereafter paid or incurred in connection with such bonds are deductible. Similarly, ordinary and necessary expenses paid or incurred in the management, conservation, or maintenance of a building devoted to rental purposes are deductible notwithstanding that there is actually no income therefrom in the taxable year, and regardless of the manner in which or the purpose for which the property in question was acquired. Expenses paid or incurred in managing, conserving, or maintaining property held for investment may be deductible under section 212 even though the property is not currently productive and there is no likelihood that the property will be sold at a profit or will otherwise be productive of income and even though the property is held merely to minimize a loss with respect thereto.

* * *

(d) Expenses, to be deductible under section 212, must be "ordinary and necessary". Thus, such expenses must be reasonable in amount and must bear a reasonable and proximate relation to the production or collection of taxable income or to the management, conservation, or maintenance of property held for the production of income.

(e) A deduction under section 212 is subject to the restrictions and limitations in part IX (section 261 and following), subchapter B, chapter 1 of the Code, relating to items not deductible. Thus, no deduction is allowable under section 212 for any amount allocable to the production or collection of one or more classes of income which are not includible in gross income, or for any amount allocable to the management, conservation, or maintenance of property held for the production of income which is not included in gross income. See section 265. Nor does section 212 allow the deduction of any expenses which are disallowed by any of the provisions of subtitle A of the Code, even though such expenses may be paid or incurred for one of the purposes specified in section 212.

(f) Among expenditures not allowable as deductions under section 212 are the following: Commuter's expenses; expenses of taking special courses or training; expenses for improving personal appearance; the cost of rental of a safe-deposit box for storing jewelry and other personal effects; expenses such as those paid or incurred in seeking employment or in placing oneself in a position to begin rendering personal services for compensation, campaign expenses of a candidate for public office, bar examination fees and other expenses paid or incurred in securing admission to the bar, and corresponding fees and expenses paid or incurred by physicians, dentists, accountants, and other taxpayers for securing the right to practice their respective professions. See, however, section 162 and the regulations thereunder.

(g) Fees for services of investment counsel, custodial fees, clerical help, office rent, and similar expenses paid or incurred by a taxpayer in connection with investments held by him are deductible under section 212 only if (1) they are paid or incurred by the taxpayer for the production or collection of income or for the management, conservation, or maintenance of investments held by him for the production of income; and (2) they are ordinary and necessary under all the circumstances, having regard to the type of investment and to the relation of the taxpayer to such investment.

(h) Ordinary and necessary expenses paid or incurred in connection with the management, conservation, or maintenance of property held for use as a residence by the taxpayer are not deductible. However, ordinary and necessary expenses paid or incurred in connection with the management, conservation, or maintenance of property held by the taxpayer as rental property are deductible even though such property was formerly held by the taxpayer for use as a home.

(i) Reasonable amounts paid or incurred by the fiduciary of an estate or trust on account of administration expenses, including fiduciaries' fees and expenses of litigation, which are ordinary and necessary in connection with the performance of the duties of administration are deductible under section 212, notwithstanding that the estate or trust is not engaged in a trade or business, except to the extent that such expenses are allocable to the production or collection of tax-exempt income. But see section 642 (g) and the regulations thereunder for disallowance of such deductions to an estate where such items are allowed as a deduction under section 2053 or 2054 in computing the net estate subject to the estate tax.

(j) Reasonable amounts paid or incurred for the services of a guardian or committee for a ward or minor, and other expenses of guardians and committees which are ordinary and necessary, in connection with the production or collection of income inuring to the ward or minor, or in connection with the management, conservation, or maintenance of property, held for the production of income, belonging to the ward or minor, are deductible.

(k) Expenses paid or incurred in defending or perfecting title to property, in recovering property (other than investment property and amounts of income which, if and when recovered, must be included in gross income), or in developing or improving property, constitute a part of the cost of the property and are not deductible expenses. Attorneys' fees paid in a suit to quiet title to lands are not deductible; but if the suit is also to collect accrued rents thereon, that portion of such fees is deductible which is properly allocable to the services rendered in collecting such rents. Expenses paid or incurred in protecting or asserting one's right to property of a decedent as heir or legatee, or as beneficiary under a testamentary trust, are not deductible.

(*l*) Expenses paid or incurred by an individual in connection with the determination, collection, or refund of any tax, whether the taxing authority be Federal, State, or municipal, and whether the tax be income, estate, gift, property, or any other tax, are deductible. Thus, expenses paid or incurred by a taxpayer for tax counsel or expenses paid or incurred in connection with the preparation of his tax returns or in connection with any proceedings involved in determining the extent of his tax liability or in contesting his tax liability are deductible.

(m) An expense (not otherwise deductible) paid or incurred by an individual in determining or contesting a liability asserted against him does not become deductible by reason of the fact that property held by him for the production of income may be required to be used or sold for the purpose of satisfying such liability.

(n) Capital expenditures are not allowable as nontrade or nonbusiness expenses. The deduction of an item otherwise allowable under section 212 will not be disallowed simply because the taxpayer was entitled under subtitle A of the Code to treat such item as a capital expenditure, rather than to deduct it as an expense. For example, see section 266. Where, however, the item may properly be treated only as a capital expenditure or where it was properly so treated under an option granted in subtitle A of the Code, no deduction is allowable under section 212; and this is true regardless of whether any basis adjustment is allowed under any other provision of the Code.

(*o*) The provisions of section 212 are not intended in any way to disallow expenses which would otherwise be allowable under section 162 and the regulations thereunder. Double deductions are not permitted. Amounts deducted under one provision of the Internal Revenue Code * * * cannot again be deducted under any other provision thereof.

(p) Frustration of public policy. The deduction of a payment will be disallowed under section 212 if the payment is of a type for which a deduction would be disallowed under section 162(c), (f), or (g) and the regulations thereunder in the case of a business expense.

[T.D. 6500, 25 FR 11402, Nov. 26, 1960, 25 FR 14021, Dec. 12, 1960, as amended by T.D. 7198, 37 FR 13685, July 13, 1972; T.D. 7345, 40 FR 7439, Feb. 20, 1975]

§ 1.213–1 Medical, dental, etc., expenses.

(a) Allowance of deduction. **(1)** Section 213 permits a deduction of payments for certain medical expenses (including expenses for medicine and drugs). Except as provided in paragraph (d) of this section (relating to special rule for decedents) a deduction is allowable only to individuals and only with respect to medical expenses actually paid during the taxable year, regardless of when the incident or event which occasioned the expenses occurred and regardless of the method of accounting employed by the taxpayer in making his income tax return. Thus, if the medical expenses are incurred but not paid during the taxable year, no deduction for such expenses shall be allowed for such year.

* * *

(e) Definitions—(1) General. **(i)** The term "medical care" includes the diagnosis, cure, mitigation, treatment, or prevention of disease. Expenses paid for "medical care" shall include those paid for the purpose of affecting any structure or function of the body or for transportation primarily for and essential to medical care. See subparagraph (4) of this paragraph for provisions relating to medical insurance.

(ii) Amounts paid for operations or treatments affecting any portion of the body, including obstetrical expenses and expenses of therapy or X-ray treatments, are deemed to be for the purpose of affecting any structure or function of the body and are therefore paid for medical care. Amounts expended for illegal operations or treatments are not deductible. Deductions for expenditures for medical care allowable under section 213 will be confined strictly to expenses incurred primarily for the prevention or alleviation of a physical or mental defect or illness. Thus, payments for the following are payments for medical care: hospital services, nursing services (including nurses' board where paid by the taxpayer), medical, laboratory, surgical, dental and other diagnostic and healing services, X-rays, medicine and drugs (as defined in subparagraph (2) of this paragraph, * * *), artificial teeth or limbs, and ambulance hire. However, an expenditure which is merely beneficial to the general health of an individual, such as an expenditure for a vacation, is not an expenditure for medical care.

(iii) Capital expenditures are generally not deductible for Federal income tax purposes. See section 263 and the regulations thereunder. However, an expenditure which otherwise qualifies as a medical expense under section 213 shall not be disqualified merely because it is a capital expenditure. For purposes of section 213 and this paragraph, a capital expenditure made by the taxpayer may qualify as a medical expense, if it has as its primary purpose the medical care (as defined in subdivisions (i) and (ii) of this subparagraph) of the taxpayer, his spouse, or his dependent. Thus, a capital expenditure which is related only to the sick person and is not related to permanent improvement or betterment of property, if it otherwise qualifies as an expenditure for medical care, shall be deductible; for example, an expenditure for eye glasses, a seeing eye dog, artificial teeth and limbs, a wheel chair, crutches, an inclinator or an air conditioner which is detachable from the property and purchased only for the use of a sick person, etc. Moreover, a capital expenditure for permanent improvement or betterment of property which would not ordinarily be for the purpose of medical care (within the meaning of this paragraph) may, nevertheless, qualify as a medical expense to the extent that the expenditure exceeds the increase in the value of the related property, if the particular expenditure is related directly to medical care. Such a situation could arise, for example, where a taxpayer is advised by a physician to install an elevator in his residence so that the taxpayer's wife who is afflicted with heart disease will not be required to climb stairs. If the cost of installing the elevator is $1,000 and the increase in the value of the residence is determined to be only $700, the difference of $300, which is the amount in excess of the value enhancement, is deductible as a medical expense. If, however, by reason of this expenditure, it is determined that the value of the residence has not been increased, the entire cost of installing the elevator would qualify as a medical expense. Expenditures made for the operation or maintenance of a capital asset are likewise deductible medical expenses if they have as their primary purpose the medical care (as defined in subdivisions (i) and (ii) of this subparagraph) of the taxpayer, his spouse, or his dependent. Normally, if a capital expenditure qualifies as a medical expense, expenditures for the operation or maintenance of the capital asset would also qualify provided that the medical reason for the capital expenditure still exists. The entire amount of such operation and maintenance expenditures qualifies, even if none or only a portion of the original cost of the capital asset itself qualified.

(iv) Expenses paid for transportation primarily for and essential to the rendition of the medical care are expenses paid for medical care. However, an amount allowable as a deduction for "transportation primarily for and essential to medical care" shall not include the cost of any meals and lodging while away from home receiving medical treatment. For example, if a doctor prescribes that a taxpayer go to a warm climate in order to alleviate a specific chronic ailment, the cost of meals and lodging while there would not be deductible. On the other hand, if the travel is undertaken merely for the general improvement of a taxpayer's health, neither the cost of transportation nor the cost of meals and lodging would be deductible. If a doctor prescribes an operation or other medical care, and the taxpayer chooses for purely personal considerations to travel to another locality (such as a resort area) for the operation or the other medical care, neither the cost of transportation nor the cost of meals and lodging (except where paid as part of a hospital bill) is deductible.

(v) The cost of in-patient hospital care (including the cost of meals and lodging therein) is an expenditure for medical care. The extent to which expenses for care in an institution other than a hospital shall constitute medical care is primarily a question of fact which depends upon the condition of the individual and the nature of the services he receives (rather than the nature of the institution). A private establishment which is regularly engaged in providing the types of care or services outlined in this subdivision shall be considered an institution for purposes of the rules provided herein. In general, the following rules will be applied:

(a) Where an individual is in an institution because his condition is such that the availability of medical care (as defined in subdivisions (i) and (ii) of this subparagraph) in such institution is a principal reason for his presence there, and meals and lodging are furnished as a necessary incident to such care, the entire cost of medical care and meals and lodging at the institution, which are furnished while the individual requires continual medical care, shall constitute an expense for medical care. For example, medical care includes the entire cost of institutional care for a person who is mentally ill and unsafe when left alone. While ordinary education is not medical care, the cost of medical care includes the cost of attending a special school for a mentally or physically handicapped individual, if his condition is such that the resources of the institution for alleviating such mental or physical handicap are a principal reason for his presence there. In such a case, the cost of attending such a special school will include the cost of meals and lodging, if supplied, and the cost of ordinary education furnished which is incidental to the special services furnished by the school. Thus, the cost of medical care includes the cost of attending a special school designed to compensate for or overcome a physical handicap, in order to qualify the individual for future normal education or for normal living, such as a school for the teaching of braille or lip reading. Similarly, the cost of care and supervision, or of treatment and training, of a mentally retarded or physically handicapped individual at an institution is within the meaning of the term "medical care".

(b) Where an individual is in an institution, and his condition is such that the availability of medical care in such institution is not a principal reason for his presence there, only that part of the cost of care in the institution as is attributable to medical care (as defined in subdivisions (i) and (ii) of this subparagraph) shall be considered as a cost of medical care; meals and lodging at the institution in such a case are not considered a cost of medical care for purposes of this section. For example, an individual is in a home for the aged for personal or family considerations and not because he requires medical or nursing attention. In such case, medical care consists only of that part of the cost for care in the home which is attributable to medical care or nursing attention furnished to him; his meals and lodging at the home are not considered a cost of medical care.

(c) It is immaterial for purposes of this subdivision whether the medical care is furnished in a Federal or State institution or in a private institution.

(vi) See section 262 and the regulations thereunder for disallowance of deduction for personal living, and family expenses not falling within the definition of medical care.

(2) Medicine and drugs. The term "medicine and drugs" shall include only items which are legally procured and which are generally accepted as falling within the category of medicine and drugs (whether or not requiring a prescription). Such term shall not include toiletries or similar preparations (such as toothpaste, shaving lotion, shaving cream, etc.) nor shall it include cosmetics (such as face creams, deodorants, hand lotions, etc., or any similar preparation used for ordinary cosmetic purposes) or sundry items. Amounts expended for items which, under this subparagraph, are excluded from the term "medicine and drugs" shall not constitute amounts expended for "medical care".

(3) Status as spouse or dependent. In the case of medical expenses for the care of a person who is the taxpayer's spouse or dependent, the deduction under section 213 is allowable if the status of such person as "spouse" or "dependent" of the taxpayer exists either at the time the medical services were rendered or at the time the expenses were paid. In determining whether such status as "spouse" exists, a taxpayer who is legally separated from his spouse under a decree of separate maintenance is not considered as married. Thus, payments made in June 1956 by A, for medical services rendered in 1955 to B, his wife, may be deducted by A for 1956 even though, before the payments were made, B may have died or in 1956 secured a divorce. Payments made in July 1956 by C, for medical services rendered to D in 1955 may be deducted by C for 1956 even though C and D were not married until June 1956.

(4) Medical insurance. **(i)(a)** For taxable years beginning after December 31, 1966, expenditures for insurance shall constitute expenses paid for medical care only to the extent that such amounts are paid for insurance covering expenses of medical care referred to in subparagraph (1) of this paragraph. In the case of an insurance contract under which amounts are payable for other than medical care (as, for example, a policy providing an indemnity for loss of income or for loss of life, limb, or sight)—

(1) No amount shall be treated as paid for insurance covering expenses of medical care referred to in subparagraph (1) of this paragraph unless the charge for such insurance is either separately stated in the contract or furnished to the policyholder by the insurer in a separate statement,

(2) The amount taken into account as the amount paid for such medical insurance shall not exceed such charge, and

(3) No amount shall be treated as paid for such medical insurance if the amount specified in the contract (or furnished to the policyholder by the insurer in a separate statement) as the charge for such insurance is unreasonably large in relation to the total charges under the contract.

For purposes of the preceding sentence, amounts will be considered payable for other than medical care under the contract if the contract provides for the waiver of premiums upon the occurrence of an event. In determining whether a separately stated charge for insurance covering expenses of medical care is unreasonably large in relation to the total premium, the relationship of the coverages under the contract together with all of the facts and circumstances shall be considered. In determining whether a contract constitutes an "insurance" contract it is irrelevant whether the benefits are payable in cash or in services. For example, amounts paid for hospitalization insurance, for membership in an association furnishing cooperative or so-called free-choice medical service, or for group hospitalization and clinical care are expenses paid for medical care. Premiums paid under Part B, Title XVIII of the Social Security Act (42 U.S.C. 1395j–1395w), relating to supplementary medical insurance benefits for the aged, are amounts paid for insurance covering expenses of medical care. Taxes imposed by any governmental unit do not, however, constitute amounts paid for such medical insurance.

* * *

(g) Reimbursement for expenses paid in prior years. (1) Where reimbursement, from insurance or otherwise, for medical expenses is received in a taxable year subsequent to a year in which a deduction was claimed on account of such expenses, the reimbursement must be included in gross income in such subsequent year to the extent attributable to (and not in excess of) deductions allowed under section 213 for any prior taxable year. See section 104, relating to compensation for injuries or sickness, and section 105(b), relating to amounts expended for medical care, and the regulations thereunder, with regard to amounts in excess of or not attributable to deductions allowed.

(2) If no medical expense deduction was taken in an earlier year, for example, if the standard deduction * * * was taken for the earlier year, the reimbursement received in the taxable year for the medical expense of the earlier year is not includible in gross income.

* * *

[T.D. 6500, 25 FR 11402, Nov. 26, 1960, as amended by T.D. 6604, 27 FR 6972, July 24, 1962; T.D. 6661, 28 FR 6629, June 27, 1963; T.D. 6761, 29 FR 13423, Sept. 29, 1964; T.D. 6946, 33 FR 2893, Feb. 13, 1968; T.D. 6985, 33 FR 19812, Dec. 27, 1968; 34 FR 254, Jan. 8, 1969; T.D. 7114, 36 FR 9020, May 18, 1971; T.D. 7317, 39 FR 23995, June 28, 1974; T.D. 7643, 44 FR 50337, Aug. 28, 1979]

§ 1.215–1T Alimony, etc., payments.

Q–1. What information is required by the Internal Revenue Service when an alimony or separate maintenance payment is claimed as a deduction by a payor?

A–1. The payor spouse must include on his/her first filed return of tax (Form 1040) for the taxable year in which the payment is made the payee's social security number, which the payee is required to furnish to the payor. * * *

[T.D. 7973, 49 FR 34458, Aug. 31, 1984]

§ 1.217–2 Deduction for moving expenses paid or incurred in taxable years beginning after December 31, 1969.

(a) Allowance of deduction—(1) In general. Section 217(a) allows a deduction from gross income for moving expenses paid or incurred by the taxpayer during the taxable year in connection with his commencement of work as an employee or as a self-employed individual at a new principal place of work. For purposes of this section, amounts are considered as being paid or incurred by an individual whether goods or services are furnished to the taxpayer directly (by an employer, a client, a customer, or similar person) or indirectly (paid to a third party on behalf of the taxpayer by an employer, a client, a customer, or similar person). A cash basis taxpayer will treat moving expenses as being paid for purposes of section 217 and this section in the year in which the taxpayer is considered to have received such payment under section 82 and § 1.82–1. No deduction is allowable under section 162 for any expenses incurred by the taxpayer in connection with moving from one residence to another residence unless such expenses are deductible under section 162 without regard to such change in residence. To qualify for the deduction under section 217 the expenses must meet the definition of the term "moving expenses" provided in section 217(b) and the taxpayer must meet the conditions set forth in section 217(c). * * *

* * *

(b) Definition of moving expenses—(1) In general. * * *

(2) Reasonable expenses. (i) The term "moving expenses" includes only those expenses which are reasonable under the circumstances of the particular move. Expenses paid or incurred in excess of a reasonable amount are not deductible. Generally, expenses paid or incurred for movement of household goods and personal effects or for travel (including meals and lodging) are reasonable only to the extent that they are paid or incurred for such movement or travel by the shortest and most direct route available from the former residence to the new residence by the conventional mode or modes of transportation actually used and in the shortest period of time commonly required to travel the distance involved by such mode. Thus, if moving or travel arrangements are made to provide a circuitous route for scenic, stopover, or other similar reasons, additional expenses resulting therefrom are not deductible since they are not reasonable nor related to the commencement of work at the new principal place of work. In addition, expenses paid or incurred for meals and lodging while traveling from the former residence to the new place of residence or to the general location of the new principal place of work and return or occupying temporary quarters in the general location of the new principal place of work are reasonable only if under the facts and circumstances involved such expenses are not lavish or extravagant.

(ii) The application of this subparagraph may be illustrated by the following example:

Example. A, an employee of the M Company works and maintains his residence in Boston, Mass. Upon receiving orders from his employer that he is to be transferred to M's Los Angeles, Calif., office, A motors to Los Angeles with his family with stopovers at various cities between Boston and Los Angeles to visit friends and relatives. In addition, A detours into Mexico for sightseeing. Because of the stopovers and tour into Mexico, A's travel time and distance are increased over what they would have been had he proceeded directly to Los Angeles. To the extent that A's route of travel between Boston and Los Angeles is in a generally southwesterly direction it may be said that he is traveling by the shortest and most direct route available by motor vehicle. Since A's excursion into Mexico is away from the usual Boston-Los Angeles route, the portion of the expenses paid or incurred attributable to such excursion is not deductible. Likewise, that portion of the expenses attributable to A's delay en route in visiting personal friends and sightseeing are not deductible.

(3) Expense of moving household goods and personal effects. Expenses of moving household goods and personal effects include expenses of transporting such goods and effects from the taxpayer's former residence to his new residence, and expenses of packing, crating, and in-transit storage and insurance for such goods and effects. Such expenses also include any costs of connecting or disconnecting utilities required because of the moving of household goods, appliances, or personal effects. Expenses of storing and insuring household goods and personal effects constitute in-transit expenses if incurred within any consecutive 30-day period after the day such goods and effects are moved from the taxpayer's former residence and prior to delivery at the taxpayer's new residence. Expenses paid or incurred in moving household goods and personal effects to the taxpayer's new residence from a place other than his former residence are allowable, but only to the extent that such expenses do not exceed the amount which would be allowable had such goods and effects been moved from the taxpayer's former residence. Expenses of moving household goods and personal effects do not include, for example, storage charges (other than in-transit), costs incurred in the acquisition of property, costs incurred and losses sustained in the disposition of property, penalties for breaking leases, mortgage penalties, expenses of refitting rugs or draperies, losses sustained on the disposal of memberships in clubs, tuition fees, and similar items. The above expenses may, however, be described in other provisions of section 217(b) and if so a deduction may be allowed for them subject to the allowable dollar limitations.

(4) Expenses of traveling from the former residence to the new place of residence. Expenses of traveling from the former residence to the new place of residence include the cost of transportation and of meals and lodging en route (including the date of arrival) from the taxpayer's former residence to his new place of residence. Expenses of meals and lodging incurred in the general location of the former residence within 1 day after the former residence is no longer suitable for occupancy because of the removal of household goods and personal effects shall be considered as expenses of traveling for purposes of this subparagraph. The date of arrival is the day the taxpayer secures lodging at the new place of residence, even if on a temporary basis. Expenses of traveling from the taxpayer's former residence to his new place of residence do not include, for example, living or other expenses following the date of arrival at the new place of residence and while waiting to enter the new residence or waiting for household goods to arrive, expenses in connection with house or apartment hunting, living expenses preceding date of departure for the new place of residence (other than expenses of meals and lodging incurred within 1 day after the former residence is no longer suitable for occupancy), expenses of trips for purposes of selling property, expenses of trips to the former residence by the taxpayer pending the move by his family to the new place of residence, or any allowance for depreciation. The above expenses may, however, be described in other provisions of section 217(b) and if so a deduction may be allowed for them subject to the allowable dollar limitations. The deduction for traveling expenses from the former residence to the new place of residence is allowable for only one trip made by the taxpayer and members of his household; however, it is not necessary that the taxpayer and all members of his household travel together or at the same time.

* * *

(8) Residence. The term "former residence" refers to the taxpayer's principal residence before his departure for his new principal place of work. The term "new residence" refers to the taxpayer's principal residence within the general location of his new principal place of work. Thus, neither term includes other residences owned or maintained by the taxpayer or members of his family or seasonal residences such as a summer beach cottage. Whether or not property is used by the taxpayer as his principal residence depends upon all the facts and circumstances in each case. Property used by the taxpayer as his principal residence may include a houseboat, a housetrailer, or similar dwelling. The term "new place of residence" generally includes the area within which the taxpayer might reasonably be expected to commute to his new principal place of work.

* * *

(d) Rules for application of section 217(c)(2)—(1) Inapplicability of minimum period of employment condition in certain cases. Section 217(d)(1) provides that the minimum period of employment condition of section 217(c)(2) does not apply in the case of a taxpayer who is unable to meet such condition by reason of—

(i) Death or disability, or

(ii) Involuntary separation (other than for willful misconduct) from the service of an employer or separation by reason of transfer for the benefit of an employer after obtaining full-time employment in which the taxpayer could reasonably have been expected to satisfy such condition.

For purposes of subdivision (i) of this paragraph disability shall be determined according to the rules in section 72(m)(7) and § 1.72–17(f). Subdivision (ii) of this subparagraph applies only where the taxpayer has obtained full-time employment in which he could reasonably have been expected to satisfy the minimum period of employment condition. A taxpayer could reasonably have been expected to satisfy the minimum period of employment condition if at the time he commences work at the new principal place of work he could have been expected, based upon the facts known to him at such time, to satisfy such condition. Thus, for example, if the taxpayer at the time of transfer was not advised by his employer that he planned to transfer him within 6 months to another principal place of work, the taxpayer could, in the absence of other factors, reasonably have been expected to satisfy the minimum employment period condition at the time of the first transfer. On the other hand, a taxpayer could not reasonably have been expected to satisfy the minimum employment condition if at the time of the commencement of the move he knew that his employer's retirement age policy would prevent his satisfying the minimum employment period condition.

(2) Election of deduction before minimum period of employment condition is satisfied. **(i)** Paragraph (2) of section 217(d) provides a rule which applies where a taxpayer paid or incurred, in a taxable year, moving expenses which would be deductible in that taxable year except that the minimum period of employment condition of section 217(c)(2) has not been satisfied before the time prescribed by law for filing the return for such taxable year. The rule provides that where a taxpayer has paid or incurred moving expenses and as of the date prescribed by section 6072 for filing his return for such taxable year (determined with regard to extensions of time for filing) there remains unexpired a sufficient portion of the 12-month or the 24-month period so that it is still possible for the taxpayer to satisfy the applicable period of employment condition, the taxpayer may elect to claim a deduction for such moving expenses on the return for such taxable year. The election is exercised by taking the deduction on the return.

(ii) Where a taxpayer does not elect to claim a deduction for moving expenses on the return for the taxable year in which such expenses were paid or incurred in accordance with subdivision (i) of this subparagraph and the applicable minimum period of employment condition of section 217(c)(2) (as well as all other requirements of section 217) is subsequently satisfied, the taxpayer may file an amended return or a claim for refund for the taxable year such moving expenses were paid or incurred on which he may claim a deduction under section 217.

(iii) The application of this subparagraph may be illustrated by the following examples:

Example (1). A is transferred by his employer from Boston, Massachusetts, to Cleveland, Ohio. He begins working there on November 1, 1970. Moving expenses are paid by A in 1970 in connection with this move. On April 15, 1971, when he files his income tax return for the year 1970, A has been a full-time employee in Cleveland for approximately 24 weeks. Although he has not satisfied the 39-week employment condition at this time, A may elect to claim his 1970 moving expenses on his 1970 income tax return as there is still sufficient time remaining before November 1, 1971, to satisfy such condition.

Example (2). Assume the same facts as in example (1), except that on April 15, 1971, A has voluntarily left his employer and is looking for other employment in Cleveland. A may not be sure he will be able to meet the 39-week employment condition by November 1, 1971.

Thus, he may if he wishes wait until such condition is met and file an amended return claiming as a deduction the expenses paid in 1970. Instead of filing an amended return A may file a claim for refund based on a deduction for such expenses. If A fails to meet the 39-week employment condition on or before November 1, 1971, no deduction is allowable for such expenses.

Example (3). B is a self-employed accountant. He moves from Rochester, N.Y., to New York, N.Y., and begins to work there on December 1, 1970. Moving expenses are paid by B in 1970 and 1971 in connection with this move. On April 15, 1971, when he files his income tax return for the year 1970, B has been performing services as a self-employed individual on a full-time basis in New York City for approximately 20 weeks. Although he has not satisfied the 78-week employment condition at this time, A may elect to claim his 1970 moving expenses on his 1970 income tax return as there is still sufficient time remaining before December 1, 1972, to satisfy such condition. On April 15, 1972, when he files his income tax return for the year 1971, B has been performing services as a self-employed individual on a full-time basis in New York City for approximately 72 weeks. Although he has not met the 78-week employment condition at this time, B may elect to claim his 1971 moving expenses on his 1971 income tax return as there is still sufficient time remaining before December 1, 1972, to satisfy such requirement.

(3) Recapture of deduction. Paragraph (3) of section 217(d) provides a rule which applies where a taxpayer has deducted moving expenses under the election provided in section 217(d)(2) prior to satisfying the applicable minimum period of employment condition and such condition cannot be satisfied at the close of a subsequent taxable year. In such cases an amount equal to the expenses deducted must be included in the taxpayer's gross income for the taxable year in which the taxpayer is no longer able to satisfy such minimum period of employment condition. Where the taxpayer has deducted moving expenses under the election provided in section 217(d)(2) for the taxable year and subsequently files an amended return for such year on which he does not claim the deduction, such expenses are not treated as having been deducted for purposes of the recapture rule of the preceding sentence.

* * *

[T.D. 7195, 37 FR 13535, July 11, 1972, 37 FR 14230, July 18, 1972, as amended by T.D. 7578, 43 FR 59355, Dec. 20, 1978; T.D. 7605, 44 FR 18970, March 30, 1979; T.D. 7689, 45 FR 20796, March 31, 1980; T.D. 7810, 47 FR 6002, Feb. 10, 1982; T.D. 8607, 60 FR 40077 (Aug. 7, 1995)]

§ 1.221–1 Deduction for interest paid on qualified education loans after December 31, 2001.

* * *

(b) Eligibility—(1) Taxpayer must have a legal obligation to make interest payments. A taxpayer is entitled to a deduction under section 221 only if the taxpayer has a legal obligation to make interest payments under the terms of the qualified education loan.

* * *

(4) Payments of interest by a third party—(i) In general. If a third party who is not legally obligated to make a payment of interest on a qualified education loan makes a payment of interest on behalf of a taxpayer who is legally obligated to make the payment, then the taxpayer is treated as receiving the payment from the third party and, in turn, paying the interest.

(ii) Examples. The following examples illustrate the rules of this paragraph (b)(4):

Example 1. Payment by employer. Student D obtains a qualified education loan to attend college. Upon Student D's graduation from college, Student D works as an intern for a non-profit organization during which time Student D's loan is in deferment and Student D makes no interest payments. As part of the internship program, the non-profit organization makes an interest payment on behalf of Student D after the deferment period. This payment is not excluded from Student D's income under section 108(f) and is treated as additional compensation includible in Student D's gross income. Assuming fulfillment of all other requirements of section 221, Student D may deduct this payment of interest for Federal income tax purposes.

Example 2. Payment by parent. Student E obtains a qualified education loan to attend college. Upon graduation from college, Student E makes legally required monthly payments of principal and interest. Student E's mother makes a required monthly payment of interest as a gift to Student E. A deduction for Student E as a dependent is not allowed on another taxpayer's tax return for that taxable year. Assuming fulfillment of all other requirements of section 221, Student E may deduct this payment of interest for Federal income tax purposes.

* * *

[T.D. 9125, 69 FR 25492, May 7, 2004]

§ 1.248–1 Election to amortize organizational expenditures.

(a) In general. Under section 248(a), a corporation may elect to amortize organizational expenditures as defined in section 248(b) and § 1.248–1(b). In the taxable year in which a corporation begins business, an electing corporation may deduct an amount equal to the lesser of the amount of the organizational expenditures of the corporation, or $5,000 (reduced (but not below zero) by the amount by which the organizational expenditures exceed $50,000). The remainder of the organizational expenditures is deducted ratably over the 180–month period beginning with the month in which the corporation begins business. All organizational expenditures of the corporation are considered in determining whether the organizational expenditures exceed $50,000, including expenditures incurred on or before October 22, 2004.

(b) Organizational expenditures defined. (1) Section 248(b) defines the term organizational expenditures. Such expenditures, for purposes of section 248 and this section, are those expenditures which are directly incident to the creation of the corporation. An expenditure, in order to qualify as an organizational expenditure, must be (i) incident to the creation of the corporation, (ii) chargeable to the capital account of the corporation, and (iii) of a character which, if expended incident to the creation of a corporation having a limited life, would be amortizable over such life. An expenditure which fails to meet each of these three tests may not be considered an organizational expenditure for purposes of section 248 and this section.

(2) The following are examples of organizational expenditures within the meaning of section 248 and this section: legal services incident to the organization of the corporation, such as drafting the corporate charter, by-laws, minutes of organizational meetings, terms of original stock certificates, and the like; necessary accounting services; expenses of temporary directors and of organizational meetings of directors or stockholders; and fees paid to the State of incorporation.

(3) The following expenditures are not organizational expenditures within the meaning of section 248 and this section:

(i) Expenditures connected with issuing or selling shares of stock or other securities, such as commissions, professional fees, and printing costs. This is so even where the particular issue of stock to which the expenditures relate is for a fixed term of years;

(ii) Expenditures connected with the transfer of assets to a corporation.

(4) Expenditures connected with the reorganization of a corporation, unless directly incident to the creation of a corporation, are not organizational expenditures within the meaning of section 248 and this section.

(c) Time and manner of making election. A corporation is deemed to have made an election under section 248(a) to amortize organizational expenditures as defined in section 248(b) and § 1.248–1(b) for the taxable year in which the corporation begins business. A corporation may choose to forgo the deemed election by affirmatively electing to capitalize its organizational expenditures on a timely filed Federal income tax return (including extensions) for the taxable year in which the corporation begins business. The election either to amortize organizational expenditures under section 248(a) or to capitalize organizational expenditures is irrevocable and applies to all organizational expenditures of the corporation. A change in the characterization of an item as an organizational expenditure is a change in method of accounting to which sections 446 and 481(a) apply if the corporation treated the item consistently for two or more taxable years. A change in the determination of the taxable year in which the corporation begins business also is treated as a change in method of accounting if the corporation amortized organizational expenditures for two or more taxable years.

(d) Determination of when corporation begins business. The deduction allowed under section 248 must be spread over a period beginning with the month in which the corporation begins business. The determination of the date the corporation begins business presents a question of fact which must be determined in each case in light of all the circumstances of the particular case. The words "begins business," however, do not have the same meaning as "in existence." Ordinarily, a corporation begins business when it starts the business operations for which it was organized; a corporation comes into existence on the date of its incorporation. Mere organizational activities, such as the obtaining of the corporate charter, are not alone sufficient to show the beginning of business. If the activities of the corporation have advanced to the extent necessary to establish the nature of its business operations, however, it will be deemed to have begun business. For example, the acquisition of operating assets which are necessary to the type of business contemplated may constitute the beginning of business.

* * *

[T.D. 6500, 25 FR 11402, Nov. 26, 1960; T.D. 9411, 73 FR 38913, July 8, 2008; T.D. 9542, 76 FR 50889, Aug. 17, 2011]

§ 1.262–1 Personal, living, and family expenses.

(a) In general. In computing taxable income, no deduction shall be allowed, except as otherwise expressly provided in chapter 1 of the Code, for personal, living, and family expenses.

(b) Examples of personal, living, and family expenses. Personal, living, and family expenses are illustrated in the following examples:

(1) Premiums paid for life insurance by the insured are not deductible. See also section 264 * * *.

(2) The cost of insuring a dwelling owned and occupied by the taxpayer as a personal residence is not deductible.

(3) Expenses of maintaining a household, including amounts paid for rent, water, utilities, domestic service, and the like, are not deductible. A taxpayer who rents a property for residential purposes, but incidentally conducts business there (his place of business being elsewhere) shall not deduct any part of the rent. If, however, he uses part of the house as his place of business, such portion of the rent and other similar expenses as is properly attributable to such place of business is deductible as a business expense.

(4) Losses sustained by the taxpayer upon the sale or other disposition of property held for personal, living, and family purposes are not deductible. But see section 165 and the regulations thereunder for deduction of losses sustained to such property by reason of casualty, etc.

(5) Expenses incurred in traveling away from home (which include transportation expenses, meals, and lodging) and any other transportation expenses are not deductible unless they qualify as expenses deductible under section 162, * * *, and paragraph (d) of § 1.162–5 (relating to trade or business expenses), section 170 * * *, section 212 * * *, section 213(e) * * *, or section 217(a) * * *. The taxpayer's costs of commuting to his place of business or employment are personal expenses and do not qualify as deductible expenses. The costs of the taxpayer's lodging not incurred in traveling away from home are personal expenses and are not deductible unless they qualify as deductible expenses under section 217. Except as permitted under section 162, 212, or 217, the costs of the taxpayer's meals not incurred in traveling away from home are personal expenses.

(6) Amounts paid as damages for breach of promise to marry, and attorney's fees and other costs of suit to recover such damages, are not deductible.

(7) Generally, attorney's fees and other costs paid in connection with a divorce, separation, or decree for support are not deductible by either the husband or the wife. However, the part of an attorney's fee and the part of the other costs paid in connection with a divorce, legal separation, written separation agreement, or a decree for support, which are properly attributable to the production or collection of amounts includible in gross income under section 71 are deductible by the wife under section 212.

(8) The cost of equipment of a member of the armed services is deductible only to the extent that it exceeds nontaxable allowances received for such equipment and to the extent that such equipment is especially required by his profession and does not merely take the place of articles required in civilian life. For example, the cost of a sword is an allowable deduction in computing taxable income, but the cost of a uniform is not. However, amounts expended by a reservist for the purchase and maintenance of uniforms which may be worn only when on active duty for training for temporary periods, when attending service school courses, or when attending training assemblies are deductible except to the extent that nontaxable allowances are received for such amounts.

(9) Expenditures made by a taxpayer in obtaining an education or in furthering his education are not deductible unless they qualify under section 162 and § 1.162–5 (relating to trade or business expenses).

* * *

[T.D. 6500, 25 FR 11402, Nov. 26, 1960, as amended by T.D. 6796, 30 FR 1041, Feb. 2, 1965; T.D. 6918, 32 FR 6681, May 2, 1967; T.D. 7207, 37 FR 20795, Oct. 4, 1972]

§ 1.263(a)–1T Capital expenditures; in general (temporary)—

(a) General rule for capital expenditures. Except as provided in chapter 1 of the Internal Revenue Code, no deduction is allowed for—

(1) Any amount paid for new buildings or for permanent improvements or betterments made to increase the value of any property or estate; or

(2) Any amount paid in restoring property or in making good the exhaustion thereof for which an allowance is or has been made.

(b) Coordination with section 263A. Section 263(a) generally requires taxpayers to capitalize an amount paid to acquire, produce, or improve real or personal tangible property. Section 263A generally prescribes the direct and indirect costs that must be capitalized to property produced by the taxpayer and property acquired for resale.

(c) **Examples of capital expenditures.** The following amounts paid are examples of capital expenditures:

(1) An amount paid to acquire or produce a unit of real or personal tangible property. See § 1.263(a)–2T.

(2) An amount paid to improve a unit of real or personal tangible property. See § 1.263(a)–3T.

(3) An amount paid to acquire or create intangibles. See § 1.263(a)–4.

(4) An amount paid or incurred to facilitate an acquisition of a trade or business, a change in capital structure of a business entity, and certain other transactions. See § 1.263(a)–5.

(5) An amount paid to acquire or create interests in land, such as easements, life estates, mineral interests, timber rights, zoning variances, or other interests in land.

* * *

(d) **Amounts paid to sell property—(1) In general.** Commissions and other transaction costs paid to facilitate the sale of property generally must be capitalized. However, in the case of dealers in property, amounts paid to facilitate the sale of property are treated as ordinary and necessary business expenses. See § 1.263(a)–5(g) for the treatment of amounts paid to facilitate the disposition of assets that constitute a trade or business.

(2) **Treatment of capitalized amount.** Amounts capitalized under paragraph (d)(1) of this section are treated as a reduction in the amount realized and generally are taken into account either in the taxable year in which the sale occurs or in the taxable year in which the sale is abandoned if a loss deduction is permissible. The capitalized amount is not added to the basis of the property and is not treated as an intangible under § 1.263(a)–4.

(3) **Examples.** The following examples, which assume the sale is not an installment sale under section 453, illustrate the rules of this paragraph (d):

Example 1. Sales costs of real property. X owns a parcel of real estate. X sells the real estate and pays legal fees, recording fees, and sales commissions to facilitate the sale. X must capitalize the fees and commissions and, in the taxable year of the sale, offset the fees and commissions against the amount realized from the sale of the real estate.

* * *

[T.D. 9564, 76 FR 81101, Dec. 27, 2011; 77 FR 74584, Dec. 17, 2012]

§ 1.263(a)–2T Amounts paid to acquire or produce tangible property (temporary).

* * *

(d) **Acquired or produced tangible property—(1) Requirement to capitalize.** Except as provided in paragraph (g) of this section (providing the de minimis rule) and in § 1.162–3T (relating to materials and supplies), a taxpayer must capitalize amounts paid to acquire or produce a unit of real or personal property (as determined under § 1.263(a)–3T(e)), including leasehold improvement property, land and land improvements, buildings, machinery and equipment, and furniture and fixtures. Amounts paid to acquire or produce a unit of real or personal property include the invoice price, transaction costs as determined under paragraph (f) of this section, and costs for work performed prior to the date that the unit of property is placed in service by the taxpayer (without regard to any applicable convention under section 168(d)). A taxpayer also must capitalize amounts paid to acquire real or personal property for resale and to produce real or personal property. See section 263A for the costs required to be capitalized to property produced by the taxpayer or to property acquired for resale.

(2) **Examples.** The rules of this section are illustrated by the following examples, in which it is assumed that the taxpayer does not apply the de minimis rule under paragraph (g) of this section:

Example 1. Acquisition of personal property. X purchases new cash registers for use in its retail store located in leased space in a shopping mall. Assume each cash register is a unit of property as determined under § 1.263(a)–3T(e) and is not a material or supply under § 1.162–3T. X must capitalize under this paragraph (d)(1) the amount paid to acquire each cash register.

Example 2. Acquisition of personal property that is a material or supply; coordination with § 1.162–3T. X operates a fleet of aircraft. In Year 1, X acquires a stock of component parts, which it intends to use to maintain and repair its aircraft. X does not make elections under § 1.162–3T(d) to treat the materials and supplies as capital expenditures. In Year 2, X uses the component parts in the repair and maintenance of its aircraft. Because the parts are materials and supplies under § 1.162–3T, X is not required to capitalize the amounts paid for the parts under this paragraph (d)(1). Rather, X must apply the rules in § 1.162–3T, governing the treatment of materials and supplies, to determine the treatment of these amounts.

Example 3. Acquisition of unit of personal property; coordination with § 1.162–3T. X operates a rental business that rents out a variety of small individual items to customers (rental items). X maintains a supply of rental items on hand to replace worn or damaged items. X purchases a large quantity of rental items to be used in its business. Assume that each of these rental items is a unit of property under § 1.263(a)–3T(e). Also assume that a portion of the rental items are materials and supplies under § 1.162–3T(c)(1). Under paragraph (d)(1) of this section, X must capitalize the amounts paid for the rental items that are not materials and supplies under § 1.162–3T(c)(1). However, X must apply the rules in § 1.162–3T to determine the treatment of the rental items that are materials and supplies under § 1.162–3T(c)(1).

Example 4. Acquisition or production cost. X purchases and produces jigs, dies, molds, and patterns for use in the manufacture of X's products. Assume that each of these items is a unit of property as determined under § 1.263(a)–3T(e) and is not a material and supply under § 1.162–3T(c)(1). X is required to capitalize under paragraph (d)(1) of this section the amounts paid to acquire and produce the jigs, dies, molds, and patterns. See section 263A for the costs required to be capitalized to the property acquired or produced by X.

Example 5. Acquisition of land. X purchases a parcel of undeveloped real estate. X must capitalize under paragraph (d)(1) of this section the amount paid to acquire the real estate. See paragraph (f) of this section for the treatment of amounts paid to facilitate the acquisition of real property.

Example 6. Acquisition of building. X purchases a building. X must capitalize under paragraph (d)(1) of this section the amount paid to acquire the building. See paragraph (f) of this section for the treatment of amounts paid to facilitate the acquisition of real property.

Example 7. Acquisition of property for resale and production of property for sale. X purchases goods for resale and produces other goods for sale. X must capitalize under paragraph (d)(1) of this section the amounts paid to acquire and produce the goods. See section 263A for the costs required to be capitalized to the property produced or property acquired for resale.

Example 8. Production of building. X constructs a building. X must capitalize under paragraph (d)(1) of this section the amount paid to construct the building. See section 263A for the costs required to be capitalized to the real property produced by X.

Example 9. Acquisition of assets constituting a trade or business. Y owns tangible and intangible assets that constitute a trade or business. X purchases all the assets of Y in a taxable transaction. X must capitalize under paragraph (d)(1) of this section the amount paid for the tangible assets of Y. See § 1.263(a)–4 for the treatment of amounts paid to acquire intangibles and § 1.263(a)–5 for the treatment of amounts paid to facilitate the acquisition of assets that constitute a trade or business. See section 1060 for special allocation rules for certain asset acquisitions.

Example 10. Work performed prior to placing the property in service. In Year 1, X purchases a building for use as a business office. Prior to placing the building in service, X incurs costs to repair cement steps, refinish wood floors, patch holes in walls, and paint the interiors and exteriors of the building. In Year 2, X places the building in service and begins using the building as its business office. Assume that the work that X performs does not constitute an improvement to the building or its structural components under § 1.263(a)–3T. Under § 1.263–3T(e)(2)(i), the building and its structural components is a single unit of property. Under paragraph (d)(1) of this section, the amounts paid must be capitalized as costs of acquiring the building because they were for work performed prior to X's placing the building in service.

Example 11. Work performed prior to placing the property in service. In January Year 1, X purchases a new machine for use in an existing production line of its manufacturing business. Assume that the machine is a unit of property under § 1.263(a)–3T(e) and is not a material or supply under § 1.162–3T. After the machine is installed, X performs a critical test on the machine to ensure that it will operate in accordance with quality standards. On November 1, Year 1, the critical test is complete, and X places the machine in service on the production line. X performs periodic quality control testing after the machine is placed in service. Under paragraph (d)(1) of this section, the amounts paid for the installation and the critical test performed before the machine is placed in service must be capitalized as costs of acquiring the machine. However, amounts paid for periodic quality control testing after X placed the machine in service are not required to be capitalized as a cost of acquiring the machine.

(e) Defense or perfection of title to property—(1) In general. Amounts paid to defend or perfect title to real or personal property are amounts paid to acquire or produce property within the meaning of this section and must be capitalized. See section 263A for the costs required to be capitalized to property produced by the taxpayer or to property acquired for resale.

(2) Examples. The following examples illustrate the rule of paragraph (e):

Example 1. Amounts paid to contest condemnation. X owns real property located in County. County files an eminent domain complaint condemning a portion of X's property to use as a roadway. X hires an attorney to contest the condemnation. The amounts that X paid to the attorney must be capitalized because they were to defend X's title to the property.

Example 2. Amounts paid to invalidate ordinance. X is in the business of quarrying and supplying for sale sand and stone in a certain municipality. Several years after X establishes its business, the municipality in which it is located passes an ordinance that prohibits the operation of X's business. X incurs attorney's fees in a successful prosecution of a suit to invalidate the municipal ordinance. X prosecutes the suit to preserve its business activities and not to defend X's title in the property. Therefore, the attorney's fees that X paid are not required to be capitalized under paragraph (e)(1) of this section. See section 263A for the rules requiring direct and allocable indirect costs (including otherwise deductible costs) to be capitalized to property produced or property acquired for resale.

Example 3. Amounts paid to challenge building line. The board of public works of a municipality establishes a building line across X's business property, adversely affecting the value of the property. X incurs legal fees in unsuccessfully litigating the establishment of the building line. The amounts X paid to the attorney must be capitalized because they were to defend X's title to the property.

(f) Transaction costs—(1) In general. A taxpayer must capitalize amounts paid to facilitate the acquisition or production of real or personal property. See section 263A for the costs required to be capitalized to property produced by the taxpayer or to property acquired for resale. See § 1.263(a)–5 for the treatment of amounts paid to facilitate the acquisition of assets that constitute a trade or business. See § 1.167(a)–5 for allocations of facilitative costs between depreciable and non-depreciable property.

(2) Scope of facilitate—(i) In general. Except as otherwise provided in this section, an amount is paid to facilitate the acquisition of real or personal property if the amount is paid in the process of investigating or otherwise pursuing the acquisition. Whether an amount is paid in the process of investigating or otherwise pursuing the acquisition is determined based on all of the facts and circumstances. In determining whether an amount is paid to facilitate an acquisition, the fact that the amount would (or would not) have been paid but for the acquisition is relevant but is not determinative. Amounts paid to facilitate an acquisition include, but are not limited to, inherently facilitative amounts specified in paragraph (f)(2)(ii) of this section.

(ii) Inherently facilitative amounts. An amount is paid in the process of investigating or otherwise pursuing the acquisition of real or personal property if the amount is inherently facilitative. An amount is inherently facilitative if the amount is paid for—

(A) Transporting the property (for example, shipping fees and moving costs);

(B) Securing an appraisal or determining the value or price of property;

(C) Negotiating the terms or structure of the acquisition and obtaining tax advice on the acquisition;

(D) Application fees, bidding costs, or similar expenses;

(E) Preparing and reviewing the documents that effectuate the acquisition of the property (for example, preparing the bid, offer, sales contract, or purchase agreement);

(F) Examining and evaluating the title of property;

(G) Obtaining regulatory approval of the acquisition or securing permits related to the acquisition, including application fees;

(H) Conveying property between the parties, including sales and transfer taxes, and title registration costs;

(I) Finders' fees or brokers' commissions, including amounts paid that are contingent on the successful closing of the acquisition;

(J) Architectural, geological, engineering, environmental, or inspection services pertaining to particular properties; or

(K) Services provided by a qualified intermediary or other facilitator of an exchange under section 1031.

(iii) Special rule for acquisitions of real property—(A) In general. Except as provided in paragraph (f)(2)(ii) of this section (relating to inherently facilitative amounts), an amount paid by the taxpayer in the process of investigating or otherwise pursuing the acquisition of real property does not facilitate the acquisition if it relates to activities performed in the process of determining whether to acquire real property and which real property to acquire.

(B) Acquisitions of real and personal property in a single transaction. An amount paid by the taxpayer in the process of investigating or otherwise pursuing the acquisition of personal property facilitates the acquisition of such personal property even if such property is acquired in a single transaction that also includes the acquisition of real property subject to the special rule set out in paragraph (f)(2)(iii)(A) of this section. A taxpayer may use a reasonable allocation to determine which costs facilitate the acquisition of personal property and which costs relate to the acquisition of real property and are subject to the special rule of paragraph (f)(2)(iii)(A) of this section.

(iv) Employee compensation and overhead costs—(A) In general. For purposes of paragraph (f) of this section, amounts paid for employee compensation (within the meaning of § 1.263(a)–4(e)(4)(ii)) and overhead are treated as amounts that do not facilitate the acquisition of real or personal property. See section 263A, however, for the treatment of employee compensation and overhead costs required to be capitalized to property produced by the taxpayer or to property acquired for resale.

(B) Election to capitalize. A taxpayer may elect to treat amounts paid for employee compensation or overhead as amounts that facilitate the acquisition of property. The election is made separately for each acquisition and applies to employee compensation or overhead, or both.* * *

(3) Treatment of transaction costs—(i) In general. All amounts paid to facilitate the acquisition or production of real or personal property are capital expenditures. Facilitative amounts allocable to real or personal property must be included in the basis of the property acquired or produced.

(ii) Treatment of inherently facilitative amounts. Inherently facilitative amounts allocable to real or personal property are capital expenditures related to such property even if the property is not eventually acquired or produced. Inherently facilitative amounts allocable to real or personal property not acquired may be allocated to those properties and recovered as appropriate in accordance with the applicable provisions of the Internal Revenue Code and the regulations thereunder (for example, sections 165, 167, or 168). See paragraph (i) of this section for the recovery of capitalized amounts.

(4) Examples. The following examples illustrate the rules of paragraph (f) of this section:

Example 1. Broker's fees to facilitate an acquisition. X decides to purchase a building in which to relocate its offices and hires a real estate broker to find a suitable building. X pays fees to the broker to find property for X to acquire. Under paragraph (f)(2)(ii)(I) of this section, X must capitalize the amounts paid to the broker because these costs are inherently facilitative of the acquisition of real property.

Example 2. Inspection and survey costs to facilitate an acquisition. X decides to purchase building A and pays amounts to third-party contractors for a termite inspection and an environmental survey of building A. Under paragraph (f)(2)(ii)(J) of this section, X must capitalize the amounts paid for the inspection and the survey of the building because these costs are inherently facilitative of the acquisition of real property.

Example 3. Moving costs to facilitate an acquisition. X purchases all the assets of Y and, in connection with the purchase, hires a transportation company to move storage tanks from Y's plant to X's plant. Under paragraph (f)(2)(ii)(A) of this section, X must capitalize the amount paid to move the storage tanks from Y's plant to X's plant because this cost is inherently facilitative to the acquisition of personal property.

Example 4. Geological and geophysical costs; coordination with other provisions. X is in the business of exploring, purchasing, and developing properties in the United States for the production of oil and gas. X considers acquiring a particular property but first incurs costs for the services of an engineering firm to perform geological and geophysical studies to determine if the property is suitable for oil or gas production. Assume that the amounts that X paid to the engineering firm constitute geological and geophysical expenditures under section 167(h). Although the amounts that X paid for the geological and geophysical services are inherently facilitative to the acquisition of real property under paragraph (f)(2)(ii)(J) of this section, X is not required to include those amounts in the basis of the real property acquired. Rather, under paragraph (c) of this section, X must capitalize these costs separately and amortize such costs as required under section 167(h) (addressing the amortization of geological and geophysical expenditures).

Example 5. Scope of facilitate. X is in the business of providing legal services to clients. X is interested in acquiring a new conference table for its office. X hires and incurs fees for an interior designer to shop for, evaluate, and make recommendations to X regarding which new table to acquire. Under paragraphs (f)(1) and (2) of this section, X must capitalize the amounts paid to the interior designer to provide these services because they are paid in the process of investigating or otherwise pursuing the acquisition of personal property.

Example 6. Transaction costs allocable to multiple properties. X, a retailer, wants to acquire land for the purpose of building a new distribution facility for its products. X considers various properties on highway A in state B. X incurs fees for the services of an architect to advise and evaluate the suitability of the sites for the type of facility that X intends to construct on the selected site. X must capitalize the architect fees as amounts paid to acquire land because these amounts are inherently facilitative to the acquisition of land under paragraph (f)(2)(ii)(J) of this section.

Example 7. Transaction costs allocable to multiple properties. X, a retailer, wants to acquire land for the purpose of building a new distribution facility for its products. X considers various properties on highway A in state B. X incurs fees for the services of an architect to prepare preliminary floor plans for a building that X could construct at any of the sites. Under these facts, the architect's fees are not inherently facilitative to the acquisition of land under paragraph (f)(2)(iii)(J) of this section but are allocable as construction costs of the building under section 263A. Therefore, X does not capitalize the architect fees as amounts paid to acquire land but instead must capitalize these costs as indirect costs allocable to the production of property under section 263A.

Example 8. Special rule for acquisitions of real property. X owns several retail stores. X decides to examine the feasibility of opening a new store in city A. In October, Year 1, X hires and incurs costs for a development consulting firm to study city A and perform market surveys, evaluate zoning and environmental requirements, and make preliminary reports and recommendations as to areas that X should consider for purposes of locating a new store. In December, Year 1, X continues to consider whether to purchase real property in city A and which property to acquire. X hires, and incurs fees for, an appraiser to perform appraisals on two different sites to determine a fair offering price for each site. In March, Year 2, X decides to acquire one of these two sites for the location of its new store. At the same time, X determines not to acquire the other site. Under paragraph (f)(2)(iii) of this section, X is not required to capitalize amounts paid to the development consultant in Year 1 because the amounts relate to activities performed in the process of determining whether to acquire real property and which real property to acquire and the amounts are not inherently facilitative costs under paragraph (f)(2)(ii) of this section. However, X must capitalize amounts paid to the appraiser in Year 1 because the appraisal costs are inherently facilitative costs under paragraph (f)(2)(ii)(B) of this section. In Year 2, X must include the appraisal costs allocable to property acquired in the basis of the property acquired and may recover the appraisal costs allocable to the property not acquired in accordance with paragraphs (f)(3)(ii) and (i) of this section.

Example 9. Employee compensation and overhead. X, a freight carrier, maintains an acquisition department whose sole function is to arrange for the purchase of vehicles and aircraft from manufacturers or other parties to be used in its freight carrying business. As provided in paragraph (f)(2)(iv)(A) of this section, X is not required to capitalize any portion of the compensation paid to employees in its acquisition department or any portion of its overhead allocable to its acquisition department. However, under paragraph (f)(2)(iv)(B) of this section, X may elect to capitalize the compensation and overhead costs allocable to the acquisition of a vehicle or aircraft by treating these amounts as costs that facilitate the acquisition of that property in its timely filed original federal income tax return for the year the amounts are paid.

(g) De minimis rule—(1) In general. Except as otherwise provided in this paragraph (g), a taxpayer is not required to capitalize under paragraph (d)(1) of this section nor treat as a material or supply under § 1.162–3T(a) amounts paid for the acquisition or production (including any amounts paid to facilitate the acquisition or production) of a unit of property (as determined under § 1.263(a)–3T(e)) or for the acquisition or production of any material or supply (as defined in § 1.162–3T(c)(1)) if—

(i) The taxpayer has an applicable financial statement (as defined in paragraph (g)(6) of this section);

(ii) The taxpayer has at the beginning of the taxable year written accounting procedures treating as an expense for non-tax purposes the amounts paid for property costing less than a certain dollar amount;

(iii) The taxpayer treats the amounts paid during the taxable year as an expense on its applicable financial statement in accordance with its written accounting procedures; and

(iv) The total aggregate of amounts paid and not capitalized under paragraph (g)(1) of this section and § 1.162–3T(f) (materials and supplies) for the taxable year are less than or equal to the greater of—

(A) 0.1 percent of the taxpayer's gross receipts for the taxable year as determined for Federal income tax purposes; or

(B) 2 percent of the taxpayer's total depreciation and amortization expense for the taxable year as determined in its applicable financial statement.

(2) Exceptions to de minimis rule. The de minimis rule in paragraph (g)(1) of this section does not apply to the following:

(i) Amounts paid for property that is or is intended to be included in inventory property; and

(ii) Amounts paid for land.

(3) Additional rules. Property to which a taxpayer applies the de minimis rule contained in paragraph (g) of this section is not treated upon sale or other disposition as a capital asset under section 1221 or as property used in the trade or business under section 1231. The cost of property to which a taxpayer properly applies the de minimis rule contained in paragraph (g) of this section is not required to be capitalized under section 263A to a separate unit of property but may be required to be capitalized as a cost of other property if incurred by reason of the production of the other property. See, for example, § 1.263A–1(e)(3)(ii)(R) requiring taxpayers to capitalize the cost of tools and equipment allocable to property produced or property acquired for resale.

(4) Election to capitalize. A taxpayer may elect not to apply the de minimis rule contained in paragraph (g)(1) of this section.* * *

(5) Materials and supplies. A taxpayer must treat amounts paid to acquire or produce a unit of property that is a material or supply as defined under § 1.162–3T(c)(1) under § 1.162–3T unless the taxpayer elects under § 1.162–3T(f) to apply the de minimis rule to that property under this paragraph (g). Property to which a taxpayer applies the de minimis rule contained in paragraph (g) of this section is not treated as a material or supply under § 1.162–3T.

* * *

(8) Examples. The following examples illustrate the rule of this paragraph (g):

Example 1. De minimis rule. X purchases 10 printers at $200 each for a total cost of $2,000. Assume that each printer is a unit of property under § 1.263(a)–3T(e) and is not a material or supply under § 1.162–3T. X has an applicable financial statement and a written policy at the beginning of the taxable year to expense amounts paid for property costing less than $500. X treats the amounts paid for the printers as an expense on its applicable financial statement. Assume that the total aggregate amounts treated as de minimis and not capitalized by X under paragraphs (g)(1)(i), (ii), and (iii) of this section, including the amounts paid for the printers, are less than or equal to the greater of 0.1 percent of total gross receipts or 2 percent of X's total financial statement depreciation under paragraph (g)(1)(iv) of this section. X is not required to capitalize the amounts paid for the 10 printers under paragraph (g)(1) of this section.

* * *

(h) Treatment of capital expenditures. Amounts required to be capitalized under this section are capital expenditures and must be taken into account through a charge to capital account or basis, or in the case of property that is inventory in the hands of a taxpayer, through inclusion in inventory costs. See section 263A for the treatment of direct and certain indirect costs of producing property or acquiring property for resale.

(i) Recovery of capitalized amounts—(1) In general. Amounts that are capitalized under this section are recovered through depreciation, cost of goods sold, or by an adjustment to basis at the time the property is placed in service, sold, used, or otherwise disposed of by the taxpayer. Cost recovery is determined by the applicable provisions of the Internal Revenue Code and regulations relating to the use, sale, or disposition of property.

(2) Examples. The following examples illustrate the rule of paragraph (i)(1) of this section. Assume that X does not apply the de minimis rule under paragraph (g) of this section.

Example 1. Recovery when property placed in service. X owns a 10-unit apartment building. The refrigerator in one of the apartments stops functioning, and X purchases a new refrigerator to replace the old one. X pays for the acquisition, delivery, and installation of the new refrigerator. Assume that the refrigerator is the unit of property, as determined under § 1.263(a)–3T(e), and is not a material or supply under § 1.162–3T. Under paragraph (d)(1) of this section, X is required to capitalize the amounts paid for the acquisition, delivery, and installation of the refrigerator. Under paragraph (i) of this section, the capitalized amounts are recovered through depreciation, which begins when the refrigerator is placed in service by X.

Example 2. Recovery when property used in the production of property. X operates a plant where it manufactures widgets. X purchases a tractor loader to move raw materials into and around the plant for use in the manufacturing process. Assume that the tractor loader is a unit of property, as determined under § 1.263(a)–3T(e), and is not a material or supply under § 1.162–3T. Under paragraph (d)(1) of this section, X is required to capitalize the amounts paid to acquire the tractor loader. Under paragraph (i) of this section, the capitalized amounts are recovered through depreciation, which begins when X places the tractor loader in service. However, because the tractor/loader is used in the production of property, under section 263A the cost recovery (that is, the depreciation) on the capitalized amounts must be capitalized to X's property produced, and, consequently, recovered through cost of goods sold. See § 1.263A–1(e)(3)(ii)(I).

* * *

[T.D. 9564, 76 FR 81102, Dec. 27, 2011; 77 FR 18687, Mar. 28, 2012; 77 FR 74584, Dec. 17, 2012]

§ 1.263(a)–3T Amounts paid to improve tangible property (temporary).

* * *

(c) Coordination with other provisions of the Internal Revenue Code—(1) In general. Nothing in this section changes the treatment of any amount that is specifically provided for under any provision of the Internal Revenue Code or the regulations other than section 162(a) or section 212 and the regulations under those sections. For example, see section 263A requiring taxpayers to capitalize the direct and indirect costs of producing property or acquiring property for resale.

(2) Materials and supplies. A material or supply as defined in § 1.162–3T(c)(1) that is acquired and used to improve a unit of tangible property is subject to this section and is not treated as a material or supply under § 1.162–3T.

(3) Exception for amounts subject to de minimis rule. A taxpayer is not required to capitalize amounts paid to acquire or produce units of property used in improvements under paragraph (d) of this section (including materials and supplies used in improvements) if these amounts are properly deducted under the de minimis rule of section § 1.263(a)–2(g).

(3) Example. The following example illustrates the rules of this paragraph (c):

Example. Railroad rolling stock. X is a railroad that properly treats amounts paid for the rehabilitation of railroad rolling stock as deductible expenses under section 263(d). X is not required to capitalize the amounts paid because nothing in this section changes the treatment of amounts specifically provided for under section 263(d).

(d) Requirement to capitalize amounts paid for improvements. Except as provided in the optional regulatory accounting method in paragraph (k) of this section or under any other accounting method published in accordance with paragraph (*l*) of this section, a taxpayer generally must capitalize the aggregate of related amounts (as defined in paragraph (f)(4) of this section) paid to improve a unit of property owned by the taxpayer. However, see paragraph (f)(1) of this section for the treatment of amounts paid to improve leased property. See section 263A for the costs required to be capitalized to property produced by the taxpayer or to property acquired for resale; section 1016 for adding capitalized amounts to the basis of the unit of property; and section 168 for the treatment of additions or improvements for depreciation purposes. For purposes of this section, a unit of property is improved if the amounts paid for activities performed after the property is placed in service by the taxpayer—

(1) Result in a betterment to the unit of property (see paragraph (h) of this section);

(2) Restore the unit of property (see paragraph (i) of this section); or

(3) Adapt the unit of property to a new or different use (see paragraph (j) of this section).

(e) Determining the unit of property—(1) In general. The unit of property rules in this paragraph (e) apply only for purposes of section 263(a) and §§ 1.263(a)–1T, 1.263(a)–2T, 1.263(a)–3T, and 1.162–3T. Unless otherwise specified, the unit of property determination is based upon the functional interdependence standard provided in paragraph (e)(3)(i) of this section. However, special rules are provided for buildings (see paragraph (e)(2) of this section), plant property (see paragraph (e)(3)(ii) of this section), network assets (see paragraph (e)(3)(iii) of this section), leased property (see paragraph (e)(2)(v) of this section for leased buildings and paragraph (e)(3)(iv) of this section for leased property other than buildings), and improvements to property (see paragraph (e)(4) of this section). Additional rules are provided if a taxpayer has assigned different MACRS classes or depreciation methods to components of property or subsequently changes the class or depreciation method of a component or other item of property (see paragraph (e)(5) of this section). Property that is aggregated or subject to a general asset account election or accounted for in a multiple asset account (that is, pooled) may not be treated as a single unit of property.

(2) Building—(i) In general. Except as otherwise provided in paragraphs (e)(4), (e)(5)(ii), and (f)(1)(ii)(B) of this section, in the case of a building (as defined in § 1.48–1(e)(1)), each building and its structural components (as defined in § 1.48–1(e)(2)) is a single unit of property ("building").

(ii) Application of improvement rules to a building. An amount is paid for an improvement to a building under paragraphs (d) and (f)(1)(iii) of this section if the amount paid results in an improvement under paragraph (h), (i), or (j) of this section to any of the following:

(A) Building structure. A building structure consists of the building (as defined in § 1.48–1(e)(1)), and its structural components (as defined in § 1.48–1(e)(2)), other than the structural components designated as buildings systems in paragraph (e)(2)(ii)(B) of this section.

(B) Building system. Each of the following structural components (as defined in § 1.48–1(e)(2)), including the components thereof, constitutes a building system that is separate from the building structure, and to which the improvement rules must be applied—

(1) Heating, ventilation, and air conditioning ("HVAC") systems (including motors, compressors, boilers, furnace, chillers, pipes, ducts, radiators);

(2) Plumbing systems (including pipes, drains, valves, sinks, bathtubs, toilets, water and sanitary sewer collection equipment, and site utility equipment used to distribute water and waste to and from the property line and between buildings and other permanent structures);

(3) Electrical systems (including wiring, outlets, junction boxes, lighting fixtures and associated connectors, and site utility equipment used to distribute electricity from property line to and between buildings and other permanent structures);

(4) All escalators;

(5) All elevators;

(6) Fire-protection and alarm systems (including sensing devices, computer controls, sprinkler heads, sprinkler mains, associated piping or plumbing, pumps, visual and audible alarms, alarm control panels, heat and smoke detection devices, fire escapes, fire doors, emergency exit lighting and signage, and fire fighting equipment, such as extinguishers, hoses);

(7) Security systems for the protection of the building and its occupants (including window and door locks, security cameras, recorders, monitors, motion detectors, security lighting, alarm systems, entry and access systems, related junction boxes, associated wiring and conduit);

(8) Gas distribution system (including associated pipes and equipment used to distribute gas to and from property line and between buildings or permanent structures); and

(9) Other structural components identified in published guidance in the Federal Register or in the Internal Revenue Bulletin (see § 601.601(d)(2)(ii)(b) of this chapter) that are excepted from the building structure under paragraph (e)(2)(ii)(A) of this section and are specifically designated as building systems under this section.

* * *

(3) Property other than building—(i) In general. Except as otherwise provided in paragraphs (e)(3), (e)(4), (e)(5), and (f)(1) of this section, in the case of real or personal property other than property described in paragraph (e)(2) of this section, all the components that are functionally interdependent comprise a single unit of property. Components of property are functionally interdependent if the placing in service of one component by the taxpayer is dependent on the placing in service of the other component by the taxpayer.

(ii) Plant property—(A) Definition. For purposes of this paragraph (e) of this section, the term plant property means functionally interdependent machinery or equipment, other than network assets, used to perform an industrial process, such as manufacturing, generation, warehousing, distribution, automated materials handling in service industries, or other similar activities.

(B) Unit of property for plant property. In the case of plant property, the unit of property determined under the general rule of paragraph (e)(3)(i) of this section is further divided into smaller units comprised of each component (or group of components) that performs a discrete and major function or operation within the functionally interdependent machinery or equipment.

* * *

(5) Additional rules—(i) Year placed in service. Notwithstanding the unit of property determination under paragraph (e)(3) of this section, a component (or a group of components) of a unit property must be treated as a separate unit of property if, at the time the unit of property is initially placed in service by the taxpayer, the taxpayer has properly treated the component as being within a different class of property under section 168(e) (MACRS classes) than the class of the unit of property of which the component is a part, or the taxpayer has properly depreciated the component using a different depreciation method than the depreciation method of the unit of property of which the component is a part.

(6) Examples. The rules of this paragraph (e) are illustrated by the following examples, in which it is assumed that the taxpayer has not made a general asset account election with regard to property or accounted for property in a multiple asset account. In addition, unless the facts specifically indicate otherwise, assume that the additional rules in paragraph (e)(5) of this section do not apply:

* * *

Example 2. Building systems. X owns a building that it uses in its retail business. The building contains two elevator banks in different locations in its building. Each elevator bank contains three elevators. X pays an amount for labor and materials for work performed on the elevators. Under paragraph (e)(2)(i) of this section, X must treat the building and its structural components as a single unit of property. As provided under paragraph (e)(2)(ii) of this section, an amount is paid for an improvement to a building if it results in an improvement to the building structure or any designated building system. Under paragraph (e)(2)(ii)(B)(5) of this section, all of the elevators, including all their components, comprise a building system. Therefore, under paragraph (e)(2)(ii) of this section, if an amount paid by X for work on the elevators results in an improvement (for example, a betterment) to the entire elevator system, X must treat these amounts as an improvement to the building.

* * *

Example 6. Plant property; discrete and major function. X is engaged in a uniform and linen rental business. X owns and operates a plant that utilizes many different machines and equipment in an assembly line-like process to treat, launder, and prepare rental items for its customers. X utilizes two laundering lines in its plant, each of which can operate independently. One line is used for uniforms and another line is used for linens. Both lines incorporate several sorters, boilers, washers, dryers, ironers, folders, and waste water treatment systems. Because the laundering equipment contained within the plant is property other than a building, the unit of property for the laundering equipment is initially determined under the general rule in paragraph (e)(3)(i) of this section and is comprised of all the components that are functionally interdependent. Under this rule, the initial units of property are each laundering line because each line is functionally independent and is comprised of components that are functionally interdependent. However, because each line is comprised of plant property under paragraph (e)(3)(ii) of this section, X must further divide these initial units of property into smaller units of property by determining the components (or groups of components) that perform discrete and major functions within the line. Under paragraph (e)(3)(ii) of this section, X must treat each sorter, boiler, washer, dryer, ironer, folder, and waste water treatment system in each line as a separate unit of property because each of these components performs a discrete and major function within the line.

* * *

Example 9. Personal property. X provides legal services to its clients. X purchased a laptop computer and a printer for its employees to use in providing legal services. When X placed the computer and printer into service, X treated the computer and printer and all their components as being within the same class of property under section 168(e) and depreciated all the components using the same depreciation method. Because the computer and printer are property other than a building, the initial units of property are determined under the general rule in paragraph (e)(3)(i) of this section and are comprised of the components that are functionally interdependent. Under paragraph (e)(3)(i) of this section, the computer and the printer are separate units of property because the computer and the printer are not components that are functionally interdependent (that is, the placing in service of the computer is not dependent on the placing in service of the printer).

* * *

Example 16. Personal property; additional rules. X is engaged in the business of transporting freight throughout the United States. To conduct its business, X owns a fleet of truck tractors and trailers. Each tractor and trailer is comprised of various components, including tires. X purchased a truck tractor with all of its components, including tires. The tractor tires have an average useful life to X of more than one year. At the time X placed the tractor in service, it treated the tractor tires as a separate asset for depreciation purposes under section 168. X properly treated the tractor (excluding the cost of the tires) as 3–year property and the tractor tires as 5–year property under section 168(e). Because X's tractor is property other than a building, the initial units of property for the tractor are determined under the general rule in paragraph (e)(3)(i) of this section, and are comprised of all the components that are functionally interdependent. Under this rule, X must treat the tractor, including its tires, as a single unit of property because the tractor and the tires are functionally interdependent (that is, the placing in service of the tires is dependent upon the placing in service of the tractor). However, under paragraph (e)(5)(i) of this section, X must treat the tractor and tires as separate units of property because X properly treated the tires as being within a different class of property under section 168(e).

* * *

(g) Safe harbor for routine maintenance on property other than buildings—(1) In general. An amount paid for routine maintenance performed on a unit of property other than a building or a structural component of a building is deemed not to improve that unit of property. Routine maintenance is the recurring activities that a taxpayer expects to perform as a result of the taxpayer's use of the unit of property to keep the unit of property in its ordinarily efficient operating condition. Routine maintenance activities include, for example, the inspection, cleaning, and testing of the unit of property, and the replacement of parts of the unit of property with comparable and commercially available and reasonable replacement parts. The activities are routine only if, at the time the unit of property is placed in service by the taxpayer, the taxpayer reasonably expects to perform the activities more than once during the class life (as defined in paragraph (g)(4) of this section) of the unit of property. Among the factors to be considered in determining whether a taxpayer is performing routine maintenance are the recurring nature of the activity, industry practice, manufacturers' recommendations, the taxpayer's experience, and the taxpayer's treatment of the activity on its applicable financial statement (as defined in paragraph (b)(4) of this section). With respect to a taxpayer that is a lessor of a unit of property, the taxpayer's use of the unit of property includes the lessee's use of the unit of property.

* * *

(3) Exceptions. Routine maintenance does not include the following:

(i) Amounts paid for the replacement of a component of a unit of property and the taxpayer has properly deducted a loss for that component (other than a casualty loss under § 1.165–7).

(ii) Amounts paid for the replacement of a component of a unit of property and the taxpayer has properly taken into account the adjusted basis of the component in realizing gain or loss resulting from the sale or exchange of the component.

(iii) Amounts paid for the repair of damage to a unit of property for which the taxpayer has taken a basis adjustment as a result of a casualty loss under section 165, or relating to a casualty event described in section 165.

(iv) Amounts paid to return a unit of property to its ordinarily efficient operating condition, if the property has deteriorated to a state of disrepair and is no longer functional for its intended use.

* * *

(5) Examples. The following examples illustrate the rules of this paragraph (g). Unless otherwise stated, assume that X has not applied the optional method of accounting for rotable and temporary spare parts under § 1.162–3T(e):

Example 1. Routine maintenance on component. **(i)** X is a commercial airline engaged in the business of transporting passengers and freight throughout the United States and abroad. To conduct its business, X owns or leases various types of aircraft. As a condition of maintaining its airworthiness certification for these aircraft, X is required by the Federal Aviation Administration (FAA) to establish and adhere to a continuous maintenance program for each aircraft within its fleet. These programs, which are designed by X and the aircraft's manufacturer and approved by the FAA, are incorporated into each aircraft's maintenance manual. The maintenance manuals require a variety of periodic maintenance visits at various intervals. One type of maintenance visit is an engine shop visit (ESV), which X expects to perform on its aircraft engines approximately every 4 years in order to keep its aircraft in its ordinarily efficient operating condition. In Year 1, X purchased a new aircraft, which included four new engines attached to the airframe. The four aircraft engines acquired with the aircraft are not materials or supplies under § 1.162–3T(c)(1)(i) because they are acquired as part of a single unit of property, the aircraft. In Year 5, X performs its first ESV on the aircraft engines. The ESV includes disassembly, cleaning, inspection, repair, replacement, reassembly, and testing of the engine and its component parts. During the ESV, the engine is removed from the aircraft and shipped to an outside vendor who performs the ESV. If inspection or testing discloses a discrepancy in a part's conformity to the specifications in X's maintenance program, the part is repaired, or if necessary, replaced with a comparable and commercially available and reasonable replacement part. After the ESVs, the engines are returned to X to be reinstalled on another aircraft or stored for later installation. Assume that the unit of property for X's aircraft is the entire aircraft, including the aircraft engines, and that the class life for X's aircraft is 12 years. Assume that none of the exceptions set out in paragraph (g)(3) of this section applies to the costs of performing the ESVs.

(ii) Because the ESVs involve the recurring activities that X expects to perform as a result of its use of the aircraft to keep the aircraft in ordinarily efficient operating condition, and consist of maintenance activities that X expects to perform more than once during the 12 year class life of the aircraft, X's ESVs are within the routine maintenance safe harbor under paragraph (g) of this section. Accordingly, the amounts paid for the ESVs are deemed not to improve the aircraft and are not required to be capitalized under paragraph (d) of this section.

Example 2. Routine maintenance after class life. Assume the same facts as in Example 1, except that in year 15, X pays amounts to perform an ESV on one of the original aircraft engines, after the end of the class life of the aircraft. Because this ESV involves the same routine maintenance activities that were performed on aircraft engines in Example 1, this ESV also is within the routine maintenance safe harbor under paragraph (g) of this section. Accordingly, the amounts paid for this ESV, even though performed after the class life of the aircraft, are deemed not to improve the aircraft and are not required to be capitalized under paragraph (d) of this section.

* * *

Example 8. Routine maintenance on non-rotable part. X is a towboat operator that owns and leases a fleet of towboats. Each towboat is equipped with two diesel-powered engines. Assume that each towboat, including its engines, is the unit of property and that a towboat has a class life of 18 years. At the time that X places its towboats into service, X is aware that approximately every three to four years, X will need to perform scheduled maintenance on the two towboat engines to keep the engines in their ordinarily efficient operating condition. This maintenance is completed while the engines are attached to the towboat and involves the cleaning and inspecting of the engines to determine which parts are within acceptable operating tolerances and can continue to be used, which parts must be reconditioned to be brought back to acceptable tolerances, and which parts must be replaced. Engine parts replaced during these procedures are replaced with comparable and commercially available and reasonable replacement parts. Assume the towboat engines are not rotable spare parts under § 1.162–3T(c)(2). In Year 1, X acquired a new towboat, including its two engines, and placed the towboat into service. In Year 5, X pays amounts to perform scheduled maintenance on both engines in the towboat. Assume that none of the exceptions set out in paragraph (g)(3) of this section apply to the scheduled maintenance costs. Because the scheduled maintenance involves recurring activities that X expects to perform more than once during the 18 year class life of the towboat, the maintenance results from X's use of the towboat and the maintenance is performed to keep the towboat in an ordinarily efficient operating condition, the scheduled maintenance on X's towboat is within the routine maintenance safe harbor under paragraph (g) of this section. Accordingly, the amounts paid for the scheduled maintenance to its towboat engines in Year 5 are deemed not to improve the towboat and are not required to be capitalized under paragraph (d) of this section.

Example 9. Routine maintenance with betterments. Assume the same facts as Example 8, except that in Year 9, X's towboat engines are due for another scheduled maintenance visit. At this time, X decides to upgrade the engines to increase their horsepower and propulsion, which would permit the towboats to tow heavier loads. Accordingly, in Year 9, X pays amounts to perform many of the same activities that it would perform during the typical scheduled maintenance activities such as cleaning, inspecting, reconditioning, and replacing minor parts, but at the same time, X incurs costs to upgrade certain engine parts to increase the towing capacity of the boats in excess of the capacity of the boats when X placed them in service. Both the scheduled maintenance procedures and the replacement of parts with new and upgraded parts are necessary to increase the horsepower of the engines and the towing capacity of the boat. Thus, the work done on the engines encompasses more than the recurring activities that X expected to perform as a result of its use of the towboats and did more than keep the towboat in its ordinarily efficient operating condition. In addition, under paragraph (f)(3)(i) of this section, the scheduled maintenance procedures directly benefit the upgrades. Therefore, the amounts that X paid in Year 9 for the maintenance and upgrade of the engines do not qualify for the routine maintenance safe harbor described under paragraph (g) of this section. These amounts must be capitalized if they result in a betterment under paragraph (h) of this section, including a material increase in the capacity of the towboat, or otherwise result in an improvement under paragraph (d) of this section.

* * *

(h) Capitalization of betterments—(1) In general. A taxpayer must capitalize amounts paid that result in the betterment of a unit of property. An amount paid results in the betterment of a unit of property only if it—

(i) Ameliorates a material condition or defect that either existed prior to the taxpayer's acquisition of the unit of property or arose during the production of the unit of property, whether or not the taxpayer was aware of the condition or defect at the time of acquisition or production;

(ii) Results in a material addition (including a physical enlargement, expansion, or extension) to the unit of property; or

(iii) Results in a material increase in capacity (including additional cubic or square space), productivity, efficiency, strength, or quality of the unit of property or the output of the unit of property.

(2) Betterments to buildings. In the case of a building, an amount results in a betterment to the unit of property if it results in a betterment to any of the properties designated in paragraphs (e)(2)(ii), (e)(2)(iii)(B), (e)(2)(iv)(B), or (e)(2)(v)(B) of this section.

(3) Application of general rule—(i) Facts and circumstances. To determine whether an amount paid results in a betterment described in paragraph (h)(1) of this section, it is appropriate to consider all the facts and circumstances including, but not limited to, the purpose of the expenditure, the physical nature of the work performed, the effect of the expenditure on the unit of property, and the taxpayer's treatment of the expenditure on its applicable financial statement (as described in paragraph (b)(4) of this section).

(ii) Unavailability of replacement parts. If a taxpayer needs to replace part of a unit of property that cannot practicably be replaced with the same type of part (for example, because of technological advancements or product enhancements), the replacement of the part with an improved, but comparable, part does not, by itself, result in a betterment to the unit of property.

(iii) Appropriate comparison—(A) In general. In cases in which a particular event necessitates an expenditure, the determination of whether an expenditure results in a betterment of the unit of property is made by comparing the condition of the property immediately after the expenditure with the condition of the property immediately prior to the circumstances necessitating the expenditure.

(B) Normal wear and tear. If the expenditure is made to correct the effects of normal wear and tear to the unit of property (including the amelioration of a condition or defect that existed prior to the taxpayer's acquisition of the unit of property resulting from normal wear and tear), the condition of the property immediately prior to the circumstances necessitating the expenditure is the condition of the property after the last time the taxpayer corrected the effects of normal wear and tear (whether the amounts paid were for maintenance or improvements) or, if the taxpayer has not previously corrected the effects of normal wear and tear, the condition of the property when placed in service by the taxpayer.

(C) Particular event. If the expenditure is made as a result of a particular event, the condition of the property immediately prior to the circumstances necessitating the expenditure is the condition of the property immediately prior to the particular event.

(4) Examples. The following examples illustrate the application of this paragraph (h) only and do not address whether capitalization is required under another provision of this section or another provision of the Internal Revenue Code (for example, section 263A):

Example 1. Amelioration of pre-existing material condition or defect. In Year 1, X purchases a store located on a parcel of land that contained underground gasoline storage tanks left by prior occupants. Assume that the parcel of land is the unit of property. The tanks had leaked, causing soil contamination. X is not aware of the contamination at the time of purchase. In Year 2, X discovers the contamination and incurs costs to remediate the soil. The remediation costs result in a betterment to the land under paragraph (h)(1)(i) of this section because X incurred the costs to ameliorate a material condition or defect that existed prior to X's acquisition of the land.

Example 2. Not amelioration of pre-existing condition or defect. X owns a building that was constructed with insulation that contained asbestos. The health dangers of asbestos were not widely known when the building was constructed. X determines that certain areas of asbestos-containing insulation had begun to deteriorate and could eventually pose a health risk to employees. Therefore, X pays an amount to remove the asbestos-containing insulation from the building structure and replace it with new insulation that is safer to employees, but no more efficient or effective than the asbestos insulation. Under paragraph (e)(2)(ii) of this section, if the amount paid results in a betterment to the building structure or any building system, X must treat the amount as an improvement to the building. Although the asbestos is determined to be unsafe under certain circumstances, the asbestos is not a preexisting or material defect of the building structure under paragraph (h)(1)(i) of this section. In addition, the removal and replacement of the asbestos does not result in a material addition to the building structure under paragraph (h)(1)(ii) of this section or result in a material increase in capacity, productivity, efficiency, strength, or quality of the building structure or the output of the building structure under paragraph (h)(1)(iii) of this section. Therefore, the amount paid to remove and replace the asbestos insulation does not result in a betterment to the building structure under paragraph (h) of this section.

Example 3. Not amelioration of pre-existing material condition or defect. (i) In January, Year 1, X purchased a used machine for use in its manufacturing operations. Assume that the machine is a unit of property and has a class life of 10 years. X placed the machine in service in January, Year 1 and at that time expected to perform manufacturer recommended scheduled maintenance on the machine every three years. The scheduled maintenance includes the cleaning and oiling of the machine, the inspection of parts for defects, and the replacement of minor items such as springs, bearings, and seals with comparable and commercially available and reasonable replacement parts. The scheduled maintenance does not result in any material additions or material increases in capacity, productivity, efficiency, strength or quality of the machine or the output of the machine. At the time X purchased the machine, it was approaching the end of a three-year scheduled maintenance period. As a result, in February, Year 1, X pays an amount to perform the manufacturer recommended scheduled maintenance to keep the machine in its ordinarily efficient operating condition.

(ii) The amount that X pays does not qualify under the routine maintenance safe harbor in paragraph (g) of this section because the cost primarily results from the prior owner's use of the property and not the taxpayer's use. X acquired the machine just before it had received its three-year scheduled maintenance. Accordingly, the amount that X pays for the scheduled maintenance results from the prior owner's use of the property and ameliorates conditions or defects that existed prior to X's ownership of the machine. Nevertheless, considering the facts and circumstances under paragraph (h)(2)(i) of this section, including the purpose and minor nature of the work performed, this amount does not ameliorate a material condition or defect in the machine under paragraph (h)(1)(i) of this section, result in a material addition to the machine under paragraph (h)(1)(ii) of this section, or result in a material increase in the capacity, productivity, efficiency, strength, or quality of the machine or the output of the machine under paragraph (h)(1)(iii) of this section. Therefore, X is not required to capitalize the amount paid for the scheduled maintenance as a betterment to the machine under this paragraph (h).

* * *

Example 5. Amelioration of material condition or defect. (i) X acquires a building for use in its business of providing assisted living services. Before and after the purchase, the building functions as an assisted living facility. However, at the time of the purchase, X is aware that the building is in a condition that is below the standards that X requires for facilities used in its business. Immediately after the acquisition and during the following two years, while X continues to use the building as an assisted living facility, X pays amounts for repairs, maintenance, and the acquisition of new property to bring the facility into the high-quality condition for which X's facilities are known. The work on X's building includes repairing damaged drywall, repainting, re-wallpapering, replacing windows, repairing and replacing doors; replacing and regrouting tile; repairing millwork; and repairing and replacing roofing materials. The work also involves the replacement of section 1245 property including window treatments, furniture, and cabinets. On its applicable financial statements, X capitalizes the costs of the repairs and maintenance to the building. The work that X performs affects only the building structure under paragraph (e)(2)(ii)(A) of this section and does not affect any of the building systems described in paragraph (e)(2)(ii)(B) of this section. Assume that each section 1245 property is a separate unit of property.

(ii) Under paragraph (e)(2)(ii) of this section, if an amount paid results in a betterment to the building structure or any building system, X must treat the amount as an improvement to the building. Considering the facts and circumstances, as required under paragraph (h)(3)(i) of this section, including the purpose of the expenditures, the effect of the expenditures on the building structure, and the treatment of the expenditures in X's applicable financial statements, the amounts that X paid for repairs and maintenance to the building structure comprises a betterment to the building structure under paragraph (h)(1)(i) of this section because the amounts ameliorate material conditions or defects that existed prior to X's acquisition of the building. Therefore, in accordance with paragraph (e)(2)(ii) of this section, X must treat the amounts paid for the betterment to the building structure as an improvement to the building and must capitalize the amounts under paragraph (d)(1) of this section. Moreover, X is required to capitalize the amounts paid to acquire and install each section 1245 property, including each window treatment, each item of furniture, and each cabinet, in accordance with § 1.263(a)–2T(d)(1).

* * *

Example 12. Not a betterment; regulatory requirement. X owns a meat processing plant. X discovers that oil is seeping through the concrete walls of the plant, creating a fire hazard. Federal meat inspectors advise X that it must correct the seepage problem or shut down its plant. To correct the problem, X pays an amount to add a concrete lining to the walls from the floor to a height of about four feet and also to add concrete to the floor of the plant. Under paragraph (e)(2)(ii) of this section, if the amount paid results in a betterment to the building structure or any building system, X must treat the amount as an improvement to the building. The event necessitating the expenditure was the seepage of the oil. Prior to the seepage, the plant did not leak and was functioning for its intended use. X is not required to treat the amount paid as a betterment under paragraph (h) of this section because it does not result in a material addition or material increase in capacity, productivity, efficiency, strength or quality of the building structure or its output compared to the condition of the structure prior to the seepage of the oil. The federal meat inspectors' requirement that X correct the seepage to continue operating the plant is not relevant in determining whether the amount paid improves the plant. See paragraph (f)(2) of this section.

Example 13. Not a betterment; replacement with same part. X owns a small retail shop. A storm damages the roof of X's shop by displacing numerous wooden shingles. X pays a contractor to replace all the wooden shingles on the roof with new wooden shingles. Under paragraph (e)(2)(ii) of this section, if the amount paid results in a betterment to the building structure or any building system, X must treat the amount as an improvement to the building. The roof is part of the building structure under paragraph (e)(2)(ii)(A) of this section. The event necessitating the expenditure was the storm. Prior to the storm, the building structure was functioning for its intended use. X is not required to treat the amount paid to replace the shingles as a betterment under paragraph (h) of this section because it does not result in a material addition, or material increase in the capacity, productivity, efficiency, strength, or quality of the building structure or the output of the building structure compared to the condition of the building structure prior to the storm.

Example 14. Not a betterment; replacement with comparable part. Assume the same facts as in Example 13, except that wooden shingles are not available on the market. X pays a contractor to replace all the wooden shingles with comparable asphalt shingles. The amount that X pays to reshingle the roof with asphalt shingles does not result in a betterment to the shop building structure, even though the asphalt shingles may be stronger than the wooden shingles. Because the wooden shingles could not practicably be replaced with new wooden shingles, the replacement of the old shingles with comparable asphalt shingles does not, by itself, result in a betterment, and therefore, an improvement, to the shop building structure under this paragraph (h).

Example 15. Betterment; replacement with improved parts. Assume the same facts as in Example 14, except that, instead of replacing the wooden shingles with asphalt shingles, X pays a contractor to replace all the wooden shingles with shingles made of lightweight composite materials that are maintenance-free and do not absorb moisture. The new shingles have a 50–year warranty and a Class A fire rating. The amount paid for these shingles results in a betterment to the shop building structure under paragraphs (h)(1)(iii) and (h)(3)(iii) of this section because it results in a material increase in the quality of the shop building structure as compared to the condition of the shop building structure prior to the storm. Therefore, in accordance with paragraph (e)(2)(ii), X must treat the amount paid for the betterment of the building structure as an improvement to the building and must capitalize the amount paid under paragraph (d)(1) of this section.

* * *

(i) Capitalization of restorations—(1) In general. A taxpayer must capitalize amounts paid to restore a unit of property, including amounts paid in making good the exhaustion for which an allowance is or has been made. An amount is paid to restore a unit of property only if it—

(i) Is for the replacement of a component of a unit of property and the taxpayer has properly deducted a loss for that component (other than a casualty loss under § 1.165–7);

(ii) Is for the replacement of a component of a unit of property and the taxpayer has properly taken into account the adjusted basis of the component in realizing gain or loss resulting from the sale or exchange of the component;

(iii) Is for the repair of damage to a unit of property for which the taxpayer has properly taken a basis adjustment as a result of a casualty loss under section 165, or relating to a casualty event described in section 165;

(iv) Returns the unit of property to its ordinarily efficient operating condition if the property has deteriorated to a state of disrepair and is no longer functional for its intended use;

(v) Results in the rebuilding of the unit of property to a like-new condition after the end of its class life as defined in paragraph (g)(4) of this section (see paragraph (i)(3) of this section); or

(vi) Is for the replacement of a part or a combination of parts that comprise a major component or a substantial structural part of a unit of property (see paragraph (i)(4) of this section).

(2) Restorations of buildings. In the case of a building, an amount is paid to restore the unit of property if it restores any of the properties designated in paragraphs (e)(2)(ii), (e)(2)(iii)(B), (e)(2)(iv)(B), (e)(2)(v)(B) of this section.

(3) Rebuild to like-new condition. For purposes of paragraph (i)(1)(v) of this section, a unit of property is rebuilt to a like-new condition if it is brought to the status of new, rebuilt, remanufactured, or similar status under the terms of any federal regulatory guideline or the manufacturer's original specifications.

(4) Replacement of a major component or a substantial structural part. To determine whether an amount is for the replacement of a part or a combination of parts that comprise a major component or a substantial structural part of the unit of property, it is appropriate to consider all the facts and circumstances. These facts and circumstances include the quantitative or qualitative significance of the part or combination of parts in relation to the unit of property. A major component or substantial structural part includes a part or combination of parts that comprise a large portion of the physical structure of the unit of property or that perform a discrete and critical function in the operation of the unit of property. However, the replacement of a minor component of the unit of property, even though such component may affect the function of the unit of property, will not generally, by itself, constitute a major component or substantial structural part.

(5) Examples. The following examples illustrate the application of this paragraph (i) only and do not address whether capitalization is required under another provision of this section or another provision of the Internal Revenue Code (for example, section 263A). Unless otherwise stated, assume that X has not properly deducted a loss for, nor taken into account the adjusted basis on a sale or exchange of, any unit of property, asset, or component of a unit of property that is replaced:

* * *

Example 6. Rebuild of property to like-new condition before end of class life. X is a Class I railroad that owns a fleet of freight cars. Freight cars have a recovery period of 7 years under section 168(c) and a class life of 14 years. Every 8 to 10 years, X rebuilds its freight cars. Ten years after X places the freight car in service, X performs a rebuild, which includes a complete disassembly, inspection, and reconditioning or replacement of components of the suspension and draft systems, trailer hitches, and other special equipment. X modifies the car to upgrade various components to the latest engineering standards. The freight car essentially is stripped to the frame, with all of its substantial components either reconditioned or replaced. The frame itself is the longest-lasting part of the car and is reconditioned. The walls of the freight car are replaced or are sandblasted and repainted. New wheels are installed on the car. All the remaining components of the car are restored before they are reassembled. At the end of the rebuild, the freight car has been restored to rebuilt condition under the manufacturer's specifications. Assume the freight car is the unit of property. X is not required to capitalize under paragraph (i)(1)(v) of this section the amounts paid to rebuild the freight car because, although the amounts paid restore the freight car to like-new condition, the amounts were not paid after the end of the class life of the freight car.

* * *

Example 8. Replacement of major component or substantial structural part; personal property. X is a common carrier that owns a fleet of petroleum hauling trucks. X pays amounts to replace the existing engine, cab, and petroleum tank with a new engine, cab, and tank. Assume the tractor of the truck (which includes the cab and the engine) is a single unit of property, and that the trailer (which contains the petroleum tank) is a separate unit of property. The new engine and cab constitute parts or combinations of parts that comprise a major component or substantial structural part of X's tractor. Therefore, the amounts paid for the replacement of those components must be capitalized under paragraph (i)(1)(vi) of this section. The new petroleum tank constitutes a part or combination of parts that comprise a major component and a substantial structural part of the trailer. Accordingly, the amounts paid for the replacement of the tank also must be capitalized under paragraph (i)(1)(vi) of this section.

Example 9. Repair performed during a restoration. Assume the same facts as in Example 8, except that, at the same time the engine and cab of the tractor are replaced, X pays amounts to paint the cab of the tractor with its company logo and to fix a broken taillight on the tractor. The repair of the broken taillight and the painting of the cab generally are deductible expenses under § 1.162–4T. However, under paragraph (f)(3)(i) of this section, a taxpayer must capitalize all the direct costs of an improvement and all the indirect costs that directly benefit or are incurred by reason of an improvement in accordance with the rules under section 263A. Repairs and maintenance that do not directly benefit or are not incurred by reason of an improvement are not required to be capitalized under section 263(a), regardless of whether they are made at the same time as an improvement. Under paragraph (f)(3)(i) of this section, X must capitalize the amounts paid to paint the cab as part of the improvement to the tractor because these amounts directly benefit and are incurred by reason of the restoration of the cab. Amounts paid to repair the broken taillight, however, are not incurred by reason of the restoration of the tractor, nor do the amounts paid directly benefit the tractor restoration, even though the repair was performed at the same time as the restoration. Thus, X must capitalize the amounts paid to paint the cab under paragraph (i)(1)(vi) and (f)(3)(i) of this section, but X is not required to capitalize the amounts paid to repair the broken taillight.

* * *

Example 12. Replacement of major component or substantial structural part; roof. X owns a large retail store. X discovers a leak in the roof of the store and hires a contractor to inspect and fix the roof. The contractor discovers that a major portion of the sheathing and rafters has rotted, and recommends the replacement of the entire roof. X pays the contractor to replace the entire roof with a new roof. Under paragraph (e)(2)(ii) of this section, if the amount paid results in a restoration of the building structure or any building system, X must treat the amount as an improvement to the building. The roof is part of the building structure under paragraph (e)(2)(ii)(A) of this section and comprises a major component or substantial structural part of X's building structure under paragraph (i)(4) of this section. Under paragraph (i)(1)(vi) of this section, X must treat the amount paid to replace the roof as a restoration because X paid the amount to replace a major component or substantial structural part of X's building structure. Therefore, in accordance with paragraph (e)(2)(ii) of this section, X must treat the amount paid to restore the building structure as an improvement to the building and must capitalize the amount paid under paragraph (d)(2) of this section.

Example 13. Replacement of major component or substantial structural part; roof. Assume the same facts as Example 12 except the contractor recommends replacement of a significant portion of the roof, but not the entire roof. Accordingly, X pays an amount to replace a large portion of the decking, insulation, and membrane of the roof of X's retail building. The portion of the roof replaced comprises a major component or substantial structural part of the building structure under paragraph (i)(4) of this section. Thus, under paragraph (i)(1)(vi) of this section, X must treat the amount paid for the roof work as a restoration of the building structure because X paid the amount to replace a major component or substantial structural part of the building structure. Therefore, in accordance with paragraph (e)(2)(ii) of this section, X must treat the amount paid as an improvement to the building and must capitalize the amount paid under paragraph (d)(2) of this section.

* * *

(j) Capitalization of amounts to adapt property to a new or different use—(1) In general. Taxpayers must capitalize amounts paid to adapt a unit of property to a new or different use. In general, an amount is paid to adapt a unit of property to a new or different use if the adaptation is not consistent with the taxpayer's intended ordinary use of the unit of property at the time originally placed in service by the taxpayer.

(2) Adapting buildings to new or different use. In the case of a building, an amount is paid to adapt the unit of property to a new or different use if it adapts to a new or different use any of the properties designated in paragraphs (e)(2)(ii), (e)(2)(iii)(B), (e)(2)(iv)(B), or (e)(2)(v)(B) of this section.

(3) Examples. The following examples illustrate solely the rules of this paragraph (j). Even if capitalization is not required in an example under this paragraph (j), the amounts paid in the example may be subject to capitalization under a different provision of this section or another provision of the Internal Revenue Code (for example, section 263A). Unless otherwise stated, assume that X has not properly deducted a loss for any unit of property, asset, or component of a unit of property that is removed and replaced.

Example 1. New or different use. X is a manufacturer and owns a manufacturing building that it has used for manufacturing since Year 1, when X placed it in service. In Year 30, X pays an amount to convert its manufacturing building into a showroom for its business. To convert the facility, X removes and replaces various structural components to provide a better layout for the showroom and its offices. X also repaints the building interiors as part of the conversion. None of the materials used are better than existing materials in the building. Under paragraph (e)(2)(ii) of this section, if the amount paid adapts the building structure to a new or different use, X must treat the amount as an improvement to the building. Under paragraph (j)(1) of this section, the amount paid to convert the manufacturing facility into a showroom adapts the building structure to a new or different use because the conversion is not consistent with X's intended ordinary use of the building structure at the time it was placed in service. Therefore, in accordance with paragraph (e)(2)(ii) of this section, X must treat the amount paid for the adaptation of the building structure as an amount that improves the building. Accordingly, X must capitalize the amount as an improvement under paragraph (d)(3) of this section.

Example 2. Not a new or different use. X owns a building consisting of twenty retail spaces. The space was designed to be reconfigured; that is, adjoining spaces could be combined into one space. One of the tenants expands its occupancy to include two adjoining retail spaces. To facilitate the new lease, X pays an amount to remove the walls between the three retail spaces. Assume that the walls between spaces are part of the building and its structural components. Under paragraph (e)(2)(ii) of this section, if the amount paid adapts the buildings structure to a new or different use, X must treat the amount as an improvement to the building. Under paragraph (j)(1) of this section, the amount paid to convert three retail spaces into one larger space for an existing tenant does not adapt X's building structure to a new or different use because the combination of retail spaces is consistent with X's intended, ordinary use of the building structure. Therefore, the amount paid by X to remove the walls does not improve the building under paragraph (d)(3) of this section.

Example 3. Not a new or different use. X owns a building consisting of twenty retail spaces. X decides to sell the building. In anticipation of selling the building, X pays an amount to repaint the interior walls and to refinish the hardwood floors. Under paragraph (e)(2)(ii) of this section, if the amount paid adapts the buildings structure to a new or different use, X must treat the amount as an improvement to the building. Preparing the building for sale does not constitute a new or different use for the building structure under paragraph (j)(1) of this section. Therefore, the amount paid to prepare the building structure for sale does not improve the building under paragraphs (d)(3) of this section.

Example 4. New or different use. X owns a parcel of land on which it previously operated a manufacturing facility. Assume that the land is the unit of property. During the course of X's operation of the manufacturing facility, the land became contaminated with wastes from its manufacturing processes. X discontinues manufacturing operations at the site, and decides to sell the property to a developer that intends to use the property for residential housing. In anticipation of selling the land, X pays an amount to cleanup the land to a standard that is required for the land to be used for residential purposes. In addition, X pays an amount to regrade the land so that it can be used for residential purposes. Amounts that X pays to cleanup wastes that were discharged in the course of X's manufacturing operations do not adapt the land to a new or different use, regardless of the extent to which the land was cleaned. Therefore, X is not required to capitalize the amount paid for the cleanup under paragraph (j)(1) of this section. However, the amount paid to regrade the land so that it can be used for residential purposes adapts the land to a new or different use that is inconsistent with X's intended ordinary use of the property at the time it was placed in service. Accordingly, the amounts paid to regrade the land must be capitalized as improvements under paragraphs (j)(1) of this section.

* * *

(m) Treatment of capital expenditures. Amounts required to be capitalized under this section are capital expenditures and must be taken into account through a charge to capital account or basis, or in the case of property that is inventory in the hands of a taxpayer, through inclusion in inventory costs. See section 263A for the treatment of direct and indirect costs of producing property or acquiring property for resale.

(n) Recovery of capitalized amounts. Amounts that are capitalized under this section are recovered through depreciation, cost of goods sold, or by an adjustment to basis at the time the property is placed in service, sold, used, or otherwise disposed of by the taxpayer. Cost recovery is determined by the applicable Internal Revenue Code and regulation provisions relating to the use, sale, or disposition of property.

[T.D. 9564, 76 FR 81107, Dec. 27, 2011; 77 FR 18687, Mar. 28, 2012; 77 FR 75484, Dec. 17, 2012]

§ 1.263(a)–4 Amounts paid to acquire or create intangibles.

(a) Overview. This section provides rules for applying section 263(a) to amounts paid to acquire or create intangibles. Except to the extent provided in paragraph (d)(8) of this section, the rules provided by this section do not apply to amounts paid to acquire or create tangible assets. Paragraph (b) of this section provides a general principle of capitalization. Paragraphs (c) and (d) of this section identify intangibles for which capitalization is specifically required under the general principle. Paragraph (e) of this section provides rules for determining the extent to which taxpayers must capitalize transaction costs. Paragraph (f) of this section provides a 12–month rule intended to simplify the application of the general principle to certain payments that create benefits of a brief duration. Additional rules and examples relating to these provisions are provided in paragraphs (g) through (n) of this section. The applicability date of the rules in this section is provided in paragraph (*o*) of this section. Paragraph (p) of this section provides rules applicable to changes in methods of accounting made to comply with this section.

(b) Capitalization with respect to intangibles—(1) In general. Except as otherwise provided in this section, a taxpayer must capitalize—

(i) An amount paid to acquire an intangible (see paragraph (c) of this section);

(ii) An amount paid to create an intangible described in paragraph (d) of this section;

(iii) An amount paid to create or enhance a separate and distinct intangible asset within the meaning of paragraph (b)(3) of this section;

(iv) An amount paid to create or enhance a future benefit identified in published guidance in the Federal Register or in the Internal Revenue Bulletin (see § 601.601(d)(2)(ii) of this chapter) as an intangible for which capitalization is required under this section; and

(v) An amount paid to facilitate (within the meaning of paragraph (e)(1) of this section) an acquisition or creation of an intangible described in paragraph (b)(1)(i), (ii), (iii) or (iv) of this section.

(2) Published guidance. Any published guidance identifying a future benefit as an intangible for which capitalization is required under paragraph (b)(1)(iv) of this section applies only to amounts paid on or after the date of publication of the guidance.

(3) Separate and distinct intangible asset—(i) Definition. The term separate and distinct intangible asset means a property interest of ascertainable and measurable value in money's worth that is subject to protection under applicable State, Federal or foreign law and the possession and control of which is intrinsically capable of being sold, transferred or pledged (ignoring any restrictions imposed on assignability) separate and apart from a trade or business. In addition, for purposes of this section, a fund (or similar account) is treated as a separate and distinct intangible asset of the taxpayer if amounts in the fund (or account) may revert to the taxpayer. The determination of whether a payment creates a separate and distinct intangible asset is made based on all of the facts and circumstances existing during the taxable year in which the payment is made.

* * *

(4) Coordination with other provisions of the Internal Revenue Code—(i) In general. Nothing in this section changes the treatment of an amount that is specifically provided for under any other provision of the Internal Revenue Code (other than section 162(a) or 212) or the regulations thereunder.

* * *

(c) Acquired intangibles—(1) In general. A taxpayer must capitalize amounts paid to another party to acquire any intangible from that party in a purchase or similar transaction. Examples of intangibles within the scope of this paragraph (c) include, but are not limited to, the following (if acquired from another party in a purchase or similar transaction):

(i) An ownership interest in a corporation, partnership, trust, estate, limited liability company, or other entity.

(ii) A debt instrument, deposit, stripped bond, stripped coupon (including a servicing right treated for federal income tax purposes as a stripped coupon), regular interest in a REMIC or FASIT, or any other intangible treated as debt for federal income tax purposes.

(iii) A financial instrument, such as—

(A) A notional principal contract;

(B) A foreign currency contract;

(C) A futures contract;

(D) A forward contract (including an agreement under which the taxpayer has the right and obligation to provide or to acquire property (or to be compensated for such property, regardless of whether the taxpayer provides or acquires the property));

(E) An option (including an agreement under which the taxpayer has the right to provide or to acquire property (or to be compensated for such property, regardless of whether the taxpayer provides or acquires the property)); and

(F) Any other financial derivative.

(iv) An endowment contract, annuity contract, or insurance contract.

(v) Non-functional currency.

(vi) A lease.

(vii) A patent or copyright.

(viii) A franchise, trademark or tradename (as defined in § 1.197–2(b)(10)).

(ix) An assembled workforce (as defined in § 1.197–2(b)(3)).

(x) Goodwill (as defined in § 1.197–2(b)(1)) or going concern value (as defined in § 1.197–2(b)(2)).

(xi) A customer list.

(xii) A servicing right (for example, a mortgage servicing right that is not treated for Federal income tax purposes as a stripped coupon).

(xiii) A customer-based intangible (as defined in § 1.197–2(b)(6)) or supplier-based intangible (as defined in § 1.197–2(b)(7)).

(xiv) Computer software.

(xv) An agreement providing either party the right to use, possess or sell an intangible described in paragraphs (c)(1)(i) through (v) of this section.

(2) Readily available software. An amount paid to obtain a nonexclusive license for software that is (or has been) readily available to the general public on similar terms and has not been substantially modified (within the meaning of § 1.197–2(c)(4)) is treated for purposes of this paragraph (c) as an amount paid to another party to acquire an intangible from that party in a purchase or similar transaction.

(3) Intangibles acquired from an employee. Amounts paid to an employee to acquire an intangible from that employee are not required to be capitalized under this section if the amounts are includible in the employee's income in connection with the performance of services under section 61 or 83. For purposes of this section, whether an individual is an employee is determined in accordance with the rules contained in section 3401(c) and the regulations thereunder.

(4) Examples. The following examples illustrate the rules of this paragraph (c):

Example 1. Debt instrument. X corporation, a commercial bank, purchases a portfolio of existing loans from Y corporation, another financial institution. X pays Y $2,000,000 in exchange for the portfolio. The $2,000,000 paid to Y constitutes an amount paid to acquire an intangible from Y and must be capitalized.

Example 2. Option. W corporation owns all of the outstanding stock of X corporation. Y corporation holds a call option entitling it to purchase from W all of the outstanding stock of X at a certain price per share. Z corporation acquires the call option from Y in exchange for $5,000,000. The $5,000,000 paid to Y constitutes an amount paid to acquire an intangible from Y and must be capitalized.

* * *

(d) Created intangibles—(1) In general. Except as provided in paragraph (f) of this section (relating to the 12–month rule), a taxpayer must capitalize amounts paid to create an intangible described in this paragraph (d). The determination of whether an amount is paid to create an intangible described in this paragraph (d) is to be made based on all of the facts and circumstances, disregarding distinctions between the labels used in this paragraph (d) to describe the intangible and the labels used by the taxpayer and other parties to the transaction.

(2) Financial interests—(i) In general. A taxpayer must capitalize amounts paid to another party to create, originate, enter into, renew or renegotiate with that party any of the following financial interests, whether or not the interest is regularly traded on an established market:

(A) An ownership interest in a corporation, partnership, trust, estate, limited liability company, or other entity.

(B) A debt instrument, deposit, stripped bond, stripped coupon (including a servicing right treated for federal income tax purposes as a stripped coupon), regular interest in a REMIC or FASIT, or any other intangible treated as debt for Federal income tax purposes.

(C) A financial instrument, such as—

(1) A letter of credit;

(2) A credit card agreement;

(3) A notional principal contract;

(4) A foreign currency contract;

(5) A futures contract;

(6) A forward contract (including an agreement under which the taxpayer has the right and obligation to provide or to acquire property (or to be compensated for such property, regardless of whether the taxpayer provides or acquires the property));

(7) An option (including an agreement under which the taxpayer has the right to provide or to acquire property (or to be compensated for such property, regardless of whether the taxpayer provides or acquires the property)); and

* * *

(vi) Examples. The following examples illustrate the rules of this paragraph (d)(2):

Example 1. Loan. X corporation, a commercial bank, makes a loan to A in the principal amount of $250,000. The $250,000 principal amount of the loan paid to A constitutes an amount paid to another party to create a debt instrument with that party under paragraph (d)(2)(i)(B) of this section and must be capitalized.

Example 2. Option. W corporation owns all of the outstanding stock of X corporation. Y corporation pays W $1,000,000 in exchange for W's grant of a 3–year call option to Y permitting Y to purchase all of the outstanding stock of X at a certain price per share. Y's payment of $1,000,000 to W constitutes an amount paid to another party to create an option with that party under paragraph (d)(2)(i)(C)(7) of this section and must be capitalized.

* * *

(3) Prepaid expenses—(i) In general. A taxpayer must capitalize prepaid expenses.

(ii) Examples. The following examples illustrate the rules of this paragraph (d)(3):

Example 1. Prepaid insurance. N corporation, an accrual method taxpayer, pays $10,000 to an insurer to obtain three years of coverage under a property and casualty insurance policy. The $10,000 is a prepaid expense and must be capitalized under this paragraph (d)(3). Paragraph (d)(2) of this section does not apply to the payment because the policy has no cash value.

Example 2. Prepaid rent. X corporation, a cash method taxpayer, enters into a 24–month lease of office space. At the time of the lease signing, X prepays $240,000. No other amounts are due under the lease. The $240,000 is a prepaid expense and must be capitalized under this paragraph (d)(3).

(4) Certain memberships and privileges—(i) In general. A taxpayer must capitalize amounts paid to an organization to obtain, renew, renegotiate, or upgrade a membership or privilege from that organization. A taxpayer is not required to capitalize under this paragraph (d)(4) an amount paid to obtain, renew, renegotiate or upgrade certification of the taxpayer's products, services, or business processes.

(ii) Examples. The following examples illustrate the rules of this paragraph (d)(4):

Example 1. Hospital privilege. B, a physician, pays $10,000 to Y corporation to obtain lifetime staff privileges at a hospital operated by Y. B must capitalize the $10,000 payment under this paragraph (d)(4).

Example 2. Initiation fee. X corporation pays a $50,000 initiation fee to obtain membership in a trade association. X must capitalize the $50,000 payment under this paragraph (d)(4).

Example 3. Product rating. V corporation, an automobile manufacturer, pays W corporation, a national quality ratings association, $100,000 to conduct a study and provide a rating of the quality and safety of a line of V's automobiles. V's payment is an amount paid to obtain a certification of V's product and is not required to be capitalized under this paragraph (d)(4).

Example 4. Business process certification. Z corporation, a manufacturer, seeks to obtain a certification that its quality control standards meet a series of international standards known as ISO 9000. Z pays $50,000 to an independent registrar to obtain a certification from the registrar that Z's quality management system conforms to the ISO 9000 standard. Z's payment is an amount paid to obtain a certification of Z's business processes and is not required to be capitalized under this paragraph (d)(4).

(5) Certain rights obtained from a governmental agency—(i) In general. A taxpayer must capitalize amounts paid to a governmental agency to obtain, renew, renegotiate, or upgrade its rights under a trademark, trade name, copyright, license, permit, franchise, or other similar right granted by that governmental agency.

(ii) Examples. The following examples illustrate the rules of this paragraph (d)(5):

Example 1. Business license. X corporation pays $15,000 to state Y to obtain a business license that is valid indefinitely. Under this paragraph (d)(5), the amount paid to state Y is an amount paid to a government agency for a right granted by that agency. Accordingly, X must capitalize the $15,000 payment.

Example 2. Bar admission. A, an individual, pays $1,000 to an agency of state Z to obtain a license to practice law in state Z that is valid indefinitely, provided A adheres to the requirements governing the practice of law in state Z. Under this paragraph (d)(5), the amount paid to state Z is an amount paid to a government agency for a right granted by that agency. Accordingly, A must capitalize the $1,000 payment.

(6) Certain contract rights—(i) In general. Except as otherwise provided in this paragraph (d)(6), a taxpayer must capitalize amounts paid to another party to create, originate, enter into, renew or renegotiate with that party—

(A) An agreement providing the taxpayer the right to use tangible or intangible property or the right to be compensated for the use of tangible or intangible property;

(B) An agreement providing the taxpayer the right to provide or to receive services (or the right to be compensated for services regardless of whether the taxpayer provides such services);

(C) A covenant not to compete or an agreement having substantially the same effect as a covenant not to compete (except, in the case of an agreement that requires the performance of services, to the extent that the amount represents reasonable compensation for services actually rendered);

(D) An agreement not to acquire additional ownership interests in the taxpayer; or

(E) An agreement providing the taxpayer (as the covered party) with an annuity, an endowment, or insurance coverage.

* * *

(vii) Examples. The following examples illustrate the rules of this paragraph (d)(6):

Example 1. New lease agreement. V seeks to lease commercial property in a prominent downtown location of city R. V pays Z, the owner of the commercial property, $50,000 in exchange for Z entering into a 10–year lease with V. V's payment is an amount paid to another party to enter into an agreement providing V the right to use tangible property. Because the $50,000 payment exceeds $5,000, no portion of the amount paid to Z is de minimis for purposes of paragraph (d)(6)(v) of this section. Under paragraph (d)(6)(i)(A) of this section, V must capitalize the entire $50,000 payment.

* * *

Example 8. Signing bonus. Employer B pays a $25,000 signing bonus to employee C to induce C to come to work for B. C can leave B's employment at any time to work for a competitor of B and is not required to repay the $25,000 bonus to B. Because C is not economically compelled to continue his employment with B, B's payment does not provide B the right to receive services from C. Accordingly, B is not required to capitalize the $25,000 payment.

* * *

(7) Certain contract terminations—(i) In general. A taxpayer must capitalize amounts paid to another party to terminate—

(A) A lease of real or tangible personal property between the taxpayer (as lessor) and that party (as lessee);

(B) An agreement that grants that party the exclusive right to acquire or use the taxpayer's property or services or to conduct the taxpayer's business (other than an intangible described in paragraph (c)(1)(i) through (iv) of this section or a financial interest described in paragraph (d)(2) of this section); or

(C) An agreement that prohibits the taxpayer from competing with that party or from acquiring property or services from a competitor of that party.

* * *

(8) Certain benefits arising from the provision, production, or improvement of real property—(i) In general. A taxpayer must capitalize amounts paid for real property if the taxpayer transfers ownership of the real property to another person (except to the extent the real property is sold for fair market value) and if the real property can reasonably be expected to produce significant economic benefits to the taxpayer after the transfer. A taxpayer also must capitalize amounts paid to produce or improve real property owned by another (except to the extent the taxpayer is selling services at fair market value to produce or improve the real property) if the real property can reasonably be expected to produce significant economic benefits for the taxpayer.

* * *

(9) Defense or perfection of title to intangible property—(i) In general. A taxpayer must capitalize amounts paid to another party to defend or perfect title to intangible property if that other party challenges the taxpayer's title to the intangible property.

* * *

(e) Transaction costs—(1) Scope of facilitate—(i) In general. Except as otherwise provided in this section, an amount is paid to facilitate the acquisition or creation of an intangible (the transaction) if the amount is paid in the process of investigating or otherwise pursuing the transaction. Whether an amount is paid in the process of investigating or otherwise pursuing the transaction is determined based on all of the facts and circumstances. In determining whether an amount is paid to facilitate a transaction, the fact that the amount would (or would not) have been paid but for the transaction is relevant, but is not determinative. An amount paid to determine the value or price of an intangible is an amount paid in the process of investigating or otherwise pursuing the transaction.

(ii) Treatment of termination payments. An amount paid to terminate (or facilitate the termination of) an existing agreement does not facilitate the acquisition or creation of another agreement under this section. See paragraph (d)(6)(iii) of this section for the treatment of termination fees paid to the other party (or parties) of a renegotiated agreement.

(iii) Special rule for contracts. An amount is treated as not paid in the process of investigating or otherwise pursuing the creation of an agreement described in paragraph (d)(2) or (d)(6) of this section if the amount relates to activities performed before the earlier of the date the taxpayer begins preparing its bid for the agreement or the date the taxpayer begins discussing or negotiating the agreement with another party to the agreement.

(2) Coordination with paragraph (d) of this section. In the case of an amount paid to facilitate the creation of an intangible described in paragraph (d) of this section, the provisions of this paragraph (e) apply regardless of whether a payment described in paragraph (d) is made.

(3) Transaction. For purposes of this section, the term transaction means all of the factual elements comprising an acquisition or creation of an intangible and includes a series of steps carried out as part of a single plan. Thus, a transaction can involve more than one invoice and more than one intangible. For example, a purchase of intangibles under one purchase agreement constitutes a single transaction, notwithstanding the fact that the acquisition involves multiple intangibles and the amounts paid to facilitate the acquisition are capable of being allocated among the various intangibles acquired.

(4) Simplifying conventions—(i) In general. For purposes of this section, employee compensation (within the meaning of paragraph (e)(4)(ii) of this section), overhead, and de minimis costs (within the meaning of paragraph (e)(4)(iii) of this section) are treated as amounts that do not facilitate the acquisition or creation of an intangible.

(ii) Employee compensation—(A) In general. The term employee compensation means compensation (including salary, bonuses and commissions) paid to an employee of the taxpayer. For purposes of this section, whether an individual is an employee is determined in accordance with the rules contained in section 3401(c) and the regulations thereunder.

(B) Certain amounts treated as employee compensation. For purposes of this section, a guaranteed payment to a partner in a partnership is treated as employee compensation. For purposes of this section, annual compensation paid to a director of a corporation is treated as employee compensation. For example, an amount paid to a director of a corporation for attendance at a regular meeting of the board of directors (or committee thereof) is treated as employee compensation for purposes of this section. However, an amount paid to a director for attendance at a special meeting of the board of directors (or committee thereof) is not treated as employee compensation. An amount paid to a person that is not an employee of the taxpayer (including the employer of the individual who performs the services) is treated as employee compensation for purposes of this section only if the amount is paid for secretarial, clerical, or similar administrative support services. In the case of an affiliated group of corporations filing a consolidated Federal income tax return, a payment by one member of the group to a second member of the group for services performed by an employee of the second member is treated as employee compensation if the services provided by the employee are provided at a time during which both members are affiliated.

(iii) De minimis costs—(A) In general. Except as provided in paragraph (e)(4)(iii)(B) of this section, the term de minimis costs means amounts (other than employee compensation and overhead) paid in the process of investigating or otherwise pursuing a transaction if, in the aggregate, the amounts do not exceed $5,000 (or such greater amount as may be set forth in published guidance). If the amounts exceed $5,000 (or such greater amount as may be set forth in published guidance), none of the amounts are de minimis costs within the meaning of this paragraph (e)(4)(iii)(A). For purposes of this paragraph (e)(4)(iii), an amount paid in the form of property is valued at its fair market value at the time of the payment. In determining the amount of transaction costs paid in the process of investigating or otherwise pursuing a transaction, a taxpayer generally must account for the specific costs paid with respect to each transaction. However, a taxpayer that reasonably expects to enter into at least 25 similar transactions during the taxable year may establish a pool of similar transactions for purposes of determining the amount of transaction costs paid in the process of investigating or otherwise pursuing the transactions in the pool. Under this pooling method, the amount of transaction costs paid in the process of investigating or otherwise pursuing each transaction included in the pool is equal to the average transaction costs paid in the process of investigating or otherwise pursuing all transactions included in the pool. A taxpayer computes the average transaction costs paid in the process of investigating or otherwise pursuing all transactions included in the pool by dividing the sum of all transaction costs paid in the process of investigating or otherwise pursuing all transactions included in the pool by the number of transactions included in the pool. See paragraph (h) of this section for additional rules relating to pooling.

(B) Treatment of commissions. The term de minimis costs does not include commissions paid to facilitate the acquisition of an intangible described in paragraphs (c)(1)(i) through (v) of this section or to facilitate the creation, origination, entrance into, renewal or renegotiation of an intangible described in paragraph (d)(2)(i) of this section.

* * *

(5) Examples. The following examples illustrate the rules of this paragraph (e):

Example 1. Costs to facilitate. In December 2005, R corporation, a calendar year taxpayer, enters into negotiations with X corporation to lease commercial property from X for a period of 25 years. R pays A, its outside legal counsel, $4,000 in December 2005 for services rendered by A during December in assisting with negotiations with X. In January 2006, R and X finalize the terms of the lease and execute the lease agreement. R pays B, another of its outside legal counsel, $2,000 in January 2006 for services rendered by B during January in drafting the lease agreement. The agreement between R and X is an agreement providing R the right to use property, as described in paragraph (d)(6)(i)(A) of this section. R's payments to its outside counsel are amounts paid to facilitate the creation of the agreement. As provided in paragraph (e)(4)(iii)(A) of this section, R must aggregate its transaction costs for purposes of determining whether the transaction costs are de minimis. Because R's aggregate transaction costs exceed $5,000, R's transaction costs are not de minimis costs within the meaning of paragraph (e)(4)(iii)(A) of this section. Accordingly, R must capitalize the $4,000 paid to A and the $2,000 paid to B under paragraph (b)(1)(v) of this section.

* * *

(f) 12-month rule—(1) In general. Except as otherwise provided in this paragraph (f), a taxpayer is not required to capitalize under this section amounts paid to create (or to facilitate the creation of) any right or benefit for the taxpayer that does not extend beyond the earlier of—

(i) 12 months after the first date on which the taxpayer realizes the right or benefit; or

(ii) The end of the taxable year following the taxable year in which the payment is made.

(2) Duration of benefit for contract terminations. For purposes of this paragraph (f), amounts paid to terminate a contract or other agreement described in paragraph (d)(7)(i) of this section prior to its expiration date (or amounts paid to facilitate such termination) create a benefit for the taxpayer that lasts for the unexpired term of the agreement immediately before the date of the termination. If the terms of a contract or other agreement described in paragraph (d)(7)(i) of this section permit the taxpayer to terminate the contract or agreement after a notice period, amounts paid by the taxpayer to terminate the contract or agreement before the end of the notice period create a benefit for the taxpayer that lasts for the amount of time by which the notice period is shortened.

(3) Inapplicability to created financial interests and self-created amortizable section 197 intangibles. Paragraph (f)(1) of this section does not apply to amounts paid to create (or facilitate the creation of) an intangible described in paragraph (d)(2) of this section (relating to amounts paid to create financial interests) or to amounts paid to create (or facilitate the creation of) an intangible that constitutes an amortizable section 197 intangible within the meaning of section 197(c).

(4) Inapplicability to rights of indefinite duration. Paragraph (f)(1) of this section does not apply to amounts paid to create (or facilitate the creation of) an intangible of indefinite duration. A right has an indefinite duration if it has no period of duration fixed by agreement or by law, or if it is not based on a period of time, such as a right attributable to an agreement to provide or receive a fixed amount of goods or services. For example, a license granted by a governmental agency that permits the taxpayer to operate a business conveys a right of indefinite duration if the license may be revoked only upon the taxpayer's violation of the terms of the license.

(5) Rights subject to renewal—(i) In general. For purposes of paragraph (f)(1) of this section, the duration of a right includes any renewal period if all of the facts and circumstances in existence during the taxable year in which the right is created indicate a reasonable expectancy of renewal.

(ii) Reasonable expectancy of renewal. The following factors are significant in determining whether there exists a reasonable expectancy of renewal:

(A) Renewal history. The fact that similar rights are historically renewed is evidence of a reasonable expectancy of renewal. On the other hand, the fact that similar rights are rarely renewed is evidence of a lack of a reasonable expectancy of renewal. Where the taxpayer has no experience with similar rights, or where the taxpayer holds similar rights only occasionally, this factor is less indicative of a reasonable expectancy of renewal.

(B) Economics of the transaction. The fact that renewal is necessary for the taxpayer to earn back its investment in the right is evidence of a reasonable expectancy of renewal. For example, if a taxpayer pays $14,000 to enter into a renewable contract with an initial 9–month term that is expected to generate income to the taxpayer of $1,000 per month, the fact that renewal is necessary for the taxpayer to earn back its $14,000 payment is evidence of a reasonable expectancy of renewal.

(C) Likelihood of renewal by other party. Evidence that indicates a likelihood of renewal by the other party to a right, such as a bargain renewal option or similar arrangement, is evidence of a reasonable expectancy of renewal. However, the mere fact that the other party will have the opportunity to renew on the same terms as are available to others is not evidence of a reasonable expectancy of renewal.

(D) Terms of renewal. The fact that material terms of the right are subject to renegotiation at the end of the initial term is evidence of a lack of a reasonable expectancy of renewal. For example, if the parties to an agreement must renegotiate price or amount, the renegotiation requirement is evidence of a lack of a reasonable expectancy of renewal.

(E) Terminations. The fact that similar rights are typically terminated prior to renewal is evidence of a lack of a reasonably expectancy of renewal.

(iii) Safe harbor pooling method. In lieu of applying the reasonable expectancy of renewal test described in paragraph (f)(5)(ii) of this section to each separate right created during a taxable year, a taxpayer that reasonably expects to enter into at least 25 similar rights during the taxable year may establish a pool of similar rights for which the initial term does not extend beyond the period prescribed in paragraph (f)(1) of this section and may elect to apply the reasonable expectancy of renewal test to that pool. See paragraph (h) of this section for additional rules relating to pooling. * * *

* * *

(6) Coordination with section 461. In the case of a taxpayer using an accrual method of accounting, the rules of this paragraph (f) do not affect the determination of whether a liability is incurred during the taxable year, including the determination of whether economic performance has occurred with respect to the liability. See § 1.461–4 for rules relating to economic performance.

(7) Election to capitalize. A taxpayer may elect not to apply the rule contained in paragraph (f)(1) of this section. An election made under this paragraph (f)(7) applies to all similar transactions during the taxable year to which paragraph (f)(1) of this section would apply (but for the election under this paragraph (f)(7)). For example, a taxpayer may elect under this paragraph (f)(7) to capitalize its costs of prepaying insurance contracts for 12 months, but may continue to apply the rule in paragraph (f)(1) to its costs of entering into nonrenewable, 12–month service contracts. A taxpayer makes the election by treating the amounts as capital expenditures in its timely filed original federal income tax return (including extensions) for the taxable year during which the amounts are paid. In the case of an affiliated group of corporations filing a consolidated return, the election is made separately with respect to each member of the group, and not with respect to the group as a whole. In the case of an S corporation or partnership, the election is made by the S corporation or by the partnership, and not by the shareholders or partners. An election made under this paragraph (f)(7) is revocable with respect to each taxable year for which made only with the consent of the Commissioner.

(8) Examples. The rules of this paragraph (f) are illustrated by the following examples, in which it is assumed (unless otherwise stated) that the taxpayer is a calendar year, accrual method taxpayer that does not have a short taxable year in any taxable year and has not made an election under paragraph (f)(7) of this section:

Example 1. Prepaid expenses. On December 1, 2005, N corporation pays a $10,000 insurance premium to obtain a property insurance policy (with no cash value) with a 1–year term that begins on February 1, 2006. The amount paid by N is a prepaid expense described in paragraph (d)(3) of this section and not paragraph (d)(2) of this section. Because the right or benefit attributable to the $10,000 payment extends beyond the end of the taxable year following the taxable year in which the payment is made, the 12–month rule provided by this paragraph (f) does not apply. N must capitalize the $10,000 payment.

Example 2. Prepaid expenses. (i) Assume the same facts as in Example 1, except that the policy has a term beginning on December 15, 2005. The 12–month rule of this paragraph (f) applies to the $10,000 payment because the right or benefit attributable to the payment neither extends more than 12 months beyond December 15, 2005 (the first date the benefit is realized by the taxpayer) nor beyond the end of the taxable year following the taxable year in which the payment is made. Accordingly, N is not required to capitalize the $10,000 payment.

(ii) Alternatively, assume N capitalizes prepaid expenses for financial accounting and reporting purposes and elects under paragraph (f)(7) of this section not to apply the 12–month rule contained in paragraph (f)(1) of this section. N must capitalize the $10,000 payment for Federal income tax purposes.

* * *

Example 10. Coordination with section 461. **(i)** U corporation leases office space from W corporation at a monthly rental rate of $2,000. On August 1, 2005, U prepays its office rent expense for the first six months of 2006 in the amount of $12,000. For purposes of this example, it is assumed that the recurring item exception provided by § 1.461–5 does not apply and that the lease between W and U is not a section 467 rental agreement as defined in section 467(d).

(ii) Under § 1.461–4(d)(3), U's prepayment of rent is a payment for the use of property by U for which economic performance occurs ratably over the period of time U is entitled to use the property. Accordingly, because economic performance with respect to U's prepayment of rent does not occur until 2006, U's prepaid rent is not incurred in 2005 and therefore is not properly taken into account through capitalization, deduction, or otherwise in 2005. Thus, the rules of this paragraph (f) do not apply to U's prepayment of its rent.

(iii) Alternatively, assume that U uses the cash method of accounting and the economic performance rules in § 1.461–4 therefore do not apply to U. The 12–month rule of this paragraph (f) applies to the $12,000 payment because the rights or benefits attributable to U's prepayment of its rent do not extend beyond December 31, 2006. Accordingly, U is not required to capitalize its prepaid rent.

Example 11. Coordination with section 461. N corporation pays R corporation, an advertising and marketing firm, $40,000 on August 1, 2005, for advertising and marketing services to be provided to N throughout calendar year 2006. For purposes of this example, it is assumed that the recurring item exception provided by § 1.461–5 does not apply. Under § 1.461–4(d)(2), N's payment arises out of the provision of services to N by R for which economic performance occurs as the services are provided. Accordingly, because economic performance with respect to N's prepaid advertising expense does not occur until 2006, N's prepaid advertising expense is not incurred in 2005 and therefore is not properly taken into account through capitalization, deduction, or otherwise in 2005. Thus, the rules of this paragraph (f) do not apply to N's payment.

(g) Treatment of capitalized costs—(1) In general. An amount required to be capitalized by this section is not currently deductible under section 162. Instead, the amount generally is added to the basis of the intangible acquired or created. See section 1012.

* * *

(h) Special rules applicable to pooling—(1) In general. Except as otherwise provided, the rules of this paragraph (h) apply to the pooling methods described in paragraph (d)(6)(v) of this section (relating to de minimis rules applicable to certain contract rights), paragraph (e)(4)(iii)(A) of this section (relating to de minimis rules applicable to transaction costs), and paragraph (f)(5)(iii) of this section (relating to the application of the 12–month rule to renewable rights).

(2) Method of accounting. A pooling method authorized by this section constitutes a method of accounting for purposes of section 446. A taxpayer that adopts or changes to a pooling method authorized by this section must use the method for the year of adoption and for all subsequent taxable years during which the taxpayer qualifies to use the pooling method unless a change to another method is required by the Commissioner in order to clearly reflect income, or unless permission to change to another method is granted by the Commissioner as provided in § 1.446–1(e).

(3) Adopting or changing to a pooling method. A taxpayer adopts (or changes to) a pooling method authorized by this section for any taxable year by establishing one or more pools for the taxable year in accordance with the rules governing the particular pooling method and the rules prescribed by this paragraph (h), and by using the pooling method to compute its taxable income for the year of adoption (or change).

(4) Definition of pool. A taxpayer may use any reasonable method of defining a pool of similar transactions, agreements or rights, including a method based on the type of customer or the type of product or service provided under a contract. However, a taxpayer that pools similar transactions, agreements or rights must include in the pool all similar transactions, agreements or rights created during the taxable year. For purposes of the pooling methods described in paragraph (d)(6)(v) of this section (relating to de minimis rules applicable to certain contract rights) and paragraph (e)(4)(iii)(A) of this section (relating to de minimis rules applicable to transaction costs), an agreement (or a transaction) is treated as not similar to other agreements (or transactions) included in the pool if the amount at issue with respect to that agreement (or transaction) is reasonably expected to differ significantly from the average amount at issue with respect to the other agreements (or transactions) properly included in the pool.

* * *

[T.D. 9107, 69 FR 435, Jan. 5, 2004]

§ 1.263(a)–5 Amounts paid or incurred to facilitate an acquisition of a trade or business, a change in the capital structure of a business entity, and certain other transactions.

(a) General rule. A taxpayer must capitalize an amount paid to facilitate (within the meaning of paragraph (b) of this section) each of the following transactions, without regard to whether the transaction is comprised of a single step or a series of steps carried out as part of a single plan and without regard to whether gain or loss is recognized in the transaction:

(1) An acquisition of assets that constitute a trade or business (whether the taxpayer is the acquirer in the acquisition or the target of the acquisition).

(2) An acquisition by the taxpayer of an ownership interest in a business entity if, immediately after the acquisition, the taxpayer and the business entity are related within the meaning of section 267(b) or 707(b) (see § 1.263(a)–4 for rules requiring capitalization of amounts paid by the taxpayer to acquire an ownership interest in a business entity, or to facilitate the acquisition of an ownership interest in a business entity, where the taxpayer and the business entity are not related within the meaning of section 267(b) or 707(b) immediately after the acquisition).

(3) An acquisition of an ownership interest in the taxpayer (other than an acquisition by the taxpayer of an ownership interest in the taxpayer, whether by redemption or otherwise).

(4) A restructuring, recapitalization, or reorganization of the capital structure of a business entity (including reorganizations described in section 368 and distributions of stock by the taxpayer as described in section 355).

(5) A transfer described in section 351 or section 721 (whether the taxpayer is the transferor or transferee).

(6) A formation or organization of a disregarded entity.

(7) An acquisition of capital.

(8) A stock issuance.

(9) A borrowing. For purposes of this section, a borrowing means any issuance of debt, including an issuance of debt in an acquisition of capital or in a recapitalization. A borrowing also includes debt issued in a debt for debt exchange under § 1.1001–3.

(10) Writing an option.

(b) Scope of facilitate—(1) In general. Except as otherwise provided in this section, an amount is paid to facilitate a transaction described in paragraph (a) of this section if the amount is paid in the process of investigating or otherwise pursuing the transaction. Whether an amount is paid in the process of investigating or otherwise pursuing the transaction is determined based on all of the facts and circumstances. In determining whether an amount is paid to facilitate a transaction, the fact that the amount would (or would not) have been paid but for the transaction is relevant, but is not determinative. An amount paid to determine the value or price of a transaction is an amount paid in the process of investigating or otherwise pursuing the transaction. An amount paid to another party in exchange for tangible or intangible property is not an amount paid to facilitate the exchange. For example, the purchase price paid to the target of an asset acquisition in exchange for its assets is not an amount paid to facilitate the acquisition. Similarly, the purchase price paid by an acquirer to the target's shareholders in exchange for their stock in a stock acquisition is not an amount paid to facilitate the acquisition of the stock. See § 1.263(a)–1, § 1.263(a)–2, and § 1.263(a)–4 for rules requiring capitalization of the purchase price paid to acquire property.

(2) Ordering rules. An amount paid in the process of investigating or otherwise pursuing both a transaction described in paragraph (a) of this section and an acquisition or creation of an intangible described in § 1.263(a)–4 is subject to the rules contained in this section, and not to the rules contained in § 1.263(a)–4. In addition, an amount required to be capitalized by § 1.263(a)–1, § 1.263(a)–2, or § 1.263(a)–4 does not facilitate a transaction described in paragraph (a) of this section.

(c) Special rules for certain costs—(1) Borrowing costs. An amount paid to facilitate a borrowing does not facilitate another transaction (other than the borrowing) described in paragraph (a) of this section.

(2) Costs of asset sales. An amount paid by a taxpayer to facilitate a sale of its assets does not facilitate another transaction (other than the sale) described in paragraph (a) of this section. For example, where a target corporation, in preparation for a merger with an acquiring corporation, sells assets that are not desired by the acquiring corporation, amounts paid to facilitate the sale of the unwanted assets are not required to be capitalized as amounts paid to facilitate the merger.

(3) Mandatory stock distributions. An amount paid in the process of investigating or otherwise pursuing a distribution of stock by a taxpayer to its shareholders does not facilitate a transaction described in paragraph (a) of this section if the divestiture of the stock (or of properties transferred to an entity whose stock is distributed) is required by law, regulatory mandate, or court order. A taxpayer is not required to capitalize (under this section or § 1.263(a)–4) an amount paid to organize (or facilitate the organization of) an entity if the entity is organized solely to receive properties that the taxpayer is required to divest by law, regulatory mandate, or court order and if the taxpayer distributes the stock of the entity to its shareholders. A taxpayer also is not required to capitalize (under this section or § 1.263(a)–4) an amount paid to transfer property to an entity if the taxpayer is required to divest itself of that property by law, regulatory mandate, or court order and if the stock of the recipient entity is distributed to the taxpayer's shareholders.

* * *

(d) Simplifying conventions—(1) In general. For purposes of this section, employee compensation (within the meaning of paragraph (d)(2) of this section), overhead, and de minimis costs (within the meaning of paragraph (d)(3) of this section) are treated as amounts that do not facilitate a transaction described in paragraph (a) of this section.

(2) Employee compensation—(i) In general. The term employee compensation means compensation (including salary, bonuses and commissions) paid to an employee of the taxpayer. For purposes of this section, whether an individual is an employee is determined in accordance with the rules contained in section 3401(c) and the regulations thereunder.

(ii) Certain amounts treated as employee compensation. For purposes of this section, a guaranteed payment to a partner in a partnership is treated as employee compensation. For purposes of this section, annual compensation paid to a director of a corporation is treated as employee compensation. For example, an amount paid to a director of a corporation for attendance at a regular meeting of the board of directors (or committee thereof) is treated as employee compensation for purposes of this section. However, an amount paid to the director for attendance at a special meeting of the board of directors (or committee thereof) is not treated as employee compensation. An amount paid to a person that is not an employee of the taxpayer (including the employer of the individual who performs the services) is treated as employee compensation for purposes of this section only if the amount is paid for secretarial, clerical, or similar administrative support services (other than services involving the preparation and distribution of proxy solicitations and other documents seeking shareholder approval of a transaction described in paragraph (a) of this section). In the case of an affiliated group of corporations filing a consolidated federal income tax return, a payment by one member of the group to a second member of the group for services performed by an employee of the second member is treated as employee compensation if the services provided by the employee are provided at a time during which both members are affiliated.

(3) De minimis costs—(i) In general. The term de minimis costs means amounts (other than employee compensation and overhead) paid in the process of investigating or otherwise pursuing a transaction described in paragraph (a) of this section if, in the aggregate, the amounts do not exceed $5,000 (or such greater amount as may be set forth in published guidance). If the amounts exceed $5,000 (or such greater amount as may be set forth in published guidance), none of the amounts are de minimis costs within the meaning of this paragraph (d)(3). For purposes of this paragraph (d)(3), an amount paid in the form of property is valued at its fair market value at the time of the payment.

(ii) Treatment of commissions. The term de minimis costs does not include commissions paid to facilitate a transaction described in paragraph (a) of this section.

* * *

(e) Certain acquisitive transactions—(1) In general. Except as provided in paragraph (e)(2) of this section (relating to inherently facilitative amounts), an amount paid by the taxpayer in the process of investigating or otherwise pursuing a covered transaction (as described in paragraph (e)(3) of this section) facilitates the transaction within the meaning of this section only if the amount relates to activities performed on or after the earlier of—

(i) The date on which a letter of intent, exclusivity agreement, or similar written communication (other than a confidentiality agreement) is executed by representatives of the acquirer and the target; or

(ii) The date on which the material terms of the transaction (as tentatively agreed to by representatives of the acquirer and the target) are authorized or approved by the taxpayer's board of directors (or committee of the board of directors) or, in the case of a taxpayer that is not a corporation, the date on which the material terms of the transaction (as tentatively agreed to by representatives of the acquirer and the target) are authorized or approved by the appropriate governing officials of the taxpayer. In the case of a transaction that does not require authorization or approval of the taxpayer's board of directors (or appropriate governing officials in the case of a taxpayer that is not a corporation) the date determined under this paragraph (e)(1)(ii) is the date on which the acquirer and the target execute a binding written contract reflecting the terms of the transaction.

(2) Exception for inherently facilitative amounts. An amount paid in the process of investigating or otherwise pursuing a covered transaction facilitates that transaction if the amount is inherently facilitative, regardless of whether the amount is paid for activities performed prior to the date determined under paragraph (e)(1) of this section. An amount is inherently facilitative if the amount is paid for—

(i) Securing an appraisal, formal written evaluation, or fairness opinion related to the transaction;

(ii) Structuring the transaction, including negotiating the structure of the transaction and obtaining tax advice on the structure of the transaction (for example, obtaining tax advice on the application of section 368);

(iii) Preparing and reviewing the documents that effectuate the transaction (for example, a merger agreement or purchase agreement);

(iv) Obtaining regulatory approval of the transaction, including preparing and reviewing regulatory filings;

(v) Obtaining shareholder approval of the transaction (for example, proxy costs, solicitation costs, and costs to promote the transaction to shareholders); or

(vi) Conveying property between the parties to the transaction (for example, transfer taxes and title registration costs).

(3) Covered transactions. For purposes of this paragraph (e), the term covered transaction means the following transactions:

(i) A taxable acquisition by the taxpayer of assets that constitute a trade or business.

(ii) A taxable acquisition of an ownership interest in a business entity (whether the taxpayer is the acquirer in the acquisition or the target of the acquisition) if, immediately after the acquisition, the acquirer and the target are related within the meaning of section 267(b) or 707(b).

(iii) A reorganization described in section 368(a)(1)(A), (B), or (C) or a reorganization described in section 368(a)(1)(D) in which stock or securities of the corporation to which the assets are transferred are distributed in a transaction which qualifies under section 354 or 356 (whether the taxpayer is the acquirer or the target in the reorganization).

* * *

(*l*) Examples. The following examples illustrate the rules of this section:

* * *

Example 4. Corporate acquisition. (i) On February 1, 2005, R corporation decides to investigate the acquisition of three potential targets: T corporation, U corporation, and V corporation. R's consideration of T, U, and V represents the consideration of three distinct transactions, any or all of which R might consummate and has the financial ability to consummate. On March 1, 2005, R enters into an exclusivity agreement with T and stops pursuing U and V. On July 1, 2005, R acquires all of the stock of T in a transaction described in section 368. R pays $1,000,000 to an investment banker and $50,000 to its outside counsel to conduct due diligence on T, U, and V; determine the value of T, U, and V; negotiate and structure the transaction with T; draft the merger agreement; secure shareholder approval; prepare SEC filings; and obtain the necessary regulatory approvals.

(ii) Under paragraph (e)(1) of this section, the amounts paid to conduct due diligence on T, U and V prior to March 1, 2005 (the date of the exclusivity agreement) are not amounts paid to facilitate the acquisition of the stock of T, U or V and are not required to be capitalized under this section. However, the amounts paid to conduct due diligence on T on and after March 1, 2005, are amounts paid to facilitate the acquisition of the stock of T and must be capitalized under paragraph (a)(2) of this section.

(iii) Under paragraph (e)(2) of this section, the amounts paid to determine the value of T, negotiate and structure the transaction with T, draft the merger agreement, secure shareholder approval, prepare SEC filings, and obtain necessary regulatory approvals are inherently facilitative amounts paid to facilitate the acquisition of the stock of T and must be capitalized, regardless of whether those activities occur prior to, on, or after March 1, 2005.

(iv) Under paragraph (e)(2) of this section, the amounts paid to determine the value of U and V are inherently facilitative amounts paid to facilitate the acquisition of U or V and must be capitalized. Because the acquisition of U, V, and T are not mutually exclusive transactions, the costs that facilitate the acquisition of U and V do not facilitate the acquisition of T. Accordingly, the amounts paid to determine the value of U and V may be recovered under section 165 in the taxable year that R abandons the planned mergers with U and V.

* * *

Example 11. Corporate acquisition; defensive measures. (i) On January 15, 2005, Y corporation, a publicly traded corporation, becomes the target of a hostile takeover attempt by Z corporation. In an effort to defend against the takeover, Y pays legal fees to seek an injunction against the takeover and investment banking fees to locate a potential "white knight" acquirer. Y also pays amounts to complete a defensive recapitalization, and pays $50,000 to an investment banker for a fairness opinion regarding Z's initial offer. Y's efforts to enjoin the takeover and locate a white knight acquirer are unsuccessful, and on March 15, 2005, Y's board of directors decides to abandon its defense against the takeover and negotiate with Z in an effort to obtain the highest possible price for its shareholders. After Y abandons its defense against the takeover, Y pays an investment banker $1,000,000 for a second fairness opinion and for services rendered in negotiating with Z.

(ii) The legal fees paid by Y to seek an injunction against the takeover are not amounts paid in the process of investigating or otherwise pursuing the transaction with Z. Accordingly, these legal fees are not required to be capitalized under this section.

(iii) The investment banking fees paid to search for a white knight acquirer do not facilitate an acquisition of Y by a white knight because none of Y's costs with respect to a white knight were inherently facilitative amounts and because Y did not reach the date described in paragraph (e)(1) of this section with respect to a white knight. Accordingly, these amounts are not required to be capitalized under this section.

(iv) The amounts paid by Y to investigate and complete the recapitalization must be capitalized under paragraph (a)(4) of this section.

(v) The $50,000 paid to the investment bankers for a fairness opinion during Y's defense against the takeover and the $1,000,000 paid to the investment bankers after Y abandons its defense against the takeover are inherently facilitative amounts with respect to the transaction with Z and must be capitalized under paragraph (a)(3) of this section.

Example 12. Corporate acquisition; acquisition by white knight. (i) Assume the same facts as in Example 11, except that Y's investment bankers identify three potential white knight acquirers: U corporation, V corporation, and W corporation. Y pays its investment bankers to conduct due diligence on the three potential white knight acquirers. On March 15, 2005, Y's board of directors approves a tentative acquisition agreement under which W agrees to acquire all of the stock of Y, and the investment bankers stop due diligence on U and V. On June 15, 2005, W acquires all of the stock of Y.

(ii) Under paragraph (e)(1) of this section, the amounts paid to conduct due diligence on U, V, and W prior to March 15, 2005 (the date of board of directors' approval) are not amounts paid to facilitate the acquisition of the stock of Y and are not required to be capitalized under this section. However, the amounts paid to conduct due diligence on W on and after March 15, 2005, facilitate the acquisition of the stock of Y and are required to be capitalized.

* * *

[T.D. 9170, 69 FR 435, Jan. 5, 2004]

§ 1.267(a)–1 Deductions disallowed.

(a) Losses. Except in cases of distributions in corporate liquidations, no deduction shall be allowed for losses arising from direct or indirect sales or exchanges of property between persons who, on the date of the sale or exchange, are within any one of the relationships specified in section 267(b). See § 1.267(b)–1.

* * *

(c) Scope of section. Section 267(a) requires that deductions for losses or unpaid expenses or interest described therein be disallowed even though the transaction in which such losses, expenses, or interest were incurred was a bona fide transaction. However, section 267 is not exclusive. No deduction for losses or unpaid expenses or interest arising in a transaction which is not bona fide will be allowed even though section 267 does not apply to the transaction.

[T.D. 6500, 25 FR 11402, Nov. 26, 1960]

§ 1.267(a)–2T Questions and answers arising under the Tax Reform Act of 1984.

* * *

(b) Questions applying section 267(a)(2) and (b) generally. The following questions and answers deal with the application of section 267(a)(2) and (b) generally:

* * *

Question 2: Does section 267(a)(2) ever apply to defer the deduction of otherwise deductible original issue discount as defined in sections 163(e) and 1271 through 1275 ("the OID rules")?

Answer 2: No. Regardless of when payment is made, an amount owed to a lender that constitutes original issue discount is included in the income of the lender periodically in accordance with the OID rules. Similarly, section 267(a)(2) does not apply to defer an otherwise deductible amount to the extent section 467 or section 7872 requires periodic inclusion of such amount in the income of the person to whom payment is to be made, even though payment has not been made.

Question 3: Does section 267(a)(2) ever apply to defer the deduction of otherwise deductible unstated interest determined to exist under section 483?

Answer 3: Yes. If section 483 recharacterizes any amount as unstated interest and the other requirements of section 267(a)(2) are met, a deduction for such unstated interest will be deferred under section 267.

Question 4: Does section 267(a)(2) ever apply to defer the deduction of otherwise deductible cost recovery, depreciation, or amortization?

Answer 4: Yes, in certain cases. In general, section 267(a)(2) does not apply to defer the deduction of otherwise deductible cost recovery, depreciation, or amortization. Notwithstanding this general rule, if the other requirements of section 267(a)(2) are met, section 267(a)(2) does apply to defer deductions for cost recovery, depreciation, or amortization of an amount owed to a related person for interest or rent or for the performance or nonperformance of services, which amount the taxpayer payor capitalized or treated as a deferred expense (unless the taxpayer payor elected to capitalize or defer the amount and section 267(a)(2) would not have deferred the deduction of such amount if the taxpayer payor had not so elected). Amounts owed for services that may be subject to this provision include, for example, amounts owed for acquisition, development, or organizational services or for covenants not to compete. In applying this rule, payments made between persons described in any of the paragraphs of section 267(b) (as modified by section 267(e)) will be closely scrutinized to determine whether they are made in respect of capitalized costs (or costs treated as deferred expenses) that are subject to deferral under section 267(a)(2), or in respect of other capitalized costs not so subject.

Question 5: If a deduction in respect of an otherwise deductible amount is deferred by section 267(a)(2) and, prior to the time the amount is includible in the gross income of the person to whom payment is to be made, such person and the payor taxpayer cease to be persons specified in any of the paragraphs of section 267(b) (as modified by section 267(e)), is the deduction allowable as of the day on which the relationship ceases?

Answer 5: No. The deduction is not allowable until the day as of which the amount is includible in the gross income of the person to whom payment of the amount is made, even though the relationship ceases to exist at an earlier time.

* * *

(c) Questions applying section 267(a) to partnerships. The following questions and answers deal with the application of section 267(a) to partnerships:

Question 1: Does section 267(a) disallow losses and defer otherwise deductible amounts at the partnership (entity) level?

Answer 1: Yes. If a loss realized by a partnership from a sale or exchange of property is disallowed under section 267(a)(1), that loss shall not enter into the computation of the partnership's taxable income. If an amount that otherwise would be deductible by a partnership is deferred by section 267(a)(2), that amount shall not enter into the computation of the partnership's taxable income until the taxable year of the partnership in which falls the day on which the amount is includible in the gross income of the person to whom payment of the amount is made.

Question 2: Does section 267(a)(1) ever apply to disallow a loss if the sale or exchange giving rise to the loss is between two partnerships even though the two partnerships are not persons specified in any of the paragraphs of section 267(b)?

Answer 2: Yes. If the other requirements of section 267(a)(1) are met, section 267(a)(1) applies to such losses arising as a result of transactions entered into after December 31, 1984 between partnerships not described in any of the paragraphs of section 267(b) as follows, and § 1.267(b)–1(b) does not apply. If the two partnerships have one or more common partners (*i.e.*, if any person owns directly, indirectly, or constructively any capital or profits interest in each of such partnerships), or if any partner in either partnership and one or more partners in the other partnership are persons specified in any of the paragraphs of section 267(b) (without modification by section 267(e)), a portion of the selling partnership's loss will be disallowed under section 267(a)(1). The amount disallowed under this rule is the greater of: (1) The amount that would be disallowed if the transaction giving rise to the loss had occurred between the selling partnership and the separate partners of the purchasing partnership (in proportion to their respective interests in the purchasing partnership); or (2) the amount that would be disallowed if such transaction had occurred between the separate partners of the selling partnership (in proportion to their respective interests in the selling partnership) and the purchasing partnership. Notwithstanding the general rule of this paragraph (c) Answer 2, no disallowance shall occur if the amount that would be disallowed pursuant to the immediately preceding sentence is less than 5 percent of the loss arising from the sale or exchange.

Question 3: Does section 267(a)(2) ever apply to defer an otherwise deductible amount if the taxpayer payor is a partnership and the person to whom payment of such amount is to be made is a partnership even though the two partnerships are not persons specified in any of the paragraphs of section 267(b) (as modified by section 267(e))?

Answer 3: Yes. If the other requirements of section 267(a)(2) are met, section 267(a)(2) applies to such amounts arising as a result of transactions entered into after December 31, 1984 between partnerships not described in any of the paragraphs of section 267(b) (as modified by section 267(e)) as follows, and § 1.267(b)–1(b) does not apply. If the two partnerships have one or more common partners (*i.e.*, if any person owns directly, indirectly, or constructively any capital or profits interest in each of such partnerships), or if any partner in either partnership and one or more partners in the other partnership are persons specified in any of the paragraphs of section 267(b) (without modification by section 267(e)), a portion of the payor partnership's otherwise allowable deduction will be deferred under section 267(a)(2). The amount deferred under this rule is the greater of: (1) The amount that would be deferred if the transaction giving rise to the otherwise allowable deduction had occurred between the payor partnership and the separate partners of the payee partnership (in proportion to their respective interests in the payee partnership); or (2) the amount that would be deferred if such transaction had occurred between the separate partners of the payor partnership (in proportion to their respective interests in the payor partnership) and the payee partnership. Notwithstanding the general rule of this paragraph (c) Answer 3, no deferral shall occur if the amount that would be deferred pursuant to the immediately preceding sentence is less than 5 percent of the otherwise allowable deduction.

Example. On May 1, 1985, partnership AB enters into a transaction whereby it accrues an otherwise deductible amount to partnership AC. AC is on the cash receipts and disbursements method of accounting. A holds a 5 percent capital and profits interest in AB and a 49 percent capital and profits interest in AC, and A's interest in each item of the income, gain, loss, deduction, and credit of each partnership is 5 percent and 49 percent, respectively. B and C are not related. Notwithstanding that AB and AC are not persons specified in section 267(b), 49 percent of the deduction in respect of such amount will be deferred under section 267(a)(2). The result would be the same if A held a 49 percent interest in AB and a 5 percent interest in AC. However, if A held more than 50 percent of the capital or profits interest of either AB or AC, the entire deduction in respect of such amount would be deferred under section 267(a)(2).

* * *

[T.D. 7991, 49 FR 46995, Nov. 30, 1984]

§ 1.267(b)–1 Relationships.

[Note: Section 267(a)(2) has been amended to defer a deduction by an accrual method taxpayer. The following regulation does not reflect that amendment. Ed.]

* * *

(b) Partnerships. **(1)** Since section 267 does not include members of a partnership and the partnership as related persons, transactions between partners and partnerships do not come within the scope of section 267. Such transactions are governed by section 707 for the purposes of which the partnership is considered to be an entity separate from the partners. See section 707 and § 1.707–1. Any transaction described in section 267(a) between a partnership and a person other than a partner shall be considered as occurring between the other person and the members of the partnership separately. Therefore, if the other person and a partner are within any one of the relationships specified in section 267(b), no deductions with respect to such transactions between the other person and the partnership shall be allowed—

(i) To the related partner to the extent of his distributive share of partnership deductions for losses or unpaid expenses or interest resulting from such transactions, and

(ii) To the other person to the extent the related partner acquires an interest in any property sold to or exchanged with the partnership by such other person at a loss, or to the extent of the related partner's distributive share of the unpaid expenses or interest payable to the partnership by the other person as a result of such transaction.

(2) The provisions of this paragraph may be illustrated by the following examples:

Example (1). A, an equal partner in the ABC partnership, personally owns all the stock of M Corporation. B and C are not related to A. The partnership and all the partners use an accrual method of accounting, and are on a calendar year. M Corporation uses the cash receipts and disbursements method of accounting and is also on a calendar year. During 1956 the partnership borrowed money from M Corporation and also sold property to M Corporation, sustaining a loss on the sale. On December 31, 1956, the partnership accrued its interest liability to the M Corporation and on April 1, 1957 (more than 2½ months after the close of its taxable year), it paid the M Corporation the amount of such accrued interest. Applying the rules of this paragraph, the transactions are considered as occurring between M Corporation and the partners separately. The sale and interest transactions considered as occurring between A and the M Corporation fall within the scope of section 267(a) and (b), but the transactions considered as occurring between partners B and C and the M Corporation do not. The latter two partners may, therefore, deduct their distributive shares of partnership deductions for the loss and the accrued interest. However, no deduction shall be allowed to A for his distributive shares of these partnership deductions. Furthermore, A's adjusted basis for his partnership interest must be decreased by the amount of his distributive share of such deductions. See section 705(a)(2).

Example (2). Assume the same facts as in example (1) of this subparagraph except that the partnership and all the partners use the cash receipts and disbursements method of accounting, and that M Corporation uses an accrual method. Assume further, that during 1956 M Corporation borrowed money from the partnership and that on a sale of property to the partnership during that year M Corporation sustained a loss. On December 31, 1956, the M Corporation accrued its interest liability on the borrowed money and on April 1, 1957 (more than 2½ months after the close of its taxable year) it paid the accrued interest to the partnership. The corporation's deduction for the accrued interest is not allowed to the extent of A's distributive share (one-third) of such interest income. M Corporation's deduction for the loss on the sale of the property to the partnership is not allowed to the extent of A's one-third interest in the purchased property.

[T.D. 6500, 25 FR 11402, Nov. 26, 1960]

§ 1.267(c)–1 Constructive ownership of stock.

(a) In general. (1) The determination of stock ownership for purposes of section 267(b) shall be in accordance with the rules in section 267(c).

(2) For an individual to be considered under section 267(c)(2) as constructively owning the stock of a corporation which is owned, directly or indirectly, by or for members of his family it is not necessary that he own stock in the corporation either directly or indirectly. On the other hand, for an individual to be considered under section 267(c)(3) as owning the stock of a corporation owned either actually, or constructively under section 267(c)(1), by or for his partner, such individual must himself actually own, or constructively own under section 267(c)(1), stock of such corporation.

(3) An individual's constructive ownership, under section 267(c)(2) or (3), of stock owned directly or indirectly by or for a member of his family, or by or for his partner, is not to be considered as actual ownership of such stock, and the individual's constructive ownership of the stock is not to be attributed to another member of his family or to another partner. However, an individual's constructive ownership, under section 267(c)(1), of stock owned directly or indirectly by or for a corporation, partnership, estate, or trust shall be considered as actual ownership of the stock, and the individual's ownership may be attributed to a member of his family or to his partner.

(4) The family of an individual shall include only his brothers and sisters, spouse, ancestors, and lineal descendants. In determining whether any of these relationships exist, full effect shall be given to a legal adoption. The term "ancestors" includes parents and grandparents, and the term "lineal descendants" includes children and grandchildren.

(b) Examples. The application of section 267(c) may be illustrated by the following examples:

Example (1). On July 1, 1957, A owned 75 percent, and AW, his wife, owned 25 percent, of the outstanding stock of the M Corporation. The M Corporation in turn owned 80 percent of the outstanding stock of the O Corporation. Under section 267(c)(1), A and AW are each considered as owning an amount of the O Corporation stock actually owned by M Corporation in proportion to their respective ownership of M Corporation stock. Therefore, A constructively owns 60 percent (75 percent of 80 percent) of the O Corporation stock and AW constructively owns 20 percent (25 percent of 80 percent) of such stock. Under the family ownership rule of section 267(c)(2), an individual is considered as constructively owning the stock actually owned by his spouse. A and AW, therefore, are each considered as constructively owning the M Corporation stock actually owned by the other. For the purpose of applying this family ownership rule, A's and AW's constructive ownership of O Corporation stock is considered as actual ownership under section 267(c)(5). Thus, A constructively owns the 20 percent of the O Corporation stock constructively owned by AW, and AW constructively owns the 60 percent of the O Corporation stock constructively owned by A. In addition, the family ownership rule may be applied to make AWF, AW's father, the constructive owner of the 25 percent of the M Corporation stock actually owned by AW. As noted above, AW's constructive ownership of 20 percent of the O Corporation stock is considered as actual ownership for purposes of applying the family ownership rule, and AWF is thereby considered the constructive owner of this stock also. However, AW's constructive ownership of the stock constructively and actually owned by A may not be considered as actual ownership for the purpose of again applying the family ownership rule to make AWF the constructive owner of these shares. The ownership of the stock in the M and O Corporations may be tabulated as follows:

Person	Stock ownership in M Corporation		Total under Section 267 (Percent)	Stock ownership in O Corporation		Total under Section 267 (Percent)
	Actual (Percent)	Constructive (Percent)		Actual (Percent)	Constructive (Percent)	
A	75	25	100	None	60–20	80
AW(A's wife)	25	75	100	None	20–60	80
AWF(AW's father)	None	25	25	None	20	20
M Corporation	......	......	......	80	None	80
O Corporation	None	None	None	......	......	......

Assuming that the M Corporation and the O Corporation make their income tax returns for calendar years, and that there was no distribution in liquidation of the M or O Corporation, and further assuming that other corporation was a personal holding company under section 542 for the calendar year 1956, no deduction is allowable with respect to losses from sales or exchanges of property made on July 1, 1957, between the two corporations. Moreover, whether or not either corporation was a personal holding company, no loss would be allowable on a sale or exchange between A or AW and either corporation. A deduction would be allowed, however, for a loss sustained in an arm's length sale or exchange between A and AWF, and between AWF and the M or O Corporation.

Example (2). On June 15, 1957, all of the stock of the N Corporation was owned in equal proportions by A and his partner, AP. Except in the case of distributions in liquidation by the N Corporation, no deduction is allowable with respect to losses from sales or exchanges of property made on June 15, 1957, between A and the N Corporation or AP and the N Corporation since each partner is considered as owning the stock owned by the other; therefore, each is considered as owning more than 50 percent in value of the outstanding stock of the N Corporation.

Example (3). On June 7, 1957, A owned no stock in X Corporation, but his wife, AW, owned 20 percent in value of the outstanding stock of X, and A's partner, AP, owned 60 percent in value of the outstanding stock of X. The partnership firm of A and AP owned no stock in X Corporation. The ownership of AW's stock is attributed to A, but not that of AP since A does not own any X Corporation stock either actually, or constructively under section 267(c)(1). A's constructive ownership of AW's stock is not the ownership required for the attribution of AP's stock. Therefore, deductions for losses from sales or exchanges of property made on June 7, 1957, between X Corporation and A or AW are allowable since neither person owned more than 50 percent in value of the outstanding stock of X, but deductions for losses from sales or exchanges between X Corporation and AP would not be allowable by section 267(a) (except for distributions in liquidation of X Corporation).

[T.D. 6500, 25 FR 11402, Nov. 26, 1960]

§ 1.267(d)–1 Amount of gain where loss previously disallowed.

(a) General rule. **(1)** If a taxpayer acquires property by purchase or exchange from a transferor who, on the transaction, sustained a loss not allowable as a deduction by reason of section 267(a)(1) * * *, then any gain realized by the taxpayer on a sale or other disposition of the property after December 31, 1953, shall be recognized only to the extent that the gain exceeds the amount of such loss as is properly allocable to the property sold or otherwise disposed of by the taxpayer.

(2) The general rule is also applicable to a sale or other disposition of property by a taxpayer when the basis of such property in the taxpayer's hands is determined directly or indirectly by reference to other property acquired by the taxpayer from a transferor through a sale or exchange in which a loss sustained by the transferor was not allowable. Therefore, section 267(d) applies to a sale or other disposition of property after a series of transactions if the basis of the property acquired in each transaction is determined by reference to the basis of the property transferred, and if the original property was acquired in a transaction in which a loss to a transferor was not allowable by reason of section 267(a)(1) * * *.

(3) The benefit of the general rule is available only to the original transferee but does not apply to any original transferee (*e.g.*, a donee) who acquired the property in any manner other than by purchase or exchange.

(4) The application of the provisions of this paragraph may be illustrated by the following examples:

Example (1). H sells to his wife, W, for $500, certain corporate stock with an adjusted basis for determining loss to him of $800. The loss of $300 is not allowable to H by reason of section 267(a)(1) and paragraph (a) of § 1.267(a)–1. W later sells this stock for $1,000. Although W's realized gain is $500 ($1,000 minus $500, her basis), her recognized gain under section 267(d) is only $200, the excess of the realized gain of $500 over the loss of $300 not allowable to H. In determining capital gain or loss W's holding period commences on the date of the sale from H to W.

Example (2). Assume the same facts as in example (1) except that W later sells her stock for $300 instead of $1,000. Her recognized loss is $200 and not $500 since section 267(d) applies only to the nonrecognition of gain and does not affect basis.

Example (3). Assume the same facts as in example (1) except that W transfers her stock as a gift to X. The basis of the stock in the hands of X for the purpose of determining gain, under the provisions of section 1015, is the same as W's, or $500. If X later sells the stock for $1,000 the entire $500 gain is taxed to him.

Example (4). H sells to his wife, W, for $5,500, farmland, with an adjusted basis for determining loss to him of $8,000. The loss of $2,500 is not allowable to H by reason of section 267(a)(1) and paragraph (a) of § 1.267(a)–1. W exchanges the farmland, held for investment purposes, with S, an unrelated individual, for two city lots, also held for investment purposes. The basis of the city lots in the hands of W ($5,500) is a substituted basis determined under section 1031(d) by reference to the basis of the farmland. Later W sells the city lots for $10,000. Although W's realized gain is $4,500 ($10,000 minus $5,500), her recognized gain under section 267(d) is only $2,000, the excess of the realized gain of $4,500 over the loss of $2,500 not allowable to H.

(b) Determination of basis and gain with respect to divisible property—(1) Taxpayer's basis. When the taxpayer acquires divisible property or property that consists of several items or classes of items by a purchase or exchange on which loss is not allowable to the transferor, the basis in the taxpayer's hands of a particular part, item, or class of such property shall be determined (if the taxpayer's basis for that part is not known) by allocating to the particular part, item, or class a portion of the taxpayer's basis for the entire property in the proportion that the fair market value of the particular part, item, or class bears to the fair market value of the entire property at the time of the taxpayer's acquisition of the property.

(2) Taxpayer's recognized gain. Gain realized by the taxpayer on sales or other dispositions after December 31, 1953, of a part, item, or class of the property shall be recognized only to the extent that such gain exceeds the amount of loss attributable to such part, item, or class of property not allowable to the taxpayer's transferor on the latter's sale or exchange of such property to the taxpayer.

(3) Transferor's loss not allowable. (i) The transferor's loss on the sale or exchange of a part, item, or class of the property to the taxpayer shall be the excess of the transferor's adjusted basis for determining loss on the part, item, or class of the property over the amount realized by the transferor on the sale or exchange of the part, item, or class. The amount realized by the transferor on the part, item, or class shall be determined (if such amount is not known) in the same manner that the taxpayer's basis for such part, item, or class is determined. See subparagraph (1) of this paragraph.

(ii) If the transferor's basis for determining loss on the part, item, or class cannot be determined, the transferor's loss on the particular part, item, or class transferred to the taxpayer shall be determined by allocating to the part, item, or class a portion of his loss on the entire property in the proportion that the fair market value of such part, item, or class bears to the fair market value of the entire property on the date of the taxpayer's acquisition of the entire property.

* * *

(c) Special rules. (1) Section 267(d) does not affect the basis of property for determining gain. Depreciation and other items which depend on such basis are also not affected.

(2) The provisions of section 267(d) shall not apply if the loss sustained by the transferor is not allowable to the transferor as a deduction by reason of section 1091, * * *, which relate to losses from wash sales of stock or securities.

(3) In determining the holding period in the hands of the transferee of property received in an exchange with a transferor with respect to whom a loss on the exchange is not allowable by reason of section 267, section 1223(2) does not apply to include the period during which the property was held by the transferor. In determining such holding period, however, section 1223(1) may apply to include the period during which the transferee held the property which he exchanged where, for example, he exchanged a capital asset in a transaction which, as to him, was nontaxable under section 1031 and the property received in the exchange has the same basis as the property exchanged.

[T.D. 6500, 25 FR 11402, Nov. 26, 1960]

§ 1.274–1 Disallowance of certain entertainment, gift and travel expenses.

Section 274 disallows in whole, or in part, certain expenditures for entertainment, gifts and travel which would otherwise be allowable under chapter 1 of the Code. The requirements imposed by section 274 are in addition to the requirements for deductibility imposed by other provisions of the Code. If a deduction is claimed for an expenditure for entertainment, gifts, or travel, the taxpayer must first establish that it is otherwise allowable as a deduction under chapter 1 of the Code before the provisions of section 274 become applicable. An expenditure for entertainment, to the extent it is lavish or extravagant, shall not be allowable as a deduction.

The taxpayer should then substantiate such an expenditure in accordance with the rules under section 274(d). * * * Section 274 is a disallowance provision exclusively, and does not make deductible any expense which is disallowed under any other provision of the Code. Similarly, section 274 does not affect the includibility of an item in, or the excludability of an item from, the gross income of any taxpayer. * * *

[T.D. 6659, 28 FR 6499, June 25, 1963; as amended by T.D. 8666, 61 FR 27005, May 30, 1996]

§ 1.274–2 Disallowance of deductions for certain expenses for entertainment, amusement, recreation, or trust.

(a) General rules—(1) Entertainment activity. Except as provided in this section, no deduction otherwise allowable under chapter 1 of the Code shall be allowed for any expenditure with respect to entertainment unless the taxpayer establishes—

(i) That the expenditure was directly related to the active conduct of the taxpayer's trade or business, or

(ii) In the case of an expenditure directly preceding or following a substantial and bona fide business discussion (including business meetings at a convention or otherwise), that the expenditure was associated with the active conduct of the taxpayer's trade or business.

Such deduction shall not exceed the portion of the expenditure directly related to (or in the case of an expenditure described in subdivision (ii) of this subparagraph, the portion of the expenditure associated with) the active conduct of the taxpayer's trade or business.

(2) Entertainment facilities. (i) * * *

* * *

(iii) Expenditures paid or incurred after December 31, 1993, with respect to a club—(a) In general. No deduction otherwise allowable under chapter 1 of the Internal Revenue Code shall be allowed for amounts paid or incurred after December 31, 1993, for membership in any club organized for business, pleasure, recreation, or other social purpose. The purposes and activities of a club, and not its name, determine whether it is organized for business, pleasure, recreation, or other social purpose. Clubs organized for business, pleasure, recreation, or other social purpose include any membership organization if a principal purpose of the organization is to conduct entertainment activities for members of the organization or their guests or to provide members or their guests with access to entertainment facilities within the meaning of paragraph (e)(2) of this section. Clubs organized for business, pleasure, recreation, or other social purpose include, but are not limited to, country clubs, golf and athletic clubs, airline clubs, hotel clubs, and clubs operated to provide meals under circumstances generally considered to be conducive to business discussion.

(b) Exceptions. Unless a principal purpose of the organization is to conduct entertainment activities for members or their guests or to provide members or their guests with access to entertainment facilities, business leagues, trade associations, chambers of commerce, boards of trade, real estate boards, professional organizations (such as bar associations and medical associations), and civic or public service organizations will not be treated as clubs organized for business, pleasure, recreation, or other social purpose.

* * *

(b) Definitions—(1) Entertainment defined—(i) In general. For purposes of this section, the term "entertainment" means any activity which is of a type generally considered to constitute entertainment, amusement, or recreation, such as entertaining at night clubs, cocktail lounges, theaters, country clubs, golf and athletic clubs, sporting events, and on hunting, fishing, vacation and similar trips, including such activity relating solely to the taxpayer or the taxpayer's family. The term "entertainment" may include an activity, the cost of which is claimed as a business expense by the taxpayer, which satisfies the personal, living, or family needs of any individual, such as providing food and beverages, a hotel suite, or an automobile to a business customer or his family. The term "entertainment" does not include activities which, although satisfying personal, living, or family needs of an individual, are clearly not regarded as constituting entertainment, such as (a) supper money provided by an employer to his employee working overtime, (b) a hotel room maintained by an employer for lodging of his employees while in business travel status, or (c) an automobile used in the active conduct of trade or business even though used for routine personal purposes such as commuting to and from work. On the other hand, the providing of a hotel room or an automobile by an employer to his employee who is on vacation would constitute entertainment of the employee.

(ii) Objective test. An objective test shall be used to determine whether an activity is of a type generally considered to constitute entertainment. Thus, if an activity is generally considered to be entertainment, it will constitute entertainment for purposes of this section and section 274(a) regardless of whether the expenditure can also be described otherwise, and even though the expenditure relates to the taxpayer alone. This objective test precludes arguments such as that "entertainment" means only entertainment of others or that an expenditure for entertainment should be characterized as an expenditure for advertising or public relations. However, in applying this test the taxpayer's trade or business shall be considered. Thus, although attending a theatrical performance would generally be considered entertainment, it would not be so considered in the case of a professional theater critic, attending in his professional capacity. Similarly, if a manufacturer of dresses conducts a fashion show to introduce his products to a group of store buyers, the show would not be generally considered to constitute entertainment. However, if an appliance distributor conducts a fashion show for the wives of his retailers, the fashion show would be generally considered to constitute entertainment.

(iii) Special definitional rules—(a) In general. Except as otherwise provided in (b) or (c) of this subdivision, any expenditure which might generally be considered either for a gift or entertainment, or considered either for travel or entertainment, shall be considered an expenditure for entertainment rather than for a gift or travel.

(b) Expenditures deemed gifts. An expenditure described in (a) of this subdivision shall be deemed for a gift to which this section does not apply if it is:

(1) An expenditure for packaged food or beverages transferred directly or indirectly to another person intended for consumption at a later time.

(2) An expenditure for tickets of admission to a place of entertainment transferred to another person if the taxpayer does not accompany the recipient to the entertainment unless the taxpayer treats the expenditure as entertainment. The taxpayer may change his treatment of such an expenditure as either a gift or entertainment at any time within the period prescribed for assessment of tax as provided in section 6501 of the Code and the regulations thereunder.

(3) Such other specific classes of expenditure generally considered to be for a gift as the Commissioner, in his discretion, may prescribe.

* * *

(c) Directly related entertainment—(1) In general. Except as otherwise provided in paragraph (d) of this section (relating to associated entertainment) or under paragraph (f) of this section (relating to business meals and other specific exceptions), no deduction shall be allowed for any expenditure for entertainment unless the taxpayer establishes that the expenditure was directly related to the active conduct of his trade or business within the meaning of this paragraph.

(2) Directly related entertainment defined. Any expenditure for entertainment, if it is otherwise allowable as a deduction under chapter 1 of the Code, shall be considered directly related to the active conduct of the taxpayer's trade or business if it meets the requirements of any one of subparagraphs (3), (4), (5), or (6) of this paragraph.

(3) Directly related in general. Except as provided in subparagraph (7) of this paragraph, an expenditure for entertainment shall be considered directly related to the active conduct of the taxpayer's trade or business if it is established that it meets all of the requirements of subdivisions (i), (ii), (iii) and (iv) of this subparagraph.

(i) At the time the taxpayer made the entertainment expenditure (or committed himself to make the expenditure), the taxpayer had more than a general expectation of deriving some income or other specific trade or business benefit (other than the goodwill of the person or persons entertained) at some indefinite future time from the making of the expenditure. A taxpayer, however, shall not be required to show that income or other business benefit actually resulted from each and every expenditure for which a deduction is claimed.

(ii) During the entertainment period to which the expenditure related, the taxpayer actively engaged in a business meeting, negotiation, discussion, or other bona fide business transaction, other than entertainment, for the purpose of obtaining such income or other specific trade or business benefit (or, at the time the taxpayer made the expenditure or committed himself to the expenditure, it was reasonable for the taxpayer to expect that he would have done so, although such was not the case solely for reasons beyond the taxpayer's control).

(iii) In light of all the facts and circumstances of the case, the principal character or aspect of the combined business and entertainment to which the expenditure related was the active conduct of the taxpayer's trade or business (or at the time the taxpayer made the expenditure or committed himself to the expenditure, it was reasonable for the taxpayer to expect that the active conduct of trade or business would have been the principal character or aspect of the entertainment, although such was not the case solely for reasons beyond the taxpayer's control). It is not necessary that more time be devoted to business than to entertainment to meet this requirement. The active conduct of trade or business is considered not to be the principal character or aspect of combined business and entertainment activity on hunting or fishing trips or on yachts and other pleasure boats unless the taxpayer clearly establishes to the contrary.

(iv) The expenditure was allocable to the taxpayer and a person or persons with whom the taxpayer engaged in the active conduct of trade or business during the entertainment or with whom the taxpayer establishes he would have engaged in such active conduct of trade or business if it were not for circumstances beyond the taxpayer's control. For expenditures closely connected with directly related entertainment, see paragraph (d)(4) of this section.

(4) Expenditures in clear business setting. An expenditure for entertainment shall be considered directly related to the active conduct of the taxpayer's trade or business if it is established that the expenditure was for entertainment occurring in a clear business setting directly in furtherance of the taxpayer's trade or business. Generally, entertainment shall not be considered to have occurred in a clear business setting unless the taxpayer clearly establishes that any recipient of the entertainment would have reasonably known that the taxpayer had no significant motive, in incurring the expenditure, other than directly furthering his trade or business. Objective rather than subjective standards will be determinative. Thus, entertainment which occurred under any circumstances described in subparagraph (7)(ii) of this paragraph ordinarily will not be considered as occurring in a clear business setting. Such entertainment will generally be considered to be socially rather than commercially motivated. Expenditures made for the furtherance of a taxpayer's trade or business in providing a "hospitality room" at a convention (described in paragraph (d)(3)(i)(b) of this section) at which goodwill is created through display or discussion of the taxpayer's products, will, however, be treated as directly related. In addition, entertainment of a clear business nature which occurred under circumstances where there was no meaningful personal or social relationship between the taxpayer and the recipients of the entertainment may be considered to have occurred in a clear business setting. For example, entertainment of business representatives and civic leaders at the opening of a new hotel or theatrical production, where the clear purpose of the taxpayer is to obtain business publicity rather than to create or maintain the goodwill of the recipients of the entertainment, would generally be considered to be in a clear business setting. Also, entertainment which has the principal effect of a price rebate in connection with the sale of the taxpayer's products generally will be considered to have occurred in a clear business setting. Such would be the case, for example, if a taxpayer owning a hotel were to provide occasional free dinners at the hotel for a customer who patronized the hotel.

* * *

(7) Expenditures generally considered not directly related. Expenditures for entertainment, even if connected with the taxpayer's trade or business, will generally be considered not directly related to the active conduct of the taxpayer's trade or business, if the entertainment occurred under circumstances where there was little or no possibility of engaging in the active conduct of trade or business. The following circumstances will generally be considered circumstances where there was little or no possibility of engaging in the active conduct of a trade or business:

(i) The taxpayer was not present;

(ii) The distractions were substantial, such as—

(a) A meeting or discussion at night clubs, theaters, and sporting events, or during essentially social gatherings such as cocktail parties, or

(b) A meeting or discussion, if the taxpayer meets with a group which includes persons other than business associates, at places such as cocktail lounges, country clubs, golf and athletic clubs, or at vacation resorts.

An expenditure for entertainment in any such case is considered not to be directly related to the active conduct of the taxpayer's trade or business unless the taxpayer clearly establishes to the contrary.

(d) Associated entertainment—(1) In general. Except as provided in paragraph (f) of this section (relating to business meals and other specific exceptions) and subparagraph (4) of this paragraph (relating to expenditures closely connected with directly related entertainment), any expenditure for entertainment which is not directly related to the active conduct of the taxpayer's trade or business will not be allowable as a deduction unless—

(i) It was associated with the active conduct of trade or business as defined in subparagraph (2) of this paragraph, and

(ii) The entertainment directly preceded or followed a substantial and bona fide business discussion as defined in subparagraph (3) of this paragraph.

(2) Associated entertainment defined. Generally, any expenditure for entertainment, if it is otherwise allowable under chapter 1 of the Code, shall be considered associated with the active conduct of the taxpayer's trade or business if the taxpayer establishes that he had a clear business purpose in making the expenditure, such as to obtain new business or to encourage the continuation of an existing business relationship. However, any portion of an expenditure allocable to a person who was not closely connected with a person who engaged in the substantial and bona fide business discussion (as defined in subparagraph (3)(i) of this paragraph) shall not be considered associated with the active conduct of the taxpayer's trade or business. The portion of an expenditure allocable to the spouse of a person who engaged in the discussion will, if it is otherwise allowable under chapter 1 of the Code, be considered associated with the active conduct of the taxpayer's trade or business.

(3) Directly preceding or following a substantial and bona fide business discussion defined—(i) Substantial and bona fide business discussion—(a) In general. Whether any meeting, negotiation or discussion constitutes a "substantial and bona fide business discussion" within the meaning of this section depends upon the facts and circumstances of each case. It must be established, however, that the taxpayer actively engaged in a business meeting, negotiation, discussion, or other bona fide business transaction, other than entertainment, for the purpose of obtaining income or other specific trade or business benefit. In addition, it must be established that such a business meeting, negotiation, discussion, or transaction was substantial in relation to the entertainment. This requirement will be satisfied if the principal character or aspect of the combined entertainment and business activity was the active conduct of business. However, it is not necessary that more time be devoted to business than to entertainment to meet this requirement.

(b) Meetings at conventions, etc. Any meeting officially scheduled in connection with a program at a convention or similar general assembly, or at a bona fide trade or business meeting sponsored and conducted by business or professional organizations, shall be considered to constitute a substantial and bona fide business discussion within the meaning of this section provided—

(1) Expenses necessary to taxpayer's attendance. The expenses necessary to the attendance of the taxpayer at the convention, general assembly, or trade or business meeting, were ordinary and necessary within the meaning of section 162 or 212;

(2) Convention program. The organization which sponsored the convention, or trade or business meeting had scheduled a program of business activities (including committee meetings or presentation of lectures, panel discussions, display of products, or other similar activities), and that such program was the principal activity of the convention, general assembly, or trade or business meeting.

(ii) Directly preceding or following. Entertainment which occurs on the same day as a substantial and bona fide business discussion (as defined in subdivision (i) of this subparagraph) will be considered to directly precede or follow such discussion. If the entertainment and the business discussion do not occur on the same day, the facts and circumstances of each case are to be considered, including the place, date and duration of the business discussion, whether the taxpayer or his business associates are from out of town, and, if so, the date of arrival and departure, and the reasons the entertainment did not take place on the day of the business discussion. For example, if a group of business associates comes from out of town to the taxpayer's place of business to hold a substantial business discussion, the entertainment of such business guests and their wives on the evening prior to, or on the evening of the day following, the business discussion would generally be regarded as directly preceding or following such discussion.

(4) Expenses closely connected with directly related entertainment. If any portion of an expenditure meets the requirements of paragraph (c)(3) of this section (relating to directly related entertainment in general), the remaining portion of the expenditure, if it is otherwise allowable under chapter 1 of the Code, shall be considered associated with the active conduct of the taxpayer's trade or business to the extent allocable to a person or persons closely connected with a person referred to in paragraph (c)(3)(iv) of this section. The spouse of a person referred to in paragraph(c)(3)(iv) of this section will be considered closely connected to such a person for purposes of this subparagraph. Thus, if a taxpayer and his wife entertain a business customer and the customer's wife under circumstances where the entertainment of the customer is considered directly related to the active conduct of the taxpayer's trade or business (within the meaning of paragraph (c)(3) of this section) the portion of the expenditure allocable to both wives will be considered associated with the active conduct of the taxpayer's trade or business under this subparagraph.

* * *

(f) Specific exceptions to application of this section—(1) In general. The provisions of paragraphs (a) through (e) of this section (imposing limitations on deductions for entertainment expenses) are not applicable in the case of expenditures set forth in subparagraph (2) of this paragraph. Such expenditures are deductible to the extent allowable under chapter 1 of the Code. This paragraph shall not be construed to affect the allowability or nonallowability of a deduction under section 162 or 212 and the regulations thereunder. The fact that an expenditure is not covered by a specific exception provided for in this paragraph shall not be determinative of the allowability or nonallowability of the expenditure under paragraphs (a) through (e) of this section. Expenditures described in subparagraph (2) of this paragraph are subject to the substantiation requirements of section 274(d) * * *.

(2) Exceptions. The expenditures referred to in subparagraph (1) of this paragraph are set forth in subdivision (i) through (ix) of this subparagraph.

* * *

(ii) Food and beverages for employees. Any expenditure by a taxpayer for food and beverages (or for use of a facility in connection therewith) furnished on the taxpayer's business premises primarily for his employees is not subject to the limitations on allowability of deductions provided for in paragraphs (a) through (e) of this section. This exception applies not only to expenditures for food or beverages furnished in a typical company cafeteria or an executive dining room, but also to expenditures with respect to the operation of such facilities. This exception applies even though guests are occasionally served in the cafeteria or dining room.

* * *

(iv) Reimbursed entertainment expenses—(a) Introductory. In the case of any expenditure for entertainment paid or incurred by one person in connection with the performance by him of services for another person (whether or not such other person is an employer) under a reimbursement or other expense allowance arrangement, the limitations on allowability of deductions provided for in paragraphs (a) through (e) of this section shall be applied only once, either (1) to the person who makes the expenditure or (2) to the person who actually bears the expense, but not to both. For purposes of this subdivision (iv), the term "reimbursement or other expense allowance arrangement" has the same meaning as it has in section 62(2)(A), but without regard to whether the taxpayer is the employee of a person for whom services are performed. If an expenditure of a type described in this subdivision properly constitutes a dividend paid to a shareholder, unreasonable compensation paid to an employee, or a personal, living or family expense, nothing in this exception prevents disallowance of the expenditure to the taxpayer under other provisions of the Code.

(b) Reimbursement arrangements between employee and employer. In the case of an expenditure for entertainment paid or incurred by an employee under a reimbursement or other expense allowance arrangement with his employer, the limitations on deductions provided for in paragraphs (a) through (e) of this section shall not apply—

(1) Employees. To the employee except to the extent his employer has treated the expenditure on the employer's income tax return as originally filed as compensation paid to the employee and as wages to such employee for purposes of withholding under chapter 24 (relating to collection of income tax at source on wages).

(2) Employers. To the employer to the extent he has treated the expenditure as compensation and wages paid to an employee in the manner provided in (b)(1) of this subdivision.

* * *

(v) Recreational expenses for employees generally. Any expenditure by a taxpayer for a recreational, social, or similar activity (or for use of a facility in connection therewith), primarily for the benefit of his employees generally, is not subject to the limitations on allowability of deductions provided for in paragraphs (a) through (e) of this section. This exception applies only to expenditures made primarily for the benefit of employees of the taxpayer other than employees who are officers, shareholders or other owners who own a 10-percent or greater interest in the business, or other highly compensated employees. For purposes of the preceding sentence, an employee shall be treated as owning any interest owned by a member of his family (within the meaning of section 267(c)(4) and the regulations thereunder). Ordinarily, this exception applies to usual employee benefit programs such as expenses of a taxpayer (a) in holding Christmas parties, annual picnics, or summer outings, for his employees generally, or (b) of maintaining a swimming pool, baseball diamond, bowling alley, or golf course available to his employees generally. Any expenditure for an activity which is made under circumstances which discriminate in favor of employees who are officers, shareholders or other owners, or highly compensated employees shall not be considered made primarily for the benefit of employees generally. On the other hand, an expenditure for an activity will not be considered outside of this exception merely because, due to the large number of employees involved, the activity is intended to benefit only a limited number of such employees at one time, provided the activity does not discriminate in favor of officers, shareholders, other owners, or highly compensated employees.

(vi) Employee, stockholder, etc. business meetings. Any expenditure by a taxpayer for entertainment which is directly related to bona fide business meetings of the taxpayer's employees, stockholders, agents, or directors held principally for discussion of trade or business is not subject to the limitations on allowability of deductions provided for in paragraphs (a) through (e) of this section. For purposes of this exception, a partnership is to be considered a taxpayer and a member of a partnership is to be considered an agent. For example, an expenditure by a taxpayer to furnish refreshments to his employees at a bona fide meeting, sponsored by the taxpayer for the principal purpose of instructing them with respect to a new procedure for conducting his business, would be within provisions of this exemption. A similar expenditure made at a bona fide meeting of stockholders of the taxpayer for the election of directors and discussion of corporate affairs would also be within the provisions of this exception. While this exception will apply to bona fide business meetings even though some social activities are provided, it will not apply to meetings which are primarily for social or nonbusiness purposes rather than for the transaction of the taxpayer's business. A meeting under circumstances where there was little or no possibility of engaging in the active conduct of trade or business (as described in paragraph (c)(7) of this section) generally will not be considered a business meeting for purposes of this subdivision. This exception will not apply to a meeting or convention of employees or agents, or similar meeting for directors, partners or others for the principal purpose of rewarding them for their services to the taxpayer. However, such a meeting or convention of employees might come within the scope of subdivisions (iii) or (v) of this subparagraph.

* * *

[T.D. 6659, 28 FR 6499, June 25, 1963, as amended by T.D. 6996, 34 FR 835, Jan. 13, 1969; T.D. 8051, 50 FR 36576, Sept. 9, 1985; T.D. 8601, 60 FR 36993, July 19, 1995; T.D. 8666, 61 FR 27005, May 30, 1996]

§ 1.274–4 Disallowance of certain foreign travel expenses.

* * *

(c) Travel in excess of 1 week. This section does not apply to an expense of travel unless the expense is for travel outside the United States away from home which exceeds 1 week. For purposes of this section, 1 week means 7 consecutive days. The day in which travel outside the United States away from home begins shall not be considered, but the day in which such travel ends shall be considered, in determining whether a taxpayer is outside the United States away from home for more than 7 consecutive days. For example, if a taxpayer departs on travel outside the United States away from home on a Wednesday morning and ends such travel the following Wednesday evening, he shall be considered as being outside the United States away from home only 7 consecutive days. In such a case, this section would not apply because the taxpayer was not outside the United States away from home for more than 7 consecutive days. However, if the taxpayer travels outside the United States away from home for more than 7 consecutive days, both the day such travel begins and the day such travel ends shall be considered a "business day" or a "nonbusiness day", as the case may be, for purposes of determining whether nonbusiness activity constituted 25 percent or more of travel time under paragraph (d) of this section and for purposes of allocating expenses under paragraph (f) of this section. For purposes of determining whether travel is outside the United States away from home, see paragraph (e) of this section.

(d) Nonbusiness activity constituting 25 percent or more of travel time—(1) In general. This section does not apply to any expense of travel outside the United States away from home unless the portion of time outside the United States away from home attributable to nonbusiness activity constitutes 25 percent or more of the total time on such travel.

(2) Allocation on per day basis. The total time traveling outside the United States away from home will be allocated on a day-by-day basis to (i) days of business activity or (ii) days of nonbusiness activity (hereinafter termed "business days" or "nonbusiness days" respectively) unless the taxpayer establishes that a different method of allocation more clearly reflects the portion of time outside the United States away from home which is attributable to nonbusiness activity. For purposes of this section, a day spent outside the United States away from home shall be deemed entirely a business day even though spent only in part on business activity if the taxpayer establishes—

(i) Transportation days. That on such day the taxpayer was traveling to or returning from a destination outside the United States away from home in the pursuit of trade or business. However, if for purposes of engaging in nonbusiness activity, the taxpayer while traveling outside the United States away from home does not travel by a reasonably direct route, only that number of days shall be considered business days as would be required for the taxpayer, using the same mode of transportation, to travel to or return from the same destination by a reasonably direct route. Also, if, while so traveling, the taxpayer interrupts the normal course of travel by engaging in substantial diversions for nonbusiness reasons of his own choosing, only that number of days shall be considered business days as equals the number of days required for the taxpayer, using the same mode of transportation, to travel to or return from the same destination without engaging in such diversion. For example, if a taxpayer residing in New York departs on an evening on a direct flight to Quebec for a business meeting to be held in Quebec the next morning, for purposes of determining whether nonbusiness activity constituted 25 percent or more of his travel time, the entire day of his departure shall be considered a business day. On the other hand, if a taxpayer travels by automobile from New York to Quebec to attend a business meeting and while en route spends 2 days in Ottawa and 1 day in Montreal on nonbusiness activities of his personal choice, only that number of days outside the United States shall be considered business days as would have been required for the taxpayer to drive by a reasonably direct route to Quebec, taking into account normal periods for rest and meals.

(ii) Presence required. That on such day his presence outside the United States away from home was required at a particular place for a specific and bona fide business purpose. For example, if a taxpayer is instructed by his employer to attend a specific business meeting, the day of the meeting shall be considered a business day even though, because of the scheduled length of the meeting, the taxpayer spends more time during normal working hours of the day on nonbusiness activity than on business activity.

(iii) Days primarily business. That during hours normally considered to be appropriate for business activity, his principal activity on such day was the pursuit of trade or business.

(iv) Circumstances beyond control. That on such day he was prevented from engaging in the conduct of trade or business as his principal activity due to circumstances beyond his control.

(v) Weekends, holidays, etc. That such day was a Saturday, Sunday, legal holiday, or other reasonably necessary standby day which intervened during that course of the taxpayer's trade or business while outside the United States away from home which the taxpayer endeavored to conduct with reasonable dispatch. For example, if a taxpayer travels from New York to London to take part in business negotiations beginning on a Wednesday and concluding on the following Tuesday, the intervening Saturday and Sunday shall be considered business days whether or not business is conducted on either of such days. Similarly, if in the above case the meetings which concluded on Tuesday evening were followed by business meetings with another business group in London on the immediately succeeding Thursday and Friday, the intervening Wednesday will be deemed a business day. However, if at the conclusion of the business meetings on Friday, the taxpayer stays in London for an additional week for personal purposes, the Saturday and Sunday following the conclusion of the business meeting will not be considered business days.

* * *

(g) Examples. The application of this section may be illustrated by the following examples:

* * *

Example (7). Taxpayer G flew from Chicago to New York where he spent 6 days on business. He then flew to London where he conducted business for 2 days. G then flew to Paris for a 5 day vacation after which he flew back to Chicago, with a scheduled landing in New York for the purpose of adding and discharging passengers. G would not have made the trip except for the business he had to conduct in London. The travel outside the United States away from home, including 2 days for travel en route, exceeded a week and the time devoted to nonbusiness activities was not less than 25 percent of the total time on such travel. The 2 days spent traveling from Chicago to New York and return, and the 6 days spent in New York are disregarded for purposes of determining whether the travel outside the United States away from home exceeded a week and whether the time devoted to nonbusiness activities was less than 25 percent of the total time outside the United States away from home. If G is unable to establish either that he did not have substantial control over the arranging of the business trip or that an opportunity for taking a personal vacation was not a major consideration in his determining to make the trip, 5/9ths (5 days devoted to nonbusiness activities out of a total 9 days outside the United States away from home on the trip) of the expenses attributable to transportation and food from New York to London and from London to New York will be disallowed (unless G establishes that a different method of allocation more clearly reflects the portion of time outside the United States away from home which is attributable to nonbusiness activity).

* * *

[T.D. 6659, 28 FR 6505, June 24, 1963, as amended by T.D. 6758, 29 FR 12768, Sept. 10, 1964]

§ 1.274–5 Substantiation requirements.

(a) and (b) [Reserved]. For further guidance, see § 1.274–5T(a) and (b).

(c) Rules of substantiation—(1) [Reserved]. For further guidance, see § 1.274–5T(c)(1).

(2) Substantiation by adequate records—(i) and (ii) [Reserved]. For further guidance, see § 1.274–5T(c)(2)(i) and (ii).

(iii) Documentary evidence—(A) Except as provided in paragraph (c)(2)(iii)(B), documentary evidence, such as receipts, paid bills, or similar evidence sufficient to support an expenditure, is required for—

(1) Any expenditure for lodging while traveling away from home, and

(2) Any other expenditure of $75 or more except, for transportation charges, documentary evidence will not be required if not readily available.

(B) The Commissioner, in his or her discretion, may prescribe rules waiving the documentary evidence requirements in circumstances where it is impracticable for such documentary evidence to be required. Ordinarily, documentary evidence will be considered adequate to support an expenditure if it includes sufficient information to establish the amount, date, place, and the essential character of the expenditure. For example, a hotel receipt is sufficient to support expenditures for business travel if it contains the following: name, location, date, and separate amounts for charges such as for lodging, meals, and telephone. Similarly, a restaurant receipt is sufficient to support an expenditure for a business meal if it contains the following: name and location of the restaurant, the date and amount of the expenditure, the number of people served, and, if a charge is made for an item other than meals and beverages, an indication that such is the case. A document may be indicative of only one (or part of one) element of an expenditure. Thus, a canceled check, together with a bill from the payee, ordinarily would establish the element of cost. In contrast, a canceled check drawn payable to a named payee would not by itself support a business expenditure without other evidence showing that the check was used for a certain business purpose.

* * *

(f) Reporting and substantiation of expenses of certain employees for travel, entertainment, gifts, and with respect to listed property—(1) through (3) [Reserved]. For further guidance, see § 1.274–5T(f)(1) through (3).

* * *

(g) Substantiation by reimbursement arrangements or per diem, mileage, and other traveling allowances—(1) In general. The Commissioner may, in his or her discretion, prescribe rules in pronouncements of general applicability under which allowances for expenses described in paragraph (g)(2) of this section will, if in accordance with reasonable business practice, be regarded as equivalent to substantiation by adequate records or other sufficient evidence, for purposes of paragraph (c) of this section, of the amount of the expenses and as satisfying, with respect to the amount of the expenses, the requirements of an adequate accounting to the employer for purposes of paragraph (f)(4) of this section. If the total allowance received exceeds the deductible expenses paid or incurred by the employee, such excess must be reported as income on the employee's return. See paragraph (j)(1) of this section relating to the substantiation of meal expenses while traveling away from home, and paragraph (j)(2) of this section relating to the substantiation of expenses for the business use of a vehicle.

(2) Allowances for expenses described. An allowance for expenses is described in this paragraph (g)(2) if it is a—

(i) Reimbursement arrangement covering ordinary and necessary expenses of traveling away from home (exclusive of transportation expenses to and from destination);

(ii) Per diem allowance providing for ordinary and necessary expenses of traveling away from home (exclusive of transportation costs to and from destination); or

(iii) Mileage allowance providing for ordinary and necessary expenses of local transportation and transportation to, from, and at the destination while traveling away from home.

* * *

(j) Authority for optional methods of computing certain expenses—(1) Meal expenses while traveling away from home. The Commissioner may establish a method under which a taxpayer may use a specified amount or amounts for meals while traveling away from home in lieu of substantiating the actual cost of meals. The taxpayer will not be relieved of the requirement to substantiate the actual cost of other travel expenses as well as the time, place, and business purpose of the travel. See paragraphs (b)(2) and (c) of this section.

(2) Use of mileage rates for vehicles expenses. The Commissioner may establish a method under which a taxpayer may use mileage rates to determine the amount of the ordinary and necessary expenses of using a vehicle for local transportation and transportation to, from, and at the destination while traveling away from home in lieu of substantiating the actual costs. The method may include appropriate limitations and conditions in order to reflect more accurately vehicle expenses over the entire period of usage. The taxpayer will not be relieved of the requirement to substantiate the amount of each business use (i.e., the business mileage), or the time and business purpose of each use. See paragraphs (b)(2) and (c) of this section.

* * *

[T.D. 8864, 65 FR 4121, Jan. 26, 2000, as amended by T.D. 9020, 67 FR 68512, Nov. 12, 2002; T.D. 9064, 68 FR 39011, July 1, 2003; T.D. 9483, 72 FR 27936, May 19, 2010]

§ 1.274–5T Substantiation requirements.

(a) In general. For taxable years beginning on or after January 1, 1986, no deduction or credit shall be allowed with respect to—

(1) Traveling away from home (including meals and lodging),

(2) Any activity which is of a type generally considered to constitute entertainment, amusement, or recreation, or with respect to a facility used in connection with such an activity, including the items specified in section 274(e),

(3) Gifts defined in section 274(b), or

(4) Any listed property (as defined in section 280F(d)(4) * * *),

unless the taxpayer substantiates each element of the expenditure or use (as described in paragraph (b) of this section) in the manner provided in paragraph (c) of this section. This limitation supersedes the doctrine founded in Cohan v. Commissioner, 39 F.2d 540 (2d Cir. 1930). The decision held that, where the evidence indicated a taxpayer incurred deductible travel or entertainment expenses but the exact amount could not be determined, the court should make a close approximation and not disallow the deduction entirely. Section 274(d) contemplates that no deduction or credit shall be allowed a taxpayer on the basis of such approximations or unsupported testimony of the taxpayer. For purposes of this section, the term "entertainment" means entertainment, amusement, or recreation, and use of a facility therefor; and the term "expenditure" includes expenses and items (including items such as losses and depreciation).

(b) Elements of an expenditure or use—(1) In general. Section 274(d) and this section contemplate that no deduction or credit shall be allowed for travel, entertainment, a gift, or with respect to listed property unless the taxpayer substantiates the requisite elements of each expenditure or use as set forth in this paragraph (b).

(2) Travel away from home. The elements to be proved with respect to an expenditure for travel away from home are—

(i) Amount. Amount of each separate expenditure for traveling away from home, such as cost of transportation or lodging, except that the daily cost of the traveler's own breakfast, lunch, and dinner and of expenditures incidental to such travel may be aggregated, if set forth in reasonable categories, such as for meals, for gasoline and oil, and for taxi fares;

(ii) Time. Dates of departure and return for each trip away from home, and number of days away from home spent on business;

(iii) Place. Destinations or locality of travel, described by name of city or town or other similar designation; and

(iv) Business purpose. Business reason for travel or nature of the business benefit derived or expected to be derived as a result of travel.

(3) Entertainment in general. The elements to be proved with respect to an expenditure for entertainment are—

(i) Amount. Amount of each separate expenditure for entertainment, except that such incidental items as taxi fares or telephone calls may be aggregated on a daily basis;

(ii) Time. Date of entertainment;

(iii) Place. Name, if any, address or location, and designation of type of entertainment, such as dinner or theater, if such information is not apparent from the designation of the place;

(iv) Business purpose. Business reason for the entertainment or nature of business benefit derived or expected to be derived as a result of the entertainment and, except in the case of business meals described in section 274(e)(1), the nature of any business discussion or activity;

(v) Business relationship. Occupation or other information relating to the person or persons entertained, including name, title, or other designation, sufficient to establish business relationship to the taxpayer.

(4) Entertainment directly preceding or following a substantial and bona fide business discussion. If a taxpayer claims a deduction for entertainment directly preceding or following a substantial and bona fide business discussion on the ground that such entertainment was associated with the active conduct of the taxpayer's trade or business, the elements to be proved with respect to such expenditure, in addition to those enumerated in paragraph (b)(3)(i), (ii), (iii), and (v) of this section are—

(i) Time. Date and duration of business discussion;

(ii) Place. Place of business discussion;

(iii) Business purpose. Nature of business discussion, and business reason for the entertainment or nature of business benefit derived or expected to be derived as the result of the entertainment;

(iv) Business relationship. Identification of those persons entertained who participated in the business discussion.

(5) Gifts. The elements to be proved with respect to an expenditure for a gift are—

(i) Amount. Cost of the gift to the taxpayer;

(ii) Time. Date of the gift;

(iii) Description. Description of the gift;

(iv) Business purpose. Business reason for the gift or nature of business benefit derived or expected to be derived as a result of the gift; and

(v) Business relationship. Occupation or other information relating to the recipient of the gift, including name, title, or other designation, sufficient to establish business relationship to the taxpayer.

(6) Listed property. The elements to be proved with respect to any listed property are—

(i) Amount—(A) Expenditures. The amount of each separate expenditure with respect to an item of listed property, such as the cost of acquisition, the cost of capital improvements, lease payments, the cost of maintenance and repairs, or other expenditures, and

(B) Uses. The amount of each business/investment use * * *, based on the appropriate measure (i.e., mileage for automobiles and other means of transportation and time for other listed property, unless the Commissioner approves an alternative method), and the total use of the listed property for the taxable period.

(ii) Time. Date of the expenditure or use with respect to listed property, and

(iii) Business or investment purpose. The business purpose for an expenditure or use with respect to any listed property * * *.

* * *

(c) Rules of substantiation—(1) In general. Except as otherwise provided * * *, a taxpayer must substantiate each element of an expenditure or use (described in paragraph (b) of this section) by adequate records or by sufficient evidence corroborating his own statement. Section 274(d) contemplates that a taxpayer will maintain and produce such substantiation as will constitute proof of each expenditure or use referred to in section 274. Written evidence has considerably more probative value than oral evidence alone. In addition, the probative value of written evidence is greater the closer in time it relates to the expenditure or use. A contemporaneous log is not required, but a record of the elements of an expenditure or of a business use of listed property made at or near the time of the expenditure or use, supported by sufficient documentary evidence, has a high degree of credibility not present with respect to a statement prepared subsequent thereto when generally there is a lack of accurate recall. Thus, the corroborative evidence required to support a statement not made at or near the time of the expenditure or use must have a high degree of probative value to elevate such statement and evidence to the level of credibility reflected by a record made at or near the time of the expenditure or use supported by sufficient documentary evidence. The substantiation requirements of section 274(d) are designed to encourage taxpayers to maintain the records, together with documentary evidence, as provided in paragraph (c)(2) of this section.

(2) Substantiation by adequate records—(i) In general. To meet the "adequate records" requirements of section 274(d), a taxpayer shall maintain an account book, diary, log, statement of expense, trip sheets, or similar record (as provided in paragraph (c)(2)(ii) of this section), and documentary evidence (as provided in paragraph (c)(2)(iii) of this section) which, in combination, are sufficient to establish each element of an expenditure or use specified in paragraph (b) of this section. It is not necessary to record information in an account book, diary, log, statement of expense, trip sheet, or similar record which duplicates information reflected on a receipt so long as the account book, etc., and receipt complement each other in an orderly manner.

(ii) Account book, diary, etc. An account book, diary, log, statement of expense, trip sheet, or similar record must be prepared or maintained in such manner that each recording of an element of an expenditure or use is made at or near the time of the expenditure or use.

(A) Made at or near the time of the expenditure or use. For purposes of this section, the phrase "made at or near the time of the expenditure or use" means the elements of an expenditure or use are recorded at a time when, in relation to the use or making of an expenditure, the taxpayer has full present knowledge of each element of the expenditure or use, such as the amount, time, place, and business purpose of the expenditure and business relationship. An expense account statement which is a transcription of an account book, diary, log, or similar record prepared or maintained in accordance with the provisions of this paragraph (c)(2)(ii) shall be considered a record prepared or maintained in the manner prescribed in the preceding sentence if such expense account statement is submitted by an employee to his employer or by an independent contractor to his client or customer in the regular course of good business practice. For example, a log maintained on a weekly basis, which accounts for use during the week, shall be considered a record made at or near the time of such use.

(B) Substantiation of business purpose. In order to constitute an adequate record of business purpose within the meaning of section 274(d) and this paragraph (c)(2), a written statement of business purpose generally is required. However, the degree of substantiation necessary to establish business purpose will vary depending upon the facts and circumstances of each case. Where the business purpose is evident from the surrounding facts and circumstances, a written explanation of such business purpose will not be required. For example, in the case of a salesman calling on customers on an established sales route, a written explanation of the business purpose of such travel ordinarily will not be required. Similarly, in the case of a business meal described in section 274(e)(1), if the business purpose of such meal is evident from the business relationship to the taxpayer of the persons entertained and other surrounding circumstances, a written explanation of such business purpose will not be required.

(C) Substantiation of business use of listed property—(1) Degree of substantiation. In order to constitute an adequate record (within the meaning of section 274(d) and this paragraph (c)(2)(ii)), which substantiates business/investment use of listed property * * *, the record must contain sufficient information as to each element of every business/investment use. However, the level of detail required in an adequate record to substantiate business/investment use may vary depending upon the facts and circumstances. For example, a taxpayer who uses a truck for both business and personal purposes and whose only business use of a truck is to make deliveries to customers on an established route may satisfy the adequate record requirement by recording the total number miles driven during the taxable year, the length of the delivery route once, and the date of each trip at or near the time of the trips. Alternatively, the taxpayer may establish the date of each trip with a receipt, record of delivery, or other documentary evidence.

(2) Written record. Generally, an adequate record must be written. However, a record of the business use of listed property, such as a computer or automobile, prepared in a computer memory device with the aid of a logging program will constitute an adequate record.

(D) Confidential information. If any information relating to the elements of an expenditure or use, such as place, business purpose, or business relationship, is of a confidential nature, such information need not be set forth in the account book, diary, log, statement of expense, trip sheet, or similar record, provided such information is recorded at or near the time of the expenditure or use and is elsewhere available to the district director to substantiate such element of the expenditure or use.

(iii) [Reserved] For further guidance, see § 1.274–5(g)

* * *

(f) Reporting and substantiation of expenses of certain employees for travel, entertainment, gifts, and with respect to listed property—(1) In general. * * *

(2) Reporting of expenses for which the employee is required to make an adequate accounting to his employer—(i) Reimbursements equal to expenses. For purposes of computing tax liability, an employee need not report on his tax return business expenses for travel, transportation, entertainment, gifts, or with respect to listed property, paid or incurred by him solely for the benefit of his employer for which he is required to, and does, make an adequate accounting to his employer * * * and which are charged directly or indirectly to the employer (for example, through credit cards) or for which the employee is paid through advances, reimbursements, or otherwise, provided that the total amount of such advances, reimbursements, and charges is equal to such expenses.

(ii) Reimbursements in excess of expenses. In case the total of the amounts charged directly or indirectly to the employer or received from the employer as advances, reimbursements, or otherwise, exceeds the business expenses paid or incurred by the employee and the employee is required to, and does, make an adequate accounting to his employer for such expenses, the employee must include such excess (including amounts received for expenditures not deductible by him) in income.

(iii) Expenses in excess of reimbursements. If an employee incurs deductible business expenses on behalf of his employer which exceed the total of the amounts charged directly or indirectly to the employer and received from the employer as advances, reimbursements, or otherwise, and the employee makes an adequate accounting to his employer, the employee must be able to substantiate any deduction for such excess with such records and supporting evidence as will substantiate each element of an expenditure (described in paragraph (b) of this section) in accordance with paragraph (c) of this section.

* * *

[T.D.7986, 49 FR 42704, Oct. 24, 1984, as amended by T.D 8009, 50 FR 7043, Feb. 20, 1985; T.D. 8061, 50 FR 46014, Nov. 6, 1985; T.D. 8063, 50 FR 52312, Dec. 23, 1985; T.D. 8451, 57 FR 57668, Dec. 7, 1992; T.D. 8715, 62 FR 13988, March 25, 1997; T.D. 8864, 65 FR 4121, Jan. 26, 2000; T.D. 9020, 67 FR 68512, Nov. 12, 2002; T.D. 9064, 68 FR 39011, July 1, 2003; T.D. 9483, 72 FR 27936, May 19, 2010]

§ 1.280A–1 *(Proposed, published 8–7–80 and 7–21–83.)* Limitations on deductions with respect to a dwelling unit which is used by the taxpayer during the taxable year as a residence.

(a) General rule. In the case of an individual, a partnership, a trust, an estate, or an electing small business corporation (as defined in section 1371(b)), no deductions which would otherwise be allowable under chapter 1 of the Code shall be allowed with respect to the use of a dwelling unit used by such person during the taxable year as a residence except as provided in section 280A and in §§ 1.280A–1 through 1.280A–3. The requirements imposed by section 280A are in addition to the requirements imposed by other provisions of the Code. If a deduction is claimed for an item attributable to a dwelling unit used by the taxpayer during the taxable year as a residence, the taxpayer must first establish that it is otherwise allowable as a deduction under chapter 1 of the Code before the provisions of section 280A become applicable. Section 1.280A–2 sets forth the rules relating to the deductibility of expenses attributable to the business use of a dwelling unit used as a residence. * * *

(b) Deductions allowable without regard to any connection with a trade or business or an income-producing activity. Deductions which are allowable without regard to any connection with a trade or business or an income-producing activity are allowed with respect to the use of dwelling units. Such deductions include the deduction for interest under section 163, the deduction for taxes under section 164, and the deduction for casualty losses under section 165.

(c) Dwelling unit—(1) In general. For purposes of this section and §§ 1.280A-2 and 1.280A-3, the term "dwelling unit" includes a house, apartment, condominium, mobile home, boat, or similar property, which provides basic living accommodations such as sleeping space, toilet, and cooking facilities. A single structure may contain more than one dwelling unit. For example, each apartment in an apartment building is a separate dwelling unit. Similarly, if the basement of a house contains basic living accommodations, the basement constitutes a separate dwelling unit. All structures and other property appurtenant to a dwelling unit which do not themselves constitute dwelling units are considered part of the unit. * * *

(2) Exception. Notwithstanding the provisions of paragraph (c)(1) of this section, the term "dwelling unit" does not include any unit or portion of a unit which is used exclusively as a hotel, motel, inn, or similar establishment. Property is so used only if it is regularly available for occupancy by paying customers and only if no person having an interest in the property is deemed under the rules of this section to have used the unit (or the portion of the unit) as a residence during the taxable year. Thus, this exception may apply to a portion of a home used to furnish lodging to tourists or to long-term boarders such as students. * * *

* * *

(e) Personal use of dwelling unit—(1) General rule. For purposes of this section and § 1.280A-2 a taxpayer shall be deemed to have used a dwelling unit for personal purposes on any day on which, for any part of the day, any portion of the unit is used—

(i) For personal purposes by the taxpayer or any other person who has an interest in the unit;

(ii) By a brother or sister (whether by the whole or half blood), spouse, ancestor, or lineal descendant of the taxpayer or of any other person who has an interest in the unit;

(iii) By any individual who uses the unit under an arrangement which enables the taxpayer to use some other dwelling unit for any period of time, whether or not a rental is charged for the use of the other unit and regardless of the length of time that the taxpayer uses the other unit; or

(iv) By any individual, other than an employee with respect to whose use section 119 (relating to meals or lodging furnished for the convenience of the employer) applies, unless for such day the dwelling unit is rented for a rental which, under the facts and circumstances, is fair rental.

For purposes of this paragraph, a person is considered to have an interest in a dwelling unit if that person holds any interest in the unit (other than a security interest or an interest under a lease for a fair rental) even if there are no immediate rights to possession and enjoyment under the interest.

(2) Rental at fair rental to other persons for use as principal residence. Notwithstanding paragraph (e)(1) of this section, a taxpayer shall not be treated as using a dwelling unit for personal purposes by reason of a rental arrangement for any day on which the taxpayer rents the dwelling unit at a fair rental to any person for use as that person's principal residence. If a taxpayer actually makes personal use of a unit on any such day, however, that personal use is taken into account because it arises other than "by reason of a rental arrangement." For purposes of the preceding sentence, a brief visit during which the taxpayer is a guest of the occupant of the unit shall not be considered personal use by the taxpayer. For the meaning of the term "principal residence," see section 1034 and § 1.1034-1(c)(3).

(3) Rental to persons having interest in the unit—(i) In general. Paragraph (e)(2) of this section shall apply in the case of a rental of a unit to a person who has an interest in the unit only if the rental is pursuant to a shared equity financing agreement.

(ii) Shared equity financing agreement. A shared equity financing agreement is any written agreement under which—

(A) Two or more persons acquire qualified ownership interests in the dwelling unit, and

(B) A person (or persons) holding one or more of the interests is—

(1) Entitled to occupy the dwelling unit for use as a principal residence, and

(2) Required to pay rent to one or more persons holding a qualified ownership interest in the unit.

(iii) Fair rental. For purposes of this paragraph (e)(3), the determination whether a unit is rented at a fair rental (within the meaning of paragraph (g) of this section) shall be made in light of all the facts and circumstances that existed at the time the agreement was entered into. The totality of rights and obligations of all parties under the agreement is taken into account in determining fair rental.

(iv) Qualified ownership interest. For purposes of this paragraph (e)(3), the term "qualified ownership interest" means an undivided interest for more than 50 years in the entire dwelling unit and appurtenant land being acquired in the transaction to which the shared equity financing agreement relates.

(v) Not necessary that all owners charge fair rental. A shared equity financing arrangement may exist even if one or more of the owners does not charge the occupant fair rental for use of the unit. Paragraph (e)(2) of this section, however, applies only to those owners who do charge fair rental.

* * *

(6) Use of the unit for repairs and maintenance. Notwithstanding the provisions of paragraph (e)(1) of this section, a dwelling unit shall not be deemed to have been used by the taxpayer for personal purposes on any day on which the principal purpose of the use of the unit is to perform repair or maintenance work on the unit. Whether the principal purpose of the use of the unit is to perform repair or maintenance work shall be determined in light of all the facts and circumstances including, but not limited to, the following: the amount of time devoted to repair and maintenance work, the frequency of the use for repair and maintenance purposes during a taxable year, and the presence and activities of companions. In no case, however, shall a day on which the taxpayer engages in repair and maintenance of the unit on a substantially full-time basis be considered a day of personal use by the taxpayer.

* * *

§ 1.280A–2 (*Proposed, published 8–7–80 and 7–21–83; portion withdrawn effective May 20, 1994.*) Deductibility of expenses attributable to business use of a dwelling unit used as a residence.

(a) Scope. This section describes the business uses of a dwelling unit used as a residence for which items may be deductible under an exception to the general rule of section 280A and explains the general conditions for the deductibility of items attributable to those uses. Deductions are allowable only to the extent provided in section 280A(c)(5) and in paragraph (i) of this section. See § 1.280A–1 for the general rules under section 280A.

(b) Use as the taxpayer's principal place of business—(1) In general. Section 280A(c)(1)(A) provides an exception to the general rule of section 280A(a) for any item to the extent that the item is allocable to a portion of the dwelling unit which is used exclusively and on a regular basis as the principal place of business for any trade or business of the taxpayer.

[(2) and (3) withdrawn effective May 20, 1994, 59 F.R. 26466]

(c) Use by patients, clients, or customers in meeting or dealing with the taxpayer in the normal course of business. Section 280A(c)(1)(B) provides an exception to the general rule of section 280A for any item to the extent the item is allocable to a portion of the dwelling unit which is used exclusively and on a regular basis as a place of business in which patients, clients, or customers meet or deal with the taxpayer in the normal course of the taxpayer's business. Property is so used only if the patients, clients, or customers are physically present on the premises; conversations with the taxpayer by telephone do not constitute use of the premises by patients, clients or customers. This exception applies only if the use of the dwelling unit by patients, clients, or customers is substantial and integral to the conduct of the taxpayer's business. Occasional meetings are insufficient to make this exception applicable.

(d) Use of a separate structure not attached to the dwelling unit in connection with the taxpayer's trade or business. Section 280A(c)(1)(C) provides an exception to the general rule of section 280A(a) for any item to the extent that the item is allocable to a separate structure which is appurtenant to, but not attached to, the dwelling unit and is used exclusively and on a regular basis in connection with the taxpayer's trade or business. An artist's studio, a florist's greenhouse, and a carpenter's workshop are examples of structures that may be within the description of this paragraph.

* * *

(g) Exclusive use requirement—(1) In general. Paragraph (b), (c), or (d) of this section may apply to the use of a portion of a dwelling unit for a taxable year only if there is no use of that portion of the unit at any time during the taxable year other than for business purposes. For purposes of section 280A(c)(1) and this section, the phrase "a portion of the dwelling unit" refers to a room or other separately identifiable space; it is not necessary that the portion be marked off by a permanent partition. Paragraph (b), (c), or (d) of this section may apply to a portion of a unit which is used for more than one business purpose. Necessary repair or maintenance does not constitute use for purposes of this paragraph.

(2) Convenience of the employer. In the case of an employee, paragraph (b), (c), or (d) shall apply to a use of a portion of a dwelling unit only if that use is for the convenience of the employer.

(h) Use on a regular basis. The determination whether a taxpayer has used a portion of a dwelling unit for a particular purpose on a regular basis must be made in light of all the facts and circumstances.

(i) Limitation on deductions—(1) In general. The deductions allowable under chapter 1 of the Code for a taxable year with respect to the use of a dwelling unit for one of the purposes described in paragraphs (b) through (f) of this section shall not exceed the gross income derived from such use of the unit during the taxable year, as determined under subparagraph (2) of this paragraph. Subparagraphs (3) and (4) of this paragraph provide rules for determining the expenses allocable to the business use of a unit. Subparagraph (5) of this paragraph prescribes the order in which deductions are allowable.

(2) Gross income derived from use of unit—(i) Only income from qualifying business use to be taken into account. For purposes of section 280A and this section, the taxpayer shall take into account, in applying the limitation on deductions, only gross income from a business use described in section 280A(c). For example, a taxpayer who teaches at school may also be engaged in a retail sales business. If the taxpayer uses a home office on a regular basis as the principal place of business for the retail sales business (a use described in section 280A(c)(1)(A)) and makes no nonbusiness use of the office, the taxpayer shall take the gross income from the use of the office for the retail sales business into account in applying the limitation on deductions. Even if the taxpayer also corrects student papers and prepares class presentations in the home office (not a use described in section 280A(c)), no portion of the taxpayer's gross income from teaching may be taken into account in applying the limitation on deductions.

(ii) More than one location. If the taxpayer engages in a business in the dwelling unit and in one or more other locations, the taxpayer shall allocate the gross income from the business to the different locations on a reasonable basis. In making this determination, the taxpayer shall take into account the amount of time that the taxpayer engages in activity related to the business at each location, the capital investment related to the business at each location, and any other facts and circumstances that may be relevant.

(iii) Exclusion of certain amounts. For purposes of section 280A(c)(5)(A) and this section, gross income derived from use of a unit means gross income from the business activity in the unit reduced by expenditures required for the activity but not allocable to use of the unit itself, such as expenditures for supplies and compensation paid to other persons. For example, a physician who uses a portion of a dwelling unit for treating patients shall compute gross income derived from use of the unit by subtracting from the gross income attributable to the business activity in the unit any expenditures for nursing and secretarial services, supplies, etc.

(3) Expenses allocable to portion of unit. The taxpayer may determine the expenses allocable to the portion of the unit used for business purposes by any method that is reasonable under the circumstances. If the rooms in the dwelling unit are of approximately equal size, the taxpayer may ordinarily allocate the general expenses for the unit according to the number of rooms used for the business purpose. The taxpayer may also allocate general expenses according to the percentage of the total floor space in the unit that is used for the business purpose. Expenses which are attributable only to certain portions of the unit, e.g., repairs to kitchen fixtures, shall be allocated in full to those portions of the unit. Expenses which are not related to the use of the unit for business purposes, e.g., expenditures for lawn care, are not taken into account for the purposes of section 280A.

* * *

(5) **Order of deductions.** Business deductions with respect to the business use of a dwelling unit are allowable in the following order and only to the following extent:

(i) The allocable portions of amounts allowable as deductions for the taxable year under chapter 1 of the Code with respect to the dwelling unit without regard to any use of the unit in trade or business, e.g., mortgage interest and real estate taxes, are allowable as business deductions to the extent of the gross income derived from use of the unit.

(ii) Amounts otherwise allowable as deductions for the taxable year under chapter 1 of the Code by reason of the business use of the dwelling unit (other than those which would result in an adjustment to the basis of property) are allowable to the extent the gross income derived from use of the unit exceeds the deductions allowed or allowable under subdivision (i) of this subparagraph.

(iii) Amounts otherwise allowable as deductions for the taxable year under chapter 1 of the Code by reason of the business use of the dwelling unit which would result in an adjustment to the basis of property are allowable to the extent the gross income derived from use of the unit exceeds the deductions allowed or allowable under subdivisions (i) and (ii) of this subparagraph.

* * *

§ 1.280A–3 (*Proposed, published 8–7–80 and 7–21–83.*) Deductibility of expenses attributable to the rental of a dwelling unit used as a residence.

(a) **Scope.** This section provides rules for determining the deductibility of expenses attributable to the rental of a dwelling unit used as a residence. Note that paragraph (c) of this section applies to any dwelling unit used by the taxpayer for personal purposes on any day during the taxable year, whether or not the taxpayer is treated as using the unit as a residence. * * *

(b) **Short rental period.** If a dwelling unit used by the taxpayer as a residence during the taxable year is actually rented for less than 15 days during the taxable year,

(1) No deduction otherwise allowable because of the rental use shall be allowed, and

(2) The rental income shall not be included in gross income.

(c) **Allocation—(1) In general.** If a taxpayer uses a dwelling unit for personal purposes on any day during the taxable year, the amount deductible by reason of the rental use of the unit during the taxable year shall not exceed an amount which bears the same relationship to the total expenses paid or incurred with respect to the unit during the taxable year as the number of days on which the unit is rented at fair rental during the year bears to the total number of days that the unit is used for any purpose during the taxable year. For purposes of section 280A(e) and this section, the fact that a unit is deemed to be used for personal purposes on a particular day does not prevent that day from being counted as a day on which the unit is rented at fair rental. Use of a unit for repair and maintenance which is disregarded under § 1.280A–1(e)(6) shall be disregarded for purposes of this paragraph.

(2) **Portion of unit rented.** If the taxpayer rents only a portion of the dwelling unit, the rule prescribed in subparagraph (1) of this paragraph shall be applied to the expenses attributable to that portion of the unit, and the days to be taken into account shall be the days on which that portion of the unit is rented at fair rental during the taxable year and the days on which that portion of the unit is used for any purpose during the taxable year. * * *

(3) **Deductions allowable without regard to rental use.** This paragraph shall not disallow any part of those deductions with respect to a dwelling unit which are allowable without regard to the rental use of the unit.

(4) **Example.** The provisions of this paragraph may be illustrated by the following example:

Example. A, an individual, owns a cottage which A rents to vacationers at fair rental for 120 days during the taxable year. A is deemed to have made personal use of the cottage on 15 of those 120 days. The unit is used for one or more purposes (other than repair or maintenance) on 160 days during the taxable year. The amount that A may claim as rental expenses may not exceed 120/160 of the total expenses paid or incurred with respect to the unit during the taxable year. If A itemizes deductions, A may claim the remaining 40/160 of items, such as mortgage interest and taxes, which are deductible without regard to the rental use of the unit.

(d) **Limitation on deductions if taxpayer has used dwelling unit as a residence—(1) In general.** The deductions allowable under chapter 1 of the Code for a taxable year with respect to the rental use of a dwelling unit which the taxpayer is treated as having used as a residence during such year shall not exceed the gross rental income from the unit for such year. * * *

(2) Gross rental income. For purposes of section 280A and this section gross rental income from a unit equals the gross receipts from rental of the unit reduced by expenditures to obtain tenants for the unit, such as realtors fees and advertising expense. The gross rental income from a unit for a taxable year includes rental income for periods during which the unit is rented at less than a fair rental as well as rental income for periods during which the unit is rented at fair rental.

(3) Order of deductions. Deductions with respect to the rental use of a dwelling unit are allowable in the following order and only to the following extent:

(i) The allocable portions of amounts otherwise allowable as deductions for the taxable year under chapter 1 of the Code with respect to the dwelling unit without regard to the rental use of the unit, e.g., mortgage interest and real estate taxes, are deductible as rental expenses to the extent of the gross rental income from the unit.

(ii) The allocable portions of amounts otherwise allowable as deductions for the taxable year under chapter 1 of the Code by reason of the rental use of the dwelling unit (other than those which would result in an adjustment to the basis of property) are allowable to the extent the gross rental income exceeds the deductions allowed or allowable under subdivision (i) of this subparagraph.

(iii) The allocable portions of amounts otherwise allowable as deductions for the taxable year under chapter 1 of the Code by reason of the rental use of the dwelling unit which would result in an adjustment to the basis of property are allowable to the extent the gross rental income exceeds the deductions allowed or allowable under subdivisions (i) and (ii) of this subparagraph.

For purposes of this subparagraph, the portion of any item which is allocable to the rental use of a unit during a taxable year shall be that amount which bears the same relationship to the total amount of the item as the number of days on which the unit is rented at a fair rental during the taxable year bears to the number of days on which the unit is used for any purpose (other than repair or maintenance) during the taxable year.

* * *

CORPORATE DISTRIBUTIONS AND ADJUSTMENTS

§ 1.301–1 Rules applicable with respect to distributions of money and other property.

(a) General. Section 301 provides the general rule for treatment of distributions on or after June 22, 1954, of property by a corporation to a shareholder with respect to its stock. The term "property" is defined in section 317(a). Such distributions, except as otherwise provided in this chapter, shall be treated as provided in section 301(c). Under section 301(c), distributions may be included in gross income, applied against and reduce the adjusted basis of the stock, treated as gain from the sale or exchange of property, or (in the case of certain distributions out of increase in value accrued before March 1, 1913) may be exempt from tax. The amount of the distributions to which section 301 applies is determined in accordance with the provisions of section 301(b). The basis of property received in a distribution to which section 301 applies is determined in accordance with the provisions of section 301(d). Accordingly, except as otherwise provided in this chapter, a distribution on or after June 22, 1954, of property by a corporation to a shareholder with respect to its stock shall be included in gross income to the extent the amount distributed is considered a dividend under section 316. For examples of distributions treated otherwise, see sections 116, 301(c)(2), 301(c)(3)(B), 301(e), 302(b), 303, and 305. See also part II (relating to distributions in partial or complete liquidation), part III (relating to corporate organizations and reorganizations), and part IV (relating to insolvency reorganizations), subchapter C, chapter 1 of the Code.

(b) Time of inclusion in gross income and of determination of fair market value. A distribution made by a corporation to its shareholders shall be included in the gross income of the distributees when the cash or other property is unqualifiedly made subject to their demands. However, if such distribution is a distribution other than in cash, the fair market value of the property shall be determined as of the date of distribution without regard to whether such date is the same as that on which the distribution is includible in gross income. For example, if a corporation distributes a taxable dividend in property (the adjusted basis of which exceeds its fair market value on December 31, 1955) on December 31, 1955, which is received by, or unqualifiedly made subject to the demand of, its shareholders on January 2, 1956, the amount to be included in the gross income of the shareholders will be the fair market value of such property on December 31, 1955, although such amount will not be includible in the gross income of the shareholders until January 2, 1956.

(c) Application of section to shareholders. Section 301 is not applicable to an amount paid by a corporation to a shareholder unless the amount is paid to the shareholder in his capacity as such.

(d) Distributions to corporate shareholders. **(1)** If the shareholder is a corporation, the amount of any distribution to be taken into account under section 301(c) shall be:

(i) The amount of money distributed,

(ii) An amount equal to the fair market value of any property distributed which consists of any obligations of the distributing corporation, stock of the distributing corporation treated as property under section 305(b), or rights to acquire such stock treated as property under section 305(b), plus

(iii) In the case of a distribution not described in subdivision (iv) of this subparagraph, an amount equal to (a) the fair market value of any other property distributed or, if lesser, (b) the adjusted basis of such other property in the hands of the distributing corporation determined immediately before the distribution and increased for any gain recognized to the distributing corporation * * *

* * *

(2) In the case of a distribution the amount of which is determined by reference to the adjusted basis described in subparagraph (1)(iii)(b) of this paragraph:

(i) That portion of the distribution which is a dividend under section 301(c)(1) may not exceed such adjusted basis, or

(ii) If the distribution is not out of earnings and profits, the amount of the reduction in basis of the shareholder's stock, and the amount of any gain resulting from such distribution, are to be determined by reference to such adjusted basis of the property which is distributed.

* * *

(e) Adjusted basis. In determining the adjusted basis of property distributed in the hands of the distributing corporation immediately before the distribution for purposes of section 301(b)(1)(B)(ii), (b)(1)(C)(i), and (d)(2)(B), the basis to be used shall be the basis for determining gain upon a sale or exchange.

(f) Examples. The application of this section (except paragraph (n)) may be illustrated by the following examples:

Example (1). On January 1, 1955, A, an individual owned all of the stock of Corporation M with an adjusted basis of $2,000. During 1955, A received distributions from Corporation M totaling $30,000, consisting of $10,000 in cash and listed securities having a basis in the hands of Corporation M and a fair market value on the date distributed of $20,000. Corporation M's taxable year is the calendar year. As of December 31, 1954, Corporation M had earnings and profits accumulated after February 28, 1913, in the amount of $26,000, and it had no earnings and profits and no deficit for 1955. Of the $30,000 received by A, $26,000 will be treated as an ordinary dividend; the remaining $4,000 will be applied against the adjusted basis of his stock; the $2,000 in excess of the adjusted basis of his stock will either be treated as gain from the sale or exchange of property (under section 301(c)(3)(A)) or, if out of increase in value accrued before March 1, 1913, will (under section 301(c)(3)(B)) be exempt from tax. If A subsequently sells his stock in Corporation M, the basis for determining gain or loss on the sale will be zero.

Example (2). The facts are the same as in Example 1 with the exceptions that the shareholder of Corporation M is Corporation W and that the securities which were distributed had an adjusted basis to Corporation M of $15,000. The distribution received by Corporation W totals $25,000 consisting of $10,000 in cash and securities with an adjusted basis of $15,000. The total $25,000 will be treated as a dividend to Corporation W since the earnings and profits of Corporation M ($26,000) are in excess of the amount of the distribution.

* * *

(g) Reduction for liabilities—(1) General rule. For the purpose of section 301, no reduction shall be made for the amount of any liability, unless the liability is assumed by the shareholder within the meaning of section 357(d).

(2) No reduction below zero. Any reduction pursuant to paragraph (g)(1) of this section shall not cause the amount of the distribution to be reduced below zero.

* * *

(j) Transfers for less than fair market value. If property is transferred by a corporation to a shareholder which is not a corporation for an amount less than its fair market value in a sale or exchange, such shareholder shall be treated as having received a distribution to which section 301 applies. In such case, the amount of the distribution shall be the difference between the amount paid for the property and its fair market value. If property is transferred in a sale or exchange by a corporation to a shareholder which is a corporation, for an amount less than its fair market value and also less than its adjusted basis, such shareholder shall be treated as having received a distribution to which section 301 applies, and—

(1) Where the fair market value of the property equals or exceeds its adjusted basis in the hands of the distributing corporation the amount of the distribution shall be the excess of the adjusted basis (increased by the amount of gain recognized * * * to the distributing corporation) over the amount paid for the property;

(2) Where the fair market value of the property is less than its adjusted basis in the hands of the distributing corporation, the amount of the distribution shall be the excess of such fair market value over the amount paid for the property. * * *

* * *

(k) Application of rule respecting transfers for less than fair market value. The application of paragraph (j) of this section may be illustrated by the following examples:

Example (1). On January 1, 1955, A, an individual shareholder of corporation X, purchased property from that corporation for $20. The fair market value of such property was $100, and its basis in the hands of corporation X was $25. The amount of the distribution determined under section 301(b) is $80. If A were a corporation, the amount of the distribution would be $5 * * * the excess of the basis of the property in the hands of corporation X over the amount received therefor. The basis of such property to corporation A would be $25. If the basis of the property in the hands of corporation X were $10, the corporate shareholder, A, would not receive a distribution. The basis of such property to corporation A would be $20. Whether or not A is a corporation, the excess of the amount paid over the basis of the property in the hands of corporation X ($20 over $10) would be a taxable gain to corporation X.

* * *

(*l*) Transactions treated as distributions. A distribution to shareholders with respect to their stock is within the terms of section 301 although it takes place at the same time as another transaction if the distribution is in substance a separate transaction whether or not connected in a formal sense. This is most likely to occur in the case of a recapitalization, a reincorporation, or a merger of a corporation with a newly organized corporation having substantially no property. For example, if a corporation having only common stock outstanding, exchanges one share of newly issued common stock and one bond in the principal amount of $10 for each share of outstanding common stock, the distribution of the bonds will be a distribution of property (to the extent of their fair market value) to which section 301 applies, even though the exchange of common stock for common stock may be pursuant to a plan of reorganization under the terms of section 368(a)(1)(E) (recapitalization) and even though the exchange of common stock for common stock may be tax free by virtue of section 354.

(m) Cancellation of indebtedness. The cancellation of indebtedness of a shareholder by a corporation shall be treated as a distribution of property.

* * *

[T.D. 6500, 25 FR 11607, Nov. 26, 1960, as amended by T.D. 6752, 29 FR 12701, Sept. 9, 1964; T.D. 7084, 36 FR 267, Jan. 8, 1971; T.D. 7209, 37 FR 20800, Oct. 5, 1972; T.D. 7238, 38 FR 20824, Aug. 3, 1973; T.D. 7293, 38 FR 32794, Nov. 28, 1973; T.D. 7556, 44 FR 1376, Jan. 5, 1979; T.D. 8586, 60 FR 2497, Jan. 10, 1995; T.D. 8924, 66 FR 723, Jan. 1, 2001; T.D. 8964, 66 FR 49278, Sept. 27, 2001; T.D. 9092, 68 FR 54336, Sept. 17, 2003]

§ 1.301–2 Application to basis (Proposed Jan. 21, 2009).

(a) Application to basis. That portion of a distribution which is not a dividend shall be applied pro rata, on a share-by-share basis, to reduce the adjusted basis of each share of stock held by the shareholder within the class of stock upon which the distribution is made. The following example illustrates this paragraph (a):

Example. (i) Facts. Corporation X, a calendar year taxpayer, has only common stock outstanding. A, an individual, owns all 100 shares; 25 were acquired on Date 1 for $25 (Block 1) and 75 were acquired on Date 2 for $175 (Block 2). On December 31, when Corporation X had earnings and profits of $100, it made a $3 distribution on each share of common stock.

(ii) Analysis. A is treated as receiving $75 of the distribution on block 1 and $225 on block 2. On Block 1, A will have a $25 dividend under section 301(c)(1), a $25 return of capital under section 301(c)(2) and a $25 gain under section 301(c)(3). On Block 2, A will have a $75 dividend under section 301(c)(1), a $150 a return of capital under section 301(c)(2) and will have a remaining basis of $25 in the shares of block 2.

* * *

§ 1.302–1 General.

(a) Under section 302(d), unless otherwise provided in subchapter C, chapter 1 of the Code, a distribution in redemption of stock shall be treated as a distribution of property to which section 301 applies if the distribution is not within any of the provisions of section 302(b). A distribution in redemption of stock shall be considered a distribution in part or full payment in exchange for the stock under section 302(a) provided paragraph (1), (2), (3), or (4) of section 302(b) applies. Section 318(a) (relating to constructive ownership of stock) applies to all redemptions under section 302 except that in the termination of a shareholder's interest certain limitations are placed on the application of section 318(a)(1) by section 302(c)(2). The term "redemption of stock" is defined in section 317(b). * * *

* * *

[T.D. 6500, 25 FR 11402, Nov. 26, 1960]

§ 1.302–2 Redemptions not taxable as dividends.

(a) In general. The fact that a redemption fails to meet the requirements of paragraph (2), (3) or (4) of section 302(b) shall not be taken into account in determining whether the redemption is not essentially equivalent to a dividend under section 302(b)(1). See, however, paragraph (b) of this section. For example, if a shareholder owns only nonvoting stock of a corporation which is not section 306 stock and which is limited and preferred as to dividends and in liquidation, and one-half of such stock is redeemed, the distribution will ordinarily meet the requirements of paragraph (1) of section 302(b) but will not meet the requirements of paragraph (2), (3) or (4) of such section. The determination of whether or not a distribution is within the phrase "essentially equivalent to a dividend" (that is, having the same effect as a distribution without any redemption of stock) shall be made without regard to the earnings and profits of the corporation at the time of the distribution. For example, if A owns all the stock of a corporation and the corporation redeems part of his stock at a time when it has no earnings and profits, the distribution shall be treated as a distribution under section 301 pursuant to section 302(d).

(b) Redemption not essentially equivalent to a dividend—(1) In general. The question whether a distribution in redemption of stock of a shareholder is not essentially equivalent to a dividend under section 302(b)(1) depends upon the facts and circumstances of each case. One of the facts to be considered in making this determination is the constructive stock ownership of such shareholder under section 318(a). All distributions in pro rata redemptions of a part of the stock of a corporation generally will be treated as distributions under section 301 if the corporation has only one class of stock outstanding. However, for distributions in partial liquidation, see section 302(e). The redemption of all of one class of stock (except section 306 stock) either at one time or in a series of redemptions generally will be considered as a distribution under section 301 if all classes of stock outstanding at the time of the redemption are held in the same proportion. Distributions in redemption of stock may be treated as distributions under section 301 regardless of the provisions of the stock certificate and regardless of whether all stock being redeemed was acquired by the stockholders from whom the stock was redeemed by purchase or otherwise.

* * *

(c) Basis adjustments. In any case in which an amount received in redemption of stock is treated as a distribution of a dividend, proper adjustment of the basis of the remaining stock will be made with respect to the stock redeemed. (For adjustments to basis required for certain redemptions of corporate shareholders that are treated as extraordinary dividends, see section 1059 and the regulations thereunder.) The following examples illustrate the application of this rule:

Example (1). A, an individual, purchased all of the stock of Corporation X for $100,000. In 1955 the corporation redeems half of the stock for $150,000, and it is determined that this amount constitutes a dividend. The remaining stock of Corporation X held by A has a basis of $100,000.

Example (2). H and W, husband and wife, each own half of the stock of Corporation X. All of the stock was purchased by H for $100,000 cash. In 1950 H gave one-half of the stock to W, the stock transferred having a value in excess of $50,000. In 1955 all of the stock of H is redeemed for $150,000, and it is determined that the distribution to H in redemption of his shares constitutes the distribution of a dividend. Immediately after the transaction, W holds the remaining stock of Corporation X with a basis of $100,000.

Example (3). The facts are the same as in Example (2) with the additional facts that the outstanding stock of Corporation X consists of 1,000 shares and all but 10 shares of the stock of H is redeemed. Immediately after the transaction, H holds 10 shares of the stock of Corporation X with a basis of $50,000, and W holds 500 shares with a basis of $50,000.

* * *

[T.D. 6500, 25 FR 11607, Nov. 26, 1960; T.D. 8724, 62 FR 38028, July 16, 1997; T.D. 9264, 71 FR 30593, May 30, 2006; T.D. 9329, 72 FR 32796, June 14, 2007]

§ 1.302–3 Substantially disproportionate redemption.

(a) Section 302(b)(2) provides for the treatment of an amount received in redemption of stock as an amount received in exchange for such stock if—

(1) Immediately after the redemption the shareholder owns less than 50 percent of the total combined voting power of all classes of stock as provided in section 302(b)(2)(B),

(2) The redemption is a substantially disproportionate redemption within the meaning of section 302(b)(2)(C), and

(3) The redemption is not pursuant to a plan described in section 302(b)(2)(D).

Section 318(a) (relating to constructive ownership of stock) shall apply both in making the disproportionate redemption test and in determining the percentage of stock ownership after the redemption. The requirements under section 302(b)(2) shall be applied to each shareholder separately and shall be applied only with respect to stock which is issued and outstanding in the hands of the shareholders. Section 302(b)(2) only applies to a redemption of voting stock or to a redemption of both voting stock and other stock. Section 302(b)(2) does not apply to the redemption solely of nonvoting stock (common or preferred). However, if a redemption is treated as an exchange to a particular shareholder under the terms of section 302(b)(2), such section will apply to the simultaneous redemption of nonvoting preferred stock (which is not section 306 stock) owned by such shareholder and such redemption will also be treated as an exchange. Generally, for purposes of this section, stock which does not have voting rights until the happening of an event, such as a default in the payment of dividends on preferred stock, is not voting stock until the happening of the specified event. Subsection 302(b)(2)(D) provides that a redemption will not be treated as substantially disproportionate if made pursuant to a plan the purpose or effect of which is a series of redemptions which result in the aggregate in a distribution which is not substantially disproportionate. Whether or not such a plan exists will be determined from all the facts and circumstances.

(b) The application of paragraph (a) of this section is illustrated by the following example:

Example. Corporation M has outstanding 400 shares of common stock of which A, B, C and D each own 100 shares or 25 percent. No stock is considered constructively owned by A, B, C or D under section 318. Corporation M redeems 55 shares from A, 25 shares from B, and 20 shares from C. For the redemption to be disproportionate as to any shareholder, such shareholder must own after the redemptions less than 20 percent (80 percent of 25 percent) of the 300 shares of stock then outstanding. After the redemptions, A owns 45 shares (15 percent), B owns 75 shares (25 percent), and C owns 80 shares (26⅔ percent). The distribution is disproportionate only with respect to A.

[T.D. 6500, 25 FR 11607, Nov. 26, 1960]

§ 1.302–4 Termination of shareholder's interest.

Section 302(b)(3) provides that a distribution in redemption of all of the stock of the corporation owned by a shareholder shall be treated as a distribution in part or full payment in exchange for the stock of such shareholder. In determining whether all of the stock of the shareholder has been redeemed, the general rule of section 302(c)(1) requires that the rules of constructive ownership provided in section 318(a) shall apply. Section 302(c)(2), however, provides that section 318(a)(1) (relating to constructive ownership of stock owned by members of a family) shall not apply where the specific requirements of section 302(c)(2) are met. The following rules shall be applicable in determining whether the specific requirements of section 302(c)(2) are met:

(a) Statement. The agreement specified in section 302(c)(2)(A)(iii) shall be in the form of a statement entitled, "STATEMENT PURSUANT TO SECTION 302(c)(2)(A)(iii) BY [INSERT NAME AND TAXPAYER IDENTIFICATION NUMBER (IF ANY) OF TAXPAYER OR RELATED PERSON, AS THE CASE MAY BE], A DISTRIBUTEE (OR RELATED PERSON) OF [INSERT NAME AND EMPLOYER IDENTIFICATION NUMBER (IF ANY) OF DISTRIBUTING CORPORATION]." The distributee must include such statement on or with the distributee's first return for the taxable year in which the distribution described in section 302(b)(3) occurs. If the distributee is a controlled foreign corporation (within the meaning of section 957), each United States shareholder (within the meaning of section 951(b)) with respect thereto must include this statement on or with its return. The distributee must represent in the statement—

(1) THE DISTRIBUTEE (OR RELATED PERSON) HAS NOT ACQUIRED, OTHER THAN BY BEQUEST OR INHERITANCE, ANY INTEREST IN THE CORPORATION (AS DESCRIBED IN SECTION 302(c)(2)(A)(i)) SINCE THE DISTRIBUTION; and

(2) THE DISTRIBUTEE (OR RELATED PERSON) WILL NOTIFY THE INTERNAL REVENUE SERVICE OF ANY ACQUISITION, OTHER THAN BY BEQUEST OR INHERITANCE, OF SUCH AN INTEREST IN THE CORPORATION WITHIN 30 DAYS AFTER THE ACQUISITION, IF THE ACQUISITION OCCURS WITHIN 10 YEARS FROM THE DATE OF THE DISTRIBUTION.

(b) Substantiation information. The distributee who files an agreement under section 302(c)(2)(A)(iii) shall retain copies of income tax returns and any other records indicating fully the amount of tax which would have been payable had the redemption been treated as a distribution subject to section 301.

(c) Stock of parent, subsidiary or successor corporation redeemed. If stock of a parent corporation is redeemed, section 302(c)(2)(A), relating to acquisition of an interest in the corporation within 10 years after termination shall be applied with reference to an interest both in the parent corporation and any subsidiary of such parent corporation. If stock of a parent corporation is sold to a subsidiary in a transaction described in section 304, section 302(c)(2)(A) shall be applicable to the acquisition of an interest in such subsidiary corporation or in the parent corporation. If stock of a subsidiary corporation is redeemed, section 302(c)(2)(A) shall be applied with reference to an interest both in such subsidiary corporation and its parent. Section 302(c)(2)(A) shall also be applied with respect to an interest in a corporation which is a successor corporation to the corporation the interest in which has been terminated.

(d) Redeemed shareholder as creditor. For the purpose of section 302(c)(2)(A)(i), a person will be considered to be a creditor only if the rights of such person with respect to the corporation are not greater or broader in scope than necessary for the enforcement of his claim. Such claim must not in any sense be proprietary and must not be subordinate to the claims of general creditors. An obligation in the form of a debt may thus constitute a proprietary interest. For example, if under the terms of the instrument the corporation may discharge the principal amount of its obligation to a person by payments, the amount or certainty of which are dependent upon the earnings of the corporation, such a person is not a creditor of the corporation. Furthermore, if under the terms of the instrument the rate of purported interest is dependent upon earnings, the holder of such instrument may not, in some cases, be a creditor.

(e) Acquisition of assets pursuant to creditor's rights. In the case of a distributee to whom section 302(b)(3) is applicable, who is a creditor after such transaction, the acquisition of the assets of the corporation in the enforcement of the rights of such creditor shall not be considered an acquisition of an interest in the corporation for purposes of section 302(c)(2) unless stock of the corporation, its parent corporation, or, in the case of a redemption of stock of a parent corporation, of a subsidiary of such corporation is acquired.

(f) Constructive ownership rules applicable. In determining whether an entire interest in the corporation has been terminated under section 302(b)(3), under all circumstances paragraphs (2), (3), (4), and (5) of section 318(a) (relating to constructive ownership of stock) shall be applicable.

(g) Avoidance of Federal income tax. Section 302(c)(2)(B) provides that section 302(c)(2)(A) shall not apply—

(1) If any portion of the stock redeemed was acquired directly or indirectly within the 10–year period ending on the date of the distribution by the distributee from a person, the ownership of whose stock would (at the time of distribution) be attributable to the distributee under section 318(a), or

(2) If any person owns (at the time of the distribution) stock, the ownership of which is attributable to the distributee under section 318(a), such person acquired any stock in the corporation directly or indirectly from the distributee within the 10–year period ending on the date of the distribution, and such stock so acquired from the distributee is not redeemed in the same transaction, unless the acquisition (described in subparagraph (1) of this paragraph) or the disposition by the distributee (described in subparagraph (2) of this paragraph) did not have as one of its principal purposes the avoidance of Federal income tax. A transfer of stock by the transferor, within the 10–year period ending on the date of the distribution, to a person whose stock would be attributable to the transferor shall not be deemed to have as one of its principal purposes the avoidance of Federal income tax merely because the transferee is in a lower income tax bracket than the transferor.

* * *

[T.D 6500, 25 FR 11607, Nov. 26, 1960, as amended by T.D. 6969, 33 FR 11997, Aug. 23, 1968; T.D. 7535, 43 FR 10686, March 15, 1978; T.D. 9264, 71 FR 30594, 30607, May 30, 2006; T.D. 9329, 72 FR 32796, 32807, June 14, 2007; 72 FR 39139, July 17, 2007]

§ 1.302–5 Redemptions under section 302(d) (Proposed Jan. 21, 2009).

(a) In general—(1) Share-by-share basis reduction. In any case in which an amount received in redemption of stock (as defined in section 317(b)) is treated as a distribution to which section 301 applies, that portion of a distribution that is not a dividend shall be applied to reduce the adjusted basis of each share held by the redeemed shareholder (as defined in paragraph (b) of this section) in the redeemed class (as defined in paragraph (b) of this section). Such reduction shall be applied pro rata, on a share-by-share basis, to all shares of the redeemed class held by the redeemed shareholder. Gain, if any, on a share shall be determined under section 301(c)(3).

(2) Deemed recapitalization. Except as provided in paragraph (a)(3) of this section, immediately following the reduction of basis as provided in section 301(c)(2) and paragraph (a)(1) of this section, all shares of the redeemed class, including the redeemed shares, held by the redeemed shareholder will be treated as surrendered in a reorganization described in section 368(a)(1)(E) in exchange for the number of shares of the redeemed class directly held by the redeemed shareholder after the redemption. The basis of the shares deemed received in the reorganization described in section 368(a)(1)(E) will be determined under the rules of section 358 and § 1.358–2.

(3) Redemption of all shares of redeemed class—(i) Remaining basis treated as loss. If all the shares of the redeemed class held by the redeemed shareholder are redeemed, an amount equal to the basis of the redeemed stock, after adjusting such basis to reflect the application of section 301(c)(2) as provided in paragraph (a)(1) of this section, will be treated as a loss on a disposition of the redeemed stock on the date of the redemption. Such loss is taken into account on the inclusion date as defined in paragraph (b) of this section.

(ii) Attributes of loss. Notwithstanding that a loss described in paragraph (a)(3)(i) of this section may be deferred and taken into account on a date later than the date of the redemption, the attributes (for example, character and source) of such loss are determined on the date of the redemption that gave rise to such loss.

(b) Definitions—(1) Redeemed shareholder. Except as provided in paragraph (c) of this section, the term redeemed shareholder means the person whose stock is redeemed in a transaction. If the redeemed shareholder is a corporation, and the assets of the redeemed shareholder are acquired in a transaction described in section 381(a) (other than transactions described in paragraph (b)(4)(ii) of this section), the acquiring corporation (within the meaning of section 381) thereafter is treated as the redeemed shareholder.

(2) Redeemed class. With respect to a shareholder whose stock has been redeemed, the term redeemed class means all of the shares of that class held by the redeemed shareholder. For this purpose, a class is defined with respect to economic rights to distributions rather than the labels attached to shares or rights with respect to corporate governance.

(3) Redeeming corporation. The term redeeming corporation means the corporation that issued the stock that is redeemed.

(4) Inclusion date—(i) Definition. The term inclusion date means the earlier of—

(A) The first date on which the redeemed shareholder would satisfy the criteria of section 302(b)(1), (2), or (3), if the facts and circumstances that exist at the end of such day had existed immediately after the redemption; or

(B) The first date on which all classes of stock of the redeeming corporation become worthless within the meaning of section 165(g). Solely for purposes of this paragraph, if the assets of the redeeming corporation (or its successor) are acquired by another corporation in a transaction described in section 381(a), the inclusion date for the redeemed shareholder is determined by treating all of the facts and circumstances that exist at the end of the day that includes the section 381 transaction (including the acquisition of the assets of the redeeming corporation or its successor) as existing immediately after the redemption. A successor for this purpose means a corporation that acquires the assets of the redeeming corporation in a transaction to which section 381(a) applies.

(ii) Special rules for corporate shareholders. If the redeemed shareholder is a corporation, the inclusion date includes the date such corporation has disposed of all of its assets in a transaction in which all gain and loss with respect its assets is recognized in whole, and the corporation ceases to exist for tax purposes. * * *

* * *

(d) Operating rules for treatment of loss attributable to basis of redeemed stock—

(1) Treatment as a deferred loss. Any loss attributable to the basis of redeemed stock under paragraph (a) of this section that has not been permitted to be taken into account under such section shall be treated as a deferred loss. The character of the deferred loss as ordinary or capital is determined at the time of the redemption.

(2) Effect of loss attributable to basis of redeemed stock on earnings and profits. If the redeemed shareholder is a corporation, any deferred loss attributable to the basis of redeemed stock is not reflected in such corporation's earnings and profits before it is taken into account pursuant to the rules of paragraph (a)(3) of this section. See, for example, §§ 1.312-6(a) and 1.312-7.

(e) Examples. For the purposes of the examples in this section, Corporations X, Y and Z are domestic corporations that file U.S. tax returns on a calendar-year basis. The examples are as follows:

Example 1. (i) Facts. A and B, husband and wife, each own 100 shares (50 percent) of the common stock of Corporation X which they hold as a capital asset. On Date 1, A acquired 50 shares for $100 (block 1) and 50 shares on Date 2 for $200 (block 2). On December 31, Corporation X, which has no current or accumulated earnings and profits, redeems all of A's block 2 shares for $300. Under section 302(d), the redemption proceeds are treated under section 301 as a recovery of basis.

(ii) Analysis. Under this section, immediately before the redemption, the distribution of property is applied on a pro rata, share-by-share basis with respect to each of the shares in the redeemed class held directly by A, the redeemed shareholder. Accordingly, A will have a $50 capital gain on block 1 ($150-100) under section 301(c)(3) and $50 of basis remaining on block 2 ($150-200). To reflect the actual number of shares held by A after the redemption, A's shares in the redeemed class, including the shares actually surrendered, will be treated as exchanged in a recapitalization under section 368(a)(1)(E). The basis in A's recapitalized shares will be determined under § 1.358-2. Accordingly, A will have 25 shares with a zero basis (attributable to block 1) and 25 shares with a basis of $50 (attributable to block 2).

Example 2. (i) Facts. The facts are the same as in Example 1, except that, Corporation X, on the following December 31, when it has no current or accumulated earnings and profits, redeems all of A's remaining 50 shares for $40. A does not file an agreement described in section 302(c)(2)(A)(iii) waiving family attribution under section 318.

(ii) Analysis. Since A is treated under section 318(a)(1) as owning B's shares, the redemption is described in section 302(d) and is treated as a distribution to which section 301 applies. As in Example 1, immediately before the redemption, the distribution is applied on a pro rata, share-by-share basis with respect to each of the shares in the redeemed class held by A. Accordingly, A recognizes a $20 gain and a $30 loss. The $30 deferred loss under § 1.302-5(a)(3) may be taken into account by A on the inclusion date (see § 1.302-5(a)(3)(ii)).

Example 3. (i) Facts. Corporation X has both common and preferred stock outstanding. A, an individual, has 100 shares of common stock with a basis of $100 and 100 shares of preferred stock with a basis of $200. The 100 shares of common stock represent voting control of Corporation X. Corporation X, when it has no current or accumulated earnings and profits, redeems all of A's preferred stock for $150. Section 302(d) applies to the redemption, and therefore the distribution is treated as a distribution of property to which section 301 applies.

(ii) Analysis. If Corporation X had declared a distribution under section 301 with respect to the redeemed preferred stock, the distribution would have been limited to the shares of common stock. Therefore, the only basis recovered under section 301(c)(2) is the basis of A's preferred stock. A has $50 in excess basis after the redemption of all its preferred stock which will not shift to the common stock held by A. Under § 1.302-5(a)(3), the excess basis will be treated as a deferred loss until the inclusion date.

Example 4. (i) Facts. Corporation Z has 100 shares of stock outstanding, 50 shares of which are owned by each of A and his son, B. A's basis in each of his shares of Corporation Z stock is $1. In Year 1, Corporation Z redeems all of A's shares of Corporation Z stock for $200. A does not file an agreement described in section 302(c)(2)(A)(iii) waiving family attribution under section 318. At the end of Year 1, Corporation Z has current and accumulated earnings and profits in excess of $200. Section 302(d) applies to the redemption, and therefore the distribution is treated as a distribution to which section 301 applies. A recognizes dividend income of $200. In Year 6, Corporation Y, a publicly traded corporation acquires all of Corporation Z's assets in exchange solely for voting stock in a reorganization described in section 368(a)(1)(C). In the reorganization, B surrenders his shares of Corporation Z stock which, at the time of the reorganization have an aggregate fair market value of $200, and receives in exchange 5,000 shares of common stock of Corporation Y representing less than one percent of the fair market value of all the stock of Y.

(ii) Analysis. Under this section, an amount equal to A's basis in the redeemed stock after the Year 1 redemption, $50, is treated as a deferred loss on a disposition of the redeemed stock on the date of the redemption. Under paragraph (b)(3) of this section, solely for purposes of determining whether a particular date on or after the date of the reorganization is the inclusion date, Corporation Y, the acquiring corporation, is treated as the redeeming corporation. If the facts and circumstances that exist at the end of the day of the reorganization had existed on the date of the redemption, the redemption would have been treated as a distribution in part or full payment in exchange for the redeemed stock pursuant to section 302(a). Therefore, the date of the reorganization is the inclusion date and A is permitted to take into account the deferred loss of $50 attributable to his basis in the redeemed stock in Year 6.

* * *

§ 1.304–2 Acquisition by related corporation (other than subsidiary).

(a) If a corporation, in return for property, acquires stock of another corporation from one or more persons, and the person or persons from whom the stock was acquired were in control of both such corporations before the acquisition, then such property shall be treated as received in redemption of stock of the acquiring corporation. The stock received by the acquiring corporation shall be treated as a contribution to the capital of such corporation. See section 362(a) for determination of the basis of such stock. The transferor's basis for his stock in the acquiring corporation shall be increased by the basis of the stock surrendered by him. (But see below in this paragraph for subsequent reductions of basis in certain cases.) As to each person transferring stock, the amount received shall be treated as a distribution of property under section 302(d), unless as to such person such amount is to be treated as received in exchange for the stock under the terms of section 302(a) or section 303. In applying section 302(b), reference shall be had to the shareholder's ownership of stock in the issuing corporation and not to his ownership of stock in the acquiring corporation (except for purposes of applying section 318(a)). In determining control and applying section 302(b), section 318(a) (relating to the constructive ownership of stock) shall be applied without regard to the 50-percent limitation contained in section 318(a)(2)(C) and (3)(C). A series of redemptions referred to in section 302(b)(2)(D) shall include acquisitions by either of the corporations of stock of the other and stock redemptions by both corporations. If section 302(d) applies to the surrender of stock by a shareholder, his basis for his stock in the acquiring corporation after the transaction (increased as stated above in this paragraph) shall not be decreased except as provided in section 301. If section 302(d) does not apply, the property received shall be treated as received in a distribution in payment in exchange for stock of the acquiring corporation under section 302(a), which stock has a basis equal to the amount by which the shareholder's basis for his stock in the acquiring corporation was increased on account of the contribution to capital as provided for above in this paragraph. Accordingly, such amount shall be applied in reduction of the shareholder's basis for his stock in the acquiring corporation. Thus, the basis of each share of the shareholder's stock in the acquiring corporation will be the same as the basis of such share before the entire transaction. The holding period of the stock which is considered to have been redeemed shall be the same as the holding period of the stock actually surrendered.

(b) In any case in which two or more persons, in the aggregate, control two corporations, section 304(a)(1) will apply to sales by such persons of stock in either corporation to the other (whether or not made simultaneously) provided the sales by each of such persons are related to each other. The determination of whether the sales are related to each other shall be dependent upon the facts and circumstances surrounding all of the sales. For this purpose, the fact that the sales may occur during a period of one or more years (such as in the case of a series of sales by persons who together control each of such corporations immediately prior to the first of such sales and immediately subsequent to the last of such sales) shall be disregarded, provided the other facts and circumstances indicate related transactions.

(c) The application of section 304(a)(1) may be illustrated by the following examples:

Example (1). Corporation X and corporation Y each have outstanding 200 shares of common stock. One-half of the stock of each corporation is owned by an individual, A, and one-half by another individual, B, who is unrelated to A. On or after August 31, 1964, A sells 30 shares of corporation X stock to corporation Y for $50,000, such stock having an adjusted basis of $10,000 to A. After the sale, A is considered as owning corporation X stock as follows: (i) 70 shares directly, and (ii) 15 shares constructively, since by virtue of his 50-percent ownership of Y he constructively owns 50 percent of the 30 shares owned directly by Y. Since A's percentage of ownership of X's voting stock after the sale (85 out of 200 shares, or 42.5%) is not less than 80 percent of his percentage of ownership of X's voting stock before the sale (100 out of 200 shares, or 50%), the transfer is not "substantially disproportionate" as to him as provided in section 302(b)(2). Under these facts, and assuming that section 302(b)(1) is not applicable, the entire $50,000 is treated as a dividend to A to the extent of the earnings and profits of corporation Y. The basis of the corporation X stock to corporation Y is $10,000, its adjusted basis to A. The amount of $10,000 is added to the basis of the stock of corporation Y in the hands of A.

* * *

Example (3). Corporation X and corporation Y each have outstanding 100 shares of common stock. A, an individual, owns one-half the stock of each corporation. B owns one-half the stock of corporation X, and C owns one-half the stock of corporation Y. A, B, and C are unrelated. A sells 30 shares of the stock of corporation X to corporation Y for $50,000, such stock having an adjusted basis of $10,000 to him. After the sale, A is considered as owning 35 shares of the stock of corporation X (20 shares directly and 15 constructively because one-half of the 30 shares owned by corporation Y are attributed to him). Since before the sale he owned 50 percent of the stock of corporation X and after the sale he owned directly and constructively only 35 percent of such stock, the redemption is substantially disproportionate as to him pursuant to the provisions of section 302(b)(2). He, therefore, realizes a gain of $40,000 ($50,000 minus $10,000). If the stock surrendered is a capital asset, such gain is long-term or short-term capital gain depending on the period of time that such stock was held. The basis to A for the stock of corporation Y is not changed as a result of the entire transaction. The basis to corporation Y for the stock of corporation X is $50,000, i.e., the basis of the transferor ($10,000), increased in the amount of gain recognized to the transferor ($40,000) on the transfer.

* * *

[T.D. 6500, 25 FR 11607, Nov. 26, 1960, as amended by T.D. 6533, 26 FR 401, Jan. 19, 1961; T.D. 6969, 33 FR 11997, Aug. 23, 1968]

§ 1.304–3 Acquisition by a subsidiary.

(a) If a subsidiary acquires stock of its parent corporation from a shareholder of the parent corporation, the acquisition of such stock shall be treated as though the parent corporation had redeemed its own stock. For the purpose of this section, a corporation is a parent corporation if it meets the 50 percent ownership requirements of section 304(c). The determination whether the amount received shall be treated as an amount received in payment in exchange for the stock shall be made by applying section 303, or by applying section 302(b) with reference to the stock of the issuing parent corporation. If such distribution would have been treated as a distribution of property (pursuant to section 302(d)) under section 301, the entire amount of the selling price of the stock shall be treated as a dividend to the seller to the extent of the earnings and profits. * * *. In such cases, the transferor's basis for his remaining stock in the parent corporation will be determined by including the amount of the basis of the stock of the parent corporation sold to the subsidiary.

(b) Section 304(a)(2) may be illustrated by the following example:

Example. Corporation M has outstanding 100 shares of common stock which are owned as follows: B, 75 shares, C, son of B, 20 shares, and D, daughter of B, 5 shares. Corporation M owns the stock of Corporation X. B sells his 75 shares of Corporation M stock to Corporation X. Under section 302(b)(3) this is a termination of B's entire interest in Corporation M and the full amount received from the sale of his stock will be treated as payment in exchange for this stock, provided he fulfills the requirements of section 302(c)(2) (relating to an acquisition of an interest in the corporations).

[T.D. 6500, 25 FR 11607, Nov. 26, 1960]

§ 1.304–4 Special rules for the use of related corporations to avoid the application of section 304.

(a) Scope and purpose. This section applies to determine the amount of a property distribution constituting a dividend (and the source thereof) under section 304(b)(2), for certain transactions involving controlled corporations. The purpose of this section is to prevent the avoidance of the application of section 304 to a controlled corporation.

(b) Amount and source of dividend. For purposes of determining the amount constituting a dividend (and source thereof) under section 304(b)(2), the following rules shall apply:

(1) Deemed acquiring corporation. A corporation (deemed acquiring corporation) shall be treated as acquiring for property the stock of a corporation (issuing corporation) acquired for property by another corporation (acquiring corporation) that is controlled by the deemed acquiring corporation, if a principal purpose for creating, organizing, or funding the acquiring corporation by any means (including through capital contributions or debt) is to avoid the application of section 304 to the deemed acquiring corporation. See paragraph (c) Example 1 of this section for an illustration of this paragraph.

(2) Deemed issuing corporation. The acquiring corporation shall be treated as acquiring for property the stock of a corporation (deemed issuing corporation) controlled by the issuing corporation if, in connection with the acquisition for property of stock of the issuing corporation by the acquiring corporation, the issuing corporation acquired stock of the deemed issuing corporation with a principal purpose of avoiding the application of section 304 to the deemed issuing corporation. See paragraph (c) Example 2 of this section for an illustration of this paragraph.

(c) Examples. The rules of this section are illustrated by the following examples:

Example 1. (i) Facts. P, a domestic corporation, wholly owns CFC1, a controlled foreign corporation with substantial accumulated earnings and profits. CFC1 is organized in Country X, which imposes a high rate of tax on the income of CFC1. P also wholly owns CFC2, a controlled foreign corporation with accumulated earnings and profits of $200x. CFC2 is organized in Country Y, which imposes a low rate of tax on the income of CFC2. P wishes to own all of its foreign corporations in a direct chain and to repatriate the cash of CFC2. In order to avoid having to obtain Country X approval for the acquisition of CFC1 (a Country X corporation) by CFC2 (a Country Y corporation) and to avoid the dividend distribution from CFC2 to P that would result if CFC2 were the acquiring corporation, P causes CFC2 to form CFC3 in Country X and to contribute $100x to CFC3. CFC3 then acquires all of the stock of CFC1 from P for $100x.

(ii) Result. Because a principal purpose for creating, organizing, or funding CFC3 (acquiring corporation) is to avoid the application of section 304 to CFC2 (deemed acquiring corporation), under paragraph (b)(1) of this section, for purposes of determining the amount of the $100x distribution constituting a dividend (and source thereof) under section 304(b)(2), CFC2 shall be treated as acquiring the stock of CFC1 (issuing corporation) from P for $100x. As a result, P receives a $100x distribution out of the earnings and profits of CFC2 to which section 301(c)(1) applies.

Example 2. (i) Facts. P, a domestic corporation, wholly owns CFC1, a controlled foreign corporation with substantial accumulated earnings and profits. The CFC1 stock has a basis of $100x. CFC1 is organized in Country X. P also wholly owns CFC2, a controlled foreign corporation with zero accumulated earnings and profits. CFC2 is organized in Country Y. P wishes to own all of its foreign corporations in a direct chain and to repatriate the cash of CFC2. In order to avoid having to obtain Country X approval for the acquisition of CFC1 (a Country X corporation) by CFC2 (a Country Y corporation) and to avoid a dividend distribution from CFC1 to P, P forms a new corporation (CFC3) in Country X and transfers the stock of CFC1 to CFC3 in exchange for CFC3 stock. P then transfers the stock of CFC3 to CFC2 in exchange for $100x.

(ii) Result. Because a principal purpose for the transfer of the stock of CFC1 (deemed issuing corporation) by P to CFC3 (issuing corporation) is to avoid the application of section 304 to CFC1, under paragraph (b)(2) of this section, for purposes of determining the amount of the $100x distribution constituting a dividend (and source thereof) under section 304(b)(2), CFC2 (acquiring corporation) shall be treated as acquiring the stock of CFC1 from P for $100x. As a result, P receives a $100x distribution out of the earnings and profits of CFC1 to which section 301(c)(1) applies.

* * *

[T.D. 9477, 74 FR 69023, Dec. 30, 2009; T.D. 9606, 77 FR 75845, Dec. 26, 2012]

§ 1.304–5 Control.

(a) Control requirement in general. Section 304(c)(1) provides that, for purposes of section 304, control means the ownership of stock possessing at least 50 percent of the total combined voting power of all classes of stock entitled to vote or at least 50 percent of the total value of shares of all classes of stock. Section 304(c)(3) makes section 318(a) (relating to constructive ownership of stock), as modified by section 304(c)(3)(B), applicable to section 304 for purposes of determining control under section 304(c)(1).

(b) Effect of section 304(c)(2)(B)—(1) In general. In determining whether the control test with respect to both the issuing and acquiring corporations is satisfied, section 304(a)(1) considers only the person or persons that—

(i) Control the issuing corporation before the transaction;

(ii) Transfer issuing corporation stock to the acquiring corporation for property; and

(iii) Control the acquiring corporation thereafter.

(2) Application. Section 317 defines property to include money, securities, and any other property except stock (or stock rights) in the distributing corporation. However, section 304(c)(2)(B) provides a special rule to extend the relevant group of persons to be tested for control of both the issuing and acquiring corporations to include the person or persons that do not acquire property, but rather solely stock from the acquiring corporation in the transaction. Section 304(c)(2)(B) provides that if two or more persons in control of the issuing corporation transfer stock of such corporation to the acquiring corporation, and if the transferors are in control of the acquiring corporation after the transfer, the person or persons in control of each corporation include each of those transferors. Because the purpose of section 304(c)(2)(B) is to include in the relevant control group the person or persons that retain or acquire acquiring corporation stock in the transaction, only the person or persons transferring stock of the issuing corporation that retain or acquire any proprietary interest in the acquiring corporation are taken into account for purposes of applying section 304(c)(2)(B).

(3) Example. This section may be illustrated by the following example.

Example. **(a)** A, the owner of 20% of T's only class of stock, transfers that stock to P solely in exchange for all of the P stock. Pursuant to the same transaction, P, solely in exchange for cash, acquires the remaining 80% of the T stock from T's other shareholder, B, who is unrelated to A and P.

(b) Although A and B together were in control of T (the issuing corporation) before the transaction and A and B each transferred T stock to P (the acquiring corporation), sections 304(a)(1) and (c)(2)(B) do not apply to B because B did not retain or acquire any proprietary interest in P in the transaction. Section 304(a)(1) also does not apply to A because A (or any control group of which A was a member) did not control T before the transaction and P after the transaction.

(c) Effective date. This section is effective on January 20, 1994.

[T.D. 8515, 59 FR 2958, Jan. 20, 1994]

§ 1.305–1 Stock dividends.

(a) In general. Under section 305, a distribution made by a corporation to its shareholders in its stock or in rights to acquire its stock is not included in gross income except as provided in section 305(b) and the regulations promulgated under the authority of section 305(c). A distribution made by a corporation to its shareholders in its stock or rights to acquire its stock which would not otherwise be included in gross income by reason of section 305 shall not be so included merely because such distribution was made out of Treasury stock or consisted of rights to acquire Treasury stock. See section 307 for rules as to basis of stock and stock rights acquired in a distribution.

(b) Amount of distribution. (1) In general, where a distribution of stock or rights to acquire stock of a corporation is treated as a distribution of property to which section 301 applies by reason of section 305(b), the amount of the distribution, in accordance with section 301(b) and § 1.301–1, is the fair market value of such stock or rights on the date of distribution. See Example (1) of § 1.305–2(b).

(2) Where a corporation which regularly distributes its earnings and profits, such as a regulated investment company, declares a dividend pursuant to which the shareholders may elect to receive either money or stock of the distributing corporation of equivalent value, the amount of the distribution of the stock received by any shareholder electing to receive stock will be considered to equal the amount of the money which could have been received instead. See Example (2) of § 1.305–2(b).

(3) For rules for determining the amount of the distribution where certain transactions, such as changes in conversion ratios or periodic redemptions, are treated as distributions under section 305(c), see Examples (6), (8), (9), and (15) of § 1.305–3(e).

(c) Adjustment in purchase price. A transfer of stock (or rights to acquire stock) or an increase or decrease in the conversion ratio or redemption price of stock which represents an adjustment of the price to be paid by the distributing corporation in acquiring property (within the meaning of section 317(a)) is not within the purview of section 305 because it is not a distribution with respect to its stock. For example, assume that on January 1, 1970, pursuant to a reorganization, corporation X acquires all the stock of corporation Y solely in exchange for its convertible preferred class B stock. Under the terms of the class B stock, its conversion ratio is to be adjusted in 1976 under a formula based upon the earnings of corporation Y over the 6–year period ending on December 31, 1975. Such an adjustment in 1976 is not covered by section 305.

(d) Definitions. (1) For purposes of this section and §§ 1.305–2 through 1.305–7, the term stock includes rights or warrants to acquire such stock.

(2) For purposes of §§ 1.305–2 through 1.305–7, the term shareholder includes a holder of rights or warrants or a holder of convertible securities.

[T.D. 7281, 38 FR 18532, July 12, 1973; 38 FR 19910, July 25, 1973; T.D. 8474, 58 FR 25557, April 27, 1993; T.D. 8471, 58 FR 26524, May 4, 1993]

§ 1.305–2 Distributions in lieu of money.

(a) In general. Under section 305(b)(1), if any shareholder has the right to an election or option with respect to whether a distribution shall be made either in money or any other property, or in stock or rights to acquire stock of the distributing corporation, then, with respect to all shareholders, the distribution of stock or rights to acquire stock is treated as a distribution of property to which section 301 applies regardless of—

(1) Whether the distribution is actually made in whole or in part in stock or in stock rights;

(2) Whether the election or option is exercised or exercisable before or after the declaration of the distribution;

(3) Whether the declaration of the distribution provides that the distribution will be made in one medium unless the shareholder specifically requests payment in the other;

(4) Whether the election governing the nature of the distribution is provided in the declaration of the distribution or in the corporate charter or arises from the circumstances of the distribution; or

(5) Whether all or part of the shareholders have the election.

(b) Examples. The application of section 305(b)(1) may be illustrated by the following examples:

Example (1). (i) Corporation X declared a dividend payable in additional shares of its common stock to the holders of its outstanding common stock on the basis of two additional shares for each share held on the record date but with the provision that, at the election of any shareholder made within a specified period prior to the distribution date, he may receive one additional share for each share held on the record date plus $12 principal amount of securities of corporation Y owned by corporation X. The fair market value of the stock of corporation X on the distribution date was $10 per share. The fair market value of $12 principal amount of securities of corporation Y on the distribution date was $11 but such securities had a cost basis to corporation X of $9.

(ii) The distribution to all shareholders of one additional share of stock of corporation X (with respect to which no election applies) for each share outstanding is not a distribution to which section 301 applies.

(iii) The distribution of the second share of stock of corporation X to those shareholders who do not elect to receive securities of corporation Y is a distribution of property to which section 301 applies, whether such shareholders are individuals or corporations. The amount of the distribution to which section 301 applies is $10 per share of stock of corporation X held on the record date (the fair market value of the stock of corporation X on the distribution date).

* * *

(v) In the case of the individual shareholders of corporation X who elects to receive such securities, the amount of the distribution to which section 301 applies is $11 per share of stock of corporation X held on the record date (the fair market value of the $12 principal amount of securities of corporation Y on the distribution date).

(vi) In the case of the corporate shareholders of corporation X electing to receive such securities, the amount of the distribution to which section 301 applies is $9 per share of stock of corporation X held on the record date (the basis of the securities of corporation Y in the hands of corporation X).

Example (2). On January 10, 1970, corporation X, a regulated investment company, declared a dividend of $1 per share on its common stock payable on February 11, 1970, in cash or in stock of corporation X of equivalent value determined as of January 22, 1970, at the election of the shareholder made on or before January 22, 1970. The amount of the distribution to which section 301 applies is $1 per share whether the shareholder elects to take cash or stock and whether the shareholder is an individual or a corporation. Such amount will also be used in determining the dividend paid deduction of corporation X and the reduction in earnings and profits of corporation X.

[T.D. 7281, 38 FR 18532, July 12, 1973]

§ 1.305–3 Disproportionate distributions.

(a) In general. Under section 305(b)(2), a distribution (including a deemed distribution) by a corporation of its stock or rights to acquire its stock is treated as a distribution of property to which section 301 applies if the distribution (or a series of distributions of which such distribution is one) has the result of (1) the receipt of money or other property by some shareholders, and (2) an increase in the proportionate interests of other shareholders in the assets or earnings and profits of the corporation. Thus, if a corporation has two classes of common stock outstanding and cash dividends are paid on one class and stock dividends are paid on the other class, the stock dividends are treated as distributions to which section 301 applies.

(b) Special rules. **(1)** As used in section 305(b)(2), the term "a series of distributions" encompasses all distributions of stock made or deemed made by a corporation which have the result of the receipt of cash or property by some shareholders and an increase in the proportionate interests of other shareholders.

(2) In order for a distribution of stock to be considered as one of a series of distributions it is not necessary that such distribution be pursuant to a plan to distribute cash or property to some shareholders and to increase the proportionate interests of other shareholders. It is sufficient if there is an actual or deemed distribution of stock (of which such distribution is one) and as a result of such distribution or distributions some shareholders receive cash or property and other shareholders increase their proportionate interests. For example, if a corporation pays quarterly stock dividends to one class of common shareholders and annual cash dividends to another class of common shareholders the quarterly stock dividends constitute a series of distributions of stock having the result of the receipt of cash or property by some shareholders and an increase in the proportionate interests of other shareholders. This is so whether or not the stock distributions and the cash distributions are steps in an overall plan or are independent and unrelated. Accordingly, all the quarterly stock dividends are distributions to which section 301 applies.

(3) There is no requirement that both elements of section 305(b)(2) (*i.e.,* receipt of cash or property by some shareholders and an increase in proportionate interests of other shareholders) occur in the form of a distribution or series of distributions as long as the result of a distribution or distributions of stock is that some shareholders' proportionate interests increase and other shareholders in fact receive cash or property. Thus, there is no requirement that the shareholders receiving cash or property acquire the cash or property by way of a corporate distribution with respect to their shares, so long as they receive such cash or property in their capacity as shareholders, if there is a stock distribution which results in a change in the proportionate interests of some shareholders and other shareholders receive cash or property. However, in order for a distribution of property to meet the requirement of section 305(b)(2), such distribution must be made to a shareholder in his capacity as a shareholder, and must be a distribution to which section 301, 356(a)(2), 871(a)(1)(A), 881(a)(1), 852(b), or 857(b) applies. (Under section 305(d)(2), the payment of interest to a holder of a convertible debenture is treated as a distribution of property to a shareholder for purposes of section 305(b)(2).) For example if a corporation makes a stock distribution to its shareholders and, pursuant to a prearranged plan with such corporation, a related corporation purchases such stock from those shareholders who want cash, in a transaction to which section 301 applies by virtue of section 304, the requirements of section 305(b)(2) are satisfied. In addition, a distribution of property incident to an isolated redemption of stock (for example, pursuant to a tender offer) will not cause section 305(b)(2) to apply even though the redemption distribution is treated as a distribution of property to which section 301, 871(a)(1)(A), 881(a)(1), or 356(a)(2) applies.

(4) Where the receipt of cash or property occurs more than 36 months following a distribution or series of distributions of stock, or where a distribution or series of distributions of stock is made more than 36 months following the receipt of cash or property, such distribution or distributions will be presumed not to result in the receipt of cash or property by some shareholders and an increase in the proportionate interest of other shareholders, unless the receipt of cash or property and the distribution or series of distributions of stock are made pursuant to a plan. For example, if, pursuant to a plan, a corporation pays cash dividends to some shareholders on January 1, 1971 and increases the proportionate interests of other shareholders on March 1, 1974, such increases in proportionate interests are distributions to which section 301 applies.

(5) In determining whether a distribution or a series of distributions has the result of a disproportionate distribution, there shall be treated as outstanding stock of the distributing corporation (i) any right to acquire such stock (whether or not exercisable during the taxable year), and (ii) any security convertible into stock of the distributing corporation (whether or not convertible during the taxable year).

(6) In cases where there is more than one class of stock outstanding, each class of stock is to be considered separately in determining whether a shareholder has increased his proportionate interest in the assets or earnings and profits of a corporation. The individual shareholders of a class of stock will be deemed to have an increased interest if the class of stock as a whole has an increased interest in the corporation.

(c) Distributions of cash in lieu of fractional shares. **(1)** Section 305(b)(2) will not apply if—

(i) A corporation declares a dividend payable in stock of the corporation and distributes cash in lieu of fractional shares to which shareholders would otherwise be entitled, or

(ii) Upon a conversion of convertible stock or securities a corporation distributes cash in lieu of fractional shares to which shareholders would otherwise be entitled.

Provided the purpose of the distribution of cash is to save the corporation the trouble, expense, and inconvenience of issuing and transferring fractional shares (or scrip representing fractional shares), or issuing full shares representing the sum of fractional shares, and not to give any particular group of shareholders an increased interest in the assets or earnings and profits of the corporation. For purposes of paragraph (c)(1)(i) of this section, if the total amount of cash distributed in lieu of fractional shares is 5 percent or less of the total fair market value of the stock distributed (determined as of the date of declaration), the distribution shall be considered to be for such valid purpose.

(2) In a case to which subparagraph (1) of this paragraph applies, the transaction will be treated as though the fractional shares were distributed as part of the stock distribution and then were redeemed by the corporation. The treatment of the cash received by a shareholder will be determined under section 302.

* * *

(e) Examples. The application of section 305(b)(2) to distributions of stock and section 305(c) to deemed distributions of stock may be illustrated by the following examples:

Example (1). Corporation X is organized with two classes of common stock, class A and class B. Each share of stock is entitled to share equally in the assets and earnings and profits of the corporation. Dividends may be paid in stock or in cash on either class of stock without regard to the medium of payment of dividends on the other class. A dividend is declared on the class A stock payable in additional shares of class A stock and a dividend is declared on class B stock payable in cash. Since the class A shareholders as a class will have increased their proportionate interests in the assets and earnings and profits of the corporation and the class B shareholders will have received cash, the additional shares of class A stock are distributions of property to which section 301 applies. This is true even with respect to those shareholders who may own class A stock and class B stock in the same proportion.

Example (2). Corporation Y is organized with two classes of stock, class A common, and class B, which is nonconvertible and limited and preferred as to dividends. A dividend is declared upon the class A stock payable in additional shares of class A stock and a dividend is declared on the class B stock payable in cash. The distribution of class A stock is not one to which section 301 applies because the distribution does not increase the proportionate interests of the class A shareholders as a class.

Example (3). Corporation K is organized with two classes of stock, class A common, and class B, which is nonconvertible preferred stock. A dividend is declared upon the class A stock payable in shares of class B stock and a dividend is declared on the class B stock payable in cash. Since the class A shareholders as a class have an increased interest in the assets and earnings and profits of the corporation, the stock distribution is treated as a distribution to which section 301 applies. If, however, a dividend were declared upon the class A stock payable in a new class of preferred stock that is subordinated in all respects to the class B stock, the distribution would not increase the proportionate interests of the class A shareholders in the assets or earnings and profits of the corporation and would not be treated as a distribution to which section 301 applies.

Example (4). (i) Corporation W has one class of stock outstanding, class A common. The corporation also has outstanding interest paying securities convertible into class A common stock which have a fixed conversion ratio that is not subject to full adjustment in the event stock dividends or rights are distributed to the class A shareholders. Corporation W distributes to the class A shareholders rights to acquire additional shares of class A stock. During the year, interest is paid on the convertible securities.

(ii) The stock rights and convertible securities are considered to be outstanding stock of the corporation and the distribution increases the proportionate interests of the class A shareholders in the assets and earnings and profits of the corporation. Therefore, the distribution is treated as a distribution to which section 301 applies. The same result would follow if, instead of convertible securities, the corporation had outstanding convertible stock. If, however, the conversion ratio of the securities or stock were fully adjusted to reflect the distribution of rights to the class A shareholders, the rights to acquire class A stock would not increase the proportionate interests of the class A shareholders in the assets and earnings and profits of the corporation and would not be treated as a distribution to which section 301 applies.

Example (5). (i) Corporation S is organized with two classes of stock, class A common and class B convertible preferred. The class B is fully protected against dilution in the event of a stock dividend or stock split with respect to the class A stock; however, no adjustment in the conversion ratio is required to be made until the stock dividends equal 3 percent of the common stock issued and outstanding on the date of the first such stock dividend except that such adjustment must be made no later than 3 years after the date of the stock dividend. Cash dividends are paid annually on the class B stock.

(ii) Corporation S pays a 1 percent stock dividend on the class A stock in 1970. In 1971, another 1 percent stock dividend is paid and in 1972 another 1 percent stock dividend is paid. The conversion ratio of the class B stock is increased in 1972 to reflect the three stock dividends paid on the class A stock. The distributions of class A stock are not distributions to which section 301 applies because they do not increase the proportionate interests of the class A shareholders in the assets and earnings and profits of the corporation.

Example (6). (i) Corporation M is organized with two classes of stock outstanding, class A and class B. Each class B share may be converted, at the option of the holder, into class A shares. During the first year, the conversion ratio is one share of class A stock for each share of class B stock. At the beginning of each subsequent year, the conversion ratio is increased by 0.05 share of class A stock for each share of class B stock. Thus, during the second year, the conversion ratio would be 1.05 shares of class A stock for each share of class B stock, during the third year, the ratio would be 1.10 shares, etc.

(ii) M pays an annual cash dividend on the class A stock. At the beginning of the second year, when the conversion ratio is increased to 1.05 shares of class A stock for each share of class B stock, a distribution of 0.05 shares of class A stock is deemed made under section 305(c) with respect to each share of class B stock, since the proportionate interests of the class B shareholders in the assets or earnings and profits of M are increased and the transaction has the effect described in section 305(b)(2). Accordingly, sections 305(b)(2) and 301 apply to the transaction.

* * *

Example (8). Corporation T has 1,000 shares of stock outstanding. C owns 100 shares. Nine other shareholders each owns 100 shares. Pursuant to a plan for periodic redemptions, T redeems up to 5 percent of each shareholder's stock each year. During the year, each of the nine other shareholders has 5 shares of his stock redeemed for cash. Thus, C's proportionate interest in the assets and earnings and profits of T is increased. Assuming that the cash received by the nine other shareholders is taxable under section 301, C is deemed under section 305(c) to have received a distribution under section 305(b)(2) of 5.25 shares of T stock to which section 301 applies. The amount of C's distribution is measured by the fair market value of the number of shares which would have been distributed to C had the corporation sought to increase his interest by 0.47 percentage points (C owned 10 percent of the T stock immediately before the redemption and 10.47 percent immediately thereafter) and the other shareholders continued to hold 900 shares (*i.e.,*)

(a) $100 \div 955 = 10.47\%$ (percent of C's ownership after redemption)

(b) $100 + x \div 1000 + x = 10.47\%$; $x = 5.25$ (additional shares considered to be distributed to C).

Since in computing the amount of additional shares deemed to be distributed to C the redemption of shares is disregarded, the redemption of shares will be similarly disregarded in determining the value of the stock of the corporation which is deemed to be distributed. Thus, in the example, 1,005.25 shares of stock are considered as outstanding after the redemption. The value of each share deemed to be distributed to C is then determined by dividing the 1,005.25 shares into the aggregate fair market value of the actual shares outstanding (955) after the redemption.

* * *

Example (10). Corporation P has 1,000 shares of stock outstanding. T owns 700 shares of the P stock and G owns 300 shares of the P stock. In a single and isolated redemption to which section 301 applies, the corporation redeems 150 shares of T's stock. Since this is an isolated redemption and is not a part of a periodic redemption plan, G is not treated as having received a deemed distribution under section 305(c) to which sections 305(b)(2) and 301 apply even though he has an increased proportionate interest in the assets and earnings and profits of the corporation.

Example (11). Corporation Q is a large corporation whose sole class of stock is widely held. However, the four largest shareholders are officers of the corporation and each owns 8 percent of the outstanding stock. In 1974, in a distribution to which section 301 applies, the corporation redeems 1.5 percent of the stock from each of the four largest shareholders in preparation for their retirement. From 1970 through 1974, the corporation distributes annual stock dividends to its shareholders. No other distributions were made to these shareholders. Since the 1974 redemptions are isolated and are not part of a plan for periodically redeeming the stock of the corporation, the shareholders receiving stock dividends will not be treated as having received a distribution under section 305(b)(2) even though they have an increased proportionate interest in the assets and earnings and profits of the corporation and whether or not the redemptions are treated as distributions to which section 301 applies.

Example (12). Corporation R has 2,000 shares of class A stock outstanding. Five shareholders own 300 shares each and five shareholders own 100 shares each. In preparation for the retirement of the five major shareholders, corporation R, in a single and isolated transaction, has a recapitalization in which each share of class A stock may be exchanged either for five shares of new class B nonconvertible preferred stock plus 0.4 share of new class C common stock, or for two shares of new class C common stock. As a result of the exchanges, each of the five major shareholders receives 1,500 shares of class B nonconvertible preferred stock and 120 shares of class C common stock. The remaining shareholders each receives 200 shares of class C common stock. None of the exchanges are within the purview of section 305.

* * *

[T.D. 7281, 38 FR 18532, July 12, 1973, 38 FR 19910, 19911, July 25, 1973, as amended by T.D. 7329, 39 FR 36860, Oct. 15, 1974; T.D. 8643, 60 FR 66134, Dec. 21, 1995]

§ 1.305-4 Distributions of common and preferred stock.

(a) In general. Under section 305(b)(3), a distribution (or a series of distributions) by a corporation which results in the receipt of preferred stock (whether or not convertible into common stock) by some common shareholders and the receipt of common stock by other common shareholders is treated as a distribution of property to which section 301 applies. For the meaning of the term "a series of distribution," see subparagraphs (1) through (6) of § 1.305-3(b).

(b) Examples. The application of section 305(b)(3) may be illustrated by the following examples:

Example (1). Corporation X is organized with two classes of common stock, class A and class B. Dividends may be paid in stock or in cash on either class of stock without regard to the medium of payment of dividends on the other class. A dividend is declared on the class A stock payable in additional shares of class A stock and a dividend is declared on class B stock payable in newly authorized class C stock which is nonconvertible and limited and preferred as to dividends. Both the distribution of class A shares and the distribution of new class C shares are distributions to which section 301 applies.

Example (2). Corporation Y is organized with one class of stock, class A common. During the year the corporation declares a dividend on the class A stock payable in newly authorized class B preferred stock which is convertible into class A stock no later than 6 months from the date of distribution at a price that is only slightly higher than the market price of class A stock on the date of distribution. Taking into account the dividend rate, redemption provisions, the marketability of the convertible stock, and the conversion price, it is reasonable to anticipate that within a relatively short period of time some shareholders will exercise their conversion rights and some will not. Since the distribution can reasonably be expected to result in the receipt of preferred stock by some common shareholders and the receipt of common stock by other common shareholders, the distribution is a distribution of property to which section 301 applies.

[T.D. 7281, 38 FR 18536, July 12, 1973]

§ 1.305-5 Distributions on preferred stock.

(a) In general. Under section 305(b)(4), a distribution by a corporation of its stock (or rights to acquire its stock) made (or deemed made under section 305(c)) with respect to its preferred stock is treated as a distribution of property to which section 301 applies unless the distribution is made with respect to convertible preferred stock to take into account a stock dividend, stock split, or any similar event (such as the sale of stock at less than the fair market value pursuant to a rights offering) which would otherwise result in the dilution of the conversion right. For purposes of the preceding sentence, an adjustment in the conversion ratio of convertible preferred stock made solely to take into account the distribution by a closed end regulated investment company of a capital gain dividend with respect to the stock into which such stock is convertible shall not be considered a "similar event." The term "preferred stock" generally refers to stock which, in relation to other classes of stock outstanding, enjoys certain limited rights and privileges (generally associated with specified dividend and liquidation priorities) but does not participate in corporate growth to any significant extent. The distinguishing feature of "preferred stock" for the purposes of section 305(b)(4) is not its privileged position as such, but that such privileged position is limited, and that such stock does not participate in corporate growth to any significant extent. However, a right to participate which lacks substance will not prevent a class of stock from being treated as preferred stock. Thus, stock which enjoys a priority as to dividends and on liquidation but which is entitled to participate, over and above such priority, with another less privileged class of stock in earnings and profits and upon liquidation, may nevertheless be treated as preferred stock for purposes of section 305 if, taking into account all the facts and circumstances, it is reasonable to anticipate at the time a distribution is made (or is deemed to have been made) with respect to such stock that there is little or no likelihood of such stock actually participating in current and anticipated earnings and upon liquidation beyond its preferred interest. Among the facts and circumstances to be considered are the prior and anticipated earnings per share, the cash dividends per share, the book value per share, the extent of preference and of participation of each class, both absolutely and relative to each other, and any other facts which indicate whether or not the stock has a real and meaningful probability of actually participating in the earnings and growth of the corporation. The determination of whether stock is preferred for purposes of section 305 shall be made without regard to any right to convert such stock into another class of stock of the corporation. The term "preferred stock", however, does not include convertible debentures.

* * *

[T.D. 7281, 38 FR 18536, July 12, 1973, as amended by T.D. 7329, 39 FR 36860, Oct. 15, 1974; T.D. 8643, 60 FR 66134, Dec. 21, 1995]

§ 1.305–6 Distributions of convertible preferred.

(a) In general. **(1)** Under section 305(b)(5), a distribution by a corporation of its convertible preferred stock or rights to acquire such stock made or considered as made with respect to its stock is treated as a distribution of property to which section 301 applies unless the corporation establishes that such distribution will not result in a disproportionate distribution as described in § 1.305–3.

(2) The distribution of convertible preferred stock is likely to result in a disproportionate distribution when both of the following conditions exist: (i) The conversion right must be exercised within a relatively short period of time after the date of distribution of the stock; and (ii) taking into account such factors as the dividend rate, the redemption provisions, the marketability of the convertible stock, and the conversion price, it may be anticipated that some shareholders will exercise their conversion rights and some will not. On the other hand, where the conversion right may be exercised over a period of many years and the dividend rate is consistent with market conditions at the time of distribution of the stock, there is no basis for predicting at what time and the extent to which the stock will be converted and it is unlikely that a disproportionate distribution will result.

(b) Examples. The application of section 305(b)(5) may be illustrated by the following examples:

Example (1). Corporation Z is organized with one class of stock, class A common. During the year the corporation declares a dividend on the class A stock payable in newly authorized class B preferred stock which is convertible into class A stock for a period of 20 years from the date of issuance. Assuming dividend rates are normal in light of existing conditions so that there is no basis for predicting the extent to which the stock will be converted, the circumstances will ordinarily be sufficient to establish that a disproportionate distribution will not result since it is impossible to predict the extent to which the class B stock will be converted into class A stock. Accordingly, the distribution of class B stock is not one to which section 301 applies.

Example (2). Corporation X is organized with one class of stock, class A common. During the year the corporation declares a dividend on the class A stock payable in newly authorized redeemable class C preferred stock which is convertible into class A common stock no later than 4 months from the date of distribution at a price slightly higher than the market price of class A stock on the date of distribution. By prearrangement with corporation X, corporation Y, an insurance company, agrees to purchase class C stock from any shareholder who does not wish to convert. By reason of this prearrangement, it is anticipated that the shareholders will either sell the class C stock to the insurance company (which expects to retain the shares for investment purposes) or will convert. As a result, some of the shareholders exercise their conversion privilege and receive additional shares of class A stock, while other shareholders sell their class C stock to corporation Y and receive cash. The distribution is a distribution to which section 301 applies since it results in the receipt of property by some shareholders and an increase in the proportionate interests of other shareholders.

[T.D. 7281, 38 FR 18538, July 12, 1973]

§ 1.305–7 Certain transactions treated as distributions.

(a) In general. Under section 305(c), a change in conversion ratio, a change in redemption price, a difference between redemption price and issue price, a redemption which is treated as a distribution to which section 301 applies, or any transaction (including a recapitalization) having a similar effect on the interest of any shareholder may be treated as a distribution with respect to any shareholder whose proportionate interest in the earnings and profits or assets of the corporation is increased by such change, difference, redemption, or similar transaction. In general, such change, difference, redemption, or similar transaction will be treated as a distribution to which sections 305(b) and 301 apply where—

(1) The proportionate interest of any shareholder in the earnings and profits or assets of the corporation deemed to have made such distribution is increased by such change, difference, redemption, or similar transaction; and

(2) Such distribution has the result described in paragraph (2), (3), (4), or (5) of section 305(b).

Where such change, difference, redemption, or similar transaction is treated as a distribution under the provisions of this section, such distribution will be deemed made with respect to any shareholder whose interest in the earnings and profits or assets of the distributing corporation is increased thereby. Such distribution will be deemed to be a distribution of the stock of such corporation made by the corporation to such shareholder with respect to his stock. * * *

* * *

(c) Recapitalizations. **(1)** A recapitalization (whether or not an isolated transaction) will be deemed to result in a distribution to which section 305(c) and this section apply if—

(i) It is pursuant to a plan to periodically increase a shareholder's proportionate interest in the assets or earnings and profits of the corporation, or

(ii) A shareholder owning preferred stock with dividends in arrears exchanges his stock for other stock and, as a result, increases his proportionate interest in the assets or earnings and profits of the corporation. An increase in a preferred shareholder's proportionate interest occurs in any case where the fair market value or the liquidation preference, whichever is greater, of the stock received in the exchange (determined immediately following the recapitalization), exceeds the issue price of the preferred stock surrendered.

(2) In a case to which subparagraph (1)(ii) of this paragraph applies, the amount of the distribution deemed under section 305(c) to result from the recapitalization is the lesser of (i) the amount by which the fair market value or the liquidation preference, whichever is greater, of the stock received in the exchange (determined immediately following the recapitalization) exceeds the issue price of the preferred stock surrendered, or (ii) the amount of the dividends in arrears.

* * *

[T.D. 7281, 38 FR 18538, July 12, 1973, as amended by T.D. 8643, 60 FR 66134, Dec. 21, 1995]

§ 1.306–1 General.

(a) Section 306 provides, in general, that the proceeds from the sale or redemption of certain stock (referred to as "section 306 stock") shall be treated either as ordinary income or as a distribution of property to which section 301 applies. Section 306 stock is defined in section 306(c) and is usually preferred stock received either as a nontaxable dividend or in a transaction in which no gain or loss is recognized. Section 306(b) lists certain circumstances in which the special rules of section 306(a) shall not apply.

(b)(1) If a shareholder sells or otherwise disposes of section 306 stock (other than by redemption or within the exceptions listed in section 306(b)), the entire proceeds received from such disposition shall be treated as ordinary income to the extent that the fair market value of the stock sold, on the date distributed to the shareholder, would have been a dividend to such shareholder had the distributing corporation distributed cash in lieu of stock. Any excess of the amount received over the sum of the amount treated as ordinary income plus the adjusted basis of the stock disposed of, shall be treated as gain from the sale of a capital asset or noncapital asset as the case may be. No loss shall be recognized. No reduction of earnings and profits results from any disposition of stock other than a redemption. The term "disposition" under section 306(a)(1) includes, among other things, pledges of stock under certain circumstances, particularly where the pledgee can look only to the stock itself as its security.

(2) Section 306(a)(1) may be illustrated by the following examples:

Example (1). On December 15, 1954, A and B owned equally all of the stock of Corporation X which files its income tax return on a calendar year basis. On that date Corporation X distributed pro rata 100 shares of preferred stock as a dividend on its outstanding common stock. On December 15, 1954, the preferred stock had a fair market value of $10,000. On December 31, 1954, the earnings and profits of Corporation X were $20,000. The 50 shares of preferred stock so distributed to A had an allocated basis to him of $10 per share or a total of $500 for the 50 shares. Such shares had a fair market value of $5,000 when issued. A sold the 50 shares of preferred stock on July 1, 1955, for $6,000. Of this amount $5,000 will be treated as ordinary income; $500 ($6,000 minus $5,500) will be treated as gain from the sale of a capital or noncapital asset as the case may be.

Example (2). The facts are the same as in Example 1 except that A sold his 50 shares of preferred stock for $5,100. Of this amount $5,000 will be treated as ordinary income. No loss will be allowed. There will be added back to the basis of the common stock of Corporation X with respect to which the preferred stock was distributed, $400, the allocated basis of $500 reduced by the $100 received.

Example (3). The facts are the same as in example 1 except that A sold 25 of his shares of preferred stock for $2,600. Of this amount $2,500 will be treated as ordinary income. No loss will be allowed. There will be added back to the basis of the common stock of Corporation X with respect to which the preferred stock was distributed, $150, the allocated basis of $250 reduced by the $100 received.

(c) The entire amount received by a shareholder from the redemption of section 306 stock shall be treated as a distribution of property under section 301. See also section 303 (relating to distribution in redemption of stock to pay death taxes).

[T.D. 6500, 25 FR 11607, Nov. 26, 1960, as amended by T.D. 7556, 43 FR 34128, Aug. 3, 1978]

§ 1.306–2 Exception.

(a) If a shareholder terminates his entire stock interest in a corporation—

(1) By a sale or other disposition within the requirements of section 306(b)(1)(A), or

(2) By redemption under section 302(b)(3) (through the application of section 306(b)(1)(B)),

the amount received from such disposition shall be treated as an amount received in part or full payment for the stock sold or redeemed. In the case of a sale, only the stock interest need be terminated. In determining whether an entire stock interest has been terminated under section 306(b)(1)(A), all of the provisions of section 318(a) (relating to constructive ownership of stock) shall be applicable. In determining whether a shareholder has terminated his entire interest in a corporation by a redemption of his stock under section 302(b)(3), all of the provisions of section 318(a) shall be applicable unless the shareholder meets the requirements of section 302(c)(2) (relating to termination of all interest in the corporation). If the requirements of section 302(c)(2) are met, section 318(a)(1) (relating to members of a family) shall be inapplicable. Under all circumstances paragraphs (2), (3), (4), and (5) of section 318(a) shall be applicable.

(b) Section 306(a) does not apply to—

(1) Redemptions of section 306 stock pursuant to a partial or complete liquidation of a corporation to which part II (section 331 and following), subchapter C, chapter 1 of the Code applies,

(2) Exchanges of section 306 stock solely for stock in connection with a reorganization or in an exchange under section 351, 355, or section 1036 (relating to exchanges of stock for stock in the same corporation) to the extent that gain or loss is not recognized to the shareholder as the result of the exchange of the stock (see paragraph (d) of § 1.306–3 relative to the receipt of other property), and

(3) A disposition or redemption, if it is established to the satisfaction of the Commissioner that the distribution, and the disposition or redemption, was not in pursuance of a plan having as one of its principal purposes the avoidance of Federal income tax. However, in the case of a prior or simultaneous disposition (or redemption) of the stock with respect to which the section 306 stock disposed of (or redeemed) was issued, it is not necessary to establish that the distribution was not in pursuance of such a plan. For example, in the absence of such a plan and of any other facts the first sentence of this subparagraph would be applicable to the case of dividends and isolated dispositions of section 306 stock by minority shareholders. Similarly, in the absence of such a plan and of any other facts, if a shareholder received a distribution of 100 shares of section 306 stock on his holdings of 100 shares of voting common stock in a corporation and sells his voting common stock before he disposes of his section 306 stock, the subsequent disposition of his section 306 stock would not ordinarily be considered a disposition one of the principal purposes of which is the avoidance of Federal income tax.

[T.D. 6500, 25 FR 11607, Nov. 26, 1960, as amended by T.D. 6969, 33 FR 11998, Aug. 23, 1968]

§ 1.306–3 Section 306 stock defined.

(a) For the purpose of subchapter C, chapter 1 of the Code, the term "section 306 stock" means stock which meets the requirements of section 306(c)(1). Any class of stock distributed to a shareholder in a transaction in which no amount is includible in the income of the shareholder or no gain or loss is recognized may be section 306 stock, if a distribution of money by the distributing corporation in lieu of such stock would have been a dividend in whole or in part. However, except as provided in section 306(g), if no part of a distribution of money by the distributing corporation in lieu of such stock would have been a dividend, the stock distributed will not constitute section 306 stock.

(b) For the purpose of section 306, rights to acquire stock shall be treated as stock. Such rights shall not be section 306 stock if no part of the distribution would have been a dividend if money had been distributed in lieu of the rights. When stock is acquired by the exercise of rights which are treated at section 306 stock, the stock acquired is section 306 stock. Upon the disposition of such stock (other than by redemption or within the exceptions listed in section 306(b)), the proceeds received from the disposition shall be treated as ordinary income to the extent that the fair market value of the stock rights, on the date distributed to the shareholder, would have been a dividend to the shareholder had the distributing corporation distributed cash in lieu of stock rights. Any excess of the amount realized over the sum of the amount treated as ordinary income plus the adjusted basis of the stock, shall be treated as gain from the sale of the stock.

(c) Section 306(c)(1)(A) provides that section 306 stock is any stock (other than common issued with respect to common) distributed to the shareholder selling or otherwise disposing thereof if, under section 305(a) (relating to distributions of stock and stock rights) any part of the distribution was not included in the gross income of the distributee.

(d) Section 306(c)(1)(B) includes in the definition of section 306 stock any stock except common stock, which is received by a shareholder in connection with a reorganization under section 368 or in a distribution or exchange under section 355 (or so much of section 356 as relates to section 355) provided the effect of the transaction is substantially the same as the receipt of a stock dividend, or the stock is received in exchange for section 306 stock. If, in a transaction to which section 356 is applicable, a shareholder exchanges section 306 stock for stock and money or other property, the entire amount of such money and of the fair market value of the other property (not limited to the gain recognized) shall be treated as a distribution of property to which section 301 applies. Common stock received in exchange for section 306 stock in a recapitalization shall not be considered section 306 stock. Ordinarily, section 306 stock includes stock which is not common stock received in pursuance of a plan of reorganization (within the meaning of section 368(a)) or received in a distribution or exchange to which section 355 (or so much of section 356 as relates to section 355) applies if cash received in lieu of such stock would have been treated as a dividend under section 356(a)(2) or would have been treated as a distribution to which section 301 applies by virtue of section 356(b) or section 302(d). The application of the preceding sentence is illustrated by the following examples:

Example (1). Corporation A, having only common stock outstanding, is merged in a statutory merger (qualifying as a reorganization under section 368(a)) with Corporation B. Pursuant to such merger, the shareholders of Corporation A received both common and preferred stock in Corporation B. The preferred stock received by such shareholders is section 306 stock.

Example (2). X and Y each own one-half of the 2,000 outstanding shares of preferred stock and one-half of the 2,000 outstanding shares of common stock of Corporation C. Pursuant to a reorganization within the meaning of section 368(a)(1)(E) (recapitalization) each shareholder exchanges his preferred stock for preferred stock of a new issue which is not substantially different from the preferred stock previously held. Unless the preferred stock exchanged was itself section 306 stock the preferred stock received is not section 306 stock.

(e) Section 306(c)(1)(C) includes in the definition of section 306 stock any stock (except as provided in section 306(c)(1)(B)) the basis of which in the hands of the person disposing of such stock, is determined by reference to section 306 stock held by such shareholder or any other person. Under this paragraph common stock can be section 306 stock. Thus, if a person owning section 306 stock in Corporation A transfers it to Corporation B which is controlled by him in exchange for common stock of Corporation B in a transaction to which section 351 is applicable, the common stock so received by him would be section 306 stock and subject to the provisions of section 306(a) on its disposition. In addition, the section 306 stock transferred is section 306 stock in the hands of Corporation B, the transferee. Section 306 stock transferred by gift remains section 306 stock in the hands of the donee. Stock received in exchange for section 306 stock under section 1036(a) (relating to exchange of stock for stock in the same corporation) or under so much of section 1031(b) as relates to section 1036(a) becomes section 306 stock and acquires, for purposes of section 306, the characteristics of the section 306 stock exchanged. The entire amount of the fair market value of the other property received in such transaction shall be considered as received upon a disposition (other than a redemption) to which section 306(a) applies. Section 306 stock ceases to be so classified if the basis of such stock is determined by reference to its fair market value on the date of the decedent-stockholder's death or the optional valuation date under section 1014.

(f) If section 306 stock which was distributed with respect to common stock is exchanged for common stock in the same corporation (whether or not such exchange is pursuant to a conversion privilege contained in section 306 stock), such common stock shall not be section 306 stock. This paragraph applies to exchanges not coming within the purview of section 306(c)(1)(B). Common stock which is convertible into stock other than common stock or into property, shall not be considered common stock. It is immaterial whether the conversion privilege is contained in the stock or in some type of collateral agreement.

(g) If there is a substantial change in the terms and conditions of any stock, then, for the purpose of this section—

(1) The fair market value of such stock shall be the fair market value at the time of distribution or the fair market value at the time of such change, whichever is higher;

(2) Such stock's ratable share of the amount which would have been a dividend if money had been distributed in lieu of stock shall be determined by reference to the time of distribution or by reference to the time of such change, whichever ratable share is higher; and

(3) Section 306(c)(2) shall be inapplicable if there would have been a dividend to any extent if money had been distributed in lieu of the stock either at the time of the distribution or at the time of such change.

* * *

[T.D. 6500, 25 FR 11607, Nov. 26, 1960, as amended by T.D. 7281, 38 FR 18540, July 12, 1973; T.D. 7556, 43 FR 34128, Aug. 3, 1978]

§ 1.307–1 General.

(a) If a shareholder receives stock or stock rights as a distribution on stock previously held and under section 305 such distribution is not includible in gross income then, except as provided in section 307(b) and § 1.307–2, the basis of the stock with respect to which the distribution was made shall be allocated between the old and new stocks or rights in proportion to the fair market values of each on the date of distribution. If a shareholder receives stock or stock rights as a distribution on stock previously held and pursuant to section 305 part of the distribution is not includible in gross income, then (except as provided in section 307(b) and § 1.307–2) the basis of the stock with respect to which the distribution is made shall be allocated between (1) the old stock and (2) that part of the new stock or rights which is not includible in gross income, in proportion to the fair market values of each on the date of distribution. The date of distribution in each case shall be the date the stock or the rights are distributed to the stockholder and not the record date. The general rule will apply with respect to stock rights only if such rights are exercised or sold.

(b) The application of paragraph (a) of this section is illustrated by the following example:

Example. A taxpayer in 1947 purchased 100 shares of common stock at $100 per share and in 1954 by reason of the ownership of such stock acquired 100 rights entitling him to subscribe to 100 additional shares of such stock at $90 a share. Immediately after the issuance of the rights, each of the shares of stock in respect of which the rights were acquired had a fair market value, ex-rights, of $110 and the rights had a fair market value of $19 each. The basis of the rights and the common stock for the purpose of determining the basis for gain or loss on a subsequent sale or exercise of the rights or a sale of the old stock is computed as follows:

100 (shares)×$100=$10,000, cost of old stock (stock in respect of which the rights were acquired).

100 (shares)×$110=$11,000, market value of old stock.

100 (rights)×$19=$1,900, market value of rights.

11,000/12,900 of $10,000=$8,527.13, cost of old stock apportioned to such stock.

1,900/12,900 of $10,000=$1,472.87, cost of old stock apportioned to rights.

If the rights are sold, the basis for determining gain or loss will be $14.7287 per right. If the rights are exercised, the basis of the new stock acquired will be the subscription price paid therefor ($90) plus the basis of the rights exercised ($14.7287 each) or $104.7287 per share. The remaining basis of the old stock for the purpose of determining gain or loss on a subsequent sale will be $85.2713 per share.

[T.D. 6500, 25 FR 11607, Nov. 26, 1960]

§ 1.307–2 Exception.

The basis of rights to buy stock which are excluded from gross income under section 305(a), shall be zero if the fair market value of such rights on the date of distribution is less than 15 percent of the fair market value of the old stock on that date, unless the shareholder elects to allocate part of the basis of the old stock to the rights as provided in paragraph (a) of § 1.307-1. The election shall be made by a shareholder with respect to all the rights received by him in a particular distribution in respect of all the stock of the same class owned by him in the issuing corporation at the time of such distribution. Such election to allocate basis to rights shall be in the form of a statement attached to the shareholder's return for the year in which the rights are received. This election, once made, shall be irrevocable with respect to the rights for which the election was made. Any shareholder making such an election shall retain a copy of the election and of the tax return with which it was filed, in order to substantiate the use of an allocated basis upon a subsequent disposition of the stock acquired by exercise.

[T.D. 6500, 25 FR 11607, Nov. 26, 1960]

§ 1.312-1 Adjustment to earnings and profits reflecting distributions by corporations.

(a) In general, on the distribution of property by a corporation with respect to its stock, its earnings, and profits (to the extent thereof) shall be decreased by—

(1) The amount of money,

(2) The principal amount of the obligations of such corporation issued in such distribution, and

(3) The adjusted basis of other property.

* * *

(b) The adjustment provided in section 312(a)(3) and paragraph (a)(3) of this section with respect to a distribution of property (other than money or its own obligations) shall be made notwithstanding the fact that such property has appreciated or depreciated in value since acquisition.

(c) The application of paragraphs (a) and (b) of this section may be illustrated by the following examples:

Example (1). Corporation A distributes to its sole shareholder property with a value of $10,000 and a basis of $5,000. It has $12,500 in earnings and profits. The reduction in earnings and profits by reason of such distribution is $5,000. Such is the reduction even though the amount of $10,000 is includible in the income of the shareholder (other than a corporation) as a dividend.

Example (2). The facts are the same as in example (1) above except that the property has a basis of $15,000 and the earnings and profits of the corporation are $20,000. The reduction in earnings and profits is $15,000. Such is the reduction even though only the amount of $10,000 is includible in the income of the shareholder as a dividend.

(d) In the case of a distribution of stock or rights to acquire stock a portion of which is includible in income by reason of section 305(b), the earnings and profits shall be reduced by the fair market value of such portion. No reduction shall be made if a distribution of stock or rights to acquire stock is not includible in income under the provisions of section 305.

(e) No adjustment shall be made in the amount of the earnings and profits of the issuing corporation upon a disposition of section 306 stock unless such disposition is a redemption.

§ 1.312-3 Liabilities.

The amount of any reductions in earnings and profits described in section 312(a) or (b) shall be * * * reduced by the amount of any liability to which the property distributed was subject and by the amount of any other liability of the corporation assumed by the shareholder in connection with such distribution, * * *.

[T.D. 6500, 25 FR 11607, Nov. 26, 1960, as amended by T.D. 6832, 30 FR 8574, July 7, 1965; T.D. 7084, 36 FR 267, Jan. 8, 1971; T.D. 7209, 37 FR 20804, Oct. 5, 1972; T.D. 8586, 60 FR 2497, Jan. 10, 1995]

§ 1.312-6 Earnings and profits.

(a) In determining the amount of earnings and profits (whether of the taxable year, or accumulated since February 28, 1913, or accumulated before March 1, 1913) due consideration must be given to the facts, and, while mere bookkeeping entries increasing or decreasing surplus will not be conclusive, the amount of the earnings and profits in any case will be dependent upon the method of accounting properly employed in computing taxable income (or net income, as the case may be). For instance, a corporation keeping its books and filing its income tax returns under subchapter E, chapter 1 of the Code, on the cash receipts and disbursements basis may not use the accrual basis in determining earnings and profits; * * *.

(b) Among the items entering into the computation of corporate earnings and profits for a particular period are all income exempted by statute, income not taxable by the Federal Government under the Constitution, as well as all items includible in gross income under section 61 or corresponding provisions of prior revenue acts. Gains and losses within the purview of section 1002 or corresponding provisions of prior revenue acts are brought into the earnings and profits at the time and to the extent such gains and losses are recognized under that section. Interest on State bonds and certain other obligations, although not taxable when received by a corporation, is taxable to the same extent as other dividends when distributed to shareholders in the form of dividends.

(c)(1) In the case of a corporation in which depletion or depreciation is a factor in the determination of income, the only depletion or depreciation deductions to be considered in the computation of the total earnings and profits are those based on cost or other basis without regard to March 1, 1913, value. In computing the earnings and profits for any period beginning after February 28, 1913, the only depletion or depreciation deductions to be considered are those based on (i) cost or other basis, if the depletable or depreciable asset was acquired subsequent to February 28, 1913, or (ii) adjusted cost or March 1, 1913, value, whichever is higher, if acquired before March 1, 1913. Thus, discovery or percentage depletion under all revenue acts for mines and oil and gas wells is not to be taken into consideration in computing the earnings and profits of a corporation. Similarly, where the basis of property in the hands of a corporation is a substituted basis, such basis, and not the fair market value of the property at the time of the acquisition by the corporation, is the basis for computing depletion and depreciation for the purpose of determining earnings and profits of the corporation.

* * *

(d) A loss sustained for a year before the taxable year does not affect the earnings and profits of the taxable year. * * *

* * *

[T.D. 6500, 25 FR 11607, Nov. 26, 1960]

§ 1.312–7 Effect on earnings and profits of gain or loss realized after February 28, 1913.

* * *

(b)(1) The gain or loss so realized increases or decreases the earnings and profits to, but not beyond, the extent to which such gain or loss was recognized in computing taxable income (or net income, as the case may be) under the law applicable to the year in which such sale or disposition was made. As used in this paragraph, the term "recognized" has reference to that kind of realized gain or loss which is recognized for income tax purposes by the statute applicable to the year in which the gain or loss was realized. For example, see section 356. A loss (other than a wash sale loss with respect to which a deduction is disallowed under the provisions of section 1091 or corresponding provisions of prior revenue laws) may be recognized though not allowed as a deduction (by reason, for example, of the operation of sections 267 and 1211 and corresponding provisions of prior revenue laws) but the mere fact that it is not allowed does not prevent decrease in earnings and profits by the amount of such disallowed loss. Wash sale losses, however, disallowed under section 1091 and corresponding provisions of prior revenue laws, are deemed nonrecognized losses and do not reduce earnings or profits. The "recognized" gain or loss for the purpose of computing earnings and profits is determined by applying the recognition provisions to the realized gain or loss computed under the provisions of section 312(f)(1) as distinguished from the realized gain or loss used in computing taxable income (or net income, as the case may be).

* * *

(c)(1) The third sentence of section 312(f)(1) provides for cases in which the adjustments, prescribed in section 1016, to the basis indicated in section 312(f)(1)(A) or (B), as the case may be, differ from the adjustments to such basis proper for the purpose of determining earnings or profits. The adjustments provided by such third sentence reflect the treatment provided by §§ 1.312–6 and 1.312–15 relative to cases where the deductions for depletion and depreciation in computing taxable income (or net income, as the case may be) differ from the deductions proper for the purpose of computing earnings and profits.

(2) The effect of the third sentence of section 312(f)(1) may be illustrated by the following examples:

* * *

Example (3). On January 1, 1973, corporation X purchased for $10,000 a depreciable asset with an estimated useful life of 20 years and no salvage value. In computing depreciation on the asset, corporation X used the declining balance method with a rate twice the straight line rate. On December 31, 1976, the asset was sold for $9,000. Under section 1016(a)(2), the basis of the asset is adjusted for depreciation allowed for the years 1973 through 1976, or a total of $3,439. Thus, X realizes a gain of $2,439 (the excess of the amount realized, $9,000, over the adjusted basis, $6,561). However, the proper adjustment to basis for the purpose of determining earnings and profits is only

$2,000, *i.e.*, the total amount which, under § 1.312–15, was applied in the computation of earnings and profits for the years 1973–76. Hence, upon sale of the asset, earnings and profits are increased by only $1,000, *i.e.*, the excess of the amount realized, $9,000, over the adjusted basis for earnings and profits purposes, $8,000.

* * *

[T.D. 6500, 25 FR 11607, Nov. 26, 1960, as amended by T.D. 7221, 37 FR 24746, Nov. 21, 1972]

§ 1.312–10 Allocation of earnings in certain corporate separations.

(a) If one corporation transfers part of its assets constituting an active trade or business to another corporation in a transaction to which section 368(a)(1)(D) applies and immediately thereafter the stock and securities of the controlled corporation are distributed in a distribution or exchange to which section 355 (or so much of section 356 as relates to section 355) applies, the earnings and profits of the distributing corporation immediately before the transaction shall be allocated between the distributing corporation and the controlled corporation. In the case of a newly created controlled corporation, such allocation generally shall be made in proportion to the fair market value of the business or businesses (and interests in any other properties) retained by the distributing corporation and the business or businesses (and interests in any other properties) of the controlled corporation immediately after the transaction. In a proper case, allocation shall be made between the distributing corporation and the controlled corporation in proportion to the net basis of the assets transferred and of the assets retained or by such other method as may be appropriate under the facts and circumstances of the case. The term "net basis" means the basis of the assets less liabilities assumed or liabilities to which such assets are subject. The part of the earnings and profits of the taxable year of the distributing corporation in which the transaction occurs allocable to the controlled corporation shall be included in the computation of the earnings and profits of the first taxable year of the controlled corporation ending after the date of the transaction.

(b) If a distribution or exchange to which section 355 applies (or so much of section 356 as relates to section 355) is not in pursuance of a plan meeting the requirements of a reorganization as defined in section 368(a)(1)(D), the earnings and profits of the distributing corporation shall be decreased by the lesser of the following amounts:

(1) The amount by which the earnings and profits of the distributing corporation would have been decreased if it had transferred the stock of the controlled corporation to a new corporation in a reorganization to which section 368(a)(1)(D) applied and immediately thereafter distributed the stock of such new corporation or,

(2) The net worth of the controlled corporation. (For this purpose the term "net worth" means the sum of the basis of all of the properties plus cash minus all liabilities.)

If the earnings and profits of the controlled corporation immediately before the transaction are less than the amount of the decrease in earnings and profits of the distributing corporation (including a case in which the controlled corporation has a deficit) the earnings and profits of the controlled corporation, after the transaction, shall be equal to the amount of such decrease. If the earnings and profits of the controlled corporation immediately before the transaction are more than the amount of the decrease in the earnings and profits of the distributing corporation, they shall remain unchanged.

(c) In no case shall any part of a deficit of a distributing corporation within the meaning of section 355 be allocated to a controlled corporation.

[T.D. 6500, 25 FR 11607, Nov. 26, 1960]

§ 1.312–11 Effect on earnings and profits of certain other tax-free exchanges, tax-free distributions, and tax-free transfers from one corporation to another.

(a) If property is transferred by one corporation to another, and, under the law applicable to the year in which the transfer was made, no gain or loss was recognized (or was recognized only to the extent of the property received other than that permitted by such law to be received without the recognition of gain), then proper adjustment and allocation of the earnings and profits of the transferor shall be made as between the transferor and the transferee. Transfers to which the preceding sentence applies include contributions to capital, transfers under section 351, transfers in connection with reorganizations under section 368, transfers in liquidations under section 332 and intercompany transfers during a period of affiliation. However, if, for example, property is transferred from one corporation to another in a transaction under section 351 or as a contribution to capital and the transfer is not followed or preceded by a reorganization, a transaction under section 302(a) involving a substantial part of the transferor's stock, or a total or partial liquidation, then ordinarily no allocation of the earnings and profits of the transferor shall be made. For specific rules as to allocation of earnings and profits in certain reorganizations under section 368 and in certain liquidations under section 332 see section 381 and the regulations thereunder. * * *

* * *

[T.D. 6500, 25 FR 11607, Nov. 26, 1960]

§ 1.312–15 Effect of depreciation on earnings and profits.

* * *

(d) Books and records. Wherever different methods of depreciation are used for taxable income and earnings and profits purposes, records shall be maintained which show the depreciation taken for earnings and profits purposes each year and which will allow computation of the adjusted basis of the property in each account using the depreciation taken for earnings and profits purposes.

[T.D. 7221, 37 FR 24746, Nov. 21, 1972; T.D. 9283, 71 FR 51746, Aug. 31, 2006]

§ 1.316–1 Dividends.

(a)(1) The term "dividend" for the purpose of subtitle A of the Code (except when used in subchapter L, chapter 1 of the Code, in any case where the reference is to dividends and similar distributions of insurance companies paid to policyholders as such) comprises any distribution of property as defined in section 317 in the ordinary course of business, even though extraordinary in amount, made by a domestic or foreign corporation to its shareholders out of either—

(i) Earnings and profits accumulated since February 28, 1913, or

(ii) Earnings and profits of the taxable year computed without regard to the amount of the earnings and profits (whether of such year or accumulated since February 28, 1913) at the time the distribution was made.

The earnings and profits of the taxable year shall be computed as of the close of such year, without diminution by reason of any distributions made during the taxable year. For the purpose of determining whether a distribution constitutes a dividend, it is unnecessary to ascertain the amount of the earnings and profits accumulated since February 28, 1913, if the earnings and profits of the taxable year are equal to or in excess of the total amount of the distributions made within such year.

(2) Where a corporation distributes property to its shareholders on or after June 22, 1954, the amount of the distribution which is a dividend to them may not exceed the earnings and profits of the distributing corporation.

(3) The rule of (2) above may be illustrated by the following example:

Example. X and Y, individuals, each own one-half of the stock of Corporation A which has earnings and profits of $10,000. Corporation A distributes property having a basis of $6,000 and a fair market value of $16,000 to its shareholders, each shareholder receiving property with a basis of $3,000 and with a fair market value of $8,000 in a distribution to which section 301 applies. The amount taxable to each shareholder as a dividend under section 301(c) is $5,000.

* * *

(e) The application of section 316 may be illustrated by the following examples:

Example (1). At the beginning of the calendar year 1955, Corporation M had an operating deficit of $200,000 and the earnings and profits for the year amounted to $100,000. Beginning on March 16, 1955, the corporation made quarterly distributions of $25,000 during the taxable year to its shareholders. Each distribution is a taxable dividend in full, irrespective of the actual or the pro rata amount of the earnings and profits on hand at any of the dates of distribution, since the total distributions made during the year ($100,000) did not exceed the total earnings and profits of the year ($100,000).

* * *

[T.D. 6500, 25 FR 11607, Nov. 26, 1960, as amended by T.D. 6625, 27 FR 12541, Dec. 19, 1962; T.D. 6949, 33 FR 5519, April 9, 1968; T.D. 7767, 46 FR 11264, Feb. 6, 1981; T.D. 7936, 49 FR 2105, Jan. 18, 1984]

§ 1.316–2 Sources of distribution in general.

(a) For the purpose of income taxation every distribution made by a corporation is made out of earnings and profits to the extent thereof and from the most recently accumulated earnings and profits. In determining the source of a distribution, consideration should be given first, to the earnings and profits of the taxable year; second, to the earnings and profits accumulated since February 28, 1913, only in the case where, and to the extent that, the distributions made during the taxable year are not regarded as out of the earnings and profits of that year; third, to the earnings and profits accumulated before March 1, 1913, only after all the earnings and profits of the taxable year and all the earnings and profits accumulated since February 28, 1913, have been distributed; and, fourth, to sources other than earnings and profits only after the earnings and profits have been distributed.

(b) If the earnings and profits of the taxable year (computed as of the close of the year without diminution by reason of any distributions made during the year and without regard to the amount of earnings and profits at the time of the distribution) are sufficient in amount to cover all the distributions made during that year, then each distribution is a taxable dividend. See § 1.316–1. If the distributions made during the taxable year consist only of money and exceed the earnings and profits of such year, then that proportion of each distribution which the total of the earnings and profits of the year bears to the total distributions made during the year shall be regarded as out of the earnings and profits of that year. The portion of each such distribution which is not regarded as out of earnings and profits of the taxable year shall be considered a taxable dividend to the extent of the earnings and profits accumulated since February 28, 1913, and available on the date of the distribution. In any case in which it is necessary to determine the amount of earnings and profits accumulated since February 28, 1913, and the actual earnings and profits to the date of a distribution within any taxable year (whether beginning before January 1, 1936, or, in the case of an operating deficit, on or after that date) cannot be shown, the earnings and profits for the year (or accounting period, if less than a year) in which the distribution was made shall be prorated to the date of the distribution not counting the date on which the distribution was made.

(c) The provisions of the section may be illustrated by the following example:

Example. At the beginning of the calendar year 1955, Corporation M had $12,000 in earnings and profits accumulated since February 28, 1913. Its earnings and profits for 1955 amounted to $30,000. During the year it made quarterly cash distributions of $15,000 each. Of each of the four distributions made, $7,500 (that portion of $15,000 which the amount of $30,000, the total earnings and profits of the taxable year, bears to $60,000, the total distributions made during the year) was paid out of the earnings and profits of the taxable year; and of the first and second distributions, $7,500 and $4,500, respectively, were paid out of the earnings and profits accumulated after February 28, 1913, and before the taxable year, as follows:

Distributions during 1955				
Date	Amount	Portion out of earnings and profits of the taxable year	Portion out of earnings accumulated since Feb. 28, 1913, and before the taxable year	Taxable amt. of each distribution
March 10	$15,000	$7,500	$7,500	$15,000
June 10	15,000	7,500	4,500	12,000
September 10	15,000	7,500	......	7,500
December 10	15,000	7,500	......	7,500
Total amount taxable as dividends	......	......	......	42,000

* * *

[T.D. 6500, 25 FR 11607, Nov. 26, 1960]

§ 1.318–1 Constructive ownership of stock; introduction.

(a) For the purposes of certain provisions of chapter 1 of the Code, section 318(a) provides that stock owned by a taxpayer includes stock constructively owned by such taxpayer under the rules set forth in such section. An individual is considered to own the stock owned, directly or indirectly, by or for his spouse (other than a spouse who is legally separated from the individual under a decree of divorce or separate maintenance), and by or for his children, grandchildren, and parents. Under section 318(a)(2) and (3), constructive ownership rules are established for partnerships and partners, estates and beneficiaries, trusts and beneficiaries, and corporations and stockholders. If any person has an option to acquire stock, such stock is considered as owned by such person. The term "option" includes an option to acquire such an option and each of a series of such options.

(b) In applying section 318(a) to determine the stock ownership of any person for any one purpose—

(1) A corporation shall not be considered to own its own stock by reason of section 318(a)(3)(C);

(2) In any case in which an amount of stock owned by any person may be included in the computation more than one time, such stock shall be included only once, in the manner in which it will impute to the person concerned the largest total stock ownership; and

(3) In determining the 50-percent requirement of section 318(a)(2)(C) and (3)(C), all of the stock owned actually and constructively by the person concerned shall be aggregated.

[T.D. 6500, 25 FR 11607, Nov. 26, 1960, as amended by T.D. 6598, 27 FR 4092, April 28, 1962; T.D. 6621, 27 FR 11877, Dec. 1, 1962; T.D. 6969, 33 FR 11999, Aug. 23, 1968]

§ 1.318–2 Application of general rules.

(a) The application of paragraph (b) of § 1.318–1 may be illustrated by the following examples:

Example (1). H, an individual, owns all of the stock of corporation A. Corporation A is not considered to own the stock owned by H in corporation A.

Example (2). H, an individual, his wife, W, and his son, S, each own one-third of the stock of the Green Corporation. For purposes of determining the amount of stock owned by H, W, or S for purposes of section 318(a)(2)(C) and (3)(C), the amount of stock held by the other members of the family shall be added pursuant to paragraph (b)(3) of § 1.318–1 in applying the 50-percent requirement of such section. H, W, or S, as the case may be, is for this purpose deemed to own 100 percent of the stock of the Green Corporation.

(b) The application of section 318(a)(1), relating to members of a family, may be illustrated by the following example:

Example. An individual, H, his wife, W, his son, S, and his grandson (S's son), G, own the 100 outstanding shares of stock of a corporation, each owning 25 shares. H, W, and S are each considered as owning 100 shares. G is considered as owning only 50 shares, that is, his own and his father's.

(c) The application of section 318(a)(2) and (3), relating to partnerships, trusts and corporations, may be illustrated by the following examples:

Example (1). A, an individual, has a 50 percent interest in a partnership. The partnership owns 50 of the 100 outstanding shares of stock of a corporation, the remaining 50 shares being owned by A. The partnership is considered as owning 100 shares. A is considered as owning 75 shares.

Example (2). A testamentary trust owns 25 of the outstanding 100 shares of stock of a corporation. A, an individual, who holds a vested remainder in the trust having a value, computed actuarially equal to 4 percent of the value of the trust property, owns the remaining 75 shares. Since the interest of A in the trust is a vested interest rather than a contingent interest (whether or not remote), the trust is considered as owning 100 shares. A is considered as owning 76 shares.

Example (3). The facts are the same as in (2), above, except that A's interest in the trust is a contingent remainder. A is considered as owning 76 shares. However, since A's interest in the trust is a remote contingent interest, the trust is not considered as owning any of the shares owned by A.

Example (4). A and B, unrelated individuals, own 70 percent and 30 percent, respectively, in value of the stock of Corporation M. Corporation M owns 50 of the 100 outstanding shares of stock of Corporation O, the remaining 50 shares being owned by A. Corporation M is considered as owning 100 shares of Corporation O, and A is considered as owning 85 shares.

Example (5). A and B, unrelated individuals, own 70 percent and 30 percent, respectively, of the stock of corporation M. A, B, and corporation M all own stock of corporation O. Since B owns less than 50 percent in value of the stock of corporation M, neither B nor corporation M constructively owns the stock of corporation O owned by the other. However, for purposes of certain sections of the Code, such as sections 304 * * *, the 50-percent limitation of section 318(a)(2)(C) and (3)(C) is disregarded or is reduced to less than 30 percent. For such purposes, B constructively owns his proportionate share of the stock of corporation O owned directly by corporation M, and corporation M constructively owns the stock of corporation O owned by B.

[T.D. 6500, 25 FR 11607, Nov. 26, 1960, as amended by T.D. 6969, 33 FR 11999, Aug. 23, 1968]

§ 1.318–3 Estates, trusts, and options.

(a) For the purpose of applying section 318(a), relating to estates, property of a decedent shall be considered as owned by his estate if such property is subject to administration by the executor or administrator for the purpose of paying claims against the estate and expenses of administration notwithstanding that, under local law, legal title to such property vests in the decedent's heirs, legatees or devisees immediately upon death. The term "beneficiary" includes any person entitled to receive property of a decedent pursuant to a will or pursuant to laws of descent and distribution. A person shall no longer be considered a beneficiary of an estate when all the property to which he is entitled has been received by him, when he no longer has a claim against the estate arising out of having been a beneficiary, and when there is only a remote possibility that it will be necessary for the estate to seek the return of property or to seek payment from him by contribution or otherwise to satisfy claims against the estate or expenses of administration. When, pursuant to the preceding sentence, a person ceases to be a beneficiary, stock owned by him shall not thereafter be considered owned by the estate, and stock owned by the estate shall not thereafter be considered owned by him. The application of section 318(a) relating to estates may be illustrated by the following examples:

Example (1). **(a)** A decedent's estate owns 50 of the 100 outstanding shares of stock of corporation X. The remaining shares are owned by three unrelated individuals, A, B, and C, who together own the entire interest in the estate. A owns 12 shares of stock of corporation X directly and is entitled to 50 percent of the estate. B owns 18 shares directly and has a life estate in the remaining 50 percent of the estate. C owns 20 shares directly and also owns the remainder interest after B's life estate.

(b) If section 318(a)(5)(C) applies (see paragraph (c)(3) of § 1.318–4), the stock of corporation X is considered to be owned as follows: the estate is considered as owning 80 shares, 50 shares directly, 12 shares constructively through A, and 18 shares constructively through B; A is considered as owning 37 shares, 12 shares directly, and 25 shares constructively (50 percent of the 50 shares owned directly by the estate); B is considered as owning 43 shares, 18 shares directly and 25 shares constructively (50 percent of the 50 shares owned directly by the estate); C is considered as owning 20 shares directly and no shares constructively. C is not considered a beneficiary of the estate under section 318(a) since he has no direct present interest in the property held by the estate nor in the income produced by such property.

(c) If section 318(a)(5)(C) does not apply, A is considered as owning nine additional shares (50 percent of the 18 shares owned constructively by the estate through B), and B is considered as owning six additional shares (50 percent of the 12 shares owned constructively by the estate through A).

Example (2). Under the will of A, Blackacre is left to B for life, remainder to C, an unrelated individual. The residue of the estate consisting of stock of a corporation is left to D. B and D are beneficiaries of the estate under section 318(a). C is not considered a beneficiary since he has no direct present interest in Blackacre nor in the income produced by such property. The stock owned by the estate is considered as owned proportionately by B and D.

(b) For the purpose of section 318(a)(2)(B) stock owned by a trust will be considered as being owned by its beneficiaries only to the extent of the interest of such beneficiaries in the trust. Accordingly, the interest of income beneficiaries, remainder beneficiaries, and other beneficiaries will be computed on an actuarial basis. Thus, if a trust owns 100 percent of the stock of Corporation A, and if, on an actuarial basis, W's life interest in the trust is 15 percent, Y's life interest is 25 percent, and Z's remainder interest is 60 percent, under this provision W will be considered to be the owner of 15 percent of the stock of Corporation A, Y will be considered to be the owner of 25 percent of such stock, and Z will be considered to be the owner of 60 percent of such stock. The factors and methods prescribed in § 20.2031–7 of this chapter (Estate Tax Regulations) for use in ascertaining the value of an interest in property for estate tax purposes shall be used in determining a beneficiary's actuarial interest in a trust for purposes of this section. See § 20.2031–7 of this chapter (Estate Tax Regulations) for examples illustrating the use of these factors and methods.

(c) The application of section 318(a) relating to options may be illustrated by the following example:

Example. A and B, unrelated individuals, own all of the 100 outstanding shares of stock of a corporation, each owning 50 shares. A has an option to acquire 25 of B's shares and has an option to acquire a further option to acquire the remaining 25 of B's shares. A is considered as owning the entire 100 shares of stock of the corporation.

[T.D. 6500, 25 FR 11607, Nov. 26, 1960, as amended by T.D. 6969, 33 FR 11999, Aug. 23, 1968]

§ 1.318–4 Constructive ownership as actual ownership; exceptions.

(a) In general. Section 318(a)(5)(A) provides that, except as provided in section 318(a)(5)(B) and (C), stock constructively owned by a person by reason of the application of section 318(a)(1), (2), (3), or (4) shall be considered as actually owned by such person for purposes of applying section 318(a)(1), (2), (3), and (4). For example, if a trust owns 50 percent of the stock of corporation X, stock of corporation Y owned by corporation X which is attributed to the trust may be further attributed to the beneficiaries of the trust.

(b) Constructive family ownership. Section 318(a)(5)(B) provides that stock constructively owned by an individual by reason of ownership by a member of his family shall not be considered as owned by him for purposes of making another family member the constructive owner of such stock under section 318(a)(1). For example, if F and his two sons, A and B, each own one-third of the stock of a corporation, under section 318(a)(1), A is treated as owning constructively the stock owned by his father but is not treated as owning the stock owned by B. Section 318(a)(5)(B) prevents the attribution of the stock of one brother through the father to the other brother, an attribution beyond the scope of section 318(a)(1) directly.

(c) Reattribution. **(1)** Section 318(a)(5)(C) provides that stock constructively owned by a partnership, estate, trust, or corporation by reason of the application of section 318(a)(3) shall not be considered as owned by it for purposes of applying section 318(a)(2) in order to make another the constructive owner of such stock. For example, if two unrelated individuals are beneficiaries of the same trust, stock held by one which is attributed to the trust under section 318(a)(3) is not reattributed from the trust to the other beneficiary. However, stock constructively owned by reason of section 318(a)(2) may be reattributed under section 318(a)(3). Thus, for example, if all the stock of corporations X and Y is owned by A, stock of corporation Z held by X is attributed to Y through A.

(2) Section 318(a)(5)(C) does not prevent reattribution under section 318(a)(2) of stock constructively owned by an entity under section 318(a)(3) if the stock is also constructively owned by the entity under section 318(a)(4). For example, if individuals A and B are beneficiaries of a trust and the trust has an option to buy stock from A, B is considered under section 318(a)(2)(B) as owning a proportionate part of such stock.

* * *

[T.D. 6500, 25 FR 11607, Nov. 26, 1960, as amended by T.D. 6969, 33 FR 11999, Aug. 23, 1968]

§ 1.331–1 Corporate liquidations.

(a) In general. Section 331 contains rules governing the extent to which gain or loss is recognized to a shareholder receiving a distribution in complete * * * liquidation of a corporation. Under section 331 * * * it is provided that amounts distributed in complete liquidation of a corporation shall be treated as in full payment in exchange for the stock. * * * If section 331 is applicable to the distribution of property by a corporation, section 301 (relating to the effects on a shareholder of distributions of property) has no application other than to a distribution in complete liquidation to which section 316(b)(2)(B) applies. * * *

(b) Gain or loss. The gain or loss to a shareholder from a distribution in * * * complete liquidation is to be determined under section 1001 by comparing the amount of the distribution with the cost or other basis of the stock. The gain or loss will be recognized to the extent provided in section 1002 and will be subject to the provisions of parts I, II, and III (section 1201 and following), subchapter P, chapter 1 of the Code.

(c) Recharacterization. A liquidation which is followed by a transfer to another corporation of all or part of the assets of the liquidating corporation or which is preceded by such a transfer may, however, have the effect of the distribution of a dividend or of a transaction in which no loss is recognized and gain is recognized only to the extent of "other property." See sections 301 and 356.

(d) Reporting requirement—(1) General rule. Every significant holder that transfers stock to the issuing corporation in exchange for property from such corporation must include on or with such holder's return for the year of such exchange the statement described in paragraph (d)(2) of this section unless—

(i) The property is part of a distribution made pursuant to a corporate resolution reciting that the distribution is made in complete liquidation of the corporation; and

(ii) The issuing corporation is completely liquidated and dissolved within one year after the distribution.

(2) Statement. If required by paragraph (d)(1) of this section, a significant holder must include on or with such holder's return a statement entitled, "STATEMENT PURSUANT TO § 1.331–1(d) BY [INSERT NAME AND TAXPAYER IDENTIFICATION NUMBER (IF ANY) OF TAXPAYER], A SIGNIFICANT HOLDER OF THE STOCK OF [INSERT NAME AND EMPLOYER IDENTIFICATION NUMBER (IF ANY) OF ISSUING CORPORATION]." * * * The statement must include—

(i) The fair market value and basis of the stock transferred by the significant holder to the issuing corporation; and

(ii) A description of the property received by the significant holder from the issuing corporation.

* * *

(e) Example. The provisions of this section may be illustrated by the following example:

Example. A, an individual who makes his income tax returns on the calendar year basis, owns 20 shares of stock of the P Corporation, a domestic corporation, 10 shares of which were acquired in 1951 at a cost of $1,500 and the remainder of 10 shares in December 1954 at a cost of $2,900. He receives in April 1955 a distribution of $250 per share in complete liquidation, or $2,500 on the 10 shares acquired in 1951, and $2,500 on the 10 shares acquired in December 1954. The gain of $1,000 on the shares acquired in 1951 is a long-term capital gain to be treated as provided in parts I, II, and III (section 1201 and following), subchapter P, chapter 1 of the Code. The loss of $400 on the shares acquired in 1954 is a short-term capital loss to be treated as provided in parts I, II, and III (section 1201 and following), subchapter P, chapter 1 of the Code.

* * *

[T.D. 6500, 25 FR 11607, Nov. 26, 1960, as amended by T.D. 6949, 33 FR 5521, April 9, 1968; T.D. 9264, 71 FR 30594, May 30, 2006; T.D. 9329, 72 FR 32797, June 14, 2007]

§ 1.332–1 Distributions in liquidation of subsidiary corporation; general.

Under the general rule prescribed by section 331 for the treatment of distributions in liquidation of a corporation, amounts received by one corporation in complete liquidation of another corporation are treated as in full payment in exchange for stock in such other corporation, and gain or loss from the receipt of such amounts is to be determined as provided in section 1001. Section 332 excepts from the general rule property received, under certain specifically described circumstances, by one corporation as a distribution in complete liquidation of the stock of another corporation and provides for the nonrecognition of gain or loss in those cases which meet the statutory requirements. Section 367 places a limitation on the application of section 332 in the case of foreign corporations. See section 334(b) for the basis for determining gain or loss from the subsequent sale of property received upon complete liquidations such as described in this section. * * *

[T.D. 6500, 25 FR 11607, Nov. 26, 1960]

§ 1.332–2 Requirements for nonrecognition of gain or loss.

(a) The nonrecognition of gain or loss is limited to the receipt of such property by a corporation which is the actual owner of stock (in the liquidating corporation) possessing at least 80 percent of the total combined voting power of all classes of stock entitled to vote and the owner of at least 80 percent of the total number of shares of all other classes of stock (except nonvoting stock which is limited and preferred as to dividends). The recipient corporation must have been the owner of the specified amount of such stock on the date of the adoption of the plan of liquidation and have continued so to be at all times until the receipt of the property. If the recipient corporation does not continue qualified with respect to the ownership of stock of the liquidating corporation and if the failure to continue qualified occurs at any time prior to the completion of the transfer of all the property, the provisions for the nonrecognition of gain or loss do not apply to any distribution received under the plan.

(b) Section 332 applies only to those cases in which the recipient corporation receives at least partial payment for the stock which it owns in the liquidating corporation. If section 332 is not applicable, see section 165(g) relative to allowance of losses on worthless securities.

(c) To constitute a distribution in complete liquidation within the meaning of section 332, the distribution must be (1) made by the liquidating corporation in complete cancellation or redemption of all of its stock in accordance with a plan of liquidation, or (2) one of a series of distributions in complete cancellation or redemption of all its stock in accordance with a plan of liquidation. Where there is more than one distribution, it is essential that a status of liquidation exist at the time the first distribution is made under the plan and that such status continue until the liquidation is completed. Liquidation is completed when the liquidating corporation and the receiver or trustees in liquidation are finally divested of all the property (both tangible and intangible). A status of liquidation exists when the corporation ceases to be a going concern and its activities are merely for the purpose of winding up its affairs, paying its debts, and distributing any remaining balance to its shareholders. A liquidation may be completed prior to the actual dissolution of the liquidating corporation. However, legal dissolution of the corporation is not required. Nor will the mere retention of a nominal amount of assets for the sole purpose of preserving the corporation's legal existence disqualify the transaction. * * *

(d) If a transaction constitutes a distribution in complete liquidation within the meaning of the Internal Revenue Code of 1954 and satisfies the requirements of section 332, it is not material that it is otherwise described under the local law. If a liquidating corporation distributes all of its property in complete liquidation and if pursuant to the plan for such complete liquidation a corporation owning the specified amount of stock in the liquidating corporation receives property constituting amounts distributed in complete liquidation within the meaning of the Code and also receives other property attributable to shares not owned by it, the transfer of the property to the recipient corporation shall not be treated, by reason of the receipt of such other property, as not being a distribution (or one of a series of distributions) in complete cancellation or redemption of all of the stock of the liquidating corporation within the meaning of section 332, even though for purposes of those provisions relating to corporate reorganizations the amount received by the recipient corporation in excess of its ratable share is regarded as acquired upon the issuance of its stock or securities in a tax-free exchange as described in section 361 and the cancellation or redemption of the stock not owned by the recipient corporation is treated as occurring as a result of a tax-free exchange described in section 354.

(e) The application of these rules may be illustrated by the following example:

Example. On September 1, 1954, the M Corporation had outstanding capital stock consisting of 3,000 shares of common stock, par value $100 a share, and 1,000 shares of preferred stock, par value $100 a share, which preferred stock was limited and preferred as to dividends and had no voting rights. On that date, and thereafter until the date of dissolution of the M Corporation, the O Corporation owned 2,500 shares of common stock of the M Corporation. By statutory merger consummated on October 1, 1954, pursuant to a plan of liquidation adopted on September 1, 1954, the M Corporation was merged into the O Corporation, the O Corporation under the plan issuing stock which was received by the other holders of the stock of the M Corporation. The receipt by the O Corporation of the properties of the M Corporation is a distribution received by the O Corporation in complete liquidation of the M Corporation within the meaning of section 332, and no gain or loss is recognized as the result of the receipt of such properties.

[T.D. 6500, 25 FR 11607, Nov. 26, 1960]

§ 1.332–3 Liquidations completed within one taxable year.

If in a liquidation completed within one taxable year pursuant to a plan of complete liquidation, distributions in complete liquidation are received by a corporation which owns the specified amount of stock in the liquidating corporation and which continues qualified with respect to the ownership of such stock until the transfer of all the property within such year is completed (see paragraph (a) of § 1.332–2), then no gain or loss shall be recognized with respect to the distributions received by the recipient corporation. In such case no waiver or bond is required of the recipient corporation under section 332.

[T.D. 6500, 25 FR 11607, Nov. 26, 1960]

§ 1.332–4 Liquidations covering more than one taxable year.

(a) If the plan of liquidation is consummated by a series of distributions extending over a period of more than one taxable year, the nonrecognition of gain or loss with respect to the distributions in liquidation shall, in addition to the requirements of § 1.332–2, be subject to the following requirements:

(1) In order for the distribution in liquidation to be brought within the exception provided in section 332 to the general rule for computing gain or loss with respect to amounts received in liquidation of a corporation, the entire property of the corporation shall be transferred in accordance with a plan of liquidation, which plan shall include a statement showing the period within which the transfer of the property of the liquidating corporation to the recipient corporation is to be completed. The transfer of all the property under the liquidation must be completed within three years from the close of the taxable year during which is made the first of the series of distributions under the plan.

* * *

(b) Pending the completion of the liquidation, if there is a compliance with paragraph (a)(1), (2), and (3) of this section and § 1.332–2 with respect to the nonrecognition of gain or loss, the income and profits tax liability of the recipient corporation for each of the years covered in whole or in part by the liquidation shall be determined without the recognition of any gain or loss on account of the receipt of the distributions in liquidation. In such determination, the basis of the property or properties received by the recipient corporation shall be determined in accordance with section 334(b). However, if the transfer of the property is not completed within the three-year period allowed by section 332 or if the recipient corporation does not continue qualified with respect to the ownership of stock of the liquidating corporation as required by that section, gain or loss shall be recognized with respect to each distribution and the tax liability for each of the years covered in whole or in part by the liquidation shall be recomputed without regard to the provisions of section 332 or section 334(b) and the amount of any additional tax due upon such recomputation shall be promptly paid.

[T.D. 6500, 25 FR 11607, Nov. 26, 1960]

§ 1.332–5 Distribution in liquidation as affecting minority interests.

Upon the liquidation of a corporation in pursuance of a plan of complete liquidation, the gain or loss of minority shareholders shall be determined without regard to section 332, since it does not apply to that part of distributions in liquidation received by minority shareholders.

[T.D. 6500, 25 FR 11607, Nov. 26, 1960]

§ 1.332–7 Indebtedness of subsidiary to parent.

If section 332(a) is applicable to the receipt of the subsidiary's property in complete liquidation, then no gain or loss shall be recognized to the subsidiary upon the transfer of such properties even though some of the properties are transferred in satisfaction of the subsidiary's indebtedness to its parent. However, any gain or loss realized by the parent corporation on such satisfaction of indebtedness, shall be recognized to the parent corporation at the time of the liquidation. For example, if the parent corporation purchased its subsidiary's bonds at a discount and upon liquidation of the subsidiary the parent corporation receives payment for the face amount of such bonds, gain shall be recognized to the parent corporation. Such gain shall be measured by the difference between the cost or other basis of the bonds to the parent and the amount received in payment of the bonds.

[T.D. 6500, 25 FR 11607, Nov. 26, 1960]

§ 1.336–1 General principles, nomenclature, and definitions for a section 336(e) election.

(a) Overview—(1) In general. Section 336(e) authorizes the promulgation of regulations under which, in certain circumstances, a sale, exchange, or distribution of the stock of a corporation may be treated as an asset sale. This section and §§ 1.336–2 through 1.336–5 provide the rules for and consequences of making such election. This section provides the definitions and nomenclature. Generally, except to the extent inconsistent with section 336(e), the results of section 336(e) should coincide with those of section 338(h)(10). Accordingly, to the extent not inconsistent with section 336(e) or these regulations, the principles of section 338 and the regulations under section 338 apply for purposes of these regulations. For example, § 1.338(h)(10)–1(d)(8), concerning the availability of the section 453 installment method, may apply with respect to section 336(e).

(2) Consistency rules. In general, the principles of § 1.338–8, concerning asset and stock consistency, apply with respect to section 336(e). However, for this purpose, the application of § 1.338–8(b)(1) is modified such that § 1.338–8(b)(1)(iii) applies to an asset if the asset is owned, immediately after its acquisition and on the disposition date, by a person or by a related person (as defined in § 1.336–1(b)(12)) to a person that acquires, by sale, exchange, distribution, or any combination thereof, five percent or more, by value, of the stock of target in the qualified stock disposition.

(b) Definitions. For purposes of §§ 1.336–1 through 1.336–5 (except as otherwise provided):

(1) Seller. The term seller means any domestic corporation that makes a qualified stock disposition of stock of another corporation. Seller includes both a transferor and a distributor of target stock. Generally, all members of a consolidated group that dispose of target stock are treated as a single seller. See § 1.336–2(g)(2).

(2) Purchaser. The term purchaser means one or more persons that acquire or receive the stock of another corporation in a qualified stock disposition. A purchaser includes both a transferee and a distributee of target stock.

(3) Target; S corporation target; old target; new target. The term target means any domestic corporation the stock of which is sold, exchanged, or distributed in a qualified stock disposition. An S corporation target is a target that is an S corporation immediately before the disposition date; any other target is a non-S corporation target. Except as the context otherwise requires, a reference to target includes a reference to an S corporation target. * * *

(4) S corporation shareholders. S corporation shareholders are the S corporation target's shareholders. Unless otherwise provided, a reference to S corporation shareholders refers both to S corporation shareholders who dispose of and those who do not dispose of their S corporation target stock.

(5) Disposed of; disposition—(i) In general. The term disposed of refers to a transfer of stock in a disposition. The term disposition means any sale, exchange, or distribution of stock, but only if—

(A) The basis of the stock in the hands of the purchaser is not determined in whole or in part by reference to the adjusted basis of such stock in the hands of the person from whom the stock is acquired or under section 1014(a) (relating to property acquired from a decedent);

(B) Except as provided in paragraph (b)(5)(ii) of this section, the stock is not sold, exchanged, or distributed in a transaction to which section 351, 354, 355, or 356 applies and is not sold, exchanged, or distributed in any transaction described in regulations in which the transferor does not recognize the entire amount of the gain or loss realized in the transaction; and

(C) The stock is not sold, exchanged, or distributed to a related person.

* * *

(6) Qualified stock disposition—(i) In general. The term qualified stock disposition means any transaction or series of transactions in which stock meeting the requirements of section 1504(a)(2) of a domestic corporation is either sold, exchanged, or distributed, or any combination thereof, by another domestic corporation or by the S corporation shareholders in a disposition, within the meaning of paragraph (b)(5) of this section, during the 12–month disposition period.

(ii) Overlap with qualified stock purchase—(A) In general. Except as provided in paragraph (b)(6)(ii)(B) of this section, a transaction satisfying the definition of a qualified stock disposition under paragraph (b)(6)(i) of this section, which also qualifies as a qualified stock purchase (as defined in section 338(d)(3)), will not be treated as a qualified stock disposition.

(B) Exception. If, as a result of the deemed sale of old target's assets pursuant to a section 336(e) election, there would be, but for paragraph (b)(6)(ii)(A) of this section, a qualified stock disposition of the stock of a subsidiary of target, then paragraph (b)(6)(ii)(A) shall not apply to the disposition of the stock of the subsidiary.

(7) 12–month disposition period. The term 12–month disposition period means the 12–month period beginning with the date of the first sale, exchange, or distribution of stock included in a qualified stock disposition.

(8) Disposition date. The term disposition date means, with respect to any corporation, the first day on which there is a qualified stock disposition with respect to the stock of such corporation.

(9) Disposition date assets. Disposition date assets are the assets of target held at the beginning of the day after the disposition date (but see § 1.338–1(d) (regarding certain transactions on the disposition date)).

(10) Domestic corporation. The term domestic corporation has the same meaning as in § 1.338–2(c)(9).

(11) Section 336(e) election. A section 336(e) election is an election to apply section 336(e) to target. A section 336(e) election is made by making an election for target under § 1.336–2(h).

(12) Related persons. Two persons are related if stock of a corporation owned by one of the persons would be attributed under section 318(a), other than section 318(a)(4), to the other. However, neither section 318(a)(2)(A) nor section 318(a)(3)(A) apply to attribute stock ownership from a partnership to a partner, or from a partner to a partnership, if such partner owns, directly or indirectly, interests representing less than five percent of the value of the partnership.

(13) Liquidation. Any reference to a liquidation is treated as a reference to the transfer described in § 1.336–2(b)(1)(iii) notwithstanding its ultimate characterization for Federal income tax purposes.

(14) Deemed asset disposition. The deemed sale of old target's assets is, without regard to its characterization for Federal income tax purposes, referred to as the deemed asset disposition.

(15) Deemed disposition tax consequences. Deemed disposition tax consequences refers to, in the aggregate, the Federal income tax consequences (generally, the income, gain, deduction, and loss) of the deemed asset disposition. Deemed disposition tax consequences also refers to the Federal income tax consequences of the transfer of a particular asset in the deemed asset disposition.

(16) 80–percent purchaser. An 80–percent purchaser is any purchaser that, after application of the attribution rules of section 318(a), other than section 318(a)(4), owns 80 percent or more of the voting power or value of target stock.

(17) Recently disposed stock. The term recently disposed stock means any stock in target that is not held by seller, a member of seller's consolidated group, or an S corporation shareholder immediately after the close of the disposition date and that was disposed of by seller, a member of seller's consolidated group, or an S corporation shareholder during the 12–month disposition period.

(18) Nonrecently disposed stock. The term nonrecently disposed stock means stock in target that is held on the disposition date by a purchaser or a person related (as described in § 1.336–1(b)(12)) to the purchaser who owns, on the disposition date, with the application of section 318(a), other than section 318(a)(4), at least 10 percent of the total voting power or value of the stock of target and that is not recently disposed stock.

(c) Nomenclature. For purposes of §§ 1.336–1 through 1.336–5, except as otherwise provided, Parent, Seller, Target, Sub, S Corporation Target, and Target Subsidiary are domestic corporations and A, B, C, and D are individuals, none of whom are related to Parent, Seller, Target, Sub, S Corporation Target, Target Subsidiary, or each other.

[T.D. 9619, 78 FR 28467, May 15, 2013]

§ 1.336–2 Availability, mechanics, and consequences of section 336(e) election.

(a) Availability of election. A section 336(e) election is available if seller or S corporation shareholder(s) dispose of stock of another corporation (target) in a qualified stock disposition (as defined in § 1.336–1(b)(6)). A section 336(e) election is irrevocable. A section 336(e) election is not available for transactions described in section 336(e) that do not constitute qualified stock dispositions.

(b) Deemed transaction—(1) Dispositions not described in section 355(d)(2) or (e)(2)—(i) Old target—deemed asset disposition—(A) In general. This paragraph (b)(1) provides the Federal income tax consequences of a section 336(e) election made with respect to a qualified stock disposition not described, in whole or in part, in section 355(d)(2) or (e)(2). For the Federal income tax consequences of a section 336(e) election made with respect to a qualified stock disposition described, in whole or in part, in section 355(d)(2) or (e)(2), see paragraph (b)(2) of this section. In general, if a section 336(e) election is made, seller (or S corporation shareholders) are treated as not having sold, exchanged, or distributed the stock disposed of in the qualified stock disposition. Instead, old target is treated as selling its assets to an unrelated person in a single transaction at the close of the disposition date (but before the deemed liquidation described in paragraph (b)(1)(iii) of this section) in exchange for the aggregate deemed asset disposition price (ADADP) as determined under § 1.336–3. ADADP is allocated among the disposition date assets in the same manner as the aggregate deemed sale price (ADSP) is allocated under §§ 1.338–6 and 1.338–7 in order to determine the amount realized from each of the sold assets. Old target realizes the deemed disposition tax consequences from the deemed asset disposition before the close of the disposition date while old target is owned by seller or the S corporation shareholders. If old target is an S corporation target, old target's S election continues in effect through the close of the disposition date (including the time of the deemed asset disposition and the deemed liquidation) notwithstanding section 1362(d)(2)(B). Also, if old target is an S corporation target (but not a qualified subchapter S subsidiary), any direct or indirect subsidiaries of old target that old target has elected to treat as qualified subchapter S subsidiaries under section 1361(b)(3) remain qualified subchapter S subsidiaries through the close of the disposition date.

(B) Gains and losses—(1) Gains. Except as provided in § 1.338(h)(10)–1(d)(8) (regarding the installment method), old target shall recognize all of the gains realized on the deemed asset disposition.

(2) Losses—(i) In general. Except as provided in paragraphs (b)(1)(i)(B)(2)(ii), (iii), and (iv) of this section, old target shall recognize all of the losses realized on the deemed asset disposition.

(ii) Stock distributions. Notwithstanding paragraphs (b)(1)(i)(A) and (b)(1)(iii)(A) of this section, for purposes of determining the amount of target's losses that are disallowed on the deemed asset disposition, seller is still treated as selling, exchanging, or distributing its target stock disposed of in the 12–month disposition period. If target's losses realized on the deemed sale of all of its assets exceed target's gains realized (a net loss), the portion of such net loss attributable to a distribution of target stock during the 12–month disposition period is disallowed. The total amount of disallowed loss and the allocation of disallowed loss is determined in the manner provided in paragraphs (b)(1)(i)(B)(2)(iii) and (iv) of this section.

* * *

(ii) New target—deemed purchase. New target is treated as acquiring all of its assets from an unrelated person in a single transaction at the close of the disposition date (but before the deemed liquidation) in exchange for an amount equal to the adjusted grossed-up basis (AGUB) as determined under § 1.336–4. New target allocates the consideration deemed paid in the transaction in the same manner as new target would under §§ 1.338–6 and 1.338–7 in order to determine the basis in each of the purchased assets. If new target qualifies as a small business corporation within the meaning of section 1361(b) and wants to be an S corporation, a new election under section 1362(a) must be made. Notwithstanding paragraph (b)(1)(iii) of this section (deemed liquidation of old target), new target remains liable for the tax liabilities of old target (including the tax liability for the deemed disposition tax consequences). For example, new target remains liable for the tax liabilities of the members of any consolidated group that are attributable to taxable years in which those corporations and old target joined in the same consolidated return. See § 1.1502–6(a).

(iii) Old target and seller—deemed liquidation—(A) In general. If old target is an S corporation, S corporation shareholders (whether or not they sell or exchange their stock) take their pro rata share of the deemed disposition tax consequences into account under section 1366 and increase or decrease their basis in target stock under section 1367. Old target and seller (or S corporation shareholders) are treated as if, before the close of the disposition date, after the deemed asset disposition described in paragraph (b)(1)(i)(A) of this section, and while target is owned by seller or S corporation shareholders, old target transferred all of the consideration deemed received from new target in the deemed asset disposition to seller or S corporation shareholders, any S corporation election for old target terminated, and old target ceased to exist. The transfer from old target to seller or S corporation shareholders is characterized for Federal income tax purposes in the same manner as if the parties had actually engaged in the transactions deemed to occur because of this section and taking into account other transactions that actually occurred or are deemed to occur. For example, the transfer may be treated as a distribution in pursuance of a plan of reorganization, a distribution in complete cancellation or redemption of all of its stock, one of a series of distributions in complete cancellation or redemption of all of its stock in accordance with a plan of liquidation, or part of a circular flow of cash. In most cases, the transfer will be treated as a distribution in complete liquidation to which sections 331 or 332 and sections 336 or 337 apply.

* * *

(iv) Seller—distribution of target stock. In the case of a distribution of target stock in a qualified stock disposition, seller (the distributor) is deemed to purchase from an unrelated person, on the disposition date, immediately after the deemed liquidation of old target, the amount of stock distributed in the qualified stock disposition (new target stock) and to have distributed such new target stock to its shareholders. Seller recognizes no gain or loss on the distribution of such stock.

(v) Seller—retention of target stock. If seller or an S corporation shareholder retains any target stock after the disposition date, seller or the S corporation shareholder is treated as purchasing the stock so retained from an unrelated person (new target stock) on the day after the disposition date for its fair market value. The holding period for the retained stock starts on the day after the disposition date. For purposes of this paragraph (b)(1)(v), the fair market value of all of the target stock equals the grossed-up amount realized on the sale, exchange, or distribution of recently disposed stock of target (see § 1.336–3(c)).

* * *

(c) Purchaser. Generally, the making of a section 336(e) election will not affect the Federal income tax consequences to which purchaser would have been subject with respect to the acquisition of target stock if a section 336(e) election was not made. Thus, notwithstanding §§ 1.336–2(b)(1)(i)(A), 1.336–2(b)(1)(iv), and 1.336–2(b)(2)(iii)(A), purchaser will still be treated as having purchased, received in an exchange, or received in a distribution, the stock of target so acquired on the date actually acquired. However, see section 1223(1)(B) with respect to the holding period for stock acquired pursuant to a distribution qualifying under section 355 (or so much of section 356 that relates to section 355). The Federal income tax consequences of the deemed asset disposition and liquidation of target may affect purchaser's consequences. For example, if seller distributes the stock of target to its shareholders in a qualified stock disposition for which a section 336(e) election is made, any increase in seller's earnings and profits as a result of old target's deemed asset disposition and liquidation into seller may increase the amount of a distribution to the shareholders constituting a dividend under section 301(c)(1).

(d) Minority shareholders—(1) In general. This paragraph (d) describes the treatment of shareholders of old target other than seller, a member of seller's consolidated group, and S corporation shareholders (whether or not they sell or exchange their stock of target). A shareholder to which this paragraph (d) applies is referred to as a minority shareholder.

(2) Sale, exchange, or distribution of target stock by a minority shareholder. A minority shareholder recognizes gain or loss (as permitted under the general principles of tax law) on its sale, exchange, or distribution of target stock.

(3) Retention of target stock by a minority shareholder. A minority shareholder who retains its target stock does not recognize gain or loss under this section with respect to its shares of target stock. The minority shareholder's basis and holding period for that target stock are not affected by the section 336(e) election. Notwithstanding this treatment of the minority shareholder, if a section 336(e) election is made, target will still be treated as disposing of all of its assets in the deemed asset disposition.

(e) Treatment consistent with an actual asset disposition. Except as otherwise provided, no provision in this section shall produce a Federal income tax result under subtitle A of the Internal Revenue Code that would not occur if the parties had actually engaged in the transactions deemed to occur because of this section, taking into account other transactions that actually occurred or are deemed to occur. See § 1.338–1(a)(2) regarding the application of other rules of law.

(f) Treatment of target under other provisions of the Internal Revenue Code. The provisions § 1.338–1(b) apply with respect to the treatment of new target after a section 336(e) election, treating any reference to section 338 or 338(h)(10) as a reference to section 336(e).

* * *

[T.D. 9619, 78 FR 28467, May 15, 2013]

§ 1.338–3 Qualification for section 338 election.

* * *

(d) Consequences of post-acquisition elimination of target where section 338 election not made—(1) Scope. The rules of this paragraph (d) apply to the transfer of target assets to the purchasing corporation (or another member of the same affiliated group as the purchasing corporation) (the transferee) following a qualified stock purchase of target stock, if the purchasing corporation does not make a section 338 election for target. Notwithstanding the rules of this paragraph (d), section 354(a) (and so much of section 356 as relates to section 354) cannot apply to any person other than the purchasing corporation or another member of the same affiliated group as the purchasing corporation unless the transfer of target assets is pursuant to a reorganization as determined without regard to this paragraph (d).

(2) Continuity of interest. By virtue of section 338, in determining whether the continuity of interest requirement of § 1.368–1(b) is satisfied on the transfer of assets from target to the transferee, the purchasing corporation's target stock acquired in the qualified stock purchase represents an interest on the part of a person who was an owner of the target's business enterprise prior to the transfer that can be continued in a reorganization.

(3) Control requirement. By virtue of section 338, the acquisition of target stock in the qualified stock purchase will not prevent the purchasing corporation from qualifying as a shareholder of the target transferor for the purpose of determining whether, immediately after the transfer of target assets, a shareholder of the transferor is in control of the corporation to which the assets are transferred within the meaning of section 368(a)(1)(D).

(4) Solely for voting stock requirement. By virtue of section 338, the acquisition of target stock in the qualified stock purchase for consideration other than voting stock will not prevent the subsequent transfer of target assets from satisfying the solely for voting stock requirement for purposes of determining if the transfer of target assets qualifies as a reorganization under section 368(a)(1)(C).

(5) Example. The following example illustrates this paragraph (d):

Example. (i) Facts. P, T, and X are domestic corporations. T and X each operate a trade or business. A and K, individuals unrelated to P, own 85 and 15 percent, respectively, of the stock of T. P owns all of the stock of X. The total adjusted basis of T's property exceeds the sum of T's liabilities plus the amount of liabilities to which T's property is subject. P purchases all of A's T stock for cash in a qualified stock purchase. P does not make an election under section 338(g) with respect to its acquisition of T stock. Shortly after the acquisition date, and as part of the same plan, T merges under applicable state law into X in a transaction that, but for the question of continuity of interest, satisfies all the requirements of section 368(a)(1)(A). In the merger, all of T's assets are transferred to X. P and K receive X stock in exchange for their T stock. P intends to retain the stock of X indefinitely.

(ii) Status of transfer as a reorganization. By virtue of section 338, for the purpose of determining whether the continuity of interest requirement of § 1.368–1(b) is satisfied, P's T stock acquired in the qualified stock purchase represents an interest on the part of a person who was an owner of T's business enterprise prior to the transfer that can be continued in a reorganization through P's continuing ownership of X. Thus, the continuity of interest requirement is satisfied and the merger of T into X is a reorganization within the meaning of section 368(a)(1)(A). Moreover, by virtue of section 338, the requirement of section 368(a)(1)(D) that a target shareholder control the transferee immediately after the transfer is satisfied because P controls X immediately after the transfer. In addition, all of T's assets are transferred to X in the merger and P and K receive the X stock exchanged therefor in pursuance of the plan of reorganization. Thus, the merger of T into X is also a reorganization within the meaning of section 368(a)(1)(D).

(iii) Treatment of T and X. Under section 361(a), T recognizes no gain or loss in the merger. Under section 362(b), X's basis in the assets received in the merger is the same as the basis of the assets in T's hands. X succeeds to and takes into account the items of T as provided in section 381.

(iv) Treatment of P. By virtue of section 338, the transfer of T assets to X is a reorganization. Pursuant to that reorganization, P exchanges its T stock solely for stock of X, a party to the reorganization. Because P is the purchasing corporation, section 354 applies to P's exchange of T stock for X stock in the merger of T into X. Thus, P recognizes no gain or loss on the exchange. Under section 358, P's basis in the X stock received in the exchange is the same as the basis of P's T stock exchanged therefor.

(v) Treatment of K. Because K is not the purchasing corporation (or an affiliate thereof), section 354 cannot apply to K's exchange of T stock for X stock in the merger of T into X unless the transfer of T's assets is pursuant to a reorganization as determined without regard to paragraph (d). Under general principles of tax law applicable to reorganizations, the continuity of interest requirement is not satisfied because P's stock purchase and the merger of T into X are pursuant to an integrated transaction in which A, the owner of 85 percent of the stock of T, received solely cash in exchange for A's T stock. See, e.g., § 1.368–1(e)(1)(i); Yoc Heating v. Commissioner, 61 T.C. 168 (1973); Kass v. Commissioner, 60 T.C. 218 (1973), aff'd, 491 F.2d 749 (3d Cir.1974). Thus, the requisite continuity of interest under § 1.368–1(b) is lacking and section 354 does not apply to K's exchange of T stock for X stock. K recognizes gain or loss, if any, pursuant to section 1001(c) with respect to its T stock.

[T.D. 8940, 66 FR 9925, Feb. 13, 2001; as amended by T.D. 9071, 68 FR 40766, July 9, 2003; T.D. 9271, 71 FR 38075, July 5, 2006]

§ 1.338–4 Aggregate deemed sale price; various aspects of taxation of the deemed asset sale.

(a) Scope. This section provides rules under section 338(a)(1) to determine the aggregate deemed sale price (ADSP) for target. ADSP is the amount for which old target is deemed to have sold all of its assets in the deemed asset sale. ADSP is allocated among target's assets in accordance with § 1.338–6 to determine the amount for which each asset is deemed to have been sold. * * *

(b) Determination of ADSP—(1) General rule. ADSP is the sum—

(i) The grossed-up amount realized on the sale to the purchasing corporation of the purchasing corporation's recently purchased target stock (as defined in section 338(b)(6)(A)); and

(ii) The liabilities of old target.

(2) Time and amount of ADSP—(i) Original determination. ADSP is initially determined at the beginning of the day after the acquisition date of target. General principles of tax law apply in determining the timing and amount of the elements of ADSP.

* * *

(c) Grossed-up amount realized on the sale to the purchasing corporation of the purchasing corporation's recently purchased target stock—(1) Determination of amount. The grossed-up amount realized on the sale to the purchasing corporation of the purchasing corporation's recently purchased target stock is an amount equal to—

(i) The amount realized on the sale to the purchasing corporation of the purchasing corporation's recently purchased target stock determined as if the selling shareholder(s) were required to use old target's accounting methods and characteristics and the installment method were not available and determined without regard to the selling costs taken into account in paragraph (c)(1)(iii) of this section;

(ii) Divided by the percentage of target stock (by value, determined on the acquisition date) attributable to that recently purchased target stock;

(iii) Less the selling costs incurred by the selling shareholders in connection with the sale to the purchasing corporation of the purchasing corporation's recently purchased target stock that reduce their amount realized on the sale of the stock (e.g., brokerage commissions and any similar costs to sell the stock).

(2) Example. The following example illustrates this paragraph (c):

Example. T has two classes of stock outstanding, voting common stock and preferred stock described in section 1504(a)(4). On March 1 of Year 1, P purchases 40 percent of the outstanding T stock from S1 for $500, 20 percent of the outstanding T stock from S2 for $225, and 20 percent of the outstanding T stock from S3 for $275. On that date, the fair market value of all the T voting common stock is $1,250 and the preferred stock $750. S1, S2, and S3 incur $40, $35, and $25 respectively of selling costs. S1 continues to own the remaining 20 percent of the outstanding T stock. The grossed-up amount realized on the sale to P of P's recently purchased T stock is calculated as follows: The total amount realized (without regard to selling costs) is $1,000 (500 + 225 + 275). The percentage of T stock by value on the acquisition date attributable to the recently purchased T stock is 50% (1,000/(1,250 + 750)). The selling costs are $100 (40 + 35 + 25). The grossed-up amount realized is $1,900 (1,000/.5–100).

(d) Liabilities of old target—(1) In general. In general, the liabilities of old target are measured as of the beginning of the day after the acquisition date. (But see § 1.338–1(d) (regarding certain transactions on the acquisition date).) In order to be taken into account in ADSP, a liability must be a liability of target that is properly taken into account in amount realized under general principles of tax law that would apply if old target had sold its assets to an unrelated person for consideration that included the discharge of its liabilities. See § 1.1001–2(a). Such liabilities may include liabilities for the tax consequences resulting from the deemed sale.

(2) Time and amount of liabilities. The time for taking into account liabilities of old target in determining ADSP and the amount of the liabilities taken into account is determined as if old target had sold its assets to an unrelated person for consideration that included the discharge of the liabilities by the unrelated person. For example, if no amount of a target liability is properly taken into account in amount realized as of the beginning of the day after the acquisition date, the liability is not initially taken into account in determining ADSP (although it may been taken into account at some later date).

(e) Deemed sale tax consequences. Gain or loss on each asset in the deemed sale is computed by reference to the ADSP allocated to that asset. ADSP is allocated under the rules of § 1.338–6. Though deemed sale tax consequences may increase or decrease ADSP by creating or reducing a tax liability, the amount of the tax liability itself may be a function of the size of the deemed sale tax consequences. Thus, these determinations may require trial and error computations.

(f) Other rules apply in determining ADSP. ADSP may not be applied in such a way as to contravene other applicable rules. For example, a capital loss cannot be applied to reduce ordinary income in calculating the tax liability on the deemed sale for purposes of determining ADSP.

* * *

[T.D. 8940, 66 FR 9925, Feb. 13, 2001; 66 FR 17466, Mar. 30, 2001]

§ 1.338–5 Adjusted grossed-up basis.

(a) Scope. This section provides rules under section 338(b) to determine the adjusted grossed-up basis (AGUB) for target. AGUB is the amount for which new target is deemed to have purchased all of its assets in the deemed purchase under section 338(a)(2). AGUB is allocated among target's assets in accordance with § 1.338–6 to determine the price at which the assets are deemed to have been purchased. * * *

(b) Determination of AGUB—(1) General rule. AGUB is the sum of—

(i) The grossed-up basis in the purchasing corporation's recently purchased target stock;

(ii) The purchasing corporation's basis in nonrecently purchased target stock; and

(iii) The liabilities of new target.

(2) Time and amount of AGUB—(i) Original determination. AGUB is initially determined at the beginning of the day after the acquisition date of target. General principles of tax law apply in determining the timing and amount of the elements of AGUB.

* * *

(c) Grossed-up basis of recently purchased stock. The purchasing corporation's grossed-up basis of recently purchased target stock (as defined in section 338(b)(6)(A)) is an amount equal to—

(1) The purchasing corporation's basis in recently purchased target stock at the beginning of the day after the acquisition date determined without regard to the acquisition costs taken into account in paragraph (c)(3) of this section;

(2) Multiplied by a fraction, the numerator of which is 100 percent minus the number that is the percentage of target stock (by value, determined on the acquisition date) attributable to the purchasing corporation's nonrecently purchased target stock, and the denominator of which is the number equal to the percentage of target stock (by value, determined on the acquisition date) attributable to the purchasing corporation's recently purchased target stock;

(3) Plus the acquisition costs the purchasing corporation incurred in connection with its purchase of the recently purchased stock that are capitalized in the basis of such stock (e.g., brokerage commissions and any similar costs incurred by the purchasing corporation to acquire the stock).

(d) Basis of nonrecently purchased stock; gain recognition election—(1) No gain recognition election. In the absence of a gain recognition election under section 338(b)(3) and this section, the purchasing corporation retains its basis in the nonrecently purchased stock.

* * *

(e) Liabilities of new target—(1) In general. The liabilities of new target are the liabilities of target as of the beginning of the day after the acquisition date (but see § 1.338–1(d) (regarding certain transactions on the acquisition date)). In order to be taken into account in AGUB, a liability must be a liability of target that is properly taken into account in basis under general principles of tax law that would apply if new target had acquired its assets from an unrelated person for consideration that included discharge of the liabilities of that unrelated person. Such liabilities may include liabilities for the tax consequences resulting from the deemed sale.

(2) Time and amount of liabilities. The time for taking into account liabilities of old target in determining AGUB and the amount of the liabilities taken into account is determined as if new target had acquired its assets from an unrelated person for consideration that included the discharge of its liabilities.

(3) Interaction with deemed sale gain. In general, see § 1.338–4(e). Although ADSP and AGUB are not necessarily linked, if an increase in the amount realized for recently purchased stock of the target is taken into account after the acquisition date, and if the tax on the deemed sale tax consequences is a liability of the target, any increase in that liability is also taken into account in determining AGUB.

* * *

[T.D. 8940, 66 FR 9925, Feb. 13, 2001; T.D. 9619, 78 FR 28467, May 15, 2013]

§ 1.338–6 Allocation of ADSP and AGUB among target assets.

(a) Scope—(1) In general. This section prescribes rules for allocating ADSP and AGUB among the acquisition date assets of a target for which a section 338 election is made.

(2) Fair market value—(i) In general. Generally, the fair market value of an asset is its gross fair market value (i.e, fair market value determined without regard to mortgages, liens, pledges, or other liabilities). However, for purposes of determining the amount of old target's deemed sale tax consequences, the fair market value of any property subject to a nonrecourse indebtedness will be treated as being not less than the amount of such indebtedness. (For purposes of the preceding sentence, a liability that was incurred because of the acquisition of the property is disregarded to the extent that such liability was not taken into account in determining old target's basis in such property.)

(ii) Transaction costs. Transaction costs are not taken into account in allocating ADSP or AGUB to assets in the deemed sale (except indirectly through their effect on the total ADSP or AGUB to be allocated).

(iii) Internal Revenue Service authority. In connection with the examination of a return, the Internal Revenue Service may challenge the taxpayer's determination of the fair market value of any asset by any appropriate method and take into account all factors, including any lack of adverse tax interests between the parties.

(b) General rule for allocating ADSP and AGUB—(1) Reduction in the amount of consideration for Class I assets. Both ADSP and AGUB, in the respective allocation of each, are first reduced by the amount of Class I acquisition date assets. Class I assets are cash and general deposit accounts (including savings and checking accounts) other than certificates of deposit held in banks, savings and loan associations, and other depository institutions. If the amount of Class I assets exceeds AGUB, new target will immediately realize ordinary income in an amount equal to such excess. The amount of ADSP or AGUB remaining after the reduction is to be allocated to the remaining acquisition date assets.

(2) Other assets—(i) In general. Subject to the limitations and other rules of paragraph (c) of this section, ADSP and AGUB (as reduced by the amount of Class I assets) are allocated among Class II acquisition date assets of target in proportion to the fair market values of such Class II assets at such time, then among Class III assets so held in such proportion, then among Class IV assets so held in such proportion, then among Class V assets so held in such proportion, then among Class VI assets so held in such proportion, and finally to Class VII assets. If an asset is described below as includible in more than one class, then it is included in such class with the lower or lowest class number (for instance, Class III has a lower class number than Class IV).

(ii) Class II assets. Class II assets are actively traded personal property within the meaning of section 1092(d)(1) and § 1.1092(d)–1 (determined without regard to section 1092(d)(3)). In addition, Class II assets include certificates of deposit and foreign currency even if they are not actively traded personal property. Class II assets do not include stock of target affiliates, whether or not of a class that is actively traded, other than actively traded stock described in section 1504(a)(4). Examples of Class II assets include U.S. government securities and publicly traded stock.

(iii) Class III assets. Class III assets are assets that the taxpayer marks to market at least annually for Federal income tax purposes and debt instruments (including accounts receivable). However, Class III assets do not include—

(A) Debt instruments issued by persons related at the beginning of the day following the acquisition date to the target under section 267(b) or 707;

(B) Contingent debt instruments subject to § 1.1275–4, § 1.483–4, or section 988, unless the instrument is subject to the non-contingent bond method of § 1.1275–4(b) or is described in § 1.988–2(b)(2)(i)(B)(2); and

(C) Debt instruments convertible into the stock of the issuer or other property.

(iv) Class IV assets. Class IV assets are stock in trade of the taxpayer or other property of a kind that would properly be included in the inventory of taxpayer if on hand at the close of the taxable year, or property held by the taxpayer primarily for sale to customers in the ordinary course of its trade or business.

(v) Class V assets. Class V assets are all assets other than Class I, II, III, IV, VI, and VII assets.

(vi) Class VI assets. Class VI assets are all section 197 intangibles, as defined in section 197, except goodwill and going concern value.

(vii) Class VII assets. Class VII assets are goodwill and going concern value (whether or not the goodwill or going concern value qualifies as a section 197 intangible).

(3) Other items designated by the Internal Revenue Service. Similar items may be added to any class described in this paragraph (b) by designation in the Internal Revenue Bulletin by the Internal Revenue Service (see § 601.601(d)(2) of this Chapter).

(c) Certain limitations and other rules for allocation to an asset—(1) Allocation not to exceed fair market value. The amount of ADSP or AGUB allocated to an asset (other than Class VII assets) cannot exceed the fair market value of that asset at the beginning of the day after the acquisition date.

(2) Allocation subject to other rules. The amount of ADSP or AGUB allocated to an asset is subject to other provisions of the Internal Revenue Code or general principles of tax law in the same manner as if such asset were transferred to or acquired from an unrelated person in a sale or exchange. For example, if the deemed asset sale is a transaction described in section 1056(a) (relating to basis limitation for player contracts transferred in connection with the sale of a franchise), the amount of AGUB allocated to a contract for the services of an athlete cannot exceed the limitation imposed by that section. As another example, section 197(f)(5) applies in determining the amount of AGUB allocated in an amortizable section 197 intangible resulting from an assumption—reinsurance transaction.

(3) Special rule for allocating AGUB when purchasing corporation has nonrecently purchased stock—(i) Scope. This paragraph (c)(3) applies if at the beginning of the day after the acquisition date—

(A) The purchasing corporation holds nonrecently purchased stock for which a gain recognition election under section 338(b)(3) and § 1.338–5(d) is not made; and

(B) The hypothetical purchase price determined under paragraph (c)(3)(ii) of this section exceeds the AGUB determined under § 1.338–5(b).

(ii) Determination of hypothetical purchase price. Hypothetical purchase price is the AGUB that would result if a gain recognition election were made.

(iii) Allocation of AGUB. Subject to the limitations in paragraphs (c)(1) and (2) of this section, the portion of AGUB (after reduction by the amount of Class I assets) to be allocated to each Class II, III,

IV, V, VI, and VII asset of target held at the beginning of the day after the acquisition date is determined by multiplying—

(A) The amount that would be allocated to such asset under the general rules of this section were AGUB equal to the hypothetical purchase price; by

(B) A fraction, the numerator of which is actual AGUB (after reduction by the amount of Class I assets) and the denominator of which is the hypothetical purchase price (after reduction by the amount of Class I assets).

(4) Liabilities taken into account in determining amount realized on subsequent disposition. In determining the amount realized on a subsequent sale or other disposition of property deemed purchased by new target, § 1.1001–2(a)(3) shall not apply to any liability that was taken into account in AGUB.

* * *

[T.D. 8940, 66 FR 9925, Feb. 13, 2001; T.D. 9158, 69 FR 55740, Sept. 16, 2004; T.D. 9358, 72 FR 51703, Sept. 11, 2007]

§ 1.338–8 Asset and stock consistency.

(a) Introduction—(1) Overview. This section implements the consistency rules of sections 338(e) and (f). Under this section, no election under section 338 is deemed made or required with respect to target or any target affiliate. Instead, the person acquiring an asset may have a carryover basis in the asset.

(2) General application. The consistency rules generally apply if the purchasing corporation acquires an asset directly from target during the target consistency period and target is a subsidiary in a consolidated group. In such a case, gain from the sale of the asset is reflected under the investment adjustment provisions of the consolidated return regulations in the basis of target stock and may reduce gain from the sale of the stock. See § 1.1502–32 (investment adjustment provisions). Under the consistency rules, the purchasing corporation generally takes a carryover basis in the asset, unless a section 338 election is made for target. Similar rules apply if the purchasing corporation acquires an asset directly from a lower-tier target affiliate if gain from the sale is reflected under the investment adjustment provisions in the basis of target stock.

(3) Extensions of the general rules. If an arrangement exists, paragraph (f) of this section generally extends the carryover basis rule to certain cases in which the purchasing corporation acquires assets indirectly from target (or a lower-tier target affiliate). To prevent avoidance of the consistency rules, paragraph (j) of this section also may extend the consistency period or the 12–month acquisition period and may disregard the presence of conduits.

* * *

(6) Stock consistency. This section limits the application of the stock consistency rules to cases in which the rules are necessary to prevent avoidance of the asset consistency rules. Following the general treatment of a section 338(h)(10) election, a sale of a corporation's stock is treated as a sale of the corporation's assets if a section 338(h)(10) election is made. Because gain from this asset sale may be reflected in the basis of the stock of a higher-tier target, the carryover basis rule may apply to the assets.

(b) Consistency for direct acquisitions—(1) General rule. The basis rules of paragraph (d) of this section apply to an asset if—

(i) The asset is disposed of during the target consistency period;

(ii) The basis of target stock, as of the target acquisition date, reflects gain from the disposition of the asset (see paragraph (c) of this section); and

(iii) The asset is owned, immediately after its acquisition and on the target acquisition date, by a corporation that acquires stock of target in the qualified stock purchase (or by an affiliate of an acquiring corporation).

(2) Section 338(h)(10) elections. For purposes of this section, if a section 338(h)(10) election is made for a corporation acquired in a qualified stock purchase—

(i) The acquisition is treated as an acquisition of the corporation's assets (see § 1.338(h)(10)–1); and

(ii) The corporation is not treated as target.

(c) Gain from disposition reflected in basis of target stock. For purposes of this section:

(1) General rule. Gain from the disposition of an asset is reflected in the basis of a corporation's stock if the gain is taken into account under

§ 1.1502–32, directly or indirectly, in determining the basis of the stock, after applying section 1503(e) and other provisions of the Internal Revenue Code.

(2) Gain not reflected if section 338 election made for target. Gain from the disposition of an asset that is otherwise reflected in the basis of target stock as of the target acquisition date is not considered reflected in the basis of target stock if a section 338 election is made for target.

(3) Gain reflected by reason of distributions. Gain from the disposition of an asset is not considered reflected in the basis of target stock merely by reason of the receipt of a distribution from a target affiliate that is not a member of the same consolidated group as the distributee. See paragraph (g) of this section for the treatment of dividends eligible for a 100 percent dividends received deduction.

* * *

(d) Basis of acquired assets—(1) Carryover basis rule. If this paragraph (d) applies to an asset, the asset's basis immediately after its acquisition is, for all purposes of the Internal Revenue Code, its adjusted basis immediately before its disposition.

(2) Exceptions to carryover basis rule for certain assets. The carryover basis rule of paragraph (d)(1) of this section does not apply to the following assets—

(i) Any asset disposed of in the ordinary course of a trade or business (see section 338(e)(2)(A));

(ii) Any asset the basis of which is determined wholly by reference to the adjusted basis of the asset in the hands of the person that disposed of the asset (see section 338(e)(2)(B));

* * *

(iv) Any asset the basis of which immediately after its acquisition would otherwise be less than its adjusted basis immediately before its disposition; and

(v) Any asset identified by the Internal Revenue Service in a revenue ruling or revenue procedure.

(3) Exception to carryover basis rule for de minimis assets. The carryover basis rules of this section do not apply to an asset if the asset is not disposed of as part of the same arrangement as the acquisition of target and the aggregate amount realized for all assets otherwise subject to the carryover basis rules of this section does not exceed $250,000.

(4) Mitigation rule—(i) General rule. If the carryover basis rules of this section apply to an asset and the asset is transferred to a domestic corporation in a transaction to which section 351 applies or as a contribution to capital and no gain is recognized, the transferor's basis in the stock of the transferee (but not the transferee's basis in the asset) is determined without taking into account the carryover basis rules of this section.

(ii) Time for transfer. This paragraph (d)(4) applies only if the asset is transferred before the due date (including extensions) for the transferor's income tax return for the year that includes the last date for which a section 338 election may be made for target.

* * *

[T.D. 8515, 59 FR 2958, Jan. 20, 1994, as amended by T.D. 8858, 65 FR 1235, Jan. 7, 2000; T.D. 8940, 66 FR 9929, Feb. 13, 2001; 66 FR 17466, Mar. 30, 2001]

§ 1.338(h)(10)–1 Deemed asset sale and liquidation.

(a) Scope. This section prescribes rules for qualification for a section 338(h)(10) election and for making a section 338(h)(10) election. This section also prescribes the consequences of such election. The rules of this section are in addition to the rules of §§ 1.338–1 through 1.338–10, and, in appropriate cases, apply instead of the rules of § 1 1.338–1 through 1.338–10.

(b) Definitions—(1) Consolidated target. A *consolidated target* is a target that is a member of a consolidated group within the meaning of § 1.1502–1(h) on the acquisition date and is not the common parent of the group on that date.

(2) Selling consolidated group. A *selling consolidated group* is the consolidated group of which the consolidated target is a member on the acquisition date.

(3) Selling affiliate; affiliated target. A *selling affiliate* is a domestic corporation that owns on the acquisition date an amount of stock in a domestic target, which amount of stock is described in section 1504(a)(2), and does not join in filing a consolidated return with the target. In such case, the target is an *affiliated target*.

(4) S corporation target. An *S corporation target* is a target that is an S corporation immediately before the acquisition date.

(5) S corporation shareholders. *S corporation shareholders* are the S corporation target's shareholders. Unless otherwise indicated, a reference to S corporation shareholders refers both to S corporation shareholders who do and those who do not sell their target stock.

(6) Liquidation. Any reference in this section to a *liquidation* is treated as a reference to the transfer described in paragraph (d)(4) of this section notwithstanding its ultimate characterization for Federal income tax purposes.

(c) Section 338(h)(10) election—(1) In general. A section 338(h)(10) election may be made for T if P acquires stock meeting the requirements of section 1504(a)(2) from a selling consolidated group, a selling affiliate, or the S corporation shareholders in a qualified stock purchase.

(2) Availability of section 338(h)(10) election in certain multi-step transactions. Notwithstanding anything to the contrary in § 1.338–3(c)(1)(i), a section 338(h)(10) election may be made for T where P's acquisition of T stock, viewed independently, constitutes a qualified stock purchase and, after the stock acquisition, T merges or liquidates into P (or another member of the affiliated group that includes P), whether or not, under relevant provisions of law, including the step transaction doctrine, the acquisition of the T stock and the merger or liquidation of T qualify as a reorganization described in section 368(a). If a section 338(h)(10) election is made in a case where the acquisition of T stock followed by a merger or liquidation of T into P qualifies as a reorganization described in section 368(a), for all Federal tax purposes, P's acquisition of T stock is treated as a qualified stock purchase and is not treated as part of a reorganization described in section 368(a).

(3) Simultaneous joint election requirement. A section 338(h)(10) election is made jointly by P and the selling consolidated group (or the selling affiliate or the S corporation shareholders) on Form 8023 in accordance with the instructions to the form. S corporation shareholders who do not sell their stock must also consent to the election. The section 338(h)(10) election must be made not later than the 15th day of the 9th month beginning after the month in which the acquisition date occurs.

(4) Irrevocability. A section 338(h)(10) election is irrevocable. If a section 338(h)(10) election is made for T, a section 338 election is deemed made for T.

(5) Effect of invalid election. If a section 338(h)(10) election for T is not valid, the section 338 election for T is also not valid.

(d) Certain consequences of section 338(h)(10) election. For purposes of subtitle A of the Internal Revenue Code (except as provided in § 1.338–1(b)(2)), the consequences to the parties of making a section 338(h)(10) election for T are as follows:

(1) P. P is automatically deemed to have made a gain recognition election for its nonrecently purchased T stock, if any. The effect of a gain recognition election includes a taxable deemed sale by P on the acquisition date of any nonrecently purchased target stock. See § 1.338–5(d).

(2) New T. The AGUB for new T's assets is determined under § 1.338–5 and is allocated among the acquisition date assets under §§ 1.338–6 and 1.338–7. Notwithstanding paragraph (d)(4) of this section (deemed liquidation of old T), new T remains liable for the tax liabilities of old T (including the tax liability for the deemed sale gain). For example, new T remains liable for the tax liabilities of the members of any consolidated group that are attributable to taxable years in which those corporations and old T joined in the same consolidated return. See § 1.1502–6(a).

(3) Old T—deemed sale—(i) In general. Old T is treated as transferring all of its assets to an unrelated person in exchange for consideration that includes the discharge of its liabilities in a single transaction at the close of the acquisition date (but before the deemed liquidation). See § 1.338–1(a) regarding the tax characterization of the deemed asset sale. Except as provided in § 1.338(h)(10)–1(d)(8) (regarding the installment method), old T recognizes all of the gain realized on the deemed transfer of its assets in consideration for the ADSP. ADSP for old T is determined under § 1.338–4 and allocated among the acquisition date assets under §§ 1.338–6 and 1.338–7. Old T realizes the deemed sale tax consequences from the deemed asset sale before the close of the acquisition date while old T is a member of the selling consolidated group (or owned by the selling affiliate or owned by the S corporation shareholders). If T is an affiliated target, or an S corporation target, the principles of

§§ 1.338–2(c)(10) and 1.338–10(a)(1), (5), and (6)(i) apply to the return on which the deemed sale tax consequences are reported. When T is an S corporation target, T's S election continues in effect through the close of the acquisition date (including the time of the deemed asset sale and the deemed liquidation) notwithstanding section 1362(d)(2)(B). Also, when T is an S corporation target (but not a qualified subchapter S subsidiary), any direct and indirect subsidiaries of T which T has elected to treat as qualified subchapter S subsidiaries under section 1361(b)(3) remain qualified subchapter S subsidiaries through the close of the acquisition date.

(ii) Tiered targets. In the case of parent-subsidiary chains of corporations making elections under section 338(h)(10), the deemed asset sale of a parent corporation is considered to precede that of its subsidiary. See § 1.338–3(b)(4)(i).

(4) Old T and selling consolidated group, selling affiliate, or S corporation shareholders—deemed liquidation; tax characterization—(i) In general. Old T is treated as if, before the close of the acquisition date, after the deemed asset sale in paragraph (d)(3) of this section, and while old T is a member of the selling consolidated group (or owned by the selling affiliate or owned by the S corporation shareholders), it transferred all of its assets to members of the selling consolidated group, the selling affiliate, or S corporation shareholders and ceased to exist. The transfer from old T is characterized for Federal income tax purposes in the same manner as if the parties had actually engaged in the transactions deemed to occur because of this section and taking into account other transactions that actually occurred or are deemed to occur. For example, the transfer may be treated as a distribution in pursuance of a plan of reorganization, a distribution in complete cancellation or redemption of all its stock, one of a series of distributions in complete cancellation or redemption of all its stock in accordance with a plan of liquidation, or part of a circular flow of cash. In most cases, the transfer will be treated as a distribution in complete liquidation to which section 336 or 337 applies.

(ii) Tiered targets. In the case of parent-subsidiary chains of corporations making elections under section 338(h)(10), the deemed liquidation of a subsidiary corporation is considered to precede the deemed liquidation of its parent.

(5) Selling consolidated group, selling affiliate, or S corporation shareholders—(i) In general. If T is an S corporation target, S corporation shareholders (whether or not they sell their stock) take their pro rata share of the deemed sale tax consequences into account under section 1366 and increase or decrease their basis in T stock under section 1367. Members of the selling consolidated group, the selling affiliate, or S corporation shareholders are treated as if, after the deemed asset sale in paragraph (d)(3) of this section and before the close of the acquisition date, they received the assets transferred by old T in the transaction described in paragraph (d)(4)(i) of this section. In most cases, the transfer will be treated as a distribution in complete liquidation to which section 331 or 332 applies.

(ii) Basis and holding period of T stock not acquired. A member of the selling consolidated group (or the selling affiliate or an S corporation shareholder) retaining T stock is treated as acquiring the stock so retained on the day after the acquisition date for its fair market value. The holding period for the retained stock starts on the day after the acquisition date. For purposes of this paragraph, the fair market value of all of the T stock equals the grossed-up amount realized on the sale to P of P's recently purchased target stock. See § 1.338–4(c).

(iii) T stock sale. Members of the selling consolidated group (or the selling affiliate or S corporation shareholders) recognize no gain or loss on the sale or exchange of T stock included in the qualified stock purchase (although they may recognize gain or loss on the T stock in the deemed liquidation).

(6) Nonselling minority shareholders other than nonselling S corporation shareholders—(i) In general. This paragraph (d)(6) describes the treatment of shareholders of old T other than the following: members of the selling consolidated group, the selling affiliate, S corporation shareholders, (whether or not they sell their stock), and P. For a description of the treatment of S corporation shareholders, see paragraph (d)(5) of this section. A shareholder to which this paragraph (d)(6) applies is called a minority shareholder.

(ii) T stock sale. A minority shareholder recognizes gain or loss on the shareholder's sale or exchange of T stock included in the qualified stock purchase.

(iii) T stock not acquired. A minority shareholder does not recognize gain or loss under this section with respect to shares of T stock retained by the shareholder. The shareholder's basis and holding period for that T stock is not affected by the section 338(h)(10) election.

(7) Consolidated return of selling consolidated group. If P acquires T in a qualified stock purchase from a selling consolidated group—

(i) The selling consolidated group must file a consolidated return for the taxable period that includes the acquisition date;

(ii) A consolidated return for the selling consolidated group for that period may not be withdrawn on or after the day that a section 338(h)(10) election is made for T; and

(iii) Permission to discontinue filing consolidated returns cannot be granted for, and cannot apply to, that period or any of the immediately preceding taxable periods during which consolidated returns continuously have been filed.

(8) Availability of the section 453 installment method. Solely for purposes of applying sections 453, 453A, and 453B, and the regulations thereunder (the installment method) to determine the consequences to old T in the deemed asset sale and to old T (and its shareholders, if relevant) in the deemed liquidation, the rules in paragraphs (d)(1) through (7) of this section are modified as follows:

(i) In deemed asset sale. Old T is treated as receiving in the deemed asset sale new T installment obligations, the terms of which are identical (except as to the obligor) to P installment obligations issued in exchange for recently purchased stock of T. Old T is treated as receiving in cash all other consideration in the deemed asset sale other than the assumption of, or taking subject to, old T liabilities. For example, old T is treated as receiving in cash any amounts attributable to the grossing-up of amount realized under § 1.338–4(c). The amount realized for recently purchased stock taken into account in determining ADSP is adjusted (and, thus, ADSP is redetermined) to reflect the amounts paid under an installment obligation for the stock when the total payments under the installment obligation are greater or less than the amount realized.

(ii) In deemed liquidation. Old T is treated as distributing in the deemed liquidation the new T installment obligations that it is treated as receiving in the deemed asset sale. The members of the selling consolidated group, the selling affiliate, or the S corporation shareholders are treated as receiving in the deemed liquidation the new T installment obligations that correspond to the P installment obligations they actually received individually in exchange for their recently purchased stock. The new T installment obligations may be recharacterized under other rules. See for example § 1.453–11(a)(2) which, in certain circumstances, treats the new T installment obligations deemed distributed by old T as if they were issued by new T in exchange for the stock in old T owned by members' of the selling consolidated group, the selling affiliate, or the S corporation shareholder. The members of the selling consolidated group, the selling affiliate, or the S corporation shareholders are treated as receiving all other consideration in the deemed liquidation in cash.

(9) Treatment consistent with an actual asset sale. No provision in section 338(h)(10) or this section shall produce a Federal income tax result under subtitle A of the Internal Revenue Code that would not occur if the parties had actually engaged in the transactions deemed to occur because of this section and taking into account other transactions that actually occurred or are deemed to occur. See, however, § 1.338–1(b)(2) for certain exceptions to this rule.

(e) Examples. The following examples illustrate the provisions of this section:

* * *

Example 11. Stock acquisition followed by upstream merger—without section 338(h)(10) election. **(i)** P owns all the stock of Y, a newly formed subsidiary. S owns all the stock of T. Each of P, S, T and Y is a domestic corporation. P acquires all of the T stock in a statutory merger of Y into T, with T surviving. In the merger, S receives consideration consisting of 50% P voting stock and 50% cash. Viewed independently of any other step, P's acquisition of T stock constitutes a qualified stock purchase. As part of the plan that includes P's acquisition of the T stock, T subsequently merges into P. Viewed independently of any other step, T's merger into P qualifies as a liquidation described in section 332. Absent the application of paragraph (c)(2) of this section, the step transaction doctrine would apply to treat P's acquisition of the T stock and T's merger into P as an acquisition by P of T's assets in a reorganization described in section 368(a). P and S do not make a section 338(h)(10) election with respect to P's purchase of the T stock.

(ii) Because P and S do not make an election under section 338(h)(10) for T, P's acquisition of the T stock and T's merger into P is treated as part of a reorganization described in section 368(a).

Example 12. Stock acquisition followed by upstream merger—with section 338(h)(10) election. **(i)** The facts are the same as in Example 11 except that P and S make a joint election under section 338(h)(10) for T.

(ii) Pursuant to paragraph (c)(2) of this section, as a result of the election under section 338(h)(10), for all Federal tax purposes, P's acquisition of the T stock is treated as a qualified stock purchase and P's acquisition of the T stock is not treated as part of a reorganization described in section 368(a).

Example 13. Stock acquisition followed by brother-sister merger—with section 338(h)(10) election. **(i)** The facts are the same as in Example 12, except that, following P's acquisition of the T stock, T merges into X, a domestic corporation that is a wholly owned subsidiary of P. Viewed independently of any other step, T's merger into X qualifies as a reorganization described in section 368(a). Absent the application of paragraph (c)(2) of this section, the step transaction doctrine would apply to treat P's acquisition of the T stock and T's merger into X as an acquisition by X of T's assets in a reorganization described in section 368(a).

(ii) Pursuant to paragraph (c)(2) of this section, as a result of the election under section 338(h)(10), for all Federal tax purposes, P's acquisition of T stock is treated as a qualified stock purchase and P's acquisition of T stock is not treated as part of a reorganization described in section 368(a).

Example 14. Stock acquisition that does not qualify as a qualified stock purchase followed by upstream merger. **(i)** The facts are the same as in Example 11, except that, in the statutory merger of Y into T, S receives only P voting stock.

(ii) Pursuant to § 1.338–3(c)(1)(i) and paragraph (c)(2) of this section, no election under section 338(h)(10) can be made with respect to P's acquisition of the T stock because, pursuant to relevant provisions of law, including the step transaction doctrine, that acquisition followed by T's merger into P is treated as a reorganization described in section 368(a)(1)(A), and that acquisition, viewed independently of T's merger into P, does not constitute a qualified stock purchase under section 338(d)(3). Accordingly, P's acquisition of the T stock and T's merger into P is treated as a reorganization described in section 368(a).

* * *

[T.D. 8940, 66 FR 9925, Feb. 13, 2001, as amended by T.D. 9071, 68 FR 40766, July 9, 2003; T.D. 9271, 71 FR 38074, July 5, 2006; T.D. 9329, 72 FR 32807, June 14, 2007]

§ 1.346–1 Partial liquidation.

(a) General. This section defines a partial liquidation. If amounts are distributed in partial liquidation such amounts are treated under section 331(a)(2) as received in part or full payment in exchange for the stock. A distribution is treated as in partial liquidation of a corporation if:

(1) The distribution is one of a series of distributions in redemption of all of the stock of the corporation pursuant to a plan of complete liquidation, or

(2) The distribution:

(i) Is not essentially equivalent to a dividend,

(ii) Is in redemption of a part of the stock of the corporation pursuant to a plan, and

(iii) Occurs within the taxable year in which the plan is adopted or within the succeeding taxable year.

An example of a distribution which will qualify as a partial liquidation under subparagraph (2) of this paragraph and section 346(a) is a distribution resulting from a genuine contraction of the corporate business such as the distribution of unused insurance proceeds recovered as a result of a fire which destroyed part of the business causing a cessation of a part of its activities. On the other hand, the distribution of funds attributable to a reserve for an expansion program which has been abandoned does not qualify as a partial liquidation within the meaning of section 346(a). A distribution to which section 355 applies (or so much of section 356 as relates to section 355) is not a distribution in partial liquidation within the meaning of section 346(a).

(b) Special requirements on termination of business. A distribution which occurs within the taxable year in which the plan is adopted or within the succeeding taxable year and which meets the requirements of subsection (b) of section 346 falls within paragraph (a)(2) of this section and within section 346(a)(2). The requirements which a distribution must meet to fall within subsection (b) of section 346 are:

(1) Such distribution is attributable to the corporation's ceasing to conduct, or consists of assets of, a trade or business which has been actively conducted throughout the five-year period immediately before the distribution, which trade or business was not acquired by the corporation within such period in a transaction in which gain or loss was recognized in whole or in part, and

(2) Immediately after such distribution by the corporation it is actively engaged in the conduct of a trade or business, which trade or business was actively conducted throughout the five-year period ending on the date of such distribution and was not acquired by the corporation within such period in a transaction in which gain or loss was recognized in whole or in part.

A distribution shall be treated as having been made in partial liquidation pursuant to section 346(b) if it consists of the proceeds of the sale of the assets of a trade or business which has been actively conducted for the five-year period and has been terminated, or if it is a distribution in kind of the assets of such a business, or if it is a distribution in kind of some of the assets of such a business and of the proceeds of the sale of the remainder of the assets of such a business. In general, a distribution which will qualify under section 346(b) may consist of, but is not limited to:

(i) Assets (other than inventory or property described in subdivision (ii) of this subparagraph) used in the trade or business throughout the five-year period immediately before the distribution (for this purpose an asset shall be considered used in the trade or business during the period of time the asset which it replaced was so used), or

(ii) Proceeds from the sale of assets described in subdivision (i) of this subparagraph, and, in addition,

(iii) The inventory of such trade or business or property held primarily for sale to customers in the ordinary course of business, if:

(a) The items constituting such inventory or such property were substantially similar to the items constituting such inventory or property during the five-year period immediately before the distribution, and

(b) The quantity of such items on the date of distribution was not substantially in excess of the quantity of similar items regularly on hand in the conduct of such business during such five-year period, or

(iv) Proceeds from the sale of inventory or property described in subdivision (iii) of this subparagraph, if such inventory or property is sold in bulk in the course of termination of such trade or business and if with respect to such inventory the conditions of subdivision (iii)(a) and (b) of this subparagraph would have been met had such inventory or property been distributed on the date of such sale.

(c) Active conduct of a trade or business. For the purpose of section 346(b)(1), a corporation shall be deemed to have actively conducted a trade or business immediately before the distribution, if:

(1) In the case of a business the assets of which have been distributed in kind, the business was operated by such corporation until the date of distribution, or

(2) In the case of a business the proceeds of the sale of the assets of which are distributed, such business was actively conducted until the date of sale and the proceeds of such sale were distributed as soon thereafter as reasonably possible.

The term "active conduct of a trade or business" shall have the same meaning in this section as in * * * § 1.355–1 [now § 1.355–3].

[T.D. 6500, 25 FR 11607, Nov. 26, 1960]

§ 1.346–2 Treatment of certain redemptions.

If a distribution in a redemption of stock qualifies as a distribution in part or full payment in exchange for the stock under both section 302(a) and this section, then only this section shall be applicable. None of the limitations of section 302 shall be applicable to such redemption.

[T.D. 6500, 25 FR 11607, Nov. 26, 1960]

§ 1.346–3 Effect of certain sales.

The determination of whether assets sold in connection with a partial liquidation are sold by the distributing corporation or by the shareholder is a question of fact to be determined under the facts and circumstances of each case.

[T.D. 6500, 25 FR 11607, Nov. 26, 1960]

§ 1.351–1 Transfer to corporation controlled by transferor.

(a)(1) Section 351(a) provides, in general, for the nonrecognition of gain or loss upon the transfer by one or more persons of property to a corporation solely in exchange for stock * * * in such corporation, if immediately after the exchange, such person or persons are in control of the corporation to which the property was transferred. As used in section 351, the phrase "one or more persons" includes individuals, trusts, estates, partnerships, associations, companies, or corporations (see section 7701(a)(1)). To be in control of the transferee corporation, such person or persons must own immediately after the transfer stock possessing at least 80 percent of the total combined voting power of all classes of stock entitled to vote and at least 80 percent of the total number of shares of all other classes of stock of such corporation (see section 368(c)). In determining control under this section, the fact that any corporate transferor distributes part or all of the stock which it receives in the exchange to its shareholders shall not be taken into account. The phrase "immediately after the exchange" does not necessarily require simultaneous exchanges by two or more persons, but comprehends a situation where the rights of the parties have been previously defined and the execution of the agreement proceeds with an expedition consistent with orderly procedure. For purposes of this section—

(i) Stock * * * issued for services rendered or to be rendered to or for the benefit of the issuing corporation will not be treated as having been issued in return for property, and

(ii) Stock * * * issued for property which is of relatively small value in comparison to the value of the stock * * * already owned (or to be received for services) by the person who transferred such property, shall not be treated as having been issued in return for property if the primary purpose of the transfer is to qualify under this section the exchanges of property by other persons transferring property.

For the purpose of section 351, stock rights or stock warrants are not included in the term "stock * * *."

(2) The application of section 351(a) is illustrated by the following examples:

Example (1). C owns a patent right worth $25,000 and D owns a manufacturing plant worth $75,000. C and D organize the R Corporation with an authorized capital stock of $100,000. C transfers his patent right to the R Corporation for $25,000 of its stock and D transfers his plant to the new corporation for $75,000 of its stock. No gain or loss to C or D is recognized.

Example (2). B owns certain real estate which cost him $50,000 in 1930, but which has a fair market value of $200,000 in 1955. He transfers the property to the N Corporation in 1955 for 78 percent of each class of stock of the corporation having a fair market value of $200,000, the remaining 22 percent of the stock of the corporation having been issued by the corporation in 1940 to other persons for cash. B realized a taxable gain of $150,000 on this transaction.

Example (3). E, an individual, owns property with a basis of $10,000 but which has a fair market value of $18,000. E also had rendered services valued at $2,000 to Corporation F. Corporation F has outstanding 100 shares of common stock all of which are held by G. Corporation F issues 400 shares of its common stock (having a fair market value of $20,000) to E in exchange for his property worth $18,000 and in compensation for the services he has rendered worth $2,000. Since immediately after the transaction, E owns 80 percent of the outstanding stock of Corporation F, no gain is recognized upon the exchange of the property for the stock. However, E realized $2,000 of ordinary income as compensation for services rendered to Corporation F.

(3) Underwritings of stock—(i) In general. For the purpose of section 351, if a person acquires stock of a corporation from an underwriter in exchange for cash in a qualified underwriting transaction, the person who acquires stock from the underwriter is treated as transferring cash directly to the corporation in exchange for stock of the corporation and the underwriter is disregarded. A qualified underwriting transaction is a transaction in which a corporation issues stock for cash in an underwriting in which either the underwriter is an agent of the corporation or the underwriter's ownership of the stock is transitory.

(ii) Effective date. This paragraph (a)(3) is effective for qualified underwriting transactions occurring on or after May 1, 1996.

(b)(1) Where property is transferred to a corporation by two or more persons in exchange for stock * * *, as described in paragraph (a) of this section, it is not required that the stock * * * received by each be substantially in proportion to his interest in the property immediately prior to the transfer. However, where the stock * * * received are received in disproportion to such interest, the entire transaction will be given tax effect in accordance with its true nature, and in appropriate cases the transaction may be treated as if the stock * * * had first been received in proportion and then some of such stock * * * had been used to make gifts (section 2501 and following), to pay compensation (section 61(a)(1)), or to satisfy obligations of the transferor of any kind.

(2) The application of paragraph (b)(1) of this section may be illustrated as follows:

Example (1). Individuals A and B, father and son, organize a corporation with 100 shares of common stock to which A transfers property worth $8,000 in exchange for 20 shares of stock, and B transfers property worth $2,000 in exchange for 80 shares of stock. No gain or loss will be recognized under section 351. However, if it is determined that A in fact made a gift to B, such gift will be subject to tax under section 2501 and following. Similarly, if B had rendered services to A (such services having no relation to the assets transferred or to the business of the corporation) and the disproportion in the amount of stock received constituted the payment of compensation by A to B, B will be taxable upon the fair market value of the 60 shares of stock received as compensation for services rendered, and A will realize gain or loss upon the difference between the basis to him of the 60 shares and their fair market value at the time of the exchange.

Example (2). Individuals C and D each transferred, to a newly organized corporation, property having a fair market value of $4,500 in exchange for the issuance by the corporation of 45 shares of its capital stock to each transferor. At the same time, the corporation issued to E, an individual, 10 shares of its capital stock in payment for organizational and promotional services rendered by E for the benefit of the corporation. E transferred no property to the corporation. C and D were under no obligation to pay for E's services. No gain or loss is recognized to C or D. E received compensation taxable as ordinary income to the extent of the fair market value of the 10 shares of stock received by him.

(c)(1) The general rule of section 351 does not apply, and consequently gain or loss will be recognized, where property is transferred to an investment company after June 30, 1967. A transfer of property after June 30, 1967, will be considered to be a transfer to an investment company if—

(i) The transfer results, directly or indirectly, in diversification of the transferors' interests, and

(ii) The transferee is (a) a regulated investment company, (b) a real estate investment trust, or (c) a corporation more than 80 percent of the value of whose assets (excluding cash and nonconvertible debt obligations from consideration) are held for investment and are readily marketable stocks or securities, or interests in regulated investment companies or real estate investment trusts.

(2) The determination of whether a corporation is an investment company shall ordinarily be made by reference to the circumstances in existence immediately after the transfer in question. However, where circumstances change thereafter pursuant to a plan in existence at the time of the transfer, this determination shall be made by reference to the later circumstances.

(3) Stocks and securities will be considered readily marketable if (and only if) they are part of a class of stock or securities which is traded on a securities exchange or traded or quoted regularly in the over-the-counter market. For purposes of subparagraph (1)(ii)(c) of this paragraph, the term "readily marketable stocks or securities" includes convertible debentures, convertible preferred stock, warrants, and other stock rights if the stock for which they may be converted or exchanged is readily marketable. Stocks and securities will be considered to be held for investment unless they are (i) held primarily for sale to customers in the ordinary course of business, or (ii) used in the trade or business of banking, insurance, brokerage, or a similar trade or business.

(4) In making the determination required under subparagraph (1)(ii)(c) of this paragraph, stock and securities in subsidiary corporations shall be disregarded and the parent corporation shall be deemed to own its ratable share of its subsidiaries' assets. A corporation shall be considered a subsidiary if the parent owns 50 percent or more of (i) the combined voting power of all classes of stock entitled to vote, or (ii) the total value of shares of all classes of stock outstanding.

(5) A transfer ordinarily results in the diversification of the transferors' interests if two or more persons transfer nonidentical assets to a corporation in the exchange. For this purpose, if any transaction involves one or more transfers of nonidentical assets which, taken in the aggregate, constitute an insignificant portion of the total value of assets transferred, such transfers shall be disregarded in determining whether diversification has occurred. If there is only one transferor (or two or more transferors of identical assets) to a newly organized corporation, the transfer will generally be treated as not resulting in diversification. If a transfer is part of a plan to achieve diversification without recognition of gain, such as a plan which contemplates a subsequent transfer, however delayed, of the corporate assets (or of the stock or securities received in the earlier exchange) to an investment company in a transaction purporting to qualify for nonrecognition treatment, the original transfer will be treated as resulting in diversification.

(6)(i) For purposes of paragraph (c)(5) of this section, a transfer of stocks and securities will not be treated as resulting in a diversification of the transferors' interests if each transferor transfers a diversified portfolio of stocks and securities. For purposes of this paragraph (c)(6), a portfolio of stocks and securities is diversified if it satisfies the 25 and 50-percent tests of section 368(a)(2)(F)(ii), applying the relevant provisions of section 368(a)(2)(F). However, Government securities are included in total assets for purposes of the denominator of the 25 and 50-percent tests (unless the Government securities are acquired to meet the 25 and 50-percent tests), but are not treated as securities of a issuer for purposes of the numerator of the 25 and 50-percent tests.

(ii) Paragraph (c)(6)(i) of this section is effective for transfers completed on or after May 2, 1996. Transfers of diversified (within the meaning of paragraph (c)(6)(i) of this section), but nonidentical, portfolios of stocks and securities completed before May 2, 1996, may be treated either—

(A) Consistent with paragraph (c)(6)(i) of this section; or

(B) As resulting in diversification of the transferors' interests.

(7) The application of subparagraph (5) of this paragraph may be illustrated as follows:

Example (1). Individuals A, B, and C organize a corporation with 101 shares of common stock. A and B each transfers to it $10,000 worth of the only class of stock of corporation X, listed on the New York Stock Exchange, in exchange for 50 shares of stock. C transfers $200 worth of readily marketable securities in corporation Y for one share of stock. In determining whether or not diversification has occurred, C's participation in the transaction will be disregarded. There is, therefore, no diversification, and gain or loss will not be recognized.

Example (2). A, together with 50 other transferors, organizes a corporation with 100 shares of stock. A transfers $10,000 worth of stock in corporation X, listed on the New York Stock Exchange, in exchange for 50 shares of stock. Each of the other 50 transferors transfers $200 worth of readily marketable securities in corporations other than X in exchange for one share of stock. In determining whether or not diversification has occurred, all transfers will be taken into account. Therefore, diversification is present, and gain or loss will be recognized.

[T.D. 6500, 25 FR 11607, Nov. 26, 1960, as amended by T.D. 6942, 32 FR 20977, Dec. 29, 1967; T.D. 8665, 61 FR 19188, May 1, 1996; T.D. 8663, 61 FR 19544, May 2, 1996]

§ 1.351–2 Receipt of property.

(a) If an exchange would be within the provisions of section 351(a) if it were not for the fact that the property received in exchange consists not only of property permitted by such subsection to be received without the recognition of gain, but also of other property or money, then the gain, if any, to the recipient shall be recognized, but in an amount not in excess of the sum of such money and the fair market value of such other property. No loss to the recipient shall be recognized.

(b) See section 357 and the regulations pertaining to that section for applicable rules as to the treatment of liabilities as "other property" in cases subject to section 351, where another party to the exchange assumes a liability, or acquires property subject to a liability.

(c) See sections 358 and 362 and the regulations pertaining to those sections for applicable rules with respect to the determination of the basis of stock, securities, or other property received in exchanges subject to section 351.

(d) See part I (section 301 and following), subchapter C, chapter 1 of the Code, and the regulations thereunder for applicable rules with respect to the taxation of dividends where a distribution by a corporation of its stock * * * in connection with an exchange subject to section 351(a) has the effect of the distribution of a taxable dividend.

* * *

[T.D. 6500, 25 FR 11607, Nov. 26, 1960, as amended by T.D. 8904, 65 FR 58650, Oct. 2, 2000]

§ 1.351–2 Rcccipt of property (Proposed Jan. 21, 2009).

(b) To determine the amount of gain recognized under section 351(b), the fair market value of each category of consideration received by each transferor is allocated to the properties transferred in proportion to each property's relative fair market value. The application of this paragraph (b) is illustrated by the following example:

Example. C transfers $2,000 in exchange for 200 shares of stock. D transfers Asset I, Asset II, and Asset III in exchange for $100 cash and 100 shares of stock. The exchange is subject to section 351. At the time of the exchange, Asset I has a fair market value of $220 and a basis of $400, Asset II has a fair market value of $330 and a basis of $200, and Asset III has a fair market value of $550 and a basis of $250. No gain or loss is recognized to C. Gain, but not loss, is recognized by D. To determine the gain recognized by D under section 351(b), the fair market value of each category of consideration received is allocated to the properties transferred in proportion to the relative fair market values of the properties transferred. Asset I represents 20 percent of the total fair market value of assets transferred (220/1100), Asset II represents 30 percent (330/1100), and Asset III represents 50 percent (550/1100). Under paragraph (b) of this section, the amount of gain recognized by D is determined by allocating a pro rata portion of each class of consideration received to each property transferred as follows: (A) $20 cash and 20 shares of stock to Asset I (20 percent of 100 shares of stock and 20 percent of $100) (B) $30 cash and 30 shares of stock to Asset II (30 percent of 100 shares of stock and 30 percent of $100); and (C) $50 cash and 50 shares of stock to Asset III (50 percent of 100 shares of stock and 50 percent of $100). D realizes a loss of $180 on Asset I, none of which is recognized, a gain of $130 on Asset II, $30 of which is recognized, and a gain of $300 on Asset III, $50 of which is recognized.

§ 1.354–1 Exchanges of stock and securities in certain reorganizations.

(a) Section 354 provides that under certain circumstances no gain or loss is recognized to a shareholder who surrenders his stock in exchange for other stock or to a security holder who surrenders his securities in exchange for stock. Section 354 also provides that under certain circumstances a security holder may surrender securities and receive securities in the same principal amount or in a lesser principal amount without the recognition of gain or loss to him. The exchanges to which section 354 applies must be pursuant to a plan of reorganization as provided in section 368(a) and the stock and securities surrendered as well as the stock and securities received must be those of a corporation which is a party to the reorganization. Section 354 does not apply to exchanges pursuant to a reorganization described in section 368(a)(1)(D) unless the transferor corporation—

(1) Transfers all or substantially all of its assets to a single corporation, and

(2) Distributes all of its remaining properties (if any) and the stock, securities and other properties received in the exchange to its shareholders or security holders in pursuance of the plan of reorganization. The fact that properties retained by the transferor corporation, or received in exchange for the properties transferred in the reorganization, are used to satisfy existing liabilities not represented by securities and which were incurred in the ordinary course of business before the reorganization does not prevent the application of section 354 to an exchange pursuant to a plan of reorganization defined in section 368(a)(1)(D).

(b) Except as provided in section 354(c) and (d), section 354 is not applicable to an exchange of stock or securities if a greater principal amount of securities is received than the principal amount of securities the recipient surrenders, or if securities are received and the recipient surrenders no securities. See, however, section 356 and regulations pertaining to such section. See also section 306 with respect to thc receipt of preferred stock in a transaction to which section 354 is applicable.

* * *

(d) The rules of section 354 may be illustrated by the following examples:

Example (1). Pursuant to a reorganization under section 368(a) to which Corporations T and W are parties, A, a shareholder in Corporation T, surrenders all his common stock in Corporation T in exchange for common stock of Corporation W. No gain or loss is recognized to A.

Example (2). Pursuant to a reorganization under section 368(a) to which Corporations X and Y (which are not railroad corporations) are parties, B, a shareholder in Corporation X, surrenders all his stock in X for stock and securities in Y. Section 354 does not apply to this exchange. See, however, section 356.

Example (3). C, a shareholder in Corporation Z * * *, surrenders all his stock in Corporation Z in exchange for securities in Corporation Z. Whether or not this exchange is in connection with a recapitalization under section 368(a)(1)(E), section 354 does not apply. See, however, section 302.

Example (4). The facts are the same as in Example 3 of this paragraph (d), except that C receives solely rights to acquire stock in Corporation Z. Section 354 does not apply.

(e) Except as provided in § 1.356–6, for purposes of section 354, the term "securities" includes rights issued by a party to the reorganization to acquire its stock. For purposes of this section and section 356(d)(2)(B), a right to acquire stock has no principal amount. For this purpose, rights to acquire stock has the same meaning as it does under sections 305 and 317(a). Other Internal Revenue Code provisions governing the treatment of rights to acquire stock may also apply to certain exchanges occurring in connection with a reorganization. See, for example, sections 83 and 421 through 424 and the regulations thereunder. This paragraph (e) applies to exchanges occurring on or after March 9, 1998.

* * *

[T.D. 6500, 25 FR 11607, Nov. 26, 1960, as amended by T.D. 7616, 44 FR 26869, May 8, 1979; T.D. 8752, 63 FR 409, Jan. 6, 1998; T.D. 8882, 65 FR 31078, May 16, 2002; T.D. 8904, 65 FR 58650, Oct. 2, 2000]

§ 1.354–1 Exchanges of stock, securities and other property in certain reorganizations (Proposed Jan. 21, 2009).

* * *

(d) Exchanges solely or partly for money or other property—(1) Determination of consideration for a share of stock or a security. In determining the consideration received for a share of stock or a security, except as otherwise provided in this paragraph (d)(1), a pro rata portion of any other property and money received shall be treated as received in exchange for each share of stock and security surrendered, based on the fair market value of such surrendered share of stock or security. However, to the extent the terms of the exchange specify the other property or money that is received in exchange for a particular share of stock or security surrendered or a particular class of stock or securities surrendered, such terms shall control provided that the terms are economically reasonable, unless the shareholder's exchange has the effect of a distribution of a dividend. If the exchange has the effect of a distribution of a dividend and the terms of an exchange specify the other property or money that is received with respect to a particular share of stock and such specification would otherwise be economically reasonable, such other property or money shall be treated as received pro rata in exchange for each share of stock within that class (as defined in section 1.302–5(b)(2)) held by the exchanging shareholder. Notwithstanding the preceding sentence, economically reasonable designations between classes of stock or securities (as opposed to within a class) shall generally control. All exchanges made by an exchanging shareholder, whether governed by section 354, 356, or 302, are taken into account to determine whether the shareholder's exchange has the effect of a distribution of a dividend.

(2) Treatment of exchanges of stock solely for money or other property. Neither section 354 nor so much of section 356 as relates to section 354 applies to a shareholder's surrender of a share of stock in exchange solely for money or other property that is not permitted to be received without the recognition of gain, even though such exchange is pursuant to a plan of reorganization described in section 368(a), and even though section 354, section 356 or both sections 354 and 356 apply to the exchange of other shares by that shareholder or other shareholders. See section 302 and the regulations under that section for the treatment of such an exchange.

(e) The rules of section 354 may be illustrated by the following examples:

* * *

Example 5. D owns shares of Class A common stock, Series 1 preferred stock, and Series 2 preferred stock in Corporation T. The Series 1 preferred stock and the Series 2 preferred stock are different classes of stock. Pursuant to a reorganization described in section 368(a) to which corporations T and V are parties, D surrenders all of D's Class A common stock in Corporation T in exchange for common stock in Corporation V, all of D's Series 1 preferred stock in Corporation T in exchange for both cash and common stock in Corporation V, and all of D's Series 2 preferred stock in Corporation T in exchange solely for cash. Section 354 applies to the exchange of the Class A common stock in Corporation T for Corporation V common stock. Section 356 applies to the exchange of Series 1 preferred stock for Corporation V common stock and cash. Neither section 354 (nor so much of section 356 as relates to section 354) applies to the exchange of Series 2 preferred stock in Corporation T solely for cash (see section 302 and regulations thereunder).

§ 1.355–1 Distribution of stock and securities of a controlled corporation.

(a) Effective/applicability date of certain sections. Except as otherwise provided, this section and §§ 1.355–2 through 1.355–4 apply to transactions occurring after February 6, 1989. For transactions occurring on or before that date, see 26 CFR 1.355–1 through 1.355–4 (revised as of April 1, 1987). This section and §§ 1.355–2 through 1.355–4, other than § 1.355–2(g) and (i), do not reflect the amendments to section 355 made by the Revenue Act of 1987, the Technical and Miscellaneous Revenue Act of 1988, and the Tax Technical Corrections Act of 2007. For the applicability date of §§ 1.355–2(g), 1.355–5, 1.355–6, and 1.355–7, see §§ 1.355–2(i), 1.355–5(e), 1.355–6(g), and 1.355–7(k), respectively.

(b) Application of section. Section 355 provides for the separation, without recognition of gain or loss to (or the inclusion in income of) the shareholders and security holders, of one or more existing businesses formerly operated, directly or indirectly, by a single corporation (the "distributing corporation"). It applies only to the separation of existing businesses that have been in active operation for at least five years (or a business that has been in active operation for at least five years into separate businesses), and which, in general, have been owned, directly or indirectly, for at least five years by the distributing corporation. A separation is achieved through the distribution by the distributing corporation of stock, or stock and securities, of one or more subsidiaries (the "controlled corporations") to its shareholders with respect to its stock or to its security holders in exchange for its securities. The controlled corporations may be preexisting or newly created subsidiaries. Throughout the regulations under section 355, the term "distribution" refers to a distribution by the distributing corporation of stock, or stock and securities, of one or more controlled corporations, unless the context indicates otherwise. Section 355 contemplates the continued operation of the business or businesses existing prior to the separation. See § 1.355–4 for types of distributions that may qualify under section 355, including pro rata distributions and non pro rata distributions. For purposes of section 355, stock rights and stock warrants are not included in the term "stock and securities."

(c) Stock rights. Except as provided in § 1.356–6, for purposes of section 355, the term securities includes rights issued by the distributing corporation or the controlled corporation to acquire the stock of that corporation. For purposes of this section and section 356(d)(2)(B), a right to acquire stock has no principal amount. For this purpose, rights to acquire stock has the same meaning as it does under sections 305 and 317(a). Other Internal Revenue Code provisions governing the treatment of rights to acquire stock may also apply to certain distributions occurring in connection with a transaction described in section 355. See, for example, sections 83 and 421 through 424 and the regulations thereunder. This paragraph (c) applies to distributions occurring on or after March 9, 1998.

* * *

[T.D. 8238, 54 FR 289, Jan. 5, 1989; T.D. 8752, 63 FR 409, Jan. 6, 1998; T.D. 8904, 65 FR 58650, Oct. 2, 2000; T.D. 9435, 73 FR 75950, Dec. 15, 2008; 74 FR 3420, Jan. 21, 2009; T.D. 9548, 76 FR 65111, Oct. 20, 2011]

§ 1.355–2 Limitations.

(a) Property distributed. Section 355 applies to a distribution only if the property distributed consists solely of stock, or stock and securities, of a controlled corporation. If additional property (including an excess principal amount of securities received over securities surrendered) is received, see section 356.

(b) Independent business purpose—(1) Independent business purpose requirement. Section 355 applies to a transaction only if it is carried out for one or more corporate business purposes. A transaction is carried out for a corporate business purpose if it is motivated, in whole or substantial part, by one or more corporate business purposes. The potential for the avoidance of Federal taxes by the distributing or controlled corporations (or a corporation controlled by either) is relevant in determining the extent to which an existing corporate business purpose motivated the distribution. The principal reason for this business purpose requirement is to provide nonrecognition treatment only to distributions that are incident to readjustments of corporate structures required by business exigencies and that effect only readjustments of continuing interests in property under modified corporate forms. This business purpose requirement is independent of the other requirements under section 355.

(2) Corporate business purpose. A corporate business purpose is a real and substantial non Federal tax purpose germane to the business of the distributing corporation, the controlled corporation, or the affiliated group (as defined in § 1.355–3(b)(4)(iv)) to which the distributing corporation belongs. A purpose of reducing non Federal taxes is not a corporate business purpose if (i) the transaction will effect a reduction in both Federal and non Federal taxes because of similarities between Federal tax law and the tax law of the other jurisdiction and (ii) the reduction of Federal taxes is greater than or substantially coextensive with the reduction of non Federal taxes. See examples (7) and (8) of paragraph (b)(5) of this section. A shareholder purpose (for example, the personal planning purposes of a shareholder) is not a corporate business purpose. Depending upon the facts of a particular case, however, a shareholder purpose for a transaction may be so nearly coextensive with a corporate business purpose as to preclude any distinction between them. In such a case, the transaction is carried out for one or more corporate business purposes. See example (2) of paragraph (b)(5) of this section.

(3) Business purpose for distribution. The distribution must be carried out for one or more corporate business purposes. See example (3) of paragraph (b)(5) of this section. If a corporate business purpose can be achieved through a nontaxable transaction that does not involve the distribution of stock of a controlled corporation and which is neither impractical nor unduly expensive, then, for purposes of paragraph (b)(1) of this section, the separation is not carried out for that corporate business purpose. See examples (3) and (4) of paragraph (b)(5) of this section. For rules with respect to the requirement of a business purpose for a transfer of assets to a controlled corporation in connection with a reorganization described in section 368(a)(1)(D), see § 1.368–1(b).

(4) Business purpose as evidence of nondevice. The corporate business purpose or purposes for a transaction are evidence that the transaction was not used principally as a device for the distribution of earnings and profits within the meaning of section 355(a)(1)(B). See paragraph (d)(3)(ii) of this section.

(5) Examples. The provisions of this paragraph (b) may be illustrated by the following examples:

Example (1). Corporation X is engaged in the production, transportation, and refining of petroleum products. In 1985, X acquires all of the properties of corporation Z, which is also engaged in the production, transportation, and refining of petroleum products. In 1991, as a result of antitrust litigation, X is ordered to divest itself of all of the properties acquired from Z. X transfers those properties to new corporation Y and distributes the stock of Y pro rata to X's shareholders. In view of the divestiture order, the distribution is carried out for a corporate business purpose. See paragraph (b)(1) of this section.

Example (2). Corporation X is engaged in two businesses: The manufacture and sale of furniture and the sale of jewelry. The businesses are of equal value. The outstanding stock of X is owned equally by unrelated individuals A and B. A is more interested in the furniture business, while B is more interested in the jewelry business. A and B decide to split up the businesses and go their separate ways. A and B anticipate that the operations of each business will be enhanced by the separation because each shareholder will be able to devote his undivided attention to the business in which he is more interested and more proficient. Accordingly, X transfers the jewelry business to new corporation Y and distributes the stock of Y to B in exchange for all of B's stock in X. The distribution is carried out for a corporate business purpose, notwithstanding that it is also carried out in part for shareholder purposes. See paragraph (b)(2) of this section.

Example (3). Corporation X is engaged in the manufacture and sale of toys and the manufacture and sale of candy. The shareholders of X wish to protect the candy business from the risks and vicissitudes of the toy business. Accordingly, X transfers the toy business to new corporation Y and distributes the stock of Y to X's shareholders. Under applicable law, the purpose of protecting the candy business from the risks and vicissitudes of the toy business is achieved as soon as X transfers the toy business to Y. Therefore, the distribution is not carried out for a corporate business purpose. See paragraph (b)(3) of this section.

Example (4). Corporation X is engaged in a regulated business in State T. X owns all of the stock of corporation Y, a profitable corporation that is not engaged in a regulated business. Commission C sets the rates that X may charge its customers, based on its total income. C has recently adopted rules according to which the total income of a corporation includes the income of a business if, and only if, the business is operated, directly or indirectly, by the corporation. Total income, for this purpose, includes the income of a wholly owned subsidiary corporation but does not include the income of a parent or "brother/sister" corporation. Under C's new rule, X's total income includes the income of Y, with the result that X has suffered a reduction of the rates that it may charge its customers. It would not be impractical or unduly expensive to create in a nontaxable transaction (such as a transaction qualifying under section 351) a holding company to hold the stock of X and Y. X distributes the stock of Y to X's shareholders. The distribution is not carried out for the purpose of increasing the rates that X may charge its customers because that purpose could be achieved through a nontaxable transaction, the creation of a holding company, that does not involve the distribution of stock of a controlled corporation and which is neither impractical nor unduly expensive. See paragraph (b)(3) of this section.

Example (5). The facts are the same as in example (4), except that C has recently adopted rules according to which the total income of a corporation includes not only the income included in example (3), but also the income of any member of the affiliated group to which the corporation belongs. In order to avoid a reduction in the rates that it may charge its customers, X distributes the stock of Y to X's shareholders. The distribution is carried out for a corporate business purpose. See paragraph (b)(3) of this section.

* * *

Example (7). The facts are the same as in Example (6)(i), except that the distribution is made to enable X to elect to become an S corporation both for Federal tax purposes and for purposes of the income tax imposed by State M. State M has tax law provisions similar to subchapter S of the Internal Revenue Code of 1986. An election to be an S corporation for Federal tax purposes will effect a substantial reduction in Federal taxes that is greater than the reduction of State M taxes pursuant to an election to be an S corporation for State M purposes. The purpose of reducing State M taxes is not a corporate business purpose. The distribution does not meet the corporate business purpose requirements. See paragraph (b)(1) and (2) of this section.

* * *

(c) Continuity of interest requirement—(1) Requirement. Section 355 applies to a separation that effects only a readjustment of continuing interests in the property of the distributing and controlled corporations. In this regard section 355 requires that one or more persons who, directly or indirectly, were the owners of the enterprise prior to the distribution or exchange own, in the aggregate, an amount of stock establishing a continuity of interest in each of the modified corporate forms in which the enterprise is conducted after the separation. This continuity of interest requirement is independent of the other requirements under section 355.

(2) Examples.

* * *

Example (2). Assume the same facts as in Example (1), except that pursuant to a plan to acquire a stock interest in X without acquiring, directly or indirectly, an interest in S, C purchased one-half of the X stock owned by A and immediately thereafter X distributed all of the S stock to B in exchange for all of B's stock in X. After the transactions, A owns 50 percent of X and B owns 100 percent of S. The distribution by X of all of the stock of S to B in exchange for all of B's stock in X will satisfy the continuity of interest requirement for section 355 because one or more persons who were the owners of X prior to the distribution (A and B) own, in the aggregate, an amount of stock establishing a continuity of interest in each of X and S after the distribution.

Example (3). Assume the same facts as in Examples (1) and (2), except that C purchased all of the X stock owned by A. After the transactions, neither A nor B own any of the stock of X, and B owns all the stock of S. The continuity of interest requirement is not met because the owners of X prior to the distribution (A and B) do not, in the aggregate, own an amount of stock establishing a continuity of interest in each of X and S after the distribution, *i.e.*, although A and B collectively have retained 50 percent of their equity interest in the former combined enterprise, they have failed to continue to own the minimum stock interest in the distributing corporation, X, that would be required in order to meet the continuity of interest requirement.

Example (4). Assume the same facts as in Examples (1) and (2), except that C purchased 80 percent of the X stock owned by A. After the transactions, A owns 20 percent of the stock of X, B owns no X stock, and B owns

100 percent of the S stock. The continuity of interest requirement is not met because the owners of X prior to the distribution (A and B) do not, in the aggregate, have a continuity of interest in each of X and S after the distribution, *i.e.,* although A and B collectively have retained 60 percent of their equity interest in the former combined enterprise, the 20 percent interest of A in X is less than the minimum equity interest in the distributing corporation, X, that would be required in order to meet the continuity of interest requirement.

(d) Device for distribution of earnings and profits—(1) In general. Section 355 does not apply to a transaction used principally as a device for the distribution of the earnings and profits of the distributing corporation, the controlled corporation, or both (a "device"). Section 355 recognizes that a tax-free distribution of the stock of a controlled corporation presents a potential for tax avoidance by facilitating the avoidance of the dividend provisions of the Code through the subsequent sale or exchange of stock of one corporation and the retention of the stock of another corporation. A device can include a transaction that effects a recovery of basis. In this paragraph (d), "exchange" includes transactions, such as redemptions, treated as exchanges under the Code. Generally, the determination of whether a transaction was used principally as a device will be made from all of the facts and circumstances, including, but not limited to, the presence of the device factors specified in paragraph (d)(2) of this section ("evidence of device"), and the presence of the nondevice factors specified in paragraph (d)(3) of this section ("evidence of nondevice"). However, if a transaction is specified in paragraph (d)(5) of this section, then it is ordinarily considered not to have been used principally as a device.

(2) Device factors—(i) In general. The presence of any of the device factors specified in this subparagraph (2) is evidence of device. The strength of this evidence depends on the facts and circumstances.

(ii) Pro rata distribution. A distribution that is pro rata or substantially pro rata among the shareholders of the distributing corporation presents the greatest potential for the avoidance of the dividend provisions of the Code and, in contrast to other types of distributions, is more likely to be used principally as a device. Accordingly, the fact that a distribution is pro rata or substantially pro rata is evidence of device.

(iii) Subsequent sale or exchange of stock—(A) In general. A sale or exchange of stock of the distributing or the controlled corporation after the distribution (a "subsequent sale or exchange") is evidence of device. Generally, the greater the percentage of the stock sold or exchanged after the distribution, the stronger the evidence of device. In addition, the shorter the period of time between the distribution and the sale or exchange, the stronger the evidence of device.

(B) Sale or exchange negotiated or agreed upon before the distribution. A subsequent sale or exchange pursuant to an arrangement negotiated or agreed upon before the distribution is substantial evidence of device.

(C) Sale or exchange not negotiated or agreed upon before the distribution. A subsequent sale or exchange not pursuant to an arrangement negotiated or agreed upon before the distribution is evidence of device.

(D) Negotiated or agreed upon before the distribution. For purposes of this subparagraph (2), a sale or exchange is always pursuant to an arrangement negotiated or agreed upon before the distribution if enforceable rights to buy or sell existed before the distribution. If a sale or exchange was discussed by the buyer and the seller before the distribution and was reasonably to be anticipated by both parties, then the sale or exchange will ordinarily be considered to be pursuant to an arrangement negotiated or agreed upon before the distribution.

(E) Exchange in pursuance of a plan of reorganization. For purposes of this subparagraph (2), if stock is exchanged for stock in pursuance of a plan of reorganization, and either no gain or loss or only an insubstantial amount of gain is recognized on the exchange, then the exchange is not treated as a subsequent sale or exchange, but the stock received in the exchange is treated as the stock surrendered in the exchange. For this purpose, gain treated as a dividend pursuant to sections 356(a)(2) and 316 shall be disregarded.

(iv) Nature and use of assets—(A) In general. The determination of whether a transaction was used principally as a device will take into account the nature, kind, amount, and use of the assets of the distributing and the controlled corporations (and corporations controlled by them) immediately after the transaction.

(B) Assets not used in a trade or business meeting the requirement of section 355(b). The existence of assets that are not used in a trade or business that satisfies the requirements of section 355(b) is evidence of device. For this purpose, assets that are not used in a trade or business that satisfies the requirements of section 355(b) include, but are not limited to, cash and other liquid assets that are not related to the reasonable needs of a business satisfying such section. The strength of the evidence of device depends on all the facts and circumstances, including, but not limited to, the ratio for each corporation of the value of assets not used in a trade or business that satisfies the requirements of section 355(b) to the value of its business that satisfies such requirements. A difference in the ratio described in the preceding sentence for the distributing and controlled corporation is ordinarily not evidence of device if the distribution is not pro rata among the shareholders of the distributing corporation and such difference is attributable to a need to equalize the value of the stock distributed and the value of the stock or securities exchanged by the distributees.

(C) Related function. There is evidence of device if a business of either the distributing or controlled corporation (or a corporation controlled by it) is (1) a "secondary business" that continues as a secondary business for a significant period after the separation, and (2) can be sold without adversely affecting the business of the other corporation (or a corporation controlled by it). A secondary business is a business of either the distributing or controlled corporation, if its principal function is to serve the business of the other corporation (or a corporation controlled by it). A secondary business can include a business transferred to a newly-created subsidiary or a business which serves a business transferred to a newly-created subsidiary. The activities of the secondary business may consist of providing property or performing services. Thus, in example (11) of § 1.355–3(c), evidence of device would be presented if the principal function of the coal mine (satisfying the requirements of the steel business) continued after the separation and the coal mine could be sold without adversely affecting the steel business. Similarly, in example (10) of § 1.355–3(c), evidence of device would be presented if the principal function of the sales operation after the separation is to sell the output from the manufacturing operation and the sales operation could be sold without adversely affecting the manufacturing operation.

(3) Nondevice factors—(i) In general. The presence of any of the nondevice factors specified in this subparagraph (3) is evidence of nondevice. The strength of this evidence depends on all of the facts and circumstances.

(ii) Corporate business purpose. The corporate business purpose for the transaction is evidence of nondevice. The stronger the evidence of device (such as the presence of the device factors specified in paragraph (d)(2) of this section), the stronger the corporate business purpose required to prevent the determination that the transaction was used principally as a device. Evidence of device presented by the transfer or retention of assets not used in a trade or business that satisfies the requirements of section 355(b) can be outweighed by the existence of a corporate business purpose for those transfers or retentions. The assessment of the strength of a corporate business purpose will be based on all of the facts and circumstances, including, but not limited to, the following factors:

(A) The importance of achieving the purpose to the success of the business;

(B) The extent to which the transaction is prompted by a person not having a proprietary interest in either corporation, or by other outside factors beyond the control of the distributing corporation; and

(C) The immediacy of the conditions prompting the transaction.

(iii) Distributing corporation publicly traded and widely held. The fact that the distributing corporation is publicly traded and has no shareholder who is directly or indirectly the beneficial owner of more than five percent of any class of stock is evidence of nondevice.

(iv) Distribution to domestic corporate shareholders. The fact that the stock of the controlled corporation is distributed to one or more domestic corporations that, if section 355 did not apply, would be entitled to a deduction under section 243(a)(1) available to corporations meeting the stock ownership requirements of section 243(c), or a deduction under section 243(a)(2) or (3) or 245(b) is evidence of nondevice.

(4) Examples. The provisions of paragraph (d)(1) through (3) of this section may be illustrated by the following examples:

* * *

Example (2). Corporation X owns and operates a fast food restaurant in State M and owns all of the stock of corporation Y, which owns and operates a fast food restaurant in State N. X and Y operate their businesses under franchises granted by D and E, respectively. X owns cash and marketable securities that exceed the reasonable needs of its business but whose value is small relative to the value of its business. E has recently changed its franchise policy and will no longer grant or renew franchises to subsidiaries (or other members of the same affiliated group) of corporations operating businesses under franchises granted by its competitors. Thus, Y will lose its franchise if it remains a subsidiary of X. The franchise is about to expire. Accordingly, X distributes the stock of Y pro rata among X's shareholders. X retains its business and transfers cash and marketable securities to Y in an amount proportional to the value of Y's business. There is no other evidence of device or evidence of nondevice. The transfer by X to Y and the retention by X of cash and marketable securities is relatively weak evidence of device because after the transfer X and Y hold cash and marketable securities in amounts proportional to the values of their businesses. The fact that the distribution is pro rata is evidence of device. A strong corporate business purpose is relatively strong evidence of nondevice. Accordingly, the transaction is considered not to have been used principally as a device. See paragraph (d)(1), (2)(ii), (iv)(A), and (B) and (3)(i) and (ii)(A), (B) and (C) of this section.

Example (3). Corporation X is engaged in a regulated business in State M and owns all of the stock of corporation Y, which is not engaged in a regulated business in State M. State M has recently amended its laws to provide that affiliated corporations operating in M may not conduct both regulated and unregulated businesses. X transfers cash not related to the reasonable needs of the business of X or Y to Y and then distributes the stock of Y pro rata among X's shareholders. As a result of the transfer of cash, the ratio of the value of its assets not used in a trade or business that satisfies the requirements of section 355(b) to the value of its business is substantially greater for Y than for X. There is no other evidence of device or evidence of nondevice. The transfer of cash by X to Y is relatively strong evidence of device because after the transfer Y holds disproportionately many assets that are not used in a trade or business that satisfies the requirements of section 355(b). The fact that the distribution is pro rata is evidence of device. The strong business purpose is relatively strong evidence of nondevice, but it does not pertain to the transfer. Accordingly, the transaction is considered to have been used principally as a device. See paragraph (d)(1), (2)(ii), (iv)(A) and (B), and (3) and (i) and (ii) of this section.

Example (4). The facts are the same as in example (3), except that, instead of transferring cash to Y, X purchases operating assets unrelated to the business of Y and transfers them to Y prior to the distribution. There is no other evidence of device or evidence of nondevice. The transaction is considered to have been used principally as a device. See paragraph (d)(1), (2)(ii), (iv)(A) and (B), and (3)(i) and (ii) of this section.

(5) Transactions ordinarily not considered as a device—(i) In general. This subparagraph (5) specifies three distributions that ordinarily do not present the potential for tax avoidance described in paragraph (d)(1) of this section. Accordingly, such distributions are ordinarily considered not to have been used principally as a device, notwithstanding the presence of any of the device factors described in paragraph (d)(2) of this section. A transaction described in paragraph (d)(5)(iii) or (iv) of this section is not protected by this subparagraph (5) from a determination that it was used principally as a device if it involves the distribution of the stock of more than one controlled corporation and facilitates the avoidance of the dividend provisions of the Code through the subsequent sale or exchange of stock of one corporation and the retention of the stock of another corporation.

(ii) Absence of earnings and profits. A distribution is ordinarily considered not to have been used principally as a device if—

(A) The distributing and controlled corporations have no accumulated earnings and profits at the beginning of their respective taxable years,

(B) The distributing and controlled corporations have no current earnings and profits as of the date of the distribution, and

(C) No distribution of property by the distributing corporation immediately before the separation would require recognition of gain resulting in current earnings and profits for the taxable year of the distribution.

(iii) Section 303(a) transactions. A distribution is ordinarily considered not to have been used principally as a device, if, in the absence of section 355, with respect to each shareholder distributee, the distribution would be a redemption to which section 303(a) applied.

(iv) Section 302(a) transactions. A distribution is ordinarily considered not to have been used principally as a device if, in the absence of section 355, with respect to each shareholder distributee, the distribution would be a redemption to which section 302(a) applied. For purposes of the preceding sentence, section 302(c)(2)(A)(ii) and (iii) shall not apply.

(v) Examples. The provisions of this subparagraph (5) may be illustrated by the following examples:

Example (1). The facts are the same as in example (3) of paragraph (d)(4) of this section, except that X and Y had no accumulated earnings and profits at the beginning of its taxable year. X and Y have no current earnings and profits as of the date of the distribution, and no distribution of property by X immediately before the separation would require recognition of gain that would result in earnings and profits for the taxable year of the distribution. The transaction is considered not to have been used principally as a device. See paragraph (d)(5)(i) and (ii) of this section.

Example (2). Corporation X is engaged in three businesses: a hotel business, a restaurant business, and a rental real estate business. Individuals A, B, and C own all of the stock of X. X transfers the restaurant business to new corporation Y and transfers the rental real estate business to new corporation Z. X then distributes the stock of Y and Z pro rata between B and C in exchange for all of their stock in X. In the absence of section 355, the distribution would be a redemption to which section 302(a) applies. Since this distribution involves the stock of more than one controlled corporation and facilitates the avoidance of the dividend provisions of the Code through the subsequent sale or exchange of stock in one corporation and the retention of the stock of another corporation, it is not protected by paragraph (d)(5)(i) and (iv) of this section from a determination that it was used principally as a device. Thus, the determination of whether the transaction was used principally as a device must be made from all the facts and circumstances, including the presence of the device factors and nondevice factors specified in paragraph (d)(2) and (3) of this section.

(e) Stock and securities distributed—(1) In general. Section 355 applies to a distribution only if the distributing corporation distributes—

(i) All of the stock and securities of the controlled corporation that it owns, or

(ii) At least an amount of the stock of the controlled corporation that constitutes control as defined in section 368(c). In such a case, all, or any part, of the securities of the controlled corporation may be distributed, and paragraph (e)(2) of this section shall apply.

(2) Additional rules. Where a part of either the stock or the securities of the controlled corporation is retained under paragraph (e)(1)(ii) of this section, it must be established to the satisfaction of the Commissioner that the retention by the distributing corporation was not in pursuance of a plan having as one of its principal purposes the avoidance of Federal income tax. Ordinarily, the corporate business purpose or purposes for the distribution will require the distribution of all of the stock and securities of the controlled corporation. If the distribution of all of the stock and securities of a controlled corporation would be treated to any extent as a distribution of "other property" under section 356, this fact tends to establish that the retention of stock or securities is in pursuance of a plan having as one of its principal purposes the avoidance of Federal income tax.

(f) Principal amount of securities—(1) Securities received. Section 355 does not apply to a distribution if, with respect to any shareholder or security holder, the principal amount of securities received exceeds the principal amount of securities surrendered, or securities are received but no securities are surrendered. In such cases, see section 356.

(2) Only stock received. If only stock is received in a distribution to which section 355(a)(1)(A) applies, the principal amount of the securities surrendered, if any, and the par value or stated value of the stock surrendered, if any, are not relevant to the application of that section.

(g) Recently acquired controlled stock under section 355(a)(3)(B)—(1) Other property. Except as provided in paragraph (g)(2) of this section, for purposes of section 355(a)(1)(A), section 355(c), and so much of section 356 as relates to section 355, stock of a controlled corporation acquired by the DSAG in a taxable transaction (as defined in paragraph (g)(4) of this section) within the five-year period ending on the date of the distribution (pre-distribution period) shall not be treated as stock of the controlled corporation but shall be treated as "other property." Transfers of controlled corporation stock that is owned by the DSAG immediately before and immediately after the transfer are disregarded and are not acquisitions for purposes of this paragraph (g)(1).

(2) Exceptions. Paragraph (g)(1) of this section does not apply to an acquisition of stock of the controlled corporation—

(i) If the controlled corporation is a DSAG member at any time after the acquisition (but prior to the distribution); or

(ii) Described in § 1.355–3(b)(4)(iii).

(3) DSAG. For purposes of this paragraph (g), a DSAG is the distributing corporation's separate affiliated group (the affiliated group which would be determined under section 1504(a) if such corporation were the common parent and section 1504(b) did not apply) that consists of the distributing corporation as the common parent and all corporations affiliated with the distributing corporation through stock ownership described in section 1504(a)(1)(B) (regardless of whether the corporations are includible corporations under section 1504(b)). For purposes of paragraph (g)(1) of this section, any reference to the DSAG is a reference to the distributing corporation if it is not the common parent of a separate affiliated group.

(4) Taxable transaction—(i) Generally. For purposes of this paragraph (g), a taxable transaction is a transaction in which gain or loss was recognized in whole or in part.

(ii) Dunn Trust and predecessor issues. [Reserved].

(5) Examples. The following examples illustrate this paragraph (g). Assume that C, D, P, and S are corporations, X is an unrelated individual, each of the transactions is unrelated to any other transaction and, but for the issue of whether C stock is treated as "other property" under section 355(a)(3)(B), the distributions satisfy all of the requirements of section 355. No inference should be drawn from any of these examples as to whether any requirements of section 355 other than section 355(a)(3)(B), as specified, are satisfied. Furthermore, the following definitions apply:

(i) Purchase is an acquisition that is a taxable transaction.

(ii) Section 368(c) stock is stock constituting control within the meaning of section 368(c).

(iii) Section 1504(a)(2) stock is stock meeting the requirements of section 1504(a)(2).

Example 1. Hot stock. For more than five years, D has owned section 368(c) stock but not section 1504(a)(2) stock of C. In year 6, D purchases additional C stock from X. However, D does not own section 1504(a)(2) stock of C after the year 6 purchase. If D distributes all of its C stock within five years after the year 6 purchase, for purposes of section 355(a)(1)(A), section 355(c), and so much of section 356 as relates to section 355, the C stock purchased in year 6 would be treated as "other property." See paragraph (g)(1) of this section.

Example 2. C becomes a DSAG member. For more than five years, D has owned section 368(c) stock but not section 1504(a)(2) stock of C. In year 6, D purchases additional C stock from X such that D's total ownership of C is section 1504(a)(2) stock. If D distributes all of its C stock within five years after the year 6 purchase, the distribution of the C stock purchased in year 6 would not be treated as "other property" because C becomes a DSAG member. See paragraph (g)(2)(i) of this section. The result would be the same if D did not own any C stock prior to year 6 and D purchased all of the C stock in year 6. See paragraph (g)(2)(i) of this section. Similarly, if D did not own any C stock prior to year 6, D purchased 20 percent of the C stock in year 6, and then acquired all of the remaining C stock in year 7, the C stock purchased in year 6 and the C stock acquired in year 7 (even if purchased) would not be treated as "other property" because C becomes a DSAG member. See paragraph (g)(2)(i) of this section.

* * *

(h) Active conduct of a trade or business. Section 355 applies to a distribution only if the requirements of § 1.355–3 (relating to the active conduct of a trade or business) are satisfied.

* * *

[T.D. 6500, 25 FR 11607, Nov. 26, 1960; T.D. 8238, 54 FR 290, Jan. 5, 1989; 54 FR 5577, Feb. 3, 1989; T.D. 8238, 57 FR 28463, June 25, 1992; T.D.9435, 73 FR 75950, Dec. 15, 2008; T.D. 9548, 76 FR 65111, Oct. 20, 2011]

§ 1.355–3 Active conduct of a trade or business.

(a) General requirements—(1) Application of section 355. Under section 355(b)(1), a distribution of stock, or stock and securities, of a controlled corporation qualifies under section 355 only if—

(i) The distributing and the controlled corporations are each engaged in the active conduct of a trade or business immediately after the distribution (section 355(b)(1)(A)), or

(ii) Immediately before the distribution, the distributing corporation had no assets other than stock or securities of the controlled corporations, and each of the controlled corporations is engaged in the active conduct of a trade or business immediately after the distribution (section 355(b)(1)(B)). A *de minimis* amount of assets held by the distributing corporation shall be disregarded for purposes of this paragraph (a)(1)(ii).

(2) Examples. Paragraph (a)(1) of this section may be illustrated by the following examples:

Example (1). Prior to the distribution, corporation X is engaged in the active conduct of a trade or business and owns all of the stock of corporation Y, which also is engaged in the active conduct of a trade or business. X distributes all of the stock of Y to X's shareholders, and each corporation continues the active conduct of its trade or business. The active business requirement of section 355(b)(1)(A) is satisfied.

Example (2). The facts are the same as in example (1), except that X transfers all of its assets other than the stock of Y to a new corporation in exchange for all of the stock of the new corporation and then distributes the stock of both controlled corporations to X's shareholders. The active business requirement of section 355(b)(1)(B) is satisfied.

(b) Active conduct of a trade or business defined—(1) In general. Section 355(b)(2) provides rules for determining whether a corporation is treated as engaged in the active conduct of a trade or business for purposes of section 355(b)(1). Under section 355(b)(2)(A), a corporation is treated as engaged in the active conduct of a trade or business if it is itself engaged in the active conduct of a trade or business or if substantially all of its assets consist of the stock, or stock and securities, of a corporation or corporations controlled by it (immediately after the distribution) each of which is engaged in the active conduct of a trade or business.

(2) Active conduct of a trade or business immediately after distribution—(i) In general. For purposes of section 355(b), a corporation shall be treated as engaged in the "active conduct of a trade or business" immediately after the distribution if the assets and activities of the corporation satisfy the requirements and limitations described in paragraph (b)(2)(ii), (iii), and (iv) of this section.

(ii) Trade or business. A corporation shall be treated as engaged in a trade or business immediately after the distribution if a specific group of activities are being carried on by the corporation for the purpose of earning income or profit, and the activities included in such group include every operation that forms a part of, or a step in, the process of earning income or profit. Such group of activities ordinarily must include the collection of income and the payment of expenses.

(iii) Active conduct. For purposes of section 355(b), the determination whether a trade or business is actively conducted will be made from all of the facts and circumstances. Generally, the corporation is required itself to perform active and substantial management and operational functions. Generally, activities performed by the corporation itself do not include activities performed by persons outside the corporation, including independent contractors. A corporation may satisfy the requirements of this subdivision (iii) through the activities that it performs itself, even though some of its activities are performed by others. Separations of real property all or substantially all of which is occupied prior to the distribution by the distributing or the controlled corporation (or by any corporation controlled directly or indirectly by either of those corporations) will be carefully scrutinized with respect to the requirements of section 355(b) and this § 1.355–3.

(iv) Limitations. The active conduct of a trade or business does not include—

(A) The holding for investment purposes of stock, securities, land, or other property, or

(B) The ownership and operation (including leasing) of real or personal property used in a trade or business, unless the owner performs significant services with respect to the operation and management of the property.

(3) Active conduct for five-year period preceding distribution. Under section 355(b)(2)(B), a trade or business that is relied upon to meet the requirements of section 355(b) must have been actively conducted throughout the five-year period ending on the date of the distribution. For purposes of this subparagraph (3)—

(i) Activities which constitute a trade or business under the tests described in paragraph (b)(2) of this section shall be treated as meeting the requirement of the preceding sentence if such activities were actively conducted throughout the 5–year period ending on the date of distribution, and

(ii) The fact that a trade or business underwent change during the five-year period preceding the distribution (for example, by the addition of new or the dropping of old products, changes in production capacity, and the like) shall be disregarded, provided that the changes are not of such a character as to constitute the acquisition of a new or different business. In particular, if a corporation engaged in the active conduct of one trade or business during that five-year period purchased, created, or otherwise acquired another trade or business in the same line of business, then the acquisition of that other business is ordinarily treated as an expansion of the original business, all of which is treated as having been actively conducted during that five-year period, unless that purchase, creation, or other acquisition effects a change of such a character as to constitute the acquisition of a new or different business.

* * *

(c) Examples. The following examples illustrate section 355(b)(2)(A) and (B) and paragraph (b)(1), (2), and (3) of this section. However, a transaction that satisfies these active business requirements will qualify under section 355 only if it satisfies the other requirements of section 355(a) and (b).

Example (1). Corporation X is engaged in the manufacture and sale of soap and detergents and also owns investment securities. X transfers the investment securities to new subsidiary Y and distributes the stocks of Y to X's shareholders. Y does not satisfy the requirements of section 355(b) because the holding of investment securities does not constitute the active conduct of a trade or business. See paragraph (b)(2)(iv)(A) of this section.

Example (2). Corporation X owns, manages, and derives rental income from an office building and also owns vacant land. X transfers the land to new subsidiary Y and distributes the stock of Y to X's shareholders. Y will subdivide the land, install streets and utilities, and sell the developed lots to various homebuilders. Y does not satisfy the requirements of section 355(b) because no significant development activities were conducted with respect to the land during the five-year period ending on the date of the distribution. See paragraph (b)(3) of this section.

Example (3). Corporation X owns land on which it conducts a ranching business. Oil has been discovered in the area, and it is apparent that oil may be found under the land on which the ranching business is conducted. X has engaged in no significant activities in connection with its mineral rights. X transfers its mineral rights to new subsidiary Y and distributes the stock of Y to X's shareholders. Y will actively pursue the development of the oil producing potential of the property. Y does not satisfy the requirements of section 355(b) because X engaged in no significant exploitation activities with respect to the mineral rights during the five-year period ending on the date of the distribution. See paragraph (b)(3) of this section.

Example (4). For more than five years, corporation X has conducted a single business of constructing sewage disposal plants and other facilities. X transfers one-half of its assets to new subsidiary Y. These assets include a contract for the construction of a sewage disposal plant in State M, construction equipment, cash, and other tangible assets. X retains a contract for the construction of a sewage disposal plant in State N, construction equipment, cash, and other intangible assets. X then distributes the stock of Y to one of X's shareholders in exchange for all of his stock of X. X and Y both satisfy the requirements of section 355(b). See paragraph (b)(3)(i) of this section.

Example (5). For the past six years, corporation X has owned and operated two factories devoted to the production of edible pork skins. The entire output of one factory is sold to one customer, C, while the output of the second factory is sold to C and a number of other customers. To eliminate errors in packaging, X opens a new factory. Thereafter, orders from C are processed and packaged at the two original factories, while the new factory handles only orders from other customers. Eight months after opening the new factory, X transfers it and related business assets to new subsidiary Y and distributes the stock of Y to X's shareholders. X and Y both satisfy the requirements of section 355(b). See paragraph (b)(3)(i) and (ii) of this section.

Example (6). Corporation X has owned and operated a men's retail clothing store in the downtown area of the City of G for nine years and has owned and operated another men's retail clothing store in a suburban area of G for seven years. X transfers the store building, fixtures, inventory, and other assets related to the operations of the suburban store to new subsidiary Y. X also transfers to Y the delivery trucks and delivery personnel that formerly served both stores. Henceforth, X will contract with a local public delivery service to make its deliveries. X retains the warehouses that formerly served both stores. Henceforth, Y will lease warehouse space from an unrelated public warehouse company. X then distributes the stock of Y to X's shareholders. X and Y both satisfy the requirements of section 355(b). See paragraph (b)(3)(i) of this section.

Example (7). For the past nine years, corporation X has owned and operated a department store in the downtown area of the City of G. Three years ago, X acquired a parcel of land in a suburban area of G and constructed a new department store on it. X transfers the suburban store and related business assets to new subsidiary Y and distributes the stock of Y to X's shareholders. After the distribution, each store has its own manager and is operated independently of the other store. X and Y both satisfy the requirements of section 355(b). See paragraph (b)(3)(i) and (ii) of this section.

Example (8). For the past six years, corporation X has owned and operated hardware stores in several states. Two years ago, X purchased all of the assets of a hardware store in State M, where X had not previously conducted business. X transfers the State M store and related business assets to new subsidiary Y and distributes the stock of Y to X's shareholders. After the distribution, the State M store has its own manager and is operated independently of the other stores. X and Y both satisfy the requirements of section 355(b). See paragraph (b)(3)(i) and (ii) of this section.

Example (9). For the past eight years, corporation X has engaged in the manufacture and sale of household products. Throughout this period, X has maintained a research department for use in connection with its manufacturing activities. The research department has 30 employees actively engaged in the development of new products. X transfers the research department to new subsidiary Y and distributes the stock of Y to X's shareholders. After the distribution, Y continues its research operations on a contractual basis with several corporations, including X. X and Y both satisfy the requirements of section 355(b). See paragraph (b)(3)(i) of this section. The result in this example is the same if, after the distribution, Y continues its research operations but furnishes its services only to X. See paragraph (b)(3)(i) of this section. However, see § 1.355–2(d)(2)(iv)(C) (related function device factor) for possible evidence of device.

Example (10). For the past six years, corporation X has processed and sold meat products. X derives income from no other source. X separates the sales function from the processing function by transferring the business assets related to the sales function and cash for working capital to new subsidiary Y. X then distributes the stock of Y to X's shareholders. After the distribution, Y purchases for resale the meat products processed by X. X and Y both satisfy the requirements of section 355(b). See paragraph (b)(3)(i) of this section. However, see § 1.355–2(d)(2)(iv)(C) (related function device factor) for possible evidence of device.

Example (11). For the past eight years, corporation X has been engaged in the manufacture and sale of steel and steel products. X owns all of the stock of corporation Y, which, for the past six years, has owned and operated a coal mine for the sole purpose of supplying X's coal requirements in the manufacture of steel. X distributes the stock of Y to X's shareholders. X and Y both satisfy the requirements of section 355(b). See paragraph (b)(3)(i) of this section. However, see § 1.355–2(d)(2)(iv)(C) (related function device factor) for possible evidence of device.

Example (12). For the past seven years, corporation X, a bank, has owned an eleven-story office building, the ground floor of which X has occupied in the conduct of its banking business. The remaining ten floors are rented to various tenants. Throughout this seven-year period, the building has been managed and maintained by employees of the bank. X transfers the building to new subsidiary Y and distributes the stock of Y to X's shareholders. Henceforth, Y will manage the building, negotiate leases, seek new tenants, and repair and maintain the building. X and Y both satisfy the requirements of section 355(b). See paragraph (b)(3) of this section.

Example (13). For the past nine years, corporation X, a bank, has owned a two-story building, the ground floor and one half of the second floor of which X has occupied in the conduct of its banking business. The other half of the second floor has been rented as storage space to a neighboring retail merchant. X transfers the building to new subsidiary Y and distributes the stock of Y to X's shareholders. After the distribution, X leases from Y the space in the building that it formerly occupied. Under the lease, X will repair and maintain its portion of the building and pay property taxes and insurance. Y does not satisfy the requirements of section 355(b) because it is not engaged in the active conduct of a trade or business immediately after the distribution. See paragraph (b)(2)(iv)(A) of this section. This example does not address the question of whether the activities of X with respect to the building prior to the separation would constitute the active conduct of a trade or business.

[T.D. 8238, 54 FR 294, Jan. 5, 1989]

§ 1.355–4 Non pro rata distributions, etc.

Section 355 provides for nonrecognition of gain or loss with respect to a distribution whether or not (a) the distribution is pro rata with respect to all of the shareholders of the distributing corporation, (b) the distribution is pursuant to a plan of reorganization within the meaning of section 368 (a)(1)(D), or (c) the shareholder surrenders stock in the distributing corporation. Under section 355, the stock of a controlled corporation may consist of common stock or preferred stock. (See, however, section 306 and the regulations thereunder.) Section 355 does not apply, however, if the substance of a transaction is merely an exchange between shareholders or security holders of stock or securities in one corporation for stock or securities in another corporation. For example, if two individuals, A and B, each own directly 50 percent of the stock of corporation X and 50 percent of the stock of corporation Y, section 355 would not apply to a transaction in which A and B transfer all of their stock of X and Y to a new corporation Z, for all of the stock of Z, and Z then distributes the stock of X to A and the stock of Y to B.

[T.D. 8238, 54 FR 296, Jan. 5, 1989]

§ 1.356–1 Receipt of additional consideration in connection with an exchange.

(a) If in any exchange to which the provisions of section 354 or section 355 would apply except for the fact that there is received by the shareholders or security holders other property (in addition to property permitted to be received without recognition of gain by such sections) or money, then—

(1) The gain, if any, to the taxpayer shall be recognized in an amount not in excess of the sum of the money and the fair market value of the other property, but,

(2) The loss, if any, to the taxpayer from the exchange or distribution shall not be recognized to any extent.

(b) For purposes of computing the gain, if any, recognized pursuant to section 356 and paragraph (a)(1) of this section, to the extent the terms of the exchange specify the other property or money that is received in exchange for a particular share of stock or security surrendered or a particular class of stock or securities surrendered, such terms shall control provided that such terms are economically reasonable. To the extent the terms of the exchange do not specify the other property or money that is received in exchange for a particular share of stock or security surrendered or a particular class of stock or securities surrendered, a pro rata portion of the other property and money received shall be treated as received in exchange for each share of stock and security surrendered, based on the fair market value of such surrendered share of stock or security.

(c) If the distribution of such other property or money by or on behalf of a corporation has the effect of the distribution of a dividend, then there shall be chargeable to each distributee (either an individual or a corporation)—

(1) As a dividend, such an amount of the gain recognized as is not in excess of the distributee's ratable share of the undistributed earnings and profits of the corporation accumulated after February 28, 1913, and

(2) As a gain from the exchange of property, the remainder of the gain so recognized.

(d) The rules of this section may be illustrated by the following examples:

Example 1. In an exchange to which the provisions of section 356 apply and to which section 354 would apply but for the receipt of property not permitted to be received without the recognition of gain or loss, A (either an individual or a corporation), received the following in exchange for a share of stock having an adjusted basis to A of $85:

One share of stock worth	$100
Cash	25
Other property (basis $25) fair market value	50
Total fair market value of consideration received	175
Adjusted basis of stock surrendered in exchange	85
Total gain	90
Gain to be recognized, limited to cash and other property received	75
A's pro rata share of earnings and profits accumulated after February 28, 1913 (taxable dividend)	30
Remainder to be treated as a gain from the exchange of property	45

Example 2. If, in Example 1, A's stock had an adjusted basis to A of $200, A would have realized a loss of $25 on the exchange, which loss would not be recognized.

Example 3. (i) Facts. J, an individual, acquired 10 shares of Class A stock of Corporation X on Date 1 for $3 each and 10 shares of Class B stock of Corporation X on Date 2 for $9 each. On Date 3, Corporation Y acquires the assets of Corporation X in a reorganization under section 368(a)(1)(A). Pursuant to the terms of the plan of reorganization, J surrenders all of J's shares of Corporation X stock for 10 shares of Corporation Y stock and $100 of cash. On the date of the exchange, the fair market value of each share of Class A stock of Corporation X is $10, the fair market value of each share of Class B stock of Corporation X is $10, and the fair market value of each share of Corporation Y stock is $10. The terms of the exchange do not specify that shares of Corporation Y stock or cash are received in exchange for particular shares of Class A stock or Class B stock of Corporation X.

(ii) Analysis. Under paragraph (b) of this section, because the terms of the exchange do not specify that the cash is received in exchange for shares of Class A or Class B stock of Corporation X, a pro rata portion of the cash received is treated as received in exchange for each share of Class A stock of Corporation X and each share of Class B stock of Corporation X based on the fair market value of the surrendered shares. Therefore, J is treated as receiving shares of Corporation Y stock with a fair market value of $50 and $50 of cash in exchange for its shares of Class A stock of Corporation X and shares of Corporation Y stock with a fair market value of $50 and $50 of cash in exchange for its shares of Class B stock of Corporation X. J realizes a gain of $70 on the exchange of shares of Class A stock, $50 of which is recognized under section 356 and paragraph (a) of this section, and J realizes a gain of $10 on the exchange of shares of Class B stock of Corporation X, all of which is recognized under section 356 and paragraph (a) of this section. Assuming that J's gain recognized is not treated as a dividend under section 356(a)(2), such gain shall be treated as gain from the exchange of property.

Example 4. (i) Facts. The facts are the same as in Example 3, except that the terms of the plan of reorganization specify that J receives 10 shares of stock of Corporation Y in exchange for J's shares of Class A stock of Corporation X and $100 of cash in exchange for J's shares of Class B stock of Corporation X.

(ii) Analysis. Under paragraph (b) of this section, because the terms of the exchange specify that J receives 10 shares of stock of Corporation Y in exchange for J's shares of Class A stock of Corporation X and $100 of cash in exchange for J's shares of Class B stock of Corporation X and such terms are economically reasonable, such terms control. J realizes a gain of $70 on the exchange of shares of Class A stock, none of which is recognized under section 356 and paragraph (a) of this section, and J realizes a gain of $10 on the exchange of shares of Class B stock of Corporation X, all of which is recognized under section 356 and paragraph (a) of this section.

(e) Section 301(b)(1)(B) and section 301(d)(2) do not apply to a distribution of "other property" to a corporate shareholder if such distribution is within the provisions of section 356.

(f) See paragraph (*l*) of § 1.301–1 for certain transactions which are not within the scope of section 356.

* * *

[T.D. 6500, 25 FR 11607, Nov. 26, 1960; T.D. 9244, 71 FR 4268, Jan. 26, 2006]

§ 1.356–2 Receipt of additional consideration not in connection with an exchange.

(a) If, in a transaction to which section 355 would apply except for the fact that a shareholder (individual or corporate) receives property permitted by section 355 to be received without the recognition of gain, together with other property or money, without the surrender of any stock or securities of the distributing corporation, then the sum of the money and the fair market value of the other property as of the date of the distribution shall be treated as a distribution of property to which the rules of section 301 (other than section 301(b) and section 301(d)) apply. See section 358 for determination of basis of such other property.

(b) Paragraph (a) of this section may be illustrated by the following examples:

Example (1). Individuals A and B each own 50 of the 100 outstanding shares of common stock of Corporation X. Corporation X owns all of the stock of Corporation Y, 100 shares. Corporation X distributes to each shareholder 50 shares of the stock of Corporation Y plus $100 cash without requiring the surrender of any shares of its own stock. The $100 cash received by each is treated as a distribution of property to which the rules of section 301 apply.

Example (2). If, in the above example, Corporation X distributes 50 shares of stock of Corporation Y to A and 30 shares of such stock plus $100 cash to B without requiring the surrender of any of its own stock, the amount of cash received by B is treated as a distribution of property to which the rules of section 301 apply.

[T.D. 6500, 25 FR 11607, Nov. 26, 1960]

§ 1.356–3 Rules for treatment of securities as "other property".

(a) As a general rule, for purposes of section 356, the term "other property" includes securities. However, it does not include securities permitted under section 354 or section 355 to be received tax free. Thus, when securities are surrendered in a transaction to which section 354 or section 355 is applicable, the characterization of the securities received as "other property" does not include securities received where the principal amount of such securities does not exceed the principal amount of securities surrendered in the transaction. If a greater principal amount of securities is received in an exchange described in section 354 (other than subsection (c) or (d) thereof) or section 355 over the principal amount of securities surrendered, the term "other property" includes the fair market value of such excess principal amount as of the date of the exchange. If no securities are surrendered in exchange, the term "other property" includes the fair market value, as of the date of receipt, of the entire principal amount of the securities received.

(b) Except as provided in § 1.356–6, for purposes of this section, a right to acquire stock that is treated as a security for purposes of section 354 or 355 has no principal amount. Thus, such right is not other property when received in a transaction to which section 356 applies (regardless of whether securities are surrendered in the exchange). This paragraph (b) applies to transactions occurring on or after March 9, 1998.

(c) In the examples in this paragraph (c), stock means common stock and warrants means rights to acquire common stock. The following examples illustrate the rules of paragraph (a) of this section:

Example (1). A, an individual, exchanged 100 shares of stock for 100 shares of stock and a security in the principal amount of $1,000 with a fair market value of $990. The amount of $990 is treated as "other property."

Example (2). B, an individual, exchanged 100 shares of stock and a security in the principal amount of $1,000 for 300 shares of stock and a security in the principal amount of $1,500. The security had a fair market value on the date of receipt of $1,575. The fair market value of the excess principal amount, or $525, is treated as "other property."

Example (3). C, an individual, exchanged a security in the principal amount of $1,000 for 100 shares of stock and a security in the principal amount of $900. No part of the security received is treated as "other property."

Example (4). D, an individual, exchanged a security in the principal amount of $1,000 for 100 shares of stock and a security in the principal amount of $1,200 with a fair market value of $1,100. The fair market value of the excess principal amount, or $183.33, is treated as "other property."

Example (5). E, an individual, exchanged a security in the principal amount of $1,000 for another security in the principal amount of $1,200 with a fair market value of $1,080. The fair market value of the excess principal amount, or $180, is treated as "other property."

Example (6). F, an individual, exchanged a security in the principal amount of $1,000 for two different securities each in the principal amount of $750. One of the securities had a fair market value of $750, the other had a fair market value of $600. One-third of the fair market value of each security ($250 and $200) is treated as "other property."

Example (7). G, an individual, exchanged stock for stock and a warrant. The warrant had no principal amount. Thus, G received no excess principal amount within the meaning of section 356(d).

Example (8). H, an individual, exchanged a warrant for stock and a warrant. The warrants had no principal amount. Thus, H received no excess principal amount within the meaning of section 356(d).

Example (9). I, an individual, exchanged a warrant for stock and a debt security. The warrant had no principal amount. The debt security had a $100 principal amount. I received $100 of excess principal amount within the meaning of section 356(d).

[T.D. 6500, 25 FR 11607, Nov. 26, 1960, as amended by T.D. 7616, 44 FR 26869, May 8, 1979; T.D. 8752, 63 FR 410, Jan. 6, 1998; T.D. 8882, 65 FR 31078, May 16, 2000]

§ 1.356–4 Exchanges for section 306 stock.

If, in a transaction to which section 356 is applicable, other property or money is received in exchange for section 306 stock, an amount equal to the fair market value of the property plus the money, if any, shall be treated as a distribution of property to which section 301 is applicable. The determination of whether section 306 stock is surrendered for other property (including money) is a question of fact to be decided under all of the circumstances of each case. Ordinarily, the other property (including money) received will first be treated as received in exchange for any section 306 stock owned by a shareholder prior to such transaction. For example, if a shareholder who owns a share of common stock (having a basis to him of $100) and a share of preferred stock which is section 306 stock (having a basis to him of $100) surrenders both shares in a transaction to which section 356 is applicable for one share of common stock having a fair market value of $80 and one $100 bond having a fair market value of $100, the bond will be deemed received in exchange for the section 306 stock and it will be treated as a distribution to which section 301 is applicable to the extent of its entire fair market value ($100).

[T.D. 6500, 25 FR 11607, Nov. 26, 1960]

§ 1.356–5 Transactions involving gift or compensation.

With respect to transactions described in sections 354, 355, or 356, but which—

(a) Result in a gift, see section 2501 and following, and the regulations pertaining thereto, or

(b) Have the effect of the payment of compensation, see section 61(a)(1), and the regulations pertaining thereto.

§ 1.356–6 Rules for treatment of nonqualified preferred stock as other property.

(a) In general. For purposes of §§ 1.354–1(e), 1.355–1(c), and 1.356–3(b), the terms stock and securities do not include—

(1) Nonqualified preferred stock, as defined in section 351(g)(2), received in exchange for (or in a distribution with respect to) stock, or a right to acquire stock, other than nonqualified preferred stock; or

(2) A right to acquire such nonqualified preferred stock, received in exchange for (or in a distribution with respect to) stock, or a right to acquire stock, other than nonqualified preferred stock.

(b) Exceptions. The following exceptions apply:

(1) Certain recapitalizations. Paragraph (a) of this section does not apply in the case of a recapitalization under section 368(a)(1)(E) of a family-owned corporation as described in section 354 (a)(2)(C)(ii)(II).

(2) Transition rule. Paragraph (a) of this section does not apply to a transaction described in section 1014 (f)(2) of the Taxpayer Relief Act of 1997 (111 Stat. 921).

(c) Effective date. This section applies to nonqualified preferred stock, or a right to acquire such stock, received in connection with a transaction occurring on or after March 9, 1998.

[T.D. 8753, 63 FR 411, Jan. 6, 1998; T.D. 8882, 65 FR 31079]

§ 1.357–1 Assumption of liability.

(a) General rule. Section 357(a) does not affect the rule that liabilities assumed are to be taken into account for the purpose of computing the amount of gain or loss realized under section 1001 upon an exchange. Section 357(a) provides, subject to the exceptions and limitations specified in section 357(b) and (c), that—

(1) Liabilities assumed are not to be treated as "other property or money" for the purpose of determining the amount of realized gain which is to be recognized under section 351, 361, * * *, if the transactions would, but for the receipt of "other property or money" have been exchanges of the type described in any one of such sections; and

(2) If the only type of consideration received by the transferor in addition to that permitted to be received by section 351, 361, * * *, consists of an assumption of liabilities, the transaction, if otherwise qualified, will be deemed to be within the provisions of section 351, 361, * * *.

(b) Application of general rule. The application of paragraph (a) of this section may be illustrated by the following example:

Example. A, an individual, transfers to a controlled corporation property with an adjusted basis of $10,000 in exchange for stock of the corporation with a fair market value of $8,000, $3,000 cash, and the assumption by the corporation of indebtedness of A amounting to $4,000. A's gain is $5,000, computed as follows:

Stock received, fair market value	$ 8,000
Cash received	3,000
Liability assumed by transferee	4,000
Total consideration received	15,000
Less: Adjusted basis of property transferred	10,000
Gain realized	5,000

Assuming that the exchange falls within section 351 as a transaction in which the gain to be recognized is limited to "other property or money" received, the gain recognized to A will be limited to the $3,000 cash received, since, under the general rule of section 357(a), the assumption of the $4,000 liability does not constitute "other property."

(c) Tax avoidance purpose. The benefits of section 357(a) do not extend to any exchange involving an assumption of liabilities where it appears that the principal purpose of the taxpayer with respect to such assumption was to avoid Federal income tax on the exchange, or, if not such purpose, was not a bona fide business purpose. In such cases, the total amount of liabilities assumed or acquired pursuant to such exchange (and not merely a particular liability with respect to which the tax avoidance purpose existed) shall, for the purpose of determining the amount of gain to be recognized upon the exchange in which the liabilities are assumed or acquired, be treated as money received by the taxpayer upon the exchange. Thus, if in the example set forth in paragraph (b) of this section, the principal purpose of the assumption of the $4,000 liability was to avoid tax on the exchange, or was not a bona fide business purpose, then the amount of gain recognized would be $5,000. In any suit or proceeding where the burden is on the taxpayer to prove that an assumption of liabilities is not to be treated as "other property or money" under section 357, which is the case if the Commissioner determines that the taxpayer's purpose with respect thereto was a purpose to avoid Federal income tax on the exchange or was not a bona fide business purpose, and the taxpayer contests such determination by litigation, the taxpayer must sustain such burden by the clear preponderance of the evidence. Thus, the taxpayer must prove his case by such a clear preponderance of all the evidence that the absence of a purpose to avoid Federal income tax on the exchange, or the presence of a bona fide business purpose, is unmistakable.

[T.D. 6500, 25 FR 11607, Nov. 26, 1960, as amended by T.D. 6528, 26 FR 399, Jan. 19, 1961]

§ 1.357–2 Liabilities in excess of basis.

(a) Section 357(c) provides in general that in an exchange to which section 351 (relating to a transfer to a corporation controlled by the transferor) is applicable, or to which section 361 (relating to the nonrecognition of gain or loss to corporations) is applicable by reason of a section 368(a)(1)(D) reorganization, if the sum of the amount of liabilities assumed plus the amount of liabilities to which the property is subject exceeds the total of the adjusted basis of the property transferred pursuant to such exchange, then such excess shall be considered as a gain from the sale or exchange of a capital asset or of property which is not a capital asset as the case may be. Thus, if an individual transfers, under section 351, properties having a total basis in his hands of $20,000, one of which has a basis of $10,000 but is subject to a mortgage of $30,000, to a corporation controlled by him, such individual will be subject to tax with respect to $10,000, the excess of the amount of the liability over the total adjusted basis of all the properties in his hands. The same result will follow whether or not the liability is assumed by the transferee. The determination of whether a gain resulting from the transfer of capital assets is long-term or short-term capital gain shall be made by reference to the holding period to the transferor of the assets transferred. An exception to the general rule of section 357(c) is made (1) for any exchange as to which under section 357(b) (relating to assumption of liabilities for tax-avoidance purposes) the entire amount of the liabilities is treated as money received * * *.

(b) The application of paragraph (a) of this section may be illustrated by the following examples:

Example (1). If all such assets transferred are capital assets and if half the assets (ascertained by reference to their fair market value at the time of the transfer) have been held for less than 1 year * * * and the remaining half for more than 1 year * * * half the excess of the amount of the liability over the total of the adjusted basis of the property transferred pursuant to the exchange shall be treated as short-term capital gain, and the remaining half shall be treated as long-term capital gain.

Example (2). If half of the assets (ascertained by reference to their fair market value at the time of the transfer) transferred are capital assets and half are assets other than capital assets, then half of the excess of the amount of the liability over the total of the adjusted basis of the property transferred pursuant to the exchange shall be treated as capital gain, and the remaining half shall be treated as gain from the sale or exchange of assets other than capital assets.

[T.D. 6500, 25 FR 11607, Nov. 26, 1960, as amended by T.D. 6528, 26 FR 399, Jan. 19, 1961; T.D. 7728, 45 FR 72650, Nov. 3, 1980]

§ 1.358–1 Basis to distributees.

(a) In the case of an exchange to which section 354 or 355 applies in which, under the law applicable to the year in which the exchange is made, only nonrecognition property is received, immediately after the transaction, the sum of the basis of all of the stock and securities received in the transaction shall be the same as the basis of all the stock and securities in such corporation surrendered in the transaction, allocated in the manner described in § 1.358–2. In the case of a distribution to which section 355 applies in which, under the law applicable to the year in which the distribution is made, only nonrecognition property is received, immediately after the transaction, the sum of the basis of all of the stock and securities with respect to which the distribution is made plus the basis of all stock and securities received in the distribution with respect to such stock and securities shall be the same as the basis of the stock and securities with respect to which the distribution is made immediately before the transaction, allocated in the manner described in § 1.358–2. In the case of an exchange to which section 351 or 361 applies in which, under the law applicable to the year in which the exchange was made, only nonrecognition property is received, the basis of all the stock and securities received in the exchange shall be the same as the basis of all property exchanged therefor. If in an exchange or distribution to which section 351, 356, or 361 applies both nonrecognition property and "other property" are received, the basis of all the property except "other property" held after the transaction shall be determined as described in the preceding three sentences decreased by the sum of the money and the fair market value of the "other property" (as of the date of the transaction) and increased by the sum of the amount treated as a dividend (if any) and the amount of the gain recognized on the exchange, but the term gain as here used does not include any portion of the recognized gain that was treated as a dividend. In any case in which a taxpayer transfers property with respect to which loss is recognized, such loss shall be reflected in determining the basis of the property received in the exchange. The basis of the "other property" is its fair market value as of the date of the transaction. See § 1.460–4(k)(3)(iv)(A) for rules relating to stock basis adjustments required where a contract accounted for using a long-term contract method of accounting is transferred in a transaction described in section 351 or a reorganization described in section 368(a)(1)(D) with respect to which the requirements of section 355 (or so much of section 356 as relates to section 355) are met.

(b) The application of paragraph (a) of this section may be illustrated by the following example:

Example. A purchased a share of stock in Corporation X in 1935 for $150. Since that date A has received distributions out of other than earnings and profits (as defined in section 316) totaling $60, so that A's adjusted basis for the stock is $90. In a transaction qualifying under section 356, A exchanged this share for one share in Corporation Y, worth $100, cash in the amount of $10, and other property with a fair market value of $30. The exchange had the effect of the distribution of a dividend. A's ratable share of the earnings and profits of Corporation X accumulated after February 28, 1913, was $5. A realized a gain of $50 on the exchange, but the amount recognized is limited to $40, the sum of the cash received and the fair market value of the other property. Of the gain recognized, $5 is taxable as a dividend, and $35 is taxable as a gain from the exchange of property. The basis to A of the one share of stock of Corporation Y is $90, that is, the adjusted basis of the one share of stock of Corporation X ($90), decreased by the sum of the cash received ($10) and the fair market value of the other property received ($30) and increased by the sum of the amount treated as a dividend ($5) and the amount treated as a gain from the exchange of property ($35). The basis of the other property received is $30.

* * *

[T.D. 6500, 25 FR 11607, Nov. 26, 1960, as amended by T.D. 6533, 26 FR 404, Jan. 19, 1965; T.D. 7616, 44 FR 26869, May 8, 1979; T.D. 8995, 67 FR 34604, May 15, 2002; T.D. 9244, 71 FR 4269, Jan. 26, 2006; 71 FR 19118, April 13, 2006; 71 FR 62556, Oct. 26, 2006]

§ 1.358–1 Basis to distributees (Proposed Jan. 21, 2009).

(a) Certain exchanges or distributions in which only nonrecognition property is received—(1) Exchanges to which section 354 or 355 applies. In the case of an exchange to which section 354 or 355 applies in which only nonrecognition property is received, the sum of the basis of all of the stock and securities received in the transaction shall be the same as the basis of all of the stock and securities in such corporation surrendered in the transaction, allocated in the manner described in § 1.358–2.

(2) Distributions to which section 355 applies. In the case of a distribution to which section 355 applies in which only nonrecognition property is received, the sum of the basis of all of the stock and securities with respect to which the distribution is made plus the basis of all of the stock and securities received in the distribution with respect to such stock and securities shall be the same as the basis of the stock and securities with respect to which the distribution is made immediately before the transaction, allocated in the manner described in § 1.358–2.

(3) Exchanges to which section 351 or 361 applies. In the case of an exchange to which section 351 or 361 applies in which only nonrecognition property is received, the basis of all of the stock and securities received in the exchange shall be the same as the basis of all of the property exchanged for such stock and securities.

(b) Certain exchanges or distributions in which both nonrecognition property and "other property" or money are received—(1) Exchanges or distributions to which section 351, 356, or 361 applies. If in an exchange or distribution to which section 351, 356, or 361 applies both nonrecognition property and "other property" or money are received, the basis of the nonrecognition property held after the transaction shall be determined as described in paragraph (a) of this section, decreased by the sum of the money and the fair market value of the "other property" (as of the date of the transaction) received and increased by the sum of the amount treated as a dividend (if any) and the amount of the gain recognized on the exchange (other than gain treated as a dividend).

(2) Cases in which loss is recognized. In any case in which a taxpayer transfers property with respect to which loss is recognized, such loss shall be reflected in determining the basis of the property received in the exchange.

(3) Basis of "other property" received. The basis of the "other property" is its fair market value as of the date of the transaction.

* * *

(d) The application of this section may be illustrated by the following example:

Example. A purchased a share of stock in Corporation X on Date 1 for $150. Since that date, A has received distributions under section 301(c)(2) totaling $60, so that A's adjusted basis for the stock is $90. In a transaction qualifying under section 356, A exchanged this share for one share in Corporation Y, with a value of $100, cash of $10, and other property with a fair market value of $30. The exchange had the effect of the distribution of a dividend. A's ratable share of the earnings and profits of Corporation X was $5. A realized a gain of $50 on the exchange ($140—$90), but the amount of gain recognized is limited to $40, the sum of the cash received and the fair market value of the other property. Of the gain recognized, $5 is taxable as a dividend, and $35 is taxable as a gain from the exchange of property. The basis to A of the one share of stock of Corporation Y is $90, that is the adjusted basis of the one share of stock of Corporation X ($90), decreased by the sum of the cash received ($10) and the fair market value of the other property received ($30) and increased by the sum of the amount treated as a dividend ($5) and the amount treated as a gain from the exchange of property ($35). The basis of the other property received is $30.

* * *

§ 1.358–2 Allocation of basis among nonrecognition property.

(a) Allocation of basis in exchanges or distributions to which section 354, 355, or 356 applies. (1) As used in this paragraph the term stock means stock which is not "other property" under section 356. The term securities means securities (including, where appropriate, fractional parts of securities) which are not "other property" under section 356. Stock, or securities, as the case may be, which differ either because they are in different corporations or because the rights attributable to them differ (although they are in the same corporation) are considered different classes of stock or securities, as the case may be, for purposes of this section.

(2)(i) If a shareholder or security holder surrenders a share of stock or a security in an exchange under the terms of section 354, 355, or 356, the basis of each share of stock or security received in the exchange shall be the same as the basis of the share or shares of stock or security or securities (or allocable portions thereof) exchanged therefor (as adjusted under § 1.358–1). If more than one share of stock or security is received in exchange for one share of stock or one security, the basis of the share of stock or security surrendered shall be allocated to the shares of stock or securities received in the exchange in proportion to the fair market value of the shares of stock or securities received. If one share of stock or security is received in exchange for more than one share of stock or security or if a fraction of a share of stock or security is received, then the basis of the shares of stock or securities surrendered must be allocated to the shares of stock or securities (or allocable portions thereof) received in a manner that reflects, to the greatest extent possible, that a share of stock or security received is received in respect of shares of stock or securities that were acquired on the same date and at the same price. To the extent it is not possible to allocate basis in this manner, the basis of the shares of stock or securities surrendered must be allocated to the shares of stock or securities (or allocable portions thereof) received in a manner that minimizes the disparity in the holding periods of the surrendered shares of stock or securities whose basis is allocated to any particular share of stock or security received.

(ii) If a shareholder or security holder surrenders a share of stock or a security in an exchange under the terms of section 354, 355, or 356, and receives shares of stock or securities of more than one class, or receives "other property" or money in addition to shares of stock or securities, then, to the extent the terms of the exchange specify that shares of stock or securities of a particular class or "other property" or money is received in exchange for a particular share of stock or security or a particular class of stock or securities, for purposes of applying the rules of this section, such terms shall control provided such terms are economically reasonable. To the extent the terms of the exchange do not specify that shares of stock or securities of a particular class or "other property" or money is received in exchange for a particular share of stock or security or a particular class of stock or securities, then, for purposes of applying the rules of paragraph (a)(2)(i) of this section, a pro rata portion of the shares of stock and securities of each class received and a pro rata portion of the "other property" and money received shall be treated as received in exchange for each share of stock and security surrendered, based on the fair market value of the stock and securities surrendered.

(iii) [Reserved]. For further guidance, see § 1.358–2T(a)(2)(iii).

(iv) If a shareholder or security holder receives one or more shares of stock or one or more securities in a distribution under the terms of section 355 (or so much of section 356 as relates to section 355), the basis of each share of stock or security of the distributing corporation (as defined in § 1.355–1(b)), as adjusted under § 1.358–1, shall be allocated between the share of stock or security of the distributing corporation with respect to which the distribution is made and the share or shares of stock or security or securities (or allocable portions thereof) received with respect to the share of stock or security of the distributing corporation in proportion to their fair market values. If one share of stock or security is received with respect to more than one share of stock or security or if a fraction of a share of stock or security is received, then the basis of each share of stock or security of the distributing corporation must be allocated to the shares of stock or securities (or allocable portions thereof) received in a manner that reflects that, to the greatest extent possible, a share of stock or security received is received with respect to shares of stock or securities acquired on the same date and at the same price. To the extent it is not possible to allocate basis in this manner, the basis of each share of stock or security of the distributing corporation must be allocated to the shares of stock or securities (or allocable portions thereof) received in a manner that minimizes the disparity in the holding periods of the shares of stock or securities with respect to which such shares of stock or securities are received.

(v) If a shareholder or security holder receives shares of stock or securities of more than one class, or receives "other property" or money in addition to stock or securities in a distribution under the terms of section 355 (or so much of section 356 as relates to section 355), then, to the extent the terms of the distribution specify that shares of stock or securities of a particular class or "other property" or money is received with respect to a particular share of stock or security of the distributing corporation or a particular class of stock or securities of the distributing corporation, for purposes of applying the rules of this section, such terms shall control provided that such terms are economically reasonable. To the extent the terms of the distribution do not specify that shares of stock or securities of a particular class or "other property" or money is received with respect to a particular share of stock or security of the distributing corporation or a particular class of stock or securities of the distributing corporation, then, for purposes of applying the rules of this section, a pro rata portion of the shares of stock and securities of each class received and a pro rata portion of the "other property" and money received shall be treated as received with respect to each share of stock and security of the distributing corporation with respect to which the distribution is made, based on the fair market value of each such share of stock or security.

(vi) If a share of stock or a security is received in exchange for, or with respect to, more than one share of stock or security and such shares or securities were acquired on different dates or at different prices, the share of stock or security received shall be divided into segments based on the relative fair market values of the shares of stock or securities surrendered in exchange for such share or security or the relative fair market values of the shares of stock or securities with respect to which the share of stock or security is received in a distribution under the terms of section 355 (or so much of section 356 as relates to section 355). Each segment shall have a basis determined under the rules of paragraph (a)(2) of this section and a corresponding holding period.

(vii) If a shareholder or security holder that purchased or acquired shares of stock or securities in a corporation on different dates or at different prices exchanges such shares of stock or securities under the terms of section 354, 355, or 356, or receives a distribution of shares of stock or securities under the terms of section 355 (or so much of section 356 as relates to section 355), and the shareholder or security holder is not able to identify which particular share of stock or security (or allocable portion of a share of stock or security) is received (or deemed received) in exchange for, or with respect to, a particular share of stock or security, the shareholder or security holder may designate which share of stock or security is received in exchange for, or with respect to, a particular share of stock or security, provided that such designation is consistent with the terms of the exchange or distribution (or an exchange deemed to have occurred pursuant to paragraph (a)(2)(iii) of this section), and the other rules of this section. In the case of an exchange under the terms of section 354 or 356 (including a deemed exchange as a result of the application of paragraph (a)(2)(iii) of this section), the designation must be made on or before the first date on which the basis of a share of stock or a security received (or deemed received in the reorganization under section 368(a)(1)(E) in the case of a transaction to which paragraph (a)(2)(iii) of this section applies) is relevant. In the case of an exchange or distribution under the terms of section 355 (or so much of section 356 as relates to section 355), the designation must be made on or before the first date on which the basis of a share of stock or a security of the distributing corporation or the controlled corporation (as defined in § 1.355–1(b)) is relevant. The basis of the shares or securities received in an exchange under the terms of section 354 or section 356, for example, is relevant when such shares or securities are sold or otherwise transferred. The designation will be binding for purposes of determining the Federal tax consequences of any sale or transfer of, or distribution with respect to, the shares or securities received. If the shareholder fails to make a designation in a case in which the shareholder is not able to identify which share of stock is received in exchange for, or with respect to, a particular share of stock, then the shareholder will not be able to identify which shares are sold or transferred for purposes of determining the basis of property sold or transferred under section 1012 and § 1.1012–1(c) and, instead, will be treated as selling or transferring the share received in respect of the earliest share purchased or acquired.

(viii) This paragraph (a)(2) shall not apply to determine the basis of a share of stock or security received by a shareholder or security holder in an exchange described in both section 351 and section 354 or section 356, if, in connection with the exchange, the shareholder or security holder exchanges property for stock or securities in an exchange to which neither section 354 nor section 356 applies or liabilities of the shareholder or security holder are assumed.

(ix) This paragraph (a)(2) shall apply to determine the basis of a share of stock or security received by a shareholder or security holder in an exchange described in both section 1036 and section 354 or section 356.

(b) Allocation of basis in exchanges to which section 351 or 361 applies. (1) As used in this paragraph (b), the term stock refers only to stock which is not "other property" under section 351 or 361 and the term securities refers only to securities which are not "other property" under section 351 or 361.

(2) If in an exchange to which section 351 or 361 applies property is transferred to a corporation and the transferor receives stock or securities of more than one class or receives both stock and securities, then the basis of the property transferred (as adjusted under § 1.358–1) shall be allocated among all of the stock and securities received in proportion to the fair market values of the stock of each class and the securities of each class.

(c) Examples. The application of paragraphs (a) and (b) of this section is illustrated by the following examples:

Example 1. (i) Facts. J, an individual, acquired 20 shares of Corporation X stock on Date 1 for $3 each and 10 shares of Corporation X stock on Date 2 for $6 each. On Date 3, Corporation Y acquires the assets of Corporation X in a reorganization under section 368(a)(1)(A). Pursuant to the terms of the plan of reorganization, J receives 2 shares of Corporation Y stock in exchange for each share of Corporation X stock. Therefore, J receives 60 shares of Corporation Y stock. Pursuant to section 354, J recognizes no gain or loss on the exchange. J is not able to identify which shares of Corporation Y stock are received in exchange for each share of Corporation X stock.

(ii) Analysis. Under paragraph (a)(2)(i) of this section, J has 40 shares of Corporation Y stock each of which has a basis of $1.50 and is treated as having been acquired on Date 1 and 20 shares of Corporation Y stock each of which has a basis of $3 and is treated as having been acquired on Date 2. Under paragraph (a)(2)(vii) of this section, on or before the date on which the basis of a share of Corporation Y stock received becomes relevant, J may designate which of the shares of Corporation Y stock have a basis of $1.50 and which have a basis of $3.

Example 2. (i) Facts. The facts are the same as in Example 1, except that instead of receiving 2 shares of Corporation Y stock in exchange for each share of Corporation X stock, J receives 1 1/2 shares of Corporation Y stock in exchange for each share of Corporation X stock. Therefore, J receives 45 shares of Corporation Y stock. Again, J is not able to identify which shares (or portions of shares) of Corporation Y stock are received in exchange for each share of Corporation X stock.

(ii) Analysis. Under paragraph (a)(2)(i) of this section, J has 30 shares of Corporation Y stock each of which has a basis of $2 and is treated as having been acquired on Date 1 and 15 shares of Corporation Y stock each of which has a basis of $4 and is treated as having been acquired on Date 2. Under paragraph (a)(2)(vii) of this section, on or before the date on which the basis of a share of Corporation Y stock received becomes relevant, J may designate which of the shares of Corporation Y stock received have a basis of $2 and which have a basis of $4.

Example 3. (i) Facts. J, an individual, acquired 10 shares of Class A stock of Corporation X on Date 1 for $3 each, 10 shares of Class A stock of Corporation X on Date

2 for $9 each, and 10 shares of Class B stock of Corporation X on Date 3 for $3 each. On Date 4, J surrenders all of J's shares of Class A stock in exchange for 20 shares of new Class C stock and 20 shares of new Class D stock in a reorganization under section 368(a)(1)(E). Pursuant to section 354, J recognizes no gain or loss on the exchange. On the date of the exchange, the fair market value of each share of Class A stock is $6, the fair market value of each share of Class C stock is $2, and the fair market value of each share of Class D stock is $4. The terms of the exchange do not specify that shares of Class C stock or shares of Class D stock of Corporation X are received in exchange for particular shares of Class A stock of Corporation X.

(ii) Analysis. Under paragraph (a)(2)(ii) of this section, because the terms of the exchange do not specify that shares of Class C stock or shares of Class D stock of Corporation X are received in exchange for particular shares of Class A stock of Corporation X, a pro rata portion of the shares of Class C stock and shares of Class D stock received will be treated as received in exchange for each share of Class A stock based on the fair market value of the surrendered shares of Class A stock. Therefore, J is treated as receiving one share of Class C stock and one share of Class D stock in exchange for each share of Class A stock. Under paragraph (a)(2)(i) of this section, J has 10 shares of Class C stock, each of which has a basis of $1 and is treated as having been acquired on Date 1 and 10 shares of Class C stock, each of which has a basis of $3 and is treated as having been acquired on Date 2. In addition, J has 10 shares of Class D stock, each of which has a basis of $2 and is treated as having been acquired on Date 1 and 10 shares of Class D stock, each of which has a basis of $6 and is treated as having been acquired on Date 2. J's basis in each share of Class B stock remains $3. Under paragraph (a)(2)(vii) of this section, on or before the date on which the basis of a share of Class C stock or Class D stock received becomes relevant, J may designate which of the shares of Class C stock have a basis of $1 and which have a basis of $3, and which of the shares of Class D stock have a basis of $2 and which have a basis of $6.

Example 4. (i) Facts. J, an individual, acquired 10 shares of Class A stock of Corporation X on Date 1 for $2 each, 10 shares of Class A stock of Corporation X on Date 2 for $4 each, and 20 shares of Class B stock of Corporation X on Date 3 for $6 each. On Date 4, Corporation Y acquires the assets of Corporation X in a reorganization under section 368(a)(1)(A). Pursuant to the terms of the plan of reorganization, J surrenders all of J's shares of Corporation X stock for 40 shares of Corporation Y stock and $200 of cash. On the date of the exchange, the fair market value of each share of Class A stock of Corporation X is $10, the fair market value of each share of Class B stock of Corporation X is $10, and the fair market value of each share of Corporation Y stock is $5. The terms of the exchange do not specify that shares of Corporation Y stock or cash are received in exchange for particular shares of Class A stock or Class B stock of Corporation X.

(ii) Analysis. Under paragraph (a)(2)(ii) of this section and under § 1.356–1(b), because the terms of the exchange do not specify that shares of Corporation Y stock or cash are received in exchange for particular shares of Class A stock or Class B stock of Corporation X, a pro rata portion of the shares of Corporation Y stock and cash received will be treated as received in exchange for each share of Class A stock and Class B stock of Corporation X surrendered based on the fair market value of such stock. Therefore, J is treated as receiving one share of Corporation Y stock and $5 of cash in exchange for each share of Class A stock of Corporation X and one share of Corporation Y stock and $5 of cash in exchange for each share of Class B stock of Corporation X. J realizes a gain of $140 on the exchange of shares of Class A stock of Corporation X, $100 of which is recognized under § 1.356–1(a). J realizes a gain of $80 on the exchange of Class B stock of Corporation X, all of which is recognized under § 1.356–1(a). Under paragraph (a)(2)(i) of this section, J has 10 shares of Corporation Y stock, each of which has a basis of $2 and is treated as having been acquired on Date 1, 10 shares of Corporation Y stock, each of which has a basis of $4 and is treated as having been acquired on Date 2, and 20 shares of Corporation Y stock, each of which has a basis of $5 and is treated as having been acquired on Date 3. Under paragraph (a)(2)(vii) of this section, on or before the date on which the basis of a share of Corporation Y stock received becomes relevant, J may designate which of the shares of Corporation Y stock received have a basis of $2, which have a basis of $4, and which have a basis of $5.

Example 5. (i) Facts. The facts are the same as in Example 4, except that the terms of the plan of reorganization specify that J receives 40 shares of stock of Corporation Y in exchange for J's shares of Class A stock of Corporation X and $200 of cash in exchange for J's shares of Class B stock of Corporation X.

(ii) Analysis. Under paragraph (a)(2)(ii) of this section and under § 1.356–1(b), because the terms of the exchange specify that J receives 40 shares of stock of Corporation Y in exchange for J's shares of Class A stock of Corporation X and $200 of cash in exchange for J's shares of Class B stock of Corporation X and such terms are economically reasonable, such terms control. J realizes a gain of $140 on the exchange of shares of Class A stock of Corporation X, none of which is recognized under § 1.356–1(a). J realizes a gain of $80 on the exchange of shares of Class B stock of Corporation X, all of which is recognized under § 1.356–1(a). Under paragraph (a)(2)(i) of this section, J has 20 shares of Corporation Y stock, each of which has a basis of $1 and is treated as having been acquired on Date 1, and 20 shares of Corporation Y stock, each of which has a basis of $2 and is treated as having been acquired on Date 2. Under paragraph (a)(2)(vii) of this section, on or before the date on which the basis of a share of Corporation Y stock received becomes relevant, J may designate which of the shares of Corporation Y stock received have a basis of $1 and which have a basis of $2.

Example 6. (i) Facts. J, an individual, acquired 10 shares of stock of Corporation X on Date 1 for $2 each, and a security issued by Corporation X to J on Date 2 with a principal amount of $100 and a basis of $100. On Date 3, Corporation Y acquires the assets of Corporation X in a reorganization under § 368(a)(1)(A). Pursuant to the terms of the plan of reorganization, J surrenders all of J's shares of Corporation X stock in exchange for 10 shares of Corporation Y stock and surrenders J's Corporation X security in exchange for a Corporation Y security. On the date of the exchange, the fair market value of each share of stock of Corporation X is $10, the fair market value of J's Corporation X security is $100, the fair market value of each share of Corporation Y stock is $10, and the fair market value and principal amount of the Corporation Y security received by J is $100.

(ii) Analysis. Under paragraph (a)(2)(ii) of this section and under § 1.354–1(a), because the terms of the exchange specify that J receives 10 shares of stock of Corporation Y in exchange for J's shares of Class A stock of Corporation X and a Corporation Y security in exchange for its Corporation X security and such terms are economically reasonable, such terms control. Pursuant to section 354, J recognizes no gain on either exchange. Under paragraph (a)(2)(i) of this section, J has 10 shares of Corporation Y stock, each of which has a basis of $2 and is treated as having been acquired on Date 1, and a security that has a basis of $100 and is treated as having been acquired on Date 2.

Example 7. (i) Facts. J, an individual, acquired 10 shares of Corporation X stock on Date 1 for $2 each and 10 shares of Corporation X stock on Date 2 for $5 each. On Date 3, Corporation Y acquires the stock of Corporation X in a reorganization under section 368(a)(1)(B). Pursuant to the terms of the plan of reorganization, J receives one share of Corporation Y stock in exchange for every 2 shares of Corporation X stock. Pursuant to section 354, J recognizes no gain or loss on the exchange. J is not able to identify which portion of each share of Corporation Y stock is received in exchange for each share of Corporation X stock.

(ii) Analysis. Under paragraph (a)(2)(i) of this section, J has 5 shares of Corporation Y stock each of which has a basis of $4 and is treated as having been acquired on Date 1 and 5 shares of Corporation Y stock each of which has a basis of $10 and is treated as having been acquired on Date 2. Under paragraph (a)(2)(vii) of this section, on or before the date on which the basis of a share of Corporation Y stock received becomes relevant, J may designate which of the shares of Corporation Y stock received have a basis of $4 and which have a basis of $10.

Example 8. (i) Facts. The facts are the same as in Example 7, except that, in addition to transferring the stock of Corporation X to Corporation Y, J transfers land to Corporation Y. In addition, after the transaction, J owns stock of Corporation Y satisfying the requirements of section 368(c). J's transfer of the Corporation X stock to Corporation Y is an exchange described in sections 351 and 354. J's transfer of land to Corporation Y is an exchange described in section 351.

(ii) Analysis. Under paragraph (a)(2)(viii) of this section, because neither section 354 nor section 356 applies to the transfer of land to Corporation Y, the rules of paragraph (a)(2) of this section do not apply to determine J's basis in the Corporation Y stock received in the transaction.

Example 9. (i) Facts. J, an individual, acquired 10 shares of Corporation X stock on Date 1 for $3 each and 10 shares of Corporation X stock on Date 2 for $6 each. On Date 3, Corporation Z, a newly formed, wholly owned subsidiary of Corporation Y, merges with and into Corporation X with Corporation X surviving. As part of the plan of merger, J receives one share of Corporation Y stock in exchange for each share of Corporation X stock. In connection with the transaction, Corporation Y assumes a liability of J. In addition, after the transaction, J owns stock of Corporation Y satisfying the requirements of section 368(c). J's transfer of the Corporation X stock to Corporation Y is an exchange described in sections 351 and 354.

(ii) Analysis. Under paragraph (a)(2)(viii) of this section, because, in connection with the transfer of the Corporation X stock to Corporation Y, Corporation Y assumed a liability of J, the rules of paragraph (a)(2) of this section do not apply to determine J's basis in the Corporation Y stock received in the transaction.

Example 10. (i) Facts. Each of Corporation X and Corporation Y has a single class of stock outstanding, all of which is owned by J, an individual. J acquired 100 shares of Corporation X stock on Date 1 for $1 each and 100 shares of Corporation Y stock on Date 2 for $2 each. On Date 3, Corporation Y acquires the assets of Corporation X in a reorganization under section 368(a)(1)(D). Pursuant to the terms of the plan of reorganization, J surrenders J's 100 shares of Corporation X stock but does not receive any additional Corporation Y stock. Immediately before the effective time of the reorganization, the fair market value of each share of Corporation X stock and each share of Corporation Y stock is $1. Pursuant to section 354, J recognizes no gain or loss.

(ii) Analysis. Under paragraph (a)(2)(iii) of this section, J is deemed to have received shares of Corporation Y stock with an aggregate fair market value of $100 in exchange for J's Corporation X shares. Given the number of outstanding shares of stock of Corporation Y and their value immediately before the effective time of the reorganization, J is deemed to have received 100 shares of stock of Corporation Y in the reorganization. Under paragraph (a)(2)(i) of this section, each of those shares has a basis of $1 and is treated as having been acquired on Date 1. Then, the stock of Corporation Y is deemed to be recapitalized in a reorganization under section 368(a)(1)(E) in which J receives 100 shares of Corporation Y stock in exchange for those shares of Corporation Y stock that J held immediately prior to the reorganization and those shares J is deemed to have received in the reorganization. Under paragraph (a)(2)(i), immediately after the reorganization, J holds 50 shares of Corporation Y stock each of which has a basis of $2 and is treated as having been acquired on Date 1 and 50 shares of Corporation Y stock each of which has a basis of $4 and is treated as having been acquired on Date 2. Under paragraph (a)(2)(vii) of this section, on or before the date on which the basis of any share of J's Corporation Y stock becomes relevant, J may designate which of the shares of Corporation Y have a basis of $2 and which have a basis of $4.

Example 11. (i) Facts. Corporation X has a single class of stock outstanding, all of which is owned by J, an individual. J acquired 100 shares of Corporation X stock on Date 1 for $1 each. Corporation Y has two classes of stock outstanding, common stock and nonvoting preferred stock. On Date 2, J acquired 100 shares of Corporation Y common stock for $2 each and 100 shares of Corporation Y preferred stock for $4 each. On Date 3, Corporation Y acquires the assets of Corporation X in a reorganization under section 368(a)(1)(D). Pursuant to the terms of the plan of reorganization, J surrenders J's 100 shares of Corporation X stock but does not receive any additional Corporation Y stock. Immediately before the effective time of the reorganization, the fair market value of each share of Corporation X stock is $10, the fair market value of each share of Corporation Y common stock is $10, and the fair market value of each share of Corporation Y preferred stock is $20. Pursuant to section 354, J recognizes no gain or loss.

(ii) Analysis. Under paragraph (a)(2)(iii) of this section, J is deemed to have received shares of Corporation Y stock with an aggregate fair market value of $1,000 in exchange for J's Corporation X shares. Consistent with the economics of the transaction and the rights associated with each class of stock of Corporation Y owned by J, J is deemed to receive additional shares of Corporation Y common stock. Because the value of the common stock indicates that the liquidation preference associated with the Corporation Y preferred stock could be satisfied even if the reorganization did not occur, it is not appropriate to deem the issuance of additional Corporation Y preferred stock. Given the number of outstanding shares of common stock of Corporation Y and their value immediately before the effective time of the reorganization, J is deemed to have received 100 shares of common stock of Corporation Y in the reorganization. Under paragraph (a)(2)(i) of this section, each of those shares has a basis of $1 and is treated as having been acquired on Date 1. Then, the common stock of Corporation Y is deemed to be recapitalized in a reorganization under section 368(a)(1)(E) in which J receives 100 shares of Corporation Y common stock in exchange for those shares of Corporation Y common stock that J held immediately prior to the reorganization and those shares of Corporation Y common stock that J is deemed to have received in the reorganization. Under paragraph (a)(2)(i), immediately after the reorganization, J holds 50 shares of Corporation Y common stock, each of which has a basis of $2 and is treated as having been acquired on Date 1, and 50 shares of Corporation Y common stock, each of which has a basis of $4 and is treated as having been acquired on Date 2. Under paragraph (a)(2)(vii) of this section, on or before the date on which the basis of any share of J's Corporation Y common stock becomes relevant, J may designate which of those shares have a basis of $2 and which have a basis of $4.

Example 12. (i) Facts. J, an individual, acquired 5 shares of Corporation X stock on Date 1 for $4 each and 5 shares of Corporation X stock on Date 2 for $8 each. Corporation X owns all of the outstanding stock of Corporation Y. The fair market value of the stock of Corporation X is $1800. The fair market value of the stock of Corporation Y is $900. In a distribution to which section 355 applies, Corporation X distributes all of the stock of Corporation Y pro rata to its shareholders. No stock of Corporation X is surrendered in connection with the distribution. In the distribution, J receives 2 shares of Corporation Y stock with respect to each share of Corporation X stock. Pursuant to section 355, J recognizes no gain or loss on the receipt of the shares of Corporation Y stock. J is not able to identify which share of Corporation Y stock is received in respect of each share of Corporation X stock.

(ii) Analysis. Under paragraph (a)(2)(iv) of this section, because J receives 2 shares of Corporation Y stock with respect to each share of Corporation X stock, the basis of each share of Corporation X stock is allocated between such share of Corporation X stock and two shares of Corporation Y stock in proportion to the fair market value of those shares. Therefore, each of the 5 shares of Corporation X stock acquired on Date 1 will have a basis of $2 and each of the 10 shares of Corporation Y stock received with respect to those shares will have a basis of $1. In addition, each of the 5 shares of Corporation X stock acquired on Date 2 will have a basis of $4 and each of the 10 shares of Corporation Y stock received with respect to those shares will have a basis of $2. Under paragraph (a)(2)(vii) of this section, on or before the date on which the basis of a share of Corporation Y stock received becomes relevant, J may designate which of the shares of Corporation Y stock have a basis of $1 and which have a basis of $2.

Example 13. (i) Facts. J, an individual, acquired 20 shares of Corporation X stock on Date 1 for $2 each and 20 shares of Corporation X stock on Date 2 for $4 each. Corporation X has 80 shares of stock outstanding. Corporation X owns 40 shares of stock of Corporation Y, which represents all of the outstanding stock of Corporation Y. The fair market value of the stock of Corporation X is $80. The fair market value of the stock of Corporation Y is $40. Corporation X distributes all of the stock of Corporation Y in a transaction to which section 355 applies. In the transaction, J surrenders 20 shares of stock of Corporation X in exchange for 20 shares of stock of Corporation Y. J retains 20 shares of Corporation X stock. Pursuant to section 355, J recognizes no gain or loss on the receipt of the shares of Corporation Y stock. J is not able to identify which shares of Corporation X stock are surrendered. In addition, J is not able to identify which shares of Corporation Y stock are received in exchange for each surrendered share of Corporation X stock.

(ii) Analysis. Under paragraph (a)(2)(i) of this section, J has 20 shares of Corporation Y stock each of which is treated as received in exchange for one share of Corporation X stock. The basis of the 20 shares of Corporation X stock that are retained by J will remain unchanged. Under paragraph (a)(2)(vii) of this section, on or before the date on which the basis of a share of Corporation X or Corporation Y stock becomes relevant, J may designate which shares of Corporation X stock J surrendered in the exchange and which share of the Corporation Y stock received is received for each share of Corporation X stock surrendered. Therefore, it is possible that a share of Corporation Y stock would have a basis of $2 and be treated as having been acquired on Date 1, or would have a basis of $4 and be treated as having been acquired on Date 2.

Example 14. (i) Facts. J, an individual, acquired 10 shares of Corporation X stock on Date 1 for $3 each, 10 shares of Corporation X stock on Date 2 for $18 each, 10 shares of Corporation X stock on Date 3 for $6 each, and 10 shares of Corporation X stock on Date 4 for $9 each. On Date 5, Corporation Y acquires the assets of Corporation X in a reorganization under section 368(a)(1)(A). Pursuant to the terms of the plan of reorganization, J receives a 3/4 share of Corporation Y stock in exchange for each share of Corporation X stock. Therefore, J receives 30 shares of Corporation X stock. Pursuant to section 354, J recognizes no gain or loss on the exchange. J is not able to identify which shares of Corporation Y stock are received in exchange for each share (or portions of shares) of Corporation X stock.

(ii) Analysis. Under paragraph (a)(2)(i) of this section, J has 7 shares of Corporation Y stock each of which has a basis of $4 and is treated as having been acquired on Date 1, 7 shares of Corporation Y stock each of which has a basis of $24 and is treated as having been acquired on Date 2, 7 shares of Corporation Y stock each of which has a basis of $8 and is treated as having been acquired on Date 3, and 7 shares of Corporation Y stock each of which has a basis of $12 and is treated as having been acquired on Date 4. In addition, J has two shares of Corporation Y stock, each of which is divided into two equal segments under paragraph (a)(2)(vi) of this section. The first of those two shares has one segment with a basis of $2 that is treated as having been acquired on Date 1 and a second segment with a basis of $12 that is treated as having been acquired on Date 2. The second of those two shares has one segment with a basis of $4 that is treated as having been acquired on Date 3 and a second segment with a basis of $6 that is treated as having been acquired on Date 4. Under paragraph (a)(2)(vii), on or before the date on which a share of Corporation Y stock received becomes relevant, J may designate which of the shares of Corporation Y stock have a basis of $4, which have a basis of $24, which have a basis of $8, which have a basis of $12, and which share has a split basis of $2 and $12, and which share has a split basis of $4 and $6.

* * *

[T.D. 6500, 25 FR 11607, Nov. 26, 1960, as amended by T.D. 7616, 44 FR 26869, May 8, 1979; T.D. 8648, 60 FR 66079, Dec. 21, 1995; T.D. 9244, 71 FR 4270, Jan. 26, 2006; T.D. 9475, 74 FR 67053, Dec. 18, 2009; T.D. 9558, 76 FR 71879, Nov. 21, 2011]

§ 1.358–2T Allocation of basis among nonrecognition property (temporary).

(a)(1) to (a)(2)(ii) [Reserved]. For further guidance, see § 1.358–2(a)(1) through (a)(2)(ii).

(iii) For purposes of this section, if a shareholder or security holder surrenders a share of stock or a security in a transaction under the terms of section 354 (or so much of section 356 as relates to section 354) in which such shareholder or security holder receives no property or property (including property permitted by section 354 to be received without the recognition of gain or "other property" or money) with a fair market value less than that of the stock or securities surrendered in the transaction, such shareholder or security holder shall be treated as follows.

(A) First, the shareholder or security holder shall be treated as receiving the stock, securities, other property, and money actually received by the shareholder or security holder in the transaction and an amount of stock of the issuing corporation (as defined in § 1.368–1(b)) that has a value equal to the excess of the value of the stock or securities the shareholder or security holder surrendered in the transaction over the value of the stock, securities, other property, and money the shareholder or security holder actually received in the transaction. If the shareholder owns only one class of stock of the issuing corporation the receipt of which would be consistent with the economic rights associated with each class of stock of the issuing corporation, the stock deemed received by the shareholder pursuant to the previous sentence shall be stock of such class. If the shareholder owns multiple classes of stock of the issuing corporation the receipt of which would be consistent with the economic rights associated with each class of stock of the issuing corporation, the stock deemed received by the shareholder shall be stock of each such class owned by the shareholder immediately prior to the transaction, in proportion to the value of the stock of each such class owned by the shareholder immediately prior to the transaction. The basis of each share of stock or security deemed received and actually received shall be determined under the rules of this section.

(B) Second, the shareholder or security holder shall then be treated as surrendering all of its shares of stock and securities in the issuing corporation, including those shares of stock or securities held immediately prior to the transaction, those shares of stock or securities actually received in the transaction, and those shares of stock deemed received pursuant to the previous sentence, in a reorganization under section 368(a)(1)(E) in exchange for the shares of stock and securities of the issuing corporation that the shareholder or security holder actually holds immediately after the transaction. The basis of each share of stock and security deemed received in the reorganization under section 368(a)(1)(E) shall be determined under the rules of this section.

(C) If an actual shareholder of the issuing corporation is deemed to receive a nominal share of stock of the issuing corporation described in § 1.368–2(*l*), such shareholder must, after allocating and adjusting the basis of the nominal share in accordance with the rules of this section and § 1.358–1, and after adjusting the basis in the nominal share for any transfers described in § 1.368–2(*l*), designate the share of stock of the issuing corporation to which the basis, if any, of the nominal share will attach.

(a)(2)(iv) to (c), Example 14 [Reserved]. For further guidance, see § 1.358–2(a)(2)(iv) through (c), Example 14.

Example 15. (i) Facts. Each of Corporation X and Corporation Y has a single class of stock outstanding, all of which is owned by J, an individual. J acquired 100 shares of Corporation X stock on Date 1 for $1.50 each. On Date 2, Corporation Y acquires the assets of Corporation X for $100 of cash, their fair market value, in a transaction described in § 1.368–2(*l*). Pursuant to the terms of the exchange, Corporation X does not receive any Corporation Y stock. Corporation X distributes the $100 of cash to J in liquidation. Pursuant to § 1.368–2(*l*), Corporation Y will be deemed to issue a nominal share of Corporation Y stock to Corporation X in addition to the $100 of cash actually exchanged for the Corporation X assets, and Corporation X will be deemed to distribute all of the consideration to J.

J will have a basis of $50 in the nominal share of Corporation Y stock under section 358(a).

(ii) Analysis. Under paragraph (a)(2)(iii) of this section, J is the actual shareholder of Corporation Y, the issuing corporation, deemed to receive the nominal share of Corporation Y stock described in § 1.368–2(*l*). Therefore, J must designate any share of Corporation Y stock to which the basis of $50 in the nominal share of Corporation Y stock will attach.

Example 16. (i) Facts. Each of Corporation X and Corporation Y has a single class of stock outstanding, all of which is owned by Corporation P. Corporation T has a single class of stock outstanding, all of which is owned by Corporation X. The corporations do not join in the filing of a consolidated return. Corporation X acquired 100 shares of Corporation T stock on Date 1 for $1.50 each. On Date 2, Corporation Y acquires the assets of Corporation T for $100 of cash, their fair market value, in a transaction described in § 1.368–2(*l*). Pursuant to the terms of the exchange, Corporation T does not receive any Corporation Y stock. Corporation T distributes the $100 of cash to Corporation X in liquidation. Pursuant to § 1.368–2(*l*), Corporation Y will be deemed to issue a nominal share of Corporation Y stock to Corporation T in addition to the $100 of cash actually exchanged for the Corporation T assets, and Corporation T will be deemed to distribute all of the consideration to Corporation X. Corporation X will have a basis of $50 in the nominal share of Corporation Y stock under section 358(a). Corporation X will be deemed to distribute the nominal share of Corporation Y stock to Corporation P. Corporation X does not recognize the loss on the deemed distribution of the nominal share to Corporation P under section 311(a). Corporation P's basis in the nominal share is zero, its fair market value, under section 301(d).

(ii) Analysis. Corporation X is deemed to receive the nominal share of Corporation Y stock described in § 1.368–2(*l*). However, under paragraph (a)(2)(iii) of this section, Corporation X is not an actual shareholder of Corporation Y, the issuing corporation. Therefore, Corporation X cannot designate any share of Corporation Y stock to which the basis, if any, of the nominal share of Corporation Y stock will attach. Furthermore, Corporation P cannot designate a share of Corporation Y stock to which basis will attach because Corporation P receives the nominal share with a basis of zero.

* * *

[T.D. 9558, 76 FR 71879, Nov. 21, 2011]

§ 1.358–2 Allocation of basis among nonrecognition property in certain exchanges or distributions (Proposed Jan. 21, 2009).

(a) Introduction—(1) Scope. This section prescribes rules for allocating basis in the case of an exchange or distribution to which section 354, 355 or 356 applies. For rules that apply to transfers of stock and other property where the transfer of stock is described in section 351 but does not qualify as a reorganization, see § 1.358–2(g). For transfers of stock described in section 361, see § 1.358–2(h).

(2) Definitions. As used in this section the term stock means stock which is not "other property" under sections 351, 356, or 361, as applicable. The term securities means securities (including, where appropriate, fractional parts of securities) which are not "other property" under sections 356 or 361, as applicable. Stock, or securities, as the case may be, which differ either because they are in different corporations or because the rights attributable to them differ (although they are in the same corporation) are considered different classes of stock or securities, as the case may be, for purposes of this section.

(b) Exchanges to which section 354, 355, or 356 applies. If a shareholder or security holder surrenders one or more shares of stock or one or more securities in an exchange under the terms of section 354, 355 or 356, the following rules apply:

(1) In general. Except as otherwise provided in this section, the basis of each share of stock or security received in the exchange shall be the same as the basis of the share or shares of stock or security or securities (or allocable portions thereof) exchanged therefor (as adjusted under § 1.358–1).

(2) More shares of stock or securities received than surrendered. If more than one share of stock or security is received in exchange for one share of stock or one security, the basis of the share of stock or security surrendered shall be allocated to the shares of stock or securities received in proportion to the fair market value of the shares of stock or securities received.

(3) Fewer shares of stock or securities received than surrendered—(i) In general. If one share of stock or security is received in exchange for more than one share of stock or security or if a fraction of a share of stock or security is received, then the basis of the shares of stock or securities surrendered must be allocated to the shares of stock or securities (or allocable portions thereof) received in a manner that reflects, to the greatest extent possible, that a share of stock or security received is received in respect of shares of stock or securities that were acquired on the same date and at the same price. To the extent it is not possible to allocate basis in this manner, the basis of the shares of stock or securities surrendered must be allocated to the shares of stock or securities (or allocable portions thereof) received in a manner that minimizes the disparity in the holding periods of the surrendered shares of stock or securities whose basis is allocated to any particular share of stock or security received.

(ii) Surrendered shares of stock or securities acquired on different dates or at different prices. If a share of stock or a security is received in exchange for more than one share of stock or security and such shares of stock or securities were acquired on different dates or at different prices, the share of stock or security received shall be divided into segments based on the relative fair market values of the shares of stock or securities surrendered in exchange for such share or security. Each segment shall have a basis determined under the rules of this section and a corresponding holding period.

(4) "Other property," money, or more than one class of stock or securities received. If a shareholder or security holder receives shares of stock or securities of more than one class, or receives "other property" or money in addition to shares of stock or securities, the rules of §§ 1.354–1(d)(1) and 1.355–1(e)(1) apply for purposes of applying the rules of this section.

(5) Pro rata exchanges to which section 355 or section 356(b) applies. If a shareholder or security holder surrenders stock in distributing (as defined in § 1.355–1(b)) for only stock in controlled and the receipt of the controlled stock would be treated, within the meaning of section 302(d), as a distribution of property to which section 301 applies if the controlled stock received were money or other property, then the basis of the shares received shall be determined under the rules of paragraph (c) of this section and not the rules of this paragraph (b). The rules of paragraph (c) and not the rules of this paragraph (b) also apply to distributions subject to section 356(b).

(c) Distributions to which section 355 applies. If a shareholder or security holder receives one or more shares of stock or one or more securities in a distribution under section 355 (or so much of section 356 as relates to section 355), the following rules apply:

(1) In general. Except as otherwise provided in this section, the basis of each share of stock or security of the distributing corporation (as defined in § 1.355–1(b)), as adjusted under § 1.358–1, shall be allocated between the share of stock or security of the distributing corporation with respect to which the distribution is made and the share or shares of stock or security or securities (or allocable portions thereof) received in proportion to their fair market values.

(2) Fewer shares of stock or securities received than with respect to which distributed—(i) In general. If one share of stock or security is received with respect to more than one share of stock or security or if a fraction of a share of stock or security is received, then the basis of each share of stock or security of the distributing corporation must be allocated to the shares of stock or securities (or allocable portions thereof) received in a manner that reflects that, to the greatest extent possible, a share of stock or security received is received with respect to shares of stock or securities acquired on the same date and at the same price. To the extent it is not possible to allocate basis in this manner, the basis of each share of stock or security of the distributing corporation must be allocated to the shares of stock or securities (or allocable portions thereof) received in a manner that minimizes the disparity in the holding periods of the shares of stock or securities with respect to which such shares of stock or securities are received.

(ii) Distribution upon shares of stock or securities acquired on different dates or at different prices. If a share of stock or a security is received with respect to more than one share of stock or security and such shares or securities were acquired on different dates or at different prices, the share of stock or security received shall be divided into segments based on the relative fair market values of the shares of stock or securities with respect to which the share of stock or security is received. Each segment shall have a basis determined under the rules of this section and a corresponding holding period.

(3) "Other property," money, or more than one class of stock or securities received. If a shareholder or security holder receives shares of stock or securities of more than one class, or receives "other property" or money in addition to stock or securities, the rules of § 1.355–1(e)(1) apply for purposes of applying the rules of this section as though the distribution were an exchange.

(d) Reorganizations in which stock is deemed received. For purposes of this section, if a shareholder or security holder surrenders a share of stock or a security in a transaction under the terms of section 354 (or so much of section 356 as relates to section 354) in which such shareholder or security holder receives no property or receives property (including property permitted by section 354 to be received without the recognition of gain or "other property" or money) with a fair market value less than that of the stock or securities surrendered in the transaction, such shareholder or security holder shall be treated as provided in paragraphs (1) and (2) of this paragraph (d).

(1) Step one: deemed issuance. First, the shareholder or security holder shall be treated as receiving the stock, securities, other property, and money actually received by the shareholder or security holder in the transaction and an amount of stock of the issuing corporation (as defined in § 1.368–1(b)) that has a value equal to the excess of the value of the stock or securities the shareholder or security holder surrendered in the transaction over the value of the stock, securities, other property, and money the shareholder or security holder actually received in the transaction. If the shareholder owns only one class of stock of the issuing corporation the receipt of which would be consistent with the economic rights associated with each class of stock of the issuing corporation, the stock deemed received by the shareholder pursuant to the previous sentence shall be stock of such class. If the shareholder owns multiple classes of stock of the issuing corporation the receipt of which would be consistent with the economic rights associated with each class of stock of the issuing corporation, the stock deemed received by the shareholder shall be stock of each such class owned by the shareholder immediately prior to the transaction, in proportion to the value of the stock of each such class owned by the shareholder immediately prior to the transaction. The basis of each share of stock or security deemed received and actually received shall be determined under the rules of this section.

(2) Step two: deemed section 368(a)(1)(E) exchange. Second, the shareholder or security holder shall then be treated as surrendering all of its shares of stock and securities in the issuing corporation, including those shares of stock or securities held immediately prior to the transaction, those shares of stock or securities actually received in the transaction, and those shares of stock deemed received pursuant to paragraph (d)(1) of this section, in a reorganization under section 368(a)(1)(E) in exchange for the shares of stock and securities of the issuing corporation that the shareholder or security holder actually holds immediately after the transaction. The basis of each share of stock and security deemed received in the reorganization under section 368(a)(1)(E) shall be determined under the rules of this section.

(e) Designating which stock or securities were received for, or with respect to, the stock or securities surrendered or distributed upon—(1) In general. If a shareholder or security holder that purchased or acquired shares of stock or securities in a corporation on different dates or at different prices exchanges such shares of stock or securities under the terms of section 354, 355, or 356, or receives a distribution of shares of stock or securities under the terms of section 355 (or so much of section 356 as relates to section 355), and the shareholder or security holder is not able to identify which particular share of stock or security (or allocable portion of a share of stock or security) is received (or deemed received) in exchange for, or with respect to, a particular share of stock or security, the shareholder or security holder may designate subject to the limitations of this section, which share of stock or security is received in exchange for, or with respect to, a particular share of stock or security, provided that such designation is consistent with the terms of the exchange or distribution (or an exchange deemed to have occurred pursuant to paragraph (d) of this section), and the other rules of this section. The designation will be binding for purposes of determining the Federal tax consequences of any sale or transfer of, or distribution with respect to, the shares or securities received.

(2) Timing for designation—(i) In exchanges under section 354 or 356. In the case of an exchange under the terms of section 354 or 356 (including a deemed exchange as a result of the application of paragraph (d) of this section), the designation must be made on or before the first date on which the basis of a share of stock or a security received (or deemed received in the reorganization under section 368(a)(1)(E) in the case of a transaction to which paragraph (d) of this section applies) is relevant. The basis of the shares or securities received in an exchange under the terms of section 354 or section 356, for example, is relevant when such shares or securities are sold or otherwise transferred.

(ii) In exchanges or distributions under section 355. In the case of an exchange or distribution under the terms of section 355 (or so much of section 356 as relates to section 355), the designation must be made on or before the first date on which the basis of a share of stock or a security of the distributing corporation or the controlled corporation (as defined in § 1.355–1(b)) is relevant.

(3) Failure to designate. If the shareholder fails to make a designation in a case in which the shareholder is not able to identify which share of stock is received in exchange for, or with respect to, a particular share of stock, then the shareholder will not be able to identify which shares are sold or transferred for purposes of determining the basis of property sold or transferred under section 1012 and § 1.1012–1(c) and, instead, will be treated as selling or transferring the share received in respect of the earliest share purchased or acquired.

(f) Applicability of section to certain overlap situations—(1) Exchanges described in both section 1036 and section 354 or 356. The rules of paragraphs (a) through (e) of this section shall apply to determine the basis of a share of stock or security received by a shareholder or security holder in an exchange described in both section 1036 and section 354 or 356.

(2) Exchanges described in both section 351 and section 354 or 356. The rules of paragraphs (a) through (e) of this section shall apply to determine the basis of a share of stock or security received by a shareholder or security holder in an exchange described in both section 351 and section 354 or 356, unless liabilities of the shareholder or security holder are assumed in connection with the exchange.

(g) Section 351 exchanges—(1) In general. Except as provided in paragraph (g)(2) of this section, if in an exchange to which section 351 applies property is transferred to a corporation and the transferor receives more than one share of stock, then the aggregate basis of the property transferred (as adjusted under § 1.358–1) shall be allocated among all of the shares of stock received in proportion to the fair market values of each share of stock.

(2) Stock and property transferred in an exchange without a liability assumption. If in an exchange to which section 351 applies stock or stock and property is transferred to a corporation and no liability is assumed by the transferee in the exchange, then the basis of the stock transferred (as adjusted under § 1.358–1) shall be allocated pursuant to paragraphs (b)(1) through (b)(3) of this section. Such rules also apply to other property, money or more than one class of stock or securities received.

(3) Transactions in which stock is deemed received. For purposes of this paragraph (g), if a shareholder transfers property to a corporation in a transaction to which section 351 applies, and such shareholder receives no property or property (including property permitted by section 351 to be received without the recognition of gain or "other property" or money) in such corporation with a fair market value less than that of the property transferred in the transaction, such shareholder shall be treated as provided in paragraphs (3)(i) and (ii) of this paragraph (g).

(i) Step one: deemed issuance. First, the shareholder shall be treated as receiving the stock, other property, and money actually received by the shareholder in the transaction and an amount of stock of the transferee corporation that has a value equal to the excess of the value of the property the shareholder transferred in the transaction over the value of the stock, other property, and money the shareholder actually received in the transaction. If the shareholder owns only one class of stock of the transferee corporation the receipt of which would be consistent with the economic rights associated with each class of stock of the transferee corporation, the stock deemed received by the shareholder pursuant to the previous sentence shall be stock of such class. If the shareholder owns multiple classes of stock of the transferee corporation the receipt of which would be consistent with the economic rights associated with each class of stock of the transferee corporation, the stock deemed received by the shareholder shall be stock of each such class owned by the shareholder immediately prior to the transaction, in proportion to the value of the stock of each such class owned by the shareholder immediately prior to the transaction.

(ii) Step two: deemed section 368(a)(1)(E) exchange. Second, the shareholder shall then be treated as surrendering all of its shares of stock in the transferee corporation, including those shares of stock held immediately prior to the transaction, those shares of stock actually received in the transaction, and those shares of stock deemed received pursuant to paragraph (3)(i) of this paragraph (g), in a reorganization under section 368(a)(1)(E) in exchange for the shares of stock of the transferee corporation that the shareholder actually holds immediately after the transaction. The basis of each share of stock deemed received in the reorganization under section 368(a)(1)(E) shall be determined under the rules of this section.

(h) Section 361 exchanges. If in an exchange to which section 361 applies property is transferred to a corporation and the transferor receives stock or securities of more than one class or receives both stock and securities, then the basis of the property transferred (as adjusted under § 1.358–1) shall be allocated among all of the stock and securities received in proportion to the fair market values of the stock of each class and the securities of each class.

(i) Examples. The application of this section is illustrated by the following examples:

Example 1. More shares of stock received than surrendered. (i) Facts. J, an individual, acquired 20 shares of Corporation X stock on Date 1 for $3 each and 10 shares of Corporation X stock on Date 2 for $6 each. On Date 3, Corporation Y acquires the assets of Corporation X in a reorganization under section 368(a)(1)(A). Pursuant to the terms of the plan of reorganization, J receives 2 shares of Corporation Y stock in exchange for each share of Corporation X stock. Therefore, J receives 60 shares of Corporation Y stock. Pursuant to section 354, J recognizes no gain or loss on the exchange. J is not able to identify which shares of Corporation Y stock are received in exchange for each share of Corporation X stock.

(ii) Analysis. Under paragraph (b)(2) of this section, J has 40 shares of Corporation Y stock each of which has a basis of $1.50 and is treated as having been acquired on Date 1 and 20 shares of Corporation Y stock each of which has a basis of $3 and is treated as having been acquired on Date 2. Under paragraph (e) of this section, on or before the date on which the basis of a share of Corporation Y stock received becomes relevant, J may designate which of the shares of corporation Y stock have a basis of $1.50 and which have a basis of $3.

Example 2. More shares of stock received than surrendered. (i) Facts. The facts are the same as in Example 1, except that instead of receiving 2 shares of Corporation Y stock in exchange for each share of Corporation X stock, J receives 1 1/2 shares of Corporation Y stock in exchange for each share of Corporation X stock. Therefore, J receives 45 shares of corporation Y stock. Again, J is not able to identify which shares (or portions of shares) of Corporation Y stock are received in exchange for each share of Corporation X stock.

(ii) Analysis. Under paragraph (b)(2) of this section, J has 30 shares of Corporation Y stock each of which has a basis of $2 and is treated as having been acquired on Date 1 and 15 shares of Corporation Y stock each of which has a basis of $4 and is treated as having been acquired on Date 2. Under paragraph (e) of this section, on or before the date on which the basis of a share of Corporation Y stock received becomes relevant, J may designate which of the shares of Corporation Y stock received have a basis of $2 and which have a basis of $4.

Example 3. More than one class of stock received. (i) Facts. J, an individual, acquired 10 shares of Class A stock of Corporation X on Date 1 for $3 each, 10 shares of Class A stock of Corporation X on Date 2 for $9 each, and 10 shares of Class B stock of Corporation X on Date 3 for $3 each. On Date 4, J surrenders all of J's shares of Class A stock in exchange for 20 shares of new Class C stock and 20 shares of new Class D stock in a reorganization under section 368(a)(1)(E). Pursuant to section 354, J recognizes no gain or loss on the exchange. On the date of the exchange, the fair market value of each share of Class A stock is $6, the fair market value of each share of Class C stock is $2, and the fair market value of each share of Class D stock is $4. The terms of the exchange do not specify that shares of Class C stock or shares of Class D stock of Corporation X are received in exchange for particular shares of Class A stock of Corporation X.

(ii) Analysis. Under paragraph (b)(4) of this section, because the terms of the exchange do not specify that shares of Class C stock or shares of Class D stock of Corporation X are received in exchange for particular shares of Class A stock of Corporation X, a pro rata portion of the shares of Class C stock and shares of Class D stock received will be treated as received in exchange for each share of Class A stock based on the fair market value of the surrendered shares of Class A stock. Therefore, J is treated as receiving one share of Class C stock and one share of Class D stock in exchange for each share of Class A stock. Under paragraph (b)(2) of this section, J has 10 shares of Class C stock, each of which has a basis of $1 and is treated as having been acquired on Date 1 and 10 shares of Class C stock, each of which has a basis of $3 and is treated as having been acquired on Date 2. In addition, J has 10 shares of Class D stock, each of which has a basis of $2 and is treated as having been acquired on Date 1 and 10 shares of Class D stock, each of which has a basis of $6 and is treated as having been acquired on Date 2. J's basis in each share of Class B stock remains $3. Under paragraph (e) of this section, on or before the date on which the basis of a share of Class C stock or Class D stock received becomes relevant, J may designate which of the shares of Class C stock have a basis of $1 and which have a basis of $3, and which of the shares of Class D stock have a basis of $2 and which have a basis of $6.

Example 4. Money received in addition to stock. (i) Facts. J, an individual, acquired 10 shares of stock of Corporation X on Date 1 for $2 each (Block 1), 10 shares of stock of Corporation X on Date 2 for $4 each (Block 2), and 20 shares of stock of Corporation X on Date 3 for $6 each (Block 3). On Date 4, Corporation Y acquires the assets of Corporation X in a reorganization under section 368(a)(1)(A). Pursuant to the terms of the plan of reorganization, J surrenders all of J's shares of Corporation X stock for 40 shares of Corporation Y stock and $200 of cash. The distribution of $200 of cash does not have the effect of a distribution of a dividend. On the date of the exchange, the fair market value of each share of stock of Corporation X is $10, and the fair market value of each share of Corporation Y stock is $5. The terms of the exchange do not specify that shares of Corporation Y stock or cash are received in exchange for particular shares of stock of Corporation X.

(ii) Analysis. Under paragraph (b)(4) of this section and under § 1.356–1(b), because the terms of the exchange do not specify that shares of Corporation Y stock or cash are received in exchange for particular shares of stock of Corporation X, a pro rata portion of the shares of Corporation Y stock and cash received will be treated as received in exchange for each share of stock of Corporation X surrendered based on the fair market value of such stock. Therefore, J is treated as receiving one share of Corporation Y stock and $5 of cash in exchange for each share of stock of Corporation X. J realizes a gain of $80 on the exchange of Block 1, $50 of which is recognized under § 1.356–1(a). J realizes a gain of $60 of the exchange of Block 2, $50 of which is recognized under § 1.356–1(a). J realizes a gain of $80 on the exchange of the Block 3 shares of stock of Corporation X, all of which is recognized under § 1.356–1(a). Under paragraph (b)(1) of this section, J has 10 shares of Corporation Y stock, each of which has a basis of $2 and is treated as having been acquired on Date 1, 10 shares of Corporation Y stock, each of which has a basis of $4 and is treated as having been acquired on Date 2, and 20 shares of Corporation Y stock, each of which has a basis of $5 and is treated as having been acquired on Date 3. Under paragraph (e) of this section, on or before the date on which the basis of a share of Corporation Y stock received becomes relevant, J may designate which of the shares of Corporation Y stock received have a basis of $2, which have a basis of $4, and which have a basis of $5.

Example 5. Money received in addition to stock. (i) Facts. The facts are the same as in Example 4, except that the terms of the plan of reorganization specify that J receives 40 shares of stock of Corporation Y in exchange for J's Block 1 and Block 2 shares of stock of Corporation X and $200 of cash in exchange for J's Block 3 shares of stock of Corporation X.

(ii) Analysis. Under paragraph (b)(4) of this section and under § 1.356–1(b), because the terms of the exchange specify that J receives 40 shares of stock of Corporation Y in exchange for J's Block 1 and Block 2 shares of stock of Corporation X and $200 of cash in exchange for J's Block 3 shares of stock of Corporation X and such terms are economically reasonable and the distribution is not dividend equivalent, such terms control. J realizes a gain of $80 on the exchange of Block 1, none of which is recognized under section 354. J realizes a gain of $60 on the exchange of Block 2, none of which is recognized under section 354. J realizes a gain of $80 on the exchange of the Block 3 shares of stock of Corporation X, all of which is recognized under section 302(a). Under paragraph (b)(2) of this section, J has 20 shares of Corporation Y stock, each of which has a basis of $1 and is treated as having been acquired on Date 1, and 20 shares of Corporation Y stock, each of which has a basis of $2 and is treated as having been acquired on Date 2. Under paragraph (e) of this section, on or before the date on which the basis of a share of Corporation Y stock received becomes relevant, J may designate which of the shares of Corporation Y stock received have a basis of $1 and which have a basis of $2.

Example 6. Stock and securities received as nonrecognition property. (i) Facts. J, an individual, acquired 10 shares of stock of Corporation X on Date 1 for $2 each, and a security issued by Corporation X to J on Date 2 with a principal amount of $100 and a basis of $100. On Date 3, Corporation Y acquires the assets of Corporation X in a reorganization under section 368(a)(1)(A). Pursuant to the terms of the plan of reorganization, J surrenders all of J's shares of Corporation X stock in exchange for 10 shares of Corporation Y stock and surrenders J's Corporation X security in exchange for a Corporation Y security. The distribution of neither the Y stock nor the Y security has the effect of a distribution of a dividend. On the date of the exchange, the fair market value of each share of stock of Corporation X is $10, the fair market value of J's Corporation X security is $100, the fair market value of each share of Corporation Y stock is $10, and the fair market value and principal amount of the Corporation Y security received by J is $100.

(ii) Analysis. Under paragraph (b)(4) of this section and under § 1.354–1(d), because the terms of the exchange specify that J receives 10 shares of stock of Corporation Y in exchange for J's shares of Class A stock of Corporation X and a Corporation Y security in exchange for its Corporation X security and such terms are economically reasonable, such terms control. Pursuant to section 354, J recognizes no gain on either exchange. Under paragraph (b)(1) of this section, J has 10 shares of Corporation Y stock, each of which has a basis of $2 and is treated as having been acquired on Date 1, and a security that has a basis of $100 and is treated as having been acquired on Date 2.

Example 7. Fewer shares of stock received than surrendered. (i) Facts. J, an individual, acquired 10 shares of Corporation X stock on Date 1 for $2 each and 10 shares of Corporation X stock on Date 2 for $5 each. On Date 3, Corporation Y acquires the stock of Corporation X in a reorganization under section 368(a)(1)(B). Pursuant to the terms of the plan of reorganization, J receives one share of Corporation Y stock in exchange for every 2 shares of Corporation X stock. Pursuant to section 354, J recognizes no gain or loss on the exchange. J is not able to identify which portion of each share of Corporation Y stock is received in exchange for each share of Corporation X stock.

(ii) Analysis. Under paragraph (b)(3) of this section, J has 5 shares of Corporation Y stock each of which has a basis of $4 and is treated as having been acquired on Date 1 and 5 shares of Corporation Y stock each of which has a basis of $10 and is treated as having been acquired on Date 2. Under paragraph (e) of this section, on or before the date on which the basis of a share of Corporation Y stock received becomes relevant, J may designate which of the shares of Corporation Y stock received have a basis of $4 and which have a basis of $10.

* * *

Example 12. Designation of stock surrendered and received. (i) Facts. J, an individual, acquired 20 shares of Corporation X stock on Date 1 for $2 each and 20 shares of Corporation X stock on Date 2 for $4 each. Corporation X has 80 shares of stock outstanding. Corporation X owns 40 shares of stock of Corporation Y, which represents all of the outstanding stock of Corporation Y. The fair market value of the stock of Corporation X is $80. The fair market value of the stock of Corporation Y is $40. Corporation X distributes all of the stock of Corporation Y in a transaction to which section 355 applies. In the transaction, J surrenders 20 shares of stock of Corporation X in exchange for 20 shares of stock of Corporation Y. J retains 20 shares of Corporation X stock. Pursuant to section 355, J recognizes no gain or loss on the receipt of the shares of Corporation Y stock. J is not able to identify which shares of Corporation X stock are surrendered. In addition, J is not able to identify which shares of Corporation Y stock are received in exchange for each surrendered share of Corporation X. In addition, the receipt of Y stock is not dividend equivalent.

(ii) Analysis. Under paragraph (b)(1) of this section, J has 20 shares of Corporation Y stock each of which is treated as received in exchange for one share of Corporation X stock. The basis of the 20 shares of Corporation X stock that are retained by J will remain unchanged. Under paragraph (e) of this section, on or before the date on which the basis of a share of Corporation X or Corporation Y stock becomes relevant, J may designate which shares of Corporation X stock J surrendered in the exchange and which share of the Corporation Y stock received is received for each share of Corporation X stock surrendered. Therefore, it is possible that a share of Corporation Y stock would have a basis of $2 and be treated as having been acquired on Date 1, or would have a basis of $4 and be treated as having been acquired on Date 2.

Example 13. Surrendered shares of stock or securities acquired on different dates or at different prices. (i) Facts. J, an individual, acquired 10 shares of Corporation X stock on Date 1 for $3 each, 10 shares of Corporation X stock on Date 2 for $18 each, 10 shares of Corporation X stock on Date 3 for $6 each, and 10 shares of Corporation X stock on Date 4 for $9 each. On Date 5, Corporation Y acquires the assets of Corporation X in a reorganization under section 368(a)(1)(A). Pursuant to the terms of the plan of reorganization, J receives a 3/4 share of Corporation Y stock in exchange for each share of Corporation X stock. Therefore, J receives 30 shares of Corporation Y stock. Pursuant to section 354, J recognizes no gain or loss on the exchange. J is not able to identify which shares of Corporation Y stock are received in exchange for each share (or portions of shares) of Corporation X stock.

(ii) Analysis. Under paragraph (b)(3) of this section, J has 7 shares of Corporation Y stock each of which has a basis of $4 and is treated as having been acquired on Date 1, 7 shares of Corporation Y stock each of which has a basis of $24 and is treated as having been acquired on Date 2, 7 shares of Corporation Y stock each of which has a basis of $8 and is treated as having been acquired on Date 3, and 7 shares of Corporation Y stock each of which has a basis of $12 and is treated as having been acquired on Date 4. In addition, J has two shares of Corporation Y stock, each of which is divided into two equal segments under paragraph (b)(3) of this section. The first of those two shares has one segment with a basis of $2 that is treated as having been acquired on Date 1 and a second segment with a basis of $12 that is treated as having been acquired on Date 2. The second of those two shares has one segment with a basis of $4 that is treated as having been acquired on Date 3 and a second segment with a basis of $6 that is treated as having been acquired on Date 4. Under paragraph (e) of this section, on or before the date on which a share of Corporation Y stock received becomes relevant, J may designate which of the shares of Corporation Y stock have a basis of $4, which have a basis of $24, which have a basis of $8, which have a basis of $12, and which share has a split basis of $2 and $12, and which share has a split basis of $4 and $6.

* * *

Example 16. Exchange described in section 351 in which only stock is received. (i) Facts. J transfers Asset I, Asset II, and 50 shares of Corporation X stock in exchange for 110 shares of Corporation Y in an exchange to which section 351 applies. At the time of the exchange, Asset I has a fair market value of $220 and a basis of $400, Asset II has a fair market value of $330 and a basis of $200, and the 50 shares of Corporation X stock each have a fair market value of $22 ($550 total) and a basis of $10 ($250 total). The fair market value of each share of Corporation Y stock is $10.

(ii) Analysis. Pursuant to section 351(a), J recognizes no gain or loss on the exchange. Under paragraph (g)(2) of this section, J has 55 shares of Corporation Y stock each of which has a basis of $10.91 ($600 total, the aggregate basis of Asset I and Asset II). Under paragraph (g)(2) of this section, J has 55 shares of Corporation Y stock each of which has a basis of $4.55 ($250 total).

Example 17. Exchange described in section 351 in which "other property" is received. (i) Facts. The facts are the same as Example 1, except J receives 100 shares of Corporation Y stock and $100 in the exchange.

(ii) Analysis. Pursuant to section 351(b), J recognizes gain, but no loss, on the exchange, but not in excess of the amount of money received. Under § 1.351–2, J realizes a loss of $180 on Asset I, none of which is recognized, a gain of $130 on Asset II, $30 of which is recognized, and a gain of $300 on shares of Corporation X stock, $50 of which is recognized. Under paragraph (g)(2) of this section, J has 50 shares of Corporation Y stock each of which has a basis of $11.60 ($580 total), and 50 shares of Corporation Y stock each of which has a basis of $5.00 ($250 total).

* * *

§ 1.358–3 Treatment of assumption of liabilities.

(a) For purposes of section 358, where a party to the exchange assumes a liability of a distributee or acquires from him property subject to a liability, the amount of such liability is to be treated as money received by the distributee upon the exchange, whether or not the assumption of liabilities resulted in a recognition of gain or loss to the taxpayer under the law applicable to the year in which the exchange was made.

(b) The application of paragraph (a) of this section may be illustrated by the following examples:

Example (1). A, an individual, owns property with an adjusted basis of $100,000 on which there is a purchase money mortgage of $25,000. On December 1, 1945, A organizes Corporation X to which he transfers the property in exchange for all the stock of Corporation X and the assumption by Corporation X of the mortgage. The capital stock of the Corporation X has a fair market value of $150,000. Under sections 351 and 357, no gain or loss is recognized to A. The basis in A's hands of the stock of Corporation X is $75,000, computed as follows:

Adjusted basis of property transferred	$100,000
Less: Amount of money received (amount of liabilities assumed)	– 25,000
Basis of Corporation X stock to A	75,000

Example (2). A, an individual, owns property with an adjusted basis of $25,000 on which there is a mortgage of $50,000. On December 1, 1954, A organizes Corporation X to which he transfers the property in exchange for all the stock of Corporation X and the assumption by Corporation X of the mortgage. The stock of Corporation X has a fair market value of $50,000. Under sections 351 and 357, gain is recognized to A in the amount of $25,000. The basis in A's hands of the stock of Corporation X is zero, computed as follows:

Adjusted basis of property transferred	$25,000
Less: Amount of money received (amount of liabilities)	− 50,000
Plus: Amount of gain recognized to taxpayer	25,000
Basis of Corporation X stock to A	0

[T.D. 6500, 25 FR 11607, Nov. 26, 1960]

§ 1.358–4 Exceptions.

(a) Plan of reorganization adopted after October 22, 1968. In the case of a plan of reorganization adopted after October 22, 1968, section 358 does not apply in determining the basis of property acquired by a corporation in connection with such reorganization by the exchange of its stock or securities (or by the exchange of stock or securities of a corporation which is in control of the acquiring corporation) as the consideration in whole or in part for the transfer of the property to it. See section 362 and the regulations pertaining to that section for rules relating to basis to corporations of property acquired in such cases.

* * *

[T.D. 6500, 25 FR 11607, Nov. 26, 1960, as amended by T.D. 7422, 41 FR 26569, June 28, 1976]

§ 1.358–5 Special rules for assumption of liabilities.

(a) In general. Section 358(h)(2)(B) does not apply to an exchange occurring on or after May 9, 2008.

* * *

[T.D. 9397, 73 FR 26321, May 9, 2008]

§ 1.358–6 Stock basis in certain triangular reorganizations.

(a) Scope. This section provides rules for computing the basis of a controlling corporation in the stock of a controlled corporation as the result of certain reorganizations involving the stock of the controlling corporation as described in paragraph (b) of this section. The rules of this section are in addition to rules under other provisions of the Internal Revenue Code and principles of law. See, e.g., section 1001 for the recognition of gain or loss by the controlled corporation on the exchange of property for the assets or stock of a target corporation in a reorganization described in section 368.

(b) Triangular reorganizations—(1) Nomenclature. For purposes of this section—

(i) P is a corporation—

(A) That is a party to a reorganization,

(B) That is in control (within the meaning of section 368(c)) of another party to the reorganization, and

(C) Whose stock is transferred pursuant to the reorganization.

(ii) S is a corporation—

(A) That is a party to the reorganization, and

(B) That is controlled by P.

(iii) T is a corporation that is another party to the reorganization.

(2) Definitions of triangular reorganizations. This section applies to the following reorganizations (which are referred to collectively as triangular reorganizations):

(i) Forward triangular merger. A forward triangular merger is a statutory merger of T and S, with S surviving, that qualifies as a reorganization under section 368(a)(1)(A) or (G) by reason of the application of section 368(a)(2)(D).

(ii) Triangular C reorganization. A triangular C reorganization is an acquisition by S of substantially all of T's assets in exchange for P stock in a transaction that qualifies as a reorganization under section 368(a)(1)(C).

(iii) Reverse triangular merger. A reverse triangular merger is a statutory merger of S and T, with T surviving, that qualifies as a reorganization under section 368(a)(1)(A) by reason of the application of section 368(a)(2)(E).

(iv) Triangular B reorganization. A triangular B reorganization is an acquisition by S of T stock in exchange for P stock in a transaction that qualifies as a reorganization under section 368(a)(1)(B).

* * *

(c) General rules. Subject to the special rule provided in paragraph (d) of this section, P's basis in the stock of S or T, as applicable, as a result of a triangular reorganization, is adjusted under the following rules—

(1) Forward triangular merger or triangular C reorganization—(i) In general. In a forward triangular merger or a triangular C reorganization, P's basis in its § stock is adjusted as if—

(A) P acquired the T assets acquired by S in the reorganization (and P assumed any liabilities which § assumed or to which the T assets acquired by S were subject) directly from T in a transaction in which P's basis in the T assets was determined under section 362(b); and

(B) P transferred the T assets (and liabilities which S assumed or to which the T assets acquired by S were subject) to S in a transaction in which P's basis in S stock was determined under section 358.

(ii) Limitation. If, in applying section 358, the amount of T liabilities assumed by S or to which the T assets acquired by S are subject equals or exceeds T's aggregate adjusted basis in its assets, the amount of the adjustment under paragraph (c)(1)(i) of this section is zero. P recognizes no gain under section 357(c) as a result of a triangular reorganization.

(2) Reverse triangular merger—(i) In general—(A) Treated as a forward triangular merger. Except as otherwise provided in this paragraph (c)(2), P's basis in its T stock acquired in a reverse triangular merger equals its basis in its S stock immediately before the transaction adjusted as if T had merged into S in a forward triangular merger to which paragraph (c)(1) of this section applies.

(B) Allocable share. If P acquires less than all of the T stock in the transaction, the basis adjustment described in paragraph (c)(2)(i)(A) of this section is reduced in proportion to the percentage of T stock not acquired in the transaction. The percentage of T stock not acquired in the transaction is determined by taking into account the fair market value of all classes of T stock.

(C) Special rule if P owns T stock before the transaction. Solely for purposes of paragraphs (c)(2)(i)(A) and (B) of this section, if P owns T stock before the transaction, P may treat that stock as acquired in the transaction or not, without regard to the form of the transaction.

(ii) Reverse triangular merger that qualifies as a section 351 transfer or section 368(a)(1)(B) reorganization. Notwithstanding paragraph (c)(2)(i) of this section, if a reorganization qualifies as both a reverse triangular merger and as a section 351 transfer or as both a reverse triangular merger and a reorganization under section 368(a)(1)(B), P can—

(A) Determine the basis in its T stock as if paragraph (c)(2)(i) of this section applies; or

(B) Determine the basis in the T stock acquired as if P acquired such stock from the former T shareholders in a transaction in which P's basis in the T stock was determined under section 362(b).

(3) Triangular B reorganization. In a triangular B reorganization, P's basis in its S stock is adjusted as if—

(i) P acquired the T stock acquired by S in the reorganization directly from the T shareholders in a transaction in which P's basis in the T stock was determined under section 362(b); and

(ii) P transferred the T stock to S in a transaction in which P's basis in its S stock was determined under section 358.

(4) Examples. The rules of this paragraph (c) are illustrated by the following examples. For purposes of these examples, P, S, and T are domestic corporations, P and S do not file consolidated returns, P owns all of the only class of S stock, the P stock exchanged in the transaction satisfies the requirements of the applicable triangular reorganization provisions, and the facts set forth the only corporate activity.

Example 1. Forward triangular merger. (a) Facts. T has assets with an aggregate basis of $60 and fair market value of $100 and no liabilities. Pursuant to a plan, P forms S with $5 cash (which S retains), and T merges into S. In the merger, the T shareholders receive P stock worth $100 in exchange for their T stock. The transaction is a reorganization to which sections 368(a)(1)(A) and (a)(2)(D) apply.

(b) Basis adjustment. Under § 1.358–6(c)(1), P's $5 basis in its S stock is adjusted as if P acquired the T assets acquired by S in the reorganization directly from T in a transaction in which P's basis in the T assets was determined under section 362(b). Under section 362(b), P would have an aggregate basis of $60 in the T assets. P is then treated as if it transferred the T assets to S in a transaction in which P's basis in the S stock was determined under section 358. Under section 358, P's $5 basis in its S stock would be increased by the $60 basis in the T assets deemed transferred. Consequently, P has a $65 basis in its S stock as a result of the reorganization.

(c) Use of pre-existing S. The facts are the same as paragraph (a) of this Example 1, except that S is an operating company with substantial assets that has been in existence for several years. P has a $110 basis in the S stock. Under § 1.358–6(c)(1), P's $110 basis in its S stock is increased by the $60 basis in the T assets deemed transferred. Consequently, P has a $170 basis in its S stock as a result of the reorganization.

(d) Mixed consideration. The facts are the same as paragraph (a) of this Example 1, except that the T shareholders receive P stock worth $80 and $20 cash from P. Under section 358, P's $5 basis in its S stock is increased by the $60 basis in the T assets deemed transferred. Consequently, P has a $65 basis in its S stock as a result of the reorganization.

(e) Liabilities. The facts are the same as paragraph (a) of this Example 1, except that T's assets are subject to

$50 of liabilities, and the T shareholders receive $50 of P stock in exchange for their T stock. Under section 358, P's basis in its S stock is increased by the $60 basis in the T assets deemed transferred and decreased by the $50 of liabilities to which the T assets acquired by S are subject. Consequently, P has a net basis adjustment of $10, and a $15 basis in its S stock as a result of the reorganization.

(f) Liabilities in excess of basis. The facts are the same as in paragraph (a) of this Example 1, except that T's assets are subject to liabilities of $90, and the T shareholders receive $10 of P stock in exchange for their T stock in the reorganization. Under § 1.358–6(c)(1)(ii), the adjustment under § 1.358–6(c) is zero if the amount of the liabilities which S assumed or to which the T assets acquired by S are subject exceeds the aggregate adjusted basis in T's assets. Consequently, P has no adjustment in its S stock, and P has a $5 basis in its S stock as a result of the reorganization.

Example 2. Reverse triangular merger. (a) Facts. T has assets with an aggregate basis of $60 and a fair market value of $100 and no liabilities. P has a $110 basis in its S stock. Pursuant to a plan, S merges into T with T surviving. In the merger, the T shareholders receive $10 cash from P and P stock worth $90 in exchange for their T stock. The transaction is a reorganization to which sections 368(a)(1)(A) and (a)(2)(E) apply.

(b) Basis adjustment. Under § 1.358–6(c)(2)(i)(A), P's basis in the T stock acquired is P's $110 basis in its S stock before the transaction, adjusted as if T had merged into S in a forward triangular merger to which § 1.358–6(c)(1) applies. In such a case, P's $110 basis in its S stock before the transaction would have been increased by the $60 basis of the T assets deemed transferred. Consequently, P has a $170 basis in its T stock immediately after the transaction.

(c) Reverse triangular merger that also qualifies under section 368(a)(1)(B). The facts relating to T are the same as in paragraph (a) of this Example 2. P, however, forms S pursuant to the plan of reorganization. The T shareholders receive $100 worth of P stock (and no cash) in exchange for their T stock. The T shareholders have an aggregate basis in their T stock of $85 immediately before the reorganization. The reorganization qualifies as both a reverse triangular merger and a reorganization under section 368(a)(1)(B). Under § 1.358–6(c)(2)(ii), P may determine its basis in its T stock either as if § 1.358–6(c)(2)(i) applied to the T stock acquired, or as if P acquired the T stock from the former T shareholders in a transaction in which P's basis in the T stock was determined under section 362(b). Accordingly, P may determine a basis in its T stock of $60 (T's net asset basis) or $85 (the T shareholders' aggregate basis in the T stock immediately before the reorganization).

(d) Allocable share in a reverse triangular merger. The facts are the same as in paragraph (a) of this Example 2, except that X, a 10% shareholder of T, does not participate in the transaction. The remaining T shareholders receive $10 cash from P and P stock worth $80 for their T stock. P owns 90% of the T stock after the transaction. Under § 1.358–6(c)(2)(i)(A), P's basis in its T stock is P's $110 basis in its S stock before the reorganization, adjusted as if T had merged into S in a forward triangular merger. In such a case, P's basis would have been adjusted by the $60 basis in the T assets deemed transferred. Under § 1.358–6(c)(2)(i)(B), however, the basis adjustment determined under § 1.358–6(c)(2)(i)(A) is reduced in proportion to the percentage of T stock not acquired by P in the transaction. The percentage of T stock not acquired in the transaction is 10%. Therefore, P reduces its $60 basis adjustment by 10%, resulting in a net basis adjustment of $54. Consequently, P has a $164 basis in its T stock as a result of the transaction.

(e) P's ownership of T stock. The facts are the same as in paragraph (a) of this Example 2, except that P owns 10% of the T stock before the transaction. P's basis in that T stock is $8. All the T shareholders other than P surrender their T stock for $10 cash from P and P stock worth $80. P does not surrender the stock in the transaction. Under § 1.358–6(c)(2)(i)(C), P may treat its T stock owned before the transaction as acquired in the transaction or not. If P treats that T stock as acquired in the transaction, P's basis in that T stock and the T stock actually acquired in the transaction equals P's $110 basis in its S stock before the transaction, adjusted by the $60 basis of the T assets deemed transferred, for a total basis of $170. If P treats its T stock as not acquired, P retains its $8 pre-transaction basis in that stock. P's basis in its other T shares equals P's $110 basis in its S stock before the transaction, adjusted by $54 (the $60 basis in the T assets deemed transferred, reduced by 10%), for a total basis of $164 in those shares. See § 1.358–6(c)(2)(i)(A) and (B). Consequently, if P treats its T shares as not acquired, P's total basis in all of its T shares is $172.

Example 3. Triangular B reorganization. (a) Facts. T has assets with a fair market value of $100 and no liabilities. The T shareholders have an aggregate basis in their T stock of $85 immediately before the reorganization. Pursuant to a plan, P forms S with $5 cash and S acquires all of the T stock in exchange for $100 of P stock. The transaction is a reorganization to which section 368(a)(1)(B) applies.

(b) Basis adjustment. Under § 1.358–6(c)(3), P adjusts its $5 basis in its S stock by treating P as if it acquired the T stock acquired by S in the reorganization directly from the T shareholders in exchange for the P stock in a transaction in which P's basis in the T stock was determined under section 362(b). Under section 362(b), P would have an aggregate basis of $85 in the T stock received by S in the reorganization. P is then treated as if it transferred the T stock to S in a transaction in which P's basis in the S stock was determined under section 358. Under section 358, P's basis in its S stock would be increased by the $85 basis in the T stock deemed transferred. Consequently, P has a $90 basis in its S stock as a result of the reorganization.

(d) Special rule for consideration not provided by P—(1) In general. The amount of P's adjustment to basis in its S or T stock, as applicable, described in paragraph (c) of this section is decreased by the fair market value of any consideration (including P stock in which gain or loss is recognized, see § 1.1032–2(c)) that is exchanged in the reorganization and that is not provided by P pursuant to the plan of reorganization. This paragraph (d) does not apply to the amount of T liabilities assumed by S or to which the T assets acquired by S are subject under paragraph (c)(1) of this section (or deemed assumed or taken subject to by S under paragraph (c)(2)(i) of this section).

(2) Limitation. P makes no adjustment to basis under this section if the decrease required under paragraph (d)(1) of this section equals or exceeds the amount of the adjustment described in paragraph (c) of this section.

(3) Example. The rules of this paragraph (d) are illustrated by the following example. For purposes of this example, P, S, and T are domestic corporations, P and S do not file consolidated returns, P owns all of the only class of S stock, the P stock exchanged in the transaction satisfies the requirements of the applicable triangular reorganization provisions, and the facts set forth the only corporate activity.

Example. (a) Facts. T has assets with an aggregate basis of $60 and fair market value of $100 and no liabilities. S is an operating company with substantial assets that has been in existence for several years. P has a $100 basis in its S stock. Pursuant to a plan, T merges into S and the T shareholders receive $70 of P stock provided by P pursuant to the plan and $30 of cash provided by S in exchange for their T stock. The transaction is a reorganization to which sections 368(a)(1)(A) and (a)(2)(D) apply.

(b) Basis adjustment. Under § 1.358–6(c)(1), P's $100 basis in its S stock is increased by the $60 basis in the T assets deemed transferred. Under § 1.358–6(d)(1), the $60 adjustment is decreased by the $30 of cash provided by S in the reorganization. Consequently, P has a net adjustment of $30 in its S stock, and P has a $130 basis in its S stock as a result of the reorganization.

(c) Appreciated asset. The facts are the same as in paragraph (a) of this Example, except that in the reorganization S provides an asset with a $20 adjusted basis and $30 fair market value instead of $30 of cash. The basis results are the same as in paragraph (b) of this Example. In addition, S recognizes $10 of gain under section 1001 on its disposition of the asset in the reorganization.

(d) Depreciated asset. The facts are the same as in paragraph (c) of this Example, except that S has a $60 adjusted basis in the asset. The basis results are the same as in paragraph (b) of this Example. In addition, S recognizes $30 of loss under section 1001 on its disposition of the asset in the reorganization.

(e) P stock. The facts are the same as in paragraph (a) of this Example, except that in the reorganization S provides P stock with a fair market value of $30 instead of $30 of cash. S acquired the P stock in an unrelated transaction several years before the reorganization. S has a $20 adjusted basis in the P stock. The basis results are the same as in paragraph (b) of this Example. In addition, S recognizes $10 of gain on its disposition of the P stock in the reorganization. See § 1.1032–2(c).

* * *

[T.D. 8648, 60 FR 66077, Dec. 21, 1995; T.D. 9243, 71 FR 4282, Jan. 26, 2006; T.D. 9424, 73 FR 53947, Sept. 17, 2008; 73 FR 62204, Oct. 20, 2008]

§ 1.361–1 Nonrecognition of gain or loss to corporations.

Section 361 provides the general rule that no gain or loss shall be recognized if a corporation, a party to a reorganization, exchanges property in pursuance of the plan of reorganization solely for stock or securities in another corporation, a party to the reorganization. This provision includes only stock and securities received in connection with a reorganization defined in section 368(a). It also includes nonvoting stock and securities in a corporation, a party to a reorganization, received in a transaction to which section 368(a)(1)(C) is applicable only by reason of section 368(a)(2)(B).

[T.D. 6500, 25 FR 11607, Nov. 26, 1960]

§ 1.362–1 Basis to corporations.

(a) In general. Section 362 provides, as a general rule, that if property was acquired on or after June 22, 1954, by a corporation (1) in connection with a transaction to which section 351 (relating to transfer of property to corporation controlled by transferor) applies, (2) as paid-in surplus or as a contribution to capital, * * *, then the basis shall be the same as it would be in the hands of the transferor, increased in the amount of gain recognized to the transferor on such transfer. * * *

(b) Exceptions. (1) In the case of a plan of reorganization adopted after October 22, 1968, section 362 does not apply if the property acquired in connection with such reorganization consists of stock or securities in a corporation a party to the reorganization, unless acquired by the exchange of stock or securities of the transferee (or of a corporation which is in control of the transferee) as the consideration in whole or in part for the transfer.

* * *

[T.D. 6500, 25 FR 11607, Nov. 26, 1960, as amended by T.D. 7422, 41 FR 26569, June 28, 1976; T.D. 8995, 67 FR 34605, May 15, 2002]

§ 1.368–1 Purpose and scope of exception of reorganization exchanges.

(a) Reorganizations. As used in the regulations under parts I, II, and III (section 301 and following), subchapter C, chapter 1 of the Code, the terms "reorganization" and "party to a reorganization" mean only a reorganization or a party to a reorganization as defined in subsections (a) and (b) of section 368. In determining whether a transaction qualifies as a reorganization under section 368(a), the transaction must be evaluated under relevant provisions of law, including the step transaction doctrine. But see §§ 1.368–2 (f) and (k) and 1.338–3(d). The preceding two sentences apply to transactions occurring after January 28, 1998, except that they do not apply to any transaction occurring pursuant to a written agreement which is binding on January 28, 1998, and at all times thereafter. With respect to insolvency reorganizations, see part IV, subchapter C, chapter 1 of the Code.

(b) Purpose. Under the general rule, upon the exchange of property, gain or loss must be accounted for if the new property differs in a material particular, either in kind or in extent, from the old property. The purpose of the reorganization provisions of the Code is to except from the general rule certain specifically described exchanges incident to such readjustments of corporate structures made in one of the particular ways specified in the Code, as are required by business exigencies and which effect only a readjustment of continuing interest in property under modified corporate forms. Requisite to a reorganization under the Internal Revenue Code are a continuity of the business enterprise through the issuing corporation under the modified corporate form as described in paragraph (d) of this section, and (except as provided in section 368(a)(1)(D)) a continuity of interest as described in paragraph (e) of this section. (For rules regarding the continuity of interest requirement under section 355, see § 1.355–2(c).) For purposes of this section, the term issuing corporation means the acquiring corporation (as that term is used in section 368(a)), except that, in determining whether a reorganization qualifies as a triangular reorganization (as defined in § 1.358–6(b)(2)), the issuing corporation means the corporation in control of the acquiring corporation. The preceding three sentences apply to transactions occurring after January 28, 1998, except that they do not apply to any transaction occurring pursuant to a written agreement which is binding on January 28, 1998, and at all times thereafter. The continuity of business enterprise requirement is described in paragraph (d) of this section. Notwithstanding the requirements of this paragraph (b), for transactions occurring on or after February 25, 2005, a continuity of the business enterprise and a continuity of interest are not required for the transaction to qualify as a reorganization under section 368(a)(1)(E) or (F). The Code recognizes as a reorganization the amalgamation (occurring in a specified way) of two corporate enterprises under a single corporate structure if there exists among the holders of the stock and securities of either of the old corporations the requisite continuity of interest in the new corporation, but there is not a reorganization if the holders of the stock and securities of the old corporation are merely the holders of short-term notes in the new corporation. In order to exclude transactions not intended to be included, the specifications of the reorganization provisions of the law are precise. Both the terms of the specifications and their underlying assumptions and purposes must be satisfied in order to entitle the taxpayer to the benefit of the exception from the general rule. Accordingly, under the Code, a short-term purchase money note is not a security of a party to a reorganization, an ordinary dividend is to be treated as an ordinary dividend, and a sale is nevertheless to be treated as a sale even though the mechanics of a reorganization have been set up.

(c) Scope. The nonrecognition of gain or loss is prescribed for two specifically described types of exchanges, viz: The exchange that is provided for in section 354(a)(1) in which stock or securities in a corporation, a party to a reorganization, are, in pursuance of a plan of reorganization, exchanged for the stock or securities in a corporation, a party to the same reorganization; and the exchange that is provided for in section 361(a) in which a corporation, a party to a reorganization, exchanges property, in pursuance of a plan of reorganization, for stock or securities in another corporation, a party to the same reorganization. Section 368(a)(1) limits the definition of the term "reorganization" to six kinds of transactions and excludes all others. From its context, the term "a party to a reorganization" can only mean a party to a transaction specifically defined as a reorganization by section 368(a). Certain rules respecting boot received in either of the two types of exchanges provided for in section 354(a)(1) and section 361(a) are prescribed in sections 356, 357, and 361(b). A special rule respecting a transfer of property with a liability in excess of its basis is prescribed in section 357(c). Under section 367 a limitation is placed on all these provisions by providing that except under specified conditions foreign corporations shall not be deemed within their scope. The provisions of the Code referred to in this paragraph are inapplicable unless there is a plan of reorganization. A plan of reorganization must contemplate the bona fide execution of one of the transactions specifically described as a reorganization in section 368(a) and for the bona fide consummation of each of the requisite acts under which nonrecognition of gain is claimed. Such transaction and such acts must be an ordinary and necessary incident of the conduct of the enterprise and must provide for a continuation of the enterprise. A scheme, which involves an abrupt departure from normal reorganization procedure in connection with a transaction on which the imposition of tax is imminent, such as a mere device that puts on the form of a corporate reorganization as a disguise for concealing its real character, and the object and accomplishment of which is the consummation of a preconceived plan having no business or corporate purpose, is not a plan of reorganization.

(d) Continuity of business enterprise—(1) General rule. Continuity of business enterprise (COBE) requires that the issuing corporation (P), as defined in paragraph (b) of this section, either continue the target corporation's (T's) historic business or use a significant portion of T's historic business assets in a business. The preceding sentence applies to transactions occurring after January 28, 1998, except that it does not apply to any transaction occurring pursuant to a written agreement which is binding on January 28, 1998, and at all times thereafter. The application of this general rule to certain transactions, such as mergers of holding companies, will depend on all facts and circumstances. The policy underlying this general rule, which is to ensure that reorganizations are limited to readjustments of continuing interests in property under modified corporate form, provides the guidance necessary to make these facts and circumstances determinations.

(2) Business continuity. (i) The continuity of business enterprise requirement is satisfied if P continues T's historic business. The fact P is in the same line of business as T tends to establish the requisite continuity, but is not alone sufficient.

(ii) If T has more than one line of business, continuity of business enterprise requires only that P continue a significant line of business.

(iii) In general, a corporation's historic business is the business it has conducted most recently. However, a corporation's historic business is not one the corporation enters into as part of a plan of reorganization.

(iv) All facts and circumstances are considered in determining the time when the plan comes into existence and in determining whether a line of business is "significant".

(3) Asset continuity. (i) The continuity of business enterprise requirement is satisfied if P uses a significant portion of T's historic business assets in a business.

(ii) A corporation's historic business assets are the assets used in its historic business. Business assets may include stock and securities and intangible operating assets such as good will, patents, and trademarks, whether or not they have a tax basis.

(iii) In general, the determination of the portion of a corporation's assets considered "significant" is based on the relative importance of the assets to operation of the business. However, all other facts and circumstances, such as the net fair market value of those assets, will be considered.

(4) Acquired assets or stock held by members of the qualified group or partnerships. The following rules apply in determining whether the COBE requirement of paragraph (d)(1) of this section is satisfied:

(i) Businesses and assets of members of a qualified group. The issuing corporation is treated as holding all of the businesses and assets of all of the members of the qualified group, as defined in paragraph (d)(4)(ii) of this section.

(ii) Qualified group. A qualified group is one or more chains of corporations connected through stock ownership with the issuing corporation, but only if the issuing corporation owns directly stock meeting the requirements of section 368(c) in at least one other corporation, and stock meeting the requirements of section 368(c) in each of the corporations (except the issuing corporation) is owned directly (or indirectly as provided in paragraph (d)(4)(iii)(D) of this section) by one of the other corporations.

(iii) Partnerships—(A) Partnership assets. Each partner of a partnership will be treated as owning the T business assets used in a business of the partnership in accordance with that partner's interest in the partnership.

(B) Partnership businesses. The issuing corporation will be treated as conducting a business of a partnership if—

(1) Members of the qualified group, in the aggregate, own an interest in the partnership representing a significant interest in that partnership business; or

(2) One or more members of the qualified group have active and substantial management functions as a partner with respect to that partnership business.

(C) Conduct of the historic T business in a partnership. If a significant historic T business is conducted in a partnership, the fact that P is treated as conducting such T business under paragraph (d)(4)(iii)(B) of this section tends to establish the requisite continuity, but is not alone sufficient.

(D) Stock attributed from certain partnerships. Solely for purposes of paragraph (d)(4)(ii) of this section, if members of the qualified group own interests in a partnership meeting requirements equivalent to section 368(c) (a section 368(c) controlled partnership), any stock owned by the section 368(c) controlled partnership shall be treated as owned by members of the qualified group. Solely for purposes of determining whether a lower-tier partnership is a section 368(c) controlled partnership, any interest in a lower-tier partnership that is owned by a section 368(c) controlled partnership shall be treated as owned by members of the qualified group.

(4) Acquired assets or stock held by members of the qualified group or partnerships. The following rules apply in determining whether the COBE requirement of paragraph (d)(1) of this section is satisfied:

(i) Businesses and assets of members of a qualified group. The issuing corporation is treated as holding all of the businesses and assets of all of the members of the qualified group, as defined in paragraph (d)(4)(ii) of this section.

(ii) Qualified group. A qualified group is one or more chains of corporations connected through stock ownership with the issuing corporation, but only if the issuing corporation owns directly stock meeting the requirements of section 368(c) in at least one other corporation, and stock meeting the requirements of section 368(c) in each of the corporations (except the issuing corporation) is owned directly (or indirectly as provided in paragraph (d)(4)(iii)(D) of this section) by one or more of the other corporations.

* * *

(5) Examples. The following examples illustrate this paragraph (d). All the corporations have only one class of stock outstanding. The preceding sentence and paragraph (d)(5) Example 6 and Example 8 through Example 13 apply to transactions occurring after January 28, 1998, except that they do not apply to any transaction occurring pursuant to a written agreement which is binding on January 28, 1998, and at all times thereafter. Paragraph (d)(5) Example 7, Example 14, and Example 15 apply to transactions occurring on or after October 25, 2007, except that they do not apply to any transaction occurring pursuant to a written agreement which is binding before October 25, 2007, and at all times after that. The examples read as follows:

Example (1). T conducts three lines of business: manufacture of synthetic resins, manufacture of chemicals for the textile industry, and distribution of chemicals. The three lines of business are approximately equal in value. On July 1, 1981, T sells the synthetic resin and chemicals distribution businesses to a third party for cash and marketable securities. On December 31, 1981, T transfers all of its assets to P solely for P voting stock. P continues the chemical manufacturing business without interruption. The continuity of business enterprise requirement is met. Continuity of business enterprise requires only that P continue one of T's three significant lines of business.

Example (2). P manufactures computers and T manufactures components for computers. T sells all of its output to P. On January 1, 1981, P decides to buy imported components only. On March 1, 1981, T merges into P. P continues buying imported components but retains T's equipment as a backup source of supply. The use of the equipment as a backup source of supply constitutes use of a significant portion of T's historic business assets, thus establishing continuity of business enterprise. P is not required to continue T's business.

Example (3). T is a manufacturer of boys' and men's trousers. On January 1, 1978, as part of a plan of reorganization, T sold all of its assets to a third party for cash and purchased a highly diversified portfolio of stocks and bonds. As part of the plan T operates an investment business until July 1, 1981. On that date, the plan of reorganization culminates in a transfer by T of all its assets to P, a regulated investment company, solely in exchange for P voting stock. The continuity of business enterprise requirement is not met. T's investment activity is not its historic business, and the stocks and bonds are not T's historic business assets.

Example (4). T manufactures children's toys and P distributes steel and allied products. On January 1, 1981, T sells all of its assets to a third party for $100,000 cash and $900,000 in notes. On March 1, 1981, T merges into P. Continuity of business enterprise is lacking. The use of the sales proceeds in P's business is not sufficient.

Example (5). T manufactures farm machinery and P operates a lumber mill. T merges into P. P disposes of T's assets immediately after the merger as part of the plan of reorganization. P does not continue T's farm machinery manufacturing business. Continuity of business enterprise is lacking.

Example (6). Use of a significant portion of T's historic business assets by the qualified group. (i) Facts. T operates an auto parts distributorship. P owns 80 percent of the stock of a holding company (HC). HC owns 80 percent of the stock of ten subsidiaries, S–1 through S–10. S–1 through S–10 each separately operate a full service gas station. Pursuant to a plan of reorganization, T merges into P and the T shareholders receive solely P stock. As part of the plan of reorganization, P transfers T's assets to HC, which in turn transfers some of the T assets to each of the ten subsidiaries. No one subsidiary receives a significant portion of T's historic business assets. Each of the subsidiaries will use the T assets in the operation of its full service gas station. No P subsidiary will be an auto parts distributor.

(ii) Continuity of business enterprise. Under paragraph (d)(4)(i) of this section, P is treated as conducting the ten gas station businesses of S–1 through S–10 and as holding the historic T assets used in those businesses. P is treated as holding all the assets and conducting the businesses of all of the members of the qualified group, which includes S–1 through S–10 (paragraphs (d)(4)(i) and (ii) of this section). No member of the qualified group continues T's historic distributorship business. However, subsidiaries S–1 through S–10 continue to use the historic T assets in a business. Even though no one corporation of the qualified group is using a significant portion of T's historic business assets in a business, the COBE requirement of paragraph (d)(1) of this section is satisfied because, in the aggregate, the qualified group is using a significant portion of T's historic business assets in a business.

Example (7). Transfers of acquired stock to members of the qualified group—continuity of business enterprise satisfied. (i) Facts. The facts are the same as Example 6, except that, instead of P acquiring the assets of T, HC acquires all of the outstanding stock of T in exchange solely for stock of P. In addition, as part of the plan of reorganization, HC transfers 10 percent of the stock of T to each of subsidiaries S–1 through S–10. T will continue to operate an auto parts distributorship. Without regard to whether the transaction satisfies the COBE requirement, the transaction qualifies as a triangular B reorganization (as defined in § 1.358–6(b)(2)(iv)).

(ii) Continuity of business enterprise. Under paragraph (d)(4)(i) of this section, P is treated as holding the assets and conducting the business of T because T is a member of the qualified group (as defined in paragraph (d)(4)(ii) of this section). The COBE requirement of paragraph (d)(1) of this section is satisfied.

Example (8). Continuation of the historic T business in a partnership satisfies continuity of business enterprise. (i) Facts. T manufactures ski boots. P owns all of the stock of S–1. S–1 owns all of the stock of S–2, and S–2 owns all of the stock of S–3. T merges into P and the T shareholders receive consideration consisting of P stock and cash. The T ski boot business is to be continued and expanded. In anticipation of this expansion, P transfers all of the T assets to S–1, S–1 transfers all of the T assets to S–2, and S–2 transfers all of the T assets to S–3. S–3 and X (an unrelated party) form a new partnership (PRS). As part of the plan of reorganization, S–3 transfers all the T assets to PRS, and S–3, in its capacity as a partner, performs active and substantial management functions for the PRS ski boot business, including making significant business decisions and regularly participating in the overall supervision, direction, and control of the employees of the ski boot business. S–3 receives a 20 percent interest in PRS. X transfers cash in exchange for an 80 percent interest in PRS.

(ii) Continuity of business enterprise. Under paragraph (d)(4)(iii)(B)(2) of this section, P is treated as conducting T's historic business because S–3 performs active and substantial management functions for the ski boot business in S–3's capacity as a partner. P is treated as holding all the assets and conducting the businesses of all of the members of the qualified group, which includes S–3 (paragraphs (d)(4)(i) and (ii) of this section). The COBE requirement of paragraph (d)(1) of this section is satisfied.

* * *

(e) Continuity of interest—(1) General rule. (i) The purpose of the continuity of interest requirement is to prevent transactions that resemble sales from qualifying for nonrecognition of gain or loss available to corporate reorganizations. Continuity of interest requires that in substance a substantial part of the value of the proprietary interests in the target corporation be preserved in the reorganization. A proprietary interest in the target corporation is preserved if, in a potential reorganization, it is exchanged for a proprietary interest in the issuing corporation (as defined in paragraph (b) of this section), it is exchanged by the acquiring corporation for a direct interest in the target corporation enterprise, or it otherwise continues as a proprietary interest in the target corporation. However, a proprietary interest in the target corporation is not preserved if, in connection with the potential reorganization, it is acquired by the issuing corporation for consideration other than stock of the issuing corporation, or stock of the issuing corporation furnished in exchange for a proprietary interest in the target corporation in the potential reorganization is redeemed. All facts and circumstances must be considered in determining whether, in substance, a proprietary interest in the target corporation is preserved. See paragraph (e)(6) of this section for rules related to when a creditor's claim against a target corporation is a proprietary interest in the corporation. For purposes of the continuity of interest requirement, a mere disposition of stock of the target corporation prior to a potential reorganization to persons not related (as defined in paragraph (e)(4) of this section determined without regard to paragraph (e)(4)(i)(A) of this section) to the target corporation or to persons not related (as defined in paragraph (e)(4) of this section) to the issuing corporation is disregarded and a mere disposition of stock of the issuing corporation received in a potential reorganization to persons not related (as defined in paragraph (e)(4) of this section) to the issuing corporation is disregarded.

(ii) For purposes of paragraph (e)(1)(i) of this section, a proprietary interest in the target corporation (other than one held by the acquiring corporation) is not preserved to the extent that consideration received prior to a potential reorganization, either in a redemption of the target corporation stock or in a distribution with respect to the target corporation stock, is treated as other property or money received in the exchange for purposes of section 356, or would be so treated if the target shareholder also had received stock of the issuing corporation in exchange for stock owned by the shareholder in the target corporation.

(2) Measuring continuity of interest—(i) In general. In determining whether a proprietary interest in the target corporation is preserved, the consideration to be exchanged for the proprietary interests in the target corporation pursuant to a contract to effect the potential reorganization shall be valued on the last business day before the first date such contract is a binding contract (the pre-signing date), if such contract provides for fixed consideration. If a portion of the consideration provided for in such a contract consists of other property identified by value, then this specified value of such other property is used for purposes of determining the extent to which a proprietary interest in the target corporation is preserved. If the contract does not provide for fixed consideration, this paragraph (e)(2)(i) is not applicable.

(ii) Binding contract—(A) In general. A binding contract is an instrument enforceable under applicable law against the parties to the instrument. The presence of a condition outside the control of the parties (including, for example, regulatory agency approval) shall not prevent an instrument from being a binding contract. Further, the fact that insubstantial terms remain to be negotiated by the parties to the contract, or that customary conditions remain to be satisfied, shall not prevent an instrument from being a binding contract.

(B) Modifications—(1) In general. If a term of a binding contract that relates to the amount or type of the consideration the target shareholders will receive in a potential reorganization is modified before the closing date of the potential reorganization, and the contract as modified is a binding contract, the date of the modification shall be treated as the first date there is a binding contract.

(2) Modification of a transaction that preserves continuity of interest. Notwithstanding paragraph (e)(2)(ii)(B)(1) of this section, a modification of a term that relates to the amount or type of consideration the target shareholders will receive in a transaction that would have resulted in the preservation of a substantial part of the value of the target corporation shareholders' proprietary interests in the target corporation if there had been no modification will not be treated as a modification if—

(i) The modification has the sole effect of providing for the issuance of additional shares of issuing corporation stock to the target corporation shareholders;

(ii) The modification has the sole effect of decreasing the amount of money or other property to be delivered to the target corporation shareholders; or

(iii) The modification has the effect of decreasing the amount of money or other property to be delivered to the target corporation shareholders and providing for the issuance of additional shares of issuing corporation stock to the target corporation shareholders.

(3) Modification of a transaction that does not preserve continuity of interest. Notwithstanding paragraph (e)(2)(ii)(B)(1) of this section, a modification of a term that relates to the amount or type of consideration the target shareholders will receive in a transaction that would not have resulted in the preservation of a substantial part of the value of the target corporation shareholders' proprietary interests in the target corporation if there had been no modification will not be treated as a modification if—

(i) The modification has the sole effect of providing for the issuance of fewer shares of issuing corporation stock to the target corporation shareholders;

(ii) The modification has the sole effect of increasing the amount of money or other property to be delivered to the target corporation shareholders; or

(iii) The modification has the effect of increasing the amount of money or other property to be delivered to the target corporation shareholders and providing for the issuance of fewer shares of issuing corporation stock to the target corporation shareholders.

(C) Tender offers. For purposes of this paragraph (e)(2), a tender offer that is subject to section 14(d) of the Securities and Exchange Act of 1934 [15 U.S.C. 78n(d)(1)] and Regulation 14D (17 CFR 240.14d–1 through 240.14d–101) and is not pursuant to a binding contract, is treated as a binding contract made on the date of its announcement, notwithstanding that it may be modified by the offeror or that it is not enforceable against the offerees. If a modification (not pursuant to a binding contract) of such a tender offer is subject to the provisions of Regulation 14d–6(c) (17 CFR 240.14d–6(c)) and relates to the amount or type of the consideration received in the tender offer, then the date of the modification shall be treated as the first date there is a binding contract.

(iii) Fixed consideration—(A) In general. A contract provides for fixed consideration if it provides the number of shares of each class of stock of the issuing corporation, the amount of money, and the other property (identified either by value or by specific description), if any, to be exchanged for all the proprietary interests in the target corporation, or to be exchanged for each proprietary interest in the target corporation. A shareholder's election to receive a number of shares of stock of the issuing corporation, money, or other property (or some combination of stock of the issuing corporation, money, or other property) in exchange for all of the shareholder's proprietary interests in the target corporation, or each of the shareholder's proprietary interests in the target corporation, will not prevent a contract from satisfying the definition of fixed consideration provided for in this paragraph (e)(2)(iii)(A).

(B) Shareholder elections. A contract that provides a target corporation shareholder with an election to receive a number of shares of stock of the issuing corporation, money, or other property (or some combination of stock of the issuing corporation, money, or other property) in exchange for all of the shareholder's proprietary interests in the target corporation, or each of the shareholder's proprietary interests in the target corporation, provides for fixed consideration if the determination of the number of shares of issuing corporation stock to be provided to the target corporation shareholder is determined using the value of the issuing corporation stock on the last business day before the first date there is a binding contract. This is the case even though the shareholder election may preclude a determination, prior to the closing date, of the number of shares of each class of the issuing corporation, the amount of money, and the other property (or the combination of shares, money and other property) to be exchanged for each proprietary interest in the target corporation.

(C) Contingent adjustments to the consideration—(1) In general. Except as provided in paragraph (e)(2)(iii)(C)(2) of this section, a contract that provides for contingent adjustments to the consideration will be treated as providing for fixed consideration if it would satisfy the requirements of paragraph (e)(2)(iii)(A) of this section without the contingent adjustment provision.

(2) Exceptions. A contract will not be treated as providing for fixed consideration if the contract provides for contingent adjustments to the consideration that prevent (to any extent) the target corporation shareholders from being subject to the economic benefits and burdens of ownership of the issuing corporation stock after the last business day before the first date the contract is a binding contract. For example, a contract will not be treated as providing for fixed consideration if the contract provides for contingent adjustments to the consideration in the event that the value of the stock of the issuing corporation, the value of the assets of the issuing corporation, or the value of any surrogate for either the value of the stock of the issuing corporation or the assets of the issuing corporation increases or decreases after the last business day before the first date there is a binding contract. Similarly, a contract will not be treated as providing for fixed consideration if the contract provides for contingent adjustments to the number of shares of the issuing corporation stock to be provided to the target corporation shareholders computed using any value of the issuing corporation shares after the last business day before the first date there is a binding contract.

(D) Escrows. Placing part of the consideration to be exchanged for proprietary interests in the target corporation in escrow to secure target's performance of customary pre-closing covenants or customary target representations and warranties will not prevent a contract from being treated as providing for fixed consideration.

(E) Anti-dilution clauses. The presence of a customary anti-dilution clause will not prevent a contract from being treated as providing for fixed consideration. However, the absence of such a clause will prevent a contract from being treated as providing for fixed consideration if the issuing corporation alters its capital structure between the first date there is an otherwise binding contract to effect the transaction and the effective date of the transaction in a manner that materially alters the economic arrangement of the parties to the binding contract. If the number of shares of the issuing corporation to be issued to the target corporation shareholders is altered pursuant to a customary anti-dilution clause, the value of the shares determined under paragraph (e)(2)(i) of this section must be adjusted accordingly.

(F) Dissenters' rights. The possibility that some shareholders may exercise dissenters' rights and receive consideration other than that provided for in the binding contract will not prevent the contract from being treated as providing for fixed consideration.

(G) Fractional shares. The fact that money may be paid in lieu of issuing fractional shares will not prevent a contract from being treated as providing for fixed consideration.

(iv) New issuances. For purposes of applying paragraph (e)(2)(i) of this section, any class of stock, securities, or indebtedness that the issuing corporation issues to the target corporation shareholders pursuant to the potential reorganization and that does not exist before the first date there is a binding contract to effect the potential reorganization is deemed to have been issued on the last business day before the first date there is a binding contract to effect the potential reorganization.

(v) Examples. For purposes of the examples in this paragraph (e)(2)(v), P is the issuing corporation, T is the target corporation, S is a wholly owned subsidiary of P, all corporations have only one class of stock outstanding, A is an individual, no transactions other than those described occur, and the transactions are not otherwise subject to recharacterization. The following examples illustrate the application of this paragraph (e)(2):

Example 1. Application of signing date rule. On January 3 of year 1, P and T sign a binding contract pursuant to which T will be merged with and into P on June 1 of year 1. Pursuant to the contract, the T shareholders will receive 40 P shares and $60 of cash in exchange for all of the outstanding stock of T. Twenty of the P shares, however, will be placed in escrow to secure customary target representations and warranties. The P stock is listed on an established market. On January 2 of year 1, the value of the P stock is $1 per share. On June 1 of year 1, T merges with and into P pursuant to the terms of the contract. On that date, the value of the P stock is $.25 per share. None of the stock placed in escrow is returned to P. Because the contract provides for the number of shares of P and the amount of money to be exchanged for all of the proprietary interests in T, under this paragraph (e)(2), there is a binding contract providing for fixed consideration as of January 3 of year 1. Therefore, whether the transaction satisfies the continuity of interest requirement is determined by reference to the value of the P stock on the pre-signing date. Because, for continuity of interest purposes, the T stock is exchanged for $40 of P stock and $60 of cash, the transaction preserves a substantial part of the value of the proprietary interest in T. Therefore, the transaction satisfies the continuity of interest requirement.

* * *

(3) Related persons acquisitions. A proprietary interest in the target corporation is not preserved if, in connection with a potential reorganization, a person related (as defined in paragraph (e)(4) of this section) to the issuing corporation acquires, for consideration other than stock of the issuing corporation, either a proprietary interest in the target corporation or stock of the issuing corporation that was furnished in exchange for a proprietary interest in the target corporation. The preceding sentence does not apply to the extent those persons who were the direct or indirect owners of the target corporation prior to the potential reorganization maintain a direct or indirect proprietary interest in the issuing corporation.

(4) Definition of related person—(i) In general. For purposes of this paragraph (e), two corporations are related persons if either—

(A) The corporations are members of the same affiliated group as defined in section 1504 (determined without regard to section 1504(b)); or

(B) A purchase of the stock of one corporation by another corporation would be treated as a distribution in redemption of the stock of the first corporation under section 304(a)(2) (determined without regard to § 1.1502–80(b)).

(ii) Special rules. The following rules apply solely for purposes of this paragraph (e)(4):

(A) A corporation will be treated as related to another corporation if such relationship exists immediately before or immediately after the acquisition of the stock involved.

(B) A corporation, other than the target corporation or a person related (as defined in paragraph (e)(4) of this section determined without regard to paragraph (e)(4)(i)(A) of this section) to the target corporation, will be treated as related to the issuing corporation if the relationship is created in connection with the potential reorganization.

* * *

(6) Creditors' claims as proprietary interests—(i) In general. A creditor's claim against a target corporation may be a proprietary interest in the target corporation if the target corporation is in a title 11 or similar case (as defined in section 368(a)(3)) or the amount of the target corporation's liabilities exceeds the fair market value of its assets immediately prior to the potential reorganization. In such cases, if any creditor receives a proprietary interest in the issuing corporation in exchange for its claim, every claim of that class of creditors and every claim of all equal and junior classes of creditors (in addition to the claims of shareholders) is a proprietary interest in the target corporation immediately prior to the potential reorganization to the extent provided in paragraph (e)(6)(ii) of this section.

* * *

(8) Examples. For purposes of the examples in this paragraph (e)(7), P is the issuing corporation, T is the target corporation, S is a wholly owned subsidiary of P, all corporations have only one class of stock outstanding, A and B are individuals, PRS is a partnership, all reorganization requirements other than the continuity of interest requirement are satisfied, and the transaction is not otherwise subject to recharacterization. The following examples illustrate the application of this paragraph (e):

Example 1. Sale of stock to third party. (i) Sale of issuing corporation stock after merger. A owns all of the stock of T. T merges into P. In the merger, A receives P stock having a fair market value of $50x and cash of $50x. Immediately after the merger, and pursuant to a preexisting binding contract, A sells all of the P stock received by A in the merger to B. Assume that there are no facts and circumstances indicating that the cash used by B to purchase A's P stock was in substance exchanged by P for T stock. Under paragraphs (e)(1) and (3) of this section, the sale to B is disregarded because B is not a person related to P within the meaning of paragraph (e)(4) of this section. Thus, the transaction satisfies the continuity of interest requirement because 50 percent of A's T stock was exchanged for P stock, preserving a substantial part of the value of the proprietary interest in T.

(ii) Sale of target corporation stock before merger. The facts are the same as paragraph (i) of this Example 1, except that B buys A's T stock prior to the merger of T into P and then exchanges the T stock for P stock having a fair market value of $50x and cash of $50x. The sale by A is disregarded. The continuity of interest requirement is satisfied because B's T stock was exchanged for P stock, preserving a substantial part of the value of the proprietary interest in T.

Example 2. Relationship created in connection with potential reorganization. Corporation X owns 60 percent of the stock of P and 30 percent of the stock of T. A owns the remaining 70 percent of the stock of T. X buys A's T stock for cash in a transaction which is not a qualified stock purchase within the meaning of section 338. T then merges into P. In the merger, X exchanges all of its T stock for additional stock of P. As a result of the issuance of the additional stock to X in the merger, X's ownership interest in P increases from 60 to 80 percent of the stock of P. X is not a person related to P under paragraph (e)(4)(i)(B) of this section, because a purchase of stock of P by X would not be treated as a distribution in redemption of the stock of P under section 304(a)(2). However, X is a person related to P under paragraphs (e)(4)(i)(A) and (ii)(B) of this section, because X becomes affiliated with P in the merger. The continuity of interest requirement is not satisfied, because X acquired a proprietary interest in T for consideration other than P stock, and a substantial part of the value of the proprietary interest in T is not preserved. See paragraph (e)(3) of this section.

* * *

Example 4. Redemptions and purchases by issuing corporation or related persons. (i) Redemption by issuing corporation. A owns 100 percent of the stock of T and none of the stock of P. T merges into S. In the merger, A receives P stock. In connection with the merger, P redeems all of the P stock received by A in the merger for cash. The continuity of interest requirement is not satisfied, because, in connection with the merger, P redeemed the stock exchanged for a proprietary interest in T, and a substantial part of the value of the proprietary interest in T is not preserved. See paragraph (e)(1) of this section.

(ii) Purchase of target corporation stock by issuing corporation. The facts are the same as paragraph (i) of this Example 4, except that, instead of P redeeming its stock, prior to and in connection with the merger of T into S, P purchases 90 percent of the T stock from A for cash. The continuity of interest requirement is not satisfied, because in connection with the merger, P acquired a proprietary interest in T for consideration other than P stock, and a substantial part of the value of the proprietary interest in T is not preserved. See paragraph (e)(1) of this section. However, see § 1.338–3(d) (which may change the result in this case by providing that, by virtue of section 338, continuity of interest is satisfied for certain parties after a qualified stock purchase).

(iii) Purchase of issuing corporation stock by person related to issuing corporation. The facts are the same as paragraph (i) of this Example 4, except that, instead of P redeeming its stock, S buys all of the P stock received by A in the merger for cash. S is a person related to P under paragraphs (e)(4)(i)(A) and (B) of this section. The continuity of interest requirement is not satisfied, because S acquired P stock issued in the merger, and a substantial part of the value of the proprietary interest in T is not preserved. See paragraph (e)(3) of this section.

Example 5. Redemption in substance by issuing corporation. A owns 100 percent of the stock of T and none of the stock of P. T merges into P. In the merger, A receives P stock. In connection with the merger, B buys all of the P stock received by A in the merger for cash. Shortly thereafter, in connection with the merger, P redeems the stock held by B for cash. Based on all the facts and circumstances, P in substance has exchanged solely cash for T stock in the merger. The continuity of interest requirement is not satisfied, because in substance P redeemed the stock exchanged for a proprietary interest in T, and a substantial part of the value of the proprietary interest in T is not preserved. See paragraph (e)(1) of this section.

* * *

Example 9. Preacquisition redemption by target corporation. T has two shareholders, A and B. P expresses an interest in acquiring the stock of T. A does not wish to own P stock. T redeems A's shares in T in exchange for cash. No funds have been or will be provided by P for this purpose. P subsequently acquires all the outstanding stock of T from B solely in exchange for voting stock of P. The cash received by A in the prereorganization redemption is not treated as other property or money under section 356, and would not be so treated even if A had received some stock of P in exchange for his T stock. The prereorganization redemption by T does not affect continuity of interest, because B's proprietary interest in T is unaffected, and the value of the proprietary interest in T is preserved.

* * *

[T.D. 6500, 25 FR 11607, Nov. 26, 1960, as amended by T.D. 7745, 45 FR 86437, Dec. 31, 1980; T.D. 8760, 63 FR 4178, Jan. 28, 1998; T.D. 8783, 63 FR 50758, Sept. 23, 1998; T.D. 8858, 65 FR 1237, Jan. 7, 2000; T.D. 8898, 65 FR 52911, Aug. 31, 2000; T.D. 8940, 66 FR 9929, Feb. 13, 2001; T.D. 9182, 70 FR 9220, Feb. 25, 2005; T.D. 9225, 70 FR 54634, Sept. 16, 2005; 70 FR 60132, Oct. 14, 2005; T.D. 9316, 72 FR 12974, Mar. 20, 2007; T.D. 9361, 72 FR 60552, Oct. 25, 2007; T.D. 9434, 73 FR 75567, Dec. 12, 2008; 73 FR 78969, Dec. 24, 2008; T.D. 9565, 76 FR 78541, Dec. 19, 2011]

§ 1.368–2 Definition of terms.

(a) The application of the term "reorganization" is to be strictly limited to the specific transactions set forth in section 368(a). The term does not embrace the mere purchase by one corporation of the properties of another corporation. The preceding sentence applies to transactions occurring after January 28, 1998, except that it does not apply to any transaction occurring pursuant to a written agreement which is binding on January 28, 1998, and at all times thereafter. If the properties are transferred for cash and deferred payment obligations of the transferee evidenced by short-term notes, the transaction is a sale and not an exchange in which gain or loss is not recognized.

(b)(1)(i) Definitions. For purposes of this paragraph (b)(1), the following terms shall have the following meanings:

(A) Disregarded entity. A disregarded entity is a business entity (as defined in § 301.7701–2(a) of this chapter) that is disregarded as an entity separate from its owner for Federal income tax purposes. Examples of disregarded entities include a domestic single member limited liability company that does not elect to be classified as a corporation for Federal income tax purposes, a corporation (as defined in § 301.7701–2(b) of this chapter) that is a qualified REIT subsidiary (within the meaning of section 856(i)(2)), and a corporation that is a qualified subchapter S subsidiary (within the meaning of section 1361(b)(3)(B)).

(B) Combining entity. A combining entity is a business entity that is a corporation (as defined in § 301.7701–2(b) of this chapter) that is not a disregarded entity.

(C) Combining unit. A combining unit is composed solely of a combining entity and all disregarded entities, if any, the assets of which are treated as owned by such combining entity for Federal income tax purposes.

(ii) Statutory merger or consolidation generally. For purposes of section 368(a)(1)(A), a statutory merger or consolidation is a transaction effected pursuant to the statute or statutes necessary to effect the merger or consolidation, in which transaction, as a result of the operation of such statute or statutes, the following events occur simultaneously at the effective time of the transaction—

(A) All of the assets (other than those distributed in the transaction) and liabilities (except to the extent such liabilities are satisfied or discharged in the transaction or are nonrecourse liabilities to which assets distributed in the transaction are subject) of each member of one or more combining units (each a transferor unit) become the assets and liabilities of one or more members of one other combining unit (the transferee unit); and

(B) The combining entity of each transferor unit ceases its separate legal existence for all purposes; provided, however, that this requirement will be satisfied even if, under applicable law, after the effective time of the transaction, the combining entity of the transferor unit (or its officers, directors, or agents) may act or be acted against, or a member of the transferee unit (or its officers, directors, or agents) may act or be acted against in the name of the combining entity of the transferor unit, provided that such actions relate to assets or obligations of the combining entity of the transferor unit that arose, or relate to activities engaged in by such entity, prior to the effective time of the transaction, and such actions are not inconsistent with the requirements of paragraph (b)(1)(ii)(A) of this section.

(iii) Examples. The following examples illustrate the rules of paragraph (b)(1) of this section. In each of the examples, except as otherwise provided, each of R, V, Y, and Z is a C corporation. X is a domestic limited liability company. Except as otherwise provided, X is wholly owned by Y and is disregarded as an entity separate from Y for Federal income tax purposes. The examples are as follows:

Example 1. Divisive transaction pursuant to a merger statute. (i) Facts. Under State W law, Z transfers some of its assets and liabilities to Y, retains the remainder of its assets and liabilities, and remains in existence for Federal income tax purposes following the transaction. The transaction qualifies as a merger under State W corporate law.

(ii) Analysis. The transaction does not satisfy the requirements of paragraph (b)(1)(ii)(A) of this section because all of the assets and liabilities of Z, the combining entity of the transferor unit, do not become the assets and liabilities of Y, the combining entity and sole member of the transferee unit. In addition, the transaction does not satisfy the requirements of paragraph (b)(1)(ii)(B) of this section because the separate legal existence of Z does not cease for all purposes. Accordingly, the transaction does not qualify as a statutory merger or consolidation under section 368(a)(1)(A).

Example 2. Merger of a target corporation into a disregarded entity in exchange for stock of the owner. (i) Facts. Under State W law, Z merges into X. Pursuant to such law, the following events occur simultaneously at the effective time of the transaction: all of the assets and liabilities of Z become the assets and liabilities of X and Z's separate legal existence ceases for all purposes. In the merger, the Z shareholders exchange their stock of Z for stock of Y.

(ii) Analysis. The transaction satisfies the requirements of paragraph (b)(1)(ii) of this section because the transaction is effected pursuant to State W law and the following events occur simultaneously at the effective time of the transaction: all of the assets and liabilities of Z, the combining entity and sole member of the transferor unit, become the assets and liabilities of one or more members of the transferee unit that is comprised of Y, the combining entity of the transferee unit, and X, a disregarded entity the assets of which Y is treated as owning for Federal income tax purposes, and Z ceases its separate legal existence for all purposes. Accordingly, the transaction qualifies as a statutory merger or consolidation for purposes of section 368(a)(1)(A).

* * *

(2) In order for the transaction to qualify under section 368(a)(1)(A) by reason of the application of section 368(a)(2)(D), one corporation (the acquiring corporation) must acquire substantially all of the properties of another corporation (the acquired corporation) partly or entirely in exchange for stock of a corporation which is in control of the acquiring corporation (the controlling corporation), provided that (i) the transaction would have qualified under section 368(a)(1)(A) if the merger had been into the controlling corporation, and (ii) no stock of the acquiring corporation is used in the transaction. The foregoing test of whether the transaction would have qualified under section 368(a)(1)(A) if the merger had been into the controlling corporation means that the general requirements of a reorganization under section 368(a)(1)(A) (such as a business purpose, continuity of business enterprise, and continuity of interest) must be met in addition to the special requirements of section 368(a)(2)(D). Under this test, it is not relevant whether the merger into the controlling corporation could have been effected pursuant to State or Federal corporation law. The term "substantially all" has the same meaning as it has in section 368(a)(1)(C). Although no stock of the acquiring corporation can be used in the transaction, there is no prohibition (other than the continuity of interest requirement) against using other property, such as cash or securities, of either the acquiring corporation or the parent or both. In addition, the controlling corporation may assume liabilities of the acquired corporation without disqualifying the transaction under section 368(a)(2)(D), and for purposes of section 357(a) the controlling corporation is considered a party to the exchange. For example, if the controlling corporation agrees to substitute its stock for stock of the acquired corporation under an outstanding employee stock option agreement, this assumption of liability will not prevent the transaction from qualifying as a reorganization under section 368(a)(2)(D) and the assumption of liability is not treated as money or other property for purposes of section 361(b). Section 368(a)(2)(D) applies whether or not the controlling corporation (or the acquiring corporation) is formed immediately before the merger, in anticipation of the merger, or after preliminary steps have been taken to merge directly into the controlling corporation. Section 368(a)(2)(D) applies only to statutory mergers occurring after October 22, 1968.

(3) For regulations under section 368(a)(2)(E), see paragraph (j) of this section.

(c) In order to qualify as a "reorganization" under section 368(a)(1)(B), the acquisition by the acquiring corporation of stock of another corporation must be in exchange solely for all or a part of the voting stock of the acquiring corporation (or, in the case of transactions occurring after December 31, 1963, solely for all or a part of the voting stock of a corporation which is in control of the acquiring corporation), and the acquiring corporation must be in control of the other corporation immediately after the transaction. If, for example, Corporation X in one transaction exchanges nonvoting preferred stock or bonds in addition to all or a part of its voting stock in the acquisition of stock of Corporation Y, the transaction is not a reorganization under section 368(a)(1)(B). Nor is a transaction a reorganization described in section 368(a)(1)(B) if stock is acquired in exchange for voting stock both of the acquiring corporation and of a corporation which is in control of the acquiring corporation. The acquisition of stock of another corporation by the acquiring corporation solely for its voting stock (or solely for voting stock of a corporation which is in control of the acquiring corporation) is permitted tax-free even though the acquiring corporation already owns some of the stock of the other corporation. Such an acquisition is permitted tax-free in a single transaction or in a series of transactions taking place over a relatively short period of time such as 12 months. For example, Corporation A purchased 30 percent of the common stock of Corporation W (the only class of stock outstanding) for cash in 1939. On March 1, 1955, Corporation A offers to exchange its own voting stock for all the stock of Corporation W tendered within 6 months from the date of the offer. Within the 6–months' period Corporation A acquires an additional 60 percent of stock of Corporation W solely for its own voting stock, so that it owns 90 percent of the stock of Corporation W. No gain or loss is recognized with respect to the exchanges of stock of Corporation A for stock of Corporation W. For this purpose, it is immaterial whether such exchanges occurred before Corporation A acquired control (80 percent) of Corporation W or after such control was acquired. If Corporation A had acquired 80 percent of the stock of Corporation W for cash in 1939, it could likewise acquire some or all of the remainder of such stock solely in exchange for its own voting stock without recognition of gain or loss.

(d) In order to qualify as a reorganization under section 368(a)(1)(C), the transaction must be one described in subparagraph (1) or (2) of this paragraph:

(1) One corporation must acquire substantially all the properties of another corporation solely in exchange for all or a part of its own voting stock, or solely in exchange for all or a part of the voting stock of a corporation which is in control of the acquiring corporation. For example, Corporation P owns all the stock of Corporation A. All the properties of Corporation W are transferred to Corporation A either solely in exchange for voting stock of Corporation P or solely in exchange for less than 80 percent of the voting stock of Corporation A. Either of such transactions constitutes a reorganization under section 368(a)(1)(C). However, if the properties of Corporation W are acquired in exchange for voting stock of both Corporation P and Corporation A, the transaction will not constitute a reorganization under section 368(a)(1)(C). In determining whether the exchange meets the requirement of "solely for voting stock", the assumption by the acquiring corporation of liabilities of the transferor corporation, or the fact that property acquired from the transferor corporation is subject to a liability, shall be disregarded. Though such an assumption does not prevent an exchange from being solely for voting stock for the purposes of the definition of a reorganization contained in section 368(a)(1)(C), it may in some cases, however, so alter the character of the transaction as to place the transaction outside the purposes and assumptions of the reorganization provisions. Section 368(a)(1)(C) does not prevent consideration of the effect of an assumption of liabilities on the general character of the transaction but merely provides that the requirement that the exchange be solely for voting stock is satisfied if the only additional consideration is an assumption of liabilities.

(2) One corporation:

(i) Must acquire substantially all of the properties of another corporation in such manner that the acquisition would qualify under (1) above, but for the fact that the acquiring corporation exchanges money, or other property in addition to such voting stock, and

(ii) Must acquire solely for voting stock (either of the acquiring corporation or of a corporation which is in control of the acquiring corporation) properties of the other corporation having a fair market value which is at least 80 percent of the fair market value of all the properties of the other corporation.

(3) For the purposes of subparagraph (2)(ii) only, a liability assumed or to which the properties are subject is considered money paid for the properties. For example, Corporation A has properties with a fair market value of $100,000 and liabilities of $10,000. In exchange for these properties, Corporation Y transfers its own voting stock, assumes the $10,000 liabilities, and pays $8,000 in cash. The transaction is a reorganization even though a part of the properties of Corporation A is acquired for cash. On the other hand, if the properties of Corporation A worth $100,000, were subject to $50,000 in liabilities, an acquisition of all the properties, subject to the liabilities, for any consideration other than solely voting stock would not qualify as a reorganization under this section since the liabilities alone are in excess of 20 percent of the fair market value of the properties. If the transaction would qualify under either subparagraph (1) or (2) of this paragraph and also under section 368(a)(1)(D), such transaction shall not be treated as a reorganization under section 368(a)(1)(C).

* * *

(4)(i) For purposes of paragraphs (d)(1) and (2)(ii) of this section, prior ownership of stock of the target corporation by an acquiring corporation will not by itself prevent the solely for voting stock requirement of such paragraphs from being satisfied. In a transaction in which the acquiring corporation has prior ownership of stock of the target corporation, the requirement of paragraph (d)(2)(ii) of this section is satisfied only if the sum of the money or other property that is distributed in pursuance of the plan of reorganization to the shareholders of the target corporation other than the acquiring corporation and to the creditors of the target corporation pursuant to section 361(b)(3), and all of the liabilities of the target corporation assumed by the acquiring corporation (including liabilities to which the properties of the target corporation are subject), does not exceed 20 percent of the value of all of the properties of the target corporation. If, in connection with a potential acquisition by an acquiring corporation of substantially all of a target corporation's properties, the acquiring corporation acquires the target corporation's stock for consideration other than the acquiring corporation's own voting stock (or voting stock of a corporation in control of the acquiring corporation if such stock is used in the acquisition of the target corporation's properties), whether from a shareholder of the target corporation or the target corporation itself, such consideration is treated, for purposes of paragraphs (d)(1) and (2) of this section, as money or other property exchanged by the acquiring corporation for the target corporation's properties. Accordingly, the transaction will not qualify under section 368(a)(1)(C) unless, treating such consideration as money or other property, the requirements of section 368(a)(2)(B) and paragraph (d)(2)(ii) of this section are met. The determination of whether there has been an acquisition in connection with a potential reorganization under section 368(a)(1)(C) of a target corporation's stock for consideration other than an acquiring corporation's own voting stock (or voting stock of a corporation in control of the acquiring corporation if such stock is used in the acquisition of the target corporation's properties) will be made on the basis of all of the facts and circumstances.

(ii) The following examples illustrate the principles of this paragraph (d)(4):

Example 1. Corporation P (P) holds 60 percent of the Corporation T (T) stock that P purchased several years ago in an unrelated transaction. T has 100 shares of stock outstanding. The other 40 percent of the T stock is owned by Corporation X (X), an unrelated corporation. T has properties with a fair market value of $110 and liabilities of $10. T transfers all of its properties to P. In exchange, P assumes the $10 of liabilities, and transfers to T $30 of P voting stock and $10 of cash. T distributes the P voting stock and $10 of cash to X and liquidates. The transaction satisfies the solely for voting stock requirement of paragraph (d)(2)(ii) of this section because the sum of $10 of cash paid to X and the assumption by P of $10 of liabilities does not exceed 20% of the value of the properties of T.

Example 2. The facts are the same as in Example 1 except that P purchased the 60 shares of T for $60 in cash in connection with the acquisition of T's assets. The transaction does not satisfy the solely for voting stock requirement of paragraph (d)(2)(ii) of this section because P is treated as having acquired all of the T assets for consideration consisting of $70 of cash, $10 of liability assumption and $30 of P voting stock, and the sum of $70 of cash and the assumption by P of $10 of liabilities exceeds 20% of the value of the properties of T.

* * *

(e) A "recapitalization," and therefore a reorganization, takes place if, for example:

(1) A corporation with $200,000 par value of bonds outstanding, instead of paying them off in cash, discharges them by issuing preferred shares to the bondholders;

(2) There is surrendered to a corporation for cancellation 25 percent of its preferred stock in exchange for no par value common stock;

(3) A corporation issues preferred stock, previously authorized but unissued, for outstanding common stock;

(4) An exchange is made of a corporation's outstanding preferred stock, having certain priorities with reference to the amount and time of payment of dividends and the distribution of the corporate assets upon liquidation, for a new issue of such corporation's common stock having no such rights;

(5) An exchange is made of an amount of a corporation's outstanding preferred stock with dividends in arrears for other stock of the corporation. However, if pursuant to such an exchange there is an increase in the proportionate interest of the preferred shareholders in the assets or earnings and profits of the corporation, then under § 1.305–7(c)(2), an amount equal to the lesser of (i) the amount by which the fair market value or liquidation preference, whichever is greater, of the stock received in the exchange (determined immediately following the recapitalization) exceeds the issue price of the preferred stock surrendered, or (ii) the amount of the dividends in arrears, shall be treated under section 305(c) as a deemed distribution to which sections 305(b)(4) and 301 apply.

(f) The term "a party to a reorganization" includes a corporation resulting from a reorganization, and both corporations, in a transaction qualifying as a reorganization where one corporation acquires stock or properties of another corporation. If a transaction otherwise qualifies as a reorganization, a corporation remains a party to the reorganization even though stock or assets acquired in the reorganization are transferred in a transaction described in paragraph (k) of this section. If a transaction otherwise qualifies as a reorganization, a corporation shall not cease to be a party to the reorganization solely by reason of the fact that part or all of the assets acquired in the reorganization are transferred to a partnership in which the transferor is a partner if the continuity of business enterprise requirement is satisfied. See § 1.368–1(d). The preceding three sentences apply to transactions occurring after January 28, 1998, except that they do not apply to any transaction occurring pursuant to a written agreement which is binding on January 28, 1998, and at all times thereafter. A corporation controlling an acquiring corporation is a party to the reorganization when the stock of such controlling corporation is used in the acquisition of properties. Both corporations are parties to the reorganization if, under statutory authority, Corporation A is merged into Corporation B. All three of the corporations are parties to the reorganization if, pursuant to statutory authority, Corporation C and Corporation D are consolidated into Corporation E. Both corporations are parties to the reorganization if Corporation F transfers substantially all its assets to Corporation G in exchange for all or a part of the voting stock of Corporation G. All three corporations are parties to the reorganization if Corporation H transfers substantially all its assets to Corporation K in exchange for all or a part of the voting stock of Corporation L, which is in control of Corporation K. Both corporations are parties to the reorganization if Corporation M transfers all or part of its assets to Corporation N in exchange for all or a part of the stock and securities of Corporation N, but only if (1) immediately after such transfer, Corporation M, or one or more of its shareholders (including persons who were shareholders immediately before such transfer), or any combination thereof, is in control of Corporation N, and (2) in pursuance of the plan, the stock and securities of Corporation N are transferred or distributed by Corporation M in a transaction in which gain or loss is not recognized under section 354 or 355, or is recognized only to the extent provided in section 356. Both Corporation O and Corporation P, but not Corporation S, are parties to the reorganization if Corporation O acquires stock of Corporation P from Corporation S in exchange solely for a part of the voting stock of Corporation O, if (1) the stock of Corporation P does not constitute substantially all of the assets of Corporation S, (2) Corporation S is not in control of Corporation O immediately after the acquisition, and (3) Corporation O is in control of Corporation P immediately after the acquisition. If a transaction otherwise qualifies as a reorganization under section 368(a)(1)(B) or as a reverse triangular merger (as defined in § 1.358–6(b)(2)(iii)), the target corporation (in the case of a transaction that otherwise qualifies as a reorganization under section 368(a)(1)(B)) or the surviving corporation (in the case of a transaction that otherwise qualifies as a reverse triangular merger) remains a party to the reorganization even though its stock or assets are transferred in a transaction described in paragraph (k) of this section. If a transaction otherwise qualifies as a forward triangular merger (as defined in § 1.358–6(b)(2)(i)), a triangular B reorganization (as defined in § 1.358–6(b)(2)(iv)), a triangular C reorganization (as defined in § 1.358–6(b)(2)(ii)), or a reorganization under section 368(a)(1)(G) by reason of section 368(a)(2)(D), the acquiring corporation remains a party to the reorganization even though its stock is transferred in a transaction described in paragraph (k) of this section. The two preceding sentences apply to transactions occurring on or after October 25, 2007, except that they do not apply to any transaction occurring pursuant to a written agreement which is binding before October 25, 2007, and at all times after that.

(g) The term "plan of reorganization" has reference to a consummated transaction specifically defined as a reorganization under section 368(a). The term is not to be construed as broadening the definition of "reorganization" as set forth in section 368(a), but is to be taken as limiting the nonrecognition of gain or loss to such exchanges or distributions as are directly a part of the transaction specifically described as a reorganization in section 368(a).

Moreover, the transaction, or series of transactions, embraced in a plan of reorganization must not only come within the specific language of section 368(a), but the readjustments involved in the exchanges or distributions effected in the consummation thereof must be undertaken for reasons germane to the continuance of the business of a corporation a party to the reorganization. Section 368(a) contemplates genuine corporate reorganizations which are designed to effect a readjustment of continuing interests under modified corporate forms.

(h) As used in section 368, as well as in other provisions of the Internal Revenue Code, if the context so requires, the conjunction "or" denotes both the conjunctive and the disjunctive, and the singular includes the plural. For example, the provisions of the statute are complied with if "stock and securities" are received in exchange as well as if "stock or securities" are received.

(i) [**Reserved**]

(j)(1) This paragraph (j) prescribes rules relating to the application of section 368(a)(2)(E).

(2) Section 368(a)(2)(E) does not apply to a consolidation.

(3) A transaction otherwise qualifying under section 368(a)(1)(A) is not disqualified by reason of the fact that stock of a corporation (the controlling corporation) which before the merger was in control of the merged corporation is used in the transaction, if the conditions of section 368(a)(2)(E) are satisfied. Those conditions are as follows:

(i) In the transaction, shareholders of the surviving corporation must surrender stock in exchange for voting stock of the controlling corporation. Further, the stock so surrendered must constitute control of the surviving corporation. Control is defined in section 368(c). The amount of stock constituting control is measured immediately before the transaction. For purposes of this subdivision (i), stock in the surviving corporation which is surrendered in the transaction (by any shareholder except the controlling corporation) in exchange for consideration furnished by the surviving corporation (and not by the controlling corporation of the merged corporation) is considered not to be outstanding immediately before the transaction. For effect on "substantially all" test of consideration furnished by the surviving corporation, see paragraph (j)(3)(iii) of this section.

(ii) Except as provided in paragraph (k) of this section, the controlling corporation must control the surviving corporation immediately after the transaction.

(iii) After the transaction, the surviving corporation must hold substantially all of its own properties and substantially all of the properties of the merged corporation (other than stock of the controlling corporation distributed in the transaction). The surviving corporation may transfer such properties as provided in paragraph (k) of this section. The term "substantially all" has the same meaning as in section 368(a)(1)(C). The "substantially all" test applies separately to the merged corporation and to the surviving corporation. In applying the "substantially all" test to the surviving corporation, consideration furnished in the transaction by the surviving corporation in exchange for its stock is property of the surviving corporation which it does not hold after the transaction. In applying the "substantially all" test to the merged corporation, assets transferred from the controlling corporation to the merged corporation in pursuance of the plan of reorganization are not taken into account. Thus, for example, money transferred from the controlling corporation to the merged corporation to be used for the following purposes is not taken into account for purposes of the "substantially all" test:

(A) To pay additional consideration to shareholders of the surviving corporation;

(B) To pay dissenting shareholders of the surviving corporation;

(C) To pay creditors of the surviving corporation;

(D) To pay reorganization expenses; or

(E) To enable the merged corporation to satisfy state minimum capitalization requirements (where the money is returned to the controlling corporation as part of the transaction).

(iv) Paragraph (j)(3)(ii) and the first two sentences of paragraph (j)(3)(iii) of this section apply to transactions occurring on or after October 25, 2007, except that they do not apply to any transaction occurring pursuant to a written agreement which is binding before October 25, 2007, and at all times thereafter. The remainder of paragraph (j)(3)(iii) of this section applies to transactions occurring after January 28, 1998, except that it does not apply to any transaction occurring pursuant to a written agreement which is binding on January 28, 1998, and at all times after that.

(4) The controlling corporation may assume liabilities of the surviving corporation without disqualifying the transaction under section 368(a)(2)(E). An assumption of liabilities of the surviving corporation by the controlling corporation is a contribution to capital by the controlling corporation to the surviving corporation. If, in pursuance of the plan of reorganization, securities of the surviving corporation are exchanged for securities of the controlling corporation, or for other securities of the surviving corporation, see sections 354 and 356.

(5) In applying section 368(a)(2)(E), it makes no difference if the merged corporation is an existing corporation, or is formed immediately before the merger, in anticipation of the merger, or after preliminary steps have been taken to otherwise acquire control of the surviving corporation.

(6) The following examples illustrate the application of this paragraph (j). In each of the examples, Corporation P owns all of the stock of Corporation S and, except as otherwise stated, Corporation T has outstanding 1,000 shares of common stock and no shares of any other class. In each of the examples, it is also assumed that the transaction qualifies under section 368(a)(1)(A) if the conditions of section 368(a)(2)(E) are satisfied.

Example (1). P owns no T stock. On January 1, 1981, S merges into T. In the merger, T's shareholders surrender 950 shares of common stock in exchange for P voting stock. The holders of the other 50 shares (who dissent from the merger) are paid in cash with funds supplied by P. After the transaction, T holds all of its own assets and all of S's assets. Based on these facts, the transaction qualifies under section 368(a)(1)(A) by reason of the application of section 368(a)(2)(E). In the transaction, former shareholders of T surrender, in exchange for P voting stock, an amount of T stock (950/1,000 shares or 95 percent) which constitutes control of T.

Example (2). The facts are the same as in example (1) except that holders of 100 shares in corporation T, who dissented from the merger, are paid in cash with funds supplied by T (and not by P or S) and in the merger. T's remaining shareholders surrender 720 shares of common stock in exchange for P voting stock and 180 shares of common stock for cash supplied by P. The requirements of section 368(a)(2)(E)(ii) are satisfied since, in the transaction, former shareholders of T surrender, in exchange for P voting stock, an amount of T stock (720/900 shares or 80 percent) which constitutes control of T. The T stock surrendered in exchange for consideration furnished by T is not considered outstanding for purposes of determining whether the amount of T stock surrendered by T shareholders for P stock constitutes control of T.

Example (3). T has outstanding 1,000 shares of common stock, 100 shares of nonvoting preferred stock, and no shares of any other class. On January 1, 1981, S merges into T. Prior to the merger, as part of the transaction, T distributes its own cash in redemption of the 100 shares of preferred stock. In the transaction, T's remaining shareholders surrender their 1,000 shares of common stock in exchange for P voting stock. The requirements of section 368(a)(2)(E)(ii) are satisfied since, in the transaction, former shareholders of T surrender, in exchange for P voting stock, an amount of T stock (1,000/1,000 shares or 100 percent) which constitutes control of T. The preferred stock surrendered in exchange for consideration furnished by T is not considered outstanding for purposes of determining whether the amount of T stock surrendered by T shareholders for P stock constitutes control of T. However, the consideration furnished by T for its stock is property of T which T does not hold after the transaction for purposes of the substantially all test in paragraph (j)(3)(iii) of this section.

Example (4). On January 1, 1971, P purchased 201 shares of T's stock. On January 1, 1981, S merges into T. In the merger, T's shareholders (other than P) surrender 799 shares of T stock in exchange for P voting stock. Based on these facts, in the transaction, former shareholders of T do not surrender, in exchange for P voting stock, an amount of T stock which constitutes control of T (799/1,000 shares being less than 80 percent). Therefore, the transaction does not qualify under section 368(a)(1)(A). However, if S is a transitory corporation, formed solely for purposes of effectuating the transaction, the transaction may qualify as a reorganization described in section 368(a)(1)(B) provided all of the applicable requirements are satisfied.

Example (5). On January 1, 1971, P purchased 200 shares of T's stock. On January 1, 1981, S merges into T. Prior to the merger, as part of the transaction, T distributes its own cash in redemption of 1 share of T stock from a T shareholder other than P. In the merger, T's remaining shareholders (other than P) surrender 799 shares of T stock in exchange for P voting stock. Based on these facts, in the transaction, former shareholders of T do not surrender, in exchange for P voting stock, an amount of T stock which constitutes control of T (799/999 shares being less than 80 percent). Therefore, the transaction does not qualify under section 368(a)(1)(A). However, if S is a transitory corporation, formed for purposes of effectuating the transaction, the transaction may qualify as a reorganization described in section 368(a)(1)(B) provided all of the applicable requirements are satisfied.

* * *

(k) Certain transfers of assets or stock in reorganizations—(1) General rule. A transaction otherwise qualifying as a reorganization under section 368(a) shall not be disqualified or recharacterized as a result of one or more subsequent transfers (or successive transfers) of assets or stock, provided that the requirements of § 1.368–1(d) are satisfied and the transfer(s) are described in either paragraph (k)(1)(i) or (k)(1)(ii) of this section. However, this paragraph (k) shall not apply to a transfer to the former shareholders of the acquired corporation (other than a former shareholder that is also the acquiring corporation) or the surviving corporation, as the case may be, to the extent it constitutes the receipt of consideration for a proprietary interest in the acquired corporation or the surviving corporation, as the case may be. Similarly, this paragraph (k) shall not apply to a transfer by the former shareholders of the acquired corporation (other than a former shareholder that is also the acquiring corporation) or the surviving corporation, as the case may be, of consideration initially received in the potential reorganization to the issuing corporation or a person related to the issuing corporation (see definition of "related person" in § 1.368–1(e)).

(i) Distributions. One or more distributions to shareholders (including distribution(s) that involve the assumption of liabilities) are described in this paragraph (k)(1)(i) if—

(A) The property distributed consists of—

(1) Assets of the acquired corporation, the acquiring corporation, or the surviving corporation, as the case may be, or an interest in an entity received in exchange for such assets in a transfer described in paragraph (k)(1)(ii) of this section;

(2) Stock of the acquired corporation provided that such distribution(s) of stock do not cause the acquired corporation to cease to be a member of the qualified group (as defined in § 1.368–1(d)(4)(ii)); or

(3) A combination thereof; and

(B) The aggregate of such distributions does not consist of—

(1) An amount of assets of the acquired corporation, the acquiring corporation (disregarding assets held prior to the potential reorganization), or the surviving corporation (disregarding assets of the merged corporation), as the case may be, that would result in a liquidation of such corporation for Federal income tax purposes; or

(2) All of the stock of the acquired corporation that was acquired in the transaction.

(ii) Transfers Other Than Distributions. One or more other transfers are described in this paragraph (k)(1)(ii) if—

(A) The transfer(s) do not consist of one or more distributions to shareholders;

(B) The property transferred consists of—

(1) Part or all of the assets of the acquired corporation, the acquiring corporation, or the surviving corporation, as the case may be;

(2) Part or all of the stock of the acquired corporation, the acquiring corporation, or the surviving corporation, as the case may be, provided that such transfer(s) of stock do not cause such corporation to cease to be a member of the qualified group (as defined in § 1.368–1(d)(4)(ii)); or

(3) A combination thereof; and

(C) The acquired corporation, the acquiring corporation, or the surviving corporation, as the case may be, does not terminate its corporate existence for Federal income tax purposes in connection with the transfer(s).

(2) Examples. The following examples illustrate the application of this paragraph (k). Except as otherwise noted, P is the issuing corporation, and T is an unrelated target corporation. All corporations have only one class of stock outstanding. T operates a bakery that supplies delectable pastries and cookies to local retail stores. The acquiring corporate group produces a variety of baked goods for nationwide distribution. Except as otherwise noted, P owns all of the stock of S–1 and 80 percent of the stock of S–4, S–1 owns 80 percent of the stock of S–2 and 50 percent of the stock of S–5, S–2 owns 80 percent of the stock of S–3, and S–4 owns the remaining 50 percent of the stock of S–5. The examples are as follows:

Example 1. Transfers of acquired assets to members of the qualified group after a reorganization under section 368(a)(1)(C). (i) Facts. Pursuant to a plan of reorganization, T transfers all of its assets to S–1 solely in exchange for P stock, which T distributes to its shareholders, and S–1's assumption of T's liabilities. In addition, pursuant to the plan, S–1 transfers all of the T assets to S–2, and S–2 transfers all of the T assets to S–3.

(ii) Analysis. Under this paragraph (k), the transaction, which otherwise qualifies as a reorganization under section 368(a)(1)(C), is not disqualified by the successive transfers of all of the T assets to S–2 and from S–2 to S–3 because the transfers are not one or more distributions to shareholders, the transfers consist of part or all of the assets of the acquiring corporation, the acquiring corporation does not terminate its corporate existence for Federal income tax purposes in connection with the transfers, and the transaction satisfies the requirements of § 1.368–1(d).

Example 2. Distribution of acquired assets to a member of the qualified group after a reorganization under section 368(a)(1)(C). (i) Facts. Pursuant to a plan of reorganization, T transfers all of its assets to S–1 solely in exchange for P stock, which T distributes to its shareholders, and S–1's assumption of T's liabilities. In addition, pursuant to the plan, S–1 distributes half of the T assets to P, and P assumes half of the T liabilities.

(ii) Analysis. Under this paragraph (k), the transaction, which otherwise qualifies as a reorganization under section 368(a)(1)(C), is not disqualified by the distribution of half of the T assets from S–1 to P, or P's assumption of half of the T liabilities from S–1, because the distribution consists of assets of the acquiring corporation, the distribution does not consist of an amount of S–1's assets that would result in a liquidation of S–1 for Federal income tax purposes (disregarding S–1's assets held prior to the acquisition of T), and the transaction satisfies the requirements of § 1.368–1(d).

Example 3. Indirect distribution of acquired assets to a member of the qualified group after a reorganization under section 368(a)(1)(C). (i) Facts. The facts are the same as Example 2, except that, instead of S–1 distributing half of the T assets to P and having P assume half of the T liabilities, S–1 contributes half of the T assets to newly formed S–6, S–6 assumes half of the T liabilities, and S–1 distributes all of the S–6 stock to P.

(ii) Analysis. Under this paragraph (k), the transaction, which otherwise qualifies as a reorganization under section 368(a)(1)(C), is not disqualified by the transfer of half of the T assets to S–6 and the distribution of the S–6 stock to P because the transfer of half of the T assets to S–6 is described in paragraph (k)(1)(ii) of this section, the distribution of the S–6 stock to P is an indirect distribution of assets of the acquiring corporation, the distribution does not consist of an amount of S–1's assets that would result in a liquidation of S–1 for Federal income tax purposes (disregarding S–1's assets held prior to the acquisition of T), and the transaction satisfies the requirements of § 1.368–1(d).

* * *

Example 7. Transfer of stock of the acquiring corporation to a member of the qualified group after a reorganization under section 368(a)(1)(A) by reason of section 368(a)(2)(D). (i) Facts. Pursuant to a plan of reorganization, S–1 acquires all of the T assets in the merger of T into S–1. In the merger, the T shareholders receive solely P stock. Also, pursuant to the plan, P transfers all of the S–1 stock to S–4.

(ii) Analysis. Under this paragraph (k), the transaction, which otherwise qualifies as a reorganization under section 368(a)(1)(A) by reason of section 368(a)(2)(D), is not disqualified by the transfer of all of the S–1 stock to S–4 because the transfer is not a distribution to shareholders, the transfer consists of part or all of the stock of the acquiring corporation, the transfer does not cause S–1 to cease to be a member of the qualified group (as defined in § 1.368–1(d)(4)(ii)), the acquiring corporation does not terminate its corporate existence for Federal income tax purposes in connection with the transfer, and the transaction satisfies the requirements of § 1.368–1(d).

* * *

Example 9. Sale of acquired assets to a member of the qualified group after a reorganization under section 368(a)(1)(C). (i) Facts. Pursuant to a plan of reorganization, T transfers all of its assets to S–1 in exchange for P stock, which T distributes to its *26325 shareholders, and S–1's assumption of T's liabilities. In addition, pursuant to the plan, S–1 sells all of the T assets to S–5 for cash equal to the fair market value of those assets.

(ii) Analysis. Under this paragraph (k), the transaction, which otherwise qualifies as a reorganization under section 368(a)(1)(C), is not disqualified by the sale of all of the T assets from S–1 to S–5 because the transfer is not a distribution to shareholders, the transfer consists of part or all of the assets of the acquiring corporation, the acquiring corporation does not terminate its corporate existence for Federal income tax purposes in connection with the transfer, and the transaction satisfies the requirements of § 1.368–1(d).

* * *

(*l*) Certain transactions treated as reorganizations described in section 368(a)(1)(D)—(1) General rule. In order to qualify as a reorganization under section 368(a)(1)(D), a corporation (transferor corporation) must transfer all or part of its assets to another corporation (transferee corporation) and immediately after the transfer the transferor corporation, or one or more of its shareholders (including persons who were shareholders immediately before the transfer), or any combination thereof, must be in control of the transferee corporation; but only if, in pursuance of the plan, stock or securities of the transferee are distributed in a transaction which qualifies under section 354, 355, or 356.

(2) Distribution requirement—(i) In general. For purposes of paragraph (*l*)(1) of this section, a transaction otherwise described in section 368(a)(1)(D) will be treated as satisfying the requirements of sections 368(a)(1)(D) and 354(b)(1)(B) notwithstanding that there is no actual issuance of stock and/or securities of the transferee corporation if the same person or persons own, directly or indirectly, all of the stock of the transferor and transferee corporations in identical proportions. In cases where no consideration is received or the value of the consideration received in the transaction is less than the fair market value of the transferor corporation's assets, the transferee corporation will be treated as issuing stock with a value equal to the excess of the fair market value of the transferor corporation's assets over the value of the consideration actually received in the transaction. In cases where the value of the consideration received in the transaction is equal to the fair market value of the transferor corporation's assets, the transferee corporation will be deemed to issue a nominal share of stock to the transferor corporation in addition to the actual consideration exchanged for the transferor corporation's assets. The nominal share of stock in the transferee corporation will then be deemed distributed by the transferor corporation to the shareholders of the transferor corporation, as part of the exchange for the stock of such shareholders. Where appropriate, the nominal share will be further transferred through chains of ownership to the extent necessary to reflect the actual ownership of the transferor and transferee corporations. Similar treatment to that of the preceding two sentences shall apply where the transferee corporation is treated as issuing stock with a value equal to the excess of the fair market value of the transferor corporation's assets over the value of the consideration actually received in the transaction.

(ii) Attribution. For purposes of paragraph (*l*)(2)(i) of this section, ownership of stock will be determined by applying the principles of section 318(a)(2) without regard to the 50 percent limitation in section 318(a)(2)(C). In addition, an individual and all members of his family described in section 318(a)(1) shall be treated as one individual.

(iii) De minimis variations in ownership and certain stock not taken into account. For purposes of paragraph (*l*)(2)(i) of this section, the same person or persons will be treated as owning, directly or indirectly, all of the stock of the transferor and transferee corporations in identical proportions notwithstanding the fact that there is a de minimis variation in shareholder identity or proportionality of ownership. Additionally, for purposes of paragraph (*l*)(2)(i) of this section, stock described in section 1504(a)(4) is not taken into account.

(iv) Exception. Paragraph (*l*)(2) of this section does not apply to a transaction otherwise described in § 1.358–6(b)(2).

(3) Examples. The following examples illustrate the principles of paragraph (*l*) of this section. For purposes of these examples, each of A, B, C, and D is an individual, T is the acquired corporation, S is the acquiring corporation, P is the parent corporation, and each of S1, S2, S3, and S4 is a direct or indirect subsidiary of P. Further, all of the requirements of section 368(a)(1)(D) other than the requirement that stock or securities be distributed in a transaction to which section 354 or 356 applies are satisfied. The examples are as follows:

Example 1. A owns all the stock of T and S. The T stock has a fair market value of $100x. T sells all of its assets to S in exchange for $100x of cash and immediately liquidates. Because there is complete shareholder identity and proportionality of ownership in T and S, under paragraph (*l*)(2)(i) of this section, the requirements of sections 368(a)(1)(D) and 354(b)(1)(B) are treated as satisfied notwithstanding the fact that no S stock is issued. Pursuant to paragraph (*l*)(2)(i) of this section, S will be deemed to issue a nominal share of S stock to T in addition to the $100x of cash actually exchanged for the T assets, and T will be deemed to distribute all such consideration to A. The transaction qualifies as a reorganization described in section 368(a)(1)(D).

Example 2. The facts are the same as in Example 1 except that C, A's son, owns all of the stock of S. Under paragraph (*l*)(2)(ii) of this section, A and C are treated as one individual. Accordingly, there is complete shareholder identity and proportionality of ownership in T and S. Therefore, under paragraph (*l*)(2)(i) of this section, the requirements of sections 368(a)(1)(D) and 354(b)(1)(B) are treated as satisfied notwithstanding the fact that no S stock is issued. Pursuant to paragraph (*l*)(2)(i) of this section, S will be deemed to issue a nominal share of S stock to T in addition to the $100x of cash actually exchanged for the T assets, and T will be deemed to distribute all such consideration to A. A will be deemed to transfer the nominal share of S stock to C. The transaction qualifies as a reorganization described in section 368(a)(1)(D).

Example 3. P owns all of the stock of S1 and S2. S1 owns all of the stock of S3, which owns all of the stock of T. S2 owns all of the stock of S4, which owns all of the stock of S. The T stock has a fair market value of $70x. T sells all of its assets to S in exchange for $70x of cash and immediately liquidates. Under paragraph (*l*)(2)(ii) of this section, there is indirect, complete shareholder identity and proportionality of ownership in T and S. Accordingly, the requirements of sections 368(a)(1)(D) and 354(b)(1)(B) are treated as satisfied notwithstanding the fact that no S stock is issued. Pursuant to paragraph (*l*)(2)(i) of this section, S will be deemed to issue a nominal share of S stock to T in addition to the $70x of cash actually exchanged for the T assets, and T will be deemed to distribute all such consideration to S3. S3 will be deemed to distribute the nominal share of S stock to S1, which, in turn, will be deemed to distribute the nominal share of S stock to P. P will be deemed to transfer the nominal share of S stock to S2, which, in turn, will be deemed to transfer such share of S stock to S4. The transaction qualifies as a reorganization described in section 368(a)(1)(D).

Example 4. A, B, and C own 34%, 33%, and 33%, respectively, of the stock of T. The T stock has a fair market value of $100x. A, B, and C each own 33% of the stock of S. D owns the remaining 1% of the stock of S. T sells all of its assets to S in exchange for $100x of cash and immediately liquidates. For purposes of determining whether the distribution requirement of sections 368(a)(1)(D) and 354(b)(1)(B) is met, under paragraph (*l*)(2)(iii) of this section, D's ownership of a de minimis amount of stock of S is disregarded and the transaction is treated as if there is complete shareholder identity and proportionality of ownership in T and S. Because there is complete shareholder identity and proportionality of ownership in T and S, under paragraph (*l*)(2)(i) of this section, the requirements of sections 368(a)(1)(D) and 354(b)(1)(B) are treated as satisfied notwithstanding the fact that no S stock is issued. Pursuant to paragraph (*l*)(2)(i) of this section, S will be deemed to issue a nominal share of S stock to T in addition to the $100x of cash actually exchanged for the T assets, T will be deemed to distribute all such consideration to A, B, and C, and the nominal S stock will be deemed transferred among the S shareholders to the extent necessary to reflect their actual ownership of S. The transaction qualifies as a reorganization described in section 368(a)(1)(D).

Example 5. The facts are the same as in Example 4 except that A, B, and C own 34%, 33%, and 33%, respectively, of the common stock of T and S. D owns preferred stock in S described in section 1504(a)(4). For purposes of determining whether the distribution requirement of sections 368(a)(1)(D) and 354(b)(1)(B) is met, under paragraph (*l*)(2)(iii) of this section, D's ownership of S stock described in section 1504(a)(4) is ignored and the transaction is treated as if there is complete shareholder identity and proportionality of ownership in T and S. Because there is complete shareholder identity and proportionality of ownership in T and S, under paragraph (*l*)(2)(i) of this section, the requirements of sections 368(a)(1)(D) and 354(b)(1)(B) are treated as satisfied notwithstanding the fact that no S stock is issued. Pursuant to paragraph (*l*)(2)(i) of this section, S will be deemed to issue a nominal share of S stock to T in addition to the $100x of cash actually exchanged for the T assets, and T will be deemed to distribute all such consideration to A, B, and C. The transaction qualifies as a reorganization described in section 368(a)(1)(D).

Example 6. A and B each own 50% of the stock of T. The T stock has a fair market value of $100x. B and C own 90% and 10%, respectively, of the stock of S. T sells all of its assets to S in exchange for $100x of cash and immediately liquidates. Because complete shareholder identity and proportionality of ownership in T and S does not exist, paragraph (*l*)(2)(i) of this section does not apply. The requirements of sections 368(a)(1)(D) and 354(b)(1)(B) are not satisfied, and the transaction does not qualify as a reorganization described in section 368(a)(1)(D).

* * *

[T.D. 6500, 25 FR 11607, Nov. 26, 1960, as amended by T.D. 7281, 38 FR 18540, July 12, 1973; T.D. 7422, 41 FR 26570, June 28, 1976; T.D. 8059, 50 FR 42689, Oct. 22, 1985; 51 FR 6400, Feb. 24, 1986; T.D. 8760, 63 FR 4182, Jan. 28, 1998; T.D. 8885, 65 FR 31805, May 19, 2000; T.D. 9038, 68 FR 3387, Jan. 24, 2003; T.D. 9242, 71 FR 4259, Jan. 26, 2006; T.D. 9259, 71 FR 23855, April 24, 2006; T.D. 9303, 71 FR 75879, Dec. 19, 2006; T.D. 9361, 72 FR 60552, Oct. 25, 2007; T.D. 9396, 73 FR 26322, May 9, 2008; T.D. 9475, 74 FR 67053, Dec. 18, 2009; 75 FR 3160, Jan. 20, 2010]

§ 1.368–3 Records to be kept and information to be filed with returns.

(a) Parties to the reorganization. The plan of reorganization must be adopted by each of the corporations that are parties thereto. Each such corporation must include a statement entitled, "STATEMENT PURSUANT TO § 1.368–3(a) BY [INSERT NAME AND EMPLOYER IDENTIFICATION NUMBER (IF ANY) OF TAXPAYER], A CORPORATION A PARTY TO A REORGANIZATION," on or with its return for the taxable year of the exchange. If any such corporation is a controlled foreign corporation (within the meaning of section 957), each United States shareholder (within the meaning of section 951(b)) with respect thereto must include this statement on or with its return. However, it is not necessary for any taxpayer to include more than one such statement on or with the same return for the same reorganization. The statement must include—

(1) The names and employer identification numbers (if any) of all such parties;

(2) The date of the reorganization;

(3) The aggregate fair market value and basis, determined immediately before the exchange, of the assets, stock or securities of the target corporation transferred in the transaction; and

(4) The date and control number of any private letter ruling(s) issued by the Internal Revenue Service in connection with this reorganization.

(b) Significant holders. Every significant holder, other than a corporation a party to the reorganization, must include a statement entitled, "STATEMENT PURSUANT TO § 1.368–3(b) BY [INSERT NAME AND TAXPAYER IDENTIFICATION NUMBER (IF ANY) OF TAXPAYER], A SIGNIFICANT HOLDER," on or with such holder's return for the taxable year of the exchange. If a significant holder is a controlled foreign corporation (within the meaning of section 957), each United States shareholder (within the meaning of section 951(b)) with respect thereto must include this statement on or with its return. The statement must include—

(1) The names and employer identification numbers (if any) of all of the parties to the reorganization;

(2) The date of the reorganization; and

(3) The fair market value, determined immediately before the exchange, of all the stock or securities of the target corporation held by the significant holder that is transferred in the transaction and such holder's basis, determined immediately before the exchange, in the stock or securities of such target corporation.

(c) Definitions. For purposes of this section:

(1) Significant holder means—

(i) A holder of stock of the target corporation that receives stock or securities in an exchange described in section 354 (or so much of section 356 as relates to section 354) if, immediately before the exchange, such holder—

(A) Owned at least five percent (by vote or value) of the total outstanding stock of the target corporation if the stock owned by such holder is publicly traded; or

(B) Owned at least one percent (by vote or value) of the total outstanding stock of the target corporation if the stock owned by such holder is not publicly traded; or

(ii) A holder of securities of the target corporation that receives stock or securities in an exchange described in section 354 (or so much of section 356 as relates to section 354) if, immediately before the exchange, such holder owned securities in such target corporation with a basis of $1,000,000 or more.

* * *

[T.D. 9329, 72 FR 32800, June 14, 2007]

ACCOUNTING PERIODS AND METHODS OF ACCOUNTING

§ 1.441–1 Period for computation of taxable income.

(a) Computation of taxable income—(1) In general. Taxable income must be computed and a return must be made for a period known as the taxable year. For rules relating to methods of accounting, the taxable year for which items of gross income are included and deductions are taken, inventories, and adjustments, see parts II and III (section 446 and following), subchapter E, chapter 1 of the Internal Revenue Code, and the regulations thereunder.

(2) Length of taxable year. Except as otherwise provided in the Internal Revenue Code and the regulations thereunder (e.g., § 1.441–2 regarding 52–53–week taxable years), a taxable year may not cover a period of more than 12 calendar months.

(b) General rules and definitions. The general rules and definitions in this paragraph (b) apply for purposes of sections 441 and 442 and the regulations thereunder.

(1) Taxable year. Taxable year means—

(i) The period for which a return is made, if a return is made for a period of less than 12 months (short period). See section 443 and the regulations thereunder;

(ii) Except as provided in paragraph (b)(1)(i) of this section, the taxpayer's required taxable year (as defined in paragraph (b)(2) of this section), if applicable;

(iii) Except as provided in paragraphs (b)(1)(i) and (ii) of this section, the taxpayer's annual accounting period (as defined in paragraph (b)(3) of this section), if it is a calendar year or a fiscal year; or

(iv) Except as provided in paragraphs (b)(1)(i) and (ii) of this section, the calendar year, if the taxpayer keeps no books, does not have an annual accounting period, or has an annual accounting period that does not qualify as a fiscal year.

(2) Required taxable year—(i) In general. Certain taxpayers must use the particular taxable year that is required under the Internal Revenue Code and the regulations thereunder (the required taxable year). For example, the required taxable year is—

* * *

(F) In the case of certain trusts, the taxable year determined under section 644;

(G) In the case of a partnership, the taxable year determined under section 706 and § 1.706–1;

* * *

(L) In the case of an S corporation, the taxable year determined under section 1378 and § 1.1378–1; or

* * *

(ii) Exceptions. Notwithstanding paragraph (b)(2)(i) of this section, the following taxpayers may have a taxable year other than their required taxable year:

(A) 52–53–week taxable years. Certain taxpayers may elect to use a 52–53–week taxable year that ends with reference to their required taxable year. See, for example, §§ 1.441–3 (PSCs), 1.706–1 (partnerships), 1.1378–1 (S corporations), and 1.1502–76(a)(1) (members of a consolidated group).

(B) Partnerships, S corporations, and PSCs. A partnership, S corporation, or PSC may use a taxable year other than its required taxable year if the taxpayer elects to use a taxable year other than its required taxable year under section 444, elects a 52–53–week taxable year that ends with reference to its required taxable year as provided in paragraph (b)(2)(ii)(A) of this section or to a taxable year elected under section 444, or establishes a business purpose to the satisfaction of the Commissioner under section 442 (such as a grandfathered fiscal year).

* * *

(3) Annual accounting period. Annual accounting period means the annual period (calendar year or fiscal year) on the basis of which the taxpayer regularly computes its income in keeping its books.

(4) Calendar year. Calendar year means a period of 12 consecutive months ending on December 31. A taxpayer who has not established a fiscal year must make its return on the basis of a calendar year.

(5) Fiscal year—(i) Definition. Fiscal year means—

(A) A period of 12 consecutive months ending on the last day of any month other than December; or

(B) A 52–53–week taxable year, if such period has been elected by the taxpayer. See § 1.441–2.

(ii) Recognition. A fiscal year will be recognized only if the books of the taxpayer are kept in accordance with such fiscal year.

* * *

(7) Books. Books include the taxpayer's regular books of account and such other records and data as may be necessary to support the entries on the taxpayer's books and on the taxpayer's return, as for example, a reconciliation of any difference between such books and the taxpayer's return. Records that are sufficient to reflect income adequately and clearly on the basis of an annual accounting period will be regarded as the keeping of books. See section 6001 and the regulations thereunder for rules relating to the keeping of books and records.

(8) Taxpayer. Taxpayer has the same meaning as the term person as defined in section 7701(a)(1) (e.g., an individual, trust, estate, partnership, association, or corporation) rather than the meaning of the term taxpayer as defined in section 7701(a)(14) (any person subject to tax).

(c) Adoption of taxable year—(1) In general. Except as provided in paragraph (c)(2) of this section, a new taxpayer may adopt any taxable year that satisfies the requirements of section 441 and the regulations thereunder without the approval of the Commissioner. A taxable year of a new taxpayer is adopted by filing its first Federal income tax return using that taxable year. The filing of an application for automatic extension of time to file a Federal income tax return (e.g., Form 7004, "Application for Automatic Extension of Time to File Corporation Income Tax Return"), the filing of an application for an employer identification number (i.e., Form SS–4, "Application for Employer Identification Number"), or the payment of estimated taxes, for a particular taxable year do not constitute an adoption of that taxable year.

(2) Approval required—(i) Taxpayers with required taxable years. A newly-formed partnership, S corporation, or PSC that wants to adopt a taxable year other than its required taxable year, a taxable year elected under section 444, or a 52–53–week taxable year that ends with reference to its required taxable year or a taxable year elected under section 444 must establish a business purpose and obtain the approval of the Commissioner under section 442.

(ii) Taxpayers without books. A taxpayer that must use a calendar year under section 441(g) and paragraph (f) of this section may not adopt a fiscal year without obtaining the approval of the Commissioner.

(d) Retention of taxable year. In certain cases, a partnership, S corporation, electing S corporation, or PSC will be required to change its taxable year unless it obtains the approval of the Commissioner under section 442, or makes an election under section 444, to retain its current taxable year. For example, a corporation using a June 30 fiscal year that either becomes a PSC or elects to be an S corporation and, as a result, is required to use the calendar year under section 441(i) or 1378, respectively, must obtain the approval of the Commissioner to retain its current fiscal year. Similarly, a partnership using a taxable year that corresponds to its required taxable year must obtain the approval of the Commissioner to retain such taxable year if its required taxable year changes as a result of a change in ownership. However, a partnership that previously established a business purpose to the satisfaction of the Commissioner to use a taxable year is not required to obtain the approval of the Commissioner if its required taxable year changes as a result of a change in ownership.

(e) Change of taxable year. Once a taxpayer has adopted a taxable year, such taxable year must be used in computing taxable income and making returns for all subsequent years unless the taxpayer obtains approval from the Commissioner to make a change or the taxpayer is otherwise authorized to change without the approval of the Commissioner under the Internal Revenue Code (e.g., section 444 or 859) or the regulations thereunder.

(f) Obtaining approval of the Commissioner or making a section 444 election. See § 1.442–1(b) for procedures for obtaining approval of the Commissioner (automatically or otherwise) to adopt, change, or retain an annual accounting period. See §§ 1.444–1T and 1.444–2T for qualifications, and 1.444–3T for procedures, for making an election under section 444.

[T.D. 8996, 67 FR 35009, May 17, 2002]

§ 1.446–1 General rule for methods of accounting.

(a) General rule. **(1)** Section 446(a) provides that taxable income shall be computed under the method of accounting on the basis of which a taxpayer regularly computes his income in keeping his books. The term "method of accounting" includes not only the overall method of accounting of the taxpayer but also the accounting treatment of any item. Examples of such over all methods are the cash receipts and disbursements method, an accrual method, combinations of such methods, and combinations of the foregoing with various methods provided for the accounting treatment of special items. These methods of accounting for special items include the accounting treatment prescribed for research and experimental expenditures, soil and water conservation expenditures, depreciation, net operating losses, etc. Except for deviations permitted or required by such special accounting treatment, taxable income shall be computed under the method of accounting on the basis of which the taxpayer regularly computes his income in keeping his books. For requirement respecting the adoption or change of accounting method, see section 446(e) and paragraph (e) of this section.

(2) It is recognized that no uniform method of accounting can be prescribed for all taxpayers. Each taxpayer shall adopt such forms and systems as are, in his judgment, best suited to his needs. However, no method of accounting is acceptable unless, in the opinion of the Commissioner, it clearly reflects income. A method of accounting which reflects the consistent application of generally accepted accounting principles in a particular trade or business in accordance with accepted conditions or practices in that trade or business will ordinarily be regarded as clearly reflecting income, provided all items of gross income and expense are treated consistently from year to year.

(3) Items of gross income and expenditures which are elements in the computation of taxable income need not be in the form of cash. It is sufficient that such items can be valued in terms of money. For general rules relating to the taxable year for inclusion of income and for taking deductions, see sections 451 and 461, and the regulations thereunder.

(4) Each taxpayer is required to make a return of his taxable income for each taxable year and must maintain such accounting records as will enable him to file a correct return. See section 6001 and the regulations thereunder. Accounting records include the taxpayer's regular books of account and such other records and data as may be necessary to support the entries on his books of account and on his return, as for example, a reconciliation of any differences between such books and his return. The following are among the essential features that must be considered in maintaining such records:

(i) In all cases in which the production, purchase, or sale of merchandise of any kind is an income-producing factor, merchandise on hand (including finished goods, work in process, raw materials, and supplies) at the beginning and end of the year shall be taken into account in computing the taxable income of the year. (For rules relating to computation of inventories, see section 263A, 471, and 472 and the regulations thereunder.)

(ii) Expenditures made during the year shall be properly classified as between capital and expense. For example, expenditures for such items as plant and equipment, which have a useful life extending substantially beyond the taxable year, shall be charged to a capital account and not to an expense account.

(iii) In any case in which there is allowable with respect to an asset a deduction for depreciation, amortization, or depletion, any expenditures (other than ordinary repairs) made to restore the asset or prolong its useful life shall be added to the asset account or charged against the appropriate reserve.

(b) Exceptions. **(1)** If the taxpayer does not regularly employ a method of accounting which clearly reflects his income, the computation of taxable income shall be made in a manner which, in the opinion of the Commissioner, does clearly reflect income.

(2) A taxpayer whose sole source of income is wages need not keep formal books in order to have an accounting method. Tax returns, copies thereof, or other records may be sufficient to establish the use of the method of accounting used in the preparation of the taxpayer's income tax returns.

(c) Permissible methods—(1) In general. Subject to the provisions of paragraphs (a) and (b) of this section, a taxpayer may compute his taxable income under any of the following methods of accounting:

(i) Cash receipts and disbursements method. Generally, under the cash receipts and disbursements method in the computation of taxable income, all items which constitute gross income (whether in the form of cash, property, or services) are to be included for the taxable year in which actually or constructively received. Expenditures are to be deducted for the taxable year in which actually made. For rules relating to constructive receipt, see § 1.451–2. For treatment of an expenditure attributable to more than one taxable year, see section 461(a) and paragraph (a)(1) of § 1.461–1.

(ii) Accrual method. **(A)** Generally, under an accrual method, income is to be included for the taxable year when all the events have occurred that fix the right to receive the income and the amount of the income can be determined with reasonable accuracy. Under such a method, a liability is incurred, and generally is taken into account for Federal income tax purposes, in the taxable year in which all the events have occurred that established the fact of the liability, the amount of the liability can be determined with reasonable accuracy, and economic performance has occurred with respect to the liability. (See paragraph (a)(2)(iii)(A) of § 1.461–1 for examples of liabilities that may not be taken into account until after the taxable year incurred, and see §§ 1.461–4 through 1.461–6 for rules relating to economic performance.) Applicable provisions of the Code, the Income Tax Regulations, and other guidance published by the Secretary prescribe the manner in which a liability that has been incurred is taken into account. For example, section 162 provides that a deductible liability generally is taken into account in the taxable year incurred through a deduction from gross income. * * *

(B) The term "liability" includes any item allowable as a deduction, cost, or expense for Federal income tax purposes. In addition to allowable deductions, the term includes any amount otherwise allowable as a capitalized cost, as a cost taken into account in computing cost of goods sold, as a cost allocable to a long-term contract, or as any other cost or expense. Thus, for example, an amount that a taxpayer expends or will expend for capital improvements to property must be incurred before the taxpayer may take the amount into account in computing its basis in the property. The term "liability" is not limited to items for which a legal obligation to pay exists at the time of payment. Thus, for example, amounts prepaid for goods or services and amounts paid without a legal obligation to do so may not be taken into account by an accrual basis taxpayer any earlier than the taxable year in which those amounts are incurred.

(C) No method of accounting is acceptable unless, in the opinion of the Commissioner, it clearly reflects income. The method used by the taxpayer in determining when income is to be accounted for will generally be acceptable if it accords with generally accepted accounting principles, is consistently used by the taxpayer from year to year, and is consistent with the Income Tax Regulations. For example, a taxpayer engaged in a manufacturing business may account for sales of the taxpayer's product when the goods are shipped, when the product is delivered or accepted, or when title to the goods passes to the customers, whether or not billed, depending on the method regularly employed in keeping the taxpayer's books.

* * *

(iv) Combinations of the foregoing methods. **(a)** In accordance with the following rules, any combination of the foregoing methods of accounting will be permitted in connection with a trade or business if such combination clearly reflects income and is consistently used. Where a combination of methods of accounting includes any special methods, such as those referred to in subdivision (iii) of this subparagraph, the taxpayer must comply with the requirements relating to such special methods. A taxpayer using an accrual method of accounting with respect to purchases and sales may use the cash method in computing all other items of income and expense. However, a taxpayer who uses the cash method of accounting in computing gross income from his trade or business shall use the cash method in computing expenses of such trade or business. Similarly, a taxpayer who uses an accrual method of accounting in computing business expenses shall use an accrual method in computing items affecting gross income from his trade or business.

(b) A taxpayer using one method of accounting in computing items of income and deductions of his trade or business may compute other items of income and deductions not connected with his trade or business under a different method of accounting.

(2) Special rules. **(i)** In any case in which it is necessary to use an inventory the accrual method of accounting must be used with regard to purchases and sales unless otherwise authorized under subdivision (ii) of this subparagraph.

(ii) No method of accounting will be regarded as clearly reflecting income unless all items of gross profit and deductions are treated with consistency from year to year. The Commissioner may authorize a taxpayer to adopt or change to a method of accounting permitted by this chapter although the method is not specifically described in the regulations in this part if, in the opinion of the Commissioner, income is clearly reflected by the use of such method. Further, the Commissioner may authorize a taxpayer to continue the use of a method of accounting consistently used by the taxpayer, even though not specifically authorized by the regulations in this part, if, in the opinion of the Commissioner, income is clearly reflected by the use of such method. See section 446(a) and paragraph (a) of this section, which require that taxable income shall be computed under the method of accounting on the basis of which the taxpayer regularly computes his income in keeping his books, and section 446(e) and paragraph (e) of this section, which require the prior approval of the Commissioner in the case of changes in accounting method.

(d) Taxpayer engaged in more than one business. **(1)** Where a taxpayer has two or more separate and distinct trades or businesses, a different method of accounting may be used for each trade or business, provided the method used for each trade or business clearly reflects the income of that particular trade or business. For example, a taxpayer may account for the operations of a personal service business on the cash receipts and disbursements method and of a manufacturing business on an accrual method, provided such businesses are separate and distinct and the methods used for each clearly reflect income. The method first used in accounting for business income and deductions in connection with each trade or business, as evidenced in the taxpayer's income tax return in which such income or deductions are first reported, must be consistently followed thereafter.

(2) No trade or business will be considered separate and distinct for purposes of this paragraph unless a complete and separable set of books and records is kept for such trade or business.

(3) If, by reason of maintaining different methods of accounting, there is a creation or shifting of profits or losses between the trades or businesses of the taxpayer (for example, through inventory adjustments, sales, purchases, or expenses) so that income of the taxpayer is not clearly reflected, the trades or businesses of the taxpayer will not be considered to be separate and distinct.

(e) Requirement respecting the adoption or change of accounting method. **(1)** A taxpayer filing his first return may adopt any permissible method of accounting in computing taxable income for the taxable year covered by such return. See section 446(c) and paragraph (c) of this section for permissible methods. Moreover, a taxpayer may adopt any permissible method of accounting in connection with each separate and distinct trade or business, the income from which is reported for the first time. See section 446(d) and paragraph (d) of this section. See also section 446(a) and paragraph (a) of this section.

(2)(i) Except as otherwise expressly provided in chapter 1 of the Code and the regulations thereunder, a taxpayer who changes the method of accounting employed in keeping his books shall, before computing his income upon such new method for purposes of taxation, secure the consent of the Commissioner. Consent must be secured whether or not such method is proper or is permitted under the Internal Revenue Code or the regulations thereunder.

(ii)(a) A change in the method of accounting includes a change in the overall plan of accounting for gross income or deductions or a change in the treatment of any material item used in such overall plan. Although a method of accounting may exist under this definition without the necessity of a pattern of consistent treatment of an item, in most instances a method of accounting is not established for an item without such consistent treatment. A material item is any item that involves the proper time for the inclusion of the item in income or the taking of a deduction. Changes in method of accounting include a change from the cash receipts and disbursement method to an accrual method, or vice versa, a change involving the method or basis used in the valuation of inventories (see sections 471 and 472 and the regulations under sections 471 and 472), a change from the cash or accrual method to a long-term contract method, or vice versa (see § 1.460–4), certain changes in computing depreciation or amortization (see paragraph (e)(2)(ii)(d) of this section), a change involving the adoption, use or discontinuance of any other specialized method of computing taxable income, such as the crop method, and a change where the Internal Revenue Code and regulations under the Internal Revenue Code specifically require that the consent of the Commissioner must be obtained before adopting such a change.

(b) A change in method of accounting does not include correction of mathematical or posting errors, or errors in the computation of tax liability (such as errors in computation of the foreign tax credit, net operating loss, percentage depletion, or investment credit). Also, a change in method of accounting does not include adjustment of any item of income or deduction that does not involve the proper time for the inclusion of the item of income or the taking of a deduction. * * *

* * *

[T.D. 6500, 25 FR 11708, Nov. 26, 1960, as amended by T.D. 7073, 35 FR 17710, Nov. 18, 1970; T.D. 7285, 38 FR 26184, Sept. 19, 1973; T.D. 8067, 51 FR 378, Jan. 6, 1986; T.D. 8131, 52 FR 10060, March 30, 1987; T.D. 8408, 57 FR 12419, Apr. 10, 1992; T.D. 8482, 58 FR 42233, Aug. 9, 1993; T.D. 8742, 62 FR 68167, Dec. 31, 1997; T.D. 9105, 69 FR 5, Jan. 2, 2004; T.D. 9307, 71 FR 78066, Dec. 28, 2006; T.D. 9354, 76 FR 45688, Aug. 1, 2011]

§ 1.446–2 Method of accounting for interest.

(a) Applicability—(1) In general. This section provides rules for determining the amount of interest that accrues during an accrual period (other than interest described in paragraph (a)(2) of this section) and for determining the portion of a payment that consists of accrued interest. For purposes of this section, interest includes original issue discount and amounts treated as interest (whether stated or unstated) in any lending or deferred payment transaction. Accrued interest determined under this section is taken into account by a taxpayer under the taxpayer's regular method of accounting (e.g., an accrual method or the cash receipts and disbursements method). Application of an exception described in paragraph (a)(2) of this section to one party to a transaction does not affect the application of this section to any other party to the transaction.

(2) Exceptions—(i) Interest included or deducted under certain other provisions. This section does not apply to interest that is taken into account under—

(A) Sections 1272(a), 1275, and 163(e) (income and deductions relating to original issue discount);

(B) Section 467(a)(2) (certain payments for the use of property or services);

(C) Sections 1276 through 1278 (market discount);

(D) Sections 1281 through 1283 (discount on certain short-term obligations);

(E) Section 7872(a) (certain loans with below-market interest rates); or

(F) Section 1.1272–3 (an election by a holder to treat all interest on a debt instrument as original issue discount).

(ii) De minimis original issue discount. This section does not apply to de minimis original issue discount (other than de minimis original issue discount treated as qualified stated interest) as determined under § 1.1273–1(d). See § 1.163–7 for the treatment of de minimis original issue discount by the issuer and §§ 1.1273–1(d) and 1.1272–3 for the treatment of de minimis original issue discount by the holder.

(b) Accrual of qualified stated interest. Qualified stated interest (as defined in § 1.1273–1(c)) accrues ratably over the accrual period (or periods) to which it is attributable and accrues at the stated rate for the period (or periods).

(c) Accrual of interest other than qualified stated interest. Subject to the modifications in paragraph (d) of this section, the amount of interest (other than qualified stated interest) that accrues for any accrual period is determined under rules similar to those in the regulations under sections 1272 and 1275 for the accrual of original issue discount. The preceding sentence applies regardless of any contrary formula agreed to by the parties.

(d) Modifications—(1) Issue price. The issue price of the loan or contract is equal to—

(i) In the case of a contract for the sale or exchange of property to which section 483 applies, the amount described in § 1.483–2(a)(1)(i) or (ii), whichever is applicable;

(ii) In the case of a contract for the sale or exchange of property to which section 483 does not apply, the stated principal amount; or

(iii) In any other case, the amount loaned.

(2) Principal payments that are not deferred payments. In the case of a contract to which section 483 applies, principal payments that are not deferred payments are ignored for purposes of determining yield and adjusted issue price.

(e) Allocation of interest to payments—(1) In general. Except as provided in paragraphs (e)(2), (e)(3), and (e)(4) of this section, each payment under a loan (other than payments of additional interest or similar charges provided with respect to amounts that are not paid when due) is treated as a payment of interest to the extent of the accrued and unpaid interest determined under paragraphs (b) and (c) of this section as of the date the payment becomes due.

(2) Special rule for points deductible under section 461(g)(2). If a payment of points is deductible by the borrower under section 461(g)(2), the payment is treated by the borrower as a payment of interest.

* * *

[T.D. 8517, 59 FR 4799, Feb. 2, 1994]

§ 1.446–4 Hedging transactions.

(a) In general. Except as provided in this paragraph (a), a hedging transaction as defined in § 1.1221–2(b) (whether or not the character of gain or loss from the transaction is determined under § 1.1221–2) must be accounted for under the rules of this section. To the extent that provisions of any other regulations governing the timing of income, deductions, gain, or loss are inconsistent with the rules of this section, the rules of this section control.

(1) Trades or businesses excepted. A taxpayer is not required to account for hedging transactions under the rules of this section for any trade or business in which the cash receipts and disbursements method of accounting is used or in which § 1.471–6 is used for inventory valuations if, for all prior taxable years ending on or after September 30, 1993, the taxpayer met the $5,000,000 gross receipts test of section 448(c) (or would have met that test if the taxpayer were a corporation or partnership). A taxpayer not required to use the rules of this section may nonetheless use a method of accounting that is consistent with these rules.

* * *

(b) Clear reflection of income. The method of accounting used by a taxpayer for a hedging transaction must clearly reflect income. To clearly reflect income, the method used must reasonably match the timing of income, deduction, gain, or loss from the hedging transaction with the timing of income, deduction, gain, or loss from the item or items being hedged. Taking gains and losses into account in the period in which they are realized may clearly reflect income in the case of certain hedging transactions. For example, where a hedge and the item being hedged are disposed of in the same taxable year, taking realized gain or loss into account on both items in that taxable year may clearly reflect income. In the case of many hedging transactions, however, taking gains and losses into account as they are realized does not result in the matching required by this section.

(c) Choice of method and consistency. For any given type of hedging transaction, there may be more than one method of accounting that satisfies the clear reflection requirement of paragraph (b) of this section. A taxpayer is generally permitted to adopt a method of accounting for a particular type of hedging transaction that clearly reflects the taxpayer's income from that type of transaction. See paragraph (e) of this section for requirements and limitations on the taxpayer's choice of method. Different methods of accounting may be used for different types of hedging transactions and for transactions that hedge different types of items. Once a taxpayer adopts a method of accounting, however, that method must be applied consistently and can only be changed with the consent of the Commissioner, as provided by section 446(e) and the regulations and procedures thereunder.

(d) Recordkeeping requirements—(1) In general. The books and records maintained by a taxpayer must contain a description of the accounting method used for each type of hedging transaction. The description of the method or methods used must be sufficient to show how the clear reflection requirement of paragraph (b) of this section is satisfied.

(2) Additional identification. In addition to the identification required by § 1.1221–2(f), the books and records maintained by a taxpayer must contain whatever more specific identification with respect to a transaction is necessary to verify the application of the method of accounting used by the taxpayer for the transaction. This additional identification may relate to the hedging transaction or to the item, items, or aggregate risk being hedged. The additional identification must be made at the time specified in § 1.1221–2(f)(2) and must be made on, and retained as part of, the taxpayer's books and records.

* * *

(e) Requirements and limitations with respect to hedges of certain assets and liabilities. In the case of certain hedging transactions, this paragraph (e) provides guidance in determining whether a taxpayer's method of accounting satisfies the clear reflection requirement of paragraph (b) of this section. Even if these rules are satisfied, however, the taxpayer's method, as actually applied to the taxpayer's hedging transactions, must clearly reflect income by meeting the matching requirement of paragraph (b) of this section.

(1) Hedges of aggregate risk—(i) In general. The method of accounting used for hedges of aggregate risk must comply with the matching requirements of paragraph (b) of this section. Even though a taxpayer may not be able to associate the hedging transaction with any particular item being hedged, the timing of income, deduction, gain, or loss from the hedging transaction must be matched with the timing of the aggregate income, deduction, gain, or loss from the items being hedged. * * *

(ii) Mark-and-spread method. The following method may be appropriate for taking into account income, deduction, gain, or loss from hedges of aggregate risk:

(A) The hedging transactions are marked to market at regular intervals for which the taxpayer has the necessary data, but not less frequently than quarterly; and

(B) The income, deduction, gain, or loss attributable to the realization or periodic marking to market of hedging transactions is taken into account over the period for which the hedging transactions are intended to reduce risk. Although the period over which the hedging transactions are intended to reduce risk may change, the period must be reasonable and consistent with the taxpayer's hedging policies and strategies.

(2) Hedges of items marked to market. In the case of a transaction that hedges an item that is marked to market under the taxpayer's method of accounting, marking the hedge to market clearly reflects income.

(3) Hedges of inventory—(i) In general. If a hedging transaction hedges purchases of inventory, gain or loss on the hedging transaction may be taken into account in the same period that it would be taken into account if the gain or loss were treated as an element of the cost of inventory. Similarly, if a hedging transaction hedges sales of inventory, gain or loss on the hedging transaction may be taken into account in the same period that it would be taken into account if the gain or loss were treated as an element of sales proceeds. If a hedge is associated with a particular purchase or sales transaction, the gain or loss on the hedge may be taken into account when it would be taken into account if it were an element of cost incurred in, or sales proceeds from, that transaction. As with hedges of aggregate risk, however, a taxpayer may not be able to associate hedges of inventory purchases or sales with particular purchase or sales transactions. In order to match the timing of income, deduction, gain, or loss from the hedge with the timing of aggregate income, deduction, gain, or loss from the hedged purchases or sales, it may be appropriate for a taxpayer to account for its hedging transactions in the manner described in paragraph (e)(1)(ii) of this section, except that the gain or loss that is spread to each period is taken into account when it would be if it were an element of cost incurred (purchase hedges), or an element of proceeds from sales made (sales hedges), during that period.

(ii) Alternative methods for certain inventory hedges. In lieu of the method described in paragraph (e)(3)(i) of this section, other simpler, less precise methods may be used in appropriate cases where the clear reflection requirement of paragraph (b) of this section is satisfied. For example:

(A) Taking into account realized gains and losses on both hedges of inventory purchases and hedges of inventory sales when they would be taken into account if the gains and losses were elements of inventory cost in the period realized may clearly reflect income in some situations, but does not clearly reflect income for a taxpayer that uses the last-in, first-out method of accounting for the inventory; and

(B) Marking hedging transactions to market with resulting gain or loss taken into account immediately may clearly reflect income even though the inventory that is being hedged is not marked to market, but only if the inventory is not accounted for under either the last-in, first-out method or the lower-of-cost-or-market method and only if items are held in inventory for short periods of time.

(4) Hedges of debt instruments. Gain or loss from a transaction that hedges a debt instrument issued or to be issued by a taxpayer, or a debt instrument held or to be held by a taxpayer, must be accounted for by reference to the terms of the debt instrument and the period or periods to which the hedge relates. A hedge of an instrument that provides for interest to be paid at a fixed rate or a qualified floating rate, for example, generally is accounted for using constant yield principles. Thus, assuming that a fixed rate or qualified floating rate instrument remains outstanding, hedging gain or loss is taken into account in the same periods in which it would be taken into account if it adjusted the yield of the instrument over the term to which the hedge relates. For example, gain or loss realized on a transaction that hedged an anticipated fixed rate borrowing for its entire term is accounted for, solely for purposes of this section, as if it decreased or increased the issue price of the debt instrument. * * *

* * *

(6) Disposition of hedged asset or liability. If a taxpayer hedges an item and disposes of, or terminates its interest in, the item but does not dispose of or terminate the hedging transaction, the taxpayer must appropriately match the built-in gain or loss on the hedging transaction to the gain or loss on the disposed item. To meet this requirement, the taxpayer may mark the hedge to market on the date it disposes of the hedged item. If the taxpayer intends to dispose of the hedging transaction within a reasonable period, however, it may be appropriate to match the realized gain or loss on the hedging transaction with the gain or loss on the disposed item. If the taxpayer intends to dispose of the hedging transaction within a reasonable period and the hedging transaction is not actually disposed of within that period, the taxpayer must match the gain or loss on the hedge at the end of the reasonable period with the gain or loss on the disposed item. For purposes of this paragraph (e)(6), a reasonable period is generally 7 days.

(7) Recycled hedges. If a taxpayer enters into a hedging transaction by recycling a hedge of a particular hedged item to serve as a hedge of a different item, as described in § 1.1221–2(d)(4), the taxpayer must match the built-in gain or loss at the time of the recycling to the gain or loss on the original hedged item, items, or aggregate risk. Income, deduction, gain, or loss attributable to the period after the recycling must be matched to the new hedged item, items, or aggregate risk under the principles of paragraph (b) of this section.

(8) Unfulfilled anticipatory transactions—(i) In general. If a taxpayer enters into a hedging transaction to reduce risk with respect to an anticipated asset acquisition, debt issuance, or obligation, and the anticipated transaction is not consummated, any income, deduction, gain, or loss from the hedging transaction is taken into account when realized.

* * *

(ii) Consummation of anticipated transaction. A taxpayer consummates a transaction for purposes of paragraph (e)(8)(i) of this section upon the occurrence (within a reasonable interval around the expected time of the anticipated transaction) of either the anticipated transaction or a different but similar transaction for which the hedge serves to reasonably reduce risk.

* * *

(f) Type or character of income and deduction. The rules of this section govern the timing of income, deduction, gain, or loss on hedging transactions but do not affect the type or character of income, deduction, gain, or loss produced by the transaction. Thus, for example, the rules of paragraph (e)(3) of this section do not affect the computation of cost of goods sold or sales proceeds for a taxpayer that hedges inventory purchases or sales. Similarly, the rules of paragraph (e)(4) of this section do not increase or decrease the interest income or expense of a taxpayer that hedges a debt instrument or a liability.

* * *

(h) Consent to change methods of accounting. The Commissioner grants consent for a taxpayer to change its methods of accounting for transactions that are entered into on or after October 1, 1994, and that are described in paragraph (a) of this section. This consent is granted only for changes for the taxable year containing October 1, 1994. The taxpayer must describe its new methods of accounting in a statement that is included in its Federal income tax return for that taxable year.

[T.D. 8554, 59 FR 36356, July 18, 1994, as amended by T.D. 8653, 61 FR 517, Jan. 8, 1996; T.D. 8674, 61 FR 30133, June 14, 1996; T.D. 8985, 67 FR 12866, Mar. 20, 2002; 67 FR 31955, May 13, 2002]

§ 1.446–5 Debt issuance costs.

(a) In general. This section provides rules for allocating debt issuance costs over the term of the debt. For purposes of this section, the term debt issuance costs means those transaction costs incurred by an issuer of debt (that is, a borrower) that are required to be capitalized under § 1.263(a)–5. If these costs are otherwise deductible, they are deductible by the issuer over the term of the debt as determined under paragraph (b) of this section.

(b) Method of allocating debt issuance costs—(1) In general. Solely for purposes of determining the amount of debt issuance costs that may be deducted in any period, these costs are treated as if they adjusted the yield on the debt. To effect this, the issuer treats the costs as if they decreased the issue price of the debt. See § 1.1273–2 to determine issue price. Thus, debt issuance costs increase or create original issue discount and decrease or eliminate bond issuance premium.

(2) Original issue discount. Any resulting original issue discount is taken into account by the issuer under the rules in § 1.163–7, which generally require the use of a constant yield method (as described in § 1.1272–1) to compute how much original issue discount is deductible for a period. However, see § 1.163–7(b) for special rules that apply if the total original issue discount on the debt is de minimis.

(3) Bond issuance premium. Any remaining bond issuance premium is taken into account by the issuer under the rules of § 1.163–13, which generally require the use of a constant yield method for purposes of allocating bond issuance premium to accrual periods.

(c) Examples. The following examples illustrate the rules of this section:

Example 1. **(i)** On January 1, 2004, X borrows $10,000,000. The principal amount of the loan ($10,000,000) is repayable on December 31, 2008, and payments of interest in the amount of $500,000 are due on December 31 of each year the loan is outstanding. X incurs debt issuance costs of $130,000 to facilitate the borrowing.

(ii) Under § 1.1273–2, the issue price of the loan is $10,000,000. However, under paragraph (b) of this section, X reduces the issue price of the loan by the debt issuance costs of $130,000, resulting in an issue price of $9,870,000. As a result, X treats the loan as having original issue discount in the amount of $130,000 (stated redemption price at maturity of $10,000,000 minus the issue price of $9,870,000). Because this amount of original issue discount is more than the de minimis amount of original issue discount for the loan determined under § 1.1273–1(d) ($125,000 ($10,000,000 x .0025 x 5)), X must allocate the original issue discount to each year based on the constant yield method described in § 1.1272–1(b). See § 1.163–7(a). Based on this method and a yield of 5.30%, compounded annually, the original issue discount is allocable to each year as follows: $23,385 for 2004, $24,625 for 2005, $25,931 for 2006, $27,306 for 2007, and $28,753 for 2008.

Example 2. **(i)** Assume the same facts as in Example 1, except that X incurs debt issuance costs of $120,000 rather than $130,000.

(ii) Under § 1.1273–2, the issue price of the loan is $10,000,000. However, under paragraph (b) of this section, X reduces the issue price of the loan by the debt issuance costs of $120,000, resulting in an issue price of $9,880,000. As a result, X treats the loan as having original issue discount in the amount of $120,000 (stated redemption price at maturity of $10,000,000 minus the issue price of $9,880,000). Because this amount of original issue discount is less than the de minimis amount of original issue discount for the loan determined under § 1.1273–1(d) ($125,000), X does not have to use the constant yield method described in § 1.1272–1(b) to allocate the original issue discount to each year. Instead, under § 1.163–7(b)(2), X can choose to allocate the original issue discount to each year on a straight-line basis over the term of the loan or in proportion to the stated interest payments ($24,000 each year). X also could choose to deduct the original issue discount at maturity of the loan. X makes its choice by reporting the original issue discount in a manner consistent with the method chosen on X's timely filed federal income tax return for 2004. If X wanted to use the constant yield method, based on a yield of 5.279%, compounded annually, the original issue discount is allocable to each year as follows: $21,596 for 2004, $22,736 for 2005, $23,937 for 2006, $25,200 for 2007, and $26,531 for 2008.

* * *

[T.D.9107,69 FR 464, Jan. 5, 2004]

§ 1.451–1 General rule for taxable year of inclusion.

(a) General rule. Gains, profits, and income are to be included in gross income for the taxable year in which they are actually or constructively received by the taxpayer unless includible for a different year in accordance with the taxpayer's method of accounting. Under an accrual method of accounting, income is includible in gross income when all the events have occurred which fix the right to receive such income and the amount thereof can be determined with reasonable accuracy. Therefore, under such a method of accounting if, in the case of compensation for services, no determination can be made as to the right to such compensation or the amount thereof until the services are completed, the amount of compensation is ordinarily income for the taxable year in which the determination can be made. Under the cash receipts and disbursements method of accounting, such an amount is includible in gross income when actually or constructively received. Where an amount of income is properly accrued on the basis of a reasonable estimate and the exact amount is subsequently determined, the difference, if any, shall be taken into account for the taxable year in which such determination is made. To the extent that income is attributable to the recovery of bad debts for accounts charged off in prior years, it is includible in the year of recovery in accordance with the taxpayer's method of accounting, regardless of the date when the amounts were charged off. For treatment of bad debts and bad debt recoveries, see sections 166 and 111 and the regulations thereunder. For rules relating to the treatment of amounts received in crop shares, see section 61 and the regulations thereunder. For the year in which a partner must include his distributive share of partnership income, see section 706(a) and paragraph (a) of § 1.706–1. If a taxpayer ascertains that an item should have been included in gross income in a prior taxable year, he should, if within the period of limitation, file an amended return and pay any additional tax due. Similarly, if a taxpayer ascertains that an item was improperly included in gross income in a prior taxable year, he should, if within the period of limitation, file claim for credit or refund of any overpayment of tax arising therefrom.

(b) Special rule in case of death. **(1)** A taxpayer's taxable year ends on the date of his death. See section 443(a)(2) * * *. In computing taxable income for such year, there shall be included only amounts properly includible under the method of accounting used by the taxpayer. However, if the taxpayer used an accrual method of accounting, amounts accrued only by reason of his death shall not be included in computing taxable income for such year. If the taxpayer uses no regular accounting method, only amounts actually or constructively received during such year shall be included. * * *

* * *

[T.D. 6500, 25 FR 11709, Nov. 26, 1960, as amended by T.D. 7001, 34 FR 997, Jan. 23, 1969; T.D. 7154, 36 FR 24996, Dec. 28, 1971; T.D. 7577, 43 FR 59357, Dec. 20, 1978; T.D. 8491, 58 FR 53135, Oct. 14, 1993; T.D. 8820, 64 FR 26851, May 18, 1999]

§ 1.451–2 Constructive receipt of income.

(a) General rule. Income although not actually reduced to a taxpayer's possession is constructively received by him in the taxable year during which it is credited to his account, set apart for him, or otherwise made available so that he may draw upon it at any time, or so that he could have drawn upon it during the taxable year if notice of intention to withdraw had been given. However, income is not constructively received if the taxpayer's control of its receipt is subject to substantial limitations or restrictions. Thus, if a corporation credits its employees with bonus stock, but the stock is not available to such employees until some future date, the mere crediting on the books of the corporation does not constitute receipt. In the case of interest, dividends, or other earnings (whether or not credited) payable in respect of any deposit or account in a bank, building and loan association, savings and loan association, or similar institution, the following are not substantial limitations or restrictions on the taxpayer's control over the receipt of such earnings:

(1) A requirement that the deposit or account, and the earnings thereon, must be withdrawn in multiples of even amounts;

(2) The fact that the taxpayer would, by withdrawing the earnings during the taxable year, receive earnings that are not substantially less in comparison with the earnings for the corresponding period to which the taxpayer would be entitled had he left the account on deposit until a later date (for example, if an amount equal to three months' interest must be forfeited upon withdrawal or redemption before maturity of a one year or less certificate of deposit, time deposit, bonus plan, or other deposit arrangement then the earnings payable on premature withdrawal or redemption would be substantially less when compared with the earnings available at maturity);

(3) A requirement that the earnings may be withdrawn only upon a withdrawal of all or part of the deposit or account. However, the mere fact that such institutions may pay earnings on withdrawals, total or partial, made during the last three business days of any calendar month ending a regular quarterly or semiannual earnings period at the applicable rate calculated to the end of such calendar month shall not constitute constructive receipt of income by any depositor or account holder in any such institution who has not made a withdrawal during such period;

(4) A requirement that a notice of intention to withdraw must be given in advance of the withdrawal. In any case when the rate of earnings payable in respect of such a deposit or account depends on the amount of notice of intention to withdraw that is given, earnings at the maximum rate are constructively received during the taxable year regardless of how long the deposit or account was held during the year or whether, in fact, any notice of intention to withdraw is given during the year. However, if in the taxable year of withdrawal the depositor or account holder receives a lower rate of earnings because he failed to give the required notice of intention to withdraw, he shall be allowed an ordinary loss in such taxable year in an amount equal to the difference between the amount of earnings previously included in gross income and the amount of earnings actually received. See section 165 and the regulations thereunder.

(b) Examples of constructive receipt. Amounts payable with respect to interest coupons which have matured and are payable but which have not been cashed are constructively received in the taxable year during which the coupons mature, unless it can be shown that there are no funds available for payment of the interest during such year. Dividends on corporate stock are constructively received when unqualifiedly made subject to the demand of the shareholder. However, if a dividend is declared payable on December 31 and the corporation followed its usual practice of paying the dividends by checks mailed so that the shareholders would not receive them until January of the following year, such dividends are not considered to have been constructively received in December. Generally, the amount of dividends or interest credited on savings bank deposits or to shareholders of organizations such as building and loan associations or cooperative banks is income to the depositors or shareholders for the taxable year when credited. However, if any portion of such dividends or interest is not subject to withdrawal at the time credited, such portion is not constructively received and does not constitute income to the depositor or shareholder until the taxable year in which the portion first may be withdrawn. Accordingly, if, under a bonus or forfeiture plan, a portion of the dividends or interest is accumulated and may not be withdrawn until the maturity of the plan, the crediting of such portion to the account of the shareholder or depositor does not constitute constructive receipt. In this case, such credited portion is income to the depositor or shareholder in the year in which the plan matures. * * * Accrued interest on unwithdrawn insurance policy dividends is gross income to the taxpayer for the first taxable year during which such interest may be withdrawn by him.

[T.D. 6500, 25 FR 11709, Nov. 26, 1960, as amended by T.D. 6723, 29 FR 5342, April 21, 1964; T.D. 7154, 36 FR 24997, Dec. 28, 1971; T.D. 7663, 44 FR 76782, Dec. 28, 1979]

§ 1.451–5 Advance payments for goods and long-term contracts.

(a) Advance payment defined. **(1)** For purposes of this section, the term "advance payment" means any amount which is received in a taxable year by a taxpayer using an accrual method of accounting for purchases and sales or a long-term contract method of accounting (described in § 1.451–3), pursuant to, and to be applied against, an agreement:

(i) For the sale or other disposition in a future taxable year of goods held by the taxpayer primarily for sale to customers in the ordinary course of his trade or business, or

(ii) For the building, installing, constructing or manufacturing by the taxpayer of items where the agreement is not completed within such taxable year.

(2) For purposes of subparagraph (1) of this paragraph:

(i) The term "agreement" includes (a) a gift certificate that can be redeemed for goods, and (b) an agreement which obligates a taxpayer to perform activities described in subparagraph (1)(i) or (ii) of this paragraph and which also contains an obligation to perform services that are to be performed as an integral part of such activities; and

(ii) Amounts due and payable are considered "received".

(3) If a taxpayer (described in subparagraph (1) of this paragraph) receives an amount pursuant to, and to be applied against, an agreement that not only obligates the taxpayer to perform the activities described in subparagraph (1)(i) and (ii) of this paragraph, but also obligates the taxpayer to perform services that are not to be performed as an integral part of such activities, such amount will be treated as an "advance payment" (as defined in subparagraph (1) of this paragraph) only to the extent such amount is properly allocable to the obligation to perform the activities described in subparagraph (1)(i) and (ii) of this paragraph. The portion of the amount not so allocable will not be considered an "advance payment" to which this section applies. If, however, the amount not so allocable is less than 5 percent of the total contract price, such amount will be treated as so allocable except that such treatment cannot result in delaying the time at which the taxpayer would otherwise accrue the amounts attributable to the activities described in subparagraph (1)(i) and (ii) of this paragraph.

(b) Taxable year of inclusion. **(1) In general.** Advance payments must be included in income either—

(i) In the taxable year of receipt; or

(ii) Except as provided in paragraph (c) of this section,

(a) In the taxable year in which properly accruable under the taxpayer's method of accounting for tax purposes if such method results in including advance payments in gross receipts no later than the time such advance payments are included in gross receipts for purposes of all of his reports (including consolidated financial statements) to shareholders, partners, beneficiaries, other proprietors, and for credit purposes, or

(b) If the taxpayer's method of accounting for purposes of such reports results in advance payments (or any portion of such payments) being included in gross receipts earlier than for tax purposes, in the taxable year in which includible in gross receipts pursuant to his method of accounting for purposes of such reports.

(2) Examples. This paragraph may be illustrated by the following examples:

Example (1). S, a retailer who uses for tax purposes and for purposes of the reports referred to in subparagraph (1)(ii)(a) of this paragraph, an accrual method of accounting under which it accounts for its sales of goods when the goods are shipped, receives advance payments for such goods. Such advance payments must be included in gross receipts for tax purposes either in the taxable year the payments are received or in the taxable year such goods are shipped (except as provided in paragraph (c) of this section).

Example (2). T, a manufacturer of household furniture, is a calendar year taxpayer who uses an accrual method of accounting pursuant to which income is accrued when furniture is shipped for purposes of its financial reports (referred to in subparagraph (1)(ii)(a) of this paragraph) and an accrual method of accounting pursuant to which the income is accrued when furniture is delivered and accepted for tax purposes. See, § 1.446–1(c)(1)(ii). In 1974, T receives an advance payment of $8,000 from X with respect to an order of furniture to be manufactured for X for a total price of $20,000. The furniture is shipped to X in December 1974, but it is not delivered to and accepted by X until January 1975. As a result of this contract, T must include the entire advance payment in its gross income for tax purposes in 1974 pursuant to subparagraph (1)(ii)(b) of this paragraph. T must include the remaining $12,000 of the gross contract price in its gross income in 1975 for tax purposes.

* * *

[T.D. 7103, 36 FR 5495, 5977, March 24, 1971, as amended by T.D. 7397, 41 FR 2641, Jan. 19, 1976; T.D. 8067, 51 FR 393, Jan. 6, 1986; T.D. 8929, 66 FR 2224, Jan. 11, 2001]

§ 1.453–1 *(Proposed, published 5-3-84.)* Installment method reporting for sales of real property and casual sales of personal property.

* * *

(f) Installment obligations received in certain nonrecognition exchanges—(1) Exchanges described in section 1031(b)—(i) In general. The provisions of paragraph (f)(1) of this section apply to exchanges described in section 1031(b) ("section 1031(b) exchanges") in which the taxpayer receives as boot (property which is "other property" under section 1031(b)) an installment obligation issued by the other party to the exchange, as well as property with respect to which no gain or loss is recognized ("permitted property" for purposes of paragraph (f)(1) of this section). However, an exchange otherwise described in section 1036 in which the receipt of an installment obligation is treated as a dividend (or would be treated as a dividend if the issuing corporation had adequate earnings and profits) is not a section 1031(b) exchange for purposes of this section.

(ii) Exclusion from payment. Receipt of permitted property will not be considered payment for purposes of paragraph (c) of this section.

(iii) Installment method determinations. In a section 1031(b) exchange, the taxpayer's basis in the property transferred by the taxpayer, including nondeductible expenses of the exchange, will first be allocated to the permitted property received by the taxpayer up to, but not in excess of, the fair market value of such property. If the taxpayer's basis exceeds the fair market value of the permitted property, that excess amount of basis is "excess basis." In making all required installment method determinations, the exchange is treated as if the taxpayer had made an installment sale of appreciated property (with a basis equal to the amount of excess basis) in which the consideration received was the installment obligation and any other boot. In a section 1031(b) exchange, only net qualifying indebtedness is taken into account in determining the amount of qualifying indebtedness * * * for this purpose, net qualifying indebtedness is the excess of—

(A) Liabilities of the taxpayer (or liabilities encumbering the property) assumed or taken subject to by the other party to the exchange as part of the consideration to the taxpayer, over

(B) The sum of any net cash paid (cash paid less any cash received) by the taxpayer in the exchange and any liability assumed or taken subject to by the taxpayer in the exchange.

Therefore, for purposes of installment method determinations, the selling price is the sum of the face value of the installment obligation (reduced by any portion of the obligation characterized as interest by section 483 or 1232), any net qualifying indebtedness, any cash received (in excess of any cash paid) by the taxpayer, and the fair market value of any other boot. The basis is the excess basis. The total contract price is the selling price less any net qualifying indebtedness that does not exceed the excess basis. Finally, payment in the year of exchange includes any net qualifying indebtedness that exceeds the excess basis.

* * *

(2) Certain exchanges described in section 356(a)—(i) In general. The provisions of paragraph (f)(2) of this section apply to exchanges described in section 356(a)(1) ("section 356(a)(1) exchanges") in which the taxpayer receives as boot (property which is "other property" under section 356(a)(1)(B)) an installment obligation issued by a qualifying corporation which is not treated as a dividend to the taxpayer. For purposes of section 453(f)(6) and paragraph (f)(2) of this section, any such section 356(a)(1) exchange shall be treated as a disposition of property by the taxpayer to the qualifying corporation and an acquisition of such property by the qualifying corporation from the taxpayer. If section 354 would apply to the exchange but for the receipt of boot, the term "qualifying corporation" means a corporation the stock of which could be received by the taxpayer in the exchange without recognition of gain or loss. If section 355 would apply to the exchange but for the receipt of boot, the term "qualifying corporation" means the distributing corporation (referred to in section 355(a)(1)(A)). Receipt of an installment obligation is treated as a dividend if section 356(a)(2) applies (determined without regard to the presence or absence of accumulated earnings and profits), or if section 356(e) (relating to certain exchanges for section 306 stock) applies to the taxpayer's receipt of the installment obligation.

(ii) Exclusion from payment. Receipt of permitted property shall not be considered payment for purposes of paragraph (c) of this section. For purposes of paragraph (f)(1) of this section, "permitted property" means property, the receipt of which does not result in recognition of gain under section 356(a)(1) (i.e., stock of a qualifying corporation).

(iii) Installment method determinations. Installment method determinations with respect to an installment obligation received in an exchange to which paragraph (f)(2) of this section applies shall be made in accordance with the rules prescribed in paragraph (f)(1)(iii) of this section. In applying such rules, a section 356(a)(1) exchange shall be treated as a section 1031(b) exchange and permitted property shall mean permitted property described in paragraph (f)(2) of this section.

* * *

(3) Other partial recognition exchanges—(i) In general. The provisions of paragraph (f)(3) of this section apply to exchanges not described in paragraph (f)(1) or (2) of this section in which a taxpayer, in exchange for appreciated property, receives both permitted property (i.e., property with respect to which no gain or loss would be recognized but which, in the hands of the taxpayer, would have as basis for determining gain or loss the same basis in whole or in part as the property exchanged) and boot that includes an installment obligation issued by the other party to the exchange. Ordinarily, the installment method rules set forth in paragraph (f)(1)(ii) and (iii) of this section will apply to an exchange described in paragraph (f)(3) of this section subject to such variations, if any, as may be required under the applicable provisions of the Code.

(ii) Exchanges to which section 351 applies. If a taxpayer receives, in an exchange to which section 351(b) applies (a "section 351(b) exchange"), an installment obligation * * *, the installment obligation is boot and the stock * * * (within the meaning of section 351(a)) * * * [is] permitted property (within the meaning of paragraph (f)(1)(ii) of this section). The taxpayer will report the installment obligation on the installment method and any other boot received will be treated as a payment made in the year of the exchange. In applying the rules of paragraph (f)(1)(iii) of this section to a section 351(b) exchange the excess basis is the amount, if any, by which the taxpayer's basis in the property transferred (plus any cash transferred) by the taxpayer exceeds the sum of the transferred liabilities which are not treated as money received under section 357 plus the fair market value of permitted property received by the taxpayer. In determining selling price and total contract price, transferred liabilities which are not treated as money received under section 357 shall be disregarded. For purposes of paragraph (f)(3)(ii) of this section, transferred liabilities are liabilities described in section 357(a)(2). Solely for the purpose of applying section 358(a)(1), the taxpayer shall be treated as if the taxpayer elected not to report receipt of the installment obligation on the installment method. Under section 362(a)(1) the corporation's basis in the property received from the taxpayer is the taxpayer's basis in the property increased by the gain recognized by the taxpayer at the time of the exchange. As the taxpayer recognizes gain on the installment method, the corporation will increase its basis in the property by an amount equal to the amount of gain recognized by the taxpayer.

(iii) Examples. The provisions of paragraph (f)(3) of this section are illustrated by the following examples. In each example, assume that adequate stated interest means both a reasonable rate of interest within the meaning of any applicable regulation promulgated under section 385 and a rate of interest not less than the test rate prescribed in the regulations under section 483, and that the debt to equity ratio of the issuing corporation is a permissible ratio under any applicable regulation promulgated under section 385.

Example (1). A owns Blackacre, unimproved real property, with a basis of $300,000. The fair market value of Blackacre is $700,000. Blackacre is encumbered by a longstanding mortgage of $200,000. A transfers Blackacre, subject to the mortgage, to newly organized X corporation. A receives in exchange all of the stock of X, worth $400,000, and a $100,000 installment obligation (bearing adequate stated interest) issued by X. A realizes $400,000 of gain on the exchange. The installment obligation calls for a single payment of the full $100,000 face amount three years following the date of issue. * * * The installment obligation is boot received by A in the exchange and the X stock is permitted property received by A in exchange. In applying the provisions of paragraph (f)(1)(ii) and (iii) of this section to a section 351(b) exchange, reference is required to section 357(a) under which the $200,000 mortgage liability is not treated as money or other property received by A in the exchange, and to section 358(a)(1) under which the basis of the X stock in the hands of A will be determined. These rules apply as follows: Neither receipt of the X stock nor relief of the mortgage encumbrance is treated as payment to A and thus A will recognize no gain in the year of the exchange. A's basis of $300,000 in Blackacre is reduced by the $200,000 mortgage from which A is deemed relieved in the exchange. The remaining basis of $100,000 is allocated to the X stock (but not in excess of the fair market value of the X stock); since the fair market value of the X stock is $400,000, the basis of the X stock in the hands of A is $100,000. Accordingly, in A's hands the installment obligation has a basis of zero. In the hands of X, the initial basis of Blackacre, determined under section 362(a), is $300,000 (the basis of the property in the hands of A), increased by the amount of gain recognized by A at the time of the transfer ($0). As A receives payments on the installment obligation and recognizes gain, X's basis in Blackacre will be increased, at that time, in an amount equal to the gain recognized by A. Thus, if the $100,000 installment obligation is paid in full on the third anniversary date, A will recognize gain of $100,000 (because A's basis in the installment obligation is zero) and X at that time will increase the basis at which it holds Blackacre by $100,000. If in the third year X had sold the property for cash before making payment on the installment obligation, X would recognize a loss of $100,000 when X paid the obligation in that amount to A on the third anniversary date.

* * *

(4) Installment obligations received as distributions in redemptions of stock pursuant to section 302(a). If a corporation redeems its stock and the redemption is treated as a distribution in part or full payment in exchange for the stock under section 302(a), then an installment obligation which meets the requirements of section 453 and is distributed in the redemption shall be reported on the installment method unless the taxpayer elects otherwise.

* * *

§ 1.453–4 Sale of real property involving deferred periodic payments.

* * *

(c) Determination of "selling price". In the sale of mortgaged property the amount of the mortgage, whether the property is merely taken subject to the mortgage or whether the mortgage is assumed by the purchaser, shall, for the purpose of determining whether a sale is on the installment plan, be included as a part of the "selling price"; and for the purpose of determining the payments and the total contract price as those terms are used in section 453, * * *, the amount of such mortgage shall be included only to the extent that it exceeds the basis of the property. The term "payments" does not include amounts received by the vendor in the year of sale from the disposition to a third person of notes given by the vendee as part of the purchase price which are due and payable in subsequent years. Commissions and other selling expenses paid or incurred by the vendor shall not reduce the amount of the payments, the total contract price, or the selling price.

[T.D. 6500, 25 FR 11715, Nov. 26, 1960]

§ 1.453–6 Deferred payment sale of real property not on installment method.

(a) Value of obligations. **(1)** * * *

(2) If the obligations received by the vendor have no fair market value, the payments in cash or other property having a fair market value shall be applied against and reduce the basis of the property sold and, if in excess of such basis, shall be taxable to the extent of the excess. Gain or loss is realized when the obligations are disposed of or satisfied, the amount thereof being the difference between the reduced basis as provided in the preceding sentence and the amount realized therefor. Only in rare and extraordinary cases does property have no fair market value.

* * *

[T.D. 6500, 25 FR 11716, Nov. 26, 1960, as amended by T.D. 6916, 32 FR 5923, April 13, 1967]

§ 1.453–9 Gain or loss on disposition of installment obligations.

(a) In general. Subject to the exceptions * * *, the entire amount of gain or loss resulting from any disposition or satisfaction of installment obligations, * * *, is recognized in the taxable year of such disposition or satisfaction and shall be considered as resulting from the sale or exchange of the property in respect of which the installment obligation was received by the taxpayer.

(b) Computation of gain or loss. **(1)** The amount of gain or loss resulting under paragraph (a) of this section is the difference between the basis of the obligation and (i) the amount realized, in the case of satisfaction at other than face value or in the case of a sale or exchange, or (ii) the fair market value of the obligation at the time of disposition, if such disposition is other than by sale or exchange.

(2) The basis of an installment obligation shall be the excess of the face value of the obligation over an amount equal to the income which would be returnable were the obligation satisfied in full.

(3) The application of subparagraphs (1) and (2) of this paragraph may be illustrated by the following examples:

Example (1). In 1960 the M Corporation sold a piece of unimproved real estate to B for $20,000. The company acquired the property in 1948 at a cost of $10,000. During 1960 the company received $5,000 cash and vendee's notes for the remainder of the selling price, or $15,000, payable in subsequent years. In 1962, before the vendee made any further payments, the company sold the notes for $13,000 in cash. The corporation makes its returns on the calendar year basis. The income to be reported for 1962 is $5,500, computed as follows:

Proceeds of sale of notes		$13,000
Selling price of property	20,000	
Cost of property	10,000	
Total profit	10,000	
Total contract price	20,000	
Percent of profit, or proportion of each payment returnable as income, $10,000 divided by $20,000, 50 percent.		
Face value of notes	15,000	
Amount of income returnable were the notes satisfied in full, 50 percent of $15,000	7,500	
Basis of obligation—excess of face value of notes over amount of income returnable were the notes satisfied in full	7,500	
Taxable income to be reported for 1962		5,500

Example (2). Suppose in example (1) the M Corporation, instead of selling the notes, distributed them in 1962 to its shareholders as a dividend, and at the time of such distribution, the fair market value of the notes was $14,000. The income to be reported for 1962 is $6,500, computed as follows:

Fair market value of notes	$14,000
Basis of obligation—excess of face value of notes over amount of income returnable were the notes satisfied in full (computed as in example (1))	7,500
Taxable income to be reported for 1962	6,500

(c) Disposition from which no gain or loss is recognized. (1)(i) * * *

* * *

(2) Where the Code provides for exceptions to the recognition of gain or loss in the case of certain dispositions, no gain or loss shall result * * * in the case of a disposition of an installment obligation. Such exceptions include: certain transfers to corporations under sections 351 and 361; contributions of property to a partnership by a partner under section 721; and distributions by a partnership to a partner under section 731 (except as provided by section 736 and section 751).

(3) Any amount received by a person in payment or settlement of an installment obligation acquired in a transaction described in subparagraphs (1) or (2) of this paragraph (other than an amount received by a stockholder with respect to an installment obligation distributed to him pursuant to section 337) shall be considered to have the character it would have had in the hands of the person from whom such installment obligation was acquired.

* * *

[T.D. 6500, 25 FR 11718, Nov. 26, 1960, as amended by T.D. 6590, 27 FR 1319, Feb. 13, 1962; T.D. 6832, 30 FR 8574, July 7, 1965; T.D. 7084, 36 FR 267, Jan. 8, 1971; T.D. 7418, 41 FR 18812, May 7, 1976; T.D. 8586, 60 FR 2497, Jan. 10, 1995]

§ 1.453–11 Installment obligations received from a liquidating corporation.

(a) In general—(1) Overview. Except as provided in section 453(h)(1)(C) (relating to installment sales of depreciable property to certain closely related persons), a qualifying shareholder (as defined in paragraph (b) of this section) who receives a qualifying installment obligation (as defined in paragraph (c) of this section) in a liquidation that satisfies section 453(h)(1)(A) treats the receipt of payments in respect of the obligation, rather than the receipt of the obligation itself, as a receipt of payment for the shareholder's stock. The shareholder reports the payments received on the installment method unless the shareholder elects otherwise in accordance with § 15a.453–1(d) of this chapter.

(2) Coordination with other provisions—(i) Deemed sale of stock for installment obligation. Except as specifically provided in section 453(h)(1)(C), a qualifying shareholder treats a qualifying installment obligation, for all purposes of the Internal Revenue Code, as if the obligation is received by the shareholder from the person issuing the obligation in exchange for the shareholder's stock in the liquidating corporation. For example, if the stock of a corporation that is liquidating is traded on an established securities market, an installment obligation distributed to a shareholder of the corporation in exchange for the shareholder's stock does not qualify for installment reporting pursuant to section 453(k)(2).

(ii) Special rules to account for the qualifying installment obligation—(A) Issue price. A qualifying installment obligation is treated by a qualifying shareholder as newly issued on the date of the distribution. The issue price of the qualifying installment obligation on that date is equal to the sum of the adjusted issue price of the obligation on the date of the distribution (as determined under § 1.1275–1(b)) and the amount of any qualified stated interest (as defined in § 1.1273–1(c)) that has accrued prior to the distribution but that is not payable until after the distribution. For purposes of the preceding sentence, if the qualifying installment obligation is subject to § 1.446–2 (e.g., a debt instrument that has unstated interest under section 483), the adjusted issue price of the obligation is determined under § 1.446–2(c) and (d).

(B) Variable rate debt instrument. If the qualifying installment obligation is a variable rate debt instrument (as defined in § 1.1275–5), the shareholder uses the equivalent fixed rate debt instrument (within the meaning of § 1.1275–5(e)(3)(ii)) constructed for the qualifying installment obligation as of the date the obligation was issued to the liquidating corporation to determine the accruals of original issue discount, if any, and interest on the obligation.

(3) Liquidating distributions treated as selling price. All amounts distributed or treated as distributed to a qualifying shareholder incident to the liquidation, including cash, the issue price of qualifying installment obligations as determined under paragraph (a)(2)(ii)(A) of this section, and the fair market value of other property (including obligations that are not qualifying installment obligations) are considered as having been received by the shareholder as the selling price (as defined in § 15a.453–1(b)(2)(ii) of this chapter) for the shareholder's stock in the liquidating corporation. For the proper method of reporting liquidating distributions received in more than one taxable year of a shareholder, see paragraph (d) of this section. An election not to report on the installment method an installment obligation received in the liquidation applies to all distributions received in the liquidation.

(4) Assumption of corporate liability by shareholders. For purposes of this section, if in the course of a liquidation a shareholder assumes secured or unsecured liabilities of the liquidating corporation, or receives property from the corporation subject to such liabilities (including any tax liabilities incurred by the corporation on the distribution), the amount of the liabilities is added to the shareholder's basis in the stock of the liquidating corporation. These additions to basis do not affect the shareholder's holding period for the stock. These liabilities do not reduce the amounts received in computing the selling price.

(5) Examples. The provisions of this paragraph (a) are illustrated by the following examples. Except as otherwise provided, assume in each example that A, an individual who is a calendar-year taxpayer, owns all of the stock of T corporation. A's adjusted tax basis in that stock is $100,000. On February 1, 1998, T, an accrual method taxpayer, adopts a plan of complete liquidation that satisfies section 453(h)(1)(A) and immediately sells all of its assets to unrelated B corporation in a single transaction. The examples are as follows:

Example (1). **(i)** The stated purchase price for T's assets is $3,500,000. In consideration for the sale, B makes a down payment of $500,000 and issues a 10–year installment obligation with a stated principal amount of $3,000,000. The obligation provides for interest payments of $150,000 on January 31 of each year, with the total principal amount due at maturity.

(ii) Assume that for purposes of section 1274, the test rate on February 1, 1998, is 8 percent, compounded semi-annually. Also assume that a semi-annual accrual period is used. Under § 1.1274–2, the issue price of the obligation on February 1, 1998, is $2,368,450. Accordingly, the obligation has $631,550 of original issue discount ($3,000,000–$2,368,450). Between February 1 and July 31, $19,738 of original issue discount and $75,000 of qualified stated interest accrue with respect to the obligation and are taken into account by T.

(iii) On July 31, 1998, T distributes the installment obligation to A in exchange for A's stock. No other property is ever distributed to A. On January 31, 1999, A receives the first annual payment of $150,000 from B.

(iv) When the obligation is distributed to A on July 31, 1998, it is treated as if the obligation is received by A in an installment sale of shares directly to B on that date. Under § 1.1275–1(b), the adjusted issue price of the obligation on that date is $2,388,188 (original issue price of $2,368,450 plus accrued original issue discount of $19,738). Accordingly, the issue price of the obligation under paragraph (a)(2)(ii)(A) of this section is $2,463,188, the sum of the adjusted issue price of the obligation on that date ($2,388,188) and the amount of accrued but unpaid qualified stated interest ($75,000).

(v) The selling price and contract price of A's stock in T is $2,463,188, and the gross profit is $2,363,188 ($2,463,188 selling price less A's adjusted tax basis of $100,000). A's gross profit ratio is thus 96 percent (gross profit of $2,363,188 divided by total contract price of $2,463,188).

(vi) Under §§ 1.446–2(e)(1) and 1.1275–2(a), $98,527 of the $150,000 payment is treated as a payment of the interest and original issue discount that accrued on the obligation from July 31, 1998, to January 31, 1999 ($75,000 of qualified stated interest and $23,527 of original issue discount). The balance of the payment ($51,473) is treated as a payment of principal. A's gain recognized in 1999 is $49,414 (96 percent of $51,473).

Example (2). **(i)** T owns Blackacre, unimproved real property, with an adjusted tax basis of $700,000. Blackacre is subject to a mortgage (underlying mortgage) of $1,100,000. A is not personally liable on the underlying mortgage and the T shares held by A are not encumbered by the underlying mortgage. The other assets of T consist of $400,000 of cash and $600,000 of accounts receivable attributable to sales of inventory in the ordinary course of business. The unsecured liabilities of T total $900,000.

(ii) On February 1, 1998, T adopts a plan of complete liquidation complying with section 453(h)(1)(A), and promptly sells Blackacre to B for a 4–year mortgage note (bearing adequate stated interest and otherwise meeting all of the requirements of section 453) in the face amount of $4 million. Under the agreement between T and B, T (or its successor) is to continue to make principal and interest payments on the underlying mortgage. Immediately thereafter, T completes its liquidation by distributing to A its remaining cash of $400,000 (after payment of T's tax liabilities), accounts receivable of $600,000, and the $4 million B note. A assumes T's $900,000 of unsecured liabilities and receives the distributed property subject to the obligation to make payments on the $1,100,000 underlying mortgage. A receives no payments from B on the B note during 1998.

(iii) Unless A elects otherwise, the transaction is reported by A on the installment method. The selling price is $5 million (cash of $400,000, accounts receivable of $600,000, and the B note of $4 million). The total contract price also is $5 million. A's adjusted tax basis in the T shares, initially $100,000, is increased by the $900,000 of unsecured T liabilities assumed by A and by the obligation (subject to which A takes the distributed property) to make payments on the $1,100,000 underlying mortgage on Blackacre, for an aggregate adjusted tax basis of $2,100,000. Accordingly, the gross profit is $2,900,000 (selling price of $5 million less aggregate adjusted tax basis of $2,100,000). The gross profit ratio is 58 percent (gross profit of $2,900,000 divided by the total contract price of $5 million). The 1998 payments to A are $1 million ($400,000 cash plus $600,000 receivables) and A recognizes gain in 1998 of $580,000 (58 percent of $1 million).

(iv) In 1999, A receives payment from B on the B note of $1 million (exclusive of interest). A's gain recognized in 1999 is $580,000 (58 percent of $1 million).

(b) Qualifying shareholder. For purposes of this section, qualifying shareholder means a shareholder to which, with respect to the liquidating distribution, section 331 applies. For example, a creditor that receives a distribution from a liquidating corporation, in exchange for the creditor's claim, is not a qualifying shareholder as a result of that distribution regardless of whether the liquidation satisfies section 453(h)(1)(A).

(c) Qualifying installment obligation—(1) In general. For purposes of this section, qualifying installment obligation means an installment obligation (other than an evidence of indebtedness described in § 15a.453–1(e) of this chapter, relating to obligations that are payable on demand or are readily tradable) acquired in a sale or exchange of corporate assets by a liquidating corporation during the 12–month period beginning on the date the plan of liquidation is adopted. See paragraph (c)(4) of this section for an exception for installment obligations acquired in respect of certain sales of inventory. Also see paragraph (c)(5) of this section for an exception for installment obligations attributable to sales of certain property that do not generally qualify for installment method treatment.

(2) Corporate assets. Except as provided in section 453(h)(1)(C), in paragraph (c)(4) of this section (relating to certain sales of inventory), and in paragraph (c)(5) of this section (relating to certain tax avoidance transactions), the nature of the assets sold by, and the tax consequences to, the selling corporation do not affect whether an installment obligation is a qualifying installment obligation. Thus, for example, the fact that the fair market value of an asset is less than the adjusted basis of that asset in the hands of the corporation; or that the sale of an asset will subject the corporation to depreciation recapture (e.g., under section 1245 or section 1250); or that the assets of a trade or business sold by the corporation for an installment obligation include depreciable property, certain marketable securities, accounts receivable, installment obligations, or cash; or that the distribution of assets to the shareholder is or is not taxable to the corporation under sections 336 and 453B, does not affect whether installment obligations received in exchange for those assets are treated as qualifying installment obligations by the shareholder. However, an obligation received by the corporation in exchange for cash, in a transaction unrelated to a sale or exchange of noncash assets by the corporation, is not treated as a qualifying installment obligation.

(3) Installment obligations distributed in liquidations described in section 453(h)(1)(E)—(i) In general. In the case of a liquidation to which section 453(h)(1)(E) (relating to certain liquidating subsidiary corporations) applies, a qualifying installment obligation acquired in respect of a sale or exchange by the liquidating subsidiary corporation will be treated as a qualifying installment obligation if distributed by a controlling corporate shareholder (within the meaning of section 368(c)) to a qualifying shareholder. The preceding sentence is applied successively to each controlling corporate shareholder, if any, above the first controlling corporate shareholder.

(ii) Examples. The provisions of this paragraph (c)(3) are illustrated by the following examples:

Example (1). **(i)** A, an individual, owns all of the stock of T corporation, a C corporation. T has an operating division and three wholly-owned subsidiaries, X, Y, and Z. On February 1, 1998, T, Y, and Z all adopt plans of complete liquidation.

(ii) On March 1, 1998, the following sales are made to unrelated purchasers: T sells the assets of its operating division to B for cash and an installment obligation. T sells the stock of X to C for an installment obligation. Y sells all of its assets to D for an installment obligation. Z sells all of its assets to E for cash. The B, C, and D installment obligations bear adequate stated interest and meet the requirements of section 453.

(iii) In June 1998, Y and Z completely liquidate, distributing their respective assets (the D installment obligation and cash) to T. In July 1998, T completely liquidates, distributing to A cash and the installment obligations respectively issued by B, C, and D. The liquidation of T is a liquidation to which section 453(h) applies and the liquidations of Y and Z into T are liquidations to which section 332 applies.

(iv) Because T is in control of Y (within the meaning of section 368(c)), the D obligation acquired by Y is treated as acquired by T pursuant to section 453(h)(1)(E). A is a qualifying shareholder and the installment obligations issued by B, C, and D are qualifying installment obligations. Unless A elects otherwise, A reports the transaction on the installment method as if the cash and installment obligations had been received in an installment sale of the stock of T corporation. Under section 453B(d), no gain or loss is recognized by Y on the distribution of the D installment obligation to T. Under sections 453B(a) and 336, T recognizes gain or loss on the distribution of the B, C, and D installment obligations to A in exchange for A's stock.

Example (2). **(i)** A, a cash-method individual taxpayer, owns all of the stock of P corporation, a C corporation. P owns 30 percent of the stock of Q corporation. The balance of the Q stock is owned by unrelated individuals. On February 1, 1998, P adopts a plan of complete liquidation and sells all of its property, other than its Q stock, to B, an unrelated purchaser for cash and an installment obligation bearing adequate stated interest. On March 1, 1998, Q adopts a plan of complete liquidation and sells all of its property to an unrelated purchaser, C, for cash and installment obligations. Q immediately distributes the cash and installment obligations to its shareholders in completion of its liquidation. Promptly thereafter, P liquidates, distributing to A cash, the B installment obligation, and a C installment obligation that P received in the liquidation of Q.

(ii) In the hands of A, the B installment obligation is a qualifying installment obligation. In the hands of P, the C installment obligation was a qualifying installment obligation. However, in the hands of A, the C installment obligation is not treated as a qualifying installment obligation because P owned only 30 percent of the stock of Q. Because P did not own the requisite 80 percent stock interest in Q, P was not a controlling corporate shareholder of Q (within the meaning of section 368(c)) immediately before the liquidation. Therefore, section 453(h)(1)(E) does not apply. Thus, in the hands of A, the C obligation is considered to be a third-party note (not a purchaser's evidence of indebtedness) and is treated as a payment to A in the year of distribution. Accordingly, for 1998, A reports as payment the cash and the fair market value of the C obligation distributed to A in the liquidation of P.

(iii) Because P held 30 percent of the stock of Q, section 453B(d) is inapplicable to P. Under sections 453B(a) and 336, accordingly, Q recognizes gain or loss on the distribution of the C obligation. P also recognizes gain or loss on the distribution of the B and C installment obligations to A in exchange for A's stock. See sections 453B and 336.

* * *

(d) Liquidating distributions received in more than one taxable year. If a qualifying shareholder receives liquidating distributions to which this section applies in more than one taxable year, the shareholder must reasonably estimate the gain attributable to distributions received in each taxable year. In allocating basis to calculate the gain for a taxable year, the shareholder must reasonably estimate the anticipated aggregate distributions. For this purpose, the shareholder must take into account distributions and other relevant events or information that the shareholder knows or reasonably could know up to the date on which the federal income tax return for that year is filed. If the gain for a taxable year is properly taken into account on the basis of a reasonable estimate and the exact amount is subsequently determined the difference, if any, must be taken into account for the taxable year in which the subsequent determination is made. However, the shareholder may file an amended return for the earlier year in lieu of taking the difference into account for the subsequent taxable year.

(e) Effective date. This section is applicable to distributions of qualifying installment obligations made on or after January 28, 1998.

[T.D. 8762, 63 FR 4168, Jan. 28, 1998]

§ 1.453–12 Allocation of unrecaptured section 1250 gain reported on the installment method.

(a) General rule. Unrecaptured section 1250 gain, as defined in section 1(h)(7), is reported on the installment method if that method otherwise applies under section 453 or 453A and the corresponding regulations. If gain from an installment sale includes unrecaptured section 1250 gain and adjusted net capital gain (as defined in section 1(h)(4)), the unrecaptured section 1250 gain is taken into account before the adjusted net capital gain.

(b) Installment payments from sales before May 7, 1997. The amount of unrecaptured section 1250 gain in an installment payment that is properly taken into account after May 6, 1997, from a sale before May 7, 1997, is determined as if, for all payments properly taken into account after the date of sale but before May 7, 1997, unrecaptured section 1250 gain had been taken into account before adjusted net capital gain.

* * *

(d) Examples. In each example, the taxpayer, an individual whose taxable year is the calendar year, does not elect out of the installment method. The installment obligation bears adequate stated interest, and the property sold is real property held in a trade or business that qualifies as both section 1231 property and section 1250 property. In all taxable years, the taxpayer's marginal tax rate on ordinary income is 28 percent. The following examples illustrate the rules of this section:

Example 1. General rule. This example illustrates the rule of paragraph (a) of this section.

(i) In 1999, A sells property for $10,000, to be paid in ten equal annual installments beginning on December 1, 1999. A originally purchased the property for $5,000, held the property for several years, and took straight-line depreciation deductions in the amount of $3,000. In each of the years 1999–2008, A has no other capital or section 1231 gains or losses.

(ii) A's adjusted basis at the time of the sale is $2,000. Of A's $8,000 of section 1231 gain on the sale of the property, $3,000 is attributable to prior straight-line depreciation deductions and is unrecaptured section 1250 gain. The gain on each installment payment is $800.

(iii) As illustrated in the table in this paragraph (iii) of this *Example*, A takes into account the unrecaptured section 1250 gain first. Therefore, the gain on A's first three payments, received in 1999, 2000, and 2001, is taxed at 25 percent. Of the $800 of gain on the fourth payment, received in 2002, $600 is taxed at 25 percent and the remaining $200 is taxed at 20 percent. The gain on A's remaining six installment payments is taxed at 20 percent. The table is as follows:

	1999	2000	2001	2002	2003	2004–2008	Total gain
Installment gain	800	800	800	800	800	4000	8000
Taxed at 25%	800	800	800	600			3000
Taxed at 20%				200	800	4000	5000
Remaining to be taxed at 25%	2200	1400	600				

* * *

Example 3, Effect of section 1231(c) recapture. This example illustrates the rule of paragraph (a) of this section when there are non-recaptured net section 1231 losses, as defined in section 1231(c)(2), from prior years as follows:

(i) The facts are the same as in *Example 1,* except that in 1999 A has non-recaptured net section 1231 losses from the previous four years of $1000.

(ii) As illustrated in the table in paragraph (iv) of this *Example 3*, in 1999, all of A's $800 installment gain is recaptured as ordinary income under section 1231(c). Under the rule described in paragraph (a) of this section, for purposes of determining the amount of unrecaptured section 1250 gain remaining to be taken into account, the $800 recaptured as ordinary income under section 1231(c) is treated as reducing unrecaptured section 1250 gain, rather than adjusted net capital gain. Therefore, A has $2200 of unrecaptured section 1250 gain remaining to be taken into account.

(iii) In 2000, A's installment gain is taxed at two rates. First, $200 is recaptured as ordinary income under section 1231(c). Second, the remaining $600 of gain on A's 2000 installment payment is taxed at 25 percent. Because the full $800 of gain reduces unrecaptured section 1250 gain, A has $1400 of unrecaptured section 1250 gain remaining to be taken into account.

(iv) The gain on A's installment payment received in 2001 is taxed at 25 percent. Of the $800 of gain on the fourth payment, received in 2002, $600 is taxed at 25 percent and the remaining $200 is taxed at 20 percent. The gain on A's remaining six installment payments is taxed at 20 percent. The table is as follows:

	1999	2000	2001	2002	2003	2004–2008	Total gain
Installment gain	800	800	800	800	800	4000	8000
Taxed at ordinary rates under section 1231(c)	800	200					1000
Taxed at 25%		600	800	600			2000
Taxed at 20%				200	800	4000	5000
Remaining non-recaptured net section 1231 losses	200						
Remaining to be taxed at 25%	2200	1400	600				

Example 4. Effect of a net section 1231 loss. This example illustrates the application of paragraph (a) of this section when there is a net section 1231 loss as follows:

(i) The facts are the same as in *Example 1* except that A has section 1231 losses of $1000 in 1999.

(ii) In 1999, A's section 1231 installment gain of $800 does not exceed A's section 1231 losses of $1000. Therefore, A has a net section 1231 loss of $200. As a result, under section 1231(a) all of A's section 1231 gains and losses are treated as ordinary gains and losses. As illustrated in the following table, A's entire $800 of installment gain is ordinary gain. Under the rule described in paragraph (a) of this section, for purposes of determining the amount of unrecaptured section 1250 gain remaining to be taken into account, A's $800 of ordinary section 1231 installment gain in 1999 is treated as reducing unrecaptured section 1250 gain. Therefore, A has $2200 of unrecaptured section 1250 gain remaining to be taken into account.

(iii) In the year 2000, A has $800 of section 1231 installment gain, resulting in a net section 1231 gain of $800. A also has $200 of non-recaptured net section 1231 losses. The $800 gain is taxed at two rates. First, $200 is taxed at ordinary rates under section 1231(c), recapturing the $200 net section 1231 loss sustained in 1999. Second, the remaining $600 of gain on A's 2000 installment payment is taxed at 25 percent. As in *Example 3,* the $200 of section 1231(c) gain is treated as reducing unrecaptured section 1250 gain, rather than adjusted net capital gain. Therefore, A has $1400 of unrecaptured section 1250 gain remaining to be taken into account.

(iv) The gain on A's installment payment received in 2001 is taxed at 25 percent, reducing the remaining unrecaptured section 1250 gain to $600. Of the $800 of gain on the fourth payment, received in 2002, $600 is taxed at 25 percent and the remaining $200 is taxed at 20 percent. The gain on A's remaining six installment payments is taxed at 20 percent. The table is as follows:

	1999	2000	2001	2002	2003	2004–2008	Total gain
Installment gain	800	800	800	800	800	4000	8000
Ordinary gain under section 1231(a)	800						800
Taxed at ordinary rates under section 1231(c)		200					200
Taxed at 25%		600	800	600			2000
Taxed at 20%				200	800	4000	5000
Net section 1231 loss	200						
Remaining to be taxed at 25%	2200	1400	600				

(e) Effective date. This section applies to installment payments properly taken into account after August 23, 1999.

[T.D. 8836, 64 FR 45874, Aug. 23, 1999]

§ 15a.453–1 Installment method reporting for sales of real property and casual sales of personal property.

(a) In general. Unless the taxpayer otherwise elects in the manner prescribed in paragraph (d)(3) of this section, income from a sale of real property or a casual sale of personal property, where any payment is to be received in a taxable year after the year of sale, is to be reported on the installment method.

(b) Installment sale defined—(1) In general. The term "installment sale" means a disposition of property (except as provided in paragraph (b)(4) of this section) where at least one payment is to be received after the close of the taxable year in which the disposition occurs. The term "installment sale" includes dispositions from which payment is to be received in a lump sum in a taxable year subsequent to the year of sale. For purposes of this paragraph, the taxable year in which payments are to be received is to be determined without regard to section 453(e) (relating to related party sales), section (f)(3) (relating to the definition of a "payment") and section (g) (relating to sales of depreciable property to a spouse or 80-percent-owned entity).

(2) Installment method defined—(i) In general. Under the installment method, the amount of any payment which is income to the taxpayer is that portion of the installment payment received in that year which the gross profit realized or to be realized bears to the total contract price (the "gross profit ratio"). See paragraph (c) of this section for rules describing installment method reporting of contingent payment sales.

(ii) Selling price defined. The term "selling price" means the gross selling price without reduction to reflect any existing mortgage or other encumbrance on the property (whether assumed or taken subject to by the buyer) and, for installment sales in taxable years ending after October 19, 1980, without reduction to reflect any selling expenses. Neither interest, whether stated or unstated, nor original issue discount is considered to be a part of the selling price. See paragraph (c) of this section for rules describing installment method reporting of contingent payment sales.

(iii) Contract price defined. The term "contract price" means the total contract price equal to selling price reduced by that portion of any qualifying indebtedness (as defined in paragraph (b)(2)(iv) of this section), assumed or taken subject to by the buyer, which does not exceed the seller's basis in the property (adjusted, for installment sales in taxable years ending after October 19, 1980, to reflect commissions and other selling expenses as provided in paragraph (b)(2)(v) of this section). See paragraph (c) of this section for rules describing installment method reporting of contingent payment sales.

(iv) Qualifying indebtedness. The term "qualifying indebtedness" means a mortgage or other indebtedness encumbering the property and indebtedness, not secured by the property but incurred or assumed by the purchaser incident to the purchaser's acquisition, holding, or operation in the ordinary course of business or investment, of the property. The term "qualifying indebtedness" does not include an obligation of the taxpayer incurred incident to the disposition of the property (e.g., legal fees relating to the taxpayer's sale of the property) or an obligation functionally unrelated to the acquisition, holding, or operating of the property (e.g., the taxpayer's medical bill). Any obligation created subsequent to the taxpayer's acquisition of the property and incurred or assumed by the taxpayer or placed as an encumbrance on the property in contemplation of disposition of the property is not qualifying indebtedness if the arrangement results in accelerating recovery of the taxpayer's basis in the installment sale.

(v) Gross profit defined. The term "gross profit" means the selling price less the adjusted basis as defined in section 1011 and the regulations thereunder. For sales in taxable years ending after October 19, 1980, in the case of sales of real property by a person other than a dealer and casual sales of personal property, commissions and other selling expenses shall be added to basis for purposes of determining the proportion of payments which is gross profit attributable to the disposition. Such additions to basis will not be deemed to affect the taxpayer's holding period in the transferred property.

(3) Payment—(i) In general. Except as provided in paragraph (e) of this section (relating to purchaser evidences of indebtedness payable on demand or readily tradable), the term "payment" does not include the receipt of evidences of indebtedness of the person acquiring the property ("installment obligation"), whether or not payment of such indebtedness is guaranteed by a third party (including a government agency). For special rules regarding the receipt of an evidence of indebtedness of a transferee of a qualified intermediary, see §§ 1.1031(b)–2(b) and 1.1031(k)–1(j)(2)(iii) of this chapter. A standby letter of credit (as defined in paragraph (b)(3)(iii) of this section) shall be treated as a third party guarantee. Payments include amounts actually or constructively received in the taxable year under an installment obligation. For a special rule regarding a transfer of property to a qualified intermediary followed by the sale of such property by the qualified intermediary, see § 1.1031(k)–1(j)(2)(ii) of this chapter. Receipt of an evidence of indebtedness which is secured directly or indirectly by cash or a cash equivalent, such as a bank certificate of deposit or a treasury note, will be treated as the receipt of payment. For a special rule regarding a transfer of property in exchange for an obligation that is secured by cash or a cash equivalent held in a qualified escrow account or a qualified trust, see § 1.1031(k)–1(j)(2)(i) of this chapter. Payment may be received in cash or other property, including foreign currency, marketable securities, and evidences of indebtedness which are payable on demand or readily tradable. However, for special rules relating to the receipt of certain property with respect to which gain is not recognized, see paragraph (f) of this section (relating to transactions described in sections 351, 356(a) and 1031). * * *, payment includes receipt of an evidence of indebtedness of a person other than the person acquiring the property from the taxpayer. For purposes of determining the amount of payment received in the taxable year, the amount of qualifying indebtedness (as defined in paragraph (b)(2)(iv) of this section) assumed or taken subject to by the person acquiring the property shall be included only to the extent that it exceeds the basis of the property (determined after adjustment to reflect selling expenses). For purposes of the preceding sentence, an arrangement under which the taxpayer's liability on qualifying indebtedness is eliminated incident to the disposition (e.g., a novation) shall be treated as an assumption of the qualifying indebtedness. If the taxpayer sells property to a creditor of the taxpayer and indebtedness of the taxpayer is cancelled in consideration of the sale, such cancellation shall be treated as payment. To the extent that cancellation is not in consideration of the sale, see §§ * * * 1.1001–2(a)(2) relating to discharges of indebtedness. If the taxpayer sells property which is encumbered by a mortgage or other indebtedness on which the taxpayer is not personally liable, and the person acquiring the property is the obligee, the taxpayer shall be treated as having received payment in the amount of such indebtedness.

(ii) Wrap-around mortgage. This paragraph (b)(3)(ii) shall apply generally to any installment sale after March 4, 1981 unless the installment sale was completed before June 1, 1981 pursuant to a written obligation binding on the seller that was executed on or before March 4, 1981. A "wrap-around mortgage" means an agreement in which the buyer initially does not assume and purportedly does not take subject to part or all of the mortgage or other indebtedness encumbering the property ("wrapped indebtedness") and, instead, the buyer issues to the seller an installment obligation the principal amount of which reflects such wrapped indebtedness. Ordinarily, the seller will use payments received on the installment obligation to service the wrapped indebtedness. The wrapped indebtedness shall be deemed to have been taken subject to even though title to the property has not passed in the year of sale and even though the seller remains liable for payments on the wrapped indebtedness. In the hands of the seller, the wrap-around installment obligation shall have a basis equal to the seller's basis in the property which was the subject of the installment sale, increased by the amount of gain recognized in the year of sale, and decreased by the amount of cash and the fair market value of other nonqualifying property received in the year of sale. For purposes of this paragraph (b)(3)(ii), the amount of any indebtedness assumed or taken subject to by the buyer (other than wrapped indebtedness) is to be treated as cash received by the seller in the year of sale. Therefore, except as otherwise required by section 483 or 1232, the gross profit ratio with respect to the wrap-around installment obligation is a fraction, the numerator of which is the face value of the obligation less the taxpayer's basis in the obligation and the denominator of which is the face value of the obligation.

(iii) Standby letter of credit. The term "standby letter of credit" means a non-negotiable, nontransferable (except together with the evidence of indebtedness which it secures) letter of credit, issued by a bank or other financial institution, which serves as a guarantee of the evidence of indebtedness which is secured by the letter of credit. Whether or not the letter of credit explicitly states it is non-negotiable and nontransferable, it will be treated as non-negotiable and nontransferable if applicable local law so provides. The mere right of the secured party (under applicable local law) to transfer the proceeds of a letter of credit shall be disregarded in determining whether the instrument qualifies as a standby letter of credit. A letter of credit is not a standby letter of credit if it may be drawn upon in the absence of default in payment of the underlying evidence of indebtedness.

(4) Exceptions. The term "installment sale" does not include, and the provisions of section 453 do not apply to, dispositions of personal property on the installment plan by a person who regularly sells or otherwise disposes of personal property on the installment plan, or to dispositions of personal property of a kind which is required to be included in the inventory of the taxpayer if on hand at the close of the taxable year. See section 453A and the regulations thereunder for rules relating to installment sales by dealers in personal property. A dealer in real property or a farmer who is not required under his method of accounting to maintain inventories may report the gain on the installment method under section 453.

(5) Examples. The following examples illustrate installment method reporting under this section:

Example (1). In 1980, A, a calendar year taxpayer, sells Blackacre, an unencumbered capital asset in A's hands, to B for $100,000: $10,000 down and the remainder payable in equal annual installments over the next 9 years, together with adequate stated interest. A's basis in Blackacre, exclusive of selling expenses, is $38,000. Selling expenses paid by A are $2,000. Therefore, the gross profit is $60,000 ($100,000 selling price—$40,000 basis inclusive of selling expenses). The gross profit ratio is 3/5 (gross profit of $60,000 divided by $100,000 contract price). Accordingly, $6,000 (3/5 of $10,000) of each $10,000 payment received is gain attributable to the sale and $4,000 ($10,000–$6,000) is recovery of basis. The interest received in addition to principal is ordinary income to A.

Example (2). C sells Whiteacre to D for a selling price of $160,000. Whiteacre is encumbered by a longstanding mortgage in the principal amount of $60,000. D will assume or take subject to the $60,000 mortgage and pay the remaining $100,000 in 10 equal annual installments together with adequate stated interest. C's basis in Whiteacre is $90,000. There are no selling expenses. The contract price is $100,000, the $160,000 selling price reduced by the mortgage of $60,000 assumed or taken subject to. Gross profit is $70,000 ($160,000 selling price less C's basis of $90,000). C's gross profit ratio is 7/10 (gross profit of $70,000 divided by $100,000 contract price). Thus, $7,000 (7/10 of $10,000) of each $10,000 annual payment is gain attributable to the sale, and $3,000 ($10,000–$7,000) is recovery of basis.

Example (3). The facts are the same as in example (2), except that C's basis in the land is $40,000. In the year of the sale C is deemed to have received payment of $20,000 ($60,000–$40,000, the amount by which the mortgage D assumed or took subject to exceeds C's basis). Since basis is fully recovered in the year of sale, the gross profit ratio is 1 ($120,000/$120,000) and C will report 100% of the $20,000 deemed payment in the year of sale and each $10,000 annual payment as gain attributable to the sale.

* * *

(c) Contingent payment sales—(1) In general. Unless the taxpayer otherwise elects in the manner prescribed in paragraph (d)(3) of this section, contingent payment sales are to be reported on the installment method. As used in this section, the term "contingent payment sale" means a sale or other disposition of property in which the aggregate selling price cannot be determined by the close of the taxable year in which such sale or other disposition occurs.

The term "contingent payment sale" does not include transactions with respect to which the installment obligation represents, under applicable principles of tax law, a retained interest in the property which is the subject of the transaction, an interest in a joint venture or a partnership, an equity interest in a corporation or similar transactions, regardless of the existence of a stated maximum selling price or a fixed payment term. * * *

This paragraph prescribes the rules to be applied in allocating the taxpayer's basis (including selling expenses except for selling expenses of dealers in real estate) to payments received and to be received in a contingent payment sale. The rules are designed appropriately to distinguish contingent payment sales for which a maximum selling price is determinable, sales for which a maximum selling price is not determinable but the time over which payments will be received is determinable, and sales for which neither a maximum selling price nor a definite payment term is determinable. In addition, rules are prescribed under which, in appropriate circumstances, the taxpayer will be permitted to recover basis under an income forecast computation.

(2) Stated maximum selling price—(i) In general. (A) Contingent payment sale will be treated as having a stated maximum selling price if, under the terms of the agreement, the maximum amount of sale proceeds that may be received by the taxpayer can be determined as of the end of the taxable year in which the sale or other disposition occurs. The stated maximum selling price shall be determined by assuming that all of the contingencies contemplated by the agreement are met or otherwise resolved in a manner that will maximize the selling price and accelerate payments to the earliest date or dates permitted under the agreement. Except as provided in paragraph (c)(2)(ii) and (7) of this section (relating to certain payment recomputations), the taxpayer's basis shall be allocated to payments received and to be received under a stated maximum selling price agreement by treating the stated maximum selling price as the selling price for purposes of paragraph (b) of this section. The stated maximum selling price, as initially determined, shall thereafter be treated as the selling price unless and until that maximum amount is reduced, whether pursuant to the terms of the original agreement, by subsequent amendment, by application of the payment recharacterization rule (described in paragraph (c)(2)(ii) of this section), or by a subsequent supervening event such as bankruptcy of the obligor. When the maximum amount is subsequently reduced, the gross profit ratio will be recomputed with respect to payments received in or after the taxable year in which an event requiring reduction occurs. If, however, application of the foregoing rules in a particular case would substantially and inappropriately accelerate or defer recovery of the taxpayer's basis, a special rule will apply. * * *

(B) The following examples illustrate the provisions of paragraph (e)(2)(i) of this section. In each example, it is assumed that application of the rules illustrated will not substantially and inappropriately defer or accelerate recovery of the taxpayer's basis.

Example (1). A sells all of the stock of X corporation to B for $100,000 payable at closing plus an amount equal to 5% of the net profits of X for each of the next nine years, the contingent payments to be made annually together with adequate stated interest. The agreement provides that the maximum amount A may receive, inclusive of the $100,000 down payment but exclusive of interest, shall be $2,000,000. A's basis in the stock of X inclusive of selling expenses, is $200,000. Selling price and contract price are considered to be $2,000,000. Gross profit is $1,800,000, and the gross profit ratio is 9/10 ($1,800,000/$2,000,000). Accordingly, of the $100,000 received by A in the year of sale, $90,000 is reportable as gain attributable to the sale and $10,000 is recovery of basis.

* * *

(3) Fixed period—(i) In general. When a stated maximum selling price cannot be determined as of the close of the taxable year in which the sale or other disposition occurs, but the maximum period over which payments may be received under the contingent sale price agreement is fixed, the taxpayer's basis (inclusive of selling expenses) shall be allocated to the taxable years in which payment may be received under the agreement in equal annual increments. In making the allocation it is not relevant whether the buyer is required to pay adequate stated interest. However, if the terms of the agreement incorporate an arithmetic component that is not identical for all taxable years, basis shall be allocated among the taxable years to accord with that component unless, taking into account all of the payment terms of the agreement, it is inappropriate to presume that payments under the contract are likely to accord with the variable component. If in any taxable year no payment is received or the amount of payment received (exclusive of interest) is less than the basis allocated to that taxable year, no loss shall be allowed unless the taxable year is the final payment year under the agreement or unless it is otherwise determined in accordance with the rules generally applicable to worthless debts that the future payment obligation under the agreement has become worthless. When no loss is allowed, the unrecovered portion of basis allocated to the taxable year shall be carried forward to the next succeeding taxable year. If application of the foregoing rules to a particular case would substantially and inappropriately defer or accelerate recovery of the taxpayer's basis, a special rule will apply. See paragraph (c)(7) of this section.

(ii) Examples. The following examples illustrate the rules for recovery of basis in a contingent payment sale in which stated maximum selling price cannot be determined but the period over which payments are to be received under the agreement is fixed. In each case, it is assumed that application of the described rules will not substantially and inappropriately defer or accelerate recovery of the taxpayer's basis.

Example (1). A sells Blackacre to B for 10 percent of Blackacre's gross yield for each of the next 5 years. A's basis in Blackacre is $5 million. Since the sales price is indefinite and the maximum selling price is not ascertainable from the terms of the contract, basis is recovered ratably over the period during which payment may be received under the contract. Thus, assuming A receives the payments (exclusive of interest) listed in the following table, A will report the following:

Year	*Payment*	*Basis Recovered*	*Gain Attributable to the Sale*
1	$1,300,000	$1,000,000	$ 300,000
2	$1,500,000	$1,000,000	$ 500,000
3	$1,400,000	$1,000,000	$ 400,000
4	$1,800,000	$1,000,000	$ 800,000
5	$2,100,000	$1,000,000	$1,100,000

Example (2). The facts are the same as in example (1), except that the payment in year 1 is only $900,000. Since the installment payment is less than the amount of basis allocated to that year, the unrecovered basis, $100,000, is carried forward to year 2.

Year	*Payment*	*Basis Recovered*	*Gain Attributable to the Sale*
1	$ 900,000	$ 900,000	–0–
2	$1,500,000	$1,100,000	$ 400,000
3	$1,400,000	$1,000,000	$ 400,000
4	$1,800,000	$1,000,000	$ 800,000
5	$2,100,000	$1,000,000	$1,100,000

Example (3). C owns all of the stock of X corporation with a basis of $100,000 (inclusive of selling expenses). D purchases the X stock from C and agrees to make four payments computed in accordance with the following formula: 40% of net profits of X in year 1, 30% in year 2, 20% in year 3, and 10% in year 4. Accordingly, C's basis is allocated as follows: $40,000 to year 1, $30,000 to year 2, $20,000 to year 3, and $10,000 to year 4.

Example (4). The facts are the same as in example (3), but the agreement also requires that D make fixed installment payments in accordance with the following schedule: no payment in year 1, $100,000 in year 2, $200,000 in year 3, $300,000 in year 4, and $400,000 in year 5. Thus, while it is reasonable to project that the contingent component of the payments will decrease each year, the fixed component of the payments will increase each year. Accordingly, C is required to allocate $20,000 of basis to each of the taxable years 1 through 5.

(4) Neither stated maximum selling price nor fixed period. If the agreement neither specifies a maximum selling price nor limits payments to a fixed period, a question arises whether a sale realistically has occurred or whether, in economic effect, payments received under the agreement are in the nature of rent or royalty income. Arrangements of this sort will be closely scrutinized. If, taking into account all of the pertinent facts, including the nature of the property, the arrangement is determined to qualify as a sale, the taxpayer's basis (including selling expenses) shall be recovered in equal annual increments over a period of 15 years commencing with the date of sale. However, if in any taxable year no payment is received or the amount of payment received (exclusive of interest) is less than basis allocated to the year, no loss shall be allowed unless it is otherwise determined in accordance with the timing rules generally applicable to worthless debts that the future payment obligation under the agreement has become worthless; instead the excess basis shall be reallocated in level amounts over the balance of the 15 year term. Any basis not recovered at the end of the 15th year shall be carried forward to the next succeeding year, and to the extent unrecovered thereafter shall be carried forward from year to year until all basis has been recovered or the future payment obligation is determined to be worthless. The general rule requiring initial level allocation of basis over 15 years shall not apply if the taxpayer can establish to the satisfaction of the Internal Revenue Service that application of the general rule would substantially and inappropriately defer recovery of the taxpayer's basis. See paragraph (c)(7) of this section. If the Service determines that initially allocating basis in level amounts over the first 15 years will substantially and inappropriately accelerate recovery of the taxpayer's basis in early years of that 15–year term, the Service may require that basis be reallocated within the 15–year term but the Service will not require that basis initially be allocated over more than 15 years. * * *

* * *

(7) Special rule to avoid substantial distortion—(i) In general. The normal basis recovery rules set forth in paragraph (c)(2) through (4) of this section may, with respect to a particular contingent payment sale, substantially and inappropriately defer or accelerate recovery of the taxpayer's basis.

(ii) Substantial and inappropriate deferral. The taxpayer may use an alternative method of basis recovery if the taxpayer is able to demonstrate prior to the due date of the return including extensions for the taxable year in which the first payment is received, that application of the normal basis recovery rule will substantially and inappropriately defer recovery of basis. To demonstrate that application of the normal basis recovery rule will substantially and inappropriately defer recovery of basis, the taxpayer must show (A) that the alternative method is a reasonable method of ratably recovering basis and, (B) that, under that method, it is reasonable to conclude that over time the taxpayer likely will recover basis at a rate twice as fast as the rate at which basis would have been recovered under the otherwise applicable normal basis recovery rule. The taxpayer must receive a ruling from the Internal Revenue Service before using an alternative method of basis recovery described in paragraph (c)(7)(ii) of this section.

The request for a ruling shall be made in accordance with all applicable procedural rules set forth in the Statement of Procedural Rules (26 CFR Part 601) and any applicable revenue procedures relating to submission of ruling requests. The request shall be submitted to the Commissioner of Internal Revenue, Attention: Assistant Commissioner (Technical), Washington, DC 20224. The taxpayer must file a request for a ruling prior to the due date for the return including extensions. In demonstrating that application of the normal basis recovery rule would substantially and inappropriately defer recovery of the taxpayer's basis, the taxpayer in appropriate circumstances may rely upon contemporaneous or immediate past relevant sales, profit, or other factual data that are subject to verification. The taxpayer ordinarily is not permitted to rely upon projections of future productivity, receipts, profits, or the like. However, in special circumstances a reasonable projection may be acceptable if the projection is based upon a specific event that already has occurred (e.g., corporate stock has been sold for future payments contingent on profits and an inadequately insured major plant facility of the corporation has been destroyed).

(iii) Substantial and inappropriate acceleration. Notwithstanding the other provisions of this paragraph, the Internal Revenue Service may find that the normal basis recovery rule will substantially and inappropriately accelerate recovery of basis. In such a case, the Service may require an alternate method of basis recovery, unless the taxpayer is able to demonstrate either (A) that the method of basis recovery required by the Service is not a reasonable method of ratable recovery, or (B) that it is not reasonable to conclude that the taxpayer over time is likely to recover basis at a rate twice as fast under the normally applicable basis recovery rule as the rate at which basis would be recovered under the method proposed by the Service. In making such demonstrations the taxpayer may rely in appropriate circumstances upon contemporaneous or immediate past relevant sales, profit, or other factual data subject to verification. In special circumstances a reasonable projection may be acceptable, but only with the consent of the Service, if the projection is based upon a specific event that has already occurred.

(iv) Subsequent recomputation. A contingent payment sale may initially and properly have been reported under the normally applicable basis recovery rule and, during the term of the agreement, circumstances may show that continued reporting on the original method will substantially and inappropriately defer or accelerate recovery of the unrecovered balance of the taxpayer's basis. In this event, the special rule provided in this paragraph is applicable.

(v) Examples. The following examples illustrate the application of the special rule of this paragraph. In examples (1) and (2) it is assumed that rulings consistent with paragraph (c)(7)(ii) of this section have been requested.

Example (1). A owns all of the stock of X corporation with a basis of $100,000. A sells the stock of X to B for a cash down payment of $1,800,000 and B's agreement to pay A an amount equal to 1% of the net profits of X in each of the next 10 years (together with adequate stated interest). The agreement further specifies that the maximum amount that may be paid to A (exclusive of interest) shall not exceed $10 million. A is able to demonstrate that current and recent profits of X have approximated $2 million annually, and that there is no reason to anticipate a major increase in the annual profits of X during the next 10 years. One percent of $2 million annual profits is $20,000, a total of $200,000 over 10 years. Under the basis recovery rule normally applicable to a maximum contingent selling price agreement, in the year of sale A would recover $18,000 of A's total $100,000 basis, and would not recover more than a minor part of the balance until the final year under the agreement. On a $2 million selling price ($200,000 plus $1,800,000 down payment), A would recover $90,000 of A's total $100,000 basis in the year of sale and 5% of each payment ($100,000/$2,000,000) received up to a maximum of $10,000 over the next ten years. Since the rate of basis recovery under the demonstrated method is more than twice the rate under the normal rule, A will be permitted to recover $90,000 basis in the year of sale.

Example (2). The facts are the same as in example (1) except that no maximum contingent selling price is stated in the agreement. Under the basis recovery rule normally applicable when no maximum amount is stated but the payment term is fixed, in the year of sale and in each subsequent year A would recover approximately $9,100 (1/11 of $100,000) of A's total basis. A will be permitted to recover $90,000 of A's total basis in the year of sale.

Example (3). The facts are the same as in example (1) except that A sells the X stock to B on the following terms: 1% of the annual net profits of X in each of the next 10 years and a cash payment of $1,800,000 in the eleventh year, all payments to be made together with adequate stated interest. No maximum contingent selling price is stated. Under the normally applicable basis recovery rule, A would recover 1/11 of A's total $100,000 basis in each of the 11 payment years under the agreement. On the facts (see example (1)), A cannot demonstrate that application of the normal rule would not substantially and inappropriately accelerate recovery of A's basis. Accordingly, A will be allowed to recover only $1,000 of A's total basis in each of the 10 contingent payment years under the agreement, and will recover the $90,000 balance of A's basis in the final year in which the large fixed cash payment will be made.

* * *

(d) Election not to report an installment sale on the installment method—(1) In general. An installment sale is to be reported on the installment method unless the taxpayer elects otherwise in accordance with the rules set forth in paragraph (d)(3) of this section.

(2) Treatment of an installment sale when a taxpayer elects not to report on the installment method—(i) In general. A taxpayer who elects not to report an installment sale on the installment method must recognize gain on the sale in accordance with the taxpayer's method of accounting. The fair market value of an installment obligation shall be determined in accordance with paragraph (d)(2)(ii) and (iii) of this section. In making such determination, any provision of contract or local law restricting the transferability of the installment obligation shall be disregarded. Receipt of an installment obligation shall be treated as a receipt of property, in an amount equal to the fair market value of the installment obligation, whether or not such obligation is the equivalent of cash. An installment obligation is considered to be property and is subject to valuation, as provided in paragraph (d)(2)(ii) and (iii) of this section, without regard to whether the obligation is embodied in a note, an executory contract, or any other instrument, or is an oral promise enforceable under local law.

(ii) Fixed amount obligations. (A) A fixed amount obligation means an installment obligation the amount payable under which is fixed. Solely for the purpose of determining whether the amount payable under an installment obligation is fixed, the provisions of section 483 and any "payment recharacterization" arrangement (as defined in paragraph (c)(2)(ii) of this section) shall be disregarded. If the fixed amount payable is stated in identified, fungible units of property the value of which will or may vary over time in relation to the United States dollar (e.g., foreign currency, ounces of gold, or bushels of wheat), such units shall be converted to United States dollars at the rate of exchange or dollar value on the date the installment sale is made. A taxpayer using the cash receipts and disbursements method of accounting shall treat as an amount realized in the year of sale the fair market value of the installment obligation. In no event will the fair market value of the installment obligation be considered to be less than the fair market value of the property sold (minus any other consideration received by the taxpayer on the sale). A taxpayer using the accrual method of accounting shall treat as an amount realized in the year of sale the total amount payable under the installment obligation. For this purpose, neither interest (whether stated or unstated) nor original issue discount is considered to be part of the amount payable. If the amount payable is otherwise fixed, but because the time over which payments may be made is contingent, a portion of the fixed amount will or may be treated as internal interest (as defined in paragraph (c)(2)(ii) of this section), the amount payable shall be determined by applying the price interest recomputation rule (described in paragraph (c)(2)(ii) of this section). Under no circumstances will an installment sale for a fixed amount obligation be considered an "open" transaction. For purposes of this (ii), remote or incidental contingencies are not to be taken into account.

(B) The following examples illustrate the provisions of paragraph (d)(2) of this section.

Example (1). A, an accrual method taxpayer, owns all of the stock of X corporation with a basis of $20 million. On July 1, 1981, A sells the stock of X corporation to B for $60 million payable on June 15, 1992. The agreement also provides that, against this fixed amount, B shall make annual prepayments (on June 15) equal to 5% of the net profits of X earned in the immediately preceding fiscal year beginning with the fiscal year ending March 31, 1982. Thus the first prepayment will be made on June 15, 1982. No stated interest is payable under the agreement and thus the unstated interest provisions of section 483 are applicable. Under section 483, no part of any payment made on June 15, 1982 (which is within one year following the July 1, 1981 sale date), will be treated as unstated interest. Under the price interest recomputation rule, it is presumed that the entire $60 million fixed amount will be paid on June 15, 1982. Accordingly, if A elects not to report the transaction on the installment method, in 1981 A must report $60 million as the amount realized on the sale and must report $40 million as gain on the sale in that year.

Example (2). The facts are the same as in example (1) except that A uses the cash receipts and disbursements method of accounting. In 1981 A must report as an amount realized on the sale the fair market value of the installment obligation and must report as gain on the sale in 1981 the excess of that amount realized over A's basis of $20 million. In no event will the fair market value of the installment obligation be considered to be less than the fair market value of the stock of X. In determining the fair market value of the installment obligation, any contractual or legal restrictions on the transferability of the installment obligation, and any remote or incidental contingencies otherwise affecting the amount payable or time of payments under the installment obligation, shall be disregarded.

(iii) Contingent payment obligations. Any installment obligation which is not a fixed amount obligation (as defined in paragraph (d)(2)(ii) of this section) is a contingent payment obligation. If an installment obligation contains both a fixed amount component and a contingent payment component, the fixed amount component shall be treated under the rules of paragraph (d)(2)(ii) of this section and the contingent amount component shall be treated under the rules of this (iii). The fair market value of a contingent payment obligation shall be determined by disregarding any restrictions on transfer imposed by agreement or under local law. The fair market value of a contingent payment obligation may be ascertained from, and in no event shall be considered to be less than, the fair market value of the property sold (less the amount of any other consideration received in the sale). Only in those rare and extraordinary cases involving sales for a contingent payment obligation in which the fair market value of the obligation (determinable under the preceding sentences) cannot reasonably be ascertained will the taxpayer be entitled to assert that the transaction is "open." Any such transaction will be carefully scrutinized to determine whether a sale in fact has taken place. A taxpayer using the cash receipts and disbursements method of accounting must report as an amount realized in the year of sale the fair market value of the contingent payment obligation. A taxpayer using the accrual method of accounting must report an amount realized in the year of sale determined in accordance with that method of accounting, but in no event less than the fair market value of the contingent payment obligation.

(3) Time and manner for making election—(i) In general. An election under paragraph (d)(1) of this section must be made on or before the due date prescribed by law (including extensions) for filing the taxpayer's return for the taxable year in which the installment sale occurs. The election must be made in the manner prescribed by the appropriate forms for the taxpayer's return for the taxable year of the sale. A taxpayer who reports an amount realized equal to the selling price including the full face amount of any installment obligation on the tax return filed for the taxable year in which the installment sale occurs will be considered to have made an effective election under paragraph (d)(1) of this section. A cash method taxpayer receiving an obligation the fair market value of which is less than the face value must make the election in the manner prescribed by appropriate instructions for the return filed for the taxable year of the sale.

(ii) Election made after the due date. Elections after the time specified in paragraph (d)(3)(i) of this section will be permitted only in those rare circumstances when the Internal Revenue Service concludes that the taxpayer had good cause for failing to make a timely election. A recharacterization of a transaction as a sale in a taxable year subsequent to the taxable year in which the transaction occurred (e.g., a transaction initially reported as a lease later is determined to have been an installment sale) will not justify a late election. No conditional elections will be permitted. * * *

(4) Revoking an election. Generally, an election made under paragraph (d)(1) is irrevocable. An election may be revoked only with the consent of the Internal Revenue Service. A revocation is retroactive. A revocation will not be permitted when one of its purposes is the avoidance of federal income taxes, or when the taxable year in which any payment was received has closed. * * *

* * *

[T.D. 7768, 46 FR 10708, Feb. 4, 1981; 46 FR 13688, Feb. 24, 1981; 46 FR 43036, Aug. 26, 1981, as amended by T.D. 7788, 46 FR 48920, Oct. 5, 1981; T.D. 8535, 59 FR 18751, Apr. 20, 1994]

§ 1.455–1 Treatment of prepaid subscription income.

[S]ection 455 permits certain taxpayers to elect with respect to a trade or business in connection with which prepaid subscription income is received, to include such income in gross income for the taxable years during which a liability exists to furnish or deliver a newspaper, magazine, or other periodical. If a taxpayer does not elect to treat prepaid subscription income under the provisions of section 455, such income is includible in gross income for the taxable year in which received by the taxpayer, unless under the method or practice of accounting used in computing taxable income such amount is to be properly accounted for as of a different period.

[T.D. 6591, 27 FR 1798, Feb. 27, 1962]

§ 1.461–1 General rule for taxable year of deduction.

(a) General rule—(1) Taxpayer using cash receipts and disbursements method. Under the cash receipts and disbursements method of accounting, amounts representing allowable deductions shall, as a general rule, be taken into account for the taxable year in which paid. Further, a taxpayer using this method may also be entitled to certain deductions in the computation of taxable income which do not involve cash disbursements during the taxable year, such as the deductions for depreciation, depletion, and losses under sections 167, 611, and 165, respectively. If an expenditure results in the creation of an asset having a useful life which extends substantially beyond the close of the taxable year, such an expenditure may not be deductible, or may be deductible only in part, for the taxable year in which made. An example is an expenditure for the construction of improvements by the lessee on leased property where the estimated life of the improvements is in excess of the remaining period of the lease. In such a case, in lieu of the allowance for depreciation provided by section 167, the basis shall be amortized ratably over the remaining period of the lease. See section 178 and the regulations thereunder for rules governing the effect to be given renewal options in determining whether the useful life of the improvements exceeds the remaining term of the lease where a lessee begins improvements on leased property after July 28, 1958, other than improvements which on such date and at all times thereafter, the lessee was under a binding legal obligation to make. See section 263 and the regulations thereunder for rules relating to capital expenditures. See section 467 and the regulations thereunder for rules under which a liability arising out of the use of property pursuant to a section 467 rental agreement is taken into account.

(2) Taxpayer using an accrual method—(i) In general. Under an accrual method of accounting, a liability (as defined in § 1.446–1(c)(1)(ii)(B)) is incurred, and generally is taken into account for Federal income tax purposes, in the taxable year in which all the events have occurred that establish the fact of the liability, the amount of the liability can be determined with reasonable accuracy, and economic performance has occurred with respect to the liability. (See paragraph (a)(2)(iii)(A) of this section for examples of liabilities that may not be taken into account until a taxable year subsequent to the taxable year incurred, and see §§ 1.461–4 through 1.461–6 for rules relating to economic performance.) Applicable provisions of the Code, the Income Tax Regulations, and other guidance published by the Secretary prescribe the manner in which a liability that has been incurred is taken into account. For example, section 162 provides that the deductible liability generally is taken into account in the taxable year incurred through a deduction from gross income. * * * The principles of this paragraph (a)(2) also apply in the calculation of earnings and profits and accumulated earnings and profits.

(ii) Uncertainty as to the amount of a liability. While no liability shall be taken into account before economic performance and all of the events that fix the liability have occurred, the fact that the exact amount of the liability cannot be determined does not prevent a taxpayer from taking into account that portion of the amount of the liability which can be computed with reasonable accuracy within the taxable year. For example, A renders services to B during the taxable year for which A charges $10,000. B admits a liability to A for $6,000 but contests the remainder. B may take into account only $6,000 as an expense for the taxable year in which the services were rendered.

(iii) Alternative timing rules. (A) If any provision of the Code requires a liability to be taken into account in a taxable year later than the taxable year provided in paragraph (a)(2)(i) of this section, the liability is taken into account as prescribed in that Code provision. See, for example, section 267 (transactions between related parties) and section 464 (farming syndicates).

(B) If the liability of a taxpayer is subject to section 170 (charitable contributions), * * *, the liability is taken into account as determined under that section and not under section 461 or the regulations thereunder. * * *

* * *

(3) Effect in current taxable year of improperly accounting for a liability in a prior taxable year. Each year's return should be complete in itself, and taxpayers shall ascertain the facts necessary to make a correct return. The expenses, liabilities, or loss of one year generally cannot be used to reduce the income of a subsequent year. A taxpayer may not take into account in a return for a subsequent taxable year liabilities that, under the taxpayer's method of accounting, should have been taken into account in a prior taxable year. If a taxpayer ascertains that a liability should have been taken into account in a prior taxable year, the taxpayer should, if within the period of limitation, file a claim for credit or refund of any overpayment of tax arising therefrom. Similarly, if a taxpayer ascertains that a liability was improperly taken into account in a prior taxable year, the taxpayer should, if within the period of limitation, file an amended return and pay any additional tax due. However, * * *, if a liability is properly taken into account in an amount based on a computation made with reasonable accuracy and the exact amount of the liability is subsequently determined in a later taxable year, the difference, if any, between such amounts shall be taken into into account for the later taxable year.

* * *

(b) Special rule in case of death. A taxpayer's taxable year ends on the date of his death. See section 443(a)(2) * * *. In computing taxable income for such year, there shall be deducted only amounts properly deductible under the method of accounting used by the taxpayer. However, if the taxpayer used an accrual method of accounting, no deduction shall be allowed for amounts accrued only by reason of his death. For rules relating to the inclusion of items of partnership deduction, loss, or credit in the return of a decedent partner, see subchapter K, chapter 1 of the Code, and the regulations thereunder.

* * *

[T.D. 6500, 25 FR 11720, Nov. 26, 1960, as amended by T.D. 6520, 25 FR 13692, Dec. 24, 1960; T.D. 6710, 29 FR 3473, March 18, 1964; T.D. 6735, 29 FR 6494, May 19, 1964; T.D. 6772, 29 FR 15753, Nov. 24, 1964; T.D. 6917, 32 FR 6682, May 2, 1967; T.D. 8408, 57 FR 12420, Apr. 10, 1992; T.D. 8482, 58 FR 42233, Aug. 9, 1993; T.D. 8554, 59 FR 36356, July 18, 1994; T.D. 8820, 64 FR 26845, May 18, 1999]

§ 1.461–2 Contested liabilities.

(a) General rule—(1) Taxable year of deduction. If—

(i) The taxpayer contests an asserted liability,

(ii) The taxpayer transfers money or other property to provide for the satisfaction of the asserted liability,

(iii) The contest with respect to the asserted liability exists after the time of the transfer, and

(iv) But for the fact that the asserted liability is contested, a deduction would be allowed for the taxable year of the transfer (or, in the case of an accrual method taxpayer, for an earlier taxable year for which such amount would be accruable),

then the deduction with respect to the contested amount shall be allowed for the taxable year of the transfer.

* * *

(3) Refunds includible in gross income. If any portion of the contested amount which is deducted under subparagraph (1) of this paragraph for the taxable year of transfer is refunded when the contest is settled, such portion is includible in gross income except as provided in § 1.111–1, relating to recovery of certain items previously deducted or credited. Such refunded amount is includible in gross income for the taxable year of receipt, or for an earlier taxable year if properly accruable for such earlier year.

(4) Examples. The provisions of this paragraph are illustrated by the following examples:

Example (1). X Corporation, which uses an accrual method of accounting, in 1964 contests $20 of a $100 asserted real property tax liability but pays the entire $100 to the taxing authority. In 1968, the contest is settled and X receives a refund of $5. X deducts $100 for the taxable year 1964, and includes $5 in gross income for the taxable year 1968 (assuming § 1.111–1 does not apply to such amount). If in 1964 X pays only $80 to the taxing authority, X deducts only $80 for 1964. The result would be the same if X Corporation used the cash method of accounting.

Example (2). Y Corporation makes its return on the basis of a calendar year and uses an accrual method of accounting. Y's real property taxes are assessed and become a lien on December 1, but are not payable until March 1 of the following year. On December 10, 1964, Y contests $20 of the $100 asserted real property tax which was assessed and became a lien on December 1, 1964. On March 1, 1965, Y pays the entire $100 to the taxing authority. In 1968, the contest is settled and Y receives a refund of $5. Y deducts $80 for the taxable year 1964, deducts $20 for the taxable year 1965, and includes $5 in gross income for the taxable year 1968 (assuming § 1.111–1 does not apply to such amount).

(b) Contest of asserted liability—(1) Asserted liability. For purposes of paragraph (a)(1) of this section, the term "asserted liability" means an item with respect to which, but for the existence of any contest in respect of such item, a deduction would be allowable under an accrual method of accounting. For example, a notice of a local real estate tax assessment and a bill received for services may represent asserted liabilities.

(2) Definition of the term "contest". Any contest which would prevent accrual of a liability under section 461(a) shall be considered to be a contest in determining whether the taxpayer satisfies paragraph (a)(1)(i) of this section. A contest arises when there is a bona fide dispute as to the proper evaluation of the law or the facts necessary to determine the existence or correctness of the amount of an asserted liability. It is not necessary to institute suit in a court of law in order to contest an asserted liability. An affirmative act denying the validity or accuracy, or both, of an asserted liability to the person who is asserting such liability, such as including a written protest with payment of the asserted liability, is sufficient to commence a contest. Thus, lodging a protest in accordance with local law is sufficient to contest an asserted liability for taxes. It is not necessary that the affirmative act denying the validity or accuracy, or both, of an asserted liability be in writing if, upon examination of all the facts and circumstances, it can be established to the satisfaction of the Commissioner that a liability has been asserted and contested.

(3) Example. The provisions of this paragraph are illustrated by the following example:

Example. O Corporation makes its return on the basis of a calendar year and uses an accrual method of accounting. O receives a large shipment of typewriter ribbons from S Company on January 30, 1964, which O pays for in full on February 10, 1964. Subsequent to their receipt, several of the ribbons prove defective because of inferior materials used by the manufacturer. On August 9, 1964, O orally notifies S and demands refund of the full purchase price of the ribbons. After negotiations prove futile and a written demand is rejected by S, O institutes an action for the full purchase price. For purposes of paragraph (a)(1)(i) of this section, S has asserted a liability against O which O contests on August 9, 1964. O deducts the contested amount for 1964.

(c) Transfer to provide for the satisfaction of an asserted liability—(1) In general. (i) A taxpayer may provide for the satisfaction of an asserted liability by transferring money or other property beyond his control to—

(A) The person who is asserting the liability;

(B) An escrowee or trustee pursuant to a written agreement (among the escrowee or trustee, the taxpayer, and the person who is asserting the liability) that the money or other property be delivered in accordance with the settlement of the contest;

(C) An escrowee or trustee pursuant to an order of the United States or of any State or political subdivision thereof or any agency or instrumentality of the foregoing, or of a court, that the money or other property be delivered in accordance with the settlement of the contest; or

(D) A court with jurisdiction over the contest.

(ii) In order for money or other property to be beyond the control of a taxpayer, the taxpayer must relinquish all authority over the money or other property.

(iii) The following are not transfers to provide for the satisfaction of an asserted liability—

(A) Purchasing a bond to guarantee payment of the asserted liability;

(B) An entry on the taxpayer's books of account;

(C) A transfer to an account that is within the control of the taxpayer;

(D) A transfer of any indebtedness of the taxpayer or of any promise by the taxpayer to provide services or property in the future; and

(E) A transfer to a person (other than the person asserting the liability) of any stock of the taxpayer or of any stock or indebtedness of a person related to the taxpayer (as defined in section 267(b)).

(2) Examples. The provisions of this paragraph are illustrated by the following examples:

Example (1). M Corporation contests a $5,000 liability asserted against it by L Company for services rendered. To provide for the contingency that it might have to pay the liability, M establishes a separate bank account in its own name. M then transfers $5,000 from its general account to such separate account. Such transfer does not qualify as a transfer to provide for the satisfaction of an asserted liability because M has not transferred the money beyond its control.

Example (2). M Corporation contests a $5,000 liability asserted against it by L Company for services rendered. To provide for the contingency that it might have to pay the liability, M transfers $5,000 to an irrevocable trust pursuant to a written agreement among the trustee, M (the taxpayer), and L (the person who is asserting the liability) that the money shall be held until the contest is settled and then disbursed in accordance with the settlement. Such transfer qualifies as a transfer to provide for the satisfaction of an asserted liability.

(d) Contest exists after transfer. In order for a contest with respect to an asserted liability to exist after the time of transfer, such contest must be pursued subsequent to such time. Thus, the contest must have been neither settled nor abandoned at the time of the transfer. A contest may be settled by a decision, judgment, decree, or other order of any court of competent jurisdiction which has become final, or by written or oral agreement between the parties. For example, Z Corporation, which uses an accrual method of accounting, in 1964 contests a $100 asserted liability. In 1967 the contested liability is settled as being $80 which Z accrues and deducts for such year. In 1968 Z pays the $80. Section 461(f) does not apply to Z with respect to the transfer because a contest did not exist after the time of such transfer.

(e) Deduction otherwise allowed—(1) In general. The existence of the contest with respect to an asserted liability must prevent (without regard to section 461(f)) and be the only factor preventing a deduction for the taxable year of the transfer (or, in the case of an accrual method taxpayer, for an earlier taxable year for which such amount would be accruable) to provide for the satisfaction of such liability. Nothing in section 461(f) or this section shall be construed to give rise to a deduction since section 461(f) and this section relate only to the timing of deductions which are otherwise allowable under the Code.

(2) Application of economic performance rules to transfers under section 461(f). **(i)** A taxpayer using an accrual method of accounting is not allowed a deduction under section 461(f) in the taxable year of the transfer unless economic performance has occurred.

(ii) Economic performance occurs for liabilities requiring payment to another person arising out of any workers compensation act or any tort, or any other liability designated in § 1.461–4(g), as payments are made to the person to which the liability is owed. Except as provided in section 468B or the regulations thereunder, economic performance does not occur when a taxpayer transfers money or other property to a trust, an escrow account, or a court to provide for the satisfaction of an asserted workers compensation, tort, or other liability designated under § 1.461–4(g) that the taxpayer is contesting unless the trust, escrow account, or court is the person to which the liability is owed or the taxpayer's payment to the trust, escrow account, or court discharges the taxpayer's liability to the claimant. Rather, economic performance occurs in the taxable year the taxpayer transfers money or other property to the person that is asserting the workers compensation, tort, or other liability designated under § 1.461–4(g) that the taxpayer is contesting or in the taxable year that payment is made from a trust, an escrow account, or a court registry funded by the taxpayer to the person to which the liability is owed.

(3) Examples. The provisions of this paragraph are illustrated by the following examples:

* * *

Example 2. Corporation X is a defendant in a class action suit for tort liabilities. In 2002, X establishes a trust for the purpose of satisfying the asserted liability and transfers $10,000,000 to the trust. The trust does not satisfy the requirements of section 468B or the regulations thereunder. In 2004, the trustee pays $10,000,000 to the plaintiffs in settlement of the litigation. Under paragraph (e)(2) of this section, economic performance with respect to X's liability to the plaintiffs occurs in 2004. X may deduct the $10,000,000 payment to the plaintiffs in 2004.

* * *

[T.D. 6772, 29 FR 15753, Nov. 24, 1964, as amended by T.D. 8408, 57 FR 12421, Apr. 10, 1992; T.D. 9095, 68 FR 65634, Nov. 21, 2003; T.D. 9140, 69 FR 43302, July 20, 2004]

§ 1.461–4 Economic performance.

(a) Introduction—(1) In general. For purposes of determining whether an accrual basis taxpayer can treat the amount of any liability (as defined in § 1.446–1(c)(1)(ii)(B)) as incurred, the all events test is not treated as met any earlier than the taxable year in which economic performance occurs with respect to the liability.

(2) Overview. Paragraph (b) of this section lists exceptions to the economic performance requirement. Paragraph (c) of this section provides cross-references to the definitions of certain terms for purposes of section 461(h) and the regulations thereunder. Paragraphs (d) through (m) of this section and § 1.461–6 provide rules for determining when economic performance occurs. Section 1.461–5 provides rules relating to an exception under which certain recurring items may be incurred for the taxable year before the year during which economic performance occurs.

(b) Exceptions to the economic performance requirement. Paragraph (a)(2)(iii)(B) of § 1.461–1 provides examples of liabilities that are taken into account under rules that operate without regard to the all events test (including economic performance).

(c) Definitions. The following cross-references identify certain terms defined for purposes of section 461(h) and the regulations thereunder.

(1) Liability. See paragraph (c)(1)(ii)(B)d of § 1.446–1 for the definition of "liability."

(2) Payment. See paragraph (g)(1)(ii) of this section for the definition of "payment."

(d) Liabilities arising out of the provision of services, property, or the use of property—(1) In general. The principles of this paragraph (d) determine when economic performance occurs with respect to liabilities arising out of the performance of services, the transfer of property, or the use of property. This paragraph (d) does not apply to liabilities described in paragraph (e) (relating to interest expense) or paragraph (g) (relating to breach of contract, workers compensation, tort, etc.) of this section. In addition, except as otherwise provided in Internal Revenue regulations, revenue procedures, or revenue rulings this paragraph (d) does not apply to amounts paid pursuant to a notional principal contract. The Commissioner may provide additional rules in regulations, revenue procedures, or revenue rulings concerning the time at which economic performance occurs for items described in this paragraph (d).

(2) Services or property provided to the taxpayer—(i) In general. Except as otherwise provided in paragraph (d)(5) of this section, if the liability of a taxpayer arises out of the providing of services or property to the taxpayer by another person, economic performance occurs as the services or property is provided.

* * *

(iii) Employee benefits—(A) In general. Except as otherwise provided in any Internal Revenue regulation, revenue procedure, or revenue ruling, the economic performance requirement is satisfied to the extent that any amount is otherwise deductible under section 404 (employer contributions to a plan of deferred compensation), * * *.

* * *

(3) Use of property provided to the taxpayer—(i) In general. Except as otherwise provided in this paragraph (d)(3) and paragraph (d)(5) of this section, if the liability of a taxpayer arises out of the use of property by the taxpayer, economic performance occurs ratably over the period of time the taxpayer is entitled to the use of the property (taking into account any reasonably expected renewal periods when necessary to carry out the purposes of section 461(h)). * * *

(ii) Exceptions—(A) Volume, frequency of use or income. If the liability of a taxpayer arises out of the use of property by the taxpayer and all or a portion of the liability is determined by reference to the frequency or volume of use of the property or the income from the property, economic performance occurs for the portion of the liability determined by reference to the frequency or volume of use of the property or the income from the property as the taxpayer uses the property or includes income from the property. See Examples 8 and 9 of paragraph (d)(7) of this section. This paragraph (d)(3)(ii) shall not apply if the District Director determines, that based on the substance of the transaction, the liability of the taxpayer for use of the property is more appropriately measured ratably over the period of time the taxpayer is entitled to the use of the property.

* * *

(4) Services or property provided by the taxpayer—(i) In general. Except as otherwise provided in paragraph (d)(5) of this section, if the liability of a taxpayer requires the taxpayer to provide services for property to another person, economic performance occurs as the taxpayer incurs costs (within the meaning of § 1.446–1(c)(1)(ii)) in connection with the satisfaction of the liability. See Examples 1 through 3 of paragraph (d)(7) of this section.

(ii) Barter transactions. If the liability of a taxpayer requires the taxpayer to provide services, property, or the use of property, and arises out of the use of property by the taxpayer, or out of the provision of services or property to the taxpayer by another person, economic performance occurs to the extent of the lesser of—

(A) The cumulative extent to which the taxpayer incurs costs (within the meaning of § 1.446–1(c)(1)(ii)) in connection with its liability to provide the services of property; or

(B) The cumulative extent to which the services or property is provided to the taxpayer.

(5) Liabilities that are assumed in connection with the sale of a trade or business—(i) In general. If, in connection with the sale or exchange of a trade or business by a taxpayer, the purchaser expressly assumes a liability arising out of the trade or business that the taxpayer but for the economic performance requirement would have been entitled to incur as of the date of the sale, economic performance with respect to that liability occurs as the amount of the liability is properly included in the amount realized on the transaction by the taxpayer. See § 1.1001–2 for rules relating to the inclusion in amount realized from a discharge of liabilities resulting from a sale or exchange.

(ii) Trade or business. For purposes of this paragraph (d)(5), a trade or business is a specific group of activities carried on by the taxpayer for the purpose of earning income or profit if every operation that is necessary to the process of earning income or profit is included in the group. Thus, for example, the group of activities generally must include the collection of income and the payment of expenses.

(iii) Tax avoidance. This paragraph (d)(5) does not apply if the District Director determines that tax avoidance is one of the taxpayer's principal purposes for the sale or exchange.

(6) Rules relating to the provision of services or property to a taxpayer. The following rules apply for purposes of this paragraph (d):

(i) Services or property provided to a taxpayer include services or property provided to another person at the direction of the taxpayer.

(ii) A taxpayer is permitted to treat services or property as provided to the taxpayer as the taxpayer makes payment to the person providing the services or property (as defined in paragraph (g)(1)(ii) of this section), if the taxpayer can reasonably expect the person to provide the services or property within 3½ months after the date of payment.

(iii) A taxpayer is permitted to treat property as provided to the taxpayer when the property is delivered or accepted, or when title to the property passes. The method used by the taxpayer to determine when property is provided is a method of accounting that must comply with the rules of § 1.446–1(e). Thus, the method of determining when property is provided must be used consistently from year to year, and cannot be changed without the consent of the Commissioner.

(iv) If different services or items of property are required to be provided to a taxpayer under a single contract or agreement, economic performance generally occurs over the time each service is provided and as each item of property is provided. However, if a service or item of property to be provided to the taxpayer is incidental to other services or property to be provided under a contract or agreement, the taxpayer is not required to allocate any portion of the total contract price to the incidental service or property. For purposes of this paragraph (d)(6)(iv), services or property is treated as incidental only if—

(A) The cost of the services or property is treated on the taxpayer's books and records as part of the cost of the other services or property provided under the contract; and

(B) The aggregate cost of the services or property does not exceed 10 percent of the total contract price.

(7) Examples. The following examples illustrate the principles of this paragraph (d). For purposes of these examples, it is assumed that the requirements of the all events test other than economic performance have been met, and that the recurring item exception is not used. Assume further that the examples do not involve section 467 rental agreements and, therefore, section 467 is not applicable. The examples are as follows:

Example 1. Services or property provided by the taxpayer. **(i)** X corporation, a calendar year, accrual method taxpayer, is an oil company. During March 1990, X enters into an oil and gas lease with Y. In November 1990, X installs a platform and commences drilling. The lease obligates X to remove its offshore platform and well fixtures upon abandonment of the well or termination of the lease. During 1998, X removes the platform and well fixtures at a cost of $200,000.

(ii) Under paragraph (d)(4)(i) of this section, economic performance with respect to X's liability to remove the offshore platform and well fixtures occurs as X incurs costs in connection with that liability. X incurs these costs in 1998 as, for example, X's employees provide X with removal services (see paragraph (d)(2) of this section). Consequently, X incurs $200,000 for the 1998 taxable year. Alternatively, assume that during 1990 X pays Z $130,000 to remove the platform and fixtures, and that Z performs these removal services in 1998. Under paragraph (d)(2) of this section, X does not incur this cost until Z performs the services. Thus, economic performance with respect to the $130,000 X pays Z occurs in 1998.

Example 2. Services or property provided by the taxpayer. **(i)** W corporation, a calendar year, accrual method taxpayer, sells tractors under a three-year warranty that obligates W to make any reasonable repairs to each tractor it sells. During 1990, W sells ten tractors. In 1992 W repairs, at a cost of $5,000, two tractors sold during 1990.

(ii) Under paragraph (d)(4)(i) of this section, economic performance with respect to W's liability to perform services under the warranty occurs as W incurs costs in connection with that liability. W incurs these costs in 1992 as, for example, replacement parts are provided to W (see paragraph (d)(2) of this section). Consequently, $5,000 is incurred by W for the 1992 taxable year.

* * *

Example 4. Services or property provided to the taxpayers. **(i)** LP1, a calendar year, accrual method limited partnership, owns the working interest in a parcel of property containing oil and gas. During December 1990, LP1 enters into a turnkey contract with Z corporation pursuant to which LP1 pays Z $200,000 and Z is required to provide a completed well by the close of 1992. In May 1992, Z commences drilling the well, and, in December 1992, the well is completed.

(ii) Under paragraph (d)(2) of this section, economic performance with respect to LP1's liability for drilling and development services provided to LP1 by Z occurs as the services are provided. Consequently, $200,000 is incurred by LP1 for the 1992 taxable year.

Example 5. Services or property provided to the taxpayer. **(i)** X corporation, a calendar year, accrual method taxpayer, is an automobile dealer. On January 15, 1990, X agrees to pay an additional $10 to Y, the manufacturer of the automobiles, for each automobile purchased by X from Y. Y agrees to provide advertising and promotional activities to X.

(ii) During 1990, X purchases from Y 1,000 new automobiles and pays to Y an additional $10,000 as provided in the agreement. Y, in turn, uses this $10,000 to provide advertising and promotional activities during 1992.

(iii) Under paragraph (d)(2) of this section, economic performance with respect to X's liability for advertising and promotional services provided to X by Y occurs as the services are provided. Consequently, $10,000 is incurred by X for the 1992 taxable year.

Example 6. Use of property provided to the taxpayer; services or property provided to the taxpayer. **(i)** V corporation, a calendar year, accrual method taxpayer, charters aircrafts. On December 20, 1990, V leases a jet aircraft from L for the four-year period that begins on January 1, 1991. The lease obligates V to pay L a base rental of $500,000 per year. In addition, the lease requires V to pay $25 to an escrow account for each hour that the aircraft is flown. The escrow account funds are held by V and are to be used by L to make necessary repairs to the aircraft. Any amount remaining in the escrow account upon termination of the lease is payable to

V. During 1991, the aircraft is flown 1,000 hours and V pays $25,000 to the escrow account. The aircraft is repaired by L in 1993. In 1994, $20,000 is released from the escrow account to pay L for the repairs.

(ii) Under paragraph (d)(3)(i) of this section, economic performance with respect to V's base rental liability occurs ratably over the period of time V is entitled to use the jet aircraft. Consequently, the $500,000 rent is incurred by V for the 1991 taxable year and for each of the next three taxable years. Under paragraph (d)(2) of this section, economic performance with respect to the liability to place amounts in escrow occurs as the aircraft is repaired. Consequently, V incurs $20,00 for the 1993 taxable year.

Example 7. Use of property provided to the taxpayer. (i) X corporation, a calendar year, accrual method taxpayer, manufactures and sells electronic circuitry. On November 15, 1990, X enters into a contract with Y that entitles X to the exclusive use of a product owned by Y for the five-year period beginning on January 1, 1991. Pursuant to the contract, X pays Y $100,000 on December 30, 1990.

(ii) Under paragraph (d)(3)(i) of this section, economic performance with respect to X's liability for the use of property occurs ratably over the period of time X is entitled to use the product. Consequently, $20,000 is incurred by X for 1991 and for each of the succeeding four taxable years.

* * *

(e) Interest. In the case of interest, economic performance occurs as the interest cost economically accrues, in accordance with the principles of relevant provisions of the Code.

* * *

(g) Certain liabilities for which payment is economic performance—(1) In general—(i) Person to which payment must be made. In the case of liabilities described in paragraphs (g)(2) through (7) of this section, economic performance occurs when, and to the extent that, payment is made to the person to which the liability is owed. Thus, except as otherwise provided in paragraph (g)(1)(iv) of this section and § 1.461–6, economic performance does not occur as a taxpayer makes payments in connection with such a liability to any other person, including a trust, escrow account, court-administered fund, or any similar arrangement, unless the payments constitute payment to the person to which the liability is owed under paragraph (g)(1)(ii)(B) of this section. Instead, economic performance occurs as payments are made from that other person or fund to the person to which the liability is owed. The amount of economic performance that occurs as payment is made from the other person or fund to the person to which the liability is owed may not exceed the amount the taxpayer transferred to the other person or fund. For special rules relating to the taxation of amounts transferred to "qualified settlement funds," see section 468B and the regulations thereunder. The Commissioner may provide additional rules in regulations, revenue procedures, and revenue rulings concerning the time at which economic performance occurs for items described in this paragraph (g).

(ii) Payment to person to which liability is owed. Paragraph (d)(6) of this section provides that for purposes of paragraph (d) of this section (relating to the provision of services or property to the taxpayer) in certain cases a taxpayer may treat services or property as provided to the taxpayer as the taxpayer makes payments to the person providing the services or property. In addition, this paragraph (g) provides that in the case of certain liabilities of a taxpayer, economic performance occurs as the taxpayer makes payment to persons specified therein. For these and all other purposes of section 461(h) and the regulations thereunder:

(A) Payment. The term *payment* has the same meaning as is used when determining whether a taxpayer using the cash receipts and disbursements method of accounting has made a payment. Thus, for example, payment includes the furnishing of cash or cash equivalents and the netting of offsetting accounts. Payment does not include the furnishing of a note or other evidence of indebtedness of the taxpayer, whether or not the evidence is guaranteed by any other instrument (including a standby letter of credit) or by any third party (including a government agency). As a further example, payment does not include a promise of the taxpayer to provide services or property in the future (whether or not the promise is evidenced by a contract or other written agreement). In addition, payment does not include an amount transferred as a loan, refundable deposit, or contingent payment.

(B) Person to which payment is made. Payment to a particular person is accomplished if paragraph (g)(1)(ii)(A) of this section is satisfied and a cash basis taxpayer in the position of that person would be treated as having actually or constructively received the amount of the payment as gross income under the principles of section 451 (without regard to section 104(a) or any other provision that specifically excludes the amount from gross income). Thus, for example, the purchase of an annuity contract or any other asset generally does not constitute payment to the person to which a liability is owed unless the ownership of the contract or other asset is transferred to that person.

(C) Liabilities that are assumed in connection with the sale of a trade or business. Paragraph (d)(5) of this section provides rules that determine when economic performance occurs in the case of liabilities that are assumed in connection with the sale of a trade or business. The provisions of paragraph (d)(5) of this section also apply to any liability described in paragraph (g)(2) through (7) of this section that the purchaser expressly assumes in connection with the sale or exchange of a trade or business by a taxpayer, provided the taxpayer (but for the economic performance requirement) would have been entitled to incur the liability as of the date of the sale.

(iii) Person. For purposes of this paragraph (g), "person" has the same meaning as in section 7701(a)(1), except that it also includes any foreign state, the United States, any State or political subdivision thereof, any possession of the United States, and any agency or instrumentality of any of the foregoing.

(iv) Assignments. If a person that has a right to receive payment in satisfaction of a liability described in paragraphs (g)(2) through (7) of this section makes a valid assignment of that right to a second person, or if the right is assigned to the second person through operation of law, then payment to the second person in satisfaction of that liability constitutes payment to the person to which the liability is owed.

(2) Liabilities arising under a workers compensation act or out of any tort, breach of contract, or violation of law. If the liability of a taxpayer requires a payment or series of payments to another person and arises under any workers compensation act or out of any tort, breach of contract, or violation of law, economic performance occurs as payment is made to the person to which the liability is owed. See Example 1 of paragraph (g)(8) of this section. For purposes of this paragraph (g)(2)—

(i) A liability to make payments for services, property, or other consideration provided under a contract is not a liability arising out of a breach of that contract unless the payments are in the nature of incidental, consequential, or liquidated damages; and

(ii) A liability arising out of a tort, breach of contract, or violation of law includes a liability arising out of the settlement of a dispute in which a tort, breach of contract, or violation of law, respectively, is alleged.

(3) Rebates and refunds. If the liability of a taxpayer is to pay a rebate, refund, or similar payment to another person (whether paid in property, money, or as a reduction in the price of goods or services to be provided in the future by the taxpayer), economic performance occurs as payment is made to the person to which the liability is owed. This paragraph (g)(3) applies to all rebates, refunds, and payments or transfers in the nature of a rebate or refund regardless of whether they are characterized as a deduction from gross income, an adjustment to gross receipts or total sales, or an adjustment or addition to cost of goods sold. In the case of a rebate or refund made as a reduction in the price of goods or services to be provided in the future by the taxpayer, "payment" is deemed to occur as the taxpayer would otherwise be required to recognize income resulting from a disposition at an unreduced price. See Example 2 of paragraph (g)(8) of this section. For purposes of determining whether the recurring item exception of § 1.461–5 applies, a liability that arises out of a tort, breach of contract, or violation of law is not considered a rebate or refund.

(4) Awards, prizes, and jackpots. If the liability of a taxpayer is to provide an award, prize, jackpot, or other similar payment to another person, economic performance occurs as payment is made to the person to which the liability is owed. See Examples 3 and 4 of paragraph (g)(8) of this section.

(5) Insurance, warranty, and service contracts. If the liability of a taxpayer arises out of the provision to the taxpayer of insurance, or a warranty or service contract, economic performance occurs as payment is made to the person to which the liability is owed. See Examples 5 through 7 of paragraph (g)(8) of this section. For purposes of this paragraph (g)(5)—

(i) A warranty or service contract is a contract that a taxpayer enters into in connection with property bought or leased by the taxpayer, pursuant to which the other party to the contract promises to replace or repair the property under specified circumstances.

(ii) The term "insurance" has the same meaning as is used when determining the deductibility of amounts paid or incurred for insurance under section 162.

(6) Taxes—(i) In general. Except as otherwise provided in this paragraph (g)(6), if the liability of a taxpayer is to pay a tax, economic performance occurs as the tax is paid to the governmental authority that imposed the tax. For purposes of this paragraph (g)(6), payment includes payments of estimated income tax and payments of tax where the taxpayer subsequently files a claim for credit or refund. In addition, for purposes of this paragraph (g)(6), a tax does not include a charge collected by a governmental authority for specific extraordinary services or property provided to a taxpayer by the governmental authority. Examples of such a charge include the purchase price of a parcel of land sold to a taxpayer by a governmental authority and a charge for labor engaged in by government employees to improve that parcel. In certain cases, a liability to pay a tax is permitted to be taken into account in the taxable year before the taxable year during which economic performance occurs under the recurring item exception of § 1.461–5. See Example 8 of paragraph (g)(8) of this section.

(ii) Licensing fees. If the liability of a taxpayer is to pay a licensing or permit fee required by a governmental authority, economic performance occurs as the fee is paid to the governmental authority, or as payment is made to any other person at the direction of the governmental authority.

(iii) Exceptions—(A) Real property taxes. If a taxpayer has made a valid election under section 461(c), the taxpayer's accrual for real property taxes is determined under section 461(c). Otherwise, economic performance with respect to a property tax liability occurs as the tax is paid, as specified in paragraph (g)(6)(i) of this section.

* * *

(7) Other liabilities. In the case of a taxpayer's liability for which economic performance rules are not provided elsewhere in this section or in any other Internal Revenue regulation, revenue ruling or revenue procedure, economic performance occurs as the taxpayer makes payments in satisfaction of the liability to the person to which the liability is owed. This paragraph (g)(7) applies only if the liability cannot properly be characterized as a liability covered by rules provided elsewhere in this section. If a liability may properly be characterized as, for example, a liability arising from the provision of services or property to, or by, a taxpayer, the determination as to when economic performance occurs with respect to that liability is made under paragraph (d) of this section and not under this paragraph (g)(7).

(8) Examples. The following examples illustrate the principles of this paragraph (g). For purposes of these examples, it is assumed that the requirements of the all events test other than economic performance have been met and, except as otherwise provided, that the recurring item exception is not used.

Example 1. Liabilities arising out of a tort. **(i)** During the period 1970 through 1975, Z corporation, a calendar year, accrual method taxpayer, manufactured and distributed industrial products that contained carcinogenic substances. In 1992, a number of lawsuits are filed against Z alleging damages due to exposure to these products. In settlement of a lawsuit maintained by A, Z agrees to purchase an annuity contract that will provide annual payments to A of $50,000 for a period of 25 years. On December 15, 1992, Z pays W, an unrelated life insurance company, $491,129 for such an annuity contract. Z retains ownership of the annuity contract.

(ii) Under paragraph (g)(2) of this section, economic performance with respect to Z's liability to A occurs as each payment is made to A. Consequently, $50,000 is incurred by Z for each taxable year that a payment is made to A under the annuity contract, (Z must also include in income a portion of amounts paid under the annuity, pursuant to section 72.) The result is the same if in 1992 Z secures its obligation with a standby letter of credit.

(iii) If Z later transfers ownership of the annuity contract to A, an amount equal to the fair market value of the annuity on the date of transfer is incurred by Z in the taxable year of the transfer (see paragraph (g)(1)(ii)(B) of this section). In addition, the transfer constitutes a transaction to which section 1001 applies.

Example 2. Rebates and refunds. **(i)** X corporation, a calendar year, accrual method taxpayer, manufactures and sells hardware products. X enters into agreements that entitle each of its distributors to a rebate (or discount on future purchases) from X based on the amount of purchases made by the distributor from X during any calendar year. During the 1992 calendar year, X becomes liable to pay a $2,000 rebate to distributor A. X pays A $1,200 of the rebate on January 15, 1993, and the remaining $800 on October 15, 1993. Assume the rebate is deductible (or allowable as an adjustment to gross receipts or cost of goods sold) when incurred.

(ii) If X does not adopt the recurring item exception described in § 1.461–5 with respect to rebates and refunds, then under paragraph (g)(3) of this section, economic performance with respect to the $2,000 rebate liability occurs in 1993. However, if X has made a proper election under § 1.461–5, and as of December 31, 1992, all events have occurred that determine the fact of the rebate liability, X incurs $1,200 for the 1992 taxable year. Because economic performance (payment) with respect to the remaining $800 does not occur until October 15, 1993 (more than 8½ months after the end of 1992), X cannot use the recurring item exception for this portion of the liability (see § 1.461–5). Thus, the $800 is not incurred by X until the 1993 taxable year. If, instead of making the cash payments to A during 1993, X adjusts the price of hardware purchased by A that is delivered to A during 1993, X's "payment" occurs as X would otherwise be required to recognize income resulting from a disposition at an unreduced price.

Example 3. Awards, prizes, and jackpots. **(i)** W corporation, a calendar year, accrual method taxpayer, produces and sells breakfast cereal. W conducts a contest pursuant to which the winner is entitled to $10,000 per year for a period of 20 years. On December 1, 1992, A is declared the winner of the contest and is paid $10,000 by W. In addition, on December 1 of each of the next nineteen years, W pays $10,000 to A.

(ii) Under paragraph (g)(4) of this section, economic performance with respect to the $200,000 contest liability occurs as each of the $10,000 payments is made by W to A. Consequently, $10,000 is incurred by W for the 1992 taxable year and for each of the succeeding nineteen taxable years.

Example 4. Awards, prizes, and jackpots. **(i)** Y corporation, a calendar year, accrual method taxpayer, owns a casino that contains progressive slot machines. A progressive slot machine provides a guaranteed jackpot amount that increases as money is gambled through the machine until the jackpot is won or until a maximum predetermined amount is reached. On July 1, 1993, the guaranteed jackpot amount on one of Y's slot machines reaches the maximum predetermined amount of $50,000. On October 1, 1994, the $50,000 jackpot is paid to B.

(ii) Under paragraph (g)(4) of this section, economic performance with respect to the $50,000 jackpot liability occurs on the date the jackpot is paid to B. Consequently, $50,000 is incurred by Y for the 1994 taxable year.

Example 5. Insurance, warranty, and service contracts. **(i)** V corporation, a calendar year, accrual method taxpayer, manufactures toys. V enters into a contract with W, an unrelated insurance company, on December 15, 1992. The contract obligates V to pay W a premium of $500,000 before the end of 1995. The contract obligates W to satisfy any liability of V resulting from claims made during 1993 or 1994 against V by any third party for damages attributable to defects in toys manufactured by V. Pursuant to the contract, V pays W a premium of $500,000 on October 1, 1995.

(ii) Assuming the arrangement constitutes insurance, under paragraph (g)(5) of this section economic performance occurs as the premium is paid. Thus, $500,000 is incurred by V for the 1995 taxable year.

* * *

Example 8. Taxes. **(i)** The laws of State A provide that every person owning personal property located in State A on the first day of January shall be liable for tax thereon and that a lien for the tax shall attach as of that date. In addition, the laws of State A provide that 60% of the tax is due on the first day of December following the lien date and the remaining 40% is due on the first day of July of the succeeding year. On January 1, 1992, X corporation, a calendar year, accrual method taxpayer, owns personal property located in State A. State A imposes a $10,000 tax on S with respect to that property on January 1, 1992. X pays State A $6,000 of the tax on December 1, 1992, and the remaining $4,000 on July 1, 1993.

(ii) Under paragraph (g)(6) of this section, economic performance with respect to $6,000 of the tax liability occurs on December 1, 1992. Consequently, $6,000 is incurred by X for the 1992 taxable year. Economic performance with respect to the remaining $4,000 of the tax liability occurs on July 1, 1993. If X has adopted the recurring item exception described in § 1.461–5 as a method of accounting for taxes, and as of December 31, 1992, all events have occurred that determine the liability of X for the remaining $4,000, X also incurs $4,000 for the 1992 taxable year. If X does not adopt the recurring item exception method, the $4,000 is not incurred by X until the 1993 taxable year.

* * *

[T.D. 8408, 57 FR 12421, Apr. 10, 1992; T.D. 8491, 58 FR 53135, Oct. 14, 1993; T.D. 8593, 60 FR 187421, Apr. 13, 1995; T.D. 8820, 64 FR 26845, May 18, 1999; T.D. 8408, 69 FR 44597, July 27, 2004]

§ 1.461–5 Recurring item exception.

(a) In general. Except as otherwise provided in paragraph (c) of this section, a taxpayer using an accrual method of accounting may adopt the recurring item exception described in paragraph (b) of this section as method of accounting for one or more types of recurring items incurred by the taxpayer. In the case of the "other payment liabilities" described in § 1.461–4(g)(7), the Commissioner may provide for the application of the recurring item exception by regulation, revenue procedure or revenue ruling.

(b) Requirements for use of the exception—(1) General rule. Under the recurring item exception, a liability is treated as incurred for a taxable year if—

(i) As of the end of that taxable year, all events have occurred that establish the fact of the liability and the amount of the liability can be determined with reasonable accuracy;

(ii) Economic performance with respect to the liability occurs on or before the earlier of—

(A) The date the taxpayer files a timely (including extensions) return for that taxable year; or

(B) The 15th day of the 9th calendar month after the close of that taxable year;

(iii) The liability is recurring in nature; and

(iv) Either—

(A) The amount of the liability is not material; or

(B) The accrual of the liability for that taxable year results in a better matching of the liability with the income to which it relates than would result from accruing the liability for the taxable year in which economic performance occurs.

(2) Amended returns. A taxpayer may file an amended return treating a liability as incurred under the recurring item exception for a taxable year if economic performance with respect to the liability occurs after the taxpayer files a return for that year, but within 8½ months after the close of that year.

(3) Liabilities that are recurring in nature. A liability is recurring if it can generally be expected to be incurred from one taxable year to the next. However, a taxpayer may treat such a liability as recurring in nature even if it is not incurred by the taxpayer in each taxable year. In addition, a liability that has never previously been incurred by a taxpayer may be treated as recurring if it is reasonable to expect that the liability will be incurred on a recurring basis in the future.

(4) Materiality requirement. For purposes of this paragraph (b):

(i) In determining whether a liability is material, consideration shall be given to the amount of the liability in absolute terms and in relation to the amount of other items of income and expense attributable to the same activity.

(ii) A liability is material if it is material for financial statement purposes under generally accepted accounting principles.

(iii) A liability that is immaterial for financial statement purposes under generally accepted accounting principles may be material for purposes of this paragraph (b).

(5) Matching requirement. (i) In determining whether the matching requirement of paragraph (b)(1)(iv)(B) of this section is satisfied, generally accepted accounting principles are an important factor, but are not dispositive.

(ii) In the case of a liability described in paragraph (g)(3) (rebates and refunds), paragraph (g)(4) (awards, prizes, and jackpots), paragraph (g)(5) (insurance, warranty, and service contracts), paragraph (g)(6) (taxes), or paragraph (h) (continuing fees under the Nuclear Waste Policy Act of 1982) of § 1.461–4, the matching requirement of paragraph (b)(1)(iv)(B) of this section shall be deemed satisfied.

(c) Types of liabilities not eligible for treatment under the recurring item exception. The recurring item exception does not apply to any liability of a taxpayer described in paragraph (e) (interest), paragraph (g)(2) (workers compensation, tort, breach of contract, and violation of law), or paragraph (g)(7) (other liabilities) of § 1.461–4. Moreover, the recurring item exception does not apply to any liability incurred by a tax shelter, as defined in section 461(i) and § 1.448–1T(b).

* * *

(e) Examples. The following examples illustrate the principles of this section:

Example 1. Requirements for use of the recurring item exception. (i) Y corporation, a calendar year, accrual method taxpayer, manufactures and distributes video cassette recorders. Y timely files its federal income tax return for each taxable year on the extended due date for the return (September 15, of the following taxable year). Y offers to refund the price of a recorder to a purchaser not satisfied with the recorder. During 1992, 100 purchasers request a refund of the $500 purchase price. Y refunds $30,000 on or before September 15, 1993, and the remaining $20,000 after such date but before the end of 1993.

(ii) Under paragraph (g)(3) of § 1.461–4, economic performance with respect to $30,000 of the refund liability occurs on September 15, 1993. Assume the refund is deductible (or allowable as an adjustment to gross receipts or cost of goods sold) when incurred. If Y does not adopt the recurring item exception with respect to rebates and refunds, the $30,000 refund is incurred by Y for the 1993 taxable year. However, if Y has properly adopted the recurring item exception method of accounting under this section, and as of December 31, 1992, all events have occurred that determine the fact of the liability for the $30,000 refund, Y incurs that amount for the 1992 taxable year. Because economic performance (payment) with respect to the remaining $20,000 occurs after September 15, 1993 (more than 8½ months after the end of 1992), that amount is not eligible for recurring item treatment under this section. Thus, the $20,000 amount is not incurred by Y until the 1993 taxable year.

Example 2. Requirements for use of the recurring item exception; amended returns. The facts are the same as in Example 2, except that Y files its income tax return for 1992 on March 15, 1993, and Y does not refund the price of any recorder before that date. Under paragraph (b)(1) of this section, the refund liability is not eligible for the recurring item exception because economic performance with respect to the refund does not occur before Y files a return for the taxable year for which the item would have been incurred under the exception. However, since economic performance occurs within 8½ months after 1992, Y may file an amended return claiming the $30,000 as incurred for its 1992 taxable year (see paragraph (b)(2) of this section).

[T.D. 8408, 57 FR 12427, Apr. 10, 1992, as amended by T.D. 8593, 60 FR 18743, Apr. 13, 1995]

§ 1.465–24 (Proposed, published 6–5–79.) Effect on amount at risk of loans for which borrower is personally liable for repayment.

(a) Creation of loan—(1) General rule. A taxpayer's amount at risk in an activity is increased by the amount of any liability incurred in the conduct of an activity for use in the activity to the extent the taxpayer is personally liable for repayment of the liability.

(2) Partnerships. **(i)** When a partnership incurs a liability in the conduct of an activity and under state law members of the partnership may be held personally liable for repayment of the liability, each partner's amount at risk is increased to the extent the partner is not protected against loss. To the extent the partner is protected against loss (such as through a right of contribution), the liability shall be treated in the same manner as amounts borrowed for which the taxpayer has no personal liability and for which no security is pledged. * * *

(ii) The application of this paragraph may be illustrated by the following example:

Example. A and B are equal general partners in partnership AB, which is engaged solely in an activity described in section 465(c)(1). AB borrows $25,000 from a bank to purchase equipment to be used in the activity. In addition to giving the bank a security interest in the newly purchased equipment, A and B each assumes personal liability for the loan. Although either A or B could be called upon by the bank to repay the entire $25,000, in such instance the partner who paid would be entitled to $12,500 from the other partner. Thus, although each is personally liable for $25,000, each is protected against loss in excess of $12,500. Accordingly, the loan increases the amount each is at risk with respect to the activity by $12,500.

* * *

§ 1.465–27 Qualified nonrecourse financing.

(a) In general. Notwithstanding any provision of section 465(b) or the regulations under section 465(b), for an activity of holding real property, a taxpayer is considered at risk for the taxpayer's share of any qualified nonrecourse financing which is secured by real property used in such activity.

(b) Qualified nonrecourse financing secured by real property—(1) In general. For purposes of section 465(b)(6) and this section, the term qualified nonrecourse financing means any financing—

(i) Which is borrowed by the taxpayer with respect to the activity of holding real property;

(ii) Which is borrowed by the taxpayer from a qualified person or represents a loan from any federal, state, or local government or instrumentality thereof, or is guaranteed by any federal, state, or local government;

(iii) For which no person is personally liable for repayment, taking into account paragraphs (b)(3), (4), and (5) of this section; and

(iv) Which is not convertible debt.

(2) Security for qualified nonrecourse financing—(i) Types of property. For a taxpayer to be considered at risk under section 465(b)(6), qualified nonrecourse financing must be secured only by real property used in the activity of holding real property. For this purpose, however, property that is incidental to the activity of holding real property will be disregarded. In addition, for this purpose, property that is neither real property used in the activity of holding real property nor incidental property will be disregarded if the aggregate gross fair market value of such property is less than 10 percent of the aggregate gross fair market value of all the property securing the financing.

(ii) Look-through rule for partnerships. For purposes of paragraph (b)(2)(i) of this section, a borrower shall be treated as owning directly its proportional share of the assets in a partnership in which the borrower owns (directly or indirectly through a chain of partnerships) an equity interest.

(3) Personal liability; partial liability. If one or more persons are personally liable for repayment of a portion of a financing, the portion of the financing for which no person is personally liable may qualify as qualified nonrecourse financing.

(4) Partnership liability. For purposes of section 465(b)(6) and this paragraph (b), the personal ability of any partnership for repayment of a financing is disregarded and, provided the requirements contained in paragraphs (b)(1)(i), (i), and (iv) of this section are satisfied, the financing will be treated as qualified nonrecourse financing secured by real property if—

(i) The only persons personally liable to repay the financing are partnerships;

(ii) Each partnership with personal liability holds only property described in paragraph (b)(2)(i) of this section (applying the principles of paragraph (b)(2)(ii) of this section in determining the property held by each partnership); and

(iii) In exercising its remedies to collect on the financing in a default or default-like situation, the lender may proceed only against property that is described in paragraph (b)(2)(i) of this section and that is held by the partnership or partnerships (applying the principles of paragraph (b)(2)(ii) of this section in determining the property held by the partnership or partnerships).

(5) Disregarded entities. Principles similar to those described in paragraph (b)(4) of this section shall apply in determining whether a financing of an entity that is disregarded for federal tax purposes under § 301.7701–3 of this chapter is treated as qualified nonrecourse financing secured by real property.

(6) Examples. The following examples illustrate the rules of this section:

Example 1. Personal liability of a partnership; incidental property. (i) X is a limited liability company that is classified as a partnership for federal tax purposes. X engages only in the activity of holding real property. In addition to real property used in the activity of holding real property, X owns office equipment, a truck, and maintenance equipment that it uses to support the activity of holding real property. X borrows $500 to use in the activity. X is personally liable on the financing, but no member of X and no other person is liable for repayment of the financing under local law. The lender may proceed against all of X's assets if X defaults on the financing.

(ii) Under paragraph (b)(2)(i) of this section, the personal property is disregarded as incidental property used in the activity of holding real property. Under paragraph (b)(4) of this section, the personal liability of X for repayment of the financing is disregarded and, provided the requirements contained in paragraphs (b)(1)(i), (ii), and (iv) of this section are satisfied, the financing will be treated as qualified nonrecourse financing secured by real property.

Example 2. Bifurcation of a financing. The facts are the same as in Example 1, except that A, a member of X, is personally liable for repayment of $100 of the financing. If the requirements contained in paragraphs (b)(1)(i), (ii), and (iv) of this section are satisfied, then under paragraph (b)(3) of this section, the portion of the financing for which A is not personally liable for repayment ($400) will be treated as qualified nonrecourse financing secured by real property.

* * *

(c) Effective date. This section is effective for any financing incurred on or after August 4, 1998. Taxpayers, however, may apply this section retroactively for financing incurred before August 4, 1998.

[T.D. 8777, 63 FR 41420, Aug. 4, 1998]

§ 1.469–2T Passive activity loss.

* * *

(d) Passive activity deductions—* * *

* * *

(6) Coordination with other limitations on deductions that apply before section 469—(i) In general. An item of deduction from a passive activity that is disallowed for a taxable year under section 704(d), 1366(d), or 465 is not a passive activity deduction for the taxable year. Paragraphs (d)(6)(ii) and (iii) of this section provide rules for determining the extent to which items of deduction from a passive activity are disallowed for a taxable year under sections 704(d), 1366(d), and 465.

(ii) Proration of deductions disallowed under basis limitations—(A) Deductions disallowed under section 704(d). If any amount of a partner's distributive share of a partnership's loss for the taxable year is disallowed under section 704(d), a ratable portion of the partner's distributive share of each item of deduction or loss of the partnership is disallowed for the taxable year. For purposes of the preceding sentence, the ratable portion of an item of deduction or loss is the amount of such item multiplied by the fraction obtained by dividing—

(1) The amount of the partner's distributive share of partnership loss that is disallowed for the taxable year; by

(2) The sum of the partner's distributive shares of all items of deduction and loss of the partnership for the taxable year.

(B) Deductions disallowed under section 1366(d). If any amount of an S corporation shareholder's pro rata share of an S corporation's loss for the taxable year is disallowed under section 1366(d), a ratable portion of the taxpayer's pro rata share of each item of deduction or loss of the S corporation is disallowed for the taxable year. For purposes of the preceding sentence, the ratable portion of an item of deduction or loss is the amount of such item multiplied by the fraction obtained by dividing—

(1) The amount of the shareholder's pro rata share of S corporation loss that is disallowed for the taxable year; by

(2) The sum of the shareholder's pro rata shares of all items of deduction and loss of the corporation for the taxable year.

* * *

[T.D. 8175, 53 FR 5711, Feb. 25, 1988; 53 FR 15494, April 29, 1988; T.D. 8253, 54 FR 20538, May 12, 1989; T.D. 8318, 55 FR 48108, Nov. 19, 1990; 55 FR 51688, Dec. 17, 1990; T.D. 8477, 58 FR 11537, Feb. 26, 1993; T.D. 8495, 58 FR 58788, Nov. 4, 1993]

§ 1.469–4 Definition of activity.

(a) Scope and purpose. This section sets forth the rules for grouping a taxpayer's trade or business activities and rental activities for purposes of applying the passive activity loss and credit limitation rules of section 469. A taxpayer's activities include those conducted through C corporations that are subject to section 469, S corporations, and partnerships.

(b) Definitions. The following definitions apply for purposes of this section—

(1) Trade or business activities. Trade or business activities are activities, other than rental activities or activities that are treated * * * as incidental to an activity of holding property for investment, that—

(i) Involve the conduct of a trade or business (within the meaning of section 162);

(ii) Are conducted in anticipation of the commencement of a trade or business; or

(iii) Involve research or experimental expenditures that are deductible under section 174 (or would be deductible if the taxpayer adopted the method described in section 174(a)).

* * *

(c) General rules for grouping activities—(1) Appropriate economic unit. One or more trade or business activities or rental activities may be treated as a single activity if the activities constitute an appropriate economic unit for the measurement of gain or loss for purposes of section 469.

(2) Facts and circumstances test. Except as otherwise provided in this section, whether activities constitute an appropriate economic unit and, therefore, may be treated as a single activity depends upon all the relevant facts and circumstances. A taxpayer may use any reasonable method of applying the relevant facts and circumstances in grouping activities. The factors listed below, not all of which are necessary for a taxpayer to treat more than one activity as a single activity, are given the greatest weight in determining whether activities constitute an appropriate economic unit for the measurement of gain or loss for purposes of section 469—

(i) Similarities and differences in types of trades or businesses;

(ii) The extent of common control;

(iii) The extent of common ownership;

(iv) Geographical location; and

(v) Interdependencies between or among the activities (for example, the extent to which the activities purchase or sell goods between or among themselves, involve products or services that are normally provided together, have the same customers, have the same employees, or are accounted for with a single set of books and records).

(3) Examples. The following examples illustrate the application of this paragraph (c).

Example 1. Taxpayer C has a significant ownership interest in a bakery and a movie theater at a shopping mall in Baltimore and in a bakery and a movie theater in Philadelphia. In this case, after taking into account all the relevant facts and circumstances, there may be more than one reasonable method for grouping C's activities. For instance, depending on the relevant facts and circumstances, the following groupings may or may not be permissible: a single activity; a movie theater activity and a bakery activity; a Baltimore activity and a Philadelphia activity; or four separate activities. Moreover, once C groups these activities into appropriate economic units, paragraph (e) of this section requires C to continue using that grouping in subsequent taxable years unless a material change in the facts and circumstances makes it clearly inappropriate.

Example 2. Taxpayer B, an individual, is a partner in a business that sells non-food items to grocery stores (partnership L). B also is a partner in a partnership that owns and operates a trucking business (partnership Q). The two partnerships are under common control. The predominant portion of Q's business is transporting goods for L, and Q is the only trucking business in which B is involved. Under this section, B appropriately treats L's wholesale activity and Q's trucking activity as a single activity.

(d) Limitation on grouping certain activities. The grouping of activities under this section is subject to the following limitations:

(1) Grouping rental activities with other trade or business activities—(i) Rule. A rental activity may not be grouped with a trade or business activity unless the activities being grouped together constitute an appropriate economic unit under paragraph (c) of this section and—

(A) The rental activity is insubstantial in relation to the trade or business activity;

(B) The trade or business activity is insubstantial in relation to the rental activity; or

(C) Each owner of the trade or business activity has the same proportionate ownership interest in the rental activity, in which case the portion of the rental activity that involves the rental of items of property for use in the trade or business activity may be grouped with the trade or business activity.

(ii) Examples. The following examples illustrate the application of paragraph (d)(1)(i) of this section:

Example 1. (i) H and W are married and file a joint return. H is the sole shareholder of an S corporation that conducts a grocery store trade or business activity. W is the sole shareholder of an S corporation that owns and rents out a building. Part of the building is rented to H's grocery store trade or business activity (the grocery store rental). The grocery store rental and the grocery store trade or business are not insubstantial in relation to each other.

(ii) Because they file a joint return, H and W are treated as one taxpayer for purposes of section 469. See § 1.469–1T(j). Therefore, the sole owner of the trade or business activity (taxpayer H–W) is also the sole owner of the rental activity. Consequently, each owner of the trade or business activity has the same proportionate ownership interest in the rental activity. Accordingly, the grocery store rental and the grocery store trade or business activity may be grouped together (under paragraph (d)(1)(i) of this section) into a single trade or business activity, if the grouping is appropriate under paragraph (c) of this section.

Example 2. Attorney D is a sole practitioner in town X. D also wholly owns residential real estate in town X that D rents to third parties. D's law practice is a trade or business activity within the meaning of paragraph (b)(1) of this section. The residential real estate is a rental activity within the meaning of § 1.469–1T(e)(3) and is insubstantial in relation to D's law practice. Under the facts and circumstances, the law practice and the residential real estate do not constitute an appropriate economic unit under paragraph (c) of this section. Therefore, D may not treat the law practice and the residential real estate as a single activity.

(2) Grouping real property rentals and personal property rentals prohibited. An activity involving the rental of real property and an activity involving the rental of personal property (other than personal property provided in connection with the real property or real property provided in connection with the personal property) may not be treated as a single activity.

(3) Certain activities of limited partners and limited entrepreneurs—(i) In general. Except as provided in this paragraph, a taxpayer that owns an interest, as a limited partner or a limited entrepreneur (as defined in section 464(e)(2)), in an activity described in section 465(c)(1), may not group that activity with any other activity. A taxpayer that owns an interest as a limited partner or a limited entrepreneur in an activity described in the preceding sentence may group that activity with another activity in the same type of business if the grouping is appropriate under the provisions of paragraph (c) of this section.

(ii) Example. The following example illustrates the application of this paragraph (d)(3):

Example. (i) Taxpayer A, an individual, owns and operates a farm. A is also a member of M, a limited liability company that conducts a cattle-feeding business. A does not actively participate in the management of M (within the meaning of section 464(e)(2)(B)). In addition, A is a limited partner in N, a limited partnership engaged in oil and gas production.

(ii) Because A does not actively participate in the management of M, A is a limited entrepreneur in M's activity. M's cattle-feeding business is described in section 465(c)(1)(B) (relating to farming) and may not be grouped with any other activity that does not involve farming. Moreover, A's farm may not be grouped with the cattle-feeding activity unless the grouping constitutes an appropriate economic unit for the measurement of gain or loss for purposes of section 469.

(iii) Because A is a limited partner in N and N's activity is described in section 465(c)(1)(D) (relating to exploring for, or exploiting, oil and gas resources), A may not group N's oil and gas activity with any other activity that does not involve exploring for, or exploiting, oil and gas activity with any other activity that does not involve exploring for, or exploiting, oil and gas resources. Thus, N's activity may not be grouped with A's farm or with M's cattle-feeding business.

(4) Other activities identified by the Commissioner. A taxpayer that owns an interest in an activity identified in guidance issued by the Commissioner as an activity covered by this paragraph (d)(4) may not group that activity with any other activity, except as provided in the guidance issued by the Commissioner.

(5) Activities conducted through section 469 entities—(i) In general. A C corporation subject to section 469, an S corporation, or a partnership (a section 469 entity) must group its activities under the rules of this section. Once the section 469 entity groups its activities, a shareholder or partner may group those activities with each other, with activities conducted directly by the shareholder or partner, and with activities conducted through other section 469 entities, in accordance with the rules of this section. A shareholder or partner may not treat activities grouped together by a section 469 entity as separate activities.

* * *

(e) Disclosure and consistency requirements—(1) Original groupings. [O]nce a taxpayer has grouped activities under this section, the taxpayer may not regroup those activities in subsequent taxable years. Taxpayers must comply with disclosure requirements that the Commissioner may prescribe with respect to both their original groupings and the addition and disposition of specific activities within those chosen groupings in subsequent taxable years.

(2) Regroupings. If it is determined that a taxpayer's original grouping was clearly inappropriate or a material change in the facts and circumstances has occurred that makes the original grouping clearly inappropriate, the taxpayer must regroup the activities and must comply with disclosure requirements that the Commissioner may prescribe.

(f) Grouping by Commissioner to prevent tax avoidance—(1) Rule. The Commissioner may regroup a taxpayer's activities if any of the activities resulting from the taxpayer's grouping is not an appropriate economic unit and a principal purpose of the taxpayer's grouping (or failure to regroup under paragraph (e) of this section) is to circumvent the underlying purposes of section 469.

(2) Example. The following example illustrates the application of this paragraph (f):

Example. **(i)** Taxpayers D, E, F, G, and H are doctors who operate separate medical practices. D invested in a tax shelter several years ago that generates passive losses and the other doctors intend to invest in real estate that will generate passive losses. The taxpayers form a partnership to engage in the trade or business of acquiring and operating X-ray equipment. In exchange for equipment contributed to the partnership, the taxpayers receive limited partnership interests. The partnership is managed by a general partner selected by the taxpayers; the taxpayers do not materially participate in its operations. Substantially all of the partnership's services are provided to the taxpayers or their patients, roughly in proportion to the doctors' interests in the partnership. Fees for the partnership's services are set at a level equal to the amounts that would be charged if the partnership were dealing with the taxpayers at arm's length and are expected to assure the partnership a profit. The taxpayers treat the partnership's services as a separate activity from their medical practices and offset the income generated by the partnership against their passive losses.

(ii) For each of the taxpayers, the taxpayer's own medical practice and the services provided by the partnership constitute an appropriate economic unit, but the services provided by the partnership do not separately constitute an appropriate economic unit. Moreover, a principal purpose of treating the medical practices and the partnership's services as separate activities is to circumvent the underlying purposes of section 469. Accordingly, the Commissioner may require the taxpayers to treat their medical practices and their interests in the partnership as a single activity, regardless of whether the separate medical practices are conducted through C corporations subject to section 469, S corporations, partnerships, or sole proprietorships. The Commissioner may assert penalties under section 6662 against the taxpayers in appropriate circumstances.

(g) Treatment of partial dispositions. A taxpayer may, for the taxable year in which there is a disposition of substantially all of an activity, treat the part disposed of as a separate activity, but only if the taxpayer can establish with reasonable certainty—

(1) The amount of deductions and credits allocable to that part of the activity for the taxable year under § 1.469–1(f)(4) (relating to carryover of disallowed deductions and credits); and

(2) The amount of gross income and of any other deductions and credits allocable to that part of the activity for the taxable year.

* * *

[T.D. 8565, 59 FR 50485, Oct. 4, 1994; T.D. 8645, 60 FR 66499, Dec. 22, 1995]

§ 1.469–5 Material participation.

(a) through (e) [Reserved]

(f) Participation—(1) In general. Except as otherwise provided in this paragraph (f), any work done by an individual (without regard to the capacity in which the individual does the work) in connection with an activity in which the individual owns an interest at the time the work is done shall be treated for purposes of this section as participation of the individual in the activity.

(f)(2) through (h)(2) [Reserved]

* * *

[T.D. 8417, 57 FR 20758, May 15, 1992]

§ 1.469–5 Material Participation. (Proposed Nov. 28, 2011)

(a) through (d) [Reserved].

(e) Treatment of an interest in a limited partnership as a limited partner—(1) In general. Except as otherwise provided in this paragraph (e), an individual shall not be treated as materially participating in any activity in which the individual owns an interest in a limited partnership as a limited partner (as defined in paragraph (e)(3)(i) of this section) for purposes of applying section 469 and the regulations thereunder to—

(i) The individual's share of any income, gain, loss, deduction, or credit from such activity that is attributable to an interest in a limited partnership as a limited partner; and

(ii) Any gain or loss from such activity recognized upon a sale or exchange of such an interest.

(2) Exceptions. Paragraph (e)(1) of this section shall not apply to an individual's share of income, gain, loss, deduction, and credit for a taxable year from any activity in which the individual would be treated as materially participating for the taxable year under paragraphs (a)(1), (a)(5), or (a)(6) of § 1.469–5T if the individual did not own an interest in a limited partnership as a limited partner (as defined in paragraph (e)(3)(i) of this section) for such taxable year.

(3) Interest in a limited partnership as a limited partner—(i) In general. Except as provided in paragraph (e)(3)(ii) of this section, for purposes of section 469(h)(2) and this paragraph (e), an interest in an entity shall be treated as an interest in a limited partnership as a limited partner if—

(A) The entity in which such interest is held is classified as a partnership for Federal income tax purposes under § 301.7701–3; and

(B) The holder of such interest does not have rights to manage the entity at all times during the entity's taxable year under the law of the jurisdiction in which the entity is organized and under the governing agreement.

(ii) Individual holding an interest other than an interest in a limited partnership as a limited partner. An individual shall not be treated as holding an interest in a limited partnership as a limited partner for the individual's taxable year if such individual also holds an interest in the partnership that is not an interest in a limited partnership as a limited partner (as defined in paragraph (e)(3)(i) of this section), such as a state-law general partnership interest, at all times during the entity's taxable year ending with or within the individual's taxable year (or the portion of the entity's taxable year during which the individual (directly or indirectly) owns such interest in a limited partnership as a limited partner).

* * *

§ 1.469–5T Material participation.

(a) In general. Except as provided in paragraphs (e) and (h)(2) of this section, an individual shall be treated, for purposes of section 469 and the regulations thereunder, as materially participating in an activity for the taxable year if and only if—

(1) The individual participates in the activity for more than 500 hours during such year;

(2) The individual's participation in the activity for the taxable year constitutes substantially all of the participation in such activity of all individuals (including individuals who are not owners of interests in the activity) for such year;

(3) The individual participates in the activity for more than 100 hours during the taxable year, and such individual's participation in the activity for the taxable year is not less than the participation in the activity of any other individual (including individuals who are not owners of interests in the activity) for such year;

(4) The activity is a significant participation activity (within the meaning of paragraph (c) of this section) for the taxable year, and the individual's aggregate participation in all significant participation activities during such year exceeds 500 hours;

(5) The individual materially participated in the activity (determined without regard to this paragraph (a)(5)) for any five taxable years (whether or not consecutive) during the ten taxable years that immediately precede the taxable year;

(6) The activity is a personal service activity (within the meaning of paragraph (d) of this section), and the individual materially participated in the activity for any three taxable years (whether or not consecutive) preceding the taxable year; or

(7) Based on all of the facts and circumstances (taking into account the rules in paragraph (b) of this section), the individual participates in the activity on a regular, continuous, and substantial basis during such year.

(b) Facts and circumstances—(1) In general. [Reserved]

(2) Certain participation insufficient to constitute material participation under this paragraph (b)—(i) Participation satisfying standards not contained in section 469. Except as provided in section 469(h)(3) and paragraph (h)(2) of this section (relating to certain retired individuals and surviving spouses in the case of farming activities), the fact that an individual satisfies the requirements of any participation standard (whether or not referred to as "material participation") under any provision (including sections 1402 and 2032A and the regulations thereunder) other than section 469 and the regulations thereunder shall not be taken into account in determining whether such individual materially participates in any activity for any taxable year for purposes of section 469 and the regulations thereunder.

(ii) Certain management activities. An individual's services performed in the management of an activity shall not be taken into account in determining whether such individual is treated as materially participating in such activity for the taxable year under paragraph (a)(7) of this section unless, for such taxable year—

(A) No person (other than such individual) who performs services in connection with the management of the activity receives compensation described in section 911(d)(2)(A) in consideration for such services; and

(B) No individual performs services in connection with the management of the activity that exceed (by hours) the amount of such services performed by such individual.

(iii) Participation less than 100 hours. If an individual participates in an activity for 100 hours or less during the taxable year, such individual shall not be treated as materially participating in such activity for the taxable year under paragraph (a)(7) of this section.

(c) Significant participation activity—(1) In general. For purposes of paragraph (a)(4) of this section, an activity is a significant participation activity of an individual if and only if such activity—

(i) Is a trade or business activity (within the meaning of § 1.469–1T(e)(2)) in which the individual significantly participates for the taxable year; and

(ii) Would be an activity in which the individual does not materially participate for the taxable year if material participation for such year were determined without regard to paragraph (a)(4) of this section.

(2) Significant participation. An individual is treated as significantly participating in an activity for a taxable year if and only if the individual participates in the activity for more than 100 hours during such year.

(d) Personal service activity. An activity constitutes a personal service activity for purposes of paragraph (a)(6) of this section if such activity involves the performance of personal services in—

(1) The fields of health, law, engineering, architecture, accounting, actuarial science, performing arts, or consulting; or

(2) Any other trade or business in which capital is not a material income-producing factor.

(e) Treatment of limited partners—(1) General rule. Except as otherwise provided in this paragraph (e), an individual shall not be treated as materially participating in any activity of a limited partnership for purposes of applying section 469 and the regulations thereunder to—

(i) The individual's share of any income, gain, loss, deduction, or credit from such activity that is attributable to a limited partnership interest in the partnership; and

(ii) Any gain or loss from such activity recognized upon a sale or exchange of such an interest.

(2) Exceptions. Paragraph (e)(1) of this section shall not apply to an individual's share of income, gain, loss, deduction, and credit for a taxable year from any activity in which the individual would be treated as materially participating for the taxable year under paragraph (a)(1), (5), or (6) of this section if the individual were not a limited partner for such taxable year.

(3) Limited partnership interest—(i) In general. Except as provided in paragraph (e)(3)(ii) of this section, for purposes of section 469(h)(2) and this paragraph (e), a partnership interest shall be treated as a limited partnership interest if—

(A) Such interest is designated a limited partnership interest in the limited partnership agreement or the certificate of limited partnership, without regard to whether the liability of the holder of such interest for obligations of the partnership is limited under the applicable State law; or

(B) The liability of the holder of such interest for obligations of the partnership is limited, under the law of the State in which the partnership is organized, to a determinable fixed amount (for example, the sum of the holder's capital contributions to the partnership and contractual obligations to make additional capital contributions to the partnership).

(ii) Limited partner holding general partner interest. A partnership interest of an individual shall not been treated as a limited partnership interest for the individual's taxable year if the individual is a general partner in the partnership at all times during the partnership's taxable year ending with or within the individual's taxable year (or the portion of the partnership's taxable year during which the individual (directly or indirectly) owns such limited partnership interest).

(f)(1) [Reserved] See § 1.469–5(f)(1) for rules relating to this paragraph.

(2) Exceptions—(i) Certain work not customarily done by owners. Work done in connection with an activity shall not be treated as participation in the activity for purposes of this section if—

(A) Such work is not of a type that is customarily done by an owner of such an activity; and

(B) One of the principal purposes for the performance of such work is to avoid the disallowance, under section 469 and the regulations thereunder, of any loss or credit from such activity.

(ii) Participation as an investor—(A) In general. Work done by an individual in the individual's capacity as an investor in an activity shall not be treated as participation in the activity for purposes of this section unless the individual is directly involved in the day-to-day management or operations of the activity.

(B) Work done in individual's capacity as an investor. For purposes of this paragraph (f)(2)(ii), work done by an individual in the individual's capacity as an investor in an activity includes—

(1) Studying and reviewing financial statements or reports on operations of the activity;

(2) Preparing or compiling summaries or analyses of the finances or operations of the activity for the individual's own use; and

(3) Monitoring the finances or operations of the activity in a nonmanagerial capacity.

(3) Participation of spouse. In the case of any person who is a married individual (within the meaning of section 7703) for the taxable year, any participation by such person's spouse in the activity during the taxable year (without regard to whether the spouse owns an interest in the activity and without regard to whether the spouses file a joint return for the taxable year) shall be treated, for purposes of applying section 469 and the regulations thereunder to such person, as participation by such person in the activity during the taxable year.

(4) Methods of proof. The extent of an individual's participation in an activity may be established by any reasonable means. Contemporaneous daily time reports, logs, or similar documents are not required if the extent of such participation may be established by other reasonable means. Reasonable means for purposes of this paragraph may include but are not limited to the identification of services performed over a period of time and the approximate number of hours spent performing such services during such period, based on appointment books, calendars, or narrative summaries.

* * *

[T.D. 8175, 53 FR 5725, Feb. 25, 1988, as amended by T.D. 8253, 54 FR 20565, May 12, 1989; T.D. 8417, 57 FR 20759, May 15, 1992; T.D. 8175, 61 FR 14247, Apr. 1, 1996]

§ 1.471–1 Need for inventories.

In order to reflect taxable income correctly, inventories at the beginning and end of each taxable year are necessary in every case in which the production, purchase, or sale of merchandise is an income-producing factor. The inventory should include all finished or partly finished goods and, in the case of raw materials and supplies, only those which have been acquired for sale or which will physically become a part of merchandise intended for sale, in which class fall containers, such as kegs, bottles, and cases, whether returnable or not, if title thereto will pass to the purchaser of the product to be sold therein. Merchandise should be included in the inventory only if title thereto is vested in the taxpayer. Accordingly, the seller should include in his inventory goods under contract for sale but not yet segregated and applied to the contract and goods out upon consignment, but should exclude from inventory goods sold (including containers), title to which has passed to the purchaser. A purchaser should include in inventory merchandise purchased (including containers), title to which has passed to him, although such merchandise is in transit or for other reasons has not been reduced to physical possession, but should not include goods ordered for future delivery, transfer of title to which has not yet been effected. (But see § 1.472–1.)

[T.D. 6500, 25 FR 11724, Nov. 26, 1960]

§ 1.471–2 Valuation of inventories.

(a) Section 471 provides two tests to which each inventory must conform:

(1) It must conform as nearly as may be to the best accounting practice in the trade or business, and

(2) It must clearly reflect the income.

(b) It follows, therefore, that inventory rules cannot be uniform but must give effect to trade customs which come within the scope of the best accounting practice in the particular trade or business. In order to clearly reflect income, the inventory practice of a taxpayer should be consistent from year to year, and greater weight is to be given to consistency than to any particular method of inventorying or basis of valuation so long as the method or basis used is in accord with §§ 1.471–1 through 1.471–11.

(c) The bases of valuation most commonly used by business concerns and which meet the requirements of section 471 are (1) cost and (2) cost or market, whichever is lower. (For inventories by dealers in securities, see § 1.471–5.) Any goods in an inventory which are unsalable at normal prices or unusable in the normal way because of damage, imperfections, shop wear, changes of style, odd or broken lots, or other similar causes, including second-hand goods taken in exchange, should be valued at bona fide selling prices less direct cost of disposition, whether subparagraph (1) or (2) of this paragraph is used, or if such goods consist of raw materials or partly finished goods held for use or consumption, they shall be valued upon a reasonable basis, taking into consideration the usability and the condition of the goods, but in no case shall such value be less than the scrap value. Bona fide selling price means actual offering of goods during a period ending not later than 30 days after inventory date. The burden of proof will rest upon the taxpayer to show that such exceptional goods as are valued upon such selling basis come within the classifications indicated above, and he shall maintain such records of the disposition of the goods as will enable a verification of the inventory to be made.

* * *

(f) The following methods, among others, are sometimes used in taking or valuing inventories, but are not in accord with the regulations in this part:

(1) Deducting from the inventory a reserve for price changes, or an estimated depreciation in the value thereof.

(2) Taking work in process, or other parts of the inventory, at a nominal price or at less than its proper value.

(3) Omitting portions of the stock on hand.

(4) Using a constant price or nominal value for so-called normal quantity of materials or goods in stock.

(5) Including stock in transit, shipped either to or from the taxpayer, the title to which is not vested in the taxpayer.

* * *

[T.D. 6500, 25 FR 11724, Nov. 26, 1960, as amended by T.D. 7285, 38 FR 26185, Sept. 19, 1973]

§ 1.471–3 Inventories at cost.

Cost means:

(a) In the case of merchandise on hand at the beginning of the taxable year, the inventory price of such goods.

(b) In the case of merchandise purchased since the beginning of the taxable year, the invoice price less trade or other discounts, except strictly cash discounts approximating a fair interest rate, which may be deducted or not at the option of the taxpayer, provided a consistent course is followed. To this net invoice price should be added transportation or other necessary charges incurred in acquiring possession of the goods. * * *

(c) In the case of merchandise produced by the taxpayer since the beginning of the taxable year, (1) the cost of raw materials and supplies entering into or consumed in connection with the product, (2) expenditures for direct labor, and (3) indirect production costs incident to and necessary for the production of the particular article, including in such indirect production costs an appropriate portion of management expenses, but not including any cost of selling or return on capital, whether by way of interest or profit. * * *

(d) In any industry in which the usual rules for computation of cost of production are inapplicable, costs may be approximated upon such basis as may be reasonable and in conformity with established trade practice in the particular industry. * * * Notwithstanding the other rules of this section, cost shall not include an amount which is of a type for which a deduction would be disallowed under section 162(c), (f), or (g) and the regulations thereunder in the case of a business expense.

[T.D. 6500, 25 FR 11725, Nov. 26, 1960, as amended by T.D. 7285, 38 FR 26185, Sept. 19, 1973; T.D. 7345, 40 FR 7439, Feb. 20, 1975; T.D. 8131, 52 FR 10060, March 30, 1987; T.D. 8482, 58 FR 42233, Aug. 9, 1993]

§ 1.471–4 Inventories at cost or market, whichever is lower.

(a) In general—(1) Market definition. Under ordinary circumstances and for normal goods in an inventory, market means the aggregate of the current bid prices prevailing at the date of the inventory of the basic elements of cost reflected in inventories of goods purchased and on hand, goods in process of manufacture, and finished manufactured goods on hand. The basic elements of cost include direct materials, direct labor, and indirect costs required to be included in inventories by the taxpayer (e.g., under section 263A and its underlying regulations for taxpayers subject to that section). For taxpayers to which section 263A applies, for example, the basic elements of cost must reflect all direct costs and all indirect costs properly allocable to goods on hand at the inventory date at the current bid price of those costs, including but not limited to the cost of purchasing, handling, and storage activities conducted by the taxpayer, both prior to and subsequent to acquisition or production of the goods. The determination of the current bid price of the basic elements of costs reflected in goods on hand at the inventory date must be based on the usual volume of particular cost elements purchased (or incurred) by the taxpayer.

(2) Fixed price contracts. Paragraph (a)(1) of this section does not apply to any goods on hand or in process of manufacture for delivery upon firm sales contracts (i.e., those not legally subject to cancellation by either party) at fixed prices entered into before the date of the inventory, under which the taxpayer is protected against actual loss. Any such goods must be inventoried at cost.

(3) Examples. The valuation principles in paragraph (a)(1) of this section are illustrated by the following examples:

Example 1. **(i)** Taxpayer A manufactures tractors. A values its inventory using cost or market, whichever is lower, under paragraph (a)(1) of this section. At the end of 1994, the cost of one of A's tractors on hand is determined as follows:

Direct materials	$ 3,000
Direct labor	4,000
Indirect costs under section 263A	3,000
Total section 263A costs (cost)	$10,000

(ii) A determines that the aggregate of the current bid prices of the materials, labor, and overhead required to reproduce the tractor at the end of 1994 are as follows:

Direct materials	$ 3,100
Direct labor	4,100
Indirect costs under section 263A	3,100
Total section 263A costs (market)	$10,300

(iii) In determining the lower of cost or market value of the tractor, A compares the cost of the tractor, $10,000, with the market value of the tractor, $10,300, in accordance with paragraph (c) of this section. Thus, under this section, A values the tractor at $10,000.

Example 2. **(i)** Taxpayer B purchases and resells several lines of shoes and is subject to section 263A. B values its inventory using cost or market, whichever is lower, under paragraph (a)(1) of this section. At the end of 1994, the cost of one pair of shoes on hand is determined as follows:

Acquisition cost	$200
Indirect costs under section 263A	10
Total section 263A costs (cost)	$210

(ii) B determines the aggregate current bid prices prevailing at the end of 1994 for the elements of cost (both direct costs and indirect costs incurred prior and subsequent to acquisition of the shoes) based on the volume of the elements usually purchased (or incurred) by B as follows:

Acquisition cost	$178
Indirect costs under section 263A	12
Total § 263A costs (market)	$190

(iii) In determining the lower of cost or market value of the shoes, B compares the cost of the pair of shoes, $210, with the market value of the shoes, $190, in accordance with paragraph (c) of this section. Thus, under this section, B values the shoes at $190.

* * *

[T.D. 6500, 25 FR 11725, Nov. 26, 1960, as amended, T.D. 8482, 58 FR 42233, Aug. 9, 1993]

§ 1.482–1 Allocation of income and deductions among taxpayers.

(a) In general—(1) Purpose and scope. The purpose of section 482 is to ensure that taxpayers clearly reflect income attributable to controlled transactions and to prevent the avoidance of taxes with respect to such transactions. Section 482 places a controlled taxpayer on a tax parity with an uncontrolled taxpayer by determining the true taxable income of the controlled taxpayer. This section sets forth general principles and guidelines to be followed under section 482. Section 1.482–2 provides rules for the determination of the true taxable income of controlled taxpayers in specific situations, including controlled transactions involving loans or advances or the use of tangible property. Sections 1.482–3 through 1.482–6 provide rules for the determination of the true taxable income of controlled taxpayers in cases involving the transfer of property. Section 1.482–7T sets forth the cost sharing provisions applicable to taxable years beginning on or after January 5, 2009. Section 1.482–8 provides examples illustrating the application of the best method rule. Finally, § 1.482–9 provides rules for the determination of the true taxable income of controlled taxpayers in cases involving the performance of services.

(2) Authority to make allocations. The district director may make allocations between or among the members of a controlled group if a controlled taxpayer has not reported its true taxable income. In such case, the district director may allocate income, deductions, credits, allowances, basis, or any other item or element affecting taxable income (referred to as allocations). The appropriate allocation may take the form of an increase or decrease in any relevant amount.

(3) Taxpayer's use of section 482. If necessary to reflect an arm's length result, a controlled taxpayer may report on a timely filed U.S. income tax return (including extensions) the results of its controlled transactions based upon prices different from those actually charged. Except as provided in this paragraph, section 482 grants no other right to a controlled taxpayer to apply the provisions of section 482 at will or to compel the district director to apply such provisions. Therefore, no untimely or amended returns will be permitted to decrease taxable income based on allocations or other adjustments with respect to controlled transactions. See § 1.6662–6T(a)(2) or successor regulations.

(b) Arm's length standard—(1) In general. In determining the true taxable income of a controlled taxpayer, the standard to be applied in every case is that of a taxpayer dealing at arm's length with an uncontrolled taxpayer. A controlled transaction meets the arm's length standard if the results of the transaction are consistent with the results that would have been realized if uncontrolled taxpayers had engaged in the same transaction under the same circumstances (arm's length result). However, because identical transactions can rarely be located, whether a transaction produces an arm's length result generally will be determined by reference to the results of comparable transactions under comparable circumstances. See § 1.482–1(d)(2) (Standard of Comparability). Evaluation of whether a controlled transaction produces an arm's length result is made pursuant to a method selected under the best method rule described in § 1.482–1(c).

(2) Arm's length methods—(i) Methods Sections 1.482–2 through 1.482–7 and 1.482–9 provide specific methods to be used to evaluate whether transactions between or among members of the controlled group satisfy the arm's length standard, and if they do not, to determine the arm's length result. This section provides general principles applicable in determining arm's length results of such controlled transactions, but do not provide methods, for which reference must be made to those other sections in accordance with paragraphs (b)(2)(ii) and (iii) of this section. Section 1.482–7 provides the specific methods to be used to evaluate whether a cost sharing arrangement as defined in § 1.482–7 produces results consistent with an arm's length result.

(ii) Selection of category of method applicable to transaction. The methods listed in § 1.482–2 apply to different types of transactions, such as transfers of property, services, loans or advances, and rentals. Accordingly, the method or methods most appropriate to the calculation of arm's length results for controlled transactions must be selected, and different methods may be applied to interrelated transactions if such transactions are most reliably evaluated on a separate basis. For example, if services are provided in connection with the transfer of property, it may be appropriate to separately apply the methods applicable to services and property in order to determine an arm's length result. But see § 1.482–1(f)(2)(i) (Aggregation of transactions). In addition, other applicable provisions of the Code may affect the characterization of a transaction, and therefore affect the methods applicable under section 482. See for example section 467.

(iii) Coordination of methods applicable to certain intangible development arrangements. Section 1.482–7 provides the specific methods to be used to determine arm's length results of controlled transactions in connection with a cost sharing arrangement as defined in § 1.482–7. Sections 1.482–4 and 1.482–9, as appropriate, provide the specific methods to be used to determine arm's length results of arrangements, including partnerships, for sharing the costs and risks of developing intangibles, other than a cost sharing arrangement covered by § 1.482–7. See also §§ 1.482–4(g) (Coordination with rules governing cost sharing arrangements) and 1.482–9(m)(3) (Coordination with rules governing cost sharing arrangements).

(c) Best method rule—(1) In general. The arm's length result of a controlled transaction must be determined under the method that, under the facts and circumstances, provides the most reliable measure of an arm's length result. Thus, there is no strict priority of methods, and no method will invariably be considered to be more reliable than others. An arm's length result may be determined under any method without establishing the inapplicability of another method, but if another method subsequently is shown to produce a more reliable measure of an arm's length result, such other method must be used. Similarly, if two or more applications of a single method provide inconsistent results, the arm's length result must be determined under the application that, under the facts and circumstances, provides the most reliable measure of an arm's length result. See § 1.482–8 for examples of the application of the best method rule. See § 1.482–7 for the applicable methods in the case of a cost sharing arrangement.

* * *

[T.D. 8552, 59 FR 34971, July 8, 1994; as amended by T.D. 9088, 68 FR 51171, Aug. 26, 2003; T.D. 9278, 71 FR 44465, Aug. 4, 2006; T.D. 9456, 74 FR 38841, Aug. 4, 2009; T.D. 9568, 76 FR 80089, Dec. 22, 2011; 77 FR 3606, Jan. 25, 2012]

§ 1.483–1 Interest on certain deferred payments.

(a) Amount constituting interest in certain deferred payment transactions—(1) In general. Except as provided in paragraph (c) of this section, section 483 applies to a contract for the sale or exchange of property if the contract provides for one or more payments due more than 1 year after the date of the sale or exchange, and the contract does not provide for adequate stated interest. In general, a contract has adequate stated interest if the contract provides for a stated rate of interest that is at least equal to the test rate (determined under § 1.483–3) and the interest is paid or compounded at least annually. Section 483 may apply to a contract whether the contract is express (written or oral) or implied. For purposes of section 483, a sale or exchange is any transaction treated as a sale or exchange for tax purposes. In addition, for purposes of section 483, property includes debt instruments and investment units, but does not include money, services, or the right to use property. For the treatment of certain obligations given in exchange for services or the use of property, see sections 404 and 467. * * *

(2) Treatment of contracts to which section 483 applies—(i) Treatment of unstated interest. If section 483 applies to a contract, unstated interest under the contract is treated as interest for tax purposes. Thus, for example, unstated interest is not treated as part of the amount realized from the sale or exchange of property (in the case of the seller), and is not included in the purchaser's basis in the property acquired in the sale or exchange.

(ii) Method of accounting for interest on contracts subject to section 483. Any stated or unstated interest on a contract subject to section 483 is taken into account by a taxpayer under the taxpayer's regular method of accounting (e.g., an accrual method or the cash receipts and disbursements method). See §§ 1.446–1, 1.451–1, and 1.461–1. For purposes of the preceding sentence, the amount of interest (including unstated interest) allocable to a payment under a contract to which section 483 applies is determined under § 1.446–2(e).

(b) Definitions—(1) Deferred payments. For purposes of the regulations under section 483, a deferred payment means any payment that constitutes all or a part of the sales price (as defined in paragraph (b)(2) of this section), and that is due more than 6 months after the date of the sale or exchange. Except as provided in section 483(c)(2) (relating to the treatment of a debt instrument of the purchaser), a payment may be made in the form of cash, stock or securities, or other property.

(2) Sales price. For purposes of section 483, the sales price for any sale or exchange is the sum of the amount due under the contract (other than stated interest) and the amount of any liability included in the amount realized from the sale or exchange. See § 1.1001–2. Thus, the sales price for any sale or exchange includes any amount of unstated interest under the contract.

(c) Exceptions to and limitations on the application of section 483—(1) In general. Sections 483(d), 1274(c)(4), and 1275(b) contain exceptions to and limitations on the application of section 483.

(2) Sales price of $3,000 or less. Section 483(d)(2) applies only if it can be determined at the time of the sale or exchange that the sales price cannot exceed $3,000, regardless of whether the sales price eventually paid for the property is less than $3,000.

(3) Other exceptions and limitations—(i) Certain transfers subject to section 1041. Section 483 does not apply to any transfer of property subject to section 1041 (relating to transfers of property between spouses or incident to divorce).

(ii) Treatment of certain obligees. Section 483 does not apply to an obligee under a contract for the sale or exchange of personal use property (within the meaning of section 1275(b)(3)) in the hands of the obligor and that evidences a below-market loan described in section 7872(c)(1).

(iii) Transactions involving certain demand loans. Section 483 does not apply to any payment under a contract that evidences a demand loan that is a below-market loan described in section 7872(c)(1).

(iv) Transactions involving certain annuity contracts. Section 483 does not apply to any payment under an annuity contract described in section 1275(a)(1)(B) (relating to annuity contracts excluded from the definition of debt instrument).

(v) Options. Section 483 does not apply to any payment under an option to buy or sell property.

* * *

(e) Aggregation rule. For purposes of section 483, all sales or exchanges that are part of the same transaction (or a series of related transactions) are treated as a single sale or exchange, and all contracts calling for deferred payments arising from the same transaction (or a series of related transactions) are treated as a single contract. This rule, however, generally only applies to contracts and to sales or exchanges involving a single buyer and a single seller.

* * *

[T.D. 8517, 59 FR 4799, Feb. 2, 1994]

§ 1.483–2 Unstated interest.

(a) In general—(1) Adequate stated interest. For purposes of section 483, a contract has unstated interest if the contract does not provide for adequate stated interest. A contract does not provide for adequate stated interest if the sum of the deferred payments exceeds—

(i) The sum of the present values of the deferred payments and the present values of any stated interest payments due under the contract; or

(ii) In the case of a cash method debt instrument (within the meaning of section 1274A(c)(2)) received in exchange for property in a potentially abusive situation (as defined in § 1.1274–3), the fair market value of the property reduced by the fair market value of any consideration other than the debt instrument, and reduced by the sum of all principal payments that are not deferred payments.

(2) Amount of unstated interest. For purposes of section 483, unstated interest means an amount equal to the excess of the sum of the deferred payments over the amount described in paragraph (a)(1)(i) or (a)(1)(ii) of this section, whichever is applicable.

(b) Operational rules—(1) In general. For purposes of paragraph (a) of this section, rules similar to those in § 1.1274–2 apply to determine whether a contract has adequate stated interest and the amount of unstated interest, if any, on the contract.

(2) Present value. For purposes of paragraph (a) of this section, the present value of any deferred payment or interest payment is determined by discounting the payment from the date it becomes due to the date of the sale or exchange at the test rate of interest applicable to the contract in accordance with § 1.483–3.

(c) Examples. The following examples illustrate the rules of this section.

Example 1. Contract that does not have adequate stated interest. On January 1, 1995, A sells B nonpublicly traded property under a contract that calls for a $100,000 payment of principal on January 1, 2005, and 10 annual interest payments of $9,000 on January 1 of each year, beginning on January 1, 1996. Assume that the test rate of interest is 9.2 percent, compounded annually. The contract does not provide for adequate stated interest because it does not provide for interest equal to 9.2 percent, compounded annually. The present value of the deferred payments is $98,727.69. As a result, the contract has unstated interest of $1,272.31 ($100,000 - $98,727.69).

Example 2. Contract that does not have adequate stated interest; no interest for initial short period. On May 1, 1996, A sells B nonpublicly traded property under a contract that calls for B to make a principal payment of $200,000 on December 31, 1998, and semiannual interest payments of $9,000, payable on June 30 and December 31 of each year, beginning on December 31, 1996. Assume that the test rate of interest is 9 percent, compounded semiannually. Even though the contract calls for a stated rate of interest no lower than the test rate of interest, the contract does not provide for adequate stated interest because the stated rate of interest does not apply for the short period from May 1, 1996, through June 30, 1996.

Example 3. Potentially abusive situation—(i) Facts. In a potentially abusive situation, a contract for the sale of nonpublicly traded personal property calls for the issuance of a cash method debt instrument (as defined in section 1274A(c)(2)) with a stated principal amount of $700,000, payable in 5 years. No other consideration is given. The debt instrument calls for annual payments of interest over its entire term at a rate of 9.2 percent, compounded annually (the test rate of interest applicable to the debt instrument). Thus, the present value of the deferred payment and the interest payments is $700,000. Assume that the fair market value of the property is $500,000.

(ii) Amount of unstated interest. A cash method debt instrument received in exchange for property in a potentially abusive situation provides for adequate stated interest only if the sum of the deferred payments under the instrument does not exceed the fair market value of the property. Because the deferred payment ($700,000) exceeds the fair market value of the property ($500,000), the debt instrument does not provide for adequate stated interest. Therefore, the debt instrument has unstated interest of $200,000.

Example 4. Variable rate debt instrument with adequate stated interest; variable rate as of the issue date greater than the test rate—(i) Facts. A contract for the sale of nonpublicly traded property calls for the issuance of a debt instrument in the principal amount of $75,000 due in 10 years. The debt instrument calls for interest payable semiannually at a rate of 3 percentage points above the yield on 6–month Treasury bills at the mid-point of the semiannual period immediately preceding each interest payment date. Assume that the interest rate is a qualified floating rate and that the debt instrument is a variable rate debt instrument within the meaning of § 1.1275–5.

(ii) Adequate stated interest. Under paragraph (b)(1) of this section, rules similar to those in § 1.1274–2(f) apply to determine whether the debt instrument has adequate stated interest. Assume that the test rate of interest applicable to the debt instrument is 9 percent, compounded semiannually. Assume also that the yield on 6–month Treasury bills on the date of the sale is 8.89 percent, which is greater than the yield on 6–month Treasury bills on the first date on which there is a binding written contract that substantially sets forth the terms under which the sale is consummated. Under § 1.1274–2(f), the debt instrument is tested for adequate stated interest as if it provided for a stated rate of interest of 11.89 percent (3 percent plus 8.89 percent), compounded semiannually, payable over its entire term. Because the test rate of interest is 9 percent, compounded semiannually, and the debt instrument is treated as providing for stated interest of 11.89 percent, compounded semiannually, the debt instrument provides for adequate stated interest.

* * *

[T.D. 8517, 59 FR 4799, Feb. 2, 1994]

§ 1.483–3 Test rate of interest applicable to a contract.

(a) General rule. For purposes of section 483, the test rate of interest for a contract is the same as the test rate that would apply under § 1.1274–4 if the contract were a debt instrument. Paragraph (b) of this section, however, provides for a lower test rate in the case of certain sales or exchanges of land between related individuals.

(b) Lower rate for certain sales or exchanges of land between related individuals—(1) Test rate. In the case of a qualified sale or exchange of land between related individuals (described in section 483(e)), the test rate is not greater than 6 percent, compounded semiannually, or an equivalent rate based on an appropriate compounding period.

(2) Special rules. The following rules and definitions apply in determining whether a sale or exchange is a qualified sale under section 483(e):

(i) Definition of family members. The members of an individual's family are determined as of the date of the sale or exchange. The members of an individual's family include those individuals described in section 267(c)(4) and the spouses of those individuals. In addition, for purposes of section 267(c)(4), full effect is given to a legal adoption, ancestor means parents and grandparents, and lineal descendants means children and grandchildren.

(ii) $500,000 limitation. Section 483(e) does not apply to the extent that the stated principal amount of the debt instrument issued in the sale or exchange, when added to the aggregate stated principal amount of any other debt instruments to which section 483(e) applies that were issued in prior qualified sales between the same two individuals during the same calendar year, exceeds $500,000. See Example 3 of paragraph (b)(3) of this section.

(iii) Other limitations. Section 483(e) does not apply if the parties to a contract include persons other than the related individuals and the parties enter into the contract with an intent to circumvent the purposes of section 483(e). In addition, if the property sold or exchanged includes any property other than land, section 483(e) applies only to the extent that the stated principal amount of the debt instrument issued in the sale or exchange is attributable to the land (based on the relative fair market values of the land and the other property).

(3) Examples. The following examples illustrate the rules of this paragraph (b).

Example 1. On January 1, 1995, A sells land to B, A's child, for $650,000. The contract for sale calls for B to make a $250,000 down payment and issue a debt instrument with a stated principal amount of $400,000. Because the stated principal amount of the debt instrument is less than $500,000, the sale is a qualified sale and section 483(e) applies to the debt instrument.

Example 2. The facts are the same as in Example 1 of paragraph (b)(3) of this section, except that on June 1, 1995, A sells additional land to B under a contract that calls for B to issue a debt instrument with a stated principal amount of $100,000. The stated principal amount of this debt instrument ($100,000) when added to the stated principal amount of the prior debt instrument ($400,000) does not exceed $500,000. Thus, section 483(e) applies to both debt instruments.

Example 3. The facts are the same as in Example 1 of paragraph (b)(3) of this section, except that on June 1, 1995, A sells additional land to B under a contract that calls for B to issue a debt instrument with a stated principal amount of $150,000. The stated principal amount of this debt instrument when added to the stated principal amount of the prior debt instrument ($400,000) exceeds $500,000. Thus, for purposes of section 483(e), the debt instrument issued in the sale of June 1, 1995, is treated as two separate debt instruments: a $100,000 debt instrument (to which section 483(e) applies) and a $50,000 debt instrument (to which section 1274, if otherwise applicable, applies).

* * *

[T.D. 8517, 59 FR 4799, Feb. 2, 1994]

CORPORATIONS USED TO AVOID INCOME TAX ON SHAREHOLDERS

§ 1.532–1 Corporations subject to accumulated earnings tax.

(a) General rule. (1) The tax imposed by section 531 applies to any domestic or foreign corporation (not specifically excepted under section 532(b) and paragraph (b) of this section) formed or availed of to avoid or prevent the imposition of the individual income tax on its shareholders, or on the shareholders of any other corporation, by permitting earnings and profits to accumulate instead of dividing or distributing them. See section 533 and § 1.533–1, relating to evidence of purpose to avoid income tax with respect to shareholders.

(2) The tax imposed by section 531 may apply if the avoidance is accomplished through the formation or use of one corporation or a chain of corporations. For example, if the capital stock of the M Corporation is held by the N Corporation, the earnings and profits of the M Corporation would not be returned as income subject to the individual income tax until such earnings and profits of the M Corporation were distributed to the N Corporation and distributed in turn by the N Corporation to its shareholders. If either the M Corporation or the N Corporation was formed or is availed of for the purpose of avoiding or preventing the imposition of the individual income tax upon the shareholders of the N Corporation, the accumulated taxable income of the corporation so formed or availed of (M or N, as the case may be) is subject to the tax imposed by section 531.

* * *

§ 1.533–1 Evidence of purpose to avoid income tax.

(a) In general. (1) The Commissioner's determination that a corporation was formed or availed of for the purpose of avoiding income tax with respect to shareholders is subject to disproof by competent evidence. Section 533(a) provides that the fact that earnings and profits of a corporation are permitted to accumulate beyond the reasonable needs of the business shall be determinative of the purpose to avoid the income tax with respect to shareholders unless the corporation, by the preponderance of the evidence, shall prove to the contrary. The burden of proving that earnings and profits have been permitted to accumulate beyond the reasonable needs of the business may be shifted to the Commissioner under section 534. * * * Section 533(b) provides that the fact that the taxpayer is a mere holding or investment company shall be prima facie evidence of the purpose to avoid income tax with respect to shareholders.

(2) The existence or nonexistence of the purpose to avoid income tax with respect to shareholders may be indicated by circumstances other than the conditions specified in section 533. Whether or not such purpose was present depends upon the particular circumstances of each case. All circumstances which might be construed as evidence of the purpose to avoid income tax with respect to shareholders cannot be outlined, but among other things, the following will be considered:

(i) Dealings between the corporation and its shareholders, such as withdrawals by the shareholders as personal loans or the expenditure of funds by the corporation for the personal benefit of the shareholders,

(ii) The investment by the corporation of undistributed earnings in assets having no reasonable connection with the business of the corporation (see § 1.537–3), and

(iii) The extent to which the corporation has distributed its earnings and profits.

The fact that a corporation is a mere holding or investment company or has an accumulation of earnings and profits in excess of the reasonable needs of the business is not absolutely conclusive against it if the taxpayer satisfies the Commissioner that the corporation was neither formed nor availed of for the purpose of avoiding income tax with respect to shareholders.

(b) General burden of proof and statutory presumptions. The Commissioner may determine that the taxpayer was formed or availed of to avoid income tax with respect to shareholders through the medium of permitting earnings and profits to accumulate. In the case of litigation involving any such determination (except where the burden of proof is on the Commissioner under section 534), the burden of proving such determination wrong by a preponderance of the evidence, together with the corresponding burden of first going forward with the evidence, is on the taxpayer under principles applicable to income tax cases generally. For the burden of proof in a proceeding before the Tax Court with respect to the allegation that earnings and profits have been permitted to accumulate beyond the reasonable needs of the business, see section 534 and §§ 1.534–2 through 1.534–4. For a definition of a holding or investment company, see paragraph (c) of this section. For determination of the reasonable needs of the business, see section 537 and §§ 1.537–1 through 1.537–3. If the taxpayer is a mere holding or investment company, and the Commissioner therefore determines that the corporation was formed or availed of for the purpose of avoiding income tax with respect to shareholders, then section 533(b) gives further weight to the presumption of correctness already arising from the Commissioner's determination by expressly providing an additional presumption of the existence of a purpose to avoid income tax with respect to shareholders. Further, if it is established (after complying with section 534 where applicable) that earnings and profits were permitted to accumulate beyond the reasonable needs of the business and the Commissioner has therefore determined that the corporation was formed or availed of for the purpose of avoiding income tax with respect to shareholders, then section 533(a) adds still more weight to the Commissioner's determination. Under such circumstances, the existence of such an accumulation is made determinative of the purpose to avoid income tax with respect to shareholders unless the taxpayer proves to the contrary by the preponderance of the evidence.

* * *

[T.D. 6500, 25 FR 11737, Nov. 26, 1960, as amended by T.D. 6652, 28 FR 4786, May 14, 1963]

§ 1.534–2 Burden of proof as to unreasonable accumulations in cases before the Tax Court.

(a) Burden of proof on Commissioner. Under the general rule provided in section 534(a), in any proceeding before the Tax Court involving a notice of deficiency based in whole or in part on the allegation that all or any part of the earnings and profits have been permitted to accumulate beyond the reasonable needs of the business, the burden of proof with respect to such allegation is upon the Commissioner if—

(1) A notification, as provided for in section 534(b) and paragraph (c) of this section, has not been sent to the taxpayer; or

(2) A notification, as provided for in section 534(b) and paragraph (c) of this section, has been sent to the taxpayer and, in response to such notification, the taxpayer has submitted a statement, as provided in section 534(c) and paragraph (d) of this section, setting forth the ground or grounds (together with facts sufficient to show the basis thereof) on which it relies to establish that all or any part of its earnings and profits have not been permitted to accumulate beyond the reasonable needs of the business. However, the burden of proof in the latter case is upon the Commissioner only with respect to the relevant ground or grounds set forth in the statement submitted by the taxpayer, and only if such ground or grounds are supported by facts (contained in the statement) sufficient to show the basis thereof.

(b) Burden of proof on the taxpayer. The burden of proof in a Tax Court proceeding with respect to an allegation that all or any part of the earnings and profits have been permitted to accumulate beyond the reasonable needs of the business is upon the taxpayer if—

(1) A notification, as provided for in section 534(b) and paragraph (c) of this section, has been sent to the taxpayer and the taxpayer has not submitted a statement, in response to such notification, as provided in section 534(c) and paragraph (d) of this section; or

(2) A statement has been submitted by the taxpayer in response to such notification, but the ground or grounds on which the taxpayer relies are not relevant to the allegation or, if relevant, the statement does not contain facts sufficient to show the basis thereof.

* * *

(d) Statement by taxpayer. **(1)** A taxpayer who has received a notification, as provided in section 534(b) and paragraph (c) of this section, that the proposed notice of deficiency includes an amount with respect to the accumulated earnings tax imposed by section 531, may, under section 534(c), submit a statement that all or any part of the earnings and profits of the corporation have not been permitted to accumulate beyond the reasonable needs of the business. Such statement shall set forth the ground or grounds (together with facts sufficient to show the basis thereof) on which the taxpayer relies to establish that there has been no accumulation of earnings and profits beyond the reasonable needs of the business. See paragraphs (a) and (b) of this section for rules concerning the effect of the statement with respect to burden of proof. See §§ 1.537–1 to 1.537–3, inclusive, relating to reasonable needs of the business.

(2) The taxpayer's statement, under section 534(c) and this paragraph, must be submitted to the Internal Revenue office which issued the notification (referred to in section 534(b) and paragraph (c) of this section) within 60 days after the mailing of such notification. If the taxpayer is unable, for good cause, to submit the statement within such 60-day period, an additional period not exceeding 30 days may be granted upon receipt in the Internal Revenue office concerned (before the expiration of the 60-day period provided herein) of a request from the taxpayer, setting forth the reasons for such request. * * *

[T.D. 6500, 25 FR 11737, Nov. 26, 1960]

§ 1.537–1 Reasonable needs of the business.

(a) In general. The term "reasonable needs of the business" includes (1) the reasonable anticipated needs of the business (including product liability loss reserves, as defined in paragraph (f) of this section), (2) the section 303 redemption needs of the business, as defined in paragraph (c) of this section, and (3) the excess business holdings redemption needs of the business as described in paragraph (d) of this section. See paragraph (e) of this section for additional rules relating to the section 303 redemption needs and the excess business holdings redemption needs of the business. An accumulation of the earnings and profits (including the undistributed earnings and profits of prior years) is in excess of the reasonable needs of the business if it exceeds the amount that a prudent businessman would consider appropriate for the present business purposes and for the reasonably anticipated future needs of the business. The need to retain earnings and profits must be directly connected with the needs of the corporation itself and must be for bona fide business purposes. For purposes of this paragraph the section 303 redemption needs of the business and the excess business holdings redemption needs of the business are deemed to be directly connected with the needs of the business and for a bona fide business purpose. See § 1.537–3 for a discussion of what constitutes the business of the corporation. The extent to which earnings and profits have been distributed by the corporation may be taken into account in determining whether or not retained earnings and profits exceed the reasonable needs of the business. See § 1.537–2, relating to grounds for accumulation of earnings and profits.

(b) Reasonable anticipated needs. **(1)** In order for a corporation to justify an accumulation of earnings and profits for reasonably anticipated future needs, there must be an indication that the future needs of the business require such accumulation, and the corporation must have specific, definite, and feasible plans for the use of such accumulation. Such an accumulation need not be used immediately, nor must the plans for its use be consummated within a short period after the close of the taxable year, provided that such accumulation will be used within a reasonable time depending upon all the facts and circumstances relating to the future needs of the business. Where the future needs of the business are uncertain or vague, where the plans for the future use of an accumulation are not specific, definite, and feasible, or where the execution of such a plan is postponed indefinitely, an accumulation cannot be justified on the grounds of reasonably anticipated needs of the business.

(2) Consideration shall be given to reasonably anticipated needs as they exist on the basis of the facts at the close of the taxable year. Thus, subsequent events shall not be used for the purpose of showing that the retention of earnings or profits was unreasonable at the close of the taxable year if all the elements of reasonable anticipation are present at the close of such taxable year. However, subsequent events may be considered to determine whether the taxpayer actually intended to consummate or has actually consummated the plans for which the earnings and profits were accumulated. In this connection, projected expansion or investment plans shall be reviewed in the light of the facts during each year and as they exist as of the close of the taxable year. If a corporation has justified an accumulation for future needs by plans never consummated, the amount of such an accumulation shall be taken into account in determining the reasonableness of subsequent accumulations.

(c) Section 303 redemption needs of the business. **(1)** The term "section 303 redemption needs" means, with respect to the taxable year of the corporation in which a shareholder of the corporation died or any taxable year thereafter, the amount needed (or reasonably anticipated to be needed) to redeem stock included in the gross estate of such shareholder but not in excess of the amount necessary to effect a distribution to which section 303 applies. For purposes of this paragraph, the term "shareholder" includes an individual in whose gross estate stock of the corporation is includable upon his death for Federal estate tax purposes.

(2) This paragraph applies to a corporation to which section 303(c) would apply if a distribution described therein were made.

(3) If stock included in the gross estate of a decedent is stock of two or more corporations described in section 303(b)(2)(B), the amount needed by each such corporation for section 303 redemption purposes under this section shall, unless the particular facts and circumstances indicate otherwise, be that amount which bears the same ratio to the amount described in section 303(a) as the fair market value of such corporation's stock included in the gross estate of such decedent bears to the fair market value of all of the stock of such corporations included in the gross estate. For example, facts and circumstances indicating that the allocation prescribed by this subparagraph is not required would include notice given to the corporations by the executor or administrator of the decedent's estate that he intends to request the redemption of stock of only one of such corporations or the redemption of stock of such corporations in a ratio which is unrelated to the respective fair market values of the stock of the corporations included in the decedent's gross estate.

* * *

[T.D. 6500, 25 FR 11737, Nov. 26, 1960, as amended by T.D. 7165, 37 FR 5022, March 9, 1972, 37 FR 5703, March 18, 1972; T.D. 7678, 44 FR 12416, Feb. 26, 1980; T.D. 8096, 51 FR 30483, Aug. 27, 1986]

§ 1.537–2 Grounds for accumulation of earnings and profits.

(a) In general. Whether a particular ground or grounds for the accumulation of earnings and profits indicate that the earnings and profits have been accumulated for the reasonable needs of the business or beyond such needs is dependent upon the particular circumstances of the case. Listed below in paragraphs (b) and (c) of this section are some of the grounds which may be used as guides under ordinary circumstances.

(b) Reasonable accumulation of earnings and profits. Although the following grounds are not exclusive, one or more of such grounds, if supported by sufficient facts, may indicate that the earnings and profits of a corporation are being accumulated for the reasonable needs of the business provided the general requirements under §§ 1.537–1 and 1.537–3 are satisfied:

(1) To provide for bona fide expansion of business or replacement of plant;

(2) To acquire a business enterprise through purchasing stock or assets;

(3) To provide for the retirement of bona fide indebtedness created in connection with the trade or business, such as the establishment of a sinking fund for the purpose of retiring bonds issued by the corporation in accordance with contract obligations incurred on issue;

(4) To provide necessary working capital for the business, such as, for the procurement of inventories;

(5) To provide for investments or loans to suppliers or customers if necessary in order to maintain the business of the corporation; or

(6) To provide for the payment of reasonably anticipated product liability losses, as defined in section 172(j), * * *.

(c) Unreasonable accumulations of earnings and profits. Although the following purposes are not exclusive, accumulations of earnings and profits to meet any one of such objectives may indicate that the earnings and profits of a corporation are being accumulated beyond the reasonable needs of the business:

(1) Loans to shareholders, or the expenditure of funds of the corporation for the personal benefit of the shareholders;

(2) Loans having no reasonable relation to the conduct of the business made to relatives or friends of shareholders, or to other persons;

(3) Loans to another corporation, the business of which is not that of the taxpayer corporation, if the capital stock of such other corporation is owned, directly or indirectly, by the shareholder or shareholders of the taxpayer corporation and such shareholder or shareholders are in control of both corporations;

(4) Investments in properties, or securities which are unrelated to the activities of the business of the taxpayer corporation; or

(5) Retention of earnings and profits to provide against unrealistic hazards.

[T.D. 6500, 25 FR 11737, Nov. 26, 1960, as amended by T.D. 8096, 51 FR 30484, Aug. 27, 1986]

§ 1.537–3 Business of the corporation.

(a) The business of a corporation is not merely that which it has previously carried on but includes, in general, any line of business which it may undertake.

(b) If one corporation owns the stock of another corporation and, in effect, operates the other corporation, the business of the latter corporation may be considered in substance, although not in legal form, the business of the first corporation. However, investment by a corporation of its earnings and profits in stock and securities of another corporation is not, of itself, to be regarded as employment of the earnings and profits in its business. Earnings and profits of the first corporation put into the second corporation through the purchase of stock or securities or otherwise, may, if a subsidiary relationship is established, constitute employment of the earnings and profits in its own business. Thus, the business of one corporation may be regarded as including the business of another corporation if such other corporation is a mere instrumentality of the first corporation; that may be established by showing that the first corporation owns at least 80 percent of the voting stock of the second corporation. If the taxpayer's ownership of stock is less than 80 percent in the other corporation, the determination of whether the funds are employed in a business operated by the taxpayer will depend upon the particular circumstances of the case. Moreover, the business of one corporation does not include the business of another corporation if such other corporation is a personal holding company, an investment company, or a corporation not engaged in the active conduct of a trade or business.

[T.D. 6500, 25 FR 11737, Nov. 26, 1960]

§ 1.543–1 Personal holding company income.

(a) General rule. The term ''personal holding company income'' means the portion of the gross income which consists of the classes of gross income described in paragraph (b) of this section. See section 543(b) * * * for special limitations on gross income and personal holding company income in cases of gains from stocks', securities', and commodities' transactions.

(b) Definitions—(1) Dividends. The term ''dividends'' includes dividends as defined in section 316 * * *.

(2) Interest. The term ''interest'' means any amounts, includible in gross income, received for the use of money loaned. However, (i) interest which constitutes ''rent'' shall not be classified as interest but shall be classified as ''rents'' (see subparagraph (10) of this paragraph) * * *.

(3) Royalties (other than mineral, oil, or gas royalties or certain copyright royalties). The term ''royalties'' (other than mineral, oil, or gas royalties or certain copyright royalties) includes amounts received for the privilege of using patents, copyrights, secret processes and formulas, good will, trade marks, trade brands, franchises, and other like property. It does not, however, include rents. * * *

(4) Annuities. The term ''annuities'' includes annuities only to the extent includible in the computation of gross income. See section 72 * * * for rules relating to the inclusion of annuities in gross income.

(5) Gains from the sale or exchange of stock or securities. **(i)** Except in the case of regular dealers in stock or securities as provided in subdivision (ii) of this subparagraph, gross income and personal holding company income include the amount by which the gains exceed the losses from the sale or exchange of stock or securities. See section 543(b)(1) * * * for provisions relating to this limitation. For this purpose, there shall be taken into account all those gains includible in gross income (including gains from liquidating dividends and other distributions from capital) and all those losses deductible from gross income which are considered under chapter 1 of the Code to be gains or losses from the sale or exchange of stock or securities. The term "stock or securities" as used in section 543(a)(2) and this subparagraph includes shares or certificates of stock, stock rights or warrants, or interest in any corporation (including any joint stock company, insurance company, association, or other organization classified as a corporation by the Code), certificates of interest or participation in any profit-sharing agreement, or in any oil, gas, or other mineral property, or lease, collateral trust certificates, voting trust certificates, bonds, debentures, certificates of indebtedness, notes, car trust certificates, bills of exchange, obligations issued by or on behalf of a State, Territory, or political subdivision thereof.

(ii) In the case of "regular dealers in stock or securities" there shall not be included gains or losses derived from the sale or exchange of stock or securities made in the normal course of business. The term "regular dealer in stock or securities" means a corporation with an established place of business regularly engaged in the purchase of stock or securities and their resale to customers. However, such corporations shall not be considered as regular dealers with respect to stock or securities which are held for investment. See section 1236 and § 1.1236–1.

(6) Gains from futures transactions in commodities. Gross income and personal holding company income include the amount by which the gains exceed the losses from futures transactions in any commodity on or subject to the rules of a board of trade or commodity exchange. * * * In general, for the purpose of determining such excess, there are included all gains and losses on futures contracts which are speculative. However, for the purpose of determining such excess, there shall not be included gains or losses from cash transactions, or gains or losses by a producer, processor, merchant, or handler of the commodity, which arise out of bona fide hedging transactions reasonably necessary to the conduct of its business in the manner in which such business is customarily and usually conducted by others. See section 1233 * * *.

(7) Estates and trusts. Under section 543(a)(4) personal holding company income includes amounts includible in computing the taxable income of the corporation under part I, subchapter J, chapter 1 of the Code (relating to estates, trusts, and beneficiaries); and any gain derived by the corporation from the sale or other disposition of any interest in an estate or trust.

(8) Personal service contracts. **(i)** Under section 543(a)(5) amounts received under a contract under which the corporation is to furnish personal services, as well as amounts received from the sale or other disposition of such contract, shall be included as personal holding company income if—

(a) Some person other than the corporation has the right to designate (by name or by description) the individual who is to perform the services, or if the individual who is to perform the services is designated (by name or by description) in the contract; and

(b) At any time during the taxable year 25 percent or more in value of the outstanding stock of the corporation is owned, directly or indirectly, by or for the individual who has performed, is to perform, or may be designated (by name or by description) as the one to perform, such services. * * * It should be noted that the stock ownership requirement of section 543(a)(5) and this subparagraph relates to the stock ownership at any time during the taxable year. * * *

(ii) If the contract, in addition to requiring the performance of services by a 25–percent stockholder who is designated or who could be designated (as specified in section 543(a)(5) and subdivision (i) of this subparagraph), requires the performance of services by other persons which are important and essential, then only that portion of the amount received under such contract which is attributable to the personal services of the 25–percent stockholder shall constitute personal holding company income. Incidental personal services of other persons employed by the corporation to facilitate the performance of the services by the 25–percent stockholder, however, shall not constitute important or essential services. Under section 482 gross income, deductions, credits, or allowances between or among organizations, trades, or businesses may be allocated if it is determined that allocation is necessary in order to prevent evasion of taxes or clearly to reflect the income of any such organizations, trades, or businesses.

* * *

(9) Compensation for use of property. Under section 543(a)(6) amounts received as compensation for the use of, or right to use, property of the corporation shall be included as personal holding company income if, at any time during the taxable year, 25 percent or more in value of the outstanding stock of the corporation is owned, directly or indirectly, by or for an individual entitled to the use of the property. Thus, if a shareholder who meets the stock ownership requirement of section 543(a)(6) and this subparagraph uses, or has the right to use, a yacht, residence, or other property owned by the corporation, the compensation to the corporation for such use, or right to use, the property constitutes personal holding company income. This is true even though the shareholder may acquire the use of, or the right to use, the property by means of a sublease or under any other arrangement involving parties other than the corporation and the shareholder. However, if the personal holding company income of the corporation (after excluding any such income described in section 543(a)(6) and this subparagraph, relating to compensation for use of property, and after excluding any such income described in section 543(a)(7) and subparagraph (10) of this paragraph, relating to rents) is not more than 10 percent of its gross income, compensation for the use of property shall not constitute personal holding company income. For purposes of the preceding sentence, in determining whether personal holding company income is more than 10 percent of gross income, copyright royalties constitute personal holding company income, regardless of whether such copyright royalties are excluded from personal holding company income under section 543(a)(9) and subparagraph (12)(ii) of this paragraph. * * * It should be noted that the stock ownership requirement of section 543(a)(6) and this subparagraph relates to the stock outstanding at any time during the entire taxable year. * * *

(10) Rents (including interest constituting rents). Rents which are to be included as personal holding company income consist of compensation (however designated) for the use, or right to use, property of the corporation. The term "rents" does not include amounts includible in personal holding company income under section 543(a)(6) and subparagraph (9) of this paragraph. The amounts considered as rents include charter fees, etc., for the use of, or the right to use, property, as well as interest on debts owed to the corporation (to the extent such debts represent the price for which real property held primarily for sale to customers in the ordinary course of the corporation's trade or business was sold or exchanged by the corporation). However, if the amount of the rents includible under section 543(a)(7) and this subparagraph constitutes 50 percent or more of the gross income of the corporation, such rents shall not be considered to be personal holding company income.

(11) Mineral, oil, or gas royalties. **(i)** The income from mineral, oil, or gas royalties is to be included as personal holding company income, unless (a) the aggregate amount of such royalties constitutes 50 percent or more of the gross income of the corporation for the taxable year and (b) the aggregate amount of deductions allowable under section 162 (other than compensation for personal services rendered by the shareholders of the corporation) equals 15 percent or more of the gross income of the corporation for the taxable year.

(ii) The term "mineral, oil, or gas royalties" means all royalties, including overriding royalties and, to the extent not treated as loans under section 636, mineral production payments, received from any interest in mineral, oil, or gas properties. The term "mineral" includes those minerals which are included within the meaning of the term "minerals" in the regulations under section 611.

(iii) The first sentence of subdivision (ii) of this subparagraph shall apply to overriding royalties received from the sublessee by the operating company which originally leased and developed the natural resource property in respect of which such overriding royalties are paid, and to mineral, oil, or gas production payments, only with respect to amounts received after September 30, 1958.

* * *

[T.D. 6500, 25 FR 11737, Nov. 26, 1960, as amended by T.D. 6739, 29 FR 7713, June 17, 1964; T.D. 7261, 38 FR 5467, March 1, 1973]

§ 1.562–1 Dividends for which the dividends paid deduction is allowable.

(a) General rule. Except as otherwise provided in section 562 (b) and (d), the term "dividend", for purposes of determining dividends eligible for the dividends paid deduction, refers only to a dividend described in section 316 (relating to definition of dividends for purposes of corporate distributions). No distribution, however, which is preferential within the meaning of section 562(c) * * * shall be eligible for the dividends paid deduction. * * * Further, for purposes if the dividends paid deduction, the term "dividend" does not include a distribution in liquidation unless the distribution is treated as a dividend under section 316(b)(2) * * *. If a dividend is paid in property (other than money) the amount of the dividends paid deduction with respect to such property shall be the adjusted basis of the property in the hands of the distributing corporation at the time of the distribution. * * *

* * *

[T.D. 6500, 25 FR 11737, Nov. 26, 1960, as amended by T.D. 6949, 33 FR 5529, April 9, 1968; T.D. 7767, 46 FR 11265, Feb. 6, 1981]

NATURAL RESOURCES

§ 1.611–1 Allowance of deduction for depletion.

(a) Depletion of mines, oil and gas wells, other natural deposits, and timber—(1) In general. Section 611 provides that there shall be allowed as a deduction in computing taxable income in the case of mines, oil and gas wells, other natural deposits, and timber, a reasonable allowance for depletion. In the case of standing timber, the depletion allowance shall be computed solely upon the adjusted basis of the property. In the case of other exhaustible natural resources the allowance for depletion shall be computed upon either the adjusted depletion basis of the property (see section 612, relating to cost depletion) or upon a percentage of gross income from the property (see section 613, relating to percentage depletion), whichever results in the greater allowance for depletion for any taxable year. In no case will depletion based upon discovery value be allowed.

* * *

(b) Economic interest. (1) Annual depletion deductions are allowed only to the owner of an economic interest in mineral deposits or standing timber. An economic interest is possessed in every case in which the taxpayer has acquired by investment any interest in mineral in place or standing timber and secures, by any form of legal relationship, income derived from the extraction of the mineral or severance of the timber, to which he must look for a return of his capital. For an exception in the case of certain mineral production payments, see section 636 and the regulations thereunder. A person who has no capital investment in the mineral deposit or standing timber does not possess an economic interest merely because through a contractual relation he possesses a mere economic or pecuniary advantage derived from production. For example, an agreement between the owner of an economic interest and another entitling the latter to purchase or process the product upon production or entitling the latter to compensation for extraction or cutting does not convey a depletable economic interest. Further, depletion deductions with respect to an economic interest of a corporation are allowed to the corporation and not to its shareholders.

(2) No depletion deduction shall be allowed the owner with respect to any timber, coal, or domestic iron ore that such owner has disposed of under any form of contract by virtue of which he retains an economic interest in such timber, coal, or iron ore, if such disposal is considered a sale of timber, coal, or domestic iron ore under section 631(b) or (c).

(c) Special rules—(1) In general. For the purpose of the equitable apportionment of depletion among the several owners of economic interests in a mineral deposit or standing timber, if the value of any mineral or timber must be ascertained as of any specific date for the determination of the basis for depletion, the values of such several interests therein may be determined separately, but, when determined as of the same date, shall together never exceed the value at that date of the mineral or timber as a whole.

(2) Leases. In the case of a lease, the deduction for depletion under section 611 shall be equitably apportioned between the lessor and lessee. In the case of a lease or other contract providing for the sharing of economic interests in a mineral deposit or standing timber, such deduction shall be computed by each taxpayer by reference to the adjusted basis of his property determined in accordance with sections 611 and 612, or computed in accordance with section 613, if applicable, and the regulations thereunder.

(3) Life tenant and remainderman. In the case of property held by one person for life with remainder to another person, the deduction for depletion under section 611 shall be computed as if the life tenant were the absolute owner of the property so that he will be entitled to the deduction during his life, and thereafter the deduction, if any, shall be allowed to the remainderman.

(4) Mineral or timber property held in trust. If a mineral property or timber property is held in trust, the allowable deduction for depletion is to be apportioned between the income beneficiaries and the trustee on the basis of the trust income from such property allocable to each, unless the governing instrument (or local law) requires or permits the trustee to maintain a reserve for depletion in any amount. In the latter case, the deduction is first allocated to the trustee to the extent that income is set aside for a depletion reserve, and any part of the deduction in excess of the income set aside for the reserve shall be apportioned between the income beneficiaries and the trustee on the basis of the trust income (in excess of the income set aside for the reserve) allocable to each. For example:

(i) If under the trust instrument of local law the income of a trust computed without regard to depletion is to be distributed to a named beneficiary, the beneficiary is entitled to the deduction to the exclusion of the trustee.

(ii) If under the trust instrument or local law the income of a trust is to be distributed to a named beneficiary, but the trustee is directed to maintain a reserve for depletion in any amount, the deduction is allowed to the trustee (except to the extent that income set aside for the reserve is less than the allowable deduction). The same result would follow if the trustee sets aside income for a depletion reserve pursuant to discretionary authority to do so in the governing instrument.

No effect shall be given to any allocation of the depletion deduction which gives any beneficiary or the trustee a share of such deduction greater than his pro rata share of the trust income, irrespective of any provisions in the trust instrument, except as otherwise provided in this paragraph when the trust instrument or local law requires or permits the trustee to maintain a reserve for depletion.

(5) Mineral or timber property held by estate. In the case of a mineral property or timber property held by an estate the deduction for depletion under section 611 shall be apportioned between the estate and the heirs, legatees, and devisees on the basis of income of the estate from such property which is allocable to each.

(d) Definitions. As used in this part, and the regulations thereunder, the term—

(1) "Property" means—(i) in the case of minerals, each separate economic interest owned in each mineral deposit in each separate tract or parcel of land or an aggregation or combination of such mineral interests permitted under section 614(b), (c), (d), or (e); and (ii) in the case of timber, an economic interest in standing timber in each tract or block representing a separate timber account (see paragraph (d) of § 1.611-3). * * * When, in the regulations under this part, either the word "mineral" or "timber" precedes the word "property", such adjectives are used only to classify the type of "property" involved. For further explanation of the term "property", see section 614 * * *.

(2) "Fair market value" of a property is that amount which would induce a willing seller to sell and a willing buyer to purchase.

(3) "Mineral enterprise" is the mineral deposit or deposits and improvements, if any, used in mining or in the production of oil and gas, and only so much of the surface of the land as is necessary for purposes of mineral extraction. The value of the mineral enterprise is the combined value of its component parts.

(4) "Mineral deposit" refers to minerals in place. When a mineral enterprise is acquired as a unit, the cost of any interest in the mineral deposit or deposits is that proportion of the total cost of the mineral enterprise which the value of the interest in the deposit or deposits bears to the value of the entire enterprise at the time of its acquisition.

(5) "Minerals" includes ores of the metals, coal, oil, gas, and all other natural metallic and nonmetallic deposits, except minerals derived from sea water, the air, or from similar inexhaustible sources. It includes but is not limited to all of the minerals and other natural deposits subject to depletion based upon a percentage of gross income from the property under section 613 and the regulations thereunder.

[T.D. 6500, 25 FR 11737, Nov. 26, 1960, as amended by T.D. 6841, 30 FR 9305, July 27, 1965; T.D. 7261, 38 FR 5467, March 1, 1973]

§ 1.611-2 Rules applicable to mines, oil and gas wells, and other natural deposits.

(a) Computation of cost depletion of mines, oil and gas wells, and other natural deposits. (1) The basis upon which cost depletion is to be allowed in respect of any mineral property is the basis provided for in section 612 and the regulations thereunder. After the amount of such basis applicable to the mineral property has been determined for the taxable year, the cost depletion for that year shall be computed by dividing such amount by the number of units of mineral remaining as of the taxable year (see subparagraph (3) of this paragraph), and by multiplying the depletion unit, so determined, by the number of units of mineral sold within the taxable year (see subparagraph (2) of this paragraph). In the selection of a unit of mineral for depletion, preference shall be given to the principal or customary unit or units paid for in the products sold, such as tons of ore, barrels of oil, or thousands of cubic feet of natural gas.

(2) As used in this paragraph, the phrase "number of units sold within the taxable year"—

(i) In the case of a taxpayer reporting income on the cash receipts and disbursements method, includes units for which payments were received within the taxable year although produced or sold prior to the taxable year, and excludes units sold but not paid for in the taxable year, and

(ii) In the case of a taxpayer reporting income on the accrual method, shall be determined from the taxpayer's inventories kept in physical quantities and in a manner consistent with his method of inventory accounting under section 471 or 472.

The phrase does not include units with respect to which depletion deductions were allowed or allowable prior to the taxable year.

(3) "The number of units of mineral remaining as of the taxable year" is the number of units of mineral remaining at the end of the year to be recovered from the property (including units recovered but not sold) plus the "number of units sold within the taxable year" as defined in this section.

(4) In the case of a natural gas well where the annual production is not metered and is not capable of being estimated with reasonable accuracy, the taxpayer may compute the cost depletion allowance in respect of such property for the taxable year by multiplying the adjusted basis of the property by a fraction, the numerator of which is equal to the decline in rock pressure during the taxable year and the denominator of which is equal to the expected total decline in rock pressure from the beginning of the taxable year to the economic limit of production. Taxpayers computing depletion by this method must keep accurate records of periodical pressure determinations.

(5) If an aggregation of two or more separate mineral properties is made during a taxable year under section 614, cost depletion for each such property shall be computed separately for that portion of the taxable year ending immediately before the effective date of the aggregation. Cost depletion with respect to the aggregated property shall be computed for that portion of the taxable year beginning on such effective date. The allowance for cost depletion for the taxable year shall be the sum of such cost depletion computations. For purposes of this paragraph, each such portion of the taxable year shall be considered as a taxable year. Similar rules shall be applied where a separate mineral property is properly removed from an existing aggregation during a taxable year. See section 614 and the regulations thereunder for rules relating to the effective date of an aggregation of mineral interests and for rules relating to the adjusted basis of an aggregation.

(6) The apportionment of the deduction among the several owners of economic interests in the mineral deposit or deposits will be made as provided in paragraph (c) of § 1.611–1.

(b) Depletion accounts of mineral property. **(1)** Every taxpayer claiming and making a deduction for depletion of mineral property shall keep a separate account in which shall be accurately recorded the cost or other basis provided by section 1012, of such property together with subsequent allowable capital additions to each account and all the other adjustments required by section 1016.

(2) Mineral property accounts shall thereafter be credited annually with the amounts of the depletion so computed in accordance with section 611 or 613 and the regulations thereunder; or the amounts of the depletion computed in shall be credited to depletion reserve accounts. No further deductions for cost depletion shall be allowed when the sum of the credits for depletion equals the cost or other basis of the property, plus allowable capital additions. However, depletion deductions may be allowable thereafter computed upon a percentage of gross income from the property. See section 613 and the regulations thereunder. In no event shall percentage depletion in excess of cost or other basis of the property be credited to the improvements account or the depreciation reserve account.

(c) Determination of mineral contents of deposits. **(1)** If it is necessary to estimate or determine with respect to any mineral deposit as of any specific date the total recoverable units (tons, pounds, ounces, barrels, thousands of cubic feet, or other measure) of mineral products reasonably known, or on good evidence believed, to have existed in place as of that date, the estimate or determination must be made according to the method current in the industry and in the light of the most accurate and reliable information obtainable. In the selection of a unit of estimate, preference shall be given to the principal unit (or units) paid for in the product marketed. The estimate of the recoverable units of the mineral products in the deposit for the purposes of valuation and depletion shall include as to both quantity and grade:

(i) The ores and minerals "in sight", "blocked out", "developed", or "assured", in the usual or conventional meaning of these terms with respect to the type of the deposits, and

(ii) "Probable" or "prospective" ores or minerals (in the corresponding sense), that is, ores or minerals that are believed to exist on the basis of good evidence although not actually known to occur on the basis of existing development. Such "probable" or "prospective" ores or minerals may be estimated:

(a) As to quantity, only in case they are extensions of known deposits or are new bodies or masses whose existence is indicated by geographical surveys or other evidence to a high degree of probability, and

(b) As to grade, only in accordance with the best indications available as to richness.

(2) If the number of recoverable units of mineral in the deposit has been previously estimated for the prior year or years, and if there has been no known change in the facts upon which the prior estimate was based, the number of recoverable units of mineral in the deposit as of the taxable year will be the number remaining from the prior estimate. However, for any taxable year for which it is ascertained either by the taxpayer or the district director from any source, such as operations or development work prior to the close of the taxable year, that the remaining recoverable mineral units as of the taxable year are materially greater or less than the number remaining from the prior estimate, then the estimate of the remaining recoverable units shall be revised, and the annual cost depletion allowance with respect to the property for the taxable year and for subsequent taxable years will be based upon the revised estimate until a change in the facts requires another revision. Such revised estimate will not, however, change the adjusted basis for depletion.

(d) Determination of fair market value of mineral properties, and improvements, if any. **(1)** If the fair market value of the mineral property and improvements at a specified date is to be determined for the purpose of ascertaining the basis, such value must be determined, subject to approval or revision by the district director, by the owner of such property and improvements in the light of the conditions and circumstances known at that date, regardless of later discoveries or developments or subsequent improvements in methods of extraction and treatment of the mineral product. The district director will give due weight and consideration to any and all factors and evidence having a bearing on the market value, such as cost, actual sales and transfers of similar properties and improvements, bona fide offers, market value of stock or shares, royalties and rentals, valuation for local or State taxation, partnership accountings, records of litigation in which the value of the property and improvements was in question, the amount at which the property and improvements may have been inventoried or appraised in probate or similar proceedings, and disinterested appraisals by approved methods.

(2) If the fair market value must be ascertained as of a certain date, analytical appraisal methods of valuation, such as the present value method will not be used:

(i) If the value of a mineral property and improvements, if any, can be determined upon the basis of cost or comparative values and replacement value of equipment, or

(ii) If the fair market value can reasonably be determined by any other method.

(e) Determination of the fair market value of mineral property by the present value method. **(1)** To determine the fair market value of a mineral property and improvements by the present value method, the essential factors must be determined for each mineral deposit. The essential factors in determining the fair market value of mineral deposits are:

(i) The total quantity of mineral in terms of the principal or customary unit (or units) paid for in the product marketed,

(ii) The quantity of mineral expected to be recovered during each operating period,

(iii) The average quality or grade of the mineral reserves,

(iv) The allocation of the total expected profit to the several processes or operations necessary for the preparation of the mineral for market,

(v) The probable operating life of the deposit in years,

(vi) The development cost,

(vii) The operating cost,

(viii) The total expected profit,

(ix) The rate at which this profit will be obtained, and

(x) The rate of interest commensurate with the risk for the particular deposit.

(2) If the mineral deposit has been sufficiently developed, the valuation factors specified in subparagraph (1) of this paragraph may be determined from past operating experience. In the application of factors derived from past experience, full allowance should be made for probable future variations in the rate of exhaustion, quality or grade of the mineral, percentage of recovery, cost of development, production, interest rate, and selling price of the product marketed during the expected operating life of the mineral deposit. Mineral deposits for which these factors cannot be determined with reasonable accuracy from past operating experience may also be valued by the present value method; but the factors must be deduced from concurrent evidence, such as the general type of the deposit, the characteristics of the district in which it occurs, the habit of the mineral deposits, the intensity of mineralization, the oil-gas ratio, the rate at which additional mineral has been disclosed by exploitation, the stage of the operating life of the deposit, and any other evidence tending to establish a reasonable estimate of the required factors.

(3) Mineral deposits of different grades, locations, and probable dates of extraction should be valued separately. The mineral content of a deposit shall be determined in accordance with paragraph (c) of this section. In estimating the average grade of the developed and prospective mineral, account should be taken of probable increases or decreases as indicated by the operating history. The rate of exhaustion of a mineral deposit should be determined with due regard to the limitations imposed by plan capacity, by the character of the deposit, by the ability to market the mineral product, by labor conditions, and by the operating program in force or reasonably to be expected for future operations. The operating life of a mineral deposit is that number of years necessary for the exhaustion of both the developed and prospective mineral content at the rate determined as above. The operating life of oil and gas wells is also influenced by the natural decline in pressure and flow, and by voluntary or enforced curtailment of production. The operating cost includes all current expense of producing, preparing, and marketing the mineral product sold (due consideration being given to taxes) exclusive of allowable capital additions, * * *, and deductions for depreciation and depletion, but including cost of repairs. This cost of repairs is not to be confused with the depreciation deduction by which the cost of improvements is returned to the taxpayer free from tax. In general, no estimates of these factors will be approved by the district director which are not supported by the operating experience of the property or which are derived from different and arbitrarily selected periods.

(4) The value of each mineral deposit is measured by the expected gross income (the number of units of mineral recoverable in marketable form multiplied by the estimated market price per unit) less the estimated operating cost, reduced to a present value as of the date for which the valuation is made at the rate of interest commensurate with the risk for the operating life, and further reduced by the value at that date of the improvements and of the capital additions, if any, necessary to realize the profits. The degree of risk is generally lowest in cases where the factors of valuation are fully supported by the operating record of the mineral enterprise before the date for which the valuation is made. On the other hand, higher risks ordinarily attach to appraisals upon any other basis.

(f) Revaluation of mineral property not allowed. No revaluation of a mineral property whose value as of any specific date has been determined and approved will be made or allowed during the continuance of the ownership under which the value was so determined and approved, except in the case of misrepresentation or fraud or gross error as to any facts known on the date as of which the valuation was made. Revaluation on account of misrepresentation or fraud or such gross error will be made only with the written approval of the Commissioner.

* * *

[T.D. 6500, 25 FR 11737, Nov. 26, 1960, as amended by T.D. 6938, 32 FR 17518, Dec. 7, 1967; T.D. 7170, 37 FR 5373, March 15, 1972]

§ 1.612–4 Charges to capital and to expense in case of oil and gas wells.

(a) Option with respect to intangible drilling and development costs. In accordance with the provisions of section 263(c), intangible drilling and development costs incurred by an operator (one who holds a working or operating interest in any tract or parcel of land either as a fee owner or under a lease or any other form of contract granting working or operating rights) in the development of oil and gas properties may at his option be chargeable to capital or to expense. This option applies to all expenditures made by an operator for wages, fuel, repairs, hauling, supplies, etc., incident to and necessary for the drilling of wells and the preparation of wells for the production of oil or gas. Such expenditures have for convenience been termed intangible drilling and development costs. They include the cost to operators of any drilling or development work (excluding amounts payable only out of production or gross or net proceeds from production, if such amounts are depletable income to the recipient, and amounts properly allocable to cost of depreciable property) done for them by contractors under any form of contract, including turnkey contracts. Examples of items to which this option applies are, all amounts paid for labor, fuel, repairs, hauling, and supplies, or any of them, which are used—

(1) In the drilling, shooting, and cleaning of wells,

(2) In such clearing of ground, draining, road making, surveying, and geological works as are necessary in preparation for the drilling of wells, and

(3) In the construction of such derricks, tanks, pipelines, and other physical structures as are necessary for the drilling of wells and the preparation of wells for the production of oil or gas.

In general, this option applies only to expenditures for those drilling and developing items which in themselves do not have a salvage value. For the purpose of this option, labor, fuel, repairs, hauling, supplies, etc., are not considered as having a salvage value, even though used in connection with the installation of physical property which has a salvage value. Included in this option are all costs of drilling and development undertaken (directly or through a contract) by an operator of an oil and gas property whether incurred by him prior or subsequent to the formal grant or assignment to him of operating rights (a leasehold interest, or other form of operating rights, or working interest); except that in any case where any drilling or development project is undertaken for the grant or assignment of a fraction of the operating rights, only that part of the costs thereof which is attributable to such fractional interest is within this option. In the excepted cases, costs of the project undertaken, including depreciable equipment furnished, to the extent allocable to fractions of the operating rights held by others, must be capitalized as the depletable capital cost of the fractional interest thus acquired.

* * *

[T.D. 6836, 30 FR 8902, July 15, 1965]

ESTATES, TRUSTS, BENEFICIARIES, AND DECEDENTS

§ 1.641(a)–0 Scope of Subchapter J.

* * *

(c) Multiple trusts. Multiple trusts that have—

(1) No substantially independent purposes (such as independent dispositive purposes),

(2) The same grantor and substantially the same beneficiary, and

(3) The avoidance or mitigation of (a) the progressive rates of tax (including mitigation as a result of deferral of tax) or (b) the minimum tax for tax preferences imposed by section 56 as their principal purpose,

shall be consolidated and treated as one trust for the purposes of subchapter J.

[T.D. 6500, 25 FR 11814, Nov. 26, 1960, as amended by T.D. 6989, 34 FR 731, Jan. 17, 1969; T.D. 7204, 37 FR 17158, Aug. 25, 1972]

§ 1.641(a)–2 Gross income of estates and trusts.

The gross income of an estate or trust is determined in the same manner as that of an individual.

Thus, the gross income of an estate or trust consists of all items of gross income received during the taxable year, including:

(a) Income accumulated in trust for the benefit of unborn or unascertained persons or persons with contingent interests;

(b) Income accumulated or held for future distribution under the terms of the will or trust;

(c) Income which is to be distributed currently by the fiduciary to the beneficiaries, and income collected by a guardian of an infant which is to be held or distributed as the court may direct;

(d) Income received by estates of deceased persons during the period of administration or settlement of the estate; and

(e) Income which, in the discretion of the fiduciary, may be either distributed to the beneficiaries or accumulated. The several classes of income enumerated in this section do not exclude others which also may come within the general purposes of section 641.

[T.D. 6500, 25 FR 11814, Nov. 26, 1960]

§ 1.641(b)–1 Computation and payment of tax; deductions and credits of estates and trusts.

Generally, the deductions and credits allowed to individuals are also allowed to estates and trusts. However, there are special rules for the computation of certain deductions and for the allocation between the estate or trust and the beneficiaries of certain credits and deductions. See section 642 and the regulations thereunder. In addition, an estate or trust is allowed to deduct, in computing its taxable income, the deductions provided by sections 651 and 661 and regulations thereunder, relating to distributions to beneficiaries.

[T.D. 6500, 25 FR 11814, Nov. 26, 1960]

§ 1.641(b)–2 Filing of returns and payment of the tax.

(a) The fiduciary is required to make and file the return and pay the tax on the taxable income of an estate or of a trust. Liability for the payment of the tax on the taxable income of an estate attaches to the person of the executor or administrator up to and after his discharge if, prior to distribution and discharge, he had notice of his tax obligations or failed to exercise due diligence in ascertaining whether or not such obligations existed. * * * Liability for the tax also follows the assets of the estate distributed to heirs, devisees, legatees, and distributees, who may be required to discharge the amount of the tax due and unpaid to the extent of the distributive shares received by them. See section 6901. The same considerations apply to trusts.

(b) The estate of an infant, incompetent, or other person under a disability, or, in general, of an individual or corporation in receivership or a corporation in bankruptcy is not a taxable entity separate from the person for whom the fiduciary is acting, in that respect differing from the estate of a deceased person or of a trust. See section 6012(b)(2) and (3) for provisions relating to the obligation of the fiduciary with respect to returns of such persons.

[T.D. 6500, 25 FR 11814, Nov. 26, 1960, as amended by T.D. 6580, 26 FR 11486, Dec. 5, 1961]

§ 1.641(b)–3 Termination of estates and trusts.

(a) The income of an estate of a deceased person is that which is received by the estate during the period of administration or settlement. The period of administration or settlement is the period actually required by the administrator or executor to perform the ordinary duties of administration, such as the collection of assets and the payment of debts, taxes, legacies, and bequests, whether the period required is longer or shorter than the period specified under the applicable local law for the settlement of estates. For example, where an executor who is also named as trustee under a will fails to obtain his discharge as executor, the period of administration continues only until the duties of administration are complete and he actually assumes his duties as trustee, whether or not pursuant to a court order. However, the period of administration of an estate cannot be unduly prolonged. If the administration of an estate is unreasonably prolonged, the estate is considered terminated for Federal income tax purposes after the expiration of a reasonable period for the performance by the executor of all the duties of administration. Further, an estate will be considered as terminated when all the assets have been distributed except for a reasonable amount which is set aside in good faith for the payment of unascertained or contingent liabilities and expenses (not including a claim by a beneficiary in the capacity of beneficiary). Notwithstanding the above, if the estate has joined in making a valid election under section 645 to treat a qualified revocable trust, as defined under section 645(b)(1), as part of the estate, the estate shall not terminate under this paragraph prior to the termination of the section 645 election period. See section 645 and the regulations thereunder for rules regarding the termination of the section 645 election period.

(b) Generally, the determination of whether a trust has terminated depends upon whether the property held in trust has been distributed to the persons entitled to succeed to the property upon termination of the trust rather than upon the technicality of whether or not the trustee has rendered his final accounting. A trust does not automatically terminate upon the happening of the event by which the duration of the trust is measured. A reasonable time is permitted after such event for the trustee to perform the duties necessary to complete the administration of the trust. Thus, if under the terms of the governing instrument, the trust is to terminate upon the death of the life beneficiary and the corpus is to be distributed to the remainderman, the trust continues after the death of the life beneficiary for a period reasonably necessary to a proper winding up of the affairs of the trust. However, the winding up of a trust cannot be unduly postponed and if the distribution of the trust corpus is unreasonably delayed, the trust is considered terminated for Federal income tax purposes after the expiration of a reasonable period for the trustee to complete the administration of the trust. Further, a trust will be considered as terminated when all the assets have been distributed except for a reasonable amount which is set aside in good faith for the payment of unascertained or contingent liabilities and expenses (not including a claim by a beneficiary in the capacity of beneficiary).

(c)(1) Except as provided in subparagraph (2) of this paragraph, during the period between the occurrence of an event which causes a trust to terminate and the time when the trust is considered as terminated under this section, whether or not the income and the excess of capital gains over capital losses of the trust are to be considered as amounts required to be distributed currently to the ultimate distributee for the year in which they are received depends upon the principles stated in § 1.651(a)–2. See § 1.663–1 et seq. for application of the separate share rule.

* * *

(d) If a trust or the administration or settlement of an estate is considered terminated under this section for Federal income tax purposes (as for instance, because administration has been unduly prolonged), the gross income, deductions, and credits of the estate or trust are, subsequent to the termination, considered the gross income, deductions, and credits of the person or persons succeeding to the property of the estate or trust.

[T.D. 6500, 25 FR 11814, Nov. 26, 1960, as amended by T.D. 9032, 67 FR 78371, Dec. 24, 2002]

§ 1.642(b)–1 Deduction for personal exemption.

In lieu of the deduction for personal exemptions provided by section 151:

(a) An estate is allowed a deduction of $600,

(b) A trust which, under its governing instrument, is required to distribute currently all of its income for the taxable year is allowed a deduction of $300, and

(c) All other trusts are allowed a deduction of $100.

A trust which, under its governing instrument, is required to distribute all of its income currently is allowed a deduction of $300, even though it also distributes amounts other than income in the taxable year and even though it may be required to make distributions which would qualify for the charitable contributions deduction under section 642(c) (and therefore does not qualify as a "simple trust" under sections 651–652). A trust for the payment of an annuity is allowed a deduction of $300 in a taxable year in which the amount of the annuity required to be paid equals or exceeds all the income of the trust for the taxable year. For the meaning of the term "income required to be distributed currently", see § 1.651(a)–2.

[T.D. 6500, 25 FR 11814, Nov. 26, 1960]

§ 1.642(c)–1 Unlimited deduction for amounts paid for a charitable purpose.

(a) In general. (1) Any part of the gross income of an estate, or trust which, pursuant to the terms of the governing instrument is paid (or treated under paragraph (b) of this section as paid) during the taxable year for a purpose specified in section 170(c) shall be allowed as a deduction to such estate or trust in lieu of the limited charitable contributions deduction authorized by section 170(a). In applying this paragraph without reference to paragraph (b) of this section, a deduction shall be allowed for an amount paid during the taxable year in respect of gross income received in a previous taxable year, but only if no deduction was allowed for any previous taxable year to the estate or trust, or in the case of a section 645 election, to a related estate, as defined under S 1.645–1(b), for the amount so paid.

(2) In determining whether an amount is paid for a purpose specified in section 170(c)(2) the provisions of section 170(c)(2)(A) shall not be taken into account. Thus, an amount paid to a corporation, trust, or community chest, fund, or foundation otherwise described in section 170(c)(2) shall be considered paid for a purpose specified in section 170(c) even though the corporation, trust, or community chest, fund, or foundation is not created or organized in the United States, any State, the District of Columbia, or any possession of the United States.

* * *

(b) Election to treat contributions as paid in preceding taxable year—(1) In general. For purposes of determining the deduction allowed under paragraph (a) of this section, the fiduciary (as defined in section 7701(a)(6)) of an estate or trust may elect under section 642(c)(1) to treat as paid during the taxable year (whether or not such year begins before January 1, 1970) any amount of gross income received during such taxable year or any preceding taxable year which is otherwise deductible under such paragraph and which is paid after the close of such taxable year but on or before the last day of the next succeeding taxable year of the estate or trust. The preceding sentence applies only in the case of payments actually made in a taxable year which is a taxable year beginning after December 31, 1969. No election shall be made, however, in respect of any amount which was deducted for any previous taxable year or which is deducted for the taxable year in which such amount is paid.

* * *

[T.D. 6500, 25 FR 11814, Nov. 26, 1960, as amended by T.D. 7357, 40 FR 23739, June 2, 1975; 40 FR 24361, June 6, 1975; T.D. 9032, 67 FR 78376, Dec. 24, 2002]

§ 1.642(c)–3 Adjustments and other special rules for determining unlimited charitable contributions deduction.

(a) Income in respect of a decedent. For purposes of §§ 1.642(c)–1 * * *, an amount received by an estate or trust which is includible in its gross income under section 691(a)(1) as income in respect of a decedent shall be included in the gross income of the estate or trust.

(b) Determination of amounts deductible under section 642(c) and the character of such amounts—(1) Reduction of charitable contributions deduction by amounts not included in gross income. If an estate, pooled income fund, or other trust pays, permanently sets aside, or uses any amount of its income for a purpose specified in section 642(c)(1), (2) or (3) and that amount includes any items of estate or trust income not entering into the gross income of the estate or trust, the deduction allowable under § 1.642(c)–1 * * * is limited to the gross income so paid, permanently set aside, or used. * * *

(2) Determination of the character of an amount deductible under section 642(c). In determining whether the amounts of income so paid, permanently set aside, or used for a purpose specified in section 642(c)(1), (2), or (3) include particular items of income of an estate or trust, whether or not included in gross income, a provision in the governing instrument or in local lawthat specifically provides the source out of which amounts are to be paid, permanently set aside, or used for such a purpose controls for Federal tax purposes to the extent such provision has economic effect independent of incom tax comsequences. See § 1.652(b)–2(b). In the absence of such specific provisions in the governing instrument, or in local law, the amount to which section 642(c) applies is deemed to consist of the same proportion of each class of the items of income of the estate or trust as the total of each class bears to the total of all classes. See § 1.643(a)–5(b) for the method of determining the allocable portion of exempt income and foreign income.

* * *

[T.D. 6500, 25 FR 11814, Nov. 26, 1960, as amended by T.D. 7357, 40 FR 23741, June 2, 1975; 40 FR 24361, June 6, 1975; T.D. 7728, 45 FR 72650, Nov. 3, 1980; T.D. 9582, 77 FR 22484, April 16, 2012]

§ 1.642(c)–5 Definition of pooled income fund.

(a) In general—(1) Application of provisions. Section 642(c)(5) prescribes certain rules for the valuation of contributions involving transfers to certain funds described in that section as pooled income funds. This section sets forth the requirements for qualifying as a pooled income fund and provides for the manner of allocating the income of the fund to the beneficiaries. Section 1.642(c)–6 provides for the valuation of a remainder interest in property transferred to a pooled income fund. * * *

(2) Tax status of fund and its beneficiaries. Notwithstanding any other provision of this chapter, a fund which meets the requirements of a pooled income fund, as defined in section 642(c)(5) and paragraph (b) of this section, shall not be treated as an association within the meaning of section 7701(a)(3). Such a fund, which need not be a trust under local law, and its beneficiaries shall be taxable under part I, subchapter J, chapter 1 of the Code, but the provisions of subpart E (relating to grantors and others treated as substantial owners) of such part shall not apply to such fund.

(3) Recognition of gain or loss on transfer to fund. No gain or loss shall be recognized to the donor on the transfer of property to a pooled income fund. In such case, the fund's basis and holding period with respect to property transferred to the fund by a donor shall be determined as provided in sections 1015(b) and 1223(2). If, however, a donor transfers property to a pooled income fund and, in addition to creating or retaining a life income interest therein, receives property from the fund, or transfers property to the fund which is subject to an indebtedness, this subparagraph shall not apply to the gain realized by reason of (i) the receipt of such property or (ii) the amount of such indebtedness, whether or not assumed by the pooled income fund, which is required to be treated as an amount realized on the transfer. For applicability of the bargain sale rules, see section 1011(b) and the regulations thereunder.

(4) Charitable contributions deduction. A charitable contributions deduction for the value of the remainder interest, as determined under § 1.642(c)–6, may be allowed under section 170, 2055, 2106, or 2522, where there is a transfer of property to a pooled income fund. For a special rule relating to the reduction of the amount of a charitable contribution of certain ordinary income property or capital gain property, see section 170(e)(1)(A) or (B)(i) and the regulations thereunder.

* * *

(b) Requirements for qualification as a pooled income fund. A pooled income fund to which this section applies must satisfy all of the following requirements:

(1) Contribution of remainder interest to charity. Each donor must transfer property to the fund and contribute an irrevocable remainder interest in such property to or for the use of a public charity, retaining for himself, or creating for another beneficiary or beneficiaries, a life income interest in the transferred property. A contingent remainder interest shall not be treated as an irrevocable remainder interest for purposes of this subparagraph.

(2) Creation of life income interest. Each donor must retain for himself for life an income interest in the property transferred to such fund, or create an income interest in such property for the life of one or more beneficiaries, each of whom must be living at the time of the transfer of the property to the fund by the donor. The term "one or more beneficiaries" includes those members of a named class who are alive and can be ascertained at the time of the transfer of the property to the fund. In the event more than one beneficiary of the income interest is designated, such beneficiaries may enjoy their shares of income concurrently, consecutively, or both concurrently and consecutively. The donor may retain the power exercisable only by will to revoke or terminate the income interest of any designated beneficiary other than the public charity. The governing instrument must specify at the time of the transfer the particular beneficiary or beneficiaries to whom the income is payable and the share of income distributable to each person so specified. The public charity to or for the use of which the remainder interest is contributed may also be designated as one of the beneficiaries of an income interest. The donor need not retain or create a life interest in all the income from the property transferred to the fund provided any income not payable under the terms of the governing instrument to an income beneficiary is contributed to, and within the taxable year in which it is received is paid to, the same public charity to or for the use of which the remainder interest is contributed. No charitable contributions deduction shall be allowed to the donor for the value of such income interest of the public charity or for the amount of any such income paid to such organization.

(3) Commingling of property required. The property transferred to the fund by each donor must be commingled with, and invested or reinvested with, other property transferred to the fund by other donors satisfying the requirements of subparagraphs (1) and (2) of this paragraph. The governing instrument of the pooled income fund must contain provision requiring compliance with the preceding sentence. The public charity to or for the use of which the remainder interest is contributed may maintain more than one pooled income fund, provided that each such find is maintained by the organization and is not a device to permit a group of donors to create a fund which may be subject to their manipulation. The fund must not include property transferred under arrangements other than those specified in section 642(c)(5) and this paragraph. However, a fund shall not be disqualified as a pooled income fund under this paragraph because any portion of its properties is invested or reinvested jointly with other properties, not a part of the pooled income fund, which are held by, or for the use of, the public charity which maintains the fund, as for example, with securities in the general endowment fund of the public charity to or for the use of which the remainder interest is contributed. Where such joint investment or reinvestment of properties occurs, records must be maintained which sufficiently identify the portion of the total fund which is owned by the pooled income fund and the income earned by, and attributable to, such portion. Such a joint investment or reinvestment of properties shall not be treated as an association or partnership for purposes of the Code. A bank which serves as trustee of more than one pooled income fund may maintain a common trust fund * * *.

(4) Prohibition against exempt securities. The property transferred to the fund by any donor must not include any securities, the income from which is exempt from tax under subtitle A of the Code, and the fund must not invest in such securities. The governing instrument of the fund must contain specific prohibitions against accepting or investing in such securities.

(5) Maintenance by charitable organization required. The fund must be maintained by the same public charity to or for the use of which the irrevocable remainder interest is contributed. The requirement of maintenance will be satisfied where the public charity exercises control directly or indirectly over the fund. For example, this requirement of control shall ordinarily be met when the public charity has the power to remove the trustee or trustees of the fund and designate a new trustee or trustees. A national organization which carries out its purposes through local organizations, chapters, or auxiliary bodies with which it has an identity of aims and purposes may maintain a pooled income fund (otherwise satisfying the requirements of this paragraph) in which one or more local organizations, chapters, or auxiliary bodies which are public charities have been named as recipients of the remainder interests. For example, a national church body may maintain a pooled income fund where donors have transferred property to such fund and contributed an irrevocable remainder interest therein to or for the use of various local churches or educational institutions of such body. The fact that such local organizations or chapters have been separately incorporated from the national organization is immaterial.

(6) Prohibition against donor or beneficiary serving as trustee. The fund must not have, and the governing instrument must prohibit the fund from having, as a trustee a donor to the fund or a beneficiary (other than the public charity to or the the use of which the remainder interest is contributed) of an income interest in any property transferred to such fund. Thus, if a donor or beneficiary (other than such public charity) directly or indirectly has general responsibilities with respect to the fund which are ordinarily exercised by a trustee, such fund does not meet the requirements of section 642(c)(5) and this paragraph. The fact that a donor of property to the fund, or a beneficiary of the fund, is a trustee, officer, director, or other official of the public charity to or for the use of which the remainder interest is contributed ordinarily will not prevent the fund from meeting the requirements of section 642(c)(5) and this paragraph.

(7) Income of beneficiary to be based on rate of return of fund. Each beneficiary entitled to income of any taxable year of the fund must receive such income in an amount determined by the rate of return earned by the fund for such taxable year with respect to his income interest, computed as provided in paragraph (c) of this section. The governing instrument of the fund shall direct the trustee to distribute income currently or within the first 65 days following the close of the taxable year in which the income is earned. Any such payment made after the close of the taxable year shall be treated as paid on the last day of the taxable year. A statement shall be attached to the return of the pooled income fund indicating the date and amount of such payments after the close of the taxable year. Subject to the provisions of part I, subchapter J, chapter 1 of the Code, the beneficiary shall include in his gross income all amounts properly paid, credited, or required to be distributed to the beneficiary during the taxable year or years of the fund ending within or with his taxable year. The governing instrument shall provide that the income interest of any designated beneficiary shall either terminate with the last regular payment which was made before the death of the beneficiary or be prorated to the date of his death.

(8) Termination of life income interest. Upon the termination of the income interest retained or created by any donor, the trustee shall sever from the fund an amount equal to the value of the remainder interest in the property upon which the income interest is based. The value of the remainder interest for such purpose may be either (i) its value as of the determination date next succeeding the termination of the income interest or (ii) its value as of the date on which the last regular payment was made before the death of the beneficiary if the income interest is terminated on such payment date. The amount so severed from the fund must either be paid to, or retained for the use of, the designated public charity, as provided in the governing instrument. However, see subparagraph (3) of this paragraph for rules relating to commingling of property.

(c) Allocation of income to beneficiary—(1) In general. Every income interest retained or created in property transferred to a pooled income fund shall be assigned a proportionate share of the annual income earned by the fund, such share, or unit of participation, being based on the fair market value of such property on the date of transfer, as provided in this paragraph.

(2) Units of participation—(i) Unit plan. **(a)** On each transfer of property by a donor to a pooled income fund, one or more units of participation in the fund shall be assigned to the beneficiary or beneficiaries of the income interest retained or created in such property, the number of units of participation being equal to the number obtained by dividing the fair market value of the property by the fair market value of a unit in the fund at the time of the transfer.

(b) The fair market value of a unit in the fund at the time of the transfer shall be determined by dividing the fair market value of all property in the fund at such time by the number of units then in the fund. The initial fair market value of a unit in a pooled income fund shall be the fair market value of the property transferred to the fund divided by the number of units assigned to the income interest in that property. The value of each unit of participation will fluctuate with each new transfer of property to the fund in relation to the appreciation or depreciation in the fair market value of the property in the fund, but all units in the fund will always have equal value.

(c) The share of income allocated to each unit of participation shall be determined by dividing the income of the fund for the taxable year by the outstanding number of units in the fund at the end of such year, except that, consistently with paragraph (b)(7) of this section, income shall be allocated to units outstanding during only part of such year by taking into consideration the period of time such units are outstanding. For this purpose the actual income of such part of the taxable year, or a prorated portion of the annual income, may be used, after making such adjustments as are reasonably necessary to reflect fluctuations during the year in the fair market value of the property in the fund.

(ii) Other plans. The governing instrument of the fund may provide any other reasonable method not described in subdivision (i) of this subparagraph for assigning units of participation in the fund and allocating income to such units which reaches a result reasonably consistent with the provisions of such subdivision.

* * *

[T.D. 7105, 36 FR 6477, April 6, 1971; 36 FR 7004, April 13, 1971, as amended by T.D. 7125, 36 FR 11032, June 8, 1971; T.D. 7357, 40 FR 23742, June 2, 1975; T.D. 7633, 44 FR 57925, Oct. 9, 1979; T.D. 9102, 69 FR 12, Jan. 2, 2004]

§ 1.642(d)–1 Net operating loss deduction.

The net operating loss deduction allowed by section 172 is available to estates and trusts generally, with the following exceptions and limitations:

(a) In computing gross income and deductions for the purposes of section 172, a trust shall exclude that portion of the income and deductions attributable to the grantor or another person under sections 671 through 678 (relating to grantors and others treated as substantial owners).

(b) An estate or trust shall not, for the purposes of section 172, avail itself of the deductions allowed by section 642(c)(relating to charitable contributions deductions) and sections 651 and 661 (relating to deductions for distributions).

[T.D. 6500, 25 FR 11814, Nov. 26, 1960]

§ 1.642(e)–1 Depreciation and depletion.

An estate or trust is allowed the deductions for depreciation and depletion, but only to the extent the deductions are not apportioned to beneficiaries under sections 167(h) [now section 167(d)] and 611(b). For purposes of sections 167(h) and 611(b), the term ''beneficiaries'' includes charitable beneficiaries. See the regulations under those sections.

[T.D. 6500, 25 FR 11814, Nov. 26, 1960, as amended by T.D. 6712, 29 FR 3655, March 24, 1964]

§ 1.642(g)–1 Disallowance of double deductions; in general.

Amounts allowable under section 2053(a)(2) (relating to administration expenses) or under section 2054 (relating to losses during administration) as deductions in computing the taxable estate of a decedent are not allowed as deductions in computing the taxable income of the estate unless there is filed a statement, in duplicate, to the effect that the items have not been allowed as deductions from the gross estate of the decedent under section 2053 or 2054 and that all rights to have such items allowed at any time as deductions under section 2053 or 2054 are waived. The statement should be filed with the return for the year for which the items are claimed as deductions or with the district director for the internal revenue district in which the return was filed, for association with the return. The statement may be filed at any time before the expiration of the statutory period of limitation applicable to the taxable year for which the deduction is sought. Allowance of a deduction in computing an estate's taxable income is not precluded by claiming a deduction in the estate tax return, so long as the estate tax deduction is not finally allowed and the statement is filed. However, after a statement is filed under section 642(g) with respect to a particular item or portion of an item, the item cannot thereafter be allowed as a deduction for estate tax purposes since the waiver operates as a relinquishment of the right to have the deduction allowed at any time under section 2053 or 2054.

[T.D. 6500, 25 FR 11814, Nov. 26, 1960]

§ 1.642(g)–2 Deductions included.

It is not required that the total deductions, or the total amount of any deduction, to which section 642(g) is applicable be treated in the same way. One deduction or portion of a deduction may be allowed for income tax purposes if the appropriate statement is filed, while another deduction or portion is allowed for estate tax purposes. Section 642(g) has no application to deductions for taxes, interest, business expenses, and other items accrued at the date of a decedent's death so that they are allowable as a deduction under section 2053(a)(3) for estate tax purposes as claims against the estate, and are also allowable under section 691(b) as deductions in respect of a decedent for income tax purposes. However, section 642(g) is applicable to deductions for interest, business expenses, and other items not accrued at the date of the decedent's death so that they are allowable as deductions for estate tax purposes only as administration expenses under section 2053(a)(2). Although deductible under section 2053(a)(3) in determining the value of the taxable estate of a decedent, medical, dental, etc., expenses of a decedent which are paid by the estate of the decedent are not deductible in computing the taxable income of the estate. See section 213(d) and the regulations thereunder for rules relating to the deductibility of such expenses in computing the taxable income of the decedent.

[T.D. 6500, 25 FR 11814, Nov. 26, 1960]

§ 1.642(h)–1 Unused loss carryovers on termination of an estate or trust.

(a) If, on the final termination of an estate or trust, a net operating loss carryover under section 172 or a capital loss carryover under section 1212 would be allowable to the estate or trust in a taxable year subsequent to the taxable year of termination but for the termination, the carryover or carryovers are allowed under section 642(h)(1) to the beneficiaries succeeding to the property of the estate or trust. See § 1.641(b)–3 for the determination of when an estate or trust terminates.

(b) The net operating loss carryover and the capital loss carryover are the same in the hands of a beneficiary as in the estate or trust, except that the capital loss carryover in the hands of a beneficiary which is a corporation is a short-term loss irrespective of whether it would have been a long-term or short-term capital loss in the hands of the estate or trust. The net operating loss carryover and the capital loss carryover are taken into account in computing taxable income, adjusted gross income, and the tax imposed by section 56 (relating to the minimum tax for tax preferences). The first taxable year of the beneficiary to which the loss shall be carried over is the taxable year of the beneficiary in which or with which the estate or trust terminates. However, for purposes of determining the number of years to which a net operating loss, or a capital loss under paragraph (a) of § 1.1212–1, may be carried over by a beneficiary, the last taxable year of the estate or trust (whether or not a short taxable year) and the first taxable year of the beneficiary to which a loss is carried over each constitute a taxable year, and, in the case of a beneficiary of an estate or trust that is a corporation, capital losses carried over by the estate or trust to any taxable year of the estate or trust beginning after December 31, 1963, shall be treated as if they were incurred in the last taxable year of the estate or trust (whether or not a short taxable year). For the treatment of the net operating loss carryover when the last taxable year of the estate or trust is the last taxable year to which such loss can be carried over, see § 1.642(h)–2.

* * *

[T.D. 6500, 25 FR 11814, Nov. 26, 1960, as amended by T.D. 6828, 30 FR 7805, June 17, 1965; T.D. 7564, 43 FR 40495, Sept. 12, 1978]

§ 1.642(h)–2 Excess deductions on termination of an estate or trust.

(a) If, on the termination of an estate or trust, the estate or trust has for its last taxable year deductions (other than the deductions allowed under section 642(b) (relating to personal exemption) or section 642(c) (relating to charitable contributions)) in excess of gross income, the excess is allowed under section 642(h)(2) as a deduction to the beneficiaries succeeding to the property of the estate or trust. The deduction is allowed only in computing taxable income and must be taken into account in computing the items of tax preference of the beneficiary; it is not allowed in computing adjusted gross income. The deduction is allowable only in the taxable year of the beneficiary in which or with which the estate or trust terminates, whether the year of termination of the estate or trust is of normal duration or is a short taxable year. For example: Assume that a trust distributes all of its assets to B and terminates on December 31, 1954. As of that date it has excess deductions, for example, because of corpus commissions on termination, of $18,000. B, who reported on the calendar year basis, could claim the $18,000 as a deduction for the taxable year 1954. However, if the deduction (when added to his other deductions) exceeds his gross income, the excess may not be carried over to the year 1955 or subsequent years.

(b) A deduction based upon a net operating loss carryover will never be allowed to beneficiaries under both paragraphs (1) and (2) of section 642(h). Accordingly, a net operating loss deduction which is allowable to beneficiaries succeeding to the property of the estate or trust under the provisions of paragraph (1) of section 642(h) cannot also be considered a deduction for purposes of paragraph (2) of section 642(h) and paragraph (a) of this section. However, if the last taxable year of the estate or trust is the last year in which a deduction on account of a net operating loss may be taken, the deduction, to the extent not absorbed in that taxable year by the estate or trust, is considered an "excess deduction" under section 642(h)(2) and paragraph (a) of this section.

(c) Any item of income or deduction, or any part thereof, which is taken into account in determining the net operating loss or capital loss carryover of the estate or trust for its last taxable year shall not be taken into account again in determining excess deductions on termination of the trust or estate within the meaning of section 642(h)(2) and paragraph (a) of this section * * *.

[T.D. 6500, 25 FR 11814, Nov. 26, 1960, as amended by T.D. 7564, 43 FR 40495, Sept. 12, 1978]

§ 1.642(h)–3 Meaning of "beneficiaries succeeding to the property of the estate or trust".

(a) The phrase "beneficiaries succeeding to the property of the estate or trust" means those beneficiaries upon termination of the estate or trust who bear the burden of any loss for which a carryover is allowed, or of any excess of deductions over gross income for which a deduction is allowed, under section 642(h).

(b) With reference to an intestate estate, the phrase means the heirs and next of kin to whom the estate is distributed, or if the estate is insolvent, to whom it would have been distributed if it had not been insolvent. If a decedent's spouse is entitled to a specified dollar amount of property before any distribution to other heirs and next of kin, and if the estate is less than that amount, the spouse is the beneficiary succeeding to the property of the estate or trust to the extent of the deficiency in amount.

(c) In the case of a testate estate, the phrase normally means the residuary beneficiaries (including a residuary trust), and not specific legatees or devisees, pecuniary legatees, or other nonresiduary beneficiaries. However, the phrase does not include the recipient of a specific sum of money even though it is payable out of the residue, except to the extent that it is not payable in full. On the other hand, the phrase includes a beneficiary (including a trust) who is not strictly a residuary beneficiary but whose devise or bequest is determined by the value of the decedent's estate as reduced by the loss or deductions in question. Thus the phrase includes:

(1) A beneficiary of a fraction of a decedent's net estate after payment of debts, expenses, etc.;

(2) A nonresiduary legatee or devisee, to the extent of any deficiency in his legacy or devise resulting from the insufficiency of the estate to satisfy it in full;

(3) A surviving spouse receiving a fractional share of an estate in fee under a statutory right of election, to the extent that the loss or deductions are taken into account in determining the share. However, the phrase does not include a recipient of dower or curtesy, or any income beneficiary of the estate or trust from which the loss or excess deduction is carried over.

(d) The principles discussed in paragraph (c) of this section are equally applicable to trust beneficiaries. A remainderman who receives all or a fractional share of the property of a trust as a result of the final termination of the trust is a beneficiary succeeding to the property of the trust. For example, if property is transferred to pay the income to A for life and then to pay $10,000 to B and distribute the balance of the trust corpus to C, C and not B is considered to be the succeeding beneficiary except to the extent that the trust corpus is insufficient to pay B $10,000.

[T.D. 6500, 25 FR 11814, Nov. 26, 1960]

§ 1.642(h)–4 Allocation.

The carryovers and excess deductions to which section 642(h) applies are allocated among the beneficiaries succeeding to the property of an estate or trust (see § 1.642(h)–3) proportionately according to the share of each in the burden of the loss or deductions. A person who qualified as a beneficiary succeeding to the property of an estate or trust with respect to one amount and does not qualify with respect to another amount is a beneficiary succeeding to the property of the estate or trust as to the amount with respect to which he qualifies. The application of this section may be illustrated by the following example:

Example. A decedent's will leaves $100,000 to A, and the residue of his estate equally to B and C. His estate is sufficient to pay only $90,000 to A, and nothing to B and C. There is an excess of deductions over gross income for the last taxable year of the estate or trust of $5,000, and a capital loss carryover of $15,000, to both of which section 642(h) applies. A is a beneficiary succeeding to the property of the estate to the extent of $10,000, and since the total of the excess of deductions and the loss carryover is $20,000, A is entitled to the benefit of one half of each item, and the remaining half is divided equally between B and C.

[T.D. 6500, 25 FR 11814, Nov. 26, 1960]

§ 1.643(a)–0 Distributable net income; deduction for distributions; in general.

The term "distributable net income" has no application except in the taxation of estates and trusts and their beneficiaries. It limits the deductions allowable to estates and trusts for amounts paid, credited, or required to be distributed to beneficiaries and is used to determine how much of an amount paid, credited, or required to be distributed to a beneficiary will be includible in his gross income. It is also used to determine the character of distributions to the beneficiaries. Distributable net income means for any taxable year, the taxable income (as defined in section 63) of the estate or trust, computed with the modifications set forth in §§ 1.643(a)–1 through 1.643(a)–7.

[T.D. 6500, 25 FR 11814, Nov. 26, 1960]

§ 1.643(a)–1 Deduction for distributions.

The deduction allowable to a trust under section 651 and to an estate or trust under section 661 for amounts paid, credited, or required to be distributed to beneficiaries is not allowed in the computation of distributable net income.

[T.D. 6500, 25 FR 11814, Nov. 26, 1960]

§ 1.643(a)–2 Deduction for personal exemption.

The deduction for personal exemption under section 642(b) is not allowed in the computation of distributable net income.

[T.D. 6500, 25 FR 11814, Nov. 26, 1960]

§ 1.643(a)–3 Capital gains and losses.

(a) In general. Except as provided in § 1.643(a)–6 and paragraph (b) of this section, gains from the sale or exchange of capital assets are ordinarily excluded from distributable net income and are not ordinarily considered as paid, credited, or required to be distributed to any beneficiary.

(b) Capital gains included in distributable net income. Gains from the sale or exchange of capital assets are included in distributable net income to the extent they are, pursuant to the terms of the governing instrument and applicable local law, or pursuant to a reasonable and impartial exercise of discretion by the fiduciary (in accordance with a power granted to the fiduciary by applicable local law or by the governing instrument if not prohibited by applicable local law)—

(1) Allocated to income (but if income under the state statute is defined as, or consists of, a unitrust amount, a discretionary power to allocate gains to income must also be exercised consistently and the amount so allocated may not be greater than the excess of the unitrust amount over the amount of distributable net income determined without regard to this subparagraph § 1.643(a)–3(b));

(2) Allocated to corpus but treated consistently by the fiduciary on the trust's books, records, and tax returns as part of a distribution to a beneficiary; or

(3) Allocated to corpus but actually distributed to the beneficiary or utilized by the fiduciary in determining the amount that is distributed or required to be distributed to a beneficiary.

(c) Charitable contributions included in distributable net income. If capital gains are paid, permanently set aside, or to be used for the purposes specified in section 642(c), so that a charitable deduction is allowed under that section in respect of the gains, they must be included in the computation of distributable net income.

(d) Capital losses. Losses from the sale or exchange of capital assets shall first be netted at the trust level against any gains from the sale or exchange of capital assets, except for a capital gain that is utilized under paragraph (b)(3) of this section in determining the amount that is distributed or required to be distributed to a particular beneficiary. See § 1.642(h)–1 with respect to capital loss carryovers in the year of final termination of an estate or trust.

(e) Examples. The following examples illustrate the rules of this section:

Example 1. Under the terms of Trust's governing instrument, all income is to be paid to A for life. Trustee is given discretionary powers to invade principal for A's benefit and to deem discretionary distributions to be made from capital gains realized during the year. During Trust's first taxable year, Trust has $5,000 of dividend income and $10,000 of capital gain from the sale of securities. Pursuant to the terms of the governing instrument and applicable local law, Trustee allocates the $10,000 capital gain to principal. During the year, Trustee distributes to A $5,000, representing A's right to trust income. In addition, Trustee distributes to A $12,000, pursuant to the discretionary power to distribute principal. Trustee does not exercise the discretionary power to deem the discretionary distributions of principal as being paid from capital gains realized during the year. Therefore, the capital gains realized during the year are not included in distributable net income and the $10,000 of capital gain is taxed to the trust. In future years, Trustee must treat all discretionary distributions as not being made from any realized capital gains.

Example 2. The facts are the same as in Example 1, except that Trustee intends to follow a regular practice of treating discretionary distributions of principal as being paid first from any net capital gains realized by Trust during the year. Trustee evidences this treatment by including the $10,000 capital gain in distributable net income on Trust's federal income tax return so that it is taxed to A. This treatment of the capital gains is a reasonable exercise of Trustee's discretion. In future years Trustee must treat all discretionary distributions as being made first from any realized capital gains.

Example 3. The facts are the same as in Example 1, except that Trustee intends to follow a regular practice of treating discretionary distributions of principal as being paid from any net capital gains realized by Trust during the year from the sale of certain specified assets or a particular class of investments. This treatment of capital gains is a reasonable exercise of Trustee's discretion.

Example 4. The facts are the same as in Example 1, except that pursuant to the terms of the governing instrument (in a provision not prohibited by applicable local law), capital gains realized by Trust are allocated to income. Because the capital gains are allocated to income pursuant to the terms of the governing instrument, the $10,000 capital gain is included in Trust's distributable net income for the taxable year.

Example 5. The facts are the same as in Example 1, except that Trustee decides that discretionary distributions will be made only to the extent Trust has realized capital gains during the year and thus the discretionary distribution to A is $10,000, rather than $12,000. Because Trustee will use the amount of any realized capital gain to determine the amount of the discretionary distribution to the beneficiary, the $10,000 capital gain is included in Trust's distributable net income for the taxable year.

Example 6. Trust's assets consist of Blackacre and other property. Under the terms of Trust's governing instrument, Trustee is directed to hold Blackacre for ten years and then sell it and distribute all the sales proceeds to A. Because Trustee uses the amount of the sales proceeds that includes any realized capital gain to determine the amount required to be distributed to A, any capital gain realized from the sale of Blackacre is included in Trust's distributable net income for the taxable year.

Example 7. Under the terms of Trust's governing instrument, all income is to be paid to A during the Trust's term. When A reaches 35, Trust is to terminate and all the principal is to be distributed to A. Because all the assets of the trust, including all capital gains, will be actually distributed to the beneficiary at the termination of Trust, all capital gains realized in the year of termination are included in distributable net income. See § 1.641(b)–3 for the determination of the year of final termination and the taxability of capital gains realized after the terminating event and before final distribution.

Example 8. The facts are the same as Example 7, except Trustee is directed to pay B $10,000 before distributing the remainder of Trust assets to A. Because the distribution to B is a gift of a specific sum of money within the meaning of section 663(a)(1), none of Trust's distributable net income that includes all of the capital gains realized during the year of termination is allocated to B's distribution.

Example 9. The facts are the same as Example 7, except Trustee is directed to distribute one-half of the principal to A when A reaches 35 and the balance to A when A reaches 45. Trust assets consist entirely of stock in corporation M with a fair market value of $1,000,000 and an adjusted basis of $300,000. When A reaches 35, Trustee sells one-half of the stock and distributes the sales proceeds to A. All the sales proceeds, including all the capital gain attributable to that sale, are actually distributed to A and therefore all the capital gain is included in distributable net income.

Example 10. The facts are the same as Example 9, except when A reaches 35, Trustee sells all the stock and distributes one-half of the sales proceeds to A. If authorized by the governing instrument and applicable state statute, Trustee may determine to what extent the capital gain is distributed to A. The $500,000 distribution to A may be treated as including a minimum of $200,000 of capital gain (and all of the principal amount of $300,000) and a maximum of $500,000 of the capital gain (with no principal). Trustee evidences the treatment by including the appropriate amount of capital gain in distributable net income on Trust's federal income tax return. If Trustee is not authorized by the governing instrument and applicable state statutes to determine to what extent the capital gain is distributed to A, one-half of the capital gain attributable to the sale is included in distributable net income.

Example 11. The applicable state statute provides that a trustee may make an election to pay an income beneficiary an amount equal to four percent of the fair market value of the trust assets, as determined at the beginning of each taxable year, in full satisfaction of that beneficiary's right to income. State statute also provides that this unitrust amount shall be considered paid first from ordinary and tax-exempt income, then from net short-term capital gain, then from net long-term capital gain, and finally from return of principal. Trust's governing instrument provides that A is to receive each year income as defined under state statute. Trustee makes the unitrust election under state statute. At the beginning of the taxable year, Trust assets are valued at $500,000. During the year, Trust receives $5,000 of dividend income and realizes $80,000 of net long-term gain from the sale of capital assets. Trustee distributes to A $20,000 (4% of $500,000) in satisfaction of A's right to income. Net long-term capital gain in the amount of $15,000 is allocated to income pursuant to the ordering rule of the state statute and is included in distributable net income for the taxable year.

Example 12. The facts are the same as in Example 11, except that neither state statute nor Trust's governing instrument has an ordering rule for the character of the unitrust amount, but leaves such a decision to the discretion of Trustee. Trustee intends to follow a regular practice of treating principal, other than capital gain, as distributed to the beneficiary to the extent that the unitrust amount exceeds Trust's ordinary and tax-exempt income. Trustee evidences this treatment by not including any capital gains in distributable net income on Trust's Federal income tax return so that the entire $80,000 capital gain is taxed to Trust. This treatment of the capital gains is a reasonable exercise of Trustee's discretion. In future years Trustee must consistently follow this treatment of not allocating realized capital gains to income.

Example 13. The facts are the same as in Example 11, except that neither state statutes nor Trust's governing instrument has an ordering rule for the character of the unitrust amount, but leaves such a decision to the discretion of Trustee. Trustee intends to follow a regular practice of treating net capital gains as distributed to the beneficiary to the extent the unitrust amount exceeds Trust's ordinary and tax-exempt income. Trustee evidences this treatment by including $15,000 of the capital gain in distributable net income on Trust's Federal income tax return. This treatment of the capital gains is a reasonable exercise of Trustee's discretion. In future years Trustee must consistently treat realized capital gain, if any, as distributed to the beneficiary to the extent that the unitrust amount exceeds ordinary and tax-exempt income.

Example 14. Trustee is a corporate fiduciary that administers numerous trusts. State statutes provide that a trustee may make an election to distribute to an income beneficiary an amount equal to four percent of the annual fair market value of the trust assets in full satisfaction of that beneficiary's right to income. Neither state statutes nor the governing instruments of any of the trusts administered by Trustee has an ordering rule for the character of the unitrust amount, but leaves such a decision to the discretion of Trustee. With respect to some trusts, Trustee intends to follow a regular practice of treating principal, other than capital gain, as distributed to the beneficiary to the extent that the unitrust amount exceeds the trust's ordinary and tax-exempt income. Trustee will evidence this treatment by not including any capital gains in distributable net income on the Federal income tax returns for those trusts. With respect to other trusts, Trustee intends to follow a regular practice of treating any net capital gains as distributed to the beneficiary to the extent the unitrust amount exceeds the trust's ordinary and tax-exempt income. Trustee will evidence this treatment by including net capital gains in distributable net income on the Federal income tax returns filed for these trusts. Trustee's decision with respect to each trust is a reasonable exercise of Trustee's discretion and, in future years, Trustee must treat the capital gains realized by each trust consistently with the treatment by that trust in prior years.

* * *

[T.D. 9102, 69 FR 12, Jan. 2, 2004]

§ 1.643(a)–4 Extraordinary dividends and taxable stock dividends.

In the case solely of a trust which qualifies under Subpart B (section 651 and following) as a "simple trust," there are excluded from distributable net income extraordinary dividends (whether paid in cash or in kind) or taxable stock dividends which are not distributed or credited to a beneficiary because the fiduciary in good faith determines that under the terms of the governing instrument and applicable local law such dividends are allocable to corpus. See section 665(e), * * *, and paragraph (b) of § 1.665(e)–1A for the treatment of such dividends upon subsequent distribution.

[T.D. 6500, 25 FR 11814, Nov. 26, 1960, as amended by T.D. 6989, 34 FR 741, Jan. 17, 1969; T.D. 7204, 37 FR 17134, Aug. 25, 1972]

§ 1.643(a)–5 Tax-exempt interest.

(a) There is included in distributable net income any tax-exempt interest excluded from gross income under section 103, reduced by disbursements allocable to such interest which would have been deductible under section 212 but for the provisions of section 265 (relating to disallowance of deductions allocable to tax-exempt income).

(b) If the estate or trust is allowed a charitable contributions deduction under section 642(c), the amounts specified in paragraph (a) of this section and § 1.643(a)–6 are reduced by the portion deemed to be included in income paid, permanently set aside, or to be used for the purposes specified in section 642(c). If the governing instrument or local law specifically provides as to the source out of which amounts are paid, permanently set aside, or to be used for such charitable purposes, the specific provisions controls for Federal tax purposes to the extent such provision has economic effect independent of inome tax consequences. See § 1.652(b)–2(b). In the absence of such specific provisions in the governing instrument or local law, an amount to which section 642(c) applies is deemed to consist of the same proportion of each class of the items of income of the estate or trust as the total of each class bears to the total of all classes. For illustrations showing the determination of the character of an amount deductible under section 642(c), see Examples 1 and 2 of § 1.662(b)–2 and § 1.662(c)–4(e).

[T.D. 6500, 25 FR 11814, Nov. 26, 1960; T.D. 9582, 77 FR 22485, April 16, 2012]

§ 1.643(b)–1 Definition of "income".

For purposes of subparts A through D, part I, subchapter J, chapter 1 of the Internal Revenue Code, "income," when not preceded by the words "taxable," "distributable net," "undistributed net," or "gross," means the amount of income of an estate or trust for the taxable year determined under the terms of the governing instrument and applicable local law. Trust provisions that depart fundamentally from traditional principles of income and principal will generally not be recognized. For example, if a trust instrument directs that all the trust income shall be paid to the income beneficiary but defines ordinary dividends and interest as principal, the trust will not be considered one that under its governing instrument is required to distribute all its income currently for purposes of section 642(b) (relating to the personal exemption) and section 651 (relating to simple trusts). Thus, items such as dividends, interest, and rents are generally allocated to income and proceeds from the sale or exchange of trust assets are generally allocated to principal. However, an allocation of amounts between income and principal pursuant to applicable local law will be respected if local law provides for a reasonable apportionment between the income and remainder beneficiaries of the total return of the trust for the year, including ordinary and tax-exempt income, capital gains, and appreciation. For example, a state statute providing that income is a unitrust amount of no less than 3% and no more than 5% of the fair market value of the trust assets, whether determined annually or averaged on a multiple year basis, is a reasonable apportionment of the total return of the trust. Similarly, a state statute that permits the trustee to make adjustments between income and principal to fulfill the trustee's duty of impartiality between the income and remainder beneficiaries is generally a reasonable apportionment of the total return of the trust. Generally, these adjustments are permitted by state statutes when the trustee invests and manages the trust assets under the state's prudent investor standard, the trust describes the amount that may or must be distributed to a beneficiary by referring to the trust's income, and the trustee after applying the state statutory rules regarding the allocation of receipts and disbursements to income and principal, is unable to administer the trust impartially. Allocations pursuant to methods prescribed by such state statutes for apportioning the total return of a trust between income and principal will be respected regardless of whether the trust provides that the income must be distributed to one or more beneficiaries or may be accumulated in whole or in part, and regardless of which alternate permitted method is actually used, provided the trust complies with all requirements of the state statute for switching methods. A switch between methods of determining trust income authorized by state statute will not constitute a recognition event for purposes of section 1001 and will not result in a taxable gift from the trust's grantor or any of the trust's beneficiaries. A switch to a method not specifically authorized by state statute, but valid under state law (including a switch via judicial decision or a binding non-judicial settlement) may constitute a recognition event to the trust or its beneficiaries for purposes of section 1001 and may result in taxable gifts from the trust's grantor and beneficiaries, based on the relevant facts and circumstances. In addition, an allocation to income of all or a part of the gains from the sale or exchange of trust assets will generally be respected if the allocation is made either pursuant to the terms of the governing instrument and applicable local law, or pursuant to a reasonable and impartial exercise of a discretionary power granted to the fiduciary by applicable local law or by the governing instrument, if not prohibited by applicable local law. This section is effective for taxable years of trusts and estates ending after January 2, 2004.

[T.D. 9102, 69 FR 12, Jan. 2, 2004]

§ 1.643(b)–2 Dividends allocated to corpus.

Extraordinary dividends or taxable stock dividends which the fiduciary, acting in good faith, determines to be allocable to corpus under the terms of the governing instrument and applicable local law are not considered "income" for purposes of Subpart A, B, C, or D, Part I, Subchapter J, Chapter 1 of the Code. * * *

[T.D. 6500, 25 FR 11814, Nov. 26, 1960, as amended by T.D. 6989, 34 FR 741, Jan. 17, 1969; T.D. 7204, 37 FR 17134, Aug. 25, 1972]

§ 1.643(c)–1 Definition of "beneficiary".

An heir, legatee, or devisee (including an estate or trust) is a beneficiary. A trust created under a decedent's will is a beneficiary of the decedent's estate. The following persons are treated as beneficiaries:

(a) Any person with respect to an amount used to discharge or satisfy that person's legal obligation as that term is used in § 1.662(a)–4.

(b) The grantor of a trust with respect to an amount applied or distributed for the support of a dependent under the circumstances specified in section 677(b) out of corpus or out of other than income for the taxable year of the trust.

(c) The trustee or cotrustee of a trust with respect to an amount applied or distributed for the support of a dependent under the circumstances specified in section 678(c) out of corpus or out of other than income for the taxable year of the trust.

[T.D. 6500, 25 FR 11814, Nov. 26, 1960]

§ 1.643(d)–2 Illustration of the provisions of section 643.

(a) The provisions of section 643 may be illustrated by the following example:

Example. **(1)** Under the terms of the trust instrument, the income of a trust is required to be currently distributed to W during her life. Capital gains are allocable to corpus and all expenses are charges against corpus. During the taxable year the trust has the following items of income and expenses:

Dividends from domestic corporations	$30,000
Extraordinary dividends allocated to corpus by the trustee in good faith	20,000
Taxable interest	10,000
Tax-exempt interest	10,000
Long-term capital gains	10,000
Trustee's commissions and miscellaneous expenses allocable to corpus	5,000

(2) The "income" of the trust determined under section 643(b) which is currently distributable to W is $50,000, consisting of dividends of $30,000, taxable interest of $10,000, and tax-exempt interest of $10,000. The trustee's commissions and miscellaneous expenses allocable to tax-exempt interest amount to $1,000 (10,000/50,000 × $5,000).

(3) The "distributable net income" determined under section 643(a) amounts to $45,000, computed as follows:

Dividends from domestic corporations		$30,000
Taxable interest		10,000
Nontaxable interest	$10,000	
Less: Expenses allocable thereto	1,000	
		9,000
Total		49,000
Less: Expenses ($5,000 less $1,000 allocable to tax-exempt interest)		$ 4,000
Distributable net income		45,000

In determining the distributable net income of $45,000, the taxable income of the trust is computed with the following modifications: No deductions are allowed for distributions to W and for personal exemption of the trust (section 643(a)(1) and (2)); capital gains allocable to corpus are excluded * * * (section 643(a)(3)); the extraordinary dividends allocated to corpus by the trustee in good faith are excluded (section 643(a)(4)); and the tax-exempt interest (as adjusted for expenses) * * * are included (section 643(a)(5) * * *).

* * *

[T.D. 6500, 25 FR 11814, Nov. 26, 1960; redesignated by T.D. 6989, 34 FR 732, Jan. 1, 1969]

§ 1.651(a)–1 Simple trusts; deduction for distributions; in general.

Section 651 is applicable only to a trust the governing instruments of which:

(a) Requires that the trust distribute all of its income currently for the taxable year, and

(b) Does not provide that any amounts may be paid, permanently set aside, or used in the taxable year for the charitable, etc., purposes specified in section 642(c),

and does not make any distribution other than of current income. A trust to which section 651 applies is referred to in this part as a "simple" trust. Trusts subject to section 661 are referred to as "complex" trusts. A trust may be a simple trust for one year and a complex trust for another year. It should be noted that under section 651 a trust qualifies as a simple trust in a taxable year in which it is required to distribute all its income currently and makes no other distributions, whether or not distributions of current income are in fact made. On the other hand a trust is not a complex trust by reason of distributions of amounts other than income unless such distributions are in fact made during the taxable year, whether or not they are required in that year.

[T.D. 6500, 25 FR 11814, Nov. 26, 1960]

§ 1.651(a)–2 Income required to be distributed currently.

(a) The determination of whether trust income is required to be distributed currently depends upon the terms of the trust instrument and the applicable local law. For this purpose, if the trust instrument provides that the trustee in determining the distributable income shall first retain a reserve for depreciation or otherwise make due allowance for keeping the trust corpus intact by retaining a reasonable amount of the current income for that purpose, the retention of current income for that purpose will not disqualify the trust from being a "simple" trust. The fiduciary must be under a duty to distribute the income currently even if, as a matter of practical necessity, the income is not distributed until after the close of the trust's taxable year. For example: Under the terms of the trust instrument, all of the income is currently distributable to A. The trust reports on the calendar year basis and as a matter of practical necessity makes distribution to A of each quarter's income on the fifteenth day of the month following the close of the quarter. The distribution made by the trust on January 15, 1955, of the income for the fourth quarter of 1954 does not disqualify the trust from treatment in 1955 under section 651, since the income is required to be distributed currently. However, if the terms of a trust require that none of the income be distributed until after the year of its receipt by the trust, the income of the trust is not required to be distributed currently and the trust is not a simple trust. For definition of the term "income" see section 643(b) and § 1.643(b)–1.

(b) It is immaterial, for purposes of determining whether all the income is required to be distributed currently, that the amount of income allocated to a particular beneficiary is not specified in the instrument. For example, if the fiduciary is required to distribute all the income currently, but has discretion to "sprinkle" the income among a class of beneficiaries, or among named beneficiaries, in such amount as he may see fit, all the income is required to be distributed currently, even though the amount distributable to a particular beneficiary is unknown until the fiduciary has exercised his discretion.

(c) If in one taxable year of a trust its income for that year is required or permitted to be accumulated, and in another taxable year its income for the year is required to be distributed currently (and no other amounts are distributed), the trust is a simple trust for the latter year. For example, a trust under which income may be accumulated until a beneficiary is 21 years old, and thereafter must be distributed currently, is a simple trust for taxable years beginning after the beneficiary reaches the age of 21 years in which no other amounts are distributed.

(d) If a trust distributes property in kind as part of its requirement to distribute currently all the income as defined under section 643(b) and the applicable regulations, the trust shall be treated as having sold the property for its fair market value on the date of distribution. If no amount in excess of the amount of income as defined under section 643(b) and the applicable regulations is distributed by the trust during the year, the trust will qualify for treatment under section 651 even though property in kind was distributed as part of a distribution of all such income. This paragraph (d) applies for taxable years of trusts ending after January 2, 2004.

[T.D. 6500, 25 FR 11814, Nov. 26, 1960; as amended by T.D. 9102, 69 FR 12, Jan. 2, 2004]

§ 1.651(a)-3 Distribution of amounts other than income.

(a) A trust does not qualify for treatment under section 651 for any taxable year in which it actually distributes corpus. For example, a trust which is required to distribute all of its income currently would not qualify as a simple trust under section 651 in the year of its termination since in that year actual distributions of corpus would be made.

(b) A trust, otherwise qualifying under section 651, which may make a distribution of corpus in the discretion of the trustee, or which is required under the terms of its governing instrument to make a distribution of corpus upon the happening of a specified event, will be disqualified for treatment under section 651 only for the taxable year in which an actual distribution of corpus is made. For example: Under the terms of a trust, which is required to distribute all of its income currently, half of the corpus is to be distributed to beneficiary A when he becomes 30 years of age. The trust reports on the calendar year basis. On December 28, 1954, A becomes 30 years of age and the trustee distributes half of the corpus of the trust to him on January 3, 1955. The trust will be disqualified for treatment under section 651 only for the taxable year 1955, the year in which an actual distribution of corpus is made.

(c) See section 661 and the regulations thereunder for the treatment of trusts which distribute corpus or claim the charitable contributions deduction provided by section 642(c).

[T.D. 6500, 25 FR 11814, Nov. 26, 1960]

§ 1.651(a)-4 Charitable purposes.

A trust is not considered to be a trust which may pay, permanently set aside, or use any amount for charitable, etc., purposes for any taxable year for which it is not allowed a charitable, etc., deduction under section 642(c). Therefore, a trust with a remainder to a charitable organization is not disqualified for treatment as a simple trust if either (a) the remainder is subject to a contingency, so that no deduction would be allowed for capital gains or other amounts added to corpus as amounts permanently set aside for a charitable, etc., purpose under section 642 (c), or (b) the trust receives no capital gains or other income added to corpus for the taxable year for which such a deduction would be allowed.

[T.D. 6500, 25 FR 11814, Nov. 26, 1960]

§ 1.651(a)-5 Estates.

Subpart B has no application to an estate.

[T.D. 6500, 25 FR 11814, Nov. 26, 1960]

§ 1.651(b)-1 Deduction for distributions to beneficiaries.

In computing its taxable income, a simple trust is allowed a deduction for the amount of income which is required under the terms of the trust instrument to be distributed currently to beneficiaries. If the amount of income required to be distributed currently exceeds the distributable net income, the deduction allowable to the trust is limited to the amount of the distributable net income. For this purpose the amount of income required to be distributed currently, or distributable net income, whichever is applicable, does not include items of trust income (adjusted for deductions allocable thereto) which are not included in the gross income of the trust. For determination of the character of the income required to be distributed currently, see § 1.652(b)-2. Accordingly, for the purposes of determining the deduction allowable to the trust under section 651, distributable net income is computed without the modifications specified in paragraphs (5), (6), and (7) of section 643(a), relating to tax-exempt interest, foreign income, and excluded dividends. For example: Assume that the distributable net income of a trust as computed under section 643(a) amounts to $99,000 but includes nontaxable income of $9,000. Then distributable net income for the purpose of determining the deduction allowable under section 651 is $90,000 ($99,000 less $9,000 nontaxable income).

[T.D. 6500, 25 FR 11814, Nov. 26, 1960]

§ 1.652(a)-1 Simple trusts; inclusion of amounts in income of beneficiaries.

Subject to the rules in §§ 1.652(a)-2 and 1.652(b)-1, a beneficiary of a simple trust includes in his gross income for the taxable year the amounts of income required to be distributed to him for such year, whether or not distributed. Thus, the income of a simple trust is includible in the beneficiary's gross income for the taxable year in which the income is required to be distributed currently even though, as a matter of practical necessity, the income is not distributed until after the close of the taxable year of the trust. * * * See § 1.652(c)-1 for treatment of amounts required to be distributed where a beneficiary and the trust have different taxable years. The term "income required to be distributed currently" includes income required to be distributed currently which is in fact used to discharge or satisfy any person's legal obligation as that term is used in § 1.662(a)–4.

[T.D. 6500, 25 FR 11814, Nov. 26, 1960]

§ 1.652(a)–2 Distributions in excess of distributable net income.

If the amount of income required to be distributed currently to beneficiaries exceeds the distributable net income of the trust (as defined in section 643(a)), each beneficiary includes in his gross income an amount equivalent to his proportionate share of such distributable net income. Thus, if beneficiary A is to receive two-thirds of the trust income and B is to receive one-third, and the income required to be distributed currently is $99,000, A will receive $66,000 and B, $33,000. However, if the distributable net income, as determined under section 643(a) is only $90,000, A will include two-thirds ($60,000) of that sum in his gross income, and B will include one-third ($30,000) in his gross income. See §§ 1.652(b)–1 and 1.652(b)–2, however, for amounts which are not includible in the gross income of a beneficiary because of their tax-exempt character.

[T.D. 6500, 25 FR 11814, Nov. 26, 1960]

§ 1.652(b)–1 Character of amounts.

In determining the gross income of a beneficiary, the amounts includible under § 1.652(a)–1 have the same character in the hands of the beneficiary as in the hands of the trust. For example, to the extent that the amounts specified in § 1.652(a)–1 consist of income exempt from tax under section 103, such amounts are not included in the beneficiary's gross income. * * * The tax treatment of amounts determined under § 1.652(a)–1 depends upon the beneficiary's status with respect to them not upon the status of the trust. Thus, if a beneficiary is deemed to have received foreign income of a foreign trust, the includibility of such income in his gross income depends upon his taxable status with respect to that income.

[T.D. 6500, 25 FR 11814, Nov. 26, 1960, as amended by T.D. 6777, 29 FR 17809, Dec. 16, 1964; T.D. 7204, 37 FR 17134, Aug. 25, 1972]

§ 1.652(b)–2 Allocation of income items.

(a) The amounts specified in § 1.652(a)–1 which are required to be included in the gross income of a beneficiary are treated as consisting of the same proportion of each class of items entering into distributable net income of the trust (as defined in section 643(a)) as the total of each class bears to such distributable net income, unless the terms of the trust specifically allocate different classes of income to different beneficiaries, or unless local law requires such an allocation. For example: Assume that under the terms of the governing instrument, beneficiary A is to receive currently one-half of the trust income and beneficiaries B and C are each to receive currently one-quarter, and the distributable net income of the trust (after allocation of expenses) consists of dividends of $10,000, taxable interest of $10,000, and tax-exempt interest of $4,000. A will be deemed to have received $5,000 of dividends, $5,000 of taxable interest, and $2,000 of tax-exempt interest; B and C will each be deemed to have received $2,500 of dividends, $2,500 of taxable interest, and $1,000 of tax-exempt interest. However, if the terms of the trust specifically allocate different classes of income to different beneficiaries, entirely or in part, or if local law requires such an allocation, each beneficiary will be deemed to have received those items of income specifically allocated to him.

(b) The terms of the trust are considered specifically to allocate different classes of income to different beneficiaries only to the extent that the allocation is required in the trust instrument, and only to the extent that it has an economic effect independent of the income tax consequences of the allocation. For example:

(1) Allocation pursuant to a provision in a trust instrument granting the trustee discretion to allocate different classes of income to different beneficiaries is not a specific allocation by the terms of the trust.

(2) Allocation pursuant to a provision directing the trustee to pay all of one income to A, or $10,000 out of the income to A, and the balance of the income to B, but directing the trustee first to allocate a specific class of income to A's share (to the extent there is income of that class and to the extent it does not exceed A's share) is not a specific allocation by the terms of the trust.

(3) Allocation pursuant to a provision directing the trustee to pay half the class of income (whatever it may be) to A, and the balance of the income to B, is a specific allocation by the terms of the trust.

[T.D. 6500, 25 FR 11814, Nov. 26, 1960]

§ 1.652(b)–3 Allocation of deductions.

Items of deduction of a trust that enter into the computation of distributable net income are to be allocated among the items of income in accordance with the following principles:

(a) All deductible items directly attributable to one class of income * * * are allocated thereto. For example, repairs to, taxes on, and other expenses directly attributable to the maintenance of rental property or the collection of rental income are allocated to rental income. See § 1.642(e)–1 for treatment of depreciation of rental property. Similarly, all expenditures directly attributable to a business carried on by a trust are allocated to the income from such business. If the deductions directly attributable to a particular class of income exceed that income, the excess is applied against other classes of income in the manner provided in paragraph (d) of this section.

(b) The deductions which are not directly attributable to a specific class of income may be allocated to any item of income (including capital gains) included in computing distributable net income, but a portion must be allocated to nontaxable income * * * pursuant to section 265 and the regulations thereunder. For example, if the income of a trust is $30,000 (after direct expenses), consisting equally of $10,000 of dividends, tax-exempt interest, and rents, and income commissions amount to $3,000, one-third ($1,000) of such commissions should be allocated to tax-exempt interest, but the balance of $2,000 may be allocated to the rents or dividends in such proportions as the trustee may elect. The fact that the governing instrument or applicable local law treats certain items of deduction as attributable to corpus or to income not included in distributable net income does not affect allocation under this paragraph. For instance, if in the example set forth in this paragraph the trust also had capital gains which are allocable to corpus under the terms of the trust instrument, no part of the deductions would be allocable thereto since the capital gains are excluded from the computation of distributable net income under section 643(a)(3).

(c) Examples of expenses which are considered as not directly attributable to a specific class of income are trustee's commissions, the rental of safe deposit boxes, and State income and personal property taxes.

(d) To the extent that any items of deduction which are directly attributable to a class of income exceed that class of income, they may be allocated to any other class of income (including capital gains) included in distributable net income in the manner provided in paragraph (b) of this section, except that any excess deductions attributable to tax-exempt income * * * may not be offset against any other class of income. See section 265 and the regulations thereunder. Thus, if the trust has rents, taxable interest, dividends, and tax-exempt interest, and the deductions directly attributable to the rents exceed the rental income, the excess may be allocated to the taxable interest or dividends in such proportions as the fiduciary may elect. However, if the excess deductions are attributable to the tax-exempt interest, they may not be allocated to either the rents, taxable interest, or dividends.

[T.D. 6500, 25 FR 11814, Nov. 26, 1960]

§ 1.652(c)–1 Different taxable years.

If a beneficiary has a different taxable year (as defined in section 441 or 442) from the taxable year of the trust, the amount he is required to include in gross income in accordance with section 652(a) and (b) is based on the income of the trust for any taxable year or years ending with or within his taxable year. This rule applies to taxable years of normal duration as well as to so-called short taxable years. Income of the trust for its taxable year or years is determined in accordance with its method of accounting and without regard to that of the beneficiary.

[T.D. 6500, 25 FR 11814, Nov. 26, 1960]

§ 1.652(c)–2 Death of individual beneficiaries.

If income is required to be distributed currently to a beneficiary, by a trust for a taxable year which does not end with or within the last taxable year of a beneficiary (because of the beneficiary's death), the extent to which the income is included in the gross income of the beneficiary for his last taxable year or in the gross income of his estate is determined by the computations under section 652 for the taxable year of the trust in which his last taxable year ends. Thus, the distributable net income of the taxable year of the trust determines the extent to which the income required to be distributed currently to the beneficiary is included in his gross income for his last taxable year or in the gross income of his estate. (Section 652(c) does not apply to such amounts.) The gross income for the last taxable year of a beneficiary on the cash basis includes only income actually distributed to the beneficiary before his death. Income required to be distributed, but in fact distributed to his estate, is included in the gross income of the estate as income in respect of a decedent under section 691. See paragraph (e) of § 1.663(c)–3 with respect to separate share treatment for the periods before and after the decedent's death. If the trust does not qualify as a simple trust for the taxable year of the trust in which the last taxable year of the beneficiary ends, see section 662(c) * * *.

[T.D. 6500, 25 FR 11814, Nov. 26, 1960]

§ 1.652(c)–3 Termination of existence of other beneficiaries.

If the existence of a beneficiary which is not an individual terminates, the amount to be included under section 652(a) in its gross income for its last taxable year is computed with reference to §§ 1.652(c)–1 and 1.652(c)–2 as if the beneficiary were a deceased individual, except that income required to be distributed prior to the termination but actually distributed to the beneficiary's successor in interest is included in the beneficiary's income for its last taxable year.

[T.D. 6500, 25 FR 11814, Nov. 26, 1960]

§ 1.652(c)–4 Illustration of the provisions of sections 651 and 652.

The rules applicable to a trust required to distribute all of its income currently to its beneficiaries may be illustrated by the following example:

Example. **(a)** Under the terms of a simple trust all of the income is to be distributed equally to beneficiaries A and B and capital gains are to be allocated to corpus. The trust and both beneficiaries file returns on the calendar year basis. No provision is made in the governing instrument with respect to depreciation. During the taxable year 1955, the trust had the following items of income and expense:

Rents	$ 25,000
Dividends of domestic corporations	50,000
Tax-exempt interest on municipal bonds	25,000
Long-term capital gains	15,000
Taxes and expenses directly attributable to rents	5,000
Trustee's commissions allocable to income account	2,600
Trustee's commissions allocable to principal account	1,300
Depreciation	5,000

(b) The income of the trust for fiduciary accounting purposes is $92,400, computed as follows:

Rents		$ 25,000
Dividends		50,000
Tax-exempt interest		25,000
Total		100,000
Deductions:		
Expenses directly attributable to rental income	$ 5,000	
Trustee's commissions allocable to income account	2,600	
		7,600
Income computed under section 643(b)		92,400

One-half ($46,200) of the income of $92,400 is currently distributable to each beneficiary.

(c) The distributable net income of the trust computed under section 643(a) is $91,100, determined as follows (cents are disregarded in the computation):

Rents		$ 25,000
Dividends		50,000
Tax-exempt interest	$25,000	
Less: Expenses allocable thereto (25,000/100,000 × $3,900)	975	
		24,025
Total		99,025
Deductions:		
Expenses directly attributable to rental income	$ 5,000	
Trustee's commissions ($3,900 less $975 allocable to tax-exempt interest)	2,925	
		7,925
Distributable net income		91,100

In computing the distributable net income of $91,100, the taxable income of the trust was computed with the following modifications: No deductions were allowed for distributions to the beneficiaries and for personal exemption of the trust (section 643(a)(1) and (2)); capital gains were excluded and no deduction under section 1202 (relating to the 50-percent deduction for long-term capital gains) was taken into account (section 643(a)(3)); the tax-exempt interest (as adjusted for expenses) and the dividend exclusion of $50 were included (section 643(a)(5) and (7)). Since all of the income of the trust is required to be currently distributed, no deduction is allowable for depreciation in the absence of specific provisions in the governing instrument providing for the keeping of the trust corpus intact. See section 167(h) [now section 167(d)] and the regulations thereunder.

(d) The deduction allowable to the trust under section 651(a) for distributions to the beneficiaries is $67,025, computed as follows:

Distributable net income computed under section 643(a) (see paragraph (c))		$ 91,100
Less:		
Tax-exempt interest as adjusted	$24,025	
Dividend exclusion	50	
		24,075
Distributable net income as determined under section 651(b)		67,025

Since the amount of the income ($92,400) required to be distributed currently by the trust exceeds the distributable net income ($67,025) as computed under section 651(b), the deduction allowable under section 651(a) is limited to the distributable net income of $67,025.

(e) The taxable income of the trust is $7,200 computed as follows:

Rents		$ 25,000
Dividends ($50,000 less $50 exclusion)		49,950
Long-term capital gains		15,000
Gross income		89,950
Deductions:		
Rental expenses	$ 5,000	
Trustee's commissions	2,925	
Capital gain deduction	7,500	
Distributions to beneficiaries	67,025	
Personal exemption	300	
		82,750
Taxable income		7,200

The trust is not allowed a deduction for the portion ($975) of the trustee's commissions allocable to tax-exempt interest in computing its taxable income.

(f) In determining the character of the amounts includible in the gross income of A and B, it is assumed that the trustee elects to allocate to rents the expenses not directly attributable to a specific item of income other than the portion ($975) of such expenses allocated to tax-exempt interest. The allocation of expenses among the items of income is shown below:

	Rents	Dividends	Tax-exempt interest	Total
Income for trust accounting purposes	$25,000	$50,000	$25,000	$100,000
Less:				
Rental expenses	5,000	......	......	5,000
Trustee's commissions	2,925	......	975	3,900
Total deductions	7,925	0	975	8,900
Character of amounts in the hands of the beneficiaries	17,075	50,000	24,025	[1] 91,100

[1] Distributable net income.

Inasmuch as the income of the trust is to be distributed equally to A and B, each is deemed to have received one-half of each item of income; that is, rents of $8,537.50, dividends of $25,000, and tax-exempt interest of $12,012.50. The dividends of $25,000 allocated to each beneficiary are to be aggregated with his other dividends (if any) for purposes of the dividend exclusion provided by section 116 and the dividend received credit allowed under section 34. Also, each beneficiary is allowed a deduction of $2,500 for depreciation of rental property attributable to the portion (one-half) of the income of the trust distributed to him.

[T.D. 6500, 25 FR 11814, Nov. 26, 1960, as amended by T.D. 6712, 29 FR 3655, March 24, 1964]

§ 1.661(a)–1 Estates and trusts accumulating income or distributing corpus; general.

Subpart C, part I, subchapter J, chapter 1 of the Code, is applicable to all decedents' estates and their beneficiaries, and to trusts and their beneficiaries other than trusts subject to the provisions of subpart B of such part I (relating to trusts which distribute current income only, or "simple" trusts). A trust which is required to distribute amounts other than income during the taxable year may be subject to subpart B, and not subpart C, in the absence of an actual distribution of amounts other than income during the taxable year. See §§ 1.651(a)–1 and 1.651(a)–3. A trust to which subpart C is applicable is referred to as a "complex" trust in this part. Section 661 has no application to amounts excluded under section 663(a).

[T.D. 6500, 25 FR 11814, Nov. 26, 1960]

§ 1.661(a)–2 Deduction for distributions to beneficiaries.

(a) In computing the taxable income of an estate or trust there is allowed under section 661(a) as a deduction for distributions to beneficiaries the sum of:

(1) The amount of income for the taxable year which is required to be distributed currently, and

(2) Any other amounts properly paid or credited or required to be distributed for such taxable year.

However, the total amount deductible under section 661(a) cannot exceed the distributable net income as computed under section 643(a) and as modified by section 661(c). See § 1.661(c)–1.

(b) The term "income required to be distributed currently" includes any amount required to be distributed which may be paid out of income or corpus (such as an annuity), to the extent it is paid out of income for the taxable year. See § 1.651(a)–2 which sets forth additional rules which are applicable in determining whether income of an estate or trust is required to be distributed currently.

(c) The term "any other amounts properly paid, credited, or required to be distributed" includes all amounts properly paid, credited, or required to be distributed by an estate or trust during the taxable year other than income required to be distributed currently. Thus, the term includes the payment of an annuity to the extent it is not paid out of income for the taxable year, and a distribution of property in kind (see paragraph (f) of this section). However, see section 663(a) and regulations thereunder for distributions which are not included. Where the income of an estate or trust may be accumulated or distributed in the discretion of the fiduciary, or where the fiduciary has a power to distribute corpus to a beneficiary, any such discretionary distribution would qualify under section 661(a)(2). The term also includes an amount applied or distributed for the support of a dependent of a grantor or of a trustee or cotrustee under the circumstances described in section 677(b) or section 678(c) out of corpus or out of other than income for the taxable year.

(d) The terms "income required to be distributed currently" and "any other amounts properly paid or credited or required to be distributed" also include any amount used to discharge or satisfy any person's legal obligation as that term is used in § 1.662(a)–4.

(e) The terms "income required to be distributed currently" and "any other amounts properly paid or credited or required to be distributed" include amounts paid, or required to be paid, during the taxable year pursuant to a court order or decree or under local law, by a decedent's estate as an allowance or award for the support of the decedent's widow or other dependent for a limited period during the administration of the estate. The term "any other amounts properly paid or credited or required to be distributed" does not include the value of any interest in real estate owned by a decedent, title to which under local law passes directly from the decedent to his heirs or devisees.

(f) Gain or loss is realized by the trust or estate (or the other beneficiaries) by reason of a distribution of property in kind if the distribution is in satisfaction of a right to receive a distribution of a specific dollar amount, of specific property other than that distributed, or of income as defined under section 643(b) and the applicable regulations, if income is required to be distributed currently. In addition, gain or loss is realized if the trustee or executor makes the election to recognize gain or loss under section 643(e). This paragraph applies for taxable years of trusts and estates ending after January 2, 2004.

[T.D. 6500, 25 FR 11814, Nov. 26, 1960; 25 FR 14021, Dec. 31, 1960, as amended by T.D. 7287, 38 FR 26912, Sept. 27, 1973; T.D. 9102, 69 FR 12, Jan. 2, 2004]

§ 1.661(b)–1 Character of amounts distributed; in general.

In the absence of specific provisions in the governing instrument for the allocation of different classes of income, or unless local law requires such an allocation, the amount deductible for distributions to beneficiaries under section 661(a) is treated as consisting of the same proportion of each class of items entering into the computation of distributable net income as the total of each class bears to the total distributable net income. For example, if a trust has distributable net income of $20,000, consisting of $10,000 each of taxable interest and royalties and distributes $10,000 to beneficiary A, the deduction of $10,000 allowable under section 661(a) is deemed to consist of $5,000 each of taxable interest and royalties, unless the trust instrument specifically provides for the distribution or accumulation of different classes of income or unless local law requires such an allocation. See also § 1.661(c)–1.

[T.D. 6500, 25 FR 11814, Nov. 26, 1960]

§ 1.661(b)–2 Character of amounts distributed when charitable contributions are made.

In the application of the rule stated in § 1.661(b)–1, the items of deduction which enter into the computation of distributable net income are allocated among the items of income which enter into the computation of distributable net income in accordance with the rules set forth in § 1.652(b)–3, except that, in the absence of specific provisions in the governing instrument, or unless local law requires a different apportionment, amounts paid, permanently set aside, or to be used for the charitable, etc., purposes specified in section 642(c) are first ratably apportioned among each class of items of income entering into the computation of the distributable net income of the estate or trust, in accordance with the rules set out in paragraph (b) of § 1.643(a)–5.

[T.D. 6500, 25 FR 11814, Nov. 26, 1960]

§ 1.661(c)–1 Limitation on deduction.

An estate or trust is not allowed a deduction under section 661(a) for any amount which is treated under section 661(b) as consisting of any item of distributable net income which is not included in the gross income of the estate or trust. For example, if in 1962, a trust, which reports on the calendar year basis, has distributable net income of $20,000, which is deemed to consist of $10,000 of dividends and $10,000 of tax-exempt interest, and distributes $10,000 to beneficiary A, the deduction allowable under section 661(a) (computed without regard to section 661(c)) would amount to $10,000 consisting of $5,000 of dividends and $5,000 of tax-exempt interest. The deduction actually allowable under section 661(a) as limited by section 661(c) is $4,975, since no deduction is allowable for the $5,000 of tax-exempt interest and the $25 deemed distributed out of the $50 of dividends excluded under section 116, items of distributable net income which are not included in the gross income of the estate or trust.

[T.D. 6500, 25 FR 11814, Nov. 26, 1960, as amended by T.D. 6777, 29 FR 17809, Dec. 16, 1964]

§ 1.662(a)–1 Inclusion of amounts in gross income of beneficiaries of estates and complex trusts; general.

There is included in the gross income of a beneficiary of an estate or complex trust the sum of:

(1) Amounts of income required to be distributed currently to him, and

(2) All other amounts properly paid, credited, or required to be distributed to him

by the estate or trust. The preceding sentence is subject to the rules contained in § 1.662(a)–2 (relating to currently distributable income), § 1.662(a)–3 (relating to other amounts distributed), and §§ 1.662(b)–1 and 1.662(b)–2 (relating to character of amounts). Section 662 has no application to amounts excluded under section 663(a).

[T.D. 6500, 25 FR 11814, Nov. 26, 1960]

§ 1.662(a)–2 Currently distributable income.

(a) There is first included in the gross income of each beneficiary under section 662(a)(1) the amount of income for the taxable year of the estate or trust required to be distributed currently to him, subject to the provisions of paragraph (b) of this section. Such amount is included in the beneficiary's gross income whether or not it is actually distributed.

(b) If the amount of income required to be distributed currently to all beneficiaries exceeds the distributable net income (as defined in section 643(a) but computed without taking into account the payment, crediting, or setting aside of an amount for which a charitable contributions deduction is allowable under section 642(c)) of the estate or trust, then there is included in the gross income of each beneficiary an amount which bears the same ratio to distributable net income (as so computed) as the amount of income required to be distributed currently to the beneficiary bears to the amount required to be distributed currently to all beneficiaries.

(c) The phrase "the amount of income for the taxable year required to be distributed currently" includes any amount required to be paid out of income or corpus to the extent the amount is satisfied out of income for the taxable year. Thus, an annuity required to be paid in all events (either out of income or corpus) would qualify as income required to be distributed currently to the extent there is income (as defined in section 643(b)) not paid, credited, or required to be distributed to other beneficiaries for the taxable year. If an annuity or a portion of an annuity is deemed under this paragraph to be income required to be distributed currently, it is treated in all respects in the same manner as an amount of income actually required to be distributed currently. The phrase "the amount of income for the taxable year required to be distributed currently" also includes any amount required to be paid during the taxable year in all events (either out of income or corpus) pursuant to a court order or decree or under local law, by a decedent's estate as an allowance or award for the support of the decedent's widow or other dependent for a limited period during the administration of the estate to the extent there is income (as defined in section 643(b)) of the estate for the taxable year not paid, credited, or required to be distributed to other beneficiaries.

(d) If an annuity is paid, credited, or required to be distributed tax free, that is, under a provision whereby the executor or trustee will pay the income tax of the annuitant resulting from the receipt of the annuity, the payment of or for the tax by the executor or trustee will be treated as income paid, credited, or required to be distributed currently to the extent it is made out of income.

(e) The application of the rules stated in this section may be illustrated by the following examples:

Example (1). **(1)** Assume that under the terms of the trust instrument $5,000 is to be paid to X charity out of income each year; that $20,000 of income is currently distributable to A; and that an annuity of $12,000 is to be paid to B out of income or corpus. All expenses are charges against income and capital gains are allocable to corpus. During the taxable year the trust had income of $30,000 (after the payment of expenses) derived from taxable interest and made the payments to X charity and distributions to A and B as required by the governing instrument.

(2) The amounts treated as distributed currently under section 662(a)(1) total $25,000 ($20,000 to A and $5,000 to B). Since the charitable contribution is out of income the amount of income available for B's annuity is only $5,000. The distributable net income of the trust computed under section 643(a) without taking into consideration the charitable contributions deduction of $5,000 as provided by section 661(a)(1), is $30,000. Since the amounts treated as distributed currently of $25,000 do not exceed the distributable net income (as modified) of $30,000, A is required to include $20,000 in his gross income and B is required to include $5,000 in his gross income under section 662(a)(1).

Example (2). Assume the same facts as in paragraph (1) of example (1), except that the trust has, in addition, $10,000 of administration expenses, commissions, etc., chargeable to corpus. The amounts treated as distributed currently under section 662(a)(1) total $25,000 ($20,000 to A and $5,000 to B), since trust income under section 643(b) remains the same as in example (1). Distributable net income of the trust computed under section 643(a) but without taking into account the charitable contributions deduction of $5,000 as provided by section 662(a)(1) is only $20,000. Since the amounts treated as distributed currently of $25,000 exceed the distributable net income (as so computed) of $20,000, A is required to include $16,000 (20,000/25,000 of $20,000) in his gross income and B is required to include $4,000 (5,000/25,000 of $20,000) in his gross income under section 662(a)(1). Because A and B are beneficiaries of amounts of income required to be distributed currently, they do not benefit from the reduction of distributable net income by the charitable contributions deduction.

[T.D. 6500, 25 FR 11814, Nov. 26, 1960; 25 FR 14021, Dec. 31, 1960, as amended by T.D. 7287, 38 FR 26912, Sept. 27, 1973]

§ 1.662(a)–3 Other amounts distributed.

(a) There is included in the gross income of a beneficiary under section 662(a)(2) any amount properly paid, credited, or required to be distributed to the beneficiary for the taxable year, other than (1) income required to be distributed currently, as determined under § 1.662(a)–2, (2) amounts excluded under section 663(a) and the regulations thereunder, and (3) amounts in excess of distributable net income (see paragraph (c) of this section). An amount which is credited or required to be distributed is included in the gross income of a beneficiary whether or not it is actually distributed.

(b) Some of the payments to be included under paragraph (a) of this section are: (1) A distribution made to a beneficiary in the discretion of the fiduciary; (2) a distribution required by the terms of the governing instrument upon the happening of a specified event; (3) an annuity which is required to be paid in all events but which is payable only out of corpus; (4) a distribution of property in kind (see paragraph (f) of § 1.661(a)–2); (5) an amount applied or distributed for the support of a dependent of a grantor or a trustee or cotrustee under the circumstances specified in section 677(b) or section 678(c) out of corpus or out of other than income for the taxable year; and (6) an amount required to be paid during the taxable year pursuant to a court order or decree or under local law, by a decedent's estate as an allowance or award for the support of the decedent's widow or other dependent for a limited period during the administration of the estate which is payable only out of corpus of the estate under the order or decree or local law.

(c) If the sum of the amounts of income required to be distributed currently (as determined under § 1.662(a)–2) and other amounts properly paid, credited, or required to be distributed (as determined under paragraph (a) of this section) exceeds distributable net income (as defined in section 643(a)), then such other amounts properly paid, credited, or required to be distributed are included in gross income of the beneficiary but only to the extent of the excess of such distributable net income over the amounts of income required to be distributed currently. If the other amounts are paid, credited, or required to be distributed to more than one beneficiary, each beneficiary includes in gross income his proportionate share of the amount includible in gross income pursuant to the preceding sentence. The proportionate share is an amount which bears the same ratio to distributable net income (reduced by amounts of income required to be distributed currently) as the other amounts (as determined under paragraphs (a) and (d) of this section) distributed to the beneficiary bear to the other amounts distributed to all beneficiaries. For treatment of excess distributions by trusts, see sections 665 to 668, inclusive, and the regulations thereunder.

(d) The application of the rules stated in this section may be illustrated by the following example:

Example. The terms of a trust require the distribution annually of $10,000 of income to A. If any income remains, it may be accumulated or distributed to B, C, and D in amounts in the trustee's discretion. He may also invade corpus for the benefit of A, B, C, or D. In the taxable year, the trust has $20,000 of income after the deduction of all expenses. Distributable net income is $20,000. The trustee distributes $10,000 of income to A. Of the remaining $10,000 of income, he distributes $3,000 each to B, C, and D, and also distributes an additional

$5,000 to A. A includes $10,000 in income under section 662(a)(1). The "other amounts distributed" amount of $14,000, includible in the income of the recipients to the extent of $10,000, distributable net income less the income currently distributable to A. A will include an additional $3,571 (5,000/14,000 × $10,000) in income under this section, and B, C, and D will each include $2,143 (3,000/14,000 × $10,000).

[T.D. 6500, 25 FR 11814, Nov. 26, 1960; 25 FR 14021, Dec. 31, 1960, as amended by T.D. 7287, 38 FR 26913, Sept. 27, 1973]

§ 1.662(a)–4 Amounts used in discharge of a legal obligation.

Any amount which, pursuant to the terms of a will or trust instrument, is used in full or partial discharge or satisfaction of a legal obligation of any person is included in the gross income of such person under section 662(a)(1) or (2), whichever is applicable, as though directly distributed to him as a beneficiary, except in cases to which section 71 (relating to alimony payments) or section 682 (relating to income of a trust in case of divorce, etc.) applies. The term "legal obligation" includes a legal obligation to support another person if, and only if, the obligation is not affected by the adequacy of the dependent's own resources. For example, a parent has a "legal obligation" within the meaning of the preceding sentence to support his minor child if under local law property or income from property owned by the child cannot be used for his support so long as his parent is able to support him. On the other hand, if under local law a mother may use the resources of a child for the child's support in lieu of supporting him herself, no obligation of support exists within the meaning of this paragraph, whether or not income is actually used for support. Similarly, since under local law a child ordinarily is obligated to support his parent only if the parent's earnings and resources are insufficient for the purpose, no obligation exists whether or not the parent's earnings and resources are sufficient. In any event the amount of trust income which is included in the gross income of a person obligated to support a dependent is limited by the extent of his legal obligation under local law. In the case of a parent's obligation to support his child, to the extent that the parent's legal obligation of support, including education, is determined under local law by the family's station in life and by the means of the parent, it is to be determined without consideration of the trust income in question.

[T.D. 6500, 25 FR 11814, Nov. 26, 1960]

§ 1.662(b)–1 Character of amounts; when no charitable contributions are made.

In determining the amount includible in the gross income of a beneficiary, the amounts which are determined under section 662(a) and §§ 1.662(a)–1 through 1.662(a)–4 shall have the same character in the hands of the beneficiary as in the hands of the estate or trust. The amounts are treated as consisting of the same proportion of each class of items entering into the computation of distributable net income as the total of each class bears to the total distributable net income of the estate or trust unless the terms of the governing instrument specifically allocate different classes of income to different beneficiaries, or unless local law requires such an allocation. For this purpose, the principles contained in § 1.652(b)–1 shall apply.

[T.D. 6500, 25 FR 11814, Nov. 26, 1960]

§ 1.662(b)–2 Character of amounts; when charitable contributions are made.

When a charitable contribution is made, the principles contained in §§ 1.652(b)–1 and 1.662(b)–1 generally apply. However, before the allocation of other deductions among the items of distributable net income, the charitable contributions deduction allowed under section 642(c) is (in the absence of specific allocation under the terms of the governing instrument or the requirement under local law of a different allocation) allocated among the classes of income entering into the computation of estate or trust income in accordance with the rules set forth in paragraph (b) of § 1.643(a)–5. In the application of the preceding sentence, for the purpose of allocating items of income and deductions to beneficiaries to whom income is required to be distributed currently, the amount of the charitable contributions deduction is disregarded to the extent that it exceeds the income of the trust for the taxable year reduced by amounts for the taxable year required to be distributed currently. The application of this section may be illustrated by the following examples (of which example (1) is illustrative of the preceding sentence):

Example (1). **(a)** A trust instrument provides that $30,000 of its income must be distributed currently to A, and the balance may either be distributed to B, distributed to a designated charity, or accumulated. Accumulated income may be distributed to B and to the charity. The trust for its taxable year has $40,000 of taxable interest and $10,000 of tax-exempt income, with no expenses. The trustee distributed $30,000 to A, $50,000 to charity X, and $10,000 to B.

(b) Distributable net income for the purpose of determining the character of the distribution to A is $30,000 (the charitable contributions deduction, for this purpose, being taken into account only to the extent of $20,000, the difference between the income of the trust for the taxable year, $50,000, and the amount required to be distributed currently, $30,000).

(c) The charitable contributions deduction taken into account, $20,000, is allocated proportionately to the items of income of the trust, $16,000 to taxable interest and $4,000 to tax-exempt income.

(d) Under section 662(a)(1), the amount of income required to be distributed currently to A is $30,000, which consists of the balance of these items, $24,000 of taxable interest and $6,000 of tax-exempt income.

(e) In determining the amount to be included in the gross income of B under section 662 for the taxable year, however, the entire charitable contributions deduction is taken into account, with the result that there is no distributable net income and therefore no amount to be included in gross income.

(f) See subpart D (section 665 and following), part I, subchapter J, chapter 1 of the Code for application of the throwback provisions to the distribution made to B.

Example (2). The net income of a trust is payable to A for life, with the remainder to a charitable organization. Under the terms of the trust instrument and local law capital gains are added to corpus. During the taxable year the trust receives dividends of $10,000 and realized a long-term capital gain of $10,000, for which a long-term capital gain deduction of $5,000 is allowed under section 1202. Since under the trust instrument and local law the capital gains are allocated to the charitable organization, and since the capital gain deduction is directly attributable to the capital gain, the charitable contributions deduction and the capital gain deduction are both allocable to the capital gain, and dividends in the amount of $10,000 are allocable to A.

[T.D. 6500, 25 FR 11814, Nov. 26, 1960]

§ 1.662(c)–1 Different taxable years.

If a beneficiary has a different taxable year (as defined in section 441 or 442) from the taxable year of an estate or trust, the amount he is required to include in gross income in accordance with section 662(a) and (b) is based upon the distributable net income of the estate or trust and the amounts properly paid, credited, or required to be distributed to the beneficiary for any taxable year or years of the estate or trust ending with or within his taxable year. This rule applies as to so-called short taxable years as well as taxable years of normal duration. Income of an estate or trust for its taxable year or years is determined in accordance with its method of accounting and without regard to that of the beneficiary.

[T.D. 6500, 25 FR 11814, Nov. 26, 1960]

§ 1.662(c)–2 Death of individual beneficiary.

If an amount specified in section 662(a)(1) or (2) is paid, credited, or required to be distributed by an estate or trust for a taxable year which does not end with or within the last taxable year of a beneficiary (because of the beneficiary's death), the extent to which the amount is included in the gross income of the beneficiary for his last taxable year or in the gross income of his estate is determined by the computations under section 662 for the taxable year of the estate or trust in which his last taxable year ends. Thus, the distributable net income and the amounts paid, credited, or required to be distributed for the taxable year of the estate or trust, determine the extent to which the amounts paid, credited, or required to be distributed to the beneficiary are included in his gross income for his last taxable year or in the gross income of his estate. (Section 662(c) does not apply to such amounts.) The gross income for the last taxable year of a beneficiary on the cash basis includes only income actually distributed to the beneficiary before his death. Income required to be distributed, but in fact distributed to his estate, is included in the gross income of the estate as income in respect of a decedent under section 691. See paragraph (e) of § 1.663(c)–3 with respect to separate share treatment for the periods before and after the death of a trust's beneficiary.

[T.D. 6500, 25 FR 11814, Nov. 26, 1960]

§ 1.662(c)–3 Termination of existence of other beneficiaries.

If the existence of a beneficiary which is not an individual terminates, the amount to be included under section 662(a) in its gross income for the last taxable year is computed with reference to §§ 1.662(c)–1 and 1.662(c)–2 as if the beneficiary were a deceased individual, except that income required to be distributed prior to the termination but actually distributed to the beneficiary's successor in interest is included in the beneficiary's income for its last taxable year.

[T.D. 6500, 25 FR 11814, Nov. 26, 1960]

§ 1.662(c)–4 Illustration of the provisions of sections 661 and 662.

The provisions of sections 661 and 662 may be illustrated in general by the following example:

Example. **(a)** Under the terms of a testamentary trust one-half of the trust income is to be distributed currently to W, the decedent's wife, for her life. The remaining trust income may, in the trustee's discretion, either be paid to D, the grantor's daughter, paid to designated charities, or accumulated. The trust is to terminate at the death of W and the principal will then be payable to D. No provision is made in the trust instrument with respect to depreciation of rental property. Capital gains are allocable to the principal account under the applicable local law. The trust and both beneficiaries file returns on the calendar year basis. The records of the fiduciary show the following items of income and deduction for the taxable year 1955:

Rents	$ 50,000
Dividends of domestic corporations	50,000
Tax-exempt interest	20,000
Partially tax-exempt interest	10,000
Capital gains (long term)	20,000
Depreciation of rental property	10,000
Expenses attributable to rental income	15,400
Trustee's commissions allocable to income account	2,800
Trustee's commissions allocable to principal account	1,100

(b) The income for trust accounting purposes is $111,800, and the trustee distributes one-half ($55,900) to W and in his discretion makes a contribution of one-quarter ($27,950) to charity X and distributes the remaining one-quarter ($27,950) to D. The total of the distributions to beneficiaries is $83,850, consisting of (1) income required to be distributed currently to W of $55,900 and (2) other amounts properly paid or credited to D of $27,950. The income for trust accounting purposes of $111,800 is determined as follows:

Rents		$ 50,000
Dividends		50,000
Tax-exempt interest		20,000
Partially tax-exempt interest		10,000
Total		130,000
Less:		
Rental expenses	$15,400	
Trustee's commissions allocable to income account	2,800	
		18,200
Income as computed under section 643(b)		111,800

(c) The distributable net income of the trust as computed under section 643(a) is $82,750, determined as follows:

Rents			$ 50,000
Dividends			50,000
Partially tax-exempt interest			10,000
Tax-exempt interest	$20,000		
Less:			
Trustee's commissions allocable thereto (20,000/130,000 of $3,900)	$ 600		
Charitable contributions allocable thereto (20,000/130,000 of $27,950)	4,300		
		4,900	
			15,100
Total			125,100
Deductions:			
Rental expenses		15,400	
Trustee's commissions ($3,900 less $600 allocated to tax-exempt interest)		3,300	
Charitable deduction ($27,950 less $4,300 attributable to tax-exempt interest)		23,650	
			42,350
Distributable net income			82,750

In computing the distributable net income of $82,750, the taxable income of the trust was computed with the following modifications: No deductions were allowed for distributions to beneficiaries and for personal exemption of the trust (section 643(a)(1) and (2)); capital gains were excluded and no deduction under section 1202 (relating to the 50 percent deduction for long-term capital gains) was taken into account (section 643(a)(3)); and the tax-exempt interest (as adjusted for expenses and charitable contributions) and the dividend exclusion of $50 were included (section 643(a)(5) and (7)).

(d) Inasmuch as the distributable net income of $82,750 as determined under section 643(a) is less than the sum of the amounts distributed to W and D of $83,850, the deduction allowable to the trust under section 661(a) is such distributable net income as modified under section 661(c) to exclude therefrom the items of income not included in the gross income of the trust, as follows:

Distributable net income		$ 82,750
Less:		
Tax-exempt interest (as adjusted for expenses and the charitable contributions)	$15,100	
Dividend exclusion allowable under section 116	50	
		15,150
Deduction allowable under section 661(a)		67,600

(e) For the purpose of determining the character of the amounts deductible under section 642(c) and section 661(a), the trustee elected to offset the trustee's commissions (other than the portion required to be allocated to tax-exempt interest) against the rental income. The following table shows the determination of the character of the amounts deemed distributed to beneficiaries and contributed to charity.

	Rents	Taxable dividends	Excluded dividends	Tax exempt interest	Partially tax exempt interest	Total
Trust income	$50,000	$49,950	$50	$20,000	$10,000	$130,000
Less:						
Charitable contribution	10,750	10,750	......	4,300	2,150	27,950

	Rents	Taxable dividends	Excluded dividends	Tax exempt interest	Partially tax exempt interest	Total
Rental expenses	15,400	....	....	....	....	15,400
Trustee's commissions	3,300	....	....	600	....	3,900
Total deductions	29,450	10,750	0	4,900	2,150	47,250
Amounts distributable to beneficiaries	20,550	39,200	50	15,100	7,850	82,750

The character of the charitable contribution is determined by multiplying the total charitable contribution ($27,950) by a fraction consisting of each item of trust income, respectively, over the total trust income, except that no part of the dividends excluded from gross income are deemed included in the charitable contribution. For example, the charitable contribution is deemed to consist of rents of $10,750 (50,000/130,000 × $27,950).

(f) The taxable income of the trust is $9,900 determined as follows:

Rental income		$ 50,000
Dividends ($50,000 less $50 exclusion)		49,950
Partially tax-exempt interest		10,000
Capital gains		20,000
Gross income		129,950
Deductions:		
Rental expenses	$15,400	
Trustee's commissions	3,300	
Charitable contributions	23,650	
Capital gain deduction	10,000	
Distributions to beneficiaries	67,600	
Personal exemption	100	
		120,050
Taxable income		9,900

(g) In computing the amount includible in W's gross income under section 662(a)(1), the $55,900 distribution to her is deemed to be composed of the following proportions of the items of income deemed to have been distributed to the beneficiaries by the trust (see paragraph (e) of this example):

Rents (20,550/82,750 × $55,900)	$ 13,882
Dividends (39,250/82,750 × $55,900)	26,515
Partially tax-exempt interest (7,850/82,750 × $55,900)	5,303
Tax-exempt interest (15,100/82,750 × $55,900)	10,200
Total	55,900

Accordingly, W will exclude $10,200 of tax-exempt interest from gross income and will receive the credits and exclusion for dividends received and for partially tax-exempt interest provided in sections 34, 116, and 35, respectively, with respect to the dividends and partially tax-exempt interest deemed to have been distributed to her, her share of the dividends being aggregated with other dividends received by her for purposes of the dividend credit and exclusion. In addition, she may deduct a share of the depreciation deduction proportionate to the trust income allocable to her; that is, one-half of the total depreciation deduction, or $5,000.

(h) Inasmuch as the sum of the amount of income required to be distributed currently to W ($55,900) and the other amounts properly paid, credited, or required to be distributed to D ($27,950) exceeds the distributable net income ($82,750) of the trust as determined under section 643(a), D is deemed to have received $26,850 ($82,750 less $55,900) for income tax purposes. The character of the amounts deemed distributed to her is determined as follows:

Rents (20,550/82,750 × $26,850)	$ 6,668
Dividends (39,250/82,750 × $26,850)	12,735
Partially tax-exempt interest (7,850/82,750 × $26,850)	2,547
Tax-exempt interest (15,100/82,750 × $26,850)	4,900
Total	26,850

Accordingly, D will exclude $4,900 of tax-exempt interest from gross income and will receive the credits and exclusion for dividends received and for partially tax-exempt interest provided in sections 34, 116, and 35, respectively, with respect to the dividends and partially tax-exempt interest deemed to have been distributed to her, her share of the dividends being aggregated with other dividends received by her for purposes of the dividend credit and exclusion. In addition, she may deduct a share of the depreciation deduction proportionate to the trust income allocable to her; that is, one-fourth of the total depreciation deduction, or $2,500.

(i) [Reserved]

(j) The remaining $2,500 of the depreciation deduction is allocated to the amount distributed to charity X and is hence nondeductible by the trust, W, or D. (See § 1.642(e)–1.)

[T.D. 6500, 25 FR 11814, Nov. 26, 1960]

§ 1.663(a)–1 Special rules applicable to sections 661 and 662; exclusions; gifts, bequests, etc.

(a) In general. A gift or bequest of a specific sum of money or of specific property, which is required by the specific terms of the will or trust instrument and is properly paid or credited to a beneficiary, is not allowed as a deduction to an estate or trust under section 661 and is not included in the gross income of a beneficiary under section 662, unless under the terms of the will or trust instrument the gift or bequest is to be paid or credited to the recipient in more than three installments. Thus, in order for a gift or bequest to be excludable from the gross income of the recipient, (1) it must qualify as a gift or bequest of a specific sum of money or of specific property (see paragraph (b) of this section), and (2) the terms of the governing instrument must not provide for its payment in more than three installments (see paragraph (c) of this section). The date when the estate came into existence or the date when the trust was created is immaterial.

(b) Definition of a gift or bequest of a specific sum of money or of specific property. **(1)** In order to qualify as a gift or bequest of a specific sum of money or of specific property under section 663(a), the amount of money or the identity of the specific property must be ascertainable under the terms of a testator's will as of the date of his death, or under the terms of an inter vivos trust instrument as of the date of the inception of the trust. For example, bequests to a decedent's son of the decedent's interest in a partnership and to his daughter of a sum of money equal to the value of the partnership interest are bequests of specific property and of a specific sum of money, respectively. On the other hand, a bequest to the decedent's spouse of money or property, to be selected by the decedent's executor, equal in value to a fraction of the decedent's "adjusted gross estate" is neither a bequest of a specific sum of money or of specific property. The identity of the property and the amount of money specified in the preceding sentence are dependent both on the exercise of the executor's discretion and on the payment of administration expenses and other charges, neither of which are facts existing on the date of the decedent's death. It is immaterial that the value of the bequest is determinable after the decedent's death before the bequest is satisfied (so that gain or loss may be realized by the estate in the transfer of property in satisfaction of it).

(2) The following amounts are not considered as gifts or bequests of a sum of money or of specific property within the meaning of this paragraph:

(i) An amount which can be paid or credited only from the income of an estate or trust, whether from the income for the year of payment or crediting, or from the income accumulated from a prior year;

(ii) An annuity, or periodic gifts of specific property in lieu of or having the effect of an annuity;

(iii) A residuary estate or the corpus of a trust; or

(iv) A gift or bequest paid in a lump sum or in not more than three installments, if the gift or bequest is required to be paid in more than three installments under the terms of the governing instrument.

(3) The provisions of subparagraphs (1) and (2) of this paragraph may be illustrated by the following examples, in which it is assumed that the gift or bequest is not required to be made in more than three installments (see paragraph (c)):

Example 1. Under the terms of a will, a legacy of $5,000 was left to A, 1,000 shares of X company stock was left to W, and the balance of the estate was to be divided equally between W and B. No provision was made in the will for the disposition of income of the estate during the period of administration. The estate had income of $25,000 during the taxable year 1954, which was accumulated and added to corpus for estate accounting purposes. During the taxable year, the executor paid the legacy of $5,000 in a lump sum to A, transferred the X company stock to W, and made no other distributions to beneficiaries. The distributions to A and W qualify for the exclusion under section 663(a)(1).

Example 2. Under the terms of a will, the testator's estate was to be distributed to A. No provision was made in the will for the distribution of the estate's income during the period of administration. The estate had income of $50,000 for the taxable year. The estate distributed to A stock with a basis of $40,000 and with a fair market value of $40,000 on the date of distribution. No other distributions were made during the year. The distribution does not qualify for the exclusion under section 663(a)(1), because it is not a specific gift to A required by the terms of the will. Accordingly, the fair market value of the property ($40,000) represents a distribution within the meaning of sections 661(a) and 662(a) (see § 1.661(a)–2(c)).

Example 3. Under the terms of a trust instrument, trust income is to be accumulated for a period of 10 years. During the eleventh year, the trustee is to distribute $10,000 to B, payable from income or corpus, and $10,000 to C, payable out of accumulated income. The trustee is to distribute the balance of the accumulated income to A. Thereafter, A is to receive all the current income until the trust terminates. Only the distribution to B would qualify for the exclusion under section 663(a)(1).

(4) A gift or bequest of a specific sum of money or of specific property is not disqualified under this paragraph solely because its payment is subject to a condition. For example, provision for a payment by a trust to beneficiary A of $10,000 when he reaches age 25, and $10,000 when he reaches age 30, with payment over to B of any amount not paid to A because of his death, is a gift to A of a specific sum of money payable in two installments, within the meaning of this paragraph, even though the exact amount payable to A cannot be ascertained with certainty under the terms of the trust instrument.

(c) Installment payments. **(1)** In determining whether a gift or bequest of a specific sum of money or of specific property, as defined in paragraph (b) of this section, is required to be paid or credited to a particular beneficiary in more than three installments—

(i) Gifts or bequests of articles for personal use (such as personal and household effects, automobiles, and the like) are disregarded.

(ii) Specifically devised real property, the title to which passes directly from the decedent to the devisee under local law, is not taken into account, since it would not constitute an amount paid, credited, or required to be distributed under section 661 (see paragraph (e) of § 1.661(a)–2).

(iii) All gifts and bequests under a decedent's will (which are not disregarded pursuant to subdivisions (i) and (ii) of this subparagraph) for which no time of payment or crediting is specified, and which are to be paid or credited in the ordinary course of administration of the decedent's estate, are considered as required to be paid or credited in a single installment.

(iv) All gifts and bequests (which are not disregarded pursuant to subdivisions (i) and (ii) of this subparagraph) payable at any one specified time under the terms of the governing instrument are taken into account as a single installment.

For purposes of determining the number of installments paid or credited to a particular beneficiary, a decedent's estate and a testamentary trust shall each be treated as a separate entity.

(2) The application of the rules stated in subparagraph (1) of this paragraph may be illustrated by the following examples:

Example (1). (i) Under the terms of a decedent's will, $10,000 in cash, household furniture, a watch, an automobile, 100 shares of X company stock, 1,000 bushels of grain, 500 head of cattle, and a farm (title to which passed directly to A under local law) are bequeathed or devised outright to A. The will also provides for the creation of a trust for the benefit of A, under the terms of which there are required to be distributed to A, $10,000 in cash and 100 shares of Y company stock when he reaches 25 years of age, $25,000 in cash and 200 shares of Y company stock when he reaches 30 years of age, and $50,000 in cash and 300 shares of Y company stock when he reaches 35 years of age.

(ii) The furniture, watch, automobile, and the farm are excluded in determining whether any gift or bequest is required to be paid or credited to A in more than three installments. These items qualify for the exclusion under section 663(a)(1) regardless of the treatment of the other items of property bequeathed to A.

(iii) The $10,000 in cash, the shares of X company stock, the grain, the cattle and the assets required to create the trust, to be paid or credited by the estate to A and the trust are considered as required to be paid or credited in a single installment to each, regardless of the manner of payment or distribution by the executor, since no time of payment or crediting is specified in the will. The $10,000 in cash and shares of Y company stock required to be distributed by the trust to A when he is 25 years old are considered as required to be paid or distributed as one installment under the trust. Likewise, the distributions to be made by the trust to A when he is 30 and 35 years old are each considered as one installment under the trust. Since the total number of installments to be made by the estate does not exceed three, all of the items of money and property distributed by the estate qualify for the exclusion under section 663(a)(1). Similarly, the three distributions by the trust qualify.

Example (2). Assume the same facts as in example (1), except that another distribution of a specified sum of money is required to be made by the trust to A when he becomes 40 years old. This distribution would also qualify as an installment, thus making four installments in all under the trust. None of the gifts to A under the trust would qualify for the exclusion under section 663(a)(1). The situation as to the estate, however, would not be changed.

Example (3). A trust instrument provides that A and B are each to receive $75,000 in installments of $25,000, to be paid in alternate years. The trustee distributes $25,000 to A in 1954, 1956, and 1958, and to B in 1955, 1957, and 1959. The gifts to A and B qualify for exclusion under section 663(a)(1), although a total of six payments is made. The gifts of $75,000 to each beneficiary are to be separately treated.

[T.D. 6500, 25 FR 11814, Nov. 26, 1960, as amended by T.D. 8849, 64 FR 72540, Dec. 28, 1999]

§ 1.663(a)–2 Charitable, etc., distributions.

Any amount paid, permanently set aside, or to be used for the charitable, etc., purposes specified in section 642(c) and which is allowable as a deduction under that section is not allowed as a deduction to an estate or trust under section 661 or treated as an amount distributed for purposes of determining the amounts includible in gross income of beneficiaries under section 662. Amounts paid, permanently set aside, or to be used for charitable, etc., purposes are deductible by estates or trusts only as provided in section 642(c). * * *

[T.D. 6500, 25 FR 11814, Nov. 26, 1960, as amended by T.D. 7428, 41 FR 34627, Aug. 16, 1976]

§ 1.663(a)–3 Denial of double deduction.

No amount deemed to have been distributed to a beneficiary in a preceding year under section 651 or 661 is included in amounts falling within section 661(a) or 662(a). For example, assume that all of the income of a trust is required to be distributed currently to beneficiary A and both the trust and A report on the calendar year basis. For administrative convenience, the trustee distributes in January and February 1956 a portion of the income of the trust required to be distributed in 1955. The portion of the income for 1955 which was distributed by the trust in 1956 may not be claimed as a deduction by the trust for 1956 since it is deductible by the trust and includible in A's gross income for the taxable year 1955.

[T.D. 6500, 25 FR 11814, Nov. 26, 1960]

§ 1.663(c)–1 Separate shares treated as separate trusts or as separate estates; in general.

(a) If a single trust (or estate) has more than one beneficiary, and if different beneficiaries have substantially separate and independent shares, their shares are treated as separate trusts (or estates) for the sole purpose of determining the amount of distributable net income allocable to the respective beneficiaries under sections 661 and 662. Application of this rule will be significant in, for example, situations in which income is accumulated for beneficiary A but a distribution is made to beneficiary B of both income and corpus in an amount exceeding the share of income that would be distributable to B had there been separate trusts (or estates). In the absence of a separate share rule B would be taxed on income which is accumulated for A. The division of distributable net income into separate shares will limit the tax liability of B. Section 663(c) does not affect the principles of applicable law in situations in which a single trust instrument creates not one but several separate trusts, as opposed to separate shares in the same trust within the meaning of this section.

(b) The separate share rule does not permit the treatment of separate shares as separate trusts (or estates) for any purpose other than the application of distributable net income. It does not, for instance, permit the treatment of separate shares as separate trusts (or estates) for purposes of:

(1) The filing of returns and payment of tax,

(2) The deduction of personal exemption under section 642(b), and

(3) The allowance to beneficiaries succeeding to the trust (or estates) property of excess deductions and unused net operating loss and capital loss carryovers on termination of the trust (or estates)under section 642(h).

(c) The separate share rule may be applicable even though separate and independent accounts are not maintained and are not required to be maintained for each share on the books of account of the trust (or estates), and even though no physical segregation of assets is made or required.

(d) Separate share treatment is not elective. Thus, if a trust (or estates) is properly treated as having separate and independent shares, such treatment must prevail in all taxable years of the trust (or estates) unless an event occurs as a result of which the terms of the trust (or estates) instrument and the requirements of proper administration require different treatment.

[T.D. 6500, 25 FR 11814, Nov. 26, 1960, as amended by T.D. 8849, 64 FR 72540, Dec. 28, 1999]

§ 1.663(c)–2 Rules of administration.

(a) When separate shares come into existence. A separate share comes into existence upon the earliest moment that a fiduciary may reasonably determine, based upon the known facts, that a separate economic interest exists.

(b) Computation of distributable net income for each separate share—(1) General rule. The amount of distributable net income for any share under section 663(c) is computed as if each share constituted a separate trust or estate. Accordingly, each separate share shall calculate its distributable net income based upon its portion of gross income that is includible in distributable net income and its portion of any applicable deductions or losses.

(2) Section 643(b) income. This paragraph (b)(2) governs the allocation of the portion of gross income includible in distributable net income that is income within the meaning of section 643(b). Such gross income is allocated among the separate shares in accordance with the amount of income that each share is entitled to under the terms of the governing instrument or applicable local law.

(3) Income in respect of a decedent. This paragraph (b)(3) governs the allocation of the portion of gross income includible in distributable net income that is income in respect of a decedent within the meaning of section 691(a) and is not income within the meaning of section 643(b). Such gross income is allocated among the separate shares that could potentially be funded with these amounts irrespective of whether the share is entitled to receive any income under the terms of the governing instrument or applicable local law. The amount of such gross income allocated to each share is based on the relative value of each share that could potentially be funded with such amounts.

(4) Gross income not attributable to cash. This paragraph (b)(4) governs the allocation of the portion of gross income includible in distributable net income that is not attributable to cash received by the estate or trust (for example, original issue discount, a distributive share of partnership tax items, and the pro rata share of an S corporation's tax items). Such gross income is allocated among the separate shares in the same proportion as section 643(b) income from the same source would be allocated under the terms of the governing instrument or applicable local law.

(5) Deductions and losses. Any deduction or any loss which is applicable solely to one separate share of the trust or estate is not available to any other share of the same trust or estate.

(c) Computations and valuations. For purposes of calculating distributable net income for each separate share, the fiduciary must use a reasonable and equitable method to make the allocations, calculations, and valuations required by paragraph (b) of this section.

[T.D. 8849, 64 FR 72540, Dec. 28, 1999]

§ 1.663(c)–3 Applicability of separate share rule to certain trusts.

(a) The applicability of the separate share rule provided by section 663(c) to trusts other than qualified revocable trusts within the meaning of sections 645(b)(1) will generally depend upon whether distributions of the trust are to be made in substantially the same manner as if separate trusts had been created. Thus, if an instrument directs a trustee to divide the testator's residuary estate into separate shares (which under applicable law do not constitute separate trusts) for each of the testator's children and the trustee is given discretion, with respect to each share, to distribute or accumulate income or to distribute principal or accumulated income, or to do both, separate shares will exist under section 663(c). In determining whether separate shares exist, it is immaterial whether the principal and any accumulated income of each share is ultimately distributable to the beneficiary of such share, to his descendants, to his appointees under a general or special power of appointment, or to any other beneficiaries (including a charitable organization) designated to receive his share of the trust and accumulated income upon termination of the beneficiary's interest in the share. Thus, a separate share may exist if the instrument provides that upon the death of the beneficiary of the share, the share will be added to the shares of the other beneficiaries of the trust.

(b) Separate share treatment will not be applied to a trust or portion of a trust subject to a power to:

(1) Distribute, apportion, or accumulate income, or

(2) Distribute corpus

to or for one or more beneficiaries within a group or class of beneficiaries, unless payment of income, accumulated income, or corpus of a share of one beneficiary cannot affect the proportionate share of income, accumulated income, or corpus of any shares of the other beneficiaries, or unless substantially proper adjustment must thereafter be made (under the governing instrument) so that substantially separate and independent shares exist.

(c) A share may be considered as separate even though more than one beneficiary has an interest in it. For example, two beneficiaries may have equal, disproportionate, or indeterminate interests in one share which is separate and independent from another share in which one or more beneficiaries have an interest. Likewise, the same person may be a beneficiary of more than one separate share.

(d) Separate share treatment may be given to a trust or portion of a trust otherwise qualifying under this section if the trust or portion of a trust is subject to a power to pay out to a beneficiary of a share (of such trust or portion) an amount of corpus in excess of his proportionate share of the corpus of the trust if the possibility of exercise of the power is remote. For example, if the trust is subject to a power to invade the entire corpus for the health, education, support, or maintenance of A, separate share treatment is applied if exercise of the power requires consideration of A's other income which is so substantial as to make the possibility of exercise of the power remote. If instead it appears that A and B have separate shares in a trust, subject to a power to invade the entire corpus for the comfort, pleasure, desire, or happiness of A, separate share treatment shall not be applied.

* * *

[T.D. 6500, 25 FR 11814, Nov. 26, 1960; 25 FR 14021, Dec. 31, 1960, as amended by T.D. 7633, 44 FR 57926, Oct. 9, 1979; T.D. 8849, 64 FR 72540, Dec. 28, 1999]

§ 1.663(c)–4 Applicability of separate share rule to estates and qualified revocable trusts.

(a) General rule. The applicability of the separate share rule provided by section 663(c) to estates and qualified revocable trusts within the meaning of section 645(b)(1) will generally depend upon whether the governing instrument and applicable local law create separate economic interests in one beneficiary or class of beneficiaries of such estate or trust. Ordinarily, a separate share exists if the economic interests of the beneficiary or class of beneficiaries neither affect nor are affected by the economic interests accruing to another beneficiary or class of beneficiaries. Separate shares include, for example, the income on bequeathed property if the recipient of the specific bequest is entitled to such income and a surviving spouse's elective share that under local law is entitled to income and appreciation or depreciation. Furthermore, a qualified revocable trust for which an election is made under section 645 is always a separate share of the estate and may itself contain two or more separate shares. Conversely, a gift or bequest of a specific sum of money or of property as defined in section 663(a)(1) is not a separate share.

(b) Special rule for certain types of beneficial interests. Notwithstanding the provisions of paragraph (a) of this section, a surviving spouse's elective share that under local law is determined as of the date of the decedent's death and is not entitled to income or any appreciation or depreciation is a separate share. Similarly, notwithstanding the provisions of paragraph (a) of this section, a pecuniary formula bequest that, under the terms of the governing instrument or applicable local law, is not entitled to income or to share in appreciation or depreciation constitutes a separate share if the governing instrument does not provide that it is to be paid or credited in more than three installments.

(c) Shares with multiple beneficiaries and beneficiaries of multiple shares. A share may be considered as separate even though more than one beneficiary has an interest in it. For example, two beneficiaries may have equal, disproportionate, or indeterminate interests in one share which is economically separate and independent from another share in which one or more beneficiaries have an interest. Moreover, the same person may be a beneficiary of more than one separate share.

[T.D. 8849, 64 FR 72544, Dec. 28, 1999]

§ 1.663(c)-5 Examples.

Section 663(c) may be illustrated by the following examples:

Example 1. **(i)** A single trust was created in 1940 for the benefit of A, B, and C, who were aged 6, 4, and 2, respectively. Under the terms of the instrument, the trust income is required to be divided into three equal shares. Each beneficiary's share of the income is to be accumulated until he becomes 21 years of age. When a beneficiary reaches the age of 21, his share of the income may thereafter be either accumulated or distributed to him in the discretion of the trustee. The trustee also has discretion to invade corpus for the benefit of any beneficiary to the extent of his share of the trust estate, and the trust instrument requires that the beneficiary's right to future income and corpus will be proportionately reduced. When each beneficiary reaches 35 years of age, his share of the trust estate shall be paid over to him. The interest in the trust estate of any beneficiary dying without issue and before he has attained the age of 35 is to be equally divided between the other beneficiaries of the trust. All expenses of the trust are allocable to income under the terms of the trust instrument.

(ii) No distributions of income or corpus were made by the trustee prior to 1955, although A became 21 years of age on June 30, 1954. During the taxable year of 1955, the trust has income from royalties of $20,000 and expenses of $5,000. The trustee in his discretion distributes $12,000 to A. Both A and the trust report on the calendar year basis.

(iii) The trust qualifies for the separate share treatment under section 663(c) and the distributable net income must be divided into three parts for the purpose of determining the amount deductible by the trust under section 661 and the amount includible in A's gross income under section 662.

(iv) The distributable net income of each share of the trust is $5,000 ($6,667 less $1,667). Since the amount ($12,000) distributed to A during 1955 exceeds the distributable net income of $5,000 allocated to his share, the trust is deemed to have distributed to him $5,000 of 1955 income and $7,000 of amounts other than 1955 income. Accordingly, the trust is allowed a deduction of $5,000 under section 661. The taxable income of the trust for 1955 is $9,900, computed as follows:

Royalties		$20,000
Deductions:		
Expenses	$ 5,000	
Distribution to A	5,000	
Personal exemption	100	
		10,100
Taxable income		9,900

(v) In accordance with section 662, A must include in his gross income for 1955 an amount equal to the portion ($5,000) of the distributable net income of the trust allocated to his share. Also, the excess distribution of $7,000 made by the trust is subject to the throwback provisions of subpart D (section 665 and following), part I, subchapter J, chapter 1 of the Code, and the regulations thereunder.

Example 2 **(i) Facts.** Testator, who dies in 2000, is survived by a spouse and two children. Testator's will contains a fractional formula bequest dividing the residuary estate between the surviving spouse and a trust for the benefit of the children. Under the fractional formula, the marital bequest constitutes 60% of the estate and the children's trust constitutes 40% of the estate. During the year, the executor makes a partial proportionate distribution of $1,000,000, ($600,000 to the surviving spouse and $400,000 to the children's trust) and makes no other distributions. The estate receives dividend income of $20,000, and pays expenses of $8,000 that are deductible on the estate's federal income tax return.

(ii) Conclusion. The fractional formula bequests to the surviving spouse and to the children's trust are separate shares. Because Testator's will provides for fractional formula residuary bequests, the income and any appreciation in the value of the estate assets are proportionately allocated between the marital share and the trust's share. Therefore, in determining the distributable net income of each share, the income and expenses must be allocated 60% to the marital share and 40% to the trust's share. The distributable net income is $7,200 (60% of income less 60% of expenses) for the marital share and $4,800 (40% of income less 40% of expenses) for the trust's share. Because the amount distributed in partial satisfaction of each bequest exceeds the distributable net income of each share, the estate's distribution deduction under section 661 is limited to the sum of the distributable net income for both shares. The estate is allowed a distribution deduction of $12,000 ($7,200 for the marital share and $4,800 for the trust's share). As a result, the estate has zero taxable income ($20,000 income less $8,000 expenses and $12,000 distribution deduction). Under section 662, the surviving spouse and the trust must include in gross income $7,200 and $4,800, respectively.

Example 3. The facts are the same as in *Example 2,* except that in 2000 the executor makes the payment to partially fund the children's trust but makes no payment to the surviving spouse. The fiduciary must use a reasonable and equitable method to allocate income and expenses to the trust's share. Therefore, depending on when the distribution is made to the trust, it may no longer be reasonable or equitable to determine the distributable net income for the trust's share by allocating to it 40% of the estate's income and expenses for the year. The computation of the distributable net income for the trust's share should take into consideration that after the partial distribution the relative size of the trust's separate share is reduced and the relative size of the spouse's separate share is increased.

Example 4 (i) Facts. Testator, who dies in 2000, is survived by a spouse and one child. Testator's will provides for a pecuniary formula bequest to be paid in not more than three installments to a trust for the benefit of the child of the largest amount that can pass free of the Federal estate tax and a bequest of the residuary to the surviving spouse. The will provides that the bequest to the child's trust is not entitled to any of the estate's income and does not participate in appreciation or depreciation in estate assets. During the 2000 taxable year, the estate receives dividend income of $200,000 and pays expenses of $15,000 that are deductible on the estate's federal income tax return. The executor partially funds the child's trust by distributing to it securities that have an adjusted basis to the estate of $350,000 and a fair market value of $380,000 on the date of distribution. As a result of this distribution, the estate realizes long-term capital gain of $30,000.

(ii) Conclusion. The estate has two separate shares consisting of a formula pecuniary bequest to the child's trust and a residuary bequest to the surviving spouse. Because, under the terms of the will, no estate income is allocated to the bequest to the child's trust, the distributable net income for that trust's share is zero. Therefore, with respect to the $380,000 distribution to the child's trust, the estate is allowed no deduction under section 661, and no amount is included in the trust's gross income under section 662. Because no distributions were made to the spouse, there is no need to compute the distributable net income allocable to the marital share. The taxable income of the estate for the 2000 taxable year is $214,400 ($200,000 (dividend income) plus $30,000 (capital gain) minus $15,000 (expenses) and minus $600 (personal exemption)).

Example 5. The facts are the same as in *Example 4,* except that during 2000 the estate reports on its federal income tax return a pro rata share of an S corporation's tax items and a distributive share of a partnership's tax items allocated on Form K–1s to the estate by the S corporation and by the partnership, respectively. Because, under the terms of the will, no estate income from the S corporation or the partnership would be allocated to the pecuniary bequest to child's trust, none of the tax items attributable to the S corporation stock or the partnership interest is allocated to the trust's separate share. Therefore, with respect to the $380,000 distribution to the trust, the estate is allowed no deduction under section 661, and no amount is included in the trust's gross income under section 662.

Example 6. The facts are the same as in *Example 4,* except that during 2000 the estate receives a distribution of $900,000 from the decedent's individual retirement account that is included in the estate's gross income as income in respect of a decedent under section 691(a). The entire $900,000 is allocated to corpus under applicable local law. Both the separate share for the child's trust and the separate share for the surviving spouse may potentially be funded with the proceeds from the individual retirement account. Therefore, a portion of the $900,000 gross income must be allocated to the trust's separate share. The amount allocated to the trust's share must be based upon the relative values of the two separate shares using a reasonable and equitable method. The estate is entitled to a deduction under section 661 for the portion of the $900,000 properly allocated to the trust's separate share, and the trust must include this amount in income under section 662.

Example 7 (i) Facts. Testator, who dies in 2000, is survived by a spouse and three adult children. Testator's will divides the residue of the estate equally among the three children. The surviving spouse files an election under the applicable state's elective share statute. Under this statute, a surviving spouse is entitled to one-third of the decedent's estate after the payment of debts and expenses. The statute also provides that the surviving spouse is not entitled to any of the estate's income and does not participate in appreciation or depreciation of the estate's assets. However, under the statute, the surviving spouse is entitled to interest on the elective share from the date of the court order directing the payment until the executor actually makes payment. During the estate's 2001 taxable year, the estate distributes to the surviving spouse $5,000,000 in partial satisfaction of the elective share and pays $200,000 of interest on the delayed payment of the elective share. During that year, the estate receives dividend income of $3,000,000 and pays expenses of $60,000 that are deductible on the estate's federal income tax return.

(ii) Conclusion. The estate has four separate shares consisting of the surviving spouse's elective share and each of the three children's residuary bequests. Because the surviving spouse is not entitled to any estate income under state law, none of the estate's gross income is allocated to the spouse's separate share for purposes of determining that share's distributable net income. Therefore, with respect to the $5,000,000 distribution, the estate is allowed no deduction under section 661, and no amount is included in the spouse's gross income under section 662. The $200,000 of interest paid to the spouse must be included in the spouse's gross income under section 61. Because no distributions were made to any other beneficiaries during the year, there is no need to compute the distributable net income of the other three separate shares. Thus, the taxable income of the estate for the 2000 taxable year is $2,939,400 ($3,000,000 (dividend income) minus $60,000 (expenses) and $600 (personal exemption)). The estate's $200,000 interest payment is a nondeductible personal interest expense described in section 1630(h).

Example 8. The will of Testator, who dies in 2000, directs the executor to distribute the X stock and all dividends therefrom to child A and the residue of the estate to child B. The estate has two separate shares consisting of the income on the X stock bequeathed to A and the residue of the estate bequeathed to B. The bequest of the X stock meets the definition of section 663(a)(1) and therefore is not a separate share. If any distributions, other than shares of the X stock, are made during the year to either A or B, then for purposes of determining the distributable net income for the separate shares, gross income attributable to dividends on the X stock must be allocated to A's separate share and any other income must be allocated to B's separate share.

Example 9. The will of Testator, who dies in 2000, directs the executor to divide the residue of the estate equally between Testator's two children, A and B. The will directs the executor to fund A's share first with the proceeds of Testator's individual retirement account. The date of death value of the estate after the payment of debts, expenses, and estate taxes is $9,000,000. During 2000, the $900,000 balance in Testator's individual retirement account is distributed to the estate. The entire $900,000 is allocated to corpus under applicable local law. This amount is income in respect of a decedent within the meaning of section 691(a). The estate has two separate shares, one for the benefit of A and one for the benefit of B. If any distributions are made to either A or B during the year, then, for purposes of determining the distributable net income for each separate share, the $900,000 of income in respect of a decedent must be allocated to A's share.

Example 10. The facts are the same as in *Example 9*, except that the will directs the executor to fund A's share first with X stock valued at $3,000,000, rather than with the proceeds of the individual retirement account. The estate has two separate shares, one for the benefit of A and one for the benefit of B. If any distributions are made to either A or B during the year, then, for purposes of determining the distributable net income for each separate share, the $900,000 of gross income attributable to the proceeds from the individual retirement account must be allocated between the two shares to the extent that they could potentially be funded with those proceeds. The maximum amount of A's share that could potentially be funded with the income in respect of decedent is $1,500,000 ($4,500,000 value of share less $3,000,000 to be funded with stock) and the maximum amount of B's share that could potentially be funded with income in respect of decedent is $4,500,000. Based upon the relative values of these amounts, the gross income attributable to the proceeds of the individual retirement account is allocated $225,000 (or one-fourth) to A's share and $675,000 (or three-fourths) to B's share.

Example 11. The will of Testator, who dies in 2000, provides that after the payment of specific bequests of money, the residue of the estate is to be divided equally among the Testator's three children, A, B, and C. The will also provides that during the period of administration one-half of the income from the residue is to be paid to a designated charitable organization. After the specific bequests of money are paid, the estate initially has three qual separate shares. One share is for the benefit of the charitable organization and A, another share is for the benefit of the charitable organization and B, and the last share is for the benefit of the charitable organization and C. During the period of administration, payments of income to the charitable organization are deductible by the estate to the extent provided in section 642(c) and are not subject to the distribution provisions of sections 661 and 662.

[T.D. 6500, 25 FR 11814, Nov. 26, 1960, as amended by T.D. 8849, 64 FR 72540, Dec. 28, 1999; 65 FR 16317, Mar. 28, 2000]

§ 1.664–1 Charitable remainder trusts.

(a) In general—(1) Introduction—(i) General description of a charitable remainder trust. Generally, a charitable remainder trust is a trust which provides for a specified distribution, at least annually, to one or more beneficiaries, at least one of which is not a charity, for life or for a term of years, with an irrevocable remainder interest to be held for the benefit of, or paid over to, charity. The specified distribution to be paid at least annually must be a sum certain which is not less than 5 percent of the initial net fair market value of all property placed in trust (in the case of a charitable remainder annuity trust) or a fixed percentage which is not less than 5 percent of the net fair market value of the trust assets, valued annually (in the case of a charitable remainder unitrust). A trust created after July 31, 1969, which is a charitable remainder trust is exempt from all of the taxes imposed by subtitle A of the Code for any taxable year of the trust, except for a taxable year beginning before January 1, 2007, in which it has unrelated business taxable income. For taxable years beginning after December 31, 2006, an excise tax, * * *, is imposed on charitable remainder trusts that have unrelated business taxable income. * * *

* * *

(2) Requirement that the trust must be either a charitable remainder annuity trust or a charitable remainder unitrust. A trust is a charitable remainder trust only if it is either a charitable remainder annuity trust in every respect or a charitable remainder unitrust in every respect. For example, a trust which provides for the payment each year to a noncharitable beneficiary of the greater of a sum certain or a fixed percentage of the annual value of the trust assets is not a charitable remainder trust inasmuch as the trust is neither a charitable remainder annuity trust (for the reason that the payment for the year may be a fixed percentage of the annual value of the trust assets which is not a "sum certain") nor a charitable remainder unitrust (for the reason that the payment for the year may be a sum certain which is not a "fixed percentage" of the annual value of the trust assets).

(3) Restrictions on investments. A trust is not a charitable remainder trust if the provisions of the trust include a provision which restricts the trustee from investing the trust assets in a manner which could result in the annual realization of a reasonable amount of income or gain from the sale or disposition of trust assets. * * *

(4) Requirement that trust must meet definition of and function exclusively as a charitable remainder trust from its creation. In order for a trust to be a charitable remainder trust, it must meet the definition of and function exclusively as a charitable remainder trust from the creation of the trust. Solely for the purposes of section 664 and the regulations thereunder, the trust will be deemed to be created at the earliest time that neither the grantor nor any other person is treated as the owner of the entire trust under subpart E, part 1, subchapter J, chapter 1, subtitle A of the Code (relating to grantors and others treated as substantial owners), but in no event prior to the time property is first transferred to the trust. For purposes of the preceding sentence, neither the grantor nor his spouse shall be treated as the owner of the trust under such subpart E merely because the grantor or his spouse is named as a recipient.

* * *

(7) Valuation of unmarketable assets—(i) In general. If unmarketable assets are transferred to or held by a trust, the trust will not be a trust with respect to which a deduction is available under section 170, 2055, 2106, or 2522, or will be treated as failing to function exclusively as a charitable remainder trust unless, whenever the trust is required to value such assets, the valuation is—

(a) Performed exclusively by an independent trustee; or

(b) Determined by a *current qualified appraisal,* as defined in § 1.170A–13(c)(3), from a *qualified appraiser,* as defined in § 1.170A–13(c)(5).

(ii) Unmarketable assets. Unmarketable assets are assets that are not cash, cash equivalents, or other assets that can be readily sold or exchanged for cash or cash equivalents. For example, unmarketable assets include real property, closely-held stock, and an unregistered security for which there is no available exemption permitting public sale.

(iii) Independent trustee. An independent trustee is a person who is not the grantor of the trust, a noncharitable beneficiary, or a related or subordinate party to the grantor, the grantor's spouse, or a noncharitable beneficiary (within the meaning of section 672(c) and the applicable regulations).

* * *

(d) Treatment of annual distributions to recipients—(1) Character of distributions—(i) Assignment of income to categories and classes at the trust level. ***(a)*** A trust's income, including income includible in gross income and other income, is assigned to one of three categories in the year in which it is required to be taken into account by the trust. These categories are—

(1) Gross income, other than gains and amounts treated as gains from the sale or other disposition of capital assets (referred to as the ordinary income category);

(2) Gains and amounts treated as gains from the sale or other disposition of capital assets (referred to as the capital gains category); and

(3) Other income (including income excluded under part III, subchapter B, chapter 1, subtitle A of the Internal Revenue Code).

(b) Items within the ordinary income and capital gains categories are assigned to different classes based on the Federal income tax rate applicable to each type of income in that category in the year the items are required to be taken into account by the trust. For example, for a trust with a taxable year ending December 31, 2004, the ordinary income category may include a class of qualified dividend income as defined in section 1(h)(11) and a class of all other ordinary income, and the capital gains category may include separate classes for short-term and long-term capital gains and losses, such as a short-term capital gain class, a 28–percent long-term capital gain class (gains and losses from collectibles and section 1202 gains), an unrecaptured section 1250 long-term capital gain class (long-term gains not treated as ordinary income that would be treated as ordinary income if section 1250(b)(1) included all depreciation), a qualified 5–year long-term capital gain class as defined in section 1(h)(9) prior to amendment by the Jobs and Growth Tax Relief Reconciliation Act of 2003 (JGTRRA), Public Law 108–27 (117 Stat. 752), and an all other long-term capital gain class. After items are assigned to a class, the tax rates may change so that items in two or more classes would be taxed at the same rate if distributed to the recipient during a particular year. If the changes to the tax rates are permanent, the undistributed items in those classes are combined into one class. If, however, the changes to the tax rates are only temporary (for example, the new rate for one class will sunset in a future year), the classes are kept separate.

(ii) Order of distributions. ***(a)*** The categories and classes of income (determined under paragraph (d)(1)(i) of this section) are used to determine the character of an annuity or unitrust distribution from the trust in the hands of the recipient irrespective of whether the trust is exempt from taxation under section 664(c) for the year of the distribution. The determination of the character of amounts distributed or deemed distributed at any time during the taxable year of the trust shall be made as of the end of that taxable year. The tax rate or rates to be used in computing the recipient's tax on the distribution shall be the tax rates that are applicable, in the year in which the distribution is required to be made, to the classes of income deemed to make up that distribution, and not the tax rates that are applicable to those classes of income in the year the income is received by the trust. The character of the distribution in the hands of the annuity or unitrust recipient is determined by treating the distribution as being made from each category in the following order:

(1) First, from ordinary income to the extent of the sum of the trust's ordinary income for the taxable year and its undistributed ordinary income for prior years.

(2) Second, from capital gain to the extent of the trust's capital gains determined under paragraph (d)(1)(iv) of this section.

(3) Third, from other income to the extent of the sum of the trust's other income for the taxable year and its undistributed other income for prior years.

(4) Finally, from trust corpus (with corpus defined for this purpose as the net fair market value of the trust assets less the total undistributed income (but not loss) in paragraphs (d)(1)(i)(a) (1) through (3) of this section).

(b) If the trust has different classes of income in the ordinary income category, the distribution from that category is treated as being made from each class, in turn, until exhaustion of the class, beginning with the class subject to the highest Federal income tax rate and ending with the class subject to the lowest Federal income tax rate. If the trust has different classes of net gain in the capital gains category, the distribution from that category is treated as being made first from the short-term capital gain class and then from each class of long-term capital gain, in turn, until exhaustion of the class, beginning with the class subject to the highest Federal income tax rate and ending with the class subject to the lowest rate. If two or more classes within the same category are subject to the same current tax rate, but at least one of those classes will be subject to a different tax rate in a future year (for example, if the current rate sunsets), the order of that class in relation to other classes in the category with the same current tax rate is determined based on the future rate or rates applicable to those classes. Within each category, if there is more than one type of income in a class, amounts treated as distributed from that class are to be treated as consisting of the same proportion of each type of income as the total of the current and undistributed income of that type bears to the total of the current and undistributed income of all types of income included in that class. For example, if rental income and interest income are subject to the same current and future Federal income tax rate and, therefore, are in the same class, a distribution from that class will be treated as consisting of a proportional amount of rental income and interest income.

(iii) Treatment of losses at the trust level— ***(a)*** **Ordinary income category.** A net ordinary loss for the current year is first used to reduce undistributed ordinary income for prior years that is assigned to the same class as the loss. Any excess loss is then used to reduce the current and undistributed ordinary income from other classes, in turn, beginning with the class subject to the highest Federal income tax rate and ending with the class subject to the lowest Federal income tax rate. If any of the loss exists after all the current and undistributed ordinary income from all classes has been offset, the excess is carried forward indefinitely to reduce ordinary income for future years and retains its class assignment. For purposes of this section, the amount of current income and prior years' undistributed income shall be computed without regard to the deduction for net operating losses provided by section 172 or 642(d).

(*b*) **Other income category.** A net loss in the other income category for the current year is used to reduce undistributed income in this category for prior years and any excess is carried forward indefinitely to reduce other income for future years.

(iv) Netting of capital gains and losses at the trust level. Capital gains of the trust are determined on a cumulative net basis under the rules of this paragraph (d)(1) without regard to the provisions of section 1212. For each taxable year, current and undistributed gains and losses within each class are netted to determine the net gain or loss for that class, and the classes of capital gains and losses are then netted against each other in the following order. First, a net loss from a class of long-term capital gain and loss (beginning with the class subject to the highest Federal income tax rate and ending with the class subject to the lowest rate) is used to offset net gain from each other class of long-term capital gain and loss, in turn, until exhaustion of the class, beginning with the class subject to the highest Federal income tax rate and ending with the class subject to the lowest rate. Second, either—

(*a*) A net loss from all the classes of long-term capital gain and loss (beginning with the class subject to the highest Federal income tax rate and ending with the class subject to the lowest rate) is used to offset any net gain from the class of short-term capital gain and loss; or

(*b*) A net loss from the class of short-term capital gain and loss is used to offset any net gain from each class of long-term capital gain and loss, in turn, until exhaustion of the class, beginning with the class subject to the highest Federal income tax rate and ending with the class subject to the lowest Federal income tax rate.

(v) Carry forward of net capital gain or loss by the trust. If, at the end of a taxable year, a trust has, after the application of paragraph (d)(1)(iv) of this section, any net loss or any net gain that is not treated as distributed under paragraph (d)(1)(ii)(a)(2) of this section, the net gain or loss is carried over to succeeding taxable years and retains its character in succeeding taxable years as gain or loss from its particular class.

(vi) Special transitional rules. To be eligible to be included in the class of qualified dividend income, dividends must meet the definition of section 1(h)(11) and must be received by the trust after December 31, 2002. Long-term capital gain or loss properly taken into account by the trust before January 1, 1997, is included in the class of all other long-term capital gains and losses. Long-term capital gain or loss properly taken into account by the trust on or after January 1, 1997, and before May 7, 1997, if not treated as distributed in 1997, is included in the class of all other long-term capital gains and losses. Long-term capital gain or loss (other than 28–percent gain (gains and losses from collectibles and section 1202 gains), unrecaptured section 1250 gain (long-term gains not treated as ordinary income that would be treated as ordinary income if section 1250(b)(1) included all depreciation), and qualified 5–year gain as defined in section 1(h)(9) prior to amendment by JGTRRA), properly taken into account by the trust before January 1, 2003, and distributed during 2003 is treated as if it were properly taken into account by the trust after May 5, 2003. Long-term capital gain or loss (other than 28–percent gain, unrecaptured section 1250 gain, and qualified 5–year gain), properly taken into account by the trust on or after January 1, 2003, and before May 6, 2003, if not treated as distributed during 2003, is included in the class of all other long-term capital gain. Qualified 5–year gain properly taken into account by the trust after December 31, 2000, and before May 6, 2003, if not treated as distributed by the trust in 2003 or a prior year, must be maintained in a separate class within the capital gains category until distributed. Qualified 5–year gain properly taken into account by the trust before January 1, 2003, and deemed distributed during 2003 is subject to the same current tax rate as deemed distributions from the class of all other long-term capital gain realized by the trust after May 5, 2003. Qualified 5–year gain properly taken into account by the trust on or after January 1, 2003, and before May 6, 2003, if treated as distributed by the trust in 2003, is subject to the tax rate in effect prior to the amendment of section 1(h)(9) by JGTRRA.

(vii) Application of section 643(a)(7). For application of the anti-abuse rule of section 643(a)(7) to distributions from charitable remainder trusts, see § 1.643(a)–8.

(viii) Examples. The following examples illustrate the rules in this paragraph (d)(1):

Example 1. (i) X, a charitable remainder annuity trust described in section 664(d)(1), is created on January 1, 2003. The annual annuity amount is $100. X's income for the 2003 tax year is as follows:

Interest income	$80
Qualified dividend income	50
Capital gains and losses	0
Tax-exempt income	0

(ii) In 2003, the year this income is received by the trust, qualified dividend income is subject to a different rate of Federal income tax than interest income and is, therefore, a separate class of income in the ordinary income category. The annuity amount is deemed to be distributed from the classes within the ordinary income category, beginning with the class subject to the highest Federal income tax rate and ending with the class subject to the lowest rate. Because during 2003 qualified dividend income is taxed at a lower rate than interest income, the interest income is deemed distributed prior to the qualified dividend income. Therefore, in the hands of the recipient, the 2003 annuity amount has the following characteristics:

Interest income	$80
Qualified dividend income	20

(iii) The remaining $30 of qualified dividend income that is not treated as distributed to the recipient in 2003 is carried forward to 2004 as undistributed qualified dividend income.

Example 2. (i) The facts are the same as in Example 1, and at the end of 2004, X has the following classes of income:

Interest income class	$ 5
Qualified dividend income class ($10 from 2004 and $30 carried forward from 2003)	40
Net short-term capital gain class	15
Net long-term capital loss in 28–percent class	(325)
Net long-term capital gain in unrecaptured section 1250 gain class	175
Net long-term capital gain in all other long-term capital gain class	350

(ii) In 2004, gain in the unrecaptured section 1250 gain class is subject to a 25–percent Federal income tax rate, and gain in the all other long-term capital gain class is subject to a lower rate. The net long-term capital loss in the 28–percent gain class is used to offset the net capital gains in the other classes of long-term capital gain and loss, beginning with the class subject to the highest Federal income tax rate and ending with the class subject to the lowest rate. The $325 net loss in the 28–percent gain class reduces the $175 net gain in the unrecaptured section 1250 gain class to $0. The remaining $150 loss from the 28–percent gain class reduces the $350 gain in the all other long-term capital gain class to $200. As in Example 1, qualified dividend income is taxed at a lower rate than interest income during 2004. The annuity amount is deemed to be distributed from all the classes in the ordinary income category and then from the classes in the capital gains category, beginning with the class subject to the highest Federal income tax rate and ending with the class subject to the lowest rate. In the hands of the recipient, the 2004 annuity amount has the following characteristics:

Interest income	$ 5
Qualified dividend income	40
Net short-term capital gain	15
Net long-term capital gain in all other long-term capital gain class	40

(iii) The remaining $160 gain in the all other long-term capital gain class that is not treated as distributed to the recipient in 2004 is carried forward to 2005 as gain in that same class.

* * *

[T.D. 7202, 37 FR 16913, Aug. 23, 1972; 37 FR 28288, Dec. 22, 1972; T.D. 7955, 49 FR 19983, May 11, 1984; T.D. 8540, 59 FR 30100, June 10, 1994; T.D. 8791, 63 FR 68188, Dec. 10, 1998; T.D. 8819, 64 FR 23187, April 29, 1999; T.D. 8926, 66 FR 1034, Jan. 5, 2001; T.D. 9190, 70 FR 12793, Mar. 16, 2005; T.D. 9403, 73 FR 35583, June 24, 2008; T.D. 9448, 74 FR 2137, May 7, 2009; T.D. 9540, 76 FR 49570, Aug. 10, 2011]

§ 1.664–2 Charitable remainder annuity trust.

(a) Description. A charitable remainder annuity trust is a trust which complies with the applicable provisions of § 1.664–1 and meets all of the following requirements:

(1) Required payment of annuity amount—(i) Payment of sum certain at least annually. The governing instrument provides that the trust will pay a sum certain not less often than annually to a person or persons described in paragraph (a)(3) of this section for each taxable year of the period specified in paragraph (a)(5) of this section.

* * *

(ii) Definition of sum certain. A sum certain is a stated dollar amount which is the same either as to each recipient or as to the total amount payable for each year of such period. For example, a provision for an amount which is the same every year to A until his death and concurrently an amount which is the same every year to B until his death, with the amount to each recipient to terminate at his death, would satisfy the above rule. Similarly, provisions for an amount to A and B for their joint lives and then to the survivor would satisfy the above rule. In the case of a distribution to an organization described in section 170(c) at the death of a recipient or the expiration of a term of years, the governing instrument may provide for a reduction of the stated amount payable after such a distribution provided that:

(a) The reduced amount payable is the same either as to each recipient or as to the total amount payable for each year of the balance of such period, and

(b) The requirements of subparagraph (2)(ii) of this paragraph are met.

(iii) Sum certain stated as a fraction or percentage. The stated dollar amount may be expressed as a fraction or a percentage of the initial net fair market value of the property irrevocably passing in trust as finally determined for Federal tax purposes. If the stated dollar amount is so expressed and such market value is incorrectly determined by the fiduciary, the requirement of this subparagraph will be satisfied if the governing instrument provides that in such event the trust shall pay to the recipient (in the case of an undervaluation) or be repaid by the recipient (in the case of an overvaluation) an amount equal to the difference between the amount which the trust should have paid the recipient if the correct value were used and the amount which the trust actually paid the recipient. Such payments or repayments must be made within a reasonable period after the final determination of such value. * * * The application of the rule permitting the stated dollar amount to be expressed as a fraction or a percentage of the initial net fair market value of the property irrevocably passing in trust as finally determined for Federal tax purposes may be illustrated by the following example:

Example. The will of X provides for the transfer of one-half of his residuary estate to a charitable remainder annuity trust which is required to pay to W for life an annuity equal to 5 percent of the initial net fair market value of the interest passing in trust as finally determined for Federal tax purposes. The annuity is to be paid on December 31 of each year computed from the date of X's death. The will also provides that if such initial net fair market value is incorrectly determined, the trust shall pay to W, in the case of an undervaluation, or be repaid by W, in the case of an overvaluation, an amount equal to the difference between the amount which the trust should have paid if the correct value were used and the amount which the trust actually paid. X dies on March 1, 1971. The executor files an estate tax return showing the value of the residuary estate as $250,000 before reduction for taxes and expenses of $50,000. The executor paid to W $4,192 ([$250,000–$50,000] × ½ × 5 percent × 306/365) on December 31, 1971. On January 1, 1972, the executor transfers one-half of the residue of the estate to the trust. The trust adopts the calendar year as its taxable year. The value of the residuary estate is finally determined for Federal tax purposes to be $240,000 ($290,000–$50,000). Accordingly, the amount which the executor should have paid to W is $5,030 ([$290,000–$50,000] × ½ × 5 percent × 306/365). Consequently, an additional amount of $838 ($5,030–$4,192) must be paid to W within a reasonable period after the final determination of value for Federal tax purposes.

* * *

(2) Minimum annuity amount—(i) General rule. The total amount payable under subparagraph (1) of this paragraph is not less than 5 percent of the initial net fair market value of the property placed in trust as finally determined for Federal tax purposes.

(ii) Reduction of annuity amount in certain cases. A trust will not fail to meet the requirements of this subparagraph by reason of the fact that it provides for a reduction of the stated amount payable upon the death of a recipient or the expiration of a term of years provided that:

(a) A distribution is made to an organization described in section 170(c) at the death of such recipient or the expiration of such term of years, and

(b) The total amounts payable each year under subparagraph (1) of this paragraph after such distribution are not less than a stated dollar amount which bears the same ratio to 5 percent of the initial net fair market value of the trust assets as the net fair market value of the trust assets immediately after such distribution bears to the net fair market value of the trust assets immediately before such distribution.

(iii) Rule applicable to inter vivos trust which does not provide for payment of minimum annuity amount. In the case where the grantor of an inter vivos trust underestimates in good faith the initial net fair market value of the property placed in trust as finally determined for Federal tax purposes and specifies a fixed dollar amount for the annuity which is less than 5 percent of the initial net fair market value of the property placed in trust as finally determined for Federal tax purposes, the trust will be deemed to have met the 5 percent requirement if the grantor or his representative consents, by appropriate agreement with the District Director, to accept an amount equal to 20 times the annuity as the fair market value of the property placed in trust for purposes of determining the appropriate charitable contributions deduction.

(3) Permissible recipients—(i) General rule. The amount described in subparagraph (1) of this paragraph is payable to or for the use of a named person or persons, at least one of which is not an organization described in section 170(c). If the amount described in subparagraph (1) of this paragraph is to be paid to an individual or individuals, all such individuals must be living at the time of the creation of the trust. A named person or persons may include members of a named class provided that, in the case of a class which includes any individual, all such individuals must be alive and ascertainable at the time of the creation of the trust unless the period for which the annuity amount is to be paid to such class consists solely of a term of years. For example, in the case of a testamentary trust, the testator's will may provide that an amount shall be paid to his children living at his death.

(ii) Power to alter amount paid to recipients. A trust is not a charitable remainder annuity trust if any person has the power to alter the amount to be paid to any named person other than an organization described in section 170(c) if such power would cause any person to be treated as the owner of the trust, or any portion thereof, if subpart E, Part 1, subchapter J, chapter 1, Subtitle A of the Code were applicable to such trust. See paragraph (a)(4) of this section for a rule permitting the retention by a grantor of a testamentary power to revoke or terminate the interest of any recipient other than an organization described in section 170(c). For example, the governing instrument may not grant the trustee the power to allocate the annuity among members of a class unless such power falls within one of the exceptions to section 674(a).

(4) Other payments. No amount other than the amount described in subparagraph (1) of this paragraph may be paid to or for the use of any person other than an organization described in section 170(c). An amount is not paid to or for the use of any person other than an organization described in section 170(c) if the amount is transferred for full and adequate consideration. The trust may not be subject to a power to invade, alter, amend, or revoke for the beneficial use of a person other than an organization described in section 170(c). Notwithstanding the preceding sentence, the grantor may retain the power exercisable only by will to revoke or terminate the interest of any recipient other than an organization described in section 170(c). The governing instrument may provide that any amount other than the amount described in subparagraph (1) of this paragraph shall be paid (or may be paid in the discretion of the trustee) to an organization described in section 170(c) provided that in the case of distributions in kind, the adjusted basis of the property distributed is fairly representative of the adjusted basis of the property available for payment on the date of payment. For example, the governing instrument may provide that a portion of the trust assets may be distributed currently, or upon the death of one or more recipients, to an organization described in section 170(c).

(5) Period of payment of annuity amount—(i) General rules. The period for which an amount described in subparagraph (1) of this paragraph is payable begins with the first year of the charitable remainder trust and continues either for the life or lives of a named individual or individuals or for a term of years not to exceed 20 years. Only an individual or an organization described in section 170(c) may receive an amount for the life of an individual. If an individual receives an amount for life, it must be solely for his life. Payment of the amount described in subparagraph (1) of this paragraph may terminate with the regular payment next preceding the termination of the period described in this subparagraph. The fact that the recipient may not receive such last payment shall not be taken into account for purposes of determining the present value of the remainder interest. In the case of an amount payable for a term of years, the length of the term of years shall be ascertainable with certainty at the time of the creation of the trust, except that the term may be terminated by the death of the recipient or by the grantor's exercise by will of a retained power to revoke or terminate the interest of any recipient other than an organization described in section 170(c). In any event, the period may not extend beyond either the life or lives of a named individual or individuals or a term of years not to exceed 20 years. For example, the governing instrument may not provide for the payment of an annuity amount to A for his life and then to B for a term of years because it is possible for the period to last longer than either the lives of recipients in being at the creation of the trust or a term of years not to exceed 20 years. On the other hand, the governing instrument may provide for the payment of an annuity amount to A for his life and then to B for his life or a term of years (not to exceed 20 years), whichever is shorter (but not longer), if both A and B are in being at the creation of the trust because it is not possible for the period to last longer than the lives of recipients in being at the creation of the trust.

(ii) Relationship to 5 percent requirement. The 5 percent requirement provided in subparagraph (2) of this paragraph must be met until the termination of all of the payments described in subparagraph (1) of this paragraph. For example, the following provisions would satisfy the above rules:

(a) An amount equal to at least 5 percent of the initial net fair market value of the property placed in trust to A and B for their joint lives and then to the survivor for his life;

(b) An amount equal to at least 5 percent of the initial net fair market value of the property placed in trust to A for life or for a term of years not longer than 20 years, whichever is longer (or shorter);

(c) An amount equal to at least 5 percent of the initial net fair market value of the property placed in trust to A for a term of years not longer than 20 years and then to B for life (provided B was living at the date of creation of the trust);

(d) An amount to A for his life and concurrently an amount to B for his life (the amount to each recipient to terminate at his death) if the amount given to each individual is not less than 5 percent of the initial net fair market value of the property placed in trust; or

(e) An amount to A for his life and concurrently an equal amount to B for his life, and at the death of the first to die, the trust to distribute one-half of the then value of its assets to an organization described in section 170(c), if the total of the amounts given to A and B is not less than 5 percent of the initial net fair market value of the property placed in trust.

(6) Permissible remaindermen—(i) General rule. At the end of the period specified in subparagraph (5) of this paragraph the entire corpus of the trust is required to be irrevocably transferred, in whole or in part, to or for the use of one or more organizations described in section 170(c) or retained, in whole or in part, for such use.

(ii) Treatment of trust. If all of the trust corpus is to be retained for such use, the taxable year of the trust shall terminate at the end of the period specified in subparagraph (5) of this paragraph and the trust shall cease to be treated as a charitable remainder trust for all purposes. If all or any portion of the trust corpus is to be transferred to or for the use of such organization or organizations, the trustee shall have a reasonable time after the period specified in subparagraph (5) of this paragraph to complete the settlement of the trust. During such time, the trust shall continue to be treated as a charitable remainder trust for all purposes, such as sections 664, 4947(a)(2), and 4947(b)(3)(B). Upon the expiration of such period, the taxable year of the trust shall terminate and the trust shall cease to be treated as a charitable remainder trust for all purposes. If the trust continues in existence, it will be subject to the provisions of section 4947(a)(1) unless the trust is exempt from taxation under section 501(a). For purposes of determining whether the trust is exempt under section 501(a) as an organization described in section 501(c)(3), the trust shall be deemed to have been created at the time it ceases to be treated as a charitable remainder trust.

(iii) Concurrent or successive remaindermen. Where interests in the corpus of the trust are given to more than one organization described in section 170(c) such interests may be enjoyed by them either concurrently or successively.

(iv) Alternative remaindermen. The governing instrument shall provide that if an organization to or for the use of which the trust corpus is to be transferred or for the use of which the trust corpus is to be retained is not an organization described in section 170(c) at the time any amount is to be irrevocably transferred to or for the use of such organization, such amount shall be transferred to or for the use of one or more alternative organizations which are described in section 170(c) at such time or retained for such use. Such alternative organization or organizations may be selected in any manner provided by the terms of the governing instrument.

(b) Additional contributions. A trust is not a charitable remainder annuity trust unless its governing instrument provides that no additional contributions may be made to the charitable remainder annuity trust after the initial contribution. For purposes of this section, all property passing to a charitable remainder annuity trust by reason of death of the grantor shall be considered one contribution.

(c) Calculation of the fair market value of the remainder interest of a charitable remainder annuity trust. For purposes of sections 170, 2055, 2106, and 2522, the fair market value of the remainder interest of a charitable remainder annuity trust (as described in this section) is the net fair market value (as of the appropriate valuation date) of the property placed in trust less the present value of the annuity. For purposes of this section, valuation date means, in general, the date on which the property is transferred to the trust by the donor regardless of when the trust is created. * * *

(d) Deduction for transfers to a charitable remainder annuity trust. For rules relating to a deduction for transfers to a charitable remainder annuity trust, see sections 170, 2055, 2106, or 2522 and the regulations thereunder. Any claim for deduction on any return for the value of a remainder interest in a charitable remainder annuity trust must be supported by a full statement attached to the return showing the computation of the present value of such interest. The deduction allowed by section 170 is limited to the fair market value of the remainder interest of a charitable remainder annuity trust regardless of whether an organization described in section 170(c) also receives a portion of the annuity. For a special rule relating to the reduction of the amount of a charitable contribution deduction with respect to a contribution of certain ordinary income property or capital gain property, see sections 170(e)(1)(A) or 170(e)(1)(B)(i) and the regulations thereunder. For rules for postponing the time for deduction of a charitable contribution of a future interest in tangible personal property, see section 170(a)(3) and the regulations thereunder.

* * *

[T.D. 7202, 37 FR 16918, Aug. 23, 1972, as amended by T.D. 7955, 49 FR 19983, May 11, 1984; T.D. 8540, 59 FR 30100, June 10, 1994; T.D. 8791, 63 FR 68188, Dec. 10, 1998; T.D. 8819, 64 FR 23187, April 29, 1999; T.D. 8926, 66 FR 1034, Jan. 5, 2001; T.D. 9448, 74 FR 21437, May 7, 2009; T.D. 9540, 76 FR 49570, Aug. 9, 2011]

§ 1.664–3 Charitable remainder unitrust.

(a) Description. A charitable remainder unitrust is a trust which complies with the applicable provisions of § 1.664–1 and meets all of the following requirements:

(1) Required payment of unitrust amount—(i) Payment of fixed percentage at least annually—(a) General rule. The governing instrument provides that the trust will pay not less often than annually a fixed percentage of the net fair market value of the trust assets determined annually to a person or persons described in paragraph (a)(3) of this section for each taxable year of the period specified in subparagraph (a)(5) of this section. * * *

(b) Income exception. Instead of the amount described in (a) of this subdivision (i), the governing instrument may provide that the trust shall pay for any year either the amount described in (1) or the total of the amounts described in (1) and (2) of this subdivision (b).

(1) The amount of trust income for a taxable year to the extent that such amount is not more than the amount required to be distributed under paragraph (a)(1)(i)(a) of this section.

(2) An amount of trust income for a taxable year that is in excess of the amount required to be distributed under paragraph (a)(1)(i)(a) of this section for such year to the extent that (by reason of paragraph (a)(1)(i)(b)(1) of this section) the aggregate of the amounts paid in prior years was less than the aggregate of such required amounts.

(3) For purposes of this paragraph (a)(1)(i)(b), trust income generally means income as defined under section 643(b) and the applicable regulations. However, trust income may not be determined by reference to a fixed percentage of the annual fair market value of the trust property, notwithstanding any contrary provision in applicable state law. Proceeds from the sale or exchange of any assets contributed to the trust by the donor must be allocated to principal and not to trust income at least to the extent of the fair market value of those assets on the date of their contribution to the trust. Proceeds from the sale or exchange of any assets purchased by the trust must be allocated to principal and not to trust income at least to the extent of the trust's purchase price of those assets. Except as provided in the two preceding sentences, proceeds from the sale or exchange of any assets contributed to the trust by the donor or purchased by the trust may be allocated to income, pursuant to the terms of the governing instrument, if not prohibited by applicable local law. A discretionary power to make this allocation may be granted to the trustee under the terms of the governing instrument but only to the extent that the state statute permits the trustee to make adjustments between income and principal to treat beneficiaries impartially.

(4) The rules in paragraph (a)(1)(i)(b)(1) and (2) of this section are applicable for taxable years ending after April 18, 1997. The rule in the first sentence of paragraph (a)(1)(i)(b)(3) is applicable for taxable years ending after April 18, 1997. The rules in the second, fourth, and fifth sentences of paragraph (a)(1)(i)(b)(3) are applicable for taxable years ending after January 2, 2004. The rule in the third sentence of paragraph (a)(1)(i)(b)(3) is applicable for sales or exchanges that occur after April 18, 1997. The rule in the sixth sentence of paragraph (a)(1)(i)(b)(3) is applicable for trusts created after January 2, 2004.

(c) Combination of methods. Instead of the amount described in paragraph (a)(1)(i)(a) or (b) of this section, the governing instrument may provide that the trust will pay not less often than annually the amount described in paragraph (a)(1)(i)(b) of this section for an initial period and then pay the amount described in paragraph (a)(1)(i)(a) of this section (calculated using the same fixed percentage) for the remaining years of the trust only if the governing instrument provides that—

(1) The change from the method prescribed in paragraph (a)(1)(i)(b) of this section to the method prescribed in paragraph (a)(1)(i)(a) of this section is triggered on a specific date or by a single event whose occurrence is not discretionary with, or within the control of, the trustees or any other persons;

(2) The change from the method prescribed in paragraph (a)(1)(i)(b) of this section to the method prescribed in paragraph (a)(1)(i)(a) of this section occurs at the beginning of the taxable year that immediately follows the taxable year during which the date or event specified under paragraph (a)(1)(i)(c)(1) of this section occurs; and

(3) Following the trust's conversion to the method described in paragraph (a)(1)(i)(a) of this section, the trust will pay at least annually to the permissible recipients the amount described only in paragraph (a)(1)(i)(a) of this section and not any amount described in paragraph (a)(1)(i)(b) of this section.

(d) Triggering event. For purposes of paragraph (a)(1)(i)(c)(1) of this section, a triggering event based on the sale of unmarketable assets as defined in § 1.664–1(a)(7)(ii), or the marriage, divorce, death, or birth of a child with respect to any individual will not be considered discretionary with, or within the control of, the trustees or any other persons.

(e) Examples. The following examples illustrate the rules in paragraph (a)(1)(i)(c) of this section. For each example, assume that the governing instrument of charitable remainder unitrust *Y* provides that *Y* will initially pay not less often than annually the amount described in paragraph (a)(1)(i)(b) of this section and then pay the amount described in paragraph (a)(1)(i)(a) of this section (calculated using the same fixed percentage) for the remaining years of the trust and that the requirements of paragraphs (a)(1)(i)(c)(2) and (3) of this section are satisfied. The examples are as follows:

Example 1. *Y* is funded with the donor's former personal residence. The governing instrument of *Y* provides for the change in method for computing the annual unitrust amount as of the first day of the year following the year in which the trust sells the residence. *Y* provides for a combination of methods that satisfies paragraph (a)(1)(i)(c) of this section.

Example 2. Y is funded with cash and an unregistered security for which there is no available exemption permitting public sale under the Securities and Exchange Commission rules. The governing instrument of *Y* provides that the change in method for computing the annual unitrust amount is triggered on the earlier of the date when the stock is sold or at the time the restrictions on its public sale lapse or are otherwise lifted. *Y* provides for a combination of methods that satisfies paragraph (a)(1)(i)(c) of this section.

Example 3. *Y* is funded with cash and with a security that may be publicly traded under the Securities and Exchange Commission rules. The governing instrument of *Y* provides that the change in method for computing the annual unitrust amount is triggered when the stock is sold. *Y* does not provide for a combination of methods that satisfies the requirements of paragraph (a)(1)(i)(c) of this section because the sale of the publicly-traded stock is within the discretion of the trustee.

Example 4. S establishes *Y* for her granddaughter, *G*, when *G* is 10 years old. The governing instrument of *Y* provides for the change in method for computing the annual unitrust amount as of the first day of the year following the year in which *G* turns 18 years old. *Y* provides for a combination of methods that satisfies paragraph (a)(1)(i)(c) of this section.

Example 5. The governing instrument of *Y* provides for the change in method for computing the annual unitrust amount as of the first day of the year following the year in which the donor is married. *Y* provides for a combination of methods that satisfies paragraph (a)(1)(i)(c) of this section.

Example 6. The governing instrument of *Y* provides that if the donor divorces, the change in method for computing the annual unitrust amount will occur as of the first day of the year following the year of the divorce. *Y* provides for a combination of methods that satisfies paragraph (a)(1)(i)(c) of this section.

Example 7. The governing instrument of *Y* provides for the change in method for computing the annual unitrust amount as of the first day of the year following the year in which the noncharitable beneficiary's first child is born. *Y* provides for a combination of methods that satisfies paragraph (a)(1)(i)(c) of this section.

Example 8. The governing instrument of *Y* provides for the change in method for computing the annual unitrust amount as of the first day of the year following the year in which the noncharitable beneficiary's father dies. *Y* provides for a combination of methods that satisfies paragraph (a)(1)(i)(c) of this section.

Example 9. The governing instrument of *Y* provides for the change in method for computing the annual unitrust amount as of the first day of the year following the year in which the noncharitable beneficiary's financial advisor determines that the beneficiary should begin receiving payments under the second prescribed payment method. Because the change in methods for paying the unitrust amount is triggered by an event that is within a person's control, *Y* does not provide for a combination of methods that satisfies paragraph (a)(1)(i)(c) of this section.

Example 10. The governing instrument of *Y* provides for the change in method for computing the annual unitrust amount as of the first day of the year following the year in which the noncharitable beneficiary submits a request to the trustee that the trust convert to the second prescribed payment method. Because the change in methods for paying the unitrust amount is triggered by an event that is within a person's control, *Y* does not provide for a combination of methods that satisfies paragraph (a)(1)(i)(c) of this section.

* * *

(ii) Definition of fixed percentage. The fixed percentage may be expressed either as a fraction or as a percentage and must be payable each year in the period specified in subparagraph (5) of this paragraph. A percentage is fixed if the percentage is the same either as to each recipient or as to the total percentage payable each year of such period. For example, provision for a fixed percentage which is the same every year to A until his death and concurrently a fixed percentage which is the same every year to B until his death, the fixed percentage to each recipient to terminate at his death, would satisfy the rule. Similarly, provision for a fixed percentage to A and B for their joint lives and then to the survivor would satisfy the rule. * * *

* * *

[T.D. 7202, 37 FR 16920, Aug. 23, 1972, as amended by T.D. 8791, 63 FR 68188, Dec. 10, 1998; T.D. 8926, 66 FR 1034, Jan. 5, 2001; T.D. 9102, 69 FR 12, Jan. 2, 2004]

§ 1.665(a)–0A Excess distributions by trusts; scope of subpart D.

(a) In general. **(1)** Subpart D (section 665 and following), part I, subchapter J, chapter 1 of the Code as amended by the Tax Reform Act of 1969, is designed to tax the beneficiary of a trust that accumulates, rather than distributes, all or part of its income currently (i.e., an accumulation trust), in most cases, as if the income had been currently distributed to the beneficiary instead of accumulated by the trusts. Accordingly, subpart D provides special rules for the treatment of amounts paid, credited, or required to be distributed by a complex trust (one that is subject to subpart C (section 661 and following) of such part I) in any year in excess of "distributable net income" (as defined in section 643(a)) for that year. Such an excess distribution is an "accumulation distribution" (as defined in section 665(b)). The special rules of subpart D are generally inapplicable to amounts paid, credited, or required to be distributed by a trust in a taxable year in which it qualifies as a simple trust (one that is subject to subpart B (section 651 and following) of such part I). * * *

(2) An accumulation distribution is deemed to consist of, first, "undistributed net income" (as defined in section 665(a)) of the trust from preceding taxable years, and, after all the undistributed net income for all preceding taxable years has been deemed distributed, "undistributed capital gain" (as defined in section 665(f)) of the trust for all preceding taxable years commencing with the first year such amounts were accumulated. An accumulation distribution of undistributed capital gain is a "capital gain distribution" (as defined in section 665(g)). To the extent an accumulation distribution exceeds the "undistributed net income" and "undistributed capital gain" so determined, it is deemed to consist of corpus.

(3) The accumulation distribution is "thrown back" to the earliest "preceding taxable year" of the trust, which, in the case of distributions made for a taxable year beginning after December 31, 1973, from a trust (other than a foreign trust created by a U.S. person), is any taxable year beginning after December 31, 1968. * * *

(4) A distribution of undistributed net income (included in an accumulation distribution) and a capital gain distribution will be included in the income of the beneficiary in the year they are actually paid, credited, or required to be distributed to him. The tax on the distribution will be approximately the amount of tax the beneficiary would have paid with respect to the distribution had the income and capital gain been distributed to the beneficiary in the year earned by the trust. An additional amount equal to the "taxes imposed on the trust" for the preceding year is also deemed distributed. To prevent double taxation, however, the beneficiary receives a credit for such taxes.

* * *

(c) Examples. Where examples contained in the regulations under subpart D refer to tax rates for years after 1968, such tax rates are not necessarily the actual rates for such years, but are only used for example purposes.

(d) Applicability to estates. Subpart D does not apply to any estate.

[T.D. 7204, 37 FR 17135, Aug. 25, 1972]

§ 1.665(a)–1A Undistributed net income.

(a) Domestic trusts. The term "undistributed net income", in the case of a trust (other than a foreign trust created by a U.S. person) means, for any taxable year beginning after December 31, 1968, the distributable net income of the trust for that year (as determined under section 643(a)), less:

(1) The amount of income required to be distributed currently and any other amounts properly paid or credited or required to be distributed to beneficiaries in the taxable year as specified in section 661(a), and

(2) The amount of taxes imposed on the trust attributable to such distributable net income, as defined in § 1.665(d)–1A. The application of the rule in this paragraph to a taxable year of a trust in which income is accumulated may be illustrated by the following example:

Example. Under the terms of the trust, $10,000 of income is required to be distributed currently to A and the trustee has discretion to make additional distributions to A. During the taxable year 1971 the trust had distributable net income of $30,100 derived from royalties and the trustee made distributions of $20,000 to A. The taxable income of the trust is $10,000 on which a tax of $2,190 is paid. The undistributed net income of the trust for the taxable year 1971 is $7,910, computed as follows:

Distributable net income		$30,100
Less:		
Income currently distributable to A	$10,000	
Other amounts distributed to A	10,000	
Taxes imposed on the trust attributable to the undistributed net income (see § 1.665(d)–1A)	2,190	
Total		22,190
Undistributed net income		7,910

[T.D. 7204, 37 FR 17136, Aug. 25, 1972]

§ 1.665(b)–1A Accumulation distributions.

(a) In general. **(1)** For any taxable year of a trust the term "accumulation distribution" means an amount by which the amounts properly paid, credited, or required to be distributed within the meaning of section 661(a)(2) (*i.e.,* all amounts properly paid, credited, or required to be distributed to the beneficiary other than income required to be distributed currently within the meaning of section 661(a)(1)) for that year exceed the distributable net income (determined under section 643(a)) of the trust, reduced (but not below zero) by the amount of income required to be distributed currently. To the extent provided in section 663(b) and the regulations thereunder, distributions made within the first 65 days following a taxable year may be treated as having been distributed on the last day of such taxable year.

(2) An accumulation distribution also includes, for a taxable year of the trust, any amount to which section 661(a)(2) and the preceding paragraph are inapplicable and which is paid, credited, or required to be distributed during the taxable year of the trust by reason of the exercise of a power to appoint, distribute, consume, or withdraw corpus of the trust or income of the trust accumulated in a preceding taxable year. No accumulation distribution is deemed to be made solely because the grantor or any other person is treated as owner of a portion of the trust by reason of an unexercised power to appoint, distributed, consume, or withdraw corpus or accumulated income of the trust. Nor will an accumulation distribution be deemed to have been made by reason of the exercise of a power that may affect only taxable income previously attributed to the holders of such power under subpart E (section 671 and following). See example 4 of paragraph (d) of this section for an example of an accumulation distribution occurring as a result of the exercise of a power of withdrawal.

(3) Although amounts properly paid or credited under section 661(a) do not exceed the income of the trust during the taxable year, an accumulation distribution may result if the amounts properly paid or credited under section 661(a)(2) exceed distributable net income reduced (but not below zero) by the amount required to be distributed currently under section 661(a)(1). This may occur, for example, when expenses, interest, taxes, or other items allocable to corpus are taken into account in determining taxable income and hence causing distributable net income to be less than the trust's income.

(b) Payments that are accumulation distributions. The following are some instances in which an accumulation distribution may arise:

(1) One trust to another. A distribution from one trust to another trust is generally an accumulation distribution. See § 1.643(c)–1. This general rule will apply regardless of whether the distribution is to an existing trust or to a newly created trust and regardless of whether the trust to which the distribution is made was created by the same person who created the trust from which the distribution is made or a different person. However, a distribution made from one trust to a second trust will be deemed an accumulation distribution by the first trust to an ultimate beneficiary of the second trust if the primary purpose of the distribution to the second trust is to avoid the capital gain distribution provisions (see section 669 and the regulations thereunder). An amount passing from one separate share of a trust to another separate share of the same trust is not an accumulation distribution. * * *

(2) Income accumulated during minority. A distribution of income accumulated during the minority of the beneficiary is generally an accumulation distribution. For example, if a trust accumulates income until the beneficiary's 21st birthday, and then distributes the income to the beneficiary, such a distribution is an accumulation distribution. * * *

(3) Amounts paid for support. To the extent that amounts forming all or part of an accumulation distribution are applied or distributed for the support of a dependent under the circumstances specified in section 677(b) or section 678(c) or are used to discharge or satisfy any person's legal obligation as that term is used in § 1.662(a)–4, such amounts will be considered as having been distributed directly to the person whose obligation is being satisfied.

* * *

[T.D. 7204, 37 FR 17137, Aug. 25, 1972]

§ 1.665(e)–1A Preceding taxable year.

* * *

(b) Simple trusts. A taxable year of a trust during which the trust was a simple trust (that is, was subject to subpart B) for the entire year shall not be considered a "preceding taxable year" unless during such year the trust received "outside income" or unless the trustee did not distribute all of the income of the trust that was required to be distributed currently for such year. In such event, undistributed net income for such year shall not exceed the greater of the "outside income" or income not distributed during such year. For purposes of this paragraph, the term "outside income" means amounts that are included in distributable net income of the trust for the year but that are not "income" of the trust as that term is defined in § 1.643(b)–1. Some examples of "outside income" are:

(1) Income taxable to the trust under section 691;

(2) Unrealized accounts receivable that were assigned to the trust; and

(3) Distributions from another trust that include distributable net income or undistributed net income of such other trust.

The term "outside income," however, does not include amounts received as distributions from an estate, other than income specified in (1) and (2), for which the estate was allowed a deduction under section 661(a). The application of this paragraph may be illustrated by the following examples:

Example (1). By his will D creates a trust for his widow W. The terms of the trust require that the income be distributed currently (*i.e.*, it is a simple trust), and authorize the trustee to make discretionary payments of corpus to W. Upon W's death the trust corpus is to be distributed to D's then living issue. The executor of D's will makes a $10,000 distribution of corpus to the trust that carries out estate income consisting of dividends and interest to the trust under section 662(a)(2). The trust reports this income as its only income on its income tax return for its taxable year in which ends the taxable year of the estate in which the $10,000 distribution was made, and pays a tax thereon of $2,106. Thus, the trust has undistributed net income of $7,894 ($10,000–$2,106). Several years later the trustee makes a discretionary corpus payment of $15,000 to W. This payment is an accumulation distribution under section 665(b). However, since the trust had no "outside income" in the year of the estate distribution, such year is not a preceding taxable year. Thus, W is not treated as receiving undistributed net income of $7,894 and taxes thereon of $2,106 for the purpose of including the same in her gross income under section 668. The result would be the same if the invasion power were not exercised and the accumulation distribution occurred as a result of the distribution of the corpus to D's issue upon the death of W.

Example (2). Trust A, a simple trust on the calendar year basis, received in 1972 extraordinary dividends or taxable stock dividends that the trustee in good faith allocated to corpus, but that are determined in 1974 to have been currently distributable to the beneficiary. See section 643(a)(4) and § 1.643(a)–4. Trust A would qualify for treatment under subpart C for 1974, the year of distribution of the extraordinary dividends or taxable stock dividends, because the distribution is not out of income of the current taxable year and is treated as another amount properly paid or credited or required to be distributed for such taxable year within the meaning of section 661(a)(2). Also, the distribution in 1974 qualifies as an accumulation distribution for the purposes of subpart D. For purposes only of such subpart D, trust A would be treated as subject to the provisions of such subpart C for 1972, the preceding taxable year in which the extraordinary or taxable stock dividends were received, and, in computing undistributed net income for 1972, the extraordinary or taxable stock dividends would be included in distributable net income under section 643(a). The rule stated in the preceding sentence would also apply if the distribution in 1974 was made out of corpus without regard to a determination that the extraordinary dividends or taxable stock dividends in question were currently distributable to the beneficiary.

[T.D. 7204, 37 FR 17141, Aug. 25, 1972]

§ 1.666(a)–1A Amount allocated.

(a) In general. In the case of a trust that is subject to subpart C of part I of subchapter J of chapter 1 of the Code (relating to estates and trusts that may accumulate income or that distribute corpus), section 666(a) prescribes rules for determining the taxable years from which an accumulation distribution will be deemed to have been made and the extent to which the accumulation distribution is considered to consist of undistributed net income. * * *

(b) Distributions by domestic trusts—(1) Taxable years beginning after December 31, 1973. An accumulation distribution made by a trust (other than a foreign trust created by a U.S. person) in any taxable year beginning after December 31, 1973, is allocated to the preceding taxable years of the trust (defined in § 1.665(e)–1A(a)(1)(ii) as those beginning after December 31, 1968) according to the amount of undistributed net income of the trust for such years. For this purpose, an accumulation distribution is first to be allocated to the earliest such preceding taxable year in which there is undistributed net income and shall then be allocated, beginning with the next earliest, to any remaining preceding taxable years of the trust. The portion of the accumulation distribution allocated to the earliest preceding taxable year is the amount of the undistributed net income for that preceding taxable year. The portion of the accumulation distribution allocated to any preceding taxable year subsequent to the earliest such preceding taxable year is the excess of the accumulation distribution over the aggregate of the undistributed net income for all earlier preceding taxable years. See paragraph (d) of this section for adjustments to undistributed net income for prior distributions. The provisions of this subparagraph may be illustrated by the following example:

Example. In 1977, a domestic trust reporting on the calendar year basis makes an accumulation distribution of $33,000. Therefore, years before 1969 are ignored. In 1969, the trust had $6,000 of undistributed net income; in 1970, $4,000; in 1971, none; in 1972, $7,000; in 1973, $5,000; in 1974, $8,000; in 1975, $6,000; and $4,000 in 1976. The accumulation distribution is deemed distributed $6,000 in 1969, $4,000 in 1970, none in 1971, $7,000 in 1972, $5,000 in 1973, $8,000 in 1974, and $3,000 in 1975.

* * *

(d) Reduction of undistributed net income for prior accumulation distributions. For the purposes of allocating to any preceding taxable year an accumulation distribution of the taxable year, the undistributed net income of such preceding taxable year is reduced by the amount from such year deemed distributed in any accumulation distribution of undistributed net income made in any taxable year intervening between such preceding taxable year and the taxable year. Accordingly, for example, if a trust has undistributed net income for 1974 and makes accumulation distributions during the taxable years 1978 and 1979, in determining that part of the 1979 accumulation distribution that is thrown back to 1974 the undistributed net income for 1974 is first reduced by the amount of the undistributed net income for 1974 deemed distributed in the 1978 accumulation distribution.

* * *

[T.D. 7204, 37 FR 17143, Aug. 25, 1972]

§ 1.666(b)–1A Total taxes deemed distributed.

(a) If an accumulation distribution is deemed under § 1.666(a)–1A to be distributed on the last day of a preceding taxable year and the amount is not less than the undistributed net income for such preceding taxable year, then an additional amount equal to the "taxes imposed on the trust attributable to the undistributed net income" (as defined in § 1.665(d)–1A(b)) for such preceding taxable year is also deemed distributed under section 661(a)(2). For example, a trust has undistributed net income of $8,000 for the taxable year 1974. The taxes imposed on the trust attributable to the undistributed net income are $3,032. During the taxable year 1977, an accumulation distribution of $8,000 is made to the beneficiary, which is deemed under § 1.666(a)–1A to have been distributed on the last day of 1974. The 1977 accumulation distribution is not less than the 1974 undistributed net income. Accordingly, the taxes of $3,032 imposed on the trust attributable to the undistributed net income for 1974 are also deemed to have been distributed on the last day of 1974. Thus, a total of $11,032 will be deemed to have been distributed on the last day of 1974.

(b) For the purpose of paragraph (a) of this section, the undistributed net income of any preceding taxable year and the taxes imposed on the trust for such preceding taxable year attributable to such undistributed net income are computed after taking into account any accumulation distributions of taxable years intervening between such preceding taxable year and the taxable year. See paragraph (d) of § 1.666(a)–1A.

[T.D. 7204, 37 FR 17145, Aug. 25, 1972]

§ 1.666(c)–1A Pro rata portion of taxes deemed distributed.

(a) If an accumulation distribution is deemed under § 1.666(a)–1A to be distributed on the last day of a preceding taxable year and the amount is less than the undistributed net income for such preceding taxable year, then an additional amount is also deemed distributed under section 661(a)(2). The additional amount is equal to the "taxes imposed on the trust attributable to the undistributed net income" (as defined in § 1.665(a)–1A(b)) for such preceding taxable year, multiplied by a fraction, the numerator of which is the amount of the accumulation distribution allocated to such preceding taxable year and the denominator of which is the undistributed net income for such preceding taxable year. * * *

(b) For the purpose of paragraph (a) of this section, the undistributed net income of any preceding taxable year and the taxes imposed on the trust for such preceding taxable year attributable to such undistributed net income are computed after taking into account any accumulation distributions of any taxable years intervening between such preceding taxable year and the taxable year. * * *

[T.D. 7204, 37 FR 17145, Aug. 25, 1972]

§ 1.666(c)–2A Illustration of the provisions of section 666(a), (b), and (c).

The application of the provisions of §§ 1.666(a)–1A, 1.666(b)–1A, and 1.666(c)–1A may be illustrated by the following examples:

Example (1). **(a)** A trust created on January 1, 1974, makes accumulation distributions as follows:

1979	$ 7,000
1980	26,000

For 1974 through 1978, the undistributed portion of distributable net income, taxes, imposed on the trust attributable to the undistributed net income, and undistributed net income are as follows:

Year	Undistributed portion of distributable net income	Taxes imposed on the trust attributable to the undistributed net income	Undistributed net income
1974	$12,100	$3,400	$ 8,700
1975	16,100	5,200	10,900
1976	6,100	1,360	4,740
1977	None	None	None
1978	10,100	2,640	7,460

The trust has no undistributed capital gain.

(b) Since the entire amount of the accumulation distribution for 1979 ($7,000) is less than the undistributed net income for 1974 ($8,700), an additional amount of $2,736 (7,000/8,700 × $3,400) is deemed distributed under section 666(c).

(c) In allocating the accumulation distribution for 1980, the amount of undistributed net income for 1974 will reflect the accumulation distribution for 1979. The undistributed net income for 1974 will then be $1,700 and the taxes imposed on the trust for 1974 will be $664, determined as follows:

Undistributed net income as of the close of 1974	$8,700
Less: Accumulation distribution (1979)	7,000
Balance (undistributed net income as of the close of 1979)	1,700
Taxes imposed on the trust attributable to the undistributed net income as of the close of 1979 (1,700/8,700 × $3,400)	664

(d) The accumulation distribution of $26,000 for 1980 is deemed to have been made on the last day of the preceding taxable years of the trust to the extent of $24,800, the total of the undistributed net income for such years, as shown in the tabulation below. In addition, $9,864, the total taxes imposed on the trust attributable to the undistributed net income for such years is also deemed to have been distributed on the last day of such years, as shown below:

Year	Undistributed net income	Taxes imposed on the trust
1974	$ 1,700	$ 664
1975	10,900	5,200
1976	4,740	1,360
1977	None	None
1978	7,460	2,640
1979	None	None

Example (2). **(a)** Under the terms of a trust instrument, the trustee has discretion to accumulate or distribute the income to X and to invade corpus for the benefit of X. The entire income of the trust is from royalties. Both X and the trust report on the calendar year basis. All of the income for 1974 was accumulated. The distributable net income of the trust for the taxable year 1974 is $20,100 and the income taxes paid by the trust for 1974 attributable to the undistributed net income are $7,260. All of the income for 1975 and 1976 was distributed and in addition the trustee made accumulation distributions within the meaning of section 665(b) of $5,420 for each year.

(b) The undistributed net income of the trust determined under section 665(a) as of the close of 1974, is $12,840, computed as follows:

Distributable net income	$20,100
Less: Taxes imposed on the trust attributable to the undistributed net income	7,260
Undistributed net income as of the close of 1974	12,840

(c) The accumulation distribution of $5,420 made during the taxable year 1975 is deemed under section 666(a) to have been made on December 31, 1974. Since this accumulation distribution is less than the 1974 undistributed net income of $12,840, a portion of the taxes imposed on the trust for 1974 is also deemed under section 666(c) to have been distributed on December 31, 1974. The total amount deemed to have been distributed to X on December 31, 1974 is $8,484, computed as follows:

Accumulation distribution	$ 5,420
Taxes deemed distributed (5,420/12,840 × $7,260)	3,064
Total	8,484

(d) After the application of the provisions of subpart D to the accumulation distribution of 1975, the undistributed net income of the trust for 1974 is $7,420, computed as follows:

Undistributed net income as of the close of 1974	$12,840
Less: 1975 accumulation distribution deemed distributed on December 31, 1974 (paragraph (c) of this example)	5,420
Undistributed net income for 1974 as of the close of 1975	7,420

(e) The taxes imposed on the trust attributable to the undistributed net income for the taxable year 1974, as adjusted to give effect to the 1975 accumulation distribution, amount to $4,196, computed as follows:

Taxes imposed on the trust attributable to undistributed net income as of the close of 1974	$ 7,260
Less: Taxes deemed distributed in 1974	3,064
Taxes attributable to the undistributed net income determined as of the close of 1975	4,196

(f) The accumulation distribution of $5,420 made during the taxable year 1976 is, under section 666(a), deemed a distribution to X on December 31, 1974, within the meaning of section 661(a)(2). Since the accumulation distribution is less than the 1974 adjusted undistributed net income of $7,420, the trust is deemed under section 666(c) also to have distributed on December 31, 1974, a portion of the taxes imposed on the trust for 1974. The total amount deemed to be distributed on December 31, 1974, with respect to the accumulation distribution made in 1976, is $8,484, computed as follows:

Accumulation distribution	$ 5,420
Taxes deemed distributed (5,420/7,420 × 4,196)	3,064
Total	8,484

(g) After the application of the provisions of subpart D to the accumulation distribution of 1976, the undistributed net income of the trust for 1974 is $2,000, computed as follows:

Undistributed net income for 1974 as of the close of 1975	$ 7,420
Less: 1976 accumulation distribution deemed distributed on December 31, 1974 (paragraph (f) of this example)	5,420
Undistributed net income for 1974 as of the close of 1976	2,000

(h) The taxes imposed on the trust attributable to the undistributed net income of the trust for the taxable year 1974, determined as of the close of the taxable year 1976, amount to $1,132 ($4,196 less $3,064).

[T.D. 7204, 37 FR 17145, Aug. 25, 1972]

§ 1.666(d)–1A Information required from trusts.

(a) Adequate records required. For all taxable years of a trust, the trustee must retain copies of the trust's income tax return as well as information pertaining to any adjustments in the tax shown as due on the return. The trustee shall also keep the records of the trust required to be retained by section 6001 and the regulations thereunder for each taxable year as to which the period of limitations on assessment of tax under section 6501 has not expired. If the trustee fails to produce such copies and records, and such failure is due to circumstances beyond the reasonable control of the trustee or any predecessor trustee, the trustee may reconstruct the amount of corpus, accumulated income, etc., from competent sources (including, to the extent permissible, Internal Revenue Service records). To the extent that an accurate reconstruction can be made for a taxable year, the requirements of this paragraph shall be deemed satisfied for such year.

(b) Rule when information is not available—(1) Accumulation distributions. If adequate records (as required by paragraph (a) of this section) are not available to determine the proper application of subpart D to an accumulation distribution made in a taxable year by a trust, such accumulation distribution shall be deemed to consist of undistributed net income earned during the earliest preceding taxable year * * * of the trust in which it can be established that the trust was in existence. If adequate records are available for some years, but not for others, the accumulation distribution shall be allocated first to the earliest preceding taxable year of the trust for which there are adequate records and then to each subsequent preceding taxable year for which there are adequate records. To the extent that the distribution is not allocated in such manner to years for which adequate records are available, it will be deemed distributed on the last day of the earliest preceding taxable year of the trust in which it is established that the trust was in existence and for which the trust has no records. The provisions of this subparagraph may be illustrated by the following example:

Example. A trust makes a distribution in 1975 of $100,000. The trustee has adequate records for 1973, 1974, and 1975. The records show that the trust is on the calendar year basis, had distributable net income in 1975 of $20,000, and undistributed net income in 1974 of $15,000, and in 1973 of $16,000. The trustee has no other records of the trust except for a copy of the trust instrument showing that the trust was established on January 1, 1965. He establishes that the loss of the records was due to circumstances beyond his control. Since the distribution is made in 1975, the earliest "preceding taxable year", * * *, in 1969. Since $80,000 of the distribution is an accumulation distribution, and $31,000 thereof is allocated to 1974 and 1973, $49,000 is deemed to have been distributed on the last day of 1969.

(2) Taxes. **(i)** If an amount is deemed under this paragraph to be undistributed net income allocated to a preceding taxable year for which adequate records are not available, there shall be deemed to be "taxes imposed on the trust" for such preceding taxable year an amount equal to the taxes that the trust would have paid if the deemed undistributed net income were the amount remaining when the taxes were subtracted from taxable income of the trust for such year. For example, assume that an accumulation distribution in 1975 of $100,000 is deemed to be undistributed net income from 1971, and that the taxable income required to produce $100,000 after taxes in 1971 would be $284,966. Therefore the amount deemed to be "taxes imposed on the trust" for such preceding taxable year is $184,966.

(ii) The credit allowed by section 667(b) shall not be allowed for any amount deemed under this subparagraph to be "taxes imposed on the trust."

[T.D. 7204, 37 FR 17146, Aug. 25, 1972]

§ 1.667(a)–1A Denial of refund to trusts.

If an amount is deemed under section 666 or 669 to be an amount paid, credited, or required to be distributed on the last day of a preceding taxable year, the trust is not allowed a refund or credit of the amount of "taxes imposed on the trust", * * *. However, such taxes imposed on the trust are allowed as a credit under section 667(b) against the tax of certain beneficiaries who are treated as having received the distributions in the preceding taxable year.

[T.D. 7204, 37 FR 17147, Aug. 25, 1972]

§ 1.671–1 Grantors and others treated as substantial owners; scope.

(a) Subpart E (section 671 and following), part I, subchapter J, chapter 1 of the Code, contains provisions taxing income of a trust to the grantor or another person under certain circumstances even though he is not treated as a beneficiary under subparts A through D (section 641 and following) of such part I. Sections 671 and 672 contain general provisions relating to the entire subpart. Sections 673 through 677 define the circumstances under which income of a trust is taxed to a grantor. These circumstances are in general as follows:

(1) If the grantor has retained a reversionary interest in the trust, within specified time limits (section 673);

(2) If the grantor or a nonadverse party has certain powers over the beneficial interests under the trust (section 674);

(3) If certain administrative powers over the trust exist under which the grantor can or does benefit (section 675).

(4) If the grantor or a nonadverse party has a power to revoke the trust or return the corpus to the grantor (section 676); or

(5) If the grantor or a nonadverse party has the power to distribute income to or for the benefit of the grantor or the grantor's spouse (section 677).

Under section 678, income of a trust is taxed to a person other than the grantor to the extent that he has the sole power to vest corpus or income in himself.

(b) Sections 671 through 677 do not apply if the income of a trust is taxable to a grantor's spouse under section 71 or 682 (relating respectively to alimony and separate maintenance payments, and the income of an estate or trust in the case of divorce, etc.).

(c) Except as provided in such subpart E, income of a trust is not included in computing the taxable income and credits of a grantor or another person solely on the grounds of his dominion and control over the trust. However, the provisions of subpart E do not apply in situations involving an assignment of future income, whether or not the assignment is to a trust. Thus, for example, a person who assigns his right to future income under an employment contract may be taxed on that income even though the assignment is to a trust over which the assignor has retained none of the controls specified in sections 671 through 677. Similarly, a bondholder who assigns his right to interest may be taxed on interest payments even though the assignment is to an uncontrolled trust. Nor are the rules as to family partnerships affected by the provisions of subpart E, even though a partnership interest is held in trust. Likewise, these sections have no application in determining the right of a grantor to deductions for payments to a trust under a transfer and leaseback arrangement. In addition, the limitation of the last sentence of section 671 does not prevent any person from being taxed on the income of a trust when it is used to discharge his legal obligation. See § 1.662(a)–4. He is then treated as a beneficiary under subparts A through D or treated as an owner under section 677 because the income is distributed for his benefit, and not because of his dominion or control over the trust.

* * *

[T.D. 6500, 25 FR 11814, Nov. 26, 1960, as amended by T.D. 7148, 36 FR 20749, Oct. 29, 1971; T.D. 7741, 45 FR 81745, Dec. 12, 1980]

§ 1.671–2 Applicable principles.

(a) Under section 671 a grantor or another person includes in computing his taxable income and credits those items of income, deduction, and credit against tax which are attributable to or included in any portion of a trust of which he is treated as the owner. Sections 673 through 678 set forth the rules for determining when the grantor or another person is treated as the owner of any portion of a trust. The rules for determining the items of income, deduction, and credit against tax that are attributable to or included in a portion of the trust are set forth in § 1.671–3.

(b) Since the principle underlying subpart E (section 671 and following), part I, subchapter J, chapter 1 of the Code, is in general that income of a trust over which the grantor or another person has retained substantial dominion or control should be taxed to the grantor or other person rather than to the trust which receives the income or to the beneficiary to whom the income may be distributed, it is ordinarily immaterial whether the income involved constitutes income or corpus for trust accounting purposes. Accordingly, when it is stated in the regulations under subpart E that "income" is attributed to the grantor or another person, the reference, unless specifically limited, is to income determined for tax purposes and not to income for trust accounting purposes. When it is intended to emphasize that income for trust accounting purposes (determined in accordance with the provisions set forth in § 1.643(b)–1 is meant, the phrase "ordinary income" is used).

(c) An item of income, deduction, or credit included in computing the taxable income and credits of a grantor or another person under section 671 is treated as if it had been received or paid directly by the grantor or other person (whether or not an individual). For example, a charitable contribution made by a trust which is attributed to the grantor (an individual) under sections 671 through 677 will be aggregated with his other charitable contributions to determine their deductibility under the limitations of section 170(b)(1). Likewise, dividends received by a trust from sources in a particular foreign country which are attributed to a grantor or another person under subpart E will be aggregated with his other income from sources within that country to determine whether the taxpayer is subject to the limitations of section 904 with respect to credit for the tax paid to that country.

(d) Items of income, deduction, and credit not attributed to or included in any portion of a trust of which the grantor or another person is treated as the owner under subpart E are subject to the provisions of subparts A through D (section 641 and following), of such part I.

(e)(1) For purposes of part I of subchapter J, chapter 1 of the Internal Revenue Code, a grantor includes any person to the extent such person either creates a trust, or directly or indirectly makes a gratuitous transfer (within the meaning of paragraph (e)(2) of this section) of property to a trust. For purposes of this section, the term *property* includes cash. If a person creates or funds a trust on behalf of another person, both persons are treated as grantors of the trust. * * * However, a person who creates a trust but makes no gratuitous transfers to the trust is not treated as an owner of any portion of the trust under sections 671 through 677 or 679. Also, a person who funds a trust with an amount that is directly reimbursed to such person within a reasonable period of time and who makes no other transfers to the trust that constitute gratuitous transfers is not treated as an owner of any portion of the trust under sections 671 through 677 or 679. * * *

(2)(i) A gratuitous transfer is any transfer other than a transfer for fair market value. A transfer of property to a trust may be considered a gratuitous transfer without regard to whether the transfer is treated as a gift for gift tax purposes.

* * *

[T.D. 6500, 25 FR 11814, Nov. 26, 1960, as amended by T.D. 8831, 64 FR 43267, Aug. 10, 1999; T.D. 8890, 65 FR 41332, July 5, 2000]

§ 1.671–3 Attribution or inclusion of income, deductions, and credits against tax.

(a) When a grantor or another person is treated under subpart E (section 671 and following) as the owner of any portion of a trust, there are included in computing his tax liability those items of income, deduction, and credit against tax attributable to or included in that portion. For example:

(1) If a grantor or another person is treated as the owner of an entire trust (corpus as well as ordinary income), he takes into account in computing his income tax liability all items of income, deduction, and credit (including capital gains and losses) to which he would have been entitled had the trust not been in existence during the period he is treated as owner.

(2) If the portion treated as owned consists of specific trust property and its income, all items directly related to that property are attributable to the portion. Items directly related to trust property not included in the portion treated as owned by the grantor or other person are governed by the provisions of subparts A through D (section 641 and following), part I, subchapter J, chapter 1 of the Code. Items that relate both to the portion treated as owned by the grantor and to the balance of the trust must be apportioned in a manner that is reasonable in the light of all the circumstances of each case, including the terms of the governing instrument, local law, and the practice of the trustee if it is reasonable and consistent.

(3) If the portion of a trust treated as owned by a grantor or another person consists of an undivided fractional interest in the trust, or of an interest represented by a dollar amount, a pro rata share of each item of income, deduction, and credit is normally allocated to the portion. Thus, where the portion owned consists of an interest in or a right to an amount of corpus only, a fraction of each item (including items allocated to corpus, such as capital gains) is attributed to the portion. The numerator of this fraction is the amount which is subject to the control of the grantor or other person and the denominator is normally the fair market value of the trust corpus at the beginning of the taxable year in question. The share not treated as owned by the grantor or other person is governed by the provisions of subparts A through D. See the last three sentences of paragraph (c) of this section for the principles applicable if the portion treated as owned consists of an interest in part of the ordinary income in contrast to an interest in corpus alone.

(b) If a grantor or another person is treated as the owner of a portion of a trust, that portion may or may not include both ordinary income and other income allocable to corpus. For example—

(1) Only ordinary income is included by reason of an interest in or a power over ordinary income alone. Thus, if a grantor is treated under section 673 as an owner by reason of a reversionary interest in ordinary income only, items of income allocable to corpus will not be included in the portion he is treated as owning. Similarly, if a grantor or another person is treated under sections 674–678 as an owner of a portion by reason of a power over ordinary income only, items of income allocable to corpus are not included in that portion. (See paragraph (c) of this section to determine the treatment of deductions and credits when only ordinary income is included in the portion.)

(2) Only income allocable to corpus is included by reason of an interest in or a power over corpus alone, if satisfaction of the interest or an exercise of the power will not result in an interest in or the exercise of a power over ordinary income which would itself cause that income to be included. For example, if a grantor has a reversionary interest in a trust which is not such as to require that he be treated as an owner under section 673, he may nevertheless be treated as an owner under section 677(a)(2) since any income allocable to corpus is accumulated for future distribution to him, but items of income included in determining ordinary income are not included in the portion he is treated as owning. Similarly, he may have a power over corpus which is such that he is treated as an owner under section 674 or 676(a), but ordinary income will not be included in the portion he owns, if his power can only affect income received after a period of time such that he would not be treated as an owner of the income if the power were a reversionary interest. (See paragraph (c) of this section to determine the treatment of deductions and credits when only income allocated to corpus is included in the portion.)

(3) Both ordinary income and other income allocable to corpus are included by reason of an interest in or a power over both ordinary income and corpus, or an interest in or a power over corpus alone which does not come within the provisions of subparagraph (2) of this paragraph. For example, if a grantor is treated under section 673 as the owner of a portion of a trust by reason of a reversionary interest in corpus, both ordinary income and other income allocable to corpus are included in the portion. Further, a grantor includes both ordinary income and other income allocable to corpus in the portion he is treated as owning if he is treated under section 674 or 676 as an owner because of a power over corpus which can affect income received within a period such that he would be treated as an owner under section 673 if the power were a reversionary interest. Similarly, a grantor or another person includes both ordinary income and other income allocable to corpus in the portion he is treated as owning if he is treated as an owner under section 675 or 678 because of a power over corpus.

(c) If only income allocable to corpus is included in computing a grantor's tax liability, he will take into account in that computation only those items of income, deductions, and credit which would not be included under subparts A through D in the computation of the tax liability of the current income beneficiaries if all distributable net income had actually been distributed to those beneficiaries. On the other hand, if the grantor or another person is treated as an owner solely because of his interest in or power over ordinary income alone, he will take into account in computing his tax liability those items which would be included in computing the tax liability of a current income beneficiary, including expenses allocable to corpus which enter into the computation of distributable net income. If the grantor or other person is treated as an owner because of his power over or right to a dollar amount of ordinary income, he will first take into account a portion of those items of income and expense entering into the computation of ordinary income under the trust instrument or local law sufficient to produce income of the dollar amount required. There will then be attributable to him a pro rata portion of other items entering into the computation of distributable net income under subparts A through D, such as expenses allocable to corpus, and a pro rata portion of credits of the trust. For examples of computations under this paragraph, see paragraph (g) of § 1.677(a)–1.

[T.D. 6500, 25 FR 11814, Nov. 26, 1960, as amended by T.D. 6989, 34 FR 742, Jan. 17, 1969]

§ 1.671–4 Method of reporting.

(a) Portion of trust treated as owned by the grantor or another person. Except as otherwise provided in paragraph (b) of this section and § 1.671–5, items of income, deduction, and credit attributable to any portion of a trust that, under the provisions of subpart E (section 671 and following), part I, subchapter J, chapter 1 of the Internal Revenue Code, is treated as owned by the grantor or another person, are not reported by the trust on Form 1041, "U.S. Income Tax Return for Estates and Trusts," but are shown on a separate statement to be attached to that form. * * *

(b) A trust all of which is treated as owned by one or more grantors or other persons—(1) In general. In the case of a trust all of which is treated as owned by one or more grantors or other persons, and which is not described in paragraph (b)(6) or (7) of this section, the trustee may, but is not required to, report by one of the methods described in this paragraph (b) rather than by the method described in paragraph (a) of this section. A trustee may not report, however, pursuant to paragraph (b)(2)(i)(A) of this section unless the grantor or other person treated as the owner of the trust provides to the trustee a complete Form W–9 or acceptable substitute Form W–9 signed under penalties of perjury. See section 3406 and the regulations thereunder for the information to include on, and the manner of executing, the Form W–9, depending upon the type of reportable payments made.

(2) A trust all of which is treated as owned by one grantor or by one other person—(i) In general. In the case of a trust all of which is treated as owned by one grantor or one other person, the trustee reporting under this paragraph (b) must either—

(A) Furnish the name and taxpayer identification number (TIN) of the grantor or other person treated as the owner of the trust, and the address of the trust, to all payors during the taxable year, and comply with the additional requirements described in paragraph (b)(2)(ii) of this section; or

(B) Furnish the name, TIN, and address of the trust to all payors during the taxable year, and comply with the additional requirements described in paragraph (b)(2)(iii) of this section.

(ii) Additional obligations of the trustee when name and TIN of the grantor or other person treated as the owner of the trust and the address of the trust are furnished to payors. (A) Unless the grantor or other person treated as the owner of the trust is the trustee or a co-trustee of the trust, the trustee must furnish the grantor or other person treated as the owner of the trust with a statement that—

(1) Shows all items of income, deduction, and credit of the trust for the taxable year;

(2) Identifies the payor of each item of income;

(3) Provides the grantor or other person treated as the owner of the trust with the information necessary to take the items into account in computing the grantor's or other person's taxable income; and

(4) Informs the grantor or other person treated as the owner of the trust that the items of income, deduction and credit and other information shown on the statement must be included in computing the taxable income and credits of the grantor or other person on the income tax return of the grantor or other person.

(B) The trustee is not required to file any type of return with the Internal Revenue Service.

(iii) Additional obligations of the trustee when name, TIN, and address of the trust are furnished to payors—(A) Obligation to file Forms 1099. The trustee must file with the Internal Revenue Service the appropriate Forms 1099, reporting the income or gross proceeds paid to the trust during the taxable year, and showing the trust as the payor and the grantor or other person treated as the owner of the trust as the payee. The trustee has the same obligations for filing the appropriate Forms 1099 as would a payor making reportable payments, except that the trustee must report each type of income in the aggregate, and each item of gross proceeds separately. See paragraph (b)(5) of this section regarding the amounts required to be included on any Forms 1099 filed by the trustee.

(B) Obligation to furnish statement. (1) Unless the grantor or other person treated as the owner of the trust is the trustee or a co-trustee of the trust, the trustee must also furnish to the grantor or other person treated as the owner of the trust a statement that—

(i) Shows all items of income, deduction, and credit of the trust for the taxable year;

(ii) Provides the grantor or other person treated as the owner of the trust with the information necessary to take the items into account in computing the grantor's or other person's taxable income; and

(iii) Informs the grantor or other person treated as the owner of the trust that the items of income, deduction and credit and other information shown on the statement must be included in computing the taxable income and credits of the grantor or other person on the income tax return of the grantor or other person.

(2) By furnishing the statement, the trustee satisfies the obligation to furnish statements to recipients with respect to the Forms 1099 filed by the trustee.

* * *

[T.D. 8633, 60 FR 66085, Dec. 21, 1995; as amended by T.D. 8668, 61 FR 19189, May 1, 1996; T.D. 9032, 67 FR 7831, Dec. 24, 2002; T.D. 9241, 71 FR 4001, Jan. 24, 2006]

§ 1.672(a)–1 Definition of adverse party.

(a) Under section 672(a) an adverse party is defined as any person having a substantial beneficial interest in a trust which would be adversely affected by the exercise or nonexercise of a power which he possesses respecting the trust. A trustee is not an adverse party merely because of his interest as trustee. A person having a general power of appointment over the trust property is deemed to have a beneficial interest in the trust. An interest is a substantial interest if its value in relation to the total value of the property subject to the power is not insignificant.

(b) Ordinarily, a beneficiary will be an adverse party, but if his right to share in the income or corpus of a trust is limited to only a part, he may be an adverse party only as to that part. Thus, if A, B, C, and D are equal income beneficiaries of a trust and the grantor can revoke with A's consent, the grantor is treated as the owner of a portion which represents three-fourths of the trust; and items of income, deduction, and credit attributable to that portion are included in determining the tax of the grantor.

(c) The interest of an ordinary income beneficiary of a trust may or may not be adverse with respect to the exercise of a power over corpus. Thus, if the income of a trust is payable to A for life, with a power (which is not a general power of appointment) in A to appoint the corpus to the grantor either during his life or by will, A's interest is adverse to the return of the corpus to the grantor during A's life, but is not adverse to a return of the corpus after A's death. In other words, A's interest is adverse as to ordinary income but is not adverse as to income allocable to corpus. Therefore, assuming no other relevant facts exist, the grantor would not be taxable on the ordinary income of the trust under section 674, 676, or 677, but would be taxable under section 677 on income allocable to corpus (such as capital gains), since it may in the discretion of a nonadverse party be accumulated for future distribution to the grantor. Similarly, the interest of a contingent income beneficiary is adverse to a return of corpus to the grantor before the termination of his interest but not to a return of corpus after the termination of his interest.

(d) The interest of a remainderman is adverse to the exercise of any power over the corpus of a trust, but not to the exercise of a power over any income interest preceding his remainder. For example, if the grantor creates a trust which provides for income to be distributed to A for 10 years and then for the corpus to go to X if he is then living, a power exercisable by X to revest corpus in the grantor is a power exercisable by an adverse party; however, a power exercisable by X to distribute part or all of the ordinary income to the grantor may be a power exercisable by a nonadverse party (which would cause the ordinary income to be taxed to the grantor).

[T.D. 6500, 25 FR 11814, Nov. 26, 1960]

§ 1.672(c)–1 Related or subordinate party.

Section 672(c) defines the term "related or subordinate party". The term, as used in sections 674(c) and 675(3), means any nonadverse party who is the grantor's spouse if living with the grantor; the grantor's father, mother, issue, brother or sister; an employee of the grantor; a corporation or any employee of a corporation in which the stock holdings of the grantor and the trust are significant from the viewpoint of voting control; or a subordinate employee of a corporation in which the grantor is an executive. For purposes of sections 674(c) and 675(3), these persons are presumed to be subservient to the grantor in respect of the exercise or nonexercise of the powers conferred on them unless shown not to be subservient by a preponderance of the evidence.

[T.D. 6500, 25 FR 11814, Nov. 26, 1960]

§ 1.672(d)–1 Power subject to condition precedent.

Section 672(d) provides that a person is considered to have a power described in subpart E (section 671 and following), part I, subchapter J, chapter 1 of the Code, even though the exercise of the power is subject to a precedent giving of notice or takes effect only after the expiration of a certain period of time. However, although a person may be considered to have such a power, the grantor will nevertheless not be treated as an owner by reason of the power if its exercise can only affect beneficial enjoyment of income received after the expiration of a period of time such that, if the power were a reversionary interest, he would not be treated as an owner under section 673. See sections 674(b)(2), 676(b), and the last sentence of section 677(a). Thus, for example, if a grantor creates a trust for the benefit of his son and retains a power to revoke which takes effect only after the expiration of 2 years from the date of exercise, he is treated as an owner from the inception of the trust. However, if the grantor retains a power to revoke, exercisable at any time, which can only affect the beneficial enjoyment of the ordinary income of a trust received after the expiration of 10 years commencing with the date of the transfer in trust, or after the death of the income beneficiary, the power does not cause him to be treated as an owner with respect to ordinary income during the first 10 years of the trust or during the income beneficiary's life, as the case may be. See section 676(b).

[T.D. 6500, 25 FR 11814, Nov. 26, 1960]

§ 1.673(a)–1 Reversionary interests; income payable to beneficiaries other than certain charitable organizations; general rule.

(a) * * *

Even though the duration of the trust may be such that the grantor is not treated as its owner under section 673, and therefore is not taxed on the ordinary income, he may nevertheless be treated as an owner under section 677(a)(2) if he has a reversionary interest in the corpus. In the latter case, items of income, deduction, and credit allocable to corpus, such as capital gains and losses, will be included in the portion he owns. * * *

* * *

[T.D. 6500, 25 FR 11814, Nov. 26, 1960, as amended by T.D. 7357, 40 FR 23742, June 2, 1975]

§ 1.674(a)–1 Power to control beneficial enjoyment; scope of section 674.

(a) Under section 674, the grantor is treated as the owner of a portion of trust if the grantor or a nonadverse party has a power, beyond specified limits, to dispose of the beneficial enjoyment of the income or corpus, whether the power is a fiduciary power, a power of appointment, or any other power. Section 674(a) states in general terms that the grantor is treated as the owner in every case in which he or a nonadverse party can affect the beneficial enjoyment of a portion of a trust, the limitations being set forth as exceptions in subsections (b), (c), and (d) of section 674. These exceptions are discussed in detail in §§ 1.674(b)–1 through 1.674(d)–1. Certain limitations applicable to section 674(b), (c), and (d) are set forth in § 1.674(d)–2. Section 674(b) describes powers which are excepted regardless of who holds them. Section 674(c) describes additional powers of trustees which are excepted if at least half the trustees are independent, and if the grantor is not a trustee. Section 674(d) describes a further power which is excepted if it is held by trustees other than the grantor or his spouse (if living with the grantor).

(b) In general terms the grantor is treated as the owner of a portion of a trust if he or a nonadverse party or both has a power to dispose of the beneficial enjoyment of the corpus or income unless the power is one of the following:

(1) Miscellaneous powers over either ordinary income or corpus. **(i)** A power that can only affect the beneficial enjoyment of income (including capital gains) received after a period of time such that the grantor would not be treated as an owner under section 673 if the power were a reversionary interest (section 674(b)(2));

(ii) A testamentary power held by anyone (other than a testamentary power held by the grantor over accumulated income) (section 674(b)(3));

(iii) A power to choose between charitable beneficiaries or to affect the manner of their enjoyment of a beneficial interest (section 674(b)(4));

(iv) A power to allocate receipts and disbursements between income and corpus (section 674(b)(8)).

(2) Powers of distribution primarily affecting only one beneficiary. **(i)** A power to distribute corpus to or for a current income beneficiary, if the distribution must be charged against the share of corpus from which the beneficiary may receive income (section 674(b)(5)(B));

(ii) A power to distribute income to or for a current income beneficiary or to accumulate it either (a) if accumulated income must either be payable to the beneficiary from whom it was withheld or as described in paragraph (b)(6) of § 1.674(b)–1 (section 674(b)(6)); (b) if the power is to apply income to the support of a dependent of the grantor, and the income is not so applied (section 674(b)(1)); or (c) if the beneficiary is under 21 or under a legal disability and accumulated income is added to corpus (section 674(b)(7)).

(3) Powers of distribution affecting more than one beneficiary. A power to distribute corpus or income to or among one or more beneficiaries or to accumulate income, either (i) if the power is held by a trustee or trustees other than the grantor, at least half of whom are independent (section 674(c)), or (ii) if the power is limited by a reasonably definite standard in the trust instrument, and in the case of a power over income, if in addition the power is held by a trustee or trustees other than the grantor and the grantor's spouse living with the grantor (section 674(b)(5)(A) and (d)). (These powers include both powers to "sprinkle" income or corpus among current beneficiaries, and powers to shift income or corpus between current beneficiaries and remaindermen; however, certain of the powers described under subparagraph (2) of this paragraph can have the latter effect incidentally.)

(c) See section 671 and §§ 1.671–2 and 1.671–3 for rules for the treatment of income, deductions, and credits when a person is treated as the owner of all or only a portion of a trust.

[T.D. 6500, 25 FR 11814, Nov. 26, 1960]

§ 1.674(b)–1 Excepted powers exercisable by any person.

(a) Paragraph (b)(1) through (8) of this section sets forth a number of powers which may be exercisable by any person without causing the grantor to be treated as an owner of a trust under section 674(a). Further, with the exception of powers described in paragraph (b)(1) of this section, it is immaterial whether these powers are held in the capacity of trustee. It makes no difference under section 674(b) that the person holding the power is the grantor, or a related or subordinate party (with the qualifications noted in paragraph (b)(1) and (3) of this section).

(b) The exceptions referred to in paragraph (a) of this section are as follows (see, however, the limitations set forth in § 1.674(d)–2):

(1) Powers to apply income to support of a dependent. Section 674(b)(1) provides, in effect, that regardless of the general rule of section 674(a), the income of a trust will not be considered as taxable to the grantor merely because in the discretion of any person (other than a grantor who is not acting as a trustee or cotrustee) it may be used for the support of a beneficiary whom the grantor is legally obligated to support, except to the extent that it is in fact used for that purpose. See section 677(b) and the regulations thereunder.

* * *

(3) Testamentary powers. Under paragraph (3) of section 674(b) a power in any person to control beneficial enjoyment exercisable only by will does not cause a grantor to be treated as an owner under section 674(a). However, this exception does not apply to income accumulated for testamentary disposition by the grantor or to income which may be accumulated for such distribution in the discretion of the grantor or a nonadverse party, or both, without the approval or consent of any adverse party. For example, if a trust instrument provides that the income is to be accumulated during the grantor's life and that the grantor may appoint the accumulated income by will, the grantor is treated as the owner of the trust. Moreover, if a trust instrument provides that the income is payable to another person for his life, but the grantor has a testamentary power of appointment over the remainder, and under the trust instrument and local law capital gains are added to corpus, the grantor is treated as the owner of a portion of the trust and capital gains and losses are included in that portion. (See § 1.671–3.)

* * *

(5) Powers to distribute corpus. Paragraph (5) of section 674(b) provides an exception to section 674(a) for powers to distribute corpus, subject to certain limitations, as follows:

(i) If the power is limited by a reasonably definite standard which is set forth in the trust instrument, it may extend to corpus distributions to any beneficiary or beneficiaries or class of beneficiaries (whether income beneficiaries or remaindermen) without causing the grantor to be treated as an owner under section 674. See section 674(b)(5)(A). It is not required that the standard consist of the needs and circumstances of the beneficiary. A clearly measurable standard under which the holder of a power is legally accountable is deemed a reasonably definite standard for this purpose. For instance, a power to distribute corpus for the education, support, maintenance, or health of the beneficiary; for his reasonable support and comfort; or to enable him to maintain his accustomed standard of living; or to meet an emergency, would be limited by a reasonably definite standard. However, a power to distribute corpus for the pleasure, desire, or happiness of a beneficiary is not limited by a reasonably definite standard. The entire context of a provision of a trust instrument granting a power must be considered in determining whether the power is limited by a reasonably definite standard. For example, if a trust instrument provides that the determination of the trustee shall be conclusive with respect to the exercise or nonexercise of a power, the power is not limited by a reasonably definite standard. However, the fact that the governing instrument is phrased in discretionary terms is not in itself an indication that no reasonably definite standard exists.

(ii) If the power is not limited by a reasonably definite standard set forth in the trust instrument, the exception applies only if distributions of corpus may be made solely in favor of current income beneficiaries, and any corpus distribution to the current income beneficiary must be chargeable against the proportionate part of corpus held in trust for payment of income to that beneficiary as if it constituted a separate trust (whether or not physically segregated). See section 674(b)(5)(B).

(iii) This subparagraph may be illustrated by the following examples:

Example (1). A trust instrument provides for payment of the income to the grantor's two brothers for life, and for payment of the corpus to the grantor's nephews in equal shares. The grantor reserves the power to distribute corpus to pay medical expenses that may be incurred by his brothers or nephews. The grantor is not treated as an owner by reason of this power because section 674(b)(5)(A) excepts a power, exercisable by any person, to invade corpus for any beneficiary, including a remainderman, if the power is limited by a reasonably definite standard which is set forth in the trust instrument. However, if the power were also exercisable in favor of a person (for example, a sister) who was not otherwise a beneficiary of the trust, section 674(b)(5)(A) would not be applicable.

Example (2). The facts are the same as in example (1) except that the grantor reserves the power to distribute any part of the corpus to his brothers or to his nephews for their happiness. The grantor is treated as the owner of the trust. Paragraph (5)(A) of section 674(b) is inapplicable because the power is not limited by a reasonably definite standard. Paragraph (5)(B) is inapplicable because the power to distribute corpus permits a distribution of corpus to persons other than current income beneficiaries.

Example (3). A trust instrument provides for payment of the income to the grantor's two adult sons in equal shares for 10 years, after which the corpus is to be distributed to his grandchildren in equal shares. The grantor reserves the power to pay over to each son up to one-half of the corpus during the 10–year period, but any such payment shall proportionately reduce subsequent income and corpus payments made to the son receiving the corpus. Thus, if one-half of the corpus is paid to one son, all the income from the remaining half is thereafter payable to the other son. The grantor is not treated as an owner under section 674(a) by reason of this power because it qualifies under the exception of section 674(b)(5)(B).

(6) Powers to withhold income temporarily. **(i)** Section 674(b)(6) excepts a power which, in general, enables the holder merely to effect a postponement in the time when the ordinary income is enjoyed by a current income beneficiary. Specifically, there is excepted a power to distribute or apply ordinary income to or for a current income beneficiary or to accumulate the income, if the accumulated income must ultimately be payable either:

(a) To the beneficiary from whom it was withheld, his estate, or his appointees (or persons designated by name, as a class, or otherwise as alternate takers in default of appointment) under a power of appointment held by the beneficiary which does not exclude from the class of possible appointees any person other than the beneficiary, his estate, his creditors, or the creditors of his estate (section 674(b)(6)(A));

(b) To the beneficiary from whom it was withheld, or if he does not survive a date of distribution which could reasonably be expected to occur within his lifetime, to his appointees (or alternate takers in default of appointment) under any power of appointment, general or special, or if he has no power of appointment to one or more designated alternate takers (other than the grantor of the grantor's estate) whose shares have been irrevocably specified in the trust instrument (section 674(b)(6)(A) and the flush material following); or

(c) On termination of the trust, or in conjunction with a distribution of corpus which is augmented by the accumulated income, to the current income beneficiaries in shares which have been irrevocably specified in the trust instrument, or if any beneficiary does not survive a date of distribution which would reasonably be expected to occur within his lifetime, to his appointees (or alternate takers in default of appointment) under any power of appointment, general or special, or if he has no power of appointment to one or more designated alternate takers (other than the grantor or the grantor's estate) whose shares have been irrevocably specified in the trust instrument (section 674(b)(6)(B) and the flush material following).

(In the application of (a) of this subdivision, if the accumulated income of a trust is ultimately payable to the estate of the current income beneficiary or is ultimately payable to his appointees or takers in default of appointment, under a power of the type described in (a) of this subdivision, it need not be payable to the beneficiary from whom it was withheld under any circumstances. Furthermore, if a trust otherwise qualifies for the exception in (a) of this subdivision the trust income will not be considered to be taxable to the grantor under section 677 by reason of the existence of the power of appointment referred to in (a) of this subdivision.) In general, the exception in section 674(b)(6) is not applicable if the power is in substance one to shift ordinary income from one beneficiary to another. Thus, a power will not qualify for this exception if ordinary income may be distributed to beneficiary A, or may be added to corpus which is ultimately payable to beneficiary B, a remainderman who is not a current income beneficiary. However, section 674(b)(6)(B), and (c) of this subdivision, permit a limited power to shift ordinary income among current income beneficiaries, as illustrated in example (1) of this subparagraph.

(ii) The application of section 674(b)(6) may be illustrated by the following examples:

Example (1). A trust instrument provides that the income shall be paid in equal shares to the grantor's two adult daughters but the grantor reserves the power to withhold from either beneficiary any part of that beneficiary's share of income and to add it to the corpus of the trust until the younger daughter reaches the age of 30 years. When the younger daughter reaches the age of 30, the trust is to terminate and the corpus is to be divided equally between the two daughters or their estates. Although exercise of this power may permit the shifting of accumulated income from one beneficiary to the other (since the corpus with the accumulations is to be divided equally) the power is excepted under section 674(b)(6)(B) and subdivision (i)(c) of this subparagraph.

Example (2). The facts are the same as in example (1), except that the grantor of the trust reserves the power to distribute accumulated income to the beneficiaries in such shares as he chooses. The combined powers are not excepted by section 674(b)(6)(B) since income accumulated pursuant to the first power is neither required to be payable only in conjunction with a corpus distribution nor required to be payable in shares specified in the trust instrument. See, however, section 674(c) and § 1.674(c)–1 for the effect of such a power if it is exercisable only by independent trustees.

Example (3). A trust provides for payment of income to the grantor's adult son with the grantor retaining the power to accumulate the income until the grantor's death, when all accumulations are to be paid to the son. If the son predeceases the grantor, all accumulations are, at the death of the grantor, to be paid to his daughter, or if she is not living, to alternate takers (which do not include the grantor's estate) in specified shares. The power is excepted under section 674(b)(6)(A) since the date of distribution (the date of the grantor's death) may, in the usual case, reasonably be expected to occur during the beneficiary's (the son's) lifetime. It is not necessary that the accumulations be payable to the son's estate or his appointees if he should predecease the grantor for this exception to apply.

(7) Power to withhold income during disability. Section 674(b)(7) provides an exception for a power which, in general, will permit ordinary income to be withheld during the legal disability of an income beneficiary or while he is under 21. Specifically, there is excepted a power, exercisable only during the existence of a legal disability of any current income beneficiary or the period during which any income beneficiary is under the age of 21 years, to distribute or apply ordinary income to or for that beneficiary or to accumulate the income and add it to corpus. To qualify under this exception it is not necessary that the income ultimately be payable to the income beneficiary from whom it was withheld, his estate, or his appointees; that is, the accumulated income may be added to corpus and ultimately distributed to others. For example, the grantor is not treated as an owner under section 674 if the income of a trust is payable to his son for life, remainder to his grandchildren, although he reserves the power to accumulate income and add it to corpus while his son is under 21.

(8) Powers to allocate between corpus and income. Paragraph (8) of section 674(b) provides that a power to allocate receipts and disbursements between corpus and income, even though expressed in broad language, will not cause the grantor to be treated as an owner under the general rule of section 674(a).

[T.D. 6500, 25 FR 11814, Nov. 26, 1960]

§ 1.674(c)–1 Excepted powers exercisable only by independent trustees.

Section 674(c) provides an exception to the general rule of section 674(a) for certain powers that are exercisable by independent trustees. This exception is in addition to those provided for under section 674(b) which may be held by any person including an independent trustee. The powers to which section 674(c) apply are powers (a) to distribute, apportion, or accumulate income to or for a beneficiary or beneficiaries, or to, for, or within a class of beneficiaries, or (b) to pay out corpus to or for a beneficiary or beneficiaries or to or for a class of beneficiaries (whether or not income beneficiaries). In order for such a power to fall within the exception of section 674(c) it must be exercisable solely (without the approval or consent of any other person) by a trustee or trustees none of whom is the grantor and no more than half of whom are related or subordinate parties who are subservient to the wishes of the grantor. (See section 672(c) for definitions of these terms.) An example of the application of section 674(c) is a trust whose income is payable to the grantor's three adult sons with power in an independent trustee to allocate without restriction the amounts of income to be paid to each son each year. Such a power does not cause the grantor to be treated as the owner of the trust. See however, the limitations set forth in § 1.674(d)–2.

[T.D. 6500, 25 FR 11814, Nov. 26, 1960]

§ 1.674(d)–1 Excepted powers exercisable by any trustee other than grantor or spouse.

Section 674(d) provides an additional exception to the general rule of section 674(a) for a power to distribute, apportion, or accumulate income to or for a beneficiary or beneficiaries or to, for, or within a class of beneficiaries, whether or not the conditions of section 674(b)(6) or (7) are satisfied, if the power is solely exercisable (without the approval or consent of any other person) by a trustee or trustees none of whom is the grantor or spouse living with the grantor, and if the power is limited by a reasonably definite external standard set forth in the trust instrument (see paragraph (b)(5) of § 1.674(b)–1 with respect to what constitutes a reasonably definite standard). See, however, the limitations set forth in § 1.674(d)–2.

[T.D. 6500, 25 FR 11814, Nov. 26, 1960]

§ 1.674(d)–2 Limitations on exceptions in section 674(b), (c), and (d).

(a) Power to remove trustee. A power in the grantor to remove, substitute, or add trustees (other than a power exercisable only upon limited conditions which do not exist during the taxable year, such as the death or resignation of, or breach of fiduciary duty by, an existing trustee) may prevent a trust from qualifying under section 674(c) or (d). For example, if a grantor has an unrestricted power to remove an independent trustee and substitute any person including himself as trustee, the trust will not qualify under section 674(c) or (d). On the other hand if the grantor's power to remove, substitute, or add trustees is limited so that its exercise could not alter the trust in a manner that would disqualify it under section 674(c) or (d), as the case may be, the power itself does not disqualify the trust. Thus, for example, a power in the grantor to remove or discharge an independent trustee on the condition that he substitute another independent trustee will not prevent a trust from qualifying under section 674(c).

(b) Power to add beneficiaries. The exceptions described in section 674(b)(5), (6), and (7), (c), and (d), are not applicable if any person has a power to add to the beneficiary or beneficiaries or to a class of beneficiaries designated to receive the income or corpus, except where the action is to provide for after-born or after-adopted children. This limitation does not apply to a power held by a beneficiary to substitute other beneficiaries to succeed to his interest in the trust (so that he would be an adverse party as to the exercise or nonexercise of that power). For example, the limitation does not apply to a power in a beneficiary of a nonspendthrift trust to assign his interest. Nor does the limitation apply to a power held by any person which would qualify as an exception under section 674(b)(3) (relating to testamentary powers).

[T.D. 6500, 25 FR 11814, Nov. 26, 1960]

§ 1.675–1 Administrative powers.

(a) General rule. Section 675 provides in effect that the grantor is treated as the owner of any portion of a trust if under the terms of the trust instrument or circumstances attendant on its operation administrative control is exercisable primarily for the benefit of the grantor rather than the beneficiaries of the trust. If a grantor retains a power to amend the administrative provisions of a trust instrument which is broad enough to permit an amendment causing the grantor to be treated as the owner of a portion of the trust under section 675, he will be treated as the owner of the portion from its inception. See section 671 and §§ 1.671–2 and 1.671–3 for rules for treatment of items of income, deduction, and credit when a person is treated as the owner of all or only a portion of a trust.

(b) Prohibited controls. The circumstances which cause administrative controls to be considered exercisable primarily for the benefit of the grantor are specifically described in paragraphs (1) through (4) of section 675 as follows:

(1) The existence of a power, exercisable by the grantor or a nonadverse party, or both, without the approval or consent of any adverse party, which enables the grantor or any other person to purchase, exchange, or otherwise deal with or dispose of the corpus or the income of the trust for less than adequate consideration in money or money's worth. Whether the existence of the power itself will constitute the holder an adverse party will depend on the particular circumstances.

(2) The existence of a power exercisable by the grantor or a nonadverse party, or both, which enables the grantor to borrow the corpus or income of the trust, directly or indirectly, without adequate interest or adequate security. However, this paragraph does not apply where a trustee (other than the grantor acting alone) is authorized under a general lending power to make loans to any person without regard to interest or security. A general lending power in the grantor, acting alone as trustee, under which he has power to determine interest rates and the adequacy of security is not in itself an indication that the grantor has power to borrow the corpus or income without adequate interest or security.

(3) The circumstance that the grantor has directly or indirectly borrowed the corpus or income of the trust and has not completely repaid the loan, including any interest, before the beginning of the taxable year. The preceding sentence does not apply to a loan which provides for adequate interest and adequate security, if it is made by a trustee other than the grantor or a related or subordinate trustee subservient to the grantor. See section 672(c) for definition of "a related or subordinate party".

(4) The existence of certain powers of administration exercisable in a nonfiduciary capacity by any nonadverse party without the approval or consent of any person in a fiduciary capacity. The term "powers of administration" means one or more of the following powers:

(i) A power to vote or direct the voting of stock or other securities of a corporation in which the holdings of the grantor and the trust are significant from the viewpoint of voting control;

(ii) A power to control the investment of the trust funds either by directing investments or reinvestments, or by vetoing proposed investments or reinvestments, to the extent that the trust funds consist of stocks or securities of corporations in which the holdings of the grantor and the trust are significant from the viewpoint of voting control; or

(iii) A power to reacquire the trust corpus by substituting other property of an equivalent value.

If a power is exercisable by a person as trustee, it is presumed that the power is exercisable in a fiduciary capacity primarily in the interests of the beneficiaries. This presumption may be rebutted only by clear and convincing proof that the power is not exercisable primarily in the interests of the beneficiaries. If a power is not exercisable by a person as trustee, the determination of whether the power is exercisable in a fiduciary or a nonfiduciary capacity depends on all the terms of the trust and the circumstances surrounding its creation and administration.

(c) Authority of trustee. The mere fact that a power exercisable by a trustee is described in broad language does not indicate that the trustee is authorized to purchase, exchange, or otherwise deal with or dispose of the trust property or income for less than an adequate and full consideration in money or money's worth, or is authorized to lend the trust property or income to the grantor without adequate interest. On the other hand, such authority may be indicated by the actual administration of the trust.

[T.D. 6500, 25 FR 11814, Nov. 26, 1960]

§ 1.676(a)–1 Power to revest title to portion of trust property in grantor; general rule.

If a power to revest in the grantor title to any portion of a trust is exercisable by the grantor or a nonadverse party, or both, without the approval or consent of an adverse party, the grantor is treated as the owner of that portion, except as provided in section 676(b) * * * If the title to a portion of the trust will revest in the grantor upon the exercise of a power by the grantor or a nonadverse party, or both, the grantor is treated as the owner of that portion regardless of whether the power is a power to revoke, to terminate, to alter or amend, or to appoint. See section 671 and §§ 1.671–2 and 1.671–3 for rules for treatment of items of income, deduction, and credit when a person is treated as the owner of all or only a portion of a trust.

[T.D. 6500, 25 FR 11814, Nov. 26, 1960]

§ 1.676(b)–1 Powers exercisable only after a period of time.

Section 676(b) provides an exception to the general rule of section 676(a) when the exercise of a power can only affect the beneficial enjoyment of the income of a trust received after the expiration of a period of time which is such that a grantor would not be treated as the owner of that portion, except as power were a reversionary interest. * * * It is immaterial for this purpose that the power is vested at the time of the transfer. However, the grantor is subject to the general rule of section 676(a) after the expiration of the period unless the power is relinquished. * * *

[T.D. 6500, 25 FR 11814, Nov. 26, 1960]

§ 1.677(a)–1 Income for benefit of grantor; general rule.

(a)(1) Scope. Section 677 deals with the treatment of the grantor of a trust as the owner of a portion of the trust because he has retained an interest in the income from that portion. For convenience, "grantor" and "spouse" are generally referred to in the masculine and feminine genders, respectively, but if the grantor is a woman the reference to "grantor" is to her and the reference to "spouse" is to her husband. Section 677 also deals with the treatment of the grantor of a trust as the owner of a portion of the trust because the income from property transferred in trust after October 9, 1969, is, or may be, distributed to his spouse or applied to the payment of premiums on policies of insurance on the life of his spouse. However, section 677 does not apply when the income of a trust is taxable to a grantor's spouse under section 71 (relating to alimony and separate maintenance payments) or section 682 (relating to income of an estate or trust in case of divorce, etc.). See section 671–1(b).

* * *

(b) Income for benefit of grantor or his spouse; general rule—(1) Property transferred in trust prior to October 10, 1969. * * *

(2) Property transferred in trust after October 9, 1969. With respect to property transferred in trust after October 9, 1969, the grantor is treated, under section 677, in any taxable year as the owner (whether or not he is treated as an owner under section 674) of a portion of a trust of which the income for the taxable year or for a period not within the exception described in paragraph (e) of this section is, or in the discretion of the grantor, or his spouse, or a nonadverse party, or any combination thereof (without the approval or consent of any adverse party other than the grantor's spouse) may be:

(i) Distributed to the grantor or the grantor's spouse;

(ii) Held or accumulated for future distribution to the grantor or the grantor's spouse; or

(iii) Applied to the payment of premiums on policies of insurance on the life of the grantor or the grantor's spouse, except policies of insurance irrevocably payable for a charitable purpose specified in section 170(c).

With respect to the treatment of a grantor as the owner of a portion of a trust solely because its income is, or may be, distributed or held or accumulated for future distribution to a beneficiary who is his spouse or applied to the payment of premiums for insurance on the spouse's life, section 677(a) applies to the income of a trust solely during the period of the marriage of the grantor to a beneficiary. In the case of divorce or separation, see sections 71 and 682 and the regulations thereunder.

(c) Constructive distribution; cessation of interest. Under section 677 the grantor is treated as the owner of a portion of a trust if he has retained any interest which might, without the approval or consent of an adverse party, enable him to have the income from that portion distributed to him at some time either actually or constructively (subject to the exception described in paragraph (e) of this section). In the case of a transfer in trust after October 9, 1969, the grantor is also treated as the owner of a portion of a trust if he has granted or retained any interest which might, without the approval or consent of an adverse party (other than the grantor's spouse), enable his spouse to have the income from the portion at some time, whether or not within the grantor's lifetime, distributed to the spouse either actually or constructively. See paragraph (b)(2) of this section for additional rules relating to the income of a trust prior to the grantor's marriage to a beneficiary. Constructive distribution to the grantor or to his spouse includes payment on behalf of the grantor or his spouse to another in obedience to his or her direction and payment of premiums upon policies of insurance on the grantor's, or his spouse's, life (other than policies of insurance irrevocably payable for charitable purposes specified in section 170(c)). If the grantor (in the case of property transferred prior to Oct. 10, 1969) or the grantor and his spouse (in the case of property transferred after Oct. 9, 1969) are divested permanently and completely of every interest described in this paragraph, the grantor is not treated as an owner under section 677 after that divesting. The word "interest" as used in this paragraph does not include the possibility that the grantor or his spouse might receive back from a beneficiary an interest in a trust by inheritance. Further, with respect to transfers in trust prior to October 10, 1969, the word "interest" does not include the possibility that the grantor might receive back from a beneficiary an interest in a trust as a surviving spouse under a statutory right of election or a similar right.

(d) Discharge of legal obligation of grantor or his spouse. Under section 677 a grantor is, in general, treated as the owner of a portion of a trust whose income is, or in the discretion of the grantor or a nonadverse party, or both, may be applied in discharge of a legal obligation of the grantor (or his spouse in the case of property transferred in trust by the grantor after October 9, 1969). However, see § 1.677(b)–1 for special rules for trusts whose income may not be applied for the discharge of any legal obligation of the grantor or the grantor's spouse other than the support or maintenance of a beneficiary (other than the grantor's spouse) whom the grantor or grantor's spouse is legally obligated to support. * * *

* * *

(g) Examples. The application of section 677(a) may be illustrated by the following examples:

Example (1). G creates an irrevocable trust which provides that the ordinary income is to be payable to him for life and that on his death the corpus shall be distributed to B, an unrelated person. Except for the right to receive income, G retains no right or power which would cause him to be treated as an owner under sections 671 through 677. Under the applicable local law capital gains must be applied to corpus. During the taxable year 1970 the trust has the following items of gross income and deductions:

Dividends	$5,000
Capital gain	1,000
Expenses allocable to income	200
Expenses allocable to corpus	100

Since G has a right to receive income he is treated as an owner of a portion of the trust under section 677. Accordingly, he should include the $5,000 of dividends, $200 income expense, and $100 corpus expense in the computation of his taxable income for 1970. He should not include the $1,000 capital gain since that is not attributable to the portion of the trust that he owns. See § 1.671–3(b). The tax consequences of the capital gain are governed by the provisions of subparts A, B, C, and D (section 641 and following), part I, subchapter J, chapter 1 of the Code. Had the trust sustained a capital loss in any amount the loss would likewise not be included in the computation of G's taxable income, but would also be governed by the provisions of such subparts.

* * *

[T.D. 6500, 25 FR 11814, Nov. 26, 1960, as amended by T.D. 7148, 36 FR 20750, Oct. 29, 1971; T.D. 8668, 61 FR 19189, May 1, 1996]

§ 1.677(b)–1 Trusts for support.

(a) Section 677(b) provides that a grantor is not treated as the owner of a trust merely because its income may in the discretion of any person other than the grantor (except when he is acting as trustee or cotrustee) be applied or distributed for the support or maintenance of a beneficiary (other than the grantor's spouse in the case of income from property transferred in trust after October 9, 1969), such as the child of the grantor, whom the grantor or his spouse is legally obligated to support. If income of the current year of the trust is actually so applied or distributed the grantor may be treated as the owner of any portion of the trust under section 677 to that extent, even though it might have been applied or distributed for other purposes. In the case of property transferred to a trust before October 10, 1969, for the benefit of the grantor's spouse, the grantor may be treated as the owner to the extent income of the current year is actually applied for the support or maintenance of his spouse.

(b) If any amount applied or distributed for the support of a beneficiary, including the grantor's spouse in the case of property transferred in trust before October 10, 1969, whom the grantor is legally obligated to support is paid out of corpus or out of income other than income of the current year, the grantor is treated as a beneficiary of the trust, and the amount applied or distributed is considered to be an amount paid within the meaning of section 661(a)(2), taxable to the grantor under section 662. Thus, he is subject to the other relevant portions of subparts A through D (section 641 and following), part I, subchapter J, chapter 1 of the Code. Accordingly, the grantor may be taxed on an accumulation distribution or a capital gain distribution under subpart D (section 665 and following) of such part I. Those provisions are applied on the basis that the grantor is the beneficiary.

(c) For the purpose of determining the items of income, deduction, and credit of a trust to be included under this section in computing the grantor's tax liability, the income of the trust for the taxable year of distribution will be deemed to have been first distributed. For example, in the case of a trust reporting on the calendar year basis, a distribution made on January 1, 1956, will be deemed to have been made out of ordinary income of the trust for the calendar year 1956 to the extent of the income for that year even though the trust had received no income as of January 1, 1956. Thus, if a distribution of $10,000 is made on January 1, 1956, for the support of the grantor's dependent, the grantor will be treated as the owner of the trust for 1956 to that extent. If the trust received dividends of $5,000 and incurred expenses of $1,000 during that year but subsequent to January 1, he will take into account dividends of $5,000 and expenses of $1,000 in computing his tax liability for 1956. In addition, the grantor will be treated as a beneficiary of the trust with respect to the $6,000 ($10,000 less distributable income of $4,000 (dividends of $5,000 less expenses of $1,000)) paid out of corpus or out of other than income of the current year. See paragraph (b) of this section.

(d) The exception provided in section 677(b) relates solely to the satisfaction of the grantor's legal obligation to support or maintain a beneficiary. Consequently, the general rule of section 677(a) is applicable when in the discretion of the grantor or nonadverse parties income of a trust may be applied in discharge of a grantor's obligations other than his obligation of support or maintenance falling within section 677(b). Thus, if the grantor creates a trust the income of which may in the discretion of a nonadverse party be applied in the payment of the grantor's debts, such as the payment of his rent or other household expenses, he is treated as an owner of the trust regardless of whether the income is actually so applied.

(e) The general rule of section 677(a), and not section 677(b), is applicable if discretion to apply or distribute income of a trust rests solely in the grantor, or in the grantor in conjunction with other persons, unless in either case the grantor has such discretion as trustee or cotrustee.

(f) The general rule of section 677(a), and not section 677(b), is applicable to the extent that income is required, without any discretionary determination, to be applied to the support of a beneficiary whom the grantor is legally obligated to support.

[T.D. 6500, 25 FR 11814, Nov. 26, 1960, as amended by T.D. 7148, 36 FR 20750, Oct. 29, 1971]

§ 1.678(a)–1 Person other than grantor treated as substantial owner; general rule.

(a) Where a person other than the grantor of a trust has a power exercisable solely by himself to vest the corpus or the income of any portion of a testamentary or inter vivos trust in himself, he is treated under section 678(a) as the owner of that portion, except as provided in section 678(b) (involving taxation of the grantor) and section 678(c) (involving an obligation of support). The holder of such a power also is treated as an owner of the trust even though he has partially released or otherwise modified the power so that he can no longer vest the corpus or income in himself, if he has retained such control of the trust as would, if retained by a grantor, subject the grantor to treatment as the owner under sections 671 to 677, inclusive. See section 671 and §§ 1.671–2 and 1.671–3 for rules for treatment of items of income, deduction, and credit where a person is treated as the owner of all or only a portion of a trust.

(b) Section 678(a) treats a person as an owner of a trust if he has a power exercisable solely by himself to apply the income or corpus for the satisfaction of his legal obligations, other than an obligation to support a dependent (see § 1.678(c)–1 subject to the limitation of section 678(b)). Section 678 does not apply if the power is not exercisable solely by himself. However, see § 1.662(a)–4 for principles applicable to income of a trust which, pursuant to the terms of the trust instrument, is used to satisfy the obligations of a person other than the grantor.

[T.D. 6500, 25 FR 11814, Nov. 26, 1960]

§ 1.678(b)–1 If grantor is treated as the owner.

Section 678(a) does not apply with respect to a power over income, as originally granted or thereafter modified, if the grantor of the trust is treated as the owner under sections 671 to 677, inclusive.

[T.D. 6500, 25 FR 11814, Nov. 26, 1960]

§ 1.678(c)–1 Trusts for support.

(a) Section 678(a) does not apply to a power which enables the holder, in the capacity of trustee or cotrustee, to apply the income of the trust to the support or maintenance of a person whom the holder is obligated to support, except to the extent the income is so applied. See paragraphs (a), (b), and (c) of § 1.677(b)–1 for applicable principles where any amount is applied for the support or maintenance of a person whom the holder is obligated to support.

(b) The general rule in section 678(a) (and not the exception in section 678(c)) is applicable in any case in which the holder of a power exercisable solely by himself is able, in any capacity other than that of trustee or cotrustee, to apply the income in discharge of his obligation of support or maintenance.

(c) Section 678(c) is concerned with the taxability of income subject to a power described in section 678(a). It has no application to the taxability of income which is either required to be applied pursuant to the terms of the trust instrument or is applied pursuant to a power which is not described in section 678(a), the taxability of such income being governed by other provisions of the Code. See § 1.662(a)–4.

[T.D. 6500, 25 FR 11814, Nov. 26, 1960]

§ 1.691(a)–1 Income in respect of a decedent.

(a) Scope of section 691. In general, the regulations under section 691 cover: (1) The provisions requiring that amounts which are not includible in gross income for the decedent's last taxable year or for a prior taxable year be included in the gross income of the estate or persons receiving such income to the extent that such amounts constitute "income in respect of a decedent"; (2) the taxable effect of a transfer of the right to such income; (3) the treatment of certain deductions and credit in respect of a decedent which are not allowable to the decedent for the taxable period ending with his death or for a prior taxable year; (4) the allowance to a recipient of income in respect of a decedent of a deduction for estate taxes attributable to the inclusion of the value of the right to such income in the decedent's estate; (5) special provisions with respect to installment obligations acquired from a decedent and with respect to the allowance of a deduction for estate taxes to a surviving annuitant under a joint and survivor annuity contract; and (6) special provisions relating to installment obligations transmitted at death when prior law applied to the transmission.

(b) General definition. In general, the term "income in respect of a decedent" refers to those amounts to which a decedent was entitled as gross income but which were not properly includible in computing his taxable income for the taxable year ending with the date of his death or for a previous taxable year under the method of accounting employed by the decedent. See the regulations under section 451. Thus, the term includes—

(1) All accrued income of a decedent who reported his income by use of the cash receipts and disbursements method;

(2) Income accrued solely by reason of the decedent's death in case of a decedent who reports his income by use of an accrual method of accounting; and

(3) Income to which the decedent had a contingent claim at the time of his death.

See sections 736 and 753 and the regulations thereunder for "income in respect of a decedent" in the case of a deceased partner.

(c) Prior decedent. The term "income in respect of a decedent" also includes the amount of all items of gross income in respect of a prior decedent, if (1) the right to receive such amount was acquired by the decedent by reason of the death of the prior decedent or by bequest, devise, or inheritance from the prior decedent and if (2) the amount of gross income in respect of the prior decedent was not properly includible in computing the decedent's taxable income for the taxable year ending with the date of his death or for a previous taxable year. See example (2) of paragraph (b) of § 1.691(a)–2.

(d) Items excluded from gross income. Section 691 applies only to the amount of items of gross income in respect of a decedent, and items which are excluded from gross income under subtitle A of the Code are not within the provisions of section 691.

* * *

[T.D. 6500, 25 FR 11814, Nov. 26, 1960, as amended by T.D. 6808, 30 FR 3435, March 16, 1965]

§ 1.691(a)–2 Inclusion in gross income by recipients.

(a) Under section 691(a)(1), income in respect of a decedent shall be included in the gross income, for the taxable year when received, of—

(1) The estate of the decedent, if the right to receive the amount is acquired by the decedent's estate from the decedent;

(2) The person who, by reason of the death of the decedent, acquires the right to receive the amount, if the right to receive the amount is not acquired by the decedent's estate from the decedent; or

(3) The person who acquires from the decedent the right to receive the amount by bequest, devise, or inheritance, if the amount is received after a distribution by the decedent's estate of such right.

These amounts are included in the income of the estate or of such persons when received by them whether or not they report income by use of the cash receipts and disbursements methods.

(b) The application of paragraph (a) of this section may be illustrated by the following examples, in each of which it is assumed that the decedent kept his books by use of the cash receipts and disbursements method.

Example (1). The decedent was entitled at the date of his death to a large salary payment to be made in equal annual installments over five years. His estate, after collecting two installments, distributed the right to the remaining installment payments to the residuary legatee of the estate. The estate must include in its gross income the two installments received by it, and the legatee must include in his gross income each of the three installments received by him.

Example (2). A widow acquired, by bequest from her husband, the right to receive renewal commissions on life insurance sold by him in his lifetime, which commissions were payable over a period of years. The widow died before having received all of such commissions, and her son inherited the right to receive the rest of the commissions. The commissions received by the widow were includible in her gross income. The commissions received by the son were not includible in the widow's gross income but must be included in the gross income of the son.

Example (3). The decedent owned a Series E United States savings bond, with his wife as co-owner or beneficiary, but died before the payment of such bond. The entire amount of interest accruing on the bond and not includible in income by the decedent, not just the amount accruing after the death of the decedent, would be treated as income to his wife when the bond is paid.

Example (4). A, prior to his death, acquired 10,000 shares of the capital stock of the X Corporation at a cost of $100 per share. During his lifetime, A had entered into an agreement with X Corporation whereby X Corporation agreed to purchase and the decedent agreed that his executor would sell the 10,000 shares of X Corporation stock owned by him at the book value of the stock at the date of A's death. Upon A's death, the shares are sold by A's executor for $500 a share pursuant to the agreement. Since the sale of stock is consummated after A's death, there is no income in respect of a decedent with respect to the appreciation in value of A's stock to the date of his death. If, in this example, A had in fact sold the stock during his lifetime but payment had not been received before his death, any gain on the sale would constitute income in respect of a decedent when the proceeds were received.

Example (5). (1) A owned and operated an apple orchard. During his lifetime, A sold and delivered 1,000 bushels of apples to X, a canning factory, but did not receive payment before his death. A also entered into negotiations to sell 3,000 bushels of apples to Y, a canning factory, but did not complete the sale before his death. After A's death, the executor received payment from X. He also completed the sale to Y and transferred to Y 1,200 bushels of apples on hand at A's death and harvested and transferred an additional 1,800 bushels. The gain from the sale of apples by A to X constitutes income in respect of a decedent when received. On the other hand, the gain from the sale of apples by the executor to Y does not.

(2) Assume that, instead of the transaction entered into with Y, A had disposed of the 1,200 bushels of harvested apples by delivering them to Z, a cooperative association, for processing and sale. Each year the association commingles the fruit received from all of its members into a pool and assigns to each member a percentage interest in the pool based on the fruit delivered by him. After the fruit is processed and the products are sold, the association distributes the net proceeds from the pool to its members in proportion to their interests in the pool. After A's death, the association made distributions to the executor with respect to A's share of the proceeds from the pool in which A had an interest. Under such circumstances, the proceeds from the disposition of the 1,200 bushels of apples constitute income in respect of a decedent.

[T.D. 6500, 25 FR 11814, Nov. 26, 1960]

§ 1.691(a)–3 Character of gross income.

(a) The right to receive an amount of income in respect of a decedent shall be treated in the hands of the estate, or by the person entitled to receive such amount by bequest, devise, or inheritance from the decedent or by reason of his death, as if it had been acquired in the transaction by which the decedent (or a prior decedent) acquired such right, and shall be considered as having the same character it would have had if the decedent (or a prior decedent) had lived and received such amount. The provisions of section 1014(a), relating to the basis of property acquired from a decedent, do not apply to these amounts in the hands of the estate and such persons. See section 1014(c).

* * *

[T.D. 6500, 25 FR 11814, Nov. 26, 1960, as amended by T.D. 6885, 31 FR 7803, June 2, 1966; T.D. 7728, 45 FR 72650, Nov. 3, 1980]

§ 1.691(a)–4 Transfer of right to income in respect of a decedent.

(a) Section 691(a)(2) provides the rules governing the treatment of income in respect of a decedent (or a prior decedent) in the event a right to receive such income is transferred by the estate or person entitled thereto by bequest, devise, or inheritance, or by reason of the death of the decedent. In general, the transferor must include in his gross income for the taxable period in which the transfer occurs the amount of the consideration, if any, received for the right or the fair market value of the right at the time of the transfer, whichever is greater. Thus, upon a sale of such right by the estate or person entitled to receive it, the fair market value of the right or the amount received upon the sale, whichever is greater, is included in the gross income of the vendor. Similarly, if such right is disposed of by gift, the fair market value of the right at the time of the gift must be included in the gross income of the donor. * * *

(b) If the estate of a decedent or any person transmits the right to income in respect of a decedent to another who would be required by section 691(a)(1) to include such income when received in his gross income, only the transferee will include such income when received in his gross income. In this situation, a transfer within the meaning of section 691(a)(2) has not occurred. This paragraph may be illustrated by the following:

(1) If a person entitled to income in respect of a decedent dies before receiving such income, only his estate or other person entitled to such income by bequest, devise, or inheritance from the latter decedent, or by reason of the death of the latter decedent, must include such amount in gross income when received.

(2) If a right to income in respect of a decedent is transferred by an estate to a specific or residuary legatee, only the specific or residuary legatee must include such income in gross income when received.

(3) If a trust to which is bequeathed a right of a decedent to certain payments of income terminates and transfers the right to a beneficiary, only the beneficiary must include such income in gross income when received.

If the transferee described in subparagraphs (1), (2), and (3) of this paragraph transfers his right to receive the amounts in the manner described in paragraph (a) of this section, the principles contained in paragraph (a) are applied to such transfer. On the other hand, if the transferee transmits his right in the manner described in this paragraph, the principles of this paragraph are again applied to such transfer.

[T.D. 6500, 25 FR 11814, Nov. 26, 1960]

§ 1.691(b)–1 Allowance of deductions and credit in respect to decedents.

(a) Under section 691(b) the expenses, interest, and taxes described in sections 162, 163, 164, and 212 for which the decedent (or a prior decedent) was liable, which were not properly allowable as a deduction in his last taxable year or any prior taxable year, are allowed when paid—

(1) As a deduction by the estate; or

(2) If the estate was not liable to pay such obligation, as a deduction by the person who by bequest, devise, or inheritance from the decedent or by reason of the death of the decedent acquires, subject to such obligation, an interest in property of the decedent (or the prior decedent).

* * * For the purposes of subparagraph (2) of this paragraph, the right to receive an amount of gross income in respect of a decedent is considered property of the decedent; on the other hand, it is not necessary for a person, otherwise within the provisions of subparagraph (2) of this paragraph, to receive the right to any income in respect of a decedent. * * * If a decedent who reported in-

come by use of the cash receipts and disbursements method owned real property on which accrued taxes had become a lien, and if such property passed directly to the heir of the decedent in a jurisdiction in which real property does not become a part of a decedent's estate, the heir, upon paying such taxes, may take the same deduction under section 164 that would be allowed to the decedent if, while alive, he had made such payment.

(b) The deduction for percentage depletion is allowable only to the person (described in section 691(a)(1)) who receives the income in respect of the decedent to which the deduction relates, whether or not such person receives the property from which such income is derived. Thus, an heir who (by reason of the decedent's death) receives income derived from sales of units of mineral by the decedent (who reported income by use of the cash receipts and disbursements method) shall be allowed the deduction for percentage depletion, computed on the gross income from such number of units as if the heir had the same economic interest in the property as the decedent. Such heir need not also receive any interest in the mineral property other than such income. If the decedent did not compute his deduction for depletion on the basis of percentage depletion, any deduction for depletion to which the decedent was entitled at the date of his death would be allowable in computing his taxable income for his last taxable year, and there can be no deduction in respect of the decedent by any other person for such depletion.

[T.D. 6500, 25 FR 11814, Nov. 26, 1960]

§ 1.691(c)–1 Deduction for estate tax attributable to income in respect of a decedent.

(a) In general. A person who is required to include in gross income for any taxable year an amount of income in respect of a decedent may deduct for the same taxable year that portion of the estate tax imposed upon the decedent's estate which is attributable to the inclusion in the decedent's estate of the right to receive such amount. The deduction is determined as follows:

(1) Ascertain the net value in the decedent's estate of the items which are included under section 691 in computing gross income. This is the excess of the value included in the gross estate on account of the items of gross income in respect of the decedent (see § 1.691(a)–1 and paragraph (c) of this section) over the deductions from the gross estate for claims which represent the deductions and credit in respect of the decedent (see § 1.691(b)–1). But see section 691(d) * * * for computation of the special value of a survivor's annuity to be used in computing the net value for estate tax purposes in cases involving joint and survivor annuities.

(2) Ascertain the portion of the estate tax attributable to the inclusion in the gross estate of such net value. This is the excess of the estate tax over the estate tax computed without including such net value in the gross estate. In computing the estate tax without including such net value in the gross estate, any estate tax deduction (such as the marital deduction) which may be based upon the gross estate shall be recomputed so as to take into account the exclusion of such net value from the gross estate. * * *

For purposes of this section, the term "estate tax" means the tax imposed under section 2001 or 2101 (or the corresponding provisions of the Internal Revenue Code of 1939), reduced by the credits against such tax. Each person including in gross income an amount of income in respect of a decedent may deduct as his share of the portion of the estate tax (computed under subparagraph (2) of this paragraph) an amount which bears the same ratio to such portion as the value in the gross estate of the right to the income included by such person in gross income (or the amount included in gross income if lower) bears to the value in the gross estate of all the items of gross income in respect of the decedent.

(b) Prior decedent. If a person is required to include in gross income an amount of income in respect of a prior decedent, such person may deduct for the same taxable year that portion of the estate tax imposed upon the prior decedent's estate which is attributable to the inclusion of the prior decedent's estate of the value of the right to receive such amount. This deduction is computed in the same manner as provided in paragraph (a) of this section and is in addition to the deduction for estate tax imposed upon the decedent's estate which is attributable to the inclusion in the decedent's estate of the right to receive such amount.

(c) Amounts deemed to be income in respect of a decedent. For purposes of allowing the deduction under section 691(c), the following items are also considered to be income in respect of a decedent under section 691(a):

* * *

(2) Amounts received by a surviving annuitant during his life expectancy period as an annuity under a joint and survivor annuity contract to the extent included in gross income under section 72. See section 691(d).

(d) Examples. Paragraphs (a) and (b) of this section may be illustrated by the following examples:

Example (1). X, an attorney who kept his books by use of the cash receipts and disbursements method, was entitled at the date of his death to a fee for services rendered in a case not completed at the time of his death, which fee was valued in his estate at $1,000, and to accrued bond interest, which was valued in his estate at $500. In all, $1,500 was included in his gross estate in respect of income described in section 691(a)(1). There were deducted as claims against his estate $150 for business expenses for which his estate was liable and $50 for taxes accrued on certain property which he owned. In all, $200 was deducted for claims which represent amounts described in section 691(b) which are allowable as deductions to his estate or to the beneficiaries of his estate. His gross estate was $185,000 and, considering deductions of $15,000 and an exemption of $60,000, his taxable estate amounted to $110,000. The estate tax on this amount is $23,700 from which is subtracted a $75 credit for State death taxes leaving an estate tax liability of $23,625. In the year following the closing of X's estate, the fee in the amount of $1,200 was collected by X's son, who was the sole beneficiary of the estate. This amount was included under section 691(a)(1)(C) in the son's gross income. The son may deduct, in computing his taxable income for such year, $260 on account of the estate tax attributable to such income, computed as follows:

(1)	(i) Value of income described in section 691(a)(1) included in computing gross estate	$ 1,500
	(ii) Deductions in computing gross estate for claims representing deductions described in section 691(b)	200
	(iii) Net value of items described in section 691(a)(1)	1,300
(2)	(i) Estate tax	23,625
	(ii) Less: Estate tax computed without including $1,300 (item (1)(iii)) in gross estate	23,235
	(iii) Portion of estate tax attributable to net value of items described in section 691(a)(1)	390
(3)	(i) Value in gross estate of items described in section 691(a)(1) received in taxable year (fee)	1,000
	(ii) Value in gross estate of all income items described in section 691(a)(1) (item (1)(i))	1,500
	(iii) Part of estate tax deductible on account of receipt of $1,200 fee (1,000/1,500 of $390)	260

Although $1,200 was later collected as the fee, only the $1,000 actually included in the gross estate is used in the above computations. However, to avoid distortion, section 691(c) provides that if the value included in the gross estate is greater than the amount finally collected, only the amount collected shall be used in the above computations. Thus, if the amount collected as the fee were only $500, the estate tax deductible on the receipt of such amount would be 500/1,500 of $390, or $130. * * *

Example (2). Assume that in example (1) the fee valued at $1,000 had been earned by prior decedent Y and had been inherited by X who died before collecting it. With regard to the son, the fee would be considered income in respect of a prior decedent. Assume further that the fee was valued at $1,000 in Y's estate, that the net value in Y's estate of items described in section 691(a)(1) was $5,000 and that the estate tax imposed on Y's estate attributable to such net value was $550. In such case, the portion of such estate tax attributable to the fee would be 1,000/5,000 of $550, or $110. When the son collects the $1,200 fee, he will receive for the same taxable year a deduction of $110 with respect to the estate tax imposed on the estate of prior decedent Y as well as the deduction of $260 (as computed in example (1)) with respect to the estate tax imposed on the estate of decedent X.

[T.D. 6500, 25 FR 11814, Nov. 26, 1960, as amended by T.D. 6887, 31 FR 8812, June 24, 1966]

§ 1.691(c)–2 Estates and trusts.

(a) In the case of an estate or trust, the deduction prescribed in section 691(c) is determined in the same manner as described in § 1.691(c)–1, with the following exceptions:

(1) If any amount properly paid, credited, or required to be distributed by an estate or trust to a beneficiary consists of income in respect of a decedent received by the estate or trust during the taxable year—

(i) Such income shall be excluded in determining the income in respect of the decedent with respect to which the estate or trust is entitled to a deduction under section 691(c), and

(ii) Such income shall be considered income in respect of a decedent to such beneficiary for purposes of allowing the deduction under section 691(c) to such beneficiary.

(2) For determination of the amount of income in respect of a decedent received by the beneficiary, see sections 652 and 662, and §§ 1.652(b)–2 and 1.662(b)–2. However, for this purpose, distributable net income as defined in section 643(a) and the regulations thereunder shall be computed without taking into account the estate tax deduction provided in section 691(c) and this section. Distributable net income as modified under the preceding sentence shall be applied for other relevant purposes of subchapter J, chapter 1 of the Code, such as the deduction provided by section 651 or 661, or subpart D, part I of subchapter J, relating to excess distributions by trusts.

(3) The rule stated in subparagraph (1) of this paragraph does not apply to income in respect of a decedent which is properly allocable to corpus by the fiduciary during the taxable year but which is distributed to a beneficiary in a subsequent year. The deduction provided by section 691(c) in such a case is allowable only to the estate or trust. If any amount properly paid, credited, or required to be distributed by a trust qualifies as a distribution under section 666, the fact that a portion thereof constitutes income in respect of a decedent shall be disregarded for the purposes of determining the deduction of the trust and of the beneficiaries under section 691(c) since the deduction for estate taxes was taken into consideration in computing the undistributed net income of the trust for the preceding taxable year.

* * *

(d) The provisions of this section may be illustrated by the following example, in which it is assumed that the estate and the beneficiary make their returns on the calendar year basis:

Example. **(1)** The fiduciary of an estate receives taxable interest of $5,500 and income in respect of a decedent of $4,500 during the taxable year. Neither the will of the decedent nor local law requires the allocation to corpus of income in respect of a decedent. The estate tax attributable to the income in respect of a decedent is $1,500. In his discretion, the fiduciary distributes $2,000 (falling within sections 661(a) and 662(a)) to a beneficiary during that year. On these facts the fiduciary and beneficiary are respectively entitled to estate tax deductions of $1,200 and $300, computed as follows:

(2) Distributable net income computed under section 643(a) without regard to the estate tax deduction under section 691(c) is $10,000, computed as follows:

Taxable interest	$ 5,500
Income in respect of a decedent	4,500
Total	10,000

(3) Inasmuch as the distributable net income of $10,000 exceeds the amount of $2,000 distributed to the beneficiary, the deduction allowable to the estate under section 661(a) and the amount taxable to the beneficiary under section 662(a) is $2,000.

(4) The character of the amounts distributed to the beneficiary under section 662(b) is shown in the following table:

	Taxable interest	Income in respect of a decedent	Total
Distributable net income	$5,500	$4,500	$10,000
Amount deemed distributed under section 662(b)	1,100	900	2,000

(5) Accordingly, the beneficiary will be entitled to an estate tax deduction of $300 (900/4,500 × $1,500) and the estate will be entitled to an estate tax deduction of $1,200 (3,600/4,500 × $1,500).

(6) The taxable income of the estate is $6,200, computed as follows:

Gross income		$10,000
Less:		
Distributions to the beneficiary	$2,000	
Estate tax deduction under section 691(c)	1,200	
Personal exemption	600	
		3,800
Taxable income		6,200

[T.D. 6500, 25 FR 11814, Nov. 26, 1960]

PARTNERS AND PARTNERSHIPS

§ 1.701–1 Partners, not partnership, subject to tax.

Partners are liable for income tax only in their separate capacities. Partnerships as such are not subject to the income tax imposed by subtitle A but are required to make returns of income under the provisions of section 6031 and the regulations thereunder. For definition of the terms "partner" and "partnership", see sections 761 and 7701(a)(2), and the regulations thereunder. * * *

[T.D. 6500, 25 FR 11814, Nov. 26, 1960]

§ 1.701–2 Anti-abuse rule.

(a) Intent of subchapter K. Subchapter K is intended to permit taxpayers to conduct joint business (including investment) activities through a flexible economic arrangement without incurring an entity-level tax. Implicit in the intent of subchapter K are the following requirements—

(1) The partnership must be bona fide and each partnership transaction or series of related transactions (individually or collectively, the transaction) must be entered into for a substantial business purpose.

(2) The form of each partnership transaction must be respected under substance over form principles.

(3) Except as otherwise provided in this paragraph (a)(3), the tax consequences under subchapter K to each partner of partnership operations and of transactions between the partner and the partnership must accurately reflect the partner's economic agreement and clearly reflect the partner's income (collectively, proper reflection of income). However, certain provisions of subchapter K and the regulations thereunder were adopted to promote administrative convenience and other policy objectives, with the recognition that the application of those provisions to a transaction could, in some circumstances, produce tax results that do not properly reflect income. Thus, the proper reflection of income requirement of this paragraph (a)(3) is treated as satisfied with respect to a transaction that satisfies paragraphs (a)(1) and (2) of this section to the extent that the application of such a provision to the transaction and the ultimate tax results, taking into account all the relevant facts and circumstances, are clearly contemplated by that provision. See, for example, paragraph (d) Example 6 of this section (relating to the value-equals-basis rule in § 1.704–1(b)(2)(iii)(c)), paragraph (d) Example 9 of this section (relating to the election under section 754 to adjust basis in partnership property), and paragraph (d) Examples 10 and 11 of this section (relating to the basis in property distributed by a partnership under section 732). See also, for example, §§ 1.704–3(e)(1) and 1.752–2(e)(4) (providing certain de minimis exceptions).

(b) Application of subchapter K rules. The provisions of subchapter K and the regulations thereunder must be applied in a manner that is consistent with the intent of subchapter K as set forth in paragraph (a) of this section (intent of subchapter K). Accordingly, if a partnership is formed or availed of in connection with a transaction a principal purpose of which is to reduce substantially the present value of the partners' aggregate federal tax liability in a manner that is inconsistent with the intent of subchapter K, the Commissioner can recast the transaction for federal tax purposes, as appropriate to achieve tax results that are consistent with the intent of subchapter K, in light of the applicable statutory and regulatory provisions and the pertinent facts and circumstances. Thus, even though the transaction may fall within the literal words of a particular statutory or regulatory provision, the Commissioner can determine, based on the particular facts and circumstances, that to achieve tax results that are consistent with the intent of subchapter K—

(1) The purported partnership should be disregarded in whole or in part, and the partnership's assets and activities should be considered, in whole or in part, to be owned and conducted, respectively, by one or more of its purported partners;

(2) One or more of the purported partners of the partnership should not be treated as a partner;

(3) The methods of accounting used by the partnership or a partner should be adjusted to reflect clearly the partnership's or the partner's income;

(4) The partnership's items of income, gain, loss, deduction, or credit should be reallocated; or

(5) The claimed tax treatment should otherwise be adjusted or modified.

(c) Facts and circumstances analysis; factors. Whether a partnership was formed or availed of with a principal purpose to reduce substantially the present value of the partners' aggregate federal tax liability in a manner inconsistent with the intent of subchapter K is determined based on all of the facts and circumstances, including a comparison of the purported business purpose for a transaction and the claimed tax benefits resulting from the transaction. The factors set forth below may be indicative, but do not necessarily establish, that a partnership was used in such a manner. These factors are illustrative only, and therefore may not be the only factors taken into account in making the determination under this section. Moreover, the weight given to any factor (whether specified in this paragraph or otherwise) depends on all the facts and circumstances. The presence or absence of any factor described in this paragraph does not create a presumption that a partnership was (or was not) used in such a manner. Factors include:

(1) The present value of the partners' aggregate federal tax liability is substantially less than had the partners owned the partnership's assets and conducted the partnership's activities directly;

(2) The present value of the partners' aggregate federal tax liability is substantially less than would be the case if purportedly separate transactions that are designed to achieve a particular end result are integrated and treated as steps in a single transaction. For example, this analysis may indicate that it was contemplated that a partner who was necessary to achieve the intended tax results and whose interest in the partnership was liquidated or disposed of (in whole or in part) would be a partner only temporarily in order to provide the claimed tax benefits to the remaining partners;

(3) One or more partners who are necessary to achieve the claimed tax results either have a nominal interest in the partnership, are substantially protected from any risk of loss from the partnership's activities (through distribution preferences, indemnity or loss guaranty agreements, or other arrangements), or have little or no participation in the profits from the partnership's activities other than a preferred return that is in the nature of a payment for the use of capital;

(4) Substantially all of the partners (measured by number or interests in the partnership) are related (directly or indirectly) to one another;

(5) Partnership items are allocated in compliance with the literal language of §§ 1.704–1 and 1.704–2 but with results that are inconsistent with the purpose of section 704(b) and those regulations. In this regard, particular scrutiny will be paid to partnerships in which income or gain is specially allocated to one or more partners that may be legally or effectively exempt from federal taxation (for example, a foreign person, an exempt organization, an insolvent taxpayer, or a taxpayer with unused federal tax attributes such as net operating losses, capital losses, or foreign tax credits);

(6) The benefits and burdens of ownership of property nominally contributed to the partnership are in substantial part retained (directly or indirectly) by the contributing partner (or a related party); or

(7) The benefits and burdens of ownership of partnership property are in substantial part shifted (directly or indirectly) to the distributee partner before or after the property is actually distributed to the distributee partner (or a related party).

(d) Examples. The following examples illustrate the principles of paragraphs (a), (b), and (c) of this section. The examples set forth below do not delineate the boundaries of either permissible or impermissible types of transactions. Further, the addition of any facts or circumstances that are not specifically set forth in an example (or the deletion of any facts or circumstances) may alter the outcome of the transaction described in the example. Unless otherwise indicated, parties to the transactions are not related to one another.

Example 1. Choice of entity; avoidance of entity-level tax; use of partnership consistent with the intent of subchapter K. (i) A and B form limited partnership PRS to conduct a bona fide business. A, the corporate general partner, has a 1% partnership interest. B, the individual limited partner, has a 99% interest. PRS is properly classified as a partnership under §§ 301.7701–2 and 301.7701–3. A and B chose limited partnership form as a means to provide B with limited liability without subjecting the income from the business operations to an entity-level tax.

(ii) Subchapter K is intended to permit taxpayers to conduct joint business activity through a flexible economic arrangement without incurring an entity-level tax. See paragraph (a) of this section. Although B has retained, indirectly, substantially all of the benefits and burdens of ownership of the money or property B contributed to PRS (see paragraph (c)(6) of this section), the decision to organize and conduct business through PRS under these circumstances is consistent with this intent. In addition, on these facts, the requirements of paragraphs (a)(1), (2), and (3) of this section have been satisfied. The Commissioner therefore cannot invoke paragraph (b) of this section to recast the transaction.

Example 2. Choice of entity; avoidance of subchapter S shareholder requirements; use of partnership consistent with the intent of subchapter K. (i) A and B form partnership PRS to conduct a bona fide business. A is a corporation that has elected to be treated as an S corporation under subchapter S. B is a nonresident alien. PRS is properly classified as a partnership under §§ 301.7701–2 and 301.7701–3. Because section 1361(b) prohibits B from being a shareholder in A, A and B chose partnership form, rather than admit B as a shareholder in A, as a means to retain the benefits of subchapter S treatment for A and its shareholders.

(ii) Subchapter K is intended to permit taxpayers to conduct joint business activity through a flexible economic arrangement without incurring an entity-level tax. See paragraph (a) of this section. The decision to organize and conduct business through PRS is consistent with this intent. In addition, on these facts, the requirements of paragraphs (a)(1), (2), and (3) of this section have been satisfied. Although it may be argued that the form of the partnership transaction should not be respected because it does not reflect its substance (inasmuch as application of the substance over form doctrine arguably could result in B being treated as a shareholder of A, thereby invalidating A's subchapter S election), the facts indicate otherwise. The shareholders of A are subject to tax on their pro rata shares of A's income (see section 1361 et seq.), and B is subject to tax on B's distributive share of partnership income (see sections 871 and 875). Thus, the form in which this arrangement is cast accurately reflects its substance as a separate partnership and S corporation. The Commissioner therefore cannot invoke paragraph (b) of this section to recast the transaction.

* * *

Example 4. Choice of entity; avoidance of gain recognition under sections 351(e) and 357(c); use of partnership consistent with the intent of subchapter K. (i) X, ABC, and DEF form limited partnership PRS to conduct a bona fide real estate management business. PRS is properly classified as a partnership under §§ 301.7701–2 and 301.7701–3. X, the general partner, is a newly formed corporation that elects to be treated as a real estate investment trust as defined in section 856. X offers its stock to the public and contributes substantially all of the proceeds from the public offering to PRS. ABC and DEF, the limited partners, are existing partnerships with substantial real estate holdings. ABC and DEF contribute all of their real property assets to PRS, subject to liabilities that exceed their respective aggregate bases in the real property contributed, and terminate under section 708(b)(1)(A). In addition, some of the former partners of ABC and DEF each have the right, beginning two years after the formation of PRS, to require the redemption of their limited partnership interests in PRS in exchange for cash or X stock (at X's option) equal to the fair market value of their respective interests in PRS at the time of the redemption. These partners are not compelled, as a legal or practical matter, to exercise their exchange rights at any time. X, ABC, and DEF chose to form a partnership rather than have ABC and DEF invest directly in X to allow ABC and DEF to avoid recognition of gain under sections 351(e) and 357(c). Because PRS would not be treated as an investment company within the meaning of section 351(e) if PRS were incorporated (so long as it did not elect under section 856), section 721(a) applies to the contribution of the real property to PRS. See section 721(b).

(ii) Subchapter K is intended to permit taxpayers to conduct joint business activity through a flexible economic arrangement without incurring an entity-level tax. See paragraph (a) of this section. The decision to organize and conduct business through PRS, thereby avoiding the tax consequences that would have resulted from contributing the existing partnerships' real estate assets to X (by applying the rules of sections 721, 731, and 752 in lieu of the rules of sections 351(e) and 357(c)), is consistent with this intent. In addition, on these facts, the requirements of paragraphs (a)(1), (2), and (3) of this section have been satisfied. Although it may be argued that the form of the transaction should not be respected because it does not reflect its substance (inasmuch as the present value of the partners' aggregate federal tax liability is substantially less than would be the case if the transaction were integrated and treated as a contribution of the encumbered assets by ABC and DEF directly to X, see paragraph (c)(2) of this section), the facts indicate otherwise. For example, the right of some of the former ABC and DEF partners after two years to exchange their PRS interests for cash or X stock (at X's option) equal to the fair market value of their PRS interest at that time would not require that right to be considered as exercised prior to its actual exercise. Moreover, X may make other real estate investments and other business decisions, including the decision to raise additional capital for those purposes. Thus, although it may be likely that some or all of the partners with the right to do so will, at some point, exercise their exchange rights, and thereby receive either cash or X stock, the form of the transaction as a separate partnership and real estate investment trust is respected under substance over form principles (see paragraph (a)(2) of this section). The Commissioner therefore cannot invoke paragraph (b) of this section to recast the transaction.

Example 5. Special allocations; dividends received deductions; use of partnership consistent with the intent of subchapter K. (i) Corporations X and Y contribute equal amounts to PRS, a bona fide partnership formed to make joint investments. PRS pays $100x for a share of common stock of Z, an unrelated corporation, which has historically paid an annual dividend of $6x. PRS specially allocates the dividend income on the Z stock to X to the extent of the London Inter–Bank Offered Rate (LIBOR) on the record date, applied to X's contribution of $50x, and allocates the remainder of the dividend income to Y. All other items of partnership income and loss are allocated equally between X and Y. The allocations under the partnership agreement have substantial economic effect within the meaning of § 1.704–1(b)(2). In addition to avoiding an entity-level tax, a principal purpose for the formation of the partnership was to invest in the Z common stock and to allocate the dividend income from the stock to provide X with a floating-rate return based on LIBOR, while permitting X and Y to claim the dividends received deduction under section 243 on the dividends allocated to each of them.

(ii) Subchapter K is intended to permit taxpayers to conduct joint business activity through a flexible economic arrangement without incurring an entity-level tax. See paragraph (a) of this section. The decision to organize and conduct business through PRS is consistent with this intent. In addition, on these facts, the requirements of paragraphs (a)(1), (2), and (3) of this section have been satisfied. Section 704(b) and § 1.704–1(b)(2) permit income realized by the partnership to be allocated validly to the partners separate from the partners' respective ownership of the capital to which the allocations relate, provided that the allocations satisfy both the literal requirements of the statute and regulations and the purpose of those provisions (see paragraph (c)(5) of this section). Section 704(e)(2) is not applicable to the facts of this example (otherwise, the allocations would be required to be proportionate to the partners' ownership of contributed capital). The Commissioner therefore cannot invoke paragraph (b) of this section to recast the transaction.

Example 6. Special allocations; nonrecourse financing; low-income housing credit; use of partnership consistent with the intent of subchapter K. (i) A and B, high-bracket taxpayers, and X, a corporation with net operating loss carryforwards, form general partnership PRS to own and operate a building that qualifies for the low-income housing credit provided by section 42. The project is financed with both cash contributions from the partners and non-recourse indebtedness. The partnership agreement provides for special allocations of income and deductions, including the allocation of all depreciation deductions attributable to the building to A and B equally in a manner that is reasonably consistent with allocations that have substantial economic effect of some other significant partnership item attributable to the building. The section 42 credits are allocated to A and B in accordance with the allocation of depreciation deductions. PRS's allocations comply with all applicable regulations, including the requirements of §§ 1.704–1(b)(2)(ii) (pertaining to economic effect) and 1.704–2(e) (requirements for allocations of nonrecourse deductions). The nonrecourse indebtedness is validly allocated to the partners under the rules of § 1.752–3, thereby increasing the basis of the partners' respective partnership interests. The basis increase created by the nonrecourse indebtedness enables A and B to deduct their distributive share of losses from the partnership (subject to all other applicable limitations under the Internal Revenue Code) against their nonpartnership income and to apply the credits against their tax liability.

(ii) At a time when the depreciation deductions attributable to the building are not treated as nonrecourse deductions under § 1.704–2(c) (because there is no net increase in partnership minimum gain during the year), the special allocation of depreciation deductions to A and B has substantial economic effect because of the value-equals-basis safe harbor contained in § 1.704–1(b)(2)(iii)(c) and the fact that A and B would bear the economic burden of any decline in the value of the building (to the extent of the partnership's investment in the building), notwithstanding that A and B believe it is unlikely that the building will decline in value (and, accordingly, they anticipate significant timing benefits through the special allocation). Moreover, in later years, when the depreciation deductions attributable to the building are treated as nonrecourse deductions under § 1.704–2(c), the special allocation of depreciation deductions to A and B is considered to be consistent with the partners' interests in the partnership under § 1.704–2(e).

(iii) Subchapter K is intended to permit taxpayers to conduct joint business activity through a flexible economic arrangement without incurring an entity-level tax. See paragraph (a) of this section. The decision to organize and conduct business through PRS is consistent with this intent. In addition, on these facts, the requirements of paragraphs (a)(1), (2), and (3) of this section have been satisfied. Section 704(b), § 1.704–1(b)(2), and § 1.704–2(e) allow partnership items of income, gain, loss, deduction, and credit to be allocated validly to the partners separate from the partners' respective ownership of the capital to which the allocations relate, provided that the allocations satisfy both the literal requirements of the statute and regulations and the purpose of those provisions (see paragraph (c)(5) of this section). Moreover, the application of the value-equals-basis safe harbor and the provisions of § 1.704–2(e) with respect to the allocations to A and B, and the tax results of the application of those provisions, taking into account all the facts and circumstances, are clearly contemplated. Accordingly, even if the allocations would not otherwise be considered to satisfy the proper reflection of income standard in paragraph (a)(3) of this section, that requirement will be treated as satisfied under these facts. Thus, even though the partners' aggregate federal tax liability may be substantially less than had the partners owned the partnership's assets directly (due to X's inability to use its allocable share of the partnership's losses and credits) (see paragraph (c)(1) of this section), the transaction is not inconsistent with the intent of subchapter K. The Commissioner therefore cannot invoke paragraph (b) of this section to recast the transaction.

* * *

Example 8. Plan to duplicate losses through absence of section 754 election; use of partnership not consistent with the intent of subchapter K. (i) A owns land with a basis of $100x and a fair market value of $60x. A would like to sell the land to B. A and B devise a plan a principal purpose of which is to permit the duplication, for a substantial period of time, of the tax benefit of A's built-in loss in the land. To effect this plan, A, C (A's brother), and W (C's wife) form partnership PRS, to which A contributes the land, and C and W each contribute $30x. All partnership items are shared in proportion to the partners' respective contributions to PRS. PRS invests the cash in an investment asset (that is not a marketable security within the meaning of section 731(c)). PRS also leases the land to B under a three-year lease pursuant to which B has the option to purchase the land from PRS upon the expiration of the lease for an amount equal to its fair market value at that time. All lease proceeds received are immediately distributed to the partners. In year 3, at a time when the values of the partnership's assets have not materially changed, PRS agrees with A to liquidate A's interest in exchange for the investment asset held by PRS. Under section 732(b), A's basis in the asset distributed equals $100x, A's basis in A's partnership interest immediately before the distribution. Shortly thereafter, A sells the investment asset to X, an unrelated party, recognizing a $40x loss.

(ii) PRS does not make an election under section 754. Accordingly, PRS's basis in the land contributed by A remains $100x. At the end of year 3, pursuant to the lease option, PRS sells the land to B for $60x (its fair market value). Thus, PRS recognizes a $40x loss on the sale, which is allocated equally between C and W. C's and W's bases in their partnership interests are reduced to $10x each pursuant to section 705. Their respective interests are worth $30x each. Thus, upon liquidation of PRS (or their interests therein), each of C and W will recognize $20x of gain. However, PRS's continued existence defers recognition of that gain indefinitely. Thus, if this arrangement is respected, C and W duplicate for their benefit A's built-in loss in the land prior to its contribution to PRS.

(iii) On these facts, any purported business purpose for the transaction is insignificant in comparison to the tax benefits that would result if the transaction were respected for federal tax purposes (see paragraph (c) of this section). Accordingly, the transaction lacks a substantial business purpose (see paragraph (a)(1) of this section). In addition, factors (1), (2), and (4) of paragraph (c) of this section indicate that PRS was used with a principal purpose to reduce substantially the partners' tax liability in a manner inconsistent with the intent of subchapter K. On these facts, PRS is not bona fide (see paragraph (a)(1) of this section), and the transaction is not respected under applicable substance over form principles (see paragraph (a)(2) of this section). Further, the tax consequences to the partners do not properly reflect the partners' income; and Congress did not contemplate application of section 754 to partnerships such as PRS, which was formed for a principal purpose of producing a double tax benefit from a single economic loss (see paragraph (a)(3) of this section). Thus, PRS has been formed and availed of with a principal purpose of reducing substantially the present value of the partners' aggregate federal tax liability in a manner inconsistent with the intent of subchapter K. Therefore (in addition to possibly challenging the transaction under judicial principles or other statutory authorities, such as the substance over form doctrine or the disguised sale rules under section 707 (see paragraph (h) of this section)), the Commissioner can recast the transaction as appropriate under paragraph (b) of this section.

Example 9. Absence of section 754 election; use of partnership consistent with the intent of subchapter K. (i) PRS is a bona fide partnership formed to engage in investment activities with contributions of cash from each partner. Several years after joining PRS, A, a partner with a capital account balance and basis in its partnership interest of $100x, wishes to withdraw from PRS. The partnership agreement entitles A to receive the balance of A's capital account in cash or securities owned by PRS at the time of withdrawal, as mutually agreed to by A and the managing general partner, P. P and A agree to distribute to A $100x worth of non-marketable securities (see section 731(c)) in which PRS has an aggregate basis of $20x. Upon distribution, A's aggregate basis in the securities is $100x under section 732(b). PRS does not make an election to adjust the basis in its remaining assets under section 754. Thus, PRS's basis in its remaining assets is unaffected by the distribution. In contrast, if a section 754 election had been in effect for the year of the distribution, under these facts section 734(b) would have required PRS to adjust the basis in its remaining assets downward by the amount of the untaxed appreciation in the distributed property, thus reflecting that gain in PRS's retained assets. In selecting the assets to be distributed, A and P had a principal purpose to take advantage of the facts that A's basis in the securities will be determined by reference to A's basis in its partnership interest under section 732(b), and because PRS will not make an election under section 754, the remaining partners of PRS will likely enjoy a federal tax timing advantage (i.e., from the $80x of additional basis in its assets that would have been eliminated if the section 754 election had been made) that is inconsistent with proper reflection of income under paragraph (a)(3) of this section.

(ii) Subchapter K is intended to permit taxpayers to conduct joint business activity through a flexible economic arrangement without incurring an entity-level tax. See paragraph (a) of this section. The decision to organize and conduct business through PRS is consistent with this intent. In addition, on these facts, the requirements of paragraphs (a)(1) and (2) of this section have been satisfied. The validity of the tax treatment of this transaction is therefore dependent upon whether the transaction satisfies (or is treated as satisfying) the proper reflection of income standard under paragraph (a)(3) of this section. A's basis in the distributed securities is properly determined under section 732(b). The benefit to the remaining partners is a result of PRS not having made an election under section 754. Subchapter K is generally intended to produce tax consequences that achieve proper reflection of income. However, paragraph (a)(3) of this section provides that if the application of a provision of subchapter K produces tax results that do not properly reflect income, but application of that provision to the transaction and the ultimate tax results, taking into account all the relevant facts and circumstances, are clearly contemplated by that provision (and the transaction satisfies the requirements of paragraphs (a)(1) and (2) of this section), then the application of that provision to the transaction will be treated as satisfying the proper reflection of income standard.

(iii) In general, the adjustments that would be made if an election under section 754 were in effect are necessary to minimize distortions between the partners' bases in their partnership interests and the partnership's basis in its assets following, for example, a distribution to a partner. The electivity of section 754 is intended to provide administrative convenience for bona fide partnerships that are engaged in transactions for a substantial business purpose, by providing those partnerships the option of not adjusting their bases in their remaining assets following a distribution to a partner. Congress clearly recognized that if the section 754 election were not made, basis distortions may result. Taking into account all the facts and circumstances of the transaction, the electivity of section 754 in the context of the distribution from PRS to A, and the ultimate tax consequences that follow from the failure to make the election with respect to the transaction, are clearly contemplated by section 754. Thus, the tax consequences of this transaction will be treated as satisfying the proper reflection of income standard under paragraph (a)(3) of this section. The Commissioner therefore cannot invoke paragraph (b) of this section to recast the transaction.

Example 10. Basis adjustments under section 732; use of partnership consistent with the intent of subchapter K. **(i)** A, B, and C are partners in partnership PRS, which has for several years been engaged in substantial bona fide business activities. For valid business reasons, the partners agree that A's interest in PRS, which has a value and basis of $100x, will be liquidated with the following assets of PRS: a nondepreciable asset with a value of $60x and a basis to PRS of $40x, and related equipment with two years of cost recovery remaining and a value and basis to PRS of $40x. Neither asset is described in section 751 and the transaction is not described in section 732(d). Under section 732(b) and (c), A's $100x basis in A's partnership interest will be allocated between the nondepreciable asset and the equipment received in the liquidating distribution in proportion to PRS's bases in those assets, or $50x to the nondepreciable asset and $50x to the equipment. Thus, A will have a $10x built-in gain in the nondepreciable asset ($60x value less $50x basis) and a $10x built-in loss in the equipment ($50x basis less $40x value), which it expects to recover rapidly through cost recovery deductions. In selecting the assets to be distributed to A, the partners had a principal purpose to take advantage of the fact that A's basis in the assets will be determined by reference to A's basis in A's partnership interest, thus, in effect, shifting a portion of A's basis from the nondepreciable asset to the equipment, which in turn would allow A to recover that portion of its basis more rapidly. This shift provides a federal tax timing advantage to A, with no offsetting detriment to B or C.

(ii) Subchapter K is intended to permit taxpayers to conduct joint business activity through a flexible economic arrangement without incurring an entity-level tax. See paragraph (a) of this section. The decision to organize and conduct business through PRS is consistent with this intent. In addition, on these facts, the requirements of paragraphs (a)(1) and (2) of this section have been satisfied. The validity of the tax treatment of this transaction is therefore dependent upon whether the transaction satisfies (or is treated as satisfying) the proper reflection of income standard under paragraph (a)(3) of this section. Subchapter K is generally intended to produce tax consequences that achieve proper reflection of income. However, paragraph (a)(3) of this section provides that if the application of a provision of subchapter K produces tax results that do not properly reflect income, but the application of that provision to the transaction and the ultimate tax results, taking into account all the relevant facts and circumstances, are clearly contemplated by that provision (and the transaction satisfies the requirements of paragraphs (a)(1) and (2) of this section), then the application of that provision to the transaction will be treated as satisfying the proper reflection of income standard.

(iii) A's basis in the assets distributed to it was determined under section 732(b) and (c). The transaction does not properly reflect A's income due to the basis distortions caused by the distribution and the shifting of basis from a nondepreciable to a depreciable asset. However, the basis rules under section 732, which in some situations can produce tax results that are inconsistent with the proper reflection of income standard (see paragraph (a)(3) of this section), are intended to provide simplifying administrative rules for bona fide partnerships that are engaged in transactions with a substantial business purpose. Taking into account all the facts and circumstances of the transaction, the application of the basis rules under section 732 to the distribution from PRS to A, and the ultimate tax consequences of the application of that provision of subchapter K, are clearly contemplated. Thus, the application of section 732 to this transaction will be treated as satisfying the proper reflection of income standard under paragraph (a)(3) of this section. The Commissioner therefore cannot invoke paragraph (b) of this section to recast the transaction.

Example 11. Basis adjustments under section 732; plan or arrangement to distort basis allocations artificially; use of partnership not consistent with the intent of subchapter K. **(i)** Partnership PRS has for several years been engaged in the development and management of commercial real estate projects. X, an unrelated party, desires to acquire undeveloped land owned by PRS, which has a value of $95x and a basis of $5x. X expects to hold the land indefinitely after its acquisition. Pursuant to a plan a principal purpose of which is to permit X to acquire and hold the land but nevertheless to recover for tax purposes a substantial portion of the purchase price for the land, X contributes $100x to PRS for an interest therein. Subsequently (at a time when the value of the partnership's assets have not materially changed), PRS distributes to X in liquidation of its interest in PRS the land and another asset with a value and basis to PRS of $5x. The second asset is an insignificant part of the economic transaction but is important to achieve the desired tax results. Under section 732(b) and (c), X's $100x basis in its partnership interest is allocated between the assets distributed to it in proportion to their bases to PRS, or $50x each. Thereafter, X plans to sell the second asset for its value of $5x, recognizing a loss of $45x. In this manner, X will, in effect, recover a substantial portion of the purchase price of the land almost immediately. In selecting the assets to be distributed to X, the partners had a principal purpose to take advantage of the fact that X's basis in the assets will be determined under section 732(b) and (c), thus, in effect, shifting a portion of X's basis economically allocable to the land that X intends to retain to an inconsequential asset that X intends to dispose of quickly. This shift provides a federal tax timing advantage to X, with no offsetting detriment to any of PRS's other partners.

(ii) Although section 732 recognizes that basis distortions can occur in certain situations, which may produce tax results that do not satisfy the proper reflection of income standard of paragraph (a)(3) of this section, the provision is intended only to provide ancillary, simplifying tax results for bona fide partnership transactions that are engaged in for substantial business purposes. Section 732 is not intended to serve as the basis for plans or arrangements in which inconsequential or immaterial assets are included in the distribution with a principal purpose of obtaining substantially favorable tax results by virtue of the statute's simplifying rules. The transaction does not properly reflect X's income due to the basis distortions caused by the distribution that result in shifting a significant portion of X's basis to this inconsequential asset. Moreover, the proper reflection of income standard contained in paragraph (a)(3) of this section is not treated as satisfied, because, taking into account all the facts and circumstances, the application of section 732 to this arrangement, and the ultimate tax consequences that would thereby result, were not clearly contemplated by that provision of subchapter K. In addition, by using a partnership (if respected), the partners' aggregate federal tax liability would be substantially less than had they owned the partnership's assets directly (see paragraph (c)(1) of this section). On these facts, PRS has been formed and availed of with a principal purpose to reduce the taxpayers' aggregate federal tax liability in a manner that is inconsistent with the intent of subchapter K. Therefore (in addition to possibly challenging the transaction under applicable judicial principles and statutory authorities, such as the disguised sale rules under section 707, see paragraph (h) of this section), the Commissioner can recast the transaction as appropriate under paragraph (b) of this section.

(e) Abuse of entity treatment.

(1) General rule. The Commissioner can treat a partnership as an aggregate of its partners in whole or in part as appropriate to carry out the purpose of any provision of the Internal Revenue Code or the regulations promulgated thereunder.

(2) Clearly contemplated entity treatment. Paragraph (e)(1) of this section does not apply to the extent that—

(i) A provision of the Internal Revenue Code or the regulations promulgated thereunder prescribes the treatment of a partnership as an entity, in whole or in part, and

(ii) That treatment and the ultimate tax results, taking into account all the relevant facts and circumstances, are clearly contemplated by that provision.

(f) Examples. The following examples illustrate the principles of paragraph (e) of this section. The examples set forth below do not delineate the boundaries of either permissible or impermissible types of transactions. Further, the addition of any facts or circumstances that are not specifically set forth in an example (or the deletion of any facts or circumstances) may alter the outcome of the transaction described in the example. Unless otherwise indicated, parties to the transactions are not related to one another.

Example 1. Aggregate treatment of partnership appropriate to carry out purpose of section

163(e)(5). **(i)** Corporations X and Y are partners in partnership PRS, which for several years has engaged in substantial bona fide business activities. As part of these business activities, PRS issues certain high yield discount obligations to an unrelated third party. Section 163(e)(5) defers (and in certain circumstances disallows) the interest deductions on this type of obligation if issued by a corporation. PRS, X, and Y take the position that, because PRS is a partnership and not a corporation, section 163(e)(5) is not applicable.

(ii) Section 163(e)(5) does not prescribe the treatment of a partnership as an entity for purposes of that section. The purpose of section 163(e)(5) is to limit corporate-level interest deductions on certain obligations. The treatment of PRS as an entity could result in a partnership with corporate partners issuing those obligations and thereby circumventing the purpose of section 163(e)(5), because the corporate partner would deduct its distributive share of the interest on obligations that would have been deferred until paid or disallowed had the corporation issued its share of the obligation directly. Thus, under paragraph (e)(1) of this section, PRS is properly treated as an aggregate of its partners for purposes of applying section 163(e)(5) (regardless of whether any party had a tax avoidance purpose in having PRS issue the obligation). Each partner of PRS will therefore be treated as issuing its share of the obligations for purposes of determining the deductibility of its distributive share of any interest on the obligations. See also section 163(i)(5)(B).

Example 2. Aggregate treatment of partnership appropriate to carry out purpose of section 1059. **(i)** Corporations X and Y are partners in partnership PRS, which for several years has engaged in substantial bona fide business activities. As part of these business activities, PRS purchases 50 shares of Corporation Z common stock. Six months later, Corporation Z announces an extraordinary dividend (within the meaning of section 1059). Section 1059(a) generally provides that if any corporation receives an extraordinary dividend with respect to any share of stock and the corporation has not held the stock for more than two years before the dividend announcement date, the basis in the stock held by the corporation is reduced by the nontaxed portion of the dividend. PRS, X, and Y take the position that section 1059(a) is not applicable because PRS is a partnership and not a corporation.

(ii) Section 1059(a) does not prescribe the treatment of a partnership as an entity for purposes of that section. The purpose of section 1059(a) is to limit the benefits of the dividends received deduction with respect to extraordinary dividends. The treatment of PRS as an entity could result in corporate partners in the partnership receiving dividends through partnerships in circumvention of the intent of section 1059. Thus, under paragraph (e)(1) of this section, PRS is properly treated as an aggregate of its partners for purposes of applying section 1059 (regardless of whether any party had a tax avoidance purpose in acquiring the Z stock through PRS). Each partner of PRS will therefore be treated as owning its share of the stock. Accordingly, PRS must make appropriate adjustments to the basis of the Corporation Z stock, and the partners must also make adjustments to the basis in their respective interests in PRS under section 705(a)(2)(B). See also section 1059(g)(1).

* * *

(h) Application of nonstatutory principles and other statutory authorities. The Commissioner can continue to assert and to rely upon applicable nonstatutory principles and other statutory and regulatory authorities to challenge transactions. This section does not limit the applicability of those principles and authorities.

(i) Scope and application. This section applies solely with respect to taxes under subtitle A of the Internal Revenue Code, and for purposes of this section, any reference to a federal tax is limited to any tax imposed under subtitle A of the Internal Revenue Code.

[T.D. 8588, 60 FR 23, Jan. 3, 1995, as amended by T.D. 8592, 60 FR 18741, Apr. 13, 1995]

§ 1.702–1 Income and credits of partner.

(a) General rule. Each partner is required to take into account separately in his return his distributive share, whether or not distributed, of each class or item of partnership income, gain, loss, deduction, or credit described in subparagraphs (1) through (9) of this paragraph. (For the taxable year in which a partner includes his distributive share of partnership taxable income, see section 706(a) and § 1.706–1(a). Such distributive share shall be determined as provided in section 704 and § 1.704–1.) Accordingly, in determining his income tax:

(1) Each partner shall take into account, as part of his gains and losses from sales or exchanges of capital assets held for not more than 1 year * * *, his distributive share of the combined net amount of such gains and losses of the partnership.

(2) Each partner shall take into account, as part of his gains and losses from sales or exchanges of capital assets held for more than 1 year * * *, his distributive share of the combined net amount of such gains and losses of the partnership.

(3) Each partner shall take into account, as part of his gains and losses from sales or exchanges of property described in section 1231 (relating to property used in the trade or business and involuntary conversions), his distributive share of the combined net amount of such gains and losses of the partnership. The partnership shall not combine such items with items set forth in subparagraph (1) or (2) of this paragraph.

(4) Each partner shall take into account, as part of the charitable contributions paid by him, his distributive share of each class of charitable contributions paid by the partnership within the partnership's taxable year. Section 170 determines the extent to which such amount may be allowed as a deduction to the partner. For the definition of the term "charitable contribution," see section 170(c).

(5) Each partner shall take into account, as part of the dividends received by him from domestic corporations, his distributive share of dividends received by the partnership * * *.

* * *

(8)(i) Each partner shall take into account separately, as part of any class of income, gain, loss, deduction, or credit, his distributive share of the following items: * * * gains and losses from wagering transactions (section 165(d)); soil and water conservation expenditures (section 175); nonbusiness expenses as described in section 212; medical, dental, etc., expenses (section 213); * * * alimony, etc., payments (section 215); amounts representing taxes and interest paid to cooperative housing corporations (section 216); intangible drilling and developments costs (section 263(c)); * * * certain mining exploration expenditures (section 617); income, gain, or loss to the partnership under section 751(b); and any items of income, gain, loss, deduction, or credit subject to a special allocation under the partnership agreement which differs from the allocation of partnership taxable income or loss generally.

(ii) Each partner must also take into account separately the partner's distributive share of any partnership item which, if separately taken into account by any partner, would result in an income tax liability for that partner, or for any other person, different from that which would result if that partner did not take the item into account separately. * * * Under section 911(a), if any partner is a bona fide resident of a foreign country who may exclude from gross income the part of the partner's distributive share which qualifies as earned income, as defined in section 911(b), the earned income of the partnership for all partners must be separately stated. * * *

(iii) Each partner shall aggregate the amount of his separate deductions or exclusions and his distributive share of partnership deductions or exclusions separately stated in determining the amount allowable to him of any deduction or exclusion under subtitle A of the Code as to which a limitation is imposed. * * *

(9) Each partner shall also take into account separately his distributive share of the taxable income or loss of the partnership, exclusive of items requiring separate computations under subparagraphs (1) through (8) of this paragraph. For limitation on allowance of a partner's distributive share of partnership losses, see section 704(d) and paragraph (d) of § 1.704–1.

(b) Character of items constituting distributive share. The character in the hands of a partner of any item of income, gain, loss, deduction, or credit described in section 702(a)(1) through (8) shall be determined as if such item were realized directly from the source from which realized by the partnership or incurred in the same manner as incurred by the partnership. For example, a partner's distributive share of gain from the sale of depreciable property used in the trade or business of the partnership shall be considered as gain from the sale of such depreciable property in the hands of the partner. * * *

(c) Gross income of a partner. (1) Where it is necessary to determine the amount or character of the gross income of a partner, his gross income shall include the partner's distributive share of the gross income of the partnership, that is, the amount of gross income of the partnership from which was derived the partner's distributive share of partnership taxable income or loss (including items described in section 702(a)(1) through (8)). * * *

* * *

(2) In determining the applicability of the 6–year period of limitation on assessment and collection provided in section 6501(e) (relating to omission of more than 25 percent of gross income), a partner's gross income includes his distributive share of partnership gross income (as described in section 6501(e)(1)(A)(i)). In this respect, the amount of partnership gross income from which was derived the partner's distributive share of any item of partnership income, gain, loss, deduction, or credit (as included or disclosed in the partner's return) is considered as an amount of gross income stated in the partner's return for the purposes of section 6501(e). For example, A, who is entitled to one-fourth of the profits of the ABCD partnership, which has $10,000 gross income and $2,000 taxable income, reports only $300 as his distributive share of partnership profits. A should have shown $500 as his distributive share of profits, which amount was derived from $2,500 of partnership gross income. However, since A included only $300 on his return without explaining in the return the difference of $200, he is regarded as having stated in his return only $1,500 ($300/$500 of $2,500) as gross income from the partnership.

(d) Partners in community property States. If separate returns are made by a husband and wife domiciled in a community property State, and only one spouse is a member of the partnership, the part of his or her distributive share of any item or items listed in paragraph (a)(1) through (9) of this section which is community property, or which is derived from community property, should be reported by the husband and wife in equal proportions.

* * *

[T.D. 6500, 25 FR 11814, Nov. 26, 1960, as amended by T.D. 6605, 27 FR 8097, Aug. 15, 1962; T.D. 6777, 29 FR 17809, Dec. 16, 1964; T.D. 6885, 31 FR 7803, June 2, 1966; T.D. 7192, 37 FR 12949, June 30, 1972; T.D. 7564, 43 FR 40496, Sept. 12, 1978; T.D. 7728, 45 FR 72650, Nov. 3, 1980; T.D. 8247, 54 FR 13680, Apr. 5, 1989; T.D. 8348, 56 FR 21952, May 13, 1991; T.D. 8348, 57 FR 4913, Feb. 10, 1992; T.D. 9008, 67 FR 48020, July 23, 2002; T.D. 9194, 70 FR 18928, Apr. 11, 2005]

§ 1.703–1 Partnership computations.

(a) Income and deductions. **(1)** The taxable income of a partnership shall be computed in the same manner as the taxable income of an individual, except as otherwise provided in this section. A partnership is required to state separately in its return the items described in section 702(a)(1) through (7) [now (a)(1) through (6)] and, in addition, to attach to its return a statement setting forth separately those items described in section 702(a)(8) [now section 702(a)(7)] which the partner is required to take into account separately in determining his income tax. See paragraph (a)(8) of § 1.702–1. The partnership is further required to compute and to state separately in its return:

(i) As taxable income under section 702(a)(9) [now section 702(a)(8)], the total of all other items of gross income (not separately stated) over the total of all other allowable deductions (not separately stated), or

(ii) As loss under section 702(a)(9),* the total of all other allowable deductions (not separately stated) over the total of all other items of gross income (not separately stated).

The taxable income or loss so computed shall be accounted for by the partners in accordance with their partnership agreement.

(2) The partnership is not allowed the following deductions:

(i) The standard deduction * * *.

(ii) The deduction for personal exemptions provided in section 151.

* * *

(iv) The deduction for charitable contributions provided in section 170. Each partner is considered as having paid within his taxable year his distributive share of any contribution or gift, payment of which was actually made by the partnership within its taxable year ending within or with the partner's taxable year. This item shall be accounted for separately by the partners as provided in section 702(a)(4). See also paragraph (b) of § 1.702–1.

(v) The net operating loss deduction provided in section 172. See § 1.702–2.

(vi) The additional itemized deductions for individuals provided in part VII, subchapter B, chapter 1 of the Code, as follows: Expenses for production of income (section 212); medical, dental, etc., expenses (section 213); * * * alimony, etc., payments (section 215); and amounts representing taxes and interest paid to cooperative housing corporation (section 216). However, see paragraph (a)(8) of § 1.702–1.

* * *

(viii) The * * * deduction for capital loss carryover provided by section 1212.

(b) Elections of the partnership—(1) General rule. Any elections (other than those described in subparagraph (2) of this paragraph) affecting the computation of income derived from a partnership shall be made by the partnership. For example, elections of methods of accounting, of computing depreciation, of treating soil and water conservation expenditures, and the option to deduct as expenses intangible drilling and development costs, shall be made by the partnership and not by the partners separately. All partnership elections are applicable to all partners equally, but any election made by a partnership shall not apply to any partner's nonpartnership interests.

* * *

[T.D. 6500, 25 FR 11814, Nov. 26, 1960, as amended by T.D. 7192, 37 FR 12949, June 30, 1972; T.D. 7332, 39 FR 44232, Dec. 23, 1974; T.D. 8348, 56 FR 21952, May 13, 1991; T.D. 8348, 57 FR 4913, Feb. 10, 1992]

§ 1.704–1 Partner's distributive share.

(a) Effect of partnership agreement. A partner's distributive share of any item or class of items of income, gain, loss, deduction, or credit of the partnership shall be determined by the partnership agreement, unless otherwise provided by section 704 and paragraphs (b) through (e) of this section. For definition of partnership agreement see section 761(c).

(b) Determination of partner's distributive share—(0) Cross-references.

Heading	Section
Cross-references	1.704–1(b)(0)
In general	1.704–1(b)(1)
Basic principles	1.704–1(b)(1)(i)
Effective dates	1.704–1(b)(1)(ii)
Generally	1.704–1(b)(1)(ii)(a)
Foreign tax expenditures	1.704–1(b)(1)(ii)(b)
[Reserved]	1.704–1(b)(1)(ii)(b)(3)
Effect of other sections	1.704–1(b)(1)(iii)
Other possible tax consequences	1.704–1(b)(1)(iv)
Purported allocations	7 1.704–1(b)(1)(v)
Section 704(c) determinations	1.704–1(b)(1)(vi)
Bottom line allocations	1.704–1(b)(1)(vii)
Substantial economic effect	1.704–1(b)(2)
Two-part analysis	1.704–1(b)(2)(i)
Economic effect	1.704–1(b)(2)(ii)
Fundamental principles	1.704–1(b)(2)(ii)(a)
Three requirements	1.704–1(b)(2)(ii)(b)
Obligation to restore deficit	1.704–1(b)(2)(ii)(c)
Alternate test for economic effect	1.704–1(b)(2)(ii)(d)
Partial economic effect	1.704–1(b)(2)(ii)(e)
Reduction of obligation to restore	1.704–1(b)(2)(ii)(f)
Liquidation defined	1.704–1(b)(2)(ii)(g)
Partnership agreement defined	1.704–1(b)(2)(ii)(h)
Economic effect equivalence	1.704–1(b)(2)(ii)(i)
Substantiality	1.704–1(b)(2)(iii)
General rules	1.704–1(b)(2)(iii)(a)
Shifting tax consequences	1.704–1(b)(2)(iii)(b)
Transitory allocations	1.704–1(b)(2)(iii)(c)
Maintenance of capital accounts	1.704–1(b)(2)(iv)
In general	1.704–1(b)(2)(iv)(a)
Basic rules	1.704–1(b)(2)(iv)(b)
Treatment of liabilities	1.704–1(b)(2)(iv)(c)
Contributed property	1.704–1(b)(2)(iv)(d)
In general	1.704–1(b)(2)(iv)(d)(1)
Contribution of promissory notes	1.704–1(b)(2)(iv)(d)(2)
Section 704(c) considerations	1.704–1(b)(2)(iv)(d)(3)
Exercise of noncompensatory option	1.704–1(b)(2)(iv)(d)(4)
Distributed property	1.704–1(b)(2)(iv)(e)
In general	1.704–1(b)(2)(iv)(e)(1)
Distribution of promissory notes	1.704–1(b)(2)(iv)(e)(2)
Revaluations of property	1.704–1(b)(2)(iv)(f)
Adjustments to reflect book value	1.704–1(b)(2)(iv)(g)
In general	1.704–1(b)(2)(iv)(g)(1)
Payables and receivables	1.704–1(b)(2)(iv)(g)(2)
Determining amount of book items	1.704–1(b)(2)(iv)(g)(3)
Determinations of fair market value	1.704–1(b)(2)(iv)(h)
In general	1.704–1(b)(2)(iv)(h)(1)
Adjustments for noncompensatory options	1.704–1(b)(2)(iv)(h)(2)
Section 705(a)(2)(B) expenditures	1.704–1(b)(2)(iv)(i)
In general	1.704–1(b)(2)(iv)(i)(1)
Expenses described in section 709	1.704–1(b)(2)(iv)(i)(2)
Disallowed losses	1.704–1(b)(2)(iv)(i)(3)
Basis adjustments to section 38 property	1.704–1(b)(2)(iv)(j)
Depletion of oil and gas properties	1.704–1(b)(2)(iv)(k)
In general	1.704–1(b)(2)(iv)(k)(1)
Simulated depletion	1.704–1(b)(2)(iv)(k)(2)
Actual depletion	1.704–1(b)(2)(iv)(k)(3)
Effect of book values	1.704–1(b)(2)(iv)(k)(4)
Transfers of partnership interests	1.704–1(b)(2)(iv)(*l*)
Section 754 elections	1.704–1(b)(2)(iv)(m)
In general	1.704–1(b)(2)(iv)(m)(1)
Section 743 adjustments	1.704–1(b)(2)(iv)(m)(2)
Section 732 adjustments	1.704–1(b)(2)(iv)(m)(3)
Section 734 adjustments	1.704–1(b)(2)(iv)(m)(4)
Limitations on adjustments	1.704–1(b)(2)(iv)(m)(5)
Partnership level characterization	1.704–1(b)(2)(iv)(n)
Guaranteed payments	1.704–1(b)(2)(iv)(*o*)
Minor discrepancies	1.704–1(b)(2)(iv)(p)
Adjustments where guidance is lacking	1.704–1(b)(2)(iv)(q)
Restatement of capital accounts	1.704–1(b)(2)(iv)(r)
Adjustments on exercise of a noncompensatory option	1.704–1(b)(2)(iv)(s)
Partner's interest in the partnership	1.704–1(b)(3)
In general	1.704–1(b)(3)(i)
Factors considered	1.704–1(b)(3)(ii)
Certain determinations	1.704–1(b)(3)(iii)
Special rules	1.704–1(b)(4)
Allocations to reflect revaluations	1.704–1(b)(4)(i)
Credits	1.704–1(b)(4)(ii)
Excess percentage depletion	1.704–1(b)(4)(iii)
Allocations attributable to nonrecourse liabilities	1.704–1(b)(4)(iv)
Allocations under section 613A(c)(7)(D)	1.704–1(b)(4)(v)
Amendments to partnership agreement	1.704–1(b)(4)(vi)
Recapture	1.704–1(b)(4)(vii)
Allocation of creditable foreign taxes	1.704–1(b)(4)(viii)
In general	1.704–1(b)(4)(viii)(a)
Creditable foreign tax expenditures (CFTEs)	1.704–1(b)(4)(viii)(b)
Income to which CFTEs relate	1.704–1(b)(4)(viii)(c)
In general	1.704–1(b)(4)(viii)(c)(1)
CFTE category	1.704–1(b)(4)(viii)(c)(2)
Net income in a CFTE category	1.704–1(b)(4)(viii)(c)(3)
Distributive shares of income	1.704–1(b)(4)(viii)(c)(4)
No net income in a CFTE category	1.704–1(b)(4)(viii)(c)(5)
Allocation and apportionment of CFTEs to CFTE categories	1.704–1(b)(4)(viii)(d)
In general	1.704–1(b)(4)(viii)(d)(1)
Timing and base differences	1.704–1(b)(4)(viii)(d)(2)
[Reserved]	1.704–1(b)(4)(viii)(d)(2)
Allocations with respect to noncompensatory options	1.704–1(b)(4)(ix)
Corrective allocations	1.704–1(b)(4)(x)
Examples	1.704–1(b)(5)

(1) In general—(i) Basic principles. Under section 704(b) if a partnership agreement does not provide for the allocation of income, gain, loss, deduction, or credit (or item thereof) to a partner, or if the partnership agreement provides for the allocation of income, gain, loss, deduction, or credit (or item thereof) to a partner but such allocation does not have substantial economic effect, then the partner's distributive share of such income, gain, loss, deduction, or credit (or item thereof) shall be determined in accordance with such partner's interest in the partnership (taking into account all facts and circumstances). If the partnership agreement provides for the allocation of income, gain, loss, deduction, or credit (or item thereof) to a partner, there are three ways in which such allocation will be respected under section 704(b) and this paragraph. First, the allocation can have substantial economic effect in accordance with paragraph (b)(2) of this section. Second, taking into account all facts and circumstances, the allocation can be in accordance with the partner's interest in the partnership. See paragraph (b)(3) of this section. Third, the allocation can be deemed to be in accordance with the partner's interest in the partnership pursuant to one of the special rules contained in paragraph (b)(4) of this section and § 1.704–2. To the extent an allocation under the partnership agreement of income, gain, loss, deduction, or credit (or item thereof) to a partner does not have substantial economic effect, is not in accordance with the partner's interest in the partnership, and is not deemed to be in accordance with the partner's interest in the partnership, such income, gain, loss, deduction, or credit (or item thereof) will be reallocated in accordance with the partner's interest in the partnership (determined under paragraph (b)(3) of this section).

* * *

(iii) Effect of other sections. The determination of a partner's distributive share of income, gain, loss, deduction, or credit (or item thereof) under section 704(b) and this paragraph is not conclusive as to the tax treatment of a partner with respect to such distributive share. For example, an allocation of loss or deduction to a partner that is respected under section 704(b) and this paragraph may not be deductible by such partner if the partner lacks the requisite motive for economic gain (see, *e.g., Goldstein v. Commissioner*, 364 F.2d 734 (2d Cir.1966)), or may be disallowed for that taxable year (and held in suspense) if the limitations of section 465 or section 704(d) are applicable. Similarly, an allocation that is respected under section 704(b) and this paragraph nevertheless may be reallocated under other provisions, such as section 482, section 704(e)(2), section 706(d) (and related assignment of income principles), and paragraph (b)(2)(ii) of § 1.751–1. If a partnership has a section 754 election in effect, a partner's distributive share of partnership income, gain, loss, or deduction may be affected as provided in § 1.743–1 (see paragraph (b)(2)(iv)(m)(2) of this section). A deduction that appears to be a nonrecourse deduction deemed to be in accordance with the partners' interests in the partnership may not be such because purported nonrecourse liabilities of the partnership in fact constitute equity rather than debt. The examples in paragraph (b)(5) of this section concern the validity of allocations under section 704(b) and this paragraph and, except as noted, do not address the effect of other sections or limitations on such allocations.

(iv) Other possible tax consequences. Allocations that are respected under section 704(b) and this paragraph may give rise to other tax consequences, such as those resulting from the application of section 61, section 83, section 751, section 2501, * * *, paragraph (b)(1) of § 1.721–1 (and related principles), and paragraph (e) of § 1.752–1. The examples in paragraph (b)(5) of this section concern the validity of allocations under section 704(b) and this paragraph and, except as noted, do not address other tax consequences that may result from such allocations.

(v) Purported allocations. Section 704(b) and this paragraph do not apply to a purported allocation if it is made to a person who is not a partner of the partnership (see section 7701(a)(2) and paragraph (d) of § 301.7701–3) or to a person who is not receiving the purported allocation in his capacity as a partner (see section 707(a) and paragraph (a) of § 1.707–1).

(vi) Section 704(c) determinations. Section 704(c) and § 1.704–3 generally require that if property is contributed by a partner to a partnership, the partners' distributive shares of income, gain, loss, and deduction, as computed for tax purposes, with respect to the property are determined so as to take account of the variation between the adjusted tax basis and fair market value of the property. Although section 704(b) does not directly determine the partners' distributive shares of tax items governed by section 704(c), the partners' distributive shares of tax items may be determined under section 704(c) and § 1.704–3 (depending on the allocation method chosen by the partnership under § 1.704–3) with reference to the partners' distributive shares of the corresponding book items, as determined under section 704(b) and this paragraph. (See paragraphs (b)(2)(iv)(d) and (b)(4)(i) of this section.) See § 1.704–3 for methods of making allocations under section 704(c), and § 1.704–3(d)(2) for a special rule in determining the amount of book items if the remedial allocation method is chosen by the partnership. See also paragraph (b)(5) Example (13)(i) of this section.

(vii) Bottom line allocations. Section 704(b) and this paragraph are applicable to allocations of income, gain, loss, deduction, and credit, allocations of specific items of income, gain, loss, deduction, and credit, and allocations of partnership net or "bottom line" taxable income and loss. An allocation to a partner of a share of partnership net or "bottom line" taxable income or loss shall be treated as an allocation to such partner of the same share of each item of income, gain, loss, and deduction that is taken into account in computing such net or "bottom line" taxable income or loss. See example (15)(i) of paragraph (b)(5) of this section.

(2) Substantial economic effect—(i) Two-part analysis. The determination of whether an allocation of income, gain, loss, or deduction (or item thereof) to a partner has substantial economic effect involves a two-part analysis that is made as of the end of the partnership taxable year to which the allocation relates. First, the allocation must have economic effect (within the meaning of paragraph (b)(2)(ii) of this section). Second, the economic effect of the allocation must be substantial (within the meaning of paragraph (b)(2)(iii) of this section).

(ii) Economic effect—(a) Fundamental principles. In order for an allocation to have economic effect, it must be consistent with the underlying economic arrangement of the partners. This means that in the event there is an economic benefit or economic burden that corresponds to an allocation, the partner to whom the allocation is made must receive such economic benefit or bear such economic burden.

(b) Three requirements. Based on the principles contained in paragraph (b)(2)(ii)(a) of this section, and except as otherwise provided in this paragraph, an allocation of income, gain, loss, or deduction (or item thereof) to a partner will have economic effect if, and only if, throughout the full term of the partnership, the partnership agreement provides—

(1) For the determination and maintenance of the partners' capital accounts in accordance with the rules of paragraph (b)(2)(iv) of this section.

(2) Upon liquidation of the partnership (or any partner's interest in the partnership), liquidating distributions are required in all cases to be made in accordance with the positive capital account balances of the partners, as determined after taking into account all capital account adjustments for the partnership taxable year during which such liquidation occurs (other than those made pursuant to this requirement (2) and requirement (3) of this paragraph (b)(2)(ii)(b)), by the end of such taxable year (or, if later, within 90 days after the date of such liquidation), and

(3) If such partner has a deficit balance in his capital account following the liquidation of his interest in the partnership, as determined after taking into account all capital account adjustments for the partnership taxable year during which such liquidation occurs (other than those made pursuant to this requirement (3)), he is unconditionally obligated to restore the amount of such deficit balance to the partnership by the end of such taxable year (or, if later, within 90 days after the date of such liquidation), which amount shall, upon liquidation of the partnership, be paid to creditors of the partnership or distributed to other partners in accordance with their positive capital account balances (in accordance with requirement (2) of this paragraph (b)(2)(ii)(b)).

For purposes of the preceding sentence, a partnership taxable year shall be determined without regard to section 706(c)(2)(A). Requirements (2) and (3) of this paragraph (b)(2)(ii)(b) are not violated if all or part of the partnership interest of one or more partners is purchased (other than in connection with the liquidation of the partnership) by the partnership or by one or more partners (or one or more persons related, within the meaning of section 267(b) (without modification by section 267(e)(1)) or section 707(b)(1), to a partner) pursuant to an agreement negotiated at arm's length by persons who at the time such agreement is entered into have materially adverse interests and if a principal purpose of such purchase and sale is not to avoid the principles of the second sentence of paragraph (b)(2)(ii)(a) of this section. In addition, requirement (2) of this paragraph (b)(2)(ii)(b) is not violated if, upon the liquidation of the partnership, the capital accounts of the partners are increased or decreased pursuant to paragraph (b)(2)(iv)(f) of this section as of the date of such liquidation and the partnership makes liquidating distributions within the time set out in that requirement (2) in the ratios of the partners' positive capital accounts, except that it does not distribute reserves reasonably required to provide for liabilities (contingent or otherwise) of the partnership and installment obligations owed to the partnership, so long as such withheld amounts are distributed as soon as practicable and in the ratios of the partners' positive capital account balances. See examples (1)(i) and (ii), (4)(i), (8)(i), and (16)(i) of paragraph (b)(5) of this section.

(c) Obligation to restore deficit. If a partner is not expressly obligated to restore the deficit balance in his capital account, such partner nevertheless will be treated as obligated to restore the deficit balance in his capital account (in accordance with requirement (3) of paragraph (b)(2)(ii)(b) of this section) to the extent of—

(1) The outstanding principal balance of any promissory note (of which such partner is the maker) contributed to the partnership by such partner (other than a promissory note that is readily tradable on an established securities market), and

(2) The amount of any unconditional obligation of such partner (whether imposed by the partnership agreement or by State or local law) to make subsequent contributions to the partnership (other than pursuant to a promissory note of which such partner is the maker),

provided that such note or obligation is required to be satisfied at a time no later than the end of the partnership taxable year in which such partner's interest is liquidated (or, if later, within 90 days after the date of such liquidation). If a promissory note referred to in the previous sentence is negotiable, a partner will be considered required to satisfy such note within the time period specified in such sentence if the partnership agreement provides that, in lieu of actual satisfaction, the partnership will retain such note and such partner will contribute to the partnership the excess, if any, of the outstanding principal balance of such note over its fair market value at the time of liquidation. See paragraph (b)(2)(iv)(d)(2) of this section. See examples (1)(ix) and (x) of paragraph (b)(5) of this section. A partner in no event will be considered obligated to restore the deficit balance in his capital account to the partnership (in accordance with requirement (3) of paragraph (b)(2)(ii)(b) of this section) to the extent such partner's obligation is not legally enforceable, or the facts and circumstances otherwise indicate a plan to avoid or circumvent such obligation. See paragraphs (b)(2)(ii)(f), (b)(2)(ii)(h), and (b)(4)(vi) of this section for other rules regarding such obligation. For purposes of this paragraph (b)(2), if a partner contributes a promissory note to the partnership during a partnership taxable year beginning after December 29, 1988 and the maker of such note is a person related to such partner (within the meaning of § 1.752–1T(h), but without regard to subdivision (4) of that section), then such promissory note shall be treated as a promissory note of which such partner is the maker.

(d) Alternate test for economic effect. If—

(1) Requirements (1) and (2) of paragraph (b)(2)(ii)(b) of this section are satisfied, and

(2) The partner to whom an allocation is made is not obligated to restore the deficit balance in his capital account to the partnership (in accordance with requirement (3) of paragraph (b)(2)(ii)(b) of this section), or is obligated to restore only a limited dollar amount of such deficit balance, and

(3) The partnership agreement contains a "qualified income offset,"

such allocation will be considered to have economic effect under this paragraph (b)(2)(ii)(d) to the extent such allocation does not cause or increase a deficit balance in such partner's capital account (in excess of any limited dollar amount of such deficit balance that such partner is obligated to restore) as of the end of the partnership taxable year to which such allocation relates. In determining the extent to which the previous sentence is satisfied, such partners's capital account also shall be reduced for—

(4) Adjustments that, as of the end of such year, reasonably are expected to be made to such partner's capital account under paragraph (b)(2)(iv)(k) of this section for depletion allowances with respect to oil and gas properties of the partnership, and

(5) Allocations of loss and deduction that, as of the end of such year, reasonably are expected to be made to such partner pursuant to section 704(e)(2), section 706(d), and paragraph (b)(2)(ii) of § 751–1, and

(6) Distributions that, as of the end of such year, reasonably are expected to be made to such partner to the extent they exceed offsetting increases to such partner's capital account that reasonably are expected to occur during (or prior to) the partnership taxable years in which such distributions reasonably are expected to be made (other than increases pursuant to a minimum gain chargeback) under paragraph (b)(4)(iv)(*e*) of this section or under § 1.704–2(f); (however, increases to a partner's capital account pursuant to a minimum gain chargeback requirement are taken into account as an offset to distributions of nonrecourse liability proceeds that are reasonably expected to be made and that are allocable to an increase in partnership minimum gain) under § 1.704–2(f).

For purposes of determining the amount of expected distributions and expected capital account increases described in (6) above, the rule set out in paragraph (b)(2)(iii)(c) of this section concerning the presumed value of partnership property shall apply. The partnership agreement contains a "qualified income offset" if, and only if, it provides that a partner who unexpectedly receives an adjustment, allocation, or distribution described in (4), (5), or (6) above, will be allocated items of income and gain (consisting of a pro rata portion of each item of partnership income, including gross income, and gain for such year) in an amount and manner sufficient to eliminate such deficit balance as quickly as possible. Allocations of items of income and gain made pursuant to the immediately preceding sentence shall be deemed to be made in accordance with the partners' interests in the partnership if requirements (1) and (2) of paragraph (b)(2)(ii)(b) of this section are satisfied. See examples (1)(iii), (iv), (v), (vi), (viii), (ix), and (x), (15), and (16)(ii) of paragraph (b)(5) of this section.

(e) Partial economic effect. If only a portion of an allocation made to a partner with respect to a partnership taxable year has economic effect, both the portion that has economic effect and the portion that is reallocated shall consist of a proportionate share of all items that made up the allocation to such partner for such year. See examples (15)(ii) and (iii) of paragraph (b)(5) of this section.

(f) Reduction of obligation to restore. If requirements (1) and (2) of paragraph (b)(2)(ii)(b) of this section are satisfied, a partner's obligation to restore the deficit balance in his capital account (or any limited dollar amount thereof) to the partnership may be eliminated or reduced as of the end of a partnership taxable year without affecting the validity of prior allocations (see paragraph (b)(4)(vi) of this section) to the extent the deficit balance (if any) in such partner's capital account, after reduction for the items described in (4), (5), and (6) of paragraph (b)(2)(ii)(d) of this section, will not exceed the partner's remaining obligation (if any) to restore the deficit balance in his capital account. See example (1)(viii) of paragraph (b)(5) of this section.

(g) Liquidation defined. For purposes of this paragraph, a liquidation of a partner's interest in the partnership occurs upon the earlier of (1) the date upon which there is a liquidation of the partnership, or (2) the date upon which there is a liquidation of the partner's interest in the partnership under paragraph (d) of § 1.761–1. For purposes of this paragraph, the liquidation of a partnership occurs upon the earlier of (3) the date upon which the partnership is terminated under section 708(b)(1), or (4) the date upon which the partnership ceases to be a going concern (even though it may continue in existence for the purpose of winding up its affairs, paying its debts, and distributing any remaining balance to its partners). Requirements (2) and (3) of paragraph (b)(2)(ii)(b) of this section will be considered unsatisfied if the liquidation of a partner's interest in the partnership is delayed after its primary business activities have been terminated (for example, by continuing to engage in a relatively minor amount of business activity, if such actions themselves do not cause the partnership to terminate pursuant to section 708(b)(1)) for a principal purpose of deferring any distribution pursuant to requirement (2) of paragraph (b)(2)(ii)(b) of this section or deferring any partner's obligations under requirement (3) of paragraph (b)(2)(ii)(b) of this section.

(h) Partnership agreement defined. For purposes of this paragraph, the partnership agreement includes all agreements among the partners, or between one or more partners and the partnership, concerning affairs of the partnership and responsibilities of partners, whether oral or written, and whether or not embodied in a document referred to by the partners as the partnership agreement. Thus, in determining whether distributions are required in all cases to be made in accordance with the partners' positive capital account balances (requirement (2) of paragraph (b)(2)(ii)(b) of this section), and in determining the extent to which a partner is obligated to restore a deficit balance in his capital account (requirement (3) of paragraph (b)(2)(ii)(b) of this section), all arrangements among partners, or between one or more partners and the partnership relating to the partnership, direct and indirect, including puts, options, and other buy-sell agreements, and any other "stop-loss" arrangement, are considered to be part of the partnership agreement. (Thus, for example, if one partner who assumes a liability of the partnership is indemnified by another partner for a portion of such liability, the indemnifying partner (depending upon the particular facts) may be viewed as in effect having a partial deficit makeup obligation as a result of such indemnity agreement.) In addition, the partnership agreement includes provisions of Federal, State, or local law that govern the affairs of the partnership or are considered under such law to be a part of the partnership agreement (see the last sentence of paragraph (c) of § 1.761–1). For purposes of this paragraph (b)(2)(ii)(h), an agreement with a partner or a partnership shall include an agreement with a person related, within the meaning of section 267(b) (without modification by section 267(e)(1)) or section 707(b)(1), to such partner or partnership. For purposes of the preceding sentence, sections 267(b) and 707(b)(1) shall be applied for partnership taxable years beginning after December 29, 1988 by (1) substituting "80 percent or more" for "more than 50 percent" each place it appears in such sections, (2) excluding brothers and sisters from the members of a person's family, and (3) disregarding section 267(f)(1)(A).

(i) Economic effect equivalence. Allocations made to a partner that do not otherwise have economic effect under this paragraph (b)(2)(ii) shall nevertheless be deemed to have economic effect, provided that as of the end of each partnership taxable year a liquidation of the partnership at the end of such year or at the end of any future year would produce the same economic results to the partners as would occur if requirements (1), (2), and (3) of paragraph (b)(2)(ii)(b) of this section had been satisfied, regardless of the economic performance of the partnership. See examples (4)(ii) and (iii) of paragraph (b)(5) of this section.

(iii) Substantiality—(a) General rules. Except as otherwise provided in this paragraph (b)(2)(iii), the economic effect of an allocation (or allocations) is substantial if there is a reasonable possibility that the allocation (or allocations) will affect substantially the dollar amounts to be received by the partners from the partnership, independent of tax consequences. Notwithstanding the preceding sentence, the economic effect of an allocation (or allocations) is not substantial if, at the time the allocation becomes part of the partnership agreement, (1) the after-tax economic consequences of at least one partner may, in present value terms, be enhanced compared to such consequences if the allocation (or allocations) were not contained in the partnership agreement, and (2) there is a strong likelihood that the after-tax economic consequences of no partner will, in present value terms, be substantially diminished compared to such consequences if the allocation (or allocations) were not contained in the partnership agreement. In determining the after-tax economic benefit or detriment to a partner, tax consequences that result from the interaction of the allocation with such partner's tax attributes that are unrelated to the partnership will be taken into account. See examples (5) and (9) of paragraph (b)(5) of this section. The economic effect of an allocation is not substantial in the two situations described in paragraphs (b)(2)(iii)(b) and (c) of this section. However, even if an allocation is not described therein, its economic effect may be insubstantial under the general rules stated in this paragraph (b)(2)(iii)(a). References in this paragraph (b)(2)(iii) to allocations include capital account adjustments made pursuant to paragraph (b)(2)(iv)(k) of this section. References in this paragraph (b)(2)(iii) to a comparison to consequences arising if an allocation (or allocations) were not contained in the partnership agreement mean that the allocation (or allocations) is determined in accordance with the partners' interests in the partnership (within the meaning of paragraph (b)(3) of this section), disregarding the allocation (or allocations) being tested under this paragraph (b)(2)(iii).

(b) Shifting tax consequences. The economic effect of an allocation (or allocations) in a partnership taxable year is not substantial if, at the time the allocation (or allocations) becomes part of the partnership agreement, there is a strong likelihood that—

(1) The net increases and decreases that will be recorded in the partners' respective capital accounts for such taxable year will not differ substantially from the net increases and decreases that would be recorded in such partners' respective capital accounts for such year if the allocations were not contained in the partnership agreement, and

(2) The total tax liability of the partners (for their respective taxable years in which the allocations will be taken into account) will be less than if the allocations were not contained in the partnership agreement (taking into account tax consequences that result from the interaction of the allocation (or allocations) with partner tax attributes that are unrelated to the partnership).

If, at the end of a partnership taxable year to which an allocation (or allocations) relates, the net increases and decreases that are recorded in the partners' respective capital accounts do not differ substantially from the net increases and decreases that would have been recorded in such partners' respective capital accounts had the allocation (or allocations) not been contained in the partnership agreement, and the total tax liability of the partners is (as described in (2) above) less than it would have been had the allocation (or allocations) not been contained in the partnership agreement, it will be presumed that, at the time the allocation (or allocations) became part of such partnership agreement, there was a strong likelihood that these results would occur. This presumption may be overcome by a showing of facts and circumstances that prove otherwise. See examples (6), (7)(ii) and (iii), and (10)(ii) of paragraph (b)(5) of this section.

(c) Transitory allocations. If a partnership agreement provides for the possibility that one or more allocations (the "original allocation(s)") will be largely offset by one or more other allocations (the "offsetting allocation(s)"), and, at the time the allocations become part of the partnership agreement, there is a strong likelihood that—

(1) The net increases and decreases that will be recorded in the partners' respective capital accounts for the taxable years to which the allocations relate will not differ substantially from the net increases and decreases that would be recorded in such partners' respective capital accounts for such years if the original allocation(s) and offsetting allocation(s) were not contained in the partnership agreement, and

(2) The total tax liability of the partners (for their respective taxable years in which the allocations will be taken into account) will be less than if the allocations were not contained in the partnership agreement (taking into account tax consequences that result from the interaction of the allocation (or allocations) with partner tax attributes that are unrelated to the partnership) the economic effect of the original allocation(s) and offsetting allocation(s) will not be substantial. If, at the end of a partnership taxable year to which an offsetting allocation(s) relates, the net increases and decreases recorded in the partners' respective capital accounts do not differ substantially from the net increases and decreases that would have been recorded in such partners' respective capital accounts had the original allocation(s) and the offsetting allocation(s) not been contained in the partnership agreement, and the total tax liability of the partners is (as described in (2) above) less than it would have been had such allocations not been contained in the partnership agreement, it will be presumed that, at the time the allocations became part of the partnership agreement, there was a strong likelihood that these results would occur. This presumption may be overcome by a showing of facts and circumstances that prove otherwise. See examples (1)(xi), (2), (3), (7), (8)(ii), and (17) of paragraph (b)(5) of this section. Notwithstanding the foregoing, the original allocation(s) and the offsetting allocation(s) will not be insubstantial (under this paragraph (b)(2)(iii)(c)) and, for purposes of paragraph (b)(2)(iii)(a), it will be presumed that there is a reasonable possibility that the allocations will affect substantially the dollar amounts to be received by the partners from the partnership if, at the time the allocations become part of the partnership agreement, there is a strong likelihood that the offsetting allocation(s) will not, in large part, be made within five years after the original allocation(s) is made (determined on a first-in, first-out basis). See example (2) of paragraph (b)(5) of this section. For purposes of applying the provisions of this paragraph (b)(2)(iii) (and paragraphs (b)(2)(ii)(d)(6) and (b)(3)(iii) of this section), the adjusted tax basis of partnership property (or, if partnership property is properly reflected on the books of the partnership at a book value that differs from its adjusted tax basis, the book value of such property) will be presumed to be the fair market value of such property, and adjustments to the adjusted tax basis (or book value) of such property will be presumed to be matched by corresponding changes in such property's fair market value. Thus, there cannot be a strong likelihood that the economic effect of an allocation (or allocations) will be largely offset by an allocation (or allocations) of gain or loss from the disposition of partnership property. See examples (1)(vi) and (xi) of paragraph (b)(5) of this section.

* * *

(iv) Maintenance of capital accounts—(a) In general. The economic effect test described in paragraph (b)(2)(ii) of this section requires an examination of the capital accounts of the partners of a partnership, as maintained under the partnership agreement. Except as otherwise provided in paragraph (b)(2)(ii)(i) of this section, an allocation of income, gain, loss, or deduction will not have economic effect under paragraph (b)(2)(ii) of this section, and will not be deemed to be in accordance with a partner's interest in the partnership under paragraph (b)(4) of this section, unless the capital accounts of the partners are determined and maintained throughout the full term of the partnership in accordance with the capital accounting rules of this paragraph (b)(2)(iv).

(b) Basic rules. Except as otherwise provided in this paragraph (b)(2)(iv), the partners' capital accounts will be considered to be determined and maintained in accordance with the rules of this paragraph (b)(2)(iv) if, and only if, each partner's capital account is increased by (1) the amount of money contributed by him to the partnership, (2) the fair market value of property contributed by him to the partnership (net of liabilities that the partnership is considered to assume or take subject to), and (3) allocations to him of partnership income and gain (or items thereof), including income and gain exempt from tax and income and gain described in paragraph (b)(2)(iv)(g) of this section, but excluding income and gain described in paragraph (b)(4)(i) of this section; and is decreased by (4) the amount of money distributed to him by the partnership, (5) the fair market value of property distributed to him by the partnership (net of liabilities that such partner is considered to assume or take subject to), (6) allocations to him of expenditures of the partnership described in section 705(a)(2)(B), and (7) allocations of partnership loss and deduction (or item thereof), including loss and deduction described in paragraph (b)(2)(iv)(g) of this section, but excluding items described in (6) above and loss or deduction described in paragraphs (b)(4)(i) or (b)(4)(iii) of this section; and is otherwise adjusted in accordance with the additional rules set forth in this paragraph (b)(2)(iv). For purposes of this paragraph, a partner who has more than one interest in a partnership shall have a single capital account that reflects all such interests, regardless of the class of interest owned by such partner (e.g., general or limited) and regardless of the time or manner in which such interests were acquired. * * *

(c) Treatment of liabilities. For purposes of this paragraph (b)(2)(iv), (1) money contributed by a partner to a partnership includes the amount of any partnership liabilities that are assumed by such partner (other than liabilities described in paragraph (b)(2)(iv)(b)(5) of this section that are assumed by a distributee partner) but does not include increases in such partner's share of partnership liabilities (see section 752(a)), and (2) money distributed to a partner by a partnership includes the amount of such partner's individual liabilities that are assumed by the partnership (other than liabilities described in paragraph (b)(2)(iv)(b)(2) of this section that are assumed by the partnership) but does not include decreases in such partner's share of partnership liabilities (see section 752(b)). For purposes of this paragraph (b)(2)(iv)(c), liabilities are considered assumed only to the extent the assuming party is thereby subjected to personal liability with respect to such obligation, the obligee is aware of the assumption and can directly enforce the assuming party's obligation, and, as between the assuming party and the party from whom the liability is assumed, the assuming party is ultimately liable.

(d) Contributed property—(1) In general. The basic capital accounting rules contained in paragraph (b)(2)(iv)(b) of this section require that a partner's capital account be increased by the fair market value of property contributed to the partnership by such partner on the date of contribution. See examples (13)(i) and (v) of paragraph (b)(5) of this section. Consistent with section 752(c), section 7701(g) does not apply in determining such fair market value.

(2) Contribution of promissory notes. Notwithstanding the general rule of paragraph (b)(2)(iv)(b)(2) of this section, except as provided in this paragraph (b)(2)(iv)(d)(2), if a promissory note is contributed to a partnership by a partner who is the maker of such note, such partner's capital account will be increased with respect to such note only when there is a taxable disposition of such note by the partnership or when the partner makes principal payments on such note. See example (1)(ix) of paragraph (b)(5) of this section. The first sentence of this paragraph (b)(2)(iv)(d)(2) shall not apply if the note referred to therein is readily tradable on an established securities market. See also paragraph (b)(2)(ii)(c) of this section. Furthermore, a partner whose interest is liquidated will be considered as satisfying his obligation to restore the deficit balance in his capital account to the extent of (i) the fair market value, at the time of contribution, of any negotiable promissory note (of which such partner is the maker) that such partner contributes to the partnership on or after the date his interest is liquidated and within the time specified in paragraph (b)(2)(ii)(b)(3) of this section, and (ii) the fair market value, at the time of liquidation, of the unsatisfied portion of any negotiable promissory note (of which such partner is the maker) that such partner previously contributed to the partnership. For purposes of the preceding sentence, the fair market value of a note will be no less than the outstanding principal balance of such note, provided that such note bears interest at a rate no less than the applicable federal rate at the time of valuation.

(3) Section 704(c) considerations. Section 704(c) and § 1.704–3 govern the determination of the partners' distributive shares of income, gain, loss, and deduction, as computed for tax purposes, with respect to property contributed to a partnership (see paragraph (b)(1)(vi) of this section). In cases where section 704(c) and § 1.704–3 apply to partnership property, the capital accounts of the partners will not be considered to be determined and maintained in accordance with the rules of this paragraph (b)(2)(iv) unless the partnership agreement requires that the partners' capital accounts be adjusted in accordance with paragraph (b)(2)(iv)(g) of this section for allocations to them of income, gain, loss, and deduction (including depreciation, depletion, amortization, or other cost recovery) as computed for book purposes, with respect to the property. See, however, § 1.704–3(d)(2) for a special rule in determining the amount of book items if the partnership chooses the remedial allocation method. See also Example (13)(i) of paragraph (b)(5) of this section. Capital accounts are not adjusted to reflect allocations under section 704(c) and § 1.704–3 (e.g., tax allocations of precontribution gain or loss).

(4) Exercise of noncompensatory options. Solely for purposes of paragraph (b)(2)(iv)(b)(2) of this section, the fair market value of the property contributed on the exercise of a noncompensatory option (as defined in § 1.721–2(f)) does not include the fair market value of the option privilege, but does include the consideration paid to the partnership to acquire the option and the fair market value of any property (other than the option) contributed to the partnership on the exercise of the option. With respect to convertible debt, the fair market value of the property contributed on the exercise of the option is the adjusted issue price of the debt and the accrued but unpaid qualified stated interest (as defined in § 1.1273–1(c)) on the debt immediately before the conversion, plus the fair market value of any property (other than the convertible debt) contributed to the partnership on the exercise of the option. See Examples 31 through 35 of paragraph (b)(5) of this section.

(e) Distributed property—(1) In general. The basic capital accounting rules contained in paragraph (b)(2)(iv)(b) of this section require that a partner's capital account be decreased by the fair market value of property distributed by the partnership (without regard to section 7701(g)) to such partner (whether in connection with a liquidation or otherwise). To satisfy this requirement, the capital accounts of the partners first must be adjusted to reflect the manner in which the unrealized income, gain, loss, and deduction inherent in such property (that has not been reflected in the capital accounts previously) would be allocated among the partners if there were a taxable disposition of such property for the fair market value of such property (taking section 7701(g) into account) on the date of distribution. See example (14)(v) of paragraph (b)(5) of this section.

(2) Distribution of promissory notes. Notwithstanding the general rule of paragraph (b)(2)(iv)(b)(5), except as provided in this paragraph (b)(2)(iv)(e)(2), if a promissory note is distributed to a partner by a partnership that is the maker of such note, such partner's capital account will be decreased with respect to such note only when there is a taxable disposition of such note by the partner or when the partnership makes principal payments on the note. The previous sentence shall not apply if a note distributed to a partner by a partnership who is the maker of such note is readily tradable on an established securities market. Furthermore, the capital account of a partner whose interest in a partnership is liquidated will be reduced to the extent of (i) the fair market value, at the time of distribution, of any negotiable promissory note (of which such partnership is the maker) that such partnership distributes to the partner on or after the date such partner's interest is liquidated and within the time specified in paragraph (b)(2)(ii)(b)(2) of this section, and (ii) the fair market value, at the time of liquidation, of the unsatisfied portion of any negotiable promissory note (of which such partnership is the maker) that such partnership previously distributed to the partner. For purposes of the preceding sentence, the fair market value of a note will be no less than the outstanding principal balance of such note, provided that such note bears interest at a rate no less than the applicable federal rate at time of valuation.

(f) Revaluations of property. A partnership agreement may, upon the occurrence of certain events, increase or decrease the capital accounts of the partners to reflect a revaluation of partnership property (including intangible assets such as goodwill) on the partnership's books. Capital accounts so adjusted will not be considered to be determined and maintained in accordance with the rules of this paragraph (b)(2)(iv) unless—

(1) The adjustments are based on the fair market value of partnership property (taking section 7701(g) into account) on the date of adjustment, as determined under paragraph (b)(2)(iv)(h) of this section. See Example 33 of paragraph (b)(5) of this section.

(2) The adjustments reflect the manner in which the unrealized income, gain, loss, or deduction inherent in such property (that has not been reflected in the capital accounts previously) would be allocated among the partners if there were a taxable disposition of such property for such fair market value on that date, and

(3) The partnership agreement requires that the partners' capital accounts be adjusted in accordance with paragraph (b)(2)(iv)(g) of this section for allocations to them of depreciation, depletion, amortization, and gain or loss, as computed for book purposes, with respect to such property, and

(4) The partnership agreement requires that the partners' distributive shares of depreciation, depletion, amortization, and gain or loss, as computed for tax purposes, with respect to such property be determined so as to take account of the variation between the adjusted tax basis and book value of such property in the same manner as under section 704(c) (see paragraph (b)(4)(i) of this section), and

(5) The adjustments are made principally for a substantial non-tax business purpose—

(i) In connection with a contribution of money or other property (other than a de minimis amount) to the partnership by a new or existing partner as consideration for an interest in the partnership, or

(ii) In connection with the liquidation of the partnership or a distribution of money or other property (other than a de minimis amount) by the partnership to a retiring or continuing partner as consideration for an interest in the partnership, or

(iii) In connection with the grant of an interest in the partnership (other than a de minimis interest) on or after May 6, 2004, as consideration for the provision of services to or for the benefit of the partnership by an existing partner acting in a partner capacity, or by a new partner acting in a partner capacity or in anticipation of being a partner, or

(iv) In connection with the issuance by the partnership of a noncompensatory option (other than an option for a de minimis partnership interest), or

(v) Under generally accepted industry accounting practices, provided substantially all of the partnership's property (excluding money) consists of stock, securities, commodities, options, warrants, futures, or similar instruments that are readily tradable on an established securities market.

See example (14) and (18) of paragraph (b)(5) of this section. If the capital accounts of the partners are not adjusted to reflect the fair market value of partnership property when an interest in the partnership is acquired from or relinquished to the partnership, paragraphs (b)(1)(iii) and (b)(1)(iv) of this section should be consulted regarding the potential tax consequences that may arise if the principles of section 704(c) are not applied to determine the partners' distributive shares of depreciation, depletion, amortization, and gain or loss as computed for tax purposes, with respect to such property.

(g) Adjustments to reflect book value—(1) In general. Under paragraphs (b)(2)(iv)(d) and (b)(2)(iv)(f) of this section, property may be properly reflected on the books of the partnership at a book value that differs from the adjusted tax basis of such property. In these circumstances, paragraphs (b)(2)(iv)(d)(3) and (b)(2)(iv)(f)(3) of this section provide that the capital accounts of the partners will not be considered to be determined and maintained in accordance with the rules of this paragraph (b)(2)(iv) unless the partnership agreement requires the partners' capital accounts to be adjusted in accordance with this paragraph (b)(2)(iv)(g) for allocations to them of depreciation, depletion, amortization, and gain or loss, as computed for book purposes, with respect to such property. In determining whether the economic effect of an allocation of book items is substantial, consideration will be given to the effect of such allocation on the determination of the partners' distributive shares of corresponding tax items under section 704(c) and paragraph (b)(4)(i) of this section. See example (17) of paragraph (b)(5) of this section. If an allocation of book items under the partnership agreement does not have substantial economic effect (as determined under paragraphs (b)(2)(ii) and (b)(2)(iii) of this section), or is not otherwise respected under this paragraph, such items will be reallocated in accordance with the partners' interests in the partnership, and such reallocation will be the basis upon which the partners' distributive shares of the corresponding tax items are determined under section 704(c) and paragraph (b)(4)(i) of this section. See examples (13), (14), and (18) of paragraph (b)(5) of this section.

(2) Payables and receivables. References in this paragraph (b)(2)(iv) and paragraph (b)(4)(i) of this section to book and tax depreciation, depletion, amortization, and gain or loss with respect to property that has an adjusted tax basis that differs from book value include, under analogous rules and principles, the unrealized income or deduction with respect to accounts receivable, accounts payable, and other accrued but unpaid items.

(3) Determining amount of book items. The partners' capital accounts will not be considered adjusted in accordance with this paragraph (b)(2)(iv)(g) unless the amount of book depreciation, depletion, or amortization for a period with respect to an item of partnership property is the amount that bears the same relationship to the book value of such property as the depreciation (or cost recovery deduction), depletion, or amortization computed for tax purposes with respect to such property for such period bears to the adjusted tax basis of such property. If such property has a zero adjusted tax basis, the book depreciation, depletion, or amortization may be determined under any reasonable method selected by the partnership.

(h) Determinations of fair market value—(1) In general. For purposes of this paragraph (b)(2)(iv), the fair market value assigned to property contributed to a partnership, property distributed by a partnership, or property otherwise revalued by a partnership, will be regarded as correct, provided that (1) such value is reasonably agreed to among the partners in arm's-length negotiations, and (2) the partners have sufficiently adverse interests. If, however, these conditions are not satisfied and the value assigned to such property is overstated or understated (by more than an insignificant amount), the capital accounts of the partners will not be considered to be determined and maintained in accordance with the rules of this paragraph (b)(2)(iv). Valuation of property contributed to the partnership, distributed by the partnership, or otherwise revalued by the partnership shall be on a property-by-property basis, except to the extent the regulations under section 704(c) permit otherwise.

(2) **Adjustments for noncompensatory options.** The value of partnership property as reflected on the books of the partnership must be adjusted to account for any outstanding noncompensatory options (as defined in § 1.721–2(f)) at the time of a revaluation of partnership property under paragraph (b)(2)(iv)(f) or (s) of this section. If the fair market value of outstanding noncompensatory options (as defined in § 1.721–2(f)) as of the date of the adjustment exceeds the consideration paid to the partnership to acquire the options, then the value of partnership property as reflected on the books of the partnership must be reduced by that excess to the extent of the unrealized income or gain in partnership property (that has not been reflected in the capital accounts previously). This reduction is allocated only to properties with unrealized appreciation in proportion to their respective amounts of unrealized appreciation. If the consideration paid to the partnership to acquire the outstanding noncompensatory options (as defined in § 1.721–2(f)) exceeds the fair market value of such options as of the date of the adjustment, then the value of partnership property as reflected on the books of the partnership must be increased by that excess to the extent of the unrealized loss in partnership property (that has not been reflected in the capital accounts previously). This increase is allocated only to properties with unrealized loss in proportion to their respective amounts of unrealized loss. However, any reduction or increase shall take into account the economic arrangement of the partners with respect to the property.

(i) Section 705(a)(2)(B) expenditures—(1) In general. The basic capital accounting rules contained in paragraph (b)(2)(iv)(b) of this section require that a partner's capital account be decreased by allocations made to such partner of expenditures described in section 705(a)(2)(B). See example (11) of paragraph (b)(5) of this section. If an allocation of these expenditures under the partnership agreement does not have substantial economic effect (as determined under paragraphs (b)(2)(ii) and (b)(2)(iii) of this section), or is not otherwise respected under this paragraph, such expenditures will be reallocated in accordance with the partners' interest in the partnership.

(2) Expenses described in section 709. Except for amounts with respect to which an election is properly made under section 709(b), amounts paid or incurred to organize a partnership or to promote the sale of (or to sell) an interest in such a partnership shall, solely for purposes of this paragraph, be treated as section 705(a)(2)(B) expenditures, and upon liquidation of the partnership no further capital account adjustments will be made in respect thereof.

(3) Disallowed losses. If a deduction for a loss incurred in connection with the sale or exchange of partnership property is disallowed to the partnership under section 267(a)(1) or section 707(b), that deduction shall, solely for purposes of this paragraph, be treated as a section 705(a)(2)(B) expenditure.

* * *

(*l*) Transfers of partnership interests. The capital accounts of the partners will not be considered to be determined and maintained in accordance with the rules of this paragraph (b)(2)(iv) unless, upon the transfer of all or a part of an interest in the partnership, the capital account of the transferor that is attributable to the transferred interest carries over to the transferee partner. (See paragraph (b)(2)(iv)(m) of this section for rules concerning the effect of a section 754 election on the capital accounts of the partners.) If the transfer of an interest in a partnership causes a termination of the partnership under section 708(b)(1)(B), the capital account of the transferee partner and the capital accounts of the other partners of the terminated partnership carry over to the new partnership that is formed as a result of the termination of the partnership under § 1.708–1(b)(1)(iv). Moreover, the deemed contribution of assets and liabilities by the terminated partnership to a new partnership and the deemed liquidation of the terminated partnership that occur under § 1.708–1(b)(1)(iv) are disregarded for purposes of this paragraph (b)(2)(iv). * * * The previous three sentence apply to terminations of partnerships under section 708(b)(1)(B) occurring on or after May 9, 1997; however, the sentences may be applied to terminations occurring on or after May 9, 1996, provided that the partnership and it partners apply the sentences to the termination in a consistent manner.

(m) Section 754 elections—(1) In general. The capital accounts of the partners will not be considered to be determined and maintained in accordance with the rules of this paragraph (b)(2)(iv) unless, upon adjustment to the adjusted tax basis of partnership property under section 732, 734, or 743, the capital accounts of the partners are adjusted as provided in this paragraph (b)(2)(iv)(m).

(2) Section 743 adjustments. In the case of a transfer of all or a part of an interest in a partnership that has a section 754 election in effect for the partnership taxable year in which such transfer occurs, adjustments to the adjusted tax basis of partnership property under section 743 shall not be reflected in the capital account of the transferee partner or on the books of the partnership, and subsequent capital account adjustments for distributions (see paragraph (b)(2)(iv)(e)(1) of this section) and for depreciation, depletion, amortization, and gain or loss with respect to such property will disregard the effect of such basis adjustment. The preceding sentence shall not apply to the extent such basis adjustment is allocated to the common basis of partnership property under paragraph (b)(1) of § 1.734–2; in these cases, such basis adjustment shall, except as provided in paragraph (b)(2)(iv)(m)(5) of this section, give rise to adjustments to the capital accounts of the partners in accordance with their interests in the partnership under paragraph (b)(3) of this section. See examples (13)(iii) and (iv) of paragraph (b)(5) of this section.

(3) Section 732 adjustments. In the case of a transfer of all or a part of an interest in a partnership that does not have a section 754 election in effect for the partnership taxable year in which such transfer occurs, adjustments to the adjusted tax basis of partnership property under section 732(d) will be treated in the capital accounts of the partners in the same manner as section 743 basis adjustments are treated under paragraph (b)(2)(iv)(m)(2) of this section.

(4) Section 734 adjustments. Except as provided in paragraph (b)(2)(iv)(m)(5) of this section, in the case of a distribution of property in liquidation of a partner's interest in the partnership by a partnership that has a section 754 election in effect for the partnership taxable year in which the distribution occurs, the partner who receives the distribution that gives rise to the adjustment to the adjusted tax basis of partnership property under section 734 shall have a corresponding adjustment made to his capital account. If such distribution is made other than in liquidation of a partner's interest in the partnership, however, except as provided in paragraph (b)(2)(iv)(m)(5) of this section, the capital accounts of the partners shall be adjusted by the amount of the adjustment to the adjusted tax basis of partnership property under section 734, and such capital account adjustment shall be shared among the partners in the manner in which the unrealized income and gain that is displaced by such adjustment would have been shared if the property whose basis is adjusted were sold immediately prior to such adjustment for its recomputed adjusted tax basis.

(5) Limitations on adjustments. Adjustments may be made to the capital account of a partner (or his successor in interest) in respect of basis adjustments to partnership property under sections 732, 734, and 743 only to the extent that such basis adjustments (i) are permitted to be made to one or more items of partnership property under section 755, and (ii) result in an increase or a decrease in the amount at which such property is carried on the partnership's balance sheet, as computed for book purposes. For example, if the book value of partnership property exceeds the adjusted tax basis of such property, a basis adjustment to such property may be reflected in a partner's capital account only to the extent such adjustment exceeds the difference between the book value of such property and the adjusted tax basis of such property prior to such adjustment.

(n) Partnership level characterization. Except as otherwise provided in paragraph (b)(2)(iv)(k) of this section, the capital accounts of the partners will not be considered to be determined and maintained in accordance with the rules of this paragraph (b)(2)(iv) unless adjustments to such capital accounts in respect of partnership income, gain, loss, deduction, and section 705(a)(2)(B) expenditures (or item thereof) are made with reference to the Federal tax treatment of such items (and in the case of book items, with reference to the Federal tax treatment of the corresponding tax items) at the partnership level, without regard to any requisite or elective tax treatment of such items at the partner level (for example, under section 58(i)). However, a partnership that incurs mining exploration expenditures will determine the Federal tax treatment of income, gain, loss, and deduction with respect to the property to which such expenditures relate at the partnership level only after first taking into account the elections made by its partners under section 617 and section 703(b)(4).

(*o*) Guaranteed payments. Guaranteed payments to a partner under section 707(c) cause the capital account of the recipient partner to be adjusted only to the extent of such partner's distributive share of any partnership deduction, loss, or other downward capital account adjustment resulting from such payment.

(p) Minor discrepancies. Discrepancies between the balances in the respective capital accounts of the partners and the balances that would be in such respective capital accounts if they had been determined and maintained in accordance with this paragraph (b)(2)(iv) will not adversely affect the validity of an allocation, provided that such discrepancies are minor and are attributable to good faith error by the partnership.

(q) Adjustments where guidance is lacking. If the rules of this paragraph (b)(2)(iv) fail to provide guidance on how adjustments to the capital accounts of the partners should be made to reflect particular adjustments to partnership capital on the books of the partnership, such capital accounts will not be considered to be determined and maintained in accordance with those rules unless such capital account adjustments are made in a manner that (1) maintains equality between the aggregate governing capital accounts of the partners and the amount of partnership capital reflected on the partnership's balance sheet, as computed for book purposes, (2) is consistent with the underlying economic arrangement of the partners, and (3) is based, wherever practicable, on Federal tax accounting principles.

* * *

(s) Adjustments on the exercise of a noncompensatory option. A partnership agreement may grant a partner, on the exercise of a noncompensatory option (as defined in § 1.721–2(f)), a right to share in partnership capital that exceeds (or is less than) the sum of the consideration paid to the partnership to acquire and exercise such option. Where such an agreement exists, capital accounts will not be considered to be determined and maintained in accordance with the rules of this paragraph (b)(2)(iv) unless the following requirements are met:

(1) In lieu of revaluing partnership property under paragraph (b)(2)(iv)(f) of this section immediately before the exercise of the option, the partnership revalues partnership property in accordance with the provisions of paragraphs (b)(2)(iv)(f)(1) through (f)(4) of this section immediately after the exercise of the option.

(2) In determining the capital accounts of the partners (including the exercising partner) under paragraph (b)(2)(iv)(s)(1) of this section, the partnership first allocates any unrealized income, gain, or loss in partnership property (that has not been reflected in the capital accounts previously) to the exercising partner to the extent necessary to reflect that partner's right to share in partnership capital under the partnership agreement, and then allocates any remaining unrealized income, gain, or loss (that has not been reflected in the capital accounts previously) to the existing partners, to reflect the manner in which the unrealized income, gain, or loss in partnership property would be allocated among those partners if there were a taxable disposition of such property for its fair market value on that date. For purposes of the preceding sentence, if the exercising partner's initial capital account as determined under § 1.704–1(b)(2)(iv)(b) and (d)(4) of this section would be less than the amount that reflects the exercising partner's right to share in partnership capital under the partnership agreement, then only income or gain may be allocated to the exercising partner from partnership properties with unrealized appreciation, in proportion to their respective amounts of unrealized appreciation. If the exercising partner's initial capital account, as determined under § 1.704–1(b)(2)(iv)(b) and (d)(4) of this section, would be greater than the amount that reflects the exercising partner's right to share in partnership capital under the partnership agreement, then only loss may be allocated to the exercising partner from partnership properties with unrealized loss, in proportion to their respective amounts of unrealized loss. However, any allocation must take into account the economic arrangement of the partners with respect to the property.

(3) If, after making the allocations described in paragraph (b)(2)(iv)(s)(2) of this section, the exercising partner's capital account does not reflect that partner's right to share in partnership capital under the partnership agreement, then the partnership reallocates partnership capital between the existing partners and the exercising partner so that the exercising partner's capital account reflects the exercising partner's right to share in partnership capital under the partnership agreement (a capital account reallocation). Any increase or decrease in the capital accounts of existing partners that occurs as a result of a capital account reallocation under this paragraph (b)(2)(iv)(s)(3) must be allocated among the existing partners in accordance with the principles of this section. See Example 32 of paragraph (b)(5) of this section.

(4) The partnership agreement requires corrective allocations so as to take into account all capital account reallocations made under paragraph (b)(2)(iv)(s)(3) of this section (see paragraph (b)(4)(x) of this section). See Example 32 of paragraph (b)(5) of this section.

(3) Partner's interest in the partnership—(i) In general. References in section 704(b) and this paragraph to a partner's interest in the partnership, or to the partner's interests in the partnership, signify the manner in which the partners have agreed to share the economic benefit or burden (if any) corresponding to the income, gain, loss, deduction, or credit (or item thereof) that is allocated. Except with respect to partnership items that cannot have economic effect (such as nonrecourse deductions of the partnership), this sharing arrangement may or may not correspond to the overall economic arrangement of the partners. Thus, a partner who has a 50 percent overall interest in the partnership may have a 90 percent interest in a particular item of income or deduction. (For example, in the case of an unexpected downward adjustment to the capital account of a partner who does not have a deficit make-up obligation that causes such partner to have a negative capital account, it may be necessary to allocate a disproportionate amount of gross income of the partnership to such partner for such year so as to bring that partner's capital account back up to zero.) The determination of a partner's interest in a partnership shall be made by taking into account all facts and circumstances relating to the economic arrangement of the partners.

(ii) Factors considered. In determining a partner's interest in the partnership, the following factors are among those that will be considered:

(a) The partners' relative contributions to the partnership,

(b) The interests of the partners in economic profits and losses (if different than that in taxable income or loss),

(c) The interests of the partners in cash flow and other non-liquidating distributions, and

(d) The rights of the partners to distributions of capital upon liquidation.

The provisions of this subparagraph (b)(3) are illustrated by examples (1)(i) and (ii), (4)(i), (5)(i) and (ii), (6), (7), (8), (10)(ii), (16)(i), and (19)(iii) of paragraph (b)(5) of this section. See paragraph (b)(4)(i) of this section concerning rules for determining the partners' interests in the partnership, with respect to certain tax items.

(iii) Certain determinations. If—

(a) Requirements (1) and (2) of paragraph (b)(2)(ii)(b) of this section are satisfied, and

(b) All or a portion of an allocation of income, gain, loss, or deduction made to a partner for a partnership taxable year does not have economic effect under paragraph (b)(2)(ii) of this section, the partners' interests in the partnership with respect to the portion of the allocation that lacks economic effect will be determined by comparing the manner in which distributions (and contributions) would be made if all partnership property were sold at book value and the partnership were liquidated immediately following the end of the taxable year to which the allocation relates with the manner in which distributions (and contributions) would be made if all partnership property were sold at book value and the partnership were liquidated immediately following the end of the prior taxable year, and adjusting the result for the items described in (4), (5), and (6) of paragraph (b)(2)(ii)(d) of this section. A determination made under this paragraph (b)(3)(iii) will have no force if the economic effect of valid allocations made in the same manner is insubstantial under paragraph (b)(2)(iii) of this section. See examples (1)(iv), (v), and (vi), and (15)(ii) and (iii) of paragraph (b)(5) of this section.

* * *

(4) Special rules—(i) Allocations to reflect revaluations. If partnership property is, under paragraphs (b)(2)(iv)(d) or (b)(2)(iv)(f) of this section, properly reflected in the capital accounts of the partners and on the books of the partnership at a book value that differs from the adjusted tax basis of such property, then depreciation, depletion, amortization, and gain or loss, as computed for book purposes, with respect to such property will be greater or less than the depreciation, depletion, amortization, and gain or loss, as computed for tax purposes, with respect to such property. In these cases the capital accounts of the partners are required to be adjusted solely for allocations of the book items to such partners (see paragraph (b)(2)(iv)(g) of this section), and the partners' shares of the corresponding tax items are not independently reflected by further adjustments to the partners' capital accounts. Thus, separate allocations of these tax items cannot have economic effect under paragraph (b)(2)(ii)(b)(1) of this section, and the partners' distributive shares of such tax items must (unless governed by section 704(c)) be determined in accordance with the partners' interest in the partnership. These tax items must be shared among the partners in a manner that takes account of the variations between the adjusted tax basis of such property and its book value in the same manner as variation between the adjusted tax basis and fair market value of property contributed to the partnership are taken into account in determining the partners' shares of tax items under section 704(c). See examples (14) and (18) of paragraph (b)(5) of this section.

* * *

(vi) Amendments to partnership agreement. If an allocation has substantial economic effect under paragraph (b)(2) of this section or is deemed to be made in accordance with the partners' interests in the partnership under paragraph (b)(4) of this section under the partnership agreement that is effective for the taxable year to which such allocation relates, and such partnership agreement thereafter is modified, both the tax consequences of the modification and the facts and circumstances surrounding the modification will be closely scrutinized to determine whether the purported modification was part of the original agreement. If it is determined that the purported modification was part of the original agreement, prior allocations may be reallocated in a manner consistent with the modified terms of the agreement, and subsequent allocations may be reallocated to take account of such modified terms. For example, if a partner is obligated by the partnership agreement to restore the deficit balance in his capital account (or any limited dollar amount thereof) in accordance with requirement (3) of paragraph (b)(2)(ii)(b) of this section and, thereafter, such obligation is eliminated or reduced (other than as provided in paragraph (b)(2)(ii)(f) of this section), or is not complied with in a timely manner, such elimination, reduction, or noncompliance may be treated as if it always were part of the partnership agreement for purposes of making any reallocations and determining the appropriate limitations period.

* * *

(5) Examples. The operation of the rules in this paragraph is illustrated by the following examples:

Example (1). **(i)** A and B form a general partnership with cash contributions of $40,000 each, which cash is used to purchase depreciable personal property at a cost of $80,000. The partnership elects under section 48(q)(4) to reduce the amount of investment tax credit in lieu of adjusting the tax basis of such property. The partnership agreement provides that A and B will have equal shares of taxable income and loss (computed without regard to cost recovery deductions) and cash flow and that all cost recovery deductions on the property will be allocated to A. The agreement further provides that the partners' capital accounts will be determined and maintained in accordance with paragraph (b)(2)(iv) of the section, but that upon liquidation of the partnership, distributions will be made equally between the partners (regardless of capital account balances) and no partner will be required to restore the deficit balance in his capital account for distribution to partners with positive capital accounts balances. In the partnership's first taxable year, it recognizes operating income equal to its operating expenses and has an additional $20,000 cost recovery deduction, which is allocated entirely to A. That A and B will be entitled to equal distributions on liquidation, even though A is allocated the entire $20,000 cost recovery deduction, indicates A will not bear the full risk of the economic loss corresponding to such deduction if such loss occurs. Under paragraph (b)(2)(ii) of this section, the allocation lacks economic effect and will be disregarded. The partners made equal contributions to the partnership, share equally in other taxable income and loss and in cash flow, and will share equally in liquidation proceeds, indicating that their actual economic arrangement is to bear the risk imposed by the potential decrease in the value of the property equally. Thus, under paragraph (b)(3) of this section the partners' interests in the partnership are equal, and the cost recovery deduction will be reallocated equally between A and B.

(ii) Assume the same facts as in (i) except that the partnership agreement provides that liquidation proceeds will be distributed in accordance with capital account balances if the partnership is liquidated during the first five years of its existence but that liquidation proceeds will be distributed equally if the partnership is liquidated thereafter. Since the partnership agreement does not provide for the requirement contained in paragraph (b)(2)(ii)(b)(2) of this section to be satisfied throughout the term of the partnership, the partnership allocations do not have economic effect. Even if the partnership agreement provided for the requirement contained in paragraph (b)(2)(ii)(b)(2) to be satisfied throughout the term of the partnership, such allocations would not have economic effect unless the requirement contained in paragraph (b)(2)(ii)(b)(3) of this section or the alternate economic effect test contained in paragraph(b)(2)(ii)(d) of this section were satisfied.

(iii) Assume the same facts as in (i) except that distributions in liquidation of the partnership (or any partner's interest) are to be made in accordance with the partners' positive capital account balances throughout the term of the partnership (as set forth in paragraph (b)(2)(ii)(b)(2) of this section). Assume further that the partnership agreement contains a qualified income offset (as defined in paragraph (b)(2)(ii)(d) of this section) and that, as of the end of each partnership taxable year, the items described in paragraphs (b)(2)(ii)(d)(4), (5), and (6) of this section are not reasonably expected to cause or increase a deficit balance in A's capital account.

	A	B
Capital account upon formation	$40,000	$40,000
Less: year 1 cost recovery deduction	(20,000)	0
Capital account at end of year 1	$20,000	$40,000

Under the alternate economic effect test contained in paragraph (b)(2)(ii)(d) of this section, the allocation of the $20,000 cost recovery deduction to A has economic effect.

(iv) Assume the same facts as in (iii) and that in the partnership's second taxable year it recognizes operating income equal to its operating expenses and has a $25,000 cost recovery deduction which, under the partnership agreement, is allocated entirely to A.

	A	B
Capital account at beginning of year 2	$20,000	$40,000
Less: year 2 cost recovery deduction	(25,000)	0
Capital account at end of year 2	($5,000)	$40,000

The allocation of the $25,000 cost recovery deduction to A satisfies that alternate economic effect test contained in paragraph (b)(2)(ii)(d) of this section only to the extent of $20,000. Therefore, only $20,000 of such allocation has economic effect, and the remaining $5,000 must be reallocated in accordance with the partners' interests in the partnership. Under the partnership agreement, if the property were sold immediately following the end of the partnership's second taxable year for $35,000 (its adjusted tax basis), the $35,000 would be distributed to B. Thus, B, and not A, bears the economic burden corresponding to $5,000 of the $25,000 cost recovery deduction allocated to A. Under paragraph (b)(3)(iii) of this section, $5,000 of such cost recovery deduction will be reallocated to B.

(v) Assume the same facts as in (iv) except that the cost recovery deduction for the partnership's second taxable year is $20,000 instead of $25,000. The allocation of such cost recovery deduction to A has economic effect under the alternate economic effect test contained in paragraph (b)(2)(ii)(d) of this section. Assume further that the property is sold for $35,000 immediately following the end of the partnership's second taxable year, resulting in a $5,000 taxable loss ($40,000 adjusted tax basis less $35,000 sales price), and the partnership is liquidated.

	A	B
Capital account at beginning of year 2	$20,000	$40,000
Less: year 2 cost recovery deduction	(20,000)	0
Capital account at end of year 2	0	$40,000
Less: loss on sale	(2,500)	(2,500)
Capital account before liquidation	($2,500)	$37,500

Under the partnership agreement the $35,000 sales proceeds are distributed to B. Since B bears the entire economic burden corresponding to the $5,000 taxable loss from the sale of the property, the allocation of $2,500 of such loss to A does not have economic effect and must be reallocated in accordance with the partners' interests in the partnership. Under paragraph (b)(3)(iii) of this section, such $2,500 loss will be reallocated to B.

(vi) Assume the same facts as in (iv) except that the cost recovery deduction for the partnership's second taxable year is $20,000 instead of $25,000, and that as of the end of the partnership's second taxable year it is reasonably expected that during its third taxable year the partnership will (1) have operating income equal to its operating expenses (but will have no cost recovery deductions), (2) borrow $10,000 (recourse) and distribute such amount $5,000 to A and $5,000 to B, and (3) thereafter sell the partnership property, repay the $10,000 liability, and liquidate. In determining the extent to which the alternate economic effect test contained in paragraph (b)(2)(ii)(d) of this section is satisfied as of the end of the partnership's second taxable year, the fair market value of partnership property is presumed to be equal to its adjusted tax basis (in accordance with paragraph (b)(2)(iii)(c) of this section). Thus, it is presumed that the selling price of such property during the partnership's third taxable year will be its $40,000 adjusted tax basis. Accordingly, there can be no reasonable expectation that there will be increases to A's capital account in the partnership's third taxable year that will offset the expected $5,000 distribution to A. Therefore, the distribution of the loan proceeds must be taken into account in determining to what extent the alternate economic effect test contained in paragraph (b)(2)(ii)(d) is satisfied.

	A	B
Capital account at beginning of year 2	$20,000	$40,000
Less: expected future distribution	(5,000)	(5,000)
Less: year 2 cost recovery deduction	(20,000)	(0)
Hypothetical capital account at end of year 2	($5,000)	$35,000

Upon sale of the partnership property, the $40,000 presumed sales proceeds would be used to repay the $10,000 liability, and the remaining $30,000 would be distributed to B. Under these circumstances the allocation of the $20,000 cost recovery deduction to A in the partnership's second taxable year satisfies the alternate economic effect test contained in paragraph (b)(2)(ii)(d) of this section only to the extent of $15,000. Under paragraph (b)(3)(iii) of this section, the remaining $5,000 of such deduction will be reallocated to B. The results in this example would be the same even if the partnership agreement also provided that any gain (whether ordinary income or capital gain) upon the sale of the property would be allocated to A to the extent of the prior allocations of cost recovery deductions to him, and, at end of the partnership's second taxable year, the partners were confident that the gain on the sale of the property in the partnership's third taxable year would be sufficient to offset the expected $5,000 distribution to A.

(vii) Assume the same facts as in (iv) except that the partnership agreement also provides that any partner with a deficit balance in his capital account following the liquidation of his interest must restore that deficit to the partnership (as set forth in paragraph (b)(2)(ii)(b)(3) of this section). Thus, if the property were sold for $35,000 immediately after the end of the partnership's second taxable year, the $35,000 would be distributed to B, A would contribute $5,000 (the deficit balance in his capital account) to the partnership, and that $5,000 would be distributed to B. The allocation of the entire $25,000 cost recovery deduction to A in the partnership's second taxable year has economic effect.

(viii) Assume the same facts as in (vii) except that A's obligation to restore the deficit balance in his capital account is limited to a maximum of $5,000. The allocation of the $25,000 cost recovery deduction to A in the partnership's second taxable year has economic effect under alternate economic effect test contained in paragraph (b)(2)(ii)(d) of this section. At the end of such year, A makes an additional $5,000 contribution to the partnership (thereby eliminating the $5,000 deficit balance in his capital account). Under paragraph (b)(2)(ii)(f) of this section, A's obligation to restore up to $5,000 of the deficit balance in his capital account may be eliminated after he contributes the additional $5,000 without affecting the validity of prior allocations.

(ix) Assume the same facts as in (iv) except that upon formation of the partnership A also contributes to the partnership his promissory note with a $5,000 principal balance. The note unconditionally obligates A to pay an additional $5,000 to the partnership at the earlier of (a) the beginning of the partnership's fourth taxable year, or (b) the end of the partnership taxable year in which A's interest is liquidated. Under paragraph (b)(2)(ii)(c) of this section, A is considered obligated to restore up to $5,000 of the deficit balance in his capital account to the partnership. Accordingly, under the alternate economic effect test contained in paragraph (b)(2)(ii)(d) of this section, the allocation of the $25,000 cost recovery deduction to A in the partnership's second taxable year has economic effect. The results in this example would be the same if (1) the note A contributed to the partnership were payable only at the end of the partnership's fourth taxable year (so that A would not be required to satisfy the note upon liquidation of his interest in the partnership), and (2) the partnership agreement provided that upon liquidation of A's interest, the partnership would retain A's note, and A would contribute to the partnership the excess of the outstanding principal balance of the note over its then fair market value.

(x) Assume the same facts as in (ix) except that A's obligation to contribute an additional $5,000 to the partnership is not evidenced by a promissory note. Instead, the partnership agreement imposes upon A the obligation to make an additional $5,000 contribution to the partnership at the earlier of (a) the beginning of the partnership's fourth taxable year, or (b) the end of the partnership taxable year in which A's interest is liquidated. Under paragraph (b)(2)(ii)(c) of this section, as a result of A's deferred contribution requirement, A is considered obligated to restore up to $5,000 of the deficit balance in his capital account to the partnership. Accordingly, under the alternate economic effect test contained in paragraph (b)(2)(ii)(d) of this section, the allocation of the $25,000 cost recovery deduction to A in the partnership's second taxable year has economic effect.

(xi) Assume the same facts as in (vii) except that the partnership agreement also provides that any gain (whether ordinary income or capital gain) upon the sale of the property will be allocated to A to the extent of the prior allocations to A of cost recovery deductions from such property, and additional gain will be allocated equally between A and B. At the time the allocations of cost recovery deductions were made to A, the partners believed there would be gain on the sale of the property in an amount sufficient to offset the allocations of cost recovery deductions to A. Nevertheless, the existence of the gain chargeback provision will not cause the economic effect of the allocations to be insubstantial under paragraph (b)(2)(iii)(c) of this section, since in testing whether the economic effect of such allocations is substantial, the recovery property is presumed to decrease in value by the amount of such deductions.

Example (2). C and D form a general partnership solely to acquire and lease machinery that is 5–year recovery property under section 168. Each contributes $100,000 and the partnership obtains an $800,000 recourse loan to purchase the machinery. The partnership elects under section 48(q)(4) to reduce the amount of investment tax credit in lieu of adjusting the tax basis of such machinery. The partnership, C and D have calendar taxable years. The partnership agreement provides that the partners' capital accounts will be determined and maintained in accordance with paragraph (b)(2)(iv) of this section, distributions in liquidation of the partnership (or any partner's interest) will be made in accordance with the partners' positive capital account balances, and any partner with a deficit balance in his capital account following the liquidation of his interest must restore that deficit to the partnership (as set forth in paragraphs (b)(2)(ii)(b)(2) and (3) of this section). The partnership agreement further provides that (a) partnership net taxable loss will be allocated 90 percent to C and 10 percent to D until such time as there is partnership net taxable income, and therefore C will be allocated 90 percent of such taxable income until he has been allocated partnership net taxable income equal to the partnership net taxable loss previously allocated to him, (b) all further partnership net taxable income or loss will be allocated equally between C and D, and (c) distributions of operating cash flow will be made equally between C and D. The partnership enters into a 12–year lease with a financially secure corporation under which the partnership expects to have a net taxable loss in each of its first 5 partnership taxable years due to cost recovery deductions with respect to the machinery and net taxable income in each of its following 7 partnership taxable years, in part due to the absence of such cost recovery deductions. There is a strong likelihood that the partnership's net taxable loss in partnership taxable years 1 through 5 will be $100,000, $90,000, $80,000, $70,000, and $60,000, respectively, and the partnership's net taxable income in partnership taxable years 6 through 12 will be $40,000, $50,000, $60,000, $70,000, $80,000, $90,000, and $100,000, respectively. Even though there is a strong likelihood that the allocations of net taxable loss in years 1 through 5 will be largely offset by other allocations in partnership taxable years 6 through 12, and even if it is assumed that the total tax liability of the partners in years 1 through 12 will be less than if the allocations had not been provided in the partnership agreement, the economic effect of the allocations will not be insubstantial under paragraph (b)(2)(iii)(c) of this section. This is because at the time such allocations became part of the partnership agreement, there was a strong likelihood that the allocations of net taxable loss in years 1 through 5 would not be largely offset by allocations of income within 5 years (determined on a first-in, first-out basis). The year 1 allocation will not be offset until years 6, 7, and 8, the year 2 allocation will not offset until years 8 and 9, the year 3 allocation will not be offset until years 9 and 10, the year 4 allocation will not be offset until years 10 and 11, and the year 5 allocation will not be offset until years 11 and 12.

Example (3). E and F enter into a partnership agreement to develop and market experimental electronic devices. E contributes $2,500 cash and agrees to devote his full-time services to the partnership. F contributes $100,000 cash and agrees to obtain a loan for the partnership for any additional capital needs. The partnership agreement provides that all deductions for research and experimental expenditures and interest on partnership loans are to be allocated to F. In addition, F will be allocated 90 percent, and E 10 percent, of partnership taxable income or loss, computed net of the deductions for such research and experimental expenditures and interest, until F has received allocations of such taxable income equal to the sum of such research and experimental expenditures, such interest expense, and his share of such taxable loss. Thereafter E and F will share all taxable income and loss equally. Operating cash flow will be distributed equally between E and F. The partnership agreement also provides that E's and F's capital accounts will be determined and maintained in accordance with paragraph (b)(2)(iv) of this section, distributions in liquidation of the partnership (or any partner's interest) will be made in accordance with the partners' positive capital account balances, and any partner with a deficit balance in his capital account following the liquidation of his interest must restore that deficit to the partnership (as set forth in paragraphs (b)(2)(ii)(b)(2) and (3) of this section). These allocations have economic effect. In addition, in view of the nature of the partnership's activities, there is not a strong likelihood at the time the allocations become part of the partnership agreement that the economic effect of the allocations to F of deductions for research and experimental expenditures and interest on partnership loans will be largely offset by allocations to F of partnership net taxable income. The economic effect of the allocations is substantial.

* * *

Example (5). **(i)** Individuals I and J are the only partners of an investment partnership. The partnership owns corporate stocks, corporate debt instruments, and tax-exempt debt instruments. Over the next several years, I expects to be in the 50 percent marginal tax bracket, and J expects to be in the 15 percent marginal tax bracket. There is a strong likelihood that in each of the next several years the partnership will realize between $450 and $550 of tax-exempt interest and between $450 and $550 of a combination of taxable interest and dividends from its investments. I and J made equal capital contributions to the partnership, and they have agreed to share equally in gains and losses from the sale of the partnership's investment securities. I and J agree, however, that rather than share interest and dividends of the partnership equally, they will allocate the partnership's tax-exempt interest 80 percent to I and 20 percent to J and will distribute cash derived from interest received on the tax-exempt bonds in the same percentages. In addition, they agree to allocate 100 percent of the partnership's taxable interest and dividends to J and to distribute cash derived from interest and dividends received on the corporate stocks and debt instruments 100 percent to J. The partnership agreement further provides that the partners' capital accounts will be determined and maintained in accordance with paragraph (b)(2)(iv) of this section, distributions in liquidation of the partnership (or any partner's interest) will be made in accordance with the partner's positive capital account balances, and any partner with a deficit balance in his capital account following the liquidation of his interest must restore that deficit to the partnership (as set forth in paragraphs (b)(2)(ii)(b)(2) and (3) of this section). The allocation of taxable interest and dividends and tax-exempt interest has economic effect, but that economic effect is not substantial under the general rules set forth in paragraph (b)(2)(iii) of this section. Without the allocation I would be allocated between $225 and $275 of tax-exempt interest and between $225 and $275 of a combination of taxable interest and dividends, which (net of Federal income taxes he would owe on such income) would give I between $337.50 and $412.50 after tax. With the allocation, however, I will be allocated between $360 and $440 of tax-exempt interest and no taxable interest and dividends, which (net of Federal income taxes) will give I between $360 and $440 after tax. Thus, at the time the allocations became part of the partnership agreement, I is expected to enhance his after-tax economic consequences as a result of the allocations. On the other hand, there is a strong likelihood that neither I nor J will substantially diminish his after-tax economic consequences as a result of the allocations. Under the combination of likely investment outcomes least favorable for J, the partnership would realize $550 of tax-exempt interest and $450 of taxable interest and dividends, giving J $492.50 after tax (which is more than the $466.25 after tax J would have received if each of such amounts had been allocated equally between the partners). Under the combination of likely investment outcomes least favorable for I, the partnership would realize $450 of tax-exempt interest and $550 of taxable interest and dividends, giving I $360 after tax (which is not substantially less than the $362.50 he would have received if each such amounts had been allocated equally between the partners). Accordingly, the allocations in the partnership agreement must be reallocated in accordance with the partners' interests in the partnership under paragraph (b)(3) of this section.

(ii) Assume the same facts as in (i). In addition, assume that in the first partnership taxable year in which the allocation arrangement described in (i) applies, the partnership realizes $450 of tax-exempt interest and $550 of taxable interest and dividends, so that, pursuant to the partnership agreement, I's capital account is credited with $360 (80 percent of the tax-exempt interest), and J's capital account is credited with $640 (20 percent of the tax-exempt interest and 100 percent of the taxable interest and dividends). The allocations of tax-exempt interest and taxable interest and dividends (which do not have substantial economic effect for the reasons stated in (i) will be disregarded and will be reallocated). Since under the partnership agreement I will receive 36 percent (360/1,000) and J will receive 64 percent (640/1,000) of the partnership's total investment income in such year, under paragraph (b)(3) of this section the partnership's tax-exempt interest and taxable interest and dividends each will be reallocated 36 percent to I and 64 percent to J.

Example (6). K and L are equal partners in a general partnership formed to acquire and operate property described in section 1231(b). The partnership, K, and L have calendar taxable years. The partnership agreement provides that the partners' capital accounts will be determined and maintained in accordance with paragraph (b)(2)(iv) of this section, that distributions in liquidation of the partnership (or any partner's interest) will be made in accordance with the partners' positive capital account balances, and that any partner with a deficit balance in his capital account following the liquidation of his interest must restore that deficit to the partnership (as set forth in paragraphs (b)(2)(ii)(b)(2) and (3) of this section). For a taxable year in which the partnership expects to incur a loss on the sale of a portion of such property, the partnership agreement is amended (at the beginning of the taxable year) to allocate such loss to K, who expects to have no gains from the sale of depreciable property described in section 1231(b) in that taxable year, and to allocate an equivalent amount of partnership loss and deduction for that year of a different character to L, who expects to have such gains. Any partnership loss and deduction in excess of these allocations will be allocated equally between K and L. The amendment is effective only for that taxable year. At the time the partnership agreement is amended, there is a strong likelihood that the partnership will incur deduction or loss in the taxable year other than loss from the sale of property described in section 1231(b) in an amount that will substantially equal or exceed the expected amount of the section 1231(b) loss. The allocations in such taxable year have economic effect. However, the economic effect of the allocations is insubstantial under the test described in paragraph (b)(2)(iii)(b) of this section because there is a strong likelihood, at the time the allocations become part of the partnership agreement, that the net increases and decreases to K's and L's capital accounts will be the same at the end of the taxable year to which they apply with such allocations in effect as they would have been in the absence of such allocations, and that the total taxes of K and L for such year will be reduced as a result of such allocations. If in fact the partnership incurs deduction or loss, other than loss from the sale of property described in section 1231(b), in an amount at least equal to the section 1231(b) loss, the loss and deduction in such taxable year will be reallocated equally between K and L under paragraph (b)(3) of this section. If not, the loss from the sale of property described in section 1231(b) and the items of deduction and other loss realized in such year will be reallocated between K and L in proportion to the net decreases in their capital accounts due to the allocation of such items under the partnership agreement.

Example (7). **(i)** M and N are partners in the MN general partnership, which is engaged in an active business. Income, gain, loss, and deduction from MN's business is allocated equally between M and N. The partnership, M, and N have calendar taxable years. Under the partnership agreement the partners' capital accounts will be determined and maintained in accordance with paragraph (b)(2)(iv) of this section, distributions in liquidation of the partnership (or any partner's interest) will be made in accordance with the partner's positive capital account balances, and any partner with a deficit balance in his capital account following the liquidation of his interest must restore that deficit to the partnership (as set forth in paragraphs (b)(2)(ii)(b)(2) and (3) of this section). In order to enhance the credit standing of the partnership, the partners contribute surplus funds to the partnership, which the partners agree to invest in equal dollar amounts of tax-exempt bonds and corporate stock for the partnership's first 3 taxable years. M is expected to be in a higher marginal tax bracket than N during those 3 years. At the time the decision to make these investments is made, it is agreed that, during the 3–year period of the investment, M will be allocated 90 percent and N 10 percent of the interest income from the tax-exempt bonds as well as any gain or loss from the sale thereof, and that M will be allocated 10 percent and N 90 percent of the dividend income from the corporate stock as well as any gain or loss from the sale thereof. At the time the allocations concerning the investments become part of the partnership agreement, there is not a strong likelihood that the gain or loss from the sale of the stock will be substantially equal to the gain or loss from the sale of the tax-exempt bonds, but there is a strong likelihood that the tax-exempt interest and the taxable dividends realized from these investments during the 3–year period will not differ substantially. These allocations have economic effect, and the economic effect of the allocations of the gain or loss on the sale of the tax-exempt bonds and corporate stock is substantial. The economic effect of the allocations of the tax-exempt interest and the taxable dividends, however, is not substantial under the test described in paragraph (b)(2)(iii)(c) of this section because there is a strong likelihood, at the time the allocations become part of the partnership agreement, that at the end of the 3–year period to which such allocations relate, the net increases and decreases to M's and N's capital accounts will be the same with such allocations as they would have been in the absence of such allocations, and that the total taxes of M and N for the taxable years to which such allocations relate will be reduced as a result of such allocations. If in fact the amounts of the tax-exempt interest and taxable dividends earned by the partnership during the 3–year period are equal, the tax-exempt interest and taxable dividends will be reallocated to the partners in equal shares under paragraph (b)(3) of this section. If not, the tax-exempt interest and taxable dividends will be reallocated between M and N in proportion to the net increases in their capital accounts during such 3–year period due to the allocation of such items under the partnership agreement.

(ii) Assume the same facts as in (i) except that gain or loss from the sale of the tax-exempt bonds and corporate stock will be allocated equally between M and N and the partnership agreement provides that the 90/10 allocation arrangement with respect to the investment income applies only to the first $10,000 of interest income from the tax-exempt bonds and the first $10,000 of dividend income from the corporate stock, and only to the first taxable year of the partnership. There is a strong likelihood at the time the 90/10 allocation of the investment income became part of the partnership agreement that in the first taxable year of the partnership, the partnership will earn more than $10,000 of tax-exempt interest and more than $10,000 of taxable dividends. The allocations of tax-exempt interest and taxable dividends provided in the partnership agreement have economic effect, but under the test contained in paragraph (b)(2)(iii)(b) of this section, such economic effect is not substantial for the same reasons stated in (i) (but applied to the 1 taxable year, rather than to a 3–year period). If in fact the partnership realizes at least $10,000 of tax-exempt interest and at least $10,000 of taxable dividends in such year, the allocations of such interest income and dividend income will be reallocated equally between M and N under paragraph (b)(3) of this section. If not, the tax-exempt interest and taxable dividends will be reallocated between M and N in proportion to the net increases in their capital accounts due to the allocations of such items under the partnership agreement.

(iii) Assume the same facts as in (ii) except that at the time the 90/10 allocation of investment income becomes part of the partnership agreement, there is not a strong likelihood that (1) the partnership will earn $10,000 or more of tax-exempt interest and $10,000 or more of taxable dividends in the partnership's first taxable year, and (2) the amount of tax-exempt interest and taxable dividends earned during such year will be substantially the same. Under these facts the economic effect of the allocations generally will be substantial. (Additional facts may exist in certain cases, however, so that the allocation is insubstantial under the second sentence of paragraph (b)(2)(iii). See example (5) above.)

* * *

Example (13). **(i)** Y and Z form a brokerage general partnership for the purpose of investing and trading in marketable securities. Y contributes cash of $10,000, and Z contributes securities of P corporation, which have an adjusted basis of $3,000 and a fair market value of $10,000. The partnership would not be an investment company under section 351(e) if it were incorporated. The partnership agreement provides that the partners' capital accounts will be determined and maintained in accordance with paragraph (b)(2)(iv) of this section, distributions in liquidation of the partnership (or any partner's interest) will be made in accordance with the partners' positive capital account balances, and any partner with a deficit balance in his capital account following the liquidation of his interest must restore that deficit to the partnership (as set forth in paragraphs (b)(2)(ii)(b)(2) and (3) of this section). The partnership uses the interim closing of the books method for purposes of section 706. The initial capital accounts of Y and Z are fixed at $10,000 each. The agreement further provides that all partnership distributions, income, gain, loss, deduction, and credit will be shared equally between Y and Z, except that the taxable gain attributable to the precontribution appreciation in the value of the securities of P corporation will be allocated to Z in accordance with section 704(c). During the partnership's first taxable year, it sells the securities of P corporation for $12,000, resulting in a $2,000 book gain ($12,000 less $10,000 book value) and a $9,000 taxable gain ($12,000 less $3,000 adjusted tax basis). The partnership has no other income, gain, loss, or deductions for the taxable year. The gain from the sale of the securities is allocated as follows:

	Y		Z	
	Tax	Book	Tax	Book
Capital account upon formation	$10,000	$10,000	$ 3,000	$10,000
Plus: gain	1,000	1,000	8,000	1,000
Capital account at end of year 1	$11,000	$11,000	$11,000	$11,000

The allocation of the $2,000 book gain, $1,000 each to Y and Z, has substantial economic effect. Furthermore, under section 704(c) the partners' distributive shares of the $9,000 taxable gain are $1,000 to Y and $8,000 to Z.

* * *

Example (14). **(i)** MC and RW form a general partnership to which each contributes $10,000. The $20,000 is invested in securities of Ventureco (which are not readily tradable on an established securities market). In each of the partnership's taxable years, it recognizes operating income equal to its operating deductions (excluding gain or loss from the sale of securities). The partnership agreement provides that the partners' capital accounts will be determined and maintained in accordance with paragraph (b)(2)(iv) of this section, distributions in liquidation of the partnership (or any partner's interest) will be made in accordance with the partners' positive capital account balances, and any partner with a deficit balance in his capital account following the liquidation of his interest must restore that deficit to the partnership (as set forth in paragraphs (b)(2)(ii)(b)(2) and (3) of this section). The partnership uses the interim closing of the books method for purposes of section 706. Assume that the Ventureco securities subsequently appreciate in value to $50,000. At that time SK makes a $25,000 cash contribution to the partnership (thereby acquiring a one-third interest in the partnership), and the $25,000 is placed in a bank account. Upon SK's admission to the partnership, the capital accounts of MC and RW (which were $10,000 each prior to SK's admission) are, in accordance with paragraph (b)(2)(iv)(f) of this section, adjusted upward (to $25,000 each) to reflect their shares of the unrealized appreciation in the Ventureco securities that occurred before SK was admitted to the partnership. Immediately after SK's admission to the partnership, the securities are sold for their $50,000 fair market value, resulting in taxable gain of $30,000 ($50,000 less $20,000 adjusted tax basis) and no book gain or loss. An allocation of the $30,000 taxable gain cannot have economic effect since it cannot properly be reflected in the partners' book capital accounts. Under paragraph (b)(2)(iv)(f) of this section and the special partners' interests in the partnership rule contained in paragraph (b)(4)(i) of this section, unless the partnership agreement provides that the $30,000 taxable gain will, in accordance with section 704(c) principles, be shared $15,000 to MC and $15,000 to RW, the partners' capital accounts will not be considered maintained in accordance with paragraph (b)(2)(iv) of this section.

	MC		RW		SK	
	Tax	Book	Tax	Book	Tax	Book
Capital account following SK's admission	$10,000	$25,000	$10,000	$25,000	$25,000	$25,000
Plus: gain	15,000	0	15,000	0	0	0
Capital account following sale	$25,000	$25,000	$25,000	$25,000	$25,000	$25,000

(ii) Assume the same facts as (i) except that after SK's admission to the partnership, the Ventureco securities appreciate in value to $74,000 and are sold, resulting in taxable gain of $54,000 ($74,000 less $20,000 adjusted tax basis) and book gain of $24,000 ($74,000 less $50,000 book value). Under the partnership agreement the $24,000 book gain (the appreciation in value occurring after SK became a partner) is allocated equally among MC, RW, and SK, and such allocations have substantial economic effect. An allocation of the $54,000 taxable gain cannot have economic effect since it cannot properly be reflected in the partners' book capital accounts. Under paragraph (b)(2)(iv)(f) of this section and the special partners' interests in the partnership rule contained in paragraph (b)(4)(i) of this section, unless the partnership agreement provides that the taxable gain will, in accordance with section 704(c) principles, be shared $23,000 to MC, $23,000 to RW, and $8,000 to SK, the partners' capital accounts will not be considered maintained in accordance with paragraph (b)(2)(iv) of this section.

	MC		RW		SK	
	Tax	Book	Tax	Book	Tax	Book
Capital account following SK's admission	$10,000	$25,000	$10,000	$25,000	$25,000	$25,000
Plus: gain	23,000	8,000	23,000	8,000	8,000	8,000
Capital account following sale	$33,000	$33,000	$33,000	$33,000	$33,000	$33,000

(iii) Assume the same facts as (i) except that after SK's admission to the partnership, the Ventureco securities depreciate in value to $44,000 and are sold, resulting in taxable gain of $24,000 ($44,000 less $20,000 adjusted tax basis) and a book loss of $6,000 ($50,000 book value less $44,000). Under the partnership agreement the $6,000 book loss is allocated equally among MC, RW, and SK, and such allocations have substantial economic effect. An allocation of the $24,000 taxable gain cannot have economic effect since it cannot properly be reflected in the partners' book capital accounts. Under paragraph (b)(2)(iv)(f) of this section and the special partners' interests in the partnership rule contained in paragraph (b)(4)(i) of this section, unless the partnership agreement provides that the $24,000 taxable gain will, in accordance with section 704(c) principles, be shared equally between MC and RW, the partners' capital accounts will not be considered maintained in accordance with paragraph (b)(2)(iv) of this section.

	MC		RW		SK	
	Tax	Book	Tax	Book	Tax	Book
Capital account following SK's admission	$10,000	$25,000	$10,000	$25,000	$25,000	$25,000
Plus: gain	12,000	0	12,000	0	0	0
Less: loss	0	(2,000)	0	(2,000)	0	(2,000)
Capital account following sale	$22,000	$23,000	$22,000	$23,000	$25,000	$2[3],000

That SK bears an economic loss of $2,000 without a corresponding taxable loss is attributable entirely to the "ceiling rule." See paragraph (c)(2) of § 1.704–1.

(iv) Assume the same facts as in (ii) except that upon the admission of SK the capital accounts of MC and RW are not each adjusted upward from $10,000 to $25,000 to reflect the appreciation in the partnership's securities that occurred before SK was admitted to the partnership. Rather, upon SK's admission to the partnership, the partnership agreement is amended to provide that the first $30,000 of taxable gain upon the sale of such securities will be allocated equally between MC and RW, and that all other income, gain, loss and deduction will be allocated equally between MC, RW, and SK. When the securities are sold for $74,000, the $54,000 of taxable gain is so allocated. These allocations of taxable gain have substantial economic effect. (If the agreement instead provides for all taxable gain (including the $30,000 taxable gain attributable to the appreciation in the securities prior to SK's admission to the partnership) to be allocated equally between MC, RW, and SK, the partners should consider whether, and to what extent, the provisions of paragraphs (b)(1)(iii) and (iv) of this section are applicable.)

* * *

Example (15). **(i)** JB and DK form a limited partnership for the purpose of purchasing residential real estate to lease. JB, the limited partner, contributes $13,500, and DK, the general partner, contributes $1,500. The partnership, which uses the cash receipts and disbursements method of accounting, purchases a building for $100,000 (on leased land), incurring a recourse mortgage of $85,000 that requires the payment of interest only for a period of 3 years. The partnership agreement provides that partnership net taxable income and loss will be allocated 90 percent to JB and 10 percent to DK, the partners' capital accounts will be determined and maintained in accordance with paragraph (b)(2)(iv) of this section, distributions in liquidation of the partnership (or any partner's interest) will be made in accordance with the partners' positive capital account balances (as set forth in paragraph (b)(2)(ii)(b)(2) of this section), and JB is not required to restore any deficit balance in his capital account, but DK is so required. The partnership agreement contains a qualified income offset (as defined in paragraph (b)(2)(ii)(d) of this section). As of the end of each of the partnership's first 3 taxable years, the items described in paragraphs (b)(2)(ii)(d)(4), (5), and (6) of this section are not reasonably expected to cause or increase a deficit balance in JB's capital account. In the partnership's first taxable year, it has rental income of $10,000, operating expenses of $2,000, interest expense of $8,000, and cost recovery deductions of $12,000. Under the partnership agreement JB and DK are allocated $10,800 and $1,200, respectively, of the $12,000 net taxable loss incurred in the partnership's first taxable year.

	JB	DK
Capital account upon formation	$13,500	$1,500
Less: year 1 net loss	(10,800)	(1,200)
Capital account at end of year 1	$2,700	$300

The alternate economic effect test contained in paragraph (b)(2)(ii)(d) of this section is satisfied as of the end of the partnership's first taxable year. Thus, the allocation made in the partnership's first taxable year has economic effect.

(ii) Assume the same facts as in (i) and that in the partnership's second taxable year it again has rental income of $10,000, operating expenses of $2,000, interest expense of $8,000, and cost recovery deductions of $12,000. Under the partnership agreement JB and DK are allocated $10,800 and $1,200, respectively, of the $12,000 net taxable loss incurred in the partnership's second taxable year.

	JB	DK
Capital account at beginning of year 1	$2,700	$300
Less: year 2 net loss	(10,800)	(1,200)
Capital account at end of year 2	($8,100)	($900)

Only $2,700 of the $10,800 net taxable loss allocated to JB satisfies the alternate economic effect test contained in paragraph (b)(2)(ii)(d) of this section as of the end of the partnership's second taxable year. The allocation of such $2,700 net taxable loss to JB (consisting of $2,250 of rental income, $450 of operating expenses, $1,800 of interest expense, and $2,700 of cost recovery deductions) has economic effect. The remaining $8,100 of net taxable loss allocated by the partnership agreement to JB must be reallocated in accordance with the partners' interests in the partnership. Under paragraph (b)(3)(iii) of this section, the determination of the partners' interests in the remaining $8,100 net taxable loss is made by comparing how distributions (and contributions) would be made if the partnership sold its property at its adjusted tax basis and liquidated immediately following the end of the partnership's first taxable year with the results of such a sale and liquidation immediately following the end of the partnership's second taxable year. If the partnership's real property were sold for its $88,000 adjusted tax basis and the partnership were liquidated immediately following the end of the partnership's first taxable year, the $88,000 sales proceeds would be used to repay the $85,000 note, and there would be $3,000 remaining in the partnership, which would be used to make liquidating distributions to DK and JB of $300 and $2,700, respectively. If such property were sold for its $76,000 adjusted tax basis and the partnership were liquidated immediately following the end of the partnership's second taxable year, DK would be required to contribute $9,000 to the partnership in order for the partnership to repay the $85,000 note, and there would be no assets remaining in the partnership to distribute. A comparison of these outcomes indicates that JB bore $2,700 and DK $9,300 of the economic burden that corresponds to the $12,000 net taxable loss. Thus, in addition to the $1,200 net taxable loss allocated to DK under the partnership agreement, $8,100 of net taxable loss will be reallocated to DK under paragraph (b)(3)(iii) of this section. Similarly, for subsequent taxable years, absent an increase in JB's capital account, all net taxable loss allocated to JB under the partnership agreement will be reallocated to DK.

(iii) Assume the same facts as in (ii) and that in the partnership's third taxable year there is rental income of $35,000, operating expenses of $2,000, interest expense of $8,000, and cost recovery deductions of $10,000. The capital accounts of the partners maintained on the books of the partnership do not take into account the reallocation to DK of the $8,100 net taxable loss in the partnership's second taxable year. Thus, an allocation of the $15,000 net taxable income, $13,500 to JB and $1,500 to DK (as dictated by the partnership agreement and as reflected in the capital accounts of the partners) does not have economic effect. The partners' interests in the partnership with respect to such $15,000 taxable gain again is made in the manner described in paragraph (b)(3)(iii) of this section. If the partnership's real property were sold for its $76,000 adjusted tax basis and the partnership were liquidated immediately following the end of the partnership's second taxable year, DK would be required to contribute $9,000 to the partnership in order for the partnership to repay the $85,000 note, and there would be no assets remaining to distribute. If such property were sold for its $66,000 adjusted tax basis and the partnership were liquidated immediately following the end of the partnership's third taxable year, the $91,000 ($66,000 sales proceeds plus $25,000 cash on hand) would be used to repay the $85,000 note and there would be $6,000 remaining in the partnership, which would be used to make liquidating distributions to DK and JB of $600 and $5,400, respectively. Accordingly, under paragraph (b)(3)(iii) of this section the $15,000 net taxable income in the partnership's third taxable year will be reallocated $9,600 to DK (minus $9,000 at end of the second taxable year to positive $600 at end of the third taxable year) and $5,400 to JB (zero at end of the second taxable year to positive $5,400 at end of the third taxable year).

* * *

(c) Contributed property; cross-reference. See § 1.704–3 for methods of making allocations that take into account precontribution appreciation or diminution in value of property contributed by a partner to a partnership.

(d) Limitation on allowance of losses. (1) A partner's distributive share of partnership loss will be allowed only to the extent of the adjusted basis (before reduction by current year's losses) of such partner's interest in the partnership at the end of the partnership taxable year in which such loss occurred. A partner's share of loss in excess of his adjusted basis at the end of the partnership taxable year will not be allowed for that year. However, any loss so disallowed shall be allowed as a deduction at the end of the first succeeding partnership taxable year, and subsequent partnership taxable years, to the extent that the partner's adjusted basis for his partnership interest at the end of any such year exceeds zero (before reduction by such loss for such year).

(2) In computing the adjusted basis of a partner's interest for the purpose of ascertaining the extent to which a partner's distributive share of partnership loss shall be allowed as a deduction for the taxable year, the basis shall first be increased under section 705(a)(1) and decreased under section 705(a)(2), except for losses of the taxable year and losses previously disallowed. If the partner's distributive share of the aggregate of items of loss specified in section 702(a)(1), (2), (3), (8), and (9) exceeds the basis of the partner's interest computed under the preceding sentence, the limitation on losses under section 704(d) must be allocated to his distributive share of each such loss. This allocation shall be determined by taking the proportion that each loss bears to the total of all such losses. For purposes of the preceding sentence, the total losses for the taxable year shall be the sum of his distributive share of losses for the current year and his losses disallowed and carried forward from prior years.

(3) For the treatment of certain liabilities of the partner or partnership, see section 752 and § 1.752–1.

(4) The provisions of this paragraph may be illustrated by the following examples:

Example (1). At the end of the partnership taxable year 1955, partnership AB has a loss of $20,000. Partner A's distributive share of this loss is $10,000. At the end of such year, A's adjusted basis for his interest in the partnership (not taking into account his distributive share of the loss) is $6,000. Under section 704(d), A's distributive share of partnership loss is allowed to him (in his taxable year within or with which the partnership taxable year ends) only to the extent of his adjusted basis of $6,000. The $6,000 loss allowed for 1955 decreases the adjusted basis of A's interest to zero. Assume that, at the end of partnership taxable year 1956, A's share of partnership income has increased the adjusted basis of A's interest in the partnership to $3,000 (not taking into account the $4,000 loss disallowed in 1955). Of the $4,000 loss disallowed for the partnership taxable year 1955, $3,000 is allowed A for the partnership taxable year 1956, thus again decreasing the adjusted basis of his interest to zero. If, at the end of partnership taxable year 1957, A has an adjusted basis of his interest of at least $1,000 (not taking into account the disallowed loss of $1,000), he will be allowed the $1,000 loss previously disallowed.

Example (2). At the end of partnership taxable year 1955, partnership CD has a loss of $20,000. Partner C's distributive share of this loss is $10,000. The adjusted basis of his interest in the partnership (not taking into account his distributive share of such loss) is $6,000. Therefore, $4,000 of the loss is disallowed. At the end of partnership taxable year 1956, the partnership has no taxable income or loss, but owes $8,000 to a bank for money borrowed. Since C's share of this liability is $4,000, the basis of his partnership interest is increased from zero to $4,000. (See sections 752 and 722, and §§ 1.752–1 and 1.722–1.) C is allowed the $4,000 loss, disallowed for the preceding year under section 704(d), for his taxable year within or with which partnership taxable year 1956 ends.

Example (3). At the end of partnership taxable year 1955, partner C has the following distributive share of partnership items described in section 702(a): Long-term capital loss, $4,000; short-term capital loss, $2,000; income as described in section 702(a)(9), $4,000. Partner C's adjusted basis for his partnership interest at the end of 1955, before adjustment for any of the above items, is $1,000. As adjusted under section 705(a)(1)(A), C's basis is increased from $1,000 to $5,000 at the end of the year. C's total distributive share of partnership loss is $6,000. Since without regard to losses, C has a basis of only $5,000, C is allowed only $5,000/$6,000 of each loss, that is, $3,333 of his long-term capital loss, and $1,667 of his short-term capital loss. C must carry forward to succeeding taxable years $667 as a long-term capital loss and $333 as a short-term capital loss.

(e) Family partnerships—(1) In general—(i) Introduction. The production of income by a partnership is attributable to the capital or services, or both, contributed by the partners. The provisions of subchapter K, chapter 1 of the Code, are to be read in the light of their relationship to section 61, which requires, inter alia, that income be taxed to the person who earns it through his own labor and skill and the utilization of his own capital.

(ii) Recognition of donee as partner. With respect to partnerships in which capital is a material income-producing factor, section 704(e)(1) provides that a person shall be recognized as a partner for income tax purposes if he owns a capital interest in such a partnership whether or not such interest is derived by purchase or gift from any other person. If a capital interest in a partnership in which capital is a material income-producing factor is created by gift, section 704(e)(2) provides that the distributive share of the donee under the partnership agreement shall be includible in his gross income, except to the extent that such distributive share is determined without allowance of reasonable compensation for services rendered to the partnership by the donor, and except to the extent that the portion of such distributive share attributable to donated capital is proportionately greater than the share of the donor attributable to the donor's capital. For rules of allocation in such cases, see subparagraph (3) of this paragraph.

(iii) Requirement of complete transfer to donee. A donee or purchaser of a capital interest in a partnership is not recognized as a partner under the principles of section 704(e)(1) unless such interest is acquired in a bona fide transaction, not a mere sham for tax avoidance or evasion purposes, and the donee or purchaser is the real owner of such interest. To be recognized, a transfer must vest dominion and control of the partnership interest in the transferee. The existence of such dominion and control in the donee is to be determined from all the facts and circumstances. A transfer is not recognized if the transferor retains such incidents of ownership that the transferee has not acquired full and complete ownership of the partnership interest. Transactions between members of a family will be closely scrutinized, and the circumstances, not only at the time of the purported transfer but also during the periods preceding and following it, will be taken into consideration in determining the bona fides or lack of bona fides of the purported gift or sale. A partnership may be recognized for income tax purposes as to some partners but not as to others.

(iv) Capital as a material income-producing factor. For purposes of section 704(e)(1), the determination as to whether capital is a material income-producing factor must be made by reference to all the facts of each case. Capital is a material income-producing factor if a substantial portion of the gross income of the business is attributable to the employment of capital in the business conducted by the partnership. In general, capital is not a material income-producing factor where the income of the business consists principally of fees, commissions, or other compensation for personal services performed by members or employees of the partnership. On the other hand, capital is ordinarily a material income-producing factor if the operation of the business requires substantial inventories or a substantial investment in plant, machinery, or other equipment.

(v) Capital interest in a partnership. For purposes of section 704(e), a capital interest in a partnership means an interest in the assets of the partnership, which is distributable to the owner of the capital interest upon his withdrawal from the partnership or upon liquidation of the partnership. The mere right to participate in the earnings and profits of a partnership is not a capital interest in the partnership.

(2) Basic tests as to ownership—(i) In general. Whether an alleged partner who is a donee of a capital interest in a partnership is the real owner of such capital interest, and whether the donee has dominion and control over such interest, must be ascertained from all the facts and circumstances of the particular case. Isolated facts are not determinative; the reality of the donee's ownership is to be determined in the light of the transaction as a whole. The execution of legally sufficient and irrevocable deeds or other instruments of gift under State law is a factor to be taken into account but is not determinative of ownership by the donee for the purposes of section 704(e). The reality of the transfer and of the donee's ownership of the property attributed to him are to be ascertained from the conduct of the parties with respect to the alleged gift and not by any mechanical or formal test. Some of the more important factors to be considered in determining whether the donee has acquired ownership of the capital interest in a partnership are indicated in subdivisions (ii) to (x), inclusive, of this subparagraph.

(ii) Retained controls. The donor may have retained such controls of the interest which he has purported to transfer to the donee that the donor should be treated as remaining the substantial owner of the interest. Controls of particular significance include, for example, the following:

(a) Retention of control of the distribution of amounts of income or restrictions on the distributions of amounts of income (other than amounts retained in the partnership annually with the consent of the partners, including the donee partner, for the reasonable needs of the business). If there is a partnership agreement providing for a managing partner or partners, then amounts of income may be retained in the partnership without the acquiescence of all the partners if such amounts are retained for the reasonable needs of the business.

(b) Limitation of the right of the donee to liquidate or sell his interest in the partnership at his discretion without financial detriment.

(c) Retention of control of assets essential to the business (for example, through retention of assets leased to the alleged partnership).

(d) Retention of management powers inconsistent with normal relationships among partners. Retention by the donor of control of business management or of voting control, such as is common in ordinary business relationships, is not by itself to be considered as inconsistent with normal relationships among partners, provided the donee is free to liquidate his interest at his discretion without financial detriment. The donee shall not be considered free to liquidate his interest unless, considering all the facts, it is evident that the donee is independent of the donor and has such maturity and understanding of his rights as to be capable of deciding to exercise, and capable of exercising, his right to withdraw his capital interest from the partnership.

The existence of some of the indicated controls, though amounting to less than substantial ownership retained by the donor, may be considered along with other facts and circumstances as tending to show the lack of reality of the partnership interest of the donee.

(iii) Indirect controls. Controls inconsistent with ownership by the donee may be exercised indirectly as well as directly, for example, through a separate business organization, estate, trust, individual, or other partnership. Where such indirect controls exist, the reality of the donee's interest will be determined as if such controls were exercisable directly.

(iv) Participation in management. Substantial participation by the donee in the control and management of the business (including participation in the major policy decisions affecting the business) is strong evidence of a donee partner's exercise of dominion and control over his interest. Such participation presupposes sufficient maturity and experience on the part of the donee to deal with the business problems of the partnership.

(v) Income distributions. The actual distribution to a donee partner of the entire amount or a major portion of his distributive share of the business income for the sole benefit and use of the donee is substantial evidence of the reality of the donee's interest, provided the donor has not retained controls inconsistent with real ownership by the donee. Amounts distributed are not considered to be used for the donee's sole benefit if, for example, they are deposited, loaned, or invested in such manner that the donor controls or can control the use or enjoyment of such funds.

(vi) Conduct of partnership business. In determining the reality of the donee's ownership of a capital interest in a partnership, consideration shall be given to whether the donee is actually treated as a partner in the operation of the business. Whether or not the donee has been held out publicly as a partner in the conduct of the business, in relations with customers, or with creditors or other sources of financing, is of primary significance. Other factors of significance in this connection include:

(a) Compliance with local partnership, fictitious names, and business registration statutes.

(b) Control of business bank accounts.

(c) Recognition of the donee's rights in distributions of partnership property and profits.

(d) Recognition of the donee's interest in insurance policies, leases, and other business contracts and in litigation affecting business.

(e) The existence of written agreements, records, or memoranda, contemporaneous with the taxable year or years concerned, establishing the nature of the partnership agreement and the rights and liabilities of the respective partners.

(f) Filing of partnership tax returns as required by law.

However, despite formal compliance with the above factors, other circumstances may indicate that the donor has retained substantial ownership of the interest purportedly transferred to the donee.

(vii) Trustees as partners. A trustee may be recognized as a partner for income tax purposes under the principles relating to family partnerships generally as applied to the particular facts of the trust-partnership arrangement. A trustee who is unrelated to and independent of the grantor, and who participates as a partner and receives distribution of the income distributable to the trust, will ordinarily be recognized as the legal owner of the partnership interest which he holds in trust unless the grantor has retained controls inconsistent with such ownership. However, if the grantor is the trustee, or if the trustee is amenable to the will of the grantor, the provisions of the trust instrument (particularly as to whether the trustee is subject to the responsibilities of a fiduciary), the provisions of the partnership agreement, and the conduct of the parties must all be taken into account in determining whether the trustee in a fiduciary capacity has become the real owner of the partnership interest. Where the grantor (or person amenable to his will) is the trustee, the trust may be recognized as a partner only if the grantor (or such other person) in his participation in the affairs of the partnership actively represents and protects the interests of the beneficiaries in accordance with the obligations of a fiduciary and does not subordinate such interests to the interests of the grantor. Furthermore, if the grantor (or person amenable to his will) is the trustee, the following factors will be given particular consideration:

(a) Whether the trust is recognized as a partner in business dealings with customers and creditors, and

(b) Whether, if any amount of the partnership income is not properly retained for the reasonable needs of the business, the trust's share of such amount is distributed to the trust annually and paid to the beneficiaries or reinvested with regard solely to the interests of the beneficiaries.

(viii) Interests (not held in trust) of minor children. Except where a minor child is shown to be competent to manage his own property and participate in the partnership activities in accordance with his interest in the property, a minor child generally will not be recognized as a member of a partnership unless control of the property is exercised by another person as fiduciary for the sole benefit of the child, and unless there is such judicial supervision of the conduct of the fiduciary as is required by law. The use of the child's property or income for support for which a parent is legally responsible will be considered a use for the parent's benefit. "Judicial supervision of the conduct of the fiduciary" includes filing of such accountings and reports as are required by law of the fiduciary who participates in the affairs of the partnership on behalf of the minor. A minor child will be considered as competent to manage his own property if he actually has sufficient maturity and experience to be treated by disinterested persons as competent to enter business dealings and otherwise to conduct his affairs on a basis of equality with adult persons, notwithstanding legal disabilities of the minor under State law.

(ix) Donees as limited partners. The recognition of a donee's interest in a limited partnership will depend, as in the case of other donated interests, on whether the transfer of property is real and on whether the donee has acquired dominion and control over the interest purportedly transferred to him. To be recognized for Federal income tax purposes, a limited partnership must be organized and conducted in accordance with the requirements of the applicable State limited-partnership law. The absence of services and participation in management by a donee in a limited partnership is immaterial if the limited partnership meets all the other requirements prescribed in this paragraph. If the limited partner's right to transfer or liquidate his interest is subject to substantial restrictions (for example, where the interest of the limited partner is not assignable in a real sense or where such interest may be required to be left in the business for a long term of years), or if the general partner retains any other control which substantially limits any of the rights which would ordinarily be exercisable by unrelated limited partners in normal business relationships, such restrictions on the right to transfer or liquidate, or retention of other control, will be considered strong evidence as to the lack of reality of ownership by the donee.

(x) Motive. If the reality of the transfer of interest is satisfactorily established, the motives for the transaction are generally immaterial. However, the presence or absence of a tax-avoidance motive is one of many factors to be considered in determining the reality of the ownership of a capital interest acquired by gift.

(3) Allocation of family partnership income—(i) In general. (a) Where a capital interest in a partnership in which capital is a material income-producing factor is created by gift, the donee's distributive share shall be includible in his gross income, except to the extent that such share is determined without allowance of reasonable compensation for services rendered to the partnership by the donor, and except to the extent that the portion of such distributive share attributable to donated capital is proportionately greater than the distributive share attributable to the donor's capital. For the purpose of section 704, a capital interest in a partnership purchased by one member of a family from another shall be considered to be created by gift from the seller, and the fair market value of the purchased interest shall be considered to be donated capital. The "family" of any individual, for the purpose of the preceding sentence, shall include only his spouse, ancestors, and lineal descendants, and any trust for the primary benefit of such persons.

(b) To the extent that the partnership agreement does not allocate the partnership income in accordance with (a) of this subdivision, the distributive shares of the partnership income of the donor and donee shall be reallocated by making a reasonable allowance for the services of the donor and by attributing the balance of such income (other than a reasonable allowance for the services, if any, rendered by the donee) to the partnership capital of the donor and donee. The portion of income, if any, thus attributable to partnership capital for the taxable year shall be allocated between the donor and donee in accordance with their respective interests in partnership capital.

(c) In determining a reasonable allowance for services rendered by the partners, consideration shall be given to all the facts and circumstances of the business, including the fact that some of the partners may have greater managerial responsibility than others. There shall also be considered the amount that would ordinarily be paid in order to obtain comparable services from a person not having an interest in the partnership.

(d) The distributive share of partnership income, as determined under (b) of this subdivision, of a partner who rendered services to the partnership before entering the Armed Forces of the United States shall not be diminished because of absence due to military service. Such distributive share shall be adjusted to reflect increases or decreases in the capital interest of the absent partner. However, the partners may by agreement allocate a smaller share to the absent partner due to his absence.

(ii) Special rules. (a) The provisions of subdivision (i) of this subparagraph, relating to allocation of family partnership income, are applicable where the interest in the partnership is created by gift, indirectly or directly. Where the partnership interest is created indirectly, the term "donor" may include persons other than the nominal transferor. This rule may be illustrated by the following examples:

Example (1). A father gives property to his son who shortly thereafter conveys the property to a partnership consisting of the father and the son. The partnership interest of the son may be considered created by gift and the father may be considered the donor of the son's partnership interest.

Example (2). A father, the owner of a business conducted as a sole proprietorship, transfers the business to a partnership consisting of his wife and himself. The wife subsequently conveys her interest to their son. In such case, the father, as well as the mother, may be considered the donor of the son's partnership interest.

Example (3). A father makes a gift to his son of stock in the family corporation. The corporation is subsequently liquidated. The son later contributes the property received in the liquidation of the corporation to a partnership consisting of his father and himself. In such case, for purposes of section 704, the son's partnership interest may be considered created by gift and the father may be considered the donor of his son's partnership interest.

(b) The allocation rules set forth in section 704(e) and subdivision (i) of this subparagraph apply in any case in which the transfer or creation of the partnership interest has any of the substantial characteristics of a gift. Thus, allocation may be required where transfer of a partnership interest is made between members of a family (including collaterals) under a purported purchase agreement, if the characteristics of a gift are ascertained from the terms of the purchase agreement, the terms of any loan or credit arrangements made to finance the purchase, or from other relevant data.

(c) In the case of a limited partnership, for the purpose of the allocation provisions of subdivision (i) of this subparagraph, consideration shall be given to the fact that a general partner, unlike a limited partner, risks his credit in the partnership business.

(4) Purchased interest—(i) In general. If a purported purchase of a capital interest in a partnership does not meet the requirements of subdivision (ii) of this subparagraph, the ownership by the transferee of such capital interest will be recognized only if it qualifies under the requirements applicable to a transfer of a partnership interest by gifts. In a case not qualifying under subdivision (ii) of this subparagraph, if payment of any part of the purchase price is made out of partnership earnings, the transaction may be regarded in the same light as a purported gift subject to deferred enjoyment of income. Such a transaction may be lacking in reality either as a gift or as a *bona fide* purchase.

(ii) Tests as to reality of purchased interests. A purchase of a capital interest in a partnership, either directly or by means of a loan or credit extended by a member of the family, will be recognized as *bona fide* if:

(a) It can be shown that the purchase has the usual characteristics of an arm's-length transaction, considering all relevant factors, including the terms of the purchase agreement (as to price, due date of payment, rate of interest, and security, if any) and the terms of any loan or credit arrangement collateral to the purchase agreement; the credit standing of the purchaser (apart from relationship to the seller) and the capacity of the purchaser to incur a legally binding obligation; or

(b) It can be shown, in the absence of characteristics of an arm's-length transaction, that the purchase was genuinely intended to promote the success of the business by securing participation of the purchaser in the business or by adding his credit to that of the other participants.

However, if the alleged purchase price or loan has not been paid or the obligation otherwise discharged, the factors indicated in (a) and (b) of this subdivision shall be taken into account only as an aid in determining whether a *bona fide* purchase or loan obligation existed.

[T.D. 6500, 25 FR 11814, Nov. 26, 1960, as amended by T.D. 6771, 29 FR 15571, Nov. 20, 1964; T.D. 8365, 50 FR 53423, Dec. 31, 1985; T.D. 8065, 51 FR 10826, March 31, 1986; T.D. 8099, 51 FR 32062, Sept. 9, 1986, corrected 52 FR 10223, March 31, 1987; amended T.D. 8237, 53 FR 53173, Dec. 30, 1988; T.D. 8385, 56 FR 66983, Dec. 27, 1991; T.D. 8500, 58 FR 67676, Dec. 22, 1993; T.D. 8717, 62 FR 25498, May 9, 1997; T.D. 9121, 69 FR 21405, April 20, 2004; T.D. 9126, 69 FR 25315, May 6, 2004; T.D. 9207, 70 FR 30334, May 23, 2005; T.D. 9292, 71 FR 61648, Oct. 19, 2006; T.D. 9398, 73 FR 28699, May 19, 2008; 73 FR 33301, June 12, 2008; T.D. 9577, 77 FR 8134, Feb. 14, 2012; T.D. 9607, 77 FR 76382, Dec. 28, 2012; T.D. 9612, 78 FR 7997, Feb. 5, 2013]

§ 1.704–2 Allocations attributable to nonrecourse liabilities.

* * *

(b) General principles and definitions—(1) Definition of and allocations of nonrecourse

deductions. Allocations of losses, deductions, or section 705(a)(2)(B) expenditures attributable to partnership nonrecourse liabilities ("nonrecourse deductions") cannot have economic effect because the creditor alone bears any economic burden that corresponds to those allocations. Thus, nonrecourse deductions must be allocated in accordance with the partners' interests in the partnership. Paragraph (e) of this section provides a test that deems allocations of nonrecourse deductions to be in accordance with the partners' interests in the partnership. If that test is not satisfied, the partners' distributive shares of nonrecourse deductions are determined under § 1.704–1(b)(3), according to the partners' overall economic interests in the partnership. See also paragraph (i) of this section for special rules regarding the allocation of deductions attributable to nonrecourse liabilities for which a partner bears the economic risk of loss (as described in paragraph (b)(4) of this section).

(2) Definition of and allocations pursuant to a minimum gain chargeback. To the extent a nonrecourse liability exceeds the adjusted tax basis of the partnership property it encumbers, a disposition of that property will generate gain that at least equals that excess ("partnership minimum gain"). An increase in partnership minimum gain is created by a decrease in the adjusted tax basis of property encumbered by a nonrecourse liability below the amount of that liability and by a partnership nonrecourse borrowing that exceeds the adjusted tax basis of the property encumbered by the borrowing. Partnership minimum gain decreases as reductions occur in the amount by which the nonrecourse liability exceeds the adjusted tax basis of the property encumbered by the liability. Allocations of gain attributable to a decrease in partnership minimum gain (a "minimum gain chargeback," as required under paragraph (f) of this section) cannot have economic effect because the gain merely offsets nonrecourse deductions previously claimed by the partnership. Thus, to avoid impairing the economic effect of other allocations, allocations pursuant to a minimum gain chargeback must be made to the partners that either were allocated nonrecourse deductions or received distributions of proceeds attributable to a nonrecourse borrowing. Paragraph (e) of this section provides a test that, if met, deems allocations of partnership income pursuant to a minimum gain chargeback to be in accordance with the partners' interests in the partnership. If property encumbered by a nonrecourse liability is reflected on the partnership's books at a value that differs from its adjusted tax basis, paragraph (d)(3) of this section provides that minimum gain is determined with reference to the property's book basis. See also paragraph (i)(4) of this section for special rules regarding the minimum gain chargeback requirement for partner nonrecourse debt.

(3) Definition of nonrecourse liability. "Nonrecourse liability" means a nonrecourse liability as defined in § 1.752–1(a)(2) or a § 1.752–7 liability (as defined in § 1.752–7(b)(3)(i)) assumed by the partnership from a partner on or after June 24, 2003.

(4) Definition of partner nonrecourse debt. "Partner nonrecourse debt" or "partner nonrecourse liability" means any partnership liability to the extent the liability is nonrecourse for purposes of § 1.1001–2, and a partner or related person (within the meaning of § 1.752–4(b)) bears the economic risk of loss under § 1.752–2 because, for example, the partner or related person is the creditor or a guarantor.

(c) Amount of nonrecourse deductions. The amount of nonrecourse deductions for a partnership taxable year equals the net increase in partnership minimum gain during the year (determined under paragraph (d) of this section), reduced (but not below zero) by the aggregate distributions made during the year of proceeds of a nonrecourse liability that are allocable to an increase in partnership minimum gain (determined under paragraph (h) of this section). See paragraph (m), Examples (1)(i) and (vi), (2), and (3) of this section. However, increases in partnership minimum gain resulting from conversions, refinancings, or other changes to a debt instrument (as described in paragraph (g)(3)) do not generate nonrecourse deductions. Generally, nonrecourse deductions consist first of certain depreciation or cost recovery deductions and then, if necessary, a pro rata portion of other partnership losses, deductions, and section 705(a)(2)(B) expenditures for that year; excess nonrecourse deductions are carried over. See paragraphs (j)(1)(ii) and (iii) of this section for more specific ordering rules. See also paragraph (m), Example (1)(iv) of this section.

(d) Partnership minimum gain—(1) Amount of partnership minimum gain. The amount of partnership minimum gain is determined by first computing for each partnership nonrecourse liability any gain the partnership would realize if it disposed of the property subject to that liability for no consideration other than full satisfaction of the liability, and then aggregating the separately computed gains. The amount of partnership minimum gain includes minimum gain arising from a conversion, refinancing, or other change to a debt instrument, as described in paragraph (g)(3) of this section, only to the extent a partner is allocated a share of that minimum gain. For any partnership taxable year, the net increase or decrease in partnership minimum gain is determined by comparing the partnership minimum gain on the last day of the immediately preceding taxable year with the partnership minimum gain on the last day of the current taxable year. See paragraph (m), Examples (1)(i) and (iv), (2), and (3) of this section.

(2) Property subject to more than one liability. (i) In general. If property is subject to more than one liability, only the portion of the property's adjusted tax basis that is allocated to a nonrecourse liability under paragraph (d)(2)(ii) of this section is used to compute minimum gain with respect to that liability.

(ii) Allocating liabilities. If property is subject to two or more liabilities of equal priority, the property's adjusted tax basis is allocated among the liabilities in proportion to their outstanding balances. If property is subject to two or more liabilities of unequal priority, the adjusted tax basis is allocated first to the liability of the highest priority to the extent of its outstanding balance and then to each liability in descending order of priority to the extent of its outstanding balance, until fully allocated. See paragraph (m), Example (1)(v) and (vii) of this section.

(3) Partnership minimum gain if there is a book/tax disparity. If partnership property subject to one or more nonrecourse liabilities is, under § 1.704–1(b)(2)(iv)(d), (f), or (r), reflected on the partnership's books at a value that differs from its adjusted tax basis, the determinations under this section are made with reference to the property's book value. See section 704(c) and § 1.704–1(b)(4)(i) for principles that govern the treatment of a partner's share of minimum gain that is eliminated by the revaluation. See also paragraph (m), Example (3) of this section.

(4) Special rule for year of revaluation. If the partners' capital accounts are increased pursuant to § 1.704–1(b)(2)(iv)(d), (f), or (r) to reflect a revaluation of partnership property subject to a nonrecourse liability, the net increase or decrease in partnership minimum gain for the partnership taxable year of the revaluation is determined by:

(i) First calculating the net decrease or increase in partnership minimum gain using the current year's book values and the prior year's partnership minimum gain amount; and

(ii) Then adding back any decrease in minimum gain arising solely from the revaluation. See paragraph (m), Example (3)(iii) of this section. If the partners' capital accounts are decreased to reflect a revaluation, the net increases or decreases in partnership minimum gain are determined in the same manner as in the year before the revaluation, but by using book values rather than adjusted tax bases. See section 7701(g) and § 1.704–1(b)(2)(iv)(f)(1) (property being revalued cannot be booked down below the amount of any nonrecourse liability to which the property is subject).

(e) Requirements to be satisfied. Allocations of nonrecourse deductions are deemed to be in accordance with the partners' interests in the partnership only if—

(1) Throughout the full term of the partnership requirements (1) and (2) of § 1.704–1(b)(2)(ii)(b) are satisfied (i.e., capital accounts are maintained in accordance with § 1.704–1(b)(2)(iv) and liquidating distributions are required to be made in accordance with positive capital account balances), and requirement (3) of either § 1.704–1(b)(2)(ii)(b) or § 1.704–1(b)(2)(ii)(d) is satisfied (i.e., partners with deficit capital accounts have an unconditional deficit restoration obligation or agree to a qualified income offset);

(2) Beginning in the first taxable year of the partnership in which there are nonrecourse deductions and thereafter throughout the full term of the partnership, the partnership agreement provides for allocations of nonrecourse deductions in a manner that is reasonably consistent with allocations that have substantial economic effect of some other significant partnership item attributable to the property securing the nonrecourse liabilities;

(3) Beginning in the first taxable year of the partnership that it has nonrecourse deductions or makes a distribution of proceeds of a nonrecourse liability that are allocable to an increase in partnership minimum gain, and thereafter throughout the full term of the partnership, the partnership agreement contains a provision that complies with the minimum gain chargeback requirement of paragraph (f) of this section; and

(4) All other material allocations and capital account adjustments under the partnership agreement are recognized under § 1.704–1(b) (without regard to whether allocations of adjusted tax basis and amount realized under section 613A(c)(7)(D) are recognized under § 1.704–1(b)(4)(v)).

(f) Minimum gain chargeback requirement—(1) In general. If there is a net decrease in partnership minimum gain for a partnership taxable year, the minimum gain chargeback requirement applies and each partner must be allocated items of partnership income and gain for that year equal to that partner's share of the net decrease in partnership minimum gain (within the meaning of paragraph (g)(2)).

(2) Exception for certain conversions and refinancings. A partner is not subject to the minimum gain chargeback requirement to the extent the partner's share of the net decrease in partnership minimum gain is caused by a recharacterization if nonrecourse partnership debt as partially or wholly recourse debt or partner nonrecourse debt, and the partner bears the economic risk of loss (within the meaning of § 1.752–2) for the liability.

(3) Exception for certain capital contributions. A partner is not subject to the minimum gain chargeback requirement to the extent the partner contributes capital to the partnership that is used to repay the nonrecourse liability or is used to increase the basis of the property subject to the nonrecourse liability, and the partner's share of the net decrease in partnership minimum gain results from the repayment or the increase to the property's basis. See paragraph (m), Example (1)(iv) of this section.

(4) Waiver for certain income allocations that fail to meet minimum gain chargeback requirement if minimum gain chargeback distorts economic arrangement. In any taxable year that a partnership has a net decrease in partnership minimum gain, if the minimum gain chargeback requirement would cause a distortion in the economic arrangement among the partners and it is not expected that the partnership will have sufficient other income to correct that distortion, the Commissioner has the discretion, if requested by the partnership, to waive the minimum gain chargeback requirement. The following facts must be demonstrated in order for a request for a waiver to be considered:

(i) The partners have made capital contributions or received net income allocations that have restored the previous nonrecourse deductions and the distributions attributable to proceeds of a nonrecourse liability; and

(ii) The minimum gain chargeback requirement would distort the partners' economic arrangement as reflected in the partnership agreement and as evidenced over the term of the partnership by the partnership's allocations and distributions and the partners' contributions.

(5) Additional exceptions. The Commissioner may, by revenue ruling, provide additional exceptions to the minimum gain chargeback requirement.

(6) Partnership items subject to the minimum gain chargeback requirement. Any minimum gain chargeback required for a partnership taxable year consists first of a pro rata portion of certain gains recognized from the disposition of partnership property subject to one or more partnership nonrecourse liabilities and income from the discharge of indebtedness relating to one or more partnership nonrecourse liabilities to which partnership property is subject, and then, if necessary, consists of a pro rata portion of the partnership's other items of income and gain for that year. If the amount of the minimum gain chargeback requirement exceeds the partnership's income and gains for the taxable year, the excess carries over. See paragraphs (j)(2)(i) and (j)(2)(iii) of this section for more specific ordering rules.

(7) Examples. The following examples illustrate the provisions in § 1.704–2(f).

Example 1. Partnership AB consists of two partners, limited partner A and general partner B. Partner A contributes $90 and Partner B contributes $10 to the partnership. The partnership agreement has a minimum gain chargeback provision and provides that, except as otherwise required by section 704(c), all losses will be allocated 90 percent to A and 10 percent to B; and that all income will be allocated first to restore previous losses and thereafter 50 percent to A and 50 percent to B. Distributions are made first to return initial capital to the partners and then 50 percent to A and 50 percent to B. Final distributions are made in accordance with capital account balances. The partnership borrows $200 on a nonrecourse basis from an unrelated third party and purchases an asset for $300. The partnership's only tax item for each of the first three years is $100 of depreciation on the asset. A's and B's shares of minimum gain (under paragraph (g) of this section) and deficit capital account balances are $180 and $20 respectively at the end of the third year. In the fourth year, the partnership earns $400 of net operating income and allocates the first $300 to restore the previous losses (i.e., $270 to A and $30 to B); the last $100 is allocated $50 each. The partnership distributes $200 of the available cash that same year; the first $100 is distributed $90 to A and $10 to B to return their capital contributions; the last $100 is distributed $50 each to reflect their ratio for sharing profits.

	A	B
Capital account on formation	$90	$10
Less: net loss in years 1–3	($270)	($30)
Capital account at end of year 3	($180)	($20)
Allocation of operating income to restore nonrecourse deductions	$180	$20
Allocation of operating income to restore capital contributions	$90	$10

	A	B
Allocation of operating income to reflect profits	$50	$50
Capital accounts after allocation of operating income	$140	$60
Distribution reflecting capital contribution	($90)	($10)
Distribution in profit-sharing ratio	($50)	($50)
Capital accounts following distribution	($0)	($0)

In the fifth year, the partnership sells the property for $300 and realizes $300 of gain. $200 of the proceeds are used to pay the nonrecourse lender. The partnership has $300 to distribute, and the partners expect to share that equally. Absent a waiver under paragraph (f)(4) of this section, the minimum gain chargeback would require the partnership to allocate the first $200 of the gain $180 to A and $20 to B, which would distort their economic arrangement. This allocation, together with the allocation of the $100 profit $50 to each partner, would result in A having a positive capital account balance of $230 and B having a positive capital account balance of $70. The allocation of income in year 4 in effect anticipated the minimum gain chargeback that did not occur until year 5. Assuming the partnership would not have sufficient other income to correct the distortion that would otherwise result, the partnership may request that the Commissioner exercise his or her discretion to waive the minimum gain chargeback requirement and recognize allocations that would allow A and B to share equally the gain on the sale of the property. These allocations would bring the partners' capital accounts to $150 each, allowing them to share the last $300 equally. The Commissioner may, in his or her discretion, permit this allocation pursuant to paragraph (f)(4) of this section because the minimum gain chargeback would distort the partners' economic arrangement over the term of the partnership as reflected in the partnership agreement and as evidenced by the partners' contributions and the partnership's allocations and distributions.

Example 2. A and B form a partnership, contribute $25 each to the partnership's capital, and agree to share all losses and profits 50 percent each. Neither partner has an unconditional deficit restoration obligation and all the requirements in paragraph (e) of this section are met. The partnership obtains a nonrecourse loan from an unrelated third party of $100 and purchases two assets, stock for $50 and depreciable property for $100. The nonrecourse loan is secured by the partnership's depreciable property. The partnership generates $20 of depreciation in each of the first five years as its only tax item. These deductions are properly treated as nonrecourse deductions and the allocation of these deductions 50 percent to A and 50 percent to B is deemed to be in accordance with the partners' interests in the partnership. At the end of year five, A and B each have a $25 deficit capital account and a $50 share of partnership minimum gain. In the beginning of year six, (at the lender's request), A guarantees the entire nonrecourse liability. Pursuant to paragraph (d)(1) of this section, the partnership has a net decrease in minimum gain of $100 and under paragraph (g)(2) of this section, A's and B's shares of that net decrease are $50 each. Under paragraph (f)(1) of this section (the minimum gain chargeback requirement), B is subject to a $50 minimum gain chargeback. Because the partnership has no gross income in year six, the entire $50 carries over as a minimum gain chargeback requirement to succeeding taxable years until their is enough income to cover the minimum gain chargeback requirement. Under the exception to the minimum gain chargeback in paragraph (f)(2) of this section, A is not subject to a minimum gain chargeback for A's $50 share of the net decrease because A bears the economic risk of loss for the liability. Instead, A's share of partner nonrecourse debt minimum gain is $50 pursuant to paragraph (i)(3) of this section. In year seven, the partnership earns $100 of net operating income and uses the money to repay the entire $100 nonrecourse debt (that A has guaranteed). Under paragraph (i)(3) of this section, the partnership has a net decrease in partner nonrecourse debt minimum gain of $50. B must be allocated $50 of the operating income pursuant to the carried over minimum gain chargeback requirement; pursuant to paragraph (i)(4) of this section, the other $50 of operating income must be allocated to A as a partner nonrecourse debt minimum gain chargeback.

(g) Shares of partnership minimum gain—(1) Partner's share of partnership minimum gain. Except as increased in paragraph (g)(3) of this section, a partner's share of partnership minimum gain at the end of any partnership taxable year equals:

(i) The sum of nonrecourse deductions allocated to that partner (and to that partner's predecessors in interest) up to that time and the distributions made to that partner (and to that partner's predecessors in interest) up to that time of proceeds of a nonrecourse liability allocable to an increase in partnership minimum gain (see paragraph (h)(1) of this section); minus

(ii) The sum of that partner's (and that partner's predecessors' in interest) aggregate share of the net decreases in partnership minimum gain plus their aggregate share of decreases resulting from revaluations of partnership property subject to one or more partnership nonrecourse liabilities.

For purposes of § 1.704–1(b)(2)(ii)(d), a partner's share of partnership minimum gain is added to the limited dollar amount, if any, of the deficit balance in the partner's capital account that the partner is obligated to restore. See paragraph (m), Examples (1)(i) and (3)(i) of this section.

(2) Partner's share of the net decrease in partnership minimum gain. A partner's share of the net decrease in partnership minimum gain is the amount of the total net decrease multiplied by the partner's percentage share of the partnership's minimum gain at the end of the immediately preceding taxable year. A partner's share of any decrease in partnership minimum gain resulting from a revaluation of partnership property equals the increase in the partner's capital account attributable to the revaluation to the extent the reduction in minimum gain is caused by the revaluation. See paragraph (m), Example (3)(ii) of this section.

(3) Conversions of recourse or partner nonrecourse debt into nonrecourse debt. A partner's share of partnership minimum gain is increased to the extent provided in this paragraph (g)(3) if a recourse or partner nonrecourse liability becomes partially or wholly nonrecourse. If a recourse liability becomes a nonrecourse liability, a partner has a share of the partnership's minimum gain that results from the conversion equal to the partner's deficit capital account (determined under § 1.704–1(b)(2)(iv)) to the extent the partner no longer bears the economic burden for the entire deficit capital account as a result of the conversion. For purposes of the preceding sentence, the determination of the extent to which a partner bears the economic burden for a deficit capital account is made by determining the consequences to the partner in the case of a complete liquidation of the partnership immediately after the conversion applying the rules described in § 1.704–1(b)(2)(iii)(c) that deem the value of partnership property to equal its basis, taking into account section 7701(g) in the case of property that secures nonrecourse indebtedness. If a partner nonrecourse debt becomes a nonrecourse liability, the partner's share of partnership minimum gain is increased to the extent the partner is not subject to the minimum gain chargeback requirement under paragraph (i)(4) of this section.

(h) Distribution of nonrecourse liability proceeds allocable to an increase in partnership minimum gain—(1) In general. If during its taxable year a partnership makes a distribution to the partners allocable to the proceeds of a nonrecourse liability, the distribution is allocable to an increase in partnership minimum gain to the extent the increase results from encumbering partnership property with aggregate nonrecourse liabilities that exceed the property's adjusted tax basis. See paragraph (m), Example (1)(vi) of this section. If the net increase in partnership minimum gain for a partnership taxable year is allocable to more than one nonrecourse liability, the net increase is allocated among the liabilities in proportion to the amount each liability contributed to the increase in minimum gain.

(2) Distribution allocable to nonrecourse liability proceeds. A partnership may use any reasonable method to determine whether a distribution by the partnership to one or more partners is allocable to proceeds of a nonrecourse liability. The rules prescribed under § 1.163–8T for allocating debt proceeds among expenditures (applying those rules to the partnership as if it were an individual) constitute a reasonable method for determining whether the nonrecourse liability proceeds are distributed to the partners and the partners to whom the proceeds are distributed.

(3) Option when there is an obligation to restore. A partnership may treat any distribution to a partner of the proceeds of a nonrecourse liability (that would otherwise be allocable to an increase in partnership minimum gain) as a distribution that is not allocable to an increase in partnership minimum gain to the extent the distribution does not cause or increase a deficit balance in the partner's capital account that exceeds the amount the partner is otherwise obligated to restore (within the meaning of § 1.704–1(b)(2)(ii)(c)) as of the end of the partnership taxable year in which the distribution occurs.

(4) Carryover to immediately succeeding taxable year. The carryover rule of this paragraph applies if the net increase in partnership minimum gain for a partnership taxable year that is allocable to a nonrecourse liability under paragraph (h)(2) of this section exceeds the distributions allocable to the proceeds of the liability ("excess allocable amount"), and all or part of the net increase in partnership minimum gain for the year is carried over as an increase in partnership minimum gain for the immediately succeeding taxable year (pursuant to paragraph (j)(1)(iii) of this section). If the carryover rule of this paragraph applies, the excess allocable amount (or the amount carried over under paragraph (j)(1)(iii) of this section, if less) is treated in the succeeding taxable year as an increase in partnership minimum gain that arose in that year as a result of incurring the nonrecourse liability to which the excess allocable amount is attributable. See paragraph (m), Example (1)(vi) of this section. If for a partnership taxable year there is an excess allocable amount with respect to more than one partnership nonrecourse liability, the excess allocable amount is allocated to each liability in proportion to the amount each liability contributed to the increase in minimum gain.

(i) Partnership nonrecourse liabilities where a partner bears the economic risk of loss—(1) In general. Partnership losses, deductions, or section 705(a)(2)(B) expenditures that are attributable to a particular partner nonrecourse liability ("partner nonrecourse deductions," as defined in paragraph (i)(2) of this section) must be allocated to the partner that bears the economic risk of loss for the liability. If more than one partner bears the economic risk of loss for a partner nonrecourse liability, any partner nonrecourse deductions attributable to that liability must be allocated among the partners according to the ratio in which they bear the economic risk of loss. If partners bear the economic risk of loss for different portions of a liability, each portion is treated as a separate partner nonrecourse liability.

(2) Definition of and determination of partner nonrecourse deductions. For any partnership taxable year, the amount of partner nonrecourse deductions with respect to a partner nonrecourse debt equals the net increase during the year in minimum gain attributable to the partner nonrecourse debt ("partner nonrecourse debt minimum gain"), reduced (but not below zero) by proceeds of the liability distributed during the year to the partner bearing the economic risk of loss for the liability that are both attributable to the liability and allocable to an increase in the partner nonrecourse debt minimum gain. See paragraph (m), Example (1)(viii) and (ix) of this section. The determination of which partnership items constitute the partner nonrecourse deductions with respect to a partner nonrecourse debt must be made in a manner consistent with the provisions of paragraphs (c) and (j)(1)(i) and (iii) of this section.

(3) Determination of partner nonrecourse debt minimum gain. For any partnership taxable year, the determination of partner nonrecourse debt minimum gain and the net increase or decrease in partner nonrecourse debt minimum gain must be made in a manner consistent with the provisions of paragraphs (d) and (g)(3) of this section.

(4) Chargeback of partner nonrecourse debt minimum gain. If during a partnership taxable year there is a net decrease in partner nonrecourse debt minimum gain, any partner with a share of that partner nonrecourse debt minimum gain (determined under paragraph (i)(5) of this section) as of the beginning of the year must be allocated items of income and gain for the year (and, if necessary, for succeeding years) equal to that partner's share of the net decrease in the partner nonrecourse debt minimum gain. A partner's share of the net decrease in partner nonrecourse debt minimum gain is determined in a manner consistent with the provisions of paragraph (g)(2) of this section. A partner is not subject to this minimum gain chargeback, however, to the extent the net decrease in partner nonrecourse debt minimum gain arises because a partner nonrecourse liability becomes partially or wholly a nonrecourse liability. The amount that would otherwise be subject to the partner nonrecourse debt minimum gain chargeback is added to the partner's share of partnership minimum gain under paragraph (g)(3) of this section. In addition, rules consistent with the provisions of paragraphs (f)(2), (3), (4), and (5) of this section apply with respect to partner nonrecourse debt in appropriate circumstances. The determination of which items of partnership income and gain must be allocated pursuant to this paragraph (i)(4) is made in a manner that is consistent with the provisions of paragraph (f)(6) of this section. See paragraph (j)(2)(ii) and (iii) of this section for more specific rules.

(5) Partner's share of partner nonrecourse debt minimum gain. A partner's share of partner nonrecourse debt minimum gain at the end of any partnership taxable year is determined in a manner consistent with the provisions of paragraphs (g)(1) and (g)(3) of this section with respect to each particular partner nonrecourse debt for which the partner bears the economic risk of loss. For purposes of § 1.704–1(b)(2)(ii)(d), a partner's share of partner nonrecourse debt minimum gain is added to the limited dollar amount, if any, of the deficit balance in the partner's capital account that the partner is obligated to restore, and the partner is not otherwise considered to have a deficit restoration obligation as a result of bearing the economic risk of loss for any partner nonrecourse debt. See paragraph (m), Example (1)(viii) of this section.

(6) Distribution of partner nonrecourse debt proceeds allocable to an increase in partner nonrecourse debt minimum gain. Rules consistent with the provisions of paragraph (h) of this section apply to distributions of the proceeds of partner nonrecourse debt.

(j) Ordering rules. For purposes of this section, the following ordering rules apply to partnership items. Notwithstanding any other provision in this section and § 1.704–1, allocations of partner nonrecourse deductions, nonrecourse deductions, and minimum gain chargebacks are made before any other allocations.

(1) Treatment of partnership losses and deductions. (i) Partner nonrecourse deductions. Partnership losses, deductions, and section 705(a)(2)(B) expenditures are treated as partner nonrecourse deductions in the amount determined under paragraph (i)(2) of this section (determining partner nonrecourse deductions) in the following order:

(A) First, depreciation or cost recovery deductions with respect to property that is subject to partner nonrecourse debt;

(B) Then, if necessary, a pro rata portion of the partnership's other deductions, losses, and section 705(a)(2)(B) items.

Depreciation or cost recovery deductions with respect to property that is subject to a partnership nonrecourse liability is first treated as a partnership nonrecourse deduction and any excess is treated as a partner nonrecourse deduction under this paragraph (j)(1)(i).

(ii) Partnership nonrecourse deductions. Partnership losses, deductions, and section 705(a)(2)(B) expenditures are treated as partnership nonrecourse deductions in the amount determined under paragraph (c) of this section (determining nonrecourse deductions) in the following order:

(A) First, depreciation or cost recovery deductions with respect to property that is subject to partnership nonrecourse liabilities;

(B) Then, if necessary, a pro rata portion of the partnership's other deductions, losses, and section 705(a)(2)(B) items.

Depreciation or cost recovery deductions with respect to property that is subject to partner nonrecourse debt is first treated as a partner nonrecourse deduction and any excess is treated as a partnership nonrecourse deduction under this paragraph (j)(1)(ii). Any other item that is treated as a partner nonrecourse deduction will in no event be treated as a partnership nonrecourse deduction.

(iii) Carryover to succeeding taxable year. If the amount of partner nonrecourse deductions or nonrecourse deductions exceeds the partnership's losses, deductions, and section 705(a)(2)(B) expenditures for the taxable year (determined under paragraphs (j)(1)(i) and (ii) of this section), the excess is treated as an increase in partner nonrecourse debt minimum gain or partnership minimum gain in the immediately succeeding partnership taxable year. See paragraph (m), Example (1)(vi) of this section.

(2) Treatment of partnership income and gains. (i) Minimum gain chargeback. Items of partnership income and gain equal to the minimum gain chargeback requirement (determined under paragraph (f) of this section) are allocated as a minimum gain chargeback in the following order:

(A) First, a pro rata portion of gain from the disposition of property subject to partnership nonrecourse liabilities and discharge of indebtedness income relating to partnership nonrecourse liabilities to which property is subject;

(B) Then, if necessary, a pro rata portion of the partnership's other items of income and gain for that year.

Gain from the disposition of property subject to partner nonrecourse debt is allocated to satisfy a minimum gain chargeback requirement for partnership nonrecourse debt only to the extent not allocated under paragraph (j)(2)(ii) of this section.

(ii) Chargeback attributable to decrease in partner nonrecourse debt minimum gain. Items of partnership income and gain equal to the partner nonrecourse debt minimum gain chargeback (determined under paragraph (i)(4) of this section) are allocated to satisfy a partner nonrecourse debt minimum gain chargeback in the following order:

(A) First, a pro rata portion of gain from the disposition of property subject to partner nonrecourse debt and discharge of indebtedness income relating to partner nonrecourse debt to which property is subject.

(B) Then, if necessary, a pro rata portion of the partnership's other items of income and gain for that year.

Gain from the disposition of property subject to a partnership nonrecourse liability is allocated to satisfy a partner nonrecourse debt minimum gain chargeback only to the extent not allocated under paragraph (j)(2)(i) of this section. An item of partnership income and gain that is allocated to satisfy a minimum gain chargeback under paragraph (f) of this section is not allocated to satisfy a minimum gain chargeback under paragraph (i)(4).

(iii) Carryover to succeeding taxable year. If a minimum gain chargeback requirement (determined under paragraphs (f) and (i)(4) of this section) exceeds the partnership's income and gains for the taxable year, the excess is treated as a minimum gain chargeback requirement in the immediately succeeding partnership taxable years until fully charged back.

(k) Tiered partnerships. For purposes of this section, the following rules determine the effect on partnership minimum gain when a partnership ("upper-tier partnership") is a partner in another partnership ("lower-tier partnership").

(1) Increase in upper-tier partnership's minimum gain. The sum of the nonrecourse deductions that the lower-tier partnership allocates to the upper-tier partnership for any taxable year of the upper-tier partnership, and the distributions made during that taxable year from the lower-tier partnership to the upper-tier partnership of proceeds of nonrecourse debt that are allocable to an increase in the lower-tier partnership's minimum gain, is treated as an increase in the upper-tier partnership's minimum gain.

(2) Decrease in upper-tier partnership's minimum gain. The upper-tier partnership's share for its taxable year of the lower-tier partnership's net decrease in its minimum gain is treated as a decrease in the upper-tier partnership's minimum gain for that taxable year.

(3) Nonrecourse debt proceeds distributed from the lower-tier partnership to the upper-tier partnership. All distributions from the lower-tier partnership to the upper-tier partnership during the upper-tier partnership's taxable year of proceeds of a nonrecourse liability allocable to an increase in the lower-tier partnership's minimum gain are treated as proceeds of a nonrecourse liability of the upper-tier partnership. The increase in the upper-tier partnership's minimum gain (under paragraph (k)(1) of this section) attributable to the receipt of those distributions is, for purposes of paragraph (h) of this section, treated as an increase in the upper-tier partnership's minimum gain arising from encumbering property of the upper-tier partnership with a nonrecourse liability of the upper-tier partnership.

(4) Nonrecourse deductions of lower-tier partnership treated as depreciation by upper-tier partnership. For purposes of paragraph (c) of this section, all nonrecourse deductions allocated by the lower-tier partnership to the upper-tier partnership for the upper-tier partnership's taxable year are treated as depreciation or cost recovery deductions with respect to property owned by the upper-tier partnership and subject to a nonrecourse liability of the upper-tier partnership with respect to which minimum gain increased during the year by the amount of the nonrecourse deductions.

(5) Coordination with partner nonrecourse debt rules. The lower-tier partnership's liabilities that are treated as the upper-tier partnership's liabilities under § 1.752–4(a) are treated as the upper-tier partnership's liabilities for purposes of applying paragraph (i) of this section. Rules consistent with the provisions of paragraphs (k)(1) through (k)(4) of this section apply to determine the allocations that the upper-tier partnership must make with respect to any liability that constitutes a nonrecourse debt for which one or more partners of the upper-tier partnership bear the economic risk of loss.

* * *

(m) Examples. The principles of this section are illustrated by the following examples:

Example 1. Nonrecourse deductions and partnership minimum gain. For Example 1, unless otherwise provided, the following facts are assumed. LP, the limited partner, and GP, the general partner, form a limited partnership to acquire and operate a commercial office building. LP contributes $180,000, and GP contributes $20,000. The partnership obtains an $800,000 nonrecourse loan and purchases the building (on leased land) for $1,000,000. The nonrecourse loan is secured only by the building, and no principal payments are due for 5 years. The partnership agreement provides that GP will be required to restore any deficit balance in GP's capital account following the liquidation of GP's interest (as set forth in § 1.704–1(b)(2)(ii)(b)(3)), and LP will not be required to restore any deficit balance in LP's capital account following the liquidation of LP's interest. The partnership agreement contains the following provisions required by paragraph (e) of this section; a qualified income offset (as defined in § 1.704–1(b)(2)(ii)(d)): a minimum gain chargeback (in accordance with paragraph (f) of this section); a provision that the partners' capital accounts will be determined and maintained in accordance with § 1.704–1(b)(2)(ii)(b)(1); and a provision that distributions will be made in accordance with partners' positive capital account balances (as set forth in § 1.704–1(b)(2)(ii)(b)(2)). In addition, as of the end of each partnership taxable year discussed herein, the items described in § 1.704–1(b)(2)(ii)(d)(4), (5), and (6) are not reasonably expected to cause or increase a deficit balance in LP's capital account. The partnership agreement provides that, except as otherwise required by its qualified income offset and minimum gain chargeback provisions, all partnership items will be allocated 90 percent to LP and 10 percent to GP until the first time when the partnership has recognized items of income and gain that exceed the items of loss and deduction it has recognized over its life, and all further partnership items will be allocated equally between LP and GP. Finally, the partnership agreement provides that all distributions, other than distributions in liquidation of the partnership or of a partner's interest in the partnership, will be made 90 percent to LP and 10 percent to GP until a total of $200,000 has been distributed, and thereafter all the distributions will be made equally to LP and GP. In each of the partnership's first 2 taxable years, it generates rental income of $95,000, operating expenses (including land lease payments) of $10,000, interest expense of $80,000, and a depreciation deduction of $90,000, resulting in a net taxable loss of $85,000 in each of those years. The allocations of these losses 90 percent to LP and 10 percent to GP have substantial economic effect.

	LP	GP
Capital account on formation	$180,000	$20,000
Less: net loss in years 1 and 2	(153,000)	(17,000)
Capital account at end of year 2	$ 27,000	$ 3,000

In the partnership's third taxable year, it again generates rental income of $95,000, operating expenses of $10,000, interest expense of $80,000, and a depreciation deduction of $90,000, resulting in net taxable loss of $85,000. The partnership makes no distributions.

(i) Calculation of nonrecourse deductions and partnership minimum gain. If the partnership were to dispose of the building in full satisfaction of the nonrecourse liability at the end of the third year, it would realize $70,000 of gain ($800,000 amount realized less $730,000 adjusted tax basis). Because the amount of partnership minimum gain at the end of the third year (and the net increase in partnership minimum gain during the year) is $70,000, there are partnership nonrecourse deductions for that year of $70,000, consisting of depreciation deductions allowable with respect to the building of $70,000. Pursuant to the partnership agreement, all partnership items comprising the net taxable loss of $85,000, including the $70,000 nonrecourse deduction, are allocated 90 percent to LP and 10 percent to GP. The allocation of these items, other than the nonrecourse deductions, has substantial economic effect.

	LP	GP
Capital account at end of year 2	$27,000	$3,000
Less: net loss in year 3 (without nonrecourse deductions)	(13,500)	(1,500)
Less: nonrecourse deductions in year 3	(63,000)	(7,000)
Capital account at end of year 3	($49,500)	($5,500)

The allocation of the $70,000 nonrecourse deduction satisfies requirement (2) of paragraph (e) of this section because it is consistent with allocations having substantial economic effect of other significant partnership items attributable to the building. Because the remaining requirements of paragraph (e) of this section are satisfied, the allocation of nonrecourse deductions is deemed to be in accordance with the partners' interests in the partnership. At the end of the partnership's third taxable year, LP's and GP's shares of partnership minimum gain are $63,000 and $7,000, respectively. Therefore, pursuant to paragraph (g)(1) of this section, LP is treated as obligated to restore a deficit capital account balance of $63,000, so that in the succeeding year LP could be allocated up to an additional $13,500 of partnership deductions, losses, and section 705(a)(2)(B) items that are not nonrecourse deductions. Even though this allocation would increase a deficit capital account balance, it would be considered to have economic effect under the alternate economic effect test contained in § 1.704–1(b)(2)(ii)(d). If the partnership were to dispose of the building in full satisfaction of the nonrecourse liability at the beginning of the partnership's fourth taxable year (and had no other economic activity in that year), the partnership minimum gain would be decreased from $70,000 to zero, and the minimum gain chargeback would require that LP and GP be allocated $63,000 and $7,000, respectively, of the gain from that disposition.

(ii) Illustration of reasonable consistency requirement. Assume instead that the partnership agreement provides that all nonrecourse deductions of the partnership will be allocated equally between LP and GP. Furthermore, at the time the partnership agreement is entered into, there is a reasonable likelihood that over the partnership's life it will realize amounts of income and gain significantly in excess of amounts of loss and deduction (other than nonrecourse deductions). The equal allocation of excess income and gain has substantial economic effect.

	LP	GP
Capital account on formation	$180,000	$20,000
Less: net loss in years 1 and 2	(153,000)	(17,000)
Less: net loss in year (without nonrecourse deductions)	(13,500)	(1,500)
Less: nonrecourse deductions in year 3	(35,000)	(35,000)
Capital account at end of year 3	($21,500)	($33,500)

The allocation of the $70,000 nonrecourse deduction equally between LP and GP satisfies requirement (2) of paragraph (e) of this section because the allocation is consistent with allocations, which will have substantial economic effect, of other significant partnership items attributable to the building. Because the remaining requirements of paragraph (e) of this section are satisfied, the allocation of nonrecourse deductions is deemed to be in accordance with the partners' interests in the partnership. The allocation of the nonrecourse deductions 75 percent to LP and 25 percent to GP (or in any other ratio between 90 percent to LP/10 percent to GP and 50 percent to LP/50 percent to GP) also would satisfy requirement (2) of paragraph (e) of this section.

(iii) Allocation of nonrecourse deductions that fails reasonable consistency requirement. Assume instead that the partnership agreement provides that LP will be allocated 99 percent, and GP 1 percent, of all nonrecourse deductions of the partnership. Allocating nonrecourse deductions this way does not satisfy requirement (2) of paragraph (e) of this section because the allocations are not reasonably consistent with allocations, having substantial economic effect, of any other significant partnership item attributable to the building. Therefore, the allocation of nonrecourse deductions will be disregarded, and the nonrecourse deductions of the partnership will be reallocated according to the partners' overall economic interests in the partnership, determined under § 1.704–1(b)(3)(ii).

(iv) Capital contribution to pay down nonrecourse debt. At the beginning of the partnership's fourth taxable year, LP contributes $144,000 and GP contributes $16,000 of additional capital to the partnership, which the partnership immediately uses to reduce the amount of its nonrecourse liability from $800,000 to $640,000. In addition, in the partnership's fourth taxable year, it generates rental income of $95,000, operating expenses of $10,000, interest expense of $64,000 (consistent with the debt reduction), and a depreciation deduction of $90,000, resulting in a net taxable loss of $69,000. If the partnership were to dispose of the building in full satisfaction of the nonrecourse liability at the end of that year, it would realize no gain ($640,000 amount realized less $640,000 adjusted tax basis). Therefore, the amount of partnership minimum gain at the end of the year is zero, which represents a net decrease in partnership minimum gain of $70,000 during the year. LP's and GP's shares of this net decrease are $63,000 and $7,000 respectively, so that at the end of the partnership's fourth taxable year, LP's and GP's shares of partnership minimum gain are zero. Although there has been a net decrease in partnership minimum gain, pursuant to paragraph (f)(3) of this section LP and GP are not subject to a minimum gain chargeback.

	LP	GP
Capital account at end of year 3	($49,000)	($5,500)
Plus: contribution	144,000	16,000
Less: net loss in year 4	(62,100)	(6,900)
Capital account at end of year 4	$32,400	$3,600
Minimum gain chargeback carryforward	0	0

(v) Loans of unequal priority. Assume instead that the building acquired by the partnership is secured by a $700,000 nonrecourse loan and a $100,000 recourse loan, subordinate in priority to the nonrecourse loan. Under paragraph (d)(2) of this section, $700,000 of the adjusted basis of the building at the end of the partnership's third taxable year is allocated to the nonrecourse liability (with the remaining $30,000 allocated to the recourse liability) so that if the partnership disposed of the building in full satisfaction of the nonrecourse liability at the end of that year, it would realize no gain ($700,000 amount realized less $700,000 adjusted tax basis). Therefore, there is no minimum gain (or increase in minimum gain) at the end of the partnership's third taxable year. If, however, the $700,000 nonrecourse loan were subordinate in priority to the $100,000 recourse loan, under paragraph (d)(2) of this section, the first $100,000 of adjusted tax basis in the building would be allocated to the recourse liability, leaving only $630,000 of the adjusted basis of the building to be allocated to the $700,000 nonrecourse loan. In that case, the balance of the $700,000 nonrecourse liability would exceed the adjusted tax basis of the building by $70,000, so that there would be $70,000 of minimum gain (and a $70,000 increase in partnership minimum gain) in the partnership's third taxable year.

(vi) Nonrecourse borrowing; distribution of proceeds in subsequent year. The partnership obtains an additional nonrecourse loan of $200,000 at the end of its fourth taxable year, secured by a second mortgage on the building, and distributes $180,000 of this cash to its partners at the beginning of its fifth taxable year. In addition, in its fourth and fifth taxable years, the partnership again generates rental income of $95,000, operating expenses of $10,000, interest expense of $80,000 ($100,000 in the fifth taxable year reflecting the interest paid on both liabilities), and a depreciation deduction of $90,000, resulting a net taxable loss of $85,000 ($105,000 in the fifth taxable year reflecting the interest paid on both liabilities). The partnership has distributed its $5,000 of operating cash flow in each year ($95,000 of rental income less $10,000 of operating expense and $80,000 of interest expense) to LP and GP at the end of each year. If the partnership were to dispose of the building in full satisfaction of both nonrecourse liabilities at the end of its fourth taxable year, the partnership would realize $360,000 of gain ($1,000,000 amount realized less $640,000 adjusted tax basis). Thus, the net increase in partnership minimum gain during the partnership's fourth taxable year is $290,000 ($360,000 of minimum gain at the end of the fourth year less $70,000 of minimum gain at the end of the third year). Because the partnership did not distribute any of the proceeds of the loan it obtained in its fourth year during that year, the potential amount of partnership nonrecourse deductions for that year is $290,000. Under paragraph (c) of this section, if the partnership had distributed the proceeds of that loan to its partners at the end of its fourth year, the partnership's nonrecourse deductions for that year would have been reduced by the amount of that distribution because the proceeds of that loan are allocable to an increase in partnership minimum gain under paragraph (h)(1) of this section. Because the nonrecourse deductions of $290,000 for the partnership's fourth taxable year exceed its total deductions for that year, all $180,000 of the partnership's deductions for that year are treated as nonrecourse deductions, and the $110,000 excess nonrecourse deductions are treated as an increase in partnership minimum gain in the partnership's fifth taxable year under paragraph (c) of this section.

	LP	GP
Capital account at end of year 3 (including cash flow distributions)	($ 63,000)	($ 7,000)
Plus: rental income in year 4	85,500	9,500
Less: nonrecourse deductions in year 4	(162,000)	(18,000)
Less: cash flow distributions in year 4	(4,500)	(500)
Capital account at end of year 4	($144,000)	($16,000)

At the end of the partnership's fourth taxable year, LP's and GP's shares of partnership minimum gain are $225,000 and $25,000, respectively (because the $110,000 excess of nonrecourse deductions is carried forward to the next year). If the partnership were to dispose of the building in full satisfaction of the nonrecourse liabilities at the end of its fifth taxable year, the partnership would realize $450,000 of gain ($1,000,000 amount realized less $550,000 adjusted tax basis). Therefore, the net increase in partnership minimum gain during the partnership's fifth taxable year is $200,000 ($110,000 deemed increase plus the $90,000 by which minimum gain at the end of the fifth year exceeds minimum gain at the end of the fourth year ($450,000 less $360,000)). At the beginning of its fifth year, the partnership distributes $180,000 of the loan proceeds (retaining $20,000 to pay the additional interest expense). Under paragraph (h) of this section, the first $110,000 of this distribution (an amount equal to the deemed increase in partnership minimum gain for the year) is considered allocable to an increase in partnership minimum gain for the year. As a result, the amount of nonrecourse deductions for the partnership's fifth taxable year is $90,000 ($200,000 net increase in minimum gain less $110,000 distribution of nonrecourse liability proceeds allocable to an increase in partnership minimum gain), and the nonrecourse deductions consist solely of the $90,000 depreciation deduction allowable with respect to the building. As a result of the distributions during the partnership's fifth taxable year, the total distributions to the partners over the partnership's life equal $205,000. Therefore, the last $5,000 distributed to the partners during the fifth year will be divided equally between them under the partnership agreement. Thus, out of the $185,000 total distribution during the partnership's fifth taxable year, the first $180,000 is distributed 90 percent to LP and 10 percent to GP, and the last $5,000 is divided equally between them.

	LP	GP
Capital account at end of year 4	($144,000)	($16,000)
Less: net loss in year 5 (without nonrecourse deductions)	(13,500)	(1,500)
Less: nonrecourse deductions in year 5	(81,000)	(9,000)
Less: distribution of loan proceeds	(162,000)	(18,000)
Less: cash flow distribution in year 5	(2,500)	(2,500)
Capital account at end of year 5	($403,000)	($47,000)

At the end of the partnership's fifth taxable year, LP's share of partnership minimum gain is $405,000 ($225,000 share of minimum gain at the end of the fourth year plus $81,000 of nonrecourse deductions for the fifth year and a $99,000 distribution of nonrecourse liability proceeds that are allocable to an increase in minimum gain) and GP's share of partnership minimum gain is $45,000 ($25,000 share of minimum gain at the end of the fourth year plus $9,000 of nonrecourse deductions for the fifth year and an $11,000 distribution of nonrecourse liability proceeds that are allocable to an increase in minimum gain).

(vii) Partner guarantee of nonrecourse debt. LP and GP personally guarantee the "first" $100,000 of the $800,000 nonrecourse loan (i.e., only if the building is worth less than $100,000 will they be called upon to make up any deficiency). Under paragraph (d)(2) of this section, only $630,000 of the adjusted tax basis of the building is allocated to the $700,000 nonrecourse portion of the loan because the collateral will be applied first to satisfy the $100,000 guaranteed portion, making it superior in priority to the remainder of the loan. On the other hand, if LP and GP were to guarantee the "last" $100,000 (i.e., if the building is worth less than $800,000, they will be called upon to make up the deficiency up to $100,000), $700,000 of the adjusted tax basis of the building would be allocated to the $700,000 nonrecourse portion of the loan because the guaranteed portion would be inferior in priority to it.

(viii) Partner nonrecourse debt. Assume instead that the $800,000 loan is made by LP, the limited partner. Under paragraph (b)(4) of this section, the $800,000 obligation does not constitute a nonrecourse liability of the partnership for purposes of this section because LP, a partner, bears the economic risk of loss for that loan within the meaning of § 1.752–2. Instead, the $800,000 loan constitutes a partner nonrecourse debt under paragraph (b)(4) of this section. In the partnership's third taxable year, partnership minimum gain would have increased by $70,000 if the debt were a nonrecourse liability of the partnership. Thus, under paragraph (i)(3) of this section, there is a net increase of $70,000 in the minimum gain attributable to the $800,000 partner nonrecourse debt for the partnership's third taxable year, and $70,000 of the $90,000 depreciation deduction from the building for the partnership's third taxable year constitutes a partner nonrecourse deduction with respect to the debt. See paragraph (i)(4) of this section. Under paragraph (i)(2) of this section, this partner nonrecourse deduction must be allocated to LP, the partner that bears the economic risk of loss for that liability.

(ix) Nonrecourse debt and partner nonrecourse debt of differing priorities. As in Example 1 (viii) of this paragraph (m), the $800,000 loan is made to the partnership by LP, the limited partner, but the loan is a purchase money loan that "wraps around" a $700,000 underlying nonrecourse note (also secured by the building) issued by LP to an unrelated person in connection with LP's acquisition of the building. Under these circumstances, LP bears the economic risk of loss with respect to only $100,000 of the liability within the meaning of § 1.752–2. See § 1.752–2(f) (Example 6). Therefore, for purposes of paragraph (d) of this section, the $800,000 liability is treated as a $700,000 nonrecourse liability of the partnership and a $100,000 partner nonrecourse debt (inferior in priority to the $700,000 liability) of the partnership for which LP bears the economic risk of loss. Under paragraph (i)(2) of this section, $70,000 of the $90,000 depreciation deduction realized in the partnership's third taxable year constitutes a partner nonrecourse deduction that must be allocated to LP.

Example 2. Netting of increases and decreases in partnership minimum gain. For Example 2 unless otherwise provided, the following facts are assumed. X and Y form a general partnership to acquire and operate residential real properties. Each partner contributes $150,000 to the partnership. The partnership obtains a $1,500,000 nonrecourse loan and purchases 3 apartment buildings (on leased land) for $720,000 ("Property A"), $540,000 ("Property B"), and $540,000 ("Property C"). The nonrecourse loan is secured only by the 3 buildings, and no principal payments are due for 5 years. In each of the partnership's first 3 taxable years, it generates rental income of $225,000, operating expenses (including land lease payments) of $50,000, interest expense of $175,000, and depreciation deductions on the 3 properties of $150,000 ($60,000 on Property A and $45,000 on each of Property B and Property C), resulting in a net taxable loss of $150,000 in each of those years. The partnership makes no distributions to X or Y.

(i) Calculation of net increases and decreases in partnership minimum gain. If the partnership were to dispose of the 3 apartment buildings in full satisfaction of its nonrecourse liability at the end of its third taxable year, it would realize $150,000 of gain ($1,500,000 amount realized less $1,350,000 adjusted tax basis). Because the amount of partnership minimum gain at the end of that year (and the net increase in partnership minimum gain during that year) is $150,000, the amount of partnership nonrecourse deductions for that year is $150,000, consisting of depreciation deductions allowable with respect to the 3 apartment buildings of $150,000. The result would be the same if the partnership obtained 3 separate nonrecourse loans that were "cross-collateralized" (i.e., if each separate loan were secured by all 3 of the apartment buildings).

(ii) Netting of increases and decreases in partnership minimum gain when there is a disposition. At the beginning of the partnership's fourth taxable year, the partnership (with the permission of the nonrecourse lender) disposes of Property A for $835,000 and uses a portion of the proceeds to repay $600,000 of the nonrecourse liability (the principal amount attributable to Property A), reducing the balance to $900,000. As a result of the disposition, the partnership realizes gain of $295,000 ($835,000 amount realized less $540,000 adjusted tax basis). If the disposition is viewed in isolation, the partnership has generated minimum gain of $60,000 on the sale of Property A ($600,000 of debt reduction less $540,000 adjusted tax basis). However, during the partnership's fourth taxable year it also generates rental income of $135,000, operating expenses of $30,000, interest expense of $105,000, and depreciation deductions of $90,000 ($45,000 on each remaining building). If the partnership were to dispose of the remaining two buildings in full satisfaction of its nonrecourse liability at the end of the partnership's fourth taxable year, it would realize gain of $180,000 ($900,000 amount realized less $720,000 aggregate adjusted tax basis), which is the amount of partnership minimum gain at the end of the year. Because the partnership minimum gain increased from $150,000 to $180,000 during the partnership's fourth taxable year, the amount of partnership nonrecourse deductions for that year is $30,000, consisting of a ratable portion of depreciation deductions allowable with respect to the two remaining apartment buildings. No minimum gain chargeback is required for the taxable year, even though the partnership disposed of one of the properties subject to the nonrecourse liability during the year, because there is no net decrease in partnership minimum gain for the year. See paragraph (f)(1) of this section.

Example 3. Nonrecourse deductions and partnership minimum gain before third partner is admitted. For purposes of Example 3, unless otherwise provided, the following facts are assumed. Additional facts are given in each of Examples 3(ii), (iii), and (iv). A and B form a limited partnership to acquire and lease machinery that is 5–year recovery property. A, the limited partner, and B, the general partner, contribute $100,000 each to the partnership, which obtains an $800,000 nonrecourse loan and purchases the machinery for $1,000,000. The nonrecourse loan is secured only by the machinery. The principal amount of the loan is to be repaid $50,000 per year during each of the partnership's first 5 taxable years, with the remaining $550,000 of unpaid principal due on the first day of the partnership's sixth taxable year. The partnership agreement contains all of the provisions required by paragraph (e) of this section, and, as of the end of each partnership taxable year discussed herein, the items described in § 1.704–1(b)(2)(ii)(d)(4), (5), and (6) are not reasonably expected to cause or increase a deficit balance in A's or B's capital account. The partnership agreement provides that, except as otherwise required by its qualified income offset and minimum gain chargeback provisions, all partnership items will be allocated equally between A and B. Finally, the partnership agreement provides that all distributions, other than distributions in liquidation of the partnership or of a partner's interest in the partnership, will be made equally between A and B. In the partnership's first taxable year it generates rental income of $130,000, interest expense of $80,000, and a depreciation deduction of $150,000, resulting in a net taxable loss of $100,000. In addition, the partnership repays $50,000 of the nonrecourse liability, reducing that liability to $750,000. Allocations of these losses equally between A and B have substantial economic effect.

	A	B
Capital account on formation	$100,000	$100,000
Less: net loss in year 1	(50,000)	(50,000)
Capital account at end of year 1	$ 50,000	$ 50,000

In the partnership's second taxable year, it generates rental income of $130,000, interest expense of $75,000, and a depreciation deduction of $220,000, resulting in a net taxable loss of $165,000. In addition, the partnership repays $50,000 of the nonrecourse liability, reducing that liability to $700,000, and distributes $2,500 of cash to each partner. If the partnership were to dispose of the machinery in full satisfaction of the nonrecourse liability at the end of that year, it would realize $70,000 of gain ($700,000 amount realized less $630,000 adjusted tax basis). Therefore, the amount of partnership minimum gain at the end of that year (and the net increase in partnership minimum gain during the year) is $70,000, and the amount of partnership nonrecourse deductions for the year is $70,000. The partnership nonrecourse deductions for its second taxable year consist of $70,000 of the depreciation deductions allowable with respect to the machinery. Pursuant to the partnership agreement, all partnership items comprising the net taxable loss of $165,000, including the $70,000 nonrecourse deduction, are allocated equally between A and B. The allocation of these items, other than the nonrecourse deductions, has substantial economic effect.

	A	B
Capital account at end of year 1	$50,000	$50,000
Less: net loss in year 2 (without nonrecourse deductions)	(47,500)	(47,500)
Less: nonrecourse deductions in year 2	(35,000)	(35,000)
Less: distribution	(2,500)	(2,500)
Capital account at end of year 2	($35,000)	($35,000)

(i) Calculation of nonrecourse deductions and partnership minimum gain. Because all of the requirements of paragraph (e) of this section are satisfied, the allocation of nonrecourse deductions is deemed to be made in accordance with the partners' interests in the partnership. At the end of the partnership's second taxable year, A's and B's shares of partnership minimum gain are $35,000 each. Therefore, pursuant to paragraph (g)(1) of this section, A and B are treated as obligated to restore deficit balances in their capital accounts of $35,000 each. If the partnership were to dispose of the machinery in full satisfaction of the nonrecourse liability at the beginning of the partnership's third taxable year (and had no other economic activity in that year), the partnership minimum gain would be decreased from $70,000 to zero. A's and B's shares of that net decrease would be $35,000 each. Upon that disposition, the minimum gain chargeback would require that A and B each be allocated $35,000 of that gain before any other allocation is made under section 704(b) with respect to partnership items for the partnership's third taxable year.

(ii) Nonrecourse deductions and restatement of capital accounts. (a) Additional facts. C is admitted to the partnership at the beginning of the partnership's third taxable year. At the time of C's admission, the fair market value of the machinery is $900,000. C contributes $100,000 to the partnership (the partnership invests $95,000 of this in undeveloped land and holds the other $5,000 in cash) in exchange for an interest in the partnership. In connection with C's admission to the partnership, the partnership's machinery is revalued on the partnership's books to reflect its fair market value of $900,000. Pursuant to § 1.704–1(b)(2)(iv)(f), the capital accounts of A and B are adjusted upwards to $100,000 each to reflect the revaluation of the partnership's machinery. This adjustment reflects the manner in which the partnership gain of $270,000 ($900,000 fair market value minus $630,000 adjusted tax basis) would be shared if the machinery were sold for its fair market value immediately prior to C's admission to the partnership.

	A	B
Capital account before C's admission	($ 35,000)	($ 35,000)
Deemed sale adjustment	135,000	135,000
Capital account adjusted for C's admission	100,000	100,000

The partnership agreement is modified to provide that, except as otherwise required by its qualified income offset and minimum gain chargeback provisions, partnership income, gain, loss, and deduction, as computed for book purposes, are allocated equally among the partners, and those allocations are reflected in the partners' capital accounts. The partnership agreement also is modified to provide that depreciation and gain or loss, as computed for tax purposes, with respect to the machinery will be shared among the partners in a manner that takes account of the variation between the property's $630,000 adjusted tax basis and its $900,000 book value, in accordance with § 1.704–1(b)(2)(iv)(f) and the special rule contained in § 1.704–1(b)(4)(i).

(b) Effect of revaluation. Because the requirements of § 1.704–1(b)(2)(iv)(g) are satisfied, the capital accounts of the partners (as adjusted) continue to be maintained in accordance with § 1.704–1(b)(2)(iv). If the partnership were to dispose of the machinery in full satisfaction of the nonrecourse liability immediately following the revaluation of the machinery, it would realize no book gain ($700,000 amount realized less $900,000 book value). As a result of the revaluation of the machinery upward by $270,000, under part (i) of paragraph (d)(4) of this section, the partnership minimum gain is reduced from $70,000 immediately prior to the revaluation to zero; but under part (ii) of paragraph (d)(4) of this section, the partnership minimum gain is increased by the $70,000 decrease arising solely from the revaluation. Accordingly, there is no net increase or decrease solely on account of the revaluation, and so no minimum gain chargeback is triggered. All future nonrecourse deductions that occur will be the nonrecourse deductions as calculated for book purposes, and will be charged to all 3 partners in accordance with the partnership agreement. For purposes of determining the partners' shares of minimum gain under paragraph (g) of this section, A's and B's shares of the decrease resulting from the revaluation are $35,000 each. However, as illustrated below, under section 704(c) principles, the tax capital accounts of A and B will eventually be charged $35,000 each, reflecting their 50 percent shares of the decrease in partnership minimum gain that resulted from the revaluation.

(iii) Allocation of nonrecourse deductions following restatement of capital accounts. (a) Additional facts. During the partnership's third taxable year, the partnership generates rental income of $130,000, interest expense of $70,000, a tax depreciation deduction of $210,000, and a book depreciation deduction (attributable to the machinery) of $300,000. As a result, the partnership has a net taxable loss of $150,000 and a net book loss of $240,000. In addition, the partnership repays $50,000 of the nonrecourse liability (after the data of C's admission), reducing the liability to $650,000 and distributes $5,000 of cash to each partner.

(b) Allocations. If the partnership were to dispose of the machinery in full satisfaction of the nonrecourse liability at the end of the year, $50,000 of book gain would result ($650,000 amount realized less $600,000 book basis). Therefore, the amount of partnership minimum gain at the end of the year is $50,000, which represents a net decrease in partnership minimum gain of $20,000 during the year. (This is so even though there would be an increase in partnership minimum gain in the partnership's third taxable year if minimum gain were computed with reference to the adjusted tax basis of the machinery.) Nevertheless, pursuant to paragraph (d)(4) of this section, the amount of nonrecourse deductions of the partnership for its third taxable year is $50,000 (the net increase in partnership minimum gain during the year determined by adding back the $70,000 decrease in partnership minimum gain attributable to the revaluation of the machinery to the $20,000 net decrease in partnership minimum gain during the year). The $50,000 of partnership nonrecourse deductions for the year consist of book depreciation deductions allowable with respect to the machinery of $50,000. Pursuant to the partnership agreement, all partnership items comprising the net book loss of $240,000, including the $50,000 nonrecourse deduction, are allocated equally among the partners. The allocation of these items, other than the nonrecourse deductions, has substantial economic effect. Consistent with the special partners' interests in the partnership rule contained in § 1.704–1(b)(4)(i), the partnership agreement provides that the depreciation deduction for tax purposes of $210,000 for the partnership's third taxable year is, in accordance with section 704(c) principles, shared $55,000 to A, $55,000 to B, and $100,000 to C.

	A		B		C	
	Tax	Book	Tax	Book	Tax	Book
Capital account at beginning of year 3	($35,000)	$100,000	($35,000)	$100,000	$100,000	$100,000
Less: nonrecourse deductions	(9,166)	(16,666)	(9,166)	(16,666)	(16,666)	(16,666)
Less: items other than nonrecourse deductions in year 3	(25,834)	(63,334)	(25,834)	(63,334)	(63,334)	(63,334)
Less: distribution	(5,000)	(5,000)	(5,000)	(5,000)	(5,000)	(5,000)
Capital account at end of year 3	($75,000)	$ 15,000	($75,000)	$ 15,000	$ 15,000	$ 15,000

Because the requirements of paragraph (e) of this section are satisfied, the allocation of the nonrecourse deduction is deemed to be made in accordance with the partners' interests in the partnership. At the end of the partnership's third taxable year, A's, B's, and C's shares of partnership minimum gain are $16,666 each.

(iv) Subsequent allocation of nonrecourse deductions following restatement of capital accounts. (a) Additional facts. The partners' capital accounts at the end of the second and third taxable years of the partnership are as stated in Example 3(iii) of this paragraph (m). In addition, during the partnership's fourth taxable year the partnership generates rental income of $130,000, interest expense of $65,000, a tax depreciation deduction of $210,000, and a book depreciation deduction (attributable to the machinery) of $300,000. As a result, the partnership has a net taxable loss of $145,000 and a net book loss of $235,000. In addition, the partnership repays $50,000 of the nonrecourse liability, reducing that liability to $600,000, and distributes $5,000 of cash to each partner.

	A		B		C	
	Tax	Book	Tax	Book	Tax	Book
Capital account at end year 3	($ 75,000)	$15,000	($ 75,000)	$15,000	$15,000	$15,000
Less: nonrecourse deductions	(45,833)	(83,333)	(45,833)	(83,333)	(83,333)	(83,333)
Plus: items other than nonrecourse deduction in year 4	12,499	5,000	12,499	5,000	5,000	5,000
Less: distribution	(5,000)	(5,000)	(5,000)	(5,000)	(5,000)	(5,000)
Capital account at end of year 4	($113,334)	($68,333)	($113,333)	($68,333)	($68,333)	($68,333)

The allocation of the $250,000 nonrecourse deduction equally among A, B, and C satisfies requirement (2) of paragraph (e) of this section. Because all of the requirements of paragraph (e) of this section are satisfied, the allocation is deemed to be in accordance with the partners' interests in the partnership. At the end of the partnership's fourth taxable year, A's, B's, and C's shares of partnership minimum gain are $100,000 each.

(v) Disposition of partnership property following restatement of capital accounts. (a) Additional facts. The partners' capital accounts at the end of the fourth taxable year of the partnership are as stated above in (iv). In addition, at the beginning of the partnership's fifth taxable year it sells the machinery for $650,000 (using $600,000 of the proceeds to repay the nonrecourse liability), resulting in a taxable gain of $440,000 ($650,000 amount realized less $210,000 adjusted tax basis) and a book gain of $350,000 ($650,000 amount realized less $300,000 book basis). The partnership has no other items of income, gain, loss, or deduction for the year.

(b) Effect of disposition. As a result of the sale, partnership minimum gain is reduced from $300,000 to zero, reducing A's, B's, and C's shares of partnership minimum gain to zero from $100,000 each. The minimum gain chargeback requires that A, B, and C each be allocated $100,000 of that gain (an amount equal to each partner's share of the net decrease in partnership minimum gain resulting from the sale) before any allocation is made to them under section 704(b) with respect to partnership items for the partnership's fifth taxable year. Thus, the allocation of the first $300,000 of book gain $100,000 to each of the partners is deemed to be in accordance with the partners' interests in the partnership under paragraph (e) of this section. The allocation of the remaining $50,000 of book gain equally among the partners has substantial economic effect. Consistent with the special partners' interests in the partnership rule contained in § 1.704–1(b)(4)(i), the partnership agreement provides that the $440,000 taxable gain is, in accordance with section 704(c) principles, allocated $161,667 to A, $161,667 to B, and $116,666 to C.

	A		B		C	
	Tax	Book	Tax	Book	Tax	Book
Capital account at end of year 4	($113,334)	($68,333)	($113,334)	($68,333)	($68,333)	($68,333)
Plus: minimum gain chargeback	138,573	100,000	138,573	100,000	100,000	100,000
Plus: additional gain	23,094	16,666	23,094	16,666	16,666	16,666
Capital account before liquidation	$ 48,333	$48,333	$ 48,333	$48,333	$48,333	$48,333

Example (4). Allocations of increase in partnership minimum gain among partnership properties. For Example 4, unless otherwise provided, the following facts are assumed. A partnership owns 4 properties, each of which is subject to a nonrecourse liability of the partnership. During a taxable year of the partnership, the following events take place. First, the partnership generates a depreciation deduction (for both book and tax purposes) with respect to Property W of $10,000 and repays $5,000 of the nonrecourse liability secured only by that property, resulting in an increase in minimum gain with respect to that liability of $5,000. Second, the partnership generates a depreciation deduction (for both book and tax purposes) with respect to Property X of $10,000 and repays none of the nonrecourse liability secured by that property, resulting in an increase in minimum gain with respect to that liability of $10,000. Third, the partnership generates a depreciation deduction (for both book and tax purposes) of $2,000 with respect to Property Y and repays $11,000 of the nonrecourse liability secured only by that property, resulting in a decrease in minimum gain with respect to that liability of $9,000 (although at the end of that year, there remains minimum gain with respect to that liability). Finally, the partnership borrows $5,000 on a nonrecourse basis, giving as the only security for that liability Property Z, a parcel of undeveloped land with an adjusted tax basis (and book value) of $2,000, resulting in a net increase in minimum gain with respect to that liability of $3,000.

(i) Allocation of increase in partnership minimum gain. The net increase in partnership minimum gain during that partnership taxable year is $9,000, so that the amount of nonrecourse deductions of the partnership for that taxable year is $9,000. Those nonrecourse deductions consist of $3,000 of depreciation deductions with respect to Property W and $6,000 of depreciation deductions with respect to Property X. See paragraph (c) of this section. The amount of nonrecourse deductions consisting of depreciation deductions is determined as follows. With respect to the nonrecourse liability secured by Property Z, for which there is no depreciation deduction, the amount of depreciation deductions that constitutes nonrecourse deductions is zero. Similarly, with respect to the nonrecourse liability secured by Property Y, for which there is no increase in minimum gain, the amount of depreciation deductions that constitutes nonrecourse deductions is zero. With respect to each of the nonrecourse liabilities secured by Properties W and X, which are secured by property for which there are depreciation deductions and for which there is an increase in minimum gain, the amount of depreciation deductions that constitutes nonrecourse deductions is determined by the following formula:

net increase in the partnership minimum gain for that taxable year × total depreciation deductions for that taxable year on the specific property securing the nonrecourse liability to the extent minimum gain increased on that liability (divided by) total depreciation deductions for that taxable year on all properties securing nonrecourse liabilities to the extent of the aggregate increase in minimum gain on all those liabilities.

Thus, for the liability secured by Property W, the amount is $9,000 times $5,000/$15,000, or $3,000. For the liability secured by Property X, the amount is $9,000 times $10,000/$15,000, or $6,000. (If one depreciable property secured two partnership nonrecourse liabilities, the amount of depreciation or book depreciation with respect to that property would be allocated among those liabilities in accordance with the method by which adjusted basis is allocated under paragraph (d)(2) of this section).

(ii) Alternative allocation of increase in partnership minimum gain among partnership properties. Assume instead that the loan secured by Property Z is $15,000 (rather than $5,000), resulting in a net increase in minimum gain with respect to that liability of $13,000. Thus, the net increase in partnership minimum gain is $19,000, and the amount of nonrecourse deductions of the partnership for that taxable year is $19,000. Those nonrecourse deductions consist of $5,000 of depreciation deductions with respect to Property W, $10,000 of depreciation deductions with respect to Property X, and a pro rata portion of the partnership's other items of deduction, loss, and section 705(a)(2)(B) expenditure for that year. The method for computing the amounts of depreciation deductions that constitute nonrecourse deductions is the same as in (i) of this Example 4 for the liabilities secured by Properties Y and Z. With respect to each of the nonrecourse liabilities secured by Properties W and X, the amount of depreciation deductions that constitutes nonrecourse deductions equals the total depreciation deductions with respect to the partnership property securing that particular liability to the extent of the increase in minimum gain with respect to that liability.

[T.D. 8385, 56 FR 66983, Dec. 27, 1991; T.D. 9207, 70 FR 30334, May 26, 2005; T.D. 9289, 71 FR 59669, Oct. 11, 2006; T.D. 9557, 76 FR 71258, Nov. 17, 2011]

§ 1.704-3 Contributed property.

(a) In general—(1) General principles. The purpose of section 704(c) is to prevent the shifting of tax consequences among partners with respect to precontribution gain or loss. Under section 704(c), a partnership must allocate income, gain, loss, and deduction with respect to property contributed by a partner to the partnership so as to take into account any variation between the adjusted tax basis of the property and its fair market value at the time of contribution. Notwithstanding any other provision of this section, the allocations must be made using a reasonable method that is consistent with the purpose of section 704(c). For this purpose, an allocation method includes the application of all of the rules of this section (e.g., aggregation rules). An allocation method is not necessarily unreasonable merely because another allocation method would result in a higher aggregate tax liability. Paragraphs (b), (c), and (d) of this section describe allocation methods that are generally reasonable. Other methods may be reasonable in appropriate circumstances. Nevertheless, in the absence of specific published guidance, it is not reasonable to use an allocation method in which the basis of property contributed to the partnership is increased (or decreased) to reflect built-in gain (or loss), or a method under which the partnership creates tax allocations of income, gain, loss, or deduction independent of allocations affecting book capital accounts. See § 1.704-3(d). Paragraph (e) of this section contains special rules and exceptions. The principles of this paragraph (a)(1), together with the methods described in paragraphs (b), (c) and (d) of this section, apply only to contributions of property that are otherwise respected. See for example § 1.701-2. Accordingly, even though a partnership's allocation method may be described in the literal language of paragraphs (b), (c) or (d) of this section, based on the particular facts and circumstances, the Commissioner can recast the contribution as appropriate to avoid tax results inconsistent with the intent of subchapter K. One factor that may be considered by the Commissioner is the use of the remedial allocation method by related partners in which allocations of remedial items of income, gain, loss or deduction are made to one partner and the allocations of offsetting remedial items are made to a related partner.

(2) Operating rules. Except as provided in paragraphs (e)(2) and (e)(3) of this section, section 704(c) and this section apply on a property-by-property basis. Therefore, in determining whether there is a disparity between adjusted tax basis and fair market value, the built-in gains and built-in losses on items of contributed property cannot be aggregated. A partnership may use different methods with respect to different items of contributed property, provided that the partnership and the partners consistently apply a single reasonable method for each item of contributed property and that the overall method or combination of methods are reasonable based on the facts and circumstances and consistent with the purpose of section 704(c). It may be unreasonable to use one method for appreciated property and another method for depreciated property. Similarly, it may be unreasonable to use the traditional method for built-in gain property contributed by a partner with a high marginal tax rate while using curative allocations for built-in gain property contributed by a partner with a low marginal tax rate. A new partnership formed as the result of the termination of a partnership under section 708(b)(1)(B) is not required to use the same method as the terminated partnership with respect to section 704(c) property deemed contributed to the new partnership by the terminated partnership under § 1.708–1(b)(1)(iv). The previous sentence applies to terminations of partnerships under section 708(b)(1)(B) occurring on or after May 9, 1997; however, the sentence may be applied to terminations occurring on or after May 9, 1996, provided that the partnership and its partners apply the sentence to the termination in a consistent manner.

(3) Definitions—(i) Section 704(c) property. Property contributed to a partnership is section 704(c) property if at the time of contribution its book value differs from the contributing partner's adjusted tax basis. For purposes of this section, book value is determined as contemplated by § 1.704–1(b). Therefore, book value is equal to fair market value at the time of contribution and is subsequently adjusted for cost recovery and other events that affect the basis of the property. For a partnership that maintains capital accounts in accordance with § 1.704–1(b)(2)(iv), the book value of property is initially the value used in determining the contributing partner's capital account under § 1.704–1(b)(2)(iv)(d), and is appropriately adjusted thereafter (e.g., for book cost recovery under §§ 1.704–1(b)(2)(iv)(g)(3) and 1.704–3(d)(2) and other events that affect the basis of the property). A partnership that does not maintain capital accounts under § 1.704–1(b)(2)(iv) must comply with this section using a book capital account based on the same principles (i.e., a book capital account that reflects the fair market value of property at the time of contribution and that is subsequently adjusted for cost recovery and other events that affect the basis of the property). Property deemed contributed to a new partnership as the result of the termination of a partnership under section 708(b)(1)(B) is treated as section 704(c) property in the hands of the new partnership only to the extent that the property was section 704(c) property in the hands of the terminated partnership immediately prior to the termination. See § 1.708–1(b)(1)(iv) for an example of the application of this rule. The previous two sentences apply to terminations of partnerships under section 708(b)(1)(B) occurring on or after May 9, 1997; however, the sentences may be applied to terminations occurring on or after May 9, 1996, provided that the partnership and its partners apply the sentences to the termination in a consistent manner.

(ii) Built-in gain and built-in loss. The built-in gain on section 704(c) property is the excess of the property's book value over the contributing partner's adjusted tax basis upon contribution. The built-in gain is thereafter reduced by decreases in the difference between the property's book value and adjusted tax basis. The built-in loss on section 704(c) property is the excess of the contributing partner's adjusted tax basis over the property's book value upon contribution. The built-in loss is thereafter reduced by decreases in the difference between the property's adjusted tax basis and book value. * * *

(4) Accounts payable and other accrued but unpaid items. Accounts payable and other accrued but unpaid items contributed by a partner using the cash receipts and disbursements method of accounting are treated as section 704(c) property for purposes of applying the rules of this section.

(5) Other provisions of the Internal Revenue Code. Section 704(c) and this section apply to a contribution of property to the partnership only if the contribution is governed by section 721, taking into account other provisions of the Internal Revenue Code. For example, to the extent that a transfer of property to a partnership is a sale under section 707, the transfer is not a contribution of property to which section 704(c) applies.

(6) Other applications of section 704(c) principles—(i) Revaluations under section 704(b). The principles of this section apply to allocations with respect to property for which differences between book value and adjusted tax basis are created when a partnership revalues partnership property pursuant to § 1.704–1(b)(2)(iv)(f) (reverse section 704(c) allocations) or 1.704–1(b)(2)(iv)(s) (reverse section 704(c) allocations). Partnerships are not required to use the same allocation method for reverse section 704(c) allocations as for contributed property, even if at the time of revaluation the property is already subject to section 704(c) and paragraph (a) of this section. In addition, partnerships are not required to use the same allocation method for reverse section 704(c) allocations each time the partnership revalues its property. A partnership that makes allocations with respect to revalued property must use a reasonable method that is consistent with the purposes of section 704(b) and (c).

(ii) Basis adjustments. A partnership making adjustments under § 1.743–1(b) or 1.751–1(a)(2) must account for built-in gain or loss under section 704(c) in accordance with the principles of this section.

(7) Transfer of a partnership interest. If a contributing partner transfers a partnership interest, built-in gain or loss must be allocated to the transferee partner as it would have been allocated to the transferor partner. If the contributing partner transfers a portion of the partnership interest, the share of built-in gain or loss proportionate to the interest transferred must be allocated to the transferee partner. * * *

(8) Special rules—(i) Disposition in a nonrecognition transaction. If a partnership disposes of section 704(c) property in a nonrecognition transaction the substituted basis property (within the meaning of section 7701(a)(42)) is treated as section 704(c) property with the same amount of built-in gain or loss as the section 704(c) property disposed of by the partnership. If gain or loss is recognized in such a transaction, appropriate adjustments must be made. The allocation method for the substituted basis property must be consistent with the allocation method chosen for the original property. If a partnership transfers an item of section 704(c) property together with other property to a corporation under section 351, in order to preserve that item's built-in gain or loss, the basis in the stock received in exchange for the section 704(c) property is determined as if each item of section 704(c) property had been the only property transferred to the corporation by the partnership. * * *

* * *

(9) Tiered partnerships. If a partnership contributes section 704(c) property to a second partnership (the lower-tier partnership), or if a partner that has contributed section 704(c) property to a partnership contributes that partnership interest to a second partnership (the upper-tier partnership), the upper-tier partnership must allocate its distributive share of lower-tier partnership items with respect to that section 704(c) property in a manner that takes into account the contributing partner's remaining built-in gain or loss. Allocations made under this paragraph will be considered to be made in a manner that meets the requirements of § 1.704–1(b)(2)(iv)(q) (relating to capital account adjustments where guidance is lacking).

(10) Anti-abuse rule—(i) In general. An allocation method (or combination of methods) is not reasonable if the contribution of property (or event that results in reverse section 704(c) allocations) and the corresponding allocation of tax items with respect to the property are made with a view to shifting the tax consequences of built-in gain or loss among the partners in a manner that substantially reduces the present value of the partners' aggregate tax liability. For purposes of this paragraph (a)(10), all references to the partners shall include both direct and indirect partners.

(ii) Definition of indirect partner. An indirect partner is any direct or indirect owner of a partnership, S corporation, or controlled foreign corporation (as defined in section 957(a) or 953(c)), or direct or indirect beneficiary of a trust or estate, that is a partner in the partnership, and any consolidated group of which the partner in the partnership is a member (within the meaning of § 1.1502–1(h)). An owner (whether directly or through tiers of entities) of a controlled foreign corporation is treated as an indirect partner only with respect to allocations of items of income, gain, loss, or deduction that enter into the computation of a United States shareholder's inclusion under section 951(a) with respect to the controlled foreign corporation, enter into any person's income attributable to a United States shareholder's inclusion under section 951(a) with respect to the controlled foreign corporation, or would enter into the computations described in this sentence if such items were allocated to the controlled foreign corporation.

(11) Contributing and noncontributing partners' recapture shares. For special rules applicable to the allocation of depreciation recapture with respect to property contributed by a partner to a partnership, see §§ 1.1245–1(e)(2) and 1.1250–1(f).

* * *

(b) Traditional method—(1) In general. This paragraph (b) describes the traditional method of making section 704(c) allocations. In general, the traditional method requires that when the partnership has income, gain, loss, or deduction attributable to section 704(c) property, it must make appropriate allocations to the partners to avoid shifting the tax consequences of the built-in gain or loss. Under this rule, if the partnership sells section 704(c) property and recognizes gain or loss, built-in gain or loss on the property is allocated to the contributing partner. If the partnership sells a portion of, or an interest in, section 704(c) property, a proportionate part of the built-in gain or loss is allocated to the contributing partner. For section 704(c) property subject to amortization, depletion, depreciation, or other cost recovery, the allocation of deductions attributable to these items takes into account built-in gain or loss on the property. For example, tax allocations to the noncontributing partners of cost recovery deductions with respect to section 704(c) property generally must, to the extent possible, equal book allocations to those partners. However, the total income, gain, loss, or deduction allocated to the partners for a taxable year with respect to a property cannot exceed the total partnership income, gain, loss, or deduction with respect to that property for the taxable year (the ceiling rule). If a partnership has no property the allocations from which are limited by the ceiling rule, the traditional method is reasonable when used for all contributed property.

(2) Examples. The following examples illustrate the principles of the traditional method.

Example 1. Operation of the traditional method—(i) Calculation of built-in gain on contribution. A and B form partnership AB and agree that each will be allocated a 50 percent share of all partnership items and that AB will make allocations under section 704(c) using the traditional method under paragraph (b) of this section. A contributes depreciable property with an adjusted tax basis of $4,000 and a book value of $10,000, and B contributes $10,000 cash. Under paragraph (a)(3) of this section, A has built-in gain of $6,000, the excess of the partnership's book value for the property ($10,000) over A's adjusted tax basis in the property at the time of contribution ($4,000).

(ii) Allocation of tax depreciation. The property is depreciated using the straight-line method over a 10–year recovery period. Because the property depreciates at an annual rate of 10 percent, B would have been entitled to a depreciation deduction of $500 per year for both book and tax purposes if the adjusted tax basis of the property equalled its fair market value at the time of contribution. Although each partner is allocated $500 of book depreciation per year, the partnership is allowed a tax depreciation deduction of only $400 per year (10 percent of $4,000). The partnership can allocate only $400 of tax depreciation under the ceiling rule of paragraph (b)(1) of this section, and it must be allocated entirely to B. In AB's first year, the proceeds generated by the equipment exactly equal AB's operating expenses. At the end of that year, the book value of the property is $9,000 ($10,000 less the $1,000 book depreciation deduction), and the adjusted tax basis is $3,600 ($4,000 less the $400 tax depreciation deduction). A's built-in gain with respect to the property decreases to $5,400 ($9,000 book value less $3,600 adjusted tax basis). Also, at the end of AB's first year, A has a $9,500 book capital account and a $4,000 tax basis in A's partnership interest. B has a $9,500 book capital account and a $9,600 adjusted tax basis in B's partnership interest.

(iii) Sale of the property. If AB sells the property at the beginning of AB's second year for $9,000, AB realizes tax gain of $5,400 ($9,000, the amount realized, less the adjusted tax basis of $3,600). Under paragraph (b)(1) of this section, the entire $5,400 gain must be allocated to A because the property A contributed has that much built-in gain remaining. If AB sells the property at the beginning of AB's second year for $10,000, AB realizes tax gain of $6,400 ($10,000, the amount realized, less the adjusted tax basis of $3,600). Under paragraph (b)(1) of this section, only $5,400 of gain must be allocated to A to account for A's built-in gain. The remaining $1,000 of gain is allocated equally between A and B in accordance with the partnership agreement. If AB sells the property for less than the $9,000 book value, AB realizes tax gain of less than $5,400, and the entire gain must be allocated to A.

(iv) Termination and liquidation of partnership. If AB sells the property at the beginning of AB's second year for $9,000, and AB engages in no other transactions that year, A will recognize a gain of $5,400, and B will recognize no income or loss. A's adjusted tax basis for A's interest in AB will then be $9,400 ($4,000, A's original tax basis, increased by the gain of $5,400). B's adjusted tax basis for B's interest in AB will be $9,600 ($10,000, B's original tax basis, less the $400 depreciation deduction in the first partnership year). If the partnership then terminates and distributes its assets ($19,000 in cash) to A and B in proportion to their capital account balances, A will recognize a capital gain of $100 ($9,500, the amount distributed to A, less $9,400, the adjusted tax basis of A's interest), B will recognize a capital loss of $100 (the excess of B's adjusted tax basis, $9,600, over the amount received, $9,500).

Example 2. Unreasonable use of the traditional method—(i) Facts. C and D form partnership CD and agree that each will be allocated a 50 percent share of all partnership items and that CD will make allocations under section 704(c) using the traditional method under paragraph (b) of this section. C contributes equipment with an adjusted tax basis of $1,000 and a book value of $10,000, with a view to taking advantage of the fact that the equipment has only one year remaining on its cost recovery schedule although its remaining economic life is significantly longer. At the time of contribution, C has a built-in gain of $9,000 and the equipment is section 704(c) property. D contributes $10,000 of cash, which CD uses to buy securities. D has substantial net operating loss carryforwards that D anticipates will otherwise expire unused. Under § 1.704–1(b)(2)(iv)(g)(3), the partnership must allocate the $10,000 of book depreciation to the partners in the first year of the partnership. Thus, there is $10,000 of book depreciation and $1,000 of tax depreciation in the partnership's first year. CD sells the equipment during the second year for $10,000 and recognizes a $10,000 gain ($10,000, the amount realized, less the adjusted tax basis of $0).

(ii) Unreasonable use of method—(A) At the beginning of the second year, both the book value and adjusted tax basis of the equipment are $0. Therefore, there is no remaining built-in gain. The $10,000 gain on the sale of the equipment in the second year is allocated $5,000 each to C and D. The interaction of the partnership's one-year write-off of the entire book value of the equipment and the use of the traditional method results in a shift of $4,000 of the precontribution gain in the equipment from C to D (D's $5,000 share of CD's $10,000 gain, less the $1,000 tax depreciation deduction previously allocated to D).

(B) The traditional method is not reasonable under paragraph (a)(10) of this section because the contribution of property is made, and the traditional method is used, with a view to shifting a significant amount of taxable income to a partner with a low marginal tax rate and away from a partner with a high marginal tax rate.

(C) Under these facts, if the partnership agreement in effect for the year of contribution had provided that tax gain from the sale of the property (if any) would always be allocated first to C to offset the effect of the ceiling rule limitation, the allocation method would not violate the anti-abuse rule of paragraph (a)(10) of this section. See paragraph (c)(3) of this section. Under other facts, (for example, if the partnership holds multiple section 704(c) properties and either uses multiple allocation methods or uses a single allocation method where one or more of the properties are subject to the ceiling rule) the allocation to C may not be reasonable.

(c) Traditional method with curative allocation—(1) In general. To correct distortions created by the ceiling rule, a partnership using the traditional method under paragraph (b) of this section may make reasonable curative allocations to reduce or eliminate disparities between book and tax items of noncontributing partners. A curative allocation is an allocation of income, gain, loss, or deduction for tax purposes that differs from the partnership's allocation of the corresponding book item. For example, if a noncontributing partner is allocated less tax depreciation than book depreciation with respect to an item of section 704(c) property, the partnership may make a curative allocation to that partner of tax depreciation from another item of partnership property to make up the difference, notwithstanding that the corresponding book depreciation is allocated to the contributing partner. A partnership may limit its curative allocations to allocations of one or more particular tax items (e.g., only depreciation from a specific property or properties) even if the allocation of those available items does not offset fully the effect of the ceiling rule.

(2) Consistency. A partnership must be consistent in its application of curative allocations with respect to each item of section 704(c) property from year to year.

(3) Reasonable curative allocations—(i) Amount. A curative allocation is not reasonable to the extent it exceeds the amount necessary to offset the effect of the ceiling rule for the current taxable year or, in the case of a curative allocation upon disposition of the property, for prior taxable years.

(ii) Timing. The period of time over which the curative allocations are made is a factor in determining whether the allocations are reasonable. Notwithstanding paragraph (c)(3)(i) of this section, a partnership may make curative allocations in a taxable year to offset the effect of the ceiling rule for a prior taxable year if those allocations are made over a reasonable period of time, such as over the property's economic life, and are provided for under the partnership agreement in effect for the year of contribution. See paragraph (c)(4) Example 3(ii)(C) of this section.

(iii) Type—(A) In general. To be reasonable, a curative allocation of income, gain, loss, or deduction must be expected to have substantially the same effect on each partner's tax liability as the tax item limited by the ceiling rule. The expectation must exist at the time the section 704(c) property is obligated to be (or is) contributed to the partnership and the allocation with respect to that property becomes part of the partnership agreement. However, the expectation is tested at the time the allocation with respect to that property is actually made if the partnership agreement is not sufficiently specific as to the precise manner in which allocations are to be made with respect to that property. Under this paragraph (c), if the item limited by the ceiling rule is loss from the sale of property, a curative allocation of gain must be expected to have substantially the same effect as would an allocation to that partner of gain with respect to the sale of the property. If the item limited by the ceiling rule is depreciation or other cost recovery, a curative allocation of income to the contributing partner must be expected to have substantially the same effect as would an allocation to that partner of partnership income with respect to the contributed property. For example, if depreciation deductions with respect to leased equipment contributed by a tax-exempt partner are limited by the ceiling rule, a curative allocation of dividend or interest income to that partner generally is not reasonable, although a curative allocation of depreciation deductions from other leased equipment to the noncontributing partner is reasonable. Similarly, under this rule, if depreciation deductions apportioned to foreign source income in a particular statutory grouping under section 904(d) are limited by the ceiling rule, a curative allocation of income from another statutory grouping to the contributing partner generally is not reasonable, although a curative allocation of income from the same statutory grouping and of the same character is reasonable.

(B) Exception for allocation from disposition of contributed property. If cost recovery has been limited by the ceiling rule, the general limitation on character does not apply to income from the disposition of contributed property subject to the ceiling rule, but only if properly provided for in the partnership agreement in effect for the year of contribution or revaluation. For example, if allocations of depreciation deductions to a noncontributing partner have been limited by the ceiling rule, a curative allocation to the contributing partner of gain from the sale of that property, if properly provided for in the partnership agreement, is reasonable for purposes of paragraph (c)(3)(iii)(A) of this section even if not of the same character.

(4) Examples. The following examples illustrate the principles of this paragraph (c).

Example 1. Reasonable and unreasonable curative allocations—(i) Facts. E and F form partnership EF and agree that each will be allocated a 50 percent share of all partnership items and that EF will make allocations under section 704(c) using the traditional method with curative allocations under paragraph (c) of this section. E contributes equipment with an adjusted tax basis of $4,000 and a book value of $10,000. The equipment has 10 years remaining on its cost recovery schedule and is depreciable using the straight-line method. At the time of contribution, E has a built-in gain of $6,000, and therefore, the equipment is section 704(c) property. F contributes $10,000 of cash, which EF uses to buy inventory for resale. In EF's first year, the revenue generated by the equipment equals EF's operating expenses. The equipment generates $1,000 of book depreciation and $400 of tax depreciation for each of 10 years. At the end of the first year EF sells all the inventory for $10,700, recognizing $700 of income. The partners anticipate that the inventory income will have substantially the same effect on their tax liabilities as income from E's contributed equipment. Under the traditional method of paragraph (b) of this section, E and F would each be allocated $350 of income from the sale of inventory for book and tax purposes and $500 of depreciation for book purposes. The $400 of tax depreciation would all be allocated to F. Thus, at the end of the first year, E and F's book and tax capital accounts would be as follows:

E		F		
Book	Tax	Book	Tax	
$10,000	$4,000	$10,000	$10,000	Initial contribution.
<500>	<0>	<500>	<400>	Depreciation.
350	350	350	350	Sales income.
9,850	4,350	9,850	9,950	

(ii) Reasonable curative allocation. Because the ceiling rule would cause a disparity of $100 between F's book and tax capital accounts, EF may properly allocate to E under paragraph (c) of this section an additional $100 of income from the sale of inventory for tax purposes. This allocation results in capital accounts at the end of EF's first year as follows:

E		F		
Book	Tax	Book	Tax	
$10,000	$4,000	$10,000	$10,000	Initial contribution.
<500>	<0>	<500>	<400>	Depreciation.
350	450	350	250	Sales income.
9,850	4,450	9,850	9,850	

(iii) Unreasonable curative allocation. (A) The facts are the same as in paragraphs (i) and (ii) of this Example 1, except that E and F choose to allocate all the income from the sale of the inventory to E for tax purposes, although they share it equally for book purposes. This allocation results in capital accounts at the end of EF's first year as follows:

E		F		
Book	Tax	Book	Tax	
$10,000	$4,000	$10,000	$10,000	Initial contribution.
<500>	<0>	<500>	<400>	Depreciation.
350	700	350	0	Sales income.
9,850	4,700	9,850	9,600	

(B) This curative allocation is not reasonable under paragraph (c)(3)(i) of this section because the allocation exceeds the amount necessary to offset the disparity caused by the ceiling rule.

Example 2. Curative allocations limited to depreciation—(i) Facts. G and H form partnership GH and agree that each will be allocated a 50 percent share of all partnership items and that GH will make allocations under section 704(c) using the traditional method with curative allocations under paragraph (c) of this section, but only to the extent that the partnership has sufficient tax depreciation deductions. G contributes property G1, with an adjusted tax basis of $3,000 and a fair market value of $10,000, and H contributes property H1, with an adjusted tax basis of $6,000 and a fair market value of $10,000. Both properties have 5 years remaining on their cost recovery schedules and are depreciable using the straight-line method. At the time of contribution, G1 has a built-in gain of $7,000 and H1 has a built-in gain of $4,000, and therefore, both properties are section 704(c) property. G1 generates $600 of tax depreciation and $2,000 of book depreciation for each of five years. H1 generates $1,200 of tax depreciation and $2,000 of book depreciation for each of 5 years. In addition, the properties each generate $500 of operating income annually. G and H are each allocated $1,000 of book depreciation for each property. Under the traditional method of paragraph (b) of this section, G would be allocated $0 of tax depreciation for G1 and $1,000 for H1, and H would be allocated $600 of tax depreciation for G1 and $200 for H1. Thus, at the end of the first year, G and H's book and tax capital accounts would be as follows:

G		H		
Book	Tax	Book	Tax	
$10,000	$3,000	$10,000	$6,000	Initial contribution.
<1,000>	<0>	<1,000>	<600>	G1 depreciation.
<1,000>	<1,000>	<1,000>	<200>	H1 depreciation.
500	500	500	500	Operating income.
8,500	2,500	8,500	5,700	

(ii) Curative allocations. Under the traditional method, G is allocated more depreciation deductions than H, even though H contributed property with a smaller disparity reflected on GH's book and tax capital accounts.

GH makes curative allocations to H of an additional $400 of tax depreciation each year, which reduces the disparities between G and H's book and tax capital accounts ratably each year. These allocations are reasonable provided the allocations meet the other requirements of this section. As a result of their agreement, at the end of the first year, G and H's capital accounts are as follows:

G		H		
Book	Tax	Book	Tax	
$10,000	$3,000	$10,000	$6,000	Initial contribution.
<1,000>	<0>	<1,000>	<600>	G1 depreciation.
<1,000>	<600>	<1,000>	<600>	H1 depreciation.
500	500	500	500	Operating income.
8,500	2,900	8,500	5,300	

Example 3. Unreasonable use of curative allocations—(i) Facts. J and K form partnership JK and agree that each will receive a 50 percent share of all partnership items and that JK will make allocations under section 704(c) using the traditional method with curative allocations under paragraph (c) of this section. J contributes equipment with an adjusted tax basis of $1,000 and a book value of $10,000, with a view to taking advantage of the fact that the equipment has only one year remaining on its cost recovery schedule although it has an estimated remaining economic life of 10 years. J has substantial net operating loss carryforwards that J anticipates will otherwise expire unused. At the time of contribution, J has a built-in gain of $9,000, and therefore, the equipment is section 704(c) property. K contributes $10,000 of cash, which JK uses to buy inventory for resale. In JK's first year, the revenues generated by the equipment exactly equal JK's operating expenses. Under § 1.704–1(b)(2)(iv)(g)(3), the partnership must allocate the $10,000 of book depreciation to the partners in the first year of the partnership. Thus, there is $10,000 of book depreciation and $1,000 of tax depreciation in the partnership's first year. In addition, at the end of the first year JK sells all of the inventory for $18,000, recognizing $8,000 of income. The partners anticipate that the inventory income will have substantially the same effect on their tax liabilities as income from J's contributed equipment. Under the traditional method of paragraph (b) of this section, J and K's book and tax capital accounts at the end of the first year would be as follows:

J		K		
Book	Tax	Book	Tax	
$10,000	$1,000	$10,000	$10,000	Initial contribution.
<5,000>	<0>	<5,000>	<1,000>	Depreciation.
4,000	4,000	4,000	4,000	Sales income.
9,000	5,000	9,000	13,000	

(ii) Unreasonable use of method. (A) The use of curative allocations under these facts to offset immediately the full effect of the ceiling rule would result in the following book and tax capital accounts at the end of JK's first year:

J		K		
Book	Tax	Book	Tax	
$10,000	$1,000	$10,000	$10,000	Initial contribution.
<5,000>	<0>	<5,000>	<1,000>	Depreciation.
4,000	8,000	4,000	0	Sales income.
9,000	9,000	9,000	9,000	

(B) This curative allocation is not reasonable under paragraph (a)(10) of this section because the contribution of property is made and the curative allocation method is used with a view to shifting a significant amount of partnership taxable income to a partner with a low marginal tax rate and away from a partner with a high marginal tax rate, within a period of time significantly shorter than the economic life of the property.

(C) The property has only one year remaining on its cost recovery schedule even though its economic life is considerably longer. Under these facts, if the partnership agreement had provided for curative allocations over a reasonable period of time, such as over the property's economic life, rather than over its remaining cost recovery period, the allocations would have been reasonable. See paragraph (c)(3)(ii) of this section. Thus, in this example, JK would make a curative allocation of $400 of sales income to J in the partnership's first year (10 percent of $4,000). J and K's book and tax capital accounts at the end of the first year would be as follows:

J		K		
Book	Tax	Book	Tax	
$10,000	$1,000	$10,000	$10,000	Initial contribution.
<5,000>	<0>	<5,000>	<1,000>	Depreciation.
4,000	4,400	4,000	3,600	Sales income.
9,000	5,400	9,000	12,600	

(d) Remedial allocation method—(1) In general. A partnership may adopt the remedial allocation method described in this paragraph to eliminate distortions caused by the ceiling rule. A partnership adopting the remedial allocation method eliminates those distortions by creating remedial items and allocating those items to its partners. Under the remedial allocation method, the partnership first determines the amount of book items under paragraph (d)(2) of this section and the partners' distributive shares of these items under section 704(b). The partnership then allocates the corresponding tax items recognized by the partnership, if any, using the traditional method described in paragraph (b)(1) of this section. If the ceiling rule (as defined in paragraph (b)(1) of this section) causes the book allocation of an item to a noncontributing partner to differ from the tax allocation of the same item to the noncontributing partner, the partnership creates a remedial item of income, gain, loss, or deduction equal to the full amount of the difference and allocates it to the noncontributing partner. The partnership simultaneously creates an offsetting remedial item in an identical amount and allocates it to the contributing partner.

(2) Determining the amount of book items. Under the remedial allocation method, a partnership determines the amount of book items attributable to contributed property in the following manner rather than under the rules of § 1.704–

1(b)(2)(iv)(g)(3). The portion of the partnership's book basis in the property equal to the adjusted tax basis in the property at the time of contribution is recovered in the same manner as the adjusted tax basis in the property is recovered (generally, over the property's remaining recovery period under section 168(i)(7) or other applicable Internal Revenue Code section). The remainder of the partnership's book basis in the property (the amount by which book basis exceeds adjusted tax basis) is recovered using any recovery period and depreciation (or other cost recovery) method (including first-year conventions) available to the partnership for newly purchased property (of the same type as the contributed property) that is placed in service at the time of contribution.

(3) Type. Remedial allocations of income, gain, loss, or deduction to the noncontributing partner have the same tax attributes as the tax item limited by the ceiling rule. The tax attributes of offsetting remedial allocations of income, gain, loss, or deduction to the contributing partner are determined by reference to the item limited by the ceiling rule. Thus, for example, if the ceiling rule limited item is loss from the sale of contributed property, the offsetting remedial allocation to the contributing partner must be gain from the sale of that property. Conversely, if the ceiling rule limited item is gain from the sale of contributed property, the offsetting remedial allocation to the contributing partner must be loss from the sale of that property. If the ceiling rule limited item is depreciation or other cost recovery from the contributed property, the offsetting remedial allocation to the contributing partner must be income of the type produced (directly or indirectly) by that property. Any partner level tax attributes are determined at the partner level. For example, if the ceiling rule limited item is depreciation from property used in a rental activity, the remedial allocation to the noncontributing partner is depreciation from property used in a rental activity and the offsetting remedial allocation to the contributing partner is ordinary income from that rental activity. Each partner then applies section 469 to the allocations as appropriate.

(4) Effect of remedial items—(i) Effect on partnership. Remedial items do not affect the partnership's computation of its taxable income under section 703 and do not affect the partnership's adjusted tax basis in partnership property.

(ii) Effect on partners. Remedial items are notional tax items created by the partnership solely for tax purposes and do not affect the partners' book capital accounts. Remedial items have the same effect as actual tax items on a partner's tax liability and on the partner's adjusted tax basis in the partnership interest.

(5) Limitations on use of methods involving remedial allocations—(i) Limitation on taxpayers. In the absence of published guidance, the remedial allocation method described in this paragraph (d) is the only reasonable section 704(c) method permitting the creation of notional tax items.

(ii) Limitation on Internal Revenue Service. In exercising its authority under paragraph (a)(10) of this section to make adjustments if a partnership's allocation method is not reasonable, the Internal Revenue Service will not require a partnership to use the remedial allocation method described in this paragraph (d) or any other method involving the creation of notional tax items.

(6) Adjustments to application of method. The Commissioner may, by published guidance, prescribe adjustments to the remedial allocation method under this paragraph (d) as necessary or appropriate. This guidance may, for example, prescribe adjustments to the remedial allocation method to prevent the duplication or omission of items of income or deduction or to reflect more clearly the partners' income or the income of a transferee of a partner.

(7) Examples. The following examples illustrate the principles of this paragraph (d).

Example 1. Remedial allocation method—(i) Facts. On January 1, L and M form partnership LM and agree that each will be allocated a 50 percent share of all partnership items. The partnership agreement provides that LM will make allocations under section 704(c) using the remedial allocation method under this paragraph (d) and that the straight-line method will be used to recover excess book basis. L contributes depreciable property with an adjusted tax basis of $4,000 and a fair market value of $10,000. The property is depreciated using the straight-line method with a 10–year recovery period and has 4 years remaining on its recovery period. M contributes $10,000, which the partnership uses to purchase land. Except for the depreciation deductions, LM's expenses equal its income in each year of the 10 years commencing with the year the partnership is formed.

(ii) Years 1 through 4. Under the remedial allocation method of this paragraph (d), LM has book depreciation for each of its first 4 years of $1,600 [$1,000 ($4,000 adjusted tax basis divided by the 4–year remaining recovery period) plus $600 ($6,000 excess of book value over tax basis, divided by the new 10–year recovery period)]. (For the purpose of simplifying the example, the partnership's book depreciation is determined without regard to any first-year depreciation conventions.) Under the partnership agreement, L and M are each allocated 50 percent ($800) of the book depreciation. M is allocated $800 of tax depreciation and L is allocated the remaining $200 of tax depreciation ($1,000 − $800). See paragraph (d)(1) of this section. No remedial allocations are made because the ceiling rule does not result in a book allocation of depreciation to M different from the tax allocation. The allocations result in capital accounts at the end of LM's first 4 years as follows:

L		M		
Book	Tax	Book	Tax	
$10,000	$4,000	$10,000	$10,000	Initial contribution
<3,200>	<800>	<3,200>	<3,200>	Depreciation
$ 6,800	$3,200	$ 6,800	$ 6,800	

(iii) Subsequent years. (A) For each of years 5 through 10, LM has $600 of book depreciation ($6,000 excess of initial book value over adjusted tax basis divided by the 10–year recovery period that commenced in year 1), but no tax depreciation. Under the partnership agreement, the $600 of book depreciation is allocated equally to L and M. Because of the application of the ceiling rule in year 5, M would be allocated $300 of book depreciation, but no tax depreciation. Thus, at the end of LM's fifth year L's and M's book and tax capital accounts would be as follows:

L		M		
Book	Tax	Book	Tax	
$6,800	$3,200	$6,800	$6,800	End of year 4
<300>		<300>		Depreciation
$6,500	$3,200	$6,500	$6,800	

(B) Because the ceiling rule would cause an annual disparity of $300 between M's allocations of book and tax depreciation, LM must make remedial allocations of $300 of tax depreciation deductions to M under the remedial allocation method for each of years 5 through 10. LM must also make an offsetting remedial allocation to L of $300 of taxable income, which must be of the same type as income produced by the property. At the end of year 5, LM's capital accounts are as follows:

L		M		
Book	Tax	Book	Tax	
$6,800	$3,200	$6,800	$6,800	End of year 4
<300>		<300>		Depreciation
	300		<300>	Remedial allocations
$6,500	$3,500	$6,500	$6,500	

(C) At the end of year 10, LM's capital accounts are as follows:

L		M		
Book	Tax	Book	Tax	
$6,500	$3,500	$6,500	$6,500	End of year 5
<1,500>		<1,500>		Depreciation
	1,500		<1,500>	Remedial allocations
$5,000	$5,000	$5,000	$5,000	

Example 2. Remedial allocations on sale—(i) Facts. N and P form partnership NP and agree that each will be allocated a 50 percent share of all partnership items. The partnership agreement provides that NP will make allocations under section 704(c) using the remedial allocation method under this paragraph (d). N contributes Blackacre (land) with an adjusted tax basis of $4,000 and a fair market value of $10,000. Because N has a built-in gain of $6,000, Blackacre is section 704(c) property. P contributes Whiteacre (land) with an adjusted tax basis and fair market value of $10,000. At the end of NP's first year, NP sells Blackacre to Q for $9,000 and recognizes a capital gain of $5,000 ($9,000 amount realized less $4,000 adjusted tax basis) and a book loss of $1,000 ($9,000 amount realized less $10,000 book basis). NP has no other items of income, gain, loss, or deduction. If the ceiling rule were applied, N would be allocated the entire $5,000 of tax gain and N and P would each be allocated $500 of book loss. Thus, at the end of NP's first year N's and P's book and tax capital accounts would be as follows:

N		P		
Book	Tax	Book	Tax	
$10,000	$4,000	$10,000	$10,000	Initial contribution
<500>	5,000	<500>		Sale of Blackacre
$ 9,500	$9,000	$ 9,500	$10,000	

(ii) Remedial allocation. Because the ceiling rule would cause a disparity of $500 between P's allocation of book and tax loss, NP must make a remedial allocation of $500 of capital loss to P and an offsetting remedial allocation to N of an additional $500 of capital gain. These allocations result in capital accounts at the end of NP's first year as follows:

N		P		
Book	Tax	Book	Tax	
$10,000	$4,000	$10,000	$10,000	Initial contribution
<500>	5,000	<500>		Sale of Blackacre
	500		<500>	Remedial allocations
$ 9,500	$9,500	$ 9,500	$ 9,500	

Example 3. Remedial allocation where built-in gain property sold for book and tax loss—(i) Facts. The facts are the same as in Example 2, except that at the end of NP's first year, NP sells Blackacre to Q for $3,000 and recognizes a capital loss of $1,000 ($3,000 amount realized less $4,000 adjusted tax basis) and a book loss of $7,000 ($3,000 amount realized less $10,000 book basis). If the ceiling rule were applied, P would be allocated the entire $1,000 of tax loss and N and P would each be allocated $3,500 of book loss. Thus, at the end of NP's first year, N's and P's book and tax capital accounts would be as follows:

N		P		
Book	Tax	Book	Tax	
$10,000	$4,000	$10,000	$10,000	Initial contribution
<3,500>	0	<3,500>	<1,000>	Sale of Blackacre
$ 6,500	$4,000	$ 6,500	$ 9,000	

(ii) Remedial allocation. Because the ceiling rule would cause a disparity of $2,500 between P's allocation of book and tax loss on the sale of Blackacre, NP must make a remedial allocation of $2,500 of capital loss to P and an offsetting remedial allocation to N of $2,500 of capital gain. These allocations result in capital accounts at the end of NP's first year as follows:

N		P		
Book	Tax	Book	Tax	
$10,000	$4,000	$10,000	$10,000	Initial contribution
<3,500>	0	<3,500>	<1,000>	Sale of Blackacre
	2,500		<2,500>	Remedial allocations
$ 6,500	$6,500	$ 6,500	$ 6,500	

(e) Exceptions and special rules—(1) Small disparities—(i) General rule. If a partner contributes one or more items of property to a partnership within a single taxable year of the partnership, and the disparity between the book value of the property and the contributing partner's adjusted tax basis in the property is a small disparity, the partnership may—

(A) Use a reasonable section 704(c) method;

(B) Disregard the application of section 704(c) to the property; or

(C) Defer the application of section 704(c) to the property until the disposition of the property.

(ii) Definition of small disparity. A disparity between book value and adjusted tax basis is a small disparity if the book value of all properties contributed by one partner during the partnership taxable year does not differ from the adjusted tax basis by more than 15 percent of the adjusted tax basis, and the total gross disparity does not exceed $20,000.

(2) Aggregation. Each of the following types of property may be aggregated for purposes of making allocations under section 704(c) and this section if contributed by one partner during the partnership taxable year.

(i) Depreciable property. All property, other than real property, that is included in the same general asset account of the contributing partner and the partnership under section 168.

(ii) Zero-basis property. All property with a basis equal to zero, other than real property.

(iii) Inventory. For partnerships that do not use a specific identification method of accounting, each item of inventory, other than qualified financial assets (as defined in paragraph (e)(3)(ii) of this section).

(3) Special aggregation rule for securities partnerships—(1) General rule. For purposes of making reverse section 704(c) allocations, a securities partnership may aggregate gains and losses from qualified financial assets using any reasonable approach that is consistent with the purpose of section 704(c). Notwithstanding paragraphs (a)(2) and (a)(6)(i) of this section, once a partnership adopts an aggregate approach, that partnership must apply the same aggregate approach to all of its qualified financial assets for all taxable years in which the partnership qualifies as a securities partnership. Paragraphs (e)(3)(iv) and (e)(3)(v) of this section describe approaches for aggregating reverse section 704(c) gains and losses that are generally reasonable. Other approaches may be reasonable in appropriate circumstances. See, however, paragraph (a)(10) of this section, which describes the circumstances under which section 704(c) methods, including the aggregate approaches described in this paragraph (e)(3), are not reasonable. A partnership using an aggregate approach must separately account for any built-in gain or loss from contributed property.

(ii) Qualified financial assets—(A) In general. A qualified financial asset is any personal property (including stock) that is actively traded. Actively traded means actively traded as defined in § 1.1092(d)–1 (defining actively traded property for purposes of the straddle rules).

(B) Management companies. For a management company, qualified financial assets also include the following, even if not actively traded: shares of stock in a corporation; notes, bonds, debentures, or other evidences of indebtedness; interest rate, currency, or equity national principal contracts; evidences of an interest in, or derivative financial instruments in, any security, currency, or commodity, including any option, forward or futures contract, or short position; or any similar financial instrument.

(C) Partnership interests. An interest in a partnership is not a qualified financial asset for purposes of this paragraph (e)(3)(ii). However, for purposes of this paragraph (e)(3), a partnership (upper-tier partnership) that holds an interest in a securities partnership (lower-tier partnership) must take into account the lower-tier partnership's assets and qualified financial assets as follows:

(1) In determining whether the upper-tier partnership qualifies as an investment partnership, the upper-tier partnership must treat its proportionate share of the lower-tier securities partnership's assets as assets of the upper-tier partnership; and

(2) If the upper-tier partnership adopts an aggregate approach under this paragraph (e)(3), the upper-tier partnership must aggregate the gains and losses from its directly held qualified financial assets with its distributive share of the gains and losses from the qualified financial assets of the lower-tier securities partnership.

(iii) Securities partnership—(A) In general. A partnership is a securities partnership if the partnership is either a management company or an investment partnership, and the partnership makes all of its book allocations in proportion to the partners' relative book capital accounts (except for reasonable special allocations to a partner that provides management services or investment advisory services to the partnership).

(B) Definitions—(1) Management company. A partnership is a management company if it is registered with the Securities and Exchange Commission as a management company under the Investment Company Act of 1940, as amended (15 U.S.C. 80a).

(2) Investment partnership. A partnership is an investment partnership if:

(i) On the date of each capital account restatement, the partnership holds qualified financial assets that constitute at least 90 percent of the fair market value of the partnership's non-cash assets; and

(ii) The partnership reasonably expects, as of the end of the first taxable year in which the partnership adopts an aggregate approach under this paragraph (e)(3), to make revaluations at least annually.

(iv) Partial netting approach. This paragraph (e)(3)(iv) describes the partial netting approach of making reverse section 704(c) allocations. See Example 1 of paragraph (e)(3)(ix) of this section for an illustration of the partial netting approach. To use the partial netting approach, the partnership must establish appropriate accounts for each partner for the purpose of taking into account each partner's share of the book gains and losses and determining each partner's share of the tax gains and losses. Under the partial netting approach, on the date of each capital account restatement, the partnership:

(A) Nets its book gains and book losses from qualified financial assets since the last capital account restatement and allocates the net amount to its partners;

(B) Separately aggregates all tax gains and all tax losses from qualified financial assets since the last capital account restatement; and

(C) Separately allocates the aggregate tax gain and aggregate tax loss to the partners in a manner that reduces the disparity between the book capital account balances and the tax capital account balances (book-tax disparities) of the individual partners.

(v) Full netting approach. This paragraph (e)(3)(v) describes the full netting approach of making reverse section 704(c) allocations on an aggregate basis. See Example 2 of paragraph (e)(3)(ix) of this section for an illustration of the full netting approach. To use the full netting approach, the partnership must establish appropriate accounts for each partner for the purpose of taking into account each partner's share of the book gains and losses and determining each partner's share of the tax gains and losses. Under the full netting approach, on the date of each capital account restatement, the partnership:

(A) Nets its book gains and book losses from qualified financial assets since the last capital account restatement and allocates the net amount to its partners;

(B) Nets tax gains and tax losses from qualified financial assets since the last capital account restatement; and

(C) Allocates the net tax gain (or net tax loss) to the partners in a manner that reduces the book-tax disparities of the individual partners.

(vi) Type of tax gain or loss. The character and other tax attributes of gain or loss allocated to the partners under this paragraph (e)(3) must:

(A) Preserve the tax attributes of each item of gain or loss realized by the partnership;

(B) Be determined under an approach that is consistently applied; and

(C) Not be determined with a view to reducing substantially the present value of the partners' aggregate tax liability.

(vii) Disqualified securities partnerships. A securities partnership that adopts an aggregate approach under this paragraph (e)(3) and subsequently fails to qualify as a securities partnership must make reverse section 704(c) allocations on an asset-by-asset basis after the date of disqualification. The partnership, however, is not required to disaggregate the book gain or book loss from qualified asset revaluations before the date of disqualification when making reverse section 704(c) allocations on or after the date of disqualification.

(viii) Transitional rule for qualified financial assets revalued after effective date. A securities partnership revaluing its qualified financial assets pursuant to § 1.704–1(b)(2)(iv)(f) on or after the effective date of this section may use any reasonable approach to coordinate with revaluations that occurred prior to the effective date of this section.

(ix) Examples. The following examples illustrate the principles of this paragraph (e)(3).

Example 1. Operation of the partial netting approach—(i) Facts. Two regulated investment companies, X and Y, each contribute $150,000 in cash to form PRS, a partnership that registers as a management company. The partnership agreement provides that book items will be allocated in accordance with the partners' relative book capital accounts, that book capital accounts will be adjusted to reflect daily revaluations of property pursuant to § 1.704–1(b)(2)(iv)(f)(5)(iii), and that reverse section 704(c) allocations will be made using the partial netting approach described in paragraph (e)(3)(iv) of this section. X and Y each have an initial book capital account of $150,000. In addition, the partnership establishes for each of X and Y a revaluation account with a beginning balance of $0. On Day 1, PRS buys Stock 1, Stock 2, and Stock 3 for $100,000 each. On Day 2, Stock 1 increases in value from $100,000 to $102,000, Stock 2 increases in value from $100,000 to $105,000, and Stock 3 declines in value from $100,000 to $98,000. At the end of Day 2, Z, a regulated investment company, joins PRS by contributing $152,500 in cash for a one-third interest in the partnership [$152,500 divided by $300,000 (initial values of stock) + $5,000 (net gain at end of Day 2) + $152,500]. PRS uses this cash to purchase Stock 4. PRS establishes a revaluation account for Z with a $0 beginning balance. As of the close of Day 3, Stock 1 increases in value from $102,000 to $105,000, and Stocks 2, 3, and 4 decrease in value from $105,000 to $102,000, from $98,000 to $96,000, and from $152,500 to $151,500, respectively. At the end of Day 3, PRS sells Stocks 2 and 3.

(ii) Book allocations—Day 2. At the end of Day 2, PRS revalues the partnership's qualified financial assets and increases X's and Y's book capital accounts by each partner's 50 percent share of the $5,000 ($2,000 + $5,000 − $2,000) net increase in the value of the partnership's assets during Day 2. PRS increases X's and Y's respective revaluation account balances by $2,500 each to reflect the amount by which each partner's book capital account increased on Day 2. Z's capital account is not affected because Z did not join PRS until the end of Day 2. At the beginning of Day 3, the partnership's accounts are as follows:

Stock 1	*Stock 2*	*Stock 3*	*Stock 4*	
$100,000	$100,000	$100,000	--	Opening Balance
2,000	5,000	(2,000)	--	Day 2 Adjustment
$102,000	$105,000	$ 98,000	$152,500	Total

X

Book	*Tax*	*Revaluation Account*	
$150,000	$150,000	$ 0	Opening Balance
2,500	0	2,500	Day 2 Adjustment
$152,500	$150,000	$ 2,500	Closing Balance

Y

Book	*Tax*	*Revaluation Account*	
$150,000	$150,000	$ 0	Opening Balance
2,500	0	2,500	Day 2 Adjustment
$152,500	$150,000	$ 2,500	Closing Balance

Z

Book	*Tax*	*Revaluation Account*	
--	--	--	Opening Balance
--	--	--	Day 2 Adjustment
$152,500	$152,500	$ 0	Closing Balance

(iii) Book and tax allocations—Day 3. At the end of Day 3, PRS decreases the book capital accounts of X, Y, and Z by $1,000 to reflect each partner's share of the $3,000 ($3,000–$3,000–$2,000–$1,000) net decrease in the value of the partnership's qualified financial assets. PRS also reduces each partner's revaluation account balance by $1,000. Accordingly, X's and Y's revaluation account balances are reduced to $1,500 each and Z's revaluation account balance is ($1,000). PRS then separately allocates the tax gain from the sale of Stock 2 and the tax loss from the sale of Stock 3. The $2,000 of tax gain recognized on the sale of Stock 2 ($102,000–$100,000) is allocated among the partners with positive revaluation account balances in accordance with the relative balances of those revaluation accounts. X's and Y's revaluation accounts have equal positive balances; thus, PRS allocates $1,000 of the gain from the sale of Stock 2 to X and $1,000 of that gain to Y. PRS allocates none of the gain from the sale to Z because

Z's revaluation account balance is negative. The $4,000 of tax loss recognized from the sale of Stock 3 ($96,000–$100,000) is allocated first to the partners with negative revaluation account balances to the extent of those balances. Because Z is the only partner with a negative revaluation account balance, the tax loss is allocated first to Z to the extent of Z's ($1,000) balance. The remaining $3,000 of tax loss is allocated among the partners in accordance with their distributive shares of the loss. Accordingly, PRS allocates $1,000 of tax loss from the sale of Stock 3 to each of X and Y. PRS also allocates an additional $1,000 of the tax loss to Z, so that Z's total share of the tax loss from the sale of Stock 3 is $2,000. PRS then reduces each partner's revaluation account balance by the amount of any tax gain allocated to that partner and increase each partner's revaluation account balance by the amount of any tax loss allocated to that partner. At the beginning of Day 4 the partnership's accounts are as follows:

Stock 1	*Stock 2*	*Stock 3*	*Stock 4*	
$100,000	$100,000	$100,000	$152,500	Opening Balance
2,000	5,000	(2,000)	--	Day 2 Adjustment
3,000	(3,000)	(2,000)	(1,000)	Day 3 Adjustment
$105,000	$102,000	$ 96,000	$151,500	Total

X and Y

Book	*Tax*	*Revaluation Account*	
$150,000	$150,000	$ 0	Opening Balance
2,500	0	2,500	Day 2 Adjustment
(1,000)	0	(1,000)	Day 3 Adjustment
$151,500	$150,000	$ 1,500	Total
0	1,000	(1,000)	Gain from Stock 2
0	(1,000)	1,000	Loss from Stock 3
$151,500	$150,000	$ 1,500	Closing Balance

Z

Book	*Tax*	*Revaluation Account*	
$152,500	$152,500	$ 0	Opening Balance
(1,000)	0	(1,000)	Day 3 Adjustment
$151,500	$152,500	($ 1,000)	Total
0	0	0	Gain from Stock 2
0	(2,000)	2,000	Loss from Stock 3
$151,500	$150,500	$ 1,000	Closing Balance

Example 2. Operation of the full netting approach—(i) Facts. The facts are the same as in Example 1, except that the partnership agreement provides that PRS will make reverse section 704(c) allocations using the full netting approach described in paragraph (e)(3)(v) of this section.

(ii) Book allocations—Days 2 and 3. PRS allocates its book gains and losses in the manner described in paragraphs (ii) and (iii) of Example 1 (the partial netting approach). Thus, at the end of Day 2, PRS increases the book capital accounts of X and Y by $2,500 to reflect the appreciation in the partnership's assets from the close of Day 1 to the close of Day 2 and records that increase in the revaluation account created for each partner. At the end of Day 3, PRS decreases the book capital accounts of X, Y, and Z by $1,000 to reflect each partner's share of the decline in value of the partnership's assets from Day 2 to Day 3 and reduces each partner's revaluation account by a corresponding amount.

(iii) Tax allocations—Day 3. After making the book adjustments described in the previous paragraph, PRS allocates its net tax gain (or net tax loss) from its sales of qualified financial assets during Day 3. To do so, PRS first determines its net tax gain (or net tax loss) recognized from its sales of qualified financial assets for the day. There is a $2,000 net tax loss ($2,000 gain from the sale of Stock 2 less $4,000 loss from the sale of Stock 3) on the sale of PRS's qualified financial assets. Because Z is the only partner with a negative revaluation account balance, the partnership's net tax loss is allocated first to Z to the extent of Z's ($1,000) revaluation account balance. The remaining net tax loss is allocated among the partners in accordance with their distributive shares of loss. Thus, PRS allocates $333.33 of the $2,000 net tax loss to each of X and Y. PRS also allocates an additional $333.33 of the net tax loss to Z, so that the total net tax loss allocation to Z is $1,333.33. PRS then increases each partner's revaluation account balance by the amount of net tax loss allocated to that partner. At the beginning of Day 4, the partnership's accounts are as follows:

Stock 1	*Stock 2*	*Stock 3*	*Stock 4*	
$100,000	$100,000	$100,000	$152,500	Opening Balance
2,000	5,000	(2,000)	--	Day 2 Adjustment
3,000	(3,000)	(2,000)	(1,000)	Day 3 Adjustment
$105,000	$102,000	$ 96,000	$151,500	Total

X and Y

Book	*Tax*	*Revaluation Account*	
$150,000	$150,000	$ 0	Opening Balance
2,500	0	2,500	Day 2 Adjustment
(1,000)	0	(1,000)	Day 3 Adjustment
$151,500	$150,000	$ 1,500	Total
0	(333)	333	Net Tax Loss–Stocks 2 & 3
$151,500	$149,667	$ 1,833	Closing Balance

Z

Book	*Tax*	*Revaluation Account*	
$152,500	$152,500	$ 0	Opening Balance
(1,000)	0	(1,000)	Day 3 Adjustment
$151,500	$152,500	($ 1,000)	Total
0	(1,333)	1,333	Net Tax Loss-Stocks 2 & 3
$151,500	$151,167	$ 333	Closing Balance

(4) Aggregation as permitted by the Commissioner. The Commissioner may, by published guidance or by letter ruling, permit:

(i) Aggregation of properties other than those described in paragraphs (e)(2) and (e)(3) of this section;

(ii) Partnerships and partners not described in paragraph (e)(3) of this section to aggregate gain and loss from qualified financial assets; and

(iii) Aggregation of qualified financial assets for purposes of making section 704(c) allocations in the same manner as that described in paragraph (e)(3) of this section.

* * *

[T.D. 8500, 58 FR 67676, Dec. 22, 1993, as amended by T.D. 8585, 59 FR 66724, Dec. 28, 1994; T.D. 8717, 62 FR 25498, May 9, 1997; T.D. 8730, 62 FR 44214, Aug. 20, 1997; T.D. 9137, 69 FR 42558, July 16, 2004; T.D. 9193, 70 FR 14394, Mar. 22, 2005; T.D. 9207, 70 FR 30334, May 26, 2005; T.D. 9193, 70 FR 45531, Aug. 8, 2005; T.D. 9485, 75 FR 32660, June 9, 2010; T.D. 9612, 78 FR 7997, Feb. 5, 2013]

§ 1.704–4 Distribution of contributed property.

[Note: The five-year period in section 704(c)(1)(B) has been extended to seven years. Ed.]

(a) Determination of gain and loss—(1) In general. A partner that contributes section 704(c) property to a partnership must recognize gain or loss under section 704(c)(1)(B) and this section on the distribution of such property to another partner within five years of its contribution to the partnership in an amount equal to the gain or loss that would have been allocated to such partner under section 704(c)(1)(A) and § 1.704–3 if the distributed property had been sold by the partnership to the distributee partner for its fair market value at the time of the distribution. See § 1.704–3(a)(3)(i) for a definition of section 704(c) property.

(2) Transactions to which section 704(c)(1)(B) applies. Section 704(c)(1)(B) and this section apply only to the extent that a distribution by a partnership is a distribution to a partner acting in the capacity of a partner within the meaning of section 731.

(3) Fair market value of property. The fair market value of the distributed section 704(c) property is the price at which the property would change hands between a willing buyer and a willing seller at the time of the distribution, neither being under any compulsion to buy or sell and both having reasonable knowledge of the relevant facts. The fair market value that a partnership assigns to distributed section 704(c) property will be regarded as correct, provided that the value is reasonably agreed to among the partners in an arm's-length negotiation and the partners have sufficiently adverse interests.

(4) Determination of five-year period—(i) General rule. The five-year period specified in paragraph (a)(1) of this section begins on and includes the date of contribution.

(ii) Section 708(b)(1)(B) terminations. A termination of the partnership under section 708(b)(1)(B) does not begin a new five-year period for each partner with respect to the built-in gain and built-in loss property that the terminated partnership is deemed to contribute to the new partnership under § 1.708–1(b)(1)(iv). See § 1.704–

3(a)(3)(ii) for the definitions of built-in gain and built-in loss on section 704(c) property. This paragraph (a)(4)(ii) applies to terminations of partnerships under section 708(b)(1)(B) occurring on or after May 9, 1997; however, this paragraph (a)(4)(ii) may be applied to terminations occurring on or after May 9, 1996, provided that the partnership and its partners apply this paragraph (a)(4)(ii) to the termination in a consistent manner.

(5) Examples. The following examples illustrate the rules of this paragraph (a). Unless otherwise specified, partnership income equals partnership expenses (other than depreciation deductions for contributed property) for each year of the partnership, the fair market value of partnership property does not change, all distributions by the partnership are subject to section 704(c)(1)(B), and all partners are unrelated.

Example 1. Recognition of gain. (i) On January 1, 1995, A, B, and C form partnership ABC as equal partners. A contributes $10,000 cash and Property A, nondepreciable real property with a fair market value of $10,000 and an adjusted tax basis of $4,000. Thus, there is a built-in gain of $6,000 on Property A at the time of contribution. B contributes $10,000 cash and Property B, nondepreciable real property with a fair market value and adjusted tax basis of $10,000. C contributes $20,000 cash.

(ii) On December 31, 1998, Property A and Property B are distributed to C in complete liquidation of C's interest in the partnership.

(iii) A would have recognized $6,000 of gain under section 704(c)(1)(A) and § 1.704–3 on the sale of Property A at the time of the distribution ($10,000 fair market value less $4,000 adjusted tax basis). As a result, A must recognize $6,000 of gain on the distribution of Property A to C. B would not have recognized any gain or loss under section 704(c)(1)(A) and § 1.704–3 on the sale of Property B at the time of distribution because Property B was not section 704(c) property. As a result, B does not recognize any gain or loss on the distribution of Property B.

Example 2. Effect of post-contribution depreciation deductions. (i) On January 1, 1995, A, B, and C form partnership ABC as equal partners. A contributes Property A, depreciable property with a fair market value of $30,000 and an adjusted tax basis of $20,000. Therefore, there is a built-in gain of $10,000 on Property A. B and C each contribute $30,000 cash. ABC uses the traditional method of making section 704(c) allocations described in § 1.704–3(b) with respect to Property A.

(ii) Property A is depreciated using the straight-line method over its remaining 10–year recovery period. The partnership has book depreciation of $3,000 per year (10 percent of the $30,000 book basis), and each partner is allocated $1,000 of book depreciation per year (one-third of the total annual book depreciation of $3,000). The partnership has a tax depreciation deduction of $2,000 per year (10 percent of the $20,000 tax basis in Property A). This $2,000 tax depreciation deduction is allocated equally between B and C, the noncontributing partners with respect to Property A.

(iii) At the end of the third year, the book value of Property A is $21,000 ($30,000 initial book value less $9,000 aggregate book depreciation) and the adjusted tax basis is $14,000 ($20,000 initial tax basis less $6,000 aggregate tax depreciation). A's remaining section 704(c)(1)(A) built-in gain with respect to Property A is $7,000 ($21,000 book value less $14,000 adjusted tax basis).

(iv) On December 31, 1997, Property A is distributed to B in complete liquidation of B's interest in the partnership. If Property A had been sold for its fair market value at the time of the distribution, A would have recognized $7,000 of gain under section 704(c)(1)(A) and § 1.704–3(b). Therefore, A recognizes $7,000 of gain on the distribution of Property A to B.

Example 3. Effect of remedial method. **(i)** On January 1, 1995, A, B, and C form partnership ABC as equal partners. A contributes Property A1, nondepreciable real property with a fair market value of $10,000 and an adjusted tax basis of $5,000, and Property A2, nondepreciable real property with a fair market value and adjusted tax basis of $10,000. B and C each contribute $20,000 cash. ABC uses the remedial method of making section 704(c) allocations described in § 1.704–3(d) with respect to Property A1.

(ii) On December 31, 1998, when the fair market value of Property A1 has decreased to $7,000, Property A1 is distributed to C in a current distribution. If Property A1 had been sold by the partnership at the time of the distribution, ABC would have recognized the $2,000 of remaining built-in gain under section 704(c)(1)(A) on the sale (fair market value of $7,000 less $5,000 adjusted tax basis). All of this gain would have been allocated to A. ABC would also have recognized a book loss of $3,000 ($10,000 original book value less $7,000 current fair market value of the property). Book loss in the amount of $2,000 would have been allocated equally between B and C. Under the remedial method, $2,000 of tax loss would also have been allocated equally to B and C to match their share of the book loss. As a result, $2,000 of gain would also have been allocated to A as an offsetting remedial allocation. A would have recognized $4,000 of total gain under section 704(c)(1)(A) on the sale of Property A1 ($2,000 of section 704(c) recognized gain plus $2,000 remedial gain). Therefore, A recognizes $4,000 of gain on the distribution of Property A1 to C under this section.

(b) Character of gain or loss—(1) General rule. Gain or loss recognized by the contributing partner under section 704(c)(1)(B) and this section has the same character as the gain or loss that would have resulted if the distributed property had been sold by the partnership to the distributee partner at the time of the distribution.

(2) Example. The following example illustrates the rule of this paragraph (b). Unless otherwise specified, partnership income equals partnership expenses (other than depreciation deductions for contributed property) for each year of the partnership, the fair market value of partnership property does not change, all distributions by the partnership are subject to section 704(c)(1)(B), and all partners are unrelated.

Example. Character of gain. **(i)** On January 1, 1995, A and B form partnership AB. A contributes $10,000 and Property A, nondepreciable real property with a fair market value of $10,000 and an adjusted tax basis of $4,000, in exchange for a 25 percent interest in partnership capital and profits. B contributes $60,000 cash for a 75 percent interest in partnership capital and profits.

(ii) On December 31, 1998, Property A is distributed to B in a current distribution. Property A is used in a trade or business of B.

(iii) A would have recognized $6,000 of gain under section 704(c)(1)(A) on a sale of Property A at the time of the distribution (the difference between the fair market value ($10,000) and the adjusted tax basis ($4,000) of the property at that time). Because Property A is not a capital asset in the hands of Partner B and B holds more than 50 percent of partnership capital and profits, the character of the gain on a sale of Property A to B would have been ordinary income under section 707(b)(2). Therefore, the character of the gain to A on the distribution of Property A to B is ordinary income.

(c) Exceptions—(1) Property contributed on or before October 3, 1989. Section 704(c)(1)(B) and this section do not apply to property contributed to the partnership on or before October 3, 1989.

(2) Certain liquidations. Section 704(c)(1)(B) and this section do not apply to a distribution of an interest in section 704(c) property to a partner other than the contributing partner in a liquidation of the partnership if—

(i) The contributing partner receives an interest in the section 704(c) property contributed by that partner (and no other property); and

(ii) The built-in gain or loss in the interest distributed to the contributing partner, determined immediately after the distribution, is equal to or greater than the built-in gain or loss on the property that would have been allocated to the contributing partner under section 704(c)(1)(A) and § 1.704–3 on a sale of the contributed property to an unrelated party immediately before the distribution.

(3) Section 708(b)(1)(B) termination. Section 704(c)(1)(B) and this section do not apply to the deemed distribution of interests in a new partnership caused by the termination of a partnership under section 708(b)(1)(B). A subsequent distribution of section 704(c) property by the new partnership to a partner of the new partnership is subject to section 704(c)(1)(B) to the same extent that distribution by the terminated partnership would have been subject to section 704(c)(1)(B). See also § 1.737–2(a) for a similar rule in the context of section 737. This paragraph (c)(3) applies to terminations of partnerships under section 708(b)(1)(B) occurring on or after May 9, 1997; however, this paragraph (c)(3) may be applied to terminations occurring on or after May 9, 1996, provided that the partnership and its partners apply this paragraph (c)(3) to the termination in a consistent manner.

(4) Complete transfer to another partnership. Section 704(c)(1)(B) and this section do not apply to a transfer by a partnership (transferor partnership) of all of its assets and liabilities to a second partnership (transferee partnership) in an exchange described in section 721, followed by a distribution of the interest in the transferee partnership in liquidation of the transferor partnership as part of the same plan or arrangement. A subsequent distribution of section 704(c) property by the transferee partnership to a partner of the transferee partnership is subject to section 704(c)(1)(B) to the same extent that a distribution by the transferor partnership would have been subject to section 704(c)(1)(B). See § 1.737–2(b) for a similar rule in the context of section 737.

(5) Incorporation of a partnership. Section 704(c)(1)(B) and this section do not apply to an incorporation of a partnership by any method of incorporation (other than a method involving an actual distribution of partnership property to the partners followed by a contribution of that property to a corporation), provided that the partnership is liquidated as part of the incorporation transaction. See § 1.737–2(c) for a similar rule in the context of section 737.

(6) Undivided interests. Section 704(c)(1)(B) and this section do not apply to a distribution of an undivided interest in property to the extent that the undivided interest does not exceed the undivided interest, if any, contributed by the distributee partner in the same property. See § 1.737–2(d)(4) for the application of section 737 in a similar context. The portion of the undivided interest in property retained by the partnership after the distribution, if any, that is treated as contributed by the distributee partner, is reduced to the extent of the undivided interest distributed to the distributee partner.

(7) Example. The following example illustrates the rule of paragraph (c)(2) of this section. Unless otherwise specified, partnership income equals partnership expenses (other than depreciation deductions for contributed property) for each year of the partnership, the fair market value of partnership property does not change, all distributions by the partnership are subject to section 704(c)(1)(B), and all partners are unrelated.

Example. **(i)** On January 1, 1995, A and B form partnership AB, as equal partners. A contributes Property A, nondepreciable real property with a fair market value and adjusted tax basis of $20,000. B contributes Property B, nondepreciable real property with a fair market value of $20,000 and an adjusted tax basis of $10,000. Property B therefore has a built-in gain of $10,000 at the time of contribution.

(ii) On December 31, 1998, the partnership liquidates when the fair market value of Property A has not changed, but the fair market value of Property B has increased to $40,000.

(iii) In the liquidation, A receives Property A and a 25 percent interest in Property B. This interest in Property B has a fair market value of $10,000 to A, reflecting the fact that A was entitled to 50 percent of the $20,000 post-contribution appreciation in Property B. The partnership distributes to B a 75 percent interest in Property B with a fair market value of $30,000. B's basis in this portion of Property B is $10,000 under section 732(b). As a result, B has a built-in gain of $20,000 in this portion of Property B immediately after the distribution ($30,000 fair market value less $10,000 adjusted tax basis). This built-in gain is greater than the $10,000 of built-in gain in Property B at the time of contribution to the partnership. B therefore does not recognize any gain on the distribution of a portion of Property B to A under this section.

(d) Special rules—(1) Nonrecognition transactions, installment obligations, contributed contracts, and capitalized costs—(i) Nonrecognition transactions. Property received by the partnership in exchange for section 704(c) property in a nonrecognition transaction is treated as the section 704(c) property for purposes of section 704(c)(1)(B) and this section to the extent that the property received is treated as section 704(c) property under § 1.704–3(a)(8). See § 1.737–2(d)(3) for a similar rule in the context of section 737.

* * *

(2) Transfers of a partnership interest. The transferee of all or a portion of the partnership interest of a contributing partner is treated as the contributing partner for purposes of section 704(c)(1)(B) and this section to the extent of the share of built-in gain or loss allocated to the transferee partner. See § 1.704–3(a)(7).

(3) Distributions of like-kind property. If section 704(c) property is distributed to a partner other than the contributing partner and like-kind property (within the meaning of section 1031) is distributed to the contributing partner no later than the earlier of (i) 180 days following the date of the distribution to the non-contributing partner, or (ii) the due date (determined with regard to extensions) of the contributing partner's income tax return for the taxable year of the distribution to the noncontributing partner, the amount of gain or loss, if any, that the contributing partner would otherwise have recognized under section 704(c)(1)(B) and this section is reduced by the amount of built-in gain or loss in the distributed like-kind property in the hands of the contributing partner immediately after the distribution. The contributing partner's basis in the distributed like-kind property is determined as if the like-kind property were distributed in an unrelated distribution prior to the distribution of any other property distributed as part of the same distribution and is determined without regard to the increase in the contributing partner's adjusted tax basis in the partnership interest under section 704(c)(1)(B) and this section. See § 1.707–3 for provisions treating the distribution of the like-kind property to the contributing partner as a disguised sale in certain situations.

(4) Example. The following example illustrates the rules of this paragraph (d). Unless otherwise specified, partnership income equals partnership expenses (other than depreciation deductions for contributed property) for each year of the partnership, the fair market value of partnership property does not change, all distributions by the partnership are subject to section 704(c)(1)(B), and all partners are unrelated.

Example. Distribution of like-kind property. **(i)** On January 1, 1995, A, B, and C form partnership ABC as equal partners. A contributes Property A, nondepreciable real property with a fair market value of $20,000 and an adjusted tax basis of $10,000. B and C each contribute $20,000 cash. The partnership subsequently buys Property X, nondepreciable real property of a like-kind to Property A with a fair market value and adjusted tax basis of $8,000. The fair market value of Property X subsequently increases to $10,000.

(ii) On December 31, 1998, Property A is distributed to B in a current distribution. At the same time, Property X is distributed to A in a current distribution. The distribution of Property X does not result in the contribution of Property A being properly characterized as a disguised sale to the partnership under § 1.707–3. A's basis in Property X is $8,000 under section 732(a)(1). A therefore has $2,000 of built-in gain in Property X ($10,000 fair market value less $8,000 adjusted tax basis).

(iii) A would generally recognize $10,000 of gain under section 704(c)(1)(B) on the distribution of Property A, the difference between the fair market value ($20,000) of the property and its adjusted tax basis ($10,000). This gain is reduced, however, by the amount of the built-in gain of Property X in the hands of A. As a result, A recognizes only $8,000 of gain on the distribution of Property A to B under section 704(c)(1)(B) and this section.

(e) Basis adjustments—(1) Contributing partner's basis in the partnership interest. The basis of the contributing partner's interest in the partnership is increased by the amount of the gain, or decreased by the amount of the loss, recognized by the partner under section 704(c)(1)(B) and this section. This increase or decrease is taken into account in determining (i) the contributing partner's adjusted tax basis under section 732 for any property distributed to the partner in a distribution that is part of the same distribution as the distribution of the contributed property, other than like-kind property described in paragraph (d)(3) of this section (pertaining to the special rule for distributions of like-kind property), and (ii) the amount of the gain recognized by the contributing partner under section 731 or section 737, if any, on a distribution of money or property to the contributing partner that is part of the same distribution as the distribution of the contributed property. For a determination of basis in a distribution subject to section 737, see § 1.737–3(a).

(2) Partnership's basis in partnership property. The partnership's adjusted tax basis in the distributed section 704(c) property is increased or decreased immediately before the distribution by the amount of gain or loss recognized by the contributing partner under section 704(c)(1)(B) and this section. Any increase or decrease in basis is therefore taken into account in determining the distributee partner's adjusted tax basis in the distributed property under section 732. For a determination of basis in a distribution subject to section 737, see § 1.737–3(b).

(3) Section 754 adjustments. The basis adjustments to partnership property made pursuant to paragraph (e)(2) of this section are not elective and must be made regardless of whether the partnership has an election in effect under section 754. Any adjustments to the bases of partnership property (including the distributed section 704(c) property) under section 734(b) pursuant to a section 754 election must be made after (and must take into account) the adjustments to basis made under paragraph (e)(2) of this section. See § 1.737–3(c)(4) for a similar rule in the context of section 737.

(4) Example. The following example illustrates the rules of this paragraph (e). Unless otherwise specified, partnership income equals partnership expenses (other than depreciation deductions for contributed property) for each year of the partnership, the fair market value of partnership property does not change, all distributions by the partnership are subject to section 704(c)(1)(B), and all partners are unrelated.

Example. Basis adjustment. **(i)** On January 1, 1995, A, B, and C form partnership ABC as equal partners. A contributes $10,000 cash and Property A, nondepreciable real property with a fair market value of $10,000 and an adjusted tax basis of $4,000. B and C each contribute $20,000 cash.

(ii) On December 31, 1998, Property A is distributed to B in a current distribution.

(iii) Under paragraph (a) of this section, A recognizes $6,000 of gain on the distribution of Property A because that is the amount of gain that would have been allocated to A under section 704(c)(1)(A) and § 1.704–3 on a sale of Property A for its fair market value at the time of the distribution (fair market value of Property A ($10,000) less its adjusted tax basis at the time of distribution ($4,000)). The adjusted tax basis of A's partnership interest is increased from $14,000 to $20,000 to reflect this gain. The partnership's adjusted tax basis in Property A is increased from $4,000 to $10,000 immediately prior to its distribution to B. B's adjusted tax basis in Property A is therefore $10,000 under section 732(a)(1).

(f) Anti-abuse rule—(1) In general. The rules of section 704(c)(1)(B) and this section must be applied in a manner consistent with the purpose of section 704(c)(1)(B). Accordingly, if a principal purpose of a transaction is to achieve a tax result that is inconsistent with the purpose of section 704(c)(1)(B), the Commissioner can recast the transaction for federal tax purposes as appropriate to achieve tax results that are consistent with the purpose of section 704(c)(1)(B) and this section. Whether a tax result is inconsistent with the purpose of section 704(c)(1)(B) and this section must be determined based on all the facts and circumstances. See § 1.737–4 for an anti-abuse rule and examples in the context of section 737.

(2) Examples. The following examples illustrate the anti-abuse rule of this paragraph (f). The examples set forth below do not delineate the boundaries of either permissible or impermissible types of transactions. Further, the addition of any facts or circumstances that are not specifically set forth in an example (or the deletion of any facts or circumstances) may alter the outcome of the transaction described in the example. Unless otherwise specified, partnership income equals partnership expenses (other than depreciation deductions for contributed property) for each year of the partnership, the fair market value of partnership property does not change, all distributions by the partnership are subject to section 704(c)(1)(B), and all partners are unrelated.

Example 1. Distribution in substance made within five-year period; results inconsistent with the purpose of section 704(c)(1)(B). **(i)** On January 1, 1995, A, B, and C form partnership ABC as equal partners. A contributes Property A, nondepreciable real property with a fair market value of $10,000 and an adjusted tax basis of $1,000. B and C each contributes $10,000 cash.

(ii) On December 31, 1998, the partners desire to distribute Property A to B in complete liquidation of B's interest in the partnership. If Property A were distributed at that time, however, A would recognize $9,000 of gain under section 704(c)(1)(B), the difference between the $10,000 fair market value and the $1,000 adjusted tax basis of Property A, because Property A was contributed to the partnership less than five years before December 31, 1998. On becoming aware of this potential gain recognition, and with a principal purpose of avoiding such gain, the partners amend the partnership agreement on December 31, 1998, and take any other steps necessary to provide that substantially all of the economic risks and benefits of Property A are borne by B as of December 31, 1998, and that substantially all of the economic risks and benefits of all other partnership property are borne by A and C. The partnership holds Property A until January 5, 2000, at which time it is distributed to B in complete liquidation of B's interest in the partnership.

(iii) The actual distribution of Property A occurred more than five years after the contribution of the property to the partnership. The steps taken by the partnership on December 31, 1998, however, are the functional equivalent of an actual distribution of Property A to B in complete liquidation of B's interest in the partnership as of that date. Section 704(c)(1)(B) requires recognition of gain when contributed section 704(c) property is in substance distributed to another partner within five years of its contribution to the partnership. Allowing a contributing partner to avoid section 704(c)(1)(B) through arrangements such as those in this Example 1 that have the effect of a distribution of property within five years of the date of its contribution to the partnership would effectively undermine the purpose of section 704(c)(1)(B) and this section. As a result, the steps taken by the partnership on December 31, 1998, are treated as causing a distribution of Property A to B for purposes of section 704(c)(1)(B) on that date, and A recognizes gain of $9,000 under section 704(c)(1)(B) and this section at that time.

(iv) Alternatively, if on becoming aware of the potential gain recognition to A on a distribution of Property A on December 31, 1998, the partners had instead agreed that B would continue as a partner with no changes to the partnership agreement or to B's economic interest in partnership operations, the distribution of Property A to B on January 5, 2000, would not have been inconsistent with the purpose of section 704(c)(1)(B) and this section. In that situation, Property A would not have been distributed until after the expiration of the five-year period specified in section 704(c)(1)(B) and this section. Deferring the distribution of Property A until the end of the five-year period for a principal purpose of avoiding the recognition of gain under section 704(c)(1)(B) and this section is not inconsistent with the purpose of section 704(c)(1)(B). Therefore, A would not have recognized gain on the distribution of Property A in that case.

Example 2. Suspension of five-year period in manner consistent with the purpose of section 704(c)(1)(B). (i) A, B, and C form partnership ABC on January 1, 1995, to conduct bona fide business activities. A contributes Property A, nondepreciable real property with a fair market value of $10,000 and an adjusted tax basis of $1,000, in exchange for a 49.5 percent interest in partnership capital and profits. B contributes $10,000 in cash for a 49.5 percent interest in partnership capital and profits. C contributes cash for a 1 percent interest in partnership capital and profits. A and B are wholly owned subsidiaries of the same affiliated group and continue to control the management of Property A by virtue of their controlling interests in the partnership. The partnership is formed pursuant to a plan a principal purpose of which is to minimize the period of time that A would have to remain a partner with a potential acquiror of Property A.

(ii) On December 31, 1997, D is admitted as a partner to the partnership in exchange for $10,000 cash.

(iii) On January 5, 2000, Property A is distributed to D in complete liquidation of D's interest in the partnership.

(iv) The distribution of Property A to D occurred more than five years after the contribution of the property to the partnership. On these facts, however, a principal purpose of the transaction was to minimize the period of time that A would have to remain partners with a potential acquiror of Property A, and treating the five-year period of section 704(c)(1)(B) as running during a time when Property A was still effectively owned through the partnership by members of the contributing affiliated group of which A is a member is inconsistent with the purpose of section 704(c)(1)(B). Prior to the admission of D as a partner, the pooling of assets between A and B, on the one hand, and C, on the other hand, although sufficient to constitute ABC as a valid partnership for federal income tax purposes, is not a sufficient pooling of assets for purposes of running the five-year period with respect to the distribution of Property A to D. Allowing a contributing partner to avoid section 704(c)(1)(B) through arrangements such as those in this Example 2 would have the effect of substantially nullifying the five-year requirement of section 704(c)(1)(B) and this section and elevating the form of the transaction over its substance. As a result, with respect to the distribution of Property A to D, the five-year period of section 704(c)(1)(B) is tolled until the admission of D as a partner on December 31, 1997. Therefore, the distribution of Property A occurred before the end of the five-year period of section 704(c)(1)(B), and A recognizes gain of $9,000 under section 704(c)(1)(B) on the distribution.

* * *

[T.D. 8642, 60 FR 66727, Dec. 26, 1995, as amended by T.D. 8717, 62 FR 25498, May 9, 1997; T.D. 9193, 70 FR 14394, Mar. 22, 2005; T.D. 9207, 70 FR 30334, May 26, 2005]

§ 1.705–1 Determination of basis of partner's interest.

(a) General rule. (1) Section 705 and this section provide rules for determining the adjusted basis of a partner's interest in a partnership. A partner is required to determine the adjusted basis of his interest in a partnership only when necessary for the determination of his tax liability or that of any other person. The determination of the adjusted basis of a partnership interest is ordinarily made as of the end of a partnership taxable year. Thus, for example, such year-end determination is necessary in ascertaining the extent to which a partner's distributive share of partnership losses may be allowed. See section 704(d). However, where there has been a sale or exchange of all or a part of a partnership interest or a liquidation of a partner's entire interest in a partnership, the adjusted basis of the partner's interest should be determined as of the date of sale or exchange or liquidation. The adjusted basis of a partner's interest in a partnership is determined without regard to any amount shown in the partnership books as the partner's "capital", "equity", or similar account. For example, A contributes property with an adjusted basis to him of $400 (and a value of $1,000) to a partnership. B contributes $1,000 cash. While under their agreement each may have a "capital account" in the partnership of $1,000, the adjusted basis of A's interest is only $400 and B's interest $1,000.

(2) The original basis of a partner's interest in a partnership shall be determined under section 722 (relating to contributions to a partnership) or section 742 (relating to transfers of partnership interests). Such basis shall be increased under section 722 by any further contributions to the partnership and by the sum of the partner's distributive share for the taxable year and prior taxable years of—

(i) Taxable income of the partnership as determined under section 703(a),

(ii) Tax-exempt receipts of the partnership, and

(iii) The excess of the deductions for depletion over the basis of the depletable property, unless the property is an oil or gas property the basis of which has been allocated to partners under section 613A(c)(7)(D).

(3) The basis shall be decreased (but not below zero) by distributions from the partnership as provided in section 733 and by the sum of the partner's distributive share for the taxable year and prior taxable years of—

(i) Partnership losses (including capital losses), and

(ii) Partnership expenditures which are not deductible in computing partnership taxable income or loss and which are not capital expenditures.

(4) The basis shall be decreased (but not below zero) by the amount of the partner's deduction for depletion allowable under section 611 for any partnership oil and gas property to the extent the deduction does not exceed the proportionate share of the adjusted basis of the property allocated to the partner under section 613A(c)(7)(D).

(5) The basis shall be adjusted (but not below zero) to reflect any gain or loss to the partner resulting from a disposition by the partnership of a domestic oil or gas property after December 31, 1974.

(6) For the effect of liabilities in determining the amount of contributions made by a partner to a partnership or the amount of distributions made by a partnership to a partner, see section 752 and § 1.752–1, relating to the treatment of certain liabilities. In determining the basis of a partnership interest on the effective date of subchapter K, chapter 1 of the Code, or any of the sections thereof, the partner's share of partnership liabilities on that date shall be included.

* * *

(b) Alternative rule. In certain cases, the adjusted basis of a partner's interest in a partnership may be determined by reference to the partner's share of the adjusted basis of partnership property which would be distributable upon termination of the partnership. The alternative rule may be used to determine the adjusted basis of a partner's interest where circumstances are such that the partner cannot practicably apply the general rule set forth in section 705(a) and paragraph (a) of this section, or where, from a consideration of all the facts, it is, in the opinion of the Commissioner, reasonable to conclude that the result produced will not vary substantially from the result obtainable under the general rule. Where the alternative rule is used, adjustments may be necessary in determining the adjusted basis of a partner's interest in a partnership. Adjustments would be required, for example, in order to reflect in a partner's share of the adjusted basis of partnership property any significant discrepancies arising as a result of contributed property, transfers of partnership interests, or distributions of property to the partners. The operation of the alternative rules may be illustrated by the following examples:

Example (1). The ABC partnership, in which A, B, and C are equal partners, owns various properties with a total adjusted basis of $1,500 and has earned and retained an additional $1,500. The total adjusted basis of partnership property is thus $3,000. Each partner's share in the adjusted basis of partnership property is one-third of this amount, or $1,000. Under the alternative rule, this amount represents each partner's adjusted basis for his partnership interest.

Example (2). Assume that partner A in example (1) of this paragraph sells his partnership interest to D for $1,250 at a time when the partnership property with an adjusted basis of $1,500 had appreciated in value to $3,000, and when the partnership also had $750 in cash. The total adjusted basis of all partnership property is

$2,250 and the value of such property is $3,750. D's basis for his partnership interest is his cost, $1,250. However, his one-third share of the adjusted basis of partnership property is only $750. Therefore, for the purposes of the alternative rule, D has an adjustment of $500 in determining the basis of his interest. This amount represents the difference between the cost of his partnership interest and his share of partnership basis at the time of his purchase. If the partnership subsequently earns and retains an additional $1,500, its property will have an adjusted basis of $3,750. D's adjusted basis for his interest under the alternative rule is $1,750, determined by adding $500, his basis adjustment to $1,250 (his one-third share of the $3,750 adjusted basis of partnership property). If the partnership distributes $250 to each partner in a current distribution, D's adjusted basis for his interest will be $1,500 ($1,000, his one-third share of the remaining basis of partnership property, $3,000, plus his basis adjustment of $500).

Example (3). Assume that BCD partnership in example (2) of this paragraph continues to operate. In 1960, D proposes to sell his partnership interest and wishes to evaluate the tax consequences of such sale. It is necessary, therefore, to determine the adjusted basis of his interest in the partnership. Assume further that D cannot determine the adjusted basis of his interest under the general rule. The balance sheet of the BCD partnership is as follows:

Assets	Adjusted basis per books	Market value
Cash	$ 3,000	$ 3,000
Receivables	4,000	4,000
Depreciable property	5,000	5,000
Land held for investment	18,000	30,000
Total	30,000	42,000
Liabilities and capital		**Per books**
Liabilities		$ 6,000
Capital accounts:		
B		4,500
C		4,500
D		15,000
Total		30,000

The $15,000 representing the amount of D's capital account does not reflect the $500 basis adjustment arising from D's purchase of his interest. See example (2) of this paragraph. The adjusted basis of D's partnership interest determined under the alternative rule is as follows:

D's share of the adjusted basis of partnership property (reduced by the amount of liabilities) at time of proposed sale	$15,000
D's share of partnership liabilities (under the partnership agreement liabilities are shared equally)	2,000
D's basis adjustment from example (2)	500
Adjusted basis of D's interest at the time of proposed sale, as determined under alternative rule	17,500

[T.D. 6500, 25 FR 11814, Nov. 26, 1960, as amended by T.D. 8437, 57 FR 43897, Sept. 22, 1992; T.D. 8986, 67 FR 15112–01, Mar. 29, 2002; T.D. 9049, 68 FR 12815, Mar. 18, 2003; T.D. 9207, 70 FR 30334, May 26, 2005]

§ 1.706–1 Taxable years of partner and partnership.

(a) Year in which partnership income is includible. (1) In computing taxable income for a taxable year, a partner is required to include the partner's distributive share of partnership items set forth in section 702 and the regulations thereunder for any partnership taxable year ending within or with the partner's taxable year. A partner must also include in taxable income for a taxable year guaranteed payments under section 707(c) that are deductible by the partnership under its method of accounting in the partnership taxable year ending within or with the partner's taxable year.

(2) The rules of this paragraph (a)(1) may be illustrated by the following example:

Example. Partner A reports income using a calendar year, while the partnership of which A is a member reports its income using a fiscal year ending May 31. The partnership reports its income and deductions under the cash method of accounting. During the partnership taxable year ending May 31, 2002, the partnership makes guaranteed payments of $120,000 to A for services and for the use of capital. Of this amount, $70,000 was paid to A between June 1 and December 31, 2001, and the remaining $50,000 was paid to A between January 1 and May 31, 2002. The entire $120,000 paid to A is includible in A's taxable income for the calendar year 2002 (together with A's distributive share of partnership items set forth in section 702 for the partnership taxable year ending May 31, 2002).

(3) If a partner receives distributions under section 731 or sells or exchanges all or part of a partnership interest, any gain or loss arising therefrom does not constitute partnership income.

(b) Taxable year—(1) Partnership treated as a taxpayer. The taxable year of a partnership must be determined as though the partnership were a taxpayer.

(2) Partnership's taxable year—(i) Required taxable year. Except as provided in paragraph (b)(2)(ii) of this section, the taxable year of a partnership must be—

(A) The majority interest taxable year, as defined in section 706(b)(4);

(B) If there is no majority interest taxable year, the taxable year of all of the principal partners of the partnership, as defined in 706(b)(3) (the principal partners' taxable year); or

(C) If there is no majority interest taxable year or principal partners' taxable year, the taxable year that produces the least aggregate deferral of income as determined under paragraph (b)(3) of this section.

(ii) Exceptions. A partnership may have a taxable year other than its required taxable year if it makes an election under section 444, elects to use a 52–53–week taxable year that ends with reference to its required taxable year or a taxable year elected under section 444, or establishes a business purpose for such taxable year and obtains approval of the Commissioner under section 442.

(3) Least aggregate deferral—(i) Taxable year that results in the least aggregate deferral of income. The taxable year that results in the least aggregate deferral of income will be the taxable year of one or more of the partners in the partnership which will result in the least aggregate deferral of income to the partners. The aggregate deferral for a particular year is equal to the sum of the products determined by multiplying the month(s) of deferral for each partner that would be generated by that year and each partner's interest in partnership profits for that year. The partner's taxable year that produces the lowest sum when compared to the other partner's taxable years is the taxable year that results in the least aggregate deferral of income to the partners. If the calculation results in more than one taxable year qualifying as the taxable year with the least aggregate deferral, the partnership may select any one of those taxable years as its taxable year. However, if one of the qualifying taxable years is also the partnership's existing taxable year, the partnership must maintain its existing taxable year. The determination of the taxable year that results in the least aggregate deferral of income generally must be made as of the beginning of the partnership's current taxable year. The director, however, may determine that the first day of the current taxable year is not the appropriate testing day and require the use of some other day or period that will more accurately reflect the ownership of the partnership and thereby the actual aggregate deferral to the partners where the partners engage in a transaction that has as its principal purpose the avoidance of the principles of this section. Thus, for example the preceding sentence would apply where there is a transfer of an interest in the partnership that results in a temporary transfer of that interest principally for purposes of qualifying for a specific taxable year under the principles of this section. For purposes of this section, deferral to each partner is measured in terms of months from the end of the partnership's taxable year forward to the end of the partner's taxable year.

(ii) Determination of the taxable year of a partner or partnership that uses a 52–53–week taxable year. For the purposes of the calculation described in paragraph (b)(3)(i) of this section, the taxable year of a partner or partnership that uses a 52–53–week taxable year must be the same year determined under the rules of section 441(f) and the regulations thereunder with respect to the inclusion of income by the partner or partnership.

(iii) Special de minimis rule. If the taxable year that results in the least aggregate deferral produces an aggregate deferral that is less than .5 when compared to the aggregate deferral of the current taxable year, the partnership's current taxable year will be treated as the taxable year with the least aggregate deferral. Thus, the partnership will not be permitted to change its taxable year.

(iv) Examples. The principles of this section may be illustrated by the following examples:

Example 1. Partnership P is on a fiscal year ending June 30. Partner A reports income on the fiscal year ending June 30 and Partner B reports income on the fiscal year ending July 31. A and B each have a 50 percent interest in partnership profits. For its taxable year beginning July 1, 1987, the partnership will be required to retain its taxable year since the fiscal year ending June 30 results in the least aggregate deferral of income to the partners. This determination is made as follows:

Test 6/30	Year end	Interest in partnership profits	Months of deferral for 6/30 year end	Interest x deferral
Partner A	6/30	.5	0	0
Partner B	7/31	.5	1	.5
Aggregate deferral				.5

Test 7/31	Year end	Interest in partnership profits	Months of deferral for 7/31 year end	Interest x deferral
Partner A	6/30	.5	11	5.5
Partner B	7/31	.5	0	0
Aggregate deferral				5.5

Example 2. The facts are the same as in Example 1 except that A reports income on the calendar year and B reports on the fiscal year ending November 30. For the partnership's taxable year beginning July 1, 1987, the partnership is required to change its taxable year to a fiscal year ending November 30 because such year results in the least aggregate deferral of income to the partners. This determination is made as follows:

Test 12/31	Year end	Interest in partnership profits	Months of deferral for 12/31 year end	Interest x deferral
Partner A	12/31	.5	0	0
Partner B	11/30	.5	11	5.5
Aggregate deferral				5.5

Test 11/30	Year end	Interest in partnership profits	Months of deferral for 11/30 year end	Interest x deferral
Partner A	12/31	.5	1	.5
Partner B	11/30	.5	0	0
Aggregate deferral				.5

Example 3. The facts are the same as in Example 2 except that B reports income on the fiscal year ending June 30. For the partnership's taxable year beginning July 1, 1987, each partner's taxable year will result in identical aggregate deferral of income. If the partnership's current taxable year was neither a fiscal year ending June 30 nor the calendar year, the partnership would select either the fiscal year ending June 30 or the calendar year as its taxable year. However, since the partnership's current taxable year ends June 30, it must retain its current taxable year. The determination is made as follows:

Test 12/31	Year end	Interest in partnership profits	Months of deferral for 12/31 year end	Interest x deferral
Partner A	12/31	.5	0	0
Partner B	6/30	.5	6	3.0
Aggregate deferral				3.0

Test 6/30	Year end	Interest in partnership profits	Months of deferral for 6/30 year end	Interest x deferral
Partner A	12/31	.5	6	3.0
Partner B	6/30	.5	0	0
Aggregate deferral				3.0

Example 4. The facts are the same as in Example 1 except that, on December 31, 1987, partner A sells a 4 percent interest in the partnership to Partner C, who reports income on the fiscal year ending June 30, and a 40 percent interest in the partnership to Partner D, who also reports income on the fiscal year ending June 30. The taxable year beginning July 1, 1987, is unaffected by the sale. However, for the taxable year beginning July 31, 1988, the partnership must determine the taxable year resulting in the least aggregate deferral as of July 1, 1988. In this case, the partnership will be required to retain its taxable year since the fiscal year ending June 30 continues to be the taxable year that results in the least aggregate deferral of income to the partners.

Example 5. The facts are the same as in Example 4 except that Partner D reports income on the fiscal year ending April 30. As in Example 4, the taxable year during which the sale took place is unaffected by the shifts in interests. However, for its taxable year beginning July 1, 1988, the partnership will be required to change its taxable year to the fiscal year ending April 30. This determination is made as follows:

Test 7/31	Year end	Interest in partnership profits	Months of deferral for 7/31 year end	Interest x deferral
Partner A	6/30	.06	11	.66
Partner B	7/31	.5	0	0
Partner C	6/30	.04	11	.44
Partner D	4/30	.4	9	3.60
Aggregate deferral				4.70

Test 6/30	Year end	Interest in partnership profits	Months of deferral for 6/30 year end	Interest x deferral
Partner A	6/30	.06	0	0
Partner B	7/31	.5	1	.5
Partner C	6/30	.04	0	0
Partner D	4/30	.4	10	4.0
Aggregate deferral				4.5

Test 4/30	Year end	Interest in partnership profits	Months of deferral for 4/30 year end	Interest x deferral
Partner A	6/30	.06	2	.12
Partner B	7/31	.5	3	1.50
Partner C	6/30	.04	2	.08
Partner D	4/30	.4	0	0
Aggregate deferral				1.70

§ 1.706–1(b)(3) Test	
Current taxable year (June 30)	4.5
Less: Taxable year producing the least aggregate deferral (April 30)	1.7
Additional aggregate deferral (greater than .5)	2.8

Example 6. (i) Partnership P has two partners, A who reports income on the fiscal year ending March 31, and B who reports income on the fiscal year ending July 31. A and B share profits equally. P has determined its taxable year under paragraph (b)(3) of this section to be the fiscal year ending March 31 as follows:

Test 3/31	Year end	Interest in partnership profits	Months of Deferral for 3/31 year end	Interest x deferral
Partner A	3/31	.5	0	0
Partner B	7/31	.5	4	2
Aggregate deferral				2

Test 7/31	Year end	Interest in partnership profits	Months of Deferral for 7/31 year end	Interest x deferral
Partner A	3/31	.5	8	4
Partner B	7/31	.5	0	0
Aggregate deferral				4

(ii) In May 1988, Partner A sells a 45 percent interest in the partnership to C, who reports income on the fiscal year ending April 30. For the taxable period beginning April 1, 1989, the fiscal year ending April 30 is the taxable year that produces the least aggregate deferral of income to the partners. However, under paragraph (b)(3)(iii) of this section the partnership is required to retain its fiscal year ending March 31. This determination is made as follows:

Test 3/31	Year end	Interest in partnership profits	Months of Deferral for 3/31 year end	Interest x deferral
Partner A	3/31	.05	0	0
Partner B	7/31	.5	4	2.0
Partner C	4/30	.45	1	.45
Aggregate deferral				2.45

Test 7/31	Year end	Interest in partnership profits	Months of Deferral for 7/31 year end	Interest x deferral
Partner A	3/31	.05	8	.40
Partner B	7/31	.5	0	0
Partner C	4/30	.45	9	4.05
Aggregate deferral				4.45

Test 4/30	Year end	Interest in partnership profits	Months of Deferral for 4/30 year end	Interest x deferral
Partner A	3/31	.05	11	.55
Partner B	7/3	.5	3	1.50
Partner C	4/30	.45	0	0
Aggregate deferral				2.05

§ 1.706–1(b)(3) Test	
Current taxable year (3/31)	2.45
Less: Taxable year producing the least aggregate deferral (4/30)	2.05
Additional aggregate deferral (less than .5)	.40

(4) Measurement of partner's profits and capital interest—

(i) In general. The rules of this paragraph (b)(4) apply in determining the majority interest taxable year, the principal partners' taxable year, and the least aggregate deferral taxable year.

(ii) Profits interest—(A) In general. For purposes of section 706(b), a partner's interest in partnership profits is generally the partner's percentage share of partnership profits for the current partnership taxable year. If the partnership does not expect to have net income for the current partnership taxable year, then a partner's interest in partnership profits instead must be the partner's percentage share of partnership net income for the first taxable year in which the partnership expects to have net income.

(B) Percentage share of partnership net income. The partner's percentage share of partnership net income for a partnership taxable year is the ratio of: the partner's distributive share of partnership net income for the taxable year, to the partnership's net income for the year. If a partner's percentage share of partnership net income for the taxable year depends on the amount or nature of partnership income for that year (due to, for example, preferred returns or special allocations of specific partnership items), then the partnership must make a reasonable estimate of the amount and nature of its income for the taxable year. This estimate must be based on all facts and circumstances known to the partnership as of the first day of the current partnership taxable year. The partnership must then use this estimate in determining the partners' interests in partnership profits for the taxable year.

(C) Distributive share. For purposes of this paragraph (b)(4)(ii), a partner's distributive share of partnership net income is determined by taking into account all rules and regulations affecting that determination, including, without limitation, sections 704(b), (c), and (e), 736, and 743.

(iii) Capital interest. Generally, a partner's interest in partnership capital is determined by reference to the assets of the partnership that the partner would be entitled to upon withdrawal from the partnership or upon liquidation of the partnership. If the partnership maintains capital accounts in accordance with § 1.704–1(b)(2)(iv), then for purposes of section 706(b), the partnership may assume that a partner's interest in partnership capital is the ratio of the partner's capital account to all partners' capital accounts as of the first day of the partnership taxable year.

* * *

(7) Adoption of taxable year. A newly-formed partnership may adopt, in accordance with § 1.441–1(c), its required taxable year, a taxable year elected under section 444, or a 52–53–week taxable year ending with reference to its required taxable year or a taxable year elected under section 444 without securing the approval of the Commissioner. If a newly-formed partnership wants to adopt any other taxable year, it must establish a business purpose and secure the approval of the Commissioner under section 442.

(8) Change in taxable year—(i) Partnerships-(A) Approval required. An existing partnership may change its taxable year only by securing the approval of the Commissioner under section

442 or making an election under section 444. However, a partnership may obtain automatic approval for certain changes, including a change to its required taxable year, pursuant to administrative procedures published by the Commissioner.

(B) Short period tax return. A partnership that changes its taxable year must make its return for a short period in accordance with section 443, but must not annualize the partnership taxable income.

(C) Change in required taxable year. If a partnership is required to change to its majority interest taxable year, then no further change in the partnership's required taxable year is required for either of the two years following the year of the change. This limitation against a second change within a three-year period applies only if the first change was to the majority interest taxable year and does not apply following a change in the partnership's taxable year to the principal partners' taxable year or the least aggregate deferral taxable year.

(ii) Partners. Except as otherwise provided in the Internal Revenue Code or the regulations thereunder (e.g., section 859 regarding real estate investment trusts or § 1.442–2(c) regarding a subsidiary changing to its consolidated parent's taxable year), a partner may not change its taxable year without securing the approval of the Commissioner under section 442. However, certain partners may be eligible to obtain automatic approval to change their taxable years pursuant to the regulations or administrative procedures published by the Commissioner. A partner that changes its taxable year must make its return for a short period in accordance with section 443.

(9) Retention of taxable year. In certain cases, a partnership will be required to change its taxable year unless it obtains the approval of the Commissioner under section 442, or makes an election under section 444, to retain its current taxable year. For example, a partnership using a taxable year that corresponds to its required taxable year must obtain the approval of the Commissioner to retain such taxable year if its required taxable year changes as a result of a change in ownership, unless the partnership previously obtained approval for its current taxable year or, if appropriate, makes an election under section 444.

(10) Procedures for obtaining approval or making a section 444 election. See § 1.442–1(b) for procedures to obtain the approval of the Commissioner (automatically or otherwise) to adopt, change, or retain a taxable year. See §§ 1.444–1T and 1.444–2T for qualifications, and § 1.444–3T for procedures, for making an election under section 444.

* * *

(c) Closing of partnership year—(1) General rule. Section 706(c) and this paragraph provide rules governing the closing of partnership years. The closing of a partnership taxable year or a termination of a partnership for Federal income tax purposes is not necessarily governed by the "dissolution", "liquidation", etc., of a partnership under State or local law. The taxable year of a partnership shall not close as the result of the death of a partner, the entry of a new partner, the liquidation of a partner's entire interest in the partnership (as defined in section 761(d)), or the sale or exchange of a partner's interest in the partnership, except in the case of a termination of a partnership and except as provided in subparagraph (2) of this paragraph. In the case of termination, the partnership taxable year closes for all partners as of the date of termination. See section 708(b) and paragraph (b) of § 1.708–1.

(2) Partner who retires or sells interest in partnership—(i) Disposition of entire interest. A partnership taxable year shall close with respect to a partner who sells or exchanges his entire interest in a partnership, and with respect to a partner whose entire interest is liquidated. However, a partnership taxable year with respect to a partner who dies shall not close prior to the end of such partnership taxable year, or the time when such partner's interest (held by his estate or other successor) is liquidated or sold or exchanged, whichever is earlier. See subparagraph (3) of this paragraph.

(ii) Inclusions in taxable income. In the case of a sale, exchange, or liquidation of a partner's entire interest in a partnership, the partner shall include in his taxable income for his taxable year within or with which his membership in the partnership ends, his distributive share of items described in section 702(a), and any guaranteed payments under section 707(c), for his partnership taxable year ending with the date of such sale, exchange, or liquidation. In order to avoid an interim closing of the partnership books, such partner's distributive share of items described in section 702(a) may, by agreement among the partners, be estimated by taking his *pro rata* part of the amount of such items he would have included in his taxable income had he remained a partner until the end of the partnership taxable year. The proration may be based on the portion of the taxable year that has elapsed prior to the sale, exchange, or liquidation, or may be determined under any other method that is reasonable. Any partner who is the transferee of such partner's interest shall include in his taxable income, as his distributive share of items described in section 702(a) with respect to the acquired interest, the *pro rata* part (determined by the method used by the transferor partner) of the amount of such items he would have included had he been a partner from the beginning of the taxable year of the partnership. The application of this subdivision may be illustrated by the following example:

Example. Assume that a partner selling his partnership interest on June 30, 1955, has an adjusted basis for his interest of $5,000 on that date; that his *pro rata* share of partnership income up to June 30 is $15,000; and that he sells his interest for $20,000. Under the provisions of section 706(c)(2), the partnership year with respect to him closes at the time of the sale. The $15,000 is includible in his income as his distributive share and, under section 705, it increases the basis of his partnership interest to $20,000, which is also the selling price of his interest. Therefore, no gain is realized on the sale of his partnership interest. The purchaser of this partnership interest shall include in his income as his distributive share his *pro rata* part of partnership income for the remainder of the partnership taxable year.

(3) Partner who dies. **(i)** When a partner dies, the partnership taxable year shall not close with respect to such partner prior to the end of the partnership taxable year. The partnership taxable year shall continue both for the remaining partners and the decedent partner. Where the death of a partner results in the termination of the partnership, the partnership taxable year shall close for all partners on the date of such termination under section 708(b)(1)(A). See also paragraph (b)(1)(i)(b) of § 1.708–1 for the continuation of a 2–member partnership under certain circumstances after the death of a partner. However, if the decedent partner's estate or other successor sells or exchanges its entire interest in the partnership, or if its entire interest is liquidated, the partnership taxable year with respect to the estate or other successor in interest shall close on the date of such sale or exchange, or the date of completion of the liquidation.

(ii) The last return of a decedent partner shall include only his share of partnership taxable income for any partnership taxable year or years ending within or with the last taxable year for such decedent partner (*i.e.*, the year ending with the date of his death). The distributive share of partnership taxable income for a partnership taxable year ending after the decedent's last taxable year is includible in the return of his estate or other successor in interest. If the estate or other successor in interest of a partner continues to share in the profits or losses of the partnership business, the distributives share thereof is includible in the taxable year of the estate or other successor in interest within or with which the taxable year of the partnership ends. See also paragraph (a)(1)(ii) of § 1.736–1. Where the estate or other successor in interest receives distributions, any gain or loss on such distributions is includible in its gross income for its taxable year in which the distribution is made.

(iii) If a partner (or a retiring partner), in accordance with the terms of the partnership agreement, designates a person to succeed to his interest in the partnership after his death, such designated person shall be regarded as a successor in interest of the deceased for purposes of this chapter. Thus, where a partner designates his widow as the successor in interest, her distributive share of income for the taxable year of the partnership ending within or with her taxable year may be included in a joint return in accordance with the provisions of sections 2 and 6013(a)(2) and (3).

(iv) If, under the terms of an agreement existing at the date of death of a partner, a sale or exchange of the decedent partner's interest in the partnership occurs upon that date, then the taxable year of the partnership with respect to such decedent partner shall close upon the date of death. See section 706(c)(2)(A)(i). The sale or exchange of a partnership interest does not, for the purpose of this rule, include any transfer of a partnership interest which occurs at death as a result of inheritance or any testamentary disposition.

(v) To the extent that any part of a distributive share of partnership income of the estate or other successor in interest of a deceased partner is attributable to the decedent for the period ending with the date of his death, such part of the distributive share is income in respect of the decedent under section 691. See section 691 and the regulations thereunder.

(vi) The provisions of this subparagraph may be illustrated by the following examples:

Example (1). B has a taxable year ending December 31 and is a member of partnership ABC, the taxable year of which ends on June 30. B dies on October 31, 1955. His estate (which as a new taxpayer may, under section 441 and the regulations thereunder, adopt any taxable year) adopts a taxable year ending October 31. The return of the decedent for the period January 1 to October 31, 1955, will include only his distributive share of taxable income of the partnership for its taxable year ending June 30, 1955. The distributive share of taxable income of the partnership for its taxable year ending June 30, 1956, arising from the interest of the decedent, will be includible in the return of the estate for its taxable year ending October 31, 1956. That part of the distributive share attributable to the decedent for the period ending with the date of his death (July 1 through October 31, 1955) is income in respect of a decedent under section 691.

Example (2). Assume the same facts as in example (1) of this subdivision, except that, prior to B's death, B and D had agreed that, upon B's death, D would purchase B's interest for $10,000. When B dies on October 31, 1955, the partnership taxable year beginning July 1, 1955, closes with respect to him. Therefore, the return for B's last taxable year (January 1 to October 31, 1955) will include his distributive share of taxable income of the partnership for its taxable year ending June 30, 1955, plus his distributive share of partnership taxable income for the period July 1 to October 31, 1955. See subdivision (iv) of this subparagraph.

Example (3). H is a member of a partnership having a taxable year ending December 31. Both H and his wife W are on a calendar year and file joint returns. H dies on March 31, 1955. Administration of the estate is completed and the estate, including the partnership interest, is distributed to W as legatee on November 30, 1955. Such distribution by the estate is not a sale or exchange of H's partnership interest. No part of the taxable income of the partnership for the taxable year ending December 31, 1955, which is allocable to H, will be included in H's taxable income for his last taxable year (January 1 through March 31, 1955) or in the taxable income of H's estate for the taxable year April 1 through November 30, 1955. The distributive share of partnership taxable income for the full calendar year that is allocable to H will be includible in the taxable income of W for her taxable year ending December 31, 1955, and she may file a joint return under sections 2 and 6013(a)(3). That part of the distributive share attributable to the decedent for the period ending with the date of his death (January 1 through March 31, 1955) is income in respect of a decedent under section 691.

* * *

(4) Disposition of less than entire interest. If a partner sells or exchanges a part of his interest in a partnership, or if the interest of a partner is reduced, the partnership taxable year shall continue to its normal end. In such case, the partner's distributive share of items which he is required to include in his taxable income under the provisions of section 702(a) shall be determined by taking into account his varying interests in the partnership during the partnership taxable year in which such sale, exchange, or reduction of interest occurred.

(5) Transfer of interest by gift. The transfer of a partnership interest by gift does not close the partnership taxable year with respect to the donor. However, the income up to the date of gift attributable to the donor's interest shall be allocated to him under section 704(e)(2).

* * *

[T.D. 6500, 25 FR 11814, Nov. 26, 1960; 25 FR 14021, Dec. 31, 1960, as amended by 38 FR 26912, Sept. 27, 1973; T.D. 8123, 52 FR 3623, Feb. 5, 1987; T.D. 8996, 67 FR 35009, May 17, 2002; T.D. 9009, 67 FR 48017, July 23, 2002; T.D. 9576, 77 FR 8124, Feb. 14, 2012]

§ 1.707–1 Transactions between partner and partnership.

(a) Partner not acting in capacity as partner. A partner who engages in a transaction with a partnership other than in his capacity as a partner shall be treated as if he were not a member of the partnership with respect to such transaction. Such transactions include, for example, loans of money or property by the partnership to the partner or by the partner to the partnership, the sale of property by the partner to the partnership, the purchase of property by the partner from the partnership, and the rendering of services by the partnership to the partner or by the partner to the partnership. Where a partner retains the ownership of property but allows the partnership to use such separately owned property for partnership purposes (for example, to obtain credit or to secure firm creditors by guaranty, pledge, or other agreement) the transaction is treated as one between a partnership and a partner not acting in his capacity as a partner. However, transfers of money or property by a partner to a partnership as contributions, or transfers of money or property by a partnership to a partner as distributions, are not transactions included within the provisions of this section. In all cases, the substance of the transaction will govern rather than its form. See paragraph (c)(3) of § 1.731–1.

(b) Certain sales or exchanges of property with respect to controlled partnerships—(1) Losses disallowed. **(i)** No deduction shall be allowed for a loss on a sale or exchange of property (other than an interest in the partnership, directly or indirectly, between a partnership and a partner who owns, directly or indirectly, more than 50 percent of the capital interest or profits interest in such partnership). A loss on a sale or exchange of property, directly or indirectly, between two partnerships in which the same persons own, directly or indirectly, more than 50 percent of the capital interest or profits interest in each partnership shall not be allowed.

(ii) If a gain is realized upon the subsequent sale or exchange by a transferee of property with respect to which a loss was disallowed under the provisions of subdivision (i) of this subparagraph, section 267(d) (relating to amount of gain where loss previously disallowed) shall apply as though the loss were disallowed under section 267(a)(1).

(2) Gains treated as ordinary income. Any gain recognized upon the sale or exchange, directly or indirectly, of property which, in the hands of the transferee immediately after the transfer, is property other than a capital asset, as defined in section 1221, shall be ordinary income if the transaction is between a partnership and a partner who owns, directly or indirectly, more than 80 percent [now 50 percent] of the capital interest or profits interest in the partnership. This rule also applies where such a transaction is between partnerships in which the same persons own, directly or indirectly, more than 80 percent * of the capital interest or profits interest in each partnership. The term "property other than a capital asset" includes (but is not limited to) trade accounts receivable, inventory, stock in trade, and depreciable or real property used in the trade or business.

(3) Ownership of a capital or profits interest. In determining the extent of the ownership by a partner, as defined in section 761(b), of his capital interest or profits interest in a partnership, the rules for constructive ownership of stock provided in section 267(c)(1), (2), (4), and (5) shall be applied for the purpose of section 707(b) and this paragraph. Under these rules, ownership of a capital or profits interest in a partnership may be attributed to a person who is not a partner as defined in section 761(b) in order that another partner may be considered the constructive owner of such interest under section 267(c). However, section 707(b)(1)(A) does not apply to a constructive owner of a partnership interest since he is not a partner as defined in section 761(b). For example, where trust T is a partner in the partnership ABT, and AW, A's wife, is the sole beneficiary of the trust, the ownership of a capital and profits interest in the partnership by T will be attributed to AW only for the purpose of further attributing the ownership of such interest to A. See section 267(c)(1) and (5). If A, B, and T are equal partners, then A will be considered as owning more than 50 percent of the capital and profits interest in the partnership, and losses on transactions between him and the partnership will be disallowed by section 707(b)(1)(A). However, a loss sustained by AW on a sale or exchange of property with the partnership would not be disallowed by section 707, but will be disallowed to the extent provided in paragraph (b) of § 1.267(b)–1. See section 267(a) and (b), and the regulations thereunder.

(c) Guaranteed payments. Payments made by a partnership to a partner for services or for the use of capital are considered as made to a person who is not a partner, to the extent such payments are determined without regard to the income of the partnership. However, a partner must include such payments as ordinary income for his taxable year within or with which ends the partnership taxable year in which the partnership deducted such payments as paid or accrued under its method of accounting. See section 706(a) and paragraph (a) of § 1.706–1. Guaranteed payments are considered as made to one who is not a member of the partnership only for the purposes of section 61(a) (relating to gross income) and section 162(a) (relating to trade or business expenses). For a guaranteed payment to be a partnership deduction, it must meet the same tests under section 162(a) as it would if the payment had been made to a person who is not a member of the partnership, and the rules of section 263 (relating to capital expenditures) must be taken into account. This rule does not affect the deductibility to the partnership of a payment described in section 736(a)(2) to a retiring partner or to a deceased partner's successor in interest. Guaranteed payments do not constitute an interest in partnership profits for purposes of sections 706(b)(3), 707(b), and 708(b). For the purposes of other provisions of the internal revenue laws, guaranteed payments are regarded as a partner's distributive share of ordinary income. Thus, a partner who receives guaranteed payments for a period during which he is absent from work because of personal injuries or sickness is not entitled to exclude such payments from his gross income under section 105(d). Similarly, a partner who receives guaranteed payments is not regarded as an employee of the partnership for the purposes of withholding of tax at source, deferred compensation plans, etc. The provisions of this paragraph may be illustrated by the following examples:

Example (1). Under the ABC partnership agreement, partner A is entitled to a fixed annual payment of $10,000 for services, without regard to the income of the partnership. His distributive share is 10 percent. After deducting the guaranteed payment, the partnership has $50,000 ordinary income. A must include $15,000 as ordinary income for his taxable year within or with which the partnership taxable year ends ($10,000 guaranteed payment plus $5,000 distributive share).

Example (2). Partner C in the CD partnership is to receive 30 percent of partnership income as determined before taking into account any guaranteed payments, but not less than $10,000. The income of the partnership is $60,000, and C is entitled to $18,000 (30 percent of $60,000) as his distributive share. No part of this amount is a guaranteed payment. However, if the partnership had income of $20,000 instead of $60,000, $6,000 (30 percent of $20,000) would be partner C's distributive share, and the remaining $4,000 payable to C would be a guaranteed payment.

Example (3). Partner X in the XY partnership is to receive a payment of $10,000 for services, plus 30 percent of the taxable income or loss of the partnership. After deducting the payment of $10,000 to partner X, the XY partnership has a loss of $9,000. Of this amount, $2,700 (30 percent of the loss) is X's distributive share of partnership loss and, subject to section 704(d), is to be taken into account by him in his return. In addition, he must report as ordinary income the guaranteed payment of $10,000 made to him by the partnership.

Example (4). Assume the same facts as in example (3) of this paragraph, except that, instead of a $9,000 loss, the partnership has $30,000 in capital gains and no other items of income or deduction except the $10,000 paid X as a guaranteed payment. Since the items of partnership income or loss must be segregated under section 702(a), the partnership has a $10,000 ordinary loss and $30,000 in capital gains. X's 30 percent distributive shares of these amounts are $3,000 ordinary loss and $9,000 capital gain. In addition, X has received a $10,000 guaranteed payment which is ordinary income to him.

[T.D. 6500, 25 FR 11814, Nov. 26, 1960; as amended by T.D. 7891, 48 FR 20049, May 4, 1983]

§ 1.707–3 Disguised sales of property to partnership; general rules.

(a) Treatment of transfers as a sale—(1) In general. Except as otherwise provided in this section, if a transfer of property by a partner to a partnership and one or more transfers of money or other consideration by the partnership to that partner are described in paragraph (b)(1) of this section, the transfers are treated as a sale of property, in whole or in part, to the partnership.

(2) Definition and timing of sale. For purposes of §§ 1.707–3 through 1.707–5, the use of the term sale (or any variation of that word) to refer to a transfer of property by a partner to a partnership and a transfer of consideration by a partnership to a partner means a sale or exchange of that property, in whole or in part, to the partnership by the partner acting in a capacity other than as a member of the partnership, rather than a contribution and distribution to which sections 721 and 731, respectively, apply. A transfer that is treated as a sale under paragraph (a)(1) this section is treated as a sale for all purposes of the Internal Revenue Code (e.g., sections 453, 483, 1001, 1012, 1031 and 1274). The sale is considered to take place on the date that, under general principles of Federal tax law, the partnership is considered the owner of the property. If the transfer of money or other consideration from the partnership to the partner occurs after the transfer of property to the partnership; the partner and the partnership are treated as if, on the date of the sale, the partnership transferred to the partner an obligation to transfer to the partner money or other consideration.

(3) Application of disguised sale rules. If a person purports to transfer property to a partnership in a capacity as a partner, the rules of this section apply for purposes of determining whether the property was transferred in a disguised sale, even if it is determined after the application of the rules of this section that such person is not a partner. If after the application of the rules of this section to a purported transfer of property to a partnership, it is determined that no partnership exists because the property was actually sold, or it is otherwise determined that the contributed property is not owned by the partnership for tax purposes, the transferor of the property is treated as having sold the property to the person (or persons) that acquired ownership of the property for tax purposes.

(4) Deemed terminations under section 708. In applying the rules of this section, transfers resulting from a termination of a partnership under section 708(b)(1)(B) are disregarded.

(b) Transfers treated as a sale—(1) In general. A transfer of property (excluding money or an obligation to contribute money) by a partner to a partnership and a transfer of money or other consideration (including the assumption of or the taking subject to a liability) by the partnership to the partner constitute a sale of property, in whole or in part, by the partner to the partnership only if based on all the facts and circumstances—

(i) The transfer of money or other consideration would not have been made but for the transfer of property; and

(ii) In cases in which the transfers are not made simultaneously, the subsequent transfer is not dependent on the entrepreneurial risks of partnership operations.

(2) Facts and circumstances. The determination of whether a transfer of property by a partner to the partnership and a transfer of money or other consideration by the partnership to the partner constitute a sale, in whole or in part, under paragraph (b)(1) of this section is made based on all the facts and circumstances in each case. The weight to be given each of the facts and circumstances will depend on the particular case. Generally, the facts and circumstances existing on the date of the earliest of such transfers are the ones considered in determining whether a sale exists under paragraph (b)(1) of this section. Among the facts and circumstances that may tend to prove the existence of a sale under paragraph (b)(1) of this section are the following:

(i) That the timing and amount of a subsequent transfer are determinable with reasonable certainty at the time of an earlier transfer;

(ii) That the transferor has a legally enforceable right to the subsequent transfer;

(iii) That the partner's right to receive the transfer of money or other consideration is secured in any manner, taking into account the period during which it is secured;

(iv) That any person has made or is legally obligated to make contributions to the partnership in order to permit the partnership to make the transfer of money or other consideration;

(v) That any person has loaned or has agreed to loan the partnership the money or other consideration required to enable the partnership to make the transfer, taking into account whether any such lending obligation is subject to contingencies related to the results of partnership operations;

(vi) That a partnership has incurred or is obligated to incur debt to acquire the money or other consideration necessary to permit it to make the transfer, taking into account the likelihood that the partnership will be able to incur that debt (considering such factors as whether any person has agreed to guarantee or otherwise assume personal liability for that debt);

(vii) That the partnership holds money or other liquid assets, beyond the reasonable needs of the business, that are expected to be available to make the transfer (taking into account the income that will be earned from those assets);

(viii) That partnership distributions, allocation or control of partnership operations is designed to effect an exchange of the burdens and benefits of ownership of property;

(ix) That the transfer of money or other consideration by the partnership to the partner is disproportionately large in relationship to the partner's general and continuing interest in partnership profits; and

(x) That the partner has no obligation to return or repay the money or other consideration to the partnership, or has such an obligation but it is likely to become due at such a distant point in the future that the present value of that obligation is small in relation to the amount of money or other consideration transferred by the partnership to the partner.

(c) Transfers made within two years presumed to be a sale—(1) In general. For purposes of this section, if within a two-year period a partner transfers property to a partnership and the partnership transfers money or other consideration to the partner (without regard to the order of the transfers), the transfers are presumed to be a sale of the property to the partnership unless the facts and circumstances clearly establish that the transfers do not constitute a sale.

(2) Disclosure of transfers made within two years. Disclosure to the Internal Revenue Service in accordance with § 1.707–8 is required if—

(i) A partner transfers property to a partnership and the partnership transfers money or other consideration to the partner with a two-year period (without regard to the order of the transfers);

(ii) The partner treats the transfers other than as a sale for tax purposes; and

(iii) The transfer of money or other consideration to the partner is not presumed to be a guaranteed payment for capital under § 1.707–4(a)(1)(ii), is not a reasonable preferred return within the meaning of § 1.707–4(a)(3), and is not an operating cash flow distribution within the meaning of § 1.707–4(b)(2).

(d) Transfers made more than two years apart presumed not to be a sale. For purposes of this section, if a transfer of money or other consideration to a partner by a partnership and the transfer of property to the partnership by that partner are more than two years apart, the transfers are presumed not to be a sale of the property to the partnership unless the facts and circumstances clearly establish that the transfers constitute a sale.

(e) Scope. This section and §§ 1.707–4 through 1.707–9 apply to contributions and distributions of property described in section 707(a)(2)(A) and transfers described in section 707(a)(2)(B) of the Internal Revenue Code.

(f) Examples. The following examples illustrate the application of this section.

Example 1. Treatment of simultaneous transfers as a sale. A transfers property X to partnership AB on April 9, 1992, in exchange for an interest in the partnership. At the time of the transfer, property X has a fair market value of $4,000,000 and an adjusted tax basis of $1,200,000. Immediately after the transfer, the partnership transfers $3,000,000 in cash to A. Assume that, under this section, the partnership's transfer of cash to A is treated as part of a sale of property X to the partnership. Because the amount of cash A receives on April 9, 1992, does not equal the fair market value of the property, A is considered to have sold a portion of property X with a value of $3,000,000 to the partnership in exchange for the cash. Accordingly, A must recognize $2,100,000 of gain ($3,000,000 amount realized less $900,000 adjusted tax basis ($1,200,000 multiplied by $3,000,000/$4,000,000)). Assuming A receives no other transfers that are treated as consideration for the sale of the property under this section, A is considered to have contributed to the partnership, in A's capacity as a partner, $1,000,000 of the fair market value of the property with an adjusted tax basis of $300,000.

Example 2. Treatment of transfers at different times as a sale. **(i)** The facts are the same as in Example 1, except that the $3,000,000 is transferred to A one year after A's transfer of property X to the partnership. Assume that under this section the partnership's transfer of cash to A is treated as part of a sale of property X to the partnership. Assume also that the applicable Federal short-term rate for April, 1992, is 10 percent, compounded semiannually.

(ii) Under paragraph (a)(2) of this section, A and the partnership are treated as if, on April 9, 1992, A sold a portion of property X to the partnership in exchange for an obligation to transfer $3,000,000 to A one year later. Section 1274 applies to this obligation because it does not bear interest and is payable more than six months after the date of the sale. As a result, A's amount realized from the receipt of the partnership's obligation will be the imputed principal amount of the partnership's obligation to transfer $3,000,000 to A, which equals $2,721,088 (the present value on April 9, 1992, of a $3,000,000 payment due one year later, determined using a discount rate of 10 percent, compounded semiannually). Therefore, A's amount realized from the receipt of the partnership's obligation is $2,721,088 (without regard to whether the sale is reported under the installment method). A is therefore considered to have sold only $2,721,088 of the fair market value of property X. The remainder of the $3,000,000 payment ($278,912) is characterized in accordance with the provisions of section 1272. Accordingly, A must recognize $1,904,761 of gain ($2,721,088 amount realized less $816,327 adjusted tax basis ($1,200,000 multiplied by $2,721,088/$4,000,000)) on the sale of property X to the partnership. The gain is reportable under the installment method of section 453 if the sale is otherwise eligible. Assuming A receives no other transfers that are treated as consideration for the sale of property under this section, A is considered to have contributed to the partnership, in A's capacity as a partner, $1,278,912 of the fair market value of property X with an adjusted tax basis of $383,673.

Example 3. Operation of presumption for transfers within two years. **(i)** C transfers undeveloped land to the CD partnership in exchange for an interest in the partnership. The partnership intends to construct a building on the land. At the time the land is transferred to the partnership, it is unencumbered and has an adjusted tax basis of $500,000 and a fair market value of $1,000,000. The partnership agreement provides that upon completing construction of the building the partnership will distribute $900,000 to C.

(ii) If, within two years of C's transfer of land to the partnership, a transfer is made to C pursuant to the provision requiring a distribution upon completion of the building, the transfer is presumed to be, under paragraph (c) of this section, part of a sale of the land to the partnership. C may rebut the presumption that the transfer is part of a sale if the facts and circumstances clearly establish that—

(A) The transfer to C would have been made without regard to C's transfer of land to the partnership; or

(B) The partnership's obligation or ability to make this transfer to C depends, at the time of the transfer to the partnership, on the entrepreneurial risks of partnership operations.

(iii) For example, if the partnership will be able to fund the transfer of cash to C only to the extent that permanent loan proceeds exceed the cost of constructing the building, the fact that excess permanent loan proceeds will be available only if the cost to complete the building is significantly less than the amount projected by a reasonable budget would be evidence that the transfer to C is not part of a sale. Similarly, a condition that limits the amount of the permanent loan to the cost of constructing the building (and thereby limits the partnership's ability to make a transfer to C) unless all or a substantial portion of the building is leased would be evidence that the transfer to C is not part of a sale, if a significant risk exists that the partnership may not be able to lease the building to that extent. Another factor that may prove that the transfer of cash to C is not part of a sale would be that, at the time the land is transferred to the partnership, no lender has committed to make a permanent loan to fund the transfer of cash to C.

(iv) Facts indicating that the transfer of cash to C is not part of a sale, however, may be offset by other factors. An offsetting factor to restrictions on the permanent loan proceeds may be that the permanent loan is to be a recourse loan and certain conditions to the loan are likely to be waived by the lender because of the creditworthiness of the partners or the value of the partnership's other assets. Similarly, the factor that no lender has committed to fund the transfer of cash to C may be offset by facts establishing that the partnership is obligated to attempt to obtain such a loan and that its ability to obtain such a loan is not significantly dependent on the value that will be added by successful completion of the building, or that the partnership reasonably anticipates that it will have (and will utilize) an alternative source to fund the transfer of cash to C if the permanent loan proceeds are inadequate.

Example 4. Operation of presumption for transfers within two years. E is a partner in the equal EF partnership. The partnership owns two parcels of unimproved real property (parcels 1 and 2). Parcels 1 and 2 are unencumbered. Parcel 1 has a fair market value of $500,000, and parcel 2 has a fair market value of $1,500,000. E transfers additional unencumbered, unimproved real property (parcel 3) with a fair market value of $1,000,000 to the partnership in exchange for an increased interest in partnership profits of 66⅔ percent. Immediately after this transfer, the partnership sells parcel 1 for $500,000 in a transaction not in the ordinary course of business. The partnership transfers the proceeds of the sale $333,333 to E and $166,667 to F in accordance with their respective partnership interests. The transfer of $333,333 to E is presumed to be, in accordance with paragraph (c) of this section, a sale, in part, of parcel 3 to the partnership. However, the facts of this example clearly establish that $250,000 of the transfer to E is not part of a sale of parcel 3 to the partnership because E would have been distributed $250,000 from the sale of parcel 1 whether or not E had transferred parcel 3 to the partnership. The transfer to E exceeds by $83,333 ($333,333 minus $250,000) the amount of the distribution that would have been made to E if E had not transferred parcel 3 to the partnership. Therefore, $83,333 of the transfer is presumed to be part of a sale of a portion of parcel 3 to the partnership by E.

Example 5. Operation of presumption for transfers more than two years apart. (i) G transfers undeveloped land to the GH partnership in exchange for an interest in the partnership. At the time the land is transferred to the partnership, it is unencumbered and has an adjusted tax basis of $500,000 and a fair market value of $1,000,000. H contributes $1,000,000 in cash in exchange for an interest in the partnership. Under the partnership agreement, the partnership is obligated to construct a building on the land. The projected construction cost is $5,000,000, which the partnership plans to fund with its $1,000,000 in cash and the proceeds of a construction loan secured by the land and improvements.

(ii) Shortly before G's transfer of the land to the partnership, the partnership secures commitments from lending institutions for construction and permanent financing. To obtain the construction loan, H guarantees completion of the building for a cost of $5,000,000. The partnership is not obligated to reimburse or indemnify H if H must make payment on the completion guarantee. The permanent loan will be funded upon completion of the building, which is expected to occur two years after G's transfer of the land. The amount of the permanent loan is to equal the lesser of $5,000,000 or 80 percent of the appraised value of the improved property at the time the permanent loan is closed. Under the partnership agreement, the partnership is obligated to apply the proceeds of the permanent loan to retire the construction loan and to hold any excess proceeds for transfer to G 25 months after G's transfer of the land to the partnership. The appraised value of the improved property at the time the permanent loan is closed is expected to exceed $5,000,000 only if the partnership is able to lease a substantial portion of the improvements by that time, and there is a significant risk that the partnership will not be able to achieve a satisfactory occupancy level. The partnership completes construction of the building for the projected cost of $5,000,000 approximately two years after G's transfer of the land. Shortly thereafter, the permanent loan is funded in the amount of $5,000,000. At the time of funding the land and building have an appraised value of $7,000,000. The partnership transfers the $1,000,000 excess permanent loan proceeds to G 25 months after G's transfer of the land to the partnership.

(iii) G's transfer of the land to the partnership and the partnership's transfer of $1,000,000 to G occurred more than two years apart. In accordance with paragraph (d) of this section, those transfers are presumed not to be a sale unless the facts and circumstances clearly establish that the transfers constitute a sale of the property, in whole or part, to the partnership. The transfer of $1,000,000 to G would not have been made but for G's transfer of the land to the partnership. In addition, at the time G transferred the land to the partnership, G had a legally enforceable right to receive a transfer from the partnership at a specified time an amount that equals the excess of the permanent loan proceeds over $4,000,000. In this case, however, there was a significant risk that the appraised value of the property would be insufficient to support a permanent loan in excess of $4,000,000 because of the risk that the partnership would not be able to achieve a sufficient occupancy level. Therefore, the facts of this example indicate that at the time G transferred the land to the partnership the subsequent transfer of $1,000,000 to G depended on the entrepreneurial risks of partnership operations. Accordingly, G's transfer of the land to the partnership is not treated as part of a sale.

Example 6. Rebuttal of presumption for transfers more than two years apart. The facts are the same as in Example 5, except that the partnership is able to secure a commitment for a permanent loan in the amount of $5,000,000 without regard to the appraised value of the improved property at the time the permanent loan is funded. Under these facts, at the time that G transferred the land to the partnership the subsequent transfer of $1,000,000 to G was not dependent on the entrepreneurial risks of partnership operations, because during the period before the permanent loan is funded, the permanent lender's obligation to make a loan in the amount necessary to fund the transfer is not subject to the contingencies related to the risks of partnership operations, and after the permanent loan is funded, the partnership holds liquid assets sufficient to make the transfer. Therefore, the facts and circumstances clearly establish that G's transfer of the land to the partnership is part of a sale.

Example 7. Operation of presumption for transfers more than two years apart. The facts are the same as in Example 6, except that H does not guarantee either that the improvements will be completed or that the cost to the partnership of completing the improvements will not exceed $5,000,000. Under these facts, if there is a significant risk that the improvements will not be completed, G's transfer of the land to the partnership will not be treated as part of a sale because the lender is required to make the permanent loan if the improvements are not completed. Similarly, the transfers will not be treated as a sale to the extent that there is a significant risk that the cost of constructing the improvements will exceed $5,000,000, because, in the absence of a guarantee of the cost of the improvements by H, the $5,000,000 proceeds of the permanent loan might not be sufficient to retire the construction loan and fund the transfer to G. In either case, the transfer of cash to G would be dependent on the entrepreneurial risks of partnership operations.

Example 8. Rebuttal of presumption for transfers more than two years apart. (i) On February 1, 1992, I, J, and K form partnership IJK. On formation of the partnership, I transfers an unencumbered office building with a fair market value of $50,000,000 and an adjusted tax basis of $20,000,000 to the partnership, and J and K each transfer United States government securities with a fair market value and an adjusted tax basis of $25,000,000 to the partnership. Substantially all of the rentable space in the office building is leased on a long-term basis. The partnership agreement provides that all items of income, gain, loss, and deduction from the office building are to be allocated 45 percent to J, 45 percent to K, and 10 percent to I. The partnership agreement also provides that all items of income, gain, loss, and deduction from the government securities are to be allocated 90 percent to I, 5 percent to J, and 5 percent to K. The partnership agreement requires that cash flow from the office building and government securities be allocated between partners in the same manner as the items of income, gain, loss, and deduction from those properties are allocated between them. The partnership agreement complies with the requirements of § 1.704–1(b)(2)(ii)(b). It is not expected that the partnership will need to resort to the government securities or the cash flow therefrom to operate the office building. At the time the partnership is formed, I, J, and K contemplated that I's interest in the partnership would be liquidated sometime after January 31, 1994, in exchange for a transfer of the government securities and cash (if necessary). On March 1, 1995, the partnership transfers cash and the government securities to I in liquidation of I's interest in the partnership. The cash transferred to I represents the excess of I's share of the appreciation in the office building since the formation of the partnership over J's and K's share of the appreciation in the government securities since they are acquired by the partnership.

(ii) I's transfer of the office building to the partnership and the partnership's transfer of the government securities and cash to I occurred more than two years apart. Therefore, those transfers are presumed not to be a sale unless the facts and circumstances clearly establish that the transfers constitute a sale. Absent I's transfer of the office building to the securities (partnership, I would not have received the government from the partnership. The facts including the amount and nature of partnership assets) indicate that, at the time that I transferred the office building to the partnership, the timing of the transfer of the government securities to I was anticipated and was not dependent on the entrepreneurial risks of partnership operations. Moreover, the facts indicate that the partnership allocations were designed to effect an exchange of the burdens and benefits of ownership of the government securities in anticipation of the transfer of those securities to I and those burdens and benefits were effectively shifted to I on formation of the partnership. Accordingly, the facts and circumstances clearly establish that I sold the office building to the partnership on February 1, 1992, in exchange for the partnership's obligation to transfer the government securities to I and to make certain other cash transfers to I.

[T.D. 8439, 57 FR 44974, Sept. 30, 1992]

§ 1.707–4 Disguised sales of property to partnership; special rules applicable to guaranteed payments, preferred returns, operating cash flow distributions, and reimbursements of preformation expenditures.

(a) Guaranteed payments and preferred returns—(1) Guaranteed payment not treated as part of a sale—(i) In general. A guaranteed payment for capital made to a partner is not treated as part of a sale of property under § 1.707–3(a) (relating to treatment of transfers as a sale). A party's characterization of a payment as a guaranteed payment for capital will not control in determining whether a payment is, in fact, a guaranteed payment for capital. The term guaranteed payment for capital means any payment to a partner by a partnership that is determined without regard to partnership income and is for the use of that partner's capital. See section 707(c). For this purpose, one or more payments are not made for the use of a partner's capital if the payments are designed to liquidate all or part of the partner's interest in property contributed to the partnership rather than to provide the partner with a return on an investment in the partnership.

(ii) Reasonable guaranteed payments. Notwithstanding the presumption set forth in § 1.707–3(c) (relating to transfers made within two years of each other), for purposes of section 707(a)(2) and the regulations thereunder a transfer of money to a partner that is characterized by the parties as a guaranteed payment for capital, is determined without regard to the income of the partnership and is reasonable (within the meaning of paragraph (a)(3) of this section) is presumed to be a guaranteed payment for capital unless the facts and circumstances clearly establish that the transfer is not a guaranteed payment for capital and is part of a sale.

(iii) Unreasonable guaranteed payments. A transfer of money to a partner that is characterized by the parties as a guaranteed payment for capital but that is not reasonable (within the meaning of paragraph (a)(3) of this section) is presumed not to be a guaranteed payment for capital unless the facts and circumstances clearly establish that the transfer is a guaranteed payment for capital. A transfer that is not a guaranteed payment for capital is subject to the rules of § 1.707–3.

(2) Presumption regarding reasonable preferred returns. Notwithstanding the presumption set forth in § 1.707–3(c) (relating to transfers made within two years of each other), a transfer of money to a partner that is characterized by the parties as a preferred return and that is reasonable (within the meaning of paragraph (a)(3) of this section) is presumed not to be part of a sale of property to the partnership unless the facts and circumstances (including the likelihood and expected timing of the subsequent allocation of income or gain to support the preferred return) clearly establish that the transfer is part of a sale. The term preferred return means a preferential distribution of partnership cash flow to a partner with respect to capital contributed to the partnership by the partner that will be matched, to the extent available, by an allocation of income or gain.

(3) Definition of reasonable preferred returns and guaranteed payments—(i) In general. A transfer of money to a partner that is characterized as a preferred return or guaranteed payment for capital is reasonable only to the extent that the transfer is made to the partner pursuant to a written provision of a partnership agreement that provides for payment for the use of capital in a reasonable amount, and only to the extent that the payment is made for the use of capital after the date on which that provision is added to the partnership agreement.

(ii) Reasonable amount. A transfer of money that is made to a partner during any partnership taxable year and is characterized as a preferred return or guaranteed payment for capital is reasonable in amount if the sum of any preferred return and any guaranteed payment for capital that is payable for that year does not exceed the amount determined by multiplying either the partner's unreturned capital at the beginning of the year or, at the partner's option, the partner's weighted average capital balance for the year (with either amount appropriately adjusted, taking into account the relevant compounding periods, to reflect any unpaid preferred return or guaranteed payment for capital that is payable to the partner) by the safe harbor interest rate for that year. The safe harbor interest rate for a partnership's taxable year equals 150 percent of the highest applicable Federal rate, at the appropriate compounding period or periods, in effect at any time from the time that the right to the preferred return or guaranteed payment for capital is first established pursuant to a binding, written agreement among the partners through the end of the taxable year. A partner's unreturned capital equals the excess of the aggregate amount of money and the fair market value of other consideration (net of liabilities) contributed by the partner to the partnership over the aggregate amount of money and the fair market value of other consideration (net of liabilities) distributed by the partnership to the partner other than transfers of money that are presumed to be guaranteed payments for capital under paragraph (a)(1)(ii) of this section, transfers of money that are reasonable preferred returns within the meaning of this paragraph (a)(3), and operating cash flow distributions within the meaning of paragraph (b)(2) of this section.

(4) Examples. The following examples illustrate the application of paragraph (a) of this section:

Example 1. Transfer presumed to be a guaranteed payment. (i) A transfers property with a fair market value of $100,000 to partnership AB. At the time of A's transfer, the partnership agreement is amended to provide that A is to receive a guaranteed payment for the use of A's capital of 10 percent (compounded annually) of the fair market value of the transferred property in each of the three years following the transfer. The partnership agreement provides that partnership net taxable income and loss will be allocated equally between partners A and B, and that partnership cash flow will be distributed in accordance with the allocation of partnership net taxable income and loss. The partnership would be allowed a deduction in the year paid if the transfers made to A are treated as guaranteed payments under section 707(c). Under the partnership agreement, that deduction would be allocated in the same manner as any other item of partnership deduction. The partnership agreement complies with the requirements of § 1.704–1(b)(2)(ii)(b). The partnership agreement does not provide for the payment of a preferred return and, other than the guaranteed payment to be paid to A, no transfer is expected to be made during the three year period following A's transfer that is not an operating cash flow distribution (within the meaning of paragraph (b)(2) of this section). Assume that the highest applicable Federal rate in effect at the time of A's transfer is eight percent compounded annually.

(ii) The transfer of money to be made to A under the partnership agreement is characterized by the parties as a guaranteed payment for capital and is determined without regard to the income of the partnership. The transfer is also reasonable within the meaning of § 1.707–4(a)(3). The transfer, therefore, is presumed to be a guaranteed payment for capital. The presumption set forth in § 1.707–3(c) (relating to transfers made within two years of each other) thus does not apply to this transfer. The transfer will not be treated as part of a sale of property to the partnership unless the facts and circumstances clearly establish that the transfer is not a guaranteed payment for capital but is part of a sale.

(iii) The presumption that the transfer is a guaranteed payment for capital is not rebutted, because there are no facts indicating that the transfer is not a guaranteed payment for the use of capital.

Example 2. Transfers characterized as guaranteed payments treated as part of a sale. (i) C and D form partnership CD. C transfers property with a fair market value of $100,000 and an adjusted tax basis of $20,000 in exchange for a partnership interest. D is responsible for managing the day-to-day operations of the partnership and makes no capital contribution to the partnership upon its formation. The partnership agreement provides that C is to receive payments characterized as guaranteed payments and determined without regard to partnership income of $8,333 per year for the first four years of partnership operations for the use of C's capital. In addition, the partnership agreement provides that—

(A) Partnership net taxable income and loss will be allocated 75 percent to C and 25 percent to D; and

(B) All partnership cash flow (determined prior to consideration of the guaranteed payment) will be distributed 75 percent to C and 25 percent to D except that guaranteed payments that the partnership is obligated to make to C are payable solely out of D's share of the partnership's cash flow.

(ii) If D's share of the partnership's cash flow is not sufficient to make the guaranteed payment to C, then D is obligated to contribute any shortfall to the partnership, even in the event the partnership is liquidated. Thus, the effect of the guaranteed payment arrangement is that the guaranteed payment to C is funded entirely by D. The partnership agreement complies with the requirements of § 1.704–1(b)(2)(ii)(b). Assume that, at the time the partnership is formed, the partnership or D could borrow $25,000 pursuant to a loan requiring equal payments of principal and interest over a four-year term at the current market interest rate of approximately 12 percent (compounded annually). Assume that the highest applicable Federal rate in effect at the time the partnership is formed is 10 percent compounded annually.

(iii) The transfer of money to be made to C under the partnership agreement is characterized by the parties as a guaranteed payment for capital and is determined without regard to the income of the partnership. The transfer is also reasonable within the meaning of § 1.707–4(a)(3). The transfer, therefore, is presumed to be a guaranteed payment for capital. The presumption set forth in § 1.707–3(c) (relating to transfers made within two years of each other) thus does not apply to this transfer. The transfer will not be treated as part of a sale of property to the partnership unless the facts and circumstances clearly establish that the transfer is not a guaranteed payment for capital and is part of a sale.

(iv) For the first four years of partnership operations, the total guaranteed payments made to C under the partnership agreement will equal $33,332. If the characterization of those payments as guaranteed payments for capital within the meaning of section 707(c) were respected, C would be allocated $24,999 of the deductions that would be claimed by the partnership for those payments, thereby leaving the balance in C's capital account approximately $25,000 less than it would have been if the guaranteed payments had not been made. The guaranteed payments thus have the effect of offsetting approximately $25,000 of the credit made to C's capital account for the property transferred to the partnership by C. C's resulting capital account is approximately equivalent to the capital account C would have had if C had only contributed 75 percent of the property to the partnership. Furthermore, the effect of D's funding the guaranteed payment to C (either through reduced distributions of cash flow to D or additional contributions) is that D's capital account is approximately equivalent to the capital account D would have had if D had contributed 25 percent of the property (or contributed cash so that the partnership could purchase the 25 percent). Moreover, a $25,000 loan requiring equal payments of principal and interest over a four-year term at the current market interest rate of 12 percent (compounded annually), would have resulted in annual payments of principal and interest of $8,230.86. Consequently, the guaranteed payments effectively place the partners in the same economic position that they would have been in had D purchased a one-quarter interest in the property from C financed at the current market rate of interest, and then C and D each contributed their share of the property to the partnership. In view of the burden the guaranteed payments place on D's right to transfers of partnership cash flow and D's legal obligation to make contributions to the partnership to the extent necessary to fund the guaranteed payments, D has effectively purchased through the partnership a one-quarter interest in the property from C.

(v) Under these facts, the presumption that the transfers to C are guaranteed payments for capital is rebutted, because the facts and circumstances clearly establish that the transfers are part of a sale and not guaranteed payments for capital. Under § 1.707–3(a), C and the partnership are treated as if C sold a one-quarter interest in the property to the partnership in exchange for a promissory note evidencing the partnership's obligation to make the guaranteed payments.

(b) Presumption regarding operating cash flow distributions—(1) In general. Notwithstanding the presumption set forth in § 1.707–3(c) (relating to transfers made within two years of each other), an operating cash flow distribution is presumed not to be part of a sale of property to the partnership unless the facts and circumstances clearly establish that the transfer is part of a sale.

(2) Operating cash flow distributions—(i) In general. One or more transfers of money by the partnership to a partner during a taxable year of the partnership are operating cash flow distributions for purposes of paragraph (b)(1) of this section to the extent that those transfers are not presumed to be guaranteed payments for capital under paragraph (a)(1)(ii) of this section, are not reasonable preferred returns within the meaning of paragraph (a)(3) of this section, are not characterized by the parties as distributions to the partner acting in a capacity other than as a partner, and to the extent they do not exceed the product of the net cash flow of the partnership from operations for the year multiplied by the lesser of the partner's percentage interest in overall partnership profits for that year or the partner's percentage interest in overall partnership profits for the life of the partnership. For purposes of the preceding sentence, the net cash flow of the partnership from operations for a taxable year is an amount equal to the taxable income or loss of the partnership arising in the ordinary course of the partnership's business and investment activities, increased by tax exempt interest, depreciation, amortization, cost recovery allowances and other noncash charges deducted in determining such taxable income and decreased by—

(A) Principal payments made on any partnership indebtedness;

(B) Property replacement or contingency reserves actually established by the partnership;

(C) Capital expenditures when made other than from reserves or from borrowings the proceeds of which are not included in operating cash flow; and

(D) Any other cash expenditures (including preferred returns) not deducted in determining such taxable income or loss.

(ii) Operating cash flow safe harbor. For any taxable year, in determining a partner's operating cash flow distributions for the year, the partner may use the partner's smallest percentage interest under the terms of the partnership agreement in any material item of partnership income or gain that may be realized by the partnership in the three-year period beginning with such taxable year. This provision is merely intended to provide taxpayers with a safe harbor and is not intended to preclude a taxpayer from using a different percentage under the rules of paragraph (b)(2)(i) of this section.

(iii) Tiered partnerships. In the case of tiered partnerships, the upper-tier partnership must take into account its share of the net cash flow from operations of the lower-tier partnership applying principles similar to those described in paragraph (b)(2)(i) of this section, so that the amount of the upper-tier partnership's operating cash flow distributions is neither overstated nor understated.

(c) Accumulation of guaranteed payments, preferred returns, and operating cash flow distributions. Guaranteed payments for capital, preferred returns, and operating cash flow distributions presumed not to be part of a sale under the rules of paragraphs (a) and (b) of this section do not lose the benefit of the presumption by reason of being retained for distribution in a later year.

(d) Exception for reimbursements of preformation expenditures. A transfer of money or other consideration by the partnership to a partner is not treated as part of a sale of property by the partner to the partnership under § 1.707–3(a) (relating to treatment of transfers as a sale) to the extent that the transfer to the partner by the partnership is made to reimburse the partner for, and does not exceed the amount of, capital expenditures that—

(1) Are incurred during the two-year period preceding the transfer by the partner to the partnership; and

(2) Are incurred by the partner with respect to—

(i) Partnership organization and syndication costs described in section 709; or

(ii) Property contributed to the partnership by the partner, but only to the extent the reimbursed capital expenditures do not exceed 20 percent of the fair market value of such property at the time of the contribution. However, the 20 percent of fair market value limitation of this paragraph (d)(2)(ii) does not apply if the fair market value of the contributed property does not exceed 120 percent of the partner's adjusted basis in the contributed property at the time of contribution.

(e) Other exceptions. The Commissioner may provide by guidance published in the Internal Revenue Bulletin that other payments or transfers to a partner are not treated as part of a sale for purposes of section 707(a)(2) and the regulations thereunder.

[T.D. 8439, 57 FR 44974, Sept. 30, 1992; 57 FR 56444, Nov. 30, 1992]

§ 1.707–5 Disguised sales of property to partnership; special rules relating to liabilities.

(a) Liability assumed or taken subject to by partnership—(1) In general. For purposes of this section and §§ 1.707–3 and 1.707–4, if a partnership assumes or takes property subject to a qualified liability (as defined in paragraph (a)(6) of this section) of a partner, the partnership is treated as transferring consideration to the partner only to the extent provided in paragraph (a)(5) of this section. By contrast, if the partnership assumes or takes property subject to a liability of the partner other than a qualified liability, the partnership is treated as transferring consideration to the partner to the extent that the amount of the liability exceeds the partner's share of that liability immediately after the partnership assumes or takes subject to the liability as provided in paragraphs (a)(2), (3) and (4) of this section.

(2) Partner's share of liability. A partner's share of any liability of the partnership is determined under the following rules:

(i) Recourse liability. A partner's share of a recourse liability of the partnership equals the partner's share of the liability under the rules of section 752 and the regulations thereunder. A partnership liability is a recourse liability to the extent that the obligation is a recourse liability under § 1.752-1(a)(1) or would be treated as a recourse liability under that section if it were treated as a partnership liability for purposes of that section.

(ii) Nonrecourse liability. A partner's share of a nonrecourse liability of the partnership is determined by applying the same percentage used to determine the partner's share of the excess nonrecourse liability under § 1.752-3(a)(3). A partnership liability is a nonrecourse liability of the partnership to the extent that the obligation is a nonrecourse liability under § 1.752-1(a)(2) or would be a nonrecourse liability of the partnership under § 1.752-1(a)(2) if it were treated as a partnership liability for purposes of that section.

(3) Reduction of partner's share of liability. For purposes of this section, a partner's share of a liability, immediately after a partnership assumes or takes subject to the liability, is determined by taking into account a subsequent reduction in the partner's share if—

(i) At the time that the partnership assumes or takes subject to a liability, it is anticipated that the transferring partner's share of the liability will be subsequently reduced; and

(ii) The reduction of the partner's share of the liability is part of a plan that has as one of its principal purposes minimizing the extent to which the assumption of or taking subject to the liability is treated as part of a sale under § 1.707-3.

(4) Special rule applicable to transfers of encumbered property to a partnership by more than one partner pursuant to a plan. For purposes of paragraph (a)(1) of this section, if the partnership assumes or takes property or properties subject to the liabilities of more than one partner pursuant to a plan, a partner's share of the liabilities assumed or taken subject to by the partnership pursuant to that plan immediately after the transfers equals the sum of that partner's shares of the liabilities (other than that partner's qualified liabilities, as defined in paragraph (a)(6) of this section) assumed or taken subject to by the partnership pursuant to the plan. This paragraph (a)(4) does not apply to any liability assumed or taken subject to by the partnership with a principal purpose of reducing the extent to which any other liability assumed or taken subject to by the partnership is treated as a transfer of consideration under paragraph (a)(1) of this section.

(5) Special rule applicable to qualified liabilities. **(i)** If a transfer of property by a partner to a partnership is not otherwise treated as part of a sale, the partnership's assumption of or taking subject to a qualified liability in connection with a transfer of property is not treated as part of a sale. If a transfer of property by a partner to the partnership is treated as part of a sale without regard to the partnership's assumption of or taking subject to a qualified liability (as defined in paragraph (a)(6) of this section) in connection with the transfer of property, the partnership's assumption of or taking subject to that liability is treated as a transfer of consideration made pursuant to a sale of such property to the partnership only to the extent of the lesser of—

(A) The amount of consideration that the partnership would be treated as transferring to the partner under paragraph (a)(1) of this section if the liability were not a qualified liability; or

(B) The amount obtained by multiplying the amount of the qualified liability by the partner's net equity percentage with respect to that property.

(ii) A partner's net equity percentage with respect to an item of property equals the percentage determined by dividing—

(A) The aggregate transfers of money or other consideration to the partner by the partnership (other than any transfer described in this paragraph (a)(5)) that are treated as proceeds realized from the sale of the transferred property; by

(B) The excess of the fair market value of the property at the time it is transferred to the partnership over any qualified liability encumbering the property or, in the case of any qualified liability described in paragraph (a)(6)(i)(C) or (D) of this section, that is properly allocable to the property.

(6) Qualified liability of a partner defined. A liability assumed or taken subject to by a partnership in connection with a transfer of property to the partnership by a partner is qualified liability of the partner only to the extent—

(i) The liability is—

(A) A liability that was incurred by the partner more than two years prior to the earlier of the date the partner agrees in writing to transfers the property or the date the partner transfers the property to the partnership and that has encumbered the transferred property throughout that two-year period;

(B) A liability that was not incurred in anticipation of the transfer of the property to a partnership, buy that was incurred by the partner within the two-year period prior to the earlier of the date the partner agrees in writing to transfer the property or the date the partner transfers the property to the partnership and that has encumbered the transferred property since it was incurred (see paragraph (a)(7) of this section for further rules regarding a liability incurred within two years of a property transfer or of a written agreement to transfer);

(C) A liability that is allocable under the rules of § 1.163–8T to capital expenditures with respect to the property; or

(D) A liability that was incurred in the ordinary course of the trade or business in which property transferred to the partnership was used or held but only if all the assets related to that trade or business are transferred other than assets that are not material to a continuation of the trade or business; and

(ii) If the liability is a recourse liability, the amount of the liability does not exceed the fair market value of the transferred property (less the amount of any other liabilities that are senior in priority and that either encumber such property or are liabilities described in paragraph (a)(6)(i)(C) or (D) of this section) at the time of the transfer.

(7) Liability incurred within two years of transfer presumed to be in anticipation of the transfer—(i) In general. For purposes of this section, if within a two-year period a partner incurs a liability (other than a liability described in paragraph (a)(6)(i)(C) or (D) of this section) and transfers property to a partnership or agrees in writing to transfer the property, and in connection with the transfer the partnership assumes or takes the property subject to the liability, the liability is presumed to be incurred in anticipation of the transfer unless the facts and circumstances clearly establish that the liability was not incurred in anticipation of the transfer.

(ii) Disclosure of transfers of property subject to liabilities incurred within two years of the transfer. If a partner treats a liability assumed or taken subject to by a partnership as a qualified liability under paragraph (a)(6)(i)(B) of this section, such treatment is to be disclosed to the Internal Revenue Service in accordance with § 1.707–8.

(b) Treatment of debt-financed transfers of consideration by partnerships—(1) In general. For purposes of § 1.707–3, if a partner transfers property to a partnership, and the partnership incurs a liability and all or a portion of the proceeds of that liability are allocable under § 1.163–8T to a transfer of money or other consideration to the partner made within 90 days of incurring the liability, the transfer of money or other consideration to the partner is taken into account only to the extent that the amount of money or the fair market value of the other consideration transferred exceeds that partner's allocable share of the partnership liability.

(2) Partner's allocable share of liability—(i) In general. A partner's allocable share of a partnership liability for purposes of paragraph (b)(1) of this section equals the amount obtained by multiplying the partner's share of the liability as described in paragraph (a)(2) of this section by the fraction determined by dividing—

(A) The portion of the liability that is allocable under § 1.163–8T to the money or other property transferred to the partner; by

(B) The total amount of the liability.

(ii) Debt-financed transfers made pursuant to a plan.—(A) In general. Except as provided in paragraph (b)(2)(iii) of this section, if a partnership transfers to more than one partner pursuant to a plan all or a portion of the proceeds of one or more partnership liabilities, paragraph (b)(1) of this section is applied by treating all of the liabilities incurred pursuant to the plan as one liability, and each partner's allocable share of those liabilities equals the amount obtained by multiplying the sum of the partner's shares of each of the respective liabilities (as defined in paragraph (a)(2) of this section) by the fraction obtained by dividing—

(1) The portion of those liabilities that is allocable under § 1.163–8T to the money or other consideration transferred to the partners pursuant to the plan; by

(2) The total amount of those liabilities.

(B) Special rule. Paragraph (b)(2)(ii)(A) of this section does not apply to any transfer of money or other property to a partner that is made with a principal purpose of reducing the extent to which any transfer is taken into account under paragraph (b)(1) of this section.

(iii) Reduction of partner's share of liability. For purposes of paragraph (b)(2) of this section, a partner's share of a liability, immediately after the partnership assumes or takes subject to the liability, is determined by taking into account a subsequent reduction in the partner's share if—

(A) It is anticipated that the partner's share of the liability that is allocable to a transfer of money or other consideration to the partner will be reduced subsequent to the transfer; and

(B) The reduction of the partner's share of the liability is part of a plan that has as one of its principal purposes minimizing the extent to which the partnership's distribution of the proceeds of the borrowing is treated as part of a sale.

(c) Refinancings. To the extent that the proceeds of a partner or partnership liability (the refinancing debt) are allocable under the rules of § 1.163–8T to payments discharging all or part of any other liability of that partner or of the partnership, as the case may be, the refinancing debt is treated as the other liability for purposes of applying the rules of this section.

(d) Share of liability where assumption accompanied by transfer of money. For purposes of §§ 1.707–3 through 1.707–5, if pursuant to a plan a partner pays or contributes money to the partnership and the partnership assumes or takes subject to one or more liabilities (other than qualified liabilities) of the partner, the amount of those liabilities that the partnership is treated as assuming or taking subject to is reduced (but not below zero) by the money transferred.

(e) Tiered partnerships and other related persons. If a lower-tier partnership succeeds to a liability of an upper-tier partnership, the liability in the lower-tier partnership retains the characterization as qualified or nonqualified that it had under these rules in the upper-tier partnership. A similar rule applies to other related party transactions involving liabilities to the extent provided by guidance published in the Internal Revenue Bulletin.

(f) Examples. The following examples illustrate the application of this section.

Example 1. Partnership's assumption of nonrecourse liability encumbering transferred property. **(i)** A and B form partnership AB, which will engage in renting office space. A transfers $500,000 in cash to the partnership, and B transfers an office building to the partnership. At the time it is transferred to the partnership, the office building has a fair market value of $1,000,000, an adjusted basis of $400,000, and is encumbered by a $500,000 liability, which B incurred 12 months earlier to finance the acquisition of other property. No facts rebut the presumption that the liability was incurred in anticipation of the transfer of the property to the partnership. Assume that this liability is a nonrecourse liability of the partnership within the meaning of section 752 and the regulations thereunder. The partnership agreement provides that partnership items will be allocated equally between A and B, including excess nonrecourse deductions under § 1.752–3(a)(3). The partnership agreement complics with the requirements of § 1.704–1(b)(2)(ii)(b).

(ii) The nonrecourse liability secured by the office building is not a qualified liability within the meaning of paragraph (a)(6) of this section. B would be allocated 50 percent of the excess nonrecourse liability under the partnership agreement. Accordingly, immediately after the partnership's assumption of that liability, B's share of the liability equals $250,000, which is equal to B's 50 percent share of the excess nonrecourse liability of the partnership as determined in accordance with B's share of partnership profits under § 1.752–3(a)(3).

(iii) The partnership's taking subject to the liability encumbering the office building is treated as a transfer of $250,000 of consideration to B (the amount by which the liability ($500,000) exceeds B's share of that liability immediately after taking subject to $250,000). B is treated as having sold $250,000 of the fair market value of the office building to the partnership in exchange for the partnership's taking subject to a $250,000 liability. This results in a gain of $150,000 ($250,000 minus ($250,000/$1,000,000 multiplied by $400,000)).

Example 2. Partnership's assumption of recourse liability encumbering transferred property. **(i)** C transfers property Y to a partnership. At the time of its transfer to the partnership, property Y has a fair market value of $10,000,000 and is subject to an $8,000,000 liability that C incurred, immediately before transferring property Y to the partnership, in order to finance other expenditures. Upon the transfer of property Y to the partnership, the partnership assumed the liability encumbering that property. The partnership assumed this liability solely to acquire property Y. Under section 752 and the regulations thereunder, immediately after the partnership's assumption of the liability encumbering property Y, the liability is a recourse liability of the partnership and C's share of that liability is $7,000,000.

(ii) Under the facts of this example, the liability encumbering property Y is not a qualified liability.

Accordingly, the partnership's assumption of the liability results in a transfer of consideration to C in connection with C's transfer of property Y to the partnership in the amount of $1,000,000 (the excess of the liability assumed by the partnership ($8,000,000) over C's share of the liability immediately after the assumption ($7,000,000)). See paragraphs (a)(1) and (2) of this section.

Example 3. Subsequent reduction of transferring partner's share of liability. **(i)** The facts are the same as in Example 2. In addition, property Y is a fully leased office building, the rental income from property Y is sufficient to meet debt service, and the remaining term of the liability is ten years. It is anticipated that, three years after the partnership's assumption of the liability, C's share of the liability under section 752 will be reduced to zero because of a shift in the allocation of partnership losses pursuant to the terms of the partnership agreement. Under the partnership agreement, this shift in the allocation of partnership losses is dependent solely on the passage of time.

(ii) Under paragraph (a)(3) of this section, if the reduction in C's share of the liability was anticipated at the time of C's transfer, and the reduction was part of a plan that has as one of its principal purposes minimizing the extent of sale treatment under § 1.707–3 (i.e., a principal purpose of allocating a large percentage of losses to C in the first three years when losses were not likely to be realized was to minimize the extent to which C's transfer would be treated as part of a sale), C's share of the liability immediately after the assumption is treated as equal to C's reduced share.

Example 4. Trade payables as qualified liabilities. **(i)** D and E form partnership DE which will engage in a consulting business that requires no overhead and minimal cash on hand for daily operating expenses. Previously, D and E, as individual sole proprietors, operated separate consulting businesses. D and E each transfer to the partnership sufficient cash to cover daily operating expenses together with the goodwill and trade payables related to each sole proprietorship. Due to uncertainty over the collection rate on the trade receivables related to their sole proprietorships, D and E agree that none of the trade receivables will be transferred to the partnership.

(ii) Under the facts of this example, all the assets related to the consulting business (other than the trade receivables) together with the trade payables were transferred to partnership DE. The trade receivables retained by D and E are not material to a continuation of the trade or business by the partnership because D and E contributed sufficient cash to cover daily operating expenses. Accordingly, the trade payables transferred to the partnership constitute qualified liability under paragraph (a)(6) of this section.

Example 5. Partnership's assumption of a qualified liability as sole consideration. **(i)** F transfers property Z to a partnership. At the time of its transfer to the partnership, property Z has a fair market value of $165,000 and an adjusted tax basis of $75,000. Also, at the time of the transfer, property Z is subject to a $75,000 liability that F incurred more than two years before transferring property Z to the partnership. The liability has been secured by property Z since it was incurred by F. Upon the transfer of property Z to the partnership, the partnership assumed the liability encumbering that property. The partnership made no other transfers to F in consideration for the transfer of property Z to the partnership. Assume that, under section 752 and the regulations thereunder, immediately after the partnership's assumption of the liability encumbering property Z, the liability is a recourse liability of the partnership and F's share of that liability is $25,000.

(ii) The $75,000 liability secured by property Z is a qualified liability of F because F incurred the liability more than two years prior to the assumption of the liability by the partnership and the liability has encumbered property Z for more than two years prior to that assumption. See paragraph (a)(6) of this section. Therefore, since no other transfer to F was made as consideration for the transfer of property Z, under paragraph (a)(5) of this section, the partnership's assumption of the qualified liability of F encumbering property Z is not treated as part of a sale.

Example 6. Partnership's assumption of a qualified liability in addition to other consideration. **(i)** The facts are the same as in Example 5, except that the partnership makes a transfer to D of $30,000 in money that is consideration for F's transfer of property Z to the partnership under § 1.707–3.

(ii) As in Example 5, the $75,000 liability secured by property Z is a qualified liability of F. Since the partnership transferred $30,000 to F in addition to assuming the qualified liability under paragraph (a)(5) of this section, the partnership's assumption of this qualified liability is treated as a transfer of additional consideration to F to the extent of the lesser of—

(A) The amount that the partnership would be treated as transferring to F if the liability were not a qualified liability ($50,000 (i.e., the excess of the $75,000 qualified liability over F's $25,000 share of that liability)); or

(B) The amount obtained by multiplying the qualified liability ($75,000) by F's net equity percentage with respect to property Z (one-third).

(iii) F's net equity percentage with respect to property Z equals the fraction determined by dividing—

(A) The aggregate amount of money or other consideration (other than the qualified liability) transferred to F and treated as part of a sale of property Z under § 1.707–3(a) ($30,000 transfer of money); by

(B) F's net equity in property Z ($90,000 (i.e., the excess of the $165,000 fair market value over the $75,000 qualified liability)).

(iv) Accordingly, the partnership's assumption of the qualified liability of F encumbering property Z is treated as a transfer of $25,000 (one-third of $75,000) of consideration to F pursuant to a sale. Therefore, F is treated as having sold $55,000 of the fair market value of property Z to the partnership in exchange for $30,000 in money and the partnership's assumption of $25,000 of the qualified liability. Accordingly, F must recognize $30,000 of gain on the sale (the excess of the $55,000 amount realized over $25,000 of F's adjusted basis for property, Z (i.e., one-third of F's adjusted basis for the property, because F is treated as having sold one-third of the property to the partnership)).

Example 7. Partnership's assumptions of liabilities encumbering properties transferred pursuant to a plan. **(i)** Pursuant to a plan, G and H transfer property 1 and property 2, respectively, to an existing partnership in exchange for interests in the partnership. At the time the properties are transferred to the partnership, property 1 has a fair market value of $10,000 and an adjusted tax basis of $6,000, and property 2 has a fair market value of $10,000 and an adjusted tax basis of $4,000. At the time properties 1 and 2 are transferred to the partnership, a $6,000 nonrecourse liability (liability 1) is secured by property 1 and a $7,000 recourse liability of F (liability 2) is secured by property 2. Properties 1 and 2 are transferred to the partnership, and the partnership takes subject to liability 1 and assumes liability 2. G and H incurred liabilities 1 and 2 immediately prior to transferring properties 1 and 2 to the partnership and used the proceeds for personal expenditures. The liabilities are not qualified liabilities. Assume that G and H are each allocated $2,000 of liability 1 in accordance with § 1.707–5(a)(2)(ii) (which determines a partner's share of a nonrecourse liability). Assume further that G's share of liability 2 is $3,500 and H's share is $0 in accordance with § 1.707–5(a)(2)(i) (which determines a partner's share of a recourse liability).

(ii) G and H transferred properties 1 and 2 to the partnership pursuant to a plan. Accordingly, the partnership's taking subject to liability 1 is treated as a transfer of only $500 of consideration to G, (the amount by which liability 1 ($6,000) exceeds G's share of liabilities 1 and 2 ($5,500)), and the partnership's assumption of liability 2 is treated as a transfer of only $5,000 of consideration to H (the amount by which liability 2 ($7,000) exceeds H's share of liabilities 1 and 2 ($2,000)). G is treated under the rule in § 1.707–3 as having sold $500 of the fair market value of property 1 in exchange for the partnership's taking subject to liability 1 and H is treated as having sold $5,000 of the fair market value of property 2 in exchange for the assumption of liability 2.

Example 8. Partnership's assumption of liability pursuant to a plan to avoid sale treatment of partnership assumption of another liability. **(i)** The facts are the same as in Example 7, except that—

(A) H transferred the proceeds of liability 2 to the partnership; and

(B) H incurred liability 2 in an attempt to reduce the extent to which the partnership's taking subject to liability 1 would be treated as a transfer of consideration to G (and thereby reduce the portion of G's transfer of property 1 to the partnership that would be treated as part of a sale).

(ii) Because the partnership assumed liability 2 with a principal purpose of reducing the extent to which the partnership's taking subject to liability 1 would be treated as a transfer of consideration to G, liability 2 is ignored in applying paragraph (a)(3) of this section. Accordingly, the partnership's taking subject to liability 1 is treated as a transfer of $4,000 of consideration to G (the amount by which liability 1 ($6,000) exceeds G's share of liability 1 ($2,000)). On the other hand, the partnership's assumption of liability 2 is not treated as a transfer of any consideration to H because H's share of that liability equals $7,000 as a result of H's transfer of $7,000 in money to the partnership.

Example 9. Partnership's assumptions of qualified liabilities encumbering properties transferred pursuant to a plan in addition to other consideration. **(i)** Pursuant to a plan, I transfers property 1 and J transfers property 2 plus $10,000 in cash to partnership IJ in exchange for equal interests in the partnership. At the time the properties are transferred to the partnership, property 1 has a fair market value of $100,000, an adjusted tax basis of $5,000, and is encumbered by a qualified liability of $50,000 (liability 1). Property 2 has a fair market value of $100,000, an adjusted tax basis of $5,000, and is encumbered by a qualified liability of $70,000 (liability 2). Pursuant to the plan, the partnership transferred to I $10,000 in cash. That amount is consideration for I's transfer of property 1 to the partnership under § 1.707–3. In accordance with § 1.707–5(a)(2), I and J are each allocated $25,000 of liability 1 and $35,000 of liability 2.

(ii) Because the partnership transferred $10,000 to I as consideration for the transfer of property, under § 1.707–5(a)(5), the partnership's assumption of liability 1 is treated as a transfer of additional consideration to I, even though liability 1 is a qualified liability, to the extent of the lesser of—

(A) The amount that the partnership would be treated as transferring to I if the liability were not a qualified liability; or

(B) The amount obtained by multiplying the qualified liability by I's net equity percentage with respect to property 1.

(iii) Because I and J transferred properties 1 and 2 to the partnership pursuant to a plan, treating I's qualified liability as a nonqualified liability under § 1.707–5(a)(5)(i)(A) enables I to apply the special rule applicable to transfers of encumbered property to a partnership by more than one partner pursuant to a plan under § 1.707–5(a)(4). Under this alternative test, the partnership's assumption of liability 1 encumbering property 1 is treated as a transfer of zero ($0) additional consideration to I pursuant to a sale. This is because the amount of liability 1 ($50,000) does not exceed the sum of I's share of liability 1 treated as a nonqualified liability ($25,000) and I's share of liability 2 ($35,000).

(iv) The alternative under § 1.707–5(a)(5)(i)(B) is the amount obtained by multiplying the qualified liability ($50,000) by I's net equity percentage with respect to property 1. I's net equity percentage with respect to property 1 equals one-fifth, the fraction determined by dividing—

(A) The aggregate amount of money or other consideration (other than the qualified liability) transferred to I and treated as part of a sale of property 1 under § 1.707–3(a) (the $10,000 transfer of money); by

(B) I's net equity in property 1 ($50,000 i.e., the excess of the $100,000 fair market value over the $50,000 qualified liability).

(v) Under this alternative test, the partnership's assumption of the qualified liability encumbering property 1 is treated as a transfer of $10,000 (one-fifth of the $50,000 qualified liability) of additional consideration to I pursuant to a sale.

(vi) Applying § 1.707–5(a)(5) to these facts, the partnership's assumption of liability 1 is treated as a transfer of additional consideration to I to the extent of the lesser of—

(A) zero; or

(B) $10,000.

(vii) Therefore, the partnership's assumption of I's qualified liability encumbering property 1 is not treated as a transfer of any additional consideration to I pursuant to a sale, and I is treated as having only received $10,000 of the fair market value of property 1 to the partnership in exchange for $10,000 in cash. Accordingly, I must recognize $9,500 of gain on the sale, that is, the excess of the $10,000 amount realized over $500 of I's adjusted tax basis for property 1 (one-tenth of I's adjusted tax basis for the property, because I is treated as having sold one-tenth of the property to the partnership). Since no other transfer to J was made as consideration for the transfer of property 2, the partnership's assumption of the qualified liability of J encumbering property 2 is not treated as part of a sale.

Example 10. Treatment of debt-financed transfers of consideration by partnership. **(i)** K transfers property Z to partnership KL in exchange for an interest therein on April 9, 1992. On September 13, 1992, the partnership incurs a liability of $20,000. On November 17, 1992, the partnership transfers $20,000 to K, and $10,000 of this transfer is allocable under the rules of § 1.163–8T to proceeds of the partnership liability incurred on September 13, 1992. The remaining $10,000 is paid from other partnership funds. Assume that, under section 752 and the corresponding regulations, the $20,000 liability incurred on September 13, 1992, is a recourse liability of the partnership and K's share of that liability is $10,000 on November 17, 1992.

(ii) Because a portion of the transfer made to K on November 17, 1992, is allocable under § 1.163–8T to proceeds of a partnership liability that was incurred by the partnership within 90 days of that transfer, K is required to take the transfer into account in applying the rules of this section and § 1.707–3 only to the extent that the amount of the transfer exceeds K's allocable share of the liability used to fund the transfer. K's allocable share of the $20,000 liability used to fund $10,000 of the transfer to K is $5,000 (K's share of the liability ($10,000)) multiplied by the fraction obtained by dividing—

(A) The amount of the liability that is allocable to the distribution to K ($10,000); by

(B) The total amount of such liability ($20,000).

(iii) Therefore, K is required to take into account only $15,000 of the $20,000 partnership transfer to K for purposes of this section and § 1.707–3. Under these facts, assuming the within-two-year presumption is not rebutted, this $15,000 transfer will be treated under the rule in § 1.707–3 as part of a sale by K of property Z to the partnership.

Example 11. Borrowing against pool of receivables. **(i)** M generates receivables which have an adjusted basis of zero in the ordinary course of its business. For M to use receivables as security for a loan, a commercial lender requires M to transfer the receivables to a partnership in which M has a 90 percent interest. In January, 1992, M transfers to the partnership receivables with a face value of $100,000. N (who is not related to M) transfers $10,000 cash to the partnership in exchange for a 10 percent interest. The partnership borrows $80,000, secured by the receivables, and makes a distribution of $72,000 of the proceeds to M and $8,000 of the proceeds to N within 90 days of incurring the liability. M's share of the liability under § 1.707–5(a)(2) is $72,000 (90 percent × $80,000).

(ii) Because the transfer of the loan proceeds to M is allocable under § 1.163–8T to proceeds of a partnership loan that was incurred by the partnership within 90 days of that transfer, M is required to take the transfer into account in applying the rules of this section and § 1.707–3 only to the extent that the amount of the transfer ($72,-000) exceeds M's allocable share of the liability used to fund the transfer. Because the distribution was a debt-financed transfer pursuant to a plan, M's allocable share of the liability is $72,000 ($72,000 × $80,000/80,000) under § 1.707–5(b)(2)(ii). Therefore, M is not required to take into account any of the loan proceeds for purposes of this section and § 1.707–3.

(iii) When the receivables are collected, M must be allocated the gain on the contributed receivables under section 704(c). However, the lender permits the partnership to distribute cash to the partners only to the extent of the value of new receivables contributed to the partnership. In 1993, M contributes additional receivables and receives a distribution of cash. The taxable income recognized by the partnership on the receivables is taxable income of the partnership arising in the ordinary course of the partnership's activities. To the extent the distribution does not exceed 90 percent (M's percentage interest in overall partnership profits) of the partnership's operating cash flow under § 1.707–4(b), the distribution to M is presumed not to be a part of a sale of receivables by M to the partnership, and the presumption is not rebutted under these facts.

[T.D. 8439, 57 FR 44974, Sept. 30, 1992]

§ 1.707–6 Disguised sales of property by partnership to partner; general rules.

(a) In general. Rules similar to those provided in § 1.707–3 apply in determining whether a transfer of property by a partnership to a partner and one or more transfers of money or other consideration by that partner to the partnership are treated as a sale of property, in whole or in part, to the partner.

(b) Special rules relating to liabilities—(1) In general. Rules similar to those provided in § 1.707–5 apply to determine the extent to which an assumption of or taking subject to a liability by a partner, in connection with a transfer of property by a partnership, is considered part of a sale. Accordingly, if a partner assumes or takes property subject to a qualified liability (as defined in paragraph (b)(2) of this section) of a partnership, the partner is treated as transferring consideration to the partnership only to the extent provided in paragraph (b). If the partner assumes or takes subject to a liability that is not a qualified liability, the amount treated as consideration transferred to the partnership is the amount that the liability assumed or taken subject to by the partner exceeds the partner's share of that liability (determined under the rules of § 1.707–5(a)(2)) immediately before the transfer. Similar to the rules provided in § 1.707–5(a)(4), if more than one partner assumes or takes subject to a liability pursuant to a plan, the amount that is treated as a transfer of consideration by each partner is the amount by which all of the liabilities (other than qualified liabilities) assumed or taken subject to by the partner pursuant to the plan exceed the partner's share of all of those liabilities immediately before the assumption or taking subject to. This paragraph (b)(1) does not apply to any liability assumed or taken subject to by a partner with a principal purpose of reducing the extent to which any other liability assumed or taken subject to by a partner is treated as a transfer of consideration under this paragraph (b).

(2) Qualified liabilities. (i) If a transfer of property by a partnership to a partner is not otherwise treated as part of a sale, the partner's assumption of or taking subject to a qualified liability is not treated as part of a sale. If a transfer of property by a partnership to the partner is treated as part of a sale without regard to the partner's assumption of or taking subject to a qualified liability, the partner's assumption of or taking subject to that liability is treated as a transfer of consideration made pursuant to a sale of such property to the partner only to the extent of the lesser of—

(A) The amount of consideration that the partner would be treated as transferring to the partnership under paragraph (b) of this section if the liability were not a qualified liability; or

(B) The amount obtained by multiplying the amount of the liability at the time of its assumption or taking subject to by the partnership's net equity percentage with respect to that property.

(ii) A partnership's net equity percentage with respect to an item of property encumbered by a qualified liability equals the percentage determined by dividing—

(A) The aggregate transfers to the partnership from the partner (other than any transfer described in this paragraph (b)(2)) that are treated as the proceeds realized from the sale of the transferred property to the partner; by

(B) The excess of the fair market value of the property at the time it is transferred to the partner over any qualified liabilities of the partnership that are assumed or taken subject to by the partner at that time.

(iii) For purposes of this section, the definition of a qualified liability is that provided in § 1.707–5(a)(6) with the following exceptions—

(A) In applying the definition, the qualified liability is one that is originally an obligation of the partnership and is assumed or taken subject to by the partner in connection with a transfer of property to the partner; and

(B) If the liability was incurred by the partnership more than two years prior to the earlier of the date the partnership agrees in writing to transfer the property or the date the partnership transfers the property to the partner, that liability is a qualified liability whether or not it has encumbered the transferred property throughout the two-year period.

(c) Disclosure rules. Similar to the rules provided in §§ 1.707–3(c)(2) and 1.707–5(a)(7)(ii), a partnership is to disclose to the Internal Revenue Service, in accordance with § 1.707–8, the facts in the following circumstances:

(1) When a partnership transfers property to a partner and the partner transfers money or other consideration to the partnership within a two-year period (without regard to the order of the transfers) and the partnership treats the transfers as other than a sale for tax purposes; and

(2) When a partner assumes or takes subject to a liability of a partnership in connection with a transfer of property by the partnership to the partner, and the partnership incurred the liability within the two-year period prior to the earlier of the date the partnership agrees in writing to the transfer of property or the date the partnership transfers the property, and the partnership treats the liability as a qualified liability under rules similar to § 1.707–5(a)(6)(i)(B).

(d) Examples. The following examples illustrate the rules of this section.

Example 1. Sale of property by partnership to partner. (i) A is a member of a partnership. The partnership transfers property X to A. At the time of the transfer, property X has a fair market value of $1,000,000. One year after the transfer, A transfers $1,100,000 to the partnership. Assume that under the rules of section 1274 the imputed principal amount of an obligation to transfer $1,100,000 one year after the transfer of property X is $1,000,000 on the date of the transfer.

(ii) Since the transfer of $1,100,000 to the partnership by A is made within two years of the transfer of property X to A, under rules similar to those provided in § 1.707–3(c), the transfers are presumed to be a sale unless the facts and circumstances clearly establish otherwise. If no facts exist that would rebut this presumption, on the date that the partnership transfers property X to A, the partnership is treated as having sold property X to A in exchange for A's obligation to transfer $1,100,000 to the partnership one year later.

Example 2. Assumption of liability by partner. **(i)** B is a member of an existing partnership. The partnership transfers property Y to B. On the date of the transfer, property Y has a fair market value of $1,000,000 and is encumbered by a nonrecourse liability of $600,000. B takes the property subject to the liability. The partnership incurred the nonrecourse liability six months prior to the transfer of property Y to B and used the proceeds to purchase an unrelated asset. Assume that, under rule of § 1.707–5(a)(2)(ii) (which determines a partner's share of a nonrecourse liability), B's share of the nonrecourse liability immediately before the transfer of property Y was $100,000.

(ii) The liability is not allocable under the rules of § 1.163–8T to capital expenditures with respect to the property transferred to B and was not incurred in the ordinary course of the trade or business in which the property transferred to the partner was used or held. Since the partnership incurred the nonrecourse liability within two years of the transfer to B, under rules similar to those provided in § 1.707–5(a)(5), the liability is presumed to be incurred in anticipation of the transfer unless the facts and circumstances clearly establish the contrary. Assuming no facts exist to rebut this presumption, the liability taken subject to by B is not a qualified liability. The partnership is treated as having received, on the date of the transfer of property Y to B, $500,000 ($600,000 liability assumed by B less B's share of the $100,000 liability immediately prior to the transfer) as consideration for the sale of one-half ($500,000/$1,000,000) of property Y to B. The partnership is also treated as having distributed to B, in B's capacity as a partner, the other one-half of property Y.

[T.D. 8439, 57 FR 44974, Sept. 30, 1992]

§ 1.707–8 Disclosure of certain information.

(a) In general. The disclosure referred to in § 1.707–3(c)(2) (regarding certain transfers made within two years of each other), § 1.707–5(a)(7)(ii) (regarding a liability incurred within two years prior to a transfer of property), and § 1.707–6(c) (relating to transfers of property from a partnership to a partner in situations analogous to those listed above) is to be made in accordance with paragraph (b) of this section.

(b) Method of providing disclosure. Disclosure is to be made on a completed Form 8275 or on a statement attached to the return of the transferor of property for the taxable year of the transfer that includes the following:

(1) A caption identifying the statement as disclosure under section 707;

(2) An identification of the item (or group of items) with respect to which disclosure is made;

(3) The amount of each item; and

(4) The facts affecting the potential tax treatment of the item (or items) under section 707.

(c) Disclosure by certain partnerships. If more than one partner transfers property to a partnership pursuant to a plan, the disclosure required by this section may be made by the partnership on behalf of all the transferors rather than by each transferor separately.

[T.D. 8439, 57 FR 44974, Sept. 30, 1992]

§ 1.708–1 Continuation of partnership.

(a) General rule. For purposes of subchapter K, chapter 1 of the Code, an existing partnership shall be considered as continuing if it is not terminated.

(b) Termination—(1) General rule. A partnership shall terminate when the operations of the partnership are discontinued and no part of any business, financial operation, or venture of the partnership continues to be carried on by any of its partners in a partnership. For example, on November 20, 1956, A and B, each of whom is a 20–percent partner in partnership ABC, sell their interests to C, who is a 60–percent partner. Since the business is no longer carried on by any of its partners in a partnership, the ABC partnership is terminated as of November 20, 1956. However, where partners DEF agree on April 30, 1957, to dissolve their partnership, but carry on the business through a winding up period ending September 30, 1957, when all remaining assets, consisting only of cash, are distributed to the partners, the partnership does not terminate because of cessation of business until September 30, 1957.

(i) Upon the death of one partner in a 2–member partnership, the partnership shall not be considered as terminated if the estate or other successor in interest of the deceased partner continues to share in the profits or losses of the partnership business.

(ii) For the continuation of a partnership where payments are being made under section 736 (relating to payments to a retiring partner or a deceased partner's successor in interest), see paragraph (a)(6) of § 1.736–1.

(2) A partnership shall terminate when 50–percent or more of the total interest in partnership capital and profits is sold or exchanged within a period of 12 consecutive months. Such sale or exchange includes a sale or exchange to another member of the partnership. However, a disposition of a partnership interest by gift (including assignment to a successor in interest), bequest, or inheritance, or the liquidation of a partnership interest, is not a sale or exchange for purposes of this subparagraph. Moreover, if the sale or exchange of an interest in a partnership (upper-tier partnership) that holds an interest in another partnership (lower-tier partnership) results in a termination of the upper-tier partnership, the upper-tier partnership is treated as exchanging its entire interest in the capital and profits of the lower-tier partnership. If the sale or exchange of an interest in an upper-tier partnership does not terminate the upper-tier partnership, the sale or exchange of an interest in the upper-tier partnership is not treated as a sale or exchange of a proportionate share of the upper-tier partnership's interest in the capital and profits of the lower-tier partnership. The previous two sentences apply to terminations of partnerships under section 708(b)(1)(B) occurring on or after May 9, 1997; however, the sentences may be applied to terminations occurring on or after May 9, 1996, provided that the partnership and its partners apply the sentences to the termination in a consistent manner. Furthermore, the contribution of property to a partnership does not constitute such a sale or exchange. See, however, paragraph (c)(3) of § 1.731–1. Fifty percent or more of the total interest in partnership capital and profits means 50 percent or more of the total interest in partnership capital plus 50–percent or more of the total interest in partnership profits. Thus, the sale of a 30–percent interest in partnership capital and a 60–percent interest in partnership profits is not the sale or exchange of 50 percent or more of the total interest in partnership capital and profits. If one or more partners sell or exchange interests aggregating 50–percent or more of the total interest in partnership capital and 50–percent or more of the total interest in partnership profits within a period of 12 consecutive months, such sale or exchange is considered as being within the provisions of this subparagraph. When interests are sold or exchanged on different dates, the percentages to be added are determined as of the date of each sale. For example, with respect to the ABC partnership, the sale by A on May 12, 1956, of a 30–percent interest in capital and profits to D, and the sale by B on March 27, 1957, of a 30–percent interest in capital and profits to E, is a sale of a 50–percent or more interest. Accordingly, the partnership is terminated as of March 27, 1957. However, if, on March 27, 1957, D instead of B, sold his 30–percent interest in capital and profits to E, there would be no termination since only one 30–percent interest would have been sold or exchanged within a 12–month period.

(3) For purposes of subchapter K, chapter 1 of the Code, a partnership taxable year closes with respect to all partners on the date on which the partnership terminates. See section 706(c)(1) and paragraph (c)(1) of § 1.706–1. The date of termination is:

(i) For purposes of section 708(b)(1)(A), the date on which the winding up of the partnership affairs is completed.

(ii) For purposes of section 708(b)(1)(B), the date of the sale or exchange of a partnership interest which, of itself or together with sales or exchanges in the preceding 12 months, transfers an interest of 50–percent or more in both partnership capital and profits.

(4) If a partnership is terminated by a sale or exchange of an interest, the following is deemed to occur: The partnership contributes all of its assets and liabilities to a new partnership in exchange for an interest in the new partnership; and, immediately thereafter, the terminated partnership distributes interests in the new partnership to the purchasing partner and the other remaining partners in proportion to their respective interests in the terminated partnership in liquidation of the terminated partnership, either for the continuation of the business by the new partnership or for its dissolution and winding up. In the latter case, the new partnership terminates in accordance with (b)(1) of this section. This paragraph (b)(1)(4) applies to terminations of partnerships under section 708(b)(1)(B) occurring on or after May 9, 1997; however, this paragraph (b)(1)(4) may be applied to terminations occurring on or after May 9, 1996, provided that the partnership and its partners apply this paragraph (b)(1)(4) to the termination in a consistent manner. The provisions of this paragraph (b)(1)(4) are illustrated by the following example:

Example. (i) A and B each contribute $10,000 cash to form AB, a general partnership, as equal partners. AB purchases depreciable Property X for $20,000. Property X increases in value to $30,000, at which time A sells its entire 50 percent interest to C for $15,000 in a transfer that terminates the partnership under section 708(b)(1)(B). At the time of the sale, Property X had an adjusted tax basis of $16,000 and a book value of $16,000 (original $20,000 tax basis and book value reduced by $4,000 of depreciation). In addition, A and B each had a capital account balance of $8,000 (original $10,000 capital account reduced by $2,000 of depreciation allocations with respect to Property X).

(ii) Following the deemed contribution of assets and liabilities by the terminated AB partnership to a new partnership (new AB) and the liquidation of the terminated AB partnership, the adjusted tax basis of Property X in the hands of new AB is $16,000. See section 723. The book value of Property X in the hands of new partnership AB is also $16,000 (the book value of Property X immediately before the termination) and B and C each have a capital account of $8,000 in new AB (the balance of their capital accounts in AB prior to the termination). See § 1.704–1(b)(2)(iv)(1) (providing that the deemed contribution and liquidation with regard to the terminated partnership are disregarded in determining the capital accounts of the partners and the books of the new partnership). Additionally, under § 301.6109–1(d)(2)(iii) of this chapter, new AB retains the taxpayer identification number of the terminated AB partnership.

(iii) Property X was not section 704(c) property in the hands of terminated AB and is therefore not treated as section 704(c) property in the hands of new AB, even though Property X is deemed contributed to new AB at a time when the fair market value of Property X ($30,000) was different from its adjusted tax basis ($16,000). See § 1.704–3(a)(3)(i) (providing that property contributed to a new partnership under § 1.708–1(b)(1)(4) is treated as section 704(c) property only to the extent that the property was section 704(c) property in the hands of the terminated partnership immediately prior to the termination).

(5) If a partnership is terminated by a sale or exchange of an interest in the partnership, a section 754 election (including a section 754 election made by the terminated partnership on its final return) that is in effect for the taxable year of the terminated partnership in which the sale occurs, applies with respect to the incoming partner. Therefore, the bases of partnership assets are adjusted pursuant to sections 743 and 755 prior to their deemed contribution to the new partnership. This paragraph (b)(1)(5) applies to terminations of partnerships under section 708(b)(1)(B) occurring on or after May 9, 1997; however, this paragraph (b)(1)(5) may be applied to terminations occurring on or after May 9, 1996, provided that the partnership and its partners apply this paragraph (b)(1)(5) to the termination in a consistent manner.

(c) Merger or consolidation—(1) General rule. If two or more partnerships merge or consolidate into one partnership, the resulting partnership shall be considered a continuation of the merging or consolidating partnership the members of which own an interest of more than 50 percent in the capital and profits of the resulting partnership. If the resulting partnership can, under the preceding sentence, be considered a continuation of more than one of the merging or consolidating partnerships, it shall, unless the Commissioner permits otherwise, be considered the continuation solely of that partnership which is credited with the contribution of assets having the greatest fair market value (net of liabilities) to the resulting partnership. Any other merging or consolidating partnerships shall be considered as terminated. If the members of none of the merging or consolidating partnerships have an interest of more than 50 percent in the capital and profits of the resulting partnership, all of the merged or consolidated partnerships are terminated, and a new partnership results.

* * *

(3) Form of a merger or consolidation—(i) Assets-over form. When two or more partnerships merge or consolidate into one partnership under the applicable jurisdictional law without undertaking a form for the merger or consolidation, or undertake a form for the merger or consolidation that is not described in paragraph (c)(3)(ii) of this section, any merged or consolidated partnership that is considered terminated under paragraph (c)(1) of this section is treated as undertaking the assets-over form for Federal income tax purposes. Under the assets-over form, the merged or consolidated partnership that is considered terminated under paragraph (c)(1) of this section contributes all of its assets and liabilities to the resulting partnership in exchange for an interest in the resulting partnership, and immediately thereafter, the terminated partnership distributes interests in the resulting partnership to its partners in liquidation of the terminated partnership.

(ii) Assets-up form. Despite the partners' transitory ownership of the terminated partnership's assets, the form of a partnership merger or consolidation will be respected for Federal income tax purposes if the merged or consolidated partnership that is considered terminated under paragraph (c)(1) of this section distributes all of its assets to its partners (in a manner that causes the partners to be treated, under the laws of the applicable jurisdiction, as the owners of such assets) in liquidation of the partners' interests in the terminated partnership, and immediately thereafter, the partners in the terminated partnership contribute the distributed assets to the resulting partnership in exchange for interests in the resulting partnership.

(4) Sale of an interest in the merging or consolidating partnership. In a transaction characterized under the assets-over form, a sale of all or part of a partner's interest in the terminated partnership to the resulting partnership that occurs as part of a merger or consolidation under section 708(b)(2)(A), as described in paragraph (c)(3)(i) of this section, will be respected as a sale of a partnership interest if the merger agreement (or another document) specifies that the resulting partnership is purchasing interests from a particular partner in the merging or consolidating partnership and the consideration that is transferred for each interest sold, and if the selling partner in the terminated partnership, either prior to or contemporaneous with the transaction, consents to treat the transaction as a sale of the partnership interest. See section 741 and § 1.741–1 for determining the selling partner's gain or loss on the sale or exchange of the partnership interest.

(5) Examples. The following examples illustrate the rules in paragraphs (c)(1) through (4) of this section:

Example 1. Partnership AB, in whose capital and profits A and B each own a 50–percent interest, and partnership CD, in whose capital and profits C and D each own a 50–percent interest, merge on September 30, 1999, and form partnership ABCD, Partners A, B, C, and D are on a calendar year, and partnership AB and partnership CD also are on a calendar year. After the merger, the partners have capital and profits interests as follows: A, 30 percent; B, 30 percent; C, 20 percent; and D, 20 percent. Since A and B together own an interest of more than 50 percent in the capital and profits of partnership ABCD, such partnership shall be considered a continuation of partnership AB and shall continue to file returns on a calendar year basis. Since C and D own an interest of less than 50 percent in the capital and profits of partnership ABCD, the taxable year of partnership CD closes as of September 30, 1999, the date of the merger, and partnership CD is terminated as of that date. Partnership ABCD is required to file a return for the taxable year January 1 to December 31, 1999, indicating thereon that, until September 30, 1999, it was partnership AB. Partnership CD is required to file a return for its final taxable year, January 1, through September 30, 1999.

Example 2. (i) Partnership X, in whose capital and profits A owns a 40–percent interest and B owns a 60–percent interest, and partnership Y, in whose capital and profits B owns a 60–percent interest and C owns a 40–percent interest, merge on September 30, 1999. The fair market value of the partnership X assets (net of liabilities) is $100X, and the fair market value of the partnership Y assets (net of liabilities) is $200X. The merger is accomplished under state law by partnership Y contributing its assets and liabilities to partnership X in exchange for interests in partnership X, with partnership Y then liquidating, distributing interests in partnership X to B and C.

(ii) B, a partner in both partnerships prior to the merger, owns a greater than 50–percent interest in the resulting partnership following the merger. Accordingly, because the fair market value of partnership Y's assets (net of liabilities) was greater than that of partnership X's, under paragraph (c)(1) of this section, partnership X will be considered to terminate in the merger. As a result, even though, for state law purposes, the transaction was undertaken with partnership Y contributing its assets and liabilities to partnership X and distributing interests in partnership X to its partners, pursuant to paragraph (c)(3)(i) of this section, for Federal income tax purposes, the transaction will be treated as if partnership X contributed its assets to partnership Y in exchange for interests in partnership Y and then liquidated, distributing interests in partnership Y to A and B.

Example 3. (i) The facts are the same as in Example 2, except that partnership X is engaged in a trade or business and has, as one of its assets, goodwill. In addition, the merger is accomplished under state law by having partnership X convey an undivided 40–percent interest in each of its assets to A and an undivided 60–percent interest in each of its assets to B, with A and B then contributing their interests in such assets to partnership Y. Partnership Y also assumes all of the liabilities of partnership X.

(ii) Under paragraph (c)(3)(ii) of this section, the form of the partnership merger will be respected so that partnership X will be treated as following the assets-up form for Federal income tax purposes.

Example 4. (i) Partnership X and partnership Y merge when the partners of partnership X transfer their partnership X interests to partnership Y in exchange for partnership Y interests. Immediately thereafter, partnership X liquidates into partnership Y. The resulting partnership is considered a continuation of partnership Y, and partnership X is considered terminated.

(ii) The partnerships are treated as undertaking the assets-over form described in paragraph (c)(3)(i) of this section because the partnerships undertook a form that is not the assets-up form described in paragraph (c)(3)(ii) of this section. Accordingly, for Federal income tax purposes, partnership X is deemed to contribute its assets and liabilities to partnership Y in exchange for interests in partnership Y, and, immediately thereafter, partnership X is deemed to have distributed the interests in partnership Y to its partners in liquidation of their interests in partnership X.

Example 5. (i) A, B, and C are partners in partnership X, D, E, and F are partners in partnership Y. Partnership X and partnership Y merge, and the resulting partnership is considered a continuation of partnership Y. Partnership X is considered terminated. Under state law, partnerships X and Y undertake the assets-over form of paragraph (c)(3)(i) of this section to accomplish the partnership merger. C does not want to become a partner in partnership Y, and partnership X does not have the resources to buy C's interest before the merger. C, partnership X, and partnership Y enter into an agreement specifying that partnership Y will purchase C's interest in partnership X for $150 before the merger, and as part of the agreement, C consents to treat the transaction in a manner that is consistent with the agreement. As part of the merger, partnership X receives from partnership Y $150 that will be distributed to C immediately before the merger, and interests in partnership Y in exchange for partnership X's assets and liabilities.

(ii) Because the merger agreement satisfies the requirements of paragraph (c)(4) of this section and C provides the necessary consent, C will be treated as selling its interest in partnership X to partnership Y for $150 before the merger. See section 741 and § 1.741–1 to determine the amount and character of C's gain or loss on the sale or exchange of its interest in partnership X.

(iii) Because the merger agreement satisfies requirements of paragraph (c)(4) of this section, partnership Y is considered to have purchased C's interest in partnership X for $150 immediately before the merger. See § 1.704–1(b)(2)(iv)(*l*) for determining partnership Y's capital account in partnership X. Partnership Y's adjusted basis of its interest in partnership X is determined under section 742 and § 1.742–1. To the extent any built-in gain or loss on section 704(c) property in partnership X would have been allocated to C (including any allocations with respect to property revaluations under section 704(b) (reverse section 704(c) allocations)), see section 704 and § 1.704–3(a)(7) for determining the built-in gain or loss or reverse section 704(c) allocations apportionable to partnership Y. Similarly, after the merger is completed, the built-in gain or loss and reverse section 704(c) allocations attributable to C's interest are apportioned to D, E, and F under section 704(c) and § 1.74–(a)(7).

(iv) Under paragraph (c)(3)(i) of this section, partnership X contributes its assets and liabilities attributable to the interests of A and B to partnership Y in exchange for interests in partnership Y; and, immediately thereafter, partnership X distributes the interests in partnership Y to A and B in liquidation of their interests in partnership Y to A and B in liquidation of their interests in partnership X. At the same time, partnership X distributes assets to partnership Y in liquidation of partnership Y's interest in partnership X. Partnership Y's bases in the distributed assets are determined under section 732(b).

(6) Prescribed form not followed in certain circumstances. (i) If any transactions described in paragraph (c)(3) or (4) of this section are part of a larger series of transactions, and the substance of the larger series of transactions is inconsistent with following the form prescribed in such paragraph, the Commissioner may disregard such form, and may recast the larger series of transactions in accordance with their substance.

(ii) Example. The following example illustrates the rules in paragraph (c)(6) of this section:

Example. A, B, and C are equal partners in partnership ABC. ABC holds no section 704(c) property. D and E are equal partners in partnership DE. B and C want to exchange their interests in ABC for all of the interests in DE. However, rather than exchanging partnership interests, DE merges with ABC by undertaking the assets-up form described in paragraph (c)(3)(ii) of this section, with D and E receiving title to the DE assets and then contributing the assets to ABC in exchange for interests in ABC. As part of a prearranged transaction, the assets acquired from DE are contributed to a new partnership, and the interests in the new partnership are distributed to B and C in complete liquidation of their interests in ABC. The merger and division in this example represent series of transactions that in substance are an exchange of interests in ABC for interests in DE. Even though paragraph (c)(3)(ii) of this section provides that the form of a merger will be respected for Federal income tax purposes if the steps prescribed under the assets-up form are followed, and paragraph (d)(3)(i) of this section provides a form that will be followed for Federal income tax purposes in the case of partnership divisions, these forms will not be respected for Federal income tax purposes under these facts, and the transactions will be recast in accordance with their substance as a taxable exchange of interests in ABC for interests in DE.

* * *

(d) Division of a partnership—(1) General rule. Upon the division of a partnership into two or more partnerships, any resulting partnership (as defined in paragraph (d)(4)(iv) of this section) or resulting partnerships shall be considered a continuation of the prior partnership (as defined in paragraph (d)(4)(ii) of this section) if the members of the resulting partnership or partnerships had an interest of more than 50 percent in the capital and profits of the prior partnership. Any other resulting partnership will not be considered a continuation of the prior partnership but will be considered a new partnership. If the members of none of the resulting partnerships owned an interest of more than 50 percent in the capital and profits of the prior partnership, none of the resulting partnerships will be considered a continuation of the prior partnership, and the prior partnership will be considered to have terminated. Where members of a partnership which has been divided into two or more partnerships do not become members of a resulting partnership which is considered a continuation of the prior partnership, such members' interests shall be considered liquidated as of the date of the division.

(2) Tax consequences—* * *

(ii) Elections. All resulting partnerships that are regarded as continuing are subject to preexisting elections that were made by the prior partnership. A subsequent election that is made by a resulting partnership does not affect the other resulting partnerships.

(3) Form of a division—(i) Assets-over form. When a partnership divides into two or more partnerships under applicable jurisdictional law without undertaking a form for the division, or undertakes a form that is not described in paragraph (d)(3)(ii) of this section, the transaction will be characterized under the assets-over form for Federal income tax purposes.

(A) Assets-over form where at least one resulting partnership is a continuation of the prior partnership. In a division under the assets-over form where at least one resulting partnership is a continuation of the prior partnership, the divided partnership (as defined in paragraph (d)(4)(i) of this section) contributes certain assets and liabilities to a recipient partnership (as defined in paragraph (d)(4)(iii) of this section) or recipient partnerships in exchange for interests in such recipient partnership or partnerships; and, immediately thereafter, the divided partnership distributes the interests in such recipient partnership or partnerships to some or all of its partners in partial or complete liquidation of the partners' interests in the divided partnership.

(B) Assets-over form where none of the resulting partnerships is a continuation of the prior partnership. In a division under the assets-over form where none of the resulting partnerships is a the continuation of the prior partnership, the prior partnership will be treated as contributing all of its assets and liabilities to new resulting partnerships in exchange for interests in the resulting partnerships; and, immediately thereafter, the prior partnership will be treated as liquidating by distributing the interests in the new resulting partnerships to the prior partnership's partners.

(ii) Assets-up form—(A) Assets-up form where the partnership distributing assets is a continuation of the prior partnership. Despite the partners' transitory ownership of some of the prior partnership's assets, the form of a partnership division will be respected for Federal income tax purposes if the divided partnership (which, pursuant to § 1.708–1(d)(4)(i), must be a continuing partnership) distributes certain assets (in a manner that causes the partners to be treated, under the laws of the applicable jurisdiction, as the owners of such assets) to some or all of its partners in partial or complete liquidation of the partners' interests in the divided partnership, and immediately thereafter, such partners contribute the distributed assets to a recipient partnership or partnerships in exchange for interests in such recipient partnership or partnerships. In order for such form to be respected for transfers to a particular recipient partnership, all assets held by the prior partnership that are transferred to the recipient partnership must be distributed to, and then contributed by, the partners of the recipient partnership.

(B) Assets-up form where none of the resulting partnerships are a continuation of the prior partnership. If none of the resulting partnerships are a continuation of the prior partnership, then despite the partners' transitory ownership of some or all of the prior partnership's assets, the form of a partnership division will be respected for Federal income tax purposes if the prior partnership distributes certain assets (in a manner that causes the partners to be treated, under the laws of the applicable jurisdiction, as the owners of such assets) to some or all of its partners in partial or complete liquidation of the partners' interests in the prior partnership, and immediately thereafter, such partners contribute the distributed assets to a resulting partnership or partnerships in exchange for interests in such resulting partnership or partnerships. In order for such form to be respected for transfers to a particular resulting partnership, all assets held by the prior partnership that are transferred to the resulting partnership must be distributed to, and then contributed by, the partners of the resulting partnership. If the prior partnership does not liquidate under the applicable jurisdictional law, then with respect to the assets and liabilities that, in form, are not transferred to a new resulting partnership, the prior partnership will be treated as transferring these assets and liabilities to a new resulting partnership under the assets-over form described in paragraph (d)(3)(i)(B) of this section.

(4) Definitions—(i) Divided partnership. For purposes of paragraph (d) of this section, the divided partnership is the continuing partnership which is treated, for Federal income tax purposes, as transferring the assets and liabilities to the recipient partnership or partnerships, either directly (under the assets-over form) or indirectly (under the assets-up form). If the resulting partnership that, in form, transferred the assets and liabilities in connection with the division is a continuation of the prior partnership, then such resulting partnership will be treated as the divided partnership. If a partnership divides into two or more partnerships and only one of the resulting partnerships is a continuation of the prior partnership, then the resulting partnership that is a continuation of the prior partnership will be treated as the divided partnership. If a partnership divides into two or more partnerships without undertaking a form for the division that is recognized under paragraph (d)(3) of this section, or if the resulting partnership that had, in form, transferred assets and liabilities is not considered a continuation of the prior partnership, and more than one resulting partnership is considered a continuation of the prior partnership, the continuing resulting partnership with the assets having the greatest fair market value (net of liabilities) will be treated as the divided partnership.

(ii) Prior partnership. For purposes of paragraph (d) of this section, the prior partnership is the partnership subject to division that exists under applicable jurisdictional law before the division.

(iii) Recipient partnership. For purposes of paragraph (d) of this section, a recipient partnership is a partnership that is treated as receiving, for Federal income tax purposes, assets and liabilities from a divided partnership, either directly (under the assets-over form) or indirectly (under the assets-up form).

(iv) Resulting partnership. For purposes of paragraph (d) of this section, a resulting partnership is a partnership resulting from the division that exists under applicable jurisdictional law after the division and that has at least two partners who were partners in the prior partnership. For example, where a prior partnership divides into two partnerships, both partnerships existing after the division are resulting partnerships.

(5) Examples. The following examples illustrate the rules in paragraphs (d)(1), (2), (3), and (4) of this section:

Example 1. Partnership ABCD is in the real estate and insurance businesses. A owns a 40–percent interest, and B, C, and D each owns a 20–percent interest, in the capital and profits of the partnership. The partnership and the partners report their income on a calendar year. On November 1, 1999, they separate the real estate and insurance businesses and form two partnerships. Partnership AB takes over the real estate business, and partnership CD takes over the insurance business. Because members of resulting partnership AB owned more than a 50–percent interest in the capital and profits of partnership ABCD (A, 40 percent, and B, 20 percent), partnership AB shall be considered a continuation of partnership ABCD. Partnership AB is required to file a return for the taxable year January 1 to December 31, 1999, indicating thereon that until November 1, 1999, it was partnership ABCD. Partnership CD is considered a new partnership formed at the beginning of the day on November 2, 1999, and is required to file a return for the taxable year it adopts pursuant to section 706(b) and the applicable regulations.

Example 2. (i) Partnership ABCD owns properties W, X, Y, and Z, and divides into partnership AB and partnership CD. Under paragraph (d)(1) of this section, partnership AB is considered a continuation of partnership ABCD and partnership CD is considered a new partnership. Partnership ABCD distributes property Y to C and titles property Y in C's name. Partnership ABCD distributes property Z to D and titles property Z in D's name. C and D then contribute properties Y and Z, respectively, to partnership CD in exchange for interests in partnership CD. Properties W and X remain in partnership AB.

(ii) Under paragraph (d)(3)(ii) of this section, partnership ABCD will be treated as following the assets-up form for Federal income tax purposes.

Example 3. (i) The facts are the same as in Example 2, except partnership ABCD distributes property Y to C and titles property Y in C's name. C then contributes property Y to partnership CD. Simultaneously, partnership ABCD contributes property Z to partnership CD in exchange for an interest in partnership CD. Immediately thereafter, partnership ABCD distributes the interest in partnership CD to D in liquidation of D's interest in partnership ABCD.

(ii) Under paragraph (d)(3)(i) of this section, because partnership ABCD did not undertake the assets-up form with respect to all of the assets transferred to partnership CD, partnership ABCD will be treated as undertaking the assets-over form in transferring the assets to partnership CD. Accordingly, for Federal income tax purposes, partnership ABCD is deemed to contribute property Y and property Z to partnership CD in exchange for interests in partnership CD, and immediately thereafter, partnership ABCD is deemed to distribute the interests in partnership CD to partner C and partner D in liquidation of their interests in partnership ABCD.

Example 4. (i) Partnership ABCD owns three parcels of property: property X, with a value of $500; property Y, with a value of $300; and property Z, with a value of $200. A and B each own a 40–percent interest in the capital and profits of partnership ABCD, and C and D each own a 10 percent interest in the capital and profits of partnership ABCD. On November 1, 1999, partnership ABCD divides into three partnerships (AB1, AB2, and CD) by contributing property X to a newly formed partnership (AB1) and distributing all interests in such partnership to A and B as equal partners, and by contributing property Z to a newly formed partnership (CD) and distributing all interests in such partnership to C and D as equal partners in exchange for all of their interests in partnership ABCD. While partnership ABCD does not transfer property Y, C and D cease to be partners in the partnership. Accordingly, after the division, the partnership holding property Y is referred to as partnership AB2.

(ii) Partnerships AB1 and AB2 both are considered a continuation of partnership ABCD, while partnership CD is considered a new partnership formed at the beginning of the day on November 2, 1999. Under paragraph (d)(3)(i)(A) of this section, partnership ABCD will be treated as following the assets-over form, with partnership ABCD contributing property X to partnership AB1 and property Z to partnership CD, and distributing the interests in such partnerships to the designated partners.

Example 5. (i) The facts are the same as in Example 4, except that partnership ABCD divides into three partnerships by operation of state law, without undertaking a form.

(ii) Under the last sentence of paragraph (d)(4)(i) of this section, partnership AB1 will be treated as the resulting partnership that is the divided partnership. Under paragraph (d)(3)(i)(A) of this section, partnership ABCD will be treated as following the assets-over form, with partnership ABCD contributing property Y to partnership AB2 and property Z to partnership CD, and distributing the interests in such partnerships to the designated partners.

Example 6. (i) The facts are the same as in Example 4, except that partnership ABCD divides into three partnerships by contributing property X to newly-formed partnership AB1 and property Y to newly-formed partnership AB2 and distributing all interests in each partnership to A and B in exchange for all of their interests in partnership ABCD.

(ii) Because resulting partnership CD is not a continuation of the prior partnership (partnership ABCD), partnership CD cannot be treated, for Federal income tax purposes, as the partnership that transferred assets (i.e., the divided partnership), but instead must be treated as a recipient partnership. Under the last sentence of paragraph (d)(4)(i) of this section, partnership AB1 will be treated as the resulting partnership that is the divided partnership. Under paragraph (d)(3)(i)(A) of this section, partnership ABCD will be treated as following the assets-over form, with partnership ABCD contributing property Y to partnership AB2 and property Z to partnership CD, and distributing the interests in such partnerships to the designated partners.

Example 7. (i) Partnership ABCDE owns Blackacre, Whiteacre, and Redacre, and divides into partnership AB, partnership CD, and partnership DE. Under paragraph (d)(1) of this section, partnership ABCDE is considered terminated (and, hence, none of the resulting partnerships are a continuation of the prior partnership) because none of the members of the new partnerships (partnership AB, partnership CD, and partnership DE) owned an interest of more than 50 percent in the capital and profits of partnership ABCDE.

(ii) Partnership ABCDE distributes Blackacre to A and B and titles Blackacre in the names of A and B. A and B then contribute Blackacre to partnership AB in exchange for interests in partnership AB. Partnership ABCDE will be treated as following the assets-up form described in paragraph (d)(3)(ii)(B) of this section for Federal income tax purposes.

(iii) Partnership ABCDE distributes Whiteacre to C and D and titles Whiteacre in the names of C and D. C and D then contribute Whiteacre to partnership CD in exchange for interests in partnership CD. Partnership ABCDE will be treated as following the assets-up form described in paragraph (d)(3)(ii)(B) of this section for Federal income tax purposes.

(iv) Partnership ABCDE does not liquidate under state law so that, in form, the assets in new partnership DE are not considered to have been transferred under state law. Partnership ABCDE will be treated as undertaking the assets-over form described in paragraph (d)(3)(i)(B) of this section for Federal income tax purposes with respect to the assets of partnership DE. Thus, partnership ABCDE will be treated as contributing Redacre to partnership DE in exchange for interests in partnership DE; and, immediately thereafter, partnership ABCDE will be treated as distributing interests in partnership DE to D and E in liquidation of their interests in partnership ABCDE. Partnership ABCDE then terminates.

(6) Prescribed form not followed in certain circumstances. If any transactions described in paragraph (d)(3) of this section are part of a larger series of transactions, and the substance of the larger series of transactions is inconsistent with following the form prescribed in such paragraph, the Commissioner may disregard such form, and may recast the larger series of transactions in accordance with their substance.

* * *

[T.D. 6500, 25 FR 11814, Nov. 26, 1960; T.D. 8717, 62 FR 25498, May 9, 1997; T.D. 8925, 66 FR 715, Jan. 4, 2001; 67 FR 57330, Sept. 10, 2002]

§ 1.709–1 Treatment of organizational expenses and syndication costs.

* * *

(b) Election to amortize organizational expenses—(1) In general. * * *

(2) Time and manner of making election. A partnership is deemed to have made an election under section 709(b) to amortize organizational expenses as defined in section 709(b)(3) and § 1.709–2(a) for the taxable year in which the partnership begins business. A partnership may choose to forgo the deemed election by affirmatively electing to capitalize its organizational expenses on a timely filed Federal income tax return (including extensions) for the taxable year in which the partnership begins business. The election either to amortize organizational expenses under section 709(b) or to capitalize organizational expenses is irrevocable and applies to all organizational expenses of the partnership. A change in the characterization of an item as an organizational expense is a change in method of accounting to which sections 446 and 481(a) apply if the partnership treated the item consistently for two or more taxable years. A change in the determination of the taxable year in which the partnership begins business also is treated as a change in method of accounting if the partnership amortized organizational expenses for two or more taxable years.

(3) Liquidation of partnership. If there is a winding up and complete liquidation of the partnership prior to the end of the amortization period, the unamortized amount of organizational expenses is a partnership deduction in its final taxable year to the extent provided under section 165 (relating to losses). However, there is no partnership deduction with respect to its capitalized syndication expenses.

* * *

[T.D. 7891, 48 FR 20048, May 4, 1983; T.D. 9411, 73 FR 38914, July 8, 2008; T.D. 9542, 76 FR 50890, Aug. 17, 2011; 76 FR 56973, Sept. 15, 2011]

§ 1.709–2 Definitions.

(a) Organizational expenses. Section 709(b)(2) of the Internal Revenue Code defines organizational expenses as expenses which:

(1) Are incident to the creation of the partnership;

(2) Are chargeable to capital account; and

(3) Are of a character which, if expended incident to the creation of a partnership having an ascertainable life, would (but for section 709(a)) be amortized over such life.

An expenditure which fails to meet one or more of these three tests does not qualify as an organizational expense for purposes of section 709(b) and this section. To satisfy the statutory requirement described in paragraph (a)(1) of this section, the expense must be incurred during the period beginning at a point which is a reasonable time before the partnership begins business and ending with the date prescribed by law for filing the partnership return (determined without regard to any extensions of time) for the taxable year the partnership begins business. In addition, the expenses must be for creation of the partnership and not for operation or starting operation of the partnership trade or business. To satisfy the statutory requirement described in paragraph (a)(3) of this section, the expense must be for an item of a nature normally expected to benefit the partnership throughout the entire life of the partnership. The following are examples of organizational expenses within the meaning of section 709 and this section: Legal fees for services incident to the organization of the partnership, such as negotiation and preparation of a partnership agreement; accounting fees for services incident to the organization of the partnership; and filing fees. The following are examples of expenses that are not organizational expenses within the meaning of section 709 and this section (regardless of how the partnership characterizes them): Expenses connected with acquiring assets for the partnership or transferring assets to the partnership; expenses connected with the admission or removal of partners other than at the time the partnership is first organized; expenses connected with a contract relating to the operation of the partnership trade or business (even where the contract is between the partnership and one of its members); and syndication expenses.

(b) Syndication expenses. Syndication expenses are expenses connected with the issuing and marketing of interests in the partnership. Examples of syndication expenses are brokerage fees; registration fees; legal fees of the underwriter or placement agent and the issuer (the general partner or the partnership) for securities advice and for advice pertaining to the adequacy of tax disclosures in the prospectus or placement memorandum for securities law purposes; accounting fees for preparation of representations to be included in the offering materials; and printing costs of the prospectus, placement memorandum, and other selling and promotional material. These expenses are not subject to the election under section 709(b) and must be capitalized.

(c) Beginning business. The determination of the date a partnership begins business for purposes of section 709 presents a question of fact that must be determined in each case in light of all the circumstances of the particular case. Ordinarily, a partnership begins business when it starts the business operations for which it was organized. The mere signing of a partnership agreement is not alone sufficient to show the beginning of business. If the activities of the partnership have advanced to the extent necessary to establish the nature of its business operations, it will be deemed to have begun business. Accordingly, the acquisition of operating assets which are necessary to the type of business contemplated may constitute beginning business for these purposes. The term "operating assets", as used herein, means assets that are in a state of readiness to be placed in service within a reasonable period following their acquisition.

[T.D. 7891, 48 FR 20049, May 4, 1983]

§ 1.721–1 Nonrecognition of gain or loss on contribution.

(a) No gain or loss shall be recognized either to the partnership or to any of its partners upon a contribution of property, including installment obligations, to the partnership in exchange for a partnership interest. This rule applies whether the contribution is made to a partnership in the process of formation or to a partnership which is already formed and operating. Section 721 shall not apply to a transaction between a partnership and a partner not acting in his capacity as a partner since such a transaction is governed by section 707. Rather than contributing property to a partnership, a partner may sell property to the partnership or may retain the ownership of property and allow the partnership to use it. In all cases, the substance of the transaction will govern, rather than its form. See paragraph (c)(3) of § 1.731–1. Thus, if the transfer of property by the partner to the partnership results in the receipt by the partner of money or other consideration, including a promissory obligation fixed in amount and time for payment, the transaction will be treated as a sale or exchange under section 707 rather than as a contribution under section 721. For the rules governing the treatment of liabilities to which contributed property is subject, see section 752 and § 1.752–1.

(b)(1) Normally, under local law, each partner is entitled to be repaid his contributions of money or other property to the partnership (at the value placed upon such property by the partnership at the time of the contribution) whether made at the formation of the partnership or subsequent thereto. To the extent that any of the partners gives up any part of his right to be repaid his contributions (as distinguished from a share in partnership profits) in favor of another partner as compensation for services (or in satisfaction of an obligation), section 721 does not apply. The value of an interest in such partnership capital so transferred to a partner as compensation for services constitutes income to the partner under section 61. The amount of such income is the fair market value of the interest in capital so transferred, either at the time the transfer is made for past services, or at the time the services have been rendered where the transfer is conditioned on the completion of the transferee's future services. The time when such income is realized depends on all the facts and circumstances, including any substantial restrictions or conditions on the compensated partner's right to withdraw or otherwise dispose of such interest. To the extent that an interest in capital representing compensation for services rendered by the decedent prior to his death is transferred after his death to the decedent's successor in interest, the fair market value of such interest is income in respect of a decedent under section 691.

(2) To the extent that the value of such interest is: (i) Compensation for services rendered to the partnership, it is a guaranteed payment for services under section 707(c); (ii) compensation for services rendered to a partner, it is not deductible by the partnership, but is deductible only by such partner to the extent allowable under this chapter.

(c) Underwritings of partnership interests—(1) In general. For the purpose of section 721, if a person acquires a partnership interest from an underwriter in exchange for cash in a qualified underwriting transaction, the person who acquires the partnership interest is treated as transferring cash directly to the partnership in exchange for the partnership interest and the underwriter is disregarded. A qualified underwriting transaction is a transaction in which a partnership issues partnership interests for cash in an underwriting in which either the underwriter is an agent of the partnership or the underwriter's ownership of the partnership interests is transitory.

* * *

(d) Debt-for-equity exchange—(1) In general. Except as otherwise provided in section 721 and the regulations under section 721, section 721 applies to a contribution of a partnership's indebtedness by a creditor to the debtor partnership in exchange for a capital or profits interest in the partnership (debt-for-equity exchange). See § 1.108–8(a) for rules in determining the debtor partnership's discharge of indebtedness income.

(2) Exception. Section 721 does not apply to a debt-for-equity exchange to the extent the transfer of the partnership interest to the creditor is in exchange for the partnership's indebtedness for unpaid rent, royalties, or interest (including accrued original issue discount) that accrued on or after the beginning of the creditor's holding period for the indebtedness. The debtor partnership will not recognize gain or loss upon the transfer of a partnership interest to a creditor in a debt-for-equity exchange for unpaid rent, royalties, or interest (including accrued original issue discount).

* * *

[T.D. 6500, 25 FR 11814, Nov. 26, 1960; T.D. 8665, 61 FR 19189, May 1, 1996; T.D. 9557, 76 FR 71259, Nov. 17, 2011]

§ 1.721–1 (*Proposed, published 5–24–2005.*) Nonrecognition of gain or loss on contributions.

* * *

(b)(1) Except as otherwise provided in this section or § 1.721–2, section 721 does not apply to the transfer of a partnership interest in connection with the performance of services or in satisfaction of an obligation. The transfer of a partnership interest to a person in connection with the performance of services constitutes a transfer of property to which section 83 and the regulations thereunder apply. To the extent that a partnership interest transferred in connection with the performance of services rendered by a decedent prior to the decedent's death is transferred after the decedent's death to the decedent's successor in interest, the fair market value of such interest is an item of income in respect of a decedent under section 691.

(2) Except as provided in section 83(h) and 1.83–6(c), no gain or loss shall be recognized by a partnership upon—

(i) The transfer or substantial vesting of a compensatory partnership interest; or

(ii) The forfeiture of a compensatory partnership interest. See § 1.704–1(b)(4)(xii) for rules regarding forfeiture allocations of partnership items that may be required in the taxable year of a forfeiture.

(3) For purposes of this section, a compensatory partnership interest is an interest in the transferring partnership that is transferred in connection with the performance of services for that partnership (either before or after the formation of the partnership), including an interest that is transferred on the exercise of a compensatory partnership option. A compensatory partnership option is an option to acquire an interest in the issuing partnership that is granted in connection with the performance of services for that partnership (either before or after the formation of the partnership).

(4) To the extent that a partnership interest is—

(i) Transferred to a partner in connection with the performance of services rendered to the partnership, it is a guaranteed payment for services under section 707(c);

(ii) Transferred in connection with the performance of services rendered to a partner, it is not deductible by the partnership, but is deductible only by such partner to the extent allowable under Chapter 1 of the Code.

(5) This paragraph (b) applies to interests that are transferred on or after the date final regulations are published in the Federal Register.

§ 1.721–2 Noncompensatory options.

(a) Exercise of a noncompensatory option—(1) In general. Notwithstanding § 1.721–1(b)(1), section 721 applies to the exercise (as defined in paragraph (g)(4) of this section) of a noncompensatory option (as defined in paragraph (f) of this section). Except as provided in paragraph (a)(2) of this section, section 721 applies to the exercise of a noncompensatory option when the holder pays the exercise price with either property or cash, regardless of whether the terms of the option require or permit cash payment. However, if the exercise price (as defined in paragraph (g)(5) of this section) of a noncompensatory option exceeds the capital account received by the option holder on the exercise of the option, then general tax principles will apply to determine the tax consequences of the transaction.

(2) Exception. Section 721 does not apply to the exercise of a noncompensatory option to the extent that the exercise price is satisfied with the partnership's obligation to the option holder for unpaid rent, royalties, or interest (including accrued original issue discount) that accrued on or after the beginning of the option holder's holding period for the obligation. The issuing partnership will not recognize gain or loss upon the transfer of a partnership interest to an exercising option holder in satisfaction of such unpaid rent, royalties, or interest (including accrued original issue discount).

(b) Transfer of property or satisfaction of an obligation in exchange for a noncompensatory option—(1) In general. Except as provided in paragraph (b)(2) of this section, section 721 does not apply to a transfer of property to a partnership in exchange for a noncompensatory option, or to the satisfaction of a partnership obligation with a noncompensatory option.

(2) Exception. Section 721 does apply to a transfer of property to a partnership in exchange for convertible equity (as defined in paragraph (g)(3) of this section).

(c) Lapse of a noncompensatory option. Section 721 does not apply to the lapse of a noncompensatory option.

(d) Cash settlement of a noncompensatory option. Section 721 does not apply to the settlement of a noncompensatory option in cash or property other than a partnership interest in the issuing partnership.

(e) Issuance of a partnership interest in satisfaction of indebtedness for interest on convertible debt. Section 721 does not apply to the transfer of a partnership interest to a noncompensatory option holder upon conversion of convertible debt in the partnership to the extent that the transfer is in satisfaction of the partnership's indebtedness for unpaid interest (including accrued original issue discount) on the convertible debt that accrued on or after the beginning of the convertible debt holder's holding period for the indebtedness. The debtor partnership will not, however, recognize gain or loss upon such conversion. For rules in determining whether a partnership interest transferred to a creditor is treated as payment of interest or accrued original issue discount, see §§ 1.446–2 and 1.1275–2, respectively.

(f) Scope. The provisions of this section apply only to noncompensatory options. For purposes of this section, the term noncompensatory option means an option (as defined in paragraph (g)(1) of this section) issued by a partnership (the issuing partnership), other than an option issued in connection with the performance of services.

(g) Definitions. The following definitions apply for the purposes of this section:

(1) Option means a contractual right to acquire an interest in the issuing partnership, including a call option, warrant, or other similar arrangement, the conversion feature of convertible debt (as defined in paragraph (g)(2) of this section), or the conversion feature of convertible equity (as defined in paragraph (g)(3) of this section). To achieve the purposes of this section, the Commissioner can treat other contractual agreements, including a futures contract, a forward contract, or a notional principal contract, as an option. A contract that otherwise constitutes an option will not fail to be treated as an option for purposes of this section merely because it may or must be settled in cash or property other than a partnership interest.

(2) Convertible debt is any indebtedness of a partnership that is convertible into an interest in the partnership that issued the debt.

(3) Convertible equity is equity in a partnership that is convertible into a different equity interest in the partnership that issued the convertible equity.

(4) Exercise means the exercise of an option in exchange for an interest in the issuing partnership or the conversion of convertible debt or convertible equity into an interest in the issuing partnership.

(5) Exercise price means, in the case of a call option, the exercise price of the call option; in the case of convertible equity, the converting partner's capital account with respect to that convertible equity, increased by the fair market value of cash or other property contributed to the partnership in connection with the conversion; and, in the case of convertible debt, the adjusted issue price (within the meaning of § 1.1275–1(b)) of the debt converted, increased by accrued but unpaid qualified stated interest on the debt and by the fair market value of cash or other property contributed to the partnership in connection with the conversion.

(h) Example. The following example illustrates the provisions of this section:

Example. In Year 1, L and M form general partnership LM with cash contributions of $5,000 each, which are used to purchase land, Property D, for $10,000. In that same year, LM issues an option to N to buy a one-third interest in LM at any time before the end of Year 3. The exercise price of the option is $5,000, payable in either cash or property. N transfers Property E with a basis of $600 and a value of $1,000 to the partnership in exchange for the option. N provides no other consideration for the option. Assume that N's option is a noncompensatory option under paragraph (f) of this section and that N is not treated as a partner with respect to the option. Under paragraph (b) of this section, section 721(a) does not apply to N's transfer of Property E to LM in exchange for the option. In accordance with § 1.1001–1, upon N's transfer of Property E to the partnership in exchange for the option, N recognizes $400 of gain. Under open transaction principles applicable to noncompensatory options, the partnership does not recognize any income for the premium (the property received in exchange for the option). The partnership has a basis of $1,000 in Property E. In Year 3, when the partnership property is valued at $16,000, N exercises the option, contributing Property F with a basis of $3,000 and a fair market value of $5,000 to the partnership. Under paragraph (a) of this section, neither the partnership nor N recognizes gain upon N's contribution of property to the partnership upon the exercise of the option. Under section 723, the partnership has a basis of $3,000 in Property F. The partnership does not recognize income for the premium (Property E) upon exercise of the option. See § 1.704–1(b)(2)(iv)(d)(4) and (s) for special rules applicable to capital account adjustments on the exercise of a noncompensatory option.

* * *

[T.D. 9612, 78 FR 8012, Feb. 5, 2013]

§ 1.722–1 Basis of contributing partner's interest.

The basis to a partner of a partnership interest acquired by a contribution of property, including money, to the partnership shall be the amount of money contributed plus the adjusted basis at the time of contribution of any property contributed. If the acquisition of an interest in partnership capital results in taxable income to a partner, such income shall constitute an addition to the basis of the partner's interest. See paragraph (b) of § 1.721–1. If the contributed property is subject to indebtedness or if liabilities of the partner are assumed by the partnership, the basis of the contributing partner's interest shall be reduced by the portion of the indebtedness assumed by the other partners, since the partnership's assumption of his indebtedness is treated as a distribution of money to the partner. Conversely, the assumption by the other partners of a portion of the contributor's indebtedness is treated as a contribution of money by them. See section 752 and § 1.752–1. * * * The provisions of this section may be illustrated by the following examples:

Example (1). A acquired a 20-percent interest in a partnership by contributing property. At the time of A's contribution, the property had a fair market value of $10,000, an adjusted basis to A of $4,000, and was subject to a mortgage of $2,000. Payment of the mortgage was assumed by the partnership. The basis of A's interest in the partnership is $2,400, computed as follows:

Adjusted basis to A of property contributed ...	$4,000
Less portion of mortgage assumed by other partners which must be treated as a distribution (80 percent of $2,000)	1,600
Basis of A's interest	2,400

Example (2). If, in example (1) of this section, the property contributed by A was subject to a mortgage of $6,000, the basis of A's interest would be zero, computed as follows:

Adjusted basis to A of property contributed ...	$4,000
Less portion of mortgage assumed by other partners which must be treated as a distribution (80 percent of $6,000)	4,800
	(800)

Since A's basis cannot be less than zero, the $800 in excess of basis, which is considered as a distribution of money under section 752(b), is treated as capital gain from the sale or exchange or a partnership interest. See section 731(a).

[T.D. 6500, 25 FR 11814, Nov. 26, 1960; T.D. 9137, 69 FR 42558, July 16, 2004]

§ 1.723–1 Basis of property contributed to partnership.

The basis to the partnership of property contributed to it by a partner is the adjusted basis of such property to the contributing partner at the time of the contribution. Since such property has the same basis in the hands of the partnership as it had in the hands of the contributing partner, the holding period of such property for the partnership includes the period during which it was held by the partner. See section 1223(2). For elective adjustments to the basis of partnership property arising from distributions or transfers of partnership interests, see sections 732(d), 734(b), and 743(b). * * *

[T.D. 6500, 25 FR 11814, Nov. 26, 1960; T.D. 9137, 69 FR 42558, July 16, 2004]

§ 1.731–1 Extent of recognition of gain or loss on distribution.

(a) Recognition of gain or loss to partner—(1) Recognition of gain. **(i)** Where money is distributed by a partnership to a partner, no gain shall be recognized to the partner except to the extent that the amount of money distributed exceeds the adjusted basis of the partner's interest in the partnership immediately before the distribution. This rule is applicable both to current distributions (i.e., distributions other than in liquidation of an entire interest) and to distributions in liquidation of a partner's entire interest in a partnership. Thus, if a partner with a basis for his interest of $10,000 receives a distribution of cash of $8,000 and property with a fair market value of $3,000, no gain is recognized to him. If $11,000 cash were distributed, gain would be recognized to the extent of $1,000. No gain shall be recognized to a distributee partner with respect to a distribution of property (other than money) until he sells or otherwise disposes of such property, except to the extent otherwise provided by section 736 (relating to payments to a retiring partner or a deceased partner's successor in interest) and section 751 (relating to unrealized receivables and inventory items). See section 731(c) and paragraph (c) of this section.

(ii) For the purposes of sections 731 and 705, advances or drawings of money or property against a partner's distributive share of income shall be treated as current distributions made on the last day of the partnership taxable year with respect to such partner.

(2) Recognition of loss. Loss is recognized to a partner only upon liquidation of his entire interest in the partnership, and only if the property distributed to him consists solely of money, unrealized receivables (as defined in section 751(c)), and inventory items (as defined in section 751(d)(2)). The term "liquidation of a partner's interest", as defined in section 761(d), is the termination of the partner's entire interest in the partnership by means of a distribution or a series of distributions. Loss is recognized to the distributee partner in such cases to the extent of the excess of the adjusted basis of such partner's interest in the partnership at the time of the distribution over the sum of—

(i) Any money distributed to him, and

(ii) The basis to the distributee, as determined under section 732, of any unrealized receivables and inventory items that are distributed to him.

If the partner whose interest is liquidated receives any property other than money, unrealized receivables, or inventory items, then no loss will be recognized. * * *

* * *

(3) Character of gain or loss. Gain or loss recognized under section 731(a) on a distribution is considered gain or loss from the sale or exchange of the partnership interest of the distributee partner, that is, capital gain or loss.

(b) Gain or loss recognized by partnership. A distribution of property (including money) by a partnership to a partner does not result in recognized gain or loss to the partnership under section 731. However, recognized gain or loss may result to the partnership from certain distributions which, under section 751(b), must be treated as a sale or exchange of property between the distributee partner and the partnership.

(c) Exceptions. **(1)** Section 731 does not apply to the extent otherwise provided by—

(i) Section 736 (relating to payments to a retiring partner or to a deceased partner's successor in interest) and

(ii) Section 751 (relating to unrealized receivables and inventory items).

For example, payments under section 736(a), which are considered as a distributive share or guaranteed payment, are taxable as such under that section.

(2) The receipt by a partner from the partnership of money or property under an obligation to repay the amount of such money or to return such property does not constitute a distribution subject to section 731 but is a loan governed by section 707(a). To the extent that such an obligation is canceled, the obligor partner will be considered to have received a distribution of money or property at the time of cancellation.

(3) If there is a contribution of property to a partnership and within a short period:

(i) Before or after such contribution other property is distributed to the contributing partner and the contributed property is retained by the partnership, or

(ii) After such contribution the contributed property is distributed to another partner,

such distribution may not fall within the scope of section 731. Section 731 does not apply to a distribution of property, if, in fact, the distribution was made in order to effect an exchange of property between two or more of the partners or between the partnership and a partner. Such a transaction shall be treated as an exchange of property.

[T.D. 6500, 25 FR 11814, Nov. 26, 1960]

§ 1.731-2 Partnership distributions of marketable securities.

(a) Marketable securities treated as money. Except as otherwise provided in section 731(c) and this section, for purposes of sections 731(a)(1) and 737, the term *money* includes marketable securities and such securities are taken into account at their fair market value as of the date of the distribution.

(b) Reduction of amount treated as money—(1) Aggregation of securities. For purposes of section 731(c)(3)(B) and this paragraph (b), all marketable securities held by a partnership are treated as marketable securities of the same class and issuer as the distributed security.

(2) Amount of reduction. The amount of the distribution of marketable securities that is treated as a distribution of money under section 731(c) and paragraph (a) of this section is reduced (but not below zero) by the excess, if any, of—

(i) The distributee partner's distributive share of the net gain, if any, which would be recognized if all the marketable securities held by the partnership were sold (immediately before the transaction to which the distribution relates) by the partnership for fair market value; over

(ii) The distributee partner's distributive share of the net gain, if any, which is attributable to the marketable securities held by the partnership immediately after the transaction, determined by using the same fair market value as used under paragraph (b)(2)(i) of this section.

(3) Distributee partner's share of net gain. For purposes of section 731(c)(3)(B) and paragraph (b)(2) of this section, a partner's distributive share of net gain is determined—

(i) By taking into account any basis adjustments under section 743(b) with respect to that partner;

(ii) Without taking into account any special allocations adopted with a principal purpose of avoiding the effect of section 731(c) and this section; and

(iii) Without taking into account any gain or loss attributable to a distributed security to which paragraph (d)(1) of this section applies.

(c) Marketable securities—(1) In general. For purposes of section 731(c) and this section, the term marketable securities is defined in section 731(c)(2).

(2) Actively traded. For purposes of section 731(c) and this section, a financial instrument is actively traded (and thus is a marketable security) if it is of a type that is, as of the date of distribution, actively traded within the meaning of section 1092(d)(1). Thus, for example, if XYZ common stock is listed on a national securities exchange, particular shares of XYZ common stock that are distributed by a partnership are marketable securities even if those particular shares cannot be resold by the distributee partner for a designated period of time.

(3) Interests in an entity—(i) Substantially all. For purposes of section 731(c)(2)(B)(v) and this section, substantially all of the assets of an entity consist (directly or indirectly) of marketable securities, money, or both only if 90 percent or more of the assets of the entity (by value) at the time of the distribution of an interest in the entity consist (directly or indirectly) of marketable securities, money, or both.

(ii) Less than substantially all. For purposes of section 731(c)(2)(B)(vi) and this section, an interest in an entity is a marketable security to the extent that the value of the interest is attributable (directly or indirectly) to marketable securities, money, or both, if less than 90 percent but 20 percent or more of the assets of the entity (by value) at the time of the distribution of an interest in the entity consist (directly or indirectly) of marketable securities, money, or both.

(4) Value of assets. For purposes of section 731(c) and this section, the value of the assets of an entity is determined without regard to any debt that may encumber or otherwise be allocable to those assets, other than debt that is incurred to acquire an asset with a principal purpose of avoiding or reducing the effect of section 731(c) and this section.

(d) Exceptions—(1) In general. Except as otherwise provided in paragraph (d)(2) of this section, section 731(c) and this section do not apply to the distribution of a marketable security if—

(i) The security was contributed to the partnership by the distributee partner;

(ii) The security was acquired by the partnership in a nonrecognition transaction, and the following conditions are satisfied—

(A) The value of any marketable securities and money exchanged by the partnership in the nonrecognition transaction is less than 20 percent of the value of all the assets exchanged by the partnership in the nonrecognition transaction; and

(B) The partnership distributed the security within five years of either the date the security was acquired by the partnership or, if later, the date the security became marketable; or

(iii) The security was not a marketable security on the date acquired by the partnership, and the following conditions are satisfied—

(A) The entity that issued the security had no outstanding marketable securities at the time the security was acquired by the partnership;

(B) The security was held by the partnership for at least six months before the date the security became marketable; and

(C) The partnership distributed the security within five years of the date the security became marketable.

(2) Anti-stuffing rule. Paragraph (d)(1) of this section does not apply to the extent that 20 percent or more of the value of the distributed security is attributable to marketable securities or money contributed (directly or indirectly) by the partnership to the entity to which the distributed security relates after the security was acquired by the partnership (other than marketable securities contributed by the partnership that were originally contributed to the partnership by the distributee partner). For purposes of this paragraph (d)(2), money contributed by the distributing partnership does not include any money deemed contributed by the partnership as a result of section 752.

(3) Successor security. Section 731(c) and this section apply to the distribution of a marketable security acquired by the partnership in a nonrecognition transaction in exchange for a security the distribution of which immediately prior to the exchange would have been excepted under this paragraph (d) only to the extent that section 731(c) and this section otherwise would have applied to the exchanged security.

(e) Investment partnerships—(1) In general. Section 731(c) and this section do not apply to the distribution of marketable securities by an investment partnership (as defined in section 731(c)(3)(C)(i)) to an eligible partner (as defined in section 731(c)(3)(C)(iii)).

(2) Eligible partner—(i) Contributed services. For purposes of section 731(c)(3)(C)(iii) and this section, a partner is not treated as a partner other than an eligible partner solely because the partner contributed services to the partnership.

(ii) Contributed partnership interests. For purposes of determining whether a partner is an eligible partner under section 731(c)(3)(C), if the partner has contributed to the investment partnership an interest in another partnership that meets the requirements of paragraph (e)(4)(i) of this section after the contribution, the contributed interest is treated as property specified in section 731(c)(3)(C)(i).

(3) Trade or business activities. For purposes of section 731(c)(3)(C) and this section, a partnership is not treated as engaged in a trade or business by reason of—

(i) Any activity undertaken as an investor, trader, or dealer in any asset described in section 731(c)(3)(C)(i), including the receipt of commitment fees, break-up fees, guarantee fees, director's fees, or similar fees that are customary in and incidental to any activities of the partnership as an investor, trader, or dealer in such assets;

(ii) Reasonable and customary management services (including the receipt of reasonable and customary fees in exchange for such management services) provided to an investment partnership (within the meaning of section 731(c)(3)(C)(i)) in which the partnership holds a partnership interest; or

(iii) Reasonable and customary services provided by the partnership in assisting the formation, capitalization, expansion, or offering of interests in a corporation (or other entity) in which the partnership holds or acquires a significant equity interest (including the provision of advice or consulting services, bridge loans, guarantees of obligations, or service on a company's board of directors), provided that the anticipated receipt of compensation for the services, if any, does not represent a significant purpose for the partnership's investment in the entity and is incidental to the investment in the entity.

(4) Partnership tiers. For purposes of section 731(c)(3)(C)(iv) and this section, a partnership (upper-tier partnership) is not treated as engaged in a trade or business engaged in by, or as holding (instead of a partnership interest) a proportionate share of the assets of, a partnership (lower-tier partnership) in which the partnership holds a partnership interest if—

(i) The upper-tier partnership does not actively and substantially participate in the management of the lower-tier partnership; and

(ii) The interest held by the upper-tier partnership is less than 20 percent of the total profits and capital interests in the lower-tier partnership.

(f) Basis rules—(1) Partner's basis—(i) Partner's basis in distributed securities. The distributee partner's basis in distributed marketable securities with respect to which gain is recognized by reason of section 731(c) and this section is the basis of the security determined under section 732, increased by the amount of such gain. Any increase in the basis of the marketable securities attributable to gain recognized by reason of section 731(c) and this section is allocated to marketable securities in proportion to their respective amounts of unrealized appreciation in the hands of the partner before such increase.

(ii) Partner's basis in partnership interest. The basis of the distributee partner's interest in the partnership is determined under section 733 as if no gain were recognized by the partner on the distribution by reason of section 731(c) and this section.

(2) Basis of partnership property. No adjustment is made to the basis of partnership property under section 734 as a result of any gain recognized by a partner, or any step-up in the basis in the distributed marketable securities in the hands of the distributee partner, by reason of section 731(c) and this section.

(g) Coordination with other sections—(1) Sections 704(c)(1)(B) and 737—(i) In general. If a distribution results in the application of sections 731(c) and one or both of sections 704(c)(1)(B) and 737, the effect of the distribution is determined by applying section 704(c)(1)(B) first, section 731(c) second, and finally section 737.

(ii) Section 704(c)(1)(B). The basis of the distributee partner's interest in the partnership for purposes of determining the amount of gain, if any, recognized by reason of section 731(c) (and for determining the basis of the marketable securities in the hands of the distributee partner) includes the increase or decrease, if any, in the partner's basis that occurs under section 704(c)(1)(B)(iii) as a result of a distribution to another partner of property contributed by the distributee partner in a distribution that is part of the same distribution as the marketable securities.

(iii) Section 737—(A) Marketable securities as other property. A distribution of marketable securities is treated as a distribution of property other than money for purposes of section 737 to the extent that the marketable securities are not treated as money under section 731(c). In addition, marketable securities contributed to the partnership are treated as property other than money in determining the contributing partner's net precontribution gain under section 737(b).

(B) Basis increase under section 737. The basis of the distributee partner's interest in the partnership for purposes of determining the amount of gain, if any, recognized by reason of section 731(c) (and for determining the basis of the marketable securities in the hands of the distributee partner) does not include the increase, if any, in the partner's basis that occurs under section 737(c)(1) as a result of a distribution of property to the distributee partner in a distribution that is part of the same distribution as the marketable securities.

(2) Section 708(b)(1)(B). If a partnership termination occurs under section 708(b)(1)(B), the successor partnership will be treated as if there had been no termination for purposes of section 731(c) and this section. Accordingly, a section 708(b)(1)(B) termination will not affect whether a partnership qualifies for any of the exceptions in paragraphs (d) and (e) of this section. In addition, a deemed distribution that may occur as a result of a section 708(b)(1)(B) termination will not be subject to section 731(c) and this section.

(h) Anti-abuse rule. The provisions of section 731(c) and this section must be applied in a manner consistent with the purpose of section 731(c) and the substance of the transaction. Accordingly, if a principal purpose of a transaction is to achieve a tax result that is inconsistent with the purpose of section 731(c) and this section, the Commissioner can recast the transaction for Federal tax purposes as appropriate to achieve tax results that are consistent with the purpose of section 731(c) and this section. Whether a tax result is inconsistent with the purpose of section 731(c) and this section must be determined based on all the facts and circumstances. For example, under the provisions of this paragraph (h)—

(1) A change in partnership allocations or distribution rights with respect to marketable securities may be treated as a distribution of the marketable securities subject to section 731(c) if the change in allocations or distribution rights is, in substance, a distribution of the securities;

(2) A distribution of substantially all of the assets of the partnership other than marketable securities and money to some partners may also be treated as a distribution of marketable securities to the remaining partners if the distribution of the other property and the withdrawal of the other partners is, in substance, equivalent to a distribution of the securities to the remaining partners; and

(3) The distribution of multiple properties to one or more partners at different times may also be treated as part of a single distribution if the distributions are part of a single plan of distribution.

(i) [Reserved]

(j) Examples. The following examples illustrate the rules of this section. Unless otherwise specified, all securities held by a partnership are marketable securities within the meaning of section 731(c); the partnership holds no marketable securities other than the securities described in the example; all distributions by the partnership are subject to section 731(a) and are not subject to sections 704(c)(1)(B), 707(a)(2)(B), 751(b), or 737; and no securities are eligible for an exception to section 731(c). The examples are as follows:

Example 1. Recognition of gain. **(i)** A and B form partnership AB as equal partners. A contributes property with a fair market value of $1,000 and an adjusted tax basis of $250. B contributes $1,000 cash. AB subsequently purchases Security X for $500 and immediately distributes the security to A in a current distribution. The basis in A's interest in the partnership at the time of distribution is $250.

(ii) The distribution of Security X is treated as a distribution of money in an amount equal to the fair market value of Security X on the date of distribution ($500). (The amount of the distribution that is treated as money is not reduced under section 731(c)(3)(B) and paragraph (b) of this section because, if Security X had been sold immediately before the distribution, there would have been no gain recognized by AB and A's distributive share of the gain would therefore have been zero.) As a result, A recognizes $250 of gain under section 731(a)(1) on the distribution ($500 distribution of money less $250 adjusted tax basis in A's partnership interest).

Example 2. Reduction in amount treated as money—in general. **(i)** A and B form partnership AB as equal partners. AB subsequently distributes Security X to A in a current distribution. Immediately before the distribution, AB held securities with the following fair market values, adjusted tax bases, and unrecognized gain or loss:

	Value	*Basis*	*Gain (Loss)*
Security *X*	100	70	30
Security *Y*	100	80	20
Security *Z*	100	110	(10)

(ii) If AB had sold the securities for fair market value immediately before the distribution to A, the partnership would have recognized $40 of net gain ($30 gain on Security X plus $20 gain on Security Y minus $10 loss on Security Z). A's distributive share of this gain would have been $20 (one-half of $40 net gain). If AB had sold the remaining securities immediately after the distribution of Security X to A, the partnership would have $10 of net gain ($20 of gain on Security Y minus $10 loss on Security Z). A's distributive share of this gain would have been $5 (one-half of $10 net gain). As a result, the distribution resulted in a decrease of $15 in A's distributive share of the net gain in AB's securities ($20 net gain before distribution minus $5 net gain after distribution).

(iii) Under paragraph (b) of this section, the amount of the distribution of Security X that is treated as a distribution of money is reduced by $15. The distribution of Security X is therefore treated as a distribution of $85 of money to A ($100 fair market value of Security X minus $15 reduction).

Example 3. Reduction in amount treated as money—carried interest. **(i)** A and B form partnership AB. A contributes $1,000 and provides substantial services to the partnership in exchange for a 60 percent interest in partnership profits. B contributes $1,000 in exchange for a 40 percent interest in partnership profits. AB subsequently distributes Security X to A in a current distribution. Immediately before the distribution, AB held securities with the following fair market values, adjusted tax bases, and unrecognized gain:

	Value	*Basis*	*Gain*
Security *X*	100	80	20
Security *Y*	100	90	10

(ii) If AB had sold the securities for fair market value immediately before the distribution to A, the partnership would have recognized $30 of net gain ($20 gain on Security X plus $10 gain on Security Y). A's distributive share of this gain would have been $18 (60 percent of $30 net gain). If AB had sold the remaining securities immediately after the distribution of Security X to A, the partnership would have $10 of net gain ($10 gain on Security Y). A's distributive share of this gain would have been $6 (60 percent of $10 net gain). As a result, the distribution resulted in a decrease of $12 in A's distributive share of the net gain in AB's securities ($18 net gain before distribution minus $6 net gain after distribution).

(iii) Under paragraph (b) of this section, the amount of the distribution of Security X that is treated as a distribution of money is reduced by $12. The distribution of Security X is therefore treated as a distribution of $88 of money to A ($100 fair market value of Security X minus $12 reduction).

Example 4. Reduction in amount treated as money—change in partnership allocations. **(i)** A is admitted to partnership ABC as a partner with a 1 percent interest in partnership profits. At the time of A's admission, ABC held no securities. ABC subsequently acquires Security X. A's interest in partnership profits is subsequently increased to 2 percent for securities acquired after the increase. A retains a 1 percent interest in all securities acquired before the increase. ABC then acquires Securities Y and Z and later distributes Security X to A in a current distribution. Immediately before the distribution, the securities held by ABC had the following fair market values, adjusted tax bases, and unrecognized gain or loss:

	Value	*Basis*	*Gain (Loss)*
Security *X*	1,000	500	500
Security *Y*	1,000	800	200
Security *Z*	1,000	1,100	(100)

(ii) If ABC had sold the securities for fair market value immediately before the distribution to A, the partnership would have recognized $600 of net gain ($500 gain on Security X plus $200 gain on Security Y minus $100 loss on Security Z). A's distributive share of this gain would have been $7 (1 percent of $500 gain on Security X plus 2 percent of $200 gain on Security Y minus 2 percent of $100 loss on Security Z).

(iii) If ABC had sold the remaining securities immediately after the distribution of Security X to A, the partnership would have $100 of net gain ($200 gain on Security Y minus $100 loss on Security Z). A's distributive share of this gain would have been $2 (2 percent of $200 gain on Security Y minus 2 percent of $100 loss on Security Z). As a result, the distribution resulted in a decrease of $5 in A's distributive share of the net gain in ABC's securities ($7 net gain before distribution minus $2 net gain after distribution).

(iv) Under paragraph (b) of this section, the amount of the distribution of Security X that is treated as a distribution of money is reduced by $5. The distribution of Security X is therefore treated as a distribution of $995 of money to A ($1000 fair market value of Security X minus $5 reduction).

Example 5. Basis consequences—distribution of marketable security. **(i)** A and B form partnership AB as equal partners. A contributes nondepreciable real property with a fair market value and adjusted tax basis of $100.

(ii) AB subsequently distributes Security X with a fair market value of $120 and an adjusted tax basis of $90 to A in a current distribution. At the time of distribution, the basis in A's interest in the partnership is $100. The amount of the distribution that is treated as money is reduced under section 731(c)(3)(B) and paragraph (b)(2) of this section by $15 (one-half of $30 net gain in Security X). As a result, A recognizes $5 of gain under section 731(a) on the distribution (excess of $105 distribution of money over $100 adjusted tax basis in A's partnership interest).

(iii) A's adjusted tax basis in Security X is $95 ($90 adjusted basis of Security X determined under section 732(a)(1) plus $5 of gain recognized by A by reason of section 731(c)). The basis in A's interest in the partnership is $10 as determined under section 733 ($100 pre-distribution basis minus $90 basis allocated to Security X under section 732).

Example 6. Basis consequences—distribution of marketable security and other property. **(i)** A and B form partnership AB as equal partners. A contributes nondepreciable real property, with a fair market value of $100 and an adjusted tax basis of $10.

(ii) AB subsequently distributes Security X with a fair market value and adjusted tax basis of $40 to A in a current distribution and, as part of the same distribution, AB distributes Property Z to A with an adjusted tax basis and fair market value of $40. At the time of distribution, the basis in A's interest in the partnership is $10. A recognizes $30 of gain under section 731(a) on the distribution (excess of $40 distribution of money over $10 adjusted tax basis in A's partnership interest).

(iii) A's adjusted tax basis in Security X is $35 ($5 adjusted basis determined under section 732(a)(2) plus $30 of gain recognized by A by reason of section 731(c)). A's basis in Property Z is $5, as determined under section 732(a)(2). The basis in A's interest in the partnership is $0 as determined under section 733 ($10 pre-distribution basis minus $10 basis allocated between Security X and Property Z under section 732).

(iv) AB's adjusted tax basis in the remaining partnership assets is unchanged unless the partnership has a section 754 election in effect. If AB made such an election, the aggregate basis of AB's assets would be increased by $70 (the difference between the $80 combined basis of Security X and Property Z in the hands of the partnership before the distribution and the $10 combined basis of the distributed property in the hands of A under section 732 after the distribution). Under section 731(c)(5), no adjustment is made to partnership property under section 734 as a result of any gain recognized by A by reason of section 731(c) or as a result of any step-up in basis in the distributed marketable securities in the hands of A by reason of section 731(c).

Example 7. Coordination with section 737. (i) A and B form partnership AB. A contributes Property A, nondepreciable real property with a fair market value of $200 and an adjusted basis of $100 in exchange for a 25 percent interest in partnership capital and profits. AB owns marketable Security X.

(ii) Within five years of the contribution of Property A, AB subsequently distributes Security X, with a fair market value of $120 and an adjusted tax basis of $100, to A in a current distribution that is subject to section 737. As part of the same distribution, AB distributes Property Y to A with a fair market value of $20 and an adjusted tax basis of $0. At the time of distribution, there has been no change in the fair market value of Property A or the adjusted tax basis in A's interest in the partnership.

(iii) If AB had sold Security X for fair market value immediately before the distribution to A, the partnership would have recognized $20 of gain. A's distributive share of this gain would have been $5 (25 percent of $20 gain). Because AB has no other marketable securities, A's distributive share of gain in partnership securities after the distribution would have been $0. As a result, the distribution resulted in a decrease of $5 in A's share of the net gain in AB's securities ($5 net gain before distribution minus $0 net gain after distribution). Under paragraph (b)(2) of this section, the amount of the distribution of Security X that is treated as a distribution of money is reduced by $5. The distribution of Security X is therefore treated as a distribution of $115 of money to A ($120 fair market value of Security X minus $5 reduction). The portion of the distribution of the marketable security that is not treated as a distribution of money ($5) is treated as other property for purposes of section 737.

(iv) A recognizes total gain of $40 on the distribution. A recognizes $15 of gain under section 731(a)(1) on the distribution of the portion of Security X treated as money ($115 distribution of money less $100 adjusted tax basis in A's partnership interest). A recognizes $25 of gain under section 737 on the distribution of Property Y and the portion of Security X that is not treated as money. A's section 737 gain is equal to the lesser of (i) A's precontribution gain ($100) or (ii) the excess of the fair market value of property received ($20 fair market value of Property Y plus $5 portion of Security X not treated as money) over the adjusted basis in A's interest in the partnership immediately before the distribution ($100) reduced (but not below zero) by the amount of money received in the distribution ($115).

(v) A's adjusted tax basis in Security X is $115 ($100 basis of Security X determined under section 732(a) plus $15 of gain recognized by reason of section 731(c)). A's adjusted tax basis in Property Y is $0 under section 732(a). The basis in A's interest in the partnership is $25 ($100 basis before distribution minus $100 basis allocated to Security X under section 732(a) plus $25 gain recognized under section 737).

(k) Effective date. This section applies to distributions made on or after December 26, 1996. However, taxpayers may apply the rules of this section to distributions made after December 8, 1994, and before December 26, 1996.

[T.D. 8707, 61 FR 67936, Dec. 26, 1996; 62 FR 8086, Feb. 21, 1997]

§ 1.732–1 Basis of distributed property other than money.

(a) Distributions other than in liquidation of a partner's interest. The basis of property (other than money) received by a partner in a distribution from a partnership, other than in liquidation of his entire interest, shall be its adjusted basis to the partnership immediately before such distribution. However, the basis of the property to the partner shall not exceed the adjusted basis of the partner's interest in the partnership, reduced by the amount of any money distributed to him in the same transaction. The provisions of this paragraph may be illustrated by the following examples:

Example (1). Partner A, with an adjusted basis of $15,000 for his partnership interest, receives in a current distribution property having an adjusted basis of $10,000 to the partnership immediately before distribution, and $2,000 cash. The basis of the property in A's hands will be $10,000. Under sections 733 and 705, the basis of A's partnership interest will be reduced by the distribution to $3,000 ($15,000 less $2,000 cash, less $10,000, the basis of the distributed property to A).

Example (2). Partner R has an adjusted basis of $10,000 for his partnership interest. He receives a current distribution of $4,000 cash and property with an adjusted basis to the partnership of $8,000. The basis of the distributed property to partner R is limited to $6,000 ($10,000, the adjusted basis of his interest, reduced by $4,000, the cash distributed).

(b) Distribution in liquidation. Where a partnership distributes property (other than money) in liquidation of a partner's entire interest in the partnership, the basis of such property to the partner shall be an amount equal to the adjusted basis of his interest in the partnership reduced by the amount of any money distributed to him in the same transaction. Application of this rule may be illustrated by the following example:

Example. Partner B, with a partnership interest having an adjusted basis to him of $12,000, retires from the partnership and receives cash of $2,000, and real property with an adjusted basis to the partnership of $6,000 and a fair market value of $14,000. The basis of the real property to B is $10,000 (B's basis for his partnership interest, $12,000, reduced by $2,000, the cash distributed).

(c) Allocation of basis among properties distributed to a partner—(1) General rule—(i) Unrealized receivables and inventory items. The basis to be allocated to properties distributed to a partner under section 732(a)(2) or (b) is allocated first to any unrealized receivables (as defined in section 751(c)) and inventory items (as defined in section 751(d)(2)) in an amount equal to the adjusted basis of each such property to the partnership immediately before the distribution. If the basis to be allocated is less than the sum of the adjusted bases to the partnership of the distributed unrealized receivables and inventory items, the adjusted basis of the distributed property must be decreased in the manner provided in paragraph (c)(2)(i) of this section. * * *

(ii) Other distributed property. Any basis not allocated to unrealized receivables or inventory items under paragraph (c)(1)(i) of this section is allocated to any other property distributed to the partner in the same transaction by assigning to each distributed property an amount equal to the adjusted basis of the property to the partnership immediately before the distribution. However, if the sum of the adjusted bases to the partnership of such other distributed property does not equal the basis to be allocated among the distributed property, any increase or decrease required to make the amounts equal is allocated among the distributed property as provided in paragraph (c)(2) of this section.

(2) Adjustment to basis allocation—(i) Decrease in basis. Any decrease to the basis of distributed property required under paragraph (c)(1) of this section is allocated first to distributed property with unrealized depreciation in proportion to each property's respective amount of unrealized depreciation before any decrease (but only to the extent of each property's unrealized depreciation). If the required decrease exceeds the amount of unrealized depreciation in the distributed property, the excess is allocated to the distributed property in proportion to the adjusted bases of the distributed property, as adjusted pursuant to the immediately preceding sentence.

(ii) Increase in basis. Any increase to the basis of distributed property required under paragraph (c)(1)(ii) of this section is allocated first to distributed property (other than unrealized receivables and inventory items) with unrealized appreciation in proportion to each property's respective amount of unrealized appreciation before any increase (but only to the extent of each property's unrealized appreciation). If the required increase exceeds the amount of unrealized appreciation in the distributed property, the excess is allocated to the distributed property (other than unrealized receivables or inventory items) in proportion to the fair market value of the distributed property.

(3) Unrealized receivables and inventory items. If the basis to be allocated upon a distribution in liquidation of the partner's entire interest in the partnership is greater than the adjusted basis to the partnership of the unrealized receivables and inventory items distributed to the partner, and if there is no other property distributed to which the excess can be allocated, the distributee partner sustains a capital loss under section 731(a)(2) to the extent of the unallocated basis of the partnership interest.

(4) Examples. The provisions of this paragraph (c) are illustrated by the following examples:

Example 1. A is a one-fourth partner in partnership PRS and has an adjusted basis in its partnership interest of $650. PRS distributes inventory items and Assets X and Y to A in liquidation of A's entire partnership interest. The distributed inventory items have a basis to the partnership of $100 and a fair market value of $200. Asset X has an adjusted basis to the partnership of $50 and a fair market value of $400. Asset Y has an adjusted basis to the partnership and a fair market value of $100. Neither Asset X nor Asset Y consists of inventory items or unrealized receivables. Under this paragraph (c), A's basis in its partnership interest is allocated first to the inventory items in an amount equal to their adjusted basis to the partnership. A, therefore, has an adjusted basis in the inventory items of $100. The remaining basis, $550, is allocated to the distributed property first in an amount equal to the property's adjusted basis to the partnership. Thus, Asset X is allocated $50 and Asset Y is allocated $100. Asset X is then allocated $350, the amount of unrealized appreciation in Asset X. Finally, the remaining basis, $50, is allocate to Assets X and Y in proportion to their fair market values: $40 to Asset X (400/500 x $50), and $10 to Asset Y (100/500 x $50). Therefore, after the distribution, A has an adjusted basis of $440 in Asset X and $110 in Asset Y.

Example 2. B is a one-fourth partner in partnership PRS and has an adjusted basis in its partnership interest of $200. PRS distributes Asset X and Asset Y to B in liquidation of its entire partnership interest. Asset X has an adjusted basis to the partnership and fair market value of $150. Asset Y has an adjusted basis to the partnership of $150 and a fair market value of $50. Neither of the assets consists of inventory items or unrealized receivables. Under this paragraph (c), B's basis is first assigned to the distributed property to the extent of the partnership's basis in each distributed property. Thus, Asset X and Asset Y are each assigned $150. Because the aggregate adjusted basis of the distributed property, $300, exceeds the basis to be allocated, $200, a decrease of $100 in the basis of the distributed property is required. Assets X and Y have unrealized depreciation of zero and $100, respectively. Thus, the entire decrease is allocated to Asset Y. After the distribution, B has an adjusted basis of $150 in Asset X and $50 in Asset Y.

Example 3. C, a partner in partnership PRS, receives a distribution in liquidation of its entire partnership interest of $6,000 cash, inventory items having an adjusted basis to the partnership of $6,000, and real property having an adjusted basis to the partnership of $4,000. C's basis in its partnership interest is $9,000. The cash distribution reduces C's basis to $3,000, which is allocated entirely to the inventory items. The real property has a zero basis in C's hands. The partnership bases carried over to C for the distributed properties are lost unless an election under section 754 is in effect requiring the partnership to adjust the bases of remaining partnership properties under section 734(b).

Example 4. Assume the same facts as in *Example 3* of this paragraph except C receives a distribution in liquidation of its entire partnership interest of $1,000 cash and inventory items having a basis to the partnership of $6,000. The cash distribution reduces C's basis to $8,000, which can be allocated only to the extent of $6,000 to the inventory items. The remaining $2,000 basis, not allocable to the distributed property, constitutes a capital loss to partner C under section 731(a)(2). If the election under section 754 is in effect, see section 734(b) for adjustment of the basis of undistributed partnership property.

(d) Special partnership basis to transferee under section 732(d). **(1)(i)** A transfer of a partnership interest occurs upon a sale or exchange of an interest or upon the death of a partner. Section 732(d) provides a special rule for the determination of the basis of property distributed to a transferee partner who acquired any part of his partnership interest in a transfer with respect to which the election under section 754 (relating to the optional adjustment to basis of partnership property) was not in effect.

(ii) Where an election under section 754 is in effect, see section 743(b) and §§ 1.743–1 and 1.732–2.

(iii) If a transferee partner receives a distribution of property (other than money) from the partnership within 2 years after he acquired his interest or part thereof in the partnership by a transfer with respect to which the election under section 754 was not in effect, he may elect to treat as the adjusted partnership basis of such property the adjusted basis such property would have if the adjustment provided in section 743(b) were in effect.

(iv) If an election under section 732(d) is made upon a distribution of property to a transferee partner, the amount of the adjustment with respect to the transferee partner is not diminished by any depletion or depreciation of that portion of the basis of partnership property which arises from the special basis adjustment under section 732(d), since depletion or depreciation on such portion for the period prior to distribution is allowed or allowable only if the optional adjustment under section 743(b) is in effect.

(v) If property is distributed to a transferee partner who elects under section 732(d), and if such property is not the same property which would have had a special basis adjustment, then such special basis adjustment shall apply to any like property received in the distribution, provided that the transferee, in exchange for the property distributed, has relinquished his interest in the property with respect to which he would have had a special basis adjustment. This rule applies whether the property in which the transferee has relinquished his interest is retained or disposed or by the partnership. * * *

* * *

(2) A transferee partner who wishes to elect under section 732(d) shall make the election with his tax return—

(i) For the year of the distribution, if the distribution includes any property subject to the allowance for depreciation, depletion, or amortization, or

(ii) For any taxable year no later than the first taxable year in which the basis of any of the distributed property is pertinent in determining his income tax, if the distribution does not include any such property subject to the allowance for depreciation, depletion or amortization.

(3) A taxpayer making an election under section 732(d) shall submit with the return in which the election is made a schedule setting forth the following:

(i) That under section 732(d) he elects to adjust the basis of property received in a distribution; and

(ii) The computation of the special basis adjustment for the property distributed and the properties to which the adjustment has been allocated. For rules of allocation, see section 755.

(4) A partner who acquired any part of his partnership interest in a transfer to which the election provided in section 754 was not in effect, is required to apply the special basis rule contained in section 732(d) to a distribution to him, whether or not made within 2 years after the transfer, if at the time of his acquisition of the transferred interest—

(i) The fair market value of all partnership property (other than money) exceeded 110 percent of its adjusted basis to the partnership.

(ii) An allocation of basis under section 732(c) upon a liquidation of his interest immediately after the transfer of the interest would have resulted in a shift of basis from property not subject to an allowance for depreciation, depletion, or amortization, to property subject to such an allowance, and

(iii) A basis adjustment under section 743(b) would change the basis to the transferee partner of the property actually distributed.

* * *

(e) Exception. When a partnership distributes unrealized receivables (as defined in section 751(c)) or substantially appreciated inventory items (as defined in section 751(d)) in exchange for any part of a partner's interest in other partnership property (including money), or, conversely, partnership property (including money) other than unrealized receivables or substantially appreciated inventory items in exchange for any part of a partner's interest in the partnership's unrealized receivables or substantially appreciated inventory items, the distribution will be treated as a sale or exchange of property under the provisions of section 751(b). In such case, section 732 (including subsection(d) thereof) applies in determining the partner's basis of the property which he is treated as having sold to or exchanged with the partnership (as constituted after the distribution). The partner is considered as having received such property in a current distribution and, immediately thereafter, as having sold or exchanged it. See section 751(b) and paragraph (b) of § 1.751–1. However, section 732 does not apply in determining the basis of that part of property actually distributed to a partner which is treated as received by him in a sale or exchange under section 751(b). Consequently, the basis of such property shall be its cost to the partner.

[T.D. 6500, 25 FR 11814, Nov. 26, 1960, as amended by T.D. 8847, 64 FR 69903, Dec. 15, 1999; T.D. 9137, 69 FR 42558, July 16, 2004]

§ 1.732–2 Special partnership basis of distributed property.

(a) Adjustments under section 734(b). In the case of a distribution of property to a partner, the partnership bases of the distributed properties shall reflect any increases or decreases to the basis of partnership property which have been made previously under section 734(b) (relating to the optional adjustment to basis of undistributed partnership property) in connection with previous distributions.

(b) Adjustments under section 743(b). In the case of a distribution of property to a partner who acquired any part of his interest in a transfer as to which an election under section 754 was in effect, then, for the purposes of section 732 (other than subsection (d) thereof), the adjusted partnership bases of the distributed property shall take into account, in addition to any adjustments under section 734(b), the transferee's special basis adjustment for the distributed property under section 743(b). The application of this paragraph may be illustrated by the following example:

Example. Partner D acquired his interest in partnership ABD from a previous partner. Since the partnership had made an election under section 754, a special basis adjustment with respect to D is applicable to the basis of partnership property in accordance with section 743(b). One of the assets of the partnership at the time D acquired his interest was property X, which is later distributed to D in a current distribution. Property X has an adjusted basis to the partnership of $1,000 and with respect to D it has a special basis adjustment of $500. Therefore, for purposes of section 732(a)(1), the adjusted basis of such property to the partnership with respect to D immediately before its distribution is $1,500. However, if property X is distributed to partner A, a nontransferee partner, its adjusted basis to the partnership for purposes of section 732(a)(1) is only $1,000. In such case, D's $500 special basis adjustment may shift over to other property. See § 1.743–1(g).

(c) Adjustments to basis of distributed inventory and unrealized receivables. Under section 732, the basis to be allocated to distributed properties shall be allocated first to any unrealized receivables and inventory items. If the distributee partner is a transferee of a partnership interest and has a special basis adjustment for unrealized receivables or inventory items under either section 743(b) or section 732(d), then the partnership adjusted basis immediately prior to distribution of any unrealized receivables or inventory items distributed to such partner shall be determined as follows: If the distributee partner receives his entire share of the fair market value of the inventory items or unrealized receivables of the partnership, the adjusted basis of such distributed property to the partnership, for the purposes of section 732, shall take into account the entire amount of any special basis adjustment which the distributee partner may have for such assets. If the distributee partner receives less than his entire share of the fair market value of partnership inventory items or unrealized receivables, then, for purposes of section 732, the adjusted basis of such distributed property to the partnership shall take into account the same proportion of the distributee's special basis adjustment for unrealized receivables or inventory items as the value of such items distributed to him bears to his entire share of the total value of all such items of the partnership. The provisions of this paragraph may be illustrated by the following example:

Example. Partner C acquired his 40–percent interest in partnership AC from a previous partner. Since the partnership had made an election under section 754, C has a special basis adjustment to partnership property under section 743(b). C retires from the partnership when the adjusted basis of his partnership interest is $3,000. He receives from the partnership in liquidation of his entire interest, $1,000 cash, certain capital assets, depreciable property, and certain inventory items and unrealized receivables. C has a special basis adjustment of $800 with respect to partnership inventory items and of $200 with respect to unrealized receivables. The common partnership basis for the inventory items distributed to him is $500 and for the unrealized receivables is zero. If the value of inventory items and the unrealized receivables distributed to C in his 40 percent share of the total value of all partnership inventory items and unrealized receivables, then, for purposes of section 732, the adjusted basis of such property in C's hands will be $1,300 for the inventory items ($500 plus $800) and $200 for the unrealized receivables (zero plus $200). The remaining basis of $500, which constitutes the basis of the capital assets and depreciable property distributed to C, is determined as follows: $3,000 (total basis) less $1,000 cash, or $2,000 (the amount to be allocated to the basis of all distributed property), less $1,500 ($800 and $200 special basis adjustments, plus $500 common partnership basis, the amount allocated to inventory items and unrealized receivables). However, if the value of the inventory items and unrealized receivables distributed to C consisted of only 20 percent of the total fair market value of such property (*i.e.*, only one-half of C's 40–percent share), then only one-half of C's special basis adjustment of $800 for partnership inventory items and $200 for unrealized receivables would be taken into account. In that case, the basis of the inventory items in C's hands would be $650 ($250, the common partnership basis for inventory items distributed to him, plus $400, one-half of C's special basis adjustment for inventory items). The basis of the unrealized receivables in C's hands would be $100 (zero plus $100, one-half of C's special basis adjustment for unrealized receivables).

[T.D. 6500, 25 FR 11814, Nov. 26, 1960, as amended by T.D. 8847, 64 FR 69903, Dec. 15, 1999]

§ 1.733–1 Basis of distributee partner's interest.

In the case of a distribution by a partnership to a partner other than in liquidation of a partner's entire interest, the adjusted basis to such partner of his interest in the partnership shall be reduced (but not below zero) by the amount of any money distributed to such partner and by the amount of the basis to him of distributed property other than money as determined under section 732 and §§ 1.732–1 and 1.732–2.

[T.D. 6500, 25 FR 11814, Nov. 26, 1960]

§ 1.734–1 Optional adjustment to basis of undistributed partnership property.

(a) General rule. A partnership shall not adjust the basis of partnership property as the result of a distribution of property to a partner, unless the election provided in section 754 (relating to optional adjustment to basis of partnership property) is in effect.

(b) Method of adjustment—(1) Increase in basis. Where an election under section 754 is in effect and a distribution of partnership property is made, whether or not in liquidation of the partner's entire interest in the partnership, the adjusted basis of the remaining partnership assets shall be increased by—

(i) The amount of any gain recognized under section 731(a)(1) to the distributee partner, or

(ii) The excess of the adjusted basis to the partnership immediately before the distribution of any property distributed (including adjustments under section 743(b) or section 732(d) when applied) over the basis under section 732 (including such special basis adjustments) of such property to the distributee partner.

* * * The provisions of this subparagraph may be illustrated by the following examples:

Example (1). Partner A has a basis of $10,000 for his one-third interest in partnership ABC. The partnership has no liabilities and has assets consisting of cash of $11,000 and property with a partnership basis of $19,000 and a value of $22,000. A receives $11,000 in cash in liquidation of his entire interest in the partnership. He has a gain of $1,000 under section 731(a)(1). If the election under section 754 is in effect, the partnership basis for the property becomes $20,000 ($19,000 plus $1,000).

Example (2). Partner D has a basis of $10,000 for his one-third interest in partnership DEF. The partnership balance sheet before the distribution shows the following:

Assets

	Adjusted basis	Value
Cash	$ 4,000	$ 4,000
Property X	11,000	11,000
Property Y	15,000	18,000
Total	30,000	33,000

Liabilities and Capital

	Adjusted basis	Value
Liabilities	$ 0	$ 0
Capital:		
D	10,000	11,000
E	10,000	11,000
F	10,000	11,000
Total	30,000	33,000

In liquidation of his entire interest in the partnership, D received property X with a partnership basis of $11,000. D's basis for property X is $10,000 under section 732(b). Where the election under section 754 is in effect, the excess of $1,000 (the partnership basis before the distribution less D's basis for property X after distribution) is added to the basis of property Y. The basis of property Y becomes $16,000 ($15,000 plus $1,000). If the distribution is made to a transferee partner who elects under section 732(d), see § 1.734–2.

(2) Decrease in basis. Where the election provided in section 754 is in effect and a distribution is made in liquidation of a partner's entire interest, the partnership shall decrease the adjusted basis of the remaining partnership property by—

(i) The amount of loss, if any, recognized under section 731(a)(2) to the distributee partner, or

(ii) The excess of the basis of the distributed property to the distributee, as determined under section 732 (including adjustments under section 743(b) or section 732(d) when applied) over the adjusted basis of such property to the partnership (including such special basis adjustments) immediately before such distribution.

The provisions of this subparagraph may be illustrated by the following examples:

Example (1). Partner G has a basis of $11,000 for his one-third interest in partnership GHI. Partnership assets consist of cash of $10,000 and property with a basis of $23,000 and a value of $20,000. There are no partnership liabilities. In liquidation of his entire interest in the partnership, G receives $10,000 in cash. He has a loss of $1,000 under section 731(a)(2). If the election under section 754 is in effect, the partnership basis for the property becomes $22,000 ($23,000 less $1,000).

Example (2). Partner J has a basis of $11,000 for his one-third interest in partnership JKL. The partnership balance sheet before the distribution shows the following:

Assets	Adjusted basis	Value
Cash	$ 5,000	$ 5,000
Property X	10,000	10,000
Property Y	18,000	15,000
Total	33,000	30,000

Liabilities and Capital	Adjusted basis	Value
Liabilities	$ 0	$ 0
Capital:		
J	11,000	10,000
K	11,000	10,000
L	11,000	10,000
Total	33,000	30,000

In liquidation of his entire interest in the partnership, J receives property X with a partnership basis of $10,000. J's basis for property X under section 732(b) is $11,000. Where the election under section 754 is in effect, the excess of $1,000 ($11,000 basis of property X to J, the distributee, less its $10,000 adjusted basis to the partnership immediately before the distribution) decreases the basis of property Y in the partnership. Thus, the basis of property Y becomes $17,000 ($18,000 less $1,000). If the distribution is made to a transferee partner who elects under section 732(d), see § 1.734–2.

(c) Allocation of basis. For allocation among the partnership properties of basis adjustments under section 734(b) and paragraph (b) of this section, see section 755 and § 1.755–1.

(d) Returns. A partnership which must adjust the bases of partnership properties under section 734 shall attach a statement to the partnership return for the year of the distribution setting forth the computation of the adjustment and the partnership properties to which the adjustment has been allocated.

(e) Recovery of adjustments to basis of partnership property—(1) Increases in basis. For purposes of section 168, if the basis of a partnership's recovery property is increased as a result of the distribution of property to a partner, then the increased portion of the basis must be taken into account as if it were newly-purchased recovery property placed in service when the distribution occurs. Consequently, any applicable recovery period and method may be used to determine the recovery allowance with respect to the increased portion of the basis. However, no change is made for purposes of determining the recovery allowance under section 168 for the portion of the basis for which there is no increase.

(2) Decreases in basis. For purposes of section 168, if the basis of a partnership's recovery property is decreased as a result of the distribution of property to a partner, then the decrease in basis must be accounted for over the remaining recovery period of the property beginning with the recovery period in which the basis is decreased.

* * *

[T.D. 6500, 25 FR 11814, Nov. 26, 1960, as amended by T.D. 8847, 64 FR 69903, Dec. 15, 1999; T.D. 9137, 69 FR 42558, July 16, 2004]

§ 1.734–2 Adjustment after distribution to transferee partner.

(a) In the case of a distribution of property by the partnership to a partner who has obtained all or part of his partnership interest by transfer, the adjustments to basis provided in section 743(b) and section 732(d) shall be taken into account in applying the rules under section 734(b). For determining the adjusted basis of distributed property to the partnership immediately before the distribution where there has been a prior transfer of a partnership interest with respect to which the election provided in section 754 or section 732(d) is in effect, see §§ 1.732–1 and 1.732–2.

(b)(1) If a transferee partner, in liquidation of his entire partnership interest, receives a distribution of property (including money) with respect to which he has no special basis adjustment, in exchange for his interest in property with respect to which he has a special basis adjustment, and does not utilize his entire special basis adjustment in determining the basis of the distributed property to him under section 732, the unused special basis adjustment of the distributee shall be applied as an adjustment to the partnership basis of the property retained by the partnership and as to which the distributee did not use his special basis adjustment. The provisions of this subparagraph may be illustrated by the following example:

Example. Upon the death of his father, partner S acquires by inheritance a half-interest in partnership ACS. Partners A and C each have a one-quarter interest. The assets of the partnership consist of $10,000 cash and land used in farming worth $10,000 with a basis of $1,000 to the partnership. Since the partnership had made the election under section 754 at the time of transfer, partner S had a special basis adjustment of $4,500 under section 743(b) with respect to his undivided half-interest in the real estate. The basis of S's partnership interest, in accordance with section 742, is $10,000. S retires from the partnership and receives $10,000 in cash in exchange for his entire interest. Since S has received no part of the real estate, his special basis adjustment of $4,500 will be allocated to the real estate, the remaining partnership property, and will increase its basis to the partnership to $5,500.

(2) The provisions of this paragraph do not apply to the extent that certain distributions are treated as sales or exchanges under section 751(b) (relating to unrealized receivables and substantially appreciated inventory items). See section 751(b) and paragraph (b) of § 1.751–1.

[T.D. 6500, 25 FR 11814, Nov. 26, 1960]

§ 1.735–1 Character of gain or loss on disposition of distributed property.

(a) Sale or exchange of distributed property—(1) Unrealized receivables. Any gain realized or loss sustained by a partner on a sale or exchange or other disposition of unrealized receivables (as defined in paragraph (c)(1) of § 1.751–1) received by him in a distribution from a partnership shall be considered gain or loss from the sale or exchange of property other than a capital asset.

(2) Inventory items. Any gain realized or loss sustained by a partner on a sale or exchange of inventory items (as defined in section 751(d)(2)) received in a distribution from a partnership shall be considered gain or loss from the sale or exchange of property other than a capital asset if such inventory items are sold or exchanged within 5 years from the date of the distribution by the partnership. The character of any gain or loss from a sale or exchange by the distributee partner of such inventory items after 5 years from the date of distribution shall be determined as of the date of such sale or exchange by reference to the character of the assets in his hands at that date (inventory items, capital assets, property used in a trade or business, etc.).

(b) Holding period for distributed property. A partner's holding period for property distributed to him by a partnership shall include the period such property was held by the partnership. The provisions of this paragraph do not apply for the purpose of determining the 5–year period described in section 735(a)(2) and paragraph (a)(2) of this section. If the property has been contributed to the partnership by a partner, then the period that the property was held by such partner shall also be included. See section 1223(2). For a partnership's holding period for contributed property, see § 1.723–1.

* * *

[T.D. 6500, 25 FR 11814, Nov. 26, 1960, as amended by T.D. 6832, 30 FR 8574, July 7, 1965]

§ 1.736–1 Payments to a retiring partner or a deceased partner's successor in interest.

(a) Payments considered as distributive share or guaranteed payment. (1)(i) Section 736 and this section apply only to payments made to a retiring partner or to a deceased partner's successor in interest in liquidation of such partner's entire interest in the partnership. See section 761(d). Section 736 and this section do not apply if the estate or other successor in interest of a deceased partner continues as a partner in its own right under local law. Section 736 and this section apply only to payments made by the partnership and not to transactions between the partners. Thus, a sale by partner A to partner B of his entire one-fourth interest in partnership ABCD would not come within the scope of section 736.

(ii) A partner retires when he ceases to be a partner under local law. However, for the purposes of subchapter K, chapter 1 of the Code, a retired partner or a deceased partner's successor will be treated as a partner until his interest in the partnership has been completely liquidated.

(2) When payments (including assumption of liabilities treated as a distribution of money under section 752) are made to a withdrawing partner, that is, a retiring partner or the estate or other successor in interest of a deceased partner, the amounts paid may represent several items. In part, they may represent the fair market value at the time of his death or retirement of the withdrawing partner's interest in all the assets of the partnership (including inventory) unreduced by partnership liabilities. Also, part of such payments may be attributable to his interest in unrealized receivables and part to an arrangement among the partners in the nature of mutual insurance. When a partnership makes such payments, whether or not related to partnership income, to retire the withdrawing partner's entire interest in the partnership, the payments must be allocated between (i) payments for the value of his interest in assets, except unrealized receivables and, under some circumstances, good will (section 736(b)), and (ii) other payments (section 736(a)). The amounts paid for his interest in assets are treated in the same manner as a distribution in complete liquidation under sections 731, 732, and, where applicable, 751. See paragraph (b)(4)(ii) of § 1.751–1. The remaining partners are allowed no deduction for these payments since they represent either a distribution or a purchase of the withdrawing partner's capital interest by the partnership (composed of the remaining partners).

(3) Under section 736(a), the portion of the payments made to a withdrawing partner for his share of unrealized receivables, good will (in the absence of an agreement to the contrary), or otherwise not in exchange for his interest in assets under the rules contained in paragraph (b) of this section will be considered either—

(i) A distributive share of partnership income, if the amount of payment is determined with regard to income of the partnership; or

(ii) A guaranteed payment under section 707(c), if the amount of the payment is determined without regard to income of the partnership.

(4) Payments, to the extent considered as a distributive share of partnership income under section 736(a)(1), are taken into account under section 702 in the income of the withdrawing partner and thus reduce the amount of the distributive shares of the remaining partners. Payments, to the extent considered as guaranteed payments under section 736(a)(2), are deductible by the partnership under section 162(a) and are taxable as ordinary income to the recipient under section 61(a). See section 707(c).

(5) The amount of any payments under section 736(a) shall be included in the income of the recipient for his taxable year with or within which ends the partnership taxable year for which the payment is a distributive share, or in which the partnership is entitled to deduct such amount as a guaranteed payment. On the other hand, payments under section 736(b) shall be taken into account by the recipient for his taxable year in which such payments are made. See paragraph (b)(4) of this section.

(6) A retiring partner or a deceased partner's successor in interest receiving payments under section 736 is regarded as a partner until the entire interest of the retiring or deceased partner is liquidated. Therefore, if one of the members of a 2–man partnership retires under a plan whereby he is to receive payments under section 736, the partnership will not be considered terminated, nor will the partnership year close with respect to either partner, until the retiring partner's entire interest is liquidated, since the retiring partner continues to hold a partnership interest in the partnership until that time. Similarly, if a partner in a 2–man partnership dies, and his estate or other successor in interest receives payments under section 736, the partnership shall not be considered to have terminated upon the death of the partner but shall terminate as to both partners only when the entire interest of the decedent is liquidated. See section 708(b).

(b) Payments for interest in partnership. **(1)** Payments made in liquidation of the entire interest of a retiring partner or deceased partner shall, to the extent made in exchange for such partner's interest in partnership property (except for unrealized receivables and good will as provided in subparagraphs (2) and (3) of this paragraph), be considered as a distribution by the partnership (and not as a distributive share or guaranteed payment under section 736(a)). Generally, the valuation placed by the partners upon a partner's interest in partnership property in an arm's length agreement will be regarded as correct. If such valuation reflects only the partner's net interest in the property (*i.e.*, total assets less liabilities), it must be adjusted so that both the value of the partner's interest in property and the basis for his interest take into account the partner's share of partnership liabilities. Gain or loss with respect to distributions under section 736(b) and this paragraph will be recognized to the distributee to the extent provided in section 731 and, where applicable, section 751.

(2) Payments made to a retiring partner or to the successor in interest of a deceased partner for his interest in unrealized receivables of the partnership in excess of their partnership basis, including any special basis adjustment for them to which such partner is entitled, shall not be considered as made in exchange for such partner's interest in partnership property. Such payments shall be treated as payments under section 736(a) and paragraph (a) of this section. For definition of unrealized receivables, see section 751(c).

(3) For the purposes of section 736(b) and this paragraph, payments made to a retiring partner or to a successor in interest of a deceased partner in exchange for the interest of such partner in partnership property shall not include any amount paid for the partner's share of good will of the partnership in excess of its partnership basis, including any special basis adjustments for it to which such partner is entitled, except to the extent that the partnership agreement provides for a reasonable payment with respect to such good will. Such payments shall be considered as payments under section 736(a). To the extent that the partnership agreement provides for a reasonable payment with respect to good will, such payments shall be treated under section 736(b) and this paragraph. Generally, the valuation placed upon good will by an arm's length agreement of the partners, whether specific in amount or determined by a formula, shall be regarded as correct.

(4) Payments made to a retiring partner or to a successor in interest of a deceased partner for his interest in inventory shall be considered as made in exchange for such partner's interest in partnership property for the purposes of section 736(b) and this paragraph. However, payments for an interest in substantially appreciated inventory items, as defined in section 751(d), are subject to the rules provided in section 751(b) and paragraph (b) of § 1.751–1. The partnership basis in inventory items as to a deceased partner's successor in interest does not change because of the death of the partner unless the partnership has elected the optional basis adjustment under section 754. But see paragraph (b)(3)(iii) of § 1.751–1.

(5) Where payments made under section 736 are received during the taxable year, the recipient must segregate that portion of each such payment which is determined to be in exchange for the partner's interest in partnership property and treated as a distribution under section 736(b) from that portion treated as a distributive share or guaranteed payment under section 736(a). Such allocation shall be made as follows—

(i) If a fixed amount (whether or not supplemented by any additional amounts) is to be received over a fixed number of years, the portion of each payment to be treated as a distribution under section 736(b) for the taxable year shall bear the same ratio to the total fixed agreed payments for such year (as distinguished from the amount actually received) as the total fixed agreed payments under section 736(b) bear to the total fixed agreed payments under section 736 (a) and (b). The balance, if any, of such amount received in the same taxable year shall be treated as a distributive share or a guaranteed payment under section 736(a)(1) or (2). However, if the total amount received in any one year is less than the amount considered as a distribution under section 736(b) for that year, then any unapplied portion shall be added to the portion of the payments for the following year or years which are to be treated as a distribution under section 736(b). For example, retiring partner W who is entitled to an annual payment of $6,000 for 10 years for his interest in partnership property, receives only $3,500 in 1955. In 1956, he receives $10,000. Of this amount, $8,500 ($6,000 plus $2,500 from 1955) is treated as a distribution under section 736(b) for 1956; $1,500, as a payment under section 736(a).

(ii) If the retiring partner or deceased partner's successor in interest receives payments which are not fixed in amount, such payments shall first be treated as payments in exchange for his interest in partnership property under section 736(b) to the extent of the value of that interest and, thereafter, as payments under section 736(a).

(iii) In lieu of the rules provided in subdivisions (i) and (ii) of this subparagraph, the allocation of each annual payment between section 736(a) and (b) may be made in any manner to which all the remaining partners and the withdrawing partner or his successor in interest agree, provided that the total amount allocated to property under section 736(b) does not exceed the fair market value of such property at the date of death or retirement.

(6) Except to the extent section 751(b) applies, the amount of any gain or loss with respect to payments under section 736(b) for a retiring or deceased partner's interest in property for each year of payment shall be determined under section 731. However, where the total of section 736(b) payments is a fixed sum, a retiring partner or a deceased partner's successor in interest may elect (in his tax return for the first taxable year for which he receives such payments), to report and to measure the amount of any gain or loss by the difference between—

(i) The amount treated as a distribution under section 736(b) in that year, and

(ii) The portion of the adjusted basis of the partner for his partnership interest attributable to such distribution (*i.e.*, the amount which bears the same proportion to the partner's total adjusted basis for his partnership interest as the amount distributed under section 736(b) in that year bears to the total amount to be distributed under section 736(b)).

A recipient who elects under this subparagraph shall attach a statement to his tax return for the first taxable year for which he receives such payments, indicating his election and showing the computation of the gain included in gross income.

(7) The provisions of this paragraph may be illustrated by the following examples:

Example (1). Partnership ABC is a personal service partnership and its balance sheet is as follows:

ASSETS

	Adjusted basis per books	Market value
Cash	$13,000	$13,000
Unrealized receivables	0	30,000
Capital and section 1231 assets	20,000	23,000
Total	33,000	66,000

LIABILITIES AND CAPITAL

	Adjusted basis per books	Market value
Liabilities	$ 3,000	$ 3,000
Capital:		
A	10,000	21,000
B	10,000	21,000
C	10,000	21,000
Total	33,000	66,000

Partner A retires from the partnership in accordance with an agreement whereby his share of liabilities ($1,000) is assumed. In addition he is to receive $9,000 in the year of retirement plus $10,000 in each of the two succeeding years. Thus, the total that A receives for his partnership interest is $30,000 ($29,000 in cash and $1,000 in liabilities assumed). Under the agreement terminating A's interest, the value of A's interest in section 736(b) partnership property is $12,000 (one-third of $36,000, the sum of $13,000 cash and $23,000, the fair market value of capital and section 1231 assets). A's share in unrealized receivables is not included in his interest in partnership property described in section 736(b). Since the basis of A's interest is $11,000 ($10,000 plus $1,000, his share of partnership liabilities), he will realize a capital gain of $1,000 ($12,000 minus $11,000) from the disposition of his interest in partnership property. The remaining $18,000 ($30,000 minus $12,000) will constitute payments under section 736(a)(2) which are taxable to A as guaranteed payments under section 707(c). The payment for the first year is $10,000, consisting of $9,000 in cash, plus $1,000 in liability assumed (section 752(b)). Thus, unless the partners agree otherwise under subparagraph (5)(iii) of this paragraph, each annual payment of $10,000 will be allocated as follows: $6,000 (18,000/30,000 of $10,000) is a section 736(a)(2) payment and $4,000 (12,000/30,000 of $10,000) is a payment for an interest in section 736(b) partnership property. (The partnership may deduct the $6,000 guaranteed payment made to A in each of the 3 years.) The gain on the payments for partnership property will be determined under section 731, as provided in subparagraph (6) of this paragraph. A will treat only $4,000 of each payment as a distribution in a series in liquidation of his entire interest and, under section 731, will have a capital gain of $1,000 when the last payment is made. However, if A so elects, as provided in subparagraph (6) of this paragraph, he may treat such gain as follows: Of each $4,000 payment attributable to A's interest in partnership property, $333 is capital gain (one-third of the total capital gain of $1,000), and $3,667 is a return of capital.

Example (2). Assume the same facts as in example (1) of this subparagraph except that the agreement between the partners provides for payments to A for three years of a percentage of annual income instead of a fixed amount. Unless the partners agree otherwise under subparagraph (5)(iii) of this paragraph, all payments received by A up to $12,000 shall be treated under section 736(b) as payments for A's interest in partnership property. His gain of $1,000 will be taxed only after he has received his full basis under section 731. Since the payments are not fixed in amount, the election provided in subparagraph (6) of this paragraph is not available. Any payments in excess of $12,000 shall be treated as a distributive share of partnership income to A under section 736(a)(1).

Example (3). Assume the same facts as in example (1) of this subparagraph except that the partnership agreement provides that the payment for A's interest in partnership property shall include payment for his interest in the good will of the partnership. At the time of A's retirement, the partners determine the value of partnership good will to be $9,000. The value of A's interest in partnership property described in section 736(b) is thus $15,000 (one-third of $45,000, the sum of $13,000 cash, plus $23,000, the value of capital and section 1231 assets, plus $9,000 good will). From the disposition of his interest in partnership property, A will realize a capital gain of $4,000 ($15,000 minus $11,000) the basis of his interest. The remaining $15,000 ($30,000 minus $15,000) will constitute payments under section 736(a)(2) which are taxable to A as guaranteed payments under section 707(c).

Example (4). Assume the same facts as in example (1) of this subparagraph except that the capital and section 1231 assets consist of an item of section 1245 property (as defined in section 1245(a)(3)). Assume further that under paragraph (c)(4) of § 1.751–1 the section 1245 property is an unrealized receivable to the extent of $2,000. Therefore, the value of A's interest in section 736(b) partnership property is only $11,333 (one-third of $34,000, the sum of $13,000 cash and $21,000, the fair market value of section 1245 property to the extent not an unrealized receivable). From the disposition of his interest in partnership property, A will realize a capital gain of $333 ($11,333 minus $11,000, the basis of his interest). The remaining $18,667 ($30,000 minus $11,333) will constitute payments under section 736(a)(2) which are taxable to A as guaranteed payments under section 707(c).

(c) Cross reference. See section 753 for treatment of payments under section 736(a) as income in respect of a decedent under section 691.

[T.D. 6500, 25 FR 11814, Nov. 26, 1960, as amended by T.D. 6832, 30 FR 8574, July 7, 1965]

§ 1.737–1 Recognition of precontribution gain.

[Note: The five-year period in section 737 has been extended to seven years. Ed.]

(a) Determination of gain—(1) In general. A partner that receives a distribution of property (other than money) must recognize gain under section 737 and this section in an amount equal to the lesser of the excess distribution (as defined in paragraph (b) of this section) or the partner's net precontribution gain (as defined in paragraph (c) of this section). Gain recognized under section 737 and this section is in addition to any gain recognized under section 731.

(2) Transactions to which section 737 applies. Section 737 and this section apply only to the extent that a distribution by a partnership is a distribution to a partner acting in the capacity of a partner within the meaning of section 731, except that section 737 and this section do not apply to the extent that section 751(b) applies to the distribution.

(b) Excess distribution—(1) Definition. The excess distribution is the amount (if any) by which the fair market value of the distributed property (other than money) exceeds the distributee partner's adjusted tax basis in the partner's partnership interest.

(2) Fair market value of property. The fair market value of the distributed property is the price at which the property would change hands between a willing buyer and a willing seller at the time of the distribution, neither being under any compulsion to buy or sell and both having reasonable knowledge of the relevant facts. The fair market value that a partnership assigns to distributed property will be regarded as correct, provided that the value is reasonably agreed to among the partners in an arm's-length negotiation and the partners have sufficiently adverse interests.

(3) Distributee partner's adjusted tax basis—(i) General rule. In determining the amount of the excess distribution, the distributee partner's adjusted tax basis in the partnership interest includes any basis adjustment resulting from the distribution that is subject to section 737 (for example, adjustments required under section 752) and from any other distribution or transaction that is part of the same distribution, except for—

(A) The increase required under section 737(c)(1) for the gain recognized by the partner under section 737; and

(B) The decrease required under section 733(2) for any property distributed to the partner other than property previously contributed to the partnership by the distributee partner. See § 1.704–4(e)(1) for a rule in the context of section 704(c)(1)(B). See also § 1.737–3(b)(2) for a special rule for determining a partner's adjusted tax basis in distributed property previously contributed by the partner to the partnership.

(ii) Advances or drawings. The distributee partner's adjusted tax basis in the partnership interest is determined as of the last day of the partnership's taxable year if the distribution to which section 737 applies is properly characterized as an advance or drawing against the partner's distributive share of income. See § 1.731–1(a)(1)(ii).

(c) Net precontribution gain—(1) General rule. The distributee partner's net precontribution gain is the net gain (if any) that would have been recognized by the distributee partner under section 704(c)(1)(B) and § 1.704–4 if all property that had been contributed to the partnership by the distributee partner within five years of the distribution and is held by the partnership immediately before the distribution had been distributed by the partnership to another partner other than a partner who owns, directly or indirectly, more than 50 percent of the capital or profits interest in the partnership. See § 1.704–4 for provisions determining a contributing partner's gain or loss under section 704(c)(1)(B) on an actual distribution of contributed section 704(c) property to another partner.

(2) Special rules—(i) Property contributed on or before October 3, 1989. Property contributed to the partnership on or before October 3, 1989, is not taken into account in determining a partner's net precontribution gain. See § 1.704–4(c)(1) for a similar rule in the context of section 704(c)(1)(B).

(ii) Section 734(b)(1)(A) adjustments. For distributions to a distributee partner of money by a partnership with a section 754 election in effect that are part of the same distribution as the distribution of property subject to section 737, for purposes of paragraph (a) and (c)(1) of this section the distributee partner's net precontribution gain is reduced by the basis adjustments (if any) made to section 704(c) property contributed by the distributee partner under section 734(b)(1)(A). See § 1.737–3(c)(4) for rules regarding basis adjustments for partnerships with a section 754 election in effect.

(iii) Transfers of a partnership interest. The transferee of all or a portion of a contributing partner's partnership interest succeeds to the transferor's net precontribution gain, if any, in an amount proportionate to the interest transferred. See § 1.704–3(a)(7) and § 1.704–4(d)(2) for similar provisions in the context of section 704(c)(1)(A) and section 704(c)(1)(B).

(iv) Section 704(c)(1)(B) gain recognized in related distribution. A distributee partner's net precontribution gain is determined after taking into account any gain or loss recognized by the partner under section 704(c)(1)(B) and § 1.704–4 (or that would have been recognized by the partner except for the like-kind exception in section 704(c)(2) and § 1.704–4(d)(3)) on an actual distribution to another partner of section 704(c) property contributed by the distributee partner that is part of the same distribution as the distribution to the distributee partner.

(v) Section 704(c)(2) disregarded. A distributee partner's net precontribution gain is determined without regard to the provisions of section 704(c)(2) and § 1.704–4(d)(3) in situations in which the property contributed by the distributee partner is not actually distributed to another partner in a distribution related to the section 737 distribution.

(d) Character of gain. The character of the gain recognized by the distributee partner under section 737 and this section is determined by, and is proportionate to, the character of the partner's net precontribution gain. For this purpose, all gains and losses on section 704(c) property taken into account in determining the partner's net precontribution gain are netted according to their character. Character is determined at the partnership level for this purpose, and any character with a net negative amount is disregarded. The character of the partner's gain under section 737 is the same as, and in proportion to, any character with a net positive amount. Character for this purpose is determined as if the section 704(c) property had been sold by the partnership to an unrelated third party at the time of the distribution and includes any item that would have been taken into account separately by the contributing partner under section 702(a) and § 1.702–1(a).

(e) Examples. The following examples illustrate the provisions of this section. Unless otherwise specified, partnership income equals partnership expenses (other than depreciation deductions for contributed property) for each year of the partnership, the fair market value of partnership property does not change, all distributions by the partnership are subject to section 737, and all partners are unrelated.

Example 1. Calculation of excess distribution and net precontribution gain. **(i)** On January 1, 1995, A, B, and C form partnership ABC as equal partners. A contributes Property A, depreciable real property with a fair market value of $30,000 and an adjusted tax basis of $20,000. B contributes Property B, nondepreciable real property with a fair market value and adjusted tax basis of $30,000. C contributes $30,000 cash.

(ii) Property A has 10 years remaining on its cost recovery schedule and is depreciated using the straight-line method. The partnership uses the traditional method for allocating items under section 704(c) described in § 1.704–3(b)(1) for Property A. The partnership has book depreciation of $3,000 per year (10 percent of the $30,000 book basis in Property A) and each partner is allocated $1,000 of book depreciation per year (one-third of the total annual book depreciation of $3,000). The partnership also has tax depreciation of $2,000 per year (10 percent of the $20,000 adjusted tax basis in Property A). This $2,000 tax depreciation is allocated equally between B and C, the noncontributing partners with respect to Property A.

(iii) At the end of 1997, the book value of Property A is $21,000 ($30,000 initial book value less $9,000 aggregate book depreciation) and its adjusted tax basis is $14,000 ($20,000 initial tax basis less $6,000 aggregate tax depreciation).

(iv) On December 31, 1997, Property B is distributed to A in complete liquidation of A's partnership interest. The adjusted tax basis of A's partnership interest at that time is $20,000. The amount of the excess distribution is $10,000, the difference between the fair market value of the distributed Property B ($30,000) and A's adjusted tax basis in A's partnership interest ($20,000). A's net precontribution gain is $7,000, the difference between the book value of Property A ($21,000) and its adjusted tax basis at the time of the distribution ($14,000). A recognizes gain of $7,000 on the distribution, the lesser of the excess distribution and the net precontribution gain.

Example 2. Determination of distributee partner's basis. **(i)** On January 1, 1995, A, B, and C form general partnership ABC as equal partners. A contributes Property A, nondepreciable real property with a fair market value of $10,000 and an adjusted tax basis of $4,000. B and C each contributes $10,000 cash.

(ii) The partnership purchases Property B, nondepreciable real property with a fair market value of $9,000, subject to a $9,000 nonrecourse liability. This nonrecourse liability is allocated equally among the partners under section 752, increasing A's adjusted tax basis in A's partnership interest from $4,000 to $7,000.

(iii) On December 31, 1998, A receives $2,000 cash and Property B, subject to the $9,000 liability, in a current distribution.

(iv) In determining the amount of the excess distribution, the adjusted tax basis of A's partnership interest is adjusted to take into account the distribution of money and the shift in liabilities. A's adjusted tax basis is therefore increased to $11,000 for this purpose ($7,000 initial adjusted tax basis, less $2,000 distribution of money, less $3,000 (decrease in A's share of the $9,000 partnership liability), plus $9,000 (increase in A's individual liabilities)). As a result of this basis adjustment, the adjusted tax basis of A's partnership interest ($11,000) is greater than the fair market value of the distributed property ($9,000) and therefore, there is no excess distribution. A recognizes no gain under section 737.

Example 3. Net precontribution gain reduced for gain recognized under section 704(c)(1)(B). **(i)** On January 1, 1995, A, B, and C form partnership ABC as equal partners. A contributes Properties A1 and A2, nondepreciable real properties located in the United States each with a fair market value of $10,000 and an adjusted tax basis of $6,000. B contributes Property B, nondepreciable real property located outside the United States, with a fair market value and adjusted tax basis of $20,000. C contributes $20,000 cash.

(ii) On December 31, 1998, Property B is distributed to A in complete liquidation of A's interest and, as part of the same distribution, Property A1 is distributed to B in a current distribution.

(iii) A's net precontribution gain before the distribution is $8,000 ($20,000 fair market value of Properties A1 and A2 less $12,000 adjusted tax basis of such properties). A recognizes $4,000 of gain under section 704(c)(1)(B) and § 1.704–4 on the distribution of Property A1 to B ($10,000 fair market value of Property A1 less $6,000 adjusted tax basis of Property A1). This gain is taken into account in determining A's excess distribution and net precontribution gain. As a result, A's net precontribution gain is reduced from $8,000 to $4,000, and the adjusted tax basis in A's partnership interest is increased by $4,000 to $16,000.

(iv) A recognizes gain of $4,000 on the receipt of Property B under section 737, an amount equal to the lesser of the excess distribution of $4,000 ($20,000 fair market value of Property B less $16,000 adjusted tax basis of A's interest in the partnership) and A's remaining net precontribution gain of $4,000.

Example 4. Character of gain. **(i)** On January 1, 1995, A, B, and C form partnership ABC as equal partners. A contributes the following nondepreciable property to the partnership:

	Fair market value	Adjusted tax basis
Property A1	$30,000	$20,000
Property A2	30,000	38,000
Property A3	10,000	9,000

(ii) The character of gain or loss on Property A1 and Property A2 is long-term, U.S.-source capital gain or loss. The character of gain on Property A3 is long-term, foreign-source capital gain. B contributes Property B, nondepreciable real property with a fair market value and adjusted tax basis of $70,000. C contributes $70,000 cash.

(iii) On December 31, 1998, Property B is distributed to A in complete liquidation of A's interest in the partnership. A recognizes $3,000 of gain under section 737, an amount equal to the excess distribution of $3,000 ($70,000 fair market value of Property B less $67,000 adjusted tax basis in A's partnership interest) and A's net precontribution gain of $3,000 ($70,000 aggregate fair market value of properties contributed by A less $67,000 aggregate adjusted tax basis of such properties).

(iv) In determining the character of A's gain, all gains and losses on property taken into account in determining A's net precontribution gain are netted according to their character and allocated to A's recognized gain under section 737 based on the relative proportions of the net positive amounts. U.S.-source and foreign-source gains must be netted separately because A would have been required to take such gains into account separately under section 702. As a result, A's net precontribution gain of $3,000 consists of $2,000 of net long-term, U.S.-source capital gain ($10,000 gain on Property A1 and $8,000 loss on Property A2) and $1,000 of net long-term, foreign-source capital gain ($1,000 gain on Property A3).

(v) The character of A's gain under paragraph (d) of this section is therefore $2,000 long-term, U.S.-source capital gain ($3,000 gain recognized under section 737 x $2,000 net long-term, U.S.-source capital gain/$3,000 total net precontribution gain) and $1,000 long-term, foreign-source capital gain ($3,000 gain recognized under section 737 x $1,000 net long-term, foreign-source capital gain/ $3,000 total net precontribution gain).

[T.D. 8642, 60 FR 66727, Dec. 26, 1995]

§ 1.737–2 Exceptions and special rules.

[Note: The five-year period in section 737 has been extended to seven years. Ed.]

(a) Section 708(b)(1)(B) terminations. Section 737 and this section do not apply to the deemed distribution of interests in a new partnership caused by the termination of a partnership under section 708(b)(1)(B). A subsequent distribution of property by the new partnership to a partner of the new partnership that was formerly a partner of the terminated partnership is subject to section 737 to the same extent that a distribution from the terminated partnership would have been subject to section 737. See also § 1.704–4(c)(3) for a similar rule in the context of section 704(c)(1)(B). This paragraph (a) applies to terminations of partnerships under section 708(b)(1)(B) occurring on or after May 9, 1997; however, this paragraph (a) may be applied to terminations occurring on or after May 9, 1996, provided that the partnership and its partners apply this paragraph (a) to the termination in a consistent manner.

(b) Transfers to another partnership—(1) Complete transfer. Section 737 and this section do not apply to a transfer by a partnership (transferor partnership) of all of its assets and liabilities to a second partnership (transferee partnership) in an exchange described in section 721, followed by a distribution of the interest in the transferee partnership in liquidation of the transferor partnership as part of the same plan or arrangement. See § 1.704–4(c)(4) for a similar rule in the context of section 704(c)(1)(B).

(2) Certain divisive transactions. Section 737 and this section do not apply to a transfer by a partnership (transferor partnership) of all of the section 704(c) property contributed by a partner to a second partnership (transferee partnership) in an exchange described in section 721, followed by a distribution as part of the same plan or arrangement of an interest in the transferee partnership (and no other property) in complete liquidation of the interest of the partner that originally contributed the section 704(c) property to the transferor partnership.

(3) Subsequent distributions. A subsequent distribution of property by the transferee partnership to a partner of the transferee partnership that was formerly a partner of the transferor partnership is subject to section 737 to the same extent that a distribution from the transferor partnership would have been subject to section 737.

(c) Incorporation of a partnership. Section 737 and this section do not apply to an incorporation of a partnership by any method of incorporation (other than a method involving an actual distribution of partnership property to the partners followed by a contribution of that property to a corporation), provided that the partnership is liquidated as part of the incorporation transaction. See § 1.704–4(c)(5) for a similar rule in the context of section 704(c)(1)(B).

(d) Distribution of previously contributed property—(1) General rule. Any portion of the distributed property that consists of property previously contributed by the distributee partner (previously contributed property) is not taken into account in determining the amount of the excess distribution or the partner's net precontribution gain. The previous sentence applies on or after May 9, 1997.

(2) Limitation for distribution of previously contributed interest in an entity. An interest in an entity previously contributed to the partnership is not treated as previously contributed property to the extent that the value of the interest is attributable to property contributed to the entity after the interest was contributed to the partnership. The preceding sentence does not apply to the extent that the property contributed to the entity was contributed to the partnership by the partner that also contributed the interest in the entity to the partnership.

(3) Nonrecognition transactions, installment sales, contributed contracts and capitalized costs—(i) Nonrecognition transactions. Property received by the partnership in exchange for contributed section 704(c) property in a nonrecognition transaction is treated as the contributed property with regard to the contributing partner for purposes of section 737 to the extent that the property received is treated as section 704(c) property under § 1.704–3(a)(8). See § 1.704–4(d)(1) for a similar rule in the context of section 704(c)(1)(B).

* * *

(4) Undivided interests. The distribution of an undivided interest in property is treated as the distribution of previously contributed property to the extent that the undivided interest does not exceed the undivided interest, if any, contributed by the distributee partner in the same property. See § 1.704–4(c)(6) for the application of section 704(c)(1)(B) in a similar context. The portion of the undivided interest in property retained by the partnership after the distribution, if any, that is treated as contributed by the distributee partner, is reduced to the extent of the undivided interest distributed to the distributee partner.

(e) Examples. The following examples illustrate the rules of this section. Unless otherwise specified, partnership income equals partnership expenses (other than depreciation deductions for contributed property) for each year of the partnership, the fair market value of partnership property does not change, all distributions by the partnership are subject to section 737, and all partners are unrelated.

Example 1. Distribution of previously contributed property. (i) On January 1, 1995, A, B, and C form partnership ABC as equal partners. A contributes the following nondepreciable real property to the partnership:

	Fair market value	Adjusted tax basis
Property A1	$20,000	$10,000
Property A2	10,000	6,000

(ii) A's total net precontribution gain on the contributed property is $14,000 ($10,000 on Property A1 plus $4,000 on Property A2). B contributes $10,000 cash and Property B, nondepreciable real property with a fair market value and adjusted tax basis of $20,000. C contributes $30,000 cash.

(iii) On December 31, 1998, Property A2 and Property B are distributed to A in complete liquidation of A's interest in the partnership. Property A2 was previously contributed by A and is therefore not taken into account in determining the amount of the excess distribution or A's net precontribution gain. The adjusted tax basis of Property A2 in the hands of A is also determined under section 732 as if that property were the only property distributed to A.

(iv) As a result of excluding Property A2 from these determinations, the amount of the excess distribution is $10,000 ($20,000 fair market value of distributed Property B less $10,000 adjusted tax basis in A's partnership interest). A's net precontribution gain is also $10,000 ($14,000 total net precontribution gain less $4,000 gain with respect to previously contributed Property A2). A therefore recognizes $10,000 of gain on the distribution, the lesser of the excess distribution and the net precontribution gain.

Example 2. Distribution of a previously contributed interest in an entity. **(i)** On January 1, 1995, A, B, and C form partnership ABC as equal partners. A contributes Property A, nondepreciable real property with a fair market value of $10,000 and an adjusted tax basis of $5,000, and all of the stock of Corporation X with a fair market value and adjusted tax basis of $500. B contributes $500 cash and Property B, nondepreciable real property with a fair market value and adjusted tax basis of $10,000. Partner C contributes $10,500 cash. On December 31, 1996, ABC contributes Property B to Corporation X in a nonrecognition transaction under section 351.

(ii) On December 31, 1998, all of the stock of Corporation X is distributed to A in complete liquidation of A's interest in the partnership. The stock is treated as previously contributed property with respect to A only to the extent of the $500 fair market value of the Corporation X stock contributed by A. The fair market value of the distributed stock for purposes of determining the amount of the excess distribution is therefore $10,000 ($10,500 total fair market value of Corporation X stock less $500 portion treated as previously contributed property). The $500 fair market value and adjusted tax basis of the Corporation X stock is also not taken into account in determining the amount of the excess distribution and the net precontribution gain.

(iii) A recognizes $5,000 of gain under section 737, the amount of the excess distribution ($10,000 fair market value of distributed property less $5,000 adjusted tax basis in A's partnership interest) and A's net precontribution gain ($10,000 fair market value of Property A less $5,000 adjusted tax basis in Property A).

Example 3. Distribution of undivided interest in property. **(i)** On January 1, 1995, A and B form partnership AB as equal partners. A contributes $500 cash and an undivided one-half interest in Property X. B contributes $500 cash and an undivided one-half interest in Property X.

(ii) On December 31, 1998, an undivided one-half interest in Property X is distributed to A in a current distribution. The distribution of the undivided one-half interest in Property X is treated as a distribution of previously contributed property because A contributed an undivided one-half interest in Property X. As a result, A does not recognize any gain under section 737 on the distribution.

[T.D. 8642, 60 FR 66727, Dec. 26, 1995; T.D. 8717, 62 FR 25498, May 9, 1997; T.D. 9193, 70 FR 14394, Mar. 22, 2005; T.D. 9207, 70 FR 30334, May 26, 2005; T.D. 9193, 70 FR 45531, Aug. 8, 2005]

§ 1.737–3 Basis adjustments; recovery rules.

[Note: The five-year period in section 737 has been extended to seven years. Ed.]

(a) Distributee partner's adjusted tax basis in the partnership interest. The distributee partner's adjusted tax basis in the partnership interest is increased by the amount of gain recognized by the distributee partner under section 737 and this section. This increase is not taken into account in determining the amount of gain recognized by the partner under section 737(a)(1) and this section or in determining the amount of gain recognized by the partner under section 731(a) on the distribution of money in the same distribution or any related distribution. See § 1.704–4(e)(1) for a determination of the distributee partner's adjusted tax basis in a distribution subject to section 704(c)(1)(B).

(b) Distributee partner's adjusted tax basis in distributed property—(1) In general. The distributee partner's adjusted tax basis in the distributed property is determined under section 732(a) or (b) as applicable. The increase in the distributee partner's adjusted tax basis in the partnership interest under paragraph (a) of this section is taken into account in determining the distributee partner's adjusted tax basis in the distributed property other than property previously contributed by the partner. See § 1.704–4(e)(2) for a determination of basis in a distribution subject to section 704(c)(1)(B).

(2) Previously contributed property. The distributee partner's adjusted tax basis in distributed property that the partner previously contributed to the partnership is determined as if it were distributed in a separate and independent distribution prior to the distribution that is subject to section 737 and § 1.737–1.

(c) Partnership's adjusted tax basis in partnership property—(1) Increase in basis. The partnership's adjusted tax basis in eligible property is increased by the amount of gain recognized by the distributee partner under section 737.

(2) Eligible property. Eligible property is property that—

(i) Entered into the calculation of the distributee partner's net precontribution gain;

(ii) Has an adjusted tax basis to the partnership less than the property's fair market value at the time of the distribution;

(iii) Would have the same character of gain on a sale by the partnership to an unrelated party as the character of any of the gain recognized by the distributee partner under section 737; and

(iv) Was not distributed to another partner in a distribution subject to section 704(c)(1)(B) and § 1.704–4 that was part of the same distribution as the distribution subject to section 737.

(3) Method of adjustment. For the purpose of allocating the basis increase under paragraph (c)(2) of this section among the eligible property, all eligible property of the same character is treated as a single group. Character for this purpose is determined in the same manner as the character of the recognized gain is determined under § 1.737–1(d). The basis increase is allocated among the separate groups of eligible property in proportion to the character of the gain recognized under section 737. The basis increase is then allocated among property within each group in the order in which the property was contributed to the partnership by the partner, starting with the property contributed first, in an amount equal to the difference between the property's fair market value and its adjusted tax basis to the partnership at the time of the distribution. For property that has the same character and was contributed in the same (or a related) transaction, the basis increase is allocated based on the respective amounts of unrealized appreciation in such properties at the time of the distribution.

(4) Section 754 adjustments. The basis adjustments to partnership property made pursuant to paragraph (c)(1) of this section are not elective and must be made regardless of whether the partnership has an election in effect under section 754. Any adjustments to the bases of partnership property (including eligible property as defined in paragraph (c)(2) of this section) under section 734(b) pursuant to a section 754 election (other than basis adjustments under section 734(b)(1)(A) described in the following sentence) must be made after (and must take into account) the adjustments to basis made under paragraph (a) and paragraph (c)(1) of this section. Basis adjustments under section 734(b)(1)(A) that are attributable to distributions of money to the distributee partner that are part of the same distribution as the distribution of property subject to section 737 are made before the adjustments to basis under paragraph (a) and paragraph (c)(1) of this section. See § 1.737–1(c)(2)(ii) for the effect, if any, of basis adjustments under section 734(b)(1)(A) on a partner's net precontribution gain. See also § 1.704–4(e)(3) for a similar rule regarding basis adjustments pursuant to a section 754 election in the context of section 704(c)(1)(B).

(d) Recovery of increase to adjusted tax basis. Any increase to the adjusted tax basis of partnership property under paragraph (c)(1) of this section is recovered using any applicable recovery period and depreciation (or other cost recovery) method (including first-year conventions) available to the partnership for newly purchased property (of the type adjusted) placed in service at the time of the distribution.

(e) Examples. The following examples illustrate the rules of this section. Unless otherwise specified, partnership income equals partnership expenses (other than depreciation deductions for contributed property) for each year of the partnership, the fair market value of partnership property does not change, all distributions by the partnership are subject to section 737, and all partners are unrelated.

Example 1. Partner's basis in distributed property. **(i)** On January 1, 1995, A, B, and C form partnership ABC as equal partners. A contributes Property A, nondepreciable real property with a fair market value of $10,000 and an adjusted tax basis of $5,000. B contributes Property B, nondepreciable real property with a fair market value and adjusted tax basis of $10,000. C contributes $10,000 cash.

(ii) On December 31, 1998, Property B is distributed to A in complete liquidation of A's interest in the partnership. A recognizes $5,000 of gain under section 737, an amount equal to the excess distribution of $5,000 ($10,000 fair market value of Property B less $5,000 adjusted tax basis in A's partnership interest) and A's net precontribution gain of $5,000 ($10,000 fair market value of Property A less $5,000 adjusted tax basis of such property).

(iii) A's adjusted tax basis in A's partnership interest is increased by the $5,000 of gain recognized under section 737. This increase is taken into account in determining A's basis in the distributed property. Therefore, A's adjusted tax basis in distributed Property B is $10,000 under section 732(b).

Example 2. Partner's basis in distributed property in connection with gain recognized under section 704(c)(1)(B). **(i)** On January 1, 1995, A, B, and C form partnership ABC as equal partners. A contributes the following nondepreciable real property located in the United States to the partnership:

	Fair market value	Adjusted tax basis
Property A1	$10,000	5,000
Property A2	10,000	2,000

(ii) B contributes $10,000 cash and Property B, nondepreciable real property located outside the United States, with a fair market value and adjusted tax basis of $10,000. C contributes $20,000 cash.

(iii) On December 31, 1998, Property B is distributed to A in a current distribution and Property A1 is distributed to B in a current distribution. A recognizes $5,000 of gain under section 704(c)(1)(B) and § 1.704-4 on the distribution of Property A1 to B, the difference between the fair market value of such property ($10,000) and the adjusted tax basis in distributed Property A1 ($5,000). The adjusted tax basis of A's partnership interest is increased by this $5,000 of gain under section 704(c)(1)(B) and § 1.704-4(e)(1).

(iv) The increase in the adjusted tax basis of A's partnership interest is taken into account in determining the amount of the excess distribution. As a result, there is no excess distribution because the fair market value of Property B ($10,000) is less than the adjusted tax basis of A's interest in the partnership at the time of distribution ($12,000). A therefore recognizes no gain under section 737 on the receipt of Property B. A's adjusted tax basis in Property B is $10,000 under section 732(a)(1). The adjusted tax basis of A's partnership interest is reduced from $12,000 to $2,000 under section 733. See Example 3 of § 1.737-1(e).

Example 3. Partnership's basis in partnership property after a distribution with section 737 gain. **(i)** On January 31, 1995, A, B, and C form partnership ABC as equal partners. A contributes the following nondepreciable property to the partnership:

	Fair market value	Adjusted tax basis
Property A1	$1,000	$ 500
Property A2	4,000	1,500
Property A3	4,000	6,000
Property A4	6,000	4,000

(ii) The character of gain or loss on Properties A1, A2, and A3 is long-term, U.S.-source capital gain or loss. The character of gain on Property A4 is long-term, foreign-source capital gain. B contributes Property B, nondepreciable real property with a fair market value and adjusted tax basis of $15,000. C contributes $15,000 cash.

(iii) On December 31, 1998, Property B is distributed to A in complete liquidation of A's interest in the partnership. A recognizes gain of $3,000 under section 737, an amount equal to the excess distribution of $3,000 ($15,000 fair market value of Property B less $12,000 adjusted tax basis in A's partnership interest) and A's net precontribution gain of $3,000 ($15,000 aggregate fair market value of the property contributed by A less $12,000 aggregate adjusted tax basis of such property).

(iv) $2,000 of A's gain is long-term, foreign-source capital gain ($3,000 total gain under section 737 x $2,000 net long-term, foreign-source capital gain/$3,000 total net precontribution gain). $1,000 of A's gain is long-term, U.S.-source capital gain ($3,000 total gain under section 737 x $1,000 net long-term, U.S.-source capital gain/$3,000 total net precontribution gain).

(v) The partnership must increase the adjusted tax basis of the property contributed by A by $3,000. All property contributed by A is eligible property. Properties A1, A2, and A3 have the same character and are grouped into a single group for purposes of allocating this basis increase. Property A4 is in a separate character group.

(vi) $2,000 of the basis increase must be allocated to long-term, foreign-source capital assets because $2,000 of the gain recognized by A was long-term, foreign-source capital gain. The adjusted tax basis of Property A4 is therefore increased from $4,000 to $6,000. $1,000 of the increase must be allocated to Properties A1 and A2 because $1,000 of the gain recognized by A is long-term, U.S.-source capital gain. No basis increase is allocated to Property A3 because its fair market value is less than its adjusted tax basis. The $1,000 basis increase is allocated between Properties A1 and A2 based on the unrealized appreciation in each asset before such basis adjustment. As a result, the adjusted tax basis of Property A1 is increased by $167 ($1,000 x $500/$3,000) and the adjusted tax basis of Property A2 is increased by $833 ($1,000 x $2,500/3,000).

[T.D. 8642, 60 FR 66727, Dec. 26, 1995; 61 FR 7214, Feb. 27, 1996]

§ 1.737-4 Anti-abuse rule.

[Note: The five-year period in section 737 has been extended to seven years. Ed.]

(a) In general. The rules of section 737 and §§ 1.737-1, 1.737-2, and 1.737-3 must be applied in a manner consistent with the purpose of section 737. Accordingly, if a principal purpose of a transaction is to achieve a tax result that is inconsistent with the purpose of section 737, the Commissioner can recast the transaction for federal tax purposes as appropriate to achieve tax results that are consistent with the purpose of section 737. Whether a tax result is inconsistent with the purpose of section 737 must be determined based on all the facts and circumstances. See § 1.704-4(f) for an anti-abuse rule and examples in the context of section 704(c)(1)(B). The anti-abuse rule and examples under section 704(c)(1)(B) and § 1.704-4(f) are relevant to section 737 and §§ 1.737-1, 1.737-2, and 1.737-3 to the extent that the net precontribution gain for purposes of section 737 is determined by reference to section 704(c)(1)(B).

(b) Examples. The following examples illustrate the rules of this section. The examples set forth below do not delineate the boundaries of either permissible or impermissible types of transactions. Further, the addition of any facts or circumstances that are not specifically set forth in an example (or the deletion of any facts or circumstances) may alter the outcome of the transaction described in the example. Unless otherwise specified, partnership income equals partnership expenses (other than depreciation deductions for contributed property) for each year of the partnership, the fair market value of partnership property does not change, all distributions by the partnership are subject to section 737, and all partners are unrelated.

Example 1. Increase in distributee partner's basis by temporary contribution; results inconsistent with the purpose of section 737. **(i)** On January 1, 1995, A, B, and C form partnership ABC as equal partners. A contributes Property A1, nondepreciable real property with a fair market value of $10,000 and an adjusted tax basis of $1,000. B contributes Property B, nondepreciable real property with a fair market value of $10,000 and an adjusted tax basis of $10,000. C contributes $10,000 cash.

(ii) On January 1, 1999, pursuant to a plan a principal purpose of which is to avoid gain under section 737, A transfers to the partnership Property A2, nondepreciable real property with a fair market value and adjusted tax basis of $9,000. A treats the transfer as a contribution to the partnership pursuant to section 721 and increases the adjusted tax basis of A's partnership interest from $1,000 to $10,000. On January 1, 1999, the partnership agreement is amended and all other necessary steps are taken so that substantially all of the economic risks and benefits of Property A2 are retained by A. On February 1, 1999, Property B is distributed to A in a current distribution. If the contribution of Property A2 is treated as a contribution to the partnership for purposes of section 737, there is no excess distribution because the fair market value of distributed Property B ($10,000) does not exceed the adjusted tax basis of A's interest in the partnership ($10,000), and therefore section 737 does not apply. A's adjusted tax basis in distributed Property B is $10,000 under section 732(a)(1) and the adjusted tax basis of A's partnership interest is reduced to zero under section 733.

(iii) On March 1, 2000, A receives Property A2 from the partnership in complete liquidation of A's interest in the partnership. A recognizes no gain on the distribution of Property A2 because the property was previously contributed property. See § 1.737-2(d).

(iv) Although A has treated the transfer of Property A2 as a contribution to the partnership that increased the adjusted tax basis of A's interest in the partnership, it would be inconsistent with the purpose of section 737 to recognize the transfer as a contribution to the partnership. Section 737 requires recognition of gain when the value of distributed property exceeds the distributee partner's adjusted tax basis in the partnership interest. Section 737 assumes that any contribution or other transaction that affects a partner's adjusted tax basis in the partnership interest is a contribution or transaction in substance and is not engaged in with a principal purpose of avoiding recognition of gain under section 737. Because the transfer of Property A2 to the partnership was not a contribution in substance and was made with a principal purpose of avoiding recognition of gain under section 737, the Commissioner can disregard the contribution of Property A2 for this purpose. As a result, A recognizes gain of $9,000 under section 737 on the receipt of Property B, an amount equal to the lesser of the excess distribution of $9,000 ($10,000 fair market value of distributed Property B less the $1,000 adjusted tax basis of A's partnership interest, determined without regard to the transitory contribution of Property A2) or A's net precontribution gain of $9,000 on Property A1.

Example 2. Increase in distributee partner's basis; section 752 liability shift; results consistent with the purpose of section 737. **(i)** On January 1, 1995, A and B form general partnership AB as equal partners. A contributes Property A, nondepreciable real property with a fair market value of $10,000 and an adjusted tax basis of $1,000. B contributes Property B, nondepreciable real property with a fair market value and adjusted tax basis of $10,000. The partnership also borrows $10,000 on a recourse basis and purchases Property C. The $10,000 liability is allocated equally between A and B under section 752, thereby increasing the adjusted tax basis in A's partnership interest to $6,000.

(ii) On December 31, 1998, the partners agree that A is to receive Property B in a current distribution. If A were to receive Property B at that time, A would recognize $4,000 of gain under section 737, an amount equal to the lesser of the excess distribution of $4,000 ($10,000 fair market value of Property B less $6,000 adjusted tax basis in A's partnership interest) or A's net precontribution gain of $9,000 ($10,000 fair market value of Property A less $1,000 adjusted tax basis of Property A).

(iii) With a principal purpose of avoiding such gain, A and B agree that A will be solely liable for the repayment of the $10,000 partnership liability and take the steps necessary so that the entire amount of the liability is allocated to A under section 752. The adjusted tax basis in A's partnership interest is thereby increased from $6,000 to $11,000 to reflect A's share of the $5,000 of liability previously allocated to B. As a result of this increase in A's adjusted tax basis, there is no excess distribution because the fair market value of distributed Property B ($10,000) is less than the adjusted tax basis of A's partnership interest. Recognizing A's increased adjusted tax basis as a result of the shift in liabilities is consistent with the purpose of section 737 and this section. Section 737 requires recognition of gain only when the value of the distributed property exceeds the distributee partner's adjusted tax basis in the partnership interest. The $10,000 recourse liability is a bona fide liability of the partnership that was undertaken for a substantial business purpose and A's and B's agreement that A will assume responsibility for repayment of that debt has substance. Therefore, the increase in A's adjusted tax basis in A's interest in the partnership due to the shift in partnership liabilities under section 752 is respected, and A recognizes no gain under section 737.

[T.D. 8642, 60 FR 66727, Dec. 26, 1995]

§ 1.741–1 Recognition and character of gain or loss on sale or exchange.

(a) The sale or exchange of an interest in a partnership shall, except to the extent section 751(a) applies, be treated as the sale or exchange of a capital asset, resulting in capital gain or loss measured by the difference between the amount realized and the adjusted basis of the partnership interest, as determined under section 705. For treatment of selling partner's distributive share up to date of sale, see section 706(c)(2). Where the provisions of section 751 require the recognition of ordinary income or loss with respect to a portion of the amount realized from such sale or exchange, the amount realized shall be reduced by the amount attributable under section 751 to unrealized receivables and substantially appreciated inventory items, and the adjusted basis of the transferor partner's interest in the partnership shall be reduced by the portion of such basis attributable to such unrealized receivables and substantially appreciated inventory items. See section 751 and § 1.751–1.

(b) Section 741 shall apply whether the partnership interest is sold to one or more members of the partnership or to one or more persons who are not members of the partnership. Section 741 shall also apply even though the sale of the partnership interest results in a termination of the partnership under section 708(b). Thus, the provisions of section 741 shall be applicable (1) to the transferor partner in a 2–man partnership when he sells his interest to the other partner, and (2) to all the members of a partnership when they sell their interests to one or more persons outside the partnership.

(c) See section 351 for nonrecognition of gain or loss upon transfer of a partnership interest to a corporation controlled by the transferor.

(d) For rules relating to the treatment of liabilities on the sale or exchange of interests in a partnership see §§ 1.752–1 and 1.1001–2.

(e) For rules relating to the capital gain or loss recognized when a partner sells or exchanges an interest in a partnership that holds appreciated collectibles or section 1250 property with section 1250 capital gain. see § 1.1(h)–1. * * *

(f) For rules relating to dividing the holding period of an interest in a partnership, see § 1.1223–3. * * *

[T.D. 6500, 25 FR 11814, Nov. 26, 1960; 25 FR 14021, Dec. 31, 1960, as amended by T.D. 7741, 45 FR 81745, Dec. 12, 1980; T.D. 8902, 65 FR 57092, Sept. 21, 2000]

§ 1.742–1 Basis of transferee partner's interest.

The basis to a transferee partner of an interest in a partnership shall be determined under the general basis rules for property provided by part II (section 1011 and following), subchapter O, chapter 1 of the Code. Thus, the basis of a purchased interest will be its cost. The basis of a partnership interest acquired from a decedent is the fair market value of the interest at the date of his death or at the alternate valuation date, increased by his estate's or other successor's share of partnership liabilities, if any, on that date, and reduced to the extent that such value is attributable to items constituting income in respect of a decedent (see section 753 and paragraph (c)(3)(v) of § 1.706–1 and paragraph (b) of § 1.753–1) under section 691. See section 1014(c). For basis of contributing partner's interest, see section 722. The basis so determined is then subject to the adjustments provided in section 705.

[T.D. 6500, 25 FR 11814, Nov. 26, 1960]

§ 1.743–1 Optional adjustment to basis of partnership property.

(a) Generally. The basis of partnership property is adjusted as a result of the transfer of an interest in a partnership by sale or exchange or on the death of a partner only if the election provided by section 754 (relating to optional adjustments to the basis of partnership property) is in effect with respect to the partnership. Whether or not the election provided in section 754 is in effect, the basis of partnership property is not adjusted as the result of a contribution of property, including money, to the partnership.

(b) Determination of adjustment. In the case of the transfer of an interest in a partnership, either by sale or exchange or as a result of the death of a partner, a partnership that has an election under section 754 in effect—

(1) Increases the adjusted basis of partnership property by the excess of the transferee's basis for the transferred partnership interest over the transferee's share of the adjusted basis to the partnership of the partnership's property; or

(2) Decreases the adjusted basis of partnership property by the excess of the transferee's share of the adjusted basis to the partnership of the partnership's property over the transferee's basis for the transferred partnership interest.

(c) Determination of transferee's basis in the transferred partnership interest. In the case of the transfer of a partnership interest by sale or exchange or as a result of the death of a partner, the transferee's basis in the transferred partnership interest is determined under section 742 and § 1.742–1. See also section 752 and §§ 1.752–1 through 1.752–5.

(d) Determination of transferee's share of the adjusted basis to the partnership of the partnership's property—

(1) Generally. A transferee's share of the adjusted basis to the partnership of partnership property is equal to the sum of the transferee's interest as a partner in the partnership's previously taxed capital, plus the transferee's share of partnership liabilities. Generally, a transferee's interest as a partner in the partnership's previously taxed capital is equal to—

(i) The amount of cash that the transferee would receive on a liquidation of the partnership following the hypothetical transaction, as defined in paragraph (d)(2) of this section (to the extent attributable to the acquired partnership interest); increased by

(ii) The amount of tax loss (including any remedial allocations under § 1.704–3(d)), that would be allocated to the transferee from the hypothetical transaction (to the extent attributable to the acquired partnership interest); and decreased by

(iii) The amount of tax gain (including any remedial allocations under § 1.704–3(d)), that would be allocated to the transferee from the hypothetical transaction (to the extent attributable to the acquired partnership interest).

(2) Hypothetical transaction defined. For purposes of paragraph (d)(1) of this section, the hypothetical transaction means the disposition by the partnership of all of the partnership's assets, immediately after the transfer of the partnership interest, in a fully taxable transaction for cash equal to the fair market value of the assets. * * *

(3) Examples. The provisions of this paragraph (d) are illustrated by the following examples:

Example 1. (i) A is a member of partnership PRS in which the partners have equal interests in capital and profits. The partnership has made an election under section 754, relating to the optional adjustment to the basis of partnership property. A sells its interest to T for $22,000. The balance sheet of the partnership at the date of sale shows the following:

Assets

	Adjusted Basis	Fair Market Value
Cash	$ 5,000	$ 5,000
Accounts receivable	10,000	10,000
Inventory	20,000	21,000
Depreciable assets	20,000	40,000
Total	$55,000	$76,000

Liabilities and Capital

	Adjusted Per Books	Fair Market Value
Liabilities	$10,000	$10,000
Capital:		
A	15,000	22,000
B	15,000	22,000
C	15,000	22,000
Total	$55,000	$76,000

(ii) The amount of the basis adjustment under section 743(b) is the difference between the basis of T's interest in the partnership and T's share of the adjusted basis to the partnership of the partnership's property. Under section 742, the basis of T's interest is $25,333 (the cash paid for A's interest, $22,000, plus $3,333, T's share of partnership liabilities). T's interest in the partnership's previously taxed capital is $15,000 ($22,000, the amount of cash T would receive if PRS liquidated immediately after the hypothetical transaction, decreased by $7,000, the amount of tax gain allocated to T from the hypothetical transaction). T's share of the adjusted basis to the partnership of the partnership's property is $18,333 ($15,000 share of previously taxed capital, plus $3,333 share of the partnership's liabilities). The amount of the basis adjustment under section 743(b) to partnership property therefore, is $7,000, the difference between $25,333 and $18,333.

Example 2. A, B, and C form partnership PRS, to which A contributes land (Asset 1) with a fair market value of $1,000 and an adjusted basis to A of $400, and B and C each contribute $1,000 cash. Each partner has $1,000 credited to it on the books of the partnership as its capital contribution. The partners share in profits equally. During the partnership's first taxable year, Asset 1 appreciates in value to $1,300. A sells its one-third interest in the partnership to T for $1,100, when an election under section 754 is in effect. The amount of tax gain that would be allocated to T from the hypothetical transaction is $700 ($600 section 704(c) built-in gain, plus one-third of the additional gain). Thus, T's interest in the partnership's previously taxed capital is $400 ($1,100, the amount of cash T would receive if PRS liquidated immediately after the hypothetical transaction, decreased by $700, T's share of gain from the hypothetical transaction). The amount of T's basis adjustment under section 743(b) to partnership property is $700 (the excess of $1,100, T's cost basis for its interest, over $400, T's share of the adjusted basis to the partnership of partnership property).

(e) Allocation of basis adjustment. For the allocation of the basis adjustment under this section among the individual items of partnership property, see section 755 and the regulations thereunder.

(f) Subsequent transfers. Where there has been more than one transfer of a partnership interest, a transferee's basis adjustment is determined without regard to any prior transferee's basis adjustment. In the case of a gift of an interest in a partnership, the donor is treated as transferring, and the donee as receiving, that portion of the basis adjustment attributable to the gifted partnership interest. The provisions of this paragraph (f) are illustrated by the following example:

Example. (i) A, B, and C form partnership PRS. A and B each contribute $1,000 cash, and C contributes land with a basis and fair market value of $1,000. When the land has appreciated in value to $1,300, A sells its interest to T1 for $1,100 (one-third of $3,300, the fair market value for the partnership property). An election under section 754 is in effect; therefore, T1 has a basis adjustment under section 743(b) of $100.

(ii) After the land has further appreciated in value to $1,600, T1 sells it interest to T2 for $1,200 (one-third of $3,600, the fair market value of the partnership property). T2 has a basis adjustment under section 743(b) of $200. This amount is determined without regard to any basis adjustment under section 743(b) that T1 may have had in the partnership assets.

(iii) During the following year, T2 makes a gift to T3 of fifty percent of T2's interest in PRS. At the time of the transfer, T2 has a $200 basis adjustment under section 743(b). T2 is treated as transferring $100 of the basis adjustment to T3 with the gift of the partnership interest.

(g) Distributions—(1) Distribution of adjusted property to the transferee—(i) Coordination with section 732. If a partnership distributes property to a transferee and the transferee has a basis adjustment for the property, the basis adjustment is taken into account under section 732. See § 1.732–2(b).

(ii) Coordination with section 734. For certain adjustments to the common basis of remaining partnership property after the distribution of adjusted property to a transferee, see § 1.734–2(b).

(2) Distribution of adjusted property to another partner—(i) Coordination with section 732. If a partner receives a distribution of property with respect to which another partner has a basis adjustment, the distributee does not take the basis adjustment into account under section 732.

(ii) Reallocation of basis. A transferee with a basis adjustment in property that is distributed to another partner reallocates the basis adjustment among the remaining items of partnership property under § 1.755–1(c).

(3) Distributions in complete liquidation of a partner's interest. If a transferee receives a distribution of property (whether or not the transferee has a basis adjustment in such property) in liquidation of its interest in the partnership, the adjusted basis to the partnership of the distributed property immediately before the distribution includes the transferee's basis adjustment for the property in which the transferee relinquished an interest (either because it remained in the partnership or was distributed to another partner). Any basis adjustment for property in which the transferee is deemed to relinquish its interest is reallocated among the properties distributed to the transferee under § 1.755–1(c).

(4) Coordination with other provisions. The rules of sections 704(c)(1)(B), 731, 737, and 751 apply before the rules of this paragraph (g).

(5) Example. The provisions of this paragraph (g) are illustrated by the following example:

Example. (i) A, B, and C are equal partners in partnership PRS. Each partner originally contributed $10,000 in cash, and PRS used the contributions to purchase five nondepreciable capital assets. PRS has no liabilities. After five years, PRS's balance sheet appears as follows:

Assets

	Adjusted Basis	Fair Market Value
Asset 1	$10,000	$10,000
Asset 2	4,000	6,000
Asset 3	6,000	6,000
Asset 4	7,000	4,000
Asset 5	3,000	13,000
Total	$30,000	$39,000

Capital

	Adjusted Per Books	Fair Market Value
Partner A	$10,000	$13,000
Partner B	10,000	13,000
Partner C	10,000	13,000
Total	$30,000	$39,000

(ii) A sells its interest to T for $13,000 when PRS has an election in effect under section 754. T receives a basis adjustment under section 743(b) in the partnership property that is equal to $3,000 (the excess of T's basis in the partnership interest, $13,000, over T's share of the adjusted basis to the partnership of partnership property, $10,000). The basis adjustment is allocated under section 755, and the partnership's balance sheet appears as follows:

Assets

	Adjusted Basis	Fair Market Value	Basis Adjustment
Asset 1	$10,000	$10,000	$ 0.00
Asset 2	4,000	6,000	666.67
Asset 3	6,000	6,000	0.00
Asset 4	7,000	4,000	(1,000.00)
Asset 5	3,000	13,000	3,333.33
Total	$30,000	$39,000	$3,000.00

Capital

	Adjusted Per Books	Fair Market Value	Special Basis
Partner T	$10,000	$13,000	$3,000
Partner B	10,000	13,000	0
Partner C	10,000	13,000	0
Total	$30,000	$39,000	$3,000

(iii) Assume that PRS distributes Asset 2 to T in partial liquidation of T's interest in the partnership. T has a basis adjustment under section 743(b) of $666.67 in Asset 2. Under paragraph (g)(1)(i) of this section, T takes the basis adjustment into account under section 732. Therefore, T will have a basis in Asset 2 of $4,666.67 following the distribution.

(iv) Assume instead that PRS distributes Asset 5 to C in complete liquidation of C's interest in PRS. T has a basis adjustment under section 743(b) of $3,333.33 in Asset 5. Under paragraph (g)(2)(i) of this section, C does not take T's basis adjustment into account under section 732. Therefore, the partnership's basis for purposes of sections 732 and 734 is $3,000. Under paragraph (g)(2)(ii) of this section, T's $3,333.33 basis adjustment is reallocated among the remaining partnership assets under § 1.755–1(c).

(v) Assume instead that PRS distributes Asset 5 to T in complete liquidation of its interest in PRS. Under paragraph (g)(3) of this section, immediately prior to the distribution of Asset 5 to T, PRS must adjust the basis of Asset 5. Therefore, immediately prior to the distribution, PRS's basis in Asset 5 is equal to $6,000, which is the sum of (A) $3,000, PRS's common basis in Asset 5, plus (B) $3,333.33, T's basis adjustment to Asset 5, plus (C) ($333.33), the sum of T's basis adjustments in Assets 2 and 4. For purposes of sections 732 and 734, therefore, PRS will be treated as having a basis in Asset 5 equal to $6,000.

* * *

(j) Effect of basis adjustment—(1) In general. The basis adjustment constitutes an adjustment to the basis of partnership property with respect to the transferee only. No adjustment is made to the common basis of partnership property. Thus, for purposes of calculating income, deduction, gain, and loss, the transferee will have a special basis for those partnership properties the bases of which are adjusted under section 743(b) and this section. The adjustment to the basis of partnership property under section 743(b) has no effect on the partnership's computation of any item under section 703.

(2) Computation of partner's distributive share of partnership items. The partnership first computes its items of income, deduction, gain, or loss at the partnership level under section 703. The partnership then allocates the partnership items among the partners, including the transferee, in accordance with section 704, and adjusts the partners' capital accounts accordingly. The partnership then adjusts the transferee's distributive share of the items of partnership income, deduction, gain, or loss, in accordance with paragraphs (j)(3) and (4) of this section, to reflect the effects of the transferee's basis adjustment under section 743(b). These adjustments to the transferee's distributive shares must be reflected on Schedules K and K–1 of the partnership's return (Form 1065). These adjustments to the transferee's distributive shares do not affect the transferee's capital account. * * *

(3) Effect of basis adjustment in determining items of income, gain, or loss—(i) In general. The amount of a transferee's income, gain, or loss from the sale or exchange of a partnership asset in which the transferee has a basis adjustment is equal to the transferee's share of the partnership's gain or loss from the sale of the asset (including any remedial allocations under § 1.704–3(d)), minus the amount of the transferee's positive basis adjustment for the partnership asset (determined by taking into account the recovery of the basis adjustment under paragraph (j)(4)(i)(B) of this section) or plus the amount of the transferee's negative basis adjustment for the partnership asset (determined by taking into account the recovery of the basis adjustment under paragraph (j)(4)(ii)(B) of this section).

(ii) Examples. The following examples illustrate the principles of this paragraph (j)(3):

Example 1. A and B form equal partnership PRS. A contributes nondepreciable property with a fair market value of $50 and an adjusted tax basis of $100. PRS will use the traditional allocation method under § 1.704–3(b). B contributes $50 cash. A sells its interest to T for $50. PRS has an election in effect to adjust the basis of partnership property under section 754. T receives a negative $50 basis adjustment under section 743(b) that, under section 755, is allocated to the nondepreciable property. PRS then sells the property for $60. PRS recognizes a book gain of $10 (allocated equally between T and B) and a tax loss of $40. T will receive an allocation of $40 of tax loss under the principles of section 704(c). However, because T has a negative $50 basis adjustment in the nondepreciable property, T recognizes a $10 gain from the partnership's sale of the property.

Example 2. A and B form equal partnership PRS. A contributes nondepreciable property with a fair market value of $100 and an adjusted tax basis of $50. B contributes $100 cash. PRS will use the traditional allocation method under § 1.704–3(b). A sells its interest to T for $100. PRS has an election in effect to adjust the basis of partnership property under section 754. Therefore, T receives a $50 basis adjustment under section 743(b) that, under section 755, is allocated to the nondepreciable property. PRS then sells the nondepreciable property for $90. PRS recognizes a book loss of $10 (allocated equally between T and B) and a tax gain of $40. T will receive an allocation of the entire $40 of tax gain under the principles of section 704(c). However, because T has a $50 basis adjustment in the property, T recognizes a $10 loss from the partnership's sale of the property.

Example 3. A and B form equal partnership PRS. PRS will make allocations under section 704(c) using the remedial allocation method described in § 1.704–3(d). A contributes nondepreciable property with a fair market value of $100 and an adjusted tax basis of $150. B contributes $100 cash. A sells its partnership interest to T for $100. PRS has an election in effect to adjust the basis of partnership property under section 754. T receives a negative $50 basis adjustment under section 743(b) that, under section 755, is allocated to the property. The partnership then sells the property for $120. The partnership recognizes a $20 book gain and a $30 tax loss. The book gain will be allocated equally between the partners. The entire $30 tax loss will be allocated to T under the principles of section 704(c). To match its $10 share of book gain, B will be allocated $10 of remedial gain, and T will be allocated an offsetting $10 of remedial loss. T was allocated a total of $40 of tax loss with respect to the property. However, because T has a negative $50 basis adjustment to the property, T recognizes a $10 gain from the partnership's sale of the property.

(4) Effect of basis adjustment in determining items of deduction—(i) Increases—(A) Additional deduction. The amount of any positive basis adjustment that is recovered by the transferee in any year is added to the transferee's distributive share of the partnership's depreciation or amortization deductions for the year. The basis adjustment is adjusted under section 1016(a)(2) to reflect the recovery of the basis adjustment.

(B) Recovery period—(*1*) In general. Except as provided in paragraph (j)(4)(i)(B)(*2*) of this section, for purposes of section 168, if the basis of a partnership's recovery property is increased as a result of the transfer of a partnership interest, then the increased portion of the basis is taken into account as if it were newly-purchased recovery property placed in service when the transfer occurs. Consequently, any applicable recovery period and method may be used to determine the recovery allowance with respect to the increased portion of the basis. However, no change is made for purposes of determining the recovery allowance under section 168 for the portion of the basis for which there is no increase.

(*2*) Remedial allocation method. If a partnership elects to use the remedial allocation method described in § 1.704–3(d) with respect to an item of the partnership's recovery property, then the portion of any increase in the basis of the item of the partnership's recovery property under section 743(b) that is attributable to section 704(c) built-in gain is recovered over the remaining recovery period for the partnership's excess book basis in the property as determined in the final sentence of § 1.704–3(d)(2). Any remaining portion of the basis increase is recovered under paragraph (j)(4)(i)(B)(*1*) of this section.

(C) Examples. The provisions of this paragraph (j)(4)(i) are illustrated by the following examples:

Example 1. **(i)** A, B, and C are equal partners in partnership PRS, which owns Asset 1, an item of depreciable property that has a fair market value in excess of its adjusted tax basis. C sells its interest in PRS to T while PRS has an election in effect under section 754. PRS, therefore, increases the basis of Asset 1 with respect to T.

(ii) Assume that in the year following the transfer of the partnership interest to T, T's distributive share of the partnership's common basis depreciation deductions from Asset 1 is $1,000. Also assume that, under paragraph (j)(4)(i)(B) of this section, the amount of the basis adjustment under section 743(b) that T recovers during the year is $500. The total amount of depreciation deductions from Asset 1 reported by T is equal to $1,500.

Example 2. **(i)** A and B form equal partnership PRS. A contributes property with an adjusted basis of $100,000 and a fair market value of $500,000. B contributes $500,000 cash. When PRS is formed, the property has five years remaining in its recovery period. The partnership's adjusted basis of $100,000 will, therefore, be recovered over the five years remaining in the property's recovery period. PRS elects to use the remedial allocation method under § 1.704–3(d) with respect to the property. If PRS had purchased the property at the time of the partnership's formation, the basis of the property would have been recovered over a 10–year period. The $400,000 of section 704(c) built-in gain will, therefore, be amortized under § 1.704–3(d) over a 10–year period beginning at the time of the partnership's formation.

(ii)(A) Except for the depreciation deductions, PRS's expenses equal its income in each year of the first two years commencing with the year the partnership is formed. After two years, A's share of the adjusted basis of partnership property is $120,000, while B's is $440,000:

Capital Accounts

	A		B	
	Book	Tax	Book	Tax
Initial Contribution	$500,000	$100,000	$500,000	$500,000
Depreciation Year 1	(30,000)		(30,000)	(20,000)
Remedial		10,000		(10,000)
	470,000	110,000	470,000	470,000
Depreciation Year 2	(30,000)		(30,000)	(20,000)
Remedial		10,000		(10,000)
	$440,000	$120,000	$440,000	$440,000

(B) A sells its interest in PRS to T for its fair market value of $440,000. A valid election under section 754 is in effect with respect to the sale of the partnership interest. Accordingly, PRS makes an adjustment, pursuant to section 743(b), to increase the basis of partnership property. Under section 743(b), the amount of the basis adjustment is equal to $320,000. Under section 755, the entire basis adjustment is allocated to the property.

(iii) At the time of the transfer, $320,000 of section 704(c) built-in gain from the property was still reflected on the partnership's books, and all of the basis adjustment is attributable to section 704(c) built-in gain. Therefore, the basis adjustment will be recovered over the remaining recovery period for the section 704(c) built-in gain under § 1.704-3(d).

(ii) Decreases—(A) Reduced deduction. The amount of any negative basis adjustment allocated to an item of depreciable or amortizable property that is recovered in any year first decreases the transferee's distributive share of the partnership's depreciation or amortization deductions from that item of property for the year. If the amount of the basis adjustment recovered in any year exceeds the transferee's distributive share of the partnership's depreciation or amortization deductions from the item of property, then the transferee's distributive share of the partnership's depreciation or amortization deductions from other items of partnership property is decreased. The transferee then recognizes ordinary income to the extent of the excess, if any, of the amount of the basis adjustment recovered in any year over the transferee's distributive share of the partnership's depreciation or amortization deductions from all items of property.

(B) Recovery period. For purposes of section 168, if the basis of an item of a partnership's recovery property is decreased as the result of the transfer of an interest in the partnership, then the decrease is recovered over the remaining useful life of the item of the partnership's recovery property. The portion of the decrease that is recovered in any year during the recovery period is equal to the product of—

(*1*) The amount of the decrease to the item's adjusted basis (determined as of the date of the transfer); multiplied by

(*2*) A fraction, the numerator of which is the portion of the adjusted basis of the item recovered by the partnership in that year, and the denominator of which is the adjusted basis of the item on the date of the transfer (determined prior to any basis adjustments).

(C) Examples. The provisions of this paragraph (j)(4)(ii) are illustrated by the following examples:

Example 1. **(i)** A, B, and C are equal partners in partnership PRS, which owns Asset 2, an item of depreciable property that has a fair market value that is less than its adjusted tax basis. C sells its interest in PRS to T while PRS has an election in effect under section 754. PRS, therefore, decreases the basis of Asset 2 with respect to T.

(ii) Assume that in the year following the transfer of the partnership interest to T, T's distributive share of the partnership's common basis depreciation deductions from Asset 2 is $1,000. Also assume that, under paragraph (j)(4)(ii)(B) of this section, the amount of the basis adjustment under section 743(b) that T recovers during the year is $500. The total amount of depreciation deductions from Asset 2 reported by T is equal to $500.

Example 2. **(i)** A and B form equal partnership PRS. A contributes property with an adjusted basis of $100,000 and a fair market value of $50,000. B contributes $50,000 cash. When PRS is formed, the property has five years remaining in its recovery period. The partnership's adjusted basis of $100,000 will, therefore, be recovered over the five years remaining in the property's recovery period. PRS uses the traditional allocation method under § 1.704-3(b) with respect to the property. As a result, B will receive $5,000 of depreciation deductions from the property in each of years 1-5, and A, as the contributing partner, will receive $15,000 of depreciation deductions in each of these years.

(ii) Except for the depreciation deductions, PRS's expenses equal its income in each of the first two years commencing with the year the partnership is formed. After two years, A's share of the adjusted basis of partnership property is $70,000, while B's is $40,000. A sells its interest in PRS to T for its fair market value of $40,000. A valid election under section 754 is in effect with respect to the sale of the partnership interest. Accordingly, PRS makes an adjustment, pursuant to section 743(b), to decrease the basis of partnership property. Under section 743(b), the amount of the adjustment is equal to ($30,000). Under section 755, the entire adjustment is allocated to the property.

(iii) The basis of the property at the time of the transfer of the partnership interest was $60,000. In each of years 3 through 5, the partnership will realize depreciation deductions of $20,000 from the property. Thus, one third of the negative basis adjustment ($10,000) will be recovered in each of years 3 through 5. Consequently, T will be allocated, for tax purposes, depreciation of $15,000 each year from the partnership and will recover $10,000 of its negative basis adjustment. Thus, T's net depreciation deduction from the partnership in each year is $5,000.

Example 3. **(i)** A, B, and C are equal partners in partnership PRS, which owns Asset 2, an item of depreciable property that has a fair market value that is less than its adjusted tax basis. C sells its interest in PRS to T while PRS has an election in effect under section 754. PRS, therefore, decreases the basis of Asset 2 with respect to T.

(ii) Assume that in the year following the transfer of the partnership interest to T, T's distributive share of the partnership's common basis depreciation deductions from Asset 2 is $500. PRS allocates no other depreciation T. Also assume that, under paragraph (j)(4)(ii)(B) of this section, the amount of the negative basis adjustment that T recovers during the year is $1,000. T will report $500 of ordinary income because the amount of the negative basis adjustment recovered during the year exceeds T's distributive share of the partnership's common basis depreciation deductions from Asset 2.

* * *

(k) Returns—(1) Statement of adjustments—(i) In general. A partnership that must adjust the bases of partnership properties under section 743(b) must attach a statement to the partnership return for the year of the transfer setting forth the name and taxpayer identification number of the transferee as well as the computation of the adjustment and the partnership properties to which the adjustment has been allocated.

* * *

(2) Requirement that transferee notify partnership—(i) Sale or exchange. A transferee that acquires, by sale or exchange, an interest in a partnership with an election under section 754 in effect for the taxable year of the transfer, must notify the partnership, in writing, within 30 days of the sale or exchange. The written notice to the partnership* * * must include* * * the amount of any liabilities assumed or taken subject to by the transferee, and the amount of any money, the fair market value of any other property delivered or to be delivered for the transferred interest in the partnership, and any other information necessary for the partnership to compute the transferee's basis.

(ii) Transfer on death. A transferee that acquires, on the death of a partner, an interest in a partnership with an election under section 754 in effect for the taxable year of the transfer, must notify the partnership, in writing, within one year of the death of the deceased partner. * * *

(3) Reliance. In making the adjustments under section 743(b) and any statement or return relating to such adjustments under this section, a partnership may rely on the written notice provided by a transferee pursuant to paragraph (k)(2) of this section to determine the transferee's basis in a partnership interest. The previous sentence shall not apply if any partner who has responsibility for federal income tax reporting by the partnership has knowledge of facts indicating that the statement is clearly erroneous.

(4) Partnership not required to make or report adjustments under section 743(b) until it has notice of the transfer. A partnership is not required to make the adjustments under section 743(b) (or any statement or return relating to those adjustments) with respect to any transfer until it has been notified of the transfer. For purposes of this section, a partnership is notified of a transfer when either—

(i) The partnership receives the written notice from the transferee required under paragraph (k)(2) of this section; or

(ii) Any partner who has responsibility for federal income tax reporting by the partnership has knowledge that there has been a transfer of a partnership interest.

(5) Effect on partnership of the failure of the transferee to comply. If the transferee fails to provide the partnership with the written notice required by paragraph (k)(2) of this section, the partnership must attach a statement to its return in the year that the partnership is otherwise notified of the transfer. This statement must set forth the name and taxpayer identification number (if ascertainable) of the transferee. In addition, the following statement must be prominently displayed in capital letters on the first page of the partnership's return for such year, and on the first page of any schedule or information statement relating to such transferee's share of income, credits, deductions, etc.: "RETURN FILED PURSUANT TO § 1.743–1(k)(5)." The partnership will then be entitled to report the transferee's share of partnership items without adjustment to reflect the transferee's basis adjustment in partnership property. If, following the filing of a return pursuant to this paragraph (k)(5), the transferee provides the applicable written notice to the partnership, the partnership must make such adjustments as are necessary to adjust the basis of partnership property (as of the date of the transfer) in any amended return otherwise to be filed by the partnership or in the next annual partnership return of income to be regularly filed by the partnership. At such time, the partnership must also provide the transferee with such information as is necessary for the transferee to amend its prior returns to properly reflect the adjustment under section 743(b).

* * *

[T.D. 8847, 64 FR 69903, Dec. 15, 1999; 65 FR 9220, Feb. 24, 2000; T.D. 9137, 69 FR 42559, July 16, 2004]

§ 1.751–1 Unrealized receivables and inventory items.

(a) Sale or exchange of interest in a partnership—(1) Character of amount realized. To the extent that money or property received by a partner in exchange for all or part of his partnership interest is attributable to his share of the value of partnership unrealized receivables or substantially appreciated inventory items, the money or fair market value of the property received shall be considered as an amount realized from the sale or exchange of property other than a capital asset. The remainder of the total amount realized on the sale or exchange of the partnership interest is realized from the sale or exchange of a capital asset under section 741. For definition of "unrealized receivables" and "inventory items which have appreciated substantially in value", see section 751(c) and (d). Unrealized receivables and substantially appreciated inventory items are hereafter in this section referred to as "section 751 property". See paragraph (e) of this section.

(2) Determination of gain or loss. The income or loss realized by a partner upon the sale or exchange of its interest in section 751 property is the amount of income or loss from section 751 property (including any remedial allocations under § 1.704–3(d)) that would have been allocated to the partner (to the extent attributable to the partnership interest sold or exchanged) if the partnership had sold all of its property in a fully taxable transaction for cash in an amount equal to the fair market value of such property (taking into account section 7701(g)) immediately prior to the partner's transfer of the interest in the partnership. Any gain or loss recognized that is attributable to section 751 property will be ordinary gain or loss. The difference between the amount of capital gain or loss that the partner would realize in the absence of section 751 and the amount of ordinary income or loss determined under this paragraph (a)(2) is the transferor's capital gain or loss on the sale of its partnership interest. * * *

(3) Statement required. A partner selling or exchanging any part of an interest in a partnership that has any section 751 property at the time of sale or exchange must submit with its income tax return for the taxable year in which the sale or exchange occurs a statement setting forth separately the following information—

(i) The date of the sale or exchange;

(ii) The amount of any gain or loss attributable to the section 751 property; and

(iii) The amount of any gain or loss attributable to capital gain or loss on the sale of the partnership interest.

(b) Certain distributions treated as sales or exchanges—(1) In general. (i) Certain distributions to which section 751(b) applies are treated in part as sales or exchanges of property between the partnership and the distributee partner, and not as distributions to which sections 731 through 736 apply. A distribution treated as a sale or exchange under section 751(b) is not subject to the provisions of section 707(b). Section 751(b) applies whether or not the distribution is in liquidation of the distributee partner's entire interest in the partnership. However, section 751(b) applies only to the extent that a partner either receives section 751 property in exchange for his relinquishing any part of his interest in other property, or receives other property in exchange for his relinquishing any part of his interest in section 751 property.

(ii) Section 751(b) does not apply to a distribution to a partner which is not in exchange for his interest in other partnership property. Thus, section 751(b) does not apply to the extent that a distribution consists of the distributee partner's share of section 751 property or his share of other property. Similarly, section 751(b) does not apply to current drawings or to advances against the partner's distributive share, or to a distribution which is, in fact, a gift or payment for services or for the use of capital. In determining whether a partner has received only his share of either section 751 property or of other property, his interest in such property remaining in the partnership immediately after a distribution must be taken into account. For example, the section 751 property in partnership ABC has a fair market value of $100,000 in which partner A has an interest of 30 percent, or $30,000. If A receives $20,000 of section 751 property in a distribution, and continues to have a 30–percent interest in the $80,000 of section 751 property remaining in the partnership after the distribution, only $6,000 ($30,000 minus $24,000 (30 percent of $80,000)) of the section 751 property received by him will be considered to be his share of such property. The remaining $14,000 ($20,000 minus $6,000) received is in excess of his share.

(iii) If a distribution is, in part, a distribution of the distributee partner's share of section 751 property, or of other property (including money) and, in part, a distribution in exchange of such properties, the distribution shall be divided for the purpose of applying section 751(b). The rules of section 751(b) shall first apply to the part of the distribution treated as a sale or exchange of such properties, and then the rules of sections 731 through 736 shall apply to the part of the distribution not treated as a sale or exchange. See paragraph (b)(4)(ii) of this section for treatment of payments under section 736(a).

(2) Distribution of section 751 property (unrealized receivables or substantially appreciated inventory items). (i) To the extent that a partner receives section 751 property in a distribution in exchange for any part of his interest in partnership property (including money) other than section 751 property, the transaction shall be treated as a sale or exchange of such properties between the distributee partner and the partnership (as constituted after the distribution).

(ii) At the time of the distribution, the partnership (as constituted after the distribution) realizes ordinary income or loss on the sale or exchange of the section 751 property. The amount of the income or loss to the partnership will be measured by the difference between the adjusted basis to the partnership of the section 751 property considered as sold to or exchanged with the partner, and the fair market value of the distributee partner's interest in other partnership property which he relinquished in the exchange. In computing the partners' distributive shares of such ordinary income or loss, the income or loss shall be allocated only to partners other than the distributee and separately taken into account under section 702(a)(8).

(iii) At the time of the distribution, the distributee partner realizes gain or loss measured by the difference between his adjusted basis for the property relinquished in the exchange (including any special basis adjustment which he may have) and the fair market value of the section 751 property received by him in exchange for his interest in other property which he has relinquished. The distributee's adjusted basis for the property relinquished is the basis such property would have had under section 732 (including subsection (d) thereof) if the distributee partner had received such property in a current distribution immediately before the actual distribution which is treated wholly or partly as a sale or exchange under section 751(b). The character of the gain or loss to the distributee partner shall be determined by the character of the property in which he relinquished his interest.

(3) Distribution of partnership property other than section 751 property. **(i)** To the extent that a partner receives a distribution of partnership property (including money) other than section 751 property in exchange for any part of his interest in section 751 property of the partnership, the distribution shall be treated as a sale or exchange of such properties between the distributee partner and the partnership (as constituted after the distribution).

(ii) At the time of the distribution, the partnership (as constituted after the distribution) realizes gain or loss on the sale or exchange of the property other than section 751 property. The amount of the gain to the partnership will be measured by the difference between the adjusted basis to the partnership of the distributed property considered as sold to or exchanged with the partner, and the fair market value of the distributee partner's interest in section 751 property which he relinquished in the exchange. The character of the gain or loss to the partnership is determined by the character of the distributed property treated as sold or exchanged by the partnership. In computing the partners' distributive shares of such gain or loss, the gain or loss shall be allocated only to partners other than the distributee and separately taken into account under section 702(a)(8).

(iii) At the time of the distribution, the distributee partner realizes ordinary income or loss on the sale or exchange of the section 751 property. The amount of the distributee partner's income or loss shall be measured by the difference between his adjusted basis for the section 751 property relinquished in the exchange (including any special basis adjustment which he may have), and the fair market value of other property (including money) received by him in exchange for his interest in the section 751 property which he has relinquished. The distributee partner's adjusted basis for the section 751 property relinquished is the basis such property would have had under section 732 (including subsection (d) thereof) if the distributee partner had received such property in a current distribution immediately before the actual distribution which is treated wholly or partly as a sale or exchange under section 751(b).

(4) Exceptions. **(i)** Section 751(b) does not apply to the distribution to a partner of property which the distributee partner contributed to the partnership. The distribution of such property is governed by the rules set forth in sections 731 through 736, relating to distributions by a partnership.

(ii) Section 751(b) does not apply to payments made to a retiring partner or to a deceased partner's successor in interest to the extent that, under section 736(a), such payments constitute a distributive share of partnership income or guaranteed payments. Payments to a retiring partner or to a deceased partner's successor in interest for his interest in unrealized receivables of the partnership in excess of their partnership basis, including any special basis adjustment for them to which such partner is entitled, constitute payments under section 736(a) and, therefore, are not subject to section 751(b). However, payments under section 736(b) which are considered as made in exchange for an interest in partnership property are subject to section 751(b) to the extent that they involve an exchange of substantially appreciated inventory items for other property. Thus, payments to a retiring partner or to a deceased partner's successor in interest under section 736 must first be divided between payments under section 736(a) and section

736(b). The section 736(b) payments must then be divided, if there is an exchange of substantially appreciated inventory items for other property, between the payments treated as a sale or exchange under section 751(b) and payments treated as a distribution under sections 731 through 736. See subparagraph (1)(iii) of this paragraph, and section 736 and § 1.736–1.

(5) Statement required. A partnership which distributes section 751 property to a partner in exchange for his interest in other partnership property, or which distributes other property in exchange for any part of the partner's interest in section 751 property, shall submit with its return for the year of the distribution a statement showing the computation of any income, gain, or loss to the partnership under the provisions of section 751(b) and this paragraph. The distributee partner shall submit with his return a statement showing the computation of any income, gain, or loss to him. Such statement shall contain information similar to that required under paragraph (a)(3) of this section.

(c) Unrealized receivables. **(1)** The term "unrealized receivables", as used in subchapter K, chapter 1 of the Code, means any rights (contractual or otherwise) to payment for—

(i) Goods delivered or to be delivered (to the extent that such payment would be treated as received for property other than a capital asset), or

(ii) Services rendered or to be rendered,

to the extent that income arising from such rights to payment was not previously includible in income under the method of accounting employed by the partnership. Such rights must have arisen under contracts or agreements in existence at the time of sale or distribution, although the partnership may not be able to enforce payment until a later time. For example, the term includes trade accounts receivable of a cash method taxpayer, and rights to payment for work or goods begun but incomplete at the time of the sale or distribution.

(2) The basis for such unrealized receivables shall include all costs or expenses attributable thereto paid or accrued but not previously taken into account under the partnership method of accounting.

(3) In determining the amount of the sale price attributable to such unrealized receivables, or their value in a distribution treated as a sale or exchange, full account shall be taken not only of the estimated cost of completing performance of the contract or agreement, but also of the time between the sale or distribution and the time of payment.

(4)(i) With respect to any taxable year of a partnership ending after September 12, 1966 (but only in respect of expenditures paid or incurred after that date), the term unrealized receivables, for purposes of this section and sections 731, 736, 741, and 751, also includes potential gain from mining property defined in section 617(f)(2). With respect to each item of partnership mining property so defined, the potential gain is the amount that would be treated as gain to which section 617(d)(1) would apply if (at the time of the transaction described in section 731, 736, 741, or 751, as the case may be) the item were sold by the partnership at its fair market value.

* * *

(iii) With respect to any taxable year of a partnership beginning after December 31, 1962, the term unrealized receivables, for purposes of this section and sections 731, 736, 741, and 751, also includes potential gain from section 1245 property. With respect to each item of partnership section 1245 property (as defined in section 1245(a)(3)), potential gain from section 1245 property is the amount that would be treated as gain to which section 1245(a)(1) would apply if (at the time of the transaction described in section 731, 736, 741, or 751, as the case may be), the item of section 1245 property were sold by the partnership at its fair market value. See § 1.1245–1(e)(1). For example, if a partnership would recognize under section 1245(a)(1) gain of $600 upon a sale of one item of section 1245 property and gain of $300 upon a sale of its only other item of such property, the potential section 1245 income of the partnership would be $900.

(iv) With respect to transfers after October 9, 1975, and to sales, exchanges, and distributions taking place after that date, the term unrealized receivables, for purposes of this section and sections 731, 736, 741, and 751, also includes potential gain from stock in certain foreign corporations as described in section 1248. With respect to stock in such a foreign corporation, the potential gain is the amount that would be treated as gain to which section 1248(a) would apply if (at the time of the transaction described in section 731, 736, 741, or 751, as the case may be) the stock were sold by the partnership at its fair market value.

(v) With respect to any taxable year of a partnership ending after December 31, 1963, the term unrealized receivables, for purposes of this section and sections 731, 736, 741, and 751, also includes potential gain from section 1250 property. With respect to each item of partnership section 1250 property (as defined in section 1250(c)), potential gain from section 1250 property is the amount that would be treated as gain to which section 1250(a) would apply if (at the time of the transaction described in section 731, 736, 741, or 751, as the case may be) the item of section 1250 property were sold by the partnership at its fair market value. See § 1.1250–1(f)(1).

(vi) With respect to any taxable year of a partnership beginning after December 31, 1969, the term unrealized receivables, for purposes of this section and sections 731, 736, 741, and 751, also includes potential gain from farm recapture property as defined in section 1251(e)(1) (as in effect before enactment of the Tax Reform Act of 1984). With respect to each item of partnership farm recapture property so defined, the potential gain is the amount which would be treated as gain to which section 1251(c) (as in effect before enactment of the Tax Reform Act of 1984) would apply if (at the time of the transaction described in section 731, 736, 741, or 751, as the case may be) the item were sold by the partnership at its fair market value.

(vii) With respect to any taxable year of a partnership beginning after December 31, 1969, the term unrealized receivables, for purposes of this section and sections 731, 736, 741, and 751, also includes potential gain from farm land as defined in section 1252(a)(2). With respect to each item of partnership farm land so defined, the potential gain is the amount that would be treated as gain to which section 1252(a)(1) would apply if (at the time of the transaction described in section 731, 736, 741, or 751, as the case may be) the item were sold by the partnership at its fair market value.

(viii) With respect to transactions which occur after December 31, 1976, in any taxable year of a partnership ending after that date, the term unrealized receivables, for purposes of this section and sections 731, 736, 741, and 751, also includes potential gain from franchises, trademarks, or trade names referred to in section 1253(a). With respect to each such item so referred to in section 1253(a), the potential gain is the amount that would be treated as gain to which section 1253(a) would apply if (at the time of the transaction described in section 731, 736, 741, or 751, as the case may be) the items were sold by the partnership at its fair market value.

(ix) With respect to any taxable year of a partnership ending after December 31, 1975, the term unrealized receivables, for purposes of this section and sections 731, 736, 741, and 751, also includes potential gain under section 1254(a) from natural resource recapture property as defined in § 1.1254–1(b)(2). With respect to each separate partnership natural resource recapture property so described, the potential gain is the amount that would be treated as gain to which section 1254(a) would apply if (at the time of the transaction described in section 731, 736, 741, or 751, as the case may be) the property were sold by the partnership at its fair market value.

(5) For purposes of subtitle A of the Internal Revenue Code, the basis of any potential gain described in paragraph (c)(4) of this section is zero.

(6)(i) If (at the time of any transaction referred to in paragraph (c)(4) of this section) a partnership holds property described in paragraph (c)(4) of this section and if—

(A) A partner had a special basis adjustment under section 743(b) in respect of the property;

(B) The basis under section 732 of the property if distributed to the partner would reflect a special basis adjustment under section 732(d); or

(C) On the date a partner acquired a partnership interest by way of a sale or exchange (or upon the death of another partner) the partnership owned the property and an election under section 754 was in effect with respect to the partnership, the partner's share of any potential gain described in paragraph (c)(4) of this section is determined under paragraph (c)(6)(ii) of this section.

(ii) The partner's share of the potential gain described in paragraph (c)(4) of this section in respect of the property to which this paragraph (c)(6)(ii) applies is that amount of gain that the partner would recognize under section 617(d)(1), 995(c), 1245(a), 1248(a), 1250(a), 1251(c) (as in effect before the Tax Reform Act of 1984), 1252(a), 1253(a), or 1254(a) (as the case may be) upon a sale of the property by the partnership, except that, for purposes of this paragraph (c)(6) the partner's share of such gain is determined in a manner that is consistent with the manner in which the partner's share of partnership property is determined; and the amount of a potential special basis adjustment under section 732(d) is treated as if it were the amount of a special basis adjustment under section

743(b). For example, in determining, for purposes of this paragraph (c)(6), the amount of gain that a partner would recognize under section 1245 upon a sale of partnership property, the items allocated under § 1.1245–1(e)(3)(ii) are allocated to the partner in the same manner as the partner's share of partnership property is determined. See § 1.1250–1(f) for rules similar to those contained in § 1.1245–1(e)(3)(ii).

(d) Inventory items which have substantially appreciated in value—(1) Substantial appreciation. [Note: Section 751(b)(3) has been amended to eliminate the 10–percent–of–fair–market test for substantial appreciation. Ed.] Partnership inventory items shall be considered to have appreciated substantially in value if, at the time of the sale or distribution, the total fair market value of all the inventory items of the partnership exceeds 120 percent of the aggregate adjusted basis for such property in the hands of the partnership (without regard to any special basis adjustment of any partner) and, in addition, exceeds 10 percent of the fair market value of all partnership property other than money. The terms "inventory items which have appreciated substantially in value" or "substantially appreciated inventory items" refer to the aggregate of all partnership inventory items. These terms do not refer to specific partnership inventory items or to specific groups of such items. For example, any distribution of inventory items by a partnership the inventory items of which as a whole are substantially appreciated in value shall be a distribution of substantially appreciated inventory items for the purposes of section 751(b), even though the specific inventory items distributed may not be appreciated in value. Similarly, if the aggregate of partnership inventory items are not substantially appreciated in value, a distribution of specific inventory items, the value of which is more than 120 percent of their adjusted basis, will not constitute a distribution of substantially appreciated inventory items. For the purpose of this paragraph, the "fair market value" of inventory items has the same meaning as "market" value in the regulations under section 471, relating to general rule for inventories.

(2) Inventory items. The term "inventory items" as used in subchapter K, chapter 1 of the Code, includes the following types of property:

(i) Stock in trade of the partnership, or other property of a kind which would properly be included in the inventory of the partnership if on hand at the close of the taxable year, or property held by the partnership primarily for sale to customers in the ordinary course of its trade or business. See section 1221(1).

(ii) Any other property of the partnership which, on sale or exchange by the partnership, would be considered property other than a capital asset and other than property described in section 1231. Thus, accounts receivable acquired in the ordinary course of business for services or from the sale of stock in trade constitute inventory items (see section 1221(4)), as do any unrealized receivables.

(iii) Any other property retained by the partnership which, if held by the partner selling his partnership interest or receiving a distribution described in section 751(b), would be considered property described in subdivision (i) or (ii) of this subparagraph. Property actually distributed to the partner does not come within the provisions of section 751(d)(2)(C) and this subdivision.

(e) Section 751 property and other property. For the purposes of this section, "section 751 property" means unrealized receivables or substantially appreciated inventory items, and "other property" means all property (including money) except section 751 property.

* * *

(g) Examples. Application of the provisions of section 751 may be illustrated by the following examples:

Example 1. (i)(A) A and B are equal partners in personal service partnership PRS. B transfers its interest in PRS to T for $15,000 when PRS's balance sheet (reflecting a cash receipts and disbursements method of accounting) is as follows:

Assets

	Adjusted Basis	Fair Market Value
Cash	$ 3,000	$ 3,000
Loans Receivable	10,000	10,000
Capital Assets	7,000	5,000
Unrealized Receivables	0	14,000
Total	20,000	32,000

Liabilities and Capital

	Adjusted Per Books	Fair Market Value
Liabilities	$ 2,000	$ 2,000
Capital:		
A	9,000	15,000
B	9,000	15,000
Total	20,000	32,000

(B) None of the assets owned by PRS is section 704(c) property, and the capital assets are nondepreciable. The total amount realized by B is $16,000, consisting of the cash received, $15,000, plus $1,000, B's share of the partnership liabilities assumed by T. See section 752. B's undivided half-interest in the partnership property includes a half-interest in the partnership's unrealized receivables items. B's basis for its partnership interest is $10,000 ($9,000, plus $1,000, B's share of partnership liabilities). If section 751(a) did not apply to the sale, B would recognize $6,000 of capital gain from the sale of the interest in PRS. However, section 751(a) does apply to the sale.

(ii) If PRS sold all of its section 751 property in a fully taxable transaction immediately prior to the transfer of B's partnership interest to T, B would have been allocated $7,000 of ordinary income from the sale of PRS's unrealized receivables. Therefore, B will recognize $7,000 of ordinary income with respect to the unrealized receivables. The difference between the amount of capital gain or loss that the partner would realize in the absence of section 751 ($6,000) and the amount of ordinary income or loss determined under paragraph (a)(2) of this section ($7,000) is the transferor's capital gain or loss on the sale of its partnership interest. In this case, B will recognize a $1,000 capital loss.

Example (2). (a) Facts. [Note: Section 751(b)(3) has been amended to eliminate the 10–percent–of–fair–market test for substantial appreciation. Ed.] Partnership ABC makes a distribution to partner C in liquidation of his entire one-third interest in the partnership. At the time of the distribution, the balance sheet of the partnership, which uses the accrual method of accounting, is as follows:

Assets

	Adjusted basis per books	Market value
Cash	$15,000	$ 15,000
Accounts receivable	9,000	9,000
Inventory	21,000	30,000
Depreciable property	42,000	48,000
Land	9,000	9,000
Total	96,000	111,000

Liabilities and Capital

	Per books	Market Value
Current liabilities	$15,000	$ 15,000
Mortgage payable	21,000	21,000
Capital:		
A	20,000	25,000
B	20,000	25,000
C	20,000	25,000
Total	96,000	111,000

The distribution received by C consists of $10,000 cash and depreciable property with a fair market value of $15,000 and an adjusted basis to the partnership of $15,000.

(b) Presence of section 751 property. The partnership has no unrealized receivables, but the dual test provided in section 751(d)(1) must be applied to determine whether the inventory items of the partnership, in the aggregate, have appreciated substantially in value. The fair market value of all partnership inventory items, $39,000 (inventory $30,000, and accounts receivable $9,000), exceeds 120 percent of the $30,000 adjusted basis of such items to the partnership. The fair market value of the inventory items, $39,000, also exceeds 10 percent of the fair market value of all partnership property other than money (10 percent of $96,000 or $9,600). Therefore, the partnership inventory items have substantially appreciated in value.

(c) The properties exchanged. Since C's entire partnership interest is to be liquidated, the provisions of section 736 are applicable. No part of the payment, however, is considered as a distributive share or as a guaranteed payment under section 736(a) because the entire payment is made for C's interest in partnership property. Therefore, the entire payment is for an interest in partnership property under section 736(b), and, to the extent applicable, subject to the rules of section 751. In the distribution, C received his share of cash ($5,000) and $15,000 in depreciable property ($1,000 less than his $16,000 share). In addition, he received other partnership property ($5,000 cash and $12,000 liabilities assumed, treated as money distributed under section 752(b)) in exchange for his interest in accounts receivable ($3,000), inventory ($10,000), land ($3,000), and the balance of his interest in depreciable property ($1,000). Section 751(b) applies only to the extent of the exchange of other property for section 751 property (*i.e.*, inventory items, which include trade accounts receivable). The section 751 property exchanged has a fair market value of $13,000 ($3,000 in accounts receivable and $10,000 in inventory). Thus, $13,000 of the total amount C received is considered as received for the sale of section 751 property.

(d) Distributee partner's tax consequences. C's tax consequences on the distribution are as follows:

(1) The section 751(b) sale or exchange. C's share of the inventory items is treated as if he received them in a current distribution, and his basis for such items is $10,000 ($7,000 for inventory and $3,000 for accounts receivable) as determined under paragraph (b)(3)(iii) of this section. Then C is considered as having sold his share of inventory items to the partnership for $13,000. Thus, on the sale of his share of inventory items, C realizes $3,000 of ordinary income.

(2) The part of the distribution not under section 751(b). Section 751(b) does not apply to the balance of the distribution. Before the distribution, C's basis for his partnership interest was $32,000 ($20,000 plus $12,000, his share of partnership liabilities). See section 752(a). This basis is reduced by $10,000, the basis attributed to the section 751 property treated as distributed to C and sold by him to the partnership. Thus, C has a basis of $22,000 for the remainder of his partnership interest. The total distribution to C was $37,000 ($22,000 in cash and liabilities assumed, and $15,000 in depreciable property). Since C received no more than his share of the depreciable property, none of the depreciable property constitutes proceeds of the sale under section 751(b). C did receive more than his share of money. Therefore, the sale proceeds, treated separately in subparagraph (1) of this paragraph of this example, must consist of money and therefore must be deducted from the money distribution. Consequently, in liquidation of the balance of C's interest, he receives depreciable property and $9,000 in money ($22,000 less $13,000). Therefore, no gain or loss is recognized to C on the distribution. Under section 732(b), C's basis for the depreciable property is $13,000 (the remaining basis of his partnership interest, $22,000, reduced by $9,000, the money received in the distribution).

(e) Partnership's tax consequences. The tax consequences to the partnership on the distribution are as follows:

(1) The section 751(b) sale or exchange. The partnership consisting of the remaining members has no ordinary income on the distribution since it did not give up any section 751 property in the exchange. Of the $22,000 money distributed (in cash and the assumption of C's share of liabilities), $13,000 was paid to acquire C's interest in inventory ($10,000 fair market value) and in accounts receivable ($3,000). Since under section 751(b) the partnership is treated as buying these properties, it has a new cost basis for the inventory and accounts receivable acquired from C. Its basis for C's share of inventory and accounts receivable is $13,000, the amount which the partnership is considered as having paid C in the exchange. Since the partnership is treated as having distributed C's share of inventory and accounts receivable to him, the partnership must decrease its basis for inventory and accounts receivable ($30,000) by $10,000, the basis of C's share treated as distributed to him, and then increase the basis for inventory and accounts receivable by $13,000 to reflect the purchase prices of the items acquired. Thus, the basis of the partnership inventory is increased from $21,000 to $24,000 in the transaction. (Note that the basis of property acquired in a section 751(b) exchange is determined under section 1012 without regard to any elections of the partnership. See paragraph (e) of § 1.732–1.) Further, the partnership realizes no capital gain or loss on the portion of the distribution treated as a sale under section 751(b) since, to acquire C's interest in the inventory and accounts receivable, it gave up money and assumed C's share of liabilities.

(2) The part of the distribution not under section 751(b). In the remainder of the distribution to C which was not in exchange for C's interest in section 751 property, C received only other property as follows: $15,000 in depreciable property (with a basis to the partnership of $15,000) and $9,000 in money ($22,000 less $13,000 treated under subparagraph (1) of this paragraph of this example). Since this part of the distribution is not an exchange of section 751 property for other property, section 751(b) does not apply. Instead, the provisions which apply are sections 731 through 736, relating to distributions by a partnership. No gain or loss is recognized to the partnership on the distribution. (See section 731(b).) Further, the partnership makes no adjustment to the basis of remaining depreciable property unless an election under section 754 is in effect. (See section 734(a).) Thus, the basis of the depreciable property before the distribution, $42,000, is reduced by the basis of the depreciable property distributed, $15,000, leaving a basis for the depreciable property in the partnership of $27,000. However, if an election under section 754 is in effect, the partnership must make the adjustment required under section 734(b) as follows: Since the adjusted basis of the distributed property to the partnership had been $15,000, and is only $13,000 in C's hands (see paragraph (d)(2) of this example), the partnership will increase the basis of the depreciable property remaining in the partnership by $2,000 (the excess of the adjusted basis to the partnership of the distributed depreciable property immediately before the distribution over its basis to the distributee). Whether or not an election under section 754 is in effect, the basis for each of the remaining partner's partnership interests will be $38,000 ($20,000 original contribution, plus $12,000, each partner's original share of the liabilities, plus $6,000, the share of C's liabilities each assumed).

(f) Partnership trial balance. A trial balance of the AB partnership after the distribution in liquidation of C's entire interest would reflect the results set forth in the schedule below. Column I shows the amounts to be reflected in the records if an election is in effect under section 754 with respect to an optional adjustment under section 734(b) to the basis of undistributed partnership property. Column II shows the amounts to be reflected in the records where an election under section 754 is not in effect. Note that in column II, the total bases for the partnership assets do not equal the total of the bases for the partnership interests.

Example (3). (a) Facts. Assume that the distribution to partner C in example (2) of this paragraph in liquidation of his entire interest in partnership ABC consists of $5,000 in cash and $20,000 worth of partnership inventory with a basis of $14,000.

	I		II	
	Sec. 754, Election in effect		Sec. 754, Election not in effect	
	Basis	Fair market value	Basis	Fair market value
Cash	$ 5,000	$ 5,000	$ 5,000	$ 5,000
Accounts receivable ..	9,000	9,000	9,000	9,000
Inventory.....	24,000	30,000	24,000	30,000
Depreciable property....	29,000	33,000	27,000	33,000
Land	9,000	9,000	9,000	9,000
	76,000	86,000	74,000	86,000
Current liabilities ...	15,000	15,000	15,000	15,000
Mortgage	21,000	21,000	21,000	21,000
Capital:				
	20,000	25,000	20,000	25,000
	20,000	25,000	20,000	25,000
	76,000	86,000	76,000	86,000

(b) Presence of section 751 property. For the same reason as stated in paragraph (b) of example (2), the partnership inventory items have substantially appreciated in value.

(c) The properties exchanged. In the distribution, C received his share of cash ($5,000) and his share of appreciated inventory items ($13,000). In addition, he received appreciated inventory with a fair market value of $7,000 (and with an adjusted basis to the partnership of $4,900) and $12,000 in money (liabilities assumed). C has relinquished his interest in $16,000 of depreciable property and $3,000 of land. Although C relinquished his interest in $3,000 of accounts receivable, such accounts receivable are inventory items and, therefore, that exchange was not an exchange of section 751 property for other property. Section 751(b) applies only to the extent of the exchange of other property for section 751 property (i.e., depreciable property or land for inventory items). Assume that the partners agree that the $7,000 of inventory in excess of C's share was received by him in exchange for $7,000 of depreciable property.

(d) Distributee partner's tax consequences. C's tax consequence on the distributions are as follows:

(1) The section 751(b) sale or exchange. C is treated as if he had received his 7/16ths share of the depreciable property in a current distribution. His basis for that share is $6,125 (42,000/48,000 of $7,000), as determined under paragraph (b)(2)(iii) of this section. Then C is considered as having sold his 7/16ths share of depreciable property to the partnership for $7,000, realizing a gain of $875.

(2) The part of the distribution not under section 751(b). Section 751(b) does not apply to the balance of the distribution. Before the distribution, C's basis for his partnership interest was $32,000 ($20,000, plus $12,000, his share of partnership liabilities). See section 752(a). This basis is reduced by $6,125, the basis of property treated as distributed to C and sold by him to the partnership. Thus, C will have a basis of $25,875 for the remainder of his partnership interest. Of the $37,000 total distribution to C, $30,000 ($17,000 in money, including liabilities assumed, and $13,000 in inventory) is not within section 751(b). Under section 732(b), C's basis for the inventory with a fair market value of $13,000 (which had an adjusted basis to the partnership of $9,100) is limited to $8,875, the amount of the remaining basis for his partnership interest, $25,875, reduced by $17,000, the money received. Thus, C's total aggregate basis for the inventory received is $15,875 ($7,000 plus $8,875), and not its $14,000 basis in the hands of the partnership.

(e) Partnership's tax consequences. The tax consequences to the partnership on the distribution are as follows:

(1) The section 751(b) sale or exchange. The partnership consisting of the remaining members has $2,100 of ordinary income on the sale of the $7,000 of inventory which had a basis to the partnership of $4,900 (21,000/30,000 of $7,000). This $7,000 of inventory was paid to acquire 7/16ths of C's interest in the depreciable property. Since, under section 751(b), the partnership is treated as buying this property from C, it has a new cost basis for such property. Its basis for the depreciable property is $42,875 ($42,000 less $6,125, the basis of the 7/16ths share considered as distributed to C, plus $7,000, the partnership purchase price for this share).

(2) The part of the distribution not under section 751(b). In the remainder of the distribution to C which was not a sale or exchange of section 751 property for other property, the partnership realizes no gain or loss. See section 731(b). Further, under section 734(a), the partnership makes no adjustment to the basis of the accounts receivable or the 9/16ths interest in depreciable property which C relinquished. However, if an election under section 754 is in effect, the partnership must make the adjustment required under section 734(b) since the adjusted basis to the partnership of the inventory distributed had been $9,100, and C's basis for such inventory after distribution is only $8,875. The basis of the inventory remaining in the partnership must be increased by $225. Whether or not an election under section 754 is in effect, the basis for each of the remaining partnership interests will be $39,050 ($20,000 original contribution, plus $12,000, each partner's original share of the liabilities, plus $6,000, the share of C's liabilities now assumed, plus $1,050, each partner's share of ordinary income realized by the partnership upon that part of the distribution treated as a sale or exchange).

Example (4). (a) Facts. Assume the same facts as in example (3) of this paragraph, except that the partners did not identify the property which C relinquished in exchange for the $7,000 of inventory which he received in excess of his share.

(b) Presence of section 751 property. For the same reasons stated in paragraph (b) of example (2) of this paragraph, the partnership inventory items have substantially appreciated in value.

(c) The properties exchanged. The analysis stated in paragraph (c) of example (3) of this paragraph is the same in this example, except that, in the absence of a specific agreement among the partners as to the properties exchanged, C will be presumed to have sold to the partnership a proportionate amount of each property in which he relinquished an interest. Thus, in the absence of an agreement, C has received $7,000 of inventory in exchange for his release of 7/19ths of the depreciable property and 7/19 ths of the land. ($7,000, fair market value of property released, over $19,000, the sum of the fair market values of C's interest in the land and C's interest in the depreciable property.)

(d) Distributee partner's tax consequences. C's tax consequences on the distribution are as follows:

(1) The section 751(b) sale or exchange. C is treated as if he had received his 7/19ths shares of the depreciable property and land in a current distribution. His basis for those shares is $6,263 (51,000/57,000 of $7,000, their fair market value), as determined under paragraph (b)(2)(iii) of this section. Then C is considered as having sold his 7/19 ths shares of depreciable property and land to the partnership for $7,000, realizing a gain of $737.

(2) The part of the distribution not under section 751(b). Section 751(b) does not apply to the balance of the distribution. Before the distribution C's basis for his partnership interest was $32,000 ($20,000 plus $12,000, his share of partnership liabilities). See section 752(a). This basis is reduced by $6,263, the bases of C's shares of depreciable property and land treated as distributed to him and sold by him to the partnership. Thus, C will have a basis of $25,737 for the remainder of his partnership interest. Of the total $37,000 distributed to C, $30,000 ($17,000 in money, including liabilities assumed, and $13,000 in inventory) is not within section 751(b). Under section 732(b), C's basis for the inventory (with a fair market value of $13,000 and an adjusted basis to the partnership of $9,100) is limited to $8,737, the amount of the remaining basis for his partnership interest ($25,737 less $17,000), money received. Thus, C's total aggregate basis for the inventory he received is $15,737 ($7,000 plus $8,737), and not the $14,000 basis it had in the hands of the partnership.

(e) Partnership's tax consequences. The tax consequences to the partnership on the distribution are as follows:

(1) The section 751(b) sale or exchange. The partnership consisting of the remaining members has $2,100 of ordinary income on the sale of $7,000 of inventory which had a basis to the partnership of $4,900 (21,000/30,000 of $7,000). This $7,000 of inventory was paid to acquire 7/19ths of C's interest in the depreciable property and land. Since, under section 751(b), the partnership is treated as buying this property from C, it has a new cost basis for such property. The bases of the depreciable property and land would be $42,737 and $9,000, respectively. The basis for the depreciable property is computed as follows: The common partnership basis of $42,000 is reduced by the $5,158 basis (42,000/48,000 of $5,895) for C's 7/19ths interest constructively distributed and increased by $5,895 (16,000/19,000 of $7,000), the part of the purchase price allocated to the depreciable property. The basis of the land would be computed in the same way. The $9,000 original partnership basis is reduced by $1,105 basis (9,000/9,000 of $1,105) of land constructively distributed to C, and increased by $1,105 (3,000/19,000 of $7,000), the portion of the purchase price allocated to the land.

(2) The part of the distribution not under section 751(b). In the remainder of the distribution to C which was not a sale or exchange of section 751 property for other property, the partnership realizes no gain or loss. See section 731(b). Further, under section 734(a), the partnership makes no adjustment to the basis of the accounts receivable or the 12/19ths interests in depreciable property and land which C relinquished. However, if an election under section 754 is in effect, the partnership must make the adjustment required under section 734(b) since the adjusted basis to the partnership of the inventory distributed had been $9,100 and C's basis for such inventory after the distribution is only $8,737. The basis of the inventory remaining in the partnership must be increased by the difference of $363. Whether or not an election under section 754 is in effect, the basis for each of the remaining partnership interests will be $39,050 ($20,000 original contribution plus $12,000, each partner's original share of the liabilities, plus $6,000, the share of C's liabilities assumed, plus $1,050, each partner's share of ordinary income realized by the partnership upon the part of the distribution treated as a sale or exchange).

Example (5). (a) Facts. Assume that partner C in example (2) of this paragraph agrees to reduce his interest in capital and profits from one-third to one-fifth for a current distribution consisting of $5,000 in cash, and $7,500 of accounts receivable with a basis to the partnership of $7,500. At the same time, the total liabilities of the partnership are not reduced. Therefore, after the distribution, C's share of the partnership liabilities has been reduced by $4,800 from $12,000 (1/3 of $36,000) to $7,200 (1/5 of $36,000).

(b) Presence of section 751 property. For the same reasons as stated in paragraph (b) of example (2) of this paragraph, the partnership inventory items have substantially appreciated in value.

(c) The properties exchanged. C's interest in the fair market value of the partnership properties before and after the distribution can be illustrated by the following table:

Item	C's interest Fair Market Value		C received		C relinquished
	One-third before	One-fifth after	Distribution of share	In excess of share	
Cash	$ 5,000	$ 2,000	$3,000	$ 2,000	......
Liabilities assumed	(12,000)	(7,200)	......	4,800	......
Inventory items:					
Accounts receivable	3,000	300	2,700	4,800	......
Inventory	10,000	6,000	......	......	$ 4,000
Depreciable property	16,000	9,600	......	......	6,400
Land	3,000	1,800	......	......	1,200
Total	25,000	12,500	5,700	11,600	11,600

Although C relinquished his interest in $4,000 of inventory and received $4,800 of accounts receivable, both items constitute section 751 property and C has received only $800 of accounts receivable for $800 worth of depreciable property or for an $800 undivided interest in land. In the absence of an agreement identifying the properties exchanged, it is presumed C received $800 for proportionate shares of his interests in both depreciable property and land. To the extent that inventory was exchanged for accounts receivable, or to the extent cash was distributed for the release of C's interest in the balance of the depreciable property and land, the transaction does not fall within section 751(b) and is a current distribution under section 732(a). Thus, the remaining $6,700 of accounts receivable are received in a current distribution.

(d) Distributee partner's tax consequences. C's tax consequences on the distribution are as follows:

(1) The section 751(b) sale or exchange. Assuming that the partners paid $800 worth of accounts receivable for $800 worth of depreciable property, C is treated as if he received the depreciable property in a current distribution, and his basis for the $800 worth of depreciable property is $700 (42,000/48,000 of $800, its fair market value), as determined under paragraph (b)(2)(iii) of this section. Then C is considered as having sold his $800 share of depreciable property to the partnership for $800. On the sale of the depreciable property, C realizes a gain of $100. If, on the other hand, the partners had agreed that C exchanged an $800 interest in the land for $800 worth of accounts receivable, C would realize no gain or loss, because under paragraph (b)(2)(iii) of this section his basis for the land sold would be $800. In the absence of an agreement, the basis for the depreciable property and land (which C is considered as having received in a current distribution and then sold back to the partnership) would be $716 (51,000/57,000 of $800). In that case, on the sale of the balance of the $800 share of depreciable property and land, C would realize $84 of gain ($800 less $716).

(2) The part of the distribution not under section 751(b). Section 751(b) does not apply to the balance of the distribution. Under section 731, C does not realize either gain or loss on the balance of the distribution. The adjustments to the basis of C's interest are illustrated in the following table:

	If accounts receivable received for depreciable property	If accounts receivable received for land	If there is no agreement
Original basis for C's interest	$32,000	$32,000	$32,000
Less basis of property distributed prior to sec. 751(b) sale or exchange	– 700	– 800	– 716
	31,300	31,200	31,284
Less money received in distribution	– 9,800	– 9,800	– 9,800
	21,500	21,400	21,484
Less basis of property received in a current distribution under sec. 732	– 6,700	– 6,700	– 6,700
Resulting basis for C's interest	14,800	14,700	14,784

C's basis for the $1,500 worth of accounts receivable which he received in the distribution will be $7,500, composed of $800 for the portion purchased in the section 751(b) exchange, plus $6,700, the basis carried over under section 732(a) for the portion received in the current distribution.

(e) Partnership's tax consequences. The tax consequences to the partnership on the distribution are as follows:

(1) The section 751(b) sale or exchange. The partnership realizes no gain or loss in the section 751 sale or exchange because it had a basis of $800 for the accounts receivable for which it received $800 worth of other property. If the partnership agreed to purchase $800 worth of depreciable property, the partnership basis of depreciable property becomes $42,100 ($42,000 less $700 basis of property constructively distributed to C, plus $800, price of property purchased). If the partnership purchased land with the accounts receivable, there would be no change in the basis of the land to the partnership because the basis of land distributed was equal to its purchase price. If there were no agreement, the basis of the depreciable property and land would be $51,084 (depreciable property, $42,084 and land $9,000). The basis for the depreciable property is computed as follows: The common partnership basis of $42,000 is reduced by the $590 basis (42,000/48,000 of $674) for C's $674 interest constructively distributed, and increased by $674 (6,400/7,600 of $800), the part of the purchase price allocated to the depreciable property. The basis of the land would be computed in the same way. The $9,000 original partnership basis is reduced by $126 basis (9,000/9,000 of $126) of the land constructively distributed to C, and increased by $126 (1,200/7,600 of $800), the portion of the purchase price allocated to the land.

(2) The part of the distribution not under section 751(b). The partnership will realize no gain or loss in the balance of the distribution under section 731. Since the property in C's hands after the distribution will have the same basis it had in the partnership, the basis of partnership property remaining in the partnership after the distribution will not be adjusted (whether or not an election under 754 is in effect).

Example (6). (a) Facts. Partnership ABC distributes to partner C, in liquidation of his entire one-third interest in the partnership, a machine which is section 1245 property with a recomputed basis (as defined in section 1245(a)(2)) of $18,000. At the time of the distribution, the balance sheet of the partnership is as follows:

ASSETS

	Adjusted basis per books	Market value
Cash	$ 3,000	$ 3,000
Machine (section 1245 property)	9,000	15,000
Land	18,000	27,000
Total	30,000	45,000

LIABILITIES AND CAPITAL

	Per books	Value
Liabilities	$ 0	$ 0
Capital:		
A	10,000	15,000
B	10,000	15,000
C	10,000	15,000
Total	30,000	45,000

(b) Presence of section 751 property. The section 1245 property is an unrealized receivable of the partnership to the extent of the potential section 1245 income in respect of the property. Since the fair market value of the property ($15,000) is lower than its recomputed basis ($18,000), the excess of the fair market value over its adjusted basis ($9,000), or $6,000, is the potential section 1245 income of the partnership in respect of the property. The partnership has no other section 751 property.

(c) The properties exchanged. In the distribution C received his share of section 751 property (potential section 1245 income of $2,000, i.e., ⅓ of $6,000) and his share of section 1245 property (other than potential section 1245 income) with a fair market value of $3,000, i.e., ⅓ of ($15,000 minus $6,000), and an adjusted basis of $3,000, i.e., ⅓ of $9,000. In addition he received $4,000 of section 751 property (consisting of $4,000 ($6,000 minus $2,000) of potential section 1245 income) and section 1245 property (other than potential section 1245 income) with a fair market value of $6,000 ($9,000 minus $3,000) and an adjusted basis of $6,000 ($9,000 minus $3,000). C relinquished his interest in $1,000 of cash and $9,000 of land. Assume that the partners agree that the $4,000 of section 751 property in excess of C's share was received by him in exchange for $4,000 of land.

(d) Distributee partner's tax consequences. C's tax consequences on the distributions are as follows:

(1) The section 751(b) sale or exchange. C is treated as if he received in a current distribution 4/9ths of his share of the land with a basis of $2,667 (18,000/27,000 × $4,000). Then C is considered as having sold his 4/9ths share of the land to the partnership for $4,000, realizing a gain of $1,333. C's basis for the remainder of his partnership interest after the current distribution is $7,333, i.e., the basis of his partnership interest before the current distribution ($10,000) minus the basis of the land treated as distributed to him ($2,667).

(2) The part of the distribution not under section 751(b). Of the $15,000 total distribution to C, $11,000

($2,000 of potential section 1245 income and $9,000 section 1245 property other than potential section 1245 income) is not within section 751(b). Under section 732(b) and (c), C's basis for his share of potential section 1245 income is zero (see paragraph (c)(5) of this section) and his basis for $9,000 of section 1245 property (other than potential section 1245 income) is $7,333, i.e., the amount of the remaining basis for his partnership interest ($7,333) reduced by the basis for his share of potential section 1245 income (zero). Thus C's total aggregate basis for the section 1245 property (fair market value of $15,000) distributed to him is $11,333 ($4,000 plus $7,333). For an illustration of the computation of his recomputed basis for the section 1245 property immediately after the distribution, see example (2) of paragraph (f)(3) of § 1.1245–4.

(e) Partnership's tax consequences. The tax consequences to the partnership on the distribution are as follows:

(1) The section 751(b) sale or exchange. Upon the sale of $4,000 potential section 1245 income, with a basis of zero, for $\frac{4}{9}$ths of C's interest in the land, the partnership consisting of the remaining members has $4,000 ordinary income under sections 751(b) and 1245(a)(1). See section 1245(b)(3) and (6)(A). The partnership's new basis for the land is $19,333, i.e., $18,000, less the basis of the $\frac{4}{9}$ths share considered as distributed to C ($2,667), plus the partnership purchase price for this share ($4,000).

(2) The part of the distribution not under section 751(b). The analysis under this subparagraph should be made in accordance with the principles illustrated in paragraph (e)(2) of examples (3), (4), and (5) of this paragraph.

[T.D. 6500, 25 FR 11814, Nov. 26, 1960, as amended by T.D. 6832, 30 FR 8575, July 7, 1965; T.D. 7084, 36 FR 268, Jan. 8, 1971; T.D. 8586, 60 FR 2497, Jan. 10, 1995; T.D. 8847, 64 FR 69903, Dec. 15, 1999; T.D. 9137, 69 FR 42559, July 16, 2004]

§ 1.752–1 Treatment of partnership liabilities.

(a) Definitions. For purposes of section 752, the following definitions apply:

(1) Recourse liability defined. A partnership liability is a recourse liability to the extent that any partner or related person bears the economic risk of loss for that liability under § 1.752–2.

(2) Nonrecourse liability defined. A partnership liability is a nonrecourse liability to the extent that no partner or related person bears the economic risk of loss for that liability under § 1.752–2.

(3) Related person. Related person means a person having a relationship to a partner that is described in § 1.752–4(b).

(4) Liability defined—(i) In general. An obligation is a liability for purposes of section 752 and the regulations thereunder (§ 1.752–1 liability), only if, when, and to the extent that incurring the obligation—

(A) Creates or increases the basis of any of the obligor's assets (including cash);

(B) Gives rise to an immediate deduction to the obligor; or

(C) Gives rise to an expense that is not deductible in computing the obligor's taxable income and is not properly chargeable to capital.

(ii) Obligation. For purposes of this paragraph and § 1.752–7, an obligation is any fixed or contingent obligation to make payment without regard to whether the obligation is otherwise taken into account for purposes of the Internal Revenue Code. Obligations include, but are not limited to, debt obligations, environmental obligations, tort obligations, contract obligations, pension obligations, obligations under a short sale, and obligations under derivative financial instruments such as options, forward contracts, futures contracts, and swaps.

(iii) Other liabilities. For obligations that are not § 1.752–1 liabilities, see §§ 1.752–6 and 1.752–7.

* * *

(b) Increase in partner's share of liabilities. Any increase in a partner's share of partnership liabilities, or any increase in a partner's individual liabilities by reason of the partner's assumption of partnership liabilities, is treated as a contribution of money by that partner to the partnership.

(c) Decrease in partner's share of liabilities. Any decrease in a partner's share of partnership liabilities, or any decrease in a partner's individual liabilities by reason of the partnership's assumption of the individual liabilities of the partner, is treated as a distribution of money by the partnership to that partner.

(d) Assumption of liability. Except as otherwise provided in paragraph (e) of this section, a person is considered to assume a liability only to the extent that:

(1) The assuming person is personally obligated to pay the liability; and

(2) If a partner or related person assumes a partnership liability, the person to whom the liability is owed knows of the assumption and can directly enforce the partner's or related person's obligation for the liability, and no other partner or person that is a related person to another partner would bear the economic risk of loss for the liability immediately after the assumption.

(e) Property subject to a liability. If property is contributed by a partner to the partnership or distributed by the partnership to a partner and the property is subject to a liability of the transferor, the transferee is treated as having assumed the liability, to the extent that the amount of the liability does not exceed the fair market value of the property at the time of the contribution or distribution.

(f) Netting of increases and decreases in liabilities resulting from same transaction. If, as a result of a single transaction, a partner incurs both an increase in the partner's share of the partnership liabilities (or the partner's individual liabilities) and a decrease in the partner's share of the partnership liabilities (or the partner's individual liabilities), only the net decrease is treated as a distribution from the partnership and only the net increase is treated as a contribution of money to the partnership. Generally, the contribution to or distribution from the partnership of property subject to a liability or the termination of the partnership under section 708(b) will require that increases and decreases in liabilities associated with the transaction be netted to determine if a partner will be deemed to have made a contribution or received a distribution as a result of the transaction. When two or more partnerships merge or consolidate under section 708(b)(2)(A), as described in § 1.708–1(c)(3)(i), increases and decreases in partnership liabilities associated with the merger or consolidation are netted by the partners in the terminating partnership and the resulting partnership to determine the effect of the merger under section 752.

(g) Example. The following example illustrates the principles of paragraphs (b), (c), (e), and (f) of this section.

Example 1. Property contributed subject to a liability; netting of increase and decrease in partner's share of liability. B contributes property with an adjusted basis of $1,000 to a general partnership in exchange for a one-third interest in the partnership. At the time of the contribution, the partnership does not have any liabilities outstanding and the property is subject to a recourse debt of $150 and has a fair market value in excess of $150. After the contribution, B remains personally liable to the creditor and none of the other partners bears any of the economic risk of loss for the liability under state law or otherwise. Under paragraph (e) of this section, the partnership is treated as having assumed the $150 liability. As a result, B's individual liabilities decrease by $150. At the same time, however, B's share of liabilities of the partnership increases by $150. Only the net increase or decrease in B's share of the liabilities of the partnership and B's individual liabilities is taken into account in applying section 752. Because there is no net change, B is not treated as having contributed money to the partnership or as having received a distribution of money from the partnership under paragraph (b) or (c) of this section. Therefore B's basis for B's partnership interest is $1,000 (B's basis for the contributed property).

Example 2. Merger or consolidation of partnerships holding property encumbered by liabilities. (i) B owns a 70 percent interest in partnership T. Partnership T's sole asset is property X, which is encumbered by a $900 liability. Partnership T's adjusted basis in property X is $600, and the value of property X is $1,000. B's adjusted basis in its partnership T interest is $420. B also owns a 20 percent interest in partnership S. Partnership S's sole asset is property Y, which is encumbered by a $100 liability. Partnership S's adjusted basis in property Y is $200, the value of property Y is $1,000, and B's adjusted basis in its partnership S interest is $40.

(ii) Partnership T and partnership S merge under section 708(b)(2)(A). Under section 708(b)(2)(A) and § 1.708–1(c)(1), partnership T is considered terminated and the resulting partnership is considered a continuation of partnership S. Partnerships T and S undertake the form described in § 1.708–1(c)(3)(i) for the partnership merger. Under § 1.708–1(c)(3)(i), partnership T contributes property X and its $900 liability to partnership S in exchange for an interest in partnership S. Immediately thereafter, partnership T distributes the interests in partnership S to its partners in liquidation of their interests in partnership T. B owns a 25 percent interest in partnership S after partnership T distributes the interests in partnership S to B.

(iii) Under paragraph (f) of this section, B nets the increases and decreases in its share of partnership liabilities associated with the merger of partnership T and partnership S. Before the merger, B's share of partnership liabilities was $650 (B had a $630 share of partnership liabilities in partnership T and a $20 share of partnership liabilities in partnership S immediately before the merger). B's share of S's partnership liabilities after the merger is $250 (25 percent of S's total partnership liabilities of $1,000). Accordingly, B has a $400 distribution from partnership S under section 752(b). Because B's adjusted basis in its partnership S interest before the deemed distribution under section 752(b) is $460 ($420 + $40), B will not recognize gain under section 731. After the merger, B's adjusted basis in its partnership S interest is $60.

(h) Sale or exchange of a partnership interest. If a partnership interest is sold or exchanged, the reduction in the transferor partner's share of partnership liabilities is treated as an amount realized under section 1001 and the regulations thereunder. For example, if a partner sells an interest in a partnership for $750 cash and transfers to the purchaser the partner's share of partnership liabilities in the amount of $250, the seller realizes $1,000 on the transaction.

(i) Bifurcation of partnership liabilities. If one or more partners bears the economic risk of loss as to part, but not all, of a partnership liability represented by a single contractual obligation, that liability is treated as two or more separate liabilities for purposes of section 752. The portion of the liability as to which one or more partners bears the economic risk of loss is a recourse liability and the remainder of the liability, if any, is a nonrecourse liability.

[T.D. 8380, 56 FR 66351, Dec. 23, 1991; as amended by T.D. 8925, 66 FR 715, Jan. 4, 2001; T.D. 9207, 70 FR 30334, May 23, 2005]

§ 1.752–2 Partner's share of recourse liabilities.

(a) In general. A partner's share of a recourse partnership liability equals the portion of that liability, if any, for which the partner or related person bears the economic risk of loss. The determination of the extent to which a partner bears the economic risk of loss for a partnership liability is made under the rules in paragraphs (b) through (k) of this section.

(b) Obligation to make a payment. (1) In general. Except as otherwise provided in this section, a partner bears the economic risk of loss for a partnership liability to the extent that, if the partnership constructively liquidated, the partner or related person would be obligated to make a payment to any person (or a contribution to the partnership) because that liability becomes due and payable and the partner or related person would not be entitled to reimbursement from another partner or person that is a related person to another partner. Upon a constructive liquidation, all of the following events are deemed to occur simultaneously:

(i) All of the partnership's liabilities become payable in full;

(ii) With the exception of property contributed to secure a partnership liability (see § 1.752–2(h)(2)), all of the partnership's assets, including cash, have a value of zero;

(iii) The partnership disposes of all of its property in a fully taxable transaction for no consideration (except relief from liabilities for which the creditors's right to repayment is limited solely to one or more assets of the partnership);

(iv) All items of income, gain, loss, or deduction are allocated among the partners; and

(v) The partnership liquidates.

(2) Treatment upon deemed disposition. For purposes of paragraph (b)(1) of this section, gain or loss on the deemed disposition of the partnership's assets is computed in accordance with the following:

(i) If the creditor's right to repayment of a partnership liability is limited solely to one or more assets of the partnership, gain or loss is recognized in an amount equal to the difference between the amount of the liability that is extinguished by the deemed disposition and the tax basis (or book value to the extent section 704(c) or § 1.704–1(b)(4)(i) applies) in those assets.

(ii) A loss is recognized equal to the remaining tax basis (or book value to the extent section 704(c) or § 1.704–1(b)(4)(i) applies) of all the partnership's assets not taken into account in paragraph (b)(2)(i) of this section.

(3) Obligations recognized. The determination of the extent to which a partner or related person has an obligation to make a payment under paragraph (b)(1) of this section is based on the facts and circumstances at the time of the determination. All statutory and contractual obligations relating to the partnership liability are taken into account for purposes of applying this section, including:

(i) Contractual obligations outside the partnership agreement such as guarantees, indemnifications, reimbursement agreements, and other obligations running directly to creditors or to other partners, or to the partnership;

(ii) Obligations to the partnership that are imposed by the partnership agreement, including the obligation to make a capital contribution and to restore a deficit capital account upon liquidation of the partnership; and

(iii) Payment obligations (whether in the form of direct remittances to another partner or a contribution to the partnership) imposed by state law, including the governing state partnership statute.

To the extent that the obligation of a partner to make a payment with respect to a partnership liability is not recognized under this paragraph (b)(3), paragraph (b) of this section is applied as if the obligation did not exist.

(4) Contingent obligations. A payment obligation is disregarded if, taking into account all the facts and circumstances, the obligation is subject to contingencies that make it unlikely that the obligation will ever be discharged. If a payment obligation would arise at a future time after the occurrence of an event that is not determinable with reasonable certainty, the obligation is ignored until the event occurs.

(5) Reimbursement rights. A partner's or related person's obligation to make a payment with respect to a partnership liability is reduced to the extent that the partner or related person is entitled to reimbursement from another partner or a person who is a related person to another partner.

(6) Deemed satisfaction of obligation. For purposes of determining the extent to which a partner or related person has a payment obligation and the economic risk of loss, it is assumed that all partners and related persons who have obligations to make payments actually perform those obligations, irrespective of their actual net worth, unless the facts and circumstances indicate a plan to circumvent or avoid the obligation. See paragraphs (j) and (k) of this section.

(c) Partner or related person as lender—(1) In general. A partner bears the economic risk of loss for a partnership liability to the extent that the partner or a related person makes (or acquires an interest in) a nonrecourse loan to the partnership and the economic risk of loss for the liability is not borne by another partner.

(2) Wrapped debt. If a partnership liability is owed to a partner or related person and that liability includes (i.e., is "wrapped" around) a nonrecourse obligation encumbering partnership property that is owed to another person, the partnership liability will be treated as two separate liabilities. The portion of the partnership liability corresponding to the wrapped debt is treated as a liability owed to another person.

(d) De minimis exceptions—(1) Partner as lender. The general rule contained in paragraph (c)(1) of this section does not apply if a partner or related person whose interest (directly or indirectly through one or more partnerships including the interest of any related person) in each item of partnership income, gain, loss, deduction, or credit for every taxable year that the partner is a partner in the partnership is 10 percent or less, makes a loan to the partnership which constitutes qualified nonrecourse financing within the meaning of section 465(b)(6) (determined without regard to the type of activity financed).

(2) Partner as guarantor. The general rule contained in paragraph (b)(1) of this section does not apply if a partner or related person whose interest (directly or indirectly through one or more partnerships including the interest of any related person) in each item of partnership income, gain, loss, deduction, or credit for every taxable year that the partner is a partner in the partnership is 10 percent or less, guarantees a loan that would otherwise be a nonrecourse loan of the partnership and which would constitute qualified nonrecourse financing within the meaning of section 465(b)(6) (without regard to the type of activity financed) if the guarantor had made the loan to the partnership.

(e) Special rule for nonrecourse liability with interest guaranteed by a partner—(1) In general. For purposes of this section, if one or more partners or related persons have guaranteed the payment of more than 25 percent of the total interest that will accrue on a partnership nonrecourse liability over its remaining term, and it is reasonable to expect that the guarantor will be required to pay substantially all of the guaranteed future interest if the partnership fails to do so, then the liability is treated as two separate partnership liabilities. If this rule applies, the partner or related person that has guaranteed the payment of interest is treated as bearing the economic risk of loss for the partnership liability to the extent of the present value of the guaranteed future interest payments. The remainder of the stated principal amount of the partnership liability constitutes a nonrecourse liability. Generally, in applying this rule, it is reasonable to expect that the guarantor will be required to pay substantially all of the guaranteed future interest if, upon a default in payment by the partnership, the lender can enforce the interest guaranty without foreclosing on the property and thereby extinguishing the underlying debt. The guarantee of interest rule continues to apply even after the point at which the amount of guaranteed interest that will accrue is less than 25 percent of the total interest that will accrue on the liability.

(2) Computation of present value. The present value of the guaranteed future interest payments is computed using a discount rate equal to either the interest rate stated in the loan documents, or if interest is imputed under either section

483 or section 1274, the applicable federal rate, compounded semi-annually. The computation takes into account any payment of interest that the partner or related person may be required to make only to the extent that the interest will accrue economically (determined in accordance with section 446 and the regulations thereunder) after the date of the interest guarantee. If the loan document contains a variable rate of interest that is an interest rate based on current values of an objective interest index, the present value is computed on the assumption that the interest determined under the objective interest index on the date of the computation will remain constant over the term of the loan. The term "objective interest index" has the meaning given to it in section 1275 and the regulations thereunder (relating to variable rate debt instruments). Examples of an objective interest index include the prime rate of a designated financial institution, LIBOR (London Interbank Offered Rate), and the applicable federal rate under section 1274(d).

(3) Safe harbor. The general rule contained in paragraph (e)(1) of this section does not apply to a partnership nonrecourse liability if the guarantee of interest by the partner or related person is for a period not in excess of the lesser of five years or one-third of the term of the liability.

(4) De minimis exception. The general rule contained in paragraph (e)(1) of this section does not apply if a partner or related person whose interest (directly or indirectly through one or more partnerships including the interest of any related person) in each item of partnership income, gain, loss, deduction, or credit for every taxable year that the partner is a partner in the partnership is 10 percent of less, guarantees the interest on a loan to that partnership which constitutes qualified nonrecourse financing within the meaning of section 465(b)(6) (determined without regard to the type of activity financed). An allocation of interest to the extent paid by the guarantor is not treated as a partnership item of deduction or loss subject to the 10 percent or less rule.

(f) Examples. The following examples illustrate the principles of paragraphs (a) through (e) of this section.

Example 1. Determining when a partner bears the economic risk of loss. A and B form a general partnership with each contributing $100 in cash. The partnership purchases an office building on leased land for $1,000 from an unrelated seller, paying $200 in cash and executing a note to the seller for the balance of $800. The note is a general obligation of the partnership, i.e., no partner has been relieved from personal liability. The partnership agreement provides that all items are allocated equally except that tax losses are specially allocated 90% to A and 10% to B and that capital accounts will be maintained in accordance with the regulations under section 704(b), including a deficit capital account restoration obligation on liquidation. In a constructive liquidation, the $800 liability becomes due and payable. All of the partnership's assets, including the building, are deemed to be worthless. The building is deemed sold for a value of zero. Capital accounts are adjusted to reflect the loss on the hypothetical disposition, as follows:

	A	B
Initial contribution	$100	$100
Loss on hypothetical sale	(900)	(100)
	($800)	$ 0

Other than the partners' obligation to fund negative capital accounts on liquidation, there are no other contractual or statutory payment obligations existing between the partners, the partnership and the lender. Therefore, $800 of the partnership liability is classified as a recourse liability because one or more partners bears the economic risk of loss for non-payment. B has no share of the $800 liability since the constructive liquidation produces no payment obligation for B. A's share of the partnership liability is $800 because A would have an obligation in that amount to make a contribution to the partnership.

Example 2. Recourse liability; deficit restoration obligation. C and D each contribute $500 in cash to the capital of a new general partnership, CD. CD purchases property from an unrelated seller for $1,000 in cash and a $9,000 mortgage note. The note is a general obligation of the partnership, i.e., no partner has been relieved from personal liability. The partnership agreement provides that profits and losses are to be divided 40% to C and 60% to D. C and D are required to make up any deficit in their capital accounts. In a constructive liquidation, all partnership assets are deemed to become worthless and all partnership liabilities become due and payable in full. The partnership is deemed to dispose of all its assets in a fully taxable transaction for no consideration. Capital accounts are adjusted to reflect the loss on the hypothetical disposition, as follows:

	C	D
Initial contribution	$ 500	$ 500
Loss on hypothetical sale	(4,000)	(6,000)
	($3,500)	($5,500)

C's capital account reflects a deficit that C would have to make up to $3,500 and D's capital account reflects a deficit that D would have to make up of $5,500. Therefore, the $9,000 mortgage note is a recourse liability because one or more partners bear the economic risk of loss for the liability. C's share of the recourse liability is $3,500 and D's share is $5,500.

Example 3. Guarantee by limited partner; partner deemed to satisfy obligation. E and F form a limited partnership. E, the general partner, contributes $2,000 and F, the limited partner, contributes $8,000 in cash to the partnership. The partnership agreement allocates losses 20% to E and 80% to F until F's capital account is reduced to zero, after which all losses are allocated to E. The partnership purchases depreciable property for $25,000 using its $10,000 cash and a $15,000 recourse loan from a bank. F guarantees payment of the $15,000 loan to the extent the loan remains unpaid after the bank has exhausted its remedies against the partnership. In a constructive liquidation, the $15,000 liability becomes due and payable. All of the partnership's assets, including the depreciable property, are deemed to be worthless. The depreciable property is deemed sold for a value of zero. Capital accounts are adjusted to reflect the loss on the hypothetical disposition, as follows:

	E	F
Initial contribution	$ 2,000	$8,000
Loss on hypothetical sale	(17,000)	(8,000)
	($15,000)	$ 0

E, as a general partner, would be obligated by operation of law to make a net contribution to the partnership of $15,000. Because E is assumed to satisfy that obligation, it is also assumed that F would not have to satisfy F's guarantee. The $15,000 mortgage is treated as a recourse liability because one or more partners bear the economic risk of loss. E's share of the liability if $15,000, and F's share is zero. This would be so even if E's net worth at the time of the determination is less than $15,000, unless the facts and circumstances indicate a plan to circumvent or avoid E's obligation to contribute to the partnership.

Example 4. Partner guarantee with right of subrogation. G, a limited partner in the GH partnership, guarantees a portion of a partnership liability. The liability is a general obligation of the partnership, i.e., no partner has been relieved from personal liability. If under state law G is subrogated to the rights of the lender, G would have the right to recover the amount G paid to the recourse lender from the general partner. Therefore, G does not bear the economic risk of loss for the partnership liability.

Example 5. Bifurcation of partnership liability; guarantee of part of nonrecourse liability. A partnership borrows $10,000, secured by a mortgage on real property. The mortgage note contains an exoneration clause which provides that in the event of default, the holder's only remedy is to foreclose on the property. The holder may not look to any other partnership asset or to any partner to pay the liability. However, to induce the lender to make the loan, a partner guarantees payment of $200 of the loan principal. The exoneration clause does not apply to the partner's guarantee. If the partner paid pursuant to the guarantee, the partner would be subrogated to the rights of the lender with respect to $200 of the mortgage debt, but the partner is not otherwise entitled to reimbursement from the partnership or any partner. For purposes of section 752, $200 of the $10,000 mortgage liability is treated as a recourse liability of the partnership and $9,800 is treated as a nonrecourse liability of the partnership. The partner's share of the recourse liability of the partnership is $200.

* * *

(g) Time-value-of-money considerations—(1) In general. The extent to which a partner or related person bears the economic risk of loss is determined by taking into account any delay in the time when a payment or contribution obligation with respect to a partnership liability is to be satisfied. If a payment obligation with respect to a partnership liability is not required to be satisfied within a reasonable time after the liability becomes due and payable, or if the obligation to make a contribution to the partnership is not required to be satisfied before the later of—

(i) The end of the year in which the partner's interest is liquidated, or

(ii) 90 days after the liquidation, the obligation is recognized only to the extent of the value of the obligation.

(2) Valuation of an obligation. The value of a payment or contribution obligation that is not required to be satisfied within the time period specified in paragraph (g)(1) of this section equals the entire principal balance of the obligation only if the obligation bears interest equal to or greater than the applicable federal rate under section 1274(d) at the time of valuation, commencing on—

(i) In the case of a payment obligation, the date that the partnership liability to a creditor or other person to whom the obligation relates becomes due and payable, or

(ii) In the case of a contribution obligation, the date of the liquidation of the partner's interest in the partnership.

If the obligation does not bear interest at a rate at least equal to the applicable federal rate at the time of valuation, the value of the obligation is discounted to the present value of all payments due from the partner or related person (i.e., the imputed principal amount computed under section 1274(b)). For purposes of making this present value determination, the partnership is deemed to have constructively liquidated as of the date on which the payment obligation is valued and the payment obligation is assumed to be a debt instrument subject to the rules of section 1274 (i.e., the debt instrument is treated as if it were issued for property at the time of the valuation).

(3) Satisfaction of obligation with partner's promissory note. An obligation is not satisfied by the transfer to the obligee of a promissory note by a partner or related person unless the note is readily tradeable on an established securities market.

(4) Example. The following example illustrates the principle of paragraph (g) of this section.

Example. Value of obligation not required to be satisfied within specified time period. A, the general partner, and B, the limited partner, each contributes $10,000 to partnership AB. AB purchases property from an unrelated seller for $20,000 in cash and a $70,000 recourse purchase money note. The partnership agreement provides that profits and losses are to be divided equally. A and B are required to make up any deficit in their capital accounts. While A is required to restore any deficit balance in A's capital account within 90 days after the date of liquidation of the partnership, B is not required to restore any deficit for two years following the date of liquidation. The deficit in B's capital account will not bear interest during that two-year period. In a constructive liquidation, all partnership assets are deemed to become worthless and all partnership liabilities become due and payable in full. The partnership is deemed to dispose of all its assets in a fully taxable transaction for no consideration. Capital accounts are adjusted to reflect the loss on the hypothetical disposition, as follows:

	A	B
Initial contribution	$10,000	$10,000
Loss on hypothetical sale	(45,000)	(45,000)
	(35,000)	(35,000)

A's and B's capital accounts each reflect deficits of $35,000. B's obligation to make a contribution pursuant to B's deficit restoration obligation is recognized only to the extent of the fair market value of that obligation at the time of the constructive liquidation because B is not required to satisfy that obligation by the later of the end of the partnership taxable year in which B's interest is liquidated or within 90 days after the date of the liquidation. Because B's obligation does not bear interest, the fair market value is deemed to equal the imputed principal amount under section 1274(b). Under section 1274(b), the imputed principal amount of a debt instrument equals the present value of all payments due under the debt instrument. Assume the applicable federal rate with respect to B's obligation is 10 percent compounded semiannually. Using this discount rate, the present value of the $35,000 payment that B would be required to make two years after the constructive liquidation to restore the deficit balance in B's capital account equals $28,795. To the extent that B's deficit restoration obligation is not recognized, it is assumed that B's obligation does not exist. Therefore, A, as the sole general partner, would be obligated by operation of law to contribute an additional $6,205 of capital to the partnership. Accordingly, under paragraph (g) of this section, B bears the economic risk of loss for $28,795 and A bears the economic risk of loss for $41,205 ($35,000 + $6,205).

(h) Partner providing property as security for partnership liability—(1) Direct pledge. A partner is considered to bear the economic risk of loss for a partnership liability to the extent of the value of any the partner's or related person's separate property (other than a direct or indirect interest in the partnership) that is pledged as security for the partnership liability.

(2) Indirect pledge. A partner is considered to bear the economic risk of loss for a partnership liability to the extent of the value of any property that the partner contributes to the partnership solely for the purpose of securing a partnership liability. Contributed property is not treated as contributed solely for the purpose of securing a partnership liability unless substantially all of the items of income, gain, loss, and deduction attributable to the contributed property are allocated to the contributing partner, and this allocation is generally greater than the partner's share of other significant items of partnership income, gain, loss, or deduction.

(3) Valuation. The extent to which a partner bears the economic risk of loss for a partnership liability as a result of a direct pledge described in paragraph (h)(1) of this section or an indirect pledge described in paragraph (h)(2) of this section is limited to the net fair market value of the property (pledged property) at the time of the pledge or contribution. If a partner provides additional pledged property, the addition is treated as a new pledge and the net fair market value of the pledged property (including but not limited to the additional property) must be determined at that time. For purposes of this paragraph (h), if pledged property is subject to one or more other obligations, those obligations must be taken into account in determining the net fair market value of pledged property at the time of the pledge or contribution.

(4) Partner's promissory note. For purposes of paragraph (h)(2) of this section, a promissory note of the partner or related person that is contributed to the partnership shall not be taken into account unless the note is readily tradeable on an established securities market.

(i) Treatment of recourse liabilities in tiered partnerships. If a partnership (the "upper-tier partnership") owns (directly or indirectly through one or more partnerships) an interest in another partnership (the "lower-tier partnership"), the liabilities of the lower-tier partnership are allocated to the upper-tier partnership in an amount equal to the sum of the following—

(1) The amount of the economic risk of loss that the upper-tier partnership bears with respect to the liabilities; and

(2) Any other amount of the liabilities with respect to which partners of the upper-tier partnership bear the economic risk of loss.

(j) Anti-abuse rules—(1) In general. An obligation of a partner or related person to make a payment may be disregarded or treated as an obligation of another person for purposes of this section if facts and circumstances indicate that a principal purpose of the arrangement between the parties is to eliminate the partner's economic risk of loss with respect to that obligation or create the appearance of the partner or related person bearing the economic risk of loss when, in fact, the substance of the arrangement is otherwise. Circumstances with respect to which a payment obligation may be disregarded include, but are not limited to, the situations described in paragraphs (j)(2) and (j)(3) of this section.

(2) Arrangements tantamount to a guarantee. Irrespective of the form of a contractual obligation, a partner is considered to bear the economic risk of loss with respect to a partnership liability, or a portion thereof, to the extent that:

(i) The partner or related person undertakes one or more contractual obligations so that the partnership may obtain a loan;

(ii) The contractual obligations of the partner or related person eliminate substantially all the risk to the lender that the partnership will not satisfy its obligations under the loan; and

(iii) One of the principal purposes of using the contractual obligations is to attempt to permit partners (other than those who are directly or indirectly liable for the obligation) to include a portion of the loan in the basis of their partnership interests.

The partners are considered to bear the economic risk of loss for the liability in accordance with their relative economic burdens for the liability pursuant to the contractual obligations. For example, a lease between a partner and a partnership which is not on commercially reasonable terms may be tantamount to a guarantee by the partner of a partnership liability.

(3) Plan to circumvent or avoid the obligation. An obligation of a partner to make a payment is not recognized if the facts and circumstances evidence a plan to circumvent or avoid the obligation.

(4) Example. The following example illustrates the principle of paragraph (j)(3) of this section.

Example. Plan to circumvent or avoid obligation. A and B form a general partnership. A, a corporation, contributes $20,000 and B contributes $80,000 to the partnership. A is obligated to restore any deficit in its partnership capital account. The partnership agreement allocates losses 20% to A and 80% to B until B's capital account is reduced to zero, after which all losses are allocated to A. The partnership purchases depreciable property for $250,000 using its $100,000 cash and a $150,000 recourse loan from a bank. B guarantees payment of the $150,000 loan to the extent the loan remains unpaid after the bank has exhausted its remedies against the partnership. A is a subsidiary, formed by a parent of a consolidated group, with capital limited to $20,000 to allow the consolidated group to enjoy the tax losses generated by the property while at the same time limiting its monetary exposure for such losses. These facts, when considered together with B's guarantee, indicate a plan to circumvent or avoid A's obligation to contribute to the partnership. The rules of section 752 must be applied as if A's obligation to contribute did not exist. Accordingly, the $150,000 liability is a recourse liability that is allocated entirely to B.

(k) Effect of a disregarded entity—(1) In general. In determining the extent to which a partner bears the economic risk of loss for a partnership liability, an obligation under paragraph (b)(1) of this section (§ 1.752–2(b)(1) payment obligation) of a business entity that is disregarded as an entity separate from its owner under sections 856(i) or 1361(b)(3) or §§ 301.7701–1 through 301.7701–3 of this chapter (disregarded entity) is taken into account only to the extent of the net value of the disregarded entity as of the allocation date (as defined in paragraph (k)(2)(iv) of this section) that is allocated to the partnership liability as determined under the rules of this paragraph (k). The rules of this paragraph (k) do not apply to a § 1.752–2(b)(1) payment obligation of a disregarded entity to the extent that the owner of the disregarded entity is otherwise required to make a payment (that satisfies the requirements of paragraph (b)(1) of this section) with respect to the obligation of the disregarded entity.

(2) Net value of a disregarded entity—(i) Definition. For purposes of this paragraph (k), the net value of a disregarded entity equals the following—

(A) The fair market value of all assets owned by the disregarded entity that may be subject to creditors' claims under local law (including the disregarded entity's enforceable rights to contributions from its owner and the fair market value of an interest in any partnership other than the partnership for which net value is being determined, but excluding the disregarded entity's interest in the partnership for which the net value is being determined and the net fair market value of property pledged to secure a liability of the partnership under paragraph (h)(1) of this section); less

(B) All obligations of the disregarded entity that do not constitute § 1.752–2(b)(1) payment obligations of the disregarded entity.

* * *

(6) Examples. The following examples illustrate the rules of this paragraph (k):

Example 1. Disregarded entity with net value of zero. (i) In 2007, A forms a wholly owned domestic limited liability company, LLC, with a contribution of $100,000. A has no liability for LLC's debts, and LLC has no enforceable right to contribution from A. Under § 301.7701–3(b)(1)(ii) of this chapter, LLC is a disregarded entity. Also in 2007, LLC contributes $100,000 to LP, a limited partnership with a calendar year taxable year, in exchange for a general partnership interest in LP, and B and C each contributes $100,000 to LP in exchange for a limited partnership interest in LP. The partnership agreement provides that only LLC is required to make up any deficit in its capital account. On January 1, 2008, LP borrows $300,000 from a bank and uses $600,000 to purchase nondepreciable property. The $300,000 debt is secured by the property and is also a general obligation of LP. LP makes payments of only interest on its $300,000 debt during 2008. LP has a net taxable loss in 2008, and under §§ 1.705–1(a) and 1.752–4(d), LP determines its partners' shares of the $300,000 debt at the end of its taxable year, December 31, 2008. As of that date, LLC holds no assets other than its interest in LP.

(ii) Because LLC is a disregarded entity, A is treated as the partner in LP for Federal tax purposes. Only LLC has an obligation to make a payment on account of the $300,000 debt if LP were to constructively liquidate as described in paragraph (b)(1) of this section. Therefore, under this paragraph (k), A is treated as bearing the economic risk of loss for LP's $300,000 debt only to the extent of LLC's net value. Because that net value is $0 on December 31, 2008, when LP determines its partners' shares of its $300,000 debt, A is not treated as bearing the economic risk of loss for any portion of LP's $300,000 debt. As a result, LP's $300,000 debt is characterized as nonrecourse under § 1.752–1(a) and is allocated as required by § 1.752–3.

Example 2. Disregarded entity with positive net value. (i) The facts are the same as in Example 1 except that on January 1, 2009, A contributes $250,000 to LLC. On January 5, 2009, LLC borrows $100,000 and LLC shortly thereafter uses the $350,000 to purchase unimproved land. LP makes payments of only interest on its $300,000 debt during 2009. As of December 31, 2009, LLC holds its interest in LP and the land, the value of which has declined to $275,000. LP has a net taxable loss in 2009, and under §§ 1.705–1(a) and 1.752–4(d), LP determines its partners' shares of the $300,000 debt at the end of its taxable year, December 31, 2009.

(ii) A's contribution of $250,000 to LLC on January 1, 2009, constitutes a more than de minimis contribution of property to LLC under paragraph (k)(2)(iii)(A) of this section and the debt incurred by LLC on January 5, 2009, is a valuation event under paragraph (k)(2)(iii)(D) of this section. Accordingly, under paragraph (k)(2)(ii) of this section, LLC's value must be redetermined as of the end of the partnership's taxable year. At that time LLC's net value is $175,000 ($275,000 land—$100,000 debt). Accordingly, $175,000 of LP's $300,000 debt will be recharacterized as recourse under § 1.752–1(a) and allocated to A under this section, and the remaining $125,000 of LP's $300,000 debt will remain characterized as nonrecourse under § 1.752–1(a) and is allocated as required by § 1.752–3.

* * *

[T.D. 8380, 56 FR 66351, Dec. 23, 1991; T.D. 9289, 71 FR 59669, Oct. 11, 2006]

§ 1.752–3 Partner's share of nonrecourse liabilities.

(a) In general. A partner's share of the nonrecourse liabilities of a partnership equals the sum of paragraphs (a)(1) through (a)(3) of this section as follows—

(1) The partner's share of partnership minimum gain determined in accordance with the rules of section 704(b) and the regulations thereunder;

(2) The amount of any taxable gain that would be allocated to the partner under section 704(c) (or in the same manner as section 704(c) in connection with a revaluation of partnership property) if the partnership disposed of (in a taxable transaction) all partnership property subject to one or more nonrecourse liabilities of the partnership in full satisfaction of the liabilities and for no other consideration; and

(3) The partner's share of the excess nonrecourse liabilities (those not allocated under paragraphs (a)(1) and (a)(2) of this section) of the partnership as determined in accordance with the partner's share of partnership profits. The partner's interest in partnership profits is determined by taking into account all facts and circumstances relating to the economic arrangement of the partners. The partnership agreement may specify the partners' interests in partnership profits for purposes of allocating excess nonrecourse liabilities provided the interests so specified are reasonably consistent with allocations (that have substantial economic effect under the section 704(b) regulations) of some other significant item of partnership income or gain. Alternatively, excess nonrecourse liabilities may be allocated among the partners in accordance with the manner in which it is reasonably expected that the deductions attributable to those nonrecourse liabilities will be allocated. Additionally, the partnership may first allocate an excess nonrecourse liability to a partner up to the amount of built-in gain that is allocable to the partner on section 704(c) property (as defined under § 1.704–3(a)(3)(ii)) or property for which reverse section 704(c) allocations are applicable (as described in § 1.704–3(a)(6)(i)) where such property is subject to the nonrecourse liability to the extent that such built-in gain exceeds the gain described in paragraph (a)(2) of this section with respect to such property. This additional method does not apply for purposes of § 1.707–5(a)(2)(ii). To the extent that a partnership uses this additional method and the entire amount of the excess nonrecourse liability is not allocated to the contributing partner, the partnership must allocate the remaining amount of the excess nonrecourse liability under one of the other methods in this paragraph (a)(3). Excess nonrecourse liabilities are not required to be allocated under the same method each year.

(b) Allocation of a single nonrecourse liability among multiple properties—(1) In general. For purposes of determining the amount of taxable gain under paragraph (a)(2) of this section, if a partnership holds multiple properties subject to a single nonrecourse liability, the partnership may allocate the liability among the multiple properties under any reasonable method. A method is not reasonable if it allocates to any item of property an amount of the liability that, when combined with any other liabilities allocated to the property, is in excess of the fair market value of the property at the time the liability is incurred. The portion of the nonrecourse liability allocated to each item of partnership property is then treated as a separate loan under paragraph (a)(2) of this section. In general, a partnership may not change the method of allocating a single nonrecourse liability under this paragraph (b) while any portion of the liability is outstanding. However, if one or more of the multiple properties subject to the liability is no longer subject to the liability, the portion of the liability allocated to that property must be reallocated among the properties still subject to the liability so that the amount of the liability allocated to any property does not exceed the fair market value of such property at the end of allocation.

(2) Reductions in principal. For purposes of this paragraph (b), when the outstanding principal of a partnership liability is reduced, the reduction of outstanding principal is allocated among the multiple properties in the same proportion that the partnership liability originally was allocated to the properties under paragraph (b)(1) of this section.

(c) Examples. The following examples illustrate the principles of paragraph (a) of this section.

Example 1. Partner's share of nonrecourse liabilities. The AB partnership purchases depreciable property for a $1,000 purchase money note that is nonrecourse liability under the rules of this section. Assume that this is the only nonrecourse liability of the partnership, and that no principal payments are due on the purchase money note for a year. The partnership agreement provides that all items of income, gain, loss, and deduction are allocated equally. Immediately after purchasing the depreciable property, the partners share the nonrecourse liability equally because they have equal interests in partnership profits. A and B are each treated as if they contributed $500 to the partnership to reflect each partner's increase in his or her share of partnership liabilities (from $0 to $500). The minimum gain with respect to an item of partnership property subject to a nonrecourse liability equals the amount of gain that would be recognized if the partnership disposed of the property in full satisfaction of the nonrecourse liability and for no other consideration. Therefore, if the partnership claims a depreciation deduction of $200 for the depreciable property for the year it acquires that property, partnership minimum gain for the year will increase by $200 (the excess of the $1,000 nonrecourse liability over the $800 adjusted tax basis of the property). See section 704(b) and the regulations thereunder. A and B each have a $100 share of partnership minimum gain at the end of that year because the depreciation deduction is treated as a nonrecourse deduction. See section 704(b) and the regulation thereunder. Accordingly, at the end of that year, A and B are allocated $100 each of the nonrecourse liability to match their shares of partnership minimum gain. The remaining $800 of the nonrecourse liability will be allocated equally between A and B ($400 each).

Example 2. Excess nonrecourse liabilities allocated consistently with reasonably expected deductions. The facts are the same as in Example 1 except that the partnership agreement provides that depreciation deductions will be allocated to A. The partners agree to allocate excess nonrecourse liabilities in accordance with the manner in which it is reasonably expected that the deductions attributable to those nonrecourse liabilities will be allocated. Assuming that the allocation of all of the depreciation deductions to A is valid under section 704(b), immediately after purchasing the depreciable property, A's share of the nonrecourse liability is $1,000. Accordingly, A is treated as if A contributed $1,000 to the partnership.

Example 3. Allocation of liability among multiple properties. (i) A and B are equal partners in a partnership (PRS). A contributes $70 of cash in exchange for a 50–percent interest in PRS. B contributes two items of property, X and Y, in exchange for a 50–percent interest in PRS. Property X has a fair market value (and book value) of $70 and an adjusted basis of $40, and is subject to a nonrecourse liability of $50. Property Y has a fair market value (and book value) of $120, an adjusted basis of $40, and is subject to a nonrecourse liability of $70. Immediately after the initial contributions, PRS refinances the two separate liabilities with a single $120 nonrecourse liability. All of the built-in gain attributable to Property X ($30) and Property Y ($80) is section 704(c) gain allocable to B.

(ii) The amount of the nonrecourse liability ($120) is less than the total book value of all of the properties that are subject to such liability ($70 + $120 = $190), so there is no partnership minimum gain. § 1.704–2(d). Accordingly, no portion of the liability is allocated pursuant to paragraph (a)(1) of this section.

(iii) Pursuant to paragraph (b)(1) of this section, PRS decides to allocate the nonrecourse liability evenly between the Properties X and Y. Accordingly, each of Properties X and Y are treated as being subject to a separate $60 nonrecourse liability for purposes of applying paragraph (a)(2) of this section. Under paragraph (a)(2) of this section, B will be allocated $20 of the liability for each of Properties X and Y (in each case, $60 liability minus $40 adjusted basis). As a result, a portion of the liability is allocated pursuant to paragraph (a)(2) of this section as follows:

Partner	Property	Tier 1	Tier 2
A	X	$0	$0
	Y	$0	$0
B	X	$0	$20
	Y	$0	$20

(iv) PRS has $80 of excess nonrecourse liability that it may allocate in any manner consistent with paragraph (a)(3) of this section. PRS determines to allocate the $80 of excess nonrecourse liabilities to the partners up to their share of the remaining section 704(c) gain on the properties, with any remaining amount of liabilities being allocated equally to A and B consistent with their equal interests in partnership profits. B has $70 of remaining section 704(c) gain ($10 on Property X and $60 on Property Y), and thus will be allocated $70 of the liability in accordance with this gain. The remaining $10 is divided equally between A and B. Accordingly, the overall allocation of the $120 nonrecourse liability is as follows:

Partner	Tier 1	Tier 2	Tier 3	Total
A	$0	$0	$5	$5
B	$0	$40	$75	$115

[T.D. 8380, 56 FR 66355, Dec. 23, 1991, as amended by T.D. 8906, 65 FR 64888, Oct. 31, 2000]

§ 1.752–4 Special rules.

(a) Tiered partnerships. An upper-tier partnership's share of the liabilities of a lower-tier partnership (other than any liability of the lower-tier partnership that is owed to the upper-tier partnership) is treated as a liability of the upper-tier partnership for purposes of applying section 752 and the regulations thereunder to the partners of the upper-tier partnership.

(b) Related person definition.—(1) In general. A person is related to a partner if the person and the partner bear a relationship to each other that is specified in section 267(b) or 707(b)(1), subject to the following modifications:

(i) Substitute "80 percent or more" for "more than 50 percent" each place it appears in those sections;

(ii) A person's family is determined by excluding brothers and sisters; and

(iii) Disregard sections 267(e)(1) and 267(f)(1)(A).

(2) Person related to more than one partner—(i) In general. If, in applying the related person rules in paragraph (b)(1) of this section, a person is related to more than one partner, paragraph (b)(1) of this section is applied by treating the person as related only to the partner with whom there is the highest percentage of related ownership. If two or more partners have the same percentage of related ownership and no other partner has a greater percentage, the liability is allocated equally among the partners having the equal percentages of related ownership.

(ii) Natural persons. For purposes of determining the percentage of related ownership between a person and a partner, natural persons who are related by virtue of being members of the same family are treated as having a percentage relationship of 100 percent with respect to each other.

(iii) Related partner exception. Notwithstanding paragraph (b)(1) of this section (which defines related person), persons owning interests directly or indirectly in the same partnership are not treated as related persons for purposes of determining the economic risk of loss borne by each of them for the liabilities of the partnership. This paragraph (iii) does not apply when determining a partner's interest under the de minimis rules in §§ 1.752–2(d) and (e).

(iv) Special rule where entity structured to avoid related person status—(A) In general. If—

(1) A partnership liability is owed to or guaranteed by another entity that is a partnership, an S corporation, a C corporation, or a trust;

(2) A partner or related person owns (directly or indirectly) a 20 percent or more ownership interest in the other entity; and

(3) A principal purpose of having the other entity act as a lender or guarantor of the liability was to avoid the determination that the partner that owns the interest bears the economic risk of loss for federal income tax purposes for all or part of the liability;

then the partner is treated as holding the other entity's interest as a creditor or guarantor to the extent of the partner's or related person's ownership interest in the entity.

(B) Ownership interest. For purposes of paragraph (b)(2)(iv)(A) of this section, a person's ownership interest in:

(1) A partnership equals the partner's highest percentage interest in any item of partnership loss or deduction for any taxable year;

(2) An S corporation equals the percentage of the outstanding stock in the S corporation owned by the shareholder;

(3) A C corporation equals the percentage of the fair market value of the issued and outstanding stock owned by the shareholder; and

(4) A trust equals the percentage of the actuarial interests owned by the beneficial owner of the trust.

(C) Example. Entity structured to avoid related person status. A, B, and C form a general partnership, ABC. A, B, and C are equal partners, each contributing $1,000 to the partnership. A and B want to loan money to ABC and have the loan treated as nonrecourse for purposes of section 752. A and B form partnership AB to which each contributes $50,000. A and B share losses equally in partnership AB. Partnership AB loans partnership ABC $100,000 on a nonrecourse basis secured by the property ABC buys with the loan. Under these facts and circumstances, A and B bear the economic risk of loss with respect to the partnership liability equally based on their percentage interest in losses of partnership AB.

(c) Limitation. The amount of an indebtedness is taken into account only once, even though a partner (in addition to the partner's liability for the indebtedness as a partner) may be separately liable therefor in a capacity other than as a partner.

(d) Time of determination. A partner's share of partnership liabilities must be determined whenever the determination is necessary in order to determine the tax liability of the partner or any other person. See § 1.705–1(a) for rules regarding when the adjusted basis of a partner's interest in the partnership must be determined.

[T.D. 8380, 56 FR 66356, Dec. 23, 1991]

§ 1.752–7 Partnership assumption of partner's § 1.752–7 liability on or after June 24, 2003.

(a) Purpose and structure. The purpose of this section is to prevent the acceleration or duplication of loss through the assumption of obligations not described in § 1.752–1(a)(4)(i) in transactions involving partnerships. Under paragraph (c) of this section, any such obligation that is assumed by a partnership from a partner in a transaction governed by section 721(a) is treated as section 704(c) property. Paragraphs (e), (f), and (g) of this section provide rules for situations where a partnership assumes such an obligation from a partner and, subsequently, that partner transfers all or part of the partnership interest, that partner receives a distribution in liquidation of the partnership interest, or another partner assumes part or all of that obligation from the partnership. These rules prevent the duplication of loss by prohibiting the partnership and any person other than the partner from whom the obligation was assumed from claiming a deduction, loss, or capital expense to the extent of the built-in loss associated with the obligation. These rules also prevent the acceleration of loss by deferring the partner's deduction or loss attributable to the obligation (if any) until the satisfaction of the § 1.752–7 liability (within the meaning of paragraph (b)(8) of this section). Paragraph (d) of this section provides a number of exceptions to paragraphs (e), (f), and (g) of this section, including a de minimis exception. Paragraph (i) provides a special rule for situations in which an amount paid to satisfy a § 1.752–7 liability is capitalized into other partnership property. Paragraph (j) of this section provides special rules for tiered partnership transactions.

* * *

[T.D. 9207, 70 FR 30344, May 26, 2005; 70 FR 39654, July 11, 2005]

§ 1.753–1 Partner receiving income in respect of decedent.

(a) Income in respect of a decedent under section 736(a). All payments coming within the provisions of section 736(a) made by a partnership to the estate or other successor in interest of a deceased partner are considered income in respect of the decedent under section 691. The estate or other successor in interest of a deceased partner shall be considered to have received income in respect of a decedent to the extent that amounts are paid by a third person in exchange for rights to future payments from the partnership under section 736(a). When a partner who is receiving payments under section 736(a) dies, section 753 applies to any remaining payments under section 736(a) made to his estate or other successor in interest.

(b) Other income in respect of a decedent. When a partner dies, the entire portion of the distributive share which is attributable to the period ending with the date of his death and which is taxable to his estate or other successor constitutes income in respect of a decedent under section 691. This rule applies even though that part of the distributive share for the period before death which the decedent withdrew is not included in the value of the decedent's partnership interest for estate tax purposes. See paragraph (c)(3) of § 1.706–1.

* * *

[T.D. 6500, 25 FR 11814, Nov. 26, 1960]

§ 1.754–1 Time and manner of making election to adjust basis of partnership property.

(a) In general. A partnership may adjust the basis of partnership property under sections 734(b) and 743(b) if it files an election in accordance with the rules set forth in paragraph (b) of this section. An election may not be filed to make the adjustments provided in either section 734(b) or section 743(b) alone, but such an election must apply to both sections. An election made under the provisions of this section shall apply to all property distributions and transfers of partnership interests taking place in the partnership taxable year for which the election is made and in all subsequent partnership taxable years unless the election is revoked pursuant to paragraph (c) of this section.

(b) Time and method of making election. **(1)** An election under section 754 and this section to adjust the basis of partnership property under sections 734(b) and 743(b), with respect to a distribution of property to a partner or a transfer of an interest in a partnership, shall be made in a written statement filed with the partnership return for the taxable year during which the distribution or transfer occurs. For the election to be valid, the return must be filed not later than the time prescribed by paragraph (e) of § 1.6031–1 (including extensions thereof) for filing the return for such taxable year (or before August 23, 1956, whichever is later). Notwithstanding the preceding two sentences, if a valid election has been made under section 754 and this section for a preceding taxable year and not revoked pursuant to paragraph (c) of this section, a new election is not required to be made. The statement required by this subparagraph shall (i) set forth the name and address of the partnership making the election, (ii) be signed by any one of the partners, and (iii) contain a declaration that the partnership elects under section 754 to apply the provisions of section 734(b) and section 743(b). * * *

(2) The principles of this paragraph may be illustrated by the following example:

Example. A, a U.S. citizen, is a member of partnership ABC, which has not previously made an election under section 754 to adjust the basis of partnership property. The partnership and the partners use the calendar year as the taxable year. A sells his interest in the partnership to D on January 1, 1971. The partnership may elect under section 754 and this section to adjust the basis of partnership property under sections 734(b) and 743(b). Unless an extension of time to make the election is obtained under the provisions of § 1.9100–1, the election must be made in a written statement filed with the partnership return for 1971 and must contain the information specified in subparagraph (1) of this paragraph. Such return must be filed by April 17, 1972 (unless an extension of time for filing the return is obtained). The election will apply to all distributions of property to a partner and transfers of an interest in the partnership occurring in 1971 and subsequent years, unless revoked pursuant to paragraph (c) of this section.

(c) Revocation of election—(1) In general. A partnership having an election in effect under this section may revoke such election with the approval of the district director for the internal revenue district in which the partnership return is required to be filed. A partnership which wishes to revoke such an election shall file with the district director for the internal revenue district in which the partnership return is required to be filed an application setting forth the grounds on which the revocation is desired. The application shall be filed not later than 30 days after the close of the partnership taxable year with respect to which revocation is intended to take effect and shall be signed by any one of the partners. Examples of situations which may be considered sufficient reason for approving an application for revocation include a change in the nature of the partnership business, a substantial increase in the assets of the partnership, a change in the character of partnership assets, or an increased frequency of retirements or shifts of partnership interests, so that an increased administrative burden would result to the partnership from the election. However, no application for revocation of an election shall be approved when the purpose of the revocation is primarily to avoid stepping down the basis of partnership assets upon a transfer or distribution.

* * *

[T.D. 6500, 25 FR 11814, Nov. 26, 1960, as amended by T.D. 7208, 37 FR 20686, Oct. 3, 1972; T.D. 8847, 64 FR 69903, Dec. 15, 1999; 65 FR 9220, Feb. 24, 2000]

§ 1.755–1 Rules for allocation of basis.

(a) In general—(1) Scope. This section provides rules for allocating basis adjustments under sections 743(b) and 734(b) among partnership property. If there is a basis adjustment to which this section applies, the basis adjustment is allocated among the partnership's assets as follows. First, the partnership must determine the value of each of its assets under paragraphs (a)(2) through (5) of this section. Second, the basis adjustment is allocated between the two classes of property described in section 755(b). These classes of property consist of capital assets and section 1231(b) property (capital gain property), and any other property of the partnership (ordinary income property). For purposes of this section, properties and potential gain treated as unrealized receivables under section 751(c) and the regulations thereunder shall be treated as separate assets that are ordinary income property. Third, the portion of the basis adjustment allocated to each class is allocated among the items within the class. Basis adjustments under section 743(b) are allocated among partnership assets under paragraph (b) of this section. Basis adjustments under section 734(b) are allocated among partnership assets under paragraph (c) of this section.

(2) Coordination of sections 755 and 1060. If there is a basis adjustment to which this section applies, and the assets of the partnership constitute a trade or business (as described in § 1.1060–1(b)(2)), then the partnership is required to use the residual method to assign values to the partnership's section 197 intangibles. To do so, the partnership must, first, determine the value of partnership assets other than section 197 intangibles under paragraph (a)(3) of this section. The partnership then must determine partnership gross value under paragraph (a)(4) of this section. Last, the partnership must assign values to the partnership's section 197 intangibles under paragraph (a)(5) of this section. For purposes of this section, the term *section 197 intangibles* includes all section 197 intangibles (as defined in section 197), as well as any goodwill or going concern value that would not qualify as a section 197 intangible under section 197.

(3) Values of properties other than section 197 intangibles. For purposes of this section, the fair market value of each item of partnership property other than section 197 intangibles shall be determined on the basis of all the facts and circumstances, taking into account section 7701(g).

(4) Partnership gross value—(i) Basis adjustments under section 743(b)—(A) In general. Except as provided in paragraph (a)(4)(ii) of this section, in the case of a basis adjustment under section 743(b), partnership gross value generally is equal to the amount that, if assigned to all partnership property, would result in a liquidating distribution to the partner equal to the transferee's basis in the transferred partnership interest immediately following the relevant transfer (reduced by the amount, if any, of such basis that is attributable to partnership liabilities).

(B) Special situations. In certain circumstances, such as where income or loss with respect to particular section 197 intangibles are allocated differently among partners, partnership gross value may vary depending on the values of particular section 197 intangibles held by the partnership. In these special situations, the partnership must assign value, first, among section 197 intangibles (other than goodwill and going concern value) in a reasonable manner that is consistent with the ordering rule in paragraph (a)(5) of this section and would cause the appropriate liquidating distribution under paragraph (a)(4)(i)(A) of this section. If the actual fair market values, determined on the basis of all the facts and circumstances, of all section 197 intangibles (other than goodwill and going concern value) is not sufficient to cause the appropriate liquidating distribution, then the fair market value of goodwill and going concern value shall be presumed to equal an amount that if assigned to goodwill and going concern value would cause the appropriate liquidating distribution.

(C) Income in respect of a decedent. Solely for the purpose of determining partnership gross value under this paragraph (a)(4)(i), where a partnership interest is transferred as a result of the death of a partner, the transferee's basis in its partnership interest is determined without regard to section 1014(c), and is deemed to be adjusted for that portion of the interest, if any, that is attributable to items representing income in respect of a decedent under section 691.

(ii) Basis adjustments under section 743(b) resulting from substituted basis transactions. This paragraph (a)(4)(ii) applies to basis adjustments under section 743(b) that result from exchanges in which the transferee's basis in the partnership interest is determined in whole or in part by reference to the transferor's basis in the interest or to the basis of other property held at any time by the transferee (substituted basis transactions). In the case of a substituted basis transaction, partnership gross value equals the value of the entire partnership as a going concern, increased by the amount of partnership liabilities at the time of the exchange giving rise to the basis adjustment.

(iii) Basis adjustments under section 734(b). In the case of a basis adjustment under section 734(b), partnership gross value equals the value of the entire partnership as a going concern immediately following the distribution causing the adjustment, increased by the amount of partnership liabilities immediately following the distribution.

(5) Determining the values of section 197 intangibles—(i) Two classes. If the aggregate value of partnership property other than section 197 intangibles (as determined in paragraph (a)(3) of this section) is equal to or greater than partnership gross value (as determined in paragraph (a)(4) of this section), then all section 197 intangibles are deemed to have a value of zero for purposes of this section. In all other cases, the aggregate value of the partnership's section 197 intangibles (the residual section 197 intangibles value) is deemed to equal the excess of partnership gross value over the aggregate value of partnership property other than section 197 intangibles. The residual section 197 intangibles value must be allocated between two asset classes in the following order—

(A) Among section 197 intangibles other than goodwill and going concern value; and

(B) To goodwill and going concern value.

(ii) Values assigned to section 197 intangibles other than goodwill and going concern value. The fair market value assigned to a section 197 intangible (other than goodwill and going concern value) shall not exceed the actual fair market value (determined on the basis of all the facts and circumstances) of that asset on the date of the relevant transfer. If the residual section 197 intangibles value is less than the sum of the actual fair market values (determined on the basis of all the facts and circumstances) of all section 197 intangibles (other than goodwill and going concern value) held by the partnership, then the residual section 197 intangibles value must be allocated among the individual section 197 intangibles (other than goodwill and going concern value) as follows. The residual section 197 intangibles value is assigned first to any section 197 intangibles (other than goodwill and going concern value) having potential gain that would be treated as unrealized receivables under the flush language of section 751(c) (flush language receivables) to the extent of the basis of those section 197 intangibles and the amount of income arising from the flush language receivables that the partnership would recognize if the section 197 intangibles were sold for their actual fair market values (determined based on all the facts and circumstances) (collectively, the flush language receivables value). If the value assigned to section 197 intangibles (other than goodwill and going concern value) is less than the flush language receivables value, then the assigned value is allocated among the properties giving rise to the flush language receivables in proportion to the flush language receivables value in those properties. Any remaining residual section 197 intangibles value is allocated among the remaining portions of the section 197 intangibles (other than goodwill and going concern value) in proportion to the actual fair market values of such portions (determined based on all the facts and circumstances).

(iii) Value assigned to goodwill and going concern value. The fair market value of goodwill and going concern value is the amount, if any, by which the residual section 197 intangibles value exceeds the aggregate value of the partnership's section 197 intangibles (other than goodwill and going concern value).

(6) Examples. The provisions of paragraphs (a)(2) through (5) are illustrated by the following examples, which assume that the partnerships have an election in effect under section 754 at the time of the transfer and that the assets of each partnership constitute a trade or business (as described in § 1.1060–1(b)(2)). Except as provided, no partnership asset (other than inventory) is property described in section 751(a), and partnership liabilities are secured by all partnership assets. The examples are as follows:

Example 1. (i) A is the sole general partner in PRS, a limited partnership having three equal partners. PRS has goodwill and going concern value, two section 197 intangibles other than goodwill and going concern value (Intangible 1 and Intangible 2), and two other assets with fair market values (determined using all the facts and circumstances) as follows: inventory worth $1,000,000 and a building (a capital asset) worth $2,000,000. The fair market value of each of Intangible 1 and Intangible 2 is $50,000. PRS has one liability of $1,000,000, for which A bears the entire risk of loss under section 752 and the regulations thereunder. D purchases A's partnership interest for $650,000, resulting in a basis adjustment under section 743(b). After the purchase, D bears the entire risk of loss for PRS's liability under section 752 and the regulations thereunder. Therefore, D's basis in its interest in PRS is $1,650,000.

(ii) D's basis in the transferred partnership interest (reduced by the amount of such basis that is attributable to partnership liabilities) is $650,000 ($1,650,000—$1,000,000). Under paragraph (a)(4)(i) of this section, partnership gross value is $2,950,000 (the amount that, if assigned to all partnership property, would result in a liquidating distribution to D equal to $650,000).

(iii) Under paragraph (a)(3) of this section, the inventory has a fair market value of $1,000,000, and the building has a fair market value of $2,000,000. Thus, the aggregate value of partnership property other than section 197 intangibles, $3,000,000, is equal to or greater than partnership gross value, $2,950,000. Accordingly, under paragraphs (a)(3) and (5) of this section, the value assigned to each of the partnership's assets is as follows: inventory, $1,000,000; building, $2,000,000; Intangibles 1 and 2, $0; and goodwill and going concern value, $0. D's section 743(b) adjustment must be allocated under paragraph (b) of this section using these assigned fair market values.

Example 2. (i) Assume the same facts as in Example 1, except that the fair market values of Intangible 1 and Intangible 2 are each $300,000, and that D purchases A's interest in PRS for $1,000,000. After the purchase, D's basis in its interest in PRS is $2,000,000.

(ii) D's basis in the transferred partnership interest (reduced by the amount of such basis that is attributable to partnership liabilities) is $1,000,000 ($2,000,000—$1,000,000). Under paragraph (a)(4)(i) of this section, partnership gross value is $4,000,000 (the amount that, if assigned to all partnership property, would result in a liquidating distribution to D equal to $1,000,000).

(iii) Under paragraph (a)(5) of this section, the residual section 197 intangibles value is $1,000,000 (the excess of partnership gross value, $4,000,000, over the aggregate value of assets other than section 197 intangibles, $3,000,000 (the sum of the value of the inventory, $1,000,000, and the value of the building, $2,000,000)). The partnership must determine the values of section 197 assets by allocating the residual section 197 intangibles value among the partnership's assets. The residual section 197 intangibles value is assigned first to section 197 intangibles other than goodwill and going concern value, and then to goodwill and going concern value. Thus, $300,000 is assigned to each of Intangible 1 and Intangible 2, and $400,000 is assigned to goodwill and going concern value (the amount by which the residual section 197 intangibles value, $1,000,000, exceeds the fair market value of section 197 intangibles other than goodwill and going concern value, $600,000). D's section 743(b) adjustment must be allocated under paragraph (b) of this section using these assigned fair market values.

Example 3. (i) Assume the same facts as in Example 1, except that the fair market values of Intangible 1 and Intangible 2 are each $300,000, and that D purchases A's interest in PRS for $750,000. After the purchase, D's basis in its interest in PRS is $1,750,000. Also assume that Intangible 1 was originally purchased for $300,000, and that its adjusted basis has been decreased to $50,000 as a result of amortization. Assume that, if PRS were to sell Intangible 1 for $300,000, it would recognize $250,000 of gain that would be treated as an unrealized receivable under the flush language in section 751(c).

(ii) D's basis in the transferred partnership interest (reduced by the amount of such basis that is attributable to partnership liabilities) is $750,000 ($1,750,000—$1,000,000). Under paragraph (a)(4)(i) of this section, partnership gross value is $3,250,000 (the amount that, if assigned to all partnership property, would result in a liquidating distribution to D equal to $750,000).

(iii) Under paragraph (a)(5) of this section, the residual section 197 intangibles value is $250,000 (the amount by which partnership gross value, $3,250,000, exceeds the aggregate value of partnership property other than section 197 intangibles, $3,000,000). Intangible 1 has potential gain that would be treated as unrealized receivables under the flush language of section 751(c). The flush language receivables value in Intangible 1 is $300,000 (the sum of PRS's basis in Intangible 1, $50,000, and the amount of ordinary income, $250,000, that the partnership would recognize if Intangible 1 were sold for its actual fair market value). Because the residual section 197 intangibles value, $250,000, is less than the flush language receivables value of Intangible 1, Intangible 1 is assigned a value of $250,000, and Intangible 2 and goodwill and going concern value are assigned a value of zero. D's section 743(b) adjustment must be allocated under paragraph (b) of this section using these assigned fair market values.

Example 4. Assume the same facts as in Example 1, except that the fair market values of Intangible 1 and Intangible 2 are each $300,000, and that A does not sell its interest in PRS. Instead, A contributes its interest in PRS to E, a newly formed corporation wholly-owned by A, in a transaction described in section 351. Assume that the contribution results in a basis adjustment under section 743(b) (other than zero). PRS determines that its value as a going concern immediately following the contribution is $3,000,000. Under paragraph (a)(4)(ii) of this section, partnership gross value is $4,000,000 (the value of PRS as a going concern, $3,000,000, increased by the partnership's liability, $1,000,000, immediately after the contribution). Under paragraph (a)(5) of this section, the residual section 197 intangibles value is $1,000,000 (the amount by which partnership gross value, $4,000,000, exceeds the aggregate value of partnership property other than section 197 intangibles, $3,000,000). Of the residual section 197 intangibles value, $300,000 is assigned to each of Intangible 1 and Intangible 2, and $400,000 is assigned to goodwill and going concern value (the amount by which the residual section 197 intangibles value, $1,000,000, exceeds the fair market value of section 197 intangibles other than goodwill and going concern value, $600,000). E's section 743(b) adjustment must be allocated under paragraph (b)(5) of this section using these assigned fair market values.

Example 5. G is the sole general partner in PRS, a limited partnership having three equal partners (G, H, and I). PRS has goodwill and going concern value, two section 197 intangibles other than goodwill and going concern value (Intangible 1 and Intangible 2), and two capital assets with fair market values (determined using all the facts and circumstances) as follows: Vacant land worth $1,000,000, and a building worth $2,000,000. The fair market value of each of Intangible 1 and Intangible 2 is $300,000. PRS has one liability of $1,000,000, for which G bears the entire risk of loss under section 752 and the regulations thereunder. PRS distributes the land to H in liquidation of H's interest in PRS. Immediately prior to the distribution, PRS's basis in the land is $800,000, and H's basis in its interest in PRS is $750,000. The distribution causes the partnership to increase the basis of its remaining property by $50,000 under section 734(b)(1)(B). PRS determines that its value as a going concern immediately following the distribution is $2,000,000. Under paragraph (a)(4)(iii) of this section, partnership gross value is $3,000,000 (the value of PRS as a going concern, $2,000,000, increased by the partnership's liability, $1,000,000, immediately after the distribution). Under paragraph (a)(5) of this section, the residual section 197 intangibles value of PRS's section 197 intangibles is $1,000,000 (the amount by which partnership gross value, $3,000,000, exceeds the aggregate value of partnership property other than section 197 intangibles, $2,000,000). Of the residual section 197 intangibles value, $300,000 is assigned to each of Intangible 1 and Intangible 2, and $400,000 is assigned to goodwill and going concern value (the amount by which the residual section 197 intangibles value, $1,000,000, exceeds the fair market value of section 197 intangibles other than goodwill and going concern value, $600,000). PRS's section 734(b) adjustment must be allocated under paragraph (c) of this section using these assigned fair market values.

(b) Adjustments under section 743(b)—(1) Generally—(i) Application. For basis adjustments under section 743(b) resulting from substituted basis transactions, paragraph (b)(5) of this section shall apply. For basis adjustments under section 743(b) resulting from all other transfers, paragraphs (b)(2) through (4) of this section shall apply. For all other transfers which result in a basis adjustment under section 743(b), paragraphs (b)(2) through (b)(4) of this section shall apply. Except as provided in paragraph (b)(5) of this section, the portion of the basis adjustment allocated to one class of property may be an increase while the portion allocated to the other class is a decrease. This would be the case even though the total amount of the basis adjustment is zero. Except as provided in paragraph (b)(5) of this section, the portion of the basis adjustment allocated to one item of property within a class may be an increase while the portion allocated to another is a decrease. This would be the case even though the basis adjustment allocated to the class is zero.

(ii) Hypothetical transaction. For purposes of paragraphs (b)(2) through (b)(4) of this section, the allocation of the basis adjustment under section 743(b) between the classes of property and among the items of property within each class are made based on the allocations of income, gain, or loss (including remedial allocations under § 1.704–3(d)) that the transferee partner would receive (to the extent attributable to the acquired partnership interest) if, immediately after the transfer of the partnership, all of the partnership's property were disposed of in a fully taxable transaction for cash in an amount equal to the fair market value of such property (the hypothetical transaction). * * *

(2) Allocations between classes of property—(i) In general. The amount of the basis adjustment allocated to the class of ordinary income property is equal to the total amount of income, gain, or loss (including any remedial allocations under § 1.704–3(d)) that would be allocated to the transferee (to the extent attributable to the acquired partnership interest) from the sale of all ordinary income property in the hypothetical transaction. The amount of the basis adjustment to capital gain property is equal to—

(A) The total amount of the basis adjustment under section 743(b); less

(B) The amount of the basis adjustment allocated to ordinary income property under the preceding sentence; provided, however, that in no event may the amount of any decrease in basis allocated to capital gain property exceed the partnership's basis (or in the case of property subject to the remedial allocation method, the transferee's share of any remedial loss under § 1.704–3(d) from the hypothetical transaction) in capital gain property. In the event that a decrease in basis allocated to capital gain property would otherwise exceed the partnership's basis in capital gain property, the excess must be applied to reduce the basis of ordinary income property.

(ii) Examples. The provisions of this paragraph (b)(2) are illustrated by the following examples:

Example 1. **(i)** A and B form equal partnership PRS. A contributes $50,000 and Asset 1, a nondepreciable capital asset with a fair market value of $50,000 and an adjusted tax basis of $25,000. B contributes $100,000. PRS uses the cash to purchase Assets 2, 3, and 4. After a year, A sells its interest in PRS to T for $120,000. At the time of the transfer, A's share of the partnership's basis in partnership assets is $75,000. Therefore, T receives a $45,000 basis adjustment.

(ii) Immediately after the transfer of the partnership interest to T, the adjusted basis and fair market value of PRS's assets are as follows:

Assets

	Adjusted Basis	Fair Market Value
Capital Gain Property:		
Asset 1	$ 25,000	$ 75,000
Asset 2	100,000	117,500
Ordinary Income Property:		
Asset 3	$ 40,000	$45,000
Asset 4	10,000	2,500
Total	$175,000	$240,000

(iii) If PRS sold all of its assets in a fully taxable transaction at fair market value immediately after the transfer of the partnership interest to T, the total amount of capital gain that would be allocated to T is equal to $46,250 ($25,000 section 704(c) built-in gain from Asset 1, plus fifty percent of the $42,500 appreciation in capital gain property). T would also be allocated a $1,250 ordinary loss from the sale of the ordinary income property.

(iv) The amount of the basis adjustment that is allocated to ordinary income property is equal to ($1,250) (the amount of the loss allocated to T from the hypothetical sale of the ordinary income property).

(v) The amount of the basis adjustment that is allocated to capital gain property is equal to $46,250 (the amount of the basis adjustment, $45,000, less ($1,250), the amount of loss allocated to T from the hypothetical sale of the ordinary income property).

Example 2. **(i)** A and B form equal partnership PRS. A and B each contribute $1,000 cash which the partnership uses to purchase Assets 1, 2, 3, and 4. After a year, A sells its partnership interest to T for $1,000. T's basis adjustment under section 743(b) is zero.

(ii) Immediately after the transfer of the partnership interest to T, the adjusted basis and fair market value of PRS's assets are as follows:

Assets

	Adjusted Basis	Fair Market Value
Capital Gain Property		
Asset 1	$ 500	$ 750
Asset 2	500	500
Ordinary Income Property:		
Asset 3	$ 500	$ 250
Asset 4	500	500
Total	$2,000	$2,000

(iii) If, immediately after the transfer of the partnership interest to T, PRS sold all of its assets in a fully taxable transaction at fair market value, T would be allocated a loss of $125 from the sale of the ordinary income property. Thus, the amount of the basis adjustment to ordinary income property is ($125). The amount of the basis adjustment to capital gain property is $125 (zero, the amount of the basis adjustment under section 743(b), less ($125), the amount of the basis adjustment allocated to ordinary income property).

(3) Allocation within the class—(i) Ordinary income property. The amount of the basis adjustment to each item of property within the class of ordinary income property is equal to—

(A) The amount of income, gain, or loss (including any remedial allocations under § 1.704–3(d)) that would be allocated to the transferee (to the extent attributable to the acquired partnership interest) from the hypothetical sale of the item; reduced by

(B) The product of—

(*1*) Any decrease to the amount of the basis adjustment to ordinary income property required pursuant to the last sentence of paragraph (b)(2)(i) of this section; multiplied by

(*2*) A fraction, the numerator of which is the fair market value of the item of property to the partnership and the denominator of which is the total fair market value of all of the partnership's items of ordinary income property.

(ii) Capital gain property. The amount of the basis adjustment to each item of property within the class of capital gain property is equal to—

(A) The amount of income, gain, or loss (including any remedial allocations under § 1.704–3(d)) that would be allocated to the transferee (to the extent attributable to the acquired partnership interest) from the hypothetical sale of the item; minus

(B) The product of—

(*1*) The total amount of gain or loss (including any remedial allocations under § 1.704–3(d)) that would be allocated to the transferee (to the extent attributable to the acquired partnership interest) from the hypothetical sale of all items of capital gain property, minus the amount of the positive basis adjustment to all items of capital gain property or plus the amount of the negative basis adjustment to capital gain property; multiplied by

(2) A fraction, the numerator of which is the fair market value of the item of property to the partnership, and the denominator of which is the fair market value of all of the partnership's items of capital gain property.

(iii) Special rules—(A) Assets in which partner has no interest. An asset with respect to which the transferee partner has no interest in income, gain, losses, or deductions shall not be taken into account in applying paragraph (b)(3)(ii)(B) of this section.

(B) Limitation in decrease of basis. In no event may the amount of any decrease in basis allocated to an item of capital gain property under paragraph (b)(3)(ii)(B) of this section exceed the partnership's adjusted basis in that item (or in the case of property subject to the remedial allocation method, the transferee's share of any remedial loss under § 1.704–3(d) from the hypothetical transaction). In the event that a decrease in basis allocated under paragraph (b)(3)(ii)(B) of this section to an item of capital gain property would otherwise exceed the partnership's adjusted basis in that item, the excess must be applied to reduce the remaining basis, if any, of other capital gain assets pro rata in proportion to the bases of such assets (as adjusted under this paragraph (b)(3)).

(iv) Examples. The provisions of this paragraph (b)(3) are illustrated by the following examples:

Example 1.(i) Assume the same facts as Example 1 in paragraph (b)(2)(ii) of this section. Of the $45,000 basis adjustment, $46,250 was allocated to capital gain property. The amount allocated to ordinary income property was ($1,250).

(ii) Asset 1 is a capital gain asset, and T would be allocated $37,500 from the sale of Asset 1 in the hypothetical transaction. Therefore, the amount of the adjustment to Asset 1 is $37,500.

(iii) Asset 2 is a capital gain asset, and T would be allocated $8,750 from the sale of Asset 2 in the hypothetical transaction. Therefore, the amount of the adjustment to Asset 2 is $8,750.

(iv) Asset 3 is ordinary income property, and T would be allocated $2,500 from the sale of Asset 3 in the hypothetical transaction. Therefore, the amount of the adjustment to Asset 3 is $2,500.

(v) Asset 4 is ordinary income property, and T would be allocated ($3,750) from the sale of Asset 4 in the hypothetical transaction. Therefore, the amount of the adjustment to Asset 4 is ($3,750.).

Example 2. (i) Assume the same facts as Example 1 in paragraph (b)(2)(ii) of this section, except that A sold its interest in PRS to T for $110,000 rather than $120,000. T, therefore, receives a basis adjustment under section 743(b) of $35,000. Of the $35,000 basis adjustment, ($1,250) is allocated to ordinary income property, and $36,250 is allocated to capital gain property.

(ii) Asset 3 is ordinary income property, and T would be allocated $2,500 from the sale of Asset 3 in the hypothetical transaction. Therefore, the amount of the adjustment to Asset 3 is $2,500.

(iii) Asset 4 is ordinary income property, and T would be allocated ($3,750) from the sale of Asset 4 in the hypothetical transaction. Therefore, the amount of the adjustment to Asset 4 is ($3,750).

(iv) Asset 1 is a capital gain asset, and T would be allocated $37,500 from the sale of Asset 1 in the hypothetical transaction. Asset 2 is a capital gain asset, and T would be allocated $8,750 from the sale of Asset 2 in the hypothetical transaction. The total amount of gain that would be allocated to T from the sale of the capital gain assets in the hypothetical transaction is $46,250, which exceeds the amount of the basis adjustment allocated to capital gain property by $10,000. The amount of the adjustment to Asset 1 is $33,604 ($37,500 minus $3,896 ($10,000 x $75,000/192,500)). The amount of the basis adjustment to Asset 2 is $2,646 ($8,750 minus $6,104 ($10,000 x $117,-500/192,500)).

(4) Income in respect of a decedent—(i) In general. Where a partnership interest is transferred as a result of the death of a partner, under section 1014(c) the transferee's basis in its partnership interest is not adjusted for that portion of the interest, if any, which is attributable to items representing income in respect of a decedent under section 691. See § 1.742–1. Accordingly, if a partnership interest is transferred as a result of the death of a partner, and the partnership holds assets representing income in respect of a decedent, no part of the basis adjustment under section 743(b) is allocated to these assets. See § 1.743–1(b).

(ii) The provisions of this paragraph (b)(4) are illustrated by the following example:

Example. (i) A and B are equal partners in personal service partnership PRS. In 2004, as a result of B's death, B's partnership interest is transferred to T when PRS's balance sheet (reflecting a cash receipts and disbursements method of accounting) is as follows (based on all the facts and circumstances):

Assets

	Adjusted Basis	Fair Market Value
Section 197 Intangible	2,000	5,000
Unrealized Receivables	0	15,000
Total	2,000	20,000

Liabilities and Capital

	Adjusted per books	Fair market value
Capital:		
A	1,000	10,000
B	1,000	10,000
Total	2,000	20,000

(ii) None of the assets owned by PRS is section 704(c) property, and the section 197 intangible is not amortizable. The fair market value of T's partnership interest on the applicable date of valuation set forth in section 1014 is $10,000. Of this amount, $2,500 is attributable to T's 50% share of the partnership's section 197 intangible, and $7,500 is attributable to T's 50% share of the partnership's unrealized receivables. The partnership's unrealized receivables represent income in respect of a decedent. Accordingly, under section 1014(c), T's basis in its partnership interest is not adjusted for that portion of the interest which is attributable to the unrealized receivables. Therefore, T's basis in its partnership interest is $2,500.

(iii) Under paragraph (a)(4)(i)(C) of this section, solely for purposes of determining partnership gross value, T's basis in its partnership interest is deemed to be $10,000. Under paragraph (a)(4)(i) of this section, partnership gross value is $20,000 (the amount that, if assigned to all partnership property, would result in a liquidating distribution to T equal to $10,000).

(iv) Under paragraph (a)(5) of this section, the residual section 197 intangibles value is $5,000 (the excess of partnership gross value, $20,000, over the aggregate value of assets other than section 197 intangibles, $15,000). The residual section 197 intangibles value is assigned first to section 197 intangibles other than goodwill and going concern value, and then to goodwill and going concern value. Thus, $5,000 is assigned to the section 197 intangible, and $0 is assigned to goodwill and going concern value. T's section 743(b) adjustment must be allocated using these assigned fair market values.

(v) At the time of the transfer, B's share of the partnership's basis in partnership assets is $1,000. Accordingly, T receives a $1,500 basis adjustment under section 743(b). Under this paragraph (b)(4), the entire basis adjustment is allocated to the partnership's section 197 intangible.

* * *

(c) Adjustments under section 734(b)—(1) Allocations between classes of property—(i) General rule. Where there is a distribution of partnership property resulting in an adjustment to the basis of the undistributed property under section 734(b)(1)(B) or (b)(2)(B), the adjustment must be allocated to remaining partnership property of a character similar to that of the distributed property with respect to which the adjustment arose. Thus, when the partnership's adjusted basis of distributed capital gain property immediately prior to distribution exceeds the basis of the property to the distributee partner (as determined under section 732), the basis of the undistributed capital gain property remaining in the partnership is increased by an amount equal to the excess. Conversely, when the basis to the distributee partner (as determined under section 732) of distributed capital gain property exceeds the partnership's adjusted basis of such property immediately prior to the distribution, the basis of the undistributed capital gain property remaining in the partnership is decreased by an amount equal to such excess. Similarly, where there is a distribution of ordinary income property, and the basis of the property to the distributee partner (as determined under section 732) is not the same as the partnership's adjusted basis of the property immediately prior to distribution, the adjustment is made only to undistributed property of the same class remaining in the partnership.

(ii) Special rule. Where there is a distribution resulting in an adjustment under section 734(b)(1)(A) or (b)(2)(A) to the basis of undistributed partnership property, the adjustment is allocated only to capital gain property.

(2) Allocations within the classes—(i) Increases. If there is an increase in basis to be allocated within a class, the increase must be allocated first to properties with unrealized appreciation in proportion to their respective amounts of unrealized appreciation before such increase (but only to the extent of each property's unrealized appreciation). Any remaining increase must be allocated among the properties within the class in proportion to their fair market values.

(ii) Decreases. If there is a decrease in basis to be allocated within a class, the decrease must be allocated first to properties with unrealized depreciation in proportion to their respective amounts of unrealized depreciation before such decrease (but only to the extent of each property's unrealized depreciation). Any remaining decrease must be allocated among the properties within the class in proportion to their adjusted bases (as adjusted under the preceding sentence).

(3) Limitation in decrease of basis. Where a decrease in the basis of partnership assets is required under section 734(b)(2) and the amount of the decrease exceeds the adjusted basis to the partnership of property of the required character, the basis of such property is reduced to zero (but not below zero).

(4) Carryover adjustment. Where, in the case of a distribution, an increase or a decrease in the basis of undistributed property cannot be made because the partnership owns no property of the character required to be adjusted, or because the basis of all the property of a like character has been reduced to zero, the adjustment is made when the partnership subsequently acquires property of a like character to which an adjustment can be made.

* * *

(6) Example. The following example illustrates this paragraph (c):

Example. **(i)** A, B, and C form equal partnership PRS. A contributes $50,000 and Asset 1, nondepreciable capital gain property with a fair market value of $50,000 and an adjusted tax basis of $25,000. B and C each contributes $100,000. PRS uses the cash to purchase Assets 2, 3, 4, 5, and 6. Assets 2 and 3 are nondepreciable capital assets and Assets 4, 5 and 6 are inventory that has not appreciated substantially in value within the meaning of section 751(b)(3). Assets 4, 5, and 6 are the only assets held by the partnership which are subject to section 751. The partnership has an election in effect under section 754. After seven years, the adjusted basis and fair market value of PRS's assets are as follows:

Assets

	Adjusted Basis	Fair Market Value
Capital Gain Property:		
Asset 1	$ 25,000	$ 75,000
Asset 2	100,000	117,500
Asset 3	50,000	60,000
Ordinary Income Property:		
Asset 4	$ 40,000	$ 45,000
Asset 5	50,000	60,000
Asset 6	10,000	2,500
Total	$275,000	$360,000

(ii) Allocation between classes. Assume that PRS distributes Assets 3 and 5 to A in complete liquidation of A's interest in the partnership. A's basis in the partnership interest was $75,000. The partnership's basis in Assets 3 and 5 was $50,000 each. A's $75,000 basis in its partnership interest is allocated between Assets 3 and 5 under sections 732(b) and (c). A will, therefore, have a basis of $25,000 in Asset 3 (capital gain property), and a basis of $50,000 in Asset 5 (section 751 property). The distribution results in a $25,000 increase in the basis of capital gain property. There is no change in the basis of ordinary income property.

(iii) Allocation within class. The amount of the basis increase to capital gain property is $25,000 and must be allocated among the remaining capital gain assets in proportion to the difference between the fair market value and basis of each. The fair market value of Asset 1 exceeds its basis by $50,000. The fair market value of Asset 2 exceeds its basis by $17,500. Therefore, the basis of Asset 1 will be increased by $18,519 ($25,000, multiplied by $50,000, divided by $67,500), and the basis of Asset 2 will be increased by $6,481 ($25,000 multiplied by $17,500, divided by $67,500).

* * *

[T.D. 8847, 64 FR 69903, Dec. 15, 1999, as amended by T.D. 9059, 68 FR 34293, June 9, 2003; T.D. 9137, 69 FR 42559, July 16, 2004]

§ 1.761–1 Terms defined.

(a) Partnership. The term "partnership" means a partnership as determined under §§ 301.7701–1, 301.7701–2, and 301.7701–3 of this chapter.

(b) Partner. The term "partner" means a member of a partnership.

(c) Partnership agreement. For the purposes of subchapter K, a partnership agreement includes the original agreement and any modifications thereof agreed to by all the partners or adopted in any other manner provided by the partnership agreement. Such agreement or modifications can be oral or written. A partnership agreement may be modified with respect to a particular taxable year subsequent to the close of such taxable year, but not later than the date (not including any extension of time) prescribed by law for the filing of the partnership return. As to any matter on which the partnership agreement, or any modification thereof, is silent, the provisions of local law shall be considered to constitute a part of the agreement.

(d) Liquidation of partner's interest. The term "liquidation of a partner's interest" means the termination of a partner's entire interest in a partnership by means of a distribution, or a series of distributions, to the partner by the partnership. A series of distributions will come within the meaning of this term whether they are made in one year or in more than one year. Where a partner's interest is to be liquidated by a series of distributions, the interest will not be considered as liquidated until the final distribution has been made. For the basis of property distributed in one liquidating distribution, or in a series of distributions in liquidation, see section 732(b). A distribution which is not in liquidation of a partner's entire interest, as defined in this paragraph, is a current distribution. Current distributions, therefore, include distributions in partial liquidation of a partner's interest, and distributions of the partner's distributive share. See paragraph (a)(1)(ii) of § 1.731–1.

(e) Distribution of partnership interest. For purposes of section 708(b)(1)(B) and § 1.708–1(b)(1)(iv), the deemed distribution of an interest in a new partnership by a partnership that terminates under section 708(b)(1)(B) is not a sale or exchange of an interest in the new partnership. However, the deemed distribution of an interest in a new partnership by a partnership that terminates under section 708(b)(1)(B) is treated as an exchange of the interest in the new partnership for purposes of section 743. This paragraph (e) applies to terminations of partnerships under section 708(b)(1)(B) occurring on or after May 9, 1997; however, this paragraph (e) may be applied to terminations occurring on or after May 9, 1996, provided that the partnership and its partners apply this paragraph (e) to the termination in a consistent manner.

[T.D. 6500, 25 FR 11814, Nov. 26, 1960, as amended by T.D. 7208, 37 FR 20686, Oct. 3, 1972; T.D. 8697, 61 FR 66584, Dec. 18, 1996; T.D. 8717, 62 FR 25498, May 9, 1997]

§ 1.761–2 Exclusion of certain unincorporated organizations from the application of all or part of subchapter K of chapter 1 of the Internal Revenue Code.

(a) Exclusion of eligible unincorporated organizations—(1) In general. Under conditions set forth in this section, an unincorporated organization described in subparagraph (2) or (3) of this paragraph may be excluded from the application of all or a part of the provisions of subchapter K of chapter 1 of the Code. Such organization must be availed of (i) for investment purposes only and not for the active conduct of a business, or (ii) for the joint production, extraction, or use of property, but not for the purpose of selling services or property produced or extracted. The members of such organization must be able to compute their income without the necessity of computing partnership taxable income. Any syndicate, group, pool, or joint venture which is classifiable as an association, or any group operating under an agreement which creates an organization classifiable as an association, does not fall within these provisions.

(2) Investing partnership. Where the participants in the joint purchase, retention, sale, or exchange of investment property—

(i) Own the property as coowners,

(ii) Reserve the right separately to take or dispose of their shares of any property acquired or retained, and

(iii) Do not actively conduct business or irrevocably authorize some person or persons acting in a representative capacity to purchase, sell, or exchange such investment property, although each separate participant may delegate authority to purchase, sell, or exchange his share of any such investment property for the time being for his account, but not for a period of more than a year, then

such group may be excluded from the application of the provisions of subchapter K under the rules set forth in paragraph (b) of this section.

(3) Operating agreements. Where the participants in the joint production, extraction, or use of property—

(i) Own the property as coowners, either in fee or under lease or other form of contract granting exclusive operating rights, and

(ii) Reserve the right separately to take in kind or dispose of their shares of any property produced, extracted, or used, and

(iii) Do not jointly sell services or the property produced or extracted, although each separate participant may delegate authority to sell his share of the property produced or extracted for the time being for his account, but not for a period of time in excess of the minimum needs of the industry, and in no event for more than 1 year, then

such group may be excluded from the application of the provisions of subchapter K under the rules set forth in paragraph (b) of this section. However, the preceding sentence does not apply to any unincorporated organization one of whose principal purposes is cycling, manufacturing, or processing for persons who are not members of the organization. * * *

* * *

[T.D. 7208, 37 FR 20687, Oct. 3, 1972; 37 FR 23161, Oct. 31, 1972, as amended by T.D. 8578, 59 FR 66181, Dec. 23, 1994; 60 FR 11028, Mar. 1, 1995]

§ 1.761–3 Certain option holders treated as partners.

(a) Noncompensatory option treated as a partnership interest—(1) General rule. A noncompensatory option (as defined in paragraph (b)(2) of this section) is treated as a partnership interest for all Federal tax purposes if, on the date of a measurement event (as defined in paragraph (c) of this section) with respect to the option—

(i) The noncompensatory option (and any agreements associated with it) provides the option holder with rights that are substantially similar to the rights afforded a partner (as determined under paragraph (d) of this section); and

(ii) There is a strong likelihood that the failure to treat the holder of the noncompensatory option as a partner would result in a substantial reduction in the present value of the partners' and noncompensatory option holder's aggregate Federal tax liabilities (as determined under paragraph (e) of this section).

(2) Continuing applicability of general principles of law. The fact that an option is not treated as a partnership interest under this section does not prevent the option from being treated as a partnership interest under general principles of Federal tax law.

(3) Timing of characterization. If a noncompensatory option is treated under this section as a partnership interest, that treatment applies, as the case may be, upon the issuance of the option, or immediately before any other measurement event that gave rise to the characterization under paragraph (a)(1) of this section.

(4) Effect of characterization. If a noncompensatory option is treated as a partnership interest under this section or under general principles of law, the option holder will be treated as a partner with respect to the partnership interest and will receive a distributive share of the partnership's income, gain, loss, deduction, or credit (or items thereof), as determined in accordance with that partner's interest in the partnership (taking into account all facts and circumstances) in accordance with § 1.704–1(b)(3). Once a noncompensatory option is treated as a partnership interest, in no event may it be characterized as an option thereafter.

(b) Definitions. For purposes of this section:

(1) Look-through entity. Look-through entity means an entity described in § 1.704–1(b)(2)(iii)(d)(2).

(2) Noncompensatory option. Noncompensatory option means an option (as defined in paragraph (b)(3) of this section) issued by a partnership, other than an option issued in connection with the performance of services. For purposes of applying this section, an option that would be a noncompensatory option under this paragraph if it had been issued by a partnership is a noncompensatory option if the option was issued by an eligible entity (as defined in § 301.7701–3(a)) that would become a partnership under § 301.7701–3(f)(2) if the noncompensatory option holder were treated as a partner. Also for purposes of applying this section, if a noncompensatory option is issued by such an eligible entity, then the eligible entity is treated as a partnership.

(3) Option. An option is a contractual right to acquire an interest in the issuing partnership, including a call option, warrant, or other similar arrangement. In addition, an option includes convertible debt (as defined in § 1.721–2(g)(2)) and convertible equity (as defined in § 1.721–2(g)(3)). To achieve the purposes of this section, the Commissioner can treat other contractual agreements, including a forward contract, a futures contract, or a notional principal contract, as an option. A contract that otherwise constitutes an option will not fail to be treated as an option for purposes of this section merely because it may or must be settled in cash or property other than a partnership interest.

(4) Underlying partnership interest. Underlying partnership interest means the interest in the issuing partnership that would be acquired by the noncompensatory option holder upon exercise of the noncompensatory option.

(c) Measurement event—(1) General rule. Except as provided in paragraph (c)(2) of this section, a measurement event with respect to a noncompensatory option is any of the following events:

(i) Issuance of the noncompensatory option;

(ii) An adjustment of the terms (modification) of the noncompensatory option or of the underlying partnership interest (as defined in paragraph (b)(4) of this section) (including an adjustment pursuant to the terms of the noncompensatory option or the underlying partnership interest);

(iii) Transfer of the noncompensatory option if either:

(A) The option may be exercised (or settled) more than 12 months after its issuance, or

(B) The transfer is pursuant to a plan in existence at the time of the issuance or modification of the noncompensatory option that has as a principal purpose the substantial reduction of the present value of the aggregate Federal tax liabilities of the partners and the noncompensatory option holder (under paragraph (a)(1)(ii) of this section);

(2) Events not treated as measurement events. A measurement event does not include the following events:

(i) A transfer of the noncompensatory option at death, between spouses or former spouses under section 1041, or in a transaction that is disregarded for Federal tax purposes;

(ii) A modification that neither materially increases the likelihood that the noncompensatory option will be exercised (as described in paragraph (d)(2) of this section) nor provides the noncompensatory option holder with partner attributes (as described in paragraph (d)(3) of this section);

(iii) A change in the strike price of a noncompensatory option or in the interests in the issuing partnership that may be issued or transferred pursuant to the noncompensatory option, made pursuant to a bona fide, reasonable adjustment formula that has the intended effect of preventing dilution of the interests of the noncompensatory option holder;

(iv) Any other event as provided in guidance published in the Internal Revenue Bulletin.

(d) Rights substantially similar to partner rights—(1) In general. A noncompensatory option provides the holder with rights that are substantially similar to the rights afforded to a partner if either the option is reasonably certain to be exercised or the option holder possesses partner attributes.

(2) Reasonable certainty of exercise—(i) General rule. The determination of whether a noncompensatory option is reasonably certain to be exercised at the time of a measurement event is based on all the facts and circumstances, including—

(A) The fair market value of the partnership interest that is the subject of the noncompensatory option;

(B) The strike price of the noncompensatory option;

(C) The term of the noncompensatory option;

(D) The volatility of the value or income of the issuing partnership or the underlying partnership interest;

(E) Anticipated distributions by the partnership during the term of the noncompensatory option;

(F) Any other special option features, such as a strike price that fluctuates;

(G) The existence of related options, including reciprocal options; and

(H) Any other arrangements affecting or undertaken with a principal purpose of affecting the likelihood that the noncompensatory option will be exercised.

(ii) Safe harbors—(A) General rule. Except as provided in paragraph (d)(2)(ii)(C) of this section, a noncompensatory option is not considered reasonably certain to be exercised if, as of the date of a measurement event with respect to the noncompensatory option—

(1) The option may be exercised no more than 24 months after the date of the measurement event and the strike price is equal to or greater than 110 percent of the fair market value of the underlying partnership interest on the date of the measurement event; or

(2) The terms of the option provide that the strike price of the option is equal to or greater than the fair market value of the underlying partnership interest on the exercise date.

(B) Options exercisable at fair market value. For purposes of paragraph (d)(2)(ii)(A) of this section, an option whose strike price is determined by a formula is considered to have a strike price equal to or greater than the fair market value of the underlying partnership interest on the exercise date if the formula is agreed upon by the parties when the option is issued in a bona fide attempt to arrive at the fair market value on the exercise date and is to be applied based on the facts and circumstances in existence on the exercise date.

(C) Exception. The safe harbors of paragraph (d)(2)(ii)(A) of this section do not apply if the parties to the noncompensatory option had a principal purpose described in paragraph (c)(1)(iii)(B) of this section with respect to a measurement event for that option (or, if multiple options were issued pursuant to a plan, a measurement event with respect to any option issued pursuant to that plan).

(D) Failure to satisfy safe harbor. Failure of an option to satisfy one of the safe harbors of paragraph (d)(2)(ii)(A) does not affect the determination of whether an option is treated as reasonably certain to be exercised.

(3) Partner attributes—(i) General rule. The determination of whether a holder of a noncompensatory option possesses partner attributes is based on all the facts and circumstances, including whether the option holder, directly or indirectly, through the option agreement or a related agreement, is provided with voting rights or managerial rights in the partnership.

(ii) Certain factors that conclusively establish partner attributes. For purposes of this section, a noncompensatory option holder has partner attributes if, based on all the facts and circumstances—

(A) The option holder is provided with rights (through the option agreement or a related agreement) that are similar to rights ordinarily afforded to a partner to participate in partnership profits through present possessory rights to share in current operating or liquidating distributions with respect to the underlying partnership interests; or

(B) The option holder, directly or indirectly, undertakes obligations (through the option agreement or a related agreement) that are similar to obligations undertaken by a partner to bear partnership losses.

(iii) Special rules. The following rules apply for purposes of paragraphs (d)(3)(i) and (d)(3)(ii) of this section:

(A) Rights in the issuing partnership possessed by a noncompensatory option holder solely by virtue of owning an interest in the issuing partnership are not taken into account, provided that those rights are no greater than the rights granted to other partners owning substantially similar interests in the partnership and who do not hold noncompensatory options in the partnership.

(B) If all of the partners owning substantially similar interests in the issuing partnership also hold noncompensatory options in the partnership, or if none of the other partners owns substantially similar interests in the partnership, then all facts and circumstances will be considered in determining whether the rights in the partnership possessed by the option holder are possessed solely by virtue of owning a partnership interest. If those rights are possessed solely by virtue of owning a partnership interest, they are not taken into account.

(C) A noncompensatory option holder will not ordinarily be considered to possess partner attributes solely because the noncompensatory option agreement significantly controls or restricts, or the noncompensatory option holder has the ability to significantly control or restrict, a partnership decision that could substantially affect the value of the underlying partnership interest. In particular, the following abilities of the option holder will not be treated as partner attributes:

(1) The ability to impose reasonable restrictions on partnership distributions or dilutive issuances of partnership equity or options while the noncompensatory option is outstanding.

(2) The ability to choose the partnership's section 704(c) method for partnership properties.

(D) When the applicable measurement event is a transfer described in paragraph (c)(1) of this section, the partner attributes of the transferee, not the transferor, are taken into account.

(E) The option holder will be treated as owning all partnership interests and noncompensatory options issued by the partnership that are owned by any person related to the option holder. For purposes of the preceding sentence, a person related to the option holder is defined as any person bearing a relationship to the option holder described in section 267(b) or 707(b).

(e) Substantial tax reduction requirement—(1) General rule. The determination of whether there is a strong likelihood that the failure to treat a noncompensatory option holder as a partner would result in a substantial reduction in the present value of the partners' and the noncompensatory option holder's aggregate Federal tax liabilities is based on all the facts and circumstances, including—

(i) The interaction of the allocations of the issuing partnership and the partners' and noncompensatory option holder's Federal tax attributes (taking into account tax consequences that result from the interaction of the allocations with the partners' and noncompensatory option holder's Federal tax attributes that are unrelated to the partnership);

(ii) The absolute amount of the Federal tax reduction;

(iii) The amount of the reduction relative to overall Federal tax liability; and

(iv) The timing of items of income and deductions.

(2) Special rules. For purposes of applying paragraph (e)(1) of this section to a partner or noncompensatory option holder that is—

(i) A look-through entity (as defined in paragraph (b)(1) of this section), the Federal tax consequences that result from the interaction of allocations of the partnership and the Federal tax attributes of any person that is an owner, or in the case of a trust or estate, the beneficiary, of an interest in such a partner or noncompensatory option holder, whether directly, or indirectly through one or more look-through entities, must be taken into account; or

(ii) A member of a consolidated group (within the meaning of § 1.1502–1(h)), the tax consequences that result from the interaction of the issuing partnership's allocations and the tax attributes of the consolidated group and the tax attributes of another member with respect to a separate return year must be taken into account.

(f) Example. The following example illustrates the provisions of this section. For purposes of the example, assume that PRS is a partnership for Federal tax purposes, none of the noncompensatory option holders or partners are related persons, and that general principles of law do not apply to treat the noncompensatory option as a partnership interest. The example reads as follows:

Example 1. Active trade or business. PRS is engaged in an active real estate business, the amount of income, gain, loss, and deductions from which cannot be predicted with any reasonable certainty. In exchange for a premium of $10x, PRS issues a noncompensatory option to A to acquire a 10 percent interest in PRS for $110x at any time during a 3–year period commencing on the date on which the option is issued. At the time of the issuance of the noncompensatory option, a 10 percent interest in PRS has a fair market value of $100x. Due to the nature of PRS's business, the value of a 10 percent PRS interest in 3 years is not reasonably predictable as of the time the noncompensatory option is issued. Assuming there are no other facts affecting the certainty of the option's exercise, it is not reasonably certain that A's option will be exercised. Therefore, assuming that A does not possess partner attributes as described in paragraph (d)(3) of this section, A's noncompensatory option is not treated as a partnership interest under paragraph (a)(1) of this section.

* * *

[T.D. 9612, 78 FR 8013, Feb. 5, 2013]

GAIN OR LOSS ON DISPOSITION OF PROPERTY

§ 1.1001–1 Computation of gain or loss.

(a) General rule. Except as otherwise provided in subtitle A of the Code, the gain or loss realized from the conversion of property into cash, or from the exchange of property for other property differing materially either in kind or in extent, is treated as income or as loss sustained. The amount realized from a sale or other disposition of property is the sum of any money received plus the fair market value of any property (other than money) received. The fair market value of property is a question of fact, but only in rare and extraordinary cases will property be considered to have no fair market value. The general method of computing such gain or loss is prescribed by section 1001(a) through (d) which contemplates that from the amount realized upon the sale or exchange there shall be withdrawn a sum sufficient to restore the adjusted basis prescribed by section 1011 and the regulations thereunder (*i.e.,* the cost or other basis adjusted for receipts, expenditures, losses, allowances, and other items chargeable against and applicable to such cost or other basis). The amount which remains after the adjusted basis has been restored to the taxpayer constitutes the realized gain. If the amount realized upon the sale or exchange is insufficient to restore to the taxpayer the adjusted basis of the property, a loss is sustained to the extent of the difference between such adjusted basis and the amount realized. The basis may be different depending upon whether gain or loss is being computed. For example, see section 1015(a) and the regulations thereunder. Section 1001(e) and paragraph (f) of this section prescribe the method of computing gain or loss upon the sale or other disposition of a term interest in property the adjusted basis (or a portion) of which is determined pursuant, or by reference, to section 1014 (relating to the basis of property acquired from a decedent) or section 1015 (relating to the basis of property acquired by gift or by a transfer in trust).

* * *

(e) Transfers in part a sale and in part a gift. **(1)** Where a transfer of property is in part a sale and in part a gift, the transferor has a gain to the extent that the amount realized by him exceeds his adjusted basis in the property. However, no loss is sustained on such a transfer if the amount realized is less than the adjusted basis. For the determination of basis of property in the hands of the transferee, see § 1.1015–4. * * *

(2) Examples. The provisions of subparagraph (1) may be illustrated by the following examples:

Example (1). A transfers property to his son for $60,000. Such property in the hands of A has an adjusted basis of $30,000 (and a fair market value of $90,000). A's gain is $30,000, the excess of $60,000, the amount realized, over the adjusted basis, $30,000. He has made a gift of $30,000, the excess of $90,000, the fair market value, over the amount realized, $60,000.

Example (2). A transfers property to his son for $30,000. Such property in the hands of A has an adjusted basis of $60,000 (and a fair market value of $90,000). A has no gain or loss, and has made a gift of $60,000, the excess of $90,000, the fair market value, over the amount realized, $30,000.

Example (3). A transfers property to his son for $30,000. Such property in A's hands has an adjusted basis of $30,000 (and a fair market value of $60,000). A has no gain and has made a gift of $30,000, the excess of $60,000, the fair market value, over the amount realized, $30,000.

Example (4). A transfers property to his son for $30,000. Such property in A's hands has an adjusted basis of $90,000 (and a fair market value of $60,000). A has sustained no loss, and has made a gift of $30,000, the excess of $60,000, the fair market value, over the amount realized, $30,000.

* * *

(g) Debt instruments issued in exchange for property.

(1) In general. If a debt instrument is issued in exchange for property, the amount realized attributable to the debt instrument is the issue price of the debt instrument as determined under § 1.1273–

2 or § 1.1274–2, whichever is applicable. If, however, the issue price of the debt instrument is determined under section 1273(b)(4), the amount realized attributable to the debt instrument is its stated principal amount reduced by any unstated interest (as determined under section 483).

(2) Certain debt instruments that provide for contingent payments. (i) In general. Paragraph (g)(1) of this section does not apply to a debt instrument subject to either § 1.483–4 or § 1.1275–4(c) (certain contingent payment debt instruments issued for nonpublicly traded property).

(ii) Special rule to determine amount realized. If a debt instrument subject to § 1.1275–4(c) is issued in exchange for property, and the income from the exchange is not reported under the installment method of section 453, the amount realized attributable to the debt instrument is the issue price of the debt instrument as determined under § 1.1274–2(g), increased by the fair market value of the contingent payments payable on the debt instrument. If a debt instrument subject to section 1.483–4 is issued in exchange for property, and the income from the exchange is not reported under the installment method of section 453, the amount realized attributable to the debt instrument is its stated principal amount, reduced by any unstated interest (as determined under section 483), and increased by the fair market value of the contingent payments payable on the debt instrument. This paragraph (g)(2)(ii), however, does not apply to a debt instrument if the fair market value of the contingent payments is not reasonably ascertainable. Only in rare and extraordinary cases will the fair market value of the contingent payments be treated as not reasonably ascertainable.

(3) Coordination with section 453. If a debt instrument is issued in exchange for property, and the income from the exchange is not reported under the installment method of section 453, this paragraph (g) applies rather than § 15a.453–1(d)(2) to determine the taxpayer's amount realized attributable to the debt instrument.

* * *

[T.D. 6500, 25 FR 11910, Nov. 26, 1960, as amended by T.D. 7142, 36 FR 18950, Sept. 24, 1971; T.D. 7207, 37 FR 20797, Oct. 5, 1972; T.D. 7213, 37 FR 21992, Oct. 18, 1972; T.D. 8517, 59 FR 4799, Feb. 2, 1994; T.D. 8674, 61 FR 30133, June 14, 1996; T.D. 9348, 72 FR 42293, Aug. 2, 2007]

§ 1.1001–2 Discharge of liabilities.

(a) Inclusion in amount realized—(1) In general. Except as provided in paragraph (a)(2) and (3) of this section, the amount realized from a sale or other disposition of property includes the amount of liabilities from which the transferor is discharged as a result of the sale or disposition.

(2) Discharge of indebtedness. The amount realized on a sale or other disposition of property that secures a recourse liability does not include amounts that are (or would be if realized and recognized) income from the discharge of indebtedness under section 61(a)(12). For situations where amounts arising from the discharge of indebtedness are not realized and recognized, see section 108 and * * *.

(3) Liability incurred on acquisition. In the case of a liability incurred by reason of the acquisition of the property, this section does not apply to the extent that such liability was not taken into account in determining the transferor's basis for such property.

(4) Special rules. For purposes of this section—

(i) The sale or other disposition of property that secures a nonrecourse liability discharges the transferor from the liability;

(ii) The sale or other disposition of property that secures a recourse liability discharges the transferor from the liability if another person agrees to pay the liability (whether or not the transferor is in fact released from liability);

(iii) A disposition of property includes a gift of the property or a transfer of the property in satisfaction of liabilities to which it is subject;

(iv) Contributions and distributions of property between a partner and a partnership are not sales or other dispositions of property; and

(v) The liabilities from which a transferor is discharged as a result of the sale or disposition of a partnership interest include the transferor's share of the liabilities of the partnership.

(b) Effect of fair market value of security. The fair market value of the security at the time of sale or disposition is not relevant for purposes of determining under paragraph (a) of this section the amount of liabilities from which the taxpayer is discharged or treated as discharged. Thus, the fact that the fair market value of the property is less than the amount of the liabilities it secures does not prevent the full amount of those liabilities from being treated as money received from the sale or other disposition of the property. However, see paragraph (a)(2) of this section for a rule relating to certain income from discharge of indebtedness.

(c) Examples. The provisions of this section may be illustrated by the following examples. In each example assume the taxpayer uses the cash receipts and disbursements method of accounting, makes a return on the basis of the calendar year, and sells or disposes of all property which is security for a given liability.

Example (1). In 1976 A purchases an asset for $10,000. A pays the seller $1,000 in cash and signs a note payable to the seller for $9,000. A is personally liable for repayment with the seller having full recourse in the event of default. In addition, the asset which was purchased is pledged as security. During the years 1976 and 1977 A takes depreciation deductions on the asset in the amount of $3,100. During this same time period A reduces the outstanding principal on the note to $7,600. At the beginning of 1978 A sells the asset. The buyer pays A $1,600 in cash and assumes personal liability for the $7,600 outstanding liability. A becomes secondarily liable for repayment of the liability. A's amount realized is $9,200 ($1,600 + $7,600). Since A's adjusted basis in the asset is $6,900 ($10,000 - $3,100) A realizes a gain of $2,300 ($9,200 - $6,900).

Example (2). Assume the same facts as in example (1) except that A is not personally liable on the $9,000 note given to the seller and in the event of default the seller's only recourse is to the asset. In addition, on the sale of the asset by A, the purchaser takes the asset subject to the liability. Nevertheless, A's amount realized is $9,200 and A's gain realized is $2,300 on the sale.

Example (3). In 1975 L becomes a limited partner in partnership GL. L contributes $10,000 in cash to GL and L's distributive share of partnership income and loss is 10 percent. L is not entitled to receive any guaranteed payments. In 1978 M purchases L's entire interest in partnership GL. At the time of the sale L's adjusted basis in the partnership interest is $20,000. At that time L's proportionate share of liabilities, of which no partner has assumed personal liability, is $15,000. M pays $10,000 in cash for L's interest in the partnership. Under section 752(d) and this section, L's share of partnership liabilities, $15,000, is treated as money received. Accordingly, L's amount realized on the sale of the partnership interest is $25,000 ($10,000 + $15,000). L's gain realized on the sale is $5,000 ($25,000–$20,000).

Example (4). In 1976 B becomes a limited partner in partnership BG. In 1978 B contributes B's entire interest in BG to a charitable organization described in section 170(c). At the time of the contribution all of the partnership liabilities are liabilities for which neither B nor G has assumed any personal liability and B's proportionate share of which is $9,000. The charitable organization does not pay any cash or other property to B, but takes the partnership interest subject to the $9,000 of liabilities. Assume that the contribution is treated as a bargain sale to a charitable organization and that under section 1011(b) $3,000 is determined to be the portion of B's basis in the partnership interest allocable to the sale. Under section 752(d) and this section, the $9,000 of liabilities is treated by B as money received, thereby making B's amount realized $9,000. B's gain realized is $6,000 ($9,000–$3,000).

Example (5). In 1975 C, an individual, creates T, an irrevocable trust. Due to certain powers expressly retained by C, T is a "grantor trust" for purposes of subpart E of part 1 of subchapter J of the Code and therefore C is treated as the owner of the entire trust. T purchases an interest in P, a partnership. C, as owner of T, deducts the distributive share of partnership losses attributable to the partnership interest held by T. In 1978, when the adjusted basis of the partnership interest held by T is $1,200, C renounces the powers previously and expressly retained that initially resulted in T being classified as a grantor trust. Consequently, T ceases to be a grantor trust and C is no longer considered to be the owner of the trust. At the time of the renunciation all of P's liabilities are liabilities on which none of the partners have assumed any personal liability and the proportionate share of which of the interest held by T is $11,000. Since prior to the renunciation C was the owner of the entire trust, C was considered the owner of all the trust property for Federal income tax purposes, including the partnership interest. Since C was considered to be the owner of the partnership interest, C not T, was considered to be the partner in P during the time T was a "grantor trust". However, at the time C renounced the powers that gave rise to T's classification as a grantor trust, T no longer qualified as a grantor trust with the result that C was no longer considered to be the owner of the trust and trust property for Federal income tax purposes. Consequently, at that time, C is considered to have transferred ownership of the interest in P to T, now a separate taxable entity, independent of its grantor C. On the transfer, C's share of partnership liabilities ($11,000) is treated as money received. Accordingly, C's amount realized is $11,000 and C's gain realized is $9,800 ($11,000–$1,200).

Example (6). In 1977 D purchases an asset for $7,500. D pays the seller $1,500 in cash and signs a note payable to the seller for $6,000. D is not personally liable for repayment but pledges as security the newly purchased asset. In the event of default, the seller's only recourse is to the asset. During the years 1977 and 1978 D takes depreciation deductions on the asset totaling $4,200 thereby reducing D's basis in the asset to $3,300 ($7,500–$4,200). In 1979 D transfers the asset to a trust which is not a "grantor trust" for purposes of subpart E of part 1 of subchapter J of the Code. Therefore D is not treated as the owner of the trust. The trust takes the asset subject to the liability and in addition pays D $750 in cash. Prior to the transfer D had reduced the amount outstanding on the liability to $4,700. D's amount realized on the transfer is $5,450 ($4,700 + $750). Since D's adjusted basis is $3,300, D's gain realized is $2,150 ($5,450–$3,300).

Example (7). In 1974 E purchases a herd of cattle for breeding purposes. The purchase price is $20,000 consisting of $1,000 cash and a $19,000 note. E is not personally liable for repayment of the liability and the seller's only recourse in the event of default is to the herd of cattle. In 1977 E transfers the herd back to the original seller thereby satisfying the indebtedness pursuant to a provision in the original sales agreement. At the time of the transfer the fair market value of the herd is $15,000 and the remaining principal balance on the note is $19,000. At that time E's adjusted basis in the herd is $16,500 due to a deductible loss incurred when a portion of the herd died as a result of disease. As a result of the indebtedness being satisfied, E's amount realized is $19,000 notwithstanding the fact that the fair market value of the herd was less than $19,000. E's realized gain is 2,500 ($19,000–$16,500).

Example (8). In 1980, F transfers to a creditor an asset with a fair market value of $6,000 and the creditor discharges $7,500 of indebtedness for which F is personally liable. The amount realized on the disposition of the asset is its fair market value ($6,000). In addition, F has income from the discharge of indebtedness of $1,500 ($7,500–$6,000).

[T.D. 7741, 45 FR 81744, Dec. 12, 1980]

§ 1.1002–1 Sales or exchanges.

(a) General rule. The general rule with respect to gain or loss realized upon the sale or exchange of property as determined under section 1001 is that the entire amount of such gain or loss is recognized except in cases where specific provisions of subtitle A of the Code provide otherwise.

(b) Strict construction of exceptions from general rule. The exceptions from the general rule requiring the recognition of all gains and losses, like other exceptions from a rule of taxation of general and uniform application, are strictly construed and do not extend either beyond the words or the underlying assumptions and purposes of the exception. Nonrecognition is accorded by the Code only if the exchange is one which satisfies both (1) the specific description in the Code of an excepted exchange, and (2) the underlying purpose for which such exchange is excepted from the general rule. The exchange must be germane to, and a necessary incident of, the investment or enterprise in hand. The relationship of the exchange to the venture or enterprise is always material, and the surrounding facts and circumstances must be shown. As elsewhere, the taxpayer claiming the benefit of the exception must show himself within the exception.

(c) Certain exceptions to general rule. Exceptions to the general rule are made, for example, by sections 351(a), 354, 361(a), 371(a)(1), 371(b)(1), 721, 1031, 1035 and 1036. These sections describe certain specific exchanges of property in which at the time of the exchange particular differences exist between the property parted with and the property acquired, but such differences are more formal than substantial. As to these, the Code provides that such differences shall not be deemed controlling, and that gain or loss shall not be recognized at the time of the exchange. The underlying assumption of these exceptions is that the new property is substantially a continuation of the old investment still unliquidated; and, in the case of reorganizations, that the new enterprise, the new corporate structure, and the new property are substantially continuations of the old still unliquidated.

(d) Exchange. Ordinarily, to constitute an exchange, the transaction must be a reciprocal transfer of property, as distinguished from a transfer of property for a money consideration only.

[T.D. 6500, 25 FR 11910, Nov. 26, 1960]

§ 1.1011–1 Adjusted basis.

The adjusted basis for determining the gain or loss from the sale or other disposition of property is the cost or other basis prescribed in section 1012 or other applicable provisions of subtitle A of the Code, adjusted to the extent provided in sections 1016, 1017, and 1018 or as otherwise specifically provided for under applicable provisions of internal revenue laws.

[T.D. 6500, 25 FR 11910, Nov. 26, 1960]

§ 1.1011–2 Bargain sale to a charitable organization.

(a) In general. **(1)** If for the taxable year a charitable contributions deduction is allowable under section 170 by reason of a sale or exchange of property, the taxpayer's adjusted basis of such property for purposes of determining gain from such sale or exchange must be computed as provided in section 1011(b) and paragraph (b) of this section. If after applying the provisions of section 170 for the taxable year, including the percentage limitations of section 170(b), no deduction is allowable under that section by reason of the sale or exchange of the property, section 1011(b) does not apply and the adjusted basis of the property is not required to be apportioned pursuant to paragraph (b) of this section. In such case the entire adjusted basis of the property is to be taken into account in determining gain from the sale or exchange, * * *. In ascertaining whether or not a charitable contributions deduction is allowable under section 170 for the taxable year for such purposes, that section is to be applied without regard to this section and the amount by which the contributed portion of the property must be reduced under section 170(e)(1) is the amount determined by taking into account the amount of gain which would have been ordinary income or long-term capital gain if the contributed portion of the property had been sold by the donor at its fair market value at the time of the sale or exchange.

(2) If in the taxable year there is a sale or exchange of property which gives rise to a charitable contribution which is carried over under section 170(b)(1)(D)(ii) or section 170(d) to a subsequent taxable year or is postponed under section 170(a)(3) to a subsequent taxable year, section 1011(b) and paragraph (b) of this section must be applied for purposes of apportioning the adjusted basis of the property for the year of the sale or exchange, whether or not such contribution is allowable as a deduction under section 170 in such subsequent year.

(3) If property is transferred subject to an indebtedness, the amount of the indebtedness must be treated as an amount realized for purposes of determining whether there is a sale or exchange to which section 1011(b) and this section apply, even though the transferee does not agree to assume or pay the indebtedness.

* * *

(b) Apportionment of adjusted basis. For purposes of determining gain on a sale or exchange to which this paragraph applies, the adjusted basis of the property which is sold or exchanged shall be that portion of the adjusted basis of the entire property which bears the same ratio to the adjusted basis as the amount realized bears to the fair market value of the entire property. The amount of such gain which shall be treated as ordinary income (or long-term capital gain) shall be that amount which bears the same ratio to the ordinary income (or long-term capital gain) which would have been recognized if the entire property had been sold by the donor at its fair market value at the time of the sale or exchange as the amount realized on the sale or exchange bears to the fair market value of the entire property at such time. The terms "ordinary income" and "long-term capital gain", as used in this section, have the same meaning as they have in paragraph (a) of § 1.170A–4. For determining the portion of the adjusted basis, ordinary income, and long-term capital gain allocated to the contributed portion of the property for purposes of applying section 170(e)(1) and paragraph (a) of § 1.170A–4 to the contributed portion of the property, and for determining the donee's basis in such contributed portion, see paragraph (c)(2) and (4) of § 1.170A–4. For determining the holding period of such contributed portion, see section 1223(2) and the regulations thereunder.

(c) Illustrations. The application of this section may be illustrated by the following examples, which are supplemented by other examples in paragraph (d) of § 1.170A–4:

Example (1). In 1970, A, a calendar-year individual taxpayer, sells to a church for $4,000 stock held for more than 6 months which has an adjusted basis of $4,000 and a fair market value of $10,000. A's contribution base for 1970, as defined in section 170(b)(1)(F), is $100,000, and during that year he makes no other charitable contributions. Thus, A makes a charitable contribution to the church of $6,000 ($10,000 value − $4,000 amount realized). Without regard to this section, A is allowed a deduction under section 170 of $6,000 for his charitable contribution to the church, since there is no reduction under section 170(e)(1) with respect to the long-term capital gain. Accordingly, under paragraph (b) of this section the adjusted basis for determining gain on the bargain sale is $1,600 ($4,000 adjusted basis × $4,000 amount realized / $10,000 value of property). A has recognized long-term capital gain of $2,400 ($4,000 amount realized − $1,600 adjusted basis) on the bargain sale.

Example (2). The facts are the same as in example (1) except that A also makes a charitable contribution in 1970 of $50,000 cash to the church. By reason of section 170(b)(1)(A), the deduction allowed under section 170 for 1970 is $50,000 for the amount of cash contributed to the church; however, the $6,000 contribution of property is carried over to 1971 under section 170(d). Under paragraphs (a)(2) and (b) of this section the adjusted basis for determining gain for 1970 on the bargain sale in that year is $1,600 ($4,000 × $4,000/$10,000). A has a recognized long-term capital gain for 1970 of $2,400 ($4,000 − $1,600) on the sale.

* * *

[T.D. 7207, 37 FR 20798, Oct. 5, 1972, as amended by T.D. 7741, 45 FR 81745, Dec. 12, 1980; T.D. 8176, 53 FR 5568, Feb. 25, 1988; T.D. 8176, 53 FR 11002, April 4, 1988; T.D. 8540, 59 FR 30100, June 10, 1994]

§ 1.1012–1 Basis of property.

(a) General rule. In general, the basis of property is the cost thereof. The cost is the amount paid for such property in cash or other property. This general rule is subject to exceptions stated in subchapter O (relating to gain or loss on the disposition of property), subchapter C (relating to corporate distributions and adjustments), subchapter K (relating to partners and partnerships), and subchapter P (relating to capital gains and losses), chapter 1 of the Code.

* * *

(c) Sale of stock—(1) In general. (i) Except as provided in paragraph (e)(2) of this section (dealing with stock for which the average basis method is permitted), if a taxpayer sells or transfers shares of stock in a corporation that the taxpayer purchased or acquired on different dates or at different prices and the taxpayer does not adequately identify the lot from which the stock is sold or transferred, the stock sold or transferred is charged against the earliest lot the taxpayer purchased or acquired to determine the basis and holding period of the stock. If the earliest lot purchased or acquired is held in a stock certificate that represents multiple lots of stock, and the taxpayer does not adequately identify the lot from which the stock is sold or transferred, the stock sold or transferred is charged against the earliest lot included in the certificate. See paragraphs (c)(2), (c)(3), and (c)(4) of this section for rules on what constitutes an adequate identification.

(ii) A taxpayer must determine the basis of identical stock (within the meaning of paragraph (e)(4) of this section) by averaging the cost of each share if the stock is purchased at separate times on the same calendar day in executing a single trade order and the broker executing the trade provides a single confirmation that reports an aggregate total cost or an average cost per share. However, the taxpayer may determine the basis of the stock by the actual cost per share if the taxpayer notifies the broker in writing of this intent. The taxpayer must notify the broker by the earlier of the date of the sale of any of the stock for which the taxpayer received the confirmation or one year after the date of the confirmation. A broker may extend the one-year period but the taxpayer must notify the broker no later than the date of sale of any of the stock.

(2) Identification of stock. An adequate identification is made if it is shown that certificates representing shares of stock from a lot which was purchased or acquired on a certain date or for a certain price were delivered to the taxpayer's transferee. Except as otherwise provided in subparagraph (3) or (4) of this paragraph, such stock certificates delivered to the transferee constitute the stock sold or transferred by the taxpayer. Thus, unless the requirements of subparagraph (3) or (4) of this paragraph are met, the stock sold or transferred is charged to the lot to which the certificates delivered to the transferee belong, whether or not the taxpayer intends, or instructs his broker or other agent, to sell or transfer stock from a lot purchased or acquired on a different date or for a different price.

(3) Identification on confirmation document. (i) Where the stock is left in the custody of a broker or other agent, an adequate identification is made if—

(a) At the time of the sale or transfer, the taxpayer specifies to such broker or other agent having custody of the stock the particular stock to be sold or transferred, and

(b) Within a reasonable time thereafter, confirmation of such specification is set forth in a written document from such broker or other agent.

Stock identified pursuant to this subdivision is the stock sold or transferred by the taxpayer, even though stock certificates from a different lot are delivered to the taxpayer's transferee.

(ii) Where a single stock certificate represents stock from different lots, where such certificate is held by the taxpayer rather than his broker or other agent, and where the taxpayer sells a part of the stock represented by such certificate through a broker or other agent, an adequate identification is made if—

(a) At the time of the delivery of the certificate to the broker or other agent, the taxpayer specifies to such broker or other agent the particular stock to be sold or transferred, and

(b) Within a reasonable time thereafter, confirmation of such specification is set forth in a written document from such broker or agent.

Where part of the stock represented by a single certificate is sold or transferred directly by the taxpayer to the purchaser or transferee instead of through a broker or other agent, an adequate identification is made if the taxpayer maintains a written record of the particular stock which he intended to sell or transfer.

* * *

[T.D. 6500, 25 FR 11910, Nov. 26, 1960, as amended by T.D. 6837, 30 FR 8787, July 13, 1965; T.D. 6887, 31 FR 8814, June 24, 1966; T.D. 6934, 32 FR 15671, 15676, Nov. 14, 1967; T.D. 6984, 33 FR 19176, Dec. 21, 1968; T.D. 7015, 34 FR 9672, June 20, 1969; T.D. 7081, 35 FR 19996, Dec. 31, 1970; T.D. 7129, 36 FR 12736, July 7, 1971; T.D. 7154, 36 FR 24997, Dec. 28, 1971; 36 FR 13208, July 16, 1971; 36 FR 24997, Dec. 28, 1971; T.D. 7213, 37 FR 21992, Oct. 18, 1972; T.D. 7568, 43 FR 47505, Oct. 16, 1978; T.D. 7728, 45 FR 72650, Nov. 3, 1980; T.D. 8517, 59 FR 4799, Feb. 2, 1994; T.D. 8674, 61 FR 30133, June 14, 1996; T.D. 9504, 75 FR 64084 (Oct. 18, 2010)]

§ 1.1014–1 Basis of property acquired from a decedent.

(a) General rule. The purpose of section 1014 is, in general, to provide a basis for property acquired from a decedent which is equal to the value placed upon such property for purposes of the Federal estate tax. Accordingly, the general rule is that the basis of property acquired from a decedent is the fair market value of such property at the date of the decedent's death, or, if the decedent's executor so elects, at the alternate valuation date prescribed in section 2032 * * *. Property acquired from a decedent includes, principally, property acquired by bequest, devise, or inheritance, and, in the case of decedents dying after December 31, 1953, property required to be included in determining the value of the decedent's gross estate under any provision of the Internal Revenue Code of 1954 or the Internal Revenue Code of 1939. The general rule governing basis of property acquired from a decedent, as well as other rules prescribed elsewhere in this section, shall have no application if the property is sold, exchanged, or otherwise disposed of before the decedent's death by the person who acquired the property from the decedent. * * *

* * *

[T.D. 6500, 25 FR 11910, Nov. 26, 1960, as amended by T.D. 6527, 26 FR 413, Jan. 19, 1961; T.D. 6887, 31 FR 8812, June 24, 1966; T.D. 7283, 38 FR 20825, Aug. 3, 1973]

§ 1.1014–2 Property acquired from a decedent.

(a) In general. The following property, except where otherwise indicated, is considered to have been acquired from a decedent and the basis thereof is determined in accordance with the general rule in § 1.1014–1:

(1) Without regard to the date of the decedent's death, property acquired by bequest, devise, or inheritance, or by the decedent's estate from the decedent, whether the property was acquired under the decedent's will or under the law governing the descent and distribution of the property of decedents. * * *

(2) Without regard to the date of the decedent's death, property transferred by the decedent during his lifetime in trust to pay the income for life to or on the order or direction of the decedent, with the right reserved to the decedent at all times before his death to revoke the trust.

(3) In the case of decedents dying after December 31, 1951, property transferred by the decedent during his lifetime in trust to pay the income for life to or on the order or direction of the decedent with the right reserved to the decedent at all times before his death to make any change in the enjoyment thereof through the exercise of a power to alter, amend, or terminate the trust.

(4) Without regard to the date of the decedent's death, property passing without full and adequate consideration under a general power of appointment exercised by the decedent by will. (See section 2041(b) for definition of general power of appointment.)

(5) In the case of decedents dying after December 31, 1947, property which represents the surviving spouse's one-half share of community property held by the decedent and the surviving spouse under the community property laws of any State, Territory, or possession of the United States or any foreign country, if at least one-half of the whole of the community interest in that property was includible in determining the value of the decedent's gross estate under part III, chapter 11 of the Internal Revenue Code of 1954 * * *. It is not necessary for the application of this subparagraph that an estate tax return be required to be filed for the estate of the decedent or that an estate tax be payable.

* * *

(b) Property acquired from a decedent dying after December 31, 1953—(1) In general. In addition to the property described in paragraph (a) of this section, and except as otherwise provided in subparagraph (3) of this paragraph, in the case of a decedent dying after December 31, 1953, property shall also be considered to have been acquired from the decedent to the extent that both of the following conditions are met: (i) The property was acquired from the decedent by reason of death, form of ownership, or other conditions (including property acquired through the exercise or non-exercise of a power of appointment), and (ii) the property is includible in the decedent's gross estate under the provisions of the Internal Revenue Code of 1954, or the Internal Revenue Code of 1939, because of such acquisition. The basis of such property in the hands of the person who acquired it from the decedent shall be determined in accordance with the general rule in § 1.1014–1. See, however, § 1.1014–6 for special adjustments if such property is acquired before the death of the decedent. See also subparagraph (3) of this paragraph for a description of property not within the scope of this paragraph.

(2) Rules for the application of subparagraph (1) of this paragraph. Except as provided in subparagraph (3) of this paragraph, this paragraph generally includes all property acquired from a decedent, which is includible in the gross estate of the decedent if the decedent died after December 31, 1953. It is not necessary for the application of this paragraph that an estate tax return be required to be filed for the estate of the decedent or that an estate tax be payable. Property acquired prior to the death of a decedent which is includible in the decedent's gross estate, such as property transferred by a decedent in contemplation of death, and property held by a taxpayer and the decedent as joint tenants or as tenants by the entireties is within the scope of this paragraph. Also, this paragraph includes property acquired through the exercise or nonexercise of a power of appointment where such property is includible in the decedent's gross estate. It does not include property not includible in the decedent's gross estate such as property not situated in the United States acquired from a nonresident who is not a citizen of the United States.

(3) Exceptions to application of this paragraph. The rules in this paragraph are not applicable to the following property:

(i) Annuities described in section 72;

* * *

(iii) Property described in any paragraph other than paragraph (9) of section 1014(b). * * *

* * *

* * *

[T.D. 6500, 25 FR 11910, Nov. 26, 1960]

§ 1.1014–3 Other basis rules.

(a) Fair market value. For purposes of this section and § 1.1014–1, the value of property as of the date of the decedent's death as appraised for the purpose of the Federal estate tax or the alternate value as appraised for such purpose, whichever is applicable, shall be deemed to be its fair market value. If no estate tax return is required to be filed under section 6018 * * *, the value of the property appraised as of the date of the decedent's death for the purpose of State inheritance or transmission taxes shall be deemed to be its fair market value and no alternate valuation date shall be applicable.

* * *

(c) Reinvestments by a fiduciary. The basis of property acquired after the death of the decedent by a fiduciary as an investment is the cost or other basis of such property to the fiduciary, and not the fair market value of such property at the death of the decedent. For example, the executor of an estate purchases stock of X company at a price of $100 per share with the proceeds of the sale of property acquired from a decedent. At the date of the decedent's death the fair market value of such stock was $98 per share. The basis of such stock to the executor or to a legatee, assuming the stock is distributed, is $100 per share.

(d) Reinvestments of property transferred during life. Where property is transferred by a decedent during life and the property is sold, exchanged, or otherwise disposed of before the decedent's death by the person who acquired the property from the decedent, the general rule stated in paragraph (a) of § 1.1014–1 shall not apply to such property. However, in such a case, the basis of any property acquired by such donee in exchange for the original property, or of any property acquired by the donee through reinvesting the proceeds of the sale of the original property, shall be the fair market value of the property thus acquired at the date of the decedent's death (or applicable alternate valuation date) if the property thus acquired is properly included in the decedent's gross estate for Federal estate tax purposes. These rules also apply to property acquired by the donee in any further exchanges or in further reinvestments. For example, on January 1, 1956, the decedent made a gift of real property to a trust for the benefit of his children, reserving to himself the power to revoke the trust at will. Prior to the decedent's death, the trustee sold the real property and invested the proceeds in stock of the Y Company at $50 per share. At the time of the decedent's death, the value of such stock was $75 per share. The corpus of the trust was required to be included in the decedent's gross estate owing to his reservation of the power of revocation. The basis of the Y company stock following the decedent's death is $75 per share. Moreover, if the trustee sold the Y Company stock before the decedent's death for $65 a share and reinvested the proceeds in Z company stock which increased in value to $85 per share at the time of the decedent's death, the basis of the Z company stock following the decedent's death would be $85 per share.

* * *

[T.D. 6500, 25 FR 11910, Nov. 26, 1960]

§ 1.1014–4 Uniformity of basis; adjustment to basis.

(a) In general. (1) The basis of property acquired from a decedent, as determined under section 1014(a), is uniform in the hands of every person having possession or enjoyment of the property at any time under the will or other instrument or under the laws of descent and distribution. The principle of uniform basis means that the basis of the property (to which proper adjustments must, of course, be made) will be the same, or uniform, whether the property is possessed or enjoyed by the executor or administrator, the heir, the legatee or devisee, or the trustee or beneficiary of a trust created by a will or an inter vivos trust. In determining the amount allowed or allowable to a taxpayer in computing taxable income as deductions for depreciation or depletion under section 1016(a)(2), the uniform basis of the property shall at all times be used and adjusted. The sale, exchange, or other disposition by a life tenant or remainderman of his interest in property will, for purposes of this section, have no effect upon the uniform basis of the property in the hands of those who acquired it from the decedent. Thus, gain or loss on sale of trust assets by the trustee will be determined without regard to the prior sale of any interest in the property. Moreover, any adjustment for depreciation shall be made to the uniform basis of the property without regard to such prior sale, exchange, or other disposition.

(2) Under the law governing wills and the distribution of the property of decedents, all titles to property acquired by bequest, devise, or inheritance relate back to the death of the decedent, even though the interest of the person taking the title was, at the date of death of the decedent, legal, equitable, vested, contingent, general, specific, residual, conditional, executory, or otherwise. Accordingly, there is a common acquisition date for all titles to property acquired from a decedent within the meaning of section 1014, and, for this reason, a common or uniform basis for all such interests. For example, if distribution of personal property left by a decedent is not made until one year after his death, the basis of such property in the hands of the legatee is its fair market value at the time when the decedent died, and not when the legatee actually received the property. If the bequest is of the residue to trustees in trust, and the executors do not distribute the residue to such trustees until five years after the death of the decedent, the basis of each piece of property left by the decedent and thus received, in the hands of the trustees, is its fair market value at the time when the decedent dies. If the bequest is to trustees in trust to pay to A during his lifetime the income of the property bequeathed, and after his death to distribute such property to the survivors of a class, and upon A's death the property is distributed to the taxpayer as the sole survivor, the basis of such property, in the hands of the taxpayer, is its fair market value at the time when the decedent died. The purpose of the Code in prescribing a general uniform basis rule for property acquired from a decedent is, on the one hand, to tax the gain, in respect of such property, to him who realizes it (without regard to the circumstances that at the death of the decedent it may have been quite uncertain whether the taxpayer would take or gain anything); and, on the other hand, not to recognize as gain any element of value resulting solely from the circumstance that the possession or enjoyment of the taxpayer was postponed. Such postponement may be, for example, until the administration of the decedent's estate is completed, until the period of the possession or enjoyment of another has terminated, or until an uncertain event has happened. It is the increase or decrease in the value of property reflected in a sale or other disposition which is recognized as the measure of gain or loss.

(3) The principles stated in subparagraphs (1) and (2) of this paragraph do not apply to property transferred by an executor, administrator or trustee, to an heir, legatee, devisee or beneficiary under circumstances such that the transfer constitutes a sale or exchange. In such a case, gain or loss must be recognized by the transferor to the extent required by the revenue laws, and the transferee acquires a basis equal to the fair market value of the property on the date of the transfer. Thus, for example, if the trustee of a trust created by will transfers to a beneficiary, in satisfaction of a specific bequest of $10,000, securities which had a fair market value of $9,000 on the date of the decedent's death (the applicable valuation date) and $10,000 on the date of the transfer, the trust realizes a taxable gain of $1,000 and the basis of the securities in the hands of the beneficiary would be $10,000. As a further example, if the executor of an estate transfers to a trust property worth $200,000, which had a fair market value of $175,000 on the date of the decedent's death (the applicable valuation date), in satisfaction of the decedent's bequest in trust for the benefit of his wife of cash or securities to be selected by the executor in an amount sufficient to utilize the marital deduction to the maximum extent authorized by law (after taking into consideration any other property qualifying for the marital deduction), capital gain in the amount of $25,000 would be realized by the estate and the basis of the property in the hands of the trustees would be $200,000. If, on the other hand, the decedent bequeathed a fraction of his residuary estate to a trust for the benefit of his wife, which fraction will not change regardless of any fluctuations in value of property in the decedent's estate after his death, no gain or loss would be realized by the estate upon transfer of property to the trust, and the basis of the property in the hands of the trustee would be its fair market value on the date of the decedent's death or on the alternate valuation date.

* * *

(c) Records. The executor or other legal representative of the decedent, the fiduciary of a trust under a will, the life tenant and every other person to whom a uniform basis under this section is applicable, shall maintain records showing in detail all deductions, distributions, or other items for which adjustment to basis is required to be made * * * and shall furnish to the district director such information with respect to those adjustments as he may require.

[T.D. 6500, 25 FR 11910, Nov. 26, 1960]

§ 1.1014–5 Gain or loss.

(a) Sale or other disposition of a life interest, remainder interest, or other interest in property acquired from a decedent. **(1)** Except as provided in paragraph (b) of this section with respect to the sale or other disposition after October 9, 1969, of a term interest in property, gain or loss from a sale or other disposition of a life interest, remainder interest, or other interest in property acquired from a decedent is determined by comparing the amount of the proceeds with the amount of that part of the adjusted uniform basis which is assignable to the interest so transferred. The adjusted uniform basis is the uniform basis of the entire property adjusted to the date of sale or other disposition of any such interest as required * * *. The uniform basis is the unadjusted basis of the entire property determined immediately after the decedent's death under the applicable sections of part II of subchapter O of chapter 1 of the Code.

(2) Except as provided in paragraph (b) of this section, the proper measure of gain or loss resulting from a sale or other disposition of an interest in property acquired from a decedent is so much of the increase or decrease in the value of the entire property as is reflected in such sale or other disposition. Hence, in ascertaining the basis of a life interest, remainder interest, or other interest which has been so transferred, the uniform basis rule contemplates that proper adjustments will be made to reflect the change in relative value of the interests on account of the passage of time.

(3) The factors set forth in the tables contained in § 20.2031–7 * * * shall be used in the manner provided therein in determining the basis of the life interest, the remainder interest, or the term certain interest in the property on the date such interest is sold. The basis of the life interest, the remainder interest, or the term certain interest is computed by multiplying the uniform basis (adjusted to the time of the sale) by the appropriate factor. In the case of the sale of a life interest or a remainder interest, the factor used is the factor (adjusted where appropriate) which appears in the life interest or the remainder interest column of the table opposite the age (on the date of the sale) of the person at whose death the life interest will terminate. In the case of the sale of a term certain interest, the factor used is the factor (adjusted where appropriate) which appears in the term certain column of the table opposite the number of years remaining (on the date of sale) before the term certain interest will terminate.

(b) Sale or other disposition of certain term interests. In determining gain or loss from the sale or other disposition after October 9, 1969, of a term interest in property (as defined in paragraph (f)(2) of § 1.1001–1) the adjusted basis of which is determined pursuant, or by reference, to section 1014 (relating to the basis of property acquired from a decedent) or section 1015 (relating to the basis of property acquired by gift or by a transfer in trust), that part of the adjusted uniform basis assignable under the rules of paragraph (a) of this section to the interest sold or otherwise disposed of shall be disregarded to the extent and in the manner provided by section 1001(e) and paragraph (f) of § 1.1001–1.

* * *

[T.D. 6500, 25 FR 11910, Nov. 26, 1960, as amended by T.D. 7142, 36 FR 18951, Sept. 24, 1971; T.D. 8540, 59 FR 30100, June 10, 1994]

§ 1.1014–6 Special rule for adjustments to basis where property is acquired from a decedent prior to his death.

(a) In general. **(1)** The basis of property described in section 1014(b)(9) which is acquired from a decedent prior to his death shall be adjusted for depreciation, obsolescence, amortization, and depletion allowed the taxpayer on such property for the period prior to the decedent's death. Thus, in general, the adjusted basis of such property will be its fair market value at the decedent's death, or the applicable alternate valuation date, less the amount allowed (determined with regard to section 1016(a)(2)(B)) to the taxpayer as deductions for exhaustion, wear and tear, obsolescence, amortization, and depletion for the period held by the taxpayer prior to the decedent's death. The deduction allowed for a taxable year in which the decedent dies shall be an amount properly allocable to that part of the year prior to his death. * * *

* * *

[T.D. 6500, 25 FR 11910, Nov. 26, 1960, as amended by T.D. 6712, 29 FR 3656, March 24, 1964; T.D. 7142, 36 FR 18952, Sept. 24, 1971]

§ 1.1015–1 Basis of property acquired by gift after December 31, 1920.

(a) General rule. **(1)** In the case of property acquired by gift after December 31, 1920 (whether by a transfer in trust or otherwise), the basis of the property for the purpose of determining gain is the same as it would be in the hands of the donor or the last preceding owner by whom it was not acquired by gift. The same rule applies in determining loss unless the basis (adjusted for the period prior to the date of gift in accordance with sections 1016 and 1017) is greater than the fair market value of the property at the time of the gift. In such case, the basis for determining loss is the fair market value at the time of the gift.

(2) The provisions of subparagraph (1) of this paragraph may be illustrated by the following example.

Example. A acquires by gift income-producing property which has an adjusted basis of $100,000 at the date of gift. The fair market value of the property at the date of gift is $90,000. A later sells the property for $95,000. In such case there is neither gain nor loss. The basis for determining loss is $90,000; therefore, there is no loss. Furthermore, there is no gain, since the basis for determining gain is $100,000.

* * *

(b) Uniform basis; proportionate parts of. Property acquired by gift has a single or uniform basis although more than one person may acquire an interest in such property. The uniform basis of the property remains fixed subject to proper adjustment for items under sections 1016 and 1017. However, the value of the proportionate parts of the uniform basis represented, for instance, by the respective interests of the life tenant and remainderman are adjustable to reflect the change in the relative values of such interest on account of the lapse of time. The portion of the basis attributable to an interest at the time of its sale or other disposition shall be determined under the rules provided in § 1.1014–5. In determining gain or loss from the sale or other disposition after October 9, 1969, of a term interest in property (as defined in § 1.1001–1(f)(2)) the adjusted basis of which is determined pursuant, or by reference, to section 1015, that part of the adjusted uniform basis assignable under the rules of § 1.1014–5(a) to the interest sold or otherwise disposed of shall be disregarded to the extent and in the manner provided by section 1001(e) and § 1.1001–1(f).

(c) Time of acquisition. The date that the donee acquires an interest in property by gift is when the donor relinquishes dominion over the property and not necessarily when title to the property is acquired by the donee. Thus, the date that the donee acquires an interest in property by gift where he is a successor in interest, such as in the case of a remainderman of a life estate or a beneficiary of the distribution of the corpus of a trust, is the date such interests are created by the donor and not the date the property is actually acquired.

(d) Property acquired by gift from a decedent dying after December 31, 1953. If an interest in property was acquired by the taxpayer by gift from a donor dying after December 31, 1953, under conditions which required the inclusion of the property in the donor's gross estate for estate tax purposes, and the property had not been sold, exchanged, or otherwise disposed of by the taxpayer before the donor's death, see the rules prescribed in section 1014 and the regulations thereunder.

(e) Fair market value. For the purposes of this section, the value of property as appraised for the purpose of the Federal gift tax, or, if the gift is not subject to such tax, its value as appraised for the purpose of a State gift tax, shall be deemed to be the fair market value of the property at the time of the gift.

* * *

(g) Records. To insure a fair and adequate determination of the proper basis under section 1015, persons making or receiving gifts of property should preserve and keep accessible a record of the facts necessary to determine the cost of the property and, if pertinent, its fair market value as of March 1, 1913, or its fair market value as of the date of the gift.

[T.D. 6500, 25 FR 11910, Nov. 26, 1960, as amended by T.D. 6693, 28 FR 12818, Dec. 3, 1963; T.D. 7142, 36 FR 18952, Sept. 24, 1971]

§ 1.1015–4 Transfers in part a gift and in part a sale.

(a) General rule. Where a transfer of property is in part a sale and in part a gift, the unadjusted basis of the property in the hands of the transferee is the sum of—

(1) Whichever of the following is the greater:

(i) The amount paid by the transferee for the property, or

(ii) The transferor's adjusted basis for the property at the time of the transfer, and

(2) The amount of increase, if any, in basis authorized by section 1015(d) for gift tax paid * * *.

For determining loss, the unadjusted basis of the property in the hands of the transferee shall not be greater than the fair market value of the property at the time of such transfer. For determination of gain or loss of the transferor, see § 1.1001–1(e) * * *. For special rule where there has been a charitable contribution of less than a taxpayer's entire interest in property, see section 170(e)(2) * * *.

(b) Examples. The rule of paragraph (a) of this section is illustrated by the following examples:

Example (1). If A transfers property to his son for $30,000, and such property at the time of the transfer has an adjusted basis of $30,000 in A's hands (and a fair market value of $60,000), the unadjusted basis of the property in the hands of the son is $30,000.

Example (2). If A transfers property to his son for $60,000, and such property at the time of transfer has an adjusted basis of $30,000 in A's hands (and a fair market value of $90,000), the unadjusted basis of such property in the hands of the son is $60,000.

Example (3). If A transfers property to his son for $30,000, and such property at the time of transfer has an adjusted basis in A's hands of $60,000 (and a fair market value of $90,000), the unadjusted basis of such property in the hands of the son is $60,000.

Example (4). If A transfers property to his son for $30,000 and such property at the time of transfer has an adjusted basis of $90,000 in A's hands (and a fair market value of $60,000), the unadjusted basis of the property in the hands of the son is $90,000. However, since the adjusted basis of the property in A's hands at the time of the transfer was greater than the fair market value at that time, for the purpose of determining any loss on a later sale or other disposition of the property by the son its unadjusted basis in his hands is $60,000.

[T.D. 6500, 25 FR 11910, Nov. 26, 1960, as amended by T.D. 6693, 28 FR 12818, Dec. 3, 1963; T.D. 7207, 37 FR 20799, Oct. 5, 1972]

§ 1.1015–5 Increased basis for gift tax paid.

* * *

(c) Special rule for increased basis for gift tax paid in the case of gifts made after December 31, 1976—(1) In general. With respect to gifts made after December 31, 1976 (other than gifts between spouses described in section 1015(e)), the increase in basis for gift tax paid is determined under section 1015(d)(6). Under section 1015(d)(6)(A), the increase in basis with respect to gift tax paid is limited to the amount (not in excess of the amount of gift tax paid) that bears the same ratio to the amount of gift tax paid as the net appreciation in value of the gift bears to the amount of the gift.

(2) Amount of gift. In general, for purposes of section 1015(d)(6)(A)(ii), the amount of the gift is determined in conformance with the provisions of paragraph (b) of this section. Thus, the amount of the gift is the amount included with respect to the gift in determining (for purposes of section 2503(a)) the total amount of gifts made during the calendar year (or calendar quarter in the case of a gift made on or before December 31, 1981), reduced by the amount of any annual exclusion allowable with respect to the gift under section 2503(b), and any deductions allowed with respect to the gift under section 2522 (relating to the charitable deduction) and section 2523 (relating to the marital deduction). Where more than one gift of a present interest in property is made to the same donee during a calendar year, the annual exclusion shall apply to the earliest of such gifts in point of time.

(3) Amount of gift tax paid with respect to the gift. In general, for purposes of section 1015(d)(6), the amount of gift tax paid with respect to the gift is determined in conformance with the provisions of paragraph (b) of this section. Where more than one gift is made by the donor in a calendar year (or quarter in the case of gifts made on or before December 31, 1981), the amount of gift tax paid with respect to any specific gift made during that period is the amount which bears the same ratio to the total gift tax paid for that period (determined after reduction for any gift tax unified credit available under section 2505) as the amount of the gift (computed as described in paragraph (c)(2) of this section) bears to the total taxable gifts for the period.

* * *

(5) Examples. Application of the provisions of this paragraph (c) may be illustrated by the following examples:

Example 1. **(i)** Prior to 1995, X exhausts X's gift tax unified credit available under section 2505. In 1995, X makes a gift to X's child Y, of a parcel of real estate having a fair market value of $100,000. X's adjusted basis in the real estate immediately before making the gift was $70,000. Also in 1995, X makes a gift to X's child Z, of a painting having a fair market value of $70,000. X timely files a gift tax return for 1995 and pays gift tax in the amount of $55,500, computed as follows:

Value of real estate transferred to Y	$100,000
Less: Annual exclusion	10,000
Included amount of gift (C)	$ 90,000
Value of painting transferred to Z	$ 70,000
Less: annual exclusion	10,000
Included amount of gift	60,000
Total included gifts (D)	$150,000
Total gift tax liability for 1995 gifts (B)	$ 55,500

(ii) The gift tax paid with respect to the real estate transferred to Y, is determined as follows:

$$\frac{\$90{,}000\ (C)}{\$150{,}000\ (D)} \times \$55{,}500\ (B) = \$33{,}300$$

(iii)(A) The amount by which Y's basis in the real property is increased is determined as follows:

$$\frac{\$30{,}000\ (\text{net appreciation})}{\$90{,}000\ (\text{amount of gift})} \times \$33{,}300 = \$11{,}100$$

(B) Y's basis in the real property is $70,000 plus $11,100, or $81,100. If x had not exhausted any of X's unified credit, no gift tax would have been paid and, as a result, Y's basis would not be increased.

* * *

[T.D. 8612, 60 FR 43531, Aug. 22, 1995]

§ 1.1016–2 Items properly chargeable to capital account.

(a) The cost or other basis shall be properly adjusted for any expenditure, receipt, loss, or other item, properly chargeable to capital account, including the cost of improvements and betterments made to the property. No adjustment shall be made in respect of any item which, under any applicable provision of law or regulation, is treated as an item not properly chargeable to capital account but is allowable as a deduction in computing net or taxable income for the taxable year. For example, in the case of oil and gas wells no adjustment may be made in respect of any intangible drilling and development expense allowable as a deduction in computing net or taxable income. * * *

(b) The application of the foregoing provisions may be illustrated by the following example:

Example. A, who makes his returns on the calendar year basis, purchased property in 1941 for $10,000. He subsequently expended $6,000 for improvements. Disregarding, for the purpose of this example, the adjustments required for depreciation, the adjusted basis of the property is $16,000. If A sells the property in 1954 for $20,000, the amount of his gain will be $4,000.

(c) Adjustments to basis shall be made for carrying charges such as taxes and interest, with respect to property (whether real or personal, improved or unimproved, and whether productive or unproductive), which the taxpayer elects to treat as chargeable to capital account under section 266, rather than as an allowable deduction. The term "taxes" for this purpose includes duties and excise taxes but does not include income taxes.

* * *

[T.D. 6500, 25 FR 11910, Nov. 26, 1960]

§ 1.1017–1 Basis reductions following a discharge of indebtedness.

(a) General rule for section 108(b)(2)(E). This paragraph (a) applies to basis reductions under section 108(b)(2)(E) that are required by section 108(a)(1)(A) or (B) because the taxpayer excluded discharge of indebtedness (COD income) from gross income. A taxpayer must reduce in the following order, to the extent of the excluded COD income (but not below zero), the adjusted bases of property held on the first day of the taxable year following the taxable year that the taxpayer excluded COD income from gross income (in proportion to adjusted basis)—

(1) Real property used in a trade or business or held for investment, other than real property described in section 1221(1), that secured the discharged indebtedness immediately before the discharge;

(2) Personal property used in a trade or business or held for investment, other than inventory, accounts receivable, and notes receivable, that secured the discharged indebtedness immediately before the discharge;

(3) Remaining property used in a trade or business or held for investment, other than inventory, accounts receivable, notes receivable, and real property described in section 1221(1);

(4) Inventory, accounts receivable, notes receivable, and real property described in section 1221(1); and

(5) Property not used in a trade or business nor held for investment.

(b) Operating rules—(1) Prior tax-attribute reduction. The amount of excluded COD income applied to reduce basis does not include any COD income applied to reduce tax attributes under sections 108(b)(2)(A) through (D) and, if applicable, section 108(b)(5). For example, if a taxpayer excludes $100 of COD income from gross income under section 108(a) and reduces tax attributes by $40 under sections 108(b)(2)(A) through (D), the taxpayer is required to reduce the adjusted bases of property by $60 ($100 − $40) under section 108(b)(2)(E).

* * *

[T.D. 8787, 63 FR 56559, Oct. 22, 1998, as amended by T.D. 9080, 68 FR 42590, July 18, 2003; T.D. 9127, 69 FR 26038, May 11, 2004; T.D. 9300, 71 FR 71042, Dec. 8, 2006]

§ 1.1031(a)-1 Property held for productive use in trade or business or for investment.

(a) In general—(1) Exchanges of property solely for property of a like kind. Section 1031(a)(1) provides an exception from the general rule requiring the recognition of gain or loss upon the sale or exchange of property. Under section 1031(a)(1), no gain or loss is recognized if property held for productive use in a trade or business or for investment is exchanged solely for property of a like kind to be held either for productive use in a trade or business or for investment. Under section 1031(a)(1), property held for productive use in a trade or business may be exchanged for property held for investment. Similarly, under section 1031(a)(1), property held for investment may be exchanged for property held for productive use in a trade or business. However, section 1031(a)(2) provides that section 1031(a)(1) does not apply to any exchange of—

(i) Stock in trade or other property held primarily for sale;

(ii) Stocks, bonds, or notes;

(iii) Other securities or evidences of indebtedness or interest;

(iv) Interests in a partnership;

(v) Certificates of trust or beneficial interests; or

(vi) Choses in action.

Section 1031(a)(1) does not apply to any exchange of interests in a partnership regardless of whether the interests exchanged are general or limited partnership interests or are interests in the same partnership or in different partnerships. An interest in a partnership that has in effect a valid election under section 761(a) to be excluded from the application of all of subchapter K is treated as an interest in each of the assets of the partnership and not as an interest in a partnership for purposes of section 1031(a)(2)(D) and paragraph (a)(1)(iv) of this section. An exchange of an interest in such a partnership does not qualify for nonrecognition of gain or loss under section 1031 with respect to any asset of the partnership that is described in section 1031(a)(2) or to the extent the exchange of assets of the partnership does not otherwise satisfy the requirements of section 1031(a).

(2) Exchanges of property not solely for property of a like kind. A transfer is not within the provisions of section 1031(a) if, as part of the consideration, the taxpayer receives money or property which does not meet the requirements of section 1031(a), but the transfer, if otherwise qualified, will be within the provisions of either section 1031(b) or (c). Similarly, a transfer is not within the provisions of section 1031(a) if, as part of the consideration, the other party to the exchange assumes a liability of the taxpayer (or acquires property from the taxpayer that is subject to a liability), but the transfer, if otherwise qualified, will be within the provisions of either section 1031(b) or (c). A transfer of property meeting the requirements of section 1031(a) may be within the provisions of section 1031(a) even though the taxpayer transfers in addition property not meeting the requirements of section 1031(a) or money. However, the nonrecognition treatment provided by section 1031(a) does not apply to the property transferred which does not meet the requirements of section 1031(a).

(b) Definition of "like kind." As used in section 1031(a), the words "like kind" have reference to the nature or character of the property and not to its grade or quality. One kind or class of property may not, under that section, be exchanged for property of a different kind or class. The fact that any real estate involved is improved or unimproved is not material, for that fact relates only to the grade or quality of the property and not to its kind or class. Unproductive real estate held by one other than a dealer for future use or future realization of the increment in value is held for investment and not primarily for sale. For additional rules for exchanges of personal property, see § 1.1031(a)–2.

(c) Examples of exchanges of property of a "like kind." No gain or loss is recognized if (1) a taxpayer exchanges property held for productive use in his trade or business, together with cash, for other property of like kind for the same use, such as a truck for a new truck or a passenger automobile for a new passenger automobile to be used for a like purpose; or (2) a taxpayer who is not a dealer in real estate exchanges city real estate for a ranch or farm, or exchanges a leasehold of a fee with 30 years or more to run for real estate, or exchanges improved real estate for unimproved real estate; or (3) a taxpayer exchanges investment property and cash for investment property of a like kind.

* * *

[T.D. 6500, 25 FR 11910, Nov. 26, 1960, as amended by T.D. 6935, 32 FR 15822, Nov. 17, 1967, and T.D. 8346, 56 FR 19937, May 1, 1991]

§ 1.1031(a)–2 Additional rules for exchanges of personal property.

(a) Introduction. Section 1.1031(a)–1(b) provides that the nonrecognition rules of section 1031 do not apply to an exchange of one kind or class of property for property of a different kind or class. This section contains additional rules for determining whether personal property has been exchanged for property of a like kind or like class. Personal properties of a like class are considered to be of a "like kind" for purposes of section 1031. In addition, an exchange of properties of a like kind may qualify under section 1031 regardless of whether the properties are also of a like class. In determining whether exchanged properties are of a like kind, no inference is to be drawn from the fact that the properties are not of a like class. Under paragraph (b) of this section, depreciable tangible personal properties are of a like class if they are either within the same General Asset Class (as defined in paragraph (b)(2) of this section) or within the same Product Class (as defined in paragraph (b)(3) of this section). Paragraph (c) of this section provides rules for exchanges of intangible personal property and nondepreciable personal property.

(b) Depreciable tangible personal property—(1) General rule. Depreciable tangible personal property is exchanged for property of a "like kind" under section 1031 if the property is exchanged for property of a like kind or like class. Depreciable tangible personal property is of a like class to other depreciable tangible personal property if the exchanged properties are either within the same General Asset Class or within the same Product Class. A single property may not be classified within more than one General Asset Class or within more than one Product Class. In addition, property classified within any General Asset Class may not be classified within a Product Class. A property's General Asset Class or Product Class is determined as of the date of the exchange.

(2) General Asset Classes. Except as provided in paragraphs (b)(4) and (b)(5) of this section, property within a General Asset Class consists of depreciable tangible personal property described in one of asset classes 00.11 through 00.28 and 00.4 of Rev. Proc. 87–56, 1987–2 C.B. 674. These General Asset Classes describe types of depreciable tangible personal property that frequently are used in many businesses. The General Asset Classes are as follows:

(i) Office furniture, fixtures, and equipment (asset class 00.11),

(ii) Information systems (computers and peripheral equipment) (asset class 00.12),

(iii) Data handling equipment, except computers (asset class 00.13),

(iv) Airplanes (airframes and engines), except those used in commercial or contract carrying of passengers or freight, and all helicopters (airframes and engines) (asset class 00.21),

(v) Automobiles, taxis (asset class 00.22),

(vi) Buses (asset class 00.23),

(vii) Light general purpose trucks (asset class 00.241),

(viii) Heavy general purpose trucks (asset class 00.242),

(ix) Railroad cars and locomotives, except those owned by railroad transportation companies (asset class 00.25),

(x) Tractor units for use over-the-road (asset class 00.26),

(xi) Trailers and trailer-mounted containers (asset class 00.27),

(xii) Vessels, barges, tugs, and similar water-transportation equipment, except those used in marine construction (asset class 00.28), and

(xiii) Industrial steam and electric generation and/or distribution systems (asset class 00.4).

(3) Product classes. Except as provided in paragraphs (b)(4) and (5) of this section, or as provided by the Commissioner in published guidance of general applicability, property within a product class consists of depreciable tangible personal property that is described in a 6-digit product class within Sectors 31, 32, and 33 (pertaining to manufacturing industries) of the North American Industry Classification System (NAICS), set forth in Executive Office of the President, Office of Management and Budget, North American Industry Classification System, United States, 2002 (NAICS Manual), as periodically updated. Copies of the NAICS Manual may be obtained from the National Technical Information Service, an agency of the U.S. Department of Commerce, and may be accessed on the internet. Sectors 31 through 33 of the NAICS Manual contain listings of specialized industries for the manufacture of described products and equipment. For this purpose, any 6-digit NAICS product class with a last digit of 9 (a miscellaneous category) is not a product class for purposes of this section. If a property is listed in more than one product class, the property is treated as listed in any one of those product classes. A property's 6-digit product class is referred to as the property's NAICS code.

* * *

(6) No inference outside of section 1031. The rules provided in this section concerning the use of general asset classes or product classes are limited to exchanges under section 1031. No inference is intended with respect to the classification of property for other purposes, such as depreciation.

(7) Examples. The application of this paragraph (b) may be illustrated by the following examples:

Example 1. Taxpayer A transfers a personal computer (asset class 00.12) to B in exchange for a printer (asset class 00.12). With respect to A, the properties exchanged are within the same General Asset Class and therefore are of a like class.

Example 2. Taxpayer C transfers an airplane (asset class 00.21) to D in exchange for a heavy general purpose truck (asset class 00.242). The properties exchanged are not of a like class because they are within different General Asset Classes. Because each of the properties is within a General Asset Class, the properties may not be classified within a Product Class. The airplane and heavy general purpose truck are also not of a like kind. Therefore, the exchange does not qualify for nonrecognition of gain or loss under section 1031.

Example 3. Taxpayer E transfers a grader to F in exchange for a scraper. Neither property is within any of the general asset classes. However, both properties are within the same product class (NAICS code 333120). The grader and scraper are of a like class and deemed to be of a like kind for purposes of section 1031.

Example 4. Taxpayer G transfers a personal computer (asset class 00.12), an airplane (asset class 00.21) and a sanding machine (NAICS code 333210), to H in exchange for a printer (asset class 00.12), a heavy general purpose truck (asset class 00.242) and a lathe (NAICS code 333210). The personal computer and the printer are of a like class because they are within the same general asset class. The sanding machine and the lathe are of a like class because they are within the same product class (although neither property is within any of the general asset classes). The airplane and the heavy general purpose truck are neither within the same general asset class nor within the same product class, and are not of a like kind.

* * *

(c) Intangible personal property and nondepreciable personal property—(1) General rule. An exchange of intangible personal property of nondepreciable personal property qualifies for nonrecognition of gain or loss under section 1031 only if the exchanged properties are of a like kind. No like classes are provided for these properties. Whether intangible personal property is of a like kind to other intangible personal property generally depends on the nature or character of the rights involved (e.g., a patent or a copyright) and also on the nature or character of the underlying property to which the intangible personal property relates.

(2) Goodwill and going concern value. The goodwill or going concern value of a business is not of a like kind to the goodwill or going concern value of another business.

(3) Examples. The application of this paragraph (c) may be illustrated by the following examples:

Example (1). Taxpayer K exchanges a copyright on a novel for a copyright on a different novel. The properties exchanged are of a like kind.

Example (2). Taxpayer J exchanges a copyright on a novel for a copyright on a song. The properties exchanged are not of a like kind.

* * *

[T.D. 8343, 56 FR 14854, Apr. 12, 1991; T.D. 9151, 69 FR 50067, Aug. 13, 2004; T.D. 9202, 70 FR 28818, May 19, 2005]

§ 1.1031(b)–1 Receipt of other property or money in tax-free exchange.

(a) If the taxpayer receives other property (in addition to property permitted to be received without recognition of gain) or money—

(1) In an exchange described in section 1031(a) of property held for investment or productive use in trade or business for property of like kind to be held either for productive use or for investment,

(2) In an exchange described in section 1035(a) of insurance policies or annuity contracts,

(3) In an exchange described in section 1036(a) of common stock for common stock, or preferred stock for preferred stock, in the same corporation and not in connection with a corporate reorganization, or

(4) In an exchange described in section 1037(a) of obligations of the United States, issued under the Second Liberty Bond Act (31 U.S.C. 774(2)), solely for other obligations issued under such Act,

the gain, if any, to the taxpayer will be recognized under section 1031(b) in an amount not in excess of the sum of the money and the fair market value of the other property, but the loss, if any, to the taxpayer from such an exchange will not be recognized under section 1031(c) to any extent.

(b) The application of this section may be illustrated by the following examples:

Example (1). A, who is not a dealer in real estate, in 1954 exchanges real estate held for investment, which he purchased in 1940 for $5,000, for other real estate (to be held for productive use in trade or business) which has a fair market value of $6,000, and $2,000 in cash. The gain from the transaction is $3,000, but is recognized only to the extent of the cash received of $2,000.

* * *

(c) Consideration received in the form of an assumption of liabilities (or a transfer subject to a liability) is to be treated as "other property or money" for the purposes of section 1031(b). Where, on an exchange described in section 1031(b), each party to the exchange either assumes a liability of the other party or acquires property subject to a liability, then, in determining the amount of "other property or money" for purposes of section 1031(b), consideration given in the form of an assumption of liabilities (or a receipt of property subject to a liability) shall be offset against consideration received in the form of an assumption of liabilities (or a transfer subject to a liability). See § 1.1031(d)–2, examples (1) and (2).

[T.D. 6500, 25 FR 11910, Nov. 26, 1960, as amended by T.D. 6935, 32 FR 15822, Nov. 17, 1967]

§ 1.1031(b)–2 Safe harbor for qualified intermediaries.

(a) In the case of simultaneous transfers of like kind properties involving a qualified intermediary * * *, the qualified intermediary is not considered the agent of the taxpayer for purposes of section 1031(a). In such a case, the transfer and receipt of property by the taxpayer is treated as an exchange.

(b) In the case of simultaneous exchanges of like-kind properties involving a qualified intermediary (as defined in § 1.1031(k)–1(g)(4)(iii)), the receipt by the taxpayer of an evidence of indebtedness of the transferee of the qualified intermediary is treated as the receipt of an evidence of indebtedness of the person acquiring property from the taxpayer for purposes of section 453 and § 15a.453–1(b)(3)(i) of this chapter.

(c) Paragraph (a) of this section applies to transfers of property made by taxpayers on or after June 10, 1991.

(d) Paragraph (b) of this section applies to transfers of property made by taxpayers on or after April 20, 1994. A taxpayer may choose to apply paragraph (b) of this section to transfers of property made on or after June 10, 1991.

[T.D. 8346, 56 FR 19937, May 1, 1991, as amended by T.D. 8535, 59 FR 18749, Apr. 20, 1994]

§ 1.1031(d)–1 Property acquired upon a tax-free exchange.

(a) If, in an exchange of property solely of the type described in section 1031, section 1035(a), section 1036(a), * * *, no part of the gain or loss was recognized under the law applicable to the year in which the exchange was made, the basis of the property acquired is the same as the basis of the property transferred by the taxpayer with proper adjustments to the date of the exchange. If additional consideration is given by the taxpayer in the exchange, the basis of the property acquired shall be the same as the property transferred increased by the amount of additional consideration given (see section 1016 and the regulations thereunder).

(b) If, in an exchange of properties of the type indicated in section 1031, section 1035(a), section

1036(a), * * *, gain to the taxpayer was recognized under the provisions of section 1031(b) or a similar provision of a prior revenue law, on account of the receipt of money in the transaction, the basis of the property acquired is the basis of the property transferred (adjusted to the date of the exchange), decreased by the amount of money received and increased by the amount of gain recognized on the exchange. The application of this paragraph may be illustrated by the following example:

Example. A, an individual in the moving and storage business, in 1954 transfers one of his moving trucks with an adjusted basis in his hands of $2,500 to B in exchange for a truck (to be used in A's business) with a fair market value of $2,400 and $200 in cash. A realizes a gain of $100 upon the exchange, all of which is recognized under section 1031(b). The basis of the truck acquired by A is determined as follows:

Adjusted basis of A's former truck	$ 2,500
Less: Amount of money received	200
Difference	2,300
Plus: Amount of gain recognized	100
Basis of truck acquired by A	$ 2,400

(c) If, upon an exchange of properties of the type described in section 1031, section 1035(a), section 1036(a), * * *, the taxpayer received other property (not permitted to be received without the recognition of gain) and gain from the transaction was recognized as required under section 1031(b), or a similar provision of a prior revenue law, the basis (adjusted to the date of the exchange) of the property transferred by the taxpayer, decreased by the amount of any money received and increased by the amount of gain recognized, must be allocated to and is the basis of the properties (other than money) received on the exchange. For the purpose of the allocation of the basis of the properties received, there must be assigned to such other property an amount equivalent to its fair market value at the date of the exchange. The application of this paragraph may be illustrated by the following example:

Example. A, who is not a dealer in real estate, in 1954 transfers real estate held for investment which he purchased in 1940 for $10,000 in exchange for other real estate (to be held for investment) which has a fair market value of $9,000, an automobile which has a fair market value of $2,000, and $1,500 in cash. A realizes a gain of $2,500, all of which is recognized under section 1031(b). The basis of the property received in exchange is the basis of the real estate A transfers ($10,000) decreased by the amount of money received ($1,500) and increased in the amount of gain that was recognized ($2,500), which results in a basis for the property received of $11,000. This basis of $11,000 is allocated between the automobile and the real estate received by A, the basis of the automobile being its fair market value at the date of the exchange, $2,000, and the basis of the real estate received being the remainder, $9,000.

(d) Section 1031(c) and, with respect to section 1031 and section 1036(a), similar provisions of prior revenue laws provide that no loss may be recognized on an exchange of properties of a type described in section 1031, section 1035(a), section 1036(a), * * *, although the taxpayer receives other property or money from the transaction. However, the basis of the property or properties (other than money) received by the taxpayer is the basis (adjusted to the date of the exchange) of the property transferred, decreased by the amount of money received. This basis must be allocated to the properties received, and for this purpose there must be allocated to such other property an amount of such basis equivalent to its fair market value at the date of the exchange.

(e) If, upon an exchange of properties of the type described in section 1031, section 1035(a), section 1036(a), * * *, the taxpayer also exchanged other property (not permitted to be transferred without the recognition of gain or loss) and gain or loss from the transaction is recognized * * *, the basis of the property acquired is the total basis of the properties transferred (adjusted to the date of the exchange) increased by the amount of gain and decreased by the amount of loss recognized on the other property. For purposes of this rule, the taxpayer is deemed to have received in exchange for such other property an amount equal to its fair market value on the date of the exchange. The application of this paragraph may be illustrated by the following example:

Example. A exchanges real estate held for investment plus stock for real estate to be held for investment. The real estate transferred has an adjusted basis of $10,000 and a fair market value of $11,000. The stock transferred has an adjusted basis of $4,000 and a fair market value of $2,000. The real estate acquired has a fair market value of $13,000. A is deemed to have received a $2,000 portion of the acquired real estate in exchange for the stock, since $2,000 is the fair market value of the stock at the time of the exchange. A $2,000 loss is recognized * * * on the exchange of the stock for real estate. No gain or loss is recognized on the exchange of the real estate since the property received is of the type permitted to be received without recognition of gain or loss. The basis of the real estate acquired by A is determined as follows:

Adjusted basis of real estate transferred	$ 10,000
Adjusted basis of stock transferred	4,000
	14,000
Less: Loss recognized on transfer of stock	2,000
Basis of real estate acquired upon the exchange	$ 12,000

[T.D. 6500, 25 FR 11910, Nov. 16, 1960, as amended by T.D. 6935, 32 FR 15823, Nov. 17, 1967]

§ 1.1031(d)–2 Treatment of assumption of liabilities.

For the purposes of section 1031(d), the amount of any liabilities of the taxpayer assumed by the other party to the exchange (or of any liabilities to which the property exchanged by the taxpayer is subject) is to be treated as money received by the taxpayer upon the exchange, whether or not the assumption resulted in a recognition of gain or loss to the taxpayer under the law applicable to the year in which the exchange was made. The application of this section may be illustrated by the following examples:

Example (1). B, an individual, owns an apartment house which has an adjusted basis in his hands of $500,000, but which is subject to a mortgage of $150,000. On September 1, 1954, he transfers the apartment house to C, receiving in exchange therefor $50,000 in cash and another apartment house with a fair market value on that date of $600,000. The transfer to C is made subject to the $150,000 mortgage. B realizes a gain of $300,000 on the exchange, computed as follows:

Value of property received	$600,000
Cash	50,000
Liabilities subject to which old property was transferred	150,000
Total consideration received	800,000
Less: Adjusted basis of property transferred	$500,000
Gain realized	$300,000

Under section 1031(b), $200,000 of the $300,000 gain is recognized. The basis of the apartment house acquired by B upon the exchange is $500,000 computed as follows:

Adjusted basis of property transferred		$500,000
Less: Amount of money received:		
Cash	$ 50,000	
Amount of liabilities subject to which property was transferred	150,000	
		200,000
Difference		300,000
Plus: Amount of gain recognized upon the exchange		200,000
Basis of property acquired upon the exchange		500,000

Example (2). **(a)** D, an individual, owns an apartment house. On December 1, 1955, the apartment house owned by D has an adjusted basis in his hands of $100,000, a fair market value of $220,000, but is subject to a mortgage of $80,000. E, an individual, also owns an apartment house. On December 1, 1955, the apartment house owned by E has an adjusted basis of $175,000, a fair market value of $250,000, but is subject to a mortgage of $150,000. On December 1, 1955, D transfers his apartment house to E, receiving in exchange therefore $40,000 in cash and the apartment house owned by E. Each apartment house is transferred subject to the mortgage on it.

(b) D realizes a gain of $120,000 on the exchange, computed as follows:

Value of property received		$250,000
Cash		40,000
Liabilities subject to which old property was transferred		80,000
Total consideration received		370,000
Less:		
Adjusted basis of property transferred	$100,000	
Liabilities to which new property is subject	150,000	
		250,000
Gain realized		120,000

For purposes of section 1031(b), the amount of "other property or money" received by D is $40,000. (Consideration received by D in the form of a transfer subject to a liability of $80,000 is offset by consideration given in the form of a receipt of property subject to a $150,000 liability. Thus, only the consideration received in the form of cash, $40,000, is treated as "other property or money" for purposes of section 1031(b).) Accordingly, under section 1031(b), $40,000 of the $120,000 gain is recognized. The basis of the apartment house acquired by D is $170,000, computed as follows:

Adjusted basis of property transferred		$100,000
Liabilities to which new property is subject		150,000
Total		250,000
Less: Amount of money received:		
Cash	$ 40,000	
Amount of liabilities subject to which property was transferred	80,000	
		120,000
Difference		$130,000
Plus: Amount of gain recognized upon the exchange		40,000
Basis of property acquired upon the exchange		$170,000

(c) E realizes a gain of $75,000 on the exchange, computed as follows:

Value of property received		$220,000
Liabilities subject to which old property was transferred		150,000
Total consideration received		370,000
Less:		
Adjusted basis of property transferred	$175,000	
Cash	40,000	
Liabilities to which new property is subject	80,000	
		295,000
Gain realized		$ 75,000

For purposes of section 1031(b), the amount of "other property or money" received by E is $30,000. (Consideration received by E in the form of a transfer subject to a liability of $150,000 is offset by consideration given in the form of a receipt of property subject to an $80,000 liability and by the $40,000 cash paid by E. Although consideration received in the form of cash or other property is not offset by consideration given in the form of an assumption of liabilities or a receipt of property subject to a liability, consideration given in the form of cash or other property is offset against consideration received in the form of an assumption of liabilities or a transfer of property subject to a liability.) Accordingly, under section 1031(b), $30,000 of the $75,000 gain is recognized. The basis of the apartment house acquired by E is $175,000, computed as follows:

Adjusted basis of property transferred		$175,000
Cash		40,000
Liabilities to which new property is subject		80,000
Total		295,000
Less: Amount of money received:		
Amount of liabilities subject to which property was transferred	$150,000	
		150,000
Difference		145,000
Plus: Amount of gain recognized upon the exchange		30,000
Basis of property acquired upon the exchange		$175,000

[T.D. 6500, 25 FR 11910, Nov. 26, 1960]

§ 1.1031(j)–1 Exchanges of multiple properties.

(a) Introduction—(1) Overview. As a general rule, the application of section 1031 requires a property-by-property comparison for computing the gain recognized and basis of property received in a like-kind exchange. This section provides an exception to this general rule in the case of an exchange of multiple properties. An exchange is an exchange of multiple properties if, under paragraph (b)(2) of this section, more than one exchange group is created. In addition, an exchange is an exchange of multiple properties if only one exchange group is created but there is more than one property being transferred or received within that exchange group. Paragraph (b) of this section provides rules for computing the amount of gain recognized in an exchange of multiple properties qualifying for nonrecognition of gain or loss under section 1031. Paragraph (c) of this section provides rules for computing the basis of properties received in an exchange of multiple properties qualifying for nonrecognition of gain or loss under section 1031.

(2) General approach. **(i)** In general, the amount of gain recognized in an exchange of multiple properties is computed by first separating the properties transferred and the properties received by the taxpayer in the exchange into exchange groups in the manner described in paragraph (b)(2) of this section. The separation of the properties transferred and the properties received in the exchange into exchange groups involves matching up properties of a like kind of like class to the extent possible. Next, all liabilities assumed by the taxpayer as part of the transaction are offset by all liabilities of which the taxpayer is relieved as part of the transaction, with the excess liabilities assumed or relieved allocated in accordance with paragraph (b)(2)(ii) of this section. Then, the rules of section 1031 and the regulations thereunder are applied separately to each exchange group to determine the amount of gain recognized in the exchange. See §§ 1.1031(b)–1 and 1.1031(c)–1. Finally, the rules of section 1031 and the regulations thereunder are applied separately to each exchange group to determine the basis of the properties received in the exchange. See §§ 1.1031(d)–1 and 1.1031(d)–2.

(ii) For purposes of this section, the exchanges are assumed to be made at arms' length, so that the aggregate fair market value of the property received in the exchange equals the aggregate fair market value of the property transferred. Thus, the amount realized with respect to the properties transferred in each exchange group is assumed to equal their aggregate fair market value.

(b) Computation of gain recognized—(1) In general. In computing the amount of gain recognized in an exchange of multiple properties, the fair market value must be determined for each property transferred and for each property received by the taxpayer in the exchange. In addition, the adjusted basis must be determined for each property transferred by the taxpayer in the exchange.

(2) Exchange groups and residual group. The properties transferred and the properties received by the taxpayer in the exchange are separated into exchange groups and a residual group to the extent provided in this paragraph (b)(2).

(i) Exchange groups. Each exchange group consists of the properties transferred and received in the exchange, all of which are of a like kind or like class. If a property could be included in more than one exchange group, the taxpayer may include the property in any of those exchange groups. Property eligible for inclusion within an exchange group does not include money or property described in section 1031(a)(2) (*i.e.*, stock in trade or other property held primarily for sale, stocks, bonds, notes, other securities or evidences of indebtedness or interest, interests in a partnership, certificates of trust or beneficial interests, or choses in action). For example, an exchange group may consist of all exchanged properties that are within the same General Asset Class or within the same Product Class (as defined in § 1.1031(a)–2(b)). Each exchange group must consist of at least one property transferred and at least one property received in the exchange.

(ii) Treatment of liabilities. **(A)** All liabilities assumed by the taxpayer as part of the exchange are offset against all liabilities of which the taxpayer is relieved as part of the exchange, regardless of whether the liabilities are recourse or nonrecourse and regardless of whether the liabilities are secured by or otherwise relate to specific property transferred or received as part of the exchange. See §§ 1.1031(b)–1(c) and 1.1031(d)–2. For purposes of this section, liabilities assumed by the taxpayer as part of the exchange consist of liabilities of the other party to the exchange assumed by the taxpayer and liabilities subject to which the other party's property is transferred in the exchange. Similarly, liabilities of which the taxpayer is relieved as part of the exchange consist of liabilities of the taxpayer assumed by the other party to the exchange and liabilities subject to which the taxpayer's property is transferred.

(B) If there are excess liabilities assumed by the taxpayer as part of the exchange (*i.e.*, the amount of liabilities assumed by the taxpayer exceeds the amount of liabilities of which the taxpayer is relieved), the excess is allocated among the exchange groups (but not to the residual group) in proportion to the aggregate fair market value of the properties received by the taxpayer in the exchange groups. The amount of excess liabilities assumed by the taxpayer that are allocated to each exchange group may not exceed the aggregate fair market value of the properties received in the exchange group.

(C) If there are excess liabilities of which the taxpayer is relieved as part of the exchange (*i.e.*, the amount of liabilities of which the taxpayer is relieved exceeds the amount of liabilities assumed by the taxpayer), the excess is treated as a Class I asset for purposes of making allocations to the residual group under paragraph (b)(2)(iii) of this section.

(D) Paragraphs (b)(2)(ii)(A), (B), and (C) of this section are applied in the same manner even if section 1031 and this section apply to only a portion of a larger transaction (such as a transaction described in section 1060(c) and § 1.1060–1T(b)). In that event, the amount of excess liabilities assumed by the taxpayer or the amount of excess liabilities of which the taxpayer is relieved is determined based on all liabilities assumed by the taxpayer and all liabilities of which the taxpayer is relieved as part of the larger transaction.

(iii) Residual group. If the aggregate fair market value of the properties transferred in all of the exchange groups differs from the aggregate fair market value of the properties received in all of the exchange groups (taking liabilities into account in the manner described in paragraph (b)(2)(ii) of this section), a residual group is created. The residual group consists of an amount of money or other property having an aggregate fair market value equal to that difference. The residual group consists of either money or other property transferred in the exchange or money or other property received in the exchange, but not both. For this purpose, other property includes property described in section 1031(a)(2) (*i.e.*, stock in trade or other property held primarily for sale, stocks, bonds, notes, other securities or evidences of indebtedness or interest, interests in a partnership, certificates of trust or beneficial interests, or choses in action), property transferred that is not of a like kind or like class with any property received, and property received that is not of a like kind or like class with any property transferred. The money and properties that are allocated to the residual group are considered to come from the following assets in the following order: first from Class I assets, then from Class II assets, then from Class III assets, and then from Class IV assets. The terms Class I assets, Class II assets, Class III assets, and Class IV assets have the same meanings as in § 1.338–6(b), to which reference is made by § 1.1060–1(c)(2). Within each Class, taxpayers may choose which properties are allocated to the residual group.

(iv) Exchange group surplus and deficiency. For each of the exchange groups described in this section, an "exchange group surplus" or "exchange group deficiency," if any, must be determined. An exchange group surplus is the excess of the aggregate fair market value of the properties received (less the amount of any excess liabilities assumed by the taxpayer that are allocated to that exchange group), in an exchange group over the aggregate fair market value of the properties transferred in that exchange group. An exchange group deficiency is the excess of the aggregate fair market value of the properties transferred in an exchange group over the aggregate fair market value of the properties received (less the amount of any excess liabilities assumed by the taxpayer that are allocated to that exchange group) in that exchange group.

(3) Amount of gain recognized.—(i) For purposes of this section, the amount of gain or loss realized with respect to each exchange group and the residual group is the difference between the aggregate fair market value of the properties transferred in that exchange group or residual group and the properties' aggregate adjusted basis. The gain realized with respect to each exchange group is recognized to the extent of the lesser of the gain realized and the amount of the exchange group deficiency, if any. Losses realized with respect to an exchange group are not recognized. See section 1031(a) and (c). The total amount of gain recognized under section 1031 in the exchange is the sum of the amount of gain recognized with respect to each exchange group. With respect to the residual group, the gain or loss realized (as determined under this section) is recognized as provided in section 1001 or other applicable provision of the Code.

(ii) The amount of gain or loss realized and recognized with respect to properties transferred by the taxpayer that are not within any exchange group or the residual group is determined under section 1001 and other applicable provisions of the Code, with proper adjustments made for all liabilities not allocated to the exchange groups or the residual group.

(c) Computation of basis of properties received. In an exchange of multiple properties qualifying for nonrecognition of gain or loss under section 1031 and this section, the aggregate basis of properties received in each of the exchange groups is the aggregate adjusted basis of the properties transferred by the taxpayer within that exchange group, increased by the amount of gain recognized by the taxpayer with respect to that exchange group, increased by the amount of the exchange group surplus or decreased by the amount of the exchange group deficiency, and increased by the amount, if any, of excess liabilities assumed by the taxpayer that are allocated to that exchange group. The resulting aggregate basis of each exchange group is allocated proportionately to each property received in the exchange group in accordance with its fair market value. The basis of each property received within the residual group (other that money) is equal to its fair market value.

(d) Examples. The application of this section may be illustrated by the following examples:

Example 1. (i) K exchanges computer A (asset class 00.12) and automobile A (asset class 00.22), both of which were held by K for productive use in its business, with W for printer B (asset class 00.12) and automobile B (asset class 00.22), both of which will be held by K for productive use in its business. K's adjusted basis and the fair market value of the exchanged properties are as follows:

	Adjusted basis	Fair market value
Computer A	$ 375	$1,000
Automobile A	1,500	4,000
Printer B		2,050
Automobile B		2,950

(ii) Under paragraph (b)(2) of this section, the properties exchanged are separated into exchange groups as follows:

(A) The first exchange group consists of computer A and printer B (both are within the same General Asset Class) and, as to K, has an exchange group surplus of $1050 because the fair market value of printer B ($2050) exceeds the fair market value of computer A ($1000) by that amount.

(B) The second exchange group consists of automobile A and automobile B (both are within the same General Asset Class) and, as to K, has an exchange group deficiency of $1050 because the fair market value of automobile A ($4000) exceeds the fair market value of automobile B ($2950) by that amount.

(iii) K recognizes gain on the exchange as follows:

(A) With respect to the first exchange group, the amount of gain realized is the excess of the fair market value of computer A ($1000) over its adjusted basis ($375), or $625. The amount of gain recognized is the lesser of the gain realized ($625) and the exchange group deficiency ($0), or $0.

(B) With respect to the second exchange group, the amount of gain realized is the excess of the fair market value of automobile A ($4000) over its adjusted basis ($1500), or $2500. The amount of gain recognized is the lesser of the gain realized ($2500) and the exchange group deficiency ($1050), or $1050.

(iv) The total amount of gain recognized by K in the exchange is the sum of the gains recognized with respect to both exchange groups ($0 + $1050), or $1050.

(v) The bases of the property received by K in the exchange, printer B and automobile B, are determined in the following manner:

(A) The basis of the property received in the first exchange group is the adjusted basis of the property transferred within the exchange group ($375), increased by the amount of gain recognized with respect to that exchange group ($0), increased by the amount of the exchange group surplus ($1050), and increased by the amount of excess liabilities assumed allocated to that exchange group ($0), or $1425. Because printer B was the only property received within the first exchange group, the entire basis of $1425 is allocated to printer B.

(B) The basis of the property received in the second exchange group is the adjusted basis of the property transferred within that exchange group ($1500), increased by the amount of gain recognized with respect to that exchange group ($1050), decreased by the amount of the exchange group deficiency ($1050), and increased by the amount of excess liabilities assumed allocated to that exchange group ($0), or $1500. Because automobile B was the only property received within the second exchange group, the entire basis of $1500 is allocated to automobile B.

* * *

[T.D. 8343, 56 FR 14855, Apr. 12, 1991; as amended by T.D. 8858, 65 FR 1235, Jan. 7, 2000; T.D. 8940, 66 FR 9929, Feb. 13, 2001; T.D. 9202, 70 FR 28820, May 19, 2005]

§ 1.1031(k)–1 Treatment of deferred exchanges.

(a) Overview. This section provides rules for the application of section 1031 and the regulations thereunder in the case of a "deferred exchange." For purposes of section 1031 and this section, a deferred exchange is defined as an exchange in which, pursuant to an agreement, the taxpayer transfers property held for productive use in a trade or business or for investment (the "relinquished property") and subsequently receives property to be held either for productive use in a trade or business or for investment (the "replacement property"). In the case of a deferred exchange, if the requirements * * * of this section (relating to identification and receipt of replacement property) are not satisfied, the replacement property received by the taxpayer will be treated as property which is not of a like kind to the relinquished property. In order to constitute a deferred exchange, the transaction must be an exchange (i.e., a transfer of property for property, as distinguished from a transfer of property for money). For example, a sale of property followed by a purchase of property of a like kind does not qualify for nonrecognition of gain or loss under section 1031 regardless of whether the identification and receipt requirements of section 1031(a)(3) * * * are satisfied. The transfer of relinquished property in a deferred exchange is not within the provisions of section 1031(a) if, as part of the consideration, the taxpayer receives money or property which does not meet the requirements of section 1031(a), but the transfer, if otherwise qualified, will be within the provisions of either section 1031(b) or (c). See § 1.1031(a)–1(a)(2). In addition, in the case of a transfer of relinquished property in a deferred exchange, gain or loss may be recognized if the taxpayer actually or constructively receives money or property which does not meet the requirements of section 1031(a) before the taxpayer actually receives like-kind replacement property. If the taxpayer actually or constructively receives money or property which does not meet the requirements of section 1031(a) in the full amount of the consideration for the relinquished property, the transaction will constitute a sale, and not a deferred exchange, even though the taxpayer may ultimately receive like-kind replacement property. For purposes of this section, property which does not meet the requirements of section 1031(a) (whether by being described in section 1031(a)(2) or otherwise) is referred to as "other property." For rules regarding actual and constructive receipt, and safe harbors therefrom, see paragraphs (f) and (g), respectively, of this section. For rules regarding the determination of gain or loss recognized and the basis of property received in a deferred exchange, see paragraph (j) of this section.

(b) Identification and receipt requirements—(1) In general. In the case of a deferred exchange, any replacement property received by the taxpayer will be treated as property which is not of a like kind to the relinquished property if—

(i) The replacement property is not "identified" before the end of the "identification period," or

(ii) The identified replacement property is not received before the end of the "exchange period."

(2) Identification period and exchange period. (i) The identification period begins on the date the taxpayer transfers the relinquished property and ends at midnight on the 45th day thereafter.

(ii) The exchange period begins on the date the taxpayer transfers the relinquished property and ends at midnight on the earlier of the 180th day thereafter or the due date (including extensions) for the taxpayer's return of the tax imposed by chapter 1 of subtitle A of the Code for the taxable year in which the transfer of the relinquished property occurs.

(iii) If, as part of the same deferred exchange, the taxpayer transfers more than one relinquished property and the relinquished properties are transferred on different dates, the identification period and the exchange period are determined by reference to the earliest date on which any of the properties are transferred.

(iv) For purposes of this paragraph (b)(2), property is transferred when the property is disposed of within the meaning of section 1001(a).

(3) Example. This paragraph (b) may be illustrated by the following example:

Example. (i) M is a corporation that files its Federal income tax return on a calendar year basis. M and C enter into an agreement for an exchange of property that requires M to transfer property X to C. Under the agreement, M is to identify like-kind replacement property which C is required to purchase and to transfer to M. M transfers property X to C on November 16, 1992.

(ii) The identification period ends at midnight on December 31, 1992, the day which is 45 days after the date of transfer of property X. The exchange period ends at midnight on March 15, 1993, the due date for M's Federal income tax return for the taxable year in which M transferred property X. However, if M is allowed the automatic six-month extension for filing its tax return, the exchange period ends at midnight on May 15, 1993, the day which is 180 days after the date of transfer of property X.

(c) Identification of replacement property before the end of the identification period—(1) In general. For purposes of paragraph (b)(1)(i) of this section (relating to the identification requirement), replacement property is identified before the end of the identification period only if the requirements of this paragraph (c) are satisfied with respect to the replacement property. However, any replacement property that is received by the taxpayer before the end of the identification period will in all events be treated as identified before the end of the identification period.

(2) Manner of identifying replacement property. Replacement property is identified only if it is designated as replacement property in a written document signed by the taxpayer and hand delivered, mailed, telecopied, or otherwise sent before the end of the identification period to either—

(i) The person obligated to transfer the replacement property to the taxpayer (regardless of whether that person is a disqualified person as defined in paragraph (k) of this section); or

(ii) Any other person involved in the exchange other than the taxpayer or a disqualified person (as defined in paragraph (k) of this section).

Examples of persons involved in the exchange include any of the parties to the exchange, an intermediary, an escrow agent, and a title company. An identification of replacement property made in a written agreement for the exchange of properties signed by all parties thereto before the end of the identification period will be treated as satisfying the requirements of this paragraph (c)(2).

(3) Description of replacement property. Replacement property is identified only if it is unambiguously described in the written document or agreement. Real property generally is unambiguously described if it is described by a legal description, street address, or distinguishable name (e.g., the Mayfair Apartment Building). Personal property generally is unambiguously described if it is described by a specific description of the particular type of property. For example, a truck generally is unambiguously described if it is described by a specific make, model, and year.

(4) Alternative and multiple properties. (i) The taxpayer may identify more than one replacement property. Regardless of the number of relinquished properties transferred by the taxpayer as part of the same deferred exchange, the maximum number of replacement properties that the taxpayer may identify is—

(A) Three properties without regard to the fair market values of the properties (the "3–property rule"), or

(B) Any number of properties as long as their aggregate fair market value as of the end of the identification period does not exceed 200 percent of the aggregate fair market value of all the relinquished properties as of the date the relinquished properties were transferred by the taxpayer (the "200–percent rule").

(ii) If, as of the end of the identification period, the taxpayer has identified more properties as replacement properties than permitted by paragraph (c)(4)(i) of this section, the taxpayer is treated as if no replacement property had been identified. The preceding sentence will not apply, however, and an identification satisfying the requirements of paragraph (c)(4)(i) of this section will be considered made, with respect to—

(A) Any replacement property received by the taxpayer before the end of the identification period, and

(B) Any replacement property identified before the end of the identification period and received before the end of the exchange period, but only if the taxpayer receives before the end of the exchange period identified replacement property the fair market value of which is at least 95 percent of the aggregate fair market value of all identified replacement properties (the "95–percent rule").

For this purpose, the fair market value of each identified replacement property is determined as of the earlier of the date the property is received by the taxpayer or the last day of the exchange period.

(iii) For purposes of applying the 3–property rule, the 200–percent rule, and the 95–percent rule, all identifications of replacement property, other than identifications of replacement property that have been revoked in the manner provided in paragraph (c)(6) of this section, are taken into account. For example, if, in a deferred exchange, B transfers property X with a fair market value of $100,000 to C and B receives like-kind property Y with a fair market value of $50,000 before the end of the identification period, under paragraph (c)(1) of this section, property Y is treated as identified by reason of being received before the end of the identification period. Thus, under paragraph (c)(4)(i) of this section, B may identify either two additional replacement properties of any fair market value or any number of additional replacement properties as long as the aggregate fair market value of the additional replacement properties does not exceed $150,000.

(5) Incidental property disregarded. **(i)** Solely for purposes of applying this paragraph (c), property that is incidental to a larger item of property is not treated as property that is separate from the larger item of property. Property is incidental to a larger item of property if—

(A) In standard commercial transactions, the property is typically transferred together with the larger item of property, and

(B) The aggregate fair market value of all of the incidental property does not exceed 15 percent of the aggregate fair market value of the larger item of property.

(ii) This paragraph (c)(5) may be illustrated by the following examples:

Example 1. For purposes of paragraph (c) of this section, a spare tire and tool kit will not be treated as separate property from a truck with a fair market value of $10,000, if the aggregate fair market value of the spare tire and tool kit does not exceed $1,500. For purposes of the 3–property rule, the truck, spare tire, and tool kit are treated as 1 property. Moreover, for purposes of paragraph (c)(3) of this section (relating to the description of replacement property), the truck, spare tire, and tool kit are all considered to be unambiguously described if the make, model, and year of the truck are specified, even if no reference is made to the spare tire and tool kit.

Example 2. For purposes of paragraph (c) of this section, furniture, laundry machines, and other miscellaneous items of personal property will not be treated as separate property from an apartment building with a fair market value of $1,000,000, if the aggregate fair market value of the furniture, laundry machines, and other personal property does not exceed $150,000. For purposes of the 3–property rule, the apartment building, furniture, laundry machines, and other personal property are treated as 1 property. Moreover, for purposes of paragraph (c)(3) of this section (relating to the description of replacement property), the apartment building, furniture, laundry machines, and other personal property are all considered to be unambiguously described if the legal description, street address, or distinguishable name of the apartment building is specified, even if no reference is made to the furniture, laundry machines, and other personal property.

* * *

(d) Receipt of identified replacement property—(1) In general. For purposes of paragraph (b)(1)(ii) of this section (relating to the receipt requirement), the identified replacement property is received before the end of the exchange period only if the requirements of this paragraph (d) are satisfied with respect to the replacement property. In the case of a deferred exchange, the identified replacement property is received before the end of the exchange period if—

(i) The taxpayer receives the replacement property before the end of the exchange period, and

(ii) The replacement property received is substantially the same property as identified.

If the taxpayer has identified more than one replacement property, section 1031(a)(3)(B) and this paragraph (d) are applied separately to each replacement property.

(2) Examples. This paragraph (d) may be illustrated by the following examples. The following facts are assumed: B, a calendar year taxpayer, and C agree to enter into a deferred exchange. Pursuant to their agreement, B transfers real property X to C on May 17, 1991. Real property X, which has been held by B for investment, is unencumbered and has a fair market value on May 17, 1991, of $100,000. On or before July 1, 1991 (the end of the identification period), B is to identify replacement property that is of a like kind to real property X. On or before November 13, 1991 (the end of the exchange period), C is required to purchase the property identified by B and to transfer that property to B. To the extent the fair market value of the replacement property transferred to B is greater or less than the fair market value of real property X, either B or C, as applicable, will make up the difference by paying cash to the other party after the date the replacement property is received by B. The replacement property is identified in a manner that satisfies paragraph (c) of this section (relating to identification of replacement property) and is of a like kind to real property X (determined without regard to section 1031(a)(3) and this section). B intends to hold any replacement property received for investment.

Example 1. **(i)** In the agreement, B identifies real properties J, K, and L as replacement properties. The agreement provides that by July 26, 1991, B will orally inform C which of the properties C is to transfer to B.

(ii) As of July 1, 1991, the fair market values of real properties J, K, and L are $75,000, $100,000, and $125,000, respectively. On July 26, 1991, B instructs C to acquire real property K. On October 31, 1991, C purchases real property K for $100,000 and transfers the property to B.

(iii) Because real property K was identified before the end of the identification period and was received before the end of the exchange period, the identification and receipt requirements of section 1031(a)(3) and this section are satisfied with respect to real property K.

Example 2. **(i)** In the agreement, B identifies real property P as replacement property. Real property P consists of two acres of unimproved land. On October 15, 1991, the owner of real property P erects a fence on the property. On November 1, 1991, C purchases real property P and transfers it to B.

(ii) The erection of the fence on real property P subsequent to its identification did not alter the basic nature or character of real property P as unimproved land. B is considered to have received substantially the same property as identified.

Example 3. **(i)** In the agreement, B identifies real property Q as replacement property. Real property Q consists of a barn on two acres of land and has a fair market value of $250,000 ($187,500 for the barn and underlying land and $87,500 for the remaining land). As of July 26, 1991, real property Q remains unchanged and has a fair market value of $250,000. On that date, at B's direction, C purchases the barn and underlying land for $187,500 and transfers it to B, and B pays $87,500 to C.

(ii) The barn and underlying land differ in basic nature or character from real property Q as a whole, B is not considered to have received substantially the same property as identified.

Example 4. **(i)** In the agreement, B identifies real property R as replacement property. Real property R consists of two acres of unimproved land and has a fair market value of $250,000. As of October 3, 1991, real property R remains unimproved and has a fair market value of $250,000. On that date, at B's direction, C purchases 1½ acres of real property R for $187,500 and transfers it to B, and B pays $87,500 to C.

(ii) The portion of real property R that B received does not differ from the basic nature or character of real property R as a whole. Moreover, the fair market value of the portion of real property R that B received ($187,500) is 75 percent of the fair market value of real property R as of the date of receipt. Accordingly, B is considered to have received substantially the same property as identified.

* * *

(f) Receipt of money or other property—(1) In general. A transfer of relinquished property in a deferred exchange is not within the provisions of section 1031(a) if, as part of the consideration, the taxpayer receives money or other property. However, such a transfer, if otherwise qualified, will be within the provisions of either section 1031(b) or (c). See § 1031(a)–1(a)(2). In addition, in the case of a transfer of relinquished property in a deferred exchange, gain or loss may be recognized if the taxpayer actually or constructively receives money or other property before the taxpayer actually receives like-kind replacement property. If the taxpayer actually or constructively receives money or other property in the full amount of the consideration for the relinquished property before the taxpayer actually receives like-kind replacement property, the transaction will constitute a sale and not a deferred exchange, even though the taxpayer may ultimately receive like-kind replacement property.

(2) Actual and constructive receipt. Except as provided in paragraph (g) of this section (relating to safe harbors), for purposes of section 1031 and this section, the determination of whether (or the extent to which) the taxpayer is in actual or constructive receipt of money or other property before the taxpayer actually receives like-kind replacement property is made under the general rules concerning actual and constructive receipt and without regard to the taxpayer's method of accounting. The taxpayer is in actual receipt of money or property at the time the taxpayer actually receives the money or property or receives the economic benefit of the money or property. The taxpayer is in constructive receipt of money or property at the time the money or property is credited to the taxpayer's account, set apart for the taxpayer, or otherwise made available so that the taxpayer may draw upon it at any time or so that the taxpayer can draw upon it if notice of intention to draw is given. Although the taxpayer is not in constructive receipt of money or property if the taxpayer's control of its receipt is subject to substantial limitations or restrictions, the taxpayer is in constructive receipt of the money or property at the time the limitations or restrictions lapse, expire, or are waived. In addition, actual or constructive receipt of money or property by an agent of the taxpayer (determined without regard to paragraph (k) of this section) is actual or constructive receipt by the taxpayer.

(3) Example. This paragraph (f) may be illustrated by the following example.

Example. **(i)** B, a calendar year taxpayer, and C agree to enter into a deferred exchange. Pursuant to the agreement, on May 17, 1991, B transfers real property X to C. Real property X, which has been held by B for investment, is unencumbered and has a fair market value on May 17, 1991, of $100,000. On or before July 1, 1991 (the end of the identification period), B is to identify replacement property that is of a like kind to real property X. On or before November 13, 1991 (the end of the exchange period), C is required to purchase the property identified by B and to transfer that property to B. At any time after May 17, 1991, and before C has purchased the replacement property, B has the right, upon notice, to demand that C pay $100,000 in lieu of acquiring and transferring the replacement property. Pursuant to the agreement, B identifies replacement property, and C purchases the replacement property and transfers it to B.

(ii) Under the agreement, B has the unrestricted right to demand the payment of $100,000 as of May 17, 1991. B is therefore in constructive receipt of $100,000 on that date. Because B is in constructive receipt of money in the full amount of the consideration for the relinquished property before B actually receives the like-kind replacement property, the transaction constitutes a sale, and the transfer of real property X does not qualify for nonrecognition of gain or loss under section 1031. B is treated as if B received the $100,000 in consideration for the sale of real property X and then purchased the like-kind replacement property.

(iii) If B's right to demand payment of the $100,000 were subject to a substantial limitation or restriction (e.g., the agreement provided that B had no right to demand payment before November 14, 1991 (the end of the exchange period)), then, for purposes of this section, B would not be in actual or constructive receipt of the money unless (or until) the limitation or restriction lapsed, expired, or was waived.

(g) Safe harbors—(1) In general. Paragraphs (g)(2) through (g)(5) of this section set forth four safe harbors the use of which will result in a determination that the taxpayer is not in actual or constructive receipt of money or other property for purposes of section 1031 and this section. More than one safe harbor can be used in the same deferred exchange, but the terms and conditions of each must be separately satisfied. For purposes of the safe harbor rules, the term "taxpayer" does not include a person or entity utilized in a safe harbor (e.g., a qualified intermediary). See paragraph (g)(8), Example 3(v), of this section.

(2) Security or guarantee arrangements. **(i)** In the case of a deferred exchange, the determination of whether the taxpayer is in actual or constructive receipt of money or other property before the taxpayer actually receives like-kind replacement property will be made without regard to the fact that the obligation of the taxpayer's transferee to transfer the replacement property to the taxpayer is or may be secured or guaranteed by one or more of the following—

(A) A mortgage, deed of trust, or other security interest in property (other than cash or a cash equivalent),

(B) A standby letter of credit which satisfies all of the requirements of § 15A.453–1(b)(3)(iii) and which may not be drawn upon in the absence of a default of the transferee's obligation to transfer like-kind replacement property to the taxpayer, or

(C) A guarantee of a third party.

(ii) Paragraph (g)(2)(i) of this section ceases to apply at the time the taxpayer has an immediate ability or unrestricted right to receive money or other property pursuant to the security or guarantee arrangement.

(3) Qualified escrow accounts and qualified trusts. **(i)** In the case of a deferred exchange, the determination of whether the taxpayer is in actual or constructive receipt of money or other property before the taxpayer actually receives like-kind replacement property will be made without regard to the fact that the obligation of the taxpayer's transferee to transfer the replacement property to the taxpayer is or may be secured by cash or a cash equivalent if the cash or cash equivalent is held in a qualified escrow account or in a qualified trust.

(ii) A qualified escrow account is an escrow account wherein—

(A) The escrow holder is not the taxpayer or a disqualified person (as defined in paragraph (k) of this section), and

(B) The escrow agreement expressly limits the taxpayer's rights to receive, pledge, borrow, or otherwise obtain the benefits of the cash or cash equivalent held in the escrow account as provided in paragraph (g)(6) of this section.

(iii) A qualified trust is a trust wherein—

(A) The trustee is not the taxpayer or a disqualified person (as defined in paragraph (k) of this section, except that for this purpose the relationship between the taxpayer and the trustee created by the qualified trust will not be considered a relationship under section 267(b)), and

(B) The trust agreement expressly limits the taxpayer's rights to receive, pledge, borrow, or otherwise obtain the benefits of the cash or cash equivalent held by the trustee as provided in paragraph (g)(6) of this section.

(iv) Paragraph (g)(3)(i) of this section ceases to apply at the time the taxpayer has an immediate ability or unrestricted right to receive, pledge, borrow, or otherwise obtain the benefits of the cash or cash equivalent held in the qualified escrow account or qualified trust. Rights conferred upon the taxpayer under state law to terminate or dismiss the escrow holder of a qualified escrow account or the trustee of a qualified trust are disregarded for this purpose.

(v) A taxpayer may receive money or other property directly from a party to the exchange, but not from a qualified escrow account or a qualified trust, without affecting the application of paragraph (g)(3)(i) of this section.

(4) Qualified intermediaries. **(i)** In the case of a taxpayer's transfer of relinquished property involving a qualified intermediary, the qualified intermediary is not considered the agent of the taxpayer for purposes of section 1031(a). In such a case, the taxpayer's transfer of relinquished property and subsequent receipt of like-kind replacement property is treated as an exchange, and the determination of whether the taxpayer is in actual or constructive receipt of money or other property before the taxpayer actually receives like-kind replacement property is made as if the qualified intermediary is not the agent of the taxpayer.

(ii) Paragraph (g)(4)(i) of this section applies only if the agreement between the taxpayer and the qualified intermediary expressly limits the taxpayer's rights to receive, pledge, borrow, or otherwise obtain the benefits of money or other property held by the qualified intermediary as provided in paragraph (g)(6) of this section.

(iii) A qualified intermediary is a person who—

(A) Is not the taxpayer or a disqualified person (as defined in paragraph (k) of this section), and

(B) Enters into a written agreement with the taxpayer (the "exchange agreement") and, as required by the exchange agreement, acquires the relinquished property from the taxpayer, transfers the relinquished property, acquires the replacement property, and transfers the replacement property to the taxpayer.

(iv) Regardless of whether an intermediary acquires and transfers property under general tax principals, solely for purposes of paragraph (g)(4)(iii)(B) of this section—

(A) An intermediary is treated as acquiring and transferring property if the intermediary acquires and transfers legal title to that property,

(B) An intermediary is treated as acquiring and transferring the relinquished property if the intermediary (either on its own behalf or as the agent of any party to the transaction) enters into an agreement with a person other than the taxpayer for the transfer of the relinquished property to that person and, pursuant to that agreement, the relinquished property is transferred to that person, and

(C) An intermediary is treated as acquiring and transferring replacement property if the intermediary (either on its own behalf or as the agent of any party to the transaction) enters into an agreement with the owner of the replacement property for the transfer of that property and, pursuant to that agreement, the replacement property is transferred to the taxpayer.

(v) Solely for purposes of paragraphs (g)(4)(iii) and (g)(4)(iv) of this section, an intermediary is treated as entering into an agreement if the rights of a party to the agreement are assigned to the intermediary and all parties to that agreement are notified in writing of the assignment on or before the date of the relevant transfer of property. For example, if a taxpayer enters into an agreement for the transfer of relinquished property and thereafter assigns its rights in that agreement to an intermediary and all parties to that agreement are notified in writing of the assignment on or before the date of the transfer of the relinquished property, the intermediary is treated as entering into that agreement. If the relinquished property is transferred pursuant to that agreement, the intermediary is treated as having acquired and transferred the relinquished property.

(vi) Paragraph (g)(4)(i) of this section ceases to apply at the time the taxpayer has an immediate ability or unrestricted right to receive, pledge, borrow, or otherwise obtain the benefits of money or other property held by the qualified intermediary. Rights conferred upon the taxpayer under state law to terminate or dismiss the qualified intermediary are disregarded for this purpose.

(vii) A taxpayer may receive money or other property directly from a party to the transaction other than the qualified intermediary without affecting the application of paragraph (g)(4)(i) of this section.

(5) Interest and growth factors. In the case of a deferred exchange, the determination of whether the taxpayer is in actual or constructive receipt of money or other property before the taxpayer actually receives the like-kind replacement property will be made without regard to the fact that the taxpayer is or may be entitled to receive any interest or growth factor with respect to the deferred exchange. The preceding sentence applies only if the agreement pursuant to which the taxpayer is or may be entitled to the interest or growth factor expressly limits the taxpayer's rights to receive the interest or growth factor as provided in paragraph (g)(6) of this section. For additional rules concerning interest or growth factors, see paragraph (h) of this section.

* * *

(k) Definition of disqualified person. **(1)** For purposes of this section, a disqualified person is a person described in paragraph (k)(2), (k)(3), or (k)(4) of this section.

(2) The person is the agent of the taxpayer at the time of the transaction. For this purpose, a person who has acted as the taxpayer's employee, attorney, accountant, investment banker or broker, or real estate agent or broker within the 2–year period ending on the date of the transfer of the first of the relinquished properties is treated as an agent of the taxpayer at the time of the transaction. Solely for purposes of this paragraph (k)(2), performance of the following services will not be taken into account—

(i) Services for the taxpayer with respect to exchanges of property intended to qualify for nonrecognition of gain or loss under section 1031; and

(ii) Routine financial, title insurance, escrow, or trust services for the taxpayer by a financial institution, title insurance company, or escrow company.

(3) The person and the taxpayer bear a relationship described in either section 267(b) or section 707(b) (determined by substituting in each section "10 percent" for "50 percent" each place it appears).

(4)(i) Except as provided in paragraph (k)(4)(ii) of this section, the person and a person described in paragraph (k)(2) of this section bear a relationship described in either section 267(b) or 707(b) (determined by substituting in each section "10 percent" for "50 percent" each place it appears).

(ii) In the case of a transfer of relinquished property made by a taxpayer on or after January 17, 2001, paragraph (k)(4)(i) of this section does not apply to a bank (as defined in section 581) or a bank affiliate if, but for this paragraph (k)(4)(ii), the bank or bank affiliate would be a disqualified person under paragraph (k)(4)(i) of this section solely because it is a member of the same controlled group (as determined under section 267(f)(1), substituting "10 percent" for "50 percent" where it appears) as a person that has provided investment banking or brokerage services to the taxpayer within the 2–year period described in paragraph (k)(2) of this section. * * *

(5) This paragraph (k) may be illustrated by the following examples. Unless otherwise provided, the following facts are assumed: On May 1, 1991, B enters into an exchange agreement (as defined in paragraph (g)(4)(iii)(B) of this section) with C whereby B retains C to facilitate an exchange with respect to real property X. On May 17, 1991, pursuant to the agreement, B executes and delivers to C a deed conveying real property X to C. C has no relationship to B described in paragraph (k)(2), (k)(3), or (k)(4) of this section.

Example 1. **(i)** C is B's accountant and has rendered accounting services to B within the 2–year period ending on May 17, 1991, other than with respect to exchanges of property intended to qualify for nonrecognition of gain or loss under section 1031.

(ii) C is a disqualified person because C has acted as B's accountant within the 2–year period ending on May 17, 1991.

(iii) If C had not acted as B's accountant within the 2–year period ending on May 17, 1991, or if C had acted as B's accountant within that period only with respect to exchanges intended to qualify for nonrecognition of gain or loss under section 1031, C would not have been a disqualified person.

Example 2. **(i)** C, which is engaged in the trade or business of acting as an intermediary to facilitate deferred exchanges, is a wholly owned subsidiary of an escrow company that has performed routine escrow services for B in the past. C has previously been retained by B to act as an intermediary in prior section 1031 exchanges.

(ii) C is not a disqualified person notwithstanding the intermediary services previously provided by C to B (see paragraph (k)(2)(i) of this section) and notwithstanding the combination of C's relationship to the escrow company and the escrow services previously provided by the escrow company to B (see paragraph (k)(2)(ii) of this section).

* * *

(m) Definition of fair market value. For purposes of this section, the fair market value of property means the fair market value of the property without regard to any liabilities secured by the property.

(n) No inference with respect to actual or constructive receipt rules outside of section 1031. The rules provided in this section relating to actual or constructive receipt are intended to be rules for determining whether there is actual or constructive receipt in the case of a deferred exchange. No inference is intended regarding the application of these rules for purposes of determining whether actual or constructive receipt exists for any other purpose.

* * *

[T.D. 8346, 56 FR 19938, May 1, 1991, as amended by T.D. 8535, 59 FR 18749, Apr. 20, 1994; T.D. 8982, 67 FR 4907, Feb. 1, 2002; T.D. 9413, 73 FR 39622, July 10, 2008]

§ 1.1032–1 Disposition by a corporation of its own capital stock.

(a) The disposition by a corporation of shares of its own stock (including treasury stock) for money or other property does not give rise to taxable gain or deductible loss to the corporation regardless of the nature of the transaction or the facts and circumstances involved. For example, the receipt by a corporation of the subscription price of shares of its stock upon their original issuance gives rise to neither taxable gain nor deductible loss, whether the subscription or issue price be equal to, in excess of, or less than, the par or stated value of such stock. Also, the exchange or sale by a corporation of its own shares for money or other property does not result in taxable gain or deductible loss, even though the corporation deals in such shares as it might in the shares of another corporation. A transfer by a corporation of shares of its own stock (including treasury stock) as compensation for services is considered, for purposes of section 1032(a), as a disposition by the corporation of such shares for money or other property.

(b) Section 1032(a) does not apply to the acquisition by a corporation of shares of its own stock except where the corporation acquires such shares in exchange for shares of its own stock (including treasury stock). See paragraph (e) of § 1.311–1, relating to treatment of acquisitions of a corporation's own stock. Section 1032(a) also does not relate to the tax treatment of the recipient of a corporation's stock.

(c) Where a corporation acquires shares of its own stock in exchange for shares of its own stock (including treasury stock) the transaction may qualify not only under section 1032(a), but also under section 368(a)(1)(E) (recapitalization) or section 305(a) (distribution of stock and stock rights).

(d) For basis of property acquired by a corporation in connection with a transaction to which section 351 applies or in connection with a reorganization, see section 362. For basis of property acquired by a corporation in a transaction to which section 1032 applies but which does not qualify under any other nonrecognition provision, see section 1012.

[T.D. 6500, 25 FR 11910, Nov. 26, 1960]

§ 1.1032–2 Disposition by a corporation of stock of a controlling corporation in certain triangular reorganizations.

(a) Scope. This section provides rules for certain triangular reorganizations described in § 1.358–6(b) when the acquiring corporation (S) acquires property or stock of another corporation (T) in exchange for stock of the corporation (P) in control of S.

(b) General nonrecognition of gain or loss. For purposes of § 1.1032–1(a), in the case of a forward triangular merger, a triangular C reorganization, or a triangular B reorganization (as described in § 1.358–6(b)), P stock provided by P to S, or directly to T or T's shareholders on behalf of S, pursuant to the plan of reorganization is treated as a disposition by P of shares of its own stock for T's assets or stock, as applicable. For rules governing the use of P stock in a reverse triangular merger, see section 361.

(c) Treatment of S. S must recognize gain or loss on its exchange of P stock as consideration in a forward triangular merger, a triangular C reorganization, or a triangular B reorganization (as described in § 1.358–6(b)), if S did not receive the P stock from P pursuant to the plan of reorganization. See § 1.358–6(d) for the effect on P's basis in its S or T stock, as applicable. For rules governing S's use of P stock in a reverse triangular merger, see section 361.

(d) Examples. The rules of this section are illustrated by the following examples. For purposes of these examples, P, S, and T are domestic corporations, P and S do not file consolidated returns, P owns all of the only class of S stock, the P stock exchanged in the transaction satisfies the requirements of the applicable reorganization provisions, and the facts set forth the only corporate activity.

Example 1. Forward triangular merger solely for P stock. (a) Facts. T has assets with an aggregate basis of $60 and fair market value of $100 and no liabilities. Pursuant to a plan, P forms S by transferring $100 of P stock to S and T merges into S. In the merger, the T shareholders receive, in exchange for their T stock, the P stock that P transferred to S. The transaction is a reorganization to which sections 368(a)(1)(A) and (a)(2)(D) apply.

(b) No gain or loss recognized on the use of P stock. Under paragraph (b) of this section, the P stock provided by P pursuant to the plan of reorganization is treated for purposes of § 1.1032–1(a) as disposed of by P for the T assets acquired by S in the merger. Consequently, neither P nor S has taxable gain or deductible loss on the exchange.

Example 2. Forward triangular merger solely for P stock provided in part by S. (a) Facts. T has assets with an aggregate basis of $60 and fair market value of $100 and no liabilities. S is an operating company with substantial assets that has been in existence for several years. S also owns P stock with a $20 adjusted basis and $30 fair market value. S acquired the P stock in an unrelated transaction several years before the reorganization. Pursuant to a plan, P transfers additional P stock worth $70 to S and T merges into S. In the merger, the T shareholders receive $100 of P stock ($70 of P stock provided by P to S as part of the plan and $30 of P stock held by S previously). The transaction is a reorganization to which sections 368(a)(1)(A) and (a)(2)(D) apply.

(b) Gain or loss recognized by S on the use of its P stock. Under paragraph (b) of this section, the $70 of P stock provided by P pursuant to the plan of reorganization is treated as disposed of by P for the T assets acquired by S in the merger. Consequently, neither P nor S has taxable gain or deductible loss on the exchange of those shares. Under paragraph (c) of this section, however, S recognizes $10 of gain on the exchange of its P stock in the reorganization because S did not receive the P stock from P pursuant to the plan of reorganization. See § 1.358–6(d) for the effect on P's basis in its S stock.

(e) Stock options. The rules of this section shall apply to an option to buy or sell P stock issued by P in the same manner as the rules of this section apply to P stock.

(f) Effective dates. This section applies to triangular reorganizations occurring on or after December 23, 1994, except for paragraph (e) of this section, which applies to transfers of stock options occurring on or after May 16, 2000.

[T.D. 8648, 60 FR 66077, Dec. 21, 1995, as amended by T.D. 8883, 65 FR 31073, May 16, 2000]

§ 1.1032–3 Disposition of stock or stock options in certain transactions not qualifying under any other nonrecognition provision.

(a) Scope. This section provides rules for certain transactions in which a corporation or a partnership (the acquiring entity) acquires money or other property (as defined in § 1.1032–1) in exchange, in whole or in part, for stock of a corporation (the issuing corporation).

(b) Nonrecognition of gain or loss—(1) General rule. In a transaction to which this section applies, no gain or loss is recognized on the disposition of the issuing corporation's stock by the acquiring entity. The transaction is treated as if, immediately before the acquiring entity disposes of the stock of the issuing corporation, the acquiring entity purchased the issuing corporation's stock from the issuing corporation for fair market value with cash contributed to the acquiring entity by the issuing corporation (or, if necessary, through intermediate corporations or partnerships). For rules that may apply in determining the issuing corporation's adjustment to basis in the acquiring entity (or, if necessary, in determining the adjustment to basis in intermediate entities), see section 358, 722, and the regulations thereunder.

(2) Special rule for actual payment for stock of the issuing corporation. If the issuing corporation receives money or other property in payment for its stock, the amount of cash deemed contributed under paragraph (b)(1) of this section is the difference between the fair market value of the issuing corporation stock and the amount of money or the fair market value of other property that the issuing corporation receives as payment.

(c) Applicability. The rules of this section apply only if, pursuant to a plan to acquire money or other property—

(1) The acquiring entity acquires stock of the issuing corporation directly or indirectly from the issuing corporation in a transaction in which, but for this section, the basis of the stock of the issuing corporation in the hands of the acquiring entity would be determined, in whole or in part, with respect to the issuing corporation's basis in the issuing corporation's stock under section 362(a) or 723 (provided that, in the case of an indirect acquisition by the acquiring entity, the transfers of issuing corporation stock through intermediate entities occur immediately after one another);

(2) The acquiring entity immediately transfers the stock of the issuing corporation to acquire money or other property (from a person other than an entity from which the stock was directly or indirectly acquired);

(3) The party receiving stock of the issuing corporation in the exchange specified in paragraph (c)(2) of this section from the acquiring entity does not receive a substituted basis in the stock of the issuing corporation within the meaning of section 7701(a)(42); and

(4) The issuing corporation stock is not exchanged for stock of the issuing corporation.

(d) Stock options. The rules of this section shall apply to an option issued by a corporation to buy or sell its own stock in the same manner as the rules of this section apply to the stock of an issuing corporation.

(e) Examples. The following examples illustrate the application of this section:

Example 1. (i) *X*, a corporation, owns all of the stock of *Y* corporation. *Y* reaches an agreement with *C*, an individual, to acquire a truck from *C* in exchange for 10 shares of *X* stock with a fair market value of $100. To effectuate *Y*'s agreement with *C*, *X* transfers to *Y* the *X* stock in a transaction in which, but for this section, the basis of the *X* stock in the hands of *Y* would be determined with respect to *X*'s basis in the *X* stock under section 362(a). *Y* immediately transfers the *X* stock to *C* to acquire the truck.

(ii) In this *Example 1*, no gain or loss is recognized on the disposition of the *X* stock by *Y*. Immediately before *Y*'s disposition of the *X* stock, *Y* is treated as purchasing the *X* stock from *X* for $100 of cash contributed to *Y* by *X*. Under section 358, *X*'s basis in its *Y* stock is increased by $100.

* * *

Example 4. (i) *X*, a corporation, owns all of the outstanding stock of *Y* corporation. *B*, an individual, is an employee of *Y*. Pursuant to an agreement between *X* and *Y* to compensate *B* for services provided to *Y*, *X* transfers to B 10 shares of *X* stock with a fair market value of $100. Under § 1.83–6(d), but for this section, the transfer of *X* stock by *X* to *B* would be treated as a contribution of the *X* stock by *X* to the capital of *Y*, and immediately thereafter, a transfer of *X* stock by *Y* to *B*. But for this section, the basis of the *X* stock in the hands of *Y* would be determined with respect to *X*'s basis in the *X* stock under section 362(a).

(ii) In this *Example 4*, no gain or loss is recognized on the deemed disposition of the *X* stock by *Y*. Immediately before *Y*'s deemed disposition of the *X* stock, *Y* is treated as purchasing the *X* stock from *X* for $100 of cash contributed to *Y* by *X*. Under section 358, *X*'s basis in its *Y* stock is increased by $100.

* * *

[T.D. 8883, 65 FR 31073, May 16, 2000]

§ 1.1033(a)–1 Involuntary conversions; nonrecognition of gain.

(a) In general. Section 1033 applies to cases where property is compulsorily or involuntarily converted. An "involuntary conversion" may be the result of the destruction of property in whole or in part, the theft of property, the seizure of property, the requisition or condemnation of property, or the threat or imminence of requisition or condemnation of property. An "involuntary conversion" may be a conversion into similar property or into money or into dissimilar property. Section 1033 provides that, under certain specified circumstances, any gain which is realized from an involuntary conversion shall not be recognized. In cases where property is converted into other property similar or related in service or use to the converted property, no gain shall be recognized regardless of when the disposition of the converted property occurred and regardless of whether or not the taxpayer elects to have the gain not recognized. In other types of involuntary conversion cases, however, the proceeds arising from the disposition of the converted property must (within the time limits specified) be reinvested in similar property in order to avoid recognition of any gain realized. Section 1033 applies only with respect to gains; losses from involuntary conversions are recognized or not recognized without regard to this section.

* * *

[T.D. 6500, 25 FR 11910, Nov. 26, 1960, as amended by T.D. 6856, 30 FR 13318, Oct. 20, 1965; T.D. 7625, 44 FR 31013, May 30, 1979; T.D. 7758, 46 FR 6925, Jan. 22, 1981]

§ 1.1033(a)–2 Involuntary conversion into similar property, into money or into dissimilar property.

(a) In general. The term "disposition of the converted property" means the destruction, theft, seizure, requisition, or condemnation of the converted property, or the sale or exchange of such property under threat or imminence of requisition or condemnation.

(b) Conversion into similar property. If property (as a result of its destruction in whole or in part, theft, seizure, or requisition or condemnation or threat or imminence thereof) is compulsorily or involuntarily converted only into property similar or related in service or use to the property so converted, no gain shall be recognized. Such nonrecognition of gain is mandatory.

(c) Conversion into money or into dissimilar property. (1) If property (as a result of its destruction in whole or in part, theft, seizure, or requisition or condemnation or threat or imminence thereof) is compulsorily or involuntarily converted into money or into property not similar or related in service or use to the converted property, the gain, if any, shall be recognized, at the election of the taxpayer, only to the extent that the amount realized upon such conversion exceeds the cost of other property purchased by the taxpayer which is similar or related in service or use to the property so converted, or the cost of stock of a corporation owning such other property which is purchased by the taxpayer in the acquisition of control of such corporation, if the taxpayer purchased such other property, or such stock, for the purpose of replacing the property so converted and during the period specified in subparagraph (3) of this paragraph. For the purposes of section 1033, the term "control" means the ownership of stock possessing at least 80 percent of the total combined voting power of all classes of stock entitled to vote and at least 80 percent of the total number of shares of all other classes of stock of the corporation.

(2) All of the details in connection with an involuntary conversion of property at a gain (including those relating to the replacement of the converted property, or a decision not to replace, or the expiration of the period for replacement) shall be reported in the return for the taxable year or years in which any of such gain is realized. An election to have such gain recognized only to the extent provided in subparagraph (1) of this paragraph shall be made by including such gain in gross income for such year or years only to such extent. If, at the time of filing such a return, the period within which the converted property must be replaced has expired, or if such an election is not desired, the gain should be included in gross income for such year or years in the regular manner. A failure to so include such gain in gross income in the regular manner shall be deemed to be an election by the taxpayer to have such gain recognized only to the extent provided in subparagraph (1) of this paragraph even though the details in connection with the conversion are not reported in such return. If, after having made an election under section 1033(a)(2), the converted property is not replaced within the required period of time, or replacement is made at a cost lower than was anticipated at the time of the election, or a decision is made not to replace, the tax liability for the year or years for which the election was made shall be recomputed. Such recomputation should be in the form of an "amended return". If a decision is made to make an election under section 1033(a)(2) after the filing of the return and the payment of the tax for the year or years in which any of the gain on an involuntary conversion is realized and before the expiration of the period within which the converted property must be replaced, a claim for credit or refund for such year or years should be filed. If the replacement of the converted property occurs in a year or years in which none of the gain on the conversion is realized, all of the details in connection with such replacement shall be reported in the return for such year or years.

(3) The period referred to in subparagraphs (1) and (2) of this paragraph is the period of time commencing with the date of the disposition of the converted property, or the date of the beginning of the threat or imminence of requisition or condemnation of the converted property, whichever is earlier, and ending 2 years * * * after the close of the first taxable year in which any part of the gain upon the conversion is realized, or at the close of such later date as may be designated pursuant to an application of the taxpayer. Such application shall be made prior to the expiration of 2 years * * * after the close of the first taxable year in which any part of the gain from the conversion is realized, unless the taxpayer can show to the satisfaction of the district director—

(i) Reasonable cause for not having filed the application within the required period of time, and

(ii) The filing of such application was made within a reasonable time after the expiration of the required period of time. The application shall contain all of the details in connection with the involuntary conversion. Such application shall be made to the district director for the internal revenue district in which the return is filed for the first taxable year in which any of the gain from the involuntary conversion is realized. No extension of time shall be granted pursuant to such application unless the taxpayer can show reasonable cause for not being able to replace the converted property within the required period of time.

See section 1033(g)(4) and § 1.1033(g)–1 for the circumstances under which, in the case of the conversion of real property held either for productive use in trade or business or for investment, the 2–year period referred to in this paragraph (c)(3) shall be extended to 3 years.

(4) Property or stock purchased before the disposition of the converted property shall be considered to have been purchased for the purpose of replacing the converted property only if such property or stock is held by the taxpayer on the date of the disposition of the converted property. Property or stock shall be considered to have been purchased only if, but for the provisions of section 1033(b), the unadjusted basis of such property or stock would be its cost to the taxpayer within the meaning of section 1012. If the taxpayer's unadjusted basis of the replacement property would be determined, in the absence of section 1033(b), under any of the exceptions referred to in section 1012, the unadjusted basis of the property would not be its cost within the meaning of section 1012. For example, if property similar or related in service or use to the converted property is acquired by gift and its basis is determined under section 1015, such property will not qualify as a replacement for the converted property.

(5) If a taxpayer makes an election under section 1033(a)(2), any deficiency, for any taxable year in which any part of the gain upon the conversion is realized, which is attributable to such gain may be assessed at any time before the expiration of three years from the date the district director with whom the return for such year has been filed is notified by the taxpayer of the replacement of the converted property or of an intention not to replace, or of a failure to replace, within the required period, notwithstanding the provisions of section 6212(c) or the provisions of any other law or rule of law which would otherwise prevent such assessment. If replacement has been made, such notification shall contain all of the details in connection with such replacement. Such notification should be made in the return for the taxable year or years in which the replacement occurs, or the intention not to replace is formed, or the period for replacement expires, if this return is filed with such district director. If this return is not filed with such district director, then such notification shall be made to such district director at the time of filing this return. If the taxpayer so desires, he may, in either event, also notify such district director before the filing of such return.

(6) If a taxpayer makes an election under section 1033(a)(2) and the replacement property or stock was purchased before the beginning of the last taxable year in which any part of the gain upon the conversion is realized, any deficiency, for any taxable year ending before such last taxable year, which is attributable to such election may be assessed at any time before the expiration of the period within which a deficiency for such last taxable year may be assessed, notwithstanding the provisions of section 6212(c) or 6501 or the provisions of any law or rule of law which would otherwise prevent such assessment.

(7) If the taxpayer makes an election under section 1033(a)(2), the gain upon the conversion shall be recognized to the extent that the amount realized upon such conversion exceeds the cost of the replacement property or stock, regardless of whether such amount is realized in one or more taxable years.

(8) The proceeds of a use and occupancy insurance contract, which by its terms insured against actual loss sustained of net profits in the business, are not proceeds of an involuntary conversion but are income in the same manner that the profits for which they are substituted would have been.

(9) There is no investment in property similar in character and devoted to a similar use if—

(i) The proceeds of unimproved real estate, taken upon condemnation proceedings, are invested in improved real estate.

(ii) The proceeds of conversion of real property are applied in reduction of indebtedness previously incurred in the purchase or a leasehold.

(iii) The owner of a requisitioned tug uses the proceeds to buy barges.

(10) If, in a condemnation proceeding, the Government retains out of the award sufficient funds to satisfy special assessments levied against the remaining portion of the plot or parcel of real estate affected for benefits accruing in connection with the condemnation, the amount so retained shall be deducted from the gross award in determining the amount of the net award.

(11) If, in a condemnation proceeding, the Government retains out of the award sufficient funds to satisfy liens (other than liens due to special assessments levied against the remaining portion of the plot or parcel of real estate affected for benefits accruing in connection with the condemnation) and mortgages against the property, and itself pays the same, the amount so retained shall not be deducted from the gross award in determining the amount of the net award. If, in a condemnation proceeding, the Government makes an award to a mortgagee to satisfy a mortgage on the condemned property, the amount of such award shall be considered as a part of the "amount realized" upon the conversion regardless of whether or not the taxpayer was personally liable for the mortgage debt. Thus, if a taxpayer has acquired property worth $100,000 subject to a $50,000 mortgage (regardless of whether or not he was personally liable for the mortgage debt) and, in a condemnation proceeding, the Government awards the taxpayer $60,000 and awards the mortgagee $50,000 in satisfaction of the mortgage, the entire $110,000 is considered to be the "amount realized" by the taxpayer.

(12) An amount expended for replacement of an asset, in excess of the recovery for loss, represents a capital expenditure and is not a deductible loss for income tax purposes.

[T.D. 6500, 25 FR 11910, Nov. 26, 1960, as amended by T.D. 6679, 28 FR 10515, Oct. 1, 1963; T.D. 7075, 35 FR 17996, Nov. 24, 1970; T.D. 7625, 44 FR 31013, May 30, 1979; T.D. 7758, 46 FR 6925, Jan. 22, 1981]

§ 1.1033(b)–1 Basis of property acquired as a result of an involuntary conversion.

* * *

(b) The provisions of the last sentence of section 1033(b) may be illustrated by the following example:

Example. A taxpayer realizes $22,000 from the involuntary conversion of his barn in 1955; the adjusted basis of the barn to him was $10,000, and he spent in the same year $20,000 for a new barn which resulted in the nonrecognition of $10,000 of the $12,000 gain on the conversion. The basis of the new barn to the taxpayer would be $10,000—the cost of the new barn ($20,000) less the amount of the gain not recognized on the conversion ($10,000). The basis of the new barn would not be a substituted basis in the hands of the taxpayer within the meaning of section 1016(b)(2). If the replacement of the converted barn had been made by the purchase of two smaller barns which, together, were similar or related in service or use to the converted barn and which cost $8,000 and $12,000, respectively, then the basis of the two barns would be $4,000 and $6,000, respectively, the total basis of the purchased property ($10,000) allocated in proportion to their respective costs (8,000/20,000 of $10,000 or $4,000; and 12,000/20,000 of $10,000, or $6,000).

[T.D. 6500, 25 FR 11910, Nov. 26, 1960; 25 FR 14021, Dec. 31, 1960; redesignated and amended by T.D. 7625, 44 FR 31013, May 30, 1979]

§ 1.1033(g)–1 Condemnation of real property held for productive use in trade or business or for investment.

(a) Special rule in general. This section provides special rules for applying section 1033 with respect to certain dispositions, occurring after December 31, 1957, of real property held either for productive use in trade or business or for investment (not including stock in trade or other property held primarily for sale). For this purpose, disposition means the seizure, requisition, or condemnation (but not destruction) of the converted property, or the sale or exchange of such property under threat or imminence of seizure, requisition, or condemnation. In such cases, for purposes of applying section 1033, the replacement of such property with property of like kind to be held either for productive use in trade or business or for investment shall be treated as property similar or related in service or use to the property so converted. For principles in determining whether the replacement property is property of like kind, see paragraph (b) of § 1.1031(a)–1.

* * *

[T.D. 6500, 25 FR 11910, Nov. 26, 1960; 25 FR 14021, Dec. 31, 1960, § 1.1033(g)–1; redesignated and amended by T.D. 7625, 44 FR 31013, May 30, 1979; 44 FR 38458, July 2, 1979; T.D. 7758, 46 FR 6925, Jan. 22, 1981; T.D. 8121, 52 FR 414, Jan. 6, 1987]

§ 1.1036–1 Stock for stock of the same corporation.

(a) Section 1036 permits the exchange, without the recognition of gain or loss, of common stock for common stock, or of preferred stock for preferred stock, in the same corporation. Section 1036 applies even though voting stock is exchanged for nonvoting stock or nonvoting stock is exchanged for voting stock. It is not limited to an exchange between two individual stockholders; it includes a transaction between a stockholder and the corporation. However, a transaction between a stockholder and the corporation may qualify not only under section 1036(a), but also under section 368(a)(1)(E) (recapitalization) or section 305(a) (distribution of stock and stock rights). The provisions of section 1036(a) do not apply if stock is exchanged for bonds, or preferred stock is exchanged for common stock, or common stock is exchanged for preferred stock, or common stock in one corporation is exchanged for common stock in another corporation. See paragraph (l) of § 1.301–1 for certain transactions treated as distributions under section 301. See paragraph (e)(5) of § 1.368–2 for certain transactions which result in deemed distributions under section 305(c) to which sections 305(b)(4) and 301 apply.

* * *

[T.D. 6500, 25 FR 11910, Nov. 26, 1960, as amended by T.D. 7281, 38 FR 18540, July 12, 1973; T.D. 8904, 65 FR 58650, Oct. 2, 2000]

§ 1.1041–1T Treatment of transfer of property between spouses or incident to divorce.

Q–1 How is the transfer of property between spouses treated under section 1041?

A–1 Generally, no gain or loss is recognized on a transfer of property from an individual to (or in trust for the benefit of) a spouse or, if the transfer is incident to a divorce, a former spouse. The following questions and answers describe more fully the scope, tax consequences and other rules which apply to transfers of property under section 1041.

(a) Scope of section 1041 in general.

Q–2 Does section 1041 apply only to transfers of property incident to divorce?

A–2 No. Section 1041 is not limited to transfers of property incident to divorce. Section 1041 applies to any transfer of property between spouses regardless of whether the transfer is a gift or is a sale or exchange between spouses acting at arm's length (including a transfer in exchange for the relinquishment of property or marital rights or an exchange otherwise governed by another nonrecognition provision of the Code). A divorce or legal separation need not be contemplated between the spouses at the time of the transfer nor must a divorce or legal separation ever occur.

Example (1). A and B are married and file a joint return. A is the sole owner of a condominium unit. A sale or gift of the condominium from A to B is a transfer which is subject to the rules of section 1041.

Example (2). A and B are married and file separate returns. A is the owner of an independent sole proprietorship, X Company. In the ordinary course of business, X Company makes a sale of property to B. This sale is a transfer of property between spouses and is subject to the rules of section 1041.

Example (3). Assume the same facts as in example (2), except that X Company is a corporation wholly owned by A. This sale is not a sale between spouses subject to the rules of section 1041. However, in appropriate circumstances, general tax principles, including the step-transaction doctrine, may be applicable in recharacterizing the transaction.

* * *

Q–4 What kinds of transfers are governed by section 1041?

A–4 Only transfers of property (whether real or personal, tangible or intangible) are governed by section 1041. Transfers of services are not subject to the rules of section 1041.

Q–5 Must the property transferred to a former spouse have been owned by the transferor spouse during the marriage?

A–5 No. A transfer of property acquired after the marriage ceases may be governed by section 1041.

(b) Transfer incident to the divorce.

Q–6 When is a transfer of property "incident to the divorce"?

A–6 A transfer of property is "incident to the divorce" in either of the following 2 circumstances—

(1) The transfer occurs not more than one year after the date on which the marriage ceases, or

(2) The transfer is related to the cessation of the marriage.

Thus, a transfer of property occurring not more than one year after the date on which the marriage ceases need not be related to the cessation of the marriage to qualify for section 1041 treatment. (See A–7 for transfers occurring more than one year after the cessation of the marriage.)

Q–7 When is a transfer of property "related to the cessation of the marriage"?

A–7 A transfer of property is treated as related to the cessation of the marriage if the transfer is pursuant to a divorce or separation instrument, as defined in section 71(b)(2), and the transfer occurs not more than 6 years after the date on which the marriage ceases. A divorce or separation instrument includes a modification or amendment to such decree or instrument. Any transfer not pursuant to a divorce or separation instrument and any transfer occurring more than 6 years after the cessation of the marriage is presumed to be not related to the cessation of the marriage. This presumption may be rebutted only by showing that the transfer was made to effect the division of property owned by the former spouses at the time of the cessation of the marriage. For example, the presumption may be rebutted by showing that (a) the transfer was not made within the one- and six-year periods described above because of factors which hampered an earlier transfer of the property, such as legal or business impediments to transfer or disputes concerning the value of the property owned at the time of the cessation of the marriage, and (b) the transfer is effected promptly after the impediment to transfer is removed.

Q–8 Do annulments and the cessations of marriages that are void *ab initio* due to violations of state law constitute divorces for purposes of section 1041?

A–8 Yes.

(c) Transfers on behalf of a spouse.

Q–9 May transfers of property to third parties on behalf of a spouse (or former spouse) qualify under section 1041?

A–9 Yes. There are three situations in which a transfer of property to a third party on behalf of a spouse (or former spouse) will qualify under section 1041, provided all other requirements of the section are satisfied. The first situation is where the transfer to the third party is required by a divorce or separation instrument. The second situation is where the transfer to the third party is pursuant to the written request of the other spouse (or former spouse). The third situation is where the transferor receives from the other spouse (or former spouse) a written consent or ratification of the transfer to the third party. Such consent or ratification must state that the parties intend the transfer to be treated as a transfer to the nontransferring spouse (or former spouse) subject to the rules of section 1041 and must be received by the transferor prior to the date of filing of the transferor's first return of tax for the taxable year in which the transfer was made. In the three situations described above, the transfer of property will be treated as made directly to the nontransferring spouse (or former spouse) and the nontransferring spouse will be treated as immediately transferring the property to the third party. The deemed transfer from the nontransferring spouse (or former spouse) to the third party is not a transaction that qualifies for nonrecognition of gain under section 1041. This A–9 shall not apply to transfers to which § 1.1041–2 applies.

(d) Tax consequences of transfers subject to section 1041.

Q–10 How is the transferor of property under section 1041 treated for income tax purposes?

A–10 The transferor of property under section 1041 recognizes no gain or loss on the transfer even if the transfer was in exchange for the release of marital rights or other consideration. This rule applies regardless of whether the transfer is of property separately owned by the transferor or is a division (equal or unequal) of community property. Thus, the result under section 1041 differs from the result in *United States v. Davis,* 370 U.S. 65 (1962).

Q–11 How is the transferee of property under section 1041 treated for income tax purposes?

A–11 The transferee of property under section 1041 recognizes no gain or loss upon receipt of the transferred property. In all cases, the basis of the transferred property in the hands of the transferee is the adjusted basis of such property in the hands of the transferor immediately before the transfer. Even if the transfer is a bona fide sale, the transferee does not acquire a basis in the transferred property equal to the transferee's costs (the fair market value). This carryover basis rule applies whether the adjusted basis of the transferred property is less than, equal to, or greater than its fair market value at the time of transfer (or the value of any consideration provided by the transferee) and applies for purposes of determining loss as well as gain upon the subsequent disposition of the property by the transferee. Thus, this rule is different from the rule applied in section 1015(a) for determining the basis of property acquired by gift.

Q–12 Do the rules described in A–10 and A–11 apply even if the transferred property is subject to liabilities which exceed the adjusted basis of the property?

A–12 Yes. For example, assume A owns property having a fair market value of $10,000 and an adjusted basis of $1,000. In contemplation of making a transfer of this property incident to a divorce from B, A borrows $5,000 from a bank, using the property as security for the borrowing. A then transfers the property to B and B assumes, or takes the property subject to, the liability to pay the $5,000 debt. Under section 1041, A recognizes no gain or loss upon the transfer of the property, and the adjusted basis of the property in the hands of B is $1,000.

* * *

(e) Notice and recordkeeping requirement with respect to transactions under section 1041.

Q–14 Does the transferor of property in a transaction described in section 1041 have to supply, at the time of the transfer, the transferee with records sufficient to determine the adjusted basis and holding period of the property at the time of the transfer and (if applicable) with notice that the property transferred under section 1041 is potentially subject to recapture of the investment tax credit?

A–14 Yes. A transferor of property under section 1041 must, at the time of the transfer, supply the transferee with records sufficient to determine the adjusted basis and holding period of the property as of the date of the transfer. In addition, in the case of a transfer of property which carries with it a potential liability for investment tax credit recapture, the transferor must, at the time of the transfer, supply the transferee with records sufficient to determine the amount and period of such potential liability. Such records must be preserved and kept accessible by the transferee.

(f) Property settlements—effective dates, transitional periods and elections.

Q–15 When does section 1041 become effective?

A–15 Generally, section 1041 applies to all transfers after July 18, 1984. However, it does not apply to transfers after July 18, 1984 pursuant to instruments in effect on or before July 18, 1984. (See A–16 with respect to exceptions to the general rule.)

Q–16 Are there any exceptions to the general rule stated in A–15 above?

A–16 Yes. Two transitional rules provide exceptions to the general rule stated in A–15. First, section 1041 will apply to transfers after July 18, 1984 under instruments that were in effect on or before July 18, 1984 if both spouses (or former spouses) elect to have section 1041 apply to such transfers. Second, section 1041 will apply to all transfers after December 31, 1983 (including transfers under instruments in effect on or before July 18, 1984) if both spouses (or former spouses) elect to have section 1041 apply. (See A–18 relating to the time and manner of making the elections under the first or second transitional rule.)

Q–17 Can an election be made to have section 1041 apply to some, but not all, transfers made after December 31, 1983, or some but not all, transfers made after July 18, 1984 under instruments in effect on or before July 18, 1984?

A–17 No. Partial elections are not allowed. An election under either of the two elective transitional rules applies to all transfers governed by that election whether before or after the election is made, and is irrevocable.

* * *

[T.D. 7973, 49 FR 34452, Aug. 31, 1984; T.D. 9035, 68 FR 1536, Jan. 13, 2003]

§ 1.1041–2 Redemptions of stock.

(a) In general—(1) Redemptions of stock not resulting in constructive distributions. Notwithstanding Q & A–9 of § 1.1041–1T(c), if a corporation redeems stock owned by a spouse or former spouse (transferor spouse), and the transferor spouse's receipt of property in respect of such redeemed stock is not treated, under applicable tax law, as resulting in a constructive distribution to the other spouse or former spouse (nontransferor spouse), then the form of the stock redemption shall be respected for Federal income tax purposes. Therefore, the transferor spouse will be treated as having received a distribution from the corporation in redemption of stock.

(2) Redemptions of stock resulting in constructive distributions. Notwithstanding Q & A–9 of § 1.1041–1T(c), if a corporation redeems stock owned by a transferor spouse, and the transferor spouse's receipt of property in respect of such redeemed stock is treated, under applicable tax law, as resulting in a constructive distribution to the nontransferor spouse, then the redeemed stock shall be deemed first to be transferred by the transferor spouse to the nontransferor spouse and then to be transferred by the nontransferor spouse to the redeeming corporation. Any property actually received by the transferor spouse from the redeeming corporation in respect of the redeemed stock shall be deemed first to be transferred by the corporation to the nontransferor spouse in redemption of such spouse's stock and then to be transferred by the nontransferor spouse to the transferor spouse.

(b) Tax consequences—(1) Transfers described in paragraph (a)(1) of this section. Section 1041 will not apply to any of the transfers described in paragraph (a)(1) of this section. See section 302 for rules relating to the tax consequences of certain redemptions; redemptions characterized as distributions under section 302(d) will be subject to section 301 if received from a Subchapter C corporation or section 1368 if received from a Subchapter S corporation.

(2) Transfers described in paragraph (a)(2) of this section. The tax consequences of each deemed transfer described in paragraph (a)(2) of this section are determined under applicable provisions of the Internal Revenue Code as if the spouses had actually made such transfers. Accordingly, section 1041 applies to any deemed transfer of the stock and redemption proceeds between the transferor spouse and the nontransferor spouse, provided the requirements of section 1041 are otherwise satisfied with respect to such deemed transfer. Section 1041, however, will not apply to any deemed transfer of stock by the nontransferor spouse to the redeeming corporation in exchange for the redemption proceeds. See section 302 for rules relating to the tax consequences of certain redemptions; redemptions characterized as distributions under section 302(d) will be subject to section 301 if received from a Subchapter C corporation or section 1368 if received from a Subchapter S corporation.

(c) Special rules in case of agreements between spouses or former spouses—(1) Transferor spouse taxable. Notwithstanding applicable tax law, a transferor spouse's receipt of property in respect of the redeemed stock shall be treated as a distribution to the transferor spouse in redemption of such stock for purposes of paragraph (a)(1) of this section, and shall not be treated as resulting in a constructive distribution to the nontransferor spouse for purposes of paragraph (a)(2) of this section, if a divorce or separation instrument, or a valid written agreement between the transferor spouse and the nontransferor spouse, expressly provides that—

(i) Both spouses or former spouses intend for the redemption to be treated, for Federal income tax purposes, as a redemption distribution to the transferor spouse; and

(ii) Such instrument or agreement supersedes any other instrument or agreement concerning the purchase, sale, redemption, or other disposition of the stock that is the subject of the redemption.

(2) Nontransferor spouse taxable. Notwithstanding applicable tax law, a transferor spouse's receipt of property in respect of the redeemed stock shall be treated as resulting in a constructive distribution to the nontransferor spouse for purposes of paragraph (a)(2) of this section, and shall not be treated as a distribution to the transferor spouse in redemption of such stock for purposes of paragraph (a)(1) of this section, if a divorce or separation instrument, or a valid written agreement between the transferor spouse and the nontransferor spouse, expressly provides that—

(i) Both spouses or former spouses intend for the redemption to be treated, for Federal income tax purposes, as resulting in a constructive distribution to the nontransferor spouse; and

(ii) Such instrument or agreement supersedes any other instrument or agreement concerning the purchase, sale, redemption, or other disposition of the stock that is the subject of the redemption.

(3) Execution of agreements. For purposes of this paragraph (c), a divorce or separation instrument must be effective, or a valid written agreement must be executed by both spouses or former spouses, prior to the date on which the transferor spouse (in the case of paragraph (c)(1) of this section) or the nontransferor spouse (in the case of paragraph (c)(2) of this section) files such spouse's first timely filed Federal income tax return for the year that includes the date of the stock redemption, but no later than the date such return is due (including extensions).

(d) Examples. The provisions of this section may be illustrated by the following examples:

Example 1. Corporation X has 100 shares outstanding. A and B each own 50 shares. A and B divorce. The divorce instrument requires B to purchase A's shares, and A to sell A's shares to B, in exchange for $100x. Corporation X redeems A's shares for $100x. Assume that, under applicable tax law, B has a primary and unconditional obligation to purchase A's stock, and therefore the stock redemption results in a constructive distribution to B. Also assume that the special rule of paragraph (c)(1) of this section does not apply. Accordingly, under paragraphs (a)(2) and (b)(2) of this section, A shall be treated as transferring A's stock of Corporation X to B in a transfer to which section 1041 applies (assuming the requirements of section 1041 are otherwise satisfied), B shall be treated as transferring the Corporation X stock B is deemed to have received from A to Corporation X in exchange for $100x in an exchange to which section 1041 does not apply and sections 302(d) and 301 apply, and B shall be treated as transferring the $100x to A in a transfer to which section 1041 applies.

Example 2. Assume the same facts as Example 1, except that the divorce instrument provides as follows: "A and B agree that the redemption will be treated for Federal income tax purposes as a redemption distribution to A." The divorce instrument further provides that it "supersedes all other instruments or agreements concerning the purchase, sale, redemption, or other disposition of the stock that is the subject of the redemption." By virtue of the special rule of paragraph (c)(1) of this section and under paragraphs (a)(1) and (b)(1) of this section, the tax consequences of the redemption shall be determined in accordance with its form as a redemption of A's shares by Corporation X and shall not be treated as resulting in a constructive distribution to B. See section 302.

Example 3. Assume the same facts as Example 1, except that the divorce instrument requires A to sell A's shares to Corporation X in exchange for a note. B guarantees Corporation X's payment of the note. Assume that, under applicable tax law, B does not have a primary and unconditional obligation to purchase A's stock, and therefore the stock redemption does not result in a constructive distribution to B. Also assume that the special rule of paragraph (c)(2) of this section does not apply. Accordingly, under paragraphs (a)(1) and (b)(1) of this section, the tax consequences of the redemption shall be determined in accordance with its form as a redemption of A's shares by Corporation X. See section 302.

Example 4. Assume the same facts as Example 3, except that the divorce instrument provides as follows: "A and B agree the redemption shall be treated, for Federal income tax purposes, as resulting in a constructive distribution to B." The divorce instrument further provides that it "supersedes any other instrument or agreement concerning the purchase, sale, redemption, or other disposition of the stock that is the subject of the redemption." By virtue of the special rule of paragraph (c)(2) of this section, the redemption is treated as resulting in a constructive distribution to B for purposes of paragraph (a)(2) of this section. Accordingly, under paragraphs (a)(2) and (b)(2) of this section, A shall be treated as transferring A's stock of Corporation X to B in a transfer to which section 1041 applies (assuming the requirements of section 1041 are otherwise satisfied), B shall be treated as transferring the Corporation X stock B is deemed to have received from A to Corporation X in exchange for a note in an exchange to which section 1041 does not apply and sections 302(d) and 301 apply, and B shall be treated as transferring the note to A in a transfer to which section 1041 applies.

* * *

[T.D. 9035, 68 FR 1534, Jan. 13, 2003]

§ 1.1060–1 Special allocation rules for certain asset acquisitions.

(a) Scope—(1) In general. This section prescribes rules relating to the requirements of section 1060, which, in the case of an applicable asset acquisition, requires the transferor (the seller) and the transferee (the purchaser) each to allocate the consideration paid or received in the transaction among the assets transferred in the same manner as amounts are allocated under section 338(b)(5) (relating to the allocation of adjusted grossed-up basis among the assets of the target corporation when a section 338 election is made). In the case of an applicable asset acquisition described in paragraph (b)(1) of this section, sellers and purchasers must allocate the consideration under the residual method, as described in §§ 1.338–6 and 1.338–7 in order to determine, respectively, the amount realized from, and the basis in, each of the transferred assets. For rules relating to distributions of partnership property or transfers of partnership interests which are subject to section 1060(d), see §-1.755–2T.

* * *

(b) Applicable asset acquisition—(1) In general. An applicable asset acquisition is any transfer, whether direct or indirect, of a group of assets if the assets transferred constitute a trade or business in the hands of either the seller or the purchaser, and except as provided in paragraph (b)(8) of this section, the purchaser's basis in the transferred assets is determined wholly by reference to the purchaser's consideration.

(2) Assets constituting a trade or business—(i) In general. For purposes of this section, a group of assets constitutes a trade or business if—

(A) The use of such assets would constitute an active trade or business under section 355; or

(B) Its character is such that goodwill or going concern value could under any circumstances attach to such group.

(ii) Goodwill or going concern value. Goodwill is the value of a trade or business attributable to the expectancy of continued customer patronage. This expectancy may be due to the name or reputation of a trade or business or any other factor. Going concern value is the additional value that attaches to property because of its existence as an integral part of an ongoing business activity. Going concern value includes the value attributable to the ability of a trade or business (or a part of a trade or business) to continue functioning or generating income without interruption notwithstanding a change in ownership. It also includes the value that is attributable to the immediate use or availability of an acquired trade or business, such as, for example, the use of the revenues or net earnings that otherwise would not be received during any period if the acquired trade or business were not available or operational.

(iii) Factors indicating goodwill or going concern value. In making the determination in this paragraph (b)(2), all the facts and circumstances surrounding the transaction are taken into account. Whether sufficient consideration is available to allocate to goodwill or going concern value after the residual method is applied is not relevant in determining whether goodwill or going concern value could attach to a group of assets. Factors to be considered include—

(A) The presence of any intangible assets (whether or not those assets are section 197 intangibles), provided, however, that the transfer of such an asset in the absence of other assets will not be a trade or business for purposes of section 1060;

(B) The existence of an excess of the total consideration over the aggregate book value of the tangible and intangible assets purchased (other than goodwill and going concern value) as shown in the financial accounting books and records of the purchaser; and

(C) Related transactions, including lease agreements, licenses, or other similar agreements between the purchaser and seller (or managers, directors, owners, or employees of the seller) in connection with the transfer.

(3) Examples. The following examples illustrate paragraphs (b)(1) and (2) of this section:

Example 1. S is a high grade machine shop that manufactures microwave connectors in limited quantities. It is a successful company with a reputation within the industry and among its customers for manufacturing unique, high quality products. Its tangible assets consist primarily of ordinary machinery for working metal and plating. It has no secret formulas or patented drawings of value. P is a company that designs, manufactures, and markets electronic components. It wants to establish an immediate presence in the microwave industry, an area in which it previously has not been engaged. P is acquiring assets of a number of smaller companies and hopes that these assets will collectively allow it to offer a broad product mix. P acquires the assets of S in order to augment its product mix and to promote its presence in the microwave industry. P will not use the assets acquired from S to manufacture microwave connectors. The assets transferred are assets that constitute a trade or business in the hands of the seller. Thus, P's purchase of S's assets is an applicable asset acquisition. The fact that P will not use the assets acquired from S to continue the business of S does not affect this conclusion.

Example 2. S, a sole proprietor who operates a car wash, both leases the building housing the car wash and sells all of the car wash equipment to P. S's use of the building and the car wash equipment constitute a trade or business. P begins operating a car wash in the building it leases from S. Because the assets transferred together with the asset leased are assets which constitute a trade or business, P's purchase of S's assets is an applicable asset acquisition.

Example 3. S, a corporation, owns a retail store business in State X and conducts activities in connection with that business enterprise that meet the active trade or business requirement of section 355. P is a minority shareholder of S. S distributes to P all the assets of S used in S's retail business in State X in complete redemption of P's stock in S held by P. The distribution of S's assets in redemption of P's stock is treated as a sale or exchange under sections 302(a) and 302(b)(3), and P's basis in the assets distributed to it is determined wholly by reference to the consideration paid, the S stock. Thus, S's distribution of assets constituting a trade or business to P is an applicable asset acquisition.

Example 4. S is a manufacturing company with an internal financial bookkeeping department. P is in the business of providing a financial bookkeeping service on a contract basis. As part of an agreement for P to begin providing financial bookkeeping services to S, P agrees to buy all of the assets associated with S's internal bookkeeping operations and provide employment to any of S's bookkeeping department employees who choose to accept a position with P. In addition to selling P the assets associated with its bookkeeping operation, S will enter into a long term contract with P for bookkeeping services. Because assets transferred from S to P, along with the related contract for bookkeeping services, are a trade or business in the hands of P, the sale of the bookkeeping assets from S to P is an applicable asset acquisition.

(4) Asymmetrical transfers of assets. A purchaser is subject to section 1060 if—**(i)** Under general principles of tax law, the seller is not treated as transferring the same assets as the purchaser is treated as acquiring; **(ii)** The assets acquired by the purchaser constitute a trade or business; and **(iii)** Except as provided in paragraph (b)(8) of this section, the purchaser's basis in the transferred assets is determined wholly by reference to the purchaser's consideration.

(5) Related transactions. Whether the assets transferred constitute a trade or business is determined by aggregating all transfers from the seller to the purchaser in a series of related transactions. Except as provided in paragraph (b)(8) of this section, all assets transferred from the seller to the purchaser in a series of related transactions are included in the group of assets among which the consideration paid or received in such series is allocated under the residual method. The principles of § 1.338–1(c) are also applied in determining which assets are included in the group of assets among which the consideration paid or received is allocated under the residual method.

(6) More than a single trade or business. If the assets transferred from a seller to a purchaser include more than one trade or business, then, in applying this section, all of the assets transferred (whether or not transferred in one transaction or a series of related transactions and whether or not part of a trade or business) are treated as a single trade or business.

(7) Covenant entered into by the seller. If, in connection with an applicable asset acquisition, the seller enters into a covenant (e.g., a covenant not to compete) with the purchaser, that covenant is treated as an asset transferred as part of a trade or business.

(8) Partial non-recognition exchanges. A transfer may constitute an applicable asset acquisition notwithstanding the fact that no gain or loss is recognized with respect to a portion of the group of assets transferred. All of the assets transferred, including the non-recognition assets, are taken into account in determining whether the group of assets constitutes a trade or business. The allocation of consideration under paragraph (c) of this section is done without taking into account either the non-recognition assets or the amount of money or other property that is treated as transferred in exchange for the non-recognition assets (together, the non-recognition exchange property). The basis in and gain or loss recognized with respect to the non-recognition exchange property are determined under such rules as would otherwise apply to an exchange of such property. The amount of the money and other property treated as exchanged for nonrecognition assets is the amount by which the fair market value of the non-recognition assets transferred by one party exceeds the fair market value of the non recognition assets transferred by the other (to the extent of the money and the fair market value of property transferred in the exchange). The money and other property that are treated as transferred in exchange for the non-recognition assets (and which are not included among the assets to which section 1060 applies) are considered to come from the following assets in the following order: first from Class I assets, then from Class II assets, then from Class III assets, then from Class IV assets, then from Class V assets, then from Class VI assets, and then from Class VII assets. For this purpose, liabilities assumed (or to which a non-recognition exchange property is subject) are treated as Class I assets. * * *

(c) Allocation of consideration among assets under the residual method—(1) Consideration. The seller's consideration is the amount, in the aggregate, realized from selling the assets in the applicable asset acquisition under section 1001(b). The purchaser's consideration is the amount, in the aggregate, of its cost of purchasing the assets in the applicable asset acquisition that is properly taken into account in basis.

(2) Allocation of consideration among assets. For purposes of determining the seller's amount realized for each of the assets sold in an applicable asset acquisition, the seller allocates consideration to all the assets sold by using the residual method under §§ 1.338–6 and 1.338–7, substituting consideration for ADSP. For purposes of determining the purchaser's basis in each of the assets purchased in an applicable asset acquisition, the purchaser allocates consideration to all the assets purchased by using the residual method under §§ 1.338–6 and 1.338–7, substituting consideration for AGUB. In allocating consideration, the rules set forth in paragraphs (c)(3) and (4) of this section apply in addition to the rules in §§ 1.338–6 and 1.338–7.

(3) Certain costs. The seller and purchaser each adjusts the amount allocated to an individual asset to take into account the specific identifiable costs incurred in transferring that asset in connection with the applicable asset acquisition (e.g., real estate transfer costs or security interest perfection costs). Costs so allocated increase, or decrease, as appropriate, the total consideration that is allocated under the residual method. No adjustment is made to the amount allocated to an individual asset for general costs associated with the applicable asset acquisition as a whole or with groups of assets included therein (e.g., non-specific appraisal fees or accounting fees). * * *

(4) Effect of agreement between parties. If, in connection with an applicable asset acquisition, the seller and purchaser agree in writing as to the allocation of any amount of consideration to, or as to the fair market value of, any of the assets, such agreement is binding on them to the extent provided in this paragraph (c)(4). Nothing in this paragraph (c)(4) restricts the Commissioner's authority to challenge the allocations or values arrived at in an allocation agreement. This paragraph (c)(4) does not apply if the parties are able to refute the allocation or valuation under the standards set forth in *Commissioner v. Danielson*, 378 F.2d 771 (3d Cir.), *cert. denied*, 389 U.S. 858 (1967) (a party wishing to challenge the tax consequences of an agreement as construed by the Commissioner must offer proof that, in an action between the parties to the agreement, would be admissible to alter that construction or show its unenforceability because of mistake, undue influence, fraud, duress, etc.).

(d) Examples. The following examples illustrate this section:

* * *

Example 2.(i) On January 1, 2001, S, a sole proprietor, sells to P, a corporation, a group of assets that constitutes a trade or business under paragraph (b)(2) of this section. S, who plans to retire immediately, also executes in P's favor a covenant not to compete. P pays S $3,000 in cash and assumes $1,000 in liabilities. Thus, the total consideration is 44,000.

(ii) On the purchase date, P and S also execute a separate agreement that states that the fair market values of the Class II, Class III, Class V, and Class VI assets S sold to P are as follows:

Asset Class	Asset	Fair Market Value
II	Actively traded securities	$ 500
	Total Class II	500
III	Accounts receivable	200
	Total Class III	200
V	Furniture and fixtures	800
	Building	800
	Land	200
	Equipment	400
	Total Class V	2,200
VI	Covenant not to compete	900
	Total Class VI	900

(iii) P and S each allocate the consideration in the transaction among the assets transferred under paragraph (c) of this section in accordance with the agreed upon fair market values of the assets, so that $500 is allocated to Class II assets, $200 is allocated to the Class III asset, $2,200 is allocated to Class V assets, $900 is allocated to Class VI assets, and $200 ($4,000 total consideration less $3,800 allocated to assets in Classes II, III, V, and VI) is allocated to the Class VII assets (goodwill and going concern value).

(iv) In connection with the examination of P's return, the Commissioner, in determining the fair market values of the assets transferred, may disregard the parties' agreement. Assume that the Commissioner correctly determines that the fair market value of the covenant not to compete was $500. Since the allocation of consideration among Class II, III, V, and VI assets results in allocations up to the fair market value limitation, the $600 of unallocated consideration resulting from the Commissioner's redetermination of the value of the covenant not to compete is allocated to Class VII assets (goodwill and going concern value).

(e) Reporting requirements—(1) Applicable asset acquisitions—(i) In general. Unless otherwise excluded from this requirement by the Commissioner, the seller and the purchaser in an applicable asset acquisition each must report information concerning the amount of consideration in the transaction and its allocation among the assets transferred. They also must report information concerning subsequent adjustments to consideration.

(ii) Time and manner of reporting—(A) In general. The seller and the purchaser each must file asset acquisition statements on Form 8594 "Asset Allocation Statement," with their income tax returns or returns of income for the taxable year that includes the first date assets are sold pursuant to an applicable asset acquisition. This reporting requirement applies to all asset acquisitions described in this section.

* * *

(B) Additional reporting requirement. When an increase or decrease in consideration is taken into account after the close of the first taxable year that includes the first date assets are sold in an applicable asset acquisition, the seller and the purchaser each must file a supplemental asset acquisition statement on Form 8594 with the income tax return or return of income for the taxable year in which the increase (or decrease) is properly taken into account.

* * *

(2) Transfers of interests in partnerships. For reporting requirements relating to the transfer of a partnership interest, see § 1.755–2(d).

[T.D. 8940, 66 FR 9925, Feb. 13, 2001, as amended by T.D. 9059, 68 FR 34293, June 9, 2003; T.D. 9158, 69 FR 55740, Sept. 16, 2004; T.D. 9358, 72 FR 51703, Sept. 11, 2007; T.D. 9377, 73 FR 3873, Jan. 23, 2008; 73 FR 14386, Mar. 18, 2008]

§ 1.1091–1 Losses from wash sales of stock or securities.

(a) A taxpayer cannot deduct any loss claimed to have been sustained from the sale or other disposition of stock or securities if, within a period beginning 30 days before the date of such sale or disposition and ending 30 days after such date (referred to in this section as the 61–day period), he has acquired (by purchase or by an exchange upon which the entire amount of gain or loss was recognized by law), or has entered into a contract or option so to acquire, substantially identical stock or securities. However, this prohibition does not apply (1) in the case of a taxpayer, not a corporation, if the sale or other disposition of stock or securities is made in connection with the taxpayer's trade or business, or (2) in the case of a corporation, a dealer in stock or securities, if the sale or other disposition of stock or securities is made in the ordinary course of its business as such dealer.

(b) Where more than one loss is claimed to have been sustained within the taxable year from the sale or other disposition of stock or securities, the provisions of this section shall be applied to the losses in the order in which the stock or securities the disposition of which resulted in the respective losses were disposed of (beginning with the earliest disposition). If the order of disposition of stock or securities disposed of at a loss on the same day cannot be determined, the stock or securities will be considered to have been disposed of in the order in which they were originally acquired (beginning with the earliest acquisition).

(c) Where the amount of stock or securities acquired within the 61–day period is less than the amount of stock or securities sold or otherwise disposed of, then the particular shares of stock or securities the loss from the sale or other disposition of which is not deductible shall be those with which the stock or securities acquired are matched in accordance with the following rule: The stock or securities acquired will be matched in accordance with the order of their acquisition (beginning with the earliest acquisition) with an equal number of the shares of stock or securities sold or otherwise disposed of.

(d) Where the amount of stock or securities acquired within the 61-day period is not less than the amount of stock or securities sold or otherwise disposed of, then the particular shares of stock or securities the acquisition of which resulted in the nondeductibility of the loss shall be those with which the stock or securities disposed of are matched in accordance with the following rule: The stock or securities sold or otherwise disposed of will be matched with an equal number of the shares of stock or securities acquired in accordance with the order of acquisition (beginning with the earliest acquisition) of the stock or securities acquired.

(e) The acquisition of any share of stock or any security which results in the nondeductibility of a loss under the provisions of this section shall be disregarded in determining the deductibility of any other loss.

(f) The word "acquired" as used in this section means acquired by purchase or by an exchange upon which the entire amount of gain or loss was recognized by law, and comprehends cases where the taxpayer has entered into a contract or option within the 61-day period to acquire by purchase or by such an exchange.

(g) For purposes of determining under this section the 61-day period applicable to a short sale of stock or securities, the principles of paragraph (a) of § 1.1233-1 for determining the consummation of a short sale shall generally apply except that the date of entering into the short sale shall be deemed to be the date of sale if, on the date of entering into the short sale, the taxpayer owns (or on or before such date has entered into a contract or option to acquire) stock or securities identical to those sold short and subsequently delivers such stock or securities to close the short sale.

(h) The following examples illustrate the application of this section:

Example (1). A, whose taxable year is the calendar year, on December 1, 1954, purchased 100 shares of common stock in the M Company for $10,000 and on December 15, 1954, purchased 100 additional shares for $9,000. On January 3, 1955, he sold the 100 shares purchased on December 1, 1954, for $9,000. Because of the provisions of section 1091, no loss from the sale is allowable as a deduction.

Example (2). A, whose taxable year is the calendar year, on September 21, 1954, purchased 100 shares of the common stock of the M Company for $5,000. On December 21, 1954, he purchased 50 shares of substantially identical stock for $2,750, and on December 27, 1954, he purchased 25 additional shares of such stock for $1,125. On January 3, 1955, he sold for $4,000 the 100 shares purchased on September 21, 1954. There is an indicated loss of $1,000 on the sale of the 100 shares. Since, within the 61-day period, A purchased 75 shares of substantially identical stock, the loss on the sale of 75 of the shares ($3,750–$3,000, or $750) is not allowable as a deduction because of the provisions of section 1091. The loss on the sale of the remaining 25 shares ($1,250–$1,000, or $250) is deductible subject to the limitations provided in sections 267 and 1211. The basis of the 50 shares purchased December 21, 1954, the acquisition of which resulted in the nondeductibility of the loss ($500) sustained on 50 of the 100 shares sold on January 3, 1955, is $2,500 (the cost of 50 of the shares sold on January 3, 1955) + $750 (the difference between the purchase price ($2,750) of the 50 shares acquired on December 21, 1954, and the selling price ($2,000) of 50 of the shares sold on January 3, 1955), or $3,250. Similarly, the basis of the 25 shares purchased on December 27, 1954, the acquisition of which resulted in the nondeductibility of the loss ($250) sustained on 25 of the shares sold on January 3, 1955, is $1,250 + $125, or $1,375. See § 1.1091-2.

* * *

[T.D. 6500, 25 FR 11910, Nov. 26, 1960, as amended by T.D. 6926, 32 FR 11468, Aug. 9, 1967]

§ 1.1091-2 Basis of stock or securities acquired in "wash sales".

(a) In general. The application of section 1091(d) may be illustrated by the following examples:

Example (1). A purchased a share of common stock of the X Corporation for $100 in 1935, which he sold January 15, 1955, for $80. On February 1, 1955, he purchased a share of common stock of the same corporation for $90. No loss from the sale is recognized under section 1091. The basis of the new share is $110; that is, the basis of the old share ($100) increased by $10, the excess of the price at which the new share was acquired ($90) over the price at which the old share was sold ($80).

Example (2). A purchased a share of common stock of the Y Corporation for $100 in 1935, which he sold January 15, 1955, for $80. On February 1, 1955, he purchased a share of common stock of the same corporation for $70. No loss from the sale is recognized under section 1091. The basis of the new share is $90; that is, the basis of the old share ($100) decreased by $10, the excess of the price at which the old share was sold ($80) over the price at which the new share was acquired ($70).

* * *

[T.D. 6500, 25 FR 11910, Nov. 26, 1960, as amended by T.D. 7129, 36 FR 12738, July 7, 1971]

§ 1.1221–1 Meaning of terms.

(a) The term "capital assets" includes all classes of property not specifically excluded by section 1221. In determining whether property is a "capital asset", the period for which held is immaterial.

(b) Property used in the trade or business of a taxpayer of a character which is subject to the allowance for depreciation provided in section 167 and real property used in the trade or business of a taxpayer is excluded from the term "capital assets". Gains and losses from the sale or exchange of such property are not treated as gains and losses from the sale or exchange of capital assets, except to the extent provided in section 1231. See § 1.1231–1. Property held for the production of income, but not used in a trade or business of the taxpayer, is not excluded from the term "capital assets" even though depreciation may have been allowed with respect to such property under section 23(*l*) of the Internal Revenue Code of 1939 before its amendment by section 121(c) of the Revenue Act of 1942 (56 Stat. 819). However, gain or loss upon the sale or exchange of land held by a taxpayer primarily for sale to customers in the ordinary course of his business, as in the case of a dealer in real estate, is not subject to the provisions of subchapter P (section 1201 and following), chapter 1 of the Code.

(c)(1) A copyright, a literary, musical, or artistic composition, and similar property are excluded from the term "capital assets" if held by a taxpayer whose personal efforts created such property, or if held by a taxpayer in whose hands the basis of such property is determined, for purposes of determining gain from a sale or exchange, in whole or in part by reference to the basis of such property in the hands of a taxpayer whose personal efforts created such property. For purposes of this subparagraph, the phrase "similar property" includes for example, such property as a theatrical production, a radio program, a newspaper cartoon strip, or any other property eligible for copyright protection (whether under statute or common law), but does not include a patent or an invention, or a design which may be protected only under the patent law and not under the copyright law.

(2) In the case of sales and other dispositions occurring after July 25, 1969, a letter, a memorandum, or similar property is excluded from the term "capital asset" if held by (i) a taxpayer whose personal efforts created such property, (ii) a taxpayer for whom such property was prepared or produced, or (iii) a taxpayer in whose hands the basis of such property is determined, for purposes of determining gain from a sale or exchange, in whole or in part by reference to the basis of such property in the hands of a taxpayer described in subdivision (i) or (ii) of this subparagraph. In the case of a collection of letters, memorandums, or similar property held by a person who is a taxpayer described in subdivision (i), (ii), or (iii) of this subparagraph as to some of such letters, memorandums, or similar property but not as to others, this subparagraph shall apply only to those letters, memorandums, or similar property as to which such person is a taxpayer described in such subdivision. For purposes of this subparagraph, the phrase "similar property" includes, for example, such property as a draft of a speech, a manuscript, a research paper, an oral recording of any type, a transcript of an oral recording, a transcript of an oral interview or of dictation, a personal or business diary, a log or journal, a corporate archive, including a corporate charter, office correspondence, a financial record, a drawing, a photograph, or a dispatch. A letter, memorandum, or property similar to a letter or memorandum, addressed to a taxpayer shall be considered as prepared or produced for him. This subparagraph does not apply to property, such as a corporate archive, office correspondence, or a financial record, sold or disposed of as part of a going business if such property has no significant value separate and apart from its relation to and use in such business; it also does not apply to any property to which subparagraph (1) of this paragraph applies (i.e., property to which section 1221(3) applied before its amendment by section 514(a) of the Tax Reform Act of 1969 (83 Stat. 643)).

(3) For purposes of this paragraph, in general, property is created in whole or in part by the personal efforts of a taxpayer if such taxpayer performs literary, theatrical, musical, artistic, or other creative or productive work which affirmatively contributes to the creation of the property, or if such taxpayer directs and guides others in the performance of such work. A taxpayer, such as corporate executive, who merely has administrative control of writers, actors, artists, or personnel and who does not substantially engage in the direction and guidance of such persons in the performance of their work, does not create property by his personal efforts. However, for purposes of subparagraph (2) of this paragraph, a letter or memorandum, or property similar to a letter or memorandum, which is prepared by personnel who are under the administrative control of a taxpayer, such as a corporate executive, shall be deemed to have been prepared or produced for him whether or not such letter, memorandum, or similar property is reviewed by him.

(4) For the application of section 1231 to the sale or exchange of property to which this paragraph applies, see § 1.1231–1. For the application of section 170 to the charitable contribution of property to which this paragraph applies, see section 170(e) and the regulations thereunder.

(d) Section 1221(4) excludes from the definition of "capital asset" accounts or notes receivable acquired in the ordinary course of trade or business for services rendered or from the sale of stock in trade or inventory or property held for sale to customers in the ordinary course of trade or business. Thus, if a taxpayer acquires a note receivable for services rendered, reports the fair market value of the note as income, and later sells the note for less than the amount previously reported, the loss is an ordinary loss. On the other hand, if the taxpayer later sells the note for more than the amount originally reported, the excess is treated as ordinary income.

* * *

[T.D. 6500, 25 FR 12003, Nov. 26, 1960, as amended by T.D. 7369, 40 FR 29840, July 16, 1975]

§ 1.1221–2 Hedging transactions.

(a) Treatment of hedging transactions—(1) In general. This section governs the treatment of hedging transactions under section 1221(a)(7). Except as provided in paragraph (g)(2) of this section, the term capital asset does not include property that is part of a hedging transaction (as defined in paragraph (b) of this section).

(2) Short sales and options. This section also governs the character of gain or loss from a short sale or option that is part of a hedging transaction. Except as provided in paragraph (g)(2) of this section, gain or loss on a short sale or option that is part of a hedging transaction (as defined in paragraph (b) of this section) is ordinary income or loss.

(3) Exclusivity. If a transaction is not a hedging transaction as defined in paragraph (b) of this section, gain or loss from the transaction is not made ordinary on the grounds that property involved in the transaction is a surrogate for a noncapital asset, that the transaction serves as insurance against a business risk, that the transaction serves a hedging function, or that the transaction serves a similar function or purpose.

* * *

(b) Hedging transaction defined. Section 1221(b)(2)(A) provides that a hedging transaction is any transaction that a taxpayer enters into in the normal course of the taxpayer's trade or business primarily—

(1) To manage risk of price changes or currency fluctuations with respect to ordinary property (as defined in paragraph (c)(2) of this section) that is held or to be held by the taxpayer;

(2) To manage risk of interest rate or price changes or currency fluctuations with respect to borrowings made or to be made, or ordinary obligations incurred or to be incurred, by the taxpayer; or

(3) To manage such other risks as the Secretary may prescribe in regulations (see paragraph (d)(6) of this section).

(c) General rules—(1) Normal course. Solely for purposes of paragraph (b) of this section, if a transaction is entered into in furtherance of a taxpayer's trade or business, the transaction is entered into in the normal course of the taxpayer's trade or business. This rule includes managing risks relating to the expansion of an existing business or the acquisition of a new trade or business.

(2) Ordinary property and obligations. Property is ordinary property to a taxpayer only if a sale or exchange of the property by the taxpayer could not produce capital gain or loss under any circumstances. Thus, for example, property used in a trade or business within the meaning of section 1231(b) (determined without regard to the holding period specified in that section) is not ordinary property. An obligation is an ordinary obligation if performance or termination of the obligation by the taxpayer could not produce capital gain or loss. For purposes of this paragraph (c)(2), the term termination has the same meaning as it does in section 1234A.

(3) Hedging an aggregate risk. The term hedging transaction includes a transaction that manages an aggregate risk of interest rate changes, price changes, and/or currency fluctuations only if all of the risk, or all but a *de minimis* amount of the risk, is with respect to ordinary property, ordinary obligations, or borrowings.

(4) Managing risk—(i) In general. Whether a transaction manages a taxpayer's risk is determined based on all of the facts and circumstances surrounding the taxpayer's business and the transaction. Whether a transaction manages a taxpayer's risk may be determined on a business unit by business unit basis (for example by treating particular groups of activities, including the assets and liabilities attributable to those activities, as separate business units), provided that the business unit is within a single entity * * *. A taxpayer's hedging strategies and policies as reflected in the taxpayer's minutes or other records are evidence of whether particular transactions were entered into primarily to manage the taxpayer's risk.

(ii) Limitation of risk management transactions to those specifically described. Except as otherwise determined by published guidance or by private letter ruling, a transaction that is not treated as a hedging transaction under paragraph (d) does not manage risk. Moreover, a transaction undertaken for speculative purposes will not be treated as a hedging transaction.

(d) Transactions that manage risk—(1) Risk reduction transactions—(i) In general. A transaction that is entered into to reduce a taxpayer's risk, manages a taxpayer's risk.

(ii) Micro and macro hedges—(A) In general. A taxpayer generally has risk of a particular type only if it is at risk when all of its operations are considered. Nonetheless, a hedge of a particular asset or liability generally will be respected as reducing risk if it reduces the risk attributable to the asset or liability and if it is reasonably expected to reduce the overall risk of the taxpayer's operations. If a taxpayer hedges particular assets or liabilities, or groups of assets or liabilities, and the hedges are undertaken as part of a program that, as a whole, is reasonably expected to reduce the overall risk of the taxpayer's operations, the taxpayer generally does not have to demonstrate that each hedge that was entered into pursuant to the program reduces its overall risk.

(B) Example. The following example illustrates the rules stated in paragraph (d)(1)(ii)(A) of this section:

Example. Corporation X manages its business operations by treating particular groups of activities, including the assets and liabilities attributable to those assets, as separate business units. A separate set of books and records is maintained with respect to the activities, assets and liabilities of separate business unit *y*. As part of a risk management program that Corporation X reasonably expects to reduce the overall risks of its business operations, Corporation X enters into hedges to reduce the risks of separate business unit *y*. Corporation X may demonstrate that the hedges reduce risk by taking into account only the activities, assets and liabilities of business unit *y*.

(iii) Written options. A written option may reduce risk. For example, in appropriate circumstances, a written call option with respect to assets held by a taxpayer or a written put option with respect to assets to be acquired by a taxpayer may be a hedging transaction. See also paragraph (d)(3) of this section.

(iv) Fixed-to-floating price hedges. Under the principles of paragraph (d)(1)(ii)(A) of this section, a transaction that economically converts a price from a fixed price to a floating price may reduce risk. For example, a taxpayer with a fixed cost for its inventory may be at risk if the price at which the inventory can be sold varies with a particular factor. Thus, for such a taxpayer a transaction that converts its fixed price to a floating price may be a hedging transaction.

(2) Interest rate conversions. A transaction that economically converts an interest rate from a fixed rate to a floating rate or that converts an interest rate from a floating rate to a fixed rate manages risk.

(3) Transactions that counteract hedging transactions. If a transaction is entered into primarily to offset all or any part of the risk management effected by one or more hedging transactions, the transaction is a hedging transaction. For example, if a written option is used to reduce or eliminate the risk reduction obtained from another position such as a purchased option, then it may be a hedging transaction.

(4) Recycling. A taxpayer may enter into a hedging transaction by using a position that was a hedge of one asset or liability as a hedge of another asset or liability (recycling).

(5) Transactions not entered into primarily to manage risk—(i) Rule. Except as otherwise determined in published guidance or private letter ruling, the purchase or sale of a debt instrument, an equity security, or an annuity contract is not a hedging transaction even if the transaction limits or reduces the taxpayer's risk with respect to ordinary property, borrowings, or ordinary obligations. In addition, the Commissioner may determine in published guidance that other transactions are not hedging transactions.

(ii) Examples. The following examples illustrate the rule stated in paragraph (d)(5)(i) of this section:

Example 1. Taxpayer borrows money and agrees to pay a floating rate of interest. Taxpayer purchases debt instruments that bear a comparable floating rate. Although taxpayer's interest rate risk from the floating rate borrowing may be reduced by the purchase of the debt instruments, the acquisition of the debt instruments is not a hedging transaction, because the transaction is not entered into primarily to manage the taxpayer's risk.

Example 2. Taxpayer undertakes obligations to pay compensation in the future. The amount of the future compensation payments is adjusted as if amounts were invested in a specified mutual fund and were increased or decreased by the earnings, gains and losses that would result from such an investment. Taxpayer invests funds in the shares of the mutual fund. Although the investment in shares of the mutual fund reduces the taxpayer's risk of fluctuation in the amount of its obligation to employees, the investment was not made primarily to manage the taxpayer's risk. Accordingly, the transaction is not a hedging transaction.

Example 3. Taxpayer provides a nonqualified retirement plan for employees that is structured like a defined contribution plan. Based on a schedule that takes into account an employee's monthly salary and years of service with the taxpayer, the taxpayer makes monthly credits to an account for each employee. Each employee may designate that the account will be treated as if it were used to pay premiums on a variable annuity contract issued by the M insurance company with a value that reflects a specified investment option. M offers a number of investment options for its variable annuity contracts. Taxpayer invests funds in M company variable annuity contracts that parallel the investment options selected by the employees. The investment is not made primarily to manage the taxpayer's risk and is not a hedging transaction.

(6) Hedges of other risks. The Commissioner may, by published guidance, determine that hedging transactions include transactions entered into to manage risks other than interest rate or price changes, or currency fluctuations.

(7) Miscellaneous provision—(i) Extent of risk management. A taxpayer may hedge all or any portion of its risk for all or any part of the period during which it is exposed to the risk.

(ii) Number of transactions. The fact that a taxpayer frequently enters into and terminates positions (even if done on a daily or more frequent basis) is not relevant to whether these transactions are hedging transactions. Thus, for example, a taxpayer hedging the risk associated with an asset or liability may frequently establish and terminate positions that hedge that risk, depending on the extent the taxpayer wishes to be hedged. Similarly, if a taxpayer maintains its level of risk exposure by entering into and terminating a large number of transactions in a single day, its transactions may nonetheless qualify as hedging transactions.

* * *

(f) Identification and recordkeeping—(1) Same-day identification of hedging transactions. Under section 1221(a)(7), a taxpayer that enters into a hedging transaction (including recycling an existing hedging transaction) must clearly identify it as a hedging transaction before the close of the day on which the taxpayer acquired, originated, or entered into the transaction (or recycled the existing hedging transaction).

(2) Substantially contemporaneous identification of hedged item—(i) Content of the identification. A taxpayer that enters into a hedging transaction must identify the item, items, or aggregate risk being hedged. Identification of an item being hedged generally involves identifying a transaction that creates risk, and the type of risk that the transaction creates. For example, if a taxpayer is hedging the price risk with respect to its June purchases of corn inventory, the transaction being hedged is the June purchase of corn and the risk is price movements in the market where the taxpayer buys its corn. For additional rules concerning the content of this identification, see paragraph (f)(3) of this section.

(ii) Timing of the identification. The identification required by this paragraph (f)(2) must be made substantially contemporaneously with entering into the hedging transaction. An identification is not substantially contemporaneous if it is made more than 35 days after entering into the hedging transaction.

(3) Identification requirements for certain hedging transactions. In the case of the hedging transactions described in this paragraph (f)(3), the identification under paragraph (f)(2) of this section must include the information specified.

(i) Anticipatory asset hedges. If the hedging transaction relates to the anticipated acquisition of assets by the taxpayer, the identification must include the expected date or dates of acquisition and the amounts expected to be acquired.

(ii) Inventory hedges. If the hedging transaction relates to the purchase or sale of inventory by the taxpayer, the identification is made by specifying the type or class of inventory to which the transaction relates. If the hedging transaction relates to specific purchases or sales, the identification must also include the expected dates of the purchases or sales and the amounts to be purchased or sold.

(iii) Hedges of debt of the taxpayer—(A) Existing debt. If the hedging transaction relates to accruals or payments under an issue of existing debt of the taxpayer, the identification must specify the issue and, if the hedge is for less than the full issue price or the full term of the debt, the amount of the issue price and the term covered by the hedge.

(B) Debt to be issued. If the hedging transaction relates to the expected issuance of debt by the taxpayer or to accruals or payments under debt that is expected to be issued by the taxpayer, the identification must specify the following information: the expected date of issuance of the debt; the expected maturity or maturities; the total expected issue price; and the expected interest provisions. If the hedge is for less than the entire expected issue price of the debt or the full expected term of the debt, the identification must also include the amount or the term being hedged. The identification may indicate a range of dates, terms, and amounts, rather than specific dates, terms, or amounts. For example, a taxpayer might identify a transaction as hedging the yield on an anticipated issuance of fixed rate debt during the second half of its fiscal year, with the anticipated amount of the debt between $75 million and $125 million, and an anticipated term of approximately 20 to 30 years.

(iv) Hedges of aggregate risk—(A) Required identification. If a transaction hedges aggregate risk as described in paragraph (c)(3) of this section, the identification under paragraph (f)(2) of this section must include a description of the risk being hedged and of the hedging program under which the hedging transaction was entered. This requirement may be met by placing in the taxpayer's records a description of the hedging program and by establishing a system under which individual transactions can be identified as being entered into pursuant to the program.

(B) Description of hedging program. A description of a hedging program must include an identification of the type of risk being hedged, a description of the type of items giving rise to the risk being aggregated, and sufficient additional information to demonstrate that the program is designed to reduce aggregate risk of the type identified. If the program contains controls on speculation (for example, position limits), the description of the hedging program must also explain how the controls are established, communicated, and implemented.

(v) Transactions that counteract hedging transactions. If the hedging transaction is described in paragraph (d)(3) of this section, the description of the hedging transaction must include an identification of the risk management transaction that is being offset and the original underlying hedged item.

(4) Manner of identification and records to be retained—(i) Inclusion of identification in tax records. The identification required by this paragraph (f) must be made on, and retained as part of, the taxpayer's books and records.

(ii) Presence of identification must be unambiguous. The presence of an identification for purposes of this paragraph (f) must be unambiguous. The identification of a hedging transaction for financial accounting or regulatory purposes does not satisfy this requirement unless the taxpayer's books and records indicate that the identification is also being made for tax purposes. The taxpayer may indicate that individual hedging transactions, or a class or classes of hedging transactions, that are identified for financial accounting or regulatory purposes are also being identified as hedging transactions for purposes of this section.

(iii) Manner of identification. The taxpayer may separately and explicitly make each identification, or, so long as paragraph (f)(4)(ii) of this section is satisfied, the taxpayer may establish a system pursuant to which the identification is indicated by the type of transaction or by the manner in which the transaction is consummated or recorded. An identification under this system is made at the later of the time that the system is established or the time that the transaction satisfies the terms of the system by being entered, or by being consummated or recorded, in the designated fashion.

(iv) Principles of paragraph (f)(4)(iii) of this section illustrated. Paragraphs (f)(4)(iv)(A) through (C) of this section illustrate the principles of paragraph (f)(4)(iii) of this section and assume that the other requirements of this paragraph (f) are satisfied.

(A) A taxpayer can make an identification by designating a hedging transaction for (or placing it in) an account that has been identified as containing only hedges of a specified item (or of specified items or specified aggregate risk).

(B) A taxpayer can make an identification by including and retaining in its books and records a statement that designates all future transactions in a specified derivative product as hedges of a specified item, items, or aggregate risk.

(C) A taxpayer can make an identification by designating a certain mark, a certain form, or a certain legend as meaning that a transaction is a hedge of a specified item (or of specified items or a specified aggregate risk). Identification can be made by placing the designated mark on a record of the transaction (for example, trading ticket, purchase order, or trade confirmation) or by using the designated form or a record that contains the designated legend.

* * *

(6) Consistency with section 1256(e)(2). Any identification for purposes of section 1256(e)(2) is also an identification for purposes of paragraph (f)(1) of this section.

(g) Effect of identification and non-identification—(1) Transactions identified—(i) In general. If a taxpayer identifies a transaction as a hedging transaction for purposes of paragraph (f)(1) of this section, the identification is binding with respect to gain, whether or not all of the requirements of paragraph (f) of this section are satisfied. Thus, gain from that transaction is ordinary income. If the transaction is not in fact a hedging transaction described in paragraph (b) of this section, however, paragraphs (a)(1) and (2) of this section do not apply and the character of loss is determined without reference to whether the transaction is a surrogate for a noncapital asset, serves as insurance against a business risk, serves a hedging function, or serves a similar function or purpose. Thus, the taxpayer's identification of the transaction as a hedging transaction does not itself make loss from the transaction ordinary.

(ii) Inadvertent identification. Notwithstanding paragraph (g)(1)(i) of this section, if the taxpayer identifies a transaction as a hedging transaction for purposes of paragraph (f) of this section, the character of the gain is determined as if the transaction had not been identified as a hedging transaction if—

(A) The transaction is not a hedging transaction (as defined in paragraph (b) of this section);

(B) The identification of the transaction as a hedging transaction was due to inadvertent error; and

(C) All of the taxpayer's transactions in all open years are being treated on either original or, if necessary, amended returns in a manner consistent with the principles of this section.

(2) Transactions not identified—(i) In general. Except as provided in paragraphs (g)(2)(ii) and (iii) of this section, the absence of an identification that satisfies the requirements of paragraph (f)(1) of this section is binding and establishes that a transaction is not a hedging transaction. Thus, subject to the exceptions, the rules of paragraphs (a)(1) and (2) of this section do not apply, and the character of gain or loss is determined without reference to whether the transaction is a surrogate for a noncapital asset, serves as insurance against a business risk, serves a hedging function, or serves a similar function or purpose.

(ii) Inadvertent error. If a taxpayer does not make an identification that satisfies the requirements of paragraph (f) of this section, the taxpayer may treat gain or loss from the transaction as ordinary income or loss under paragraph (a)(1) or (2) of this section if—

(A) The transaction is a hedging transaction (as defined in paragraph (b) of this section);

(B) The failure to identify the transaction was due to inadvertent error; and

(C) All of the taxpayer's hedging transactions in all open years are being treated on either original or, if necessary, amended returns as provided in paragraphs (a)(1) and (2) of this section.

(iii) Anti-abuse rule. If a taxpayer does not make an identification that satisfies all the requirements of paragraph (f) of this section but the taxpayer has no reasonable grounds for treating the transaction as other than a hedging transaction, then gain from the transaction is ordinary. The reasonableness of the taxpayer's failure to identify a transaction is determined by taking into consideration not only the requirements of paragraph (b) of this section but also the taxpayer's treatment of the transaction for financial accounting or other purposes and the taxpayer's identification of similar transactions as hedging transactions.

* * *

[T.D. 8985, 67 FR 12863, Mar. 20, 2002; T.D. 9264, 71 FR 30591, May 30, 2006; T.D. 9329, 72 FR 32804, June 14, 2007]

§ 1.1223–1 Determination of period for which capital assets are held.

(a) The holding period of property received in an exchange by a taxpayer includes the period for which the property which he exchanged was held by him, if the property received has the same basis in whole or in part for determining gain or loss in the hands of the taxpayer as the property exchanged. However, this rule shall apply, in the case of exchanges after March 1, 1954, only if the property exchanged was at the time of the exchange a capital asset in the hands of the taxpayer or property used in his trade or business as defined in section 1231(b). For the purposes of this paragraph, the term "exchange" includes the following transactions: (1) An involuntary conversion described in section 1033, and (2) a distribution to which section 355 (or so much of section 356 as relates to section 355) applies. Thus, if property acquired as the result of a compulsory or involuntary conversion of other property of the taxpayer has under section 1033(c) the same basis in whole or in part in the hands of the taxpayer as the property so converted, its acquisition is treated as an exchange and the holding period of the newly acquired property shall include the period during which the converted property was held by the taxpayer. Thus, also, where stock of a controlled corporation is received by a taxpayer pursuant to a distribution to which section 355 (or so much of section 356 as relates to section 355) applies, the distribution is treated as an exchange and the period for which the taxpayer has held the stock of the controlled corporation shall include the period for which he held the stock of the distributing corporation with respect to which such distribution was made.

(b) The holding period of property in the hands of a taxpayer shall include the period during which the property was held by any other person, if such property has the same basis in whole or in part in the hands of the taxpayer for determining gain or loss from a sale or exchange as it would have in the hands of such other person. For example, the period for which property acquired by gift after December 31, 1920, was held by the donor must be included in determining the period for which the property was held by the taxpayer if, under the provisions of section 1015, such property has, for the purpose of determining gain or loss from the sale or exchange, the same basis in the hands of the taxpayer as it would have in the hands of the donor.

* * *

(d) If the acquisition of stock or securities resulted in the nondeductibility (under section 1091, relating to wash sales) of the loss from the sale or other disposition of substantially identical stock or securities, the holding period of the newly acquired securities shall include the period for which the taxpayer held the securities with respect to which the loss was not allowable.

* * *

(i) If shares of stock in a corporation are sold from lots purchased at different dates or at different prices and the identity of the lots cannot be determined, the rules prescribed by the regulations under section 1012 for determining the cost or other basis of such stocks so sold or transferred shall also apply for the purpose of determining the holding period of such stock.

* * *

[T.D. 6500, 25 FR 12005, Nov. 26, 1960, as amended by T.D. 7238, 37 FR 28717, Dec. 29, 1972; T.D. 7728, 45 FR 72650, Nov. 3, 1980]

§ 1.1223–3 Rules relating to the holding periods of partnership interests.

(a) In general. A partner shall not have a divided holding period in an interest in a partnership unless:

(1) The partner acquired portions of an interest at different times; or

(2) The partner acquired portions of the partnership interest in exchange for property transferred at the same time but resulting in different holding periods (e.g. section 1223).

(b) Accounting for holding periods of an interest in a partnership—(1) General rule. The portion of a partnership interest to which a holding period relates shall be determined by reference to a fraction, the numerator of which is the fair market value of the portion of the partnership interest received in the transaction to which the holding period relates, and the denominator of which is the fair market value of the entire partnership interest (determined immediately after the transaction).

(2) Special rule. For purposes of applying paragraph (b)(1) of this section to determine the holding period of a partnership interest (or portion thereof) that is sold or exchanged (or with respect to which gain or loss is recognized upon a distribution under section 731), if a partner makes one or more contributions of cash to the partnership and receives one or more distributions of cash from the partnership during the one-year period ending on the date of the sale or exchange (or distribution with respect to which gain or loss is recognized under section 731), the partner may reduce the cash contributions made during the year by cash distributions received on a last-in-first-out basis, treating all cash distributions as if they were received immediately before the sale or exchange (or at the time of the distribution with respect to which gain or loss is recognized under section 731).

(3) Deemed contributions and distributions. For purposes of paragraphs (b)(1) and (2) of this section, deemed contributions of cash under section 752(a) and deemed distributions of cash under section 752(b) shall be disregarded to the same extent that such amounts are disregarded under § 1.704–1(b)(2)(iv)(c).

(4) Adjustment with respect to contributed section 751 assets. For purposes of applying paragraph (b)(1) of this section to determine the holding period of a partnership interest (or portion thereof) that is sold or exchanged, if a partner receives a portion of the partnership interest in exchange for property described in section 751(c) or (d) (section 751 assets) within the one-year period ending on the date of the sale or exchange of all or a portion of the partner's interest in the partnership, and the partner recognizes ordinary income or loss on account of such a section 751 asset in a fully taxable transaction (either as a result of the sale of all or part of the partner's interest in the partnership or the sale by the partnership of the section 751 asset), the contribution of the section 751 asset during the one-year period shall be disregarded. However, if, in the absence of this paragraph, a partner would not be treated as having held any portion of the interest for more than one year (e.g., because the partner's only contributions to the partnership are contributions of section 751 assets or section 751 assets and cash within the prior one-year period), this adjustment is not available.

(5) Exception. The Commissioner may prescribe by guidance published in the Internal Revenue Bulletin (see § 601.601(d)(2) of this chapter) a rule disregarding certain cash contributions (including contributions of a *de minimis* amount of cash) in applying paragraph (b)(1) of this section to determine the holding period of a partnership interest (or portion thereof) that is sold or exchanged.

(c) Sale or exchange of all or a portion of an interest in a partnership—(1) Sale or exchange of entire interest in a partnership. If a partner sells or exchanges the partner's entire interest in a partnership, any capital gain or loss recognized shall be divided between long-term and short-term capital gain or loss in the same proportions as the holding period of the interest in the partnership is divided between the portion of the interest held for more than one year and the portion of the interest held for one year or less.

(2) Sale or exchange of a portion of an interest in a partnership. * * *

(ii) Other partnerships. If a partner has a divided holding period in a partnership interest, * * * then the holding period of the transferred interest shall be divided between long-term and short-term capital gain or loss in the same proportions as the long-term and short-term capital gain or loss that the transferor partner would realize if the entire interest in the partnership were transferred in a fully taxable transaction immediately before the actual transfer.

(d) Distributions—(1) In general. Except as provided in paragraph (b)(2) of this section, a partner's holding period in a partnership interest is not affected by distributions from the partnership.

(2) Character of capital gain or loss recognized as a result of a distribution from a partnership. If a partner is required to recognize capital gain or loss as a result of a distribution from a partnership, then the capital gain or loss recognized shall be divided between long-term and short-term capital gain or loss in the same proportions as the long-term and short-term capital gain or loss that the distributee partner would realize if such partner's entire interest in the partnership were transferred in a fully taxable transaction immediately before the distribution.

(e) Section 751(c) assets. For purposes of this section, properties and potential gain treated as unrealized receivables under section 751(c) shall be treated as separate assets that are not capital assets as defined in section 1221 or property described in section 1231.

(f) Examples. The provisions of this section are illustrated by the following examples:

Example 1. Division of holding period—contribution of money and a capital asset. (i) A contributes

$5,000 of cash and a nondepreciable capital asset *A* has held for two years to a partnership (*PRS*) for a 50% interest in *PRS*. *A*'s basis in the capital asset is $5,000, and the fair market value of the asset is $10,000. After the exchange, *A*'s basis in *A*'s interest in *PRS* is $10,000, and the fair market value of the interest is $15,000. *A* received one-third of the interest in *PRS* for a cash payment of $5,000 ($5,000/$15,000). Therefore, *A*'s holding period in one-third of the interest received (attributable to the contribution of money to the partnership) begins on the day after the contribution. *A* received two-thirds of the interest in *PRS* in exchange for the capital asset ($10,000/$15,000). Accordingly, pursuant to section 1223(1), *A* has a two-year holding period in two-thirds of the interest received in *PRS*.

(ii) Six months later, when *A*'s basis in *PRS* is $12,000 (due to a $2,000 allocation of partnership income to *A*), *A* sells the interest in *PRS* for $17,000. Assuming *PRS* holds no inventory or unrealized receivables (as defined under section 751(c)) and no collectibles or section 1250 property, *A* will realize $5,000 of capital gain. As determined above, one-third of A's interest in *PRS* has a holding period of one year or less, and two-thirds of *A*'s interest in *PRS* has a holding period equal to two years and six months. Therefore, one-third of the capital gain will be short-term capital gain, and two-thirds of the capital gain will be long-term capital gain.

Example 2. Division of holding period—contribution of section 751 asset and a capital asset. A contributes inventory with a basis of $2,000 and a fair market value of $6,000 and a capital asset which A has held for more than one year with a basis of $4,000 and a fair market value of $6,000, and B contributes cash of $12,000 to form a partnership (AB). As a result of the contribution, one-half of A's interest in AB is treated as having been held for more than one year under section 1223(1). Six months later, A transfers one-half of A's interest in AB to C for $6,000, realizing a gain of $3,000. If AB were to sell all of its section 751 property in a fully taxable transaction immediately before A's transfer of the partnership interest, A would be allocated $4,000 of ordinary income on account of the inventory. Accordingly, A will recognize $2,000 of ordinary income and $1,000 of capital gain ($3,000—$2,000) on account of the transfer to C. Because A recognizes ordinary income on account of the inventory that was contributed to AB within the one year period ending on the date of the sale, the inventory will be disregarded in determining the holding period of A's interest in AB. All of the capital gain will be long-term.

Example 3. Netting of cash contributions and distributions. **(i)** On January 1, 2000, A holds a 50 percent interest in the capital and profits of a partnership (PS). The value of A's PS interest is $900, and A's holding period in the entire interest is long-term. On January 2, 2000, when the value of A's PS interest is still $900, A contributes $100 to PS. On June 1, 2000, A receives a distribution of $40 cash from the partnership. On September 1, 2000, when the value of A's interest in PS is $1,350, A contributes an additional $230 cash to PS, and on October 1, 2000, A receives another $40 cash distribution from PS. A sells A's entire partnership interest on November 1, 2000, for $1,600. A's adjusted basis in the PS interest at the time of the sale is $1,000.

(ii) For purposes of netting cash contributions and distributions in determining the holding period of A's interest in PS, A is treated as having received a distribution of $80 on November 1, 2000. Applying that distribution on a last-in-first-out basis to reduce prior contributions during the year, the contribution made on September 1, 2000, is reduced to $150 ($230—$80). The holding period then is determined as follows: Immediately after the contribution of $100 on January 2, 2000, A's holding period in A's PS interest is 90 percent long-term ($900/($900 + $100)) and 10 percent short-term ($100/($900 + $100)). The contribution of $150 on September 1, 2000, causes 10 percent of A's partnership interest ($150/($1,350 + $150)) to have a short-term holding period. Accordingly, immediately after the contribution on September 1, 2000, A's holding period in A's PS interest is 81 percent long-term (.90 x .90) and 19 percent short-term ((.10 x .90) + .10). Accordingly, $486 ($600 x .81) of the gain from A's sale of the PS interest is long-term capital gain, and $114 ($600 x .19) is short-term capital gain.

Example 4. Division of holding period when capital account is increased by contribution. A, B, C, and D are equal partners in a partnership (PRS), and the fair market value of a 25 percent interest in PRS is $100. A, B, C, and D each contribute an additional $100 to partnership capital, thereby increasing the fair market value of each partner's interest to $200. As a result of the contribution, each partner has a new holding period in the portion of the partner's interest in PRS that is attributable to the contribution. That portion equals 50 percent ($100/$200) of each partner's interest in PRS.

Example 5. Sale or exchange of a portion of an interest in a partnership. **(i)** A, B, and C form an equal partnership (PRS). In connection with the formation, A contributes $5,000 in cash and a capital asset (capital asset 1) with a fair market value of $5,000 and a basis of $2,000; B contributes $7,000 in cash and a capital asset (capital asset 2) with a fair market value of $3,000 and a basis of $3,000; and C contributes $10,000 in cash. At the time of the contribution, A had held the contributed property for two years. Six months later, when A's basis in PRS is $7,000, A transfers one-half of A's interest in PRS to T for $7,000 at a time when PRS's balance sheet (reflecting a cash receipts and disbursements method of accounting) is as follows:

ASSETS

	Adjusted Basis	Market Value
Cash	$22,000	$22,000
Unrealized Receivables	0	6,000
Capital Asset 1	2,000	5,000
Capital Asset 2	3,000	9,000
Capital Assets	5,000	14,000
Total	$27,000	$42,000

(ii) Although at the time of the transfer A has not held A's interest in PRS for more than one year, 50 percent of the fair market value of A's interest in PRS was received in exchange for a capital asset with a long-term holding period. Therefore, 50 percent of A's interest in PRS has a long-term holding period.

(iii) If PRS were to sell all of its section 751 property in a fully taxable transaction immediately before A's transfer of the partnership interest, A would be allocated $2,000 of ordinary income. One-half of that amount ($1,000) is attributable to the portion of A's interest in PRS transferred to T. Accordingly, A will recognize $1,000 ordinary income and $2,500 ($3,500—$1,000) of capital gain on account of the transfer to T of one-half of A's interest in PRS. Fifty percent ($1,250) of that gain is long-term capital gain and 50 percent ($1,250) is short-term capital gain.

* * *

Example 7. Disproportionate distribution. In 1997, A and B each contribute cash of $50,000 to form and become equal partners in a partnership (PRS). More than one year later, A receives a distribution worth $22,000 from PRS, which reduces A's interest in PRS to 36 percent. After the distribution, B owns 64 percent of PRS. The holding periods of A and B in their interests in PRS are not affected by the distribution.

Example 8. Gain or loss as a result of a distribution—(i) On January 1, 1996, A contributes property with a basis of $10 and a fair market value of $10,000 in exchange for an interest in a partnership (ABC). On September 30, 2000, when A's interest in ABC is worth $12,000 (and the basis of A's partnership interest is still $10), A contributes $12,000 cash in exchange for an additional interest in ABC. A is allocated a loss equal to $10,000 by ABC for the taxable year ending December 31, 2000, thereby reducing the basis of A's partnership interest to $2,010. On February 1, 2001, ABC makes a cash distribution to A of $10,000. ABC holds no inventory or unrealized receivables. (Assume that A is allocated no gain or loss for the taxable year ending December 31, 2001, so that the basis of A's partnership interest does not increase or decrease as a result of such allocations.)

(ii) The netting rule contained in paragraph (b)(2) of this section provides that, in determining the holding period of A's interest in ABC, the cash contribution made on September 30, 2000, must be reduced by the distribution made on February 1, 2001. Accordingly, for purposes of determining the holding period of A's interest in ABC, A is treated as having made a cash contribution of $2,000 ($12,000—$10,000) to ABC on September 30, 2000. A's holding period in one-seventh of A's interest in ABC ($2,000 cash contributed over the $14,000 value of the entire interest (determined as if only $2,000 were contributed rather than $12,000)) begins on the day after the cash contribution. A recognizes $7,990 of capital gain as a result of the distribution. See section 731(a)(1). One-seventh of the capital gain recognized as a result of the distribution is short-term capital gain, and six-sevenths of the capital gain is long-term capital gain. After the distribution, A's basis in the interest in PRS is $0, and the holding period for the interest in PRS continues to be divided in the same proportions as before the distribution.

* * *

[T.D. 8902, 65 FR 57092, Sept. 21, 2000]

§ 1.1231–1 Gains and losses from the sale or exchange of certain property used in the trade or business.

* * *

(d) Extent to which gains and losses are taken into account. All gains and losses to which section 1231 applies must be taken into account in determining whether and to what extent the gains exceed the losses. For the purpose of this computation, the provisions of section 1211 limiting the deduction of capital losses do not apply, and no losses are excluded by that section. With that exception, gains are included in the computations under section 1231 only to the extent that they are taken into account in computing gross income, and losses are included only to the extent that they are taken into account in computing taxable income. The following are examples of gains and losses not included in the computations under section 1231:

(1) Losses of a personal nature which are not deductible by reason of section 165(c) or (d), such as losses from the sale of property held for personal use;

(2) Losses which are not deductible under section 267 (relating to losses with respect to transactions between related taxpayers) or section 1091 (relating to losses from wash sales);

(3) Gain on the sale of property (to which section 1231 applies) reported for any taxable year on the installment method under section 453, except to the extent the gain is to be reported under section 453 for the taxable year; and

(4) Gains and losses which are not recognized * * *, such as those to which sections 1031 through 1036, relating to common nontaxable exchanges, apply.

* * *

[T.D. 6500, 25 FR 12006, Nov. 26, 1960, as amended by T.D. 6841, 30 FR 9309, July 27, 1965; T.D. 7141, 36 FR 18792, Sept. 22, 1971; T.D. 7369, 40 FR 29841, July 16, 1975; T.D. 7728, 45 FR 72650, Nov. 3, 1980; T.D. 7829, 47 FR 38515, Sept. 1, 1982]

§ 1.1233–1 Gains and losses from short sales.

(a) General. (1) For income tax purposes, a short sale is not deemed to be consummated until delivery of property to close the short sale. Whether the recognized gain or loss from a short sale is capital gain or loss or ordinary gain or loss depends upon whether the property so delivered constitutes a capital asset in the hands of the taxpayer.

(2) Thus, if a dealer in securities makes a short sale of X Corporation stock, ordinary gain or loss results on closing of the short sale if the stock used to close the short sale was stock which he held primarily for sale to customers in the ordinary course of his trade or business. If the stock used to close the short sale was a capital asset in his hands, or if the taxpayer in this example was not a dealer, a capital gain or loss would result.

(3) Generally, the period for which a taxpayer holds property delivered to close a short sale determines whether long-term or short-term capital gain or loss results.

(4) Thus, if a taxpayer makes a short sale of shares of stock and covers the short sale by purchasing and delivering shares which he held for not more than 1 year * * *, the recognized gain or loss would be considered short-term capital gain or loss. If the short sale is made through a broker and the broker borrows property to make a delivery, the short sale is not deemed to be consummated until the obligation of the seller created by the short sale is finally discharged by delivery of property to the broker to replace the property borrowed by the broker.

(5) For rules for determining the date of sale for purposes of applying under section 1091 the 61–day period applicable to a short sale of stock or securities at a loss, see paragraph (g) of § 1.1091–1.

* * *

[T.D. 6500, 25 FR 12011, Nov. 26, 1960, as amended by T.D. 6494, 25 FR 9372, Sept. 30, 1960, T.D. 6926, 32 FR 11468, Aug. 9, 1967; T.D. 7728, 45 FR 72650, Nov. 3, 1980]

§ 1.1236–1 Dealers in securities.

(a) Capital gains. Section 1236(a) provides that gain realized by a dealer in securities from the sale or exchange of a security (as defined in paragraph (c) of this section) shall not be considered as gain from the sale or exchange of a capital asset unless:

(1) The security is, before the expiration of the thirtieth day after the date of its acquisition, clearly identified in the dealer's records as a security held for investment * * *; and

(2) The security is not held by the dealer primarily for sale to customers in the ordinary course of his trade or business at any time after the identification referred to in subparagraph (1) of this paragraph has been made.

Unless both of these requirements are met, the gain is considered as gain from the sale of assets held by the dealer primarily for sale to customers in the course of his business.

(b) Ordinary losses. Section 1236(b) provides that a loss sustained by a dealer in securities from the sale or exchange of a security shall not be considered a loss from the sale or exchange of property which is not a capital asset if at any time after November 19, 1951, the security has been clearly identified in the dealer's records as a security held for investment. Once a security has been identified after November 19, 1951, as being held by the dealer for investment, it shall retain that character for purposes of determining loss on its ultimate disposition, even though at the time of its disposition the dealer holds it primarily for sale to his customers in the ordinary course of his business. * * *

(c) Definitions—(1) Security. For the purposes of this section, the term "security" means any share of stock in any corporation, any certificate of stock or interest in any corporation, any note, bond, debenture, or other evidence of indebtedness, or any evidence of any interest in, or right to subscribe to or purchase, any of the foregoing.

(2) Dealer in securities. For definition of a "dealer in securities", see the regulations under section 471.

(d) Identification of security in dealer's records. **(1)** A security is clearly identified in the dealer's records as a security held for investment when there is an accounting separation of the security from other securities, as by making appropriate entries in the dealer's books of account to distinguish the security from inventories and to designate it as an investment and by (i) indicating with such entries, to the extent feasible, the individual serial number of, or other characteristic symbol imprinted upon, the individual security, or (ii) adopting any other method of identification satisfactory to the Commissioner.

* * *

[T.D. 6500, 25 FR 12015, Nov. 26, 1960, as amended by T.D. 6726, 29 FR 5667, April 29, 1964]

§ 1.1237–1 Real property subdivided for sale.

(a) General rule—(1) Introductory. This section provides a special rule for determining whether the taxpayer holds real property primarily for sale to customers in the ordinary course of his business under section 1221(1). This rule is to permit taxpayers qualifying under it to sell real estate from a single tract held for investment without the income being treated as ordinary income merely because of subdividing the tract or of active efforts to sell it. * * *

(2) When subdividing and selling activities are to be disregarded. When its conditions are met, section 1237 provides that if there is no other substantial evidence that a taxpayer holds real estate primarily for sale to customers in the ordinary course of his business, he shall not be considered a real estate dealer holding it primarily for sale merely because he has (i) subdivided the tract into lots (or parcels) and (ii) engaged in advertising, promotion, selling activities or the use of sales agents in connection with the sale of lots in such subdivision. Such subdividing and selling activities shall be disregarded in determining the purpose for which the taxpayer held real property sold from a subdivision whenever it is the only substantial evidence indicating that the taxpayer has ever held the real property sold primarily for sale to customers in the ordinary course of his business.

(3) When subdividing and selling activities are to be taken into account. When other substantial evidence tends to show that the taxpayer held real property for sale to customers in the ordinary course of his business, his activities in connection with the subdivision and sale of the property sold shall be taken into account in determining the purpose for which the taxpayer held both the subdivided property and any other real property. For example, such other evidence may consist of the taxpayer's selling activities in connection with other property in prior years during which he was engaged in subdividing or selling activities with respect to the subdivided tract, his intention in prior years (or at the time of acquiring the property subdivided) to hold the tract primarily for sale in his business, his subdivision of other tracts in the same year, his holding other real property for sale to customers in the same year, or his construction of a permanent real estate office which he could use in selling other real property. On the other hand, if the only evidence of the taxpayer's purpose in holding real property consisted of not more than one of the following, in the year in question, such fact would not be considered substantial other evidence:

(i) Holding a real estate dealer's license;

(ii) Selling other real property which was clearly investment property;

(iii) Acting as a salesman for a real estate dealer, but without any financial interest in the business; or

(iv) Mere ownership of other vacant real property without engaging in any selling activity whatsoever with respect to it.

If more than one of the above exists, the circumstances may or may not constitute substantial evidence that the taxpayer held real property for sale in his business, depending upon the particular facts in each case.

(4) Section 1237 not exclusive. **(i)** The rule in section 1237 is not exclusive in its application. Section 1237 has no application in determining whether or not real property is held by a taxpayer primarily for sale in his business if any requirement under the section is not met. Also, even though the conditions of section 1237 are met, the rules of section 1237 are not applicable if without regard to section 1237 the real property sold would not have been considered real property held primarily for sale to customers in the ordinary course of his business. Thus, the district director may at all times conclude from convincing evidence that the taxpayer held the real property solely as an investment. Furthermore, whether or not the conditions of section 1237 are met, the section has no application to losses realized upon the sale of realty from subdivided property.

* * *

[T.D. 6500, 25 FR 12016, Nov. 26, 1960]

§ 1.1241–1 Cancellation of lease or distributor's agreement.

(a) In general. Section 1241 provides that proceeds received by lessees or distributors from the cancellation of leases or of certain distributorship agreements are considered as amounts received in exchange therefor. Section 1241 applies to leases of both real and personal property. Distributorship agreements to which section 1241 applies are described in paragraph (c) of this section. Section 1241 has no application in determining whether or not a cancellation not qualifying under that section is a sale or exchange. Further, section 1241 has no application in determining whether or not a lease or a distributorship agreement is a capital asset, even though its cancellation qualifies as an exchange under section 1241.

(b) Definition of "cancellation". The term "cancellation" of a lease or a distributor's agreement, as used in section 1241, means a termination of all the contractual rights of a lessee or distributor with respect to particular premises or a particular distributorship, other than by the expiration of the lease or agreement in accordance with its terms. A payment made in good faith for a partial cancellation of a lease or a distributorship agreement is recognized as an amount received for cancellation under section 1241 if the cancellation relates to a severable economic unit, such as a portion of the premises covered by a lease, a reduction in the unexpired term of a lease or distributorship agreement, or a distributorship in one of several areas or of one of several products. Payments made for other modifications of leases or distributorship agreements, however, are not recognized as amounts received for cancellation under section 1241.

(c) **Amounts received upon cancellation of a distributorship agreement.** Section 1241 applies to distributorship agreements only if they are for marketing or marketing and servicing of goods. It does not apply to agreements for selling intangible property or for rendering personal services as, for example, agreements establishing insurance agencies or agencies for the brokerage of securities. Further, it applies to a distributorship agreement only if the distributor has made a substantial investment of capital in the distributorship. The substantial capital investment must be reflected in physical assets such as inventories of tangible goods, equipment, machinery, storage facilities, or similar property. An investment is not considered substantial for purposes of section 1241 unless it consists of a significant fraction or more of the facilities for storing, transporting, processing, or otherwise dealing with the goods distributed, or consists of a substantial inventory of such goods. The investment required in the maintenance of an office merely for clerical operations is not considered substantial for purposes of this section. Furthermore, section 1241 shall not apply unless a substantial amount of the capital or assets needed for carrying on the operations of a distributorship are acquired by the distributor and actually used in carrying on the distributorship at some time before the cancellation of the distributorship agreement. It is immaterial for the purposes of section 1241 whether the distributor acquired the assets used in performing the functions of the distributorship before or after beginning his operations under the distributorship agreement. It is also immaterial whether the distributor is a retailer, wholesaler, jobber, or other type of distributor. The application of this paragraph may be illustrated by the following examples:

Example (1). Taxpayer is a distributor of various food products. He leases a warehouse including cold storage facilities and owns a number of motor trucks. In 1955 he obtains the exclusive rights to market certain frozen food products in his State. The marketing is accomplished by using the warehouse and trucks acquired before he entered into the agreement and entails no additional capital. Payments received upon the cancellation of the agreement are treated under section 1241 as though received upon the sale or exchange of the agreement.

Example (2). Assume that the taxpayer in example (1) entered into an exclusive distributorship agreement with the producer under which the taxpayer merely solicits orders through his staff of salesmen, the goods being shipped direct to the purchasers. Payments received upon the cancellation of the agreement would not be treated under section 1241 as though received upon the sale or exchange of the agreement.

Example (3). Taxpayer is an exclusive distributor for M city of certain frozen food products which he distributes to frozen-food freezer and locker customers. The terms of his distributorship do not make it necessary for him to have any substantial investment in inventory. Taxpayer rents a loading platform for a nominal amount, but has no warehouse space. Orders for goods from customers are consolidated by the taxpayer and forwarded to the producer from time to time. Upon receipt of these goods, taxpayer allocates them to the individual orders of customers and delivers them immediately by truck. Although it would require a fleet of fifteen or twenty trucks to carry out this operation, the distributor uses only one truck of his own and hires cartage companies to deliver the bulk of the merchandise to the customers. Payments received upon the cancellation of the distributorship agreement in such a case would not be considered received upon the sale or exchange of the agreement under section 1241 since the taxpayer does not have facilities for the physical handling of more than a small fraction of the goods involved in carrying on the distributorship and, therefore, does not have a substantial capital investment in the distributorship. On the other hand, if the taxpayer had acquired and used a substantial number of the trucks necessary for the deliveries to his customers, payments received upon the cancellation of the agreement would be considered received in exchange therefor under section 1241.

[T.D. 6500, 25 FR 12021, Nov. 26, 1960]

§ 1.1244(a)–1 Loss on small business stock treated as ordinary loss.

(a) **In general.** Subject to certain conditions and limitations, section 1244 provides that a loss on the sale or exchange (including a transaction treated as a sale or exchange, such as worthlessness) of "section 1244 stock" which would otherwise be treated as a loss from the sale or exchange of a capital asset shall be treated as a loss from the sale or exchange of an asset which is not a capital asset (referred to in this section and §§ 1.1244(b)–1 to 1.1244(e)–1, inclusive, as an "ordinary loss"). Such a loss shall be allowed as a deduction from gross income in arriving at adjusted gross income. The requirements that must be satisfied in order that stock may be considered section 1244 stock are described in §§ 1.1244(c)–1 and 1.1244(c)–2. These requirements relate to the stock itself and the corporation issuing such stock. In addition, the taxpayer who claims an ordinary loss deduction pursuant to section 1244 must satisfy the requirements of paragraph (b) of this section.

(b) Taxpayers entitled to ordinary loss. The allowance of an ordinary loss deduction for a loss of section 1244 stock is permitted only to the following two classes of taxpayers:

(1) An individual sustaining the loss to whom the stock was issued by a small business corporation, or

(2) An individual who is a partner in a partnership at the time the partnership acquired the stock in an issuance from a small business corporation and whose distributive share of partnership items reflects the loss sustained by the partnership. The ordinary loss deduction is limited to the lesser of the partner's distributive share at the time of the issuance of the stock or the partner's distributive share at the time the loss is sustained.

In order to claim a deduction under section 1244 the individual, or the partnership, sustaining the loss must have continuously held the stock from the date of issuance. A corporation, trust, or estate is not entitled to ordinary loss treatment under section 1244 regardless of how the stock was acquired. An individual who acquires stock from a shareholder by purchase, gift, devise, or in any other manner is not entitled to an ordinary loss under section 1244 with respect to this stock. Thus, ordinary loss treatment is not available to a partner to whom the stock is distributed by the partnership. Stock acquired through an investment banking firm, or other person, participating in the sale of an issue may qualify for ordinary loss treatment only if the stock is not first issued to the firm or person. Thus, for example, if the firm acts as a selling agent for the issuing corporation the stock may qualify. On the other hand, stock purchased by an investment firm and subsequently resold does not qualify as section 1244 stock in the hands of the person acquiring the stock from the firm.

(c) Examples. The provisions of paragraph (b) of this section may be illustrated by the following examples:

Example (1). A and B, both individuals, and C, a trust, are equal partners in a partnership to which a small business corporation issues section 1244 stock. The partnership sells the stock at a loss. A's and B's distributive share of the loss may be treated as an ordinary loss pursuant to section 1244, but C's distributive share of the loss may not be so treated.

Example (2). The facts are the same as in example (1) except that the section 1244 stock is distributed by the partnership to partner A and he subsequently sells the stock at a loss. Section 1244 is not applicable to the loss since A did not acquire the stock by issuance from the small business corporation.

[T.D. 6495, 25 FR 9675, Oct. 8, 1960, as amended by T.D. 7779, 46 FR 29467, June 18, 1981]

§ 1.1244(c)–1 Section 1244 stock defined.

* * *

(d) Issued for money or other property. (1) The stock must be issued to the taxpayer for money or other property transferred by the taxpayer to the corporation. However, stock issued in exchange for stock or securities, including stock or securities, of the issuing corporation, cannot qualify as section 1244 stock, except as provided in § 1.1244(d)–3, relating to certain cases where stock is issued in exchange for section 1244 stock. Stock issued for services rendered or to be rendered to, or for the benefit of, the issuing corporation does not qualify as section 1244 stock. Stock issued in consideration for cancellation of indebtedness of the corporation shall be considered issued in exchange for money or other property unless such indebtedness is evidenced by a security, or arises out of the performance of personal services.

(2) The following examples illustrate situations where stock fails to qualify as section 1244 stock as a result of the rules in subparagraph (1) of this paragraph:

Example (1). A taxpayer owns stock of Corporation X issued to him prior to July 1, 1958. Under a plan adopted in 1977, he exchanges his stock for a new issuance of stock of Corporation X. The stock received by the taxpayer in the exchange may not qualify as section 1244 stock even if the corporation has adopted a valid plan and is a small business corporation.

Example (2). A taxpayer owns stock in Corporation X. Corporation X merges into Corporation Y. In exchange for his stock, Corporation Y issues shares of its stock to the taxpayer. The stock in Corporation Y does not qualify as section 1244 stock even if the stock exchanged by the taxpayer did qualify.

Example (3). Corporation X transfers part of its business assets to Corporation Y, a new corporation, and all of the stock of Corporation Y is issued directly to the shareholders of Corporation X. Since the Corporation Y stock was not issued to the shareholders for a transfer by them of money or other property, none of the Corporation Y stock in the hands of the shareholders can qualify.

(e) Gross receipts. (1)(i)(a) Except as provided in subparagraph (2) of this paragraph, stock will not qualify under section 1244, if 50 percent or more of the gross receipts of the corporation, for the period consisting of the five most recent taxable years of the corporation ending before the date the loss on such stock is sustained by the shareholders, is derived from royalties, rents, dividends, interest, annuities, and sales or exchanges of stock or securities. If the corporation has not been in existence for five taxable years ending before such date, the percentage test referred to in the preceding sentence applies to the period of the taxable years ending before such date during which the corporation has been in existence; and if the loss is sustained during the first taxable year of the corporation such test applies to the period beginning with the first day of such taxable year and ending on the day before the loss is sustained. The test under this paragraph shall be made on the basis of total gross receipts, except that gross receipts from the sales or exchanges of stock or securities shall be taken into account only to the extent of gains therefrom. The term "gross receipts" as used in section 1244(c)(1)(C) is not synonymous with "gross income". Gross receipts means the total amount received or accrued under the method of accounting used by the corporation in computing its taxable income. Thus, the total amount of receipts is not reduced by returns and allowances, cost, or deductions. For example, gross receipts will include the total amount received or accrued during the corporation's taxable year from the sale or exchange * * * of any kind of property, from investments, and for services rendered by the corporation. However, gross receipts does not include amounts received in nontaxable sales or exchanges * * * except to the extent that gain is recognized by the corporation, nor does that term include amounts received as a loan, as a repayment of a loan, as a contribution to capital, or on the issuance by the corporation of its own stock.

(b) The meaning of the term "gross receipts" as used in section 1244(c)(1)(C) may be further illustrated by the following examples:

Example (1). A corporation on the accrual method sells property (other than stock or securities) and receives payment partly in money and partly in the form of a note payable at a future time. The amount of the money and the face amount of the note would be considered gross receipts in the taxable year of the sale and would not be reduced by the adjusted basis of the property, the costs of sale, or any other amount.

* * *

Example (3). A corporation which regularly sells personal property on the installment plan elects to report its taxable income from the sale of property (other than stock or securities) on the installment method in accordance with section 453. The installment payments actually received in a given taxable year of the corporation shall be included in gross receipts for such year.

(ii) The term "royalties" as used in subdivision (i) of this subparagraph means all royalties, including mineral, oil, and gas royalties (whether or not the aggregate amount of such royalties constitutes 50 percent or more of the gross income of the corporation for the taxable year), and amounts received for the privilege of using patents, copyrights, secret processes and formulas, good will, trademarks, trade brands, franchises, and other like property. The term "royalties" does not include amounts received upon the disposal of timber, coal, or domestic iron ore with a retained economic interest to which the special rules of section 631(b) and (c) apply or amounts received from the transfer of patent rights to which section 1235 applies. For the definition of "mineral, oil, or gas royalties", see paragraph (b)(11)(ii) and (iii) of § 1.543–1. For purposes of this subdivision, the gross amount of royalties shall not be reduced by any part of the cost of the rights under which they are received or by any amount allowable as a deduction in computing taxable income.

(iii) The term "rents" as used in subdivision (i) of this subparagraph means amounts received for the use of, or right to use, property (whether real or personal) of the corporation, whether or not such amounts constitute 50 percent or more of the gross income of the corporation for the taxable year. The term "rents" does not include payments for the use or occupancy of rooms or other space where significant services are also rendered to the occupant, such as for the use or occupancy of rooms or other quarters in hotels, boarding houses, or apartment houses furnishing hotel services, or in tourist homes, motor courts, or motels. Generally, services are considered rendered to the occupant if they are primarily for his convenience and are other than those usually or customarily rendered in connection with the rental of rooms or other space for occupancy only. The supplying of maid service, for example, constitutes such services; whereas the furnishing of heat and light, the cleaning of public entrances, exits, stairways, and lobbies, the collection of trash, etc., are not considered as services rendered to the occupant. Payments for the use or occupancy of entire private residences or living quarters in duplex or multiple housing units, of offices in an office building, etc., are generally "rents" under section 1244(c)(1)(C). Payments for the parking of automobiles ordinarily do not constitute rents. Payments for the warehousing of goods or for the use of personal property do not constitute rents if significant services are rendered in connection with such payments.

(iv) The term "dividends" as used in subdivision (i) of this subparagraph includes dividends as defined in section 316, amounts required to be included in gross income under section 551 (relating to foreign personal holding company income taxed to United States shareholders), and consent dividends determined as provided in section 565.

(v) The term "interest" as used in subdivision (i) of this subparagraph means any amounts received for the use of money (including tax-exempt interest).

(vi) The term "annuities" as used in subdivision (i) of this subparagraph means the entire amount received as an annuity under an annuity, endowment, or life insurance contract, regardless of whether only part of such amount would be includible in gross income under section 72.

(vii) For purposes of subdivision (i) of this subparagraph, gross receipts from the sales or exchanges of stock or securities are taken into account only to the extent of gains therefrom. Thus, the gross receipts from the sale of a particular share of stock will be the excess of the amount realized over the adjusted basis of such share. If the adjusted basis should equal or exceed the amount realized on the sale or exchange of a certain share of stock, bond, etc., there would be no gross receipts resulting from the sale of such security. Losses on sales or exchanges of stock or securities do not offset gains on the sales or exchanges of other stock or securities for purposes of computing gross receipts from such sales or exchanges. Gross receipts from the sale or exchange of stocks and securities include gains received from such sales or exchanges by a corporation even though such corporation is a regular dealer in stocks and securities. For the meaning of the term "stocks or securities", see paragraph (b)(5)(i) of § 1.543–1.

(2) The requirement of subparagraph (1) of this paragraph need not be satisfied if for the applicable period the aggregate amount of deductions allowed to the corporation exceeds the aggregate amount of its gross income. But for this purpose the deductions allowed by section 172, relating to the net operating loss deduction, and by sections 242, 243, 244, and 245, relating to certain special deductions for corporations, shall not be taken into account. Notwithstanding the provisions of this subparagraph and of subparagraph (1) of this paragraph, pursuant to the specific delegation of authority granted in section 1244(e) to prescribe such regulations as may be necessary to carry out the purposes of section 1244, ordinary loss treatment will not be available with respect to stock of a corporation which is not largely an operating company within the five most recent taxable years (or such lesser period as the corporation is in existence) ending before the date of the loss. Thus, for example, assume that a person who is not a dealer in real estate forms a corporation which issues stock to him which meets all the formal requirements of section 1244 stock. The corporation then acquires a piece of unimproved real estate which it holds as an investment. The property declines in value and the stockholder sells his stock at a loss. The loss does not qualify for ordinary loss treatment under section 1244 but must be treated as a capital loss.

(3) In applying subparagraphs (1) and (2) of this paragraph to a successor corporation in a reorganization described in section 368(a)(1)(F), such corporation shall be treated as the same corporation as its predecessor. * * *

* * *

[T.D. 6495, 25 FR 9676, Oct. 8, 1960, as amended by T.D. 6508, 25 FR 12345, Dec. 2, 1960; T.D. 6637, 28 FR 1765, Feb. 26, 1963; T.D. 6841, 30 FR 9309, July 27, 1965; T.D. 7779, 46 FR 29465, June 18, 1981]

§ 1.1244(c)–2 Small business corporation defined.

* * *

(b) Post–November 1978 stock—(1) Amount received by corporation for stock. Capital receipts of a small business corporation may not exceed $1,000,000. For purposes of this paragraph the term "capital receipts" means the aggregate dollar amount received by the corporation for its stock, as a contribution to capital, and as paid-in surplus. If the $1,000,000 limitation is exceeded, the rules of subparagraph (2) of this paragraph (b) apply. In making these determinations, (i) property is taken into account at its adjusted basis to the corporation (for determining gain) as of the date received by the corporation, and (ii) this aggregate amount is reduced by the amount of any liability to which the property was subject and by the amount of any liability assumed by the corporation at the time the property was received. Capital receipts are not reduced by distributions to shareholders, even though the distributions may be capital distributions.

(2) Requirement of designation in event $1,000,000 limitation exceeded. **(i)** If capital receipts exceed $1,000,000, the corporation shall designate as section 1244 stock certain shares of post-November 1978 common stock issued for money or other property in the transitional year. For purposes of this paragraph, the term "transitional year" means the first taxable year in which capital receipts exceed $1,000,000 and in which the corporation issues stock. This designation shall be made in accordance with the rules of subdivision (iii) of this paragraph (b)(2). The amount received for designated stock shall not exceed $1,000,000, less amounts received (i) in exchange for stock in years prior to the transitional year; (ii) as contributions to capital in years prior to the transitional year; and (iii) as paid-in surplus in years prior to the transitional year.

(ii) Post–November 1978 common stock issued for money or other property before the transitional year qualifies as section 1244 stock without affirmative designation by the corporation. Post–November 1978 common stock issued after the transitional year does not qualify as section 1244 stock.

(iii) The corporation shall make the designation required by subdivision (i), of this paragraph (b)(2) not later than the 15th day of the third month following the close of the transitional year. However, in the case of post-November 1978 common stock issued on or before June 2, 1981, the corporation shall make the required designation by August 3, 1981 or by the 15th day of the 3rd month following the close of the transitional year, whichever is later. The designation shall be made by entering the numbers of the qualifying share certificates on the corporation's records. If the shares do not bear serial numbers or other identifying numbers or letters, or are not represented by share certificates, the corporation shall make an alternative designation in writing at the time of issuance, or, in the case of post-November 1978 common stock issued on or before June 2, 1981, by August 3, 1981. This alternative designation may be made in any manner sufficient to identify the shares qualifying for section 1244 treatment. If the corporation fails to make a designation by share certificate number or an alternative written designation as described, the rules of subparagraph (3) of this paragraph (b) apply.

(3) Allocation of section 1244 benefit in event corporation fails to designate qualifying shares. If a corporation issues post-November 1978 stock in the transitional year and fails to designate certain shares of post-November 1978 common stock as section 1244 stock in accordance with the rules of subparagraph (2) of this paragraph (b), the following rules apply:

(i) Section 1244 treatment is extended to losses sustained on post-November 1978 common stock issued for money or other property in taxable years before the transitional year and is withheld from losses sustained on post-November 1978 stock issued in taxable years after the transitional year.

(ii) Post–1958 capital received before the transitional year is subtracted from $1,000,000.

(iii) Subject to the annual limitation described in § 1.1244(b)–1, an ordinary loss on post-November 1978 common stock issued for money or other property in the transitional year is allowed in an amount which bears the same ratio to the total loss sustained by the individual as:

(A) The amount described in § 1.1244(c)–2(b)(3)(ii) bears to

(B) The total amount of money and other property received by the corporation in exchange for stock, as a contribution to capital, and as paid-in surplus in the transitional year.

* * *

[T.D. 6495, 25 FR 9678, Oct. 8, 1960, as amended by T.D. 7779, 46 FR 29470, June 2, 1981; T.D. 7837, 47 FR 42729, Sept. 29, 1982; 60 FR 16575, Mar. 31, 1995]

§ 1.1245–1 General rule for treatment of gain from dispositions of certain depreciable property.

(a) General. **(1)** In general, section 1245(a)(1) provides that, upon a disposition of an item of section 1245 property, the amount by which the lower of (i) the "recomputed basis" of the property, or (ii) the amount realized on a sale, exchange, or involuntary conversion (or the fair market value of the property on any other disposition), exceeds the adjusted basis of the property shall be treated as gain from the sale or exchange of property which is neither a capital asset nor property described in section 1231 (that is, shall be recognized as ordinary income). The amount of such gain shall be determined separately for each item of section 1245 property. In general, the term "recomputed basis" means the adjusted basis of property plus all adjustments reflected in such adjusted basis on account of depreciation allowed or allowable for all periods after December 31, 1961. See section 1245(a)(2) and § 1.1245–2. Generally, the ordinary income treatment applies even though in the absence of section 1245 no gain would be recognized under the Code. * * *

* * *

(3) For purposes of this section and §§ 1.1245–2 through 1.1245–6, the term "disposition" includes a sale in a sale-and-leaseback transaction and a transfer upon the foreclosure of a security interest, but such term does not include a mere transfer of title to a creditor upon creation of a security interest or to a debtor upon termination of a security interest. Thus, for example, a disposition occurs upon a sale of property pursuant to a conditional sales contract even though the seller retains legal title to the property for purposes of security but a disposition does not occur when the seller ultimately gives up his security interest following payment by the purchaser.

* * *

(5) In case of a sale, exchange, or involuntary conversion of section 1245 and non-section 1245 property in one transaction, the total amount realized upon the disposition shall be allocated between the section 1245 property and the non-section 1245 property in proportion to their respective fair market values. In general, if a buyer and seller have adverse interests as to the allocation of the amount realized between the section 1245 property and the non-section 1245 property, any arm's length agreement between the buyer and the seller will establish the allocation. In the absence of such an agreement, the allocation shall be made by taking into account the appropriate facts and circumstances. Some of the facts and circumstances which shall be taken into account to the extent appropriate include, but are not limited to, a comparison between the section 1245 property and all the property disposed of in such transaction of (i) the original cost and reproduction cost of construction, erection, or production, (ii) the remaining economic useful life, (iii) state of obsolescence, and (iv) anticipated expenditures to maintain, renovate, or to modernize.

(b) Sale, exchange, or involuntary conversion. **(1)** In the case of a sale, exchange, or involuntary conversion of section 1245 property, the gain to which section 1245(a)(1) applies is the amount by which (i) the lower of the amount realized upon the disposition of the property or the recomputed basis of the property, exceeds (ii) the adjusted basis of the property.

(2) The provisions of this paragraph may be illustrated by the following examples:

Example (1). On January 1, 1964, Brown purchases section 1245 property for use in his manufacturing business. The property has a basis for depreciation of $3,300. After taking depreciation deductions of $1,300 (the amount allowable), Brown realizes after selling expenses the amount of $2,900 upon sale of the property on January 1, 1969. Brown's gain is $900 ($2,900 amount realized minus $2,000 adjusted basis). Since the amount realized upon disposition of the property ($2,900) is lower than its recomputed basis ($3,300, i.e., $2,000 adjusted basis plus $1,300 in depreciation deductions), the entire gain is treated as ordinary income under section 1245(a)(1) and not as gain from the sale or exchange of property described in section 1231.

Example (2). Assume the same facts as in example (1) except that Brown exchanges the section 1245 property for land which has a fair market value of $3,700, thereby realizing a gain of $1,700 ($3,700 amount realized minus $2,000 adjusted basis). Since the recomputed basis of the property ($3,300) is lower than the amount realized upon its disposition ($3,700), the excess of recomputed basis over adjusted basis, or $1,300, is treated as ordinary income under section 1245(a)(1). The remaining $400 of the gain may be treated as gain from the sale or exchange of property described in section 1231.

(c) Other dispositions. **(1)** In the case of a disposition of section 1245 property other than by way of a sale, exchange, or involuntary conversion, the gain to which section 1245(a)(1) applies is the amount by which (i) the lower of the fair market value of the property on the date of disposition or the recomputed basis of the property, exceeds (ii) the adjusted basis of the property. If property is transferred by a corporation to a shareholder for an amount less than its fair market value in a sale or exchange, for purposes of applying section 1245 such transfer shall be treated as a disposition other than by way of a sale, exchange, or involuntary conversion.

* * *

(d) Losses. Section 1245(a)(1) does not apply to losses. Thus, section 1245(a)(1) does not apply if a loss is realized upon a sale, exchange, or involuntary conversion of property, all of which is considered section 1245 property, nor does the section apply to a disposition of such property other than by way of sale, exchange, or involuntary conversion if at the time of the disposition the fair market value of such property is not greater than its adjusted basis.

(e) Treatment of partnership and partners. **(1)** The manner of determining the amount of gain recognized under section 1245(a)(1) to a partnership may be illustrated by the following example:

Example. A partnership sells for $63 section 1245 property which has an adjusted basis to the partnership of $30 and a recomputed basis to the partnership of $60. The partnership recognizes under section 1245(a)(1) gain of $30, i.e., the lower of the amount realized ($63) or recomputed basis ($60), minus adjusted basis ($30). This result would not be changed if one or more partners had, in respect of the property, a special basis adjustment described in section 743(b) or had taken depreciation deductions in respect of such special basis adjustment.

(2)(i) Unless paragraph (e)(3) of this section applies, a partner's distributive share of gain recognized under section 1245(a)(1) by the partnership is equal to the lesser of the partner's share of total gain from the disposition of the property (gain limitation) or the partner's share of depreciation or amortization with respect to the property (as determined under paragraph (e)(2)(ii) of this section). Any gain recognized under section 1245(a)(1) by the partnership that is not allocated under the first sentence of this paragraph (e)(2)(i) (excess depreciation recapture) is allocated among the partners whose shares of total gain from the disposition of the property exceed their shares of depreciation or amortization with respect to the property. Excess depreciation recapture is allocated among those partners in proportion to their relative shares of the total gain (including gain recognized under section 1245(a)(1)) from the disposition of the property that is allocated to the partners who are not subject to the gain limitation. See Example 2 of paragraph (e)(2)(iii) of this section.

(ii)(A) Subject to the adjustments described in paragraphs (e)(2)(ii)(B) and (e)(2)(ii)(C) of this section, a partner's share of depreciation or amortization with respect to property equals the total amount of allowed or allowable depreciation or amortization previously allocated to that partner with respect to the property.

(B) If a partner transfers a partnership interest, a share of depreciation or amortization must be allocated to the transferee partner as it would have been allocated to the transferor partner. If the partner transfers a portion of the partnership interest, a share of depreciation or amortization proportionate to the interest transferred must be allocated to the transferee partner.

(C)(1) A partner's share of depreciation or amortization with respect to property contributed by the partner includes the amount of depreciation or amortization allowed or allowable to the partner for the period before the property is contributed.

(2) A partner's share of depreciation or amortization with respect to property contributed by a partner is adjusted to account for any curative allocations. (See § 1.704–3(c) for a description of the traditional method with curative allocations.) The contributing partner's share of depreciation or amortization with respect to the contributed property is decreased (but not below zero) by the amount of any curative allocation of ordinary income to the contributing partner with respect to that property and by the amount of any curative allocation of deduction or loss (other than capital loss) to the noncontributing partners with respect to that property. A noncontributing partner's share of depreciation or amortization with respect to the contributed property is increased by the noncontributing partner's share of any curative allocation of ordinary income to the contributing partner with respect to that property and by the amount of any curative allocation of deduction or loss (other than capital loss) to the noncontributing partner with respect to that property. The partners' shares of depreciation or amortization with respect to property from which curative allocations of depreciation or amortization are taken is determined without regard to those curative allocations. See Example 3(iii) of paragraph (e)(2)(iii) of this section.

(3) A partner's share of depreciation or amortization with respect to property contributed by a partner is adjusted to account for any remedial allocations. (See § 1.704–3(d) for a description of the remedial allocation method.) The contributing partner's share of depreciation or amortization with respect to the contributed property is decreased (but not below zero) by the amount of any remedial allocation of income to the contributing partner with respect to that property. A noncontributing partner's share of depreciation or amortization with respect to the contributed property is increased by the amount of any remedial allocation of depreciation or amortization to the noncontributing partner with respect to that property. See Example 3(iv) of paragraph (e)(2)(iii) of this section.

(4) If, under paragraphs (e)(2)(ii)(C)(2) and (e)(2)(ii)(C)(3) of this section, the partners' shares of depreciation or amortization with respect to a contributed property exceed the adjustments reflected in the adjusted basis of the property under § 1.1245–2(a) at the partnership level, then the partnership's gain recognized under section 1245(a)(1) with respect to that property is allocated among the partners in proportion to their relative shares of depreciation or amortization (subject to any gain limitation that might apply).

(5) This paragraph (e)(2)(ii)(C) also applies in determining a partner's share of depreciation or amortization with respect to property for which differences between book value and adjusted tax basis are created when a partnership revalues partnership property pursuant to § 1.704–1(b)(2)(iv)(f).

(iii) Examples. The application of this paragraph (e)(2) may be illustrated by the following examples:

Example (1). Recapture allocations. (i) Facts. A and B each contribute $5,000 cash to form AB, a general partnership. The partnership agreement provides that depreciation deductions will be allocated 90 percent to A and 10 percent to B, and, on the sale of depreciable property, A will first be allocated gain to the extent necessary to equalize A's and B's capital accounts. Any remaining gain will be allocated 50 percent to A and 50 percent to B. In its first year of operations, AB purchases depreciable equipment for $5,000. AB depreciates the equipment over its 5–year recovery period and elects to use the straight-line method. In its first year of operations, AB's operating income equals its expenses (other than depreciation). (To simplify this example, AB's depreciation deductions are determined without regard to any first-year depreciation conventions.)

(ii) Year 1. In its first year of operations, AB has $1,000 of depreciation from the partnership equipment. In accordance with the partnership agreement, AB allocates 90 percent ($900) of the depreciation to A and 10 percent ($100) of the depreciation to B. At the end of the year, AB sells the equipment for $5,200, recognizing $1,200 of gain ($5,200 amount realized less $4,000 adjusted tax basis). In accordance with the partnership agreement, the first $800 of gain is allocated to A to equalize the partners' capital accounts, and the remaining $400 of gain is allocated $200 to A and $200 to B.

(iii) Recapture allocations. $1,000 of the gain from the sale of the equipment is treated as section 1245(a)(1) gain. Under paragraph (e)(2)(i) of this section, each partner's share of the section 1245(a)(1) gain is equal to the lesser of the partner's share of total gain recognized on the sale of the equipment or the partner's share of total depreciation with respect to the equipment. Thus, A's share of the section 1245(a)(1) gain is $900 (the lesser of A's share of the total gain ($1,000) and A's share of depreciation ($900)). B's share of the section 1245(a)(1) gain is $100 (the lesser of B's share of the total gain ($200) and B's share of depreciation ($100)). Accordingly, $900 of the $1,000 of total gain allocated to A is treated as ordinary income and $100 of the $200 of total gain allocated to B is treated as ordinary income.

Example (2). Recapture allocation subject to gain limitation. (i) Facts. A, B, and C form general partnership ABC. The partnership agreement provides that depreciation deductions will be allocated equally among the partners, but that gain from the sale of depreciable property will be allocated 75 percent to A and 25 percent to B. ABC purchases depreciable personal property for $300 and subsequently allocates $100 of depreciation deductions each to A, B, and C, reducing the adjusted tax basis of the property to $0. ABC then sells the property for $440. ABC allocates $330 of the gain to A (75 percent of $440) and allocates $110 of the gain to B (25 percent of $440). No gain is allocated to C.

(ii) Application of gain limitation. Each partner's share of depreciation with respect to the property is $100. C's share of the total gain from the disposition of the property, however, is $0. As a result, under the gain limitation provision in paragraph (e)(2)(i) of this section, C's share of section 1245(a)(1) gain is limited to $0.

(iii) Excess depreciation recapture. Under paragraph (e)(2)(i) of this section, the $100 of section 1245(a)(1) gain that cannot be allocated to C under the gain limitation provision (excess depreciation recapture) is allocated to A and B (the partners not subject to the gain limitation at the time of the allocation) in proportion to their relative shares of total gain from the disposition of the property. A's relative share of the total gain allocated to A and B is 75 percent ($330 of $440 total gain). B's relative share of the total gain allocated to A and B is 25 percent ($110 of $440 total gain). However, under the gain limitation provision of paragraph (e)(2)(i) of this section, B cannot be allocated 25 percent of the excess depreciation recapture ($25) because that would result in a total allocation of $125 of depreciation recapture to B (a $100 allocation equal to B's share of depreciation plus a $25 allocation of excess depreciation recapture), which is in excess of B's share of the total gain from the disposition of the property ($110). Therefore, only $10 of excess depreciation recapture is allocated to B and the remaining $90 of excess depreciation recapture is allocated to A. A is not subject to the gain limitation because A's share of the total gain ($330) still exceeds A's share of section 1245(a)(1) gain ($190). Accordingly, all $110 of the total gain allocated to B is treated as ordinary income ($100 share of depreciation allocated to B plus $10 of excess depreciation recapture) and $190 of the total gain allocated to A is treated as ordinary income ($100 share of depreciation allocated to A plus $90 of excess depreciation recapture).

Example (3). Determination of partners' shares of depreciation with respect to contributed property. (i) Facts. C and D form partnership CD as equal partners. C contributes depreciable personal property C1 with an adjusted tax basis of $800 and a fair market value of $2,800. Prior to the contribution, C claimed $200 of depreciation from C1. At the time of the contribution, C1 is depreciable under the straight-line method and has four years remaining on its 5–year recovery period. D contributes $2,800 cash, which CD uses to purchase depreciable personal property D1, which is depreciable over seven years under the straight-line method. (To simplify the example, all depreciation is determined without regard to any first-year depreciation conventions.)

(ii) Traditional method. C1 generates $700 of book depreciation (1/4 of $2,800 book value) and $200 of tax depreciation (1/4 of $800 adjusted tax basis) each year. C and D will each be allocated $350 of book depreciation from C1 in year 1. Under the traditional method of making section 704(c) allocations, D will be allocated the entire $200 of tax depreciation from C1 in year 1. D1 generates $400 of book and tax depreciation each year (1/7 of $2,800 book value and adjusted tax basis). C and D will each be allocated $200 of book and tax depreciation from D1 in year 1. As a result, after the first year of partnership operations, C's share of depreciation with respect to C1 is $200 (the depreciation taken by C prior to contribution) and D's share of depreciation with respect to C1 is $200 (the amount of tax depreciation allocated to D). C and D each have a $200 share of depreciation with respect to D1. At the end of four years, C's share of depreciation with respect to C1 will be $200 (the depreciation taken by C prior to contribution) and D's share of depreciation with respect to C1 will be $800 (four years of $200 depreciation per year). At the end of four years, C and D will each have an $800 share of depreciation with respect to D1 (four years of $200 depreciation per year).

(iii) Effect of curative allocations. (A) Year 1. If the partnership elects to make curative allocations under § 1.704–3(c) using depreciation from D1, the results will be the same as under the traditional method, except that $150 of the $200 of tax depreciation from D1 that would be allocated to C under the traditional method will be allocated to D as additional depreciation with respect to C1. As a result, after the first year of partnership operations, C's share of depreciation with respect to C1 will be reduced to $50 (the total depreciation taken by C prior to contribution ($200) decreased by the amount of the curative allocation to D ($150)). D's share of depreciation with respect to C1 will be $350 (the depreciation allocated to D under the traditional method ($200) increased by the amount of the curative allocation to D ($150)). C and D will each have a $200 share of depreciation with respect to D1.

(B) Year 4. At the end of four years, C's share of depreciation with respect to C1 will be reduced to $0 (the total depreciation taken by C prior to contribution ($200) decreased, but not below zero, by the amount of the curative allocations to D ($600)), and D's share of depreciation with respect to C1 will be $1,400 (the total depreciation allocated to D under the traditional method ($800) increased by the amount of the curative allocations to D ($600)). However, CD's section 1245(a)(1) gain with respect to C1 will not be more than $1,000 (CD's tax depreciation ($800) plus C's tax depreciation prior to contribution ($200)). Under paragraph (e)(2)(ii)(C)(*4*) of this section, because the partners' shares of depreciation with respect to C1 exceed the adjustments reflected in the property's adjusted basis, CD's section 1245(a)(1) gain will be allocated in proportion to the partners' relative shares of depreciation with respect to C1. Because C's share of depreciation with respect to C1 is $0, and D's share of depreciation with respect to C1 is $1,400, all of CD's $1,000 of section 1245(a)(1) gain will be allocated to D. At the end of four years, C and D will each have an $800 share of depreciation with respect to D1 (four years of $200 depreciation per year).

(iv) Effect of remedial allocations. (A) Year 1. If the partnership elects to make remedial allocations under § 1.704–3(d), there will be $600 of book depreciation from C1 in year 1. (Under the remedial allocation method, the amount by which C1's book basis ($2,800) exceeds its tax basis ($800) is depreciated over a 5–year life, rather than a 4–year life.) C and D will each be allocated one-half ($300) of the total book depreciation. As under the traditional method, D will be allocated all $200 of tax depreciation from C1. Because the ceiling rule would cause a disparity of $100 between D's book and tax allocations of depreciation, D will also receive a $100 remedial allocation of depreciation with respect to C1, and C will receive a $100 remedial allocation of income with respect to C1. As a result, after the first year of partnership operations, D's share of depreciation with respect to C1 is $300 (the depreciation allocated to D under the traditional method ($200) increased by the amount of the remedial allocation ($100)). C's share of depreciation with respect to C1 is $100 (the total depreciation taken by C prior to contribution ($200) decreased by the amount of the remedial allocation of income ($100)). C and D will each have a $200 share of depreciation with respect to D1.

(B) Year 5. At the end of five years, C's share of depreciation with respect to C1 will be $0 (the total depreciation taken by C prior to contribution ($200) decreased, but not below zero, by the total amount of the remedial allocations of income to C ($600)). D's share of depreciation with respect to C1 will be $1,400 (the total depreciation allocated to D under the traditional method ($800) increased by the total amount of the remedial allocations of depreciation to D ($600)). However, CD's section 1245(a)(1) gain with respect to C1 will not be more than $1,000 (CD's tax depreciation ($800) plus C's tax depreciation prior to contribution ($200)). Under paragraph (e)(2)(ii)(C)(*4*) of this section, because the partners' shares of depreciation with respect to C1 exceed the adjustments reflected in the property's adjusted basis, CD's section 1245(a)(1) gain will be allocated in proportion to the partners' relative shares of depreciation with respect to C1. Because C's share of depreciation with respect to C1 is $0, and D's share of depreciation with respect to C1 is $1,400, all of CD's $1,000 of section 1245(a)(1) gain will be allocated to D. At the end of five years, C and D will each have a $1,000 share of depreciation with respect to D1 (five years of $200 depreciation per year).

(iv) Effective date. This paragraph (e)(2) is effective for properties acquired by a partnership on or after August 20, 1997. However, partnerships may rely on this paragraph (e)(2) for properties acquired before August 20, 1997 and disposed of on or after August 20, 1997.

(3)(i) If (*a*) a partner had a special basis adjustment under section 743(b) in respect of section 1245 property, or (*b*) on the date he acquired his partnership interest by way of a sale or exchange (or upon death of another partner) the partnership owned section 1245 property and an election under section 754 (relating to optional adjustment to basis of partnership property) was in effect with respect to the partnership, then the amount of gain recognized under section 1245(a)(1) by him upon a disposition by the partnership of such property shall be determined under this subparagraph.

(ii) There shall be allocated to such partner, in the same proportion as the partnership's total gain is allocated to him as his distributive share under section 704, a portion of (*a*) the common partnership adjusted basis for the property, and (*b*) the amount realized by the partnership upon the disposition, or, if nothing is realized, the fair market value of the property. There shall also be allocated to him, in the same proportion as the partnership's gain recognized under section 1245(a)(1) is allocated under subparagraph (2) of this paragraph as his distributive share of such gain, a portion of "the adjustments reflected in the adjusted basis" (as defined in paragraph (a)(2) of § 1.1245–2) of such property. If on the date he acquired his partnership interest by way of a sale or exchange the partnership owned such property and an election under section 754 was in effect, then for purposes of the preceding sentence the amount of the adjustments reflected in the adjusted basis of such property on such date shall be deemed to be zero. For special rules relating to the amount of adjustments reflected in the adjusted basis of property after partnership transactions, see paragraph (c)(6) of § 1.1245–2.

(iii) The partner's adjusted basis in respect of the property shall be deemed to be (a) the portion of the partnership's adjusted basis for the property allocated to the partner under subdivision (ii) of this subparagraph, (b) increased by the amount of any special basis adjustment described in section 743(b)(1) (or decreased by the amount of any special basis adjustment described in section 743(b)(2) which the partner may have in respect of the property on the date the partnership disposed of the property).

(iv) The partner's recomputed basis in respect of the property shall be deemed to be (a) the sum of the partner's adjusted basis for the property, as determined in subdivision (iii) of this subparagraph, plus the amount of "the adjustments reflected in the adjusted basis" (as defined in paragraph (a)(2) of § 1.1245–2) for the property allocated to the partner under subdivision (ii) of this subparagraph, (b) increased by the amount by which any special basis adjustment described in section 743(b)(1) (or decreased by the amount by which any special basis adjustment described in section 743(b)(2)) in respect of the property was reduced, but only to the extent such amount was applied to adjust the amount of the deductions allowed or allowable to the partner for depreciation or amortization of section 1245 property attributable to periods referred to in paragraph (a)(2) of § 1.1245–2. The terms "allowed or allowable," "depreciation or amortization," and "attributable to periods" shall have the meanings assigned to these terms in paragraph (a) of § 1.1245–2.

(4) The application of subparagraph (3) of this paragraph may be illustrated by the following example:

Example. A, B, and C each hold a one-third interest in calendar year partnership ABC. On December 31, 1962, the firm holds section 1245 property which has an adjusted basis of $30,000 and a recomputed basis of $33,000. Depreciation deductions in respect of the property for 1962 were $3,000. On January 1, 1963, when D purchases C's partnership interest, the election under section 754 is in effect and a $5,000 special basis adjustment is made in respect of D to his one-third share of the common partnership adjusted basis for the property. For 1963 and 1964 the partnership deducts $6,000 as depreciation in respect of the property, thereby reducing its adjusted basis to $24,000, and D deducts $2,800, i.e., his distributive share of partnership depreciation ($2,000) plus depreciation in respect of his special basis adjustment ($800). On March 15, 1965, the partnership sells the property for $48,000. Since the partnership's recomputed basis for the property ($33,000, i.e., $24,000 adjusted basis plus $9,000 in depreciation deductions) is lower than the amount realized upon the sale ($48,000), the excess of recomputed basis over adjusted basis, or $9,000, is treated as partnership gain under section 1245(a)(1). D's distributive share of such gain is $3,000 (1/3 of $9,000). However, the amount of gain recognized by D under section 1245 (a)(1) is only $2,800, determined as follows:

(1) Adjusted basis:		
D's portion of partnership adjusted basis (1/3 of $24,000)	$8,000	
D's special basis adjustment as of December 31, 1964 ($5,000 minus $800)	4,200	
D's adjusted basis		$12,200
(2) Recomputed basis:		
D's adjusted basis		12,200
D's portion of partnership depreciation for 1963 and 1964, i.e., for periods after he acquired his partnership interest (1/3 of $6,000)	2,000	
Depreciation for 1963 and 1964 in respect of D's special basis adjustment	800	
D's recomputed basis		15,000
(3) D's portion of amount realized by partnership (1/3 of $48,000)		16,000
(4) Gain recognized to D under section 1245(a)(1), i.e., the lower of (2) or (3), minus (1)		2,800

[T.D. 6832, 30 FR 8576, July 7, 1965, as amended by T.D. 7084, 36 FR 268, Jan. 8, 1971; T.D. 7141, 36 FR 18793, Sept. 22, 1971; T.D. 8730, 62 FR 44214, Aug. 20, 1997]

§ 1.1245–2 Definition of recomputed basis.

(a) General rule—(1) Recomputed basis defined. The term "recomputed basis" means, with respect to any property, an amount equal to the sum of:

(i) The adjusted basis of the property, as defined in section 1011, plus

(ii) The amount of the adjustments reflected in the adjusted basis.

(2) Definition of adjustments reflected in adjusted basis. The term "adjustments reflected in the adjusted basis" means:

(i) With respect to any property other than property described in subdivision (ii), (iii), or (iv) of this subparagraph, the amount of the adjustments attributable to periods after December 31, 1961,

(ii) With respect to an elevator or escalator, the amount of the adjustments attributable to periods after June 30, 1963,

(iii) With respect to livestock (described in subparagraph (4) of § 1.1245–3(a)), the amount of the adjustments attributable to periods after December 31, 1969, or

(iv) [Reserved]

which are reflected in the adjusted basis of such property on account of deductions allowed or allowable for depreciation or amortization (within the meaning of subparagraph (3) of this paragraph). For cases where the taxpayer can establish that the amount allowed for any period was less than the amount allowable, see subparagraph (7) of this paragraph. * * *

(3) Meaning of "depreciation or amortization." **(i)** For purposes of subparagraph (2) of this paragraph, the term "depreciation or amortization" includes allowances (and amounts treated as allowances) for depreciation (or amortization in lieu thereof) * * * Thus, for example, such term includes a reasonable allowance for exhaustion, wear and tear (including a reasonable allowance for obsolescence) under section 167, an expense allowance (additional first-year depreciation allowance for property placed in service before January 1, 1981) under section 179 * * * and a deduction for depreciation of improvements under section 611 (relating to depletion). For further examples, the term "depreciation or amortization" includes periodic deductions referred to in § 1.162–11 in respect of a specified sum paid for the acquisition of a leasehold and in respect of the cost to a lessee of improvements on property of which he is the lessee. However, such term does not include deductions for the periodic payment of rent.

(ii) The provisions of this subparagraph may be illustrated by the following example:

Example. On January 1, 1966, Smith purchases for $1,000, and places in service, an item of property described in section 1245(a)(3)(A). Smith deducts an additional first-year allowance for depreciation under section 179 of $200. Accordingly, the basis of the property for purposes of depreciation is $800 on January 1, 1966. Between that date and January 1, 1974, Smith deducts $640 in depreciation (the amount allowable) with respect to the property, thereby reducing its adjusted basis to $160. Since this adjusted basis reflects deductions for depreciation and amortization (within the meaning of this subparagraph) amounting to $840 ($200 plus $640), the recomputed basis of the property is $1,000 ($160 plus $840).

(4) Adjustments of other taxpayers or in respect of other property. **(i)** For purposes of subparagraph (2) of this paragraph, the adjustments reflected in adjusted basis on account of depreciation or amortization which must be taken into account in determining recomputed basis are not limited to those adjustments on account of depreciation or amortization with respect to the property disposed of, nor are such adjustments limited to those on account of depreciation or amortization allowed or allowable to the taxpayer disposing of such property. Except as provided in subparagraph (7) of this paragraph, all such adjustments are taken into account, whether the deductions were allowed or allowable in respect of the same or other property and whether to the taxpayer or to any other person. For manner of determining the amount of adjustments reflected in the adjusted basis of property immediately after certain dispositions, see paragraph (c) of this section.

(ii) The provisions of this subparagraph may be illustrated by the following example:

Example. On January 1, 1966, Jones purchases machine X for use in his trade or business. The machine, which is section 1245 property, has a basis for depreciation of $10,000. After taking depreciation deductions of $2,000 (the amount allowable), Jones transfers the machine to his son as a gift on January 1, 1968. Since the exception for gifts in section 1245(b)(1) applies, Jones does not recognize gain under section 1245(a)(1). The son's adjusted basis for the machine is $8,000. On January 1, 1969, after taking a depreciation deduction of $1,000 (the amount allowable), the son exchanges machine X for machine Y in a like kind exchange described in section 1031. Since the exception for like kind exchanges in section 1245(b)(4) applies, the son does not recognize gain under section 1245(a)(1). The son's adjusted basis for machine Y is $7,000. In 1969, the son takes a depreciation deduction of $1,000 (the amount allowable) in respect of machine Y. The son sells machine Y on June 30, 1970. No depreciation was allowed or allowable for 1970, the year of the sale. The recomputed basis of machine Y on June 30, 1070, is determined in the following manner:

Adjusted basis		$ 6,000
Adjustments reflected in the adjusted basis:		
Depreciation deducted by Jones for 1966 and 1967 on machine X	2,000	
Depreciation deducted by son for 1968 on machine X	1,000	
Depreciation deducted by son for 1969 on machine Y	1,000	
Total adjustments reflected in the adjusted basis		$ 4,000
Recomputed basis		10,000

* * *

(7) Depreciation or amortization allowed or allowable. For purposes of determining recomputed basis, generally all adjustments (for periods after December 31, 1961, or, in the case of property described in subparagraph (2)(ii), (iii), or (iv) of this paragraph, for periods after the applicable date) attributable to allowed or allowable depreciation or amortization must be taken into account. See section 1016(a)(2) and the regulations thereunder for the meaning of "allowed" and "allowable". However, if a taxpayer can establish by adequate records or other sufficient evidence that the amount allowed for depreciation or amortization for any period was less than the amount allowable for such period, the amount to be taken into account for such period shall be the amount allowed. No adjustment is to be made on account of the tax imposed by section 56 (relating to the minimum tax for tax preferences). See paragraph (b) of this section (relating to records to be kept and information to be filed). For example, assume that in the year 1967 it becomes necessary to determine the recomputed basis of property, the $500 adjusted basis of which reflects adjustments of $1,000 with respect to depreciation deductions allowable for periods after December 31, 1961. If the taxpayer can establish by adequate records or other sufficient evidence that he had been allowed deductions amounting to only $800 for the period, then in determining recomputed basis the amount added to adjusted basis with respect to the $1,000 adjustments to basis for the period will be only $800.

* * *

(c) Adjustments reflected in adjusted basis immediately after certain acquisitions—(1) Zero. **(i)** If on the date a person acquires property his basis for the property is determined solely by reference to its cost (within the meaning of section 1012), then on such date the amount of the adjustments reflected in his adjusted basis for the property is zero.

(ii) If on the date a person acquires property his basis for the property is determined solely by reason of the application of section 301(d) (relating to basis of property received in corporate distribution) or section 334(a) (relating to basis of property received in a liquidation in which gain or loss is recognized), then on such date the amount of the adjustments reflected in his adjusted basis for the property is zero.

* * *

(iv) If as of the date a person acquires property from a decedent such person's basis is determined, by reason of the application of section 1014(a), solely by reference to the fair market value of the property on the date of the decedent's death or on the applicable date provided in section 2032 (relating to alternate valuation date), then on such date the amount of the adjustments reflected in his adjusted basis for the property is zero.

(2) Gifts and certain tax-free transactions. **(i)** If property is disposed of in a transaction described in subdivision (ii) of this subparagraph, then the amount of the adjustments reflected in the adjusted basis of the property in the hands of a transferee immediately after the disposition shall be an amount equal to:

(a) The amount of the adjustments reflected in the adjusted basis of the property in the hands of the transferor immediately before the disposition, minus

(b) The amount of any gain taken into account under section 1245(a)(1) by the transferor upon the disposition.

(ii) The transactions referred to in subdivision (i) of this subparagraph are:

(a) A disposition which is in part a sale or exchange and in part a gift (see paragraph (a)(3) of § 1.1245–4).

(b) A disposition (other than a disposition to which section 1245(b)(6)(A) applies) which is described in section 1245(b)(3) (relating to certain tax-free transactions), or

* * *

(iii) The provisions of this subparagraph may be illustrated by the following example:

Example. Jones transfers section 1245 property to a corporation in exchange for stock of the corporation and $1,000 cash in a transaction which qualifies under section 351 (relating to transfer to a corporation controlled by transferor). Before the exchange the amount of the adjustments reflected in the adjusted basis of the property is $3,000. Upon the exchange $1,000 gain is recognized under section 1245(a)(1). Immediately after the exchange, the amount of the adjustments reflected in the adjusted basis of the property in the hands of the corporation is $2,000 (that is, $3,000 minus $1,000).

* * *

(4) Property received in a like kind exchange, involuntary conversion, or F.C.C. transaction. **(i)** If property is acquired in a transaction described in subdivision (ii) of this subparagraph then immediately after the acquisition (and before applying subparagraph (5) of this paragraph, if applicable) the amount of the adjustments reflected in the adjusted basis of the property acquired shall be an amount equal to:

(a) The amount of the adjustments reflected in the adjusted basis of the property disposed of immediately before the disposition, minus

(b) The sum of (1) the amount of any gain recognized under section 1245(a)(1) upon the disposition, plus (2) the amount of gain (if any) referred to in subparagraph (5)(ii) of this paragraph.

(ii) The transactions referred to in subdivision (i) of this subparagraph are:

(a) A disposition which is a like kind exchange or an involuntary conversion to which section 1245(b)(4) applies, or

* * *

(iii) The provisions of subdivisions (i) and (ii) of this subparagraph may be illustrated by the following examples:

Example (1). Smith exchanges machine A for machine B and $1,000 cash in a like kind exchange. Gain of $1,000 is recognized under section 1245(a)(1). If before the exchange the amount of the adjustments reflected in the adjusted basis of machine A was $5,000, the amount of adjustments reflected in the adjusted basis of machine B after the exchange is $4,000 (that is, $5,000 minus $1,000).

Example (2). Assume the same facts as in example (1) except that machine A is destroyed by fire, that $5,000 in insurance proceeds are received of which $4,000 is used to purchase machine B, and that Smith properly elects under section 1033(a)(3)(A) to limit recognition of gain. The result is the same as in example (1), that is, the amount of adjustments reflected in the adjusted basis of machine B is $4,000 ($5,000 minus $1,000).

(iv) If more than one item of section 1245 property is acquired in a transaction referred to in subdivision (i) of this subparagraph, the total amount of the adjustments reflected in the adjusted bases of the items acquired shall be allocated to such items in proportion to their respective adjusted bases.

* * *

[T.D. 6832, 30 FR 8578, July 7, 1965, as amended by T.D. 7084, 36 FR 268, Jan. 8, 1971; T.D. 7141, 36 FR 18793, Sept. 22, 1971; 36 FR 19160, Sept. 30, 1971; T.D. 7564, 43 FR 40496, Sept. 12, 1978; T.D. 8121, 52 FR 414, Jan. 6, 1987]

§ 1.1245–3 Definition of section 1245 property.

* * *

(b) Personal property defined. The term "personal property" means:

(1) Tangible personal property (as defined in paragraph (c) of § 1.48–1, relating to the definition of "section 38 property" for purposes of the investment credit), and

(2) Intangible personal property.

* * *

[T.D. 6832, 30 FR 8580, July 7, 1965, as amended by T.D. 7141, 36 FR 18794, Sept. 22, 1971]

§ 1.1245–4 Exceptions and limitations.

(a) Exception for gifts—(1) General rule. Section 1245(b)(1) provides that no gain shall be recognized under section 1245(a)(1) upon a disposition by gift. For purposes of this paragraph, the term "gift" means, except to the extent that subparagraph (3) of this paragraph applies, a transfer of property which, in the hands of the transferee, has a basis determined under the provisions of section 1015(a) or (d) (relating to basis of property acquired by gifts). For reduction in amount of charitable contribution in case of a gift of section 1245 property, see section 170(e) and the regulations thereunder.

* * *

(3) Disposition in part a sale or exchange and in part a gift. Where a disposition of property is in part a sale or exchange and in part a gift, the gain to which section 1245(a)(1) applies is the amount by which (i) the lower of the amount realized upon the disposition of the property or the recomputed basis of the property, exceeds (ii) the adjusted basis of the property. * * *

(4) Example. The provisions of subparagraph (3) of this paragraph may be illustrated by the following example:

Example. **(i)** Smith transfers section 1245 property, which he has held in excess of 1 year * * * to his son for $60,000. Immediately before the transfer the property in the hands of Smith has an adjusted basis of $30,000, a fair market value of $90,000, and a recomputed basis of $110,000. Since the amount realized upon disposition of the property ($60,000) is lower than its recomputed basis ($110,000), the excess of the amount realized over adjusted basis, or $30,000, is treated as ordinary income under section 1245(a)(1) and not as gain from the sale or exchange of property described in section 1231. Smith has made a gift of $30,000 ($90,000 fair market value minus $60,000 amount realized) to which section 1245(a)(1) does not apply.

(ii) Immediately before the transfer, the amount of adjustments reflected in the adjusted basis of the property was $80,000. Under paragraph (c)(2) of § 1.1245–2, $50,000 of adjustments are reflected in the adjusted basis of the property immediately after the transfer, that is, $80,000 of such adjustments immediately before the transfer, minus $30,000 gain taken into account under section 1245(a)(1) upon the transfer. Thus, the recomputed basis of the property in the hands of the son is $110,000.

(b) Exception for transfers at death—(1) General rule. Section 1245(b)(2) provides that, except as provided in section 691 (relating to income in respect of a decedent), no gain shall be recognized under section 1245(a)(1) upon a transfer at death. For purposes of this paragraph, the term "transfer at death" means a transfer of property which, in the hands of the transferee, has a basis determined under the provisions of section 1014(a) (relating to basis of property acquired from a decedent) because of the death of the transferor. * * *

* * *

(c) Limitation for certain tax-free transactions—(1) Limitation on amount of gain. Section 1245(b)(3) provides that upon a transfer of property described in subparagraph (2) of this paragraph, the amount of gain taken into account by the transferor under section 1245(a)(1) shall not exceed the amount of gain recognized to the transferor on the transfer (determined without regard to section 1245). For purposes of this subparagraph, in case of a transfer of both section 1245 property and non-section 1245 property in one transaction, the amount realized from the disposition of the section 1245 property (as determined under paragraph (a)(5) of § 1.1245–1) shall be deemed to consist of that portion of the fair market value of each property acquired which bears the same ratio to the fair market value of such acquired property as the amount realized from the disposition of the section 1245 property bears to the total amount realized. The preceding sentence shall be applied solely for purposes of computing the portion of the total gain (determined without regard to section 1245) which shall be recognized as ordinary income under section 1245(a)(1). * * *

(2) Transfers covered. The transfers referred to in subparagraph (1) of this paragraph are transfers of property in which the basis of the property in the hands of the transferee is determined by reference to its basis in the hands of the transferor by reason of the application of any of the following provisions:

(i) Section 332 (relating to distributions in complete liquidation of an 80–percent–or–more controlled subsidiary corporation). See subparagraph (3) of this paragraph.

(ii) Section 351 (relating to transfer to a corporation controlled by transferor).

(iii) Section 361 (relating to exchanges pursuant to certain corporate reorganizations).

* * *

(vi) Section 721 (relating to transfers to a partnership in exchange for a partnership interest).

(vii) Section 731 (relating to distributions by a partnership to a partner). For special carryover basis rule, see section 1245(b)(6)(A) * * *.

(3) Complete liquidation of subsidiary. In the case of a distribution in complete liquidation of an 80–percent–or–more controlled subsidiary to which section 332 applies, the limitation provided in section 1245(b)(3) is confined to instances in which the basis of the property in the hands of the transferee is determined, under section 334(b)(1), by reference to its basis in the hands of the transferor. Thus, for example, the limitation of section 1245(b)(3) may apply in respect of a liquidating distribution of section 1245 property by an 80–percent–or–more controlled corporation to the parent corporation, but does not apply in respect of a liquidating distribution of section 1245 property to a minority shareholder. Section 1245(b)(3) does not apply to a liquidating distribution of property by an 80–percent–or–more controlled subsidiary to its parent if the parent's basis for the property is determined, under section 334(b)(2), by reference to its basis for the stock of the subsidiary.

(4) Examples. The provisions of this paragraph may be illustrated by the following examples:

Example (1). Section 1245 property, which is owned by Smith, has a fair market value of $10,000, a recomputed basis of $8,000, and an adjusted basis of $4,000. Smith transfers the property to a corporation in exchange for stock in the corporation worth $9,000 plus $1,000 in cash in a transaction qualifying under section 351. Without regard to section 1245, Smith would recognize $1,000 gain under section 351(b), and the corporation's basis for the property would be determined under section 362(a) by reference to its basis in the hands of Smith. Since the recomputed basis of the property disposed of ($8,000) is lower than the amount realized ($10,000), the excess of recomputed basis over adjusted basis ($4,000), or $4,000, would be treated as ordinary income under section 1245(a)(1) if the provisions of section 1245(b)(3) did not apply. However, section 1245(b)(3) limits the gain taken into account by Smith under section 1245(a)(1) to $1,000. If, instead, Smith transferred the property to the corporation solely in exchange for stock of the corporation worth $10,000, then, because of the application of section 1245(b)(3), Smith would not take any gain into account under section 1245(a)(1). If, however, Smith transferred the property to the corporation for stock worth $5,000 and $5,000 cash, only $4,000 of the $5,000 gain under section 351(b) would be treated as ordinary income under section 1245(a)(1).

Example (2). Assume the same facts as in example (1) except that Smith contributes the property to a new partnership in which he has a one-half interest. Since, without regard to section 1245, no gain would be recognized to Smith under section 721, and by reason of the application of section 721 the partnership's basis for the property would be determined under section 723 by reference to its basis in the hands of Smith, the application of section 1245(b)(3) results in no gain being taken into account by Smith under section 1245(a)(1).

Example (3). Assume the same facts as in example (2) except that the property is subject to a $9,000 mortgage. Since under section 752(b) (relating to decrease in partner's liabilities) Smith is treated as receiving a distribution in money of $4,500 (one-half of liability assumed by partnership), and since the basis of Smith's partnership interest is $4,000 (the adjusted basis of the contributed property), the $4,500 distribution results in his realizing $500 gain under section 731(a) (relating to distributions by a partnership), determined without regard to section 1245. Accordingly, the application of section 1245(b)(3) limits the gain taken into account by Smith under section 1245(a)(1) to $500.

(d) Limitation for like kind exchanges and involuntary conversions—(1) General rule. Section 1245(b)(4) provides that if property is disposed of and gain (determined without regard to section 1245) is not recognized in whole or in part under section 1031 (relating to like kind exchanges) or section 1033 (relating to involuntary conversions), then the amount of gain taken into account by the transferor under section 1245(a)(1) shall not exceed the sum of:

(i) The amount of gain recognized on such disposition (determined without regard to section 1245), plus

(ii) The fair market value of property acquired which is not section 1245 property and which is not taken into account under subdivision (i) of this subparagraph (that is, the fair market value of non-section 1245 property acquired which is qualifying property under section 1031 or 1033, as the case may be).

(2) Examples. The provisions of subparagraph (1) of this paragraph may be illustrated by the following examples:

Example (1). Smith exchanges machine A for machine B in a like kind exchange as to which no gain is recognized under section 1031(a). Both machines are section 1245 property. No gain is recognized under section 1245(a)(1) because of the limitation contained in section 1245(b)(4). The result would be the same if machine A were involuntarily converted into machine B in a transaction as to which no gain is recognized under section 1033(a)(1).

Example (2). Jones owns property A, which is section 1245 property, with an adjusted basis of $100,000 and a recomputed basis of $116,000. The property is destroyed by fire and Jones receives $117,000 of insurance proceeds. Thus, the amount of gain under section 1245(a)(1), determined without regard to section 1245(b)(4), would be $16,000. He uses $105,000 of the proceeds to purchase section 1245 property similar or related in service or use to property A, and $9,000 of the proceeds to purchase stock in the acquisition of control of a corporation owning property similar or related in service or use to property A. Both acquisitions qualify under section 1033(a)(3)(A). Jones properly elects under section 1033(a)(3)(A) and the regulations thereunder to limit recognition of gain to the amount by which the amount realized from the conversion exceeds the cost of the stock and other property acquired to replace the converted property. Since $3,000 of the gain is recognized (without regard to section 1245) under section 1033(a)(3) (that is, $117,000 minus $114,000), and since the stock purchased for $9,000 is not section 1245 property and was not taken into account in determining the gain under section 1033, section 1245(b)(4) limits the amount of the gain taken into account under section 1245(a)(1) to $12,000 (that is, $3,000 plus $9,000). If, instead of purchasing $9,000 in stock, Jones purchases $9,000 worth of property which is section 1245 property similar or related in use to the destroyed property, section 1245(b)(4) would limit the amount of gain taken into account under section 1245(a)(1) to $3,000.

* * *

(f) Limitation for property distributed by a partnership—(1) In general. For purposes of section 1245(b)(3) (relating to certain tax-free transactions), the basis of section 1245 property distributed by a partnership to a partner shall be deemed to be determined by reference to the adjusted basis of such property to the partnership.

(2) Adjustments reflected in the adjusted basis. If section 1245 property is distributed by a partnership to a partner, then, for purposes of determining the recomputed basis of the property in the hands of the distributee, the amount of the adjustments reflected in the adjusted basis of the property immediately after the distribution shall be an amount equal to:

(i) The potential section 1245 income (as defined in paragraph (c)(4) of § 1.751–1) of the partnership in respect of the property immediately before the distribution, reduced by

(ii) The portion of such potential section 1245 income which is recognized as ordinary income to the partnership under paragraph (b)(2)(ii) of § 1.751–1.

(3) Examples. The provisions of this paragraph may be illustrated by the following examples:

Example (1). **(i)** A machine, which is section 1245 property owned by partnership ABC, has an adjusted basis of $9,000, a recomputed basis of $18,000, and a fair market value of $15,000. Since the fair market value of the machine is lower than its recomputed basis, the potential section 1245 income in respect of the machine is the excess of fair market value over adjusted basis, or $6,000. The partnership distributes the machine to C in a complete liquidation of his partnership interest to which section 736(a) does not apply. C, who had originally contributed the machine to the partnership, has a basis for his partnership interest of $10,000. Since section 751(b)(2)(A) provides that section 751(b)(1) does not apply to a distribution of property to the partner who contributed the property, no gain would be recognized to the partnership under section 731(b) (without regard to the application of section 1245). By reason of the application of section 731, C's basis for the property would, under section 732(b), be equal to his basis for his interest in the partnership, or $10,000.

(ii) Since section 731 applies to the distribution, and since subparagraph (1) of this paragraph provides that, for purposes of section 1245(b)(3), C's basis for the property is deemed to be determined by reference to the adjusted basis of the property to the partnership, the gain taken into account under section 1245(a)(1) by the partnership is limited by section 1245(b)(3) so as not to exceed the amount of gain which would be recognized to the partnership if section 1245 did not apply. Accordingly, the partnership does not recognize any gain under section 1245(a)(1) upon the distribution.

(iii) Immediately after the distribution, the amount of the adjustments reflected in the adjusted basis of the property is equal to $6,000 (that is, the potential section 1245 income of the partnership in respect of the property before the distribution, $6,000, minus the gain recognized by the partnership under section 751(b), zero). Accordingly, C's recomputed basis for the property is $16,000 (that is, adjusted basis, $10,000, plus adjustments reflected in the adjusted basis, $6,000).

Example (2). Assume the same facts as in example (1) except that the machine had been purchased by the partnership. Assume further that upon the distribution, the partnership recognizes $4,000 gain as ordinary income under section 751(b). Under section 1245(b)(3), gain to be taken into account under section 1245(a)(1) by the partnership is limited to $4,000. Immediately after the distribution, the amount of adjustments reflected in the adjusted basis of the property is $2,000 (that is, potential section 1245 income of the partnership, $6,000, minus gain recognized to the partnership under section 751(b), $4,000). Thus, if the adjusted basis of the machine in the hands of C were $11,333 (see, for example, the computation in paragraph (d)(2) of example (6) of paragraph (g) of § 1.751–1), the recomputed basis of the machine would be $13,333 ($11,333 plus $2,000).

* * *

[T.D. 6832, 30 FR 8581, July 7, 1965, as amended by T.D. 7084, 36 FR 268, Jan. 8, 1971; T.D. 7207, 37 FR 20799, Oct. 14, 1972; T.D. 7728, 45 FR 72650, Nov. 3, 1980; T.D. 7927, 48 FR 55847, Dec. 16, 1983]

§ 1.1245–6 Relation of section 1245 to other sections.

(a) General. The provisions of section 1245 apply notwithstanding any other provision of subtitle A of the Code. Thus, unless an exception or limitation under section 1245(b) applies, gain under section 1245(a)(1) is recognized notwithstanding any contrary nonrecognition provision or income characterizing provision. For example, since section 1245 overrides section 1231 (relating to property used in the trade or business), the gain recognized under section 1245(a)(1) upon a disposition will be treated as ordinary income and only the remaining gain, if any, from the disposition may be considered as gain from the sale or exchange of a capital asset if section 1231 is applicable. See example (2) of paragraph (b)(2) of § 1.1245–1. * * *

* * *

(d) Installment method. **(1)** Gain from a disposition to which section 1245(a)(1) applies may be reported under the installment method if such method is otherwise available under section 453 of the Code. In such case, the income (other than interest) on each installment payment shall be deemed to consist of gain to which section 1245(a)(1) applies until all such gain has been reported, and the remaining portion (if any) of such income shall be deemed to consist of gain to which section 1245(a)(1) does not apply. For treatment of amounts as interest on certain deferred payments, see section 483.

(2) The provisions of this paragraph may be illustrated by the following example:

Example. Jones contracts to sell an item of section 1245 property for $10,000 to be paid in 10 equal payments of $1,000 each, plus a sufficient amount of interest so that section 483 does not apply. He properly elects under section 453 to report under the installment method gain of $2,000 to which section 1245(a)(1) applies and gain of $1,000 to which section 1231 applies. Accordingly, $300 of each of the first 6 installment payments and $200 of the seventh installment payment is ordinary income under section 1245(a)(1), and $100 of the seventh installment payment and $300 of each of the last 3 installment payments is gain under section 1231.

* * *

(f) Treatment of gain not recognized under section 1245. Section 1245 does not prevent gain which is not recognized under section 1245 from being considered as gain under another provision of the Code, such as, for example, * * *, section 341(f) (relating to collapsible corporations), section 357(c) (relating to liabilities in excess of basis), * * *, or section 1239 (relating to gain from sale of depreciable property between certain related persons). Thus, for example, if section 1245 property, which has an adjusted basis of $1,000 and a recomputed basis of $1,500, is sold for $1,750 in a transaction to which section 1239 applies, $500 of the gain would be recognized under section 1245(a)(1) and the remaining $250 of the gain would be treated as ordinary income under section 1239.

[T.D. 6832, 30 FR 8584, July 7, 1965, as amended by T.D. 7084, 36 FR 269, Jan. 8, 1971; T.D. 7400, 41 FR 5101, Feb. 4, 1976]

§ 1.1250–1 Gain from dispositions of certain depreciable realty.

(a) Dispositions after December 31, 1969—(1) Ordinary income. **(i)** In general, section 1250(a)(1) provides that, upon a disposition of an item of section 1250 property after December 31, 1969, the applicable percentage of the lower of:

(a) The additional depreciation (as defined in § 1.1250–2) attributable to periods after December 31, 1969 in respect of the property, or

(b) The excess of the amount realized on a sale, exchange, or involuntary conversion (or the fair market value of the property on any other disposition) over the adjusted basis of the property,

shall be treated as gain from the sale or exchange of property which is neither a capital asset nor property described in section 1231 (that is, shall be recognized as ordinary income). The amount of such gain shall be determined separately for each item (see subparagraph (2)(ii) of this paragraph) of section 1250 property. If the amount determined under (b) of this subdivision exceeds the amount determined under (a) of this subdivision, then such excess shall be treated as provided in subdivision (ii) of this subparagraph. For relation of section 1250 to other provisions, see paragraph (c) of this section.

(ii) If the amount determined under subdivision (i)(b) of this subparagraph exceeds the amount determined under subdivision (i)(a) of this subparagraph, then the applicable percentage of the lower of:

(a) The additional depreciation attributable to periods before January 1, 1970, or

(b) Such excess,

shall also be recognized as ordinary income.

(iii) If gain would be recognized upon a disposition of an item of section 1250 property under subdivisions (i) and (ii) of this subparagraph, and if section 1250(d) applies, then the gain recognized shall be considered as recognized first under subdivision (i) of this subparagraph. * * *

(2) Meaning of terms. **(i)** For purposes of section 1250, the term "disposition" shall have the same meaning as in paragraph (a)(3) of § 1.1245–1. "Section 1250 property" is, in general, depreciable real property other than section 1245 property. See paragraph (e) of this section. See paragraph (d)(1) of this section for meaning of the term "applicable percentage." * * *

(ii) For purposes of applying section 1250, the facts and circumstances of each disposition shall be considered in determining what is the appropriate item of section 1250 property. In general, a building is an item of section 1250 property, but in an appropriate case more than one building may be treated as a single item. For example, if two or more buildings or structures on a single tract or parcel (or contiguous tracts or parcels) of land are operated as an integrated unit (as evidenced by their actual operation, management, financing, and accounting), they may be treated as a single item of section 1250 property. * * *

(3) Sale, exchange, or involuntary conversion after December 31, 1969. **(i)** In the case of a disposition of section 1250 property by a sale, exchange, or involuntary conversion after December 31, 1969, the gain to which section 1250(a)(1) applies is the applicable percentage for the property (determined under paragraph (d)(1) of this section) multiplied by the lower of (a) the additional depreciation in respect of the property attributable to periods after December 31, 1969, or (b) the excess (referred to as "gain realized") of the amount realized over the adjusted basis of the property.

(ii) In addition to gain recognized under section 1250(a)(1) and subdivision (i) of this subparagraph, gain may also be recognized under section 1250(a)(2) and this subdivision if the gain realized exceeds the additional depreciation attributable to periods after December 31, 1969. In such a case, the amount of gain recognized under section 1250(a)(2) and this subdivision is the applicable percentage for the property (determined under paragraph (d)(2) of this section) multiplied by the lower of (a) the additional depreciation attributable to periods before January 1, 1970, or (b) the excess (referred to as "remaining gain") of the gain realized over the additional depreciation attributable to periods after December 31, 1969.

* * *

(4) Other dispositions after December 31, 1969. **(i)** In the case of a disposition of section 1250 property after December 31, 1969, other than by way of a sale, exchange, or involuntary conversion, the gain to which section 1250(a)(1) applies is the applicable percentage for the property (determined under paragraph (d)(1) of this section) multiplied by the lower of (a) the additional depreciation in respect of the property attributable to periods after December 31, 1969, or (b) the excess (referred to as "potential gain") of the fair market value of the property over its adjusted basis. In addition, if the potential gain exceeds the additional depreciation attributable to periods after December 31, 1969, then the gain to which section 1250(a)(2) applies is the applicable percentage for the property (determined under paragraph (d)(2) of this section) multiplied by the lower of (c) the additional depreciation attributable to periods before January 1, 1970, or (d) the excess (referred to as "remaining potential gain") of the potential gain over the additional depreciation attributable to periods after December 31, 1969. If property is transferred by a corporation to a shareholder for an amount less than its fair market value in a sale or exchange, for purposes of applying section 1250 such transfer shall be treated as a disposition other than by way of a sale, exchange, or involuntary conversion.

(ii) The provisions of this subparagraph may be illustrated by the following examples:

Example (1). Section 1250 property having an adjusted basis of $500,000 and a fair market value of $550,000 is distributed by a corporation to a stockholder in complete liquidation of the corporation after December 31, 1969, and thus the potential gain is $50,000. At the time of the liquidation, the additional depreciation for the property attributable to periods after December 31, 1969, is $80,000 and the applicable percentage is 100 percent (paragraph (d)(1)(i)(e) of this section). Since the potential gain of $50,000 is lower than the additional depreciation attributable to periods after December 31, 1969 ($80,000), the amount of gain recognized as ordinary income under section 1250(a)(1) is $50,000 (that is, 100 percent of $50,000) even though in the absence of section 1250, section 336 would preclude recognition of gain to the corporation.

Example (2). The facts are the same as in example (1) except that the fair market value of the property is $650,000, and thus the potential gain is $150,000. Since the additional depreciation attributable to periods after December 31, 1969 ($80,000), is lower than the potential gain of $150,000, the amount of gain recognized as ordinary income under section 1250(a)(1) is $80,000 (that is, 100 percent of $80,000). In addition, section 1250(a)(2) applies since there is remaining potential gain of $70,000, that is, potential gain ($150,000) minus additional depreciation attributable to periods after December 31, 1969 ($80,000). The additional depreciation attributable to periods before January 1, 1970, is $90,000 and the applicable percentage under paragraph (d)(2) of this section is 50 percent. Since the remaining potential gain of $70,000 is lower than the additional depreciation attributable to periods before January 1, 1970 ($90,000), the amount of gain recognized as ordinary income under section 1250(a)(2) is $35,000 (that is, 50 percent of $70,000). * * *

(5) Instances of nonapplication. **(i)** Section 1250(a)(1) does not apply to losses. Thus, section 1250(a)(1) does not apply if a loss is realized upon a sale, exchange, or involuntary conversion of property, all of which is considered section 1250 property, nor does the section apply to a disposition of such property other than by way of sale, exchange, or involuntary conversion if at the time of the disposition the fair market value of such property is not greater than its adjusted basis.

(ii) In general, in the case of section 1250 property with a holding period under section 1223 of more than 1 year, section 1250(a)(1) does not apply if for periods after December 31, 1969, there are no "depreciation adjustments in excess of straight line" (as computed under section 1250(b) and paragraph (b) of § 1.1250–2).

(6) Allocation rules. **(i)** In the case of a sale, exchange, or involuntary conversion of section 1250 property and nonsection 1250 property in one transaction after December 31, 1969, the total amount realized upon the disposition shall be allocated between the section 1250 property and the other property in proportion to their respective fair market values. Such allocation shall be made in accordance with the principles set forth in paragraph (a)(5) of § 1.1245–1 (relating to allocation between section 1245 property and nonsection 1245 property).

(ii) If an item of section 1250 property has two (or more) applicable percentages because one subdivision of paragraph (d)(1)(i) of this section applies to one portion of the taxpayer's holding period (determined under § 1.1250–4) and another subdivision of such paragraph applies with respect to another such portion, then the gain realized on a sale, exchange, or involuntary conversion, or the potential gain in the case of any other disposition, shall be allocated to each such portion of the taxpayer's holding period after December 31, 1969, in the same proportion as the additional depreciation with respect to such item for such portion bears to the additional depreciation with respect to such item for the entire holding period after December 31, 1969.

* * *

(c) Relation of section 1250 to other provisions—(1) General. The provisions of section 1250 apply notwithstanding any other provision of subtitle A of the Code. See section 1250(i). Thus, unless an exception or limitation under section 1250(d) * * * applies, gain under section 1250(a) is recognized notwithstanding any contrary nonrecognition provision or income characterizing provision. For example, since section 1250 overrides section 1231 (relating to property used in the trade or business), the gain recognized under section 1250(a) upon a disposition will be treated as ordinary income and only the remaining gain, if any, from the disposition may be considered as gain from the sale or exchange of a capital asset if section 1231 is applicable. * * *

* * *

(4) Treatment of gain not recognized under section 1250. Section 1250 does not prevent gain which is not recognized under section 1250 from being considered as gain under another provision of the Code, such as, for example, section 1239 (relating to gain from sale of depreciable property between certain related persons). Thus, for example, if section 1250 property which has an adjusted basis of $10,000 is sold for $17,500 in a transaction to which section 1239 applies, and if $5,000 of the gain would be recognized under section 1250(a) then the remaining $2,500 of the gain would be treated as ordinary income under section 1239.

* * *

(6) Installment method. Gain from a disposition to which section 1250(a) applies may be reported under the installment method if such method is otherwise available under section 453 of the Code. In such case, the income (other than interest) on each installment payment shall be deemed to consist of gain to which section 1250(a) applies until all such gain has been reported, and the remaining portion (if any) of such income shall be deemed to consist of other gain. For treatment of amounts as interest on certain deferred payments, see section 483.

(d) Applicable percentage—(1) Definition for purposes of section 1250(a)(1). * * *

* * *

(4) Full month. For purposes of this paragraph, the term "full month" (or "full months") means the period beginning on a date in 1 month and terminating on the date before the corresponding date in the next succeeding month (or in another succeeding month), or, if a particular succeeding month does not have such a corresponding date, terminating on the last day of such particular succeeding month.

* * *

(e) Section 1250 property—(1) Definition. The term "section 1250 property" means any real property (other than section 1245 property, as defined in section 1245(a)(3) * * *) which is or has been property of a character subject to the allowance for depreciation provided in section 167. See section 1250(c).

(2) Character of property. For purposes of subparagraph (1) of this paragraph, the term "is or has been property of a character subject to the allowance for depreciation provided in section 167" shall have the same meaning as when used in paragraph (a)(1) and (3) of § 1.1245–3. Thus, if a father uses a house in his trade or business during a period after December 31, 1963, and then gives the house to his son as a gift for the son's personal use, the house is section 1250 property in the hands of the son. For exception to the application of section 1250(a) upon disposition of a principal residence, see section 1250(d)(7).

(3) Real property. **(i)** For purposes of subparagraph (1) of this paragraph, the term "real property" means any property which is not personal property within the meaning of paragraph (b) of § 1.1245–3. The term section 1250 property includes three types of depreciable real property. The first type is intangible real property. For purposes of this paragraph, a leasehold of land or of section 1250 property is intangible real property, and accordingly such a leasehold is section 1250 property. However, a fee simple interest in land is not depreciable, and therefore is not section 1250 property. * * * The third type is all other tangible real property except (a) "property described in section 1245(a)(3)(B)" * * * and (b) property described in section 1245(a)(3)(D). An elevator or escalator (within the meaning of section 1245(a)(3)(C)) is not section 1250 property.

* * *

[T.D. 7084, 36 FR 271, Jan. 8, 1971, as amended by T.D. 7193, 37 FR 12953, June 30, 1972]

§ 1.1250–2 Additional depreciation defined.

(a) In general—(1) Definition for purposes of section 1250(b)(1). Except as otherwise provided in paragraph (e) of this section, for purposes of section 1250(b)(1), the term "additional depreciation" means:

(i) In the case of property which at the time of disposition has a holding period under section 1223 of not more than 1 year, the "depreciation adjustments" (as defined in paragraph (d) of this section) in respect of such property for periods after December 31, 1963, and

(ii) In the case of property which at the time of disposition has a holding period under section 1223 of more than 1 year, the depreciation adjustments in excess of straight line for periods after December 31, 1963, computed under paragraph (b)(1) of this section.

* * *

(b) Computation of depreciation adjustments in excess of straight line—(1) General rule. For purposes of paragraph (a)(1) of this section, depreciation adjustments in excess of straight line shall be, in the case of any property, the excess of (i) the sum of the "depreciation adjustments" (as defined in paragraph (d) of this section) in respect of the property attributable to periods after December 31, 1963, over (ii) the sum such adjustments would have been for such periods if such adjustments had been determined for the entire period the property was held under the straight line method of depreciation (or, if applicable, under the lease-renewal-period provision in paragraph (c) of this section). Depreciation in excess of straight line may arise, for example, if the declining balance method, the sum of the years-digits method, or the units of production method is used, or for another example, if the cost of a leasehold improvement or of a leasehold is depreciated over a period which does not take into account certain renewal periods referred to in paragraph (c) of this section. * * *

* * *

[T.D. 7084, 36 FR 273, Jan. 8, 1971, as amended by T.D. 7193, 37 FR 12956, June 30, 1972]

§ 1.1250–4 Holding period.

(a) General. In general, for purposes only of determining the applicable percentage (as defined in sec. 1250(1)(C) and (2)(B)) of section 1250 property, the holding period of the property shall be determined under the rules of section 1250(e) and this section and not under the rules of section 1223. * * * Section 1250(e) does not affect the determination of the amount of additional depreciation in respect of section 1250 property.

(b) Beginning of holding period. **(1)** For the purpose of determining the applicable percentage, in the case of property acquired by the taxpayer (other than by means of a transaction referred to in paragraph (c) or (d) of this section), the holding period of the property shall begin on the day after the date of its acquisition. See section 1250(e)(1)(A). Thus, for example, if a taxpayer purchases section 1250 property on January 1, 1965, the holding period of the property begins on January 2, 1965. If he sells the property on October 1, 1966, the holding period on the day of the sale is 21 full months, and, accordingly, the applicable percentage is 99 percent. This result would not be changed even if the property initially had been used solely as the taxpayer's residence for a portion of the 21–month period. If, however, the property were sold on September 30, 1966, the holding period would be only 20 full months.

* * *

[T.D. 7084, 36 FR 281, Jan. 8, 1971, as amended by T.D. 7400, 41 FR 5103, Feb. 4, 1976]

§ 1.1258–1 Netting rule for certain conversion transactions.

(a) Purpose. The purpose of this section is to provide taxpayers with a method to net certain gains and losses from positions of the same conversion transaction before determining the amount of gain treated as ordinary income under section 1258(a).

(b) Netting of gain and loss for identified transactions—(1) In general. If a taxpayer disposes of or terminates all the positions of an identified netting transaction (as defined in paragraph (b)(2) of this section) within a 14–day period in a single taxable year, all gains and losses on those positions taken into account for federal tax purposes within that period (other than built-in losses as defined in paragraph (c) of this section) are netted solely for purposes of determining the amount of gain treated as ordinary income under section 1258(a). For purposes of the preceding sentence, a taxpayer is treated as disposing of any position that is treated as sold under any provision of the Code or regulations thereunder (for example, under section 1256(a)(1)).

(2) Identified netting transaction. For purposes of this section, an identified netting transaction is a conversion transaction (as defined in section 1258(c)) that the taxpayer identifies as an identified netting transaction on its books and records. Identification of each position of the conversion transaction must be made before the close of the day on which the position becomes part of the conversion transaction. No particular form of identification is necessary, but all the positions of a single conversion transaction must be identified as part of the same transaction and must be distinguished from all other positions.

(c) Definition of built-in loss. For purposes of this section, built-in loss means—

(1) Built-in loss as defined in section 1258(d)(3)(B); and

(2) If a taxpayer realizes gain or loss on any one position of a conversion transaction (for example, under section 1256), as of the date that gain or loss is realized, any unrecognized loss in any other position of the conversion transaction that is not disposed of, terminated, or treated as sold under any provision of the Code or regulations thereunder within 14 days of and within the same taxable year as the realization event.

(d) Examples. These examples illustrate this section:

Example 1. Identified netting transaction with simultaneous actual dispositions. (i) On December 1, 1995, A purchases 1,000 shares of XYZ stock for $100,000 and enters into a forward contract to sell 1,000 shares of XYZ stock on November 30, 1997, for $110,000. The XYZ stock is actively traded as defined in § 1.1092(d)–1(a) and is a capital asset in A's hands. A maintains books and records on which, on December 1, 1995, it identifies the two positions as all the positions of a single conversion transaction. A owns no other XYZ stock. On December 1, 1996, when the applicable imputed income amount for the transaction is $7,000, A sells the 1,000 shares of XYZ stock for $95,000. On the same day, A terminates its forward contract with its counterparty, receiving $10,200. No dividends were received on the stock during the time it was part of the conversion transaction.

(ii) The XYZ stock and forward contract are positions of a conversion transaction. Under section 1258(c)(1), substantially all of A's expected return from the overall transaction is attributable to the time value of the net investment in the transaction. Under section 1258(c)(2)(B), the transaction is an applicable straddle as defined in section 1258(d)(1).

(iii) A disposed of or terminated all the positions of the conversion transaction within 14 days and within the same taxable year as required by paragraph (b)(1) of this section. The transaction is an identified netting transaction because it meets the identification requirement of paragraph (b)(2) of this section. Solely for purposes of section 1258(a), the $5,000 loss realized ($100,000 basis less $95,000 amount realized) on the disposition of the XYZ stock is netted against the $10,200 gain recognized on the disposition of the forward contract. Thus, the net gain from the conversion transaction for purposes of section 1258(a) is $5,200 ($10,200 gain less $5,000 loss). Only the $5,200 net gain is recharacterized as ordinary income under section 1258(a) even though the applicable imputed income amount is $7,000. For federal tax purposes other than section 1258(a), A has recognized a $10,200 gain on the disposition of the forward contract ($5,200 of which is treated as ordinary income) and realized a separate $5,000 loss on the sale of the XYZ stock.

Example 2. Identified netting transaction with built-in loss. (i) The facts are the same as in Example 1, except that A had purchased the XYZ stock for $104,000 on May 15, 1995. The XYZ stock had a fair market value of $100,000 on December 1, 1995, the date it became part of a conversion transaction.

(ii) The results are the same as in Example 1, except that A has built-in loss (in addition to the $5,000 loss that arose economically during the period of the conversion transaction), as defined in section 1258(d)(3)(B), of $4,000 on the XYZ stock. That $4,000 built-in loss is not netted against the $10,200 gain on the forward contract for purposes of section 1258(a). Thus, the net gain from the conversion transaction for purposes of section 1258(a) is $5,200, the same as in Example 1. The $4,000 built-in loss is recognized and has a character determined without regard to section 1258.

* * *

[T.D. 8649, 60 FR 66083, Dec. 21, 1995]

§ 1.1272–1 Current Inclusion of OID in income.

(a) Overview—(1) In general. Under section 1272(a)(1), a holder of a debt instrument includes accrued OID in gross income (as interest), regardless of the holder's regular method of accounting. * * *

(2) Debt instruments not subject to OID inclusion rules. Sections 1272(a)(2) and 1272(c) list exceptions to the general inclusion rule of section 1272(a)(1). For purposes of section 1272(a)(2)(E) (relating to certain loans between natural persons), a loan does not include a stripped bond or stripped coupon within the meaning of section 1286(e), and the rule in section 1272(a)(2)(E)(iii), which treats a husband and wife as 1 person, does not apply to loans made between a husband and wife.

(b) Accrual of OID—(1) Constant yield method. * * *, the amount of OID includible in the income of a holder of a debt instrument for any taxable year is determined using the constant yield method as described under this paragraph (b)(1).

(i) Step one: Determine the debt instrument's yield to maturity. The yield to maturity or yield of a debt instrument is the discount rate that, when used in computing the present value of all principal and interest payments to be made under the debt instrument, produces an amount equal to the issue price of the debt instrument. The yield must be constant over the term of the debt instrument and, when expressed as a percentage, must be calculated to at least two decimal places. See paragraph (c) of this section for rules relating to the yield of certain debt instruments subject to contingencies.

(ii) Step two: Determine the accrual periods. An accrual period is an interval of time over which the accrual of OID is measured. Accrual periods may be of any length and may vary in length over the term of the debt instrument, provided that each accrual period is no longer than 1 year and each scheduled payment of principal or interest occurs either on the final day of an accrual period or on the first day of an accrual period. In general, the computation of OID is simplest if accrual periods correspond to the intervals between payment dates provided by the terms of the debt instrument. In computing the length of accrual periods, any reasonable counting convention may be used (e.g., 30 days per month/360 days per year).

(iii) Step three: Determine the OID allocable to each accrual period. Except as provided in paragraph (b)(4) of this section, the OID allocable to an accrual period equals the product of the adjusted issue price of the debt instrument * * * at the beginning of the accrual period and the yield of the debt instrument, less the amount of any qualified stated interest allocable to the accrual period. In performing this calculation, the yield must be stated appropriately taking into account the length of the particular accrual period. * * *

(iv) Step four: Determine the daily portions of OID. The daily portions of OID are determined by allocating to each day in an accrual period the ratable portion of the OID allocable to the accrual period. The holder of the debt instrument includes in income the daily portions of OID for each day during the taxable year on which the holder held the debt instrument.

* * *

(4) Special rules for determining the OID allocable to an accrual period. The following rules apply to determine the OID allocable to an accrual period under paragraph (b)(1)(iii) of this section.

(i) Unpaid qualified stated interest allocable to an accrual period. In determining the OID allocable to an accrual period, if an interval between payments of qualified stated interest contains more than 1 accrual period—

(A) The amount of qualified stated interest payable at the end of the interval (including any qualified stated interest that is payable on the first day of the accrual period immediately following the interval) is allocated on a pro rata basis to each accrual period in the interval; and

(B) The adjusted issue price at the beginning of each accrual period in the interval must be increased by the amount of any qualified stated interest that has accrued prior to the first day of the accrual period but that is not payable until the end of the interval. * * *

(ii) Final accrual period. The OID allocable to the final accrual period is the difference between the amount payable at maturity (other than a payment of qualified stated interest) and the adjusted issue price at the beginning of the final accrual period.

(iii) Initial short accrual period. If all accrual periods are of equal length, except for either an initial shorter accrual period or an initial and a final shorter accrual period, the amount of OID allocable to the initial accrual period may be computed using any reasonable method. * * *

(iv) Payment on first day of an accrual period. The adjusted issue price at the beginning of an accrual period is reduced by the amount of any payment (other than a payment of qualified stated interest) that is made on the first day of the accrual period.

* * *

(g) Basis adjustment. The basis of a debt instrument in the hands of the holder is increased by the amount of OID included in the holder's gross income and decreased by the amount of any payment from the issuer to the holder under the debt instrument other than a payment of qualified stated interest. * * *

* * *

[T.D. 8517, 59 FR 4799, Feb. 2, 1994, as amended by T.D. 8674, 61 FR 30133, June 14, 1996; T.D. 9612, 78 FR 7997, Feb. 5, 2013]

§ 1.1272–3 Election by a holder to treat all interest on a debt instrument as OID.

(a) Election. A holder of a debt instrument may elect to include in gross income all interest that accrues on the instrument by using the constant yield method described in paragraph (c) of this section. For purposes of this election, interest includes stated interest, acquisition discount, OID, de minimis OID, market discount, de minimis market discount, and unstated interest, as adjusted by any amortizable bond premium or acquisition premium.

* * *

[T.D. 8517, 59 FR 4799, Feb. 2, 1994]

§ 1.1273–1 Definition of OID.

* * *

(b) Stated redemption price at maturity. A debt instrument's stated redemption price at maturity is the sum of all payments provided by the debt instrument other than qualified stated interest payments. If the payment schedule of a debt instrument is determined under § 1.1272–1(c) (relating to certain debt instruments subject to contingencies), that payment schedule is used to determine the instrument's stated redemption price at maturity.

(c) Qualified stated interest—(1) Definition—(i) In general. Qualified stated interest is stated interest that is unconditionally payable in cash or in property (other than debt instruments of the issuer), or that will be constructively received under section 451, at least annually at a single fixed rate (within the meaning of paragraph (c)(1)(iii) of this section).

* * *

(iii) Single fixed rate—(A) In general. Interest is payable at a single fixed rate only if the rate appropriately takes into account the length of the interval between payments. Thus, if the interval between payments varies during the term of the debt instrument, the value of the fixed rate on which a payment is based generally must be adjusted to reflect a compounding assumption that is consistent with the length of the interval preceding the payment. See Example 1 in paragraph (f) of this section.

(B) Special rule for certain first and final payment intervals. Notwithstanding paragraph (c)(1)(iii)(A) of this section, if a debt instrument provides for payment intervals that are equal in length throughout the term of the instrument, except that the first or final payment interval differs in length from the other payment intervals, the first or final interest payment is considered to be made at a fixed rate if the value of the rate on which the payment is based is adjusted in any reasonable manner to take into account the length of the interval. * * *

* * *

(4) Stated interest in excess of qualified stated interest. To the extent that stated interest payable under a debt instrument exceeds qualified stated interest, the excess is included in the debt instrument's stated redemption price at maturity.

(5) Short-term obligations. In the case of a debt instrument with a term that is not more than 1 year from the date of issue, no payments of interest are treated as qualified stated interest payments.

* * *

(d) De minimis OID—(1) In general. If the amount of OID with respect to a debt instrument is less than the de minimis amount, the amount of OID is treated as zero, and all stated interest (including stated interest that would otherwise be characterized as OID) is treated as qualified stated interest.

(2) De minimis amount. The de minimis amount is an amount equal to 0.0025 multiplied by the product of the stated redemption price at maturity and the number of complete years to maturity from the issue date.

(3) Installment obligations. In the case of an installment obligation (as defined in paragraph (e)(1) of this section), paragraph (d)(2) of this section is applied by substituting for the number of complete years to maturity the weighted average maturity (as defined in paragraph (e)(3) of this section). Alternatively, in the case of a debt instrument that provides for payments of principal no more rapidly than a self-amortizing installment obligation (as defined in paragraph (e)(2) of this section), the de minimis amount defined in paragraph (d)(2) of this section may be calculated by substituting 0.00167 for 0.0025.

(4) Special rule for interest holidays, teaser rates, and other interest shortfalls—(i) In general. This paragraph (d)(4) provides a special rule to determine whether a debt instrument with a teaser rate (or rates), an interest holiday, or any other interest shortfall has de minimis OID. This rule applies if—

(A) The amount of OID on the debt instrument is more than the de minimis amount as otherwise determined under paragraph (d) of this section; and

(B) All stated interest provided for in the debt instrument would be qualified stated interest under paragraph (c) of this section except that for 1 or more accrual periods the interest rate is below the rate applicable for the remainder of the instrument's term (e.g., if as a result of an interest holiday, none of the stated interest is qualified stated interest).

(ii) Redetermination of OID for purposes of the de minimis test. For purposes of determining whether a debt instrument described in paragraph (d)(4)(i) of this section has de minimis OID, the instrument's stated redemption price at maturity is treated as equal to the instrument's issue price plus the greater of the amount of foregone interest or the excess (if any) of the instrument's stated principal amount over its issue price. The amount of foregone interest is the amount of additional stated interest that would be required to be payable on the debt instrument during the period of the teaser rate, holiday, or shortfall so that all stated interest would be qualified stated interest under paragraph (c) of this section. * * * In addition, for purposes of computing the de minimis amount of OID, the weighted average maturity of the debt instrument is determined by treating all stated interest payments as qualified stated interest payments.

(5) Treatment of de minimis OID by holders—(i) Allocation of de minimis OID to principal payments. The holder of a debt instrument includes any de minimis OID (other than de minimis OID treated as qualified stated interest under paragraph (d)(1) of this section, such as de minimis OID attributable to a teaser rate or interest holiday) in income as stated principal payments are made. The amount includible in income with respect to each principal payment equals the product of the total amount of de minimis OID on the debt instrument and a fraction, the numerator of which is the amount of the principal payment made and the denominator of which is the stated principal amount of the instrument.

(ii) Character of de minimis OID—(A) De minimis OID treated as gain recognized on retirement. Any amount of de minimis OID includible in income under this paragraph (d)(5) is treated as gain recognized on retirement of the debt instrument. See section 1271 to determine whether a retirement is treated as an exchange of the debt instrument.

(B) Treatment of de minimis OID on sale or exchange. Any gain attributable to de minimis OID that is recognized on the sale or exchange of a debt instrument is capital gain if the debt instrument is a capital asset in the hands of the seller.

* * *

(e) Definitions—(1) Installment obligation. An installment obligation is a debt instrument that provides for the payment of any amount other than qualified stated interest before maturity.

(2) Self-amortizing installment obligation. A self-amortizing installment obligation is an obligation that provides for equal payments composed of principal and qualified stated interest that are unconditionally payable at least annually during the entire term of the debt instrument with no significant additional payment required at maturity.

(3) Weighted average maturity. The weighted average maturity of a debt instrument is the sum of the following amounts determined for each payment under the instrument (other than a payment of qualified stated interest)—

(i) The number of complete years from the issue date until the payment is made; multiplied by

(ii) A fraction, the numerator of which is the amount of the payment and the denominator of which is the debt instrument's stated redemption price at maturity.

(f) Examples. The following examples illustrate the rules of this section.

Example 1. Qualified stated interest—(i) Facts. On January 1, 1995, A purchases at original issue, for $100,000, a debt instrument that matures on January 1, 1999, and has a stated principal amount of $100,000, payable at maturity. The debt instrument provides for interest payments of $8,000 on January 1, 1996, and January 1, 1997, and quarterly interest payments of $1,942.65, beginning on April 1, 1997.

(ii) Amount of qualified stated interest. The annual payments of $8,000 and the quarterly payments of $1,942.65 are payable at a single fixed rate because 8 percent, compounded annually, is equivalent to 7.77 percent, compounded quarterly. Consequently, all stated interest payments under the debt instrument are qualified stated interest payments.

Example 2. Qualified stated interest with short initial payment interval. On October 1, 1994, A purchases at original issue, for $100,000, a debt instrument that matures on January 1, 1998, and has a stated principal amount of $100,000, payable at maturity. The debt instrument provides for an interest payment of $2,000 on January 1, 1995, and interest payments of $8,000 on January 1, 1996, January 1, 1997, and January 1, 1998. Under paragraph (c)(1)(iii)(B) of this section, all stated interest payments on the debt instrument are computed at a single fixed rate and are qualified stated interest payments.

Example 3. Stated interest in excess of qualified stated interest—(i) Facts. On January 1, 1995, B purchases at original issue, for $100,000, C corporation's 5–year debt instrument. The debt instrument provides for a principal payment of $100,000, payable at maturity, and calls for annual interest payments of $10,000 for the first 3 years and annual interest payments of $10,600 for the last 2 years.

(ii) Payments in excess of qualified stated interest. All of the first three interest payments and $10,000 of each of the last two interest payments are qualified stated interest payments within the meaning of paragraph (c)(1) of this section. Under paragraph (c)(4) of this section, the remaining $600 of each of the last two interest payments is included in the stated redemption price at maturity, so that the stated redemption price at maturity is $101,200. Pursuant to paragraph (e)(3) of this section, the weighted average maturity of the debt instrument is 4.994 years {(4 years × $600/$101,200) + (5 years × $100,600/$101,200)}. The de minimis amount, or one-fourth of 1 percent of the stated redemption price at maturity multiplied by the weighted average maturity, is $1,263.50. Because the actual amount of discount, $1,200, is less than the de minimis amount, the instrument is treated as having no OID, and, under paragraph (d)(1) of this section, all of the interest payments are treated as qualified stated interest payments.

* * *

[T.D. 8517, 59 FR 4799, Feb. 2, 1994, as amended by T.D. 8674, 61 FR 30133, June 14, 1996; T.D. 9599, 77 FR 56333, Sept. 13, 2012]

§ 1.1273–2 Determination of issue price and issue date.

(a) Debt instruments issued for money—(1) Issue price. If a substantial amount of the debt instruments in an issue is issued for money, the issue price of each debt instrument in the issue is the first price at which a substantial amount of the debt instruments is sold for money. Thus, if an issue consists of a single debt instrument that is issued for money, the issue price of the debt instrument is the amount paid for the instrument. For example, in the case of a debt instrument evidencing a loan to a natural person, the issue price of the instrument is the amount loaned. * * *

* * *

(2) Issue date. The issue date of an issue described in paragraph (a)(1) of this section is the first settlement date or closing date, whichever is applicable, on which a substantial amount of the debt instruments in the issue is sold for money.

* * *

[T.D. 8517, 59 FR 4799, Feb. 2, 1994; T.D. 9599, 77 FR 56333, Sept. 13, 2012; T.D. 9612, 78 FR 7997, Feb. 5, 2013]

§ 1.1274–1 Debt instruments to which section 1274 applies.

(a) In general. Subject to the exceptions and limitations in paragraph (b) of this section, section 1274 and this section apply to any debt instrument issued in consideration for the sale or exchange of property. For purposes of section 1274, property includes debt instruments and investment units, but does not include money, services, or the right to use property. For the treatment of certain obligations given in exchange for services or the use of property, see sections 404 and 467. For purposes of this paragraph (a), money includes functional currency and, in certain circumstances, nonfunctional currency. * * *

(b) Exceptions—(1) Debt instrument with adequate stated interest and no OID. Section 1274 does not apply to a debt instrument if—

(i) All interest payable on the instrument is qualified stated interest;

(ii) The stated rate of interest is at least equal to the test rate of interest * * *;

(iii) The debt instrument is not issued in a potentially abusive situation (as defined in § 1.1274–3); and

(iv) No payment from the buyer-borrower to the seller-lender designated as points or interest is made at the time of issuance of the debt instrument.

(2) Exceptions under sections 1274(c)(1)(B), 1274(c)(3), 1274A(c), and 1275(b)(1)—(i) In general. Sections 1274(c)(1)(B), 1274(c)(3), 1274A(c), and 1275(b)(1) describe certain transactions to which section 1274 does not apply. This paragraph (b)(2) provides certain rules to be used in applying those exceptions.

(ii) Special rules for certain exceptions under section 1274(c)(3)—(A) Determination of sales price for certain sales of farms. For purposes of section 1274(c)(3)(A), the determination as to whether the sales price cannot exceed $1,000,000 is made without regard to any other exception to, or limitation on, the applicability of section 1274 (e.g., without regard to the special rules regarding sales of principal residences and land transfers between related persons). In addition, the sales price is determined without regard to section 1274 and without regard to any stated interest. The sales price includes the amount of any liability included in the amount realized from the sale or exchange. See § 1.1001–2.

(B) Sales involving total payments of $250,000 or less. Under section 1274(c)(3)(C), the determination of the amount of payments due under all debt instruments and the amount of other consideration to be received is made as of the date of the sale or exchange or, if earlier, the contract date. If the precise amount due under any debt instrument or the precise amount of any other consideration to be received cannot be determined as of that date, section 1274(c)(3)(C) applies only if it can be determined that the maximum of the aggregate amount of payments due under the debt instruments and other consideration to be received cannot exceed $250,000. For purposes of section 1274(c)(3)(C), if a liability is assumed or property is taken subject to a liability, the aggregate amount of payments due includes the outstanding principal balance or adjusted issue price (in the case of an obligation originally issued at a discount) of the obligation.

* * *

(3) Other exceptions to section 1274—(i) Holders of certain below-market instruments. Section 1274 does not apply to any holder of a debt instrument that is issued in consideration for the sale or exchange of personal use property (within the meaning of section 1275(b)(3)) in the hands of the issuer and that evidences a below-market loan described in section 7872(c)(1).

(ii) Transactions involving certain demand loans. Section 1274 does not apply to any debt instrument that evidences a demand loan that is a below-market loan described in section 7872(c)(1).

(iii) Certain transfers subject to section 1041. Section 1274 does not apply to any debt instrument issued in consideration for a transfer of property subject to section 1041 (relating to transfers of property between spouses or incident to divorce).

(c) Examples. The following examples illustrate the rules of this section.

Example 1. Single stated rate paid semiannually. A debt instrument issued in consideration for the sale of nonpublicly traded property in a transaction that is not a potentially abusive situation calls for the payment of a principal amount of $1,000,000 at the end of a 10–year term and 20 semiannual interest payments of $60,000. Assume that the test rate of interest is 12 percent, compounded semiannually. The debt instrument is not subject to section 1274 because it provides for interest equal to the test rate and all interest payable on the instrument is qualified stated interest.

Example 2. Sale of farm for debt instrument with contingent interest—(i) Facts. On July 1, 1995, A, an individual, sells to B land used as a farm within the meaning of section 6420(c)(2). As partial consideration for the sale, B issues a debt instrument calling for a single $500,000 payment due in 10 years unless profits from the land in each of the 10 years preceding maturity of the debt instrument exceed a specified amount, in which case B is to make a payment of $1,200,000. The debt instrument does not provide for interest.

(ii) Total payments may exceed $1,000,000. Even though the total payments ultimately payable under the contract may be less than $1,000,000, at the time of the sale or exchange it cannot be determined that the sales price cannot exceed $1,000,000. Thus, the sale of the land used as a farm is not an excepted transaction described in section 1274(c)(3)(A).

Example 3. Sale between related parties subject to section 483(e)—(i) Facts. On July 1, 1995, A, an individual, sells land (not used as a farm within the meaning of section 6420(c)(2)) to A's child B for $650,000. In consideration for the sale, B issues a 10–year debt instrument to A that calls for a payment of $650,000. No other consideration is given. The debt instrument does not provide for interest.

(ii) Treatment of debt instrument. For purposes of section 483(e), the $650,000 debt instrument is treated as two separate debt instruments: a $500,000 debt instrument and a $150,000 debt instrument. The $500,000 debt instrument is subject to section 483(e), and accordingly is covered by the exception from section 1274 described in section 1274(c)(3)(F). Because the amount of the payments due as consideration for the sale exceeds $250,000, however, the $150,000 debt instrument is subject to section 1274.

[T.D. 8517, 59 FR 4799, Feb. 2, 1994]

§ 1.1274–2 Issue price of debt instruments to which section 1274 applies.

(a) In general. If section 1274 applies to a debt instrument, section 1274 and this section determine the issue price of the debt instrument. For rules relating to the determination of the amount and timing of OID to be included in income, see section 1272 and the regulations thereunder.

(b) Issue price—(1) Debt instruments that provide for adequate stated interest; stated principal amount. The issue price of a debt instrument that provides for adequate stated interest is the stated principal amount of the debt instrument. For purposes of section 1274, the stated principal amount of a debt instrument is the aggregate amount of all payments due under the debt instrument, excluding any amount of stated interest. * * *

(2) Debt instruments that do not provide for adequate stated interest; imputed principal amount. The issue price of a debt instrument that does not provide for adequate stated interest is the imputed principal amount of the debt instrument.

(3) Debt instruments issued in a potentially abusive situation; fair market value. Notwithstanding paragraphs (b)(1) and (b)(2) of this section, in the case of a debt instrument issued in a potentially abusive situation (as defined in § 1.1274–3), the issue price of the debt instrument is the fair market value of the property received in exchange for the debt instrument, reduced by the fair market value of any consideration other than the debt instrument issued in consideration for the sale or exchange.

(c) Determination of whether a debt instrument provides for adequate stated interest—(1) In general. A debt instrument provides for adequate stated interest if its stated principal amount is less than or equal to its imputed principal amount. Imputed principal amount means the sum of the present values, as of the issue date, of all payments, including payments of stated interest, due under the debt instrument * * *. If a debt instrument has a single fixed rate of interest that is paid or compounded at least annually, and that rate is equal to or greater than the test rate, the debt instrument has adequate stated interest.

(2) Determination of present value. The present value of a payment is determined by discounting the payment from the date it becomes due to the date of the sale or exchange at the test rate of interest. To determine present value, a compounding period must be selected, and the test rate must be based on the same compounding period.

* * *

[T.D. 8517, 59 FR 4799, Feb. 2, 1994, as amended by T.D. 8674, 61 FR 30133, June 14, 1996]

§ 1.1274–3 Potentially abusive situations defined.

(a) In general. For purposes of section 1274, a potentially abusive situation means—

(1) A tax shelter (as defined in section 6662(d)(2)(C)(ii)); or

(2) Any other situation involving—

(i) A recent sales transaction;

(ii) Nonrecourse financing;

(iii) Financing with a term in excess of the useful life of the property; or

(iv) A debt instrument with clearly excessive interest.

(b) Operating rules—(1) Debt instrument exchanged for nonrecourse financing. Nonrecourse financing does not include an exchange of a nonrecourse debt instrument for an outstanding recourse or nonrecourse debt instrument.

(2) Nonrecourse debt with substantial down payment. Nonrecourse financing does not include a sale or exchange of a real property interest financed by a nonrecourse debt instrument if, in addition to the nonrecourse debt instrument, the purchaser makes a down payment in money that equals or exceeds 20 percent of the total stated purchase price of the real property interest. For purposes of the preceding sentence, a real property interest means any interest, other than an interest solely as a creditor, in real property.

(3) Clearly excessive interest. Interest on a debt instrument is clearly excessive if the interest, in light of the terms of the debt instrument and the creditworthiness of the borrower, is clearly greater than the arm's length amount of interest that would have been charged in a cash lending transaction between the same two parties.

* * *

(c) Other situations to be specified by Commissioner. The Commissioner may designate in the Internal Revenue Bulletin situations that, although described in paragraph (a)(2) of this section, will not be treated as potentially abusive because they do not have the effect of significantly misstating basis or amount realized * * *.

(d) Consistency rule. The issuer's determination that the debt instrument is or is not issued in a potentially abusive situation is binding on all holders of the debt instrument. However, the issuer's determination is not binding on a holder who explicitly discloses a position that is inconsistent with the issuer's determination. Unless otherwise prescribed by the Commissioner, the disclosure must be made on a statement attached to the holder's timely filed Federal income tax return for the taxable year that includes the acquisition date of the debt instrument. * * *

[T.D. 8517, 59 FR 4799, Feb. 2, 1994; T.D. 9599, 77 FR 56333, Sept. 13, 2012]

§ 1.1274-4 Test rate.

(a) Determination of test rate of interest—(1) In general—(i) Test rate is the 3-month rate. Except as provided in paragraph (a)(2) of this section, the test rate of interest for a debt instrument issued in consideration for the sale or exchange of property is the 3-month rate.

(ii) The 3-month rate. Except as provided in paragraph (a)(1)(iii) of this section, the 3-month rate is the lower of—

(A) The lowest applicable Federal rate (based on the appropriate compounding period) in effect during the 3-month period ending with the first month in which there is a binding written contract that substantially sets forth the terms under which the sale or exchange is ultimately consummated; or

(B) The lowest applicable Federal rate (based on the appropriate compounding period) in effect during the 3-month period ending with the month in which the sale or exchange occurs.

(iii) Special rule if there is no binding written contract. If there is no binding written contract that substantially sets forth the terms under which the sale or exchange is ultimately consummated, the 3-month rate is the lowest applicable Federal rate (based on the appropriate compounding period) in effect during the 3-month period ending with the month in which the sale or exchange occurs.

(2) Test rate for certain debt instruments—(i) Sale-leaseback transactions. Under section 1274(e) (relating to certain sale-leaseback transactions), the test rate is 110 percent of the 3-month rate determined under paragraph (a)(1) of this section. For purposes of section 1274(e)(3), related party means a person related to the transferor within the meaning of section 267(b) or 707(b)(1).

(ii) Qualified debt instrument. Under section 1274A(a), the test rate for a qualified debt instrument is no greater than 9 percent, compounded semiannually, or an equivalent rate based on an appropriate compounding period.

* * *

(b) Applicable Federal rate. Except as otherwise provided in this section, the applicable Federal rate for a debt instrument is based on the term of the instrument (i.e., short-term, mid-term, or long-term). See section 1274(d)(1). The Internal Revenue Service publishes the applicable Federal rates for each month in the Internal Revenue Bulletin (see § 601.601(d)(2)(ii) of this chapter). The applicable Federal rates are based on the yield to maturity of outstanding marketable obligations of the United States of similar maturities during the one month period ending on the 14th day of the month preceding the month for which the rates are applicable.

* * *

[T.D. 8517, 59 FR 4799, Feb. 2, 1994]

READJUSTMENT OF TAX BETWEEN YEARS AND SPECIAL LIMITATIONS

§ 1.1341-1 Restoration of amounts received or accrued under claim of right.

(a) In general. **(1)** If, during the taxable year, the taxpayer is entitled under other provisions of chapter 1 of the Internal Revenue Code of 1954 to a deduction of more than $3,000 because of the restoration to another of an item which was included in the taxpayer's gross income for a prior taxable year (or years) under a claim of right, the tax imposed by chapter 1 of the Internal Revenue Code of 1954 for the taxable year shall be the tax provided in paragraph (b) of this section.

(2) For the purpose of this section "income included under a claim of right" means an item included in gross income because it appeared from all the facts available in the year of inclusion that the taxpayer had an unrestricted right to such item, and "restoration to another" means a restoration resulting because it was established after the close of such prior taxable year (or years) that the taxpayer did not have an unrestricted right to such item (or portion thereof).

(3) For purposes of determining whether the amount of a deduction described in section 1341(a)(2) exceeds $3,000 for the taxable year, there shall be taken into account the aggregate of all such deductions with respect to each item of income (described in section 1341(a)(1)) of the same class.

(b) Determination of tax. **(1)** Under the circumstances described in paragraph (a) of this section, the tax imposed by chapter 1 of the Internal Revenue Code * * * for the taxable year shall be the lesser of:

(i) The tax for the taxable year computed under section 1341(a)(4), that is, with the deduction taken into account, or

(ii) The tax for the taxable year computed under section 1341(a)(5), that is, without taking such deduction into account, minus the decrease in tax * * * for the prior taxable year (or years) which would result solely from the exclusion from gross income of all or that portion of the income included under a claim of right to which the deduction is attributable. For the purpose of this subdivision, the amount of the decrease in tax is not limited to the amount of the tax for the taxable year. See paragraph (i) of this section where the decrease in tax for the prior taxable year (or years) exceeds the tax for the taxable year.

* * *

(c) Application to deductions which are capital in nature. Section 1341 and this section shall also apply to a deduction which is capital in nature otherwise allowable in the taxable year. If the deduction otherwise allowable is capital in nature, the determination of whether the taxpayer is entitled to the benefits of section 1341 and this section shall be made without regard to the net capital loss limitation imposed by section 1211. For example, if a taxpayer restores $4,000 in the taxable year and such amount is a long-term capital loss, the taxpayer will, nevertheless, be considered to have met the $3,000 deduction requirement for purposes of applying this section, although the full amount of the loss might not be allowable as a deduction for the taxable year. However, if the tax for the taxable year is computed with the deduction taken into account, the deduction allowable will be subject to the limitation on capital losses provided in section 1211, and the capital loss carryover provided in section 1212.

* * *

(e) Method of accounting. The provisions of section 1341 and this section shall be applicable in the case of a taxpayer on the cash receipts and disbursements method of accounting only to the taxable year in which the item of income included in a prior year (or years) under a claim of right is actually repaid. However, in the case of a taxpayer on the cash receipts and disbursements method of accounting who constructively received an item of income under a claim of right and included such item of income in gross income in a prior year (or years), the provisions of section 1341 and this section shall be applicable to the taxable year in which the taxpayer is required to relinquish his right to receive such item of income. Such provisions shall be applicable in the case of other taxpayers only to the taxable year which is the proper taxable year (under the method of accounting used by the taxpayer in computing taxable income) for taking into account the deduction resulting from the restoration of the item of income included in a prior year (or years) under a claim of right. For example, if the taxpayer is on an accrual method of accounting, the provisions of this section shall apply to the year in which the obligation properly accrues for the repayment of the item included under a claim of right.

(f) Inventory items, stock in trade, and property held primarily for sale in the ordinary course of trade or business. (1) Except for amounts specified in subparagraphs (2) and (3) of this paragraph, the provisions of section 1341 and this section do not apply to deductions attributable to items which were included in gross income by reason of the sale or other disposition of stock in trade of the taxpayer (or other property of a kind which would properly have been included in the inventory of the taxpayer if on hand at the close of the prior taxable year) or property held by the taxpayer primarily for sale to customers in the ordinary course of the taxpayer's trade or business. This section is, therefore, not applicable to sales returns and allowances and similar items.

* * *

(h) Legal fees and other expenses. Section 1341 and this section do not apply to legal fees or other expenses incurred by a taxpayer in contesting the restoration of an item previously included in income. This rule may be illustrated by the following example:

Example. A sold his personal residence to B in a prior taxable year and realized a capital gain on the sale. C claimed that under an agreement with A he was entitled to a 5-percent share of the purchase price since he brought the parties together and was instrumental in closing the sale. A rejected C's demand and included the entire amount of the capital gain in gross income for the year of sale. C instituted action and in the taxable year judgment is rendered against A who pays C the amount involved. In addition, A pays legal fees in the taxable year which were incurred in the defense of the action. Section 1341 applies to the payment of the 5-percent share of the purchase price to C. However, the payment of the legal fees, whether or not otherwise deductible, does not constitute an item restored for purposes of section 1341(a) and paragraph (a) of this section.

(i) Refunds. If the decrease in tax for the prior taxable year (or years) determined under section 1341(a)(5)(B) and paragraph (b)(1)(ii) of this section exceeds the tax imposed by chapter 1 of the Code for the taxable year computed without the deduction, and for taxable years beginning after December 31, 1961, if such excess is greater than the decrease in tax for the taxable year (or years) to which the net operating loss described in section 1341(b)(4)(A) and paragraph (b)(1)(iii) of this section is carried back, such excess shall be considered to be a payment of tax for the taxable year of restoration. Such payment is deemed to have been made on the last day prescribed by law for the payment of tax for the taxable year and shall be refunded or credited in the same manner as if it were an overpayment of tax for such taxable year. However, no interest shall be allowed or paid if such an excess results from the application of section 1341(a)(5)(B) in the case of a deduction described in paragraph (f)(3) of this section (relating to payments or repayments pursuant to price redetermination). * * *

[T.D. 6500, 25 FR 12049, Nov. 26, 1960, as amended by T.D. 6617, 27 FR 10824, Nov. 7, 1962; T.D. 6747, 29 FR 9790, July 21, 1964; T.D. 7244, 37 FR 28897, Dec. 30, 1972; T.D. 7564, 43 FR 40496, Sept. 12, 1978; T.D. 8677, 61 FR 33321, June 27, 1996]

TAX TREATMENT OF S CORPORATIONS AND THEIR SHAREHOLDERS

§ 1.1361–1 S corporation defined.

(a) In general. For purposes of this title, with respect to any taxable year—(1) The term S corporation means a small business corporation (as defined in paragraph (b) of this section) for which an election under section 1362(a) is in effect for that taxable year.

(2) The term C corporation means a corporation that is not an S corporation for that taxable year.

(b) Small business corporation defined—(1) In general. * * *

* * *

(3) Treatment of restricted stock. For purposes of subchapter S, stock that is issued in connection with the performance of services (within the meaning of section 1.83–3(f)) and that is substantially nonvested (within the meaning of section 1.83–3(b)) is not treated as outstanding stock of the corporation, and the holder of that stock is not treated as a shareholder solely by reason of holding the stock, unless the holder makes an election with respect to the stock under section 83(b). In the event of such an election, the stock is treated as outstanding stock of the corporation, and the holder of the stock is treated as a shareholder for purposes of subchapter S. See paragraphs (*l*)(1) and (3) of this section for rules for determining whether substantially nonvested stock with respect to which an election under section 83(b) has been made is treated as a second class of stock.

(4) Treatment of deferred compensation plans. For purposes of subchapter S, an instrument, obligation, or arrangement is not outstanding stock if it—

(i) Does not convey the right to vote;

(ii) Is an unfunded and unsecured promise to pay money or property in the future;

(iii) Is issued to an individual who is an employee in connection with the performance of services for the corporation or to an individual who is an independent contractor in connection with the performance of services for the corporation (and is not excessive by reference to the services performed); and

(iv) Is issued pursuant to a plan with respect to which the employee or independent contractor is not taxed currently on income.

A deferred compensation plan that has a current payment feature (e.g., payment of dividend equivalent amounts that are taxed currently as compensation) is not for that reason excluded from this paragraph (b)(4).

(5) Treatment of straight debt. For purposes of subchapter S, an instrument or obligation that satisfies the definition of straight debt in paragraph (*l*)(5) of this section is not treated as outstanding stock.

* * *

(*l*) Classes of stock—(1) General rule. A corporation that has more than one class of stock does not qualify as a small business corporation. Except as provided in paragraph (*l*)(4) of this section (relating to instruments, obligations, or arrangements treated as a second class of stock), a corporation is treated as having only one class of stock if all outstanding shares of stock of the corporation confer identical rights to distribution and liquidation proceeds. Differences in voting rights among shares of stock of a corporation are disregarded in determining whether a corporation has more than one class of stock. Thus, if all shares of stock of an S corporation have identical rights to distribution and liquidation proceeds, the corporation may have voting and nonvoting common stock, a class of stock that may vote only on certain issues, irrevocable proxy agreements, or groups of shares that differ with respect to rights to elect members of the board of directors.

(2) Determination of whether stock confers identical rights to distribution and liquidation proceeds—(i) In general. The determination of whether all outstanding shares of stock confer identical rights to distribution and liquidation proceeds is made based on the corporate charter, articles of incorporation, bylaws, applicable state law, and binding agreements relating to distribution and liquidation proceeds (collectively, the governing provisions). A commercial contractual agreement, such as a lease, employment agreement, or loan agreement, is not a binding agreement relating to distribution and liquidation proceeds and thus is not a governing provision unless a principal purpose of the agreement is to circumvent the one class of stock requirement of section 1361(b)(1)(D) and this paragraph (*l*). Although a corporation is not treated as having more than one class of stock so long as the governing provisions provide for identical distribution and liquidation rights, any distributions (including actual, constructive, or deemed distributions) that differ in timing or amount are to be given appropriate tax effect in accordance with the facts and circumstances.

(ii) State law requirements for payment and withholding of income tax. State laws may require a corporation to pay or withhold state income taxes on behalf of some or all of the corporation's shareholders. Such laws are disregarded in determining whether all outstanding shares of stock of the corporation confer identical rights to distribution and liquidation proceeds, within the meaning of paragraph (*l*)(1) of this section, provided that, when the constructive distributions resulting from the payment or withholding of taxes by the corporation are taken into account, the outstanding shares confer identical rights to distribution and liquidation proceeds. A difference in timing between the constructive distributions and the actual distributions to the other shareholders does not cause the corporation to be treated as having more than one class of stock.

(iii) Buy-sell and redemption agreements—(A) In general. Buy-sell agreements among shareholders, agreements restricting the transferability of stock, and redemption agreements are disregarded in determining whether a corporation's outstanding shares of stock confer identical distribution and liquidation rights unless—

(1) A principal purpose of the agreement is to circumvent the one class of stock requirement of section 1361(b)(1)(D) and this paragraph (*l*), and

(2) The agreement establishes a purchase price that, at the time the agreement is entered into, is significantly in excess of or below the fair market value of the stock.

Agreements that provide for the purchase or redemption of stock at book value or at a price between fair market value and book value are not considered to establish a price that is significantly in excess of or below the fair market value of the stock and, thus, are disregarded in determining whether the outstanding shares of stock confer identical rights. For purposes of this paragraph (*l*)(2)(iii)(A), a good faith determination of fair market value will be respected unless it can be shown that the value was substantially in error and the determination of the value was not performed with reasonable diligence. Although an agreement may be disregarded in determining whether shares of stock confer identical distribution and liquidation rights, payments pursuant to the agreement may have income or transfer tax consequences.

(B) Exception for certain agreements. Bona fide agreements to redeem or purchase stock at the time of death, divorce, disability, or termination of employment are disregarded in determining whether a corporation's shares of stock confer identical rights. In addition, if stock that is substantially nonvested (within the meaning of section 1.83–3(b)) is treated as outstanding under these regulations, the forfeiture provisions that cause the stock to be substantially nonvested are disregarded. Furthermore, the Commissioner may provide by Revenue Ruling or other published guidance that other types of bona fide agreements to redeem or purchase stock are disregarded.

(C) Safe harbors for determinations of book value. A determination of book value will be respected if—

(1) The book value is determined in accordance with Generally Accepted Accounting Principles (including permitted optional adjustments); or

(2) The book value is used for any substantial nontax purpose.

(iv) Distributions that take into account varying interests in stock during a taxable year. A governing provision does not, within the meaning of paragraph (*l*)(2)(i) of this section, alter the rights to liquidation and distribution proceeds conferred by an S corporation's stock merely because the governing provision provides that, as a result of a change in stock ownership, distributions in a taxable year are to be made on the basis of the shareholders' varying interests in the S corporation's income in the current or immediately preceding taxable year. If distributions pursuant to the provision are not made within a reasonable time after the close of the taxable year in which the varying interests occur, the distributions may be recharacterized depending on the facts and circumstances, but will not result in a second class of stock.

* * *

(vi) Examples. The application of paragraph (*l*)(2) of this section may be illustrated by the following examples. In each of the examples, the S corporation requirements of section 1361 are satisfied except as otherwise stated, the corporation has in effect an S election under section 1362, and the corporation has only the shareholders described.

Example 1. Determination of whether stock confers identical rights to distribution and liquidation proceeds. **(i)** The law of State A requires that permission be obtained from the State Commissioner of Corporations before stock may be issued by a corporation. The Commissioner grants permission to S, a corporation, to issue its stock subject to the restriction that any person who is issued stock in exchange for property, and not cash, must waive all rights to receive distributions until the shareholders who contributed cash for stock have received distributions in the amount of their cash contributions.

(ii) The condition imposed by the Commissioner pursuant to state law alters the rights to distribution and liquidation proceeds conferred by the outstanding stock of S so that those rights are not identical. Accordingly, under paragraph (*l*)(2)(i) of this section, S is treated as having more than one class of stock and does not qualify as a small business corporation.

Example 2. Distributions that differ in timing. **(i)** S, a corporation, has two equal shareholders, A and B. Under S's bylaws, A and B are entitled to equal distributions. S distributes $50,000 to A in the current year, but does not distribute $50,000 to B until one year later. The circumstances indicate that the difference in timing did not occur by reason of a binding agreement relating to distribution or liquidation proceeds.

(ii) Under paragraph (*l*)(2)(i) of this section, the difference in timing of the distributions to A and B does not cause S to be treated as having more than one class of stock. However, section 7872 or other recharacterization principles may apply to determine the appropriate tax consequences.

Example 3. Treatment of excessive compensation. **(i)** S, a corporation, has two equal shareholders, C and D, who are each employed by S and have binding employment agreements with S. The compensation paid by S to C under C's employment agreement is reasonable. The compensation paid by S to D under D's employment agreement, however, is found to be excessive. The facts and circumstances do not reflect that a principal purpose to D's employment agreement is to circumvent the one class of stock requirement of section 1361(b)(1)(D) and this paragraph (*l*).

(ii) Under paragraph (*l*)(2)(i) of this section, the employment agreements are not governing provisions. Accordingly, S is not treated as having more than one class of stock by reason of the employment agreements, even though S is not allowed a deduction for the excessive compensation paid to D.

Example 4. Agreement to pay fringe benefits. (i) S, a corporation, is required under binding agreements to pay accident and health insurance premiums on behalf of certain of its employees who are also shareholders. Different premium amounts are paid by S for each employee-shareholder. The facts and circumstances do not reflect that a principal purpose of the agreements is to circumvent the one class of stock requirement of section 1361(b)(1)(D) and this paragraph (*l*).

(ii) Under paragraph (*l*)(2)(i) of this section, the agreements are not governing provisions. Accordingly, S is not treated as having more than one class of stock by reason of the agreements. In addition, S is not treated as having more than one class of stock by reason of the payment of fringe benefits.

Example 5. Below-market corporation-shareholder loan. (i) E is a shareholder of S, a corporation. S makes a below-market loan to E that is a corporation-shareholder loan to which section 7872 applies. Under section 7872, E is deemed to receive a distribution with respect to S stock by reason of the loan. The facts and circumstances do not reflect that a principal purpose of the loan is to circumvent the one class of stock requirement of section 1361(b)(1)(D) and this paragraph (*l*).

(ii) Under paragraph (*l*)(2)(i) of this section, the loan agreement is not a governing provision. Accordingly, S is not treated as having more than one class of stock by reason of the below-market loan to E.

Example 6. Agreement to adjust distributions for state tax burdens. (i) S, a corporation, executes a binding agreement with its shareholders to modify its normal distribution policy by making upward adjustments of its distributions to those shareholders who bear heavier state tax burdens. The adjustments are based on a formula that will give the shareholders equal after-tax distributions.

(ii) The binding agreement relates to distribution or liquidation proceeds. The agreement is thus a governing provision that alters the rights conferred by the outstanding stock of S to distribution proceeds so that those rights are not identical. Therefore, under paragraph (*l*)(2)(i) of this section, S is treated as having more than one class of stock.

Example 7. State law requirements for payment and withholding of income tax. (i) The law of State X requires corporations to pay state income taxes on behalf of nonresident shareholders. The law of State X does not require corporations to pay state income taxes on behalf of resident shareholders. S is incorporated in State X. S's resident shareholders have the right (for example, under the law of State X or pursuant to S's bylaws or a binding agreement) to distributions that take into account the payments S makes on behalf of its nonresident shareholders.

(ii) The payment by S of state income taxes on behalf of its nonresident shareholders are generally treated as constructive distributions to those shareholders. Because S's resident shareholders have the right to equal distributions, taking into account the constructive distributions to the nonresident shareholders, S's shares confer identical rights to distribution proceeds. Accordingly, under paragraph (*l*)(2)(ii) of this section, the state law requiring S to pay state income taxes on behalf of its nonresident shareholders is disregarded in determining whether S has more than one class of stock.

(iii) The same result would follow if the payments of state income taxes on behalf of nonresident shareholders are instead treated as advances to those shareholders and the governing provisions require the advances to be repaid or offset by reductions in distributions to those shareholders.

Example 8. Redemption agreements. (i) F, G, and H are shareholders of S, a corporation. F is also an employee of S. By agreement, S is to redeem F's shares on the termination of F's employment.

(ii) On these facts, under paragraph (*l*)(2)(iii)(B) of this section, the agreement is disregarded in determining whether all outstanding shares of S's stock confer identical rights to distribution and liquidation proceeds.

Example 9. Analysis of redemption agreements. (i) J, K, and L are shareholders of S, a corporation. L is also an employee of S. L's shares were not issued to L in connection with the performance of services. By agreement, S is to redeem L's shares for an amount significantly below their fair market value on the termination of L's employment or if S's sales fall below certain levels.

(ii) Under paragraph (*l*)(2)(iii)(B) of this section, the portion of the agreement providing for redemption of L's stock on termination of employment is disregarded. Under paragraph (*l*)(2)(iii)(A), the portion of the agreement providing for redemption of L's stock if S's sales fall below certain levels is disregarded unless a principal purpose of that portion of the agreement is to circumvent the one class of stock requirement of section 1361(b)(1)(D) and this paragraph (*l*).

(3) Stock taken into account. Except as provided in paragraphs (b)(3), (4), and (5) of this section (relating to restricted stock, deferred compensation plans, and straight debt), in determining whether all outstanding shares of stock confer identical rights to distribution and liquidation proceeds, all outstanding shares of stock of a corporation are taken into account. For example, substantially nonvested stock with respect to which an election under section 83(b) has been made is taken into account in determining whether a corporation has a second class of stock, and such stock is not treated as a second class of stock if the stock confers rights to distribution and liquidation proceeds that are identical, within the meaning of paragraph (*l*)(1) of this section, to the rights conferred by the other outstanding shares of stock.

(4) Other instruments, obligations, or arrangements treated as a second class of stock—(i) In general. Instruments, obligations, or arrangements are not treated as a second class of stock for purposes of this paragraph (*l*) unless they are described in paragraph (*l*)(5)(ii) or (iii) of this section. However, in no event are instruments, obligations, or arrangements described in paragraph (b)(4) of this section (relating to deferred compensation plans), paragraphs (*l*)(4)(iii)(B) and (C) of this section (relating to the exceptions and safe harbor for options), paragraph (*l*)(4)(ii)(B) of this section (relating to the safe harbors for certain short-term unwritten advances and proportionally-held debt), or paragraph (*l*)(5) of this section (relating to the safe harbor for straight debt), treated as a second class of stock for purposes of this paragraph (*l*).

(ii) Instruments, obligations, or arrangements treated as equity under general principles—(A) In general. Except as provided in paragraph (*l*)(4)(i) of this section, any instrument, obligation, or arrangement issued by a corporation (other than outstanding shares of stock described in paragraph (*l*)(3) of this section), regardless of whether designated as debt, is treated as a second class of stock of the corporation—

(1) If the instrument, obligation, or arrangement constitutes equity or otherwise results in the holder being treated as the owner of stock under general principles of Federal tax law; and

(2) A principal purpose of issuing or entering into the instrument, obligation, or arrangement is to circumvent the rights to distribution or liquidation proceeds conferred by the outstanding shares of stock or to circumvent the limitation on eligible shareholders contained in paragraph (b)(1) of this section.

(B) Safe harbor for certain short-term unwritten advances and proportionately held obligations—(1) Short-term unwritten advances. Unwritten advances from a shareholder that do not exceed $10,000 in the aggregate at any time during the taxable year of the corporation, are treated as debt by the parties, and are expected to be repaid within a reasonable time are not treated as a second class of stock for that taxable year, even if the advances are considered equity under general principles of Federal tax law. The failure of an unwritten advance to meet this safe harbor will not result in a second class of stock unless the advance is considered equity under paragraph (*l*)(4)(ii)(A)(1) of this section and a principal purpose of the advance is to circumvent the rights of the outstanding shares of stock or the limitation on eligible shareholders under paragraph (*l*)(4)(ii)(A)(2) of this section.

(2) Proportionately-held obligations. Obligations of the same class that are considered equity under general principles of Federal tax law, but are owned solely by the owners of, and in the same proportion as, the outstanding stock of the corporation, are not treated as a second class of stock. Furthermore, an obligation or obligations owned by the sole shareholder of a corporation are always held proportionately to the corporation's outstanding stock. The obligations that are considered equity that do not meet this safe harbor will not result in a second class of stock unless a principal purpose of the obligations is to circumvent the rights of the outstanding shares of stock or the limitation on eligible shareholders under paragraph (*l*)(4)(ii)(A)(2) of this section.

(iii) Certain call options, warrants or similar instruments—(A) In general. Except as otherwise provided in this paragraph (*l*)(4)(iii), a call option, warrant, or similar instrument (collectively, call option) issued by a corporation is treated as a second class of stock of the corporation if, taking into account all the facts and circumstances, the call option is substantially certain to be exercised (by the holder or a potential transferee) and has a strike price substantially below the fair market value of the underlying stock on the date that the call option is issued, transferred by a person who is an eligible shareholder under paragraph (b)(1) of this section to a person who is not an eligible shareholder under paragraph (b)(1) of this section, or materially modified. For purposes of this paragraph (*l*)(4)(iii), if an option is issued in connection with a loan and the time period in which the option can be exercised is extended in connection with (and consistent with) a modification of the terms of the loan, the extension of the time period in which the option may be exercised is not considered a material modification. In addition, a call option does not have a strike price substantially below fair market value if the price at the time of exercise cannot, pursuant to the terms of the instrument, be substantially below the fair market value of the underlying stock at the time of exercise.

(B) Certain exceptions. (1) A call option is not treated as a second class of stock for purposes of this paragraph (*l*) if it is issued to a person that is actively and regularly engaged in the business of lending and issued in connection with a commercially reasonable loan to the corporation. This paragraph (*l*)(4)(iii)(B)(1) continues to apply if the call option is transferred with the loan (or if a portion of the call option is transferred with a corresponding portion of the loan). However, if the call option is transferred without a corresponding portion of the loan, this paragraph (*l*)(4)(iii)(B)(*1*) ceases to apply. Upon that transfer, the call option is tested under paragraph (*l*)(4)(iii)(A) (notwithstanding anything in that paragraph to the contrary) if, but for this paragraph, the call option would have been treated as a second class of stock on the date it was issued.

(2) A call option that is issued to an individual who is either an employee or an independent contractor in connection with the performance of services for the corporation or a related corporation (and that is not excessive by reference to the services performed) is not treated as a second class of stock for purposes of this paragraph (*l*) if—

(i) The call option is nontransferable within the meaning of section 1.83–3(d); and

(ii) The call option does not have a readily ascertainable fair market value as defined in section 1.83–7(b) at the time the option is issued.

If the call option becomes transferable, this paragraph (*l*)(4)(iii)(B)(*2*) ceases to apply. Solely for purposes of this paragraph (*l*)(4)(iii)(B)(*2*), a corporation is related to the issuing corporation if more than 50 percent of the total voting power and total value of its stock is owned by the issuing corporation.

(3) The Commissioner may provide other exceptions by Revenue Ruling or other published guidance.

(C) Safe harbor for certain options. A call option is not treated as a second class of stock if, on the date the call option is issued, transferred by a person who is an eligible shareholder under paragraph (b)(1) of this section to a person who is not an eligible shareholder under paragraph (b)(1) of this section, or materially modified, the strike price of the call option is at least 90 percent of the fair market value of the underlying stock on that date. For purposes of this paragraph (*l*)(4)(iii)(C), a good faith determination of fair market value by the corporation will be respected unless it can be shown that the value was substantially in error and the determination of the value was not performed with reasonable diligence to obtain a fair value. Failure of an option to meet this safe harbor will not necessarily result in the option being treated as a second class of stock.

(iv) Convertible debt. A convertible debt instrument is considered a second class of stock if—

(A) It would be treated as a second class of stock under paragraph (*l*)(4)(ii) of this section (relating to instruments, obligations, or arrangements treated as equity under general principles); or

(B) It embodies rights equivalent to those of a call option that would be treated as a second class of stock under paragraph (*l*)(4)(iii) of this section (relating to certain call options, warrants, and similar instruments).

(v) Examples. The application of this paragraph (*l*)(4) may be illustrated by the following examples. In each of the examples, the S corporation requirements of section 1361 are satisfied except as otherwise stated, the corporation has in effect an S election under section 1362, and the corporation has only the shareholders described.

Example 1. Transfer of call option by eligible shareholder to ineligible shareholder. **(i)** S, a corporation, has 10 shareholders. S issues call options to A, B, and C, individuals who are U.S. residents. A, B, and C are not shareholders, employees, or independent contractors of S. The options have a strike price of $40 and are issued on a date when the fair market value of S stock is also $40. A year later, P, a partnership, purchases A's option. On the date of transfer, the fair market value of S stock is $80.

(ii) On the date the call option is issued, its strike price is not substantially below the fair market value of the S stock. Under paragraph (*l*)(4)(iii)(A) of this section, whether a call option is a second class of stock must be redetermined if the call option is transferred by a person who is an eligible shareholder under paragraph (b)(1) of this section to a person who is not an eligible shareholder under paragraph (b)(1) of this section. In this case, A is an eligible shareholder of S under paragraph (b)(1) of this section, but P is not. Accordingly, the option is retested on the date it is transferred to D.

(iii) Because on the date the call option is transferred to P its strike price is 50% of the fair market value, the strike price is substantially below the fair market value of the S stock. Accordingly, the call option is treated as a second class of stock as of the date it is transferred to P if, at that time, it is determined that the option is substantially certain to be exercised. The determination of whether the option is substantially certain to be exercised is made on the basis of all the facts and circumstances.

Example 2. Call option issued in connection with the performance of services. **(i)** E is a bona fide employee of S, a corporation. S issues to E a call option in connection with E's performance of services. At the time the call option is issued, it is not transferable and does not have a readily ascertainable fair market value. However, the call option becomes transferable before it is exercised by E.

(ii) While the option is not transferable, under paragraph (*l*)(4)(iii)(B)(*2*) of this section it is not treated as a second class of stock, regardless of its strike price. When the option becomes transferable, that paragraph ceases to apply, and the general rule of paragraph (*l*)(4)(iii)(A) of this section applies. Accordingly, if the option is materially modified or is transferred to a person who is not an eligible shareholder under paragraph (b)(1) of this section, and on the date of such modification or transfer, the option is substantially certain to be exercised and has a strike price substantially below the fair market value of the underlying stock, the option is treated as a second class of stock.

(iii) If E left S's employment before the option became transferable, the exception provided by paragraph (*l*)(4)(iii)(B)(2) would continue to apply until the option became transferable.

(5) Straight debt safe harbor—(i) In general. Notwithstanding paragraph (*l*)(4) of this section, straight debt is not treated as a second class of stock. For purposes of section 1361(c)(5) and this section, the term straight debt means a written unconditional obligation, regardless of whether embodied in a formal note, to pay a sum certain on demand, or on a specified due date, which—

(A) Does not provide for an interest rate or payment dates that are contingent on profits, the borrower's discretion, the payment of dividends with respect to common stock, or similar factors;

(B) Is not convertible (directly or indirectly) into stock or any other equity interest of the S corporation; and

(C) Is held by an individual (other than a nonresident alien), an estate, or a trust described in section 1361(c)(2).

(ii) Subordination. The fact that an obligation is subordinated to other debt of the corporation does not prevent the obligation from qualifying as straight debt.

(iii) Modification or transfer. An obligation that originally qualifies as straight debt ceases to so qualify if the obligation—

(A) Is materially modified so that it no longer satisfies the definition of straight debt; or

(B) Is transferred to a third party who is not an eligible shareholder under paragraph (b)(1) of this section.

(iv) Treatment of straight debt for other purposes. An obligation of an S corporation that satisfies the definition of straight debt in paragraph (*l*)(5)(i) of this section is not treated as a second class of stock even if it is considered equity under general principles of Federal tax law. Such an obligation is generally treated as debt and when so treated is subject to the applicable rules governing indebtedness for other purposes of the Code. Accordingly, interest paid or accrued with respect to a straight debt obligation is generally treated as interest by the corporation and the recipient and does not constitute a distribution to which section 1368 applies. However, if a straight debt obligation bears a rate of interest that is unreasonably high, an appropriate portion of the interest may be recharacterized and treated as a payment that is not interest. Such a recharacterization does not result in a second class of stock.

(v) Treatment of C corporation debt upon conversion to S status. If a C corporation has outstanding an obligation that satisfies the definition of straight debt in paragraph (*l*)(5)(i) of this section, but that is considered equity under general principles of Federal tax law, the obligation is not treated as a second class of stock for purposes of this section if the C corporation converts to S status. In addition, the conversion from C corporation status to S corporation status is not treated as an exchange of debt for stock with respect to such an instrument.

(6) Inadvertent terminations. See section 1362(f) and the regulations thereunder for rules relating to inadvertent terminations in cases where the one class of stock requirement has been inadvertently breached.

* * *

[T.D. 8419, 57 FR 22646, May 29, 1992, as amended by T.D. 8600, 60 FR 37578, July 21, 1995; T.D. 8940, 66 FR 9925, Feb. 13, 2001, T.D. 9078, 68 FR 42251, July 17, 2003; T.D. 9422, 73 FR 47526, Aug. 14, 2008]

§ 1.1362–1 Election to be an S corporation.

(a) In general. Except as provided in § 1.1362–5, a small business corporation as defined in section 1361 may elect to be an S corporation under section 1362(a). An election may be made only with the consent of all of the shareholders of the corporation at the time of the election. See § 1.1362–6(a) for rules concerning the time and manner of making this election.

(b) Years for which election is effective. An election under section 1362(a) is effective for the entire taxable year of the corporation for which it is made and for all succeeding taxable years of the corporation, until the election is terminated.

[T.D. 8449, 57 FR 55445, Nov. 25, 1992]

§ 1.1362–2 Termination of election.

(a) Termination by revocation—(1) In general. An election made under section 1362(a) is terminated if the corporation revokes the election for any taxable year of the corporation for which the election is effective, including the first taxable year. A revocation may be made only with the consent of shareholders who, at the time the revocation is made, hold more than one-half of the number of issued and outstanding shares of stock (including non-voting stock) of the corporation. See § 1.1362–6(a) for rules concerning the time and manner of revoking an election made under section 1362(a).

(2) When effective—(i) In general. Except as provided in paragraph (a)(2)(ii) of this section, a revocation made during the taxable year and before the 16th day of the third month of the taxable year is effective on the first day of the taxable year and a revocation made after the 15th day of the third month of the taxable year is effective for the following taxable year. If a corporation makes an election to be an S corporation that is to be effective beginning with the next taxable year and revokes its election on or before the first day of the next taxable year, the corporation is deemed to have revoked its election on the first day of the next taxable year.

(ii) Revocations specifying a prospective revocation date. If a corporation specifies a date for revocation and the date is expressed in terms of a stated day, month, and year that is on or after the date the revocation is filed, the revocation is effective on and after the date so specified.

(3) Effect on taxable year of corporation. In the case of a corporation that revokes its election to be an S corporation effective on the first day of the first taxable year for which its election is to be effective, any statement made with the election regarding a change in the corporation's taxable year has no effect.

(4) Rescission of a revocation. A corporation may rescind a revocation made under paragraph (a)(2) of this section at any time before the revocation becomes effective. A rescission may be made only with the consent of each person who consented to the revocation and by each person who became a shareholder of the corporation within the period beginning on the first day after the date the revocation was made and ending on the date on which the rescission is made. See § 1.1362–6(a) for rules concerning the time and manner of rescinding a revocation.

(b) Termination by reason of corporation ceasing to be a small business corporation—(1) In general. If a corporation ceases to be a small business corporation, as defined in section 1361(b), at any time on or after the first day of the first taxable year for which its election under section 1362(a) is effective, the election terminates. In the event of a termination under this paragraph (b)(1), the corporation should attach to its return for the taxable year in which the termination occurs a notification that a termination has occurred and the date of the termination.

(2) When effective. If an election terminates because of a specific event that causes the corporation to fail to meet the definition of a small business corporation, the termination is effective as of the date on which the event occurs. If a corporation makes an election to be an S corporation that is effective beginning with the following taxable year and is not a small business corporation on the first day of that following taxable year, the election is treated as having terminated on that first day. If a corporation is a small business corporation on the first day of the taxable year for which its election is effective, its election does not terminate even if the corporation was not a small business corporation during all or part of the period beginning after the date the election was made and ending before the first day of the taxable year for which the election is effective.

(3) Effect on taxable year of corporation. In the case of a corporation that fails to meet the definition of a small business corporation on the first day of the first taxable year for which its election to be an S corporation is to be effective, any statement made with the election regarding a change in the corporation's taxable year has no effect.

(c) Termination by reason of excess passive investment income—(1) In general. A corporation's election under section 1362(a) terminates if the corporation has subchapter C earnings and profits at the close of each of three consecutive taxable years and, for each of those taxable years, has passive investment income in excess of 25 percent of gross receipts. See section 1375 for the tax imposed on excess passive investment income.

(2) When effective. A termination under this paragraph (c) is effective on the first day of the first taxable year beginning after the third consecutive year in which the S corporation had excess passive investment income.

(3) Subchapter C earnings and profits. For purposes of this paragraph (c), subchapter C earnings and profits of a corporation are the earnings and profits of any corporation, including the S corporation or an acquired or predecessor corporation, for any period with respect to which an election under section 1362(a) (or under section 1372 of prior law) was not in effect. The subchapter C earnings and profits of an S corporation are modified as required by section 1371(c).

(4) Gross receipts—(i) In general. For purposes of this paragraph (c), gross receipts generally means the total amount received or accrued under the method of accounting used by the corporation in computing its taxable income and is not reduced by returns and allowances, cost of goods sold, or deductions.

(ii) Special rules for sales of capital assets, stock and securities—(A) Sales of capital assets. For purposes of this paragraph (c), gross receipts from the sales or exchanges of capital assets (as defined in section 1221), other than stock and securities, are taken into account only to the extent of capital gain net income (as defined in section 1222).

(B) Sales of stock or securities—(1) In general. For purposes of this paragraph (c), gross receipts from the sales or exchanges of stock or securities are taken into account only to the extent of gains therefrom. In addition, for purposes of computing gross receipts from sales or exchanges of stock or securities, losses do not offset gains.

(2) Treatment of certain liquidations. Gross receipts from the sales or exchanges of stock or securities do not include amounts described in section 1362(d)(3)(D)(iv), relating to the treatment of certain liquidations. For purposes of section 1362(d)(3)(D)(iv), stock of the liquidating corporation owned by an S corporation shareholder is not treated as owned by the S corporation.

(3) Definition of stock or securities. For purposes of this paragraph (c), stock or securities includes shares or certificates of stock, stock rights or warrants, or an interest in any corporation (including any joint stock company, insurance company, association, or other organization classified as a corporation under section 7701); an interest as a limited partner in a partnership; certificates of interest or participation in any profit-sharing agreement, or in any oil, gas, or other mineral property, or lease; collateral trust certificates; voting trust certificates; bonds; debentures; certificates of indebtedness; notes; car trust certificates; bills of exchange; or obligations issued by or on behalf of a State, Territory, or political subdivision thereof.

(4) General partner interests—(i) In general. Except as provided in paragraph (c)(4)(ii)(B)(4)(ii) of this section, if an S corporation disposes of a general partner interest, the gain on the disposition is treated as gain from the sale of stock or securities to the extent of the amount the S corporation would have received as a distributive share of gain from the sale of stock or securities held by the partnership if all of the stock and securities held by the partnership had been sold by the partnership at fair market value at the time the S corporation disposes of the general partner interest. In applying this rule, the S corporation's distributive share of gain from the sale of stock or securities held by the partnership is not reduced to reflect any loss that would be recognized from the sale of stock or securities held by the partnership. In the case of tiered partnerships, the rules of this section apply by looking through each tier.

(ii) Exception. An S corporation that disposes of a general partner interest may treat the disposition, for purposes of this paragraph (c), in the same manner as the disposition of an interest as a limited partner.

(iii) Other exclusions from gross receipts. For purposes of this paragraph (c), gross receipts do not include—

(A) Amounts received in nontaxable sales or exchanges except to the extent that gain is recognized by the corporation on the sale or exchange; or

(B) Amounts received as a loan, as a repayment of a loan, as a contribution to capital, or on the issuance by the corporation of its own stock.

(5) Passive investment income—(i) In general. In general, passive investment income means gross receipts (as defined in paragraph (c)(4) of this section) derived from royalties, rents, dividends, interest, annuities, and gains from the sales or exchanges of stock or securities.

(ii) Definitions. For purposes of this paragraph (c)(5), the following definitions apply:

(A) Royalties—(1) In general. Royalties means all royalties, including mineral, oil, and gas royalties, and amounts received for the privilege of using patents, copyrights, secret processes and formulas, good will, trademarks, tradebrands, franchises, and other like property. The gross amount of royalties is not reduced by any part of the cost of the rights under which the royalties are received or by any amount allowable as a deduction in computing taxable income.

(2) Royalties derived in the ordinary course of a trade or business. Royalties does not include royalties derived in the ordinary course of a trade or business of franchising or licensing property. Royalties received by a corporation are derived in the ordinary course of a trade or business of franchising or licensing property only if, based on all the facts and circumstances, the corporation—

(i) Created the property; or

(ii) Performed significant services or incurred substantial costs with respect to the development or marketing of the property.

(3) Copyright, mineral, oil and gas, and active business computer software royalties. Royalties does not include copyright royalties, nor mineral, oil and gas royalties if the income from those royalties would not be treated as personal holding company income under section 543(a)(3) and (a)(4) if the corporation were a C corporation; amounts received upon disposal of timber, coal, or domestic iron ore with respect to which the special rules of section 631(b) and (c) apply; and active business computer software royalties as defined under section 543(d) (without regard to paragraph (d)(5) of section 543).

(B) Rents—(1) In general. Rents means amounts received for the use of, or right to use, property (whether real or personal) of the corporation.

(2) Rents derived in the active trade or business of renting property. Rents does not include rents derived in the active trade or business of renting property. Rents received by a corporation are derived in an active trade or business of renting property only if, based on all the facts and circumstances, the corporation provides significant services or incurs substantial costs in the rental business. Generally, significant services are not rendered and substantial costs are not incurred in connection with net leases. Whether significant services are performed or substantial costs are incurred in the rental business is determined based upon all the facts and circumstances including, but not limited to, the number of persons employed to provide the services and the types and amounts of costs and expenses incurred (other than depreciation).

(3) Produced film rents. Rents does not include produced film rents as defined under section 543(a)(5).

(4) Income from leasing self-produced tangible property. Rents does not include compensation, however designated, for the use of, or right to use, any real or tangible personal property developed, manufactured, or produced by the taxpayer, if during the taxable year the taxpayer is engaged in substantial development, manufacturing, or production of real or tangible personal property of the same type.

(C) Dividends. Dividends includes dividends as defined in section 316, amounts to be included in gross income under section 551 (relating to foreign personal holding company income taxed to U.S. shareholders), and consent dividends as provided in section 565. See paragraphs (c)(5)(iii)(B) and (C) of this section for special rules for the treatment of certain dividends and certain payments to a patron of a cooperative. See § 1.1362–8 for the special rules regarding the treatment of dividends received by an S corporation from a C corporation in which the S corporation holds stock meeting the requirements of section 1504(a)(2).

(D) Interest—(1) In general. Interest means any amount received for the use of money (including tax-exempt interest and amounts treated as interest under section 483, 1272, 1274, or 7872). See paragraph (c)(5)(iii)(B) of this section for a special rule for the treatment of interest derived in certain businesses.

(2) Interest on obligations acquired in the ordinary course of a trade or business. Interest does not include interest on any obligation acquired from the sale of property described in section 1221(1) or the performance of services in the ordinary course of a trade or business of selling the property or performing the services.

(E) Annuities. Annuities means the entire amount received as an annuity under an annuity, endowment, or life insurance contract, if any part of the amount would be includible in gross income under section 72.

(F) Gross receipts from the sale of stock or securities. Gross receipts from the sales or exchanges of stock or securities, as described in paragraph (c)(4)(ii)(B) of this section, are passive investment income to the extent of gains therefrom. See paragraph (c)(5)(iii)(B) of this section for a special rule for the treatment of gains derived in certain businesses.

(G) Identified income. Passive investment income does not include income identified by the Commissioner by regulations, revenue ruling, or revenue procedure as income derived in the ordinary course of a trade or business for purposes of this section.

(iii) Special rules. For purposes of this paragraph (c)(5), the following special rules apply:

(A) Options or commodities dealers. In the case of an options dealer or commodities dealer, passive investment income does not include any gain or loss (in the normal course of the taxpayer's activity of dealing in or trading section 1256 contracts) from any section 1256 contract or property related to the contract. Options dealer, commodities dealer, and section 1256 contract have the same meaning as in section 1362(d)(3)(E)(ii).

(B) Treatment of certain lending, financing and other business—(1) In general. Passive investment income does not include gross receipts that are directly derived in the ordinary course of a trade or business of—

(i) Lending or financing;

(ii) Dealing in property;

(iii) Purchasing or discounting accounts receivable, notes, or installment obligations; or

(iv) Servicing mortgages.

(2) Directly derived. For purposes of this paragraph (c)(5)(iii)(B), gross receipts directly derived in the ordinary course of business includes gain (as well as interest income) with respect to loans originated in a lending business, or interest income (as well as gain) from debt obligations of a dealer in such obligations. However, interest earned from the investment of idle funds in short-term securities does not constitute gross receipts directly derived in the ordinary course of business. Similarly, a dealer's income or gain from an item of property is not directly derived in the ordinary course of its trade or business if the dealer held the property for investment at any time before the income or gain is recognized.

(C) Payment to a patron of a cooperative. Passive investment income does not include amounts included in the gross income of a patron of a cooperative (within the meaning of section 1381(a), without regard to paragraph (2)(A) or (C) of section 1381(a)) by reason of any payment or allocation to the patron based on patronage occurring in the case of a trade or business of the patron.

(6) Examples. The principles of paragraphs (c)(4) and (c)(5) of this section are illustrated by the following examples. Unless otherwise provided in an example, S is an S corporation with subchapter C earnings and profits, and S's gross receipts from operations are gross receipts not derived from royalties, rents, dividends, interest, annuities, or gains from the sales or exchanges of stock or securities. S is a calendar year taxpayer and its first taxable year as an S corporation is 1993.

Example 1. Sales of capital assets, stock and securities. **(i)** S uses an accrual method of accounting and sells:

(1) A depreciable asset, held for more than 6 months, which is used in the corporation's business;

(2) A capital asset (other than stock or securities) for a gain;

(3) A capital asset (other than stock or securities) for a loss; and

(4) Securities.

S receives payment for each asset partly in money and partly in the form of a note payable at a future time, and elects not to report the sales on the installment method.

(ii) The amount of money and the face amount (or issue price if different) of the note received for the business asset are considered gross receipts in the taxable year of sale and are not reduced by the adjusted basis of the property, costs of sale, or any other amount. With respect to the sales of the capital assets, gross receipts include the cash down payment and face amount (or issue price if different) of any notes, but only to the extent of S's capital gain net income. In the case of the sale of the securities, gross receipts include the cash down payment and face amount (or issue price if different) of the notes, but only to the extent of gain on the sale. In determining gross receipts from sales of securities, losses are not netted against gains.

Example 2. Long-term contract reported on percentage-of-completion method. S has a long-term contract as defined in § 1.460–1(b)(1) with respect to which it reports income according to the percentage-of-completion method as described in § 1.460–4(b). The portion of the gross contract price which corresponds to the percentage of the entire contract which has been completed during the taxable year is included in S's gross receipts for the year.

Example 3. Income reported on installment sale method. For its 1993 taxable year, S sells personal property on the installment plan and elects to report its taxable income from the sale of the property (other than property qualifying as a capital asset or stock or securities) on the installment method in accordance with section 453. The installment payment actually received in a given taxable year of S is included in gross receipts for the year.

Example 4. Partnership interests. In 1993, S and two of its shareholders contribute cash to form a general partnership, PRS. S receives a 50 percent interest in the capital and profits of PRS. S formed PRS to indirectly invest in marketable stocks and securities. The only assets of PRS are the stock and securities, and certain real and tangible personal property. In 1994, S needs cash in its business and sells its partnership interest at a gain rather than having PRS sell the marketable stock or securities that have appreciated. Under paragraph (c)(4)(ii)(B)(4) of this section, the gain on S's disposition of its interest is PRS is treated as gain from the sale or exchange of stock or securities to the extent of the amount the distributive share of gain S would have received from the sale of stock or securities held by PRS if PRS sold all of its stock or securities at fair market value at the time S disposed of its interest in PRS.

Example 5. Royalties derived in ordinary course of trade or business. **(i)** In 1993, S has gross receipts of $75,000. Of this amount, $5,000 is from royalty payments with respect to Trademark A, $8,000 is from royalty payments with respect to Trademark B, and $62,000 is gross receipts from operations. S created Trademark A, but S did not create Trademark B or perform significant services or incur substantial costs with respect to the development or marketing of Trademark B.

(ii) Because S created Trademark A, the royalty payments with respect to Trademark A are derived in the ordinary course of S's business and are not included within the definition of royalties for purposes of determining S's passive investment income. However, the royalty payments with respect to Trademark B are included within the definition of royalties for purposes of determining S's passive investment income. See paragraph (c)(5)(ii)(A) of this section. S's passive investment income for the year is $8,000, and S's passive investment income percentage for the taxable year is 10.67% ($8,000/$75,000). This does not exceed 25 percent of S's gross receipts and consequently the three-year period described in section 1362(d)(3) does not begin to run.

Example 6. Dividends; gain on sale of stock derived in the ordinary course of trade or business. **(i)** In 1993, S receives dividends of $10,000 on stock of corporations P and O, recognizes a gain of $25,000 on sale of the P stock, and recognizes a loss of $12,000 on sale of the O stock. S held the P and O stock for investment, rather than for sale in the ordinary course of a trade or business. S has gross receipts from operations and from gain on the sale of stock in the ordinary course of its trade or business of $110,000.

(ii) S's gross receipts are calculated as follows:

$110,000	Gross receipts from operations and from gain on the sale of stock in the ordinary course of a trade or business
10,000	Gross dividend receipts
25,000	Gain on sale of P stock (Loss on O stock not taken into account
145,000	Total gross receipts

(iii) S's passive investment income is determined as follows:

$ 10,000	Gross dividend receipts
25,000	Gain on sale of P stock (Loss on O stock not taken into account
35,000	Total passive investment income

(iv) S's passive investment income percentage for its first year as an S corporation is 24.1% ($35,000/$145,000). This does not exceed 25 percent of S's gross receipts and consequently the three-year period described in section 1362(d)(3) does not begin to run.

Example 7. Interest on accounts receivable netting of gain on sale of real property investments. **(i)** In 1993, S receives $6,000 of interest on accounts receivable arising from S's sales of inventory property. S also received dividends with respect to stock held for investment of $1,500. In addition, S sells two parcels of real property (Property J and Property K) that S had purchased and held for investment. S sells Property J, in which S has a basis of $5,000, for $10,000 (a gain of $5,000). S sells Property K, in which S has a basis of $12,000, for $9,000 (a loss of $3,000). S has gross receipts from operations of $90,000.

(ii) S's gross receipts are calculated as follows:

$ 90,000	Gross receipts from operations
6,000	Gross interest receipts
1,500	Gross dividend receipts
2,000	Net gain on sale of real property investments
99,500	Total gross receipts

(iii) Under paragraph (c)(5)(ii)(D) of this section, S's gross interest receipts are not passive investment income. In addition, gain on the sale of real property ($2,000) is not passive investment income. S's passive investment income includes only the $1,500 of gross dividend receipts. Accordingly, S's passive investment income percentage for its first year as an S corporation is 1.51% ($1,500/$99,500). This does not exceed 25 percent of S's gross receipts and consequently the three-year period described in section 1362(d)(3) does not begin to run.

Example 8. Interest received in the ordinary course of a lending business. **(i)** In 1993, S has gross receipts of $100,000 from loans and investments made in the ordinary course of S's mortgage banking business. This includes, for example, mortgage servicing fees, interest earned on mortgages prior to sale of the mortgages, and gain on sale of mortgages. In addition, S receives, from the investment of idle funds in short-term securities, $15,000 of gross interest income and $5,000 of gain.

(ii) S's gross receipts are calculated as follows:

$100,000	Gross receipts from operations
15,000	Gross interest receipts
5,000	Gain on sale of securities
120,000	Total gross receipts

(iii) S's passive investment income is determined as follows:

$ 15,000	Gross interest receipts
5,000	Gain on sale of securities
20,000	Total passive investment income

(iv) S's passive investment income percentage for its first year as an S corporation is 16.67% ($20,000/ $120,000). This does not exceed 25 percent of S's gross receipts and consequently the three-year period described in section 1362(d)(3) does not begin to run.

[T.D. 8449, 57 FR 55445, Nov. 25, 1992, as amended by T.D. 8869, 65 FR 3843, Jan. 25, 2000; T.D. 8995, 67 FR 34603, May 15, 2002]

§ 1.1362–3 Treatment of S termination year.

(a) In general. If an S election terminates under section 1362(d) on a date other than the first day of a taxable year of the corporation, the corporation's taxable year in which the termination occurs is an S termination year. The portion of the S termination year ending at the close of the day prior to the termination is treated as a short taxable year for which the corporation is an S corporation (the S short year). The portion of the S termination year beginning on the day the termination is effective is treated as a short taxable year for which the corporation is a C corporation (the C short year). Except as provided in paragraphs (b) and (c)(1) of this section, the corporation allocates income or loss for the entire year on a pro rata basis as described in section 1362(e)(2). To the extent that income or loss is not allocated on a pro rata basis under this section, items of income, gain, loss, deduction, and credit are assigned to each short taxable year on the basis of the corporation's normal method of accounting as determined under section 446. * * *

(b) Allocations other than pro rata—(1) Elections under section 1362(e)(3). The pro rata allocation rules of section 1362(e)(2) do not apply if the corporation elects to allocate its S termination year income on the basis of its normal tax accounting method. This election may be made only with the consent of each person who is a shareholder in the corporation at any time during the S short year and of each person who is a shareholder in the corporation on the first day of the C short year. See § 1.1362–6(a) for rules concerning the time and manner of making this election.

(2) Purchase of stock treated as an asset purchase. The pro rata allocation rules of section 1362(e)(2) do not apply with respect to any item resulting from the application of section 338.

(3) 50 percent change in ownership during S termination year. The pro rata allocation rules of section 1362(e)(2) do not apply if at any time during the S termination year, as a result of sales or exchanges of stock in the corporation during that year, there is a change in ownership of 50 percent or more of the issued and outstanding shares of stock of the corporation. If stock has already been sold or exchanged during the S termination year, subsequent sales or exchanges of that stock are not taken into account for purposes of this paragraph (b)(3).

(c) Special rules—(1) S corporation that is a partner in a partnership. For purposes of section 706(c) only, the termination of the election of an S corporation that is a partner in a partnership during any portion of the S short year under § 1.1362–2(a) or (b), is treated as a sale or exchange of the corporation's entire interest in the partnership on the last day of the S short year, if—

(i) The pro rata allocation rules do not apply to the corporation; and

(ii) Any taxable year of the partnership ends with or within the C short year.

(2) Tax for the C short year. The taxable income for the C short year is determined on an annualized basis as described in section 1362(e)(5).

(3) Each short year treated as taxable year. Except as otherwise provided in paragraph (c)(4) of this section, the S and C short years are treated as two separate years for purposes of all provisions of the Internal Revenue Code.

(4) Year for carryover purposes. The S and C short years are treated as one year for purposes of determining the number of taxable years to which any item may be carried back or forward by the corporation.

(5) Due date for S short year return. The date by which the return for the S short year must be filed is the same as the date by which the return for the C short year must be filed (including extensions).

(6) Year in which income from S short year is includible. A shareholder must include in taxable income the shareholder's pro rata share of the items described in section 1366(a) for the S short year for the taxable year with or within which the S termination year ends.

(d) Examples. The provisions of this section are illustrated by the following examples:

Example 1. S termination year not created. **(i)** On January 1, 1993, the first day of its taxable year, a subchapter C corporation had three eligible shareholders. During 1993, the corporation properly elected to be treated as an S corporation effective January 1, 1994, the first day of the succeeding taxable year. Subsequently, a transfer of some of the stock in the corporation was made to an ineligible shareholder. The ineligible shareholder still holds the stock on January 1, 1994.

(ii) The corporation fails to meet the definition of a small business corporation on January 1, 1994, and its election is treated as having terminated on that date. See § 1.1362–2(b)(2) for the termination rules. Because the corporation ceases to be a small business corporation on the first day of a taxable year, an S termination year is not created. In addition, if the corporation in the future meets the definition of a small business corporation and desires to elect to be treated as an S corporation, the corporation is automatically granted consent to reelect before the expiration of the 5–year waiting period. See § 1.1362–5 for special rules concerning automatic consent to reelect.

Example 2. More than 50 percent change in ownership during S short year. A, an individual, owns all 100 outstanding shares of stock of S, a calendar year S corporation. On January 31, 1993, A sells 60 shares of S stock to B, an individual. On June 1, 1993, A sells 5 shares of S stock to PRS, a partnership. S ceases to be a small business corporation on June 1, 1993, and pursuant to section 1362(d)(2), its election terminates on that date. Because there was a more than 50 percent change in ownership of the issued and outstanding shares of S stock, S must assign the items of income, loss, deduction, or credit for the S termination year to the two short taxable years on the basis of S's normal method of accounting under the rules of paragraph (b)(3) of this section.

Example 3. More than 50 percent change in ownership during C short year. A, an individual, owns all 100 outstanding shares of stock of S, a calendar year S corporation. On June 1, 1993, A sells 5 shares of S stock to PRS, a partnership. S ceases to be a small business corporation on that date and pursuant to section 1362(d)(3), its election terminates on that date. On July 1, 1993, A sells 60 shares of S stock to B, an individual. Since there was a more than 50 percent change in ownership of the issued and outstanding shares of S stock during the S termination year, S must assign the items of income, loss, deduction, or credit for the S termination year to the two short taxable years on the basis of S's normal method of accounting under the rules of paragraph (b)(3) of this section.

Example 4. Stock acquired other than by sale or exchange. C and D are shareholders in S, a calendar year S corporation. Each owns 50 percent of the issued and outstanding shares of the corporation on December 31, 1993. On March 1, 1994, C makes a gift of his entire shareholder interest to T, a trust not permitted as a shareholder under section 1361(c)(2). S ceases to be a small business corporation on March 1, 1994, and pursuant to section 1362(d)(2), its S corporation election terminates effective on that date. As a result of the gift, T owns 50 percent of S's issued and outstanding stock. However, because T acquired the stock by gift from C rather than by sale or exchange, there has not been a more than 50 percent change in ownership by sale or exchange of S that would cause the rules of paragraph (b)(3) of this section to apply.

[T.D. 8449, 57 FR 55445, Nov. 25, 1992, as amended by T.D. 8842, 64 FR 61205, Nov. 9, 1999; T.D. 9137, 69 FR 42551, July 16, 2004]

§ 1.1362–6 Elections and consents.

(a) Time and manner of making elections—(1) In general. An election statement made under this section must identify the election being made, set forth the name, address, and taxpayer identification number of the corporation, and be signed by a person authorized to sign the return required to be filed under section 6037.

(2) Election to be an S corporation—(i) Manner of making election. A small business corporation makes an election under section 1362(a) to be an S corporation by filing a completed Form 2553. The election form must be filed with the service center designated in the instructions applicable to Form 2553. The election is not valid unless all shareholders of the corporation at the time of the election consent to the election in the manner provided in paragraph (b) of this section. However, once a valid election is made, new shareholders need not consent to that election.

(ii) Time of making election—(A) In general. The election described in paragraph (a)(2)(i) of this section may be made by a small business corporation at any time during the taxable year that immediately precedes the taxable year for which the election is to be effective, or during the taxable year for which the election is to be effective provided that the election is made before the 16th day of the third month of the year. If a corporation makes an election for a taxable year, and the election meets all the requirements of this section but is made during the period beginning after the 15th day of the third month of the taxable year, the election is treated as being made for the following taxable year provided that the corporation meets all the requirements of section 1361(b) at the time the election is made. For taxable years of 2½ months or less, an election made before the 16th day of the third month after the first day of the taxable year is treated as made during that year.

(B) Elections made during the first 2½ months treated as made for the following taxable year. A timely election made by a small business corporation during the taxable year for which it is intended to be effective is nonetheless treated as made for the following taxable year if—

(1) The corporation is not a small business corporation during the entire portion of the taxable year which occurs before the date the election is made; or

(2) Any person who held stock in the corporation at any time during the portion of the taxable year which occurs before the time the election is made, and who does not hold stock at the time the election is made, does not consent to the election.

(C) Definition of month and beginning of the taxable year. Month means a period commencing on the same numerical day of any calendar month as the day of the calendar month on which the taxable year began and ending with the close of the day preceding the numerically corresponding day of the succeeding calendar month or, if there is no corresponding day, with the close of the last day of the succeeding calendar month. In addition, the taxable year of a new corporation begins on the date that the corporation has shareholders, acquires assets, or begins doing business, whichever is the first to occur. The existence of incorporators does not necessarily begin the taxable year of a new corporation.

(iii) Examples. The provisions of this section are illustrated by the following examples:

Example 1. Effective election; no prior taxable year. A calendar year small business corporation begins its first taxable year on January 7, 1993. To be an S corporation beginning with its first taxable year, the corporation must make the election set forth in this section during the period that begins January 7, 1993, and ends before March 22, 1993. Because the corporation had no taxable year immediately preceding the taxable year for which the election is to be effective, an election made earlier than January 7, 1993, will not be valid.

Example 2. Effective election; taxable year less than 2½ months. A calendar year small business corporation begins its first taxable year on November 8, 1993. To be an S corporation beginning with its first taxable year, the corporation must make the election set forth in this section during the period that begins November 8, 1993, and ends before January 23, 1994.

Example 3. Election effective for the following taxable year; ineligible shareholder. On January 1, 1993, two individuals and a partnership own all of the stock of a calendar year subchapter C corporation. On January 31, 1993, the partnership dissolved and distributed its shares in the corporation to its five partners, all individuals. On February 28, 1993, the seven shareholders of the corporation consented to the corporation's election of subchapter S status. The corporation files a properly completed Form 2533 on March 2, 1993. The corporation is not eligible to be a subchapter S corporation for the 1993 taxable year because during the period of the taxable year prior to the election it had an ineligible shareholder. However, under paragraph (a)(2)(ii)(B) of this section, the election is treated as made for the corporation's 1994 taxable year.

(3) Revocation of S election—(i) Manner of revoking election. To revoke an election, the corporation files a statement that the corporation revokes the election made under section 1362(a). The statement must be filed with the service center where the election was properly filed. The revocation statement must include the number of shares of stock (including non-voting stock) issued and outstanding at the time the revocation is made. A revocation may be made only with the consent of shareholders who, at the time the revocation is made, hold more than one-half of the number of issued and outstanding shares of stock (including non-voting stock) of the corporation. Each shareholder who consents to the revocation must consent in the manner required under paragraph (b) of this section. In addition, each consent should indicate the number of issued and outstanding shares of stock (including non-voting stock) held by each shareholder at the time of the revocation.

(ii) Time of revoking election. For rules concerning when a revocation is effective, see § 1.1362–2(a)(2).

(iii) Examples. The principles of this paragraph (a)(3) are illustrated by the following examples:

Example 1. Revocation; consent of shareholders owning more than one-half of issued and outstanding shares. A calendar year S corporation has issued an outstanding 40,000 shares of class A voting common stock and 20,000 shares of class B non-voting common stock. The corporation wishes to revoke its election of subchapter S status. Shareholders owning 11,000 shares of class A stock sign revocation consents. Shareholders owning 20,000 shares of class B stock sign revocation consents. The corporation has obtained the required shareholder consent to revoke its subchapter S election because shareholders owning more than one-half of the total number of issued and outstanding shares of stock of the corporation consented to the revocation.

Example 2. Effective prospective revocation. In June 1993, a calendar year S corporation determines that it will revoke its subchapter S election effective August 1, 1993. To do so it must file its revocation statement with consents attached on or before August 1, 1993, and the statement must indicate that the revocation is intended to be effective August 1, 1993.

(4) Rescission of revocation—(i) Manner of rescinding a revocation. To rescind a revocation, the corporation files a statement that the corporation rescinds the revocation made under section 1362(d)(1). The statement must be filed with the service center where the revocation was properly filed. A rescission may be made only with the consent (in the manner required under paragraph (b)(1) of this section) of each person who consented to the revocation and of each person who became a shareholder of the corporation within the period beginning on the first day after the date the revocation was made and ending on the date on which the rescission is made.

(ii) Time of rescinding a revocation. If the rescission statement is filed before the revocation becomes effective and is filed with proper service center, the rescission is effective on the date it is so filed.

(5) Election not to apply pro rata allocation. To elect not to apply the pro rata allocation rules to an S termination year, a corporation files a statement that it elects under section 1362(e)(3) not to apply the rules provided in section 1362(e)(2). In addition to meeting the requirements of paragraph (a)(1) of this section, the statement must set forth the cause of the termination and the date thereof. The statement must be filed with the corporation's return for the C short year. This election may be made only with the consent of all persons who are shareholders of the corporation at any time during the S short year and all persons who are shareholders of the corporation on the first day of the C short year (in the manner required under paragraph (b)(1) of this section).

(b) Shareholders' consents—(1) Manner of consents in general. A shareholder's consent required under paragraph (a) of this section must be in the form of a written statement that sets forth the name, address, and taxpayer identification number of the shareholder, the number of shares of stock owned by the shareholder, the date (or dates) on which the stock was acquired, the date on which the shareholder's taxable year ends, the name of the S corporation, the corporation's taxpayer identification number, and the election to which the shareholder consents. The statement must be signed by the shareholder under penalties of perjury. Except as provided in paragraph (b)(3)(iii) of this section, the election of the corporation is not valid if any required consent is not filed in accordance with the rules contained in this paragraph (b). The consent statement should be attached to the corporation's election statement.

(2) Persons required to consent. The following rules apply in determining persons required to consent:

(i) Community interest in stock. When stock of the corporation is owned by husband and wife as community property (or the income from the stock is community property), or is owned by tenants in common, joint tenants, or tenants by the entirety, each person having a community interest in the stock or income therefrom and each tenant in common, joint tenant and tenant by the entirety must consent to the election.

(ii) Minor. The consent of a minor must be made by the minor or by the legal representative of the minor (or by a natural or an adoptive parent of the minor if no legal representative has been appointed).

(iii) Estate. The consent of an estate must be made by an executor or administrator thereof, or by any other fiduciary appointed by testamentary instrument or appointed by the court having jurisdiction over the administration of the estate.

(iv) Trusts. In the case of a trust described in section 1361(c)(2)(A) (including a trust treated under section 1361(d)(1)(A) as a trust described in section 1361(c)(2)(A)(i) and excepting an electing small business trust described in section 1361(c)(2)(A)(v)(ESBT)), only the person treated as the shareholder for purposes of section 1361(b)(1) must consent to the election. When stock of the corporation is held by a trust, both husband and wife must consent to any election if the husband and wife have a community interest in the trust property. See paragraph (b)(2)(i) of this section for rules concerning community interests in S corporation stock. In the case of an ESBT, the trustee and owner of any portion of the trust that consists of the stock in one or more S corporations . . . must consent to the election. If there is more than one trustee, the trustee or trustees with authority to legally bind the trust must consent to the S corporation election.

(3) Special rules for consent of shareholder to election to be an S corporation—(i) In general. The consent of a shareholder to an election by a small business corporation under section 1362(a) may be made on Form 2553 or on a separate statement in the manner described in paragraph (b)(1) of this section. In addition, the separate statement must set forth the name, address, and taxpayer identification number of the corporation. A shareholder's consent is binding and may not be withdrawn after a valid election is made by the corporation. Each person who is a shareholder (including any person who is treated as a shareholder under section 1361(c)(2)(B) at the time the election is made) must consent to the election. If the election is made before the 16th day of the third month of the taxable year and is intended to be effective for that year, each person who was a shareholder (including any person who was treated as a shareholder under section 1361(c)(2)(B)) at any time during the portion of that year which occurs before the time the election is made, and who is not a shareholder at the time the election is made, must also consent to the election. If the election is to be effective for the following taxable year, no consent need be filed by any shareholder who is not a shareholder on the date of the election. Any person who is considered to be a shareholder under applicable State law solely by virtue of his or her status as an incorporator is not treated as a shareholder for purposes of this paragraph (b)(3)(i).

(ii) Examples. The principles of this section are illustrated by the following examples:

Example 1. Effective election; shareholder consents. On January 1, 1993, the first day of its taxable year, a subchapter C corporation had 15 shareholders. On January 30, 1993, two of the C corporation's shareholders, A and B, both individuals, sold their shares in the corporation to P, Q, and R, all individuals. On March 1, 1993, the corporation filed its election to be an S corporation for the 1993 taxable year. The election will be effective (assuming the other requirements of section 1361(b) are met) provided that all of the shareholders as of March 1, 1993, as well as former shareholders A and B, consent to the election.

Example 2. Consent of new shareholder unnecessary. On January 1, 1993, three individuals own all of the stock of a calendar year subchapter C corporation. On April 15, 1993, the corporation, in accordance with paragraph (a)(2) of this section, files a properly completed Form 2553. The corporation anticipates that the election will be effective beginning January 1, 1994, the first day of the succeeding taxable year. On October 1, 1993, the three shareholders collectively sell 75% of their shares in the corporation to another individual. On January 1, 1994, the corporation's shareholders are the three original individuals and the new shareholder. Because the election was valid and binding when made, it is not necessary for the new shareholder to consent to the election. The corporation's subchapter S election is effective on January 1, 1994 (assuming the other requirements of section 1361(b) are met).

(iii) Extension of time for filing consents to an election—(A) In general. An election that is timely filed for any taxable year and that would be valid except for the failure of any shareholder to file a timely consent is not invalid if consents are filed as required under paragraph (b)(3)(iii)(B) of this section and it is shown to the satisfaction of the district director or director of the service center with which the corporation files its income tax return that—

(1) There was reasonable cause for the failure to file the consent;

(2) The request for the extension of time to file a consent is made within a reasonable time under the circumstances; and

(3) The interests of the Government will not be jeopardized by treating the election as valid.

(B) Required consents. Consents must be filed within the extended period of time as may be granted by the Internal Revenue Service, by all persons who—

(1) Were shareholders of the corporation at any time during the period beginning as of the date of the invalid election and ending on the date on which an extension of time is granted in accordance with this paragraph (b)(3)(iii); and

(2) Have not previously consented to the election.

[T.D. 8449, 57 FR 55445, Nov. 25, 1992, as amended by T.D. 8994, 67 FR 34388, May 14, 2002]

§ 1.1363–1 Effect of election on corporation.

(a) Exemption of corporation from income tax—(1) In general. Except as provided in this paragraph (a), a small business corporation that makes a valid election under section 1362(a) is exempt from the taxes imposed by chapter 1 of the Internal Revenue Code with respect to taxable years of the corporation for which the election is in effect.

(2) Corporate level taxes. An S corporation is not exempt from the tax imposed by section 1374 (relating to the tax imposed on certain built-in gains), or section 1375 (relating to the tax on excess passive investment income). See also section 1363(d) (relating to the recapture of LIFO benefits) for the rules regarding the payment by an S corporation of LIFO recapture amounts.

(b) Computation of corporate taxable income. The taxable income of an S corporation is computed as described in section 1363(b).

(c) Elections of the S corporation—(1) In general. Any elections (other than those described in paragraph (c)(2) of this section) affecting the computation of items derived from an S corporation are made by the corporation. For example, elections of methods of accounting, of computing depreciation, of treating soil and water conservation expenditures, and the option to deduct as expenses intangible drilling and development costs, are made by the corporation and not by the shareholders separately. All corporate elections are applicable to all shareholders.

(2) Exceptions. **(i)** Each shareholder's pro rata share of expenses described in section 617 paid or accrued by the S corporation is treated according to the shareholder's method of treating those expenses, notwithstanding the treatment of the expenses by the corporation.

(ii) Each shareholder may elect to amortize that shareholder's pro rata share of any qualified expenditure described in section 59(e) paid or accrued by the S corporation.

(iii) Each shareholder's pro rata share of taxes described in section 901 paid or accrued by the S corporation to foreign countries or possessions of the United States (according to its method of treating those taxes) is treated according to the shareholder's method of treating those taxes, and each shareholder may elect to use the total amount either as a credit against tax or as a deduction from income.

* * *

[T.D. 8449, 57 FR 55445, Nov. 25, 1992]

§ 1.1366–1 Shareholder's share of items of an S corporation.

(a) Determination of shareholder's tax liability—(1) In general. An S corporation must report, and a shareholder is required to take into account in the shareholder's return, the shareholder's pro rata share, whether or not distributed, of the S corporation's items of income, loss, deduction, or credit described in paragraphs (a)(2), (3), and (4) of this section. A shareholder's pro rata share is determined in accordance with the provisions of section 1377(a) and the regulations thereunder. The shareholder takes these items into account in determining the shareholder's taxable income and tax liability for the shareholder's taxable year with or within which the taxable year of the corporation ends. If the shareholder dies (or if the shareholder is an estate or trust and the estate or trust terminates) before the end of the taxable year of the corporation, the shareholder's pro rata share of these items is taken into account on the shareholder's final return. For the limitation on allowance of a shareholder's pro rata share of S corporation losses or deductions, see section 1366(d) and § 1.1366–2.

(2) Separately stated items of income, loss, deduction, or credit. Each shareholder must take into account separately the shareholder's pro rata share of any item of income (including tax-exempt income), loss, deduction, or credit of the S corporation that if separately taken into account by any shareholder could affect the shareholder's tax liability for that taxable year differently than if the shareholder did not take the item into account separately. The separately stated items of the S corporation include, but are not limited to, the following items—

(i) The corporation's combined net amount of gains and losses from sales or exchanges of capital assets grouped by applicable holding periods, by applicable rate of tax under section 1(h), and by any other classification that may be relevant in determining the shareholder's tax liability;

(ii) The corporation's combined net amount of gains and losses from sales or exchanges of property described in section 1231 (relating to property used in the trade or business and involuntary conversions), grouped by applicable holding periods, by applicable rate of tax under section 1(h), and by any other classification that may be relevant in determining the shareholder's tax liability;

(iii) Charitable contributions, grouped by the percentage limitations of section 170(b), paid by the corporation within the taxable year of the corporation;

(iv) The taxes described in section 901 that have been paid (or accrued) by the corporation to foreign countries or to possessions of the United States;

(v) Each of the corporation's separate items involved in the determination of credits against tax allowable under part IV of subchapter A (section 21 and following) of the Internal Revenue Code, except for any credit allowed under section 34 (relating to certain uses of gasoline and special fuels);

(vi) Each of the corporation's separate items of gains and losses from wagering transactions (section 165(d)); soil and water conservation expenditures (section 175); deduction under an election to expense certain depreciable business expenses (section 179); medical, dental, etc., expenses (section 213); the additional itemized deductions for individuals provided in part VII of subchapter B (section 212 and following) of the Internal Revenue Code;

and any other itemized deductions for which the limitations on itemized deductions under sections 67 or 68 applies;

(vii) Any of the corporation's items of portfolio income or loss, and expenses related thereto, as defined under section 469;

(viii) The corporation's tax-exempt income. For purposes of subchapter S, tax-exempt income is income that is permanently excludible from gross income in all circumstances in which the applicable provision of the Internal Revenue Code applies. For example, income that is excludible from gross income under section 101 (certain death benefits) or section 103 (interest on state and local bonds) is tax-exempt income, while income that is excludible from gross income under section 108 (income from discharge of indebtedness) or section 109 (improvements by lessee on lessor's property) is not tax-exempt income;

(ix) The corporation's adjustments described in sections 56 and 58, and items of tax preference described in section 57; and

(x) Any item identified in guidance (including forms and instructions) issued by the Commissioner as an item required to be separately stated under this paragraph (a)(2).

(3) Nonseparately computed income or loss. Each shareholder must take into account separately the shareholder's pro rata share of the nonseparately computed income or loss of the S corporation. For this purpose, *nonseparately computed income or loss* means the corporation's gross income less the deductions allowed to the corporation under chapter 1 of the Internal revenue Code, determined by excluding any item requiring separate computation under paragraph (a)(2) of this section.

(4) Separate activities requirement. An S corporation must report, and each shareholder must take into account in the shareholder's return, the shareholder's pro rata share of an S corporation's items of income, loss, deduction, or credit described in paragraphs (a)(2) and (3) of this section for each of the corporation's activities as defined in section 469 and the regulations thereunder.

(5) Aggregation of deductions or exclusions for purposes of limitations—(i) In general. A shareholder aggregates the shareholder's separate deductions or exclusions with the shareholder's pro rata share of the S corporation's separately stated deductions or exclusions in determining the amount of any deduction or exclusion allowable to the shareholder under subtitle A of the Internal Revenue Code as to which a limitation is imposed.

(ii) Example. The provisions of paragraph (a)(5)(i) of this section are illustrated by the following example:

Example. In 1999, Corporation M, an S corporation, purchases and places in service section 179 property costing $10,000. Corporation M elects to expense the entire cost of the property. Shareholder A owns 50 percent of the stock of Corporation M. Shareholder A's pro rata share of this item after Corporation M applies the section 179(b) limitations is $5,000. Because the aggregate amount of Shareholder A's pro rata share and separately acquired section 179 expense may not exceed $19,000 (the aggregate maximum cost that may be taken into account under section 179(a) for the applicable taxable year), Shareholder A may elect to expense up to $14,000 of separately acquired section 179 property that is purchased and placed in service in 1999, subject to the limitations of section 179(b).

(b) Character of items constituting pro rata share—(1) In general. Except as provided in paragraph (b)(2) or (3) of this section, the character of any item of income, loss, deduction, or credit described in section 1366(a)(1)(A) or (B) and paragraph (a) of this section is determined for the S corporation and retains that character in the hands of the shareholder. For example, if an S corporation has capital gain on the sale or exchange of a capital asset, a shareholder's pro rata share of that gain will also be characterized as a capital gain regardless of whether the shareholder is otherwise a dealer in that type of property. Similarly, if an S corporation engages in an activity that is not for profit (section 183), a shareholder's pro rata share of the S corporation's deductions will be characterized as not for profit. Also, if an S corporation makes a charitable contribution to an organization qualifying under section 170(b)(1)(A), a shareholder's pro rata share of the S corporation's charitable contribution will be characterized as made to an organization qualifying under section 170(b)(1)(A).

(2) Exception for contribution of noncapital gain property. If an S corporation is formed or availed of by any shareholder or group of shareholders for a principal purpose of selling or exchanging contributed property that in the hands of the shareholder or shareholders would not have produced capital gain if sold or exchanged by the shareholder or shareholders, then the gain on the sale or exchange of the property recognized by the corporation is not treated as a capital gain.

(3) Exception for contribution of capital loss property. If an S corporation is formed or availed of by any shareholder or group of shareholders for a principal purpose of selling or exchanging contributed property that in the hands of the shareholder or shareholders would have produced capital loss if sold or exchanged by the shareholder or shareholders, then the loss on the sale or exchange of the property recognized by the corporation is treated as a capital loss to the extent that, immediately before the contribution, the adjusted basis of the property in the hands of the shareholder or shareholders exceeded the fair market value of the property.

(c) Gross income of a shareholder—(1) In general. Where it is necessary to determine the amount or character of the gross income of a shareholder, the shareholder's gross income includes the shareholder's pro rata share of the gross income of the S corporation. The shareholder's pro rata share of the gross income of the S corporation is the amount of gross income of the corporation used in deriving the shareholder's pro rata share of S corporation taxable income or loss (including items described in section 1366(a)(1)(A) or (B) and paragraph (a) of this section). For example, a shareholder is required to include the shareholder's pro rata share of S corporation gross income in computing the shareholder's gross income for the purposes of determining the necessity of filing a return (section 6012(a)) and the shareholder's gross income derived from farming (sections 175 and 6654(i)).

* * *

(d) Shareholders holding stock subject to community property laws. If a shareholder holds S corporation stock that is community property, then the shareholder's pro rata share of any item or items listed in paragraphs (a)(2), (3), and (4) of this section with respect to that stock is reported by the husband and wife in accordance with community property rules.

* * *

[T.D. 8852, 64 FR 71641, Dec. 22, 1999]

§ 1.1366–2 Limitations on deduction of pass-through items of an S corporation to its shareholders.

(a) In general—(1) Limitation on losses and deductions. The aggregate amount of losses and deductions taken into account by a shareholder under § 1.1366–1(a)(2), (3), and (4) for any taxable year of an S corporation cannot exceed the sum of—

(i) The adjusted basis of the shareholder's stock in the corporation (as determined under paragraph (a)(3)(i) of this section); and

(ii) The adjusted basis of any indebtedness of the corporation to the shareholder (as determined under paragraph (a)(3)(ii) of this section).

(2) Carryover of disallowance. A shareholder's aggregate amount of losses and deductions for a taxable year in excess of the sum of the adjusted basis of the shareholder's stock in an S corporation and of any indebtedness of the S corporation to the shareholder is not allowed for the taxable year. However, any disallowed loss or deduction retains its character and is treated as incurred by the corporation in the corporation's first succeeding taxable year, and subsequent taxable years, with respect to the shareholder. For rules on determining the adjusted bases of stock of an S corporation and indebtedness of the corporation to the shareholder, see paragraphs (a)(3)(i) and (ii) of this section.

(3) Basis limitation amount—(i) Stock portion. A shareholder generally determines the adjusted basis of stock for purposes of paragraphs (a)(1)(i) and (2) of this section (limiting losses and deductions) by taking into account only increases in basis under section 1367(a)(1) for the taxable year and decreases in basis under section 1367(a)(2)(A), (D) and (E) (relating to distributions, noncapital, nondeductible expenses, and certain oil and gas depletion deductions) for the taxable year. In so determining this loss limitation amount, the shareholder disregards decreases in basis under section 1367(a)(2)(B) and (C) (for losses and deductions, including losses and deductions previously disallowed) for the taxable year. However, if the shareholder has in effect for the taxable year an election under § 1.1367–1(g) to decrease basis by items of loss and deduction prior to decreasing basis by noncapital, nondeductible expenses and certain oil and gas depletion deductions, the shareholder also disregards decreases in basis under section 1367(a)(2)(D) and (E). This basis limitation amount for stock is determined at the time prescribed under § 1.1367–1(d)(1) for adjustments to the basis of stock.

(ii) Indebtedness portion. A shareholder determines the shareholder's adjusted basis in indebtedness of the corporation for purposes of paragraphs (a)(1)(ii) and (2) of this section (limiting losses and deductions) without regard to any adjustment under section 1367(b)(2)(A) for the taxable year. This basis limitation amount for indebtedness is determined at the time prescribed under § 1.1367–2(d)(1) for adjustments to the basis of indebtedness.

(4) Limitation on losses and deductions allocated to each item. If a shareholder's pro rata share of the aggregate amount of losses and deductions specified in § 1.1366–1(a)(2), (3), and (4) exceeds the sum of the adjusted basis of the shareholder's stock in the corporation (determined in accordance with paragraph (a)(3)(i) of this section) and the adjusted basis of any indebtedness of the corporation to the shareholder (determined in accordance with paragraph (a)(3)(ii) of this section), then the limitation on losses and deductions under section 1366(d)(1) must be allocated among the shareholder's pro rata share of each loss or deduction. The amount of the limitation allocated to any loss or deduction is an amount that bears the same ratio to the amount of the limitation as the loss or deduction bears to the total of the losses and deductions. For this purpose, the total of losses and deductions for the taxable year is the sum of the shareholder's pro rata share of losses and deductions for the taxable year, and the losses and deductions disallowed and carried forward from prior years pursuant to section 1366(d)(2).

(5) Nontransferability of losses and deductions—(i) In general. Except as provided in paragraph (a)(5)(ii) of this section, any loss or deduction disallowed under paragraph (a)(1) of this section is personal to the shareholder and cannot in any manner be transferred to another person. If a shareholder transfers some but not all of the shareholder's stock in the corporation, the amount of any disallowed loss or deduction under this section is not reduced and the transferee does not acquire any portion of the disallowed loss or deduction. If a shareholder transfers all of the shareholder's stock in the corporation, any disallowed loss or deduction is permanently disallowed.

(ii) Exceptions for transfers of stock under section 1041(a). If a shareholder transfers stock of an S corporation after December 31, 2004, in a transfer described in section 1041(a), any loss or deduction with respect to the transferred stock that is disallowed to the transferring shareholder under paragraph (a)(1) of this section shall be treated as incurred by the corporation in the following taxable year with respect to the transferee spouse or former spouse. The amount of any loss or deduction with respect to the stock transferred shall be determined by prorating any losses or deductions disallowed under paragraph (a)(1) of this section for the year of the transfer between the transferor and the spouse or former spouse based on the stock ownership at the beginning of the following taxable year. If a transferor claims a deduction for losses in the taxable year of transfer, then under paragraph (a)(4) of this section, if the transferor's pro rata share of the losses and deductions in the year of transfer exceeds the transferor's basis in stock and the indebtedness of the corporation to the transferor, then the limitation must be allocated among the transferor spouse's pro rata share of each loss or deduction, including disallowed losses and deductions carried over from the prior year.

(iii) Examples. The following examples illustrates the provisions of paragraph (a)(5)(ii) of this section:

Example 1. A owns all 100 shares in X, a calendar year S corporation. For X's taxable year ending December 31, 2006, A has zero basis in the shares and X does not have any indebtedness to A. For the 2006 taxable year, X had $100 in losses that A cannot use because of the basis limitation in section 1366(d)(1) and that are treated as incurred by the corporation with respect to A in the following taxable year. Halfway through the 2007 taxable year, A transfers 50 shares to B, A's former spouse in a transfer to which section 1041(a) applies. In the 2007 taxable year, X has $80 in losses. On A's 2007 individual income tax return, A may use the entire $100 carryover loss from 2006, as well as A's share of the $80 2007 loss determined under section 1377(a) ($60), assuming A acquires sufficient basis in the X stock. On B's 2007 individual income tax return, B may use B's share of the $80 2007 loss determined under section 1377(a) ($20), assuming B has sufficient basis in the X stock. If any disallowed 2006 loss is disallowed to A under section 1366(d)(1) in 2007, that loss is prorated between A and B based on their stock ownership at the beginning of 2008. On B's 2008 individual income tax return, B may use that loss, assuming B acquires sufficient basis in the X stock. If neither A nor B acquires any basis during the 2007 taxable year, then as of the beginning of 2008, the corporation will be treated as incurring $50 of loss with respect to A and $50 of loss with respect to B for the $100 of disallowed 2006 loss, and the corporation will be treated as incurring $60 of loss with respect to A and $20 with respect to B for the $80 of disallowed 2007 loss.

Example 2. Assume the same facts as Example 1, except that during the 2007 taxable year, A acquires $10 of basis in A's shares in X. For the 2007 taxable year, A may claim a $10 loss deduction, which represents $6.25 of the disallowed 2006 loss of $100 and $3.75 of A's 2007 loss of $60. The disallowed 2006 loss is reduced to $93.75. As of the beginning of 2008, the corporation will be treated as incurring half of the remaining $93.75 of loss with respect to A and half of that loss with respect to B for the remaining $93.75 of disallowed 2006 loss, and if B does not acquire any basis during 2007, the corporation will be treated as incurring $56.25 of loss with respect to A and $20 with respect to B for the remaining disallowed 2007 loss.

(6) Basis of stock acquired by gift. For purposes of section 1366(d)(1)(A) and paragraphs (a)(1)(i) and (2) of this section, the basis of stock in a corporation acquired by gift is the basis of the stock that is used for purposes of determining loss under section 1015(a).

(b) Special rules for carryover of disallowed losses and deductions to post-termination transition period described in section 1377(b)—(1) In general. If, for the last taxable year of a corporation for which it was an S corporation, a loss or deduction was disallowed to a shareholder by reason of the limitation in paragraph (a) of this section, the loss or deduction is treated under section 1366(d)(3) as incurred by that shareholder on the last day of any post-termination transition period (within the meaning of section 1377(b)).

(2) Limitation on losses and deductions. The aggregate amount of losses and deductions taken into account by a shareholder under paragraph (b)(1) of this section cannot exceed the adjusted basis of the shareholder's stock in the corporation determined at the close of the last day of the post-termination transition period. For this purpose, the adjusted basis of a shareholder's stock in the corporation is determined at the close of the last day of the post-termination transition period without regard to any reduction required under paragraph (b)(4) of this section. If a shareholder disposes of a share of stock prior to the close of the last day of the post-termination transition period, the adjusted basis of that share is its basis as of the close of the day of disposition. Any losses and deductions in excess of a shareholder's adjusted stock basis are permanently disallowed. For purposes of section 1366(d)(3)(B) and this paragraph (b)(2), the basis of stock in a corporation acquired by gift is the basis of the stock that is used for purposes of determining loss under section 1015(a).

(3) Limitation on losses and deductions allocated to each item. If the aggregate amount of losses and deductions treated as incurred by the shareholder under paragraph (b)(1) of this section exceeds the adjusted basis of the shareholder's stock determined under paragraph (b)(2) of this section, the limitation on losses and deductions under section 1366(d)(3)(B) must be allocated among each loss or deduction. The amount of the limitation allocated to each loss or deduction is an amount that bears the same ratio to the amount of the limitation as the amount of each loss or deduction bears to the total of all the losses and deductions.

(4) Adjustment to the basis of stock. The shareholder's basis in the stock of the corporation is reduced by the amount allowed as a deduction by reason of this paragraph (b). For rules regarding adjustments to the basis of a shareholder's stock in an S corporation, see § 1.1367–1.

(c) Carryover of disallowed losses and deductions in the case of liquidations, reorganizations, and divisions—(1) Liquidations and reorganizations. If a corporation acquires the assets of an S corporation in a transaction to which section 381(a) applies, any loss or deduction disallowed under paragraph (a) of this section with respect to a shareholder of the distributor or transferor S corporation is available to that shareholder as a shareholder of the acquiring corporation. Thus, where the acquiring corporation is an S corporation, a loss or deduction of a shareholder of the distributor or transferor S corporation disallowed prior to or during the taxable year of the transaction is treated as incurred by the acquiring S corporation with respect to that shareholder if the shareholder is a shareholder of the acquiring S corporation after the transaction. Where the acquiring corporation is a C corporation, a post-termination transition period arises the day after the last day that an S corporation was in existence and the rules provided in paragraph (b) of this section apply with respect to any shareholder of the acquired S corporation that is also a shareholder of the acquiring C corporation after the transaction. See the special rules under section 1377 for the availability of the post-termination transition period if the acquiring corporation is a C corporation.

(2) Corporate separations to which section 368(a)(1)(D) applies. If an S corporation transfers a portion of its assets constituting an active trade or business to another corporation in a transaction to which section 368(a)(1)(D) applies, and immediately thereafter the stock and securities of the controlled corporation are distributed in a distribution or exchange to which section 355 (or so much of section 356 as relates to section 355) applies, any loss or deduction disallowed under paragraph (a) of this section with respect to a shareholder of the distributing S corporation immediately before the transaction is allocated between the distributing corporation and the controlled corporation with respect to the shareholder. Such allocation shall be made according to any reasonable method, including a method based on the relative fair market value of the shareholder's stock in the distributing and controlled corporations immediately after the distribution, a method based on the relative adjusted basis of the assets in the distributing and controlled corporations immediately after the distribution, or, in the case of losses and deductions clearly attributable to either the distributing or controlled corporation, any method that allocates such losses and deductions accordingly.

[T.D. 8852, 64 FR 71641, Dec. 22, 1999; T.D. 9422, 73 FR 47531, Aug. 14, 2008]

§ 1.1366–3 Treatment of family groups.

(a) In general. Under section 1366(e), if an individual, who is a member of the family of one or more shareholders of an S corporation, renders services for, or furnishes capital to, the corporation without receiving reasonable compensation, the Commissioner shall prescribe adjustments to those items taken into account by the individual and the shareholders as may be necessary to reflect the value of the services rendered or capital furnished. For these purposes, in determining the reasonable value for services rendered, or capital furnished, to the corporation, consideration will be given to all the facts and circumstances, including the amount that ordinarily would be paid in order to obtain comparable services or capital from a person (other than a member of the family) who is not a shareholder in the corporation. In addition, for purposes of section 1366(e), if a member of the family of one or more shareholders of the S corporation holds an interest in a pass-through entity (e.g., a partnership, S corporation, trust, or estate), that performs services for, or furnishes capital to, the S corporation without receiving reasonable compensation, the Commissioner shall prescribe adjustments to the pass-through entity and the corporation as may be necessary to reflect the value of the services rendered or capital furnished. For purposes of section 1366(e), the term *family* of any shareholder includes only the shareholder's spouse, ancestors, lineal descendants, and any trust for the primary benefit of any of these persons.

(b) Examples. The provisions of this section may be illustrated by the following examples:

Example 1. The stock of an S corporation is owned 50 percent by F and 50 percent by T, the minor son of F. For the taxable year, the corporation has items of taxable income equal to $70,000. Compensation of $10,000 is paid by the corporation to F for services rendered during the taxable year, and no compensation is paid to T, who rendered no services. Based on all the relevant facts and circumstances, reasonable compensation for the services rendered by F would be $30,000. In the discretion of the Internal Revenue Service, up to an additional $20,000 of the $70,000 of the corporation's taxable income, for tax purposes, may be allocated to F as compensation for services rendered. If the Internal Revenue Service allocates $20,000 of the corporation's taxable income to F as compensation for services, taxable income of the corporation would be reduced by $20,000 to $50,000 of which F and T each would be allocated $25,000. F would have $30,000 of total compensation paid by the corporation for services rendered.

Example 2. The stock of an S corporation is owned by A and B. For the taxable year, the corporation has paid compensation to a partnership that rendered services to the corporation during the taxable year. The spouse of A is a partner in that partnership. Consequently, if based on all the relevant facts and circumstances the partnership did not receive reasonable compensation for the services rendered to the corporation, the Internal Revenue Service, in its discretion, may make adjustments to those items taken into account by the partnership and the corporation as may be necessary to reflect the value of the services rendered.

[T.D. 8852, 64 FR 71641, Dec. 22, 1999]

§ 1.1366–4 Special rules limiting the pass through of certain items of an S corporation to its shareholders.

* * *

(b) Reduction in pass through for tax imposed on built-in gains. For purposes of § 1.1366–1(a), if for any taxable year of the S corporation a tax is imposed on the corporation under section 1374, the amount of the tax imposed is treated as a loss sustained by the S corporation during the taxable year. The character of the deemed loss is determined by allocating the loss proportionately among the recognized built-in gains items giving rise to the tax and attributing the character of each recognized built-in gain item to the allocable portion of the loss.

(c) Reduction in pass through for tax imposed on excess net passive income. For purposes of § 1.1366–1(a), if for any taxable year of the S corporation a tax is imposed on the corporation under section 1375, each item of passive investment income shall be reduced by an amount that bears the same ratio the amount of the tax as the net amount of the item bears to the total passive investment income for that taxable year.

[T.D. 8852, 64 FR 71641, Dec. 22, 1999; 68 FR 12471, Mar. 9, 2000]

§ 1.1367–1 Adjustments to basis of shareholder's stock in an S corporation.

(a) In general—(1) Adjustments under section 1367. This section provides rules relating to adjustments required by section 1367 to the basis of a shareholder's stock in an S corporation. Paragraph (b) of this section provides rules concerning increases in the basis of a shareholder's stock, and paragraph (c) of this section provides rules concerning decreases in the basis of a shareholder's stock.

(2) Applicability of other Internal Revenue Code provisions. In addition to the adjustments required by section 1367 and this section, the basis of stock is determined or adjusted under other applicable provisions of the Internal Revenue Code.

(b) Increase in basis of stock—(1) In general. Except as provided in § 1.1367–2(c) (relating to restoration of basis of indebtedness to the shareholder), the basis of a shareholder's stock in an S corporation is increased by the sum of the items described in section 1367(a)(1). The increase in basis described in section 1367(a)(1)(C) for the excess of the deduction for depletion over the basis of the property subject to depletion does not include the depletion deduction attributable to oil or gas property. See section 613(A)(c)(11).

(2) Amount of increase in basis of individual shares. The basis of a shareholder's share of stock is increased by an amount equal to the shareholder's pro rata portion of the items described in section 1367(a)(1) that is attributable to that share, determined on a per share, per day basis in accordance with section 1377(a).

(c) Decrease in basis of stock—(1) In general. The basis of a shareholder's stock in an S corporation is decreased (but not below zero) by the sum of the items described in section 1367(a)(2).

(2) Noncapital, nondeductible expenses. For purposes of section 1367(a)(2)(D), expenses of the corporation not deductible in computing its taxable income and not properly chargeable to a capital account (noncapital, nondeductible expenses) are only those items for which no loss or deduction is allowable and do not include items the deduction for which is deferred to a later taxable year. Examples of noncapital, nondeductible expenses include (but are not limited to) the following: illegal bribes, kickbacks, and other payments not deductible under section 162(c); fines and penalties not deductible under section 162(f); expenses and interest relating to tax-exempt income under section 265, losses for which the deduction is disallowed under section 267(a)(1); the portion of meals and entertainment expenses disallowed under section 274; and the two-thirds portion of treble damages paid for violating antitrust laws not deductible under section 162.

(3) Amount of decrease in basis of individual shares. The basis of a shareholder's share of stock is decreased by an amount equal to the shareholder's pro rata portion of the passthrough items and distributions described in section 1367(a)(2) attributable to that share, determined on a per share, per day basis in accordance with section 1377(a). If the amount attributable to a share exceeds its basis, the excess is applied to reduce (but not below zero) the remaining bases of all other shares of stock in the corporation owned by the shareholder in proportion to the remaining basis of each of those shares.

(d) Time at which adjustments to basis of stock are effective—(1) In general. The adjustments described in section 1367(a) to the basis of a shareholder's stock are determined as of the close of the corporation's taxable year, and the adjustments generally are effective as of that date. However, if a shareholder disposes of stock during the corporation's taxable year, the adjustments with respect to that stock are effective immediately prior to the disposition.

(2) Adjustment for nontaxable item. An adjustment for a nontaxable item is determined for the taxable year in which the item would have been includible or deductible under the corporation's method of accounting for federal income tax purposes if the item had been subject to federal income taxation.

(3) Effect of election under section 1377(a)(2) or § 1.1368–1(g)(2). If an election under section 1377(a)(2) (to terminate the year in the case of the termination of a shareholder's interest) or under § 1.1368–1(g)(2) (to terminate the year in the case of a qualifying disposition) is made with respect to the taxable year of a corporation, this paragraph (d) applies as if the taxable year consisted of separate taxable years, the first of which ends at the close of the day on which either the shareholder's interest is terminated or a qualifying disposition occurs, whichever the case may be.

* * *

(f) Ordering rules for taxable years beginning on or after August 18, 1998. For any taxable year of a corporation beginning on or after August 18, 1998, except as provided in paragraph (g) of this section, the adjustments required by section 1367(a) are made in the following order—

(1) Any increase in basis attributable to the income items described in section 1367(a)(1)(A) and (B), and the excess of the deductions for depletion described in section 1367(a)(1)(C);

(2) Any decrease in basis attributable to a distribution by the corporation described in section 1367(a)(2)(A);

(3) Any decrease in basis attributable to noncapital, nondeductible expenses described in section 1367(a)(2)(D), and the oil and gas depletion deduction described in section 1367(a)(2)(E); and

(4) Any decrease in basis attributable to items of loss or deduction described in section 1367(a)(2)(B) and (C).

(g) Elective ordering rule. A shareholder may elect to decrease basis under paragraph (e)(3) or (f)(4) of this section, whichever applies, prior to decreasing basis under paragraph (e)(2) or (f)(3) of this section, whichever applies. If a shareholder makes this election, any amount described in paragraph (e)(2) or (f)(3) of this section, whichever applies, that is in excess of the shareholder's basis in stock and indebtedness is treated, solely for purposes of this section, as an amount described in paragraph (e)(2) or (f)(3) of this section, whichever applies, in the succeeding taxable year. A shareholder makes the election under this paragraph by attaching a statement to the shareholder's timely filed original or amended return that states that the shareholder agrees to the carryover rule of the preceding sentence. Once a shareholder makes an election under this paragraph with respect to an S corporation, the shareholder must continue to use the rules of this paragraph for that S corporation in future taxable years unless the shareholder receives the permission of the Commissioner.

(h) Examples. The following examples illustrate the principles of § 1.1367–1. In each example, the corporation is a calendar year S corporation:

* * *

Example 2. Adjustments to basis of stock for taxable years beginning on or after August 18, 1998. **(i)** On December 31, 2001, A owns a block of 50 shares of stock with an adjusted basis per share of $6 in Corporation S. On December 31, 2001, A purchases for $400 an additional block of 50 shares of stock with an adjusted basis of $8 per share. Thus, A holds 100 shares of stock for each day of the 2002 taxable year. For S's 2002 taxable year, A's pro rata share of the amount of items described in section 1367(a)(1)(A) (relating to increases in basis of stock) is $300, A's pro rata share of the amount of the items described in section 1367(a)(2)(B) (relating to decreases in basis of stock attributable to items of loss and deduction) is $300, and A's pro rata share of the amount of the items described in section 1367(a)(2)(D) (relating to decreases in basis of stock attributable to noncapital, nondeductible expenses) is $200. S makes a distribution to A in the amount of $100 during 2002.

(ii) Pursuant to the ordering rules of paragraph (f) of this section, A first increases the basis of each share of stock by $3 ($300/100 shares) and then decreases the basis of each share by $1 ($100/100 shares) for the distribution. A next decreases the basis of each share by $2 ($200/100 shares) for the noncapital, nondeductible expenses and then decreases the basis of each share by $3 (300/100 shares) for the items of loss. Thus, on January 1, 2003, A has a basis of $3 per share in the original block of 50 shares ($6 + $3 – $1 – $2 – $3) and a basis of $5 per share in the second block of 100 shares ($8 + $3 – $1 – $2 – $3).

Example 3. Adjustments attributable to basis of individual shares of stock. **(i)** On December 31, 1993, B owns one share of S corporation's 10 outstanding shares of stock. The basis of B's share is $30. On July 2, 1994, B purchases from another shareholder two shares for $25 each. During 1994, S corporation has no income or deductions but incurs a loss of $365. Under section 1377(a)(1)(A) and paragraph (c)(3) of this section, the amount of the loss assigned to each day of S's taxable year is $1.00 ($365/365 days). For each day, $.10 is allocated to each outstanding share ($1.00 amount of loss assigned to each day/10 shares).

(ii) B owned one share for 365 days and, therefore, reduces the basis of that share by the amount of loss attributable to it, i.e., $36.50 ($.10 × 365 days). B owned two shares for 182 days and, therefore, reduces the basis of each of those shares by the amount of the loss attributable to each, i.e., $18.20 ($.10 × 182 days).

(iii) The bases of the shares are decreased as follows:

Share	Original basis	Decrease	Adjusted basis	Excess basis reduction
No. 1	$30.00	$36.50	$ 0	$6.50
No. 2	25.00	18.20	6.80	0
No. 3	25.00	18.20	6.80	0
Total remaining basis...........	......	......	13.60	.....

(iv) Because the decrease in basis attributable to share No. 1 exceeds the basis of share No. 1 by $6.50 ($36.50 – $30.00), the excess is applied to reduce the bases of shares No. 2 and No. 3 in proportion to their remaining bases. Therefore, the bases of share No. 2 and share No. 3 are each decreased by an additional $3.25 ($6.50 × $6.80/$13.60). After this decrease, Share No. 1 has a basis of zero, Share No. 2 has a basis of $3.55, and Share No. 3 has a basis of $3.55.

* * *

Example 5. Effects of section 1377(a)(2) election and distribution on basis of stock for taxable years beginning on or after August 18, 1998. (i) The facts are the same as in *Example 4*, except that all of the events occur in 2001 rather than in 1994 and except as follows: On June 30, 2001, B sells 25 shares of her stock for $5,000 to D and 25 shares back to Corporation S for $5,000. Under section 1377(a)(2)(B) and § 1.1377–1(b)(2), B, C, and D are affected shareholders because B has transferred shares to Corporations S and D. Pursuant to section 1377(a)(2)(A) and § 1.1377–1(b)(1), B, C, and D, the affected shareholders, and Corporation S agree to treat the taxable year 2001 as if it consisted of two separate taxable years for all affected shareholders for the purposes set forth in § 1.1377–1(b)(3)(i).

(ii) On June 30, 2001, B and C, pursuant to the ordering rules of paragraph (f)(1) of this section, increase the basis of each share by $60 ($6,000/100 shares) for the nonseparately computed income. Then B and C reduce the basis of each share by $120 ($12,000/100 shares) for the distribution. Finally, B and C decrease the basis of each share by $40 ($4,000/100 shares) for the separately stated deduction item.

(iii) The basis of the stock of B is reduced from $120 to $20 per share ($120 + $60—$120—$40). Prior to accounting for the separately stated deduction item, the basis of the stock of C is reduced from $80 to $20 ($80 $60—$120). Finally, because the period from January 1 through June 30, 2001 is treated under § 1.1377–1(b)(3)(i) as a separate taxable year for purposes of making adjustments to the basis of stock, under section 1366(d) and § 1.1366–2(a)(2), C may deduct only $20 per share of the remaining $40 of the separately stated deduction item, and the basis of the stock of C is reduced from $20 per share to $0 per share. Under section 1366 and § 1.1366–2(a)(2), C's remaining separately stated deduction item of $20 per share is treated as having been incurred in the first succeeding taxable year of Corporation S, which, for this purpose, begins on July 1, 2001.

(i) [Reserved]

(j) Adjustments for items of income in respect of a decedent. The basis determined under section 1014 of any stock in an S corporation is reduced by the portion of the value of the stock that is attributable to items constituting income in respect of a decedent. For the determination of items realized by an S corporation constituting income in respect of a decedent, see sections 1367(b)(4)(A) and 691 and applicable regulations thereunder. For the determination of the allowance of a deduction for the amount of estate tax attributable to income in respect of a decedent, see section 691(c) and applicable regulations thereunder.

[T.D. 8508, 59 FR 12, Jan. 3, 1994, as amended by T.D. 8852, 64 FR 71641, Dec. 22, 1999; 65 FR 12471, Mar. 9, 2000]

§ 1.1367–2 Adjustments to basis of indebtedness to shareholder.

(a) In general—(1) Adjustments under section 1367. This section provides rules relating to adjustments required by subchapter S to the basis of indebtedness (including open account debt as described in paragraph (a)(2) of this section) of an S corporation to a shareholder. The basis of indebtedness of the S corporation to a shareholder is reduced as provided in paragraph (b) of this section and restored as provided in paragraph (c) of this section in accordance with the timing rules in paragraph (d) of this section.

* * *

(b) Reduction in basis of indebtedness—(1) General rule. If, after making the adjustments required by section 1367(a)(1) for any taxable year of the S corporation, the amounts specified in section 1367(a)(2)(B), (C), (D), and (E) (relating to losses, deductions, noncapital, nondeductible expenses, and certain oil and gas depletion deductions) exceed the basis of a shareholder's stock in the corporation, the excess is applied to reduce (but not below zero) the basis of any indebtedness of the S corporation to the shareholder held by the shareholder at the close of the corporation's taxable year. Any such indebtedness that has been satisfied by the corporation, or disposed of or forgiven by the shareholder, during the taxable year, is not held by the shareholder at the close of that year and is not subject to basis reduction.

(2) Termination of shareholder's interest in corporation during taxable year. If a shareholder terminates his or her interest in the corporation during the taxable year, the rules of this paragraph (b) are applied with respect to any indebtedness of the S corporation held by the shareholder immediately prior to the termination of the shareholder's interest in the corporation.

(3) Multiple indebtedness. If a shareholder holds more than one indebtedness at the close of the corporation's taxable year or, if applicable, immediately prior to the termination of the shareholder's interest in the corporation, the reduction in basis is applied to each indebtedness in the same proportion that the basis of each indebtedness bears to the aggregate bases of the indebtedness to the shareholder.

(c) Restoration of basis—(1) General rule. If, for any taxable year of an S corporation beginning after December 31, 1982, there has been a reduction in the basis of an indebtedness of the S corporation to a shareholder under section

1367(b)(2)(A), any net increase in any subsequent taxable year of the corporation is applied to restore that reduction. For purposes of this section, net increase with respect to a shareholder means the amount by which the shareholder's pro rata share of the items described in section 1367(a)(1) (relating to income items and excess deduction for depletion) exceed the items described in section 1367(a)(2) (relating to losses, deductions, noncapital, nondeductible expenses, certain oil and gas depletion deductions, and certain distributions) for the taxable year. These restoration rules apply only to indebtedness held by a shareholder as of the beginning of the taxable year in which the net increase arises. The reduction in basis of indebtedness must be restored before any net increase is applied to restore the basis of a shareholder's stock in an S corporation. In no event may the shareholder's basis of indebtedness be restored above the adjusted basis of the indebtedness under section 1016(a), excluding any adjustments under section 1016(a)(17) for prior taxable years, determined as of the beginning of the taxable year in which the net increase arises.

(2) Multiple indebtedness. If a shareholder holds more than one indebtedness (including any open account debt and any debt treated as a single indebtedness under paragraph (a)(2)(ii) of this section) as of the beginning of an S corporation's taxable year, any net increase is applied first to restore the reduction of basis in any indebtedness repaid (in whole or in part) in that taxable year to the extent necessary to offset any gain that would otherwise be realized on the repayment. Any remaining net increase is applied to restore each outstanding indebtedness (including any open account debt and any debt treated as a single indebtedness under paragraph (a)(2)(ii) of this section) in proportion to the amount that the basis of each outstanding indebtedness has been reduced under section 1367(b)(2)(A) and paragraph (b) of this section and not restored under section 1367(b)(2)(B) and this paragraph (c).

(d) Time at which adjustments to basis of indebtedness are effective—(1) In general. The amounts of the adjustments to basis of indebtedness (including open account debt) provided in section 1367(b)(2) and this section are determined as of the close of the S corporation's taxable year, and the adjustments are generally effective as of the close of the S corporation's taxable year. However, if the shareholder is not a shareholder in the S corporation at that time, these adjustments are effective immediately before the shareholder terminates his or her interest in the S corporation. Except as provided in paragraph (d)(2) of this section, if a debt is disposed of or repaid in whole or in part before the close of the taxable year, the basis of that indebtedness is restored under paragraph (c) of this section, effective immediately before the disposition or the first repayment on the debt during the taxable year. To the extent any indebtedness of the S corporation to the shareholder is disposed of or repaid (in whole or in part) during the taxable year and the shareholder's basis in that indebtedness has been reduced under paragraph (b) of this section and is not restored completely under paragraph (c) of this section, the disposition or repayment is a recognition event effective immediately before the indebtedness is disposed of or repaid (in whole or in part).

(2) Open account debt—(i) In general. All advances and repayments on open account debt (as described in paragraph (a)(2)(i) of this section) during the S corporation's taxable year are netted at the close of the S corporation's taxable year to determine the amount of any net advance or net repayment. The net advance or net repayment is combined with the outstanding aggregate principal balance of the existing open account debt and that amount is carried forward to the beginning of the subsequent taxable year as the outstanding aggregate principal amount of the open account debt * * *.

(3) Effect of election under section 1377(a)(2) or § 1.1368–1(g)(2). If an election is made under section 1377(a)(2) (to terminate the year in the case of the termination of a shareholder's interest) or under § 1.1368–1(g)(2) (to terminate the year in the case of a qualifying disposition), this paragraph (d) applies as if the taxable year consisted of separate taxable years, the first of which ends at the close of the day on which the shareholder either terminates his or her interest in the corporation or disposes of a substantial amount of stock, whichever the case may be.

(e) Examples. The following examples illustrate the principles of § 1.1367–2. In each example, the corporation is a calendar year S corporation. The lending transactions described in the examples do not result in foregone interest (within the meaning of section 7872(e)(2)), original issue discount (within the meaning of section 1273), or total unstated interest (within the meaning of section 483(b)).

Example 1. Reduction in basis of indebtedness. **(i)** A has been the sole shareholder in Corporation S since 1992. In 1993, A loans S $1,000 (Debt No. 1), which is evidenced by a ten-year promissory note in the face amount of $1,000. In 1996, A loans S $5,000 (Debt No. 2), which is evidenced by a demand promissory note. On December 31, 1996, the basis of A's stock is zero; the basis of Debt No. 1 has been reduced under paragraph (b) of this section to $0; and the basis of Debt No. 2 has been reduced to $1,000. On January 1, 1997, A loans S $4,000 (Debt No. 3), which is evidenced by a demand promissory note. For S's 1997 taxable year, the sum of the amounts specified in section 1367(a)(1) (in this case, nonseparately computed income and the excess deduction for depletion) is $6,000, and the sum of the amounts specified in section 1367(a)(2)(B), (D), and (E) (in this case, items of separately stated deductions and losses, noncapital, nondeductible expenses, and certain oil and gas depletion deductions—there is no nonseparately computed loss) is $10,000. Corporation S makes no payments to A on any of the loans during 1997.

(ii) The $4,000 excess of loss and deduction items is applied to reduce the basis of each indebtedness in proportion to the basis of that indebtedness over the aggregate bases of the indebtedness to the shareholder (determined immediately before any adjustment under section 1367(b)(2)(A) and paragraph (b) of this section is effective for the taxable year). Thus, the basis of Debt No. 2 is reduced in an amount equal to $800 ($4,000 (excess) × $1,000 (basis of Debt No. 2)/$5,000 (total basis of all debt)). Similarly, the basis in Debt No. 3 is reduced in an amount equal to $3,200 ($4,000 × $4,000/$5,000). Accordingly, on December 31, 1997, A's basis in his stock is zero and his bases in the three debts are as follows:

Debt	1/1/96 basis	12/31/96 reduction	1/1/97 basis	12/31/97 reduction	1/1/98 basis
No. 1	$1,000	$1,000	$ 0	$ 0	$ 0
No. 2	5,000	4,000	1,000	800	200
No. 3	......	......	4,000	3,200	800

Example 2. Restoration of basis of indebtedness. **(i)** The facts are the same as in Example 1. On July 1, 1998, S completely repays Debt No. 3, and, for S's 1998 taxable year, the net increase (within the meaning of paragraph (c) of this section) with respect to A equals $4,500.

(ii) The net increase is applied first to restore the bases in the debts held on January 1, 1998, before any of the net increase is applied to increase A's basis in his shares of S stock. The net increase is applied to restore first the reduction of basis in indebtedness repaid in 1998. Any remaining net increase is applied to restore the bases of the outstanding debts in proportion to the amount that each of these outstanding debts have been reduced previously under paragraph (b) of this section and have not been restored. As of December 31, 1998, the total reduction in A's debts held on January 1, 1998 equals $9,000. Thus, the basis of Debt No. 3 is restored by $3,200 (the amount of the previous reduction) to $4,000. A's basis in Debt No. 3 is treated as restored immediately before that debt is repaid. Accordingly, A does not realize any gain on the repayment. The remaining net increase of $1,300 ($4,500 − $3,200) is applied to restore the bases of Debt No. 1 and Debt No. 2. As of December 31, 1998, the total reduction in these outstanding debts is $5,800 ($9,000 − $3,200). The basis of Debt No. 1 is restored in an amount equal to $224 ($1,300 × $1,000/$5,800). Similarly, the basis in Debt No. 2 is restored in an amount equal to $1,076 ($1,300 × $4,800/$5,800). On December 31, 1998, A's basis in his S stock is zero and his bases in the two remaining debts are as follows:

Original basis	Amount reduced	1/1/98 basis	Amount restored	12/31/98 basis
$1,000	$1,000	$ 0	$ 224	$ 224
5,000	4,800	200	1,076	1,276

Example 3. Full restoration of basis in indebtedness when debt is repaid in part during the taxable year. **(i)** C has been a shareholder in Corporation S since 1992. In 1997, C loans S $1,000. S issues its note to C in the amount of $1,000, of which $950 is payable on March 1, 1998, and $50 is payable on March 1, 1999. On December 31, 1997, C's basis in all her shares of S stock is zero and her basis in the note has been reduced under paragraph (b) of this section to $900. For 1998, the net increase (within the meaning of paragraph (c) of this section) with respect to C is $300.

(ii) Because C's basis of indebtedness was reduced in a prior taxable year under § 1.1367–2(b), the net increase for 1998 is applied to restore this reduction. The restored basis cannot exceed the adjusted basis of the debt as of the beginning of the first day of 1998, excluding prior adjustments under section 1367, or $1,000. Therefore, $100 of the $300 net increase is applied to restore the basis of the debt from $900 to $1,000 effective immediately before the repayment on March 1, 1998. The remaining net increase of $200 increases C's basis in her stock.

Example 4. Determination of net increase—distribution in excess of increase in basis. **(i)** D has been the sole shareholder in Corporation S since 1990. On January 1, 1996, D loans S $10,000 in return for a note from S in the amount of $10,000 of which $5,000 is payable on each of January 1, 2000, and January 1, 2001. On December 31, 1997, the basis of D's shares of S stock is zero, and his basis in the note has been reduced under paragraph (b) of this section to $8,000. During 1998, the sum of the items under section 1367(a)(1) (relating to increases in basis of stock) with respect to D equals $10,000 (in this case, nonseparately computed income), and the sum of the items under section 1367(a)(2)(B), (C), (D), and (E) (relating to decreases in basis of stock) with respect to D equals $0. During 1998, S also makes distributions to D totaling $11,000. This distribution is an item that reduces basis of stock under section 1367(a)(2)(A) and must be taken into account for purposes of determining whether there is a net increase for the taxable year. Thus, for 1998, there is no net increase with respect to D because the amount of the items provided in section 1367(a)(1) do not exceed the amount of the items provided in section 1367(a)(2).

(ii) Because there is no net increase with respect to D for 1998, none of the 1997 reduction in D's basis in the indebtedness is restored. The $10,000 increase in basis under section 1367(a)(1) is applied to increase D's basis in his S stock. Under section 1367(a)(2)(A), the $11,000 distribution with respect to D's stock reduces D's basis in his shares of S stock to $0. See section 1368 and § 1.1368–1(c) and (d) for the tax treatment of the $1,000 distribution in excess of D's basis.

Example 5. Distributions less than increase in basis. (i) The facts are the same as in Example 4, except that in 1998 S makes distributions to D totaling $8,000. On these facts, for 1998, there is a net increase with respect to D of $2,000 (the amount by which the items provided in section 1367(a)(1) exceed the amount of the items provided in section 1367(a)(2)).

(ii) Because there is a net increase of $2,000 with respect to D for 1998, $2,000 of the $10,000 increase in basis under section 1367(a)(1) is first applied to restore D's basis in the indebtedness to $10,000 ($8,000 + $2,000). Accordingly, on December 31, 1998, D has a basis in his shares of S stock of $0 ($0 + $8,000 (increase in basis remaining after restoring basis in indebtedness)— $8,000 (distribution)) and a basis in the note of $10,000.

* * *

[T.D. 8508, 59 FR 12, Jan. 3, 1994; T.D. 9428, 73 FR 67389, Nov. 14, 2008; 73 FR 71545, Nov. 25, 2008]

§ 1.1368–1 Distributions by S corporations.

(a) In general. This section provides rules for distributions made by an S corporation with respect to its stock which, but for section 1368(a) and this section, would be subject to section 301(c) and other rules of the Internal Revenue Code that characterize a distribution as a dividend.

(b) Date distribution made. For purposes of section 1368, a distribution is taken into account on the date the corporation makes the distribution, regardless of when the distribution is treated as received by the shareholder.

(c) S corporation with no earnings and profits. A distribution made by an S corporation that has no accumulated earnings and profits as of the end of the taxable year of the S corporation in which the distribution is made is treated in the manner provided in section 1368(b).

(d) S corporation with earnings and profits—(1) General treatment of distribution. Except as provided in paragraph (d)(2) of this section, a distribution made with respect to its stock by an S corporation that has accumulated earnings and profits as of the end of the taxable year of the S corporation in which the distribution is made is treated in the manner provided in section 1368(c). See section 316 and § 1.316–2 for provisions relating to the allocation of earnings and profits among distributions.

(2) Previously taxed income. This paragraph (d)(2) applies to distributions by a corporation that has both accumulated earnings and profits and previously taxed income (within the meaning of section 1375(d)(2), as in effect prior to its amendment by the Subchapter S Revision Act of 1982, and the regulations thereunder) with respect to one or more shareholders. In the case of such a distribution, that portion remaining after the application of section 1368(c)(1) (relating to distributions from the accumulated adjustments account (AAA) as defined in § 1.1368–2(a)) is treated in the manner provided in section 1368(b) (relating to S corporations without earnings and profits) to the extent that portion is a distribution of money and does not exceed the shareholder's net share immediately before the distribution of the corporation's previously taxed income. The AAA and the earnings and profits of the corporation are not decreased by that portion of the distribution. Any distribution remaining after the application of this paragraph (d)(2) is treated in the manner provided in section 1368(c)(2) and (3).

(e) Certain adjustments taken into account—* * *.

(2) Taxable years beginning on or after August 18, 1998. For any taxable year of the corporation beginning on or after August 18, 1998, paragraphs (c) and (d) of this section are applied only after taking into account—

(i) The adjustments to the basis of the shares of a shareholder's stock described in section 1367(a)(1) (relating to increases in basis of stock) for the S corporation's taxable year; and

(ii) The adjustments to the AAA required by section 1368(e)(1)(A) (but without regard to the adjustments for distributions under § 1.1368–2(a)(3)(iii)) for the S corporation's taxable year. Any net negative adjustment (as defined in section 1368(e)(1)(C)(ii)) for the taxable year shall not be taken into account.

(f) Elections relating to source of distributions—(1) In general. An S corporation may modify the application of paragraphs (c) and (d) of this section by electing (pursuant to paragraph (f)(5) of this section)—

(i) To distribute earnings and profits first as described in paragraph (f)(2) of this section;

(ii) To make a deemed dividend as described in paragraph (f)(3) of this section; or

(iii) To forego previously taxed income as described in paragraph (f)(4) of this section.

(2) Election to distribute earnings and profits first—(i) In general. An S corporation with accumulated earnings and profits may elect under this paragraph (f)(2) for any taxable year to distribute earnings and profits first as provided in section 1368(e)(3). Except as provided in paragraph (f)(2)(ii) of this section, distributions made by an S corporation making this election are treated as made first from earnings and profits under section 1368(c)(2) and second from the AAA under section 1368(c)(1). Any remaining portion of the distribution is treated in the manner provided in section 1368(b). This election is effective for all distributions made during the year for which the election is made.

(ii) Previously taxed income. If a corporation to which paragraph (d)(2) of this section (relating to corporations with previously taxed income) applies makes the election provided in this paragraph (f)(2) for the taxable year, and does not make the election to forego previously taxed income under paragraph (f)(4) of this section, distributions by the S corporation during the taxable year are treated as made first, from previously taxed income under paragraph (d)(2) of this section; second, from earnings and profits under section 1368(c)(2); and third, from the AAA under section 1368(c)(1). Any portion of a distribution remaining after the previously taxed income, earnings and profits, and the AAA are exhausted is treated in the manner provided in section 1368(b).

(iii) Corporation with subchapter C and subchapter S earnings and profits. If an S corporation that makes the election provided in this paragraph (f)(2) has both subchapter C earnings and profits (as defined in section 1362(d)(3)(B)) and subchapter S earnings and profits in a taxable year of the corporation in which the distribution is made, the distribution is treated as made first from subchapter C earnings and profits, and second from subchapter S earnings and profits. Subchapter S earnings and profits are earnings and profits accumulated in a taxable year beginning before January 1, 1983 (or in the case of a qualified casualty insurance electing small business corporation or a qualified oil corporation, earnings and profits accumulated in any taxable year), for which an election under subchapter S of chapter 1 of the Internal Revenue Code was in effect.

(3) Election to make a deemed dividend. An S corporation may elect under this paragraph (f)(3) to distribute all or part of its subchapter C earnings and profits through a deemed dividend. If an S corporation makes the election provided in this paragraph (f)(3), the S corporation will be considered to have made the election provided in paragraph (f)(2) of this section (relating to the election to distribute earnings and profits first). The amount of the deemed dividend may not exceed the subchapter C earnings and profits of the corporation on the last day of the taxable year, reduced by any actual distributions of subchapter C earnings and profits made during the taxable year. The amount of the deemed dividend is considered, for all purposes of the Internal Revenue Code, as if it were distributed in money to the shareholders in proportion to their stock ownership, received by the shareholders, and immediately contributed by the shareholders to the corporation, all on the last day of the corporation's taxable year.

(4) Election to forego previously taxed income. An S corporation may elect to forego distributions of previously taxed income. If such an election is made, paragraph (d)(2) of this section (relating to corporations with previously taxed income) does not apply to any distribution made during the taxable year. Thus, distributions by a corporation that makes the election to forego previously taxed income for a taxable year under this paragraph (f)(4) and does not make the election to distribute earnings and profits first under paragraph (f)(2) of this section are treated in the manner provided in section 1368(c) (relating to distributions by corporations with earnings and profits). Distributions by a corporation that makes both the election to distribute earnings and profits first under paragraph (f)(2) of this section and the election to forego previously taxed income under this paragraph (f)(4), are treated in the manner provided in paragraph (f)(2)(i) of this section.

(5) Time and manner of making elections—(i) For earnings and profits. If an election is made under paragraph (f)(2) of this section to distribute earnings and profits first, see section 1368(e)(3) regarding the consent required by shareholders.

(ii) For previously taxed income and deemed dividends. If an election is made to forego previously taxed income under paragraph (f)(4) of this section or to make a deemed dividend under paragraph (f)(3) of this section, consent by each "affected shareholder," as defined in section 1368(e)(3)(B), is required.

(iii) Corporate statement regarding elections. A corporation makes an election for a taxable year under § 1.1368–1(f) by attaching a statement to a timely filed (including extensions) original or amended return required to be filed under section 6037 for that taxable year. * * *

(iv) Irrevocable elections. The elections under this paragraph (f) are irrevocable and are effective only for the taxable year for which they are made. * * *

* * *

[T.D. 8508, 59 FR 12, Jan. 3, 1994, as amended by T.D. 8696, 61 FR 67454, Dec. 23, 1996; T.D. 8852, 64 FR 71641, Dec. 22, 1999; T.D. 9100, 68 FR 70701, Dec. 19, 2003; T.D. 9300, 71 FR 71040, Dec. 8, 2006]

§ 1.1368–2 Accumulated adjustments account (AAA).

(a) Accumulated adjustments account—(1) In general. The accumulated adjustments account is an account of the S corporation and is not apportioned among shareholders. The AAA is relevant for all taxable years beginning on or after January 1, 1983, for which the corporation is an S corporation. On the first day of the first year for which the corporation is an S corporation, the balance of the AAA is zero. The AAA is increased in the manner provided in paragraph (a)(2) of this section and is decreased in the manner provided in paragraph (a)(3) of this section. For the adjustments to the AAA in the case of redemptions, liquidations, reorganizations, and corporate separations, see paragraph (d) of this section.

(2) Increases to the AAA. The AAA is increased for the taxable year of the corporation by the sum of the following items with respect to the corporation for the taxable year:

(i) The items of income described in section 1366(a)(1)(A) other than income that is exempt from tax,

(ii) Any nonseparately computed income determined under section 1366(a)(1)(B); and

(iii) The excess of the deductions for depletion over the basis of property subject to depletion unless the property is an oil or gas property the basis of which has been allocated to shareholders under section 613A(c)(11).

(3) Decreases to the AAA—(i) In general. The AAA is decreased for the taxable year of the corporation by the sum of the following items with respect to the corporation for the taxable year—

(A) The items of loss or deduction described in section 1366(a)(1)(A);

(B) Any nonseparately computed loss determined under section 1366(a)(1)(B);

(C) Any expense of the corporation not deductible in computing its taxable income and not properly chargeable to a capital account, other than—

(1) Federal taxes attributable to any taxable year in which the corporation was a C corporation; and

(2) Expenses related to income that is exempt from tax; and

(D) The sum of the shareholders' deductions for depletion for any oil or gas property held by the corporation described in section 1367(a)(2)(E).

(ii) Extent of allowable reduction. The AAA may be decreased under paragraph (a)(3)(i) of this section below zero. The AAA is decreased by noncapital, nondeductible expenses under paragraph (a)(3)(i)(C) of this section even though a portion of the noncapital, nondeductible expenses is not taken into account by a shareholder under § 1.1367–1(g) (relating to the elective ordering rule). The AAA is also decreased by the entire amount of any loss or deduction even though a portion of the loss or deduction is not taken into account by a shareholder under section 1366(d)(1) or is otherwise not currently deductible under the Internal Revenue Code. However, in any subsequent taxable year in which the loss, deduction, or noncapital, nondeductible expense is treated as incurred by the corporation with respect to the shareholder under section 1366(d)(2) or § 1.1367–1(g) (or in which the loss or deduction is otherwise allowed to the shareholder), no further adjustment is made to the AAA.

(iii) Decrease to the AAA for distributions. The AAA is decreased (but not below zero) by any portion of a distribution to which section 1368(b) or (c)(1) applies.

* * *

(5) Ordering rules for the AAA for taxable years beginning on or after August 18, 1998. For any taxable year of the S corporation beginning on or after August 18, 1998, the adjustments to the AAA are made in the following order—

(i) The AAA is increased under paragraph (a)(2) of this section before it is decreased under paragraph (a)(3)(i) of this section for the taxable year;

(ii) The AAA is decreased under paragraph (a)(3)(i) of this section (without taking into account any net negative adjustment (as defined in section 1368(e)(1)(C)(ii)) before it is decreased under paragraph (a)(3)(iii) of this section);

(iii) The AAA is decreased (but not below zero) by any portion of an ordinary distribution to which section 1368(b) or (c)(1) applies;

(iv) The AAA is decreased by any net negative adjustment (as defined in section 1368(e)(1)(C)(ii)); and

(v) The AAA is adjusted (whether negative or positive) for redemption distributions under paragraph (d)(1) of this section.

(b) Distributions in excess of the AAA—(1) In general. A portion of the AAA (determined under paragraph (b)(2) of this section) is allocated to each of the distributions made for the taxable year if—

(i) An S corporation makes more than one distribution of property with respect to its stock during the taxable year of the corporation (including an S short year as defined under section 1362(e)(1)(A));

(ii) The AAA has a positive balance at the close of the year; and

(iii) The sum of the distributions made during the corporation's taxable year exceeds the balance of the AAA at the close of the year.

(2) Amount of the AAA allocated to each distribution. The amount of the AAA allocated to each distribution is determined by multiplying the balance of the AAA at the close of the current taxable year by a fraction, the numerator of which is the amount of the distribution and the denominator of which is the amount of all distributions made during the taxable year. For purposes of this paragraph (b)(2), the term all distributions made during the taxable year does not include any distribution treated as from earnings and profits or previously taxed income pursuant to an election made under section 1368(e)(3) and § 1.1368-1(f)(2). See paragraph (d)(1) of this section for rules relating to the adjustments to the AAA for redemptions and distributions in the year of a redemption.

(c) Distribution of money and loss property—(1) In general. The amount of the AAA allocated to a distribution under this section must be further allocated (under paragraph (c)(2) of this section) if the distribution—

(i) Consists of property the adjusted basis of which exceeds its fair market value on the date of the distribution and money;

(ii) Is a distribution to which § 1.1368-1(d)(1) applies; and

(iii) Exceeds the amount of the corporation's AAA properly allocable to that distribution.

(2) Allocating the AAA to loss property. The amount of the AAA allocated to the property other than money is equal to the amount of the AAA allocated to the distribution multiplied by a fraction, the numerator of which is the fair market value of the property other than money on the date of distribution and the denominator of which is the amount of the distribution. The amount of the AAA allocated to the money is equal to the amount of the AAA allocated to the distribution reduced by the amount of the AAA allocated to the property other than money.

(d) Adjustment in the case of redemptions, liquidations, reorganizations, and divisions—(1) Redemptions—(i) General rule. In the case of a redemption distribution by an S corporation that is treated as an exchange under section 302(a) or section 303(a) (a redemption distribution), the AAA of the corporation is adjusted in an amount equal to the ratable share of the corporation's AAA (whether negative or positive) attributable to the redeemed stock as of the date of the redemption.

(ii) Special rule for years in which a corporation makes both ordinary and redemption distributions. In any year in which a corporation makes one or more distributions to which section 1368(a) applies (ordinary distributions) and makes one or more redemption distributions, the AAA of the corporation is adjusted first for any ordinary distributions and then for any redemption distributions.

(iii) Adjustments to earnings and profits. Earnings and profits are adjusted under section 312 independently of any adjustments made to the AAA.

(2) Liquidations and reorganizations. An S corporation acquiring the assets of another S corporation in a transaction to which section 381(a) applies will succeed to and merge its AAA (whether positive or negative) with the AAA (whether positive or negative) of the distributor or transferor S corporation as of the close of the date of distribution or transfer. Thus, the AAA of the acquiring corporation after the transaction is the sum of the AAAs of the corporations prior to the transaction.

(3) Corporate separations to which section 368(a)(1)(D) applies. If an S corporation with accumulated earnings and profits transfers a part of its assets constituting an active trade or business to another corporation in a transaction to which section 368(a)(1)(D) applies, and immediately thereafter the stock and securities of the controlled corporation are distributed in a distribution or exchange to which section 355 (or so much of section 356 as relates to section 355) applies, the AAA of the distributing corporation immediately before the transaction is allocated between the distributing corporation and the controlled corporation in a manner similar to the manner in which the earnings and profits of the distributing corporation are allocated under section 312(h). See § 1.312–10(a).

* * *

[T.D. 8508, 59 FR 12, Jan. 3, 1994, as amended by T.D. 8852, 64 FR 71641, Dec. 22, 1999; T.D. 8869, 65 FR 3843, Jan. 25, 2000]

§ 1.1368–3 Examples.

The principles of §§ 1.1368–1 and 1.1368–2 are illustrated by the examples below. In each example Corporation S is a calendar year corporation:

* * *

Example 2. Distributions by S corporations without earnings and profits for taxable years beginning on or after August 18, 1998. (i) Corporation S, an S corporation, has no earnings and profits as of January 1, 2001, the first day of its 2001 taxable year. S's sole shareholder, A, holds 10 shares of S stock with a basis of $1 per share as of that date. On March 1, 2001, S makes a distribution of $38 to A. The balance in Corporation S's AAA is $100. For S's 2001 taxable year, A's pro rata share of the amount of the items described in section 1367(a)(1) (relating to increases in basis of stock) is $50. A's pro rata share of the amount of the items described in section 1367(a)(2)(B) through (D) (relating to decreases in basis of stock for items other than distributions) is $26, $20 of which is attributable to items described in section 1367(a)(2)(B) and (C) and $6 of which is attributable to items described in section 1367(a)(2)(D) (relating to decreases in basis attributable to noncapital, nondeductible expenses).

(ii) Under section 1368(d)(1) and § 1.1368–1(e)(1) and (2), the adjustments to the basis of A's stock in S described in sections 1367(a)(1) are made before the distribution rules of section 1368 are applied. Thus, A's basis per share in the stock is $6.00 ($1 + [$50/10]) before taking into account the distribution. Under section 1367(a)(2)(A), the basis of A's stock is decreased by distributions to A that are not includible in A's income. Under § 1.1367–1(c)(3), the amount of the distribution that is attributable to each share of A's stock is $3.80 ($38 distribution/10 shares). Thus, A's basis per share in the stock is $2.20 ($6.00 − $3.80), after taking into account the distribution. Under section 1367(a)(2)(D), the basis of each share of A's stock in S after taking into account the distribution, $2.20, is decreased by $.60 ($6 noncapital, nondeductible expenses/10). Thus, A's basis per share after taking into account the nondeductible, noncapital expenses is $1.60. Under section 1367(a)(2)(B) and (C), A's basis per share is further decreased by $2 ($20 items described in section 1367(a)(2)(B) and (C)/10 shares). However, basis may not be reduced below zero. Therefore, the basis of each share of A's stock is reduced to zero. As of January 1, 2002, A has a basis of $0 in his hares of S stock. Pursuant to section 1366(d)(2), the $.40 of loss in excess of A's basis in each of his shares of S stock is treated as incurred by the corporation in the succeeding taxable year with respect to A.

* * *

Example 4. Distributions by S corporations with earnings and profits and no net negative adjustment for taxable years beginning on or after August 18, 1998. (i) Corporation S, an S corporation, has accumulated earnings and profits of $1,000 and a balance in the AAA of $2,000 on January 1, 2001. S's sole shareholder B holds 100 shares of stock with a basis of $20 per share as of January 1, 2001. On April 1, 2001, S makes a distribution of $1,500 to B. B's pro rata share of the income earned by S during 2001 is $2,000 and B's pro rata share of S's losses is $1,500. For the taxable year ending December 31, 2001, S does not have a net negative adjustment as defined in section 1368(e)(1)(C). S does not make the election under section 1368(e)(1)(C). S does not make the election under section 1368(e)(3) and § 1.1368–1(f)(2) to distribute its earnings and profits before its AAA.

(ii) The AAA is increased from $2,000 to $4,000 for the $2,000 of income earned during the 2001 taxable year. The AAA is decreased from $4,000 to $2,500 for the $1,500 of losses. The AAA is decreased from $2,500 to $1,000 for the portion of the distribution ($1,500) to B that does not exceed the AAA.

(iii) As of December 31, 2001, B's basis in his stock is $10 ($20 + $20) ($2,000 income/100 shares)—$15 ($1,500 distribution/100 shares)—$15 ($1,500 loss/100 shares).

Example 5. Distributions by S corporations with earnings and profits and net negative adjustment for taxable years beginning on or after August 18, 1998. (i) Corporation S, an S corporation, has accumulated earnings and profits of $1,000 and a balance in the AAA of $2,000 on January 1, 2001. S's sole shareholder B holds 100 shares of stock with a basis of $20 per share as of January 1, 2001. On April 1, 2001, S makes a distribution of $2,000 to B. B's pro rata share of the income earned by S during 2001 is $2,000 and B's pro rata share of S's losses is $3,500. For the taxable year ending December 31, 2001, S has a net negative adjustment as defined in section 1368(e)(1)(C). S does not make the election under section

1368(e)(3) and § 1.1368–1(f)(2) to distribute its earnings and profits before its AAA.

(ii) The AAA is increased from $2,000 to $4,000 for the $2,000 of income earned during the 2001 taxable year. Because under section 1368(e)(1)(C)(ii) and § 1.1368–2(a)(ii), the net negative adjustment is not taken into account, the AAA is decreased from $4,000 to $2,000 for the portion of the losses ($2,000) that does not exceed the income earned during the 2001 taxable year. The AAA is reduced from $2,000 to zero for the portion of the distribution to B ($2,000) that does not exceed the AAA. The AAA is decreased from zero to a negative $1,500 for the portion of the $3,500 of loss that exceeds the $2,000 of income earned during the 2001 taxable year.

(iii) Under § 1.1367–1(c)(1), the basis of a shareholder's share in an S corporation stock may not be reduced below zero. Accordingly, as of December 31, 2001, B's basis per share in his stock is zero ($20 + $20 income − $20 distribution − $35 loss). Pursuant to section 1366(d)(2), the $15 of loss in excess of B's basis in each of his shares of S stock is treated as incurred by the corporation in the succeeding taxable year with respect to B.

Example 6. Election in case of disposition of substantial amount of stock. **(i)** Corporation S, and S corporation, has earnings and profits of $3,000 and a balance in the AAA of $1,000 on January 1, 1997. C, an individual and the sole shareholder of Corporation S, has 100 shares of S stock with a basis of $10 per share. On July 3, 1997, C sells 50 shares of his S stock to D, an individual, for $250. For 1997, S has taxable income of $1,000, of which $500 was earned on or before July 3, 1997, and $500 earned after July 3, 1997. During its 1997 taxable year, S distributes $1,000 to C on February 1 and $1,000 to each of C and D on August 1. S does not make the election under section 1368(e)(3) and § 1.1368–1(f)(2) to distribute its earnings and profits before its AAA. S makes the election under § 1.1368–1(g)(2) to treat its taxable year as if it consisted of separate taxable years, the first of which ends at the close of July 3, 1997, the date of the qualifying disposition.

(ii) Under section § 1.1368–1(g)(2), for the period ending on July 3, 1997, S's AAA is $500 ($1,000 (AAA as of January 1, 1997) + $500 (income earned from January 1, 1997 through July 3, 1997) − $1,000 (distribution made on February 1, 1997)). C's bases in his shares of stock is decreased to $5 per share ($10 (original basis) + $5 (increase per share for income) − $10 (decrease per share for distribution)).

(iii) The AAA is adjusted at the end of the taxable year for the period July 4 through December 31, 1997. It is increased from $500 (AAA as of the close of July 3, 1997) to $1,000 for the income earned during this period and is decreased by $1,000, the portion of the distribution ($2,000 in total) made to C and D on August 1 that does not exceed the AAA. The $1,000 portion of the distribution that remains after the AAA is reduced to zero is attributable to earnings and profits. Therefore C and D each have a dividend of $500, which does not affect their basis or S's AAA. The earnings and profits account is reduced from $3,000 to $2,000.

(iv) As of December 31, 1997, C and D have bases in their shares of stock of zero ($5 (basis as of July 4) + $5 ($500 income/100 shares) − $10 ($1,000 distribution/100 shares)). C and D each will report $500 as dividend income, which does not affect their basis or S's AAA.

Example 7. Election to distribute earnings and profits first. **(i)** Corporation S has been a calendar year C corporation since 1975. For 1982, S elects for the first time to be taxed under subchapter S, and during 1982 has $60 of earnings and profits. As of December 31, 1995, S has an AAA of $10 and earnings and profits of $160, consisting of $100 of subchapter C earnings and profits and $60 of subchapter S earnings and profits. For 1996, S has $200 of taxable income and the AAA is increased to $210 (before taking distributions into account). During 1996, S distributes $240 to its shareholders. With its 1996 tax return, S properly elects under section 1368(e)(3) and § 1.1368–1(f)(2) to distribute its earnings and profits before its AAA.

(ii) Because S elected to distribute its earnings and profits before its AAA, the first $100 of the distribution is characterized as a distribution from subchapter C earnings and profits; the next $60 of the distribution is characterized as a distribution from subchapter S earnings and profits. Because $160 of the distribution is from earnings and profits, the shareholders of S have a $160 dividend. The remaining $80 of the distribution is a distribution from S's AAA and is treated by the shareholders as a return of capital or gain from the sale or exchange of property, as appropriate, under § 1.1368–1(d)(1). S's AAA, as of December 31, 1996, equals $130 ($210 − $80).

Example 8. Distributions in excess of the AAA. **(i)** On January 1, 1995, Corporation S has $40 of earnings and profits and a balance in the AAA of $100. S has two shareholders, E and F, each of whom own 50 shares of S's stock. For 1995, S has taxable income of $50, which increases the AAA to $150 as of December 31, 1995 (before taking into account distributions made during 1995). On February 1, 1995, S distributes $60 to each shareholder. On September 1, 1995, S distributes $30 to each shareholder. S does not make the election under section 1368(e)(3) and § 1.1368–1(f)(2) to distribute its earnings and profits before its AAA.

(ii) The sum of the distributions exceed S's AAA. Therefore, under § 1.1368–2(b), a portion of S's $150 balance in the AAA as of December 31, 1995, is allocated to each of the February 1 and September 1 distributions based on the respective sizes of the distributions. Accordingly, S must allocate $100 ($150 (AAA) × ($120 (February 1 distribution)/$180 (the sum of the distributions))) of the AAA to the February 1 distribution, and $50 ($150 × ($60/$180)) to the September 1 distribution. The portions of the distributions to which the AAA is allocated are treated by the shareholder as a return of capital or gain from the sale or exchange of property, as appropriate. The remainder of the two distributions is treated as a dividend to the extent that it does not exceed S's earnings and profits. E and F must each report $10 of dividend income for the February 1 distribution. For the September 1 distribution, E and F must each report $5 of dividend income.

Example 9. Ordinary and redemption distributions in the same taxable year. **(i)** On January 1, 1995, Corporation S, an S corporation, has $20 of earnings and profits and a balance in the AAA of $10. S has two shareholders, G and H, each of whom owns 50 shares of S's stock. For 1995, S has taxable income of $16, which increases the AAA to $26 as of December 31, 1995 (before taking into account distributions made during 1995). On

February 1, 1995, S distributes $10 to each shareholder. On December 31, 1995, S redeems for $13 all of shareholder G's stock in a redemption that is treated as a sale or exchange under section 302(a).

(ii) The sum of the ordinary distributions does not exceed S's AAA. Therefore, S must reduce the $26 balance in the AAA by $20 for the February 1 ordinary distribution. The portions of the distribution by which the AAA is reduced are treated by the shareholders as a return of capital or gain from the sale or exchange of property. S must adjust the remaining AAA, $6, in an amount equal to the ratable share of the remaining AAA attributable to the redeemed stock, or $3 (50% × $6).

(iii) S also must adjust the earnings and profits of $20 in an amount equal to the ratable share of the earnings and profits attributable to the redeemed stock. Therefore, S adjusts the earnings and profits by $10 (50% × $20), the ratable share of the earnings and profits attributable to the redeemed stock.

[T.D. 8508, 59 FR 12, Jan. 3, 1994, as amended by T.D. 8852, 64 FR 71641, Dec. 22, 1999]

§ 1.1374–1 General rules and definitions.

(a) Computation of tax. The tax imposed on the income of an S corporation by section 1374(a) for any taxable year during the recognition period is computed as follows—

(1) Step One: Determine the net recognized built-in gain of the corporation for the taxable year under section 1374(d)(2) and § 1.1374–2;

(2) Step Two: Reduce the net recognized built-in gain (but not below zero) by any net operating loss and capital loss carryforward allowed under section 1374(b)(2) and § 1.1374–5;

(3) Step Three: Compute a tentative tax by applying the rate of tax determined under section 1374(b)(1) for the taxable year to the amount determined under paragraph (a)(2) of this section;

(4) Step Four: Compute the final tax by reducing the tentative tax (but not below zero) by any credit allowed under section 1374(b)(3) and § 1.1374–6.

(b) Anti-trafficking rules. If section 382, 383, or 384 would have applied to limit the use of a corporation's recognized built-in loss or section 1374 attributes at the beginning of the first day of the recognition period if the corporation had remained a C corporation, these sections apply to limit their use in determining the S corporation's pre-limitation amount, taxable income limitation, net unrealized built-in gain limitation, deductions against net recognized built-in gain, and credits against the section 1374 tax.

(c) Section 1374 attributes. Section 1374 attributes are the loss carryforwards allowed under section 1374(b)(2) as a deduction against net recognized built-in gain and the credit and credit carryforwards allowed under section 1374(b)(3) as a credit against the section 1374 tax.

(d) Recognition period. The recognition period is the 10–year (120–month) period beginning on the first day the corporation is an S corporation or the day an S corporation acquires assets in a section 1374(d)(8) transaction. For example, if the first day of the recognition period is July 14, 1996, the last day of the recognition period is July 13, 2006. If the recognition period for certain assets ends during an S corporation's taxable year (for example, because the corporation was on a fiscal year as a C corporation and changed to a calendar year as an S corporation or because an S corporation acquired assets in a section 1374(d)(8) transaction during a taxable year), the S corporation must determine its prelimitation amount (as defined in § 1.1374–2(a)(1)) for the year as if the corporation's books were closed at the end of the recognition period.

(e) Predecessor corporation. For purposes of section 1374(c)(1), if the basis of an asset of the S corporation is determined (in whole or in part) by reference to the basis of the asset (or any other property) in the hands of another corporation, the other corporation is a predecessor corporation of the S corporation.

[T.D. 8579, 59 FR 66458, Dec. 27, 1994]

§ 1.1374–2 Net recognized built-in gain.

(a) In general. An S corporation's net recognized built-in gain for any taxable year is the least of—

(1) Its taxable income determined by using all rules applying to C corporations and considering only its recognized built-in gain, recognized built-in loss, and recognized built-in gain carryover (pre-limitation amount);

(2) Its taxable income determined by using all rules applying to C corporations as modified by section 1375(b)(1)(B) (taxable income limitation); and

(3) The amount by which its net unrealized built-in gain exceeds its net recognized built-in gain for all prior taxable years (net unrealized built-in gain limitation).

(b) Allocation rule. If an S corporation's pre-limitation amount for any taxable year exceeds its net recognized built-in gain for that year, the S corporation's net recognized built-in gain consists of a ratable portion of each item of income, gain, loss, and deduction included in the pre-limitation amount.

(c) Recognized built-in gain carryover. If an S corporation's net recognized built-in gain for any taxable year is equal to its taxable income limitation, the amount by which its pre-limitation amount exceeds its taxable income limitation is a recognized built-in gain carryover included in its pre-limitation amount for the succeeding taxable year. The recognized built-in gain carryover consists of that portion of each item of income, gain, loss, and deduction not included in the S corporation's net recognized built-in gain for the year the carryover arose, as determined under paragraph (b) of this section.

(d) Accounting methods. In determining its taxable income for pre-limitation amount and taxable income limitation purposes, a corporation must use the accounting method(s) it uses for tax purposes as an S corporation.

(e) Example. The rules of this section are illustrated by the following example.

Example. Net recognized built-in gain. X is a calendar year C corporation that elects to become an S corporation on January 1, 1996. X has a net unrealized built-in gain of $50,000 and no net operating loss or capital loss carryforwards. In 1996, X has a pre-limitation amount of $20,000, consisting of ordinary income of $15,000 and capital gain of $5,000, a taxable income limitation of $9,600, and a net unrealized built-in gain limitation of $50,000. Therefore, X's net recognized built-in gain for 1996 is $9,600, because that is the least of the three amounts described in paragraph (a) of this section. Under paragraph (b) of this section, X's net recognized built-in gain consists of recognized built-in ordinary income of $7,200 [$15,000 x ($9,600/$20,000) = $7,200] and recognized built-in capital gain of $2,400 [$5,000 x ($9,600/$20,000) = $2,400]. Under paragraph (c) of this section, X has a recognized built-in gain carryover to 1997 of $10,400 ($20,000 - $9,600 = $10,400), consisting of $7,800 ($15,000 - $7,200 = $7,800) of recognized built-in ordinary income and $2,600 ($5,000 - $2,400 = $2,600) of recognized built-in capital gain.

[T.D. 8579, 59 FR 66458, Dec. 27, 1994]

§ 1.1374–3 Net unrealized built-in gain.

(a) In general. An S corporation's net unrealized built-in gain is the total of the following—

(1) The amount that would be the amount realized if, at the beginning of the first day of the recognition period, the corporation had remained a C corporation and had sold all its assets at fair market value to an unrelated party that assumed all its liabilities; decreased by

(2) Any liability of the corporation that would be included in the amount realized on the sale referred to in paragraph (a)(1) of this section, but only if the corporation would be allowed a deduction on payment of the liability; decreased by

(3) The aggregate adjusted bases of the corporation's assets at the time of the sale referred to in paragraph (a)(1) of this section; increased or decreased by

(4) The corporation's section 481 adjustments that would be taken into account on the sale referred to in paragraph (a)(1) of this section; and increased by

(5) Any recognized built-in loss that would not be allowed as a deduction under section 382, 383, or 384 on the sale referred to in paragraph (a)(1) of this section.

* * *

(c) Examples. The following examples illustrate the rules of this section:

Example 1. Computation of net unrealized built-in gain. X, a calendar year C corporation using the cash method, elects to become an S corporation on January 1, 1996. On December 31, 1995, X has assets and liabilities as follows:

	FMV	*Basis*
Assets:		
Factory	$ 500,000	$900,000
Accounts Receivable	300,000	0
Goodwill	250,000	0
Total	$1,050,000	$900,000
Liabilities	*Amount*	
Mortgage	$ 200,000	
Accounts Payable	100,000	
Total	$ 300,000	

(b) Further, X must include a total of $60,000 in taxable income in 1996, 1997, and 1998 under section 481(a).

(ii) If, on December 31, 1995, X sold all its assets to a third party that assumed all its liabilities, X's amount realized would be $1,050,000 ($750,000 cash received + $300,000 liabilities assumed = $1,050,000). Thus, X's net unrealized built-in gain is determined as follows:

Amount realized	$1,050,000
Deduction allowed	(100,000)
Basis of X's assets	(900,000)
Section 481 adjustments	60,000
Net unrealized built-in gain	$ 110,000

* * *

[T.D. 8579, 59 FR 66458, Dec. 27, 1994; as amended by T.D. 9182, 70 FR 8727, Feb. 23, 2005]

§ 1.1374–4 Recognized built-in gain or loss.

(a) Sales and exchanges—(1) In general. Section 1374(d)(3) or 1374(d)(4) applies to any gain or loss recognized during the recognition period in a transaction treated as a sale or exchange for federal income tax purposes.

(2) Oil and gas property. For purposes of paragraph (a)(1) of this section, an S corporation's adjusted basis in oil and gas property equals the sum of the shareholders' adjusted bases in the property as determined in section 613A(c)(11)(B).

(3) Examples. The rules of this paragraph (a) are illustrated by the following examples.

Example 1. Production and sale of oil. X is a C corporation that purchased a working interest in an oil and gas property for $100,000 on July 1, 1993. X elects to become an S corporation effective January 1, 1996. On that date, the working interest has a fair market value of $250,000 and an adjusted basis of $50,000, but no oil has as yet been extracted. In 1996, X begins production of the working interest, sells oil that it has produced to a refinery for $75,000, and includes that amount in gross income. Under paragraph (a)(1) of this section, the $75,000 is not recognized built-in gain because as of the beginning of the recognition period X held only a working interest in the oil and gas property (since the oil had not yet been extracted from the ground), and not the oil itself.

Example 2. Sale of oil and gas property. Y is a C corporation that elects to become an S corporation effective January 1, 1996. Y has two shareholders, A and B. A and B each own 50 percent of Y's stock. In addition, Y owns a royalty interest in an oil and gas property with a fair market value of $300,000 and an adjusted basis of $200,000. Under section 613A(c)(11)(B), Y's $200,000 adjusted basis in the royalty interest is allocated $100,000 to A and $100,000 to B. During 1996, A and B take depletion deductions with respect to the royalty interest of $10,000 and $15,000, respectively. As of January 1, 1997, A and B have a basis in the royalty interest of $90,000 and $85,000, respectively. On January 1, 1997, Y sells the royalty interest for $250,000. Under paragraph (a)(1) of this section, Y has gain recognized and recognized built-in gain of $75,000 ($250,000 − ($90,000 + $85,000) = $75,000) on the sale.

(b) Accrual method rule—(1) Income items. Except as otherwise provided in this section, any item of income properly taken into account during the recognition period is recognized built-in gain if the item would have been properly included in gross income before the beginning of the recognition period by an accrual method taxpayer (disregarding any method of accounting for which an election by the taxpayer must be made unless the taxpayer actually used the method when it was a C corporation).

(2) Deduction items. Except as otherwise provided in this section, any item of deduction properly taken into account during the recognition period is recognized built-in loss if the item would have been properly allowed as a deduction against gross income before the beginning of the recognition period to an accrual method taxpayer (disregarding any method of accounting for which an election by the taxpayer must be made unless the taxpayer actually used the method when it was a C corporation). In determining whether an item would have been properly allowed as a deduction against gross income by an accrual method taxpayer for purposes of this paragraph, section 461(h)(2)(C) and § 1.461–4(g) (relating to liabilities for tort, worker's compensation, breach of contract, violation of law, rebates, refunds, awards, prizes, jackpots, insurance contracts, warranty contracts, service contracts, taxes, and other liabilities) do not apply.

(3) Examples. The rules of this paragraph (b) are illustrated by the following examples.

Example 1. Accounts receivable. X is a C corporation using the cash method that elects to become an S corporation effective January 1, 1996. On January 1, 1996, X has $50,000 of accounts receivable for services rendered before that date. On that date, the accounts receivable have a fair market value of $40,000 and an adjusted basis of $0. In 1996, X collects $50,000 on the accounts receivable and includes that amount in gross income. Under paragraph (b)(1) of this section, the $50,000 included in gross income in 1996 is recognized built-in gain because it would have been included in gross income before the beginning of the recognition period if X had been an accrual method taxpayer. However, if X instead disposes of the accounts receivable for $45,000 on July 1, 1996, in a transaction treated as a sale or exchange for federal income tax purposes, X would have recognized built-in gain of $40,000 on the disposition.

Example 2. Contingent liability. Y is a C corporation using the cash method that elects to become an S corporation effective January 1, 1996. In 1995, a lawsuit was filed against Y claiming $1,000,000 in damages. In 1996, Y loses the lawsuit, pays a $500,000 judgment, and properly claims a deduction for that amount. Under paragraph (b)(2) of this section, the $500,000 deduction allowed in 1996 is not recognized built-in loss because it would not have been allowed as a deduction against gross income before the beginning of the recognition period if Y had been an accrual method taxpayer (even disregarding section 461(h)(2)(C) and § 1.461–4(g)).

Example 3. Deferred payment liabilities. X is a C corporation using the cash method that elects to become an S corporation on January 1, 1996. In 1995, X lost a lawsuit and became obligated to pay $150,000 in damages. Under section 461(h)(2)(C), this amount is not allowed as a deduction until X makes payment. In 1996, X makes payment and properly claims a deduction for the amount of the payment. Under paragraph (b)(2) of this section, the $150,000 deduction allowed in 1996 is recognized built-in loss because it would have been allowed as a deduction against gross income before the beginning of the recognition period if X had been an accrual method taxpayer (disregarding section 461(h)(2)(C) and § 1.461–4(g)).

Example 4. Deferred prepayment income. Y is a C corporation using an accrual method that elects to become an S corporation effective January 1, 1996. In 1995, Y received $2,500 for services to be rendered in 1996, and properly elected to include the $2,500 in gross income in 1996 under Rev.Proc. 71–21, 1971–2 C.B. 549 (see § 601.601(d)(2)(ii)(b) of this chapter). Under paragraph (b)(1) of this section, the $2,500 included in gross income in 1996 is not recognized built-in gain because it would not have been included in gross income before the beginning of the recognition period by an accrual method taxpayer using the method that Y actually used before the beginning of the recognition period.

Example 5. Change in method. X is a C corporation using an accrual method that elects to become an S corporation effective January 1, 1996. In 1995, X received $5,000 for services to be rendered in 1996, and properly included the $5,000 in gross income. In 1996, X properly elects to include the $5,000 in gross income in 1996 under Rev.Proc. 71–21, 1971–2 C.B. 549 (see § 601.601(d)(2)(ii)(b) of this chapter). As a result of the change in method of accounting, X has a $5,000 negative section 481(a) adjustment. Under paragraph (b)(1) of this section, the $5,000 included in gross income in 1996 is recognized built-in gain because it would have been included in gross income before the beginning of the recognition period by an accrual method taxpayer using the method that X actually used before the beginning of the recognition period. In addition, the $5,000 negative section 481(a) adjustment is recognized built-in loss because it relates to an item (the $5,000 X received for services in 1995) attributable to periods before the beginning of the recognition period under the principles for determining recognized built-in gain or loss in this section. See paragraph (d) of this section for rules regarding section 481(a) adjustments.

(c) Section 267(a)(2) and 404(a)(5) deductions—(1) Section 267(a)(2). Notwithstanding paragraph (b)(2) of this section, any amount properly deducted in the recognition period under section 267(a)(2), relating to payments to related parties, is recognized built-in loss to the extent—

(i) All events have occurred that establish the fact of the liability to pay the amount, and the exact amount of the liability can be determined, as of the beginning of the recognition period; and

(ii) The amount is paid—

(A) In the first two and one-half months of the recognition period; or

(B) To a related party owning, under the attribution rules of section 267, less than 5 percent, by voting power and value, of the corporation's stock, both as of the beginning of the recognition period and when the amount is paid.

(2) Section 404(a)(5). Notwithstanding paragraph (b)(2) of this section, any amount properly deducted in the recognition period under section 404(a)(5), relating to payments for deferred compensation, is recognized built-in loss to the extent—

(i) All events have occurred that establish the fact of the liability to pay the amount, and the exact amount of the liability can be determined, as of the beginning of the recognition period; and

(ii) The amount is not paid to a related party to which section 267(a)(2) applies.

(3) Examples. The rules of this paragraph (c) are illustrated by the following examples.

Example 1. Fixed annuity. X is a C corporation that elects to become an S corporation effective January 1, 1996. On December 31, 1995, A is age 60, has provided services to X as an employee for 20 years, and is a vested participant in X's unfunded nonqualified retirement plan. Under the plan, A receives $1,000 per month upon retirement until death. The plan provides no additional benefits. A retires on December 31, 1997, after working for X for 22 years. A at no time is a shareholder of X. X's deductions under section 404(a)(5) in the recognition period on paying A the $1,000 per month are recognized built-in loss because all events have occurred that establish the fact of the liability to pay the amount, and the exact amount of the liability can be determined, as of the beginning of the recognition period.

Example 2. Increase in annuity for working beyond 20 years. The facts are the same as Example 1, except that under the plan A receives $1,000 per month, plus $100 per month for each year A works for X beyond 20 years, upon retirement until death. X's deductions on paying A the $1,000 per month are recognized built-in loss. However, X's deductions on paying A the $200 per month for the two years A worked for X beyond 20 years are not recognized built-in loss because all events have not occurred that establish the fact of the liability to pay the amount, and the exact amount of the liability cannot be determined, as of the beginning of the recognition period.

Example 3. Cost of living adjustment. The facts are the same as Example 1, except that under the plan A receives $1,000 per month, plus annual cost of living adjustments, upon retirement until death. X's deductions under section 404(a)(5) on paying A the $1,000 per month are recognized built-in loss. However, X's deductions under section 404(a)(5) on paying A the annual cost of living adjustment are not recognized built-in loss because all events have not occurred that establish the fact of the liability to pay the amount, and the exact amount of the liability cannot be determined, as of the beginning of the recognition period.

(d) Section 481(a) adjustments—(1) In general. Any section 481(a) adjustment taken into account in the recognition period is recognized built-in gain or loss to the extent the adjustment relates to items attributable to periods before the beginning of the recognition period under the principles for determining recognized built-in gain or loss in this section. The principles for determining recognized built-in gain or loss in this section include, for example, the accrual method rule under paragraph (b) of this section.

(2) Examples. The rules of this paragraph (d) are illustrated by the following examples.

Example 1. Omitted item attributable to prerecognition period. X is a C corporation that elects to become an S corporation effective January 1, 1996. X improperly capitalizes repair costs and recovers the costs through depreciation of the related assets. In 1999, X properly changes to deducting repair costs as they are incurred. Under section 481(a), the basis of the related assets are reduced by an amount equal to the excess of the repair costs incurred before the year of change over the repair costs recovered through depreciation before the year of change. In addition, X has a negative section 481(a) adjustment equal to the basis reduction. Under paragraph (d)(1) of this section, the portion of X's negative section 481(a) adjustment relating to the repair costs incurred before the recognition period is recognized built-in loss because those repair costs are items attributable to periods before the beginning of the recognition period under the principles for determining recognized built-in gain or loss in this section.

Example 2. Duplicated item attributable to prerecognition period. Y is a C corporation that elects to become an S corporation effective January 1, 1996. Y improperly uses an accrual method without regard to the economic performance rules of section 461(h) to account for worker's compensation claims. As a result, Y takes deductions when claims are filed. In 1999, Y properly changes to an accrual method with regard to the economic performance rules under section 461(h)(2)(C) for worker's compensation claims. As a result, Y takes deductions when claims are paid. The positive section 481(a) adjustment resulting from the change is equal to the amount of claims filed, but unpaid, before the year of change. Under paragraph (b)(2) of this section, the deduction allowed in the recognition period for claims filed, but unpaid, before the recognition period is recognized built-in loss because a deduction was allowed for those claims before the recognition period under an accrual method without regard to section 461(h)(2)(C). Under paragraph (d)(1) of this section, the portion of Y's positive section 481(a) adjustment relating to claims filed, but unpaid, before the recognition period is recognized built-in gain because those claims are items attributable to periods before the beginning of the recognition period under the principles for determining recognized built-in gain or loss in this section.

* * *

(f) Discharge of indebtedness and bad debts. Any item of income or deduction properly taken into account during the first year of the recognition period as discharge of indebtedness income under section 61(a)(12) or as a bad debt deduction under section 166 is recognized built-in gain or loss if the item arises from a debt owed by or to an S corporation at the beginning of the recognition period.

* * *

(h) Installment method—(1) In general. If a corporation sells an asset before or during the recognition period and reports the income from the sale using the installment method under section 453 during or after the recognition period, that income is subject to tax under section 1374.

(2) Limitation on amount subject to tax. For purposes of paragraph (h)(1) of this section, the taxable income limitation under § 1.1374–2(a)(2) is equal to the amount by which the S corporation's net recognized built-in gain would have been increased from the year of the sale to the earlier of the year the income is reported under the installment method or the last year of the recognition period, assuming all income from the sale had been reported in the year of the sale and all provisions of section 1374 applied. For purposes of the preceding sentence, if the corporation sells the asset before the recognition period, the income from the sale that is not reported before the recognition period is treated as having been reported in the first year of the recognition period.

(3) Rollover rule. If the limitation in paragraph (h)(2) of this section applies, the excess of the amount reported under the installment method over the amount subject to tax under the limitation is treated as if it were reported in the succeeding taxable year(s), but only for succeeding taxable year(s) in the recognition period. The amount reported in the succeeding taxable year(s) under the preceding sentence is reduced to the extent that the amount not subject to tax under the limitation in paragraph (h)(2) of this section was not subject to tax because the S corporation had an excess of recognized built-in loss over recognized built-in gain in the taxable year of the sale and succeeding taxable year(s) in the recognition period.

(4) Use of losses and section 1374 attributes. If income is reported under the installment method by an S corporation for a taxable year after the recognition period and the income is subject to tax under paragraph (h)(1) of this section, the S corporation's section 1374 attributes may be used to the extent their use is allowed under all applicable provisions of the Code in determining the section 1374 tax. However, the S corporation's loss recognized for a taxable year after the recognition period that would have been recognized built-in loss if it had been recognized in the recognition period may not be used in determining the section 1374 tax.

(5) Examples. The rules of this paragraph (h) are illustrated by the following examples.

Example 1. Rollover rule. X is a C corporation that elects to become an S corporation effective January 1, 1996. On that date, X sells Blackacre with a basis of $0 and a value of $100,000 in exchange for a $100,000 note bearing a market rate of interest payable on January 1, 2001. X does not make the election under section 453(d) and, therefore, reports the $100,000 gain using the installment method under section 453. In the year 2001, X has income of $100,000 on collecting the note, unexpired C year attributes of $0, recognized built-in loss of $0, current losses of $100,000, and taxable income of $0. If X had reported the $100,000 gain in 1996, X's net recognized built-in gain from 1996 through 2001 would have been $75,000 greater than otherwise. Under paragraph (h) of this section, X has $75,000 net recognized built-in gain subject to tax under section 1374. X also must treat the $25,000 excess of the amount reported, $100,000, over the amount subject to tax, $75,000, as income reported under the installment method in the succeeding taxable year(s) in the recognition period, except to the extent X establishes that the $25,000 was not subject to tax under section 1374 in the year 2001 because X had an excess of recognized built-in loss over recognized built-in gain in the taxable year of the sale and succeeding taxable year(s) in the recognition period.

Example 2. Use of losses. Y is a C corporation that elects to become an S corporation effective January 1, 1996. On that date, Y sells Whiteacre with a basis of $0 and a value of $250,000 in exchange for a $250,000 note bearing a market rate of interest payable on January 1, 2006. Y does not make the election under section 453(d) and, therefore, reports the $250,000 gain using the installment method under section 453. In the year 2006, Y has income of $250,000 on collecting the note, unexpired C year attributes of $0, loss of $100,000 that would have been recognized built-in loss if it had been recognized in the recognition period, current losses of $150,000, and taxable income of $0. If Y had reported the $250,000 gain in 1996, X's net recognized built-in gain from 1996 through 2005 (that is, during the recognition period) would have been $225,000 greater than otherwise. Under paragraph (h) of this section, X has $225,000 net recognized built-in gain subject to tax under section 1374.

Example 3. Use of section 1374 attribute. Z is a C corporation that elects to become an S corporation effective January 1, 1996. On that date, Z sells Greenacre with a basis of $0 and a value of $500,000 in exchange for a $500,000 note bearing a market rate of interest payable on January 1, 2011. Z does not make the election under section 453(d) and, therefore, reports the $500,000 gain using the installment method under section 453. In the year 2011, Z has income of $500,000 on collecting the note, loss of $0 that would have been recognized built-in loss if it had been recognized in the recognition period, current losses of $0, taxable income of $500,000, and a minimum tax credit of $60,000 arising in 1995. None of Z's minimum tax credit is limited under sections 53(c) or 383. If Z had reported the $500,000 gain in 1996, Z's net recognized built-in gain from 1996 through 2005 (that is, during the recognition period) would have been $350,000 greater than otherwise. Under paragraph (h) of this section, Z has $350,000 net recognized built-in gain subject to tax under section 1374, a tentative section 1374 tax of $122,500 ($350,000 × .35 = $122,500), and a section 1374 tax after using its minimum tax credit arising in 1995 of $62,250 ($122,500 − $60,000 = $62,250).

(i) Partnership interests—(1) In general. If an S corporation owns a partnership interest at the beginning of the recognition period or transfers property to a partnership in a transaction to which section 1374(d)(6) applies during the recognition period, the S corporation determines the effect on net recognized built-in gain from its distributive share of partnership items as follows—

(i) Step One: Apply the rules of section 1374(d) to the S corporation's distributive share of partnership items of income, gain, loss, or deduction included in income or allowed as a deduction under the rules of subchapter K to determine the extent to which it would have been treated as recognized built-in gain or loss if the partnership items had originated in and been taken into account directly by the S corporation (partnership 1374 items);

(ii) Step Two: Determine the S corporation's net recognized built-in gain without partnership 1374 items;

(iii) Step Three: Determine the S corporation's net recognized built-in gain with partnership 1374 items; and

(iv) Step Four: If the amount computed under Step Three (paragraph (i)(1)(iii) of this section) exceeds the amount computed under Step Two (paragraph (i)(1)(ii) of this section), the excess (as limited by paragraph (i)(2)(i) of this section) is the S corporation's partnership RBIG, and the S corporation's net recognized built-in gain is the sum of the amount computed under Step Two (paragraph (i)(1)(ii) of this section) plus the partnership RBIG. If the amount computed under Step Two (paragraph (i)(1)(ii) of this section) exceeds the amount computed under Step Three (paragraph (i)(1)(iii) of this section), the excess (as limited by paragraph (i)(2)(ii) of this section) is the S corporation's partnership RBIL, and the S corporation's net recognized built-in gain is the remainder of the amount computed under Step Two (paragraph (i)(1)(ii) of this section) after subtracting the partnership RBIL.

(2) Limitations—(i) Partnership RBIG. An S corporation's partnership RBIG for any taxable year may not exceed the excess (if any) of the S corporation's RBIG limitation over its partnership RBIG for prior taxable years. The preceding sentence does not apply if a corporation forms or avails of a partnership with a principal purpose of avoiding the tax imposed under section 1374.

(ii) Partnership RBIL. An S corporation's partnership RBIL for any taxable year may not exceed the excess (if any) of the S corporation's RBIL limitation over its partnership RBIL for prior taxable years.

(3) Disposition of partnership interest. If an S corporation disposes of its partnership interest, the amount that may be treated as recognized built-in gain may not exceed the excess (if any) of the S corporation's RBIG limitation over its partnership RBIG during the recognition period. Similarly, the amount that may be treated as recognized built-in loss may not exceed the excess (if any) of the S corporation's RBIL limitation over its partnership RBIL during the recognition period.

(4) RBIG and RBIL limitations—(i) Sale of partnership interest. An S corporation's RBIG or RBIL limitation is the total of the following—

(A) The amount that would be the amount realized if, at the beginning of the first day of the recognition period, the corporation had remained a C corporation and had sold its partnership interest (and any assets the corporation contributed to the partnership during the recognition period) at fair market value to an unrelated party; decreased by

(B) The corporation's adjusted basis in the partnership interest (and any assets the corporation contributed to the partnership during the recognition period) at the time of the sale referred to in paragraph (i)(4)(i)(A) of this section; and increased or decreased by

(C) The corporation's allocable share of the partnership's section 481(a) adjustments at the time of the sale referred to in paragraph (i)(4)(i)(A) of this section.

(ii) Amounts of limitations. If the result in paragraph (i)(4)(i) of this section is a positive amount, the S corporation has a RBIG limitation equal to that amount and a RBIL limitation of $0, but if the result in paragraph (i)(4)(i) of this section is a negative amount, the S corporation has a RBIL limitation equal to that amount and a RBIG limitation of $0.

(5) Small interest exception—(i) In general. Paragraph (i)(1) of this section does not apply to a taxable year in the recognition period if the S corporation's partnership interest represents less than 10 percent of the partnership's capital and profits at all times during the taxable year and prior taxable years in the recognition period, and the fair market value of the S corporation's partnership interest as of the beginning of the recognition period is less than $100,000.

(ii) Contributed assets. For purposes of paragraph (i)(5)(i) of this section, if the S corporation contributes any assets to the partnership during the recognition period and the S corporation held the assets as of the beginning of the recognition period, the fair market value of the S corporation's partnership interest as of the beginning of the recognition period is determined as if the assets were contributed to the partnership before the beginning of the recognition period (using the fair market value of each contributed asset as of the beginning of the recognition period). The contribution does not affect whether paragraph (i)(5)(i) of this section applies for taxable years in the recognition period before the taxable year in which the contribution was made.

(iii) Anti-abuse rule. Paragraph (i)(5)(i) of this section does not apply if a corporation forms or avails of a partnership with a principal purpose of avoiding the tax imposed under section 1374.

(6) Section 704(c) gain or loss. Solely for purposes of section 1374, an S corporation's section 704(c) gain or loss amount with respect to any asset is not reduced during the recognition period, except for amounts treated as recognized built-in gain or loss with respect to that asset under this paragraph.

(7) Disposition of distributed partnership asset. If on the first day of the recognition period an S corporation holds an interest in a partnership that holds an asset and during the recognition period the partnership distributes the asset to the S corporation that thereafter disposes of the asset, the asset is treated as having been held by the S corporation on the first day of the recognition period and as having the fair market value and adjusted basis in the hands of the S corporation that it had in the hands of the partnership on that day.

(8) Examples. The rules of this paragraph (i) are illustrated by the following examples.

Example 1. Pre-conversion partnership interest. X is a C corporation that elects to become an S corporation on January 1, 1996. On that date, X owns a 50 percent interest in partnership P and P owns (among other assets) Blackacre with a basis of $25,000 and a value of $45,000. In 1996, P buys Whiteacre for $50,000. In 1999, P sells Blackacre for $55,000 and recognizes a gain of $30,000 of which $15,000 is included in X's distributive share. P also sells Whiteacre in 1999 for $42,000 and recognizes a loss of $8,000 of which $4,000 is included in X's distributive share. Under this paragraph and section 1374(d)(3), X's $15,000 gain is presumed to be recognized built-in gain and thus treated as a partnership 1374 item, but this presumption is rebutted if X establishes that P's gain would have been only $20,000 ($45,000 – $25,000 = $20,000) if Blackacre had been sold on the first day of the recognition period. In such a case, only X's distributive share of the $20,000 built-in gain, $10,000, would be treated as a partnership 1374 item. Under this paragraph and section 1374(d)(4), X's $4,000 loss is not treated as a partnership 1374 item because P did not hold Whiteacre on the first day of the recognition period.

Example 2. Post-conversion contribution. Y is a C corporation that elects to become an S corporation on January 1, 1996. On that date, Y owns (among other assets) Blackacre with a basis of $100,000 and a value of $200,000. On January 1, 1998, when Blackacre has a basis of $100,000 and a value of $200,000, Y contributes Blackacre to partnership P for a 50 percent interest in P. On January 1, 2000, P sells Blackacre for $300,000 and recognizes a gain of $200,000 on the sale ($300,000 – $100,000 = $200,000). P is allocated $100,000 of the gain under section 704(c), and another $50,000 of the gain for its fifty percent share of the remainder, for a total of $150,000. Under this paragraph and section 1374(d)(3), if Y establishes that P's gain would have been only $100,000 ($200,000 – $100,000 = $100,000) if Blackacre had been sold on the first day of the recognition period, Y would treat only $100,000 as a partnership 1374 item.

Example 3. RBIG limitation of $100,000 or $50,000. X is a C corporation that elects to become an S corporation on January 1, 1996. On that date, X owns a 50 percent interest in partnership P with a RBIG limitation of $100,000 and a RBIL limitation of $0. P owns (among other assets) Blackacre with a basis of $50,000 and a value of $200,000. In 1996, P sells Blackacre for $200,000 and recognizes a gain of $150,000 of which $75,000 is included in X's distributive share and treated as a partnership 1374 item. X's net recognized built-in gain for 1996 computed without partnership 1374 items is $35,000 and with partnership 1374 items is $110,000. Thus, X has a partnership RBIG of $75,000 except as limited under paragraph (i)(2)(i) of this section. Because X's RBIG limitation is $100,000, X's partnership RBIG of $75,000 is not limited and X's net recognized built-in gain for the year is $110,000 ($35,000 + $75,000 = $110,000). However, if X had a RBIG limitation of $50,000 instead of $100,000, X's partnership RBIG would be limited to $50,000 under paragraph (i)(2)(i) of this section and X's net recognized built-in gain would be $85,000 ($35,000 + $50,000 = $85,000).

Example 4. RBIL limitation of $60,000 or $40,000. Y is a C corporation that elects to become an S corporation on January 1, 1996. On that date, Y owns a 50 percent interest in partnership P with a RBIG limitation of $0 and a RBIL limitation of $60,000. P owns (among other assets) Blackacre with a basis of $225,000 and a value of $125,000. In 1996, P sells Blackacre for $125,000 and recognizes a loss of $100,000 of which $50,000 is included in Y's distributive share and treated as a partnership 1374 item. Y's net recognized built-in gain for 1996 computed without partnership 1374 items is $75,000 and with partnership 1374 items is $25,000. Thus, Y has a partnership RBIL of $50,000 for the year except as limited under paragraph (i)(2)(ii) of this section. Because Y's RBIL limitation is $60,000, Y's partnership RBIL for the year is not limited and Y's net recognized built-in gain for the year is $25,000 ($75,000 – $50,000 = $25,000). However, if Y had a RBIL limitation of $40,000 instead of $60,000, Y's partnership RBIL would be limited to $40,000 under paragraph (i)(2)(ii) of this section and Y's net recognized built-in gain for the year would be $35,000 ($75,000 – $40,000 = $35,000).

Example 5. RBIG limitation of $0. **(i)** X is a C corporation that elects to become an S corporation on January 1, 1996. X owns a 50 percent interest in partnership P with a RBIG limitation of $0 and a RBIL limitation of $25,000.

(a) In 1996, P's partnership 1374 items are—

(1) Ordinary income of $25,000; and

(2) Capital gain of $75,000.

(b) X itself has—

(1) Recognized built-in ordinary income of $40,000; and

(2) Recognized built-in capital loss of $90,000.

(ii) X's net recognized built-in gain for 1996 computed without partnership 1374 items is $40,000 and with partnership 1374 items is $65,000 ($40,000 + $25,000 = $65,000). Thus, X's partnership RBIG is $25,000 for the year except as limited under paragraph (i)(2)(i) of this section. Because X's RBIG limitation is $0, X's partnership RBIG of $25,000 is limited to $0 and X's net recognized built-in gain for the year is $40,000.

Example 6. RBIL limitation of $0. **(i)** Y is a C corporation that elects to become an S corporation on January 1, 1996. Y owns a 50 percent interest in partnership P with a RBIG limitation of $60,000 and a RBIL limitation of $0.

(a) In 1996, P's partnership 1374 items are—

(1) Ordinary income of $25,000; and

(2) Capital loss of $90,000.

(b) Y itself has—

(1) recognized built-in ordinary income of $40,000; and

(2) recognized built-in capital gain of $75,000.

(ii) Y's net recognized built-in gain for 1996 computed without partnership 1374 items is $115,000 ($40,000 + $75,000 = $115,000) and with partnership 1374 items is $65,000 ($40,000 + $25,000 = $65,000). Thus, Y's partnership RBIL is $50,000 for the year except as limited under paragraph (i)(2)(ii) of this section. Because Y's RBIL limitation is $0, Y's partnership RBIL of $50,000 is limited to $0 and Y's net recognized built-in gain is $115,000.

Example 7. Disposition of partnership interest. X is a C corporation that elects to become an S corporation on January 1, 1996. On that date, X owns a 50 percent interest in partnership P with a RBIG limitation of $200,000 and a RBIL limitation of $0. P owns (among other assets) Blackacre with a basis of $20,000 and a value of $140,000. In 1996, P sells Blackacre for $140,000 and recognizes a gain of $120,000 of which $60,000 is included in X's distributive share and treated as a partnership 1374 item. X's net recognized built-in gain for 1996 computed without partnership 1374 items is $95,000 and with partnership 1374 items is $155,000. Thus, X has a partnership RBIG of $60,000. In 1999, X sells its entire interest in P for $350,000 and recognizes a gain of $250,000. Under paragraph (i)(3) of this section, X's recognized built-in gain on the sale is limited by its RBIG limitation to $140,000 ($200,000 − $60,000 = $140,000).

Example 8. Section 704(c) case. Y is a C corporation that elects to become an S corporation on January 1, 1996. On that date, Y contributes Asset 1, 5-year property with a value of $40,000 and a basis of $0, and an unrelated party contributes $40,000 in cash, each for a 50 percent interest in partnership P. The partnership adopts the traditional method under § 1.704-3(b). If P sold Asset 1 for $40,000 immediately after it was contributed by Y, P's $40,000 gain would be allocated to Y under section 704(c). Instead, Asset 1 is sold by P in 1999 for $36,000 and P recognizes gain of $36,000 ($36,000 − $0 = $36,000) on the sale. However, because book depreciation of $8,000 per year has been taken on Asset 1 in 1996, 1997, and 1998, Y is allocated only $16,000 of P's $36,000 gain ($40,000 − (3 × $8,000) = ($16,000 − $0) = $16,000) under section 704(c). The remaining $20,000 of P's $36,000 gain ($36,000 − $16,000 = $20,000) is allocated 50 percent to each partner under section 704(b). Thus, a total of $26,000 ($16,000 + $10,000 = $26,000) of P's $36,000 gain is allocated to Y. However, under paragraph (i)(6) of this section, Y treats $36,000 as a partnership 1374 item on P's sale of Asset 1.

Example 9. Disposition of distributed partnership asset. X is a C corporation that elects to become an S corporation on January 1, 1996. On that date, X owns a fifty percent interest in partnership P and P owns (among other assets) Blackacre with a basis of $20,000 and a value of $40,000. On January 1, 1998, P distributes Blackacre to X, when Blackacre has a basis of $20,000 and a value of $50,000. Under section 732(a)(1), X has a transferred basis of $20,000 in Blackacre. On January 1, 1999, X sells Blackacre for $60,000 and recognizes a gain of $40,000. Under paragraph (i)(7) of this section and section 1374(d)(3), X has recognized built-in gain from the sale of $20,000, the amount of built-in gain in Blackacre on the first day of the recognition period.

[T.D. 8579, 59 FR 66458, Dec. 27, 1994; T.D. 8995, 67 FR 34603, May 15, 2002]

§ 1.1374-5 Loss carryforwards.

(a) In general. The loss carryforwards allowed as deductions against net recognized built-in gain under section 1374(b)(2) are allowed only to the extent their use is allowed under the rules applying to C corporations. Any other loss carryforwards, such as charitable contribution carryforwards under section 170(d)(2), are not allowed as deductions against net recognized built-in gain.

(b) Example. The rules of this section are illustrated by the following example.

Example. Section 382 limitation. X is a C corporation that has an ownership change under section 382(g)(1) on January 1, 1994. On that date, X has a fair market value of $500,000, NOL carryforwards of $400,000, and a net unrealized built-in gain under section 382(h)(3)(A) of $0. Assume X's section 382 limitation under section 382(b)(1) is $40,000. X elects to become an S corporation on January 1, 1998. On that date, X has NOL carryforwards of $240,000 (having used $160,000 of its pre-change net operating losses in its 4 preceding taxable years) and a section 1374 net unrealized built-in gain of $250,000. In 1998, X has net recognized built-in gain of $100,000. X may use $40,000 of its NOL carryforwards as a deduction against its $100,000 net recognized built-in gain, because X's section 382 limitation is $40,000.

[T.D. 8579, 59 FR 66458, Dec. 27, 1994]

§ 1.1374-7 Inventory.

(a) Valuation. The fair market value of the inventory of an S corporation on the first day of the recognition period equals the amount that a willing buyer would pay a willing seller for the inventory in a purchase of all the S corporation's assets by a buyer that expects to continue to operate the S corporation's business. For purposes of the preceding sentence, the buyer and seller are presumed not to be under any compulsion to buy or sell and to have reasonable knowledge of all relevant facts.

(b) Identity of dispositions. The inventory method used by an S corporation for tax purposes must be used to identify whether the inventory it disposes of during the recognition period is inventory it held on the first day of that period. Thus, a corporation using the LIFO method does not dispose of inventory it held on the first day of the recognition period unless the carrying value of its inventory for a taxable year during that period is less than the carrying value of its inventory on the first day of the recognition period (determined using the LIFO method as described in section 472). However, if a corporation changes its method of accounting for inventory (for example, from the FIFO method to the LIFO method or from the LIFO method to the FIFO method) with a principal purpose of avoiding the tax imposed under section

1374, it must use its former method to identify its dispositions of inventory.

[T.D. 8579, 59 FR 66458, Dec. 27, 1994]

§ 1.1374–8 Section 1374(d)(8) transactions.

(a) In general. If any S corporation acquires any asset in a transaction in which the S corporation's basis in the asset is determined (in whole or in part) by reference to a C corporation's basis in the assets (or any other property) (a section 1374(d)(8) transaction), section 1374 applies to the net recognized built-in gain attributable to the assets acquired in any section 1374(d)(8) transaction.

* * *

(c) Separate determination of tax. For purposes of the tax imposed under section 1374(d)(8), a separate determination of tax is made with respect to the assets the S corporation acquires in one section 1374(d)(8) transaction from the assets the S corporation acquires in another section 1374(d)(8) transaction and from the assets the corporation held when it became an S corporation. Thus, an S corporation's section 1374 attributes when it became an S corporation may only be used to reduce the section 1374 tax imposed on dispositions of assets the S corporation held at that time. Similarly, an S corporation's section 1374 attributes acquired in a section 1374(d)(8) transaction may only be used to reduce a section 1374 tax imposed on dispositions of assets the S corporation acquired in the same transaction. * * *

(d) Taxable income limitation. For purposes of paragraph (a) of this section, an S corporation's taxable income limitation under § 1.1374–2(a)(2) for any taxable year is allocated between or among each of the S corporation's separate determinations of net recognized built-in gain for that year (determined without regard to the taxable income limitation) based on the ratio of each of those determinations to the sum of all of those determinations.

(e) Examples. The rules of this section are illustrated by the following examples.

Example 1. Separate determination of tax. **(i)** X is a C corporation that elected to become an S corporation effective January 1, 1986 (before section 1374 was amended in the Tax Reform Act of 1986). X has a net operating loss carryforward of $20,000 arising in 1985 when X was a C corporation. On January 1, 1996, Y (an unrelated C corporation) merges into X in a transaction to which section 368(a)(1)(A) applies. Y has no loss carryforwards, credits, or credit carryforwards. The assets X acquired from Y are subject to tax under section 1374 and have a net unrealized built-in gain of $150,000.

(ii) In 1996, X has a pre-limitation amount of $50,000 on dispositions of assets acquired from Y and a taxable income limitation of $100,000 (because only one group of assets is subject to section 1374, there is no allocation of the taxable income limitation). As a result, X has a net recognized built-in gain on those assets of $50,000. X's $20,000 net operating loss carryforward may not be used as a deduction against its $50,000 net recognized built-in gain on the assets X acquired from Y. Therefore, X has a section 1374 tax of $17,500 ($50,000 × .35 = $17,500, assuming a 35 percent tax rate) for its 1996 taxable year.

Example 2. Allocation of taxable income limitation. **(i)** Y is a C corporation that elects to become an S corporation effective January 1, 1996. The assets Y holds when it becomes an S corporation have a net unrealized built-in gain of $5,000. Y has no loss carryforwards, credits, or credit carryforwards. On January 1, 1997, Z (an unrelated C corporation) merges into Y in a transaction to which section 368(a)(1)(A) applies. Z has no loss carryforwards, credits, or credit carryforwards. The assets Y acquired from Z are subject to tax under section 1374 and have a net unrealized built-in gain of $80,000.

(ii) In 1997, Y has a pre-limitation amount on the assets it held when it became an S corporation of $15,000, a pre-limitation amount on the assets Y acquired from Z of $15,000, and a taxable income limitation of $10,000. However, because the assets Y held on becoming an S corporation have a net unrealized built-in gain of $5,000, its net recognized built-in gain on those assets is limited to $5,000 before taking into account the taxable income limitation. Y's taxable income limitation of $10,000 is allocated between the assets Y held on becoming an S corporation and the assets Y acquired from Z for purposes of determining the net recognized built-in gain from each pool of assets. Thus, Y's net recognized built-in gain on the assets Y held on becoming an S corporation is $2,500 [$10,000 × ($5,000/$20,000) = $2,500]. Y's net recognized built-in gain on the assets Y acquired from Z is $7,500 [$10,000 × ($15,000/$20,000) = $7,500]. Therefore, Y has a section 1374 tax of $3,500 [($2,500 + $7,500) × .35 = $3,500, assuming a 35 percent tax rate] for its 1997 taxable year.

[T.D. 8579, 59 FR 66458, Dec. 27, 1994]

§ 1.1374–9 Anti-stuffing rule.

If a corporation acquires an asset before or during the recognition period with a principal purpose of avoiding the tax imposed under section 1374, the asset and any loss, deduction, loss carryforward, credit, or credit carryforward attributable to the asset is disregarded in determining the S corporation's pre-limitation amount, taxable income limitation, net unrealized built-in gain limitation, deductions against net recognized built-in gain, and credits against the section 1374 tax.

[T.D. 8579, 59 FR 66458, Dec. 27, 1994]

§ 1.1374–10 Effective date and additional rules.

* * *

(b) Additional rules. This paragraph (b) provides rules applicable to certain S corporations, assets, or transactions to which §§ 1.1374–1 through 1.1374–9 do not apply.

(1) Certain transfers to partnerships. If a corporation transfers an asset to a partnership in a transaction to which section 721(a) applies and the transfer is made in contemplation of an S election or during the recognition period, section 1374 applies on a disposition of the asset by the partnership as if the S corporation had disposed of the asset itself. This paragraph (b)(1) applies as of the effective date of section 1374, unless the recognition period with respect to the contributed asset is pursuant to an S election or a section 1374(d)(8) transaction occurring on or after December 27, 1994.

(2) Certain inventory dispositions. For purposes of section 1374(d)(2)(A), the inventory method used by the taxpayer for tax purposes (FIFO, LIFO, etc.) must be used to identify whether goods disposed of following conversion to S corporation status were held by the corporation at the time of conversion. Thus, for example, a corporation using the LIFO inventory method will not be subject to the built-in gain tax with respect to sales of inventory except to the extent that a LIFO layer existing prior to the beginning of the first taxable year as an S corporation is invaded after the beginning of that year. This paragraph (b)(2) applies as of the effective date of section 1374, unless the recognition period with respect to the inventory is pursuant to an S election or a section 1374(d)(8) transaction occurring on or after December 27, 1994.

(3) Certain contributions of built-in loss assets. If a built-in loss asset (that is, an asset with an adjusted tax basis in excess of its fair market value) is contributed to a corporation within 2 years before the earlier of the beginning of its first taxable year as an S corporation, or the filing of its S election, the loss inherent in the asset will not reduce net unrealized built-in gain, as defined in section 1374(d)(1), unless the taxpayer demonstrates a clear and substantial relationship between the contributed property and the conduct of the corporation's current or future business enterprises. This paragraph (b)(3) applies as of the effective date of section 1374, unless the recognition period with respect to the contributed asset is pursuant to an S election or a section 1374(d)(8) transaction occurring on or after December 27, 1994.

(4) Certain installment sales—(i) In general. If a taxpayer sells an asset either prior to or during the recognition period and recognizes income either during or after the recognition period from the sale under the installment method, the income will, when recognized, be taxed under section 1374 to the extent it would have been so taxed in prior taxable years if the selling corporation had made the election under section 453(d) not to report the income under the installment method. For purposes of determining the extent to which the income would have been subject to tax if the section 453(d) election had not been made, the taxable income limitation of section 1374(d)(2)(A)(ii) and the built-in gain carryover rule of section 1374(d)(2)(B) will be taken into account. This paragraph (b)(4) applies for installment sales occurring on or after March 26, 1990, and before December 27, 1994.

(ii) Examples. The rules of this paragraph (b)(4) are illustrated by the following examples.

Example 1. In year 1 of the recognition period under section 1374, a corporation realizes a gain of $100,000 on the sale of an asset with built-in gain. The corporation is to receive full payment for the asset in year 11. Because the corporation does not make an election under section 453(d), all $100,000 of the gain from the sale is reported under the installment method in year 11. If the corporation had made an election under section 453(d) with respect to the sale, the gain would have been recognized in year 1 and, taking into account the corporation's income and gains from other sources, application of the taxable income limitation of section 1374(d)(2)(A)(ii) and the built-in gain carryover rule of section 1374(d)(2)(B) would have resulted in $40,000 of the gain being subject to tax during the recognition period under section 1374. Therefore, $40,000 of the gain recognized in year 11 is subject to tax under section 1374.

Example 2. In year 1 of the recognition period under section 1374, a corporation realizes a gain of $100,000 on the sale of an asset with built-in gain. The corporation is to receive full payment for the asset in year 6. Because the corporation does not make an election under section 453(d), all $100,000 of the gain from the sale is reported under the installment method in year 6. If the corporation had made an election under section 453(d) with respect to the sale, the gain would have been recognized in year 1 and, taking into account the corporation's income and gains from other sources, application of the taxable income limitation of section 1374(d)(2)(A)(ii) and the built-in gain carryover rule of section 1374(d)(2)(B) would have resulted in all of the gain being subjected to tax under section 1374 in years 1 through 5. Therefore, notwithstanding that the taxable income limitation of section 1374(d)(2)(A)(ii) might otherwise limit the taxation of the gain recognized in year 6, the entire $100,000 of gain will be subject to tax under section 1374 when it is recognized in year 6.

* * *

[T.D. 8579, 59 FR 66458, Dec. 27, 1994; as amended by T.D. 9180, 70 FR 8727, Feb. 23, 2005; T.D. 9236, 70 FR 75730, Dec. 21, 2005]

§ 1.1375–1 Tax imposed when passive investment income of corporation having Subchapter C earnings and profits exceed 25 percent of gross receipts.

(a) General rule. For taxable years beginning after 1981, section 1375(a) imposes a tax on the income of certain S corporations that have passive investment income. In the case of a taxable year beginning during 1982, an electing small business corporation may elect to have the rules under this section not apply. See the regulations under section 1362 for rules on the election. For purposes of this section, the term "S corporation" shall include an electing small business corporation under prior law. This tax shall apply to an S corporation for a taxable year if the S corporation has—

(1) Subchapter C earnings and profits at the close of such taxable year, and

(2) Gross receipts more than 25 percent of which are passive investment income.

If the S corporation has no Subchapter C earnings and profits at the close of the taxable year (because, for example, such earnings and profits were distributed in accordance with section 1368), the tax shall not be imposed even though the S corporation has passive investment income for the taxable year. If the tax is imposed, the tax shall be computed by multiplying the excess net passive income (as defined in paragraph (b) of this section) by the highest rate of tax specified in section 11(b).

(b) Definitions—(1) Excess net passive income—(i) In general. The term "excess net passive income" is defined in section 1375(b)(1), and can be expressed by the following formula:

$$ENPI = NPI \times \frac{PII - (.25 \times GR)}{PII}$$

Where:

ENPI=excess net passive income

NPI=net passive income

PII=passive investment income

GR=total gross receipts

(ii) Limitation. The amount of the excess net passive income for any taxable year shall not exceed the corporation's taxable income for the taxable year (determined in accordance with section 1374(d) and § 1.1374–1(d)).

(2) Net passive income. The term "net passive income" means—

(i) Passive investment income, reduced by

(ii) The deductions allowable under Chapter 1 of the Internal Revenue Code * * * which are directly connected (within the meaning of paragraph (b)(3) of this section) with the production of such income (other than deductions allowable under section 172 and Part VIII of Subchapter B).

(3) Directly connected—(i) In general. For purposes of paragraph (b)(2)(ii) of this section to be directly connected with the production of income, an item of deduction must have proximate and primary relationship to the income. Expenses, depreciation, and similar items attributable solely to such income qualify for deduction.

(ii) Allocation of deduction. If an item of deduction is attributable (within the meaning of paragraph (b)(3)(i) of this section) in part to passive investment income and in part to income other than passive investment income, the deduction shall be allocated between the two types of items on a reasonable basis. The portion of any deduction so allocated to passive investment income shall be treated as proximately and primarily related to such income.

(4) Other definitions. The terms "subchapter C earnings and profits," "passive investment income," and "gross receipts" shall have the same meaning given these terms in section 1362(d)(3) and the regulations thereunder.

(c) Special rules—(1) Disallowance of credits. No credit is allowed under Part IV of Subchapter A of Chapter 1 of the Code (other than section 34) against the tax imposed by section 1375(a) and this section.

(2) Coordination with section 1374. If any gain—

(i) is taken into account in determining passive income for purposes of this section, and

(ii) is taken into account under section 1374,

the amount of such gain taken into account under section 1374(b) and § 1.1374–1(b)(1) and (2) in determining the amount of tax shall be reduced by the portion of the excess net passive income for the taxable year which is attributable (on a pro rata basis) to such gain. For purposes of the preceding sentence, the portion of excess net passive income for the taxable year which is attributable to such capital gain is equal to the amount determined by multiplying the excess net passive income by the following fraction:

$$\frac{NCG-E}{NPI}$$

Where:

NCG=net capital gain

NPI=net passive income

E=Expense attributable to net capital gain

(d) Waiver of tax in certain cases—(1) In general. If an S corporation establishes to the satisfaction of the Commissioner that—

(i) It determined in good faith that it had no Subchapter C earnings and profits at the close of the taxable year, and

(ii) During a reasonable period of time after it was determined that it did have Subchapter C earnings and profits at the close of such taxable year such earnings and profits were distributed,

the Commissioner may waive the tax imposed by section 1375 for such taxable year. The S corporation has the burden of establishing that under the relevant facts and circumstances the Commissioner should waive the tax. For example, if an S corporation establishes that in good faith and using due diligence it determined that it had no Subchapter C earnings and profits at the close of a taxable year, but it was later determined on audit that it did have Subchapter C earnings and profits at the close of such taxable year, and if the corporation establishes that it distributed such earnings and profits within a reasonable time after the audit, it may be appropriate for the Commissioner to waive the tax on passive income for such taxable year.

(2) Corporation's request for a waiver. A request for waiver of the tax imposed by section 1375 shall be made in writing to the district director and shall contain all relevant facts to establish that the requirements of paragraph (d)(1) of this section are met. Such request shall contain a description of how and on what date the S corporation in good faith and using due diligence determined that it had no Subchapter C earnings and profits at the close of the taxable year, a description of how and on what date it was determined that the S corporation had Subchapter C earnings and profits at the close of the year and a description (including dates) of any steps taken to distribute such earnings and profits. If the earnings and profits have not yet been distributed, the request shall contain a timetable for distribution and an explanation of why such timetable is reasonable. On the date the waiver is to become effective, all Subchapter C earnings and profits must have been distributed.

(e) Reduction in pass-thru for tax imposed on excess net passive income. See section 1366(f)(3) for a special rule reducing each item of the corporation's passive investment income for purposes of section 1366(a) if a tax is imposed on the corporation under section 1375.

(f) Examples. The following example illustrates the principles of this section:

Example (1). Assume Corporation M, an S corporation, has for its taxable year total gross receipts of $200,000, passive investment income of $100,000, $60,000 of which is interest income, and expenses directly connected with the production of such interest income in the amount of $10,000. Assume also that at the end of the taxable year Corporation M has Subchapter C earnings and profits. Since more than 25 percent of the Corporation M's total gross receipts are passive investment income, and since Corporation M has Subchapter C earnings and profits at the end of the taxable year, Corporation M will be subject to the tax imposed by section 1375. The amount of excess net passive investment income is $45,000 ($90,000 + ($50,000/$100,000)). Assume that the other $40,000 of passive investment income is attributable to net capital gain and that there are no expenses directly connected with such gain. Under these facts, $20,000 of the excess net passive income is attributable to the net capital gain ($45,000 + ($40,000/$90,000)). Accordingly, the amount of gain taken into account under section 1374(b)(1) and the taxable income of Corporation M under section 1374(b)(2) shall be reduced by $20,000.

Example (2). Assume an S corporation with Subchapter C earnings and profits has tax-exempt income of $400, its only passive income, gross receipts of $1,000 and taxable income of $250 and there are no expenses associated with the tax-exempt income. The corporation's excess net income for the taxable year would total $150 (400 + ((400–250)/400)). This amount is subject to the tax imposed by section 1375, notwithstanding that such amount is otherwise tax-exempt income.

[T.D. 8104, 51 FR 34203, Sept. 26, 1986, 52 FR 9162, March 23, 1987; T.D. 8419, 57 FR 22653, May 29, 1992]

§ 1.1378–1 Taxable year of S corporation.

(a) In general. The taxable year of an S corporation must be a permitted year. A permitted year is the required taxable year (i.e., a taxable year ending on December 31), a taxable year elected under section 444, a 52–53–week taxable year ending with reference to the required taxable year or a taxable year elected under section 444, or any other taxable year for which the corporation establishes a business purpose to the satisfaction of the Commissioner under section 442.

(b) Adoption of taxable year. An electing S corporation may adopt, in accordance with § 1.441–1(c), its required taxable year, a taxable year elected under section 444, or a 52–53–week taxable year ending with reference to its required taxable year or a taxable year elected under section 444 without the approval of the Commissioner. See § 1.441–1. An electing S corporation that wants to adopt any other taxable year, must establish a business purpose and obtain the approval of the Commissioner under section 442.

(c) Change in taxable year—(1) Approval required. An S corporation or electing S corporation that wants to change its taxable year must obtain the approval of the Commissioner under section 442 or make an election under section 444. However, an S corporation or electing S corporation may obtain automatic approval for certain changes, including a change to its required taxable year, pursuant to administrative procedures published by the Commissioner.

(2) Short period tax return. An S corporation or electing S corporation that changes its taxable year must make its return for a short period in accordance with section 443, but must not annualize the corporation's taxable income.

(d) Retention of taxable year. In certain cases, an S corporation or electing S corporation will be required to change its taxable year unless it obtains the approval of the Commissioner under section 442, or makes an election under section 444, to retain its current taxable year. For example, a corporation using a June 30 fiscal year that elects to be an S corporation and, as a result, is required to use the calendar year must obtain the approval of the Commissioner to retain its current fiscal year.

(e) Procedures for obtaining approval or making a section 444 election—(1) In general. See § 1.442–1(b) for procedures to obtain the approval of the Commissioner (automatically or otherwise) to adopt, change, or retain a taxable year. See §§ 1.444–1T and 1.444–2T for qualifications, and 1.444–3T for procedures, for making an election under section 444.

(2) Special rules for electing S corporations. An electing S corporation that wants to adopt, change to, or retain a taxable year other than its required taxable year must request approval of the Commissioner on Form 2553, "Election by a Small Business Corporation," when the election to be an S corporation is filed pursuant to section 1362(b) and § 1.1362–6. See § 1.1362–6(a)(2)(i) for the manner of making an election to be an S corporation. If such corporation receives permission to adopt, change to, or retain a taxable year other than its required taxable year, the election to be an S corporation will be effective. Denial of the request renders the election ineffective unless the corporation agrees that, in the event the request to adopt, change to, or retain a taxable year other than its required taxable year is denied, it will adopt, change to, or retain its required taxable year or, if applicable, make an election under section 444.

* * *

[T.D. 8996, 67 FR 35009, May 17, 2002]

ESTATE TAX

§ 20.0–2 General description of tax.

(a) Nature of tax. The Federal estate tax is neither a property tax nor an inheritance tax. It is a tax imposed upon the transfer of the entire taxable estate and not upon any particular legacy, devise, or distributive share. Escheat of a decedent's property to the State for lack of heirs is a transfer which causes the property to be included in the decedent's gross estate.

(b) Method of determining tax; estate of citizen or resident—(1) In general. Subparagraphs (2) to (5) of this paragraph contain a general description of the method to be used in determining the Federal estate tax imposed upon the transfer of the estate of a decedent who was a citizen or resident of the United States at the time of his death.

(2) Gross estate. The first step in determining the tax is to ascertain the total value of the decedent's gross estate. The value of the gross estate includes the value of all property to the extent of the interest therein of the decedent at the time of his death. * * * In addition, the gross estate may include property in which the decedent did not have an interest at the time of his death. A decedent's gross estate for Federal estate tax purposes may therefore be very different from the same decedent's estate for local probate purposes. Examples of items which may be included in a decedent's gross estate and not in his probate estate are the following: certain property transferred by the decedent during his lifetime without adequate consideration; property held jointly by the decedent and others; property over which the decedent had a general power of appointment; proceeds of certain policies of insurance on the decedent's life; annuities; and dower or curtesy of a surviving spouse or a statutory estate in lieu thereof. For a detailed explanation of the method of ascertaining the value of the gross estate, see sections 2031 through 2044, and the regulations thereunder.

(3) Taxable estate. The second step in determining the tax is to ascertain the value of the decedent's taxable estate. The value of the taxable estate is determined by subtracting from the value of the gross estate the authorized exemption and deductions. Under various conditions and limitations, deductions are allowable for expenses, indebtedness, taxes, losses, charitable transfers, and transfers to a surviving spouse. For a detailed explanation of the method of ascertaining the value of the taxable estate, see sections 2051 through 2056, and the regulations thereunder.

(4) Gross estate tax. The third step is the determination of the gross estate tax. This is accomplished by the application of certain rates to the value of the decedent's taxable estate. In this connection, see section 2001 and the regulations thereunder.

(5) Net estate tax payable. The final step is the determination of the net estate tax payable. This is done by subtracting from the gross estate tax the authorized credits against tax. Under certain conditions and limitations, credits are allowable for the following (computed in the order stated below):

(i) State death taxes paid in connection with the decedent's estate (section 2011);

(ii) Gift taxes paid on inter-vivos transfers by the decedent of property included in his gross estate (section 2012);

(iii) Foreign death taxes paid in connection with the decedent's estate (section 2014); and

(iv) Federal estate taxes paid on transfers of property to the decedent (section 2013). Sections 2015 and 2016 contain certain further rules for the application of the credits for State and foreign death taxes. Sections 25.2701–5 and 25.2702–6 of this chapter contain rules that provide additional adjustments to mitigate double taxation in cases where the amount of the decedent's gift was previously determined under the special valuation provisions of sections 2701 and 2702. For a detailed explanation of the credits against tax, see sections 2011 through 2016, * * *.

* * *

[T.D. 6296, 23 FR 4529, June 24, 1958, as amended by T.D. 6684, 28 FR 11408, Oct. 24, 1963; T.D. 7296, 38 FR 34191, Dec. 12, 1973; T.D. 8395, 57 FR 4254, Feb. 4, 1992]

§ 20.2010–1T Unified credit against estate tax; in general (temporary).

* * *

(d) Explanation of terms. The explanation of terms in this section applies to this section and to §§ 20.2010–2T and 20.2010–3T.

(1) Applicable credit amount. The term applicable credit amount refers to the allowable credit against estate tax imposed by section 2001 and gift tax imposed by section 2501. The applicable credit amount equals the amount of the tentative tax that would be determined under section 2001(c) if the amount on which such tentative tax is to be computed were equal to the applicable exclusion amount. The applicable credit amount is determined by applying the unified rate schedule in section 2001(c) to the applicable exclusion amount.

(2) Applicable exclusion amount. The applicable exclusion amount equals the sum of the basic exclusion amount and, in the case of a surviving spouse, the deceased spousal unused exclusion (DSUE) amount.

(3) Basic exclusion amount. The basic exclusion amount is the sum of—

(i) For any decedent dying in calendar year 2011, $5,000,000; and

(ii) For any decedent dying after calendar year 2011, $5,000,000 multiplied by the cost-of-living adjustment determined under section 1(f)(3) for that calendar year by substituting "calendar year 2010" for "calendar year 1992" in section 1(f)(3)(B) and by rounding to the nearest multiple of $10,000.

(4) Deceased spousal unused exclusion (DSUE) amount. The term DSUE amount refers, generally, to the unused portion of a decedent's applicable exclusion amount to the extent this amount does not exceed the basic exclusion amount in effect in the year of the decedent's death. For rules on computing the DSUE amount, see §§ 20.2010–2T(c) and 20.2010–3T(b).

(5) Last deceased spouse. The term last deceased spouse means the most recently deceased individual who, at that individual's death after December 31, 2010, was married to the surviving spouse. See §§ 20.2010–3T(a) and 25.2505–2T(a) of this chapter for additional rules pertaining to the identity of the last deceased spouse for purposes of determining the applicable exclusion amount of the surviving spouse.

(e) Effective/applicability date. Paragraphs (d)(2), (d)(3), (d)(4), and (d)(5) of this section apply to the estates of decedents dying in calendar year 2011 or a subsequent year in which the applicable exclusion amount is determined under section 2010(c) of the Internal Revenue Code by adding the basic exclusion amount and, in the case of a surviving spouse, the DSUE amount. Paragraphs (a), (b), (c), and (d)(1) of this section apply to the estates of decedents dying on or after June 15, 2012.

(f) Expiration date. The applicability of this section expires on or before June 15, 2015.

[T.D. 9593, 77 FR 36157, June 18, 2012]

§ 20.2010–2T Portability provisions applicable to estate of a decedent survived by a spouse (temporary).

(a) Election required for portability. To allow a decedent's surviving spouse to take into account that decedent's deceased spousal unused exclusion (DSUE) amount, the executor of the decedent's estate must elect portability of the DSUE amount on a timely-filed Form 706, "United States Estate (and Generation–Skipping Transfer) Tax Return" (estate tax return). This election is referred to in this section and in § 20.2010–3T as the portability election.

(1) Timely filing required. An estate that elects portability will be considered, for purposes of Subtitle B and Subtitle F of the Internal Revenue Code (Code), to be required to file a return under section 6018(a). Accordingly, the due date of an estate tax return required to elect portability is 9 months after the decedent's date of death or the last day of the period covered by an extension (if an extension of time for filing has been obtained). See §§ 20.6075–1 and 20.6081–1 for additional rules relating to the time for filing estate tax returns.

(2) Portability election upon filing of estate tax return. Upon the timely filing of a complete and properly-prepared estate tax return, an executor of an estate of a decedent (survived by a spouse) will have elected portability of the decedent's DSUE amount unless the executor chooses not to elect portability and satisfies the requirement in paragraph (a)(3)(i) of this section. See paragraph (a)(7) of this section for the return requirements related to the portability election.

(3) Portability election not made; requirements for election not to apply. The executor of the estate of a decedent (survived by a spouse) will not make or be considered to make the portability election if either of the following applies:

(i) The executor states affirmatively on a timely-filed estate tax return, or in an attachment to that estate tax return, that the estate is not electing portability under section 2010(c)(5). The manner in which the executor may make this affirmative statement on the estate tax return will be as set forth in the instructions issued with respect to such form ("Instructions for Form 706").

(ii) The executor does not timely file an estate tax return in accordance with paragraph (a)(1) of this section.

(4) Election irrevocable. An executor of the estate of a decedent (survived by a spouse) who timely files an estate tax return may make and may supersede a portability election previously made, provided that the estate tax return reporting the decision not to make a portability election is filed on or before the due date of the return, including extensions actually granted. However, see paragraph (a)(6) of this section when contrary elections are made by more than one person permitted to make the election. The portability election, once made, becomes irrevocable once the due date of the estate tax return, including extensions actually granted, has passed.

(5) Estates eligible to make the election. An executor may elect portability on behalf of the estate of a decedent (survived by a spouse) if the decedent dies in calendar year 2011 or during a subsequent period in which portability of a DSUE amount is in effect. However, an executor of the estate of a nonresident decedent who was not a citizen of the United States at the time of death may not elect portability on behalf of that decedent, and the timely filing of such a decedent's estate tax return will not constitute the making of a portability election.

(6) Persons permitted to make the election—(i) Appointed executor. An executor or administrator of the estate of a decedent (survived by a spouse) that is appointed, qualified, and acting within the United States, within the meaning of section 2203 (an appointed executor), may file the estate tax return on behalf of the estate of the decedent and, in so doing, elect portability of the decedent's DSUE amount. An appointed executor also may elect not to have portability apply pursuant to paragraph (a)(3) of this section.

(ii) Non-appointed executor. If there is no appointed executor, any person in actual or constructive possession of any property of the decedent (a non-appointed executor) may file the estate tax return on behalf of the estate of the decedent and, in so doing, elect portability of the decedent's DSUE amount, or, by complying with paragraph (a)(3) of this section, may elect not to have portability apply. A portability election made by a non-appointed executor cannot be superseded by a contrary election made by another non-appointed executor of that same decedent's estate (unless such other non-appointed executor is the successor of the non-appointed executor who made the election). See § 20.6018–2 for additional rules relating to persons permitted to file the estate tax return.

(7) Requirements of return—(i) General rule. An estate tax return will be considered complete and properly-prepared for purposes of this section if it is prepared in accordance with the instructions issued for the estate tax return (Instructions for Form 706) and if the requirements of §§ 20.6018–2, 20.6018–3, and 20.6018–4 are satisfied. However, see paragraph (a)(7)(ii) of this section for reduced requirements applicable to certain property of certain estates.

(ii) Reporting of value not required for certain property—(A) In general. A special rule applies with respect to certain property of estates in which the executor is not required to file an estate tax return under section 6018(a), as determined without regard to paragraph (a)(1) of this section. With respect to such an estate, for bequests, devises, or transfers of property included in the gross estate, the value of which is deductible under section 2056 or 2056A (marital deduction property) or under section 2055(a) (charitable deduction property), an executor is not required to report a value for such property on the estate tax return (except to the extent provided in this paragraph (a)(7)(ii)(A)) and will be required to report only the description, ownership, and/or beneficiary of such property, along with all other information necessary to establish the right of the estate to the deduction in accordance with §§ 20.2056(a)–1(b)(i) through (iii) and 20.2055–1(c), as applicable. However, this rule does not apply to marital deduction property or charitable deduction property if—

(1) The value of such property relates to, affects, or is needed to determine, the value passing from the decedent to another recipient;

(2) The value of such property is needed to determine the estate's eligibility for the provisions of sections 2032, 2032A, 6166, or another provision of the Code;

(3) Less than the entire value of an interest in property includible in the decedent's gross estate is marital deduction property or charitable deduction property; or

(4) A partial disclaimer or partial qualified terminable interest property (QTIP) election is made with respect to a bequest, devise, or transfer of property includible in the gross estate, part of which is marital deduction property or charitable deduction property.

(B) Statement required on the return. Paragraph (a)(7)(ii)(A) of this section applies only if the executor exercises due diligence to estimate the fair market value of the gross estate, including the property described in paragraph (a)(7)(ii)(A) of this section. The Instructions for Form 706 will provide ranges of dollar values, and the executor must identify on the estate tax return an amount corresponding to the particular range within which falls the executor's best estimate of the total gross estate. Until such time as the prescribed form for the estate tax return expressly includes this estimate in the manner described in the preceding sentence, the executor must include the executor's best estimate, rounded to the nearest $250,000, on or attached to the estate tax return, signed under penalties of perjury.

* * *

(b) Computation required for portability election—(1) General rule. In addition to the requirements described in paragraph (a) of this section, an executor of a decedent's estate must include a computation of the DSUE amount on the estate tax return to elect portability and thereby allow the decedent's surviving spouse to take into account that decedent's DSUE amount. See paragraph (b)(2) of this section for a transitional rule when the estate tax return form prescribed by the Internal Revenue Service (IRS) does not show expressly the computation of the DSUE amount. See paragraph (c) of this section for rules on computing the DSUE amount.

* * *

(c) Computation of the DSUE amount—(1) General rule. Subject to paragraphs (c)(2) through (c)(4) of this section, the DSUE amount of a decedent with a surviving spouse is the lesser of the following amounts—

(i) The basic exclusion amount in effect in the year of the death of the decedent; or

(ii) The excess of—

(A) The decedent's applicable exclusion amount; over

(B) The sum of the amount of the taxable estate and the amount of the adjusted taxable gifts of the decedent, which together is the amount on which the tentative tax on the decedent's estate is determined under section 2001(b)(1).

* * *

(5) Examples. The following examples illustrate the application of this paragraph (c):

Example 1. Computation of DSUE amount. (i) Facts. In 2002, having made no prior taxable gift, Husband (H) makes a taxable gift valued at $1,000,000 and reports the gift on a timely-filed gift tax return. Because the amount of the gift is equal to the applicable exclusion amount for that year ($1,000,000), $345,800 is allowed as a credit against the tax, reducing the gift tax liability to zero. H dies on September 29, 2011, survived by Wife (W). H and W are US citizens and neither has any prior marriage. H's taxable estate is $1,000,000. The executor of H's estate timely files H's estate tax return and elects portability, thereby allowing W to benefit from H's DSUE amount.

(ii) Application. The executor of H's estate computes H's DSUE amount to be $3,000,000 (the lesser of the $5,000,000 basic exclusion amount in 2011, or the excess of H's $5,000,000 applicable exclusion amount over the sum of the $1,000,000 taxable estate and the $1,000,000 amount of adjusted taxable gifts).

* * *

(d) Authority to examine returns of decedent. The IRS may examine returns of a decedent in determining the decedent's DSUE amount, regardless of whether the period of limitations on assessment has expired for that return. See § 20.2010–3T(d) for additional rules relating to the IRS's authority to examine returns. See also section 7602 for the IRS's authority, when ascertaining the correctness of any return, to examine any returns that may be relevant or material to such inquiry.

* * *

[T.D. 9593, 77 FR 36157, June 18, 2012]

§ 20.2010–3T Portability provisions applicable to the surviving spouse's estate (temporary).

(a) Surviving spouse's estate limited to DSUE amount of last deceased spouse—(1) In general. A deceased spousal unused exclusion (DSUE) amount of a decedent, computed under § 20.2010–2T(c), is included in determining a surviving spouse's applicable exclusion amount under section 2010(c)(2), provided—

(i) Such decedent is the last deceased spouse of such surviving spouse within the meaning of § 20.2010–1T(d)(5) on the date of the death of the surviving spouse; and

(ii) The executor of the decedent's estate elected portability (see § 20.2010–2T(a) and (b) for applicable requirements).

(2) No DSUE amount available from last deceased spouse. If the last deceased spouse of such surviving spouse had no DSUE amount, or if the executor of such a decedent's estate did not make a portability election, the surviving spouse's estate has no DSUE amount (except as provided in paragraph (b)(1)(ii) of this section) to be included in determining the applicable exclusion amount, even if the surviving spouse previously had a DSUE amount available from another decedent who, prior to the death of the last deceased spouse, was the last deceased spouse of such surviving spouse. See paragraph (b) of this section for a special rule in the case of multiple deceased spouses and a previously-applied DSUE amount.

(3) Identity of last deceased spouse unchanged by subsequent marriage or divorce. A decedent is the last deceased spouse (as defined in § 20.2010–1T(d)(5)) of a surviving spouse even if, on the date of the death of the surviving spouse, the surviving spouse is married to another (then-living) individual. If a surviving spouse marries again and that marriage ends in divorce or an annulment, the subsequent death of the divorced spouse does not end the status of the prior deceased spouse as the last deceased spouse of the surviving spouse. The divorced spouse, not being married to the surviving spouse at death, is not the last deceased spouse as that term is defined in § 20.2010–1T(d)(5).

(b) Special rule in case of multiple deceased spouses and previously-applied DSUE amount—(1) In general. A special rule applies to compute the DSUE amount included in the applicable exclusion amount of a surviving spouse who previously has applied the DSUE amount of one or more deceased spouses to taxable gifts in accordance with § 25.2505–2T(b) and (c) of this chapter. If a surviving spouse has applied the DSUE amount of one or more last deceased spouses to the surviving spouse's transfers during life, and if any of those last deceased spouses is different from the surviving spouse's last deceased spouse as defined in § 20.2010–1T(d)(5) at the time of the surviving spouse's death, then the DSUE amount to be included in determining the applicable exclusion amount of the surviving spouse at the time of the surviving spouse's death is the sum of—

(i) The DSUE amount of the surviving spouse's last deceased spouse as described in paragraph (a)(1) of this section; and

(ii) The DSUE amount of each other deceased spouse of the surviving spouse, to the extent that such amount was applied to one or more taxable gifts of the surviving spouse.

(2) Example. The following example, in which all described individuals are US citizens, illustrates the application of this paragraph (b):

Example. (i) Facts. Husband 1 (H1) dies on January 15, 2011, survived by Wife (W). Neither has made any taxable gifts during H1's lifetime. H1's executor elects portability of H1's DSUE amount. The DSUE amount of H1 as computed on the estate tax return filed on behalf of H1's estate is $5,000,000. On December 31, 2011, W makes taxable gifts to her children valued at $2,000,000. W reports the gifts on a timely-filed gift tax return. W is considered to have applied $2,000,000 of H1's DSUE amount to the amount of taxable gifts, in accordance with § 25.2505–2T(c), and, therefore, W owes no gift tax. W has an applicable exclusion amount remaining in the amount of $8,000,000 ($3,000,000 of H1's remaining DSUE amount plus W's own $5,000,000 basic exclusion amount). After the death of H1, W marries Husband 2 (H2). H2 dies in June 2012. H2's executor elects portability of H2's DSUE amount, which is properly computed on H2's estate tax return to be $2,000,000. W dies in October 2012.

(ii) Application. The DSUE amount to be included in determining the applicable exclusion amount available to W's estate is $4,000,000, determined by adding the $2,000,000 DSUE amount of H2 and the $2,000,000 DSUE amount of H1 that was applied by W to W's 2011 taxable gifts. Thus, W's applicable exclusion amount is $9,000,000.

(c) Date DSUE amount taken into consideration by surviving spouse's estate—(1) General rule. A portability election made by an executor of a decedent's estate (see § 20.2010–2T(a) and (b) for applicable requirements) applies as of the date of the decedent's death. Thus, the decedent's DSUE amount is included in the applicable exclusion amount of the decedent's surviving spouse under section 2010(c)(2) and will be applicable to transfers made by the surviving spouse after the decedent's death. However, such decedent's DSUE amount will not be included in the applicable exclusion amount of the surviving spouse, even if the surviving spouse had made a transfer in reliance on the availability or computation of the decedent's DSUE amount:

(i) If the executor of the decedent's estate supersedes the portability election by filing a subsequent estate tax return in accordance with § 20.2010–2T(a)(4);

(ii) To the extent that the DSUE amount subsequently is reduced by a valuation adjustment or the correction of an error in calculation; or

(iii) To the extent that the surviving spouse cannot substantiate the DSUE amount claimed on the surviving spouse's return.

* * *

(d) Authority to examine returns of deceased spouses. For the purpose of determining the DSUE amount to be included in the applicable exclusion amount of the surviving spouse, the Internal Revenue Service (IRS) may examine returns of each of the surviving spouse's deceased spouses whose DSUE amount is claimed to be included in the surviving spouse's applicable exclusion amount, regardless of whether the period of limitations on assessment has expired for any such return. The IRS's authority to examine returns of a deceased spouse applies with respect to each transfer by the surviving spouse to which a DSUE amount is or has been applied. Upon examination, the IRS may adjust or eliminate the DSUE amount reported on such a return; however, the IRS may assess additional tax on that return only if that tax is assessed within the period of limitations on assessment under section 6501 applicable to the tax shown on that return. See also section 7602 for the IRS's authority, when ascertaining the correctness of any return, to examine any returns that may be relevant or material to such inquiry. For purposes of these examinations to determine the DSUE amount, the surviving spouse is considered to have a material interest that is affected by the return information of the deceased spouse within the meaning of section 6103(e)(3).

* * *

[T.D. 9593, 77 FR 36160, June 18, 2012]

§ 20.2013–1 Credit for tax on prior transfers.

(a) In general. A credit is allowed under section 2013 against the Federal estate tax imposed on the present decedent's estate for Federal estate tax paid on the transfer of property to the present decedent from a transferor who died within ten years before, or within two years after, the present decedent's death. See § 20.2013–5 for definition of the terms "property" and "transfer". There is no requirement that the transferred property be identified in the estate of the present decedent or that the property be in existence at the time of the decedent's death. It is sufficient that the transfer of the property was subjected to Federal estate tax in the estate of the transferor and that the transferor died within the prescribed period of time. The executor must submit such proof as may be requested by the district director in order to establish the right of the estate to the credit.

(b) Limitations on credit. The credit for tax on prior transfers is limited to the smaller of the following amounts:

(1) The amount of the Federal estate tax attributable to the transferred property in the transferor's estate, computed as set forth in § 20.2013–2; or

(2) The amount of the Federal estate tax attributable to the transferred property in the decedent's estate, computed as set forth in § 20.2013–3.

Rules for valuing property for purposes of the credit are contained in § 20.2013–4.

(c) Percentage reduction. If the transferor died within the two years before, or within the two years after, the present decedent's death, the credit is the smaller of the two limitations described in paragraph (b) of this section. If the transferor predeceased the present decedent by more than two years, the credit is a certain percentage of the smaller of the two limitations described in paragraph (b) of this section, determined as follows:

(1) 80 percent, if the transferor died within the third or fourth years preceding the present decedent's death;

(2) 40 percent, if the transferor died within the fifth or sixth years preceding the present decedent's death;

(3) 40 percent, if the transferor died within the seventh or eighth years preceding the present decedent's death; and

(4) 20 percent, if the transferor died within the ninth or tenth years preceding the present decedent's death.

The word "within" as used in this paragraph means "during". Therefore, if a death occurs on the second anniversary of another death, the first death is considered to have occurred within the two years before the second death. If the credit for tax on prior transfers relates to property received from two or more transferors, the provisions of this paragraph are to be applied separately with respect to the property received from each transferor. See paragraph (d) of example (2) in § 20.2013–6.

(d) Examples. For illustrations of the application of this section, see examples (1) and (2) set forth in § 20.2013–6.

[T.D. 6296, 23 FR 4529, June 24, 1958]

§ 20.2013–2 "First limitation".

(a) The amount of the Federal estate tax attributable to the transferred property in the transferor's estate is the "first limitation." Thus, the credit is limited to an amount, A, which bears the same ratio to B (the "transferor's adjusted Federal estate tax", computed as described in paragraph (b) of this section) as C (the value of the property transferred (see § 20.2013–4)) bears to D (the "transferor's adjusted taxable estate", computed as described in paragraph (c) of this section). Stated algebraically, the "first limitation" (A) equals:

Value of transferred property (C) / "Transferor's adjusted taxable estate" (D) x "Transferor's adjusted Federal estate tax" (B).

(b) For purposes of the ratio stated in paragraph (a) of this section, the "transferor's adjusted Federal estate tax" referred to as factor "B" is the amount of the Federal estate tax paid with respect to the transferor's estate plus:

(1) Any credit allowed the transferor's estate for gift tax under section 2012, or the corresponding provisions of prior law; and

(2) Any credit allowed the transferor's estate, under section 2013, for tax on prior transfers, but only if the transferor acquired property from a person who died within 10 years before the death of the present decedent.

(c)(1) For purposes of the ratio stated in paragraph (a) of this section, the "transferor's adjusted taxable estate" referred to as factor "D" is the amount of the transferor's taxable estate (or net estate) decreased by the amount of any "death taxes" paid with respect to his gross estate and increased by the amount of the exemption allowed in computing his taxable estate (or net estate). The amount of the transferor's taxable estate (or net estate) is determined in accordance with the provisions of § 20.2051–1 in the case of a citizen or resident of the United States or of § 20.2106–1 in the case of a nonresident not a citizen of the United States (or the corresponding provisions of prior regulations). The term "death taxes" means the Federal estate tax plus all other estate, inheritance, legacy, succession, or similar death taxes imposed by, and paid to, any taxing authority, whether within or without the United States. However, only the net amount of such taxes paid is taken into consideration.

(2) The amount of the exemption depends upon the citizenship and residence of the transferor at the time of his death. Except in the case of a decedent described in section 2209 (relating to certain residents of possessions of the United States who are considered nonresidents not citizens), if the decedent was a citizen or resident of the United States, the exemption is the $60,000 authorized by section 2052 (or the corresponding provisions of prior law). If the decedent was a nonresident not a citizen of the United States, or is considered under section 2209 to have been such a nonresident, the exemption is the $30,000 or $2,000, as the case may be, authorized by section 2106(a)(3) (or the corresponding provisions of prior law), or such larger amount as is authorized by section 2106(a)(3)(B) or may have been allowed as an exemption pursuant to the prorated exemption provisions of an applicable death tax convention. See § 20.2052–1 and paragraph (a)(3) of § 20.2106–1.

(d) If the credit for tax on prior transfers relates to property received from two or more transferors, the provisions of this section are to be applied separately with respect to the property received from each transferor. See paragraph (b) of example (2) in § 20.2013–6.

(e) For illustrations of the application of this section, see examples (1) and (2) set forth in § 20.2013–6.

[T.D. 6296, 23 FR 4529, June 24, 1958; 25 FR 14021, Dec. 31, 1960, as amended at T.D. 7296, 38 FR 34191, Dec. 12, 1973]

§ 20.2013–3 "Second limitation".

(a) The amount of the Federal estate tax attributable to the transferred property in the present decedent's estate is the "second limitation". Thus, the credit is limited to the difference between—

(1) The net estate tax payable (see paragraph (b)(5) or (c), as the case may be, of § 20.0–2) with respect to the present decedent's estate, determined without regard to any credit for tax on prior transfers under section 2013 or any credit for foreign death taxes claimed under the provisions of a death tax convention, and

(2) The net estate tax determined as provided in subparagraph (1) of this paragraph but computed by subtracting from the present decedent's gross estate the value of the property transferred (see § 20.2013–4), and by making only the adjustment indicated in paragraph (b) of this section if a charitable deduction is allowable to the estate of the present decedent.

(b) If a charitable deduction is allowable to the estate of the present decedent under the provisions of section 2055 or section 2106 (a)(2)(for estates of nonresidents not citizens), for purposes of determining the tax described in paragraph (a)(2) of this section, the charitable deduction otherwise allowable is reduced by an amount, E, which bears the same ratio to F (the charitable deduction otherwise allowable) as G (the value of the transferred property (see § 20.2013–4)) bears to H (the value of the present decedent's gross estate reduced by the amount of the deductions for expenses, indebtedness, taxes, losses, etc., allowed under the provisions of sections 2053 and 2054 or section 2106(a)(1) (for estates of nonresidents not citizens)). See paragraph (c)(2) of example (1) and paragraph (c)(2) of example (2) in § 20.2013–6.

(c) If the credit for tax on prior transfers relates to property received from two or more transferors, the property received from all transferors is aggregated in determining the limitation on credit under this section (the "second limitation"). However, the limitation so determined is apportioned to the property received from each transferor in the ratio that the property received from each transferor bears to the total property received from all transferors. See paragraph (c) of example (2) in § 20.2013–6.

(d) For illustrations of the application of this section, see examples (1) and (2) set forth in § 20.2013–6.

[T.D. 6296, 23 FR 4529, June 24, 1958; 25 FR 14021, Dec. 31, 1960, as amended at T.D. 7296, 38 FR 34191, Dec. 12, 1973]

§ 20.2013–4 Valuation of property transferred.

(a) For purposes of section 2013 and §§ 20.2013–1 to 20.2013–6, the value of the property transferred to the decedent is the value at which the property was included in the transferor's gross estate for the purpose of the Federal estate tax (see sections 2031, 2032, 2103, and 2107, and the regulations thereunder) reduced as indicated in paragraph (b) of this section. If the decedent received a life estate or a remainder or other limited interest in property that was included in a transferor decedent's gross estate, the value of the interest is determined as of the date of the transferor's death on the basis of recognized valuation principles (see §§ 20.2031–7 (or, for certain prior periods, § 20.2031–7A) and 20.7520–1 through 20.7520–4). The application of this paragraph may be illustrated by the following examples:

Example (1). A died on January 1, 1953, leaving Blackacre to B. The property was included in A's gross estate at a value of $100,000. On January 1, 1955, B sold Blackacre to C for $150,000. B died on February 1, 1955. For purposes of computing the credit against the tax imposed on B's estate, the value of the property transferred to B is $100,000.

Example (2). A died on January 1, 1953, leaving Blackacre to B for life and, upon B's death, remainder to C. At the time of A's death, B was 56 years of age. The property was included in A's gross estate at a value of $100,000. The part of that value attributable to the life estate is $44,688 and the part of that value attributable to the remainder is $55,312 (see § 20.2031–7A(b)). B died on January 1, 1955, and C died on January 1, 1956. For purposes of computing the credit against the tax imposed on B's estate, the value of the property transferred to B is $44,688. For purposes of computing the credit against the tax imposed on C's estate, the value of the property transferred to C is $55,312.

(b) In arriving at the value of the property transferred to the decedent, the value at which the property was included in the transferor's gross estate (see paragraph (a) of this section) is reduced as follows:

(1) By the amount of the Federal estate tax and any other estate, inheritance, legacy, or succession taxes which were payable out of the property transferred to the decedent or which were payable by the decedent in connection with the property transferred to him. For example, if under the transferor's will or local law all death taxes are to be paid out of other property with the result that the decedent receives a bequest free and clear of all death taxes, no reduction is to be made under this subparagraph;

(2) By the amount of any marital deduction allowed the transferor's estate under section 2056 (or under section 812(e) of the Internal Revenue Code of 1939) if the decedent was the spouse of the transferor at the time of the transferor's death;

(3)(i) By the amount of administration expenses in accordance with the principles of § 20.2056(b)–4(d).

(ii) This paragraph (b)(3) applies to transfers from estates of decedents dying on or after December 3, 1999; and

(4)(i) By the amount of any encumbrance on the property or by the amount of any obligation imposed by the transferor and incurred by the decedent with respect to the property, to the extent such charges would be taken into account if the amount of a gift to the decedent of such property were being determined.

(ii) For purposes of this subparagraph, an obligation imposed by the transferor and incurred by the decedent with respect to the property includes a bequest, etc., in lieu of the interest of the surviving spouse under community property laws, unless the interest was, immediately prior to the transferor's death, a mere expectancy. However, an obligation imposed by the transferor and incurred by the decedent with respect to the property does not include a bequest, devise, or other transfer in lieu of dower, curtesy, or of a statutory estate created in lieu of dower or curtesy, or of other marital rights in the transferor's property or estate.

(iii) The application of this subparagraph may be illustrated by the following examples:

Example (1). The transferor devised to the decedent real estate subject to a mortgage. The value of the property transferred to the decedent does not include the amount of the mortgage. If, however, the transferor by his will directs the executor to pay off the mortgage, such payment constitutes an additional amount transferred to the decedent.

Example (2). The transferor bequeathed certain property to the decedent with a direction that the decedent pay $1,000 to X. The value of the property transferred to the decedent is the value of the property reduced by $1,000.

Example (3). The transferor bequeathed certain property to his wife, the decedent, in lieu of her interest in property held by them as community property under the law of the State of their residence. The wife elected to relinquish her community property interest and to take the bequest. The value of the property transferred to the decedent is the value of the property reduced by the value of the community property interest relinquished by the wife.

Example (4). The transferor bequeathed to the decedent his entire residuary estate, out of which certain claims were to be satisfied. The entire distributable income of the transferor's estate (during the period of its administration) was applied toward the satisfaction of these claims and the remaining portion of the claims was satisfied by the decedent out of his own funds. Thus, the decedent received a larger sum upon settlement of the transferor's estate than he was actually bequeathed. The value of the property transferred to the decedent is the value at which such property was included in the transferor's gross estate, reduced by the amount of the estate income and the decedent's own funds paid out in satisfaction of the claims.

[T.D. 6296, 23 FR 4529, June 24, 1958, as amended by T.D. 7077, 35 FR 18461, Dec. 4, 1970; T.D. 7296, 38 FR 34191, Dec. 12, 1973; T.D. 8522, 59 FR 9646, March 1, 1994; T.D. 8540, 59 FR 30151, June 10, 1994; T.D. 8846, 64 FR 67764, Dec. 3, 1999]

§ 20.2013–5 "Property" and "transfer" defined.

(a) For purposes of section 2013 and §§ 20.2013–1 to 20.2013–6, the term "property" means any beneficial interest in property, including a general power of appointment (as defined in section 2041) over property. Thus, the term does not include an interest in property consisting merely of a bare legal title, such as that of a trustee. Nor does the term include a power of appointment over property which is not a general power of appointment (as defined in section 2041). Examples of property, as described in this paragraph, are annuities, life estates, estates for terms of years, vested or contingent remainders and other future interests.

(b) In order to obtain the credit for tax on prior transfers, there must be a transfer of property described in paragraph (a) of this section by or from the transferor to the decedent. The term "transfer" of property by or from a transferor means any passing of property or an interest in property under circumstances which were such that the property or interest was included in the gross estate of the transferor. In this connection, if the decedent receives property as a result of the exercise or nonexercise of a power of appointment, the donee of the power (and not the creator) is deemed to be the transferor of the property if the property subject to the power is includible in the donee's gross estate under section 2041 (relating to powers of appointment). Thus, notwithstanding the designation by local law of the capacity in which the decedent takes, property received from the transferor includes interests in property held by or devolving upon the decedent: (1) As spouse under dower or curtesy laws or laws creating an estate in lieu of dower or curtesy; (2) as surviving tenant of a tenancy by the entirety or joint tenancy with survivorship rights; (3) as beneficiary of the proceeds of life insurance; (4) as survivor under an annuity contract; (5) as donee (possessor) of a general power of appointment (as defined in section 2041); (6) as appointee under the exercise of a general power of appointment (as defined in section 2041); or (7) as remainderman under the release or nonexercise of a power of appointment by reason of which the property is included in the gross estate of the donee of the power under section 2041.

(c) The application of this section may be illustrated by the following example:

Example: A devises Blackacre to B, as trustee, with directions to pay the income therefore to C, his son, for life. Upon C's death, Blackacre is to be sold. C is given a general testamentary power, to appoint one-third of the proceeds, and a testamentary power, which is not a general power, to appoint the remaining two-thirds of the proceeds, to such of the issue of his sister D as he should choose. D has a daughter, E, and a son, F. Upon his death, C exercised his general power by appointing one-third of the proceeds to D and his special power by appointing two-thirds of the proceeds to E. Since B's interest in Blackacre as a trustee is not a beneficial interest, no part of it is "property" for purpose of the credit in B's estate. On the other hand, C's life estate and his testamentary power over the one-third interest in the remainder constitute "property" received from A for purpose of the credit in C's estate. Likewise, D's one-third interest in the remainder received through the exercise of C's general power of appointment is "property" received from C for purpose of the credit in D's estate. No credit is allowed E's estate for the property which passed to her from C since the property was not included in C's gross estate. On the other hand, no credit is allowed in E's estate for property passing to her from A since her interest was not susceptible of valuation at the time of A's death (see § 20.2013–4).

[T.D. 6296, 23 FR 4529, June 24, 1958; 25 FR 14021, Dec. 31, 1960]

§ 20.2031–1 Definition of gross estate; valuation of property.

(a) Definition of gross estate. Except as otherwise provided in this paragraph the value of the gross estate of a decedent who was a citizen or resident of the United States at the time of his death is the total value of the interests described in sections 2033 through 2044. * * * The contents of sections 2033 through 2044 are, in general, as follows:

(1) Sections 2033 and 2034 are concerned mainly with interests in property passing through the decedent's probate estate. Section 2033 includes in the decedent's gross estate any interest that the decedent had in property at the time of his death. Section 2034 provides that any interest of the decedent's surviving spouse in the decedent's property, such as dower or curtesy, does not prevent the inclusion of such property in the decedent's gross estate.

(2) Sections 2035 through 2038 deal with interests in property transferred by the decedent during his life under such circumstances as to bring the interests within the decedent's gross estate. * * * Section 2036 provides for the inclusion of transferred property with respect to which the decedent retained the income or the power to designate who shall enjoy the income. Section 2037 includes in the decedent's gross estate certain transfers under which the beneficial enjoyment of the property could be obtained only by surviving the decedent. Section 2038 provides for the inclusion of transferred property if the decedent had at the time of his death the power to change the beneficial enjoyment of the property. It should be noted that there is considerable overlap in the application of sections 2036 through 2038 with respect to reserved powers, so that transferred property may be includible in the decedent's gross estate in varying degrees under more than one of those sections.

(3) Sections 2039 through 2042 deal with special kinds of property and powers. Sections 2039 and 2040 concern annuities and jointly held property respectively. Section 2041 deals with powers held by the decedent over the beneficial enjoyment of property not originating with the decedent. Section 2042 concerns insurance under policies on the life of the decedent.

(4) Section 2043 concerns the sufficiency of consideration for transfers made by the decedent during his life. This has a bearing on the amount to be included in the decedent's gross estate under sections 2035 through 2038, and 2041. * * *

(b) Valuation of property in general. The value of every item of property includible in a decedent's gross estate under sections 2031 through 2044 is its fair market value at the time of the decedent's death, except that if the executor elects the alternate valuation method under section 2032, it is the fair market value thereof at the date, and with the adjustments, prescribed in that section. The fair market value is the price at which the property would change hands between a willing buyer and a willing seller, neither being under any compulsion to buy or to sell and both having reasonable knowledge of relevant facts. The fair market value of a particular item of property includible in the decedent's gross estate is not to be determined by a forced sale price. Nor is the fair market value of an item of property to be determined by the sale price of the item in a market other than that in which such item is most commonly sold to the public, taking into account the location of the item wherever appropriate. Thus, in the case of an item of property includible in the decedent's gross estate, which is generally obtained by the public in the retail market, the fair market value of such an item of property is the price at which the item or a comparable item would be sold at retail. For example, the fair market value of an automobile (an article generally obtained by the public in the retail market) includible in the decedent's gross estate is the price for which an automobile of the same or approximately the same description, make, model, age, condition, etc., could be purchased by a member of the general public and not the price for which the particular automobile of the decedent would be purchased by a dealer in used automobiles. Examples of items of property which are generally sold to the public at retail may be found in §§ 20.2031–6 and 20.2031–8. The value is generally to be determined by ascertaining as a basis the fair market value as of the applicable valuation date of each unit of property. For example, in the case of shares of stock or bonds, such unit of property is generally a share of stock or a bond. Livestock, farm machinery, harvested and growing crops must generally be itemized and the value of each item separately returned. Property shall not be returned at the value at which it is assessed for local tax purposes unless that value represents the fair market value as of the applicable valuation date. All relevant facts and elements of value as of the applicable valuation date shall be considered in every case. The value of items of property which were held by the decedent for sale in the course of a business generally should be reflected in the value of the business. For valuation of interests in businesses, see § 20.2031–3. See § 20.2031–2 and §§ 20.2031–4 through 20.2031–8 for further information concerning the valuation of other particular kinds of property. For certain circumstances under which the sale of an item of property at a price below its fair market value may result in a deduction for the estate, see paragraph (d)(2) of § 20.2053–3.

* * *

[T.D. 6296, 23 FR 4529, June 24, 1958, as amended by T.D. 6684, 28 FR 11408, Oct. 24, 1963; T.D. 6826, 30 FR 7708, June 15, 1965]

§ 20.2031–2 Valuation of stocks and bonds.

(a) In general. The value of stocks and bonds is the fair market value per share or bond on the applicable valuation date.

(b) Based on selling prices. **(1)** In general, if there is a market for stocks or bonds, on a stock exchange, in an over-the-counter market, or otherwise, the mean between the highest and lowest quoted selling prices on the valuation date is the fair market value per share or bond. If there were no sales on the valuation date but there were sales on dates within a reasonable period both before and after the valuation date, the fair market value is determined by taking a weighted average of the means between the highest and lowest sales on the nearest date before and the nearest date after the valuation date. The average is to be weighted inversely by the respective numbers of trading days between the selling dates and the valuation date. If the stocks or bonds are listed on more than one exchange, the records of the exchange where the stocks or bonds are principally dealt in should be employed if such records are available in a generally available listing or publication of general circulation. In the event that such records are not so available and such stocks or bonds are listed on a composite listing of combined exchanges available in a generally available listing or publication of general circulation, the records of such combined exchanges should be employed. In valuing listed securities, the executor should be careful to consult accurate records to obtain values as of the applicable valuation date. If quotations of unlisted securities are obtained from brokers, or evidence as to their sale is obtained from officers of the issuing companies, copies of the letters furnishing such quotations or evidence of sale should be attached to the return.

(2) If it is established with respect to bonds for which there is a market on a stock exchange, that the highest and lowest selling prices are not available for the valuation date in a generally available listing or publication of general circulation but that closing selling prices are so available, the fair market value per bond is the mean between the quoted closing selling price on the valuation date and the quoted closing selling price on the trading day before the valuation date. If there were no sales on the trading day before the valuation date but there were sales on a date within a reasonable period before the valuation date, the fair market value is determined by taking a weighted average of the quoted closing selling price on the valuation date and the quoted closing selling price on the nearest date before the valuation date. The closing selling price for the valuation date is to be weighted by the number of trading days between the previous selling date and the valuation date. If there were no sales within a reasonable period before the valuation date but there were sales on the valuation date, the fair market value is the closing selling price on such valuation date. If there were no sales on the valuation date but there were sales on dates within a reasonable period both before and after the valuation date, the fair market value is determined by taking a weighted average of the quoted closing selling prices on the nearest date before and the nearest date after the valuation date. The average is to be weighted inversely by the respective numbers of trading days between the selling dates and the valuation date. If the bonds are listed on more than one exchange, the records of the exchange where the bonds are principally dealt in should be employed. In valuing listed securities, the executor should be careful to consult accurate records to obtain values as of the applicable valuation date.

(3) The application of this paragraph may be illustrated by the following examples:

Example (1). Assume that sales of X Company common stock nearest the valuation date (Friday, June 15) occurred two trading days before (Wednesday, June 13) and three trading days after (Wednesday, June 20) and on these days the mean sale prices per share were $10 and $15, respectively. The price of $12 is taken as representing the fair market value of a share of X Company common stock as of the valuation date

$$[(3 \times 10) + (2 \times 15)]/5.$$

Example (2). Assume the same facts as in example (1) except that the mean sale prices per share on June 13, and June 20 were $15 and $10, respectively. The price of $13 is taken as representing the fair market value of a share of X Company common stock as of the valuation date

$$[(3 \times 15) + (2 \times 10)]/5.$$

Example (3). Assume the decedent died on Sunday, October 7, and that Saturday and Sunday were not trading days. If sales of X Company common stock occurred on Friday, October 5, at mean sale prices per share of $20 and on Monday, October 8, at mean sale prices per share of $23, the price of $21.50 is taken as representing the fair market value of a share of X Company common stock as of the valuation date

$$[(1 \times 20) + (23 \times 1)]/2.$$

Example (4). Assume that on the valuation date (Tuesday, April 3, 1973) the closing selling price of a listed bond was $25 per bond and that the highest and lowest selling prices are not available in a generally available listing or publication of general circulation for that date. Assume further, that the closing selling price of the same listed bond was $21 per bond on the day before the valuation date (Monday, April 2, 1973). Thus, under paragraph (b)(2) of this section the price of $23 is taken as representing the fair market value per bond as of the valuation date

$$(25 + 21)/2.$$

Example (5). Assume the same facts as in example (4) except that there were no sales on the day before the valuation date. Assume further, that there were sales on Thursday, March 29, 1973, and that the closing selling price on that day was $23. The price of $24.50 is taken as representing the fair market value per bond as of the valuation date

$$[(1 \times 23) + (3 \times 25)]/4.$$

Example (6). Assume that no bonds were traded on the valuation date (Friday, April 20). Assume further, that sales of bonds nearest the valuation date occurred two trading days before (Wednesday, April 18) and three trading days after (Wednesday, April 25) the valuation date and that on these two days the closing selling prices per bond were $29 and $22, respectively. The highest and lowest selling prices are not available for these dates in a generally available listing or publication of general circulation. Thus, under paragraph (b)(2) of this section, the price of $26.20 is taken as representing the fair market value of a bond as of the valuation date

$$[(3 \times 29) + (2 \times 22)]/5.$$

(c) Based on bid and asked prices. If the provisions of paragraph (b) of this section are inapplicable because actual sales are not available during a reasonable period beginning before and ending after the valuation date, the fair market value may be determined by taking the mean between the bona fide bid and asked prices on the valuation date, or if none, by taking a weighted average of the means between the bona fide bid and asked prices on the nearest trading date before and the nearest trading date after the valuation date, if both such nearest dates are within a reasonable period. The average is to be determined in the manner described in paragraph (b) of this section.

(d) Based on incomplete selling prices or bid and asked prices. If the provisions of paragraphs (b) and (c) of this section are inapplicable because no actual sale prices or bona fide bid and asked prices are available on a date within a reasonable period before the valuation date, but such prices are available on a date within a reasonable period after the valuation date, or vice versa, then the mean between the highest and lowest available sale prices or bid and asked prices may be taken as the value.

(e) Where selling prices or bid and asked prices do not reflect fair market value. If it is established that the value of any bond or share of stock determined on the basis of selling or bid and asked prices as provided under paragraphs (b), (c), and (d) of this section does not reflect the fair market value thereof, then some reasonable modification of that basis or other relevant facts and elements of value are considered in determining the fair market value. Where sales at or near the date of death are few or of a sporadic nature, such sales alone may not indicate fair market value. In certain exceptional cases, the size of the block of stock to be valued in relation to the number of shares changing hands in sales may be relevant in determining whether selling prices reflect the fair market value of the block of stock to be valued. If the executor can show that the block of stock to be valued is so large in relation to the actual sales on the existing market that it could not be liquidated in a reasonable time without depressing the market, the price at which the block could be sold as such outside the usual market, as through an underwriter, may be a more accurate indication of value than market quotations. Complete data in support of any allowance claimed due to the size of the block of stock being valued shall be submitted with the return. On the other hand, if the block of stock to be valued represents a controlling interest, either actual or effective, in a going business, the price at which other lots change hands may have little relation to its true value.

(f) Where selling prices or bid and asked prices are unavailable. If the provisions of paragraphs (b), (c), and (d) of this section are inapplicable because actual sale prices and bona fide bid and asked prices are lacking, then the fair market value is to be determined by taking the following factors into consideration:

(1) In the case of corporate or other bonds, the soundness of the security, the interest yield, the date of maturity, and other relevant factors; and

(2) In the case of shares of stock, the company's net worth, prospective earning power and dividend-paying capacity, and other relevant factors.

Some of the "other relevant factors" referred to in subparagraphs (1) and (2) of this paragraph are: The good will of the business; the economic outlook in the particular industry; the company's position in the industry and its management; the degree of control of the business represented by the block of stock to be valued; and the values of securities of corporations engaged in the same or similar lines of business which are listed on a stock exchange. However, the weight to be accorded such comparisons or any other evidentiary factors considered in the determination of a value depends upon the facts of each case. In addition to the relevant factors described above, consideration shall also be given to nonoperating assets, including proceeds of life insurance policies payable to or for the benefit of the company, to the extent such nonoperating assets have not been taken into account in the determination of net worth, prospective earning power and dividend-earning capacity. Complete financial and other data upon which the valuation is based should be submitted with the return, including copies of reports of any examinations of the company made by accountants, engineers, or any technical experts as of or near the applicable valuation date.

(g) Pledged securities. The full value of securities pledged to secure an indebtedness of the decedent is included in the gross estate. If the decedent had a trading account with a broker, all securities belonging to the decedent and held by the broker at the date of death must be included at their fair market value as of the applicable valuation date. Securities purchased on margin for the decedent's account and held by a broker must also be returned at their fair market value as of the applicable valuation date. The amount of the decedent's indebtedness to a broker or other person with whom securities were pledged is allowed as a deduction from the gross estate in accordance with the provisions of § 20.2053–1 * * *.

(h) Securities subject to an option or contract to purchase. Another person may hold an option or a contract to purchase securities owned by a decedent at the time of his death. The effect, if any, that is given to the option or contract price in determining the value of the securities for estate tax purposes depends upon the circumstances of the particular case. Little weight will be accorded a price contained in an option or contract under which the decedent is free to dispose of the underlying securities at any price he chooses during his lifetime. Such is the effect, for example, of an agreement on the part of a shareholder to purchase whatever shares of stock the decedent may own at the time of his death. Even if the decedent is not free to dispose of the underlying securities at other than the option or contract price, such price will be disregarded in determining the value of the securities unless it is determined under the circumstances of the particular case that the agreement represents a bona fide business arrangement and not a device to pass the decedent's shares to the natural objects of his bounty for less than an adequate and full consideration in money or money's worth. See section 2703 and the regulations at § 25.2703 of this chapter for special rules involving options and agreements (including contracts to purchase) entered into (or substantially modified after) October 8, 1990.

(i) Stock sold "ex-dividend." In any case where a dividend is declared on a share of stock before the decedent's death but payable to stock holders of record on a date after his death and the stock is selling "ex-dividend" on the date of the decedent's death, the amount of the dividend is added to the ex-dividend quotation in determining the fair market value of the stock as of the date of the decedent's death.

(j) Application of chapter 14. See section 2701 and the regulations at § 25.2701 of this chapter for special rules for valuing the transfer of an interest in a corporation and for the treatment of unpaid qualified payments at the death of the transferor or an applicable family member. See section 2704(b) and the regulations at § 25.2704–2 of this chapter for special valuation rules involving certain restrictions on liquidation rights created after October 8, 1990.

[T.D. 6296, 23 FR 4529, June 24, 1958; 25 FR 14021, Dec. 31, 1960, as amended by T.D. 7312, 39 FR 14948, April 29, 1974; T.D. 7327, 39 FR 35354, Oct. 1, 1974; T.D. 7432, 41 FR 38769, Sept. 13, 1976; T.D. 8395, 57 FR 4254, Feb. 4, 1992]

§ 20.2031–3 Valuation of interests in businesses.

The fair market value of any interest of a decedent in a business, whether a partnership or a proprietorship, is the net amount which a willing purchaser whether an individual or a corporation, would pay for the interest to a willing seller, neither being under any compulsion to buy or to sell and both having reasonable knowledge of relevant facts. The net value is determined on the basis of all relevant factors including—

(a) A fair appraisal as of the applicable valuation date of all the assets of the business, tangible and intangible, including good will;

(b) The demonstrated earning capacity of the business; and

(c) The other factors set forth in paragraphs (f) and (h) of § 20.2031–2 relating to the valuation of corporate stock, to the extent applicable.

Special attention should be given to determining an adequate value of the good will of the business in all cases in which the decedent has not agreed, for an adequate and full consideration in money or money's worth, that his interest passes at his death to, for example, his surviving partner or partners. Complete financial and other data upon which the valuation is based should be submitted with the return, including copies of reports of examinations of the business made by accountants, engineers, or any technical experts as of or near the applicable valuation date. See section 2701 and the regulations at § 25.2701 of this chapter for special rules for valuing the transfer of an interest in a partnership and for the treatment of unpaid qualified payments at the death of the transferor or an applicable family member. See section 2703 and the regulations at § 25.2703 of this chapter for special rules involving options and agreements (including contracts to purchase) entered into (or substantially modified after) October 8, 1990. See section 2704(b) and the regulations at § 25.2704–2 of this chapter for special valuation rules involving certain restrictions on liquidation rights created after October 8, 1990.

[T.D. 8395, 57 FR 4254, Feb. 4, 1992]

§ 20.2031–4 Valuation of notes.

The fair market value of notes, secured or unsecured, is presumed to be the amount of unpaid principal, plus interest accrued to the date of death, unless the executor establishes that the value is lower or that the notes are worthless. However, items of interest shall be separately stated on the estate tax return. If not returned at face value, plus accrued interest, satisfactory evidence must be submitted that the note is worth less than the unpaid amount (because of the interest rate, date of maturity, or other cause), or that the note is uncollectible, either in whole or in part (by reason of the insolvency of the party or parties liable, or for other cause), and that any property pledged or mortgaged as security is insufficient to satisfy the obligation.

[T.D. 6296, 23 FR 4529, June 24, 1958, 25 FR 14021, Dec. 31, 1960]

§ 20.2031–5 Valuation of cash on hand or on deposit.

The amount of cash belonging to the decedent at the date of his death, whether in his possession or in the possession of another, or deposited with a bank, is included in the decedent's gross estate. If bank checks outstanding at the time of the decedent's death and given in discharge of bona fide legal obligations of the decedent incurred for an adequate and full consideration in money or money's worth are subsequently honored by the bank and charged to the decedent's account, the balance remaining in the account may be returned, but only if the obligations are not claimed as deductions from the gross estate.

[T.D. 6296, 23 FR 4529, June 24, 1958, 25 FR 14021, Dec. 31, 1960]

§ 20.2031–6 Valuation of household and personal effects.

(a) General rule. The fair market value of the decedent's household and personal effects is the price which a willing buyer would pay to a willing seller, neither being under any compulsion to buy or to sell and both having reasonable knowledge of relevant facts. A room by room itemization of household and personal effects is desirable. All the articles should be named specifically, except that a number of articles contained in the same room, none of which has a value in excess of $100, may be grouped. A separate value should be given for each article named. In lieu of an itemized list, the executor may furnish a written statement, containing a declaration that it is made under penalties of perjury, setting forth the aggregate value as appraised by a competent appraiser or appraisers of recognized standing and ability, or by a dealer or dealers in the class of personalty involved.

(b) Special rule in cases involving a substantial amount of valuable articles. Notwithstanding the provisions of paragraph (a) of this section, if there are included among the household and personal effects articles having marked artistic or intrinsic value of a total value in excess of $3,000 (*e.g.*, jewelry, furs, silverware, paintings, etchings, engravings, antiques, books, statuary, vases, oriental rugs, coin or stamp collections), the appraisal of an expert or experts, under oath, shall be filed with the return. The appraisal shall be accompanied by a written statement of the executor containing a declaration that it is made under the penalties of perjury as to the completeness of the itemized list of such property and as to the disinterested character and the qualifications of the appraiser or appraisers.

(c) Disposition of household effects prior to investigation. If it is desired to effect distribution or sale of any portion of the household or personal effects of the decedent in advance of an investigation by an officer of the Internal Revenue Service, information to that effect shall be given to the district director. The statement to the district director shall be accompanied by an appraisal of such property, under oath, and by a written statement of the executor, containing a declaration that it is made under the penalties of perjury, regarding the completeness of the list of such property and the qualifications of the appraiser, as heretofore described. If a personal inspection by an officer of the Internal Revenue Service is not deemed necessary, the executor will be so advised. This procedure is designed to facilitate disposition of such property and to obviate future expense and inconvenience to the estate by affording the district director an opportunity to make an investigation should one be deemed necessary prior to sale or distribution.

(d) Additional rules if an appraisal involved. If, pursuant to paragraphs (a), (b), and (c) of this section, expert appraisers are employed, care should be taken to see that they are reputable and of recognized competency to appraise the particular class of property involved. In the appraisal, books in sets by standard authors should be listed in separate groups. In listing paintings having artistic value, the size, subject, and artist's name should be stated. In the case of oriental rugs, the size, make, and general condition should be given. Sets of silverware should be listed in separate groups. Groups or individual pieces of silverware should be weighed and the weights given in troy ounces. In arriving at the value of silverware, the appraisers should take into consideration its antiquity, utility, desirability, condition, and obsolescence.

§ 20.2031–7 Valuation of annuities, interests for life or term of years, and remainder or reversionary interests.

(a) In general. Except as otherwise provided in paragraph (b) of this section and § 20.7520–3(b) (pertaining to certain limitations on the use of prescribed tables), the fair market value of annuities, life estates, terms of years, remainders, and reversionary interests for estates of decedents is the present value of such interests, determined under paragraph (d) of this section. The regulations in this and in related sections provide tables with standard actuarial factors and examples that illustrate how to use the tables to compute the present value of ordinary annuity, life, and remainder interests in property. These sections also refer to standard and special actuarial factors that may be necessary to compute the present value of similar interests in more unusual fact situations.

(b) Commercial annuities and insurance contracts. The value of annuities issued by companies regularly engaged in their sale, and of insurance policies on the lives of persons other than the decedent, is determined under § 20.2031–8. See § 20.2042–1 with respect to insurance policies on the decedent's life.

(c) Actuarial valuations. The present value of annuities, life estates, terms of years, remainders, and reversions for estates of decedents for which the valuation date of the gross estate is on or after May 1, 2009, is determined under paragraph (d) of this section.* * *

(d) Actuarial valuations on or after May 1, 2009—(1) In general. Except as otherwise provided in paragraph (b) of this section and § 20.7520–3(b) (pertaining to certain limitations on the use of prescribed tables), if the valuation date for the gross estate of the decedent is on or after May 1, 2009, the fair market value of annuities, life estates, terms of years, remainders, and reversionary interests is the present value determined by use of standard or special section 7520 actuarial factors. These factors are derived by using the appropriate section 7520 interest rate and, if applicable, the mortality component for the valuation date of the interest that is being valued. For purposes of the computations described in this section, the age of an individual is the age of that individual at the individual's nearest birthday. See §§ 20.7520–1 through 20.7520–4.

(2) Specific interests—(i) Charitable remainder trusts.* * *

(ii) Ordinary remainder and reversionary interests. If the interest to be valued is to take effect after a definite number of years or after the death of one individual, the present value of the interest is computed by multiplying the value of the property by the appropriate remainder interest actuarial factor (that corresponds to the applicable section 7520 interest rate and remainder interest period) in Table B (for a term certain) or in Table S (for one measuring life), as the case may be. Table B is contained in paragraph (d)(6) of this section and Table S (for one measuring life when the valuation date is on or after May 1, 2009) is contained in paragraph (d)(7) of this section and in Internal Revenue Service Publication 1457. See § 20.2031–7A containing Table S for valuation of interests before May 1, 2009. For information about obtaining actuarial factors for other types of remainder interests, see paragraph (d)(4) of this section.

(iii) Ordinary term-of-years and life interests. If the interest to be valued is the right of a person to receive the income of certain property, or to use certain nonincome-producing property, for a term of years or for the life of one individual, the present value of the interest is computed by multiplying the value of the property by the appropriate term-of-years or life interest actuarial factor (that corresponds to the applicable section 7520 interest rate and term-of-years or life interest period). Internal Revenue Service Publication 1457 includes actuarial factors for a remainder interest after a term of years in Table B and after the life of one individual in Table S (for one measuring life when the valuation date is on or after May 1, 2009). However, term-of-years and life interest actuarial factors are not included in Table B in paragraph (d)(6) of this section or Table S in paragraph (d)(7) of this section (or in § 20.2031–7A). If Internal Revenue Service Publication 1457 (or any other reliable source of term-of-years and life interest actuarial factors) is not conveniently available, an actuarial factor for the interest may be derived mathematically. This actuarial factor may be derived by subtracting the correlative remainder factor (that corresponds to the applicable section 7520 interest rate and the term of years or the life) in Table B (for a term of years) in paragraph (d)(6) of this section or in Table S (for the life of one individual) in paragraph (d)(7) of this section, as the case may be, from 1.000000. For information about obtaining actuarial factors for other types of term-of-years and life interests, see paragraph (d)(4) of this section.

(iv) Annuities. (A) If the interest to be valued is the right of a person to receive an annuity that is payable at the end of each year for a term of years or for the life of one individual, the present value of the interest is computed by multiplying the aggregate amount payable annually by the appropriate annuity actuarial factor (that corresponds to the applicable section 7520 interest rate and annuity period). Internal Revenue Publication 1457 includes actuarial factors for a remainder interest in Table B (after an annuity payable for a term of years) and in Table S (after an annuity payable for the life of one individual when the valuation date is on or after May 1, 2009).* * *

* * *

(5) Examples. The provisions of this section are illustrated by the following examples:

Example 1. Remainder payable at an individual's death. The decedent, or the decedent's estate, was entitled to receive certain property worth $50,000 upon the death of A, to whom the income was bequeathed for life. At the time of the decedent's death, A was 47 years and 5 months old. In the month in which the decedent died, the section 7520 rate was 6.2 percent. Under Table S in paragraph (d)(7) of this section, the remainder factor at 6.2 percent for determining the present value of the remainder interest due at the death of a person aged 47, the number of years nearest A's actual age at the decedent's death, is .18672. The present value of the remainder interest at the date of the decedent's death is, therefore, $9,336.00 ($50,000 x .18672).

* * *

Example 3. Annuity payable for an individual's life. A purchased an annuity for the benefit of both A and B. Under the terms of the annuity contract, at A's death, a survivor annuity of $10,000 per year payable in equal semiannual installments made at the end of each interval is payable to B for life. At A's death, B was 45 years and 7 months old. Also, at A's death, the section 7520 rate was 4.8 percent. Under Table S in paragraph (d)(7) of this section, the factor at 4.8 percent for determining the present value of the remainder interest at the death of a person age 46 (the number of years nearest B's actual age) is .24774. By converting the factor to an annuity factor, as described in paragraph (d)(2)(iv)(A) of this section, the factor for the present value of an annuity payable until the death of a person age 46 is 15.6721 (1.000000 minus .24774, divided by .048). The adjustment factor from Table K in paragraph (d)(6) of this section at an interest rate of 4.8 percent for semiannual annuity payments made at the end of the period is 1.0119. The present value of the annuity at the date of A's death is, therefore, $158,585.98 ($10,000 x 15.6721 x 1.0119).

Example 4. Annuity payable for a term of years. The decedent, or the decedent's estate, was entitled to receive an annuity of $10,000 per year payable in equal quarterly installments at the end of each quarter throughout a term certain. At the time of the decedent's death, the section 7520 rate was 9.8 percent. A quarterly payment had been made immediately prior to the decedent's death and payments were to continue for 5 more years. Under Table B in paragraph (d)(6) of this section for the interest rate of 9.8 percent, the factor for the present value of a remainder interest due after a term of 5 years is .626597. Converting the factor to an annuity factor, as described in paragraph (d)(2)(iv)(A) of this section, the factor for the present value of an annuity for a term of 5 years is 3.8102 (1.000000 minus .626597, divided by .098). The adjustment factor from Table K in paragraph (d)(6) of this section at an interest rate of 9.8 percent for quarterly annuity payments made at the end of the period is 1.0360.

The present value of the annuity is, therefore, $39,473.67 ($10,000 x 3.8102 x 1.0360).

(6) Actuarial Table B, Table J, and Table K where the valuation date is after April 30, 1989. Except as provided in § 20.7520–3(b) (pertaining to certain limitations on prescribed tables), for determination of the present value of an interest that is dependent on a term of years, the tables in this paragraph (d)(6) must be used in the application of the provisions of this section when the section 7520 interest rate component is between 4.2 and 14 percent.

TABLE B.—TERM CERTAIN REMAINDER FACTORS APPLICABLE AFTER APRIL 30, 1989

	Interest rate									
Years	4.2%	4.4%	4.6%	4.8%	5.0%	5.2%	5.4%	5.6%	5.8%	6.0%
1	.959693	.957854	.956023	.954198	.952381	.950570	.948767	.946970	.945180	.943396
2	.921010	.917485	.913980	.910495	.907029	.903584	.900158	.896752	.893364	.889996
3	.883887	.878817	.873786	.868793	.863838	.858920	.854040	.849197	.844390	.839619
4	.848260	.841779	.835359	.829001	.822702	.816464	.810285	.804163	.798100	.792094
5	.814069	.806302	.798623	.791031	.783526	.776106	.768771	.761518	.754348	.747258
6	.781257	.772320	.763501	.754801	.746215	.737744	.729384	.721135	.712994	.704961
7	.749766	.739770	.729925	.720230	.710681	.701277	.692015	.682893	.673908	.665057
8	.719545	.708592	.697825	.687242	.676839	.666613	.656561	.646679	.636964	.627412
9	.690543	.678728	.667137	.655765	.644609	.633663	.622923	.612385	.602045	.591898
10	.662709	.650122	.637798	.625730	.613913	.602341	.591009	.579910	.569041	.558395
11	.635997	.622722	.609750	.597071	.584679	.572568	.560729	.549157	.537846	.526788
12	.610362	.596477	.582935	.569724	.556837	.544266	.532001	.520035	.508361	.496969
13	.585760	.571339	.557299	.543630	.530321	.517363	.504745	.492458	.480492	.468839
14	.562150	.547259	.532790	.518731	.505068	.491790	.478885	.466343	.454151	.442301
15	.539491	.524195	.509360	.494972	.481017	.467481	.454350	.441612	.429255	.417265
16	.517746	.502102	.486960	.472302	.458112	.444374	.431072	.418194	.405723	.393646
17	.496877	.480941	.465545	.450670	.436297	.422408	.408987	.396017	.383481	.371364
18	.476849	.460671	.445071	.430028	.415521	.401529	.388033	.375016	.362458	.350344
19	.457629	.441256	.425498	.410332	.395734	.381681	.368153	.355129	.342588	.330513
20	.439183	.422659	.406786	.391538	.376889	.362815	.349291	.336296	.323807	.311805
21	.421481	.404846	.388897	.373605	.358942	.344881	.331396	.318462	.306056	.294155
22	.404492	.387783	.371794	.356494	.341850	.327834	.314417	.301574	.289278	.277505
23	.388188	.371440	.355444	.340166	.325571	.311629	.298309	.285581	.273420	.261797
24	.372542	.355785	.339813	.324586	.310068	.296225	.283025	.270437	.258431	.246979
25	.357526	.340791	.324869	.309719	.295303	.281583	.268525	.256096	.244263	.232999
26	.343115	.326428	.310582	.295533	.281241	.267664	.254768	.242515	.230873	.219810
27	.329285	.312670	.296923	.281998	.267848	.254434	.241715	.229654	.218216	.207368
28	.316012	.299493	.283866	.269082	.255094	.241857	.229331	.217475	.206253	.195630
29	.303275	.286870	.271382	.256757	.242946	.229902	.217582	.205943	.194947	.184557
30	.291051	.274780	.259447	.244997	.231377	.218538	.206434	.195021	.184260	.174110
31	.279319	.263199	.248038	.233776	.220359	.207736	.195858	.184679	.174158	.164255
32	.268061	.252106	.237130	.223069	.209866	.197468	.185823	.174886	.164611	.154957
33	.257256	.241481	.226702	.212852	.199873	.187707	.176303	.165612	.155587	.146186
34	.246887	.231304	.216732	.203103	.190355	.178429	.167270	.156829	.147058	.137912
35	.236935	.221556	.207201	.193801	.181290	.169609	.158701	.148512	.138996	.130105
36	.227385	.212218	.198089	.184924	.172657	.161225	.150570	.140637	.131376	.122741
37	.218220	.203274	.189377	.176454	.164436	.153256	.142856	.133179	.124174	.115793
38	.209424	.194707	.181049	.168373	.156605	.145681	.135537	.126116	.117367	.109239
39	.200983	.186501	.173087	.160661	.149148	.138480	.128593	.119428	.110933	.103056
40	.192882	.178641	.165475	.153302	.142046	.131635	.122004	.113095	.104851	.097222
41	.185107	.171112	.158198	.146281	.135282	.125128	.115754	.107098	.099103	.091719
42	.177646	.163900	.151241	.139581	.128840	.118943	.109823	.101418	.093670	.086527
43	.170486	.156992	.144590	.133188	.122704	.113064	.104197	.096040	.088535	.081630
44	.163614	.150376	.138231	.127088	.116861	.107475	.098858	.090947	.083682	.077009
45	.157019	.144038	.132152	.121267	.111297	.102163	.093793	.086124	.079094	.072650
46	.150690	.137968	.126340	.115713	.105997	.097113	.088988	.081557	.074758	.068538
47	.144616	.132153	.120784	.110413	.100949	.092312	.084429	.077232	.070660	.064658
48	.138787	.126583	.115473	.105356	.096142	.087749	.080103	.073136	.066786	.060998
49	.133193	.121248	.110395	.100530	.091564	.083412	.075999	.069258	.063125	.057546
50	.127824	.116138	.105540	.095926	.087204	.079289	.072106	.065585	.059665	.054288
51	.122672	.111243	.100898	.091532	.083051	.075370	.068411	.062107	.056394	.051215
52	.117728	.106555	.096461	.087340	.079096	.071644	.064907	.058813	.053302	.048316

Years	Interest rate 4.2%	4.4%	4.6%	4.8%	5.0%	5.2%	5.4%	5.6%	5.8%	6.0%
53	.112982	.102064	.092219	.083340	.075330	.068103	.061581	.055695	.050380	.045582
54	.108428	.097763	.088164	.079523	.071743	.064737	.058426	.052741	.047618	.043001
55	.104058	.093642	.084286	.075880	.068326	.061537	.055433	.049944	.045008	.040567
56	.099864	.089696	.080580	.072405	.065073	.058495	.052593	.047296	.042541	.038271
57	.095839	.085916	.077036	.069089	.061974	.055604	.049898	.044787	.040208	.036105
58	.091976	.082295	.073648	.065924	.059023	.052855	.047342	.042412	.038004	.034061
59	.088268	.078826	.070409	.062905	.056212	.050243	.044916	.040163	.035921	.032133
60	.084710	.075504	.067313	.060024	.053536	.047759	.042615	.038033	.033952	.030314

TABLE B.—TERM CERTAIN REMAINDER FACTORS APPLICABLE AFTER APRIL 30, 1989

Years	Interest rate 6.2%	6.4%	6.6%	6.8%	7.0%	7.2%	7.4%	7.6%	7.8%	8.0%
1	.941620	.939850	.938086	.936330	.934579	.932836	.931099	.929368	.927644	.925926
2	.886647	.883317	.880006	.876713	.873439	.870183	.866945	.863725	.860523	.857339
3	.834885	.830185	.825521	.820892	.816298	.811738	.807211	.802718	.798259	.793832
4	.786144	.780249	.774410	.768626	.762895	.757218	.751593	.746021	.740500	.735030
5	.740248	.733317	.726464	.719687	.712986	.706360	.699808	.693328	.686920	.680583
6	.697032	.689208	.681486	.673864	.666342	.658918	.651590	.644357	.637217	.630170
7	.656339	.647752	.639292	.630959	.622750	.614662	.606694	.598845	.591111	.583490
8	.618022	.608789	.599711	.590786	.582009	.573379	.564892	.556547	.548340	.540269
9	.581942	.572170	.562581	.553170	.543934	.534868	.525971	.517237	.508664	.500249
10	.547968	.537754	.527750	.517950	.508349	.498944	.489731	.480704	.471859	.463193
11	.515977	.505408	.495075	.484972	.475093	.465433	.455987	.446750	.437717	.428883
12	.485854	.475007	.464423	.454093	.444012	.434173	.424569	.415196	.406046	.397114
13	.457490	.446436	.435669	.425181	.414964	.405012	.395316	.385870	.376666	.367698
14	.430781	.419582	.408695	.398109	.387817	.377810	.368078	.358615	.349412	.340461
15	.405632	.394344	.383391	.372762	.362446	.352434	.342717	.333285	.324130	.315242
16	.381951	.370624	.359654	.349028	.338735	.328763	.319103	.309745	.300677	.291890
17	.359653	.348331	.337386	.326805	.316574	.306682	.297117	.287867	.278921	.270269
18	.338656	.327379	.316498	.305997	.295864	.286084	.276645	.267534	.258739	.250249
19	.318885	.307687	.296902	.286514	.276508	.266870	.257584	.248638	.240018	.231712
20	.300268	.289179	.278520	.268272	.258419	.248946	.239836	.231076	.222651	.214548
21	.282739	.271785	.261276	.251191	.241513	.232225	.223311	.214755	.206541	.198656
22	.266232	.255437	.245099	.235197	.225713	.216628	.207925	.199586	.191596	.183941
23	.250689	.240073	.229924	.220222	.210947	.202078	.193598	.185489	.177733	.170315
24	.236054	.225632	.215689	.206201	.197147	.188506	.180259	.172387	.164873	.157699
25	.222273	.212060	.202334	.193072	.184249	.175845	.167839	.160211	.152943	.146018
26	.209297	.199305	.189807	.180779	.172195	.164035	.156275	.148895	.141877	.135202
27	.197078	.187317	.178056	.169269	.160930	.153017	.145507	.138379	.131611	.125187
28	.185572	.176049	.167031	.158491	.150402	.142740	.135482	.128605	.122088	.115914
29	.174739	.165460	.156690	.148400	.140563	.133153	.126147	.119521	.113255	.107328
30	.164537	.155507	.146989	.138951	.131367	.124210	.117455	.111079	.105060	.099377
31	.154932	.146154	.137888	.130104	.122773	.115868	.109362	.103233	.097458	.092016
32	.145887	.137362	.129351	.121820	.114741	.108085	.101827	.095942	.090406	.085200
33	.137370	.129100	.121342	.114064	.107235	.100826	.094811	.089165	.083865	.078889
34	.129350	.121335	.113830	.106802	.100219	.094054	.088278	.082867	.077797	.073045
35	.121798	.114036	.106782	.100001	.093663	.087737	.082196	.077014	.072168	.067635
36	.114688	.107177	.100171	.093634	.087535	.081844	.076532	.071574	.066946	.062625
37	.107992	.100730	.093969	.087673	.081809	.076347	.071259	.066519	.062102	.057986
38	.101688	.094671	.088151	.082090	.076457	.071219	.066349	.061821	.057609	.053690
39	.095751	.088977	.082693	.076864	.071455	.066436	.061778	.057454	.053440	.049713
40	.090161	.083625	.077573	.071970	.066780	.061974	.057521	.053396	.049573	.046031
41	.084897	.078595	.072770	.067387	.062412	.057811	.053558	.049625	.045987	.042621
42	.079941	.073867	.068265	.063097	.058329	.053929	.049868	.046120	.042659	.039464
43	.075274	.069424	.064038	.059079	.054513	.050307	.046432	.042862	.039572	.036541
44	.070880	.065248	.060074	.055318	.050946	.046928	.043233	.039835	.036709	.033834
45	.066742	.061323	.056354	.051796	.047613	.043776	.040254	.037021	.034053	.031328
46	.062845	.057635	.052865	.048498	.044499	.040836	.037480	.034406	.031589	.029007
47	.059176	.054168	.049592	.045410	.041587	.038093	.034898	.031976	.029303	.026859
48	.055722	.050910	.046522	.042519	.038867	.035535	.032493	.029717	.027183	.024869
49	.052469	.047848	.043641	.039812	.036324	.033148	.030255	.027618	.025216	.023027
50	.049405	.044970	.040939	.037772	.033948	.030922	.028170	.025668	.023392	.021321
51	.046521	.042265	.038405	.034903	.031727	.028845	.026229	.023855	.021699	.019742
52	.043805	.039722	.036027	.032681	.029651	.026907	.024422	.022170	.020129	.018280

Years	6.2%	6.4%	6.6%	6.8%	7.0%	7.2%	7.4%	7.6%	7.8%	8.0%
	Interest rate									
53	.041248	.037333	.033796	.030006	.027711	.025100	.022739	.020604	.018673	.016925
54	.038840	.035087	.031704	.028652	.025899	.023414	.021172	.019149	.017322	.015672
55	.036572	.032977	.029741	.026828	.024204	.021842	.019714	.017796	.016068	.014511
56	.034437	.030993	.027900	.025119	.022621	.020375	.018355	.016539	.014906	.013436
57	.032427	.029129	.026172	.023520	.021141	.019006	.017091	.015371	.013827	.012441
58	.030534	.027377	.024552	.022023	.019758	.017730	.015913	.014285	.012827	.011519
59	.028751	.025730	.023320	.020620	.018465	.016539	.014817	.013276	.011899	.010666
60	.027073	.024183	.021606	.019307	.017257	.015428	.013796	.012339	.011380	.009876

* * *

(7) Actuarial Table S and Table 2000CM where the valuation date is on or after May 1, 2009. Except as provided in § 20.7520–2(b) (pertaining to certain limitations on the use of prescribed tables), for determination of the present value of an interest that is dependent on the termination of a life interest, Table 2000CM and Table S (single life remainder factors applicable where the valuation date is on or after May 1, 2009) contained in this paragraph (d)(7) and Table J and Table K contained in paragraph (d)(6) of this section, must be used in the application of the provisions of this section when the section 7520 interest rate component is between 0.2 and 14 percent.

* * *

TABLE S. BASED ON LIFE TABLE 2000CM SINGLE LIFE REMAINDER FACTORS APPLICABLE ON OR AFTER MAY 1, 2009

Age	4.2%	4.4%	4.6%	4.8%	5.0%	5.2%	5.4%	5.6%	5.8%	6.0%
	Interest Rate									
0	.06083	.05483	.04959	.04501	.04101	.03749	.03441	.03170	.02931	.02721
1	.05668	.05049	.04507	.04034	.03618	.03254	.02934	.02652	.02403	.02183
2	.05858	.05222	.04665	.04178	.03750	.03373	.03042	.02750	.02492	.02264
3	.06072	.05420	.04848	.04346	.03904	.03516	.03173	.02871	.02603	.02366
4	.06303	.05634	.05046	.04530	.04075	.03674	.03319	.03006	.02729	.02483
5	.06547	.05861	.05258	.04726	.04258	.03844	.03478	.03153	.02866	.02610
6	.06805	.06102	.05482	.04935	.04453	.04026	.03647	.03312	.03014	.02749
7	.07074	.06353	.05717	.05155	.04658	.04217	.03826	.03479	.03171	.02895
8	.07356	.06617	.05964	.05386	.04875	.04421	.04017	.03658	.03338	.03053
9	.07651	.06895	.06225	.05631	.05105	.04637	.04220	.03849	.03518	.03222
10	.07960	.07185	.06499	.05889	.05347	.04865	.04435	.04052	.03709	.03402
11	.08283	.07490	.06786	.06160	.05603	.05106	.04663	.04267	.03912	.03594
12	.08620	.07808	.07087	.06444	.05871	.05360	.04903	.04494	.04127	.03798
13	.08967	.08137	.07397	.06738	.06149	.05623	.05152	.04729	.04351	.04010
14	.09321	.08472	.07715	.07038	.06433	.05892	.05406	.04971	.04579	.04227
15	.09680	.08812	.08036	.07342	.06721	.06164	.05664	.05214	.04810	.04445
16	.10041	.09154	.08360	.07649	.07011	.06438	.05923	.05459	.05041	.04664
17	.10409	.09502	.08689	.07960	.07305	.06716	.06185	.05707	.05276	.04886
18	.10782	.09855	.09024	.08276	.07604	.06998	.06452	.05959	.05514	.05111
19	.11164	.10217	.09366	.08600	.07910	.07288	.06726	.06218	.05758	.05341
20	.11559	.10592	.09721	.08937	.08228	.07589	.07010	.06487	.06012	.05582
21	.11965	.10977	.10087	.09283	.08557	.07900	.07305	.06765	.06276	.05831
22	.12383	.11376	.10465	.09642	.08897	.08223	.07610	.07055	.06550	.06090
23	.12817	.11789	.10859	.10016	.09252	.08559	.07930	.07358	.06837	.06363
24	.13270	.12221	.11270	.10408	.09625	.08914	.08267	.07678	.07141	.06651
25	.13744	.12674	.11703	.10821	.10019	.09289	.08625	.08018	.07465	.06960
26	.14239	.13149	.12158	.11256	.10435	.09686	.09003	.08380	.07810	.07288
27	.14758	.13647	.12636	.11714	.10873	.10106	.09405	.08764	.08177	.07639
28	.15300	.14169	.13137	.12195	.11335	.10549	.09829	.09171	.08567	.08012
29	.15864	.14712	.13660	.12698	.11819	.11013	.10275	.09598	.08977	.08406
30	.16448	.15275	.14203	.13222	.12323	.11498	.10742	.10047	.09408	.08820
31	.17053	.15861	.14769	.13768	.12849	.12006	.11230	.10517	.09860	.09255
32	.17680	.16468	.15357	.14336	.13398	.12535	.11741	.11009	.10335	.09712

33	.18330	.17099	.15968	.14927	.13970	.13088	.12275	.11525	.10832	.10192
34	.19000	.17750	.16599	.15539	.14562	.13661	.12829	.12061	.11350	.10693
35	.19692	.18423	.17253	.16174	.15178	.14258	.13408	.12621	.11892	.11217
36	.20407	.19119	.17931	.16833	.15818	.14879	.14009	.13204	.12457	.11764
37	.21144	.19838	.18631	.17515	.16481	.15523	.14635	.13811	.13046	.12335
38	.21904	.20582	.19357	.18222	.17170	.16193	.15287	.14444	.13661	.12932
39	.22687	.21348	.20105	.18952	.17882	.16887	.15962	.15102	.14300	.13554
40	.23493	.22137	.20878	.19707	.18619	.17606	.16663	.15784	.14965	.14201
41	.24322	.22950	.21674	.20487	.19381	.18350	.17390	.16493	.15656	.14873
42	.25173	.23786	.22494	.21290	.20168	.19120	.18141	.17227	.16372	.15572
43	.26049	.24648	.23342	.22122	.20982	.19918	.18922	.17990	.17118	.16301
44	.26950	.25535	.24214	.22979	.21824	.20742	.19730	.18781	.17892	.17057
45	.27874	.26447	.25112	.23862	.22692	.21595	.20566	.19600	.18694	.17843
46	.28824	.27385	.26038	.24774	.23589	.22476	.21431	.20450	.19527	.18659
47	.29798	.28349	.26989	.25712	.24513	.23386	.22326	.21328	.20390	.19505
48	.30797	.29338	.27967	.26678	.25466	.24325	.23250	.22238	.21283	.20383
49	.31822	.30355	.28974	.27674	.26449	.25294	.24206	.23179	.22210	.21294
50	.32876	.31401	.30011	.28701	.27465	.26298	.25196	.24156	.23172	.22242
51	.33958	.32477	.31079	.29759	.28513	.27335	.26221	.25168	.24170	.23226
52	.35068	.33582	.32178	.30851	.29595	.28407	.27282	.26216	.25206	.24249
53	.36206	.34717	.33308	.31974	.30710	.29513	.28378	.27301	.26279	.25309
54	.37371	.35880	.34467	.33127	.31857	.30651	.29507	.28420	.27388	.26406
55	.38559	.37067	.35652	.34308	.33032	.31820	.30668	.29572	.28529	.27537
56	.39765	.38275	.36859	.35512	.34232	.33014	.31855	.30751	.29699	.28697
57	.40990	.39502	.38086	.36739	.35455	.34233	.33068	.31957	.30898	.29887
58	.42231	.40747	.39333	.37985	.36700	.35474	.34304	.33188	.32121	.31103
59	.43490	.42011	.40600	.39253	.37968	.36740	.35567	.34446	.33374	.32348
60	.44768	.43296	.41890	.40546	.39261	.38033	.36858	.35733	.34656	.33625
61	.46064	.44600	.43200	.41860	.40578	.39351	.38175	.37048	.35968	.34933
62	.47373	.45920	.44527	.43194	.41915	.40690	.39514	.38387	.37305	.36267
63	.48696	.47253	.45870	.44544	.43271	.42049	.40876	.39749	.38666	.37625
64	.50030	.48601	.47229	.45911	.44645	.43428	.42258	.41133	.40051	.39010
65	.51377	.49963	.48603	.47295	.46037	.44827	.43662	.42540	.41460	.40420
66	.52750	.51352	.50007	.48711	.47464	.46262	.45103	.43987	.42911	.41872
67	.54144	.52765	.51436	.50154	.48919	.47727	.46578	.45468	.44397	.43363
68	.55554	.54196	.52885	.51619	.50398	.49218	.48079	.46978	.45915	.44887
69	.56976	.55640	.54349	.53102	.51896	.50731	.49603	.48513	.47458	.46438
70	.58407	.57095	.55826	.54598	.53410	.52260	.51147	.50069	.49025	.48013
71	.59848	.58561	.57316	.56109	.54940	.53808	.52710	.51646	.50615	.49614
72	.61294	.60035	.58815	.57632	.56484	.55371	.54291	.53243	.52225	.51237
73	.62741	.61512	.60318	.59160	.58035	.56943	.55882	.54851	.53849	.52876
74	.64183	.62983	.61818	.60686	.59586	.58516	.57476	.56464	.55480	.54523
75	.65612	.64444	.63309	.62204	.61129	.60083	.59065	.58074	.57109	.56169
76	.67026	.65891	.64786	.63710	.62661	.61640	.60646	.59676	.58731	.57810
77	.68423	.67321	.66248	.65201	.64181	.63186	.62215	.61269	.60345	.59444
78	.69800	.68733	.67692	.66676	.65684	.64717	.63772	.62849	.61948	.61068
79	.71156	.70124	.69116	.68132	.67170	.66230	.65312	.64414	.63537	.62680
80	.72487	.71490	.70516	.69563	.68632	.67721	.66830	.65959	.65106	.64272
81	.73791	.72830	.71890	.70970	.70069	.69188	.68325	.67481	.66654	.65844
82	.75065	.74140	.73235	.72348	.71479	.70628	.69794	.68977	.68176	.67391
83	.76308	.75419	.74548	.73695	.72858	.72037	.71232	.70443	.69669	.68909
84	.77516	.76664	.75828	.75008	.74203	.73413	.72638	.71877	.71130	.70396

85	.78689	.77873	.77072	.76285	.75512	.74753	.74008	.73275	.72556	.71849
86	.79825	.79044	.78278	.77524	.76783	.76055	.75340	.74636	.73944	.73264
87	.80921	.80176	.79443	.78722	.78014	.77316	.76630	.75956	.75292	.74638
88	.81978	.81268	.80569	.79880	.79203	.78536	.77880	.77234	.76598	.75971
89	.82994	.82317	.81651	.80995	.80349	.79712	.79085	.78467	.77859	.77259
90	.83967	.83324	.82690	.82065	.81450	.80843	.80244	.79655	.79073	.78500
91	.84898	.84288	.83685	.83091	.82505	.81928	.81358	.80795	.80241	.79693
92	.85787	.85208	.84636	.84072	.83515	.82966	.82423	.81888	.81360	.80838
93	.86632	.86083	.85541	.85006	.84477	.83955	.83440	.82931	.82428	.81931
94	.87435	.86915	.86402	.85894	.85393	.84898	.84409	.83925	.83447	.82975
95	.88197	.87705	.87219	.86739	.86265	.85795	.85331	.84872	.84419	.83970
96	.88915	.88451	.87991	.87537	.87088	.86643	.86203	.85768	.85338	.84912
97	.89593	.89154	.88720	.88290	.87865	.87444	.87028	.86616	.86208	.85804
98	.90232	.89818	.89408	.89002	.88600	.88202	.87808	.87418	.87031	.86649
99	.90835	.90444	.90057	.89674	.89294	.88918	.88546	.88177	.87811	.87449
100	.91397	.91028	.90663	.90301	.89942	.89587	.89234	.88885	.88539	.88196
101	.91930	.91583	.91238	.90897	.90558	.90223	.89890	.89560	.89233	.88908
102	.92424	.92096	.91771	.91448	.91128	.90811	.90496	.90184	.89875	.89568
103	.92914	.92605	.92300	.91996	.91695	.91397	.91100	.90806	.90514	.90225
104	.93364	.93074	.92786	.92501	.92217	.91935	.91656	.91379	.91103	.90830
105	.93809	.93537	.93266	.92998	.92731	.92467	.92204	.91943	.91683	.91426
106	.94365	.94115	.93867	.93621	.93376	.93133	.92892	.92651	.92413	.92176
107	.94994	.94771	.94549	.94328	.94108	.93890	.93673	.93457	.93242	.93028
108	.96010	.95830	.95651	.95472	.95295	.95118	.94942	.94767	.94593	.94420
109	.97985	.97893	.97801	.97710	.97619	.97529	.97438	.97348	.97259	.97170

TABLE S. BASED ON LIFE TABLE 2000CM SINGLE LIFE
REMAINDER FACTORS
APPLICABLE ON OR AFTER MAY 1, 2009

Interest Rate

Age	6.2%	6.4%	6.6%	6.8%	7.0%	7.2%	7.4%	7.6%	7.8%	8.0%
0	.02534	.02370	.02223	.02093	.01978	.01874	.01782	.01699	.01625	.01559
1	.01989	.01817	.01664	.01528	.01406	.01298	.01202	.01115	.01037	.00967
2	.02061	.01882	.01722	.01580	.01454	.01340	.01239	.01148	.01066	.00993
3	.02156	.01969	.01802	.01654	.01521	.01403	.01297	.01201	.01115	.01038
4	.02264	.02069	.01896	.01741	.01602	.01478	.01367	.01267	.01176	.01095
5	.02383	.02180	.01999	.01838	.01693	.01563	.01446	.01341	.01246	.01161
6	.02512	.02301	.02113	.01944	.01793	.01657	.01535	.01424	.01325	.01235
7	.02650	.02430	.02234	.02058	.01900	.01758	.01630	.01514	.01410	.01315
8	.02798	.02570	.02365	.02182	.02017	.01868	.01734	.01613	.01503	.01404
9	.02957	.02720	.02507	.02316	.02143	.01988	.01848	.01721	.01606	.01502
10	.03128	.02881	.02659	.02460	.02280	.02118	.01971	.01838	.01718	.01608
11	.03309	.03053	.02823	.02615	.02428	.02258	.02105	.01966	.01839	.01725
12	.03503	.03237	.02997	.02781	.02585	.02408	.02248	.02103	.01971	.01850
13	.03704	.03428	.03179	.02954	.02750	.02565	.02398	.02246	.02108	.01982
14	.03909	.03623	.03364	.03130	.02918	.02726	.02551	.02392	.02248	.02116
15	.04117	.03820	.03551	.03308	.03087	.02886	.02704	.02538	.02387	.02249
16	.04324	.04016	.03737	.03484	.03254	.03046	.02855	.02682	.02524	.02379
17	.04533	.04214	.03924	.03661	.03422	.03205	.03007	.02826	.02661	.02509
18	.04746	.04415	.04114	.03841	.03592	.03366	.03159	.02970	.02798	.02639
19	.04963	.04620	.04309	.04025	.03766	.03530	.03315	.03117	.02937	.02772
20	.05191	.04835	.04512	.04217	.03948	.03702	.03478	.03272	.03083	.02910
21	.05427	.05058	.04723	.04416	.04137	.03881	.03647	.03432	.03235	.03054
22	.05672	.05291	.04943	.04625	.04334	.04067	.03823	.03599	.03394	.03205
23	.05930	.05535	.05174	.04844	.04542	.04265	.04010	.03777	.03562	.03364
24	.06204	.05795	.05421	.05078	.04764	.04476	.04211	.03967	.03743	.03536
25	.06497	.06074	.05687	.05331	.05005	.04705	.04429	.04174	.03940	.03724
26	.06811	.06373	.05972	.05603	.05264	.04952	.04665	.04400	.04155	.03929
27	.07146	.06694	.06278	.05895	.05543	.05219	.04920	.04644	.04389	.04153
28	.07503	.07036	.06605	.06209	.05844	.05507	.05196	.04908	.04642	.04396
29	.07881	.07398	.06953	.06542	.06163	.05814	.05490	.05191	.04913	.04656
30	.08279	.07780	.07319	.06894	.06502	.06138	.05802	.05491	.05202	.04933
31	.08697	.08182	.07707	.07267	.06860	.06483	.06134	.05810	.05509	.05229
32	.09137	.08606	.08115	.07660	.07239	.06848	.06485	.06148	.05835	.05543
33	.09601	.09053	.08546	.08075	.07639	.07234	.06858	.06508	.06182	.05878
34	.10084	.09520	.08996	.08511	.08059	.07640	.07249	.06886	.06547	.06231
35	.10590	.10009	.09470	.08968	.08501	.08067	.07662	.07285	.06933	.06605
36	.11120	.10522	.09966	.09448	.08966	.08517	.08098	.07706	.07341	.06999
37	.11674	.11059	.10486	.09952	.09454	.08990	.08556	.08150	.07771	.07416
38	.12254	.11621	.11032	.10481	.09968	.09487	.09039	.08618	.08225	.07856
39	.12857	.12208	.11601	.11035	.10505	.10009	.09545	.09110	.08702	.08320
40	.13487	.12820	.12196	.11613	.11067	.10555	.10076	.09626	.09204	.08807
41	.14142	.13458	.12817	.12217	.11655	.11127	.10632	.10167	.09730	.09319
42	.14823	.14122	.13464	.12848	.12269	.11725	.11214	.10734	.10282	.09856
43	.15535	.14816	.14141	.13508	.12913	.12353	.11826	.11330	.10863	.10422
44	.16274	.15538	.14847	.14196	.13585	.13008	.12466	.11954	.11472	.11016

45	.17042	.16290	.15581	.14914	.14286	.13694	.13135	.12608	.12110	.11640
46	.17842	.17073	.16348	.15664	.15020	.14411	.13836	.13293	.12780	.12294
47	.18672	.17886	.17145	.16445	.15784	.15159	.14568	.14010	.13481	.12980
48	.19534	.18732	.17974	.17258	.16581	.15940	.15334	.14759	.14215	.13699
49	.20429	.19612	.18838	.18106	.17413	.16757	.16134	.15544	.14984	.14453
50	.21362	20529	.19740	.18993	.18284	.17612	.16974	.16368	.15793	.15247
51	.22332	.21484	.20680	.19917	.19194	.18506	.17853	.17232	.16642	.16080
52	.23341	.22479	.21660	.20883	20144	.19442	.18774	.18138	.17533	.16957
53	.24388	.23513	.22681	.21889	.21136	.20419	.19737	.19087	.18467	.17876
54	.25473	24585	.23739	.22935	.22168	.21437	.20741	.20076	.19442	.18837
55	.26593	.25693	.24835	.24017	.23238	.22494	.21784	.21105	.20458	.19838
56	.27742	.26831	.25962	.25132	.24340	.23583	.22860	.22169	.21508	.20875
57	.28922	.28001	.27121	.26280	.25476	.24707	.23971	.23267	.22593	.21947
58	.30129	.29199	.28309	.27457	.26642	.25862	.25114	.24398	.23712	.23053
59	.31367	.30428	.29529	.28667	.27842	.27051	.26293	.25565	.24867	.24197
60	.32638	.31691	.30784	.29914	.29079	.28278	.27509	.26771	.26062	.25380
61	.33940	.32987	.32073	.31195	.30352	.29542	.28763	.28015	.27295	.26603
62	.35269	.34311	.33391	.32506	.31656	.30837	.30050	.29293	.28564	.27862
63	.36625	.35663	.34738	.33847	.32990	.32165	.31370	.30604	.29867	.29155
64	.38007	.37043	.36113	.35218	.34356	.33524	.32723	.31950	.31204	.30484
65	.39417	.38451	.37519	.36620	.35753	.34917	.34110	.33330	.32577	.31850
66	.40871	.39905	.38972	.38071	.37201	.36361	.35550	.34765	.34006	.33273
67	.42365	.41400	.40468	.39567	.38696	.37853	.37038	.36250	.35487	.34749
68	.43892	.42931	.42001	.41101	.40230	.39387	.38570	.37780	.37014	.36272
69	.45450	.44493	.43567	.42670	.41800	.40958	.40141	.39350	.38582	.37837
70	.47033	.46083	.45162	.44269	.43403	.42563	.41748	.40957	.40189	.39443
71	.48644	.47702	.46788	.45901	.45040	.44203	.43391	.42602	.41835	.41090
72	.50278	.49347	.48441	.47562	.46707	.45877	.45069	.44284	.43520	.42776
73	.51930	.51010	.50115	.49245	.48399	.47575	.46774	.45994	.45234	.44494
74	.53591	.52684	.51802	.50943	.50106	.49291	.48497	.47724	.46970	.46235
75	.55253	.54361	.53492	.52645	.51820	.51015	.50230	.49465	.48719	.47991
76	.56912	.56036	.55182	.54349	.53536	.52742	.51968	.51213	.50475	.49754
77	.58565	.57706	.56868	.56050	.55251	.54471	.53708	.52964	.52236	.51525
78	.60209	.59369	.58549	.57747	.56963	.56197	.55448	.54715	.53999	.53298
79	.61841	.61021	.60219	.59435	.58668	.57917	.57182	.56463	.55760	.55071
80	.63456	.62657	.61875	.61109	.60359	.59625	.58906	.58202	.57512	.56836
81	.65050	.64273	.63512	.62766	.62034	.61318	.60616	.59927	.59252	.58590
82	.66621	.65867	.65127	.64401	.63690	.62992	.62308	.61636	.60977	.60330
83	.68164	.67433	.66716	.66012	.65321	.64642	.63976	.63322	.62680	.62050
84	.69676	.68969	.68275	.67593	.66923	.66265	.65618	.64983	.64358	.63745
85	.71154	.70472	.69801	.69141	.68493	.67856	.67229	.66613	.66007	.65412
86	.72595	.71937	.71290	.70654	.70028	.69412	.68806	.68210	.67623	.67046
87	.73995	.73362	.72740	.72127	.71523	.70929	.70344	.69768	.69201	.68642
88	.75354	.74746	.74148	.73558	.72978	.72406	.71842	.71287	.70739	.70200
89	.76668	.76085	.75511	.74945	.74387	.73837	.73295	.72761	.72234	.71714
90	.77934	.77377	.76827	.76284	.75749	.75222	.74701	.74188	.73681	.73181
91	.79153	.78620	.78094	.77575	.77063	.76558	.76059	.75566	.75080	.74600
92	.80323	.79814	.79312	.78816	.78326	.77843	.77365	.76894	.76428	.75967

93	.81440	.80956	.80477	.80004	.79536	.79074	.78618	.78166	.77721	.77280
94	.82508	.82047	.81591	.81140	.80694	.80253	.79817	.79387	.78961	.78539
95	.83526	.83088	.82654	.82225	.81800	.81380	.80965	.80554	.80148	.79746
96	.84491	.84074	.83662	.83254	.82850	.82450	.82055	.81663	.81276	.80892
97	.85405	.85009	.84617	.84230	.83846	.83466	.83089	.82717	.82348	.81982
98	.86270	.85895	.85523	.85155	.84791	.84430	.84072	.83718	.83367	.83019
99	.87090	.86735	.86382	.86033	.85687	.85345	.85005	.84668	.84335	.84004
100	.87856	.87519	.87185	.86854	.86526	.86201	.85878	.85559	.85242	.84927
101	.88587	.88268	.87952	.87638	.87327	.87019	.86713	.86409	.86109	.85810
102	.89263	.88961	.88662	.88364	.88069	.87777	.87487	.87199	.86913	.86629
103	.89938	.89653	.89370	.89089	.88810	.88534	.88259	.87987	.87717	.87448
104	.90558	.90289	.90021	.89756	.89492	.89231	.88971	.88713	.88456	.88202
105	.91170	.90916	.90664	.90413	.90164	.89917	.89672	.89428	.89186	.88945
106	.91940	.91706	.91474	.91242	.91013	.90784	.90558	.90332	.90108	.89885
107	.92816	.92605	.92395	.92186	.91978	.91772	.91567	.91362	.91159	.90957
108	.94247	.94075	.93904	.93734	.93565	.93396	.93229	.93062	.92895	.92730
109	.97081	.96992	.96904	.96816	.96729	.96642	.96555	.96468	.96382	.96296

[T.D. 8540, 59 FR 30152, June 10, 1994 T.D. 8819, 64 FR 23212, April 30, 1999; T.D. 8886, 65 FR 36929, June 12, 2000; T.D. 9448, 74 FR 21484, May 7, 2009; T.D. 9540, 76 FR 49612, Aug. 10, 2011]

§ 20.2031–8 Valuation of certain life insurance and annuity contracts; valuation of shares in an open-end investment company.

(a) Valuation of certain life insurance and annuity contracts. **(1)** The value of a contract for the payment of an annuity, or an insurance policy on the life of a person other than the decedent, issued by a company regularly engaged in the selling of contracts of that character is established through the sale by that company of comparable contracts. An annuity payable under a combination annuity contract and life insurance policy on the decedent's life (*e.g.*, a "retirement income" policy with death benefit) under which there was no insurance element at the time of the decedent's death (see paragraph (d) of § 20.2039–1) is treated like a contract for the payment of an annuity for purposes of this section.

(2) As valuation of an insurance policy through sale of comparable contracts is not readily ascertainable when, at the date of the decedent's death, the contract has been in force for some time and further premium payments are to be made, the value may be approximated by adding to the interpolated terminal reserve at the date of the decedent's death the proportionate part of the gross premium last paid before the date of the decedent's death which covers the period extending beyond that date. If, however, because of the unusual nature of the contract such an approximation is not reasonably close to the full value of the contract, this method may not be used.

(3) The application of this section may be illustrated by the following examples. In each case involving an insurance contract, it is assumed that there are no accrued dividends or outstanding indebtedness on the contract.

Example (1). X purchased from a life insurance company a joint and survivor annuity contract under the terms of which X was to receive payments of $1,200 annually for his life and, upon X's death, his wife was to receive payments of $1,200 annually for her life. Five years after such purchase, when his wife was 50 years of age, X died. The value of the annuity contract at the date of X's death is the amount which the company would charge for an annuity providing for the payment of $1,200 annually for the life of a female 50 years of age.

Example (2). Y died holding the incidents of ownership in a life insurance policy on the life of his wife. The policy was one on which no further payments were to be made to the company (*e.g.*, a single premium policy or a paid-up policy). The value of the insurance policy at the date of Y's death is the amount which the company would charge for a single premium contract of the same specified amount on the life of a person of the age of the insured.

Example (3). Z died holding the incidents of ownership in a life insurance policy on the life of his wife. The policy was an ordinary life policy issued nine years and four months prior to Z's death and at a time when Z's wife was 35 years of age. The gross annual premium is $2,811 and the decedent died four months after the last premium due date. The value of the insurance policy at the date of Z's death is computed as follows:

Terminal reserve at end of tenth year	$14,601.00
Terminal reserve at end of ninth year	12,965.00
Increase	1,636.00
One-third of such increase (Z having died four months following the last preceding premium date) is	545.33
Terminal reserve at end of ninth year	12,965.00
Interpolated terminal reserve at date of Z's death	13,510.33
Two-thirds of gross premium (2/3 × $2,811)	1,874.00
Value of the insurance policy	$15,384.33

(b) Valuation of shares in an open-end investment company. **(1)** The fair market value of a share in an open-end investment company (commonly known as a "mutual fund") is the public redemption price of a share. In the absence of an affirmative showing of the public redemption price in effect at the time of death, the last public redemption price quoted by the company for the date of death shall be presumed to be the applicable public redemption price. If the alternate valuation method under 2032 is elected, the last public redemption price quoted by the company for the alternate valuation date shall be the applicable redemption price. If there is no public redemption price quoted by the company for the applicable valuation date (*e.g.*, the valuation date is a Saturday, Sunday, or holiday), the fair market value of the mutual fund share is the last public redemption price quoted by the company for the first day preceding the applicable valuation date for which there is a quotation. In any case where a dividend is declared on a share in an open-end investment company before the decedent's death but payable to shareholders of record on a date after his death and the share is quoted "exdividend" on the date of the decedent's death, the amount of the dividend is added to the ex-dividend quotation in determining the fair market value of the share as of the date of the decedent's death. As used in this paragraph, the term "open-end investment company" includes only a company which on the applicable valuation date was engaged in offering its shares to the public in the capacity of an open-end investment company.

* * *

[T.D. 6680, 28 FR 10872, Oct. 10, 1963, as amended by T.D. 7319, 39 FR 26723, July 23, 1974]

§ 20.2032–1 Alternate valuation.

(a) In general. In general, section 2032 provides for the valuation of a decedent's gross estate at a date other than the date of the decedent's death. More specifically, if an executor elects the alternate valuation method under section 2032, the property included in the decedent's gross estate on the date of his death is valued as of whichever of the following dates is applicable:

(1) Any property distributed, sold, exchanged, or otherwise disposed of within 6 months * * * after the decedent's death is valued as of the date on which it is first distributed, sold, exchanged, or otherwise disposed of;

(2) Any property not distributed, sold, exchanged, or otherwise disposed of within 6 months * * * after the decedent's death is valued as of the date 6 months * * * after the date of the decedent's death;

(3) Any property, interest, or estate which is affected by mere lapse of time is valued as of the date of the decedent's death, but adjusted for any difference in its value not due to mere lapse of time as of the date 6 months * * * after the decedent's death, or as of the date of its distribution, sale, exchange, or other disposition, whichever date first occurs.

(b) Method and effect of election—(1) In general. The election to use the alternate valuation method is made on the return of tax imposed by section 2001. For purposes of this paragraph (b), the term return of tax imposed by section 2001 means the last estate tax return filed by the executor on or before the due date of the return (including extensions of time to file actually granted) or, if a timely return is not filed, the first estate tax return filed by the executor after the due date, provided the return is filed no later than 1 year after the due date (including extensions of time to file actually granted). Once the election is made, it is irrevocable, provided that an election may be revoked on a subsequent return filed on or before the due date of the return (including extensions of time to file actually granted). The election may be made only if it will decrease both the value of the gross estate and the sum (reduced by allowable credits) of the estate tax and the generation-skipping transfer tax payable by reason of the decedent's death with respect to the property includible in the decedent's gross estate. If the election is made, the alternate valuation method applies to all property included in the gross estate and cannot be applied to only a portion of the property.

(2) Protective election. If, based on the return of tax as filed, use of the alternate valuation method would not result in a decrease in both the value of the gross estate and the sum (reduced by allowable credits) of the estate tax and the generation-skipping transfer tax liability payable by reason of the decedent's death with respect to the property includible in the decedent's gross estate, a protective election may be made to use the alternate valuation method if it is subsequently determined that such a decrease would occur. A protective election is made on the return of tax imposed by section 2001. The protective election is irrevocable as of the due date of the return (including extensions of time actually granted). The protective election becomes effective on the date on which it is determined that use of the alternate valuation method would result in a decrease in both the value of the gross estate and in the sum (reduced by allowable credits) of the estate tax and generation-skipping transfer tax liability payable by reason of the decedent's death with respect to the property includible in the decedent's gross estate.

(3) Requests for extension of time to make the election. A request for an extension of time to make the election or protective election pursuant to §§ 301.9100–1 and 301.9100–3 of this chapter will not be granted unless the return of tax imposed by section 2001 is filed no later than 1 year after the due date of the return (including extensions of time actually granted).

(c) Meaning of "distributed, sold, exchanged, or otherwise disposed of". **(1)** The phrase "distributed, sold, exchanged, or otherwise disposed of" comprehends all possible ways by which property ceases to form a part of the gross estate. For example, money on hand at the date of the decedent's death which is thereafter used in the payment of funeral expenses, or which is thereafter invested, falls within the term "otherwise disposed of." The term also includes the surrender of a stock certificate for corporate assets in complete or partial liquidation of a corporation pursuant to section 331. The term does not, however, extend to transactions which are mere changes in form. Thus, it does not include a transfer of assets to a corporation in exchange for its stock in a transaction with respect to which no gain or loss would be recognizable for income tax purposes under section 351. Nor does it include an exchange of stock or securities in a corporation for stock or securities in the same corporation or another corporation in a transaction, such as a merger, recapitalization, reorganization or other transaction described in section 368(a) or 355, with respect to which no gain or loss is recognizable for income tax purposes under section 354 or 355.

(2) Property may be "distributed" either by the executor, or by a trustee of property included in the gross estate under section 2035 through 2038, or section 2041. Property is considered as "distributed" upon the first to occur of the following:

(i) The entry of an order or decree of distribution, if the order or decree subsequently becomes final;

(ii) The segregation or separation of the property from the estate or trust so that it becomes unqualifiedly subject to the demand or disposition of the distributee; or

(iii) The actual paying over or delivery of the property to the distributee.

(3) Property may be "sold, exchanged, or otherwise disposed of" by: (i) The executor; (ii) a trustee or other donee to whom the decedent during his lifetime transferred property included in his gross estate under sections 2035 through 2038, or section 2041; (iii) an heir or devisee to whom title to property passes directly under local law; (iv) a surviving joint tenant or tenant by the entirety; or (v) any other person. If a binding contract for the sale, exchange, or other disposition of property is entered into, the property is considered as sold, exchanged, or otherwise disposed of on the effective date of the contract, unless the contract is not subsequently carried out substantially in accordance with its terms. The effective date of a contract is normally the date it is entered into (and not the date it is consummated, or the date legal title to the property passes) unless the contract specifies a different effective date.

(d) "Included property" and "excluded property". If the executor elects the alternate valuation method under section 2032, all property interests existing at the date of decedent's death which form a part of his gross estate as determined under sections 2033 through 2044 are valued in accordance with the provisions of this section. Such property interests are referred to in this section as "included property". Furthermore, such property interests remain "included property" for the purpose of valuing the gross estate under the alternate valuation method even though they change in form during the alternate valuation period by being actually received, or disposed of, in whole or in part, by the estate. On the other hand, property earned or accrued (whether received or not) after the date of the decedent's death and during the alternate valuation period with respect to any property interest existing at the date of the decedent's death, which does not represent a form of "included property" itself or the receipt of "included property" is excluded in valuing the gross estate under the alternate valuation method. Such property is referred to in this section as "excluded property". Illustrations of "included property" and "excluded property" are contained in the subparagraphs (1) to (4) of this paragraph:

(1) Interest-bearing obligations. Interest-bearing obligations, such as bonds or notes, may comprise two elements of "included property" at the date of the decedent's death, namely, (i) the principal of the obligation itself, and (ii) interest accrued to the date of death. Each of these elements is to be separately valued as of the applicable valuation date. Interest accrued after the date of death and before the subsequent valuation date constitutes "excluded property". However, any part payment or principal made between the date of death and the subsequent valuation date, or any advance payment of interest for a period after the subsequent valuation date made during the alternate valuation period which has the effect of reducing the value of the principal obligation as of the subsequent valuation date, will be included in the gross estate, and valued as of the date of such payment.

(2) Leased property. The principles set forth in subparagraph (1) of this paragraph with respect to interest-bearing obligations also apply to leased realty or personalty which is included in the gross estate and with respect to which an obligation to pay rent has been reserved. Both the realty or personalty itself and the rents accrued to the date of death constitute "included property", and each is to be separately valued as of the applicable valuation date. Any rent accrued after the date of death and before the subsequent valuation date is "excluded property". Similarly, the principle applicable with respect to interest paid in advance is equally applicable with respect to advance payments of rent.

(3) Noninterest-bearing obligations. In the case of noninterest-bearing obligations sold at a discount, such as savings bonds, the principal obligation and the discount amortized to the date of death are property interests existing at the date of death and constitute "included property". The obligation itself is to be valued at the subsequent valuation date without regard to any further increase in value due to amortized discount. The additional discount amortized after death and during the alternate valuation period is the equivalent of interest accruing during that period and is, therefore, not to be included in the gross estate under the alternate valuation method.

(4) Stock of a corporation. Shares of stock in a corporation and dividends declared to stockholders of record on or before the date of the decedent's death and not collected at the date of death constitute "included property" of the estate. On the other hand, ordinary dividends out of earnings and profits (whether in cash, shares of the corporation, or other property) declared to stockholders of record after the date of the decedent's death are "excluded property" and are not to be valued under the alternate valuation method. If, however, dividends are declared to stockholders of record after the date of the decedent's death with the effect that the shares of stock at the subsequent valuation date do not reasonably represent the same "included property" of the gross estate as existed at the date of the decedent's death, the dividends are "included property", except to the extent that they are out of earnings of the corporation after the date of the decedent's death. For example, if a corporation makes a distribution in partial liquidation to stockholders of record during the alternate valuation period which is not accompanied by a surrender of a stock certificate for cancellation, the amount of the distribution received on stock included in the gross estate is itself "included property", except to the extent that the distribution was out of earnings and profits since the date of the decedent's death. Similarly, if a corporation, in which the decedent owned a substantial interest and which possessed at the date of the decedent's death accumulated earnings and profits equal to its paid-in capital, distributed all of its accumulated earnings and profits as a cash dividend to shareholders of record during the alternate valuation period, the amount of the dividends received on stock includible in the gross estate will be included in the gross estate under the alternate valuation method. Likewise, a stock dividend distributed under such circumstances is "included property".

* * *

(f) Mere lapse of time. In order to eliminate changes in value due only to mere lapse of time, section 2032(a)(3) provides that any interest or estate "affected by mere lapse of time" is included in a decedent's gross estate under the alternate valuation method at its value as of the date of the decedent's death, but with adjustment for any difference in its value as of the subsequent valuation date not due to mere lapse of time. Properties, interests, or estates which are "affected by mere lapse of time" include patents, estates for the life of a person other than the decedent, remainders, reversions, and other like properties, interests, or estates. The phrase "affected by mere lapse of time" has no reference to obligations for the payment of money, whether or not interest-bearing, the value of which changes with the passing of time. However, such an obligation, like any other property, may become affected by lapse of time when made the subject of a bequest or transfer which itself is creative of an interest or estate so affected. * * *

* * *

(g) Effect of election on deductions. If the executor elects the alternate valuation method under section 2032, any deduction for administration expenses under section 2053(b) (pertaining to property not subject to claims) or losses under section 2054 * * * is allowed only to the extent that it is not otherwise in effect allowed in determining the value of the gross estate. Furthermore, the amount of any charitable deduction under section 2055 * * * or the amount of any marital deduction under section 2056 is determined by the value of the property with respect to which the deduction is allowed as of the date of the decedent's death, adjusted, however, for any difference in its value as of the date 6 months * * * after death, or as of the date of its distribution, sale, exchange, or other disposition, whichever first occurs. However, no such adjustment may take into account any difference in value due to lapse of time or to the occurrence or nonoccurrence of a contingency.

* * *

[T.D. 6296, 23 FR 4529, June 24, 1958, as amended by T.D. 7238, 37 FR 28718, Dec. 29, 1972; T.D. 7955, 49 FR 19995, May 11, 1984; T.D. 8540, 59 FR 30100, June 10, 1994; T.D. 8819, 64 FR 23187, April 29, 1999; T.D. 9172, 70 FR 295, Jan. 4, 2005; T.D. 9448, 74 FR 21437, May 7, 2009; 74 FR 27080, June 8, 2009]

§ 20.2033–1 Property in which the decedent had an interest.

(a) In general. The gross estate of a decedent who was a citizen or resident of the United States at the time of his death includes under section 2033 the value of all property, whether real or personal, tangible or intangible, and wherever situated, beneficially owned by the decedent at the time of his death. (For certain exceptions in the case of real property situated outside the United States, see paragraphs (a) and (c) of § 20.2031–1.) Real property is included whether it came into the possession and control of the executor or administrator or passed directly to heirs or devisees. Various statutory provisions which exempt bonds, notes, bills, and certificates of indebtedness of the Federal Government or its agencies and the interest thereon from taxation are generally not applicable to the estate tax, since such tax is an excise tax on the transfer of property at death and is not a tax on the property transferred.

(b) Miscellaneous examples. A cemetery lot owned by the decedent is part of his gross estate, but its value is limited to the salable value of that part of the lot which is not designed for the interment of the decedent and the members of his family. Property subject to homestead or other exemptions under local law is included in the gross estate. Notes or other claims held by the decedent are likewise included even though they are cancelled by the decedent's will. Interest and rents accrued at the date of the decedent's death constitute a part of the gross estate. Similarly, dividends which are payable to the decedent or his estate by reason of the fact that on or before the date of the decedent's death he was a stockholder of record (but which have not been collected at death) constitute a part of the gross estate.

[T.D. 6296, 23 FR 4529, June 24, 1958, as amended by T.D. 6684, 28 FR 11409, Oct. 24, 1963]

§ 20.2034–1 Dower or curtesy interests.

A decedent's gross estate includes under section 2034 any interest in property of the decedent's surviving spouse existing at the time of the decedent's death as dower or curtesy, or any interest created by statute in lieu thereof (although such other interest may differ in character from dower or curtesy). Thus, the full value of property is included in the decedent's gross estate, without deduction of such an interest of the surviving husband or wife, and without regard to when the right to such an interest arose.

[T.D. 6296, 23 FR 4529, June 24, 1958]

§ 20.2036–1 Transfers with retained life estate.

(a) In general. A decedent's gross estate includes under section 2036 the value of any interest in property transferred by the decedent after March 3, 1931, whether in trust or otherwise, except to the extent that the transfer was for an adequate and full consideration in money or money's worth (see § 20.2043–1), if the decedent retained or reserved—

(1) For his life;

(2) For any period not ascertainable without reference to his death (if the transfer was made after June 6, 1932); or

(3) For any period which does not in fact end before his death:

(i) The use, possession, right to income, or other enjoyment of the transferred property.

(ii) The right, either alone or in conjunction with any other person or persons, to designate the person or persons who shall possess or enjoy the transferred property or its income (except that, if the transfer was made before June 7, 1932, the right to designate must be retained by or reserved to the decedent alone).

(b) Meaning of terms. (1) A reservation by the decedent "for any period not ascertainable without reference to his death" may be illustrated by the following examples:

(i) A decedent reserved the right to receive the income from transferred property in quarterly payments, with the proviso that no part of the income between the last quarterly payment and the date of the decedent's death was to be received by the decedent or his estate; and

(ii) A decedent reserved the right to receive the income, annuity, or other payment from transferred property after the death of another person who was in fact enjoying the income, annuity, or other payment at the time of the decedent's death. In such a case, the amount to be included in the decedent's gross estate under this section does not include the value of the outstanding interest of the other person as determined in paragraphs (c)(1)(i) and (c)(2)(ii) of this section. See also, paragraphs (c)(1)(ii) Example 1 and (c)(2)(iv) Example 8 of this section. If the other person predeceased the decedent, the reservation by the decedent may be considered to be either for life, or for a period that does not in fact end before death.

(2) The "use, possession, right to the income, or other enjoyment of the transferred property" is considered as having been retained by or reserved to the decedent to the extent that the use, possession, right to the income, or other enjoyment is to be applied toward the discharge of a legal obligation of the decedent, or otherwise for his pecuniary benefit. The term "legal obligation" includes a legal obligation to support a dependent during the decedent's lifetime.

(3) The phrase "right * * * to designate the person or persons who shall possess or enjoy the transferred property or the income therefrom" includes a reserved power to designate the person or persons to receive the income from the transferred property, or to possess or enjoy nonincome-producing property, during the decedent's life or during any other period described in paragraph (a) of this section. With respect to such a power, it is immaterial (i) whether the power was exercisable alone or only in conjunction with another person or persons, whether or not having an adverse interest; (ii) in what capacity the power was exercisable by the decedent or by another person or persons in conjunction with the decedent; and (iii) whether the exercise of the power was subject to a contingency beyond the decedent's control which did not occur before his death (e.g., the death of another person during the decedent's lifetime). The phrase, however, does not include a power over the transferred property itself which does not affect the enjoyment of the income received or earned during the decedent's life. (See, however, section 2038 for the inclusion of property in the gross estate on account of such a power.) Nor does the phrase apply to a power held solely by a person other than the decedent. But, for example, if the decedent reserved the unrestricted power to remove or discharge a trustee at any time and appoint himself as trustee, the decedent is considered as having the powers of the trustee.

(c) Retained or reserved interest—(1) Amount included in gross estate—(i) In general. If the decedent retained or reserved an interest or right with respect to all of the property transferred by him, the amount to be included in his gross estate under section 2036 is the value of the entire property, less only the value of any outstanding income interest which is not subject to the decedent's interest or right and which is actually being enjoyed by another person at the time of the decedent's death. If the decedent retained or reserved an interest or right with respect to a part only of the property transferred by him, the amount to be included in his gross estate under section 2036 is only a corresponding proportion of the amount described in the preceding sentence. An interest or right is treated as having been retained or reserved if at the time of the transfer there was an understanding, express, or implied, that the interest or right would later be conferred. If this section applies to an interest retained by the decedent in a trust or otherwise and the terms of the trust or other governing instrument provide that, after the decedent's death, payments the decedent was receiving during life are to continue to be made to the decedent's estate for a specified period (as opposed to payments that were payable to the decedent prior to the decedent's death but were not actually paid until after the decedent's death), such payments that become payable after the decedent's death are not includible in the decedent's gross estate under section 2033 because they are properly reflected in the value of the trust corpus included under this section. Payments that become payable to the decedent prior to the decedent's date of death, but are not paid until after the decedent's date of death, are includible in the decedent's gross estate under section 2033.

(ii) Examples. The application of paragraph (c)(1)(i) of this section is illustrated in the following examples:

Example 1. Decedent (D) creates an irrevocable inter vivos trust. The terms of the trust provide that all of the trust income is to be paid to D and D's child, C, in equal shares during their joint lives and, on the death of the first to die of D and C, all of the trust income is to be paid to the survivor. On the death of the survivor of D and C, the remainder is to be paid to another individual, F. Subsequently, D dies survived by C. Fifty percent of the value of the trust corpus is includible in D's gross estate under section 2036(a)(1) because, under the terms of the trust, D retained the right to receive one-half of the trust income for D's life. In addition, the excess (if any) of the value of the remaining 50 percent of the trust corpus, over the present value of C's outstanding life estate in that 50 percent of trust corpus, also is includible in D's gross estate under section 2036(a)(1), because D retained the right to receive all of the trust income for such time as D survived C. If C had predeceased D, then 100 percent of the trust corpus would have been includible in D's gross estate.

Example 2. D transferred D's personal residence to D's child (C), but retained the right to use the residence for a term of years. D dies during the term. At D's death, the fair market value of the personal residence is includible in D's gross estate under section 2036(a)(1) because D retained the right to use the residence for a period that did not in fact end before D's death.

(2) Retained annuity, unitrust, and other income interests in trusts—(i) In general. This paragraph (c)(2) applies to a grantor's retained use of an asset held in trust or a retained annuity, unitrust, or other interest in any trust (other than a trust constituting an employee benefit) including without limitation the following (collectively referred to in this paragraph (c)(2) as "trusts"): Certain charitable remainder trusts (collectively CRTs) such as a charitable remainder annuity trust (CRAT) within the meaning of section 664(d)(1), a charitable remainder unitrust (CRUT) within the meaning of section 664(d)(2) or (d)(3), and any charitable remainder trust that does not qualify under section 664(d), whether because the CRT was created prior to 1969, there was a defect in the drafting of the CRT, there was no intention to qualify the CRT for the charitable deduction, or otherwise; other trusts established by a grantor (collectively GRTs) such as a grantor retained annuity trust (GRAT) paying out a qualified annuity interest within the meaning of § 25.2702–3(b) of this chapter, a grantor retained unitrust (GRUT) paying out a qualified unitrust interest within the meaning of § 25.2702–3(c) of this chapter; and various other forms of grantor retained income trusts (GRITs) whether or not the grantor's retained interest is a qualified interest as defined in section 2702(b), including without limitation a qualified personal residence trust (QPRT) within the meaning of § 25.2702–5(c) of this chapter and a personal residence trust (PRT) within the meaning of § 25.2702–5(b) of this chapter. If a decedent transferred property into such a trust and retained or reserved the right to use such property, or the right to an annuity, unitrust, or other interest in such trust with respect to the property decedent so transferred for decedent's life, any period not ascertainable without reference to the decedent's death, or for a period that does not in fact end before the decedent's death, then the decedent's right to use the property or the retained annuity, unitrust, or other interest (whether payable from income and/or principal) constitutes the retention of the possession or enjoyment of, or the right to the income from, the property for purposes of section 2036. The portion of the trust's corpus includible in the decedent's gross estate for Federal estate tax purposes is that portion of the trust corpus necessary to provide the decedent's retained use or retained annuity, unitrust, or other payment (without reducing or invading principal). In the case of a retained annuity or unitrust, the portion of the trust's corpus includible in the decedent's gross estate is that portion of the trust corpus necessary to generate sufficient income to satisfy the retained annuity or unitrust (without reducing or invading principal), using the interest rates provided in section 7520 and the adjustment factors prescribed in § 20.2031–7 (or § 20.2031–7A), if applicable. The computation is illustrated in paragraph (c)(2)(iv), Examples 1, 2, and 3 of this section. The portion of the trust's corpus includible in the decedent's gross estate under section 2036, however, shall not exceed the fair market value of the trust's corpus at the decedent's date of death.

(ii) Decedent's retained annuity following a current annuity interest of another person. If the decedent retained the right to receive an annuity or other payment (rather than income) after the death of the current recipient of that interest, then the amount includible in the decedent's gross estate under this section is the amount of trust corpus required to produce sufficient income to satisfy the entire annuity or other payment the decedent would have been entitled to receive if the decedent had survived the current recipient (thus, also including the portion of that entire amount payable to the decedent before the current recipient's death), reduced by the present value of the current recipient's interest. However, the amount includible shall not be less than the amount of corpus required to produce sufficient income to satisfy the annuity or other payment the decedent was entitled, at the time of the decedent's death, to receive for each year. In addition, in no event shall the amount includible exceed the value of the trust corpus on the date of death. Finally, in calculating the present value of the current recipient's interest, the exhaustion of trust corpus test described in § 20.7520–3(b)(2) (exhaustion test) is not to be applied, even in cases where § 20.7520–3(b)(2) would otherwise require it to be applied. The following steps implement this computation.

(A) *Step 1:* Determine the fair market value of the trust corpus on the decedent's date of death.

(B) *Step 2:* Determine, in accordance with paragraph (c)(2)(i) of this section, the amount of corpus required to generate sufficient income to pay the annuity, unitrust, or other payment (determined on the date of the decedent's death) payable to the decedent for the trust year in which the decedent's death occurred.

(C) *Step 3:* Determine, in accordance with paragraph (c)(2)(i) of this section, the amount of corpus required to generate sufficient income to pay the annuity, unitrust, or other payment that the decedent would have been entitled to receive for each trust year if the decedent had survived the current recipient.

(D) *Step 4:* Determine the present value of the current recipient's annuity, unitrust, or other payment (without applying the exhaustion test).

(E) *Step 5:* Reduce the amount determined in Step 3 by the amount determined in Step 4, but not to below the amount determined in Step 2.

(F) *Step 6:* The amount includible in the decedent's gross estate under this section is the lesser of the amounts determined in Step 5 and Step 1.

* * *

(iv) Examples. The application of paragraphs (c)(2)(i), (c)(2)(ii), and (c)(2)(iii) of this section is illustrated in the following examples:

Example 1. (i) Decedent (D) transferred $100,000 to an inter vivos trust that qualifies as a CRAT under section 664(d)(1). The trust agreement provides for an annuity of $7,500 to be paid each year to D for D's life, then to D's child (C) for C's life, with the remainder to be distributed upon the survivor's death to N, a charitable organization described in sections 170(c), 2055(a), and 2522(a). The annuity is payable to D or C, as the case may be, annually on each December 31st. D dies in September 2006, survived by C who was then age 40. On D's death, the value of the trust assets was $300,000 and the section 7520 interest rate was 6 percent. D's executor does not elect to use the alternate valuation date.

(ii) The amount of corpus with respect to which D retained the right to the income, and thus the amount includible in D's gross estate under section 2036, is that amount of corpus necessary to yield the annual annuity payment to D (without reducing or invading principal). In this case, the formula for determining the amount of corpus necessary to yield the annual annuity payment to D is: annual annuity / section 7520 interest rate = amount includible under section 2036. The amount of corpus necessary to yield the annual annuity is $7,500 / .06 = $125,000. Therefore, $125,000 is includible in D's gross estate under section 2036(a)(1). (The result would be the same if D had retained an interest in the CRAT for a term of years and had died during the term. The result also would be the same if D had irrevocably relinquished D's annuity interest less than 3 years prior to D's death because of the application of section 2035.) If, instead, the trust agreement had provided that D could revoke C's annuity interest or change the identity of the charitable remainderman, see section 2038 with regard to the portion of the trust to be included in the gross estate on account of such a retained power to revoke. Under the facts presented, section 2039 does not apply to include any amount in D's gross estate by reason of this retained annuity. See § 20.2039–1(e).

Example 2. (i) D transferred $100,000 to a GRAT in which D's annuity is a qualified interest described in section 2702(b). The trust agreement provides for an annuity of $12,000 per year to be paid to D for a term of ten years or until D's earlier death. The annuity amount is payable in twelve equal installments at the end of each month. At the expiration of the term of years or on D's earlier death, the remainder is to be distributed to D's child (C). D dies prior to the expiration of the ten-year term. On the date of D's death, the value of the trust assets is $300,000 and the section 7520 interest rate is 6 percent. D's executor does not elect to use the alternate valuation date.

(ii) The amount of corpus with respect to which D retained the right to the income, and thus the amount includible in D's gross estate under section 2036, is that amount of corpus necessary to yield the annual annuity payment to D (without reducing or invading principal). In this case, the formula for determining the amount of corpus necessary to yield the annual annuity payment to D is: annual annuity (adjusted for monthly payments) / section 7520 interest rate = amount includible under section 2036. The Table K adjustment factor for monthly annuity payments in this case is 1.0272. Thus, the amount of corpus necessary to yield the annual annuity is ($12,000 x 1.0272) / .06 = $205,440. Therefore, $205,440 is includible in D's gross estate under section 2036(a)(1). If, instead, the trust agreement had provided that the annuity was to be paid to D during D's life and to D's estate for the balance of the 10–year term if D died during that term, then the portion of trust corpus includible in D's gross estate would still be as calculated in this paragraph. It is not material whether payments are made to D's estate after D's death. Under the facts presented, section 2039 does not apply to include any amount in D's gross estate by reason of this retained annuity. See § 20.2039–1(e).

Example 3. **(i)** In 2000, D created a CRUT within the meaning of section 664(d)(2). The trust instrument directs the trustee to hold, invest, and reinvest the corpus of the trust and to pay to D for D's life, and then to D's child (C) for C's life, in equal quarterly installments payable at the end of each calendar quarter, an amount equal to 6 percent of the fair market value of the trust as valued on December 15 of the prior taxable year of the trust. At the termination of the trust, the then-remaining corpus, together with any and all accrued income, is to be distributed to N, a charitable organization described in sections 170(c), 2055(a), and 2522(a). D dies in 2006, survived by C, who was then age 55. The value of the trust assets on D's death was $300,000. D's executor does not elect to use the alternate valuation date and, as a result, D's executor does not choose to use the section 7520 interest rate for either of the two months prior to D's death.

(ii) The amount of the corpus with respect to which D retained the right to the income, and thus the amount includible in D's gross estate under section 2036(a)(1), is that amount of corpus necessary to yield the unitrust payments. In this case, such amount of corpus is determined by dividing the trust's equivalent income interest rate by the section 7520 rate (which was 6 percent at the time of D's death). The equivalent income interest rate is determined by dividing the trust's adjusted payout rate by the excess of 1 over the adjusted payout rate. Based on § 1.664–4(e)(3) of this chapter, the appropriate adjusted payout rate for the trust at D's death is 5.786 percent (6 percent x .964365). Thus, the equivalent income interest rate is 6.141 percent (5.786 percent / (1—5.786 percent)). The ratio of the equivalent interest rate to the assumed interest rate under section 7520 is 102.35 percent (6.141 percent / 6 percent). Because this exceeds 100 percent, D's retained payout interest exceeds a full income interest in the trust, and D effectively retained the income from all the assets transferred to the trust. Accordingly, because D retained for life an interest at least equal to the right to all income from all the property transferred by D to the CRUT, the entire value of the corpus of the CRUT is includible in D's gross estate under section 2036(a)(1). (The result would be the same if D had retained, instead, an interest in the CRUT for a term of years and had died during the term.) Under the facts presented, section 2039 does not apply to include any amount in D's gross estate by reason of D's retained unitrust interest. See § 20.2039–1(e).

(iii) If, instead, D had retained the right to a unitrust amount having an adjusted payout for which the corresponding equivalent interest rate would have been less than the 6 percent assumed interest rate of section 7520, then a correspondingly reduced proportion of the trust corpus would be includible in D's gross estate under section 2036(a)(1). Alternatively, if the interest retained by D was instead only one-half of the 6 percent unitrust interest, then the amount included in D's estate would be the amount needed to produce a 3 percent unitrust interest. All of the results in this Example 3 would be the same if the trust had been a GRUT instead of a CRUT.

Example 4. During life, D established a 15–year GRIT for the benefit of individuals who are not members of D's family within the meaning of section 2704(c)(2). D retained the right to receive all of the net income from the GRIT, payable annually, during the GRIT's term. D dies during the GRIT's term. D's executor does not elect to use the alternate valuation date. In this case, the GRIT's corpus is includible in D's gross estate under section 2036(a)(1) because D retained the right to receive all of the income from the GRIT for a period that did not in fact end before D's death. If, instead, D had retained the right to receive 60 percent of the GRIT's net income, then 60 percent of the GRIT's corpus would have been includible in D's gross estate under section 2036. Under the facts presented, section 2039 does not apply to include any amount in D's gross estate by reason of D's retained interest. See § 20.2039–1(e).

Example 5. In 2003, D transferred $10X to a pooled income fund that conforms to Rev. Proc. 88–53, 1988–2 CB 712 (1988) in exchange for 1 unit in the fund. D is to receive all of the income from that 1 unit during D's life. Upon D's death, D's child (C), is to receive D's income interest for C's life. In 2008, D dies. D's executor does not elect to use the alternate valuation date. In this case, the fair market value of D's 1 unit in the pooled income fund is includible in D's gross estate under section 2036(a)(1) because D retained the right to receive all of the income from that unit for a period that did not in fact end before D's death. See § 601.601(d)(2)(ii)(b) of this chapter.

Example 6. D transferred D's personal residence to a trust that met the requirements of a qualified personal residence trust (QPRT) as set forth in § 25.2702–5(c) of this chapter. Pursuant to the terms of the QPRT, D retained the right to use the residence for 10 years or until D's prior death. D dies before the end of the term. D's executor does not elect to use the alternate valuation date. In this case, the fair market value of the QPRT's assets on the date of D's death are includible in D's gross estate under section 2036(a)(1) because D retained the right to use the residence for a period that did not in fact end before D's death.

* * *

Example 8. **(i)** D creates an irrevocable inter vivos trust. The terms of the trust provide that an annuity of $10,000 per year is to be paid to D and C, D's child, in equal shares during their joint lives. On the death of the first to die of D and C, the entire $10,000 annuity is to be paid to the survivor for life. On the death of the survivor of D and C, the remainder is to be paid to another individual, F. Subsequently, D dies survived by C. On D's date of death, the fair market value of the trust is $120,000 and the section 7520 rate is 7 percent. At the date of D's death, the amount of trust corpus needed to produce D's annuity interest ($5,000 per year) is $71,429 ($5,000/0.07). In addition, assume the present value of C's right to receive $5,000 annually for the remainder of C's life is $40,000. The portion of the trust corpus includible in D's gross estate under section 2036(a)(1) is $102,857, determined as follows:

(ii) Step 1: Fair market value of corpus: $120,000

(iii) Step 2: Corpus required to produce D's date of death annuity ($5,000/0.07): $71,429

(iv) Step 3: Corpus required to produce D's annuity if D had survived C ($10,000/0.07): $142,857

(v) Step 4: Present value of C's interest: $40,000

(vi) Step 5: The amount determined in Step 3, reduced by the amount determined in Step 4, but not to below the amount determined in Step 2 ($142,857—$40,000, but not less than $71,429): $102,857

(vii) Step 6: The lesser of the amounts determined in Steps 5 and 1 ($102,857 or $120,000): $102,857

* * *

[T.D. 6296, 23 FR 4529, June 24, 1958, as amended by T.D. 6501, 25 FR 10869, Nov. 16, 1960; T.D. 9414, 73 FR 40177, July 14, 2008; 73 FR 44648, July 31, 2008; T.D. 9555, 76 FR 69128, Nov. 8, 2011]

§ 20.2037–1 Transfers taking effect at death.

(a) In general. A decedent's gross estate includes under section 2037 the value of any interest in property transferred by the decedent after September 7, 1916, whether in trust or otherwise, except to the extent that the transfer was for an adequate and full consideration in money or money's worth (see § 20.2043–1), if—

(1) Possession or enjoyment of the property could, through ownership of the interest, have been obtained only by surviving the decedent,

* * *

(3) The value of the reversionary interest immediately before the decedent's death exceeded 5 percent of the value of the entire property.

(b) Condition of survivorship. As indicated in paragraph (a) of this section, the value of an interest in transferred property is not included in a decedent's gross estate under section 2037 unless possession or enjoyment of the property could, through ownership of such interest, have been obtained only by surviving the decedent. Thus, property is not included in the decedent's gross estate if, immediately before the decedent's death, possession or enjoyment of the property could have been obtained by any beneficiary either by surviving the decedent or through the occurrence of some other event such as the expiration of a term of years. However, if a consideration of the terms and circumstances of the transfer as a whole indicates that the "other event" is unreal and if the death of the decedent does, in fact, occur before the "other event", the beneficiary will be considered able to possess or enjoy the property only by surviving the decedent. Notwithstanding the foregoing, an interest in transferred property is not includible in a decedent's gross estate under section 2037 if possession or enjoyment of the property could have been obtained by any beneficiary during the decedent's life through the exercise of a general power of appointment (as defined in section 2041) which in fact was exercisable immediately before the decedent's death. See examples (5) and (6) in paragraph (e) of this section.

(c) Retention of reversionary interest. **(1)** As indicated in paragraph (a) of this section, the value of an interest in transferred property is not included in a decedent's gross estate under section 2037 unless the decedent had retained a reversionary interest in the property, and the value of the reversionary interest immediately before the death of the decedent exceeded 5 percent of the value of the property.

(2) For purposes of section 2037, the term "reversionary interest" includes a possibility that property transferred by the decedent may return to him or his estate and a possibility that property transferred by the decedent may become subject to a power of disposition by him. The term is not used in a technical sense, but has reference to any reserved right under which the transferred property shall or may be returned to the grantor. Thus, it encompasses an interest arising either by the express terms of the instrument of transfer or by operation of law. (See, however, paragraph (f) of this section with respect to transfers made before October 8, 1949.) The term "reversionary interest" does not include rights to income only, such as the right to receive the income from a trust after the death of another person. (However, see section 2036 for the inclusion of property in the gross estate on account of such rights.) Nor does the term "reversionary interest" include the possibility that the decedent during his lifetime might have received back an interest in transferred property by inheritance through the estate of another person. Similarly, a statutory right of a spouse to receive a portion of whatever estate a decedent may leave at the time of his death is not a "reversionary interest".

(3) For purposes of this section, the value of the decedent's reversionary interest is computed as of the moment immediately before his death, without regard to whether or not the executor elects the alternate valuation method under section 2032 and without regard to the fact of the decedent's death. The value is ascertained in accordance with recognized valuation principles for determining the value for estate tax purposes of future or conditional interests in property. (See §§ 20.2031–1, 20.2031–7, and 20.2031–9). For example, if the decedent's reversionary interest was subject to an outstanding life estate in his wife, his interest is valued according to the actuarial rules set forth in § 20.2031–7. On the other hand, if the decedent's reversionary interest was contingent on the death of his wife without issue surviving and if it cannot be shown that his wife is incapable of having issue (so that his interest is not subject to valuation according to the actuarial rules in § 20.2031–7), his interest is valued according to the general rules set forth in § 20.2031–1. A possibility that the decedent may be able to dispose of property under certain conditions is considered to have the same value as a right of the decedent to the return of the property under those same conditions.

(4) In order to determine whether or not the decedent retained a reversionary interest in transferred property of a value in excess of 5 percent, the value of the reversionary interest is compared with the value of the transferred property, including interests therein which are not dependent upon survivorship of the decedent. For example, assume that the decedent, A, transferred property in trust with the income payable to B for life and with the remainder payable to C if A predeceases B, but with the property to revert to A if B predeceases A. Assume further that A does, in fact, predecease B. The value of A's reversionary interest immediately before his death is compared with the value of the trust corpus, without deduction of the value of B's outstanding life estate. If, in the above example, A had retained a reversionary interest in one-half only of the trust corpus, the value of his reversionary interest would be compared with the value of one-half of the trust corpus, again without deduction of any part of the value of B's outstanding life estate.

(d) Transfers partly taking effect at death. If separate interests in property are transferred to one or more beneficiaries, paragraphs (a) to (c) of this section are to be separately applied with respect to each interest. For example, assume that the decedent transferred an interest in Blackacre to A which could be possessed or enjoyed only by surviving the decedent, and that the decedent transferred an interest in Blackacre to B which could be possessed or enjoyed only on the occurrence of some event unrelated to the decedent's death. Assume further that the decedent retained a reversionary interest in Blackacre of a value in excess of 5 percent. Only the value of the interest transferred to A is includible in the decedent's gross estate. Similar results would obtain if possession or enjoyment of the entire property could have been obtained only by surviving the decedent, but the decedent had retained a reversionary interest in a part only of such property.

(e) Examples. The provisions of paragraphs (a) to (d) of this section may be further illustrated by the following examples. * * *

Example (1). The decedent transferred property in trust with the income payable to his wife for life and, at her death, remainder to the decedent's then surviving children, or if none, to the decedent or his estate. Since each beneficiary can possess or enjoy the property without surviving the decedent, no part of the property is includible in the decedent's gross estate under section 2037, regardless of the value of the decedent's reversionary interest. (However, see section 2033 for inclusion of the value of the reversionary interest in the decedent's gross estate.)

Example (2). The decedent transferred property in trust with the income to be accumulated for the decedent's life, and at his death, principal and accumulated income to be paid to the decedent's then surviving issue, or, if none, to A or A's estate. Since the decedent retained no reversionary interest in the property, no part of the property is includible in the decedent's gross estate, even though possession or enjoyment of the property could be obtained by the issue only by surviving the decedent.

Example (3). The decedent transferred property in trust with the income payable to his wife for life and with the remainder payable to the decedent or, if he is not living at his wife's death, to his daughter or her estate. The daughter cannot obtain possession or enjoyment of the property without surviving the decedent. Therefore, if the decedent's reversionary interest immediately before his death exceeded 5 percent of the value of the property, the value of the property, less the value of the wife's outstanding life estate, is includible in the decedent's gross estate.

Example (4). The decedent transferred property in trust with the income payable to his wife for life and with the remainder payable to his son or, if the son is not living at the wife's death, to the decedent or, if the decedent is not then living, to X or X's estate. Assume that the decedent was survived by his wife, his son, and X. Only X cannot obtain possession or enjoyment of the property without surviving the decedent. Therefore, if the decedent's reversionary interest immediately before his death exceeded 5 percent of the value of the property, the value of X's remainder interest (with reference to the time immediately after the decedent's death) is includible in the decedent's gross estate.

Example (5). The decedent transferred property in trust with the income to be accumulated for a period of 20 years or until the decedent's prior death, at which time the principal and accumulated income was to be paid to the decedent's son if then surviving. Assume that the decedent does, in fact, die before the expiration of the 20–year period. If, at the time of the transfer, the decedent was 30 years of age, in good health, etc., the son will be considered able to possess or enjoy the property without surviving the decedent. If, on the other hand, the decedent was 70 years of age at the time of the transfer, the son will not be considered able to possess or enjoy the property without surviving the decedent. In this latter case, if the value of the decedent's reversionary interest (arising by operation of law) immediately before his death exceeded 5 percent of the value of the property, the value of the property is includible in the decedent's gross estate.

Example (6). The decedent transferred property in trust with the income to be accumulated for his life and, at his death, the principal and accumulated income to be paid to the decedent's then surviving children. The decedent's wife was given the unrestricted power to alter, amend, or revoke the trust. Assume that the wife survived the decedent but did not, in fact, exercise her power during the decedent's lifetime. Since possession or enjoyment of the property could have been obtained by the wife during the decedent's lifetime under the exercise of a general power of appointment, which was, in fact, exercisable immediately before the decedent's death, no part of the property is includible in the decedent's gross estate.

* * *

[T.D. 6296, 23 FR 4529, June 24, 1958]

§ 20.2038–1 Revocable transfers.

(a) In general. A decedent's gross estate includes under section 2038 the value of any interest in property transferred by the decedent, whether in trust or otherwise, if the enjoyment of the interest was subject at the date of the decedent's death to any change through the exercise of a power by the decedent to alter, amend, revoke, or terminate, * * *. However, section 2038 does not apply—

(1) To the extent that the transfer was for an adequate and full consideration in money or money's worth (see § 20.2043–1);

(2) If the decedent's power could be exercised only with the consent of all parties having an interest (vested or contingent) in the transferred property, and if the power adds nothing to the rights of the parties under local law; or

(3) To a power held solely by a person other than the decedent. But, for example, if the decedent had the unrestricted power to remove or discharge a trustee at any time and appoint himself trustee, the decedent is considered as having the powers of the trustee. However, this result would not follow if he only had the power to appoint himself trustee under limited conditions which did not exist at the time of his death. (See last two sentences of paragraph (b) of this section.)

Except as provided in this paragraph, it is immaterial in what capacity the power was exercisable by the decedent or by another person or persons in conjunction with the decedent; whether the power was exercisable alone or only in conjunction with another person or persons, whether or not having an adverse interest * * *; and at what time or from what source the decedent acquired his power * * *. Section 2038 is applicable to any power affecting the time or manner of enjoyment of property or its income, even though the identity of the beneficiary is not affected. For example, section 2038 is applicable to a power reserved by the grantor of a trust to accumulate income or distribute it to A, and to distribute corpus to A, even though the remainder is vested in A or his estate, and no other person has any beneficial interest in the trust. However, only the value of an interest in property subject to a power to which section 2038 applies is included in the decedent's gross estate under section 2038.

(b) Date of existence of power. A power to alter, amend, revoke, or terminate will be considered to have existed at the date of the decedent's death even though the exercise of the power was subject to a precedent giving of notice or even though the alteration, amendment, revocation, or termination would have taken effect only on the expiration of a stated period after the exercise of the power, whether or not on or before the date of the decedent's death notice had been given or the power had been exercised. In determining the value of the gross estate in such cases, the full value of the property transferred subject to the power is discounted for the period required to elapse between the date of the decedent's death and the date upon which the alteration, amendment, revocation, or termination could take effect. In this connection, see especially § 20.2031–7. However, section 2038 is not applicable to a power the exercise of which was subject to a contingency beyond the decedent's control which did not occur before his death (*e.g.*, the death of another person during the decedent's life). See, however, section 2036(a)(2) for the inclusion of property in the decedent's gross estate on account of such a power.

* * *

[T.D. 6296, 23 FR 4529, June 24, 1958, as amended by T.D. 6600, 27 FR 4985, May 29, 1962]

§ 20.2039–1 Annuities.

(a) In general. A decedent's gross estate includes under section 2039(a) and (b) the value of an annuity or other payment receivable by any beneficiary by reason of surviving the decedent under certain agreements or plans to the extent that the value of the annuity or other payment is attributable to contributions made by the decedent or his employer. Sections 2039(a) and (b), however, have no application to an amount which constitutes the proceeds of insurance under a policy on the decedent's life. * * *

The fact that an annuity or other payment is not includible in a decedent's gross estate under section 2039(a) and (b) does not mean that it is not includible under some other section of part III of subchapter A of chapter 11. * * *

(b) Agreements or plans to which section 2039(a) and (b) applies. (1) Section 2039(a) and (b) applies to the value of an annuity or other payment receivable by any beneficiary under any form of contract or agreement entered into after March 3, 1931, under which—

(i) An annuity or other payment was payable to the decedent, either alone or in conjunction with another person or persons, for his life or for any period not ascertainable without reference to his death or for any period which does not in fact end before his death, or

(ii) The decedent possessed, for his life or for any period not ascertainable without reference to his death or for any period which does not in fact end before his death, the right to receive such an annuity or other payment, either alone or in conjunction with another person or persons.

The term "annuity or other payment" as used with respect to both the decedent and the beneficiary has reference to one or more payments extending over any period of time. The payments may be equal or unequal, conditional or unconditional, periodic or sporadic. The term "contract or agreement" includes any arrangement, understanding or plan, or any combination of arrangements, understandings or plans arising by reason of the decedent's employment. An annuity or other payment "was payable" to the decedent if, at the time of his death, the decedent was in fact receiving an annuity or other payment, whether or not he had an enforceable right to have payments continued. The decedent "possessed the right to receive" an annuity or other payment if, immediately before his death, the decedent had an enforceable right to receive payments at some time in the future, whether or not, at the time of his death, he had a present right to receive payments. In connection with the preceding sentence, the decedent will be regarded as having had "an enforceable right to receive payments at some time in the future" so long as he had complied with his obligations under the contract or agreement up to the time of his death. For the meaning of the phrase "for his life or for any period not ascertainable without reference to his death or for any period which does not in fact end before his death", see section 2036 and § 20.2036–1.

(2) The application of this paragraph is illustrated and more fully explained in the following examples. In each example: (i) it is assumed that all transactions occurred after March 3, 1931, and (ii) the amount stated to be includible in the decedent's gross estate is determined in accordance with the provisions of paragraph (c) of this section.

Example (1). The decedent purchased an annuity contract under the terms of which the issuing company agreed to pay an annuity to the decedent for his life and, upon his death, to pay a specified lump sum to his designated beneficiary. The decedent was drawing his annuity at the time of his death. The amount of the lump sum payment to the beneficiary is includible in the decedent's gross estate under section 2039(a) and (b).

Example (2). Pursuant to a retirement plan, the employer made contributions to a fund which was to provide the employee, upon his retirement at age 60, with an annuity for life, and which was to provide the employee's wife, upon his death after retirement, with a similar annuity for life. The benefits under the plan were completely forfeitable during the employee's life, but upon his death after retirement, the benefits to the wife were forfeitable only upon her remarriage. The employee had no right to originally designate or to ever change the employer's designation of the surviving beneficiary. The retirement plan at no time met the requirements of section 401(a) (relating to qualified plans). Assume that the employee died at age 61 after the employer started payment of his annuity as described above. The value of the wife's annuity is includible in the decedent's gross estate under section 2039(a) and (b). Includibility in this case is based on the fact that the annuity to the decedent "was payable" at the time of his death. The fact that the decedent's annuity was forfeitable is of no consequence since, at the time of his death, he was in fact receiving payments under the plan. Nor is it important that the decedent had no right to choose the surviving beneficiary. The element of forfeitability in the wife's annuity may be taken into account only with respect to the valuation of the annuity in the decedent's gross estate.

Example (3). Pursuant to a retirement plan, the employer made contributions to a fund which was to provide the employee, upon his retirement at age 60, with an annuity of $100 per month for life, and which was to provide his designated beneficiary, upon the employee's death after retirement, with a similar annuity for life. The plan also provided that (a) upon the employee's separation from service before retirement, he would have a nonforfeitable right to receive a reduced annuity starting at age 60, and (b) upon the employee's death before retirement, a lump sum payment representing the amount of the employer's contributions credited to the employee's account would be paid to the designated beneficiary. The plan at no time met the requirements of section 401(a) (relating to qualified plans). Assume that the employee died at age 49 and that the designated beneficiary was paid the specified lump sum payment. Such amount is includible in the decedent's gross estate under section 2039(a) and (b). Since immediately before his death, the employee had an enforceable right to receive an annuity commencing at age 60, he is considered to have "possessed the right to receive" an annuity as that term is used in section 2039(a). If, in this example, the employee would not be entitled to any benefits in the event of his separation from service before retirement for any reason other than death, the result would be the same so long as the decedent had complied with his obligations under the contract up to the time of his death. In such case, he is considered to have had, immediately before his death, an enforceable right to receive an annuity commencing at age 60.

Example (4). Pursuant to a retirement plan, the employee made contributions to a fund which was to provide the employee, upon his retirement at age 60, with an annuity for life, and which was to provide his designated beneficiary, upon the employee's death after retirement, with a similar annuity for life. The plan provided, however, that no benefits were payable in the event of the employee's death before retirement. The retirement plan at no time met the requirements of section 401(a) (relating to qualified plans). Assume that the employee died at age 59 but that the employer nevertheless started payment of an annuity in a slightly reduced amount to the designated beneficiary. The value of the annuity is not includible in the decedent's gross estate under section 2039(a) and (b). Since the employee died before reaching the retirement age, the employer was under no obligation to pay the annuity to the employee's designated beneficiary. Therefore, the annuity was not paid under a "contract or agreement" as that term is used in section 2039(a). If, however, it can be established that the employer has consistently paid an annuity under such circumstances, the annuity will be considered as having been paid under a "contract or agreement".

Example (5). The employer made contributions to a retirement fund which were credited to the employee's individual account. Under the plan, the employee was to receive one-half the amount credited to his account upon his retirement at age 60, and his designated beneficiary was to receive the other one-half upon the employee's death after retirement. If the employee should die before reaching the retirement age, the entire amount credited to his account at such time was to be paid to the designated beneficiary. The retirement plan at no time met the requirements of section 401(a) (relating to qualified plans). Assume that the employee received one-half the amount credited to his account upon reaching the retirement age and that he died shortly thereafter. Since the employee received all that he was entitled to receive under the plan before his death, no amount was payable to him for his life or for any period not ascertainable without reference to his death, or for any period which did not in fact end before his death. Thus, the amount of the payment to the designated beneficiary is not includible in the decedent's gross estate under section 2039(a) and (b). If, in this example, the employee died before reaching the retirement age, the amount of the payment to the designated beneficiary would be includible in the decedent's gross estate under section 2039(a) and (b). In this latter case, the decedent possessed the right to receive lump sum payment for a period which did not in fact end before his death.

Example (6). The employer made contributions to two different funds set up under two different plans. One plan was to provide the employee upon his retirement at age 60, with an annuity for life, and the other plan was to provide the employee's designated beneficiary, upon the employee's death, with a similar annuity for life. Each plan was established at a different time and each plan was administered separately in every respect. Neither plan at any time met the requirements of section 401(a) (relating to qualified plans). The value of the designated beneficiary's annuity is includible in the employee's gross estate. All rights and benefits accruing to an employee and to others by reason of the employment (except rights and benefits accruing under certain plans meeting the requirements of section 401(a) (see S 20.2039–2)) are considered together in determining whether or not section 2039(a) and (b) applies. The scope of section 2039(a) and (b) cannot be limited by indirection.

(c) Amount includible in the gross estate. The amount to be included in a decedent's gross estate under section 2039(a) and (b) is an amount which bears the same ratio to the value at the decedent's death of the annuity or other payment receivable by the beneficiary as the contribution made by the decedent, or made by his employer (or former employer) for any reason connected with his employment, to the cost of the contract or agreement bears to its total cost. * * * The application of this paragraph may be illustrated by the following examples:

Example (1). On January 1, 1945, the decedent and his wife each contributed $15,000 to the purchase price of an annuity contract under the terms of which the issuing company agreed to pay an annuity to the decedent and his wife for their joint lives and to continue the annuity to the survivor for his life. Assume that the value of the survivor's annuity at the decedent's death (computed under § 20.2031–8) is $20,000. Since the decedent contributed one-half of the cost of the contract, the amount to be included in his gross estate under section 2039(a) and (b) is $10,000.

* * *

(d) Insurance under policies on the life of the decedent. If an annuity or other payment receivable by a beneficiary under a contract or agreement is in substance the proceeds of insurance under a policy on the life of the decedent, section 2039(a) and (b) does not apply. For the extent to which such an annuity or other payment is includable in a decedent's gross estate, see section 2042 and § 20.2042–1. A combination annuity contract and life insurance policy on the decedent's life (*e.g.*, a "retirement income" policy with death benefits) which matured during the decedent's lifetime so that there was no longer an insurance element under the contract at the time of the decedent's death is subject to the provisions of section 2039(a) and (b). On the other hand, the treatment of a combination annuity contract and life insurance policy on the decedent's life which did not mature during the decedent's lifetime depends upon the nature of the contract at the time of the decedent's death. The nature of the contract is generally determined by the relation of the reserve value of the policy to the value of the death benefit at the time of the decedent's death. If the decedent dies before the reserve value equals the death benefit, there is still an insurance element under the contract. The contract is therefore considered, for estate tax purposes, to be an insurance policy subject to the provisions of section 2042. However, if the decedent dies after the reserve value equals the death benefit, there is no longer an insurance element under the contract. The contract is therefore considered to be a contract for an annuity or other payment subject to the provisions of section 2039(a) and (b) or some other section of part III of subchapter A of chapter 11. Notwithstanding the relation of the reserve value to the value of the death benefit, a contract under which the death benefit could never exceed the total premiums paid, plus interest, contains no insurance element.

Example. Pursuant to a retirement plan established January 1, 1945, the employer purchased a contract from an insurance company which was to provide the employee, upon his retirement at age 65, with an annuity of $100 per month for life, and which was to provide his designated beneficiary, upon the employee's death after retirement, with a similar annuity for life. The contract further provided that if the employee should die before reaching the retirement age, a lump sum payment of $20,000 would be paid to his designated beneficiary in lieu of the annuity described above. The plan at no time met the requirements of section 401(a) (relating to qualified plans). Assume that the reserve value of the contract at the retirement age would be $20,000. If the employee died after reaching the retirement age, the death benefit to the designated beneficiary would constitute an annuity, the value of which would be includable in the employee's gross estate under section 2039(a) and (b). If, on the other hand, the employee died before reaching his retirement age, the death benefit to the designated beneficiary would constitute insurance under a policy on the life of the decedent since the reserve value would be less than the death benefit. Accordingly, its includability would depend upon section 2042 and § 20.2042–1.

(e) No application to certain trusts. Section 2039 shall not be applied to include in a decedent's gross estate all or any portion of a trust (other than a trust constituting an employee benefit, but including those described in the following sentence) if the decedent retained a right to use property of the trust or retained an annuity, unitrust, or other interest in the trust, in either case as described in section 2036. Such trusts include without limitation the following (collectively referred to in this paragraph (e) as "trusts"): Certain charitable remainder trusts (collectively CRTs) such as a charitable remainder annuity trust (CRAT) within the meaning of section 664(d)(1), a charitable remainder unitrust (CRUT) within the meaning of section 664(d)(2) or (d)(3), and any other charitable remainder trust that does not qualify under section 664(d), whether because the CRT was created prior to 1969, there was a defect in the drafting of the CRT, there was no intention to qualify the CRT for the charitable deduction, or otherwise; other trusts established by a grantor (collectively GRTs) such as a grantor retained annuity trust (GRAT) paying out a qualified annuity interest within the meaning of § 25.2702–3(b) of this chapter, a grantor retained unitrust (GRUT) paying out a qualified unitrust interest within the meaning of § 25.2702–3(c) of this chapter; and various forms of grantor retained income trusts (GRITs) whether or not the grantor's retained interest is a qualified interest as defined in section 2702(b), including without limitation a qualified personal residence trust (QPRT) within the meaning of § 25.2702–5(c) of this chapter and a personal residence trust (PRT) within the meaning of § 25.2702–5(b) of this chapter. For purposes of determining the extent to which a retained interest causes all or a portion of a trust to be included in a decedent's gross estate, see § 20.2036–1(c)(1), (2), and (3).

* * *

[T.D. 6296, 23 FR 4529, June 24, 1958; 25 FR 14021, Dec. 31, 1960, as amended by T.D. 7416, 41 FR 14514, April 6, 1976; T.D. 9414, 73 FR 40178, July 14, 2008]

§ 20.2040–1 Joint interests.

(a) In general. A decedent's gross estate includes under section 2040 the value of property held jointly at the time of the decedent's death by the decedent and another person or persons with right of survivorship, as follows:

(1) To the extent that the property was acquired by the decedent and the other joint owner or owners by gift, devise, bequest, or inheritance, the decedent's fractional share of the property is included.

(2) In all other cases, the entire value of the property is included except such part of the entire value as is attributable to the amount of the consideration in money or money's worth furnished by the other joint owner or owners. See § 20.2043–1 with respect to adequacy of consideration. Such part of the entire value is that portion of the entire value of the property at the decedent's death (or at the alternate valuation date described in section 2032) which the consideration in money or money's worth furnished by the other joint owner or owners bears to the total cost of acquisition and capital additions.

In determining the consideration furnished by the other joint owner or owners, there is taken into account only that portion of such consideration which is shown not to be attributable to money or other property acquired by the other joint owner or owners from the decedent for less than a full and adequate consideration in money or money's worth.

The entire value of jointly held property is included in a decedent's gross estate unless the executor submits facts sufficient to show that property was not acquired entirely with consideration furnished by the decedent, or was acquired by the decedent and the other joint owner or owners by gift, bequest, devise, or inheritance.

(b) Meaning of "property held jointly". Section 2040 specifically covers property held jointly by the decedent and any other person (or persons), property held by the decedent and spouse as tenants by the entirety, and a deposit of money, or a bond or other instrument, in the name of the decedent and any other person and payable to either or the survivor. The section applies to all classes of property, whether real or personal, and regardless of when the joint interests were created. Furthermore, it makes no difference that the survivor takes the entire interest in the property by right of survivorship and that no interest therein forms a part of the decedent's estate for purposes of administration. The section has no application to property held by the decedent and any other person (or persons) as tenants in common.

(c) Examples. The application of this section may be explained in the following examples in each of which it is assumed that the other joint owner or owners survived the decedent:

(1) If the decedent furnished the entire purchase price of the jointly held property, the value of the entire property is included in his gross estate;

(2) If the decedent furnished a part only of the purchase price, only a corresponding portion of the value of the property is so included;

(3) If the decedent furnished no part of the purchase price, no part of the value of the property is so included;

(4) If the decedent, before the acquisition of the property by himself and the other joint owner, gave the latter a sum of money or other property which thereafter became the other joint owner's entire contribution to the purchase price, then the value of the entire property is so included, notwithstanding the fact that the other property may have appreciated in value due to market conditions between the time of the gift and the time of the acquisition of the jointly held property;

(5) If the decedent, before the acquisition of the property by himself and the other joint owner, transferred to the latter for less than an adequate and full consideration in money or money's worth other income-producing property, the income from which belonged to and became the other joint owner's entire contribution to the purchase price, then the value of the jointly held property less that portion attributable to the income which the other joint owner did furnish is included in the decedent's gross estate;

(6) If the property originally belonged to the other joint owner and the decedent purchased his interest from the other joint owner, only that portion of the value of the property attributable to the consideration paid by the decedent is included;

(7) If the decedent and his spouse acquired the property by will or gift as tenants by the entirety, one-half of the value of the property is included in the decedent's gross estate; and

(8) If the decedent and his two brothers acquired the property by will or gift as joint tenants, one-third of the value of the property is so included.

[T.D. 6296, 23 FR 4529, June 24, 1958]

§ 20.2041–1 Powers of appointment; in general.

(a) Introduction. A decedent's gross estate includes under section 2041 the value of property in respect of which the decedent possessed, exercised, or released certain powers of appointment. This section contains rules of general application; * * * § 20.2041–3 sets forth specific rules applicable to powers of appointment created after October 21, 1942.

(b) Definition of "power of appointment"—(1) In general. The term "power of appointment" includes all powers which are in substance and effect powers of appointment regardless of the nomenclature used in creating the power and regardless of local property law connotations. For example, if a trust instrument provides that the beneficiary may appropriate or consume the principal of the trust, the power to consume or appropriate is a power of appointment. Similarly, a power given to a decedent to affect the beneficial enjoyment of trust property or its income by altering, amending, or revoking the trust instrument or terminating the trust is a power of appointment. If the community property laws of a State confer upon the wife a power of testamentary disposition over property in which she does not have a vested interest she is considered as having a power of appointment. A power in a donee to remove or discharge a trustee and appoint himself may be a power of appointment. For example, if under the terms of a trust instrument, the trustee or his successor has the power to appoint the principal of the trust for the benefit of individuals including himself, and the decedent has the unrestricted power to remove or discharge the trustee at any time and appoint any other person including himself, the decedent is considered as having a power of appointment. However, the decedent is not considered to have a power of appointment if he only had the power to appoint a successor, including himself, under limited conditions which did not exist at the time of his death, without an accompanying unrestricted power of removal. Similarly, a power to amend only the administrative provisions of a trust instrument, which cannot substantially affect the beneficial enjoyment of the trust property or income, is not a power of appointment. The mere power of management, investment, custody of assets, or the power to allocate receipts and disbursements as between income and principal, exercisable in a fiduciary capacity, whereby the holder has no power to enlarge or shift any of the beneficial interests therein except as an incidental consequence of the discharge of such fiduciary duties is not a power of appointment. Further, the right in a beneficiary of a trust to assent to a periodic accounting, thereby relieving the trustee from further accountability, is not a power of appointment if the right of assent does not consist of any power or right to enlarge or shift the beneficial interest of any beneficiary therein.

(2) Relation to other sections. For purposes of §§ 20.2041–1 to 20.2041–3, the term "power of appointment" does not include powers reserved by the decedent to himself within the concept of sections 2036 through 2038. (See §§ 20.2036–1 to 20.2038–1.) No provision of section 2041 or of §§ 20.2041–1 to 20.2041–3 is to be construed as in any way limiting the application of any other section of the Internal Revenue Code or of these regulations. The power of the owner of a property interest already possessed by him to dispose of his interest, and nothing more, is not a power of appointment, and the interest is includable in his gross estate to the extent it would be includable under section 2033 or some other provision of part III of subchapter A of chapter 11. For example, if a trust created by S provides for payment of the income to A for life with power in A to appoint the remainder by will and, in default of such appointment for payment of the income to A's widow, W, for her life and for payment of the remainder to A's estate, the value of A's interest in the remainder is includable in his gross estate under section 2033 regardless of its includability under section 2041.

(3) Powers over a portion of property. If a power of appointment exists as to part of an entire group of assets or only over a limited interest in property, section 2041 applies only to such part or interest. For example, if a trust created by S provides for the payment of income to A for life, then to W for life, with power in A to appoint the remainder by will and in default of appointment for payment of the remainder to B or his estate, and if A dies before W, section 2041 applies only to the value of the remainder interest excluding W's life estate. If A dies after W, section 2041 would apply to the value of the entire property. If the power were only over one-half the remainder interest, section 2041 would apply only to one-half the value of the amounts described above.

(c) Definition of "general power of appointment"—(1) In general. The term "general power of appointment" as defined in section 2041(b)(1) means any power of appointment exercisable in favor of the decedent, his estate, his creditors, or the creditors of his estate, except (i) joint powers, to the extent provided in §§ 20.2041–2 and 20.2041–3, and (ii) certain powers limited by an ascertainable standard, to the extent provided in subparagraph (2) of this paragraph. A power of appointment exercisable to meet the estate tax, or any other taxes, debts, or charges which are enforceable against the estate, is included within the meaning of a power of appointment exercisable in favor of the decedent's estate, his creditors, or the creditors of his estate. A power of appointment exercisable for the purpose of discharging a legal obligation of the decedent or for his pecuniary benefit is considered a power of appointment exercisable in favor of the decedent or his creditors. However, for purposes of §§ 20.2041–1 to 20.2041–3, a power of appointment not otherwise considered to be a general power of appointment is not treated as a general power of appointment merely by reason of the fact that an appointee may, in fact, be a creditor of the decedent or his estate. A power of appointment is not a general power if by its terms it is either—

(a) Exercisable only in favor of one or more designated persons or classes other than the decedent or his creditors, or the decedent's estate or the creditors of his estate, or

(b) Expressly not exercisable in favor of the decedent or his creditors, or the decedent's estate or the creditors of his estate.

A decedent may have two powers under the same instrument, one of which is a general power of appointment and the other of which is not. For example, a beneficiary may have a power to withdraw trust corpus during his life, and a testamentary power to appoint the corpus among his descendants. The testamentary power is not a general power of appointment.

(2) Powers limited by an ascertainable standard. A power to consume, invade, or appropriate income or corpus, or both, for the benefit of the decedent which is limited by an ascertainable standard relating to the health, education, support, or maintenance of the decedent is, by reason of section 2041(b)(1)(A), not a general power of appointment. A power is limited by such a standard if the extent of the holder's duty to exercise and not to exercise the power is reasonably measurable in terms of his needs for health, education, or support (or any combination of them). As used in this subparagraph, the words "support" and "maintenance" are synonymous and their meaning is not limited to the bare necessities of life. A power to use property for the comfort, welfare, or happiness of the holder of the power is not limited by the requisite standard. Examples of powers which are limited by the requisite standard are powers exercisable for the holder's "support," "support in reasonable comfort," "maintenance in health and reasonable comfort," "support in his accustomed manner of living," "education, including college and professional education," "health," and "medical, dental, hospital and nursing expenses and expenses of invalidism." In determining whether a power is limited by an ascertainable standard, it is immaterial whether the beneficiary is required to exhaust his other income before the power can be exercised.

* * *

(d) Definition of "exercise". Whether a power of appointment is in fact exercised may depend upon local law. For example, the residuary clause of a will may be considered under local law as an exercise of a testamentary power of appointment in the absence of evidence of a contrary intention drawn from the whole of the testator's will. However, regardless of local law, a power of appointment is considered as exercised for purposes of section 2041 even though the exercise is in favor of the taker in default of appointment, and irrespective of whether the appointed interest and the interest in default of appointment are identical or whether the appointee renounces any right to take under the appointment. A power of appointment is also considered as exercised even though the disposition cannot take effect until the occurrence of an event after the exercise takes place, if the exercise is irrevocable and, as of the time of the exercise, the condition was not impossible of occurrence. For example, if property is left in trust to A for life, with a power in B to appoint the remainder by will, and B dies before A, exercising his power by appointing the remainder to C if C survives A, B is considered to have exercised his power if C is living at B's death. On the other hand, a testamentary power of appointment is not considered as exercised if it is exercised subject to the occurrence during the decedent's life of an express or implied condition which did not in fact occur. Thus, if in the preceding example, C dies before B, B's power of appointment would not be considered to have been exercised. Similarly, if a trust provides for income to A for life, remainder as A appoints by will, and A appoints a life estate in the property to B and does not otherwise exercise his power, but B dies before A, A's power is not considered to have been exercised.

(e) Time of creation of power. A power of appointment created by will is, in general, considered as created on the date of the testator's death. * * * A power of appointment created by an inter vivos instrument is considered as created on the date the instrument takes effect. Such a power is not considered as created at some future date merely because it is not exercisable on the date the instrument takes effect, or because it is revocable, or because the identity of its holders is not ascertainable until after the date the instrument takes effect. However, if the holder of a power exercises it by creating a second power, the second power is considered as created at the time of the exercise of the first. * * *

* * *

[T.D. 6296, 23 FR 4529, June 24, 1958, as amended by T.D. 6582, 26 FR 11861, Dec. 12, 1961]

§ 20.2041–3 Powers of appointment created after October 21, 1942.

(a) In general. (1) Property subject to a power of appointment created after October 21, 1942, is includable in the gross estate of the holder of the power under varying conditions depending on whether the power is (i) general in nature, (ii) possessed at death, or (iii) exercised or released. See paragraphs (b), (c), and (d) of § 20.2041–1 for the definition of various terms used in this section. See paragraph (c) of this section for the rules applicable to determine the extent to which joint powers created after October 21, 1942, are to be treated as general powers of appointment.

(2) If the power is a general power of appointment, the value of an interest in property subject to such a power is includable in a decedent's gross estate under section 2041(a)(2) if either—

(i) The decedent has the power at the time of his death (and the interest exists at the time of his death), or

(ii) The decedent exercised or released the power, or the power lapsed, under the circumstances and to the extent described in paragraph (d) of this section.

(3) If the power is not a general power of appointment, the value of property subject to the power is includable in the holder's gross estate under section 2041(a)(3) only if it is exercised to create a further power under certain circumstances (see paragraph (e) of this section).

(b) Existence of power at death. For purposes of section 2041(a)(2), a power of appointment is considered to exist on the date of a decedent's death even though the exercise of the power is subject to the precedent giving of notice, or even though the exercise of the power takes effect only on the expiration of a stated period after its exercise, whether or not on or before the decedent's death notice has been given or the power has been exercised. However, a power which by its terms is exercisable only upon the occurrence during the decedent's lifetime of an event or a contingency which did not in fact take place or occur during such time is not a power in existence on the date of the decedent's death. For example, if a decedent was given a general power of appointment exercisable only after he reached a certain age, only if he survived another person, or only if he died without descendants, the power would not be in existence on the date of the decedent's death if the condition precedent to its exercise had not occurred.

(c) Joint powers created after October 21, 1942. The treatment of a power of appointment created after October 21, 1942, which is exercisable only in conjunction with another person is governed by section 2041(b)(1)(C), which provides as follows:

(1) Such a power is not considered a general power of appointment if it is not exercisable by the decedent except with the consent or joinder of the creator of the power.

(2) Such power is not considered a general power of appointment if it is not exercisable by the decedent except with the consent or joinder of a person having a substantial interest in the property subject to the power which is adverse to the exercise of the power in favor of the decedent, his estate, his creditors, or the creditors of his estate. An interest adverse to the exercise of a power is considered as substantial if its value in relation to the total value of the property subject to the power is not insignificant. For this purpose, the interest is to be valued in accordance with the actuarial principles set forth in § 20.2031-7 or, if it is not susceptible to valuation under those provisions, in accordance with the general principles set forth in § 20.2031-1. A taker in default of appointment under a power has an interest which is adverse to an exercise of the power. A coholder of the power has no adverse interest merely because of his joint possession of the power nor merely because he is a permissible appointee under a power. However, a coholder of a power is considered as having an adverse interest where he may possess the power after the decedent's death and may exercise it at that time in favor of himself, his estate, his creditors, or the creditors of his estate. Thus, for example, if X, Y, and Z held a power jointly to appoint among a group of persons which includes themselves and if on the death of X the power will pass to Y and Z jointly, then Y and Z are considered to have interests adverse to the exercise of the power in favor of X. Similarly, if on Y's death the power will pass to Z, Z is considered to have an interest adverse to the exercise of the power in favor of Y. The application of this subparagraph may be further illustrated by the following additional examples in each of which it is assumed that the value of the interest in question is substantial:

Example (1). The decedent and R were trustees of a trust under the terms of which the income was to be paid to the decedent for life and then to M for life, and the remainder was to be paid to R. The trustees had power to distribute corpus to the decedent. Since R's interest was substantially adverse to an exercise of the power in favor of the decedent the latter did not have a general power of appointment. If M and the decedent were the trustees, M's interest would likewise have been adverse.

Example (2). The decedent and L were trustees of a trust under the terms of which the income was to be paid to L for life and then to M for life, and the remainder was to be paid to the decedent. The trustees had power to distribute corpus to the decedent during L's life. Since L's interest was adverse to an exercise of the power in favor of the decedent, the decedent did not have a general power of appointment. If the decedent and M were the trustees, M's interest would likewise have been adverse.

Example (3). The decedent and L were trustees of a trust under the terms of which the income was to be paid to L for life. The trustees could designate whether corpus was to be distributed to the decedent or to A after L's death. L's interest was not adverse to an exercise of the power in favor of the decedent, and the decedent therefore had a general power of appointment.

(3) A power which is exercisable only in conjunction with another person, and which after application of the rules set forth in subparagraphs (1) and (2) of this paragraph constitutes a general power of appointment, will be treated as though the holders of the power who are permissible appointees of the property were joint owners of property subject to the power. The decedent, under this rule, will be treated as possessed of a general power of appointment over an aliquot share of the property to be determined with reference to the number of joint holders, including the decedent, who (or whose estates or creditors) are permissible appointees. Thus, for example, if X, Y, and Z hold an unlimited power jointly to appoint among a group of persons, including themselves, but on the death of X the power does not pass to Y and Z jointly, then Y and Z are not considered to have interests adverse to the exercise of the power in favor of X. In this case X is considered to possess a general power of appointment as to one-third of the property subject to the power.

(d) Releases, lapses, and disclaimers of general powers of appointment. **(1)** Property subject to a general power of appointment created after October 21, 1942, is includable in the gross estate of a decedent under section 2041(a)(2) even though he does not have the power at the date of his death, if during his life he exercised or released the power under circumstances such that, if the property subject to the power had been owned and transferred by the decedent, the property would be includable in the decedent's gross estate under section 2035, 2036, 2037, or 2038. Further, section 2041(b)(2) provides that the lapse of a power of appointment is considered to be a release of the power to the extent set forth in subparagraph (3) of this paragraph. A release of a power of appointment need not be formal or express in character. * * * If a general power of appointment created after October 21, 1942, is partially released, a subsequent exercise or release of the power under circumstances described in the first sentence of this subparagraph, or its possession at death will nevertheless cause the property subject to the power to be included in the gross estate of the holder of the power.

* * *

(3) The failure to exercise a power of appointment created after October 21, 1942, within a specified time, so that the power lapses, constitutes a release of the power. However, section 2041(b)(2) provides that such a lapse of a power of appointment during any calendar year during the decedent's life is treated as a release for purposes of inclusion of property in the gross estate under section 2041(a)(2) only to the extent that the property which could have been appointed by exercise of the lapsed power exceeds the greater of (i) $5,000 or (ii) 5 percent of the aggregate value, at the time of the lapse, of the assets out of which, or the proceeds of which, the exercise of the lapsed power could have been satisfied. For example, assume that A transferred $200,000 worth of securities in trust providing for payment of income to B for life with remainder to B's issue. Assume further that B was given a noncumulative right to withdraw $10,000 a year from the principal of the trust fund (which neither increased nor decreased in value prior to B's death). In such case, the failure of B to exercise his right of withdrawal will not result in estate tax with respect to the power to withdraw $10,000 which lapses each year before the year of B's death. At B's death there will be included in his gross estate the $10,000 which he was entitled to withdraw for the year in which his death occurs less any amount which he may have taken during that year. However, if in the above example B had possessed the right to withdraw $15,000 of the principal annually, the failure to exercise such power in any year will be considered a release of the power to the extent of the excess of the amount subject to withdrawal over 5 percent of the trust fund (in this example, $5,000, assuming that the trust fund is worth $200,000 at the time of the lapse). Since each lapse is treated as though B had exercised dominion over the trust property by making a transfer of principal reserving the income therefrom for his life, the value of the trust property (but only to the extent of the excess of the amount subject to withdrawal over 5 percent of the trust fund) is includable in B's gross estate (unless before B's death he has disposed of his right to the income under circumstances to which sections 2035 through 2038 would not be applicable). The extent to which the value of the trust property is included in the decedent's gross estate is determined as provided in subparagraph (4) of this paragraph.

(4) The purpose of section 2041(b)(2) is to provide a determination, as of the date of the lapse of the power, of the proportion of the property over which the power lapsed which is an exempt disposition for estate tax purposes and the proportion which, if the other requirements of sections 2035 through 2038 are satisfied, will be considered as a taxable disposition. Once the taxable proportion of any disposition at the date of lapse has been determined, the valuation of that proportion as of the date of the decedent's death (or, if the executor has elected the alternate valuation method under section 2032, the value as of the date therein provided), is to be ascertained in accordance with the principles which are applicable to the valuation of transfers of property by the decedent under the corresponding provisions of sections 2035 through 2038. For example, if the life beneficiary of a trust had a right exercisable only during one calendar year to draw down $50,000 from the corpus of a trust, which he did not exercise, and if at the end of the year the corpus was worth $800,000, the taxable portion over which the power lapsed is $10,000 (the excess of $50,000 over 5 percent of the corpus), or 1/80 of the total value. On the decedent's death, if the total value of the corpus of the trust (excluding income accumulated after the lapse of the power) on the applicable valuation date was $1,200,000, $15,000 (1/80 of $1,200,000) would be includable in the decedent's gross estate. However, if the total value was then $600,000, only $7,500 (1/80 of $600,000) would be includable.

(5) If the failure to exercise a power, such as a right of withdrawal, occurs in more than a single year, the proportion of the property over which the power lapsed which is treated as a taxable disposition will be determined separately for each such year. The aggregate of the taxable proportions for all such years, valued in accordance with the above principles, will be includable in the gross estate by reason of the lapse. The includable amount, however, shall not exceed the aggregate value of the assets out of which, or the proceeds of which, the exercise of the power could have been satisfied, valued as of the date of the decedent's death (or, if the executor has elected the alternate valuation method under section 2032, the value as of the date therein provided).

(6)(i) A disclaimer or renunciation of a general power of appointment created in a transfer made after December 31, 1976, is not considered to be the release of the power if the disclaimer or renunciation is a qualified disclaimer as described in section 2518 and the corresponding regulations. For rules relating to when the transfer creating the power occurs, see § 25.2518–2(c)(3) of this chapter. If the disclaimer or renunciation is not a qualified disclaimer, it is considered a release of the power by the disclaimant.

(ii) The disclaimer or renunciation of a general power of appointment created in a taxable transfer before January 1, 1977, in the person disclaiming is not considered to be a release of the power. The disclaimer or renunciation must be unequivocal and effective under local law. A disclaimer is a complete and unqualified refusal to accept the rights to which one is entitled. There can be no disclaimer or renunciation of a power after its acceptance. In the absence of facts to the contrary, the failure to renounce or disclaim within a reasonable time after learning of its existence will be presumed to constitute an acceptance of the power. In any case where a power is purported to be disclaimed or renounced as to only a portion of the property subject to the power, the determination as to whether or not there has been a complete and unqualified refusal to accept the rights to which one is entitled will depend on all the facts and circumstances of the particular case, taking into account the recognition and effectiveness of such a disclaimer under local law. Such rights refer to the incidents of the power and not to other interests of the decedent in the property. If effective under local law, the power may be disclaimed or renounced without disclaiming or renouncing such other interests.

(iii) The first and second sentences of paragraph (d)(6)(i) of this section are applicable for transfers creating the power to be disclaimed made on or after December 31, 1997.

(e) Successive powers. **(1)** Property subject to a power of appointment created after October 21, 1942, which is not a general power, is includable in the gross estate of the holder of the power under section 2041(a)(3) if the power is exercised, and if both of the following conditions are met:

(i) If the exercise is (a) by will, or (b) by a disposition which is of such nature that if it were a transfer of property owned by the decedent, the property would be includable in the decedent's gross estate under sections 2035 through 2037; and

(ii) If the power is exercised by creating another power of appointment which, under the terms of the instruments creating and exercising the first power and under applicable local law, can be validly exercised so as to (a) postpone the vesting of any estate or interest in the property for a period ascertainable without regard to the date of the creation of the first power, or (b) (if the applicable rule against perpetuities is stated in terms of suspension of ownership or of the power of alienation, rather than of vesting) suspend the absolute ownership or the power of alienation of the property for a period ascertainable without regard to the date of the creation of the first power.

(2) For purposes of the application of section 2041(a)(3), the value of the property subject to the second power of appointment is considered to be its value unreduced by any precedent or subsequent interest which is not subject to the second power. Thus, if a decedent has a power to appoint by will $100,000 to a group of persons consisting of his children and grandchildren and exercises the power by making an outright appointment of $75,000 and by giving one appointee a power to appoint $25,000, no more than $25,000 will be includable in the decedent's gross estate under section 2041(a)(3). If, however, the decedent appoints the income from the entire fund to a beneficiary for life with power in the beneficiary to appoint the remainder by will, the entire $100,000 will be includable in the decedent's gross estate under section 2041(a)(3) if the exercise of the second power can validly postpone the vesting of any estate or interest in the property or can suspend the absolute ownership or power of alienation of the property for a period ascertainable without regard to the date of the creation of the first power.

* * *

[T.D. 6296, 23 FR 4529, June 24, 1958; T.D. 8095, 51 FR 28367, Aug. 7, 1986; T.D. 8744, 62 FR 68183, Dec. 31, 1997]

§ 20.2042–1 Proceeds of life insurance.

(a) In general. **(1)** Section 2042 provides for the inclusion in a decedent's gross estate of the proceeds of insurance on the decedent's life (i) receivable by or for the benefit of the estate (see paragraph (b) of this section) and (ii) receivable by other beneficiaries (see paragraph (c) of this section). The term "insurance" refers to life insurance of every description, including death benefits paid by fraternal beneficial societies operating under the lodge system.

(2) Proceeds of life insurance which are not includable in the gross estate under section 2042 may, depending upon the facts of the particular case, be includable under some other section of part III of subchapter A of chapter 11. * * * Section 2042 has no application to the inclusion in the gross estate of the value of rights in an insurance policy on the life of a person other than the decedent, or the value of rights in a combination annuity contract and life insurance policy on the decedent's life (*i.e.,* a "retirement income" policy with death benefit or an "endowment" policy) under which there was no insurance element at the time of the decedent's death (see paragraph (d) of § 20.2039–1).

(3) Except as provided in paragraph (c)(6), the amount to be included in the gross estate under section 2042 is the full amount receivable under the policy. If the proceeds of the policy are made payable to a beneficiary in the form of an annuity for life or for a term of years, the amount to be included in the gross estate is the one sum payable at death under an option which could have been exercised either by the insured or by the beneficiary, or if no option was granted, the sum used by the insurance company in determining the amount of the annuity.

(b) Receivable by or for the benefit of the estate. **(1)** Section 2042 requires the inclusion in the gross estate of the proceeds of insurance on the decedent's life receivable by the executor or administrator, or payable to the decedent's estate. It makes no difference whether or not the estate is specifically named as the beneficiary under the terms of the policy. Thus, if under the terms of an insurance policy the proceeds are receivable by another beneficiary but are subject to an obligation, legally binding upon the other beneficiary, to pay taxes, debts, or other charges enforceable against the estate, then the amount of such proceeds required for the payment in full (to the extent of the beneficiary's obligation) of such taxes, debts, or other charges is includable in the gross estate. Similarly, if the decedent purchased an insurance policy in favor of another person or a corporation as collateral security for a loan or other accommodation, its proceeds are considered to be receivable for the benefit of the estate. The amount of the loan outstanding at the date of the decedent's death, with interest accrued to that date, will be deductible in determining the taxable estate. See § 20.2053–4.

(2) If the proceeds of an insurance policy made payable to the decedent's estate are community assets under the local community property law and, as a result, one-half of the proceeds belongs to the decedent's spouse, then only one-half of the proceeds is considered to be receivable by or for the benefit of the decedent's estate.

(c) Receivable by other beneficiaries. **(1)** Section 2042 requires the inclusion in the gross estate of the proceeds of insurance on the decedent's life not receivable by or for the benefit of the estate if the decedent possessed at the date of his death any of the incidents of ownership in the policy, exercisable either alone or in conjunction with any other person. However, if the decedent did not possess any of such incidents of ownership at the time of his death nor transfer them in contemplation of death, no part of the proceeds would be includible in his gross estate under section 2042. Thus, if the decedent owned a policy of insurance on his life and, 4 years before his death, irrevocably assigned his entire interest in the policy to his wife retaining no reversionary interest therein (see subparagraph (3) of this paragraph), the proceeds of the policy would not be includible in his gross estate under section 2042.

(2) For purposes of this paragraph, the term "incidents of ownership" is not limited in its meaning to ownership of the policy in the technical legal sense. Generally speaking, the term has reference to the right of the insured or his estate to the economic benefits of the policy. Thus, it includes the power to change the beneficiary, to surrender or cancel the policy, to assign the policy, to revoke an assignment, to pledge the policy for a loan, or to obtain from the insurer a loan against the surrender value of the policy, etc. See subparagraph (6) of this paragraph for rules relating to the circumstances under which incidents of ownership held by a corporation are attributable to a decedent through his stock ownership.

(3) The term "incidents of ownership" also includes a reversionary interest in the policy or its proceeds, whether arising by the express terms of the policy or other instrument or by operation of law, but only if the value of the reversionary interest immediately before the death of the decedent exceeded 5 percent of the value of the policy.

As used in this subparagraph, the term "reversionary interest" includes a possibility that the policy or its proceeds may return to the decedent or his estate and a possibility that the policy or its proceeds may become subject to a power of disposition by him. In order to determine whether or not the value of a reversionary interest immediately before the death of the decedent exceeded 5 percent of the value of the policy, the principles contained in paragraph (c)(3) and (4) of § 20.2037–1, insofar as applicable, shall be followed under this subparagraph. In that connection, there must be specifically taken into consideration any incidents of ownership held by others immediately before the decedent's death which would affect the value of the reversionary interest. For example, the decedent would not be considered to have a reversionary interest in the policy of a value in excess of 5 percent if the power to obtain the cash surrender value existed in some other person immediately before the decedent's death and was exercisable by such other person alone and in all events. The terms "reversionary interest" and "incidents of ownership" do not include the possibility that the decedent might receive a policy or its proceeds by inheritance through the estate of another person, or as a surviving spouse under a statutory right of election or a similar right.

(4) A decedent is considered to have an "incident of ownership" in an insurance policy on his life held in trust if, under the terms of the policy, the decedent (either alone or in conjunction with another person or persons) has the power (as trustee or otherwise) to change the beneficial ownership in the policy or its proceeds, or the time or manner of enjoyment thereof, even though the decedent has no beneficial interest in the trust. Moreover, assuming the decedent created the trust, such a power may result in the inclusion in the decedent's gross estate under section 2036 or 2038 of other property transferred by the decedent to the trust if, for example, the decedent has the power to surrender the insurance policy and if the income otherwise used to pay premiums on the policy would become currently payable to a beneficiary of the trust in the event that the policy were surrendered.

(5) As an additional step in determining whether or not a decedent possessed any incidents of ownership in a policy or any part of a policy, regard must be given to the effect of the State or other applicable law upon the terms of the policy. For example, assume that the decedent purchased a policy of insurance on his life with funds held by him and his surviving wife as community property, designating their son as beneficiary but retaining the right to surrender the policy. Under the local law, the proceeds upon surrender would have inured to the marital community. Assuming that the policy is not surrendered and that the son receives the proceeds on the decedent's death, the wife's transfer of her one-half interest in the policy was not considered absolute before the decedent's death. Upon the wife's prior death, one-half of the value of the policy would have been included in her gross estate. Under these circumstances, the power of surrender possessed by the decedent as agent for his wife with respect to one-half of the policy is not, for purposes of this section, an "incident of ownership", and the decedent is, therefore, deemed to possess an incident of ownership in only one-half of the policy.

(6) In the case of economic benefits of a life insurance policy on the decedent's life that are reserved to a corporation of which the decedent is the sole or controlling stockholder, the corporation's incidents of ownership will not be attributed to the decedent through his stock ownership to the extent the proceeds of the policy are payable to the corporation. Any proceeds payable to a third party for a valid business purpose, such as in satisfaction of a business debt of the corporation, so that the net worth of the corporation is increased by the amount of such proceeds, shall be deemed to be payable to the corporation for purposes of the preceding sentence. See § 20.2031–2(f) for a rule providing that the proceeds of certain life insurance policies shall be considered in determining the value of the decedent's stock. Except as hereinafter provided with respect to a group-term life insurance policy, if any part of the proceeds of the policy are not payable to or for the benefit of the corporation, and thus are not taken into account in valuing the decedent's stock holdings in the corporation for purposes of section 2031, any incidents of ownership held by the corporation as to that part of the proceeds will be attributed to the decedent through his stock ownership where the decedent is the sole or controlling stockholder. Thus, for example, if the decedent is the controlling stockholder in a corporation, and the corporation owns a life insurance policy on his life, the proceeds of which are payable to the decedent's spouse, the incidents of ownership held by the corporation will be attributed to the decedent through his stock ownership and the proceeds will be included in his gross estate under section 2042. If in this example the policy proceeds had been payable 40 percent to decedent's spouse and 60 percent to the corporation, only 40 percent of the proceeds would be included in decedent's gross estate under section 2042. For purposes of this subparagraph, the decedent will not be deemed to be the controlling stockholder of a corporation unless, at the time of his death, he owned stock possessing more than 50 percent of the total combined voting power of the corporation. Solely for purposes of the preceding sentence, a decedent shall be considered to be the owner of only the stock with respect to which legal title was held, at the time of his death, by (i) the decedent (or his agent or nominee); (ii) the decedent and another person jointly (but only the proportionate number of shares which corresponds to the portion of the total consideration which is considered to be furnished by the decedent for purposes of section 2040 and the regulations thereunder); and (iii) by a trustee of a voting trust (to the extent of the decedent's beneficial interest therein) or any other trust with respect to which the decedent was treated as an owner under subpart E, part I, subchapter J, chapter 1 of the Code immediately prior to his death. In the case of group-term life insurance, as defined in the regulations under section 79, the power to surrender or cancel a policy held by a corporation shall not be attributed to any decedent through his stock ownership.

[T.D. 6296, 23 FR 4529, June 24, 1958; 25 FR 14021, Dec. 31, 1960, as amended by T.D. 7312, 39 FR 14949, April 29, 1974; T.D. 7623, 44 FR 28800, May 17, 1979]

§ 20.2043–1 Transfers for insufficient consideration.

(a) In general. The transfers, trusts, interests, rights or powers enumerated and described in sections 2035 through 2038 and section 2041 are not subject to the Federal estate tax if made, created, exercised, or relinquished in a transaction which constituted a bona fide sale for an adequate and full consideration in money or money's worth. To constitute a bona fide sale for an adequate and full consideration in money or money's worth, the transfer must have been made in good faith, and the price must have been an adequate and full equivalent reducible to a money value. If the price was less than such a consideration, only the excess of the fair market value of the property (as of the applicable valuation date) over the price received by the decedent is included in ascertaining the value of his gross estate.

* * *

[T.D. 6296, 23 FR 4529, June 24, 1958]

§ 20.2044–1 Certain property for which marital deduction was previously allowed.

(a) In general. Section 2044 generally provides for the inclusion in the gross estate of property in which the decedent had a qualifying income interest for life and for which a deduction was allowed under section 2056(b)(7) or 2523(f). The value of the property included in the gross estate under section 2044 is not reduced by the amount of any section 2503(b) exclusion that applied to the transfer creating the interest. See section 2207A, regarding the right of recovery against the persons receiving the property that is applicable in certain cases.

(b) Passed from. For purposes of section 1014 and chapters 11 and 13 of subtitle B of the Internal Revenue Code, property included in a decedent's gross estate under section 2044 is considered to have been acquired from or to have passed from the decedent to the person receiving the property upon the decedent's death. Thus, for example, the property is treated as passing from the decedent for purposes of determining the availability of the charitable deduction under section 2055, the marital deduction under section 2056, and special use valuation under section 2032A. In addition, the tax imposed on property includible under section 2044 is eligible for the installment payment of estate tax under section 6166.

(c) Presumption. Unless established to the contrary, section 2044 applies to the entire value of the trust at the surviving spouse's death. If a marital deduction is taken on either the estate or gift tax return with respect to the transfer which created the qualifying income interest, it is presumed that the deduction was allowed for purposes of section 2044. To avoid the inclusion of property in the decedent-spouse's gross estate under this section, the executor of the spouse's estate must establish that a deduction was not taken for the transfer which created the qualifying income interest. For example, to establish that a deduction was not taken, the executor may produce a copy of the estate or gift tax return filed with respect to the transfer by the first spouse or the first spouse's estate establishing that no deduction was taken under section 2523(f) or section 2056(b)(7). In addition, the executor may establish that no return was filed on the original transfer by the decedent because the value of the first spouse's gross estate was below the threshold requirement for filing under section 6018. Similarly, the executor could establish that the transfer creating the decedent's qualifying income interest for life was made before the effective date of section 2056(b)(7) or section 2523(f).

(d) Amount included—(1) In general. The amount included under this section is the value of the entire interest in which the decedent had a qualifying income interest for life, determined as of the date of the decedent's death (or the alternate valuation date, if applicable). If, in connection with the transfer of property that created the decedent's qualifying income interest for life, a deduction was allowed under section 2056(b)(7) or section 2523(f) for less than the entire interest in the property (i.e., for a fractional or percentage share of the entire interest in the transferred property), the amount includible in the decedent's gross estate under this section is equal to the fair market value of the entire interest in the property on the date of the decedent's death (or the alternate valuation date, if applicable) multiplied by the fractional or percentage share of the interest for which the deduction was taken.

(2) Inclusion of income. If any income from the property for the period between the date of the transfer creating the decedent-spouse's interest and the date of the decedent–spouse's death has not been distributed before the decedent-spouse's death, the undistributed income is included in the decedent-spouse's gross estate under this section to the extent that the income is not so included under any other section of the Internal Revenue Code.

(3) Reduction of includible share in certain cases. If only a fractional or percentage share is includible under this section, the includible share is appropriately reduced if—

(i) The decedent-spouse's interest was in a trust and distributions of principal were made to the spouse during the spouse's lifetime;

(ii) The trust provides that the distributions are to be made from the qualified terminable interest share of the trust; and

(iii) The executor of the decedent-spouse's estate can establish the reduction in that share based on the fair market value of the trust assets at the time of each distribution.

(4) Interest in previously severed trust. If the decedent-spouse's interest was in a trust consisting of only qualified terminable interest property and the trust was severed (in compliance with § 20.2056(b)–7(b) or § 25.2523(f)–1(b) of this chapter) from a trust that, after the severance, held only property that was not qualified terminable interest property, only the value of the property in the severed portion of the trust is includible in the decedent-spouse's gross estate.

(e) Examples. The following examples illustrate the principles in paragraphs (a) through (d) of this section, where the decedent, D, was survived by spouse, S.

Example 1. Inclusion of trust subject to election. Under D's will, assets valued at $800,000 in D's gross estate (net of debts, expenses and other charges, including death taxes, payable from the property) passed in trust with income payable to S for life. Upon S's death, the trust principal is to be distributed to D's children. D's executor elected under section 2056(b)(7) to treat the entire trust property as qualified terminable interest property and claimed a marital deduction of $800,000. S made no disposition of the income interest during S's lifetime under section 2519. On the date of S's death, the fair market value of the trust property was $740,000. S's executor did not elect the alternate valuation date. The amount included in S's gross estate pursuant to section 2044 is $740,000.

Example 2. Inclusion of trust subject to partial election. The facts are the same as in Example 1, except that D's executor elected under section 2056(b)(7) with respect to only 50 percent of the value of the trust ($400,000). Consequently, only the equivalent portion of the trust is included in S's gross estate; i.e., $370,000 (50 percent of $740,000).

Example 3. Spouse receives qualifying income interest in a fraction of trust income. Under D's will, assets valued at $800,000 in D's gross estate (net of debts, expenses and other charges, including death taxes, payable from the property) passed in trust with 20 percent of the trust income payable to S for S's life. The will provides that the trust principal is to be distributed to D's children upon S's death. D's executor elected to deduct, pursuant to section 2056(b)(7), 50 percent of the amount for which the election could be made; i.e., $80,000 (50 percent of 20 percent of $800,000). Consequently, on the death of S, only the equivalent portion of the trust is included in S's gross estate; i.e., $74,000 (50 percent of 20 percent of $740,000).

Example 4. Distribution of corpus during spouse's lifetime. The facts are the same as in Example 3, except that S was entitled to receive all the trust income but the executor of D's estate elected under section 2056(b)(7) with respect to only 50 percent of the value of the trust ($400,000). Pursuant to authority in the will, the trustee made a discretionary distribution of $100,000 of principal to S in 1995 and charged the entire distribution to the qualified terminable interest share. Immediately prior to the distribution, the fair market value of the trust property was $1,100,000 and the qualified terminable interest portion of the trust was 50 percent. Immediately after the distribution, the qualified terminable interest portion of the trust was 45 percent ($450,000 divided by $1,000,000). Provided S's executor can establish the relevant facts, the amount included in S's gross estate is $333,000 (45 percent of $740,000).

Example 5. Spouse assigns a portion of income interest during life. Under D's will, assets valued at $800,000 in D's gross estate (net of debts, expenses and other charges, including death taxes, payable from the property) passed in trust with all the income payable to S, for S's life. The will provides that the trust principal is to be distributed to D's children upon S's death. D's executor elected under section 2056(b)(7) to treat the entire trust property as qualified terminable interest property and claimed a marital deduction of $800,000. During the term of the trust, S transfers to C the right to 40 percent of the income from the trust for S's life. Because S is treated as transferring the entire remainder interest in the trust corpus under section 2519 (as well as 40 percent of the income interest under section 2511), no part of the trust is includible in S's gross estate under section 2044. However, if S retains until death an income interest in 60 percent of the trust corpus (which corpus is treated pursuant to section 2519 as having been transferred by S for both gift and estate tax purposes), 60 percent of the property will be includible in S's gross estate under section 2036(a) and a corresponding adjustment is made in S's adjusted taxable gifts.

Example 6. Inter vivos trust subject to election under section 2523(f). D transferred $800,000 to a trust providing that trust income is to be paid annually to S, for S's life. The trust provides that upon S's death, $100,000 of principal is to be paid to X charity and the remaining principal distributed to D's children. D elected to treat all of the property transferred to the trust as qualified terminable interest property under section 2523(f). At the time of S's death, the fair market value of the trust is $1,000,000. S's executor does not elect the alternate valuation date. The amount included in S's gross estate is $1,000,000; i.e., the fair market value at S's death of the entire trust property. The $100,000 that passes to X charity on S's death is treated as a transfer by S to X charity for purposes of section 2055. Therefore, S's estate is allowed a charitable deduction for the $100,000 transferred from the trust to the charity to the same extent that a deduction would be allowed by section 2055 for a bequest by S to X charity.

Example 7. Spousal interest in the form of an annuity. D died prior to October 24, 1992, the effective date of the Energy Policy Act of 1992 (Pub.L. 102–486). See § 20.2056(b)–7(e). Under D's will, assets valued at $500,000 in D's gross estate (net of debts, expenses and other charges, including death taxes, payable from the property) passed in trust pursuant to which an annuity of $20,000 a year was payable to S for S's life. Trust income not paid to S as an annuity is to be accumulated in the trust and may not be distributed during S's lifetime. D's estate deducted $200,000 under section 2056(b)(7) and § 20.2056(b)–7(e)(2). S did not assign any portion of S's interest during S's life. At the time of S's death, the value of the trust property is $800,000. S's executor does not elect the alternate valuation date. The amount included in S's gross estate pursuant to section 2044 is $320,000 ([$200,000/$500,000] × $800,000).

Example 8. Inclusion of trust property when surviving spouse dies before first decedent's estate tax return is filed. D dies on July 1, 1997. Under the terms of D's will, a trust is established for the benefit of D's spouse, S. The will provides that S is entitled to receive the income from that portion of the trust that the executor elects to treat as qualified terminable interest property. The remaining portion of the trust passes as of D's date of death to a trust for the benefit of C, D's child. The trust terms otherwise provide S with a qualifying income interest for life under section 2056(b)(7)(B)(ii). S dies on February 10, 1998. On April 1, 1998, D's executor files D's estate tax return on which an election is made to treat a portion of the trust as qualified terminable interest property under section 2056(b)(7). S's estate tax return is filed on November 10, 1998. The value on the date of S's death of the portion of the trust for which D's executor made a QTIP election is includible in S's gross estate under section 2044.

[T.D. 8522, 59 FR 9642, Mar. 1, 1994; T.D. 8779, 63 FR 44391, Aug. 18, 1998]

§ 20.2046–1 Disclaimed property.

(a) This section shall apply to the disclaimer or renunciation of an interest in the person disclaiming by a transfer made after December 31, 1976. For rules relating to when the transfer creating the interest occurs, see § 25.2518–2(c)(3) and (c)(4) of this chapter. If a qualified disclaimer is made with respect to such a transfer, the Federal estate tax provisions are to apply with respect to the property interest disclaimed as if the interest had never been transferred to the person making the disclaimer. See section 2518 and the corresponding regulations for rules relating to a qualified disclaimer.

(b) The first and second sentences of this section are applicable for transfers creating the interest to be disclaimed made on or after December 31, 1997.

[T.D. 8095, 51 FR 28368, Aug. 7, 1986; T.D. 8744, 62 FR 68183, Dec. 31, 1997]

§ 20.2053–1 Deductions for expenses, indebtedness, and taxes; in general.

(a) General rule. In determining the taxable estate of a decedent who was a citizen or resident of the United States at death, there are allowed as deductions under section 2053(a) and (b) amounts falling within the following two categories (subject to the limitations contained in this section and in §§ 20.2053–2 through 20.2053–10)—

(1) First category. Amounts which are payable out of property subject to claims and which are allowable by the law of the jurisdiction, whether within or without the United States, under which the estate is being administered for—

(i) Funeral expenses;

(ii) Administration expenses;

(iii) Claims against the estate (including taxes to the extent set forth in § 20.2053–6 and charitable pledges to the extent set forth in § 20.2053–5); and

(iv) Unpaid mortgages on, or any indebtedness in respect of, property, the value of the decedent's interest in which is included in the value of the gross estate undiminished by the mortgage or indebtedness.

As used in this subparagraph, the phrase "allowable by the law of the jurisdiction" means allowable by the law governing the administration of decedents' estates. The phrase has no reference to amounts allowable as deductions under a law which imposes a State death tax. See further §§ 20.2053–2 through 20.2053–7.

(2) Second category. Amounts representing expenses incurred in administering property which is included in the gross estate but which is not subject to claims and which—

(i) Would be allowed as deductions in the first category if the property being administered were subject to claims; and

(ii) Were paid before the expiration of the period of limitation for assessment provided in section 6501.

See further § 20.2053–8.

(b) Provisions applicable to both categories—(1) In general. If the item is not one of those described in paragraph (a) of this section, it is not deductible merely because payment is allowed by the local law. If the amount which may be expended for the particular purpose is limited by the local law no deduction in excess of that limitation is permissible.

(2) Bona fide requirement—(i) In general. Amounts allowed as deductions under section 2053(a) and (b) must be expenses and claims that are bona fide in nature. No deduction is permissible to the extent it is founded on a transfer that is essentially donative in character (a mere cloak for a gift or bequest) except to the extent the deduction is for a claim that would be allowable as a deduction under section 2055 as a charitable bequest.

(ii) Claims and expenses involving family members. Factors indicative (but not necessarily determinative) of the bona fide nature of a claim or expense involving a family member of a decedent, a related entity, or a beneficiary of a decedent's estate or revocable trust, in relevant instances, may include, but are not limited to, the following—

(A) The transaction underlying the claim or expense occurs in the ordinary course of business, is negotiated at arm's length, and is free from donative intent.

(B) The nature of the claim or expense is not related to an expectation or claim of inheritance.

(C) The claim or expense originates pursuant to an agreement between the decedent and the family member, related entity, or beneficiary, and the agreement is substantiated with contemporaneous evidence.

(D) Performance by the claimant is pursuant to the terms of an agreement between the decedent and the family member, related entity, or beneficiary and the performance and the agreement can be substantiated.

(E) All amounts paid in satisfaction or settlement of a claim or expense are reported by each party for Federal income and employment tax purposes, to the extent appropriate, in a manner that is consistent with the reported nature of the claim or expense.

(iii) Definitions. The following definitions apply for purposes of this paragraph (b)(2):

(A) Family members include the spouse of the decedent; the grandparents, parents, siblings, and lineal descendants of the decedent or of the decedent's spouse; and the spouse and lineal descendants of any such grandparent, parent, and sibling. Family members include adopted individuals.

(B) A related entity is an entity in which the decedent, either directly or indirectly, had a beneficial ownership interest at the time of the decedent's death or at any time during the three-year period ending on the decedent's date of death. Such an entity, however, shall not include a publicly-traded entity nor shall it include a closely-held entity in which the combined beneficial interest, either direct or indirect, of the decedent and the decedent's family members, collectively, is less than 30 percent of the beneficial ownership interests (whether voting or non-voting and whether an interest in stock, capital and/or profits), as determined at the time a claim described in this section is being asserted. Notwithstanding the foregoing, an entity in which the decedent, directly or indirectly, had any managing interest (for example, as a general partner of a partnership or as a managing member of a limited liability company) at the time of the decedent's death shall be considered a related entity.

(C) Beneficiaries of a decedent's estate include beneficiaries of a trust of the decedent.

(3) Court decrees and settlements—(i) Court decree. If a court of competent jurisdiction over the administration of an estate reviews and approves expenditures for funeral expenses, administration expenses, claims against the estate, or unpaid mortgages (referred to in this section as a "claim or expense"), a final judicial decision in that matter may be relied upon to establish the amount of a claim or expense that is otherwise deductible under section 2053 and these regulations provided that the court actually passes upon the facts on which deductibility depends. If the court does not pass upon those facts, its decree may not be relied upon to establish the amount of the claim or expense that is otherwise deductible under section 2053. It must appear that the court actually passed upon the merits of the claim. This will be presumed in all cases of an active and genuine contest. If the result reached appears to be unreasonable, this is some evidence that there was not such a contest, but it may be rebutted by proof to the contrary. Any amount meeting the requirements of this paragraph (b)(3)(i) is deductible to the extent it actually has been paid or will be paid, subject to any applicable limitations in this section.

(ii) Claims and expenses where court approval not required under local law. A deduction for the amount of a claim or expense that is otherwise deductible under section 2053 and these regulations will not be denied under section 2053 solely because a local court decree has not been entered with respect to such amount, provided that no court decree is required under applicable law to determine the amount or allowability of the claim or expense.

(iii) Consent decree. A local court decree rendered by consent may be relied on to establish the amount of a claim or expense that is otherwise deductible under section 2053 and these regulations provided that the consent resolves a bona fide issue in a genuine contest. Consent given by all parties having interests adverse to that of the claimant will be presumed to resolve a bona fide issue in a genuine contest. Any amount meeting the requirements of this paragraph (b)(3)(iii) is deductible to the extent it actually has been paid or will be paid, subject to any applicable limitations in this section.

(iv) Settlements. A settlement may be relied on to establish the amount of a claim or expense (whether contingent or noncontingent) that is otherwise deductible under section 2053 and these regulations, provided that the settlement resolves a bona fide issue in a genuine contest and is the product of arm's-length negotiations by parties having adverse interests with respect to the claim or expense. A deduction will not be denied for a settlement amount paid by an estate if the estate can establish that the cost of defending or contesting the claim or expense, or the delay associated with litigating the claim or expense, would impose a higher burden on the estate than the payment of the amount paid to settle the claim or expense. Nevertheless, no deduction will be allowed for amounts paid in settlement of an unenforceable claim. For this purpose, to the extent a claim exceeds an applicable limit under local law, the claim is deemed to be unenforceable. However, as long as the enforceability of the claim is at issue in a bona fide dispute, the claim will not be deemed to be unenforceable for this purpose. Any amount meeting the requirements of this paragraph (b)(3)(iv) is deductible to the extent it actually has been paid or will be paid, subject to any applicable limitations in this section.

(v) Additional rules. Notwithstanding paragraph (b)(3)(i) through (iv) of this section, additional rules may apply to the deductibility of certain claims and expenses. See § 20.2053–2 for additional rules regarding the deductibility of funeral expenses. See § 20.2053–3 for additional rules regarding the deductibility of administration expenses. See § 20.2053–4 for additional rules regarding the deductibility of claims against the estate. See § 20.2053–7 for additional rules regarding the deductibility of unpaid mortgages.

(4) Examples. Unless otherwise provided, assume that the amount of any claim or expense is paid out of property subject to claims and is paid within the time prescribed for filing the "United States Estate (and Generation–Skipping Transfer) Tax Return," Form 706. The following examples illustrate the application of this paragraph (b):

Example 1. Consent decree at variance with the law of the State. Decedent's (D's) estate is probated in State. D's probate estate is valued at $100x. State law provides that the executor's commission shall not exceed 3 percent of the probate estate. A consent decree is entered allowing the executor's commission in the amount of $5x. The estate pays the executor's commission in the amount of $5x. For purposes of section 2053, the executor may deduct only $3x of the $5x expense paid for the executor's commission because the amount approved by the consent decree in excess of $3x is in excess of the applicable limit for executor's commissions under local law. Therefore, for purposes of section 2053, the consent decree may not be relied upon to establish the amount of the expense for the executor's commission.

Example 2. Decedent's (D's) estate is probated in State. State law grants authority to an executor to administer an estate without court approval, so long as notice of and a right to object to a proposed action is provided to interested persons. The executor of D's estate (E) proposes to sell property of the estate in order to pay the debts of D. E gives requisite notice to all interested parties and no interested person objects. E sells the real estate and pays a real estate commission of $20x to a professional real estate agent. The amount of the real estate commission paid does not exceed the applicable limit under State law. Provided that the sale of the property was necessary to pay D's debts, expenses of administration, or taxes, to preserve the estate, or to effect distribution, the executor may deduct the $20x expense for the real estate commission under section 2053 even though no court decree was entered approving the expense.

Example 3. Claim by family member. For a period of three years prior to D's death, D's niece (N) provides accounting and bookkeeping services on D's behalf. N is a CPA and provides similar accounting and bookkeeping services to unrelated clients. At the end of each month, N presents an itemized bill to D for services rendered. The fees charged by N conform to the prevailing market rate for the services rendered and are comparable to the fees N charges other clients for similar services. The amount due is timely paid each month by D and is properly reported for Federal income and employment tax purposes by N. In the six months prior to D's death, D's poor health prevents D from making payments to N for the amount due. After D's death, N asserts a claim against the estate for $25x, an amount representing the amount due for the six-month period prior to D's death. D's estate pays $25x to N in satisfaction of the claim before the return is timely filed and N properly reports the $25x received by E for income tax purposes. Barring any other relevant facts or circumstances, E may rely on the following factors to establish that the claim is bona fide: (1) N's claim for services rendered arose in the ordinary course of business, as N is a CPA performing similar services for other clients; (2) the fees charged were deemed to be negotiated at arm's length, as the fees were consistent with the fees N charged for similar services to unrelated clients; (3) the billing records and the records of D's timely payments to N constitute contemporaneous evidence of an agreement between D and N for N's bookkeeping services; and (4) the amount of the payments to N is properly reported by N for Federal income and employment tax purposes. E may deduct the amount paid to N in satisfaction of the claim.

(c) Provision applicable to first category only. Deductions of the first category (described in paragraph (a)(1) of this section) are limited under section 2053(a) to amounts which would be property allowable out of property subject to claims by the law of the jurisdiction under which the decedent's estate is being administered. Further, the total allowable amount of deductions of the first category is limited by section 2053(c)(2) to the sum of—

(1) The value of property included in the decedent's gross estate and subject to claims, plus

(2) Amounts paid, out of property not subject to claims against the decedent's estate, within 9 months (15 months in the case of the estate of a decedent dying before January 1, 1971) after the decedent's death (the period within which the estate tax return must be filed under section 6075), or within any extension of time for filing the return granted under section 6081.

The term "property subject to claims" is defined in section 2053(c)(2) as meaning the property includible in the gross estate which, or the avails of which, under the applicable law, would bear the burden of the payment of these deductions in the final adjustment and settlement of the decedent's estate. However, for the purposes of this definition, the value of property subject to claims is first reduced by the amount of any deduction allowed under section 2054 for any losses from casualty or theft incurred during the settlement of the estate attributable to such property. The application of this paragraph may be illustrated by the following examples:

Example (1). The only item in the gross estate is real property valued at $250,000 which the decedent and his surviving spouse held as tenants by the entirety. Under the local law this real property is not subject to claims. Funeral expenses of $1,200 and debts of the decedent in the amount of $1,500 are allowable under local law. Before the prescribed date for filing the estate tax return, the surviving spouse paid the funeral expenses and $1,000 of the debts. The remaining $500 of the debts was paid by her after the prescribed date for filing the return. The total amount allowable as deductions under section 2053 is limited to $2,200, the amount paid prior to the prescribed date for filing the return.

Example (2). The only two items in the gross estate were a bank deposit of $20,000 and insurance in the amount of $150,000. The insurance was payable to the decedent's surviving spouse and under local law was not subject to claims. Funeral expenses of $1,000 and debts in the amount of $29,000 were allowable under local law. A son was executor of the estate and before the prescribed date for filing the estate tax return he paid the funeral expenses of $9,000 of the debts, using therefor $5,000 of the bank deposit and $5,000 supplied by the surviving spouse. After the prescribed date for filing the return, the executor paid the remaining $20,000 of the debts, using for that purpose the $15,000 left in the bank account plus an additional $5,000 supplied by the surviving spouse. The total amount allowable as deductions under section 2053 is limited to $25,000 ($20,000 of property subject to claims plus the $5,000 additional amount which, before the prescribed date for filing the return, was paid out of property not subject to claims).

(d) Amount deductible—(1) General rule. To take into account properly events occurring after the date of a decedent's death in determining the amount deductible under section 2053 and these regulations, the deduction for any claim or expense described in paragraph (a) of this section is limited to the total amount actually paid in settlement or satisfaction of that item (subject to any applicable limitations in this section). However, see paragraph (d)(4) of this section for the rules for deducting certain ascertainable amounts; see § 20.2053–4(b) and (c) for the rules regarding the deductibility of certain claims against the estate; and see § 20.2053–7 for the rules regarding the deductibility of unpaid mortgages and other indebtedness.

(2) Application of post-death events. In determining whether and to what extent a deduction under section 2053 is allowable, events occurring after the date of a decedent's death will be taken into consideration—

(i) Until the expiration of the applicable period of limitations on assessment prescribed in section 6501 (including without limitation at all times during which the running of the period of limitations is suspended); and

(ii) During subsequent periods, in determining the amount (if any) of an overpayment of estate tax due in connection with a claim for refund filed within the time prescribed in section 6511(a).

(3) Reimbursements. A deduction is not allowed to the extent that a claim or expense described in paragraph (a) of this section is or could be compensated for by insurance or otherwise could be reimbursed. If the executor is able to establish that only a partial reimbursement could be collected, then only that portion of the potential reimbursement that reasonably could have been expected to be collected will reduce the estate's deductible portion of the total claim or expense. An executor may certify that the executor neither knows nor reasonably should have known of any available reimbursement for a claim or expense described in section 2053(a) or (b) on the estate's United States Estate (and Generation–Skipping Transfer) Tax Return (Form 706), in accordance with the instructions for that form. A potential reimbursement will not reduce the deductible amount of a claim or expense to the extent that the executor, on Form 706 and in accordance with the instructions for that form, provides a reasonable explanation for his or her reasonable determination that the burden of necessary collection efforts in pursuit of a right of reimbursement would outweigh the anticipated benefit from those efforts. Nevertheless, even if a reasonable explanation is provided, subsequent events (including without limitation an actual reimbursement) occurring within the period described in § 20.2053–1(d)(2) will be considered in determining the amount (if any) of a reduction under this paragraph (d)(3) in the deductible amount of a claim or expense.

(4) Exception for certain ascertainable amounts—(i) General rule. A deduction will be allowed for a claim or expense that satisfies all applicable requirements even though it is not yet paid, provided that the amount to be paid is ascertainable with reasonable certainty and will be paid. For example, executors' commissions and attorneys' fees that are not yet paid, and that meet the requirements for deductibility under § 20.2053–3(b) and (c), respectively, are deemed to be ascertainable with reasonable certainty and may be deducted if such expenses will be paid. However, no deduction may be taken upon the basis of a vague or uncertain estimate. To the extent a claim or expense is contested or contingent, such a claim or expense cannot be ascertained with reasonable certainty.

(ii) Effect of post-death events. A deduction under this paragraph (d)(4) will be allowed to the extent the Commissioner is reasonably satisfied that the amount to be paid is ascertainable with reasonable certainty and will be paid. In making this determination, the Commissioner will take into account events occurring after the date of a decedent's death. To the extent the amount for which a deduction was claimed does not satisfy the requirements of this paragraph (d)(4), and is not otherwise deductible, the deduction will be disallowed by the Commissioner. If a deduction is claimed on Form 706 for an amount that is not yet paid and the deduction is disallowed in whole or in part (or if no deduction is claimed on Form 706), then if the claim or expense subsequently satisfies the requirements of this paragraph (d)(4) or is paid, relief may be sought by filing a claim for refund. To preserve the estate's right to claim a refund for amounts becoming deductible after the expiration of the period of limitation for the filing of a claim for refund, a protective claim for refund may be filed in accordance with paragraph (d)(5) of this section.

(5) Protective claim for refund—(i) In general. A protective claim for refund under this section may be filed at any time before the expiration of the period of limitation prescribed in section 6511(a) for the filing of a claim for refund to preserve the estate's right to claim a refund by reason of claims or expenses that are not paid or do not otherwise meet the requirements of deductibility under section 2053 and these regulations until after the expiration of the period of limitation for filing a claim for refund. Such a protective claim shall be made in accordance with guidance that may be provided from time to time by publication in the Internal Revenue Bulletin (see § 601.601(d)(2)(ii)(b)). Although the protective claim need not state a particular dollar amount or demand an immediate refund, a protective claim must identify each outstanding claim or expense that would have been deductible under section 2053(a) or (b) if such item already had been paid and must describe the reasons and contingencies delaying the actual payment of the claim or expense. Action on protective claims will proceed after the executor has notified the Commissioner within a reasonable period that the contingency has been resolved and that the amount deductible under § 20.2053–1 has been established.

(ii) Effect on marital and charitable deduction. To the extent that a protective claim for refund is filed with respect to a claim or expense that would have been deductible under section 2053(a) or (b) if such item already had been paid and that is payable out of a share that meets the requirements for a charitable deduction under section 2055 or a marital deduction under section 2056 or section 2056A, or from a combination thereof, neither the charitable deduction nor the marital deduction shall be reduced by the amount of such claim or expense until the amount is actually paid or meets the requirements of paragraph (d)(4) of this section for deducting certain ascertainable amounts or the requirements of § 20.2053–4(b) or (c) for deducting certain claims against the estate.

(6) [Reserved]

(7) Examples. Assume that the amounts described in section 2053(a) are payable out of property subject to claims and are allowable by the law of the jurisdiction governing the administration of the estate, whether the applicable jurisdiction is within or outside of the United States. Assume that the claims against the estate are not deductible under § 20.2053–4(b) or (c). Also assume, unless otherwise provided, that none of the limitations on the amount of the deduction described in this section apply to the deduction claimed under section 2053. The following examples illustrate the application of this paragraph (d):

Example 1. Amount of expense ascertainable. Decedent's (D's) estate was probated in State. State law provides that the personal representative shall receive compensation equal to 2.5 percent of the value of the probate estate. The executor (E) may claim a deduction for estimated fees equal to 2.5 percent of D's probate estate on the Form 706 filed for D's estate under the rule for deducting certain ascertainable amounts set forth in paragraph (d)(4) of this section, provided that the estimated amount will be paid. However, the Commissioner will disallow the deduction upon examination of the estate's Form 706 to the extent that the amount for which a deduction was claimed no longer satisfies the requirements of paragraph (d)(4) of this section. If this occurs, E may file a protective claim for refund in accordance with paragraph (d)(5) of this section in order to preserve the estate's right to claim a refund for the amount of the fee that is subsequently paid or that subsequently meets the requirements of paragraph (d)(4) of this section for deducting certain ascertainable amounts.

Example 2. Amount of claim not ascertainable. Prior to death, Decedent (D) is sued by Claimant (C) for $100x in a tort proceeding and responds asserting affirmative defenses available to D under applicable local law. C and D are unrelated. D subsequently dies and D's Form 706 is due before a final judgment is entered in the case. The executor of D's estate (E) may not claim a deduction with respect to C's claim on D's Form 706 under the special rule contained in paragraph (d)(4) of this section because the deductible amount cannot be ascertained with reasonable certainty. However, E may file a timely protective claim for refund in accordance with paragraph (d)(5) of this section in order to preserve the estate's right to subsequently claim a refund at the time a final judgment is entered in the case and the claim is either paid or meets the requirements of paragraph (d)(4) of this section for deducting certain ascertainable amounts.

Example 3. Amount of claim payable out of property qualifying for marital deduction. The facts are the same as in Example 2 except that the applicable credit amount, under section 2010, against the estate tax was fully consumed by D's lifetime gifts, D is survived by Spouse (S), and D's estate passes entirely to S in a bequest that qualifies for the marital deduction under section 2056. Even though any amount D's estate ultimately pays with respect to C's claim will be paid from the assets qualifying for the marital deduction, in filing Form 706, E need not reduce the amount of the marital deduction claimed on D's Form 706. Instead, pursuant to the protective claim for refund filed by E, the marital deduction will be reduced by the claim once a final judgment is entered in the case. At that time, a deduction will be allowed for the amount that is either paid or meets the requirements of paragraph (d)(4) of this section for deducting certain ascertainable amounts.

(e) Disallowance of double deductions. See section 642(g) and § 1.642(g)–1 with respect to the disallowance for income tax purposes of certain deductions unless the right to take such deductions for estate tax purposes is waived.

(f) Effective/applicability date. This section applies to the estates of decedents dying on or after October 20, 2009.

[T.D. 6296, 23 FR 4529, June 24, 1958, as amended by T.D. 7238, 37 FR 28719, Dec. 29, 1972; T.D. 9468, 74 FR 53657, Oct. 20, 2009; 74 FR 61525, Nov. 25, 2009]

§ 20.2053–2 Deduction for funeral expenses.

Such amounts for funeral expenses are allowed as deductions from a decedent's gross estate as (a) are actually expended, (b) would be properly allowable out of property subject to claims under the laws of the local jurisdiction, and (c) satisfy the requirements of paragraph (c) of § 20.2053–1. A reasonable expenditure for a tombstone, monument, or mausoleum, or for a burial lot, either for the decedent or his family, including a reasonable expenditure for its future care, may be deducted under this heading, provided such an expenditure is allowable by the local law. Included in funeral expenses is the cost of transportation of the person bringing the body to the place of burial.

[T.D. 6296, 23 FR 4529, June 24, 1958]

§ 20.2053–3 Deduction for expenses of administering estate.

(a) In general. The amounts deductible from a decedent's gross estate as "administration expenses" of the first category (see paragraphs (a) and (c) of § 20.2053–1) are limited to such expenses as are actually and necessarily, incurred in the administration of the decedent's estate; that is, in the collection of assets, payment of debts, and distribution of property to the persons entitled to it. The expenses contemplated in the law are such only as attend the settlement of an estate and the transfer of the property of the estate to individual beneficiaries or to a trustee, whether the trustee is the executor or some other person. Expenditures not essential to the proper settlement of the estate, but incurred for the individual benefit of the heirs, legatees, or devisees, may not be taken as deductions. Administration expenses include (1) executor's commissions; (2) attorney's fees; and (3) miscellaneous expenses. Each of these classes is considered separately in paragraphs (b) through (d) of this section.

(b) Executor's commissions. (1) Executors' commissions are deductible to the extent permitted by § 20.2053–1 and this section, but no deduction may be taken if no commissions are to be paid. In addition, the amount of the commissions claimed as a deduction must be in accordance with the usually accepted standards and practice of allowing such an amount in estates of similar size and character in the jurisdiction in which the estate is being administered, or any deviation from the usually accepted standards or range of amounts (permissible under applicable local law) must be justified to the satisfaction of the Commissioner.

(2) A bequest or devise to the executor in lieu of commissions is not deductible. If, however, the terms of the will set forth the compensation payable to the executor for services to be rendered in the administration of the estate, a deduction may be taken to the extent that the amount so fixed does not exceed the compensation allowable by the local law or practice and to the extent permitted by § 20.2053–1.

(3) Except to the extent that a trustee is in fact performing services with respect to property subject to claims which would normally be performed by an executor, amounts paid as trustees' commissions do not constitute expenses of administration under the first category, and are only deductible as expenses of the second category to the extent provided in § 20.2053–8.

(c) Attorney's fees. (1) Attorney's fees are deductible to the extent permitted by § 20.2053–1 and this section. Further, the amount of the fees claimed as a deduction may not exceed a reasonable remuneration for the services rendered, taking into account the size and character of the estate, the law and practice in the jurisdiction in which the estate is being administered, and the skill and expertise of the attorneys.

(2) A deduction for attorneys' fees incurred in contesting an asserted deficiency or in prosecuting a claim for refund should be claimed at the time the deficiency is contested or the refund claim is prosecuted. A deduction for reasonable attorney's fees actually incurred in contesting an asserted deficiency or in prosecuting a claim for refund will be allowed to the extent permitted by § 20.2053–1 even though the deduction, as such, was not claimed on the estate tax return or in the claim for refund. A deduction for these fees shall not be denied, and the sufficiency of a claim for refund shall not be questioned, solely by reason of the fact that the amount of the fees to be paid was not established at the time that the right to the deduction was claimed.

(3) Attorneys' fees incurred by beneficiaries incident to litigation as to their respective interests are not deductible if the litigation is not essential to the proper settlement of the estate within the meaning of paragraph (a) of this section. An attorney's fee not meeting this test is not deductible as an administration expense under section 2053 and this section, even if it is approved by a probate court as an expense payable or reimbursable by the estate.

(d) Miscellaneous administration expenses. **(1)** Miscellaneous administration expenses include such expenses as court costs, surrogates' fees, accountants' fees, appraisers' fees, clerk hire, etc. Expenses necessarily incurred in preserving and distributing the estate, including the cost of storing or maintaining property of the estate if it is impossible to effect immediate distribution to the beneficiaries, are deductible to the extent permitted by § 20.2053–1. Expenses for preserving and caring for the property may not include outlays for additions or improvements; nor will such expenses be allowed for a longer period than the executor is reasonably required to retain the property.

(2) Expenses for selling property of the estate are deductible to the extent permitted by § 20.2053–1 if the sale is necessary in order to pay the decedent's debts, expenses of administration, or taxes, to preserve the estate, or to effect distribution. The phrase "expenses for selling property" includes brokerage fees and other expenses attending the sale, such as the fees of an auctioneer if it is reasonably necessary to employ one. Where an item included in the gross estate is disposed of in a bona fide sale (including a redemption) to a dealer in such items at a price below its fair market value, for purposes of this paragraph there shall be treated as an expense for selling the item whichever of the following amounts is the lesser: (i) The amount by which the fair market value of the property on the applicable valuation date exceeds the proceeds of the sale, or (ii) the amount by which the fair market value of the property on the date of the sale exceeds the proceeds of the sale. The principles used in determining the value at which an item of property is included in the gross estate shall be followed in arriving at the fair market value of the property for purposes of this paragraph. See §§ 20.2031–1 through 20.2031–9.

(3) Expenses incurred in defending the estate against claims described in section 2053(a)(3) are deductible to the extent permitted by § 20.2053–1 if the expenses are incurred incident to the assertion of defenses to the claim available under the applicable law, even if the estate ultimately does not prevail. For purposes of this paragraph (d)(3), "expenses incurred in defending the estate against claims" include costs relating to the arbitration and mediation of contested issues, costs associated with defending the estate against claims (whether or not enforceable), and costs associated with reaching a negotiated settlement of the issues.

(e) Effective/applicability date. This section applies to the estates of decedents dying on or after October 20, 2009.

[T.D. 6296, 23 FR 4529, June 24, 1958, as amended by T.D. 6826, 30 FR 7708, June 15, 1965; 44 FR 23525, April 20, 1979; T.D. 9468, 74 FR 53660, Oct. 20, 2009]

§ 20.2053–4 Deduction for claims against the estate.

(a) In general—(1) General rule. For purposes of this section, liabilities imposed by law or arising out of contracts or torts are deductible if they meet the applicable requirements set forth in

§ 20.2053–1 and this section. To be deductible, a claim against a decedent's estate must represent a personal obligation of the decedent existing at the time of the decedent's death. Except as otherwise provided in paragraphs (b) and (c) of this section and to the extent permitted by § 20.2053–1, the amounts that may be deducted as claims against a decedent's estate are limited to the amounts of bona fide claims that are enforceable against the decedent's estate (and are not unenforceable when paid) and claims that—

(i) Are actually paid by the estate in satisfaction of the claim; or

(ii) Meet the requirements of § 20.2053–1(d)(4) for deducting certain ascertainable amounts.

(2) Effect of post-death events. Events occurring after the date of a decedent's death shall be considered in determining whether and to what extent a deduction is allowable under section 2053. See § 20.2053–1(d)(2).

(b) Exception for claims and counterclaims in related matter—(1) General rule. If a decedent's gross estate includes one or more claims or causes of action and there are one or more claims against the decedent's estate in the same or a substantially-related matter, or, if a decedent's gross estate includes a particular asset and there are one or more claims against the decedent's estate integrally related to that particular asset, the executor may deduct on the estate's United States Estate (and Generation–Skipping Transfer) Tax Return (Form 706) the current value of the claim or claims against the estate, even though payment has not been made, provided that—

(i) Each such claim against the estate otherwise satisfies the applicable requirements set forth in § 20.2053–1;

(ii) Each such claim against the estate represents a personal obligation of the decedent existing at the time of the decedent's death;

(iii) Each such claim is enforceable against the decedent's estate (and is not unenforceable when paid);

(iv) The value of each such claim against the estate is determined from a "qualified appraisal" performed by a "qualified appraiser" within the meaning of section 170 of the Internal Revenue Code and the corresponding regulations;

(v) The value of each such claim against the estate is subject to adjustment for post-death events; and

(vi) The aggregate value of the related claims or assets included in the decedent's gross estate exceeds 10 percent of the decedent's gross estate.

(2) Limitation on deduction. The deduction under this paragraph (b) is limited to the value of the related claims or particular assets included in decedent's gross estate.

(3) Effect of post-death events. If, under this paragraph (b), a deduction is claimed on Form 706 for a claim against the estate and, during the period described in § 20.2053–1(d)(2), the claim is paid or meets the requirements of § 20.2053–1(d)(4) for deducting certain ascertainable amounts, the claimed deduction is subject to adjustment to reflect, and may not exceed, the amount paid on the claim or the amount meeting the requirements of § 20.2053–1(d)(4). If, under this paragraph (b), a deduction is claimed on Form 706 for a claim against the estate and, during the period described in § 20.2053–1(d)(2), the claim remains unpaid (and does not meet the requirements of § 20.2053–1(d)(4) for deducting certain ascertainable amounts), the claimed deduction is subject to adjustment to reflect, and may not exceed, the current valuation of the claim. A valuation of the claim will be considered current if it reflects events occurring after the decedent's death. With regard to any amount in excess of the amount deductible under this paragraph (b), an estate may preserve the estate's right to claim a refund for claims that are paid or that meet the requirements of § 20.2053–(1)(d)(4) after the expiration of the period of limitation for filing a claim for refund by filing a protective claim for refund in accordance with the rules in § 20.2053–1(d)(5).

(c) Exception for claims totaling not more than $500,000—(1) General rule. An executor may deduct on Form 706 the current value of one or more claims against the estate even though payment has not been made on the claim or claims to the extent that—

(i) Each such claim against the estate otherwise satisfies the applicable requirements for deductibility set forth in § 20.2053–1;

(ii) Each such claim against the estate represents a personal obligation of the decedent existing at the time of the decedent's death;

(iii) Each such claim is enforceable against the decedent's estate (and is not unenforceable when paid);

(iv) The value of each such claim against the estate is determined from a "qualified appraisal" performed by a "qualified appraiser" within the meaning of section 170 of the Internal Revenue Code and the corresponding regulations;

(v) The total amount deducted by the estate under this paragraph (c) does not exceed $500,000;

(vi) The full value of each claim, rather than just a portion of that amount, must be deductible under this paragraph (c) and, for this purpose, the full value of each such claim is deemed to be the unpaid amount of that claim that is not deductible after the application of §§ 20.2053–1 and 20.2053–4(b); and

(vii) The value of each claim deducted under this paragraph (c) is subject to adjustment for post-death events.

(2) Effect of post-death events. If, under this paragraph (c), a deduction is claimed for a claim against the estate and, during the period described in § 20.2053–1(d)(2), the claim is paid or meets the requirements of § 20.2053–1(d)(4) for deducting certain ascertainable amounts, the amount of the allowable deduction for that claim is subject to adjustment to reflect, and may not exceed, the amount paid on the claim or the amount meeting the requirements of § 20.2053–1(d)(4). If, under this paragraph (c), a deduction is claimed for a claim against the estate and, during the period described in § 20.2053–1(d)(2), the claim remains unpaid (and does not meet the requirements of § 20.2053–1(d)(4) for deducting certain ascertainable amounts), the amount of the allowable deduction for that claim is subject to adjustment to reflect, and may not exceed, the current value of the claim. The value of the claim will be considered current if it reflects events occurring after the decedent's death. To claim a deduction for amounts in excess of the amount deductible under this paragraph (c), the estate may preserve the estate's right to claim a refund for claims that are not paid or that do not meet the requirements of § 20.2053–1(d)(4) until after the expiration of the period of limitation for the filing of a claim for refund by filing a protective claim for refund in accordance with the rules in § 20.2053–1(d)(5).

(3) Examples. The following examples illustrate the application of this paragraph (c). Assume that the value of each claim is determined from a "qualified appraisal" performed by a "qualified appraiser" and reflects events occurring after the death of the decedent (D). Also assume that each claim represents a personal obligation of D that existed at D's death, that each claim is enforceable against the decedent's estate (and is not unenforceable when paid), and that each claim otherwise satisfies the requirements for deductibility of § 20.2053–1.

Example 1. There are three claims against the estate of the decedent (D) that are not paid and are not deductible under § 20.2053–1(d)(4) or paragraph (b) of this section: $25,000 of Claimant A, $35,000 of Claimant B, and $1,000,000 of Claimant C. The executor of D's estate (E) may not claim a deduction under this paragraph with respect to any portion of the claim of Claimant C because the value of that claim exceeds $500,000. E may claim a deduction under this paragraph for the total amount of the claims filed by Claimant A and Claimant B ($60,000) because the aggregate value of the full amount of those claims does not exceed $500,000.

Example 2. There are three claims against the estate of the decedent (D) that are not paid and are not deductible under § 20.2053–1(d)(4) or paragraph (b) of this section; specifically, a separate $200,000 claim of each of three claimants, A, B and C. The executor of D's estate (E) may claim a deduction under this paragraph for any two of these three claims because the aggregate value of the full amount of any two of the claims does not exceed $500,000. E may not deduct any part of the value of the remaining claim under this paragraph because the aggregate value of the full amount of all three claims would exceed $500,000.

Example 3. As a result of an automobile accident involving the decedent (D) and A, D's gross estate includes a claim against A that is valued at $750,000. In the same matter, A files a counterclaim against D's estate that is valued at $1,000,000. A's claim against D's estate is not paid and is not deductible under § 20.2053–1(d)(4). All other section 2053 claims and expenses of D's estate have been paid and are deductible. The executor of D's estate (E) deducts $750,000 of A's claim against the estate under § 20.2053–4(b). E may claim a deduction under this paragraph (c) for the total value of A's claim not deducted under § 20.2053–4(b), or $250,000. If, instead, the value of A's claim against D's estate is $1,500,000, so that the amount not deductible under § 20.2053–4(b) exceeds $500,000, no deduction is available under this paragraph (c).

(d) Special rules—(1) Potential and unmatured claims. Except as provided in § 20.2053–1(d)(4) and in paragraphs (b) and (c) of this section, no estate tax deduction may be taken for a claim against the decedent's estate while it remains a potential or unmatured claim. Claims that later mature may be deducted (to the extent permitted by § 20.2053–1) in connection with a timely claim for refund. To preserve the estate's right to claim a refund for claims that mature and become deductible after the expiration of the period of limitation for filing a claim for refund, a protective claim for refund may be filed in accordance with § 20.2053–

1(d)(5). See § 20.2053–1(b)(3) for rules relating to the treatment of court decrees and settlements.

(2) Contested claims. Except as provided in paragraphs (b) and (c) of this section, no estate tax deduction may be taken for a claim against the decedent's estate to the extent the estate is contesting the decedent's liability. Contested claims that later mature may be deducted (to the extent permitted by § 20.2053–1) in connection with a claim for refund filed within the time prescribed in section 6511(a). To preserve the estate's right to claim a refund for claims that mature and become deductible after the expiration of the period of limitation for filing a claim for refund, a protective claim for refund may be filed in accordance with § 20.2053–1(d)(5). See § 20.2053–1(b)(3) for rules relating to the treatment of court decrees and settlements.

(3) Claims against multiple parties. If the decedent or the decedent's estate is one of two or more parties against whom the claim is being asserted, the estate may deduct only the portion of the total claim due from and paid by the estate, reduced by the total of any reimbursement received from another party, insurance, or otherwise. The estate's deductible portion also will be reduced by the contribution or other amount the estate could have collected from another party or an insurer but which the estate declines or fails to attempt to collect. See further § 20.2053–1(d)(3).

(4) Unenforceable claims. Claims that are unenforceable prior to or at the decedent's death are not deductible, even if they are actually paid. Claims that become unenforceable during the administration of the estate are not deductible to the extent that they are paid (or will be paid) after they become unenforceable. However, see § 20.2053–1(b)(3)(iv) regarding a claim whose enforceability is at issue.

(5) Claims founded upon a promise. Except with regard to pledges or subscriptions (see § 20.2053–5), section 2053(c)(1)(A) provides that the deduction for a claim founded upon a promise or agreement is limited to the extent that the promise or agreement was bona fide and in exchange for adequate and full consideration in money or money's worth; that is, the promise or agreement must have been bargained for at arm's length and the price must have been an adequate and full equivalent reducible to a money value.

(6) Recurring payments—(i) Noncontingent obligations. If a decedent is obligated to make recurring payments on an enforceable and certain claim that satisfies the requirements for deductibility under this section and the payments are not subject to a contingency, the amount of the claim will be deemed ascertainable with reasonable certainty for purposes of the rule for deducting certain ascertainable amounts set forth in § 20.2053–1(d)(4). If the recurring payments will be paid, a deduction will be allowed under the rule for deducting certain ascertainable amounts set forth in § 20.2053–1(d)(4) (subject to any applicable limitations in § 20.2053–1). Recurring payments for purposes of this section exclude those payments made in connection with a mortgage or indebtedness described in and governed by § 20.2053–7. If a decedent's obligation to make a recurring payment is contingent on the death or remarriage of the claimant and otherwise satisfies the requirements of this paragraph (d)(6)(i), the amount of the claim (measured according to actuarial principles, using factors set forth in the transfer tax regulations or otherwise provided by the IRS) will be deemed ascertainable with reasonable certainty for purposes of the rule for deducting certain ascertainable amounts set forth in § 20.2053–1(d)(4).

(ii) Contingent obligations. If a decedent has a recurring obligation to pay an enforceable and certain claim but the decedent's obligation is subject to a contingency or is not otherwise described in paragraph (d)(6)(i) of this section, the amount of the claim is not ascertainable with reasonable certainty for purposes of the rule for deducting certain ascertainable amounts set forth in § 20.2053–1(d)(4). Accordingly, the amount deductible is limited to amounts actually paid by the estate in satisfaction of the claim in accordance with § 20.2053–1(d)(1) (subject to any applicable limitations in § 20.2053–1).

(iii) Purchase of commercial annuity to satisfy recurring obligation to pay. If a decedent has a recurring obligation (whether or not contingent) to pay an enforceable and certain claim and the estate purchases a commercial annuity from an unrelated dealer in commercial annuities in an arm's-length transaction to satisfy the obligation, the amount deductible by the estate (subject to any applicable limitations in § 20.2053–1) is the sum of—

(A) The amount paid for the commercial annuity, to the extent that the amount paid is not refunded, or expected to be refunded, to the estate;

(B) Any amount actually paid to the claimant by the estate prior to the purchase of the commercial annuity; and

(C) Any amount actually paid to the claimant by the estate in excess of the annuity amount as is necessary to satisfy the recurring obligation.

(7) Examples. The following examples illustrate the application of paragraph (d) of this section. Except as is otherwise provided in the examples, assume—

(i) A claim satisfies the applicable requirements set forth in § 20.2053-1 and paragraph (a) of this section, is payable from property subject to claims, and the amount of the claim is not subject to any other applicable limitations in § 20.2053-1;

(ii) A claim is not deductible under paragraphs (b) or (c) of this section as an exception to the general rule contained in paragraph (a) of this section; and

(iii) The claimant (C) is not a family member, related entity or beneficiary of the estate of decedent (D) and is not the executor (E).

Example 1. Contested claim, single defendant, no decision. D is sued by C for $100x in a tort proceeding and responds asserting affirmative defenses available to D under applicable local law. D dies and E is substituted as defendant in the suit. D's Form 706 is due before a judgment is reached in the case. D's gross estate exceeds $100x. E may not take a deduction on Form 706 for the claim against the estate. However, E may claim a deduction under § 20.2053-3(c) or § 20.2053-3(d)(3) for expenses incurred in defending the estate against the claim if the expenses have been paid in accordance with § 20.2053-1(d)(1) or if the expenses meet the requirements of § 20.2053-1(d)(4) for deducting certain ascertainable amounts. E may file a protective claim for refund before the expiration of the period of limitation prescribed in section 6511(a) in order to preserve the estate's right to claim a refund, if the amount of the claim will not be paid or cannot be ascertained with reasonable certainty by the expiration of this limitation period. If payment is subsequently made pursuant to a court decision or a settlement, the payment, as well as expenses incurred incident to the claim and not previously deducted, may be deducted and relief may be sought in connection with a timely-filed claim for refund.

Example 2. Contested claim, single defendant, final court decree and payment. The facts are the same as in Example 1 except that, before the Form 706 is timely filed, the court enters a decision in favor of C, no timely appeal is filed, and payment is made. E may claim a deduction on Form 706 for the amount paid in satisfaction of the claim against the estate pursuant to the final decision of the local court, including any interest accrued prior to D's death. In addition, E may claim a deduction under § 20.2053-3(c) or § 20.2053-3(d)(3) for expenses incurred in defending the estate against the claim and in processing payment of the claim if the expenses have been paid in accordance with § 20.2053-1(d)(1) or if the expenses meet the requirements of § 20.2053-1(d)(4) for deducting certain ascertainable amounts.

Example 3. Contested claim, single defendant, settlement and payment. The facts are the same as in Example 1 except that a settlement is reached between E and C for $80x and payment is made before Form 706 is timely filed. E may claim a deduction on Form 706 for the amount paid to C ($80x) in satisfaction of the claim against the estate. In addition, E may claim a deduction under § 20.2053-3(c) or § 20.2053-3(d)(3) for expenses incurred in defending the estate, reaching a settlement, and processing payment of the claim if the expenses have been paid in accordance with § 20.2053-1(d)(1) or if the expenses meet the requirements of § 20.2053-1(d)(4) for deducting certain ascertainable amounts.

Example 4. Contested claim, multiple defendants. The facts are the same as in Example 1 except that the suit filed by C lists D and an unrelated third-party (K) as defendants. If the claim against the estate is not resolved prior to the time the Form 706 is filed, E may not take a deduction for the claim on Form 706. If payment is subsequently made of D's share of the claim pursuant to a court decision holding D liable for 40 percent of the amount due and K liable for 60 percent of the amount due, then E may claim a deduction for the amount paid in satisfaction of the claim against the estate representing D's share of the liability as assigned by the court decree ($40x), plus any interest on that share accrued prior to D's death. If the court decision finds D and K jointly and severally liable for the entire $100x and D's estate pays the entire $100x but could have reasonably collected $50x from K in reimbursement, E may claim a deduction of $50x together with the interest on $50x accrued prior to D's death. In both instances, E also may claim a deduction under § 20.2053-3(c) or § 20.2053-3(d)(3) for expenses incurred and not previously deducted in defending the estate against the claim and processing payment of the amount due from D if the expenses have been paid in accordance with § 20.2053-1(d)(1) or if the expenses meet the requirements of § 20.2053-1(d)(4) for deducting certain ascertainable amounts.

Example 5. Contested claim, multiple defendants, settlement and payment. The facts are the same as in Example 1 except that the suit filed by C lists D and an unrelated third-party (K) as defendants. D's estate settles with C for $10x and payment is made before Form 706 is timely filed. E may take a deduction on Form 706 for the amount paid to C ($10x) in satisfaction of the claim against the estate. In addition, E may claim a deduction under § 20.2053-3(c) or § 20.2053-3(d)(3) for expenses incurred in defending the estate, reaching a settlement, and processing payment of the claim if the expenses have been paid in accordance with § 20.2053-1(d)(1) or if the expenses meet the requirements of § 20.2053-1(d)(4) for deducting certain ascertainable amounts.

Example 6. Mixed claims. During life, D contracts with C to perform specific work on D's home for $75x. Under the contract, additional work must be approved in advance by D. C performs additional work and sues D for $100x for work completed including the $75x agreed to in the contract. D dies and D's Form 706 is due before a judgment is reached in the case. E accepts liability of $75x but contests liability of $25x. E may take a deduction of

$75x on Form 706 if the amount has been paid or meets the requirements of § 20.2053–1(d)(4) for deducting certain ascertainable amounts. In addition, E may claim a deduction under § 20.2053–3(c) or § 20.2053–3(d)(3) for expenses incurred in defending the estate against the claim if the expenses have been paid or if the expenses meet the requirements of § 20.2053–1(d)(4) for deducting certain ascertainable amounts. E may file a protective claim for refund before the expiration of the period of limitation prescribed in section 6511(a) in order to preserve the estate's right to claim a refund for any amount in excess of $75x that is subsequently paid to resolve the claim against the estate. To the extent that any unpaid expenses incurred in defending the estate against the claim are not deducted as an ascertainable amount pursuant to § 20.2053–1(d)(4), they may be included in the protective claim for refund.

Example 7. Claim having issue of enforceability. D is sued by C for $100x in a tort proceeding in which there is an issue as to whether the claim is barred by the applicable period of limitations. After D's death but prior to the decision of the court, a settlement meeting the requirements of § 20.2053–1(b)(3)(iv) is reached between E and C in the amount of $50x. E pays C this amount before the Form 706 is timely filed. E may take a deduction on Form 706 for the amount paid to C ($50x) in satisfaction of the claim. If, subsequent to E's payment to C, facts develop to indicate that the claim was, in fact, unenforceable, the deduction will not be denied provided the enforceability of the claim was at issue in a bona dispute at the time of the payment. See § 20.2053–1(b)(3)(iv). A deduction may be available under § 20.2053–3(d)(3) for expenses incurred in defending the estate, reaching a settlement, and processing payment of the claim if the expenses have been paid in accordance with § 20.2053–1(d)(1) or if the expenses meet the requirements of § 20.2053–1(d)(4) for deducting certain ascertainable amounts.

Example 8. Noncontingent and recurring obligation to pay, binding on estate. D's property settlement agreement incident to D's divorce, signed three years prior to D's death, obligates D or D's estate to pay to S, D's former spouse, $20x per year until S's death or remarriage. Prior to D's death, D made payments in accordance with the agreement and, after D's death, E continues to make the payments in accordance with the agreement. D's obligation to pay S under the property settlement agreement is deemed to be a claim against the estate that is ascertainable with reasonable certainty for purposes of § 20.2053–1(d)(4). To the extent the obligation to make the recurring payment is a claim that will be paid, E may deduct the amount of the claim (measured according to actuarial principles, using factors set forth in the transfer tax regulations or otherwise provided by the IRS) under the rule for deducting certain ascertainable amounts set forth in § 20.2053–1(d)(4).

Example 9. Recurring obligation to pay, estate purchases a commercial annuity in satisfaction. D's settlement agreement with T, the claimant in a suit against D, signed three years prior to D's death, obligates D or D's estate to pay to T $20x per year for 10 years, provided that T does not reveal the details of the claim or of the settlement during that period. D dies in Year 1. In Year 2, D's estate purchases a commercial annuity from an unrelated issuer of commercial annuities, XYZ, to fund the obligation to T. E may deduct the entire amount paid to XYZ to obtain the annuity, even though the obligation to T was contingent.

(e) Interest on claim—(1) Subject to any applicable limitations in § 20.2053–1, the interest on a deductible claim is itself deductible as a claim under section 2053 to the extent of the amount of interest accrued at the decedent's death (even if the executor elects the alternate valuation method under section 2032), but only to the extent of the amount of interest actually paid or meeting the requirements of § 20.2053–1(d)(4) for deducting certain ascertainable amounts.

(2) Post-death accrued interest may be deductible in appropriate circumstances either as an estate tax administration expense under section 2053 or as an income tax deduction.

(f) Effective/applicability date. This section applies to the estates of decedents dying on or after October 20, 2009.

[T.D. 6296, 23 FR 4529, June 24, 1958; T.D. 9468, 74 FR 53660, Oct. 20, 2009; 74 FR 61525, Nov. 25, 2009]

§ 20.2053–7 Deduction for unpaid mortgages.

A deduction is allowed from a decedent's gross estate of the full unpaid amount of a mortgage upon, or of any other indebtedness in respect of, any property of the gross estate, including interest which had accrued thereon to the date of death, provided the value of the property, undiminished by the amount of the mortgage or indebtedness, is included in the value of the gross estate. If the decedent's estate is liable for the amount of the mortgage or indebtedness, the full value of the property subject to the mortgage or indebtedness must be included as part of the value of the gross estate; the amount of the mortgage or indebtedness being in such case allowed as a deduction. But if the decedent's estate is not so liable, only the value of the equity of redemption (or the value of the property, less the mortgage or indebtedness) need be returned as part of the value of the gross estate. In no case may the deduction on account of the mortgage or indebtedness exceed the liability therefor contracted bona fide and for an adequate and full consideration in money or money's worth. See § 20.2043–1. Only interest accrued to the date of the decedent's death is allowable even though the alternate valuation method under section 2032 is selected. In any case where real property situated outside the United States no deduction may be taken of any mortgage thereon or any other indebtedness does not form a part of the gross estate, in respect thereof.

[T.D. 6296, 23 FR 4529, June 24, 1958, as amended by T.D. 6684, 28 FR 11409, Oct. 24, 1963]

§ 20.2053–8 Deduction for expenses in administering property not subject to claims.

(a) Expenses incurred in administering property included in a decedent's gross estate but not subject to claims fall within the second category of deductions set forth in § 20.2053–1, and may be allowed as deductions if they—

(1) Would be allowed as deductions in the first category if the property being administered were subject to claims; and

(2) Were paid before the expiration of the period of limitation for assessment provided in section 6501.

Usually, these expenses are incurred in connection with the administration of a trust established by a decedent during his lifetime. They may also be incurred in connection with the collection of other assets or the transfer or clearance of title to other property included in a decedent's gross estate for estate tax purposes but not included in his probate estate.

(b) These expenses may be allowed as deductions only to the extent that they would be allowed as deductions under the first category if the property were subject to claims. See § 20.2053–3. The only expenses in administering property not subject to claims which are allowed as deductions are those occasioned by the decedent's death and incurred in settling the decedent's interest in the property or vesting good title to the property in the beneficiaries. Expenses not coming within the description in the preceding sentence but incurred on behalf of the transferees are not deductible.

(c) The principles set forth in paragraphs (b), (c), and (d) of § 20.2053–3 (relating to the allowance of executor's commissions, attorney's fees, and miscellaneous administration expenses of the first category) are applied in determining the extent to which trustee's commissions, attorney's and accountant's fees, and miscellaneous administration expenses are allowed in connection with the administration of property not subject to claims.

(d) The application of this section may be illustrated by the following examples:

Example (1). In 1940, the decedent made an irrevocable transfer of property to the X Trust Company, as trustee. The instrument of transfer provided that the trustee should pay the income from the property to the decedent for the duration of his life and upon his death, distribute the corpus of the trust among designated beneficiaries. The property was included in the decedent's gross estate under the provisions of section 2036. Three months after the date of death, the trustee distributed the trust corpus among the beneficiaries, except for $6,000 which it withheld. The amount withheld represented $5,000 which it retained as trustee's commissions in connection with the termination of the trust and $1,000 which it had paid to an attorney for representing it in connection with the termination. Both the trustee's commissions and the attorney's fees were allowable under the law of the jurisdiction in which the trust was being administered, were reasonable in amount, and were in accord with local custom. Under these circumstances, the estate is allowed a deduction of $6,000.

Example (2). In 1945, the decedent made an irrevocable transfer of property to Y Trust Company, as trustee. The instrument of transfer provided that the trustee should pay the income from the property to the decedent during his life. If the decedent's wife survived him, the trust was to continue for the duration of her life, with Y Trust Company and the decedent's son as co-trustees, and with income payable to the decedent's wife for the duration of her life. Upon the death of both the decedent and his wife, the corpus is to be distributed among designated remaindermen. The decedent was survived by his wife. The property was included in the decedent's gross estate under the provisions of section 2036. In accordance with local custom, the trustee made an accounting to the court as of the date of the decedent's death. Following the death of the decedent, a controversy arose among the remaindermen as to their respective rights under the instrument of transfer, and a suit was brought in court to which the trustee was made a party. As part of the accounting, the court approved the following expenses which the trustee had paid within 3 years following the date of death: $10,000, trustee's commissions; $5,000, accountant's fees; $25,000, attorney's fees; and $2,500, representing fees paid to the guardian of a remainderman who was a minor. The trustee's commissions and accountant's fees were for services in connection with the usual issues involved in a trust accounting as also were one-half of the attorney's and guardian's fees. The remainder of the attorney's and guardian's fees were for services performed in connection with the suit brought by the remaindermen. The amount allowed as a deduction is the $28,750 ($10,000, trustee's commissions; $5,000, accountant's fees; $12,500, attorney's fees; and $1,250, guardian's fees) incurred as expenses in connection with the usual issues involved in a trust accounting. The remaining expenses are not allowed as deductions since they were incurred on behalf of the transferees.

* * *

[T.D. 6296, 23 FR 4529, June 24, 1958]

§ 20.2054–1 Deduction for losses from casualties or theft.

A deduction is allowed for losses incurred during the settlement of the estate arising from fires, storms, shipwrecks, or other casualties, or from theft, if the losses are not compensated for by insurance or otherwise. If the loss is partly compensated for, the excess of the loss over the compensation may be deducted. Losses which are not of the nature described are not deductible. In order to be deductible a loss must occur during the settlement of the estate. If a loss with respect to an asset occurs after its distribution to the distributee it may not be deducted. Notwithstanding the foregoing, no deduction is allowed under this section if the estate has waived its right to take such a deduction pursuant to the provisions of section 642(g) in order to permit its allowance for income tax purposes. * * *

[T.D. 6296, 23 FR 4529, June 24, 1958]

§ 20.2055–1 Deduction for transfers for public, charitable, and religious uses; in general.

(a) General rule. A deduction is allowed under section 2055(a) from the gross estate of a decedent who was a citizen or resident of the United States at the time of his death for the value of property included in the decedent's gross estate and transferred by the decedent during his lifetime or by will—

(1) To or for the use of the United States, any State, Territory, any political subdivision thereof, or the District of Columbia, for exclusively public purposes;

(2) To or for the use of any corporation or association organized and operated exclusively for religious, charitable, scientific, literary, or educational purposes (including the encouragement of art and for the prevention of cruelty to children or animals), if no part of the net earnings of the corporation or association inures to the benefit of any private stockholder or individual (other than as a legitimate object of such purposes), if the organization is not disqualified for tax exemption under section 501(c)(3) by reason of attempting to influence legislation, and if, in the case of transfers made after December 31, 1969, it does not participate in, or intervene in (including the publishing or distributing of statements), any political campaign on behalf of or in opposition to any candidate for public office;

(3) To a trustee or trustees, or a fraternal society, order, or association operating under the lodge system, if the transferred property is to be used exclusively for religious, charitable, scientific, literary, or educational purposes (or for the prevention of cruelty to children or animals), if no substantial part of the activities of such transferee is carrying on propaganda, or otherwise attempting, to influence legislation, and if, in the case of transfers made after December 31, 1969, such transferee does not participate in, or intervene in (including the publishing or distributing of statements), any political campaign on behalf of any candidate for public office; or

(4) To or for the use of any veterans' organization incorporated by act of Congress, or of any of its departments, local chapters, or posts, no part of the net earnings of which inures to the benefit of any private shareholder or individual.

The deduction is not limited, in the case of estates of citizens or residents of the United States, to transfers to domestic corporations or associations, or to trustees for use within the United States. Nor is the deduction subject to percentage limitations such as are applicable to the charitable deduction under the income tax. An organization will not be considered to meet the requirements of subparagraph (2) or (3) of this paragraph if such organization engages in any activity which would cause it to be classified as an "action" organization * * *. * * *

* * *

(c) Submission of evidence. In establishing the right of the estate to the deduction authorized by section 2055, the executor should submit the following with the return:

(1) A copy of any instrument in writing by which the decedent made a transfer of property in his lifetime the value of which is required by statute to be included in his gross estate, for which a deduction under section 2055 is claimed. If the instrument is of record the copy should be certified, and if not of record, the copy should be verified.

(2) A written statement by the executor containing a declaration that it is made under penalties of perjury and stating whether any action has been instituted to construe or to contest the decedent's will or any provision thereof affecting the charitable deduction claimed and whether, according to his information and belief, any such action is designed or contemplated.

The executor shall also submit such other documents or evidence as may be requested by the district director.

* * *

[T.D. 6296, 23 FR 4529, June 24, 1958; 25 FR 14021, Dec. 31, 1960, as amended by T.D. 8318, 39 FR 25452, July 11, 1974; T.D. 8308, 55 FR 35593, Aug. 31, 1990]

§ 20.2055-2 Transfers not exclusively for charitable purposes.

(a) Remainders and similar interests. If a trust is created or property is transferred for both a charitable and a private purpose, deduction may be taken of the value of the charitable beneficial interest only insofar as that interest is presently ascertainable, and hence severable from the non-charitable interest. * * *

(b) Transfers subject to a condition or a power. (1) If, as of the date of a decedent's death, a transfer for charitable purposes is dependent upon the performance of some act or the happening of a precedent event in order that it might become effective, no deduction is allowable unless the possibility that the charitable transfer will not become effective is so remote as to be negligible. If an estate or interest has passed to, or is vested in, charity at the time of a decedent's death and the estate or interest would be defeated by the subsequent performance of some act or the happening of some event, the possibility of occurrence of which appeared at the time of the decedent's death to be so remote as to be negligible, the deduction is allowable. If the legatee, devisee, donee, or trustee is empowered to divert the property or fund, in whole or in part, to a use or purpose which would have rendered it, to the extent that it is subject to such power, not deductible had it been directly so bequeathed, devised, or given by the decedent, the deduction will be limited to that portion, if any, of the property or fund which is exempt from an exercise of the power.

(2) The application of this paragraph may be illustrated by the following examples:

Example (1). In 1965, A dies leaving certain property in trust in which charity is to receive the income for the life of his widow. The assets placed in trust by the decedent consist of stock in a corporation the fiscal policies of which are controlled by the decedent and his family. The trustees of the trust and the remaindermen are members of the decedent's family, and the governing instrument contains no adequate guarantee of the request income to the charitable organization. Under such circumstances, no deduction will be allowed. Similarly, if the trustees are not members of the decedent's family but have no power to sell or otherwise dispose of the closely held stock, or otherwise insure the requisite enjoyment of income to the charitable organization, no deduction will be allowed.

Example (2). C dies leaving a tract of land to a city government for as long as the land is used by the city for a public park. If the city accepts the tract and if, on the date of C's death, the possibility that the city will not use the land for a public park is so remote as to be negligible, a deduction will be allowed.

(c) Disclaimers—(1) Decedents dying after December 31, 1976. In the case of a bequest, devise, or transfer made by a decedent dying after December 31, 1976, the amount of a bequest, devise or transfer for which a deduction is allowable under section 2055 includes an interest which falls into the bequest, devise or transfer as the result of either—

(i) A qualified disclaimer (see section 2518 and the corresponding regulations for rules relating to a qualified disclaimer), or

(ii) The complete termination of a power to consume, invade, or appropriate property for the benefit of an individual by reason of the death of such individual or for any other reason, if the termination occurs within the period of time (including extensions) for filing the decedent's Federal estate tax return and before such power has been exercised.

* * *

(d) Payments in compromise. If a charitable organization assigns or surrenders a part of a transfer to it pursuant to a compromise agreement in settlement of a controversy, the amount so assigned or surrendered is not deductible as a transfer to that charitable organization.

(e) Limitation applicable to decedents dying after December 31, 1969—(1) Disallowance of deduction—(i) In general. In the case of decedents dying after December 31, 1969, where an interest in property passes or has passed from the decedent for charitable purposes and an interest (other than an interest which is extinguished upon the decedent's death) in the same property passes or has passed from the decedent for private purposes (for less than an adequate and full consideration in money or money's worth) after October 9, 1969, no deduction is allowed under section 2055 for the value of the interest which passes or has passed for charitable purposes unless the interest in property is a deductible interest described in subparagraph (2) of this paragraph. The principles of section 2056 and the regulations thereunder shall apply for purposes of determining under this paragraph (e)(1)(i) whether an interest in property passes or has passed from the decedent. If however, as of the date of a decedent's death, a transfer for a private purpose is dependent upon the performance of some act on the happening of a precedent event in order that it might become effective, an interest in property will be considered to pass for a private purpose unless the possibility of occurrence of such act or event is so remote as to be negligible. The application of this paragraph (e)(1)(i) may be illustrated by the following examples, in each of which it is assumed that the interest in property which passes for private purposes does not pass for an adequate and full consideration in money or money's worth:

Example (1). In 1973, H creates a trust which is to pay the income of the trust to W for her life, the reversionary interest in the trust being retained by H. H predeceases W in 1975. H's will provide that the residue of his estate (including the reversionary interest in the trust) is to be transferred to charity. For purposes of this paragraph (e)(1)(i), interests in the same property have passed from H for charitable purposes and for private purposes.

Example (2). In 1973, H creates a trust which is to pay the income of the trust to W for her life and upon termination of the life estate to transfer the remainder to S. S predeceases W in 1975. S's will provides that the residue of his estate (including the remainder interest in the trust) is to be transferred to charity. For purposes of this paragraph (e)(1)(i), interests in the same property have not passed from H or S for charitable purposes and for private purposes.

Example (3). H transfers Blackacre to A by gift, reserving the right to the rentals of Blackacre for a term of 20 years. H dies within the 20–year term, bequeathing the right to the remaining rentals to charity. For purposes of this paragraph (e)(1)(i), the term "property" refers to Blackacre, and the right to rentals from Blackacre consist of an interest in Blackacre. An interest in Blackacre has passed from H for charitable purposes and for private purposes.

Example (4). H bequeaths the residue of his estate in trust for the benefit of A and a charity. An annuity of $5,000 a year is to be paid to charity for 20 years. Upon termination of the 20–year term the corpus is to be distributed to A if living. However, if A should die during the 20–year term, the corpus is to be distributed to charity upon termination of the term. An interest in the residue of the estate has passed from H for charitable purposes. In addition, an interest in the residue of the estate has passed from H for private purposes, unless the possibility that A will survive the 20–year term is so remote as to be negligible.

Example (5). H bequeaths the residue of his estate in trust. Under the terms of the trust an annuity of $5,000 a year is to be paid to charity for 20 years. Upon termination of the term, the corpus is to pass to such of A's children and their issue as A may appoint. However, if A should die during the 20–year term without exercising the power of appointment, the corpus is to be distributed to charity upon termination of the term. Since the possible appointees include private persons, an interest in the residue of the estate is considered to have passed from H for private purposes.

Example (6). H devises Blackacre to X Charity. Under applicable local law, W, H's widow, is entitled to elect a dower interest in Blackacre. W elects to take her dower interest in Blackacre. For purposes of this paragraph (e)(1)(i), interests in the same property have passed from H for charitable purposes and for private purposes. If, however, W does not elect to take her dower interest in Blackacre, then, for purposes of this paragraph (e)(1)(i), interests in the same property have not passed from H for charitable purposes and for private purposes.

* * *

(2) Deductible interests. A deductible interest for purposes of subparagraph (1) of this paragraph is a charitable interest in property where—

(i) Undivided portion of decedent's entire interest. The charitable interest is an undivided portion, not in trust, of the decedent's entire interest in property. An undivided portion of a decedent's entire interest in property must consist of a fraction or percentage of each and every substantial interest or right owned by the decedent in such property and must extend over the entire term of the decedent's interest in such property and in other property into which such property is converted. For example, if the decedent transferred a life estate in an office building to his wife for her life and retained a reversionary interest in the office building, the devise by the decedent of one-half of that reversionary interest to charity while his wife is still alive will not be considered the transfer of a deductible interest; because an interest in the same property has already passed from the decedent for private purposes, the reversionary interest will not be considered the decedent's entire interest in the property. If, on the other hand, the decedent had been given a life estate in Blackacre for the life of his wife and the decedent had no other interest in Blackacre at any time during his life, the devise by the decedent of one-half of that life estate to charity would be considered the transfer of a deductible interest; because the life estate would be considered the decedent's entire interest in the property, the devise would be of an undivided portion of such entire interest. An undivided portion of a decedent's entire interest in the property includes an interest in property whereby the charity is given the right, as a tenant in common with the decedent's devisee or legatee, to possession, dominion, and control of the property for a portion of each year appropriate to its interest in such property. However, except as provided in paragraphs (e)(2)(ii), (iii), and (iv) of this section, for purposes of this subdivision a charitable contribution of an interest in property not in trust where the decedent transfers some specific rights to one party and transfers other substantial rights to another party will not be considered a contribution of an undivided portion of the decedent's entire interest in property. A bequest to charity made on or before December 17, 1980, of an open space easement in gross in perpetuity shall be considered the transfer to charity of an undivided portion of the decedent's entire interest in the property. * * *

(ii) Remainder interest in personal residence. The charitable interest is a remainder interest, not in trust, in a personal residence. Thus, for example, if the decedent devises to charity a remainder interest in a personal residence and bequeaths to his surviving spouse a life estate in such property, the value of the remainder interest is deductible under section 2055. For purposes of this subdivision, the term "personal residence" means any property which was used by the decedent as his personal residence even though it was not used as his principal residence. For example, a decedent's vacation home may be a personal residence for purposes of this subdivision. The term "personal residence" also includes stock owned by the decedent as a tenant-stockholder in a cooperative housing corporation (as those terms are defined in section 216(b)(1) and (2)) if the dwelling which the decedent was entitled to occupy as such stockholder was used by him as his personal residence.

(iii) Remainder interest in a farm. The charitable interest is a remainder interest, not in trust, in a farm. Thus, for example, if the decedent devises to charity a remainder interest in a farm and bequeaths to his daughter a life estate in such property, the value of the remainder interest is deductible under section 2055. For purposes of this subdivision, the term "farm" means any land used by the decedent or his tenant for the production of crops, fruits, or other agricultural products or for the sustenance of livestock. The term "livestock" includes cattle, hogs, horses, mules, donkeys, sheep, goats, captive furbearing animals, chickens, turkeys, pigeons, and other poultry. A farm includes the improvements thereon.

(iv) Qualified conservation contribution. The charitable interest is a qualified conservation contribution. * * *

(v) Charitable remainder trusts and pooled income funds. The charitable interest is a remainder interest in a trust which is a charitable remainder annuity trust, as defined in section 664(d)(1) and § 1.664–2 of this chapter; a charitable remainder unitrust, as defined in section 664(d)(2) and (3) and § 1.664–3 of this chapter; or a pooled income fund, as defined in section 642(c)(5) and § 1.642(c)–5 of this chapter. The charitable organization to or for the use of which the remainder interest passes must meet the requirements of both section 2055(a) and section 642(c)(5)(A), section 664(d)(1)(C), or section 664(d)(2)(C), whichever applies. For example, the charitable organization to which the remainder interest in a charitable remainder annuity trust passes may not be a foreign corporation.

(vi) Guaranteed annuity interest. **(a)** The charitable interest is a guaranteed annuity interest, whether or not such interest is in trust. For purposes of this subdivision (vi), the term "guaranteed annuity interest" means the right pursuant to the instrument of transfer to receive a guaranteed annuity. A guaranteed annuity is an arrangement under which a determinable amount is paid periodically, but not less often than annually, for a specified term of years or for the life or lives of certain individuals, each of whom must be living at the date of death of the decedent and can be ascertained at such date. Only one or more of the following individuals may be used as measuring lives: the decedent's spouse, and an individual who, with respect to all remainder beneficiaries (other than charitable organizations described in section 170, 2055, or 2522), is either a lineal ancestor or the spouse of a lineal ancestor of those beneficiaries. A trust will satisfy the requirement that all noncharitable remainder beneficiaries are lineal descendants of the individual who is the measuring life, or that individual's spouse, if there is less than a 15% probability that individuals who are not lineal descendants will receive any trust corpus. This probability must be computed, based on the current applicable Life Table contained in § 20.2031–7, as of the date of the decedent's death taking into account the interests of all primary and contingent remainder beneficiaries who are living at that time. An interest payable for a specified term of years can qualify as a guaranteed annuity interest even if the governing instrument contains a savings clause intended to ensure compliance with a rule against perpetuities. The savings clause must utilize a period for vesting of 21 years after the deaths of measuring lives who are selected to maximize, rather than limit, the term of the trust. The rule in this paragraph that a charitable interest may be payable for the life or lives of only certain specified individuals does not apply in the case of a charitable guaranteed annuity interest payable under a charitable remainder trust described in section 664. An amount is determinable if the exact amount which must be paid under the conditions specified in the instrument of transfer can be ascertained as of the appropriate valuation date. For example, the amount to be paid may be a stated sum for a term of years, or for the life of the decedent's spouse at the expiration of which it may be changed by a specified amount, but it may not be redetermined by reference to a fluctuating index such as the cost of living index. In further illustration, the amount to be paid may be expressed in terms of a fraction or a percentage of the net fair market value, as finally determined for Federal estate tax purposes, of the residue of the estate on the appropriate valuation date, or it may be expressed in terms of a fraction or percentage of the cost of living index on the appropriate valuation date.

(b) A charitable interest is a guaranteed annuity interest only if it is a guaranteed annuity interest in every respect. For example, if the charitable interest is the right to receive from a trust each year a payment equal to the lesser of a sum certain or a fixed percentage of the net fair market value of the trust assets, determined annually, such interest is not a guaranteed annuity interest.

(c) Where a charitable interest in the form of a guaranteed annuity interest is not in trust, the interest will be considered a guaranteed annuity interest only if it is to be paid by an insurance company or by an organization regularly engaged in issuing annuity contracts.

(d) Where a charitable interest in the form of a guaranteed annuity interest is in trust, the governing instrument of the trust may provide that income of the trust which is in excess of the amount required to pay the guaranteed annuity interest shall be paid to or for the use of a charity. * * *

* * *

(vii) Unitrust interest. (a) The charitable interest is a unitrust interest, whether or not such interest is in trust. For purposes of this subdivision (vii), the term "unitrust interest" means the right pursuant to the instrument of transfer to receive payment, not less often than annually, of a fixed percentage of the net fair market value, determined annually, of the property which funds the unitrust interest. In computing the net fair market value of the property which funds the unitrust interest, all assets and liabilities shall be taken into account without regard to whether particular items are taken into account in determining the income from the property. The net fair market value of the property which funds the unitrust interest may be determined on any one date during the year or by taking the average of valuations made on more than one date during the year, provided that the same valuation date or dates and valuation methods are used each year. Where the charitable interest is a unitrust interest to be paid by a trust and the governing instrument of the trust does not specify the valuation date or dates, the trustee shall select such date or dates and shall indicate his selection on the first return on Form 1041 which the trust is required to file. Payments under a unitrust interest may be paid for a specified term of years or for the life or lives of certain individuals, each of whom must be living at the date of death of the decedent and can be ascertained at such date. Only one or more of the following individuals may be used as measuring lives: the decedent's spouse, and an individual who, with respect to all remainder beneficiaries (other than charitable organizations described in section 170, 2055, or 2522), is either a lineal ancestor or the spouse of a lineal ancestor of those beneficiaries. A trust will satisfy the requirement that all noncharitable remainder beneficiaries are lineal descendants of the individual who is the measuring life, or that individual's spouse, if there is less than a 15% probability that individuals who are not lineal descendants will receive any trust corpus. This probability must be computed, based on the current applicable Life Table contained in § 20.2031–7, as of the date of the decedent's death taking into account the interests of all primary and contingent remainder beneficiaries who are living at that time. An interest payable for a specified term of years can qualify as a unitrust interest even if the governing instrument contains a savings clause intended to ensure compliance with a rule against perpetuities. The savings clause must utilize a period for vesting of 21 years after the deaths of measuring lives who are selected to maximize, rather than limit, the term of the trust. The rule in this paragraph that a charitable interest may be payable for the life or lives of only certain specified individuals does not apply in the case of a charitable unitrust interest payable under a charitable remainder trust described in section 664.

(b) A charitable interest is a unitrust interest only if it is a unitrust interest in every respect. For example, if the charitable interest is the right to receive from a trust each year a payment equal to the lesser of a sum certain or a fixed percentage of the net fair market value of the trust assets, determined annually, such interest is not a unitrust interest.

(c) Where a charitable interest in the form of a unitrust interest is not in trust, the interest will be considered a unitrust interest only if it is to be paid by an insurance company or by an organization regularly engaged in issuing interests otherwise meeting the requirements of a unitrust interest.

(d) Where a charitable interest in the form of a unitrust interest is in trust, the governing instrument of the trust may provide that income of the trust which is in excess of the amount required to pay the unitrust interest shall be paid to or for the use of a charity. * * *

* * *

[T.D. 6296, 23 FR 4529, June 24, 1958, as amended by T.D. 7238, 37 FR 28719, Dec. 29, 1972; T.D. 7318, 39 FR 25453, July 11, 1974, 39 FR 26154, July 17, 1974; T.D. 7340, 40 FR 1240, Jan. 7, 1975; T.D. 7955, 49 FR 19996, May 11, 1984; T.D. 7957, 49 FR 20811, May 17, 1984; T.D. 8069, 51 FR 1507, Jan. 14, 1986; 51 FR 32071, Sept. 9, 1986; T.D. 8540, 59 FR 30100, June 10, 1994; T.D. 8819, 64 FR 23187, April 29, 1999; T.D. 8886, 65 FR 36943, June 12, 2000; T.D. 8923, 66 FR 1040, Jan. 5, 2001; T.D. 9068, 68 FR 40130, July 7, 2003; T.D. 9448, 74 FR 21437, May 7, 2009; T.D. 9540, 76 FR 49570, Aug. 10, 2011]

§ 20.2055–3 Effect of death taxes and administration expenses.

(a) Death taxes. * * *

(b) Administration expenses—(1) Definitions—(i) Management expenses. Estate management expenses are expenses that are incurred in connection with the investment of estate assets or with their preservation or maintenance during a reasonable period of administration. Examples of these expenses could include investment advisory fees, stock brokerage commissions, custodial fees, and interest.

(ii) Transmission expenses. Estate transmission expenses are expenses that would not have been incurred but for the decedent's death and the consequent necessity of collecting the decedent's assets, paying the decedent's debts and death taxes, and distributing the decedent's property to those who are entitled to receive it. Estate transmission expenses include any administration expense that is not a management expense. Examples of these expenses could include executor commissions and attorney fees (except to the extent of commissions or fees specifically related to investment, preservation, or maintenance of the assets), probate fees, expenses incurred in construction proceedings and defending against will contests, and appraisal fees.

(iii) Charitable share. The charitable share is the property or interest in property that passed from the decedent for which a deduction is allowable under section 2055(a) with respect to all or part of the property interest. The charitable share includes, for example, bequests to charitable organizations and bequests to a charitable lead unitrust or annuity trust, a charitable remainder unitrust or annuity trust, a charitable remainder unitrust or annuity trust, and a pooled income fund, described in section 2055(e)(2). The charitable share also includes the income produced by the property or interest in property during the period of administration if the income, under the terms of the governing instrument or applicable local law, is payable to the charitable organization or is to be added to the principal of the property interest passing in whole or in part to the charitable organization.

(2) Effect of transmission expenses. For purposes of determining the charitable deduction, the value of the charitable share shall be reduced by the amount of the estate transmission expenses paid from the charitable share.

(3) Effect of management expenses attributable to the charitable share. For purposes of determining the charitable deduction, the value of the charitable share shall not be reduced by the amount of the estate management expenses attributable to and paid from the charitable share. Pursuant to section 2056(b)(9), however, the amount of the allowable charitable deduction shall be reduced by the amount of any such management expenses that are deducted under section 2053 on the decedent's federal estate tax return.

(4) Effect of management expenses not attributable to the charitable share. For purposes of determining the charitable deduction, the value of the charitable share shall be reduced by the amount of the estate management expenses paid from the charitable share but attributable to a property interest not included in the charitable share.

(5) Example. The following example illustrates the application of this paragraph (b):

Example. The decedent, who dies in 2000, leaves his residuary estate, after the payment of debts, expenses, and estate taxes, to a charitable remainder unitrust that satisfies the requirements of section 664(d). During the period of administration, the estate incurs estate transmission expenses of $400,000. The residue of the estate (the charitable share) must be reduced by the $400,000 of transmission expenses and by the Federal and State estate taxes before the present value of the remainder interest passing to charity can be determined in accordance with the provisions of § 1.664–4 of this chapter. Because the estate taxes are payable out of the residue, the computation of the estate taxes and the allowable charitable deduction are interrelated. See paragraph (a)(2) of this section.

(6) Cross reference. See § 20.2056(b)–4(d) for additional examples applicable to the treatment of administration expenses under this paragraph (b).

* * *

[T.D. 8846, 64 FR 67763, Dec. 2, 1999; 64 FR 71022, Dec. 20, 1999]

§ 20.2055–6 Disallowance of double deduction in the case of qualified terminable interest property.

No deduction is allowed from the decedent's gross estate under section 2055 for property with respect to which a deduction is allowed by reason of section 2056(b)(7). See section 2056(b)(9) and § 20.2056(b)–9.

[T.D. 8522, 59 FR 9642, Mar. 1, 1994]

§ 20.2056(a)–1 Marital deduction; in general.

(a) In general. A deduction is allowed under section 2056 from the gross estate of a decedent for the value of any property interest which passes from the decedent to the decedent's surviving spouse if the interest is a deductible interest as defined in § 20.2056(a)–2. With respect to decedents dying in certain years, a deduction is allowed under section 2056 only to the extent that the total of the deductible interests does not exceed the applicable limitations set forth in paragraph (c) of this section. The deduction allowed under section 2056 is referred to as the marital deduction. See also sections 2056(d) and 2056A for special rules applicable in the case of decedents dying after November 10, 1988, if the decedent's surviving spouse is not a citizen of the United States at the time of the decedent's death. In such cases, the marital deduction may not be allowed unless the property passes to a qualified domestic trust as described in section 2056A(a).

(b) Requirements for marital deduction—(1) In general. To obtain the marital deduction with respect to any property interest, the executor must establish the following facts—

(i) The decedent was survived by a spouse (see § 20.2056(c)–2(e));

(ii) The property interest passed from the decedent to the spouse (see §§ 20.2056(b)–5 through 20.2056(b)–8 and 20.2056(c)–1 through 20.2056(c)–3);

(iii) The property interest is a deductible interest (see § 20.2056(a)–2); and

(iv) The value of the property interest (see § 20.2056(b)–4).

(2) Burden of establishing requisite facts. The executor must provide the facts relating to any applicable limitation on the amount of the allowable marital deduction under § 20.2056(a)–1(c), and must submit proof necessary to establish any fact required under paragraph (b)(1), including any evidence requested by the district director.

* * *

[T.D. 8522, 59 FR 9642, Mar. 1, 1994]

§ 20.2056(a)–2 Marital deduction; "deductible interests" and "nondeductible interests".

(a) In general. Property interests which passed from a decedent to his surviving spouse fall within two general categories: (1) Those with respect to which the marital deduction is authorized, and (2) those with respect to which the marital deduction is not authorized. These categories are referred to in this section and other sections of the regulations under section 2056 as "deductible interests" and "nondeductible interests", respectively (see paragraph (b) of this section). Subject to any applicable limitations set forth in § 20.2056(a)–1(c), the amount of the marital deduction is the aggregate value of the deductible interests.

(b) Deductible interests. An interest passing to a decedent's surviving spouse is a "deductible interest" if it does not fall within one of the following categories of "nondeductible interests";

(1) Any property interest which passed from the decedent to his surviving spouse is a "nondeductible interest" to the extent it is not included in the decedent's gross estate.

(2) If a deduction is allowed under section 2053 (relating to deductions for expenses and indebtedness) by reason of the passing of a property interest from the decedent to his surviving spouse, such interest is, to the extent of the deduction under section 2053, a "nondeductible interest." Thus, a property interest which passed from the decedent to his surviving spouse in satisfaction of a deductible claim of the spouse against the estate is, to the extent of the claim, a "nondeductible interest" (see

§ 20.2056(b)–4). Similarly, amounts deducted under section 2053(a)(2) for commissioners allowed to the surviving spouse as executor are "nondeductible interests". As to the valuation, for the purpose of the marital deduction, of any property interest which passed from the decedent to his surviving spouse subject to a mortgage or other encumbrance, see § 20.2056(b)–4.

(3) If during settlement of the estate a loss deductible under section 2054 occurs with respect to a property interest, then that interest is, to the extent of the deductible loss, a "nondeductible interest" for the purpose of the marital deduction.

(4) A property interest passing to a decedent's surviving spouse which is a "terminable interest", as defined in § 20.2056(b)–1, is a "nondeductible interest" to the extent specified in that section.

[T.D. 6296, 23 FR 4529, June 24, 1958, as amended by T.D. 8522, 59 FR 9642, Mar. 1, 1994]

§ 20.2056(b)–1 Marital deduction; limitation in case of life estate or other "terminable interest".

(a) In general. Section 2056(b) provides that no marital deduction is allowed with respect to certain property interests, referred to generally as "terminable interests", passing from a decedent to his surviving spouse. The phrase "terminable interest" is defined in paragraph (b) of this section. However, the fact that an interest in property passing to a decedent's surviving spouse is a "terminable interest" makes it nondeductible only (1) under the circumstances described in paragraph (c) of this section, and (2) if it does not come within one of the exceptions referred to in paragraph (d) of this section.

(b) "Terminable interests". A "terminable interest" in property is an interest which will terminate or fail on the lapse of time or on the occurrence or the failure to occur of some contingency. Life estates, terms for years, annuities, patents, and copyrights are therefore terminable interests. However, a bond, note, or similar contractual obligation, the discharge of which would not have the effect of an annuity or a term for years, is not a terminable interest.

(c) Nondeductible terminable interests. **(1)** A property interest which constitutes a terminable interest, as defined in paragraph (b) of this section, is nondeductible if—

(i) Another interest in the same property passed from the decedent to some other person for less than an adequate and full consideration in money or money's worth, and

(ii) By reason of its passing, the other person or his heirs or assigns may possess or enjoy any part of the property after the termination or failure of the spouse's interest.

(2) Even though a property interest which constitutes a terminable interest is not nondeductible by reason of the rules stated in subparagraph (1) of this paragraph, such an interest is nondeductible if—

(i) The decedent has directed his executor or a trustee to acquire such an interest for the decedent's surviving spouse (see further paragraph (f) of this section), or

(ii) Such an interest passing to the decedent's surviving spouse may be satisfied out of a group of assets which includes a nondeductible interest (see further § 20.2056(b)–2). In this case, however, full nondeductibility may not result.

(d) Exceptions. A property interest passing to a decedent's surviving spouse is deductible (if it is not otherwise disqualified under § 20.2056(a)–2) even though it is a terminable interest, and even though an interest therein passed from the decedent to another person, if it is a terminable interest only because—

(1) It is conditioned on the spouse's surviving for a limited period, in the manner described in § 20.2056(b)–3;

(2) It is a right to income for life with a general power of appointment, meeting the requirements set forth in § 20.2056(b)–5;

(3) It consists of life insurance or annuity payments held by the insurer with a general power of appointment in the spouse, meeting the requirements set forth in § 20.2056(b)–6;

(4) It is qualified terminable interest property, meeting the requirements set forth in § 20.2056(b)–7; or

(5) It is an interest in a qualified charitable remainder trust in which the spouse is the only noncharitable beneficiary, meeting the requirements set forth in § 20.2056(b)–8.

(e) Miscellaneous principles. **(1)** In determining whether an interest passed from the decedent to some other person, it is immaterial whether interests in the same property passed to the decedent's spouse and another person at the same time, or under the same instrument.

(2) In determining whether an interest in the same property passed from the decedent both to his surviving spouse and to some other person, a distinction is to be drawn between "property", as such term is used in section 2056, and an "interest in property". The term "property" refers to the underlying property in which various interests exist; each such interest is not for this purpose to be considered as "property".

(3) Whether or not an interest is nondeductible because it is a terminable interest is to be determined by reference to the property interests which actually passed from the decedent. Subsequent conversions of the property are immaterial for this purpose. Thus, where a decedent bequeathed his estate to his wife for life with remainder to his children, the interest which passed to his wife is a nondeductible interest, even though the wife agrees with the children to take a fractional share of the estate in fee in lieu of the life interest in the whole, or sells the life estate for cash, or acquires the remainder interest of the children either by purchase or gift.

(4) The terms passed from the decedent, passed from the decedent to his surviving spouse and passed from the decedent to a person other than his surviving spouse are defined in §§ 20.2056(c)–1 through 20.2056(c)–3.

(f) Direction to acquire a terminable interest. No marital deduction is allowed with respect to a property interest which a decedent directs his executor or a trustee to covert after his death into a terminable interest for his surviving spouse. The marital deduction is not allowed even though no interest in the property subject to the terminable interest passes to another person and even though the interest would otherwise come within the exceptions described in §§ 20.2056(b)–5 and 20.2056(b)–6 (relating to life estates and life insurance and annuity payments with powers of appointment). However, a general investment power, authorizing investments in both terminable interests and other property, is not a direction to invest in a terminable interest.

(g) Examples. The application of this section may be illustrated by the following examples. In each example, it is assumed that the executor made no election under section 2056(b)(7) (even if under the specific facts the election would have been available), that any property interest passing from the decedent to a person other than the surviving spouse passed for less than full and adequate consideration in money or money's worth, and that section 2056(b)(8) is inapplicable.

Example (1). H (the decedent) devised real property to W (his surviving wife) for life, with remainder to A and his heirs. The interest which passed from H to W is a nondeductible interest since it will terminate upon her death and A (or his heirs or assigns) will thereafter possess or enjoy the property.

Example (2). H bequeathed the residue of his estate in trust for the benefit of W and A. The trust income is to be paid to W for life, and upon her death the corpus is to be distributed to A or his issue. However, if A should die without issue, leaving W surviving, the corpus is then to be distributed to W. The interest which passed from H to W is a nondeductible interest since it will terminate in the event of her death if A or his issue survive, and A or his issue will thereafter possess or enjoy the property.

Example (3). H during his lifetime purchased an annuity contract providing for payments to himself for life and then to W for life if she should survive him. Upon the death of the survivor of H and W, the excess, if any, of the cost of the contract over the annuity payments theretofore made was to be refunded to A. The interest which passed from H to W is a nondeductible interest since A may possess or enjoy a part of the property following the termination of the interest of W. If, however, the contract provided for no refund upon the death of the survivor of H and W, or provided that any refund was to go to the estate of the survivor, then the interest which passed from H to W is (to the extent it is included in H's gross estate) a deductible interest.

Example (4). H, in contemplation of death, transferred a residence to A for life with remainder to W provided W survives A, but if W predeceases A, the property is to pass to B and his heirs. If it is assumed that H died during A's lifetime, and the value of the residence was included in determining the value of his gross estate, the interest which passed from H to W is a nondeductible interest since it will terminate if W predeceases A and the property will thereafter be possessed or enjoyed by B (or his heirs or assigns). This result is not affected by B's assignment of his interest during H's lifetime, whether made in favor of W or another person, since the term "assigns" (as used in section 2056(b)(1)(B)) includes such an assignee. However, if it is assumed that A predeceased H, the interest of B in the property was extinguished, and, viewed as of the time of the subsequent death of H, the interest which passed from him to W is the entire interest in the property and, therefore, a deductible interest.

Example (5). H transferred real property to A by gift (reserving the right to the rentals) of the property for a term of 20 years. H died within the 20–year term, bequeathing the right to the remaining rentals to a trust for the benefit of W. The terms of the trust satisfy the five conditions stated in § 20.2056(b)–5, so that the property interest which passed in trust is considered to have passed from H to W. However, the interest is a nondeductible interest since it will terminate upon the expiration of the term and A will thereafter possess or enjoy the property.

Example (6). H bequeathed a patent to W and A as tenants in common. In this case, the interest of W will terminate upon the expiration of the term of the patent, but possession or enjoyment of the property by A must necessarily cease at the same time. Therefore, since A's possession or enjoyment cannot outlast the termination of W's interest, the latter is a deductible interest.

Example (7). A decedent bequeathed $100,000 to his wife, subject to a direction to his executor to use the bequest for the purchase of an annuity for the wife. The bequest is a nondeductible interest.

Example (8). Assume that pursuant to local law an allowance for support is payable to the decedent's surviving spouse during the period of the administration of the decedent's estate, but that upon her death or remarriage during such period her right to any further allowance will terminate. Assume further that the surviving spouse is sole beneficiary of the decedent's estate. Under such circumstances, the allowance constitutes a deductible interest since any part of the allowance not receivable by the surviving spouse during her lifetime will pass to her estate under the terms of the decedent's will. If, in this example, the decedent bequeathed only one-third of his residuary estate to his surviving spouse, then two-thirds of the allowance for support would constitute a nondeductible terminable interest.

[T.D. 6296, 23 FR 4529, June 24, 1958, as amended by T.D. 8522, 59 FR 9642, Mar. 1, 1994]

§ 20.2056(b)–2 Marital deduction; interest in unidentified assets.

(a) In general. Section 2056(b)(2) provides that if an interest passing to a decedent's surviving spouse may be satisfied out of assets (or their proceeds) which include a particular asset that would be a nondeductible interest if it passed from the decedent to his spouse, the value of the interest passing to the spouse is reduced, for the purpose of the marital deduction, by the value of the particular asset.

(b) Application of section 2056(b)(2). In order for section 2056(b)(2) to apply, two circumstances must coexist, as follows:

(1) The property interest which passed from the decedent to his surviving spouse must be payable out of a group of assets included in the gross estate. Examples of property interests payable out of a group of assets are a general legacy, a bequest of the residue of the decedent's estate or of a proportion of the residue, and a right to a share of the corpus of a trust upon its termination.

(2) The group of assets out of which the property interest is payable must include one or more particular assets which, if passing specifically to the surviving spouse, would be nondeductible interests. Therefore, section 2056(b)(2) is not applicable merely because the group of assets includes a terminable interest, but would only be applicable if the terminable interest were nondeductible under the provisions of § 20.2056(b)–1.

(c) Interest nondeductible if circumstances present. If both of the circumstances set forth in paragraph (b) of this section are present, the property interest payable out of the group of assets is (except as to any excess of its value over the aggregate value of the particular asset or assets which would not be deductible if passing specifically to the surviving spouse) a nondeductible interest.

(d) Example. The application of this section may be illustrated by the following example:

Example. A decedent bequeathed one-third of the residue of his estate to his wife. The property passing under the decedent's will included a right to the rentals of an office building for a term of years, reserved by the decedent under a deed of the building by way of gift to his son. The decedent did not make a specific bequest of the right to such rentals. Such right, if passing specifically to the wife, would be a nondeductible interest (see example (5) of paragraph (g) of § 20.2056(b)–1). It is assumed that the value of the bequest of one-third of the residue of the estate to the wife was $85,000, and that the right to the rentals was included in the gross estate at a value of $60,000. If the decedent's executor had the right under the decedent's will or local law to assign the entire lease in satisfaction of the bequest, the bequest is a nondeductible interest to the extent of $60,000. If the executor could only assign a one-third interest in the lease in satisfaction of the bequest, the bequest is a nondeductible interest to the extent of $20,000. If the decedent's will provided that his wife's bequest could not be satisfied with a nondeductible interest, the entire bequest is a deductible interest. If, in this example, the asset in question had been foreign real estate not included in the decedent's gross estate, the results would be the same.

[T.D. 6296, 23 FR 4529, June 24, 1958, as amended by T.D. 8522, 59 FR 9642, Mar. 1, 1994]

§ 20.2056(b)–3 Marital deduction; interest of spouse conditioned on survival for limited period.

(a) In general. Generally, no marital deduction is allowable if the interest passing to the surviving spouse is a terminable interest as defined in paragraph (b) of § 20.2056(b)(1). However, section 2056(b)(3) provides an exception to this rule so as to allow a deduction if (1) the only condition under which it will terminate is the death of the surviving spouse within 6 months after the decedent's death, or her death as a result of a common disaster which also resulted in the decedent's death, and (2) the condition does not in fact occur.

(b) Six months' survival. If the only condition which will cause the interest taken by the surviving spouse to terminate is the death of the surviving spouse and the condition is of such nature that it can occur only within 6 months following the decedent's death, the exception provided by section

2056(b)(3) will apply, provided the condition does not in fact occur. However, if the condition (unless it relates to death as a result of a common disaster) is one which may occur either within the 6–month period or thereafter, the exception provided by section 2056(b)(3) will not apply.

(c) Common disaster. If a property interest passed from the decedent to his surviving spouse subject to the condition that she does not die as a result of a common disaster which also resulted in the decedent's death, the exception provided by section 2056(b)(3) will not be applied in the final audit of the return if there is still a possibility that the surviving spouse may be deprived of the property interest by operation of the common disaster provision as given effect by the local law.

(d) Examples. The application of this section may be illustrated by the following examples:

Example (1). A decedent bequeathed his entire estate to his spouse on condition that she survive him by 6 months. In the event his spouse failed to survive him by 6 months, his estate was to go to his niece and her heirs. The decedent was survived by his spouse. It will be observed that, as of the time of the decedent's death, it was possible that the niece would, by reason of the interest which passed to her from the decedent possess or enjoy the estate after the termination of the interest which passed to the spouse. Hence, under the general rule set forth in § 20.2056(b)–1, the interest which passed to the spouse would be regarded as a nondeductible interest. If the surviving spouse in fact died within 6 months after the decedent's death, that general rule is to be applied, and the interest which passed to the spouse is a nondeductible interest. However, if the spouse in fact survived the decedent by 6 months, thus extinguishing the interest of the niece, the case comes within the exception provided by section 2056(b)(3), and the interest which passed to the spouse is a deductible interest. (It is assumed for the purpose of this example that no other factor which would cause the interest to be nondeductible is present.)

Example (2). The facts are the same as in example (1) except that the will provided that the estate was to go to the niece either in case the decedent and his spouse should both die as a result of a common disaster, or in case the spouse should fail to survive the decedent by 3 months. It is assumed that the decedent was survived by his spouse. In this example, the interest which passed from the decedent to his surviving spouse is to be regarded as a nondeductible interest if the surviving spouse in fact died either within 3 months after the decedent's death or as a result of a common disaster which also resulted in the decedent's death. However, if the spouse in fact survived the decedent by 3 months, and did not thereafter die as a result of a common disaster which also resulted in the decedent's death, the exception provided under section 2056(b)(3) will apply and the interest will be deductible.

Example (3). The facts are the same as in example (1) except that the will provided that the estate was to go to the niece if the decedent and his spouse should both die as a result of a common disaster and if the spouse failed to survive the decedent by 3 months. If the spouse in fact survived the decedent by 3 months, the interest of the niece is extinguished, and the interest passing to the spouse is a deductible interest.

Example (4). A decedent devised and bequeathed his residuary estate to his wife if she was living on the date of distribution of his estate. The devise and bequest is a nondeductible interest even though distribution took place within 6 months after the decedent's death and the surviving spouse in fact survived the date of distribution.

[T.D. 6296, 23 FR 4529, June 24, 1958]

§ 20.2056(b)–4 Marital deduction; valuation of interest passing to surviving spouse.

(a) In general. The value, for the purpose of the marital deduction, of any deductible interest which passed from the decedent to his surviving spouse is to be determined as of the date of the decedent's death, except that if the executor elects the alternate valuation method under section 2032 the valuation is to be determined as of the date of the decedent's death but with the adjustment described in paragraph (a)(3) of § 20.2032–1. The marital deduction may be taken only with respect to the net value of any deductible interest which passed from the decedent to his surviving spouse, the same principles being applicable as if the amount of a gift to the spouse were being determined. In determining the value of the interest in property passing to the spouse account must be taken of the effect of any material limitations upon her right to income from the property. An example of a case in which this rule may be applied is a bequest of property in trust for the benefit of the decedent's spouse but the income from the property from the date of the decedent's death until distribution of the property to the trustee is to be used to pay expenses incurred in the administration of the estate.

(b) Property interest subject to an encumbrance or obligation. If a property interest passed from the decedent to his surviving spouse subject to a mortgage or other encumbrance, or if an obligation is imposed upon the surviving spouse by the decedent in connection with the passing of a property interest, the value of the property interest is to be reduced by the amount of the mortgage, other encumbrance, or obligation. However, if under the terms of the decedent's will or under local law the executor is required to discharge, out of other assets of the decedent's estate, a mortgage or other encumbrance on property passing from the decedent to his surviving spouse, or is required to reimburse the surviving spouse for the amount of the mortgage or other encumbrance, the payment or reimbursement constitutes an additional interest passing to the surviving spouse. The passing of a property interest subject to the imposition of an obligation by the decedent does not include a bequest, devise, or transfer in lieu of dower, curtesy, or of a statutory estate created in lieu of dower or curtesy, or of other marital rights in the decedent's property or estate. The passing of a property interest subject to the imposition of an obligation by the decedent does, however, include a bequest, etc., in lieu of the interest of his surviving spouse under community property laws unless such interest was, immediately prior to the decedent's death, a mere expectancy. The following examples are illustrative of property interests which passed from the decedent to his surviving spouse subject to the imposition of an obligation by the decedent:

Example (1). A decedent devised a residence valued at $25,000 to his wife, with a direction that she pay $5,000 to his sister. For the purpose of the marital deduction, the value of the property interest passing to the wife is only $20,000.

Example (2). A decedent devised real property to his wife in satisfaction of a debt owing to her. The debt is a deductible claim under section 2053. Since the wife is obligated to relinquish the claim as a condition to acceptance of the devise, the value of the devise is, for the purpose of the marital deduction, to be reduced by the amount of the claim.

Example (3). A decedent bequeathed certain securities to his wife in lieu of her interest in property held by them as community property under the law of the State of their residence. The wife elected to relinquish her community property interest and to take the bequest. For the purpose of the marital deduction, the value of the bequest is to be reduced by the value of the community property interest relinquished by the wife.

(c) Effect of death taxes. **(1)** In the determination of the value of any property interest which passed from the decedent to his surviving spouse, there must be taken into account the effect which the Federal estate tax, or any estate, succession, legacy, or inheritance tax, has upon the net value to the surviving spouse of the property interest.

(2) For example, assume that the only bequest to the surviving spouse is $100,000 and the spouse is required to pay a State inheritance tax in the amount of $1,500. If no other death taxes affect the net value of the bequest, the value, for the purpose of the marital deduction, is $98,500.

(3) As another example, assume that a decedent devised real property to his wife having a value for Federal estate tax purposes of $100,000 and also bequeathed to her a nondeductible interest for life under a trust. The State of residence valued the real property at $90,000 and the life interest at $30,000, and imposed an inheritance tax (at graduated rates) of $4,800 with respect to the two interests. If it is assumed that the inheritance tax on the devise is required to be paid by the wife, the amount of tax to be ascribed to the devise is:

$$(90{,}000 \div 120{,}000) \times \$4{,}800 = \$3{,}600.$$

Accordingly, if no other death taxes affect the net value of the bequest, the value, for the purpose of the marital deduction, is $100,000 less $3,600, or $96,400.

(4) If the decedent bequeaths his residuary estate, or a portion of it, to his surviving spouse, and his will contains a direction that all death taxes shall be payable out of the residuary estate, the value of the bequest, for the purpose of the marital deduction, is based upon the amount of the residue as reduced pursuant to such direction, if the residuary estate, or a portion of it, is bequeathed to the surviving spouse, and by the local law the Federal estate tax is payable out of the residuary estate, the value of the bequest, for the purpose of the marital deduction, may not exceed its value as reduced by the Federal estate tax. Methods of computing the deduction, under such circumstances, are set forth in supplemental instructions to the estate tax return.

(d) Effect of administration expenses—(1) Definitions—(i) Management expenses. Estate management expenses are expenses that are incurred in connection with the investment of estate assets or with their preservation or maintenance during a reasonable period of administration. Examples of these expenses could include investment advisory fees, stock brokerage commissions, custodial fees, and interest.

(ii) Transmission expenses. Estate transmission expenses are expenses that would not have been incurred but for the decedent's death and the consequent necessity of collecting the decedent's assets, paying the decedent's debts and death taxes, and distributing the decedent's property to those who are entitled to receive it. Estate transmission expenses include any administration expense that is not a management expense. Examples of these expenses could include executor commissions and attorney fees (except to the extent of commissions or fees specifically related to investment, preservation, or maintenance of the assets), probate fees, expenses incurred in construction proceedings and defending against will contests, and appraisal fees.

(iii) Marital share. The marital share is the property or interest in property that passed from the decedent for which a deduction is allowable under section 2056(a). The marital share includes the income produced by the property or interest in property during the period of administration if the income, under the terms of the governing instrument or applicable local law, is payable to the surviving spouse or is to be added to the principal of the property interest passing to, or for the benefit of, the surviving spouse.

(2) Effect of transmission expenses. For purposes of determining the marital deduction, the value of the marital share shall be reduced by the amount of the estate transmission expenses paid from the marital share.

(3) Effect of management expenses attributable to the marital share. For purposes of determining the marital deduction, the value of the marital share shall not be reduced by the amount of the estate management expenses attributable to and paid from the marital share. Pursuant to section 2056(b)(9), however, the amount of the allowable marital deduction shall be reduced by the amount of any such management expenses that are deducted under section 2053 on the decedent's Federal estate tax return.

(4) Effect of management expenses not attributable to the marital share. For purposes of determining the marital deduction, the value of the marital share shall be reduced by the amount of the estate management expenses paid from the marital share but attributable to a property interest not included in the marital share.

(5) Examples. The following examples illustrate the application of this paragraph (d):

Example 1. The decedent dies after 2006 having made no lifetime gifts. The decedent makes a bequest of shares of ABC Corporation stock to the decedent's child. The bequest provides that the child is to receive the income from the shares from the date of the decedent's death. The value of the bequeathed shares on the decedent's date of death is $3,000,000. The residue of the estate is bequeathed to a trust for which the executor properly makes an election under section 2056(b)(7) to treat as qualified terminable interest property. The value of the residue on the decedent's date of death, before the payment of administration expenses and Federal and State estate taxes, is $6,000,000. Under applicable local law, the executor has the discretion to pay administration expenses from the income or principal of the residuary estate. All estate taxes are to be paid from the residue. The State estate tax equals the State death tax credit available under section 2011. During the period of administration, the estate incurs estate transmission expenses of $400,000, which the executor charges to the residue. For purposes of determining the marital deduction, the value of the residue is reduced by the Federal and State estate taxes and by the estate transmission expenses. If the transmission expenses are deducted on the Federal estate tax return, the marital deduction is $3,500,000 ($6,000,000 minus $400,000 transmission expenses and minus $2,100,000 Federal and State estate taxes). If the transmission expenses are deducted on the estate's Federal income tax return rather than on the estate tax return, the marital deduction is $3,011,111 ($6,000,000 minus $400,000 transmission expenses and minus $2,588,889 Federal and State estate taxes).

Example 2. The facts are the same as in *Example 1*, except that, instead of incurring estate transmission expenses, the estate incurs estate management expenses of $400,000 in connection with the residue property passing for the benefit of the spouse. The executor charges these management expenses to the residue. In determining the value of the residue passing to the spouse for marital deduction purposes, a reduction is made for Federal and State estate taxes payable from the residue but no reduction is made for the estate management expenses. If the management expenses are deducted on the estate's income tax return, the net value of the property passing to the spouse is $3,900,000 ($6,000,000 minus $2,100,000 Federal and State estate taxes). A marital deduction is claimed for that amount, and the taxable estate is $5,100,000.

Example 3. The facts are the same as in *Example 1*, except that the estate management expenses of $400,000 are incurred in connection with the bequest of ABC Corporation stock to the decedent's child. The executor charges these management expenses to the residue. For purposes of determining the marital deduction, the value of the residue is reduced by the Federal and State estate taxes and by the management expenses. The management expenses reduce the value of the residue because they are charged to the property passing to the spouse even though they were incurred with respect to stock passing to the child. If the management expenses are deducted on the estate's Federal income tax return, the marital deduction is $3,011,111 ($6,000,000 minus $400,000 management expenses and minus $2,588,889 Federal and State estate taxes). If the management expenses are deducted on the estate's Federal estate tax return, rather than on the estate's Federal income tax return, the marital deduction is $3,500,000 ($6,000,000 minus $400,000 management expenses and minus $2,100,000 in Federal and State estate taxes).

Example 4. The decedent, who dies in 2000, has a gross estate of $3,000,000.

Included in the gross estate are proceeds of $150,000 from a policy insuring the decedent's life and payable to the decedent's child as beneficiary. The applicable credit amount against the tax was fully consumed by the decedent's lifetime gifts. Applicable State law requires the child to pay any estate taxes attributable to the life insurance policy. Pursuant to the decedent's will, the rest of the decedent's estate passes outright to the surviving spouse. During the period of administration, the estate incurs estate management expenses of $150,000 in connection with the property passing to the spouse. The value of the property passing to the spouse is $2,850,000 ($3,000,-000 less the insurance proceeds of $150,000 passing to the child). For purposes of determining the marital deduction, if the management expenses are deducted on the estate's income tax return, the marital deduction is $2,850,000 ($3,000,000 less $150,000) and there is a resulting taxable estate of $150,000 ($3,000,000 less a marital deduction of $2,850,000). Suppose, instead, the management expenses of $150,000 are deducted on the estate's estate tax return under section 2053 as expenses of administration. In such a situation, claiming a marital deduction of $2,850,000 would be taking a deduction for the same $150,000 in property under both sections 2053 and 2056 and would shield from estate taxes the $150,000 in insurance proceeds passing to the decedent's child. Therefore, in accordance with section 2056(b)(9), the marital deduction is limited to $2,700,000, and the resulting taxable estate is $150,000.

Example 5. The decedent dies after 2006 having made no lifetime gifts. The value of the decedent's residuary estate on the decedent's date of death is $3,000,000, before the payment of administration expenses and Federal and State estate taxes. The decedent's will provides a formula for dividing the decedent's residuary estate between two trusts to reduce the estate's Federal estate taxes to zero. Under the formula, one trust, for the benefit of the decedent's child, is to be funded with that amount of property equal in value to so much of the applicable exclusion amount under section 2010 that would reduce the estate's Federal estate tax to zero. The other trust, for the benefit of the surviving spouse, satisfies the requirements of section 2056(b)(7) and is to be funded with the remaining property in the estate. The State estate tax equals the State death tax credit available under section 2011. During the period of administration, the estate incurs transmission expenses of $200,000. The transmission expenses of $200,000 reduce the value of the residue to $2,800,000. If the transmission expenses are deducted on the Federal estate tax return, then the formula divides the residue so that the value of the property passing to the child's trust is $1,000,000 and the value of the property passing to the marital trust is $1,800,000. The allowable marital deduction is $1,800,000. The applicable exclusion amount shields from Federal estate tax the entire $1,000,000 passing to the child's trust so that the amount of Federal and State estate taxes is zero. Alternatively, if the transmission expenses are deducted on the estate's Federal income tax return, the formula divides the residue so that the value of the property passing to the child's trust is $800,000 and the value of the property passing to the marital trust is $2,000,000. The allowable marital deduction is $2,000,000. The applicable exclusion amount shields from Federal estate tax the entire $800,000 passing to the child's trust so that the amount of Federal and State estate taxes remains zero.

Example 6. The facts are the same as in Example 5, except that the decedent's will provides that the child's trust is to be funded with that amount of property equal in value to the applicable exclusion amount under section 2010 allowable to the decedent's estate. The residue of the estate, after the payment of any debts, expenses, and Federal and State estate taxes, is to pass to the marital trust. The applicable exclusion amount in this case is $1,000,000, so the value of the property passing to the child's trust is $1,000,000. After deducting the $200,000 of transmission expenses, the residue of the estate is $1,800,000 less any estate taxes. If the transmission expenses are deducted on the Federal estate tax return, the allowable marital deduction is $1,800,000, the taxable estate is zero, and the Federal and State estate taxes are zero. Alternatively, if the transmission expenses are deducted on the estate's Federal income tax return, the net value of the property passing to the spouse is $1,657,874 ($1,800,000 minus $142,106 estate taxes). A marital deduction is claimed for that amount, the taxable estate is $1,342,106, and the Federal and State estate taxes total $142,106.

Example 7. The decedent, who dies in 2000, makes an outright pecuniary bequest of $3,000,000 to the decedent's surviving spouse, and the residue of the estate, after the payment of all debts, expenses, and Federal and State estate taxes, passes to the decedent's child. Under the terms of the governing instrument and applicable local law, a beneficiary of a pecuniary bequest is not entitled to any income on the bequest. During the period of administration, the estate pays estate transmission expenses from the income earned by the property that will be distributed to the surviving spouse in satisfaction of the pecuniary bequest. The income earned on this property is not part of the marital share. Therefore, the allowable marital deduction is $3,000,000, unreduced by the amount of the estate transmission expenses.

* * *

(e) Remainder interests. If the income from property is made payable to another individual for life, or for a term of years, with remainder absolutely to the surviving spouse or to her estate, the marital deduction is based upon the present value of the remainder. * * *

[T.D. 6296, 23 FR 4529, June 24, 1958, as amended by T.D. 8522, 59 FR 9642, Mar. 1, 1994; T.D. 8540, 59 FR 30100, June 10, 1994; T.D. 8846, 64 FR 67763, Dec. 2, 1999; 64 FR 71022, Dec. 15, 1999]

§ 20.2056(b)–5 Marital deduction; life estate with power of appointment in surviving spouse.

(a) In general. Section 2056(b)(5) provides that if an interest in property passes from the decedent to his surviving spouse (whether or not in trust) and the spouse is entitled for life to all the income from the entire interest or all the income from a specific portion of the entire interest, with a power in her to appoint the entire interest or the specific portion, the interest which passes to her is a deductible interest, to the extent that it satisfies all five of the conditions set forth below (see paragraph (b) of this section if one or more of the conditions is satisfied as to only a portion of the interest):

(1) The surviving spouse must be entitled for life to all of the income from the entire interest or a specific portion of the entire interest, or to a specific portion of all the income from the entire interest.

(2) The income payable to the surviving spouse must be payable annually or at more frequent intervals.

(3) The surviving spouse must have the power to appoint the entire interest or the specific portion to either herself or her estate.

(4) The power in the surviving spouse must be exercisable by her alone and (whether exercisable by will or during life) must be exercisable in all events.

(5) The entire interest or the specific portion must not be subject to a power in any other person to appoint any part to any person other than the surviving spouse.

(b) Specific portion; deductible amount. If either the right to income or the power of appointment passing to the surviving spouse pertains only to a specific portion of a property interest passing from the decedent, the marital deduction is allowed only to the extent that the rights in the surviving spouse meet all of the five conditions described in paragraph (a) of this section. While the rights over the income and the power must coexist as to the same interest in property, it is not necessary that the rights over the income or the power as to such interest be in the same proportion. However, if the rights over income meeting the required conditions set forth in paragraph (a)(1) and (2) of the section extend over a smaller share of the property interest than the share with respect to which the power of appointment requirements set forth in paragraph (a)(3) through (5) of this section are satisfied, the deductible interest is limited to the smaller share. Correspondingly, if a power of appointment meeting all the requirements extends to a smaller portion of the property interest than the portion over which the income rights pertain, the deductible interest cannot exceed the value of the portion to which such power of appointment applies. Thus, if the decedent leaves to his surviving spouse the right to receive annually all of the income from a particular property interest and a power of appointment meeting the specifications prescribed in paragraph (a)(3) through (5) of this section as to only one-half of the property interest, then only one-half of the property interest is treated as a deductible interest. Correspondingly, if the income interest of the spouse satisfying the requirements extends to only one-fourth of the property interest and a testamentary power of appointment satisfying the requirements extends to all of the property interest, then only one-fourth of the interest in the spouse qualifies as a deductible interest. Further, if the surviving spouse has no right to income from a specific portion of a property interest but a testamentary power of appointment which meets the necessary conditions over the entire interest, then none of the interest qualifies for the deduction. In addition, if, from the time of the decedent's death, the surviving spouse has a power of appointment meeting all of the required conditions over three-fourths of the entire property interest and the prescribed income rights over the entire interest, but with a power in another person to appoint one-half of the entire interest, the value of the interest in the surviving spouse over only one-half of the property interest will qualify as a deductible interest.

(c) Meaning of specific portion—(1) In general. Except as provided in paragraphs (c)(2) and (c)(3) of this section, a partial interest in property is not treated as a specific portion of the entire interest. In addition, any specific portion of an entire interest in property is nondeductible to the extent the specific portion is subject to invasion for the benefit of any person other than the surviving spouse, except in the case of a deduction allowable under section 2056(b)(5), relating to the exercise of a general power of appointment by the surviving spouse.

(2) Fraction or percentage share. Under section 2056(b)(10), a partial interest in property is treated as a specific portion of the entire interest if the rights of the surviving spouse in income, and the required rights as to the power described in § 20.2056(b)–5(a), constitute a fractional or percentage share of the entire property interest, so that the surviving spouse's interest reflects its proportionate share of the increase or decrease in the value of the entire property interest to which the income rights and the power relate. Thus, if the spouse's right to income and the spouse's power extend to a specified fraction or percentage of the property, or the equivalent, the interest is in a specific portion of the property. In accordance with paragraph (b) of this section, if the spouse has the right to receive the income from a specific portion of the trust property (after applying paragraph (c)(3) of this section) but has a power of appointment over a different specific portion of the property (after applying paragraph (c)(3) of this section), the marital deduction is limited to the lesser specific portion.

(3) Special rule in the case of estates of decedents dying on or before October 24, 1992, and certain decedents dying after October 24, 1992, with wills or revocable trusts executed on or prior to that date.

(i) In the case of estates of decedents within the purview of the effective date and transitional rules contained in paragraphs (c)(3)(ii) and (iii) of this section:

(A) A specific sum payable annually, or at more frequent intervals, out of the property and its income that is not limited by the income of the property is treated as the right to receive the income from a specific portion of the property. The specific portion, for purposes of paragraph (c)(2) of this section, is the portion of the property that, assuming the interest rate generally applicable for the valuation of annuities at the time of the decedent's death, would produce income equal to such payments. However, a pecuniary amount payable annually to a surviving spouse is not treated as a right to the income from a specific portion of the trust property for purposes of this paragraph (c)(3)(i)(A) if any person other than the surviving spouse may receive, during the surviving spouse's lifetime, any distribution of the property. To determine the applicable interest rate for valuing annuities, see sections 2031 and 7520 and the regulations under those sections.

(B) The right to appoint a pecuniary amount out of a larger fund (or trust corpus) is considered the right to appoint a specific portion of such fund or trust for purposes of paragraph (c)(2) in an amount equal to such pecuniary amount.

(ii) The rules contained in paragraphs (c)(3)(i)(A) and (B) of this section apply with respect to estates of decedents dying on or before October 24, 1992.

(iii) The rules contained in paragraphs (c)(3)(i)(A) and (B) of this section apply in the case of decedents dying after October 24, 1992, if property passes to the spouse pursuant to a will or revocable trust agreement executed on or before October 24, 1992, and either—

(A) On that date, the decedent was under a mental disability to change the disposition of the property and did not regain competence to dispose of such property before the date of death; or

(B) The decedent dies prior to October 24, 1995.

(iv) Notwithstanding paragraph (c)(3)(iii) of this section, paragraphs (c)(3)(i)(A) and (B) of this section do not apply if the will or revocable trust is amended after October 24, 1992, in any respect that increases the amount of the transfer qualifying for the marital deduction or alters the terms by which the interest so passes to the surviving spouse of the decedent.

(4) Local law. A partial interest in property is treated as a specific portion of the entire interest if it is shown that the surviving spouse has rights under local law that are identical to those the surviving spouse would have acquired had the partial interest been expressed in terms satisfying the requirements of paragraph (c)(2) (or paragraph (c)(3) if applicable) of this section.

(5) Examples. The following examples illustrate the application of paragraphs (a) through (c)(4) of this section:

Example 1. Spouse entitled to the lesser of an annuity or a fraction of trust income. The decedent, D, died prior to October 24, 1992. D bequeathed in trust 500 identical shares of X company stock, valued for estate tax purposes at $500,000. The trust provides that during the lifetime of D's spouse, S, the trustee is to pay annually to S the lesser of one-half of the trust income or $20,000. Any trust income not paid to S is to be accumulated in the trust and may not be distributed during S's lifetime. S has a testamentary general power of appointment over the entire trust principal. The applicable interest rate for valuing annuities as of D's date of death under section 7520 is 10 percent. For purposes of paragraphs (a) through (c) of this section, S is treated as receiving all of the income from the lesser of—

(i) One half of the stock ($250,000); or

(ii) $200,000, the specific portion of the stock which, as determined in accordance with § 20.2056(b)–5(c)(3)(i)(A), would produce annual income of $20,000 (20,000/.10). Accordingly, the marital deduction is limited to $200,000 (200,000/500,000 or ⅖ of the value of the trust).

Example 2. Spouse possesses power and income interest over different specific portions of trust. The facts are the same as in Example 1 except that S's testamentary general power of appointment is exercisable over only ¼ of the trust principal. Consequently, under section 2056(b)(5), the marital deduction is allowable only for the value of ¼ of the trust ($125,000); i.e., the lesser of the value of the portion with respect to which S is deemed to be entitled to all of the income (⅖ of the trust or $200,000), or the value of the portion with respect to which S possesses the requisite power of appointment (¼ of the trust or $125,000).

Example 3. Power of appointment over pecuniary amount. The decedent, D, died prior to October 24, 1992. D bequeathed property valued at $400,000 for estate tax purposes in trust. The trustee is to pay annually to D's spouse, S, one-fourth of the trust income. Any trust income not paid to S is to be accumulated in the trust and may not be distributed during S's lifetime. The will gives S a testamentary general power of appointment over the sum of $160,000. Because D died prior to October 24, 1992, S's power of appointment over $160,000 is treated as a power of appointment over a specific portion of the entire trust interest. The marital deduction allowable under section 2056(b)(5) is limited to $100,000; that is, the lesser of—

(1) The value of the trust corpus ($400,000);

(2) The value of the trust corpus over which S has a power of appointment ($160,000); or

(3) That specific portion of the trust with respect to which S is entitled to all the income ($100,000).

Example 4. Power of appointment over shares of stock constitutes a power over a specific portion.

Under D's will, 250 shares of Y company stock were bequeathed in trust pursuant to which all trust income was payable annually to S, D's spouse, for life. S was given a testamentary general power of appointment over 100 shares of stock. The trust provides that if the trustee sells the Y company stock, S's general power of appointment is exercisable with respect to the sale proceeds or the property in which the proceeds are reinvested. Because the amount of property represented by a single share of stock would be altered if the corporation split its stock, issued stock dividends, made a distribution of capital, etc., a power to appoint 100 shares at the time of S's death is not necessarily a power to appoint the entire interest that the 100 shares represented on the date of D's death. If it is shown that, under local law, S has a general power to appoint not only the 100 shares designated by D but also 100/250 of any distributions by the corporation that are included in trust principal, the requirements of paragraph (c)(2) of this section are satisfied and S is treated as having a general power to appoint 100/250 of the entire interest in the 250 shares. In that case, the marital deduction is limited to 40 percent of the trust principal. If local law does not give S that power, the 100 shares would not constitute a specific portion under § 20.2056(b)–5(c) (including § 20.2056(b)–5(c)(3)(i)(B)). The nature of the asset is such that a change in the capitalization of the corporation could cause an alteration in the original value represented by the shares at the time of D's death and, thus, it does not represent a specific portion of the trust.

(d) Meaning of entire interest. Because a marital deduction is allowed for each separate qualifying interest in property passing from the decedent to the decedent's surviving spouse (subject to any applicable limitations in § 20.2056(a)–1(c)), for purposes of paragraphs (a) and (b) of this section, each property interest with respect to which the surviving spouse received any rights is considered separately in determining whether the surviving spouse's rights extend to the entire interest or to a specific portion of the entire interest. A property interest which consists of several identical units of property (such as a block of 250 shares of stock, whether the ownership is evidenced by one or several certificates) is considered one property interest, unless certain of the units are to be segregated and accorded different treatment, in which case each segregated group of items is considered a separate property interest. The bequest of a specified sum of money constitutes the bequest of a separate property interest if immediately following distribution by the executor and thenceforth it, and the investments made with it, must be so segregated or accounted for as to permit its identification as a separate item of property. The application of this paragraph may be illustrated by the following examples:

Example (1). The decedent transferred to a trustee three adjoining farms, Blackacre, Whiteacre, and Greenacre. His will provided that during the lifetime of the surviving spouse the trustee should pay her all of the income from the trust. Upon her death, all of Blackacre, a one-half interest in Whiteacre, and a one-third interest in Greenacre were to be distributed to the person or persons appointed by her in her will. The surviving spouse is considered as being entitled to all of the income from the entire interest in Blackacre, all of the income from the entire interest in Whiteacre, and all of the income from the entire interest in Greenacre. She also is considered as having a power of appointment over the entire interest in Blackacre, over one-half of the entire interest in Whiteacre, and over one-third of the entire interest in Greenacre.

Example (2). The decedent bequeathed $250,000 to C, as trustee. C is to invest the money and pay all of the income from the investments to W, the decedent's surviving spouse, annually. W was given a general power, exercisable by will, to appoint one-half of the corpus of the trust. Here, immediately following distribution by the executor, the $250,000 will be sufficiently segregated to permit its identification as a separate item, and the $250,000 will constitute an entire property interest. Therefore, W has a right to income and a power of appointment such that one-half of the entire interest is a deductible interest.

Example (3). The decedent bequeathed 100 shares of Z corporation stock to D, as trustee. W, the decedent's surviving spouse, is to receive all of the income of the trust annually and is given a general power, exercisable by will, to appoint out of the trust corpus the sum of $25,000. In this case the $25,000 is not, immediately following distribution, sufficiently segregated to permit its identification as a separate item of property in which the surviving spouse has the entire interest. Therefore, the $25,000 does not constitute the entire interest in a property for the purpose of paragraphs (a) and (b) of this section.

(e) Application of local law. In determining whether or not the conditions set forth in paragraph (a)(1) through (5) of this section are satisfied by the instrument of transfer, regard is to be had to the applicable provisions of the law of the jurisdiction under which the interest passes and, if the transfer is in trust, the applicable provisions of the law governing the administration of the trust. For example, silence of a trust instrument as to the frequency of payment will not be regarded as a failure to satisfy the condition set forth in paragraph (a)(2) of this section that income must be payable to the surviving spouse annually or more frequently unless the applicable law permits payment to be made less frequently than annually. The principles outlined in this paragraph and paragraphs (f) and (g) of this section which are applied in determining whether transfers in trust meet such conditions are equally applicable in ascertaining whether, in the case of interests not in trust, the surviving spouse has the equivalent in rights over income and over the property.

(f) Right to income. **(1)** If an interest is transferred in trust, the surviving spouse is "entitled for life to all of the income from the entire interest or a specific portion of the entire interest", for the purpose of the condition set forth in paragraph (a)(1) of this section, if the effect of the trust is to give her substantially that degree of beneficial enjoyment of the trust property during her life which the principles of the law of trusts accord to a person who is unqualifiedly designated as the life beneficiary of a trust. Such degree of enjoyment is given only if it was the decedent's intention, as manifested by the terms of the trust instrument and the surrounding circumstances, that the trust should produce for the surviving spouse during her life such an income, or that the spouse should have such use of the trust property as is consistent with the value of the trust corpus and with its preservation. The designation of the spouse as sole income beneficiary for life of the entire interest or a specific portion of the entire interest will be sufficient to qualify the trust unless the terms of the trust and the surrounding circumstances considered as a whole evidence an intention to deprive the spouse of the requisite degree of enjoyment. In determining whether a trust evidences that intention, the treatment required or permitted with respect to individual items must be considered in relation to the entire system provided for the administration of the trust. In addition, the surviving spouse's interest shall meet the condition set forth in paragraph (a)(1) of this section if the spouse is entitled to income as determined by applicable local law that provides for a reasonable apportionment between the income and remainder beneficiaries of the total return of the trust and that meets the requirements of § 1.643(b)–1 of this chapter.

(2) If the over-all effect of a trust is to give to the surviving spouse such enforceable rights as will preserve to her the requisite degree of enjoyment, it is immaterial whether that result is effected by rules specifically stated in the trust instrument, or, in their absence, by the rules for the management of the trust property and the allocation of receipts and expenditures supplied by the State law. For example, a provision in the trust instrument for amortization of bond premium by appropriate periodic charges to interest will not disqualify the interest passing in trust even though there is no State law specifically authorizing amortization, or there is a State law denying amortization which is applicable only in the absence of such a provision in the trust instrument.

(3) In the case of a trust, the rules to be applied by the trustee in allocation of receipts and expenses between income and corpus must be considered in relation to the nature and expected productivity of the assets passing in trust, the nature and frequency of occurrence of the expected receipts, and any provisions as to change in the form of investments. If it is evident from the nature of the trust assets and the rules provided for management of the trust that the allocation to income of such receipts as rents, ordinary cash dividends, and interest will give to the spouse the substantial enjoyment during life required by the statute, provisions that such receipts as stock dividends and proceeds from the conversion of trust assets shall be treated as corpus will not disqualify the interest passing in trust. Similarly, provision for a depletion charge against income in the case of trust assets which are subject to depletion will not disqualify the interest passing in trust, unless the effect is to deprive the spouse of the requisite beneficial enjoyment. The same principle is applicable in the case of depreciation, trustees' commissions, and other charges.

(4) Provisions granting administrative powers to the trustee will not have the effect of disqualifying an interest passing in trust unless the grant of powers evidences the intention to deprive the surviving spouse of the beneficial enjoyment required by the statute. Such an intention will not be considered to exist if the entire terms of the instrument are such that the local courts will impose reasonable limitations upon the exercise of the powers. Among the powers which if subject to reasonable limitations will not disqualify the interest passing in trust are the power to determine the allocation or apportionment of receipts and disbursements between income and corpus, the power to apply the income or corpus for the benefit of the spouse, and the power to retain the assets passing to the trust. For example, a power to retain trust assets which consist substantially of unproductive property will not disqualify the interest if the applicable rules for the administration of the trust require, or permit the spouse to require, that the trustee either make the property productive or convert it within a reasonable time. Nor will such a power disqualify the interest if the applicable rules for administration of the trust require the trustee to use the degree of judgment and care in the exercise of the power which a prudent man would use if he were owner of the trust assets. Further, a power to retain a residence or other property for the personal use of the spouse will not disqualify the interest passing in trust.

(5) An interest passing in trust will not satisfy the condition set forth in paragraph (a)(1) of this section that the surviving spouse be entitled to all the income if the primary purpose of the trust is to safeguard property without providing the spouse with the required beneficial enjoyment. Such trusts include not only trusts which expressly provide for the accumulation of the income but also trusts which indirectly accomplish a similar purpose. For example, assume that the corpus of a trust consists substantially of property which is not likely to be income producing during the life of the surviving spouse and that the spouse cannot compel the trustee to convert or otherwise deal with the property as described in subparagraph (4) of this paragraph. An interest passing to such a trust will not qualify unless the applicable rules for the administration require, or permit the spouse to require, that the trustee provide the required beneficial enjoyment such as by payments to the spouse out of other assets of the trust.

(6) If a trust is created during the decedent's life, it is immaterial whether or not the interest passing in trust satisfied the conditions set forth in paragraph (a)(1) through (5) of this section prior to the decedent's death. If a trust may be terminated during the life of the surviving spouse, under her exercise of a power of appointment or by distribution of the corpus to her, the interest passing in trust satisfies the condition set forth in paragraph (a)(1) of this section (that the spouse be entitled to all the income) if she (i) is entitled to the income until the trust terminates, or (ii) has the right, exercisable in all events, to have the corpus distributed to her at any time during her life.

(7) An interest passing in trust fails to satisfy the condition set forth in paragraph (a)(1) of this section, that the spouse be entitled to all the income, to the extent that the income is required to be accumulated in whole or in part or may be accumulated in the discretion of any person other than the surviving spouse; to the extent that the consent of any person other than the surviving spouse is required as a condition precedent to distribution of the income; or to the extent that any person other than the surviving spouse has the power to alter the terms of the trust so as to deprive her of her right to the income. An interest passing in trust will not fail to satisfy the condition that the spouse be entitled to all the income merely because its terms provide that the right of the surviving spouse to the income shall not be subject to assignment, alienation, pledge, attachment or claims of creditors.

(8) In the case of an interest passing in trust, the terms "entitled for life" and "payable annually or at more frequent intervals," as used in the conditions set forth in paragraph (a)(1) and (2) of this section, require that under the terms of the trust the income referred to must be currently (at least annually; see paragraph (e) of this section) distributable to the spouse or that she must have such command over the income that it is virtually hers. Thus, the conditions in paragraph (a)(1) and (2) of this section are satisfied in this respect if, under the terms of the trust instrument, the spouse has the right exercisable annually (or more frequently) to require distribution to herself of the trust income, and otherwise the trust income is to be accumulated and added to corpus. Similarly, as respects the income for the period between the last distribution date and the date of the spouse's death, it is sufficient if that income is subject to the spouse's power to appoint. Thus, if the trust instrument provides that income accrued or undistributed on the date of the spouse's death is to be disposed of as if it had been received after her death, and if the spouse has a power of appointment over the trust corpus, the power necessarily extends to the undistributed income.

(9) An interest is not to be regarded as failing to satisfy the conditions set forth in paragraph (a)(1) and (2) of this section (that the spouse be entitled to all the income and that it be payable annually or more frequently) merely because the spouse is not entitled to the income from estate assets for the period before distribution of those assets by the executor, unless the executor is, by the decedent's will, authorized or directed to delay distribution beyond the period reasonably required for administration of the decedent's estate. As to the valuation of the property interest passing to the spouse in trust where the right to income is expressly postponed, see § 20.2056(b)–4.

(g) Power of appointment in surviving spouse. **(1)** The conditions set forth in paragraph (a)(3) and (4) of this section, that is, that the surviving spouse must have a power of appointment exercisable in favor of herself or her estate and exercisable alone and in all events are not met unless the power of the surviving spouse to appoint the entire interest or a specific portion of it falls within one of the following categories:

(i) A power so to appoint fully exercisable in her own favor at any time following the decedent's death (as, for example, an unlimited power to invade); or

(ii) A power so to appoint exercisable in favor of her estate. Such a power, if exercisable during life, must be fully exercisable at any time during life, or, if exercisable by will, must be fully exercisable irrespective of the time of her death (subject in either case to the provisions of § 20.2053(b)–3, relating to interests conditioned on survival for a limited period); or

(iii) A combination of the powers described under subdivisions (i) and (ii) of this subparagraph. For example, the surviving spouse may, until she attains the age of 50 years, have a power to appoint to herself and thereafter have a power to appoint to her estate. However, the condition that the spouse's power must be exercisable in all events is not satisfied unless irrespective of when the surviving spouse may die the entire interest or a specific portion of it will at the time of her death be subject to one power or the other (subject to the exception in § 20.2053(b)–3, relating to interests contingent on survival for a limited period).

(2) The power of the surviving spouse must be a power to appoint the entire interest or a specific portion of it as unqualified owner (and free of the trust if a trust is involved, or free of the joint tenancy if a joint tenancy is involved) or to appoint the entire interest or a specific portion of it as a part of her estate (and free of the trust if a trust is involved), that is, in effect, to dispose of it to whomsoever she pleases. Thus, if the decedent devised property to a son and the surviving spouse as joint tenants with right of survivorship and under local law the surviving spouse has a power of severance exercisable without consent of the other joint tenant, and by exercising this power could acquire a one-half interest in the property as a tenant in common, her power of severance will satisfy the conditions set forth in paragraph (a)(3) of this section that she have a power of appointment in favor of herself or her estate. However, if the surviving spouse entered into a binding agreement with the decedent to exercise the power only in favor of their issue, that condition is not met. An interest passing in trust will not be regarded as failing to satisfy the condition merely because takers in default of the surviving spouse's exercise of the power are designated by the decedent. The decedent may provide that, in default of exercise of the power, the trust shall continue for an additional period.

(3) A power is not considered to be a power exercisable by a surviving spouse alone and in all events as required by paragraph (a)(4) of this section if the exercise of the power in the surviving spouse to appoint the entire interest or a specific portion of it to herself or to her estate requires the joinder or consent of any other person. The power is not "exercisable in all events", if it can be terminated during the life of the surviving spouse by any event other than her complete exercise or release of it. Further, a power is not "exercisable in all events" if it may be exercised for a limited purpose only. For example, a power which is not exercisable in the event of the spouse's remarriage is not exercisable in all events. Likewise, if there are any restrictions, either by the terms of the instrument or under applicable local law, on the exercise of a power to consume property (whether or not held in trust) for the benefit of the spouse, the power is not exercisable in all events. Thus, if a power of invasion is exercisable only for the spouse's support, or only for her limited use, the power is not exercisable in all events. In order for a power of invasion to be exercisable in all events, the surviving spouse must have the unrestricted power exercisable at any time during her life to use all or any part of the property subject to the power, and to dispose of it in any manner, including the power to dispose of it by gift (whether or not she has power to dispose of it by will).

(4) The power in the surviving spouse is exercisable in all events only if it exists immediately following the decedent's death. For example, if the power given to the surviving spouse is exercisable during life, but cannot be effectively exercised before distribution of the assets by the executor, the power is not exercisable in all events. Similarly, if the power is exercisable by will, but cannot be effectively exercised in the event the surviving spouse dies before distribution of the assets by the executor, the power is not exercisable in all events. However, an interest will not be disqualified by the mere fact that, in the event the power is exercised during administration of the estate, distribution of the property to the appointee will be delayed for the period of administration. If the power is in existence at all times following the decedent's death, limitations of a formal nature will not disqualify an interest. Examples of formal limitations on a power exercisable during life are requirements that an exercise must be in a particular form, that it must be filed with a trustee during the spouse's life, that reasonable notice must be given, or that reasonable intervals must elapse between successive partial exercises. Examples of formal limitations on a power exercisable by will are that it must be exercised by a will executed by the surviving spouse after the decedent's death or that exercise must be by specific reference to the power.

(5) If the surviving spouse has the requisite power to appoint to herself or her estate, it is immaterial that she also has one or more lesser powers. Thus, if she has a testamentary power to appoint to her estate, she may also have a limited power of withdrawal or of appointment during her life. Similarly, if she has an unlimited power of withdrawal, she may have a limited testamentary power.

(h) Requirement of survival for a limited period. A power of appointment in the surviving spouse will not be treated as failing to meet the requirements of paragraph (a)(3) of this section even though the power may terminate, if the only conditions which would cause the termination are those described in paragraph (a) of § 20.2056(b)–3, and if those conditions do not in fact occur. Thus, the entire interest or a specific portion of it will not be disqualified by reason of the fact that the exercise of the power in the spouse is subject to a condition of survivorship described in § 20.2056(b)–3 if the terms of the condition, that is, the survivorship of the surviving spouse, or the failure to die in a common disaster, are fulfilled.

(i) [Reserved]

(j) Existence of a power in another. Paragraph (a)(5) of this section provides that a transfer described in paragraph (a) is nondeductible to the extent that the decedent created a power in the trustee or in any other person to appoint a part of the interest to any person other than the surviving spouse. However, only powers in other persons which are in opposition to that of the surviving spouse will cause a portion of the interest to fail to satisfy the condition set forth in paragraph (a)(5) of this section. Thus, a power in a trustee to distribute corpus to or for the benefit of a surviving spouse will not disqualify the trust. Similarly, a power to distribute corpus to the spouse for the support of minor children will not disqualify the trust if she is legally obligated to support such children. The application of this paragraph may be illustrated by the following examples:

Example (1). Assume that a decedent created a trust, designating his surviving spouse as income beneficiary for life with an unrestricted power in the spouse to appoint the corpus during her life. The decedent further provided that in the event the surviving spouse should die without having exercised the power, the trust should continue for the life of his son with a power in the son to appoint the corpus. Since the power in the son could become exercisable only after the death of the surviving spouse, the interest is not regarded as failing to satisfy the condition set forth in paragraph (a)(5) of this section.

Example (2). Assume that the decedent created a trust, designating his surviving spouse as income beneficiary for life and as donee of a power to appoint by will the entire corpus. The decedent further provided that the trustee could distribute 30 percent of the corpus to the decedent's son when he reached the age of 35 years. Since the trustee has a power to appoint 30 percent of the entire interest for the benefit of a person other than the surviving spouse, only 70 percent of the interest placed in trust satisfied the condition set forth in paragraph (a)(5) of this section. If, in this case, the surviving spouse had a power, exercisable by her will, to appoint only one-half of the corpus as it was constituted at the time of her death, it should be noted that only 35 percent of the interest placed in the trust would satisfy the condition set forth in paragraph (a)(3) of this section.

[T.D. 6296, 23 FR 4529, June 24, 1958, as amended by T.D. 8522, 59 FR 9642, Mar. 1, 1994; T.D. 9102, 69 FR 12, Jan. 2, 2004]

§ 20.2056(b)–6 Marital deduction; life insurance or annuity payments with power of appointment in surviving spouse.

(a) In general. Section 2056(b)(6) provides that an interest in property passing from a decedent to his surviving spouse, which consists of proceeds held by an insurer under the terms of a life insurance, endowment, or annuity contract, is a ''deductible interest'' to the extent that is satisfied all five of the following conditions (see paragraph (b) of this section if one or more of the conditions is satisfied as to only a portion of the proceeds):

(1) The proceeds, or a specific portion of the proceeds, must be held by the insurer subject to an agreement either to pay the entire proceeds or a specific portion thereof in installments, or to pay interest thereon, and all or a specific portion of the installments or interest payable during the life of the surviving spouse must be payable only to her.

(2) The installments or interest payable to the surviving spouse must be payable annually, or more frequently, commencing not later than 13 months after the decedent's death.

(3) The surviving spouse must have the power to appoint all or a specific portion of the amounts so held by the insurer to either herself or her estate.

(4) The power in the surviving spouse must be exercisable by her alone and (whether exercisable by will or during life) must be exercisable in all events.

(5) The amounts or the specific portion of the amounts payable under such contract must not be subject to a power in any other person to appoint any part thereof to any person other than the surviving spouse.

(b) Specific portion; deductible interest. If the right to receive interest or installment payments or the power of appointment passing to the surviving spouse pertains only to a specific portion of the proceeds held by the insurer, the marital deduction is allowed only to the extent that the rights of the surviving spouse in the specific portion meet the five conditions described in paragraph (a) of this section. While the rights to interest, or to receive payment in installments, and the power must coexist as to the proceeds of the same contract, it is not necessary that the rights to each be in the same proportion. If the rights to interest meeting the required conditions set forth in paragraph (a)(1) and (2) of this section extend over a smaller share of the proceeds than the share with respect to which the power of appointment requirements set forth in paragraph (a)(3) through (5) of this section are satisfied, the deductible interest is limited to the smaller share. Similarly, if the portion of the proceeds payable in installments is a smaller portion of the proceeds than the portion to which the power of appointment meeting such requirements relates, the deduction is limited to the smaller portion. In addition, if a power of appointment meeting all the requirements extends to a smaller portion of the proceeds than the portion over which the interest or installment rights pertain, the deductible interest cannot exceed the value of the portion to which such power of appointment applies. Thus, if the contract provides that the insurer is to retain the entire proceeds and pay all of the interest thereon annually to the surviving spouse and if the surviving spouse has a power of appointment meeting the specifications prescribed in paragraph (a)(3) through (5) of this section, as to only one-half of the proceeds held, then only one-half of the proceeds may be treated as a deductible interest. Correspondingly, if the rights of the spouse to receive installment payments or interest satisfying the requirements extend to only one-fourth of the proceeds and a testamentary power of appointment satisfying the requirements of paragraph (a)(3) through (5) of this section extends to all of the proceeds, then only one-fourth of the proceeds qualifies as a deductible interest. Further, if the surviving spouse has no right to installment payments (or interest) over any portion of the proceeds but a testamentary power of appointment which meets the necessary conditions over the entire remaining proceeds, then none of the proceeds qualifies for the deduction. In addition, if, from the time of the decedent's death, the surviving spouse has a power of appointment meeting all of the required conditions over three-fourths of the proceeds and the right to receive interest from the entire proceeds, but with a power in another person to appoint one-half of the entire proceeds, the value of the interest in the surviving spouse over only one-half of the proceeds will qualify as a deductible interest.

(c) Applicable principles. **(1)** The principles set forth in paragraph (c) of § 20.2056(b)–5 for determining what constitutes a "specific portion of the entire interest" for the purpose of section 2056(b)(5) are applicable in determining what constitutes a "specific portion of all such amounts" for the purpose of section 2056(b)(6). However, the interest in the proceeds passing to the surviving spouse will not be disqualified by the fact that the installment payments or interest to which the spouse is entitled or the amount of the proceeds over which the power of appointment is exercisable may be expressed in terms of a specific sum rather than a fraction or a percentage of the proceeds provided it is shown that such sums are a definite or fixed percentage or fraction of the total proceeds.

(2) The provisions of paragraph (a) of this section are applicable with respect to a property interest which passed from the decedent in the form of proceeds of a policy of insurance upon the decedent's life, a policy of insurance upon the life of a person who predeceased the decedent, a matured endowment policy, or an annuity contract, but only in case the proceeds are to be held by the insurer. With respect to proceeds under any such contract which are to be held by a trustee, with power of appointment in the surviving spouse, see § 20.2056(b)–5. As to the treatment of proceeds not meeting the requirements of § 20.2056(b)–5 or of this section, see § 20.2056(a)–2.

(3) In the case of a contract under which payments by the insurer commenced during the decedent's life, it is immaterial whether or not the conditions in subparagraphs (1) through (5) of paragraph (a) of this section were satisfied prior to the decedent's death.

(d) Payments of installments or interest. The conditions in subparagraphs (1) and (2) of paragraph (a) of this section relative to the payments of installments or interest to the surviving spouse are satisfied if, under the terms of the contract, the spouse has the right exercisable annually (or more frequently) to require distribution to herself of installments of the proceeds or a specific portion thereof, as the case may be, and otherwise such proceeds or interest are to be accumulated and held by the insurer pursuant to the terms of the contract. A contract which otherwise requires the insurer to make annual or more frequent payments to the surviving spouse following the decedent's death, will not be disqualified merely because the surviving spouse must comply with certain formalities in order to obtain the first payment. For example, the contract may satisfy the conditions in subparagraphs (1) and (2) of paragraph (a) of this section even though it requires the surviving spouse to furnish proof of death before the first payment is made. The condition in paragraph (a)(1) of this section is satisfied where interest on the proceeds or a specific portion thereof is payable, annually or more frequently, for a term, or until the occurrence of a specified event, following which the proceeds or a specific portion thereof are to be paid in annual or more frequent installments.

(e) Powers of appointment. **(1)** In determining whether the terms of the contract satisfy the conditions in subparagraph (3), (4), or (5) of paragraph (a) of this section relating to a power of appointment in the surviving spouse or any other person, the principles stated in § 20.2056(b)–5 are applicable. As stated in § 20.2056(b)–5, the surviving spouse's power to appoint is "exercisable in all events" only if it is in existence immediately following the decedent's death, subject, however, to the operation of § 20.2056(b)–3 relating to interests conditioned on survival for a limited period.

(2) For examples of formal limitations on the power which will not disqualify the contract, see paragraph (g)(4) of § 20.2056(b)–5. If the power is exercisable from the moment of the decedent's death, the contract is not disqualified merely because the insurer may require proof of the decedent's death as a condition to making payment to the appointee. If the submission of proof of the decedent's death is a condition to the exercise of the power, the power will not be considered "exercisable in all events" unless in the event the surviving spouse had died immediately following the decedent, her power to appoint would have been considered to exist at the time of her death, within the meaning of section 2041(a)(2). See paragraph (b) of § 20.2041–3.

(3) It is sufficient for the purposes of the condition in paragraph (a)(3) of this section that the surviving spouse have the power to appoint amounts held by the insurer to herself or her estate if the surviving spouse has the unqualified power, exercisable in favor of herself or her estate, to appoint amounts held by the insurer which are payable after her death. Such power to appoint need not extend to installments or interest which will be paid to the spouse during her life. Further, the power to appoint need not be a power to require payment in a single sum. For example, if the proceeds of a policy are payable in installments, and if the surviving spouse has the power to direct that all installments payable after her death be paid to her estate, she has the requisite power.

(4) It is not necessary that the phrase "power to appoint" be used in the contract. For example, the condition in paragraph (a)(3) of this section that the surviving spouse have the power to appoint amounts held by the insurer to herself or her estate is satisfied by terms of a contract which give the surviving spouse a right which is, in substance and effect, a power to appoint to herself or her estate, such as a right to withdraw the amount remaining in the fund held by the insurer, or a right to direct that any amount held by the insurer under the contract at her death shall be paid to her estate.

[T.D. 6296, 23 FR 4529, June 24, 1958]

§ 20.2056(b)–7 Election with respect to life estate for surviving spouse.

(a) In general. Subject to section 2056(d), a marital deduction is allowed under section 2056(b)(7) with respect to estates of decedents dying after December 31, 1981, for qualified terminable interest property as defined in paragraph (b) of this section. All of the property for which a deduction is allowed under this paragraph (a) is treated as passing to the surviving spouse (for purposes of § 20.2056(a)–1), and no part of the property is treated as passing to any person other than the surviving spouse (for purposes of § 20.2056(b)–1).

(b) Qualified terminable interest property—(1) In general. Section 2056(b)(7)(B)(i) provides the definition of qualified terminable interest property.

(i) Terminable interests described in section 2056(b)(1)(C) cannot qualify as qualified terminable interest property. Thus, if the decedent directs the executor to purchase a terminable interest with estate assets, the terminable interest acquired will not qualify as qualified terminable interest property.

(ii) For purposes of section 2056(b)(7)(B)(i), the term property generally means the entire interest in property (within the meaning of § 20.2056(b)–5(d)) or a specific portion of the entire interest (within the meaning of § 20.2056(b)–5(c)).

(2) Property for which an election may be made—(i) In general. The election may relate to all or any part of property that meets the requirements of section 2056(b)(7)(B)(i), provided that any partial election must be made with respect to a fractional or percentage share of the property so that the elective portion reflects its proportionate share of the increase or decrease in value of the entire property for purposes of applying sections 2044 or 2519. The fraction or percentage may be defined by formula.

(ii) Division of trusts—(A) In general. A trust may be divided into separate trusts to reflect a partial election that has been made, or is to be made, if authorized under the governing instrument or otherwise permissible under local law. Any such division must be accomplished no later than the end of the period of estate administration. If, at the time of the filing of the estate tax return, the trust has not yet been divided, the intent to divide the trust must be unequivocally signified on the estate tax return.

(B) Manner of dividing and funding trust. The division of the trust must be done on a fractional or percentage basis to reflect the partial election. However, the separate trusts do not have to be funded with a pro rata portion of each asset held by the undivided trust.

(C) Local law. A trust may be divided only if the fiduciary is required, either by applicable local law or by the express or implied provisions of the governing instrument, to divide the trust on the basis of the fair market value of the assets of the trust at the time of the division.

(3) Persons permitted to make the election. The election referred to in section 2056(b)(7)(B)(i)(III) must be made by the executor that is appointed, qualified, and acting within the United States, within the meaning of section 2203, regardless of whether the property with respect to which the election is to be made is in the executor's possession. If there is no executor appointed, qualified, and acting within the United States, the election may be made by any person with respect to property in the actual or constructive possession of that person and may also be made by that person with respect to other property not in the actual or constructive possession of that person if the person in actual or constructive possession of such other property does not make the election. For example, in the absence of an appointed executor, the trustee of an inter vivos trust (that is included in the gross estate of the decedent) can make the election.

(4) Manner and time of making the election—(i) In general. The election referred to in section 2056(b)(7)(B)(i)(III) and (v) is made on the return of tax imposed by section 2001 (or section 2101). For purposes of this paragraph, the term return of tax imposed by section 2001 means the last estate tax return filed by the executor on or before the due date of the return, including extensions or, if a timely return is not filed, the first estate tax return filed by the executor after the due date.

(ii) Election irrevocable. The election, once made, is irrevocable, provided that an election may be revoked or modified on a subsequent return filed on or before the due date of the return, including extensions actually granted. If an executor appointed under local law has made an election on the return of tax imposed by section 2001 (or section 2101) with respect to one or more properties, no subsequent election may be made with respect to other properties included in the gross estate after the return of tax imposed by section 2001 is filed. An election under section 2056(b)(7)(B)(v) is separate from any elections made under section 2056A(a)(3).

(c) Protective elections—(1) In general. A protective election may be made to treat property as qualified terminable interest property only if, at the time the federal estate tax return is filed, the executor of the decedent's estate reasonably believes that there is a bona fide issue that concerns whether an asset is includible in the decedent's gross estate, or the amount or nature of the property the surviving spouse is entitled to receive, i.e., whether property that is includible is eligible for the qualified terminable interest property election. The protective election must identify either the specific asset, group of assets, or trust to which the election applies and the specific basis for the protective election.

(2) Protective election irrevocable. The protective election, once made on the return of tax imposed by section 2001, cannot be revoked. For example, if a protective election is made on the basis that a bona fide question exists regarding the inclusion of a trust corpus in the gross estate and it is later determined that the trust corpus is so includible, the protective election becomes effective with respect to the trust corpus and cannot thereafter be revoked.

(d) Qualifying income interest for life—(1) In general. Section 2056(b)(7)(B)(ii) provides the definition of qualifying income interest for life. For purposes of section 2056(b)(7)(B)(ii)(II), the surviving spouse is included within the prohibited class of powerholders referred to therein. A power under applicable local law that permits the trustee to adjust between income and principal to fulfill the trustee's duty of impartiality between the income and remainder beneficiaries that meets the requirements of § 1.643(b)–1 of this chapter will not be considered a power to appoint trust property to a person other than the surviving spouse.

(2) Entitled for life to all income. The principles of § 20.2056(b)–5(f), relating to whether the spouse is entitled for life to all of the income from the entire interest, or a specific portion of the entire interest, apply in determining whether the surviving spouse is entitled for life to all of the income from the property regardless of whether the interest passing to the spouse is in trust.

(3) Contingent income interests. (i) An income interest for a term of years, or a life estate subject to termination upon the occurrence of a specified event (e.g., remarriage), is not a qualifying income interest for life. However, a qualifying income interest for life that is contingent upon the executor's election under section 2056(b)(7)(B)(v) will not fail to be a qualifying income interest for life because of such contingency or because the portion of the property for which the election is not made passes to or for the benefit of persons other than the surviving spouse. This paragraph (d)(3)(i) applies with respect to estates of decedents whose estate tax returns are due after February 18, 1997. This paragraph (d)(3)(i) also applies to estates of decedents whose estate tax returns were due on or before February 18, 1997, that meet the requirements of paragraph (d)(3)(ii) of this section.

(ii) Estates of decedents whose estate tax returns were due on or before February 18, 1997, that did not make the election under section 2056(b)(7)(B)(v) because the surviving spouse's income interest in the property was contingent upon the election or because the nonelected portion of the property was to pass to a beneficiary other than the surviving spouse are granted an extension of time to make the QTIP election if the following requirements are satisfied:

(A) The period of limitations on filing a claim for credit or refund under section 6511(a) has not expired.

(B) A claim for credit or refund is filed on form 843 with a revised Recapitulation and Schedule M, Form 706 (or 706NA) that signifies the QTIP election. Reference to this section should be made on the Form 843.

(C) The following statement is included with the Form 843: "The undersigned certifies that the property with respect to which the QTIP election is being made will be included in the gross estate of the surviving spouse as provided in section 2044 of the Internal Revenue Code, in determining the federal estate tax liability on the spouse's death." The statement must be signed, under penalties of perjury, by the surviving spouse, the surviving spouse's legal representative (if the surviving spouse is legally incompetent), or the surviving spouse's executor (if the surviving spouse is deceased).

(4) Income between last distribution date and date of spouse's death. An income interest does not fail to constitute a qualifying income interest for life solely because income between the last distribution date and the date of the surviving spouse's death is not required to be distributed to the surviving spouse or to the estate of the surviving spouse. See § 20.2044–1 relating to the inclusion of such undistributed income in the gross estate of the surviving spouse.

(5) Pooled income funds. An income interest in a pooled income fund described in section 642(c)(5) constitutes a qualifying income interest for life for purposes of section 2056(b)(7)(B)(ii).

(6) Power to distribute principal to spouse. An income interest in a trust will not fail to constitute a qualifying income interest for life solely because the trustee has a power to distribute principal to or for the benefit of the surviving spouse. The fact that property distributed to a surviving spouse may be transferred by the spouse to another person does not result in a failure to satisfy the requirement of section 2056(b)(7)(B)(ii)(II). However, if the surviving spouse is legally bound to transfer the distributed property to another person without full and adequate consideration in money or money's worth, the requirement of section 2056(b)(7)(B)(ii)(II) is not satisfied.

(e) Annuities payable from trusts in the case of estates of decedents dying on or before October 24, 1992, and certain decedents dying after October 24, 1992, with wills or revocable trusts executed on or prior to that date—(1) In general. In the case of estates of decedents within the purview of the effective date and transitional rules contained in § 20.2056(b)–7(e)(5), a surviving spouse's lifetime annuity interest payable from a trust or other group of assets passing from the decedent is treated as a qualifying income interest for life for purposes of section 2056(b)(7)(B)(ii).

(2) Deductible interest. The deductible interest, for purposes of § 20.2056(a)–2(b), is the specific portion of the property that, assuming the applicable interest rate for valuing annuities, would produce income equal to the minimum amount payable annually to the surviving spouse. If, based on the applicable interest rate, the entire property from which the annuity may be satisfied is insufficient to produce income equal to the minimum annual payment, the value of the deductible interest is the entire value of the property. The value of the deductible interest may not exceed the value of the property from which the annuity is payable. If the annual payment may increase, the increased amount is not taken into account in valuing the deductible interest.

(3) Distributions permissible only to surviving spouse. An annuity interest is not treated as a qualifying income interest for life for purposes of section 2056(b)(7)(B)(ii) if any person other than the surviving spouse may receive, during the surviving spouse's lifetime, any distribution of the property or its income (including any distribution under an annuity contract) from which the annuity is payable.

(4) Applicable interest rate. To determine the applicable interest rate for valuing annuities, see sections 2031 and 7520 and the regulations under those sections.

* * *

(f) Joint and survivor annuities. [Reserved]

(g) Application of local law. The provisions of local law are taken into account in determining whether the conditions of section 2056(b)(7)(B)(ii)(I) are satisfied. For example, silence of a trust instrument as to the frequency of payment is not regarded as a failure to satisfy the requirement that the income must be payable to the surviving spouse annually or more frequently unless applicable local law permits payments less frequently.

(h) Examples. The following examples illustrate the application of paragraphs (a) through (g) of this section. In each example, it is assumed that the decedent, D, was survived by S, D's spouse and that, unless stated otherwise, S is not the trustee of any trust established for S's benefit.

Example 1. Life estate in residence. D owned a personal residence valued at $250,000 for estate tax purposes. Under D's will, the exclusive and unrestricted right to use the residence (including the right to continue to occupy the property as a personal residence or to rent the property and receive the income) passes to S for life. At S's death, the property passes to D's children. Under applicable local law, S must consent to any sale of the property. If the executor elects to treat all of the personal residence as qualified terminable interest property, the deductible interest is $250,000, the value of the residence for estate tax purposes.

Example 2. Power to make property productive. D's will established a trust funded with property valued for estate tax purposes at $500,000. The assets include both income producing assets and non-productive assets. S was given the power, exercisable annually, to require distribution of all of the trust income to herself. No trust property may be distributed during S's lifetime to any person other than S. Applicable local law permits S to require that the trustee either make the trust property productive or sell the property and reinvest in productive property within a reasonable time after D's death. If the executor elects to treat all of the trust as qualified terminable interest property, the deductible interest is $500,000. If the executor elects to treat only 20 percent of the trust as qualified terminable interest property, the deductible interest is $100,000, i.e., 20 percent of $500,000.

Example 3. Power of distribution over fraction of trust income. The facts are the same as in Example 2 except that S is given the right exercisable annually for S's lifetime to require distribution to herself of only 50 percent of the trust income for life. The remaining trust income is to be accumulated or distributed among S and the decedent's children in the trustee's discretion. The maximum amount that D's executor may elect to treat as qualified terminable interest property is $250,000; i.e., the estate tax value of the trust ($500,000) multiplied by the percentage of the trust in which S has a qualifying income interest for life (50 percent). If D's executor elects to treat only 20 percent of the portion of the trust in which S has a qualifying income interest as qualified terminable interest property, the deductible interest is $50,000, i.e., 20 percent of $250,000.

Example 4. Power to distribute trust corpus to other beneficiaries. D's will established a trust providing that S is entitled to receive at least annually all the trust income. The trustee is given the power to use annually during S's lifetime $5,000 from the trust for the maintenance and support of S's minor child, C. Any such distribution does not necessarily relieve S of S's obligation to support and maintain C. S does not have a qualifying income interest for life in any portion of the trust because the bequest fails to satisfy the condition that no person have a power, other than a power the exercise of which takes effect only at or after S's death, to appoint any part of the property to any person other than S. The trust would also be nondeductible under section 2056(b)(7) if S, rather than the trustee, held the power to appoint a portion of the principal to C. However, in the latter case, if S made a qualified disclaimer (within the meaning of section 2518) of the power to appoint to C, the trust could qualify for the marital deduction pursuant to section 2056(b)(7), assuming that the power is personal to S and S's disclaimer terminates the power. Similarly, in either case, if C made a qualified disclaimer of C's right to receive distributions from the trust, the trust would qualify under section 2056(b)(7), assuming that C's disclaimer effectively negates the trustee's power under local law.

Example 5. Spouse's income interest terminable on remarriage. D's will established a trust providing that all of the trust income is payable at least annually to S for S's lifetime, provided that, if S remarries, S's interest in the trust will pass to X. The trust is not deductible under section 2056(b)(7). S's income interest is not a qualifying income interest for life because it is not for life but, rather, is terminable upon S's remarriage.

Example 6. Spouse's qualifying income interest for life contingent on executor's election. D's will established a trust providing that S is entitled to receive the income, payable at least annually, from that portion of the trust that the executor elects to treat as qualified terminable interest property. The portion of the trust which the executor does not elect to treat as qualified terminable interest property passes as of D's date of death to a trust for the benefit of C, D's child. Under these facts, the executor is not considered to have a power to appoint any part of the trust property to any person other than S during S's life.

Example 7. Formula partial election. D's will established a trust funded with the residue of D's estate. Trust income is to be paid annually to S for life, and the principal is to be distributed to D's children upon S's death. S has the power to require that all the trust property be made productive. There is no power to distribute trust property during S's lifetime to any person other than S. D's executor elects to deduct a fractional share of the residuary estate under section 2056(b)(7). The election specifies that the numerator of the fraction is the amount of deduction necessary to reduce the Federal estate tax to zero (taking into account final estate tax values) and the denominator of the fraction is the final estate tax value of the residuary estate (taking into account any specific bequests or liabilities of the estate paid out of the residuary estate). The formula election is of a fractional share. The value of the share qualifies for the marital deduction even though the executor's determinations to claim administration expenses as estate or income tax deductions and the final estate tax values will affect the size of the fractional share.

Example 8. Formula partial election. The facts are the same as in Example 7 except that, rather than defining a fraction, the executor's formula states: "I elect to treat as qualified terminable interest property that portion of the residuary trust, up to 100 percent, necessary to reduce the Federal estate tax to zero, after taking into account the available unified credit, final estate tax values and any liabilities and specific bequests paid from the residuary estate." The formula election is of a fractional share. The share is equivalent to the fractional share determined in Example 7.

Example 9. Severance of QTIP trust. D's will established a trust funded with the residue of D's estate. Trust income is to be paid annually to S for life, and the principal is to be distributed to D's children upon S's death. S has the power to require that all of the trust property be made productive. There is no power to distribute trust property during S's lifetime to any person other than S. D's will authorizes the executor to make the election under section 2056(b)(7) only with respect to the minimum amount of property necessary to reduce estate taxes on D's estate to zero, authorizes the executor to divide the residuary estate into two separate trusts to reflect the election, and authorizes the executor to charge any payment of principal to S to the qualified terminable interest trust. S is the sole beneficiary of both trusts during S's lifetime. The authorizations in the will do not adversely affect the allowance of the marital deduction. Only the property remaining in the marital deduction trust, after payment of principal to S, is subject to inclusion in S's gross estate under section 2044 or subject to gift tax under section 2519.

Example 10. Payments to spouse from individual retirement account. S is the life beneficiary of sixteen remaining annual installments payable from D's individual retirement account. The terms of the account provide for the payment of the account balance in nineteen annual installments that commenced when D reached age 70½. Each installment is equal to all the income earned on the remaining principal in the account plus a share of the remaining principal equal to 1/19 in the first year, 1/18 in the second year, 1/17 in the third year, etc. Under the terms of the account, S has no right to withdraw any other amounts from the account. Any payments remaining after S's death pass to D's children. S's interest in the account qualifies as a qualifying income interest for life under section 2056(b)(7)(B)(ii), without regard to the provisions of section 2056(b)(7)(C).

Example 11. Spouse's interest in trust in the form of an annuity. D died prior to October 24, 1992. D's will established a trust funded with income producing property valued at $500,000 for estate tax purposes. The trustee is required by the trust instrument to pay $20,000 a year to S for life. Trust income in excess of the annuity amount is to be accumulated in the trust and may not be distributed during S's lifetime. S's lifetime annuity interest is treated as a qualifying income interest for life. If the executor elects to treat the entire portion of the trust in which S has a qualifying income interest as qualified terminable interest property, the value of the deductible interest is (assuming that 10 percent is the applicable interest rate under section 7520 for valuing annuities on the appropriate valuation date) $200,000, because that amount would yield an income to S of $20,000 a year.

Example 12. Value of spouse's annuity exceeds value of trust corpus. The facts are the same as in Example 11 except that the trustee is required to pay S $70,000 a year for life. If the executor elects to treat the entire portion of the trust in which S has a qualifying income interest as qualified terminable interest property, the value of the deductible interest is $500,000, which is the lesser of the entire value of the property ($500,000), or the amount of property that (assuming a 10 percent interest rate) would yield an income to S of $70,000 a year ($700,000).

Example 13. Pooled income fund. D's will provides for a bequest of $200,000 to a pooled income fund described in section 642(c)(5), designating S as the income beneficiary for life. If D's executor elects to treat the entire $200,000 as qualified terminable interest property, the deductible interest is $200,000.

Example 14. Funding severed QTIP trusts. D's will established a trust satisfying the requirements of section 2056(b)(7). Pursuant to the authority in D's will and § 20.2056(b)–7(b)(2)(ii), D's executor indicates on the

Federal estate tax return that an election under section 2056(b)(7) is being made with respect to 50 percent of the trust, and that the trust will subsequently be divided to reflect the partial election on the basis of the fair market value of the property at the time of the division. D's executor funds the trust at the end of the period of estate administration. At that time, the property available to fund the trusts consists of 100 shares of X Corporation stock with a current value of $400,000 and 200 shares of Y Corporation stock with a current value of $400,000. D may fund each trust with the stock of either or both corporations, in any combination, provided that the aggregate value of the stock allocated to each trust is $400,000.

[T.D. 8522, 59 FR 9642, Mar. 1, 1994; as amended by T.D. 8779, 63 FR 44391, Aug. 18, 1998; T.D. 9102, 69 FR 12, Jan. 2, 2004]

§ 20.2056(b)–8 Special rule for charitable remainder trusts.

(a) In general—(1) Surviving spouse only noncharitable beneficiary. With respect to estates of decedents dying after December 31, 1981, subject to section 2056(d), if the surviving spouse of the decedent is the only noncharitable beneficiary of a charitable remainder annuity trust or a charitable remainder unitrust described in section 664 (qualified charitable remainder trust), section 2056(b)(1) does not apply to the interest in the trust that is transferred to the surviving spouse. Thus, the value of the annuity or unitrust interest passing to the spouse qualifies for a marital deduction under section 2056(b)(8) and the value of the remainder interest qualifies for a charitable deduction under section 2055. If an interest in property qualifies for a marital deduction under section 2056(b)(8), no election may be made with respect to the property under section 2056(b)(7). For purposes of this section, the term non-charitable beneficiary means any beneficiary of the qualified charitable remainder trust other than an organization described in section 170(c).

(2) Interest for life or term of years. The surviving spouse's interest need not be an interest for life to qualify for a marital deduction under section 2056(b)(8). However, for purposes of section 664, an annuity or unitrust interest payable to the spouse for a term of years cannot be payable for a term that exceeds 20 years.

(3) Payment of state death taxes. A deduction is allowed under section 2056(b)(8) even if the transfer to the surviving spouse is conditioned on the spouse's payment of state death taxes, if any, attributable to the qualified charitable remainder trust. See § 20.2056(b)–4(c) for the effect of such a condition on the amount of the deduction allowable.

(b) Charitable remainder trusts where the surviving spouse is not the only noncharitable beneficiary. In the case of a charitable remainder trust where the decedent's spouse is not the only noncharitable beneficiary (for example, where the noncharitable interest is payable to the decedent's spouse for life and then to another individual for life), the qualification of the interest as qualified terminable interest property is determined solely under section 2056(b)(7) and not under section 2056(b)(8). Accordingly, if the decedent died on or before October 24, 1992, or the trust otherwise comes within the purview of the transitional rules contained in § 20.2056(b)–7(e)(5), the spousal annuity or unitrust interest may qualify under § 20.2056(b)–(7)(e) as a qualifying income interest for life.

[T.D. 8522, 59 FR 9642, Mar. 1, 1994]

§ 20.2056(b)–9 Denial of double deduction.

The value of an interest in property may not be deducted for Federal estate tax purposes more than once with respect to the same decedent. For example, where a decedent transfers a life estate in a farm to the spouse with a remainder to charity, the entire property is, pursuant to the executor's election under section 2056(b)(7), treated as passing to the spouse. The entire value of the property qualifies for the marital deduction. No part of the value of the property qualifies for a charitable deduction under section 2055 in the decedent's estate.

[T.D. 8522, 59 FR 9642, Mar. 1, 1994]

§ 20.2056(c)–1 Marital deduction; definition of "passed from the decedent".

(a) In general. The following rules are applicable in determining the person to whom any property interest "passed from the decedent":

(1) Property interests devolving upon any person (or persons) as surviving coowner with the decedent under any form of joint ownership under which the right of survivorship existed are considered as having passed from the decedent to such person (or persons).

(2) Property interests at any time subject to the decedent's power to appoint (whether alone or in conjunction with any person) are considered as having passed from the decedent to the appointee under his exercise of the power, or, in case of the lapse, release or nonexercise of the power, as having passed from the decedent to the taker in default of exercise.

(3) The dower or curtesy interest (or statutory interest in lieu thereof) of the decedent's surviving spouse is considered as having passed from the decedent to his spouse.

(4) The proceeds of insurance upon the life of the decedent are considered as having passed from the decedent to the person who, at the time of the decedent's death, was entitled to receive the proceeds.

(5) Any property interest transferred during life, bequeathed or devised by the decedent, or inherited from the decedent, is considered as having passed to the person to whom he transferred, bequeathed, or devised the interest, or to the person who inherited the interest from him.

(6) The survivor's interest in an annuity or other payment described in section 2039 (see §§ 20.2039–1 and 20.2039–2) is considered as having passed from the decedent to the survivor only to the extent that the value of such interest is included in the decedent's gross estate under that section. If only a portion of the entire annuity or other payment is included in the decedent's gross estate and the annuity or other payment is payable to more than one beneficiary, then the value of the interest considered to have passed to each beneficiary is that portion of the amount payable to each beneficiary that the amount of the annuity or other payment included in the decedent's gross estate bears to the total value of the annuity or other payment payable to all beneficiaries.

(b) Expectant interest in property under community property laws. If before the decedent's death the decedent's surviving spouse had merely an expectant interest in property held by her and the decedent under community property laws, that interest is considered as having passed from the decedent to the spouse. * * *

[T.D. 6296, 23 FR 4529, June 24, 1958, as amended by T.D. 8522, 59 FR 9642, Mar. 1, 1994]

§ 20.2056(c)–2 Marital deduction; definition of "passed from the decedent to his surviving spouse".

(a) In general. In general, the definition stated in § 20.2056(c)–1 is applicable in determining the property interests which "passed from the decedent to his surviving spouse". Special rules are provided, however, for the following:

(1) In the case of certain interests with income for life to the surviving spouse with power of appointment in her (see § 20.2056(b)–5);

(2) In the case of certain interests with income for life to the surviving spouse that the executor elects to treat as qualified terminable interest property (see § 20.2056(b)–7);

(3) In the case of proceeds held by the insurer under a life insurance, endowment, or annuity contract with power of appointment in the surviving spouse (see § 20.2056(b)–6);

(4) In case of the disclaimer of an interest by the surviving spouse or by any other person (see § 20.2056(d)–1);

(5) In case of an election by the surviving spouse (see paragraph (c) of this section); and

(6) In case of a controversy involving the decedent's will, see paragraph (d) of this section.

A property interest is treated as passing to the surviving spouse only if it passes to the spouse as beneficial owner, except to the extent otherwise provided in §§ 20.2056(b)–5 through 20.2056(b)–7. For this purpose, where a property interest passed from the decedent in trust, such interest is considered to have passed from him to his surviving spouse to the extent of her beneficial interest therein. The deduction may not be taken with respect to a property interest which passed to such spouse merely as trustee, or subject to a binding agreement by the spouse to dispose of the interest in favor of a third person. An allowance or award paid to a surviving spouse pursuant to local law for her support during the administration of the decedent's estate constitutes a property interest passing from the decedent to his surviving spouse. In determining whether or not such an interest is deductible, however, see generally the terminable interest rules of § 20.2056(b)–1 and especially example (8) of paragraph (g) of that section.

(b) Examples. The following illustrate the provisions of paragraph (a) of this section:

(1) A property interest bequeathed in trust by H (the decedent) is considered as having passed from him to W (his surviving spouse)—

(i) If the trust income is payable to W for life and upon her death the corpus is distributable to her executors or administrators;

(ii) If W is entitled to the trust income for a term of years following which the corpus is to be paid to W or her estate;

(iii) If the trust income is to be accumulated for a term of years or for W's life and the augmented fund paid to W or her estate; or

(iv) If the terms of the transfer satisfy the requirements of § 20.2056(b)–5 or 20.2056(b)–7.

(2) If H devised property—

(i) To A for life with remainder absolutely to W or her estate, the remainder interest is considered to have passed from H to W;

(ii) To W for life with remainder to her estate, the entire property is considered as having passed from H to W; or

(iii) Under conditions which satisfy the provisions of § 20.2056(b)–5 or 20.2056(b)–7, the entire property is considered as having passed from H to W.

(3) Proceeds of insurance upon the life of H are considered as having passed from H to W if the terms of the contract—

(i) Meet the requirements of § 20.2056(b)–6;

(ii) Provide that the proceeds are payable to W in a lump sum;

(iii) Provide that the proceeds are payable in installments to W for life and after her death any remaining installments are payable to her estate;

(iv) Provide that interest on the proceeds is payable to W for life and upon her death the principal amount is payable to her estate; or

(v) Provide that the proceeds are payable to a trustee under an arrangement whereby the requirements of section 2056(b)(5) or 20.2056(b)–7 are satisfied.

(c) Effect of election by surviving spouse. This paragraph contains rules applicable if the surviving spouse may elect between a property interest offered to her under the decedent's will or other instrument and a property interest to which she is otherwise entitled (such as dower, a right in the decedent's estate, or her interest under community property laws) of which adverse disposition was attempted by the decedent under the will or other instrument. If the surviving spouse elects to take against the will or other instrument, then the property interests offered thereunder are not considered as having "passed from the decedent to his surviving spouse" and the dower or other property interest retained by her is considered as having so passed (if it otherwise so qualifies under this section). If the surviving spouse elects to take under the will or other instrument, then the dower or other property interest relinquished by her is not considered as having "passed from the decedent to his surviving spouse" (irrespective of whether it otherwise comes within the definition stated in paragraph (a) of this section) and the interest taken under the will or other instrument is considered as having so passed (if it otherwise so qualifies). As to the valuation of the property interest taken under the will or other instrument, see paragraph (b) of § 20.2056(b)–4.

(d) Will contests. (1) If as a result of a controversy involving the decedent's will, or involving any bequest or devise thereunder, his surviving spouse assigns or surrenders a property interest in settlement of the controversy, the interest so assigned or surrendered is not considered as having "passed from the decedent to his surviving spouse."

(2) If as a result of the controversy involving the decedent's will, or involving any bequest or devise thereunder, a property interest is assigned or surrendered to the surviving spouse, the interest so acquired will be regarded as having "passed from the decedent to his surviving spouse" only if the assignment or surrender as a bona fide recognition of enforceable rights of the surviving spouse in the decedent's estate. Such a bona fide recognition will be presumed where the assignment or surrender was pursuant to a decision of a local court upon the merits in an adversary proceeding following a genuine and active contest. However, such a decree will be accepted only to the extent that the court passed upon the facts upon which deductibility of the property interest depends. If the assignment or surrender was pursuant to a decree rendered by consent, or pursuant to an agreement not to contest the will or not to probate the will, it will not necessarily be accepted as a bona fide evaluation of the rights of the spouse.

(e) Survivorship. If the order of deaths of the decedent and his spouse cannot be established by proof, a presumption (whether supplied by local law, the decedent's will, or otherwise) that the decedent was survived by his spouse will be recognized as satisfying paragraph (b)(1) of § 20.2056(a)–1, but only to the extent that it has the effect of giving to the spouse an interest in property includible in her gross estate under part III of subchapter A of chapter 11. Under these circumstances, if an estate tax return is required to be filed for the estate of the decedent's spouse, the marital deduction will not be allowed in the final audit of the estate tax return of the decedent's estate with respect to any property interest which has not been finally determined to be includible in the gross estate of his spouse.

[T.D. 6296, 23 FR 4529, June 24, 1958, as amended by T.D. 8522, 59 FR 9642, Mar. 1, 1994]

§ 20.2056(d)–1 Marital deduction; special rules for marital deduction if surviving spouse is not a United States citizen.

Rules pertaining to the application of section 2056(d), including certain transition rules, are contained in §§ 20.2056A–1 through 20.2056A–13.

[T.D. 8612, 60 FR 43531, Aug. 22, 1995]

§ 20.2056(d)–2 Marital deduction; effect of disclaimers of post-December 31, 1976 transfers.

(a) Disclaimer by a surviving spouse. If a surviving spouse disclaims an interest in property passing to such spouse from the decedent, which interest was created in a transfer made after December 31, 1976, the effectiveness of the disclaimer will be determined by section 2518 and the corresponding regulations. For rules relating to when the transfer creating the interest occurs, see § 25.2518–2(c)(3) and (c)(4) of this chapter. If a qualified disclaimer is determined to have been made by the surviving spouse, the property interest disclaimed is treated as if such interest had never been transferred to the surviving spouse.

(b) Disclaimer by a person other than a surviving spouse. If an interest in property passes from a decedent to a person other than the surviving spouse, and the interest is created in a transfer made after December 31, 1976, and—

(1) The person other than the surviving spouse makes a qualified disclaimer with respect to such interest; and

(2) The surviving spouse is entitled to such interest in property as a result of such disclaimer, the disclaimed interest is treated as passing directly from the decedent to the surviving spouse. For rules relating to when the transfer creating the interest occurs, see s25.2518–2(c)(3) and (c)(4) of this chapter.

(c) Effective date. The first and second sentences of paragraphs (a) and (b) of this section are applicable for transfers creating the interest to be disclaimed made on or after December 31, 1997.

[T.D. 8095, 51 FR 28368, Aug. 7, 1986; T.D. 8744, 62 FR 68183, Dec. 31, 1997]

§ 20.2056A–1 Restrictions on allowance of marital deduction if surviving spouse is not a United States citizen.

(a) General rule. [T]he federal estate tax marital deduction is not allowed for property passing to or for the benefit of a surviving spouse who is not a United States citizen at the date of the decedent's death (whether or not the surviving spouse is a resident of the United States) unless—

(1) The property passes from the decedent to (or pursuant to)—

(i) A qualified domestic trust (QDOT) described in section 2056A and § 20.2056A–2;

(ii) A trust that, although not meeting all of the requirements for a QDOT, is reformed after the decedent's death to meet the requirements of a QDOT (see § 20.2056A–4(a));

(iii) The surviving spouse not in trust (e.g., by outright bequest or devise, by operation of law, or pursuant to the terms of an annuity or other similar plan or arrangement) and, prior to the date that the estate tax return is filed and on or before the last date prescribed by law that the QDOT election may be made (no more than one year after the time prescribed by law, including extensions, for filing the return), the surviving spouse either actually transfers the property to a QDOT or irrevocably assigns the property to a QDOT (see § 20.2056A–4(b)); or

(iv) A plan or other arrangement that would have qualified for the marital deduction but for section 2056(d)(1)(A), and whose payments are not assignable or transferable to a QDOT, if the requirements of § 20.2056A–4(c) are met; and

(2) The executor makes a timely QDOT election under § 20.2056A–3.

(b) Marital deduction allowed if resident spouse becomes citizen. For purposes of section 2056(d)(1) and paragraph (a) of this section, the surviving spouse is treated as a citizen of the United States at the date of the decedent's death if the requirements of section 2056(d)(4) are satisfied. For purposes of section 2056(d)(4)(A) and notwithstanding § 20.2056A–3(a), a return filed prior to the due date (including extensions) is considered filed on the last date that the return is required to be filed (including extensions), and a late return filed at any time after the due date is considered filed on the date that it is actually filed. A surviving spouse is a resident only if the spouse is a resident under chapter 11 of the Internal Revenue Code. See § 20.0–1(b)(1). The status of the spouse as a resident under section 7701(b) is not relevant to this determination except to the extent that the income tax residency of the spouse is pertinent in applying § 20.0–1(b)(1).

(c) Special rules in the case of certain transfers subject to estate and gift tax treaties. Under section 7815(d)(14) of the Omnibus Budget Reconciliation Act of 1989 (Pub.L. 101–239, 103 Stat. 2106) certain special rules apply in the case of transfers governed by certain estate and gift tax treaties to which the United States is a party. In the case of the estate of, or gift by, an individual who was not a citizen or resident of the United States but was a resident of a foreign country with which the United States has a tax treaty with respect to estate, inheritance, or gift taxes, the amendments made by section 5033 of the Technical and Miscellaneous Revenue Act of 1988 (Pub.L. 100–647, 102 Stat. 3342) do not apply to the extent such amendments would be inconsistent with the provisions of such treaty relating to estate, inheritance, or gift tax marital deductions. Under this rule, the estate may choose either the statutory deduction under section 2056A or the marital deduction allowed under the treaty. Thus, the estate may not avail itself of both the marital deduction under the treaty and the marital deduction under the QDOT provisions of section 2056A and chapter 11 of the Internal Revenue Code with respect to the remainder of the marital property that is not deductible under the treaty.

[T.D. 8612, 60 FR 43531, Aug. 22, 1995]

§ 20.2056A–2 Requirements for qualified domestic trust.

(a) In general. In order to qualify as a qualified domestic trust (QDOT), the requirements of paragraphs (b) and (c) of this section, and the requirements of § 20.2056A–2T(d), must be satisfied. The executor of the decedent's estate and the U.S. Trustee shall establish in such manner as may be prescribed by the Commissioner on the estate tax return and applicable instructions that these requirements have been satisfied or are being complied with. In order to constitute a QDOT, the trust must be maintained under the laws of a state of the United States or the District of Columbia, and the administration of the trust must be governed by the laws of a particular state of the United States or the District of Columbia. For purposes of this paragraph (a), a trust is maintained under the laws of a state of the United States or the District of Columbia if the records of the trust (or copies thereof) are kept in that state (or the District of Columbia). The trust may be established pursuant to an instrument executed under either the laws of a state of the United States or the District of Columbia or pursuant to an instrument executed under the laws of a foreign jurisdiction, such as a foreign will or trust, provided that such foreign instrument designates the law of a particular state of the United States or the District of Columbia as governing the administration of the trust, and such designation is effective under the law of the designated jurisdiction. In addition, the trust must constitute an ordinary trust, as defined in § 301.7701–4(a) of this chapter, and not any other type of entity. For purposes of this paragraph, a trust will not fail to constitute an ordinary trust solely because of the nature of the assets transferred to that trust, regardless of its classification under §§ 301.7701–2 through 301.7701–4 of this chapter.

(b) Qualified marital interest requirements—(1) Property passing to QDOT. If property passes from a decedent to a QDOT, the trust must qualify for the federal estate tax marital deduction under section 2056(b)(5) (life estate with power of appointment), section 2056(b)(7) (qualified terminable interest property, including joint and survivor annuities under section 2056(b)(7)(C)), or section 2056(b)(8) (surviving spouse is the only noncharitable beneficiary of a charitable remainder trust), or meet the requirements of an estate trust as defined in § 20.2056(c)–2(b)(1)(i) through (iii).

(2) Property passing outright to spouse. If property does not pass from a decedent to a QDOT, but passes to a noncitizen surviving spouse in a form that meets the requirements for a marital deduction without regard to section 2056(d)(1)(A), and that is not described in paragraph (b)(1) of this section, the surviving spouse must either actually transfer the property, or irrevocably assign the property, to a trust (whether created by the decedent, the decedent's executor or by the surviving spouse) that meets the requirements of paragraph (c) of this section and the requirements of § 20.2056A-2T(d) (pertaining, respectively, to statutory requirements and regulatory requirements imposed to ensure collection of tax) prior to the filing of the estate tax return for the decedent's estate and on or before the last date prescribed by law that the QDOT election may be made (see § 20.2056A–3(a)).

(3) Property passing under a nontransferable plan or arrangement. If property does not pass from a decedent to a QDOT, but passes under a plan or other arrangement that meets the requirements for a marital deduction without regard to section 2056(d)(1)(A) and whose payments are not assignable or transferable (see § 20.2056A–4(c)), the property is treated as meeting the requirements of this section, and the requirements of § 20.2056A–2T(d), if the requirements of § 20.2056A–4(c) are satisfied. In addition, where an annuity or similar arrangement is described above except that it is assignable or transferable, see § 20.2056A–4(b)(7).

(c) Statutory requirements. The requirements of section 2056A(a)(1)(A) and (B) must be satisfied. For purposes of that section, a domestic corporation is a corporation that is created or organized under the laws of the United States or under the laws of any state of the United States or the District of Columbia. The trustee required under that section is referred to herein as the "U.S. Trustee".

* * *

[T.D. 8612, 60 FR 43531, Aug. 22, 1995; T.D. 8686, 61 FR 60551, Nov. 29, 1996]

§ 20.2056A–3 QDOT election.

(a) General rule. Subject to the time period prescribed in section 2056A(d), the election to treat a trust as a QDOT must be made on the last federal estate tax return filed before the due date (including extensions of time to file actually granted) or, if a timely return is not filed, on the first federal estate tax return filed after the due date. The election, once made, is irrevocable.

(b) No partial elections. An election to treat a trust as a QDOT may not be made with respect to a specific portion of an entire trust that would otherwise qualify for the marital deduction but for the application of section 2056(d). However, if the trust is actually severed in accordance with the applicable requirements of § 20.2056(b)–7(b)(2)(ii) prior to the due date for the election, a QDOT election may be made for any one or more of the severed trusts.

(c) Protective elections. A protective election may be made to treat a trust as a QDOT only if at the time the federal estate tax return is filed, the executor of the decedent's estate reasonably believes that there is a bona fide issue that concerns either the residency or citizenship of the decedent, the citizenship of the surviving spouse, whether an asset is includible in the decedent's gross estate, or the amount or nature of the property the surviving spouse is entitled to receive. For example, if at the time the federal estate tax return is filed either the estate is involved in a bona fide will contest, there is uncertainty regarding the inclusion in the gross estate of an asset which, if includible, would be eligible for the QDOT election, or there is uncertainty regarding the status of the decedent as a resident alien or a nonresident alien for estate tax purposes, or a similar uncertainty regarding the citizenship status of the surviving spouse, a protective QDOT election may be made. The protective election is in addition to, and is not in lieu of, the requirements set forth in § 20.2056A–4. The protective QDOT election must be made on a written statement signed by the executor under penalties of perjury and must be attached to the return described in paragraph (a) of this section, and must identify the specific assets to which the protective election refers and the specific basis for the protective election. However, the protective election may otherwise be defined by means of a formula (such as the minimum amount necessary to reduce the estate tax to zero). Once made, the protective election is irrevocable. For example, if a protective election is made because a bona fide question exists as to the includibility of an asset in the decedent's gross estate and it is later finally determined that the asset is so includible, the protective election becomes effective with respect to the asset and cannot thereafter be revoked.

(d) Manner of election. The QDOT election under paragraph (a) of this section is made in the form and manner set forth in the decedent's estate tax return, including applicable instructions.

[T.D. 8612, 60 FR 43531, Aug. 22, 1995]

§ 20.2056A–4 Procedures for conforming marital trusts and nontrust marital transfers to the requirements of a qualified domestic trust.

(a) Marital trusts—(1) In general. If an interest in property passes from the decedent to a trust for the benefit of a noncitizen surviving spouse and if the trust otherwise qualifies for a marital deduction but for the provisions of section 2056(d)(1)(A), the property interest is treated as passing to the surviving spouse in a QDOT if the trust is reformed, either in accordance with the terms of the decedent's will or trust agreement or pursuant to a judicial proceeding, to meet the requirements of a QDOT. For this purpose, the requirements of a QDOT include all of the applicable requirements set forth in § 20.2056A–2, and the requirements of § 20.2056A–2T(d). A reformation pursuant to the terms of the decedent's will or trust instrument must be completed by the time prescribed (including extensions) for filing the decedent's estate tax return. For purposes of this paragraph (a), a return filed prior to the due date (including extensions) is considered filed on the last date that the return is required to be filed (including extensions), and a late return filed at any time after the due date is considered filed on the date that it is actually filed.

(2) Judicial reformations. In general, a reformation pursuant to a judicial proceeding is permitted under this section if the reformation is commenced on or before the due date (determined with regard to extensions actually granted) for filing the return of tax imposed by chapter 11 of the Internal Revenue Code, regardless of the date that the return is actually filed. The reformation (either pursuant to a judicial proceeding or otherwise) must result in a trust that is effective under local law. The reformed trust may be revocable by the spouse, or otherwise be subject to the spouse's general power of appointment, provided that no person (including the spouse) has the power to amend the trust during the continued existence of the trust such that it would no longer qualify as a QDOT. Prior to the time that the judicial reformation is completed, the trust must be treated as a QDOT. Thus, the trustee of the trust is responsible for filing the Form 706–QDT, paying any section 2056A estate tax that becomes due, and filing the annual statement required under § 20.2056A–2T(d)(3), if applicable. Failure to comply with these requirements may cause the trust to be subject to the anti-abuse rule under § 20.2056A–2T(d)(1)(iv). In addition, if the judicial reformation is terminated prior to the time that the reformation is completed, the estate of the decedent is required to pay the increased estate tax imposed on the decedent's estate (plus interest and any applicable penalties) that becomes due at the time of such termination as a result of the failure of the trust to comply with section 2056(d). See section 6511 as to applicable time periods for credit or refund of tax.

(3) Tolling of statutory assessment period. For the tolling of the statute of limitations in the case of a judicial reformation, see section 2056(d)(5)(B).

(b) Nontrust marital transfers—(1) In general. Under section 2056(d)(2)(B), if an interest in property passes outright from a decedent to a noncitizen surviving spouse either by testamentary bequest or devise, by operation of law, or pursuant to an annuity or other similar plan or arrangement, and such property interest otherwise qualifies for a marital deduction except that it does not pass in a QDOT, solely for purposes of section 2056(d)(2)(A), the property is treated as passing to the surviving spouse in a QDOT if the property interest is either actually transferred to a QDOT before the estate tax return is filed and on or before the last date prescribed by law that the QDOT election may be made, or is assigned to a QDOT under an enforceable and irrevocable written assignment made on or before the date on which the return is filed and on or before the last date prescribed by law that the QDOT election may be made. The transfer or assignment of property to a QDOT may be made by the surviving spouse, the surviving spouse's legal representative (if the surviving spouse is incompetent), or the personal representative of the surviving spouse's estate (if the surviving spouse has died). The QDOT to which the property is transferred may be created by the decedent (during life or by will), by the surviving spouse, or by the executor. For purposes of section 2056(d)(2)(B), if no property other than the property passing to the surviving spouse from the decedent is transferred to the QDOT, the transferee QDOT need not be in a form such that the property transferred to the QDOT would qualify for a marital deduction under section 2056(a). However, if other property is or has been transferred to the QDOT, 100 percent of the value of the transferee QDOT must qualify for the marital deduction under section 2056. For example, if the decedent, a U.S. citizen, bequeaths property to a trust that does not satisfy the requirements of section 2056(b)(5) or (7), or to a trust that does not qualify as an estate trust under § 20.2056(c)–2(b)(1)(i)–(iii), that trust cannot be used as a transferee QDOT by the surviving spouse, since after that trust is fully funded the portion of the value of the trust attributable to property bequeathed to the trust by the decedent will not qualify for a marital deduction under section 2056. Similarly, if the decedent, a nonresident not a citizen of the United States, bequeaths foreign situs assets to a trust created under his will, the surviving spouse may not transfer U.S. situs assets passing to the spouse outside of the will to that trust under this paragraph. See § 20.2056A–3(c) with respect to protective elections. See § 20.2056A–3(a) with respect to the time limitations for making the QDOT election.

(2) Form of transfer or assignment. A transfer or assignment of property to a QDOT must be in writing and otherwise be in accordance with all local law requirements for such assignment or transfer. The transfer or assignment may be of a specific asset or a group of assets, or a fractional share of either, or may be of a pecuniary amount. A transfer or assignment of less than an entire interest in an asset or a group of assets may be expressed by means of a formula (such as the minimum amount necessary to reduce the estate tax to zero). In the case of a transfer, a copy of the trust instrument evidencing the transfer must be submitted with the decedent's estate tax return. In the case of an assignment, a copy of the assignment must be submitted with the decedent's estate tax return.

(3) Assets eligible for transfer or assignment. If a transfer or assignment is of a specific asset or group of assets, only assets included in the decedent's gross estate and passing from the decedent to the spouse (or the proceeds from the sale, exchange or conversion of such assets) may be transferred or assigned to the QDOT. The noncitizen surviving spouse may not transfer or assign to the QDOT property owned by the surviving spouse at the time of the decedent's death in lieu of property included in the decedent's gross estate that passes to the spouse (or in lieu of the proceeds from the sale, exchange or conversion of such includible assets). In addition, if only a portion of an asset is includible in the decedent's gross estate, the spouse may only transfer the portion that is so includible to the transferee trust under this paragraph (b)(3).

(4) Pecuniary assignment—special rules. If the assignment is expressed in the form of a pecuniary amount (such as a fixed dollar amount or a formula designed to reduce the decedent's estate tax to zero), the assignment must specify that—

(i) Assets actually transferred to the QDOT in satisfaction of the assignment have an aggregate fair market value on the date of actual transfer to the QDOT amounting to no less than the amount of the pecuniary transfer or assignment; or

(ii) The assets actually transferred to the QDOT be fairly representative of appreciation or depreciation in the value of all property available for transfer to the QDOT between the valuation date and the date of actual transfer to the QDOT, if the assignment is to be satisfied by accounting for the assets on the basis of their fair market value as of some date before the date of actual transfer to the QDOT.

(5) Transfer tax treatment of transfer or assignment. Property assigned or transferred to a QDOT pursuant to section 2056(d)(2)(B) is treated as passing from the decedent to a QDOT solely for purposes of section 2056(d)(2)(A). For all other purposes (e.g., income, gift, estate, generation-skipping transfer tax, and section 1491 excise tax), the surviving spouse is treated as the transferor of the property to the QDOT. However, the spouse is not considered the transferor of property to a QDOT if the transfer by the spouse constitutes a transfer that satisfies the requirements of section 2518(c)(3). For a special exception to the valuation rules of section 2702 in the case of a transfer by the surviving spouse to a QDOT, see § 25.2702–1(c)(8) of this chapter.

(6) Period for completion of transfer. Property irrevocably assigned but not actually transferred to the QDOT before the estate tax return is filed must actually be conveyed and transferred to the QDOT under applicable local law before the administration of the decedent's estate is completed. If there is no administration of the decedent's estate (because for example, none of the decedent's assets are subject to probate under local law), the conveyance must be made on or before the date that is one year after the due date (including extensions) for filing the decedent's estate tax return. If an actual transfer to the QDOT is not timely made, section 2056(d)(1)(A) applies and the marital deduction is not allowed. The executor of the decedent's estate (or other authorized legal representative) may request a private letter ruling from the Internal Revenue Service requesting an extension of the time for completing the conveyance or waiving the actual conveyance under specified circumstances under § 301.9100–1(a) of this chapter.

(7) Retirement accounts and annuities—(i) In general. An assignment otherwise in compliance with this paragraph (b) of rights under annuities or other similar arrangements that are assignable and thus, are not described in paragraph (c) of this section, is treated as a transfer of such property to the QDOT regardless of the method of payment actually elected under such annuity or plan.

(ii) Individual retirement annuities. Individual retirement annuities described in section 408(b) are not assignable pursuant to section 408(b)(1) and thus, do not come within the purview of this paragraph (b)(7). See the procedures provided in paragraph (c) of this section.

(iii) Individual retirement accounts. Unless the terms of the account provide otherwise, individual retirement accounts described in section 408(a) are assignable and subject to the provisions of this paragraph (b)(7). However, under paragraph (c) of this section, the surviving spouse may treat an individual retirement account as nonassignable and, therefore, eligible for the procedures in paragraph (c) of this section if the spouse timely complies with the requirements in paragraph (c) of this section.

(iv) Other effects of assignment. The provisions of this paragraph (b)(7) apply solely for purposes of qualifying the annuity or account under the rules of § 20.2056A-2 and this section. See, for example, section 408(d) and 4980A regarding the consequences of an assignment for purposes other than this paragraph (b)(7).

(8) Protective assignment. A protective assignment of property to a QDOT may be made only if, at the time the federal estate tax return is filed, the executor of the decedent's estate reasonably believes that there is a bona fide issue that concerns either the residency or citizenship of the decedent, the citizenship of the surviving spouse, whether all or a portion of an asset is includible in the decedent's gross estate, or the amount or nature of the property the surviving spouse is entitled to receive. For example, if at the time the federal estate tax return is filed, either the estate is involved in a bona fide will contest, there is uncertainty regarding the inclusion in the gross estate of an asset which, if includible, would be eligible for the QDOT election, or there is uncertainty regarding the status of the decedent as a resident alien or a nonresident alien for estate tax purposes, or a similar uncertainty regarding the citizenship status of the surviving spouse, a protective assignment may be made. The protective assignment must be made on a written statement signed by the assignor under penalties of perjury on or before the date prescribed under paragraph (b)(1) of this section, and must identify the specific assets to which the assignment refers and the specific basis for the protective assignment. However, the protective assignment may otherwise be defined by means of a formula (such as the minimum amount necessary to reduce the estate tax to zero). Once made, the protective assignment cannot be revoked. For example, if a protective assignment is made because a bona fide question exists as to the includibility of an asset in the decedent's gross estate and it is later finally determined that the asset is so includible, the protective assignment becomes effective with respect to the asset and cannot thereafter be revoked. Protective assignments are, in all events, subject to paragraph (b)(6) of this section. A copy of the protective assignment must be submitted with the decedent's estate tax return.

(c) Nonassignable annuities and other arrangements—(1) Definition and general rule. For purposes of this section, a nonassignable annuity or other arrangement means a plan, annuity, or other arrangement (whether qualified or not qualified under part I of subchapter D of chapter 1 of subtitle A of the Internal Revenue Code) that qualifies for the marital deduction but for section 2056(d)(1)(A), and whose payments are not assignable or transferable to the QDOT under either federal law (see, e.g., section 401(a)(13)), state law, foreign law, or the terms of the plan or arrangement itself. For purposes of this paragraph (c), a surviving spouse's interest as beneficiary of an individual retirement annuity described in section 408(b) is a nonassignable annuity or other arrangement. See section 408(b)(1). For purposes of this paragraph (c), a surviving spouse's interest as beneficiary of an individual retirement account described in section 408(a), although assignable under that section, is considered to be a nonassignable annuity or other arrangement eligible for the procedures contained in this paragraph (c), at the option of the surviving spouse, if the requirements of this paragraph are otherwise satisfied. See paragraph (b)(7) of this section if the spouse elects to treat the account as assignable. In the case of a plan, annuity, or other arrangement which is not assignable or transferable (or is treated as such), the property passing under the plan from the decedent is treated as meeting the requirements § 20.2056A-2, and the requirements of § 20.2056A- 2T(d) (pertaining, respectively, to general requirements, qualified marital interest requirements, statutory requirements, and requirements to ensure collection of the tax) if the requirements of either paragraph (c)(2) or (3) of this section are satisfied. Thus, the property will be treated as passing in the form of a QDOT, notwithstanding that the spouse does not irrevocably transfer or assign the annuity or other payment to the QDOT as provided in paragraph (b) of this section. The Commissioner will prescribe by administrative guidance the extent, if any, to which the provisions of this paragraph (c) apply to a rollover from a qualified trust to an eligible retirement plan within the meaning of section 402(c) or a distribution from an individual retirement account or an individual retirement annuity that is paid into an individual retirement account or an individual retirement annuity within the meaning of section 408(d)(3).

(2) Agreement to remit section 2056A estate tax on corpus portion of each annuity payment. The requirements of this paragraph (c)(2) are satisfied if—

(i) The noncitizen surviving spouse agrees to pay on an annual basis, as described in paragraph (c)(6)(i) of this section, the estate tax imposed under section 2056A(b)(1) due on the corpus portion, as defined in paragraph (c)(4) of this section, of each nonassignable annuity or other payment received under the plan or arrangement. However, for purposes of this paragraph (c)(2), if the financial circumstances of the spouse are such that an amount equal to all or a portion of the corpus portion of a nonassignable annuity payment received by the spouse would be subject to a hardship exemption (as defined in § 20.2056A–5(c)) if paid from a QDOT, then all or a corresponding part of the corpus portion will be exempt from the tax payment requirement under this paragraph (c)(2);

(ii) The executor of the decedent's estate files with the estate tax return the Information Statement described in paragraph (c)(5) of this section;

(iii) The executor files with the estate tax return the Agreement To Pay Section 2056A Estate Tax described in paragraph (c)(6) of this section; and

(iv) The executor makes the election under § 20.2056A–3 with respect to the nonassignable annuity or other payment.

(3) Agreement to roll over corpus portion of annuity payment to QDOT. The requirements of this paragraph (c)(3) are satisfied if—

(i) The noncitizen surviving spouse agrees to roll over and transfer, within the time prescribed under paragraph (c)(7)(i) of this section, the corpus portion of each annuity payment to a QDOT, whether the QDOT is created by the decedent's will, the executor of the decedent's estate, or the surviving spouse. However, for purposes of this section, if the financial circumstances of the spouse are such that an amount equal to all or a portion of the corpus portion of a nonassignable annuity payment received by the spouse would be subject to a hardship exemption (as defined in § 20.2056A–5(c)) if paid from a QDOT, then all or a corresponding part of the corpus portion will be exempt from the rollover requirement under this paragraph (c)(3);

(ii) A QDOT for the benefit of the surviving spouse is established prior to the date that the estate tax return is filed and on or prior to the last date prescribed by law that the QDOT election may be made;

(iii) The executor of the decedent's estate files with the estate tax return the Information Statement described in paragraph (c)(5) of this section;

(iv) The executor files with the estate tax return the Agreement To Roll Over Annuity Payments described in paragraph (c)(7) of this section; and

(v) The executor makes the election under § 20.2056A–3 with respect to the nonassignable annuity or other payment. See § 20.2056A–5(c)(3)(iv)(A), regarding distributions from the QDOT reimbursing the spouse for income taxes paid (either by actual payment or withholding) by the spouse with respect to amounts transferred to the QDOT pursuant to this paragraph (c)(3).

* * *

[T.D. 8612, 60 FR 43531, Aug. 22, 1995, as amended by T.D. 8819, 64 FR 23187, April 29, 1999; T.D. 9448, 74 FR 21437, May 7, 2009; T.D. 9540, 76 FR 49570, Aug. 10, 2011]

§ 20.2056A–5 Imposition of section 2056A estate tax.

(a) In general. An estate tax is imposed under section 2056A(b)(1) on the occurrence of a taxable event, as defined in section 2056A(b)(9). The tax is generally equal to the amount of estate tax that would have been imposed if the amount involved in the taxable event had been included in the decedent's taxable estate and had not been deductible under section 2056. See section 2056A(b)(3) and paragraph (c) of this section for certain exceptions from taxable events.

(b) Amounts subject to tax—(1) Distribution of principal during the spouse's lifetime. If a taxable event occurs during the noncitizen surviving spouse's lifetime, the amount on which the section 2056A estate tax is imposed is the amount of money and the fair market value of the property that is the subject of the distribution (including property distributed from the trust pursuant to the exercise of a power of appointment), including any amount withheld from the distribution by the U.S. Trustee to pay the tax. If, however, the tax is not withheld by the U.S. Trustee but is paid by the U.S.

Trustee out of other assets of the QDOT, an amount equal to the tax so paid is treated as an additional distribution to the spouse in the year that the tax is paid.

(2) Death of surviving spouse. If a taxable event occurs as a result of the death of the surviving spouse, the amount subject to tax is the fair market value of the trust assets on the date of the spouse's death (or alternate valuation date if applicable). See also section 2032A. Any corpus portion amounts, within the meaning of § 20.2056A–4(c)(4)(i), remaining in a QDOT upon the surviving spouse's death, are subject to tax under section 2056A(b)(1)(B), as well as any residual payments resulting from a nonassignable plan or arrangement that, upon the surviving spouse's death, are payable to the spouse's estate or to successor beneficiaries.

(3) Trust ceases to qualify as QDOT. If a taxable event occurs as a result of the trust ceasing to qualify as a QDOT (for example, the trust ceases to have at least one U.S. Trustee), the amount subject to tax is the fair market value of the trust assets on the date of disqualification.

(c) Distributions and dispositions not subject to tax—(1) Distributions of principal on account of hardship. Section 2056A(b)(3)(B) provides an exemption from the section 2056A estate tax for distributions to the surviving spouse on account of hardship. A distribution of principal is treated as made on account of hardship if the distribution is made to the spouse from the QDOT in response to an immediate and substantial financial need relating to the spouse's health, maintenance, education, or support, or the health, maintenance, education, or support of any person that the surviving spouse is legally obligated to support. A distribution is not treated as made on account of hardship if the amount distributed may be obtained from other sources that are reasonably available to the surviving spouse; e.g., the sale by the surviving spouse of personally owned, publicly traded stock or the cashing in of a certificate of deposit owned by the surviving spouse. Assets such as closely held business interests, real estate and tangible personalty are not considered sources that are reasonably available to the surviving spouse. Although a hardship distribution of principal is exempt from the section 2056A estate tax, it must be reported on Form 706–QDT even if it is the only distribution that occurred during the filing period. See § 20.2056A–11 regarding filing requirements for Form 706–QDT.

(2) Distributions of income to the surviving spouse. Section 2056A(b)(3)(A) provides an exemption from the section 2056A estate tax for distributions of income to the surviving spouse. In general, for purposes of section 2056A(b)(3)(A), the term income has the same meaning as is provided in section 643(b), except that income does not include capital gains. In addition, income does not include any other item that would be allocated to corpus under applicable local law governing the administration of trusts irrespective of any specific trust provision to the contrary. However, distributions made to the surviving spouse as the income beneficiary in conformance with applicable local law that defines the term income as a unitrust amount (or permits a right to income to be satisfied by such an amount), or that permits the trustee to adjust between principal and income to fulfill the trustee's duty of impartiality between income and principal beneficiaries, will be considered distributions of trust income if applicable local law provides for a reasonable apportionment between the income and remainder beneficiaries of the total return of the trust and meets the requirements of § 1.643(b)–1 of this chapter. In cases where there is no specific statutory or case law regarding the allocation of such items under the law governing the administration of the QDOT, the allocation under this paragraph (c)(2) will be governed by general principles of law (including but not limited to any uniform state acts, such as the Uniform Principal and Income Act, or any Restatements of applicable law). Further, except as provided in this paragraph (c)(2) or in administrative guidance published by the Internal Revenue Service, income does not include items constituting income in respect of a decedent (IRD) under section 691. However, in cases where a QDOT is designated by the decedent as a beneficiary of a pension or profit sharing plan described in section 401(a) or an individual retirement account or annuity described in section 408, the proceeds of which are payable to the QDOT in the form of an annuity, any payments received by the QDOT may be allocated between income and corpus using the method prescribed under § 20.2056A–4(c) for determining the corpus and income portion of an annuity payment.

(3) Certain miscellaneous distributions and dispositions. Certain miscellaneous distributions and dispositions of trust assets are exempt from the section 2056A estate tax, including but not limited to the following—

(i) Payments for ordinary and necessary expenses of the QDOT (including bond premiums and letter of credit fees);

(ii) Payments to applicable governmental authorities for income tax or any other applicable tax imposed on the QDOT (other than a payment of the section 2056A estate tax due on the occurrence of a taxable event as described in paragraph (b) of this section);

(iii) Dispositions of trust assets by the trustees (such as sales, exchanges, or pledging as collateral) for full and adequate consideration in money or money's worth; and

(iv) Pursuant to section 2056A(b)(15), amounts paid from the QDOT to reimburse the surviving spouse for any tax imposed on the spouse under Subtitle A of the Internal Revenue Code on any item of income of the QDOT to which the surviving spouse is not entitled under the terms of the trust. Such distributions include (but are not limited to) amounts paid from the QDOT to reimburse the spouse for income taxes paid by the spouse (either by actual payment or through withholding) with respect to amounts received from a nonassignable annuity or other arrangement that are transferred by the spouse to a QDOT pursuant to § 20.2056A–4(c)(3); and income taxes paid by the spouse (either by actual payment or through withholding) with respect to amounts received in a lump sum distribution from a qualified plan if the lump sum distribution is assigned by the surviving spouse to a QDOT. For purposes of this paragraph (c)(3)(iv), the amount of attributable tax eligible for reimbursement is the difference between the actual income tax liability of the spouse and the spouse's income tax liability determined as if the item had not been included in the spouse's gross income in the applicable taxable year.

[T.D. 8612, 60 FR 43531, Aug. 22, 1995, as amended by T.D. 9102, 69 FR 12, Jan. 2, 2004]

§ 20.2056A–10 Surviving spouse becomes citizen after QDOT established.

(a) Section 2056A estate tax no longer imposed under certain circumstances. Section 2056A(b)(12) provides that a QDOT is no longer subject to the imposition of the section 2056A estate tax if the surviving spouse becomes a citizen of the United States and the following conditions are satisfied—

(1) The spouse either was a United States resident (for the definition of resident for this purpose, see § 20.2056A–1(b)) at all times after the death of the decedent and before becoming a United States citizen, or no taxable distributions are made from the QDOT before the spouse becomes a United States citizen (regardless of the residency status of the spouse); and

(2) The U.S. Trustee(s) of the QDOT notifies the Internal Revenue Service and certifies in writing that the surviving spouse has become a United States citizen. Notice is to be made by filing a final Form 706–QDT on or before April 15th of the calendar year following the year in which the surviving spouse becomes a United States citizen, unless an extension of time for filing is granted under section 6081.

(b) Special election by spouse. If the surviving spouse becomes a United States citizen and the spouse is not a United States resident at all times after the death of the decedent and before becoming a United States citizen, and a tax was previously imposed under section 2056A(b)(1)(A) with respect to any distribution from the QDOT before the surviving spouse becomes a United States citizen, the estate tax imposed under section 2056A(b)(1) does not apply to distributions after the spouse becomes a citizen if—

(1) The spouse elects to treat any taxable distribution from the QDOT prior to the spouse's election as a taxable gift made by the spouse for purposes of section 2001(b)(1)(B) (referring to adjusted taxable gifts), and for purposes of determining the amount of the tax imposed by section 2501 on actual taxable gifts made by the spouse during the year in which the spouse becomes a citizen or in any subsequent year;

(2) The spouse elects to treat any previous reduction in the section 2056A estate tax by reason of the decedent's unified credit (under either section 2010 or section 2102(c)) as a reduction in the spouse's unified credit under section 2505 for purposes of determining the amount of the credit allowable with respect to taxable gifts made by the surviving spouse during the taxable year in which the spouse becomes a citizen, or in any subsequent year; and

(3) The elections referred to in this paragraph (b) are made by timely filing a Form 706–QDT on or before April 15th of the year following the year in which the surviving spouse becomes a citizen (unless an extension of time for filing is granted under section 6081) and attaching notification of the election to the return.

[T.D. 8612, 60 FR 43531, Aug. 22, 1995]

§ 20.2203–1 Definition of executor.

The term "executor" means the executor or administrator of the decedent's estate. However, if there is no executor or administrator appointed, qualified and acting within the United States, the term means any person in actual or constructive possession of any property of the decedent. The term "person in actual or constructive possession of any property of the decedent" includes, among others, the decedent's agents and representatives; safe-deposit companies, warehouse companies, and other custodians of property in this country; brokers holding, as collateral, securities belonging to the decedent; and debtors of the decedent in this country.

[T.D. 6296, 23 FR 4529, June 24, 1958]

§ 20.2207A–1 Right of recovery of estate taxes in the case of certain marital deduction property.

(a) In general—(1) Right of recovery from person receiving the property. If the gross estate includes the value of property that is includible by reason of section 2044 (relating to certain property in which the decedent had a qualifying income interest for life under sections 2056(b)(7) or 2523(f)), the estate of the surviving spouse is entitled to recover from the person receiving the property (as defined in paragraph (d) of this section) the amount of Federal estate tax attributable to that property. The right of recovery arises when the Federal estate tax with respect to the property includible in the gross estate by reason of section 2044 is paid by the estate. There is no right of recovery from any person for the property received by that person for which a deduction was allowed from the gross estate if no tax is attributable to that property.

(2) Failure to exercise right of recovery. Failure of an estate to exercise a right of recovery under this section upon a transfer subject to section 2044 is treated as a transfer for Federal gift tax purposes of the unrecovered amounts from the persons who would benefit from the recovery to the persons from whom the recovery could have been obtained. See § 25.2511–1 of this chapter. The transfer is considered made when the right of recovery is no longer enforceable under applicable law. A delay in the exercise of the right of recovery without payment of sufficient interest is a below-market loan. Section 1.7872–5T of the Temporary Income Tax regulations describes factors that are used to determine, based on the facts and circumstances of a particular case, whether a loan otherwise subject to imputation under section 7872 (relating to the treatment of below-market loans) is exempted from its provisions.

(3) Waiver of right of recovery. The provisions of § 20.2207A–1(a)(2) do not apply to the extent that the surviving spouse's will provides that a recovery shall not be made or to the extent that the beneficiaries cannot otherwise compel recovery. Thus, e.g., if the surviving spouse gives the executor of the estate discretion to waive the right of recovery and the executor waives the right, no gift occurs under § 25.2511–1 of this chapter if the persons who would benefit from the recovery cannot compel the executor to exercise the right of recovery.

(b) Amount of estate tax attributable to property includible under section 2044. The amount of Federal estate tax attributable to property includible in the gross estate under section 2044 is the amount by which the total Federal estate tax (including penalties and interest attributable to the tax) under chapter 11 of the Internal Revenue Code that has been paid, exceeds the total Federal estate tax (including penalties and interest attributable to the tax) under chapter 11 of the Internal Revenue Code that would have been paid if the value of the property includible in the gross estate by reason of section 2044 had not been so included.

(c) Amount of estate tax attributable to a particular property. An estate's right of recovery with respect to a particular property is an amount equal to the amount determined in paragraph (b) of this section multiplied by a fraction. The numerator of the fraction is the value for Federal estate tax purposes of the particular property included in the gross estate by reason of section 2044, less any deduction allowed with respect to the property. The denominator of the fraction is the total value of all properties included in the gross estate by reason of section 2044, less any deductions allowed with respect to those properties.

(d) Person receiving the property. If the property is in a trust at the time of the decedent's death, the person receiving the property is the trustee and any person who has received a distribution of the property prior to the expiration of the right of recovery if the property does not remain in trust. This paragraph (d) does not affect the right, if any, under local law, of any person with an interest in property to reimbursement or contribution from another person with an interest in the property.

(e) Example. The following example illustrates the application of paragraphs (a) through (d) of this section.

Example. D died in 1994. D's will created a trust funded with certain income producing assets included in D's gross estate at $1,000,000. The trust provides that all the income is payable to D's wife, S, for life, remainder to be divided equally among their four children. In computing D's taxable estate, D's executor deducted, pursuant to section 2056(b)(7), $1,000,000. Assume that S received no other property from D and that S died in 1996. Assume further that S made no section 2519 disposition of the property, that the property was included in S's gross estate at a value of $1,080,000, and that S's will contained no provision regarding section 2207A(a). The tax attributable to the property is equal to the amount by which the total Federal estate tax (including penalties and interest) paid by S's estate exceeds the Federal estate tax (including penalties and interest) that would have been paid if S's gross estate had been reduced by $1,080,000. That amount of tax may be recovered by S's estate from the trust. If, at the time S's estate seeks reimbursement, the trust has been distributed to the four children, S's estate is also entitled to recover the tax from the children.

[T.D. 8522, 59 FR 9642, Mar. 1, 1994, as amended by T.D. 9077, 68 FR 42593, July 18, 2003]

GIFT TAX

§ 25.0–1 Introduction.

* * *

(b) Nature of tax. The gift tax is not a property tax. It is a tax imposed upon the transfer of property by individuals. It is not applicable to transfers by corporations or persons other than individuals. However, see paragraph (h)(1) of § 25.2511–1 with respect to the extent to which a transfer by or to a corporation is considered a transfer by or to its shareholders.

(c) Scope of regulations—(1) Determination of tax liability. Subchapter A of Chapter 12 of the Code pertains to the determination of tax liability. The regulations pursuant to Subchapter A are set forth in §§ 25.2501–1 through 25.2504–2. Sections 25.2701–5 and 25.2702–6 contain rules that provide additional adjustments to mitigate double taxation where the amount of the transferor's property was previously determined under the special valuation provisions of sections 2701 and 2702.

(2) Transfer. Subchapter B of chapter 12 and chapter 14 of the Internal Revenue Code pertain to the transfers which constitute the making of gifts and the valuation of those transfers. The regulations pursuant to subchapter B are set forth in §§ 25.2511–1 through 25.2518–3. The regulations pursuant to chapter 14 are set forth in §§ 25.2701–1 through 25.2704–3.

* * *

[T.D. 6334, 23 FR 8904, Nov. 15, 1958, as amended by T.D. 6542, 26 FR 548, Jan. 20, 1961; T.D. 7238, 37 FR 28725, Dec. 29, 1972; 45 FR 6089, Jan. 25, 1980; T.D. 7910, 48 FR 40371, Sept. 7, 1983; T.D. 8395, 57 FR 4254, Feb. 4, 1992]

§ 25.2207A–1 Right of recovery of gift taxes in the case of certain marital deduction property.

(a) In general. If an individual is treated as transferring an interest in property by reason of section 2519, the individual or the individual's estate is entitled to recover from the person receiving the property (as defined in paragraph (e) of this section) the amount of gift tax attributable to that property. The value of property to which this paragraph (a) applies is the value of all interests in the property other than the qualifying income interest. There is no right of recovery from any person for the property received by that person for which a deduction was allowed from the total amount of gifts, if no Federal gift tax is attributable to the property. The right of recovery arises at the time the Federal gift tax is actually paid by the transferor subject to section 2519.

(b) Failure of a person to exercise the right of recovery. (1) The failure of a person to exercise a right of recovery provided by section 2207A(b) upon a lifetime transfer subject to section 2519 is treated as a transfer for Federal gift tax purposes of the unrecovered amounts to the person(s) from whom the recovery could have been obtained. See § 25.2511–1. The transfer is considered to be made when the right to recovery is no longer enforceable under applicable law and is treated as a gift even if recovery is impossible. A delay in the exercise of the right of recovery without payment of sufficient interest is a below-market loan. Section 1.7872–5T of this chapter describes factors that are used to determine, based on the facts and circumstances of a particular case, whether a loan otherwise subject to imputation under section 7872 (relating to the treatment of below-market loans) is exempted from its provisions.

(2) The transferor subject to section 2519 may execute a written waiver of the right of recovery arising under section 2207A before that right of recovery becomes unenforceable. If a waiver is executed, the transfer of the unrecovered amounts by the transferor is considered to be made on the later of—

(i) The date of the valid and irrevocable waiver rendering the right of recovery no longer enforceable; or

(ii) The date of the payment of the tax by the transferor.

(c) Amount of gift tax attributable to all properties. The amount of Federal gift tax attributable to all properties includible in the total amount of gifts under section 2519 made during the calendar year is the amount by which the total Federal gift tax for the calendar year (including penalties and interest attributable to the tax) under chapter 12 of the Internal Revenue Code which has been paid, exceeds the total Federal gift tax for the calendar year (including penalties and interest attributable to the tax) under chapter 12 of the Internal Revenue Code which would have been paid if the value of the properties includible in the total amount of gifts by reason of section 2519 had not been included.

(d) Amount of gift tax attributable to a particular property. A person's right of recovery with respect to a particular property is an amount equal to the amount determined in paragraph (c) of this section multiplied by a fraction. The numerator of the fraction is the value of the particular property included in the total amount of gifts made during the calendar year by reason of section 2519, less any deduction allowed with respect to the property. The denominator of the fraction is the total value of all properties included in the total amount of gifts made during the calendar year by reason of section 2519, less any deductions allowed with respect to those properties.

(e) Person receiving the property. If the property is in a trust at the time of the transfer, the person receiving the property is the trustee, and any person who has received a distribution of the property prior to the expiration of the right of recovery if the property does not remain in trust. This paragraph (e) does not affect the right, if any, under local law, of any person with an interest in property to reimbursement or contribution from another person with an interest in the property.

(f) Example. The following example illustrates the application of paragraphs (a) through (e) of this section.

Example. D created an inter vivos trust during 1994 with certain income producing assets valued at $1,000,000. The trust provides that all income is payable to D's wife, S, for S's life, with the remainder at S's death to be divided equally among their four children. In computing taxable gifts during calendar year 1994, D deducted, pursuant to section 2523(f), $1,000,000 from the total amount of gifts made. In addition, assume that S received no other transfers from D and that S made a gift during 1996 of the entire life interest to one of the children, at which time the value of trust assets was $1,080,000 and the value of S's life interest was $400,000. Although the entire value of the trust assets ($1,080,000) is, pursuant to sections 2511 and 2519, included in the total amount of S's gifts for calendar year 1996, S is only entitled to reimbursement for the Federal gift tax attributable to the value of the remainder interest, that is, the Federal gift tax attributable to $680,000 ($1,080,000 less $400,000). The Federal gift tax attributable to $680,000 is equal to the amount by which the total Federal gift tax (including penalties and interest) paid for the calendar year exceeds the federal gift tax (including penalties and interest) that would have been paid if the total amount of gifts during 1996 had been reduced by $680,000. That amount of tax may be recovered by S from the trust.

[T.D. 8522, 59 FR 9642, Mar. 1, 1994, as amended by T.D. 9077, 68 FR 42593, July 18, 2003]

§ 25.2502–1 Rate of tax.

(a) Computation of tax. The rate of tax is determined by the total of all gifts made by the donor during the calendar period and all the preceding calendar periods since June 6, 1932. See § 25.2502–1(c)(1) for the definition of "calendar period" and § 25.2502–1(c)(2) for the definition of "preceding calendar periods." The following six steps are to be followed in computing the tax:

(1) First step. Ascertain the amount of the "taxable gifts" (as defined in § 25.2503–1) for the calendar period for which the return is being prepared.

(2) Second step. Ascertain "the aggregate sum of the taxable gifts for each of the preceding calendar periods" (as defined in § 25.2504–1), considering only those gifts made after June 6, 1932.

(3) Third step. Ascertain the total amount of the taxable gifts which is the sum of the amounts determined in the first and second steps. See § 25.2702–6 for an adjustment to the total amount of an individual's taxable gifts where the individual's current taxable gifts include the transfer of certain interests in trust that were previously valued under the provisions of section 2702.

(4) Fourth step. Compute the tentative tax on the total amount of taxable gifts (as determined in the third step) using the rate schedule in effect at the time the gift (for which the return is being filed) is made.

(5) Fifth step. Compute the tentative tax on the aggregate sum of the taxable gifts for each of the preceding calendar periods (as determined in the second step), using the same rate schedule set forth in the fourth step of this paragraph (a).

(6) Sixth step. Subtract the amount determined in the fifth step from the amount determined in the fourth step. The amount remaining is the gift tax for the calendar period for which the return is being prepared.

(b) Rate of tax. The tax is computed in accordance with the rate schedule in effect at the time the gift was made as set forth in section 2001(c) or corresponding provisions of prior law.

(c) Definitions. **(1)** The term "calendar period" means:

(i) Each calendar year for the calendar years 1932 (but only that portion of such year after June 6, 1932) through 1970;

(ii) Each calendar quarter for the first calendar quarter of the calendar year 1971 through the last calendar quarter of calendar year 1981; or

(iii) Each calendar year for the calendar year 1982 and each succeeding calendar year.

(2) The term "preceding calendar periods" means all calendar periods ending prior to the calendar period for which the tax is being computed.

* * *

[T.D. 6334, 23 FR 8904, Nov. 15, 1958, as amended by T.D. 7238, 37 FR 28725, Dec. 29, 1972; T.D. 7910, 48 FR 40371, Sept. 7, 1983; T.D. 8395, 57 FR 4255, Feb. 4, 1992]

§ 25.2503–1 General definitions of "taxable gifts" and of "total amount of gifts."

The term "taxable gifts" means the "total amount of gifts" made by the donor during the "calendar period" (as defined in § 25.2502–1(c)(1)) less the deductions provided for in sections * * * 2522, and 2523 (* * * charitable, etc., gifts and the marital deduction, respectively). The term "total amount of gifts" means the sum of the values of the gifts made during the calendar period less the amounts excludable under section 2503(b). * * * The entire value of any gift of a future interest in property must be included in the total amount of gifts for the calendar period in which the gift is made. See § 25.2503–3.

[T.D. 7238, 37 FR 28727, Dec. 29, 1972, as amended by T.D. 7910, 48 FR 40371, Sept. 7, 1983]

§ 25.2503–2 Exclusions from gifts.

(a) Gifts made after December 31, 1981. Except as provided in paragraph (f) of this section (involving gifts to a noncitizen spouse), the first $10,000 of gifts made to any one donee during the calendar year 1982 or any calendar year thereafter, except gifts of future interests in property as defined in §§ 25.2503–3 and 25.2503–4, is excluded in determining the total amount of gifts for the calendar year. In the case of a gift in trust the beneficiary of the trust is the donee.

* * *

(f) Special rule in the case of gifts made on or after July 14, 1988, to a spouse who is not a United States citizen—(1) In general. Subject to the special rules set forth at § 20.2056A–1(c) of this chapter, in the case of gifts made on or after July 14, 1988, if the donee of the gift is the donor's spouse and the donee spouse is not a citizen of the United States at the time of the gift, the first $100,000 of gifts made during the calendar year to the donee spouse (except gifts of future interests) is excluded in determining the total amount of gifts for the calendar year. The rule of this paragraph (f) applies regardless of whether the donor is a citizen or resident of the United States for purposes of chapter 12 of the Internal Revenue Code.

(2) Gifts made after June 29, 1989. In the case of gifts made after June 29, 1989, the $100,000 exclusion provided in paragraph (f)(1) of this section applies only if the gift in excess of the otherwise applicable annual exclusion is in a form that qualifies for the gift tax marital deduction under section 2523(a) but for the provisions of section 2523(i)(1) (disallowing the marital deduction if the donee spouse is not a United States citizen.) See § 25.2523(i)–1(d), Example 4.

(3) Effective date. This paragraph (f) is effective with respect to gifts made after August 22, 1995.

[T.D. 6334, 23 FR 8904, Nov. 15, 1958, as amended by T.D. 7238, 37 FR 28727, Dec. 29, 1972; T.D. 7910, 48 FR 40371, Sept. 7, 1983; T.D. 7978, 49 FR 38541, Oct. 1, 1984; T.D. 8612, 60 FR 43531, Aug. 22, 1995]

§ 25.2503–3 Future interests in property.

(a) No part of the value of a gift of a future interest may be excluded in determining the total amount of gifts made during the "calendar period" (as defined in § 25.2502–1(c)(1)). "Future interest" is a legal term, and includes reversions, remainders, and other interests or estates, whether vested or contingent, and whether or not supported by a particular interest or estate, which are limited to commence in use, possession, or enjoyment at some future date or time. The term has no reference to such contractual rights as exist in a bond, note (though bearing no interest until maturity), or in a policy of life insurance, the obligations of which are to be discharged by payments in the future. But a future interest or interests in such contractual obligations may be created by the limitations contained in a trust or other instrument of transfer used in effecting a gift.

(b) An unrestricted right to the immediate use, possession, or enjoyment of property or the income from property (such as a life estate or term certain) is a present interest in property. An exclusion is allowable with respect to a gift of such an interest (but not in excess of the value of the interest). If a donee has received a present interest in property, the possibility that such interest may be diminished by the transfer of a greater interest in the same property to the donee through the exercise of a power is disregarded in computing the value of the present interest, to the extent that no part of such interest will at any time pass to any other person (see example (4) of paragraph (c) of this section). For an exception to the rule disallowing an exclusion for gifts of future interests in the case of certain gifts to minors, see § 25.2503–4.

(c) The operation of this section may be illustrated by the following examples:

Example (1). Under the terms of a trust created by A the trustee is directed to pay the net income to B, so long as B shall live. The trustee is authorized in his discretion to withhold payments of income during any period he deems advisable and add such income to the trust corpus. Since B's right to receive the income payments is subject to the trustee's discretion, it is not a present interest and no exclusion is allowable with respect to the transfer in trust.

Example (2). C transfers certain insurance policies on his own life to a trust created for the benefit of D. Upon C's death the proceeds of the policies are to be invested and the net income therefrom paid to D during his lifetime. Since the income payments to D will not begin until after C's death the transfer in trust represents a gift of a future interest in property against which no exclusion is allowable.

Example (3). Under the terms of a trust created by E the net income is to be distributed to E's three children in such shares as the trustee, in his uncontrolled discretion deems advisable. While the terms of the trust provide that all of the net income is to be distributed, the amount of income any one of the three beneficiaries will receive rests entirely within the trustee's discretion and cannot be presently ascertained. Accordingly, no exclusions are allowable with respect to the transfers to the trust.

Example (4). Under the terms of a trust the net income is to be paid to F for life, with the remainder payable to G on F's death. The trustee has the uncontrolled power to pay over the corpus to F at any time. Although F's present right to receive the income may be terminated, no other person has the right to such income interest. Accordingly, the power in the trustee is disregarded in determining the value of F's present interest. The power would not be disregarded to the extent that the trustee during F's life could distribute corpus to persons other than F.

Example (5). The corpus of a trust created by J consists of certain real property, subject to a mortgage. The terms of the trust provide that the net income from the property is to be used to pay the mortgage. After the mortgage is paid in full the net income is to be paid to K during his lifetime. Since K's right to receive the income payments will not begin until after the mortgage is paid in full the transfer in trust represents a gift of a future interest in property against which no exclusion is allowable.

Example (6). L pays premiums on a policy of insurance on his life, all the incidents of ownership in the policy (including the right to surrender the policy) are vested in M. The payment of premiums by L constitutes a gift of a present interest in property.

[T.D. 6334, 23 FR 8904, Nov. 15, 1958, as amended by T.D. 7238, 37 FR 28727, Dec. 29, 1972; T.D. 7910, 48 FR 40371, Sept. 7, 1983]

§ 25.2503–4 Transfer for the benefit of a minor.

(a) Section 2503(c) provides that no part of a transfer for the benefit of a donee who has not attained the age of 21 years on the date of the gift will be considered a gift of a future interest in property if the terms of the transfer satisfy all of the following conditions:

(1) Both the property itself and its income may be expended by or for the benefit of the donee before he attains the age of 21 years;

(2) Any portion of the property and its income not disposed of under subparagraph (1) of this paragraph will pass to the donee when he attains the age of 21 years; and

(3) Any portion of the property and its income not disposed of under subparagraph (1) of this paragraph will be payable either to the estate of the donee or as he may appoint under a general power of appointment as defined in section 2514(c) if he dies before attaining the age of 21 years.

(b) Either a power of appointment exercisable by the donee by will or a power of appointment exercisable by the donee during his lifetime will satisfy the conditions set forth in paragraph (a)(3) of this section. However, if the transfer is to qualify for the exclusion under this section, there must be no restrictions of substance (as distinguished from formal restrictions of the type described in paragraph (g)(4) of § 25.2523(e)–1) by the terms of the instrument of transfer on the exercise of the power by the donee. However, if the minor is given a power of appointment exercisable during lifetime or is given a power of appointment exercisable by will, the fact that under the local law a minor is under a disability to exercise an *inter vivos* power or to execute a will does not cause the transfer to fail to satisfy the conditions of section 2503(c). Further, a transfer does not fail to satisfy the conditions of section 2503(c) by reason of the mere fact that—

(1) There is left to the discretion of a trustee the determination of the amounts, if any, of the income or property to be expended for the benefit of the minor and the purpose for which the expenditure is to be made, provided there are no substantial restrictions under the terms of the trust instrument on the exercise of such discretion;

(2) The donee, upon reaching age 21, has the right to extend the term of the trust; or

(3) The governing instrument contains a disposition of the property or income not expended during the donee's minority to persons other than the donee's estate in the event of the default of appointment by the donee.

(c) A gift to a minor which does not satisfy the requirements of section 2503(c) may be either a present or a future interest under the general rules of § 25.2503–3. Thus, for example, a transfer of property in trust with income required to be paid annually to a minor beneficiary and corpus to be distributed to him upon his attaining the age of 21 is a gift of a present interest with respect to the right to income but is a gift of a future interest with respect to the right to corpus.

[T.D. 6334, 23 FR 8904, Nov. 15, 1958]

§ 25.2503–6 Exclusion for certain qualified transfer for tuition or medical expenses.

(a) In general. Section 2503(e) provides that any qualified transfer after December 31, 1981, shall not be treated as a transfer of property by gift for purposes of chapter 12 of subtitle B of the Code. Thus, a qualified transfer on behalf of any individual is excluded in determining the total amount of gifts in calendar year 1982 and subsequent years. This exclusion is available in addition to the $10,000 annual gift tax exclusion. Furthermore, an exclusion for a qualified transfer is permitted without regard to the relationship between the donor and the donee.

(b) Qualified transfers—(1) Definition. For purposes of this paragraph, the term "qualified transfer" means any amount paid on behalf of an individual—

(i) As tuition to a qualifying educational organization for the education or training of that individual, or

(ii) To any person who provides medical care with respect to that individual as payment for the qualifying medical expenses arising from such medical care.

(2) Tuition expenses. For purposes of paragraph (b)(1)(i) of this section, a qualifying educational organization is one which normally maintains a regular faculty and curriculum and normally has a regularly enrolled body of pupils or students in attendance at the place where its educational activities are regularly carried on. See section 170(b)(1)(A)(ii) and the regulations thereunder. The unlimited exclusion is permitted for tuition expenses of full-time or part-time students paid directly to the qualifying educational organization providing the education. No unlimited exclusion is permitted for amounts paid for books, supplies, dormitory fees, board, or other similar expenses which do not constitute direct tuition costs.

(3) Medical expenses. For purposes of paragraph (b)(1)(ii) of this section, qualifying medical expenses are limited to those expenses defined in section 213(d) * * * and include expenses incurred for the diagnosis, cure, mitigation, treatment or prevention of disease, or for the purpose of affecting any structure or function of the body or for transportation primarily for and essential to medical care. In addition, the unlimited exclusion from the gift tax includes amounts paid for medical insurance on behalf of any individual. The unlimited exclusion from the gift tax does not apply to amounts paid for medical care that are reimbursed by the donee's insurance. Thus, if payment for a medical expense is reimbursed by the donee's insurance company, the donor's payment for that expense, to the extent of the reimbursed amount, is not eligible for the unlimited exclusion from the gift tax and the gift is treated as having been made on the date the reimbursement is received by the donee.

(c) Examples. The provisions of paragraph (b) of this section may be illustrated by the following examples.

Example (1). In 1982, A made a tuition payment directly to a foreign university on behalf of B. A had no legal obligation to make this payment. The foreign university is described in section 170(b)(1)(A)(ii) of the Code. A's tuition payment is exempt from the gift tax under section 2503(e) of the Code.

Example (2). A transfers $100,000 to a trust the provisions of which state that the funds are to be used for tuition expenses incurred by A's grandchildren. A's transfer to the trust is a completed gift for Federal gift tax purposes and is not a direct transfer to an educational organization as provided in paragraph (b)(2) of this section and does not qualify for the unlimited exclusion from gift tax under section 2503(e).

Example (3). C was seriously injured in an automobile accident in 1982. D, who is unrelated to C, paid C's various medical expenses by checks made payable to the physician. D also paid the hospital for C's hospital bills. These medical and hospital expenses were types described in section 213 of the Code and were not reimbursed by insurance or otherwise. Because the medical and hospital bills paid in 1982 for C were medical expenses within the meaning of section 213 of the Code, and since they were paid directly by D to the person rendering the medical care, they are not treated as transfers subject to the gift tax.

Example (4). Assume the same facts as in example (3) except that instead of making the payments directly to the medical service provided, D reimbursed C for the medical expenses which C had previously paid. The payments made by D to C do not qualify for the exclusion under section 2503(e) of the Code and are subject to the gift tax on the date the reimbursement is received by C to the extent the reimbursement and all other gifts from D to C during the year of the reimbursement exceed the $10,000 annual exclusion provided in section 2503(b).

[T.D. 7978, 49 FR 38541, Oct. 1, 1984; T.D. 1978, 49 FR 39843, Oct. 11, 1984]

§ 25.2504–1 Taxable gifts for preceding calendar periods.

(a) In order to determine the correct gift tax liability for any calendar period it is necessary to ascertain the correct amount, if any, of the aggregate sum of the taxable gifts for each of the "preceding calendar periods" (as defined in § 25.2502–1(c)(2)). See paragraph (a) of § 25.2502–1. The term "aggregate sum of the taxable gifts for each of the preceding calendar periods" means the correct aggregate of such gifts, not necessarily that returned for those calendar periods and in respect of which tax was paid. All transfers that constituted gifts in prior calendar periods under the laws, including the provisions of law relating to exclusions from gifts, in effect at the time the transfers were made are included in determining the amount of taxable gifts for preceding calendar periods. The deductions other than for the specific exemption (see paragraph (b) of this section) allowed by the laws in effect at the time the transfers were made also are taken into account in determining the aggregate sum of the taxable gifts for preceding calendar periods. The deductions other than for the specific exemption (see paragraph (b) of this section) allowed by the laws in effect at the time the transfers were made also are taken into account in determining the aggregate sum of the taxable gifts for preceding calendar periods. (The allowable exclusion from a gift is $5,000 for years before 1939, $4,000 for the calendar years 1939 through 1942, $3,000 for the calendar years 1943 through 1981, and $10,000 thereafter.)

(b) In determining the aggregate sum of the taxable gifts for the "preceding calendar periods" (as defined in § 25.2502–1(c)(2)), the total of the amounts allowed as deductions for the specific exemption, under section 2521 (as in effect prior to its repeal by the Tax Reform Act of 1976) and the corresponding provisions of prior laws, shall not exceed $30,000. Thus, if the only prior gifts by a donor were made in 1940 and 1941 (at which time the specific exemption allowable was $40,000), and if in the donor's returns for those years the donor claimed deductions totaling $40,000 for the specific exemption and reported taxable gifts totaling $110,000, then in determining the aggregate sum of the taxable gifts for the preceding calendar periods, the deductions for the specific exemption cannot exceed $30,000, and the donor's taxable gifts for such periods will be $120,000 (instead of the $110,000 reported on the donor's returns). (The allowable deduction for the specific exemption was $50,000 for calendar years before 1936, $40,000 for calendar years 1936 through 1942, and $30,000 for 1943 through 1976.)

(c) If the donor and the donor's spouse consented to have gifts made to third parties considered as made one-half by each spouse, pursuant to the provisions of section 2513 or section 1000(f) of the Internal Revenue Code of 1939 (which corresponds to Section 2513), these provisions shall be taken into account in determining the aggregate sum of the taxable gifts for the preceding calendar periods (under paragraph (a) of this section).

(d) If interpretations of the gift tax law in preceding calendar periods resulted in the erroneous inclusion of property for gift tax purposes that should have been excluded, or the erroneous exclusion of property that should have been included, adjustments must be made in order to arrive at the correct aggregate of taxable gifts for the preceding calendar periods (under paragraph (a) of this section). However, see section 1000(e) and (g) of the 1939 Code relating to certain discretionary trusts and reciprocal trusts. However, see § 25.2504–2(b) regarding certain gifts made after August 5, 1997.

[T.D. 6334, 23 FR 8904, Nov. 15, 1958, as amended by T.D. 7238, 37 FR 28727, Dec. 29, 1972; T.D. 7910, 48 FR 40373, Sept. 7, 1983; T.D. 8845, 64 FR 67770, Dec. 3, 1999]

§ 25.2504–2 Determination of gifts for preceding calendar periods.

(a) Gifts made before August 6, 1997. If the time has expired within which a tax may be assessed under chapter 12 of the Internal Revenue Code (or under corresponding provisions of prior laws) on the transfer of property by gift made during a preceding calendar period, as defined in § 25.2502–1(c)(2), the gift was made prior to August 6, 1997, and a tax has been assessed or paid for such prior calendar period, the value of the gift, for purposes of arriving at the correct amount of the taxable gifts for the preceding calendar periods (as defined under § 25.2504–1(a)), is the value used in computing the tax for the last preceding calendar period for which a tax was assessed or paid under chapter 12 of the Internal Revenue Code or the corresponding provisions of prior laws. However, this rule does not apply where no tax was paid or assessed for the prior calendar period. Furthermore, this rule does not apply to adjustments involving issues other than valuation. See § 25.2504–1(d).

(b) Gifts made or section 2701(d) taxable events occurring after August 5, 1997. If the time has expired under section 6501 within which a gift tax may be assessed under chapter 12 of the Internal Revenue Code (or under corresponding provisions of prior laws) on the transfer of property by gift made during a preceding calendar period, as defined in § 25.2502–1(c)(2), or with respect to an increase in taxable gifts required under section 2701(d) and § 25.2701–4, and the gift was made, or the section 2701(d) taxable event occurred, after August 5, 1997, the amount of the taxable gift or the amount of the increase in taxable gifts, for purposes of determining the correct amount of taxable gifts for the preceding calendar periods (as defined in § 25.2504–1(a)), is the amount that is finally determined for gift tax purposes (within the meaning of § 20.2001–1(c) of this chapter) and such amount may not be thereafter adjusted. The rule of this paragraph (b) applies to adjustments involving all issues relating to the gift including valuation issues and legal issues involving the interpretation of the gift tax law. For purposes of determining if the time has expired within which a gift tax may be assessed, see § 301.6501(c)–1(e) and (f) of this chapter.

(c) Examples. The following examples illustrate the rules of paragraphs (a) and (b) of this section:

Example 1. (i) Facts. In 1996, A transferred closely-held stock in trust for the benefit of B, A's child. A timely filed a Federal gift tax return reporting the 1996 transfer to B. No gift tax was assessed or paid as a result of the gift tax annual exclusion and the application of A's available unified credit. In 2001, A transferred additional closely-held stock to the trust. A's Federal gift tax return reporting the 2001 transfer was timely filed and the transfer was adequately disclosed under § 301.6501(c)–1(f)(2) of this chapter. In computing the amount of taxable gifts, A claimed annual exclusions with respect to the transfers in 1996 and 2001. In 2003, A transfers additional property to B and timely files a Federal gift tax return reporting the gift.

(ii) Application of the rule limiting adjustments to prior gifts. Under section 2504(c), in determining A's 2003 gift tax liability, the amount of A's 1996 gift can be adjusted for purposes of computing prior taxable gifts, since that gift was made prior to August 6, 1997, and therefore, the provisions of paragraph (a) of this section apply. Adjustments can be made with respect to the valuation of the gift and legal issues presented (for example, the availability of the annual exclusion with respect to the gift). However, A's 2001 transfer was adequately disclosed on a timely filed gift tax return and, thus, under paragraph (b) of this section, the amount of the 2001 taxable gift by A may not be adjusted (either with respect to the valuation of the gift or any legal issue) for purposes of computing prior taxable gifts in determining A's 2003 gift tax liability.

Example 2. (i) Facts. In 1996, A transferred closely-held stock to B, A's child. A timely filed a Federal gift tax return reporting the 1996 transfer to B and paid gift tax on the value of the gift reported on the return. On August 1, 1997, A transferred additional closely-held stock to B in exchange for a promissory note signed by B. Also, on September 10, 1997, A transferred closely-held stock to C, A's other child. On April 15, 1998, A timely filed a gift tax return for 1997 reporting the September 10, 1997, transfer to C and, under § 301.6501(c)–1(f)(2) of this chapter, adequately disclosed that transfer and paid gift tax with respect to the transfer. However, A believed that the transfer to B on August 1, 1997, was for full and adequate consideration and A did not report the transfer to B on the 1997 Federal gift tax return. In 2002, A transfers additional property to B and timely files a Federal gift tax return reporting the gift.

(ii) Application of the rule limiting adjustments to prior gifts. Under section 2504(c), in determining A's 2002 gift tax liability, the value of A's 1996 gift cannot be adjusted for purposes of computing the value of prior taxable gifts, since that gift was made prior to August 6, 1997, and a timely filed Federal gift tax return was filed on which a gift tax was assessed and paid. However, A's prior taxable gifts can be adjusted to reflect the August 1, 1997, transfer because, although a gift tax return for 1997 was timely filed and gift tax was paid, under § 301.6501(c)–1(f) of this chapter the period for assessing gift tax with respect to the August 1, 1997, transfer did not commence to run since that transfer was not adequately disclosed on the 1997 gift tax return. Accordingly, a gift tax may be assessed with respect to the August 1, 1997, transfer and the amount of the gift would be reflected in prior taxable gifts for purposes of computing A's gift tax liability for 2002. A's September 10, 1997, transfer to C was adequately disclosed on a timely filed gift tax return and, thus, under paragraph (b) of this section, the amount of the September 10, 1997, taxable gift by A may not be adjusted for purposes of computing prior taxable gifts in determining A's 2002 gift tax liability.

Example 3. (i) Facts. In 1994, A transferred closely-held stock to B and C, A's children. A timely filed a Federal gift tax return reporting the 1994 transfers to B and C and paid gift tax on the value of the gifts reported on the return. Also in 1994, A transferred closely-held stock to B in exchange for a bona fide promissory note signed by B. A believed that the transfer to B in exchange for the promissory note was for full and adequate consideration and A did not report that transfer to B on the 1994 Federal gift tax return. In 2002, A transfers additional property to B and timely files a Federal gift tax return reporting the gift.

(ii) Application of the rule limiting adjustments to prior gifts. Under section 2504(c), in determining A's 2002 gift tax liability, the value of A's 1994 gifts cannot be adjusted for purposes of computing prior taxable gifts because those gifts were made prior to August 6, 1997, and a timely filed Federal gift tax return was filed with respect to which a gift tax was assessed and paid, and the period of limitations on assessment has expired. The provisions of paragraph (a) of this section apply to the 1994 transfers. However, for purposes of determining A's adjusted taxable gifts in computing A's estate tax liability, the gifts may be adjusted. See § 20.2001–1(a) of this chapter.

(d) Effective dates. paragraph (a) of this section applies to transfers of property by gift made prior to August 6, 1997. Paragraphs (b) and (c) of this section apply to transfers of property by gift made after August 5, 1997, if the gift tax return for the calendar period in which the transfer is reported is filed after December 3, 1999.

[T.D. 6334, 23 FR 8904, Nov. 15, 1958, as amended by T.D. 7238, 37 FR 28728, Dec. 29, 1972; T.D. 7910, 48 FR 40374, Sept. 7, 1983; T.D. 8845, 64 FR 67770, Dec. 3, 1999]

§ 25.2505–2T Gifts made by a surviving spouse having a DSUE amount available (temporary).

(a) Donor who is surviving spouse is limited to DSUE amount of last deceased spouse—(1) In general. In computing a surviving spouse's gift tax liability with regard to a transfer subject to the tax imposed by section 2501 (taxable gift), a deceased spousal unused exclusion (DSUE) amount of a decedent, computed under § 20.2010–2T(c) of this chapter, is included in determining the surviving spouse's applicable exclusion amount under section 2010(c)(2), provided:

(i) Such decedent is the last deceased spouse of such surviving spouse within the meaning of § 20.2010–1T(d)(5) of this chapter at the time of the surviving spouse's taxable gift; and

(ii) The executor of the decedent's estate elected portability (see § 20.2010–2T(a) and (b) of this chapter for applicable requirements).

(2) No DSUE amount available from last deceased spouse. If on the date of the surviving spouse's taxable gift the last deceased spouse of such surviving spouse had no DSUE amount or if the executor of the estate of such last deceased spouse did not elect portability, the surviving spouse has no DSUE amount (except as and to the extent provided in paragraph (c)(1)(ii) of this section) to be included in determining his or her applicable exclusion amount, even if the surviving spouse previously had a DSUE amount available from another decedent who, prior to the death of the last deceased spouse, was the last deceased spouse of such surviving spouse. See paragraph (c) of this section for a special rule in the case of multiple deceased spouses.

(3) Identity of last deceased spouse unchanged by subsequent marriage or divorce. A decedent is the last deceased spouse (as defined in § 20.2010–1T(d)(5) of this chapter) of a surviving spouse even if, on the date of the surviving spouse's taxable gift, the surviving spouse is married to another (then-living) individual. If a surviving spouse marries again and that marriage ends in divorce or an annulment, the subsequent death of the divorced spouse does not end the status of the prior deceased spouse as the last deceased spouse of the surviving spouse. The divorced spouse, not being married to the surviving spouse at death, is not the last deceased spouse as that term is defined in § 20.2010–1T(d)(5) of this chapter.

(b) Manner in which DSUE amount is applied. If a donor who is a surviving spouse makes a taxable gift and a DSUE amount is included in determining the surviving spouse's applicable exclusion amount under section 2010(c)(2), such surviving spouse will be considered to apply such DSUE amount to the taxable gift before the surviving spouse's own basic exclusion amount.

(c) Special rule in case of multiple deceased spouses and previously-applied DSUE amount—(1) In general. A special rule applies to compute the DSUE amount included in the applicable exclusion amount of a surviving spouse who previously has applied the DSUE amount of one or more deceased spouses. If a surviving spouse applied the DSUE amount of one or more last deceased spouses to the surviving spouse's previous lifetime transfers, and if any of those last deceased spouses is different from the surviving spouse's last deceased spouse as defined in § 20.2010–1T(d)(5) of this chapter at the time of the current taxable gift by the surviving spouse, then the DSUE amount to be included in determining the applicable exclusion amount of the surviving spouse that will be applicable at the time of the current taxable gift is the sum of—

(i) The DSUE amount of the surviving spouse's last deceased spouse as described in paragraph (a)(1) of this section; and

(ii) The DSUE amount of each other deceased spouse of the surviving spouse to the extent that such amount was applied to one or more previous taxable gifts of the surviving spouse.

* * *

[T.D. 9593, 77 FR 36161, June 18, 2012]

§ 25.2511–1 Transfers in general.

(a) The gift tax applies to a transfer by way of gift whether the transfer is in trust or otherwise, whether the gift is direct or indirect, and whether the property is real or personal, tangible or intangible. For example, a taxable transfer may be effected by the creation of a trust, the forgiving of a debt, the assignment of a judgment, the assignment of the benefits of an insurance policy, or the transfer of cash, certificates of deposit, or Federal, State or municipal bonds. Statutory provisions which exempt bonds, notes, bills and certificates of indebtedness of the Federal Government or its agencies and the interest thereon from taxation are not applicable to the gift tax, since the gift tax is an excise tax on the transfer, and is not a tax on the subject of the gift.

* * *

(c)(1) The gift tax also applies to gifts indirectly made. Thus, any transaction in which an interest in property is gratuitously passed or conferred upon another, regardless of the means or device employed, constitutes a gift subject to tax. See further § 25.2512–8 relating to transfers for insufficient consideration. However, in the case of a transfer creating an interest in property (within the meaning of § 25.2518–2(c)(3) and (c)(4)) made after December 31, 1976, this paragraph (c)(1) shall not apply to the donee if, as a result of a qualified disclaimer by the donee, the interest passes to a different donee. Nor shall it apply to a donor if, as a result of a qualified disclaimer by the donee, a completed transfer of an interest in property is not effected. See section 2518 and the corresponding regulations for rules relating to a qualified disclaimer.

* * *

(3) The fourth sentence of paragraph (c)(1) of this section is applicable for transfers creating an interest to be disclaimed made on or after December 31, 1997.

(d) If a joint income tax return is filed by a husband and wife for a taxable year, the payment by one spouse of all or part of the income tax liability for such year is not treated as resulting in a transfer that is subject to gift tax. The same rule is applicable to the payment of gift tax for a "calendar period" (as defined in § 25.2502–1(c)(1)) in the case of a husband and wife who have consented to have the gifts made considered as made half by each of them in accordance with the provisions of section 2513.

(e) If a donor transfers by gift less than his entire interest in property, the gift tax is applicable to the interest transferred. The tax is applicable, for example, to the transfer of an undivided half interest in property, or to the transfer of a life estate when the grantor retains the remainder interest, or vice versa. However, if the donor's retained interest is not susceptible of measurement on the basis of generally accepted valuation principles, the gift tax is applicable to the entire value of the property subject to the gift. Thus if a donor, aged 65 years, transfers a life estate in property to A, aged 25 years, with remainder to A's issue, or in default of issue, with reversion to the donor, the gift tax will normally be applicable to the entire value of the property.

* * *

(g)(1) Donative intent on the part of the transferor is not an essential element in the application of the gift tax to the transfer. The application of the tax is based on the objective facts of the transfer and the circumstances under which it is made, rather than on the subjective motives of the donor. However, there are certain types of transfers to which the tax is not applicable. It is applicable only to a transfer of a beneficial interest in property. It is not applicable to a transfer of bare legal title to a trustee. A transfer by a trustee of trust property in which he has no beneficial interest does not constitute a gift by the trustee (but such a transfer may constitute a gift by the creator of the trust, if until the transfer he had the power to change the beneficiaries by amending or revoking the trust). The gift tax is not applicable to a transfer for a full and adequate consideration in money or money's worth, or to ordinary business transactions, described in § 25.2512–8.

(2) If a trustee has a beneficial interest in trust property, a transfer of the property by the trustee is not a taxable transfer if it is made pursuant to a fiduciary power the exercise or nonexercise of which is limited by a reasonably fixed or ascertainable standard which is set forth in the trust instrument. A clearly measurable standard under which the holder of a power is legally accountable is such a standard for this purpose. For instance, a power to distribute corpus for the education, support, maintenance, or health of the beneficiary; for his reasonable support and comfort; to enable him to maintain his accustomed standard of living; or to meet an emergency, would be such a standard. However, a power to distribute corpus for the pleasure, desire, or happiness of a beneficiary is not such a standard. The entire context of a provision of a trust instrument granting a power must be considered in determining whether the power is limited by a reasonably definite standard. For example, if a trust instrument provides that the determination of the trustee shall be conclusive with respect to the exercise or nonexercise of a power, the power is not limited by a reasonably definite standard. However, the fact that the governing instrument is phrased in discretionary terms is not in itself an indication that no such standard exists.

(h) The following are examples of transactions resulting in taxable gifts and in each case it is assumed that the transfers were not made for an adequate and full consideration in money or money's worth:

(1) A transfer of property by a corporation to B is a gift to B from the stockholders of the corporation. If B himself is a stockholder, the transfer is a gift to him from the other stockholders but only to the extent it exceeds B's own interest in such amount as a shareholder. A transfer of property by B to a corporation generally represents gifts by B to the other individual shareholders of the corporation to the extent of their proportionate interests in the corporation. However, there may be an exception to this rule, such as a transfer made by an individual to a charitable, public, political or similar organization which may constitute a gift to the organization as a single entity, depending upon the facts and circumstances in the particular case.

(2) The transfer of property to B if there is imposed upon B the obligation of paying a commensurate annuity to C is a gift to C.

(3) The payment of money or the transfer of property to B in consideration of B's promise to render a service to C is a gift to C, or to both B and C, depending on whether the service to be rendered to C is or is not an adequate and full consideration in money or money's worth for that which is received by B. See section 2512(b) and the regulations thereunder.

(4) If A creates a joint bank account for himself and B (or a similar type of ownership by which A can regain the entire fund without B's consent), there is a gift to B when B draws upon the account for his own benefit, to the extent of the amount drawn without any obligation to account for a part of the proceeds to A. Similarly, if A purchases a United States savings bond registered as payable to "A or B," there is a gift to B when B surrenders the bond for cash without any obligation to account for a part of the proceeds to A.

(5) If A with his own funds purchases property and has the title conveyed to himself and B as joint owners, with rights of survivorship (other than a joint ownership described in example (4)), but which rights may be defeated by either party severing his interest, there is a gift to B in the amount of half the value of the property. * * *

(6) If A is possessed of a vested remainder interest in property, subject to being divested only in the event he should fail to survive one or more individuals or the happening of some other event, an irrevocable assignment of all or any part of his interest would result in a transfer includible for Federal gift tax purposes. * * *

(7) If A, without retaining a power to revoke the trust or to change the beneficial interests therein, transfers property in trust whereby B is to receive the income for life and at his death the trust is to terminate and the corpus is to be returned to A, provided A survives, but if A predeceases B the corpus is to pass to C, A has made a gift equal to the total value of the property less the value of his retained interest. * * *

(8) If the insured purchases a life insurance policy, or pays a premium on a previously issued policy, the proceeds of which are payable to a beneficiary or beneficiaries other than his estate, and with respect to which the insured retains no reversionary interest in himself or his estate and no power to revest the economic benefits in himself or his estate or to change the beneficiaries or their proportionate benefits (or if the insured relinquishes by assignment, by designation of a new beneficiary or otherwise, every such power that was retained in a previously issued policy), the insured has made a gift of the value of the policy, or to the extent of the premium paid, even though the right of the assignee or beneficiary to receive the benefits is conditioned upon his surviving the insured. For the valuation of life insurance policies see § 25.2512–6.

(9) Where property held by a husband and wife as community property is used to purchase insurance upon the husband's life and a third person is revocably designated as beneficiary and under the State law the husband's death is considered to make absolute the transfer by the wife, there is a gift by the wife at the time of the husband's death of half the amount of the proceeds of such insurance.

(10) If under a pension plan (pursuant to which he has an unqualified right to an annuity) an employee has an option to take either a retirement annuity for himself alone or a smaller annuity for himself with a survivorship annuity payable to his wife, an irrevocable election by the employee to take the reduced annuity in order that an annuity may be paid, after the employee's death, to his wife results in the making of a gift. * * *

[T.D. 6334, 23 FR 8904, Nov. 15, 1958, as amended by T.D. 6542, 26 FR 550, Jan. 20, 1961; T.D. 7150, 36 FR 22900, Dec. 2, 1971; T.D. 7238, 37 FR 28728, Dec. 29, 1972; T.D. 7296, 38 FR 34202, Dec. 12, 1973; T.D. 7910, 48 FR 40371, Sept. 7, 1983; T.D. 8095, 51 FR 28369, Aug. 7, 1986; T.D. 8540, 59 FR 30100, June 10, 1994; T.D. 8744, 62 FR 68183, Dec. 31, 1997]

§ 25.2511-2 Cessation of donor's dominion and control.

(a) The gift tax is not imposed upon the receipt of the property by the donee, nor is it necessarily determined by the measure of enrichment resulting to the donee from the transfer, nor is it conditioned upon ability to identify the donee at the time of the transfer. On the contrary, the tax is a primary and personal liability of the donor, is an excise upon his act of making the transfer, is measured by the value of the property passing from the donor, and attaches regardless of the fact that the identity of the donee may not then be known or ascertainable.

(b) As to any property, or part thereof or interest therein, of which the donor has so parted with dominion and control as to leave in him no power to change its disposition, whether for his own benefit or for the benefit of another, the gift is complete. But if upon a transfer of property (whether in trust or otherwise) the donor reserves any power over its disposition, the gift may be wholly incomplete, or may be partially complete and partially incomplete, depending upon all the facts in the particular case. Accordingly, in every case of a transfer of property subject to a reserved power, the terms of the power must be examined and its scope determined. For example, if a donor transfers property to another in trust to pay the income to the donor or accumulate it in the discretion of the trustee, and the donor retains a testamentary power to appoint the remainder among his descendants, no portion of the transfer is a completed gift. On the other hand, if the donor had not retained the testamentary power of appointment, but instead provided that the remainder should go to X or his heirs, the entire transfer would be a completed gift. However, if the exercise of the trustee's power in favor of the grantor is limited by a fixed or ascertainable standard (see paragraph (g)(2) of § 25.2511-1), enforceable by or on behalf of the grantor, then the gift is incomplete to the extent of the ascertainable value of any rights thus retained by the grantor.

(c) A gift is incomplete in every instance in which a donor reserves the power to revest the beneficial title to the property in himself. A gift is also incomplete if and to the extent that a reserved power gives the donor the power to name new beneficiaries or to change the interests of the beneficiaries as between themselves unless the power is a fiduciary power limited by a fixed or ascertainable standard. Thus, if an estate for life is transferred but, by an exercise of a power, the estate may be terminated or cut down by the donor to one of less value, and without restriction upon the extent to which the estate may be so cut down, the transfer constitutes an incomplete gift. If in this example the power was confined to the right to cut down the estate for life to one for a term of five years, the certainty of an estate for not less than that term results in a gift to that extent complete.

(d) A gift is not considered incomplete, however, merely because the donor reserves the power to change the manner or time of enjoyment. Thus, the creation of a trust the income of which is to be paid annually to the donee for a period of years, the corpus being distributable to him at the end of the period, and the power reserved by the donor being limited to a right to require that, instead of the income being so payable, it should be accumulated and distributed with the corpus to the donee at the termination of the period, constitutes a completed gift.

(e) A donor is considered as himself having a power if it is exercisable by him in conjunction with any person not having a substantial adverse interest in the disposition of the transferred property or the income therefrom. A trustee, as such, is not a person having an adverse interest in the disposition of the trust property or its income.

(f) The relinquishment or termination of a power to change the beneficiaries of transferred property, occurring otherwise than by the death of the donor (the statute being confined to transfers by living donors), is regarded as the event that completes the gift and causes the tax to apply. For example, if A transfers property in trust for the benefit of B and C but reserves the power as trustee to change the proportionate interests of B and C, and if A thereafter has another person appointed trustee in place of himself, such later relinquishment of the power by A to the new trustee completes the gift of the transferred property, whether or not the new trustee has a substantial adverse interest. The receipt of income or of other enjoyment of the transferred property by the transferee or by the beneficiary (other than by the donor himself) during the interim between the making of the initial transfer and the relinquishment or termination of the power operates to free such income or other enjoyment from the power, and constitutes a gift of such income or of such other enjoyment taxable as of the "calendar period" (as defined in § 25.2502–1(c)(1)) of its receipt. If property is transferred in trust to pay the income to A for life with remainder to B, powers to distribute corpus to A, and to withhold income from A for future distribution to B, are powers to change the beneficiaries of the transferred property.

(g) If a donor transfers property to himself as trustee (or to himself and some other person, not possessing a substantial adverse interest, as trustees), and retains no beneficial interest in the trust property and no power over it except fiduciary powers, the exercise or nonexercise of which is limited by a fixed or ascertainable standard, to change the beneficiaries of the transferred property, the donor has made a completed gift and the entire value of the transferred property is subject to the gift tax.

(h) If a donor delivers a properly indorsed stock certificate to the donee or the donee's agent, the gift is completed for gift tax purposes on the date of delivery. If the donor delivers the certificate to his bank or broker as his agent, or to the issuing corporation or its transfer agent, for transfer into the name of the donee, the gift is completed on the date the stock is transferred on the books of the corporation.

(i) [Reserved]

(j) If the donor contends that a power is of such nature as to render the gift incomplete, and hence not subject to the tax as of the "calendar period" (as defined in § 25.2502–1(c)(1)) of the initial transfer, see § 301.6501(c)–1(f)(5) of this chapter (Adequate disclosure of incomplete transfers. Ed.)

* * *

[T.D. 6334, 23 FR 8904, Nov. 15, 1958, as amended by T.D. 7238, 37 FR 28728, Dec. 29, 1972; T.D. 7910, 48 FR 40371, Sept. 7, 1983; T.D. 8845, 64 FR 67767, Dec. 3, 1999]

§ 25.2512–1 Valuation of property; in general.

Section 2512 provides that if a gift is made in property, its value at the date of the gift shall be considered the amount of the gift. The value of the property is the price at which such property would change hands between a willing buyer and a willing seller, neither being under any compulsion to buy or to sell, and both having reasonable knowledge of relevant facts. The value of a particular item of property is not the price that a forced sale of the property would produce. Nor is the fair market value of an item of property the sale price in a market other than that in which such item is most commonly sold to the public, taking into account the location of the item wherever appropriate. Thus, in the case of an item of property made the subject of a gift, which is generally obtained by the public in the retail market, the fair market value of such an item of property is the price at which the item or a comparable item would be sold at retail. For example, the value of an automobile (an article generally obtained by the public in the retail market) which is the subject of a gift, is the price for which an automobile of the same or approximately the same description, make, model, age, condition, etc., could be purchased by a member of the general public and not the price for which the particular automobile of the donor would be purchased by a dealer in used automobiles. * * * See section 2701 and the regulations at § 25.2701 for special rules for valuing transfers of an interest in a corporation or a partnership and for the treatment of unpaid qualified payments at the subsequent transfer of an applicable retained interest by the transferor or by an applicable family member. See section 2704(b) and the regulations at § 25.2704–2 for special valuation rules where an interest in property is subject to an applicable restriction.

[T.D. 6334, 23 FR 8904, Nov. 15, 1958, as amended by T.D. 6826, 30 FR 7709, June 15, 1965; T.D. 8395, 57 FR 4255, Feb. 4, 1992]

§ 25.2512–2 Stocks and bonds.

(a) In general. The value of stocks and bonds is the fair market value per share or bond on the date of the gift.

(b) Based on selling prices. **(1)** In general, if there is a market for stocks or bonds, on a stock exchange, in an over-the-counter market or otherwise, the mean between the highest and lowest quoted selling prices on the date of the gift is the fair market value per share or bond. If there were no sales on the date of the gift but there were sales on dates within a reasonable period both before and after the date of the gift, the fair market value is determined by taking a weighted average of the means between the highest and lowest sales on the nearest date before and the nearest date after the date of the gift. The average is to be weighted inversely by the respective numbers of trading days between the selling dates and the date of the gift. If the stocks or bonds are listed on more than one exchange, the records of the exchange where the stocks or bonds are principally dealt in should be employed if such records are available in a generally available listing or publication of general circulation. In the event that such records are not so available and such stocks or bonds are listed on a composite listing of combined exchanges available in a generally available listing or publication of general circulation, the records of such combined exchanges should be employed. In valuing listed securities, the donor should be careful to consult accurate records to obtain values as of the date of the gift. If quotations of unlisted securities are obtained from brokers, or evidence as to their sale is obtained from the officers of the issuing companies, copies of letters furnishing such quotations or evidence of sale should be attached to the return.

(2) If it is established with respect to bonds for which there is a market on a stock exchange, that the highest and lowest selling prices are not available for the date of the gift in a generally available listing or publication of general circulation but that closing prices are so available, the fair market value per bond is the mean between the quoted closing selling price on the date of the gift and the quoted closing selling price on the trading day before the date of the gift. If there were no sales on the trading day before the date of the gift but there were sales on dates within a reasonable period before the date of the gift, the fair market value is determined by taking a weighted average of the quoted closing selling prices on the date of the gift and the nearest date before the date of the gift. The closing selling price for the date of the gift is to be weighted by the respective number of trading days between the previous selling date and the date of the gift. If there were no sales within a reasonable period before the date of the gift but there were sales on the date of the gift, the fair market value is the closing selling price on the date of the gift. If there were no sales on the date of the gift but there were sales within a reasonable period both before and after the date of the gift, the fair market value is determined by taking a weighted average of the quoted closing selling prices on the nearest date before and the nearest date after the date of the gift. The average is to be weighed inversely by the respective numbers of trading days between the selling dates and the date of the gift. If the bonds are listed on more than one exchange, the records of the exchange where the bonds are principally dealt in should be employed. In valuing listed securities, the donor should be careful to consult accurate records to obtain values as of the date of the gift.

* * *

(c) Based on bid and asked prices. If the provisions of paragraph (b) of this section are inapplicable because actual sales are not available during reasonable period beginning before and ending after the date of the gift, the fair market value may be determined by taking the mean between the bona fide bid and asked prices on the date of the gift, or if none, by taking a weighted average of the means between the bona fide bid and asked prices on the nearest trading date before and the nearest trading date after the date of the gift, if both such nearest dates are within a reasonable period. The average is to be determined in the manner described in paragraph (b) of this section.

(d) Where selling prices and bid and asked prices are not available for dates both before and after the date of gift. If the provisions of paragraphs (b) and (c) of this section are inapplicable because no actual sale prices or quoted bona fide bid and asked prices are available on a date within a reasonable period before the date of the gift, but such prices are available on a date within a reasonable period after the date of the gift, or vice versa, then the mean between the highest and lowest available sale prices or bid and asked prices may be taken as the value.

(e) Where selling prices or bid and asked prices do not represent fair market value. In cases in which it is established that the value per bond or share of any security determined on the basis of the selling or bid and asked prices as provided under paragraphs (b), (c), and (d) of this section does not represent the fair market value thereof, then some reasonable modification of the value determined on that basis or other relevant facts and elements of value shall be considered in determining fair market value. Where sales at or near the date of the gift are few or of a sporadic nature, such sales alone may not indicate fair market value. In certain exceptional cases, the size of the block of securities made the subject of each separate gift in relation to the number of shares changing hands in sales may be relevant in determining whether selling prices reflect the fair market value of the block of stock to be valued. If the donor can show that the block of stock to be valued, with reference to each separate gift, is so large in relation to the actual sales on the existing market that it could not be liquidated in a reasonable time without depressing the market, the price at which the block could be sold as such outside the usual market, as through an underwriter, may be a more accurate indication of value than market quotations. Complete data in support of any allowance claimed due to the size of the block of stock being valued should be submitted with the return. On the other hand, if the block of stock to be valued represents a controlling interest, either actual or effective, in a going business, the price at which other lots change hands may have little relation to its true value.

(f) Where selling prices or bid and asked prices are unavailable. If the provisions of paragraphs (b), (c), and (d) of this section are inapplicable because actual sale prices and bona fide bid and asked prices are lacking, then the fair market value is to be determined by taking the following factors into consideration:

(1) In the case of corporate or other bonds, the soundness of the security, the interest yield, the date of maturity, and other relevant factors; and

(2) In the case of shares of stock, the company's net worth, prospective earning power and dividend-paying capacity, and other relevant factors.

Some of the "other relevant factors" referred to in subparagraphs (1) and (2) of this paragraph are: The goodwill of the business; the economic outlook in the particular industry; the company's position in the industry and its management; the degree of control of the business represented by the block of stock to be valued; and the values of securities of corporations engaged in the same or similar lines of business which are listed on a stock exchange. However, the weight to be accorded such comparisons or any other evidentiary factors considered in the determination of a value depends upon the facts of each case. Complete financial and other data upon which the valuation is based should be submitted with the return, including copies of reports of any examinations of the company made by accountants, engineers, or any technical experts as of or near the date of the gift.

[T.D. 6334, 23 FR 8904, Nov. 15, 1958; 25 FR 14021, Dec. 31, 1960, as amended by T.D. 7327, 39 FR 35355, Oct. 1, 1974; T.D. 7432, 41 FR 38769, Sept. 13, 1976]

§ 25.2512–3 Valuation of interest in businesses.

(a) Care should be taken to arrive at an accurate valuation of any interest in a business which the donor transfers without an adequate and full consideration in money or money's worth. The fair market value of any interest in a business, whether a partnership or a proprietorship, is the net amount which a willing purchaser, whether an individual or a corporation, would pay for the interest to a willing seller, neither being under any compulsion to buy or to sell and both having reasonable knowledge of the relevant facts. The net value is determined on the basis of all relevant factors including—

(1) A fair appraisal as of the date of the gift of all the assets of the business, tangible and intangible, including good will;

(2) The demonstrated earning capacity of the business; and

(3) The other factors set forth in paragraph (f) of § 25.2512–2 relating to the valuation of corporate stock, to the extent applicable.

Special attention should be given to determining an adequate value of the good will of the business. Complete financial and other data upon which the valuation is based should be submitted with the return, including copies of reports of examinations of the business made by accountants, engineers, or any technical experts as of or near the date of the gift.

[T.D. 6334, 23 FR 8904, Nov. 15, 1958]

§ 25.2512–4 Valuation of notes.

The fair market value of notes, secured or unsecured, is presumed to be the amount of unpaid principal, plus accrued interest to the date of the gift, unless the donor establishes a lower value. Unless returned at face value, plus accrued interest, it must be shown by satisfactory evidence that the note is worth less than the unpaid amount (because of the interest rate, or date of maturity, or other cause), or that the note is uncollectible in part (by reason of the insolvency of the party or parties liable, or for other cause), and that the property, if any, pledged or mortgaged as security is insufficient to satisfy it.

[T.D. 6334, 23 FR 8904, Nov. 15, 1958]

§ 25.2512–5 Valuation of annuities, unitrust interests, interests for life or term of years, and remainder or reversionary interests.

(a) In general. Except as otherwise provided in paragraph (b) of this section and § 25.7520–3(b), the fair market value of annuities, unitrust interests, life estates, terms of years, remainders, and reversions transferred by gift is the present value of the interests determined under paragraph (d) of this section. Section 20.2031–7 of this chapter (Estate Tax Regulations) and related sections provide tables with standard actuarial factors and examples that illustrate how to use the tables to compute the present value of ordinary annuity, life, and remainder interests in property. These sections also refer to standard and special actuarial factors that may be necessary to compute the present value of similar interests in more unusual fact situations. These factors and examples are also generally applicable for gift tax purposes in computing the values of taxable gifts.

(b) Commercial annuities and insurance contracts. The value of life insurance contracts and contracts for the payment of annuities issued by companies regularly engaged in their sale is determined under § 25.2512–6.

(c) Actuarial valuations. The present value of annuities, unitrust interests, life estates, terms of years, remainders, and reversions transferred by gift on or after May 1, 2009, is determined under paragraph (d) of this section.* * *

(d) Actuarial valuations on or after May 1, 2009—(1) In general. Except as otherwise provided in paragraph (b) of this section and § 25.7520–3(b) (relating to exceptions to the use of prescribed tables under certain circumstances), if the valuation date for the gift is on or after May 1, 2009, the fair market value of annuities, life estates, terms of years, remainders, and reversions transferred on or after May 1, 2009, is the present value of such interests determined under paragraph (d)(2) of this section and by use of standard or special section 7520 actuarial factors. These factors are derived by using the appropriate section 7520 interest rate and, if applicable, the mortality component for the valuation date of the interest that is being valued. See §§ 25.7520–1 through 25.7520–4.* * *

(2) Specific interests. When the donor transfers property in trust or otherwise and retains an interest therein, generally, the value of the gift is the value of the property transferred less the value of the donor's retained interest. However, if the donor transfers property after October 8, 1990, to or for the benefit of a member of the donor's family, the value of the gift is the value of the property transferred less the value of the donor's retained interest as determined under section 2702. If the donor assigns or relinquishes an annuity, life estate, remainder, or reversion that the donor holds by virtue of a transfer previously made by the donor or another, the value of the gift is the value of the interest transferred. However, see section 2519 for a special rule in the case of the assignment of an income interest by a person who received the interest from a spouse.

* * *

(ii) Ordinary remainder and reversionary interests. If the interest to be valued is to take effect after a definite number of years or after the death of one individual, the present value of the interest is computed by multiplying the value of the property by the appropriate remainder interest actuarial factor (that corresponds to the applicable section 7520 interest rate and remainder interest period) in Table B (for a term certain) or in Table S (for one measuring life), as the case may be. Table B is contained in § 20.2031–7(d)(6) of this chapter and Table S (for one measuring life when the valuation date is on or after May 1, 2009) is included in § 20.2031–7(d)(7) and Internal Revenue Service Publication 1457. See § 20.2031–7A containing Table S for valuation of interests before May 1, 2009. For information about obtaining actuarial factors for other types of remainder interests, see paragraph (d)(4) of this section.

(iii) Ordinary term-of-years and life interests. If the interest to be valued is the right of a person to receive the income of certain property, or to use certain nonincome-producing property, for a term of years or for the life of one individual, the present value of the interest is computed by multiplying the value of the property by the appropriate term-of-years or life interest actuarial factor (that corresponds to the applicable section 7520 interest rate and term-of-years or life interest period). Internal Revenue Service Publication 1457 includes actuarial factors for a remainder interest after a term of years in Table B and after the life of one individual in Table S (for one measuring life when the valuation date is on or after May 1, 2009). However, term-of-years and life interest actuarial factors are not included in Table B in § 20.2031–7(d)(6) of this chapter or Table S in § 20.2031–7(d)(7) (or in § 20.2031–7A).* * *

(iv) Annuities. (A) If the interest to be valued is the right of a person to receive an annuity that is payable at the end of each year for a term of years or for the life of one individual, the present value of the interest is computed by multiplying the aggregate amount payable annually by the appropriate annuity actuarial factor (that corresponds to the applicable section 7520 interest rate and annuity period). Internal Revenue Service Publication 1457 includes actuarial factors in Table B (for a remainder interest after an annuity payable for a term of years) and in Table S (for a remainder interest after an annuity payable for the life of one individual when the valuation date is on or after May 1, 2009). However, annuity actuarial factors are not included in Table B in § 20.2031–7(d)(6) of this chapter or Table S in § 20.2031–7(d)(7) (or in § 20.2031–7A).* * *

(4) Publications and actuarial computations by the Internal Revenue Service. Many standard actuarial factors not included in § 20.2031–7(d)(6) or § 20.2031–7(d)(7) of this chapter are included in Internal Revenue Service Publication 1457, "Actuarial Valuations Version 3A" (2009). Internal Revenue Service Publication 1457 also includes examples that illustrate how to compute many special factors for more unusual situations. A copy of this publication is available, at no charge, electronically via the IRS Internet site at http://www.irs.gov. If a special factor is required in the case of a completed gift, the Internal Revenue Service may furnish the factor to the donor upon a request for a ruling. The request for a ruling must be accompanied by a recitation of the facts including a statement of the date of birth for each measuring life, the date of the gift, any other applicable dates, and a copy of the will, trust, or other relevant documents. A request for a ruling must comply with the instructions for requesting a ruling published periodically in the Internal Revenue Bulletin * * * and include payment of the required user fee.

* * *

[T.D. 8540, 59 FR 30174, June 10, 1994; T.D. 8819, 64 FR 23224, April 30, 1999; T.D. 8886, 65 FR 36940, June 12, 2000; 65 FR 39470, June 26, 2000; 65 FR 52163, Aug. 28, 2000; 65 FR 58222, Sept. 28, 2000; T.D. 9448, 74 FR 21512, May 7, 2009; T.D. 9540, 76 FR 49639, Aug. 10, 2011]

§ 25.2512–6 Valuation of certain life insurance and annuity contracts; valuation of shares in an open-end investment company.

(a) Valuation of certain life insurance and annuity contracts. The value of a life insurance contract or of a contract for the payment of an annuity issued by a company regularly engaged in the selling of contracts of that character is established through the sale of the particular contract by the company, or through the sale by the company of comparable contracts. As valuation of an insurance policy through sale of comparable contracts is not readily ascertainable when the gift is of a contract which has been in force for some time and on which further premium payments are to be made, the value may be approximated by adding to the interpolated terminal reserve at the date of the gift the proportionate part of the gross premium last paid before the date of the gift which covers the period extending beyond that date. If, however, because of the unusual nature of the contract such approximation is not reasonably close to the full value, this method may not be used. * * *

* * *

(b) Valuation of shares in an open-end investment company. (1) The fair market value of a share in an open-end investment company (commonly known as a "mutual fund") is the public redemption price of a share. In the absence of an affirmative showing of the public redemption price in effect at the time of the gift, the last public redemption price quoted by the company for the date of the gift shall be presumed to be the applicable public redemption price. If there is no public redemption price quoted by the company for the date of the gift (*e.g.,* the date of the gift is a Saturday, Sunday, or holiday), the fair market value of the mutual fund share is the last public redemption price quoted by the company for the first day preceding the date of the gift for which there is a quotation. As used in this paragraph the term "open-end investment company" includes only a company which on the date of the gift was engaged in offering its shares to the public in the capacity of an open-end investment company.

* * *

[T.D. 6334, 23 FR 8904, Nov. 15, 1958, as amended by T.D. 6542, 26 FR 549, Jan. 20, 1961; T.D. 6680, 28 FR 10872, Oct. 10, 1963; T.D. 7319, 39 FR 26723, July 23, 1974]

§ 25.2512–8 Transfers for insufficient consideration.

Transfers reached by the gift tax are not confined to those only which, being without a valuable consideration, accord with the common law concept of gifts, but embrace as well sales, exchanges, and other dispositions of property for a consideration to the extent that the value of the property transferred by the donor exceeds the value in money or money's worth of the consideration given therefor. However, a sale, exchange, or other transfer of property made in the ordinary course of business (a transaction which is bona fide, at arm's length, and free from any donative intent), will be considered as made for an adequate and full consideration in money or money's worth. A consideration not reducible to a value in money or money's worth, as love and affection, promise of marriage, etc., is to be wholly disregarded, and the entire value of the property transferred constitutes the amount of the gift. Similarly, a relinquishment or promised relinquishment of dower or curtesy, or of a statutory estate created in lieu of dower or curtesy, or of other marital rights in the spouse's property or estate, shall not be considered to any extent a consideration "in money or money's worth." See, however, section 2516 and the regulations thereunder with respect to certain transfers incident to a divorce. See also sections 2701, 2702, 2703 and 2704 and the regulations at §§ 25.2701–0 through 25.2704–3 for special rules for valuing transfers of business interests, transfers in trust, and transfers pursuant to options and purchase agreements.

[T.D. 6334, 23 FR 8904, Nov. 15, 1958; T.D. 8395, 57 FR 4255, Feb. 4, 1992]

§ 25.2513–1 Gifts by husband or wife to third party considered as made one-half by each.

(a) A gift made by one spouse to a person other than his (or her) spouse may, for the purpose of the gift tax, be considered as made one-half by his spouse, but only if at the time of the gift each spouse was a citizen or resident of the United States. For purposes of this section, an individual is to be considered as the spouse of another individual only if he was married to such individual at the time of the gift and does not remarry during the remainder of the "calendar period" (as defined in § 25.2502–1(c)(1)).

(b) The provisions of this section will apply to gifts made during a particular "calendar period" (as defined in § 25.2502–1(c)(1)) only if both spouses signify their consent to treat all gifts made to third parties during that calendar period by both spouses while married to each other as having been made one-half by each spouse. As to the manner and time for signifying consent, see § 25.2513–2. Such consent, if signified with respect to any calendar period, is effective with respect to all gifts made to third parties during such calendar period except as follows:

(1) If the consenting spouses were not married to each other during a portion of the calendar period, the consent is not effective with respect to any gifts made during such portion of the calendar period. Where the consent is signified by an executor or administrator of a deceased spouse, the consent is not effective with respect to gifts made by the surviving spouse during the portion of the calendar period that his spouse was deceased.

(2) If either spouse was a nonresident not a citizen of the United States during any portion of the calendar period, the consent is not effective with respect to any gift made during that portion of the calendar period.

(3) The consent is not effective with respect to a gift by one spouse of a property interest over which he created in his spouse a general power of appointment (as defined in section 2514(c)).

(4) If one spouse transferred property in part to his spouse and in part to third parties, the consent is effective with respect to the interest transferred to third parties only insofar as such interest is ascertainable at the time of the gift and hence severable from the interest transferred to his spouse. See § 25.2512–5 for the principles to be applied in the valuation of annuities, life estates, terms for years, remainders and reversions.

(5) The consent applies alike to gifts made by one spouse alone and to gifts made partly by each spouse, provided such gifts were to third parties and do not fall within any of the exceptions set forth in subparagraphs (1) through (4) of this paragraph. The consent may not be applied only to a portion of the property interest constituting such gifts. For example, a wife may not treat gifts made by her spouse from his separate property to third parties as having been made one-half by her if her spouse does not consent to treat gifts made by her to third parties during the same calendar period as having been made one-half by him. If the consent is effectively signified on either the husband's return or the wife's return, all gifts made by the spouses to third parties (except as described in subparagraphs (1) through (4) of this paragraph), during the calendar period will be treated as having been made one-half by each spouse.

(c) If a husband and wife consent to have the gifts made to third party donees considered as made one-half by each spouse, and only one spouse makes gifts during the "calendar period" (as defined in § 25.2502–1(c)(1)), the other spouse is not required to file a gift tax return provided: (1) The total value of the gifts made to each third party donee since the beginning of the calendar year is not in excess of $20,000 ($6,000 for calendar years prior to 1982), and (2) no portion of the property transferred constitutes a gift of a future interest. If a transfer made by either spouse during the calendar period to a third-party represents a gift of a future interest in property and the spouses consent to have the gifts considered as made one-half by each, a gift tax return for such calendar period must be filed by each spouse regardless of the value of the transfer. (See § 25.2503–3 for the definition of a future interest.)

* * *

[T.D. 6334, 23 FR 8904, Nov. 15, 1958, as amended by T.D. 7238, 37 FR 28729, Dec. 29, 1972; T.D. 7910, 48 FR 40371, Sept. 7, 1983]

§ 25.2513–2 Manner and time of signifying consent.

(a)(1) Consent to the application of the provisions of section 2513 with respect to a "calendar period" (as defined in § 25.2502–1(c)(1)) shall, in order to be effective, be signified by both spouses. If both spouses file gift tax returns within the time for signifying consent, it is sufficient if—

(i) The consent of the husband is signified on the wife's return, and the consent of the wife is signified on the husband's return;

(ii) The consent of each spouse is signified on his own return; or

(iii) The consent of both spouses is signified on one of the returns.

If only one spouse files a gift tax return within the time provided for signifying consent, the consent of both spouses shall be signified on that return. However, wherever possible, the notice of the consent is to be shown on both returns and it is preferred that the notice be executed in the manner described in subdivision (i) of this subparagraph. * * * If one spouse files more than one gift tax return for a calendar period on or before the due date of the return, the last return so filed shall, for the purpose of determining whether a consent has been signified, be considered as the return. * * *

* * *

(c) The executor or administrator of a deceased spouse, or the guardian or committee of a legally incompetent spouse, as the case may be, may signify the consent.

(d) If the donor and spouse consent to the application of section 2513, the return or returns for the "calendar period" (as defined in § 25.2502–1(c)(1)) must set forth, to the extent provided thereon, information relative to the transfers made by each spouse.

[T.D. 6334, 23 FR 8904, Nov. 15, 1958, as amended by T.D. 7238, 37 FR 28730, Dec. 29, 1972; T.D. 7910, 48 FR 40371, Sept. 7, 1983]

§ 25.2513–4 Joint and several liability for tax.

If consent to the application of the provisions of section 2513 is signified as provided in § 25.2513–2, and not revoked as provided in § 25.2513–3, the liability with respect to the entire gift tax of each spouse for such "calendar period" (as defined in § 25.2502–1(c)(1)) is joint and several. See paragraph (d) of § 25.2511–1.

[T.D. 6334, 23 FR 8904, Nov. 15, 1958, as amended by T.D. 7238, 37 FR 28730, Dec. 29, 1972; T.D. 7910, 48 FR 40371, Sept. 7, 1983]

§ 25.2514–1 Transfers under power of appointment.

(a) Introductory. (1) Section 2514 treats the exercise of a general power of appointment created on or before October 21, 1942, as a transfer of property for purposes of the gift tax. The section also treats as a transfer of property the exercise or complete release of a general power of appointment created after October 21, 1942, and under certain circumstances the exercise of a power of appointment (not a general power of appointment) created after October 21, 1942, by the creation of another power of appointment. See paragraph (d) of § 25.2514–3. Under certain circumstances, also, the failure to exercise a power of appointment created after October 21, 1942, within a specified time, so that the power lapses, constitutes a transfer of property. * * *

(b) Definition of "power of appointment"—(1) In general. The term "power of appointment" includes all powers which are in substance and effect powers of appointment received by the donee of the power from another person, regardless of the nomenclature used in creating the power and regardless of local property law connotations. For example, if a trust instrument provides that the beneficiary may appropriate or consume the principal of the trust, the power to consume or appropriate is a power of appointment. Similarly, a power given to a donee to affect the beneficial enjoyment of a trust property or its income by altering, amending or revoking the trust instrument or terminating the trust is a power of appointment. A power in a donee to remove or discharge a trustee and appoint himself may be a power of appointment. For example, if under the terms of a trust instrument, the trustee or his successor has the power to appoint the principal of the trust for the benefit of individuals including himself, and A, another person, has the unrestricted power to remove or discharge the trustee at any time and appoint any other person, including himself, A is considered as having a power of appointment. However, he would not be considered to have a power of appointment if he only had the power to appoint a successor, including himself, under limited conditions which did not exist at the time of exercise, release or lapse of the trustee's power, without an accompanying unrestricted power of removal. Similarly, a power to amend only the administrative provisions of a trust instrument, which cannot substantially affect the beneficial enjoyment of the trust property or income, is not a power of appointment. The mere power of management, investment, custody of assets, or the power to allocate receipts and disbursements as between income and principal, exercisable in a fiduciary capacity, whereby the holder has no power to enlarge or shift any of the beneficial interests therein except as an incidental consequence of the discharge of such fiduciary duties is not a power of appointment. Further, the right in a beneficiary of a trust to assent to a periodic accounting, thereby relieving the trustee from further accountability, is not a power of appointment if the right of assent does not consist of any power or right to enlarge or shift the beneficial interest of any beneficiary therein.

(2) Relation to other sections. For purposes of §§ 25.2514–1 through 25.2514–3, the term "power of appointment" does not include powers reserved by a donor to himself. No provision of section 2514 or of §§ 25.2514–1 through 25.2514–3 is to be construed as in any way limiting the application of any other section of the Internal Revenue Code or of these regulations. The power of the owner of a property interest already possessed by him to dispose of his interest, and nothing more, is not a power of appointment, and the interest is includible in the amount of his gifts to the extent it would be includible under section 2511 or other provisions of the Internal Revenue Code. For example, if a trust created by S provides for payment of the income to A for life with power in A to appoint the entire trust property by deed during her lifetime to a class consisting of her children, and a further power to dispose of the entire corpus by will to anyone, including her estate, and A exercises the inter vivos power in favor of her children, she has necessarily made a transfer of her income interest which constitutes a taxable gift under section 2511(a), without regard to section 2514. This transfer also results in a relinquishment of her general power to appoint by will which constitutes a transfer under section 2514 if the power was created after October 21, 1942.

(3) Powers over a portion of property. If a power of appointment exists as to part of an entire group of assets or only over a limited interest in property, section 2514 applies only to such part or interest.

(c) Definition of "general power of appointment"—(1) In general. The term "general power of appointment" as defined in section 2514(c) means any power of appointment exercisable in favor of the person possessing the power (referred to as the "possessor"), his estate, his creditors, or the creditors of his estate, except (i) joint powers, to the extent provided in §§ 25.2514–2 and 25.2514–3 and (ii) certain powers limited by an ascertainable standard, to the extent provided in subparagraph (2) of this paragraph. A power of appointment exercisable to meet the estate tax, or any other taxes, debts, or charges which are enforceable against the possessor or his estate, is included within the meaning of a power of appointment exercisable in favor of the possessor, his estate, his creditors, or the creditors of his estate. A power of appointment exercisable for the purpose of discharging a legal obligation of the possessor or for his pecuniary benefit is considered a power of appointment exercisable in favor of the possessor or his creditors. However, for purposes of §§ 25.2514–1 through 25.2514–3, a power of appointment not otherwise considered to be a general power of appointment is not treated as a general power of appointment merely by reason of the fact that an appointee may, in fact, be a creditor of the possessor or his estate. A power of appointment is not a general power if by its terms it is either—

(a) Exercisable only in favor of one or more designated persons or classes other than the possessor or his creditors, or the possessor's estate, or the creditors of his estate, or

(b) Expressly not exercisable in favor of the possessor or his creditors, the possessor's estate, or the creditors of his estate.

A beneficiary may have two powers under the same instrument, one of which is a general power of appointment and the other of which is not. For example, a beneficiary may have a general power to withdraw a limited portion of trust corpus during his life, and a further power exercisable during his lifetime to appoint the corpus among his children. The latter power is not a general power of appointment (but its exercise may result in the exercise of the former power; see paragraph (d) of this section).

(2) Powers limited by an ascertainable standard. A power to consume, invade, or appropriate income or corpus, or both, for the benefit of the possessor which is limited by an ascertainable standard relating to the health, education, support, or maintenance of the possessor is, by reason of section 2514(c)(1), not a general power of appointment. A power is limited by such a standard if the extent of the possessor's duty to exercise and not to exercise the power is reasonably measurable in terms of his needs for health, education, or support (or any combination of them). As used in this subparagraph, the words "support" and "maintenance" are synonymous and their meaning is not limited to the bare necessities of life. A power to use property for the comfort, welfare, or happiness of the holder of the power is not limited by the requisite standard. Examples of powers which are limited by the requisite standard are powers exercisable for the holder's "support," "support in reasonable comfort," "maintenance in health and reasonable comfort," "support in his accustomed manner of living," "education, including college and professional education," "health," and "medical, dental, hospital and nursing expenses and expenses of invalidism." In determining whether a power is limited by an ascertainable standard, it is immaterial whether the beneficiary is required to exhaust his other income before the power can be exercised.

* * *

(d) Definition of "exercise." Whether a power of appointment is in fact exercised may depend upon local law. However, regardless of local law, a power of appointment is considered as exercised for purposes of section 2514 even though the exercise is in favor of the taker in default of appointment, and irrespective of whether the appointed interest and the interest in default of appointment are identical or whether the appointee renounces any right to take under the appointment. A power of appointment is also considered as exercised even though the disposition cannot take effect until the occurrence of an event after the exercise takes place, if the exercise is irrevocable and, as of the time of the exercise, the condition was not impossible of occurrence. For example, if property is left in trust to A for life, with a power in A to appoint the remainder by an instrument filed with the trustee during his life, and A exercises his power by appointing the remainder to B in the event that B survives A, A is considered to have exercised his power if the exercise was irrevocable. Furthermore, if a person holds both a presently exercisable general power of appointment and a presently exercisable nongeneral power of appointment over the same property, the exercise of the nongeneral power is considered the exercise of the general power only to the extent that immediately after the exercise of the nongeneral power the amount of money or property subject to being transferred by the exercise of the general power is decreased. For example, assume A has a noncumulative annual power to withdraw the greater of $5,000 or 5 percent of the value of a trust having a value of $300,000 and a lifetime nongeneral power to appoint all or a portion of the trust corpus to A's child or grandchildren. If A exercises the nongeneral power by appointing $150,000 to A's child, the exercise of the nongeneral power is treated as the exercise of the general power to the extent of $7,500 (maximum exercise of general power before the exercise of the nongeneral power, 5% of $300,000 or $15,000, less maximum exercise of the general power after the exercise of the nongeneral power, 5% of $150,000 or $7,500).

(e) Time of creation of power. A power of appointment created by will is, in general, considered as created on the date of the testator's death. * * * A power of appointment created by an inter vivos instrument is considered as created on the date the instrument takes effect. Such a power is not considered as created at some future date merely because it is not exercisable on the date the instrument takes effect, or because it is revocable, or because the identity of its holders is not ascertainable until after the date the instrument takes effect. However, if the holder of a power exercises it by creating a second power, the second power is considered as created at the time of the exercise of the first. The application of this paragraph may be illustrated by the following examples:

Example (1). A created a revocable trust before October 22, 1942, providing for payment of income to B for life with remainder as B shall appoint by deed or will. Even though A dies after October 21, 1942, without having exercised his power of revocation, B's power of appointment is considered a power created before October 22, 1942.

Example (2). C created an irrevocable inter vivos trust before October 22, 1942, naming T as trustee and providing for payment of income to D for life with remainder to E. T was given the power to pay corpus to D and the power to appoint a successor trustee. If T resigns after October 21, 1942, and appoints D as successor trustee, D is considered to have a power of appointment created before October 22, 1942.

Example (3). F created an irrevocable inter vivos trust before October 22, 1942, providing for payment of income to G for life with remainder as G shall appoint by deed or will, but in default of appointment income to H for life with remainder as H shall appoint by deed or will. If G died after October 21, 1942, without having exercised his power of appointment, H's power of appointments is considered a power created before October 22, 1942, even though it was only a contingent interest until G's death.

Example (4). If in example (3) above G had exercised by will his power of appointment, by creating a similar power in J, J's power of appointment would be considered a power created after October 21, 1942.

[T.D. 6334, 23 FR 8904, Nov. 15, 1958, as amended by T.D. 6582, 26 FR 11861, Dec. 12, 1961; T.D. 7757, 46 FR 6929, Jan. 22, 1981]

§ 25.2514–3 Powers of appointment created after October 21, 1942.

(a) In general. The exercise, release, or lapse (except as provided in paragraph (c) of this section) of a general power of appointment created after October 21, 1942, is deemed to be a transfer of property by the individual possessing the power. The exercise of a power of appointment that is not a general power is considered to be a transfer if it is exercised to create a further power under certain circumstances (see paragraph (d) of this section). See paragraph (c) of § 25.2514–1 for the definition of various terms used in this section. See paragraph (b) of this section for the rules applicable to determine the extent to which joint powers created after October 21, 1942, are to be treated as general powers of appointment.

(b) Joint powers created after October 21, 1942. The treatment of a power of appointment created after October 21, 1942, which is exercisable only in conjunction with another person is governed by section 2514(c)(3), which provides as follows:

(1) Such a power is not considered as a general power of appointment if it is not exercisable by the possessor except with the consent or joinder of the creator of the power.

(2) Such power is not considered as a general power of appointment if it is not exercisable by the possessor except with the consent or joinder of a person having a substantial interest in the property subject to the power which is adverse to the exercise of the power in favor of the possessor, his estate, his creditors, or the creditors of his estate. An interest adverse to the exercise of a power is considered as substantial if its value in relation to the total value of the property subject to the power is not insignificant. For this purpose, the interest is to be valued in accordance with the actuarial principles set forth in § 25.2512–5 or, if it is not susceptible to valuation under those provisions, in accordance with the general principles set forth in § 25.2512–1. A taker in default of appointment under a power has an interest which is adverse to an exercise of the power. A coholder of the power has no adverse interest merely because of his joint possession of the power nor merely because he is a permissible appointee under a power. However, a coholder of a power is considered as having an adverse interest where he may possess the power after the possessor's death and may exercise it at that time in favor of himself, his estate, his creditors, or the creditors of his estate. Thus, for example, if X, Y, and Z held a power jointly to appoint among a group of persons which includes themselves and if on the death of X the power will pass to Y and Z jointly, then Y and Z are considered to have interests adverse to the exercise of the power in favor of X. Similarly, if on Y's death the power will pass to Z, Z is considered to have an interest adverse to the exercise of the power in favor of Y. The application of this subparagraph may be further illustrated by the following examples in each of which it is assumed that the value of the interest in question is substantial:

Example (1). The taxpayer and R are trustees of a trust under which the income is to be paid to the taxpayer for life and then to M for life, and R is remainderman. The trustees have power to distribute corpus to the taxpayer. Since R's interest is substantially adverse to an exercise of the power in favor of the taxpayer, the latter does not have a general power of appointment. If M and the taxpayer were trustees, M's interest would likewise be adverse.

Example (2). The taxpayer and L are trustees of a trust under which the income is to be paid to L for life and then to M for life, and the taxpayer is remainderman. The trustees have power to distribute corpus to the taxpayer during L's life. Since L's interest is adverse to an exercise of the power in favor of the taxpayer, the taxpayer does not have a general power of appointment. If the taxpayer and M were trustees, M's interest would likewise be adverse.

Example (3). The taxpayer and L are trustees of a trust under which the income is to be paid to L for life. The trustees can designate whether corpus is to be distributed to the taxpayer or to A after L's death. L's interest is not adverse to an exercise of the power in favor of the taxpayer, and the taxpayer therefore has a general power of appointment.

(3) A power which is exercisable only in conjunction with another person, and which after application of the rules set forth in subparagraphs (1) and (2) of this paragraph, constitutes a general power of appointment, will be treated as though the holders of the power who are permissible appointees of the property were joint owners of property subject to the power. The possessor, under this rule, will be treated as possessed of a general power of appointment over an aliquot share of the property to be determined with reference to the number of joint holders, including the possessor, who (or whose estates or creditors) are permissible appointees. Thus, for example, if X, Y, and Z hold an unlimited power jointly to appoint among a group of persons, including themselves, but on the death of X the power does not pass to Y and Z jointly, then Y and Z are not considered to have interests adverse to the exercise of the power in favor of X. In this case, X is considered to possess a general power of appointment as to one-third of the property subject to the power.

(c) Partial releases, lapses, and disclaimers of general powers of appointment created after October 21, 1942—(1) Partial release of power. The general principles set forth in § 25.2511–2 for determining whether a donor of property (or of a property right or interest) has divested himself of all or any portion of his interest therein to the extent necessary to effect a completed gift are applicable in determining whether a partial release of a power of appointment constitutes a taxable gift. Thus, if a general power of appointment is partially released so that thereafter the donor may still appoint among a limited class of persons not including himself the partial release does not effect a complete gift, since the possessor of the power has retained the right to designate the ultimate beneficiaries of the property over which he holds the power and since it is only the termination of such control which completes a gift.

* * *

(3) Power partially released after May 31, 1951. If a general power of appointment created after October 21, 1942, was partially released after May 31, 1951, the subsequent exercise, release or a lapse of the power at any time thereafter, will constitute the exercise or release of a general power of appointment for gift tax purposes.

(4) Release or lapse of power. A release of a power of appointment need not be formal or express in character. For example, the failure to exercise a general power of appointment created after October 21, 1942, within a specified time so that the power lapses, constitutes a release of the power. In any case where the possessor of a general power of appointment is incapable of validly exercising or releasing a power, by reason of minority, or otherwise, and the power may not be validly exercised or released on his behalf, the failure to exercise or release the power is not a lapse of the power. If a trustee has in his capacity as trustee a power which is considered as a general power of appointment, his resignation or removal as trustee will cause a lapse of his power. However, section 2514(e) provides that a lapse during any calendar year is considered as a release so as to be subject to the gift tax only to the extent that the property which could have been appointed by exercise of the lapsed power of appointment exceeds the greater of (i) $5,000, or (ii) 5 percent of the aggregate value, at the time of the lapse, of the assets out of which, or the proceeds of which, the exercise of the lapsed power could be satisfied. For example, if an individual has a noncumulative right to withdraw $10,000 a year from the principal of a trust fund, the failure to exercise this right of withdrawal in a particular year will not constitute a gift if the fund at the end of the year equals or exceeds $200,000. If, however, at the end of the particular year the fund should be worth only $100,000, the failure to exercise the power will be considered a gift to the extent of $5,000, the excess of $10,000 over 5 percent of a fund of $100,000. Where the failure to exercise a power, such as a right of withdrawal, occurs in more than a single year, the value of the taxable transfer will be determined separately for each year.

(5) Disclaimer of power created after December 31, 1976. A disclaimer or renunciation of a general power of appointment created in a transfer made after December 31, 1976, is not considered a release of the power for gift tax purposes if the disclaimer or renunciation is a qualified disclaimer as described in section 2518 and the corresponding regulations. For rules relating to when a transfer creating the power occurs, see § 25.2518–2(c)(3). If the disclaimer or renunciation is not a qualified disclaimer, it is considered a release of the power.

(6) Disclaimer of power created before January 1, 1977. A disclaimer or renunciation of a general power of appointment created in a taxable transfer before January 1, 1977, in the person disclaiming is not considered a release of the power. The disclaimer or renunciation must be unequivocal and effective under local law. A disclaimer is a complete and unqualified refusal to accept the rights to which one is entitled. There can be no disclaimer or renunciation of a power after its acceptance. In the absence of facts to the contrary, the failure to renounce or disclaim within a reasonable time after learning of the existence of a power shall be presumed to constitute an acceptance of the power. In any case where a power is purported to be disclaimed or renounced as to only a portion of the property subject to the power, the determination as to whether there has been a complete and unqualified refusal to accept the rights to which one is entitled will depend on all the facts and circumstances of the particular case, taking into account the recognition and effectiveness of such a disclaimer under local law. Such rights refer to the incidents of the power and not to other interests of the possessor of the power in the property. If effective under local law, the power may be disclaimed or renounced without disclaiming or renouncing such other interests.

(7) The first and second sentences of paragraph (c)(5) of this section are applicable for transfers creating the power to be disclaimed made on or after December 31, 1997.

(d) Creation of another power in certain cases. Paragraph (d) of section 2514 provides that there is a transfer for purposes of the gift tax of the value of property (or of property rights or interests) with respect to which a power of appointment, which is not a general power of appointment, created after October 21, 1942, is exercised by creating another power of appointment which, under the terms of the instruments creating and exercising the first power and under applicable local law, can be validly exercised so as to (1) postpone the vesting of any estate or interest in the property for a period ascertainable without regard to the date of the creation of the first power, or (2) (if the applicable rule against perpetuities is stated in terms of suspensions of ownership or of the power of alienation, rather than of vesting) suspend the absolute ownership or the power of alienation of the property for a period ascertainable without regard to the date of the creation of the first power. For the purpose of section 2514(d), the value of the property subject to the second power of appointment is considered to be its value unreduced by any precedent or subsequent interest which is not subject to the second power. Thus, if a donor has a power to appoint $100,000 among a group consisting of his children or grandchildren and during his lifetime exercises the power by making an outright appointment of $75,000 and by giving one appointee a power to appoint $25,000, no more than $25,000 will be considered a gift under section 2514(d). If, however, the donor appoints the income from the entire fund to a beneficiary for life with power in the beneficiary to appoint the remainder, the entire $100,000 will be considered a gift under section 2514(d), if the exercise of the second power can validly postpone the vesting of any estate or interest in the property or can suspend the absolute ownership or power of alienation of the property for a period ascertainable without regard to the date of the creation of the first power.

(e) Examples. The application of this section may be further illustrated by the following examples in each of which it is assumed, unless otherwise stated, that S has transferred property in trust after October 21, 1942, with the remainder payable to R at L's death, and that neither L nor R has any interest in or power over the enjoyment of the trust property except as is indicated separately in each example:

Example (1). The income is payable to L for life. L has the power to cause the income to be paid to R. The exercise of the right constitutes the making of a transfer of property under section 2511. L's power does not constitute a power of appointment since it is only a power to dispose of his income interest, a right otherwise possessed by him.

Example (2). The income is to be accumulated during L's life. L has the power to have the income distributed to himself. If L's power is limited by an ascertainable standard (relating to health, etc.) as defined in paragraph (c)(2) of § 25.2514–1, the lapse of such power will not constitute a transfer of property for gift tax purposes. If L's power is not so limited, its lapse or release during L's lifetime may constitute a transfer of property for gift tax purposes. See especially paragraph (c)(4) of § 25.2514–3.

Example (3). The income is to be paid to L for life. L has a power, exercisable at any time, to cause the corpus to be distributed to himself. L has a general power of appointment over the remainder interest, the release of which constitutes a transfer for gift tax purposes of the remainder interest. If in this example L had a power to cause the corpus to be distributed only to X, L would have a power of appointment which is not a general power of appointment, the exercise or release of which would not constitute a transfer of property for purposes of the gift tax. Although the exercise or release of the nongeneral power is not taxable under this section, see § 25.2514–1(b)(2) for the gift tax consequences of the transfer of the life income interest.

Example (4). The income is payable to L for life. R has the right to cause the corpus to be distributed to L at any time. R's power is not a power of appointment, but merely a right to dispose of his remainder interest, a right already possessed by him. In such a case, the exercise of the right constitutes the making of a transfer of property under section 2511 of the value, if any, of his remainder interest. See paragraph (e) of § 25.2511–1.

Example (5). The income is to be paid to L. R has the right to appoint the corpus to himself at any time. R's general power of appointment over the corpus includes a general power to dispose of L's income interest therein. The lapse or release of R's general power over the income interest during his life may constitute the making of a transfer of property. See especially paragraph (c)(4) of § 25.2514–3.

[T.D. 6334, 23 FR 8904, Nov. 15, 1958, as amended by T.D. 7238, 37 FR 28730, Dec. 29, 1972; T.D. 7776, 46 FR 27642, May 21, 1981; T.D. 7910, 48 FR 40371, Sept. 7, 1983; T.D. 8095, 51 FR 28370, Aug. 7, 1986; T.D. 8744, 62 FR 68185, Dec. 31, 1997]

§ 25.2518–2 Requirements for a qualified disclaimer.

(a) In general. For the purposes of section 2518(a), a disclaimer shall be a qualified disclaimer only if it satisfies the requirements of this section. In general, to be a qualified disclaimer—

(1) The disclaimer must be irrevocable and unqualified:

(2) The disclaimer must be in writing;

(3) The writing must be delivered to the person specified in paragraph (b)(2) of this section within the time limitations specified in paragraph (c)(1) of this section;

(4) The disclaimant must not have accepted the interest disclaimed or any of its benefits; and

(5) The interest disclaimed must pass either to the spouse of the decedent or to a person other than the disclaimant without any direction on the part of the person making the disclaimer.

(b) Writing—(1) Requirements. A disclaimer is a qualified disclaimer only if it is in writing. The writing must identify the interest in property disclaimed and be signed either by the disclaimant or by the disclaimant's legal representative.

(2) Delivery. The writing described in paragraph (b)(1) of this section must be delivered to the transferor of the interest, the transferor's legal representative, the holder of the legal title to the property to which the interest relates, or the person in possession of such property.

(c) Time limit—(1) In general. A disclaimer is a qualified disclaimer only if the writing described in paragraph (b)(1) of this section is delivered to the persons described in paragraph (b)(2) of this section no later than the date which is 9 months after the later of—

(i) The date on which the transfer creating the interest in the disclaimant is made, or

(ii) The day on which the disclaimant attains age 21.

(2) A timely mailing of a disclaimer treated as a timely delivery. Although section 7502 and the regulations under that section apply only to documents to be filed with the Service, a timely mailing of a disclaimer to the person described in paragraph (b)(2) of this section is treated as a timely delivery if the mailing requirements under paragraphs (c)(1), (c)(2) and (d) of § 301.7502–1 are met. Further, if the last day of the period specified in paragraph (c)(1) of this section falls on Saturday, Sunday or a legal holiday * * *, then the delivery of the writing described in paragraph (b)(1) of this section shall be considered timely if delivery is made on the first succeeding day which is not Saturday, Sunday or a legal holiday. See paragraph (d)(3) of this section for rules applicable to the exception for individuals under 21 years of age.

(3) Transfer. (i) For purposes of the time limitation described in paragraph (c)(1)(i) of this section, the 9–month period for making a disclaimer generally is to be determined with reference to the transfer creating the interest in the disclaimant. With respect to inter vivos transfers, a transfer creating an interest occurs when there is a completed gift for Federal gift tax purposes regardless of whether a gift tax is imposed on the completed gift. Thus, gifts qualifying for the gift tax annual exclusion under section 2503(b) are regarded as transfers creating an interest for this purpose. With respect to transfers made by a decedent at death or transfers that become irrevocable at death, the transfer creating the interest occurs on the date of the decedent's death, even if an estate tax is not imposed on the transfer. For example, a bequest of foreign-situs property by a nonresident alien decedent is regarded as a transfer creating an interest in property even if the transfer would not be subject to estate tax. If there is a transfer creating an interest in property during the transferor's lifetime and such interest is later included in the transferor's gross estate for estate tax purposes (or would have been included if such interest were subject to estate tax), the 9–month period for making the qualified disclaimer is determined with reference to the earlier transfer creating the interest. In the case of a general power of appointment, the holder of the power has a 9–month period after the transfer creating the power in which to disclaim. If a person to whom any interest in property passes by reason of the exercise, release, or lapse of a general power desires to make a qualified disclaimer, the disclaimer must be made within a 9–month period after the exercise, release, or lapse regardless of whether the exercise, release, or lapse is subject to estate or gift tax. In the case of a nongeneral power of appointment, the holder of the power, permissible appointees, or takers in default of appointment must disclaim within a 9–month period after the original transfer that created or authorized the creation of the power. If the transfer is for the life of an income beneficiary with succeeding interests to other persons, both the life tenant and the other remaindermen, whether their interests are vested or contingent, must disclaim no later than 9 months after the original transfer creating an interest. In the case of a remainder interest in property which an executor elects to treat as qualified terminable interest property under section 2056(b)(7), the remainderman must disclaim within 9 months of the transfer creating the interest, rather than 9 months from the date such interest is subject to tax under section 2044 or 2519. A person who receives an interest in property as the result of a qualified disclaimer of the interest must disclaim the previously disclaimed interest no later than 9 months after the date of the transfer creating the interest in the preceding disclaimant. Thus, if A were to make a qualified disclaimer of a specific bequest and as a result of the qualified disclaimer the property passed as part of the residue, the beneficiary of the residue could make a qualified disclaimer no later than 9 months after the date of the testator's death. See paragraph (d)(3) of this section for the time limitation rule with reference to recipients who are under 21 years of age.

(ii) Sentences 1 through 10 and 12 of paragraph (c)(3)(i) of this section are applicable for transfers creating the interest to be disclaimed made on or after December 31, 1997.

(4) Joint property—(i) Interests in joint tenancy with right of survivorship or tenancies by the entirety. Except as provided in paragraph (c)(4)(iii) of this section (with respect to joint bank, brokerage, and other investment accounts), in the case of an interest in a joint tenancy with right of survivorship or a tenancy by the entirety, a qualified disclaimer of the interest to which the disclaimant succeeds upon creation of the tenancy must be made no later than 9 months after the creation of the tenancy regardless of whether such interest can be unilaterally severed under local law. A qualified disclaimer of the survivorship interest to which the survivor succeeds by operation of law upon the death of the first joint tenant to die must be made no later than 9 months after the death of the first joint tenant to die regardless of whether such interest can be unilaterally severed under local law and, except as provided in paragraph (c)(4)(ii) of this section (with respect to certain tenancies created on or after July 14, 1988), such interest is deemed to be a one-half interest in the property. (See, however, section 2518(b)(2)(B) for a special rule in the case of disclaimers by persons under age 21.) This is the case regardless of the portion of the property attributable to consideration furnished by the disclaimant and regardless of the portion of the property that is included in the decedent's gross estate under section 2040 and regardless of whether the interest can be unilaterally severed under local law. See paragraph (c)(5), Examples (7) and (8), of this section.

(ii) Certain tenancies in real property between spouses created on or after July 14, 1988. In the case of a joint tenancy between spouses or a tenancy by the entirety in real property created on or after July 14, 1988, to which section 2523(i)(3) applies (relating to the creation of a tenancy where the spouse of the donor is not a United States citizen), the surviving spouse may disclaim any portion of the joint interest that is includible in the decedent's gross estate under section 2040. See paragraph (c)(5), Example (9), of this section.

(iii) Special rule for joint bank, brokerage, and other investment accounts (e.g., accounts held at mutual funds) established between spouses or between persons other than husband and wife. In the case of a transfer to a joint bank, brokerage, or other investment account (e.g., an account held at a mutual fund), if a transferor may unilaterally regain the transferor's own contributions to the account without the consent of the other cotenant, such that the transfer is not a completed gift under § 25.2511–1(h)(4), the transfer creating the survivor's interest in the decedent's share of the account occurs on the death of the deceased cotenant. Accordingly, if a surviving joint tenant desires to make a qualified disclaimer with respect to funds contributed by a deceased cotenant, the disclaimer must be made within 9 months of the cotenant's death. The surviving joint tenant may not disclaim any portion of the joint account attributable to consideration furnished by that surviving joint tenant. See paragraph (c)(5), Examples (12), (13), and (14), of this section, regarding the treatment of disclaimed interests under sections 2518, 2033 and 2040.

(iv) Effective date. This paragraph (c)(4) is applicable for disclaimers made on or after December 31, 1997.

(5) Examples. The provisions of paragraphs (c)(1) through (c)(4) of this section may be illustrated by the following examples. For purposes of the following examples, assume that all beneficiaries are over 21 years of age.

Example (1). On May 13, 1978, in a transfer which constitutes a completed gift for Federal gift tax purposes, A creates a trust in which B is given a lifetime interest in the income from the trust. B is also given a nongeneral testamentary power of appointment over the corpus of the trust. The power of appointment may be exercised in favor of any of the issue of A and B. If there are no surviving issue at B's death or if the power is not exercised, the corpus is to pass to E. On May 13, 1978, A and B have two surviving children, C and D. If A, B, C or D wishes to make a qualified disclaimer, the disclaimer must be made no later than 9 months after May 13, 1978.

Example (2). Assume the same facts as in example (1) except that B is given a general power of appointment over the corpus of the trust. B exercises the general power of appointment in favor of C upon B's death on June 17, 1989. C may make a qualified disclaimer no later than 9 months after June 17, 1989. If B had died without exercising the general power of appointment, E could have made a qualified disclaimer no later than 9 months after June 17, 1989.

Example (3). F creates a trust on April 1, 1978, in which F's child G is to receive the income from the trust for life. Upon G's death, the corpus of the trust is to pass to G's child H. If either G or H wishes to make a qualified disclaimer, it must be made no later than 9 months after April 1, 1978.

Example (4). A creates a trust on February 15, 1978, in which B is named the income beneficiary for life. The trust further provides that upon B's death the proceeds of the trust are to pass to C, if then living. If C predeceases D, the proceeds shall pass to D or D's estate. To have timely disclaimers for purposes of section 2518, B, C, and D must disclaim their respective interests no later than 9 months after February 15, 1978.

Example (5). A, a resident of State Q, dies on January 10, 1979, devising certain real property to B. The disclaimer laws of State Q require that a disclaimer be made within a reasonable time after a transfer. B disclaims the entire interest in real property on November 10, 1979. Although B's disclaimer may be effective under State Q law, it is not a qualified disclaimer under section 2518 because the disclaimer was made later than 9 months after the taxable transfer to B.

Example (6). A creates a revocable trust on June 1, 1980, in which B and C are given the income interest for life. Upon the death of the last income beneficiary, the remainder interest is to pass to D. The creation of the trust is not a completed gift for Federal gift tax purposes, but each distribution of trust income to B and C is a completed gift at the date of distribution. B and C disclaim each income distribution no later than 9 months after the date of the particular distribution. In order to disclaim an income distribution in the form of a check, the recipient must return the check to the trustee uncashed along with a written disclaimer. A dies on September 1, 1982, causing the trust to become irrevocable, and the trust corpus is includible in A's gross estate for Federal estate tax purposes under section 2038. If B or C wishes to make a qualified disclaimer of his income interest, he must do so no later than 9 months after September 1, 1982. If D wishes to make a qualified disclaimer of his remainder interest, he must do so no later than 9 months after September 1, 1982.

Example (7). On February 1, 1990, A purchased real property with A's funds. Title to the property was conveyed to "A and B, as joint tenants with right of survivorship." Under applicable state law, the joint interest is unilaterally severable by either tenant. B dies on May 1, 1998, and is survived by A. On January 1, 1999, A disclaims the one-half survivorship interest in the property to which A succeeds as a result of B's death. Assuming that the other requirements of section 2518(b) are satisfied, A has made a qualified disclaimer of the one-half survivorship interest (but not the interest retained by A upon the creation of the tenancy, which may not be disclaimed by A). The result is the same whether or not A and B are married and regardless of the proportion of consideration furnished by A and B in purchasing the property.

Example (8). Assume the same facts as in Example (7) except that A and B are married and title to the property was conveyed to "A and B, as tenants by the entirety." Under applicable state law, the tenancy cannot be unilaterally severed by either tenant. Assuming that the other requirements of section 2518(b) are satisfied, A has made a qualified disclaimer of the one-half survivorship interest (but not the interest retained by A upon the creation of the tenancy, which may not be disclaimed by A). The result is the same regardless of the proportion of consideration furnished by A and B in purchasing the property.

Example (9). On March 1, 1989, H and W purchase a tract of vacant land which is conveyed to them as tenants by the entirety. The entire consideration is paid by H. W is not a United States citizen. H dies on June 1, 1998. W can disclaim the entire joint interest because this is the interest includible in H's gross estate under section 2040(a). Assuming that W's disclaimer is received by the executor of H's estate no later than 9 months after June 1, 1998, and the other requirements of section 2518(b) are satisfied, W's disclaimer of the property would be a qualified disclaimer. The result would be the same if the property was held in joint tenancy with right of survivorship that was unilaterally severable under local law.

Example (10). In 1986, spouses A and B purchased a personal residence taking title as tenants by the entirety. B dies on July 10, 1998. A wishes to disclaim the one-half undivided interest to which A would succeed by right of survivorship. If A makes the disclaimer, the property interest would pass under B's will to their child C. C, an adult, and A resided in the residence at B's death and will continue to reside there in the future. A continues to own a one-half undivided interest in the property. Assuming that the other requirements of section 2518(b) are satisfied, A may make a qualified disclaimer with respect to the one-half undivided survivorship interest in the residence if A delivers the written disclaimer to the personal representative of B's estate by April 10, 1999, since A is not deemed to have accepted the interest or any of its benefits prior to that time and A's occupancy of the residence after B's death is consistent with A's retained undivided ownership interest. The result would be the same if the property was held in joint tenancy with right of survivorship that was unilaterally severable under local law.

Example (11). H and W, husband and wife, reside in state X, a community property state. On April 1, 1978, H and W purchase real property with community funds. The property is not held by H and W as jointly owned property with rights of survivorship. H and W hold the property until January 3, 1985, when H dies. H devises his portion of the property to W. On March 15, 1985, W disclaims the portion of the property devised to her by H. Assuming all the other requirements of section 2518(b) have been met, W has made a qualified disclaimer of the interest devised to her by H. However, W could not disclaim the interest in the property that she acquired on April 1, 1978.

Example (12). On July 1, 1990, A opens a bank account that is held jointly with B, A's spouse, and transfers $50,000 of A's money to the account. A and B are United States citizens. A can regain the entire account without B's consent, such that the transfer is not a completed gift under § 25.2511–1(h)(4). A dies on August 15, 1998, and B disclaims the entire amount in the bank account on October 15, 1998. Assuming that the remaining requirements of section 2518(b) are satisfied, B made a qualified disclaimer under section 2518(a) because the disclaimer was made within 9 months after A's death at which time B had succeeded to full dominion and control over the account. Under state law, B is treated as predeceasing A with respect to the disclaimed interest. The disclaimed account balance passes through A's probate estate and is no longer joint property includible in A's gross estate under section 2040. The entire account is, instead, includible in A's gross estate under section 2033. The result would be the same if A and B were not married.

Example (13). The facts are the same as Example (12), except that B, rather than A, dies on August 15, 1998. A may not make a qualified disclaimer with respect to any of the funds in the bank account, because A furnished the funds for the entire account and A did not relinquish dominion and control over the funds.

Example (14). The facts are the same as Example (12), except that B disclaims 40 percent of the funds in the account. Since, under state law, B is treated as predeceasing A with respect to the disclaimed interest, the 40 percent portion of the account balance that was disclaimed passes as part of A's probate estate, and is no longer characterized as joint property. This 40 percent portion of the account balance is, therefore, includible in A's gross estate under section 2033. The remaining 60 percent of the account balance that was not disclaimed retains its character as joint property and, therefore, is includible in A's gross estate as provided in section 2040(b). Therefore, 30 percent (1/2 x60 percent) of the account balance is includible in A's gross estate under section 2040(b), and a total of 70 percent of the aggregate account balance is includible in A's gross estate. If A and B were not married, then the 40 percent portion of the account subject to the disclaimer would be includible in A's gross estate as provided in section 2033 and the 60 percent portion of the account not subject to the disclaimer would be includible in A's gross estate as provided in section 2040(a), because A furnished all of the funds with respect to the account.

(d) No acceptance of benefits—(1) Acceptance. A qualified disclaimer cannot be made with respect to an interest in property if the disclaimant has accepted the interest or any of its benefits, expressly or impliedly, prior to making the disclaimer. Acceptance is manifested by an affirmative act which is consistent with ownership of the interest in property. Acts indicative of acceptance include using the property or the interest in property; accepting dividends, interest, or rents from the property; and directing others to act with respect to the property or interest in property. However, merely taking delivery of an instrument of title, without more, does not constitute acceptance. Moreover, a disclaimant is not considered to have accepted property merely because under applicable local law title to the property vests immediately in the disclaimant upon the death of a decedent. The acceptance of one interest in property will not, by itself, constitute an acceptance of any other separate interests created by the transferor and held by the disclaimant in the same property. In the case of residential property, held in joint tenancy by some or all of the residents, a joint tenant will not be considered to have accepted the joint interest merely because the tenant resided on the property prior to disclaiming his interest in the property. The exercise of a power of appointment to any extent by the donee of the power is an acceptance of its benefits. In addition, the acceptance of any consideration in return for making the disclaimer is an acceptance of the benefits of the entire interest disclaimed.

(2) Fiduciaries. If a beneficiary who disclaims an interest in property is also a fiduciary, actions taken by such person in the exercise of fiduciary powers to preserve or maintain the disclaimed property shall not be treated as an acceptance of such property or any of its benefits. Under this rule, for example, an executor who is also a beneficiary may direct the harvesting of a crop or the general maintenance of a home. A fiduciary, however, cannot retain a wholly discretionary power to direct the enjoyment of the disclaimed interest. For example, a fiduciary's disclaimer of a beneficial interest does not meet the requirements of a qualified disclaimer if the fiduciary exercised or retains a discretionary power to allocate enjoyment of that interest among members of a designated class. See paragraph (e) of this section for rules relating to the effect of directing the redistribution of disclaimed property.

(3) Under 21 years of age. A beneficiary who is under 21 years of age has until 9 months after his twenty-first birthday in which to make a qualified disclaimer of his interest in property. Any actions taken with regard to an interest in property by a beneficiary or a custodian prior to the beneficiary's twenty-first birthday will not be an acceptance by the beneficiary of the interest.

(4) Examples. The provisions of paragraphs (d)(1), (2) and (3) of this section may be illustrated by the following examples:

Example (1). On April 9, 1977, A established a trust for the benefit of B, then age 22. Under the terms of the trust, the current income of the trust is to be paid quarterly to B. Additionally, one half the principal is to be distributed to B when B attains the age of 30 years. The balance of the principal is to be distributed to B when B attains the age of 40 years. Pursuant to the terms of the trust, B received a distribution of income on June 30, 1977. On August 1, 1977, B disclaimed B's right to receive both the income from the trust and the principal of the trust, B's disclaimer of the income interest is not a qualified disclaimer for purposes of section 2518(a) because B accepted income prior to making the disclaimer. B's disclaimer of the principal, however, does satisfy section 2518(b)(3). See also § 25.2518–3 for rules relating to the disclaimer of less than an entire interest in property.

Example (2). B is the recipient of certain property devised to B under the will of A. The will stated that any disclaimed property was to pass to C. B and C entered into negotiations in which it was declined that B would disclaim all interest in the real property that was devised to B. In exchange, C promised to let B live in the family home for life. B's disclaimer is not a qualified disclaimer for purposes of section 2518(a) because B accepted consideration for making the disclaimer.

Example (3). A received a gift of Blackacre on December 25, 1978. A never resided on Blackacre but when property taxes on Blackacre became due on July 1, 1979, A paid them out of personal funds. On August 15, 1979, A disclaimed the gift of Blackacre. Assuming all the requirements of section 2518 (b) have been met, A has made a qualified disclaimer of Blackacre. Merely paying the property taxes does not constitute an acceptance of Blackacre even though A's personal funds were used to pay the taxes.

Example (4). A died on February 15, 1978. Pursuant to A's will, B received a farm in State Z. B requested the executor to sell the farm and to give the proceeds to B. The executor then sold the farm pursuant to B's request. B then disclaimed $50,000 of the proceeds from the sale of the farm. B's disclaimer is not a qualified disclaimer. By requesting the executor to sell the farm B accepted the farm even though the executor may not have been legally obligated to comply with B's request. See also § 25.2518–3 for rules relating to the disclaimer of less than an entire interest in property.

Example (5). Assume the same facts as in example (4) except that instead of requesting the executor to sell the farm, B pledged the farm as security for a short-term loan which was paid off prior to distribution of the estate. B then disclaimed his interest in the farm. B's disclaimer is not a qualified disclaimer. By pledging the farm as security for the loan, B accepted the farm.

Example (6). A delivered 1,000 shares of stock in Corporation X to B as a gift on February 1, 1980. A had the shares registered in B's name on that date. On April 1, 1980, B disclaimed the interest in the 1,000 shares. Prior to making the disclaimer, B did not pledge the shares, accept any dividends or otherwise commit any acts indicative of acceptance. Assuming the remaining requirements of section 2518 are satisfied, B's disclaimer is a qualified disclaimer.

Example (7). On January 1, 1980, A created an irrevocable trust in which B was given a testamentary general power of appointment over the trust's corpus. B executed a will on June 1, 1980, in which B provided for the exercise of the power of appointment. On September 1, 1980, B disclaimed the testamentary power of appointment. Assuming the remaining requirements of section 2518(b) are satisfied, B's disclaimer of the testamentary power of appointment is a qualified disclaimer.

* * *

(e) Passage without direction by the disclaimant of beneficial enjoyment of disclaimed interest—(1) In general. A disclaimer is not a qualified disclaimer unless the disclaimed interest passes without any direction on the part of the disclaimant to a person other than the disclaimant (except as provided in paragraph (e)(2) of this section). If there is an express or implied agreement that the disclaimed interest in property is to be given or bequeathed to a person specified by the disclaimant, the disclaimant shall be treated as directing the transfer of the property interest. The requirements of a qualified disclaimer under section 2518 are not satisfied if—

(i) The disclaimant, either alone or in conjunction with another, directs the redistribution or transfer of the property or interest in property to another person (or has the power to direct the redistribution or transfer of the property or interest in property to another person unless such power is limited by an ascertainable standard); or

(ii) The disclaimed property or interest in property passes to or for the benefit of the disclaimant as a result of the disclaimer (except as provided in paragraph (e)(2) of this section).

If a power of appointment is disclaimed, the requirements of this paragraph (e)(1) are satisfied so long as there is no direction on the part of the disclaimant with respect to the transfer of the interest subject to the power or with respect to the transfer of the power to another person. A person may make a qualified disclaimer of a beneficial interest in property even if after such disclaimer the disclaimant has a fiduciary power to distribute to designated beneficiaries, but only if the power is subject to an ascertainable standard. See examples (11) and (12) of paragraph (e)(5) of this section.

(2) Disclaimer by surviving spouse. In the case of a disclaimer made by a decedent's surviving spouse with respect to property transferred by the decedent, the disclaimer satisfies the requirements of this paragraph (e) if the interest passes as a result of the disclaimer without direction on the part of the surviving spouse either to the surviving spouse or to another person. If the surviving spouse, however, retains the right to direct the beneficial enjoyment of the disclaimed property in a transfer that is not subject to Federal estate and gift tax (whether as trustee or otherwise), such spouse will be treated as directing the beneficial enjoyment of the disclaimed property, unless such power is limited by an ascertainable standard. See examples (4), (5), and (6) in paragraph (e)(5) of this section.

(3) Partial failure of disclaimer. If a disclaimer made by a person other than the surviving spouse is not effective to pass completely an interest in property to a person other than the disclaimant because—

(i) The disclaimant also has a right to receive such property as an heir at law, residuary beneficiary, or by any other means; and

(ii) The disclaimant does not effectively disclaim these rights, the disclaimer is not a qualified disclaimer with respect to the portion of the disclaimed property which the disclaimant has a right to receive. If the portion of the disclaimed interest in property which the disclaimant has a right to receive is not severable property or an undivided portion of the property, then the disclaimer is not a qualified disclaimer with respect to any portion of the property. Thus, for example, if a disclaimant who is not a surviving spouse receives a specific bequest of a fee simple interest in property and as a result of the disclaimer of the entire interest, the property passes to a trust in which the disclaimant has a remainder interest, then the disclaimer will not be a qualified disclaimer unless the remainder interest in the property is also disclaimed. See § 25.2518–3(a)(1)(ii) for the definition of severable property.

(4) Effect of precatory language. Precatory language in a disclaimer naming takers of disclaimed property will not be considered as directing the redistribution or transfer of the property or interest in property to such persons if the applicable State law gives the language no legal effect.

(5) Examples. The provisions of this paragraph (e) may be illustrated by the following examples:

Example (1). A, a resident of State X, died on July 30, 1978. Pursuant to A's will, B, A's son and heir at law, received the family home. In addition, B and C each received 50 percent of A's residuary estate. B disclaimed the home. A's will made no provision for the distribution of property in the case of a beneficiary's disclaimer. Therefore, pursuant to the disclaimer laws of State X, the disclaimed property became part of the residuary estate. Because B's 50 percent share of the residuary estate will be increased by 50 percent of the value of the family home, the disclaimed property will not pass solely to another person. Consequently, B's disclaimer of the family home is a qualified disclaimer only with respect to the 50 percent portion that passes solely to C. Had B also disclaimed B's 50 percent interest in the residuary estate, the disclaimer would have been a qualified disclaimer under section 2518 of the entire interest in the home (assuming the remaining requirements of a qualified disclaimer were satisfied). Similarly, if under the laws of State X, the disclaimer has the effect of divesting B of all interest in the home, both as devisee and as a beneficiary of the residuary estate, including any property resulting from its sale, the disclaimer would be a qualified disclaimer of B's entire interest in the home.

Example (2). D, a resident of State Y, died testate on June 30, 1978. E, an heir at law of D, received specific bequests of certain severable personal property from D. E disclaimed the property transferred by D under the will. The will made no provision for the distribution of property in the case of a beneficiary's disclaimer. The disclaimer laws of State Y provide that such property shall pass to the decedent's heirs at law in the same manner as if the disclaiming beneficiary had died immediately before the testator's death. Because State Y's law treats E as predeceasing D, the property disclaimed by E does not pass to E as an heir at law or otherwise. Consequently, if the remaining requirements of section 2518(b) are satisfied, E's disclaimer is a qualified disclaimer under section 2518(a).

Example (3). Assume the same facts as in example (2) except that State Y has no provision treating the disclaimant as predeceasing the testator. E's disclaimer satisfies section 2518(b)(4) only to the extent that E does not have a right to receive the property as an heir at law. Had E disclaimed both the share E received under D's will and E's intestate share, the requirement of section 2518(b)(4) would have been satisfied.

Example (4). B died testate on February 13, 1980. B's will established both a marital trust and a nonmarital trust. The decedent's surviving spouse, A, is an income beneficiary of the martial trust and has a testamentary general power of appointment over its assets. A is also an income beneficiary of the nonmarital trust, but has no power to appoint or invade the corpus. The provisions of the will specify that any portion of the marital trust disclaimed is to be added to the nonmarital trust. A disclaimed 30 percent of the marital trust. (See § 25.2518–3(b) for rules relating to the disclaimer of an undivided portion of an interest in property.) Pursuant to the will, this portion of the marital trust property was transferred to the nonmarital trust without any direction on the part of A. This disclaimer by A satisfies section 2518(b)(4).

Example (5). Assume the same facts as in example (4) except that A, the surviving spouse, has both an income interest in the nonmarital trust and a testamentary nongeneral power to appoint among designated beneficiaries. This power is not limited by an ascertainable standard. The requirements of section 2518(b)(4) are not satisfied unless A also disclaims the nongeneral power to appoint the portion of the trust corpus that is attributable to the property that passed to the nonmarital trust as a result of A's disclaimer. Assuming that the fair market value of the disclaimed property on the date of the disclaimer is $250,000 and that the fair market value of the nonmarital trust (including the disclaimed property) immediately after the disclaimer is $750,000, A must disclaim the power to appoint one-third of the nonmarital trust's corpus. The result is the same regardless of whether the nongeneral power is testamentary or inter vivos.

Example (6). Assume the same facts as in example (4) except that A has both an income interest in the nonmarital trust and a power to invade corpus if needed for A's health or maintenance. In addition, an independent trustee has power to distribute to A any portion of the corpus which the trustee determines to be desirable for A's happiness. Assuming the other requirements of section 2518 are satisfied, A may make a qualified disclaimer of interests in the marital trust without disclaiming any of A's interests in the nonmarital trust.

Example (7). B died testate on June 1, 1980. B's will created both a marital trust and a nonmarital trust. The decedent's surviving spouse, C, is an income beneficiary of the marital trust and has a testamentary general power of appointment over its assets. C is an income beneficiary of the nonmarital trust, and additionally has the noncumulative right to withdraw yearly the greater of $5,000 or 5 percent of the aggregate value of the principal. The provisions of the will specify that any portion of the marital trust disclaimed is to be added to the nonmarital trust. C disclaims 50 percent of the marital trust corpus. Pursuant to the will, this amount is transferred to the nonmarital trust. Assuming the remaining requirements of section 2518(b) are satisfied, C's disclaimer is a qualified disclaimer.

Example (8). A, a resident of State X, died on July 19, 1979. A was survived by a spouse B, and three children, C, D, and E. Pursuant to A's will, B received one-half of A's estate and the children received equal shares of the remaining one-half of the estate. B disclaimed the entire interest B had received. The will made no provisions for the distribution of property in the case of a beneficiary's disclaimer. The disclaimer laws of State X provide that under these circumstances disclaimed property passes to the decedent's heirs at law in the same manner as if the disclaiming beneficiary had died immediately before the testator's death. As a result, C, D, and E are A's only remaining heirs at law, and will divide the disclaimed property equally among themselves. B's disclaimer includes language stating that "it is my intention that C, D, and E will share equally in the division of this property as a result of my disclaimer." State X considers these to be precatory words and gives them no legal effect. B's disclaimer meets all other requirements imposed by State X on disclaimers, and is considered an effective disclaimer under which the property will vest solely in C, D, and E in equal shares without any further action required by B. Therefore, B is not treated as directing the redistribution or transfer of the property. If the remaining requirements of section 2518 are met, B's disclaimer is a qualified disclaimer.

Example (9). C died testate on January 1, 1979. According to C's will, D was to receive ⅓ of the residuary estate with any disclaimed property going to E. D was also to receive a second ⅓ of the residuary estate with any disclaimed property going to F. Finally, D was to receive a final ⅓ of the residuary estate with any disclaimed property going to G. D specifically states that he is disclaiming the interest in which the disclaimed property is designated to pass to E. D has effectively directed that the disclaimed property will pass to E and therefore D's disclaimer is not a qualified disclaimer under section 2518(a).

Example (10). Assume the same facts as in example (9) except that C's will also states that D was to receive Blackacre and Whiteacre. C's will further provides that if D disclaimed Blackacre then such property was to pass to E and that if D disclaimed Whiteacre then Whiteacre was to pass to F. D specifically disclaims Blackacre with the intention that it pass to E. Assuming the other requirements of section 2518 are met, D has made a qualified disclaimer of Blackacre. Alternatively, D could disclaim an undivided portion of both Blackacre and Whiteacre. Assuming the other requirements of section 2518 are met, this would also be a qualified disclaimer.

Example (11). G creates an irrevocable trust on February 16, 1983, naming H, I and J as the income beneficiaries for life and F as the remainderman. F is also named the trustee and as trustee has the discretionary power to invade the corpus and make discretionary distributions to H, I or J during their lives. F disclaims the remainder interest on August 8, 1983, but retains his discretionary power to invade the corpus. F has not made a qualified disclaimer because F retains the power to direct enjoyment of the corpus and the retained fiduciary power is not limited by an ascertainable standard.

Example (12). Assume the same facts as in example (11) except that F may only invade the corpus to make distributions for the health, maintenance or support of H, I or J during their lives. If the other requirements of section 2518(b) are met, F has made a qualified disclaimer of the remainder interest because the retained fiduciary power is limited by an ascertainable standard.

[T.D. 8095, 51 FR 28371, Aug. 7, 1986; T.D. 8744, 62 FR 68183, Dec. 31, 1997]

§ 25.2518-3 Disclaimer of less than an entire interest.

(a) Disclaimer of a partial interest—(1) In general—(i) Interest. If the requirements of this section are met, the disclaimer of all or an undivided portion of any separate interest in property may be a qualified disclaimer even if the disclaimant has another interest in the same property. In general, each interest in property that is separately created by the transferor is treated as a separate interest. For example, if an income interest in securities is bequeathed to A for life, then to B for life, with the remainder interest in such securities bequeathed to A's estate, and if the remaining requirements of section 2518(b) are met, A could make a qualified disclaimer of either the income interest or the remainder, or an undivided portion of either interest. A could not, however, make a qualified disclaimer of the income interest for a certain number of years. Further, where local law merges interests separately created by the transferor, a qualified disclaimer will be allowed only if there is a disclaimer of the entire merged interest or an undivided portion of such merged interest. See example (12) in paragraph (d) of this section. See § 25.2518–3(b) for rules relating to the disclaimer of an undivided portion. Where the merger of separate interests would occur but for the creation by the transferor of a nominal interest (as defined in paragraph (a)(1)(iv) of this section), a qualified disclaimer will be allowed only if there is a disclaimer of all the separate interests, or an undivided portion of all such interests, which would have merged but for the nominal interest.

(ii) Severable property. A disclaimant shall be treated as making a qualified disclaimer of a separate interest in property if the disclaimer relates to severable property and the disclaimant makes a disclaimer which would be a qualified disclaimer if such property were the only property in which the disclaimant had an interest. If applicable local law does not recognize a purported disclaimer of severable property, the disclaimant must comply with the requirements of paragraph (c)(1) of § 25.2518–1 in order to make a qualified disclaimer of the severable property. Severable property is property which can be divided into separate parts each of which, after severance, maintains a complete and independent existence. For example, a legatee of shares of corporate stock may accept some shares of the stock and make a qualified disclaimer of the remaining shares.

(iii) Powers of appointment. A power of appointment with respect to property is treated as a separate interest in such property and such power of appointment with respect to all or an undivided portion of such property may be disclaimed independently from any other interests separately created by the transferor in the property if the requirements of section 2518(b) are met. See example (21) of paragraph (d) of this section. Further, a disclaimer of a power of appointment with respect to property is a qualified disclaimer only if any right to direct the beneficial enjoyment of the property which is retained by the disclaimant is limited by an ascertainable standard. See example (9) of paragraph (d) of this section.

(iv) Nominal interest. A nominal interest is an interest in property created by the transferor that—

(A) Has an actuarial value * * * of less than 5 percent of the total value of the property at the time of the taxable transfer creating the interest,

(B) Prevents the merger under local law or two or more other interests created by the transferor, and

(C) Can be clearly shown from all the facts and circumstances to have been created primarily for the purpose of preventing the merger of such other interests.

Factors to be considered in determining whether an interest is created primarily for the purpose of preventing merger include (but are not limited to) the following: the relationship between the transferor and the interest holder; the age difference between the interest holder and the beneficiary whose interests would have merged; the interest holder's state of health at the time of the taxable transfer; and, in the case of a contingent remainder, any other factors which indicate that the possibility of the interest vesting as a fee simple is so remote as to be negligible.

(2) In trust. A disclaimer is not a qualified disclaimer under section 2518 if the beneficiary disclaims income derived from specific property transferred in trust while continuing to accept income derived from the remaining properties in the same trust unless the disclaimer results in such property being removed from the trust and passing, without any direction on the part of the disclaimant, to persons other than the disclaimant or to the spouse of the decedent. Moreover, a disclaimer of both an income interest and a remainder interest in specific trust assets is not a qualified disclaimer if the beneficiary retains interests in other trust property unless, as a result of the disclaimer, such assets are removed from the trust and pass, without any direction on the part of the disclaimant, to persons other than the disclaimant or to the spouse of the decedent. The disclaimer of an undivided portion of an interest in a trust may be a qualified disclaimer. See also paragraph (b) of this section for rules relating to the disclaimer of an undivided portion of an interest in property.

(b) Disclaimer of undivided portion. A disclaimer of an undivided portion of a separate interest in property which meets the other requirements of a qualified disclaimer under section 2518(b) and the corresponding regulations is a qualified disclaimer. An undivided portion of a disclaimant's separate interest in property must consist of a fraction or percentage of each and every substantial interest or right owned by the disclaimant in such property and must extend over the entire term of the disclaimant's interest in such property and in other property into which such property is converted. A disclaimer of some specific rights while retaining other rights with respect to an interest in the property is not a qualified disclaimer of an undivided portion of the disclaimant's interest in property. Thus, for example, a disclaimer made by the devisee of a fee simple interest in Blackacre is not a qualified disclaimer if the disclaimant disclaims a remainder interest in Blackacre but retains a life estate.

(c) Disclaimer of a pecuniary amount. A disclaimer of a specific pecuniary amount out of a pecuniary or nonpecuniary bequest or gift which satisfies the other requirements of a qualified disclaimer under section 2518(b) and the corresponding regulations is a qualified disclaimer provided that no income or other benefit of the disclaimed amount inures to the benefit of the disclaimant either prior to or subsequent to the disclaimer. Thus, following the disclaimer of a specific pecuniary amount from a bequest or gift, the amount disclaimed and any income attributable to such amount must be segregated from the portion of the gift or bequest that was not disclaimed. Such a segregation of assets making up the disclaimer of a pecuniary amount must be made on the basis of the fair market value of the assets on the date of the disclaimer or on a basis that is fairly representative of value changes that may have occurred between the date of transfer and the date of the disclaimer. A pecuniary amount distributed to the disclaimant from the bequest or gift prior to the disclaimer shall be treated as a distribution of corpus from the bequest or gift. However, the acceptance of a distribution from the gift or bequest shall also be considered to be an acceptance of a proportionate amount of income earned by the bequest or gift. The proportionate share of income considered to be accepted by the disclaimant shall be determined at the time of the disclaimer according to the following formula:

$$\frac{\text{Total amount of distributions received by the disclaimant out of the gift or bequest}}{\text{Total value of the gift or bequest on the date of transfer}} \times \text{Total amount of income earned by the gift or bequest between date of transfer and date of disclaimer.}$$

See examples (17), (18), and (19) in § 25.2518–3(d) for illustrations of the rules set forth in this paragraph (c).

(d) Examples. The provisions of this section may be illustrated by the following examples:

Example (1). A, a resident of State Q, died on August 1, 1978. A's will included specific bequests of 100 shares of stock in X corporation; 200 shares of stock in Y corporation; 500 shares of stock in Z corporation; personal effects consisting of paintings, home furnishings, jewelry, and silver, and a 500 acre farm consisting of a residence, various outbuildings, and 500 head of cattle. The laws of State Q provide that a disclaimed interest passes in the same manner as if the disclaiming beneficiary had died immediately before the testator's death. Pursuant to A's will, B was to receive both the personal effects and the farm. C was to receive all the shares of stock in Corporation X and Y and D was to receive all the shares of stock in Corporation Z. B disclaimed 2 of the paintings and all the jewelry, C disclaimed 50 shares of Y corporation stock, and D disclaimed 100 shares of Z corporation stock. If the remaining requirements of section 2518(b) and the corresponding regulations are met, each of these disclaimers is a qualified disclaimer for purposes of section 2518(a).

Example (2). Assume the same facts as in example (1) except that D disclaimed the income interest in the shares of Z corporation stock while retaining the remainder interest in such shares. D's disclaimer is not a qualified disclaimer.

Example (3). Assume the same facts as in example (1) except that B disclaimed 300 identified acres of the 500 acres. Assuming that B's disclaimer meets the remaining requirements of section 2518(b), it is a qualified disclaimer.

Example (4). Assume the same facts as in example (1) except that A devised the income from the farm to B for life and the remainder interest to C. B disclaimed 40 percent of the income from the farm. Assuming that it meets the remaining requirements of section 2518(b), B's disclaimer of an undivided portion of the income is a qualified disclaimer.

Example (5). E died on September 13, 1978. Under the provisions of E's will, E's shares of stock in X, Y, and Z corporations were to be transferred to a trust. The trust provides that all income is to be distributed currently to F and G in equal parts until F attains the age of 45 years. At that time the corpus of the trust is to be divided equally between F and G. F disclaimed the income arising from the shares of X stock. G disclaimed 20 percent of G's interest in the trust. F's disclaimer is not a qualified disclaimer because the X stock remains in the trust. If the remaining requirements of section 2518(b) are met, G's disclaimer is a qualified disclaimer.

Example (6). Assume the same facts as in example (5) except that F disclaimed both the income interest and the remainder interest in the shares of X stock. F's disclaimer results in the X stock being transferred out of the trust to G without any direction on F's part. F's disclaimer is a qualified disclaimer under section 2518(b).

Example (7). Assume the same facts as in example (5) except that F is only an income beneficiary of the trust. The X stock remains in the trust after F's disclaimer of the income arising from the shares of X stock. F's disclaimer is not a qualified disclaimer under section 2518.

Example (8). Assume the same facts as in example (5) except that F disclaimed the entire income interest in the trust while retaining the interest F has in corpus. Alternatively, assume that G disclaimed G's entire corpus interest while retaining G's interest in the income from the trust. If the remaining requirements of section 2518(b) are met, either disclaimer will be a qualified disclaimer.

Example (9). G creates an irrevocable trust on May 13, 1980, with H, I, and J as the income beneficiaries. In addition, H, who is the trustee, holds the power to invade corpus for H's health, maintenance, support and happiness and a testamentary power of appointment over the corpus. In the absence of the exercise of the power of appointment, the property passes to I and J in equal shares. H disclaimed the power to invade corpus for H's health, maintenance, support and happiness. Because H retained the testamentary power to appoint the property in the corpus, H's disclaimer is not a qualified disclaimer. If H also disclaimed the testamentary power of appointment, H's disclaimer would have been a qualified disclaimer.

Example (10). E creates an irrevocable trust on May 1, 1980, in which D is the income beneficiary for life. Subject to the trustee's discretion, E's children, A, B, and C, have the right to receive corpus during D's lifetime. The remainder passes to D if D survives A, B, C, and all their issue. D also holds an inter vivos power to appoint the trust corpus to A, B, and C. On September 1, 1980, D disclaimed the remainder interest. D's disclaimer is not a qualified disclaimer because D retained the power to direct the use and enjoyment of corpus during D's life.

Example (11). Under H's will, a trust is created from which W is to receive all of the income for life. The trustee has the power to invade the trust corpus for the support or maintenance of D during the life of W. The trust is to terminate at W's death, at which time the trust property is to be distributed to D. D makes a timely disclaimer of the right to corpus during W's lifetime, but does not disclaim the remainder interest. D's disclaimer is a qualified disclaimer assuming the remaining requirements of section 2518 are met.

Example (12). Under the provisions of G's will A received a life estate in a farm, and was the sole beneficiary of property in the residuary estate. The will also provided that the remainder interest in the farm pass to the residuary estate. Under local law A's interests merged to give A a fee simple in the farm. A made a timely disclaimer of the life estate. A's disclaimer of a partial interest is not a qualified disclaimer under section 2518(a). If A makes a disclaimer of the entire merged interest in the farm or an undivided portion of such merged interest then A would be making a qualified disclaimer assuming all the other requirements of section 2518(b) are met.

* * *

[T.D. 8095, 51 FR 28375, Aug. 7, 1986, as amended by T.D. 8540, 59 FR 30100, June 10, 1994]

§ 25.2519–1 Dispositions of certain life estates.

(a) In general. If a donee spouse makes a disposition of all or part of a qualifying income interest for life in any property for which a deduction was allowed under section 2056(b)(7) or section 2523(f) for thc transfer creating the qualifying income interest, the donee spouse is treated for purposes of chapters 11 and 12 of subtitle B of the Internal Revenue Code as transferring all interests in property other than the qualifying income interest. For example, if the donee spouse makes a disposition of part of a qualifying income interest for life in trust corpus, the spouse is treated under section 2519 as making a transfer subject to chapters 11 and 12 of the entire trust other than the qualifying income interest for life. Therefore, the donee spouse is treated as making a gift under section 2519 of the entire trust less the qualifying income interest, and is treated for purposes of section 2036 as having transferred the entire trust corpus, including that portion of the trust corpus from which the retained income interest is payable. A transfer of all or a portion of the income interest of the spouse is a transfer by the spouse under section 2511. See also section 2702 for special rules applicable in valuing the gift made by the spouse under section 2519.

(b) Presumption. Unless the donee spouse establishes to the contrary, section 2519 applies to the entire trust at the time of the disposition. If a deduction is taken on either the estate or gift tax return with respect to the transfer which created the qualifying income interest, it is presumed that the deduction was allowed for purposes of section 2519. To avoid the application of section 2519 upon a transfer of all or part of the donee spouse's income interest, the donee spouse must establish that a deduction was not taken for the transfer of property which created the qualifying income interest. For example, to establish that a deduction was not taken, the donee spouse may produce a copy of the estate or gift tax return filed with respect to the transfer creating the qualifying income interest for life establishing that no deduction was taken under section 2056(b)(7) or section 2523(f). In addition, the donee spouse may establish that no return was filed on the original transfer by the donor spouse because the value of the first spouse's gross estate was below the threshold requirement for filing under section 6018. Similarly, the donee spouse could establish that the transfer creating the qualifying income interest for life was made before the effective date of section 2056(b)(7) or section 2523(f), whichever is applicable.

(c) Amount treated as a transfer—(1) In general. The amount treated as a transfer under this section upon a disposition of all or part of a qualifying income interest for life in qualified terminable interest property is equal to the fair market value of the entire property subject to the qualifying income interest, determined on the date of the disposition (including any accumulated income and not reduced by any amount excluded from total gifts under section 2503(b) with respect to the transfer creating the interest), less the value of the qualifying income interest in the property on the date of the disposition. The gift tax consequences of the disposition of the qualifying income interest are determined separately under § 25.2511–2. See paragraph (c)(4) of this section for the effect of gift tax that the donee spouse is entitled to recover under section 2207A.

(2) Disposition of interest in property with respect to which a partial election was made. If, in connection with the transfer of property that created the spouse's qualifying income interest for life, a deduction was allowed under section 2056(b)(7) or section 2523(f) for less than the entire interest in the property (i.e., for a fractional or percentage share of the entire interest in the transferred property) the amount treated as a transfer by the donee spouse under this section is equal to the fair market value of the entire property subject to the qualifying income interest on the date of the disposition, less the value of the qualifying income interest for life, multiplied by the fractional or percentage share of the interest for which the deduction was taken.

(3) Reduction for distributions charged to nonelective portion of trust. The amount determined under paragraph (c)(2) of this section (if applicable) is appropriately reduced if—

(i) The donee spouse's interest is in a trust and distributions of principal have been made to the donee spouse;

(ii) The trust provides that distributions of principal are made first from the qualified terminable interest share of the trust; and

(iii) The donee spouse establishes the reduction in that share based on the fair market value of the trust assets at the time of each distribution.

(4) Effect of gift tax entitled to be recovered under section 2207A on the amount of the transfer. The amount treated as a transfer under paragraph (c)(1) of this section is further reduced by the amount the donee spouse is entitled to recover under section 2207A(b) (relating to the right to recover gift tax attributable to the remainder interest). If the donee spouse is entitled to recover gift tax under section 2207A(b), the amount of gift tax recoverable and the value of the remainder interest treated as transferred under section 2519 are determined by using the same interrelated computation applicable for other transfers in which the transferee assumes the gift tax liability. The gift tax consequences of failing to exercise the right of recovery are determined separately under § 25.2207A–1(b).

(5) Interest in previously severed trust. If the donee spouse's interest is in a trust consisting of only qualified terminable interest property, and the trust was previously severed (in compliance with § 20.2056(b)–7(b)(2)(ii) of this chapter or § 25.2523(f)–l(b)(3)(ii)) from a trust that, after the severance, held only property that was not qualified terminable interest property, only the value of the property in the severed portion of the trust at the time of the disposition is treated as transferred under this section.

(d) Identification of property transferred. If only part of the property in which a donee spouse has a qualifying income interest for life is qualified terminable interest property, the donee spouse is, in the case of a disposition of all or part of the income interest within the meaning of section 2519, deemed to have transferred a pro rata portion of the entire qualified terminable interest property for purposes of this section.

(e) Exercise of power of appointment. The exercise by any person of a power to appoint qualified terminable interest property to the donee spouse is not treated as a disposition under section 2519, even though the donee spouse subsequently disposes of the appointed property.

(f) Conversion of qualified terminable interest property. The conversion of qualified terminable interest property into other property in which the donee spouse has a qualifying income interest for life is not, for purposes of this section, treated as a disposition of the qualifying income interest. Thus, the sale and reinvestment of assets of a trust holding qualified terminable interest property is not a disposition of the qualifying income interest, provided that the donee spouse continues to have a qualifying income interest for life in the trust after the sale and reinvestment. Similarly, the sale of real property in which the spouse possesses a legal life estate and thus meets the requirements of qualified terminable interest property, followed by the transfer of the proceeds into a trust which also meets the requirements of qualified terminable interest property, or by the reinvestment of the proceeds in income producing property in which the donee spouse has a qualifying income interest for life, is not considered a disposition of the qualifying income interest. On the other hand, the sale of qualified terminable interest property, followed by the payment to the donee spouse of a portion of the proceeds equal to the value of the donee spouse's income interest, is considered a disposition of the qualifying income interest.

(g) Examples. The following examples illustrate the application of paragraphs (a) through (f) of this section. Except as provided otherwise in the examples, assume that the decedent, D, was survived by spouse, S, that in each example the section 2503(b) exclusion has already been fully utilized for each year with respect to the donee in question, that section 2503(e) is not applicable to the amount deemed transferred, and that the gift taxes on the amount treated as transferred under paragraph (c) are offset by S's unified credit. The examples are as follows:

Example 1. Transfer of the spouse's life estate in residence. Under D's will, a personal residence valued for estate tax purposes at $250,000 passes to S for life, and after S's death to D's children. D's executor made a valid election to treat the property as qualified terminable interest property. During 1995, when the fair market value of the property is $300,000 and the value of S's life interest in the property is $100,000, S makes a gift of S's entire interest in the property to D's children. Pursuant to section 2519, S makes a gift in the amount of $200,000 (i.e., the fair market value of the qualified terminable interest property of $300,000 less the fair market value of S's qualifying income interest in the property of $100,000). In addition, under section 2511, S makes a gift of $100,000 (i.e., the fair market value of S's income interest in the property). See § 25.2511–2.

Example 2. Sale of spouse's life estate. The facts are the same as in Example 1 except that during 1995, S sells S's interest in the property to D's children for $100,000. Pursuant to section 2519, S makes a gift of $200,000 ($300,000 less $100,000 value of the qualifying income interest in the property). S does not make a gift of the income interest under section 2511, because the consideration received for S's income interest is equal to the value of the income interest.

Example 3. Transfer of income interest in trust subject to partial election. D's will established a trust valued for estate tax purposes at $500,000, all of the income of which is payable annually to S for life. After S's death, the principal of the trust is to be distributed to D's children. Assume that only 50 percent of the trust was treated as qualified terminable interest property. During 1995, S makes a gift of all of S's interest in the trust to D's children at which time the fair market value of the trust is $400,000 and the fair market value of S's life income interest in the trust is $100,000. Pursuant to section 2519, S makes a gift of $150,000 (the fair market value of the qualified terminable interest property, 50 percent of $400,000, less the $50,000 income interest in the qualified terminable interest property). S also makes a gift pursuant to section 2511 of $100,000 (i.e., the fair market value of S's life income interest).

Example 4. Transfer of a portion of income interest in trust subject to a partial election. The facts are the same as in Example 3 except that S makes a gift of only 40 percent of S's interest in the trust. Pursuant to section 2519, S makes a gift of $150,000 (i.e., the fair market value of the qualified terminable interest property, 50 percent of $400,000, less the $50,000 value of S's qualified income interest in the qualified terminable interest property). S also makes a gift pursuant to section 2511 of $40,000 (i.e., the fair market value of 40 percent of S's life income interest). See also section 2702 for additional rules that may affect the value of the total amount of S's gift under section 2519 to take into account the fact that S's 30 percent retained income interest attributable to the qualifying income interest is valued at zero under that section, thereby increasing the value of S's section 2519 gift to $180,000. In addition, under § 25.2519–1(d), S's disposition of 40 percent of the income interest is deemed to be a transfer of a pro rata portion of the qualified terminable interest property. Thus, assuming no further lifetime dispositions by S, 30 percent (60 percent of 50 percent) of the trust property is included in S's gross estate under section 2036 and an adjustment is made to S's adjusted taxable gifts under section 2001(b)(1)(B). If S later disposes of all or a portion of the retained income interest, see § 25.2702–6.

Example 5. Transfer of a portion of spouse's interest in a trust from which corpus was previously distributed to the spouse. D's will established a trust valued for estate tax purposes at $500,000, all of the income of which is payable annually to S for life. The trustee is granted the discretion to distribute trust principal to S. All appointments of principal must be made from the portion of the trust subject to the section 2056(b)(7) election. After S's death, the principal of the trust is to be distributed to D's children. The executor makes the section 2056(b)(7) election with respect to 50 percent of the trust. In 1994, pursuant to the terms of D's will, the trustee distributed $50,000 of principal to S and charged the entire distribution to the qualified terminable interest portion of the trust.

§Immediately prior to the distribution, the value of the entire trust was $550,000 and the value of the qualified terminable interest portion was $275,000 (50 percent of $550,000). Provided S can establish the above facts, the qualified terminable interest portion of the trust immediately after the distribution is $225,000 or 45 percent of the value of the trust ($225,000/$500,000). In 1996, when the value of the trust is $400,000 and the value of S's income interest is $100,000, S makes a transfer of 40 percent of S's income interest. S's gift under section 2519 is $135,000; i.e., the fair market value of the qualified terminable interest property, 45 percent of $400,000 ($180,-000), less the value of the income interest in the qualified terminable interest property, $45,000 (45 percent of $100,000). S also makes a gift under section 2511 of $40,000; i.e., the fair market value of 40 percent of S's income interest. S's disposition of 40 percent of the income interest is deemed to be a transfer under section 2519 of the entire 45 percent portion of the remainder subject to the section 2056(b)(7) election. Since S retained 60 percent of the income interest, 27 percent (60 percent of 45 percent) of the trust property is includible in S's gross estate under section 2036. See also section 2702 and Example 4 as to the principles applicable in valuing S's gift under section 2702 and adjusted taxable gifts upon S's subsequent death.

Example 6. Transfer of spousal annuity payable from trust. D died prior to October 24, 1992. D's will established a trust valued for estate tax purposes at $500,000. The trust instrument required the trustee to pay an annuity to S of $20,000 a year for life. All the trust income other than the amounts paid to S as an annuity are to be accumulated in the trust and may not be distributed during S's lifetime to any person other than S. After S's death, the principal of the trust is to be distributed to D's children. Because D died prior to the effective date of section 1941 of the Energy Policy Act of 1992, S's annuity interest qualifies as a qualifying income interest for life. Under § 20.2056(b)–7(e) of this chapter, based on an applicable 10 percent interest rate, 40 percent of the property, or $200,000, is the value of the deductible interest. During 1996, S makes a gift of the annuity interest to D's children at which time the fair market value of the trust is $800,000 and the fair market value of S's annuity interest in the trust is $100,000. Pursuant to section 2519, S is treated as making a gift of $220,000 (the fair market value of the qualified terminable interest property, 40 percent of $800,000 ($320,000), less the $100,000 annuity interest in the qualified terminable interest property). S is also treated pursuant to section 2511 as making a gift of $100,000 (the fair market value of S's annuity interest).

[T.D. 8522, 59 FR 9642, Mar. 1, 1994, as amended by T.D. 9077, 68 FR 42593, July 18, 2003]

§ 25.2523(a)–1 Gift to spouse; in general.

(a) In general. In determining the amount of taxable gifts for the calendar quarter (with respect to gifts made after December 31, 1970, and before January 1, 1982), or calendar year (with respect to gifts made before January 1, 1971, or after December 31, 1981), a donor may deduct the value of any property interest transferred by gift to a donee who at the time of the gift is the donor's spouse, except as limited by paragraphs (b) and (c) of this section. See § 25.2502–1(c)(1) for the definition of calendar quarter. This deduction is referred to as the marital deduction. In the case of gifts made prior to July 14, 1988, no marital deduction is allowed with respect to a gift if, at the time of the gift, the donor is a nonresident not a citizen of the United States. Further, in the case of gifts made on or after July 14, 1988, no marital deduction is allowed (regardless of the donor's citizenship or residence) for transfers to a spouse who is not a citizen of the United States at the time of the transfer. However, for certain special rules applicable in the case of estate and gift tax treaties, see section 7815(d)(14) of Public Law 101–239. The donor must submit any evidence necessary to establish the donor's right to the marital deduction.

(b) "Deductible interests" and "nondeductible interests"—(1) In general. The property interests transferred by a donor to his spouse consist of either transfers with respect to which the marital deduction is authorized (as described in subparagraph (2) of this paragraph) or transfers with respect to which the marital deduction is not authorized (as described in subparagraph (3) of this paragraph). These transfers are referred to in this section and in §§ 25.2523(b)–1 through 25.2523(f)–1 as "deductible interests" and "nondeductible interests", respectively.

(2) "Deductible interest". A property interest transferred by a donor to his spouse is a "deductible interest" if it does not fall within either class of "nondeductible interests" described in subparagraph (3) of this paragraph.

(3) "Nondeductible interests". (i) A property interest transferred by a donor to his spouse is a "terminable interest", as defined in § 25.2523(b)–1, is a "nondeductible interest" to the extent specified in that section.

(ii) Any property interest transferred by a donor to the donor's spouse is a nondeductible interest to the extent it is not required to be included in a gift tax return for a calendar quarter (for gifts made after December 31, 1970, and before January 1, 1982) or calendar year (for gifts made before January 1, 1971, or after December 31, 1981).

* * *

[T.D. 6334, 23 FR 8904, Nov. 15, 1958, as amended by T.D. 7012, 34 FR 7691, May 15, 1969; T.D. 7238, 37 FR 28733, Dec. 29, 1972; T.D. 7955, 49 FR 19998, May 11, 1984; T.D. 8522, 59 FR 9658, March 1, 1994; T.D. 8540, 59 FR 30103, June 10, 1994; 60 FR 16382, March 30, 1995]

§ 25.2523(b)–1 Life estate or other terminable interest.

(a) In general. (1) The provisions of section 2523(b) generally disallow a marital deduction with respect to certain property interests (referred to generally as terminable interests and defined in paragraph (a)(3) of this section) transferred to the donee spouse under the circumstances described in paragraph (a)(2) of this section, unless the transfer comes within the purview of one of the exceptions set forth in § 25.2523(d)–1 (relating to certain joint interests); § 25.2523(e)–1 (relating to certain life estates with powers of appointment); § 25.2523(f)–1 (relating to certain qualified terminable interest property); or § 25.2523(g)–1 (relating to certain qualified charitable remainder trusts).

(2) If a donor transfers a terminable interest in property to the donee spouse, the marital deduction is disallowed with respect to the transfer if the donor spouse also—

(i) Transferred an interest in the same property to another donee (see paragraph (b) of this section), or

(ii) Retained an interest in the same property in himself (see paragraph (c) of this section), or

(iii) Retained a power to appoint an interest in the same property (see paragraph (9d) of this section).

Notwithstanding the preceding sentence, the marital deduction is disallowed under these circumstances only if the other donee, the donor, or the possible appointee, may, by reason of the transfer or retention, possess or enjoy any part of the property after the termination or failure of the interest therein transferred to the donee spouse.

(3) For purposes of this section, a distinction is to be drawn between "property," as such term is used in section 2523, and an "interest in property." The "property" referred to is the underlying property in which various interests exist; each such interest is not, for this purpose, to be considered as "property." A "terminable interest" in property is an interest which will terminate or fail on the lapse of time or on the occurrence or failure to occur of some contingency. Life estates, terms for years, annuities, patents, and copyrights are therefore terminable interests. However, a bond, note, or similar contractual obligation, the discharge of which would not have the effect of an annuity or term for years, is not a terminable interest.

* * *

(c) Interest in property which the donor may possess or enjoy. (1) Section 2523(b) provides that no marital deduction is allowed with respect to the transfer to the donee spouse of a "terminable interest" in property, if—

(i) The donor retained in himself an interest in the same property, and

(ii) By reason of such retention, the donor (or his heirs or assigns) may possess or enjoy any part of the property after the termination or failure of the interest transferred to the donee spouse. However, as to a transfer to the donee spouse as sole joint tenant with the donor or as tenant by the entirety, see § 25.2523(d)–1.

(2) In general, the principles illustrated by the examples under paragraph (b) of this section are applicable in determining whether the marital deduction may be taken with respect to a property interest transferred to the donee spouse subject to the retention by the donor of an interest in the same property. The application of this paragraph may be further illustrated by the following example, in which it is assumed that the donor made no election under sections 2523(f)(2)(C) and (f)(4).

Example. The donor purchased three annuity contracts for the benefit of his wife and himself. The first contract provided for payments to the wife for life, with refund to the donor in case the aggregate payments made to the wife were less than the cost of the contract. The second contract provided for payments to the donor for life, and then to the wife for life if she survived the donor. The third contract provided for payments to the donor and his wife for their joint lives and then to the survivor of them for life. No marital deduction may be taken with respect to the gifts resulting from the purchases of the contracts since, in the case of each contract, the donor may possess or enjoy a part of the property after the termination or failure of the interest transferred to the wife.

(d) Interest in property over which the donor retained a power to appoint. (1) Section 2523(b) provides that no marital deduction is allowed with respect to the transfer to the donee spouse of a terminable interest in property if—

(i) The donor had, immediately after the transfer, a power to appoint an interest in the same property, and

(ii) The donor's power was exercisable (either alone or in conjunction with any person) in such manner that the appointee may possess or enjoy any part of the property after the termination or failure of the interest transferred to the donee spouse.

(2) For the purposes of section 2523(b), the donor is to be considered as having, immediately after the transfer to the donee spouse, such a power to appoint even though the power cannot be exercised until after the lapse of time, upon the occurrence of an event or contingency, or upon the failure of an event or contingency to occur. It is immaterial whether the power retained by the donor was a taxable power of appointment under section 2514.

(3) The principles illustrated by the examples under paragraph (b) of this section are generally applicable in determining whether the marital deduction may be taken with respect to a property interest transferred to the donee spouse subject to retention by the donor of a power to appoint an interest in the same property. The application of this paragraph may be further illustrated by the following example:

Example. The donor, having a power of appointment over certain property, appointed a life estate to his spouse. No marital deduction may be taken with respect to such transfer, since, if the retained power to appoint the remainder interest is exercised, the appointee thereunder may possess or enjoy the property after the termination or failure of the interest taken by the donee spouse.

[T.D. 6334, 23 FR 8904, Nov. 15, 1958; T.D. 8522, 59 FR 9659, March 1, 1994]

§ 25.2523(e)–1 Marital deduction; life estate with power of appointment in donee spouse.

* * *

(c) Meaning of specific portion—(1) In general. Except as provided in paragraphs (c)(2) and (c)(3) of this section, a partial interest in property is not treated as a specific portion of the entire interest. In addition, any specific portion of an entire interest in property is nondeductible to the extent the specific portion is subject to invasion for the benefit of any person other than the donee spouse, except in the case of a deduction allowable under section 2523(e), relating to the exercise of a general power of appointment by the donee spouse.

(2) Fraction or percentage share. Under section 2523(e), a partial interest in property is treated as a specific portion of the entire interest if the rights of the donee spouse in income, and the required rights as to the power described in § 25.2523(e)–1(a), constitute a fractional or percentage share of the entire property interest, so that the donee spouse's interest reflects its proportionate share of the increase or decrease in the value of the entire property interest to which the income rights and the power relate. Thus, if the spouse's right to income and the spouse's power extend to a specified fraction or percentage of the property, or its equivalent, the interest is in a specific portion of the property. In accordance with paragraph (b) of this section, if the spouse has the right to receive the income from a specific portion of the trust property (after applying paragraph (c)(3) of this section) but has a power of appointment over a different specific portion of the property (after applying paragraph (c)(3) of this section), the marital deduction is limited to the lesser specific portion.

(3) Special rule in the case of gifts made on or before October 24, 1992. In the case of gifts within the purview of the effective date rule contained in paragraph (c)(3)(iii) of this section:

(i) A specific sum payable annually, or at more frequent intervals, out of the property and its income that is not limited by the income of the property is treated as the right to receive the income from a specific portion of the property. The specific portion, for purposes of paragraph (c)(2) of this section, is the portion of the property that, assuming the interest rate generally applicable for the valuation of annuities at the time of the donor's gift, would produce income equal to such payments. However, a pecuniary amount payable annually to a donee spouse is not treated as a right to the income from a specific portion of trust property for purposes of this paragraph (c)(3)(i) if any person other than the donee spouse may receive, during the donee spouse's lifetime, any distribution of the property. To determine the applicable interest rate for valuing annuities, see sections 2512 and 7520 and the regulations under those sections.

(ii) The right to appoint a pecuniary amount out of a larger fund (or trust corpus) is considered the right to appoint a specific portion of such fund or trust in an amount equal to such pecuniary amount.

(iii) The rules contained in paragraphs (c)(3)(i) and (ii) of this section apply with respect to gifts made on or before October 24, 1992.

(4) Local law. A partial interest in property is treated as a specific portion of the entire interest if it is shown that the donee spouse has rights under local law that are identical to those the donee spouse would have acquired had the partial interest been expressed in terms satisfying the requirements of paragraph (c)(2) of this section (or paragraph (c)(3) of this section if applicable).

(5) Examples. The following examples illustrate the application of paragraphs (b) and (c) of this section, where D, the donor, transfers property to D's spouse, S:

Example 1. Spouse entitled to the lesser of an annuity or a fraction of trust income. Prior to October 24, 1992, D transferred in trust 500 identical shares of

X Company stock, valued for gift tax purposes at $500,000. The trust provided that during the lifetime of D's spouse, S, the trustee is to pay annually to S the lesser of one-half of the trust income or $20,000. Any trust income not paid to S is to be accumulated in the trust and may not be distributed during S's lifetime. S has a testamentary general power of appointment over the entire trust principal. The applicable interest rate for valuing annuities as of the date of D's gift under section 7520 is 10 percent. For purposes of paragraphs (a) through (c) of this section, S is treated as receiving all of the income from the lesser of one-half of the stock ($250,000), or $200,000, the specific portion of the stock which, as determined in accordance with § 25.2523(e)–1(c)(3)(i) of this chapter, would produce annual income of $20,000 (20,000/.10). Accordingly, the marital deduction is limited to $200,000 (200,000/500,000 or ⅖ of the value of the trust.)

Example 2. Spouse possesses power and income interest over different specific portions of trust. The facts are the same as in Example 1 except that S's testamentary general power of appointment is exercisable over only ¾ of the trust principal. Consequently, under section 2523(e), the marital deduction is allowable only for the value of ¼ of the trust ($125,000); i.e., the lesser of the value of the portion with respect to which S is deemed to be entitled to all of the income (⅖ of the trust or $200,000), or the value of the portion with respect to which S possesses the requisite power of appointment (¼ of the trust or $125,000).

Example 3. Power of appointment over shares of stock constitutes a power over a specific portion. D transferred 250 identical shares of Y company stock to a trust under the terms of which trust income is to be paid annually to S, during S's lifetime, S was given a testamentary general power of appointment over 100 shares of stock. The trust provides that if the trustee sells the Y company stock, S's general power of appointment is exercisable with respect to the sale proceeds or the property in which the proceeds are reinvested. Because the amount of property represented by a single share of stock would be altered if the corporation split its stock, issued stock dividends, made a distribution of capital, etc., a power to appoint 100 shares at the time of S's death is not necessarily a power to appoint the entire interest that the 100 shares represented on the date of D's gift. If it is shown that, under local law, S has a general power to appoint not only the 100 shares designated by D but also 100/250 of any distributions by the corporation that are included in trust principal, the requirements of paragraph (c)(2) of this section are satisfied and S is treated as having a general power to appoint 100/250 of the entire interest in the 250 shares. In that case, the marital deduction is limited to 40 percent of the trust principal. If local law does not give S that power, the 100 shares would not constitute a specific portion under § 25.2523(e)–1(c) (including § 25.2523(e)–1(c)(3)(ii)). The nature of the asset is such that a change in the capitalization of the corporation could cause an alteration in the original value represented by the shares at the time of the transfer and is thus not a specific portion of the trust.

* * *

(f) Right to income. (1) If an interest is transferred in trust, the donee spouse is "entitled for life to all of the income from the entire interest or a specific portion of the entire interest," for the purpose of the condition set forth in paragraph (a)(1) of this section, if the effect of the trust is to give her substantially that degree of beneficial enjoyment of the trust property during her life which the principles of the law of trust accord to a person who is unqualifiedly designated as the life beneficiary of a trust. Such degree of enjoyment is given only if it was the donor's intention, as manifested by the terms of the trust instrument and the surrounding circumstances, that the trust should produce for the donee spouse during her life such an income, or that the spouse should have such use of the trust property as is consistent with the value of the trust corpus and with its preservation. The designation of the spouse as sole income beneficiary for life of the entire interest or a specific portion of the entire interest will be sufficient to qualify the trust unless the terms of the trust and the surrounding circumstances considered as a whole evidence an intention to deprive the spouse of the requisite degree of enjoyment. In determining whether a trust evidences that intention, the treatment required or permitted with respect to individual items must be considered in relation to the entire system provided for the administration of the trust. In addition, the spouse's interest shall meet the condition set forth in paragraph (a)(1) of this section if the spouse is entitled to income as defined or determined by applicable local law that provides for a reasonable apportionment between the income and remainder beneficiaries of the total return of the trust and that meets the requirements of § 1.643(b)–1 of this chapter.

(2) If the over-all effect of a trust is to give to the donee spouse such enforceable rights as will preserve to her the requisite degree of enjoyment, it is immaterial whether that result is effected by rules specifically stated in the trust instrument, or, in their absence, by the rules for the management of the trust property and the allocation of receipts and expenditures supplied by the State law. For example, a provision in the trust instrument for amortization of bond premium by appropriate periodic charges to interest will not disqualify the interest transferred in trust even though there is no State law specifically authorizing amortization or there is a State law denying amortization which is applicable only in the absence of such a provision in the trust instrument.

(3) In the case of a trust, the rules to be applied by the trustee in allocation of receipts and expenses between income and corpus must be considered in relation to the nature and expected productivity of the assets transferred in trust, the nature and frequency of occurrence of the expected receipts, and any provisions as to change in the form of investments. If it is evident from the nature of the trust assets and the rules provided for management of the trust that the allocation to income of such receipts as rents, ordinary cash dividends and interest will give to the spouse the substantial enjoyment during life required by the statute, provisions that such receipts as stock dividends and proceeds from the conversion of trust assets shall be treated as corpus will not disqualify the interest transferred in trust. Similarly, provision for a depletion charge against income in the case of trust assets which are subject to depletion will not disqualify the interest transferred in trust, unless the effect is to deprive the spouse of the requisite beneficial enjoyment. The same principle is applicable in the case of depreciation, trustees' commissions, and other charges.

(4) Provisions granting administrative powers to the trustees will not have the effect of disqualifying an interest transferred in trust unless the grant of powers evidences the intention to deprive the donee spouse of the beneficial enjoyment required by the statute. Such an intention will not be considered to exist if the entire terms of the instrument are such that the local courts will impose reasonable limitations upon the exercise of the powers. Among the powers which if subject to reasonable limitations will not disqualify the interest transferred in trust are the power to determine the allocation or apportionment of receipts and disbursements between income and corpus, the power to apply the income or corpus for the benefit of the spouse, and the power to retain the assets transferred to the trust. For example, a power to retain trust assets which consist substantially of unproductive property will not disqualify the interest if the applicable rules for the administration of the trust require, or permit the spouse to require, that the trustee either make the property productive or convert it within a reasonable time. Nor will such a power disqualify the interest if the applicable rules for administration of the trust require the trustee to use the degree of judgment and care in the exercise of the power which a prudent man would use if he were owner of the trust assets. Further, a power to retain a residence for the spouse or other property for the personal use of the spouse will not disqualify the interest transferred in trust.

* * *

(g) Power of appointment in donee spouse. **(1)** The conditions set forth in paragraph (a)(3) and (4) of this section, that is, that the donee spouse must have a power of appointment exercisable in favor of herself or her estate and exercisable alone and in all events, are not met unless the power of the donee spouse to appoint the entire interest or a specific portion of it falls within one of the following categories:

(i) A power so to appoint fully exercisable in her own favor at any time during her life (as, for example, an unlimited power to invade); or

(ii) A power so to appoint exercisable in favor of her estate. Such a power, if exercisable during life, must be fully exercisable at any time during life, or if exercisable by will, must be fully exercisable irrespective of the time of her death; or

(iii) A combination of the powers described under subdivisions (i) and (ii) of this subparagraph. For example, the donee spouse may, until she attains the age of 50 years, have a power to appoint to herself and thereafter have a power to appoint to her estate. However, the condition that the spouse's power must be exercisable in all events is not satisfied unless irrespective of when the donee spouse may die the entire interest or a specific portion of it will at the time of her death be subject to one power or the other.

(2) The power of the donee spouse must be a power to appoint the entire interest or a specific portion of it as unqualified owner (and free of the trust if a trust is involved, or free of the joint tenancy if a joint tenancy is involved) or to appoint the entire interest or a specific portion of it as a part of her estate (and free of the trust if a trust is involved), that is, in effect, to dispose of it to whomsoever she pleases. Thus, if the donor transferred property to a son and the donee spouse as joint tenants with right of survivorship and under local law the donee spouse has a power of severance exercisable without consent of the other joint tenant, and by exercising this power could acquire a one-half interest in the property as a tenant in common, her power of severance will satisfy the condition set forth in paragraph (a)(3) of this section that she have a power of appointment in favor of herself or her estate. However, if the donee spouse entered into a binding agreement with the donor to exercise the power only in favor of their issue, that condition is not met. An interest transferred in trust will not be regarded as failing to satisfy the condition merely because takers in default of the donee spouse's exercise of the power are designated by the donor. The donor may provide that, in default of exercise of the power, the trust shall continue for an additional period.

(3) A power is not considered to be a power exercisable by a donee spouse alone and in all events as required by paragraph (a)(4) of this section if the exercise of the power in the donee spouse to appoint the entire interest or a specific portion of it to herself or to her estate requires the joinder or consent of any other person. The power is not "exercisable in all events", if it can be terminated during the life of the donee spouse by any event other than her complete exercise or release of it. Further, a power is not "exercisable in all events" if it may be exercised for a limited purpose only. For example, a power which is not exercisable in the event of the spouse's remarriage is not exercisable in all events. Likewise, if there are any restrictions, either by the terms of the instrument or under applicable local law, on the exercise of a power to consume property (whether or not held in trust) for the benefit of the spouse, the power is not exercisable in all events. Thus, if a power of invasion is exercisable only for the spouse's support, or only for her limited use, the power is not exercisable in all events. In order for a power of invasion to be exercisable in all events, the donee spouse must have the unrestricted power exercisable at any time during her life to use all or any part of the property subject to the power, and to dispose of it in any manner, including the power to dispose of it by gift (whether or not she has power to dispose of it by will).

(4) If the power is in existence at all times following the transfer of the interest, limitations of a formal nature will not disqualify the interest. Examples of formal limitations on a power exercisable during life are requirements that an exercise must be in a particular form, that it must be filed with a trustee during the spouse's life, that reasonable notice must be given, or that reasonable intervals must elapse between successive partial exercises. Examples of formal limitations on a power exercisable by will are that it must be exercised by a will executed by the donee spouse after the making of the gift or that exercise must be by specific reference to the power.

(5) If the donee spouse has the requisite power to appoint to herself or her estate, it is immaterial that she also has one or more lesser powers. Thus, if she has a testamentary power to appoint to her estate, she may also have a limited power of withdrawal or of appointment during her life. Similarly, if she has an unlimited power of withdrawal, she may have a limited testamentary power.

* * *

[T.D. 6334, 23 FR 8904, Nov. 15, 1958, as amended by T.D. 6542, 26 FR 552, Jan. 20, 1961; T.D. 8522, 59 FR 9642, Mar. 1, 1994; T.D. 9102, 69 FR 12, Jan. 2, 2004]

§ 25.2523(f)–1 Election with respect to life estate transferred to donee spouse.

(a) In general. **(1)** With respect to gifts made after December 31, 1981, subject to section 2523(i), a marital deduction is allowed under section 2523(a) for transfers of qualified terminable interest property. Qualified terminable interest property is terminable interest property described in section 2523(b)(1) that satisfies the requirements of section 2523(f)(2) and this section. Terminable interests that are described in section 2523(b)(2) cannot qualify as qualified terminable interest property. Thus, if the donor retains a power described in section 2523(b)(2) to appoint an interest in qualified terminable interest property, no deduction is allowable under section 2523(a) for the property.

(2) All of the property for which a deduction is allowed under this paragraph (a) is treated as passing to the donee spouse (for purposes of § 25.2523(a)–1), and no part of the property is treated as retained by the donor or as passing to any person other than the donee spouse (for purposes of § 25.2523(b)–1(b)).

(b) Qualified terminable interest property—(1) Definition. Section 2523(f)(2) provides the definition of qualified terminable interest property.

(2) Meaning of property. For purposes of section 2523(f)(2), the term property generally means an entire interest in property (within the meaning of § 25.2523(e)–1(d)) or a specific portion of the entire interest (within the meaning of § 25.2523(e)–1(c)).

(3) Property for which the election may be made—(i) In general. The election may relate to all or any part of property that meets the requirements of section 2523(f)(2)(A) and (B), provided that any partial election must be made with respect to a fractional or percentage share of the property so that the elective portion reflects its proportionate share of the increase or decrease in the entire property for purposes of applying sections 2044 or 2519. Thus, if the interest of the donee spouse in a trust (or other property in which the spouse has a qualifying income interest) meets the requirements of this section, the election may be made under section 2523(f)(2)(C) with respect to a part of the trust (or other property) only if the election relates to a defined fraction or percentage of the entire trust (or other property) or specific portion thereof within the meaning of § 25.2523(e)–1(c). The fraction or percentage may be defined by formula.

(ii) Division of trusts. If the interest of the donee spouse in a trust meets the requirements of this section, the trust may be divided into separate trusts to reflect a partial election that has been made, if authorized under the terms of the governing instrument or otherwise permissible under local law. A trust may be divided only if the fiduciary is required, either by applicable local law or by the express or implied provisions of the governing instrument, to divide the trust according to the fair market value of the assets of the trust at the time of the division. The division of the trusts must be done on a fractional or percentage basis to reflect the partial election. However, the separate trusts do not have to be funded with a pro rata portion of each asset held by the undivided trust.

(4) Manner and time of making election. (i) An election under section 2523(f)(2)(C) (other than a deemed election with respect to a joint and survivor annuity as described in section 2523(f)(6)), is made on a gift tax return for the calendar year in which the interest is transferred. The return must be filed within the time prescribed by section 6075(b) (determined without regard to section 6019(a)(2)), including any extensions authorized under section 6075(b)(2) (relating to an automatic extension of time for filing a gift tax return where the donor is granted an extension of time to file the income tax return).

(ii) If the election is made on a return for the calendar year that includes the date of death of the donor, the return (as prescribed by section 6075(b)(3)) must be filed no later than the time (including extensions) for filing the estate tax return. The election, once made, is irrevocable.

(c) Qualifying income interest for life—(1) In general. For purposes of this section, the term qualifying income interest for life is defined as provided in section 2056(b)(7)(B)(ii) and § 20.2056(b)–7(d)(1).

(i) Entitled for life to all the income. The principles outlined in § 25.2523(e)–1(f) (relating to whether the spouse is entitled for life to all of the income from the entire interest or a specific portion of the entire interest) apply in determining whether the donee spouse is entitled for life to all the income from the property, regardless of whether the interest passing to the donee spouse is in trust. An income interest granted for a term of years, or a life estate subject to termination upon the occurrence of a specified event (e.g., divorce) is not a qualifying income interest for life.

(ii) Income between last distribution date and date of spouse's death. An income interest does not fail to constitute a qualifying income interest for life solely because income for the period between the last distribution date and the date of the donee spouse's death is not required to be distributed to the estate of the donee spouse. See § 20.2044–1 of this chapter relating to the inclusion of such undistributed income in the gross estate of the donee spouse.

(iii) Pooled income funds. An income interest in a pooled income fund described in section 642(c)(5) constitutes a qualifying income interest for life for purposes of this section.

(iv) Distribution of principal for the benefit of the donee spouse. An income interest does not fail to constitute a qualifying income interest for life solely because the trustee has a power to distribute principal to or for the benefit of the donee spouse. The fact that property distributed to a donee spouse may be transferred by the spouse to another person does not result in a failure to satisfy the requirement of section 2056(b)(7)(B)(ii)(II). However, if the governing instrument requires the donee spouse to transfer the distributed property to another person without full and adequate consideration in money or money's worth, the requirement of section 2056(b)(7)(B)(ii)(II) is not satisfied.

(2) Immediate right to income. In order to constitute a qualifying income interest for life, the donee spouse must be granted the immediate right to receive the income from the property. Thus, an income interest does not constitute a qualifying income interest for life if the donee spouse receives the right to trust income commencing at some time in the future, e.g., on the termination of a preceding life income interest of the donor spouse.

(3) Annuities payable from trusts in the case of gifts made on or before October 24, 1992. (i) In the case of gifts made on or before

October 24, 1992, a donee spouse's lifetime annuity interest payable from a trust or other group of assets passing from the donor is treated as a qualifying income interest for life for purposes of section 2523(f)(2)(B). The deductible interest, for purposes of § 25.2523(a)–1(b), is the specific portion of the property that, assuming the applicable interest rate for valuing annuities at the time the annuity interest is transferred, would produce income equal to the minimum amount payable annually to the donee spouse. If, based on the applicable interest rate, the entire property from which the annuity may be satisfied is insufficient to produce income equal to the minimum annual payment, the value of the deductible interest is the entire value of the property. The value of the deductible interest may not exceed the value of the property from which the annuity is payable. If the annual payment may increase, the increased amount is not taken into account in valuing the deductible interest.

(ii) An annuity interest is not treated as a qualifying income interest for life for purposes of section 2523(f)(2)(B) if any person other than the donee spouse may receive during the donee spouse's lifetime, any distribution of the property or its income from which the annuity is payable.

(iii) To determine the applicable interest rate for valuing annuities, see sections 2512 and 7520 and the regulations under those sections.

(4) Joint and survivor annuities. [Reserved]

(d) Treatment of interest retained by the donor spouse—(1) In general. Under section 2523(f)(5)(A), if a donor spouse retains an interest in qualified terminable interest property, any subsequent transfer by the donor spouse of the retained interest in the property is not treated as a transfer for gift tax purposes. Further, the retention of the interest until the donor spouse's death does not cause the property subject to the retained interest to be includable in the gross estate of the donor spouse.

(2) Exception. Under section 2523(f)(5)(B), the rule contained in paragraph (d)(1) of this section does not apply to any property after the donee spouse is treated as having transferred the property under section 2519, or after the property is includable in the gross estate of the donee spouse under section 2044.

(e) Application of local law. The provisions of local law are taken into account in determining whether or not the conditions of section 2523(f)(2)(A) and (B), and the conditions of paragraph (c) of this section, are satisfied. For example, silence of a trust instrument on the frequency of payment is not regarded as a failure to satisfy the requirement that the income must be payable to the donee spouse annually or more frequently unless applicable local law permits payments less frequently to the donee spouse.

(f) Examples. The following examples illustrate the application of this section, where D, the donor, transfers property to D's spouse, S. Unless stated otherwise, it is assumed that S is not the trustee of any trust established for S's benefit:

Example 1. Life estate in residence. D transfers by gift a personal residence valued at $250,000 on the date of the gift to S and D's children, giving S the exclusive and unrestricted right to use the property (including the right to continue to occupy the property as a personal residence or rent the property and receive the income for her lifetime). After S's death, the property is to pass to D's children. Under applicable local law, S's consent is required for any sale of the property. If D elects to treat all of the transferred property as qualified terminable interest property, the deductible interest is $250,000, the value of the property for gift tax purposes.

Example 2. Power to make property productive. D transfers assets having a fair market value of $500,000 to a trust pursuant to which S is given the right exercisable annually to require distribution of all the trust income to S. No trust property may be distributed during S's lifetime to any person other than S. The assets used to fund the trust include both income producing assets and nonproductive assets. Applicable local law permits S to require that the trustee either make the trust property productive or sell the property and reinvest the proceeds in productive property within a reasonable time after the transfer. If D elects to treat the entire trust as qualified terminable interest property, the deductible interest is $500,000. If D elects to treat only 20 percent of the trust as qualified terminable interest property, the deductible interest is $100,000; i.e., 20 percent of $500,000.

Example 3. Power of distribution over fraction of trust income. The facts are the same as in Example 2 except that S is given the power exercisable annually to require distribution to S of only 50 percent of the trust income for life. The remaining trust income may be accumulated or distributed among D's children and S in the trustee's discretion. The maximum amount that D may elect to treat as qualified terminable interest property is $250,000; i.e., the value of the trust for gift tax purposes ($500,000) multiplied by the percentage of the trust in which S has a qualifying income interest for life (50 percent). If D elects to treat only 20 percent of the portion of the trust in which S has a qualifying income interest as qualified terminable interest property, the deductible interest is $50,000; i.e., 20 percent of $250,000.

Example 4. Power to distribute trust corpus to other beneficiaries. D transfers $500,000 to a trust providing that all the trust income is to be paid to D's spouse, S, during S's lifetime. The trustee is given the power to use annually $5,000 from the trust for the maintenance and support of S's minor child, C. Any such distribution does not necessarily relieve S of S's obligation to support and maintain C. S does not have a qualifying income interest for life in any portion of the trust because the gift fails to satisfy the condition in sections 2523(f)(3) and 2056(b)(7)(B)(ii)(II) that no person have a power, other than a power the exercise of which takes effect only at or after S's death, to appoint any part of the property to any person other than S. The trust would also be nondeductible under section 2523(f) if S, rather than the trustee, were given the power to appoint a portion of the principal to C. However, in the latter case, if S made a qualified disclaimer (within the meaning of section 2518) of the power to appoint to C, the trust could qualify for the marital deduction pursuant to section 2523(f), assuming that the power was personal to S and S's disclaimer terminates the power. Similarly, if C made a qualified disclaimer of the right to receive distributions from the trust, the trust would qualify under section 2523(f) assuming that C's disclaimer effectively negates the trustee's power under local law.

Example 5. Spouse's interest terminable on divorce. The facts are the same as in Example 3 except that if S and D divorce, S's interest in the trust will pass to C. S's income interest is not a qualifying income interest for life because it is terminable upon S's divorce. Therefore, no portion of the trust is deductible under section 2523(f).

Example 6. Spouse's interest in trust in the form of an annuity. Prior to October 24, 1992, D established a trust funded with income producing property valued for gift tax purposes at $800,000. The trustee is required by the trust instrument to pay $40,000 a year to S for life. Any income in excess of the annuity amount is to be accumulated in the trust and may not be distributed during S's lifetime. S's lifetime annuity interest is treated as a qualifying income interest for life. If D elects to treat the entire portion of the trust in which S has a qualifying income interest as qualified terminable interest property, the value of the deductible interest is $400,000, because that amount would yield an income to S of $40,000 a year (assuming a 10 percent interest rate applies in valuing annuities at the time of the transfer).

Example 7. Value of spouse's annuity exceeds value of trust corpus. The facts are the same as in Example 6, except that the trustee is required to pay S $100,000 a year for S's life. If D elects to treat the entire portion of the trust in which S has a qualifying income interest for life as qualified terminable interest property, the value of the deductible interest is $800,000, which is the lesser of the entire value of the property ($800,000) or the amount of property that (assuming a 10 percent interest rate) would yield an income to S of $100,000 a year ($1,000,000).

Example 8. Transfer to pooled income fund. D transfers $200,000 on June 1, 1994, to a pooled income fund (described in section 642(c)(5)) designating S as the only life income beneficiary. If D elects to treat the entire $200,000 as qualified terminable interest property, the deductible interest is $200,000.

Example 9. Retention by donor spouse of income interest in property. On October 1, 1994, D transfers property to an irrevocable trust under the terms of which trust income is to be paid to D for life, then to S for life and, on S's death, the trust corpus is to be paid to D's children. Because S does not possess an immediate right to receive trust income, S's interest does not qualify as a qualifying income interest for life under section 2523(f)(2). Further, under section 2702(a)(2) and § 25.2702–2(b), D is treated for gift tax purposes as making a gift with a value equal to the entire value of the property. If D dies in 1996 survived by S, the trust corpus will be includible in D's gross estate under section 2036. However, in computing D's estate tax liability, D's adjusted taxable gifts under section 2001(b)(1)(B) are adjusted to reflect the inclusion of the gifted property in D's gross estate. In addition, if S survives D, the trust property is eligible for treatment as qualified terminable interest property under section 2056(b)(7) in D's estate.

Example 10. Retention by donor spouse of income interest in property. On October 1, 1994, D transfers property to an irrevocable trust under the terms of which trust income is to be paid to S for life, then to D for life and, on D's death, the trust corpus is to be paid to D's children. D elects under section 2523(f) to treat the property as qualified terminable interest property. D dies in 1996, survived by S. S subsequently dies in 1998. Under § 2523(f)–1(d)(1), because D elected to treat the transfer as qualified terminable interest property, no part of the trust corpus is includible in D's gross estate because of D's retained interest in the trust corpus. On S's subsequent death in 1998, the trust corpus is includible in S's gross estate under section 2044.

Example 11. Retention by donor spouse of income interest in property. The facts are the same as in Example 10, except that S dies in 1996 survived by D, who subsequently dies in 1998. Because D made an election under section 2523(f) with respect to the trust, on S's death the trust corpus is includible in S's gross estate under section 2044. Accordingly, under section 2044(c), S is treated as the transferor of the property for estate and gift tax purposes. Upon D's subsequent death in 1998, because the property was subject to inclusion in S's gross estate under section 2044, the exclusion rule in § 25.2523(f)–1(d)(1) does not apply under § 25.2523(f)–1(d)(2). However, because S is treated as the transferor of the property, the property is not subject to inclusion in D's gross estate under section 2036 or section 2038. If the executor of S's estate made a section 2056(b)(7) election with respect to the trust, the trust is includible in D's gross estate under section 2044 upon D's later death.

[T.D. 8522, 59 FR 9642, Mar. 1, 1994]

§ 25.2523(g)–1 Special rule for charitable remainder trusts.

(a) In general. **(1)** With respect to gifts made after December 31, 1981, subject to section 2523(i), if the donor's spouse is the only noncharitable beneficiary (other than the donor) of a charitable remainder annuity trust or charitable remainder unitrust described in section 664 (qualified charitable remainder trust), section 2523(b) does not apply to the interest in the trust transferred to the donee spouse. Thus, the value of the annuity or unitrust interest passing to the spouse qualifies for a marital deduction under section 2523(g) and the value of the remainder interest qualifies for a charitable deduction under section 2522.

(2) A marital deduction for the value of the donee spouse's annuity or unitrust interest in a qualified charitable remainder trust to which section 2523(g) applies is allowable only under section 2523(g). Therefore, if an interest in property qualifies for a marital deduction under section 2523(g), no election may be made with respect to the property under section 2523(f).

(3) The donee spouse's interest need not be an interest for life to qualify for a marital deduction under section 2523(g). However, for purposes of section 664, an annuity or unitrust interest payable to the spouse for a term of years cannot be payable for a term that exceeds 20 years or the trust does not qualify under section 2523(g).

(4) A deduction is allowed under section 2523(g) even if the transfer to the donee spouse is conditioned on the donee spouse's payment of state death taxes, if any, attributable to the qualified charitable remainder trust.

(5) For purposes of this section, the term noncharitable beneficiary means any beneficiary of the qualified charitable remainder trust other than an organization described in section 170(c).

(b) Charitable remainder trusts where the donee spouse and the donor are not the only noncharitable beneficiaries. In the case of a charitable remainder trust where the donor and the donor's spouse are not the only noncharitable beneficiaries (for example, where the noncharitable interest is payable to the donor's spouse for life and then to another individual (other than the donor) for life), the qualification of the interest as qualified terminable interest property is determined solely under section 2523(f) and not under section 2523(g). Accordingly, if the transfer to the trust is made prior to October 24, 1992, the spousal annuity or unitrust interest may qualify under § 25.2523(f)–(1)(c)(3) as a qualifying income interest for life.

[T.D. 8522, 59 FR 9642, Mar. 1, 1994]

§ 25.2523(h)–1 Denial of double deduction.

The value of an interest in property may not be deducted for Federal gift tax purposes more than once with respect to the same donor. For example, assume that D, a donor, transferred a life estate in a farm to D's spouse, S, with a remainder to charity and that D elects to treat the property as qualified terminable interest property. The entire value of the property is deductible under section 2523(f). No part of the value of the property qualifies for a charitable deduction under section 2522 for gift tax purposes.

[T.D. 8522, 59 FR 9642, Mar. 1, 1994]

§ 25.2523(i)–1 Disallowance of marital deduction when spouse is not a United States citizen.

(a) In general. Subject to § 20.2056A–1(c) of this chapter, section 2523(i)(1) disallows the marital deduction if the spouse of the donor is not a citizen of the United States at the time of the gift. If the spouse of the donor is a citizen of the United States at the time of the gift, the gift tax marital deduction under section 2523(a) is allowed regardless of whether the donor is a citizen or resident of the United States at the time of the gift, subject to the otherwise applicable rules of section 2523.

(b) Exception for certain joint and survivor annuities. Paragraph (a) does not apply to disallow the marital deduction with respect to any transfer resulting in the acquisition of rights by a noncitizen spouse under a joint and survivor annuity described in section 2523(f)(6).

(c) Increased annual exclusion—(1) In general. In the case of gifts made from a donor to the donor's spouse for which a marital deduction is not allowable under this section, if the gift otherwise qualifies for the gift tax annual exclusion under section 2503(b), the amount of the annual exclusion under section 2503(b) is $100,000 in lieu of $10,000. However, in the case of gifts made after June 29, 1989, in order for the increased annual exclusion to apply, the gift in excess of the otherwise applicable annual exclusion under section 2503(b) must be in a form that qualifies for the marital deduction but for the disallowance provision of section 2523(i)(1). See paragraph (d), Example 4, of this section.

(2) Status of donor. The $100,000 annual exclusion for gifts to a noncitizen spouse is available regardless of the status of the donor. Accordingly, it is immaterial whether the donor is a citizen, resident or a nonresident not a citizen of the United States, as long as the spouse of the donor is not a citizen of the United States at the time of the gift and the conditions for allowance of the increased annual exclusion have been satisfied. See § 25.2503–2(f).

(d) Examples. The principles outlined in this section are illustrated in the following examples. Assume in each of the examples that the donee, S, is D's spouse and is not a United States citizen at the time of the gift.

Example 1. Outright transfer of present interest. In 1995, D, a United States citizen, transfers to S, outright, 100 shares of X corporation stock valued for federal gift tax purposes at $130,000. The transfer is a gift of a present interest in property under section 2503(b). Additionally, the gift qualifies for the gift tax marital deduction except for the disallowance provision of section 2523(i)(1). Accordingly, $100,000 of the $130,000 gift is excluded from the total amount of gifts made during the calendar year by D for gift tax purposes.

Example 2. Transfer of survivor benefits. In 1995, D, a United States citizen, retires from employment in the United States and elects to receive a reduced retirement annuity in order to provide S with a survivor annuity upon D's death. The transfer of rights to S in the joint and survivor annuity is a gift by D for gift tax purposes. However, under paragraph (b) of this section, the gift qualifies for the gift tax marital deduction even though S is not a United States citizen.

Example 3. Transfer of present interest in trust property. In 1995, D, a resident alien, transfers property valued at $500,000 in trust to S, who is also a resident alien. The trust instrument provides that the trust income is payable to S at least quarterly and S has a testamentary general power to appoint the trust corpus. The transfer to S qualifies for the marital deduction under section 2523 but for the provisions of section 2523(i)(1). Because S has a life income interest in the trust, S has a present interest in a portion of the trust. Accordingly, D may exclude the present value of S's income interest (up to $100,000) from D's total 1995 calendar year gifts.

Example 4. Transfer of present interest in trust property. The facts are the same as in Example 3, except that S does not have a testamentary general power to appoint the trust corpus. Instead, D's child, C, has a remainder interest in the trust. If S were a United States citizen, the transfer would qualify for the gift tax marital deduction if a qualified terminable interest property election was made under section 2523(f)(4). However, because S is not a U.S. citizen, D may not make a qualified terminable interest property election. Accordingly, the gift does not qualify for the gift tax marital deduction but for the disallowance provision of section 2523(i)(1). The $100,000 annual exclusion under section 2523(i)(2) is not available with respect to D's transfer in trust and D may not exclude the present value of S's income interest in excess of $10,000 from D's total 1995 calendar year gifts.

Example 5. Spouse becomes citizen after transfer. D, a United States citizen, transfers a residence valued at $350,000 on December 20, 1995, to D's spouse, S, a resident alien. On January 31, 1996, S becomes a naturalized United States citizen. On D's federal gift tax return for 1995, D must include $250,000 as a gift ($350,000 transfer less $100,000 exclusion). Although S becomes a citizen in January, 1996, S is not a citizen of the United States at the time the transfer is made. Therefore, no gift tax marital deduction is allowable. However, the transfer does qualify for the $100,000 annual exclusion.

[T.D. 8612, 60 FR 43531, Aug. 22, 1995]

TAX ON GENERATION SKIPPING TRANSFERS

§ 26.2601–1 Effective dates.

(a) Transfers subject to the generation-skipping transfer tax—(1) In general. Except as otherwise provided in this section, the provisions of chapter 13 of the Internal Revenue Code of 1986 (Code) apply to any generation-skipping transfer (as defined in section 2611) made after October 22, 1986.

(2) Certain transfers treated as if made after October 22, 1986. Solely for purposes of chapter 13, an inter vivos transfer is treated as if it were made on October 23, 1986, if it was—

(i) Subject to chapter 12 (regardless of whether a tax was actually incurred or paid); and

(ii) Made after September 25, 1985, but before October 23, 1986. For purposes of this paragraph, the value of the property transferred shall be the value of the property on the date the property was transferred.

(3) Certain trust events treated as if occurring after October 22, 1986. For purposes of chapter 13, if an inter vivos transfer is made to a trust after September 25, 1985, but before October 23, 1986, any subsequent distribution from the trust or termination of an interest in the trust that occurred before October 23, 1986, is treated as occurring immediately after the deemed transfer on October 23, 1986. If more than one distribution or termination occurs with respect to a trust, the events are treated as if they occurred on October 23, 1986, in the same order as they occurred. See paragraph (b)(1)(iv)(B) of this section for rules determining the portion of distributions and terminations subject to tax under chapter 13. This paragraph (a)(3) does not apply to transfers to trusts not subject to chapter 13 by reason of the transition rules in paragraphs (b) (2) and (3) of this section. The provisions of this paragraph (a)(3) do not apply in determining the value of the property under chapter 13.

(4) Example. The following example illustrates the principle that paragraph (a)(2) of this section is not applicable to transfers under a revocable trust that became irrevocable by reason of the transferor's death after September 25, 1985, but before October 23, 1986:

Example. T created a revocable trust on September 30, 1985, that became irrevocable when T died on October 10, 1986. Although the trust terminated in favor of a grandchild of T, the transfer to the grandchild is not treated as occurring on October 23, 1986, pursuant to paragraph (a)(2) of this section because it is not an inter vivos transfer subject to chapter 12. The transfer is not subject to chapter 13 because it is in the nature of a testamentary transfer that occurred prior to October 23, 1986.

(b) Exceptions—(1) Irrevocable trusts—(i) In general. The provisions of chapter 13 do not apply to any generation-skipping transfer under a trust (as defined in section 2652(b)) that was irrevocable on September 25, 1985. The rule of the preceding sentence does not apply to a pro rata portion of any generation-skipping transfer under an irrevocable trust if additions are made to the trust after September 25, 1985. See paragraph (b)(1)(iv) of this section for rules for determining the portion of the trust that is subject to the provisions of chapter 13. Further, the rule in the first sentence of this paragraph (b)(1)(i) does not apply to a transfer of property pursuant to the exercise, release, or lapse of a general power of appointment that is treated as a taxable transfer under chapter 11 or chapter 12. The transfer is made by the person holding the power at the time the exercise, release, or lapse of the power becomes effective, and is not considered a transfer under a trust that was irrevocable on September 25, 1985. See paragraph (b)(1)(v)(B) of this section regarding the treatment of the release, exercise, or lapse of a power of appointment that will result in a constructive addition to a trust. See § 26.2652–1(a) for the definition of a transferor.

(ii) Irrevocable trust defined—(A) In general. Unless otherwise provided in either paragraph (b)(1)(ii)(B) or (C) of this section, any trust (as defined in section 2652(b)) in existence on September 25, 1985, is considered an irrevocable trust.

(B) Property includible in the gross estate under section 2038. For purposes of this chapter a trust is not an irrevocable trust to the extent that, on September 25, 1985, the settlor held a power with respect to such trust that would have caused the value of the trust to be included in the settlor's gross estate for Federal estate tax purposes by reason of section 2038 (without regard to powers relinquished before September 25, 1985) if the settlor had died on September 25, 1985. A trust is considered subject to a power on September 25, 1985, even though the exercise of the power was subject to the precedent giving of notice, or even though the exercise could take effect only on the expiration of a stated period, whether or not on or before September 25, 1985, notice had been given or the power had been exercised. A trust is not considered subject to a power if the power is, by its terms, exercisable only on the occurrence of an event or contingency not subject to the settlor's control (other than the death of the settlor) and if the event or contingency had not in fact taken place on September 25, 1985.

(C) Property includible in the gross estate under section 2042. A policy of insurance on an individual's life that is treated as a trust under section 2652(b) is not considered an irrevocable trust to the extent that, on September 25, 1985, the insured possessed any incident of ownership (as defined in § 20.2042–1(c) of this chapter, and without regard to any incidents of ownership relinquished before September 25, 1985), that would have caused the value of the trust, (i.e., the insurance proceeds) to be included in the insured's gross estate for Federal estate tax purposes by reason of section 2042, if the insured had died on September 25, 1985.

(D) Examples. The following examples illustrate the application of this paragraph (b)(1):

Example 1. Section 2038 applicable. On September 25, 1985, T, the settlor of a trust that was created before September 25, 1985, held a testamentary power to add new beneficiaries to the trust. T held no other powers over any portion of the trust. The testamentary power held by T would have caused the trust to be included in T's gross estate under section 2038 if T had died on September 25, 1985. Therefore, the trust is not an irrevocable trust for purposes of this section.

Example 2. Section 2038 not applicable when power held by a person other than settlor. On September 25, 1985, S, the spouse of the settlor of a trust in existence on that date, had an annual right to withdraw a portion of the principal of the trust. The trust was otherwise irrevocable on that date. Because the power was not held by the settlor of the trust, it is not a power described in section 2038. Thus, the trust is considered an irrevocable trust for purposes of this section.

Example 3. Section 2038 not applicable. In 1984, T created a trust and retained the right to expand the class of remaindermen to include any of T's afterborn grandchildren. As of September 25, 1985, all of T's grandchildren were named remaindermen of the trust. Since the exercise of T's power was dependent on there being afterborn grandchildren who were not members of the class of remaindermen, a contingency that did not exist on September 25, 1985, the trust is not considered subject to the power on September 25, 1985, and is an irrevocable trust for purposes of this section. The result is not changed even if grandchildren are born after September 25, 1985, whether or not T exercises the power to expand the class of remaindermen.

Example 4. Section 2042 applicable. On September 25, 1985, T purchased an insurance policy on T's own life and designated child, C, and grandchild, GC, as the beneficiaries. T retained the power to obtain from the insurer a loan against the surrender value of the policy. T's insurance policy is a trust (as defined in section 2652(b)) for chapter 13 purposes. The trust is not considered an irrevocable trust because, on September 25, 1985, T possessed an incident of ownership that would have caused the value of the policy to be included in T's gross estate under section 2042 if T had died on that date.

Example 5. Trust partially irrevocable. In 1984, T created a trust naming T's grandchildren as the income and remainder beneficiaries. T retained the power to revoke the trust as to one-half of the principal at any time prior to T's death. T retained no other powers over the trust principal. T did not die before September 25, 1985, and did not exercise or release the power before that date. The half of the trust not subject to T's power to revoke is an irrevocable trust for purposes of this section.

(iii) Trust containing qualified terminable interest property—(A) In general. For purposes of chapter 13, a trust described in paragraph (b)(1)(ii) of this section that holds qualified terminable interest property by reason of an election under section 2056(b)(7) or section 2523(f) (made either on, before or after September 25, 1985) is treated in the same manner as if the decedent spouse or the donor spouse (as the case may be) had made an election under section 2652(a)(3). Thus, transfers from such trusts are not subject to chapter 13, and the decedent spouse or the donor spouse (as the case may be) is treated as the transferor of such property. The rule of this paragraph (b)(1)(iii) does not apply to that portion of the trust that is subject to chapter 13 by reason of an addition to the trust occurring after September 25, 1985. See § 26.2652–2(a) for rules where an election under section 2652(a)(3) is made. See § 26.2652–2(c) for rules where a portion of a trust is subject to an election under section 2652(a)(3).

(B) Examples. The following examples illustrate the application of this paragraph (b)(1)(iii):

Example 1. QTIP election made after September 25, 1985. On March 28, 1985, T established a trust. The trust instrument provided that the trustee must distribute all income annually to T's spouse, S, during S's life. Upon S's death, the remainder is to be distributed to GC, the grandchild of T and S. On April 15, 1986, T elected under section 2523(f) to treat the property in the trust as qualified terminable interest property. On December 1, 1987, S died and soon thereafter the trust assets were distributed to GC. Because the trust was irrevocable on September 25, 1985, the transfer to GC is not subject to tax under chapter 13. T is treated as the transferor with respect to the transfer of the trust assets to GC in the same manner as if T had made an election under section 2652(a)(3) to reverse the effect of the section 2523(f) election for chapter 13 purposes.

Example 2. Section 2652(a)(3) election deemed to have been made. Assume the same facts as in Example 1, except the trust instrument provides that after S's death all income is to be paid annually to C, the child of T and S. Upon C's death, the remainder is to be distributed to GC. C died on October 1, 1992, and soon thereafter the trust assets are distributed to GC. Because the trust was irrevocable on September 25, 1985, the termination of C's interest is not subject to chapter 13.

(iv) Additions to irrevocable trusts—(A) In general. If an addition is made after September 25, 1985, to an irrevocable trust which is excluded from chapter 13 by reason of paragraph (b)(1) of this section, a pro rata portion of subsequent distributions from (and terminations of interests in property held in) the trust is subject to the provisions of chapter 13. If an addition is made, the trust is thereafter deemed to consist of two portions, a portion not subject to chapter 13 (the non-chapter 13 portion) and a portion subject to chapter 13 (the chapter 13 portion), each with a separate inclusion ratio (as defined in section 2642(a)). The non-chapter 13 portion represents the value of the assets of the trust as it existed on September 25, 1985. The applicable fraction (as defined in section 2642(a)(2)) for the non-chapter 13 portion is deemed to be 1 and the inclusion ratio for such portion is 0. The chapter 13 portion of the trust represents the value of all additions made to the trust after September 25, 1985. The inclusion ratio for the chapter 13 portion is determined under section 2642. This paragraph (b)(1)(iv)(A) requires separate portions of one trust only for purposes of determining inclusion ratios. For purposes of chapter 13, a constructive addition under paragraph (b)(1)(v) of this section is treated as an addition. See paragraph (b)(4) of this section for exceptions to the additions rule of this paragraph (b)(1)(iv). See § 26.2654-1(a)(2) for rules treating additions to a trust by an individual other than the initial transferor as a separate trust for purposes of chapter 13.

(B) Terminations of interests in and distributions from trusts. Where a termination or distribution described in section 2612 occurs with respect to a trust to which an addition has been made, the portion of such termination or distribution allocable to the chapter 13 portion is determined by reference to the allocation fraction, as defined in paragraph (b)(1)(iv)(C) of this section. In the case of a termination described in section 2612(a) with respect to a trust, the portion of such termination that is subject to chapter 13 is the product of the allocation fraction and the value of the trust (to the extent of the terminated interest therein). In the case of a distribution described in section 2612(b) from a trust, the portion of such distribution that is subject to chapter 13 is the product of the allocation fraction and the value of the property distributed.

(C) Allocation fraction—(1) In general. The allocation fraction allocates appreciation and accumulated income between the chapter 13 and non-chapter 13 portions of a trust. The numerator of the allocation fraction is the amount of the addition (valued as of the date the addition is made), determined without regard to whether any part of the transfer is subject to tax under chapter 11 or chapter 12, but reduced by the amount of any Federal or state estate or gift tax imposed and subsequently paid by the recipient trust with respect to the addition. The denominator of the allocation fraction is the total value of the entire trust immediately after the addition. For purposes of this paragraph (b)(1)(iv)(C), the total value of the entire trust is the fair market value of the property held in trust (determined under the rules of section 2031), reduced by any amount attributable to or paid by the trust and attributable to the transfer to the trust that is similar to an amount that would be allowable as a deduction under section 2053 if the addition had occurred at the death of the transferor, and further reduced by the same amount that the numerator was reduced to reflect Federal or state estate or gift tax incurred by and subsequently paid by the recipient trust with respect to the addition. Where there is more than one addition to principal after September 25, 1985, the portion of the trust subject to chapter 13 after each such addition is determined pursuant to a revised fraction. In each case, the numerator of the revised fraction is the sum of the value of the chapter 13 portion of the trust immediately before the latest addition, and the amount of the latest addition. The denominator of the revised fraction is the total value of the entire trust immediately after the addition. If the transfer to the trust is a generation- skipping transfer, the numerator and denominator are reduced by the amount of the generation-skipping transfer tax, if any, that is imposed by chapter 13 on the transfer and actually recovered from the trust. The allocation fraction is rounded off to five decimal places (.00001).

(2) Examples. The following examples illustrate the application of paragraph (b)(1)(iv) of this section. In each of the examples, assume that the recipient trust does not pay any Federal or state transfer tax by reason of the addition.

Example 1. Post September 25, 1985, addition to trust. (i) On August 16, 1980, T established an irrevocable trust. Under the trust instrument, the trustee is required to distribute the entire income annually to T's child, C, for life, then to T's grandchild, GC, for life. Upon GC's death, the remainder is to be paid to GC's issue. On October 1, 1986, when the total value of the entire trust is $400,000, T transfers $100,000 to the trust. The allocation fraction is computed as follows:

$$\frac{\text{Value of addition}}{\text{Total value of trust}} = \frac{\$100{,}000}{\$400{,}000 + \$100{,}000} = .2$$

(ii) Thus, immediately after the transfer, 20 percent of the value of future generation-skipping transfers under the trust will be subject to chapter 13.

Example 2. Effect of expenses. Assume the same facts as in Example 1, except immediately prior to the transfer on October 1, 1986, the fair market value of the individual assets in the trust totaled $400,000. Also, assume that the trust had accrued and unpaid debts, expenses, and taxes totaling $300,000. Assume further that the entire $300,000 represented amounts that would be deductible under section 2053 if the trust were includible in the transferor's gross estate. The numerator of the allocation fraction is $100,000 and the denominator of the allocation fraction is $200,000 (($400,000–$300,000) + $100,000). Thus, the allocation fraction is .5 ($100,000/ $200,000) and 50 percent of the value of future generation-skipping transfers will be subject to chapter 13.

Example 3. Multiple additions. (i) Assume the same facts as in Example 1, except on January 30, 1988, when the total value of the entire trust is $600,000, T transfers an additional $40,000 to the trust. Before the transfer, the value of the portion of the trust that was attributable to the prior addition was $120,000 ($600,- 000x.2). The new allocation fraction is computed as follows:

$$\frac{\text{Total value of additions}}{\text{Total value of trust}} = \frac{\$120{,}000 + \$40{,}000}{\$600{,}000 + \$40{,}000} = \frac{\$160{,}000}{\$640{,}000} = .25$$

(ii) Thus, immediately after the transfer, 25 percent of the value of future generation-skipping transfers under the trust will be subject to chapter 13.

Example 4. Allocation fraction at time of generation-skipping transfer. Assume the same facts as in Example 3, except on March 1, 1989, when the value of the trust is $800,000, C dies. A generation-skipping transfer occurs at C's death because of the termination of C's life estate. Therefore, $200,000 ($800,000 x.25) is subject to tax under chapter 13.

(v) Constructive additions—(A) Powers of Appointment. Except as provided in paragraph (b)(1)(v)(B) of this section, where any portion of a trust remains in the trust after the post-September 25, 1985, release, exercise, or lapse of a power of appointment over that portion of the trust, and the release, exercise, or lapse is treated to any extent as a taxable transfer under chapter 11 or chapter 12, the value of the entire portion of the trust subject to the power that was released, exercised, or lapsed is treated as if that portion had been withdrawn and immediately retransferred to the trust at the time of the release, exercise, or lapse. The creator of the power will be considered the transferor of the addition except to the extent that the release, exercise, or lapse of the power is treated as a taxable transfer under chapter 11 or chapter 12. See § 26.2652–1 for rules for determining the identity of the transferor of property for purposes of chapter 13.

(B) Special rule for certain powers of appointment. The release, exercise, or lapse of a power of appointment (other than a general power of appointment as defined in section 2041(b)) is not treated as an addition to a trust if—

(1) Such power of appointment was created in an irrevocable trust that is not subject to chapter 13 under paragraph (b)(1) of this section; and

(2) In the case of an exercise, the power of appointment is not exercised in a manner that may postpone or suspend the vesting, absolute ownership or power of alienation of an interest in property for a period, measured from the date of creation of the trust, extending beyond any life in being at the date of creation of the trust plus a period of 21 years plus, if necessary, a reasonable period of gestation (the perpetuities period). For purposes of this paragraph (b)(1)(v)(B)(2), the exercise of a power of appointment that validly postpones or suspends the vesting, absolute ownership or power of alienation of an interest in property for a term of years that will not exceed 90 years (measured from the date of creation of the trust) will not be considered an exercise that postpones or suspends vesting, absolute ownership or the power of alienation beyond the perpetuities period. If a power is exercised by creating another power, it is deemed to be exercised to whatever extent the second power may be exercised.

(C) Constructive addition if liability is not paid out of trust principal. Where a trust described in paragraph (b)(1) of this section is relieved of any liability properly payable out of the assets of such trust, the person or entity who actually satisfies the liability is considered to have made a constructive addition to the trust in an amount equal to the liability. The constructive addition occurs when the trust is relieved of liability (e.g., when the right of recovery is no longer enforceable). But see § 26.2652–1(a)(3) for rules involving the application of section 2207A in the case of an election under section 2652(a)(3).

(D) Examples. The following examples illustrate the application of this paragraph (b)(1)(v):

Example 1. Lapse of a power of appointment. On June 19, 1980, T established an irrevocable trust with a corpus of $500,000. The trust instrument provides that the trustee shall distribute the entire income from the trust annually to T's spouse, S, during S's life. At S's death, the remainder is to be distributed to T and S's grandchild, GC. T also gave S a general power of appointment over one-half of the trust assets. On December 21, 1989, when the value of the trust corpus is $1,500,000, S died without having exercised the general power of appointment. The value of one-half of the trust corpus, $750,000 ($1,500,000 x .5) is included in S's gross estate under section 2041(a) and is subject to tax under Chapter 11. Because the value of one-half of the trust corpus is subject to tax under Chapter 11 with respect to S's estate, S is treated as the transferor of that property for purposes of Chapter 13 (see section 2652(a)(1)(A)). For purposes of the generation-skipping transfer tax, the lapse of S's power of appointment is treated as if $750,000 ($1,500,000 x .5) had been distributed to S and then transferred back to the trust. Thus, S is considered to have added $750,000 ($1,500,000 x .5) to the trust at the date of S's death. Because this constructive addition occurred after September 25, 1985, 50 percent of the corpus of the trust became subject to Chapter 13 at S's death.

Example 2. Multiple actual additions. On June 19, 1980, T established an irrevocable trust with a principal of $500,000. The trust instrument provides that the trustee shall distribute the entire income from the trust annually to T's spouse, S, during S's life. At S's death, the remainder is to be distributed to GC, the grandchild of T and S. On October 1, 1985, when the trust assets were valued at $800,000, T added $200,000 to the trust. After the transfer on October 1, 1985, the allocation fraction was .2 ($200,000/$1,000,000). On December 21, 1989, when the value of the trust principal is $1,000,000, T adds $1,000,000 to the trust. After this addition, the new allocation fraction is 0.6 ($1,200,000/$2,000,000). The numerator of the fraction is the value of that portion of trust assets that were subject to chapter 13 immediately prior to the addition (by reason of the first addition), $200,000 (.2 x $1,000,000), plus the value of the second transfer, $1,000,000, which equals $1,200,000. The denominator of the fraction, $2,000,000, is the total value of the trust assets immediately after the second transfer. Thus, 60 percent of the principal of the trust becomes subject to chapter 13.

Example 3. Entire portion of trust subject to lapsed power is treated as an addition. On September 25, 1985, B possessed a general power of appointment over the assets of an irrevocable trust that had been created by T in 1980. Under the terms of the trust, B's power lapsed on July 20, 1987. For Federal gift tax purposes, B is treated as making a gift of ninety-five percent (100%—5%) of the value of the principal (see section 2514). However, because the entire trust was subject to the power of appointment, 100 percent (that portion of the trust subject to the power) of the assets of the trust are treated as a constructive addition. Thus, the entire amount of all generation-skipping transfers occurring pursuant to the trust instrument after July 20, 1987, are subject to chapter 13.

Example 4. Exercise of power of appointment in favor of another trust. On March 1, 1985, T established an irrevocable trust as defined in paragraph (b)(1)(ii) of this section. Under the terms of the trust instrument, the trustee is required to distribute the entire income annually to T's child, C, for life, then to T's grandchild, GC, for life. GC has the power to appoint any or all of the trust assets to Trust 2 which is an irrevocable trust (as defined in paragraph (b)(1)(ii) of this section) that was established on August 1, 1985. The terms of Trust 2's governing instrument provide that the trustee shall pay income to T's great grandchild, GGC, for life. Upon GGC's death, the remainder is to be paid to GGC's issue. GGC was alive on March 1, 1985, when Trust 1 was created. C died on April 1, 1986. On July 1, 1987, GC exercised the power of appointment. The exercise of GC's power does not subject future transfers from Trust 2 to tax under chapter 13 because the exercise of the power in favor of Trust 2 does not suspend the vesting, absolute ownership, or power of alienation of an interest in property for a period, measured from the date of creation of Trust 1, extending beyond the life of GGC (a beneficiary under Trust 2 who was in being at the date of creation of Trust 1) plus a period of 21 years. The result would be the same if Trust 2 had been created after the effective date of chapter 13.

Example 5. Exercise of power of appointment in favor of another trust. Assume the same facts as in Example 4, except that GGC was born on March 28, 1986. The valid exercise of GC's power in favor of Trust 2 causes the principal of Trust 1 to be subject to chapter 13, because GGC was not born until after the creation of Trust 1. Thus, such exercise may suspend the vesting, absolute ownership, or power of alienation of an interest in the trust principal for a period, measured from the date of creation of Trust 1, extending beyond the life of GGC (a beneficiary under Trust 2 who was not a life in being at the date of creation of Trust 1).

Example 6. Extension for the longer of two periods. Prior to the effective date of chapter 13, GP established an irrevocable trust under which the trust income was to be paid to GP's child, C, for life. C was given a testamentary power to appoint the remainder in further trust for the benefit of C's issue. In default of C's exercise of the power, the remainder was to pass to charity. C died on February 3, 1995, survived by a child who was alive when GP established the trust. C exercised the power in a manner that validly extends the trust in favor of C's issue until the latter of May 15, 2064 (80 years from the date the trust was created), or the death of C's child plus 21 years. C's exercise of the power is a constructive addition to the trust because the exercise may extend the trust for a period longer than the permissible periods of either the life of C's child (a life in being at the creation of the trust) plus 21 years or a term not more than 90 years measured from the creation of the trust. On the other hand, if C's exercise of the power could extend the trust based only on the life of C's child plus 21 years or only for a term of 80 years from the creation of the trust (but not the later of the two periods) then the exercise of the power would not have been a constructive addition to the trust.

Example 7. Extension for the longer of two periods. The facts are the same as in Example 6 except local law provides that the effect of C's exercise is to extend the term of the trust until May 15, 2064, whether or not C's child predeceases that date by more than 21 years. C's exercise is not a constructive addition to the trust because C exercised the power in a manner that cannot postpone or suspend vesting, absolute ownership, or power of alienation for a term of years that will exceed 90 years. The result would be the same if the effect of C's exercise is either to extend the term of the trust until 21 years after the death of C's child or to extend the term of the trust until the first to occur of May 15, 2064 or 21 years after the death of C's child.

(vi) Appreciation and income. Except to the extent that the provisions of paragraphs (b)(1)(iv) and (v) of this section allocate subsequent appreciation and accumulated income between the original trust and additions thereto, appreciation in the value of the trust and undistributed income added thereto are not considered an addition to the principal of a trust.

(2) Transition rule for wills or revocable trusts executed before October 22, 1986—(i) In general. The provisions of chapter 13 do not apply to any generation-skipping transfer under a will or revocable trust executed before October 22, 1986, provided that—

(A) The document in existence on October 21, 1986, is not amended at any time after October 21, 1986, in any respect which results in the creation of, or an increase in the amount of, a generation-skipping transfer;

(B) In the case of a revocable trust, no addition is made to the revocable trust after October 21, 1986, that results in the creation of, or an increase in the amount of, a generation-skipping transfer; and

(C) The decedent dies before January 1, 1987.

(ii) Revocable trust defined. For purposes of this section, the term revocable trust means any trust (as defined in section 2652(b)) except to the extent that, on October 22, 1986, the trust—

(A) Was an irrevocable trust described in paragraph (b)(1) of this section; or

(B) Would have been an irrevocable trust described in paragraph (b)(1) of this section had it not been created or become irrevocable after September 25, 1985, and before October 22, 1986.

(iii) Will or revocable trust containing qualified terminable interest property. The rules contained in paragraph (b)(1)(iii) of this section apply to any will or revocable trust within the scope of the transition rule of this paragraph (b)(2).

(iv) Amendments to will or revocable trust. For purposes of this paragraph (b)(2), an amendment to a will or a revocable trust in existence on October 21, 1986, is not considered to result in the creation of, or an increase in the amount of, a generation-skipping transfer where the amendment is—

(A) Basically administrative or clarifying in nature and only incidentally increases the amount transferred; or

(B) Designed to ensure that an existing bequest or transfer qualifies for the applicable marital or charitable deduction for estate, gift, or generation-skipping transfer tax purposes and only incidentally increases the amount transferred to a skip person or to a generation-skipping trust.

(v) Creation of, or increase in the amount of, a GST. In determining whether a particular amendment to a will or revocable trust creates, or increases the amount of, a generation-skipping transfer for purposes of this paragraph (b)(2), the effect of the instrument(s) in existence on October 21, 1986, is measured against the effect of the instrument(s) in existence on the date of death of the decedent or on the date of any prior generation-skipping transfer. If the effect of an amendment cannot be immediately determined, it is deemed to create, or increase the amount of, a generation-skipping transfer until a determination can be made.

(vi) Additions to revocable trusts. Any addition made after October 21, 1986, but before the death of the settlor, to a revocable trust subjects all subsequent generation-skipping transfers under the trust to the provisions of chapter 13. Any addition made to a revocable trust after the death of the settlor (if the settlor dies before January 1, 1987) is treated as an addition to an irrevocable trust. See paragraph (b)(1)(v) of this section for rules involving constructive additions to trusts. See paragraph (b)(1)(v)(B) of this section for rules providing that certain transfers to trusts are not treated as additions for purposes of this section.

(vii) Examples. The following examples illustrate the application of paragraph (b)(2)(iv) of this section:

(A) Facts applicable to Examples 1 through 5. In each of Examples 1 through 5 assume that T executed a will prior to October 22, 1986, and that T dies on December 31, 1986.

Example 1. Administrative change. On November 1, 1986, T executes a codicil to T's will removing one of the co-executors named in the will. Although the codicil may have the effect of lowering administrative costs and thus increasing the amount transferred, it is considered administrative in nature and thus does not cause generation-skipping transfers under the will to be subject to chapter 13.

Example 2. Effect of amendment not immediately determinable. On November 1, 1986, T executes a codicil to T's will revoking a bequest of $100,000 to C, a non-skip person (as defined under section 2613(b)) and causing that amount to be added to a residuary trust held for a skip person. The amendment is deemed to increase the amount of a generation-skipping transfer and prevents any transfers under the will from qualifying under paragraph (b)(2)(i) of this section. If, however, C dies before T and under local law the property would have been added to the residue in any event because the bequest would have lapsed, the codicil is not considered an amendment that increases the amount of a generation-skipping transfer.

Example 3. Refund of tax paid because of amendment. T's will provided that an amount equal to the maximum allowable marital deduction would pass to T's spouse with the residue of the estate passing to a trust established for the benefit of skip persons. On October 23, 1986, the will is amended to provide that the marital share passing to T's spouse shall be the lesser of the maximum allowable marital deduction or the minimum amount that will result in no estate tax liability for T's estate. The amendment may increase the amount of a generation-skipping transfer. Therefore, any generation-skipping transfers under the will are subject to tax under chapter 13. If it becomes apparent that the amendment does not increase the amount of a generation-skipping transfer, a claim for refund may be filed with respect to any generation-skipping transfer tax that was paid within the period set forth in section 6511. For example, it would become apparent that the amendment did not result in an increase in the residue if it is subsequently determined that the maximum marital deduction and the minimum amount that will result in no estate tax liability are equal in amount.

Example 4. An amendment that increases a generation-skipping transfer causes complete loss of exempt status. T's will provided for the creation of two trusts for the benefit of skip persons. On November 1, 1986, T executed a codicil to the will specifically increasing the amount of a generation-skipping transfer under the will. All transfers made pursuant to the will or either of the trusts created thereunder are precluded from qualifying under the transition rule of paragraph (b)(2)(i) of this section and are subject to tax under chapter 13.

Example 5. Corrective action effective. Assume that T in Example 4 later executes a second codicil deleting the increase to the generation-skipping transfer. Because the provision increasing a generation-skipping transfer does not become effective, it is not considered an amendment to a will in existence on October 22, 1986.

(B) Facts applicable to Examples 6 through 8. T created a trust on September 30, 1985, in which T retained the power to revoke the transfer at any time prior to T's death. The trust provided that, upon the death of T, the income was to be paid to T's spouse, W, for life and then to A, B, and C, the children of T's sibling, S, in equal shares for life, with one-third of the principal to be distributed per stirpes to each child's surviving issue upon the death of the child. The trustee has the power to make discretionary distributions of trust principal to T's sibling, S.

Example 6. Amendment that affects only a person who is not a skip person. A became disabled, and T modified the trust on December 1, 1986, to increase A's share of the income. Since the amendment does not result in the creation of, or increase in the amount of, a generation-skipping transfer, transfers pursuant to the trust are not subject to chapter 13.

Example 7. Amendment that adds a skip person. Assume that T amends the trust to add T's grandchild, D, as an income beneficiary. The trust will be subject to the provisions of chapter 13 because the amendment creates a generation-skipping transfer.

Example 8. Refund of tax paid during interim period when effect of amendment is not determinable. Assume that T amends the trust to provide that the issue of S are to take a one-fourth share of the principal per stirpes upon S's death. Because the distribution to be made upon S's death may involve skip persons, the amendment is considered an amendment that creates or increases the amount of a generation-skipping transfer until a determination can be made. Accordingly, any distributions from (or terminations of interests in) such trust are subject to chapter 13 until it is determined that no skip person has been added to the trust. At that time, a claim for refund may be filed within the period set forth in section 6511 with respect to any generation-skipping transfer tax that was paid.

(3) Transition rule in the case of mental incompetency—(i) In general. If an individual was under a mental disability to change the disposition of his or her property continuously from October 22, 1986, until the date of his or her death, the provisions of chapter 13 do not apply to any generation-skipping transfer-(A) Under a trust (as defined in section 2652(b)) to the extent such trust consists of property, or the proceeds of property, the value of which was included in the gross estate of the individual (other than property transferred by or on behalf of the individual during the individual's life after October 22, 1986); or

(B) Which is a direct skip (other than a direct skip from a trust) that occurs by reason of the death of the individual.

(ii) Mental disability defined. For purposes of this paragraph (b)(2), the term mental disability means mental incompetence to execute an instrument governing the disposition of the individual's property, whether or not there was an adjudication of incompetence and regardless of whether there has been an appointment of a guardian, fiduciary, or other person charged with either the care of the individual or the care of the individual's property.

(iii) Decedent who has not been adjudged mentally incompetent. **(A)** If there has not been a court adjudication that the decedent was mentally incompetent on or before October 22, 1986, the executor must file, with Form 706, either—

(1) A certification from a qualified physician stating that the decedent was—

(i) mentally incompetent at all times on and after October 22, 1986; and

(ii) did not regain competence to modify or revoke the terms of the trust or will prior to his or her death; or

(2) Sufficient other evidence demonstrating that the decedent was mentally incompetent at all times on and after October 22, 1986, as well as a statement explaining why no certification is available from a physician; and

(3) Any judgment or decree relating to the decedent's incompetency that was made after October 22, 1986.

(B) Such items in paragraphs (b)(3)(iii)(A)(1), (2) and (3) of this section will be considered relevant, but not determinative, in establishing the decedent's state of competency.

(iv) Decedent who has been adjudged mentally incompetent. If the decedent has been adjudged mentally incompetent on or before October 22, 1986, a copy of the judgment or decree, and any modification thereof, must be filed with the Form 706.

(v) Rule applies even if another person has power to change trust terms. In the case of a transfer from a trust, this paragraph (b)(3) applies even though a person charged with the care of the decedent or the decedent's property has the power to revoke or modify the terms of the trust, provided that the power is not exercised after October 22, 1986, in a manner that creates, or increases the amount of, a generation-skipping transfer. See paragraph (b)(2)(iv) of this section for rules concerning amendments that create or increase the amount of a generation-skipping transfer.

(vi) Example. The following example illustrates the application of paragraph (b)(3)(v) of this section:

Example. T was mentally incompetent on October 22, 1986, and remained so until death in 1993. Prior to becoming incompetent, T created a revocable generation-skipping trust that was includible in T's gross estate. Prior to October 22, 1986, the appropriate court issued an order under which P, who was thereby charged with the care of T's property, had the power to modify or revoke the revocable trust. Although P exercised the power after October 22, 1986, and while T was incompetent, the power was not exercised in a manner that created, or increased the amount of, a generation-skipping transfer. Thus, the existence and exercise of P's power did not cause the trust to lose its exempt status under paragraph (b)(3) of this section. The result would be the same if the court order was issued after October 22, 1986.

* * *

(5) Exceptions to additions rule—(i) In general. Any addition to a trust made pursuant to an instrument or arrangement covered by the transition rules in paragraph (b)(1), (2) or (3) of this section is not treated as an addition for purposes of this section. Moreover, any property transferred inter vivos to a trust is not treated as an addition if the same property would have been added to the trust pursuant to an instrument covered by the transition rules in paragraph (b)(2) or (3) of this section.

(ii) Examples. The following examples illustrate the application of paragraph (b)(4)(i) of this section:

Example 1. Addition pursuant to terms of exempt instrument. On December 31, 1980, T created an irrevocable trust having a principal of $100,000. Under the terms of the trust, the principal was to be held for the benefit of T's grandchild, GC. Pursuant to the terms of T's will, a document entitled to relief under the transition rule of paragraph (b)(2) of this section, the residue of the estate was paid to the trust. Because the addition to the trust was paid pursuant to the terms of an instrument (T's will) that is not subject to the provisions of chapter 13 because of paragraph (b)(2) of this section, the payment to the trust is not considered an addition to the principal of the trust. Thus, distributions to or for the benefit of GC, are not subject to the provisions of chapter 13.

Example 2. Property transferred inter vivos that would have been transferred to the same trust by the transferor's will. T is the grantor of a trust that was irrevocable on September 25, 1985. T's will, which was executed before October 22, 1986, and not amended thereafter, provides that, upon T's death, the entire estate will pour over into T's trust. On October 1, 1985, T transfers $100,000 to the trust. While T's will otherwise qualifies for relief under the transition rule in paragraph (b)(2) of this section, the transition rule is not applicable unless T dies prior to January 1, 1987. Thus, if T dies after December 31, 1986, the transfer is treated as an addition to the trust for purposes of any distribution made from the trust after the transfer to the trust on October 1, 1985. If T dies before January 1, 1987, the entire trust (as well as any distributions from or terminations of interests in the trust prior to T's death) is exempt, under paragraph (b)(2) of this section, from chapter 13 because the $100,000 would have been added to the trust under a will that would have qualified under paragraph (b)(2) of this section. In either case, for any generation-skipping transfers made after the transfer to the trust on October 1, 1985, but before T's death, the $100,000 is treated as an addition to the trust and a proportionate amount of the trust is subject to chapter 13.

Example 3. Pour over to a revocable trust. T and S are the settlors of separate revocable trusts with equal values. Both trusts were established for the benefit of skip persons (as defined in section 2613). S dies on December 1, 1985, and under the provisions of S's trust, the principal pours over into T's trust. If T dies before January 1, 1987, the entire trust is excluded under paragraph (b)(2) of this section from the operation of chapter 13. If T dies after December 31, 1986, the entire trust is subject to the generation-skipping transfer tax provisions because T's trust is not a trust described in paragraph (b)(1) or (2) of this section. In the latter case, the fact that S died before January 1, 1987, is irrelevant because the principal of S's trust was added to a trust that never qualified under the transition rules of paragraph (b)(1) or (2) of this section.

Example 4. Pour over to exempt trust. Assume the same facts as in Example 3, except upon the death of S on December 1, 1985, S's trust continues as an irrevocable trust and that the principal of T's trust is to be paid over upon T's death to S's trust. Again, if T dies before January 1, 1987, S's entire trust falls within the provisions of paragraph (b)(2) of this section. However, if T dies after December 31, 1986, the pour-over is considered an addition to the trust. Therefore, S's trust is not a trust excluded under paragraph (b)(2) of this section because an addition is made to the trust.

Example 5. Lapse of a general power of appointment. S, the spouse of the settlor of an irrevocable trust that was created in 1980, had, on September 25, 1985, a general power of appointment over the trust assets. The trust provides that should S fail to exercise the power of appointment the property is to remain in the trust. On October 21, 1986, S executed a will under which S failed to exercise the power of appointment. If S dies before January 1, 1987, without having exercised the power in a manner which results in the creation of, or increase in the amount of, a generation-skipping transfer (or amended the will in a manner that results in the creation of, or increase in the amount of, a generation-skipping transfer), transfers pursuant to the trust or the will are not subject to chapter 13 because the trust is an irrevocable trust and the will qualifies under paragraph (b)(2) of this section.

Example 6. Lapse of general power of appointment held by intestate decedent. Assume the same facts as in Example 5, except on October 22, 1986, S did not have a will and that S dies after that date. Upon S's death, or upon the prior exercise or release of the power, the value of the entire trust is treated as having been distributed to S, and S is treated as having made an addition to the trust in the amount of the entire principal. Any distribution or termination pursuant to the trust occurring after S's death is subject to chapter 13. It is immaterial whether S's death occurs before January 1, 1987, since paragraph (b)(2) of this section is only applicable where a will or revocable trust was executed before October 22, 1986.

* * *

[T.D. 8644, 60 FR 66898, Dec. 27, 1995; 61 FR 29653, June 12, 1996; 61 FR 43656, Aug. 26, 1996; T.D. 8912, 65 FR 79738, Dec. 20, 2000; 66 FR 11108, Feb. 22, 2001; 66 FR 12834, Feb. 28, 2001; T.D. 9102, 69 FR 21, Jan. 2, 2004]

§ 26.2611–1 Generation-skipping transfer defined.

A generation-skipping transfer (GST) is an event that is either a direct skip, a taxable distribution, or a taxable termination. See § 26.2612–1 for the definition of these terms. The determination as to whether an event is a GST is made by reference to the most recent transfer subject to the estate or gift tax. See § 26.2652–1(a)(2) for determining whether a transfer is subject to Federal estate or gift tax.

[T.D. 8644, 60 FR 66898, Dec. 27, 1995]

§ 26.2612–1 Definitions.

(a) Direct skip—A direct skip is a transfer to a skip person that is subject to Federal estate or gift tax. If property is transferred to a trust, the transfer is a direct skip only if the trust is a skip person. Only one direct skip occurs when a single transfer of property skips two or more generations. See paragraph (d) of this section for the definition of skip person. See § 26.2652–1(b) for the definition of trust. See § 26.2632–1(c)(4) for the time that a direct skip occurs if the transferred property is subject to an estate tax inclusion period.

(b) Taxable termination—(1) In general. Except as otherwise provided in this paragraph (b), a taxable termination is a termination (occurring for any reason) of an interest in trust unless—

(i) A transfer subject to Federal estate or gift tax occurs with respect to the property held in the trust at the time of the termination;

(ii) Immediately after the termination, a person who is not a skip person has an interest in the trust; or

(iii) At no time after the termination may a distribution, other than a distribution the probability of which occurring is so remote as to be negligible (including a distribution at the termination of the trust) be made from the trust to a skip person. For this purpose, the probability that a distribution will occur is so remote as to be negligible only if it can be ascertained by actuarial standards that there is less than a 5 percent probability that the distribution will occur.

(2) Partial termination. If a distribution of a portion of trust property is made to a skip person by reason of a termination occurring on the death of a lineal descendant of the transferor, the termination is a taxable termination with respect to the distributed property.

(3) Simultaneous terminations. A simultaneous termination of two or more interests creates only one taxable termination.

(c) Taxable distribution—(1) In general. A taxable distribution is a distribution of income or principal from a trust to a skip person unless the distribution is a taxable termination or a direct skip. If any portion of GST tax (including penalties and interest thereon) imposed on a distributee is paid from the distributing trust, the payment is an additional taxable distribution to the distributee. For purposes of chapter 13, the additional distribution is treated as having been made on the last day of the calendar year in which the original taxable distribution is made. If Federal estate or gift tax is imposed on any individual with respect to an interest in property held by a trust, the interest in property is treated as having been distributed to the individual to the extent that the value of the interest is subject to Federal estate or gift tax. See § 26.2652–1(a)(6) Example 5, regarding the treatment of the lapse of a power of appointment as a transfer to a trust.

(2) Look-through rule not to apply. Solely for purposes of determining whether any transfer from a trust to another trust is a taxable distribution, the rules of section 2651(e)(2) do not apply. If the transferring trust and the recipient trust have the same transferor, see § 26.2642–4(a)(1) and (2) for rules for recomputing the applicable fraction of the recipient trust.

(d) Skip person. A skip person is—

(1) An individual assigned to a generation more than one generation below that of the transferor (determined under the rules of section 2651); or

(2) A trust if—

(i) All interests in the trust are held by skip persons; or

(ii) No person holds an interest in the trust and no distributions, other than a distribution the probability of which occurring is so remote as to be negligible (including distributions at the termination of the trust), may be made after the transfer to a person other than a skip person. For this purpose, the probability that a distribution will occur is so remote as to be negligible only if it can be ascertained by actuarial standards that there is less than a 5 percent probability that the distribution will occur.

(e) Interest in trust—(1) In general. An interest in trust is an interest in property held in trust as defined in section 2652(c) and these regulations. An interest in trust exists if a person—

(i) Has a present right to receive trust principal or income;

(ii) Is a permissible current recipient of trust principal or income and is not described in section 2055(a); or

(iii) Is described in section 2055(a) and the trust is a charitable remainder annuity trust or unitrust (as defined in section 664(d)) or a pooled income fund (as defined in section 642(c)(5)).

(2) Exceptions—(i) Support obligations. In general, an individual has a present right to receive trust income or principal if trust income or principal may be used to satisfy the individual's support obligations. However, an individual does not have an interest in a trust merely because a support obligation of that individual may be satisfied by a distribution that is either within the discretion of a fiduciary or pursuant to provisions of local law substantially equivalent to the Uniform Gifts (Transfers) to Minors Act.

(ii) Certain interests disregarded. An interest which is used primarily to postpone or avoid the GST tax is disregarded for purposes of chapter 13. An interest is considered as used primarily to postpone or avoid the GST tax if a significant purpose for the creation of the interest is to postpone or avoid the tax.

(3) Disclaimers. An interest does not exist to the extent it is disclaimed pursuant to a disclaimer that constitutes a qualified disclaimer under section 2518.

(f) Examples. The following examples illustrate the provisions of this section.

Example 1. Direct skip. T gratuitously conveys Blackacre to T's grandchild. Because the transfer is a transfer to a skip person of property subject to Federal gift tax, it is a direct skip.

Example 2. Direct skip of more than one generation. T gratuitously conveys Blackacre to T's great-grandchild. The transfer is a direct skip. Only one GST tax is imposed on the direct skip although two generations are skipped by the transfer.

Example 3. Withdrawal power in trust. T transfers $50,000 to a new trust providing that trust income is to be paid to T's child, C, for life and, on C's death, the trust principal is to be paid to T's descendants. Under the terms of the trust, T grants four grandchildren the right to withdraw $10,000 from the trust for a 60 day period following the transfer. Since C, who is not a skip person, has an interest in the trust, the trust is not a skip person. T's transfer to the trust is not a direct skip.

Example 4. Taxable termination. T establishes an irrevocable trust under which the income is to be paid to T's child, C, for life. On the death of C, the trust principal is to be paid to T's grandchild, GC. Since C has an interest in the trust, the trust is not a skip person and the transfer to the trust is not a direct skip. If C dies survived by GC, a taxable termination occurs at C's death because C's interest in the trust terminates and thereafter the trust property is held by a skip person who occupies a lower generation than C.

Example 5. Direct skip of property held in trust. T establishes a testamentary trust under which the income is to be paid to T's surviving spouse, S, for life and the remainder is to be paid to a grandchild of T and S. T's executor elects to treat the trust as qualified terminable interest property under section 2056(b)(7). The transfer to the trust is not a direct skip because S, a person who is not a skip person, holds a present right to receive income from the trust. Upon S's death, the trust property is included in S's gross estate under section 2044 and passes directly to a skip person. The GST occurring at that time is a direct skip because it is a transfer subject to chapter 11. The fact that the interest created by T is terminated at S's death is immaterial because S becomes the transferor at the time of the transfer subject to chapter 11.

Example 6. Taxable termination. T establishes an irrevocable trust for the benefit of T's child, C, T's grandchild, GC, and T's great-grandchild, GGC. Under the terms of the trust, income and principal may be distributed to any or all of the living beneficiaries at the discretion of the trustee. Upon the death of the second beneficiary to die, the trust principal is to be paid to the survivor. C dies first. A taxable termination occurs at that time because, immediately after C's interest terminates, all interests in the trust are held by skip persons (GC and GGC).

Example 7. Taxable termination resulting from distribution. The facts are the same as in Example 6, except twenty years after C's death the trustee exercises its discretionary power and distributes the entire principal to GGC. The distribution results in a taxable termination because GC's interest in the trust terminates as a result of the distribution of the entire trust property to GGC, a skip person. The result would be the same if the trustee retained sufficient funds to pay the GST tax due by reason of the taxable termination, as well as any expenses of winding up the trust.

Example 8. Simultaneous termination of interests of more than one beneficiary. T establishes an irrevocable trust for the benefit of T's child, C, T's grandchild, GC, and T's great-grandchild, GGC. Under the terms of the trust, income and principal may be distributed to any or all of the living beneficiaries at the discretion of the trustee. Upon the death of C, the trust property is to be distributed to GGC if then living. If C is survived by both GC and GGC, both C's and GC's interests in the trust will terminate on C's death. However, because both interests will terminate at the same time and as a result of one event, only one taxable termination occurs.

Example 9. Partial taxable termination. T creates an irrevocable trust providing that trust income is to be paid to T's children, A and B, in such proportions as the trustee determines for their joint lives. On the death of the first child to die, one-half of the trust principal is to be paid to T's then living grandchildren. The balance of the trust principal is to be paid to T's grandchildren on the death of the survivor of A and B. If A predeceases B, the distribution occurring on the termination of A's interest in the trust is a taxable termination and not a taxable distribution. It is a taxable termination because the distribution is a distribution of a portion of the trust that occurs as a result of the death of A, a lineal descendant of T. It is immaterial that a portion of the trust continues and that B, a person other than a skip person, thereafter holds an interest in the trust.

Example 10. Taxable distribution. T establishes an irrevocable trust under which the trust income is payable to T's child, C, for life. When T's grandchild, GC, attains 35 years of age, GC is to receive one-half of the principal. The remaining one-half of the principal is to be distributed to GC on C's death. Assume that C survives until GC attains age 35. When the trustee distributes one-half of the principal to GC on GC's 35th birthday, the distribution is a taxable distribution because it is a distribution to a skip person and is neither a taxable termination nor a direct skip.

Example 11. Exercise of withdrawal right as taxable distribution. The facts are the same as in Example 10, except GC holds a continuing right to withdraw trust principal and after one year GC withdraws $10,000. The withdrawal by GC is not a taxable termination because the withdrawal does not terminate C's interest in the trust. The withdrawal by GC is a taxable distribution to GC.

Example 12. Interest in trust. T establishes an irrevocable trust under which the income is to be paid to T's child, C, for life. On the death of C, the trust principal is to be paid to T's grandchild, GC. Because C has a present right to receive income from the trust, C has an interest in the trust. Because GC cannot currently receive distributions from the trust, GC does not have an interest in the trust.

Example 13. Support obligation. T establishes an irrevocable trust for the benefit of T's grandchild, GC. The trustee has discretion to distribute property for GC's support without regard to the duty or ability of GC's parent, C, to support GC. Because GC is a permissible current recipient of trust property, GC has an interest in the trust. C does not have an interest in the trust because the potential use of the trust property to satisfy C's support obligation is within the discretion of a fiduciary. C would be treated as having an interest in the trust if the trustee was required to distribute trust property for GC's support.

[T.D. 8644, 60 FR 66898, Dec. 27, 1995, as corrected by Announcement 96–72, 61 FR 29653, June 12, 1996; T.D. 9214, 70 FR 41142, July 18, 2005]

§ 26.2613–1 Skip person.

For the definition of skip person see § 26.2612–1(d).

[T.D. 8644, 60 FR 66898, Dec. 27, 1995]

§ 26.2632–1 Allocation of GST exemptions.

(a) General rule. Except as otherwise provided in this section, an individual or the individual's executor may allocate the individual's $1 million GST exemption at any time from the date of the transfer through the date for filing the individual's Federal estate tax return (including any extensions for filing that have been actually granted). If no estate tax return is required to be filed, the GST exemption may be allocated at any time through the date a Federal estate tax return would be due if a return were required to be filed (including any extensions actually granted). If property is held in trust, the allocation of GST exemption is made to the entire trust rather than to specific trust assets. If a transfer is a direct skip to a trust, the allocation of GST exemption to the transferred property is also treated as an allocation of GST exemption to the trust for purposes of future GSTs with respect to the trust by the same transferor.

(b) Lifetime allocations—(1) Automatic allocation to direct skips—(i) In general. If a direct skip occurs during the transferor's lifetime, the transferor's GST exemption not previously allocated (unused GST exemption) is automatically allocated to the transferred property (but not in excess of the fair market value of the property on the date of the transfer). The transferor may prevent the automatic allocation of GST exemption by describing on a timely-filed United States Gift (and Generation–Skipping Transfer) Tax Return (Form 709) the transfer and the extent to which the automatic allocation is not to apply. In addition, a timely-filed Form 709 accompanied by payment of the GST tax (as shown on the return with respect to the direct skip) is sufficient to prevent an automatic allocation of GST exemption with respect to the transferred property. See paragraph (c)(4) of this section for special rules in the case of direct skips treated as occurring at the termination of an estate tax inclusion period.

(ii) Time for filing Form 709. A Form 709 is timely filed if it is filed on or before the date required for reporting the transfer if it were a taxable gift (i.e., the date prescribed by section 6075(b), including any extensions to file actually granted (the due date)). Except as provided in paragraph (b)(1)(iii) of this section, the automatic allocation of GST exemption (or the election to prevent the allocation, if made) is irrevocable after the due date. An automatic allocation of GST exemption is effective as of the date of the transfer to which it relates. Except as provided above, a Form 709 need not be filed to report an automatic allocation.

(iii) Transitional rule. An election to prevent an automatic allocation of GST exemption filed on or before January 26, 1996, becomes irrevocable on July 24, 1996.

(2) Automatic allocation to indirect skips made after December 31, 2000—(i) In general. An indirect skip is a transfer of property to a GST trust as defined in section 2632(c)(3)(B) provided that the transfer is subject to gift tax and does not qualify as a direct skip. In the case of an indirect skip made after December 31, 2000, to which section 2642(f) (relating to transfers subject to an estate tax inclusion period (ETIP)) does not apply, the transferor's unused GST exemption is automatically allocated to the property transferred (but not in excess of the fair market value of the property on the date of the transfer). The automatic allocation pursuant to this paragraph is effective whether or not a Form 709 is filed reporting the transfer, and is effective as of the date of the transfer to which it relates. An automatic allocation is irrevocable after the due date of the Form 709 for the calendar year in which the transfer is made. In the case of an indirect skip to which section 2642(f) does apply, the indirect skip is deemed to be made at the close of the ETIP and the GST exemption is deemed to be allocated at that time. In either case, except as otherwise provided in paragraph (b)(2)(ii) of this section, the automatic allocation of exemption applies even if an allocation of exemption is made to the indirect skip in accordance with section 2632(a).

(ii) Prevention of automatic allocation. Except as otherwise provided in forms or other guidance published by the Service, the transferor may prevent the automatic allocation of GST exemption with regard to an indirect skip (including indirect skips to which section 2642(f) may apply) by making an election, as provided in paragraph (b)(2)(iii) of this section. Notwithstanding paragraph (b)(2)(iii)(B) of this section, the transferor may also prevent the automatic allocation of GST exemption with regard to an indirect skip by making an affirmative allocation of GST exemption on a Form 709 filed at any time on or before the due date for timely filing (within the meaning of paragraph (b)(1)(ii) of this section) of an amount that is less than (but not equal to) the value of the property transferred as reported on that return, in accordance with the provisions of paragraph (b)(4) of this section. See paragraph (b)(4)(iii) Example 6 of this section. Any election out of the automatic allocation rules under this section has no effect on the application of the automatic allocation rules applicable after the transferor's death under section 2632(e) and paragraph (d) of this section.

(iii) Election to have automatic allocation rules not apply—(A) In general. A transferor may prevent the automatic allocation of GST exemption (elect out) with respect to any transfer or transfers constituting an indirect skip made to a trust or to one or more separate shares that are treated as separate trusts under § 26.2654–1(a)(1) (collectively referred to hereinafter as a trust). In the case of a transfer treated under section 2513 as made one-half by the transferor and one-half by the transferor's spouse, each spouse shall be treated as a separate transferor who must satisfy separately the requirements of paragraph (b)(2)(iii)(B) to elect out with respect to the transfer. A transferor may elect out with respect to—

(1) One or more prior-year transfers subject to section 2642(f) (regarding ETIPs) made by the transferor to a specified trust or trusts;

(2) One or more (or all) current-year transfers made by the transferor to a specified trust or trusts;

(3) One or more (or all) future transfers made by the transferor to a specified trust or trusts;

(4) All future transfers made by the transferor to all trusts (whether or not in existence at the time of the election out); or

(5) Any combination of paragraphs (b)(2)(iii)(A)(1) through (4) of this section.

(B) Manner of making an election out. Except as otherwise provided in forms or other guidance published by the IRS, an election out is made as described in this paragraph (b)(2)(iii)(B). To elect out, the transferor must attach a statement (election out statement) to a Form 709 filed within the time period provided in paragraph (b)(2)(iii)(C) of this section (whether or not any transfer was made in the calendar year for which the Form 709 was filed, and whether or not a Form 709 otherwise would be required to be filed for that year). See paragraph (b)(4)(iv) Example 7 of this section. The election out statement must identify the trust (except for an election out under paragraph (b)(2)(iii)(A)(4) of this section), and specifically must provide that the transferor is electing out of the automatic allocation of GST exemption with respect to the described transfer or transfers. Prior-year transfers that are subject to section 2642(f), and to which the election out is to apply, must be specifically described or otherwise identified in the election out statement. Further, unless the election out is made for all transfers made to the trust in the current year and/or in all future years, the current-year transfers and/or future transfers to which the election out is to apply must be specifically described or otherwise identified in the election out statement.

(C) Time for making an election out. To elect out, the Form 709 with the attached election out statement must be filed on or before the due date for timely filing (within the meaning of paragraph (b)(1)(ii) of this section) of the Form 709 for the calendar year in which—

(1) For a transfer subject to section 2642(f), the ETIP closes; or

(2) For all other elections out, the first transfer to be covered by the election out was made.

(D) Effect of election out. An election out does not affect the automatic allocation of GST exemption to any transfer not covered by the election out statement. Except for elections out for transfers described in paragraph (b)(2)(iii)(A)(1) of this section that are specifically described in an election out statement, an election out does not apply to any prior-year transfer to a trust, including any transfer subject to an ETIP (even if the ETIP closes after the election is made). An election out does not prevent the transferor from allocating the transferor's available GST exemption to any transfer covered by the election out, either on a timely filed Form 709 reporting the transfer or at a later date in accordance with the provisions of paragraph (b)(4) of this section. An election out with respect to future transfers remains in effect unless and until terminated. Once an election out with respect to future transfers is made, a transferor need not file a Form 709 in future years solely to prevent the automatic allocation of the GST exemption to any future transfer covered by the election out.

(E) Termination of election out. Except as otherwise provided in forms or other guidance published by the IRS, an election out may be terminated as described in this paragraph (b)(2)(iii)(E). Pursuant to this section, a transferor may terminate an election out made on a Form 709 for a prior year, to the extent that election out applied to future transfers or to a transfer subject to section 2642(f). To terminate an election out, the transferor must attach a statement (termination statement) to a Form 709 filed on or before the due date of the Form 709 for the calendar year in which is made the first transfer to which the election out is not to apply (whether or not any transfer was made in the calendar year for which the Form 709 was filed, and whether or not a Form 709 otherwise would be required to be filed for that year). The termination statement must identify the trust (if applicable), describe the prior election out that is being terminated, specifically provide that the prior election out is being terminated, and either describe the extent to which the prior election out is being terminated or describe any current-year transfers to which the election out is not to apply. Consequently, the automatic allocation rules contained in section 2632(c)(1) will apply to any current-year transfer described on the termination statement and, except as otherwise provided in this paragraph, to all future transfers that otherwise would have been covered by the election out. The termination of an election out does not affect any transfer, or any election out, that is not described in the termination statement. The termination of an election out will not revoke the election out for any prior-year transfer, except for a prior-year transfer subject to section 2642(f) for which the election out is revoked on a timely filed Form 709 for the calendar year in which the ETIP closes or for any prior calendar year. The termination of an election out does not preclude the transferor from making another election out in the same or any subsequent year.

(3) Election to treat trust as a GST trust—(i) In general. A transferor may elect to treat any trust as a GST trust (GST trust election), without regard to whether the trust is subject to section 2642(f), with respect to—

(A) Any current-year transfer (or any or all current-year transfers) by the electing transferor to the trust;

(B) Any selected future transfers by the electing transferor to the trust;

(C) All future transfers by the electing transferor to the trust; or

(D) Any combination of paragraphs (b)(3)(i)(A) through (C) of this section.

(ii) Time and manner of making GST trust election. Except as otherwise provided in forms or other guidance published by the Internal Revenue Service, a GST trust election is made as described in this paragraph (b)(3)(ii). To make a GST trust election, the transferor must attach a statement (GST trust election statement) to a Form 709 filed on or before the due date for timely filing (within the meaning of paragraph (b)(1)(ii) of this section) of the Form 709 for the calendar year in which the first transfer to be covered by the GST trust election is made (whether or not any transfer was made in the calendar year for which the Form 709 was filed, and whether or not a Form 709 otherwise would be required to be filed for that year). The GST trust election statement must identify the trust, specifically describe or otherwise clearly identify the transfers to be covered by the election, and specifically provide that the transferor is electing to have the trust treated as a GST trust with respect to the covered transfers.

(iii) Effect of GST trust election. Except as otherwise provided in this paragraph, a GST trust election will cause all transfers made by the electing transferor to the trust that are subject to the election to be deemed to be made to a GST trust as defined in section 2632(c)(3)(B). Thus, the electing transferor's unused GST exemption may be allocated automatically to such transfers in accordance with paragraph (b)(2) of this section. A transferor may prevent the automatic allocation of GST exemption to future transfers to the trust either by terminating the GST trust election in accordance with paragraph (b)(3)(iv) of this section (in the case of trusts that would not otherwise be treated as GST trusts) or by electing out of the automatic allocation of GST exemption in accordance with paragraph (b)(2) of this section.

(iv) Termination of GST trust election. Except as otherwise provided in forms or other guidance published by the Service, a GST trust election may be terminated as described in this paragraph (b)(3)(iv). A transferor may terminate a GST trust election made on a Form 709 for a prior year, to the extent that election applied to future transfers or to a transfer subject to section 2642(f). To terminate a GST trust election, the transferor must attach a statement (termination statement) to a Form 709 filed on or before the due date for timely filing (within the meaning of paragraph (b)(1)(ii) of this section) a Form 709 for the calendar year: in which is made the electing transferor's first transfer to which the GST trust election is not to apply; or that is the first calendar year for which the GST trust election is not to apply, even if no transfer is made to the trust during that year. The termination statement must identify the trust, describe the current-year transfer (if any), and provide that the prior GST trust election is terminated. Accordingly, if the trust otherwise does not satisfy the definition of a GST trust, the automatic allocation rules contained in section 2632(c)(1) will not apply to the described current-year transfer or to any future transfers made by the transferor to the trust, unless and until another election under this paragraph (b)(3) is made.

(4) Allocation to other transfers—(i) In general. An allocation of GST exemption to property transferred during the transferor's lifetime, other than in a direct skip, is made on Form 709. The allocation must clearly identify the trust to which the allocation is being made, the amount of GST exemption allocated to it, and if the allocation is late or if an inclusion ratio greater than zero is claimed, the value of the trust assets at the effective date of the allocation. See paragraph (b)(4)(ii) of this section. The allocation should also state the inclusion ratio of the trust after the allocation. Except as otherwise provided in this paragraph, an allocation of GST exemption may be made by a formula; e.g., the allocation may be expressed in terms of the amount necessary to produce an inclusion ratio of zero. However, formula allocations made with respect to charitable lead annuity trusts are not valid except to the extent they are dependent on values as finally determined for Federal estate or gift tax purposes. With respect to a timely allocation, an allocation of GST exemption becomes irrevocable after the due date of the return. Except as provided in § 26.2642–3 (relating to charitable lead annuity trusts), an allocation of GST exemption to a trust is void to the extent the amount allocated exceeds the amount necessary to obtain an inclusion ratio of zero with respect to the trust. See § 26.2642–1 for the definition of inclusion ratio. An allocation is also void if the allocation is made with respect to a trust that has no GST potential with respect to the transferor making the allocation, at the time of the allocation. For this purpose, a trust has GST potential even if the possibility of a GST is so remote as to be negligible.

(ii) Effective date of allocation—(A) In general. **(1)** Except as otherwise provided, an allocation of GST exemption is effective as of the date of any transfer as to which the Form 709 on which it is made is a timely filed return (a timely allocation). If more than one timely allocation is made, the earlier allocation is modified only if the later allocation clearly identifies the transfer and the nature and extent of the modification. Except as provided in paragraph (d)(1) of this section, an allocation to a trust made on a Form 709 filed after the due date for reporting a transfer to the trust (a late allocation) is effective on the date the Form 709 is filed and is deemed to precede in point of time any taxable event occurring on such date. For purposes of this paragraph (b)(4)(ii), the Form 709 is deemed filed on the date it is postmarked to the Internal Revenue Service address as directed in forms or other guidance published by the Service. See § 26.2642–2 regarding the effect of a late allocation in determining the inclusion ratio, etc. See paragraph (c)(1) of this section regarding allocation of GST exemption to property subject to an estate tax inclusion period. If it is unclear whether an allocation of GST exemption on a Form 709 is a late or a timely allocation to a trust, the allocation is effective in the following order—

(i) To any transfer to the trust disclosed on the return as to which the return is a timely return;

(ii) As a late allocation; and

(iii) To any transfer to the trust not disclosed on the return as to which the return would be a timely return.

(2) A late allocation to a trust may be made on a Form 709 that is timely filed with respect to another transfer. A late allocation is irrevocable when made.

(B) Amount of allocation. If other transfers exist with respect to which GST exemption could be allocated under paragraphs (b)(4)(ii)(A)(1)(ii) and (iii), any GST exemption allocated under paragraph (b)(4)(ii)(A)(1)(i) of this section is allocated in an amount equal to the value of the transferred property as reported on the Form 709. Thus, if the GST exemption allocated on the Form 709 exceeds the value of the transfers reported on that return that have generation-skipping potential, the initial allocation under paragraph (b)(4)(ii)(A)(1)(i) of this section is in the amount of the value of those transfers as reported on that return. Any remaining amount of GST exemption allocated on that return is then allocated pursuant to paragraphs (b)(4)(ii)(A)(1)(ii) and (iii) of this section, notwithstanding any subsequent upward adjustment in value of the transfers reported on the return.

(iii) Examples. The following examples illustrate the provisions of this paragraph (b):

Example 1. Modification of allocation of GST exemption. On December 1, 2003, T transfers $100,000 to an irrevocable GST trust described in section 2632(c)(3)(B). The transfer to the trust is not a direct skip. The date prescribed for filing the gift tax return reporting the taxable gift is April 15, 2004. On February 10, 2004, T files a Form 709 on which T properly elects out of the automatic allocation rules contained in section 2632(c)(1) with respect to the transfer in accordance with paragraph (b)(2)(iii) of this section, and allocates $50,000 of GST exemption to the trust. On April 13th of the same year, T files an additional Form 709 on which T confirms the election out of the automatic allocation rules contained in section 2632(c)(1) and allocates $100,000 of GST exemption to the trust in a manner that clearly indicates the intention to modify and supersede the prior allocation with respect to the 2003 transfer. The allocation made on the April 13 return supersedes the prior allocation because it is made on a timely-filed Form 709 that clearly identifies the trust and the nature and extent of the modification of GST exemption allocation. The allocation of $100,000 of GST exemption to the trust is effective as of December 1, 2003. The result would be the same if the amended Form 709 decreased the amount of the GST exemption allocated to the trust.

Example 2. Modification of allocation of GST exemption. The facts are the same as in Example 1 except, on July 8, 2004, T files a Form 709 attempting to reduce the earlier allocation. The return filed on July 8, 2004, is not a timely filed return. The $100,000 GST exemption allocated to the trust, as amended on April 13, 2004, remains in effect because an allocation, once made, is irrevocable and may not be modified after the last date on which a timely filed Form 709 may be filed.

Example 3. Effective date of late allocation of GST exemption. On November 15, 2003, T transfers $100,000 to an irrevocable GST trust described in section 2632(c)(3)(B). The transfer to the trust is not a direct skip.

The date prescribed for filing the gift tax return reporting the taxable gift is April 15, 2004. On February 10, 2004, T files a Form 709 on which T properly elects out of the automatic allocation rules contained in section 2632(c)(1) in accordance with paragraph (b)(2)(iii) of this section with respect to that transfer. On December 1, 2004, T files a Form 709 and allocates $50,000 to the trust. The allocation is effective as of December 1, 2004.

Example 4. Effective date of late allocation of GST exemption. T transfers $100,000 to an irrevocable GST trust on December 1, 2003, in a transfer that is not a direct skip. On April 15, 2004, T files a Form 709 on which T properly elects out of the automatic allocation rules contained in section 2632(c)(1) with respect to the entire transfer in accordance with paragraph (b)(2)(iii) of this section and T does not make an allocation of any GST exemption on the Form 709. On September 1, 2004, the trustee makes a taxable distribution from the trust to T's grandchild in the amount of $30,000. Immediately prior to the distribution, the value of the trust assets was $150,000. On the same date, T allocates GST exemption to the trust in the amount of $50,000. The allocation of GST exemption on the date of the transfer is treated as preceding in point of time the taxable distribution. At the time of the GST, the trust has an inclusion ratio of .6667 (1—(50,000/150,000)).

Example 5. Automatic allocation to split-gift. On December 1, 2003, T transfers $50,000 to an irrevocable GST Trust described in section 2632(c)(3)(B). The transfer to the trust is not a direct skip. On April 30, 2004, T and T's spouse, S, each files an initial gift tax return for 2003, on which they consent, pursuant to section 2513, to have the gift treated as if one-half had been made by each. In spite of being made on a late-filed gift tax return for 2003, the election under section 2513 is valid because neither spouse had filed a timely gift tax return for that year. Previously, neither T nor S filed a timely gift tax return electing out of the automatic allocation rules contained in section 2632(c)(1). As a result of the election under section 2513, which is retroactive to the date of T's transfer, T and S are each treated as the transferor of one-half of the property transferred in the indirect skip. Thus, $25,000 of T's unused GST exemption and $25,000 of S's unused GST exemption is automatically allocated to the trust. Both allocations are effective on and after the date that T made the transfer. The result would be the same if T's transfer constituted a direct skip subject to the automatic allocation rules contained in section 2632(b).

Example 6. Partial allocation of GST exemption. On December 1, 2003, T transfers $100,000 to an irrevocable GST trust described in section 2632(c)(3)(B). The transfer to the trust is not a direct skip. The date prescribed for filing the gift tax return reporting the taxable gift is April 15, 2004. On February 10, 2004, T files a Form 709 on which T allocates $40,000 of GST exemption to the trust. By filing a timely Form 709 on which a partial allocation is made of $40,000, T effectively elected out of the automatic allocation rules for the remaining value of the transfer for which T did not allocate GST exemption.

(iv) Example. The following example illustrates language that may be used in the statement required under paragraph (b)(2)(iii) of this section to elect out of the automatic allocation rules under various scenarios:

Example 1. On March 1, 2006, T transfers $100,000 to Trust B, a GST trust described in section 2632(c)(3)(B). Subsequently, on September 15, 2006, T transfers an additional $75,000 to Trust B. No other transfers are made to Trust B in 2006. T attaches an election out statement to a timely filed Form 709 for calendar year 2006. Except with regard to paragraph (v) of this Example 1, the election out statement identifies Trust B as required under paragraph (b)(2)(iii)(B) of this section, and contains the following alternative election statements:

(i) "T hereby elects that the automatic allocation rules will not apply to the $100,000 transferred to Trust B on March 1, 2006." The election out of the automatic allocation rules will be effective only for T's March 1, 2006, transfer and will not apply to T's $75,000 transfer made on September 15, 2006.

(ii) "T hereby elects that the automatic allocation rules will not apply to any transfers to Trust B in 2006." The election out of the automatic allocation rules will be effective for T's transfers to Trust B made on March 1, 2006, and September 15, 2006.

(iii) "T hereby elects that the automatic allocation rules will not apply to any transfers to Trust B made by T in 2006 or to any additional transfers T may make to Trust B in subsequent years." The election out of the automatic allocation rules will be effective for T's transfers to Trust B in 2006 and for all future transfers to be made by T to Trust B, unless and until T terminates the election out of the automatic allocation rules.

(iv) "T hereby elects that the automatic allocation rules will not apply to any transfers T has made or will make to Trust B in the years 2006 through 2008." The election out of the automatic allocation rules will be effective for T's transfers to Trust B in 2006 through 2008. T's transfers to Trust B after 2008 will be subject to the automatic allocation rules, unless T elects out of those rules for one or more years after 2008. T may terminate the election out of the automatic allocation rules for 2007, 2008, or both in accordance with the termination rules of paragraph (b)(2)(iii)(E) of this section. T may terminate the election out for one or more of the transfers made in 2006 only on a later but still timely filed Form 709 for calendar year 2006.

(v) "T hereby elects that the automatic allocation rules will not apply to any current or future transfer that T may make to any trust." The election out of the automatic allocation rules will be effective for all of T's transfers (current-year and future) to Trust B and to any and all other trusts (whether such trusts exist in 2006 or are created in a later year), unless and until T terminates the election out of the automatic allocation rules. T may terminate the election out with regard to one or more (or all) of the transfers covered by the election out in accordance with the termination rules of paragraph (b)(2)(iii)(E) of this section.

(c) Special rules during an estate tax inclusion period—(1) In general—(i) Automatic allocations with respect to direct skips and indirect skips. A direct skip or an indirect skip that is subject to an estate tax inclusion period (ETIP) is deemed to have been made only at the close of the ETIP. The transferor may prevent the automatic allocation of GST exemption to a direct skip or an indirect skip by electing out of the automatic allocation rules at any time prior to the due date of the Form 709 for the calendar year in which the close of the ETIP occurs (whether or not any transfer was made in the calendar year for which the Form 709 was filed, and whether or not a Form 709 otherwise would be required to be filed for that year). See paragraph (b)(2)(i) of this section regarding the automatic allocation of GST exemption to an indirect skip subject to an ETIP.

(ii) Other allocations. An affirmative allocation of GST exemption cannot be revoked, but becomes effective as of (and no earlier than) the date of the close of the ETIP with respect to the trust. If an allocation has not been made prior to the close of the ETIP, an allocation of exemption is effective as of the close of the ETIP during the transferor's lifetime if made by the due date for filing the Form 709 for the calendar year in which the close of the ETIP occurs (timely ETIP return). An allocation of exemption is effective in the case of the close of the ETIP by reason of the death of the transferor as provided in paragraph (d) of this section.

(iii) Portion of trust subject to ETIP. If any part of a trust is subject to an ETIP, the entire trust is subject to the ETIP. See § 26.2642–1(b)(2) for rules determining the inclusion ratio applicable in the case of GSTs during an ETIP.

(2) Estate tax inclusion period defined—(i) In general. An ETIP is the period during which, should death occur, the value of transferred property would be includible (other than by reason of section 2035) in the gross estate of—

(A) The transferor; or

(B) The spouse of the transferor.

(ii) Exceptions—(A) For purposes of paragraph (c)(2) of this section, the value of transferred property is not considered as being subject to inclusion in the gross estate of the transferor or the spouse of the transferor if the possibility that the property will be included is so remote as to be negligible. A possibility is so remote as to be negligible if it can be ascertained by actuarial standards that there is less than a 5 percent probability that the property will be included in the gross estate.

(B) For purposes of paragraph (c)(2) of this section, the value of transferred property is not considered as being subject to inclusion in the gross estate of the spouse of the transferor, if the spouse possesses with respect to any transfer to the trust, a right to withdraw no more than the greater of $5,000 or 5 percent of the trust corpus, and such withdrawal right terminates no later than 60 days after the transfer to the trust.

(C) The rules of this paragraph (c)(2) do not apply to qualified terminable interest property with respect to which the special election under § 26.2652–2 has been made.

(3) Termination of an ETIP. An ETIP terminates on the first to occur of—

(i) The death of the transferor;

(ii) The time at which no portion of the property is includible in the transferor's gross estate (other than by reason of section 2035) or, in the case of an individual who is a transferor solely by reason of an election under section 2513, the time at which no portion would be includible in the gross estate of the individual's spouse (other than by reason of section 2035);

(iii) The time of a GST, but only with respect to the property involved in the GST; or

(iv) In the case of an ETIP arising by reason of an interest or power held by the transferor's spouse under subsection (c)(2)(i)(B) of this section, at the first to occur of—

(A) The death of the spouse; or

(B) The time at which no portion of the property would be includible in the spouse's gross estate (other than by reason of section 2035).

(4) Treatment of direct skips. If property transferred to a skip person is subject to an ETIP, the direct skip is treated as occurring on the termination of the ETIP.

(5) Examples. The following examples illustrate the rules of this section as they apply to the termination of an ETIP during the lifetime of the transferor. In each example assume that T transfers $100,000 to an irrevocable trust:

Example 1. Allocation of GST exemption during ETIP. The trust instrument provides that trust income is to be paid to T for 9 years or until T's prior death. The trust principal is to be paid to T's grandchild on the termination of T's income interest. If T dies within the 9–year period, the value of the trust principal is includible in T's gross estate under section 2036(a). Thus, the trust is subject to an ETIP. T files a timely Form 709 reporting the transfer and allocating $100,000 of GST exemption to the trust. The allocation of GST exemption to the trust is not effective until the termination of the ETIP.

Example 2. Effect of prior allocation on termination of ETIP. The facts are the same as in Example 1, except the trustee has the power to invade trust principal on behalf of T's grandchild, GC, during the term of T's income interest. In year 4, when the value of the trust is $200,000, the trustee distributes $15,000 to GC. The distribution is a taxable distribution. The ETIP with respect to the property distributed to GC terminates at the time of the taxable distribution. See paragraph (c)(3)(iii) of this section. Solely for purposes of determining the trust's inclusion ratio with respect to the taxable distribution, the prior $100,000 allocation of GST exemption (as well as any additional allocation made on a timely ETIP return) is effective immediately prior to the taxable distribution. See § 26.2642–1(b)(2). The trust's inclusion ratio with respect to the taxable distribution is therefore .50 (1—(100,-000/200,000)).

Example 3. Split-gift transfers subject to ETIP. The trust instrument provides that trust income is to be paid to T for 9 years or until T's prior death. The trust principal is to be paid to T's grandchild on the termination of T's income interest. T files a timely Form 709 reporting the transfer. T's spouse, S, consents to have the gift treated as made one-half by S under section 2513. Because S is treated as transferring one-half of the property to T's grandchild, S becomes the transferor of one-half of the trust for purposes of chapter 13. Because the value of the trust would be includible in T's gross estate if T died immediately after the transfer, S's transfer is subject to an ETIP. If S should die prior to the termination of the trust, S's executor may allocate S's GST exemption to the trust, but only to the portion of the trust for which S is treated as the transferor. However, the allocation does not become effective until the earlier of the expiration of T's income interest or T's death.

Example 4. Transfer of retained interest as ETIP termination. The trust instrument provides that trust income is to be paid to T for 9 years or until T's prior death. The trust principal is to be paid to T's grandchild on the termination of T's income interest. Four years after the initial transfer, T transfers the income interest to T's sibling. The ETIP with respect to the trust terminates on T's transfer of the income interest because, after the transfer, the trust property would not be includible in T's gross estate (other than by reason of section 2035) if T died at that time.

Example 5. Election out of automatic allocation of GST exemption for trust subject to an ETIP. On December 1, 2003, T transfers $100,000 to Trust A, an irrevocable GST trust described in section 2632(c)(3) that is subject to an estate tax inclusion period (ETIP). T made no other gifts in 2003. The ETIP terminates on December 31, 2008. T timely files a gift tax return (Form 709) reporting the gift on April 15, 2004. On May 15, 2006, T files a Form 709 on which T properly elects out of the automatic allocation rules contained in section 2632(c)(1) with respect to the December 1, 2003, transfer to Trust A in accordance with paragraph (b)(2)(iii) of this section. Because the indirect skip is not deemed to occur until December 31, 2008, T's election out of automatic GST allocation filed on May 15, 2006, is timely, and will be effective as of December 31, 2008 (unless revoked on a Form 709 filed on or before the due date of a Form 709 for calendar year 2008).

(d) Allocations after the transferor's death—(1) Allocation by executor. Except as otherwise provided in this paragraph (d), an allocation of a decedent's unused GST exemption by the executor of the decedent's estate is made on the appropriate United States Estate (and Generation-Skipping Transfer) Tax Return (Form 706 or Form 706NA) filed on or before the date prescribed for filing the return by section 6075(a) (including any extensions actually granted (the due date)). An allocation of GST exemption with respect to property included in the gross estate of a decedent is effective as of the date of death. A timely allocation of GST exemption by an executor with respect to a lifetime transfer of property that is not included in the transferor's gross estate is made on a Form 709. A late allocation of GST exemption by an executor, other than an allocation that is deemed to be made under section 2632(b)(1) or (c)(1), with respect to a lifetime transfer of property is made on Form 706, Form 706NA, or Form 709 (filed on or before the due date of the transferor's estate tax return) and applies as of the date the allocation is filed. An allocation of GST exemption to a trust (whether or not funded at the time the Form 706 or Form 706NA is filed) is effective if the notice of allocation clearly identifies the trust and the amount of the decedent's GST exemption allocated to the trust. An executor may allocate the decedent's GST exemption by use of a formula. For purposes of this section, an allocation is void if the allocation is made for a trust that has no GST potential with respect to the transferor for whom the allocation is being made, as of the date of the transferor's death. For this purpose, a trust has GST potential even if the possibility of a GST is so remote as to be negligible.

(2) Automatic allocation after death. A decedent's unused GST exemption is automatically allocated on the due date for filing Form 706 or Form 706NA to the extent not otherwise allocated by the decedent's executor on or before that date. The automatic allocation occurs whether or not a return is actually required to be filed. Unused GST exemption is allocated pro rata (subject to the rules of § 26.2642–2(b)), on the basis of the value of the property as finally determined for purposes of chapter 11 (chapter 11 value), first to direct skips treated as occurring at the transferor's death. The balance, if any, of unused GST exemption is allocated pro rata (subject to the rules of § 26.2642–2(b)) on the basis of the chapter 11 value of the nonexempt portion of the trust property (or in the case of trusts that are not included in the gross estate, on the basis of the date of death value of the trust) to trusts with respect to which a taxable termination may occur or from which a taxable distribution may be made. The automatic allocation of GST exemption is irrevocable, and an allocation made by the executor after the automatic allocation is made is ineffective. No automatic allocation of GST exemption is made to a trust that will have a new transferor with respect to the entire trust prior to the occurrence of any GST with respect to the trust. In addition, no automatic allocation of GST exemption is made to a trust if, during the nine month period ending immediately after the death of the transferor—

(i) No GST has occurred with respect to the trust; and

(ii) At the end of such period no future GST can occur with respect to the trust.

(e) Effective dates. This section is applicable as provided in § 26.2601–1(c), with the following exceptions:

(1) Paragraphs (b)(2) and (b)(3), the third sentence of paragraph (b)(4)(i), the fourth sentence of paragraph (b)(4)(ii)(A)(1), paragraphs (b)(4)(iii) and (b)(4)(iv), and the fourth sentence of paragraph (d)(1) of this section, which will apply to elections made on or after July 13, 2004; and

(2) Paragraph (c)(1), and Example 5 of paragraph (c)(5), which will apply to elections made on or after June 29, 2005.

[T.D. 8644, 60 FR 66912, Dec. 27, 1995; 61 FR 29654, June 12, 1996; T.D. 9208, 70 FR 37260, June 29, 2005]

§ 26.2641–1 Applicable rate of tax.

The rate of tax applicable to any GST (applicable rate) is determined by multiplying the maximum Federal estate tax rate in effect at the time of the GST by the inclusion ratio (as defined in § 26.2642–1). For this purpose, the maximum Federal estate tax rate is the maximum rate set forth under section 2001(c) (without regard to section 2001(c)(2)).

[T.D. 8644, 60 FR 66898, Dec. 27, 1995]

§ 26.2642–1 Inclusion ratio.

(a) In general. Except as otherwise provided in this section, the inclusion ratio is determined by subtracting the applicable fraction (rounded to the nearest one-thousandth (.001)) from 1. In rounding the applicable fraction to the nearest one-thousandth, any amount that is midway between one one-thousandth and another one-thousandth is rounded up to the higher of those two amounts.

(b) Numerator of applicable fraction—(1) In general. Except as otherwise provided in this paragraph (b), and in §§ 26.2642–3 (providing a special rule for charitable lead annuity trusts) and 26.2642–4 (providing rules for the redetermination of the applicable fraction), the numerator of the applicable fraction is the amount of GST exemption allocated to the trust (or to the transferred property in the case of a direct skip not in trust).

(2) GSTs occurring during an ETIP—(i) In general. For purposes of determining the inclusion ratio with respect to a taxable termination or a taxable distribution that occurs during an ETIP, the numerator of the applicable fraction is the sum of—

(A) The GST exemption previously allocated to the trust (including any allocation made to the trust prior to any taxable termination or distribution) reduced (but not below zero) by the nontax amount of any prior GSTs with respect to the trust; and

(B) Any GST exemption allocated to the trust on a timely ETIP return filed after the termination of the ETIP. See § 26.2632–1(c)(5) Example 2.

(ii) Nontax amount of a prior GST. **(1)** The nontax amount of a prior GST with respect to the trust is the amount of the GST multiplied by the applicable fraction attributable to the trust at the time of the prior GST.

(2) For rules regarding the allocation of GST exemption to property during an ETIP, see § 26.2632–1(c).

(c) Denominator of applicable fraction—(1) In general. Except as otherwise provided in this paragraph (c) and in §§ 26.2642–3 and 26.2642–4, the denominator of the applicable fraction is the value of the property transferred to the trust (or transferred in a direct skip not in trust) (as determined under § 26.2642–2) reduced by the sum of—

(i) Any Federal estate tax and any State death tax incurred by reason of the transfer that is chargeable to the trust and is actually recovered from the trust;

(ii) The amount of any charitable deduction allowed under section 2055, 2106, or 2522 with respect to the transfer; and

(iii) In the case of a direct skip, the value of the portion of the transfer that is a nontaxable gift. See paragraph (c)(3) of this section for the definition of nontaxable gift.

(2) Zero denominator. If the denominator of the applicable fraction is zero, the inclusion ratio is zero.

(3) Nontaxable gifts. Generally, for purposes of chapter 13, a transfer is a nontaxable gift to the extent the transfer is excluded from taxable gifts by reason of section 2503(b) (after application of section 2513) or section 2503(e). However, a transfer to a trust for the benefit of an individual is not a nontaxable gift for purposes of this section unless—

(i) Trust principal or income may, during the individual's lifetime, be distributed only to or for the benefit of the individual; and

(ii) The assets of the trust will be includible in the gross estate of the individual if the individual dies before the trust terminates.

(d) Examples. The following examples illustrate the provisions of this section. See § 26.2652–2(d) Examples 2 and 3 for illustrations of the computation of the inclusion ratio where the special (reverse QTIP) election may be applicable.

Example 1. Computation of the inclusion ratio. T transfers $100,000 to a newly-created irrevocable trust providing that income is to be accumulated for 10 years. At the end of 10 years, the accumulated income is to be distributed to T's child, C, and the trust principal is to be paid to T's grandchild. T allocates $40,000 of T's GST exemption to the trust on a timely-filed gift tax return. The applicable fraction with respect to the trust is .40 ($40,000 (the amount of GST exemption allocated to the trust) over $100,000 (the value of the property transferred to the trust)). The inclusion ratio is .60 (1—.40). If the maximum Federal estate tax rate is 55 percent at the time of a GST, the rate of tax applicable to the transfer (applicable rate) will be .333 (55 percent (the maximum estate tax rate) x .60 (the inclusion ratio)).

Example 2. Gift entirely nontaxable. On December 1, 1996, T transfers $10,000 to an irrevocable trust for the benefit of T's grandchild, GC. GC possesses a right to withdraw any contributions to the trust such that the entire transfer qualifies for the annual exclusion under section 2503(b). Under the terms of the trust, the income is to be paid to GC for 10 years or until GC's prior death. Upon the expiration of GC's income interest, the trust principal is payable to GC or GC's estate. The transfer to the trust is a direct skip. T made no prior gifts to or for the benefit of GC during 1996. The entire $10,000 transfer is a nontaxable transfer. For purposes of computing the tax on the direct skip, the denominator of the applicable fraction is zero, and thus, the inclusion ratio is zero.

Example 3. Gift nontaxable in part. T transfers $12,000 to an irrevocable trust for the benefit of T's grandchild, GC. Under the terms of the trust, the income is to be paid to GC for 10 years or until GC's prior death. Upon the expiration of GC's income interest, the trust principal is payable to GC or GC's estate. Further, GC has the right to withdraw $10,000 of any contribution to the trust such that $10,000 of the transfer qualifies for the annual exclusion under section 2503(b). The amount of the nontaxable transfer is $10,000. Solely for purposes of computing the tax on the direct skip, T's transfer is divided into two portions. One portion is equal to the amount of the nontaxable transfer ($10,000) and has a zero inclusion ratio; the other portion is $2,000 ($12,000—$10,000). With respect to the $2,000 portion, the denominator of the applicable fraction is $2,000. Assuming that T has sufficient GST exemption available, the numerator of the applicable fraction is $2,000 (unless T elects to have the automatic allocation provisions not apply). Thus, assuming T does not elect to have the automatic allocation not apply, the applicable fraction is one ($2,000/$2,000 = 1) and the inclusion ratio is zero (1 − 1 = 0).

Example 4. Gift nontaxable in part. Assume the same facts as in Example 3, except T files a timely Form 709 electing that the automatic allocation of GST exemption not apply to the $12,000 transferred in the direct skip. T's transfer is divided into two portions, a $10,000 portion with a zero inclusion ratio and a $2,000 portion with an applicable fraction of zero (0/$2,000 = 0) and an inclusion ratio of one (1 − 0 = 1).

[T.D. 8644, 60 FR 66898, Dec. 27, 1995]

§ 26.2642–2 Valuation.

(a) Lifetime transfers—(1) In general. For purposes of determining the denominator of the applicable fraction, the value of property transferred during life is its fair market value on the effective date of the allocation of GST exemption. In the case of a timely allocation under § 26.2632–1(b)(2)(ii), the denominator of the applicable fraction is the fair market value of the property as finally determined for purposes of chapter 12.

(2) Special rule for late allocations during life. If a transferor makes a late allocation of GST exemption to a trust, the value of the property transferred to the trust is the fair market value of the trust assets determined on the effective date of the allocation of GST exemption. Except as otherwise provided in this paragraph (a)(2), if a transferor makes a late allocation of GST exemption to a trust, the transferor may, solely for purposes of determining the fair market value of the trust assets, elect to treat the allocation as having been made on the first day of the month during which the late allocation is made (valuation date). An election under this paragraph (a)(2) is not effective with respect to a life insurance policy or a trust holding a life insurance policy, if the insured individual has died. An allocation subject to the election contained in this paragraph (a)(2) is not effective until it is actually filed with the Internal Revenue Service. The election is made by stating on the Form 709 on which the allocation is made—

(i) That the election is being made;

(ii) The applicable valuation date; and

(iii) The fair market value of the trust assets on the valuation date.

(b) Transfers at death—(1) In general. Except as provided in paragraphs (b)(2) and (3) of this section, in determining the denominator of the applicable fraction, the value of property included in the decedent's gross estate is its value for purposes of chapter 11. In the case of qualified real property with respect to which the election under section 2032A is made, the value of the property is the value determined under section 2032A provided the recapture agreement described in section 2032A(d)(2) filed with the Internal Revenue Service specifically provides for the signatories' consent to the imposition of, and personal liability for, additional GST tax in the event an additional estate tax is imposed under section 2032A(c). See § 26.2642–4(a)(4). If the recapture agreement does not contain these provisions, the value of qualified real property as to which the election under section 2032A is made is the fair market value of the property determined without regard to the provisions of section 2032A.

(2) Special rule for pecuniary payments—(i) In general. If a pecuniary payment is satisfied with cash, the denominator of the applicable fraction is the pecuniary amount. If property other than cash is used to satisfy a pecuniary payment, the denominator of the applicable fraction is the pecuniary amount only if payment must be made with property on the basis of the value of the property on—

(A) The date of distribution; or

(B) A date other than the date of distribution, but only if the pecuniary payment must be satisfied on a basis that fairly reflects net appreciation and depreciation (occurring between the valuation date and the date of distribution) in all of the assets from which the distribution could have been made.

(ii) Other pecuniary amounts payable in kind. The denominator of the applicable fraction with respect to any property used to satisfy any other pecuniary payment payable in kind is the date of distribution value of the property.

(3) Special rule for residual transfers after payment of a pecuniary payment—(i) In general. Except as otherwise provided in this paragraph (b)(3), the denominator of the applicable fraction with respect to a residual transfer of property after the satisfaction of a pecuniary payment is the estate tax value of the assets available to satisfy the pecuniary payment reduced, if the pecuniary payment carries appropriate interest (as defined in paragraph (b)(4) of this section), by the pecuniary amount. The denominator of the applicable fraction with respect to a residual transfer of property after the satisfaction of a pecuniary payment that does not carry appropriate interest is the estate tax value of the assets available to satisfy the pecuniary payment reduced by the present value of the pecuniary payment. For purposes of this paragraph (b)(3)(i), the present value of the pecuniary payment is determined by using—

(A) The interest rate applicable under section 7520 at the death of the transferor; and

(B) The period between the date of the transferor's death and the date the pecuniary amount is paid.

(ii) Special rule for residual transfers after pecuniary payments payable in kind. The denominator of the applicable fraction with respect to any residual transfer after satisfaction of a pecuniary payment payable in kind is the date of distribution value of the property distributed in satisfaction of the residual transfer, unless the pecuniary payment must be satisfied on the basis of the value of the property on—

(A) The date of distribution; or

(B) A date other than the date of distribution, but only if the pecuniary payment must be satisfied on a basis that fairly reflects net appreciation and depreciation (occurring between the valuation date and the date of distribution) in all of the assets from which the distribution could have been made.

(4) Appropriate interest—(i) In general. For purposes of this section and § 26.2654–1 (relating to certain trusts treated as separate trusts), appropriate interest means that interest must be payable from the date of death of the transferor (or from the date specified under applicable State law requiring the payment of interest) to the date of payment at a rate—

(A) At least equal to—

(1) The statutory rate of interest, if any, applicable to pecuniary bequests under the law of the State whose law governs the administration of the estate or trust; or

(2) If no such rate is indicated under applicable State law, 80 percent of the rate that is applicable under section 7520 at the death of the transferor; and

(B) Not in excess of the greater of—

(1) The statutory rate of interest, if any, applicable to pecuniary bequests under the law of the State whose law governs the administration of the trust; or

(2) 120 percent of the rate that is applicable under section 7520 at the death of the transferor.

(ii) Pecuniary payments deemed to carry appropriate interest. For purposes of this paragraph (b)(4), if a pecuniary payment does not carry appropriate interest, the pecuniary payment is considered to carry appropriate interest to the extent—

(A) The entire payment is made or property is irrevocably set aside to satisfy the entire pecuniary payment within 15 months of the transferor's death; or

(B) The governing instrument or applicable local law specifically requires the executor or trustee to allocate to the pecuniary payment a pro rata share of the income earned by the fund from which the pecuniary payment is to be made between the date of death of the transferor and the date of payment. For purposes of paragraph (b)(4)(ii)(A) of this section, property is irrevocably set aside if it is segregated and held in a separate account pending distribution.

(c) Examples. The following examples illustrate the provisions of this section:

Example 1. T transfers $100,000 to a newly-created irrevocable trust on December 15, 1996. The trust provides that income is to be paid to T's child for 10 years. At the end of the 10–year period, the trust principal is to be paid to T's grandchild. T does not allocate any GST exemption to the trust on the gift tax return reporting the transfer. On November 15, 1997, T files a Form 709 allocating $50,000 of GST exemption to the trust. Because the allocation was made on a late filed return, the value of the property transferred to the trust is determined on the date the allocation is filed (unless an election is made pursuant to paragraph (a)(2) of this section to value the trust property as of the first day of the month in which the allocation document is filed with the Internal Revenue Service). On November 15, 1997, the value of the trust property is $150,000. Effective as of November 15, 1997, the applicable fraction with respect to the trust is .333 ($50,000 (the amount of GST exemption allocated to the trust) over $150,000 (the value of the trust principal on the effective date of the GST exemption allocation)), and the inclusion ratio is .667 (1.0.–333).

Example 2. The facts are the same as in Example 1, except the value of the trust property is $80,000 on November 15, 1997. The applicable fraction is .625 ($50,000 over $80,000) and the inclusion ratio is .375 (1.0 – .625).

Example 3. T transfers $100,000 to a newly-created irrevocable trust on December 15, 1996. The trust provides that income is to be paid to T's child for 10 years. At the end of the 10–year period, the trust principal is to be paid to T's grandchild. T does not allocate any GST exemption to the trust on the gift tax return reporting the transfer. On November 15, 1997, T files a Form 709 allocating $50,000 of GST exemption to the trust. T elects to value the trust principal on the first day of the month in which the allocation is made pursuant to the election provided in paragraph (a)(2) of this section. Because the late allocation is made in November, the value of the trust is determined as of November 1, 1997.

[T.D. 8644, 60 FR 66898, Dec. 27, 1995, as corrected by Announcement 96–72, 61 FR 29653, June 12, 1996]

§ 26.2642–3 Special rule for charitable lead annuity trusts.

(a) In general. In determining the applicable fraction with respect to a charitable lead annuity trust—

(1) The numerator is the adjusted generation-skipping transfer tax exemption (adjusted GST exemption); and

(2) The denominator is the value of all property in the trust immediately after the termination of the charitable lead annuity.

(b) Adjusted GST exemption defined. The adjusted GST exemption is the amount of GST exemption allocated to the trust increased by an amount equal to the interest that would accrue if an amount equal to the allocated GST exemption were invested at the rate used to determine the amount of the estate or gift tax charitable deduction, compounded annually, for the actual period of the charitable lead annuity. If a late allocation is made to a charitable lead annuity trust, the adjusted GST exemption is the amount of GST exemption allocated to the trust increased by the interest that would accrue if invested at such rate for the period beginning on the date of the late allocation and extending for the balance of the actual period of the charitable lead annuity. The amount of GST exemption allocated to a charitable lead annuity trust is not reduced even though it is ultimately determined that the allocation of a lesser amount of GST exemption would have resulted in an inclusion ratio of zero. For purposes of chapter 13, a charitable lead annuity trust is any trust providing an interest in the form of a guaranteed annuity described in § 25.2522(c)–3(c)(2)(vi) of this chapter for which the transferor is allowed a charitable deduction for Federal estate or gift tax purposes.

(c) Example. The following example illustrates the provisions of this section:

Example. T creates a charitable lead annuity trust for a 10–year term with the remainder payable to T's grandchild. T timely allocates an amount of GST exemption to the trust which T expects will ultimately result in a zero inclusion ratio. However, at the end of the charitable lead interest, because the property has not appreciated to the extent T anticipated, the numerator of the applicable fraction is greater than the denominator. The inclusion ratio for the trust is zero. No portion of the GST exemption allocated to the trust is restored to T or to T's estate.

[T.D. 8644, 60 FR 66898, Dec. 27, 1995]

§ 26.2642–4 Redetermination of applicable fraction.

(a) In general. The applicable fraction for a trust is redetermined whenever additional exemption is allocated to the trust or when certain changes occur with respect to the principal of the trust. Except as otherwise provided in this paragraph (a), the numerator of the redetermined applicable fraction is the sum of the amount of GST exemption currently being allocated to the trust (if any) plus the value of the nontax portion of the trust, and the denominator of the redetermined applicable fraction is the value of the trust principal immediately after the event occurs. The nontax portion of a trust is determined by multiplying the value of the trust assets, determined immediately prior to the event, by the then applicable fraction.

(1) Multiple transfers to a single trust. If property is added to an existing trust, the denominator of the redetermined applicable fraction is the value of the trust immediately after the addition reduced as provided in § 26.2642–1(c).

(2) Consolidation of separate trusts. If separate trusts created by one transferor are consolidated, a single applicable fraction for the consolidated trust is determined. The numerator of the redetermined applicable fraction is the sum of the nontax portions of each trust immediately prior to the consolidation.

(3) Property included in transferor's gross estate. If the value of property held in a trust created by the transferor, with respect to which an allocation was made at a time that the trust was not subject to an ETIP, is included in the transferor's gross estate, the applicable fraction is redetermined if additional GST exemption is allocated to the property. The numerator of the redetermined applicable fraction is an amount equal to the nontax portion of the property immediately after the death of the transferor increased by the amount of GST exemption allocated by the executor of the transferor's estate to the trust. If additional GST exemption is not allocated to the trust, then, except as provided in this paragraph (a)(3), the applicable fraction immediately before death is not changed, if the trust was not subject to an ETIP at the time GST exemption was allocated to the trust. In any event, the denominator of the applicable fraction is reduced to reflect any federal or state, estate or inheritance taxes paid from the trust.

(4) Imposition of recapture tax under section 2032A—(i) If an additional estate tax is imposed under section 2032A and if the section 2032A election was effective (under § 26.2642–2(b)) for purposes of the GST tax, the applicable fraction with respect to the property is redetermined as of the date of death of the transferor. In making the redetermination, any available GST exemption not allocated at the death of the transferor (or at a prior recapture event) is automatically allocated to the property. The denominator of the applicable fraction is the fair market value of the property at the date of the transferor's death reduced as provided in § 26.2642–1(c) and further reduced by the amount of the additional GST tax actually recovered from the trust.

(ii) The GST tax imposed with respect to any taxable termination, taxable distribution, or direct skip occurring prior to the recapture event is recomputed based on the applicable fraction as redetermined. Any additional GST tax as recomputed is due and payable on the date that is six months after the event that causes the imposition of the additional estate tax under section 2032A. The additional GST tax is remitted with Form 706–A and is reported by attaching a statement to Form 706–A showing the computation of the additional GST tax.

(iii) The applicable fraction, as redetermined under this section, is also used in determining any GST tax imposed with respect to GSTs occurring after the date of the recapture event.

(b) Examples. The following examples illustrate the principles of this section:

Example 1. Allocation of additional exemption. T transfers $200,000 to an irrevocable trust under which the income is payable to T's child, C, for life. Upon the termination of the trust, the remainder is payable to T's grandchild, GC. At a time when no ETIP exists with respect to the trust property, T makes a timely allocation of $100,000 of GST exemption, resulting in an inclusion ratio of .50. Subsequently, when the entire trust property is valued at $500,000, T allocates an additional $100,000 of T's unused GST exemption to the trust. The inclusion ratio of the trust is recomputed at that time. The numerator of the applicable fraction is $350,000 ($250,000 (the nontax portion as of the date of the allocation) plus $100,000 (the GST exemption currently being allocated)). The denominator is $500,000 (the date of allocation fair market value of the trust). The inclusion ratio is .30 (1—.70).

Example 2. Multiple transfers to a trust, allocation both timely and late. On December 10, 1993, T transfers $10,000 to an irrevocable trust that does not satisfy the requirements of section 2642(c)(2). T makes identical transfers to the trust on December 10, 1994,

1995, 1996, and on January 15, 1997. Immediately after the transfer on January 15, 1997, the value of the trust principal is $40,000. On January 14, 1998, when the value of the trust principal is $50,000, T allocates $30,000 of GST exemption to the trust. T discloses the 1997 transfer on the Form 709 filed on January 14, 1998. Thus, T's allocation is a timely allocation with respect to the transfer in 1997, $10,000 of the allocation is effective as of the date of that transfer, and, on and after January 15, 1997, the inclusion ratio of the trust is .75 (1—($10,000/$40,000)). The balance of the allocation is a late allocation with respect to prior transfers to the trust and is effective as of January 14, 1998. In redetermining the inclusion ratio as of that date, the numerator of the redetermined applicable fraction is $32,500 ($12,500 (.25 x $50,000), the nontax portion of the trust on January 14, 1998) plus $20,000 (the amount of GST exemption allocated late to the trust). The denominator of the new applicable fraction is $50,000 (the value of the trust principal at the time of the late allocation).

Example 3. Excess allocation. **(i)** T creates an irrevocable trust for the benefit of T's child and grandchild in 1996 transferring $50,000 to the trust on the date of creation. T allocates no GST exemption to the trust on the Form 709 reporting the transfer. On July 1, 1997 (when the value of the trust property is $60,000), T transfers an additional $40,000 to the trust.

(ii) On April 15, 1998, when the value of the trust is $150,000, T files a Form 709 reporting the 1997 transfer and allocating $150,000 of GST exemption to the trust. The allocation is a timely allocation of $40,000 with respect to the 1997 transfer and is effective as of that date. Thus, the applicable fraction for the trust as of July 1, 1997 is .40 ($40,000/$100,000 ($40,000 + $60,000)).

(iii) The allocation is also a late allocation of $90,000, the amount necessary to attain a zero inclusion ratio on April 15, 1998, computed as follows: $60,000 (the nontax portion immediately prior to the allocation (.40 x $150,000)) plus $90,000 (the additional allocation necessary to produce a zero inclusion ratio based on a denominator of $150,000)/$150,000 equals one and, thus, an inclusion ratio of zero. The balance of the allocation, $20,000 ($150,000 less the timely allocation of $40,000 less the late allocation of $90,000) is void.

Example 4. Undisclosed transfer. **(i)** The facts are the same as in Example 3, except that on February 1, 1998 (when the value of the trust is $150,000), T transfers an additional $50,000 to the trust and the value of the entire trust corpus on April 15, 1998 is $220,000. The Form 709 filed on April 15, 1998 does not disclose the 1998 transfer. Under the rule in § 26.2632–1(b)(2)(ii), the allocation is effective first as a timely allocation to the 1997 transfer; second, as a late allocation to the trust as of April 15, 1998; and, finally as a timely allocation to the February 1, 1998 transfer. As of April 15, 1998, $55,000, a pro rata portion of the trust assets, is considered to be the property transferred to the trust on February 1, 1998 (($50,000/$200,000) x $220,000). The balance of the trust, $165,000, represents prior transfers to the trust.

(ii) As in Example 3, the allocation is a timely allocation as to the 1997 transfer (and the applicable fraction as of July 1, 1997 is .40) and a late allocation as of 1998. The amount of the late allocation is $99,000, computed as follows: (.40 x $165,000 plus $99,000)/$165,000 = one.

(iii) The balance of the allocation, $11,000 ($150,000 less the timely allocation of $40,000 less the late allocation of $99,000) is a timely allocation as of February 1, 1998. The applicable fraction with respect to the trust, as of February 1, 1998, is .355, computed as follows: $60,000 (the nontax portion of the trust immediately prior to the February 1, 1998 transfer (.40 x $150,000)) plus $11,000 (the amount of the timely allocation to the 1998 transfer)/$200,000 (the value of the trust on February 1, 1998, after the transfer on that date) = $71,000/$200,000 = .355.

(iv) The applicable fraction with respect to the trust, as of April 15, 1998, is .805 computed as follows: $78,100 (the nontax portion immediately prior to the allocation (.355 x $220,000)) plus $99,000 (the amount of the late allocation)/ $220,000 = $177,100/$220,000 = .805.

Example 5. Redetermination of inclusion ratio on ETIP termination. **(i)** T transfers $100,000 to an irrevocable trust. The trust instrument provides that trust income is to be paid to T for 9 years or until T's prior death. The trust principal is to be paid to T's grandchild, GC, on the termination of T's income interest. The trustee has the power to invade trust principal for the benefit of GC during the term of T's income interest. The trust is subject to an ETIP while T holds the retained income interest. T files a timely Form 709 reporting the transfer and allocates $100,000 of GST exemption to the trust. In year 4, when the value of the trust is $200,000, the trustee distributes $15,000 to GC. The distribution is a taxable distribution. Because of the existence of the ETIP, the inclusion ratio with respect to the taxable distribution is determined immediately prior to the occurrence of the GST. Thus, the inclusion ratio applicable to the year 4 GST is .50 (1—($100,000/$200,000)).

(ii) In year 5, when the value of the trust is again $200,000, the trustee distributes another $15,000 to GC. Because the trust is still subject to the ETIP in year 5, the inclusion ratio with respect to the year 5 GST is again computed immediately prior to the GST. In computing the new inclusion ratio, the numerator of the applicable fraction is reduced by the nontax portion of prior GSTs occurring during the ETIP. Thus, the numerator of the applicable fraction with respect to the GST in year 5 is $92,500 ($100,000—(.50 x $15,000)) and the inclusion ratio applicable with respect to the GST in year 5 is .537 (1—($92,500/$200,000) = .463). Any additional GST exemption allocated on a timely ETIP return with respect to the GST in year 5 is effective immediately prior to the transfer.

[T.D. 8644, 60 FR 66898, Dec. 27, 1995, as corrected by Announcement 96–72, 61 FR 29653, June 12, 1996]

§ 26.2642–5 Finality of inclusion ratio.

(a) Direct skips. The inclusion ratio applicable to a direct skip becomes final when no additional GST tax (including additional GST tax payable as a result of a cessation, etc. of qualified use under section 2032A(c)) may be assessed with respect to the direct skip.

(b) Other GSTs. With respect to taxable distributions and taxable terminations, the inclusion ratio for a trust becomes final, on the later of—

(1) The expiration of the period for assessment with respect to the first GST tax return filed using that inclusion ratio (unless the trust is subject to an election under section 2032A in which case the applicable date under this subsection is the expiration of the period of assessment of any additional GST tax due as a result of a cessation, etc. of qualified use under section 2032A); or

(2) The expiration of the period for assessment of Federal estate tax with respect to the estate of the transferor. For purposes of this paragraph (b)(2), if an estate tax return is not required to be filed, the period for assessment is determined as if a return were required to be filed and as if the return were timely filed within the period prescribed by section 6075(a).

[T.D. 8644, 60 FR 66898, Dec. 27, 1995, as corrected by Announcement 96–90, 61 FR 43656, Aug. 26, 1996]

§ 26.2651–1 Generation assignment.

(a) Special rule for persons with a deceased parent—(1) In general. This paragraph (a) applies for purposes of determining whether a transfer to or for the benefit of an individual who is a descendant of a parent of the transferor (or the transferor's spouse or former spouse) is a generation-skipping transfer. If that individual's parent, who is a lineal descendant of the parent of the transferor (or the transferor's spouse or former spouse), is deceased at the time the transfer (from which an interest of such individual is established or derived) is subject to the tax imposed on the transferor by chapter 11 or 12 of the Internal Revenue Code, the individual is treated as if that individual were a member of the generation that is one generation below the lower of—

(i) The transferor's generation; or

(ii) The generation assignment of the individual's youngest living lineal ancestor who is also a descendant of the parent of the transferor (or the transferor's spouse or former spouse).

(2) Special rules—(i) Corresponding generation adjustment. If an individual's generation assignment is adjusted with respect to a transfer in accordance with paragraph (a)(1) of this section, a corresponding adjustment with respect to that transfer is made to the generation assignment of each—

(A) Spouse or former spouse of that individual;

(B) Descendant of that individual; and

(C) Spouse or former spouse of each descendant of that individual.

(ii) Continued application of generation assignment. If a transfer to a trust would be a generation-skipping transfer but for paragraph (a)(1) of this section, any generation assignment determined under this paragraph (a) continues to apply in determining whether any subsequent distribution from (or termination of an interest in) the portion of the trust attributable to that transfer is a generation-skipping transfer.

(iii) Ninety-day rule. For purposes of paragraph (a)(1) of this section, any individual who dies no later than 90 days after a transfer occurring by reason of the death of the transferor is treated as having predeceased the transferor.

(iv) Local law. A living person is not treated as having predeceased the transferor solely by reason of a provision of applicable local law; e.g., an individual who disclaims is not treated as a predeceased parent solely because state law treats a disclaimant as having predeceased the transferor for purposes of determining the disposition of the disclaimed property.

(3) Established or derived. For purposes of section 2651(e) and paragraph (a)(1) of this section, an individual's interest is established or derived at the time the transferor is subject to transfer tax on the property. See § 26.2652–1(a) for the definition of a transferor. If the same transferor, on more than one occasion, is subject to transfer tax imposed by either chapter 11 or 12 of the Internal Revenue Code on the property so transferred (whether the same property, reinvestments thereof, income thereon, or any or all of these), then the relevant time for determining whether paragraph (a)(1) of this section applies is the earliest time at which the transferor is subject to the tax imposed by either chapter 11 or 12 of the Internal Revenue Code. For purposes of section 2651(e) and paragraph (a)(1) of this section, the interest of a remainder beneficiary of a trust for which an election under section 2523(f) or section 2056(b)(7) (QTIP election) has been made will be deemed to have been established or derived, to the extent of the QTIP election, on the date as of which the value of the trust corpus is first subject to tax under section 2519 or section 2044. The preceding sentence does not apply to a trust, however, to the extent that an election under section 2652(a)(3) (reverse QTIP election) has been made for the trust because, to the extent of a reverse QTIP election, the spouse who established the trust will remain the transferor of the trust for generation-skipping transfer tax purposes.

(4) Special rule in the case of additional contributions to a trust. If a transferor referred to in paragraph (a)(1) of this section contributes additional property to a trust that existed before the application of paragraph (a)(1), then the additional property is treated as being held in a separate trust for purposes of chapter 13 of the Internal Revenue Code. The provisions of § 26.2654–1(a)(2), regarding treatment as separate trusts, apply as if different transferors had contributed to the separate portions of the single trust. Additional subsequent contributions from that transferor will be added to the new share that is treated as a separate trust.

(b) Limited application to collateral heirs. Paragraph (a) of this section does not apply in the case of a transfer to any individual who is not a lineal descendant of the transferor (or the transferor's spouse or former spouse) if the transferor has any living lineal descendant at the time of the transfer.

(c) Examples. The following examples illustrate the provisions of this section:

Example 1. T establishes an irrevocable trust, Trust, providing that trust income is to be paid to T's grandchild, GC, for 5 years. At the end of the 5–year period or on GC's prior death, Trust is to terminate and the principal is to be distributed to GC if GC is living or to GC's children if GC has died. The transfer that occurred on the creation of the trust is subject to the tax imposed by chapter 12 of the Internal Revenue Code and, at the time of the transfer, T's child, C, who is a parent of GC, is deceased. GC is treated as a member of the generation that is one generation below T's generation. As a result, GC is not a skip person and Trust is not a skip person. Therefore, the transfer to Trust is not a direct skip. Similarly, distributions to GC during the term of Trust and at the termination of Trust will not be GSTs.

Example 2. On January 1, 2004, T transfers $100,000 to an irrevocable inter vivos trust that provides T with an annuity payable for four years or until T's prior death. The annuity satisfies the definition of a qualified interest under section 2702(b). When the trust terminates, the corpus is to be paid to T's grandchild, GC. The transfer is subject to the tax imposed by chapter 12 of the Internal Revenue Code and, at the time of the transfer, T's child, C, who is a parent of GC, is living. C dies in 2006. In this case, C was alive at the time the transfer by T was subject to the tax imposed by chapter 12 of the Internal Revenue Code. Therefore, section 2651(e) and paragraph (a)(1) of this section do not apply. When the trust subsequently terminates, the distribution to GC is a taxable termination that is subject to the GST tax to the extent the trust has an inclusion ratio greater than zero. See section 2642(a).

Example 3. T dies testate in 2002, survived by T's spouse, S, their children, C1 and C2, and C1's child, GC. Under the terms of T's will, a trust is established for the benefit of S and of T and S's descendants. Under the terms of the trust, all income is payable to S during S's lifetime and the trustee may distribute trust corpus for S's health, support and maintenance. At S's death, the corpus is to be distributed, outright, to C1 and C2. If either C1 or C2 has predeceased S, the deceased child's share of the corpus is to be distributed to that child's then-living descendants, per stirpes. The executor of T's estate makes the election under section 2056(b)(7) to treat the trust property as qualified terminable interest property (QTIP) but does not make the election under section 2652(a)(3) (reverse QTIP election). In 2003, C1 dies survived by S and GC. In 2004, S dies, and the trust terminates. The full fair market value of the trust is includible in S's gross estate under section 2044 and S becomes the transferor of the trust under section 2652(a)(1)(A). GC's interest is considered established or derived at S's death, and because C1 is deceased at that time, GC is treated as a member of the generation that is one generation below the generation of the transferor, S. As a result, GC is not a skip person and the transfer to GC is not a direct skip.

Example 4. The facts are the same as in Example 3. However, the executor of T's estate makes the election under section 2652(a)(3) (reverse QTIP election) for the entire trust. Therefore, T remains the transferor because, for purposes of chapter 13 of the Internal Revenue Code, the election to be treated as qualified terminable interest property is treated as if it had not been made. In this case, GC's interest is established or derived on T's death in 2002. Because C1 was living at the time of T's death, the predeceased parent rule under section 2651(e) does not apply, even though C1 was deceased at the time the transfer from S to GC was subject to the tax under chapter 11 of the Internal Revenue Code. When the trust terminates, the distribution to GC is a taxable termination that is subject to the GST tax to the extent the trust has an inclusion ratio greater than zero. See section 2642(a).

Example 5. T establishes an irrevocable trust providing that trust income is to be paid to T's grandniece, GN, for 5 years or until GN's prior death. At the end of the 5–year period or on GN's prior death, the trust is to terminate and the principal is to be distributed to GN if living, or if GN has died, to GN's then-living descendants, per stirpes. S is a sibling of T and the parent of N. N is the parent of GN. At the time of the transfer, T has no living lineal descendant, S is living, N is deceased, and the transfer is subject to the gift tax imposed by chapter 12 of the Internal Revenue Code. GN is treated as a member of the generation that is one generation below T's generation because S, GN's youngest living lineal ancestor who is also a descendant of T's parent, is in T's generation. As a result, GN is not a skip person and the transfer to the trust is not a direct skip. In addition, distributions to GN during the term of the trust and at the termination of the trust will not be GSTs.

Example 6. On January 1, 2004, T transfers $50,000 to a great-grandniece, GGN, who is the great-grandchild of B, a brother of T. At the time of the transfer, T has no living lineal descendants and B's grandchild, GN, who is a parent of GGN and a child of B's living child, N, is deceased. GGN will be treated as a member of the generation that is one generation below the lower of T's generation or the generation assignment of GGN's youngest living lineal ancestor who is also a descendant of the parent of the transferor. In this case, N is GGN's youngest living lineal ancestor who is also a descendant of the parent of T. Because N's generation assignment is lower than T's generation, GGN will be treated as a member of the generation that is one generation below N's generation assignment (i.e., GGN will be treated as a member of her parent's generation). As a result, GGN remains a skip person and the transfer to GGN is a direct skip.

Example 7. T has a child, C. C and C's spouse, S, have a 20–year-old child, GC. C dies and S subsequently marries S2. S2 legally adopts GC. T transfers $100,000 to GC. Under section 2651(b)(1), GC is assigned to the generation that is two generations below T. However, since GC's parent, C, is deceased at the time of the transfer, GC will be treated as a member of the generation that is one generation below T. As a result, GC is not a skip person and the transfer to GC is not a direct skip.

[T.D. 9214, 70 FR 41142, July 18, 2005]

§ 26.2651–2 Individual assigned to more than 1 generation.

(a) In general. Except as provided in paragraph (b) or (c) of this section, an individual who would be assigned to more than 1 generation is assigned to the youngest of the generations to which that individual would be assigned.

(b) Exception. Notwithstanding paragraph (a) of this section, an adopted individual (as defined in this paragraph) will be treated as a member of the generation that is one generation below the adoptive parent for purposes of determining whether a transfer to the adopted individual from the adoptive parent (or the spouse or former spouse of the adoptive parent, or a lineal descendant of a grandparent of the adoptive parent) is subject to chapter 13 of the Internal Revenue Code. For purposes of this paragraph (b), an adopted individual is an individual who is—

(1) Legally adopted by the adoptive parent;

(2) A descendant of a parent of the adoptive parent (or the spouse or former spouse of the adoptive parent);

(3) Under the age of 18 at the time of the adoption; and

(4) Not adopted primarily for the purpose of avoiding GST tax. The determination of whether an adoption is primarily for GST tax-avoidance purposes is made based upon all of the facts and circumstances. The most significant factor is whether there is a bona fide parent/child relationship between the adoptive parent and the adopted individual, in which the adoptive parent has fully assumed all significant responsibilities for the care and raising of the adopted child. Other factors may include (but are not limited to), at the time of the adoption—

(i) The age of the adopted individual (for example, the younger the age of the adopted individual, or the age of the youngest of siblings who are all adopted together, the more likely the adoption will not be considered primarily for GST tax-avoidance purposes); and

(ii) The relationship between the adopted individual and the individual's parents (for example, objective evidence of the absence or incapacity of the parents may indicate that the adoption is not primarily for GST tax-avoidance purposes).

(c) Special rules—(1) Corresponding generation adjustment. If an individual's generation assignment is adjusted with respect to a transfer in accordance with paragraph (b) of this section, a corresponding adjustment with respect to that transfer is made to the generation assignment of each—

(i) Spouse or former spouse of that individual;

(ii) Descendant of that individual; and

(iii) Spouse or former spouse of each descendant of that individual.

(2) Continued application of generation assignment. If a transfer to a trust would be a generation-skipping transfer but for paragraph (b) of this section, any generation assignment determined under paragraph (b) or (c) of this section continues to apply in determining whether any subsequent distribution from (or termination of an interest in) the portion of the trust attributable to that transfer is a generation-skipping transfer.

(d) Example. The following example illustrates the provisions of this section:

Example. T has a child, C. C has a 20–year-old child, GC. T legally adopts GC and transfers $100,000 to GC. GC's generation assignment is determined by section 2651(b)(1) and GC is assigned to the generation that is two generations below T. In addition, because T has legally adopted GC, GC is generally treated as a child of T under state law. Under these circumstances, GC is an individual who is assigned to more than one generation and the exception in § 26.2651–2(b) does not apply. Thus, the special rule under section 2651(f)(1) applies and GC is assigned to the generation that is two generations below T. GC remains a skip person with respect to T and the transfer to GC is a direct skip.

[T.D. 9214, 70 FR 41143, July 18, 2005]

§ 26.2651–3 Effective dates.

(a) In general. The rules of §§ 26.2651–1 and 26.2651–2 are applicable for terminations, distributions, and transfers occurring on or after July 18, 2005.

(b) Transition rule. In the case of transfers occurring after December 31, 1997, and before July 18, 2005, taxpayers may rely on any reasonable interpretation of section 2651(e). For this purpose, these final regulations, as well as the proposed regulations issued on September 3, 2004 (69 FR 53862), are treated as a reasonable interpretation of the statute.

[T.D. 9214, 70 FR 41143, July 18, 2005]

§ 26.2652–1 Transferor defined; other definitions.

(a) Transferor defined—(1) In general. Except as otherwise provided in paragraph (a)(3) of this section, the individual with respect to whom property was most recently subject to Federal estate or gift tax is the transferor of that property for purposes of chapter 13. An individual is treated as transferring any property with respect to which the individual is the transferor. Thus, an individual may be a transferor even though there is no transfer of property under local law at the time the Federal estate or gift tax applies. For purposes of this paragraph, a surviving spouse is the transferor of a qualified domestic trust created by the deceased spouse that is included in the surviving spouse's gross estate, provided the trust is not subject to the election described in § 26.2652–2 (reverse QTIP election). A surviving spouse is also the transferor of a qualified domestic trust created by the surviving spouse pursuant to section 2056(d)(2)(B).

(2) Transfers subject to Federal estate or gift tax. For purposes of this chapter, a transfer is subject to Federal gift tax if a gift tax is imposed under section 2501(a) (without regard to exemptions, exclusions, deductions, and credits). A transfer is subject to Federal estate tax if the value of the property is includible in the decedent's gross estate as determined under section 2031 or section 2103.

(3) Special rule for certain QTIP trusts. Solely for purposes of chapter 13, if a transferor of qualified terminable interest property (QTIP) elects under § 26.2652–2(a) to treat the property as if the QTIP election had not been made (reverse QTIP election), the identity of the transferor of the property is determined without regard to the application of sections 2044, 2207A, and 2519.

(4) Split-gift transfers. In the case of a transfer with respect to which the donor's spouse makes an election under section 2513 to treat the gift as made one-half by the spouse, the electing spouse is treated as the transferor of one-half of the entire value of the property transferred by the donor, regardless of the interest the electing spouse is actually deemed to have transferred under section 2513. The donor is treated as the transferor of one-half of the value of the entire property. See § 26.2632–1(c)(5) Example 3, regarding allocation of GST exemption with respect to split-gift transfers subject to an ETIP.

(5) Examples. The following examples illustrate the principles of this paragraph (a):

Example 1. Identity of transferor. T transfers $100,000 to a trust for the sole benefit of T's grandchild. The transfer is subject to Federal gift tax because a gift tax is imposed under section 2501(a) (without regard to exemptions, exclusions, deductions, and credits). Thus, for purposes of chapter 13, T is the transferor of the $100,000. It is immaterial that a portion of the transfer is excluded from the total amount of T's taxable gift by reason of section 2503(b).

Example 2. Gift splitting and identity of transferor. The facts are the same as in Example 1, except T's spouse, S, consents under section 2513 to split the gift with T. For purposes of chapter 13, S and T are each treated as a transferor of $50,000 to the trust.

Example 3. Change of transferor on subsequent transfer tax event. T transfers $100,000 to a trust providing that all the net trust income is to be paid to T's spouse, S, for S's lifetime. T elects under section 2523(f) to treat the transfer as a transfer of qualified terminable interest property, and T does not make the reverse QTIP election under section 2652(a)(3). On S's death, the trust property is included in S's gross estate under section 2044. Thus, S becomes the transferor at the time of S's death.

Example 4. Effect of transfer of an interest in trust on identity of the transferor. T transfers $100,000 to a trust providing that all of the net income is to be paid to T's child, C, for C's lifetime. At C's death, the trust property is to be paid to T's grandchild. C transfers the income interest to X, an unrelated party, in a transfer that is a completed transfer for Federal gift tax purposes. Because C's transfer is a transfer of a term interest in the trust that does not affect the rights of other parties with respect to the trust property, T remains the transferor with respect to the trust.

Example 5. Effect of lapse of withdrawal right on identity of transferor. T transfers $10,000 to a new trust providing that the trust income is to be paid to T's child, C, for C's life and, on the death of C, the trust principal is to be paid to T's grandchild, GC. The trustee has discretion to distribute principal for GC's benefit during C's lifetime. C has a right to withdraw $10,000 from the trust for a 60–day period following the transfer. Thereafter, the power lapses. C does not exercise the withdrawal right. The transfer by T is subject to Federal gift tax because a gift tax is imposed under section 2501(a) (without regard to exemptions, exclusions, deductions, and credits) and, thus, T is treated as having transferred the entire $10,000 to the trust. On the lapse of the withdrawal right, C becomes a transferor to the extent C is treated as having made a completed transfer for purposes of chapter 12. Therefore, except to the extent that the amount with respect to which the power of withdrawal lapses exceeds the greater of $5,000 or 5% of the value of the trust property, T remains the transferor of the trust property for purposes of chapter 13.

Example 6. Effect of reverse QTIP election on identity of the transferor. T establishes a testamentary trust having a principal of $500,000. Under the terms of the trust, all trust income is payable to T's surviving spouse, S, during S's lifetime. T's executor makes an election to treat the trust property as qualified terminable interest property and also makes the reverse QTIP election. For purposes of chapter 13, T is the transferor with respect to the trust. On S's death, the then full fair market value of the trust is includible in S's gross estate under section 2044. However, because of the reverse QTIP election, S does not become the transferor with respect to the trust; T continues to be the transferor.

Example 7. Effect of reverse QTIP election on constructive additions. The facts are the same as in Example 6, except the inclusion of the QTIP trust in S's gross estate increased the Federal estate tax liability of S's estate by $200,000. The estate does not exercise the right of recovery from the trust granted under section 2207A. Under local law, the beneficiaries of S's residuary estate (which bears all estate taxes under the will) could compel the executor to exercise the right of recovery but do not do so. Solely for purposes of chapter 13, the beneficiaries of the residuary estate are not treated as having made an addition to the trust by reason of their failure to exercise their right of recovery. Because of the reverse QTIP election, for GST purposes, the trust property is not treated as includible in S's gross estate and, under those circumstances, no right of recovery exists.

Example 8. Effect of reverse QTIP election on constructive additions. S, the surviving spouse of T, dies testate. At the time of S's death, S was the beneficiary of a trust with respect to which T's executor made a QTIP election under section 2056(b)(7). Thus, the trust is includible in S's gross estate under section 2044. T's executor also made the reverse QTIP election with respect to the trust. S's will provides that all death taxes payable with respect to the trust are payable from S's residuary estate. Since the transferor of the property is determined without regard to section 2044 and section 2207A, S is not treated as making a constructive addition to the trust by reason of the tax apportionment clause in S's will.

Example 9. Split-gift transfers. T transfers $100,000 to an inter vivos trust that provides T with an annuity payable for ten years or until T's prior death. The annuity satisfies the definition of a qualified interest under section 2702(b). When the trust terminates, the corpus is to be paid to T's grandchild, GC. T's spouse, S, consents under section 2513 to have the gift treated as made one-half by S. Under section 2513, only the actuarial value of the gift to GC is eligible to be treated as made one-half by S. However, because S is treated as the donor of one-half of the gift to GC, S becomes the transferor of one-half of the entire trust ($50,000) for purposes of Chapter 13.

(b) Trust defined—(1) In general. A trust includes any arrangement (other than an estate) that has substantially the same effect as a trust. Thus, for example, arrangements involving life estates and remainders, estates for years, and insurance and annuity contracts are trusts. Generally, a transfer as to which the identity of the transferee is contingent upon the occurrence of an event is a transfer in trust; however, a transfer of property included in the transferor's gross estate, as to which the identity of the transferee is contingent upon an event that must occur within 6 months of the transferor's death, is not considered a transfer in trust solely by reason of the existence of the contingency.

(2) Examples. The following examples illustrate the provisions of this paragraph (b):

Example 1. Uniform gifts to minors transfers. T transfers cash to an account in the name of T's child, C, as custodian for C's child, GC (who is a minor), under a state statute substantially similar to the Uniform Gifts to Minors Act. For purposes of chapter 13, the transfer to the custodial account is treated as a transfer to a trust.

Example 2. Contingent transfers. T bequeaths $200,000 to T's child, C, provided that if C does not survive T by more than 6 months, the bequest is payable to T's grandchild, GC. C dies 4 months after T. The bequest is not a transfer in trust because the contingency that determines the recipient of the bequest must occur within 6 months of T's death. The bequest to GC is a direct skip.

Example 3. Contingent transfers. The facts are the same as in Example 2, except C must survive T by 18 months to take the bequest. The bequest is a transfer in trust for purposes of chapter 13, and the death of C is a taxable termination.

(c) Trustee defined. The trustee of a trust is the person designated as trustee under local law or, if no such person is so designated, the person in actual or constructive possession of property held in trust.

(d) Executor defined. For purposes of chapter 13, the executor is the executor or administrator of the decedent's estate. However, if no executor or administrator is appointed, qualified or acting within the United States, the executor is the fiduciary who is primarily responsible for payment of the decedent's debts and expenses. If there is no such executor, administrator or fiduciary, the executor is the person in actual or constructive possession of the largest portion of the value of the decedent's gross estate.

(e) Interest in trust. See § 26.2612–1(e) for the definition of interest in trust.

[T.D. 8644, 60 FR 66918, Dec. 27, 1995; 61 FR 29654, June 12, 1996; T.D. 8720, 62 FR 27498, May 20, 1997]

§ 26.2652–2 Special election for qualified terminable interest property.

(a) In general. If an election is made to treat property as qualified terminable interest property (QTIP) under section 2523(f) or section 2056(b)(7), the person making the election may, for purposes of chapter 13, elect to treat the property as if the QTIP election had not been made (reverse QTIP election). An election under this section is irrevocable. An election under this section is not effective unless it is made with respect to all of the property in the trust to which the QTIP election applies. See, however, § 26.2654–1(b)(1). Property that qualifies for a deduction under section 2056(b)(5) is not eligible for the election under this section.

(b) Time and manner of making election. An election under this section is made on the return on which the QTIP election is made. If a protective QTIP election is made, no election under this section is effective unless a protective reverse QTIP election is also made.

(c) Transitional rule. If a reverse QTIP election is made with respect to a trust prior to December 27, 1995, and GST exemption has been allocated to that trust, the transferor (or the transferor's executor) may elect to treat the trust as two separate trusts, one of which has a zero inclusion ratio by reason of the transferor's GST exemption previously allocated to the trust. The separate trust with the zero inclusion ratio consists of that fractional share of the value of the entire trust equal to the value of the nontax portion of the trust under § 26.2642–4(a). The reverse QTIP election is treated as applying only to the trust with the zero inclusion ratio. An election under this paragraph (c) is made by attaching a statement to a copy of the return on which the reverse QTIP election was made under section 2652(a)(3). The statement must indicate that an election is being made to treat the trust as two separate trusts and must identify the values of the two separate trusts. The statement is to be filed in the same place in which the original return was filed and must be filed before June 24, 1996. A trust subject to the election described in this paragraph is treated as a trust that was created by two transferors. See § 26.2654–1(a)(2) for special rules involving trusts with multiple transferors.

(d) Examples. The following examples illustrate the provisions of this section:

Example 1. Special (reverse QTIP) election under section 2652(a)(3). T transfers $1,000,000 to a trust providing that all trust income is to be paid to T's spouse, S, for S's lifetime. On S's death, the trust principal is payable to GC, a grandchild of S and T. T elects to treat all of the transfer as a transfer of QTIP and also makes the reverse QTIP election for all of the property. Because of the reverse QTIP election, T continues to be treated as the transferor of the property after S's death for purposes of chapter 13. A taxable termination rather than a direct skip occurs on S's death.

Example 2. Election under transition rule. In 1994, T died leaving $4 million in trust for the benefit of T's surviving spouse, S. On January 16, 1995, T's executor filed T's Form 706 on which the executor elects to treat the entire trust as qualified terminable interest property. The executor also makes a reverse QTIP election. The reverse QTIP election is effective with respect to the entire trust even though T's executor could allocate only $1 million of GST exemption to the trust. T's executor may elect to treat the trust as two separate trusts, one having a value of 25% of the value of the single trust and an inclusion ratio of zero, but only if the election is made prior to June 24, 1996. If the executor makes the transitional election, the other separate trust, having a value of 75% of the value of the single trust and an inclusion ratio of one, is not treated as subject to the reverse QTIP election.

Example 3. Denominator of the applicable fraction of QTIP trust. T bequeaths $1,500,000 to a trust in which T's surviving spouse, S, receives an income interest for life. Upon the death of S, the property is to remain in trust for the benefit of C, the child of T and S. Upon C's death, the trust is to terminate and the trust property paid to the descendants of C. The bequest qualifies for the estate tax marital deduction under section 2056(b)(7) as QTIP. The executor does not make the reverse QTIP election under section 2652(a)(3). As a result, S becomes the transferor of the trust at S's death when the value of the property in the QTIP trust is included in S's gross estate under section 2044. For purposes of computing the applicable fraction with respect to the QTIP trust upon S's death, the denominator of the fraction is reduced by any Federal estate tax (whether imposed under section 2001, 2101 or 2056A(b)) and State death tax attributable to the trust property that is actually recovered from the trust.

[T.D. 8644, 60 FR 66898, Dec. 27, 1995]

§ 26.2653–1 Taxation of multiple skips.

(a) General rule. If property is held in trust immediately after a GST, solely for purposes of determining whether future events involve a skip person, the transferor is thereafter deemed to occupy the generation immediately above the highest generation of any person holding an interest in the trust immediately after the transfer. If no person holds an interest in the trust immediately after the GST, the transferor is treated as occupying the generation above the highest generation of any person in existence at the time of the GST who then occupies the highest generation level of any person who may subsequently hold an interest in the trust. See § 26.2612–1(e) for rules determining when a person has an interest in property held in trust.

(b) Examples. The following examples illustrate the provisions of this section:

Example 1. T transfers property to an irrevocable trust for the benefit of T's grandchild, GC, and great-grandchild, GGC. During GC's life, the trust income may be distributed to GC and GGC in the trustee's absolute discretion. At GC's death, the trust property passes to GGC. Both GC and GGC have an interest in the trust for purposes of chapter 13. The transfer by T to the trust is a direct skip, and the property is held in trust immediately after the transfer. After the direct skip, the transferor is treated as being one generation above GC, the highest generation individual having an interest in the trust. Therefore, GC is no longer a skip person and distributions to GC are not taxable distributions. However, because GGC occupies a generation that is two generations below the deemed generation of T, GGC is a skip person and distributions of trust income to GGC are taxable distributions.

Example 2. T transfers property to an irrevocable trust providing that the income is to be paid to T's child, C, for life. At C's death, the trust income is to be accumulated for 10 years and added to principal. At the end of the 10–year accumulation period, the trust income is to be paid to T's grandchild, GC, for life. Upon GC's death, the trust property is to be paid to T's great-grandchild, GGC, or to GGC's estate. A GST occurs at C's death. Immediately after C's death and during the 10–year accumulation period, no person has an interest in the trust within the meaning of section 2652(c) and § 26.2612–1(e) because no one can receive current distributions of income or principal. Immediately after C's death, T is treated as occupying the generation above the generation of GC (the trust beneficiary in existence at the time of the GST who then occupies the highest generation level of any person who may subsequently hold an interest in the trust). Thus, subsequent income distributions to GC are not taxable distributions.

[T.D. 8644, 60 FR 66898, Dec. 27, 1995]

§ 26.2654–1 Certain trusts treated as separate trusts.

(a) Single trust treated as separate trusts—(1) Substantially separate and independent shares—(i) In general. If a single trust consists solely of substantially separate and independent shares for different beneficiaries, the share attributable to each beneficiary (or group of beneficiaries) is treated as a separate trust for purposes of Chapter 13. The phrase "substantially separate and independent shares" generally has the same meaning as provided in § 1.663(c)–3. However, except as provided in paragraph (a)(1)(iii) of this section, a portion of a trust is not a separate share unless such share exists from and at all times after the creation of the trust. For purposes of this paragraph (a)(1), a trust is treated as created at the date of death of the grantor if the trust is includible in its entirety in the grantor's gross estate for Federal estate tax purposes. Further, except with respect to shares or trusts that are treated as separate trusts under local law, treatment of a single trust as separate trusts under this paragraph (a)(1) does not permit treatment of those portions as separate trusts for purposes of filing returns and payment of tax or for purposes of computing any other tax imposed under the Internal Revenue Code. Also, additions to, and distributions from, such trusts are allocated pro rata among the separate trusts, unless the governing instrument expressly provides otherwise. See § 26.2642–6 and paragraph (b) of this section regarding the treatment, for purposes of Chapter 13, of separate trusts resulting from the discretionary severance of a single trust.

(ii) Certain pecuniary amounts. For purposes of this section, if a person holds the current right to receive a mandatory (i.e., nondiscretionary and noncontingent) payment of a pecuniary amount at the death of the transferor from an inter vivos trust that is includible in the transferor's gross estate, or a testamentary trust, the pecuniary amount is a separate and independent share if—

(A) The trustee is required to pay appropriate interest (as defined in § 26.2642–2(b)(4)(i) and (ii)) to the person; and

(B) If the pecuniary amount is payable in kind on the basis of value other than the date of distribution value of the assets, the trustee is required to allocate assets to the pecuniary payment in a manner that fairly reflects net appreciation or depreciation in the value of the assets in the fund available to pay the pecuniary amount measured from the valuation date to the date of payment.

(iii) Mandatory severances. For purposes of this section, if the governing instrument of a trust requires the division or severance of a single trust into separate trusts upon the future occurrence of a particular event not within the discretion of the trustee or any other person, and if the trusts resulting from such a division or severance are recognized as separate trusts under applicable state law, then each resulting trust is treated as a separate trust for purposes of Chapter 13. * * *

(2) Multiple transferors with respect to single trust—(i) In general. If there is more than one transferor with respect to a trust, the portions of the trust attributable to the different transferors are treated as separate trusts for purposes of chapter 13. Treatment of a single trust as separate trusts under this paragraph (a)(2) does not permit treatment of those portions as separate trusts for purposes of filing returns and payment of tax or for purposes of computing any other tax imposed under the Internal Revenue Code. Also, additions to, and distributions from, such trusts are allocated pro rata among the separate trusts unless otherwise expressly provided in the governing instrument.

(ii) Addition by a transferor. If an individual makes an addition to a trust of which the individual is not the sole transferor, the portion of the single trust attributable to each separate trust is determined by multiplying the fair market value of the single trust immediately after the contribution by a fraction. The numerator of the fraction is the value of the separate trust immediately after the contribution. The denominator of the fraction is the fair market value of all the property in the single trust immediately after the transfer.

(3) Severance of a single trust. A single trust treated as separate trusts under paragraphs (a)(1) or (2) of this section may be divided at any time into separate trusts to reflect that treatment. For this purpose, the rules of paragraph (b)(1)(ii)(C) of this section apply with respect to the severance and funding of the severed trusts.

(4) Allocation of exemption—(i) In general. With respect to a separate share treated as a separate trust under paragraph (a)(1) or (2) of this section, an individual's GST exemption is allocated to the separate trust. See § 26.2632–1 for rules concerning the allocation of GST exemption.

(ii) Automatic allocation to direct skips. If the transfer is a direct skip to a trust that occurs during the transferor's lifetime and is treated as a transfer to separate trusts under paragraphs (a)(1) or (a)(2) of this section, the transferor's GST exemption not previously allocated is automatically allocated on a pro rata basis among the separate trusts. The transferor may prevent an automatic allocation of GST exemption to a separate share of a single trust by describing on a timely-filed United States Gift (and Generation–Skipping Transfer) Tax Return (Form 709) the transfer and the extent to which the automatic allocation is not to apply to a particular share. See § 26.2632–1(b) for rules for avoiding the automatic allocation of GST exemption.

(5) Examples. The following examples illustrate the principles of this section (a):

Example 1. Separate shares as separate trusts. T transfers $100,000 to a trust under which income is to be paid in equal shares for 10 years to T's child, C, and T's grandchild, GC (or their respective estates). The trust does not permit distributions of principal during the term of the trust. At the end of the 10–year term, the trust principal is to be distributed to C and GC in equal shares. The shares of C and GC in the trust are separate and independent and, therefore, are treated as separate trusts. The result would not be the same if the trust permitted distributions of principal unless the distributions could only be made from a one-half separate share of the initial trust principal and the distributee's future rights with respect to the trust are correspondingly reduced. T may allocate part of T's GST exemption under section 2632(a) to the share held for the benefit of GC.

Example 2. Separate share rule inapplicable. The facts are the same as in Example 1, except the trustee holds the discretionary power to distribute the income in any proportion between C and GC during the last year of the trust. The shares of C and GC in the trust are not separate and independent shares throughout the entire term of the trust and, therefore, are not treated as separate trusts for purposes of chapter 13.

Example 3. Pecuniary payment as separate share. T creates a lifetime revocable trust providing that on T's death $500,000 is payable to T's spouse, S, with the balance of the principal to be held for the benefit of T's grandchildren. The value of the trust is includible in T's gross estate upon T's death. Under the terms of the trust, the payment to S is required to be made in cash, and under local law S is entitled to receive interest on the payment at an annual rate of 6 percent, commencing immediately upon T's death. For purposes of chapter 13, the trust is treated as created at T's death, and the $500,000 payable to S from the trust is treated as a separate share. The result would be the same if the payment to S could be satisfied using noncash assets at their value on the date of distribution. Further, the result would be the same if the decedent's probate estate poured over to the revocable trust on the decedent's death and was then distributed in accordance with the terms of the trust.

Example 4. Pecuniary payment not treated as separate share. The facts are the same as in Example 3, except the bequest to S is to be paid in noncash assets valued at their values as finally determined for Federal estate tax purposes. Neither the trust instrument nor local law requires that the assets distributed in satisfaction of the bequest fairly reflect net appreciation or depreciation in all the assets from which the bequest may be funded. S's $500,000 bequest is not treated as a separate share and the trust is treated as a single trust for purposes of chapter 13.

Example 5. Multiple transferors to single trust. A transfers $100,000 to an irrevocable generation-skipping trust; B simultaneously transfers $50,000 to the same trust. As of the time of the transfers, the single trust is treated as two trusts for purposes of chapter 13. Because A contributed ⅔ of the value of the initial corpus, ⅔ of the single trust principal is treated as a separate trust created by A. Similarly, because B contributed ⅓ of the value of the initial corpus, ⅓ of the single trust is treated as a separate trust created by B. A or B may allocate their GST exemption under section 2632(a) to the respective separate trusts.

Example 6. Additional contributions. A transfers $100,000 to an irrevocable generation-skipping trust; B simultaneously transfers $50,000 to the same trust. When the value of the single trust has increased to $180,000, A contributes an additional $60,000 to the trust. At the time of the additional contribution, the portion of the single trust attributable to each grantor's separate trust must be redetermined. The portion of the single trust attributable to A's separate trust immediately after the contribution is ¾ (((⅔ x $180,000) + $60,000)/$240, 000). The portion attributable to B's separate trust after A's addition is ¼.

Example 7. Distributions from a separate share. The facts are the same as in Example 6, except that, after A's second contribution, $50,000 is distributed to a beneficiary of the trust. Absent a provision in the trust instrument that charges the distribution against the contribution of either A or B, ¾ of the distribution is treated as made from the separate trust of which A is the transferor and ¼ from the separate trust of which B is the transferor.

Example 8. Subsequent mandatory division into separate trusts. T creates an irrevocable trust that provides the trustee with the discretionary power to distribute income or corpus to T's children and grandchildren. The trust provides that, when T's youngest child reaches age 21, the trust will be divided into separate shares, one share for each child of T. The income from a respective child's share will be paid to the child during the child's life, with the remainder passing on the child's death to such child's children (grandchildren of T). The separate shares that come into existence when the youngest child reaches age 21 will be recognized as of that date as separate trusts for purposes of Chapter 13. The inclusion ratio of the separate trusts will be identical to the inclusion ratio of the trust before the severance. Any allocation of GST tax exemption to the trust after T's youngest child reaches age 21 may be made to any one or more of the separate shares. The result would be the same if the trust instrument provided that the trust was to be divided into separate trusts when T's youngest child reached age 21, provided that the severance and funding of the separate trusts meets the requirements of this section.

(b) Division of a trust included in the gross estate—(1) In general. The severance of a trust that is included in the transferor's gross estate (or created under the transferor's will) into two or more trusts is recognized for purposes of chapter 13 if—

(i) The trust is severed pursuant to a direction in the governing instrument providing that the trust is to be divided upon the death of the transferor; or

(ii) The governing instrument does not require or otherwise direct severance but the trust is severed pursuant to discretionary authority granted either under the governing instrument or under local law; and

(A) The terms of the new trusts provide in the aggregate for the same succession of interests and beneficiaries as are provided in the original trust;

(B) The severance occurs (or a reformation proceeding, if required, is commenced) prior to the date prescribed for filing the Federal estate tax return (including extensions actually granted) for the estate of the transferor; and

(C) Either—

(1) The new trusts are severed on a fractional basis. If severed on a fractional basis, the separate trusts need not be funded with a pro rata portion of each asset held by the undivided trust. The trusts may be funded on a nonpro rata basis provided funding is based on either the fair market value of the assets on the date of funding or in a manner that fairly reflects the net appreciation or depreciation in the value of the assets measured from the valuation date to the date of funding; or

(2) If the severance is required (by the terms of the governing instrument) to be made on the basis of a pecuniary amount, the pecuniary payment is satisfied in a manner that would meet the requirements of paragraph (a)(1)(ii) of this section if it were paid to an individual.

(2) Special rule. If a court order severing the trust has not been issued at the time the Federal estate tax return is filed, the executor must indicate on a statement attached to the return that a proceeding has been commenced to sever the trust and describe the manner in which the trust is proposed to be severed. A copy of the petition or other instrument used to commence the proceeding must also be attached to the return. If the governing instrument of a trust or local law authorizes the severance of the trust, a severance pursuant to that authorization is treated as meeting the requirement of paragraph (b)(1)(ii)(B) of this section if the executor indicates on the Federal estate tax return that separate trusts will be created (or funded) and clearly sets forth the manner in which the trust is to be severed and the separate trusts funded.

(3) Allocation of exemption. An individual's GST exemption under § 2632 may be allocated to the separate trusts created pursuant to this section at the discretion of the executor or trustee.

(4) Examples. The following examples illustrate the provisions of this section (b):

Example 1. Severance of single trust. T's will establishes a testamentary trust providing that income is to be paid to T's spouse for life. At the spouse's death, one-half of the corpus is to be paid to T's child, C, or C's estate (if C fails to survive the spouse) and one-half of the corpus is to be paid to T's grandchild, GC, or GC's estate (if GC fails to survive the spouse). If the requirements of paragraph (b) of this section are otherwise satisfied, T's executor may divide the testamentary trust equally into two separate trusts, one trust providing an income interest to spouse for life with remainder to C, and the other trust with an income interest to spouse for life with remainder to GC. Furthermore, if the requirements of paragraph (b) of this section are satisfied, the executor or trustee may further divide the trust for the benefit of GC. GST exemption may be allocated to any of the divided trusts.

Example 2. Severance of revocable trust. T creates an inter vivos revocable trust providing that, at T's death and after payment of all taxes and administration expenses, the remaining corpus will be divided into two trusts. One trust, for the benefit of T's spouse, is to be funded with the smallest amount that, if qualifying for the marital deduction, will reduce the estate tax to zero. The other trust, for the benefit of T's descendants, is to be funded with the balance of the revocable trust corpus. The trust corpus is includible in T's gross estate. Each trust is recognized as a separate trust for purposes of chapter 13.

* * *

[T.D. 8644, 60 FR 66921, Dec. 27, 1995; 61 FR 29654, June 12, 1996; 61 FR 43656, Aug. 26, 1996; T.D. 9348, 72 FR 42297, Aug. 2, 2007; T.D. 9421, 73 FR 44652, July 31, 2008]

SPECIAL VALUATION RULES

§ 25.2701–1 Special valuation rules in the case of transfers of certain interests in corporations and partnerships.

(a) In general—(1) Scope of section 2701. Section 2701 provides special valuation rules to determine the amount of the gift when an individual transfers an equity interest in a corporation or partnership to a member of the individual's family. For section 2701 to apply, the transferor or an applicable family member (as defined in paragraph (d)(2) of this section) must, immediately after the transfer, hold an applicable retained interest (a type of equity interest defined in § 25.2701–2(b)(1)). If certain subsequent payments with respect to the applicable retained interest do not conform to the assumptions used in valuing the interest at the time of the initial transfer, § 25.2701–4 provides a special rule to increase the individual's later taxable gifts or taxable estate. Section 25.2701–5 provides an adjustment to mitigate the effects of double taxation when an applicable retained interest is subsequently transferred.

(2) Effect of section 2701. If section 2701 applies to a transfer, the amount of the transferor's gift, if any, is determined using a subtraction method of valuation (described in § 25.2701–3). Under this method, the amount of the gift is determined by subtracting the value of any family-held applicable retained interests and other non-transferred equity interests from the aggregate value of family-held interests in the corporation or partnership (the "entity"). Generally, in determining the value of any applicable retained interest held by the transferor or an applicable family member—

(i) Any put, call, or conversion right, any right to compel liquidation, or any similar right is valued at zero if the right is an "extraordinary payment right" (as defined in § 25.2701–2(b)(2));

(ii) Any distribution right in a controlled entity (e.g., a right to receive dividends) is valued at zero unless the right is a "qualified payment right" (as defined in § 25.2701–2(b)(6)); and

(iii) Any other right (including a qualified payment right) is valued as if any right valued at zero did not exist but otherwise without regard to section 2701.

(3) Example. The following example illustrates rules of this paragraph (a).

Example. A, an individual, holds all the outstanding stock of S Corporation. A exchanges A's shares in S for 100 shares of 10–percent cumulative preferred stock and 100 shares of voting common stock. A transfers the common stock to A's child. Section 2701 applies to the transfer because A has transferred an equity interest (the common stock) to a member of A's family, and immediately thereafter holds an applicable retained interest (the preferred stock). A's preferred stock is valued under the rules of section 2701. A's gift is determined under the subtraction method by subtracting the value of A's preferred stock from the value of A's interest in S immediately prior to the transfer.

(b) Transfers and other triggering events—(1) Completed transfers. Section 2701 applies to determine the existence and amount of any gift, whether or not the transfer would otherwise be a taxable gift under chapter 12 of the Internal Revenue Code. For example, section 2701 applies to a transfer that would not otherwise be a gift under chapter 12 because it was a transfer for full and adequate consideration.

(2) Transactions treated as transfers—(i) In general. Except as provided in paragraph (b)(3) of this section, for purposes of section 2701, transfer includes the following transactions:

(A) A contribution to the capital of a new or existing entity;

(B) A redemption, recapitalization, or other change in the capital structure of an entity (a "capital structure transaction"), if—

(1) The transferor or an applicable family member receives an applicable retained interest in the capital structure transaction;

(2) The transferor or an applicable family member holding an applicable retained interest before the capital structure transaction surrenders an equity interest that is junior to the applicable retained interest (a "subordinate interest") and receives property other than an applicable retained interest; or

(3) The transferor or an applicable family member holding an applicable retained interest before the capital structure transaction surrenders an equity interest in the entity (other than a subordinate interest) and the fair market value of the applicable retained interest is increased; or

(C) The termination of an indirect holding in an entity (as defined in § 25.2701-6) (or a contribution to capital by an entity to the extent an individual indirectly holds an interest in the entity), if—

(1) The property is held in a trust as to which the indirect holder is treated as the owner under subchapter J of chapter 1 of the Internal Revenue Code; or

(2) If the termination (or contribution) is not treated as a transfer under paragraph (b)(2)(i)(C)(1) of this section, to the extent the value of the indirectly-held interest would have been included in the value of the indirect holder's gross estate for Federal estate tax purposes if the indirect holder died immediately prior to the termination.

(ii) Multiple attribution. For purposes of paragraph (b)(2)(i)(C) of this section, if the transfer of an indirect holding in property is treated as a transfer with respect to more than one indirect holder, the transfer is attributed in the following order:

(A) First, to the indirect holder(s) who transferred the interest to the entity (without regard to section 2513);

(B) Second, to the indirect holder(s) possessing a presently exercisable power to designate the person who shall possess or enjoy the property;

(C) Third, to the indirect holder(s) presently entitled to receive the income from the interest;

(D) Fourth, to the indirect holder(s) specifically entitled to receive the interest at a future date; and

(E) Last, to any other indirect holder(s) proportionally.

(3) Excluded transactions. For purposes of section 2701, a transfer does not include the following transactions:

(i) A capital structure transaction, if the transferor, each applicable family member, and each member of the transferor's family holds substantially the same interest after the transaction as that individual held before the transaction. For this purpose, common stock with non-lapsing voting rights and nonvoting common stock are interests that are substantially the same;

(ii) A shift of rights occurring upon the execution of a qualified disclaimer described in section 2518; and

(iii) A shift of rights occurring upon the release, exercise, or lapse of a power of appointment other than a general power of appointment described in section 2514, except to the extent the release, exercise, or lapse would otherwise be a transfer under chapter 12.

(c) Circumstances in which section 2701 does not apply. To the extent provided, section 2701 does not apply in the following cases:

(1) Marketable transferred interests. Section 2701 does not apply if there are readily available market quotations on an established securities market for the value of the transferred interests.

(2) Marketable retained interests. Section 25.2701-2 does not apply to any applicable retained interest if there are readily available market quotations on an established securities market for the value of the applicable retained interests.

(3) Interests of the same class. Section 2701 does not apply if the retained interest is of the same class of equity as the transferred interest or if the retained interest is of a class that is proportional to the class of the transferred interest. A class is the same class as (or is proportional to the class of) the transferred interest if the rights are identical (or proportional) to the rights of the transferred interest, except for non-lapsing differences in voting rights (or, for a partnership, non-lapsing differences with respect to management and limitations on liability). For purposes of this section, non-lapsing provisions necessary to comply with partnership allocation requirements of the Internal Revenue Code (e.g., section 704(b)) are non-lapsing differences with respect to limitations on liability. A right that lapses by reason of Federal or State law is treated as a non-lapsing right unless the Secretary determines, by regulation or by published revenue ruling, that it is necessary to treat such a right as a lapsing right to accomplish the purposes of section 2701. An interest in a partnership is not an interest in the same class as the transferred interest if the transferor or applicable family members have the right to alter the liability of the transferee.

(4) Proportionate transfers. Section 2701 does not apply to a transfer by an individual to a member of the individual's family of equity interests to the extent the transfer by that individual results in a proportionate reduction of each class of equity interest held by the individual and all applicable family members in the aggregate immediately before the transfer. Thus, for example, section 2701 does not apply if P owns 50 percent of each class of equity interest in a corporation and transfers a portion of each class to P's child in a manner that reduces each interest held by P and any applicable family members, in the aggregate, by 10 percent even if the transfer does not proportionately reduce P's interest in each class. See § 25.2701–6 regarding indirect holding of interests.

(d) Family definitions—(1) Member of the family. A member of the family is, with respect to any transferor—

(i) The transferor's spouse;

(ii) Any lineal descendant of the transferor or the transferor's spouse; and

(iii) The spouse of any such lineal descendant.

(2) Applicable family member. An applicable family member is, with respect to any transferor—

(i) The transferor's spouse;

(ii) Any ancestor of the transferor or the transferor's spouse; and

(iii) The spouse of any such ancestor.

(3) Relationship by adoption. For purposes of section 2701, any relationship by legal adoption is the same as a relationship by blood.

(e) Examples. The following examples illustrate provisions of this section:

Example 1. P, an individual, holds all the outstanding stock of X Corporation. Assume the fair market value of P's interest in X immediately prior to the transfer is $1.5 million. X is recapitalized so that P holds 1,000 shares of $1,000 par value preferred stock bearing an annual cumulative dividend of $100 per share (the aggregate fair market value of which is assumed to be $1 million) and 1,000 shares of voting common stock. P transfers the common stock to P's child. Section 2701 applies to the transfer because P has transferred an equity interest (the common stock) to a member of P's family and immediately thereafter holds an applicable retained interest (the preferred stock). P's right to receive annual cumulative dividends is a qualified payment right and is valued for purposes of section 2701 at its fair market value of $1,000,000. The amount of P's gift, determined using the subtraction method of § 25.2701–3, is $500,000 ($1,500,000 minus $1,000,000).

Example 2. The facts are the same as in Example 1, except that the preferred dividend right is noncumulative. Under § 25.2701–2, P's preferred dividend right is valued at zero because it is a distribution right in a controlled entity, but is not a qualified payment right. All of P's other rights in the preferred stock are valued as if P's dividend right does not exist but otherwise without regard to section 2701. The amount of P's gift, determined using the subtraction method, is $1,500,000 ($1,500,000 minus $0). P may elect, however, to treat the dividend right as a qualified payment right as provided in § 25.2701–2(c)(2).

[T.D. 8395, 57 FR 4255, Feb. 4, 1992, as amended by T.D. 8536, 59 FR 23152, May 5, 1994]

§ 25.2701–2 Special valuation rules for applicable retained interests.

(a) In general. In determining the amount of a gift under § 25.2701–3, the value of any applicable retained interest (as defined in paragraph (b)(1) of this section) held by the transferor or by an applicable family member is determined using the rules of chapter 12, with the modifications prescribed by this section. See § 25.2701–6 regarding the indirect holding of interests.

(1) Valuing an extraordinary payment right. Any extraordinary payment right (as defined in paragraph (b)(2) of this section) is valued at zero.

(2) Valuing a distribution right. Any distribution right (as defined in paragraph (b)(3) of this section) in a controlled entity is valued at zero, unless it is a qualified payment right (as defined in paragraph (b)(6) of this section). Controlled entity is defined in paragraph (b)(5) of this section.

(3) Special rule for valuing a qualified payment right held in conjunction with an extraordinary payment right. If an applicable retained interest confers a qualified payment right and one or more extraordinary payment rights, the value of all these rights is determined by assuming that each extraordinary payment right is exercised in a manner that results in the lowest total value being determined for all the rights, using a consistent set of assumptions and giving due regard to the entity's net worth, prospective earning power, and other relevant factors (the "lower of" valuation rule). See §§ 20.2031–2(f) and 20.2031–3 for rules relating to the valuation of business interests generally.

(4) Valuing other rights. Any other right (including a qualified payment right not subject to the prior paragraph) is valued as if any right valued at zero does not exist and as if any right valued under the lower of rule is exercised in a manner consistent with the assumptions of that rule but otherwise without regard to section 2701. Thus, if an applicable retained interest carries no rights that are valued at zero or under the lower of rule, the value of the interest for purposes of section 2701 is its fair market value.

(5) Example. The following example illustrates rules of this paragraph (a).

Example. P, an individual, holds all 1,000 shares of X Corporation's $1,000 par value preferred stock bearing an annual cumulative dividend of $100 per share and holds all 1,000 shares of X's voting common stock. P has the right to put all the preferred stock to X at any time for $900,000. P transfers the common stock to P's child and immediately thereafter holds the preferred stock. Assume that at the time of the transfer, the fair market value of X is $1,500,000, and the fair market value of P's annual cumulative dividend right is $1,000,000. Because the preferred stock confers both an extraordinary payment right (the put right) and a qualified payment right (i.e., the right to receive cumulative dividends), the lower of rule applies and the value of these rights is determined as if the put right will be exercised in a manner that results in the lowest total value being determined for the rights (in this case, by assuming that the put will be exercised immediately). The value of P's preferred stock is $900,000 (the lower of $1,000,000 or $900,000). The amount of the gift is $600,000 ($1,500,000 minus $900,000).

(b) Definitions—(1) Applicable retained interest. An applicable retained interest is any equity interest in a corporation or partnership with respect to which there is either—

(i) An extraordinary payment right (as defined in paragraph (b)(2) of this section), or

(ii) In the case of a controlled entity (as defined in paragraph (b)(5) of this section), a distribution right (as defined in paragraph (b)(3) of this section).

(2) Extraordinary payment right. Except as provided in paragraph (b)(4) of this section, an extraordinary payment right is any put, call, or conversion right, any right to compel liquidation, or any similar right, the exercise or nonexercise of which affects the value of the transferred interest. A call right includes any warrant, option, or other right to acquire one or more equity interests.

(3) Distribution right. A distribution right is the right to receive distributions with respect to an equity interest. A distribution right does not include—

(i) Any right to receive distributions with respect to an interest that is of the same class as, or a class that is subordinate to, the transferred interest;

(ii) Any extraordinary payment right; or

(iii) Any right described in paragraph (b)(4) of this section.

(4) Rights that are not extraordinary payment rights or distribution rights. Mandatory payment rights, liquidation participation rights, rights to guaranteed payments of a fixed amount under section 707(c), and non-lapsing conversion rights are neither extraordinary payment rights nor distribution rights.

(i) Mandatory payment right. A mandatory payment right is a right to receive a payment required to be made at a specific time for a specific amount. For example, a mandatory redemption right in preferred stock requiring that the stock be redeemed at its fixed par value on a date certain is a mandatory payment right and therefore not an extraordinary payment right or a distribution right. A right to receive a specific amount on the death of the holder is a mandatory payment right.

(ii) Liquidation participation rights. A liquidation participation right is a right to participate in a liquidating distribution. If the transferor, members of the transferor's family, or applicable family members have the ability to compel liquidation, the liquidation participation right is valued as if the ability to compel liquidation—

(A) Did not exist, or

(B) If the lower of rule applies, is exercised in a manner that is consistent with that rule.

(iii) Right to a guaranteed payment of a fixed amount under section 707(c). The right to a guaranteed payment of a fixed amount under section 707(c) is the right to a guaranteed payment (within the meaning of section 707(c)) the amount of which is determined at a fixed rate (including a rate that bears a fixed relationship to a specified market interest rate). A payment that is contingent as to time or amount is not a guaranteed payment of a fixed amount.

(iv) Non-lapsing conversion right—(A) Corporations. A non-lapsing conversion right, in the case of a corporation, is a non-lapsing right to convert an equity interest in a corporation into a fixed number or a fixed percentage of shares of the same class as the transferred interest (or into an interest that would be of the same class but for non-lapsing differences in voting rights), that is subject to proportionate adjustments for changes in the equity ownership of the corporation and to adjustments similar to those provided in section 2701(d) for unpaid payments.

(B) Partnerships. A non-lapsing conversion right, in the case of a partnership, is a non-lapsing right to convert an equity interest in a partnership into a specified interest (other than an interest represented by a fixed dollar amount) of the same class as the transferred interest (or into an interest that would be of the same class but for non-lapsing differences in management rights or limitations on liability) that is subject to proportionate adjustments for changes in the equity ownership of the partnership and to adjustments similar to those provided in section 2701(d) for unpaid payments.

(C) Proportionate adjustments in equity ownership. For purposes of this paragraph (b)(4), an equity interest is subject to proportionate adjustments for changes in equity ownership if, in the case of a corporation, proportionate adjustments are required to be made for splits, combinations, reclassifications, and similar changes in capital stock, or, in the case of a partnership, the equity interest is protected from dilution resulting from changes in the partnership structure.

(D) Adjustments for unpaid payments. For purposes of this paragraph (b)(4), an equity interest is subject to adjustments similar to those provided in section 2701(d) if it provides for—

(1) Cumulative payments;

(2) Compounding of any unpaid payments at the rate specified in § 25.2701–4(c)(2); and

(3) Adjustment of the number or percentage of shares or the size of the interest into which it is convertible to take account of accumulated but unpaid payments.

(5) Controlled entity—(i) In general. For purposes of section 2701, a controlled entity is a corporation or partnership controlled, immediately before a transfer, by the transferor, applicable family members, and any lineal descendants of the parents of the transferor or the transferor's spouse. See § 25.2701–6 regarding indirect holding of interests.

(ii) Corporations—(A) In general. In the case of a corporation, control means the holding of at least 50 percent of the total voting power or total fair market value of the equity interests in the corporation.

(B) Voting rights. Equity interests that carry no right to vote other than on liquidation, merger, or a similar event are not considered to have voting rights for purposes of this paragraph (b)(5)(ii). Generally, a voting right is considered held by an individual to the extent that the individual, either alone or in conjunction with any other person, is entitled to exercise (or direct the exercise of) the right. However, if an equity interest carrying voting rights is held in a fiduciary capacity, the voting rights are not considered held by the fiduciary, but instead are considered held by each beneficial owner of the interest and by each individual who is a permissible recipient of the income from the interest. A voting right does not include a right to vote that is subject to a contingency that has not occurred, other than a contingency that is within the control of the individual holding the right.

(iii) Partnerships. In the case of any partnership, control means the holding of at least 50 percent of either the capital interest or the profits interest in the partnership. Any right to a guaranteed payment under section 707(c) of a fixed amount is disregarded in making this determination. In addition, in the case of a limited partnership, control means the holding of any equity interest as a general partner. See § 25.2701–2(b)(4)(iii) for the definition of a right to a guaranteed payment of a fixed amount under section 707(c).

(6) Qualified payment right—(i) In general. A qualified payment right is a right to receive qualified payments. A qualified payment is a distribution that is—

(A) A dividend payable on a periodic basis (at least annually) under any cumulative preferred stock, to the extent such dividend is determined at a fixed rate;

(B) Any other cumulative distribution payable on a periodic basis (at least annually) with respect to an equity interest, to the extent determined at a fixed rate or as a fixed amount; or

(C) Any distribution right for which an election has been made pursuant to paragraph (c)(2) of this section.

(ii) Fixed rate. For purposes of this section, a payment rate that bears a fixed relationship to a specified market interest rate is a payment determined at a fixed rate.

(c) Qualified payment elections—(1) Election to treat a qualified payment right as

other than a qualified payment right. Any transferor holding a qualified payment right may elect to treat all rights held by the transferor of the same class as rights that are not qualified payment rights. An election may be a partial election, in which case the election must be exercised with respect to a consistent portion of each payment right in the class as to which the election has been made.

(2) Election to treat other distribution rights as qualified payment rights. Any individual may elect to treat a distribution right held by that individual in a controlled entity as a qualified payment right. An election may be a partial election, in which case the election must be exercised with respect to a consistent portion of each payment right in the class as to which the election has been made. An election under this paragraph (c)(2) will not cause the value of the applicable retained interest conferring the distribution right to exceed the fair market value of the applicable retained interest (determined without regard to section 2701). The election is effective only to the extent—

(i) Specified in the election, and

(ii) That the payments elected are permissible under the legal instrument giving rise to the right and are consistent with the legal right of the entity to make the payment.

(3) Elections irrevocable. Any election under paragraph (c)(1) or (c)(2) of this section is revocable only with the consent of the Commissioner.

(4) Treatment of certain payments to applicable family members. Any payment right described in paragraph (b)(6) of this section held by an applicable family member is treated as a payment right that is not a qualified payment right unless the applicable family member elects (pursuant to paragraph (c)(2) of this section) to treat the payment right as a qualified payment right. An election may be a partial election, in which case the election must be exercised with respect to a consistent portion of each payment right in the class as to which the election has been made.

(5) Time and manner of elections. Any election under paragraph (c)(1) or (c)(2) of this section is made by attaching a statement to the Form 709, Federal Gift Tax Return, filed by the transferor on which the transfer is reported. An election filed after the time of the filing of the Form 709 reporting the transfer is not a valid election. An election filed as of April 6, 1992, for transfers made prior to its publication is effective. The statement must—

(i) Set forth the name, address, and taxpayer identification number of the electing individual and of the transferor, if different;

(ii) If the electing individual is not the transferor filing the return, state the relationship between the individual and the transferor;

(iii) Specifically identify the transfer disclosed on the return to which the election applies;

(iv) Describe in detail the distribution right to which the election applies;

(v) State the provision of the regulation under which the election is being made; and

(vi) If the election is being made under paragraph (c)(2) of this section—

(A) State the amounts that the election assumes will be paid, and the times that the election assumes the payments will be made;

(B) Contain a statement, signed by the electing individual, in which the electing individual agrees that—

(1) If payments are not made as provided in the election, the individual's subsequent taxable gifts or taxable estate will, upon the occurrence of a taxable event (as defined in § 25.2701–4(b)), be increased by an amount determined under § 25.2701–4(c), and

(2) The individual will be personally liable for any increase in tax attributable thereto.

(d) Examples. The following examples illustrate provisions of this section:

Example 1. On March 30, 1991, P transfers nonvoting common stock of X Corporation to P's child, while retaining $100 par value voting preferred stock bearing a cumulative annual dividend of $10. Immediately before the transfer, P held 100 percent of the stock. Because X is a controlled entity (within the meaning of paragraph (b)(5) of this section), P's dividend right is a distribution right that is subject to section 2701. See § 25.2701–2(b)(3). Because the distribution right is an annual cumulative dividend, it is a qualified payment right. See § 25.2701–2(b)(6).

Example 2. The facts are the same as in Example 1, except that the dividend right is non-cumulative. P's dividend right is a distribution right in a controlled entity, but is not a qualified payment right because the dividend is non-cumulative. Therefore, the non-cumulative dividend right is valued at zero under § 25.2701–2(a)(2). If the corporation were not a controlled entity, P's dividend right would be valued without regard to section 2701.

Example 3. The facts are the same as in Example 1. Because P holds sufficient voting power to compel liquidation of X, P's right to participate in liquidation is an extraordinary payment right under paragraph (b)(2) of this section. Because P holds an extraordinary payment right in conjunction with a qualified payment right (the right to receive cumulative dividends), the lower of rule applies.

Example 4. The facts are the same as in Example 1, except that immediately before the transfer, P, applicable family members of P, and members of P's family, hold 60 percent of the voting rights in X. Assume that 80 percent of the vote is required to compel liquidation of any interest in X. P's right to participate in liquidation is not an extraordinary payment right under paragraph (b)(2) of this section, because P and P's family cannot compel liquidation of X. P's preferred stock is an applicable retained interest that carries no rights that are valued under the special valuation rules of section 2701. Thus, in applying the valuation method of § 25.2701–3, the value of P's preferred stock is its fair market value determined without regard to section 2701.

Example 5. L holds 10–percent non-cumulative preferred stock and common stock in a corporation that is a controlled entity. L transfers the common stock to L's child. L holds no extraordinary payment rights with respect to the preferred stock. L elects under paragraph (c)(2) of this section to treat the noncumulative dividend right as a qualified payment right consisting of the right to receive a cumulative annual dividend of 5 percent. Under § 25.2701–2(c)(2), the value of the distribution right pursuant to the election is the lesser of—

(A) The fair market value of the right to receive a cumulative 5–percent dividend from the corporation, giving due regard to the corporation's net worth, prospective earning power, and dividend-paying capacity; or

(B) The value of the distribution right determined without regard to section 2701 and without regard to the terms of the qualified payment election.

[T.D. 8395, 57 FR 4255, Feb. 4, 1992]

§ 25.2701–3 Determination of amount of gift.

(a) Overview—(1) In general. The amount of the gift resulting from any transfer to which section 2701 applies is determined by a subtraction method of valuation. Under this method, the amount of the transfer is determined by subtracting the values of all family-held senior equity interests from the fair market value of all family-held interests in the entity determined immediately before the transfer. The values of the senior equity interests held by the transferor and applicable family members generally are determined under section 2701. Other family-held senior equity interests are valued at their fair market value. The balance is then appropriately allocated among the transferred interests and other family-held subordinate equity interests. Finally, certain discounts and other appropriate reductions are provided, but only to the extent permitted by this section.

(2) Definitions. The following definitions apply for purposes of this section.

(i) Family-held. Family-held means held (directly or indirectly) by an individual described in § 25.2701–2(b)(5)(i).

(ii) Senior equity interest. Senior equity interest means an equity interest in the entity that carries a right to distributions of income or capital that is preferred as to the rights of the transferred interest.

(iii) Subordinate equity interest. Subordinate equity interest means an equity interest in the entity as to which an applicable retained interest is a senior equity interest.

(b) Valuation methodology. The following methodology is used to determine the amount of the gift when section 2701 applies.

(1) Step 1—Valuation of family-held interest—(i) In general. Except as provided in paragraph (b)(1)(ii) of this section determine the fair market value of all family-held equity interests in the entity immediately after the transfer. The fair market value is determined by assuming that the interests are held by one individual, using a consistent set of assumptions.

(ii) Special rule for contributions to capital. In the case of a contribution to capital, determine the fair market value of the contribution.

(2) Step 2—Subtract the value of senior equity interests—(i) In general. If the amount determined in Step 1 of paragraph (b)(1) of this section is not determined under the special rule for contributions to capital, from that value subtract the following amounts:

(A) An amount equal to the sum of the fair market value of all family-held senior equity interests, (other than applicable retained interests held by the transferor or applicable family members) and the fair market value of any family-held equity interests of the same class or a subordinate class to the transferred interests held by persons other than the transferor, members of the transferor's family, and applicable family members of the transferor. The fair market value of an interest is its pro rata share of the fair market value of all family-held senior equity interests of the same class (determined, immediately after the transfer, as is all family-held senior equity interests were held by one individual); and

(B) The value of all applicable retained interests held by the transferor or applicable family members (other than an interest received as consideration for the transfer) determined under § 25.2701-2, taking into account the adjustment described in paragraph (b)(5) of this section.

(ii) Special rule for contributions to capital. If the value determined in Step 1 of paragraph (b)(1) of this section is determined under the special rule for contributions to capital, subtract the value of any applicable retained interest received in exchange for the contribution to capital determined under § 25.2701-2.

(3) Step 3—Allocate the remaining value among the transferred interests and other family-held subordinate equity interests. The value remaining after Step 2 is allocated among the transferred interests and other subordinate equity interests held by the transferor, applicable family members, and members of the transferor's family. If more than one class of family-held subordinate equity interest exists, the value remaining after Step 2 is allocated, beginning with the most senior class of subordinate equity interest, in the manner that would most fairly approximate their value if all rights valued under section 2701 at zero did not exist (or would be exercised in a manner consistent with the assumptions of the rule of § 25.2702-2(a)(4), if applicable). If there is no clearly appropriate method of allocating the remaining value pursuant to the preceding sentence, the remaining value (or the portion remaining after any partial allocation pursuant to the preceding sentence) is allocated to the interests in proportion to their fair market values determined without regard to section 2701.

(4) Step 4—Determine the amount of the gift—(i) In general. The amount allocated to the transferred interests in Step 3 is reduced by the amounts determined under this paragraph (b)(4).

(ii) Reduction for minority or similar discounts. Except as provided in § 25.2701-3(c), if the value of the transferred interest (determined without regard to section 2701) would be determined after application of a minority or similar discount with respect to the transferred interest, the amount of the gift determined under section 2701 is reduced by the excess, if any, of—

(A) A pro rata portion of the fair market value of the family-held interests of the same class (determined as if all voting rights conferred by family-held equity interests were held by one person who had no interest in the entity other than the family-held interests of the same class, but otherwise without regard to section 2701), over

(B) The value of the transferred interest (without regard to section 2701).

(iii) Adjustment for transfers with a retained interest. If the value of the transferor's gift (determined without regard to section 2701) would be reduced under section 2702 to reflect the value of a retained interest, the value determined under section 2701 is reduced by the same amount.

(iv) Reduction for consideration. The amount of the transfer (determined under section 2701) is reduced by the amount of consideration in money or money's worth received by the transferor, but not in excess of the amount of the gift (determined without regard to section 2701). The value of consideration received by the transferor in the form of an applicable retained interest in the entity is determined under section 2701 except that, in the case of a contribution to capital, the *Step 4* value of such an interest is zero.

(5) Adjustment in Step 2—(i) In general. For purposes of paragraph (b)(2) of this section, if the percentage of any class of applicable retained interest held by the transferor and by applicable family members (including any interest received as consideration for the transfer) exceeds the family interest percentage, the excess is treated as a family-held interest that is not held by the transferor or an applicable family member.

(ii) Family interest percentage. The family interest percentage is the highest ownership percentage (determined on the basis of relative fair market values) of family-held interests in—

(A) Any class of subordinate equity interest; or

(B) All subordinate equity interests, valued in the aggregate.

(c) Minimum value rule—(1) In general. If section 2701 applies to the transfer of an interest in an entity, the value of a junior equity interest is not less than its pro-rata portion of 10 percent of the sum of—

(i) The total value of all equity interests in the entity, and

(ii) The total amount of any indebtedness of the entity owed to the transferor and applicable family members.

(2) Junior equity interest. For purposes of paragraph (c)(1) of this section, junior equity interest means common stock or, in the case of a partnership, any partnership interest under which the rights to income and capital are junior to the rights of all other classes of partnership interests. Common stock means the class or classes of stock that, under the facts and circumstances, are entitled to share in the reasonably anticipated residual growth in the entity.

(3) Indebtedness—(i) In general. For purposes of paragraph (c)(1) of this section, indebtedness owed to the transferor (or an applicable family member) does not include—

(A) Short-term indebtedness incurred with respect to the current conduct of the entity's trade or business (such as amounts payable for current services);

(B) Indebtedness owed to a third party solely because it is guaranteed by the transferor or an applicable family member; or

(C) Amounts permanently set aside in a qualified deferred compensation arrangement, to the extent the amounts are unavailable for use by the entity.

(ii) Leases. A lease of property is not indebtedness, without regard to the length of the lease term, if the lease payments represent full and adequate consideration for use of the property. Lease payments are considered full and adequate consideration if a good faith effort is made to determine the fair rental value under the lease and the terms of the lease conform to the value so determined. Arrearages with respect to a lease are indebtedness.

(d) Examples. The application of the subtraction method described in this section is illustrated by the following Examples:

Example 1. Corporation X has outstanding 1,000 shares of $1,000 par value voting preferred stock, each share of which carries a cumulative annual dividend of 8 percent and a right to put the stock to X for its par value at any time. In addition, there are outstanding 1,000 shares of non-voting common stock. A holds 600 shares of the preferred stock and 750 shares of the common stock. The balance of the preferred and common stock is held by B, a person unrelated to A. Because the preferred stock confers both a qualified payment right and an extraordinary payment right, A's rights are valued under the "lower of" rule of § 25.2701–2(a)(3). Assume that A's rights in the preferred stock are valued at $800 per share under the "lower of" rule (taking account of A's voting rights). A transfers all of A's common stock to A's child. The method for determining the amount of A's gift is as follows—

Step 1: Assume the fair market value of all the family-held interests in X, taking account of A's control of the corporation, is determined to be $1 million.

Step 2: From the amount determined under Step 1, subtract $480,000 (600 shares × $800 (the section 2701 value of A's preferred stock, computed under the "lower of" rule of § 25.2701–2(a)(3))).

Step 3: The result of Step 2 is a balance of $520,000. This amount is fully allocated to the 750 shares of family-held common stock.

Step 4: Because no consideration was furnished for the transfer, the adjustment under *Step 4* is limited to the amount of any appropriate minority or similar discount. Before the application of *Step 4* the amount of A's gift is $520,000.

Example 2. The facts are the same as in Example 1, except that prior to the transfer A holds only 50 percent of the common stock and B holds the remaining 50 percent. Assume that the fair market value of A's 600 shares of preferred stock is $600,000.

Step 1: Assume that the result of this step (determining the value of the family-held interest) is $980,000.

Step 2: From the amount determined under Step 1, subtract $500,000 ($400,000, the value of 500 shares of A's preferred stock determined under section 2701 plus $100,000, the fair market value of A's other 100 shares of preferred stock determined without regard to section 2701 pursuant to the valuation adjustment determined under paragraph (b)(5) of this section). The adjustment in step 2 applies in this example because A's percentage ownership of the preferred stock (60 percent) exceeds the family interest percentage of the common stock (50 percent). Therefore, 100 shares of A's preferred stock are valued at fair market value, or $100,000 (100 × $1,000). The balance of A's preferred stock is valued under section 2701 at $400,000 (500 shares × $800). The value of A's preferred stock for purposes of section 2701 equals $500,000 ($100,000 plus $400,000).

Step 3: The result of Step 2 is $480,000 ($980,000 minus $500,000) which is allocated to the family-held common stock. Because A transferred all of the family-held subordinate equity interests, all of the value determined under Step 2 is allocated to the transferred shares.

Step 4: The adjustment under Step 4 is the same as in Example 1. Thus, the amount of the gift is $480,000.

Example 3. Corporation X has outstanding 1,000 shares of $1,000 par value non-voting preferred stock, each share of which carries a cumulative annual dividend of 8 percent and a right to put the stock to X for its par value at any time. In addition, there are outstanding 1,000 shares of voting common stock. A holds 600 shares of the preferred stock and 750 shares of the common stock. The balance of the preferred and common stock is held by B, a person unrelated to A. Assume further that steps one through three, as in Example 1, result in

$520,000 being allocated to the family-held common stock and that A transfers only 75 shares of A's common stock. The transfer fragments A's voting interest. Under Step 4, an adjustment is appropriate to reflect the fragmentation of A's voting rights. The amount of the adjustment is the difference between 10 percent (75/750) of the fair market value of A's common shares and the fair market value of the transferred shares, each determined as if the holder thereof had no other interest in the corporation.

Example 4. On December 31, 1990, the capital structure of Y corporation consists of 1,000 shares of voting common stock held three-fourths by A and one-fourth by A's child, B. On January 15, 1991, A transfers 250 shares of common stock to Y in exchange for 300 shares of nonvoting, noncumulative 8% preferred stock with a section 2701 value of zero. Assume that the fair market value of Y is $1,000,000 at the time of the exchange and that the exchange by A is for full and adequate consideration in moneys' worth. However, for purposes of section 2701, if a subordinate equity interest is transferred in exchange for an applicable retained interest, consideration in the exchange is determined with reference to the section 2701 value of the senior interest. Thus, A is treated as transferring the common stock to the corporation for no consideration. Immediately after the transfer, B is treated as holding one-third (250/750) of the common stock and A is treated as holding two-thirds (500/750). The amount of the gift is determined as follows:

Step 1. Because Y is held exclusively by A and B, the Step 1 value is $1,000,000.

Step 2. The result of Step 2 is $1,000,000 ($1,000,000 − 0).

Step 3. The amount allocated to the transferred common stock is $250,000 (250/100 × $1,000,000). That amount is further allocated in proportion to the respective holdings of A and B in the common stock ($166,667 and $83,333, respectively).

Step 4. There is no Step 4 adjustment because the section 2701 value of the consideration received by A was zero and no minority discount would have been involved in the exchange. Thus, the amount of the gift is $83,333. If the section 2701 value of the applicable retained interested were $100,000, the *Step 4* adjustment would have been a $33,333 reduction for consideration received ((250/750) × $100,000).

Example 5. The facts are the same as in Example 4, except that on January 6, 1992, when the fair market value of Y is still $1,000,000, A transfers A's remaining 500 shares of common stock to Y in exchange for 2500 shares of preferred stock. The second transfer is also for full and adequate consideration in money or money's worth. The result of Step 2 is the same—$1,000,000.

Step 3. The amount allocated to the transferred common stock is $666,667 (500/750 × $1,000,000). Since A holds no common stock immediately after the transfer, A is treated as transferring the entire interest to the other shareholder (B). Thus, $666,667 is fully allocated to the shares held by B.

Step 4. There is no Step 4 adjustment because the section 2701 value of the consideration received by A was zero and no minority discount would have been involved in the exchange. Thus, the amount of the gift is $666,667.

[T.D. 8395, 57 FR 4259, Feb. 4, 1992; 57 FR 11264, April 2, 1992]

§ 25.2701–4 Accumulated qualified payments.

(a) In general. If a taxable event occurs with respect to any applicable retained interest conferring a distribution right that was previously valued as a qualified payment right (a "qualified payment interest"), the taxable estate or taxable gifts of the individual holding the interest are increased by the amount determined under paragraph (c) of this section.

(b) Taxable event—(1) In general. Except as otherwise provided in this section, taxable event means the transfer of a qualified payment interest, either during life or at death, by the individual in whose hands the interest was originally valued under section 2701 (the "interest holder") or by any individual treated pursuant to paragraph (b)(3) of this section in the same manner as the interest holder. Except as provided in paragraph (a)(2) of this section, any termination of an individual's rights with respect to a qualified payment interest is a taxable event. Thus, for example, if an individual is treated as indirectly holding a qualified payment interest held by a trust, a taxable event occurs on the earlier of—

(i) The termination of the individual's interest in the trust (whether by death or otherwise), or

(ii) The termination of the trust's interest in the qualified payment interest (whether by disposition or otherwise).

(2) Exception. If, at the time of a termination of an individual's rights with respect to a qualified payment interest, the value of the property would be includible in the individual's gross estate for Federal estate tax purposes if the individual died immediately after the termination, a taxable transfer does not occur until the earlier of—

(i) The time the property would no longer be includible in the individual's gross estate (other than by reason of section 2035), or

(ii) The death of the individual.

(3) Individual treated as interest holder—(i) In general. If a taxable event involves the transfer of a qualified payment interest by the interest holder (or an individual treated as the interest holder) to an applicable family member of the individual who made the transfer to which section 2701 applied (other than the spouse of the individual transferring the qualified payment interest), the transferee applicable family member is treated in the same manner as the interest holder with respect to late or unpaid qualified payments first due after the taxable event. Thus, for example, if an interest holder transfers during life a qualified payment interest to an applicable family member, that transfer is a taxable event with respect to the interest holder whose taxable gifts are increased for the year of the transfer as provided in paragraph (c) of this section. The transferee is treated thereafter in the same manner as the interest holder with respect to late or unpaid qualified payments first due after the taxable event.

(ii) Transfers to spouse—(A) In general. If an interest holder (or an individual treated as the interest holder) transfers a qualified payment interest, the transfer is not a taxable event to the extent a marital deduction is allowed with respect to the transfer under sections 2056, 2106(a)(3), or 2523 or, in the case of a transfer during the individual's lifetime, to the extent the spouse furnishes consideration for the transfer. If this exception applies, the transferee spouse is treated as if he or she were the holder of the interest from the date the transferor spouse acquired the interest. If the deduction for a transfer to a spouse is allowable under section 2056(b)(8) or 2523(g) (relating to charitable remainder trusts), the transferee spouse is treated as the holder of the entire interest passing to the trust.

(B) Marital bequests. If the selection of property with which a marital bequest is funded is discretionary, a transfer of a qualified payment interest will not be considered a transfer to the surviving spouse unless—

(1) The marital bequest is funded with the qualified payment interest before the due date for filing the decedent's Federal estate tax return (including extensions actually granted) (the "due date"), or

(2) The executor—

(i) Files a statement with the return indicating the extent to which the marital bequest will be funded with the qualified payment interest, and

(ii) Before the date that is one year prior to the expiration of the period of limitations on assessment of the Federal estate tax, notifies the District Director having jurisdiction over the return of the extent to which the bequest was funded with the qualified payment interest (or the extent to which the qualified payment interest has been permanently set aside for that purpose).

(C) Purchase by the surviving spouse. For purposes of this section, the purchase (before the date prescribed for filing the decedent's estate tax return, including extensions actually granted) by the surviving spouse (or a trust described in section 2056(b)(7)) of a qualified payment interest held (directly or indirectly) by the decedent immediately before death is considered a transfer with respect to which a deduction is allowable under section 2056 or section 2106(a)(3), but only to the extent that the deduction is allowed to the estate. For example, assume that A bequeaths $50,000 to A's surviving spouse, B, in a manner that qualifies for deduction under section 2056, and that subsequent to A's death B purchases a qualified payment interest from A's estate for $200,000, its fair market value. The economic effect of the transaction is the equivalent of a bequest by A to B of the qualified payment interest, one-fourth of which qualifies for the marital deduction. Therefore, for purposes of this section, one-fourth of the qualified payment interest purchased by B ($50,000 ÷ $200,000) is considered a transfer of an interest with respect to which a deduction is allowed under 2056. If the purchase by the surviving spouse is not made before the due date of the decedent's return, the purchase of the qualified payment interest will not be considered a bequest for which a marital deduction is allowed unless the executor—

(1) Files a statement with the return indicating the qualified payment interests to be purchased by the surviving spouse (or a trust described in section 2056(b)(7)), and

(2) Before the date that is one year prior to the expiration of the period of limitations on assessment of the Federal estate tax, notifies the District Director having jurisdiction over the return that the purchase of the qualified payment interest has been made (or that the funds necessary to purchase the qualified payment interest have been permanently set aside for that purpose).

(c) Amount of increase—(1) In general. Except as limited by paragraph (c)(6) of this section, the amount of the increase to an individual's taxable estate or taxable gifts is the excess, if any, of—

(i) The sum of—

(A) The amount of qualified payments payable during the period beginning on the date of the transfer to which section 2701 applied (or, in the case of an individual treated as the interest holder, on the date the interest of the prior interest holder terminated) and ending on the date of the taxable event; and

(B) The earnings on those payments, determined hypothetically as if each payment were paid on its due date and reinvested as of that date at a yield equal to the appropriate discount rate (as defined below); over

(ii) The sum of—

(A) The amount of the qualified payments actually paid during the same period;

(B) The earnings on those payments, determined hypothetically as if each payment were reinvested as of the date actually paid at a yield equal to the appropriate discount rate; and

(C) To the extent required to prevent double inclusion, by an amount equal to the sum of—

(1) The portion of the fair market value of the qualified payment interest solely attributable to any right to receive unpaid qualified payments determined as of the date of the taxable event;

(2) The fair market value of any equity interest in the entity received by the individual in lieu of qualified payments and held by the individual at the taxable event, and

(3) The amount by which the individual's aggregate taxable gifts were increased by reason of the failure of the individual to enforce the right to receive qualified payments.

(2) Due date of qualified payments. With respect to any qualified payment, the "due date" is that date specified in the governing instrument as the date on which payment is to be made. If no date is specified in the governing instrument, the due date is the last day of each calendar year.

(3) Appropriate discount rate. The appropriate discount rate is the discount rate that was applied in determining the value of the qualified payment right at the time of the transfer to which section 2701 applied.

(4) Application of payments. For purposes of this section, any payment of an unpaid qualified payment is applied in satisfaction of unpaid qualified payments beginning with the earliest unpaid qualified payment. Any payment in excess of the total of all unpaid qualified payments is treated as a prepayment of future qualified payments.

(5) Payment. For purposes of this paragraph (c), the transfer of a debt obligation bearing compound interest from the due date of the payment at a rate not less than the appropriate discount rate is a qualified payment if the term of the obligation (including extensions) does not exceed four years from the date issued. A payment in the form of an equity interest in the entity is not a qualified payment. Any payment of a qualified payment made (or treated as made) either before or during the four-year period beginning on the due date of the payment but before the date of the taxable event is treated as having been made on the due date.

(6) Limitation—(i) In general. The amount of the increase to an individual's taxable estate or taxable gifts is limited to the applicable percentage of the excess, if any, of—

(A) The sum of—

(1) The fair market value of all outstanding equity interests in the entity that are subordinate to the applicable retained interest, determined as of the date of the taxable event without regard to any accrued liability attributable to unpaid qualified payments; and

(2) Any amounts expended by the entity to redeem or otherwise acquire any such subordinate interest during the period beginning on the date of the transfer to which section 2701 applied (or, in the case of an individual treated as an interest holder, on the date the interest of the prior interest holder terminated) and ending on the date of the taxable event (reduced by any amounts received on the resale or issuance of any such subordinate interest during the same period); over

(B) The fair market value of all outstanding equity interests in the entity that are subordinate to the applicable retained interest, determined as of the date of the transfer to which section 2701 applied (or, in the case of an individual treated as an interest holder, on the date the interest of the prior interest holder terminated).

(ii) Computation of limitation. For purposes of computing the limitation applicable under this paragraph (c)(6), the aggregate fair market value of the subordinate interests in the entity are determined without regard to § 25.2701-3(c).

(iii) Applicable percentage. The applicable percentage is determined by dividing the number of shares or units of the applicable retained interest held by the interest holder (or an individual treated as the interest holder) on the date of the taxable event by the total number of such shares or units outstanding on the same date. If an individual holds applicable retained interests in two or more classes of interests, the applicable percentage is equal to the largest applicable percentage determined with respect to any class. For example, if T retains 40 percent of the class A preferred and 60 percent of the class B preferred in a corporation, the applicable percentage with respect to T's holdings is 60 percent.

(d) Taxpayer election—(1) In general. An interest holder (or individual treated as an interest holder) may elect to treat as a taxable event the payment of an unpaid qualified payment occurring more than four years after its due date. Under this election, the increase under paragraph (c) of this section is determined only with respect to that payment and all previous payments for which an election was available but not made. Payments for which an election applies are treated as having been paid on their due dates for purposes of subsequent taxable events. The election is revocable only with the consent of the Commissioner.

(2) Limitation not applicable. If a taxable event occurs by reason of an election described in paragraph (d)(1) of this section, the limitation described in paragraph (c)(6) of this section does not apply.

(3) Time and manner of election—(i) Timely-filed returns. The election may be made by attaching a statement to a Form 709, Federal Gift Tax Return, filed by the recipient of the qualified payment on a timely basis for the year in which the qualified payment is received. In that case, the taxable event is deemed to occur on the date the qualified payment is received.

(ii) Election on late returns. The election may be made by attaching a statement to a Form 709, Federal Gift Tax Return, filed by the recipient of the qualified payment other than on a timely basis for the year in which the qualified payment is received. In that case, the taxable event is deemed to occur on the first day of the month immediately preceding the month in which the return is filed. If an election, other than an election on a timely return, is made after the death of the interest holder, the taxable event with respect to the decedent is deemed to occur on the later of—

(A) The date of the recipient's death, or

(B) The first day of the month immediately preceding the month in which the return is filed.

(iii) Requirements of statement. The statement must—

(A) Provide the name, address, and taxpayer identification number of the electing individual and the interest holder, if different;

(B) Indicate that a taxable event election is being made under paragraph (d) of this section;

(C) Disclose the nature of the qualified payment right to which the election applies, including the due dates of the payments, the dates the payments were made, and the amounts of the payments;

(D) State the name of the transferor, the date of the transfer to which section 2701 applied, and the discount rate used in valuing the qualified payment right; and

(E) State the resulting amount of increase in taxable gifts.

(4) Example. The following example illustrates the rules of this paragraph (d).

Example. A holds cumulative preferred stock that A retained in a transfer to which section 2701 applied. No dividends were paid in years 1 through 5 following the transfer. In year 6, A received a qualified payment that, pursuant to paragraph (c)(3) of this section, is considered to be in satisfaction of the unpaid qualified payment for year 1. No election was made to treat that payment as a taxable event. In year 7, A receives a qualified payment that, pursuant to paragraph (c)(4) of this section, is considered to be in satisfaction of the unpaid qualified payment for year 2. A elects to treat the payment in year 7 as a taxable event. The election increases A's taxable gifts in year 7 by the amount computed under paragraph (c) of this section with respect to the payments due in both year 1 and year 2. For purposes of any future taxable events, the payments with respect to years 1 and 2 are treated as having been made on their due dates.

[T.D. 8395, 57 FR 4261, Feb. 4, 1992]

§ 25.2701-5 Adjustments to mitigate double taxation.

(a) Reduction of transfer tax base—(1) In general. This section provides rules under which an individual (the initial transferor) making a transfer subject to section 2701 (the initial transfer) is entitled to reduce his or her taxable gifts or adjusted taxable gifts (the reduction). The amount of the reduction is determined under paragraph (b) of this section. See paragraph (e) of this section if section 2513 (split gifts) applied to the initial transfer.

(2) Federal gift tax modification. If, during the lifetime of the initial transferor, the holder of a section 2701 interest (as defined in paragraph (a)(4) of this section) transfers the interest to or for the benefit of an individual other than the initial transferor or an applicable family member of the initial transferor in a transfer subject to Federal estate or gift tax, the initial transferor may reduce the amount on which the initial transferor's tentative tax is computed under section 2502(a). The reduction is first applied on any gift tax return required to be filed for the calendar year in which the section 2701 interest is transferred; any excess reduction is carried forward and applied in each succeeding calendar year until the reduction is exhausted. The amount of the reduction that is used in a calendar year is the amount of the initial transferor's taxable gifts for that year. Any excess reduction remaining at the death of the initial transferor may be applied by the executor of the initial transferor's estate as provided under paragraph (a)(3) of this section. See paragraph (a)(4) of this section for the definition of a section 2701 interest. See § 25.2701–6 for rules relating to indirect ownership of equity interests transferred to trusts and other entities.

(3) Federal estate tax modification. Except as otherwise provided in this paragraph (a)(3), in determining the Federal estate tax with respect to an initial transferor, the executor of the initial transferor's estate may reduce the amount on which the decedent's tentative tax is computed under section 2001(b) (or section 2101(b)) by the amount of the reduction (including any excess reduction carried forward under paragraph (a)(2) of this section). The amount of the reduction under this paragraph (a)(3) is limited to the amount that results in zero Federal estate tax with respect to the estate of the initial transferor.

(4) Section 2701 interest. A section 2701 interest is an applicable retained interest that was valued using the special valuation rules of section 2701 at the time of the initial transfer. However, an interest is a section 2701 interest only to the extent the transfer of that interest effectively reduces the aggregate ownership of such class of interest by the initial transferor and applicable family members of the initial transferor below that held by such persons at the time of the initial transfer (or the remaining portion thereof).

(b) Amount of reduction. Except as otherwise provided in paragraphs (c)(3)(iv) (pertaining to transfers of partial interests) and (e) (pertaining to initial split gifts) of this section, the amount of the reduction is the lesser of—

(1) The amount by which the initial transferor's taxable gifts were increased as a result of the application of section 2701 to the initial transfer; or

(2) The amount (determined under paragraph (c) of this section) duplicated in the transfer tax base at the time of the transfer of the section 2701 interest (the duplicated amount).

(c) Duplicated amount—(1) In general. The duplicated amount is the amount by which the transfer tax value of the section 2701 interest at the time of the subsequent transfer exceeds the value of that interest determined under section 2701 at the time of the initial transfer. If, at the time of the initial transfer, the amount allocated to the transferred interest under § 25.2701–3(b)(3) (Step 3 of the valuation methodology) is less than the entire amount available for allocation at that time, the duplicated amount is a fraction of the amount described in the preceding sentence. The numerator of the fraction is the amount allocated to the transferred interest at the time of the initial transfer (pursuant to § 25.2701–3(b)(3)) and the denominator of the fraction is the amount available for allocation at the time of the initial transfer (determined after application of § 25.2701–3(b)(2)).

(2) Transfer tax value—In general. Except as provided in paragraph (c)(3) of this section, for purposes of paragraph (c)(1) of this section the transfer tax value of a section 2701 interest is the value of that interest as finally determined for Federal transfer tax purposes under chapter 11 or chapter 12, as the case may be (including the right to receive any distributions thereon (other than qualified payments)), reduced by the amount of any deduction allowed with respect to the section 2701 interest to the extent that the deduction would not have been allowed if the section 2701 interest were not included in the transferor's total amount of gifts for the calendar year or the transferor's gross estate, as the case may be. Rules similar to the rules of section 691(c)(2)(C) are applicable to determine the extent that a deduction would not be allowed if the section 2701 interest were not so included.

(3) Special transfer tax value rules—(i) Transfers for consideration. Except as provided in paragraph (c)(3)(iii) of this section, if, during the life of the initial transferor, a section 2701 interest is transferred to or for the benefit of an individual other than the initial transferor or an applicable family member of the initial transferor for consideration in money or money's worth, or in a transfer that is treated as a transfer for consideration in money or money's worth, the transfer of the section 2701 interest is deemed to occur at the death of the initial transferor. In this case, the estate of the initial transferor is entitled to a reduction in the same manner as if the initial transferor's gross estate included a section 2701 interest having a chapter 11 value equal to the amount of consideration in money or money's worth received in the exchange (determined as of the time of the exchange).

(ii) Interests held by applicable family members at date of initial transferor's death. If a section 2701 interest in existence on the date of the initial transferor's death is held by an applicable family member and, therefore, is not included in the gross estate of the initial transferor, the section 2701 interest is deemed to be transferred at the death of the initial transferor to or for the benefit of an individual other than the initial transferor or an applicable family member of the initial transferor. In this case, the transfer tax value of that interest is the value that the executor of the initial transferor's estate can demonstrate would be determined under chapter 12 if the interest were transferred immediately prior to the death of the initial transferor.

(iii) Nonrecognition transactions. If an individual exchanges a section 2701 interest in a nonrecognition transaction (within the meaning of section 7701(a)(45)), the exchange is not treated as a transfer of a section 2701 interest and the transfer tax value of that interest is determined as if the interest received in exchange is the section 2701 interest.

(iv) Transfer of less than the entire section 2701 interest. If a transfer is a transfer of less than the entire section 2701 interest, the amount of the reduction under paragraph (a)(2) or (a)(3) of this section is reduced proportionately.

(v) Multiple classes of section 2701 interest. For purposes of paragraph (b) of this section, if more than one class of section 2701 interest exists, the amount of the reduction is determined separately with respect to each such class.

(vi) Multiple initial transfers. If an initial transferor has made more than one initial transfer, the amount of the reduction with respect to any section 2701 interest is the sum of the reductions computed under paragraph (b) of this section with respect to each such initial transfer.

(d) Examples. The following examples illustrate the provisions of paragraphs (a) through (c) of this section.

Facts. (1) In general. (i) P, an individual, holds 1,500 shares of $1,000 par value preferred stock of X corporation (bearing an annual noncumulative dividend of $100 per share that may be put to X at any time for par value) and 1,000 shares of voting common stock of X. There is no other outstanding common stock of X.

(ii) On January 15, 1991, when the aggregate fair market value of the preferred stock is $1,500,000 and the aggregate fair market value of the common stock is $500,000, P transfers common stock to P's child. The fair market value of P's interest in X (common and preferred) immediately prior to the transfer is $2,000,000, and the section 2701 value of the preferred stock (the section 2701 interest) is zero. Neither P nor P's spouse, S, made gifts prior to 1991.

(2) Additional facts applicable to Examples 1 through 3. P's transfer consists of all 1,000 shares of P's common stock. With respect to the initial transfer, the amount remaining after Step 2 of the subtraction method of § 25.2701–3 is $2,000,000 ($2,000,000 minus zero), all of which is allocated to the transferred stock. P's aggregate taxable gifts for 1991 (including the section 2701 transfer) equal $2,500,000.

(3) Additional facts applicable to Examples 4 and 5. P's initial transfer consists of one-half of P's common stock. With respect to the initial transfer in this case, only $1,000,000 (one-half of the amount remaining after Step 2 of the subtraction method of § 25.2701–3) is allocated to the transferred stock. P's aggregate taxable gifts for 1991 (the section 2701 transfer and P's other transfers) equal $2,500,000.

Example 1. Inter vivos transfer of entire section 2701 interest. **(i)** On October 1, 1994, at a time when the value of P's preferred stock is $1,400,000, P transfers all of the preferred stock to P's child. In computing P's 1994 gift tax, P, as the initial transferor, is entitled to reduce the amount on which P's tentative tax is computed under section 2502(a) by $1,400,000.

(ii) The amount of the reduction computed under paragraph (b) of this section is the lesser of $1,500,000 (the amount by which the initial transferor's taxable gifts were increased as a result of the application of section 2701 to the initial transfer) or $1,400,000 (the duplicated amount). The duplicated amount is 100 percent (the portion of the section 2701 interest subsequently transferred) times $1,400,000 (the amount by which the gift tax value of the preferred stock ($1,400,000 at the time of the subsequent transfer) exceeds zero (the section 2701 value of the preferred stock at the time of the initial transfer)).

(iii) The result would be the same if the preferred stock had been held by P's parent, GM, and GM had, on October 1, 1994, transferred the preferred stock to or for the benefit of an individual other than P or an applicable family member of P. In that case, in computing the tax on P's 1994 and subsequent transfers, P would be entitled to reduce the amount on which P's tentative tax is computed under section 2502(a) by $1,400,000. If the value of P's 1994 gifts is less than $1,400,000, P is entitled to claim the excess adjustment in computing the tax with respect to P's subsequent transfers.

Example 2. Transfer of section 2701 interest at death of initial transferor. (i) P continues to hold the preferred stock until P's death. The chapter 11 value of the preferred stock at the date of P's death is the same as the fair market value of the preferred stock at the time of the initial transfer. In computing the Federal estate tax with respect to P's estate, P's executor is entitled to a reduction of $1,500,000 under paragraph (a)(3) of this section.

(ii) The result would be the same if P had sold the preferred stock to any individual other than an applicable family member at a time when the value of the preferred stock was $1,500,000. In that case, the amount of the reduction is computed as if the preferred stock were included in P's gross estate at a fair market value equal to the sales price. If the value of P's taxable estate is less than $1,500,000, the amount of the adjustment available to P's executor is limited to the actual value of P's taxable estate.

(iii) The result would also be the same if the preferred stock had been held by P's parent, GM, and at the time of P's death, GM had not transferred the preferred stock.

Example 3. Transfer of after-acquired preferred stock. On September 1, 1992, P purchases 100 shares of X preferred stock from an unrelated party. On October 1, 1994, P transfers 100 shares of X preferred stock to P's child. In computing P's 1994 gift tax, P is not entitled to reduce the amount on which P's tentative tax is computed under section 2502(a) because the 1994 transfer does not reduce P's preferred stock holding below that held at the time of the initial transfer. See paragraph (a)(4) of this section.

Example 4. Inter vivos transfer of entire section 2701 interest. (i) On October 1, 1994, at a time when the value of P's preferred stock is $1,400,000, P transfers all of the preferred stock to P's child. In computing P's 1994 gift tax, P, as the initial transferor, is entitled to reduce the amount on which P's tentative tax is computed under section 2502(a) by $700,000.

(ii) The amount of the reduction computed under paragraph (b) of this section is the lesser of $750,000 (($1,500,000 × .5 ($1,000,000 over $2,000,000)) the amount by which the initial transferor's taxable gifts were increased as a result of the application of section 2701 to the initial transfer) or $700,000 (($1,400,000 × .5) the duplicated amount). The duplicated amount is 100 percent (the portion of the section 2701 interest subsequently transferred) times $700,000; e.g., one-half (the fraction representing the portion of the common stock transferred in the initial transfer ($1,000,000/$2,000,000)) of the amount by which the gift tax value of the preferred stock at the time of the subsequent transfer ($1,400,000) exceeds zero (the section 2701 value of the preferred stock at the time of the initial transfer).

Example 5. Subsequent transfer of less than the entire section 2701 interest. On October 1, 1994, at a time when the value of P's preferred stock is $1,400,000, P transfers only 250 of P's 1,000 shares of preferred stock to P's child. In this case, the amount of the reduction computed under paragraph (b) is $175,000 (one-fourth (250/1,000) of the amount of the reduction available if P had transferred all 1,000 shares of preferred stock).

(e) Computation of reduction if initial transfer is split under section 2513—(1) In general. If section 2513 applies to the initial transfer (a split initial transfer), the special rules of this paragraph (e) apply.

(2) Transfers during joint lives. If there is a split initial transfer and the corresponding section 2701 interest is transferred during the joint lives of the donor and the consenting spouse, for purposes of determining the reduction under paragraph (a)(2) of this section each spouse is treated as if the spouse was the initial transferor of one-half of the split initial transfer.

(3) Transfers at or after death of either spouse—(i) In general. If there is a split initial transfer and the corresponding section 2701 interest is transferred at or after the death of the first spouse to die, the reduction under paragraph (a)(2) or (a)(3) of this section is determined as if the donor spouse was the initial transferor of the entire initial transfer.

(ii) Death of donor spouse. Except as provided in paragraph (e)(3)(iv) of this section, the executor of the estate of the donor spouse in a split initial transfer is entitled to compute the reduction as if the donor spouse was the initial transferor of the section 2701 interest otherwise attributable to the consenting spouse. In this case, if the consenting spouse survives the donor spouse—

(A) The consenting spouse's aggregate sum of taxable gifts used in computing each tentative tax under section 2502(a) (and, therefore, adjusted taxable gifts under section 2001(b)(1)(B) (or section 2101(b)(1)(B)) and the tax payable on the consenting spouse's prior taxable gifts under section 2001(b)(2) (or section 2101(b)(2))) is reduced to eliminate the remaining effect of the section 2701 interest; and

(B) Except with respect to any excess reduction carried forward under paragraph (a)(2) of this section, the consenting spouse ceases to be treated as the initial transferor of the section 2701 interest.

(iii) Death of consenting spouse. If the consenting spouse predeceases the donor spouse, except for any excess reduction carried forward under paragraph (a)(2) of this section, the reduction with respect to any section 2701 interest in the split initial transfer is not available to the estate of the consenting spouse (regardless of whether the interest is included in the consenting spouse's gross estate). Similarly, if the consenting spouse predeceases the donor spouse, no reduction is available to the consenting spouse's adjusted taxable gifts under section 2001(b)(1)(B) (or section 2101(b)(1)(B)) or to the consenting spouse's gift tax payable under section 2001(b)(2) (or section 2101(b)(2)). See paragraph (a)(2) of this section for rules involving transfers by an applicable family member during the life of the initial transferor.

(iv) Additional limitation on reduction. If the donor spouse (or the estate of the donor spouse) is treated under this paragraph (e) as the initial transferor of the section 2701 interest otherwise attributable to the consenting spouse, the amount of additional reduction determined under paragraph (b) of this section is the amount determined under that paragraph with respect to the consenting spouse. If a reduction was previously available to the consenting spouse under this paragraph (e), the amount determined under this paragraph (e)(3)(iv) with respect to the consenting spouse is determined as if the consenting spouse's taxable gifts in the split initial transfer had been increased only by that portion of the increase that corresponds to the remaining portion of the section 2701 interest. The amount of the additional reduction (i.e., the amount determined with respect to the consenting spouse) is limited to the amount that results in a reduction in the donor spouse's Federal transfer tax no greater than the amount of the increase in the consenting spouse's gift tax incurred by reason of the section 2701 interest (or the remaining portion thereof).

(f) Examples. The following examples illustrate the provisions of paragraph (e) of this section. The examples assume the facts set out in this paragraph (f).

Facts. (1) In each example assume that P, an individual, holds 1,500 shares of $1,000 par value preferred stock of X corporation (bearing an annual noncumulative dividend of $100 per share that may be put to X at any time for par value) and 1,000 shares of voting common stock of X. There is no other outstanding stock of X. The annual exclusion under section 2503 is not allowable with respect to any gift.

(2) On January 15, 1991, when the aggregate fair market value of the preferred stock is $1,500,000 and the aggregate fair market value of the common stock is $500,000, P transfers all 1,000 shares of the common stock to P's child. Section 2701 applies to the initial transfer because P transferred an equity interest (the common stock) to a member of P's family and immediately thereafter held an applicable retained interest (the preferred stock). The fair market value of P's interest in X immediately prior to the transfer is $2,000,000 and the section 2701 value of the preferred stock (the section 2701 interest) is zero. With respect to the initial transfer, the amount remaining after Step 2 of the subtraction method of § 25.2701–3 was $2,000,000 ($2,000,000 minus zero), all of which is allocated to the transferred stock. P had made no gifts prior to 1991. The sum of P's aggregate taxable gifts for the calendar year 1991 (including the section 2701 transfer) is $2,500,000. P's spouse, S, made no gifts prior to 1991.

(3) P and S elected pursuant to section 2513 to treat one-half of their 1991 gifts as having been made by each spouse. Without the application of section 2701, P and S's aggregate gifts would have been $500,000 and each spouse would have paid no gift tax because of the application of the unified credit under section 2505. However, because of the application of section 2701, both P and S are each treated as the initial transferor of aggregate taxable gifts in the amount of $1,250,000 and, after the application of the unified credit under section 2505, each paid $255,500 in gift tax with respect to their 1991 transfers. On October 1, 1994, at a time when the value of the preferred stock is the same as at the time of the initial transfer, P transfers the preferred stock (the section 2701 interest) to P's child.

Example 1. Inter vivos transfer of entire section 2701 interest. P transfers all of the preferred stock to P's child. P and S are each entitled to a reduction of $750,000 in computing their 1994 gift tax. P is entitled to the reduction because P subsequently transferred the one-half share of the section 2701 interest as to which P was the initial transferor to an individual who was not an applicable family member of P. S is entitled to the reduction because P, an applicable family member with respect to S, transferred the one-half share of the section 2701 interest as to which S was the initial transferor to an individual other than S or an applicable family member of S. S may claim the reduction against S's 1994 gifts. If S's 1994 taxable gifts are less than $750,000, S may claim the remaining amount of the reduction against S's next succeeding lifetime transfers.

Example 2. Inter vivos transfer of portion of section 2701 interest. P transfers one-fourth of the preferred stock to P's child. In this case, P and S are each entitled to a reduction of $187,500, the corresponding portion of the reduction otherwise available to each spouse (one-fourth of $750,000).

Example 3. Transfer at death of donor spouse. P, the donor spouse in the section 2513 election, dies on October 1, 1994, while holding all of the preferred stock. The executor of P's estate is entitled to a reduction in the computation of the tentative tax under section 2001(b). Since no reduction had been previously available with respect to the section 2701 interest, P's estate is entitled to a full reduction of $750,000 with respect to the one-half share of the preferred stock as to which P was the initial transferor. In addition, P's estate is entitled to an additional reduction of up to $750,000 for the remaining section 2701 interest as to which S was the initial transferor. The reduction for the consenting spouse's remaining section 2701 interest is limited to that amount that will produce a tax saving in P's Federal estate tax of $255,500, the amount of gift tax incurred by S by reason of the application of section 2701 to the split initial transfer.

Example 4. Transfer after death of donor spouse. The facts are the same as in Example 3, except that S acquires the preferred stock from P's estate and subsequently transfers the preferred stock to S's child. S is not entitled to a reduction because S ceased to be an initial transferor upon P's death (and S's prior taxable gifts were automatically adjusted at that time to the level that would have existed had the split initial transfer not been subject to section 2701).

Example 5. Death of donor spouse after inter vivos transfer. **(i)** P transfers one-fourth of the preferred stock to P's child. In this case, P and S are each entitled to a reduction of $187,500, the corresponding portion of the reduction otherwise available to each spouse (one-fourth of $750,000). S may claim the reduction against S's 1994 or subsequent transfers. P dies on November 1, 1994.

(ii) P's executor is entitled to include, in computing the reduction available to P's estate, the remaining reduction to which P is entitled and an additional amount of up to $562,500 ($750,000 minus $187,500, the amount of the remaining reduction attributable to the consenting spouse determined immediately prior to P's death). The amount of additional reduction available to P's estate cannot exceed the amount that will reduce P's estate tax by $178,625, the amount that S's 1991 gift tax would have been increased if the application of section 2701 had increased S's taxable gifts by only $562,500 ($750,000 − $187,500).

(g) Double taxation otherwise avoided. No reduction is available under this section if—

(1) Double taxation is otherwise avoided in the computation of the estate tax under section 2001 (or section 2101); or

(2) A reduction was previously taken under the provisions of section 2701(e)(6) with respect to the same section 2701 interest and the same initial transfer.

* * *

[T.D. 8536, 59 FR 23152, May 5, 1994]

§ 25.2701-6 Indirect holding of interests.

(a) In general—(1) Attribution to individuals. For purposes of section 2701, an individual is treated as holding an equity interest to the extent the interest is held indirectly through a corporation, partnership, estate, trust, or other entity. If an equity interest is treated as held by a particular individual in more than one capacity, the interest is treated as held by the individual in the manner that attributes the largest total ownership of the equity interest. An equity interest held by a lower-tier entity is attributed to higher-tier entities in accordance with the rules of this section. For example, if an individual is a 50-percent beneficiary of a trust that holds 50 percent of the preferred stock of a corporation, 25 percent of the preferred stock is considered held by the individual under these rules.

(2) Corporations. A person is considered to hold an equity interest held by or for a corporation in the proportion that the fair market value of the stock the person holds bears to the fair market value of all the stock in the corporation (determined as if each class of stock were held separately by one individual). This paragraph applies to any entity classified as a corporation or as an association taxable as a corporation for federal income tax purposes.

(3) Partnerships. A person is considered to hold an equity interest held by or for a partnership in the proportion that the fair market value of the larger of the person's profits interest or capital interest in the partnership bears to the total fair market value of the corresponding profits interests or capital interests in the partnership, as the case may be (determined as if each class were held by one individual). This paragraph applies to any entity classified as a partnership for federal income tax purposes.

(4) Estates, trusts and other entities—(i) In general. A person is considered to hold an equity interest held by or for an estate or trust to the extent the person's beneficial interest therein may be satisfied by the equity interest held by the estate or trust, or the income or proceeds thereof, assuming the maximum exercise of discretion in favor of the person. A beneficiary of an estate or trust who cannot receive any distribution with respect to an equity interest held by the estate or trust, including the income therefrom or the proceeds from the disposition thereof, is not considered the holder of the equity interest. Thus, if stock held by a decedent's estate has been specifically bequeathed to one beneficiary and the residue of the estate has been bequeathed to other beneficiaries, the stock is considered held only by the beneficiary to whom it was specifically bequeathed. However, any person who may receive distributions from a trust is considered to hold an equity interest held by the trust if the distributions may be made from current or accumulated income from or the proceeds from the disposition of the equity interest, even though under the terms of the trust the interest can never be distributed to that person. This paragraph applies to any entity that is not classified as a corporation, an association taxable as a corporation, or a partnership for federal income tax purposes.

(ii) Special rules—(A) Property is held by a decedent's estate if the property is subject to claims against the estate and expenses of administration.

(B) A person holds a beneficial interest in a trust or an estate so long as the person may receive distributions from the trust or the estate other than payments for full and adequate consideration.

(C) An individual holds an equity interest held by or for a trust if the individual is considered an owner of the trust (a "grantor trust") under subpart E, part I, subchapter J of the Internal Revenue Code (relating to grantors and others treated as substantial owners). However, if an individual is treated as the owner of only a fractional share of a grantor trust because there are multiple grantors, the individual holds each equity interest held by the trust, except to the extent that the fair market value of the interest exceeds the fair market value of the fractional share.

(5) Multiple attribution—(i) Applicable retained interests. If this section attributes an applicable retained interest to more than one individual in a class consisting of the transferor and one or more applicable family members, the interest is attributed within that class in the following order—

(A) If the interest is held in a grantor trust, to the individual treated as the holder thereof;

(B) To the transferor;

(C) To the transferor's spouse; or

(D) To each applicable family member on a pro rata basis.

(ii) Subordinate equity interests. If this section attributes a subordinate equity interest to more than one individual in a class consisting of the transferor, applicable family members, and members of the transferor's family, the interest is attributed within that class in the following order—

(A) To the transferee;

(B) To each member of the transferor's family on a pro rata basis;

(C) If the interest is held in a grantor trust, to the individual treated as the holder thereof;

(D) To the transferor;

(E) To the transferor's spouse; or

(F) To each applicable family member on a pro rata basis.

(b) Examples. The following examples illustrate the provisions of this section:

Example 1. A, an individual, holds 25 percent by value of each class of stock of Y Corporation. Persons unrelated to A hold the remaining stock. Y holds 50 percent of the stock of Corporation X. Under paragraph (a)(2) of this section, Y's interests in X are attributed proportionately to the shareholders of Y. Accordingly, A is considered to hold a 12.5 percent (25 percent × 50 percent) interest in X.

Example 2. Z Bank's authorized capital consists of 100 shares of common stock and 100 shares of preferred stock. A holds 60 shares of each (common and preferred) and A's child, B, holds 40 shares of common stock. Z holds the balance of its own preferred stock, 30 shares as part of a common trust fund it maintains and 10 shares permanently set aside to satisfy a deferred obligation. For purposes of section 2701, A holds 60 shares of common stock and 66 shares of preferred stock in Z, 60 shares of each class directly and 6 shares of preferred stock indirectly (60 percent of the 10 shares set aside to fund the deferred obligation).

Example 3. An irrevocable trust holds a 10–percent general partnership interest in Partnership Q. One-half of the trust income is required to be distributed to O Charity. The other one-half of the income is to be distributed to D during D's life and thereafter to E for such time as E survives D. D holds one-half of the trust's interest in Q by reason of D's present right to receive one-half of the trust's income, and E holds one-half of the trust's interest in Q by reason of E's future right to receive one-half of the trust's income. Nevertheless, no family member is treated as holding more than one-half of the trust's interest in Q because at no time will either D or E actually hold, in the aggregate, any right with respect to income or corpus greater than one-half.

Example 4. An irrevocable trust holds a 10–percent general partnership interest in Partnership M. One-half of the trust income is to be paid to D for D's life. The remaining income may, in the trustee's discretion, be accumulated or paid to or for the benefit of a class that includes D's child F, in such amounts as the trustee determines. On the death of the survivor of D and F, the trust corpus is required to be distributed to O Charity. The trust's interest in M is held by the trust's beneficiaries to the extent that present and future income or corpus may be distributed to them. Accordingly, D holds one-half of the trust's interest in M because D is entitled to receive one-half of the trust income currently. F holds the entire value of the interest because F is a member of the class eligible to receive the entire trust income for such time as F survives D. See paragraph (a)(5) of this section for rules applicable in the case of multiple attribution.

Example 5. The facts are the same as in Example 4, except that all the income is required to be paid to O Charity for the trust's initial year. The result is the same as in Example 4.

[T.D. 8395, 57 FR 4263, Feb. 4, 1992]

§ 25.2701–7 Separate interests.

The Secretary may, by regulation, revenue ruling, notice, or other document of general application, prescribe rules under which an applicable retained interest is treated as two or more separate interests for purposes of section 2701. In addition, the Commissioner may, by ruling issued to a taxpayer upon request, treat any applicable retained interest as two or more separate interests as may be necessary and appropriate to carry out the purposes of section 2701.

[T.D. 8395, 57 FR 4264, Feb. 4, 1992]

§ 25.2702–1 Special valuation rules in the case of transfers of interests in trust.

(a) Scope of section 2702. Section 2702 provides special rules to determine the amount of the gift when an individual makes a transfer in trust to (or for the benefit of) a member of the individual's family and the individual or an applicable family member retains an interest in the trust. Section 25.2702–4 treats certain transfers of property as transfers in trust. Certain transfers, including transfers to a personal residence trust, are not subject to section 2702. See paragraph (c) of this section. Member of the family is defined in § 25.2702–2(a)(1). Applicable family member is defined in § 25.2701–1(d)(2).

(b) Effect of section 2702. If section 2702 applies to a transfer, the value of any interest in the trust retained by the transferor or any applicable family member is determined under § 25.2702–2(b). The amount of the gift, if any, is then determined by subtracting the value of the interests retained by the transferor or any applicable family member from the value of the transferred property. If the retained interest is not a qualified interest (as defined in § 25.2702–3), the retained interest is generally valued at zero, and the amount of the gift is the entire value of the property.

(c) Exceptions to section 2702. Section 2702 does not apply to the following transfers.

(1) Incomplete gift. A transfer no portion of which would be treated as a completed gift without regard to any consideration received by the transferor. If a transfer is wholly incomplete as to an undivided fractional share of the property transferred (without regard to any consideration received by the transferor), for purposes of this paragraph the transfer is treated as incomplete as to that share.

(2) Personal residence trust. A transfer in trust that meets the requirements of § 25.2702–5.

(3) Charitable remainder trust. (i) For transfers made on or after May 19, 1997, a transfer to a pooled income fund described in section 642(c)(5); a transfer to a charitable remainder annuity trust described in section 664(d)(1); a transfer to a charitable remainder unitrust described in section 664(d)(2) if under the terms of the governing instrument the unitrust amount can be computed only under section 664(d)(2)(A); and a transfer to a charitable remainder unitrust if under the terms of the governing instrument the unitrust amount can be computed under section 664(d)(2) and (3) and either there are only two consecutive noncharitable beneficial interests and the transferor holds the second of the two interests, or the only permissible recipients of the unitrust amount are the transferor, the transferor's U.S. citizen spouse, or both the transferor and the transferor's U.S. citizen spouse.

(ii) For transfers made before May 19, 1997, a transfer in trust if the remainder interest in the trust qualifies for a deduction under section 2522.

(4) Pooled income fund. A transfer of property to a pooled income fund (as defined in section 642(c)(5)).

(5) Charitable lead trust. A transfer in trust if the only interest in the trust, other than the remainder interest or a qualified annuity or unitrust interest, is an interest that qualifies for deduction under section 2522.

(6) Certain assignments of remainder interests. The assignment of a remainder interest if the only retained interest of the transferor or an applicable family member is as the permissible recipient of distributions of income in the sole discretion of an independent trustee (as defined in section 674(c)).

(7) Certain property settlements. A transfer in trust if the transfer of an interest to a spouse is deemed to be for full and adequate consideration by reason of section 2516 (relating to certain property settlements) and the remaining interests in the trust are retained by the other spouse.

(8) Transfer or assignment to a Qualified Domestic Trust. A transfer or assignment (as described in section 2056(d)(2)(B)) by a noncitizen surviving spouse of property to a Qualified Domestic Trust under the circumstances described in § 20.2056A–4(b) of this chapter, where the surviving spouse retains an interest in the transferred property that is not a qualified interest and the transfer is not described in sections 2702(a)(3)(A)(ii) or 2702(c)(4).

[T.D. 8395, 57 FR 4265, Feb. 4, 1992, as amended by T.D. 8612, 60 FR 43531, Aug. 22, 1995; T.D. 8791, 63 FR 68188, Dec. 10, 1998]

§ 25.2702–2 Definitions and valuation rules.

(a) Definitions. The following definitions apply for purposes of section 2702 and the regulations thereunder.

(1) Member of the family. With respect to any individual, member of the family means the individual's spouse, any ancestor or lineal descendant of the individual or the individual's spouse, any brother or sister of the individual, and any spouse of the foregoing.

(2) Transfer in trust. A transfer in trust includes a transfer to a new or existing trust and an assignment of an interest in an existing trust. Transfer in trust does not include—

(i) The exercise, release or lapse of a power of appointment over trust property that is not a transfer under chapter 12; or

(ii) The execution of a qualified disclaimer (as defined in section 2518).

(3) Retained. Retained means held by the same individual both before and after the transfer in trust. In the case of the creation of a term interest, any interest in the property held by the transferor immediately after the transfer is treated as held both before and after the transfer.

(4) Interest. An interest in trust includes a power with respect to a trust if the existence of the power would cause any portion of a transfer to be treated as an incomplete gift under chapter 12.

(5) Holder. The holder is the person to whom the annuity or unitrust interest is payable during the fixed term of that interest. References to holder shall also include the estate of that person.

(6) Qualified interest. Qualified interest means a qualified annuity interest, a qualified unitrust interest, or a qualified remainder interest. If a transferor retains a power to revoke a qualified annuity interest or qualified unitrust interest of the transferor's spouse, then the revocable qualified annuity or unitrust interest of the transferor's spouse is treated as a retained qualified interest of the transferor. In order for the transferor to be treated as having retained a qualified interest under the preceding sentence, the interest of the transferor's spouse (the successor holder) must be an interest that meets the requirements of a qualified annuity interest in accordance with § 25.2702–3(b) and (d), or a qualified unitrust interest in accordance with § 25.2702–3(c) and (d), but for the transferor's retained power to revoke the interest.

(7) Qualified annuity interest. Qualified annuity interest means an interest that meets all the requirements of § 25.2702–3(b) and (d).

(8) Qualified unitrust interest. Qualified unitrust interest means an interest that meets all the requirements of § 25.2702–3(c) and (d).

(9) Qualified remainder interest. Qualified remainder interest means an interest that meets all the requirements of § 25.2702–3(f).

(10) Governing instrument. Governing instrument means the instrument or instruments creating and governing the operation of the trust arrangement.

(b) Valuation of retained interests—(1) In general. Except as provided in paragraphs (b)(2) and (c) of this section, the value of any interest retained by the transferor or an applicable family member is zero.

(2) Qualified interest. The value of a qualified annuity interest and a qualified remainder interest following a qualified annuity interest are determined under section 7520. The value of a qualified unitrust interest and a qualified remainder interest following a qualified unitrust interest are determined as if they were interests described in section 664.

(c) Valuation of a term interest in certain tangible property—(1) In general. If section 2702 applies to a transfer in trust of tangible property described in paragraph (c)(2) of this section ("tangible property"), the value of a retained term interest (other than a qualified interest) is not determined under section 7520 but is the amount the transferor establishes as the amount a willing buyer would pay a willing seller for the interest, each having reasonable knowledge of the relevant facts and neither being under any compulsion to buy or sell. If the transferor cannot reasonably establish the value of the term interest pursuant to this paragraph (c)(1), the interest is valued at zero.

(2) Tangible property subject to rule—(i) In general. Except as provided in paragraph (c)(2)(ii) of this section, paragraph (c)(1) of this section applies only to tangible property—

(A) For which no deduction for depreciation or depletion would be allowable if the property were used in a trade or business or held for the production of income; and

(B) As to which the failure to exercise any rights under the term interest would not increase the value of the property passing at the end of the term interest.

(ii) Exception for de minimis amounts of depreciable property. In determining whether property meets the requirements of this paragraph (c)(2) at the time of the transfer in trust, improvements that would otherwise cause the property not to qualify are ignored if the fair market value of the improvements, in the aggregate, do not exceed 5 percent of the fair market value of the entire property.

(3) Evidence of value of property. The best evidence of the value of any term interest to which this paragraph (c) applies is actual sales or rentals that are comparable both as to the nature and character of the property and the duration of the term interest. Little weight is accorded appraisals in the absence of such evidence. Amounts determined under section 7520 are not evidence of what a willing buyer would pay a willing seller for the interest.

(4) Conversion of property—(i) In general. Except as provided in paragraph (c)(4)(iii) of this section, if a term interest in property is valued under paragraph (c)(1) of this section, and during the term the property is converted into property a term interest in which would not qualify for valuation under paragraph (c)(1) of this section, the conversion is treated as a transfer for no consideration for purposes of chapter 12 of the value of the unexpired portion of the term interest.

(ii) Value of unexpired portion of term interest. For purposes of paragraph (c)(4)(i) of this section, the value of the unexpired portion of a term interest is the amount that bears the same relation to the value of the term interest as of the date of conversion (determined under section 7520 using the rate in effect under section 7520 on the date of the original transfer and the fair market value of the property as of the date of the original transfer) as the value of the term interest as of the date of the original transfer (determined under paragraph (c)(1) of this section) bears to the value of the term interest as of the date of the original transfer (determined under section 7520).

(iii) Conversion to qualified annuity interest. The conversion of tangible property previously valued under paragraph (c)(1) of this section into property a term interest in which would not qualify for valuation under paragraph (c)(1) of this section is not a transfer of the value of the unexpired portion of the term interest if the interest thereafter meets the requirements of a qualified annuity interest. The rules of § 25.2702–5(d)(8) (including governing instrument requirements) apply for purposes of determining the amount of the annuity payment required to be made and the determination of whether the interest meets the requirements of a qualified annuity interest.

(5) Additions or improvements to property—(i) Additions or improvements substantially affecting nature of property. If an addition or improvement is made to property a term interest in which was valued under paragraph (c)(1) of this section, and the addition or improvement affects the nature of the property to such an extent that the property would not be treated as property meeting the requirements of paragraph (c)(2) of this section if the property had included the addition or improvement at the time it was transferred, the entire property is deemed, for purposes of paragraph (c)(4) of this section, to convert (effective as of the date the addition or improvement is commenced) into property a term interest in which would not qualify for valuation under paragraph (c)(1) of this section.

(ii) Other additions or improvements. If an addition or improvement is made to property, a term interest in which was valued under paragraph (c)(1) of this section, and the addition or improvement does not affect the nature of the property to such an extent that the property would not be treated as property meeting the requirements of paragraph (c)(2) of this section if the property had included the addition or improvement at the time it was transferred, the addition or improvement is treated as an additional transfer (effective as of the date the addition or improvement is commenced) subject to § 25.2702–2(b)(1).

(d) Examples. **(1)** The following examples illustrate the rules of § 25.2702–1 and § 25.2702–2. Each example assumes that all applicable requirements of those sections not specifically described in the example are met.

Example 1. A transfers property to an irrevocable trust, retaining the right to receive the income of the trust for 10 years. On the expiration of the 10–year term, the trust is to terminate and the trust corpus is to be paid to A's child. However, if A dies during the 10–year term, the entire trust corpus is to be paid to A's estate. Each retained interest is valued at zero because it is not a qualified interest. Thus, the amount of A's gift is the fair market value of the property transferred to the trust.

Example 2. A transfers property to an irrevocable trust, retaining a 10–year annuity interest that meets the requirements set forth in § 25.2702–3 for a qualified annuity interest. Upon expiration of the 10–year term, the trust is to terminate and the trust corpus is to be paid to A's child. The amount of A's gift is the fair market value of the property transferred to the trust less the value of the retained qualified annuity interest determined under section 7520.

Example 3. D transfers property to an irrevocable trust under which the income is payable to D's spouse for life. Upon the death of D's spouse, the trust is to terminate and the trust corpus is to be paid to D's child. D retains no interest in the trust. Although the spouse is an applicable family member of D under section 2702, the spouse has not retained an interest in the trust because the spouse did not hold the interest both before and after the transfer. Section 2702 does not apply because neither the transferor nor an applicable family member has retained an interest in the trust. The result is the same whether or not D elects to treat the transfer as a transfer of qualified terminable interest property under section 2056(b)(7).

Example 4. A transfers property to an irrevocable trust, under which the income is to be paid to A for life. Upon termination of the trust, the trust corpus is to be distributed to A's child. A also retains certain powers over principal that cause the transfer to be wholly incomplete for federal gift tax purposes. Section 2702 does not apply because no portion of the transfer would be treated as a completed gift.

Example 5. The facts are the same as in Example 4, except that the trust is divided into separate fractional shares and A's retained powers apply to only one of the shares. Section 2702 applies except with respect to the share of the trust as to which A's retained powers cause the transfer to be an incomplete gift.

(2) The following facts apply for Examples 6 through 8 (examples illustrating § 25.2702–2(c)—tangible property exception):

Facts. A transfers a painting having a fair market value of $2,000,000 to A's child, B, retaining the use of the painting for 10 years. The painting does not possess an ascertainable useful life. Assume that the painting would not be depreciable if it were used in a trade or business or held for the production of income. Assume that the value of A's term interest, determined under section 7520, is $1,220,000, and that A establishes that a willing buyer of A's interest would pay $500,000 for the interest.

Example 6. A's term interest is not a qualified interest under § 25.2702–3. However, because of the nature of the property, A's failure to exercise A's rights with regard to the painting would not be expected to cause the value of the painting to be higher than it would otherwise be at the time it passes to B. Accordingly, A's interest is valued under § 25.2702–2(c)(1) at $500,000. The amount of A's gift is $1,500,000, the difference between the fair market value of the painting and the amount determined under § 25.2702–2(c)(1).

Example 7. Assume that the only evidence produced by A to establish the value of A's 10–year term interest is the amount paid by a museum for the right to use a comparable painting for 1 year. A asserts that the value of the 10–year term is 10 times the value of the 1–year term. A has not established the value of the 10–year term interest because a series of short-term rentals the aggregate duration of which equals the duration of the actual term interest does not establish what a willing buyer would pay a willing seller for the 10–year term interest. However, the value of the 10–year term interest is not less than the value of the 1–year term because it can be assumed that a willing buyer would pay no less for a 10–year term interest than a 1–year term interest.

Example 8. Assume that after 24 months A and B sell the painting for $2,000,000 and invest the proceeds in a portfolio of securities. A continues to hold an income interest in the securities for the duration of the 10–year term. Under § 25.2702–2(c)(4) the conversion of the painting into a type of property a term interest in which would not qualify for valuation under § 25.2702–2(c)(1) is treated as a transfer by A of the value of the unexpired portion of A's original term interest, unless the property is thereafter held in a trust meeting the requirements of a qualified annuity interest. Assume that the value of A's remaining term interest in $2,000,000 (determined under section 7520 using the section 7520 rate in effect on the date of the original transfer) is $1,060,000. The value of the unexpired portion of A's interest is $434,426, the amount that bears the same relation to $1,060,000 as $500,000 (the value of A's interest as of the date of the original transfer determined under paragraph (c)(1) of this section) bears to $1,220,000 (the value of A's interest as of the date of the original transfer determined under section 7520).

[T.D. 8395, 57 FR 4265, Feb. 4, 1992; as amended by T.D. 9181, 70 FR 9222, Feb. 25, 2005]

§ 25.2702–3 Qualified interests.

(a) In general. This section provides rules for determining if an interest is a qualified annuity interest, a qualified unitrust interest, or a qualified remainder interest.

(b) Special rules for qualified annuity interests. An interest is a qualified annuity interest only if it meets the requirements of this paragraph and paragraph (d) of this section.

(1) Payment of annuity amount—(i) In general. A qualified annuity interest is an irrevocable right to receive a fixed amount. The annuity amount must be payable to (or for the benefit of) the holder of the annuity interest at least annually. A right of withdrawal, whether or not cumulative, is not a qualified annuity interest. Issuance of a note, other debt instrument, option, or other similar financial arrangement, directly or indirectly, in satisfaction of the annuity amount does not constitute payment of the annuity amount.

(ii) Fixed amount. A fixed amount means—

(A) A stated dollar amount payable periodically, but not less frequently than annually, but only to the extent the amount does not exceed 120 percent of the stated dollar amount payable in the preceding year; or

(B) A fixed fraction or percentage of the initial fair market value of the property transferred to the trust, as finally determined for federal tax purposes, payable periodically but not less frequently than annually, but only to the extent the fraction or percentage does not exceed 120 percent of the fixed fraction or percentage payable in the preceding year.

(iii) Income in excess of the annuity amount. An annuity interest does not fail to be a qualified annuity interest merely because the trust permits income in excess of the amount required to pay the annuity amount to be paid to or for the benefit of the holder of the qualified annuity interest. Nevertheless, the right to receive the excess income is not a qualified interest and is not taken into account in valuing the qualified annuity interest.

(2) Incorrect valuations of trust property. If the annuity is stated in terms of a fraction or percentage of the initial fair market value of the trust property, the governing instrument must contain provisions meeting the requirements of § 1.664-2(a)(1)(iii) of this chapter (relating to adjustments for any incorrect determination of the fair market value of the property in the trust).

(3) Period for payment of annuity amount. The annuity amount may be payable based on either the anniversary date of the creation of the trust or the taxable year of the trust. In either situation, the annuity amount may be paid annually or more frequently, such as semi-annually, quarterly, or monthly. If the payment is made based on the anniversary date, proration of the annuity amount is required only if the last period during which the annuity is payable to the grantor is a period of less than 12 months. If the payment is made based on the taxable year, proration of the annuity amount is required for each short taxable year of the trust during the grantor's term. The prorated amount is the annual annuity amount multiplied by a fraction, the numerator of which is the number of days in the short period and the denominator of which is 365 (366 if February 29 is a day included in the numerator).

(4) Payment of the annuity amount in certain circumstances. An annuity amount payable based on the anniversary date of the creation of the trust must be paid no later than 105 days after the anniversary date. An annuity amount payable based on the taxable year of the trust may be paid after the close of the taxable year, provided the payment is made no later than the date by which the trustee is required to file the Federal income tax return of the trust for the taxable year (without regard to extensions). If the trustee reports for the taxable year pursuant to § 1.671-(b) of this chapter, the annuity payment must be made no later than the date by which the trustee would have been required to file the Federal income tax return of the trust for the taxable year (without regard to extensions) had the trustee reported pursuant to § 1.671-4(a) of this chapter.

(5) Additional contributions prohibited. The governing instrument must prohibit additional contributions to the trust.

(c) Special rules for qualified unitrust interests. An interest is a qualified unitrust interest only if it meets the requirements of this paragraph and paragraph (d) of this section.

(1) Payment of unitrust amount—(i) In general. A qualified unitrust interest is an irrevocable right to receive payment periodically, but not less frequently than annually, of a fixed percentage of the net fair market value of the trust assets, determined annually. For rules relating to computation of the net fair market value of the trust assets see § 25.2522(c)-3(c)(2)(vii). The unitrust amount must be payable to (or for the benefit of) the holder of the unitrust interest at least annually. A right of withdrawal, whether or not cumulative, is not a qualified unitrust interest. Issuance of a note, other debt instrument, option, or other similar financial arrangement, directly or indirectly, in satisfaction of the unitrust amount does not constitute payment of the unitrust amount.

(ii) Fixed percentage. A fixed percentage is a fraction or percentage of the net fair market value of the trust assets, determined annually, payable periodically but not less frequently than annually, but only to the extent the fraction or percentage does not exceed 120 percent of the fixed fraction or percentage payable in the preceding year.

(iii) Income in excess of unitrust amount. A unitrust interest does not fail to be a qualified unitrust interest merely because the trust permits income in excess of the amount required to pay the unitrust amount to be paid to or for the benefit of the holder of the qualified unitrust interest. Nevertheless, the right to receive the excess income is not a qualified interest and is not taken into account in valuing the qualified unitrust interest.

(2) Incorrect valuations of trust property. The governing instrument must contain provisions meeting the requirements of § 1.664–3(a)(1)(iii) of this chapter (relating to the incorrect determination of the fair market value of the property in the trust).

(3) Period for payment of unitrust amount. The unitrust amount may be payable based on either the anniversary date of the creation of the trust or the taxable year of the trust. In either situation, the unitrust amount may be paid annually or more frequently, such as semi-annually, quarterly, or monthly. If the payment is made based on the anniversary date, proration of the unitrust amount is required only if the last period during which the annuity is payable to the grantor is a period of less than 12 months. If the payment is made based on the taxable year, proration of the unitrust amounts is required for each short taxable year of the trust during the grantor's term. The prorated amount is the annual unitrust amount multiplied by a fraction, the numerator of which is the number of days in the short period and the denominator of which is 365 (366 if February 29 is a day included in the numerator).

(4) Payment of the unitrust amount in certain circumstances. A unitrust amount payable based on the anniversary date of the creation of the trust must be paid no later than 105 days after the anniversary date. A unitrust amount payable based on the taxable year of the trust may be paid after the close of the taxable year, provided the payment is made no later than the date by which he trustee is required to file the Federal income tax return of the trust for the taxable year (without regard to extensions). If the trustee reports for the taxable year pursuant to § 1.671–4(b) of this chapter, the unitrust payment must be made no later than the date by which the trustee would have been required to file the Federal income tax return of the trust for the taxable year (without regard to extensions) had the trustee reported pursuant to § 1.671–4(a) of this chapter.

(d) Requirements applicable to qualified annuity interests and qualified unitrust interests—(1) In general. To be a qualified annuity or unitrust interest, an interest must be a qualified annuity interest in every respect or a qualified unitrust interest in every respect. For example, if the interest consists of the right to receive each year a payment equal to the lesser of a fixed amount of the initial trust assets or a fixed percentage of the annual value of the trust assets, the interest is not a qualified interest. If, however, the interest consists of the right to receive each year a payment equal to the greater of a stated dollar amount or a fixed percentage of the initial trust assets or a fixed percentage of the annual value of the trust assets, the interest is a qualified interest that is valued at the greater of the two values. To be a qualified interest, the interest must meet the definition of and function exclusively as a qualified interest from the creation of the trust.

(2) Contingencies. A holder's qualified interest must be payable in any event to or for the benefit of the holder for the fixed term of that interest. Thus, payment of the interest cannot be subject to any contingency other than either the survival of the holder until the commencement, or throughout the term, of that holder's interest, or, in the case of a revocable interest described in § 25.2702–2(a)(6), the transferor's right to revoke the qualified interest of that transferor's spouse.

(3) Amounts payable to other persons. The governing instrument must prohibit distributions from the trust to or for the benefit of any person other than the holder of the qualified annuity or unitrust interest during the term of the qualified interest.

(4) Term of the annuity or unitrust interest. Term of the annuity or unitrust interest. The governing instrument must fix the term of the annuity or unitrust and the term of the interest must be fixed and ascertainable at the creation of the trust. The term must be for the life of the holder, for a specified term of years, or for the shorter (but not the longer) of those periods. Successive term interests for the benefit of the same individual are treated as the same term interest.

(5) Commutation. The governing instrument must prohibit commutation (prepayment) of the interest of the holder.

(6) Use of debt obligations to satisfy the annuity or unitrust payment obligation—(i) In general. In the case of a trust created on or after September 20, 1999, the trust instrument must prohibit the trustee from issuing a note, other debt instrument, option, or other similar financial arrangement in satisfaction of the annuity or unitrust payment obligation.

(ii) Special rule in the case of a trust created prior to September 20, 1999. In the case of a trust created prior to September 20, 1999, the interest will be treated as a qualified interest under section 2702(b) if—

(A) Notes, other debt instruments, options, or similar financial arrangements are not issued after September 20, 1999, to satisfy the annuity or unitrust payment obligation; and

(B) Any notes or any other debt instruments that were issued to satisfy the annual payment obligation on or prior to September 20, 1999, are paid in full by December 31, 1999, and any option or similar financial arrangement issued to satisfy the annual payment obligation is terminated by December 31, 1999, such that the grantor receives cash or other trust assets in satisfaction of the payment obligation. For purposes of the preceding sentence, an option will be considered terminated only if the grantor receives cash or other trust assets equal in value to the greater of the required annuity or unitrust payment plus interest computed under section 7520 of the Internal Revenue Code, or the fair market value of the option.

(e) Examples. The following examples illustrate the rules of paragraphs (b), (c), and (d) of this section. Each example assumes that all applicable requirements for a qualified interest are met unless otherwise specifically stated.

Example 1. A transfers property to an irrevocable trust, retaining the right to receive the greater of $10,000 or the trust income in each year for a term of 10 years. Upon expiration of the 10–year term, the trust is to terminate and the entire trust corpus is to be paid to A's child, provided that if A dies within the 10–year term the trust corpus is to be paid to A's estate. A's annual payment right is a qualified annuity interest to the extent of the right to receive $10,000 per year for 10 years or until A's prior death, and is valued under section 7520 without regard to the right to receive any income in excess of $10,000 per year. The contingent reversion is valued at zero. The amount of A's gift is the fair market value of the property transferred to the trust less the value of the qualified annuity interest.

Example 2. U transfers property to an irrevocable trust, retaining the right to receive $10,000 in each of years 1 through 3, $12,000 in each of years 4 through 6, and $15,000 in each of years 7 through 10. The interest is a qualified annuity interest to the extent of U's right to receive $10,000 per year in years 1 through 3, $12,000 in years 4 through 6, $14,400 in year 7, and $15,000 in years 8 through 10, because those amounts represent the lower of the amount actually payable each year or an amount that does not exceed 120 percent of the stated dollar amount for the preceding year.

Example 3. S transfers property to an irrevocable trust, retaining the right to receive $50,000 in each of years 1 through 3 and $10,000 in each of years 4 through 10. S's entire retained interest is a qualified annuity interest.

Example 4. R transfers property to an irrevocable trust retaining the right to receive annually an amount equal to the lesser of 8 percent of the initial fair market value of the trust property or the trust income for the year. R's annual payment right is not a qualified annuity interest to any extent because R does not have the irrevocable right to receive a fixed amount for each year of the term.

Example 5. A transfers property to an irrevocable trust, retaining the right to receive 5 percent of the net fair market value of the trust property, valued annually, for 10 years. If A dies within the 10–year term, the unitrust amount is to be paid to A's estate for the balance of the term. The interest of A (and A's estate) to receive the unitrust amount for the specified term of 10 years in all events is a qualified unitrust interest for a term of 10 years.

Example 6. The facts are the same as in Example 5, except that if A dies within the 10–year term the unitrust amount will be paid to A's estate for an additional 35 years. As in Example 5, the interest of A (and A's estate) to receive the unitrust amount for a specified term of 10 years in all events is a qualified unitrust interest for a term of 10 years. However, the right of A's estate to continue to receive the unitrust amount after the expiration of the 10–year term if A dies within that 10–year period is not fixed and ascertainable at the creation of the interest and is not a qualified unitrust interest.

Example 7. B transfers property to an irrevocable trust retaining the right to receive annually an amount equal to 8 percent of the initial fair market value of the trust property for 10 years. Upon expiration of the 10–year term, the trust is to terminate and the entire trust corpus is to be paid to B's child. The governing instrument provides that income in excess of the annuity amount may be paid to B's child in the trustee's discretion. B's interest is not a qualified annuity interest to any extent because a person other than the individual holding the term interest may receive distributions from the trust during the term.

Example 8. A transfers property to an irrevocable trust, retaining the right to receive an annuity equal to 6 percent of the initial net fair market value of the trust property for 10 years, or until A's prior death. At the expiration of the 10–year term, or on A's death prior to the expiration of the 10–year term, the annuity is to be paid to B, A's spouse, if then living, for 10 years or until B's prior death. A retains an inter vivos and testamentary power to revoke B's interest during the initial 10–year term. If not exercised by A during the initial 10–year term (whether during A's life or on A's death), A's right to revoke B's interest will lapse upon either A's death during the 10–year term, or the expiration of A's 10–year term (assuming A survives the term). Upon expiration of B's interest (or on the expiration of A's interest if A revokes B's interest or if B predeceases A), the trust terminates and the trust corpus is payable to A's child. Because A has made a completed gift of the remainder interest, the transfer of property to the trust is not incomplete as to all interests in the property and section 2702 applies. A's annuity interest (A's right to receive the annuity for 10 years, or until A's prior death) is a retained interest that is a qualified annuity interest under paragraphs (b) and (d) of this section. In addition, because A has retained the power to revoke B's interest, B's interest is treated as an interest retained by A for purposes of section 2702. B's successive annuity interest otherwise satisfies the requirements for a qualified interest contained in paragraph (d) of this section, but for A's power to revoke. The term of B's interest is specified in the governing instrument and is fixed and ascertainable at the creation of the trust, and B's right to receive the annuity is contingent only on B's survival, and A's power to revoke. Following the expiration of A's interest, the annuity is to be paid for a 10–year term or for B's (the successor holder's) life, whichever is shorter. Accordingly, A is treated as retaining B's revocable qualified annuity interest pursuant to § 25.2702–2(a)(6). Because both A's interest and B's interest are treated as qualified interests retained by A, the value of the gift is the value of the property transferred to the trust less the value of both A's qualified interest and B's qualified interest (subject to A's power to revoke), each valued as a single-life annuity. If A survives the 10–year term without having revoked B's interest, then A's power to revoke lapses and A will make a completed gift to B at that time. Further, if A revokes B's interest prior to the commencement of that interest, A is treated as making an additional completed gift at that time to A's child. In either case, the amount of the gift would be the present value of B's interest determined under section 7520 and the applicable regulations, as of the date the revocation power lapses or the interest is revoked. See § 25.2511–2(f).

Example 9. **(i)** A transfers property to an irrevocable trust, retaining the right to receive 6 percent of the initial net fair market value of the trust property for 10 years, or until A's prior death. If A survives the 10–year term, the trust terminates and the trust corpus is payable to A's child. If A dies prior to the expiration of the 10–year term, the annuity is payable to B, A's spouse, if then living, for the balance of the 10–year term, or until B's prior death. A retains the right to revoke B's interest. Upon expiration of B's interest (or upon A's death if A revokes B's interest or if B predeceases A), the trust terminates and the trust corpus is payable to A's child. As is the case in Example 8, A's retained annuity interest (A's right to receive the annuity for 10 years, or until A's prior death) is a qualified annuity interest under paragraphs (b) and (d) of this section. However, B's interest does not meet the requirements of paragraph (d) of this section. The term of B's annuity is not fixed and ascertainable at the creation of the trust, because it is not payable for the life of B, a specified term of years, or for the shorter of those periods. Rather, B's annuity is payable for an unspecified period that will depend upon the number of years left in the original term after A's death. Further, B's annuity is payable only if A dies prior to the expiration of the 10–year term. Thus, payment of B's annuity is not dependent solely on B's survival, but rather is dependent on A's failure to survive.

(ii) Accordingly, the amount of the gift is the fair market value of the property transferred to the trust reduced by the value of A's qualified interest (A's right to receive the stated annuity for 10 years or until A's prior death). B's interest is not a qualified interest and is thus valued at zero under section 2702.

(f) Qualified remainder interest—(1) Requirements. An interest is a qualified remainder interest only if it meets all of the following requirements:

(i) It is a qualified remainder interest in every respect.

(ii) It meets the definition of and functions exclusively as a qualified interest from the creation of the interest.

(iii) It is non-contingent. For this purpose, an interest is non-contingent only if it is payable to the beneficiary or the beneficiary's estate in all events.

(iv) All interests in the trust, other than non-contingent remainder interests, are qualified annuity interests or qualified unitrust interests. Thus, an interest is a qualified remainder interest only if the governing instrument does not permit payment of income in excess of the annuity or unitrust amount to the holder of the qualified annuity or unitrust interest.

(2) Remainder interest. Remainder interest is the right to receive all or a fractional share of the trust property on termination of all or a fractional share of the trust. Remainder interest includes a reversion. A transferor's right to receive an amount that is a stated or pecuniary amount is not a remainder interest. Thus, the right to receive the original value of the trust corpus (or a fractional share) is not a remainder interest.

(3) Examples. The following examples illustrate rules of this paragraph (f). Each example assumes that all applicable requirements of a qualified interest are met unless otherwise specifically stated.

Example 1. A transfers property to an irrevocable trust. The income of the trust is payable to A's child for life. On the death of A's child, the trust is to terminate and the trust corpus is to be paid to A. A's remainder interest is not a qualified remainder interest because the interest of A's child is neither a qualified annuity interest nor a qualified unitrust interest.

Example 2. The facts are the same as in Example 1, except that A's child has the right to receive the greater of the income of the trust or $10,000 per year. A's remainder interest is not a qualified remainder interest because the right of A's child to receive income in excess of the annuity amount is not a qualified interest.

Example 3. A transfers property to an irrevocable trust. The trust provides a qualified annuity interest to A's child for 12 years. An amount equal to the initial value of the trust corpus is to be paid to A at the end of that period and the balance is to be paid to A's grandchild. A's interest is not a qualified remainder interest because the amount A is to receive is not a fractional share of the trust property.

Example 4. U transfers property to an irrevocable trust. The trust provides a qualified unitrust interest to U's child for 15 years, at which time the trust terminates and the trust corpus is paid to U or, if U is not then living, to U's child. Because U's remainder interest is contingent, it is not a qualified remainder interest.

[T.D. 8395, 57 FR 4267, Feb. 4, 1992, as amended by T.D. 8536, 59 FR 23152, May 5, 1994; T.D. 8633, 60 FR 66085, Dec. 21, 1995; T.D. 8899, 65 FR 53587, Sept. 1, 2000; T.D. 9181, 70 FR 9222, Feb. 25, 2005]

§ 25.2702–4 Certain property treated as held in trust.

(a) In general. For purposes of section 2702, a transfer of an interest in property with respect to which there are one or more term interests is treated as a transfer in trust. A term interest is one of a series of successive (as contrasted with concurrent) interests. Thus, a life interest in property or an interest in property for a term of years is a term interest. However, a term interest does not include a fee interest in property merely because it is held as a tenant in common, a tenant by the entireties, or a joint tenant with right of survivorship.

(b) Leases. A leasehold interest in property is not a term interest to the extent the lease is for full and adequate consideration (without regard to section 2702). A lease will be considered for full and adequate consideration if, under all the facts and circumstances as of the time the lease is entered into or extended, a good faith effort is made to determine the fair rental value of the property and the terms of the lease conform to the value so determined.

(c) Joint purchases. Solely for purposes of section 2702, if an individual acquires a term interest in property and, in the same transaction or series of transactions, one or more members of the individual's family acquire an interest in the same property, the individual acquiring the term interest is treated as acquiring the entire property so acquired, and transferring to each of those family members the interests acquired by that family member in exchange for any consideration paid by that family member. For purposes of this paragraph (c), the amount of the individual's gift will not exceed the amount of consideration furnished by that individual for all interests in the property.

(d) Examples. The following examples illustrate rules of this section:

Example 1. A purchases a 20–year term interest in an apartment building and A's child purchases the remainder interest in the property. A and A's child each provide the portion of the purchase price equal to the value of their respective interests in the property determined under section 7520. Solely for purposes of section 2702, A is treated as acquiring the entire property and transferring the remainder interest to A's child in exchange for the portion of the purchase price provided by A's child. In determining the amount of A's gift, A's retained interest is valued at zero because it is not a qualified interest.

Example 2. K holds rental real estate valued at $100,000. K sells a remainder interest in the property to K's child, retaining the right to receive the income from the property for 20 years. Assume the purchase price paid by K's child for the remainder interest is equal to the value of the interest determined under section 7520. K's retained interest is not a qualified interest and is therefore valued at zero. K has made a gift in the amount of $100,000 less the consideration received from K's child.

Example 3. G and G's child each acquire a 50 percent undivided interest as tenants in common in an office building. The interests of G and G's child are not term interests to which section 2702 applies.

Example 4. B purchases a life estate in property from R, B's grandparent, for $100 and B's child purchases the remainder interest for $50. Assume that the value of the property is $300, the value of the life estate determined under section 7520 is $250 and the value of the remainder interest is $50. B is treated as acquiring the entire property and transferring the remainder interest to B's child. However, the amount of B's gift is $100, the amount of consideration ($100) furnished by B for B's interest.

Example 5. H and W enter into a written agreement relative to their marital and property rights that requires W to transfer property to an irrevocable trust, the terms of which provide that the income of the trust will be paid to H for 10 years. On the expiration of the 10–year term, the trust is to terminate and the trust corpus is to be paid to W. H and W divorce within two years after the agreement is entered into. Pursuant to section 2516, the transfer to H would otherwise be deemed to be for full and adequate consideration. Section 2702 does not apply to the acquisition of the term interest by H because no member of H's family acquired an interest in the property in the same transaction or series of transactions. The result would not be the same if, on the termination of H's interest in the trust, the trust corpus were distributable to the children of H and W rather than W.

[T.D. 8395, 57 FR 4269, Feb. 4, 1992]

§ 25.2702–5 Personal residence trusts.

(a)(1) In general. Section 2702 does not apply to a transfer in trust meeting the requirements of this section. A transfer in trust meets the requirements of this section only if the trust is a personal residence trust (as defined in paragraph (b) of this section). A trust meeting the requirements of a qualified personal residence trust (as defined in paragraph (c) of this section) is treated as a personal residence trust. A trust of which the term holder is the grantor that otherwise meets the requirements of a personal residence trust (or a qualified personal residence trust) is not a personal residence trust (or a qualified personal residence trust) if, at the time of transfer, the term holder of the trust already holds term interests in two trusts that are personal residence trusts (or qualified personal residence trusts) of which the term holder was the grantor. For this purpose, trusts holding fractional interests in the same residence are treated as one trust.

(2) Modification of trust. A trust that does not comply with one or more of the regulatory requirements under paragraph (b) or (c) of this section will, nonetheless, be treated as satisfying these requirements if the trust is modified, by judicial reformation (or nonjudicial reformation if effective under state law), to comply with the requirements. In the case of a trust created after December 31, 1996, the reformation must be commenced within 90 days after the due date (including extensions) for the filing of the gift tax return reporting the transfer of the residence under section 6075 and must be completed within a reasonable time after commencement. If the reformation is not completed by the due date (including extensions) for filing the gift tax return, the grantor or grantor's spouse must attach a statement to the gift tax return stating that the reformation has been commenced or will be commenced within the 90–day period. In the case of a trust created before January 1, 1997, the reformation must be commenced within 90 days after December 23, 1997 and must be completed within a reasonable time after commencement.

(b) Personal residence trust—(1) In general. A personal residence trust is a trust the governing instrument of which prohibits the trust from holding, for the original duration of the term interest, any asset other than one residence to be used or held for use as a personal residence of the term holder and qualified proceeds (as defined in paragraph (b)(3) of this section). A residence is held for use as a personal residence of the term holder so long as the residence is not occupied by any other person (other than the spouse or a dependent of the term holder) and is available at all times for use by the term holder as a personal residence. A trust does not meet the requirements of this section if, during the original duration of the term interest, the residence may be sold or otherwise transferred by the trust or may be used for a purpose other than as a personal residence of the term holder. In addition, the trust does not meet the requirements of this section unless the governing instrument prohibits the trust from selling or transferring the residence, directly or indirectly, to the grantor, the grantor's spouse, or an entity controlled by the grantor or the grantor's spouse, at any time after the original duration of the term interest during which the trust is a grantor trust. For purposes of the preceding sentence, a sale or transfer to another grantor trust of the grantor or the grantor's spouse is considered a sale or transfer to the grantor or the grantor's spouse; however, a distribution (for no consideration) upon or after the expiration of the original duration of the term interest to another grantor trust of the grantor or the grantor's spouse pursuant to the express terms of the trust will not be considered a sale or transfer to the grantor or the grantor's spouse if such other grantor trust prohibits the sale or transfer of the property to the grantor, the grantor's spouse, or an entity controlled by the grantor or the grantor's spouse. In the event the grantor dies prior to the expiration of the original duration of the term interest, this paragraph (b)(1) does not apply to the distribution (for no consideration) of the residence to any person (including the grantor's estate) pursuant to the express terms of the trust or pursuant to the exercise of a power retained by the grantor under the terms of the trust. Further, this paragraph (b)(1) does not apply to any outright distribution (for no consideration) of the residence to the grantor's spouse after the expiration of the original duration of the term interest pursuant to the express terms of the trust. For purposes of this paragraph (b)(1), a grantor trust is a trust treated as owned in whole or in part by the grantor or the grantor's spouse pursuant to sections 671 through 678, and control is defined in s 25.2701–2(b)(5)(ii) and (iii). Expenses of the trust whether or not attributable to trust principal may be paid directly by the term holder of the trust.

(2) Personal residence—(i) In general. For purposes of this paragraph (b), a personal residence of a term holder is either—

(A) The principal residence of the term holder (within the meaning of section 1034);

(B) One other residence of the term holder (within the meaning of section 280A(d)(1) but without regard to section 280A(d)(2)); or

(C) An undivided fractional interest in either.

(ii) Additional property. A personal residence may include appurtenant structures used by the term holder for residential purposes and adjacent land not in excess of that which is reasonably appropriate for residential purposes (taking into account the residence's size and location). The fact that a residence is subject to a mortgage does not affect its status as a personal residence. The term personal residence does not include any personal property (e.g., household furnishings).

(iii) Use of residence. A residence is a personal residence only if its primary use is as a residence of the term holder when occupied by the term holder. The principal residence of the term holder will not fail to meet the requirements of the preceding sentence merely because a portion of the residence is used in an activity meeting the requirements of section 280A(c)(1) or (4) (relating to deductibility of expenses related to certain uses), provided that such use is secondary to use of the residence as a residence. A residence is not used primarily as a residence if it is used to provide transient lodging and substantial services are provided in connection with the provision of lodging (e.g. a hotel or a bed and breakfast). A residence is not a personal residence if, during any period not occupied by the term holder, its primary use is other than as a residence.

(iv) Interests of spouses in the same residence. If spouses hold interests in the same residence (including community property interests), the spouses may transfer their interests in the residence (or a fractional portion of their interests in the residence) to the same personal residence trust, provided that the governing instrument prohibits any person other than one of the spouses from holding a term interest in the trust concurrently with the other spouse.

(3) Qualified proceeds. Qualified proceeds means the proceeds payable as a result of damage to, or destruction or involuntary conversion (within the meaning of section 1033) of, the residence held by a personal residence trust, provided that the governing instrument requires that the proceeds (including any income thereon) be reinvested in a personal residence within two years from the date on which the proceeds are received.

(c) Qualified personal residence trust—(1) In general. A qualified personal residence trust is a trust meeting all the requirements of this paragraph (c). These requirements must be met by provisions in the governing instrument, and these governing instrument provisions must by their terms continue in effect during the existence of any term interest in the trust.

(2) Personal residence—(i) In general. For purposes of this paragraph (c), a personal residence of a term holder is either—

(A) The principal residence of the term holder (within the meaning of section 1034);

(B) One other residence of the term holder (within the meaning of section 280A(d)(1) but without regard to section 280A(d)(2)); or

(C) An undivided fractional interest in either.

(ii) Additional property. A personal residence may include appurtenant structures used by the term holder for residential purposes and adjacent land not in excess of that which is reasonably appropriate for residential purposes (taking into account the residence's size and location). The fact that a residence is subject to a mortgage does not affect its status as a personal residence. The term personal residence does not include any personal property (e.g., household furnishings).

(iii) Use of residence. A residence is a personal residence only if its primary use is as a residence of the term holder when occupied by the term holder. The principal residence of the term holder will not fail to meet the requirements of the preceding sentence merely because a portion of the residence is used in an activity meeting the requirements of section 280A(c)(1) or (4) (relating to deductibility of expenses related to certain uses), provided that such use is secondary to use of the residence as a residence. A residence is not used primarily as a residence if it is used to provide transient lodging and substantial services are provided in connection with the provision of lodging (e.g., a hotel or a bed and breakfast). A residence is not a personal residence if, during any period not occupied by the term holder, its primary use is other than as a residence. A residence is not a personal residence if, during any period not occupied by the term holder, its primary use is other than as a residence.

(iv) Interests of spouses in the same residence. If spouses hold interests in the same residence (including community property interests), the spouses may transfer their interests in the residence (or a fractional portion of their interests in the residence) to the same qualified personal residence trust, provided that the governing instrument prohibits any person other than one of the spouses from holding a term interest in the trust concurrently with the other spouse.

(3) Income of the trust. The governing instrument must require that any income of the trust be distributed to the term holder not less frequently than annually.

(4) Distributions from the trust to other persons. The governing instrument must prohibit distributions of corpus to any beneficiary other than the transferor prior to the expiration of the retained term interest.

(5) Assets of the trust—(i) In general. Except as otherwise provided in paragraphs (c)(5)(ii) and (c)(8) of this section, the governing instrument must prohibit the trust from holding, for the entire term of the trust, any asset other than one residence to be used or held for use (within the meaning of paragraph (c)(7)(i) of this section) as a personal residence of the term holder (the "residence").

(ii) Assets other than personal residence. Except as otherwise provided, the governing instrument may permit a qualified personal residence trust to hold the following assets (in addition to the residence) in the amounts and in the manner described in this paragraph (c)(5)(ii):

(A) Additions of cash for payment of expenses, etc.—(1) Additions. The governing instrument may permit additions of cash to the trust, and may permit the trust to hold additions of cash in a separate account, in an amount which, when added to the cash already held in the account for such purposes, does not exceed the amount required:

(i) For payment of trust expenses (including mortgage payments) already incurred or reasonably expected to be paid by the trust within six months from the date the addition is made;

(ii) For improvements to the residence to be paid by the trust within six months from the date the addition is made; and

(iii) For purchase by the trust of the initial residence, within three months of the date the trust is created, provided that no addition may be made for this purpose, and the trust may not hold any such addition, unless the trustee has previously entered into a contract to purchase that residence; and

(iv) For purchase by the trust of a residence to replace another residence, within three months of the date the addition is made, provided that no addition may be made for this purpose, and the trust may not hold any such addition, unless the trustee has previously entered into a contract to purchase that residence.

(2) Distributions of excess cash. If the governing instrument permits additions of cash to the trust pursuant to paragraph (c)(5)(ii)(A)(1) of this section, the governing instrument must require that the trustee determine, not less frequently than quarterly, the amounts held by the trust for payment of expenses in excess of the amounts permitted by that paragraph and must require that those amounts be distributed immediately thereafter to the term holder. In addition, the governing instrument must require, upon termination of the term holder's interest in the trust, any amounts held by the trust for the purposes permitted by paragraph (c)(5)(ii)(A)(1) of this section that are not used to pay trust expenses due and payable on the date of termination (including expenses directly related to termination) be distributed outright to the term holder within 30 days of termination.

(B) Improvements. The governing instrument may permit improvements to the residence to be added to the trust and may permit the trust to hold such improvements, provided that the residence, as improved, meets the requirements of a personal residence.

(C) Sale proceeds. The governing instrument may permit the sale of the residence (except as set forth in paragraph (c)(9) of this section) and may permit the trust to hold proceeds from the sale of the residence, in a separate account.

(D) Insurance and insurance proceeds. The governing instrument may permit the trust to hold one or more policies of insurance on the residence. In addition, the governing instrument may permit the trust to hold, in a separate account, proceeds of insurance payable to the trust as a result of damage to or destruction of the residence. For purposes of this paragraph, amounts (other than insurance proceeds payable to the trust as a result of damage to or destruction of the residence) received as a result of the involuntary conversion (within the meaning of section 1033) of the residence are treated as proceeds of insurance.

(6) Commutation. The governing instrument must prohibit commutation (prepayment) of the term holder's interest.

(7) Cessation of use as a personal residence—(i) In general. The governing instrument must provide that a trust ceases to be a qualified personal residence trust if the residence ceases to be used or held for use as a personal residence of the term holder. A residence is held for use as a personal residence of the term holder so long as the residence is not occupied by any other person (other than the spouse or a dependent of the term holder) and is available at all times for use by the term holder as a personal residence. See § 25.2702–5(c)(8) for rules governing disposition of assets of a trust as to which the trust has ceased to be a qualified personal residence trust.

(ii) Sale of personal residence. The governing instrument must provide that the trust ceases to be a qualified personal residence trust upon sale of the residence if the governing instrument does not permit the trust to hold proceeds of sale of the residence pursuant to paragraph (c)(5)(ii)(C) of this section. If the governing instrument permits the trust to hold proceeds of sale pursuant to that paragraph, the governing instrument must provide that the trust ceases to be a qualified personal residence trust with respect to all proceeds of sale held by the trust not later than the earlier of—

(A) The date that is two years after the date of sale;

(B) The termination of the term holder's interest in the trust; or

(C) The date on which a new residence is acquired by the trust.

(iii) Damage to or destruction of personal residence—(A) In general. The governing instrument must provide that, if damage or destruction renders the residence unusable as a residence, the trust ceases to be a qualified personal residence trust on the date that is two years after the date of damage or destruction (or the date of termination of the term holder's interest in the trust, if earlier) unless, prior to such date—

(1) Replacement of or repairs to the residence are completed; or

(2) A new residence is acquired by the trust.

(B) Insurance proceeds. For purposes of this paragraph (C)(7)(iii), if the governing instrument permits the trust to hold proceeds of insurance received as a result of damage to or destruction of the residence pursuant to paragraph (c)(5)(ii)(D) of this section, the governing instrument must contain provisions similar to those required by paragraph (c)(7)(ii) of this section.

(8) Disposition of trust assets on cessation as personal residence trust—(i) In general. The governing instrument must provide that, within 30 days after the date on which the trust has ceased to be a qualified personal residence trust with respect to certain assets, either—

(A) The assets be distributed outright to the term holder;

(B) The assets be converted to and held for the balance of the term holder's term in a separate share of the trust meeting the requirements of a qualified annuity interest; or

(C) In the trustee's sole discretion, the trustee may elect to comply with either paragraph (c)(8)(i)(A) or (B) of this section pursuant to their terms.

(ii) Requirements for conversion to a qualified annuity interest—(A) Governing instrument requirements. For assets subject to this paragraph (c)(8) to be converted to and held as a qualified annuity interest, the governing instrument must contain all provisions required by § 25.2702–3 with respect to a qualified annuity interest.

(B) Effective date of annuity. The governing instrument must provide that the right of the term holder to receive the annuity amount begins on the date of sale of the residence, the date of damage to or destruction of the residence, or the date on which the residence ceases to be used or held for use as a personal residence, as the case may be ("the cessation date"). Notwithstanding the preceding sentence, the governing instrument may provide that the trustee may defer payment of any annuity amount otherwise payable after the cessation date until the date that is 30 days after the assets are converted to a qualified annuity interest under paragraph (c)(8)(i)(B) of this section ("the conversion date"); provided that any deferred payment must bear interest from the cessation date at a rate not less than the section 7520 rate in effect on the cessation date. The governing instrument may permit the trustee to reduce aggregate deferred annuity payments by the amount of income actually distributed by the trust to the term holder during the deferral period.

(C) Determination of annuity amount—(1) In general. The governing instrument must require that the annuity amount be no less than the amount determined under this paragraph (C).

(2) Entire trust ceases to be a qualified personal residence trust. If, on the conversion date, the assets of the trust do not include a residence used or held for use as a personal residence, the annuity may not be less than an amount determined by dividing the lesser of the value of all interests retained by the term holder (as of the date of the original transfer or transfers) or the value of all the trust assets (as of the conversion date) by an annuity factor determined—

(i) For the original term of the term holder's interest; and

(ii) At the rate used in valuing the retained interest at the time of the original transfer.

(3) Portion of trust continues as qualified personal residence trust. If, on the conversion date, the assets of the trust include a residence used or held for use as a personal residence, the annuity must not be less than the amount determined under paragraph (c)(8)(ii)(C)(2) of this section multiplied by a fraction. The numerator of the fraction is the excess of the fair market value of the trust assets on the conversion date over the fair market value of the assets as to which the trust continues as a qualified personal residence trust, and the denominator of the fraction is the fair market value of the trust assets on the conversion date.

(9) Sale of residence to grantor, grantor's spouse, or entity controlled by grantor or grantor's spouse. The governing instrument must prohibit the trust from selling or transferring the residence, directly or indirectly, to the grantor, the grantor's spouse, or an entity controlled by the grantor or the grantor's spouse during the retained term interest of the trust, or at any time after the retained term interest that the trust is a grantor trust. For purposes of the preceding sentence, a sale or transfer to another grantor trust of the grantor or the grantor's spouse is considered a sale or transfer to the grantor or the grantor's spouse; however, a distribution (for no consideration) upon or after the expiration of the retained term interest to another grantor trust of the grantor or the grantor's spouse pursuant to the express terms of the trust will not be considered a sale or transfer to the grantor or the grantor's spouse if such other grantor trust prohibits the sale or transfer of the property to the grantor, the grantor's spouse, or an entity controlled by the grantor or the grantor's spouse. In the event the grantor dies prior to the expiration of the retained term interest, this paragraph (c)(9) does not apply to the distribution (for no consideration) of the residence to any person (including the grantor's estate) pursuant to the express terms of the trust or pursuant to the exercise of a power retained by the grantor under the terms of the trust. Further, this paragraph (c)(9) does not apply to an outright distribution (for no consideration) of the residence to the grantor's spouse after the expiration of the retained trust term pursuant to the express terms of the trust. For purposes of this paragraph (c)(9), a grantor trust is a trust treated as owned in whole or in part by the grantor or the grantor's spouse pursuant to sections 671 through 678, and control is defined in § 25.2701–2(b)(5)(ii) and (iii).

(d) Examples. The following examples illustrate rules of this section. Each example assumes that all applicable requirements of a personal residence trust (or qualified personal residence trust) are met unless otherwise stated.

Example (1). C maintains C's principal place of business in one room of C's principal residence. The room meets the requirements of section 280A(c)(1) for deductibility of expenses related to such use. The residence is a personal residence.

Example (2). L owns a vacation condominium that L rents out for six months of the year, but which is treated as L's residence under section 280A(d)(1) because L occupies it for at least 18 days per year. L provides no substantial services in connection with the rental of the condominium. L transfers the condominium to an irrevocable trust, the terms of which meet the requirements of a qualified personal residence trust. L retains the right to use the condominium during L's lifetime. The trust is a qualified personal residence trust.

Example (3). W owns a 200–acre farm. The farm includes a house, barns, equipment buildings, a silo, and enclosures for confinement of farm animals. W transfers the farm to an irrevocable trust, retaining the use of the farm for 20 years, with the remainder to W's child. The trust is not a personal residence trust because the farm includes assets not meeting the requirements of a personal residence.

Example (4). A transfers A's principal residence to an irrevocable trust, retaining the right to use the residence for a 20–year term. The governing instrument of the trust does not prohibit the trust from holding personal property. The trust is not a qualified personal residence trust.

Example (5). T transfers a personal residence to a trust that meets the requirements of a qualified personal residence trust, retaining a term interest in the trust for 10 years. During the period of T's retained term interest, T is forced for health reasons to move to a nursing home. T's spouse continues to occupy the residence. If the residence is available at all times for T's use as a residence during the term (without regard to T's ability to actually use the residence), the residence continues to be held for T's use and the trust does not cease to be a qualified personal residence trust. The residence would cease to be held for use as a personal residence of T if the trustee rented the residence to an unrelated party, because the residence would no longer be available for T's use at all times.

Example (6). T transfers T's personal residence to a trust that meets the requirements of a qualified personal residence trust, retaining the right to use the residence for 12 years. On the date the residence is transferred to the trust, the fair market value of the residence is $100,000. After 6 years, the trustee sells the residence, receiving net proceeds of $250,000, and invests the proceeds of sale in common stock. After an additional eighteen months, the common stock has paid $15,000 in dividends and has a fair market value of $260,000. On that date, the trustee purchases a new residence for $200,000. On the purchase of the new residence, the trust ceases to be a qualified personal residence trust with respect to any amount not reinvested in the new residence. The governing instrument of the trust provides that the trustee, in the trustee's sole discretion, may elect either to distribute the excess proceeds or to convert the proceeds into a qualified annuity interest. The trustee elects the latter option. The amount of the annuity is the amount of the annuity that would be payable if no portion of the sale proceeds had been reinvested in a personal residence multiplied by a fraction. The numerator of the fraction is $60,000 (the amount remaining after reinvestment) and the denominator of the fraction is $260,000 (the fair market value of the trust assets on the conversion date). The obligation to pay the annuity commences on the date of sale, but payment of the annuity that otherwise would have been payable during the period between the date of sale and the date on which the trust ceased to be a qualified personal residence trust with respect to the excess proceeds may be deferred until 30 days after the date on which the new residence is purchased. Any amount deferred must bear compound interest from the date the annuity is payable at the section 7520 rate in effect on the date of sale. The $15,000 of income distributed to the term holder during that period may be used to reduce the annuity amount payable with respect to that period if the governing instrument so provides and thus reduce the amount on which compound interest is computed.

[T.D. 8395, 57 FR 4269, Feb. 4, 1992; T.D. 8395, 57 FR 11265, April 2, 1992; T.D. 8743, 62 FR 66988, Dec. 23, 1997]

§ 25.2702–6 Reduction in taxable gifts.

(a) Transfers of retained interests in trust—(1) Inter vivos transfers. If an individual subsequently transfers by gift an interest in trust previously valued (when held by that individual) under § 25.2702–2(b)(1) or (c), the individual is entitled to a reduction in aggregate taxable gifts. The amount of the reduction is determined under paragraph (b) of this section. Thus, for example, if an individual transferred property to an irrevocable trust, retaining an interest in the trust that was valued at zero under § 25.2702–2(b)(1), and the individual later transfers the retained interest by gift, the individual is entitled to a reduction in aggregate taxable gifts on the subsequent transfer. For purposes of this section, aggregate taxable gifts means the aggregate sum of the individual's taxable gifts for the calendar year determined under section 2502(a)(1).

(2) Testamentary transfers. If either—

(i) A term interest in trust is included in an individual's gross estate solely by reason of section 2033, or

(ii) A remainder interest in trust is included in an individual's gross estate,

and the interest was previously valued (when held by that individual) under § 25.2702–2(b)(1) or (c), the individual's estate is entitled to a reduction in the individual's adjusted taxable gifts in computing the Federal estate tax payable under section 2001. The amount of the reduction is determined under paragraph (b) of this section.

(3) Gift splitting on subsequent transfer. If an individual who is entitled to a reduction in aggregate taxable gifts (or adjusted taxable gifts) subsequently transfers the interest in a transfer treated as made one-half by the individual's spouse under section 2513, the individual may assign one-half of the amount of the reduction to the consenting spouse. The assignment must be attached to the Form 709 on which the consenting spouse reports the split gift.

(b) Amount of reduction—(1) In general. The amount of the reduction in aggregate taxable gifts (or adjusted taxable gifts) is the lesser of—

(i) The increase in the individual's taxable gifts resulting from the interest being valued at the time of the initial transfer under § 25.2702–2(b)(1) or (c); or

(ii) The increase in the individual's taxable gifts (or gross estate) resulting from the subsequent transfer of the interest.

(2) Treatment of annual exclusion. For purposes of determining the amount under paragraph (b)(1)(ii) of this section, the exclusion under section 2503(b) applies first to transfers in that year other than the transfer of the interest previously valued under § 25.2702–2(b)(1) or (c).

(3) Overlap with section 2001. Notwithstanding paragraph (b)(1) of this section, the amount of the reduction is reduced to the extent section 2001 would apply to reduce the amount of an individual's adjusted taxable gifts with respect to the same interest to which paragraph (b)(1) of this section would otherwise apply.

(c) Examples. The rules of this section are illustrated by the following examples. The following facts apply for Examples 1–4:

Facts. In 1992, X transferred property to an irrevocable trust retaining the right to receive the trust income for life. On the death of X, the trust is to terminate and the trust corpus is to be paid to X's child, C. X's income interest had a value under section 7520 of $40,000 at the time of the transfer; however, because X's retained interest was not a qualified interest, it was valued at zero under § 25.2702–2(b)(1) for purposes of determining the amount of X's gift. X's taxable gifts in 1992 were therefore increased by $40,000. In 1993, X transfers the income interest to C for no consideration.

Example 1. Assume that the value under section 7520 of the income interest on the subsequent transfer to C is $30,000. If X makes no other gifts to C in 1993, X is entitled to a reduction in aggregate taxable gifts of $20,000, the lesser of the amount by which X's taxable gifts were increased as a result of the income interest being valued at zero on the initial transfer ($40,000) or the amount by which X's taxable gifts are increased as a result of the subsequent transfer of the income interest ($30,000 minus $10,000 annual exclusion).

Example 2. Assume that in 1993, 4 months after X transferred the income interest to C, X transferred $5,000 cash to C. In determining the increase in taxable gifts occurring on the subsequent transfer, the annual exclusion under section 2503(b) is first applied to the cash gift. X is entitled to a reduction in aggregate taxable gifts of $25,000, the lesser of the amount by which X's taxable gifts were increased as a result of the income interest being valued at zero on the initial transfer ($40,000) or the amount by which X's taxable gifts are increased as a result of the subsequent transfer of the income interest ($25,000) ($30,000 + $5,000) – ($10,000 annual exclusion).

Example 3. Assume that the value under section 7520 of the income interest on the subsequent transfer to C is $55,000. X is entitled to reduce aggregate taxable gifts by $40,000, the lesser of the amount by which X's taxable gifts were increased as a result of the income interest being valued at zero on the initial transfer ($40,000) or the amount by which X's taxable gifts are increased as a result of the subsequent transfer of the income interest ($55,000 minus $10,000 annual exclusion = $45,000).

Example 4. Assume that X and X's spouse, S, split the subsequent gift to C. X is entitled to assign one-half the reduction to S. If the assignment is made, each is entitled to reduce aggregate taxable gifts by $17,500, the lesser of their portion of the increase in taxable gifts on the initial transfer by reason of the application of section 2702 ($20,000) and their portion of the increase in taxable gifts on the subsequent transfer of the retained interest ($27,500 – $10,000 annual exclusion).

Example 5. In 1992, A transfers property to an irrevocable trust, retaining the right to receive the trust income for 10 years. On the expiration of the 10–year term, the trust is to terminate and the trust corpus is to be paid to A's child, B. Assume that A's term interest has a value under section 7520 of $20,000 at the time of the transfer; however, because A's retained interest was not a qualified interest, it was valued at zero under § 25.2702–2(b)(1) for purposes of determining the amount of A's gift. Assume also that A and A's spouse, S, split the gift of the remainder interest under section 2513. In 1993, A transfers A's term interest to D, A's other child, for no consideration. A is entitled to reduce A's aggregate taxable gifts on the transfer. Assume that A and S also split the subsequent gift to D, and that A dies one month after making the subsequent transfer of the term interest and S dies six months later. The gift of the term interest is included in A's gross estate under section 2035(d)(2). To the extent S's taxable gifts are reduced pursuant to section 2001(e), S is entitled to no reduction in aggregate or adjusted taxable gifts under this section.

Example 6. T transfers property to an irrevocable trust retaining the power to direct the distribution of trust income for 10 years among T's descendants in whatever shares T deems appropriate. On the expiration of the 10–year period, the trust corpus is to be paid in equal shares to T's children. T's transfer of the remainder interest is a completed gift. Because T's retained interest is not a qualified interest, it is valued at zero under § 25.2702–2(b)(1) and the amount of T's gift is the fair market value of the property transferred to the trust. The distribution of income each year is not a transfer of a retained interest in trust. Therefore, T is not entitled to reduce aggregate taxable gifts as a result of the distributions of income from the trust.

Example 7. The facts are the same as in Example 6, except that after 3 years T exercises the right to direct the distribution of trust income by assigning the right to the income for the balance of the term to T's child, C. The exercise is a transfer of a retained interest in trust for purposes of this section. T is entitled to reduce aggregate taxable gifts by the lesser of the increase in taxable gifts resulting from the application of section 2702 to the initial transfer or the increase in taxable gifts resulting from the transfer of the retained interest in trust.

Example 8. In 1992, V purchases an income interest for 10 years in property in the same transaction or series of transactions in which G, V's child, purchases the remainder interest in the same property. V dies in 1997 still holding the term interest, the value of which is includible in V's gross estate under section 2033. V's estate would be entitled to a reduction in adjusted taxable gifts in the amount determined under paragraph (b) of this section.

[T.D. 8395, 57 FR 4272, Feb. 4, 1992]

§ 25.2703-1 Property subject to restrictive arrangements.

(a) Disregard of rights or restrictions—(1) In general. For purposes of subtitle B (relating to estate, gift, and generation-skipping transfer taxes), the value of any property is determined without regard to any right or restriction relating to the property.

(2) Right or restriction. For purposes of this section, right or restriction means—

(i) Any option, agreement, or other right to acquire or use the property at a price less than fair market value (determined without regard to the option, agreement, or right); or

(ii) Any restriction on the right to sell or use the property.

(3) Agreements, etc. containing rights or restrictions. A right or restriction may be contained in a partnership agreement, articles of incorporation, corporate bylaws, a shareholders' agreement, or any other agreement. A right or restriction may be implicit in the capital structure of an entity.

(4) Qualified easements. A perpetual restriction on the use of real property that qualified for a charitable deduction under either section 2522(d) or section 2055(f) of the Internal Revenue Code is not treated as a right or restriction.

(b) Exceptions—(1) In general. This section does not apply to any right or restriction satisfying the following three requirements—

(i) The right or restriction is a bona fide business arrangement;

(ii) The right or restriction is not a device to transfer property to the natural objects of the transferor's bounty for less than full and adequate consideration in money or money's worth; and

(iii) At the time the right or restriction is created, the terms of the right or restriction are comparable to similar arrangements entered into by persons in an arm's length transaction.

(2) Separate requirements. Each of the three requirements described in paragraph (b)(1) of this section must be independently satisfied for a right or restriction to meet this exception. Thus, for example, the mere showing that a right or restriction is a bona fide business arrangement is not sufficient to establish that the right or restriction is not a device to transfer property for less than full and adequate consideration.

(3) Exception for certain rights or restrictions. A right or restriction is considered to meet each of the three requirements described in paragraph (b)(1) of this section if more than 50 percent by value of the property subject to the right or restriction is owned directly or indirectly (within the meaning of § 25.2701-6) by individuals who are not members of the transferor's family. In order to meet this exception, the property owned by those individuals must be subject to the right or restriction to the same extent as the property owned by the transferor. For purposes of this section, members of the transferor's family include the persons described in § 25.2701-2(b)(5) and any other individual who is a natural object of the transferor's bounty. Any property held by a member of the transferor's family under the rules of § 25.2701-6 (without regard to § 25.2701-6(a)(5)) is treated as held only by a member of the transferor's family.

(4) Similar arrangement—(i) In general. A right or restriction is treated as comparable to similar arrangements entered into by persons in an arm's length transaction if the right or restriction is one that could have been obtained in a fair bargain among unrelated parties in the same business dealing with each other at arm's length. A right or restriction is considered a fair bargain among unrelated parties in the same business if it conforms with the general practice of unrelated parties under negotiated agreements in the same business. This determination generally will entail consideration of such factors as the expected term of the agreement, the current fair market value of the property, anticipated changes in value during the term of the arrangement, and the adequacy of any consideration given in exchange for the rights granted.

(ii) Evidence of general business practice. Evidence of general business practice is not met by showing isolated comparables. If more than one valuation method is commonly used in a business, a right or restriction does not fail to evidence general business practice merely because it uses only one of the recognized methods. It is not necessary that the terms of a right or restriction parallel the terms of any particular agreement. If comparables are difficult to find because the business is unique, comparables from similar businesses may be used.

(5) Multiple rights or restrictions. If property is subject to more than one right or restriction described in paragraph (a)(2) of this section, the failure of a right or restriction to satisfy the requirements of paragraph (b)(1) of this section does not cause any other right or restriction to fail to satisfy those requirements if the right or restriction otherwise meets those requirements. Whether separate provisions are separate rights or restrictions, or are integral parts of a single right or restriction, depends on all the facts and circumstances.

(c) Substantial modification of a right or restriction—(1) In general. A right or restriction that is substantially modified is treated as a right or restriction created on the date of the modification. Any discretionary modification of a right or restriction, whether or not authorized by the terms of the agreement, that results in other than a de minimis change to the quality, value, or timing of the rights of any party with respect to property that is subject to the right or restriction is a substantial modification. If the terms of the right or restriction require periodic updating, the failure to update is presumed to substantially modify the right or restriction unless it can be shown that updating would not have resulted in a substantial modification. The addition of any family member as a party to a right or restriction (including by reason of a transfer of property that subjects the transferee family member to a right or restriction with respect to the transferred property) is considered a substantial modification unless the addition is mandatory under the terms of the right or restriction or the added family member is assigned to a generation (determined under the rules of section 2651 of the Internal Revenue Code) no lower than the lowest generation occupied by individuals already party to the right or restriction.

(2) Exceptions. A substantial modification does not include—

(i) A modification required by the terms of a right or restriction;

(ii) A discretionary modification of an agreement conferring a right or restriction if the modification does not change the right or restriction;

(iii) A modification of a capitalization rate used with respect to a right or restriction if the rate is modified in a manner that bears a fixed relationship to a specified market interest rate; and

(iv) A modification that results in an option price that more closely approximates fair market value.

(d) Examples. The following examples illustrate the provisions of this section:

Example 1. T dies in 1992 owning title to Blackacre. In 1991, T and T's child entered into a lease with respect to Blackacre. At the time the lease was entered into, the terms of the lease were not comparable to leases of similar property entered into among unrelated parties. The lease is a restriction on the use of the property that is disregarded in valuing the property for Federal estate tax purposes.

Example 2. T and T's child, C, each own 50 percent of the outstanding stock of X corporation. T and C enter into an agreement in 1987 providing for the disposition of stock held by the first to die at the time of death. The agreement also provides certain restrictions with respect to lifetime transfers. In 1992, as permitted (but not required) under the agreement, T transfers one-half of T's stock to T's spouse, S. S becomes a party to the agreement between T and C by reason of the transfer. The transfer is the addition of a family member to the right or restriction. However, it is not a substantial modification of the right or restriction because the added family member would be assigned to a generation under section 2651 of the Internal Revenue Code no lower than the generation occupied by C.

Example 3. The facts are the same as in Example 2. In 1993, the agreement is amended to reflect a change in the company's name and a change of address for the company's registered agent. These changes are not a substantial modification of the agreement conferring the right or restriction because the right or restriction has not changed.

[T.D. 8395, 57 FR 4273, Feb. 4, 1992]

§ 25.2704–1 Lapse of certain rights.

(a) Lapse treated as transfer—(1) In general. The lapse of a voting right or a liquidation right in a corporation or partnership (an "entity") is a transfer by the individual directly or indirectly holding the right immediately prior to its lapse (the "holder") to the extent provided in paragraphs (b) and (c) of this section. This section applies only if the entity is controlled by the holder and members of the holder's family immediately before and after the lapse. The amount of the transfer is determined under paragraph (d) of this section. If the lapse of a voting right or a liquidation right occurs during the holder's lifetime, the lapse is a transfer by gift. If the lapse occurs at the holder's death, the lapse is a transfer includible in the holder's gross estate.

(2) Definitions. The following definitions apply for purposes of this section.

(i) Control. Control has the meaning given it in § 25.2701–2(b)(5).

(ii) Member of the family. Member of the family has the meaning given it in § 25.2702–2(a)(1).

(iii) Directly or indirectly held. An interest is directly or indirectly held only to the extent the value of the interest would have been includible in the gross estate of the individual if the individual had died immediately prior to the lapse.

(iv) Voting right. Voting right means a right to vote with respect to any matter of the entity. In the case of a partnership, the right of a general partner to participate in partnership management is a voting right. The right to compel the entity to acquire all or a portion of the holder's equity interest in the entity by reason of aggregate voting power is treated as a liquidation right and is not treated as a voting right.

(v) Liquidation right. Liquidation right means a right or ability to compel the entity to acquire all or a portion of the holder's equity interest in the entity, including by reason of aggregate voting power, whether or not its exercise would result in the complete liquidation of the entity.

(vi) Subordinate. Subordinate has the meaning given it in § 25.2701–3(a)(2)(iii).

(3) Certain temporary lapses. If a lapsed right may be restored only upon the occurrence of a future event not within the control of the holder or members of the holder's family, the lapse is deemed to occur at the time the lapse becomes permanent with respect to the holder, i.e. either by a transfer of the interest or otherwise.

(4) Source of right or lapse. A voting right or a liquidation right may be conferred by and may lapse by reason of a State law, the corporate charter or bylaws, an agreement, or other means.

(b) Lapse of voting right. A lapse of a voting right occurs at the time a presently exercisable voting right is restricted or eliminated.

(c) Lapse of liquidation right—(1) In general. A lapse of a liquidation right occurs at the time a presently exercisable liquidation right is restricted or eliminated. Except as otherwise provided, a transfer of an interest that results in the lapse of a liquidation right is not subject to this section if the rights with respect to the transferred interest are not restricted or eliminated. However, a transfer that results in the elimination of the transferor's right or ability to compel the entity to acquire an interest retained by the transferor that is subordinate to the transferred interest is a lapse of a liquidation right with respect to the subordinate interest.

(2) Exceptions. Section 2704(a) does not apply to the lapse of a liquidation right under the following circumstances.

(i) Family cannot obtain liquidation value—(A) In general. Section 2704(a) does not apply to the lapse of a liquidation right to the extent the holder (or the holder's estate) and members of the holder's family cannot immediately after the lapse liquidate an interest that the holder held directly or indirectly and could have liquidated prior to the lapse.

(B) Ability to liquidate. Whether an interest can be liquidated immediately after the lapse is determined under the State law generally applicable to the entity, as modified by the governing instruments of the entity, but without regard to any restriction described in section 2704(b). Thus, if, after any restriction described in section 2704(b) is disregarded, the remaining requirements for liquidation under the governing instruments are less restrictive than the State law that would apply in the absence of the governing instruments, the ability to liquidate is determined by reference to the governing instruments.

(ii) Rights valued under section 2701. Section 2704(a) does not apply to the lapse of a liquidation right previously valued under section 2701 to the extent necessary to prevent double taxation (taking into account any adjustment available under § 25.2701–5).

(iii) Certain changes in State law. Section 2704(a) does not apply to the lapse of a liquidation right that occurs solely by reason of a change in State law. For purposes of this paragraph, a change in the governing instrument of an entity is not a change in State law.

(d) Amount of transfer. The amount of the transfer is the excess, if any, of—

(1) The value of all interests in the entity owned by the holder immediately before the lapse (determined immediately after the lapse as if the lapsed right was nonlapsing); over

(2) The value of the interests described in the preceding paragraph immediately after the lapse (determined as if all such interests were held by one individual).

(e) Application to similar rights. [Reserved]

(f) Examples. The following examples illustrate the provisions of this section:

Example 1. Prior to D's death, D owned all the preferred stock of Corporation Y and D's children owned all the common stock. At that time, the preferred stock had 60 percent of the total voting power and the common stock had 40 percent. Under the corporate by-laws, the voting rights of the preferred stock terminated on D's death. The value of D's interest immediately prior to D's death (determined as if the voting rights were nonlapsing) was $100X. The value of that interest immediately after death would have been $90X if the voting rights had been nonlapsing. The decrease in value reflects the loss in value resulting from the death of D (whose involvement in Y was a key factor in Y's profitability). Section 2704(a) applies to the lapse of voting rights on D's death. D's gross estate includes an amount equal to the excess, if any, of $90X over the fair market value of the preferred stock determined after the lapse of the voting rights.

Example 2. Prior to D's death, D owned all the preferred stock of Corporation Y. The preferred stock and the common stock each carried 50 percent of the total voting power of Y. D's children owned 40 percent of the common stock and unrelated parties own the remaining 60 percent. Under the corporate by-laws, the voting rights of the preferred stock terminate on D's death. Section 2704(a) does not apply to the lapse of D's voting rights because members of D's family do not control Y after the lapse.

Example 3. The by-laws of Corporation Y provide that the voting rights of any transferred shares of the single outstanding class of stock are reduced to ½ vote per share after the transfer but are fully restored to the transferred shares after 5 years. D owned 60 percent of the shares prior to death and members of D's family owned the balance. On D's death, D's shares pass to D's children and the voting rights are reduced pursuant to the by-laws. Section 2704(a) applies to the lapse of D's voting rights. D's gross estate includes an amount equal to the excess, if any, of the fair market value of D's stock (determined immediately after D's death as though the voting rights had not been reduced and would not be reduced) over the stock's fair market value immediately after D's death.

Example 4. D owns 84 percent of the single outstanding class of stock of Corporation Y. The by-laws require at least 70 percent of the vote to liquidate Y. D gives one-half of D's stock in equal shares to D's three children (14 percent to each). Section 2704(a) does not apply to the loss of D's ability to liquidate Y, because the voting rights with respect to the corporation are not restricted or eliminated by reason of the transfer.

Example 5. D and D's two children, A and B, are partners in Partnership X. Each has a 3⅓ percent general partnership interest and a 30 percent limited partnership interest. Under State law, a general partner has the right to participate in partnership management. The partnership agreement provides that when a general partner withdraws or dies, X must redeem the general partnership interest for its liquidation value. Also, under the agreement any general partner can liquidate the partnership. A limited partner cannot liquidate the partnership and a limited partner's capital interest will be returned only when the partnership is liquidated. A deceased limited partner's interest continues as a limited partnership interest. D dies, leaving his limited partnership interest to D's spouse. Because of a general partner's right to dissolve the partnership, a limited partnership interest has a greater fair market value when held in conjunction with a general partnership interest than when held alone. Section 2704(a) applies to the lapse of D's liquidation right because after the lapse, members of D's family could liquidate D's limited partnership interest. D's gross estate includes an amount equal to the excess of the value of all D's interests in X immediately before D's death (determined immediately after D's death but as though the liquidation right had not lapsed and would not lapse) over the fair market value of all D's interests in X immediately after D's death.

Example 6. The facts are the same as in Example 5, except that under the partnership agreement D is the only general partner who holds a unilateral liquidation right. Assume further that the partnership agreement contains a restriction described in section 2704(b) that prevents D's family members from liquidating D's limited partnership interest immediately after D's death. Under State law, in the absence of the restriction in the partnership agreement, D's family members could liquidate the partnership. The restriction on the family's ability to liquidate is disregarded and the amount of D's gross estate is increased by reason of the lapse of D's liquidation right.

Example 7. D owns all the stock of Corporation X, consisting of 100 shares of non-voting preferred stock and 100 shares of voting common stock. Under the by-laws, X can only be liquidated with the consent of at least 80 percent of the voting shares. D transfers 30 shares of common stock to D's child. The transfer is not a lapse of a liquidation right with respect to the common stock because the voting rights that enabled D to liquidate prior to the transfer are not restricted or eliminated. The transfer is not a lapse of a liquidation right with respect to the retained preferred stock because the preferred stock is not subordinate to the transferred common stock.

Example 8. D owns all of the single class of stock of Corporation Y. D recapitalizes Y, exchanging D's common stock for voting common stock and non-voting, non-cumulative preferred stock. The preferred stock carries a right to put the stock for its par value at any time during the next 10 years. D transfers the common stock to D's grandchild in a transfer subject to section 2701. In determining the amount of D's gift under section 2701, D's retained put right is valued at zero. D's child, C, owns the preferred stock when the put right lapses. Section 2704(a) applies to the lapse, without regard to the application of section 2701, because the put right was not valued under section 2701 in the hands of C.

Example 9. A and A's two children are equal general and limited partners in Partnership Y. Under the partnership agreement, each general partner has a right to liquidate the partnership at any time. Under State law that would apply in the absence of contrary provisions in the partnership agreement, the death or incompetency of a general partner terminates the partnership. However, the partnership agreement provides that the partnership does not terminate on the incompetence or death of a general partner, but that an incompetent partner cannot exercise rights as a general partner during any period of incompetency. A partner's full rights as general partner are restored if the partner regains competency. A becomes incompetent. The lapse of A's voting right on becoming incompetent is not subject to section 2704(a) because it may be restored to A in the future. However, if A dies while incompetent, a lapse subject to section 2704(a) is deemed to occur at that time because the lapsed right cannot thereafter be restored to A.

[T.D. 8395, 57 FR 4274, Feb. 4, 1992]

§ 25.2704–2 Transfers subject to applicable restrictions.

(a) In general. If an interest in a corporation or partnership (an "entity") is transferred to or for the benefit of a member of the transferor's family, any applicable restriction is disregarded in valuing the transferred interest. This section applies only if the transferor and members of the transferor's family control the entity immediately before the transfer. For the definition of control, see § 25.2701–2(b)(5). For the definition of member of the family, see § 25.2702–2(a)(1).

(b) Applicable restriction defined. An applicable restriction is a limitation on the ability to liquidate the entity (in whole or in part) that is more restrictive than the limitations that would apply under the State law generally applicable to the entity in the absence of the restriction. A restriction is an applicable restriction only to the extent that either the restriction by its terms will lapse at any time after the transfer, or the transferor (or the transferor's estate) and any members of the transferor's family can remove the restriction immediately after the transfer. Ability to remove the restriction is determined by reference to the State law that would apply but for a more restrictive rule in the governing instruments of the entity. See § 25.2704–1(c)(1)(B) for a discussion of the term "State law." An applicable restriction does not include a commercially reasonable restriction on liquidation imposed by an unrelated person providing capital to the entity for the entity's trade or business operations whether in the form of debt or equity. An unrelated person is any person whose relationship to the transferor, the transferee, or any member of the family of either is not described in section 267(b) of the Internal Revenue Code, provided that for purposes of this section the term "fiduciary of a trust" as used in section 267(b) does not include a bank as defined in section 581 of the Internal Revenue Code. A restriction imposed or required to be imposed by Federal or State law is not an applicable restriction. An option, right to use property, or agreement that is subject to section 2703 is not an applicable restriction.

(c) Effect of disregarding an applicable restriction. If an applicable restriction is disregarded under this section, the transferred interest is valued as if the restriction does not exist and as if the rights of the transferor are determined under the State law that would apply but for the restriction. For example, an applicable restriction with respect to preferred stock will be disregarded in determining the amount of a transfer of common stock under section 2701.

(d) Examples. The following examples illustrate the provisions of this section:

Example 1. D owns a 76 percent interest and each of D's children, A and B, owns a 12 percent interest in General Partnership X. The partnership agreement requires the consent of all the partners to liquidate the partnership. Under the State law that would apply in the absence of the restriction in the partnership agreement, the consent of partners owning 70 percent of the total partnership interests would be required to liquidate X. On D's death, D's partnership interest passes to D's child, C. The requirement that all the partners consent to liquidation is an applicable restriction. Because A, B and C (all members of D's family), acting together after the transfer, can remove the restriction on liquidation, D's interest is valued without regard to the restriction; i.e., as though D's interest is sufficient to liquidate the partnership.

Example 2. D owns all the preferred stock in Corporation X. The preferred stock carries a right to liquidate X that cannot be exercised until 1999. D's children, A and B, own all the common stock of X. The common stock is the only voting stock. In 1994, D transfers the preferred stock to D's child, A. The restriction on D's right to liquidate is an applicable restriction that is disregarded. Therefore, the preferred stock is valued as though the right to liquidate were presently exercisable.

Example 3. D owns 60 percent of the stock of Corporation X. The corporate by-laws provide that the corporation cannot be liquidated for 10 years after which time liquidation requires approval by 60 percent of the voting interests. In the absence of the provision in the by-laws, State law would require approval by 80 percent of the voting interests to liquidate X. D transfers the stock to a trust for the benefit of D's child, A, during the 10–year period. The 10–year restriction is an applicable restriction and is disregarded. Therefore, the value of the stock is determined as if the transferred block could currently liquidate X.

Example 4. D and D's children, A and B, are partners in Limited Partnership Y. Each has a 3.33 percent general partnership interest and a 30 percent limited partnership interest. Any general partner has the right to liquidate the partnership at any time. As part of a loan agreement with a lender who is related to D, each of the partners agree that the partnership may not be liquidated without the lender's consent while any portion of the loan remains outstanding. During the term of the loan agreement, D transfers one-half of both D's partnership interests to each of A and B. Because the lender is a related party, the requirement that the lender consent to liquidation is an applicable restriction and the transfers of D's interests are valued as if such consent were not required.

Example 5. D owns 60 percent of the preferred and 70 percent of the common stock in Corporation X. The remaining stock is owned by individuals unrelated to D. The preferred stock carries a put right that cannot be exercised until 1999. In 1995, D transfers the common stock to D's child in a transfer that is subject to section 2701. The restriction on D's right to liquidate is an applicable restriction that is disregarded in determining the amount of the gift under section 2701.

[T.D. 8395, 57 FR 4276, Feb. 4, 1992; 57 FR 11264, Apr. 2, 1992]

PROCEDURE AND ADMINISTRATION

§ 1.6031(a)–1 Return of partnership income.

(a) Domestic partnerships—(1) Return required. Except as provided in paragraphs (a)(3) and (c) of this section, every domestic partnership must file a return of partnership income under section 6031 (partnership return) for each taxable year on the form prescribed for the partnership return. The partnership return must be filed for the taxable year of the partnership regardless of the taxable years of the partners. For taxable years of a partnership and of a partner, see section 706 and § 1.706–1. For the rules governing partnership statements to partners and nominees, see § 1.6031(b)–1T. For the rules requiring disclosure of certain transactions, see § 1.6011–4T.

(2) Content of return. The partnership return must contain the information required by the prescribed form and the accompanying instructions.

(3) Special rule. (i) A partnership that has no income, deductions, or credits for federal income tax purposes for a taxable year is not required to file a partnership return for that year.

* * *

(4) Failure to file. For the consequences of a failure to comply with the requirements of section 6031(a) and this paragraph (a), see sections 6229(a), * * *, 6698, and 7203.

* * *

(c) Partnerships excluded from the application of subchapter K of the Internal Revenue Code—(1) Wholly excluded—(i) Year of election. An eligible partnership as described in § 1.761–2(a) that elects to be excluded from all the provisions of subchapter K of chapter 1 of the Internal Revenue Code in the manner specified by § 1.761–2(b) (2)(i) must timely file the form prescribed for the partnership return for the taxable year for which the election is made. In lieu of the information otherwise required, the return must contain or be accompanied by the information required by § 1.761–2(b)(2)(i).

(ii) Subsequent years. Except as otherwise provided in paragraph (c)(1)(i) of this section, an eligible partnership that elects to be wholly excluded from the application of subchapter K is not required to file a partnership return.

* * *

(e) Procedural requirements—(1) Place for filing. The return of a partnership must be filed with the service center prescribed in the relevant IRS revenue procedure, publication, form, or instructions to the form * * *.

(2) Time for filing. The return of a partnership must be filed on or before the fifteenth day of the fourth month following the close of the taxable year of the partnership.

* * *

[T.D. 8841, 64 FR 61498, Nov. 12, 1999, as amended by T.D. 9094, 68 FR 63733, Nov. 10, 2003; 68 FR 70584, Dec. 18, 2003; T.D. 9123, 69 FR 24078, May 3, 2004; T.D. 9177, 70 FR 7176, Feb. 11, 2005]

§ 20.6081–1 Extension of time for filing the return.

* * *

(b) Automatic extension. An estate will be allowed an automatic 6–month extension of time beyond the date prescribed in section 6075(a) to file Form 706, "United States Estate (and Generation–Skipping Transfer) Tax Return," if Form 4768 is filed on or before the due date for filing Form 706 and in accordance with the procedures under paragraph (a) of this section.

* * *

[T.D. 6296, 23 FR 4529, June 24, 1958, as amended by T.D. 6711, 29 FR 3656, March 24, 1964; T.D. 7238, 37 FR 28722, Dec. 29, 1972; T.D. 7710, 45 FR 50745, July 31, 1980; T.D. 8957, 66 FR 38546, July 25, 2001]

§ 1.6662–3 Negligence or disregard of rules or regulations.

* * *

(b) Definitions and rules—(1) Negligence. The term "negligence" includes any failure to make a reasonable attempt to comply with the provisions of the internal revenue laws or to exercise ordinary and reasonable care in the preparation of a tax return. "Negligence" also includes any failure by the taxpayer to keep adequate books and records or to substantiate items properly. * * * Negligence is strongly indicated where—

(i) A taxpayer fails to include on an income tax return an amount of income shown on an information return, * * *;

(ii) A taxpayer fails to make a reasonable attempt to ascertain the correctness of a deduction, credit or exclusion on a return which would seem to a reasonable and prudent person to be "too good to be true" under the circumstances;

(iii) A partner fails to comply with the requirements of section 6222, which requires that a partner treat partnership items on its return in a manner that is consistent with the treatment of such items on the partnership return (or notify the Secretary of the inconsistency); or

(iv) A shareholder fails to comply with the requirements of section 6242, which requires that an S corporation shareholder treat subchapter S items on its return in a manner that is consistent with the treatment of such items on the corporation's return (or notify the Secretary of the inconsistency).

(2) Disregard of rules or regulations. The term disregard includes any careless, reckless or intentional disregard of rules or regulations. The term "rules or regulations" includes the provisions of the Internal Revenue Code, temporary or final Treasury regulations issued under the Code, and revenue rulings or notices (other than notices of proposed rulemaking) issued by the Internal Revenue Service and published in the Internal Revenue Bulletin. A disregard of rules or regulations is "careless" if the taxpayer does not exercise reasonable diligence to determine the correctness of a return position that is contrary to the rule or regulation. A disregard is "reckless" if the taxpayer makes little or no effort to determine whether a rule or regulation exists, under circumstances which demonstrate a substantial deviation from the standard of conduct that a reasonable person would observe. A disregard is "intentional" if the taxpayer knows of the rule or regulation that is disregarded. Nevertheless, a taxpayer who takes a position (other than with respect to a reportable transaction, as defined in § 1.6011–4(b) or § 1.6011–4T(b), as applicable) contrary to a revenue ruling or a notice has not disregarded the ruling or notice if the contrary position has a realistic possibility of being sustained on its merits.

* * *

[T.D. 8381, 56 FR 67498, Dec. 31, 1991, as amended by T.D. 8617, 60 FR 45661, Sept. 1, 1995; T.D. 9059, 68 FR 75126, Dec. 30, 2003]

§ 1.6662–4 Substantial understatement of income tax.

* * *

(d) Substantial authority—(1) Effect of having substantial authority. If there is substantial authority for the tax treatment of an item, the item is treated as if it were shown properly on the return for the taxable year in computing the amount of the tax shown on the return. Thus, for purposes of section 6662(d), the tax attributable to the item is not included in the understatement for that year. * * *

(2) Substantial authority standard. The substantial authority standard is an objective standard involving an analysis of the law and application of the law to relevant facts. * * *

(3) Determination of whether substantial authority is present—(i) Evaluation of authorities. There is substantial authority for the tax treatment of an item only if the weight of the authorities supporting the treatment is substantial in relation to the weight of authorities supporting contrary treatment. All authorities relevant to the tax treatment of an item, including the authorities contrary to the treatment, are taken into account in determining whether substantial authority exists. The weight of authorities is determined in light of the pertinent facts and circumstances in the manner prescribed by paragraph (d)(3)(ii) of this section. There may be substantial authority for more than one position with respect to the same item. Because the substantial authority standard is an objective standard, the taxpayer's belief that there is substantial authority for the tax treatment of an item is not relevant in determining whether there is substantial authority for that treatment.

(ii) Nature of analysis. The weight accorded an authority depends on its relevance and persuasiveness, and the type of document providing the authority. For example, a case or revenue ruling having some facts in common with the tax treatment at issue is not particularly relevant if the authority is materially distinguishable on its facts, or is otherwise inapplicable to the tax treatment at issue. An authority that merely states a conclusion ordinarily is less persuasive than one that reaches its conclusion by cogently relating the applicable law to pertinent facts. The weight of an authority from which information has been deleted, such as a private letter ruling, is diminished to the extent that the deleted information may have affected the authority's conclusions. The types of document also must be considered. For example, a revenue ruling is accorded greater weight than a private letter ruling addressing the same issue. An older private letter ruling, technical advice memorandum, general counsel memorandum or action on decision generally must be accorded less weight than a more recent one. Any document described in the preceding sentence that is more than 10 years old generally is accorded very little weight. However, the persuasiveness and relevance of a document, viewed in light of subsequent developments, should be taken into account along with the age of the document. There may be substantial authority for the tax treatment of an item despite the absence of certain types of authority. Thus, a taxpayer may have substantial authority for a position that is supported only by a well-reasoned construction of the applicable statutory provision.

(iii) Types of authority. Except in cases described in paragraph (d)(3)(iv) of this section concerning written determinations, only the following are authority for purposes of determining whether there is substantial authority for the tax treatment of an item: Applicable provisions of the Internal Revenue Code and other statutory provisions; proposed, temporary and final regulations construing such statutes; revenue rulings and revenue procedures; tax treaties and regulations thereunder, and Treasury Department and other official explanations of such treaties; court cases; congressional intent as reflected in committee reports, joint explanatory statements of managers included in conference committee reports, and floor statements made prior to enactment by one of a bill's managers; General Explanations of tax legislation prepared by the Joint Committee on Taxation (the Blue Book); private letter rulings and technical advice memoranda issued after October 31, 1976; actions on decisions and general counsel memoranda issued after March 12, 1981 (as well as general counsel memoranda published in pre–1955 volumes of the Cumulative Bulletin); Internal Revenue Service information or press releases; and notices, announcements and other administrative pronouncements published by the Service in the Internal Revenue Bulletin. Conclusions reached in treatises, legal periodicals, legal opinions or opinions rendered by tax professionals are not authority. The authorities underlying such expressions of opinion where applicable to the facts of a particular case, however, may give rise to substantial authority for the tax treatment of an item. Notwithstanding the preceding list of authorities, an authority does not continue to be an authority to the extent it is overruled or modified, implicitly or explicitly, by a body with the power to overrule or modify the earlier authority. In the case of court decisions, for example, a district court opinion on an issue is not an authority if overruled or reversed by the United States Court of Appeals for such district. However, a Tax Court opinion is not considered to be overruled or modified by a court of appeals to which a taxpayer does not have a right of appeal, unless the Tax Court adopts the holding of the court of appeals. Similarly, a private letter ruling is not authority if revoked or if inconsistent with a subsequent proposed regulation, revenue ruling or other administrative pronouncement published in the Internal Revenue Bulletin.

(iv) Special rules—(A) Written determinations. There is substantial authority for the tax treatment of an item by a taxpayer if the treatment is supported by the conclusion of a ruling or a determination letter (as defined in § 301.6110–2(d) and (e)) issued to the taxpayer, by the conclusion of a technical advice memorandum in which the taxpayer is named, or by an affirmative statement in a revenue agent's report with respect to a prior taxable year of the taxpayer ("written determinations"). The preceding sentence does not apply, however, if—

(1) There was a misstatement or omission of a material fact or the facts that subsequently develop are materially different from the facts on which the written determination was based, or

(2) The written determination was modified or revoked after the date of issuance by—

(i) A notice to the taxpayer to whom the written determination was issued,

(ii) The enactment of legislation or ratification of a tax treaty,

(iii) A decision of the United States Supreme Court,

(iv) The issuance of temporary or final regulations, or

(v) The issuance of a revenue ruling, revenue procedure, or other statement published in the Internal Revenue Bulletin.

Except in the case of a written determination that is modified or revoked on account of § 1.6662–4(d)(3)(iv)(A)(1), a written determination that is modified or revoked as described in § 1.6662–4(d)(3)(iv)(A)(2) ceases to be authority on the date, and to the extent, it is so modified or revoked. * * *

(B) Taxpayer's jurisdiction. The applicability of court cases to the taxpayer by reason of the taxpayer's residence in a particular jurisdiction is not taken into account in determining whether there is substantial authority for the tax treatment of an item. Notwithstanding the preceding sentence, there is substantial authority for the tax treatment of an item if the treatment is supported by controlling precedent of a United States Court of Appeals to which the taxpayer has a right of appeal with respect to the item.

(C) When substantial authority determined. There is substantial authority for the tax treatment of an item if there is substantial authority at the time the return containing the item is filed or there was substantial authority on the last day of the taxable year to which the return relates.

* * *

[T.D. 8381, 56 FR 67499, Dec. 31, 1991, as amended by T.D. 8617, 60 FR 45661, Sept. 1, 1995; T.D. 9059, 68 FR 75126, Dec. 30, 2003]

§ 1.7520–1 Valuation of annuities, unitrust interests, interests for life or terms of years, and remainder or reversionary interests.

(a) General actuarial valuations. (1) Except as otherwise provided in this section and in § 1.7520–3 (relating to exceptions to the use of prescribed tables under certain circumstances), in the case of certain transactions after April 30, 1989, subject to income tax, the fair market value of annuities, interests for life or for a term of years (including unitrust interests), remainders, and reversions is their present value determined under this section. * * *

(b) Components of valuation—(1) Interest rate component—(i) Section 7520 Interest rate. The section 7520 interest rate is the rate of return, rounded to the nearest two-tenths of one percent, that is equal to 120 percent of the applicable Federal mid-term rate, compounded annually, for purposes of section 1274(d)(1), for the month in which the valuation date falls. In rounding the rate to the nearest two-tenths of a percent, any rate that is midway between one two-tenths of a percent and another is rounded up to the higher of those two rates. For example, if 120 percent of the applicable Federal mid-term rate is 10.30, the section 7520 interest rate component is 10.4. The section 7520 interest rate is published monthly by the Internal Revenue Service in the Internal Revenue Bulletin * * *.

(2) Mortality component. The mortality component reflects the mortality data most recently available from the United States census. As new mortality data becomes available after each decennial census, the mortality component described in this section will be revised and the revised mortality component tables will be published in the regulations at that time. For transactions with valuation dates on or after May 1, 2009, the mortality component table (Table 2000CM) is contained in § 20.2031–7(d)(7) of this chapter. See § 20.2031–7A for mortality component tables applicable to transactions for which the valuation date falls before May 1, 2009.

(c) Tables. The present value on the valuation date of an annuity, life estate, term of years, remainder, or reversion is computed by using the section 7520 interest rate component that is described in paragraph (b)(1) of this section and the mortality component that is described in paragraph (b)(2) of this section. Actuarial factors for determining these present values are included in tables in these regulations and in publications by the Internal Revenue Service. If a special factor is required in order to value an interest, the Internal Revenue Service will furnish the factor upon a request for a ruling. The request for a ruling must be accompanied by a recitation of the facts, including the date of birth for each measuring life and copies of relevant instruments. A request for a ruling must comply with the instructions for requesting a ruling published periodically in the Internal Revenue Bulletin * * *.

(1) Regulation sections containing tables with interest rates between 0.2 and 14 percent for valuation dates on or after May 1, 2009. Section 1.642(c)–6(e)(6) contains Table S used for determining the present value of a single life remainder interest in a pooled income fund as defined in § 1.642(c)–5. See § 1.642(c)–6A for actuarial factors for one life applicable to valuation dates before May 1, 2009. Section 1.664–4(e)(6) contains Table F (payout factors) and Table D (actuarial factors used in determining the present value of a remainder interest postponed for a term of years). Section 1.664–4(e)(7) contains Table U(1) (unitrust single life remainder factors). These tables are used in determining the present value of a remainder interest in a charitable remainder unitrust as defined in § 1.664–3. See § 1.664–4A for unitrust single life remainder factors applicable to valuation dates before May 1, 2009. Section 20.2031–7(d)(6) of this chapter contains Table B (actuarial factors used in determining the present value of an interest for a term of years), Table J (term certain annuity beginning-of-interval adjustment factors), and Table K (annuity end-of-interval adjustment factors). Section 20.2031–7(d)(7) contains Table S (single life remainder factors), and Table 2000CM (mortality components). These tables are used in determining the present value of annuities, life estates, remainders, and reversions. See § 20.2031–7A for single life remainder factors for one life and mortality components applicable to valuation dates before May 1, 2009.

(2) Internal Revenue Service publications containing tables with interest rates between 0.2 and 22 percent for valuation dates on or after May 1, 2009. The following documents are available, at no charge, electronically via the IRS Internet site at http://www.irs.gov:

(i) Internal Revenue Service Publication 1457, "Actuarial Valuations Version 3A" (2009). This publication includes tables of valuation factors, as well as examples that show how to compute other valuation factors, for determining the present value of annuities, life estates, terms of years, remainders, and reversions, measured by one or two lives. These factors must also be used in the valuation of interests in a charitable remainder annuity trust as defined in § 1.664–2 and a pooled income fund as defined in § 1.642(c)–5.

(ii) Internal Revenue Service Publication 1458, "Actuarial Valuations Version 3B" (2009). This publication includes term certain tables and tables of one and two life valuation factors for determining the present value of remainder interests in a charitable remainder unitrust as defined in § 1.664–3.

(iii) Internal Revenue Service Publication 1459, "Actuarial Valuations Version 3C" (2009). This publication includes tables for computing depreciation adjustment factors. See § 1.170A–12.

(d) Effective/applicability date. This section applies on and after May 1, 2009.

[T.D. 8540, 59 FR 30100, June 10, 1994, as amended by T.D. 8819, 64 FR 23187, April 29, 1999; T.D. 8886, 65 FR 36908, June 12, 2000; T.D. 9448, 74 FR 21437, May 7, 2009; T.D. 9540, 76 FR 49570, Aug. 10, 2011]

§ 1.7520–2 Valuation of charitable interests.

(a) In general—(1) Valuation. Except as otherwise provided in this section and in § 1.7520–3 (relating to exceptions to the use of prescribed tables under certain circumstances), the fair market value of annuities, interests for life or for a term of years, remainders, and reversions for which an income tax charitable deduction is allowable is the present value of such interests determined under § 1.7520–1.

(2) Prior-month election rule. If any part of the property interest transferred qualifies for an income tax charitable deduction under section 170(c), the taxpayer may elect (under paragraph (b) of this section) to compute the present value of the interest transferred by use of the section 7520 interest rate for the month during which the interest is transferred or the section 7520 interest rate component for either of the 2 months preceding the month during which the interest is transferred. Paragraph (b) of this section explains how a prior-month election is made. The interest rate for the month so elected is the applicable section 7520 interest rate. If the actuarial factor for either or both of the 2 months preceding the month during which the interest is transferred is based on a mortality experience that is different from the mortality experience at the date of the transfer and if the taxpayer elects to use the section 7520 rate for a prior month with the different mortality experience, the taxpayer must use the actuarial factor derived from the mortality experience in effect during the month of the section 7520 rate elected. All actuarial computations relating to the transfer must be made by applying the interest rate component and the mortality component of the month elected by the taxpayer.

(3) Transfers of more than one interest in the same property. If a taxpayer transfers more than one interest in the same property at the same time, for purposes of valuing the transferred interests, the taxpayer must use the same interest rate and mortality component for each interest in the property transferred. If more than one interest in the same property is transferred in two or more separate transfers at different times, the value of each interest is determined by the use of the interest rate component and mortality component in effect during the month of the transfer of that interest or, if applicable under paragraph (a)(2) of this section, either of the two months preceding the month of thc transfer.

(4) Information required with tax return. The following information must be attached to the income tax return (or to the amended return) if the taxpayer claims a charitable deduction for the present value of a temporary or remainder interest in property—

(i) A complete description of the interest that is transferred, including a copy of the instrument of transfer;

(ii) The valuation date of the transfer;

(iii) The names and identification numbers of the beneficiaries of the transferred interest;

(iv) The names and birthdates of any measuring lives, a description of any relevant terminal illness condition of any measuring life, and (if applicable) an explanation of how any terminal illness condition was taken into account in valuing the interest; and

(v) A computation of the deduction showing the applicable section 7520 interest rate that is used to value the transferred interest.

(5) Place for filing returns. See section 6091 of the Internal Revenue Code and the regulations thereunder for the place for filing the return or other document required by this section.

(b) Election of interest rate component—(1) Time for making election. A taxpayer makes a prior-month election under paragraph (a)(2) of this section by attaching the information described in paragraph (b)(2) of this section to the taxpayer's income tax return or to an amended return for that year that is filed within 24 months after the later of the date the original return for the year was filed or the due date for filing the return.

(2) Manner of making election. A statement that the prior-month election under section 7520(a) of the Internal Revenue Code is being made and that identifies the elected month must be attached to the income tax return (or to the amended return).

(3) Revocability. The prior-month election may be revoked by filing an amended return within 24 months after the later of the date the original return of tax for the year was filed or the due date for filing the return. The revocation must be filed in the place referred to in paragraph (a)(5) of this section.

* * *

[T.D. 8540, 59 FR 30100, June 10, 1994]

§ 1.7520-3 Limitation on the application of section 7520.

(a) Internal Revenue Code sections to which section 7520 does not apply. Section 7520 of the Internal Revenue Code does not apply for purposes of—

(1) Part I, subchapter D of subtitle A (section 401 et seq.), relating to the income tax treatment of certain qualified plans. (However, section 7520 does apply to the estate and gift tax treatment of certain qualified plans and for purposes of determining excess accumulations under section 4980A);

(2) Sections 72 and 101(b), relating to the income taxation of life insurance, endowment, and annuity contracts, unless otherwise provided for in the regulations under sections 72, 101, and 1011 * * *;

(3) Sections 83 and 451, unless otherwise provided for in the regulations under those sections;

* * *

(7) Section 7872, relating to income and gift taxation of interest-free loans and loans with below-market interest rates, unless otherwise provided for in the regulations under section 7872; or

(8) Section 2702(a)(2)(A), relating to the value of a nonqualified retained interest upon a transfer of an interest in trust to or for the benefit of a member of the transferor's family; and

(9) Any other sections of the Internal Revenue Code to the extent provided by the Internal Revenue Service in revenue rulings or revenue procedures. * * *

(b) Other limitations on the application of section 7520—(1) In general—(i) Ordinary beneficial interests. For purposes of this section:

(A) An ordinary annuity interest is the right to receive a fixed dollar amount at the end of each year during one or more measuring lives or for some other defined period. A standard section 7520 annuity factor for an ordinary annuity interest represents the present worth of the right to receive $1.00 per year for a defined period, using the interest rate prescribed under section 7520 for the appropriate month. If an annuity interest is payable more often than annually or is payable at the beginning of each period, a special adjustment must be made in any computation with a standard section 7520 annuity factor.

(B) An ordinary income interest is the right to receive the income from, or the use of, property during one or more measuring lives or for some other defined period. A standard section 7520 income factor for an ordinary income interest represents the present worth of the right to receive the use of $1.00 for a defined period, using the interest rate prescribed under section 7520 for the appropriate month.

(C) An ordinary remainder or reversionary interest is the right to receive an interest in property at the end of one or more measuring lives or some other defined period. A standard section 7520 remainder factor for an ordinary remainder or reversionary interest represents the present worth of the right to receive $1.00 at the end of a defined period, using the interest rate prescribed under section 7520 for the appropriate month.

(ii) Certain restricted beneficial interests. A restricted beneficial interest is an annuity, income, remainder, or reversionary interest that is subject to a contingency, power, or other restriction, whether the restriction is provided for by the terms of the trust, will, or other governing instrument or is caused by other circumstances. In general, a standard section 7520 annuity, income, or remainder factor may not be used to value a restricted beneficial interest. However, a special section 7520 annuity, income, or remainder factor may be used to value a restricted beneficial interest under some circumstances. See paragraph (b)(4) Example 2 of this section, which illustrates a situation where a special section 7520 actuarial factor is needed to take into account the shorter life expectancy of the terminally ill measuring life. See § 1.7520–1(c) for requesting a special factor from the Internal Revenue Service.

(iii) Other beneficial interests. If, under the provisions of this paragraph (b), the interest rate and mortality components prescribed under section 7520 are not applicable in determining the value of any annuity, income, remainder, or reversionary interest, the actual fair market value of the interest (determined without regard to section 7520) is based on all of the facts and circumstances if and to the extent permitted by the Internal Revenue Code provision applicable to the property interest.

(2) Provisions of governing instrument and other limitations on source of payment—(i) Annuities. A standard section 7520 annuity factor may not be used to determine the present value of an annuity for a specified term of years or the life of one or more individuals unless the effect of the trust, will, or other governing instrument is to ensure that the annuity will be paid for the entire defined period. In the case of an annuity payable from a trust or other limited fund, the annuity is not considered payable for the entire defined period if, considering the applicable section 7520 interest rate at the valuation date of the transfer, the annuity is expected to exhaust the fund before the last possible annuity payment is made in full. For this purpose, it must be assumed that it is possible for each measuring life to survive until age 110. For example, for a fixed annuity payable annually at the end of each year, if the amount of the annuity payment (expressed as a percentage of the initial corpus) is less than or equal to the applicable section 7520 interest rate at the date of the transfer, the corpus is assumed to be sufficient to make all payments. If the percentage exceeds the applicable section 7520 interest rate and the annuity is for a definite term of years, multiply the annual annuity amount by the Table B term certain annuity factor, as described in § 1.7520–1(c)(1), for the number of years of the defined period. If the percentage exceeds the applicable section 7520 interest rate and the annuity is payable for the life of one or more individuals, multiply the annual annuity amount by the Table B annuity factor for 110 years minus the age of the youngest individual. If the result exceeds the limited fund, the annuity may exhaust the fund, and it will be necessary to calculate a special section 7520 annuity factor that takes into account the exhaustion of the trust or fund. This computation would be modified, if appropriate, to take into account annuities with different payment terms. See § 25.7520–3(b)(2)(v) Example 5 of this chapter, which provides an illustration involving an annuity trust that is subject to exhaustion.

(ii) Income and similar interests—(A) Beneficial enjoyment. A standard section 7520 income factor for an ordinary income interest may not be used to determine the present value of an income or similar interest in trust for a term of years or for the life of one or more individuals unless the effect of the trust, will, or other governing instrument is to provide the income beneficiary with that degree of beneficial enjoyment of the property during the term of the income interest that the principles of the law of trusts accord to a person who is unqualifiedly designated as the income beneficiary of a trust for a similar period of time. This degree of beneficial enjoyment is provided only if it was the transferor's intent, as manifested by the provisions of the governing instrument and the surrounding circumstances, that the trust provide an income interest for the income beneficiary during the specified period of time that is consistent with the value of the trust corpus and with its preservation. In determining whether a trust arrangement evidences that intention, the treatment required or permitted with respect to individual items must be considered in relation to the entire system provided for in the administration of the subject trust. Similarly, in determining the present value of the right to use tangible property (whether or not in trust) for one or more measuring lives or for some other specified period of time, the interest rate component prescribed under section 7520 and § 1.7520–1 may not be used unless, during the specified period, the effect of the trust, will or other governing instrument is to provide the beneficiary with that degree of use, possession, and enjoyment of the property during the term of interest that applicable state law accords to a person who is unqualifiedly designated as a life tenant or term holder for a similar period of time.

(B) Diversions of income and corpus. A standard section 7520 income factor for an ordinary income interest may not be used to value an income interest or similar interest in property for a term of years or for one or more measuring lives if—

(1) The trust, will, or other governing instrument requires or permits the beneficiary's income or other enjoyment to be withheld, diverted, or accumulated for another person's benefit without the consent of the income beneficiary; or

(2) The governing instrument requires or permits trust corpus to be withdrawn from the trust for another person's benefit during the income beneficiary's term of enjoyment without the consent of and accountability to the income beneficiary for such diversion.

(iii) Remainder and reversionary interests. A standard section 7520 remainder interest factor for an ordinary remainder or reversionary interest may not be used to determine the present value of a remainder or reversionary interest (whether in trust or otherwise) unless, consistent with the preservation and protection that the law of trusts would provide for a person who is unqualifiedly designated as the remainder beneficiary of a trust for a similar duration, the effect of the administrative and dispositive provisions for the interest or interests that precede the remainder or reversionary interest is to assure that the property will be adequately preserved and protected (e.g., from erosion, invasion, depletion, or damage) until the remainder or reversionary interest takes effect in possession and enjoyment. This degree of preservation and protection is provided only if it was the transferor's intent, as manifested by the provisions of the arrangement and the surrounding circumstances, that the entire disposition provide the remainder or reversionary beneficiary with an undiminished interest in the property transferred at the time of the termination of the prior interest.

(iv) Pooled income fund interests. In general, pooled income funds are created and administered to achieve a special rate of return. A beneficial interest in a pooled income fund is not ordinarily valued using a standard section 7520 income or remainder interest factor. The present value of a beneficial interest in a pooled income fund is determined according to rules and special remainder factors prescribed in § 1.642(c)–6 and, when applicable, the rules set forth in paragraph (b)(3) of this section, if the individual who is the measuring life is terminally ill at the time of the transfer.

(3) Mortality component. The mortality component prescribed under section 7520 may not be used to determine the present value of an annuity, income interest, remainder interest, or reversionary interest if an individual who is a measuring life is terminally ill at the time of the transaction. For purposes of this paragraph (b)(3), an individual who is known to have an incurable illness or other deteriorating physical condition is considered terminally ill if there is at least a 50 percent probability that the individual will die within 1 year. However, if the individual survives for eighteen months or longer after the date of the transaction, that individual shall be presumed to have not been terminally ill at the time of the transaction unless the contrary is established by clear and convincing evidence.

(4) Examples. The provisions of this paragraph (b) are illustrated by the following examples:

Example 1. Annuity funded with unproductive property. The taxpayer transfers corporation stock worth $1,000,000 to a trust. The trust provides for a 6 percent ($60,000 per year) annuity in cash or other property to be paid to a charitable organization for 25 years and for the remainder to be distributed to the donor's child. The trust specifically authorizes, but does not require, the trustee to retain the shares of stock. The section 7520 interest rate for the month of the transfer is 8.2 percent. The corporation has paid no dividends on this stock during the past 5 years, and there is no indication that this policy will change in the near future. Under applicable state law, the corporation is considered to be a sound investment that satisfies fiduciary standards. Therefore, the trust's sole investment in this corporation is not expected to adversely affect the interest of either the annuitant or the remainder beneficiary. Considering the 6 percent annuity payout rate and the 8.2 percent section 7520 interest rate, the trust corpus is considered sufficient to pay this annuity for the entire 25–year term of the trust, or even indefinitely. Although it appears that neither beneficiary would be able to compel the trustee to make the trust corpus produce investment income, the annuity interest in this case is considered to be an ordinary annuity interest, and the standard section 7520 annuity factor may be used to determine the present value of the annuity. In this case, the section 7520 annuity factor would represent the right to receive $1.00 per year for a term of 25 years.

Example 2. Terminal illness. The taxpayer transfers property worth $1,000,000 to a charitable remainder unitrust described in section 664(d)(2) and § 1.664–3. The trust provides for a fixed-percentage 7 percent unitrust benefit (each annual payment is equal to 7 percent of the trust assets as valued at the beginning of each year) to be paid quarterly to an individual beneficiary for life and for the remainder to be distributed to a charitable organization. At the time the trust is created, the individual beneficiary is age 60 and has been diagnosed with an incurable illness and there is at least a 50 percent probability of the individual dying within 1 year. Assuming the presumption in paragraph (b)(3) of this section does not apply, because there is at least a 50 percent probability that this beneficiary will die within 1 year, the standard section 7520 unitrust remainder factor for a person age 60 from the valuation tables may not be used to determine the present value of the charitable remainder interest. Instead, a special unitrust remainder factor must be computed that is based on the section 7520 interest rate and that takes into account the projection of the individual beneficiary's actual life expectancy.

(5) Additional limitations. Section 7520 does not apply to the extent as may otherwise be provided by the Commissioner.

* * *

[T.D. 8540, 59 FR 30100, June 10, 1994, as amended by T.D. 8630, 60 FR 63913, Dec. 13, 1995]

§ 20.7520–3 Limitation on the application of section 7520.

* * *

(b) Other limitations on the application of section 7520—(1) In general—(i) Ordinary beneficial interests. For purposes of this section:

(A) An ordinary annuity interest is the right to receive a fixed dollar amount at the end of each year during one or more measuring lives or for some other defined period. A standard section 7520 annuity factor for an ordinary annuity interest represents the present worth of the right to receive $1.00 per year for a defined period, using the interest rate prescribed under section 7520 for the appropriate month. If an annuity interest is payable more often than annually or is payable at the beginning of each period, a special adjustment must be made in any computation with a standard section 7520 annuity factor.

(B) An ordinary income interest is the right to receive the income from or the use of property during one or more measuring lives or for some other defined period. A standard section 7520 income factor for an ordinary income interest represents the present worth of the right to receive the use of $1.00 for a defined period, using the interest rate prescribed under section 7520 for the appropriate month.

(C) An ordinary remainder or reversionary interest is the right to receive an interest in property at the end of one or more measuring lives or some other defined period. A standard section 7520 remainder factor for an ordinary remainder or reversionary interest represents the present worth of the right to receive $1.00 at the end of a defined period, using the interest rate prescribed under section 7520 for the appropriate month.

(ii) Certain restricted beneficial interests. A restricted beneficial interest is an annuity, income, remainder, or reversionary interest that is subject to any contingency, power, or other restriction, whether the restriction is provided for by the terms of the trust, will, or other governing instrument or is caused by other circumstances. In general, a standard section 7520 annuity, income, or remainder factor may not be used to value a restricted beneficial interest. However, a special section 7520 annuity, income, or remainder factor may be used to value a restricted beneficial interest under some circumstances. See paragraphs (b)(2)(v) Example 4 and (b)(4) Example 1 of this section, which illustrate situations where special section 7520 actuarial factors are needed to take into account limitations on beneficial interests. See § 20.7520–1(c) for requesting a special factor from the Internal Revenue Service.

(iii) Other beneficial interests. If, under the provisions of this paragraph (b), the interest rate and mortality components prescribed under section 7520 are not applicable in determining the value of any annuity, income, remainder, or reversionary interest, the actual fair market value of the interest (determined without regard to section 7520) is based on all of the facts and circumstances if and to the extent permitted by the Internal Revenue Code provision applicable to the property interest.

(2) Provisions of governing instrument and other limitations on source of payment—(i) Annuities. A standard section 7520 annuity factor may not be used to determine the present value of an annuity for a specified term of years or the life of one or more individuals unless the effect of the trust, will, or other governing instrument is to ensure that the annuity will be paid for the entire defined period. In the case of an annuity payable from a trust or other limited fund, the annuity is not considered payable for the entire defined period if, considering the applicable section 7520 interest rate at the valuation date of the transfer, the annuity is expected to exhaust the fund before the last possible annuity payment is made in full. For this purpose, it must be assumed that it is possible for each measuring life to survive until age 110. For example, for a fixed annuity payable annually at the end of each year, if the amount of the annuity payment (expressed as a percentage of the initial corpus) is less than or equal to the applicable section 7520 interest rate at the date of the transfer, the corpus is assumed to be sufficient to make all payments. If the percentage exceeds the applicable section 7520 interest rate and the annuity is for a definite term of years, multiply the annual annuity amount by the Table B term certain annuity factor, as described in § 20.7520-1(c)(1), for the number of years of the defined period. If the percentage exceeds the applicable section 7520 interest rate and the annuity is payable for the life of one or more individuals, multiply the annual annuity amount by the Table B annuity factor for 110 years minus the age of the youngest individual. If the result exceeds the limited fund, the annuity may exhaust the fund, and it will be necessary to calculate a special section 7520 annuity factor that takes into account the exhaustion of the trust or fund. This computation would be modified, if appropriate, to take into account annuities with different payment terms. See § 25.7520-3(b)(2)(v) Example 5 of this chapter, which provides an illustration involving an annuity trust that is subject to exhaustion.

(ii) Income and similar interests—(A) Beneficial enjoyment. A standard section 7520 income factor for an ordinary income interest may not be used to determine the present value of an income or similar interest in trust for a term of years, or for the life of one or more individuals, unless the effect of the trust, will, or other governing instrument is to provide the income beneficiary with that degree of beneficial enjoyment of the property during the term of the income interest that the principles of the law of trusts accord to a person who is unqualifiedly designated as the income beneficiary of a trust for a similar period of time. This degree of beneficial enjoyment is provided only if it was the transferor's intent, as manifested by the provisions of the governing instrument and the surrounding circumstances, that the trust provide an income interest for the income beneficiary during the specified period of time that is consistent with the value of the trust corpus and with its preservation. In determining whether a trust arrangement evidences that intention, the treatment required or permitted with respect to individual items must be considered in relation to the entire system provided for in the administration of the subject trust. Similarly, in determining the present value of the right to use tangible property (whether or not in trust) for one or more measuring lives or for some other specified period of time, the interest rate component prescribed under section 7520 and § 1.7520-1 of this chapter may not be used unless, during the specified period, the effect of the trust, will or other governing instrument is to provide the beneficiary with that degree of use, possession, and enjoyment of the property during the term of interest that applicable state law accords to a person who is unqualifiedly designated as a life tenant or term holder for a similar period of time.

(B) Diversions of income and corpus. A standard section 7520 income factor for an ordinary income interest may not be used to value an income interest or similar interest in property for a term of years, or for one or more measuring lives, if—

(1) The trust, will, or other governing instrument requires or permits the beneficiary's income or other enjoyment to be withheld, diverted, or accumulated for another person's benefit without the consent of the income beneficiary; or

(2) The governing instrument requires or permits trust corpus to be withdrawn from the trust for another person's benefit without the consent of the income beneficiary during the income beneficiary's term of enjoyment and without accountability to the income beneficiary for such diversion.

(iii) Remainder and reversionary interests. A standard section 7520 remainder interest factor for an ordinary remainder or reversionary interest may not be used to determine the present value of a remainder or reversionary interest (whether in trust or otherwise) unless, consistent with the preservation and protection that the law of trusts would provide for a person who is unqualifiedly designated as the remainder beneficiary of a trust for a similar duration, the effect of the administrative and dispositive provisions for the interest or interests that precede the remainder or reversionary interest is to assure that the property will be adequately preserved and protected (e.g., from erosion, invasion, depletion, or damage) until the remainder or reversionary interest takes effect in possession and enjoyment. This degree of preservation and protection is provided only if it was the transferor's intent, as manifested by the provisions of the arrangement and the surrounding circumstances, that the entire disposition provide the remainder or reversionary beneficiary with an undiminished interest in the property transferred at the time of the termination of the prior interest.

(iv) Pooled income fund interests. In general, pooled income funds are created and administered to achieve a special rate of return. A beneficial interest in a pooled income fund is not ordinarily valued using a standard section 7520 income or remainder interest factor. The present value of a beneficial interest in a pooled income fund is determined according to rules and special remainder factors prescribed in § 1.642(c)–6 of this chapter and, when applicable, the rules set forth under paragraph (b)(3) of this section if the individual who is the measuring life is terminally ill at the time of the transfer.

(v) Examples. The provisions of this paragraph (b)(2) are illustrated by the following examples:

Example 1. Unproductive property. A died, survived by B and C. B died two years after A. A's will provided for a bequest of corporation stock in trust under the terms of which all of the trust income was paid to B for life. After the death of B, the trust terminated and the trust property was distributed to C. The trust specifically authorized, but did not require, the trustee to retain the shares of stock. The corporation paid no dividends on this stock during the 5 years before A's death and the 2 years before B's death. There was no indication that this policy would change after A's death. Under applicable state law, the corporation is considered to be a sound investment that satisfies fiduciary standards. The facts and circumstances, including applicable state law, indicate that B did not have the legal right to compel the trustee to make the trust corpus productive in conformity with the requirements for a lifetime trust income interest under applicable local law. Therefore, B's life income interest in this case is considered nonproductive. Consequently, B's income interest may not be valued actuarially under this section.

Example 2. Beneficiary's right to make trust productive. The facts are the same as in Example 1, except that the trustee is not specifically authorized to retain the shares of stock. Further, the terms of the trust specifically provide that B, the life income beneficiary, may require the trustee to make the trust corpus productive consistent with income yield standards for trusts under applicable state law. Under that law, the minimum rate of income that a productive trust may produce is substantially below the section 7520 interest rate for the month of A's death. In this case, because B has the right to compel the trustee to make the trust productive for purposes of applicable local law during the beneficiary's lifetime, the income interest is considered an ordinary income interest for purposes of this paragraph, and the standard section 7520 life income interest factor may be used to determine the present value of B's income interest.

Example 3. Discretionary invasion of corpus. The decedent, A, transferred property to a trust under the terms of which all of the trust income is to be paid to A's child for life and the remainder of the trust is to be distributed to a grandchild. The trust authorizes the trustee without restriction to distribute corpus to A's surviving spouse for the spouse's comfort and happiness. In this case, because the trustee's power to invade trust corpus is unrestricted, the exercise of the power could result in the termination of the income interest at any time. Consequently, the income interest is not considered an ordinary income interest for purposes of this paragraph, and may not be valued actuarially under this section.

Example 4. Limited invasion of corpus. The decedent, A, bequeathed property to a trust under the terms of which all of the trust income is to be paid to A's child for life and the remainder is to be distributed to A's grandchild. The trust authorizes the child to withdraw up to $5,000 per year from the trust corpus. In this case, the child's power to invade trust corpus is limited to an ascertainable amount each year. Annual invasions of any amount would be expected to progressively diminish the property from which the child's income is paid. Consequently, the income interest is not considered an ordinary income interest for purposes of this paragraph, and the standard section 7520 income interest factor may not be used to determine the present value of the income interest. Nevertheless, the present value of the child's income interest is ascertainable by making a special actuarial calculation that would take into account not only the initial value of the trust corpus, the section 7520 interest rate for the month of the transfer, and the mortality component for the child's age, but also the assumption that the trust corpus will decline at the rate of $5,000 each year during the child's lifetime. The child's right to receive an amount not in excess of $5,000 per year may be separately valued in this instance and, assuming the trust corpus would not exhaust before the child would attain age 110, would be considered an ordinary annuity interest.

Example 5. Power to consume. The decedent, A, devised a life estate in 3 parcels of real estate to A's surviving spouse with the remainder to a child, or, if the child doesn't survive, to the child's estate. A also conferred upon the spouse an unrestricted power to consume the property, which includes the right to sell part or all of the property and to use the proceeds for the spouse's support, comfort, happiness, and other purposes. Any portion of the property or its sale proceeds remaining at the death of the surviving spouse is to vest by operation of law in the child at that time. The child predeceased the surviving spouse. In this case, the surviving spouse's power to consume the corpus is unrestricted, and the exercise of the power could entirely exhaust the remainder interest during the life of the spouse. Consequently, the remainder interest that is includible in the child's estate is not considered an ordinary remainder interest for purposes of this paragraph and may not be valued actuarially under this section.

(3) Mortality component—(i) Terminal illness. Except as provided in paragraph (b)(3)(ii) of this section, the mortality component prescribed under section 7520 may not be used to determine the present value of an annuity, income interest, remainder interest, or reversionary interest if an individual who is a measuring life is terminally ill at the time of the decedent's death. For purposes of this paragraph (b)(3), an individual who is known to have an incurable illness or other deteriorating physical condition is considered terminally ill if there is at least a 50 percent probability that the individual will die within 1 year. However, if the individual survives for eighteen months or longer after the date of the decedent's death, that individual shall be presumed to have not been terminally ill at the date of death unless the contrary is established by clear and convincing evidence.

(ii) Terminal illness exceptions. In the case of the allowance of the credit for tax on a prior transfer under section 2013, if a final determination of the federal estate tax liability of the transferor's estate has been made under circumstances that required valuation of the life interest received by the transferee, the value of the property transferred, for purposes of the credit allowable to the transferee's estate, shall be the value determined previously in the transferor's estate. Otherwise, for purposes of section 2013, the provisions of paragraph (b)(3)(i) of this section shall govern in valuing the property transferred. The value of a decedent's reversionary interest under sections 2037(b) and 2042(2) shall be determined without regard to the physical condition, immediately before the decedent's death, of the individual who is the measuring life.

(iii) Death resulting from common accidents. The mortality component prescribed under section 7520 may not be used to determine the present value of an annuity, income interest, remainder interest, or reversionary interest if the decedent, and the individual who is the measuring life, die as a result of a common accident or other occurrence.

(4) Examples. The provisions of paragraph (b)(3) of this section are illustrated by the following examples:

Example 1. Terminal illness. The decedent bequeaths $1,000,000 to a trust under the terms of which the trustee is to pay $103,000 per year to a charitable organization during the life of the decedent's child. Upon the death of the child, the remainder in the trust is to be distributed to the decedent's grandchild. The child, who is age 60, has been diagnosed with an incurable illness, and there is at least a 50 percent probability of the child dying within 1 year. Assuming the presumption provided for in paragraph (b)(3)(i) of this section does not apply, the standard life annuity factor for a person age 60 may not be used to determine the present value of the charitable organization's annuity interest because there is at least a 50 percent probability that the child, who is the measuring life, will die within 1 year. Instead, a special section 7520 annuity factor must be computed that takes into account the projection of the child's actual life expectancy.

Example 2. Deaths resulting from common accidents, etc. The decedent's will establishes a trust to pay income to the decedent's surviving spouse for life. The will provides that, upon the spouse's death or, if the spouse fails to survive the decedent, upon the decedent's death the trust property is to pass to the decedent's children. The decedent and the decedent's spouse die simultaneously in an accident under circumstances in which it was impossible to determine who survived the other. Even if the terms of the will and applicable state law presume that the decedent died first with the result that the property interest is considered to have passed in trust for the benefit of the spouse for life, after which the remainder is to be distributed to the decedent's children, the spouse's life income interest may not be valued by use of the mortality component described under section 7520. The result would be the same even if it was established that the spouse survived the decedent.

(5) Additional limitations. Section 7520 does not apply to the extent as may otherwise be provided by the Commissioner.

* * *

[T.D. 8540, 59 FR 30170, June 10, 1990, as amended by T.D. 8630, 60 FR 63913, Dec. 13, 1995]

§ 25.7520–3 Limitation on the application of section 7520.

* * *

(b) Other limitations on the application of section 7520—(1) In general—(i) Ordinary beneficial interests. For purposes of this section:

(A) An ordinary annuity interest is the right to receive a fixed dollar amount at the end of each year during one or more measuring lives or for some other defined period. A standard section 7520 annuity factor for an ordinary annuity interest represents the present worth of the right to receive $1.00 per year for a defined period, using the interest rate prescribed under section 7520 for the appropriate month. If an annuity interest is payable more often than annually or is payable at the beginning of each period, a special adjustment must be made in any computation with a standard section 7520 annuity factor.

(B) An ordinary income interest is the right to receive the income from or the use of property during one or more measuring lives or for some other defined period. A standard section 7520 income factor for an ordinary income interest represents the present worth of the right to receive the use of $1.00 for a defined period, using the interest rate prescribed under section 7520 for the appropriate month. However, in the case of certain gifts made after October 8, 1990, if the donor does not retain a qualified annuity, unitrust, or reversionary interest, the value of any interest retained by the donor is considered to be zero if the remainder beneficiary is a member of the donor's family. See § 25.2702–2.

(C) An ordinary remainder or reversionary interest is the right to receive an interest in property at the end of one or more measuring lives or some other defined period. A standard section 7520 remainder factor for an ordinary remainder or reversionary interest represents the present worth of the right to receive $1.00 at the end of a defined period, using the interest rate prescribed under section 7520 for the appropriate month.

(ii) Certain restricted beneficial interests. A restricted beneficial interest is an annuity, income, remainder, or reversionary interest that is subject to any contingency, power, or other restriction, whether the restriction is provided for by the terms of the trust, will, or other governing instrument or is caused by other circumstances. In general, a standard section 7520 annuity, income, or remainder factor may not be used to value a restricted beneficial interest. However, a special section 7520 annuity, income, or remainder factor may be used to value a restricted beneficial interest under some circumstances. See paragraphs (b)(2)(v) Example 5 and (b)(4) of this section, which illustrate situations in which special section 7520 actuarial factors are needed to take into account limitations on beneficial interests. See § 25.7520–1(c) for requesting a special factor from the Internal Revenue Service.

(iii) Other beneficial interests. If, under the provisions of this paragraph (b), the interest rate and mortality components prescribed under section 7520 are not applicable in determining the value of any annuity, income, remainder, or reversionary interest, the actual fair market value of the interest (determined without regard to section 7520) is based on all of the facts and circumstances if and to the extent permitted by the Internal Revenue Code provision applicable to the property interest.

(2) Provisions of governing instrument and other limitations on source of payment—(i) Annuities. A standard section 7520 annuity factor may not be used to determine the present value of an annuity for a specified term of years or the life of one or more individuals unless the effect of the trust, will, or other governing instrument is to ensure that the annuity will be paid for the entire defined period. In the case of an annuity payable from a trust or other limited fund, the annuity is not considered payable for the entire defined period if, considering the applicable section 7520 interest rate on the valuation date of the transfer, the annuity is expected to exhaust the fund before the last possible annuity payment is made in full. For this purpose, it must be assumed that it is possible for each measuring life to survive until age 110. For example, for a fixed annuity payable annually at the end of each year, if the amount of the annuity payment (expressed as a percentage of the initial corpus) is less than or equal to the applicable section 7520 interest rate at the date of the transfer, the corpus is assumed to be sufficient to make all payments. If the percentage exceeds the applicable section 7520 interest rate and the annuity is for a definite term of years, multiply the annual annuity amount by the Table B term certain annuity factor, as described in § 25.7520–1(c)(1), for the number of years of the defined period. If the percentage exceeds the applicable section 7520 interest rate and the annuity is payable for the life of one or more individuals, multiply the annual annuity amount by the Table B annuity factor for 110 years minus the age of the youngest individual. If the result exceeds the limited fund, the annuity may exhaust the fund, and it will be necessary to calculate a special section 7520 annuity factor that takes into account the exhaustion of the trust or fund. This computation would be modified, if appropriate, to take into account annuities with different payment terms.

(ii) Income and similar interests—(A) Beneficial enjoyment. A standard section 7520 income factor for an ordinary income interest is not to be used to determine the present value of an income or similar interest in trust for a term of years or for the life of one or more individuals unless the effect of the trust, will, or other governing instrument is to provide the income beneficiary with that degree of beneficial enjoyment of the property during the term of the income interest that the principles of the law of trusts accord to a person who is unqualifiedly designated as the income beneficiary of a trust for a similar period of time. This degree of beneficial enjoyment is provided only if it was the transferor's intent, as manifested by the provisions of the governing instrument and the surrounding circumstances, that the trust provide an income interest for the income beneficiary during the specified period of time that is consistent with the value of the trust corpus and with its preservation. In determining whether a trust arrangement evidences that intention, the treatment required or permitted with respect to individual items must be considered in relation to the entire system provided for in the administration of the subject trust. Similarly, in determining the present value of the right to use tangible property (whether or not in trust) for one or more measuring lives or for some other specified period of time, the interest rate component prescribed under section 7520 and s 1.7520–1 of this chapter may not be used unless, during the specified period, the effect of the trust, will or other governing instrument is to provide the beneficiary with that degree of use, possession, and enjoyment of the property during the term of interest that applicable state law accords to a person who is unqualifiedly designated as a life tenant or term holder for a similar period of time.

(B) Diversions of income and corpus. A standard section 7520 income factor for an ordinary income interest may not be used to value an income interest or similar interest in property for a term of years, or for one or more measuring lives, if—

(1) The trust, will, or other governing instrument requires or permits the beneficiary's income or other enjoyment to be withheld, diverted, or accumulated for another person's benefit without the consent of the income beneficiary; or

(2) The governing instrument requires or permits trust corpus to be withdrawn from the trust for another person's benefit without the consent of the income beneficiary during the income beneficiary's term of enjoyment and without accountability to the income beneficiary for such diversion.

(iii) Remainder and reversionary interests. A standard section 7520 remainder interest factor for an ordinary remainder or reversionary interest may not be used to determine the present value of a remainder or reversionary interest (whether in trust or otherwise) unless, consistent with the preservation and protection that the law of trusts would provide for a person who is unqualifiedly designated as the remainder beneficiary of a trust for a similar duration, the effect of the administrative and dispositive provisions for the interest or interests that precede the remainder or reversionary interest is to assure that the property will be adequately preserved and protected (e.g., from erosion, invasion, depletion, or damage) until the remainder or reversionary interest takes effect in possession and enjoyment. This degree of preservation and protection is provided only if it was the transferor's intent, as manifested by the provisions of the arrangement and the surrounding circumstances, that the entire disposition provide the remainder or reversionary beneficiary with an undiminished interest in the property transferred at the time of the termination of the prior interest.

(iv) Pooled income fund interests. In general, pooled income funds are created and administered to achieve a special rate of return. A beneficial interest in a pooled income fund is not ordinarily valued using a standard section 7520 income or remainder interest factor. The present value of a beneficial interest in a pooled income fund is determined according to rules and special remainder factors prescribed in § 1.642(c)–6 of this chapter and, when applicable, the rules set forth under paragraph (b)(3) of this section if the individual who is the measuring life is terminally ill at the time of the transfer.

(v) Examples. The provisions of this paragraph (b)(2) are illustrated by the following examples:

Example 1. Unproductive property. The donor transfers corporation stock to a trust under the terms of which all of the trust income is payable to A for life. Considering the applicable federal rate under section 7520 and the appropriate life estate factor for a person A's age, the value of A's income interest, if valued under this section, would be $10,000. After A's death, the trust is to terminate and the trust property is to be distributed to B. The trust specifically authorizes, but does not require, the trustee to retain the shares of stock. The corporation has paid no dividends on this stock during the past 5 years, and there is no indication that this policy will change in the near future. Under applicable state law, the corporation is considered to be a sound investment that satisfies fiduciary standards. The facts and circumstances, including applicable state law, indicate that the income beneficiary would not have the legal right to compel the trustee to make the trust corpus productive in conformity with the requirements for a lifetime trust income interest under applicable local law. Therefore, the life income interest in this case is considered nonproductive. Consequently, A's income interest may not be valued actuarially under this section.

Example 2. Beneficiary's right to make trust productive. The facts are the same as in Example 1, except that the trustee is not specifically authorized to retain the shares of corporation stock. Further, the terms of the trust specifically provide that the life income beneficiary may require the trustee to make the trust corpus productive consistent with income yield standards for trusts under applicable state law. Under that law, the minimum rate of income that a productive trust may produce is substantially below the section 7520 interest rate on the valuation date. In this case, because A, the income beneficiary, has the right to compel the trustee to make the trust productive for purposes of applicable local law during A's lifetime, the income interest is considered an ordinary income interest for purposes of this paragraph, and the standard section 7520 life income factor may be used to determine the value of A's income interest. However, in the case of gifts made after October 8, 1990, if the donor was the life income beneficiary, the value of the income interest would be considered to be zero in this situation. See § 25.2702–2.

Example 3. Annuity trust funded with unproductive property. The donor, who is age 60, transfers corporation stock worth $1,000,000 to a trust. The trust will pay a 6 percent ($60,000 per year) annuity in cash or other property to the donor for 10 years or until the donor's prior death. Upon the termination of the trust, the trust property is to be distributed to the donor's child. The section 7520 rate for the month of the transfer is 8.2 percent. The corporation has paid no dividends on the stock during the past 5 years, and there is no indication that this policy will change in the near future. Under applicable state law, the corporation is considered to be a sound investment that satisfies fiduciary standards. Therefore, the trust's sole investment in this corporation is not expected to adversely affect the interest of either the annuity beneficiary or the remainder beneficiary. Considering the 6 percent annuity payout rate and the 8.2 percent section 7520 interest rate, the trust corpus is considered sufficient to pay this annuity for the entire 10–year term of the trust, or even indefinitely. The trust specifically authorizes, but does not require, the trustee to retain the shares of stock. Although it appears that neither beneficiary would be able to compel the trustee to make the trust corpus produce investment income, the annuity interest in this case is considered to be an ordinary annuity interest, and a section 7520 annuity factor may be used to determine the present value of the annuity. In this case, the section 7520 annuity factor would represent the right to receive $1.00 per year for a term of 10 years or the prior death of a person age 60.

Example 4. Unitrust funded with unproductive property. The facts are the same as in Example 3, except that the donor has retained a unitrust interest equal to 7 percent of the value of the trust property, valued as of the beginning of each year. Although the trust corpus is nonincome-producing, the present value of the donor's retained unitrust interest may be determined by using the section 7520 unitrust factor for a term of years or a prior death.

* * *

(3) Mortality component. The mortality component prescribed under section 7520 may not be used to determine the present value of an annuity, income interest, remainder interest, or reversionary interest if an individual who is a measuring life dies or is terminally ill at the time the gift is completed. For purposes of this paragraph (b)(3), an individual who is known to have an incurable illness or other deteriorating physical condition is considered terminally ill if there is at least a 50 percent probability that the individual will die within 1 year. However, if the individual survives for eighteen months or longer after the date the gift is completed, that individual shall be presumed to have not been terminally ill at the date the gift was completed unless the contrary is established by clear and convincing evidence.

(4) [Reserved]. For further guidance, see § 25.7520–3T(b)(4).

(5) Additional limitations. Section 7520 does not apply to the extent as may otherwise be provided by the Commissioner.

* * *

[T.D. 8540, 59 FR 30170, June 10, 1994, as amended by T.D. 8630, 60 FR 63913, Dec. 13, 1995; T.D. 8819, 64 FR 23187, April 29, 1999; T.D. 9448, 74 FR 21437, May 7, 2009; T.D. 9540, 76 FR 49570, Aug. 10, 2011]

§ 301.7701–1 Classification of organizations for federal tax purposes.

(a) Organizations for federal tax purposes—(1) In general. The Internal Revenue Code prescribes the classification of various organizations for federal tax purposes. Whether an organization is an entity separate from its owners for federal tax purposes is a matter of federal tax law and does not depend on whether the organization is recognized as an entity under local law.

(2) Certain joint undertakings give rise to entities for federal tax purposes. A joint venture or other contractual arrangement may create a separate entity for federal tax purposes if the participants carry on a trade, business, financial operation, or venture and divide the profits therefrom. For example, a separate entity exists for federal tax purposes if co-owners of an apartment building lease space and in addition provide services to the occupants either directly or through an agent. Nevertheless, a joint undertaking merely to share expenses does not create a separate entity for federal tax purposes. For example, if two or more persons jointly construct a ditch merely to drain surface water from their properties, they have not created a separate entity for federal tax purposes. Similarly, mere co-ownership of property that is maintained, kept in repair, and rented or leased does not constitute a separate entity for federal tax purposes. For example, if an individual owner, or tenants in common, of farm property lease it to a farmer for a cash rental or a share of the crops, they do not necessarily create a separate entity for federal tax purposes.

(3) Certain local law entities not recognized. An entity formed under local law is not always recognized as a separate entity for federal tax purposes. For example, an organization wholly owned by a State is not recognized as a separate entity for federal tax purposes if it is an integral part of the State. Similarly, tribes incorporated under section 17 of the Indian Reorganization Act of 1934, as amended, 25 U.S.C. 477, or under section 3 of the Oklahoma Indian Welfare Act, as amended, 25 U.S.C. 503, are not recognized as separate entities for federal tax purposes.

(4) Single owner organizations. Under §§ 301.7701-2 and 301.7701-3, certain organizations that have a single owner can choose to be recognized or disregarded as entities separate from their owners.

* * *

(e) State. For purposes of this section and § 301.7701-2, the term State includes the District of Columbia.

* * *

[32 FR 15241, Nov. 3, 1967, as amended by T.D. 7515, 42 FR 55612, Oct. 18, 1977; T.D. 8697, 61 FR 66584, Dec. 18, 1996; T.D. 9153, 69 FR 49809, Aug. 12, 2004; T.D. 9246, 71 FR 4815, Jan. 30, 2006; T.D. 9441, 74 FR 340, Jan. 5, 2009; T.D. 9568, 76 FR 80082, Dec. 22, 2011]

§ 301.7701-2 Business entities; definitions.

(a) Business entities. For purposes of this section and § 301.7701-3, a *business entity* is any entity recognized for federal tax purposes (including an entity with a single owner that may be disregarded as an entity separate from its owner under § 301.7701-3) that is not properly classified as a trust under § 301.7701-4 or otherwise subject to special treatment under the Internal Revenue Code. A business entity with two or more members is classified for federal tax purposes as either a corporation or a partnership. A business entity with only one owner is classified as a corporation or is disregarded; if the entity is disregarded, its activities are treated in the same manner as a sole proprietorship, branch, or division of the owner.

* * *

(b) Corporations. For federal tax purposes, the term *corporation* means—

(1) A business entity organized under a Federal or State statute, or under a statute of a federally recognized Indian tribe, if the statute describes or refers to the entity as incorporated or as a corporation, body corporate, or body politic;

(2) An association (as determined under § 301.7701-3);

(3) A business entity organized under a State statute, if the statute describes or refers to the entity as a joint-stock company or joint-stock association;

(4) An insurance company;

(5) A State-chartered business entity conducting banking activities, if any of its deposits are insured under the Federal Deposit Insurance Act, as amended, 12 U.S.C. 1811 et seq., or a similar federal statute;

(6) A business entity wholly owned by a State or any political subdivision thereof, * * *;

(7) A business entity that is taxable as a corporation under a provision of the Internal Revenue Code other than section 7701(a)(3); and

(8) Certain foreign entities—(i) In general. Except as provided in paragraphs (b)(8)(ii) and (d) of this section, the following business entities formed in the following jurisdictions:

American Samoa, Corporation

Argentina, Sociedad Anonima

Australia, Public Limited Company

Austria, Aktiengesellschaft

Barbados, Limited Company

Belgium, Societe Anonyme

Belize, Public Limited Company

Bolivia, Sociedad Anonima

Brazil, Sociedade Anonima

Bulgaria, Aktsionerno Druzhestvo

Canada, Corporation and Company

Chile, Sociedad Anonima

People's Republic of China, Gufen Youxian Gongsi

Republic of China (Taiwan), Ku-fen Yu-hsien Kung-szu

Colombia, Sociedad Anonima

Costa Rica, Sociedad Anonima

Cyprus, Public Limited Company

Czech Republic, Akciova Spolecnost

Denmark, Aktieselskab

Ecuador, Sociedad Anonima or Compania Anonima

Egypt, Sharikat Al–Mossahamah

El Salvador, Sociedad Anonima

Estonia, Aktsiaselts

European Economic Area/European Union, Societas Europaea

Finland, Julkinen Osakeyhito/Publikt Aktiebolag

France, Societe Anonyme

Germany, Aktiengesellschaft

Greece, Anonymos Etairia

Guam, Corporation

Guatemala, Sociedad Anonima

Guyana, Public Limited Company

Honduras, Sociedad Anonima

Hong Kong, Public Limited Company

Hungary, Reszvenytarsasag

Iceland, Hlutafelag

India, Public Limited Company

Indonesia, Perseroan Terbuka

Ireland, Public Limited Company

Israel, Public Limited Company

Italy, Societa per Azioni

Jamaica, Public Limited Company

Japan, Kabushiki Kaisha

Kazakstan, Ashyk Aktsionerlik Kogham

Republic of Korea, Chusik Hoesa

Latvia, Akciju Sabiedriba

Liberia, Corporation

Liechtenstein, Aktiengesellschaft

Lithuania, Akcine Bendroves

Luxembourg, Societe Anonyme

Malaysia, Berhad

Malta, Public Limited Company

Mexico, Sociedad Anonima

Morocco, Societe Anonyme

Netherlands, Naamloze Vennootschap

New Zealand, Limited Company

Nicaragua, Compania Anonima

Nigeria, Public Limited Company

Northern Mariana Islands, Corporation

Norway, Allment Aksjeselskap

Pakistan, Public Limited Company

Panama, Sociedad Anonima

Paraguay, Sociedad Anonima

Peru, Sociedad Anonima

Philippines, Stock Corporation

Poland, Spolka Akcyjna

Portugal, Sociedade Anonima

Puerto Rico, Corporation

Romania, Societe pe Actiuni

Russia, Otkrytoye Aktsionernoy Obshchestvo

Saudi Arabia, Sharikat Al–Mossahamah

Singapore, Public Limited Company

Slovak Republic, Akciova Spolocnost

Slovenia, Delniska Druzba

South Africa, Public Limited Company

Spain, Sociedad Anonima

Surinam, Naamloze Vennootschap

Sweden, Publika Aktiebolag

Switzerland, Aktiengesellschaft

Thailand, Borisat Chamkad (Mahachon)

Trinidad and Tobago, Public Limited Company

Tunisia, Societe Anonyme

Turkey, Anonim Sirket

Ukraine, Aktsionerne Tovaristvo Vidkritogo Tipu

United Kingdom, Public Limited Company

United States Virgin Islands, Corporation

Uruguay, Sociedad Anonima

Venezuela, Sociedad Anonima or Compania Anonima

* * *

(iv) Limited companies. For purposes of this paragraph (b)(8), any reference to a Limited Company includes, as the case may be, companies limited by shares and companies limited by guarantee.

(v) Multilingual countries. Different linguistic renderings of the name of an entity listed in paragraph (b)(8)(i) of this section shall be disregarded. For example, an entity formed under the laws of Switzerland as a Societe Anonyme will be a corporation and treated in the same manner as an Aktiengesellschaft.

(c) Other business entities. For federal tax purposes—

(1) The term *partnership* means a business entity that is not a corporation under paragraph (b) of this section and that has at least two members.

(2) Wholly owned entities—(i) In general. Except as otherwise provided in this paragraph (c), a business entity that has a single owner and is not a corporation under paragraph (b) of this section is disregarded as an entity separate from its owner.

(ii) Special rule for certain business entities. If the single owner of a business entity is a bank (as defined in section 581), * * *, then the special rules applicable to banks under the Internal Revenue Code will continue to apply to the single owner as if the wholly owned entity were a separate entity. * * *

* * *

[32 FR 15241, Nov. 3, 1967, as amended by T.D. 7515, 42 FR 55612, Oct. 18, 1977; T.D. 7889, 48 FR 18804, April 26, 1983; T.D. 8475, 58 FR 28501, May 14, 1993; T.D. 8697, 61 FR 66584, Dec. 18, 1996; T.D. 8844, 64 FR 66580, Nov. 29, 1999; T.D. 9012, 67 FR 49862, Aug. 1, 2002; T.D. 9093, 68 FR 60286, Oct. 22, 2003; T.D. 9153, 69 FR 49809, Aug. 12, 2004; T.D. 9183, 70 FR 9220, Feb. 25, 2005; T.D. 9197, 70 FR 19697, April 14, 2005; T.D. 9235, 70 FR 74658, Dec. 15, 2005; T.D. 9246, 71 FR 4817, Jan. 30, 2006; T.D. 9356, 72 FR 45891, Aug. 16, 2007; T.D. 9388, 73 FR 15064, Mar. 21, 2008; T.D. 9433, 73 FR 72345, Nov. 28, 2008; T.D. 9462, 74 FR 46903, Sept. 14, 2009; T.D. 9553, 76 FR 66182, Oct. 26, 2011; T.D. 9554, 76 FR 67365, Nov. 1, 2011; T.D. 9596, 77 FR 37806, June 25, 2012]

§ 301.7701–3 Classification of certain business entities.

(a) In general. A business entity that is not classified as a corporation under § 301.7701–2(b)(1), (3), (4), (5), (6), (7), or (8) (an *eligible entity*) can elect its classification for federal tax purposes as provided in this section. An eligible entity with at least two members can elect to be classified as either an association (and thus a corporation under § 301.7701–2(b)(2)) or a partnership, and an eligible entity with a single owner can elect to be classified as an association or to be disregarded as an entity separate from its owner. Paragraph (b) of this section provides a default classification for an eligible entity that does not make an election. Thus, elections are necessary only when an eligible entity chooses to be classified initially as other than the default classification or when an eligible entity chooses to change its classification. An entity whose classification is determined under the default classification retains that classification (regardless of any changes in the members' liability that occurs at any time during the time that the entity's classification is relevant as defined in paragraph (d) of this section) until the entity makes an election to change that classification under paragraph (c)(1) of this section. Paragraph (c) of this section provides rules for making express elections. Paragraph (d) of this section provides special rules for foreign eligible entities. Paragraph (e) of this section provides special rules for classifying entities resulting from partnership terminations and divisions under section 708(b). Paragraph (f) of this section sets forth the effective date of this section and a special rule relating to prior periods.

(b) Classification of eligible entities that do not file an election—(1) Domestic eligible entities. Except as provided in paragraph (b)(3) of this section, unless the entity elects otherwise, a domestic eligible entity is—

(i) A partnership if it has two or more members; or

(ii) Disregarded as an entity separate from its owner if it has a single owner.

(2) Foreign eligible entities—(i) In general. Except as provided in paragraph (b)(3) of this section, unless the entity elects otherwise, a foreign eligible entity is—

(A) A partnership if it has two or more members and at least one member does not have limited liability;

(B) An association if all members have limited liability; or

(C) Disregarded as an entity separate from its owner if it has a single owner that does not have limited liability.

(ii) Definition of limited liability. For purposes of paragraph (b)(2)(i) of this section, a member of a foreign eligible entity has limited liability if the member has no personal liability for the debts of or claims against the entity by reason of being a member. This determination is based solely on the statute or law pursuant to which the entity is organized, except that if the underlying statute or law allows the entity to specify in its organizational documents whether the members will have limited liability, the organizational documents may also be relevant. For purposes of this section, a member has personal liability if the creditors of the entity may seek satisfaction of all or any portion of the debts or claims against the entity from the member as such. A member has personal liability for purposes of this paragraph even if the member makes an agreement under which another person (whether or not a member of the entity) assumes such liability or agrees to indemnify that member for any such liability.

(3) Existing eligible entities—(i) In general. Unless the entity elects otherwise, an eligible entity in existence prior to the effective date of this section will have the same classification that the entity claimed under §§ 301.7701-1 through 301.7701-3 as in effect on the date prior to the effective date of this section; except that if an eligible entity with a single owner claimed to be a partnership under those regulations, the entity will be disregarded as an entity separate from its owner under this paragraph (b)(3)(i). For special rules regarding the classification of such entities for periods prior to the effective date of this section, see paragraph (f)(2) of this section.

(ii) Special rules. For purposes of paragraph (b)(3)(i) of this section, a foreign eligible entity is treated as being in existence prior to the effective date of this section only if the entity's classification was relevant (as defined in paragraph (d) of this section) at any time during the sixty months prior to the effective date of this section. * * *

(c) Elections—(1) Time and place for filing—(i) In general. Except as provided in paragraphs (c)(1)(iv) and (v) of this section, an eligible entity may elect to be classified other than as provided under paragraph (b) of this section, or to change its classification, by filing Form 8832, Entity Classification Election, with the service center designated on Form 8832. An election will not be accepted unless all of the information required by the form and instructions, including the taxpayer identifying number of the entity, is provided on Form 8832. See § 301.6109-1 for rules on applying for and displaying Employer Identification Numbers.

* * *

(iii) Effective date of election. An election made under paragraph (c)(1)(i) of this section will be effective on the date specified by the entity on Form 8832 or on the date filed if no such date is specified on the election form. The effective date specified on Form 8832 can not be more than 75 days prior to the date on which the election is filed and can not be more than 12 months after the date on which the election is filed. If an election specifies an effective date more than 75 days prior to the date on which the election is filed, it will be effective 75 days prior to the date it was filed. If an election specifies an effective date more than 12 months from the date on which the election is filed, it will be effective 12 months after the date it was filed. If an election specifies an effective date before January 1, 1997, it will be effective as of January 1, 1997. If a purchasing corporation makes an election under section 338 regarding an acquired subsidiary, an election under paragraph (c)(1)(i) of this section for the acquired subsidiary can be effective no earlier than the day after the acquisition date (within the meaning of section 338(h)(2)).

(iv) Limitation. If an eligible entity makes an election under paragraph (c)(1)(i) of this section to change its classification (other than an election made by an existing entity to change its classification as of the effective date of this section), the entity cannot change its classification by election again during the sixty months succeeding the effective date of the election. However, the Commissioner may permit the entity to change its classification by election within the sixty months if more than fifty percent of the ownership interests in the entity as of the effective date of the subsequent election are owned by persons that did not own any interests in the entity on the filing date or on the effective date of the entity's prior election. An election by a newly formed eligible entity that is effective on the date of formation is not considered a change for purposes of this paragraph (c)(1)(iv).

(v) Deemed elections—

* * *

(C) S corporations. An eligible entity that timely elects to be an S corporation under section 1362(a)(1) is treated as having made an election under this section to be classified as an association, provided that (as of the effective date of the election under section 1362(a)(1)) the entity meets all other requirements to qualify as a small business corporation under section 1361(b). Subject to § 301.7701–3(c)(1)(iv), the deemed election to be classified as an association will apply as of the effective date of the S corporation election and will remain in effect until the entity makes a valid election, under § 301.7701–3(c)(1)(i), to be classified as other than an association.

* * *

(2) Authorized signatures—(i) In general. An election made under paragraph (c)(1)(i) of this section must be signed by—

(A) Each member of the electing entity who is an owner at the time the election is filed; or

(B) Any officer, manager, or member of the electing entity who is authorized (under local law or the entity's organizational documents) to make the election and who represents to having such authorization under penalties of perjury.

(ii) Retroactive elections. For purposes of paragraph (c)(2)(i) of this section, if an election under paragraph (c)(1)(i) of this section is to be effective for any period prior to the time that it is filed, each person who was an owner between the date the election is to be effective and the date the election is filed, and who is not an owner at the time the election is filed, must also sign the election.

(iii) Changes in classification. For paragraph (c)(2)(i) of this section, if an election under paragraph (c)(1)(i) of this section is made to change the classification of an entity, each person who was an owner on the date that any transactions under paragraph (g) of this section are deemed to occur, and who is not an owner at the time the election is filed, must also sign the election. * * *.

(d) Special rules for foreign eligible entities—(1) Definition of relevance—(i) General rule. For purposes of this section, a foreign eligible entity's classification is relevant when its classification affects the liability of any person for federal tax or information purposes. * * *

* * *

(e) Coordination with section 708(b). Except as provided in § 301.7701–2(d)(3) (regarding termination of grandfather status for certain foreign business entities), an entity resulting from a transaction described in section 708(b)(1)(B) (partnership termination due to sales or exchanges) or section 708(b)(2)(B) (partnership division) is a partnership.

(f) Changes in number of members of an entity—(1) Associations. The classification of an eligible entity as an association is not affected by any change in the number of members of the entity.

(2) Partnerships and single member entities. An eligible entity classified as a partnership becomes disregarded as an entity separate from its owner when the entity's membership is reduced to one member. A single member entity disregarded as an entity separate from its owner is classified as a partnership when the entity has more than one member. If an elective classification change under paragraph (c) of this section is effective at the same time as a membership change described in this paragraph (f)(2), the deemed transactions in paragraph (g) of this section resulting from the elective change preempt the transactions that would result from the change in membership.

(3) Effect on sixty month limitation. A change in the number of members of an entity does not result in the creation of a new entity for purposes of the sixty month limitation on elections under paragraph (c)(1)(iv) of this section.

(4) Examples. The following examples illustrate the application of this paragraph (f):

Example 1. A, a U.S. person, owns a domestic eligible entity that is disregarded as an entity separate from its owner. On January 1, 1998, B, a U.S. person, buys a 50 percent interest in the entity from A. Under this paragraph (f), the entity is classified as a partnership when B acquires an interest in the entity. However, A and B elect to have the entity classified as an association effective on January 1, 1998. Thus, B is treated as buying shares of stock on January 1, 1998. (Under paragraph (c)(1)(iv) of this section, this election is treated as a change in classification so that the entity generally cannot change its classification by election again during the sixty months succeeding the effective date of the election.) Under paragraph (g)(1) of this section, A is treated as contributing the assets and liabilities of the entity to the newly formed association immediately before the close of December 31, 1997. Because A does not retain control of the association as required by section 351, A's contribution will be a taxable event. Therefore, under section 1012, the association will take a fair market value basis in the assets contributed by A, and A will have a fair market value basis in the stock received. A will have no additional gain upon the sale of stock to B, and B will have a cost basis in the stock purchased from A.

* * *

(g) Elective changes in classification—(1) Deemed treatment of elective change—(i) Partnership to association. If an eligible entity classified as a partnership elects under paragraph (c)(1)(i) of this section to be classified as an association, the following is deemed to occur: The partnership contributes all of its assets and liabilities to the association in exchange for stock in the association, and immediately thereafter, the partnership liquidates by distributing the stock of the association to its partners.

(ii) Association to partnership. If an eligible entity classified as an association elects under paragraph (c)(1)(i) of this section to be classified as a partnership, the following is deemed to occur: The association distributes all of its assets and liabilities to its shareholders in liquidation of the association, and immediately thereafter, the shareholders contribute all of the distributed assets and liabilities to a newly formed partnership.

(iii) Association to disregarded entity. If an eligible entity classified as an association elects under paragraph (c)(1)(i) of this section to be disregarded as an entity separate from its owner, the following is deemed to occur: The association distributes all of its assets and liabilities to its single owner in liquidation of the association.

(iv) Disregarded entity to an association. If an eligible entity that is disregarded as an entity separate from its owner elects under paragraph (c)(1)(i) of this section to be classified as an association, the following is deemed to occur: The owner of the eligible entity contributes all of the assets and liabilities of the entity to the association in exchange for stock of the association.

(2) Effect of elective changes—(i) In general. The tax treatment of a change in the classification of an entity for federal tax purposes by election under paragraph (c)(1)(i) of this section is determined under all relevant provisions of the Internal Revenue Code and general principles of tax law, including the step transaction doctrine.

(ii) Adoption of plan of liquidation. For purposes of satisfying the requirement of adoption of a plan of liquidation under section 332, unless a formal plan of liquidation that contemplates the election to be classified as a partnership or to be disregarded as an entity separate from its owner is adopted on an earlier date, the making, by an association, of an election under paragraph (c)(1)(i) of this section to be classified as a partnership or to be disregarded as an entity separate from its owner is considered to be the adoption of a plan of liquidation immediately before the deemed liquidation described in paragraph (g)(1)(ii) or (iii) of this section.

* * *

(3) Timing of election—(i) In general. An election under paragraph (c)(1)(i) of this section that changes the classification of an eligible entity for federal tax purposes is treated as occurring at the start of the day for which the election is effective. Any transactions that are deemed to occur under this paragraph (g) as a result of a change in classification are treated as occurring immediately before the close of the day before the election is effective. For example, if an election is made to change the classification of an entity from an association to a partnership effective on January 1, the deemed transactions specified in paragraph (g)(1)(ii) of this section (including the liquidation of the association) are treated as occurring immediately before the close of December 31 and must be reported by the owners of the entity on December 31. Thus, the last day of the association's taxable year will be December 31 and the first day of the partnership's taxable year will be January 1.

* * *

(h) Effective date—(1) In general.

* * *

(2) Prior treatment of existing entities. In the case of a business entity that is not described in § 301.7701–2(b)(1), (3), (4), (5), (6), or (7), and that was in existence prior to January 1, 1997, the entity's claimed classification(s) will be respected for all periods prior to January 1, 1997, if—

(i) The entity had a reasonable basis (within the meaning of section 6662) for its claimed classification;

(ii) The entity and all members of the entity recognized the federal tax consequences of any change in the entity's classification within the sixty months prior to January 1, 1997; and

(iii) Neither the entity nor any member was notified in writing on or before May 8, 1996, that the classification of the entity was under examination (in which case the entity's classification will be determined in the examination).

* * *

[32 FR 15241, Nov. 3, 1967; T.D. 8632, 60 FR 65566, Dec. 20, 1995; T.D. 8697, 61 FR 66590, Dec. 18, 1996; 62 FR 11769, March 13, 1997; T.D. 8767, 63 FR 14619, March 26, 1998; T.D 8844, 64 FR 66580, Nov. 29, 1999; T.D. 8970, 66 FR 64911, Dec. 17, 2001; T.D. 9093, 68 FR 60286, Oct. 22, 2003; T.D. 9100, 68 FR 70709, Dec. 19, 2003; T.D. 9139, 69 FR 43317, July 20, 2004; T.D. 9153, 69 FR 49811, Aug. 12, 2004; T.D. 9203, 70 FR 29452, May 23, 2005; T.D. 9300, 71 FR 71040, Dec. 8, 2006]

§ 301.7701–4 Trusts.

(a) Ordinary trusts. In general, the term "trust" as used in the Internal Revenue Code refers to an arrangement created either by a will or by an inter vivos declaration whereby trustees take title to property for the purpose of protecting or conserving it for the beneficiaries under the ordinary rules applied in chancery or probate courts. Usually the beneficiaries of such a trust do no more than accept the benefits thereof and are not the voluntary planners or creators of the trust arrangement. However, the beneficiaries of such a trust may be the persons who create it and it will be recognized as a trust under the Internal Revenue Code if it was created for the purpose of protecting or conserving the trust property for beneficiaries who stand in the same relation to the trust as they would if the trust had been created by others for them. Generally speaking, an arrangement will be treated as a trust under the Internal Revenue Code if it can be shown that the purpose of the arrangement is to vest in trustees responsibility for the protection and conservation of property for beneficiaries who cannot share in the discharge of this responsibility and, therefore, are not associates in a joint enterprise for the conduct of business for profit.

(b) Business trusts. There are other arrangements which are known as trusts because the legal title to property is conveyed to trustees for the benefit of beneficiaries, but which are not classified as trusts for purposes of the Internal Revenue Code because they are not simply arrangements to protect or conserve the property for the beneficiaries. These trusts, which are often known as business or commercial trusts, generally are created by the beneficiaries simply as a device to carry on a profit-making business which normally would have been carried on through business organizations that are classified as corporations or partnerships under the Internal Revenue Code. However, the fact that the corpus of the trust is not supplied by the beneficiaries is not sufficient reason in itself for classifying the arrangement as an ordinary trust rather than as an association or partnership. The fact that any organization is technically cast in the trust form, by conveying title to property to trustees for the benefit of persons designated as beneficiaries, will not change the real character of the organization if the organization is more properly classified as a business entity under § 301.7701–2.

(c) Certain investment trusts—(1) An "investment" trust will not be classified as a trust if there is a power under the trust agreement to vary the investment of the certificate holders. See Commissioner v. North American Bond Trust, 122 F.2d 545 (2d Cir.1941), cert. denied, 314 U.S. 701 (1942). An investment trust with a single class of ownership interests, representing undivided beneficial interests in the assets of the trust, will be classified as a trust if there is no power under the trust agreement to vary the investment of the certificate holders. An investment trust with multiple classes of ownership interests ordinarily will be classified as a business entity under § 301.7701–2; however, an investment trust with multiple classes of ownership interests, in which there is no power under the trust agreement to vary the investment of the certificate holders, will be classified as a trust if the trust is formed to facilitate direct investment in the assets of the trust and the existence of multiple classes of ownership interests is incidental to that purpose.

(2) The provisions of paragraph (c)(1) of this section may be illustrated by the following examples:

Example (1). A corporation purchases a portfolio of residential mortgages and transfers the mortgages to a bank under a trust agreement. At the same time, the bank as trustee delivers to the corporation certificates evidencing rights to payments from the pooled mortgages; the corporation sells the certificates to the public. The trustee holds legal title to the mortgages in the pool for the benefit of the certificate holders but has no power to reinvest proceeds attributable to the mortgages in the pool or to vary investments in the pool in any other manner. There are two classes of certificates. Holders of class A certificates are entitled to all payments of mortgage principal, both scheduled and prepaid, until their certificates are retired; holders of class B certificates receive payments of principal only after all class A certificates have been retired. The different rights of the class A and class B certificates serve to shift to the holders of the class A certificates, in addition to the earlier scheduled payments of principal, the risk that mortgages in the pool will be prepaid so that the holders of the class B certificates will have "call protection" (freedom from premature termination of their interests on account of prepayments). The trust thus serves to create investment interests with respect to the mortgages held by the trust that differ significantly from direct investment in the mortgages. As a consequence, the existence of multiple classes of trust ownership is not incidental to any purpose of the trust to facilitate direct investment, and, accordingly, the trust is classified as a business entity under § 301.7701-2.

Example (2). Corporation M is the originator of a portfolio of residential mortgages and transfers the mortgages to a bank under a trust agreement. At the same time, the bank as trustee delivers to M certificates evidencing rights to payments from the pooled mortgages. The trustee holds legal title to the mortgages in the pool for the benefit of the certificate holders, but has no power to reinvest proceeds attributable to the mortgages in the pool or to vary investments in the pool in any other manner. There are two classes of certificates. Holders of class C certificates are entitled to receive 90 percent of the payments of principal and interest on the mortgages; class D certificate holders are entitled to receive the other ten percent. The two classes of certificates are identical except that, in the event of a default on the underlying mortgages, the payment rights of class D certificate holders are subordinated to the rights of class C certificate holders. M sells the class C certificates to investors and retains the class D certificates. The trust has multiple classes of ownership interests, given the greater security provided to holders of class C certificates. The interests of certificate holders, however, are substantially equivalent to undivided interests in the pool of mortgages, coupled with a limited recourse guarantee running from M to the holders of class C certificates. In such circumstances, the existence of multiple classes of ownership interests is incidental to the trust's purpose of facilitating direct investment in the assets of the trust. Accordingly, the trust is classified as a trust.

Example (3). A promoter forms a trust in which shareholders of a publicly traded corporation can deposit their stock. For each share of stock deposited with the trust, the participant receives two certificates that are initially attached, but may be separated and traded independently of each other. One certificate represents the right to dividends and the value of the underlying stock up to a specified amount; the other certificate represents the right to appreciation in the stock's value above the specified amount. The separate certificates represent two different classes of ownership interest in the trust, which effectively separate dividend rights on the stock held by the trust from a portion of the right to appreciation in the value of such stock. The multiple classes of ownership interests are designed to permit investors, by transferring one of the certificates and retaining the other, to fulfill their varying investment objectives of seeking primarily either dividend income or capital appreciation from the stock held by the trust. Given that the trust serves to create investment interests with respect to the stock held by the trust that differ significantly from direct investment in such stock, the trust is not formed to facilitate direct investment in the assets of the trust. Accordingly, the trust is classified as a business entity under § 301.7701-2.

Example (4). Corporation N purchases a portfolio of bonds and transfers the bonds to a bank under a trust agreement. At the same time, the trustee delivers to N certificates evidencing interests in the bonds. These certificates are sold to public investors. Each certificate represents the right to receive a particular payment with respect to a specific bond. Under section 1286, stripped coupons and stripped bonds are treated as separate bonds for federal income tax purposes. Although the interest of each certificate holder is different from that of each other certificate holder, and the trust thus has multiple classes of ownership, the multiple classes simply provide each certificate holder with a direct interest in what is treated under section 1286 as a separate bond. Given the similarity of the interests acquired by the certificate holders to the interests that could be acquired by direct investment, the multiple classes of trust interests merely facilitate direct investment in the assets held by the trust. Accordingly, the trust is classified as a trust.

(d) Liquidating trusts. Certain organizations which are commonly known as liquidating trusts are treated as trusts for purposes of the Internal Revenue Code. An organization will be considered a liquidating trust if it is organized for the primary purpose of liquidating and distributing the assets transferred to it, and if its activities are all reasonably necessary to, and consistent with, the accomplishment of that purpose. A liquidating trust is treated as a trust for purposes of the Internal Revenue Code because it is formed with the objective of liquidating particular assets and not as an organization having as its purpose the carrying on of a profit-making business which normally would be conducted through business organizations classified as corporations or partnerships. However, if the liquidation is unreasonably prolonged or if the liquidation purpose becomes so obscured by business activities that the declared purpose of liquidation can be said to be lost or abandoned, the status of the organization will no longer be that of a liquidating trust. Bondholders' protective committees, voting trusts, and other agencies formed to protect the interests of security holders during insolvency, bankruptcy, or corporate reorganization proceedings are analogous to liquidating trusts but if subsequently utilized to further the control or profitable operation of a going business on a permanent continuing basis, they will lose their classification as trusts for purposes of the Internal Revenue Code.

* * *

[32 FR 15241, Nov. 3, 1967; T.D. 8080, 51 FR 9952, March 24, 1986; T.D. 8668, 61 FR 19189, May 1, 1996; T.D. 8697, 61 FR 66584, Dec. 18, 1996]

§ 301.7701–6 Definitions; person, fiduciary.

(a) Person. The term person includes an individual, a corporation, a partnership, a trust or estate, a joint-stock company, an association, or a syndicate, group, pool, joint venture, or other unincorporated organization or group. The term also includes a guardian, committee, trustee, executor, administrator, trustee in bankruptcy, receiver, assignee for the benefit of creditors, conservator, or any person acting in a fiduciary capacity.

(b) Fiduciary—(1) In general. Fiduciary is a term that applies to persons who occupy positions of peculiar confidence toward others, such as trustees, executors, and administrators. A fiduciary is a person who holds in trust an estate to which another has a beneficial interest, or receives and controls income of another, as in the case of receivers. A committee or guardian of the property of an incompetent person is a fiduciary.

(2) Fiduciary distinguished from agent. There may be a fiduciary relationship between an agent and a principal, but the word agent does not denote a fiduciary. An agent having entire charge of property, with authority to effect and execute leases with tenants entirely on his own responsibility and without consulting his principal, merely turning over the net profits from the property periodically to his principal by virtue of authority conferred upon him by a power of attorney, is not a fiduciary within the meaning of the Internal Revenue Code. In cases when no legal trust has been created in the estate controlled by the agent and attorney, the liability to make a return rests with the principal.

* * *

[32 FR 15241, Nov. 3, 1967; T.D. 8697, 61 FR 66584, Dec. 18, 1996]

§ 1.7872–1 *(Proposed, published 8–20–85.)* Introduction.

(a) Statement of purpose. Section 7872 generally treats certain loans in which the interest rate charged is less than the applicable Federal rate as economically equivalent to loans bearing interest at the applicable Federal rate, coupled with a payment by the lender to the borrower sufficient to fund all or part of the payment of interest by the borrower. Such loans are referred to as "below-market loans." See s 1.7872–3 for detailed definitions of below-market loans and the determination of the applicable Federal rate. Accordingly, section 7872 recharacterizes a below-market loan as two transactions:

(1) An arm's-length transaction in which the lender makes a loan to the borrower in exchange for a note requiring the payment of interest at the applicable Federal rate; and

(2) A transfer of funds by the lender to the borrower ("imputed transfer").

The timing and the characterization of the amount of the imputed transfer by the lender to the borrower are determined in accordance with the substance of the transaction. The timing and the amount of the imputed interest payment (the excess of the amount of interest required to be paid using the applicable Federal rate, over the amount of interest required to be paid according to the loan agreement) by the borrower to the lender depend on the character of the imputed transfer by the lender to the borrower and whether the loan is a term loan or a demand loan. If the imputed transfer by the lender is characterized as a gift, the provisions of chapter 12 of the Internal Revenue Code, relating to gift tax, also apply. All imputed transfers under section 7872 (e.g., interest, compensation, gift) are characterized in accordance with the substance of the transaction, and, except as otherwise provided in the regulations under section 7872, are treated as so characterized for all purposes of the Code. For example, for purposes of section 170, an interest-free loan to a charity referred to in section 170 for which interest is imputed under section 7872, is treated as an interest bearing loan coupled with periodic gifts to the charity in the amount of the imputed transfer, for purposes of section 170. In addition, all applicable information and reporting requirements (e.g., reporting on Form W-2 and Form 1099) must be satisfied.

* * *

§ 1.7872-2 *(Proposed, published 8-20-85.)* Definition of loan.

(a) In general—(1) "Loan" interpreted broadly. For purposes of section 7872, the term "loan" includes generally any extension of credit (including, for example, a purchase money mortgage) and any transaction under which the owner of money permits another person to use the money for a period of time after which the money is to be transferred to the owner or applied according to an express or implied agreement with the owner. The term "loan" is interpreted broadly to implement the anti-abuse intent of the statute. An integrated series of transactions which is the equivalent of a loan is treated as a loan. A payment for property, goods, or services under a contract, however, is not a loan merely because one of the payor's remedies for breach of the contract is recovery of the payment. Similarly, a bona fide prepayment made in a manner consistent with normal commercial practices for services, property, or the use of property, generally, is not a loan; see section 461 and the regulations thereunder for the treatment of certain prepaid expenses and for the special rules of sections 461(h) and (i). However, a taxpayer's characterization of a transaction as a prepayment or as a loan is not conclusive. Transactions will be characterized for tax purposes according to their economic substance, rather than the terms used to describe them. * * *

(2) Limitations on applicability of section 7872—(i) In general. Section 7872 applies only to certain below-market loans (as defined in section 7872(e)(1)). * * * Certain below-market loans within these categories, however, are exempt from the provisions of section 7872. * * *

(ii) Loans to which section 483 or 1274 applies. Generally, section 7872 does not apply to any loan which is given in consideration for the sale or exchange of property (within the meaning of section 1274(c)(1)) or paid on account of the sale or exchange of property (within the meaning of section 483(c)(1)), even if the rules of those sections do not apply by reason of exceptions or safe harbor provisions. Any transaction, however, which otherwise is described in section 7872(c)(1)(A), (B), or (C), and is—

(A) A debt instrument that is issued in exchange for property and that is payable on demand,

(B) A debt instrument described in section 1273(b)(3), or

(C) A debt instrument described in section 1275(b), * * *.

is not subject to sections 483 and 1274 and is subject to 7872.

(iii) Relation to section 482. If a below-market loan subject to section 7872 would also be subject to section 482 if the Commissioner chose to apply section 482 to the loan transaction, then section 7872 will be applied first. If the Commissioner chooses to apply section 482, then the loan transaction is subject to section 482 in addition to section 7872.

(3) Loan proceeds transferred over time. In general, each extension of credit or transfer of money by a lender to a borrower is treated as a separate loan. Accordingly, if the loan agreement provides that the lender will transfer the loan proceeds to the borrower in installments, each installment payment is treated as a separate loan. Similarly, in the case of a loan in which the transfer of the loan proceeds to the borrower is subject to a draw-down restriction, each draw-down of loan proceeds is treated as a separate loan.

* * *

§ 1.7872-4 *(Proposed, published 8-20-85.)* Types of below-market loans.

(a) In general. Section 7872 applies only to certain categories of below-market loans. These categories are gift loans, compensation-related loans, corporation-shareholder loans, tax avoidance loans, and certain other loans classified in the regulations under section 7872 as significant tax effect loans (i.e., loans whose interest arrangements have a significant effect on any Federal tax liability of the lender or the borrower.)

(b) Gift loans—(1) In general. The term "gift loan" means any below-market loan in which the foregoing of interest is in the nature of a gift within the meaning of Chapter 12 of the Internal Revenue Code (whether or not the lender is a natural person).

* * *

(c) Compensation-related loans—(1) In general. A compensation-related loan is a below-market loan that is made in connection with the performance of services, directly or indirectly, between—

(i) An employer and an employee,

(ii) An independent contractor and a person for whom such independent contractor provides services, or

(iii) A partnership and a partner if the loan is made in consideration for services performed by the partner acting other than in his capacity as a member of the partnership.

The imputed transfer (amount of money treated as transferred) by the lender to the borrower is compensation. For purposes of this section, the term "in connection with the performance of services" has the same meaning as the term has for purposes of section 83. A loan from a qualified pension, profit-sharing, or stock bonus plan to a participant of the plan is not, directly or indirectly, a compensation-related loan.

(2) Loan in part in exchange for services. Except as provided in paragraph (d)(2) of this section (relating to a loan from a corporation to an employee who is also a shareholder of the corporation), a loan which is made in part in exchange for services and in part for other reasons is treated as a compensation-related loan for purposes of section 7872(c)(3) only if more than 25 percent of the amount loaned is attributable to the performance of services. If 25 percent or less of the amount loaned is attributable to the performance of services, the loan is not subject to section 7872 by reason of being a compensation-related loan. The loan may, however, be subject to section 7872 by reason of being a below-market loan characterized other than as a compensation-related loan (e.g., corporation-shareholder loan or tax avoidance loan). If—

(i) A loan is characterized as a "compensation-related" loan under this paragraph (c),

(ii) Less than 100 percent of the amount loaned is attributable to the performance of services, and

(iii) The portion of the amount loaned that is not attributable to the performance of services is not subject to section 7872, then the amounts of imputed transfer (as defined in § 1.7872–1(a)(2)) and imputed transfer (as defined in § 1.7872–1(a)) are determined only with respect to that part of the loan which is attributable to services. All of the facts and circumstances surrounding the loan agreement and the relationship between the lender and the borrower are taken into account in determining the portion of the loan made in exchange for services.

(3) Third-party lender as agent. A below-market loan by an unrelated third-party lender to an employee is treated as attributable to the performance of services if, taking into account all the facts and circumstances, the transaction is in substance a loan by the employer made with the aid of a third-party lender acting as an agent of the employer. Among the facts and circumstances which indicate whether such a loan has been made is whether the employer bears the risk of default at and immediately after the time the loan is made. The principles of this paragraph (c)(3) also apply with respect to a below-market loan by an unrelated third-party lender to an independent contractor.

(4) Special rule for continuing care facilities. Any loan to a continuing care facility will not be treated, in whole or in part, as a compensation-related loan.

* * *

(d) Corporation-shareholder loans—(1) In general. A below-market loan is a corporation-shareholder loan if the loan is made directly or indirectly between a corporation and any shareholder of the corporation. The amount of money treated as transferred by the lender to the borrower is a distribution of money (characterized according to section 301 or in the case of an S corporation, section 1368) if the corporation is the lender, or a contribution to capital if the shareholder is the lender.

(2) Special rule. A below-market loan—

(i) From a publicly held corporation to an employee of the corporation who is also a shareholder owning directly or indirectly more than 0.5 percent of the total voting power of all classes of stock entitled to vote or more than 0.5 percent of the total value of shares of all other classes of stock or 0.5 percent of the total value of shares of all classes of stock (including voting stock) of the corporation; or

(ii) From a corporation that is not a publicly held corporation to an employee of the corporation who is also a shareholder owning directly or indirectly more than 5 percent of the total voting power of all classes of stock entitled to vote or more than 5 percent of the total number of shares of all other classes of stock or 5 percent of the total value of shares of all classes of stock (including voting stock) of the corporation;

will be presumed to be a corporation-shareholder loan, in the absence of clear and convincing evidence that the loan is made solely in connection with the performance of services. For purposes of determining the percentage of direct and indirect stock ownership, the constructive ownership rules of section 267(c) apply.

* * *

(e) Tax avoidance loan—(1) In general. A tax avoidance loan is any below-market loan one of the principal purposes for the interest arrangements of which is the avoidance of Federal tax with respect to either the borrower or the lender, or both. For purposes of this rule, tax avoidance is a principal purpose of the interest arrangements if a principal factor in the decision to structure the transaction as a below-market loan (rather than, for example, as a market interest rate loan and a payment by the lender to the borrower) is to reduce the Federal tax liability of the borrower or the lender or both. The purpose for entering into the transaction (for example, to make a gift or to pay compensation) is irrelevant in determining whether a principal purpose of the interest arrangements of the loan is the avoidance of Federal tax.

* * *

(g) Indirect loans—(1) In general. If a below-market loan is made between two persons and, based on all the facts and circumstances, the effect of the loan is to make a gift or a capital contribution or a distribution of money (under section 301 or in the case of an S corporation, section 1368), or to pay compensation to a third person (“indirect participant”), or is otherwise attributable to the relationship of the lender or borrower to the indirect participant, the loan is restructured as two or more successive below-market loans (“deemed loans”) for purposes of section 7872, as follows:

(i) A deemed below-market loan made by the named lender to the indirect participant; and

(ii) A deemed below-market loan made by the indirect participant to the borrower. Section 7872 is applied separately to each deemed loan, and each deemed loan is treated as having the same provisions as the original loan between the lender and the borrower. Thus, for example, if a father makes an interest-free loan to his daughter’s corporation, the loan is restructured as a below-market loan from father to daughter (deemed gift loan) and a second below-market loan from daughter to corporation (deemed corporation-shareholder loan). Similarly, if a corporation makes an interest-free loan to another commonly controlled corporation, the loan is restructured as a below-market loan from the lending corporation to the common parent corporation and a second below-market loan from the parent corporation to the borrowing corporation.

(2) Special rule for intermediaries. If a lender and a borrower use another person, such as an individual, a trust, a partnership, or a corporation, as an intermediary or middleman in a loan transaction and a purpose for such use is to avoid the application of section 7872(c)(1)(A), (B), or (C), the intermediary will be ignored and the loan will be treated as made directly between the lender and the borrower. Thus, for example, if a father and a son arrange their below-market loan transaction by having the father make a below-market loan to the father’s partnership, followed by a second below-market loan (with substantially identical terms and conditions as the first loan) made by the partnership to the son, the two below-market loans will be restructured as one below-market loan from the father to the son.

§ 1.7872–5T Exempted loans.

(a) In general—(1) General rule. Except as provided in paragraph (a)(2) of this section, notwithstanding any other provision of section 7872 and the regulations thereunder, section 7872 does not apply to the loans listed in paragraph (b) of this section because the interest arrangements do not have a significant effect on the Federal tax liability of the borrower or the lender.

(2) No exemption for tax avoidance loans. If a taxpayer structures a transaction to be a loan described in paragraph (b) of this section and one of the principal purposes of so structuring the transaction is the avoidance of Federal tax, then the transaction will be recharacterized as a tax avoidance loan as defined in section 7872(c)(1)(D).

(b) List of exemptions. Except as provided in paragraph (a) of this section, the following transactions are exempt from section 7872:

(1) Loans which are made available by the lender to the general public on the same terms and conditions and which are consistent with the lender's customary business practice;

(2) Accounts or withdrawable shares with a bank (as defined in section 581), or an institution to which section 591 applies, or a credit union, made in the ordinary course of its business;

(3) Acquisitions of publicly traded debt obligations for an amount equal to the public trading price at the time of acquisition;

(4) Loans made by a life insurance company * * * in the ordinary course of its business, to an insured, under a loan right contained in a life insurance policy and in which the cash surrender values are used as collateral for the loans;

(5) Loans subsidized by the Federal, State (including the District of Columbia), or Municipal government (or any agency or instrumentality thereof), and which are made available under a program of general application to the public;

(6) Employee-relocation loans that meet the requirements of paragraph (c)(1) of this section;

(7) Obligations the interest on which is excluded from gross income under section 103;

(8) Obligations of the United States government;

* * *

(14) Loans the interest arrangements of which the taxpayer is able to show have no significant effect on any Federal tax liability of the lender or the borrower, as described in paragraph (c)(3) of this section; and

(15) Loans, described in revenue rulings or revenue procedures issued under section 7872(g)(1)(C), if the Commissioner finds that the factors justifying an exemption for such loans are sufficiently similar to the factors justifying the exemptions contained in this section.

(c) Special rules—(1) Employee-relocation loans—(i) Mortgage loans. In the case of a compensation-related loan to an employee, where such loan is secured by a mortgage on the new principal residence (within the meaning of section 217 and the regulations thereunder) of the employee, acquired in connection with the transfer of that employee to a new principal place of work (which meets the requirements in section 217(c) and the regulations thereunder), the loan will be exempt from section 7872 if the following conditions are satisfied:

(A) The loan is a demand loan or is a term loan the benefits of the interest arrangements of which are not transferable by the employee and are conditioned on the future performance of substantial services by the employee;

(B) The employee certifies to the employer that the employee reasonably expects to be entitled to and will itemize deductions for each year the loan is outstanding; and

(C) The loan agreement requires that the loan proceeds be used only to purchase the new principal residence of the employee.

(ii) Bridge loans. In the case of a compensation-related loan to an employee which is not described in paragraph (c)(1)(i) of this section, and which is used to purchase a new principal residence (within the meaning of section 217 and the regulations thereunder) of the employee acquired in connection with the transfer of that employee to a new principal place of work (which meets the requirements in section 217(c) and the regulations thereunder), the loan will be exempt from section 7872 if the following conditions are satisfied:

(A) The conditions contained in paragraphs (c)(1)(i)(A), (B), and (C) of this section;

(B) The loan agreement provides that the loan is payable in full within 15 days after the date of the sale of the employee's immediately former principal residence;

(C) The aggregate principal amount of all outstanding loans described in this paragraph (c)(1)(ii) to an employee is no greater than the employer's reasonable estimate of the amount of the equity of the employee and the employee's spouse in the employee's immediately former principal residence, and

(D) The employee's immediately former principal residence is not converted to business or investment use.

* * *

(3) Loans without significant tax effect. Whether a loan will be considered to be a loan the interest arrangements of which have a significant effect on any Federal tax liability of the lender or the borrower will be determined according to all of the facts and circumstances. Among the factors to be considered are—

(i) Whether items of income and deduction generated by the loan offset each other;

(ii) the amount of such items;

(iii) the cost to the taxpayer of complying with the provisions of section 7872 if such section were applied; and

(iv) any non-tax reasons for deciding to structure the transaction as a below-market loan rather than a loan with interest at a rate equal to or greater than the applicable Federal rate and a payment by the lender to the borrower.

[T.D. 8045, 50 FR 33520, Aug. 20, 1985; T.D. 8093, 51 FR 25033, July 10, 1986; 51 FR 28553, Aug. 8, 1986; T.D. 8204, 53 FR 18282, May 23, 1988]

APPENDIX

Rev.Proc. 87–57

1987-2 C.B. 687

* * *

SECTION 1. PURPOSE

.01 This revenue procedure provides guidance to taxpayers and Service personnel in computing depreciation allowances for tangible property under section 168 of the Internal Revenue Code, as amended by section 201(a) of the Tax Reform Act of 1986 (the Act), 1986–3 (Vol. 1) C.B. 38. This revenue procedure describes the applicable depreciation methods, applicable recovery periods, and applicable conventions that must be used in computing depreciation allowances under section 168.

.02 Sections 2–7 of this revenue procedure prescribe the manner of computing depreciation allowances. Section 8 of this revenue procedure contains various tables that may be used by certain taxpayers in lieu of computing allowances in the manner described in sections 2–7.

* * *

SEC. 8. OPTIONAL TABLES

.01 This section contains optional depreciation tables that may be used by certain taxpayers in computing annual depreciation allowances under section 168 of the Code. The depreciation tables may be used with respect to any item of property placed in service in a taxable year. For all items of property placed in service in a taxable year for which the depreciation tables are not used, depreciation allowances must be computed in the manner prescribed in sections 2–7 of this revenue procedure.

.02 The optional depreciation tables specify schedules of annual depreciation rates to be applied to the *unadjusted basis* of property in each taxable year. If a taxpayer uses a table to compute the annual depreciation allowance for any item of property, the taxpayer must use the table to compute the annual depreciation allowances for the entire recovery period of such property. However, a taxpayer may not continue to use the table if there are any adjustments to the basis of the property for reasons other than (1) depreciation allowed or allowable or (2) an addition or an improvement to such property that is subject to depreciation as a separate item of property. Use of the tables in this revenue procedure to compute depreciation allowances does not require the filing of any notice with the Internal Revenue Service.

Taxpayers use the appropriate table for any property based on the depreciation system, the applicable depreciation method, the applicable recovery period, and the applicable convention. The tables list the percentage depreciation rates to be applied to the unadjusted basis of property in each taxable year.

In Tables 1–5, for the general depreciation system, the listed depreciation rates reflect the 200 percent declining balance method switching to the straight line method for property with applicable recovery periods of 3, 5, 7 or 10 years and the 150 percent declining balance method switching to straight line method for property with applicable recovery periods of 15 and 20 years.

* * *

APPENDIX

Table 1. General Depreciation System
Applicable Depreciation Method: 200 or 150 Percent
Declining Balance Switching to Straight Line
Applicable Recovery Periods: 3, 5, 7, 10, 15, 20 years
Applicable Convention: Half-year

If the Rccovery Year is:	and the Recovery Period is: 3–year	5–year	7–year	10–year	15–year	20–year
	the Depreciation Rate is:					
1	33.33	20.00	14.29	10.00	5.00	3.750
2	44.45	32.00	24.49	18.00	9.50	7.219
3	14.81	19.20	17.49	14.40	8.55	6.677
4	7.41	11.52	12.49	11.52	7.70	6.177
5		11.52	8.93	9.22	6.93	5.713
6		5.76	8.92	7.37	6.23	5.285
7			8.93	6.55	5.90	4.888
8			4.46	6.55	5.90	4.522
9				6.56	5.91	4.462
10				6.55	5.90	4.461
11				3.28	5.91	4.462
12					5.90	4.461
13					5.91	4.462
14					5.90	4.461
15					5.91	4.462
16					2.95	4.461
17						4.462
18						4.461
19						4.462
20						4.461
21						2.231

APPENDIX

Instructions for Form 4562

Department of Treasury, Internal Revenue Service

Table C—General Depreciation System **Convention:** Mid-month

Method: Straight line **Recovery period:** 27.5 years

The month in the 1st recovery year the property is placed in service:

Year	1	2	3	4	5	6	7	8	9	10	11	12
1	3.485%	3.182%	2.879%	2.576%	2.273%	1.970%	1.667%	1.364%	1.061%	0.758%	0.455%	0.152%
2–9	3.636%	3.636%	3.636%	3.636%	3.636%	3.636%	3.636%	3.636%	3.636%	3.636%	3.636%	3.636%
10, 12, 14, 16, 18, 20, 22, 24, 26	3.637%	3.637%	3.637%	3.637%	3.637%	3.637%	3.636%	3.636%	3.636%	3.636%	3.636%	3.636%
11, 13, 15, 17, 19, 21, 23, 25, 27	3.636%	3.636%	3.636%	3.636%	3.636%	3.636%	3.637%	3.637%	3.637%	3.637%	3.637%	3.637%
28	1.97%	2.273%	2.576%	2.879%	3.182%	3.485%	3.636%	3.636%	3.636%	3.636%	3.636%	3.636%

Table E—General Depreciation System **Convention:** Mid-month

Method: Straight line **Recovery period:** 39 years

The month in the 1st recovery year the property is placed in service:

Year	1	2	3	4	5	6	7	8	9	10	11	12
1	2.461%	2.247%	2.033%	1.819%	1.605%	1.391%	1.177%	0.963%	0.749%	0.535%	0.321%	0.107%
2–39	2.564%	2.564%	2.564%	2.564%	2.564%	2.564%	2.564%	2.564%	2.564%	2.564%	2.564%	2.564%
40	0.107%	0.321%	0.535%	0.749%	0.963%	1.177%	1.391%	1.605%	1.819%	2.033%	2.247%	2.461%

Actuarial Values
Book Aleph

IRS Publication 1457
(7–1999)

Table S (4.0)
Single Life Factors Based on Life Table 90CM
Interest at 4.0 Percent

Age	Annuity	Life Estate	Remainder	Age	Annuity	Life Estate	Remainder
0	23.1342	.92537	.07463	43	17.8507	.71403	.28597
1	23.2822	.93129	.06871	44	17.6137	.70455	.29545
2	23.2307	.92923	.07077	45	17.3707	.69483	.30517
3	23.1714	.92686	.07314	46	17.1215	.68486	.31514
4	23.1071	.92429	.07571	47	16.8668	.67467	.32533
5	23.0386	.92154	.07846	48	16.6064	.66426	.33574
6	22.9665	.91866	.08134	49	16.3405	.65362	.34638
7	22.8908	.91563	.08437	50	16.0685	.64274	.35726
8	22.8119	.91248	.08752	51	15.7910	.63164	.36836
9	22.7291	.90916	.09084	52	15.5087	.62035	.37965
10	22.6422	.90569	.09431	53	15.2217	.60887	.39113
11	22.5517	.90207	.09793	54	14.9304	.59722	.40278
12	22.4574	.89830	.10170	55	14.6347	.58539	.41461
13	22.3606	.89442	.10558	56	14.3348	.57339	.42661
14	22.2624	.89050	.10950	57	14.0308	.56123	.43877
15	22.1635	.88654	.11346	58	13.7238	.54895	.45105
16	22.0642	.88257	.11743	59	13.4146	.53658	.46342
17	21.9641	.87856	.12144	60	13.1036	.52414	.47586
18	21.8626	.87450	.12550	61	12.7904	.51162	.48838
19	21.7586	.87034	.12966	62	12.4743	.49897	.50103
20	21.6513	.86605	.13395	63	12.1553	.48621	.51379
21	21.5402	.86161	.13839	64	11.8339	.47336	.52664
22	21.4257	.85703	.14297	65	11.5104	.46042	.53958
23	21.3072	.85229	.14771	66	11.1843	.44737	.55263
24	21.1843	.84737	.15263	67	10.8550	.43420	.56580
25	21.0566	.84226	.15774	68	10.5231	.42092	.57908
26	20.9241	.83696	.16304	69	10.1896	.40758	.59242
27	20.7861	.83145	.16855	70	9.8560	.39424	.60576
28	20.6434	.82574	.17426	71	9.5236	.38094	.61906
29	20.4957	.81983	.18017	72	9.1932	.36773	.63227
30	20.3432	.81373	.18627	73	8.8655	.35462	.64538
31	20.1859	.80744	.19256	74	8.5395	.34158	.65842
32	20.0236	.80094	.19906	75	8.2142	.32857	.67143
33	19.8559	.79423	.20577	76	7.8889	.31556	.68444
34	19.6829	.78732	.21268	77	7.5637	.30255	.69745
35	19.5040	.78016	.21984	78	7.2393	.28957	.71043
36	19.3196	.77278	.22722	79	6.9175	.27670	.72330
37	19.1293	.76517	.23483	80	6.6006	.26403	.73597
38	18.9327	.75731	.24269	81	6.2908	.25163	.74837
39	18.7300	.74920	.25080	82	5.9892	.23957	.76043
40	18.5206	.74082	.25918	83	5.6958	.22783	.77217
41	18.3042	.73217	.26783	84	5.4085	.21634	.78366
42	18.0809	.72324	.27676	85	5.1258	.20503	.79497
				86	4.8501	.19400	.80600

Age	Annuity	Life Estate	Remainder	Age	Annuity	Life Estate	Remainder
87	4.5845	.18338	.81662	89	4.0839	.16336	.83664
88	4.3291	.17317	.82683				

* * *

TABLE S (6.0)
SINGLE LIFE FACTORS BASED ON LIFE TABLE 90CM
INTEREST AT 6.0 PERCENT

Age	Annuity	Life Estate	Remainder	Age	Annuity	Life Estate	Remainder
0	16.1278	.96767	.03233	45	13.5237	.81142	.18858
1	16.2522	.97513	.02487	46	13.3792	.80275	.19725
2	16.2395	.97437	.02563	47	13.2298	.79379	.20621
3	16.2220	.97332	.02668	48	13.0751	.78451	.21549
4	16.2016	.97209	.02791	49	12.9152	.77491	.22509
5	16.1787	.97072	.02928	50	12.7497	.76498	.23502
6	16.1540	.96924	.03076	51	12.5787	.75472	.24528
7	16.1273	.96764	.03236	52	12.4027	.74416	.25584
8	16.0988	.96593	.03407	53	12.2219	.73331	.26669
9	16.0680	.96408	.03592	54	12.0363	.72218	.27782
10	16.0350	.96210	.03790	55	11.8459	.71075	.28925
11	15.9997	.95998	.04002	56	11.6505	.69903	.30097
12	15.9624	.95774	.04226	57	11.4505	.68703	.31297
13	15.9236	.95542	.04458	58	11.2463	.67478	.32522
14	15.8844	.95306	.04694	59	11.0387	.66232	.33768
15	15.8450	.95070	.04930	60	10.8279	.64967	.35033
16	15.8060	.94836	.05164	61	10.6136	.63682	.36318
17	15.7669	.94601	.05399	62	10.3951	.62371	.37629
18	15.7274	.94364	.05636	63	10.1723	.61034	.38966
19	15.6867	.94120	.05880	64	9.9456	.59674	.40326
20	15.6441	.93865	.06135	65	9.7151	.58291	.41709
21	15.5995	.93597	.06403	66	9.4804	.56882	.43118
22	15.5530	.93318	.06682	67	9.2407	.55444	.44556
23	15.5041	.93025	.06975	68	8.9967	.53980	.46020
24	15.4526	.92716	.07284	69	8.7490	.52498	.47506
25	15.3981	.92389	.07611	70	8.4988	.50993	.49007
26	15.3407	.92044	.07956	71	8.2473	.49484	.50516
27	15.2797	.91678	.08322	72	7.9951	.47971	.52029
28	15.2157	.91294	.08706	73	7.7429	.46457	.53543
29	15.1484	.90891	.09109	74	7.4898	.44939	.55061
30	15.0780	.90468	.09532	75	7.2349	.43409	.56591
31	15.0044	.90026	.09974	76	6.9775	.41865	.58135
32	14.9274	.89565	.10435	77	6.7177	.40306	.59694
33	14.8467	.89080	.10920	78	6.4560	.38736	.61264
34	14.7623	.88574	.11426	79	6.1941	.37164	.62836
35	14.6737	.88042	.11958	80	5.9340	.35604	.64396
36	14.5810	.87486	.12514	81	5.6778	.34067	.65933
37	14.4841	.86904	.13096	82	5.4265	.32559	.67441
38	14.3824	.86295	.13705	83	5.1801	.31081	.68919
39	14.2761	.85656	.14344	84	4.9372	.29623	.70377
40	14.1646	.84987	.15013	85	4.6961	.28177	.71823
41	14.0475	.84285	.15715	86	4.4592	.26755	.73245
42	13.9249	.83550	.16450	87	4.2294	.25376	.74624
43	13.7967	.82780	.17220	88	4.0070	.24042	.75958
44	13.6628	.81977	.18023				

Age	Annuity	Life Estate	Remainder
89	3.7920	.22752	.77248

* * *

TABLE S (8.0)
SINGLE LIFE FACTORS BASED ON LIFE TABLE 90CM
INTEREST AT 8.0 PERCENT

Age	Annuity	Life Estate	Remainder
0	12.2534	.98027	.01973
1	12.3540	.98832	.01168
2	12.3516	.98813	.01187
3	12.3460	.98768	.01232
4	12.3385	.98708	.01292
5	12.3295	.98636	.01364
6	12.3193	.98555	.01445
7	12.3080	.98464	.01536
8	12.2956	.98365	.01635
9	12.2818	.98255	.01745
10	12.2666	.98133	.01867
11	12.2500	.98000	.02000
12	12.2320	.97856	.02144
13	12.2133	.97706	.02294
14	12.1945	.97556	.02444
15	12.1759	.97407	.02593
16	12.1580	.97264	.02736
17	12.1403	.97123	.02877
18	12.1228	.96983	.03017
19	12.1048	.96839	.03161
20	12.0859	.96687	.03313
21	12.0658	.96527	.03473
22	12.0448	.96358	.03642
23	12.0224	.96179	.03821
24	11.9985	.95988	.04012
25	11.9728	.95782	.04218
26	11.9453	.95562	.04438
27	11.9155	.95324	.04676
28	11.8839	.95071	.04929
29	11.8502	.94802	.05198
30	11.8146	.94517	.05483
31	11.7769	.94215	.05785
32	11.7371	.93897	.06103
33	11.6949	.93559	.06441
34	11.6502	.93202	.06798
35	11.6027	.92821	.07179
36	11.5524	.92419	.07581
37	11.4992	.91994	.08006
38	11.4426	.91541	.08459
39	11.3827	.91062	.08938
40	11.3191	.90553	.09447
41	11.2514	.90011	.09989
42	11.1794	.89436	.10564
43	11.1033	.88826	.11174
44	11.0227	.88181	.11819
45	10.9380	.87504	.12496
46	10.8491	.86793	.13207
47	10.7563	.86050	.13950
48	10.6591	.85273	.14727
49	10.5577	.84461	.15539
50	10.4515	.83612	.16388
51	10.3407	.82725	.17275
52	10.2256	.81804	.18196
53	10.1061	.80849	.19151
54	9.9824	.79860	.20140
55	9.8543	.78834	.21166
56	9.7217	.77773	.22227
57	9.5845	.76676	.23324
58	9.4434	.75547	.24453
59	9.2987	.74390	.25610
60	9.1507	.73206	.26794
61	8.9991	.71993	.28007
62	8.8431	.70745	.29255
63	8.6826	.69461	.30539
64	8.5179	.68143	.31857
65	8.3490	.66792	.33208
66	8.1754	.65403	.34597
67	7.9965	.63972	.36028
68	7.8126	.62501	.37499
69	7.6243	.60994	.39006
70	7.4325	.59460	.40540
71	7.2381	.57905	.42095
72	7.0418	.56334	.43666
73	6.8439	.54751	.45249
74	6.6438	.53151	.46849
75	6.4407	.51526	.48474
76	6.2338	.49870	.50130
77	6.0231	.48185	.51815
78	5.8091	.46473	.53527
79	5.5930	.44744	.55256
80	5.3768	.43015	.56985
81	5.1624	.41299	.58701
82	4.9506	.39605	.60395
83	4.7417	.37934	.62066
84	4.5342	.36273	.63727
85	4.3268	.34614	.65386
86	4.1214	.32971	.67029

Age	Annuity	Life Estate	Remainder	Age	Annuity	Life Estate	Remainder
87	3.9210	.31368	.68632	89	3.5360	.28288	.71712
88	3.7258	.29806	.70194				

* * *

TABLE B

ANNUITY, INCOME, AND REMAINDER INTERESTS FOR A TERM CERTAIN INTEREST RATE 4.0%

Years	Annuity	Income Interest	Remainder	Years	Annuity	Income Interest	Remainder
1	0.9615	.038462	.961538	32	17.8736	.714942	.285058
2	1.8861	.075444	.924556	33	18.1476	.725906	.274094
3	2.7751	.111004	.888996	34	18.4112	.736448	.263552
4	3.6299	.145196	.854804	35	18.6646	.746585	.253415
5	4.4518	.178073	.821927	36	18.9083	.756331	.243669
6	5.2421	.209685	.790315	37	19.1426	.765703	.234297
7	6.0021	.240082	.759918	38	19.3679	.774715	.225285
8	6.7327	.269310	.730690	39	19.5845	.783379	.216621
9	7.4353	.297413	.702587	40	19.7928	.791711	.208289
10	8.1109	.324436	.675564	41	19.9931	.799722	.200278
11	8.7605	.350419	.649581	42	20.1856	.807425	.192575
12	9.3851	.375403	.624597	43	20.3708	.814832	.185168
13	9.9856	.399426	.600574	44	20.5488	.821954	.178046
14	10.5631	.422525	.577475	45	20.7200	.828802	.171198
15	11.1184	.444735	.555265	46	20.8847	.835386	.164614
16	11.6523	.466092	.533908	47	21.0429	.841717	.158283
17	12.1657	.486627	.513373	48	21.1951	.847805	.152195
18	12.6593	.506372	.493628	49	21.3415	.853659	.146341
19	13.1339	.525358	.474642	50	21.4822	.859287	.140713
20	13.5903	.543613	.456387	51	21.6175	.864699	.135301
21	14.0292	.561166	.438834	52	21.7476	.869903	.130097
22	14.4511	.578045	.421955	53	21.8727	.874907	.125093
23	14.8568	.594274	.405726	54	21.9930	.879718	.120282
24	15.2470	.609879	.390121	55	22.1086	.884344	.115656
25	15.6221	.624883	.375117	56	22.2198	.888793	.111207
26	15.9828	.639311	.360689	57	22.3267	.893070	.106930
27	16.3296	.653183	.346817	58	22.4296	.897183	.102817
28	16.6631	.666523	.333477	59	22.5284	.901137	.098863
29	16.9837	.679349	.320651	60	22.6235	.904940	.095060
30	17.2920	.691681	.308319				
31	17.5885	.703540	.296460				

INTEREST RATE 6.0%

Years	Annuity	Income Interest	Remainder	Years	Annuity	Income Interest	Remainder
1	0.9434	.056604	.943396	10	7.3601	.441605	.558395
2	1.8334	.110004	.889996				
3	2.6730	.160381	.839619	11	7.8869	.473212	.526788
4	3.4651	.207906	.792094	12	8.3838	.503031	.496969
5	4.2124	.252742	.747258	13	8.8527	.531161	.468839
				14	9.2950	.557699	.442301
6	4.9173	.295039	.704961	15	9.7122	.582735	.417265
7	5.5824	.334943	.665057				
8	6.2098	.372588	.627412	16	10.1059	.606354	.393646
9	6.8017	.408102	.591898	17	10.4773	.628636	.371364

Years	Annuity	Income Interest	Remainder	Years	Annuity	Income Interest	Remainder
18	10.8276	.649656	.350344	39	14.9491	.896944	.103056
19	11.1581	.669487	.330513	40	15.0463	.902778	.097222
20	11.4699	.688195	.311805				
21	11.7641	.705845	.294155	41	15.1380	.908281	.091719
22	12.0416	.722495	.277505	42	15.2245	.913473	.086527
23	12.3034	.738203	.261797	43	15.3062	.918370	.081630
24	12.5504	.753021	.246979	44	15.3832	.922991	.077009
25	12.7834	.767001	.232999	45	15.4558	.927350	.072650
26	13.0032	.780190	.219810	46	15.5244	.931462	.068538
27	13.2105	.792632	.207368	47	15.5890	.935342	.064658
28	13.4062	.804370	.195630	48	15.6500	.939002	.060998
29	13.5907	.815443	.184557	49	15.7076	.942454	.057546
30	13.7648	.825890	.174110	50	15.7619	.945712	.054288
31	13.9291	.835745	.164255	51	15.8131	.948785	.051215
32	14.0840	.845043	.154957	52	15.8614	.951684	.048316
33	14.2302	.853814	.146186	53	15.9070	.954418	.045582
34	14.3681	.862088	.137912	54	15.9500	.956999	.043001
35	14.4982	.869895	.130105	55	15.9905	.959433	.040567
36	14.6210	.877259	.122741	56	16.0288	.961729	.038271
37	14.7368	.884207	.115793	57	16.0649	.963895	.036105
38	14.8460	.890761	.109239	58	16.0990	.965939	.034061
				59	16.1311	.967867	.032133
				60	16.1614	.969686	.030314

INTEREST RATE
8.0%

Years	Annuity	Income Interest	Remainder	Years	Annuity	Income Interest	Remainder
1	0.9259	.074074	.925926	27	10.9352	.874813	.125187
2	1.7833	.142661	.857339	28	11.0511	.884086	.115914
3	2.5771	.206168	.793832	29	11.1584	.892672	.107328
4	3.3121	.264970	.735030	30	11.2578	.900623	.099377
5	3.9927	.319417	.680583				
6	4.6229	.369830	.630170	31	11.3498	.907984	.092016
7	5.2064	.416510	.583490	32	11.4350	.914800	.085200
8	5.7466	.459731	.540269	33	11.5139	.921111	.078889
9	6.2469	.499751	.500249	34	11.5869	.926955	.073045
10	6.7101	.536807	.463193	35	11.6546	.932365	.067635
11	7.1390	.571117	.428883	36	11.7172	.937375	.062625
12	7.5361	.602886	.397114	37	11.7752	.942014	.057986
13	7.9038	.632302	.367698	38	11.8289	.946310	.053690
14	8.2442	.659539	.340461	39	11.8786	.950287	.049713
15	8.5595	.684758	.315242	40	11.9246	.953969	.046031
16	8.8514	.708110	.291890	41	11.9672	.957379	.042621
17	9.1216	.729731	.270269	42	12.0067	.960536	.039464
18	9.3719	.749751	.250249	43	12.0432	.963459	.036541
19	9.6036	.768288	.231712	44	12.0771	.966166	.033834
20	9.8181	.785452	.214548	45	12.1084	.968672	.031328
21	10.0168	.801344	.198656	46	12.1374	.970993	.029007
22	10.2007	.816059	.183941	47	12.1643	.973141	.026849
23	10.3711	.829685	.170315	48	12.1891	.975131	.024869
24	10.5288	.842301	.157699	49	12.2122	.976973	.023027
25	10.6748	.853982	.146018	50	12.2335	.978679	.021321
26	10.8100	.864798	.135202	51	12.2532	.980258	.019742
				52	12.2715	.981720	.018280

APPENDIX

Years	Annuity	Income Interest	Remainder	Years	Annuity	Income Interest	Remainder
53	12.2884	.983075	.016925	57	12.3445	.987559	.012441
54	12.3041	.984328	.015672	58	12.3560	.988481	.011519
55	12.3186	.985489	.014511	59	12.3667	.989334	.010666
56	12.3321	.986564	.013436	60	12.3766	.990124	.009876

Rev. Proc. 2012–41

2012–2 C.B. 539

Table of Contents

SECTION 1. PURPOSE

This revenue procedure sets forth inflation-adjusted items for 2013.

SECTION 2. CHANGES

* Omitted entirely.

APPENDIX

This revenue procedure does not include the following items: the tax rate tables under § 1 of the Internal Revenue Code (Code), the adoption credit under § 23, the child tax credit under § 24, the Hope Scholarship and Lifetime Learning Credits under § 25A, the earned income credit under § 32, the standard deduction under § 63, the overall limitation on itemized deductions under § 68, the qualified transportation fringe benefit under § 132(f), the adoption assistance exclusion under § 137, the personal exemption under § 151, the election to expense certain depreciable assets under § 179, the interest on education loans under § 221, and the unified credit against estate tax for estates of decedents under § 2010(c). Those items will be addressed in future guidance.

SECTION 3. 2013 ADJUSTED ITEMS

.01 *Unearned Income of Minor Children Taxed as if Parent's Income (the "Kiddie Tax").* For taxable years beginning in 2013, the amount in § 1(g)(4)(A)(ii)(I), which is used to reduce the net unearned income reported on the child's return that is subject to the "kiddie tax," is $1,000. This $1,000 amount is the same as the amount provided in § 63(c)(5)(A), as adjusted for inflation. The same $1,000 amount is used for purposes of § 1(g)(7) (that is, to determine whether a parent may elect to include a child's gross income in the parent's gross income and to calculate the "kiddie tax"). For example, one of the requirements for the parental election is that a child's gross income is more than the amount referenced in § 1(g)(4)(A)(ii)(I) but less than 10 times that amount; thus, a child's gross income for 2013 must be more than $1,000 but less than $10,000.

* * *

.04 *Alternative Minimum Tax Exemption for a Child Subject to the "Kiddie Tax."* For taxable years beginning in 2013, for a child to whom the § 1(g) "kiddie tax" applies, the exemption amount under §§ 55 and 59(j) for purposes of the alternative minimum tax under § 55 may not exceed the sum of (1) the child's earned income for the taxable year, plus (2) $7,150.

* * *

.06 *Income from United States Savings Bonds for Taxpayers Who Pay Qualified Higher Education Expenses.* For taxable years beginning in 2013, the exclusion under § 135, regarding income from United States savings bonds for taxpayers who pay qualified higher education expenses, begins to phase out for modified adjusted gross income above $112,050 for joint returns and $74,700 for other returns. The exclusion is completely phased out for modified adjusted gross income of $142,050 or more for joint returns and $89,700 or more for other returns.

* * *

.11 *Eligible Long-Term Care Premiums.* For taxable years beginning in 2013, the limitations under § 213(d)(10), regarding eligible long-term care premiums includible in the term "medical care," are as follows:

Attained Age Before the Close of the Taxable Year	Limitation on Premiums
40 or less	$360
More than 40 but not more than 50	$680
More than 50 but not more than 60	$1,360
More than 60 but not more than 70	$3,640
More than 70	$4,550

.12 *Medical Savings Accounts.*

(1) *Self-only coverage.* For taxable years beginning in 2013, the term "high deductible health plan" as defined in § 220(c)(2)(A) means, for self-only coverage, a health plan that has an annual deductible that is not less than $2,150 and not more than $3,200, and under which the annual out-of-pocket expenses required to be paid (other than for premiums) for covered benefits do not exceed $4,300.

(2) *Family coverage.* For taxable years beginning in 2013, the term "high deductible health plan" means, for family coverage, a health plan that has an annual deductible that is not less than $4,300 and not more than $6,450, and under which the annual out-of-pocket expenses required to be paid (other than for premiums) for covered benefits do not exceed $7,850.

* * *

.17 *Foreign Earned Income Exclusion.* For taxable years beginning in 2013, the foreign earned income exclusion amount under § 911(b)(2)(D)(i) is $97,600.

.18 *Valuation of Qualified Real Property in Decedent's Gross Estate*. For an estate of a decedent dying in calendar year 2013, if the executor elects to use the special use valuation method under § 2032A for qualified real property, the aggregate decrease in the value of qualified real property resulting from electing to use § 2032A for purposes of the estate tax cannot exceed $1,070,000.

.19 *Annual Exclusion for Gifts*.

(1) For calendar year 2013, the first $14,000 of gifts to any person (other than gifts of future interests in property) are not included in the total amount of taxable gifts under § 2503 made during that year.

(2) For calendar year 2013, the first $143,000 of gifts to a spouse who is not a citizen of the United States (other than gifts of future interests in property) are not included in the total amount of taxable gifts under §§ 2503 and 2523(i)(2) made during that year.

* * *

Rev. Proc. 2013–15

2013–1 C.B. 444

Table of Contents

SECTION 1. PURPOSE

This revenue procedure sets forth inflation adjusted items for 2013. It also includes some items whose values for 2013 are specified in the American Taxpayer Relief Act of 2012, Pub. L. No. 112–240, 126 Stat. 2313 (ATRA): the beginning of the new 39.6 percent income brackets; the beginning income levels for the limitation on certain itemized deductions; and the beginning income levels for the phaseout of personal exemptions. This revenue procedure also modifies and supersedes section 3.12 of Rev. Proc. 2011–52, 2011–45 I.R.B. 701 to reflect a statutory amendment to § 132(f)(2) made by ATRA. Other inflation adjusted items for 2013 are set forth in Rev. Proc. 2012–41, 2012–45 I.R.B. 539 (dated November 5, 2012).

SECTION 2. 2013 ADJUSTED ITEMS

.01 *Tax Rate Tables*. For taxable years beginning in 2013, the tax rate tables under § 1 are as follows:

TABLE 1—Section 1(a)—Married Individuals Filing Joint Returns and Surviving Spouses

If Taxable Income Is:	*The Tax Is*:
Not over $17,850	10% of the taxable income
Over $17,850 but not over $72,500	$1,785 plus 15% of the excess over $17,850

Over $72,500 but not over $146,400	$9,982.50 plus 25% of the excess over $72,500
Over $146,400 but not over $223,050	$28,457.50 plus 28% of the excess over $146,400
Over $223,050 but not over $398,350	$49,919.50 plus 33% of the excess over $223,050
Over $398,350 but not over $450,000	$107,768.50 plus 35% of the excess over $398,350
Over $450,000	$125,846 plus 39.6% of the excess over $450,000

TABLE 2—Section 1(b)—Heads of Households

If Taxable Income Is:	*The Tax Is*:
Not over $12,750	10% of the taxable income
Over $12,750 but not over $48,600	$1,275 plus 15% of the excess over $12,750
Over $48,600 but not over $125,450	$6,652.50 plus 25% of the excess over $48,600
Over $125,450 but not over $203,150	$25,865 plus 28% of the excess over $125,450
Over $203,150 but not over $398,350	$47,621 plus 33% of the excess over $203,150
Over $398,350 but not over $425,000	$112,037 plus 35% of the excess over $398,350
Over $425,000	$121,364.50 plus 39.6% of the excess over $425,000

TABLE 3—Section 1 (c)—Unmarried Individuals (other than Surviving Spouses and Heads of Households)

If Taxable Income Is:	*The Tax Is*:
Not over $8,925	10% of the taxable income
Over $8,925 but not over $36,250	$892.50 plus 15% of the excess over $8,925
Over $36,250 but not over $87,850	$4,991.25 plus 25% of the excess over $36,250
Over $87,850 but not over $183,250	$17,891.25 plus 28% of the excess over $87,850
Over $183,250 but not over $398,350	$44,603.25 plus 33% of the excess over $183,250
Over $398,350 but not over $400,000	$115,586.25 plus 35% of the excess over $398,350
Over $400,000	$116,163.75 plus 39.6% of the excess over $400,000

TABLE 4—Section 1 (d)—Married Individuals Filing Separate Returns

If Taxable Income Is:	*The Tax Is*:
Not over $8,925	10% of the taxable income
Over $8,925 but not over $36,250	$892.50 plus 15% of the excess over $8,925
Over $36,250 but not over $73,200	$4,991.25 plus 25% of the excess over $36,250
Over $73,200 but not over $111,525	$14,228.75 plus 28% of the excess over $73,200
Over $111,525 but not over $199,175	$24,959.75 plus 33% of the excess over $111,525
Over $199,175 but not over $225,000	$53,884.25 plus 35% of the excess over $199,175
Over $225,000	$62,923 plus 39.6% of the excess over $225,000

TABLE 5—Section 1(e)—Estates and Trusts

If Taxable Income Is:	*The Tax Is*:
Not over $2,450	15% of the taxable income
Over $2,450 but not over $5,700	$367.50 plus 25% of the excess over $2,450
Over $5,700 but not over $8,750	$1,180 plus 28% of the excess over $5,700
Over $8,750 but not over $11,950	$2,034 plus 33% of the excess over $8,750
Over $11,950	$3,090 plus 39.6% of the excess over $11,950

* * *

.03 *Child Tax Credit.* For taxable years beginning in 2013, the value used in § 24(d)(1)(B)(i) to determine the amount of credit under § 24 that may be refundable is $3,000.

.04 *Hope Scholarship, American Opportunity, and Lifetime Learning Credits.*

(1) For taxable years beginning in 2013, the Hope Scholarship Credit under § 25A(b)(1), as increased under § 25A(i) (the American Opportunity Tax Credit), is an amount equal to 100 percent of qualified tuition and related expenses not in excess of $2,000 plus 25 percent of those expenses in excess of $2,000, but not in excess of $4,000. Accordingly, the maximum Hope Scholarship Credit allowable under § 25A(b)(1) for taxable years beginning in 2013 is $2,500.

(2) For taxable years beginning in 2013, a taxpayer's modified adjusted gross income in excess of $80,000 ($160,000 for a joint return) is used to determine the reduction under § 25A(d)(2) in the amount of the Hope Scholarship Credit otherwise allowable under § 25A(a)(1). For taxable years beginning in 2013, a taxpayer's modified adjusted gross income in excess of $53,000 ($107,000 for a joint return) is used to determine the reduction under § 25A(d)(2) in the amount of the Lifetime Learning Credit otherwise allowable under § 25A(a)(2).

.05 *Earned Income Credit.*

(1) *In general.* For taxable years beginning in 2013, the following amounts are used to determine the earned income credit under § 32(b). The "earned income amount" is the amount of earned income at or above which the maximum amount of the earned income credit is allowed. The "threshold phaseout amount" is the amount of adjusted gross income (or, if greater, earned income) above which the maximum amount of the credit begins to phase out. The "completed phaseout amount" is the amount of adjusted gross income (or, if greater, earned income) at or above which no credit is allowed. The threshold phaseout amounts and the completed phaseout amounts shown in the table below for married taxpayers filing a joint return include the increase provided in § 32(b)(3)(B)(i), as adjusted for inflation for taxable years beginning in 2013.

Item	*Number of Qualifying Children* One	Two	Three or More	None
Earned Income Amount	$9,560	$13,430	$13,430	$6,370
Maximum Amount of Credit	$3,250	$5,372	$6,044	$487
Threshold Phaseout Amount (Single, Surviving Spouse, or Head of Household)	$17,530	$17,530	$17,530	$7,970
Completed Phaseout Amount (Single, Surviving Spouse, or Head of Household)	$37,870	$43,038	$46,227	$14,340
Threshold Phaseout Amount (Married Filing Jointly)	$22,870	$22,870	$22,870	$13,310
Completed Phaseout Amount (Married Filing Jointly)	$43,210	$48,378	$51,567	$19,680

The instructions for the Form 1040 series provide tables showing the amount of the earned income credit for each type of taxpayer.

(2) *Excessive Investment Income.* For taxable years beginning in 2013, the earned income tax credit is not allowed under § 32(i) if the aggregate amount of certain investment income exceeds $3,300.

.06 *Exemption Amounts for Alternative Minimum Tax.* For taxable years beginning in 2013, the exemption amounts under § 55(d)(1) are:

Joint Returns or Surviving Spouses	$80,800
Unmarried Individuals (other than Surviving Spouses)	$51,900
Married Individuals Filing Separate Returns	$40,400
Estates and Trusts	$23,100

For taxable years beginning in 2013, under § 55(b)(1), the excess taxable income above which the 28 percent tax rate applies is:

Married Individuals Filing Separate Returns	$89,750
Joint Returns, Unmarried Individuals (other than surviving spouses), and Estates and Trusts	$179,500

For taxable years beginning in 2013, the amounts used under § 55(d)(3) to determine the phaseout of the exemption amounts are:

Joint Returns or a Surviving Spouses	$153,900
Unmarried Individuals (other than Surviving Spouses)	$115,400
Married Individuals Filing Separate Returns and Estates and Trusts	$76,950

.07 *Standard Deduction.*

(1) *In general.* For taxable years beginning in 2013, the standard deduction amounts under § 63(c)(2) are as follows:

Filing Status	*Standard Deduction*

APPENDIX

Married Individuals Filing Joint Returns and Surviving Spouses (§ 1(a))	$12,200
Heads of Households (§ 1(b))	$8,950
Unmarried Individuals (other than Surviving Spouses and Heads of Households) (§ 1(c))	$6,100
Married Individuals Filing Separate Returns (§ 1(d))	$6,100

(2) *Dependent.* For taxable years beginning in 2013, the standard deduction amount under § 63(c)(5) for an individual who may be claimed as a dependent by another taxpayer cannot exceed the greater of (1) $1,000, or (2) the sum of $350 and the individual's earned income.

(3) *Aged or blind.* For taxable years beginning in 2013, the additional standard deduction amount under § 63(f) for the aged or the blind is $1,200. The additional standard deduction amount is increased to $1,500 if the individual is also unmarried and not a surviving spouse.

.08 *Overall Limitation on Itemized Deductions.* For taxable years beginning in 2013, the applicable amounts under § 68(b) are $300,000 in the case of a joint return or a surviving spouse, $275,000 in the case of a head of household, $250,000 in the case of an individual who is not married and who is not a surviving spouse or head of household, and $150,000 in the case of a married individual filing a separate return.

.09 *Qualified Transportation Fringe Benefit.* For taxable years beginning in 2013, the monthly limitation under § 132(f)(2)(A) regarding the aggregate fringe benefit exclusion amount for transportation in a commuter highway vehicle and any transit pass is $245. The monthly limitation under § 132(f)(2)(B) regarding the fringe benefit exclusion amount for qualified parking is $245.

* * *

.11 *Personal Exemption.*

(1) For taxable years beginning in 2013, the personal exemption amount under § 151(d) is $3,900.

(2) *Phaseout.* For taxable years beginning in 2013, the personal exemption phases out for taxpayers with the following adjusted gross income amounts:

Filing Status	*AGI—Beginning of Phaseout*	*AGI—Completed Phaseout*
Married Individuals Filing Joint Returns and Surviving Spouses (§ 1(a))	$300,000	$422,500
Heads of Households (§ 1(b))	$275,000	$397,500
Unmarried Individuals (other than Surviving Spouses and Heads of Households) (§ 1(c))	$250,000	$372,500
Married Individuals Filing Separate Returns (§ 1(d))	$150,000	$211,250

.12 *Interest on Education Loans.* For taxable years beginning in 2013, the $2,500 maximum deduction for interest paid on qualified education loans under § 221 begins to phase out under § 221(b)(2)(B) for taxpayers with modified adjusted gross income in excess of $60,000 ($125,000 for joint returns), and is completely phased out for taxpayers with modified adjusted gross income of $75,000 or more ($155,000 or more for joint returns).

.13 *Unified Credit Against Estate Tax.* For an estate of any decedent dying during calendar year 2013, the basic exclusion amount is $5,250,000 for determining the amount of the unified credit against estate tax under § 2010.

* * *

Rev. Proc. 2012–26

2012–1 C.B. 933

SECTION 1. PURPOSE

This revenue procedure provides the 2013 inflation adjusted amounts for Health Savings Accounts (HSAs) as determined under § 223 of the Internal Revenue Code.

SECTION 2. 2013 INFLATION ADJUSTED ITEMS

Annual contribution limitation. For calendar year 2013, the annual limitation on deductions under § 223(b)(2)(A) for an individual with self-only coverage under a high deductible health plan is $3,250. For calendar year 2013, the annual limitation on deductions under § 223(b)(2)(B) for an individual with family coverage under a high deductible health plan is $6,450.

High deductible health plan. For calendar year 2013, a "high deductible health plan" is defined under § 223(c)(2)(A) as a health plan with an annual deductible that is not less than $1,250 for self-only coverage or $2,500 for family coverage, and the annual out-of-pocket expenses (deductibles, co-payments, and other amounts, but not premiums) do not exceed $6,250 for self-only coverage or $12,500 for family coverage.

* * *

Notice 2012–67

2012–2 C.B. 671

Section 415 of the Internal Revenue Code (the Code) provides for dollar limitations on benefits and contributions under qualified retirement plans. Section 415(d) requires that the Commissioner annually adjust these limits for cost-of-living increases. Other limitations applicable to deferred compensation plans are also affected by these adjustments under § 415. Under § 415(d), the adjustments are to be made pursuant to adjustment procedures which are similar to those used to adjust benefit amounts under § 215(i)(2)(A) of the Social Security Act.

The limitations that are adjusted by reference to § 415(d) generally will change for 2013 because the increase in the cost-of-living index met the statutory thresholds that trigger their adjustment. For example, the limitation under § 402(g)(1) on the exclusion for elective deferrals described in § 402(g)(3) is increased from $17,000 to $17,500 for 2013. This limitation affects elective deferrals to § 401(k) plans, § 403(b) plans, and the Federal Government's Thrift Savings Plan, among other plans.

Cost-of-Living Adjusted Limits for 2013

Effective January 1, 2013, the limitation on the annual benefit under a defined benefit plan under § 415(b)(1)(A) is increased from $200,000 to $205,000.

For a participant who separated from service before January 1, 2013, the participant's limitation under a defined benefit plan under § 415(b)(1)(B) is computed by multiplying the participant's compensation limitation, as adjusted through 2012, by 1.0170.

The limitation for defined contribution plans under § 415(c)(1)(A) is increased in 2013 from $50,000 to $51,000.

The Code provides that various other dollar amounts are to be adjusted at the same time and in the same manner as the dollar limitation of § 415(b)(1)(A). After taking into account the applicable rounding rules, the amounts for 2013 are as follows:

The limitation under § 402(g)(1) on the exclusion for elective deferrals described in § 402(g)(3) is increased from $17,000 to $17,500.

The annual compensation limit under §§ 401(a)(17), 404(1), 408(k)(3)(C), and 408(k)(6)(D)(ii) is increased from $250,000 to $255,000.

The dollar limitation under § 416(i)(*l*)(A)(i) concerning the definition of key employee in a top-heavy plan remains unchanged at $165,000.

The dollar amount under § 409(*o*)(*l*)(C)(ii) for determining the maximum account balance in an employee stock ownership plan subject to a 5–year distribution period is increased from $1,015,000 to $1,035,000, while the dollar amount used to determine the lengthening of the 5–year distribution period is increased from $200,000 to $205,000.

The limitation used in the definition of highly compensated employee under § 414(q)(*l*)(B) remains unchanged at $115,000.

The dollar limitation under § 414(v)(2)(B)(i) for catch-up contributions to an applicable employer plan other than a plan described in § 401(k)(11) or 408(p) for individuals aged 50 or over remains unchanged at $5,500. The dollar limitation under § 414(v)(2)(B)(ii) for catch-up contributions to an applicable employer plan described in § 401(k)(11) or 408(p) for individuals aged 50 or over remains unchanged at $2,500.

The annual compensation limitation under § 401(a)(17) for eligible participants in certain governmental plans that, under the plan as in effect on July 1, 1993, allowed cost-of-living adjustments to the compensation limitation under the plan under § 401(a)(17) to be taken into account, is increased from $375,000 to $380,000.

The compensation amount under § 408(k)(2)(C) regarding simplified employee pensions (SEPs) remains unchanged at $550.

The limitation under § 408(p)(2)(E) regarding SIMPLE retirement accounts is increased from $11,500 to $12,000.

The limitation on deferrals under § 457(e)(15) concerning deferred compensation plans of state and local governments and tax-exempt organizations is increased from $17,000 to $17,500.

The compensation amount under § 1.61–21(f)(5)(i) of the Income Tax Regulations concerning the definition of "control employee" for fringe benefit valuation purposes remains unchanged at $100,000. The compensation amount under § 1.61–21(f)(5)(iii) remains unchanged at $205,000.

The Code also provides that several pension-related amounts are to be adjusted using the cost-of-living adjustment under § 1(f)(3). After taking the applicable rounding rules into account, the amounts for 2013 are as follows:

The adjusted gross income limitation under § 25B(b)(*l*)(A) for determining the retirement savings contribution credit for married taxpayers filing a joint return is increased from $34,500 to $35,500; the limitation under § 25B(b)(*l*)(B) is increased from $37,500 to $38,500; and the limitation under § 25B(b)(*l*)(C) and (D) is increased from $57,500 to $59,000.

The adjusted gross income limitation under § 25B(b)(*l*)(A) for determining the retirement savings contribution credit for taxpayers filing as head of household is increased from $25,875 to $26,625; the limitation under § 25B(b)(*l*)(B) is increased from $28,125 to $28,875; and the limitation under § 25B(b)(*l*)(C) and (D) is increased from $43,125 to $44,250.

The adjusted gross income limitation under § 25B(b)(*l*)(A) for determining the retirement savings contribution credit for all other taxpayers is increased from $17,250 to $17,750; the limitation under § 25B(b)(*l*)(B) is increased from $18,750 to $19,250; and the limitation under § 25B(b)(*l*)(C) and (D) is increased from $28,750 to $29,500.

The deductible amount under § 219(b)(5)(A) for an individual making qualified retirement contributions is increased from $5,000 to $5,500.

The applicable dollar amount under § 219(g)(3)(B)(i) for determining the deductible amount of an IRA contribution for taxpayers who are active participants filing a joint return or as a qualifying widow(er) is increased from $92,000 to $95,000. The applicable dollar amount under § 219(g)(3)(B)(ii) for all other taxpayers (other than married taxpayers filing separate returns) is increased from $58,000 to $59,000. The applicable dollar amount under § 219(g)(7)(A) for a taxpayer who is not an active participant but whose spouse is an active participant is increased from $173,000 to $178,000.

The adjusted gross income limitation under § 408A(c)(3)(B)(ii)(I) for determining the maximum Roth IRA contribution for married taxpayers filing a joint return or as a qualifying widow(er) is increased from $173,000 to $178,000. The adjusted gross income limitation under § 408A(c)(3)(B)(ii)(II) for all other taxpayers (other than married taxpayers filing separate returns) is increased from $110,000 to $112,000.

The dollar amount under § 430(c)(7)(D)(i)(II) used to determine excess employee compensation with respect to a single-employer defined benefit pension plan for which the special election under § 430(c)(2)(D) has been made is increased from $1,039,000 to $1,066,000.

* * *

APPENDIX

Notice 2012–72

2012–2 C.B. 673

* * *

SECTION 2. STANDARD MILEAGE RATES

The standard mileage rate for transportation or travel expenses is 56.5 cents per mile for all miles of business use (business standard mileage rate). See section 4 of Rev. Proc. 2010–51.

The standard mileage rate is 14 cents per mile for use of an automobile in rendering gratuitous services to a charitable organization under § 170. See section 5 of Rev. Proc. 2010–51.

The standard mileage rate is 24 cents per mile for use of an automobile (1) for medical care described in § 213, or (2) as part of a move for which the expenses are deductible under § 217. See section 5 of Rev. Proc. 2010–51.

* * *

TOPICAL INDEX

(References are to Code sections)

†